Stanley Gibbons
Stamp Catalogue

Commonwealth & British Empire Stamps 1840–1952

107th edition

Stanley Gibbons Ltd
London and Ringwood

By Appointment to Her Majesty The Queen
Stanley Gibbons Ltd, London
Philatelists

Published by **Stanley Gibbons Ltd**
Editorial, Publications Sales Offices and Distribution Centre:
Parkside, Christchurch Road, Ringwood, Hants BH24 3SH

ISBN: 0-85259-564-6

Item No. 2813 (05)

Printed in Great Britain by Unwin Brothers Ltd., Old Woking, Surrey

Preface to the 2005 Edition

STRENGTHENING MARKET

Those who are following the progress of the SG100™ stamp price index in *Gibbons Stamp Monthly* or who have visited any of the major auction houses around the world will know that the market for fine stamps has strengthened considerably over the past couple of years.

As always, some areas and periods have seen more activity than others, while the rule for those who look to stamps to provide them with something more than just 'the finest hobby on earth' continue to seek scarce stamps in very fine condition, pushing the market for such material well ahead of that for the most popular and frequently 'traded' stamps, which go to make up the SG100™ Stamp Price Index.

Following the complete re-setting of this catalogue last year, our prime objective has been to publish an increased number of the new series of catalogues devoted to single countries or groups of Commonwealth Countries from SG 1 to date. These have allowed the re-evaluation of prices for more modern stamps of some countries for the first time in three years and the results seem to have been proving popular with collectors, especially now that they are being presented in a traditional 'bound' style.

The production of these catalogues continues and we welcome comments or news of unlisted items from post-1953 Commonwealth countries to be incorporated in those listings when we come to prepare them.

As for this 1840–1952 catalogue, we have continued to remove the odd discrepancies which arose from last year's re-set and to replace some more of the black and white illustrations. We are particularly grateful to Richard Lockyer OBE for kindly allowing us to take illustrations of many King George VI and also a few King George V varieties from his collection.

As in the previous edition, countries have been arranged so that they appear under the names current in 1952. This means that British Solomon Islands is used instead of Solomon Islands and Virgin Islands is used instead of British Virgin Islands. Colonies that amalgamated into larger territories or dominions are grouped together before the united country, while dependent territories appear after the main listings. Thus the Australian states appear before Australia itself, with Nauru, New Guinea and Papua after it.

A complete two page contents list appears in the Catalogue Introduction and there is a full index at the end of the volume.

PRICES

As mentioned here last year, one of the major benefits accruing from our new production systems is that, while repricing each new edition of this and all Stanley Gibbons Catalogues, remains a lengthy and painstaking process, late amendments can now be made a matter of days before a catalogue is put to press, allowing some of the results of recent auctions to be reflected in the prices quoted.

As might be expected, there are a vast number of price changes in this new edition nearly all of them in an upward direction.

In many cases, movements this year are a continuation of trends already established in previous editions of this catalogue. Thus varieties and errors continue to appreciate, with many of the watermark varieties and plate flaws listed in previous editions marked up, while some of those previously listed without a price are now provided with one.

'Used abroad' prices which have been revised this time include **Great Britain used in Ascension, India used in Bahrain** and **Zanzibar**, **Falkland Islands used in the Dependencies** and **Hong Kong used in the British Post Offices in China and Japan**.

Interest in the stamps of **Australia** continues to increase and once again we are indebted to Simon Dunkerley for his guidance on pricing this section. Significant increases are recorded among the watermark errors and early booklets and the stamps of the states have again been revised. The early issues of **New South Wales** have received particular attention.

Asian countries also continue to advance with numerous price increases in **Brunei, Burma, Ceylon, Hong Kong, India and States, Malaya, North Borneo, Pakistan** and **Sarawak.**

In Africa, **Gold Coast, British East Africa, Morocco Agencies, Rhodesia,** the **Nyasaland** keyplates **Somaliland, Griqualand West, Natal, Uganda** and **Zanzibar** see significant gains, while the Indian Ocean territories of **Mauritius, Seychelles** and the **Maldives** are all moving up.

Prices for **Antigua, Bahamas, Barbados, Bermuda, British Guiana, Cayman Islands, Grenada, St. Kitts, Nevis, Trinidad** and the **Turks and Caicos Islands** are all clearly hardening, while other areas which show greater than average numbers of increases include **Bahrain, Newfoundland** and **Prince Edward Island**, **Cyprus**, the **Falkland Islands, Fiji, Ireland, Malta** and **New Zealand**.

Once again the World War I occupation issues have been marked up with **New Guinea**, **Batum, Bushire, Iraq, Long Island, Tanganyika** and **Togo** standing out.

Collectors who do not use the *Great Britain Concise Catalogue* may also be surprised at some of the increases to the **Great Britain** section of this catalogue since the previous edition. The demand for scarce to rare Great Britain material in fine condition has been significant in recent months with the prices achieved at auction being reflected in some significant rises. All indications are that this trend is set to continue in the coming months.

To meet the challenge of this rising market, the popular lists of alterations and additions to catalogue prices have returned to the pages of *Gibbons Stamp Monthly*. Collectors keen to keep an eye on the market should place a regular order.

REVISIONS TO THIS EDITION.

Among the new varieties added to this edition are two more examples of the 1935 Silver Jubilee 'frame printed double, one albino', a further selection of watermark varieties and some additional plate flaws – the **Ascension** 'Mountaineer', the **Gibraltar** 'Ape on Rock' and the **Malta** 'Flag on Citadel', among others.

New varieties have been added and revisions made to the listings of **Queensland** on the advice of Alan Griffiths. These include the relisting of the 1867 1d., 2d. and 6d., clean-cut perf 13, the separate listing of the two transfers of the 1866 lithographed 4d. and the provision of notes on the two plates of the 2d. Chalon head to assist in separating the printings of that value up to 1879. Some of the previously listed varieties are now illustrated and there is a new note on the late use of fiscal stamps for postal purposes.

In **Tasmania** two major varieties have been added to the 1871–91 typographed stamps and the sideways watermarked stamps of **Victoria**, previously footnoted, have now been listed and in some cases priced. Many cases of inverted watermarks on the stamps of the Australian states continue to be reported. Readers' attention is drawn to the note regarding these above the New South Wales listings, explaining why the vast majority of these are omitted.

Notes regarding the direction of some of the early sideways watermarks of **Australia** have been expanded and four of the major plate varieties on the King George V 1d. stamps have been added with the help of Colin Mount. Following further research by David Banwell and Dr. R. F. Parsons, a further Die II cliché has been discovered on the 1929 and 1932 9d. Kangaroo stamp. It is now clear that the substitutions took place during the 'third watermark' period but, since examples on this watermark could only be identified in pairs with Die IIB stamps, they have not been listed there.

The listings of the **Nauru** overprints on Great Britain seahorses have been revised, following discussions with Keith Buckingham.

Following recent research and advice from Sir John Inglefield Watson and Brian Hurst of the Bechuanalands and Botswana Society, some new varieties have been added to the **Bechuanaland** listings.

In **Prince Edward Island** a note has been added regarding the perforator gauging exactly 11¼, following the article on the subject by Alan Griffiths, published in the *London Philatelist*.

John Hillson has provided illustrations of one currently listed and two new varieties on the 'Small Queens' of **Canada**. It is hoped that the description of the 5c. on 6c. re-entry will assist in the correct identification of this celebrated variety.

For the **Falkland Islands** the four shades of the King George VI 10s. value are now separately listed, as is the 'thick serif' variety on the 1933 Centenary 1d. The 'Gap in the 80th parallel' or 'Broken arc' varieties on the 'Thick Map' set of the **Falkland Islands Dependencies**, footnoted for many years, are now individually listed and priced.

An extended note has been added regarding the **Fiji** Queen Victoria 5s. stamp and its reprints following the publication of Ross Duberal's researches by the Pacific Islands Study Circle, while David Gillis has advised on the clarification of the booklet listings and those of **Pitcairn Island**.

Two dies have been identified and listed for the 1948–50 3a.4p. of **Cochin**, following the listing of both the 2p. dies from this set last year.

There have been several additions to the **Malaya** listings thanks to Keith Elliot, Rob Holley and other members of the Malaya Study Group. The lists of stamps from one state, put on sale in others during the 1941 shortages have also been revised.

Many other additions and amendments have been made throughout the catalogue. We are grateful to individual collectors, members of the trade and specialist study circles for their continuing advice and support. Without this assistance this catalogue could not continue to develop and we welcome all such approaches as we embark on the preparation of the 2006 edition.

Finally a personal thanks to my colleagues in Ringwood, London and Nailsea for all their help during my first year as Catalogue Editor. Without their contributions, support and advice the publication of this catalogue could not have been achieved. Thank you all.

Hugh Jefferies
Catalogue Editor

Stanley Gibbons Holdings Plc Addresses

STANLEY GIBBONS LIMITED, STANLEY GIBBONS AUCTIONS

399 Strand, London WC2R 0LX
Auction Room and Specialist Stamp Departments. Open Monday–Friday 9.30 a.m. to 5 p.m.
Shop. Open Monday–Friday 9 a.m. to 5.30 p.m. and Saturday 9.30 a.m. to 5.30 p.m.
Telephone 020 7836 8444, Fax 020 7836 7342, E-mail: enquiries@stanleygibbons.co.uk and Internet: www.stanleygibbons.com for all departments

STANLEY GIBBONS PUBLICATIONS

Parkside, Christchurch Road, Ringwood, Hants BH24 3SH.
Telephone 01425 472363 (24 hour answer phone service), Fax 01425 470247 and E-mail info@stanleygibbons.co.uk
Publications Mail Order. FREEPHONE 0800 611622. Monday–Friday 8.30 a.m. to 5 p.m.

FRASER'S

(a division of Stanley Gibbons Ltd)
399 Strand, London WC2R 0LX
Autographs, photographs, letters and documents.
Monday–Friday 9 a.m. to 5.30 p.m. and Saturday 10 a.m. to 4 p.m.
Telephone 020 7836 8444, Fax 020 7836 7342 E-mail: info@frasersautographs.co.uk and Internet: www.frasersautographs.com

STANLEY GIBBONS PUBLICATIONS OVERSEAS REPRESENTATION

Stanley Gibbons Publications are represented overseas by the following sole distributors (*), distributors (**) or licensees (***).

Australia

Lighthouse Philatelic (Aust.) Pty Ltd*
Locked Bag 5900
Botany DC
New South Wales 2019
Australia

Stanley Gibbons (Australia) Pty Ltd***
Level 6, 36 Clarence Street
Sydney N.S.W. 2000
Australia

Belgium and Luxembourg**

Davo c/o Philac
Rue du Midi 48
Bruxelles 1000
Belgium

Canada*

Lighthouse Publications (Canada) Ltd
255 Duke Street
Montreal
Quebec
Canada H3C 2M2

Denmark**

Samlerforum/Davo
Ostergade 3
DK 7470 Karup
Denmark

Finland**

Davo
c/o Kapylan Merkkiky
Pohjolankatu 1
00610 Helsinki
Finland

France*

Davo France (Casteilla)
10 Rue Leon Foucault
78184 St Quentin Yvelines Cesex
France

Hong Kong**

Po-on Stamp Service
GPO Box 2498
Hong Kong

Israel**

Capital Stamps
PO Box 3769
Jerusalem 91036
Israel

Italy*

Ernesto Marini Srl
Via Struppa 300
1-16165 Genova GE
Italy

Japan**

Japan Philatelic Co Ltd
PO Box 2
Suginami-Minami
Tokyo
Japan

Netherlands*

Davo Publications
PO Box 411
7400 AK Deventer
Netherlands

New Zealand***

Mowbray Collectables
PO Box 80
Wellington
New Zealand

Norway**

Davo Norge A/S
PO Box 738 Sentrum
N-01 05 Oslo
Norway

Singapore**

Stamp Inc Collectibles Pte Ltd
10 Ubi Crescent
#01-43 Ubi Tech Park
Singapore 408564

Sweden*

Chr Winther Sorensen AB
Box 43
S-310 Knaered
Sweden

Switzerland**

Phila Service
Burgstrasse 160
CH 4125 Riehen
Switzerland

Stanley Gibbons Stamp Catalogue Complete List of Parts

Commonwealth & British Empire 1840–1952
(Annual plus range of one-country catalogues)

2 Austria & Hungary (6th edition, 2002)
Austria, U.N. (Vienna), Hungary

3 Balkans (4th edition, 1998)
Albania, Bosnia & Herzegovina, Bulgaria, Croatia, Greece & Islands, Macedonia, Rumania, Slovenia, Yugoslavia

4 Benelux (5th edition, 2003)
Belgium & Colonies, Luxembourg, Netherlands & Colonies

5 Czechoslovakia and Poland (6th edition, 2002)
Czechoslovakia, Czech Republic, Slovakia, Poland

6 France (5th edition, 2001)
France, Colonies, Post Offices, Andorra, Monaco

7 Germany (6th edition, 2002)
Germany, States, Colonies, Post Offices

8 Italy & Switzerland (6th edition, 2003)
Italy & Colonies, Liechtenstein, San Marino, Switzerland, U.N. (Geneva), Vatican City

9 Portugal & Spain (4th edition, 1996)
Andorra, Portugal & Colonies, Spain & Colonies

10 Russia (5th edition, 1999)
Russia, Armenia, Azerbaijan, Belarus, Estonia, Georgia, Kazakhstan, Kyrgyzstan, Latvia, Lithuania, Moldova, Tajikistan, Turkmenistan, Ukraine, Uzbekistan, Mongolia

11 Scandinavia (5th edition, 2001)
Aland Islands, Denmark, Faroe Islands, Finland, Greenland, Iceland, Norway, Sweden

12 Africa since Independence A–E (2nd edition, 1983)
Algeria, Angola, Benin, Burundi, Cameroun, Cape Verde, Central African Republic, Chad, Comoro Islands, Congo, Djibouti, Equatorial Guinea, Ethiopia

13 Africa since Independence F–M (1st edition, 1981)
Gabon, Guinea, Guinea-Bissau, Ivory Coast, Liberia, Libya, Malagasy Republic, Mali, Mauritania, Morocco, Mozambique

14 Africa since Independence N–Z (1st edition, 1981)
Niger Republic, Rwanda, St. Thomas & Prince, Senegal, Somalia, Sudan, Togo, Tunisia, Upper Volta, Zaire

15 Central America (2nd edition, 1984)
Costa Rica, Cuba, Dominican Republic, El Salvador, Guatemala, Haiti, Honduras, Mexico, Nicaragua, Panama

16 Central Asia (3rd edition, 1992)
Afghanistan, Iran, Turkey

17 China (6th edition, 1998)
China, Taiwan, Tibet, Foreign P.O.'s, Hong Kong, Macao

18 Japan & Korea (4th edition, 1997)
Japan, Korean Empire, South Korea, North Korea

19 Middle East (5th edition, 1996)
Bahrain, Egypt, Iraq, Israel, Jordan, Kuwait, Lebanon, Oman, Qatar, Saudi Arabia, Syria, U.A.E., Yemen

20 South America (3rd edition, 1989)
Argentina, Bolivia, Brazil, Chile, Colombia, Ecuador, Paraguay, Peru, Surinam, Uruguay, Venezuela

21 South-East Asia (4th edition, 2004)
Bhutan, Cambodia, Indo-China, Indonesia, Laos, Myanmar, Nepal, Philippines, Thailand, Timor, Vietnam

22 United States (5th edition, 2000)
U.S. & Possessions, Marshall Islands, Micronesia, Palau, U.N. (New York, Geneva, Vienna)

GREAT BRITAIN SPECIALISED CATALOGUES

Volume 1 Queen Victoria (13th edition, 2004)
Volume 2 King Edward VII to King George VI (11th edition, 1999)
Volume 3 Queen Elizabeth II Pre-decimal Issues (10th edition, 1998)
Volume 4 Queen Elizabeth II Decimal Definitive Issues (9th edition, 2000)
Volume 5 Queen Elizabeth II Decimal Special Issues (3rd edition, 1998, with 1998–99 and 2000/1 Supplements)

THEMATIC CATALOGUES

Collect Aircraft on Stamps (out of print)
Collect Birds on Stamps (5th edition, 2003)
Collect Chess on Stamps (2nd edition, 1999)
Collect Fish on Stamps (1st edition, 1999)
Collect Fungi on Stamps (2nd edition, 1997)
Collect Motor Vehicles on Stamps (1st edition, 2004)
Collect Railways on Stamps (3rd edition, 1999)
Collect Shells on Stamps (1st edition, 1995)
Collect Ships on Stamps (3rd edition, 2001)

Stamps Added

The following are the catalogue numbers of stamps listed in this edition for the first time.

Great Britain. 90c, O11b

British Post Offices Abroad. Z88a

Ascension. 4b, 39ba, 39ca, 41aa, 41ba, 41ca, 42da

Australia—New South Wales. O22a, O55a, D2a

Queensland. 26a, 26b, 27b, 27c, 28b, 28c, 33a, 33b, 34a, 34b, 35a, 35b, 37, 38, 40, 41, 42, 47a, 47b, 48a, 48b, 53b, 54, 54a, 54b, 55b, 56b, 128ab

Tasmania. 146b, 146f, 150b, 154a, 160b, 164d, 165b, 171a, 173b

Victoria. 180a, 331a, 332b, 336b, 340c, 341a, 357b, 361a, 366a, 385bb, 387e, 388b, 422b, 424e, 437d, 454b, 462a

Commonwealth of Australia. 1cw, 2daw, 21cg, 21ch, 21ci, 21cj, 44aa, 47bb, 47bc, 47bd, 47be, 48bw, 49c, 49d, 49e, 49f, 50c, 50d, 50e, 50f, 57c, 57d, 57e, 57f, 76a, 76b, 76c, 76d, 82a, 82b, 82c, 82d, 83a, 83b, 83c, 83d, 86a, 86b, 86c, 86d, 95aa, 95ab, 95ac, 95ad, D120w

Nauru. 4c, 17s

New Guinea. 67bb, 67bc, 67bd, 67be, 103ab, 103ac, 103ad, 103ae, 120a, 120b, 120c, 120d

Bahrain. Z8a, Z67a, Z124a

Barbados. 75w, 211y, 213a

Bechuanaland. 2a, 5b, 6b, 7a, 31d, 32b, 38d, 39c, 39e, 41b, 70a, D6b

Bermuda. 60a, 76w, 76y, 76ys

British Guiana. 223x

Canada—Newfoundland. 211ca

Prince Edward Island. 26a, 26b, 26c, 26d, 26e, 28d

Dominion of Canada. 75d, 85a

Ceylon. 63bw, 166aw, 207w

Dominica. 166a, 122c

Falkland Islands. 128a, 162a, 162b, 162c

Falkland Islands Dependencies. G1a, G2a, G3a, G4a, G5a, G6a, G6ea, G7a, G8a

Fiji. 26a

Gibraltar. 66x, 86b, 124aa

Hong Kong. 111w

British Post Offices in China. Z300

India. 180w, 195c, 236bw, 279w, O146bw, O147w

Indian Convention States—Jind. O25c

Patiala. O51w

Indian Feudatory States—Bundi. 21a, 35a

Cochin. 116b, O14a, O15a, O99c

Hydrabad. 1d, 4a, 14ca, 36bc, O39db, O40ca, O43h

Kishangarh. 22ac

Morvi. 17b

Soruth. 7a

Travancore. 31b

Travancore-Cochin. O1h

Iraq—Issues for Baghdad. 11ba

Issues for Iraq. 8a, 46w

Jamaica. 96w

Kenya, Uganda and Tanganyika—British East Africa. 63c

Kenya, Uganda and Tanganyika. 29w, 129a

Leeward Islands. 65w

Madagascar. 58b, 58c

Malaya—Straits Settlements. 65w, 155as, 194w, 198aw, 201w, 202aw, 253g

Federated Malay States. 43dy, 55a, 58a, 60b, 68x

Johore. 17b, 19w, 63a

Kedah. 6y, 21a, 22a, 29a, 47a, 54a

Perak. 19a, 66a, 105a, 105ba, O2c

Selangor. 31w, 42a

Siamese Posts in Northern Malaya. Z266

Malta. 21w, 27w, 221bb, 238b

Mauritius. 113a, 117d

New Zealand. 265b, SB7a, D31x

Niue. 72a, 73a, 74a

Western Samoa. 182bw

North Borneo—Labuan. 8x, 9y, 13y, 17y, 72d, 99b

North Borneo. D8c

Pakistan. 1w

Rhodesia. 75ac, 78d, 187b, 188a, 253a

St. Helena. 16x, 29x

St. Lucia. 161a

St. Vincent. 60d

Sierra Leone. 55d

South Africa–Cape of Good Hope. 59aw

Natal. 55x

Orange Free State. 13b

Transvaal. 173b, 234c

Union of South Africa. 46ca, O37a

Southern Rhodesia. 61b

South West Africa. 102a

Sudan. O35a

Swaziland. 48a

Tanganyika. M44a, 105a

Tonga. 34/5, 37Ai, 37Bg

Trinidad and Tobago. 189b, 189c

Turks Is. 11f, 11g

Uganda. 19a

Virgin Islands. 3a

Zanzibar. Z41a, 21m

Catalogue Numbers Altered

The table below is a cross-reference of those catalogue numbers which have been altered in this edition.

Old	New
Great Britain	
90c	90d
90ca	90da
Z63b	*Deleted*
Australia—New South Wales	
O22a	O22b
O22b	O22c
O22ba	O22ca
O22c	O22d
D2a	D2b
D2b	D2c
D2c	D2d
D2d	D2e
D2e	D2f
Queensland	
34a	35
35	36
35a	36a
53s	56s
57s	58s
128ab	128ac
142a	143a
Tasmania	
146b	146c
146ba	146ca
146c	146d
146ca	146da
146d	146e
Victoria	
180a	180b
180b	180c
180c	180d
180d	180e
180e	180f
180f	180g
422ab	422c
454ab	454c
454b	454d
Nauru	
21c	*Deleted*
24c	*Deleted*
Bechuanaland	
5b	5c
6b	6c
38d	38e
38e	38f
39c	39d
39d	39f
39e	39g
D6b	D6c
D6ba	D6ca
D6bb	D6cb

Old	New
British Levant	
S4a	*Deleted*
Canada—Prince Edward Island	
31c	*Deleted*
Falkland Islands Dependencies	
G1a	G1aa
G2a	G2aa
G3a	G3aa
G4a	G4aa
G5a	G5aa
G6a	G6aa
G6ea	G6eaa
G7a	G7aa
G8a	G8aa
Fiji	
26aa	26b
26a	26c
26b	26d
26c	26e
26d	26f
26e	26g
Indian Convention States—Gwalior	
O52a	O52ba
Indian Feudatory States—Cochin	
O32b	*Deleted*
Malaya—Straits Settlements	
198a	198b
202a	202b
202as	202bs
202b	202c
202bs	202cs
202c	202d
243g	*Deleted*
Perak	
19a	19ab
105a	105b
Mauritius	
60a	59a
New Hebrides	
68/78	*Deleted*
D11/15	*Deleted*
F81/91	*Deleted*
FD92/6	*Deleted*

Old	New
New Zealand	
256b	256c
256ba	256ca
256bb	256cb
256bc	256cc
256bd	256cd
256c	256d
256ca	256da
North Borneo—Labuan	
99b	99c
Rhodesia	
51c	*Deleted*
85d	*Deleted*
Sierra Leone	
39c	*Deleted*
South Africa—Cape of Good Hope	
SB1	*Deleted*
SB2	SB1
New Republic	
79da	*Deleted*
81ca	*Deleted*
Transvaal	
173b	173c
173ba	173ca
173c	173d
Sudan	
3a	*Deleted*
4a	*Deleted*
SB3	*Deleted*
SB4	SB3
Virgin Islands	
22ab	22b

Contents

CONTENTS

General Philatelic Information

and Guidelines to the Scope of Part 1 (British Commonwealth) Catalogue

The notes which follow seek to reflect current practice in compiling the Part 1 (British Commonwealth) Catalogue.

It scarcely needs emphasising that the Stanley Gibbons Stamp Catalogue has a very long history and that the vast quantity of information it contains has been carefully built up by successive generations through the work of countless individuals. Philately is never static and the Catalogue has evolved and developed over the years. These notes relate to the current criteria upon which a stamp may be listed or priced. It should be recognised that these criteria have developed over time and may have differed somewhat in the early years of this catalogue. These notes are not intended to suggest that we plan to make wholesale changes to the listing of classic issues in order to bring them into line with today's listing policy, they are designed to inform catalogue users as to the policies currently in operation.

PRICES

The prices quoted in this Catalogue are the estimated selling prices of Stanley Gibbons Ltd at the time of publication. They are, unless it is specifically stated otherwise, for examples in fine condition for the issue concerned. Superb examples are worth more; those of a lower quality considerably less.

All prices are subject to change without prior notice and Stanley Gibbons Ltd may from time to time offer stamps below catalogue price. Individual low value stamps sold at 399, Strand are liable to an additional handling charge. Purchasers of new issues are asked to note the prices charged for them contain an element for the service rendered and so may exceed the prices shown when the stamps are subsequently catalogued. Postage and handling charges are extra.

No guarantee is given to supply all stamps priced, since it is not possible to keep every catalogued item in stock. Commemorative issues may, at times, only be available in complete sets and not as individual values.

Quotation of prices. The prices in the left-hand column are for unused stamps and those in the right-hand column are for used.

A dagger (†) denotes that the item listed does not exist in that condition and a blank, or dash, that it exists, or may exist, but we are unable to quote a price.

Prices are expressed in pounds and pence sterling. One pound comprises 100 pence (£1 = 100p).

The method of notation is as follows: pence in numerals (e.g. 10 denotes ten pence); pounds and pence, up to £100, in numerals (e.g. 4.25 denotes four pounds and twenty-five pence); prices above £100 are expressed in whole pounds with the '£' sign shown.

Unused stamps. Great Britain and Commonwealth: the prices for unused stamps of Queen Victoria to King George V are for lightly hinged examples. Unused prices for King Edward VIII and King George VI issues are for unmounted mint.

Some stamps from the King George VI period are often difficult to find in unmounted mint condition. In such instances we would expect that collectors would need to pay a high proportion of the price quoted to obtain mounted mint examples. Generally speaking lightly mounted mint stamps from this reign, issued before 1945, are in considerable demand.

Used stamps. The used prices are normally for stamps postally used but may be for stamps cancelled-to-order where this practice exists.

A pen-cancellation on early issues can sometimes correctly denote postal use. Instances are individually noted in the Catalogue in explanation of the used price given.

Prices quoted for bisects on cover or large piece are for those dated during the period officially authorised.

Stamps not sold unused to the public (e.g. some official stamps) are priced used only.

The use of 'unified' designs, that is stamps inscribed for both postal and fiscal purposes, results in a number of stamps of very high face value. In some instances these may not have been primarily intended for postal purposes, but if they are so inscribed we include them. We only price such items used, however, where there is evidence of normal postal usage.

Cover prices. To assist collectors, cover prices are quoted for issues up to 1945 at the beginning of each country.

The system gives a general guide in the form of a factor by which the corresponding used price of the basic loose stamp should be multiplied when found in fine average condition on cover.

Care is needed in applying the factors and they relate to a cover which bears a single of the denomination listed; if more than one denomination is present the most highly priced attracts the multiplier and the remainder are priced at the simple figure for used singles in arriving at a total.

The cover should be of non-philatelic origin; bearing the correct postal rate for the period and distance involved and cancelled with the markings normal to the offices concerned. Purely philatelic items have a cover value only slightly greater than the catalogue value for the corresponding used stamps. This applies generally to those high-value stamps used philatelically rather than in the normal course of commerce. Low-value stamps, e.g. ¼d. and ½d., are desirable when used as a single rate on cover and merit an increase in 'multiplier' value.

First day covers in the period up to 1945 are not within the scope of the system and the multiplier should not be used. As a special category of philatelic usage, with wide variations in valuation according to scarcity, they require separate treatment.

Oversized covers, difficult to accommodate on an album page, should be reckoned as worth little more than the corresponding value of the used stamps. The condition of a cover also affects its value. Except for 'wreck covers', serious damage or soiling reduce the value where the postal markings and stamps are ordinary ones. Conversely, visual appeal adds to the value and this can include freshness of appearance, important addresses, old-fashioned but legible handwriting, historic town-names, etc.

The multipliers are a base on which further value would be added to take account of the cover's postal historical importance in demonstrating such things as unusual, scarce or emergency cancels, interesting routes, significant postal markings, combination usage, the development of postal rates, and so on.

For Great Britain, rather than multiplication factors, the cover price is shown as a third column, following the prices for unused and used stamps. It is hoped to extend these prices beyond King Edward VII in subsequent editions.

Minimum price. The minimum catalogue price quoted is 10p. For individual stamps prices between 10p. and 45p. are provided as a guide for catalogue users. The lowest price charged for individual stamps or sets purchased from Stanley Gibbons Ltd is 50p.

Set prices. Set prices are generally for one of each value, excluding shades and varieties, but including major colour changes. Where there are alternative shades, etc., the cheapest is usually included. The number of stamps in the set is always stated for clarity. The mint prices for sets containing *se-tenant* pieces are based on the prices quoted for such combinations, and not on those for the individual stamps.

Varieties. Where plate or cylinder varieties are priced in a used condition the price quoted is for a fine used example with the cancellation well clear of the listed flaw.

Specimen stamps. The pricing of these items is explained under that heading.

Stamp booklets. Prices are for complete assembled booklets in fine condition with those issued before 1945 showing normal wear and tear. Incomplete booklets and those which have been 'exploded' will, in general, be worth less than the figure quoted.

Repricing. Collectors will be aware that the market factors of supply and demand directly influence the prices quoted in this Catalogue. Whatever the scarcity of a particular stamp, if there is no one in the market who wishes to buy it cannot be expected to achieve a high price. Conversely, the same item actively sought by numerous potential buyers may cause the price to rise.

All the prices in this Catalogue are examined during the preparation of each new edition by the expert staff of Stanley Gibbons and repriced as necessary. They take many factors into account, including supply and demand, and are in close touch with the international stamp market and the auction world.

Commonwealth cover prices and advice on postal history material originally provided by Edward B Proud.

GUARANTEE

All stamps are guaranteed originals in the following terms:

If not as described, and returned by the purchaser, we undertake to refund the price paid to us in the original transaction. If any stamp is certified as genuine by the Expert Committee of the Royal Philatelic Society, London, or by BPA Expertising Ltd, the purchaser shall not be entitled to make any claim against us for any error, omission or mistake in such certificate.

Consumers' statutory rights are not affected by the above guarantee.

The recognised Expert Committees in this country are those of the Royal Philatelic Society, 41 Devonshire Place, London W1G 6JY, and BPA Expertising Ltd, PO Box 137, Leatherhead, Surrey KT22 0RG. They do not undertake valuations under any circumstances and fees are payable for their services.

CONDITION GUIDE

To assist collectors in assessing the true value of items they are considering buying or in reviewing stamps already in their collections, we now offer a more detailed guide to the condition of stamps on which this catalogue's prices are based

For a stamp to be described as 'Fine', it should be sound in all respects, without creases, bends, wrinkles, pin holes, thins or tears. If perforated, all perforation 'teeth' should be intact, it should not suffer from fading, rubbing or toning and it should be of clean, fresh appearance.

Margins on imperforate stamps: These should be even on all sides and should be at least as wide as half the distance between that stamp and the next. To have one or more margins of less than this width, would normally preclude a stamp from being described as 'Fine'. It should be remembered that some early stamps were positioned very close together on the printing plate and in such cases 'Fine' margins would necessarily be narrow. On the other hand, some plates were laid down to give a substantial gap between individual stamps and in such cases margins would be expected to be much wider.

An 'average' four-margin example would have a narrower margin on one or more sides and should be priced accordingly, while a stamp with wider, yet even, margins than 'Fine' would merit the description 'Very Fine' or 'Superb' and, if available, would command a price in excess of that quoted in the catalogue.

Gum: Since the prices for stamps of King Edward VIII and King George VI are for 'unmounted' or 'never hinged' mint, it should be anticipated that even stamps from these reigns which have been very lightly mounted should be available at a discount from catalogue price, the more obvious the hinge marks, the greater the discount,

Catalogue prices for stamps issued prior to King Edward VIII's reign are for mounted mint, so unmounted examples would be worth a premium, Hinge marks on 20th century stamps should not be too obtrusive, and should be at least in the lightly hinged category. For 19th century stamps more obvious hinging would be acceptable, but stamps should still carry a large part of their original gum—'Large part o.g.'—in order to be described as 'Fine'.

Centring: Ideally, the stamp's image should appear in the exact centre of the perforated area, giving equal margins on all sides. 'Fine' centring would be close to this ideal with any deviation having an effect on the value of the stamp. As in the case if the margins on imperforate stamps, it should be borne in mind that the space between some early stamps was very narrow, so it was very difficult to achieve accurate perforation, especially when the technology was in its infancy. Thus, poor centring would have a less damaging effect on the value of a 19th century stamp than on a 20th century example, but the premium put on a perfectly centred specimen would be greater.

Cancellations: Early cancellation devices were designed to 'obliterate' the stamp in order to prevent it being reused and this is still an important objective for today's postal administrations. Stamp collectors, on the other hand, prefer postmarks to be lightly applied, clear, and to leave as much as possible of the design visible. Dated, circular cancellations have long been 'the postmark of choice', but the definition of a 'Fine' cancellation will depend upon the types of cancellation in use at the time a stamp was current—it is clearly illogical to seek a circular datestamp. on a Penny Black.

'Fine', by definition, will be superior to 'Average', so, in terms of cancellation quality, if one begins by identifying what 'Average' looks like, then one will be half way to identifying 'Fine'. The illustrations will give some guidance on mid-19th century and mid-20th century cancellations of Great Britain, but types of cancellation in general use in each country and in each period will determine the appearance of 'Fine'.

As for the factors discussed above, anything less than 'Fine' will result in a downgrading of the stamp concerned, while a very fine or superb cancellation will be worth a premium.

Combining the factors: To merit the description 'Fine', a stamp should be fine in every respect, but a small deficiency in one area might be made up for in another by a factor meriting an 'Extremely Fine' description.

Some early issues are so seldom found in what would normally be considered to be 'Fine' condition, the catalogue prices are for a slightly lower grade, with 'Fine' examples being worth a premium. In such cases a note to this effect is given in the catalogue, while elsewhere premiums are given for well-centred, lightly cancelled examples.

It should be emphasised that stamps graded at less than fine remain collectable and, in the case of more highly priced stamps will continue to hold a value. Nevertheless, buyers should always bear condition in mind.

MARGINS ON IMPERFORATE STAMPS

Superb

Very fine

Fine

Average

Poor

GUM

Unmounted

Very lightly mounted

Lightly mounted

Mounted/large part original gum (o.g.)

Heavily mounted/ small part o.g.

CENTRING

Superb

Very fine

Fine

Average

Poor

CANCELLATIONS

Superb

Very fine

Fine

Average

Poor

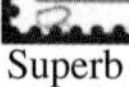
Superb

Very fine

Fine

Average

Poor

THE CATALOGUE IN GENERAL

Contents. The Catalogue is confined to adhesive postage stamps, including miniature sheets. For particular categories the rules are:

(a) Revenue (fiscal) stamps or telegraph stamps are listed only where they have been expressly authorised for postal duty.

(b) Stamps issued only precancelled are included, but normally issued stamps available additionally with precancel have no separate precancel listing unless the face value is changed.

(c) Stamps prepared for use but not issued, hitherto accorded full listing, are nowadays foot-noted with a price (where possible).

(d) Bisects (trisects, etc.) are only listed where such usage was officially authorised.

(e) Stamps issued only on first day covers or in presentation packs and not available separately are not listed but may be priced in a footnote.

(f) New printings are only included in this Catalogue where they show a major philatelic variety, such as a change in shade, watermark or paper. Stamps which exist with or without imprint dates are listed separately; changes in imprint dates are mentioned in footnotes.

(g) Official and unofficial reprints are dealt with by footnote.

(h) Stamps from imperforate printings of modern issues which occur perforated are covered by footnotes, but are listed where widely available for postal use.

Exclusions. The following are excluded: (a) non-postal revenue or fiscal stamps; (b) postage stamps used fiscally; (c) local carriage labels and private local issues; (d) bogus or phantom stamps; (f) railway or airline letter fee stamps, bus or road transport company labels; (g) cut-outs; (h) all types of non-postal labels and souvenirs; (i) documentary labels for the postal service, e.g. registration, recorded delivery, air-mail etiquettes, etc.; (j) privately applied embellishments to official issues and privately commissioned items generally; (k) stamps for training postal officers.

Full listing. 'Full listing' confers our recognition and implies allotting a catalogue number and (wherever possible) a price quotation.

In judging status for inclusion in the catalogue broad considerations are applied to stamps. They must be issued by a legitimate postal authority, recognised by the government concerned, and must be adhesives valid for proper postal use in the class of service for which they are inscribed. Stamps, with the exception of such categories as postage dues and officials, must be available to the general public, at face value, in reasonable quantities without any artificial restrictions being imposed on their distribution.

For errors and varieties the criterion is legitimate (albeit inadvertent) sale through a postal administration in the normal course of business. Details of provenance are always important; printers' waste and deliberately manufactured material are excluded.

Certificates. In assessing unlisted items due weight is given to Certificates from recognised Expert Committees and, where appropriate, we will usually ask to see them.

Date of issue. Where local issue dates differ from dates of release by agencies, 'date of issue' is the local date. Fortuitous stray usage before the officially intended date is disregarded in listing.

Catalogue numbers. Stamps of each country are catalogued chronologically by date of issue. Subsidiary classes are placed at the end of the country, as separate lists, with a distinguishing letter prefix to the catalogue number, e.g. D for postage due, O for official and E for express delivery stamps.

The catalogue number appears in the extreme left column. The boldface Type numbers in the next column are merely cross-references to illustrations.

Once published in the Catalogue, numbers are changed as little as possible; really serious renumbering is reserved for the occasions when a complete country or an entire issue is being rewritten. The edition first affected includes cross-reference tables of old and new numbers.

Our catalogue numbers are universally recognised in specifying stamps and as a hallmark of status.

Illustrations. Stamps are illustrated at three-quarters linear size. Stamps not illustrated are the same size and format as the value shown, unless otherwise indicated. Stamps issued only as miniature sheets have the stamp alone illustrated but sheet size is also quoted. Overprints, surcharges, watermarks and postmarks are normally actual size. Illustrations of varieties are often enlarged to show the detail. Stamp booklet covers are illustrated half-size, unless otherwise indicated.

Designers. Designers' names are quoted where known, though space precludes naming every individual concerned in the production of a set. In particular, photographers supplying material are usually named only where they also make an active contribution in the design stage; posed photographs of reigning monarchs are, however, an exception to this rule.

CONTACTING THE CATALOGUE EDITOR

The editor is always interested in hearing from people who have new information which will improve or correct the Catalogue. As a general rule he must see and examine the actual stamps before they can be considered for listing; photographs or photocopies are insufficient evidence.

Submissions should be made in writing to the Catalogue Editor, Stanley Gibbons Publications at the Ringwood office. The cost of return postage for items submitted is appreciated, and this should include the registration fee if required.

Where information is solicited purely for the benefit of the enquirer, the editor cannot undertake to reply if the answer is already contained in these published notes or if return postage is omitted. Written communications are greatly preferred to enquiries by telephone and the editor regrets that he or his staff cannot see personal callers without a prior appointment being made. Correspondence may be subject to delay during the production period of each new edition.

The editor welcomes close contact with study circles and is interested, too, in finding reliable local correspondents who will verify and supplement official information in countries where this is deficient.

We regret we do not give opinions as to the genuineness of stamps, nor do we identify stamps or number them by our Catalogue.

TECHNICAL MATTERS

The meanings of the technical terms used in the catalogue will be found in our *Philatelic Terms Illustrated*.

References below to (more specialised) listings are to be taken to indicate, as appropriate, the Stanley Gibbons *Great Britain Specialised Catalogue* in five volumes or the *Great Britain Concise Catalogue*.

1. Printing

Printing errors. Errors in printing are of major interest to the Catalogue. Authenticated items meriting consideration would include: background, centre or frame inverted or omitted; centre or subject transposed; error of colour; error or omission of value; double prints and impressions; printed both sides; and so on. Designs *tête-bêche*, whether intentionally or by accident, are listable. *Se-tenant* arrangements of stamps are recognised in the listings or footnotes. Gutter pairs (a pair of stamps separated by blank margin) are not included in this volume. Colours only partially omitted are not listed. Stamps with embossing omitted are reserved for our more specialised listings.

Printing varieties. Listing is accorded to major changes in the printing base which lead to completely new types. In recess-printing this could be a design re-engraved; in photogravure or photolithography a screen altered in whole or in part. It can also encompass flat-bed and rotary printing if the results are readily distinguishable.

To be considered at all, varieties must be constant.

Early stamps, produced by primitive methods, were prone to numerous imperfections; the lists reflect this, recognising re-entries, retouches, broken frames, misshapen letters, and so on. Printing technology has, however, radically improved over the years, during which time photogravure and lithography have become predominant. Varieties nowadays are more in the nature of flaws and these, being too specialised for this general catalogue, are almost always outside the scope. The development of our range of specialised catalogues allows us now to list those items which have philatelic significance in their appropriate volume.

In no catalogue, however, do we list such items as: dry prints, kiss prints, doctor-blade flaws, colour shifts or registration flaws (unless they lead to the complete omission of a colour from an individual stamp), lithographic ring flaws, and so on. Neither do we recognise fortuitous happenings like paper creases or confetti flaws.

Overprints (and surcharges). Overprints of different types qualify for separate listing. These include overprints in different colours; overprints from different printing processes such as litho and typo; overprints in totally different typefaces, etc. Major errors in machine-printed overprints are important and listable. They include: overprint inverted or omitted; overprint double (treble, etc.); overprint diagonal; overprint double, one inverted; pairs with one overprint omitted, e.g. from a radical shift to an adjoining stamp; error of colour; error of type fount; letters inverted or omitted, etc. If the overprint is handstamped, few of these would qualify and a distinction is drawn. We continue, however, to list pairs of stamps where one has a handstamped overprint and the other has not.

Varieties occurring in overprints will often take the form of broken letters, slight differences in spacing, rising spaces, etc. Only the most important would be considered for footnote mention.

Sheet positions. If space permits we quote sheet positions of listed varieties and authenticated data is solicited for this purpose.

De La Rue plates. The Catalogue classifies the general plates used by De La Rue for printing British Colonial stamps as follows:

VICTORIAN KEY TYPE

Die I

1. The ball of decoration on the second point of the crown appears as a dark mass of lines.
2. Dark vertical shading separates the front hair from the bun.
3. The vertical line of colour outlining the front of the throat stops at the sixth line of shading on the neck.
4. The white space in the coil of the hair above the curl is roughly the shape of a pin's head.

Die II

1. There are very few lines of colour in the ball and it appears almost white.
2. A white vertical strand of hair appears in place of the dark shading.
3. The line stops at the eighth line of shading.
4. The white space is oblong, with a line of colour partially dividing it at the left end.

Plates numbered 1 and 2 are both Die I. Plates 3 and 4 are Die II.

GEORGIAN KEY TYPE

Die I

A. The second (thick) line below the name of the country is cut slanting, conforming roughly to the shape of the crown on each side.
B. The labels of solid colour bearing the words "POSTAGE" and "& REVENUE" are square at the inner top corners.
C. There is a projecting "bud" on the outer spiral of the ornament in each of the lower corners.

Die II

A. The second line is cut vertically on each side of the crown.
B. The labels curve inwards at the top.
C. There is no "bud" in this position.

Unless otherwise stated in the lists, all stamps with watermark Multiple Crown CA (w **8**) are Die I while those with watermark Multiple Crown Script CA (w **9**) are Die II. The Georgian Die II was introduced in April 1921 and was used for Plates 10 to 22 and 26 to 28. Plates 23 to 25 were made from Die I by mistake.

2. Paper

All stamps listed are deemed to be on (ordinary) paper of the wove type and white in colour; only departures from this are normally mentioned.

Types. Where classification so requires we distinguish such other types of paper as, for example, vertically and horizontally laid; wove and laid bâtonné; card(board); carton; cartridge; glazed; granite; native; pelure; porous; quadrillé; ribbed; rice; and silk thread.

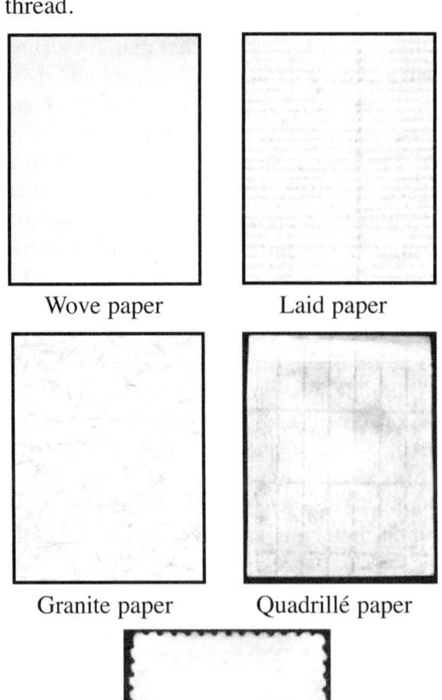
Wove paper Laid paper
Granite paper Quadrillé paper
Burelé band

The various makeshifts for normal paper are listed as appropriate. The varieties of double paper and joined paper are recognised. The security device of a printed burelé band on the back of a stamp, as in early Queensland, qualifies for listing.

Descriptive terms. The fact that a paper is handmade (and thus probably of uneven thickness) is mentioned where necessary. Such descriptive terms as "hard" and "soft"; "smooth" and "rough"; "thick", "medium" and "thin" are applied where there is philatelic merit in classifying papers.

Coloured, very white and toned papers. A coloured paper is one that is coloured right through (front and back of the stamp). In the Catalogue the colour of the paper is given in italics, thus:
black/*rose* = black design on rose paper.

Papers have been made specially white in recent years by, for example, a very heavy coating of chalk. We do not classify shades of whiteness of paper as distinct varieties. There does exist, however, a type of paper from early days called toned. This is off-white, often brownish or buffish, but it cannot be assigned any definite colour. A toning effect brought on by climate, incorrect storage or gum staining is disregarded here, as this was not the state of the paper when issued.

"Ordinary" and "Chalk-surfaced" papers. The availability of many postage stamps for revenue purposes made necessary some safeguard against the illegitimate re-use of stamps with removable cancellations. This was at first secured by using fugitive inks and later by printing on paper surfaced by coatings containing either chalk or china clay, both of which made it difficult to remove any form of obliteration without damaging the stamp design.

This catalogue lists these chalk-surfaced paper varieties from their introduction in 1905. Where no indication is given, the paper is "ordinary".

Our chalk-surfaced paper is specifically one which shows a black mark when touched with a silver wire. The paper used during the Second World War for high values, as in Bermuda, the Leeward Islands, etc., was thinly coated with some kind of surfacing which does not react to silver and is therefore regarded (and listed) as "ordinary". Stamps on chalk-surfaced paper can easily lose this coating through immersion in water.

Another paper introduced during the War as a substitute for chalk-surfaced is rather thick, very white and glossy and shows little or no watermark, nor does it show a black line when touched with silver. In the Bahamas high values this paper might be mistaken for the chalk-surfaced (which is thinner and poorer-looking) but for the silver test.

Some modern coated papers show little or no reaction to the silver test and, therefore, cannot be classed as chalk-surfaced.

Green and yellow papers. Issues of the First World War and immediate postwar period occur on green and yellow papers and these are given separate Catalogue listing. The original coloured papers (coloured throughout) gave way to surface-coloured papers, the stamps having "white backs"; other stamps show one colour on the front and a different one at the back. Because of the numerous variations a grouping of colours is adopted as follows:

YELLOW PAPERS

(1) The original *yellow* paper (throughout), usually bright in colour. The gum is often sparse, of harsh consistency and dull-looking. Used 1912–1920.

(2) The *white-backs*. Used 1913–1914.

(3) A bright *lemon* paper. The colour must have a pronounced greenish tinge, different from the "yellow" in (1). As a rule, the gum on stamps using this lemon paper is plentiful, smooth and shiny, and the watermark shows distinctly. Care is needed with stamps printed in green on yellow paper (1) as it may appear that the paper is this lemon. Used 1914–1916.

(4) An experimental *orange-buff* paper. The colour must have a distinct brownish tinge. It is not to be confused with a muddy yellow (1) nor the misleading appearance (on the surface) of stamps printed in red on yellow paper where an engraved plate has been insufficiently wiped. Used 1918–1921.

(5) An experimental *buff* paper. This lacks the brownish tinge of (4) and the brightness of the yellow shades. The gum is shiny when compared with the matt type used on (4). Used 1919–1920.

(6) A *pale yellow* paper that has a creamy tone to the yellow. Used from 1920 onwards.

GREEN PAPERS

(7) The original "green" paper, varying considerably through shades of blue-green and yellow-green, the front and back sometimes differing. Used 1912–1916.

(8) The *white backs*. Used 1913–1914.

(9) A paper blue-green on the surface with *pale olive* back. The back must be markedly paler than the front and this and the pronounced olive tinge to the back distinguish it from (7). Used 1916–1920.

(10) Paper with a vivid green surface, commonly called *emerald-green*; it has the olive back of (9). Used 1920.

(11) Paper with *emerald-green* both back and front. Used from 1920 onwards.

3. Perforation and Rouletting

Perforation gauge. The gauge of a perforation is the number of holes in a length of 2 cm. For correct classification the size of the holes (large or small) may need to be distinguished; in a few cases the actual number of holes on each edge of the stamp needs to be quoted.

Measurement. The Gibbons *Instanta* gauge is the standard for measuring perforations. The stamp is viewed against a dark background with the transparent gauge put on top of it. Though the gauge measures to decimal accuracy, perforations read from it are generally quoted in the Catalogue to the nearest half. For example:

Just over perf $12\frac{3}{4}$ to just under $13\frac{1}{4}$ = perf 13
Perf $13\frac{1}{4}$ exactly, rounded up = perf $13\frac{1}{2}$
Just over perf $13\frac{1}{4}$ to just under $13\frac{3}{4}$ = perf $13\frac{1}{2}$
Perf $13\frac{3}{4}$ exactly, rounded up = perf 14

However, where classification depends on it, actual quarter-perforations are quoted.

Notation. Where no perforation is quoted for an issue it is imperforate. Perforations are usually abbreviated (and spoken) as follows, though sometimes they may be spelled out for clarity. This notation for rectangular stamps (the majority) applies to diamond shapes if "top" is read as the edge to the top right.

P 14: perforated alike on all sides (read: "perf 14").

P 14×15: the first figure refers to top and bottom, the second to left and right sides (read: "perf 14 by 15"). This is a compound perforation. For an upright triangular stamp the first figure refers to the two sloping sides and second to the base. In inverted triangulars the base is first and the second figure to the sloping sides.

P 14–15: perforation measuring anything between 14 and 15: the holes are irregularly spaced, thus the gauge may vary along a single line or even along a single edge of the stamp (read: "perf 14 to 15").

P 14 *irregular*: perforated 14 from a worn perforator, giving badly aligned holes irregularly spaced (read: "irregular perf 14").

P comp(ound) 14×15: two gauges in use but not necessarily on opposite sides of the stamp. It could be one side in one gauge and three in the other; or two adjacent sides with the same gauge. (Read: "perf compound of 14 and 15".) For three gauges or more, abbreviated as "*P* 12, 14½, 15 *or compound*" for example.

P 14, 14½: perforated approximately 14¼ (read: "perf 14 or 14¼"). It does *not* mean two stamps, one perf 14 and the other perf 14½. This obsolescent notation is gradually being replaced in the Catalogue.

Imperf: imperforate (not perforated)

Imperf×*P* 14: imperforate at top ad bottom and perf 14 at sides.

P 14×*imperf*: perf 14 at top and bottom and imperforate at sides.

Such headings as "*P* 13×14 (*vert*) and *P* 14×13 (*horiz*)" indicate which perforations apply to which stamp format—vertical or horizontal.

Some stamps are additionally perforated so that a label or tab is detachable; others have been perforated for use as two halves. Listings are normally for whole stamps, unless stated otherwise.

Imperf×perf

Other terms. Perforation almost always gives circular holes; where other shapes have been used they are specified, e.g. square holes; lozenge perf. Interrupted perfs are brought about by the omission of pins at regular intervals. Perforations merely simulated by being printed as part of the design are of course ignored. With few exceptions, privately applied perforations are not listed.

In the 19th century perforations are often described as clean cut (clean, sharply incised holes), intermediate or rough (rough holes, imperfectly cut, often the result of blunt pins).

Perforation errors and varieties. Authenticated errors, where a stamp normally perforated is accidentally issued imperforate, are listed provided no traces of perforation (blind holes or indentations) remain. They must be provided as pairs, both stamps wholly imperforate, and are only priced in that form.

Stamps imperforate between stamp and sheet margin are not listed in this catalogue, but such errors on Great Britain stamps will be found in the *Great Britain Specialised Catalogue*.

Pairs described as "imperforate between" have the line of perforations between the two stamps omitted.

Imperf between (*horiz pair*): a horizontal pair of stamps with perfs all around the edges but none between the stamps.

Imperf between (*vert pair*): a vertical pair of stamps with perfs all around the edges but none between the stamps.

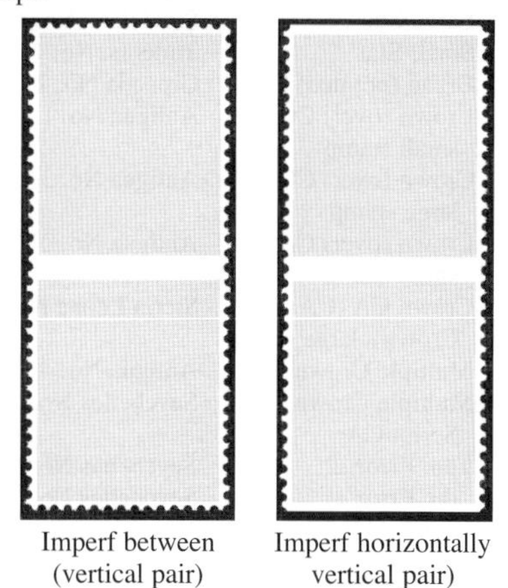

Imperf between (vertical pair) | Imperf horizontally vertical pair)

Where several of the rows have escaped perforation the resulting varieties are listable. Thus:

Imperf vert (*horiz pair*): a horizontal pair of stamps perforated top and bottom; all three vertical directions are imperf—the two outer edges and between the stamps.

Imperf horiz (*vert pair*): a vertical pair perforated at left and right edges; all three horizontal directions are imperf—the top, bottom and between the stamps.

Straight edges. Large sheets cut up before issue to post offices can cause stamps with straight edges, i.e. imperf on one side or on two sides at right angles. They are not usually listable in this condition and are worth less than corresponding stamps properly perforated all round. This does not, however, apply to certain stamps, mainly from coils and booklets, where straight edges on various sides are the manufacturing norm affecting every stamp. The listings and notes make clear which sides are correctly imperf.

Malfunction. Varieties of double, misplaced or partial perforation caused by error or machine malfunction are not listable, neither are freaks, such as perforations placed diagonally from paper folds, nor missing holes caused by broken pins.

Types of perforating. Where necessary for classification, perforation types are distinguished.

These include:

Line perforation from one line of pins punching single rows of holes at a time.

Comb perforation from pins disposed across the sheet in comb formation, punching out holes at three sides of the stamp a row at a time.

Harrow perforation applied to a whole pane or sheet at one stroke.

Rotary perforation from toothed wheels operating across a sheet, then crosswise.

Sewing machine perforation. The resultant condition, clean-cut or rough, is distinguished where required.

Pin-perforation is the commonly applied term for pin-roulette in which, instead of being punched out, round holes are pricked by sharp-pointed pins and no paper is removed.

Mixed perforation occurs when stamps with defective perforations are re-perforated in a different gauge.

Punctured stamps. Perforation holes can be punched into the face of the stamp. Patterns of small holes, often in the shape of initial letters, are privately applied devices against pilferage. These (perfins) are outside the scope except for Australia, Canada, Cape of Good Hope, Papua and Sudan where they were used as official stamps by the national administration. Identification devices, when officially inspired, are listed or noted; they can be shapes, or letters or words formed from holes, sometimes converting one class of stamp into another.

Rouletting. In rouletting the paper is cut, for ease of separation, but none is removed. The gauge is measured, when needed, as for perforations. Traditional French terms descriptive of the type of cut are often used and types include:

Arc roulette (*percé en arc*). Cuts are minute, spaced arcs, each roughly a semicircle.

Cross roulette (*percé en croix*). Cuts are tiny diagonal crosses.

Line roulette (*percé en ligne* or *en ligne droite*). Short straight cuts parallel to the frame of the stamp. The commonest basic roulette. Where not further described, "roulette" means this type.

Rouletted in colour or coloured roulette (*percé en lignes colorées* or *en lignes de coleur*). Cuts with coloured edges, arising from notched rule inked simultaneously with the printing plate.

Saw-tooth roulette (*percé en scie*). Cuts applied zigzag fashion to resemble the teeth of a saw.

Serpentine roulette (*percé en serpentin*). Cuts as sharply wavy lines.

Zigzag roulette (*percé en zigzags*). Short straight cuts at angles in alternate directions, producing sharp points on separation. US usage favours "serrate(d) roulette" for this type.

Pin-roulette (originally *percé en points* and now *perforés trous d'epingle*) is commonly called pin-perforation in English.

4. Gum

All stamps listed are assumed to have gum of some kind; if they were issued without gum this is stated. Original gum (o.g.) means that which was present on the stamp as issued to the public. Deleterious climates and the presence of certain chemicals can cause gum to crack and, with early stamps, even make the paper deteriorate. Unscrupulous fakers are adept in removing it and regumming the stamp to meet the unreasoning demand often made for "full o.g." in cases where such a thing is virtually impossible.

5. Watermarks

Stamps are on unwatermarked paper except where the heading to the set says otherwise.

Detection. Watermarks are detected for Catalogue description by one of four methods: (1) holding stamps to the light; (2) laying stamps face down on a dark background; (3) adding a few drops of petroleum ether 40/60 to the stamp laid face down in a watermark tray; (4) by use of the Morley-Bright Detector, or other equipment, which work by revealing the thinning of the paper at the watermark. (Note that petroleum ether is highly inflammable in use and can damage photogravure stamps.)

Listable types. Stamps occurring on both watermarked and unwatermarked papers are different types and both receive full listing.

Single watermarks (devices occurring once on every stamp) can be modified in size and shape as between different issues; the types are noted but not usually separately listed. Fortuitous absence of watermark from a single stamp or its gross displacement would not be listable.

To overcome registration difficulties the device may be repeated at close intervals (a *multiple watermark*), single stamps thus showing parts of several devices. Similarly, a large *sheet watermark* (or *all-over watermark*) covering numerous stamps can be used. We give informative notes and illustrations for them. The designs may be such that numbers of stamps in the sheet automatically lack watermark: this is not a listable variety. Multiple and all-over watermarks sometimes undergo modifications, but if the various types are difficult to distinguish from single stamps notes are given but not separate listings.

Papermakers' watermarks are noted where known but not listed separately, since most stamps in the sheet will lack them. Sheet watermarks which are nothing more than officially adopted papermakers' watermarks are, however, given normal listing.

Marginal watermarks, falling outside the pane of stamps, are ignored except where misplacement caused the adjoining row to be affected, in which case they are footnoted.

Watermark errors and varieties. Watermark errors are recognised as of major importance. They comprise stamps intended to be on unwatermarked paper but issued watermarked by mistake, or stamps printed on paper with the wrong watermark. Varieties showing letters omitted from the watermark are also included, but broken or deformed bits on the dandy roll are not listed unless they represent repairs.

Watermark positions. The diagram shows how watermark position is described in the Catalogue. Paper has a side intended for printing and watermarks are usually impressed so that they read normally when looked through from that printed side. However, since philatelists customarily detect watermarks by looking at the back of the stamp the watermark diagram also makes clear what is actually seen.

Illustrations in the Catalogue are of watermarks in normal positions (from the front of the stamps) and are actual size where possible.

Differences in watermark position are collectable varieties. This Catalogue now lists inverted, sideways inverted and reversed watermark varieties on Commonwealth stamps from the 1860s onwards except where the watermark position is completely haphazard.

Great Britain inverted and sideways inverted watermarks can be found in the *Great Britain Specialised Catalogue* and the *Great Britain Concise Catalogue*.

Where a watermark comes indiscriminately in various positions our policy is to cover this by a general note: we do not give separate listings because the watermark position in these circumstances has no particular philatelic importance.

AS DESCRIBED (Read through front of stamp)		AS SEEN DURING WATERMARK DETECTION (Stamp face down and back examined)
GvR	Normal	
	Inverted	
	Reversed	GvR
	Inverted and reversed	
	Sideways	
	Sideways inverted	

Standard types of watermark. Some watermarks have been used generally for various British possessions rather than exclusively for a single colony. To avoid repetition the Catalogue classifies 11 general types, as under, with references in the headings throughout the listings being given either in words or in the form ("*W* w **9**") (meaning "watermark type w **9**"). In those cases where watermark illustrations appear in the listings themselves, the respective reference reads, for example, *W* **153**, thus indicating that the watermark will be found in the normal sequence of illustrations as (type) **153**.

The general types are as follows, with an example of each quoted.

W	*Description*	*Example*
w **1**	Large Star	St. Helena No. 1
w **2**	Small Star	Turks Is. No. 4
w **3**	Broad (pointed) Star	Grenada No. 24
w **4**	Crown (over) CC, small stamp	Antigua No. 13
w **5**	Crown (over) CC, large stamp	Antigua No. 31
w **6**	Crown (over) CA, small stamp	Antigua No. 21
w **7**	Crown CA (CA over Crown), large stamp	Sierra Leone No. 54
w **8**	Multiple Crown CA	Antigua No. 41
w **9**	Multiple Crown Script CA	Seychelles No. 158
w **9***a*	do. Error	Seychelles No. 158a
w **9***b*	do. Error	Seychelles No. 158b
w **10**	V over Crown	N.S.W. No. 327
w **11**	Crown over A	N.S.W. No. 347

CC in these watermarks is an abbreviation for "Crown Colonies" and CA for "Crown Agents". Watermarks w **1**, w **2** and w **3** are on stamps printed by Perkins, Bacon; w **4** onwards on stamps from De La Rue and other printers.

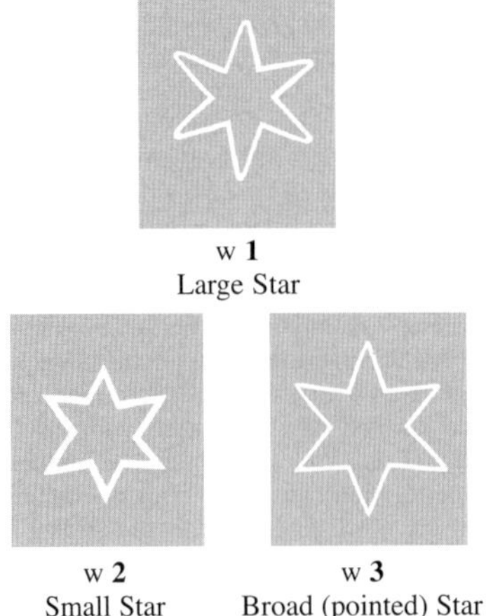

w **1**
Large Star

w **2**
Small Star

w **3**
Broad (pointed) Star

Watermark w **1**, *Large Star*, measures 15 to 16 mm across the star from point to point and about 27 mm from centre to centre vertically between stars in the sheet. It was made for long stamps like Ceylon 1857 and St. Helena 1856.

Watermark w **2**, *Small Star* is of similar design but measures 12 to 13½mm from point to point and 24 mm from centre to centre vertically. It was for use with ordinary-size stamps such as Grenada 1863–71.

When the Large Star watermark was used with the smaller stamps it only occasionally comes in the centre of the paper. It is frequently so misplaced as to show portions of two stars above and below and this eccentricity will very often help in determining the watermark.

Watermark w **3**, *Broad (pointed) Star*, resembles w **1** but the points are broader.

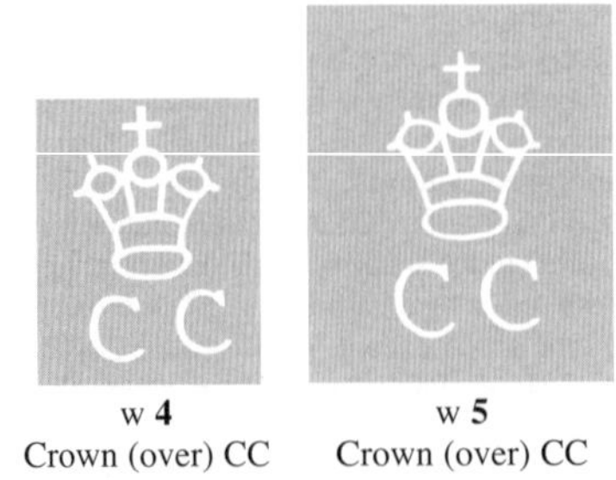

w **4**
Crown (over) CC

w **5**
Crown (over) CC

Two *Crown (over) CC* watermarks were used: w **4** was for stamps of ordinary size and w **5** for those of larger size.

w **6**
Crown (over) CA

w **7**
CA over Crown

Two watermarks of *Crown CA* type were used, w **6** being for stamps of ordinary size. The other, w **7**, is properly described as CA over Crown. It was specially made for paper on which it was intended to print long fiscal stamps: that some were used postally accounts for the appearance of w **7** in the Catalogue. The watermark occupies twice the space of the ordinary Crown CA watermark, w **6**. Stamps of normal size printed on paper with w **7** watermark show it sideways; it takes a horizontal pair of stamps to show the entire watermark.

w **8**
Multiple Crown CA

w **9**
Multiple Crown Script CA

Multiple watermarks began in 1904 with w **8**, *Multiple Crown CA*, changed from 1921 to w **9**, *Multiple Crown Script CA*. On stamps of ordinary size portions of two or three watermarks appear and on the large-sized stamps a greater number can be observed. The change to letters in script character with w **9** was accompanied by a Crown of distinctly different shape.

It seems likely that there were at least two dandy rolls for each Crown Agents watermark in use at any one time with a reserve roll being employed when the normal one was withdrawn for maintenance or repair. Both the Mult Crown CA and the Mult Script CA types exist with one or other of the letters omitted from individual impressions. It is possible that most of these occur from the reserve rolls as they have only been found on certain issues. The MCA watermark experienced such problems during the early 1920s and the Script over a longer period from the early 1940s until 1951.

During the 1920s damage must also have occurred on one of the Crowns as a substituted Crown has been found on certain issues. This is smaller than the normal and consists of an oval base joined to two upright ovals with a circle positioned between their upper ends. The upper line of the Crown's base is omitted, as are the left and right-hand circles at the top and also the cross over the centre circle.

Substituted Crown

The *Multiple Crown Script CA* watermark, w **9**, is known with two errors, recurring among the 1950–52 printings of several territories. In the first a crown has fallen away from the dandy-roll that impresses the watermark into the paper pulp. It gives w **9***a*, *Crown missing*, but this omission has been found in both "Crown only" (*illustrated*) and "Crown CA" rows. The resulting faulty paper was used for Bahamas, Johore, Seychelles and the postage due stamps of nine colonies.

w **9***a*: Error, Crown missing

w **9***b*: Error, St. Edward's Crown

When the omission was noticed a second mishap occurred, which was to insert a wrong crown in the space, giving w **9***b*, *St. Edward's Crown*. This produced varieties in Bahamas, Perlis, St. Kitts-Nevis and Singapore and the incorrect crown likewise occurs in "Crown only" and "Crown CA" rows.

w **10**
V over Crown

w **11**
Crown over A

Resuming the general types, two watermarks found in issues of several Australian States are: w **10**, *V over Crown*, and w **11**, *Crown over A*.

6. Colours

Stamps in two or three colours have these named in order of appearance, from the centre moving outwards. Four colours or more are usually listed as multicoloured.

In compound colour names the second is the predominant one, thus:

orange-red = a red tending towards orange;

red-orange = an orange containing more red than usual.

Standard colours used. The 200 colours most used for stamp identification are given in the Stanley Gibbons Stamp Colour Key. The Catalogue has used the Stamp Colour Key as standard for describing new issues for some years. The names are also introduced as lists are rewritten, though exceptions are made for those early issues where traditional names have become universally established.

Determining colours. When comparing actual stamps with colour samples in the Stamp Colour Key, view in a good north daylight (or its best substitute: fluorescent "colour-matching" light). Sunshine is not recommended. Choose a solid portion of the stamp design; if available, marginal markings such as solid bars of colour or colour check dots are helpful. Shading lines in the design can be misleading as they appear lighter than solid colour. Postmarked portions of a stamp appear darker than normal. If more than one colour is present, mask off the extraneous ones as the eye tends to mix them.

Errors of colour. Major colour errors in stamps or overprints which qualify for listing are: wrong colours; one colour inverted in relation to the rest; albinos (colourless impressions), where these have Expert Committee certificates; colours completely omitted, but only on unused stamps (if found on used stamps the information is footnoted) and with good credentials, missing colours being frequently faked.

Colours only partially omitted are not recognised, Colour shifts, however spectacular, are not listed.

Shades. Shades in philately refer to variations in the intensity of a colour or the presence of differing amounts of other colours. They are particularly significant when they can be linked to specific printings. In general, shades need to be quite marked to fall within the scope of this Catalogue; it does not favour nowadays listing the often numerous shades of a stamp, but chooses a single applicable colour name which will indicate particular groups of outstanding shades. Furthermore, the listings refer to colours as issued; they may deteriorate into something different through the passage of time.

Modern colour printing by lithography is prone to marked differences of shade, even within a single run, and variations can occur within the same sheet. Such shades are not listed.

Aniline colours. An aniline colour meant originally one derived from coal-tar; it now refers more widely to colour of a particular brightness suffused on the surface of a stamp and showing through clearly on the back.

Colours of overprints and surcharges. All overprints and surcharges are in black unless stated otherwise in the heading or after the description of the stamp.

7. Specimen Stamps

Originally, stamps overprinted SPECIMEN were circulated to postmasters or kept in official records, but after the establishment of the Universal Postal Union supplies were sent to Berne for distribution to the postal administrations of member countries.

During the period 1884 to 1928 most of the stamps of British Crown Colonies required for this purpose were overprinted SPECIMEN in various shapes and sizes by their printers from typeset formes. Some locally produced provisionals were handstamped locally, as were sets prepared for presentation. From 1928 stamps were punched with holes forming the word SPECIMEN, each firm of printers using a different machine or machines. From 1948 the stamps supplied for UPU distribution were no longer punctured.

Stamps of some other Commonwealth territories were overprinted or handstamped locally, while stamps of Great Britain and those overprinted for use in overseas postal agencies (mostly of the higher denominations) bore SPECIMEN overprints and handstamps applied by the Inland Revenue or the Post Office.

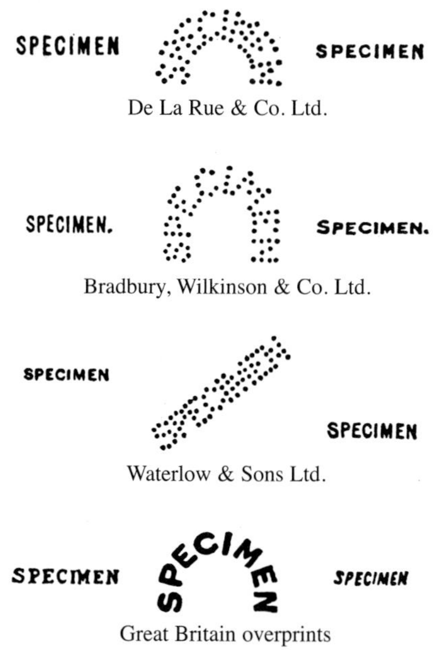

De La Rue & Co. Ltd.

Bradbury, Wilkinson & Co. Ltd.

Waterlow & Sons Ltd.

Great Britain overprints

Some of the commoner types of overprints or punctures are illustrated here. Collectors are warned that dangerous forgeries of the punctured type exist.

The *Part 1 (British Commonwealth) Catalogue* records those Specimen overprints or perforations intended for distribution by the UPU to member countries. In addition the Specimen overprints of Australia and its dependent territories, which were sold to collectors by the Post Office, are also included.

Various Perkins Bacon issues exist obliterated with a "CANCELLED" within an oval of bars handstamp.

Perkins Bacon "CANCELLED" Handstamp

This was applied to six examples of those issues available in 1861 which were then given to members of Sir Rowland Hill's family. 75 different stamps (including four from Chile) are recorded with this handstamp although others may possibly exist. The unauthorised gift of these "CANCELLED" stamps to the Hill family was a major factor in the loss of the Agent General for the Crown Colonies (the forerunner of the Crown Agents) contracts by Perkins Bacon in the following year. Where examples of these scarce items are known to be in private hands the catalogue provides a price.

For full details of these stamps see *CANCELLED by Perkins Bacon* by Peter Jaffé (published by Spink in 1998).

All other Specimens are outside the scope of this volume.

Specimens are not quoted in Great Britain as they are fully listed in the Stanley Gibbons *Great Britain Specialised Catalogue*.

In specifying type of specimen for individual high-value stamps, "H/S" means handstamped, "Optd" is overprinted and "Perf" is punctured. Some sets occur mixed, e.g. "Optd/Perf". If unspecified, the type is apparent from the date or it is the same as for the lower values quoted as a set.

Prices. Prices for stamps up to £1 are quoted in sets; higher values are priced singly. Where specimens exist in more than one type the price quoted is for the cheapest. Specimen stamps have rarely survived even as pairs; these and strips of three, four or five are worth considerably more than singles.

8. Coil Stamps

Stamps issued only in coil form are given full listing. If stamps are issued in both sheets and coils the coil stamps are listed separately only where there is some feature (e.g. perforation or watermark sideways) by which singles can be distinguished. Coil strips containing different stamps *se-tenant* are also listed.

Coil join pairs are too random and too easily faked to permit of listing; similarly ignored are coil stamps which have accidentally suffered an extra row of perforations from the claw mechanism in a malfunctioning vending machine.

9. Stamp Booklets

Stamp booklets (with the exception of those from Great Britain for which see the current edition of the *Great Britain Concise Catalogue*) are now listed in this catalogue.

Single stamps from booklets are listed if they are distinguishable in some way (such as watermark or perforation) from similar sheet stamps.

Booklet panes are listed where they contain stamps of different denominations *se-tenant*, where stamp-size labels are included, or where such panes are otherwise identifiable. Booklet panes are placed in the listing under the lowest denomination present.

Particular perforations (straight edges) are covered by appropriate notes.

10. Miniature Sheets and Sheetlets

We distinguish between "miniature sheets" and "sheetlets" and this affects the catalogue numbering. An item in sheet form that is postally valid, containing a single stamp, pair, block or set of stamps, with wide, inscribed and/or decorative margins, is a *miniature sheet* if it is sold at post offices as an indivisable entity. As such the Catalogue allots a single **MS** number and describes what stamps make it up. The *sheetlet* or *small sheet* differs in that the individual stamps are intended to be purchased separately for postal purposes. For sheetlets, all the component postage stamps are numbered individually and the composition explained in a footnote. Note that the definitions refer to post office sale—not how items may be subsequently offered by stamp dealers.

11. Forgeries and Fakes

Forgeries. Where space permits, notes are considered if they can give a concise description that will permit unequivocal detection of a forgery, Generalised warnings, lacking detail, are not nowadays inserted, since their value to the collector is problematic.

Fakes. Unwitting fakes are numerous, particularly "new shades" which are colour changelings brought about by exposure to sunlight, soaking in water contaminated with dyes from adherent paper, contact with oil and dirt from a pocketbook, and so on. Fraudulent operators, in addition, can offer to arrange: removal of hinge marks; repairs of thins on white or coloured papers; replacement of missing margins or perforations; reperforating in true or false gauges; removal of fiscal cancellations; rejoining of severed pairs, strips and blocks; and (a major hazard) regumming. Collectors can only be urged to purchase from reputable sources and to insist upon Expert Committee certification where there is any kind of doubt.

The Catalogue can consider footnotes about fakes where these are specific enough to assist in detection.

Abbreviations

Printers

A.B.N. Co.	American Bank Note Co, New York.
B.A.B.N.	British American Bank Note Co. Ottawa
B.W.	Bradbury Wilkinson & Co, Ltd.
C.B.N.	Canadian Bank Note Co, Ottawa.
Continental B.N. Co.	Continental Bank Note Co.
Courvoisier	Imprimerie Courvoisier S.A., La-Chaux-de-Fonds, Switzerland.
D.L.R.	De La Rue & Co, Ltd, London.
Enschedé	Joh. Enschedé en Zonen, Haarlem, Netherlands.
Harrison	Harrison & Sons, Ltd. London
P.B.	Perkins Bacon Ltd, London.
Waterlow	Waterlow & Sons, Ltd, London.

General Abbreviations

Alph	Alphabet
Anniv	Anniversary
Comp	Compound (perforation)
Des	Designer; designed
Diag	Diagonal; diagonally
Eng	Engraver; engraved
F.C.	Fiscal Cancellation
H/S	Handstamped
Horiz	Horizontal; horizontally
Imp, Imperf	Imperforate
Inscr	Inscribed
L	Left
Litho	Lithographed
mm	Millimetres
MS	Miniature sheet
N.Y.	New York
Opt(d)	Overprint(ed)
P or P-c	Pen-cancelled
P, Pf or Perf	Perforated
Photo	Photogravure
Pl	Plate
Pr	Pair
Ptd	Printed
Ptg	Printing
R	Right
R.	Row
Recess	Recess-printed
Roto	Rotogravure
Roul	Rouletted
S	Specimen (overprint)
Surch	Surcharge(d)
T.C.	Telegraph Cancellation
T	Type
Typo	Typographed
Un	Unused
Us	Used
Vert	Vertical; vertically
W or wmk	Watermark
Wmk s	Watermark sideways

(†) = Does not exist

(–) (or blank price column) = Exists, or may exist, but no market price is known.

/ between colours means "on" and the colour following is that of the paper on which the stamp is printed.

Colours of Stamps

Bl (blue); blk (black); brn (brown); car, carm (carmine); choc (chocolate); clar (claret); emer (emerald); grn (green); ind (indigo); mag (magenta); mar (maroon); mult (multicoloured); mve (mauve); ol (olive); orge (orange); pk (pink); pur (purple); scar (scarlet); sep (sepia); turq (turquoise); ultram (ultramarine); verm (vermilion); vio (violet); yell (yellow).

Colour of Overprints and Surcharges

(B.) = blue, (Blk.) = black, (Br.) = brown, (C.) = carmine, (G.) = green, (Mag.) = magenta, (Mve.) = mauve, (Ol.) = olive, (O.) = orange, (P.) = purple, (Pk.) = pink, (R.) = red, (Sil.) = silver, (V.) = violet, (Vm.) or (Verm.) = vermilion, (W.) = white, (Y.) = yellow.

Arabic Numerals

As in the case of European figures, the details of the Arabic numerals vary in different stamp designs, but they should be readily recognised with the aid of this illustration.

International Philatelic Glossary

English	*French*	*German*	*Spanish*	*Italian*
Agate	Agate	Achat	Agata	Agata
Air stamp	Timbre de la poste aérienne	Flugpostmarke	Sello de correo aéreo	Francobollo per posta aerea
Apple Green	Vert-pomme	Apfelgrün	Verde manzana	Verde mela
Barred	Annulé par barres	Balkenentwertung	Anulado con barras	Sbarrato
Bisected	Timbre coupé	Halbiert	Partido en dos	Frazionato
Bistre	Bistre	Bister	Bistre	Bistro
Bistre-brown	Brun-bistre	Bisterbraun	Castaño bistre	Bruno-bistro
Black	Noir	Schwarz	Negro	Nero
Blackish Brown	Brun-noir	Schwärzlichbraun	Castaño negruzco	Bruno nerastro
Blackish Green	Vert foncé	Schwärzlichgrün	Verde negruzco	Verde nerastro
Blackish Olive	Olive foncé	Schwärzlicholiv	Oliva negruzco	Oliva nerastro
Block of four	Bloc de quatre	Viererblock	Bloque de cuatro	Bloco di quattro
Blue	Bleu	Blau	Azul	Azzurro
Blue-green	Vert-bleu	Blaugrün	Verde azul	Verde azzuro
Bluish Violet	Violet bleuâtre	Bläulichviolett	Violeta azulado	Violtto azzurrastro
Booklet	Carnet	Heft	Cuadernillo	Libretto
Bright Blue	Bleu vif	Lebhaftblau	Azul vivo	Azzurro vivo
Bright Green	Vert vif	Lebhaftgrün	Verde vivo	Verde vivo
Bright Purple	Mauve vif	Lebhaftpurpur	Púrpura vivo	Porpora vivo
Bronze Green	Vert-bronze	Bronzegrün	Verde bronce	Verde bronzo
Brown	Brun	Braun	Castaño	Bruno
Brown-lake	Carmin-brun	Braunlack	Laca castaño	Lacca bruno
Brown-purple	Pourpre-brun	Braunpurpur	Púrpura castaño	Porpora bruno
Brown-red	Rouge-brun	Braunrot	Rojo castaño	Rosso bruno
Buff	Chamois	Sämisch	Anteado	Camoscio
Cancellation	Oblitération	Entwertung	Cancelación	Annullamento
Cancelled	Annulé	Gestempelt	Cancelado	Annullato
Carmine	Carmin	Karmin	Carmín	Carminio
Carmine-red	Rouge-carmin	Karminrot	Rojo carmín	Rosso carminio
Centred	Centré	Zentriert	Centrado	Centrato
Cerise	Rouge-cerise	Kirschrot	Color de ceresa	Color Ciliegia
Chalk-surfaced paper	Papier couché	Kreidepapier	Papel estucado	Carta gessata
Chalky Blue	Bleu terne	Kreideblau	Azul turbio	Azzurro smorto
Charity stamp	Timbre de bienfaisance	Wohltätigkeitsmarke	Sello de beneficenza	Francobollo di beneficenza
Chestnut	Marron	Kastanienbraun	Castaño rojo	Marrone
Chocolate	Chocolat	Schokolade	Chocolate	Cioccolato
Cinnamon	Cannelle	Zimtbraun	Canela	Cannella
Claret	Grenat	Weinrot	Rojo vinoso	Vinaccia
Cobalt	Cobalt	Kobalt	Cobalto	Cobalto
Colour	Couleur	Farbe	Color	Colore
Comb-perforation	Dentelure en peigne	Kammzähnung, Reihenzähnung	Dentado de peine	Dentellatura e pettine
Commemorative stamp	Timbre commémoratif	Gedenkmarke	Sello conmemorativo	Francobollo commemorativo
Crimson	Cramoisi	Karmesin	Carmesí	Cremisi
Deep Blue	Blue foncé	Dunkelblau	Azul oscuro	Azzurro scuro
Deep bluish Green	Vert-bleu foncé	Dunkelbläulichgrün	Verde azulado oscuro	Verde azzurro scuro
Design	Dessin	Markenbild	Diseño	Disegno
Die	Matrice	Urstempel. Type, Platte	Cuño	Conio, Matrice
Double	Double	Doppelt	Doble	Doppio
Drab	Olive terne	Trüboliv	Oliva turbio	Oliva smorto
Dull Green	Vert terne	Trübgrün	Verde turbio	Verde smorto
Dull purple	Mauve terne	Trübpurpur	Púrpura turbio	Porpora smorto
Embossing	Impression en relief	Prägedruck	Impresión en relieve	Impressione a relievo
Emerald	Vert-eméraude	Smaragdgrün	Esmeralda	Smeraldo
Engraved	Gravé	Graviert	Grabado	Inciso
Error	Erreur	Fehler, Fehldruck	Error	Errore
Essay	Essai	Probedruck	Ensayo	Saggio
Express letter stamp	Timbre pour lettres par exprès	Eilmarke	Sello de urgencia	Francobollo per espresso
Fiscal stamp	Timbre fiscal	Stempelmarke	Sello fiscal	Francobollo fiscale
Flesh	Chair	Fleischfarben	Carne	Carnicino
Forgery	Faux, Falsification	Fälschung	Falsificación	Falso, Falsificazione
Frame	Cadre	Rahmen	Marco	Cornice

INTERNATIONAL PHILATELIC GLOSSARY

English	*French*	*German*	*Spanish*	*Italian*
Granite paper	Papier avec fragments de fils de soie	Faserpapier	Papel con filamentos	Carto con fili di seta
Green	Vert	Grün	Verde	Verde
Greenish Blue	Bleu verdâtre	Grünlichblau	Azul verdoso	Azzurro verdastro
Greenish Yellow	Jaune-vert	Grünlichgelb	Amarillo verdoso	Giallo verdastro
Grey	Gris	Grau	Gris	Grigio
Grey-blue	Bleu-gris	Graublau	Azul gris	Azzurro grigio
Grey-green	Vert gris	Graugrün	Verde gris	Verde grigio
Gum	Gomme	Gummi	Goma	Gomma
Gutter	Interpanneau	Zwischensteg	Espacio blanco entre dos grupos	Ponte
Imperforate	Non-dentelé	Geschnitten	Sin dentar	Non dentellato
Indigo	Indigo	Indigo	Azul indigo	Indaco
Inscription	Inscription	Inschrift	Inscripción	Dicitura
Inverted	Renversé	Kopfstehend	Invertido	Capovolto
Issue	Émission	Ausgabe	Emisión	Emissione
Laid	Vergé	Gestreift	Listado	Vergato
Lake	Lie de vin	Lackfarbe	Laca	Lacca
Lake-brown	Brun-carmin	Lackbraun	Castaño laca	Bruno lacca
Lavender	Bleu-lavande	Lavendel	Color de alhucema	Lavanda
Lemon	Jaune-citron	Zitrongelb	Limón	Limone
Light Blue	Bleu clair	Hellblau	Azul claro	Azzurro chiaro
Lilac	Lilas	Lila	Lila	Lilla
Line perforation	Dentelure en lignes	Linienzähnung	Dentado en linea	Dentellatura lineare
Lithography	Lithographie	Steindruck	Litografía	Litografia
Local	Timbre de poste locale	Lokalpostmarke	Emisión local	Emissione locale
Lozenge roulette	Percé en losanges	Rautenförmiger Durchstich	Picadura en rombos	Perforazione a losanghe
Magenta	Magenta	Magentarot	Magenta	Magenta
Margin	Marge	Rand	Borde	Margine
Maroon	Marron pourpré	Dunkelrotpurpur	Púrpura rojo oscuro	Marrone rossastro
Mauve	Mauve	Malvenfarbe	Malva	Malva
Multicoloured	Polychrome	Mehrfarbig	Multicolores	Policromo
Myrtle Green	Vert myrte	Myrtengrün	Verde mirto	Verde mirto
New Blue	Bleu ciel vif	Neublau	Azul nuevo	Azzurro nuovo
Newspaper stamp	Timbre pour journaux	Zeitungsmarke	Sello para periódicos	Francobollo per giornali
Obliteration	Oblitération	Abstempelung	Matasello	Annullamento
Obsolete	Hors (de) cours	Ausser Kurs	Fuera de curso	Fuori corso
Ochre	Ocre	Ocker	Ocre	Ocra
Official stamp	Timbre de service	Dienstmarke	Sello de servicio	Francobollo di servizio
Olive-brown	Brun-olive	Olivbraun	Castaño oliva	Bruno oliva
Olive-green	Vert-olive	Olivgrün	Verde oliva	Verde oliva
Olive-grey	Gris-olive	Olivgrau	Gris oliva	Grigio oliva
Olive-yellow	Jaune-olive	Olivgelb	Amarillo oliva	Giallo oliva
Orange	Orange	Orange	Naranja	Arancio
Orange-brown	Brun-orange	Orangebraun	Castaño naranja	Bruno arancio
Orange-red	Rouge-orange	Orangerot	Rojo naranja	Rosso arancio
Orange-yellow	Jaune-orange	Orangegelb	Amarillo naranja	Giallo arancio
Overprint	Surcharge	Aufdruck	Sobrecarga	Soprastampa
Pair	Paire	Paar	Pareja	Coppia
Pale	Pâle	Blass	Pálido	Pallido
Pane	Panneau	Gruppe	Grupo	Gruppo
Paper	Papier	Papier	Papel	Carta
Parcel post stamp	Timbre pour colis postaux	Paketmarke	Sello para paquete postal	Francobollo per pacchi postali
Pen-cancelled	Oblitéré à plume	Federzugentwertung	Cancelado a pluma	Annullato a penna
Percé en arc	Percé en arc	Bogenförmiger Durchstich	Picadura en forma de arco	Perforazione ad arco
Percé en scie	Percé en scie	Bogenförmiger Durchstich	Picado en sierra	Foratura a sega
Perforated	Dentelé	Gezähnt	Dentado	Dentellato
Perforation	Dentelure	Zähnung	Dentar	Dentellatura
Photogravure	Photogravure, Heliogravure	Rastertiefdruck	Fotograbado	Rotocalco
Pin perforation	Percé en points	In Punkten durchstochen	Horadado con alfileres	Perforato a punti
Plate	Planche	Platte	Plancha	Lastra, Tavola
Plum	Prune	Pflaumenfarbe	Color de ciruela	Prugna
Postage Due stamp	Timbre-taxe	Portomarke	Sello de tasa	Segnatasse
Postage stamp	Timbre-poste	Briefmarke, Freimarke, Postmarke	Sello de correos	Francobollo postale
Postal fiscal stamp	Timbre fiscal-postal	Stempelmarke als Postmarke verwendet	Sello fiscal-postal	Fiscale postale

English	*French*	*German*	*Spanish*	*Italian*
Postmark	Oblitération postale	Poststempel	Matasello	Bollo
Printing	Impression, Tirage	Druck	Impresión	Stampa, Tiratura
Proof	Épreuve	Druckprobe	Prueba de impresión	Prova
Provisionals	Timbres provisoires	Provisorische Marken. Provisorien	Provisionales	Provvisori
Prussian Blue	Bleu de Prusse	Preussischblau	Azul de Prusia	Azzurro di Prussia
Purple	Pourpre	Purpur	Púrpura	Porpora
Purple-brown	Brun-pourpre	Purpurbraun	Castaño púrpura	Bruno porpora
Recess-printing	Impression en taille douce	Tiefdruck	Grabado	Incisione
Red	Rouge	Rot	Rojo	Rosso
Red-brown	Brun-rouge	Rotbraun	Castaño rojizo	Bruno rosso
Reddish Lilac	Lilas rougeâtre	Rötlichlila	Lila rojizo	Lilla rossastro
Reddish Purple	Poupre-rouge	Rötlichpurpur	Púrpura rojizo	Porpora rossastro
Reddish Violet	Violet rougeâtre	Rötlichviolett	Violeta rojizo	Violetto rossastro
Red-orange	Orange rougeâtre	Rotorange	Naranja rojizo	Arancio rosso
Registration stamp	Timbre pour lettre chargée (recommandée)	Einschreibemarke	Sello de certificado lettere	Francobollo per raccomandate
Reprint	Réimpression	Neudruck	Reimpresión	Ristampa
Reversed	Retourné	Umgekehrt	Invertido	Rovesciato
Rose	Rose	Rosa	Rosa	Rosa
Rose-red	Rouge rosé	Rosarot	Rojo rosado	Rosso rosa
Rosine	Rose vif	Lebhaftrosa	Rosa vivo	Rosa vivo
Roulette	Percage	Durchstich	Picadura	Foratura
Rouletted	Percé	Durchstochen	Picado	Forato
Royal Blue	Bleu-roi	Königblau	Azul real	Azzurro reale
Sage green	Vert-sauge	Salbeigrün	Verde salvia	Verde salvia
Salmon	Saumon	Lachs	Salmón	Salmone
Scarlet	Écarlate	Scharlach	Escarlata	Scarlatto
Sepia	Sépia	Sepia	Sepia	Seppia
Serpentine roulette	Percé en serpentin	Schlangenliniger Durchstich	Picado a serpentina	Perforazione a serpentina
Shade	Nuance	Tönung	Tono	Gradazione de colore
Sheet	Feuille	Bogen	Hoja	Foglio
Slate	Ardoise	Schiefer	Pizarra	Ardesia
Slate-blue	Bleu-ardoise	Schieferblau	Azul pizarra	Azzurro ardesia
Slate-green	Vert-ardoise	Schiefergrün	Verde pizarra	Verde ardesia
Slate-lilac	Lilas-gris	Schierferlila	Lila pizarra	Lilla ardesia
Slate-purple	Mauve-gris	Schieferpurpur	Púrpura pizarra	Porpora ardesia
Slate-violet	Violet-gris	Schieferviolett	Violeta pizarra	Violetto ardesia
Special delivery stamp	Timbre pour exprès	Eilmarke	Sello de urgencia	Francobollo per espressi
Specimen	Spécimen	Muster	Muestra	Saggio
Steel Blue	Bleu acier	Stahlblau	Azul acero	Azzurro acciaio
Strip	Bande	Streifen	Tira	Striscia
Surcharge	Surcharge	Aufdruck	Sobrecarga	Soprastampa
Tête-bêche	Tête-bêche	Kehrdruck	Tête-bêche	Tête-bêche
Tinted paper	Papier teinté	Getöntes Papier	Papel coloreado	Carta tinta
Too-late stamp	Timbre pour lettres en retard	Verspätungsmarke	Sello para cartas retardadas	Francobollo per le lettere in ritardo
Turquoise-blue	Bleu-turquoise	Türkisblau	Azul turquesa	Azzurro turchese
Turquoise-green	Vert-turquoise	Türkisgrün	Verde turquesa	Verde turchese
Typography	Typographie	Buchdruck	Tipografia	Tipografia
Ultramarine	Outremer	Ultramarin	Ultramar	Oltremare
Unused	Neuf	Ungebraucht	Nuevo	Nuovo
Used	Oblitéré, Usé	Gebraucht	Usado	Usato
Venetian Red	Rouge-brun terne	Venezianischrot	Rojo veneciano	Rosso veneziano
Vermilion	Vermillon	Zinnober	Cinabrio	Vermiglione
Violet	Violet	Violett	Violeta	Violetto
Violet-blue	Bleu-violet	Violettblau	Azul violeta	Azzurro violetto
Watermark	Filigrane	Wasserzeichen	Filigrana	Filigrana
Watermark sideways	Filigrane couché liegend	Wasserzeichen	Filigrana acostado	Filigrana coricata
Wove paper	Papier ordinaire, Papier uni	Einfaches Papier	Papel avitelado	Carta unita
Yellow	Jaune	Gelb	Amarillo	Giallo
Yellow-brown	Brun-jaune	Gelbbraun	Castaño amarillo	Bruno giallo
Yellow-green	Vert-jaune	Gelbgrün	Verde amarillo	Verde giallo
Yellow-olive	Olive-jaunâtre	Gelboliv	Oliva amarillo	Oliva giallastro
Yellow-orange	Orange jaunâtre	Gelborange	Naranja amarillo	Arancio giallastro
Zig-zag roulette	Percé en zigzag	Sägezahnartiger Durchstich	Picado en zigzag	Perforazione a zigzag

Specialist Philatelic Societies

Requests for inclusion on this page should be sent to the Catalogue Editor.

Great Britain Philatelic Society
Membership Secretary – Mr. A. G. Lajer
The Old Post Office, Hurst,
Berks RG10 0TR

Great Britain Decimal Stamp Book Study Circle
Membership Secretary – Mr. A. J. Wilkins
3 Buttermere Close, Brierley Hill,
West Midlands DY5 3SD

Great Britain Collectors' Club
Secretary – Mr. Parker A. Bailey Jr
13 Greenwood Road, Merrimack,
NH03054 U.S.A.

Channel Islands Specialists Society
Membership Secretary – Mr. R. Osborne
7 Overlord Close, Broxbourne,
Herts EN10 7TG

Aden & Somaliland Study Group
UK Representative – Mr M. Lacey
P.O. Box 9, Winchester, Hampshire
SO22 5RF

Ascension Study Circle
Secretary – Dr. R. C. F. Baker
Greys, Tower Road, Whitstable,
Kent CT5 2ER

Australian States Study Circle
Royal Sydney Philatelic Club
Honorary Secretary – Mr. B. Palmer
G.P.O. Box 1751, Sydney,
N.S.W. 1043 Australia

British Society of Australian Philately
Secretary – Mr. A. J. Griffiths
c/o The British Philatelic Centre,
107 Charterhouse Street, London EC1M 6PT

Society of Australasian Specialists/Oceania
Secretary – Mr. S. Leven
P.O. Box 24764, San Jose, CA 95154-4764
U.S.A.

Bechuanalands and Botswana Society
Membership Secretary – Mr. N. Midwood
69 Porlock Lane, Furzton,
Milton Keynes MK4 1JY

Bermuda Collectors Society
Secretary – Mr. T. J. McMahon
P.O. Box 1949, Stuart, FL 34995 U.S.A.

British Caribbean Philatelic Study Group
Overseas Director – Mr. D. N. Druett
Pennymead Auctions, 1 Brewerton Street,
Knaresborough, North Yorkshire HG5 8AZ

British West Indies Study Circle
Membership Secretary – Mr. P. G. Boulton
84 Tangier Road, Richmond,
Surrey TW10 5DN

Burma—a new society is being organised—for current details write to G. M. Rosamond,
35 Church Hill, Winchmore Hill,
London N21 1LN

Canadian Philatelic Society of Great Britain
Secretary – Mr. J. M. Wright
12 Milchester House, Staveley Road
Meads, Eastbourne, East Sussex BN20 7JX

Ceylon Study Circle
Secretary – Mr. R. W. P. Frost
42 Lonsdale Road, Cannington, Bridgwater,
Somerset TA5 2JS

Cyprus Study Circle
Membership Secretary – Mr. J. Wigmore
19 Riversmeet, Appledore, Bideford,
North Devon EX39 1RE

East Africa Study Circle
Honorary Secretary – Mr. K. Hewitt
16 Ashleigh Road, Solihull, B91 1AE

Falklands Islands Study Group
Membership Secretary – Mr. D. W. A. Jeffery
38 Bradstock Road, Stoneleigh, Epsom,
Surrey KT17 2LH

Hong Kong Study Circle
Membership Secretary – Mr. P. V. Ball
37 Hart Court, Newcastle-under-Lyme,
Staffordshire ST5 2AL

Indian Ocean Study Circle
Secretary – Mr. K. B. Fitton
50 Firlands, Weybridge, Surrey KT13 0HR

India Study Circle
Secretary – Mr. C. Haines
134a North View Road, London N8 7LP

Irish Philatelic Circle
General Secretary – Mr. F. McDonald
63 Rafters Road, Drimnagh, Dublin 12,
Ireland

King George V Silver Jubilee Study Circle
Secretary – Mr. N. Levinge
80 Towcester Road, Northampton NN4 8LQ

King George VI Collectors Society
Secretary – Mr. J. L. Shaw MBE
17 Balcaskie Road, Eltham
London SE9 1HQ

Kiribati and Tuvalu Philatelic Society
Honorary Secretary – Mr. M. J. Shaw
88 Stoneleigh Avenue, Worcester Park,
Surrey KT4 8XY

Malaya Study Group
Membership Secretary – Mr. K. Elliot
78 Howard Road, Queens Park,
Bournemouth, Dorset BH8 9ED

Malta Study Circle
Honorary Secretary – Mr. D. Crookes
9a Church Street,
Durham DH1 3DG

New Zealand Society of Great Britain
General Secretary – Mr. K. C. Collins
13 Briton Crescent, Sanderstead,
Surrey CR2 0JN

Orange Free State Study Circle
Secretary – Mr. J. R. Stroud
28 Oxford Street, Burnham-on-Sea,
Somerset TA8 1LQ

Pacific Islands Study Circle
Honorary Secretary – Mr. J. D. Ray
24 Woodvale Avenue, London SE25 4AE

Papuan Philatelic Society
Secretary – Mr. D. C. Ashton
71 Lowerside, Ham, Plymouth,
Devon PL2 2HU

Pitcairn Islands Study Group (U.K.)
Honorary Secretary – Mr. D. Sleep
6 Palace Gardens, 100 Court Road, Eltham,
London SE9 5NS

Rhodesian Study Circle
Secretary – Mr. R. G. Barnett
2 Cox Ley, Hatfield Heath,
Bishop's Stortford CM22 7ER

St. Helena, Ascension and Tristan da Cunha Philatelic Society
Secretary – Mr. J. Havill
205 N. Murray Blvd., #221, Colorado Springs,
CO 80916 U.S.A.

Sarawak Specialists Society
(also Brunei, North Borneo and Labuan)
Secretary – Dr. J. Higgins
31 Grimston Road, Kings Lynn,
Norfolk PE30 3HT

South African Collectors' Society
General Secretary – Mr. C. Oliver
Telephone 020 8940 9833

Philatelic Society of Sri Lanka
Secretary – Mr. H. Goonawardena, J.P.
44A Hena Road, Mt. Lavinia 10370,
Sri Lanka

Sudan Study Group
Secretary – Mr. N. D. Collier
34 Padleys Lane, Burton Joyce,
Nottingham NG14 5BZ

Transvaal Study Circle
Secretary – Mr. J. Woolgar
132 Dale Street, Chatham, Kent ME4 6QH

West Africa Study Circle
Secretary – Mr. J. Powell
23 Brook Street, Edlesborough, Dunstable,
Bedfordshire LU6 2JG

Select Bibliography

The literature on British Commonwealth stamps is vast, but works are often difficult to obtain once they are out of print. The selection of books below has been made on the basis of authority together with availability to the general reader, either as new or secondhand. Very specialised studies, and those covering aspects of postal history to which there are no references in the catalogue, have been excluded.

The following abbreviations are used to denote publishers:
CRL–Christie's Robson Lowe; HH–Harry Hayes; PB–Proud Bailey Co. Ltd. and Postal History Publications Co.; PC–Philip Cockrill; RPSL–Royal Philatelic Society, London; SG–Stanley Gibbons Ltd.

Where no publisher is quoted, the book is published by its author.

GENERAL
Encyclopaedia of British Empire Postage Stamps. Vols 1–6. Edited Robson Lowe. (CRL, 1951–1991)
Specimen Stamps of the Crown Colonies 1857–1948. Marcus Samuel. (RPSL, 1976 and 1984 Supplement)
Cancelled by Perkins Bacon. P. Jaffé. (Spink & Son Ltd., 1998)
U.P.U. Specimen Stamps. J. Bendon. (1988)
King George V Key Plates of the Imperium Postage and Revenue Design. P. Fernbank (West Africa Study Circle, 1997)
Silver Jubilee of King George V Stamps Handbook. A.J. Ainscough. (Ainweel Developments, 1985)
The Commemorative Stamps of the British Commonwealth. H.D.S. Haverbeck. (Faber, 1955)
The Printings of King George VI Colonial Stamps. W.J.W. Potter & Lt-Col R.C.M. Shelton. (1952 and later facsimile edition)
King George VI Large Key Type Stamps of Bermuda, Leeward Islands, Nyasaland. R.W. Dickgiesser and E.P. Yendall. (Triad Publications, 1985)
Madame Joseph Forged Postmarks. D. Worboys (RPSL, 1994)
G.B. Used Abroad: Cancellations and Postal Markings. J. Parmenter. (The Postal History Society, 1993)

GREAT BRITAIN
For extensive bibliographies see *G.B. Specialised Catalogues. Vols 1–5*.
Stamps and Postal History of the Channel Islands. W. Newport. (Heineman, 1972)

ADEN
The Postal History of British Aden 1839–67. Major R.W. Pratt. (PB, 1985)

ASCENSION
Ascension. The Stamps and Postal History. J.H. Attwood. (CRL, 1981)

AUSTRALIA
The Postal History of New South Wales 1788–1901. Edited J.S. White (Philatelic Association of New South Wales, 1988)
South Australia. The Long Stamps 1902-12. J.R.W. Purves. (Royal Philatelic Society of Victoria, 1978)
The Departmental Stamps of South Australia. A.R. Butler. (RPSL, 1978)
A Priced Listing of the Departmental Stamps of South Australia. A.D. Presgrave (2nd edition, 1999)
Stamps and Postal History of Tasmania. W.E.Tinsley. (RPSL, 1986)
The Pictorial Stamps of Tasmania 1899–1912. K.E. Lancaster. (Royal Philatelic Society of Victoria, 1986)
The Stamps of Victoria. G. Kellow. (B. & K. Philatelic Publishing, 1990)
Western Australia, The Stamps and Postal History. Edited M. Hamilton and B. Pope. (W. Australian Study Group, 1979)
Postage Stamps and Postal History of Western Australia. Vols 1–3. M. Juhl. (1981–83)
The Chapman Collection of Australian Commonwealth Stamps. R. Chapman. (Royal Philatelic Society of Victoria, 1999)
The Postal History of British New Guinea and Papua 1885–1942. R. Lee. (CRL, 1983)
Norfolk Island. A Postal and Philatelic History, 1788–1969. P. Collas & R. Breckon. (B. & K. Philatelic Publishing, 1997)

BAHAMAS
The Postage Stamps and Postal History of the Bahamas. H.G.D. Gisburn. (SG, 1950 and later facsimile edition)

BARBADOS
The Stamps of Barbados. E.A. Bayley. (1989)
Advanced Barbados Philately. H.F. Deakin. (B.W.I. Study Circle, 1997)

BASUTOLAND
The Cancellations and Postal Markings of Basutoland/Lesotho Post Offices. A.H. Scott. (Collectors Mail Auctions (Pty) Ltd., 1980)

BATUM.
British Occupation of Batum. P.T. Ashford. (1989)

BECHUANALAND.
The Postage Stamps, Postal Stationery and Postmarks of the Bechuanalands. H.R. Holmes. (RPSL, 1971)

BERMUDA
The Postal History and Stamps of Bermuda. M.H. Ludington. (Quarterman Publications Inc., 1978)
The King George V High-value Stamps of Bermuda, 1917–1938. M. Glazer. (Calaby Publishers, 1994)

BRITISH GUIANA
The Postage Stamps and Postal History of British Guiana. W.A. Townsend and F.G. Howe. (RPSL, 1970)

BRITISH HONDURAS
The Postal History of British Honduras. E.B. Proud. (PB, 1999)

BRITISH OCCUPATION OF GERMAN COLONIES
G.R.I. R.M. Gibbs. (CRL, 1989)

BRITISH POSTAL AGENCIES IN EASTERN ARABIA
The Postal Agencies in Eastern Arabia and the Gulf. N. Donaldson (HH, 1975) and Supplement (Bridger & Kay Guernsey Ltd., 1994)

BRITISH SOLOMON ISLANDS
British Solomon Islands Protectorate. Its Postage Stamps and Postal History. H.G.D. Gisburn. (T. Sanders (Philatelist) Ltd., 1956)

BRITISH WEST AFRICA
The Postal History and Handstamps of British West Africa. C. McCaig. (CRL, 1978)

BURMA
Burma Postal History. G. Davis and D. Martin. (CRL, 1971 and 1987 Supplement).
The Postal History of Burma. E.B. Proud. (PB, 2002)

CAMEROONS
The Postal Arrangements of the Anglo-French Cameroons Expeditionary Force 1914–16. R.J. Maddocks. (1996)

CANADA
The Postage Stamps and Postal History of Newfoundland. W.S. Boggs. (Quarterman Publications Inc., 1975)
Stamps of British North America. F. Jarrett. (Quarterman Publications Inc., 1975)
The Postage Stamps and Postal History of Canada. W.S. Boggs. (Quarterman Publications Inc., 1974)
The First Decimal Issue of Canada 1859–68. G. Whitworth. (RPSL, 1966)
The Five Cents Beaver Stamp of Canada. G. Whitworth. (RPSL, 1985)
The Small Queens of Canada. J. Hillson. (CRL, 1989)
Canada Small Queens Re-Appraised. J. Hillson. (Canadian Philatelic Society of Great Britain, 1999)
The Edward VII Issue of Canada. G.C. Marler. (National Postal Museum, Canada, 1975)
The Admiral Issue of Canada. G.C. Marler. (American Philatelic Society, 1982)

CYPRUS
Cyprus 1353–1986. W. Castle. (CRL 3rd edition, 1987)

DOMINICA
Dominica Postal History, Stamps and Postal Stationery to 1935. E.V. Toeg. (B.W.I. Study Circle, 1994)

EGYPT
Egypt Stamps & Postal History. P.A.S. Smith. (James Bendon, 1999)

FALKLAND ISLANDS
The Postage Stamps of the Falkland Islands and Dependencies. B.S.H. Grant. (SG, 1952 and later fasimile edition)
The Falkland Islands Philatelic Digest. Nos. 1 & 2. M. Barton and R. Spafford. (HH, 1975 and 1979)
The De La Rue Definitives of the Falkland Islands 1901–29. J.P. Bunt. (1986 and 1996 Supplement)
The Falkland Islands. The 1891 Provisionals. M. Barton. (BPA Expertising Educational Trust, 2002)
The War Stamp Overprints of the Falkland Islands 1918–20. J.P. Bunt. (1981)
The Falkland Islands. Printings of the Pictorial Issue of 1938–49. C.E. Glass . (CRL, 1979)

FIJI
Fiji Philatelics. D.E.F. Alford. (Pacific Islands Study Circle, 1994)
Fiji Queen Victoria One Shilling and Five Shillings Postage Stamps 1881–1902. R.F. Duberal. (Pacific Islands Study Circle, 2003)
The Postal History of Fiji 1911–1952. J.G. Rodger. (Pacific Islands Study Circle, 1991)

GAMBIA
The Stamps and Postal History of the Gambia. Edited J.O. Andrew. (CRL, 1985)
The Postal History of the Gambia. E.B. Proud. (PB, 1994)

GIBRALTAR
Posted in Gibraltar. W. Hine-Haycock. (CRL, 1978 and 1983 Supplement)
Gibraltar. The Postal History and Postage Stamps. Vol 1 (to 1885). G. Osborn. (Gibraltar Study Circle, 1995)

The Postal History of Gibraltar. R.J.M. Garcia & E.B. Proud. (PB, 1998)

GOLD COAST
The Postal History of the Gold Coast. E.B. Proud. (PB, 1995)
The Postal Services of the Gold Coast, 1901–1957. Edited M. Ensor. (West Africa Study Circle, 1998)

HONG KONG
The Philatelic History of Hong Kong. Vol 1. (Hong Kong Study Circle, 1984)
Hong Kong Postage Stamps of the Queen Victoria Period. R.N. Gurevitch. (1993)
Hong Kong. The 1898 10c. on 30c. Provisional Issue. A.M. Chu. (1998)
British Post Offices in the Far East. E.B. Proud. (PB, 1991)
Cancellations of the Treaty Ports of Hong Kong. H. Schoenfeld. (1988)
The Crown Colony of Wei Hai Wei. M. Goldsmith and C.W. Goodwyn. (RPSL, 1985)

INDIA
C.E.F. The China Expeditionary Force 1900–1923. D.S. Virk, J.C. Hume, D. Lang, G. Sattin. (Philatelic Congress of India, 1992)
India Used Abroad. V.S. Dastur. (Mysore Philatelics, 1982)
The Indian Postal Agencies in the Persian Gulf Area. A. Parsons. (Sahara Publications Ltd., 2001)
A Handbook on Gwalior Postal History and Stamps. V.K. Gupta. (1980)
The Stamps of Jammu & Kashmir. F. Staal. (The Collectors Club, 1983)
Sorath Stamps and Postal History. R.A. Malaviya. (Ravi Prakashan, 1999)

IRAQ
The Postal History of Iraq. P.C. Pearson and E.B. Proud. (PB, 1996)

IRELAND
Irish Stamp Booklets 1931–1991. C.I. Dulin. (1998)

JAMAICA
Encyclopaedia of Jamaican Philately. Vol 1. D. Sutcliffe & S. Jarvis. (1997); *Vol 6*. S. Jarvis. (2001) (B.W.I. Study Circle)
Jamaica, the Definitive and Commemorative Stamps and Postal Stationery of the Reign of King George VI. H.A.H. James. (The King George VI Collectors Society, 1999)

KENYA
British East Africa. The Stamps and Postal Stationery. J. Minns. (RPSL, 1982 and 1990 Supplement)
The Postal History of Kenya. E.B. Proud. (PB, 1992)

LEEWARD ISLANDS
The Leeward Islands – Notes for Philatelists. M.N. Oliver. (B.W.I. Study Circle, 2000)

MALAYA
The Postal History of British Malaya. Vols 1–3. E.B. Proud. (PB, 2nd edition, 2000)
The Postage Stamps of Federated Malay States. W.A. Reeves. (Malaya Study Group, 1978)
Kedah and Perlis. D.R.M. Holley. (Malaya Study Group, 1995)
Kelantan. Its Stamps and Postal History. W.A. Reeves and B.E. Dexter. (Malaya Study Group, 1992)
The Postal History of the Occupation of Malaya and British Borneo 1941–1945. E.B. Proud and M.D. Rowell. (PB, 1992)

MALTA
Malta. The Postal History and Postage Stamps. Edited R.E. Martin. (CRL, 1980 and 1985 Supplement)

MAURITIUS
The Postal History and Stamps of Mauritius. P. Ibbotson. (RPSL, 1991); Revisions and additions Supplement (Indian Ocean Study Circle, 1995)
The Postal History of Mauritius. E.B Proud. (PB, 2001)

MONTSERRAT
Montserrat to 1965. L.E. Britnor. (B.W.I. Study Circle, 2nd edition, 1998)

MOROCCO AGENCIES
British Post Offices and Agencies in Morocco 1857–1907 and Local Posts 1891–1914. R.K. Clough. (Gibraltar Study Circle, 1984)

NEW ZEALAND
The Postage Stamps of New Zealand. Vols I–VII. (Royal Philatelic Society of New Zealand, 1939–98)
The Early Cook Islands Post Office. A.R. Burge. (Hawthorn Press, 1978)
The Postal History and Postage Stamps of the Tokelau/Union Islands. A.H. Burgess. (Pacific Islands Study Circle, 2nd edition, 1998)
A Postal History of the Samoan Islands (Parts Iand II). Edited R. Burge. (Royal Philatelic Society of New Zealand, 1987–89)

NIGERIA
The Stamps and Postal History of the Niger Territories and the Niger Coast Protectorate. M.P. Nicholson. (PC, 1982)
The Local Bisects and Surcharges of the Oil Rivers and Niger Coast 1893–94. M.P. Nicholson. (PC, 1982)
The Stamps and Postal History of Southern Nigeria. M.P. Nicholson. (PC, 1982)
The Postal Services of the British Nigeria Region. J. Ince and J. Sacher. (RPSL, 1992)
The Postal History of Nigeria. E.B. Proud. (PB, 1995)

NORTH BORNEO
A Concise Guide to the Queen Issues of Labuan. R. Price. (Sarawak Specialists Society, 1991)
The Stamps and Postal History of North Borneo. Parts 1-3. L.H. Shipman and P.K. Cassells. (Sarawak Specialists Society, 1976–88)
The Postal History of British Borneo. E.B. Proud. (PB, 2003)

NYASALAND
The Postal History of Nyasaland. E.B. Proud. (PB, 1997)

PALESTINE
The Stamps & Postal Stationery of Palestine Mandate 1918–1948. D. Dorfman. (Edward G. Rosen, 2001)

PITCAIRN ISLANDS
Pitcairn Islands Philately. D.E. Hume. (2nd edition, 1999)

RHODESIA
Mashonaland. A Postal History 1890–96. Dr. A.R. Drysdall and D. Collis. (CRL, 1990)
Rhodesia. A Postal History. R.C. Smith. (1967 and 1970 Supplement)

ST. HELENA
St. Helena, Postal History and Stamps. E. Hibbert. (CRL, 1979)

ST. KITTS-NEVIS
A Study of the King George VI Stamps of St. Kitts-Nevis. P.L. Baldwin. (Murray Payne Ltd. 2nd edition 1997)
The Philately of Nevis. F. Borromeo. (British West Indies Study Circle, 2001)

SARAWAK
The Stamps and Postal History of Sarawak. W.A. Forrester-Wood. (Sarawak Specialists Society, 1959 and 1970 Supplement)
Sarawak: The Issues of 1871 and 1875. W. Batty-Smith and W. Watterson.

SEYCHELLES
Seychelles Postal History and Postage Stamps to 1976. S. Hopson & B.M. McCloy. (Indian Ocean Study Circle, 2002)

SIERRA LEONE
The Postal Service of Sierra Leone. P.O. Beale. (RPSL, 1988)
The Postal History of Sierra Leone. E.B. Proud. (PB, 1994)
Sierra Leone King George VI Definitive Stamps. F. Walton. (West Africa Study Circle, 2001)

SOUTH AFRICA
Postmarks of the Cape of Good Hope. R. Goldblatt. (Reijger Publishers (Pty) Ltd., 1984)
Stamps of the Orange Free State. Parts 1–3. G.D. Buckley & W.B. Marriott. (O.F.S. Study Circle, 1967–80)
Transvaal Philately. Edited I.B. Mathews. (Reijger Publishers (Pty) Ltd., 1986)
Transvaal. The Provisional Issues of the First British Occupation. Dr. A.R. Drysdall. (James Bendon, 1994)
The Wherewithal of Wolmaransstad. H. Birkhead and J. Groenewald. (Philatelic Foundation of Southern Africa, 1999)

SOUTH WEST AFRICA
The Overprinted Stamps of South West Africa to 1930. N. Becker. (Philatelic Holdings (Pty) Ltd., 1990)

SUDAN
Sudan. The Stamps and Postal Stationery of 1867 to 1970. E.C.W. Stagg. (HH, 1977)
The Camel Postman 1898–1998. R. Stock. (Sudan Study Group, 2001)

TANGANYIKA
The Postal History of Tanganyika. 1915–1961. E.B. Proud. (PB, 1989)

TOGO
Togo–The Postal History of the Anglo-French Occupation 1914–22. J. Martin and F. Walton. (West Africa S.C., 1995)

TRANSJORDAN
The Stamps of Jordan 1920–1965. A.H. Najjar. (Sahara Publications Ltd., 1998)

TRINIDAD AND TOBAGO
The Postal History of Trinidad and Tobago. J.C. Aleong and E.B. Proud. (PB, 1997)

TRISTAN DA CUNHA
The History and Postal History of Tristan da Cunha. G. Crabb. (1980)

TURKS AND CAICOS ISLANDS
Turks Islands and Caicos Islands to 1950. J.J. Challis. (Roses Caribbean Philatelic Society, 1983)

UGANDA
The Postal History of Uganda and Zanzibar. E.B. Proud. (PB, 1993)

ZANZIBAR
Zanzibar 1895–1904. T.W. Hall. (Reprint, East Africa Study Circle, 2002)

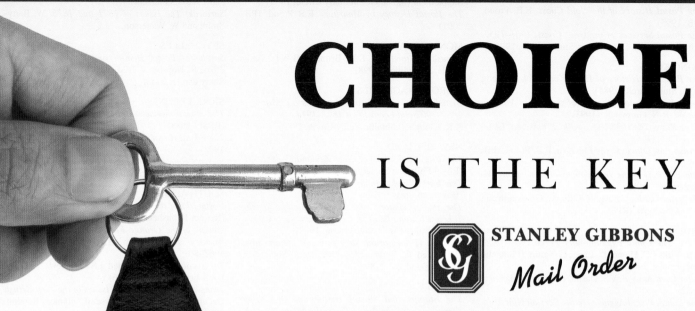

Great Britain

STAMPS ON COVER. Prices are quoted, as a third price column, for those Victorian and Edwardian issues usually found used on cover. In general these prices refer to the cheapest version of each basic stamp with other shades, plates or varieties, together with unusual frankings and postmarks, being worth more.

UNITED KINGDOM OF GREAT BRITAIN AND IRELAND

QUEEN VICTORIA
20 June 1837—22 January 1901

MULREADY ENVELOPES AND LETTER SHEETS, so called from the name of the designer, William Mulready, were issued concurrently with the first British adhesive stamps

1d. black

Envelopes.	£250 *unused*;	£325 *used*.
Letter Sheets:	£225 *unused*;	£300 *used*.

2d. blue

Envelopes.	£325 *unused*;	£900 *used*.
Letter Sheets:	£300 *unused*;	£850 *used*.

LINE-ENGRAVED ISSUES

GENERAL NOTES

Brief notes on some aspects of the line-engraved stamps follow, but for further information and a full specialist treatment of these issues collectors are recommended to consult Volume 1 of the Stanley Gibbons *Great Britain Specialised Catalogue*.

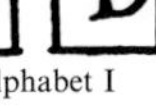

Alphabet I — Alphabet II

Alphabet III — Alphabet IV

Typical Corner Letters of the four Alphabets

Alphabets. Four different styles were used for the corner letters on stamps prior to the issue with letters in all four corners, these being known to collectors as:

Alphabet I. Used for all plates made from 1840 to the end of 1851. Letters small.

Alphabet II. Plates from 1852 to mid-1855. Letters larger, heavier and broader.

Alphabet III. Plates from mid-1855 to end of period. Letters tall and more slender.

Alphabet IV. 1861. 1d. Die II, Plates 50 and 51 only. Letters were hand-engraved instead of being punched on the plate. They are therefore inconsistent in shape and size but generally larger and outstanding.

While the general descriptions and the illustrations of typical letters given above may be of some assistance, only long experience and published aids can enable every stamp to be allocated to its particular Alphabet without hesitation, as certain letters in each are similar to those in one of the others.

Blue Paper. The blueing of the paper of the earlier issues is believed to be due to the presence of prussiate of potash in the printing ink, or in the paper, which, under certain conditions, tended to colour the paper when the sheets were damped for printing. An alternative term is bleuté paper.

Corner Letters. The corner letters on the early British stamps were intended as a safeguard against forgery, each stamp in the sheet having a different combination of letters. Taking the first 1d. stamp, printed in 20 horizontal rows of 12, as an example, the lettering is as follows:

Row 1. A A, A B, A C, etc. to A L.
Row 2. B A, B B, B C, etc. to B L.
and so on to
Row 20. T A, T B, T C, etc. to T L.

On the stamps with four corner letters, those in the upper corners are in the reverse positions to those in the lower corners. Thus in a sheet of 240 (12 × 20) the sequence is:

Row 1.	A A A A	B A A B	C A A C	etc. to	L A A L
Row 2.	A B B A	B B B B	C B B C	etc. to	L B B L
	and so on to				
Row 20.	A T T A	B T T B	C T T C	etc. to	L T T L

Placing letters in all four corners was not only an added precaution against forgery but was meant to deter unmarked parts of used stamps being pieced together and passed off as an unused whole.

Dies. The first die of the 1d. was used for making the original die of the 2d., both the No Lines and White Lines issues. In 1855 the 1d. Die I was amended by retouching the head and deepening the lines on a transferred impression of the original. This later version, known to collectors as Die II, was used for making the dies for the 1d. and 2d. with letters in all four corners and also for the 1½d.

The two dies are illustrated above No. 17 in the catalogue.

Double letter

Guide line in corner

Guide line through value

Double Corner Letters. These are due to the workman placing his letter-punch in the wrong position at the first attempt, when lettering the plate, and then correcting the mistake; or to a slight shifting of the punch when struck. If a wrong letter was struck in the first instance, traces of a wrong letter may appear in a corner in addition to the correct one. A typical example is illustrated.

Guide Lines and Dots. When laying down the impressions of the design on the early plates, fine vertical and horizontal guidelines were marked on the plates to assist the operative. These were usually removed from the gutter margins, but could not be removed from the stamp impressions without damage to the plate, so that in such cases they appear on the printed stamps, sometimes in the corners, sometimes through "POSTAGE" or the value. Typical examples are illustrated.

Guide dots or cuts were similarly made to indicate the spacing of the guide lines. These too sometimes appear on the stamps.

Ivory Head

"Ivory Head." The so-called "ivory head" variety is one in which the Queen's Head shows white on the back of the stamp. It arises from the comparative absence of ink in the head portion of the design, with consequent absence of blueing. (*See* "Blued Paper" note above.)

Line-engraving. In this context "line-engraved" is synonymous with recess-printing, in which the engraver cuts recesses in a plate and printing (the coloured areas) is from these recesses. "Line-engraved" is the traditional philatelic description for these stamps; other equivalent terms found are "engraving in *taille-douce*" (French) or in "*intaglio*" (Italian).

Plates. Until the introduction of the stamps with letters in all four corners, the number of the plate was not indicated in the design of the stamp, but was printed on the sheet margin. By long study of identifiable blocks and the minor variations in the design, coupled with the position of the corner letters, philatelists are now able to allot many of these stamps to their respective plates. Specialist collectors often endeavour to obtain examples of a given stamp printed from its different plates and our catalogue accordingly reflects this depth of detail.

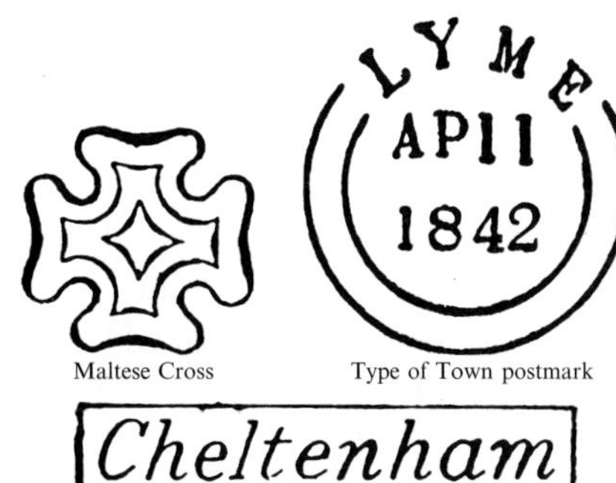

Maltese Cross — Type of Town postmark

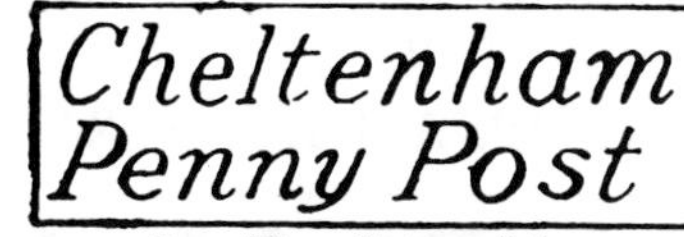

Type of Penny Post cancellation

Example of 1844 type postmark

Postmarks. The so-called "Maltese Cross" design was the first employed for obliterating British postage stamps and was in use from 1840 to 1844. Being hand-cut, the obliterating stamps varied greatly in detail and some distinctive types can be allotted to particular towns or offices. Local types, such as those used at Manchester, Norwich, Leeds, etc., are keenly sought. A red ink was first employed, but was superseded by black, after some earlier experiments, in February 1841. Maltese Cross obliterations in other colours are rare.

Obliterations of this type, numbered 1 to 12 in the centre, were used at the London Chief Office in 1843 and 1844.

Some straight-line cancellations were in use in 1840 at the Penny Post receiving offices, normally applied on the envelope, the adhesives then being obliterated at the Head Office. They are nevertheless known, with or without Maltese Cross, on the early postage stamps.

In 1842 some offices in S.W. England used dated postmarks in place of the Maltese Cross, usually on the back of the letter since they were not originally intended as obliterators. These town postmarks have likewise been found on adhesives.

In 1844 the Maltese Cross design was superseded by numbered obliterators of varied type, one of which is illustrated. They are naturally comparatively scarce on the first 1d. and 2d. stamps. Like the Maltese Cross they are found in various colours, some of which are rare.

Re-entry

"Union Jack" re-entry

Re-entries. Re-entries on the plate show as a doubling of part of the design of the stamp generally at top or bottom. Many re-entries are very slight while others are most marked. A typical one is illustrated.

The "*Union Jack*" *re-entry*, so called owing to the effect of the re-entry on the appearance of the corner stars (*see illustration*) occurs on stamp L K of Plate 75 of the 1d. red, Die I.

T A (T L)

M A (M L)

Varieties of Large Crown Watermark

I Two states of Large Crown Watermark

II

Watermarks. Two watermark varieties, as illustrated, consisting of crowns of entirely different shape, are found in sheets of the Large Crown paper and fall on stamps lettered M A and T A (or M L and T L when the paper is printed on the wrong side). Both varieties are found on the 1d. rose-red of 1857, while the M A (M L) variety comes also on some plates of the 1d. of 1864 (Nos. 43, 44) up to about Plate 96. On the 2d. the T A (T L) variety is known on plates 8 and 9, and the M A (M L) on later prints of plate 9. These varieties may exist inverted, or inverted reversed, on stamps lettered A A and A L and H A and H L, and some are known.

In 1861 a minor alteration was made in the Large Crown watermark by the removal of the two vertical strokes, representing *fleurs-de-lis*, which projected upwards from the uppermost of the three horizontal curves at the base of the Crown. Hence two states are distinguishable, as illustrated.

CONDITION—IMPERFORATE LINE-ENGRAVED ISSUES

The prices quoted for the 1840 and 1841 imperforate Line-engraved issues are for "fine" examples. As condition is most important in assessing the value of a stamp, the following definitions will assist collectors in the evaluation of individual examples.

Four main factors are relevant when considering quality.

(a) **Impression**. This should be clean and the surface free of any rubbing or unnatural blurring which would detract from the appearance.

(b) **Margins**. This is perhaps the most difficult factor to evaluate. Stamps described as "fine", the standard adopted in this catalogue for pricing purposes, should have margins of the recognised width, defined as approximately one half of the distance between two adjoining unsevered stamps. Stamps described as "very fine" or "superb" should have margins which are proportionately larger than those of a "fine" stamp. Examples with close margins should not, generally, be classified as "fine".

(c) **Cancellation**. On a "fine" stamp this should be reasonably clear and not noticeably smudged. A stamp described as "superb" should have a neat cancellation, preferably centrally placed or to the right.

(d) **Appearance**. Stamps, at the prices quoted, should always be without any tears, creases, bends or thins and should not be toned on either the front or back. Stamps with such defects are worth only a proportion of the catalogue price.

Good

Fine

Very Fine

Superb

The above actual size illustrations of 1840 1d. blacks show the various grades of quality. When comparing these illustrations it should be assumed that they are all from the same plate and that they are free of any hidden defects.

PRINTERS. Nos. 1/53*a* were recess-printed by Perkins, Bacon & Petch, known from 1852 as Perkins, Bacon & Co.

1

1a

2 Small Crown

(Eng Charles and Frederick Heath)

1840 (6 May). *Letters in lower corners.* Wmk Small Crown. W **2**. Imperf.

			Un	Used	Used on cover
1	**1**	1d. intense black	£5500	£300	
2		1d. black	£4500	£225	£400
3		1d. grey-black (worn plate)	£5250	£325	
4	**1a**	2d. deep full blue	£13000	£650	
5		2d. blue	£10000	£500	£1100
6		2d. pale blue	£13000	£550	

The 1d. stamp in black was printed from Plates 1 to 11. Plate 1 exists in two states (known to collectors as 1*a* and 1*b*), the latter being the result of extensive repairs.

Repairs were also made to Plates 2, 5, 6, 8, 9, 10 and 11, and certain impressions exist in two or more states.

The so-called "Royal reprint" of the ld. black was made in 1864, from Plate 66, Die II, on paper with Large Crown watermark, inverted. A printing was also made in carmine, on paper with the same watermark, normal.

For 1d. black with "VR" in upper corners *see* No. Vl under Official Stamps.

The 2d. stamps were printed from Plates 1 and 2.

Plates of 1d. black

Plate	*Un*	*Used*
1*a*	£6000	£250
1*b*	£4500	£225
2	£4500	£225
3	£5750	£275
4	£4500	£250
5	£4500	£225
6	£4500	£225
7	£4750	£250
8	£5250	£300
9	£6250	£350
10	£7750	£500
11	£8500	£3000

Varieties of 1d. black.

			Un	*Used*
.	On *bleuté* paper (Plates 1 to 8)	*from*	—	£350
.	Double letter in corner	*from*	£4750	£250
b.	Re-entry		£5000	£275
c.	"PB" re-entry (Plate 5, 3rd state)		—	£4500
c.	Large letters in each corner (E J, I L, J C and P A) (Plate 1*b*)	*from*	£4750	£375
.	Guide line in corner		£4750	£250
.	Guide line through value		£4750	£275
.	Watermark inverted		£7000	£800
.	Obliterated by Maltese Cross			
		In red	—	£250
		In black	—	£225
		In blue	—	£3750
		In magenta	—	£1250
		In yellow	—	—
.	Obliterated by Maltese Cross with number in centre	*from*		
		No. 1	—	£3500
		No. 2	—	£3500
		No. 3	—	£3500
		No. 4	—	£3500
		No. 5	—	£3500
		No. 6	—	£3500
		No. 7	—	£3500
		No. 8	—	£3500
		No. 9	—	£3500
		No. 10	—	£3500
		No. 11	—	£3500
		No. 12	—	£3500
	Obliterated "Penny Post" in black (without Maltese Cross)	*from*	—	£1900

			Un	*Used*
j.	Obliterated by town postmark (without Maltese Cross)			
	In black	*from*	—	£2500
	In yellow	*from*	—	£15000
	In red	*from*	—	£2500
k.	Obliterated by 1844 type postmark in black	*from*	—	£650

Plates of 2d. blue

Plate		*Un*	*Used*
1	*Shades from*	£10000	£500
2	*Shades from*	£12000	£550

Varieties of 2d. blue.

			Un	*Used*
a.	Double letter in corner		—	£550
aa.	Re-entry		—	£600
b.	Guide line in corner		—	£525
c.	Guide line through value		—	£525
d.	Watermark inverted	*from*	£16000	£2500
e.	Obliterated by Maltese Cross			
		In red	—	£550
		In black	—	£500
		In blue	—	£4750
		In magenta	—	£4000
f.	Obliterated by Maltese Cross with number in centre	*from*		
		No. 1	—	£4000
		No. 2	—	£4000
		No. 3	—	£4250
		No. 4	—	£4000
		No. 5	—	£4000
		No. 6	—	£4250
		No. 7	—	£4250
		No. 8	—	£4250
		No. 9	—	£4750
		No. 10	—	£4250
		No. 11	—	£4250
		No. 12	—	£3750
g.	Obliterated "Penny Post" in black (without Maltese Cross)	*from*	—	£2250
h.	Obliterated by town postmark (without Maltese Cross) in black	*from*	—	£2500
i.	Obliterated by 1844 type postmark			
	In black	*from*	—	£1250
	In blue	*from*	—	£5250

1841 (10 Feb). *Printed from "black" plates.* Wmk W **2**. Paper more or less blued. Imperf.

			Un	Used	Used on cover
7	**1**	1d. red-brown (*shades*)	£950	75·00	£175
		a. "PB" re-entry (Plate 5, 3rd state)	—	£1500	

The first printings of the 1d. in red-brown were made from Plates 1*b*, 2, 5 and 8 to 11 used for the 1d. black.

1d. red-brown from "black" plates.

Plate	*Un*	*Used*
1*b*	£4000	£250
2	£2750	£200
5	£950	£110
8	£950	90·00
9	£950	90·00
10	£950	90·00
11	£700	75·00

1841 (late Feb). *Plate 12 onwards.* Wmk W **2**. Paper more or less blued. Imperf.

			Un	Used	Used on cover
8	**1**	1d. red-brown	£250	15·00	25·00
8*a*		1d. red-brown on very blue paper	£300	15·00	
9		1d. pale red-brown (worn plates)	£350	25·00	
10		1d. deep red-brown	£400	30·00	
11		1d. lake-red	£2000	£425	
12		1d. orange-brown	£750	£125	

Error. No letter "A" in right lower corner (Stamp B(A), *Plate 77)*

12*a*	**1**	1d. red-brown	—	£7500

The error "No letter A in right corner" was due to the omission to insert this letter on stamp B A of Plate 77. The error was discovered some months after the plate was registered and was then corrected.

There are innumerable variations in the colour and shade of the 1d. "red" and those given in the above list represent colour groups each covering a wide range.

Varieties of 1d. red-brown, etc.

			Un	*Used*
b.	Re-entry	*from*	—	50·00
c.	Double letter in corner	*from*		25·00
d.	Double Star (Plate 75) "Union Jack" re-entry		£10000	£1500
e.	Guide line in corner		—	18·00
f.	Guide line through value		—	22·00
g.	Thick outer frame to stamp		—	22·00
h.	Ivory head		£275	22·00
i.	Watermark inverted		£950	£175
j.	Left corner letter "S" inverted (Plates 78, 105, 107)	*from*	—	£100
k.	P converted to R (Plates 30/1, 33, 83, 86)	*from*	—	60·00
l.	Obliterated by Maltese Cross			
		In red	—	£2500
		In black	—	40·00
		In blue	—	£350
m.	Obliterated by Maltese Cross with number in centre			
		No. 1	—	£100
		No. 2	—	£100
		No. 3	—	£125
		No. 4	—	£300
		No. 5	—	£100
		No. 6	—	80·00
		No. 7	—	80·00
		No. 8	—	80·00
		No. 9	—	£100
		No. 10	—	£150
		No. 11	—	£175
		No. 12	—	£200
n.	Obliterated "Penny Post" in black (without Maltese Cross)		—	£400
o.	Obliterated by town postmark (without Maltese Cross)			
	In black	*from*	—	£350
	In blue	*from*	—	£800
	In green	*from*	—	£1200
	In yellow	*from*	—	—
	In red	*from*	—	£4500
p.	Obliterated by 1844 type postmark			
	In blue	*from*	—	£150
	In red	*from*	—	£3000
	In green	*from*	—	£750
	In violet	*from*	—	£1400
	In black	*from*	—	15·00

Stamps with thick outer frame to the design are from plates on which the frame-lines have been strengthened or recut, particularly Plates 76 and 90.

For "Union Jack" re-entry *see* General Notes to Line-engraved Issues.

In "P converted to R" the corner letter "R" is formed from the "P", the distinctive long tail having been hand-cut.

KEY TO LINE-ENGRAVED ISSUES

S.G. Nos	*Description*	*Date*	*Wmk*	*Perf*	*Die*	*Alpha-bet*
	THE IMPERFORATE ISSUES					
1/3	1d. black	6.5.40	SC	Imp	I	I
4/6	2d. no lines	8.5.40	SC	Imp	I	I
	PAPER MORE OR LESS BLUED					
7	1d. red-brown	Feb 1841	SC	Imp	I	I
8/12	1d. red-brown	Feb 1841	SC	Imp	I	I
8/12	1d. red-brown	6.2.52	SC	Imp	I	II
13/15	2d. white lines	13.3.41	SC	Imp	I	I
	THE PERFORATED ISSUES					
	ONE PENNY VALUE					
16*a*	1d. red-brown	1848	SC	Roul	I	I
16*b*	1d. red-brown	1850	SC	16	I	I
16*c*	1d. red-brown	1853	SC	16	I	II
17/18	1d. red-brown	Feb 1854	SC	16	I	II
22	1d. red-brown	Jan 1855	SC	14	I	II
24/5	1d. red-brown	28.2.55	SC	14	II	II
21	1d. red-brown	1.3.55	SC	16	II	II
26	1d. red-brown	15.5.55	LC	16	II	II
29/33	1d. red-brown	Aug 1855	LC	14	II	Ill
	NEW COLOURS ON WHITE PAPER					
37/41	1d. rose-red	Nov 1856	LC	14	II	III
36	1d. rose-red	26.12.57	LC	16	II	III
42	1d. rose-red	1861	LC	14	II	IV
	TWO PENCE VALUE					
19, 20	2d. blue	1.3.54	SC	16	I	I
23	2d. blue	22.2.55	SC	14	I	I
23*a*	2d. blue	5.7.55	SC	14	I	II
20*a*	2d. blue	18.8.55	SC	16	I	II
27	2d. blue	20.7.55	LC	16	I	II
34	2d. blue	20.7.55	LC	14	I	II
35	2d. blue	2.7.57	LC	14	I	III
36*a*	2d. blue	1.2.58	LC	16	I	III
	LETTERS IN ALL FOUR CORNERS					
48/9	½d. rose-red	1.10.70	W **9**	14	—	
43/4	1d. rose-red	1.4.64	LC	14	II	
53*a*	1½d rosy mauve	1860	LC	14	II	
51/3	1½d. rose-red	1.10.70	LC	14	II	
45	2d. blue	July 1858	LC	14	II	
46/7	2d. thinner lines	7.7.69	LC	14	II	

Watermarks: SC = Small Crown, T **2**. LC = Large Crown, T **4**.

Dies: See notes above No. 17 in the catalogue.

Alphabets: See General Notes to this section.

3 White lines added

1841 (13 Mar)–**51**. *White lines added.* Wmk W **2**. Paper more or less blued. Imperf.

			Un	Used	Used on cover
13	**3**	2d. pale blue	£2500	80·00	
14		2d. blue	£2250	70·00	£225
15		2d. deep full blue	£2500	80·00	
15*aa*		2d. violet-blue (1851)	£12000	£800	

The 2d. stamp with white lines was printed from Plates 3 and 4.

No. 15*aa* came from Plate 4 and the price quoted is for examples on thicker, lavender tinted paper.

Plates of 2d. blue

Plate		*Un*	*Used*
3	*Shades from*	£2250	80·00
4	*Shades from*	£2250	70·00

Varieties of 2d. blue

		Un	*Used*
a.	Guide line in corner	—	85·00
b.	Guide line through value	£2500	85·00
bb.	Double letter in corner	—	90·00
be.	Re-entry	£3000	£110
c.	Ivory head	£2500	80·00
d.	Watermark inverted	£4000	£350
e.	Obliterated by Maltese Cross		
	In red	—	£11000
	In black	—	£150
	In blue	—	£2250
f.	Obliterated by Maltese Cross with number in centre		
	No. 1	—	£350
	No. 2	—	£350
	No. 3	—	£350
	No. 4	—	£325
	No. 5	—	£475
	No. 6	—	£350
	No. 7	—	£650
	No. 8	—	£500
	No. 9	—	£650
	No. 10	—	£700
	No. 11	—	£475
	No. 12	—	£275
g.	Obliterated by town postmark (without Maltese Cross)		
	In black *from*	—	£750
	In blue *from*	—	£1250
h.	Obliterated by 1844 type postmark		
	In black *from*	—	70·00
	In blue *from*	—	£500
	In red *from*	—	£8500
	In green *from*	—	£1500

1841 (Apr). *Trial printing (unissued) on Dickinson silk-thread paper.* No wmk. Imperf.

16 **1** 1d. red-brown (Plate 11) £3000

Eight sheets were printed on this paper, six being gummed, two ungummed, but we have only seen examples without gum.

1848. Wmk Small Crown, W **2**. *Rouletted approx 11½ by Henry Archer.*

16*a* **1** 1d. red-brown (Plates 70, 71) £6500

1850. Wmk Small Crown, W **2**. P 16 by Henry Archer.

16*b* **1** 1d. red-brown (Alph 1) (from Plates 90-101) . . . *from* £1000 £350 £850

Stamps on cover dated prior to February 1854 are worth a premium of 50% over the price on cover quoted above.

1853. *Government Trial Perforation.* Wmk Small Crown. W **2**.

16*c* **1** 1d. red-brown (P 16) (Alph II) (*on cover*) . . . . † £9000

SEPARATION TRIALS. Although the various trials of machines for rouletting and perforating were unofficial, Archer had the consent of the authorities in making his experiments, and sheets so experimented upon were afterwards used by the Post Office.

As Archer ended his experiments in 1850 and plates with corner letters Alphabet II did not come into issue until 1852, perforated stamps with corner letters of Alphabet I may safely be assumed to be Archer productions, if genuine.

The Government trial perforation is believed to have been done on Archer's machines after they had been purchased in 1853. As Alphabet II was by that time in use, the trials can only be distinguished from the perforated stamps listed below by being dated prior to 24 February 1854, the date when the perforated stamps were officially issued.

Die I Alphabet I, stamps from plates 74 and 113 perforated 14 have been recorded for many years, but it is now generally recognised that the type of comb machine used, producing one extension hole in the side margins, cannot be contemporary with other trials of this period.

Die I

Die II

4 Large Crown

Die I: The features of the portrait are lightly shaded and consequently lack emphasis.

Die II (Die I retouched): The lines of the features have been deepened and appear stronger.

The eye is deeply shaded and made more lifelike. The nostril and lips are more clearly defined. the latter appearing much thicker. A strong downward stroke of colour marks the corner of the mouth. There is a deep indentation of colour between lower lip and chin. The band running from the back of the ear to the chignon has a bolder horizontal line below it than in Die I.

The original die (Die I) was used to provide roller dies for the laying down of all the line-engraved stamps from 1840 to 1855. In that year a new master die was laid down (by means of a Die I roller die) and the impression was retouched by hand engraving by William Humphrys. This retouched die, always known to philatelists as Die II, was from that time used for preparing all new roller dies.

One Penny. The numbering of the 1d. plates recommenced at 1 on the introduction of Die II. Plates 1 to 21 were Alphabet II from which a scarce plum shade exists. Corner letters of Alphabet III appear on Plate 22 and onwards.

As an experiment, the corner letters were engraved by hand on Plates 50 and 51 in 1856, instead of being punched (Alphabet IV), but punching was again resorted to from Plate 52 onwards. Plates 50 and 51 were not put into use until 1861.

Two Pence. Unlike the 1d. the old sequence of plate numbers continued. Plates 3 and 4 of the 2d. had corner letters of Alphabet I, Plate 5 Alphabet II and Plate 6 Alphabet III. In Plate 6 the white lines are thinner than before.

1854–57. *Paper more or less blued.*

(a) Wmk Small Crown, W **2**. P 16.

			Un	*Used**	*Used on cover*
17	**1**	1d. red-brown (Die I) (24.2.54)	£250	18·00	40·00
		a. Imperf three sides (horiz pair)	†	—	
18		1d. yellow brown (Die I)	£300	40·00	
19	**3**	2d. deep blue (Plate 4) (12.3.54)	£2500	85·00	£130
		a. Imperf three sides (horiz pair)	†	—	
20		2d. pale blue (Plate 4)	£2500	90·00	
20*a*		2d. blue (Plate 5) (18.8.55)	£4500	£250	£400
21	**1**	1d. red-brown (Die II) (22.2.55)	£275	50·00	90·00
		a. Imperf			

(b) Wmk Small Crown, W **2**. P 14.

22	**1**	1d. red-brown (Die I) (1.55)	£450	60·00	£110
23	**3**	2d. blue (Plate 4) (22.2.55)	£4500	£180	£275
23*a*		2d. blue (Plate 5) (4.7.55)	£5500	£250	£350
		b. Imperf (Plate 5)			
24	**1**	1d. red-brown (Die II) (27.2.55)	£400	45·00	75·00
24*a*		1d. deep red-brown (very blue paper) (Die II)	£475	70·00	
25		1d. orange-brown (Die II)	£1200	£125	

(c) Wmk Large Crown, W **4**. P 16.

26	**1**	1d. red-brown (Die II) (15.5.55)	£700	80·00	£150
		a. Imperf (Plate 7)			
27	**3**	2d. blue (Plate 5) (20.7.55)	£6000	£325	£400
		a. Imperf	—	£4000	

(d) Wmk Large Crown, W **4**. P 14.

29	**1**	1d. red-brown (Die II) (6.55)	£180	15·00	30·00
		a. Imperf (*shades*) (Plates 22, 24, 25, 32, 43)	£1500	£1200	
30		1d. brick-red (Die II)	£250	35·00	
31		1d. plum (Die II) (2.56)	£1500	£500	
32		1d. brown-rose (Die II)	£250	35·00	
33		1d. orange-brown (Die II) (3.57)	£375	40·00	
34	**3**	2d. blue (Plate 5) (20.7.55)	£1750	50·00	£130
35		2d. blue (Plate 6) (2.7.57)	£2000	50·00	£130
		a. Imperf	—	£4000	
		b. Imperf horiz (vert pair)	†	—	

*17/35a **For well-centred, lightly used +125%.**

1856–58. Wmk Large Crown, W **4**. Paper no longer blued.

(a) P 16.

36	**1**	1d. rose-red (Die II) (26.12.57)	£1250	60·00	£130
36*a*	**3**	2d. blue (Plate 6) (1.2.58)	£6000	£300	£400

(b) *Die II.* P 14.

37	**1**	1d. red-brown (11.56)	£700	£175	£450
38		1d. pale red (9.4.57)	75·00	15·00	
		a. Imperf	£1200	£850	
39		1d. pale rose (3.57)	75·00	25·00	
40		1d. rose-red (9.57)	40·00	9·00	20·00
		a. Imperf	£1200	£850	
		b. Imperf vert (horiz pair)	†	—	
41		1d. deep rose-red (7.57)	90·00	12·00	

1861. *Letters engraved on plate instead of punched (Alphabet IV).*

42	**1**	1d. rose-red (Die II) (Plates 50 and 51)	£200	30·00	50·00
		a. Imperf	—	£2250	

*36/42a **For well-centred, lightly used +125%.**

In both values, varieties may be found as described in the preceding issues—ivory heads, inverted watermarks, re-entries, and double letters in corners.

The change of perforation from 16 to 14 was decided upon late in 1854 since the closer holes of the former gauge tended to cause the sheets of stamps to break up when handled, but for a time both gauges were in concurrent use. Owing to faulty alignment of the impressions on the plates and to shrinkage of the paper when damped, badly perforated stamps are plentiful in the line-engraved issues.

5

6

Showing position of the plate number on the 1d. and 2d. values. (Plate 170 shown)

1858–79. *Letters in all four corners.* Wmk Large Crown, W **4**. Die II (1d. and 2d.). P 14.

			Un	*Used**	*Used on cover*
43	**5**	1d. rose-red (1.4.64)	15·00	2·00	6·00
44		1d. lake-red	15·00	2·00	
		a. Imperf from	£1600	£1250	

*43/4a **For well-centred, lightly used +125%.**

Plate	*Un*	*Used*	*Plate*	*Un*	*Used*
71	35·00	3·00	150	15·00	2·00
72	40·00	4·00	151	60·00	9·00
73	40·00	3·00	152	60·00	5·50
74	40·00	2·00	153	£100	9·00
76	35·00	2·00	154	50·00	2·00
77	—	£120000	155	50·00	2·25
78	90·00	2·00	156	45·00	2·00
79	30·00	2·00	157	50·00	2·00
80	45·00	2·00	158	30·00	2·00
81	45·00	2·25	159	30·00	2·00
82	90·00	4·00	160	30·00	2·00
83	£110	7·00	161	60·00	7·00
84	60·00	2·25	162	50·00	7·00
85	40·00	2·25	163	50·00	3·00
86	50·00	4·00	164	50·00	3·00
87	30·00	2·00	165	45·00	2·00
88	£130	8·00	166	45·00	6·00
89	40·00	2·00	167	45·00	2·00
90	40·00	2·00	168	50·00	8·00
91	55·00	6·00	169	60·00	7·00
92	35·00	2·00	170	35·00	2·00
93	50·00	2·00	171	15·00	2·00
94	45·00	5·00	172	30·00	2·00
95	40·00	2·00	173	70·00	9·00
96	45·00	2·00	174	30·00	2·00
97	40·00	3·50	175	60·00	3·50
98	50·00	6·00	176	60·00	2·25
99	55·00	5·00	177	40·00	2·00
100	60·00	2·25	178	60·00	3·50
101	60·00	9·00	179	50·00	2·25
102	45·00	2·00	180	60·00	5·00
103	50·00	3·50	181	45·00	2·00
104	75·00	5·00	182	90·00	5·00
105	90·00	7·00	183	55·00	3·00
106	55·00	2·00	184	30·00	2·25
107	60·00	7·00	185	50·00	3·00
108	80·00	2·25	186	65·00	2·25
109	85·00	3·50	187	50·00	2·00
110	60·00	9·00	188	70·00	10·00
111	50·00	2·25	189	70·00	7·00
112	70·00	2·25	190	50·00	6·00
113	50·00	12·00	191	30·00	7·00
114	£250	12·00	192	50·00	2·00
115	90·00	2·25	193	30·00	2·00
116	75·00	9·00	194	50·00	8·00
117	45·00	2·00	195	50·00	8·00
118	50·00	2·00	196	50·00	5·00
119	45·00	2·00	197	55·00	9·00
120	15·00	2·00	198	40·00	6·00
121	40·00	9·50	199	55·00	6·00
122	15·00	2·00	200	60·00	2·00
123	40·00	2·00	201	30·00	5·00
124	28·00	2·00	202	60·00	8·00
125	40·00	2·00	203	30·00	16·00
127	55·00	2·25	204	55·00	2·25
129	40·00	8·00	205	55·00	3·00
130	55·00	2·25	206	55·00	9·00
131	65·00	16·00	207	60·00	9·00
132	£130	22·00	208	55·00	16·00
133	£110	9·00	209	50·00	9·00
134	15·00	2·00	210	65·00	12·00
135	95·00	26·00	211	70·00	20·00
136	90·00	20·00	212	60·00	11·00
137	28·00	2·25	213	60·00	11·00
138	18·00	2·00	214	65·00	18·00
139	60·00	16·00	215	65·00	18·00
140	18·00	2·00	216	70·00	18·00
141	£110	9·00	217	70·00	7·00
142	70·00	24·00	218	65·00	8·00
143	60·00	15·00	219	90·00	70·00
144	95·00	20·00	220	40·00	7·00
145	30·00	2·25	221	70·00	16·00
146	40·00	6·00	222	80·00	40·00
147	50·00	3·00	223	90·00	60·00
148	40·00	3·00	224	£100	50·00
149	40·00	6·00	225	£1750	£650

Error. Imperf. Issued at Cardiff (Plate 116).

			Un	*Used*
44*b*	**5**	1d. rose-red (18.1.70)	£4000	£2000

The following plate numbers are also known imperf and used (No. 44a); 72, 79, 80, 81, 82, 83, 84, 85, 86, 87, 88, 90, 91, 92, 93, 96, 97, 98, 100, 101, 102, 103, 104, 105, 107, 108, 109, 112, 113, 114, 116, 117, 120, 121, 122, 136, 137, 142, 146, 148, 158, 162, 164, 166, 171, 174, 191 and 202.

The numbering of this series of 1d. red plates follows after that of the previous 1d. stamp, last printed from Plate 68.

Plates 69, 70, 75, 126 and 128 were prepared for this issue but rejected owing to defects, and stamps from these plates do not exist, so that specimens which appear to be from these plates (like many of those which optimistic collectors believe to be from Plate 77) bear other plate numbers. Owing to faulty engraving or printing it is not always easy to identify the plate number. Plate 77 was also rejected but some stamps printed from it were used. One specimen is in the Tapling Collection and six or seven others are known. Plates 226 to 228 were made but not used.

Specimens from most of the plates are known with inverted watermark. The variety of watermark described in the General Notes to this section occurs on stamp M A (or M L) on plates up to about 96 (*Prices from* £110 *used*).

Re-entries in this issue are few, the best being on stamps M K and T K of Plate 71 and on S L and T L, Plate 83.

			Un	*Used**	*Used on cover*
45	**6**	2d. blue (thick lines) (7.58)	£275	10·00	35·00
		a. Imperf (Plate 9)	—	£3750	
		Plate			
		7	£1000	45·00	
		8	£900	32·00	
		9	£275	10·00	
		12	£1500	£110	
46		2d. blue (thin lines) (1.7.69)	£300	20·00	50·00
47		2d. deep blue (thin lines)	£300	20·00	
		a. Imperf (Plate 13)	£4500		
		Plate			
		13	£300	20·00	
		14	£375	25·00	
		15	£350	25·00	

*45/7 **For well-centred, lightly used +125%.**

Plates 10 and 11 of the 2d. were prepared but rejected. Plates 13 to 15 were laid down from a new roller impression on which the white lines were thinner.

There are some marked re-entries and repairs, particularly on Plates 7, 8, 9 and 12.

SELLING YOUR COLLECTION?

Warwick and Warwick have an expanding requirement for world collections, single country collections, single items, covers, proof material and specialised collections, especially G.B. Our customer base is increasing dramatically and we need an ever larger supply of quality material to keep pace with demand. The market for quality material has never been stronger and if you are considering the sale of your collection, now is the time to act.

FREE VALUATIONS

We will provide a free professional and without obligation valuation of your collection. Either we will make you a fair, binding private treaty offer, or we will recommend inclusion of your property in our next public auction.

FREE TRANSPORTATION

We can arrange insured transportation of your collection to our Warwick offices completely free of charge. If you decline our offer we ask you to cover the return carriage costs only.

FREE VISITS

Visits by our valuers are possible anywhere in the country or abroad, usually within 48 hours, in order to value larger collections. Please phone for details.

EXCELLENT PRICES

Because of the strength of our customer base we are in a position to offer prices that we feel sure will exceed your expectations.

ACT NOW

Telephone today with details of your property. E-mail or fax us if you prefer.

Get the experts on your side.

Warwick & Warwick

www.warwickandwarwick.com

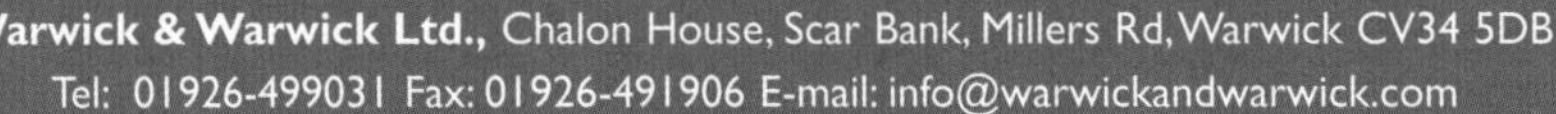

Stamps with inverted watermark may be found and also the T A (T L) and M A (M L) watermark varieties (*see* General Notes to this section).

Though the paper is normally white, some printings showed blueing and stamps showing the "ivory head" may therefore be found.

7

Showing the plate number (9)

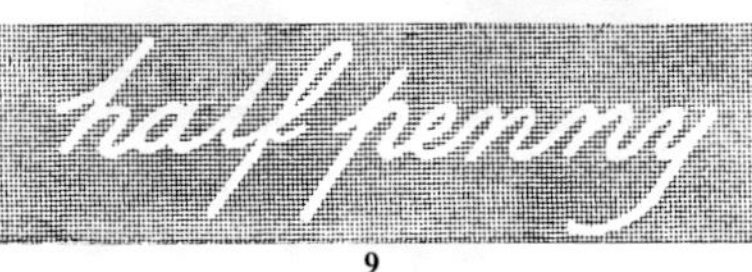
9

1870 (1 Oct). Wmk W **9**, extending over three stamps. P 14.

			Un	*Used**	*Used on cover*
48	**7**	½d. rose-red	85·00	15·00	55·00
49		½d. rose	85·00	15·00	
		a. Imperf (Plates 1, 4, 5, 6, 8, 14) *from*	£1500	£1000	
		Plate			
		1	£180	70·00	
		3	£140	35·00	
		4	£120	25·00	
		5	85·00	15·00	
		6	90·00	15·00	
		8	£225	90·00	
		9	£3250	£600	
		10	£100	15·00	
		11	90·00	15·00	
		12	90·00	15·00	
		13	90·00	15·00	
		14	90·00	15·00	
		15	£140	35·00	
		19	£160	50·00	
		20	£190	70·00	

49/9a **For well-centred, lightly used +200%**

The ½d. was printed in sheets of 480 (24 × 20) so that the check letters run from A A / A A to X T / T X.

Plates 2, 7, 16, 17 and 18 were not completed while Plates 21 and 22, though made, were not used.

Owing to the method of perforating, the outer side of stamps in either the A or X row (ie the left or right side of the sheet) is imperf.

Stamps may be found with watermark inverted or reversed, or without watermark, the latter due to misplacement of the paper when printing.

8

Position of plate Number

1870 (1 Oct). Wmk W **4**. P 14.

			Un	*Used**	*Used on cover*
51	**8**	1½d. rose-red	£350	45·00	£200
52		1½d. lake-red	£350	45·00	
		a. Imperf (Plates 1 and 3) *from*	£3000	†	
		Plate			
		(1)	£500	65·00	
		3	£350	40·00	
		Error of lettering. OP–PC *for* CP–PC *(Plate 1).*			
53	**8**	1½d. rose-red	£8000	£900	
		Prepared for use in 1860 but not issued; blued paper.			
53*a*	**8**	1½d. rosy mauve (Plate 1)	£3500		
		b. Error of lettering, OP-PC for CP-PC	—	†	

51/3 **For well-centred, lightly used +125%.**

Owing to a proposed change in the postal rates, 1½d. stamps were first printed in 1860, in rosy mauve, No. 53*a*, but the change was not approved and the greater part of the stock was destroyed, though three or four postally used examples have been recorded.

In 1870 a 1½d. stamp was required and was issued in rose-red.

Plate 1 did not have the plate number in the design of the stamps, but on stamps from Plate 3 the number will be found in the frame as shown above.

Plate 2 was defective and was not used.

The error of lettering OP-PC on Plate 1 was apparently not noticed by the printers, and therefore not corrected.

EMBOSSED ISSUES

Volume 1 of the Stanley Gibbons *Great Britain Specialised Catalogue* gives further detailed information on the embossed issues.

PRICES. The prices quoted are for cut-square stamps with average to fine embossing. Stamps with exceptionally clear embossing are worth more.

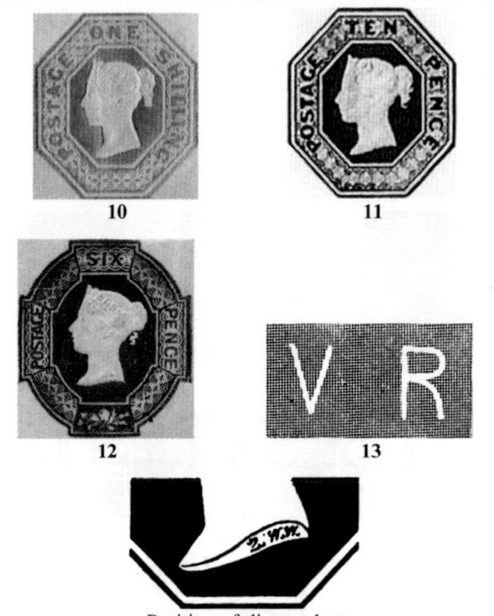
10 11 12 13

Position of die number

(Primary die engraved at the Royal Mint by William Wyon. Stamps printed at Somerset House)

1847–54. Imperf. (*For paper and wmk see footnote.*)

			Un	*Used*	*Used on cover*
54	**10**	1s. pale green (11.9.47)	£7000	£500	£800
55		1s. green	£7000	£550	
56		1s. deep green	£7500	£550	
		Die 1 (1847)	£7000	£500	
		Die 2 (1854)	£7500	£575	
57	**11**	10d. brown (6.11.48)	£4500	£900	£1500
		Die 1 (1848)	£5000	£900	
		Die 2 (1850)	£4500	£900	
		Die 3 1853)	£5000	£900	
		Die 4 (1854)	£5000	£900	
		Die 5			
58	**12**	6d. mauve (1.3.54)	£5250	£675	
59		6d. dull lilac	£5250	£675	£900
60		6d. purple	£5250	£675	
61		6d. violet	£6500	£1750	

The 1s. and 10d. are on "Dickinson" paper with "silk" threads (actually a pale blue twisted cotton yarn). The 6d. is on paper watermarked V R in single-lined letters, W **13**, which may be found in four ways—upright, inverted, upright reversed, and inverted reversed, upright reversed being the most common.

The die numbers are indicated on the base of the bust. Only Die 1 (1 WW) of the 6d. was used for the adhesive stamps. The 10d. is from Die 1 (W.W.1 on stamps), and Dies 2 to 5 (2 W.W., 3 W.W., 4 W.W. and 5 W.W.) but the number and letters on stamps from Die 1 are seldom clear and many specimens are known without any trace of them. Because of this the stamp we previously listed as "No die number" has been deleted. That they are from Die I is proved by the existence of blocks showing stamps with and without the die number. The 1s. is from Dies 1 and 2 (W.W.1, W.W.2).

The normal arrangement of the "silk" threads in the paper was in pairs running down each vertical row of the sheet, the space between the threads of each pair being approximately 5 mm and between pairs of threads 20 mm. Varieties due to misplacement of the paper in printing show a single thread on the first stamp from the sheet margin and two threads 20 mm apart on the other stamps of the row. Faulty manufacture is the cause of stamps with a single thread in the middle.

Through bad spacing of the impressions, which were handstruck, all values may be found with two impressions more or less overlapping. Owing to the small margin allowed for variation of spacing, specimens with good margins on all sides are not common.

Double impressions are known of all values.

Later printings of the 6d. had the gum tinted green to enable the printer to distinguish the gummed side of the paper.

SURFACE-PRINTED ISSUES

GENERAL NOTES

Volume 1 of the Stanley Gibbons *Great Britain Specialised Catalogue* gives further detailed information on the surface-printed issues.

"Abnormals". The majority of the great rarities in the surface-printed group of issues are the so-called "abnormals", whose existence is due to the practice of printing six sheets from every plate as soon as made, one of which was kept for record purposes at Somerset House, while the others were perforated and usually issued. If such plates were not used for general production or if, before they came into full use, a change of watermark or colour took place, the six sheets originally printed would differ from the main issue in plate, colour or watermark and, if issued, would be extremely rare.

The abnormal stamps of this class listed in this Catalogue and distinguished, where not priced, by an asterisk (*), are:

No.		
78	3d.	Plate 3 (with white dots)
152	4d.	vermilion, Plate 16
153	4d.	sage-green, Plate 17
109	6d.	mauve, Plate 10
124/*a*	6d.	chestnut and 6d. pale chestnut, Plate 12
145	6d.	pale buff, Plate 13
88	9d.	Plate 3 (hair lines)
98	9d.	Plate 5 (*see* footnote to No. 98)
113	10d.	Plate 2
91	1s.	Plate 3 ("Plate 2")
148/50	1s.	green, Plate 14
120	2s.	blue, Plate 3

Those which may have been issued, but of which no specimens are known, are 2½d. wmk Anchor, Plates 4 and 5; 3d. wmk Emblems, Plate 5; 3d. wmk Spray, Plate 21; 6d. grey, wmk Spray, Plate 18; 8d. orange, Plate 2; 1s. wmk Emblems, Plate 5; 5s. wmk Maltese Cross, Plate 4.

The 10d. Plate 1, wmk Emblems (No. 99), is sometimes reckoned among the abnormals, but was an error, due to the use of the wrong paper.

Corner Letters. With the exception of the 4d., 6d. and 1s. of 1855–57, the ½d., 1½d., 2d. and 5d. of 1880, the 1d. lilac of 1881 and the £5 (which had letters in lower corners only, and in the reverse order to the normal), all the surface-printed stamps issued prior to 1887 had letters in all four corners, as in the later line-engraved stamps. The arrangement is the same, the letters running in sequence right across and down the sheets, whether these were divided into ones or not. The corner letters existing naturally depend on the number of stamps in the sheet and their arrangement.

Imprimaturs and Imperforate Stamps. The Post Office retained in their records (now in the National Postal Museum) one imperforate sheet from each plate, known as the Imprimatur (or officially approved) sheet. Some stamps were removed from time to time for presentation purposes and have come on to the market, but these tmperforates are not listed as they were not issued. Full details can be found in Volume I of the *Great Britain Specialised Catalogue*.

However, other imperforate stamps are known to have been issued and these are listed where it has been possible to prove that they do not come from the Imprimatur sheets. It is therefore advisable to purchase these only when acccompanied by an Expert Committee certificate of genuineness.

Plate Numbers. All stamps from No. 75 to No. 163 bear in their designs either the plate number or, in one or two earlier instances, some other indication by which one plate can be distinguished from another. With the aid of these and of the corner letters it is thus possible to "reconstruct" a sheet of stamps from any plate of any issue or denomination.

Surface-printing. In this context the traditional designation "surface-printing" is synonymous with typo(graphy)—a philatelic term—or letterpress—the printers' term—as meaning printing from (the surface of) raised type. It is also called relief-printing, as the image is in relief (in French, *en épargne*), unwanted parts of the design having been cut away. Duplicate impressions can be electrotyped or stereotyped from an original die, the resulting *clichés* being locked together to form the printing plate.

Wing Margins. As the vertical gutters (spaces) between the panes, into which sheets of stamps of most values were divided until the introduction of the Imperial Crown watermark, were perforated through the centre with a single row of holes, instead of each vertical row of stamps on the inner side of the panes having its own line of perforation as is now usual, a proportion of the stamps in each sheet have what is called a "wing margin" about 5 mm wide on one or other side.

The stamps with "wing margins" are the watermark Emblems and Spray of Rose series (3d., 6d., 9d., 10d., 1s. and 2s.) with letters D, E, H or I in S.E. corner, and the watermark Garter series (4d. and 8d.) with letters F or G in S.E. corner. Knowledge of this lettering will enable collectors to guard against stamps with wing margin cut down and reperforated, but note that wing margin stamps of Nos. 62 to 73 are also to be found re-perforated.

PRINTERS. The issues of Queen Victoria, Nos. 62/214, were typo by Thomas De La Rue & Co.

PERFORATIONS. All the surface-printed issues of Queen Victoria are Perf 14, with the exception of Nos. 126/9.

KEY TO SURFACE-PRINTED ISSUES 1855–83

S.G. Nos	*Description*	*Watermark*	*Date of Issue*
	NO CORNER LETTERS		
62	4d. carmine	Small Garter	31.7.55
63/5	4d. carmine	Medium Garter	25.2.56
66/*a*	4d. carmine	Large Garter	Jan 1857
69/70	6d. lilac	Emblems	21.10.56
71/3	1s. green	Emblems	1.11.56
	SMALL WHITE CORNER LETTERS		
75/7	3d. carmine	Emblems	1.5.62
78	3d. carmine (dots)	Emblems	Aug 1862
79/82	4d. red	Large Garter	15.1.62
83/5	6d. lilac	Emblems	1.12.62
86/8	9d. bistre	Emblems	15.1.62
89/91	1s. green	Emblems	1.12.62
	LARGE WHITE CORNER LETTERS		
92	3d. rose	Emblems	1.3.65
102/3	3d. rose	Spray	July 1867
93/4	4d. vermilion	Large Garter	4.7.65
96/7	6d. lilac	Emblems	7.3.65
104/7	6d. lilac	Spray	21.6.67
108/9	6d. lilac	Spray	8.3.69
122/4	6d. chestnut	Spray	12.4.72
125	6d. grey	Spray	24.4.73
98	9d. straw	Emblems	30.10.65
110/11	9d. straw	Spray	3.10.67
99	10d. brown	Emblems	11.11.67
112/14	10d. brown	Spray	1.7.67
101	1s. green	Emblems	19.1.65
115/17	1s. green	Spray	13.7.67
118/20*b*	2s. blue	Spray	1.7.67
121	2s. brown	Spray	27.2.80
126/7	5s. rose	Cross	1.7.67
128	10s. grey	Cross	26.9.78
129	£1 brown-lilac	Cross	26.9.78
130, 134	5s. rose	Anchor	25.11.82
131, 135	10s. grey-green	Anchor	Feb 1883
132, 136	£1 brown-lilac	Anchor	Dec 1882
133, 137	£5 orange	Anchor	21.3.82
	LARGE COLOURED CORNER LETTERS		
166	1d. Venetian red	Crown	1.1.80
138/9	2½d. rosy mauve	Anchor	1.7.75
141	2½d. rosy mauve	Orb	1.5.76
142	2½d. blue	Orb	5.2.80
157	2½d. blue	Crown	23.3.81
143/4	3d. rose	Spray	5.7.73
158	3d. rose	Crown	Jan 1881
159	3d. on 3d. lilac	Crown	1.1.83
152	4d. vermilion	Large Garter	1.3.76
153	4d. sage-green	Large Garter	12.3.77
154	4d. brown	Large Garter	15.8.80
160	4d. brown	Crown	9.12.80

145	6d. buff	Spray	15.3.73
146/7	6d. grey	Spray	20.3.74
161	6d. grey	Crown	1.1.81
162	6d. on 6d. lilac	Crown	1.1.83
156*a*	8d. purple-brown	Large Garter	July 1876
156	8d. orange	Large Garter	11.9.76
148/50	1s. green	Spray	1.9.73
151	1s. brown	Spray	14.10.80
163	1s. brown	Crown	24.5.81

Watermarks:		
	Anchor	W **40, 47**
	Cross	W **39**
	Crown	W **49**
	Emblems	W **20**
	Large Garter	W **17**
	Medium Garter	W **16**
	Orb	W **48**
	Small Garter	W **15**
	Spray	W **33**

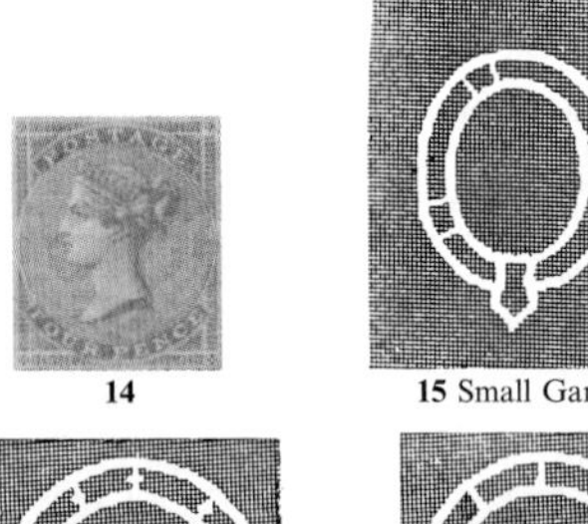

14 **15** Small Garter

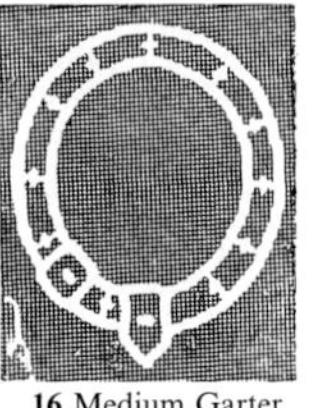

16 Medium Garter

17 Large Garter

1855–57. *No corner letters.*

(a) Wmk Small Garter, W **15**. *Highly glazed, deeply blued paper* (31 July 1855).

			Un	*Used**	*Used on cover*
62	**14**	4d. carmine (*shades*)	£4000	£325	£500
		a. Paper slightly blued	£4250	£325	
		b. White paper	—	£600	

(b) Wmk Medium Garter, W **16**.

(i) Thick, blued highly glazed paper (25 February 1856).

63	**14**	4d. carmine (*shades*)	£4750	£375	£500
		a. White paper	£3750		

(ii) Ordinary thin white paper (September 1856).

64	**14**	4d. pale carmine	£3500	£300	£375
		a. Stamp printed double	†	—	

(iii) Ordinary white paper, specially prepared ink (1 November 1856).

65	**14**	4d. rose or deep rose	£3750	£325	£425

(c) Wmk Large Garter, W **17**. *Ordinary white paper* (January 1857).

66	**14**	4d. rose-carmine	£1100	90·00	£150
		a. Rose	£1000	90·00	
		b. Thick glazed paper	£2500	£225	

*62/6b **For well-centred, lightly used +125%.**

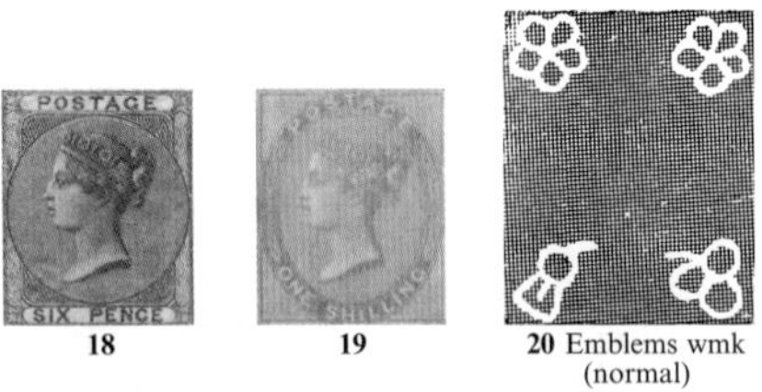

18 **19** **20** Emblems wmk (normal)

20a Wmk error, three roses and shamrock

20b Wmk error, three roses and thistle

(d) Wmk Emblems, W **20**.

			Un	*Used**	*Used on cover*
69	**18**	6d. deep lilac (21.10.56)	£1000	£110	
70		6d. pale lilac	£800	85·00	£150
		a. Azure paper	£3250	£500	
		b. Thick paper	£2000	£275	
		c. Error. Wmk W **20a**			
71	**19**	1s. deep green (1.11.56)	£2000	£275	
72		1s. green	£1000	£250	£300
73		1s. pale green	£1000	£250	
		a. Azure paper	—	£900	
		b. Thick paper	—	£275	
		c. Imperf	†	—	

*69/73b **For well-centred, lightly used +125%.**

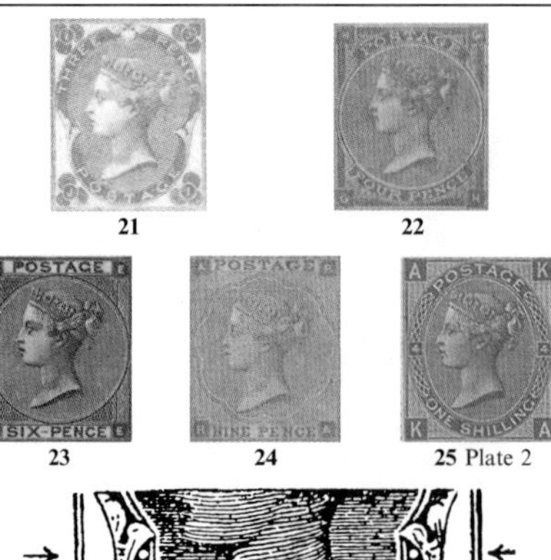

21 **22** **23** **24** **25** Plate 2

A. White dots added

B. Hair lines

1862–64. *A small uncoloured letter in each corner,* the 4d. wmk Large Garter. W **17**, the others Emblems, W **20**.

			Un	*Used**	*Used on cover*
75	**21**	3d. deep carmine-rose (Plate 2) (1.5.62)	£2500	£325	
76		3d. bright carmine-rose	£1400	£225	£400
77		3d. pale carmine-rose	£1400	£225	
		b. Thick paper	—	£325	
78		3d. rose (with white dots, Type A, Plate 3) (8.62)	£17500	£6000	
		a. Imperf (Plate 3)	£3250		
79	**22**	4d. bright red (Plate 3) (15.1.62)	£1200	£100	
80		4d. pale red	£1000	80·00	£175
81		4d. bright red (Hair lines, Type B, Plate 4) (16.10.63)	£1250	90·00	
82		4d. pale red (Hair lines, Type B, Plate 4)	£1100	80·00	£180
		a. Imperf (Plate 4)	£3000		
83	**23**	6d. deep lilac (Plate 3) (1.12.62)	£1300	£100	
84		6d. lilac	£1250	80·00	£150
		a. Azure paper	—	£700	
		b. Thick paper	—	£200	
		c. Error. Shamrock missing from wmk (stamp TF)			
		d. Error. Wmk W **20b** (stamp TF)	—	£5750	
85		6d. lilac (Hair lines, Plate 4) (20.4.64)	£1600	£160	£250
		a. Imperf	£2750		
		c. Thick paper	£2000	£200	
		d. Error. Wmk W **20b** (stamp TF)			
86	**24**	9d. bistre (Plate 2) (15.1.62)	£2500	£300	£425
87		9d. straw	£2500	£275	
		a. On azure paper			
		b. Thick paper	£3250	£350	
		c. Error. Watermark W **20b** (stamp TF)	†	—	
88		9d. bistre (Hair lines, Plate 3) (5.62)	£10000	£6500	
89	**25**	1s. deep green (Plate No. 1 = Plate 2) (1.12.62)	£2250	£300	
90		1s. green (Plate No. 1 = Plate 2)	£1500	£150	£225
		a. "K" in lower left corner in white circle (stamp KD)	£5000	£800	
		aa. "K" normal (stamp KD)	—	£1100	
		b. On azure paper			
		c. Error. Wmk **20b** (stamp TF)			
		d. Thick paper	—	£250	
		da. Thick paper, "K" in circle as No. 90a	—	£1900	
91		1s. deep green (Plate No. 2 = Plate 3)	£17500		
		a. Imperf	£3000		

*75/91 **For well-centred, lightly used +125%.**

The 3d. as Type **21**, but with network background in the spandrels which is found overprinted SPECIMEN, was never issued.

The plates of this issue may be distinguished as follows:

3d.	Plate 2.	No white dots.
	Plate 3.	White dots as Illustration A.
4d.	Plate 3.	No hair lines. Roman I next to lower corner letters.
	Plate 4.	Hair lines in corners. (Illustration B.). Roman II.
6d.	Plate 3.	No hair lines.
	Plate 4.	Hair lines in corners.
9d.	Plate 2.	No hair lines.
	Plate 3.	Hair lines in corners. Beware of faked lines.
1s.	Plate 2.	Numbered 1 on stamps.
	Plate 3.	Numbered 2 on stamps and with hair lines.

The 9d. on azure paper (No. 87a) is very rare, only one confirmed example being known.

The variety "K" in circle, No. 90a, is believed to be due to a damaged letter having been cut out and replaced. It is probable that the punch was driven in too deeply, causing the flange to penetrate the surface, producing an indentation showing as an uncoloured circle.

The watermark variety "three roses and a shamrock" illustrated in W **20a** was evidently due to the substitution of an extra rose for the thistle in a faulty watermark bit. It is found on stamp TA of Plate 4 of the 3d., Plates 1 (No. 70c), 3, 5 and 6 of the 6d., Plate 4 of the 9d. and Plate 4 of the 1s.

Similar problems occurred on stamp TF of the 6d. and 9d. Here the shamrock emblem became detached and a used example of the 6d. (No. 84) is known showing it omitted. It was replaced by a third rose (W **20b**) and this variety exists on the 6d. (Nos. 84/5 and 97) and 9d. (Nos. 87 and 98).

26

27

28 (with hyphen) **28a** (without hyphen)

29

30

31

1865–67. *Large uncoloured corner letters.* Wmk Large Garter (4d.) others Emblems.

			Un	*Used**	*Used on cover*
92	**26**	3d. rose (Plate 4) (1.3.65)	£1000	£100	£17[illegible]
		a. Error. Wmk W **20a**	£1950	£650	
		b. Thick paper	£900	£125	
93	**27**	4d. dull vermilion (4.7.65)	£500	80·00	
94		4d. vermilion	£425	50·00	£11[illegible]
		a. Imperf (Plates 11, 12)	£1300		
		Plate			
		7 (1865)	£500	80·00	
		8 (1866)	£450	50·00	
		9 (1867)	£450	50·00	
		10 (1868)	£500	90·00	
		11 (1869)	£450	50·00	
		12 (1870)	£425	50·00	
		13 (1872)	£450	50·00	
		14 (1873)	£500	80·00	
96	**28**	6d. deep lilac (with hyphen) (7.3.65)	£750	90·00	
97		6d. lilac (with hyphen)	£650	75·00	£11[illegible]
		a. Thick paper	£750	£100	
		b. Stamp doubly printed (Pl 6)	—	£10000	
		c. Error. Wmk W **20a** (Pl 5, 6) *from*	—	£700	
		d. Error. Wmk W **20b** (Plate 5)			
		Plate			
		5 (1865)	£650	75·00	
		6 (1867)	£2000	£140	
98	**29**	9d. straw (Plate 4) (30.10.65)	£1800	£375	£50[illegible]
		a. Thick paper	£2000	£500	
		b. Error. Wmk W **20a**	—	£700	
		c. Error. Wmk W **20b** (stamp TF)			
99	**30**	10d. red-brown (Pl 1) (11.11.67)	†	£25000	
101	**31**	1s. green (Plate 4) (19.1.65)	£1200	£150	£20[illegible]
		a. Error. Wmk **W20a**	—	£750	
		b. Thick paper	£1300	£240	
		c. Imperf between (vert pair)	—	£7000	

*92/101c **For well-centred, lightly used +100%.**

From mid-1866 to about the end of 1871 4d. stamps of this issu[e] appeared generally with watermark inverted.

Unused examples of No. 98 from Plate 5 exist, but this was neve[r] put to press and all evidence points to such stamps originating fro[m] a portion of the Imprimatur sheet which was perforated by De L[a] Rue in 1887 for insertion in albums to be presented to members [of] the Stamp Committee (*Price* £18000 *un*).

The 10d. stamps, No. 99, were printed in *error* on pap[er] watermarked "Emblems" instead of on "Spray of Rose".

32

33 Spray of Rose

34

1867–80. Wmk Spray of Rose, W **33**.

			Un	*Used**	*Used on cover*
102	**26**	3d. deep rose (12.7.67)	£700	£150	
103		3d. rose	£350	45·00	75·[illegible]
		a. Imperf (Plates 5, 6, 8) *from*	£1900		
		Plate			
		4 (1867)	£700	£150	
		5 (1868)	£350	45·00	
		6 (1870)	£375	45·00	
		7 (1871)	£450	50·00	
		8 (1872)	£425	45·00	
		9 (1872)	£425	50·00	
		10 (1873)	£450	90·00	

104	**28**	6d. lilac (with hyphen) (Plate 6) (21.6.67)	£850	75·00	£140
		a. Imperf			
105		6d. deep lilac (with hyphen) (Plate 6)	£850	75·00	
106		6d. purple (with hyphen) (Pl 6)	£850	£100	
107		6d. right violet (with hyphen) (Plate 6) (22.7.68)	£850	80·00	
108	**28a**	6d. dull violet (without hyphen) (Plate 8) (8.3.69)	£500	75·00	
109		6d. mauve (without hyphen)	£450	75·00	£100
		a. Imperf (Plate Nos. 8 and 9)	£3500	£2500	
		Plate			
		8 (1869, mauve)	£450	75·00	
		9 (1870, mauve)	£450	75·00	
		10 (1869, mauve)	*	£17500	
110	**29**	9d. straw (Plate No. 4) (3.10.67)	£1250	£200	£325
111		9d. pale straw (Plate No. 4)	£1100	£200	
		a. Imperf (Plate 4)	£3800		
112	**30**	10d. red-brown (1.7.67)	£1850	£275	£450
113		10d. pale red-brown	£1850	£300	
114		10d. deep red-brown	£2500	£400	
		a. Imperf (Plate 1)	£4500		
		Plate			
		1 (1867)	£1850	£275	
		2 (1867)	£17500	£6000	
115	**31**	1s. deep green (13.7.67)	£650	35·00	
117		1s. green	£550	32·00	50·00
		a. Imperf between (horiz pair) (Plate 7)			
		b. Imperf (Plate 4)	£2250	£1300	
		Plate			
		4 (1867)	£650	35·00	
		5 (1871)	£625	35·00	
		6 (1871)	£950	35·00	
		7 (1873)	£900	60·00	
118	**32**	2s. dull blue (1.7.67)	£1800	£125	£600
119		2s. deep blue	£1800	£125	
		a. Imperf (Plate 1)	£5000		
120		2s. pale blue	£2500	£180	
		aa. Imperf (Plate 1)	£5000		
120*a*		2s. cobalt	£10000	£2000	
120*b*		2s. milky blue	£8500	£1200	
		Plate			
		1 (1867)	£1800	£125	
		3 (1868)	*	£6000	
121		2s. brown (Plate No. 1) (27.2.80)	£12000	£2500	
		a. Imperf	£10000		
		b. No watermark	†	—	

*102/21 **For well-centred, lightly used +75%.**

Examples of the 1s. from Plates 5 and 6 *without* watermark are postal forgeries used at the Stock Exchange Post Office in the early 1870's.

1872–73. *Uncoloured letters in corners.* Wmk Spray, W **33**.

			Un	Used*	Used on cover
122	**34**	6d. deep chestnut (Plate II) (12.4.72)	£700	70·00	90·00
122*a*		6d. chestnut (Plate II) (22.5.72)	£600	45·00	
122*b*		6d. pale chestnut (Plate II) (1872)	£500	45·00	
123		6d. pale buff (19.10.72)	£550	75·00	£200
		Plate			
		11 (1872, pale buff)	£550	75·00	
		12 (1872, pale buff)	£1500	£200	
124		6d. chestnut (Plate 12) (1872)	*	£2500	
124*a*		6d. pale chestnut (Plate 12) (1872)	*	£2500	
125		6d. grey (Plate 12) (24.4.73)	£1250	£200	£240
		a. Imperf	£3000		

*122/5 **For well-centred, lightly used +50%.**

35

36

37

38

39 Maltese Cross

40 Large Anchor

1867–83. *Uncoloured letters in corners.*

(a) Wmk Maltese Cross, W **39**. P 15½ × 15.

			Un	Used*
126	**35**	5s. rose (1.7.67)	£4500	£550
127		5s. pale rose	£4500	£550
		a. Imperf (Plate 1)	£7000	
		Plate		
		1 (1867)	£4500	£550
		2 (1874)	£6500	£850
128	**36**	10s. greenish grey (Plate 1) (26.9.78)	£35000	£2000
129	**37**	£1 brown-lilac (Plate 1) (26.9.78)	£42000	£3000

(b) Wmk Anchor, W **40**. P 14.

(i) Blued paper.

130	**35**	5s. rose (Plate 4) (25.11.82)	£12000	£3000
131	**36**	10s. grey-green (Plate 1) (2.83)	£50000	£3500
132	**37**	£1 brown-lilac (Plate 1) (12.82)	£65000	£7000
133	**38**	£5 orange (Plate 1) (21.3.82)	£30000	£9000

(ii) White paper.

134	**35**	5s. rose (Plate 4)	£10000	£2400
135	**36**	10s. greenish grey (Plate 1)	£50000	£2800
136	**37**	£1 brown-lilac (Plate 1)	£70000	£5500
137	**38**	£5 orange (Plate 1)	£7000	£3500

*126/37 **For well-centred, lightly used +75%.**

41

42

43

44

45

46

47 Small Anchor

48 Orb

1873–80. *Large coloured letters in the corners.*

(a) Wmk Anchor, W **47**.

			Un	Used*	Used on cover
138	**41**	2½d. rosy mauve (*blued paper*) (1.7.75)	£625	£110	
		a. Imperf			
		Plate			
		1 (*blued paper*) (1875)	£625	£110	
		2 (*blued paper*) (1875)	£4500	£950	
		3 (*blued paper*) (1875)	—	£4000	
139		2½d. rosy mauve (white paper)	£450	75·00	£125
		Plate			
		1 (*white paper*) (1875)	£450	75·00	
		2 (*white paper*) (1875)	£450	75·00	
		3 (*white paper*) (1875)	£700	£110	

Error of Lettering L H—F L for L H—H L (Plate 2).

140	**41**	2½d. rosy mauve	£12500	£1700	

(b) Wmk Orb, W **48**.

141	**41**	2½d. rosy mauve (1.5.76)	£380	45·00	70·00
		Plate			
		3 (1876)	£850	90·00	
		4 (1876)	£380	45·00	
		5 (1876)	£380	45·00	
		6 (1876)	£380	45·00	
		7 (1877)	£380	45·00	
		8 (1877)	£380	45·00	
		9 (1877)	£380	45·00	
		10 (1878)	£420	60·00	
		11 (1878)	£380	45·00	
		12 (1878)	£380	45·00	
		13 (1878)	£380	45·00	
		14 (1879)	£380	45·00	
		15 (1879)	£380	45·00	
		16 (1879)	£380	45·00	
		17 (1880)	£1100	£220	
142		2½d. blue (5.2.80)	£350	50·00	70·00
		Plate			
		17 (1880)	£350	50·00	
		18 (1880)	£375	35·00	
		19 (1880)	£350	35·00	
		20 (1880)	£350	35·00	

(c) Wmk Spray, W **33**.

143	**42**	3d. rose (5.7.73)	£325	35·00	50·00
144		3d. pale rose	£400	35·00	
		Plate			
		11 (1873)	£325	35·00	
		12 (1873)	£380	35·00	
		14 (1874)	£400	35·00	
		15 (1874)	£325	35·00	
		16 (1875)	£325	35·00	
		17 (1875)	£380	35·00	
		18 (1875)	£380	35·00	
		19 (1876)	£325	35·00	
		20 (1879)	£380	60·00	
145	**43**	6d. pale buff (Plate 13) (15.3.73)	*	£12000	
146		6d. deep grey (20.3.74)	£350	50·00	80·00
147		6d. grey	£350	50·00	
		Plate			
		13 (1874)	£350	50·00	
		14 (1875)	£350	50·00	
		15 (1876)	£350	50·00	
		16 (1878)	£350	50·00	
		17 (1880)	£500	£100	
148	**44**	1s. deep green (1.9.73)	£500	85·00	
150		1s. green	£425	70·00	£140
		Plate			
		8 (1873)	£500	85·00	
		9 (1874)	£500	85·00	
		10 (1874)	£500	90·00	
		11 (1875)	£500	90·00	
		12 (1875)	£425	70·00	
		13 (1876)	£425	70·00	
		14 (—)	*	£20000	
151		1s. orange-brown (Plate 13) (14.10.80)	£2850	£475	£650

(d) Wmk Large Garter, W **17**.

152	**45**	4d. vermilion (1.3.76)	£1400	£325	£500
		Plate			
		15 (1876)	£1400	£325	
		16 (1877)	*	£18500	
153		4d. sage-green (12.3.77)	£800	£225	£350
		Plate			
		15 (1877)	£800	£225	
		16 (1877)	£700	£200	
		17 (1877)	*	£12500	
154		4d. grey-brown (Plate 17) (15.8.80)	£1250	£325	£600
		a. Imperf	£5250		
156	**46**	8d. orange (Plate 1) (11.9.76)	£900	£250	£300

*138/56 **For well-centred, lightly used +100%.**

1876 (July). *Prepared for use but not issued.*

156*a*	**46**	8d. purple-brown (Plate 1)	£5500

49 Imperial Crown

3d
..

(50)

1880–83. Wmk Imperial Crown. W **49**.

			Un	Used*	Used on cover
157	**41**	2½d. blue (23.3.81)	£325	25·00	40·00
		Plate			
		21 (1881)	£375	30·00	
		22 (1881)	£325	30·00	
		23 (1881)	£325	25·00	
158	**42**	3d. rose (3.81)	£375	70·00	£125
		Plate			
		20 (1881)	£425	£110	
		21 (1881)	£375	70·00	
159	**50**	3d.on 3d. lilac (C.) (Plate 21) (1.1.83)	£375	£125	£325
160	**45**	4d. grey-brown (8.12.80)	£300	50·00	£120
		Plate			
		17 (1880)	£300	50·00	
		18 (1882)	£300	50·00	
161	**43**	6d. grey (1.1.81)	£300	55·00	80·00
		Plate			
		17 (1881)	£350	55·00	
		18 (1882)	£300	55·00	
162	**50**	6d.on 6d. lilac (C.) (Plate 18) (1.1.83)	£400	£120	£300
		a. Slanting dots (various) *from*	£600	£250	
		b. Opt double	—	£8000	
163	**44**	1s. orange-brown (24.5.81)	£400	£110	£300
		Plate			
		13 (1881)	£475	£110	
		14 (1881)	£400	£110	

*157/63 **For well-centred, lightly used +75%.**

The 1s. Plate 14 (line perf 14) exists in purple, but was not issued in this shade (*Price* £4500 *unused*). Examples were included in a few of the Souvenir Albums prepared for members of the "Stamp Committee of 1884".

52

53

54 55

56

1880–81. Wmk Imperial Crown, W **49**.

No.	Type	Description	*Un*	*Used**	*Used on cover*
164	**52**	½d. deep green (14.10.80)	40·00	10·00	20·00
		a. Imperf	£1200		
		b. No watermark	£5000		
165		½d. pale green	40·00	15·00	
166	**53**	1d. Venetian red (1.1.80)	20·00	10·00	18·00
		a. Imperf	£1300		
167	**54**	1½d. Venetian red (14.10.80)	£150	40·00	£120
168	**55**	2d. pale rose (8.12.80)	£200	80·00	£150
168*a*		2d. deep rose	£225	80·00	
169	**56**	5d. indigo (15.3.81)	£575	£100	£200
		a. Imperf	£2500	£2000	

*164/9 **For well-centred, lightly used +75%.**

Two used examples of the 1d. value have been reported on the Orb (fiscal) watermark.

Die I

57

Die II

1881. Wmk Imperial Crown. W **49**.

No.	Type	Description	*Un*	*Used**	*Used on cover*
		(a) 14 dots in each corner, Die I (12 July).			
170	**57**	1d. lilac	£175	28·00	45·00
171		1d. pale lilac	£175	28·00	
		(b) 16 dots in each corner, Die II (13 December).			
172	**57**	1d. lilac	2·50	2·00	3·00
172*a*		1d. bluish lilac	£250	80·00	
173		1d. deep purple	2·50	2·00	
		a. Printed both sides	£700	†	
		b. Frame broken at bottom	£750	£275	
		c. Printed on gummed side	£650	†	
		d. Imperf three sides (pair)	£4500	†	
		e. Printed both sides but impression on back inverted	£750	†	
		f. No watermark	£2500	†	
		g. Blued paper	£3250		
174		1d. mauve	2·50	1·50	
		a. Imperf (pair)	£2200		

*170/4 **For well-centred, lightly used +50%.**

1d. stamps with the words "PEARS SOAP" printed on the back in *orange, blue* or *mauve* price *from* £500, *unused.*

The variety "frame broken at bottom" (No. 173b) shows a white space just inside the bottom frame-line from between the "N" and "E" of "ONE" to below the first "N" of "PENNY", breaking the pearls and cutting into the lower part of the oval below "PEN".

KEY TO SURFACE-PRINTED ISSUES 1880–1900

S.G. Nos.	*Description*	*Date of Issue*
164/5	½d. green	14.10.80
187	½d. slate-blue	1.4.84
197/*e*	½d. vermilion	1.1.87
213	½d. blue-green	17.4.1900
166	1d. Venetian red	1.1.80
170/1	1d. lilac, Die I	12.7.81
172/4	1d. lilac, Die II	12.12.81
167	1½d. Venetian red	14.10.80
188	1½d. lilac	1.4.84
198	1½d. purple and green	1.1.87
168/*a*	2d. rose	8.12.80
189	2d. lilac	1.4.84
199/200	2d. green and red	1.1.87
190	2½d.lilac	1.4.84
201	2½d purple on blue paper	1.1.87
191	3d. lilac	1.4.84
202/4	3d. purple on yellow paper	1.1.87
192	4d. dull green	1.4.84
205/*a*	4d. green and brown	1.1.87
206	4½d. green and carmine	15.9.92
169	5d. indigo	15.3.81
193	5d. dull green	1.4.84
207	5d. purple and blue, Die I	1.1.87
207*a*	5d. purple and blue, Die II	1888
194	6d. dull green	1.4.84
208/*a*	6d. purple on rose-red paper	1.1.87
195	9d. dull green	1.8.83
209	9d. purple and blue	1.1.87
210/*b*	10d. purple and carmine	24.2.90
196	1s. dull green	1.4.84
211	1s. green	1.1.87
214	1s. green and carmine	11.7.1900
175	2s.6d. lilac on blued paper	2.7.83
178/9	2s.6d. lilac	1884
176	5s. rose on blued paper	1.4.84
180/1	5s. rose	1884
177/*a*	10s. ultramarine on blued paper	1.4.84
182/3*a*	10s. ultramarine	1884
185	£1 brown-lilac, wmk Crowns	1.4.84
186	£1 brown-lilac, wmk Orbs	6.1.88
212	£1 green	28.1.91

Note that the £5 value used with the above series is listed as Nos. 133 and 137.

58

59

60

1883–84. *Coloured letters in the corners.* Wmk Anchor, W **40**.

No.	Type	Description	*Un*	*Used**
		(a) Blued paper.		
175	**58**	2s.6d. lilac (2.7.83)	£3750	£950
176	**59**	5s. rose (1.4.84)	£7500	£2500
177	**60**	10s. ultramarine (1.4.84)	£26000	£6000
177*a*		10s. cobalt (5.84)	£32000	£9000
		(b) White paper.		
178	**58**	2s.6d. lilac	£400	£125
179		2s.6d. deep lilac	£400	£125
		a. Error. On blued paper	£5000	£2000
180	**59**	5s. rose	£800	£180
181		5s. crimson	£700	£180
182	**60**	10s. cobalt	£20000	£6000
183		10s. ultramarine	£1500	£450
183*a*		10s. pale ultramarine	£1700	£450

*175/83*a* **For well-centred, lightly used +50%.**

For No. 180 perf 12 *see* second note below No. 196.

61

Broken frames, Plate 2

1884 (1 April). Wmk Three Imperial Crowns, W **49**.

No.	Type	Description	*Un*	*Used**
185	**61**	£1 brown-lilac	£20000	£2000
		a. Frame broken	£28000	£3250

1888 (Jan). Wmk Three Orbs, W **48**.

No.	Type	Description	*Un*	*Used**
186	**61**	£1 brown-lilac	£45000	£3250
		a. Frame broken	£48000	£5000

*185/6a **For well-centred, lightly used +50%.**

The December 1887 printing of the £1 brown-lilac was produced on paper watermarked Three Orbs in error. The decision was taken to issue date stamps for normal postal use and the earliest recorded postmark is 6 January 1888 at Leadenhall Street, London EC.

The broken-frame varieties, Nos. 185a and 186a, are on Plate 2 stamps JC and TA, as illustrated. *See also* No. 212a.

62 63 64 65 66

1883 (1 Aug). *(9d.) or* **1884** (1 April) *(others).* Wmk Imperial Crown, W **49** (sideways on horiz designs).

No.	Type	Description	*Un*	*Used**	*Used on cover*
187	**52**	½d. slate-blue	20·00	7·00	12·00
		a. Imperf	£1250		
188	**62**	1½d. lilac	90·00	35·00	£100
		a. Imperf	£1250		
189	**63**	2d. lilac	£150	65·00	£110
		a. Imperf	£1500		
190	**64**	2½d. lilac	70·00	12·00	24·00
		a. Imperf	£1500		
191	**65**	3d. lilac	£180	85·00	£125
		a. Imperf	£1500		
192	**66**	4d. dull green	£400	£175	£250
		a. Imperf	£1800		
193	**62**	5d. dull green	£400	£175	£250
		a. Imperf	£1800		
194	**63**	6d. dull green	£425	£200	£275
		a. Imperf	£1800		
195	**64**	9d. dull green (1.8.83)	£800	£375	£1500
196	**65**	1s. dull green	£750	£200	£450
		a. Imperf	£3000		

*187/96 **For well-centred, lightly used +100%**

The above prices are for stamps in the true dull green colour. Stamps which have been soaked, causing the colour to run, are virtually worthless.

Stamps of the above set and No. 180 are also found perf 12; these are official perforations, but were never issued. A second variety of the 5d. is known with a line instead of a stop under the "d" in the value; this was never issued and is therefore only known *unused* (*Price* £12000).

71 72 73 74 75 76 77 78 79 80 81 82

Die I Die II

Die I: Square dots to right of "d".
Die II: Thin vertical lines to right of "d".

1887 (1 Jan)–**92**. *"Jubilee" issue. New types. The bicoloured stamp have the value tablets, or the frames including the value tablets, i the second colour.* Wmk Imperial Crown, W **49** (Three Crowns o £1).

No.	Type	Description	*Un*	*Used**	*Used on cover*
197	**71**	½d. vermillion	1·50	1·00	6·0
		a. Printed on gummed side	£1700	£1300	
		b. Printed both sides			
		c. Doubly printed	£9000		
		d. Imperf	£1600		
197*e*		½d. orange-vermilion	1·50	1·00	
198	**72**	1½d. dull purple and pale green	15·00	7·00	22·0
		a. Purple part of design double	—	£6000	
199	**73**	2d. green and scarlet	£350	£225	
200		2d. grey-green and carmine	28·00	12·00	24·0
201	**74**	2½d. purple/*blue*	22·00	3·00	6·0
		a. Printed on gummed side	£3250	†	
		b. Imperf three sides	£2750		
		c. Imperf	£3000		
202	**75**	3d. purple/*yellow*	22·00	3·25	30·0
		a. Imperf	£4500		
203		3d. deep purple/*yellow*	22·00	3·25	
204		3d. purple/*orange* (1890)	£750	£475	
205	**76**	4d. green and purple-brown	30·00	13·00	35·0
		aa. Imperf	—	£5000	
205*a*		4d. green and deep brown	30·00	13·00	
206	**77**	4½d. green and carmine (15.9.92)	10·00	40·00	75·0
206*a*		4½d. green & deep brt carmine	£475	£400	
207	**78**	5d. dull purple and blue (Die I)	£600	£475	75·0
207*a*		5d. dull pur & bl (Die II) (1888)	35·00	11·00	40·0

No.	Type	Description	Un	Used*	Used on cover
208	79	6d. purple/*rose-red*	30·00	10·00	75·00
208*a*		6d. deep purple/*rose-red*	30·00	11·00	
209	80	9d. dull purple and blue	60·00	40·00	£200
210	81	10d. dull purple and carmine (*shades*) 24.2.90)	45·00	38·00	£225
		aa. Imperf	£1800	£6000	
210*a*		10d. dull purple & dp dull carm	£400	£200	
210*b*		10d. dull purple and scarlet	60·00	45·00	
211	82	1s. dull green	£200	60·00	£125
212	61	£1 green (28.1.91)	£2500	£600	
		a. Frame broken	£5500	£1600	

*197/212a **For well-centred, lightly used +50%.**

The broken-frame varieties, No. 212a, are on Plate 2 stamps JC or TA, as illustrated above No. 185.

½d. stamps with "PEARS SOAP" printed on the back in *orange*, *blue* or *mauve*, price *from* £475 each.

No used price is quoted for No. 204 as it is not possible to authenticate the paper colour on stamps in used condition.

1900. *Colours changed.* Wmk Imperial Crown, W **49**.

No.	Type	Description	Un	Used*	Used on cover
213	71	½d. blue-green (17.4)	1·75	2·00	6·00
		a. Printed on gummed side	—	†	
		b. Imperf	£3000		
214	82	1s. green and carmine (11.7)	50·00	£125	£750
197/214 *Set of* 14			£500	£325	

*213/14 **For well-centred, lightly used +50%.**

The ½d., No. 213, in bright blue, is a colour changeling caused by a constituent of the ink used for some months in 1900.

KING EDWARD VII
22 January 1901–6 May 1910

PRINTINGS. Distinguishing De La Rue printings from the provisional printings of the same values made by Harrison & Sons Ltd. or at Somerset House may prove difficult in some cases. For very full guidance Volume 2 of the Stanley Gibbons *Great Britain Specialised Catalogue* should prove helpful.

Note that stamps perforated 15 × 14 must be Harrison; the 2½d., 3d. and 4d. in this perforation are useful reference material, their shades and appearance in most cases matching the Harrison perf 14 printings.

Except for the 6d. value, all stamps on chalk-surfaced paper were printed by De La Rue.

Of the stamps on ordinary paper, the De La Rue impressions are usually clearer and of a higher finish than those of the other printers. The shades are markedly different except in some printings of the 4d., 6d. and 7d. and in the 5s., 10s. and £1.

Used stamps in good, clean, unrubbed condition and with dated postmarks can form the basis of a useful reference collection, the dates often assisting in the assignment to the printers.

USED STAMPS. For well-centred, lightly used examples of King Edward VII stamps, add the following percentages to the used prices quoted below:
De La Rue printings (Nos. 215/66)—3d. values +35%, 4d. orange + 100%, 6d. +75%, 7d. and 1s. +25%, all other values + 50%.
Harrison printings (Nos. 267/86)—all values and perforations +75%.
Somerset House printings (Nos. 287/320)—1s. values +25%, all other values +50%.

83 84 85 86 87 88 89 90 91 92 93 94

95

96

97

(Des E. Fuchs)

1902 (1 Jan)–**10**. *Printed by De La Rue & Co.* Wmk Imperial Crown (½d. to 1s.): Anchor (2s.6d. to 10s.); Three Crowns (£1). *Ordinary paper*. P 14.

No.	Type	Description	Un	Used*	Used on cover
215	83	½d. dull blue-green (1.1.02)	2·00	1·50	2·50
216		½d. blue-green	2·00	1·50	
217		½d. pale yellowish green (26.11.04)	2·00	1·50	2·50
218		½d. yellowish green	2·00	1·50	
		a. Booklet pane. Five stamps plus St. Andrew's Cross label (6.06)	£350		
		b. Doubly printed (bottom row on one pane) (Control H9)	£25000	£17500	
219		1d. scarlet (1.1.02)	2·00	1·50	2·50
220		1d. bright scarlet	2·00	1·50	
		a. Imperf (pair)	£12000		
221	84	1½d. dull purple & green (21.3.02)	35·00	18·00	
222		1½d. slate-purple and green	38·00	18·00	28·00
223		1½d. pale dull pur & green (*chalk-surfaced paper*) (8.05)	40·00	18·00	
224		1½d. slate-purple & bluish green (*chalk-surfaced paper*)	40·00	15·00	
225	85	2d. yellowish green & carmine-red (25.3.02)	45·00	18·00	30·00
226		2d. grey-grn & carm-red (1904)	45·00	20·00	
227		2d. pale grey-green & carm-red (*chalk-surfaced paper*) (4.06)	40·00	24·00	
228		2d. pale grey-green & scar (*chalk-surfaced paper*) (1909)	40·00	24·00	
229		2d. dull blue-green & carm (*chalk-surfaced paper*) (1907)	70·00	45·00	
230	86	2½d. ultramarine (1.1.02)	20·00	10·00	20·00
231		2½d. pale ultramarine	20·00	10·00	
232	87	3d. dull pur/*orge-yell* (20.3.02)	40·00	12·00	30·00
		a. Chalk-surfaced paper (3.06)	£150	70·00	
232*b*		3d. deep purple/*orange-yellow*	40·00	12·00	
232*c*		3d. pale reddish pur/*orge-yell* (*chalk-surfaced paper*) (3.06)	£150	60·00	
233		3d. dull reddish pur/*yell* (*lemon back*) (*chalk-surfaced paper*)	£150	75·00	
233*b*		3d. pale purple/*lemon* (*chalk-surfaced paper*)	35·00	15·00	
234		3d. pur/*lemon* (*chalk-surfaced paper*)	35·00	15·00	
235	88	4d. green & grey-brn (27.3.02)	50·00	30·00	
236		4d. green and chocolate-brown	50·00	30·00	
		a. Chalk-surfaced paper (1.06)	40·00	18·00	40·00
238		4d. dp green & choc-brn (*chalk-surfaced paper*) (1.06)	40·00	18·00	
239		4d. brown-orange (1.11.09)	£150	£130	
240		4d. pale orange (12.09)	20·00	15·00	35·00
241		4d. orange-red (12.09)	20·00	15·00	
242	89	5d. dull pur & ultram (14.5.02)	55·00	20·00	50·00
		a. Chalk-surfaced paper (5.06)	50·00	20·00	
244		5d. slate-pur & ultram (*chalk-surfaced paper*) (5.06)	50·00	20·00	
245	83	6d. pale dull purple (1.1.02)	35·00	18·00	45·00
		a. Chalk-surfaced paper (1.06)	35·00	18·00	
246		6d. slate-purple	35·00	18·00	
248		6d. dull purple (*chalk-surfaced paper*) (1.06)	35·00	18·00	
249	90	7d. grey-black (4.5.10)	10·00	18·00	£175
249*a*		7d. deep grey-black	£110	£100	
250	91	9d. dull pur & ultram (7.4.02)	80·00	60·00	£175
		a. Chalk-surfaced paper (6.05)	80·00	60·00	
251		9d. slate-purple & ultramarine	80·00	60·00	
		a. Chalk-surfaced paper (6.05)	80·00	60·00	
254	92	10d. dull purple & carm (3.7.02)	80·00	60·00	£190
		a. No cross on crown	£300	£200	
		b. Chalk-surfaced paper (9.06)	80·00	60·00	
255		10d. slate-purple & carm (*chalk-surfaced paper*) (9.06)	80·00	60·00	
		a. No cross on crown	£300	£200	
256		10d. dull purple & scarlet (*chalk-surfaced paper*) (9.10)	80·00	60·00	
		a. No cross on crown	£300	£200	
257	93	1s. dull green & carm (24.3.02)	80·00	35·00	£120
		a. Chalk-surfaced paper (9.05)	80·00	35·00	
259		1s. dull green & scarlet (*chalk-surfaced paper*) (9.10)	80·00	50·00	
260	94	2s.6d. lilac (5.4.02)	£220	£120	£600
261		2s.6d. pale dull purple (*chalk-surfaced paper*) (7.10.05)	£225	£150	
262		2s.6d. dull pur (*chalk-surfaced paper*)	£225	£150	
263	95	5s. bright carmine (5.4.02)	£350	£200	£700
264		5s. deep bright carmine	£350	£200	
265	96	10s. ultramarine (5.4.02)	£600	£450	
266	97	£1 dull blue-green (16.6.02)	£1500	£650	

97a

1910 (May). *Prepared for use by De La Rue but not issued.* Wmk Imperial Crown, W **49**. P 14.

No.	Type	Description	Un
266*a*	97a	2d. Tyrian plum	£40000

One example of this stamp is known used, but it was never issued to the public.

1911. *Printed by Harrison & Sons. Ordinary paper.* Wmk Imperial Crown.

(a) P 14.

No.	Type	Description	Un	Used	Used on cover
267	83	½d. dull yellow-green (3.5.11)	2·50	1·50	4·00
268		½d. dull green	2·75	1·50	
269		½d. deep dull green	11·00	4·00	
270		½d. pale bluish green	40·00	40·00	
		a. Booklet pane. Five stamps plus St. Andrew's Cross label	£500		
		b. Wmk sideways	—	£15000	
		c. Imperf (pair)	£17000	†	
271		½d. brt green (fine impression) (6.11)	£225	£140	
272		1d. rose-red (3.5.11)	8·00	12·00	15·00
		a. No wmk	40·00	40·00	
273		1d. deep rose-red	8·00	12·00	
274		1d. rose-carmine	55·00	30·00	
275		1d. aniline pink (5.11)	£550	£300	
275*a*		1d. aniline rose	£180	£140	
276	86	2½d. bright blue (10.7.11)	45·00	30·00	50·00
277	87	3d. purple/*lemon* (12.9.11)	65·00	£180	£500
277*a*		3d. grey/*lemon*	£3000		
278	88	4d. bright orange (12.7.11)	65·00	50·00	£175
		(b) P 15 × 14.			
279	83	½d. dull green (30.10.11)	40·00	45·00	£100
279*a*		½d. deep dull green	40·00	45·00	
280		1d. rose-red (4.10.11)	38·00	25·00	
281		1d. rose-carmine	15·00	15·00	30·00
282		1d. pale rose-carmine	22·00	15·00	
283	86	2½d. bright blue (14.10.11)	22·00	15·00	30·00
284		2½d. dull blue	22·00	15·00	
285	87	3d. purple/*lemon* (22.9.11)	45·00	15·00	40·00
285*a*		3d. grey/*lemon*	£2250		
286	88	4d. bright orange (11.11.11)	30·00	15·00	65·00
279/86 *Set of* 5			£130	90·00	

1911–13. *Printed at Somerset House. Ordinary paper.* Wmk as 1902–1910. P 14.

No.	Type	Description	Un	Used	Used on cover
287	84	1½d. reddish purple and bright green (13.7.11)	40·00	35·00	
288		1½d. dull purple and green	25·00	28·00	50·00
289		1½d. slate-purple & grn (9.12)	28·00	28·00	
290	85	2d. dp dull green & red (8.8.11)	25·00	20·00	40·00
291		2d. deep dull green & carmine	25·00	20·00	
292		2d. grey-green & bright carmine (carmine shows clearly on back) (11.3.12)	25·00	25·00	
293	89	5d. dull reddish purple and bright blue (7.8.11)	30·00	20·00	65·00
294		5d. deep dull reddish purple and bright blue	28·00	20·00	
295	83	6d. royal purple (31.10.11)	50·00	85·00	
296		6d. bright magenta (*chalk-surfaced paper*) (31.10.11)	£4500		
297		6d. dull purple	30·00	20·00	70·00

No.	Type	Description	Un	Used	
298		6d. reddish purple (11.11)	30·00	25·00	
		a. No cross on crown (*various shades*)	£500		
299		6d. very dp reddish pur (11.11)	40·00	40·00	
300		6d. dark purple (3.12)	30·00	35·00	
301		6d. dull purple ("Dickinson" coated paper) (3.13)	£140	£140	
303		6d. deep plum (7.13)	28·00	70·00	
		a. No cross on crown	£575		
305	**90**	7d. slate-grey (1.8.12)	15·00	22·00	£175
306	**91**	9d. reddish purple and light blue (24.7.11)	80·00	75·00	
306*a*		9d. deep dull reddish purple & deep bright blue (9.11)	80·00	75·00	
307		9d. dull reddish purple & blue (10.11)	60·00	60·00	£175
307*a*		9d. deep plum and blue (7.13)	60·00	60·00	
308		9d. slate-pur & cobalt-bl (3.12)	95·00	£100	
309	**92**	10d. dull purple & scar (9.10.11)	80·00	75·00	
310		10d. dull reddish pur & aniline pink	£250	£225	
311		10d. dull reddish purple & carm (5.12)	60·00	60·00	£225
		a. No cross on crown	£750		
312	**93**	1s. dark green & scar (13.7.11)	90·00	60·00	
313		1s. dp green & scar (9.10.11)	60·00	35·00	
314		1s. green & carmine (15.4.12)	50·00	35·00	£125
315	**94**	2s.6d. dull greyish purple (15.9.11)	£550	£350	
316		2s.6d. dull reddish purple	£200	£140	£400
317		2s.6d. dark purple	£200	£140	
318	**95**	5s. carmine (29.2.12)	£250	£175	£600
319	**96**	10s. blue (14.1.12)	£700	£500	
320	**97**	£1 deep green (3.9.11)	£1500	£700	

*No. 301 was on an experimental coated paper which does not respond to the silver test.

KING GEORGE V
6 May 1910–20 January 1936

Further detailed information on the issues of King George V will be found in Volume 2 of the Stanley Gibbons *Great Britain Specialised Catalogue.*

PRINTERS. Types **98** to **102** were typographed by Harrison & Sons Ltd, with the exception of certain preliminary printings made at Somerset House and distinguishable by the controls "A.11 ", B.11" or "B.12" (the Harrison printings do not have a full stop after the letter). The booklet stamps, Nos. 334/7 and 344/5 were printed by Harrisons only.

WATERMARK VARIETIES. Many British stamps to 1967 exist without watermark owing to misplacement of the paper, and with either inverted, reversed, or inverted and reversed watermarks. A proportion of the low-value stamps issued in booklets have the watermark inverted in the normal course of printing.

Low values with *watermark sideways* are normally from stamp rolls used in machines with sideways delivery or, from June 1940, certain booklets.

STAMPS WITHOUT WATERMARK. Stamps found without watermark, due to misplacement of the sheet in relation to the dandy roll, are not listed here, but will be found in the *Great Britain Specialised Catalogue.*

The 1½d. and 5d. 1912–22, and 2d. and 2½d., 1924–26, listed here, are from *whole* sheets completely without watermark.

98

99

For type differences with T **101/2** *see* notes below the latter.

Die A

Die B

Dies of Halfpenny

Die A. The three upper scales on the body of the right hand dolphin form a triangle; the centre jewel of the cross inside the crown is suggested by a comma.

Die B. The three upper scales are incomplete; the centre jewel is suggested by a crescent.

Die A

Die B

Dies of One Penny

Die A. The second line of shading on the ribbon to the right of the crown extends right across the wreath; the line nearest to the crown on the right hand ribbon shows as a short line at the bottom of the ribbon.

Die B. The second line of shading is broken in the middle; the first line is little more than a dot.

(Des Bertram Mackennal and G. W. Eve. Head from photograph by W. & D. Downey. Die eng J. A. C. Harrison)

1911–12. Wmk Imperial Crown, W **49**. P 15 × 14.

No.	Type	Description	*Un*	*Used*
321	**98**	½d. pale green (Die A) (22.6.11)	5·00	4·00
322		½d. green (Die A) (22.6.11)	5·00	4·00
		a. Error. Perf 14 (8.11)	£11000	£600
323		½d. bluish green (Die A)	£300	£180
324		½d. yellow-green (Die B)	8·00	1·50
325		½d. bright green (Die B)	4·50	1·50
		a. Wmk sideways	—	£3500
326		½d. bluish green (Die B)	£160	£100
327	**99**	1d. carmine-red (Die A) (22.6.11)	4·50	2·50
		c. Wmk sideways	†	—
328		1d. pale carmine (Die A) (22.6.11)	14·00	3·00
		a. No cross on crown	£400	£275
329		1d. carmine (Die B)	7·00	3·00
330		1d. pale carmine (Die B)	10·00	4·00
		a. No cross on crown	£500	£350
331		1d. rose-pink (Die B)	£100	40·00
332		1d. scarlet (Die B) (6.12)	25·00	18·00
333		1d. aniline scarlet (Die B)	£175	£100

For note on the aniline scarlet No. 333 *see* below No. 343.

100 Simple Cypher

1912 (Aug). *Booklet stamps.* Wmk Royal Cypher ("Simple"), W **100**. P 15 × 14.

No.	Type	Description	Un	Used
334	**98**	½d. pale green (Die B)	40·00	40·00
335		½d. green (Die B)	40·00	40·00
336	**99**	1d. scarlet (Die B)	30·00	30·00
337		1d. bright scarlet (Die B)	30·00	30·00

101

102

103 Multiple Cypher

Type differences

½d. In T **98** the ornament above "P" of "HALFPENNY" has two thin lines of colour and the beard is undefined. In T **101** the ornament has one thick line and the beard is well defined.

1d. In T **99** the body of the lion is unshaded and in T **102** it is shaded.

1912 (1 Jan). Wmk Imperial Crown, W **49**. P 15 × 14.

No.	Type	Description	Un	Used
338	**101**	½d. deep green	15·00	8·00
339		½d. green	8·00	4·00
340		½d. yellow-green	8·00	4·00
		a. No cross on crown	£100	50·00
341	**102**	1d. bright scarlet	5·00	2·00
		a. No cross on crown	80·00	50·00
		b. Printed double, one albino	£180	
342		1d. scarlet	5·00	2·00
343		1d. aniline scarlet*	£175	£100
		a. No cross on crown	£1000	

*Our prices for the aniline scarlet 1d. stamps, Nos. 333 and 343, are for specimens in which the colour is suffused on the surface of the stamp and shows through clearly on the back. Specimens without these characteristics but which show "aniline" reactions under the quartz lamp are relatively common.

1912 (Aug). Wmk Royal Cypher ("Simple"), W **100**. P 15 × 14.

No.	Type	Description	Un	Used
344	**101**	½d. green	7·00	3·00
		a. No cross on crown	£100	50·00
345	**102**	1d. scarlet	8·00	3·00
		a. No cross on crown	£100	50·00

1912 (Sept–Oct). Wmk Royal Cypher ("Multiple"), W **103**. P 15 × 14.

No.	Type	Description	Un	Used
346	**101**	½d. green (Oct)	12·00	8·00
		a. No cross on crown	£100	60·00
		b. Imperf	£130	
		c. Wmk sideways	†	£2200
		d. Printed on gummed side	—	†
347		½d. yellow-green	15·00	8·00
348		½d. pale green	15·00	8·00
349	**102**	1d. bright scarlet	18·00	10·00
350		1d. scarlet	18·00	10·00
		a. No cross on crown	£120	50·00
		b. Imperf	£130	
		c. Wmk sideways	£130	£150
		d. Wmk sideways. No cross on crown	£750	

104

105

106

No. 357a

No. 357ab

No.357ac

107

108

Die I

Die II

Dies of 2d.

Die I.— Inner frame-line at top and sides close to solid of background. *Four* complete lines of shading between top of head and oval frame-line. These four lines do *not* extend to the oval itself. White line round "TWOPENCE" thin.

Die II.— Inner frame-line farther from solid of background. *Three* lines between top of head and extending to the oval. White line round "TWOPENCE" thicker.

(Des Bertram Mackennal (heads) and G. W. Eve (frames). Coinage head (½, 1½, 2, 3 and 4d.); large medal head (1d., 2½d.); intermediate medal head (5d. to 1s.); small medal head used for fiscal stamps. Dies eng J. A. C. Harrison)

(Typo by Harrison & Sons Ltd., except the 6d. printed by the Stamping Department of the Board of Inland Revenue, Somerset House. The latter also made printings of the following which can only be distinguished by the controls: ½d. B.13; 1½d. A.12; 2d. C.13; 2½d. A.12; 3d. A.12, B.13, C.13; 4d. B.13; 5d. B.13; 7d. C.13; 8d. C.13; 9d. agate B.13; 10d. C.13; 1s. C.13)

1912–24. Wmk Royal Cypher, W **100**. *Chalk-surfaced paper (6d.).* P 15 × 14.

No.	Type	Description	Un	Used
351	**105**	½d. green (1.13)	1·00	1·00
		a. Partial double print (half of bottom row from Control G15)	£16000	†
		b. Gummed both sides		
352		½d. bright green	1·00	1·00
353		½d. deep green	4·00	2·00
354		½d. yellow-green	5·00	3·00
355		½d. very yellow (Cyprus) green (1914)	£4000	†
356		½d. blue-green	40·00	25·00
357	**104**	1d. bright scarlet (8.10.12)	1·00	1·00
		a. "Q" for "O" (R. 1/4) (Control E14)	£150	£140
		ab. "Q" for "O" (R. 4/11) (Control T22)	£350	£175
		ac. Reversed "Q" for "O" (R. 15/9) (Control T22)	£300	£225
		ad. Inverted "Q" for "O" (R. 20/3)	£375	£225
		b. *Tête-bêche* (pair)	£50000	†
358		1d. vermilion	5·00	2·50
359		1d. pale rose-red	15·00	2·50
360		1d. carmine-red	11·00	5·00
361		1d. scarlet-vermilion	£125	50·00
		a. Printed on back†	£275	†
362	**105**	1½d. red-brown (15.10.12)	4·00	1·50
		a. "PENCF" (R. 15/12)	£180	£150
		b. Booklet pane. Four stamps plus two printed labels (2.24)	£450	
363		1½d. chocolate-brown	9·00	2·00
		a. Without wmk	£175	£110
364		1½d. chestnut	5·00	1·00
		a. "PENCF" (R. 15/12)	£100	80·00
365		1½d. yellow-brown	20·00	16·00
366	**106**	2d. orange-yellow (Die I) (20.8.12)	7·00	3·00
367		2d. reddish orange (Die I) (11.13)	6·00	3·00
368		2d. orange (Die I)	6·00	3·00
369		2d. bright orange (Die I)	5·00	3·00
370		2d. orange (Die II) (9.21)	5·00	3·50
371	**104**	2½d. cobalt-blue (18.10.12)	12·00	4·00
371*a*		2½d. bright blue (1914)	12·00	4·00
372		2½d. blue	12·00	4·00
373		2½d. indigo-blue* (1920)	£1700	£100
373*a*		2½d. dull Prussian blue* (1921)	£700	£60

No.	Type	Description	Unused	Used
374	**106**	3d. dull reddish violet (9.10.12)	12·00	2·00
375		3d. violet	7·00	3·00
376		3d. bluish violet (11.13)	7·00	2·00
377		3d. pale violet	7·00	2·00
378		4d. deep grey-green (15.1.13)	35·00	10·00
379		4d. grey-green	15·00	2·00
380		4d. pale grey-green	25·00	5·00
381	**107**	5d. brown (30.6.13)	15·00	5·00
382		5d. yellow-brown	15·00	5·00
		a. Without wmk	£500	
383		5d. bistre-brown	£100	50·00
384		6d. dull purple (1.8.13)	25·00	10·00
385		6d. reddish purple (8.13)	15·00	7·00
		a. Perf 14 (9.20)	90·00	£110
386		6d. deep reddish purple	20·00	5·00
387		7d. olive (8.13)	20·00	10·00
388		7d. bronze-green (1915)	60·00	25·00
389		7d. sage-green (1917)	60·00	15·00
390		8d. black/*yellow* (1.8.13)	32·00	11·00
391		8d. black/*yellow-buff* (*granite*) (5.17)	40·00	15·00
392	**108**	9d. agate (30.6.13)	20·00	6·00
		a. Printed double, one albino		
393		9d. deep agate	25·00	6·00
393*a*		9d. olive-green (9.22)	£100	30·00
393*b*		9d. pale olive-green	£100	40·00
394		10d. turquoise-blue (1.8.13)	22·00	20·00
394*a*		10d. deep turquoise-blue	70·00	25·00
395		1s. bistre (1.8.13)	20·00	4·00
396		1s. bistre-brown	35·00	12·00
351/95 *Set of* 15			£260	95·00

Imperf stamps of this issue exist but may be war-time colour trials.

†The impression of No. 361a is set sideways and is very pale.

Nos. 362a and 364a occur on Plates 12 and 29 and are known from Controls L18, M18, M19, O19 and Q21. The flaws were corrected by 1921.

*No. 373 comes from Control O20 and also exists on toned paper. No. 373*a* comes from Control R21 and also exists on toned paper, but both are unlike the rare Prussian blue shade of the 1935 2½d. Jubilee issue.

See also Nos. 418/29.

For the 2d., T **106** bisected, see note under Guernsey, War Occupation Issues.

1913 (1 Aug). Wmk Royal Cypher ("Multiple"). W **103**. P 15 × 14.

No.	Type	Description	Unused	Used
397	**105**	½d. bright green	£150	£180
		a. Wmk sideways	†	£18000
398	**104**	1d. dull scarlet	£225	£225

Both these stamps were originally issued in rolls only. Subsequently sheets were found, so that horizontal pairs and blocks are known but are of considerable rarity.

109

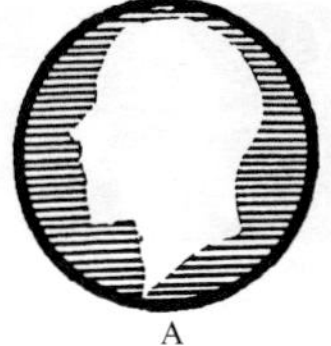

A

110 Single Cypher

Major Re-entries on 2s.6d.

Nos. 400a and 408a

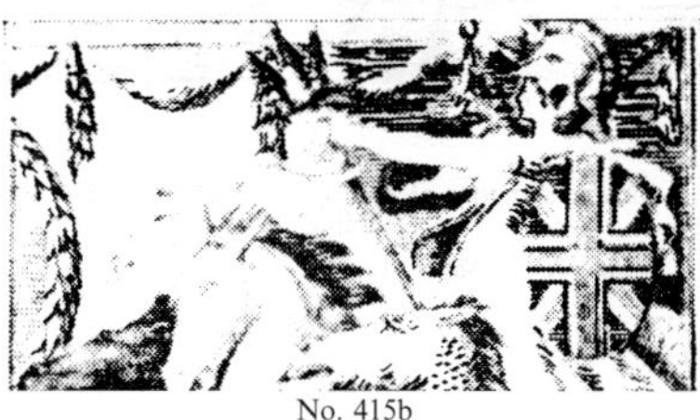

No. 415b

(Des Bertram Mackennal. Dies eng J. A. C. Harrison. Recess)

High values, so-called "Sea Horses" design: T **109**. *Background around portrait consists of horizontal lines, Type A*. Wmk Single Cypher, W **110**. P 11 × 12.

1913 (30 June–Aug). *Printed by Waterlow Bros & Layton.*

No.	Description	Unused	Used
9	2s.6d. deep sepia-brown	£240	£160
0	2s.6d. sepia-brown	£225	£140
	a. Re-entry (R. 2/1)	£800	£525
1	5s. rose-carmine	£325	£275
2	10s. indigo-blue (1 Aug)	£550	£375
3	£1 green (1 Aug)	£1500	£950
4	£1 dull blue-green (1 Aug)	£1500	£1000

399/404 **For well-centred, lightly used +35%.**

1915 (Oct–Dec). *Printed by De La Rue & Co.*

No.	Description	Unused	Used
405	2s.6d. deep yellow-brown	£250	£190
406	2s.6d. yellow-brown	£225	£190
	a. Re-entry (R. 2/1)		
407	2s.6d. pale brown	£225	£190
	a. Re-entry (R. 2/1)	£900	£550
408	2s.6d. sepia (seal-brown)	£225	£190
409	5s. bright carmine	£375	£300
410	5s. pale carmine	£450	£280
411	10s. deep blue (Dec)	£1900	£875
412	10s. blue	£1500	£700
413	10s. pale blue	£1600	£700

*405/13 **For well-centred, lightly used + 45%.**

Nos. 406/7 were produced from the original Waterlow plates as were all De La Rue 5s. and 10s. printings. Examples of Nos. 406/7, 410 and 411 occur showing degrees of plate wear.

1918 (Dec)–**19**. *Printed by Bradbury, Wilkinson & Co, Ltd.*

No.	Description	Unused	Used
413*a*	2s.6d. olive-brown	£100	65·00
414	2s.6d. chocolate-brown	£125	70·00
415	2s.6d. reddish brown	£125	70·00
415*a*	2s.6d. pale brown	£110	65·00
	b. Major re-entry (R. 1/2)	£650	£350
416	5s. rose-red (1.19)	£250	£110
417	10s. dull grey-blue (1.19)	£350	£160
399/417 *Set of* 4		£2100	£1200

*413*a*/17 **For well-centred, lightly used +35%.**

DISTINGUISHING PRINTINGS. Note that the £1 value was only printed by Waterlow.

Waterlow and De La Rue stamps measure exactly 22 mm vertically. In the De La Rue printings the gum is usually patchy and yellowish, and the colour of the stamp, particularly in the 5s., tends to show through the back. The holes of the perforation are smaller than those of the other two printers, but there is a thick perforation tooth at the top of each vertical side.

In the Bradbury Wilkinson printings the height of the stamp is 22¾ or 23 mm due to the use of curved plates. On most of the 22¾ mm high stamps a minute coloured guide dot appears in the margin just above the middle of the upper frame-line.

For (1934) re-engraved Waterlow printings *see* Nos. 450/2.

UNITED KINGDOM OF GREAT BRITAIN AND NORTHERN IRELAND

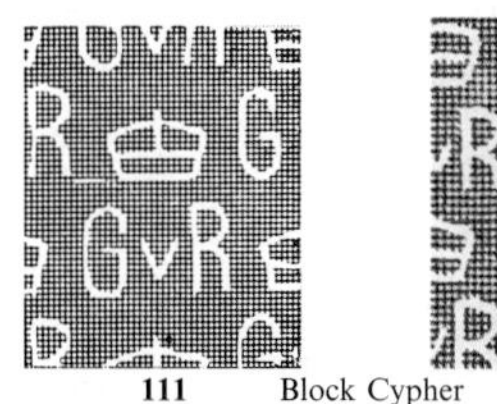

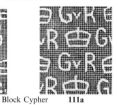

111 Block Cypher 111a

The watermark Type **111a**, as compared with Type **111**, differs as follows: Closer spacing of horizontal rows (12½ mm instead of 14½ mm). Letters shorter and rounder. Watermark thicker.

(Typo by Waterlow & Sons, Ltd (all values except 6d.) and later, 1934–35, by Harrison & Sons, Ltd (all values). Until 1934 the 6d. was printed at Somerset House where a printing of the 1½d. was also made in 1926 (identifiable only by control E.26). Printings by Harrisons in 1934–35 can be identified, when in mint condition, by the fact that the gum shows a streaky appearance vertically, the Waterlow gum being uniformly applied, but Harrisons also used up the balance of the Waterlow "smooth gum" paper)

1924 (Feb)–**26**. Wmk Block Cypher, W **111**. P 15 × 14.

No.	Type	Description	Unused	Used
418	**105**	½d. green	1·00	1·00
		a. Wmk sideways (5.24)	6·00	3·25
		b. Doubly printed	£7500	†
419	**104**	1d. scarlet	1·00	1·00
		a. Wmk sideways	15·00	15·00
		b. Experimental paper, W **111***a* (10.24)	22·00	
		c. Partial double print, one inverted	£6500	
		d. Inverted "Q" for "O" (R. 20/3)	£375	
420	**105**	1½d. red-brown	1·00	1·00
		a. *Tête-bêche* (pair)	£375	£750
		b. Wmk sideways (8.24)	7·00	3·50
		c. Printed on the gummed side	£400	†
		d. Booklet pane. Four stamps plus two printed labels (3.24)	£125	
		e. Ditto. Wmk sideways	£5000	
		f. Experimental paper, W **111***a* (10.24)	60·00	70·00
		g. Double impression	£10000	†
421	**106**	2d. orange (Die II) (7.24)	2·50	2·50
		a. No wmk	£675	
		b. Wmk sideways (7.26)	70·00	80·00
		c. Partial double print	£14000	†
422	**104**	2½d. blue (10.24)	5·00	3·00
		a. No wmk	£1100	
		b. Wmk sideways	†	£5500
423	**106**	3d. violet (10.24)	10·00	2·50
424		4d. grey-green (11.24)	12·00	2·50
		a. Printed on the gummed side	£1750	†
425	**107**	5d. brown (11.24)	20·00	3·00
426		6d. reddish purple (*chalk-surfaced paper*) (9.24)	12·00	2·50
426*a*		6d. purple (6.26)	3·00	1·50
427	**108**	9d. olive-green (12.24)	12·00	3·50
428		10d. turquoise-blue (11.24)	35·00	40·00
429		1s. bistre-brown (10.24)	22·00	3·00
418/29 *Set of* 12			£110	60·00

There are numerous shades in this issue.

The 6d. on both chalk-surfaced and ordinary papers was printed by both Somerset House and Harrisons. The Harrisons printings have streaky gum, differ slightly in shade, and that on chalk-surfaced paper is printed in a highly fugitive ink. The prices quoted are for the commonest (Harrison) printing in each case.

The dandy roll to produce watermark Type **111***a* was provided by Somerset House in connection with experiments in paper composition undertaken during 1924–25. These resulted in a change from rag only paper to that made from a mixture including esparto and sulphite.

112

(Des H. Nelson. Eng J. A. C. Harrison, Recess Waterlow)

1924–25. *British Empire Exhibition*. W **111**. P 14.

(a) Dated "1924" *(23.4.24).*

No.	Type	Description	Unused	Used
430	**112**	1d. scarlet	10·00	11·00
431		1½d. brown	15·00	15·00

(b) Dated "1925" *(9.5.25).*

No.	Type	Description	Unused	Used
432	**112**	1d. scarlet	15·00	30·00
433		1½d. brown	40·00	70·00

113

114

115

116 St. George and the Dragon

117

(Des J. Farleigh (T **113** and **115**), E. Linzell (T **114**) and H. Nelson (T **116**). Eng C. G. Lewis (T **113**), T. E. Storey (T **115**), both at the Royal Mint; J. A. C. Harrison, of Waterlow (T **114** and **116**). Typo by Waterlow from plates made at the Royal Mint, except T **116**, recess by Bradbury, Wilkinson from die and plate of their own manufacture)

1929 (10 May). *Ninth U.P.U. Congress, London.*

(a) W **11**. P 15 × 14.

No.	Type	Description	Unused	Used
434	**113**	½d. green	2·25	2·25
		a. Wmk sideways	35·00	35·00
435	**114**	1d. scarlet	2·25	2·25
		a. Wmk sideways	60·00	60·00
436		1½d. purple-brown	2·25	1·75
		a. Wmk sideways	35·00	35·00
		b. Booklet pane. Four stamps plus two printed labels	£225	
437	**115**	2½d. blue	10·00	10·00

(b) W **117**. P 12.

No.	Type	Description	Unused	Used
438	**116**	£1 black	£750	£550
434/7 *Set of* 4 (*to* 2½d.)			15·00	14·50

PRINTERS. All subsequent issues were printed in photogravure by Harrison and Sons Ltd *except where otherwise stated.*

118 119 120

121 122

1934–36. W **111**. P 15 × 14.

No.	Type	Description	Unused	Used
439	**118**	½d. green (19.11.34)	50	50
		a. Wmk sideways	7·00	3·50
		b. Imperf three sides	£1800	
440	**119**	1d. scarlet (24.9.34)	50	50
		a. Imperf (pair)	£1500	
		b. Printed on the gummed side	£500	†
		c. Wmk sideways	12·00	6·00
		d. Double impression	†	£15000
		e. Imperf between (pair)	£2500	
		f. Imperf three sides (pair)	£1700	

No.	Type	Description	Unused	Used
441	**118**	1½d. red-brown (20.8.34)	50	50
		a. Imperf (pair)	£325	
		b. Imperf three sides (lower stamp in vert pair)	£1000	
		c. Imperf between (horiz pair)		
		d. Wmk sideways	6·00	4·00
		e. Booklet pane. Four stamps plus two printed labels (1.35)	£100	
442	**120**	2d. orange (21.1.35)	75	75
		a. Imperf (pair)	£2000	
		b. Wmk sideways	90·00	60·00
443	**119**	2½d. ultramarine (18.3.35)	1·50	1·25
444	**120**	3d. violet (18.3.35)	1·50	1·25
445		4d. deep grey-green (2.12.35)	2·00	1·25
446	**121**	5d. yellow-brown (17.2.36)	6·00	2·75
447	**122**	9d. deep olive-green (2.12.35)	12·00	2·25
448		10d. turquoise-blue (24.2.36)	15·00	10·00
449		1s. bistre-brown (24.2.36)	15·00	1·25
		a. Double impression	—	†
439/49 *Set of* 11			50·00	20·00

Owing to the need for wider space for the perforations the size of the designs of the ½d. and 2d. were once, and the 1d. and 1½d. twice, reduced from that of the first printings.

There are also numerous minor variations, due to the photographic element in the process.

The ½d. imperf three sides, No. 439b, is known in a block of four, from a sheet, to which the bottom pair is imperf at top and sides.

For No. 442 bisected, see Guernsey, War Occupation Issues.

B

123

(Eng J. A. C. Harrison. Recess Waterlow)

1934 (16 Oct). *T* **109** *(re-engraved). Background around portrait consists of horizontal and diagonal lines. Type B.* W **110**. P 11 × 12.

No.	Type	Description	Unused	Used
450	**109**	2s.6d. chocolate-brown	70·00	40·00
451		5s. bright rose-red	£160	85·00
452		10s. indigo	£340	80·00
450/2 *Set of* 3			£525	£190

There are numerous other minor differences in the design of this issue.

(Des B. Freedman)

1935 (7 May). *Silver Jubilee.* W **111**. P 15 × 14.

No.	Type	Description	Unused	Used
453	**123**	½d. green	75	50
454		1d. scarlet	1·25	1·50
455		1½d. red-brown	75	50
456		2½d. blue	4·50	5·50
456*a*		2½d. Prussian blue	£6000	£6000
453/6 *Set of* 4			6·00	7·00

The 1½d. and 2½d. values differ from T **123** in the emblem in the panel at right.

Four sheets of No. 456*a*, printed in the wrong shade, were issued in error by the Post Office Stores Department on 25 June 1935. It is known that three of the sheets were sold from the sub-office at 134 Fore Street, Upper Edmonton, London. between that date and 4 July.

KING EDWARD VIII
20 January–10 December 1936

Further detailed information on the stamps of King Edward VIII will be found in Volume 2 of the Stanley Gibbons *Great Britain Specialised Catalogue*.

124

125

(Des H. Brown, adapted Harrison using a photo by Hugh Cecil)

1936. W **125**. P 15 × 14.

No.	Type	Description	Unused	Used
457	**124**	1d. green (1.9.36)	30	30
		a. Double impression		
458		1d. scarlet (14.9.36)	60	50
459		1½d. red-brown (1.9.36)	30	30
		a. Booklet pane. Four stamps plus two printed labels (10.36)	60·00	
460		2½d. bright blue (1.9.36)	30	85
457/60 *Set of* 4			1·25	1·75

KING GEORGE VI
11 December 1936–6 February 1952

Further detailed information on the stamps of King George VI will be found in Volume 2 of the Stanley Gibbons *Great Britain Specialised Catalogue*.

126 King George VI and Queen Elizabeth

(Des E. Dulac)

1937 (13 May). *Coronation.* W **127**. P 15 × 14.

No.	Type	Description	Unused	Used
461	**126**	1½d. maroon	30	30

127

128

129

130

King George VI and National Emblems

(Des T **128/9**, E. Dulac (head) and E. Gill (frames). T **130**, E. Dulac (whole stamp))

1937–47. W **127**. P 15 × 14.

No.	Type	Description	Unused	Used
462	**128**	½d. green (10.5.37)	30	25
		a. Wmk sideways (1.38)	50	50
		ab. Booklet pane of 4 (6.40)	38·00	
463		1d. scarlet (10.5.37)	30	25
		a. Wmk sideways (2.38)	20·00	9·00
		ab. Booklet pane of 4 (6.40)	95·00	
464		1½d. red-brown (30.7.37)	20	25
		a. Wmk sideways (2.38)	1·00	1·25
		b. Booklet pane. Four stamps plus two printed labels (8.37)	55·00	
		c. Imperf three sides (pair)		
465		2d. orange (31.1.38)	75	50
		a. Wmk sideways (2.38)	70·00	38·00
		b. Bisected (on cover)	†	40·00
466		2½d. ultramarine (10.5.37)	30	25
		a. Wmk sideways (6.40)	70·00	32·00
		b. *Tête-bêche* (horiz pair)	£12000	
467		3d. violet (31.1.38)	3·75	1·00
468	**129**	4d. grey-green (21.11.38)	60	75
		a. Imperf (pair)	£4500	
		b. Imperf three sides (horiz pair)	£5250	
469		5d. brown (21.11.38)	2·50	85
		a. Imperf (pair)	£5500	
		b. Imperf three sides (horiz pair)	£4750	
470		6d. purple (30.1.39)	1·25	60
471	**130**	7d. emerald-green (27.2.39)	4·50	60
		a. Imperf three sides (horiz pair)	£5000	
472		8d. bright carmine (27.2.39)	4·00	80
473		9d. deep olive-green (1.5.39)	5·75	80
474		10d. turquoise-blue (1.5.39)	6·00	80
		aa. Imperf (pair)	£6000	
474*a*		11d. plum (29.12.47)	2·00	2·75
475		1s. bistre-brown (1.5.39)	7·00	75
462/75 *Set of* 15			35·00	10·00

For later printings of the lower values in apparently lighter shades and different colours, see Nos. 485/90 and 503/8.

No. 465b was authorised for use in Guernsey. See notes on War Occupation Issues.

Nos. 468b and 469b are perforated at foot only and each occurs in the same sheet as Nos. 468a and 469a.

No. 471a is also perforated at foot only, but occurs on the top row of a sheet.

131 King George VI

132 King George VI

133

(Des E. Dulac (T **131**) and Hon. G. R. Bellew (T **132**). Eng J. A. C. Harrison. Recess Waterlow)

1939–48. W **133**. P 14.

No.	Type	Description	Unused	Used
476	**131**	2s.6d. brown (4.9.39)	35·00	6·00
476*a*		2s.6d. yellow-green (9.3.42)	4·50	1·50
477		5s. red (21.8.39)	9·00	2·00
478	**132**	10s. dark blue (30.10.39)	£225	20·00
478*a*		10s. ultramarine (30.11.42)	20·00	5·00
478*b*		£1 brown (1.10.48)	7·00	26·00
476/8b *Set of* 6			£275	55·00

134 Queen Victoria and King George VI.

(Des H. L. Palmer)

1940 (6 May). *Centenary of First Adhesive Postage Stamps.* W **127**. P 14½ × 14.

No.	Type	Description	Unused	Used
479	**134**	½d. green	30	30
480		1d. scarlet	1·00	40
481		1½d. red-brown	50	75
482		2d. orange	1·00	40
		a. Bisected (on cover)	†	30·00
483		2½d. ultramarine	2·25	50
484		3d. violet	3·00	3·50
479/84 *Set of* 6			7·00	5·25

No. 482a was authorised for use in Guernsey. See notes on War Occupation Issues.

1941–42. *Head as Nos. 462/7, but with lighter background to provide a more economic use of the printing ink.* W **127**. P 15 × 14.

No.	Type	Description	Unused	Used
485	**128**	½d. pale green (1.9.41)	30	30
		a. *Tête-bêche* (horiz pair)	£10000	
		b. Imperf (pair)	£4500	
486		1d. pale scarlet (11.8.41)	30	30
		a. Wmk sideways (10.42)	4·00	4·50
		b. Imperf (pair)	£6000	
		c. Imperf three sides (horiz pair)	£6000	
487		1½d. pale red-brown (28.9.42)	50	80
488		2d. pale orange (6.10.41)	50	50
		a. Wmk sideways (6.42)	28·00	19·00
		b. *Tête-bêche* (horiz pair)	£10000	
		c. Imperf (pair)	£5000	
		d. Imperf pane*	£15000	
489		2½d. light ultramarine (21.7.41)	30	30
		a. Wmk sideways (8.42)	15·00	12·00
		b. *Tête-bêche* (horiz pair)	£10000	
		c. Imperf (pair)	£4000	
		d. Imperf pane*	£10000	
		e. Imperf three sides (horiz pair)	£6000	
490		3d. pale violet (3.11.41)	2·00	1·00
485/90 *Set of* 6			3·50	2·75

The *tête-bêche* varieties are from defectively made-up stamp booklets.

Nos. 486c and 489e are perforated at foot only and occur in the same sheets as Nos. 486b and 489c.

*BOOKLET ERRORS. Those listed as "imperf panes" show one row of perforations either at the top or at the bottom of the pane of 6.

WATERMARK VARIETIES. Please note that *inverted watermarks* are outside the scope of this listing but are fully listed in the *Great Britain Specialised* and *Great Britain Concise Catalogues*. See also the notes about watermarks at the beginning of the King George V section.

135

136 Symbols of Peace and Reconstruction

(Des H. L. Palmer (T **135**) and R. Stone (T **136**))

1946 (11 June). *Victory.* W **127**. P 15 × 14.

No.	Type	Description	Unused	Used
491	**135**	2½d. ultramarine	20	1
492	**136**	3d. violet	20	4

137

138 King George VI and Queen Elizabeth

(Des G. Knipe and Joan Hassall from photographs by Dorothy Wilding)

1948 (26 Apr). *Royal Silver Wedding.* W **127**. P 15 × 14 (2½d.) or 14 × 15 (£1).

No.	Type	Description	Unused	Used
493	**137**	2½d. ultramarine	35	
494	**138**	£1 blue	40·00	40·

1948 (10 May). Stamps of 1d. and 2½d. showing seaweed-gatheri[ng] were on sale at eight Head Post Offices in Great Britain, but we[re] primarily for use in the Channel Islands and are listed there (s[ee] after Great Britain Postal Fiscals).

139 Globe and Laurel Wreath

140 "Speed"

141 Olympic Symbol

142 Winged Victory

(Des P. Metcalfe (T **139**), A. Games (T **140**), S. D. Scott (T **141**) and E. Dulac (T **142**))

1948 (29 July). *Olympic Games.* W **127**. P 15 × 14.

495	**139**	2½d. ultramarine	35	10
496	**140**	3d. violet	35	55
497	**141**	6d. bright purple	75	40
498	**142**	1s. brown	1·40	1·60
495/8 *Set of* 4			2·50	2·40

143 Two Hemispheres

144 U.P.U. Monument, Berne

145 Goddess Concordia, Globe and Points of Compass

146 Posthorn and Globe

(Des Mary Adshead (T **143**), P. Metcalfe (T **144**), H. Fleury (T **145**) and Hon. G. R. Bellew (T **146**))

1949 (10 Oct). *75th Anniv of Universal Postal Union.* W **127**. P 15 × 14.

499	**143**	2½d. ultramarine	15	10
500	**144**	3d. violet	15	50
501	**145**	6d. bright purple	25	50
502	**146**	1s. brown	60	1·25
499/502 *Set of* 4			1·00	2·10

1950–52. *4d. as Nos. 468 and others as Nos. 485/9, but colours changed.* W **127**. P 15 × 14.

503	**128**	½d. pale orange (3.5.51)	30	30
		a. Imperf (pair)	£4000	
		b. *Tête-bêche* (horiz pair)	£10000	
		c. Imperf pane	£12000	
504		1d. light ultramarine (3.5.51)	30	30
		a. Wmk sideways (5.51)	1·10	1·25
		b. Imperf (pair)	£3000	
		c. Imperf three sides (horiz pair)	£4000	
		d. Booklet pane. Three stamps plus three printed labels (3.52)	18·00	
		e. Ditto. Partial *tête-bêche* pane	£6000	
505		1½d. pale green (3.5.51)	65	60
		a. Wmk sideways (9.51)	3·25	5·00
506		2d. pale red-brown (3.5.51)	75	40
		a. Wmk sideways (5.51)	1·75	2·00
		b. *Tête-bêche* (horiz pair)	£10000	
		c. Imperf three sides (horiz pair)	£4000	
507		2½d. pale scarlet (3.5.51)	60	40
		a. Wmk sideways (5.51)	1·75	1·75
		b. *Tête-bêche* (hoiz pair)		
508	**129**	4d. light ultramarine (2.10.50)	2·00	1·75
		a. Double impression	†	£7000
503/8 *Set of* 6			4·00	3·25

No. 504c is perforated at foot only and occurs in the same sheet as No. 504b.

No. 506c is also perforated at foot only.

*BOOKLET ERRORS. Those listed as "imperf panes" show one row of perforations either at the top or at the bottom of the pane of 6.

147 H.M.S. *Victory*

148 White Cliffs of Dover

149 St. George and the Dragon

150 Royal Coat of Arms

(Des Mary Adshead (T **147/8**), P. Metcalfe (T **149/50**). Recess Waterlow)

951 (3 May). W **133**. P 11 × 12.

09	**147**	2s.6d. yellow-green	2·00	1·00
10	**148**	5s. red	40·00	1·50
11	**149**	10s. ultramarine	10·00	8·50
12	**150**	£1 brown	48·00	20·00
09/12 *Set of* 4			90·00	27·00

151 "Commerce and Prosperity"

152 Festival Symbol

(Des E. Dulac (T **151**), A. Games (T **152**))

1951 (3 May). *Festival of Britain.* W **127**. P 15 × 14.

513	**151**	2½d. scarlet	15	20
514	**152**	4d. ultramarine	30	65

STAMP BOOKLETS

For a full listing of Great Britain stamp booklets see the *Great Britain Concise Catalogue* published each Spring.

POSTAGE DUE STAMPS

PERFORATIONS. All postage due stamps to No. D39 are perf 14 × 15.

D 1

D 2

(Des G. Eve. Typo Somerset House (early trial printings of ½d., 1d., 2d. and 5d.; all printings of 1s.) or Harrison (later printings of all values except 1s.)).

1914 (20 Apr)–**22**. W **100** (Simple Cypher) sideways.

D1	D **1**	½d. emerald	50	25
D2		1d. carmine	50	25
		a. Pale carmine	75	50
D3		1½d. chestnut (1922)	48·00	20·00
D4		2d. agate	50	25
D5		3d. violet (1918)	5·00	75
		a. Bluish violet	6·00	2·75
D6		4d. dull grey-green (12.20)	18·00	5·00
D7		5d. brownish cinnamon	6·00	3·50
D8		1s. bright blue (1915)	40·00	4·75
		a. Deep bright blue	40·00	5·00
D1/8 *Set of* 8			£110	32·00

The 1d. is known bisected from various offices between 1914 and 1924, the 2d. bisected for use as a 1d. between 1918 and 1923, the 3d. bisected for use as a 1½d. in 1922 at Warminster and trisected for use as a 1d. in 1921 at Malvern.

(Typo Waterlow)

1924. *As 1914–22, but on thick chalk-surfaced paper.*

D9	D **1**	1d. carmine	2·25	3·50

(Typo Waterlow and (from 1934) Harrison)

1924–31. W **111** (Black Cypher) sideways.

D10	D **1**	½d. emerald (6.25)	1·25	75
D11		1d. carmine (4.25)	60	25
D12		1½d. chestnut (10.24)	45·00	18·00
D13		2d. agate (7.24)	1·00	25
D14		3d. dull violet (10.24)	1·50	25
		a. Printed on gummed side	75·00	†
		b. Experimental paper W **111***a*	38·00	35·00
D15		4d. dull grey-green (10.24)	15·00	3·00
D16		5d. brownish cinnamon (1.31)	32·00	28·00
D17		1s. deep blue (9.24)	10·00	1·00
D18	D **2**	2s. 6d. purple/*yellow* (5.24)	45·00	2·00
D10/18 *Set of* 9			£140	48·00

The 1d. is known bisected from various offices between 1925 and 1932 and the 2d. exists bisected to make up the 2½d. rate at Perranwell Station, Cornwall, in 1932.

1936–37. W **125** (E 8 R) sideways.

D19	D **1**	½d. emerald (6.37)	7·50	8·00
D20		1d. carmine (5.37)	1·50	2·00
D21		2d. agate (5.37)	8·00	11·00
D22		3d. dull violet (3.37)	1·50	2·25
D23		4d. dull grey-green (12.36)	35·00	35·00
D24		5d. brownish cinnamon (11.36)	55·00	25·00
		a. Yellow-brown (1937)	16·00	23·00
D25		1s. deep blue (12.36)	11·00	9·00
D26	D **2**	2s.6d. purple/*yellow* (5.37)	£300	9·00
D19/26 *Set of* 8 *(cheapest)*			£350	90·00

The 1d. is known bisected at Solihull in 1937.

1937–38. W **127** (G VI R) sideways.

D27	D **1**	½d. emerald (5.38)	9·00	5·00
D28		1d. carmine (5.38)	3·00	75
D29		2d. agate (5.38)	2·50	75
D30		3d. violet (12.37)	12·00	1·00
D31		4d. dull grey-green (9.37)	75·00	13·00
D32		5d. yellow-brown (11.38)	14·00	75
D33		1s. deep blue (10.37)	75·00	2·00
D34	D **2**	2s.6d. purple/*yellow* (9.38)	75·00	2·50
D27/34 *Set of* 8			£250	23·00

The 2d. is known bisected at various offices between 1951 and 1954.

DATES OF ISSUE. The dates for Nos. D35/9 arc those on which stamps were first issued by the Supplies Department to postmasters.

1951–52. *Colours changed and new value (1½d.).* W **127**(G VI R) sideways.

D35	D **1**	½d. orange (18.9.51)	1·00	3·00
D36		1d. violet-blue (6.6.51)	1·50	1·50
D37		1½d. green (11.2.52)	1·75	3·00
D38		4d. blue (14.8.51)	32·00	12·00
D39		1s. ochre (6.12.51)	38·00	14·00
D35/9 *Set of* 5			70·00	30·00

The 1d. is known bisected at Capel, Dorking in 1952 and at Camberley in 1954.

OFFICIAL STAMPS

In 1840 the 1d. black (Type **1**), with "V R" in the upper corners, was prepared for official use, but never issued for postal purposes. Obliterated specimens are those which were used for experimental trials of obliterating inks, or those that passed through the post by oversight.

V 1

1840. *Prepared for use but not issued; "V" "R" in upper corners. Imperf.*

			Un	*Used*	*Used on cover*
V1	V **1**	1d. black	£10000	£16000	

The following Official stamps would be more correctly termed Departmental stamps as they were exclusively for the use of certain government departments. Until 1882 official mail used ordinary postage stamps purchased at post offices, the cash being refunded once a quarter. Later the government departments obtained Official stamps by requisition.

Official stamps were on sale to the public for a short time at Somerset House but they were not sold from post offices. The system of only supplying the Government departments was open to abuse so that all Official stamps were withdrawn on 13 May 1904.

OVERPRINTS, PERFORATIONS, WATERMARKS. All Official stamps were overprinted by Thomas De La Rue & Co. and are perf 14. They are on Crown watermarked paper unless otherwise stated.

INLAND REVENUE

These stamps were used by revenue officials in the provinces, mail to and from Head Office passing without a stamp. The London Office used these stamps only for foreign mail.

I.R.
OFFICIAL
(O **1**)

I. R.
OFFICIAL
(O **2**)

Optd with Types O **1** (½d. to 1s.) or O **2** (others)

1882–1901. *Stamps of Queen Victoria.*

(a) Issues of 1880–81.

		Un	*Used**	*Used on cover*
O 1	½d. deep green (1.11.82)	60·00	20·00	60·00
O 2	½d. pale green	60·00	20·00	
O 3	1d. lilac (Die II) (1.10.82)	4·00	2·00	20·00
	a. Optd in blue-black	£150	50·00	
	b. "OFFICIAL" omitted	—	£5000	
O 4	6d. grey (Plate 18) (3.11.82)	£250	65·00	

No. O3 with the lines of the overprint transposed is an essay.

(b) Issues of 1884–1888.

O 5	½d. slate-blue (8.5.85)	60·00	22·00	90·00
O 6	2½d. lilac (12.3.85)	£250	80·00	£850
O 7	1s. dull green (12.3.85)	£3500	£850	
O 8	5s. rose (*blued paper*) (wmk Anchor) (12.3.85)	£3750	£1500	
O 9	5s. rose (wmk Anchor) (3.90)	£2500	£750	
	a. Raised stop after "R"	£3000	£850	
	b. Optd in blue-black	£3500	£850	
O 9*c*	10s. cobalt (*blued paper*) (wmk Anchor) (12.3.85)	£8000	£2000	
O 9*d*	10s. ultramarine (*blued paper*) (wmk Anchor) (12.3.85)	£7500	£2500	
O10	10s. ultram (wmk Anchor) (3.90)	£3750	£1000	
	a. Raised stop after "R"	£4250	£1500	
	b. Optd in blue-black	£4500	£1500	
O11	£1 brown-lilac (wmk Crowns) (12.3.85)	£27000	£14000	
	a. Frame broken	£32000		
	b. Optd in blue-black			
O12	£1 brown-lilac (wmk Orbs) (3.90)	£40000	£20000	
	a. Frame broken	£45000		

(c) issues of 1887–92.

O13	½d. vermilion (15.5.88)	5·00	2·00	60·00
	a. Without "I.R."	£2500		
	b. Imperf	£1700		
	c. Opt double (imperf)	£2000		
O14	2½d. purple/*blue* (2.92)	£100	10·00	£300
O15	1s. dull green (9.89)	£350	£125	£2000
O16	£1 green (6.92)	£5500	£950	
	a. No stop after "R"	—	£1500	
	b. Frame broken	£8000	£2000	

Nos. O3, O13, O15 and O16 may be found showing worn impressions of the overprints with thicker letters.

(d) Issues of 1887 and 1900.

O17	½d. blue-green (4.01)	10·00	6·00	£200
O18	6d. purple/*rose-red* (1.7.01)	£250	60·00	
O19	1s. green and carmine (12.01)	£1400	£450	

*O1/19 **For well-centred, lightly used +35%.**

1902–04. *Stamps of King Edward VII. Ordinary paper.*

O20	½d. blue-green (4.2.02)	22·00	3·00	£110
O21	1d. scarlet (4.2.02)	15·00	2·00	75·00
O22	2½d. ultramarine (19.2.02)	£500	£125	
O23	6d. pale dull purple (14.3.04)	£120000	£70000	
O24	1s. dull green & carmine (29.4.02)	£1250	£250	
O25	5s. bright carmine (29.4.02)	£7500	£4500	
	a. Raised stop after "R"	£8000	£5000	
O26	10s. ultramarine (29.4.02)	£35000	£18000	
	a. Raised stop after "R"	£40000	£20000	

No.	Description	Un	Used	Used on cover
O27	£1 dull blue-green (29.4.02)	£25000	£12000	

OFFICE OF WORKS

These were issued to Head and Branch (local) offices in London and to Branch (local) offices at Birmingham, Bristol, Edinburgh, Glasgow, Leeds, Liverpool, Manchester and Southampton. The overprints on stamps of value 2d. and upwards were created later in 1902, the 2d. for registration fees and the rest for overseas mail.

O. W.

OFFICIAL

(O 3)

Optd with Type O **3**

1896 (24 Mar)–**02**. *Stamps of Queen Victoria.*

No.	Description	Un	Used	Used on cover
O31	½d. vermilion	£150	75·00	£400
O32	½d. blue-green (2.02)	£200	£100	
O33	1d. lilac (Die II)	£250	75·00	£500
O34	5d. dull purple and blue (II) (29.4.02)	£1250	£400	
O35	10d. dull purple and carmine (28.5.02)	£2000	£600	

1902 (11 Feb)–**03**. *Stamps of King Edward VII. Ordinary paper.*

No.	Description	Un	Used	Used on cover
O36	½d. blue-green (2.02)	£500	£150	£1500
O37	1d. scarlet	£500	£150	£350
O38	2d. yellowish green & carmine-red (27.4.02)	£1000	£300	£2000
O39	2½d. ultramarine (29.4.02)	£1250	£500	£2250
O40	10d. dull purple & carmine (28.5.03)	£12000	£4250	

*O31/40 **For well-centred, lightly used +25%.**

ARMY

Letters to and from the War Office in London passed without postage. The overprinted stamps were distributed to District and Station Paymasters nationwide, including Cox and Co., the Army Agents, who were paymasters to the Household Division.

ARMY OFFICIAL (O 4) ARMY OFFICIAL (O 5) ARMY OFFICIAL (O 6)

1896 (1 Sept)–**01**. *Stamps of Queen Victoria optd with Type* O **4** *(½d., 1d.) or* O **5** *(2½d., 6d.).*

No.	Description	Un	Used	Used on cover
O41	½d. vermilion	3·50	1·50	40·00
	a. "OFFICIAL" (R. 13/7)	£100	50·00	
	b. Lines of opt transposed	£1750		
O42	½d. blue-green (6.00)	3·50	6·00	
O43	1d. lilac (Die II)	3·50	2·50	65·00
	a. "OFFICIAL" (R. 13/7)	£100	50·00	
O44	2½d. purple/*blue*	15·00	8·00	£450
O45	6d. purple/*rose-red* (20.9.01)	50·00	30·00	£975

Nos. O41a and O43a occur on sheets overprinted by Forme 1.

1902–03. *Stamps of King Edward VII optd with Type* O **4** *(Nos. O48/50) or Type* O **6** *(No. O52). Ordinary paper.*

No.	Description	Un	Used	Used on cover
O48	½d. blue-green (11.2.02)	5·00	2·00	90·00
O49	1d. scarlet (11.2.02)	5·00	2·00	90·00
	a. "ARMY" omitted	†	—	
O50	6d. pale dull purple (23.8.02)	£120	50·00	
O52	6d. pale dull purple (12.03)	£1250	£450	

GOVERNMENT PARCELS

These stamps were issued to all departments, including the Head Office, for use on parcels weighing over 3 lb. Below this weight government parcels were sent by letter post to avoid the 55% of the postage paid from accruing to the railway companies, as laid down by parcel-post regulations. Most government parcels stamps suffered heavy postmarks in use.

GOVT PARCELS

(O 7)

Optd as Type O **7**

1883 (1 Aug)–**86**. *Stamps of Queen Victoria.*

No.	Description	Un	Used*
O61	1½d. lilac (1.5.86)	£200	45·00
	a. No dot under "T"	£275	55·00
	b. Dot to left of "T"	£250	55·00
O62	6d. dull green (1.5.86)	£1200	£400
O63	9d. dull green	£1000	£400
O64	1s. orange-brown (wmk Crown, Pl 13)	£600	£100
	a. No dot under "T"	£850	£125
	b. Dot to left of "T"	£850	£125
O64*c*	1s. orange-brown (Pl 14)	£1000	£200
	ca. No dot under "T"	£1100	£225
	cb. Dot to left of "T"		

1887–90. *Stamps of Queen Victoria.*

No.	Description	Un	Used*
O65	1½d. dull purple and pale green (29.10.87)	50·00	5·00
	a. No dot under "T"	70·00	10·00
	b. Dot to right of "T"	70·00	10·00
	c. Dot to left of "T"	70·00	10·00
O66	6d. purple/*rose-red* (19.12.87)	£100	18·00
	a. No dot under "T"	£140	22·00
	b. Dot to right of "T"	£140	22·00
	c. Dot to left of "T"	£140	22·00
O67	9d. dull purple and blue (21.8.88)	£150	25·00
O68	1s. dull green (25.3.90)	£250	£100
	a. No dot under "T"	£300	£120
	b. Dot to right of "T"	£300	£120
	c. Dot to left of "T"	£325	£120
	d. Optd in blue-black		

1891–1900. *Stamps of Queen Victoria.*

No.	Description	Un	Used*
O69	1d. lilac (Die II) (18.6.97)	50·00	10·00
	a. No dot under "T"	65·00	25·00
	b. Dot to left of "T"	65·00	25·00
	c. Opt inverted	£2500	£1200
	d. Ditto. Dot to left of "T"	£2750	£1400
O70	2d. grey-green and carmine (24.10.91)	£100	15·00
	a. No dot under "T"	£140	25·00
	b. Dot to left of "T"	£140	25·00
O71	4½d. green and carmine (29.9.92)	£160	£125
	b. Dot to right of "T"		
O72	1s. green and carmine (11.00)	£250	90·00
	a. Opt inverted †	†	£5000

*O61/72 **For well-centred, lightly used +100%.**

The "no dot under T" variety occurred on R. 12/3 and 20/2. The "dot to left of T" comes four times in the sheet on R. 2/7, 6/7, 7/9 and 12/9. The best example of the "dot to right of T" is on R. 20/1. All three varieties were corrected around 1897.

1902. *Stamps of King Edward VII. Ordinary paper.*

No.	Description	Un	Used*
O74	1d. scarlet (30.10.02)	30·00	12·00
O75	2d. yellowish green & carmine-red (29.4.02)	90·00	22·00
O76	6d. pale dull purple (19.2.02)	£160	25·00
	a. Opt double, one albino	£9000	
O77	9d. dull purple and ultramarine (28.8.02)	£350	75·00
O78	1s. dull green and carmine (17.12.02)	£550	£125

BOARD OF EDUCATION

BOARD OF EDUCATION

(O 8)

Optd with Type O **8**

1902 (19 Feb). *Stamps of Queen Victoria.*

No.	Description	Un	Used	Used on Cover
O81	5d. dull purple and blue (II)	£1000	£225	
O82	1s. green and carmine	£3000	£1800	

1902 (19 Feb)–**04**. *Stamps of King Edward VII. Ordinary paper.*

No.	Description	Un	Used	Used on Cover
O83	½d. blue-green	£100	35·00	£350
O84	1d. scarlet	£100	35·00	£375
O85	2½d. ultramarine	£1500	£110	
O86	5d. dull purple & ultram (6.2.04)	£6000	£2000	
O87	1s. dull green & carmine (23.12.02)	£60000		

ROYAL HOUSEHOLD

R.H. OFFICIAL

(O 9)

1902. *Stamps of King Edward VII optd with Type* O **9**. *Ordinary paper.*

No.	Description	Un	Used	Used on Cover
O91	½d. blue-green (29.4.02)	£200	£140	£750
O92	1d. scarlet (19.2.02)	£175	£120	£600

ADMIRALTY

ADMIRALTY OFFICIAL (O 10) ADMIRALTY OFFICIAL (O 11) (with different "M")

1903 (1 Apr). *Stamps of King Edward VII optd with Type* O **10**. *Ordinary paper.*

No.	Description	Un	Used	Used on Cover
O101	½d. blue-green	15·00	12·00	
O102	1d. scarlet	10·00	6·00	£275
O103	1½d. dull purple and green	£110	70·00	
O104	2d. yellowish green & carmine-red	£185	85·00	
O105	2½d. ultramarine	£200	70·00	
O106	3d. purple/*yellow*	£185	70·00	

1903–04. *Stamps of King Edward VII optd with Type* O **11**. *Ordinary paper.*

No.	Description	Un	Used	Used on Cover
O107	½d. blue-green (9.03)	30·00	15·00	£450
O108	1d. scarlet (12.03)	30·00	15·00	£100
O109	1½d. dull purple and green (2.04)	£500	£300	
O110	2d. yellowish green and carmine red (3.04)	£750	£325	
O111	2½d. ultramarine (3.04)	£850	£500	
O112	3d. dull purple/*orange-yell* (12.03)	£600	£160	

Stamps of various issues perforated with a Crown and initials ("H.M.O.W.", "O.W.", "B.T." or "S.O.") or with initials only ("H.M.S.O." or "D.S.I.R.") have also been used for official purposes, but these are outside the scope of the catalogue.

POSTAL FISCAL STAMPS

PRICES. Prices in the used column are for stamps with genuine postal cancellations dated from the time when they were authorised for use as postage stamps. Beware of stamps with fiscal cancellations removed and fraudulent postmarks applied.

VALIDITY. The 1d. Surface-printed stamps were authorised for postal use from 1 June 1881 and at the same time the 1d. postage issue, No. 166, was declared valid for fiscal purposes. The 3d. and 6d. values, together with the Embossed issues were declared valid for postal purposes by another Act effective from 1 January 1883.

SURFACE-PRINTED ISSUES

(Typo Thomas De La Rue & Co)

F **1** Rectangular Buckle

F **2**

F **3** Octagonal Buckle

F **4**

F **5** Double-lined Anchor

F **6** Single-lined Anchor

1853–57. P 15½ × 15.

(a) Wmk F **5** *(inverted) (1853–55).*

No.	Type	Description	Un	Used	Used on cover
F1	F **1**	1d. light blue (10.10.53)	30·00	40·00	£16
F2	F **2**	1d. ochre (10.53)	95·00	£110	£42
		a. *Tête-bêche* (in block of four)	£15000		
F3	F **3**	1d. pale turquoise-blue (12.53)	25·00	38·00	£22
F4		1d. light blue/*blue* (12.53)	65·00	65·00	£37
F5	F **4**	1d. reddish lilac/*blue glazed paper* (25.3.55)	95·00	£100	£32

Only one example is known of No. F2a outside the National Postal Museum and the Royal Collection.

(b) Wmk F **6** *(1856–57).*

No.	Type	Description	Un	Used	Used on cover
F6	F **4**	1d. reddish lilac (*shades*)	8·50	7·00	£12
F7		1d. reddish lilac/*bluish* (*shades*) (1857)	8·50	7·00	£12

INLAND REVENUE

(F 7)

1860 (3 Apr). *No. F7 optd with Type* F **7**, *in red.*

No.	Type	Description	Un	Used	Used on cover
F8	F **4**	1d. dull reddish lilac/*blue*	£625	£525	£100

BLUE PAPER. In the following issues we no longer distinguis between bluish and white paper. There is a range of papers fro white or greyish to bluish.

F **8**

F **9**

F 10

1860–67. *Bluish to white Paper.* P 15½ × 15.

(a) Wmk F **6** *(1860).*

F 9	F **8**	1d. reddish lilac (May)	10·00	10·00	£125
F10	F **9**	3d. reddish lilac (June)	£325	£200	£375
F11	F **10**	6d. reddish lilac (Oct)	£150	£125	£325

(b) W **40**. (Anchor 16 mm high) *(1864).*

F12	F **8**	1d. pale reddish lilac (Nov)	8·50	8·50	£125
F13	F **9**	3d. pale reddish lilac	£185	£125	£375
F14	F **10**	6d. pale reddish lilac	£150	£125	£325

(c) W **40** (Anchor 18 mm high) *(1867).*

F15	F **8**	1d. reddish lilac	16·00	16·00	£185
F16	F **9**	3d. reddish lilac	85·00	80·00	£325
F17	F **10**	6d. reddish lilac	75·00	60·00	£210

For stamps perf 14, see Nos. F24/7.

F 11

F 12

Four Dies of Type F 12

Nos. F19/21 show "O" of "ONE" circular. No. F22 (Die 4) shows a horizontal oval

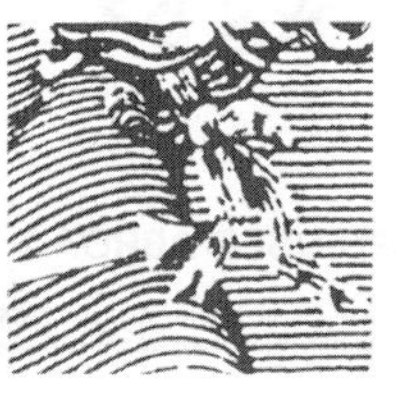

Die 1. Four lines of shading in left band of ribbon opposite "Y" of "PENNY", small ornaments and heavy shading under chin

Die 2. Two lines of shading in left band of ribbon. Clear line of shading under chin. Small ornaments

Die 3. Ornaments larger and joined; line of shading under chin extended half way down neck

Die 4. Ornaments much larger; straight line of shading continued to bottom of neck

1867–81. *White to bluish paper.* P 14.

(a) W **47** (Small Anchor).

F18	F **11**	1d. purple (1.9.67)	15·00	15·00	£100
F19	F **12**	1d. purple (Die 1) (6.68)	4·50	5·00	£100
F20		1d. purple (Die 2) (6.76)	18·00	13·00	£225
F21		1d. purple (Die 3) (3.77)	9·00	9·00	£150
F22		1d. purple (Die 4) (7.78)	6·00	6·00	95·00

(b) W **48** (Orb).

F23	F **12**	1d. purple (Die 4) (1.81)	6·00	3·00	80·00

1881. *White to bluish paper.* P 14.

(a) W **40** *(Anchor 18 mm high) (Jan).*

F24	F **9**	3d. reddish lilac	£600	£325	£675
F25	F **10**	6d. reddish lilac	£275	£130	£325

(b) W **40** *(Anchor 20 mm high) (May).*

F26	F **9**	3d. reddish lilac	£450	£250	£500
F27	F **10**	6d. reddish lilac	£250	£130	£325

ISSUES EMBOSSED IN COLOUR

(Made at Somerset House)

The embossed stamps were struck from dies not appropriated to any special purpose on paper which had the words "INLAND REVENUE" previously printed, and thus became available for payment of any duties for which no special stamps had been provided.

The die letters are included in the embossed designs and holes were drilled for the insertion of plugs showing figures indicating dates of striking.

F 13

F 14

INLAND REVENUE
(F 15)

INLAND REVENUE
(F 16)

1860 (3 Apr)–**71**. *Types* F **13/14** *and similar types embossed on bluish paper. Underprint Type* F **15**. No wmk. Imperf.

		Un	*Used*
F28	2d. pink (Die A) (1.1.71)	£500	
F29	3d. pink (Die C)	£125	
	a. *Tête-bêche* (vert pair)	£1000	
F30	3d. pink (Die D)	£500	
F31	6d. pink (Die T)		
F32	6d. pink (Die U)	£250	
	a. *Tête-bêche* (vert pair)		
F33	9d. pink (Die C) (1.1.71)	£625	
F34	1s. pink (Die E) (28.6.61)	£500	
	a. *Tête-bêche* (vert pair)		
F35	1s. pink (Die F) (28.6.61)	£180	
	a. *Tête-bêche* (vert pair)	£750	
F36	2s. pink (Die K) (6.8.61)	£500	
F37	2s.6d. pink (Die N) (28.6.61)		
F38	2s.6d. pink (Die O) (28.6.61)	£250	

1871 (Aug). *As last but perf 12½.*

F39	2d. pink (Die A)	£325	
F42	9d. pink (Die C)	£750	
F43	1s. pink (Die E)	£500	
F44	1s. pink (Die F)	£425	
F45	2s.6d. pink (Die O)	£250	

1874 (Nov). *Types as before embossed on white paper. Underprint Type* F **16**, *in green.* W **47** (Small Anchor). P 12½.

F46	2d. pink (Die A)		
F47	9d. pink (Die C)		
F48	1s. pink (Die F)	£500	
F49	2s.6d. pink (Die O)		

It is possible that the 2d., 9d. and 2s.6d. may not exist with the thin underprint, Type F **16**, in this shade

1875 (Nov)–**80**. *As last but colour changed and on white or bluish paper.*

F50	2d. vermilion (Die A) (1880)	£375	
F51	9d. vermilion (Die C) (1876)	£500	
F52	1s. vermilion (Die E)	£325	
F53	1s. vermilion (Die F)	£750	
F54	2s.6d. vermilion (Die O) (1878)	£325	

1882 (Oct). *As last but* W **48** *(Orbs).*

F55	2d. vermilion (Die A)		
F56	9d. vermilion (Die C)		
F57	1s. vermilion (Die E)		
F58	2s.6d. vermilion (Die O)	£650	£500

Although specimen overprints of Nos. F55/7 are known there is some doubt if these values were issued.

The sale of Inland Revenue stamps up to the 2s. value ceased from 30 December 1882 and stocks were called in and destroyed. The 2s.6d. value remained on sale until 2 July 1883 when it was replaced by the 2s.6d. "Postage & Revenue" stamp. Inland Revenue stamps still in the hands of the public continued to be accepted for revenue and postal purposes.

TELEGRAPH STAMPS. A priced listing of the Post Office telegraph stamps appears in Volume 1 of the Stanley Gibbons *Great Britain Specialised Catalogue*. The last listing for the private telegraph companies in the Part 1 Catalogue was in the 1940 edition and for military telegraphs the 1941 edition.

CHANNEL ISLANDS

GENERAL ISSUE

C **1** Gathering Vraic

C **2** Islanders gathering Vraic

(Des J. R. R. Stobie (1 d.) or from drawing by E. Blampied (2½d.). Photo Harrison)

1948 (10 May). *Third Anniv of Liberation.* W **127** of Great Britain. P15 × 14.

C1	C **1**	1d. scarlet	25	30
C2	C **2**	2½d. ultramarine	25	30

Supplies of these stamps were also available from eight head post offices on the mainland of Great Britain.

GUERNSEY

WAR OCCUPATION ISSUES

Stamps issued under the authority of the Guernsey States during the German Occupation

BISECTS. On 24 December 1940 authority was given, by Post Office notice, that prepayment of penny postage could be effected by using half a British 2d. stamp, diagonally bisected. Such stamps were first used on 27 December 1940.

The 2d. stamps generally available were those of the Postal Centenary issue, 1940 (S.G. 482) and the first colour of the King George VI issue (S.G. 465). These are listed under Nos. 482a and 465b. A number of the 2d. King George V, 1912–22, and of the King George V photogravure stamp (S.G. 442) which were in the hands of philatelists, were also bisected and used.

1

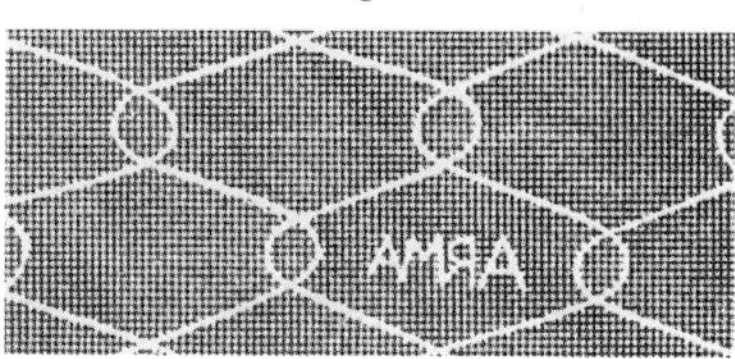

1a Loops (*half actual size*)

(Des E. W. Vaudin. Typo Guernsey Press Co Ltd)

1941–44. *Rouletted.*

(a) White paper. No wmk.

1	**1**	½d. light green (7.4.41)	3·00	1·75
		a. Emerald-green (6.41)	3·50	1·50
		b. Bluish green (11.41)	30·00	13·00
		c. Bright green (2.42)	18·00	9·00
		d. Dull green (9.42)	3·00	1·75
		e. Olive-green (2.43)	25·00	10·00
		f. Pale yellowish green (7.43 and later) (*shades*)	3·00	1·50
		g. Imperf (pair)	£200	
		h. Imperf between (horiz pair)	£700	
		i. Imperf between (vert pair)	£800	
2		1d. scarlet (18.2.41)	2·00	90
		a. Pale vermilion (7.43) (etc.)	2·50	75
		b. Carmine (1943)	2·00	75
		c. Imperf (pair)	£150	75·00
		d. Imperf between (horiz pair)	£700	
		da. Imperf vert (centre stamp of horiz strip of 3)		
		e. Imperf between (vert pair)	£800	
		f. Printed double (scarlet shade)	£100	
3		2½d. ultramarine (12.4.44)	3·25	4·00
		a. Pale ultramarine (7.44)	3·25	5·00
		b. Imperf (pair)	£500	
		c. Imperf between (horiz pair)	£1000	

(b) Bluish French bank-note paper. W **1a** (sideways).

4	**1**	½d. bright green (11.3.42)	20·00	18·00
5		1d. scarlet (9.4.42)	10·00	16·00

The dates given for the shades of Nos. 1/3 are the months in which they were printed as indicated on the printer's imprints. Others are issue dates.

JERSEY

WAR OCCUPATION ISSUES

Stamps issued under the authority of the Jersey States during the German Occupation

1

(Des Major N. V. L. Rybot. Typo Jersey Evening Post, St. Helier)

1941–43. *White paper (thin to thick).* No wmk. P 11.

1	1	½d. bright green (29.1.42)	4·00	3·25
		a. Imperf between (vert pair)	£800	
		b. Imperf between (horiz pair)	£700	
		c. Imperf (pair)	£250	
		d. On greyish paper (1.43)	5·50	5·50
2		1d. scarlet (1.4.41)	4·50	2·50
		a. Imperf between (vert pair)	£800	
		b. Imperf between (horiz pair)	£700	
		c. Imperf (pair)	£275	
		d. On chalk-surfaced paper	42·00	38·00
		e. On greyish paper (1.43)	5·50	5·75

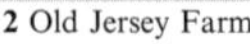

2 Old Jersey Farm

3 Portelet Bay

4 Corbière Lighthouse

5 Elizabeth Castle

6 Mont Orgueil Castle

7 Gathering Vraic (seaweed)

(Des E. Blampied. Eng H. Cortot. Typo French Govt Works, Paris)

1943–44. No wmk. P 13½.

3	2	½d. green (1 June)	7·50	5·50
		a. Rough, grey paper (6.10.43)	7·50	5·50
4	3	1d. scarlet (1 June)	2·00	75
		a. On newsprint (28.2.44)	2·50	75
5	4	1½d. brown (8 June)	3·50	3·25
6	5	2d. orange-yellow (8 June)	4·75	3·25
7	6	2½d. blue (29 June)	2·00	1·00
		a. On newsprint (25.2.44)	1·00	1·10
		ba. Thin paper*	£225	
8	7	3d. violet (29 June)	1·25	3·00
3/8 *Set of* 6			18·00	15·00

*On No. 7ba the design shows clearly through the back of the stamp.

British Post Offices Abroad

The origins of the network of Post Offices, Postal Agencies and Packet Agents can be recognised from the 18th century, but the system did not become established until the expansion of trade, following the end of the Napoleonic Wars in 1815.

Many offices were provided in newly acquired dependent territories, and were then, eventually, transferred from the control of the British Post Office to the evolving local administrations.

Those in foreign countries, nearly always based on existing British Consular appointments, were mostly connected to the network of British Packet lines which had been re-established in 1814. They tended to survive until the country in which they were situated established its own efficient postal service or joined the U.P.U. The term "Post Office Agent" was employed by the British G.P.O. and "Packet Agent" by the shipping lines to describe similar functions.

Listed in this section are the Crowned-circle handstamps and G.B. stamps used in the Post Offices and Agencies situated in foreign countries. Those for the territories within the scope of this catalogue will be found under the following headings:

Prices. Catalogue prices quoted in this section, and throughout the volume, covering Crowned-circle handstamps and stamps of Great Britain used abroad are for used examples with the cancellation or handstamp clearly legible. Poor impressions of the cancellations and handstamps are worth much less than the prices quoted.

They also take into account the fact that many identifiable cancellations of the post offices abroad render the stamps they obliterate in less than 'fine' condition. As a result, some stamps listed in this section are priced at less than the same items used in Great Britain, where the prices are for fine examples. Lightly cancelled stamps used in offices abroad would be worth a premium over the prices quoted.

CROWNED-CIRCLE HANDSTAMPS

Following the introduction, in 1840, of adhesive stamps in Great Britain there was considerable pressure from a number of the dependent territories for the British Post Office to provide something similar for their use.

Such suggestions were resisted, however, because of supposed operational problems, but the decision was taken, in connection with an expansion of the Packet Service, to issue a uniform series of handstamps and date stamps to the offices abroad, both in the dependent territories and in foreign countries.

Under the regulations circulated in December 1841, letters and packets forwarded through these offices to the United Kingdom or any of its territories were to be sent unpaid, the postage being collected on delivery. Where this was not possible, for example from a British colony to a foreign country or between two foreign ports, then a *crowned-circle handstamp* was to be applied with the postage, paid in advance, noted alongside in manuscript.

Examples of these handstamps were supplied over twenty years from 1842, but many continued to fulfil other functions long after the introduction of adhesive stamps in the colony concerned.

Our listings cover the use of these handstamps for their initial purpose and the prices quoted are for examples used on cover during the pre-adhesive period.

In most instances the dates quoted are those on which the handstamp appears in the G.P.O. Record Books, but it seems to have been normal for the handstamps to be sent to the office concerned immediately following this registration.

Many of the handstamps were individually cut by hand, so that each has its own characteristics, but for the purposes of the listing they have been grouped into nine Types as shown in the adjacent column. No attempt has been made to identify them by anything but the most major differences, so that minor differences in size and in the type of the crown have been ignored.

DOUBLE CIRCLE

CC 1 CC 1a

Curved "PAID"

CC 1b CC 1c

Curved "PAID"

CC 2

Straight "PAID"

SINGLE CIRCLE

CC 3

CC 4

Straight "PAID"

CC 5

Curved "PAID"

CC 6 Straight "PAID"

CC 7 Curved "PAID"

GREAT BRITAIN STAMPS USED ABROAD

Prices quoted are for single stamps not on cover unless otherwise stated. Stamps on cover are worth considerably more in most cases.

In many instances obliterators allocated to post offices abroad were, at a later date re-allocated to offices at home. Postmarks on issues later than those included in our lists can therefore safely be regarded as *not* having been "used abroad".

INDEX

C28 Montevideo (Uruguay)	GB25
C30 Valparaiso (Chile)	GB20
C35 Panama (Colombia)	GB21
G36 Arica (Peru)	GB23
C37 Caldera (Chile)	GB20
C38 Callao (Peru)	GB23
C39 Cobija (Bolivia)	GB20
C40 Coquimbo (Chile)	GB20
C41 Guayaquil (Ecuador)	GB22
C42 Islay (Peru)	GB24
C43 Paita (Peru)	GB24
C51 St. Thomas (Danish West Indies)	GB22
C56 (or 65) Carthagena (Colombia)	GB21
C57 Greytown (Nicaragua)	GB23
C58 Havana (Cuba)	GB21
C59 Jacmel (Haiti)	GB22
C60 La Guayra (Venezuela)	GB25
C61 San Juan (Porto Rico)	GB24
C62 Santa Martha (Colombia)	GB21
C63 Tampico (Mexico)	GB23
C65 (see C56)	GB21
C79 (Mailboats)	GB26
C81 Bahia (Brazil)	GB20
C82 Pernambuco (Brazil)	GB20
C83 Rio de Janeiro (Brazil)	GB20
C86 Porto Plata (Dominican Republic)	GB22
C87 St. Domingo (Dominican Republic)	GB22
C88 St. Jago de Cuba (Cuba)	GB21
Crimea (Army)	GB24
D22 Ciudad Bolivar (Venezuela)	GB25
D26 (Mailboats)	GB26
D65 Pisagua? (Peru)	GB24
D74 Pisco and Chincha Islands (Peru)	GB24
D87 Iquique (Peru)	GB24
E53 Port-au-Prince (Haiti)	GB22
E88 Colon (Colombia)	GB21
Egypt (Army)	121
F69 Savanilla (Colombia)	GB21
F83 Arroyo (Porto Rico)	GB24
F84 Aguadilla (Porto Rico)	GB24
F85 Mayaguez (Porto Rico)	GB24
F87 Smyrna (British Levant)	76
F88 Ponce (Porto Rico)	GB24
Forcados River (Niger Coast Protectorate) (Nigeria)	282
G Gibraltar	133
G06 Beyrout (British Levant)	75
Ionian Islands	201
Lokoja, Niger Company Territories (Nigeria)	284
M Malta	244
Old Calabar River, Niger Coast Protectorate (Nigeria)	282
Opobo River. Niger Coast Protectorate (Nigeria)	282
S. Stamboul (British Levant)	76
Salonica (British Levant)	76
South Africa (Army)	340
247. Fernando Poo	GB22
582 Naguabo (Porto Rico)	GB24
942, 969, 974, 975, 981, 982 Cyprus	113
Wavy lines Malta	244

TYPES OF OBLITERATOR FOR GREAT BRITAIN STAMPS USED ABROAD

HORIZONTAL OVAL

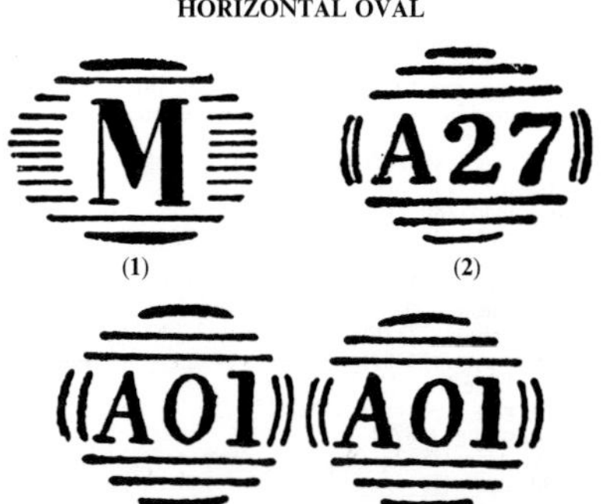

(1) (2)

(3)

(4)

(5)

(6)

(7)

VERTICAL OVAL

(8) (9)

(10)

(11)

(12)

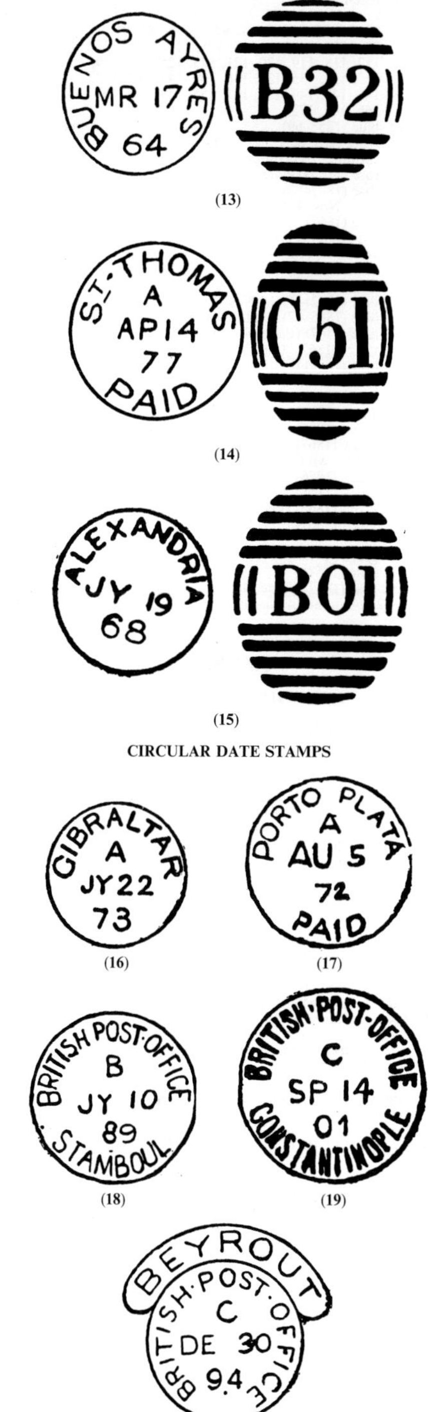

(13)

(14)

(15)

CIRCULAR DATE STAMPS

(16) (17)

(18) (19)

(20)

ARGENTINE REPUBLIC

BUENOS AYRES

The first regular monthly British mail packet service was introduced in 1824, replacing a private arrangement which had previously existed for some years.

Great Britain stamps were used from 1860 until the office closed at the end of June 1873. Until 1878 the British Consul continued to sell stamps which were used in combination with an Argentine value prepaying the internal rate. The British stamps on such covers were cancelled on arrival in England.

CROWNED-CIRCLE HANDSTAMPS

CC1 CC 7 BUENOS AYRES (Black or R.) (5.1.1851) . . . . *Price on cover* £700

Stamps of GREAT BRITAIN *cancelled* "B 32" *as in Types* **2**, **12** *or* **13**.

1860–73.

Z 1 1d. rose-red (1857) . . . . 40·00

Z 2 1d. rose-red (1864) *From* 35·00
Plate Nos. 71, 72, 73, 74, 76, 78, 79, 80, 81, 82, 85, 87, 89, 90, 91, 92, 93, 94, 95, 96, 97, 99, 101, 103, 104, 107, 108, 110, 112, 113, 114, 117, 118, 119, 120, 121, 123, 125, 127, 129, 130, 131, 135, 136, 138, 139, 140, 142, 143, 145, 147, 149, 150, 151, 155, 159, 163, 164, 166, 169, 172.
Z 3 2d. blue (1858–69) *From* 40·00
Plate Nos. 8, 9, 12, 13, 14.
Z 4 3d. carmine-rose (1862) £225
Z 5 3d. rose (1865) (Plate No. 4) 80·00
Z 6 3d. rose (1867–73) *From* 40·00
Plate Nos. 4, 5, 6, 7, 8, 9, 10.
Z 7 4d. rose (1857) 90·00
Z 8 4d. red (1862) (Plate Nos. 3, 4) 80·00
Z 9 4d. vermilion (1865–73) *From* 45·00
Plate Nos. 7, 8, 9, 10, 11, 12, 13.
Z10 6d. lilac (1856) 80·00
Z11 6d. lilac (1862) (Plate Nos. 3, 4)
Z12 6d. lilac (1865–67) (Plate Nos. 5, 6) *From* 70·00
Z13 6d. lilac (1867) (Plate No. 6) 80·00
Z14 6d. violet (1867–70) (Plate Nos. 6, 8, 9) *From* 65·00
Z15 6d. buff (1872) (Plate No. 11) 75·00
Z16 6d. chestnut (1872) (Plate No. 11) 40·00
Z17 9d. bistre (1862) £275
Z18 9d. straw (1862) £250
Z19 9d. straw (1865) £425
Z20 9d. straw (1867) £275
Z21 10d. red-brown (1867) £275
Z22 1s. green (1856) £250
Z23 1s. green (1862) £150
Z24 1s. green (1865) (Plate No. 4) £140
Z25 1s. green (1867–73) (Plate Nos. 4, 5, 6, 7) *From* 40·00
Z26 1s. green (1873–77) (Plate No. 8)
Z27 2s. blue (1867) £130
Z28 5s. rose (1867) (Plate No. 1) £400

A "B 32" obliteration was later used by Mauritius on its own stamps.

AZORES

ST. MICHAELS (SAN MIGUEL)

A British Postal Agency existed at Ponta Delgada, the chief port of the island, to operate with the services of the Royal Mail Steam Packet Company.

CROWNED-CIRCLE HANDSTAMPS

CC1 CC **1b** ST MICHAELS (27.5.1842)

BOLIVIA

COBIJA

It is believed that the British Postal Agency opened in 1862. The stamps of Great Britain were used between 1865 and 1878. They can be found used in combination with Bolivia adhesive stamps paying the local postage. The Agency closed in 1881, the town having been occupied by Chile in 1879

CROWNED-CIRCLE HANDSTAMPS

CC1 CC **4** COBIJA (29.3.1862)

Stamps of GREAT BRITAIN *cancelled* "C 39" *as Types* **4**, **8** or **12**.

1865–78.
Z 1 1d. rose-red (Plate Nos. 93, 95)
Z 2 2d. blue (1858–69) (Plate No. 14)
Z 3 3d. rose (1867–73) (Plate No. 6)
Z 4 3d. rose (1873–76) (Plate Nos. 16, 19)
Z 5 4d. sage-green (1877) (Plate No. 15) £450
Z 6 6d. violet (1867–70) (Plate No. 9) £425
Z 7 6d. buff (1872) (Plate No. 11)
Z 8 6d. grey (1874–76) (Plate Nos. 13, 14, 15, 16) £350
Z 9 1s. green (1867–73) (Plate Nos. 4, 5) £350
Z10 1s. green (1873–77) (Plate Nos. 10, 11 , 12, 13) £350
Z11 2s. blue (1867) £350
Z12 5s. rose (1867–74) (Plate No. 2) £700

BRAZIL

The first packets ran to Brazil in 1808 when the Portuguese royal family went into exile at Rio de Janeiro. The Agencies at Bahia and Pernambuco did not open until 1851. All three agencies used the stamps of Great Britain from 1866 and these can be found used in combination with Brazil adhesive stamps paying the local postage. The agencies closed on 30 June 1874

BAHIA

CROWNED-CIRCLE HANDSTAMPS

CC1 CC **7** BAHIA (Black, G. *or* R.) (6.1.1851) *Price on cover* £2500

Stamps of GREAT BRITAIN *cancelled* "C 81" *as Type* **12**.

1866–74.
Z 1 1d. rose-red (1864–79) *From* 40·00
Plate Nos. 90, 93, 96, 108, 113, 117, 135, 140, 147, 155.
Z 2 1½d. lake-red (1870–74) (Plate No. 3) £100
Z 3 2d. blue (1858–59) (Plate Nos. 9, 12, 13, 14) 60·00
Z 4 3d. rose (1865) (Plate No. 4)
Z 5 3d. rose (1867–73) (Plate Nos. 4, 6, 8, 9, 10) 50·00
Z 6 3d. rose (1873–79) (Plate No. 11)
Z 7 4d. vermilion (1865–73) *From* 45·00
Plate Nos. 8, 9, 10, 11, 12, 13.
Z 8 6d. lilac (1865–67) (Plate No. 5)
Z 9 6d. lilac (1867) (Plate No. 6) 80·00
Z10 6d. violet (1867–70) (Plate Nos. 6, 8, 9) *From* 65·00
Z11 6d. buff (1872–73) (Plate Nos. 11, 12) *From* 90·00
Z12 6d. chestnut (1872) (Plate No. 11) 90·00
Z13 6d. grey (1873) (Plate No. 12)
Z14 6d. grey (1874–76) (Plate No. 13)
Z15 9d. straw (1865) £375
Z16 9d. straw (1867) £225
Z17 1s. green (1865) (Plate No. 4) £150
Z18 1s. green (1867–73) (Plate Nos. 4, 5, 6, 7) *From* 45·00
Z19 1s. green (1873–77) (Plate Nos. 8, 9) 75·00
Z20 2s. blue (1867) £225
Z21 5s. rose (1867) (Plate No. 1) £400

PERNAMBUCO

CROWNED-CIRCLE HANDSTAMPS

CC2 CC **7** PERNAMBUCO (Black *or* R.) (6.1.1851) *Price on cover* £2500

Stamps of GREAT BRITAIN *cancelled* "C 82" *as Type* **12** *or with circular date stamp as Type* **16**.

1866–74.
Z22 1d. rose-red (1864–79) *From* 40·00
Plate Nos. 85, 108, 111, 130, 131, 132, 149, 157, 159, 160, 187.
Z23 2d. blue (1858–69) *From* 50·00
Plate Nos. 9, 12, 13, 14.
Z23*a* 3d. rose (1865) (Plate No. 4) 80·00
Z24 3d. rose (1867–73) (Plate Nos. 4, 5, 6, 7, 10) 50·00
Z25 3d. rose (1873–77) (Plate No. 11)
Z26 4d. vermilion (1865–73) *From* 45·00
Plate Nos. 9, 10, 11, 12, 13, 14.
Z27 6d. lilac (1865–67) (Plate Nos. 5, 6)
Z28 6d. lilac (1867) (Plate No. 6) 70·00
Z29 6d. violet (1867–70) (Plate Nos. 8, 9) *From* 65·00
Z30 6d. buff (1872–73) (Plate Nos. 11, 12) *From* 70·00
Z31 6d. chestnut (1872) (Plate No. 11) 50·00
Z32 6d. grey (1873) (Plate No. 12)
Z33 9d. straw (1865) £375
Z34 9d. straw (1867) £200
Z35 10d. red-brown (1867) £275
Z36 1s. green (1865) (Plate No. 4) £150
Z37 1s. green (1867–73) (Plate Nos. 4, 5, 6, 7) *From* 45·00
Z38 2s. blue (1867) £225
Z39 5s. rose (1867–74) (Plate Nos. 1, 2) *From* £425

RIO DE JANEIRO

CROWNED-CIRCLE HANDSTAMPS

CC3 CC **7** RIO DE JANEIRO (Black, B., G. *or* R.) (6.1.1851) *Price on cover* £450

Stamps of GREAT BRITAIN *cancelled* "C 83" *as Type* **12**.

1866–74.
Z40 1d. rose-red (1857) 40·00
Z41 1d. rose-red (1864–79) *From* 35·00
Plate Nos. 71, 76, 80, 82, 86, 94, 103, 113, 117, 119, 123, 130, 132, 134, 135, 146, 148, 159, 161, 166, 185, 200, 204.
Z42 2d. blue (1858–69) *From* 35·00
Plate Nos. 9, 12, 13, 14.
Z43 3d. rose (1867–73) *From* 40·00
Plate Nos. 4, 5, 6, 7, 8, 9.
Z44 3d. rose (1873–77) (Plate No. 11)
Z45 4d. vermilion (1865–73) *From* 45·00
Plate Nos. 8, 9, 10, 11, 12, 13, 14.
Z46 6d. lilac (1865–67) (Plate No. 5) 90·00
Z47 6d. lilac (1867) (Plate No. 6) 70·00
Z48 6d. violet (1867–70) (Plate Nos. 6, 8, 9) *From* 65·00
Z49 6d. buff (1872) (Plate No. 11) 70·00
Z50 6d. chestnut (1872) (Plate No. 11) 40·00
Z51 6d. grey (1873) (Plate No. 12)
Z52 9d. straw (1865) £350
Z53 9d. straw (1867) £180
Z54 10d. red-brown (1867) £250
Z55 1s. green (1865) (Plate No. 4) £130
Z56 1s. green (1867–73) (Plate Nos. 4, 5, 6, 7) *From* 40·00
Z57 1s. green (1873–77) (Plate Nos. 8, 9) 65·00
Z58 2s. blue (1867) £120
Z59 5s. rose (1867–74) (Plate Nos. 1, 2) *From* £375

CAPE VERDE ISLANDS

The British Packet Agency at St. Vincent opened in 1851 as part of the revised service to South America. The agency was closed by 1860.

CROWNED-CIRCLE HANDSTAMPS

CC1 CC **6** ST. VINCENT C.DE.V. (6.1.1851)

CHILE

The British Postal Agency at Valparaiso opened on 7 May 1846, to be followed by further offices at Caldera (1858) and Coquimbo (1863). The stamps of Great Britain were introduced in 1865 and can be found used in combination with Chile adhesives paying the local postage. All three offices closed on 31 March 1881 when Chile joined the U.P.U.

CALDERA

Stamps of GREAT BRITAIN *cancelled* "C 37" *as in Type* **4**.

1865–81.
Z 1 1d. rose-red (1864–79) *From* 50·00
Plate Nos. 71, 72, 88, 90, 95, 160, 195.
Z 2 1½d. lake-red (1870–74) (Plate No. 3)
Z 3 2d. blue (1858–69) (Plate No. 9) 55·00
Z 4 3d. rose (1865) (Plate No. 4) 80·00
Z 5 3d. rose (1867–73) (Plate Nos. 5, 7) 60·00
Z 6 3d. rose (1873–76) *From* 50·00
Plate Nos. 11, 12, 16, 17, 18, 19.
Z 7 4d. red (1862) (Plate No. 4)
Z 8 4d. vermilion (1865–73) *From* 50·00
Plate Nos. 8, 11, 12, 13, 14.
Z 9 4d. sage-green (1877) (Plate No. 16)
Z10 6d. lilac (1862) (Plate No. 4) 90·00
Z11 6d. lilac (1865–67) (Plate Nos. 5, 6) *From* £120
Z12 6d. violet (1867–70) (Plate Nos. 6, 8, 9) *From* 80·00
Z13 6d. buff (1872) (Plate No. 11)
Z14 6d. chestnut (1872) (Plate No. 11)
Z15 6d. grey (1873) (Plate No. 12)
Z16 6d. grey (1874–80) *From* 50·00
Plate Nos. 13, 14, 15, 16, 17.
Z17 8d. orange (1876) £325
Z18 9d. straw (1867) £225
Z19 10d. red-brown (1867) £250
Z20 1s. green (1865) (Plate No. 4)
Z21 1s. green 1867–73 (Plate Nos. 4, 5, 6) *From* 50·0
Z22 1s. green (1873–77) *From* 75·0
Plate Nos. 8, 10, 11, 12, 13.
Z23 2s. blue (1867) £20
Z23*a* 2s. cobalt (1867)
Z24 2s. brown (1880) £170
Z25 5s. rose (1867–74) (Plate No. 2) £42

COQUIMBO

Stamps of GREAT BRITAIN *cancelled* "C 40" *as in Type* **4** *o* *with circular date stamp as Type* **16**.

1865–81.
Z26 ½d. rose-red (1870–79) (Plate No. 14)
Z27 1d. rose-red (1857)
Z28 1d. rose-red (1864–79) (Plate Nos. 85, 204)
Z29 2d. blue (1858–69) (Plate Nos. 9, 14)
Z30 3d. rose (1865)
Z31 3d. rose (1872) (Plate No. 8)
Z32 3d. rose (1873–76) (Plate Nos. 18, 19) *From* 50·0
Z33 4d. red (1863) (Plate No. 4) (*Hair lines*)
Z34 4d. vermilion (1865–73) (Plate Nos. 12, 14) 55·0
Z35 4d. sage-green (1877) (Plate Nos. 15, 16) *From* £18
Z36 6d. lilac (1862) (Plate Nos. 3, 4) *From* 75·0
Z37 6d. lilac (1865–67) (Plate No. 5)
Z38 6d. lilac (1867) (Plate No. 6) 70·0
Z39 6d. violet (1867–70) (Plate Nos. 6, 8, 9) *From* 65·0
Z40 6d. buff (1872–73) (Plate Nos. 11, 12) *From* 70·0
Z41 6d. chestnut (1872) (Plate No. 11)
Z42 6d. grey (1873) (Plate No. 12) £19
Z43 6d. grey (1874–76) *From* 50·0
Plate Nos. 13, 14, 15, 16.
Z44 8d. orange (1876)
Z45 9d. straw (1862) £27
Z46 9d. straw (1867) £20
Z47 10d. red-brown (1867)
Z48 1s. green (1865) (Plate No. 4) £15
Z49 1s. green (1867–73) (Plate Nos. 4, 5, 6) 50·0
Z50 1s. green (1873–77) *From* 70·0
Plate Nos. 8, 10, 11, 12, 13.
Z51 2s. blue (1867) £15
Z51*a* 2s. cobalt (1867)
Z52 2s. brown (1880) £170
Z53 5s. rose (1867–74) (Plate Nos. 1, 2) *From* £42

VALPARAISO

CROWNED-CIRCLE HANDSTAMPS

CC1 CC **1** VALPARAISO (R.) (*without stop*) (13.1.1846) *Price on cover* £3
CC2 VALPARAISO. (R.) (*with stop*) (16.7.1846) *Price on cover* £4

Stamps of GREAT BRITAIN *cancelled* "C 30", *as in Types* **12** *a* **14** (*without* "PAID" *before* 1870) *or with circular date stamp* *Type* **16**.

1865–81.
Z54 ½d. rose-red (1870–79) *From* 60·
Plate Nos. 6,11, 12, 13, 14.
Z55 1d. rose-red (1864–79) *From* 30·
Plate Nos. 80, 84, 85, 89, 91, 101, 106, 113, 116, 122, 123, 138, 140, 141, 146, 148, 149, 152, 157, 158, 162, 167, 175, 178, 181, 185, 186, 187, 189, 190, 195, 197, 198, 199, 200, 201, 207, 209, 210, 211, 212, 213, 214, 215, 217.
Z56 1½d. lake-red (1870–74) (Plate Nos, 1, 3) *From* 60·
Z57 2d. blue (1858–69) (Plate Nos. 9, 13, 14, 15) 40·
Z58 2½d. rosy mauve (1875), white paper £1
Plate No. 2.
Z59 2½d. rosy mauve (1876) (Plate Nos. 4, 8) £1
Z60 3d. carmine-rose (1862)
Z61 3d. rose (1865) (Plate No. 4)
Z62 3d. rose (1867–73) *From* 45·
Plate Nos. 5, 6, 7, 8, 9, 10.
Z63 3d. rose (1873–76) *From* 35·
Plate Nos. 11, 12, 14, 16, 17, 18, 19.
Z63*a* 4d. red (1862) (Plate Nos. 3, 4)
Z64 4d. vermilion (1865–73) *From* 45·
Plate Nos. 9, 10, 11, 12, 13, 14.
Z65 4d. vermilion (1876) (Plate No. 15) £2
Z66 4d. sage-green (1877) (Plate Nos. 15, 16) *From* £1
Z67 4d. grey-brown (1880) wmk Large Garter
Plate No. 17.
Z68 6d. lilac (1862) (Plate Nos. 3, 4) *From* 75·
Z69 6d. lilac (1865) (Plate Nos. 5, 6)
Z70 6d. lilac (1867) (Plate No. 6)
Z71 6d. violet (1867–70) (Plate Nos. 6, 8, 9) *From* 65·
Z72 6d. buff (1872–73) (Plate Nos. 11, 12) *From* 70·
Z73 6d. chestnut (1872) (Plate No. 11) 40·
Z74 6d. grey (1873) (Plate No. 12) £1
Z75 6d. grey (1874–80) *From* 40·
Plate Nos. 13, 14, 15, 16, 17.
Z76 6d. grey (1881) (Plate No. 17)
Z77 8d. orange (1876) £2
Z78 9d. straw (1862)
Z79 9d. straw (1865)
Z80 9d. straw (1867) £1
Z81 10d. red-brown (1867) £2

Z82 1s. green (1865) (Plate No. 4)
Z83 1s. green (1867–73) From 35·00
Plate Nos. 4, 5, 6, 7.
Z84 1s. green (1873–77) From 60·00
Plate Nos. 8, 9, 10, 11, 12, 13.
Z85 1s. orange-brown (1880) (Plate No. 13) £350
Z86 2s. blue (1867) £110
Z86*a* 2s. cobalt (1867) £1400
Z87 2s. brown (1880) £1700
Z88 5s. rose (1867–74) (Plate Nos. 1, 2) From £350
Z89 10s. grey-green (1878) (wmk Cross) £2500
Z90 £1 brown-lilac (1878) (wmk Cross) £3500

1880.
Z91 1d. Venetian red 70·00
Z92 1½d. Venetian red £110

COLOMBIA

The system of British Postal Agencies in the area was inaugurated by the opening of the Carthagena office in 1825. In 1842 agencies at Chagres, Panama and Santa Martha were added to the system. A further office opened at Colon in 1852, this port also being known as Aspinwall. During 1872 the system was further enlarged by an office at Savanilla, although this agency was later, 1878, transferred to Barranquilla.

Stamps of Great Britain were supplied to Carthagena, Panama and Santa Martha in 1865, Colon in 1870 and Savanilla in 1872. Combination covers with Colombia stamps paying the local postage are known from Santa Martha and Savanilla as are similar covers from Panama showing Costa Rica and El Salvador stamps.

All offices, except Chagres which had ceased to operate in 1855, closed for public business on 30 June 1881. Colon and Panama continued to exist as transit offices to deal with the mail across the isthmus. Both finally closed on 31 March 1921.

CARTHAGENA

CROWNED-CIRCLE HANDSTAMPS

CC1 CC **1b** CARTHAGENA (R.) (15.1.1841)
CC2 CC **1** CARTHAGENA (1.7.1846) *Price on cover* £900

Stamps of GREAT BRITAIN **cancelled** "C 56" *as in Type* **4**.

1865–81.
Z 1 ½d. rose-red (1870–79) (Plate No. 10)
Z 2 1d. rose-red (1864–79) From 50·00
Plate Nos. 78, 87, 100, 111, 113, 117, 119, 125, 172, 189, 217.
Z 3 2d. blue (1858–69) (Plate Nos. 9, 14) From 50·00
Z 4 3d. rose (1865) (Plate No. 4)
Z 5 3d. rose (1865–68) (Plate Nos. 4, 5)
Z 6 3d. rose (1873–79) (Plate Nos. 12, 17, 18) From 50·00
Z 7 4d. vermilion (1865–73) From 50·00
Plate Nos. 7, 8, 9, 10, 11, 12, 13, 14.
Z 8 4d. vermilion (1876) (Plate No. 15) £275
Z 9 4d. sage-green (1877) (Plate Nos. 15, 16) From £180
Z10 6d. lilac (1865–67) (Plate Nos. 5, 6)
Z11 6d. violet (1867–70) (Plate Nos. 6, 8) From 70·00
Z12 6d. grey (1873) (Plate No. 12) £190
Z13 6d. grey (1874–76) From 50·00
Plate Nos. 13, 14, 15, 16.
Z14 8d. orange (1876) £275
Z15 9d. straw (1865)
Z16 1s. green (1865)
Z17 1s. green (1867–73) (Plate Nos. 4, 5, 7) From 55·00
Z18 1s. green (1873–77) From 65·00
Plate Nos. 8, 9, 10, 11, 12, 13.
Z19 1s. orange-brown (1880)
Z20 2s. blue (1867) £200
Z21 5s. rose (1867) (Plate No. 1) £450

Cancelled "C 65" *(incorrect handstamp, supplied in error) as* **T 12**.

1866–81.
Z22 ½d. rose-red (1870–79) (Plate No. 10)
Z23 1d. rose-red (1864–79) From 70·00
Plate Nos. 100, 106, 111, 123.
Z23*a* 1½d. lake-red (1870) (Plate No. 3)
Z24 2d. blue (1858–69) (Plate No. 9) 70·00
Z25 2d. rose (1880)
Z26 2½d. blue (1880) (Plate No. 19)
Z27 3d. rose (1867–73) (Plate No. 9)
Z28 3d. rose (1873–79) (Plate Nos. 14, 17, 19, 20)
Z29 4d. vermilion (1865–73) From 55·00
Plate Nos. 7, 8, 9, 11, 12, 13 14.
Z30 4d. vermilion (1876) (Plate No. 15) £275
Z31 4d. sage-green (1877) (Plate Nos. 15, 16) From £180
Z32 6d. violet (1867–70) (Plate Nos. 6, 8) 80·00
Z33 6d. pale buff (1872) (Plate No. 11)
Z34 6d. grey (1873) (Plate No. 12) £190
Z35 6d. grey (1874–80) From 55·00
Plate Nos. 13, 14, 15, 16, 17.
Z36 8d. orange (1876) £325
Z37 9d. straw (1865) £350
Z38 1s. green (1865) (Plate No. 4) £120
Z39 1s. green (1867) (Plate Nos. 4, 5, 6, 7) From 60·00
Z40 1s. green (1873–77) From 70·00
Plate Nos. 8, 11, 12, 13.
Z41 1s. orange-brown (1880)
Z42 2s. blue (1867) £350
Z43 2s. brown (1880) £2000
Z44 5s. rose (1867) (Plate Nos. 1, 2) From £475

CHAGRES

CROWNED-CIRCLE HANDSTAMPS

CC3 CC **1** CHAGRES (16.9.1846)

COLON

CROWNED-CIRCLE HANDSTAMPS

CC4 CC **5** COLON (R.) (21.6.1854) *Price on cover* £4250

Stamps of GREAT BRITAIN *cancelled* "E 88" *as in Type* **12** *or with two types of circular date stamp as Type* **16**, *one with* "COLON" *straight.*

1870–81.
Z45 1d. rose-red (1864–79) From 45·00
Plate Nos. 107, 121, 122, 123, 125, 127, 130, 131, 133, 136, 138, 142, 150, 151, 152, 153, 155, 156, 157, 158, 160, 169, 170, 171, 174, 176, 178, 179, 184, 187, 188, 194, 195, 201, 209, 213, 214, 217.
Z46 1d. Venetian red (1880) 65·00
Z47 1½d. lake-red (1870–74) (Plate No. 3) 90·00
Z48 2d. blue (1858–69) (Plate Nos. 14, 15) 45·00
Z49 2d. pale rose (1880)
Z50 3d. rose (1867–73) (Plate Nos. 6, 9)
Z51 3d. rose (1873–76) From 50·00
Plate Nos. 11, 12, 16, 18, 19, 20.
Z52 4d. vermilion (1865–73) From 50·00
Plate Nos. 10, 11, 12, 13 14.
Z53 4d. vermilion (1876) (Plate No. 15)
Z54 4d. sage-green (1877) (Plate Nos. 15, 16) From £180
Z55 4d. grey-brown (1880) wmk Large Garter £300
Plate No. 17.
Z56 4d. grey-brown (1880) wmk Crown 70·00
Plate No. 17.
Z57 6d. violet (1867–70) (Plate Nos. 6, 8, 9)
Z58 6d. buff (1872) (Plate No. 11)
Z59 6d. chestnut (1872) (Plate No. 11) 60·00
Z60 6d. grey (1873) (Plate No. 12)
Z61 6d. grey (1874–80) From 50·00
Plate Nos. 13, 14, 15, 16, 17.
Z62 8d. orange (1876)
Z63 9d. straw (1867) £180
Z63*a* 10d. red-brown (1867)
Z64 1s. green (1867–73) From 45·00
Plate Nos. 4, 5, 6, 7.
Z65 1s. green (1873–77) From 60·00
Plate Nos. 8, 9, 10, 11, 12, 13.
Z66 1s. orange-brown (1880) (Plate 13) £350
Z67 1s. orange-brown (1881) (Plate 13) £125
Z68 2s. blue (1867) £140
Z69 2s. brown (1880) £1700
Z70 5s. rose (1867) (Plate Nos. 1, 2) From £400

PANAMA

CROWNED-CIRCLE HANDSTAMPS

CC5 CC **1** PANAMA (R.) (24.8.1846) *Price on cover* £1700

Stamps of GREAT BRITAIN *cancelled* "C 35" *as in Type* **4**, **11** *or as* **14** *with "PANAMA" straight.*

1865–81.
Z 71 ½d. rose-red (1870–79) From 45·00
Plate Nos. 10, 11, 12, 13, 14, 15, 19.
Z 72 1d. rose-red (1864–79) From 30·00
Plate Nos. 71, 72, 76, 81, 85, 87, 88, 89, 93, 95, 96, 101, 104, 114, 122, 124, 130, 138, 139, 142, 159, 168, 171, 172, 174, 177, 179, 180, 184, 185, 187, 189, 191, 192, 193, 196, 197, 200, 203, 204, 205, 207, 208, 209, 210, 211, 213, 214, 215, 218, 224.
Z 73 1½d. lake-red (1870–74) (Plate No. 3) 60·00
Z 74 2d. blue (1858–69) From 35·00
Plate Nos. 9, 12, 13, 14, 15.
Z 75 2½d. rosy mauve (1875) (Plate No. 1) £150
Z 76 2½d. rosy mauve (1876–80) (Plate Nos. 4, 12, 16) £110
Z 77 2½d. blue (1880) (Plate No. 19)
Z 78 2½d. blue (1881) (Plate Nos. 22, 23)
Z 79 3d. carmine-rose (1862) £225
Z 80 3d. rose (1865) (Plate No. 4)
Z 81 3d. rose (1867–73) From 45·00
Plate Nos. 4, 5, 6, 7, 8, 9.
Z 82 3d. rose (1873–76) From 35·00
Plate Nos. 12, 14, 15, 16, 17, 18, 19, 20.
Z 83 3d. rose (1881) (Plate Nos. 20, 21)
Z 84 4d. red (1863) (Plate No. 4) (*Hair lines*) 85·00
Z 85 4d. vermilion (1865–73) From 45·00
Plate Nos. 7, 8, 9, 10, 11, 12, 13, 14.
Z 86 4d. vermilion (1876) (Plate No. 15) £275
Z 87 4d. sage-green (1877) (Plate Nos. 15, 16) From £180
Z 88 4d. grey-brown (1880) *wmk* Crown From 50·00
Plate Nos. 17 18.
Z 89 6d. lilac (1862) (Plate Nos. 3, 4) From 75·00
Z 90 6d. lilac (1865–67) (Plate Nos. 5, 6) From 70·00
Z 91 6d. lilac (1867) (Plate No. 6)
Z 92 6d. violet (1867–70) (Plate Nos. 6, 8, 9) 65·00
Z 93 6d. buff (1872–73) (Plate Nos. 11, 12) From 70·00
Z 94 6d. chestnut (Plate No. 11) 45·00
Z 95 6d. grey (1873) (Plate No. 12) £190
Z 96 6d. grey (1874–80) From 45·00
Plate Nos. 13, 14, 15, 16, 17.
Z 97 6d. grey (1881) (Plate No. 17) 65·00
Z 98 8d. orange (1876) £225
Z 99 9d. straw (1862) £250
Z100 9d. straw (1867) £225
Z101 10d. red-brown (1867) £250
Z102 1s. green (1865) (Plate No. 4) £130
Z103 1s. green (1867–73) From 40·00
Plate Nos. 4, 5, 6, 7.
Z104 1s. green (1873–77) From 55·00
Plate Nos. 8, 9, 10, 11, 12, 13.
Z105 1s. orange-brown (1880) (Plate No. 13) £350
Z106 1s. orange-brown (1881) (Plate No. 13) £100
Z107 2s. blue (1867) £120
Z108 2s. brown (1880) £1700
Z109 5s. rose (1867–74) (Plate Nos. 1, 2) From £400

1880.
Z110 1d. Venetian red 40·00
Z111 2d. rose 90·00
Z112 5d. indigo £140

Later stamps cancelled "C 35" are believed to originate from sailors' letters or other forms of maritime mail.

SANTA MARTHA

CROWNED-CIRCLE HANDSTAMPS

CC6 CC **1b** SANTA MARTHA (R.) (15.12.1841) *Price on cover* £1700

Stamps of GREAT BRITAIN *cancelled* "C 62" *as in Type* **4**.

1865–81.
Z113 ½d. rose-red (1870–79) (Plate No. 6) 80·00
Z114 1d. rose-red (1864–79) (Plate No. 106) 60·00
Z115 2d. blue (1858–69) (Plate Nos. 9, 13) 80·00
Z116 4d. vermilion (1865–73) From 55·00
Plate Nos. 7, 8, 9, 11, 12, 13, 14.
Z117 4d. sage-green (1877) (Plate No. 15) £180
Z118 4d. grey-brown (1880) wmk Large Garter £300
Plate No. 17.
Z119 4d. grey-brown (1880) wmk Crown 70·00
Plate No. 17.
Z120 6d. lilac (1865–67) (Plate No. 5) 80·00
Z121 6d. grey (1873) (Plate No. 12)
Z122 6d. grey (1874–76) (Plate No. 14)
Z123 8d. orange (1876) £275
Z123*a* 9d. bistre (1862)
Z124 1s. green (1865) (Plate No. 4) £150
Z125 1s. green (1867–73) (Plate Nos. 5, 7) From 70·00
Z126 1s. green (1873–77) (Plate No. 8)
Z127 2s. blue (1867) £275
Z128 5s. rose (1867) (Plate No. 2) £475

SAVANILLA (BARRANQUILLA)

Stamps of GREAT BRITAIN *cancelled* "F 69" *as in Type* **12**.

1872–81.
Z129 ½d. rose-red (1870–79) (Plate No. 6) 80·00
Z130 1d. rose-red (1864–79) (Plate Nos. 122, 171) 60·00
Z131 1½d. lake-red (1870–74) Plate No. 3) £100
Z132 3d. rose (1867–73) (Plate No. 7)
Z133 3d. rose (1873–76) (Plate No. 20) 90·00
Z134 3d. rose (1881) (Plate No. 20) 90·00
Z135 4d. verm (1865–73) From 55·00
Plate Nos. 12, 13, 14.
Z136 4d. vermilion (1876) (Plate No. 15) £275
Z137 4d. sage-green (1877) (Plate Nos. 15, 16) From £200
Z138 4d. grey-brown (1880) wmk Large Garter £350
Plate No. 17.
Z139 4d. grey-brown (1880) wmk Crown 70·00
Plate No. 17.
Z140 6d. buff (1872) (Plate No. 11)
Z141 6d. grey (1878) (Plate Nos. 16, 17) From 75·00
Z142 8d. orange (1876) £275
Z143 1s. green (1867–73) (Plate Nos. 5,7) 55·00
Z144 1s. green (1873–77) (Plate Nos. 8, 11, 12, 13) 75·00
Z145 1s. orange-brown (1880) £350
Z146 2s. blue (1867) £200
Z147 5s. rose (1867–74) (Plate No. 2) £475

CUBA

The British Postal Agency at Havana opened in 1762, the island then being part of the Spanish Empire. A further office, at St. Jago de Cuba, was added in 1841.

Great Britain stamps were supplied to Havana in 1865 and to St. Jago de Cuba in 1866. They continued in use until the offices closed on 30 May 1877.

HAVANA

CROWNED-CIRCLE HANDSTAMPS

1890.
CC1 CC **1b** HAVANA (13.11.1841) *Price on cover* £900
CC2 CC **1c** HAVANA (1848) *Price on cover* £900
CC3 CC **2** HAVANA (14.7.1848) *Price on cover* £750

Stamps of GREAT BRITAIN *cancelled* "C 58" *as in Type* **4**, *or as Type* **14** *but with* "HAVANA" *straight.*

1865–77.
Z 1 ½d. rose-red (1870) (Plate Nos. 6, 12) 60·00
Z 2 1d. rose-red (1864–79) 50·00
Plate Nos. 86, 90, 93, 115, 120, 123, 144, 146, 171, 174, 208.
Z 3 2d. blue (1858–69) (Plate Nos. 9, 14, 15) 60·00
Z 4 3d. rose (1867–73) (Plate No. 4) £125
Z 5 3d. rose (1873–76) (Plate Nos. 18, 19)
Z 6 4d. vermilion (1865–73) From 60·00
Plate Nos. 7, 8, 10, 11, 12, 13, 14.
Z 7 4d. vermilion (1876) (Plate No. 15) £275
Z 8 6d. lilac (1865) (with hyphen) (Plate No. 5)
Z 9 6d. grey (1874–76) (Plate No. 15)
Z10 8d. orange (1876)
Z11 9d. straw (1867) £225
Z12 10d. red-brown (1867) £250
Z13 1s. green (1865) (Plate No. 4) £150
Z14 1s. green (1867–73) (Plate Nos. 4, 5, 7) From 60·00
Z15 1s. green (1873–77) (Plate Nos. 10, 12, 13) From 80·00
Z16 2s. blue (1867) £175
Z17 5s. rose (1867–74) (Plate Nos. 1, 2) From £425

ST. JAGO DE CUBA

CROWNED-CIRCLE HANDSTAMPS

CC4 CC **1b** ST JAGO-DE-CUBA (R.) (15.12.1841) *Price on cover* £5500

Stamps of GREAT BRITAIN *cancelled* "C 88" *as Type* **12**.

1866–77.
Z18 ½d. rose-red (1870–79) (Plate Nos. 4, 6, 14)
Z19 1d. rose-red (1864–79) From £120
Plate Nos. 100, 105, 106, 109, 111, 120, 123, 138, 144, 146, 147, 148, 171, 208.
Z20 1½d. lake-red (1870–74) (Plate No. 3)
Z21 2d. blue (1858–69) (Plate Nos. 9, 12, 13, 14) £120
Z22 3d. rose (1867) (Plate No. 5)

No.	Stamp		Price
Z23	4d. vermilion (1865–73) Plate Nos. 9, 10, 11, 12, 13, 14.	*From*	£120
Z24	4d. vermilion (1876) (Plate No. 15)		£450
Z25	6d. violet (1867–70) (Plate Nos. 6, 8, 9)	*From*	£300
Z26	6d. buff (Plate No. 11)		
Z27	9d. straw (1865)		
Z27*a*	9d. straw (1867)		
Z28	10d. red-brown (1867)		£425
Z29	1s. green (1867–73) (Plate Nos. 4, 5, 6)	*From*	£275
Z30	1s. green (1873–77) (Plate Nos. 9, 10, 12, 13)		
Z31	2s. blue (1867)		
Z32	5s. rose (1867) (Plate 1)		

DANISH WEST INDIES

ST. THOMAS

The British Postal Agency at St. Thomas opened in January 1809 and by 1825 was the office around which many of the packet routes were organised.

Great Britain stamps were introduced on 3 July 1865 and can be found used in combination with Danish West Indies adhesives paying the local postage.

Following a hurricane in October 1867 the main British packet office was moved to Colon in Colombia.

The British Post Office at St. Thomas closed to the public on I September 1877, but continued to operate as a transit office for a further two years

CROWNED-CIRCLE HANDSTAMPS

CC1	CC **1**	ST. THOMAS (R.) (20.2.49) *Price on cover*	£450
CC2	CC **6**	ST. THOMAS (R.) (1.5.1855) *Price on cover*	£1500

Stamps of GREAT BRITAIN *cancelled* "C 51" *as in Types* **4**, **12** *or* **14**.

1865–79.

No.	Stamp		Price
Z 1	½d. rose-red (1870–79) Plate Nos. 5, 6, 8, 10, 11, 12.		35·00
Z 2	1d. rose-red (1857)		
Z 3	1d. rose-red (1864–79) Plate Nos. 71, 72, 79, 81, 84, 85, 86, 87, 88, 89, 90, 93, 94, 95, 96, 97, 98, 99, 100, 101, 102, 105, 106, 107, 108, 109, 110, 111, 112, 113, 114, 116, 117, 118, 119, 120, 121, 122, 123, 124, 125, 127, 129, 130, 131, 133, 134, 136, 137, 138, 139, 140, 141, 142, 144, 145, 146, 147, 148, 149, 150, 151, 152, 154, 155, 156, 157, 158, 159, 160, 161, 162, 163, 164, 165, 166, 167, 169, 170, 171, 172, 173, 174, 175, 176, 177, 178, 179, 180, 181, 182, 184, 185, 186, 187, 189, 190, 197.	*From*	25·00
Z 4	1½d. lake-red (1870–74) (Plate Nos. 1, 3)		60·00
Z 5	2d. blue (1858–69) Plate Nos. 9, 12, 13, 14, 15.	*From*	30·00
Z 6	3d. rose (1865) (Plate No. 4)		80·00
Z 7	3d. rose (1867–73) Plate Nos. 4, 5, 6, 7, 8, 9, 10.	*From*	40·00
Z 8	3d. rose (1873–76) Plate Nos. 11, 12, 14, 15, 16, 17, 18, 19.	*From*	30·00
Z 9	4d. red (1862) (Plate Nos. 3, 4)		70·00
Z10	4d. vermilion (1865–73) Plate Nos. 7, 8, 9, 10, 11, 12, 13, 14.	*From*	45·00
Z11	4d. vermilion (1876) (Plate No. 15)		£275
Z12	4d. sage-green (1877) (Plate Nos. 15, 16)	*From*	£180
Z14	6d. lilac (1864) (Plate No. 4)		£140
Z15	6d. lilac (1865–67) (Plate Nos. 5, 6)	*From*	70·00
Z16	6d. lilac (1867) (Plate No. 6)		70·00
Z17	6d. violet (1867–70) (Plate Nos. 6, 8, 9)	*From*	65·00
Z18	6d. buff (1872–73) (Plate Nos. 11, 12)	*From*	70·00
Z19	6d. chestnut (1872) (Plate No. 11)		40·00
Z20	6d. grey (1873) (Plate No. 12)		£190
Z21	6d. grey (1874–76) Plate Nos. 13, 14, 15, 16.	*From*	40·00
Z22	8d. orange (1876)		£250
Z23	9d. straw (1862)		£225
Z24	9d. bistre (1862)		£250
Z25	9d. straw (1865)		£350
Z26	9d. straw (1867)		£180
Z27	10d. red-brown (1867)		£250
Z28	1s. green (1865) (Plate No. 4)		£130
Z29	1s. green (1867–73) (Plate Nos. 4, 5, 6, 7)	*From*	30·00
Z30	1s. green (1873–77) Plate Nos, 8, 9, 10, 11, 12, 13.	*From*	55·00
Z31	2s. blue (1867)		£120
Z32	5s. rose (1867–74) (Plate Nos. 1, 2)	*From*	£400

DOMINICAN REPUBLIC

British Postal Agencies may have existed in the area before 1867, but it is only from that year that details can be found concerning offices at Porto Plata and St. Domingo. Both were closed in 1871, but re-opened in 1876.

Although postmarks were supplied in 1866 it seems likely that Great Britain stamps were not sent until the offices re-opened in 1876.

Covers exist showing Great Britain stamps used in combination with those of Dominican Republic with the latter paying the local postage. Both agencies finally closed in 1881.

PORTO PLATA

Stamps of GREAT BRITAIN *cancelled* "C 86" *or circular date stamp as in Types* **8** *or* **17**.

1876–81.

No.	Stamp		Price
Z 1	½d. rose-red (1870–79) Plate Nos. 10, 12, 14.	*From*	70·00
Z 2	1d. rose-red (1864–79) Plate Nos. 123, 130, 136, 146, 151, 178, 199, 200, 205, 217.	*From*	55·00
Z 3	1½d. lake-red (1870–74) (Plate No. 3)		£100
Z 4	2d. blue (1858–69) (Plate Nos. 14, 15)		70·00
Z 5	2½d. rosy mauve (1876–79) Plate Nos. 13, 14.	*From*	£140
Z 6	3d. rose (1873–76) (Plate No. 18)		80·00
Z 7	4d. vermilion (1873) (Plate No. 14)		80·00
Z 8	4d. vermilion (1876) (Plate No. 15)		£300
Z 9	4d. sage-green (1877) (Plate No. 15)		£200
Z10	6d. violet (1867–70) (Plate No. 8)		
Z11	6d. grey (1874–76) (Plate No. 15)		70·00
Z12	8d. orange (1876)		£300
Z13	1s. green (1867–73) (Plate Nos. 4, 7)	*From*	60·00
Z14	1s. green (1873–77) Plate Nos. 11, 12, 13.	*From*	70·00
Z15	2s. blue (1867)		£220
Z15*a*	5s. rose (1867–83) (Plate No. 2)		

ST. DOMINGO

Stamps of GREAT BRITAIN *cancelled* "C 87" *or circular date stamp as in Types* **12** *or* **16**.

1876–81.

No.	Stamp		Price
Z16	½d. rose-red (1870–79) Plate Nos. 5, 6, 8, 10, 11, 13.	*From*	80·00
Z17	1d. rose-red (1864–79) Plate Nos. 146, 154, 171, 173, 174, 176, 178, 186, 190, 197, 220.	*From*	60·00
Z18	1½d. lake-red (1870–74) (Plate No. 3)		£100
Z19	2d. blue (1858–69) (Plate Nos. 13, 14)		90·00
Z20	3d. rose (1873–76) (Plate No. 18)		
Z21	4d. vermilion (1865–73) Plate Nos. 11, 12, 14.	*From*	90·00
Z22	4d. vermilion (1876) (Plate No. 15)		£325
Z23	4d. sage-green (1877) (Plate No. 15)		£225
Z24	6d. grey (1874–76) (Plate No. 15)		
Z25	9d. straw (1867)		
Z26	1s. green (1867) (Plate No. 4)		
Z27	1s. green (1873–77) Plate Nos. 10, 11, 12, 13.	*From*	80·00
Z28	2s. blue (1867)		

ECUADOR

GUAYAQUIL

The first British Postal Agent in Guayaquil was appointed in 1848.

Great Britain stamps were supplied in 1865 and continued to be used until the agency closed on 30 June 1880. They can be found used in combination with stamps of Ecuador with the latter paying the local postage.

Stamps of GREAT BRITAIN *cancelled* "C 41" *as Type* **4**.

1865–80.

No.	Stamp		Price
Z 1	½d. rose-red (1870–79) (Plate Nos. 5, 6)		55·00
Z 2	1d. rose-red (1857)		
Z 3	1d. rose-red (1864–79) Plate Nos. 74, 78, 85, 92, 94, 105, 110, 115, 133, 140, 145, 166, 174, 180, 216.	*From*	40·00
Z 4	1½d. lake-red (1870–74) (Plate No. 3)		80·00
Z 5	2d. blue (1858–69) (Plate Nos. 9, 13, 14)	*From*	40·00
Z 6	3d. carmine-rose (1862)		£225
Z 7	3d. rose (1865) (Plate No. 4)		90·00
Z 8	3d. rose (1867–73) (Plate Nos. 6, 7, 9, 10)	*From*	45·00
Z 9	3d. rose (1873–76) Plate Nos. 11, 12, 15, 16, 17, 18, 19, 20.	*From*	45·00
Z10	4d. red (1862) (Plate Nos. 3, 4)		90·00
Z11	4d. vermilion (1865–73) Plate Nos. 7, 8, 9, 10, 11, 12, 13, 14.	*From*	45·00
Z12	4d. vermilion (1876) (Plate No. 15)		£275
Z13	4d. sage-green (1877) (Plate Nos. 15, 16)	*From*	£180
Z14	6d. lilac (1864) (Plate No. 4)		£140
Z15	6d. lilac (1865–67) (Plate Nos. 5, 6)	*From*	70·00
Z16	6d. lilac (1867) (Plate No. 6)		
Z17	6d. violet (1867–70) (Plate Nos. 6, 8, 9)	*From*	65·00
Z18	6d. buff (1872–73) (Plate Nos. 11,12)	*From*	75·00
Z19	6d. chestnut (1872) (Plate No. 11)		
Z20	6d. grey (1873) (Plate No. 12)		
Z21	6d. grey (1874–76) Plate Nos. 13, 14, 15, 16.	*From*	45·00
Z22	8d. orange (1876)		£275
Z23	9d. straw (1862)		£225
Z24	9d. straw (1867)		£180
Z25	10d. red-brown (1867)		£250
Z26	1s. green (1865) (Plate No. 4)		£150
Z27	1s. green (1867–73) (Plate Nos. 4, 5, 6, 7)	*From*	40·00
Z28	1s. green (1873–77) Plate Nos. 8, 9, 10, 11, 12, 13.	*From*	70·00
Z29	2s. blue (1867)		£140
Z30	2s. brown (1880)		£2000
Z31	5s. rose (1867–74) (Plate Nos. 1, 2)	*From*	£400

FERNANDO PO

The British government leased naval facilities on this Spanish island from 1827 until 1834. A British Consul was appointed in 1849 and a postal agency was opened on 1 April 1858.

The use of Great Britain stainps was authorised in 1858, but a cancellation was not supplied until 1874. The office remained open until 1877.

CROWNED-CIRCLE HANDSTAMPS

CC1	CC **4**	FERNANDO-PO (R.) (19.2.1859) *Price on cover*	£5000

Stamps of GREAT BRITAIN *cancelled* "247" *as Type* **9**.

1874–77.

No.	Stamp		Price
Z1	4d. vermilion (1865–72) (Plate Nos. 13, 14)		
Z2	4d. vermilion (1876) (Plate No. 15)		
Z3	6d. grey (1874–76) (Plate Nos. 13, 14, 15, 16)		

GUADELOUPE

A British Packet Agency was established on Guadeloupe on 1 October 1848 and continued to function until 1874.

No. CC1 is often found used in conjunction with French Colonies (General Issues) adhesive stamps.

A similar packet agency existed on Martinique from 1 October 1848 until 1879, but no crowned-circle handstamp was issued for it.

CROWNED-CIRCLE HANDSTAMPS

CC1	CC **1**	GUADALOUPE (R., B. or Black) (9.3.1849) *Price on cover*	£1800

HAITI

The original British Postal Agencies in Haiti date from 1830 when it is known a Packet Agency was established at Jacmel. An office at Port-au-Prince followed in 1842, both these agencies remaining in operation until 30 June 1881.

During this period short-lived agencies also operated in the following Haitian towns: Aux Cayes (1848 to 1863, Cap Haitien (1842 to 1863), Gonaives (1849 to 1857) and St. Marc (1854 to 1861). A further agency may have operated at Le Mole around the year 1841.

Great Britain stamps were supplied to Jacmel in 1865 and to Port-au-Prince in 1869.

CAP HAITIEN

CROWNED-CIRCLE HANDSTAMPS

CC1	CC **1b**	CAPE-HAITIEN (R.) (31.12.1841)	

JACMEL

CROWNED-CIRCLE HANDSTAMPS

CC2	CC **1b**	JACMEL (R.) (29.6.1843) *Price on cover*	£800

Stamps of GREAT BRITAIN *cancelled* "C 59" *as Type* **4** *or with circular date stamp as Type* **16**, *but with* "JACMEL" *straight*.

1865–81.

No.	Stamp		Price
Z 1	½d. rose-red (1870–79) Plate Nos. 4, 5, 6, 10, 11, 12, 14, 15.	*From*	55·00
Z 2	1d. rose-red (1864–79) Plate Nos. 74, 81, 84, 87, 95, 106, 107, 109, 122, 136, 137, 139, 148, 150, 151, 152, 156, 157, 159, 160, 162, 164, 166, 167, 170, 171, 179, 181, 183, 184, 186, 187, 189, 192, 194, 198, 200, 204, 206, 215, 219.	*From*	40·00
Z 3	1½d. lake-red (1870–74) (Plate No. 3)		60·00
Z 4	2d. blue (1858–69) (Plate Nos. 9, 13, 14, 15)		40·00
Z 5	2½d. rosy mauve (1876) (Plate No. 4)		
Z 6	3d. rose (1867–73) Plate Nos. 5, 6, 7, 8, 9, 10.	*From*	45·00
Z 7	3d. rose (1873–76) Plate Nos. 11, 12, 14, 16, 17, 18, 19.		45·00
Z 8	4d. red (1863) (Plate No. 4) (*Hair lines*)		90·00
Z 9	4d. vermilion (1865–73) Plate Nos. 7, 8, 9, 10, 11, 12, 13, 14.	*From*	45·00
Z10	4d. vermilion (1876) (Plate No. 15)		£275
Z11	4d. sage-green (1877) (Plate Nos. 15, 16)	*From*	£180
Z12	4d. grey-brown (1880) *wmk* Large Garter Plate No. 17.		£300
Z13	4d. grey-brown (1880) *wmk* Crown Plate No. 17.		50·00
Z14	6d. lilac (1867) (Plate Nos. 5, 6)		75·00
Z15	6d. violet (1867–70) (Plate Nos. 8, 9)		70·00
Z16	6d. buff (1872–73) (Plate Nos. 11, 12)	*From*	75·00
Z17	6d. chestnut (1872) (Plate No. 11)		
Z18	6d. grey (1873) (Plate No. 12)		
Z19	6d. grey (1874–76) Plate Nos. 13, 14, 15, 16, 17.	*From*	50·00
Z20	8d. orange (1876)		£275
Z21	9d. straw (1862)		£225
Z22	9d. straw (1867)		£180
Z23	10d. red-brown (1867)		£250
Z24	1s. green (1865) (Plate No. 4)		£130
Z25	1s. green (1867–73) (Plate Nos. 4, 5, 6, 7)	*From*	40·00
Z26	1s. green (1873–77) Plate Nos. 8, 9, 10, 11, 12, 13.	*From*	60·00
Z27	1s. orange-brown (1880) (Plate No. 13)		£350
Z28	2s. blue (1867)		£120
Z29	2s. brown (1880)		£2000
Z30	5s. rose (1867–74) (Plate Nos. 1, 2)	*From*	£400

1880.

No.	Stamp		Price
Z31	½d. green (1880)		40·00
Z32	1d. Venetian red		40·00
Z33	1½d. Venetian red		60·00
Z34	2d. rose		90·00

PORT-AU-PRINCE

CROWNED-CIRCLE HANDSTAMPS

CC3	CC **1b**	PORT-AU-PRINCE (R.) (29.6.1843) *Price on cover*	£2000

Stamps of GREAT BRITAIN *cancelled* "E 53" *as in Types* **8**, **12** *or* **16**.

1869–81.

No.	Stamp		Price
Z35	½d. rose-red (1870–79) Plate Nos. 5, 6, 10, 11, 12, 13, 14.	*From*	55·00
Z36	1d. rose-red (1864–79) Plate Nos. 87, 134, 154, 159, 167, 171, 173, 174, 177, 183, 187, 189, 193, 199, 200, 201, 202, 206, 209, 210, 218, 219.	*From*	40·00
Z37	1½d. lake-red (1870–74) (Plate No. 3)		75·00
Z38	2d. blue (1858–69) (Plate Nos. 9, 14, 15)		45·00
Z40	2½d. rosy mauve (1876–79) (Plate Nos. 3, 9)	*From*	80·00
Z41	3d. rose (1867–73) (Plate Nos. 6, 7)		
Z42	3d. rose (1873–79) (Plate Nos. 17, 18, 20)	*From*	45·00
Z43	4d. vermilion (1865–73) Plate Nos. 11, 12, 13, 14.	*From*	45·00
Z44	4d. vermilion (1876) (Plate No. 15)		£275
Z45	4d. sage-green (1877) (Plate Nos. 15, 16)	*From*	£180

Z46 4d. grey-brown (1880) wmk £300
Large Garter Plate No. 17.
Z47 4d. grey-brown (1880) wmk Crown . . . . 50·00
Plate No. 17.
Z48 6d. grey (1874–76) (Plate Nos. 15, 16) . . . . .
Z49 8d. orange (1876) £250
Z50 1s. green (1867–73) (Plate Nos. 4, 5, 6, 7) *From* 40·00
Z51 1s. green (1873–77) . . . . *From* 60·00
Plate Nos. 8, 9, 10, 11, 12, 13.
Z52 1s. orange-brown (1880) (Plate No. 13) £350
Z53 1s. orange-brown (1880) (Plate No. 13) £110
Z54 2s. blue (1867) £120
Z55 2s. brown (1880) £2000
Z56 5s. rose (1867–74) (Plate Nos. 1, 2) . . . *From* £400
Z57 10s. greenish grey (1878) £2800

1880.
Z58 ½d. green . . . . 40·00
Z59 1d. Venetian red . . . . 40·00
Z60 1½d. Venetian red . . . . 55·00
Z61 2d. rose . . . . 90·00

MACAO

A British Consular Post Office opened in 1841. It had been preceded by the Macao Boat Office, possibly a private venture, which operated in the 1830s. The office closed when the consulate closed on 30 September 1845, but was back in operation by 1854.

The Agency continued to function, in conjunction with the Hong Kong Post Office, until 28 February 1884 when Portugal joined the U.P.U.

CROWNED-CIRCLE HANDSTAMPS

Z 2

CC1 – PAID AT MACAO (crowned-oval 20 mm wide) (R.) (1844) . . . . . *Price on cover* £20000
CC2 **Z 2** Crown and Macao (1881) . . . .

No. CC2 with the Crown removed was used by the Portuguese post office in Macao as a cancellation until 1890.

A locally-cut mark, as Type CC **2**, inscribed "PAGO EM MACAO" is known on covers between 1870 and 1877. It was probably used by the Portuguese postmaster to send letters via the British Post Office (*Price* £10000).

MADEIRA

The British Packet Agency on this Portuguese island was opened in 1767 and was of increased importance from 1808 following the exile of the Portuguese royal family to Brazil. The South American packets ceased to call in 1858. It appears to have closed sometime around 1860.

CROWN-CIRCLE HANDSTAMPS

CC1 CC **1b** MADEIRA (R.) (28.2.1842)
Price on cover £16000

MEXICO

The British Postal Agency at Vera Cruz opened in 1825, following the introduction of the Mexican Packet service. No handstamps were supplied, however, until 1842, when a similar agency at Tampico was set up.

Great Britain stamps were used at Tampico from 1867, but, apparently, were never sent to the Vera Cruz office. Combination covers exist showing the local postage paid by Mexican adhesives. The Agency at Vera Cruz closed in 1874 and that at Tampico in 1876.

TAMPICO

CROWNED-CIRCLE HANDSTAMPS

CC1 CC **1b** TAMPICO (R.) (13.11.1841)
Price on cover £1600

No. CC1 may be found on cover, used in conjunction with Mexico adhesive stamps.

Stamps of GREAT BRITAIN *cancelled* "C 63" *as Type* **4**.

1867–76.
Z1 1d. rose-red (1864–79) . . . . *From* £100
Plate Nos. 81, 89, 103, 117, 139, 147.
Z2 2d. blue (1858–69) (Plate Nos. 9, 14) £140
Z3 4d. vermilion (1865–73) . . . . *From* 80·00
Plate Nos. 7, 8, 10, 11, 12, 13, 14.
Z4 1s. green (1867–73) (Plate Nos. 4, 5, 7, 8) £120
Z5 2s. blue (1867) £375

VERA CRUZ

CROWNED-CIRCLE HANDSTAMPS

CC2 CC **1b** VERA CRUZ (R.) (13.11.1841)
Price on cover £1600
CC3 VERA CRUZ (Black) (*circa* 1845)
Price on cover £800

NICARAGUA

GREYTOWN

British involvement on the Mosquito Coast of Nicaragua dates from 1655 when contacts were first made with the indigenous Misquito Indians. A formal alliance was signed in 1740 and the area was considered as a British dependency until the Spanish authorities negotiated a withdrawal in 1786.

The Misquitos remained under British protection, however, and, following the revolutionary period in the Spanish dominions, this eventually led to the appropriation, by the Misquitos with British backing, of the town of San Juan del Norte, later renamed Greytown.

The port was included in the Royal West Indian Mail Steam Packet Company's mail network from January 1842, forming part of the Jamaica District. This arrangement only lasted until September of that year, however, although packets were once again calling at Greytown by November 1844. Following the discovery of gold in California the office increased in importance, owing to the overland traffic, although the first distinctive postmark is not recorded in use until February 1856.

A subsidiary agency, without its own postmark, operated at Bluefields from 1857 to 1863.

The British Protectorate over the Misquitos ended in 1860, but the British Post Office at Greytown continued to operate, being supplied with Great Britain stamps in 1865. These are occasionally found used in combination with Nicaragua issues, which had only internal validity.

The British Post Office at Greytown closed on 1 May 1882 when the Republic of Nicaragua joined the U.P.U.

CROWNED-CIRCLE HANDSTAMPS

Z 1

CC1 **Z 1** GREYTOWN (R.) (14.4.1859) . . . . . .

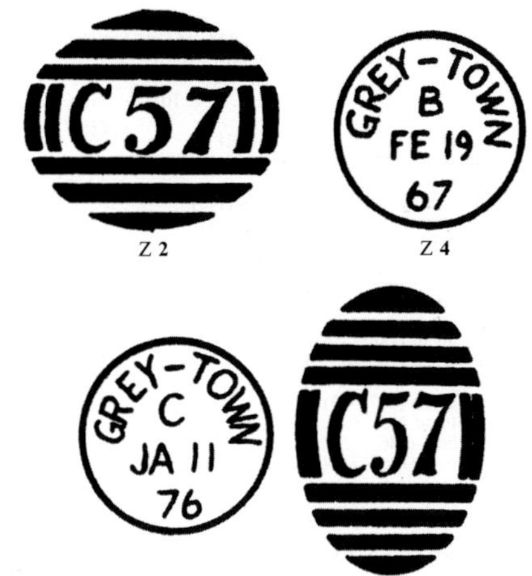

Z 2 Z 4

Z 3

Stamps of GREAT BRITAIN *cancelled* "C 57" *as in Types* **Z 2** (*issued* 1865), **Z 3** (*issued* 1875), *or with circular postmark as Type* **Z 4** (*issued* 1864).

1865–82.
Z 1 ½d. rose-red (1870–79) (Plate Nos. 5, 10, 11) . . . 75·00
Z 2 1d. rose-red (1864–79) . . . . 45·00
Plate Nos. 180, 197, 210.
Z 3 1½d. lake-red (1870) (Plate No. 3) . . . . 70·00
Z 4 2d. blue (1858–69) (Plate Nos. 9, 14, 15) . . . .
Z 5 3d. rose (1873–76) (Plate Nos. 17, 18, 19, 20) . . 50·00
Z 6 3d. rose (1881) (Plate No. 20) . . . .
Z 7 4d. vermilion (1865–73) . . . . *From* 50·00
Plate Nos. 8, 10, 11, 12, 13, 14.
Z 8 4d. vermilion (1876) (Plate No. 15) £275
Z 9 4d. sage-green (1877) (Plate Nos. 15, 16) . . . . *From* £180
Z10 4d. grey-brown (1880) wmk Large Garter £300
Plate No. 17.
Z11 4d. grey-brown (1880) wmk Crown . . . . 80·00
Plate No. 17.
Z12 6d. grey (1874–76) (Plate Nos. 14, 15, 16) . . . . 85·00
Z13 8d. orange (1876) £250
Z14 1s. green (1865) (Plate No. 4) . . . .
Z15 1s. green (1867–73) (Plate Nos. 6, 7) . . . . . .
Z16 1s. green (1873–77) . . . . *From* 60·00
Plate Nos. 8, 10, 12, 13.
Z17 1s. orange-brown (1880) (Plate No. 13) £350
Z18 1s. orange-brown (1881) (Plate No. 13) £100
Z19 2s. blue (1867) £150
Z20 2s. brown (1880) £2000
Z21 5s. rose (1867–74) (Plate Nos. 1, 2) . . . *From* £400
Z22 5s. rose (1882) (Plate No. 4), *blue paper* £1400
Z23 10s. greenish grey (1878) £2500

1880.
Z24 1d. Venetian red . . . . 50·00
Z25 1½d. Venetian red . . . . 50·00

PERU

British Agencies in Peru date from 1846 when offices were established at Arica and Callao. The network was later expanded to include agencies at Paita (1848), Pisco (1868) and Iquique and Islay (both 1869). This last office was transferred to Mollendo in 1877.

It is believed that a further agency existed at Pisagua, but no details exist.

Great Britain stamps were supplied from 1865 and are often found in combination with Peru adhesives which paid the local postal tax.

The Postal Agency at Pisco closed in 1870 and the remainder in 1879, the towns of Arica, Iquique and Pisagua passing to Chile by treaty in 1883.

ARICA

CROWNED-CIRCLE HANDSTAMPS

CC1 CC **1** ARICA (Black or R.) (5.11.1850)
Price on cover £3750

Stamps of Great Britain *cancelled* "C 36" *as Types* **4**, **12** *and* **14** (*with* "ARICA" *straight*) *or with circular date stamp as Type* **16**, *but with* "ARICA" *straight*.

1865–79.
Z 1 ½d. rose-red (1870–79) . . . . *From* 70·00
Plate Nos. 5, 6, 10, 11, 13.
Z 2 1d. rose-red (1864–79) . . . . *From* 50·00
Plate Nos. 102, 139, 140, 163, 167.
Z 3 1½d. lake-red (1870–74) (Plate No. 3) . . . . . .
Z 4 2d. blue (1858–69) (Plate No. 14) . . . . 70·00
Z 5 3d. rose (1867–73) (Plate Nos. 5, 9) . . . . . .
Z 6 3d. rose (1873–76) . . . . *From* 50·00
Plate Nos. 11, 12, 17, 18, 19.
Z 7 4d. vermilion (1865–73) . . . . *From* 50·00
Plate Nos. 10, 11, 12, 13, 14.
Z 8 4d. vermilion (1876) (Plate No. 15) . . . . . .
Z 9 4d. sage-green (1877) (Plate Nos. 15, 16) £180
Z10 6d. lilac (1862) (Plate Nos. 3, 4) . . . .
Z11 6d. lilac (1865–67) (Plate No. 5) . . . .
Z12 6d. violet (1867–70) (Plate Nos. 6, 8, 9) *From* 75·00
Z13 6d. buff (1872) (Plate No. 11) . . . . 90·00
Z14 6d. chestnut (1872) (Plate No.11) . . . . 90·00
Z15 6d. grey (1873) (Plate No. 12) £190
Z16 6d. grey (1874–76) . . . . *From* 50·00
Plate Nos. 13, 14, 15, 16.
Z17 8d. orange (1876) . . . .
Z18 9d. straw (1862) . . . .
Z19 9d. straw (1865) . . . .
Z20 9d. straw (1867) £180
Z21 10d. red-brown (1867) . . . .
Z22 1s. green (1862) . . . .
Z23 1s. green (1865) . . . .
Z24 1s. green (1867–73) (Plate Nos. 4, 5, 6, 7) *From* 50·00
Z25 1s. green (1873–77) . . . . *From* 65·00
Plate Nos. 8, 9, 10, 11, 12, 13.
Z26 2s. blue (1867) £160
Z27 5s. rose (1867–74) (Plate Nos. 1, 2) . . . *From* £400

CALLAO

CROWNED-CIRCLE HANDSTAMPS

CC2 CC **1** CALLAO (R.) (13.1.1846)
Price on cover £600

A second version of No. CC 2, showing "PAID" more curved, was supplied in July 1847.

No. CC2 can be found used on covers from 1865 showing the local postage paid by a Peru adhesive.

Stamps of GREAT BRITAIN *cancelled* "C 38" *as in Types* **4**, **12** *and* **14** (*with* "CALLAO" *straight*) *or with circular date stamp as Type* **5**.

1865–79.
Z28 ½d. rose-red (1870–79) . . . . *From* 40·00
Plate Nos. 5, 6, 10, 11, 12, 13, 14.
Z29 1d. rose-red (1864–79) . . . . *From* 30·00
Plate Nos. 74, 88, 89, 93, 94, 97, 108, 123, 127, 128, 130, 134, 137, 139, 140, 141, 143, 144, 145, 146, 148, 149, 156, 157, 160, 163, 167, 171, 172, 173, 175, 176, 180, 181, 182, 183, 185, 187, 190, 193, 195, 198, 199, 200, 201, 204, 206, 209, 210, 212, 213, 215.
Z30 1½d. lake-red (1870–74) (Plate No. 3) . . . . . .
Z31 2d. blue (1858–69) . . . . *From* 30·00
Plate Nos. 9, 12, 13, 14, 15.
Z32 3d. carmine-rose (1862) . . . .
Z33 3d. rose (1865) (Plate No. 4) . . . . 80·00
Z34 3d. rose (1867–73) . . . . *From* 40·00
Plate Nos. 5, 6, 7, 8, 9, 10.
Z35 3d. rose (1873–76) . . . . *From* 40·00
Plate Nos. 11, 12, 14, 15, 16, 17, 18, 19.
Z36 4d. red (1862) (Plate Nos. 3, 4) . . . .
Z37 4d. vermilion (1865–73) . . . . *From* 35·00
Plate Nos. 8, 10, 11, 12, 13, 14.
Z38 4d. vermilion (1876) (Plate No. 15) £275
Z39 4d. sage-green (1877) (Plate Nos. 15, 16) £180
Z40 6d. lilac (1862) (Plate Nos. 3, 4) . . . .
Z40*a* 6d. lilac (1865) (Plate No. 5) . . . .
Z41 6d. lilac (1867) . . . .
Z42 6d. violet (1867–70) . . . . *From* 65·00
Plate Nos. 6, 8, 9.
Z43 6d. buff (1872–73) (Plate Nos. 11, 12) *From* 65·00
Z44 6d. chestnut (1872) (Plate No. 11) . . . . 45·00
Z45 6d. grey (1873) (Plate No. 12) £190
Z46 6d. grey (1874–80) . . . . *From* 45·00
Plate Nos. 13, 14, 15, 16.
Z47 8d. orange (1876) £250
Z48 9d. straw (1862) . . . .
Z49 9d. straw (1865) £350
Z50 9d. straw (1867) £180
Z51 10d. red-brown (1867) £250
Z52 1s. green (1865) . . . .
Z53 1s. green (1867–73) . . . . *From* 35·00
Plate Nos. 4, 5, 6, 7.
254 1s. green (1873–77) . . . . *From* 50·00
Plate Nos. 8, 9, 10, 11, 12, 13.
Z55 2s. blue (1867) £110
Z56 5s. rose (1867–74) (Plate Nos. 1, 2) . . *From* £400

IQUIQUE

Stamps of GREAT BRITAIN *cancelled* "D 87" *as Type* **12**.

1865–79.
Z57 ½d. rose-red (1870–79) (Plate Nos. 5, 6, 13, 14) . . 70·00
Z58 1d. rose-red (1864–79) . . . . . . 45·00
Plate Nos. 76, 179, 185, 205.
Z59 2d. blue (1858–69) (Plate Nos. 9, 12, 13, 14) . . . 45·00
Z60 3d. rose (1867–73) (Plate Nos. 5, 6, 7, 8, 9) *From* 55·00
Z61 3d. rose (1873–76) (Plate Nos. 12, 18, 19) . . . 70·00
Z62 4d. vermilion (1865–73) . . . *From* 60·00
Plate Nos. 12, 13, 14.
Z63 4d. vermilion (1876) (Plate No. 15) . . . £275
Z64 4d. sage-green (1877) (Plate Nos. 15, 16) . . . *From* £180
Z65 6d. mauve (1869) (Plate Nos. 8, 9) . . .
Z66 6d. buff (1872–73) (Plate Nos. 11, 12) . . *From* £100
Z67 6d. chestnut (1872) (Plate No. 11) . . .
Z68 6d. grey (1873) (Plate No. 12) . . . £190
Z69 6d. grey (1874–76) (Plate Nos. 13, 14, 15, 16) . . 75·00
Z70 8d. orange (1876) . . . £300
Z71 9d. straw (1867) . . . £180
Z72 10d. red-brown (1867) . . .
Z73 1s. green (1867–73) (Plate Nos. 4, 6, 7) *From* 55·00
Z74 1s. green (1873–77) . . . *From* 75·00
Plate Nos. 8, 9, 10, 11, 12, 13.
Z75 2s. blue (1867) . . . £200

ISLAY (*later* MOLLENDO)

CROWNED-CIRCLE HANDSTAMPS

CC4 CC **1** ISLAY (Black or R.) (23.10.1850)
Price on cover £4500

Stamps of GREAT BRITAIN *cancelled* "C 42" *as Type* **4** *or with circular date stamp as Type* **16**.

1865–79.
Z76 1d. rose-red (1864–79) . . . *From* 50·00
Plate Nos. 78, 84, 87, 88, 96, 103, 125, 134.
Z77 1½d. lake-red (1870–74) (Plate No. 3) . . .
Z78 2d. blue (1858–69) (Plate Nos. 9, 13, 15) . . . 50·00
Z79 3d. carmine-rose (1862) . . .
Z80 3d. rose (1865) . . . 80·00
Z81 3d. rose (1867–73) (Plate Nos. 4, 5, 6, 10) *From* 55·00
Z82 4d. red (1862) (Plate Nos. 3, 4) . . . 90·00
Z83 4d. vermilion (1865–73) . . . *From* 55·00
Plate Nos. 9, 10, 11, 12, 13.
Z84 4d. vermilion (1876) (Plate No. 15) . . .
Z85 4d. sage-green (1877) (Plate Nos. 15, 16) *From* £180
Z86 6d. lilac (1862) (Plate Nos, 3, 4) *From* 80·00
Z87 6d. lilac (1865) (Plate No. 5) . . . 75·00
Z88 6d. violet (1867–70) (Plate Nos. 6, 8, 9) . . . *From* 75·00
Z88*a* 6d. chestnut (1872) (Plate No. 11) . . .
Z89 6d. buff (1873) (Plate No. 12) . . .
Z90 6d. grey (1873) (Plate No. 12) . . .
Z91 6d. grey (1874–76) . . . *From* 60·00
Plate Nos. 13, 14, 15, 16.
Z92 9d. straw (1865) . . . £350
Z93 9d. straw (1867) . . . £180
Z94 10d. red-brown (1867) . . . £250
Z95 1s. green (1865) (Plate No. 4) . . .
Z96 1s. green (1867–73) (Plate Nos. 4, 5, 6, 7) *From* 55·00
Z97 1s. green (1873–77) . . . *From* 75·00
Plate Nos. 8, 10, 12, 13.
Z98 2s. blue (1867) . . .
Z99 5s. rose (1867) (Plate No. 1) . . .

PAITA

CROWNED-CIRCLE HANDSTAMPS

CC5 CC **1** PAITA (Black or R.) (5.11.1850)
Price on cover £4500

Stamps of GREAT BRITAIN *cancelled* "C 43" *as Type* **4** *or with circular date stamp as Type* **16** *showing* "PAYTA" *straight*.

1865–79.
Z100 1d. rose-red (1864–79) (Plate Nos. 127, 147) . . 60·00
Z101 2d. blue (1858–69) (Plate Nos. 9, 14) . . . 60·00
Z102 3d. rose (1867–73) (Plate Nos. 5, 6) . . . 70·00
Z103 3d. rose (1876) (Plate Nos. 17, 18, 19) . . . 70·00
Z104 4d. vermilion (1865–73) . . . *From* 70·00
Plate Nos. 10, 11, 12, 13, 14.
Z105 4d. sage-green (1877) (Plate No. 15) . . .
Z106 6d. lilac (1862) (Plate No. 3) . . . £100
Z107 6d. lilac (1865–67) (Plate Nos. 5, 6) . . *From* 90·00
Z108 6d. violet (1867–70) (Plate Nos. 6, 8, 9) . . . *From* 80·00
Z109 6d. buff (1872–73) (Plate Nos. 11, 12) *From* 90·00
Z110 6d. chestnut (Plate No. 11) . . . 70·00
Z111 6d. grey (1873) . . .
Z112 6d. grey (1874–76) (Plate Nos. 13, 14, 15) . . .
Z113 9d. straw (1862) . . .
Z114 10d. red-brown (1867) . . . £300
Z115 1s. green (1865) (Plate No. 4) . . .
Z116 1s. green (1867–73) (Plate No. 4) . . . 70·00
Z117 1s. green (1873–77) (Plate Nos. 8, 9, 10, 13) . . 80·00
Z118 2s. blue (1867) . . . £250
Z119 5s. rose (1867) (Plate No. 1) . . . £550

PISAGUA(?)

Stamp of GREAT BRITAIN *cancelled* "D 65" *as Type* **12**.

Z120 2s. blue (1867) . . .

PISCO AND CHINCHA ISLANDS

Stamps of GREAT BRITAIN *cancelled* "D 74" *as Type* **12**.

1865–70.
Z121 2d. blue (1858–69) (Plate No. 9) . . .
Z122 4d. vermilion (1865–73) (Plate Nos. 10, 12) . . . £500
Z123 6d. violet (1868) (Plate No. 6) . . . £1000
Z124 1s. green (1867) (Plate No. 4) . . .
Z125 2s. blue (1867) . . . £1200

PORTO RICO

A British Postal Agency operated at San Juan from 1844. On 24 October 1872 further offices were opened at Aguadilla, Arroyo, Mayaguez and Ponce, with Naguabo added three years later.

Great Britain stamps were used from 1865 to 1877, but few letters appear to have used the San Juan postal agency between 1866 and 1873 due to various natural disasters and the hostile attitude of the local authorities. All the British Agencies closed on 1 May 1877.

AGUADILLA

Stamps of GREAT BRITAIN *cancelled* "F 84" *as Type* **8**.

1873–77.
Z 1 ½d. rose-red (1870) (Plate No. 6) . . . 80·00
Z 2 1d. rose-red (1864–79) . . . 50·00
Plate Nos. 119, 122, 139, 149, 156, 160.
Z 3 2d. blue (1858–69) (Plate No. 14) . . .
Z 4 3d. rose (1867–73) (Plate Nos. 7, 8, 9) . . .
Z 5 3d. rose (1873–76) (Plate No. 12) . . .
Z 6 4d. vermilion (1865–73) . . . *From* 60·00
Plate Nos. 12, 13, 14.
Z 7 4d. vermilion (1876) (Plate No. 15) . . . £275
Z 7*a* 6d. pale buff (1872–73) (Plate No. 11) . . .
Z 8 6d. grey (1874–76) (Plate Nos. 13, 14) . . .
Z 9 9d. straw (1867) . . . £325
Z10 10d. red-brown (1867) . . . £275
Z11 1s. green (1867–73) (Plate Nos. 4, 5, 6, 7) *From* 55·00
Z12 1s. green (1873–77) . . . *From* 65·00
Plate Nos. 8, 9, 10, 11, 12.
Z13 2s. blue (1867) . . . £225

ARROYO

Stamps of GREAT BRITAIN *cancelled* "F 83" *as Type* **8** *or with circular date stamps as Types* **17** *and* **18**.

1873–77.
Z14 ½d. rose-red 1870) (Plate No. 5) . . . 55·00
Z15 1d. rose-red (1864–79) . . . 50·00
Plate Nos. 149, 150, 151, 156, 164, 174, 175.
Z16 1½d. lake-red (1870) (Plate Nos. 1, 3) . . .
Z17 2d. blue (1858–69) (Plate No. 14) . . .
Z18 3d. rose (1867–73) (Plate Nos. 5, 7, 10) *From* 55·00
Z19 3d. rose 1873–76 . . . *From* 60·00
Plate Nos. 11, 12, 14, 16, 18.
Z20 4d. verm (1865–73) (Plate Nos. 12, 13, 14) *From* 50·00
Z21 4d. vermilion (1876) (Plate No. 15) . . . £275
Z22 6d. chestnut (1872) (Plate No. 11) . . . 60·00
Z23 6d. pale buff (1872) (Plate No. 11) . . . 75·00
Z23*a* 6d. grey (1873) (Plate No. 12) . . .
Z24 6d. grey (1874–76) (Plate Nos. 13, 14, 15) . . . 55·00
Z25 9d. straw (1867) . . . £275
Z26 10d. red-brown (1867) . . . £275
Z27 1s. green (1865) (Plate No. 4) . . .
Z28 1s. green (1867–73) (Plate Nos. 4, 5, 6, 7) *From* 55·00
Z29 1s. green (1873–77) . . . *From* 65·00
Plate Nos. 8, 9, 10, 11, 12, 13.
Z30 2s. blue (1867) . . . £200
Z31 5s. rose (1867–74) (Plate No. 2) . . .

MAYAGUEZ

Stamps of GREAT BRITAIN *cancelled* "F 85" *as Type* **8**.

1873–77.
Z32 ½d. rose-red (1870) . . . *From* 50·00
Plate Nos. 4, 5, 6, 8, 10, 11.
Z33 1d. rose-red (1864–79) . . . *From* 35·00
Plate Nos. 76, 120, 121, 122, 124, 134, 137, 140, 146, 149, 150, 151, 154, 155, 156, 157, 160, 167, 170, 171, 174, 175, 176, 178, 180, 182, 185, 186, 189.
Z34 1½d. lake-red (1870–74) (Plate Nos. 1, 3) . . . 45·00
Z35 2d. blue (1858–69) (Plate Nos. 13, 14, 15) . . . 45·00
Z36 3d. rose (1867–73) (Plate Nos. 7, 8, 9, 10) *From* 50·00
Z37 3d. rose (1873–76) . . . *From* 45·00
Plate Nos. 11, 12, 14, 15, 16, 17, 18, 19.
Z38 4d. vermilion (1865–73) . . . *From* 45·00
Plate Nos. 11, 12, 13, 14.
Z39 4d. vermilion (1876) (Plate No. 15) . . . £275
Z40 4d. sage-green (1877) (Plate No. 15) . . .
Z41 6d. mauve (1870) (Plate No. 9) . . .
Z42 6d. buff (1872) (Plate No. 11) . . . 75·00
Z43 6d. chestnut (1872) (Plate No. 11) . . . 65·00
Z44 6d. grey (1873) (Plate No. 12) . . .
Z45 6d. grey (1874–80) . . . *From* 45·00
Plate Nos. 13, 14, 15, 16.
Z46 8d. orange (1876) . . . £275
Z47 9d. straw (1867) . . . £200
Z48 10d. red-brown (1867) . . . £275
Z49 1s. green (1867–73) (Plate Nos. 4, 5, 6, 7) *From* 40·00
Z50 1s. green (1873–77) . . . *From* 55·00
Plate Nos. 8, 9, 10, 11, 12.
Z51 2s. blue (1867) . . . £160
Z52 5s. rose (1867–74) (Plate Nos. 1, 2) . . .

NAGUABO

Stamps of GREAT BRITAIN *cancelled* "582" *as Type* **9**.

1875–77.
Z53 ½d. rose-red (1870–79) (Plate Nos. 5. 12, 14) . . .
Z54 1d. rose-red (1864–79) (Plate Nos. 150, 159, 165) £275
Z55 3d. rose (1873–76) (Plate Nos. 17, 18) . . . £450
Z56 4d. vermilion (1872–73) (Plate Nos. 13, 14) *From* £425
Z57 4d. vermilion (1876) (Plate No. 15) . . .
Z58 6d. grey (1874–76) (Plate Nos. 14, 15) . . .
Z59 9d. straw (1867) . . .
Z60 10d. red-brown (1867) . . . £800
Z61 1s. green (1873–77) (Plate Nos. 11, 12) . . .
Z62 2s. dull blue (1867) (Plate No. 1) . . . £600

PONCE

Stamps of GREAT BRITAIN *cancelled* "F 88" *as Type* **8**.

1873–77.
Z63 ½d. rose-red (1870) (Plate Nos. 5, 10, 12) . . . 50·00
Z64 1d. rose-red (1864–79) . . . *From* 40·00
Plate Nos. 120, 121, 122, 123, 124, 146, 148, 154, 156, 157, 158, 160, 167, 171, 174, 175, 179, 186, 187.
Z65 1½d. lake-red (1870–74) (Plate No. 3) . . . £100
Z66 2d. blue (1858–69) (Plate Nos. 13, 14) . . . 50·00
Z67 3d. rose (1867–73) (Plate Nos. 7, 8, 9) . . .
Z68 3d. rose (1873–76) . . . 45·00
Plate Nos. 12, 16, 17, 18, 19.
Z69 4d. vermilion (1865–73) . . . *From* 50·00
Plate Nos. 8, 9, 12, 13, 14.
Z70 4d. vermilion (1876) (Plate No. 15) . . . £275
Z71 4d. sage-green (1877) (Plate Nos. 15, 16) . . . *From* £18
Z72 6d. buff (1872–73) (Plate Nos. 11, 12) . . *From* 70·0
Z73 6d. chestnut (1872) (Plate No. 11) . . . 60·0
Z74 6d. grey (1873) (Plate No. 12) . . .
Z75 6d. grey (1874–76) (Plate Nos. 13, 14, 15) *From* 50·0
Z76 9d. straw (1867) . . . £22
Z77 10d. red-brown (1867) . . . £27
Z78 1s. green (1867–73) (Plate Nos. 4, 6, 7) . . . 45·0
Z79 1s. green (1873–77) . . . *From* 55·0
Plate Nos. 8, 9. 10, 11, 12, 13.
Z80 2s. blue (1867) . . .
Z81 5s. rose (1867–74) (Plate Nos. 1, 2) . . . *From* £35

SAN JUAN

CROWNED-CIRCLE HANDSTAMPS

CC1 CC **1** SAN JUAN PORTO RICO (R. *or* Black) (25.5.1844) . . . *Price on cover* £60

No. CC1 may be found on cover, used in conjunction with Spanish colonial adhesive stamps paying the local postage.

Stamps of GREAT BRITAIN *cancelled* "C 61" *as in Types* **4**, **8**, **1** *or* **14** (*without* "PAID").

1865–77.
Z 82 ½d. rose-red (1870) (Plate Nos. 5, 10, 15) *From* 45·0
Z 83 1d. rose-red (1857) . . .
Z 84 1d. rose-red (1864–79) . . . *From* 35·0
Plate Nos. 73, 74, 81, 84, 90, 94, 100, 101, 102, 107, 117, 122, 124, 125, 127, 130, 137, 138, 139, 140, 145, 146, 149, 153, 156, 159, 160, 162, 163, 169, 171, 172, 173, 174, 175, 179, 180, 182, 186.
Z 85 1½d. lake-red (1870–74) (Plate Nos. 1, 3) . . . *From* 60·0
Z 86 2d. blue (1858–69) (Plate Nos. 9, 13, 14) *From* 35·0
Z 87 3d. rose (1865) (Plate No. 4) . . . 80·0
Z 88 3d. rose (1867–73) . . . *From* 45·0
Plate Nos. 5, 6, 7, 8, 9, 10.
Z 89 3d. rose (1873–76) . . . *From* 40·0
Plate Nos. 11, 12, 14, 15, 16, 17, 18.
Z 90 4d. vermilion (1865–73) . . . *From* 45·0
Plate Nos. 7, 8, 9, 10, 11, 12, 13, 14.
Z 91 4d. vermilion (1876) (Plate No. 15) . . . £27
Z 92 6d. lilac (1865–67) (Plate Nos. 5, 6) . . *From* 70·0
Z 93 6d. lilac (1867) (Plate No. 6) . . . 70·0
Z 94 6d. violet (1867–70) (Plate Nos. 6, 8, 9) . . . *From* 65·0
Z 95 6d. buff (1872–73) (Plate Nos. 11, 12) *From* 70·0
Z 96 6d. chestnut (1872) (Plate No. 11) . . . 45·0
Z 97 6d. grey (1873) (Plate No. 12) . . .
Z 98 6d. grey (1874–76) (Plate Nos. 13, 14, 15) *From* 45·0
Z 99 9d. straw (1862) . . . £22
Z100 9d. straw (1865) . . . £35
Z101 9d. straw (1867) . . . £18
Z102 10d. red-brown (1867) . . . £25
Z103 1s. green (1865) (Plate No. 4) . . . £13
Z104 1s. green (1867–73) (Plate Nos. 4, 5, 6, 7) *From* 40·0
Z105 1s. green (1873–77) . . . *From* 55·0
Plate Nos. 8, 9, 10, 11, 12, 13.
Z106 2s. blue (1867) . . . £12
Z107 5s. rose (1867) (Plate Nos. 1, 2) . . . *From* £40

RUSSIA

ARMY FIELD OFFICES IN THE CRIMEA

1854–57.

Crown between Stars.
Z 1 1d. red-brown (1841), imperf . . . £6
Z 2 1d. red-brown (1854), Die I, wmk Small Crown, perf 16 . . .
Z 3 1d. red-brown (1855), Die II, wmk Small Crown, perf 16 . . . £1

Z 4 1d. red-brown, Die I, wmk Small Crown, perf 14
Z 5 1d. red-brown (1855), Die II, Small Crown, perf 14
Z 6 2d. blue (1841) imperf £1100
Z 7 2d. blue, Small Crown (1854), perf 16 (Plate No. 4)
Z 8 1s. green (1847), embossed £1800

Star between Cyphers.

Z 9 1d. red-brown (1841), imperf
Z10 1d. red-brown (1854), Die I, wmk Small Crown, perf 16 70·00
Z11 1d. red-brown (1855), Die II, wmk Small Crown, perf 16 70·00
Z12 1d. red-brown (1855), Die I, wmk Small Crown, perf 14 70·00
Z13 1d. red-brown (1855), Die II, wmk Small Crown, perf 14 70·00
Z14 1d. red-brown (1855), Die II, wmk Large Crown, perf 16 90·00
Z15 1d. red-brown (1855), Die II, wmk Large Crown, perf 14 42·00
Z16 2d. blue (1841), imperf £1250
Z17 2d. blue (1854), wmk Small Crown, perf 16. *From* £130
Plate Nos. 4, 5.
Z18 2d. blue (1855), wmk Small Crown, perf 14. £175
Plate No. 4.
Z19 2d. blue (1855), wmk Large Crown, perf 16. £200
Plate No. 5.
Z20 2d. blue (1855), wmk Large Crown, perf 14. £120
Plate No. 5.
Z21 4d. rose (1857) £800
Z22 6d. violet (1854), embossed £1400
Z23 1s. green (1847), embossed £1400

SPAIN

Little is known about the operation of British Packet Agencies in Spain, other than the dates recorded for the various postal markings in the G.P.O. Proof Books. The Agency at Corunna is said to date from the late 17th century when the Spanish packets for South America were based there. No. CC1 was probably issued in connection with the inauguration of the P. & O. service to Spain in 1843. The Spanish port of call was changed to Vigo in 1846 and the office at Corunna was then closed. Teneriffe became a port-of-call for the South American packets in 1817 and this arrangement continued until 1858.

CORUNNA

CROWNED-CIRCLE HANDSTAMPS

CC1 CC **1b** CORUNNA (28.2.1842)
Although recorded in the G.P.O. Proof Books no example of No. CC1 on cover is known.

TENERIFFE (CANARY ISLANDS)

CROWNED-CIRCLE HANDSTAMPS

CC2 CC **7** TENERIFFE (6.1.1851) *Price on cover* £3500
CC3 CC **4** TENERIFFE (23.10.1857) *Price on cover* £3500

No. CC2/3 can be found used on covers from Spain to South America with the rate from Spain to Teneriffe paid in Spanish adhesive stamps.

UNITED STATES OF AMERICA

The network of British Packet Agencies, to operate the trans-Atlantic Packet system, was re-established in 1814 after the War of 1812.

The New York Agency opened in that year to be followed by further offices at Boston, Charleston (South Carolina), New Orleans, Savannah (Georgia) (all in 1842), Mobile (Alabama) (1848) and San Francisco (1860). Of these agencies Charleston and Savannah closed the same year (1842) as did New Orleans, although the latter was re-activated from 1848 to 1850. Mobile closed 1850, Boston in 1865, New York in 1882 and San Francisco, for which no postal markings have been recorded, in 1883.

Although recorded in the G.P.O. Proof Books no actual examples of the Crowned-circle handstamps for Charleston, Mobile, New Orleans and Savannah are known on cover.

The G.P.O. Proof Books record, in error, a Crowned-circle handstamp for St. Michaels, Maryland. This handstamp was intended for the agency on San Miguel in the Azores.

CHARLESTON

CROWNED-CIRCLE HANDSTAMPS

CC1 CC **1b** CHARLESTON (15.12.1841)

MOBILE

CROWNED-CIRCLE HANDSTAMPS

CC2 CC **1b** MOBILE (15.12.1841)

NEW ORLEANS

CROWNED-CIRCLE HANDSTAMPS

CC3 CC **1b** NEW ORLEANS (15.12.1841)
CC4 CC **1** NEW ORLEANS (27.4.1848)

NEW YORK

CROWNED-CIRCLE HANDSTAMPS

CC5 CC **1b** NEW YORK (R.) (15.12.1841) *Price on cover* £25000

SAVANNAH

CROWNED-CIRCLE HANDSTAMPS

CC6 CC **1b** SAVANNAH (15.12.1841)

URUGUAY

MONTEVIDEO

British packets commenced calling at Montevideo in 1824 on passage to and from Buenos Aires.

Great Britain stamps were in use from 1864. Combination covers exist with the local postage paid by Uruguay adhesive stamps. The agency was closed on 31 July 1873.

CROWNED-CIRCLE HANDSTAMPS

CC1 CC **5** MONTEVIDEO (Black or R.) (6.1.1851) *Price on cover* £900

Stamps of GREAT BRITAIN *cancelled* "C 28" *as Type* **4**.

1864–73.
Z 1 1d. rose-red (1864) 50·00
Plate Nos. 73, 92, 93, 94, 119, 148, 154, 157, 171.
Z 2 2d. blue (1858–69) (Plate Nos. 9, 13) 50·00
Z 3 3d. rose (1865) (Plate No. 4)
Z 4 3d. rose (1867–71) (Plate Nos. 4, 5, 7) *From* 45·00
Z 6 4d. rose (1857)
Z 7 4d. red (1862) (Plate No. 4)
Z 8 4d. vermilion (1865–70) *From* 45·00
Plate Nos. 7, 8, 9, 10, 11, 12.
Z 9 6d. lilac (1856)
Z10 6d. lilac (1862) (Plate No. 4)
Z11 6d. lilac (1865–67) (Plate Nos. 5, 6) *From* 80·00
Z12 6d. lilac (1867) (Plate No. 6)
Z13 6d. violet (1867–70) (Plate Nos. 8, 9) *From* 75·00
Z14 6d. buff (1872)
Z15 6d. chestnut (1872)
Z16 9d. straw (1862)
Z17 9d. straw (1865)
Z18 9d. straw (1867) £225
Z19 10d. red-brown (1867) £275
Z20 1s. green (1862) £150
Z21 1s. green (1865) (Plate No. 4) £130
Z22 1s. green (1867–73) (Plate Nos. 4, 5) *From* 45·00
Z23 2s. blue (1867) £180
Z24 5s. rose (1867) (Plate No. 1) £400

VENEZUELA

British Postal Agencies were initially opened at La Guayra and Porto Cabello on 1 January 1842. Further offices were added at Maracaibo in 1842 and Ciudad Bolivar during January 1868. Porto Cabello closed in 1858 and Maracaibo was also short-lived. The remaining offices closed at the end of 1879 when Venezuela joined the U.P.U.

Great Britain stamps were used at La Guayra from 1865 and at Ciudad Bolivar from its establishment in 1868. They can be found used in combination with Venezuela adhesives paying the local postage.

CIUDAD BOLIVAR

Stamps of GREAT BRITAIN *cancelled* "D 22" *as Type* **12**, *or circular date stamps as Types* **16** *or* **17**.

1868–79.
Z 1 1d. rose-red (1864–79) (Plate No. 133) £120
Z 2 2d. blue (1858–69) (Plate No. 13)
Z 3 3d. rose (1867–73) (Plate No. 5)
Z 4 3d. rose (1873–79) (Plate No. 11) £140
Z 5 4d. vermilion (1865–73) *From* £125
Plate Nos. 9, 11, 12, 14.
Z 6 4d. sage-green (1877) (Plate Nos. 15, 16) *From* £325
Z 7 4d. grey-brown (1880) wmk Crown (Plate No. 17) £600
Z 8 9d. straw (1867)
Z 9 10d. red-brown (1867)
Z10 1s. green (1867–73) (Plate Nos. 4, 5, 7) *From* £175
Z11 1s. green (1873–77) (Plate Nos. 10, 12, 13) *From* £250
Z12 2s. blue (1867) £600
Z13 5s. rose (1867–74) (Plate Nos. 1, 2) *From* £950

LA GUAYRA

CROWNED-CIRCLE HANDSTAMPS

CC1 CC **1b** LA GUAYRA (R.) (15.12.1841) *Price on cover* £1200

Stamps of GREAT BRITAIN *cancelled* "C 60" *as Type* **4**, *circular date stamp as Types* **16** *and* **17** *or with No.* CC1.

1865–80.
Z14 ½d. rose-red (1870) Plate No. 6)
Z15 1d. rose-red (1864–79) *From* 50·00
Plate Nos. 81, 92, 96, 98, 111, 113, 115, 131, 138, 144, 145, 154, 177, 178, 180, 196.
Z16 1½d. lake-red (1870–74) (Plate No. 3)
Z17 2d. blue (1858–69) (Plate Nos. 13, 14) 50·00
Z18 3d. rose (1873–76) *From* 55·00
Plate Nos. 14, 15, 17, 18, 19.
Z19 4d. vermilion (1865–73) *From* 50·00
Plate Nos. 7, 9, 11, 12, 13, 14.
Z20 4d. vermilion (1876) (Plate No. 15) £275
Z21 4d. sage-green (1877) (Plate Nos. 15, 16) *From* £180
Z22 6d. lilac (1865) (Plate No. 5)
Z23 6d. violet (1867–70) (Plate Nos. 6, 8)
Z24 6d. buff (1872–73) (Plate Nos. 11, 12) *From* 90·00
Z25 6d. grey (1873) (Plate No. 12) £190
Z26 6d. grey (1874–76) (Plate Nos. 13, 14, 15, 16) 50·00
Z27 8d. orange (1876) £275
Z28 9d. straw (1862)
Z29 9d. straw (1867)
Z30 10d. red-brown (1867)
Z31 1s. green (1865) (Plate No. 4) £130
Z32 1s. green (1867–73) (Plate Nos. 4, 7)
Z33 1s. green (1873–77) *From* 50·00
Plate Nos. 8, 9, 10, 11, 12, 13.
Z34 2s. blue (1867) £200
Z35 5s. rose (1867–74) (Plate No. 1, 2) *From* £400

MARACAIBO

CROWNED-CIRCLE HANDSTAMPS

CC2 CC **1b** MARACAIBO (31.12.1841)
No examples of No. CC2 on cover have been recorded.

PORTO CABELLO

CROWNED-CIRCLE HANDSTAMPS

CC3 CC **1b** PORTO-CABELLO (R.) (15.12.1841) *Price on cover* £3000

MAIL BOAT OBLITERATIONS

The following cancellations were supplied to G.P.O. sorters operating on ships holding mail contracts from the British Post Office. They were for use on mail posted on board, but most examples occur on letters from soldiers and sailors serving overseas which were forwarded to the mailboats without postmarks.

P. & O. MEDITERRANEAN AND FAR EAST MAILBOATS

The first such cancellation, "A 17" as Type **2**, was issued to the Southampton–Alexandria packet in April 1858, but no examples have been recorded.

The G.P.O. Proof Book also records "B 16", in Type **2**, as being issued for marine sorting in November 1859, but this postmark was subsequently used by the Plymouth and Bristol Sorting Carriage.

Sorting on board P. & O. packets ceased in June 1870 and many of the cancellation numbers were subsequently reallocated using Types **9**, **11** or **12**.

Stamps of GREAT BRITAIN *cancelled* "A 80" *as Type* **2**.

1859 (Mar)–**70.**
Z1 1d. rose-red (1857). Die II, wmk Large Crown, perf 14 35·00
Z2 6d. lilac (1856) £125

Stamps of GREAT BRITAIN *cancelled* "A 81" *as Type* **2**.

1859 (Mar)–**70.**
Z 3 1d. rose-red (1857), Die II, wmk Large Crown, *perf* 14 35·00
Z 4 1d. rose-red (1864–79) *From* 30·00
Plate Nos, 84, 85, 86, 91, 97.
Z 5 2d. blue (1858–69) (Plate No. 9) 40·00
Z 6 4d. red (1862) (Plate No. 4) £100
Z 7 4d. vermilion (1865–73) (Plate No. 8) 50·00
Z 8 6d. lilac (1856) £125
Z 9 6d. lilac (1862) (Plate No. 3) £100
Z10 6d. lilac (1865–67) (Plate Nos. 5, 6) *From* 85·00
Z11 6d. lilac (1867) (Plate No. 6) 80·00
Z12 6d. violet (1867–70) (Plate Nos. 6, 8) *From* 65·00
Z13 10d. red-brown (1867) £400
Z14 1s. red-brown (1856) £225

Stamps of GREAT BRITAIN *cancelled* "A 82" *as Type* **2**.

1859 (Mar)–**70.**
Z15 1d. rose-red (1857), Die II, wmk Large Crown, perf 14 40·00
Z16 2d. blue (1858) (Plate No. 7) 45·00
Z17 4d. rose (1856) £180
Z18 6d. lilac 1856) £160
Z19 6d. lilac (1865–67) (Plate Nos. 5. 6) *From* £110
Z20 6d. lilac (1867) (Plate No. 6) 90·00

Stamps of GREAT BRITAIN *cancelled* "A 83" *as Type* **2**.

1859 (Apr)–**70.**
Z21 1d. rose-red (1857), Die II, wmk Large Crown, perf 14 35·00
Z22 1d. rose-red (1864–79) *From* 30·00
Plate Nos. 73, 74, 84, 91, 109.
Z23 3d. carmine-rose (1862) £225
Z24 4d. rose (1857) £160
Z25 4d. red (1862) 90·00
Z26 4d. vermilion (1865–73) (Plate Nos. 9, 10) *From* 50·00
Z27 6d. lilac (1856) £125
Z28 6d. lilac (1862) £100
Z29 6d. lilac (1865–67) (Plate Nos. 5, 6) *From* 85·00
Z30 6d. violet (1867–70) (Plate Nos. 6, 8) *From* 65·00
Z31 10d. red-brown (1867) £400
Z32 1s. green (1862) £225

Stamps of GREAT BRITAIN *cancelled* "A 84" *as Type* **2**.

1859 (Apr)–**70.**
Z33 1d. rose-red (1857), Die II, wmk Large Crown, perf 14 90·00

Stamps of GREAT BRITAIN *cancelled* "A 85" *as Type* **2**.

1859 (Apr)–**70.**
Z34 1d. rose-red (1857), Die II, wmk Large Crown, perf 14 35·00
Z35 1d. rose-red (1864–79) *From* 30·00
Plate Nos. 79, 97, 103.
Z36 3d. carmine-rose (1862) £225
Z37 4d. red (1862) 90·00
Z38 6d. lilac (1856) £125
Z39 6d. lilac (1862) (Plate Nos. 3, 4) *From* £100
Z40 6d. lilac (1865–67) (Plate No. 5) 85·00
Z41 6d. lilac (1867) (Plate No. 6) 70·00
Z42 1s. green (1862) £250

Stamps of GREAT BRITAIN *cancelled* "A 86" *as Type* **2**.

1859 (Apr)–**70**.

Z43 1d. rose-red (1857), Die II, wmk Large Crown, perf 14 . . . 35·00
Z44 1d. rose-red (1864–79) . . . *From* 30·00
Plate Nos. 73, 84, 94, 97, 114, 118.
Z45 3d. rose (1865) . . . £200
Z46 3d. rose (1867–73) (Plate Nos. 4, 5) . . . *From* 65·00
Z47 4d. rose (1857) . . . £160
Z48 4d. red (1862) (Plate No. 4) . . . 90·00
Z49 4d. vermilion (1865–73) (Plate No. 10) . . . 70·00
Z50 6d. lilac (1856) . . . £125
Z51 6d. lilac (1862) (Plate Nos. 3, 4) . . . *From* £100
Z52 6d. lilac (1865–67) (Plate Nos. 5, 6) . . . *From* 85·00
Z53 6d. lilac (1867) (Plate Nos. 6, 8) . . . *From* 65·00
Z54 10d. red-brown (1867) . . . £375
Z55 1s. green (1862) . . . £225

Stamps of GREAT BRITAIN *cancelled* "A 87" *as Type* **2**.

1859 (Apr)–**70**.

Z56 1d. rose-red (1857), Die II, wmk Large Crown, perf 14 . . . 45·00
Z57 4d. rose (1856) . . . £200
Z58 6d. lilac (1867) (Plate No. 6) . . . £100

Stamps of GREAT BRITAIN *cancelled* "A 88" *as Type* **2**.

1859 (Apr)–**70**.

Z59 1d. rose-red (1857), Die II, wmk Large Crown, perf 14 . . . 35·00
Z60 1d. rose-red (1864–79) . . . *From* 30·00
Plate Nos. 74, 80, 85.
Z61 4d. rose (1857) . . . £175
Z62 4d. red (1862) . . . £100
Z63 4d. vermilion (1865–73) (Plate No. 8) . . . 50·00
Z64 6d. lilac (1856)
Z65 6d. lilac (1862) (Plate No. 4) . . . £125
Z66 6d. lilac (1865–67) (Plate No. 5) . . . £100
Z67 6d. lilac (1867) (Plate No. 6) . . . 85·00
Z68 6d. violet (1867–70) (Plate No. 8) . . . 65·00
Z69 10d. red-brown (1867) . . . £425
Z70 1s. green (1856) . . . £250

Stamps of GREAT BRITAIN *cancelled* "A 89" *as Type* **2**.

1859 (Apr)–**70**.

Z71 1d. rose-red (1857), Die II, wmk Large Crown, perf 14 . . . 90·00
Z72 6d. lilac (1856) . . . £250

Stamps of GREAT BRITAIN *cancelled* "A 90" *as Type* **2**.

1859 (June)–**70**.

Z73 1d. rose-red (1857), Die II, wmk Large Crown, perf 14 . . . 55·00
Z74 4d. rose (1856)
Z75 6d. lilac (1856) . . . £200
Z76 6d. lilac (1865–67) (Plate Nos. 5, 6) . . . *From* £125
Z77 9d. straw (1867)

Stamps of GREAT BRITAIN *cancelled* "A 99" *as Type* **2**.

1859 (June)–**70**.

Z78 1d. rose-red (1857), Die II, wmk Large Crown, perf 14 . . . 35·00
Z79 1d. rose-red (1864–79) . . . *From* 30·00
Plate Nos. 93, 97, 99, 118.
Z80 4d. rose (1857) . . . £160
Z81 4d. red (1862) . . . 90·00
Z82 4d. vermilion (1865–73) (Plate No. 11) . . . 50·00
Z83 6d. lilac (1856)
Z84 6d. lilac (1862) . . . £125
Z85 6d. lilac (1865–67) (Plate Nos. 5, 6) . . . *From* £100
Z86 10d. red-brown (1867) . . . £400

Stamps of GREAT BRITAIN *cancelled* "B 03" *as Type* **2**.

1859 (Aug)–**70**.

Z87 1d. rose-red (1857), Die II, wmk Large Crown, perf 14 . . . 45·00
Z88 1d. rose-red (1864–79) (Plate Nos. 109, 116) . . . *From* 35·00
Z89 3d. rose (1865) (Plate No. 4) . . . 80·00
Z90 6d. lilac (1856) . . . £140
Z91 6d. lilac (1867) (Plate No. 6) . . . £110
Z92 6d. violet (1867–70) (Plate Nos. 6, 8) . . . *From* 80·00
Z93 10d. red-brown (1867) . . . £450

Stamps of GREAT BRITAIN *cancelled* "B 12" *as Type* **2**.

1859 (Oct)–**70**.

Z 94 1d. rose-red (1857), Die II, wmk Large Crown, perf 14 . . . 45·00
Z 95 1d. rose-red (1864–79) (Plate No. 94) . . . 35·00
Z 96 3d. rose (1865) (Plate No. 4) . . . 80·00
Z 97 4d. red (1862) . . . £100
Z 98 4d. vermilion (1865–73) (Plate No. 8) . . . 65·00
Z 99 6d. lilac (1856)
Z100 6d. lilac (1862) . . . £140
Z101 6d. lilac (1865–67) (Plate Nos. 5, 6) . . . *From* £110
Z102 6d. violet (1867–70) (Plate No. 8) . . . 75·00

Stamps of GREAT BRITAIN *cancelled* "B 56" *as Type* **2**.

1861 (July)–**70**.

Z103 1d. rose-red (1864–70) (Plate No. 84) . . . 35·00
Z104 2d. blue (1858–69) (Plate No. 9) . . . 50·00
Z105 4d. red (1862) (Plate No. 4) . . . £100
Z106 4d. vermilion (1865–73) (Plate Nos. 7, 8) . . . 55·00
Z107 6d. lilac (1862) (Plate Nos. 3, 4) . . . *From* £120
Z108 6d. lilac (1865–67) (Plate Nos. 5, 6) . . . *From* £100
Z109 6d. violet (1867–71) (Plate Nos. 6, 8) . . . *From* 80·00

Stamps of GREAT BRITAIN *cancelled* "B 57" *as Type* **2**.

1861 (July)–**70**.

Z110 1d. rose-red (1857), Die II, wmk Large Crown, perf 14 . . . 40·00
Z111 1d. rose-red (1864–79) (Plate No. 81) . . . 35·00
Z112 2d. blue (1858–69) (Plate No. 9) . . . 50·00
Z113 4d. red (1862) . . . £100
Z114 4d. vermilion (1865–73) (Plate Nos. 7, 8) . . . 55·00
Z115 6d. lilac (1865–67) (Plate Nos. 5, 6) . . . *From* £100

Stamps of GREAT BRITAIN *cancelled* "C 79" *as Type* **12**.

1866 (June)–**70**.

Z116 6d. violet (1867–70) (Plate Nos. 6, 8) . . . *From* 75·00
Z117 10d. red-brown (1867) . . . £375

CUNARD LINE ATLANTIC MAILBOATS

These were all issued in June 1859. No examples arc known used after August 1868. "B 61" is recorded as being issued in March 1862, but no examples are known. Cancellation numbers were subsequently reallocated to offices in Great Britain or, in the case of "A 91", the British Virgin Islands.

Stamps of GREAT BRITAIN *cancelled* "A 91" *as Type* **2**.

1859 (June)–**68**.

Z130 1d. rose-red (1857), Die II, wmk Large Crown, perf 14 . . . 60·00
Z131 1d. rose-red (1864–79) (Plate No. 121) . . . 50·00
Z132 2d. blue (1855), wmk Small Crown, perf 14
Z133 2d. blue (1858–69) (Plate Nos. 8, 9) . . . 75·00
Z134 4d. rose (1857) . . . £200
Z135 4d. red (1862) . . . £110
Z136 6d. lilac (1856) . . . £150
Z137 6d. lilac (1862) . . . £125
Z138 6d. lilac (1865–67) . . . £100
Z139 9d. straw (1862)
Z140 1s. green (1856) . . . £275

Stamps of GREAT BRITAIN *cancelled* "A 92" *as Type* **2**.

1859 (June)–**68**.

Z141 1d. rose-red (1857), Die II, wmk Large Crown, perf 14 . . . 60·00
Z142 1d. rose-red (1864–79) (Plate Nos. 93, 97) . . . *From* 50·00
Z143 6d. lilac (1856) . . . £150
Z144 6d. lilac (1862) (Plate No. 3) . . . £125
Z145 6d. lilac (1865–67) (Plate Nos. 5, 6) . . . *From* £100

Stamps of GREAT BRITAIN *cancelled* "A 93" *as Type* **2**.

1859 (June)–**68**.

Z146 1d. rose-red (1857), Die II, wmk Large Crown, perf 14 . . . 60·00
Z147 1d. rose-red (1864–79) (Plate No. 85) . . . 50·00
Z148 6d. lilac (1856) . . . £150
Z149 6d. lilac (1865–67) (Plate No. 6) . . . £130
Z150 10d. red-brown (1867) . . . £425

Stamps of GREAT BRITAIN *cancelled* "A 94" *as Type* **2**.

1859 (June)–**68**.

Z151 1d. rose-red (1857), Die II, wmk Large Crown, perf 14 . . . 75·00
Z152 1d. rose-red (1864–79) (Plate Nos. 74, 97) . . . 60·00
Z153 4d. vermilion (1865–73) (Plate No. 7) . . . 85·00
Z154 6d. lilac (1856) . . . £160
Z155 6d. lilac (1862) . . . £140
Z156 6d. lilac (1865–67) (Plate Nos. 5, 6) . . . *From* £120

Stamps of GREAT BRITAIN *cancelled* "A 95" *as Type* **2**.

1859 (June)–**68**.

Z157 1d. rose-red (1857), Die II, wmk Large Crown, perf 14 . . . 55·00
Z158 1d. rose-red (1864–79) . . . *From* 45·00
Plate Nos. 72, 89, 97.
Z159 3d. rose (1867–73) (Plate No. 5) . . . 75·00
Z160 4d. red (1862) . . . £110
Z161 4d. vermilion (1865–73) (Plate No. 8) . . . 60·00
Z162 6d. lilac (1862) . . . £150
Z163 6d. lilac (1865–67) (Plate No. 5) . . . £125
Z164 6d. lilac (1867) (Plate No. 6) . . . £110
Z165 1s. green (1856) . . . £225

Stamps of GREAT BRITAIN *cancelled* "A 96" *as Type* **2**.

1859 (June)–**68**.

Z166 1d. rose-red (1857), Die II, wmk Large Crown, perf 14 . . . 60·00
Z167 4d. vermilion (1865–73) (Plate No. 7) . . . 80·00
Z168 6d. lilac (1856) . . . £150
Z169 1s. green (1856) . . . £250

Stamps of GREAT BRITAIN *cancelled* "A 97" *as Type* **2**.

1859 (June)–**68**.

Z170 1d. rose-red (1857), Die II, wmk Large Crown, perf 14 . . . 60·00
Z171 1d. rose-red (1864–79) (Plate No. 71) . . . 50·00
Z172 4d. Ted (1862) (Plate No. 3) . . . £120

Stamps of GREAT BRITAIN *cancelled* "A 98" *as Type* **2**.

1859 (June)–**68**.

Z173 1d. rose-red (1857), Die II, wmk Large Crown, perf 14 . . . 60·00
Z174 4d. red (1862) . . . £120
Z175 6d. lilac (1856) . . . £160
Z176 6d. lilac (1862) (Plate No. 4) . . . £140
Z177 6d. lilac (1865–67) (Plate Nos. 5, 6) . . . *From* £100

ALLAN LINE ATLANTIC MAILBOATS

British G.P.O. sorters worked on these Canadian ships between November 1859 and April 1860. Cancellations as Type **2** numbered "B 17", "B 18", "B 27", "B 28", "B 29" and "B 30" were issued to them, but have not been reported used on Great Britain stamps during this period. All were subsequently reallocated to British post offices.

SPANISH WEST INDIES MAILBOATS

"D 26" was supplied for use by British mail clerks employed on ships of the Herrara Line operating between St. Thomas (Danish West Indies), Cuba, Dominican Republic and Porto Rico.

Stamps of GREAT BRITAIN *cancelled* "D 26" *as Type* **12**.

1868–**71**.

Z190 1d. rose-red (1864–79) (Plate Nos. 98, 125)
Z191 4d. vermilion (1865–73) (Plate Nos. 9, 10, 11) . . . £600
Z192 6d. violet (1867–70) (Plate No. 8)
Z193 1s. green (1867) (Plate No. 4)

Aden

The first post office in Aden opened during January 1839, situated in what became known as the Crater district. No stamps were initially available, but, after the office was placed under the Bombay Postal Circle, stocks of the 1854 ½a. and 1a. stamps were placed on sale in Aden from 10 October 1854. Supplies of the 2a. and 4a. values did not arrive until December. Most Indian issues from the 1854 lithographs up to 1935 Silver Jubilee set can be found with Aden postmarks.

During January 1858 a further office, Aden Steamer Point, was opened in the harbour area and much of the business was transferred to it by 1869. The original Aden post office, in Crater, was renamed Aden Cantonment, later to be changed again to Aden Camp.

The first cancellation used with the Indian stamps was a plain diamond of dots. This type was also used elsewhere so that attribution to Aden is only possible when on cover. Aden was assigned "124" in the Indian postal number system, with the sub-office at Aden, Steamer Point being "132". After a short period "124" was used at both offices. It should be noted that "132" was also used at an office in India, although the two can be identified by the spacing and shape of the numerals, as can the two versions of "124".

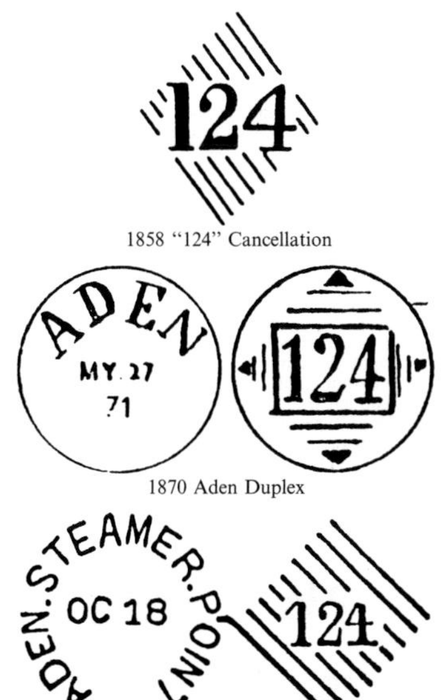

1858 "124" Cancellation

1870 Aden Duplex

1872 Aden Steamer Point Duplex

Both post offices used "124" until 1871 when Aden Cantonment was assigned "125", only to have this swiftly amended to "124A" in the same year.

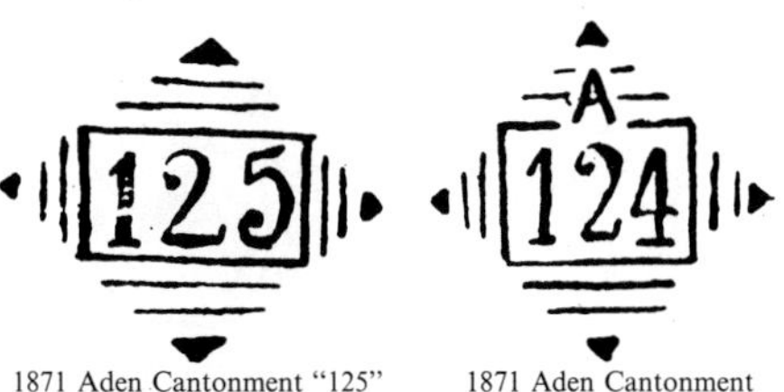

1871 Aden Cantonment "125" Cancellation

1871 Aden Cantonment "124A" Cancellation

Cancellations inscribed "Aden Steamer Point" disappear after 1874 and this office was then known simply as Aden. Following this change the office was given number "B-22" under the revised Indian P.O. scheme and this number appears as a major part of the cancellations from 1875 to 1886, either on its own or as part of a duplex, Aden Camp, the alternative name for the Cantonment office, became "B-22/1".

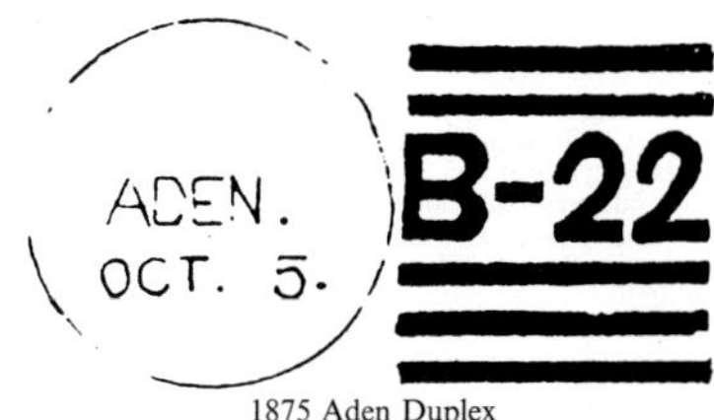

1875 Aden Duplex

Squared-circle types for Aden and Aden Cantonment were introduced in 1884 and 1888 to be in turn replaced by standard Indian double and single circle from 1895 onwards.

A number of other post offices were opened between 1891 and 1937:

Dthali (*opened* 1903, *initially using* "EXPERIMENTAL P.O. B-84" *postmark; closed* 1907)
Kamaran (*opened c* 1915, *but no civilian postmarks known before* 1925)
Khormaksar (*opened* 1892; *closed* 1915; *reopened* 1925)
Maalla (*opened* 1923; *closed* 1931)
Nobat-Dakim (*opened* 1904, *initially using* "EXPERIMENTAL P.O. B-84" *postmark; closed* 1905)
Perim (*opened* 1915; *closed* 1936)
Sheikh Othman (*opened* 1891; *closed* 1915; *reopened* 1922; *closed* 1937)

PRICES FOR STAMPS ON COVER TO 1945	
Nos. 1/15	*from* × 6
Nos. 16/27	*from* × 3

(Currency. 12 pies = 1 anna; 16 annas = 1 rupee)

1 Dhow

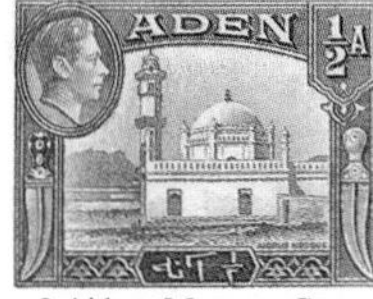

3 Aidrus Mosque, Crater

(Recess D.L.R.)

1937 (1 Apr). Wmk Mult Script CA sideways. P 13 × 12.

No.	Type	Description	Unused	Used
1	1	½a. yellow-green	3·75	2·00
2		9p. deep green	3·75	2·50
3		1a. sepia	3·75	80
4		2a. scarlet	3·75	2·25
5		2½a. bright blue	4·00	1·00
6		3a. carmine	10·00	7·00
7		3½a. grey-blue	7·50	3·00
8		8a. pale purple	24·00	6·50
9		1r. brown	38·00	7·50
10		2r. yellow	55·00	19·00
11		5r. deep purple	£100	70·00
12		10r. olive-green	£325	£350
1/12		*Set of* 12	£500	£425
1s/12s		Perf "Specimen" *Set of* 12	£350	

1937 (12 May). *Coronation. As Nos. 95/7 of Antigua, but ptd by D.L.R.* P 14.

No.	Description	Unused	Used
13	1a. sepia	65	1·25
14	2½a. light blue	75	1·40
15	3½a. grey-blue	1·00	2·75
13/15	*Set of* 3	2·25	4·75
13s/15s	Perf "Specimen" *Set of* 3	80·00	

(Recess Waterlow)

1939 (19 Jan)–**48**. *Horiz designs as T* **3**. Wmk Mult Script CA. P 12½.

No.	Description	Unused	Used
16	½a. yellowish green	50	60
	a. Bluish green (13.9.48)	2·50	4·00
17	¾a. red-brown	1·50	1·25
18	1a. pale blue	20	40
19	1½a. scarlet	55	60
20	2a. sepia	20	25
21	2½a. deep ultramarine	40	30
22	3a. sepia and carmine	60	25
23	8a. red-orange	55	40
23*a*	14a. sepia and light blue (15.1.45)	2·50	1·00
24	1r. emerald-green	2·50	2·00
25	2r. deep blue and magenta	4·75	2·25
26	5r. red-brown and olive-green	13·00	8·00
27	10r. sepia and violet	30·00	11·00
16/27	*Set of* 13	50·00	25·00
16s/27s	Perf "Specimen" *Set of* 13	£190	

Designs:—½a., 2a., Type **3**; ¾a., 5r. Adenese Camel Corps; 1a., 2r. The Harbour; 1½a., 1r. Adenese Dhow; 2½a., 8a. Mukalla; 3a., 14a., 10r. "Capture of Aden, 1839" (Capt. Rundle).

Accent over "D" (R. 7/1, later corrected)

1946 (15 Oct). *Victory. As Nos. 110/11 of Antigua.*

No.	Description	Unused	Used
28	1½a. carmine	15	1·25
	a. Accent over "D"	24·00	
29	2½a. blue	15	50
	w. Wmk inverted	£550	
28s/9s	Perf "Specimen" *Set of* 2	60·00	

1949 (7 Jan). *Royal Silver Wedding. As Nos. 112/13 of Antigua.*

No.	Description	Unused	Used
30	1½a. scarlet (P 14 × 15)	40	1·25
31	10r. mauve (P 11½ × 11)	27·00	32·00

1949 (10 Oct). *75th Anniv of U.P.U. As Nos. 114/17 of Antigua, surch with new values by Waterlow.*

No.	Description	Unused	Used
32	2½a. on 20c. ultramarine	50	1·50
33	3a. on 30c. carmine-red	1·75	1·50
34	8a. on 50c. orange	1·10	1·50
35	1r. on 1s. blue	1·60	2·75
32/5	*Set of* 4	4·50	6·50

(New Currency. 100 cents = 1 shilling)

5
CENTS
(12)

1951 (1 Oct). *Nos. 18 and 20/7 surch with new values, in cents or shillings, as T* **12**, *or in one line between bars (30c.) by Waterlow.*

No.	Description	Unused	Used
36	5c. on 1a. pale blue	15	40
37	10c. on 2a. sepia	15	45
38	15c. on 2½a. deep ultramarine	20	1·25
	a. Surch double	£750	
39	20c. on 3a. sepia and carmine	30	40
40	30c. on 8a. red-orange (R.)	30	65
41	50c. on 8a. red-orange	30	35
42	70c. on 14a. sepia and light blue	2·00	1·50
43	1s. on 1r. emerald-green	35	30
44	2s. on 2r. deep blue and magenta	9·00	2·75
	a. Surch albino	£500	
45	5s. on 5r. red-brown and olive-green	16·00	10·00
46	10s. on 10r. sepia and violet	25·00	11·00
36/46	*Set of* 11	48·00	26·00

ADEN PROTECTORATE STATES

KATHIRI STATE OF SEIYUN

The stamps of ADEN were used in Kathiri State of Seiyun from 22 May 1937 until 1942. A further office was opened at Tarim on 11 December 1940.

PRICES FOR STAMPS ON COVER TO 1945	
Nos. 1/11	*from* × 10

1 Sultan of Seiyun

2 Seiyun

(Recess D.L.R.)

1942 (July–Oct). *Designs as T* **1/2**. Wmk Mult Script CA. *T* **1**, perf 14; others, perf 12 × 13 (vert) or 13 × 12 (horiz).

No.	Description	Unused	Used
1	½a. blue-green	20	60
2	¾a. brown	40	1·00
3	1a. blue	70	60
4	1½a. carmine	70	80
5	2a. sepia	40	80
6	2½a. blue	1·25	1·00
7	3a. sepia and carmine	1·75	2·25
8	8a. red	1·25	50
9	1r. green	3·75	1·75
10	2r. blue and purple	7·00	10·00
11	5r. brown and green	22·00	17·00
1/11	*Set of* 11	35·00	32·00
1s/11s	Perf "Specimen" *Set of* 11	£150	

Designs:—½ to 1a. Type **1**. *Vert as T* **2**—2a. Tarim; 2½a. Mosque, Seiyun; 1r. South Gate, Tarim; 5r. Mosque entrance, Tarim. *Horiz as T* **2**—3a. Fortress, Tarim; 8a. Mosque, Seiyun; 2r. A Kathiri house.

VICTORY
ISSUE
8TH JUNE 1946
(10)

1946 (15 Oct). *Victory. No. 4 optd with T* **10**, *and No. 6 optd similarly but in four lines, by De La Rue.*

No.	Description	Unused	Used
12	1½a. carmine	10	65
13	2½a. blue (R.)	10	10
	a. Opt inverted	£500	
12s/13s	Perf "Specimen" *Set of* 2	60·00	

No. 13 is known with overprint double but the second impression is almost coincident with the first.

1949 (17 Jan). *Royal Silver Wedding. As Nos. 112/13 of Antigua.*

No.	Description	Unused	Used
14	1½a. scarlet	30	2·00
15	5r. green	16·00	9·00

1949 (10 Oct). *75th Anniv of U.P.U. As Nos. 114/17 of Antigua, surch with new values by Waterlow.*

No.	Description	Unused	Used
16	2½a. on 20c. ultramarine	15	50
17	3a. on 30c. carmine-red	1·25	1·00
18	8a. on 50c. orange	25	1·00
19	1r. on 1s. blue	30	1·00
16/19	*Set of* 4	1·75	3·25

5 CTS (11) **50 CENTS** (12) **5/-** (13)

1951 (1 Oct). *Currency changed. Nos. 3 and 5/11 surch as T* **11** *(5c.),* **12** *(10c. ("CTS"), 15c. ("CTS"), 20c. and 50c.) or* **13** *(1s. to 5s.), by Waterlow.*

No.	Description	Unused	Used
20	5c. on 1a. blue (R.)	15	80
21	10c. on 2a. sepia	30	60
22	15c. on 2½a. blue	15	1·00
23	20c. on 3a. sepia and carmine	20	1·75
24	50c. on 8a. red	20	60
25	1s. on 1r. green	50	2·00
26	2s. on 2r. blue and purple	3·25	24·00
27	5s. on 5r. brown and green	20·00	35·00
20/27	*Set of* 8	22·00	60·00

QU'AITI STATE IN HADHRAMAUT

The stamps of ADEN were used in Qu'aiti State in Hadhramaut from 22 April 1937 until 1942. The main post office was at Mukalla. Other offices existed at Du'an (*opened* 1940), Gheil Ba Wazir (*opened* 1942), Haura (*opened* 1940), Shibam (*opened* 1940) and Shihr (*opened* 1939).

PRICES FOR STAMPS ON COVER TO 1945	
Nos. 1/11	*from* × 6

I. ISSUES INSCR "SHIHR AND MUKALLA".

1 Sultan of Shihr and Mukalla

2 Mukalla Harbour

VICTORY
ISSUE
8TH JUNE
1946
(10)

(Recess D.L.R.)

1942 (July)–**46**. *Designs as T* **1** *(½ to 1a.) or T* **2** *(others)*. Wmk Mult Script CA. P 14 (½ to 1a.), 12 × 13 (1½, 2, 3a. and 1r.) or 13 × 12 (others).

1 ½a. blue-green . . . 80 50
a. Olive-green (12.46) . . . 25·00 35·00
2 ¾a. brown . . . 1·50 30
3 1a. blue . . . 1·00 1·00
4 1½a. carmine . . . 1·50 50
5 2a. sepia . . . 1·50 1·75
6 2½a. blue . . . 50 30
7 3a. sepia and carmine . . . 1·00 75
8 8a. red . . . 50 40
9 1r. green . . . 4·00 3·00
a. "A" of "CA" missing from wmk . . . † £800
10 2r. blue and purple . . . 12·00 8·00
11 5r. brown and green . . . 15·00 11·00
1/11 *Set of* 11 . . . 35·00 24·00
1s/11s Perf "Specimen" *Set of* 11 . . . £150

Designs: *Vert*—2a. Gateway of Shihr; 3a. Outpost of Mukalla; 1r. Du'an. *Horiz*—2½a. Shibam; 8a. 'Einat; 2r. Mosque in Hureidha; 5r. Meshhed.

1946 (15 Oct). *Victory. No. 4 optd. with T* **10** *and No. 6 optd similarly, but to three lines, by De La Rue.*

12 1½a. carmine . . . 15 1·00
13 2½a. blue (R.) . . . 15 15
12s/13s Perf "Specimen" *Set of* 2 . . . 60·00

1949 (17 Jan). *Royal Silver Wedding. As Nos. 112/13 of Antigua.*

14 1½a. scarlet . . . 50 3·25
15 5r. green . . . 16·00 9·00

1949 (10 Oct). *75th Anniv of U.P.U. As Nos. 114/17 of Antigua, surch with new values by Waterlow.*

16 2½a. on 20c. ultramarine . . . 15 20
17 3a. on 30c. carmine-red . . . 1·10 50
18 8a. on 50c. orange . . . 25 60
19 1r. on 1s. blue . . . 30 50
a. Surch omitted . . . £1500
16/19 *Set of* 4 . . . 1·60 1·60

1951 (1 Oct). *Currency changed. Surch with new values in cents or shillings as T* **11** *(5c.),* **12** *(10c. ("CTS"), 15c., 20c. and 50c.) or* **13** *(1s. to 5s.) of Seiyun, by Waterlow.*

20 5c. on 1a. blue (R.) . . . 15 15
21 10c. on 2a. sepia . . . 15 15
22 15c. on 2½a. blue . . . 15 15
23 20c. on 3a. sepia and carmine . . . 30 50
a. Surch double, one albino . . . £225
24 50c. on 8a. red . . . 50 1·50
25 1s. on 1r. green . . . 2·00 30
26 2s. on 2r. blue and purple . . . 7·50 14·00
27 5s. on 5r. brown and green . . . 12·00 21·00
20/27 *Set of* 8 . . . 20·00 35·00

Aitutaki
see after New Zealand

Antigua

It is believed that the first postmaster for Antigua was appointed under Edward Dummer's scheme in 1706. After the failure of his service, control of the overseas mails passed to the British G.P.O. Mail services before 1850 were somewhat haphazard, until St. John's was made a branch office of the British G.P.O. in 1850. A second office, at English Harbour, opened in 1857.

The stamps of Great Britain were used between May 1858 and the end of April 1860, when the island postal service became the responsibility of the local colonial authorities. In the interim period, between the take-over and the appearance of Antiguan stamps, the crowned-circle handstamps were again utilised and No. CC1 can be found used as late as 1869.

For illustrations of the handstamp and postmark types see BRITISH POST OFFICES ABROAD notes, following GREAT BRITAIN.

ST. JOHN'S.

CROWNED-CIRCLE HANDSTAMPS.

CC1 CC **1** ANTIGUA (St. John's) (9.3.1850) (R.)
Price on cover £600

Stamps of GREAT BRITAIN *cancelled* "A 02" *as Type* **2**.

1858–60.

Z1 1d. rose-red (1857), P 14 . . . £500
Z2 2d. blue (1855), P 14 (Plate No. 6) . . . £900
Z3 2d. blue (1858) (Plate Nos. 7, 8, 9) . . . £600
Z4 4d. rose (1857) . . . £500
Z5 6d. lilac (1856) . . . £160
Z6 1s. green (1856) . . . £1700

ENGLISH HARBOUR.

CROWNED-CIRCLE HANDSTAMPS.

CC2 CC **3** ENGLISH HARBOUR (10.12.1857)
Price on cover £5000

Stamps of GREAT BRITAIN *cancelled* "A 18" *as Type* **2**.

1858–60.

Z 7 2d. blue (1858) (Plate No. 7) . . . £5000
Z 8 4d. rose (1857) . . . £5000
Z 9 6d. lilac . . . £2000
Z10 1s. green (1856)

PRICES FOR STAMPS ON COVER TO 1945		
No.	1	*from* × 8
Nos.	2/4	†
Nos.	5/10	*from* × 15
Nos.	13/14	*from* × 20
No.	15	*from* × 50
Nos.	16/18	*from* × 30
Nos.	19/23	*from* × 12
No.	24	*from* × 40
Nos.	25/30	*from* × 10
Nos.	31/51	*from* × 4
Nos.	52/4	*from* × 10
Nos.	55/61	*from* × 4
Nos.	62/80	*from* × 3
Nos.	81/90	*from* × 4
Nos.	91/4	*from* × 5
Nos.	95/7	*from* × 4
Nos.	98/109	*from* × 3

CROWN COLONY

1

3

(Eng C. Jeens after drawing by Edward Corbould. Recess P.B.)

1862 (Aug). No wmk.

(a) Rough perf 14 to 16.

1 **1** 6d. blue-green . . . £800 £500

(b) P 11 to 12½.

2 **1** 6d. blue-green . . . £5000

(c) P 14 to 16 × 11 to 12½.

3 **1** 6d. blue-green . . . £2750

(d) P 14 to 16 compound with 11 to 12½.

4 **1** 6d. blue-green . . . £3000

Nos. 2/4 may be trial perforations. They are not known used.

1863 (Jan)–**67**. Wmk Small Star. W w **2** (sideways on 6d.). Rough perf 14 to 16.

5 **1** 1d. rosy mauve . . . £130 50·00
6 1d. dull rose (1864) . . . £100 38·00
a. Imperf between (vert pair) . . . £18000
7 1d. vermilion (1867) . . . £180 23·00
a. Imperf between (horiz pair) . . . £18000
b. Wmk sideways . . . £250 38·00
8 6d. green (*shades*) . . . £475 23·00
a. Wmk upright . . . — £100
9 6d. dark green . . . £550 23·00
10 6d. yellow-green . . . £3250 80·00

Caution is needed in buying No. 10 as some of the shades of No. 8 verge on yellow-green.

The 1d. rosy mauve exists showing trial perforations of 11 to 12½ and 14 to 16.

(Recess D.L.R. from P.B. plates)

1872. Wmk Crown CC. P 12½.

13 **1** 1d. lake . . . £140 15·00
w. Wmk inverted
x. Wmk reversed . . . £140 15·00
y. Wmk inverted and reversed
14 1d. scarlet . . . £170 19·00
w. Wmk inverted . . . £200 50·00
x. Wmk reversed
15 6d. blue-green . . . £500 9·50
w. Wmk inverted . . . — 65·00
x. Wmk reversed . . . £500 12·00
y. Wmk inverted and reversed

1876. Wmk Crown CC. P 14.

16 **1** 1d. lake . . . £140 9·00
a. Bisected (½d.) (1883) (on cover) . . . † £4000
x. Wmk reversed
17 1d. lake-rose . . . £140 9·00
w. Wmk inverted . . . £180 60·00
x. Wmk reversed
y. Wmk inverted and reversed
18 6d. blue-green . . . £350 13·00
w. Wmk inverted . . . † 85·00
x. Wmk reversed . . . £350 14·00
y. Wmk inverted and reversed . . . — 55·00

(Recess (T **1**); typo (T **3**) De La Rue & Co).

1879. Wmk Crown CC. P 14.

19 **3** 2½d. red-brown . . . £600 £160
a. Large "2" in "2½" with slanting foot . . . £8000 £2250
20 4d. blue . . . £250 15·00

Top left triangle detached (Pl 2 R. 3/3 of right panel)

1882. Wmk Crown CA. P 14.

21 **3** ½d. dull green . . . 2·75 14·00
a. Top left triangle detached . . . £225
22 2½d. red-brown . . . £170 55·00
a. Large "2" in "2½" with slanting foot . . . £2750 £1100
23 4d. blue . . . £275 15·00
a. Top left triangle detached . . . — £550

1884. Wmk Crown CA. P 12.

24 **1** 1d. carmine-red . . . 50·00 15·00
w. Wmk inverted
y. Wmk inverted and reversed

The 1d. scarlet is a colour changeling.

1884–86. Wmk Crown CA. P 14

25 **1** 1d. carmine-red . . . 1·75 3·25
x. Wmk reversed . . . — 20·00
y. Wmk inverted and reversed
26 1d. rose . . . 55·00 12·00
27 **3** 2½d. ultramarine (1886) . . . 6·50 12·00
a. Large "2" in "2½" with slanting foot . . . £160 £250
b. Top left triangle detached . . . £375
s. Optd "Specimen" . . . 45·00
28 4d. chestnut (1886) . . . 2·25 3·00
a. Top left triangle detached . . . £225
s. Optd "Specimen" . . . 45·00
29 **1** 6d. deep green . . . 60·00 £120
30 **3** 1s. mauve (1886) . . . £160 £130
a. Top left triangle detached . . . £1200
s. Optd "Specimen" . . . 70·00

Nos. 25 and 26 postmarked "A 12" in place of "A 02" were used in St. Christopher.

2½ 2½ 2½
A B C

The variety "Large '2' in '2½' with slanting foot" occurs on the first stamp of the seventh row in both left (A) and right (B) panes (in which positions the "NN" of "PENNY" have three vertical strokes shortened) and on the first stamp of the third row of the right-hand pane (C). The "2" varies slightly in each position.

From 31 October 1890 until July 1903 Leeward Islands general issues were used. Subsequently both general issues and the following separate issues were in concurrent use until July 1956, when the general Leewards Island stamps were withdrawn.

4

5

(Typo D.L.R.)

1903 (July)–**07**. Wmk Crown CC. *Ordinary paper*. P 14.

31 **4** ½d. grey-black and grey-green . . . 3·75 6·5
32 1d. grey-black and rose-red . . . 6·50 1·2
33 2d. dull purple and brown . . . 7·50 24·0
34 2½d. grey-black and blue . . . 9·00 15·0
a. Chalk-surfaced paper (1907) . . . 26·00 60·0
35 3d. grey-green and orange-brown . . . 11·00 20·0
36 6d. purple and black . . . 32·00 48·0
w. Wmk inverted . . . £130
37 1s. blue and dull purple . . . 45·00 55·0
a. Chalk-surfaced paper (1907) . . . 55·00 £12
38 2s. grey-green and pale violet . . . 75·00 95·0
39 2s.6d. grey-black and purple . . . 18·00 55·0
40 **5** 5s. grey-green and violet . . . 70·00 £10
a. Chalk-surfaced paper (1907) . . . £100 £14
31/40 *Set of* 10 . . . £250 £35
31s/40s Optd "Specimen" *Set of* 10 . . . £150

1908–17. Wmk Mult Crown CA. *Chalk-surfaced paper* (2d., 3d. t 2s.). P 14.

41 **4** ½d. green . . . 2·75 4·5
s. Optd "Specimen" . . . 18·00
w. Wmk inverted
42 ½d. blue-green (1917) . . . 3·75 6·5
43 1d. red (1909) . . . 6·00 2·2
s. Optd "Specimen" . . . 30·00
44 1d. scarlet (5.8.15) . . . 7·00 3·2
w. Wmk inverted
45 2d. dull purple and brown (1912) . . . 4·75 29·0
46 2½d. ultramarine . . . 12·00 16·0
a. Blue . . . 17·00 21·0
s. Optd "Specimen" . . . 25·00
47 3d. grey-green and orange-brown (1912) . . . 6·50 19·0

48 6d. purple and black (1911) . . . . . 7·50 40·00
49 1s. blue and dull purple . . . . 15·00 70·00
50 2s. grey-green and violet (1912) . . . . 80·00 85·00
41/50 *Set of* 8 . . . . £120 £225

1913. *As T* **5**, *but portrait of George V.* Wmk Mult Crown CA. *Chalk-surfaced paper.* P 14.
51 5s. grey-green and violet . . . . 70·00 £110
s. Optd "Specimen" . . . . 60·00

WAR STAMP
(7) **8**

1918 (Sept)–**17**. *No. 41 optd in London with T* **7**.
52 **4** ½d. green (Bk.) . . . . 2·00 2·50
53 ½d. green (R.) (1.10.17) . . . . 1·50 2·50

1918 (July). *Optd with T* **7**. Wmk Mult Crown CA. P 14.
54 **4** 1½d. orange . . . . 1·00 1·25
52s/4s Optd "Specimen" *Set of* 3 . . . . 70·00

(Typo D.L.R.)

1921–29. P 14.

(a) Wmk Mult Crown CA. *Chalk-surfaced paper.*
55 **8** 3d. purple/*pale yellow* . . . . 4·50 12·00
56 4d. grey-black and red/*pale yellow* (1922) . . . . 2·25 5·50
57 1s. black/*emerald* . . . . 4·25 9·00
y. Wmk inverted and reversed £225
58 2s. purple and blue/*blue* . . . . 13·00 19·00
59 2s.6d. black and red/*blue* . . . . 17·00 50·00
50 5s. green and red/*pale yellow* (1922) . . 8·50 50·00
51 £1 purple and black/*red* (1922) £190 £300
55/61 *Set of* 7 . . . . £225 £400
55s/61s Optd "Specimen" *Set of* 7 . . . . £170

(b) Wmk Mult Script CA. *Chalk-surfaced paper* (3d. to 4s.).
52 **8** ½d. dull green . . . . 2·50 50
53 1d. carmine-red . . . . 2·75 50
54 1d. bright violet (1923) . . . . 4·50 1·50
a. Mauve . . . . 12·00 7·00
55 1d. bright scarlet (1929) . . . . 19·00 3·50
57 1½d. dull orange (1922) . . . . 3·50 7·00
58 1½d. carmine-red (1926) . . . . 5·00 1·75
59 1½d. pale red-brown (1929) . . . . . . 3·00 60
70 2d. grey (1922) . . . . 3·00 75
a. Wmk sideways . . . . † £1500
71 2½d. bright blue (1922) . . . . 6·50 17·00
72 2½d. orange-yellow (1923) . . . . 2·50 17·00
73 2½d. ultramarine (1927) . . . . 5·50 5·50
74 3d. purple/*pale yellow* (1925) . . . . . 5·00 8·50
75 6d. dull and bright purple (1922) . . . . 4·00 6·50
76 1s. black/*emerald* (1929) . . . . 6·00 8·00
77 2s. purple and blue/*blue* (1927) . . . . 10·00 55·00
78 2s.6d. black and red/*blue* (1927) . . . . 26·00 28·00
79 3s. green and violet (1922) . . . . . . 35·00 90·00
80 4s. grey-black and red (1922) . . . . . 48·00 65·00
2/80 *Set of* 16 . . . . £150 £275
2s/80s Optd or Perf (Nos. 65, 69, 76) Specimen" *Set of* 18 . . . . £325

9 Old Dockyard, English Harbour

10 Government House, St. John's

Des Mrs. J. Goodwin (5s.), Waterlow (others). Recess Waterlow)

932 (27 Jan). *Tercentenary. T* **9/10** *and similar designs.* Wmk Mult Script CA. P 12½.
1 **9** ½d. green . . . . 2·75 7·50
2 1d. scarlet . . . . 3·25 7·50
3 1½d. brown . . . . 3·25 4·75
4 **10** 2d. grey . . . . 4·25 18·00
5 2½d. deep blue . . . . 4·25 8·50
6 3d. orange . . . . 4·25 12·00
7 – 6d. violet . . . . 15·00 12·00
8 – 1s. olive-green . . . . 19·00 27·00
9 – 2s.6d. claret . . . . 40·00 65·00
0 5s. black and chocolate . . . . 95·00 £130
1/90 *Set of* 10 . . . . £170 £250
1s/90s Perf "Specimen" *Set of* 10 . . . . £200
Designs: *Horiz*—6d., 1s., 2s.6d. Nelson's *Victory*. *Vert*—5s. Sir Thomas Warner's *Concepcion*.
Examples of all values are known showing a forged St. Johns postmark dated "MY 18 1932".

13 Windsor Castle

(Des H. Fleury. Recess D.L.R.)

935 (6 May). *Silver Jubilee.* Wmk Mult Script CA. P 13½ × 14.
1 **13** 1d. deep blue and carmine . . . . . . 2·00 3·00
f. Diagonal line by turret . . . . . 65·00
2 1½d. ultramarine and grey . . . . 2·75 55
3 2½d. brown and deep blue . . . . 6·50 1·25
g. Dot to left of chapel £160

94 1s. slate and purple . . . . 8·50 12·00
a. Frame printed double, one albino . . . .
h. Dot by flagstaff £225
91/4 *Set of* 4 . . . . 18·00 15·00
91s/4s Perf "Specimen" *Set of* 4 . . . . 80·00
For illustrations of plate varieties see Omnibus section following Zanzibar.

14 King George VI and Queen Elizabeth

(Des D.L.R. Recess B.W.)

1937 (12 May). *Coronation.* Wmk Mult Script CA. P 11 × 11½.
95 **14** 1d. carmine . . . . 60 1·25
96 1½d. yellow-brown . . . . 60 1·50
97 2½d. blue . . . . 1·50 1·75
95/7 *Set of* 3 . . . . 2·40 4·00
95s/7s Perf "Specimen" *Set of* 3 . . . . 60·00

15 English Harbour

16 Nelson's Dockyard

(Recess Waterlow)

1938 (15 Nov)–**51**. *T* **15**, **16** *and similar designs.* Wmk Mult Script CA. P 12½.
98 **15** ½d. green . . . . 40 1·25
99 **16** 1d. scarlet . . . . 3·00 2·00
a. Red (8.42 and 11.47) . . . . . . 4·00 2·75
100 1½d. chocolate-brown . . . . 6·50 1·00
a. Dull reddish brown (12.43) . . . 2·75 1·75
b. Lake-brown (7.49) . . . . 32·00 13·00
101 **15** 2d. grey 75 50
a. Slate-grey (6.51) . . . . 8·50 5·00
102 **16** 2½d. deep ultramarine . . . . 1·00 80
103 – 3d. orange . . . . 1·00 1·00
104 – 6d. violet . . . . 3·00 1·25
105 – 1s. black and brown . . . . 4·75 1·50
a. Black and red-brown (7.49) . . . 32·00 11·00
ab. Frame ptd double, once albino . . £3500
106 – 2s.6d. brown-purple . . . . 48·00 12·00
a. Maroon (8.42) . . . . 24·00 12·00
107 – 5s. olive-green . . . . 14·00 7·50
108 **16** 10s. magenta (1.4.48) . . . . 16·00 27·00
109 – £1 slate-green (1.4.48) . . . . 25·00 38·00
98/109 *Set of* 12 . . . . 80·00 85·00
98s/109s Perf "Specimen" *Set of* 12 . . . . . . £180
Designs: *Horiz*—3d., 2s.6d., £1 Fort James. *Vert*—6d., 1s., 5s. St. John's Harbour.

17 Houses of Parliament, London

(Des and recess D.L.R.)

1946 (1 Nov). *Victory.* Wmk Mult Script CA. P 13½ × 14.
110 **17** 1½d. brown 20 10
111 3d. red-orange 20 50
110s/11s Perf "Specimen" *Set of* 2 . . . . 60·00

18 King George VI and Queen Elizabeth

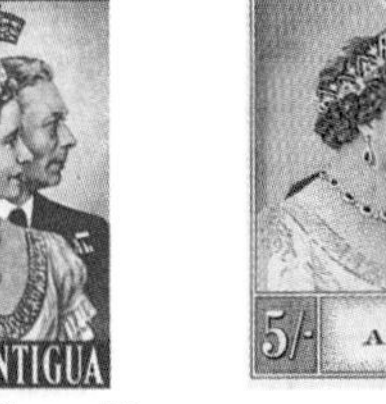

19

(Des and photo Waterlow (T **18**). Design recess; name typo B.W. (T **19**))

1949 (3 Jan). *Royal Silver Wedding.* Wmk Mult Script CA.
112 **18** 2½d. ultramarine (P 14 × 15) . . . . . 40 2·00
113 **19** 5s. grey-olive (P 11½ × 11) . . . . . 8·50 8·50

20 Hermes, Globe and Forms of Transport

21 Hemispheres, Jet-powered Vickers Viking Airliner and Steamer

22 Hermes and Globe

23 U.P.U. Monument

(Recess Waterlow (T **20**, **23**). Designs recess, name typo B.W. (T **21/2**))

1949 (10 Oct). *75th Anniv of Universal Postal Union.* Wmk Mult Script CA.
114 **20** 2½d. ultramarine (P 13½–14) 40 50
115 **21** 3d. orange (P 11 × 11½) . . . . . . 1·75 2·25
116 **22** 6d. purple (P 11 × 11½) . . . . . . 45 1·75
117 **23** 1s. red-brown (P 13½–14) . . . . . 45 1·25
114/17 *Set of* 4 . . . . 2·75 5·25

(New Currency. 100 cents = 1 West Indian, later Eastern Caribbean, dollar)

24 Arms of University

25 Princess Alice

(Recess Waterlow)

1951 (16 Feb). *Inauguration of B.W.I. University College.* Wmk Mult Script CA. P 14 × 14½.
118 **24** 3c. black and brown . . . . 45 1·00
119 **25** 12c. black and violet . . . . 80 1·25

BARBUDA

DEPENDENCY OF ANTIGUA.

PRICES FOR STAMPS ON COVER TO 1945	
Nos. 1/11	*from* × 5

BARBUDA
(1)

1922 (13 July). *Stamps of Leeward Islands optd with T* **1**. *All Die II. Chalk-surfaced paper (3d. to 5s.).*

(a) Wmk Mult Script CA
1 **11** ½d. deep green . . . . 1·50 9·50
2 1d. bright scarlet . . . . 1·50 9·50
x. Wmk reversed £600
3 **10** 2d. slate-grey . . . . 1·50 7·00
x. Wmk reversed . . . . 60·00
4 **11** 2½d. bright blue . . . . 1·50 7·50
w. Wmk inverted . . . . 25·00 80·00
5 6d. dull and bright purple . . . . 2·00 18·00
6 **10** 2s. purple and blue/*blue* . . . . 14·00 48·00
7 3s. bright green and violet . . . . . . 32·00 75·00
8 4s. black and red (R.) . . . . 40·00 75·00

(b) Wmk Mult Crown CA.
9 **10** 3d. purple/*pale yellow* . . . . 1·75 12·00
10 **12** 1s. black/*emerald* (R.) . . . . 1·50 8·00
11 5s. green and red/*pale yellow* . . . . . 65·00 £130
1/11 *Set of* 11 . . . . £130 £325
1s/11s Optd "Specimen" *Set of* 11 . . . . £225
Examples of all values are known showing a forged Barbuda postmark of "JU 1 23".

Stocks of the overprinted stamps were exhausted by October 1925 and issues of Antigua were then used in Barbuda until 1968.

Ascension

DEPENDENCY OF ST. HELENA

Ascension, first occupied in 1815, was retained as a Royal Navy establishment from 1816 until 20 October 1922 when it became a dependency of St. Helena by Letters Patent.

Under Post Office regulations of 1850 (ratings) and 1854 (officers) mail from men of the Royal Navy serving abroad had the postage repaid in Great Britain stamps, supplies of which were issued to each ship. Great Britain stamps used on Ascension before 1860 may have been provided by the naval officer in charge of the postal service.

The British G.P.O. assumed responsibility for such matters in 1860, but failed to send any stamps to the island until January 1867.

Until about 1880 naval mail, which made up most early correspondence, did not have the stamps cancelled until arrival in England. The prices quoted for Nos. Z1/3 and Z6 are for examples on cover showing the Great Britain stamps cancelled on arrival and an Ascension postmark struck elsewhere on the front of the envelope.

The use of British stamps ceased in December 1922.

The following postmarks were used on Great Britain stamps from Ascension:

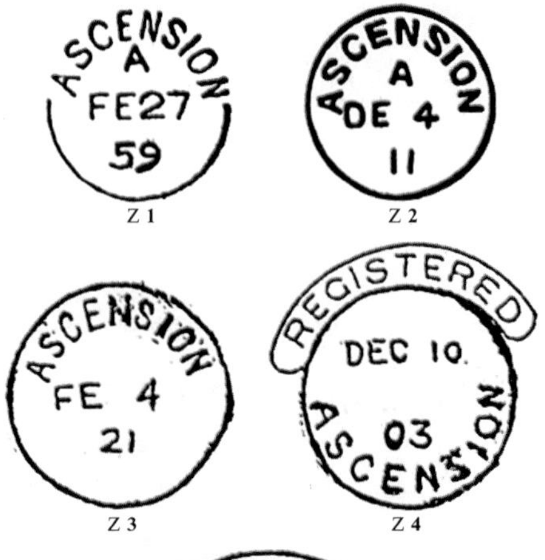

Z 1 Z 2

Z 3 Z 4

Z 5

Postmark Type	*Approx Period of use*	*Diameter*	*Index Letter*
Z 1	1862	20 mm	A
Z 2	1864–1872	20 mm	A
	1872–1878	21½ mm	A
	1879–1889	19½mm	A
	1891–1894	21½ mm	C
	1894–1902	22 mm	A
	1903–1907	20½ mm	A
	1908–1920	21 mm	A or none
	1909–1920	23 mm	C sideways (1909), none (1910–11), B (1911–20)
Z 3	1920–1922	24 mm	none
Z 4	1897–1903 Reg'd	23 mm	none
Z 5	1900–1902 Reg'd	28 mm	C
	1903–1904 Reg'd	29 mm	A

Postmark Type Z **1** appears in the G.P.O. proof book for 1858, but the first recorded use is 3 November 1862.

Forged postmarks exist. Those found most frequently are genuine postmarks of the post-1922 period with earlier date slugs fraudulently inserted, namely a 20 mm postmark as Type Z **2** (because of the shape of the "O" in "ASCENSION" this is often known as the Square O postmark) and a 24 mm postmark as Type Z **3** but with the index letter A.

Stamps of GREAT BRITAIN *cancelled with Types* Z **2/5**. *Prices quoted for Nos.* Z 1/6 *are for complete covers.*

Line-engraved issues.

Z1	1d. red-brown (1855)	£4000
Z2	1d. rose-red (1864–79) *From*	£1800
	Plate Nos. 71, 74, 76, 78, 83, 85, 96, 100, 102, 103, 104, 122, 134, 138, 154, 155, 157, 160, 168, 178	

Surface-printed issues (1856–1883).

Z2*a*	6d. lilac (1856)	
Z3	6d. lilac (1865) (Plate No. 5)	£4000
Z4	1s. green (1865) (Plate No. 4)	
Z5	1s. green (1867) (Plate No. 7)	
Z6	6d. grey (1874) (Plate Nos. 15, 16)	£3250
Z6*a*	6d.on 6d. lilac (1883)	
Z7	1d. lilac (1881) (16 dots)	42·00

1887–92.

Z 8	½d. vermilion	65·00
Z 9	1½d. purple and green	£300
Z10	2d. green and carmine	£140
Z11	2½d. purple/*blue*	65·00
Z12	3d. purple/*yellow*	£275
Z13	4d. green and brown	£200
Z14	4½d. green and carmine	£500
Z15	5d. dull purple and blue	£200
Z16	6d. purple/*rose-red*	£170
Z17	9d. purple and blue	£450
Z17*a*	10d. dull purple and carmine	£550
Z18	1s. green	£475

1900.

Z19	½d. blue-green	65·00
Z20	1s. green and carmine	£500

1902–11. *King Edward VII issues*

Z21	½d. green	42·00
Z22	1d. red	20·00
Z23	1½d. purple and green	£140
Z24	2d. green and carmine	95·00
Z25	2½d. blue	95·00
Z26	3d. purple/*yellow*	£140
Z27	4d. green and brown	£425
Z28	4d. orange (1909)	£160
Z29	5d. purple and ultramarine	£160
Z30	6d. purple	£150
Z31	7d. grey-black (1910)	£275
Z32	9d. purple and ultramarine (1910)	£275
Z32*a*	10d. dull purple and scarlet	£350
Z33	1s. green and carmine	95·00
Z33*a*	2s.6d. dull reddish purple (1911)	£600
Z34	5s. carmine	£850
Z35	10s. ultramarine	£1400
Z35*a*	£1 green	£3250

1911–12. *T* **98/9** *of Great Britain.*

Z36	½d. green (Die A)	80·00
Z37	½d. yellow-green (Die B)	42·00
Z38	1d. scarlet (Die B)	48·00

1912. *T* **101/2** *of Great Britain.*

Z38*a*	½d. green	48·00
Z38*b*	1d. scarlet	48·00

1912–22.

Z39	½d. green (1913)	38·00
Z40	1d. scarlet	22·00
Z41	1½d. red-brown	50·00
Z42	2d. orange (Die I)	45·00
Z42*a*	2d. orange (Die II) (1921)	£375
Z43	2½d. blue	60·00
Z44	3d. violet	80·00
Z45	4d. grey-green (1913)	£100
Z46	5d. brown (1913)	£100
Z47	6d. purple (1913)	90·00
Z47*a*	7d. green (1913)	£350
Z47*b*	8d. black/*yellow* (1913)	£375
Z48	9d. agate (1913)	£325
Z49	9d. olive-green (1922)	£750
Z50	10d. turquoise-blue (1913)	£325
Z51	1s. bistre (1913)	£120
Z52	2s.6d. brown (1918)	£900
Z53	5s. rose-red (1919)	£1400

Supplies of some values do not appear to have been sent to the island and known examples originate from maritime or, in the case of high values, philatelic mail.

PRICES FOR STAMPS ON COVER	
Nos. 1/34	*from* × 5
Nos. 35/7	*from* × 10
Nos. 38/47	*from* × 6

ASCENSION
(1)

Line through "P" of "POSTAGE" (R. 3/6)

Blot on scroll (R. 3/10)

1922 (2 Nov). *Stamps of St. Helena, showing Government House or the Wharf, optd with T* **1** *by D.L.R.*

(a) Wmk Mult Script CA.

1	½d. black and green	4·50	17·00
	x. Wmk reversed	£600	
2	1d. green	4·50	16·00
3	1½d. rose-scarlet	15·00	48·00
4	2d. black and grey	15·00	13·00
	a. Line through "P" of "POSTAGE"	£250	£250
	b. Blot on scroll	£200	£200
5	3d. bright blue	13·00	17·00
6	8d. black and dull purple	26·00	48·00
7	2s. black and blue/*blue*	85·00	£120
8	3s. black and violet	£120	£160

(b) Wmk Mult Crown CA.

9	1s. black/*green* (R.)	28·00	48·00
1/9	*Set of* 9	£275	£400
1s/9s	*Set of* 9	£600	

Nos. 1, 4 and 6/8 are on special printings which were not issued without overprint.

Examples of all values are known showing a forged Ascension postmark dated "MY 24 23".

PLATE FLAWS ON THE 1924–33 ISSUE. Many constant plate varieties exist on both the vignette and duty plates of this issue.

The three major varieties are illustrated and listed below.

This issue utilised the same vignette plate as the St. Helena 1922–37 set so that these flaws occur there also.

2 Badge of St. Helena

Broken mainmast. Occurs on R. 2/1 of all values.

Torn flag. Occurs on R. 4/6 of all values except the 5d. Retouched on sheets of ½d. and 1d. printed after 1927.

Cleft rock. Occurs on R. 5/1 of all values.

Broken scroll. Occurs on R. 1/4 of 1½d. only

(Typo D.L.R.)

1924 (20 Aug)–**33**. Wmk Mult Script CA. *Chalk-surfaced pape* P 14.

10	**2**	½d. grey-black and black	3·50	13·
		a. Broken mainmast	75·00	£14
		b. Torn flag	£110	£17
		c. Cleft rock	65·00	£13
11		1d. grey-black and deep blue-green	5·50	8·
		a. Broken mainmast	85·00	£1
		b. Torn flag	£100	£1
		c. Cleft rock	75·00	£1
11*d*		1d. grey-black & brt blue-green (1933)	90·00	£4
		da. Broken mainmast	£425	
		dc. Cleft rock	£400	
12		1½d. rose-red	7·50	26·
		a. Broken mainmast	90·00	£1
		b. Torn flag	90·00	£1
		c. Cleft rock	75·00	£1
		d. Broken scroll	£100	£1
13		2d. grey-black and grey	14·00	7·
		a. Broken mainmast	£110	£1
		b. Torn flag	£130	£1
		c. Cleft rock	95·00	£1
14		3d. blue	8·00	14·
		a. Broken mainmast	95·00	£1
		b. Torn flag	95·00	£1
		c. Cleft rock	80·00	£1

15 4d. grey-black and black/*yellow* . . . 48·00 80·00
a. Broken mainmast £250 £375
b. Torn flag £250 £375
c. Cleft rock £200 £300
15*d* 5d. purple and olive-green (8.27) . . . 10·00 21·00
da. Broken mainmast £150 £225
dc. Cleft rock £130 £180
16 6d. grey-black and bright purple . . . 48·00 90·00
a. Broken mainmast £300 £400
b. Torn flag £300 £400
c. Cleft rock £250 £350
17 8d. grey-black and bright violet . . . 15·00 42·00
a. Broken mainmast £150 £250
b. Torn flag £150 £250
c. Cleft rock £120 £225
18 1s. grey-black and brown . . . . . . 20·00 50·00
a. Broken mainmast £180 £275
b. Torn flag £180 £275
c. Cleft rock £160 £250
19 2s. grey-black and blue/*blue* . . . . . 55·00 85·00
a. Broken mainmast £325 £425
b. Torn flag £325 £425
c. Cleft rock £275 £375
20 3s. grey-black and black/*blue* . . . . 80·00 90·00
a. Broken mainmast £450 £550
b. Torn flag £450 £550
c. Cleft rock £400 £475
10/20 *Set of* 12 . . . . £275 £450
10s/20s Optd "Specimen" *Set of* 12 . . . . . . £550

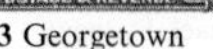

3 Georgetown **4** Ascension Island

"Teardrops" flaw (R. 4/5)

(Des and recess D.L.R.)

1934 (2 July). *T* **3/4** *and similar designs.* Wmk Mult Script CA. P 14.
21 **3** ½d. black and violet 90 80
22 **4** 1d. black and emerald . . . . 1·75 1·25
a. Teardrops flaw . . . . 65·00 65·00
23 – 1½d. black and scarlet . . . . 1·75 2·25
24 **4** 2d. black and orange . . . . 1·75 2·50
a. Teardrops flaw . . . . 80·00 £100
25 – 3d. black and ultramarine . . . . . . 1·75 1·50
26 – 5d. black and blue . . . . 2·25 3·25
27 **4** 8d. black and sepia . . . . 4·25 4·75
a. Teardrops flaw £160 £190
28 – 1s. black and carmine . . . . 18·00 7·00
29 **4** 2s.6d. black and bright purple . . . . 45·00 35·00
a. Teardrops flaw £550 £550
30 – 5s. black and brown . . . . 45·00 55·00
21/30 *Set of* 10 . . . . £110 £100
21s/30s Perf "Specimen" *Set of* 10 . . . . . . £325

Designs: *Horiz*—1½d. The Pier; 3d. Long Beach; 5d. Three Sisters; 1s. Sooty Tern and Wideawake Fair; 5s. Green Mountain.

1935 (6 May). *Silver Jubilee. As Nos. 91/4 of Antigua, but ptd by Waterlow.* P 11 × 12.
31 1½d. deep blue and scarlet . . . . 3·50 7·00
l. Kite and horizontal log £170
32 2d. ultramarine and grey . . . . 11·00 23·00
l. Kite and horizontal log £300
33 5d. green and indigo . . . . 17·00 24·00
k. Kite and vertical log £225 £275
l. Kite and horizontal log £375
34 1s. slate and purple . . . . 23·00 27·00
l. Kite and horizontal log £425 £475
31/4*Set of* 4 . . . . 48·00 70·00
31s/4s Perf "Specimen" *Set of* 4 . . . . £225

For illustrations of plate varieties see Omnibus section following Zanzibar.

1937 (19 May). *Coronation. As Nos. 95/7 of Antigua, but printed by D.L.R.* P 14.
35 1d. green . . . . 50 1·25
36 2d. orange . . . . 1·00 50
37 3d. bright blue . . . . 1·00 50
35/7 *Set of* 3 . . . . 2·25 2·00
35s/7s Perf "Specimen" *Set of* 3 . . . . £200

10 The Pier

Long centre bar to "E" in "GEORGETOWN" (R. 2/3)

"Mountaineer" flaw (R. 4/4)

"Davit" flaw (R. 5/1) (all ptgs of 1½d. and 2s.6d.)

(Recess D.L.R.)

1938 (12 May)–**53**. *Horiz designs as King George V issue, but modified and with portrait of King George VI as in T* **10**. Wmk Mult Script CA. P 13½.
38 **3** ½d. black and violet . . . . 3·50 1·25
a. Long centre bar to E £150
b. Perf 13. *Black and bluish violet* (17.5.44) . . . . 70 1·75
ba. Long centre bar to E . . . . . . 65·00
39 – 1d. black and green . . . . 40·00 8·00
39*a* – 1d. black and yellow-orange (8.7.40) . . . . 14·00 9·00
b. Perf 13 (5.42) 45 60
ba. Mountaineer flaw . . . . 60·00
c. Perf 14 (17.2.49) . . . . 70 16·00
ca. Mountaineer flaw . . . . 80·00
39*d* – 1d. black and green, P 13 (1.6.49) . . 60 1·00
40 **10** 1½d. black and vermilion . . . . . . 4·50 1·40
a. Davit flaw £250
b. Perf 13 (17.5.44) 85 80
ba. Davit flaw £110
c. Perf 14 (17.2.49) . . . . 1·25 13·00
ca. Davit flaw £140
40*d* 1½d. black and rose-carmine, P 14 (1.6.49) 55 80
da. Davit flaw £100
db. Black and carmine . . . . 7·00 5·00
dba. Davit flaw £275
e. Perf 13 (25.2.53) . . . . 45 6·50
ea. Davit flaw . . . . 95·00
41 – 2d. black and red-orange . . . . . . 4·00 1·00
a. Perf 13 (17.5.44) 80 40
aa. Mountaineer flaw . . . . 80·00
b. Perf 14 (17.2.49) . . . . 1·25 35·00
ba. Mountaineer flaw £110
41*c* – 2d. black and scarlet, P 14 (1.6.49) . . 1·00 1·50
ca. Mountaineer flaw £100
42 – 3d. black and ultramarine . . . . . £100 27·00
42*a* – 3d. black and grey (8.7.40) . . . . . 18·00 1·00
b. Perf 13 (17.5.44) 70 80
42*c* – 4d. black and ultramarine (8.7.40) . . 16·00 3·25
d. Perf 13 (17.5.44) . . . . 4·50 3·00
da. Mountaineer flaw £180
43 – 6d. black and blue . . . . 9·00 2·00
a. Perf 13 (17.5.44) . . . . 9·00 5·00
44 **3** 1s. black and sepia . . . . 17·00 1·90
a. Perf 13 (17.5.44) . . . . 4·75 2·00
45 **10** 2s.6d. black and deep carmine . . . 42·00 9·50
a. Frame printed double, once albino £3000
b. Davit flaw £800 £375
c. Perf 13 (17.5.44) . . . . 27·00 32·00
ca. Davit flaw £700
46 – 5s. black and yellow-brown . . . . 95·00 8·50
a. Perf 13 (17.5.44) . . . . 38·00 27·00
47 – 10s. black and bright purple . . . . £110 42·00
a. Perf 13 (17.5.44) . . . . 42·00 55·00
38/47a *Set of* 16 . . . . £250 95·00
38s/47s Perf "Specimen" *Set of* 13 . . . . . . £600

Designs: *Horiz*—1d. (Nos. 39/c), 2d., 4d. Green Mountain; 1d. (No. 39d), 6d., 10s. Three Sisters; 3d., 5s. Long Beach.

1946 (21 Oct). *Victory. As Nos. 110/11 of Antigua.*
48 2d. red-orange 40 75
49 4d. blue 40 50
48s/9s Perf "Specimen" *Set of* 2 . . . . £200

1948 (20 Oct). *Royal Silver Wedding. As Nos. 112/13 of Antigua.*
50 3d. black 50 30
51 10s. bright purple . . . . 45·00 42·00

1949 (10 Oct). *75th Anniv of Universal Postal Union. As Nos. 114/17 of Antigua.*
52 3d. carmine . . . . 1·00 1·75
53 4d. deep blue . . . . 3·50 1·25
54 6d. olive . . . . 2·00 3·25
55 1s. blue-black . . . . 2·00 1·50
52/5 *Set of* 4 . . . . 7·50 7·00

Australia

The Australian colonies of New South Wales, Queensland, South Australia, Tasmania, Victoria and Western Australia produced their own issues before federation in 1901. Stamps inscribed for the individual states continued in use after federation until the end of December 1912.

INVERTED WATERMARKS. The stamp printers in the various Australian colonies paid little attention to the position of the watermark in the sheets they produced so that some entire printings had the watermark inverted, some 50% upright and 50% inverted while on others the inverted watermarks were restricted to odd sheets. In such circumstances it is impossible to provide adequate prices for such items so only those inverted watermarks occurring on stamps printed in Great Britain are included in the following listings.

NEW SOUTH WALES

PRICES FOR STAMPS ON COVER		
Nos.	1/83	*from* × 2
Nos.	84/7	*from* × 3
No.	88	—
Nos.	89/96	*from* × 2
Nos.	97/8	—
Nos.	99/101	*from* × 2
Nos.	102/13	*from* × 3
No.	114	*from* × 10
Nos.	115/17	*from* × 2
Nos.	118/27	*from* × 3
Nos.	131/53	*from* × 2
Nos.	154/70	*from* × 3
Nos.	171/81	—
Nos.	186/202	*from* × 2
Nos.	203/6	*from* × 10
Nos.	207/21	*from* × 5
Nos.	222/37	*from* × 6
Nos.	238/42	—
Nos.	243/4	*from* × 6
Nos.	253/64	*from* × 10
Nos.	265/8	*from* × 15
Nos.	269/70	*from* × 2
Nos.	271/3	*from* × 10
Nos.	280/1	*from* × 2
Nos.	288/97	*from* × 10
Nos.	298/312	*from* × 12
Nos.	313/31	*from* × 10
No.	332	—
Nos.	333/49	*from* × 12
No.	350	—
Nos.	351/63	*from* × 12
No.	O1	—
Nos.	O2/12	*from* × 4
Nos.	O13/18	—
Nos.	O19/34	*from* × 20
Nos.	O35/8	—
Nos.	O39/47	*from* × 40
Nos.	O48/53	—
Nos.	O54/8	*from* × 20
No.	O59	—
Nos.	D1/7	*from* × 50
Nos.	D8/10	—
Nos.	D11/15	*from* × 50

EMBOSSED LETTER SHEETS AND ENVELOPES. From 1 November 1838 the Sydney G.P.O. supplied letter sheets pre-stamped with an albino embossing, as illustrated, at 1½d. each or 1s.3d. per dozen. From January 1841 the price was reduced to 1s. per dozen. The public were also able to present their own stationery for embossing. The circular design measures approximately 29 mm in diameter, and examples are known on laid or wove paper of varying colours. Embossing continued until 1 May 1852 after which the Post Office refused to carry mail which was not franked with postage stamps. The die was used for reprints in 1870 and 1898 before it was destroyed later the same year.

A 1

PRINTERS. The early issues of New South Wales were printed on a press supervised by the Inspector of Stamps. On 1 January 1857 this responsibility passed to the Government printer who produced all subsequent issues, *unless otherwise stated.*

SPECIMEN OVERPRINTS. Those listed are from U.P.U. distributions between 1892 and 1903. Further "Specimen" overprints exist, but these were used for other purposes. From 1891 examples of some of these Specimens, together with cancelled stamps, were sold to collectors by the N.S.W. Post Office.

NEW SOUTH WALES USED IN NEW CALEDONIA. From October 1859 mail for Europe from New Caledonia was routed via Sydney and franked with New South Wales stamps in combination with local issues. Such N.S.W. stamps were cancelled on arrival in Sydney.

1

2

(Eng Robert Clayton, Sydney)

1850 (1 Jan). *T* **1**. *Plate I. No clouds.*

(a) Soft yellowish paper.

1 1d. crimson-lake . . . £4500 £450
2 1d. carmine . . . £4250 £400
3 1d. reddish rose . . . £4000 £375
4 1d. brownish red . . . £4250 £400

(b) Hard bluish paper.

5 1d. pale red . . . £4000 £375
6 1d. dull lake . . . £4250 £400

1850 (Aug). *T* **2**. *Plate I re-engraved by H. C. Jervis, commonly termed Plate II. With clouds.*

(a) Hard toned white to yellowish paper.

7 1d. vermilion . . . £2750 £300
8 1d. dull carmine . . . £2750 £300
a. No trees on hill (R. 2/2) . . . £4750 £475
b. Hill unshaded (R. 2/3) . . . £4750 £475
c. Without clouds (R. 3/5) . . . £4750 £475

(b) Hard greyish or bluish paper.

9 1d. crimson-lake . . . £2750 £300
10 1d. gooseberry-red . . . £3250 £475
11 1d. dull carmine . . . £2500 £275
12 1d. brownish red . . . £2500 £275
a. No trees on hill (R. 2/2) . . . £4750 £475
b. Hill unshaded (R. 2/3) . . . £4750 £475
c. Without clouds (R. 3/5) . . . £4750 £475

(c) Laid paper.

13 1d. carmine . . . £4250 £475
14 1d. vermilion . . . £4750 £450
a. No trees on hill (R. 2/2) . . . — £800
b. Hill unshaded (R. 2/3) . . . — £800
c. Without clouds (R. 3/5) . . . — £800

The varieties quoted with the letters "a", "b", "c" of course exist in each shade; the prices quoted are for the commonest shade, and the same applies to the following portions of this list.

Nos. 1/14 were printed in sheets of 25 (5 × 5).

LAID PAPER. Nos. 13/14, 34/5, 38 and 43*d*/*e* can be found showing parts of the papermaker's watermark (T. H. SAUNDERS 1847 in double-lined capitals and the figure of Britannia seated in an oval beneath a crown).

3

4

A (Pl I)

Illustrations A, B, C, and D are sketches of the lower part of the inner circular frame, showing the characteristic variations of each plate.

(Eng John Carmichael)

1850 (1 Jan). *Plate I. Vertical-lined background. T* **3**.

(a) Early impressions, full details of clouds, etc.

15 2d. greyish blue . . . £4750 £400
16 2d. deep blue . . . — £450
a. Double lines on bale (R. 2/7) . . . — £650

(b) Intermediate impressions.

16*b* 2d. greyish blue . . . £3250 £275
16*c* 2d. deep blue . . . £3500 £325

(c) Later impressions, clouds, etc., mostly gone, T **4**.

17 2d. greyish blue . . . £2500 £150
18 2d. dull blue . . . £2000 £140

(d) Stamps in the lower row partially retouched (end Jan).

19 2d. greyish blue . . . £3000 £225
20 2d. dull blue . . . £3250 £275

5

B (Pl II)

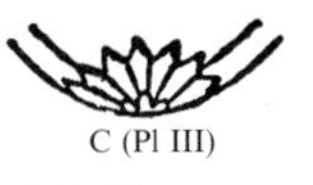
C (Pl III)

(Plate entirely re-engraved by H. C. Jervis)

1850 (Apr). *T* **5**. *Plate II. Horizontal-lined background. Bale on left side supporting the seated figure, dated. Dot in centre of the star In each corner.*

(a) Early impressions.

21 2d. indigo . . . £3750 £275
22 2d. lilac-blue . . . — £1000
23 2d. grey-blue . . . £3750 £225
24 2d. bright blue . . . £3750 £225
a. Fan as in Pl III, but with shading outside (R. 1/1) . . . — £375
b. Fan as in Pl III, but without shading, and inner circle intersects the fan (R. 1/2) . . . — £375
c. Fan as B, but inner circle intersects fan (R. 1/3) . . . — £375
d. No whip and inner circle intersects fan (R. 1/4) . . . — £375
e. No whip (R. 1/8, 2/8) . . . — £300
f. Pick and shovel omitted (R. 1/10) . . . — £375
g. "CREVIT" omitted (R. 2/1) . . . — £600

(b) Worn impressions.

25 2d. dull blue . . . £2000 £130
26 2d. Prussian blue . . . £2000 £170
a. Fan as in Pl III, but with shading outside (R. 1/1) . . . — £300
b. Fan as in Pl III, but without shading, and inner circle intersects the fan (R. 1/2) . . . — £300
c. Fan as B, but inner circle intersects fan (R. 1/3) . . . — £300
d. No whip and inner circle intersects fan (R. 1/4) . . . — £300
e. No whip (R. 1/8, 2/8) . . . £2750 £225
f. Pick and shovel omitted (R. 1/10) . . . — £300
g. "CREVIT" omitted (R. 2/1) . . . — £400

(c) Bottom row retouched with dots and dashes in lower spandrels (from July).

27 2d. Prussian blue . . . £3000 £225
28 2d. dull blue . . . £2750 £150
e. No whip (R. 2/8) . . . — £250
g. "CREVIT" omitted (R. 2/1) . . . — £375

(Plate re-engraved a second time by H.C. Jervis)

1850 (Sept). *Plate III. Bale not dated and single-lined, except on No. 30c which is doubled-lined. No dots in stars.*

29 2d. ultramarine . . . £2500 £170
30 2d. deep blue . . . £2500 £170
a. No whip (R. 2/3, 2/7) . . . — £250
b. Fan with 6 segments (R. 2/8) . . . — £375
c. Double lines on bale (R. 1/7, 1/10, 1/12) . . . — £225

(Plate re-engraved a third time by H. C. Jervis)

1851 (Jan). *Plate IV. Double-lined bale, and circle in centre of each star.*

(a) Hard bluish grey wove paper.

31 2d. ultramarine . . . £3000 £160
32 2d. Prussian blue . . . £2500 £130
33 2d. bright blue . . . £2750 £150
a. Hill not shaded (R. 1/12) . . . — £225
b. Fan with 6 segments (R. 2/8) . . . — £225
c. No clouds (R. 2/10) . . . — £225
d. Retouch (R. 2/1) . . . — £300
e. No waves (R. 1/9, 2/5) . . . — £190

(b) Stout yellowish vertically laid paper.

34 2d. ultramarine . . . £3250 £170
35 2d. Prussian blue . . . £3500 £180
a. Hill not shaded (R. 1/12) . . . — £250
b. Fan with 6 segments (R. 2/8) . . . — £250
c. No clouds (R. 2/10) . . . — £250
d. Retouch (R. 2/1) . . . — £325
e. No waves (R. 1/9, 2/5) . . . — £200
f. "PENOE" (R. 1/10, 2/12) . . . — £250

The retouch, Nos. 33d and 35d., occurs outside the left margin line on R. 2/1.

6

D (Pl V)

7

(Plate re-engraved a fourth time by H. C. Jervis)

1851 (Apr). *T* **6**. *Plate V. Pearl in fan.*

(a) Hard greyish wove paper.

36 2d. ultramarine . . . £2750 £140
37 2d. dull blue . . . £2750 £140
a. Pick and shovel omitted (R. 2/5) . . . — £250
b. Fan with 6 segments (R. 2/8) . . . — £250

(b) Stout yellowish vertically laid paper.

38 2d. dull ultramarine . . . £4000 £300
a. Pick and shovel omitted (R. 2/5) . . . — £425
b. Fan with 6 segments (R. 2/8) . . . — £425

Nos. 15/38 were printed in sheets of 24 (12 × 2), although the existence of an inter-panneau *tête-bêche* pair from Plate II indicates that the printer applied two impressions of the plate to each sheet of paper. The two panes were normally separated before issue. The original plate I was re-cut four times to form Plates II to V. An interesting variety occurs on R. 1/9-11 and 2/7 in all five plates. It consists of ten loops of the engine-turning on each side of the design instead of the normal nine loops.

(Eng H. C. Jervis)

1850. *T* **7**.

(a) Soft yellowish wove paper.

39 3d. yellow-green . . . £3000 £250
40 3d. myrtle green . . . £10000 £1000
41 3d. emerald-green . . . £3500 £275
a. No whip (R. 4/3–4) . . . — £375
b. "SIGIIIUM" for "SIGILLUM" (R. 5/3) . . . — £450

(b) Bluish to grey wove paper.

42 3d. yellow-green . . . £2500 £225
43 3d. emerald-green . . . £3000 £225
b. No whip (R. 4/3–4) . . . — £300
c. "SIGIIIUM" for "SIGILLUM" (R. 5/3) . . . — £375

(c) Yellowish to bluish laid paper.

43*d* 3d. bright green . . . £5500 £500
43*e* 3d. yellowish green . . . £5000 £450
f. No whip (R. 4/3–4) . . . — £650
g. "SIGIIIUM" for "SIGILLUM" (R. 5/3) . . . — £750

Nos. 39/43*e* were printed in sheets of 25 (5 × 5).

A used example of No. 42 is known printed double, one albino.

8

9

(Des A. W. Manning from sketch by W. T. Levine; eng on steel by John Carmichael, Sydney)

1851 (18 Dec)–**52**. Imperf.

(a) Thick yellowish paper.

44 **8** 1d. carmine . . . £1800 £200
a. No leaves right of "SOUTH" (R. 1/7, 3/1) . . . — £375
b. Two leaves right of "SOUTH" (R. 2/5) . . . — £500
c. "WALE" (R. 1/9) . . . — £500

(b) Bluish medium wove paper (1852).

45 **8** 1d. carmine . . . £1000 £130
46 1d. scarlet . . . £1000 £130
47 1d. vermilion . . . £900 £110
48 1d. brick-red . . . £900 £110
a. No leaves right of "SOUTH" (R. 1/7, 3/1) . . . £2000 £225
b. Two leaves right of "SOUTH" (R. 2/5) . . . — £300
c. "WALE" (R. 1/9) . . . — £300

(c) Thick vertically laid bluish paper (1852?).

49 **8** 1d. orange-brown . . . £3000 £350
50 1d. claret . . . £3000 £375
a. No leaves right of "SOUTH" (R. 1/7, 3/1) . . . — £600
b. Two leaves right of "SOUTH" (R. 2/5) . . . — £700
c. "WALE" (R. 1/9) . . . — £700

Nos. 44/50 were printed in sheets of 50 (10 × 5)

(Eng John Carmichael (Nos. 51/9), H. C. Jervis (Nos. 60/4))

1851 (24 July)–**55**. Imperf.

(a) Plate I.

(i) Thick yellowish wove paper.

51 **8** 2d. ultramarine . . . £850 85·0

(ii) Fine impressions, blue to greyish medium paper.

52 **8** 2d. ultramarine . . . £750 30·0
53 2d. chalky blue . . . £650 30·0
54 2d. dark blue . . . £650 30·0
55 2d. greyish blue . . . £650 30·0

(iii) Worn plate, blue to greyish medium paper.

56 **8** 2d. ultramarine . . . £450 30·0
57 2d. Prussian blue . . . £450 30·0

(iv) Worn plate, blue wove medium paper.

58 **8** 2d. ultramarine . . . £350 30·0
59 2d. Prussian blue . . . £325 30·0

(b) Plate II. Stars in corners (Oct 1853).

(i) Bluish medium to thick wove paper.

60 **9** 2d. deep ultramarine . . . £1000 £11
61 2d. indigo . . . £1100 90·0
a. "WAEES" (R. 3/3) . . . — £37

(ii) Worn plate, hard blue wove paper.

62 **9** 2d. deep Prussian blue . . . £1000 £10
a. "WAEES" (R. 3/3) . . . — £37

(c) Plate III, being Plate I (T **8***) re-engraved by H. C. Jervi Background of crossed lines (Sept 1855).*

(i) Medium bluish wove paper.

63 – 2d. Prussian blue . . . £475 60·0
a. "WALES" partly covered with wavy lines (R. 1/3) . . . — £19

(ii) Stout white wove paper.

64 – 2d. Prussian blue . . . £475 60·
a. "WALES" partly covered with wavy lines (R. 1/3) . . . — £19

Nos. 51/64 were printed in sheets of 50 (10 × 5).

(Eng John Carmichael)

1852 (3 Dec). Imperf.

(a) Medium greyish blue wove paper.

No.	Type	Description	Unused	Used
65	**8**	3d. deep green	£1600	£200
66		3d. green	£1300	£140
67		3d. dull yellow-green	£1200	£100
		a. "WAEES" with centre bar of first "E" missing (R. 4/7)	—	£350

(b) Thick blue wove paper.

No.	Type	Description	Unused	Used
69	**8**	3d. emerald-green	£1600	£225
71		3d. blue-green	£1600	£225
		a. "WAEES" with centre bar of first "E" missing (R. 4/7)	—	£600

Nos. 65/71 were printed in sheets of 50 (10 × 5).

1852 (Apr)–**53**. Imperf.

(a) Plate I.

(i) Medium white wove paper.

No.	Type	Description	Unused	Used
72	**8**	6d. vandyke-brown	—	£900
		a. "WALLS" (R. 2/3)	—	£1600

(ii) Medium bluish grey wove paper.

No.	Type	Description	Unused	Used
73	**8**	6d. vandyke-brown	£1700	£250
74		6d. yellow-brown	£1800	£275
75		6d. chocolate-brown	£1700	£250
76		6d. grey-brown	£1600	£250
		a. "WALLS" (R. 2/3)	—	£600

(b) Plate I re-engraved by H. C. Jervis. Coarse background (June 1853).

No.	Type	Description	Unused	Used
77	–	6d. brown	£1800	£300
78	–	6d. grey-brown	£1700	£300

Examples of the 6d. in vandyke-brown on thick yellowish paper are proofs.

Nos. 72/6 and 77/8 were printed in sheets of 25 (5 × 5).

(Eng H. C. Jervis)

1853 (May). Imperf. *Medium bluish paper.*

No.	Type	Description	Unused	Used
79	8	8d. dull yellow	£4000	£600
80		8d. orange-yellow	£4000	£600
81		8d. orange	£4250	£650
		a. No bow at back of head (R. 1/9)	—	£1400
		b. No leaves right of "SOUTH" (R. 3/1)	—	£1400
		c. No lines in spandrel (R. 2/2, 3/2, 4/2)	—	£850

Nos. 79/81 were issued in sheets of 50 (10 × 5).

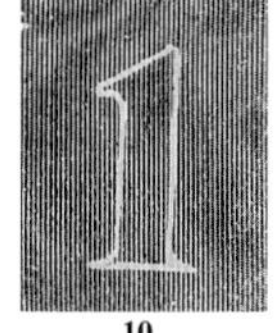

10

NOTE. All watermarked stamps from No. 82 to No. 172 have double-lined figures, as T **10**.

1854 (Jan–Mar). *Yellowish wove paper.* Wmk "**1**", "**2**", or "**3**" as T **10**, to match face value. Imperf.

No.	Type	Description	Unused	Used
82	**8**	1d. red-orange (Feb)	£200	19·00
83		1d. orange-vermilion	£200	19·00
		a. No leaves right of "SOUTH" (R. 1/7, 3/1)	£400	85·00
		b. Two leaves right of "SOUTH" (R. 2/5)	£550	£120
		c. "WALE" (R. 1/9)	£550	£120
84	–	2d. ultramarine (Pl III) (Jan)	£140	11·00
85	–	2d. Prussian blue (Pl III)	£140	11·00
86	–	2d. chalky blue (Pl III)	£140	8·50
		a. "WALES" partly covered by wavy lines (R. 1/3)	£475	50·00
87	**8**	3d. yellow-green (Mar)	£250	29·00
		a. "WAEES" with centre bar of first "E" missing (R. 4/7)	—	£120
		b. Error. Wmk "**2**"	£3000	£1500

Nos. 82/7 were printed in sheets of 50 (10 × 5).

11

12

13

14

6d. and 1s. des E. H. Corbould after sketches by T. W. Levinge.
(Printed by New South Wales Govt Ptg Dept from Perkins Bacon plates)

1854 (1 Feb)–**59**. Wmk "**5**", "**6**", "**8**" or "**12**" to match face value. Imperf.

No.	Type	Description	Unused	Used
88	**11**	5d. dull green (1.12.55)	£1000	£600
89	**12**	6d. deep slate	£600	35·00
		a. Wmk sideways	†	£750
90		6d. greenish grey	£450	35·00
91		6d. slate-green	£450	35·00
		a. Printed both sides		
92		6d. bluish grey	£500	55·00
93		6d. fawn	£550	95·00
		a. Wmk "**8**" (15.8.59)	£1700	£110
94		6d. grey	£500	55·00
95		6d. olive-grey	£500	35·00
96		6d. greyish brown	£500	35·00
		a. Wmk "**8**" (15.8.59)	£1700	£110
		ab. Wmk sideways	—	£350
97	**13**	8d. golden yellow (1.12.55)	£4500	£1000
98		8d. dull yellow-orange	£4000	£950
99	**14**	1s. rosy vermilion (2.54)	£800	70·00
		a. Wmk "**8**" (20.6.57)	£2250	£180
100		1s. pale red	£800	70·00
101		1s. brownish red	£850	80·00

Nos. 93a, 96a and 99a come from printings made when supplies of the correct numeral watermarks were unavailable.

Plate proofs of the 6d. in red-brown and of the 1s. in deep blue on unwatermarked paper exist handstamped "CANCELLED" in oval of bars (see note on Perkins Bacon "CANCELLED" in Catalogue introduction) (*Price £5500 each*).

For further examples of Types **11/14** on different watermarks see Nos. 141/53, 160/70, 215, 218, 231/3, 236 and 329.

15

16

(Eng John Carmichael)

1856 (1 Jan)–**59**. *For Registered Letters.* No wmk. Imperf.

(a) Soft medium yellowish paper.

No.	Type	Description	Unused	Used
102	**15**	(6d.) vermilion and Prussian blue	£800	£170
		a. Frame printed on back	£3500	£2250
103		(6d.) salmon and indigo	£800	£190
104		(6d.) orange and Prussian blue	£800	£225
105		(6d.) orange and indigo	£800	£200

(b) Hard medium bluish wove paper, with manufacturer's wmk in sans-serif, double-lined capitals across sheet and only showing portions of letters on a few stamps in a sheet.

No.	Type	Description	Unused	Used
106	**15**	(6d.) orange and Prussian blue (4.59)	£950	£180

For further examples of Type **15** on different watermarks see Nos. 119/27.

(Printed by New South Wales Govt Ptg Dept from plates engraved by Perkins, Bacon & Co)

1856 (7 Jan)–**60**. Wmk "**1**", "**2**" or "**3**" to match face value. Imperf.

(a) Recess.

No.	Type	Description	Unused	Used
107	**16**	1d. orange-vermilion (6.4.56)	£160	22·00
		a. Error. Wmk "**2**"	†	£5000
108		1d. carmine-vermilion	£160	22·00
109		1d. orange-red	£160	22·00
		a. Printed on both sides	£1800	£1800
110		2d. deep turquoise-blue (Pl I)	£150	9·00
111		2d. ultramarine (Pl I)	£140	9·00
112		2d. blue (Pl 1)	£140	9·00
		a. Major retouch (1858)	£1800	£450
		b. Error. Wmk "**1**"	†	£5000
		c. Wmk "**5**" (3.57)	£475	60·00
		d. Error. Wmk "**8**"		
113		2d. pale blue (Pl I)	£140	9·00
114		2d. blue (Pl II) (1.60)	£500	50·00
115		3d. yellow-green (10.10.56)	£800	80·00
116		3d. bluish green	£850	85·00
117		3d. dull green	£850	85·00
		a. Error, Wmk "**2**"	—	£3000

(b) Lithographic transfer of Plate I.

No.	Type	Description	Unused	Used
118	**16**	2d. pale blue (3.8.59)	—	£750
		a. Retouched	—	£2500

For further examples of Type **16** on different watermarks see Nos. 131/40, 154/8, 171/2, 211/12, 226/8 and 327/8.

Two plates were used for the 2d. The 2d. Plate I was retouched, on a total of ten positions, several times as No. 112a. Stamps from Plate II are wider apart and are more regularly spaced. There is also a white patch between "A" of "WALES" and the back of the Queen's head.

On the 3d. the value is in block letters on a white background. No. 112c comes from a printing made when supplies of the "2" paper were unavailable. Of the errors there are only two known of both Nos. 112b and 112d, all used. One example of each is in the Royal Collection.

The 1d. exists privately rouletted 10, a used pair of which is known postmarked 15 May 1861.

No. 114 was mainly used at post offices in Queensland.

STAMPS WITH STRAIGHT EDGES. Stamps between Nos. 119 and 243 can be found with one or two sides imperforate. These come from the outside rows which were not perforated between the stamps and the sheet margins.

1860 (Feb)–**63**. *For Registered Letters.*

(a) P 12.

(i) Hard medium bluish wove paper with manufacturer's wmk in sans-serif, double-lined capitals across sheet, showing portions of letters on a few stamps.

No.	Type	Description	Unused	Used
119	**15**	(6d.) orange and Prussian blue	£400	55·00
120		(6d.) orange and indigo	£375	60·00

(ii) Coarse, yellowish wove paper with manufacturer's wmk in Roman capitals (Feb 1860).

No.	Type	Description	Unused	Used
121	**15**	(6d.) rose-red and Prussian blue	£300	40·00
122		(6d.) rose-red and indigo	£375	85·00
123		(6d.) salmon and indigo		

(b) P 13. *(i) Coarse, yellowish wove paper with manufacturer's wmk in Roman capitals (1862).*

No.	Type	Description	Unused	Used
124	**15**	(6d.) rose-red and Prussian blue	£300	55·00

(ii) Yellowish wove paper. Wmk "**6**" (May 1863).

No.	Type	Description	Unused	Used
125	**15**	(6d.) rose-red and Prussian blue	£110	21·00
126		(6d.) rose-red and indigo	£170	28·00
127		(6d.) rose-red and pale blue	85·00	19·00
		a. Double impression of frame	—	£500

1860 (14 Feb)–**72**. Wmk double-lined figure of value.

(a) P 12.

No.	Type	Description	Unused	Used
131	**16**	1d. orange-red	£180	16·00
		a. Imperf between (pair)		
		b. Double impression		
132		1d. scarlet	£120	16·00
133		2d. pale blue (Pl I)	£500	£140
		a. Retouched	—	£1300
134		2d. greenish blue (Pl II)	£100	10·00
136		2d. Prussian blue (Pl II)	£100	11·00
		a. Error. Wmk "**1**"	—	£2750
		b. Retouched (*shades*)	—	£400
137		2d. Prussian blue (Pl I) (3.61)	£130	12·00
138		2d. dull blue (Pl I)	£120	11·00
139		3d. yellow-green (1860)	£1000	55·00
140		3d. blue-green	£550	42·00
141	**11**	5d. dull green (1863)	£160	55·00
142		5d. yellowish green (1863)	£160	55·00
143	**12**	6d. grey-brown	£300	45·00
144		6d. olive-brown	£300	55·00
145		6d. greenish grey	£375	45·00
146		6d. fawn	£350	65·00
147		6d. mauve	£325	35·00
148		6d. violet	£300	16·00
		a. Imperf between (pair)		
149	**13**	8d. lemon-yellow	—	£1400
150		8d. orange	£2500	£650
151		8d. red-orange	£2500	£650
152	**14**	1s. brownish red	£475	48·00
153		1s. rose-carmine	£475	48·00
		a. Imperf between (pair)		

(b) P 13.

No.	Type	Description	Unused	Used
154	**16**	1d. scarlet (1862)	75·00	10·00
155		1d. dull red	75·00	10·00
156		3d. blue-green (12.62)	48·00	11·00
157		3d. yellow-green	60·00	8·50
		a. Wmk "**6**" (7.72)	£110	12·00
158		3d. dull green	60·00	8·00
		a. Wmk "**6**" (7.72)	£110	15·00
160	**11**	5d. bluish green (12.63)	55·00	17·00
161		5d. bright yellow-green (8.65)	95·00	38·00
162		5d. sea-green (1866)	55·00	20·00
162*a*		5d. dark bluish green (11.70)	42·00	20·00
163	**12**	6d. reddish purple (Pl I) (7.62)	95·00	6·00
164		6d. mauve	95·00	6·00
165		6d. purple (Pl II) (1864)	65·00	4·75
		a. Wmk "**5**" (7.66)	£350	25·00
		ab. Wmk "**5**" sideways	†	£1000
		b. Wmk "**12**" (12.66 and 1868)	£300	20·00
166		6d. violet	65·00	6·50
		a. Wmk "**5**" (7.66)	—	30·00
167		6d. aniline mauve	£900	£120
167*a*	**13**	8d. red-orange (1862)	£160	55·00
167*b*		8d. yellow-orange	£180	40·00
167*c*		8d. bright yellow	£160	40·00
168	**14**	1s. rose-carmine (1862)	95·00	7·50
169		1s. carmine	90·00	8·00
170		1s. crimson-lake	85·00	8·00

(c) Perf compound 12 × 13.

No.	Type	Description	Unused	Used
171	**16**	1d. scarlet (1862)	—	£1700
172		2d. dull blue (1.62)	£2000	£180

No. 133 was made by perforating a small remaining stock of No. 113. Nos. 137/8 were printed from the original plate after its return from London, where it had been repaired.

Nos. 157a, 158a and 165a/b come from printings made when supplies of paper with the correct face value were unavailable.

For later printings in these types, with different watermarks and perforations, see Nos. 195, 211/2, 215, 218, 226/8, 231/3, 236, 269/70 and 327/9.

24

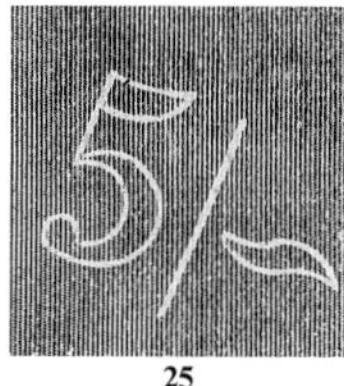

25

(Des E. H. Corbould, R.I.)

1861–88. W **25**. Various perfs.

No.	Type	Description	Unused	Used
174	**24**	5s. dull violet, P 12 (1861)	£1200	£325
		a. Perf 13 (1861)	£200	32·00
175		5s. royal purple, P 13 (1872)	£350	55·00
176		5s. deep rose-lilac, P 13 (1875)	£120	32·00
177		5s. deep purple, P 13 (1880)	£190	48·00
		a. Perf 10 (1882)	£190	55·00
178		5s. rose-lilac, P 10 (1883)	£140	48·00
179		5s. purple, P 12 (1885)	—	55·00
		a. Perf 10 × 12 (1885)	—	£140
180		5s. reddish purple, P 10 (1886)	£140	48·00
		a. Perf 12 × 10 (1887)	£300	55·00
181		5s. rose-lilac, P 11 (1888)	—	£140

This value was replaced by Nos. 261, etc. in 1888 but reissued in 1897, *see* Nos. 297*c*/*e*.

26

27

28

(Printed by De La Rue & Co, Ltd, London and perf at Somerset House, London)

1862–65. *Surfaced paper.* P 14.

		(i) W **27**.		
186	**26**	1d. dull red (Pl I) (1.4.64)	£100	45·00
		(ii) No wmk.		
187	**26**	1d. dull red (Pl II) (1.65)	85·00	38·00
188	**28**	2d. pale blue (25.3.62)	90·00	45·00

(Printed from the De La Rue plates in the Colony)

1862 (12 Apr). Wmk double-lined "**2**" (No. 189) or "**5**" (No. 190). P 13.

189	**28**	2d. blue	65·00	9·50
		a. Perf 12	£150	32·00
		b. Perf 12 × 13	£450	£200
190		2d. dull blue (9.62)	70·00	11·00

29

1863–69. W **29**. P 13.

191	**26**	1d. pale red (3.69)	£110	16·00
192	**28**	2d. pale blue (4.63)	15·00	1·00
		a. Perf 12		
193		2d. cobalt-blue	15·00	1·00
194		2d. Prussian blue	26·00	3·75

1864–65. W **27**. P 13.

195	**16**	1d. pale red (6.64)	48·00	17·00
196	**26**	1d. dark red-brown (Pl I)	£160	18·00
197		1d. brownish red (Pl II)	25·00	3·00
		a. Imperf between (horiz pair)	†	£750
198		1d. brick-red (Pl II)	25·00	3·00
		a. Highly surfaced paper (1865)	£200	
199	**28**	2d. pale blue	£140	4·00

Plates I and II were made from the same die; they can only be distinguished by the colour or by the marginal inscription.

1865–66. *Thin wove paper.* No wmk. P 13.

200	**26**	1d. brick-red	£120	22·00
201		1d. brownish red	£120	22·00
202	**28**	2d. pale blue (11.65)	70·00	3·75

32

34

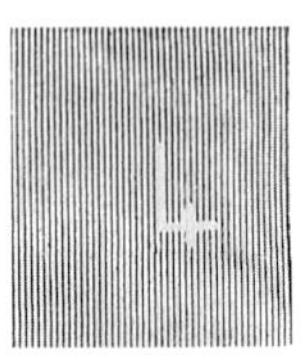
33

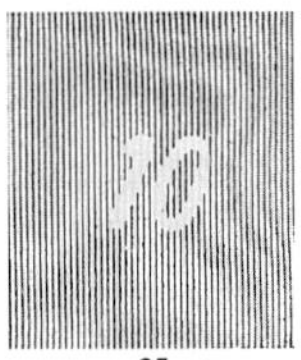
35

1867 (Sept)–**93**. W **33** and **35**.

203	**32**	4d. red-brown, P 13	50·00	4·00
204		4d. pale red-brown, P 13	50·00	4·00
205	**34**	10d. lilac, P 13	13·00	4·00
		a. Imperf between (horiz pair)	£750	
		s. Optd "Specimen"	25·00	
206		10d. lilac, P 11 (1893)	13·00	4·00
		a. Perf 10	15·00	5·00
		b. Perf 10 × 11 or 11 × 10	20·00	7·50
		c. Perf 12 × 11	£110	15·00

36

37

38

NINEPENCE
(39)

From 1871 to 1903 the 9d. is formed from the 10d. by a black surch. (T **39**), 15 mm long on Nos. 219 to 220g, and 13½ mm long on subsequent issues.

1871–1902. W **36**.

207	**26**	1d. dull red, P 13 (8.71)	8·00	75
		a. Imperf vert (horiz pair)	†	£850
208		1d. salmon, P 13 (1878)	8·00	75
		a. Perf 10 (6.80)	£250	30·00
		b. Perf 10 × 13 (6.80)	50·00	5·50
		ba. Perf 13 × 10	20·00	60
		c. Scarlet. Perf 10 (4.82)	—	£180
209	**28**	2d. Prussian-blue, P 13 (11.71)	11·00	65
		a. Perf 11 × 12, comb (11.84)	£250	40·00
		b. Imperf between (vert pair)	†	—
210		2d. pale blue, P 13 (1876)	11·00	65
		a. Perf 10 (6.80)	£250	22·00
		b. Perf 10 × 13 (6.80)	£100	15·00
		ba. Perf 13 × 10	11·00	65
		c. Surfaced paper. Perf 13		
211	**16**	3d. yellow-green, P 13 (3.74)	24·00	3·25
		a. Perf 10 (6.80)	65·00	7·00
		b. Perf 11 (1902)	£150	£100
		c. Perf 12 (5.85)	—	£150
		d. Perf 10 × 12 or 12 × 10 (5.85)	£150	32·00
		e. Perf 11 × 12 (1902)	£120	32·00
212		3d. bright green, P 10 (6.80)	£120	12·00
		a. Perf 13 × 10 (6.80)	£110	16·00
		b. Perf 13		
213	**32**	4d. pale red-brown, P 13 (8.77)	60·00	8·50
214		4d. red-brown, P 13	60·00	8·00
		a. Perf 10 (6.80)	£180	50·00
		b. Perf 10 × 13 (6.80)	£100	20·00
		ba. Perf 13 × 10	75·00	4·25
215	**11**	5d. bluish green, P 10 (8.84)	18·00	13·00
		a. Perf 12 (5.85)	£250	£100
		b. Perf 10 × 13 or 13 × 10		
		c. Perf 10 × 12 (5.85)	£120	42·00
		ca. Perf 12 × 10	32·00	14·00
216	**37**	6d. bright mauve, P 13 (1.1.72)	50·00	1·50
		a. Imperf between (horiz pair)	†	£750
217		6d. pale lilac, P 13 (1878)	50·00	1·50
		a. Perf 10 (6.80)	£180	12·00
		b. Perf 10 × 13 (6.80)	80·00	15·00
		ba. Perf 13 × 10	55·00	1·50
		c. Imperf between (horiz pair). Perf 13 × 10	†	£750
218	**13**	8d. yellow, P 13 (3.77)	£110	17·00
		a. Perf 10 (6.80)	£275	26·00
		b. Perf 13 × 10 (6.80)	£180	24·00
219	**34**	9d.on 10d. pale red-brown, P 13 (8.71)	28·00	4·50
220		9d.on 10d. red-brown, P 13 (1878)	28·00	7·00
		a. Perf 10 (6.80)	12·00	6·00
		b. Perf 12 (5.85)	12·00	6·00
		c. Perf 11 (12.85)	30·00	7·00
		ca. Surch in both black and blue (12.85)	£140	
		d. Perf 12 × 10 (5.85)	£250	£160
		e. Perf 10 × 11 or 11 × 10 (12.85)	50·00	11·00
		f. Perf 12 × 11 (12.85)	14·00	5·50
		g. Perf 12 × 11, comb (1.84)	14·00	5·50
		gs. Optd "Specimen"	25·00	
221	**38**	1s. black, P 13 (1.4.76)	80·00	4·25
		a. Perf 10 (6.80)	£200	13·00
		b. Perf 10 × 13 (6.80)	£240	20·00
		ba. Perf 13 × 10	£170	6·50
		c. Perf 11		
		d. Imperf between (vert pair)	†	£950
		e. Imperf (pair)	†	£850

Collectors should note that the classification of perforations is that adopted by the Royal Philatelic Society, London. "Perf 12" denotes the perforation formerly called "11½, 12" and "perf 13" that formerly called "12½, 13".

BISECTS. Between 1887 and 1913 various 1d. and 2d. stamps can be found vertically or diagonally bisected. This was unauthorised.

40

1882 (Apr)–**97**. W **40**.

222	**26**	1d. salmon, P 10	16·00	50
		a. Perf 13		
		b. Perf 10 × 13		
		ba. Perf 13 × 10	40·00	1·50
223		1d. orange *to* scarlet, P 13	£800	£400
		a. Perf 10	10·00	30
		ab. Imperf between (horiz pair)		
		b. Perf 10 × 13	£120	7·00
		c. Perf 10 × 12 or 12 × 10 (4.85)	£250	65·00
		d. Perf 11 × 10 (12.85)	£450	£120
		e. Perf 12 × 11 (12.85)	—	£120
		f. Perf 11 × 12, comb (1.84)	5·50	30
		h. Perf 11 (12.85)	—	£130
224	**28**	2d. pale blue, P 13	£450	90·00
		a. Perf 10	20·00	30
		b. Perf 10 × 13	65·00	2·50
		ba. Perf 13 × 10		
225		2d. Prussian blue, P 10	28·00	30
		b. Perf 12 (4.85)	—	£225
		c. Perf 11 (12.85)	—	£100
		d. Perf 12 × 11 (12.85)	£400	£100
		e. Perf 10 × 12 (4.85)	£225	65·00
		ca. Perf 12 × 10	£400	£100
		f. Perf 10 × 11 or 11 × 10 (12.85)	£450	£150
		g. Perf 11 × 12, comb (1.84)	12·00	30
		ga. Printed double	†	£500
226	**16**	3d. yellow-green, P 10 (1886)	8·50	80
		a. Double impression	†	£1000
		b. Wmk sideways		
		bs. Optd "Specimen"	25·00	
		c. Perf 10 × 12	£160	35·00
		ca. Perf 12 × 10	£120	15·00
		d. Perf 11	6·00	1·00
		da. Imperf vert (horiz pair)	£250	
		e. Perf 11 × 12 or 12 × 11	6·00	1·00
		f. Perf 12	9·00	1·50
		g. Imperf (pair)	£180	
227		3d. bluish green, P 10	8·00	80
		a. Wmk sideways	50·00	10·00
		b. Perf 11	8·00	1·25
		c. Perf 10 × 11	18·00	1·75
		ca. Perf 11 × 10	£100	35·00
		d. Perf 11 × 12 or 12 × 11	7·00	1·50
		e. Perf 10 × 12 or 12 × 10	35·00	3·00
228		3d. emerald-green, P 10 (1893)	55·00	7·50
		a. Wmk sideways	—	16·00
		b. Perf 10 × 11	55·00	3·50
		ba. Perf 11 × 10	£120	38·00
		c. Perf 10 × 12	50·00	3·50
		ca. Perf 12 × 10	75·00	6·00
		d. Perf 12 × 11	—	11·00
229	**32**	4d. red-brown, P 10	50·00	3·25
		a. Perf 10 × 12 (4.85)	—	£160
		b. Perf 11 × 12, comb (1.84)	50·00	1·75
230		4d. dark brown, P 10	50·00	3·00
		a. Perf 12 (4.85)	£300	£180
		b. Perf 10 × 12 (4.85)	£200	60·00
		ba. Perf 12 × 10	£300	£150
		c. Perf 11 × 12, comb (1.84)	35·00	1·50
231	**11**	5d. dull green, P 10 (1890)	18·00	1·50
		as. Optd. "Specimen"	25·00	
		b. Perf 11 × 10	50·00	
		c. Perf 12 × 10 (4.85)	80·00	4·00
232		5d. bright green, P 10	42·00	5·00
		b. Perf 10 × 11 (12.85)	50·00	4·50
		ba. Perf 11 × 10	50·00	6·00
		c. Perf 10 × 12 (4.85)	£150	32·00
		ca. Perf 12 × 10	£100	70·00
233		5d. blue-green, P 10	12·00	1·00
		a. Perf 12 (4.85)	15·00	1·25
		ab. Wmk sideways	50·00	
		b. Perf 11 (12.85)	9·00	1·00
		c. Perf 10 × 11 (12.85)	35·00	1·75
		d. Perf 11 × 12 or 12 × 11 (12.85)	9·00	1·00
		da. Wmk sideways (P 11 × 12)	55·00	20·00
		e. Imperf (pair)	£275	
234	**37**	6d. pale lilac, P 10	48·00	1·25
		a. Perf 10 × 13 or 13 × 10	—	£300
		b. Perf 10 × 12 or 12 × 10 (4.85)	50·00	1·50
235		6d. mauve, P 10	48·00	1·25
		a. Perf 12 (4.85)	80·00	10·00
		b. Perf 11 (12.85)	80·00	8·00
		c. Perf 10 × 12 (4.85)	50·00	8·00
		ca. Perf 12 × 10	48·00	2·25
		cb. Imperf between (horiz pair)	†	£750
		d. Perf 11 × 12 (12.85)	80·00	12·00
		da. Perf 12 × 11	48·00	1·60
		e. Perf 11 × 10 (12.85)	55·00	2·25
236	**13**	8d. yellow, P 10 (1883)	£100	15·00
		a. Perf 12 (4.85)	£170	27·00
		b. Perf 11 (12.85)	£100	20·00
		c. Perf 10 × 12 (4.85)	£130	40·00
		ca. Perf 12 × 10	£100	32·00
236*d*	**34**	9d.on 10d. red-brn, P 11 × 12 (28.2.97)	8·00	7·00
		das. Optd "Specimen"	25·00	
		db. Perf 12	11·00	9·00
		dc. Perf 11	11·00	10·00
		dca. Surch double	£200	£170
236*e*		10d. violet, P 11 × 12 (1897)	12·00	6·50
		eas. Optd "Specimen"	25·00	
		eb. Perf 12 × 11½	12·00	6·50
		ec. Perf 12	15·00	7·50
		ed. Perf 11	22·00	9·00
237	**38**	1s. black, P 10	65·00	3·50
		a. Perf 11 (12.85)	£200	10·00
		b. Perf 10 × 12	—	£250
		c. Perf 10 × 13		
		ca. Perf 13 × 10	£200	22·00
		d. Perf 11 × 12, comb (1.84)	65·00	3·50

41

42

1885–86. W **41** (sideways).

		(i) Optd "POSTAGE", *in black.*		
238	**42**	5s. lilac and green, P 13 (15.10.85)		
		a. Perf 10		
		b. Perf 12 × 10	£425	90·
239		10s. lilac and claret, P 13 (17.5.86)		
		a. Perf 12	£850	£2
240		£1 lilac and claret, P 13 (17.5.86)	—	£30
		a. Perf 12	£3250	
		(ii) Overprinted in blue.		
241	**42**	10s. mauve and claret, P 10	£750	£2
		as. Optd "Specimen"	60·00	
		b. Perf 12	£225	65·
		c. Perf 12 × 11		
242		£1 rose-lilac and claret, P 12 × 10	£3250	£18

1886–87. W **41**.

243	**26**	1d. scarlet, P 10 (12.86)	16·00	5·
		a. Perf 11 × 12, comb	5·50	2·
244	**28**	2d. deep blue, P 10 (12.87)	48·00	7·
		a. Perf 11 × 12, comb	15·00	2·
		b. Imperf		

45 View of Sydney

46 Emu

47 Captain Cook

48 Queen Victoria and Arms of Colony

49 Superb Lyrebird

50 Eastern Grey Kangaroo

51 Map of Australia

52 Capt. Arthur Phillip, first Governor and Lord Carrington, Governor in 1888

(Des M. Tannenberg (1d., 6d.), Miss Devine (2d., 8d.), H. Barraclough (4d.), Govt Ptg Office (1s.), C. Turner (5s.), Mrs. F. Stoddard (20s.). Eng W. Bell).

888 (1 May)–**89**. *Centenary of New South Wales.*

(a) W **40**. P 11 × 12.

53	**45**	1d. lilac (9.7.88)	4·50	65
		a. Perf 12 × 11½	18·00	90
		b. Perf 12	6·50	30
		c. Imperf (pair)		
		d. Mauve	5·00	30
		da. Imperf between (pair)		
		db. Perf 12 × 11½	7·50	50
		dc. Perf 12	7·50	50
54	**46**	2d. Prussian blue (1.9.88)	8·00	30
		a. Imperf (pair)	£120	
		b. Imperf between (pair)	£450	
		c. Perf 12 × 11½	12·00	30
		d. Perf 12	11·00	30
		e. Chalky blue	7·50	30
		ea. Perf 12 × 11½		
		eb. Perf 12	10·00	50
55	**47**	4d. purple-brown (8.10.88)	12·00	3·25
		a. Perf 12 × 11½	35·00	7·50
		b. Perf 12	28·00	3·25
		c. Perf 11	£300	95·00
		d. Red-brown	10·00	3·25
		da. Perf 12 × 11½	13·00	2·75
		db. Perf 12	13·00	2·75
		e. Orange-brown, P 12 × 11½	17·00	3·25
		f. Yellow-brown, P 12 × 11½	15·00	3·50
56	**48**	6d. carmine (26.11.88)	22·00	3·50
		a. Perf 12 × 11½	26·00	4·00
		b. Perf 12	22·00	8·50
57	**49**	8d. lilac-rose (17.1.89)	19·00	3·75
		a. Perf 12 × 11½	42·00	12·00
		b. Perf 12	19·00	4·00
		c. Magenta	75·00	10·00
		ca. Perf 12 × 11½	19·00	4·00
		cb. Perf 12	19·00	4·25
58	**50**	1s. maroon (21.2.89)	25·00	1·50
		a. Perf 12 × 11½	27·00	1·50
		b. Perf 12	29·00	1·50
		c. Violet-brown	25·00	1·75
		ca. Imperf (pair)	£600	
		cb. Perf 12 × 11½	48·00	2·25
		cc. Perf 12	48·00	1·75
3s/8s Optd "Specimen" *Set of* 6			£160	

(b) W **41**. P 11 × 12.

9	**45**	1d. lilac (1888)	19·00	
		a. Mauve	17·00	2·00
0	**46**	2d. Prussian blue (1888)	60·00	3·00

(c) W **25** (sideways on 5s.) P 10.

1	**51**	5s. deep purple (13.3.89)	£190	48·00
		a. Deep violet	£190	48·00
2	**52**	20s. cobalt-blue (27.4.88)	£250	£120

Nos. 255c and 261/2 are line perforated, the remainder are comb.

A postal forgery exists of the 2d. on unwatermarked paper and rforated 11.

53

54

90. W **53** (5s.) or **54** (20s.). P 10.

3	**51**	5s. lilac	£150	29·00
		a. Perf 11	£200	42·00
		ab. Imperf between (horiz pair)		
		b. Perf 12	£300	48·00
		c. Perf 10 × 11 or 11 × 10	£190	29·00
		d. Mauve	£190	29·00
		da. Perf 11	£190	42·00
4	**52**	20s. cobalt-blue	£325	£130
		a. Perf 11	£275	75·00
		b. Perf 11 × 10		
		c. Ultramarine, P 11	£225	75·00
		ca. Perf 12	£250	£130
		cb. Perf 11 × 12 or 12 × 11	£180	75·00
s/4s Optd "Specimen" *Set of* 2			£180	

55 Allegorical figure of Australia

Halfpenny
(56)

SEVEN-PENCE
HALFPENNY
(57)

1890 (22 Dec). W **40**.

265	**55**	2½d. ultramarine, P 11 × 12 comb	4·00	50
		as. Optd "Specimen"	25·00	
		b. Perf 12 × 11½, comb	45·00	
		c. Perf 12, comb	8·00	50

1891 (5 Jan). *Surch as T* **56** *and* **57**. W **40**.

266	**26**	½d.on 1d. grey, P 11 × 12 *comb*	3·00	4·00
		a. Surch omitted		
		b. Surch double	£275	
267	**37**	7½d.on 6d. brown, P 10	5·50	3·50
		a. Perf 11	5·00	3·00
		b. Perf 12	6·50	3·50
		c. Perf 11 × 12 or 12 × 11	5·50	3·50
		d. Perf 10 × 12	6·00	3·50
268	**38**	12½d.on 1s. red, P 10	12·00	11·00
		a. "HALFPENCE" omitted		
		b. Perf 11	13·00	11·00
		c. Perf 11 × 12, comb	12·00	10·00
		d. Perf 12 × 11½, comb	11·00	10·00
		e. Perf 12, comb	15·00	10·00
266/8s Optd "Specimen" *Set of* 3			70·00	

1891 (1 July). Wmk "10" as W **35**. P 10.

269	**16**	3d. green	12·00	80·00
270		3d. dark green	5·00	17·00

58

Type I. Narrow "H" in "HALF"

1892 (21 Mar)–**99**. *Type I.* W **40**.

271	**58**	½d. grey, P 10	25·00	1·50
		a. Perf 11	70·00	6·00
		b. Perf 10 × 12 or 12 × 10	65·00	8·50
		c. Perf 11 × 12	2·25	20
		cs. Optd "Specimen"	20·00	
		d. Perf 12	2·50	20
272		½d. slate, P 11 × 12 (1897)	2·25	20
		a. Perf 12 × 11½	2·25	20
		b. Perf 12	2·50	20
		c. Imperf between (horiz pair). Perf 11 × 12	£500	
273		½d. bluish green, P 11 × 12 (1.99)	3·25	20
		a. Perf 12 × 11½	2·00	20
		b. Perf 12	3·25	20

The perforations 11 × 12, 12 × 11½, 12, are from comb machines.

The die for Type **58** was constructed from an electro taken from the die of the De La Rue 1d., Type **26**, with "ONE" replaced by "HALF" and two "½" plugs added to the bottom corners. These alterations proved to be less hard-wearing than the remainder of the die and defects were visible by the 1905 plate of No. 333. It seems likely that repairs were undertaken before printing from the next plate in late 1907 which produced stamps as Type II.

59

1894–1904. *Optd* "POSTAGE" *in blue.* W **59** (sideways).

274	**42**	10s. mauve and claret, P 10	£325	£140
275		10s. violet and claret, P 12	£170	48·00
		a. Perf 11	£300	90·00
		b. Perf 12 × 11	£200	60·00
276		10s. violet and aniline crimson, P 12 × 11	£200	55·00
		a. Chalk-surfaced paper (1903)		
		b. Perf 12	£300	85·00
277		10s. violet and rosine (*chalk-surfaced paper*), P 12 (1904)	£200	80·00
		a. Perf 11	£225	85·00
		b. Perf 12 × 11	£200	50·00
278		10s. violet and claret (*chalk-surfaced paper*), P 12 × 11 (1904)	£250	90·00
279		£1 violet and claret, P 12 × 11		

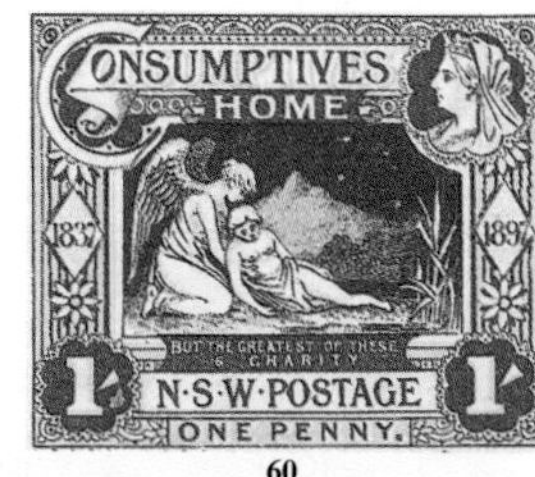

60

61

(Des C. Turner. Litho Govt Printing Office, Sydney)

1897. *Diamond Jubilee and Hospital Charity. T* **60/1**. W **40**. P 12 × 11 (1d.) or 11 (2½d.).

280	**60**	1d.(1s.) green and brown (22.6)	40·00	40·00
281	**61**	2½d. (2s.6d.),gold, carmine & blue (28.6)	£170	£170
280s/1s Optd "Specimen" *Set of* 2			£200	

These stamps, sold at 1s. and 2s.6d. respectively, paid postage of 1d. and 2½d. only, the difference being given to a Consumptives' Home.

62

63

64

Dies of the 1d.

Die I

Die II

1d. Die I. The first pearl on the crown on the left side is merged into the arch, the shading under the fleur-de-lis is indistinct, the "S" of "WALES" is open.

Die II. The first pearl is circular, the vertical shading under the fleur-de-lis clear, the "S" of "WALES" not so open.

Dies of the 2½d.

Die I

Die II

2½d. Die I. There are 12 radiating lines in the star on the Queen's breast.

Die II. There are 16 radiating lines in the star and the eye is nearly full of colour.

(Des D. Souter (2d., 2½d.). Eng W. Amor)

1897 (22 June)–**99**. W **40** (sideways on 2½d.). P 12 × 11 (2½d.) or 11 × 12 (others)

288	**62**	1d. carmine (Die I)	2·25	10
		a. Perf 12 × 11½	2·50	10
		s. Optd "Specimen"	20·00	
289		1d. scarlet (Die I)	2·50	10
		a. Perf 12 × 11½	4·75	40
		b. Perf 12	4·75	50
		ba. Imperf horiz (vert pair)	£275	
290		1d. rose-carmine (Die II) (10.97)	2·25	10
		a. Perf 12 × 11½	2·00	10
		b. Perf 12	2·00	10
		c. Imperf between (pair)	£450	
291		1d. salmon-red (Die II) (P 12 × 11½)	2·00	10
		a. Perf 12	4·00	40
292	**63**	2d. deep dull blue	3·75	20
		a. Perf 12 × 11½	3·75	20
		b. Perf 12	6·00	20
		s. Optd "Specimen"	20·00	
293		2d. cobalt-blue	5·00	20
		a. Perf 12 × 11½	3·50	20
		b. Perf 12	5·00	20
294		2d. ultramarine (1.12.97)	3·75	10
		a. Perf 12 × 11½	2·75	10
		b. Perf 12	2·75	10
		c. Imperf between (pair)		
		s. Optd "Specimen"	22·00	
295	**64**	2½d. purple (Die I)	10·00	1·75
		a. Perf 11½ × 12	12·00	1·25
		b. Perf 11	12·00	2·75
		s. Optd "Specimen"	20·00	
296		2½d. deep violet (Die II) (11.97)	9·00	1·25
		a. Perf 11½ × 12	12·00	1·25
		b. Perf 12	8·00	1·25
297		2½d. Prussian blue (17.1.99)	8·00	1·75
		a. Perf 11½ × 12	4·25	1·75
		b. Perf 12	3·50	1·75

The perforations 11 × 12, 12 × 11½ and 12 are from comb machines, the perforation 11 is from a single-line machine.

1897. *Reissue of T* **24**. W **25**. P 11.

297*c*		5s. reddish purple (*shades*)	48·00	13·00
		ca. Imperf between (horiz pair)	£5000	
		d. Perf 12	65·00	22·00
		e. Perf 11 × 12 or 12 × 11	50·00	19·00

1898–99. W **40**. P 11 × 12.

No.	Type	Description	Unused	Used
297*f*	**48**	6d. emerald-green	32·00	11·00
		fa. Perf 12 × 11½	25·00	9·00
		fb. Perf 12	23·00	9·00
		fs. Optd "Specimen"	22·00	
297*g*		6d. orange-yellow (1899)	16·00	4·50
		ga. Perf 12 × 11½	15·00	4·00
		gb. Perf 12	25·00	6·00
		gc. Yellow, P 12 × 11½	16·00	2·75

1899 (Oct). *Chalk-surfaced paper.* W **40** (sideways on 2½d.). P 12 × 11½ or 11½ × 12 (2½d.), comb.

No.	Type	Description	Unused	Used
298	**58**	½d. blue-green (Type I)	1·00	40
		a. Imperf (pair)	85·00	£100
299	**62**	1d. carmine (Die II)	2·25	10
		a. Imperf horiz (vert pair)	£375	
		b. Perf 11		
300		1d. scarlet (Die II)	1·25	10
301		1d. salmon-red (Die II)	2·75	10
		a. Imperf (pair)	95·00	£110
302	**63**	2d. cobalt-blue	2·50	20
		a. Imperf (pair)	95·00	
		b. Imperf horiz (vert pair)	£550	
303	**64**	2½d. Prussian blue (Die II)	3·50	70
		a. Imperf (pair)	£120	
303*b*	**47**	4d. red-brown	13·00	5·00
		c. Imperf (pair)	£300	
304		4d. orange-brown	10·00	4·50
305	**48**	6d. deep orange	12·00	2·50
		a. Imperf (pair)	£225	
306		6d. orange-yellow	11·00	2·50
307		6d. emerald-green	75·00	22·00
		a. Imperf (pair)	£275	
308	**49**	8d. magenta	21·00	3·50
309	**34**	9d.on 10d. dull brown	8·00	7·00
		a. Surcharge double	£120	£140
		b. Without surcharge	£130	
310		10d. violet	14·00	6·00
311	**50**	1s. maroon	24·00	1·75
312		1s. purple-brown	24·00	2·25
		a. Imperf (pair)	£275	

65 The spacing between the Crown and "NSW" is 1 mm in T **65** as against 2 mm in T **40**

66 Superb Lyrebird

67

1902–03. *Chalk-surfaced paper.* W **65** (sideways on 2½d.). P 12 × 11½ or 11½ × 12 (2½d.), comb

No.	Type	Description	Unused	Used
313	**58**	½d. blue-green (Type I)	4·25	40
		a. Perf 12 × 11	4·25	
314	**62**	1d. carmine (Die II)	2·50	20
		a. Perf 11	†	—
315	**63**	2d. cobalt-blue	3·25	30
		a. Perf 11	†	—
316	**64**	2½d. dark blue (Die II)	6·00	20
317	**47**	4d. orange-brown	30·00	8·00
318	**48**	6d. yellow-orange	18·00	2·50
319		6d. orange	18·00	2·50
320		6d. orange-buff	25·00	2·50
321	**49**	8d. magenta	21·00	3·50
322	**34**	9d.on 10d. brownish orange	9·50	3·75
323		10d. violet	18·00	6·00
324	**50**	1s. maroon	30·00	1·00
325		1s. purple-brown	32·00	1·00
326	**66**	2s.6d. green (1903)	42·00	18·00
		s. Optd "Specimen"	38·00	

1903–08. W **65**.

No.	Type	Description	Unused	Used
327	**16**	3d. yellow-green, P 11	9·00	90
		b. Perf 12	8·00	90
		ba. Imperf between (horiz pair)		
		c. Perf 11 × 12 or 12 × 11	8·00	90
328		3d. dull green, P 12	25·00	2·50
		a. Perf 11 × 12 or 12 × 11	10·00	1·50
		b. Perf 11		
329	**11**	5d. dark blue-green, P 11 × 12 or 12 × 11	8·00	1·25
		a. Wmk sideways	22·00	6·50
		b. Perf 11	18·00	1·25
		ba. Wmk sideways		
		c. Perf 12	27·00	3·75
		ca. Wmk sideways	40·00	13·00
		d. Imperf (pair)	£160	

(Typo Victoria Govt Printer, Melbourne)

1903 (18 July). Wmk double-lined V over Crown. W w **10**.

No.	Type	Description	Unused	Used
330	**67**	9d. brown & ultram, P 12¼ × 12½, *comb*	14·00	3·00
		s. Optd "Specimen"	29·00	
331		9d. brown & dp blue, P 12¼ × 12½, *comb*	14·00	3·00
332		9d. brown and blue, P 11	£650	£350

Type II. Broad "H" in "HALF"

68

1905 (1 Oct)–**10**. W **68** (sideways on 2½d.). Chalk-surfaced paper. P 12 × 11½ or 11½ × 12 (2½d.) comb, unless otherwise stated.

No.	Type	Description	Unused	Used
333	**58**	½d. blue-green (Type I)	2·75	20
		a. Perf 11½ × 11		
		b. Type II (1908)	2·50	20
		ba. Perf 11½ × 11	2·50	
334	**62**	1d. rose-carmine (Die II)	2·00	10
		a. Double impression	£250	
		b. Perf 11½ × 11	2·25	
335	**63**	2d. deep ultramarine	2·00	10
		b. Perf 11½ × 11	2·25	
336		2d. milky blue (1910)	2·00	10
		da. Perf 11	50·00	
		db. Perf 11½ × 11		
337	**64**	2½d. Prussian blue (Die II)	4·00	2·00
338	**47**	4d. orange-brown	10·00	3·50
339		4d. red-brown	12·00	3·50
340	**48**	6d. dull yellow	13·00	2·25
		a. Perf 11½ × 11	22·00	
341		6d. orange-yellow	13·00	2·25
		a. Perf 11 × 11½	28·00	
342		6d. deep orange	12·00	2·25
		a. Perf 11	£225	
343		6d. orange-buff	12·00	2·25
		a. Perf 11½ × 11	22·00	3·25
344	**49**	8d. magenta	22·00	4·50
345		8d. lilac-rose	22·00	5·00
346	**34**	10d. violet	14·00	4·50
		a. Perf 11½ × 11	13·00	4·00
		b. Perf 11	13·00	4·00
347	**50**	1s. maroon	24·00	1·75
348		1s. purple-brown (1908)	27·00	1·75
349	**66**	2s.6d. blue-green	48·00	20·00
		a. Perf 11½ × 11	32·00	18·00
		b. Perf 11	32·00	22·00

69

1905 (Dec). W **69**. *Chalk-surfaced paper.* P 11.

No.	Type	Description	Unused	Used
350	**52**	20s. cobalt-blue	£180	65·00
		a. Perf 12	£225	75·00
		b. Perf 11 × 12 or 12 × 11	£160	60·00

(Typo Victoria Govt Printer, Melbourne)

1906 (Sept). Wmk double-lined "A" and Crown, W w **11**. P 12 × 12½ comb.

No.	Type	Description	Unused	Used
351	**67**	9d. brown and ultramarine	9·50	1·75
		a. Perf 11	65·00	42·00
352		9d. yellow-brown and ultramarine	9·50	1·75

1907 (July). W w **11** (sideways on 2½d.). P 12 × 11½ or 11½ × 12 (2½d.), comb, unless otherwise stated

No.	Type	Description	Unused	Used
353	**58**	½d. blue-green (Type I)	4·25	1·50
354	**62**	1d. dull rose (Die II)	7·00	1·00
355	**63**	2d. cobalt-blue	7·00	1·00
356	**64**	2½d. Prussian blue (Die II)	45·00	80·00
357	**47**	4d. orange-brown	13·00	12·00
358	**48**	6d. orange-buff	30·00	16·00
359		6d. dull yellow	29·00	16·00
360	**49**	8d. magenta	19·00	16·00
361	**34**	10d. violet, P 11	24·00	38·00
362	**50**	1s. purple-brown	35·00	8·00
		a. Perf 11		
363	**66**	2s.6d. blue-green	50·00	30·00

STAMP BOOKLETS.

There are very few surviving examples of Nos. SB1/4. Listings are provided for those believed to have been issued with prices quoted for those known to still exist.

1904 (May)–**19**. *Black on red cover with map of Australia on front and picture of one of six different State G.P.O.'s on back. Stapled.*

SB1 £1 booklet containing two hundred and forty 1d. in four blocks of 30 and two blocks of 60
- a. Red on pink cover (1909)
- b. Blue on pink cover

1904 (May). *Black on grey cover as No. SB1. Stapled.*

SB2 £1 booklet containing one hundred and twenty 2d. in four blocks of 30

1910 (May). *Black on cream cover inscribed* "COMMONWEALTH OF AUSTRALIA/POSTMASTER-GENERAL'S DEPARTMENT". *Stapled.*

SB3 2s. booklet containing eleven ½d. (No. 333), either in block of 6 plus block of 5 or block of 11, and eighteen 1d. (No.334), either in three blocks of 6 or block of 6 plus block of 12 . . . £3000

Unsold stock of No. SB3 was uprated with one additional ½d. in May 1911.

1911 (Aug). *Red on pink cover as No. SB3. Stapled.*

SB4 2s. booklet containing twelve ½d. (No. 333), either in two blocks of 6 or block of 12, and eighteen 1d. (No. 334) either in three blocks of 6 or 1 block of 6 plus block of 12 . . . £2500

OFFICIAL STAMPS

O S (O 1) **O S** (O 2) **O S** (O 3)

The space between the letters is normally 7 mm as illustrated, except on the 5d. and 8d. (11–11½ mm), 5s. (12 mm) and 20s. (14 mm). Later printings of the 3d., W **40**, are 5½ mm, and these are listed. Varieties in the settings are known on the 1d. (8 and 8½ mm), 2d. (8½ mm) and 3d. (9 mm).

Varieties of Type O 1 exist with "O" sideways.

Nos. O1/35 *overprinted with Type* O **1**

1879. Wmk double-lined "**6**". P 13.

No.	Type	Description	Unused	Used
O1	**16**	3d. dull green	—	£47

1879 (Oct)–**85**. W **36**. P 13.

No.	Type	Description	Unused	Used
O 2	**26**	1d. salmon	16·00	2·5
		a. Perf 10 (5.81)	£180	30·0
		b. Perf 13 × 10 (1881)	30·00	4·0
O 3	**28**	2d. blue	20·00	2·0
		a. Perf 10 (7.81)	£225	32·0
		b. Perf 10 × 13 (1881)	50·00	24·0
		ba. Perf 13 × 10	29·00	3·0
		d. Perf 11 × 12 (11.84?)	—	£22
O 4	**16**	3d. dull green (R.) (12.79)	£475	£27
O 5		3d. dull green (3.80)	£250	55·0
		a. Perf 10 (1881)	£150	50·0
		b. Yellow-green. Perf 10 (10.81)	£150	27·0
		ba. Perf 13 × 10 (1881)	£150	27·0
		bb. Perf 12 (4.85)	£200	50·0
		be. Perf 10 × 12 or 12 × 10 (4.85)	£200	50·0
O 6	**32**	4d. red-brown	£170	8·0
		a. Perf 10 (1881)	—	£22
		b. Perf 10 × 13 (1881)	£225	90·0
		ba. Perf 13 × 10	£160	12·0
O 7	**11**	5d. green, P 10 (8.84)	18·00	16·0
O 8	**37**	6d. pale lilac	£225	7·0
		a. Perf 10 (1881)	£350	42·0
		b. Perf 13 × 10 (1881)	£170	42·0
O 9	**13**	8d. yellow (R.) (12.79)	—	£22
O10		8d. yellow (1880)	—	23·0
		a. Perf 10 (1881)	£300	75·0
O11	**34**	9d.on 10d. brown, P 10 (30.5.80)	£475	
		s. Optd "Specimen"	60·00	
O12	**38**	1s. black (R.)	£250	9·0
		a. Perf 10 (1881)	—	18·0
		b. Perf 10 × 13 (1881)	—	28·0
		ba. Perf 13 × 10	—	11·0

Other stamps are known with red overprint but their status is in doubt.

1880–88. W **25**.

No.	Type	Description	Unused	Used
		(a) P 13.		
O13	**24**	5s. deep purple (15.2.80)	£475	95·0
		a. Royal purple	—	£30
		b. Deep rose-lilac	£475	95·0
		(b) P 10.		
O14	**24**	5s. deep purple (9.82)	£475	£17
		a. Opt double	£2500	£15
		b. Rose-lilac (1883)	£350	£1
		(c) P 10 × 12.		
O15	**24**	5s. purple (10.86)		
		(d) P 12 × 10.		
O16	**24**	5s. reddish purple (1886)	£450	£1
		(e) P 12.		
O17	**24**	5s. purple	†	£5
		(f) P 11.		
O18	**24**	5s. rose-lilac (1888)	£200	85·

1880 (31 May). W **35**. P 13.

No.	Type	Description	Unused	Used
O18*a*	**34**	10d. lilac	£170	£1
		ab. Perf 10 and 11, compound	£250	£2
		ac. Perf 10	£250	
		aca. Opt double, one albino		
		as. Optd "Specimen"	60·00	

1882–85. W **40**. P 10.

No.	Type	Description	Unused	Used
O19	**26**	1d. salmon	17·00	2·
		a. Perf 13 × 10	—	£1
O20		1d. orange *to* scarlet	10·00	1·
		a. Perf 10 × 13	—	£1
		b. Perf 11 × 12, comb (1.84)	8·50	1·
		c. Perf 10 × 12 or 12 × 10 (4.85)	—	£1
		d. Perf 12 × 11 (12.85)		
O21	**28**	2d. blue	9·00	1·
		a. Perf 10 × 13 or 13 × 10	£190	75
		c. Perf 11 × 12, comb (1.84)	8·00	1
		ca. Opt double	—	£2
		e. Perf 12 × 11 (12.85)		
O22	**16**	3d. yellow-green (7 *mm*)	7·50	3
		a. Wmk sideways		
		b. Perf 12 (4.85)	£120	80
		c. Perf 12 × 10 (4.85)		
		ca. Opt double	†	£4
		d. Perf 12 × 11		
O23		3d. bluish green (7 *mm*)	9·00	3
		a. Perf 12 (4.85)	£120	80
		b. Perf 12 × 10 (4.85)		
		c. Perf 10 × 11 (12.85)		
O24		3d. yellow-green (5½ *mm*)	8·50	3
		a. Wmk sideways	35·00	23
		as. Optd "Specimen"	35·00	
		b. Perf 10 × 12 or 12 × 10 (4.85)	11·00	3
		c. Perf 10 × 11 or 11 × 10 (12.85)		
O25		3d. bluish green (5½ *mm*)	7·50	4
		a. Wmk sideways		
		b. Perf 10 × 12 or 12 × 10 (4.85)	6·50	4
		c. Perf 10 × 11 or 11 × 10 (12.85)	5·00	3
O26	**32**	4d. red-brown	30·00	4
		a. Perf 11 × 12, comb (1.84)	12·00	3
		b. Perf 10 × 12 (4.85)	—	70
O27		4d. dark brown	15·00	3
		a. Perf 11 × 12, comb (1.84)	13·00	3
		b. Perf 12 (4.85)	£200	£
		c. Perf 10 × 12 (4.85)	£200	90
O28	**11**	5d. dull green	13·00	15
		a. Perf 12 × 10 (4.85)		
		s. Optd "Specimen"	35·00	
O29		5d. blue-green	14·00	17
		a. Perf 12 (4.85)	£100	
		b. Perf 10 × 11	14·00	16
		c. Perf 11	—	£

O30 **37** 6d. pale lilac . . . . . 20·00 5·50
a. Perf 11 (12.85) . . . . . 23·00 5·50
O31 6d. mauve . . . . . 20·00 6·00
a. Perf 12 (4.85) . . . . . — 45·00
b. Perf 10 × 12 or 12 × 10 (4.85) . . 20·00 5·50
d. Perf 11 × 10 (12.85) . . . . 20·00 6·00
e. Perf 11 × 12 . . . . .
ea. Perf 12 × 11 (12.85) . . . . 55·00 15·00
O32 **13** 8d. yellow . . . . . 22·00 11·00
a. Perf 12 (4.85) . . . . . £130 38·00
b. Perf 10 × 12 or 12 × 10 (4.85) . . 22·00 10·00
ba. Opt double . . . . . † —
d. Perf 11 (12.85) . . . . . 22·00 13·00
da. Opt double . . . . .
db. Opt treble . . . . . † —
O33 **38** 1s. black (R.) . . . . . 25·00 8·00
a. Perf 10 × 13 . . . . . — 55·00
b. Perf 11 × 12, comb (1.84) . . . 25·00 8·00
ba. Opt double . . . . . — £250

1886–57. W **41**. P 10.
O34 **26** 1d. scarlet . . . . . 45·00 4·50
O35 **28** 2d. deep blue . . . . .
a. Perf 11 × 12, comb . . . . .

1887–90. *Nos. 241/2 optd in black.*

(a) With Type O **1**.
O36 **42** 10s. mauve and claret, P 12 (1890) . . — £1800

(b) With Type O **2** (30 April 1889).
O37 **42** 10s. mauve and claret P 12 . . . £2000 £800
as. Optd "Specimen" . . . . 80·00
b. Perf 10 . . . . . £3500 £1800

(c) With Type O **3** (7 Jan 1887).
O38 **42** £1 mauve and claret, P 12 × 10 . . £8500 £5000

Only nine examples of No. O38 are recorded, three of which are mint. One of the used stamps, in the Royal Collection, shows overprint Type O **3** double.

1888 (17 July)–**90**. *Optd as Type* O **1**.

(a) W **40**. P 11 × 12.
O39 **45** 1d. lilac . . . . . 2·75 65
a. Perf 12 . . . . . 2·75 65
b. Mauve . . . . . 2·75 65
ba. Perf 12 . . . . . 2·75 65
O40 **46** 2d. Prussian blue (15.10.88) . . . 4·50 40
a. Perf 12 . . . . . 4·50 40
O41 **47** 4d. purple-brown (10.10.89) . . . 11·00 3·75
a. Perf 12 . . . . . 14·00 4·00
b. Perf 11 . . . . .
c. Red-brown . . . . . 11·00 3·75
ca. Opt double . . . . . † —
cb. Perf 12 . . . . . 14·00 4·00
O42 **48** 6d. carmine (16.1.89) . . . . 8·50 5·50
a. Perf 12 . . . . . 12·00 5·50
O43 **49** 8d. lilac-rose (1890) . . . . 21·00 12·00
a. Perf 12 . . . . . 27·00 15·00
O44 **50** 1s. maroon (9.1.90) . . . . 20·00 4·00
a. Perf 12 . . . . . 20·00 4·00
b. Purple-brown . . . . . 20·00 4·00
ba. Opt double . . . . .
bb. Perf 12 . . . . . 20·00 4·00
O39s/44s Optd "Specimen" *Set of* 6 . . . £200

(b) W **41**. P 11 × 12 (1889).
O45 **45** 1d. mauve . . . . .
O46 **46** 2d. blue . . . . .

(c) W **25**. P 10.
O47 **51** 5s. deep purple (R.) (9.1.90) . . . £750 £500
O48 **52** 20s. cobalt-blue (10.3.90) . . . £1900 £800

1890 (15 Feb)–**91**. *Optd as Type* O **1**. W **53** (5s.) or **54** (20s.). P 10.
O49 **51** 5s. lilac £325 £120
a. Mauve . . . . . £170 70·00
b. Dull lilac, P 12 . . . . £475 £130
O50 **52** 20s. cobalt-blue (3.91) £1900 £600
O49s/50s Optd "Specimen" *Set of* 2 . . . £200

1891 (Jan). *Optd as Type* O **1**. W **40**.

(a) On No. 265. P 11 × 12.
O54 **55** 2½d. ultramarine . . . . . 9·00 8·00

(b) On Nos. 266/8.
O55 **26** ½d.on 1d. grey, P 11 × 12 . . . 55·00 55·00
a. Opt double . . . . .
O56 **37** 7½d.on 6d. brown, P 10 . . . 35·00 40·00
O57 **38** 12½d.on 1s. red, P 11 × 12 . . . 60·00 70·00
O54s/7s Optd "Specimen" *Set of* 4 . . . £140

1892 (May). *No. 271 optd as Type* O **1**. P 10.
O58 **58** ½d. grey . . . . . 7·00 16·00
a. Perf 11 × 12 . . . . . 5·00 11·00
as. Optd "Specimen" . . . . 30·00
b. Perf 12 . . . . . 6·50 11·00
c. Perf 12 × 11½ . . . . . 15·00 13·00

Official stamps were withdrawn from the government departments on 31 December 1894.

POSTAGE DUE STAMPS

D **1**

(Dies eng by A. Collingridge. Typo Govt Printing Office, Sydney)

1891 (1 Jan)–**92**. W **40**. P 10.
D 1 **D 1** ½d. green (21.1.92) . . . . 4·00 3·50
D 2 1d. green . . . . . 9·00 1·50
a. Imperf vert (horiz pair) . . .
b. Perf 11 . . . . . 8·00 1·50
c. Perf 12 . . . . . 18·00 3·25
d. Perf 12 × 10 . . . . . 24·00 2·50
e. Perf 10 × 11 . . . . . 12·00 2·00
f. Perf 11 × 12 or 12 × 11 . . . 8·00 1·50
D 3 2d. green . . . . . 12·00 2·00
a. Perf 11 . . . . . 12·00 2·00
b. Perf 12 . . . . . — 11·00
c. Perf 12 × 10 . . . . . 22·00 3·75
d. Perf 10 × 11 . . . . . 13·00 2·25
e. Perf 11 × 12 or 12 × 11 . . . 12·00 1·75
f. Wmk sideways . . . . . 20·00 9·00
D 4 3d. green . . . . . 22·00 5·00
a. Perf 10 × 11 . . . . . 22·00 5·00
D 5 4d. green . . . . . 14·00 2·00
a. Perf 11 . . . . . 15·00 2·00
b. Perf 10 × 11 . . . . . 14·00 2·00
D 6 6d. green . . . . . 25·00 5·50
D 7 8d. green . . . . . 75·00 17·00
D 8 5s. green . . . . . £130 45·00
a. Perf 11 . . . . . £275 85·00
b. Perf 11 × 12 . . . . . — £275
D 9 10s. green (early 1891) . . . £250 65·00
a. Perf 12 × 10 . . . . . £250 £130
D10 20s. green (early 1891) . . . £400 £100
a. Perf 12 . . . . . £450
b. Perf 12 × 10 . . . . . £250 £170
D1s/10s Optd "Specimen" *Set of* 10 . . . £180

Used prices for 10s. and 20s. are for cancelled-to-order stamps. Postally used examples are rare.

1900. *Chalk-surfaced paper.* W **40**. P 11.
D11 **D 1** ½d. emerald-green . . . . .
D12 1d. emerald-green . . . . 9·50 3·25
a. Perf 12 . . . . . 24·00 7·00
b. Perf 11 × 12 or 12 × 11 . . . 9·50 2·25
D13 2d. emerald-green . . . . 12·00 3·75
a. Perf 12 . . . . . — 30·00
b. Perf 11 × 12 or 12 × 11 . . . 10·00 3·75
D14 3d. emerald-green, P 11 × 12 or 12 × 11 . . . . . 35·00 10·00
D15 4d. emerald-green (7.00) . . . 19·00 4·50

New South Wales became part of the Commonwealth of Australia on 1 January 1901.

QUEENSLAND

The area which later became Queensland was previously part of New South Wales known as the Moreton Bay District. The first post office, at Brisbane, was opened in 1834 and the use of New South Wales stamps from the District became compulsory from 1 May 1854.

Queensland was proclaimed a separate colony on 10 December 1859, but continued to use New South Wales issues until 1 November 1860.

Post Offices opened in the Moreton Bay District before 10 December 1859, and using New South Wales stamps, were

Office	*Opened*	*Numeral Cancellation*
Brisbane	1834	95
Burnett's Inn/ Goode's Inn/ Nanango	1850	108
Callandoon	1850	74
Condamine	1856	151
Dalby	1854	133
Drayton	1846	85
Gayndah	1850	86
Gladstone	1854	131
Goode's Inn	1858	108
Ipswich	1846	87
Maryborough	1849	96
Rockhampton	1858	201
Surat	1852	110
Taroom	1856	152
Toowoomba	1858	214
Warwick	1848	81

PRICES FOR STAMPS ON COVER

Nos.	1/3	*from* × 2
Nos.	4/56	*from* × 3
Nos.	57/8	—
Nos.	59/73	*from* × 4
Nos.	74/82	*from* × 2
Nos.	83/109	*from* × 3
Nos.	110/13	*from* × 2
Nos.	116/17	*from* × 3
Nos.	118/27	—
Nos.	128/50	*from* × 4
Nos.	151/65	—
Nos.	166/78	*from* × 10
Nos.	179/83	*from* × 4
Nos.	184/206	*from* × 15
No.	207	—
Nos.	208/28	*from* × 15
No.	229	*from* × 100
No.	230	—
Nos.	231/54	*from* × 15
Nos.	256/62*c*	*from* × 10
Nos.	264*a*/*b*	*from* × 2
Nos.	265/6	*from* × 20
Nos.	270/4	—
Nos.	281/5	*from* × 10
Nos.	286/308	*from* × 12
Nos.	309/13	—
Nos.	F1/37	—

PERKINS BACON "CANCELLED". For notes on these handstamps, showing "CANCELLED" between horizontal bars forming an oval, see Catalogue Introduction.

1   2 Large Star   3 Small Star

(Dies eng W. Humphrys. Recess P.B.)

1860. W **2**.

(a) Imperf.
1 **1** 1d. carmine-rose £2750 £800
2 2d. blue £6000 £1600
3 6d. green £4000 £800

(b) Clean-cut perf 14–15½.
4 **1** 1d. carmine-rose £1300 £250
5 2d. blue £500 £100
a. Imperf between (horiz pair) . . . † —
6 6d. green (15 Nov) . . . . . £550 65·00

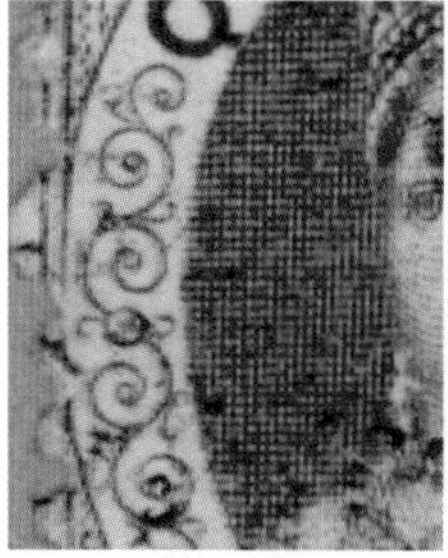

3d. re-entry

3d. retouch (R.2/8)

The 3d. re-entry which occurs on one stamp in the second row, shows doubling of the left-hand arabesque and the retouch has redrawn spandrel dots under "EN" of "PENCE", a single dot in the centre of the circle under "E" and the bottom outer frame line closer to the spandrel's frame line.

1860–61. W 3.

(a) Clean-cut perf 14–15½.
7 **1** 2d. blue £500 £100
a. Imperf between (horiz pair) . . . † £1400
8 3d. brown (15.4.61) . . . . £300 65·00
a. Re-entry . . . . . — £225
b. Retouch . . . . . — £225
9 6d. green . . . . . £600 65·00
10 1s. violet (15.11.60) (H/S "CANCELLED" in oval £6000) . . £550 85·00
11 "REGISTERED" (6d.) olive-yellow (1.61) (H/S "CANCELLED" in oval £6000) . . . . £375 80·00
a. Imperf between (pair) . . . £3250

(b) Clean-cut perf 14 at Somerset House (7.61).
12 **1** 1d. carmine-rose (H/S "CANCELLED" in oval £5000) . . . . £130 42·00
13 2d. blue (H/S "CANCELLED" in oval £5000) . . . . . £350 55·00

(c) Rough perf 14–15½ (9.61).
14 **1** 1d. carmine-rose . . . . . 75·00 32·00
15 2d. blue . . . . . £120 28·00
a. Imperf between (horiz pair) . . . £2250
16 3d. brown . . . . . 50·00 32·00
a. Imperf vert (horiz pair) . . . £2250
b. Re-entry £225 £120
c. Retouch (R. 2/8) . . . . — £120
17 6d. deep green (H/S "CANCELLED" in oval £6000) . . . . £150 27·00
18 6d. yellow-green . . . . . £250 27·00
19 1s. violet . . . . . £400 80·00
20 "REGISTERED" (6d.) orange-yellow 65·00 38·00

The perforation of No. 8 is that known as "intermediate between clean-cut and rough", No. 20 can also be found with a similar perforation.

Line through design

(Printed and perforated by Thomas Ham, Brisbane)

1862–67. *Thick toned paper.* No wmk.

(a) P 13 rough perforations (1862–63).
21 **1** 1d. Indian red (16.12.62) . . . £300 60·00
22 1d. orange-vermilion (2.63) . . . 70·00 12·00
a. Imperf (pair) . . . . . — £800
b. Imperf between (horiz pair) . . . † —
23 2d. pale blue (16.12.62) . . . 95·00 27·00
24 2d. blue . . . . . 50·00 9·00
a. Imperf (pair) . . . . . — £800
b. Imperf between (horiz pair) . . . † £1300
c. Imperf between (vert pair) . . . £2000
25 3d. brown . . . . . 70·00 32·00
a. Re-entry . . . . . — £120
b. Retouch (R. 2/8) . . . . — £120
26 6d. apple green (17.4.63) . . . £110 15·00
a. Line through design at right . . . — 75·00
b. Line through design at left . . . — 75·00

No.	Type	Description	Unused	Used
27		6d. yellow-green	£100	12·00
		a. Imperf between (horiz pair)	†	£1500
		b. Line through design at right	—	65·00
		c. Line through design at left	—	65·00
28		6d. pale bluish green	£160	28·00
		a. Imperf (pair)	—	£850
		b. Line through design at right	—	£120
		c. Line through design at left	—	£120
29		1s. grey (14.7.63)	£170	22·00
		a. Imperf between (horiz pair)	†	£1600
		b. Imperf between (vert pair)	†	—
		s. Handstamped "Specimen"	40·00	

The top or bottom row of perforations was sometimes omitted from the sheet, resulting in stamps perforated on three sides only.

Prior to the plates being printed from in Brisbane, damage occurred to the 6d. plate in the form of a scratch across two adjoining stamps. The position of the pair in the plate is not yet recorded. One joined pair is known.

This flaw was not corrected until around 1869 when, after plate cleaning, only faint traces remain. These are hard to see.

(b) P 12½ × 13 rough (1863–67).

No.	Type	Description	Unused	Used
30	1	1d. orange-vermilion	70·00	27·00
31		2d. blue	60·00	20·00
32		3d. brown	75·00	25·00
		a. Re-entry	—	£110
		b. Retouch (R. 2/8)	—	£110
33		6d. apple green	£110	35·00
		a. Line through design at right	—	£150
		b. Line through design at left	—	£150
34		6d. yellow-green	£110	35·00
		a. Line through design at right	—	£150
		b. Line through design at left	—	£150
35		6d. pale bluish green		
		a. Line through design at right		
		b. Line through design at left		
36		1s. grey	£225	38·00
		a. Imperf between (horiz pair)		

This paper was used again for a very limited printing in 1867 which can be properly regarded as the First Government Printing. The perforations were now clean-cut. The designs and the background to the head are very well defined, the plates having been cleaned when transferred to the Government Printing Office.

(c) P 13 Clean-cut (1867).

No.	Description	Unused	Used
37	1d. orange-vermilion	70·00	20·00
38	2d. blue	50·00	9·00
40	6d. apple green	£120	15·00
41	6d. yellow-green	£120	18·00
42	6d. deep green		

Previously listed and then removed, the significance of this issue has been reassessed and it is now re-listed under this paper.

Copies of the 3d. and 1s. have been identified with these characteristics but there are no records of them being printed at this time.

1864–65. W 3.

(a) P 13.

No.	Type	Description	Unused	Used
44	1	1d. orange-vermilion (1.65)	65·00	24·00
		a. Imperf between (horiz pair)	£650	
45		2d. pale blue (1.65)	65·00	16·00
46		2d. deep blue	65·00	16·00
		a. Imperf between (vert pair)	£1300	
		b. Bisected (1d.) (on cover)	†	£2500
47		6d. yellow-green (1.65)	£120	22·00
		a. Line through design at right	—	£100
		b. Line through design at left	—	£100
48		6d. deep green	£140	22·00
		a. Line through design at right	—	£100
		b. Line through design at left	—	£100
49		"REGISTERED" (6d.) orge-yell (21.6.64)	85·00	35·00
		a. Double printed	£900	
		b. Imperf		

(b) P 12½ × 13.

No.	Type	Description	Unused	Used
50	1	1d. orange-vermilion	95·00	48·00
50*a*		2d. deep blue	£120	48·00

The "REGISTERED" stamp was reprinted in 1895. See note below No. 82.

1866 (24 Jan). Wmk "QUEENSLAND/POSTAGE—POSTAGE/STAMPS—STAMPS" in three lines in script capitals with double wavy lines above and below the wmk and single wavy lines with projecting sprays between each line of words. There are ornaments ("fleurons") between "POSTAGE" "POSTAGE" and between "STAMPS" "STAMPS". Single stamps only show a portion of one or two letters of this wmk.

(a) P 13.

No.	Type	Description	Unused	Used
51	1	1d. orange-vermilion	£140	27·00
52		2d. blue	55·00	17·00

(b) P 12½ × 13.

No.	Type	Description	Unused	Used
52*a*	1	1d. orange-vermilion	£170	48·00
52*b*		2d. blue	£170	48·00

1866. *Lithographed on thick paper. No wmk.* P 13.

The 4d. was lithographed from two separate transfers from the 3d. plate and the 5s. was taken from the 1s. plate.

First transfer

Double transfer

First Transfer (Sept 1866) "FOUR" in taller thin letters.

No.	Description	Unused	Used
53	4d. reddish lilac (*shades*)	£180	20·00
	a. Re-entry	—	£100
	b. Double transfer	—	£100
54	4d. grey-lilac (*shades*)	£180	20·00
	a. Re-entry	—	£100
	b. Double transfer	—	£100

Second transfer

Second Transfer (Feb 1867) "FOUR" in shorter letters.

No.	Description	Unused	Used
55	4d. lilac (*shades*)	£150	18·00
	a. Retouch (R. 2/8)	—	90·00
	b. "FOUR" missing	—	£225
56	4d. grey-lilac (*shades*)	£150	18·00
	a. Retouch (R. 2/8)	—	90·00
	b. "FOUR" missing	—	£225
	s. Handstamped "Specimen"	45·00	
57	5s. bright rose	£400	£100
58	5s. pale rose	£325	75·00
	a. Imperf between (vert pair)	†	£1500
	s. Handstamped "Specimen"	55·00	

The alterations in values were made by hand on the stones and there are minor varieties in the shape and position of the letters.

4

2d. Pl II. Dot by "U"

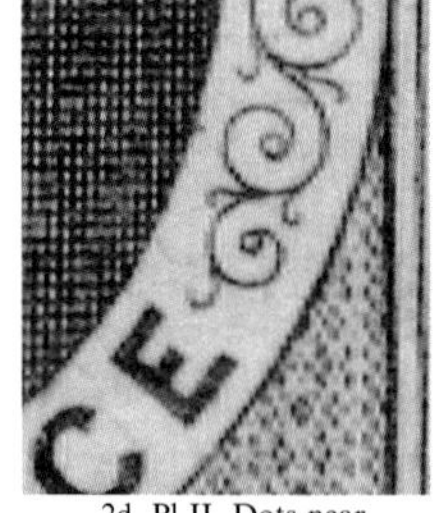

2d. Pl II. Dots near arabesque

1868–74. *Wmk small truncated Star,* W **4** *on each stamp, and the word "QUEENSLAND" in single-lined Roman capitals four times in each sheet. A second plate of the 2d. denomination was sent by Perkins, Bacon to the Colony in 1872 and it was first printed from in August of that year. The new plate is helpful in separating many of the 2d. printings up to 1879.*

No.	Type	Description	Unused	Used
59	1	1d. orange-vermilion (18.1.71)	45·00	4·50
60		2d. pale blue (3.4.68) (Pl I)	45·00	4·50
61		2d. blue (18.1.71) (Pl I)	40·00	2·75
62		2d. bright blue (Pl I)	50·00	2·75
63		2d. greenish blue (Pl I)	85·00	2·50
64		2d. dark blue (Pl I)	45·00	2·50
		a. Imperf		
65		3d. olive-green (27.2.71)	85·00	6·00
		a. Re-entry	—	40·00
		b. Retouch (R. 2/8)	—	40·00
66		3d. greenish grey	£100	5·50
		a. Re-entry	—	38·00
		b. Retouch (R. 2/8)	—	38·00
67		3d. brown	80·00	5·50
		a. Re-entry	—	38·00
		b. Retouch (R. 2/8)	—	38·00
68		6d. yellow-green (10.11.71)	£140	7·00
69		6d. green	£130	10·00
70		6d. deep green	£170	17·00
71		1s. greenish grey (13.11.72)	£375	40·00
72		1s. brownish grey	£375	40·00
73		1s. mauve (19.2.74)	£225	22·00
59s/73s		H/S "Specimen" *Set of 5*	£180	

(b) P 12 (about Feb 1874).

No.	Type	Description	Unused	Used
74	1	1d. orange-vermilion	£325	24·00
75		2d. blue (Pl II)	£750	42·00
76		3d. greenish grey	—	£170
		a. Re-entry		
		b. Retouch (R. 2/8)		
77		3d. brown	£450	£170
		a. Re-entry		
		b. Retouch (R. 2/8)		
78		6d. green	£1200	40·00
79		1s. mauve	£475	42·00

(c) P 13 × 12.

No.	Type	Description	Unused	Used
80	1	1d. orange-vermilion	—	£170
81		2d. blue (Pl II)	£1000	40·00
82		3d. greenish grey	—	£275

Plate II of the 2d. may be identified by a smudged dot to the left of "U" in "QUEEN" and tiny dots near the lower curl of the right arabesque.

Reprints were made in 1895 of all five values on Wmk W **4**, and perforated 13; the colours are:—1d. orange and brownish orange, 2d. deep dull blue (Pl II), 3d. brown, 6d green, 1s. red-violet and dull violet. The "Registered" was also reprinted with these on the same paper, but perforated 12. One sheet of the 2d. reprint is known to have had the perforations missing between the fourth and fifth vertical rows.

5

6

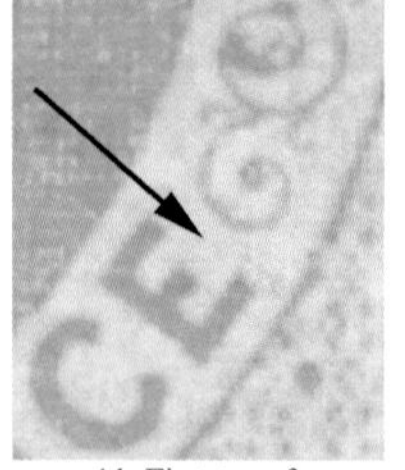

4d. First transfer

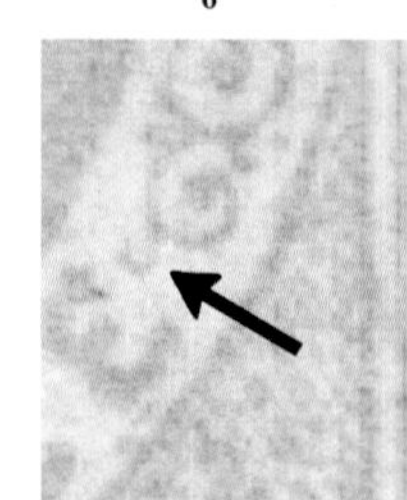

4d. Second transfer

The first transfer of the 4d. was taken from the 3d. plate, identified by the lack of the curl at the foot of the arabesque, the second was from Plate II of the 2d.

(4d., litho. Other values recess)

1868–78. Wmk Crown and Q. W **5**.

(a) P 13 (1868–75).

No.	Type	Description	Unused	Used
83	1	1d. orange-vermilion (10.11.68)	55·00	4·50
		a. Imperf (pair)	£250	
84		1d. pale rose-red (4.11.74)	55·00	8·50
85		1d. deep rose-red	95·00	9·00
86		2d. pale blue (20.11.68) (Pl I)	50·00	1·75
87		2d. deep blue (4.11.74) (Pl II)	42·00	4·50
		a. Imperf (pair)	£350	
		b. Imperf between (vert pair)	†	—
88		3d. brown (11.6.75)	75·00	12·00
		a. Re-entry	—	65·00
		b. Retouch (R. 2/8)	—	65·00
89		4d. yellow (*shades*) (1st transfer) (1.1.75)	£800	50·00
		s. Handstamped "Specimen"	65·00	
90		6d. deep green (9.4.69)	£120	9·00
91		6d. yellow-green	£100	6·50
92		6d. pale apple-green (1.1.75)	£130	9·00
		a. Imperf (pair)	£350	
93		1s. mauve	£200	40·0

(b) P 12 (1876–78).

No.	Type	Description	Unused	Used
94	1	1d. deep orange-vermilion	38·00	5·0
95		1d. pale orange-vermilion	40·00	5·0
		a. Imperf between (vert pair)	†	—
96		1d. rose-red	48·00	10·0
97		1d. flesh	65·00	10·0
98		2d. pale blue (Pl II)	85·00	15·0
99		2d. bright blue (Pl II)	32·00	1·0
100		2d. deep blue (Pl II)	35·00	1·5
101		3d. brown	65·00	9·0
		a. Re-entry	—	50·0
		b. Retouch (R. 2/8)	—	50·0
102		4d. yellow (*shades*) (1st transfer)	£650	25·0
103		4d. buff-yellow (*shades*) (2nd transfer)	£650	24·0
104		6d. deep green	£140	7·5
105		6d. green	£130	4·2
106		6d. yellow-green	£140	4·5
107		6d. apple-green	£150	7·0
108		1s. mauve	48·00	9·0
109		1s. purple	£140	5·0
		a. Imperf between (vert pair)	†	—

(c) P 13 × 12 or 12 × 13.

No.	Type	Description	Unused	Used
110	1	1d. orange-vermilion	—	£15
110*a*		1d. rose-red	—	£18
111		2d. deep blue (Pl II)	£1100	£25
112		4d. yellow	—	£30
113		6d. deep green	—	£30

(d) P 12½ × 13 (1868).

No.	Type	Description	Unused	Used
114	1	1d. orange-vermilion	—	£35
115		2d. deep blue (Pl I)	—	£35
115*a*		6d. yellow-green		

(e) P 12½ (1868).

No.	Type	Description	Unused	Used
115*b*	1	2d. deep blue (Pl I)		

Reprints of the above were made in 1895 on thicker pape Wmk. W **6**, perf 12. The colours are:—1d. vermilion-red, 2d. dee dull blue and pale ultramarine, 3d. brown, 6d. dull yellow-green an 1s. lilac-grey.

1879. No wmk. P 12.

No.	Type	Description	Unused	Used
116	1	6d. pale emerald-green	£200	26·
		a. Imperf between (horiz pair)	†	£9
117		1s. mauve (*fiscal cancel* £5)	£120	55·

No. 117 has a very indistinct lilac *burelé* band at back.

Nos. 116/17 can be found showing portions of a papermaker watermark, either T. H. Saunders & Co or A. Pirie & Sons.

1881. *Lithographed from transfers from the 1s. die.* Wmk Crown ar Q, W **6**. P 12.

No.	Type	Description	Unused	Used
118	1	2s. pale blue (6 Apr)	95·00	27·
119		2s. blue (*fiscal cancel* £4)	95·00	27·
		a. Imperf vert (horiz pair)		
120		2s. deep blue (*fiscal cancel* £4)	£110	27·
121		2s.6d. dull scarlet (28 Aug)	£150	55·
122		2s.6d. bright scarlet (*fiscal cancel* £4)	£180	55·
123		5s. pale yellow-ochre (28 Aug)	£200	85·
124		5s. yellow-ochre (*fiscal cancel* £5)	£200	85·
125		10s. reddish brown (Mar)	£425	£1
		a. Imperf	£475	
126		10s. bistre-brown	£425	£1
127		20s. rose (*fiscal cancel* £7)	£1000	£1

Of the 2s. and 20s. stamps there are five types of each, and of t other values ten types of each.

Beware of fiscally used copies that have been cleaned and provided with forged postmarks.

7

Die I

Die II

Dies I and II often occur in the same sheet.
Die I. The white horizontal inner line of the triangle in the upper right-hand corner merges into the outer white line of the oval above the "L".
Die II. The same line is short and does not touch the inner oval.

1879–80. *Typo.* P 12.

(a) Wmk Crown and Q. W **5**.

128 **7** 1d. reddish brown (Die I) (15.5.79) . . 80·00 21·00
a. Die II . . . . . £120 21·00
ab. Imperf between (horiz pair) . . . .
ac. "QOEENSLAND" £1000 £180
129 1d. orange-brown (Die I) . . . . . £120 21·00
130 2d. blue (Die I) (10.4.79) . . . . . 70·00 11·00
a. "PENGE" (R. 12/6) £650 £110
b. "QUEENSbAND" (R. 5/6) . . . . — £110
c. "QU" joined . . . . . — £110
131 4d. orange-yellow (6.6.79) . . . . . £450 48·00

(b) No wmk, with lilac *burelé* band on back.

132 **7** 1d. reddish brown (Die I) (21.10.79) . . £350 48·00
a. Die II . . . . . £375 75·00
ab. "QOEENSLAND" . . . . . — £1500
133 2d. blue (Die I) (21.10.79) . . . . . £400 26·00
a. "PENGE" (R. 12/6) £3500 £650
b. "QUEENSbAND" (R. 5/6) . . . .

(c) Wmk Crown and Q. W **6**.

134 **7** 1d. reddish brown (Die I) (31.10.79) . . 42·00 6·00
a. Imperf between (pair) . . . . . † £550
b. Die II . . . . . 55·00 6·00
ba. "QOEENSLAND" . . . . . £250 45·00
bb. Imperf between (pair) . . . . . † £550
135 1d. dull orange (Die I) . . . . . 24·00 4·00
a. Die II . . . . . 27·00 4·00
ab. "QOEENSLAND" . . . . . 75·00 22·00
136 1d. scarlet (Die I) (7.3.81) . . . . . 20·00 2·25
a. Die II . . . . . 22·00 2·75
ab. "QOEENSLAND" . . . . . 95·00 26·00
137 2d. blue (Die I) (10.4.79) . . . . . 35·00 1·50
a. "PENGE" . . . . . £140 40·00
b. "QUEENSbAND" . . . . . £140 40·00
c. Die II . . . . . 40·00 3·25
138 2d. grey-blue (Die I) . . . . . 35·00 1·25
a. "PENGE" . . . . . £140 40·00
b. "QUEENSbAND" . . . . . £140 40·00
c. Die II . . . . . 40·00 3·25
139 2d. bright blue (Die I) . . . . . 40·00 1·25
a. "PENGE" . . . . . £150 40·00
b. "QUEENSbAND" . . . . . £150 40·00
c. Imperf between (pair) £750
d. Die II . . . . . 42·00 3·25
140 2d. deep blue (Die I) . . . . . 42·00 1·00
a. "PENGE" . . . . . £160 40·00
b. "QUEENSbAND" . . . . . £160 40·00
c. Die II . . . . . 35·00 4·75
141 4d. orange-yellow . . . . . £150 10·00
a. Imperf between (pair) . . . . .
142 6d. deep green . . . . . 80·00 4·50
143 6d. yellow-green . . . . . 85·00 4·50
a. Imperf between (pair) . . . . .
144 1s. deep violet (3.80) . . . . . 75·00 5·00
145 1s. pale lilac . . . . . 65·00 6·00

The variety "QO" is No. 48 in the first arrangement, and No. 44 in a later arrangement on the sheets.

All these values have been seen imperf and unused, but we have no evidence that any of them were used in this condition.

The above were printed in sheets of 120, from plates made up of 30 groups of four electrotypes. There are four different types in each group, and two such groups of four are known of the 1d. and 2d., thus giving eight varieties of these two values. There was some resetting of the first plate of the 1d., and there are several plates of the 2d.; the value in the first plate of the latter value is in thinner letters, and in the last plate three types in each group of four have the "TW" of "TWO" joined, the letters of "PENCE" are larger and therefore much closer together, and in one type the "O" of "TWO" is oval, that letter being circular in the other types.

(8)

9

10

1880 (21 Feb). *Surch with T* **8**.

151 **7** ½d. on 1d. (No. 134) (Die I) £225 £140
a. Die II £550 £400
ab. "QOEENSLAND" £1300 £900

Examples with "Half-penny" reading downwards are forged surcharges.

£1 Re-entry (R. 1/2) £1 Retouch (R. 6/8)

(Eng H. Bourne. Recess Govt Printing Office, Brisbane, from plates made by B.W.)

1882 (13 Apr)–**95**. P 12.

(a) *W* **5** (twice sideways). *Thin paper.*

152 **9** 2s. bright blue (14.4.82) . . . . . £100 28·00
153 2s.6d. vermilion (12.7.82) . . . . . 80·00 20·00
154 5s. rose . . . . . 75·00 22·00
155 10s. brown (12.7.82) . . . . . £140 40·00
156 £1 deep green (30.5.83) £325 £130
a. Re-entry (R. 1/2) . . . . . — £225
b. Retouch (R. 6/4) . . . . . — £225
152s/6s (*ex* 2s. 6d.) H/S "Specimen" *Set of* 4 . . £160

(b) W **10**. *Thick paper* (10.11.86).

157 **9** 2s. bright blue . . . . . £120 30·00
158 2s.6d. vermilion . . . . . 42·00 22·00
159 5s. rose . . . . . 40·00 30·00
160 **9** 10s. brown . . . . . £100 45·00
161 £1 deep green . . . . . £200 60·00
a. Re-entry (R. 1/2) . . . . . — £120
b. Retouch (R. 6/4) . . . . . — £120

(c) W **6** (twice sideways). *Thin paper* (1895).

162 **9** 2s.6d. vermilion . . . . . 45·00 30·00
163 5s. rose . . . . . 50·00 20·00
164 10s. brown . . . . . £300 80·00
165 £1 deep green . . . . . £225 85·00
a. Re-entry (R. 1/2) . . . . . — £150
b. Retouch (R. 6/4) . . . . . — £150

The re-entry on the £1 shows as a double bottom frame line and the retouch occurs alongside the bottom right numeral.

See also Nos. 270/1, 272/4 and 309/12.

11

12

In T **12** the shading lines do not extend entirely across, as in T **11**, thus leaving a white line down the front of the throat and point of the bust.

4d. "PENGE" for "PENCE" (R. 8/1)

4d. "EN" joined in "PENCE" (R. 4/6)

1882 (1 Aug)–**91**. W **6**.

(a) P 12.

166 **11** 1d. pale vermilion-red (23.11.82) . . . 4·00 50
a. Double impression . . . . .
167 1d. deep vermilion-red . . . . . 4·00 50
168 2d. blue . . . . . 6·00 50
a. Imperf between (horiz pair) . . .
169 4d. pale yellow (18.4.83) . . . . . 16·00 2·25
a. "PENGE" for "PENCE" . . . . £150 45·00
b. "EN" joined in "PENCE" . . . . £100 30·00
c. Imperf (11.91) . . . . .
170 6d. green (6.11.82) . . . . . 11·00 1·50
171 1s. violet (6.2.83) . . . . . 22·00 2·75
172 1s. lilac . . . . . 11·00 2·75
173 1s. deep mauve . . . . . 11·00 2·50
174 1s. pale mauve . . . . . 12·00 2·50
a. Imperf . . . . . † —

(b) P 9½ × 12 (1884).

176 **11** 1d. pale red . . . . . £120 35·00
177 2d. blue . . . . . £375 55·00
178 1s. mauve . . . . . £200 45·00

The above were printed from plates made up of groups of four electrotypes as previously. In the 1d. the words of value are followed by a full stop. There are four types of the 4d., 6d. and 1s., eight types of the 1d., and twelve types of the 2d.

No. 169c is from a sheet used at Roma post office and comes cancelled with the "46" numeral postmark.

1887 (5 May)–**91**. W **6**.

(a) P 12.

179 **12** 1d. vermilion-red . . . . . 3·50 60
180 2d. blue . . . . . 6·50 60
a. Oval white flaw on Queen's head behind diadem (R. 12/5) . . . . . 25·00 7·50
181 2s. deep brown (12.3.89) . . . . . 70·00 38·00
182 2s. pale brown . . . . . 60·00 30·00

(b) P 9½ × 12.

183 **12** 2d. blue . . . . . £350 55·00

These are from new plates; four types of each value grouped as before. The 1d. is without stop. In all values No. 2 in each group of four has the "L" and "A" of "QUEENSLAND" joined at the foot, and No. 3 of the 2d. has "P" of word "PENCE" with a long downstroke.

The 2d. is known bisected and used as a 1d. value.

13

14

1890–94. W **6** (sideways on ½d.). P 12½, 13 (comb machine).

184 **13** ½d. pale green . . . . . 4·75 1·50
185 ½d. deep green . . . . . 4·00 1·50
186 ½d. deep blue-green . . . . . 4·00 1·50
187 **12** 1d. vermilion-red . . . . . 3·25 20
a. Imperf (pair) £140 £140
b. Oval broken by tip of bust (R. 10/3) . . . . . 26·00 5·00
c. Double impression . . . . . † £325
188 2d. blue (old plate) . . . . . 6·00 20
189 2d. pale blue (old plate) . . . . . 6·00 20
190 2d. pale blue (retouched plate) . . . 5·50 40
a. "FWO" for "TWO" (R. 8/7) . . . — 22·00
191 **14** 2½d. carmine . . . . . 12·00 1·50
192 **12** 3d. brown . . . . . 9·00 2·75
193 **11** 4d. yellow . . . . . 13·00 2·50
a. "PENGE" for "PENCE" . . . . 65·00 22·00
b. "EN" joined in "PENCE" . . . 48·00 16·00
194 4d. orange . . . . . 18·00 2·50
a. "PENGE" for "PENCE" . . . . 80·00 22·00
b. "EN" joined in "PENCE" . . . 60·00 16·00
195 4d. lemon . . . . . 20·00 2·50
a. "PENGE" for "PENCE" . . . . 90·00 28·00
b. "EN" joined in "PENCE" . . . 70·00 20·00
196 6d. green . . . . . 10·00 1·50
197 **12** 2s. red-brown . . . . . 40·00 18·00
198 2s. pale brown . . . . . 48·00 20·00

This issue is perforated by a new vertical comb machine, gauging about 12¾ × 12¾. The 3d. is from a plate similar to those of the last issue, No. 2 in each group of four types having "L" and "A" joined at the foot. The ½d. and 2½d. are likewise in groups of four types, but the differences are very minute. In the retouched plate of the 2d. the letters "L" and "A" no longer touch in No. 2 of each group and the "P" in No. 3 is normal.

1895. *A. Thick paper.* W **10**.

(a) P 12½, 13.

202 **12** 1d. vermilion-red (16.1.95) . . . . . 3·50 30
a. Oval broken by tip of bust (R. 10/3) . . . . . 29·00 5·00
203 1d. red-orange . . . . . 3·50 30
a. Oval broken by tip of bust (R. 10/3) . . . . . 29·00 5·00
204 2d. blue (retouched plate) (16.1.95) . . 4·00 30
a. "FWO" for "TWO" (R. 8/7) . . . 65·00 22·00

(b) P 12.

205 **11** 1s. mauve (8.95) . . . . . 13·00 5·00

B. Unwmkd paper; with blue burelé band at back. P 12½, 13.

206 **12** 1d. vermilion-red (19.2.95) . . . . . 2·50 40
a. Oval broken by tip of bust (R. 10/3) . . . . . 22·00 5·00
b. "PE" of "PENNY" omitted (R. 1/2) £160 £130
206*c* 1d. red-orange . . . . . 2·50 40

C. Thin paper. Crown and Q faintly impressed. P 12½, 13.

207 **12** 2d. blue (retouched plate) (6.95) . . . 12·00
a. "FWO" for "TWO" (R. 8/7) . . . £100

15

16

17

18

1895–96. *A.* W **6** (sideways on ½d.).

(a) P 12½, 13.

208 **15** ½d. green (11.5.95) . . . . . 1·40 75
a. Double impression . . . . .
209 ½d. deep green . . . . . 1·40 75
a. Printed both sides £110
210 **16** 1d. orange-red (28.2.95) . . . . . 3·25 20
211 1d. pale red . . . . . 4·00 20
212 2d. blue (19.6.95) . . . . . 10·00 45
213 **17** 2½d. carmine (8.95) . . . . . 14·00 3·75
214 2½d. rose . . . . . 15·00 3·75
215 **18** 5d. purple-brown (10.95) . . . . . 16·00 3·75

(b) P 12.

217 **16** 1d. red (8.95) . . . . . 42·00 15·00
218 2d. blue (8.95) . . . . . 42·00 15·00

B. Thick paper. W **10** (sideways) (part only on each stamp).

(a) P 12½, 13.

219 **15** ½d. green (6.8.95) . . . . . 2·75 1·75
220 ½d. deep green . . . . . 2·75 1·75

(b) P 12.

221 **15** ½d. green . . . . . 18·00
222 ½d. deep green . . . . . 18·00

C. No wmk; *with blue burelé band at back.*

(a) P 12½, 13.

223 **15** ½d. green (1.8.95) . . . . . 4·50 2·50
a. Without *burelé* band . . . . . 45·00
224 ½d. deep green . . . . . 4·50

(b) P 12.

225 **15** ½d. green . . . . . 18·00
a. Without *burelé* band . . . . . 75·00

Nos. 223a and 225a are from the margins of the sheet.

D. Thin paper, with Crown and Q faintly impressed. P 12½, 13.

227 **15** ½d. green . . . . . 1·75 2·50
228 **16** 1d. orange-red . . . . . 3·25 1·75

19

1896–1902. W **6**. P 12½, 13.
229 **19** 1d. vermilion . . . . 11·00 50
230 6d. green (1902) . . . . † £9000
Only used examples of No. 230 are known, mostly with readable postmarks from 1902. It is suggested that an electrotype of this unissued design was inadvertently entered in a plate of No. 249.

20

21

22

23

24

25

"Cracked plate"

Die I

Die II

Two Dies of 4d.:

Die I. Serif of horizontal bar on lower right 4d. is clear of vertical frame line.
Die II. Serif joins vertical frame line.

1897–08. *Figures in all corners.* W **6** (sideways on ½d.). P 12½, 13.
231 **20** ½d. deep green . . . . 3·75 4·75
a. Perf 12 . . . . — £120
232 **21** 1d. orange-vermilion . . . . 2·25 15
233 1d. vermilion . . . . 2·25 15
a. Perf 12 (1903) . . . . 3·50 80
234 2d. blue . . . . 3·00 15
a. Cracked plate . . . . 70·00 22·00
b. Perf 12 (1903) . . . . £1000 6·00
235 2d. deep blue . . . . 3·00 15
a. Cracked plate . . . . 70·00 22·00
236 **22** 2½d. rose (10.98) . . . . 17·00 20·00
237 2½d. purple/*blue* (20.1.99) . . . . 9·50 2·00
238 2½d. brown-purple/*blue* . . . . 9·50 2·00
239 2½d. slate/*blue* (5.08) . . . . 12·00 3·50
240 **21** 3d. brown (10.98) . . . . 10·00 2·00
241 3d. deep brown . . . . 8·00 2·00
242 3d. reddish brown (1906) . . . . 8·00 2·00
243 3d. grey-brown (1907) . . . . 12·00 2·00
244 4d. yellow (Die I) (10.98) . . . . 9·00 2·00
a. Die II . . . . 24·00 4·00
245 4d. yellow-buff (Die I) . . . . 9·00 2·00
a. Die II . . . . 22·00 4·00
246 **23** 5d. purple-brown . . . . 8·50 2·00
247 5d. dull brown (1906) . . . . 9·50 2·75
248 5d. black-brown (1907) . . . . 11·00 3·00
249 **21** 6d. green (1.4.98) . . . . 8·00 1·75
250 6d. yellow-green . . . . 7·00 1·75
251 **24** 1s. pale mauve (1.7.99) . . . . 13·00 2·25
252 1s. dull mauve . . . . 13·00 2·25
253 1s. bright mauve . . . . 15·00 3·00
254 **25** 2s. turquoise-green . . . . 30·00 22·00
The 1d. perf 12 × 9½ exists used and unused but their status has not yet been established.
The cracked plate variety on the 2d. developed during 1901 and shows as a white break on the Queen's head and neck. The electro was later replaced.

1897–98. W **6**

(a) Zigzag roulette in black.
(b) The same but plain.
(c) Roulette *(a)* and also *(b)*.
(d) Roulette *(b)* and perf 12½, 13.
(e) Roulette *(a)* and perf 12½, 13.
(f) Compound of *(a)*, *(b)*, and perf 12½, 13.
256 **21** 1d. vermilion *(a)* . . . . 13·00 9·00
257 1d. vermilion *(b)* . . . . 6·00 3·75
258 1d. vermilion *(c)* . . . . 13·00 16·00
259 1d. vermilion *(d)* . . . . 8·50 5·50
260 1d. vermilion *(e)* . . . . 65·00 85·00
261 1d. vermilion *(f)* . . . . 85·00 90·00

26

27

(Des M. Kellar)

1899–1906. W **6**. P 12½, 13.
262 **26** ½d. deep green . . . . 3·00 1·25
a. Grey-green . . . . 2·50 1·25
b. Green (P 12) (1903) . . . . 3·25 1·25
c. Pale green (1906) . . . . 3·00 1·25
Stamps of T **26** without wmk, are proofs.

(Des F. Elliott)

1900 (19 Jun). *Charity. T* **27** *and horiz design showing Queen Victoria in medallion inscr* "PATRIOTIC FUND 1900". W **6**. P 12.
264*a* 1d. (6d.) claret £120 £110
264*b* 2d. (1s.) violet £300 £275
These stamps, sold at 6d. and 1s. respectively, paid postage of 1d. and 2d. only, the difference being contributed to a Patriotic Fund.

28

QUEENSLAND A   QUEENSLAND B

TWO TYPES OF "QUEENSLAND". Three different duty plates, each 120 (12 x 10), were produced for Type **28**. The first contained country inscriptions as Type A and was only used for No. 265. The second duty plate used for Nos. 265/6 and 282/4 contained 117 examples as Type A and 3 as Type B occurring on R. 1/6, R. 2/6 and R. 3/6. The third plate, used for Nos. 266, 283, 284 and 285 had all inscriptions as Type B.

(Typo Victoria Govt Printer, Melbourne)

1903 (4 Jul)–**05**. W w **10**. P 12½.
265 **28** 9d. brown and ultramarine (A) . . . . 20·00 3·25
266 9d. brown and ultramarine (B) (1905) . . . . 20·00 3·25

1903 (Oct). *As Nos. 162 and 165.* W **6** (twice sideways). P 12½, 13 (irregular line).
270 **9** 2s.6d. vermilion . . . . £100 38·00
271 £1 deep green £1500 £550
a. Re-entry (R. 1/2) . . . . — £900
b. Retouch (R. 6/4) . . . . — £900

(Litho Govt Ptg Office, Brisbane, from transfers of the recess plates).

1905 (Nov)–**06**. W **6** (twice sideways).

(a) P 12½, 13 (irregular line).
272 **9** £1 deep green £750 £130
a. Re-entry (R. 1/2) . . . . — £225
b. Retouch (R. 6/4) . . . . — £225

(b) P 12.
273 **9** 5s. rose (7.06) . . . . 90·00 70·00
274 £1 deep green (7.06) £350 £100
a. Re-entry (R. 1/2) £600 £180
b. Retouch (R. 6/4) £600 £180

30

32

Redrawn types of T **21**

T **30**. The head is redrawn, the top of the crown is higher and touches the frame, as do also the back of the chignon and the point of the bust. The forehead is filled in with lines of shading, and the figures in the corners appear to have been redrawn also.
T **32**. The forehead is plain (white instead of shaded), and though the top of the crown is made higher, it does not touch the frame; but the point of the bust and the chignon still touch. The figure in the right lower corner does not touch the line below, and has not the battered appearance of that in the first redrawn type. The stamps are very clearly printed, the lines of shading being distinct.

1906 (Sept). W **6**. P 12½, 13 (comb).
281 **30** 2d. dull blue (*shades*) . . . . 9·00 3·50

(Typo Victoria Govt Printer, Melbourne)

1906 (Sept)–**10**. Wmk Crown and double-lined A, W w **11**.

(a) P 12 × 12½.
282 **28** 9d. brown and ultramarine (A) . . . . 40·00 3·75
283 9d. brown and ultramarine (B) . . . . 13·00 3·50
283*a* 9d. pale brown and blue (A) . . . . 40·00 4·25
284 9d. pale brown and blue (B) . . . . 13·00 3·75

(b) P 11 (1910).
285 **28** 9d. brown and blue (B) £4500 £350

33

1907–11. W **33**.

(a) P 12½, 13 (comb).
286 **26** ½d. deep green . . . . 1·75 2·50
287 ½d. deep blue-green . . . . 1·75 2·50
288 **21** 1d. vermilion . . . . 2·75 30
a. Imperf (pair) £225
289 **30** 2d. dull blue . . . . 6·50 1·00
289*a* 2d. bright blue (3.08) . . . . 14·00 6·50
290 **32** 2d. bright blue (4.08) . . . . 3·25 30
291 **21** 3d. pale brown (8.08) . . . . 13·00 2·00
292 3d. bistre-brown . . . . 12·00 2·50
293 4d. yellow (Die I) . . . . 11·00 2·50
a. Die II . . . . 32·00 4·75
294 4d. grey-black (Die I) (4.09) . . . . 15·00 3·75
a. Die II . . . . 38·00 7·50
295 **23** 5d. dull brown . . . . 11·00 5·00
295*a* 5d. sepia (12.09) . . . . 15·00 6·00
296 **21** 6d. yellow-green . . . . 11·00 3·75
297 6d. bright green . . . . 12·00 4·00
298 **24** 1s. violet (1908) . . . . 12·00 2·75
299 1s. bright mauve . . . . 13·00 2·75
300 **25** 2s. turquoise-green (8.08) . . . . 35·00 20·00
Stamps of this issue also exist with the irregular line perforation 12½, 13. This was used when the comb perforation was under repair.

(b) P 13 × 11 to 12½ (May 1911).
301 **26** ½d. deep green . . . . 5·50 5·50
302 **21** 1d. vermilion . . . . 6·50 2·25
303 **32** 2d. blue . . . . 8·00 4·00
304 **21** 3d. bistre-brown . . . . 14·00 8·00
305 4d. grey-black . . . . 45·00 30·00
306 **23** 5d. dull brown . . . . 21·00 30·00
307 **21** 6d. yellow-green . . . . 21·00 30·00
308 **23** 1s. violet . . . . 38·00 32·00
The perforation (*b*) is from a machine introduced to help cope with the demands caused by the introduction of penny postage. The three rows at top (or bottom) of the sheet show varieties gauging 13 × 11½, 13 × 11, and 13 × 12, respectively, these are obtainable in strips of three showing the three variations.

(Litho Govt Ptg Office, Brisbane)

1907 (Oct)–**12**. W **33** (twice sideways). P 12½, 13 (irregular line).
309 **9** 2s.6d. vermilion . . . . 42·00 38·00
a. Dull orange (1910) . . . . 65·00 65·00
b. Reddish orange (1912) £170 £200
310 5s. rose (12.07) . . . . 60·00 40·00
a. Deep rose (1910) . . . . 70·00 60·00
b. Carmine-red (1912) £170 £250
311 10s. blackish brown . . . . £110 60·00
a. Sepia (1912) £350
312 £1 bluish green £225 £100
a. Re-entry (R. 1/2) £425 £180
b. Retouch (R. 6/4) £425 £180
c. Deep bluish green (1910) £425 £275
ca. Re-entry (R. 1/2) . . . . — £450
cb. Retouch (R. 6/4) . . . . — £450
d. Deep yellowish green (1912) £1500
da. Re-entry (R. 1/2) . . . .
db. Retouch (R. 6/4) £3000
The 1912 printings are on thinner, whiter paper.
The lithographic stone used for Nos. 272/4 and 309/12 took the full sheet of 30 so the varieties on the £1 recess-printed version also appear on the stamps printed by lithography.

1911. W **33**. Perf irregular compound, 10½ to 12½.
313 **21** 1d. vermilion £850 £550
This was from another converted machine, formerly used for perforating Railway stamps. The perforation was very unsatisfactory and only one or two sheets were sold.

STAMP BOOKLETS

There are very few surviving examples of Nos. SB1/4. Listings are provided for those believed to have been issued with prices quoted for those known to still exist.

1904 (1 Jan)–**09**. *Black on a red cover as No. SB1 of New South Wales. Stapled.*
SB1 £1 booklet containing two hundred and forty 1d. in four blocks of 30 and two blocks of 60 . . . .
a. Red on pink cover (1909) . . . .
b. Blue on pink cover £1000C

1904 (1 Jan). *Black on grey cover as No. SB1. Stapled.*
SB2 £1 booklet containing one hundred and twenty 2d. in four blocks of 30 . . . .

1910 (May). *Black on cream cover as No. SB3 of New South Wales Stapled.*
SB3 2s. booklet containing eleven ½d. (No. 301), either in block of 6 plus block of 5 or block of 11 and eighteen 1d. (No. 302), either in three blocks of 6 or block of 6 plus block of 12 . . . .
Unsold stock of No. SB3 was uprated with one additional ½d. in May 1911.

1911 (Aug). *Red on pink cover as No. SB3. Stapled*
SB4 2s. booklet containing twelve ½d. (No. 301), either in two blocks of 6 or block of 12, and eighteen 1d. (No. 302), either in three blocks of 6 or block of 6 plus block of 12 . . . . £275
a. Red on white £275

POSTAL FISCALS

Authorised for use from 1 January 1880 until 1 July 1892

CANCELLATIONS. Beware of stamps which have had pen-cancellations cleaned off and then had faked postmarks applied. Used prices quoted are for postally used examples between the above dates.

F 1

F 2

1866–68.

A. No wmk. P 13.

No.	Type	Description	Unused	Used
F1	F 1	1d. blue	45·00	11·00
F2		6d. deep violet	50·00	50·00
F3		1s. blue-green	60·00	27·00
F4		2s. brown	£120	80·00
F5		2s.6d. dull red	£120	65·00
F6		5s. yellow	£275	90·00
F6*a*		6s. light brown	£600	
F7		10s. green	£425	£160
F8		20s. rose	£600	£250

B. Wmk F **2**. P 13.

No.	Type	Description	Unused	Used
F 9	F 1	1d. blue	25·00	27·00
F10		6d. deep violet	50·00	50·00
F11		6d. blue	£110	80·00
F12		1s. blue-green	60·00	42·00
F13		2s. brown	£120	60·00
F13*a*		5s. yellow	£275	95·00
F14		10s. green	£450	£160
F15		20s. rose	£600	£250

F 3

F 3a

1871–72. P 12 or 13.

A. Wmk Large Crown and Q, Wmk F **3a**.

No.	Type	Description	Unused	Used
F16	F 3	1d. mauve	18·00	8·00
F17		6d. red-brown	42·00	22·00
F18		1s. green	50·00	22·00
F19		2s. blue	70·00	27·00
F20		2s.6d. brick-red	£100	55·00
F21		5s. orange-brown	£140	65·00
F22		10s. brown	£300	£110
F23		20s. rose	£500	£170

B. No wmk. *Blue burelé band at back.*

No.	Type	Description	Unused	Used
F24	F 3	1d. mauve	22·00	9·50
F25		6d. red-brown	42·00	22·00
F26		6d. mauve	95·00	45·00
F27		1s. green	50·00	22·00
F28		2s. blue	85·00	65·00
F29		2s.6d. vermilion	£130	60·00
F30		5s. yellow-brown	£170	70·00
F31		10s. brown	£325	£130
F32		20s. rose	£500	£170

F 4

F 5

1878–79.

A. No wmk. *Lilac burelé band at back.* P 12.

No.	Type	Description	Unused	Used
F33	F 4	1d. violet	65·00	24·00

B. Wmk Crown and Q, W **5**. P 12.

No.	Type	Description	Unused	Used
F34	F 4	1d. violet	26·00	18·00

Stamps as Type F **5** may not have been issued until after 1 July 1892 when the proper use of duty stamps for postal service was terminated but there are several examples which appear to have genuinely passed through the post during the 1890's. Unless they are dated during 1892 their postal use was certainly unauthorised although they may have been accepted.

Queensland became part of the Commonwealth of Australia on 1 January 1901.

SOUTH AUSTRALIA

PRICES FOR STAMPS ON COVER

Nos.	1/3	*from* × 3
No.	4	†
Nos.	5/12	*from* × 2
Nos.	13/18	*from* × 3
Nos.	19/43	*from* × 4
Nos.	44/9*b*	—
Nos.	50/110	*from* × 3
No.	111	—
Nos.	112/34	*from* × 6
Nos.	135/45	*from* × 3
Nos.	146/66	*from* × 5
Nos.	167/70*a*	*from* × 10
Nos.	171/2*a*	—
Nos.	173/94*a*	*from* × 12
Nos.	195/208	—
Nos.	229/31	*from* × 12
No.	232	—
Nos.	233/42	*from* × 12
Nos.	268/75	*from* × 30
Nos.	276/9	—
Nos.	280/8	*from* × 30
Nos.	289/92	—
Nos.	293/304	*from* × 15
No.	305	—
Nos.	O1/13	—
Nos.	O14/36	*from* × 20
Nos.	O37/42	*from* × 5
Nos.	O43/4	*from* × 50
Nos.	O45/7	—
Nos.	O48/52	*from* × 30
No.	O53	—
Nos.	O54/85	*from* × 50
Nos.	O86/7	—

SPECIMEN OVERPRINTS. Those listed are from U.P.U. distributions between 1889 and 1895. Further "Specimen" overprints exist, but these were used for other purposes.

PERKINS BACON "CANCELLED". For notes on these handstamps, showing "CANCELLED" between horizontal bars forming an oval, see Catalogue Introduction.

1

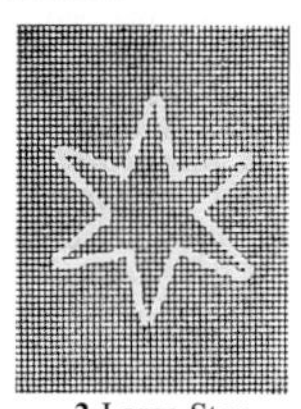
2 Large Star

(Eng Wm Humphrys. Recess P.B.)

1855 (1 Jan). *Printed in London.* W **2**. Imperf.

No.	Type	Description	Unused	Used
1	1	1d. dark green (Oct 1855) (H/S "CANCELLED" in oval £6000)	£3250	£425
2		2d. rose-carmine (*shades*) (1 Nov) (H/S "CANCELLED" in oval £4500)	£550	80·00
3		6d. deep blue (Oct 1855) (H/S "CANCELLED" in oval £4500)	£2250	£160

Prepared and sent to the Colony, but not issued.

No.	Type	Description	Unused	Used
4	1	1s. vio (H/S "CANCELLED" in oval £7500)	£5500	

A printing of 500,000 of these 1s. stamps was delivered, but, as the colour was liable to be confused with that of the 6d. stamp, this stock was destroyed on 5 June 1857. It is believed that surviving examples of No. 4 come from Perkins Bacon remainders which came on to the market in the late 1890s.

Proofs of the 1d. and 6d. without wmk exist, and these are found with forged star watermarks added, and are sometimes offered as originals.

For reprints of the above and later issues, see note after No. 194.

1856–58. *Printed by Printer of Stamps, Adelaide, from Perkins, Bacon plates.* W **2**. Imperf.

No.	Type	Description	Unused	Used
5	1	1d. deep yellow-green (15.6.58)	£5500	£500
6		1d. yellow-green (11.10.58)	£4500	£600
7		2d. orange-red (23.4.56)	£1500	80·00
8		2d. blood-red (14.11.56)	£1300	60·00
		a. Printed on both sides	†	£850
9		2d. red (shades) (29.10.57)	£650	40·00
		a. Printed on both sides	†	£650
10		6d. slate-blue (7.57)	£2500	£170
11		1s. red-orange (8.7.57)	—	£500
12		1s. orange (11.6.58)	£4500	£400

1858–59. Rouletted. *(This first rouletted issue has the same colours as the local imperf issue).* W **2**.

No.	Type	Description	Unused	Used
13	1	1d. yellow-green (8.1.59)	£550	55·00
14		1d. light yellow-green (18.3.59)	£550	60·00
		a. Imperf between (pair)		
15		2d. red (17.2.59)	£120	20·00
		a. Printed on both sides	†	£650
17		6d. slate-blue (12.12.58)	£425	30·00
18		1s. orange (18.3.59)	£900	40·00
		a. Printed on both sides	†	£1200

3

4

(5)

1860–69. Second rouletted issue, *printed (with the exception of No. 24) in colours only found rouletted or perforated. Surch with T* **5** *(Nos. 35/7).* W **2**.

No.	Type	Description	Unused	Used
19	1	1d. bright yellow-green (22.4.61)	48·00	29·00
20		1d. dull blue-green (17.12.63)	45·00	27·00
21		1d. sage-green	60·00	35·00
22		1d. Pale sage-green (27.5.65)	48·00	
23		1d. deep green (1864)	£250	70·00
24		1d. deep yellow-green (1869)	95·00	
24*a*		2d. pale red	75·00	4·00
		b. Printed on both sides	†	£400
25		2d. pale vermilion (3.2.63)	60·00	4·00
26		2d. bright vermilion (19.8.64)	55·00	3·25
		a. Imperf between (horiz pair)	£800	£350
27	3	4d. dull violet (24.1.67)	70·00	18·00
28	1	6d. violet-blue (19.3.60)	£160	7·00
29		6d. greenish blue (11.2.63)	80·00	4·00
30		6d. dull ultramarine (25.4.64)	75·00	4·00
		a. Imperf between (horiz pair)	†	£350
31		6d. violet-ultramarine (11.4.68)	£160	6·00
32		6d. dull blue (26.8.65)	£110	6·50
		a. Imperf between (pair)	†	£650
33		6d. Prussian blue (7.9.69)	£600	50·00
33*a*		6d. indigo	—	55·00
34	4	9d. grey-lilac (24.12.60)	60·00	9·00
		a. Imperf between (horiz pair)	†	£1100
35		10d.on 9d. orange-red (B.) (20.7.66)	£225	35·00
36		10d.on 9d. yellow (B.) (29.7.67)	£250	27·00
37		10d.on 9d. yellow (Blk.) (14.8.69)	£1600	40·00
		a. Surch inverted at the top	†	£3000
		b. Printed on both sides	†	£900
		c. Roul × perf 10	†	—
38	1	1s. yellow (25.10.61)	£475	28·00
		a. Imperf between (vert pair)	†	£1300
39		1s. grey-brown (10.4.63)	£170	17·00
40		1s. dark grey-brown (26.5.63)	£150	17·00
41		1s. chestnut (25.8.63)	£160	11·00
42		1s. lake-brown (27.3.65)	£120	12·00
		a. Imperf between (horiz pair)	†	£475
43	3	2s. rose-carmine (24.1.67)	£180	27·00
		a. Imperf between (vert pair)	†	£850

1868–71. *Remainders of old stock subsequently perforated by the 11½–12½ machine.*

(a) Imperf stamps. P 11½–12½.

No.	Type	Description	Unused	Used
44	1	2d. pale vermilion (Feb 1868)	—	£900
45		2d. vermilion (18.3.68)	—	£1000

(b) Rouletted stamps. P 11½–12½.

No.	Type	Description	Unused	Used
46	1	1d. bright green (9.11.69)	—	£475
47		2d. pale vermilion (15.8.68)	£1500	£425
48		6d. Prussian blue (8.11.69)	—	£225
		aa. Horiz pair perf all round, roul between		
48*a*		6d. indigo	—	£325
49	4	9d. grey-lilac (29.3.71)	£1600	£180
		a. Perf × roulette	—	£200
49*b*	1	1s. lake-brown (23.5.70)		

1867–70. W **2**. P 11½–12½ × roulette.

No.	Type	Description	Unused	Used
50	1	1d. pale bright green (2.11.67)	£160	22·00
51		1d. bright green (1868)	£140	22·00
52		1d. grey-green (26.1.70)	£160	24·00
		a. Imperf between (horiz pair)		
53		1d. blue-green (29.11.67)	£200	40·00
54	3	4d. dull violet (July 1868)	£1600	£150
55		4d. dull purple (1869)	—	£100
56	1	6d. bright pale blue (29.5.67)	£475	19·00
57		6d. Prussian blue (30.7.67)	£425	19·00
		a. Printed on both sides		
58		6d. indigo (1.8.69)	£550	25·00
59	4	10d.on 9d. yellow (B.) (2.2.69)	£700	35·00
		a. Printed on both sides	—	£650
60	1	1s. chestnut (April 1868)	£275	18·00
61		1s. lake-brown (3.3.69)	£275	18·00

NOTE. The stamps perf 11½, 12½, or compound of the two, are here combined in one list, as both perforations are on the one machine, and all the varieties may be found in each sheet of stamps. This method of classifying the perforations by the machines is by far the most simple and convenient.

3-PENCE
(6)
7 (= Victoria W **19**)

1868–79. *Surch with T* **6** *(Nos. 66/8).* W **2**. P 11½–12½.

No.	Type	Description	Unused	Used
62	1	1d. pale bright green (8.2.68)	£160	27·00
63		1d. grey-green (18.2.68)	£130	45·00
64		1d. dark green (20.3.68)	70·00	22·00
		a. Printed on both sides		
65		1d. deep yellow-green (28.6.72)	65·00	22·00
		a. Imperf between (horiz)	†	£600
66	3	3d.on 4d. Prussian blue (Blk.) (7.2.71)	—	£800
67		3d.on 4d. sky-blue (Blk.) (12.8.70)	£300	13·00
		a. Imperf		
		b. Rouletted	—	£650
68		3d.on 4d. deep ultramarine (Blk.) (9.72)	80·00	9·00
		a. Surch double	†	£3500
		b. Additional surch on back	†	£2750
		c. Surch omitted	£16000	£9000
70		4d. dull purple (1.2.68)	70·00	15·00
		a. Imperf between (horiz pair)	†	—
71		4d. dull violet (1868)	65·00	8·00
72	1	6d. bright pale blue (23.2.68)	£325	11·00
73		6d. Prussian blue (29.9.69)	95·00	7·00
		a. Perf 11½ × imperf (horiz pair)	†	£600
74		6d. indigo (1869)	£130	17·00
75	4	9d. claret (7.72)	£110	8·00
76		9d. bright mauve (1.11.72)	£110	8·00
		a. Printed on both sides	†	£400
77		9d. red-purple (15.1.74)	70·00	8·00
78		10d.on 9d. yellow (B.) (15.8.68)	£1100	35·00
		a. Wmk Crown and S A (W **10**) (1868)	—	£900
79		10d.on 9d. yellow (Blk.) (13.9.69)	£250	40·00
80	1	1s. lake-brown (9.68)	£160	11·00
81		1s. chestnut (8.10.72)	£130	17·00
82		1s. dark red-brown	£100	11·00
83		1s. red-brown (6.1.69)	£110	11·00
84	3	2s. pale rose-pink (10.10.69)	£1000	£160
85		2s. deep rose-pink (8.69)	—	£110
86		2s. crimson-carmine (16.10.69)	85·00	18·00

87 2s. carmine (1869) . . . . 75·00 12·00
a. Printed on both sides . . . . † £350

No. 68c comes from two sheets on which, it is believed, some stamps showed the surcharge omitted and others the surcharge double. One of the used examples of No. 68c is known postmarked in 1875 and many of the others in 1879.

No. 78a was a trial printing made to test the perforating machine on the new D.L.R. paper.

1870–71. W **2**. P 10.

88 **1** 1d. grey-green (6.70) . . . . £130 16·00
89 1d. pale bright green (9.8.70) . . . . £130 16·00
90 1d. bright green (1871) . . . . £110 16·00
91 **3** 3d.on 4d. dull ultramarine (R.) (6.8.70) . . . . £475 75·00
92 3d.on 4d. pale ultram (Blk.) (14.2.71) . . . . £300 19·00
93 3d.on 4d. ultramarine (Blk.) (14.8.71) . . . . £120 21·00
93*a* 3d.on 4d. Prussian blue (Blk.) (16.12.71)
94 4d. dull lilac (1870) . . . . £120 11·00
95 4d. dull purple (1871) . . . . £110 11·00
96 **1** 6d. bright blue (19.6.70) . . . . £180 17·00
97 6d. indigo (11.10.71) . . . . £250 16·00
98 1s. chestnut (4.1.71) . . . . £160 24·00

1870–73. W **2**. P 10 × 11½–12½, 11½–12½ × 10, or compound.

99 **1** 1d. pale bright green (11.10.70) . . . . £150 14·00
a. Printed on both sides
100 1d. grey-green . . . . £140 15·00
101 1d. deep green (19.6.71) . . . . 80·00 10·00
102 **3** 3d.on 4d. pale ultram (Blk.) (9.11.70) . . . . £225 48·00
103 4d. dull lilac (11.5.72) . . . . — 20·00
104 4d. slate-lilac (5.3.73) . . . . £130 18·00
105 **1** 6d. Prussian blue (2.3.70) . . . . £150 8·00
106 6d. bright Prussian blue (26.10.70) . . . . £160 10·00
107 **4** 10d.on 9d. yellow (Blk.) (1.70) . . . . £130 26·00
108 **1** 1s. chestnut (17.6.71) . . . . £225 45·00
109 **3** 2s. rose-pink (24.4.71) . . . . — £190
110 2s. carmine (2.3.72) . . . . £140 32·00

1871 (17 July). W **7**. P 10.

111 **3** 4d. dull lilac £2000 £225
a. Printed on both sides . . . . † £2000

8 Broad Star

8 PENCE

(9)

1876–1900. *Surch with T* **9** *(Nos. 118/21)*. W **8**.

(a) P 11½–12½.

112 **3** 3d.on 4d. ultramarine (1.6.79) . . . . 80·00 19·00
a. Surch double . . . . † £1300
113 4d. violet-slate (15.3.79) . . . . £110 14·00
114 4d. plum (16.4.80) . . . . 55·00 6·50
115 4d. deep mauve (8.6.82) . . . . 55·00 5·50
116 **1** 6d. indigo (2.12.76) . . . . £110 4·50
a. Imperf between (horiz pair) . . . . † —
117 6d. Prussian blue (7.78) . . . . 70·00 4·00
118 **4** 8d.on 9d. brown-orange (7.76) . . . . 85·00 7·00
119 8d.on 9d. burnt umber (1880) . . . . 90·00 7·00
120 8d.on 9d. brown (9.3.80) . . . . 90·00 7·00
a. Imperf between (vert pair) £600
121 8d.on 9d. grey-brown (10.5.81) . . . . 75·00 7·00
a. Surch double . . . . — £500
122 9d. purple (9.3.80) . . . . 55·00 8·00
a. Printed on both sides . . . . — £375
123 9d. rose-lilac (21.8.80) . . . . 16·00 3·25
124 9d. rose-lilac (large holes) (26.5.00) . . . . 10·00 3·50
125 **1** 1s. red-brown (3.11.77) . . . . 50·00 2·75
a. Imperf between (horiz pair) . . . . † £400
126 1s. reddish lake-brown (1880) . . . . 48·00 3·00
127 1s. lake-brown (9.1.83) . . . . 55·00 2·75
a. Printed double
128 1s. Vandyke brown (1891) . . . . 65·00 8·00
129 1s. dull brown (1891) . . . . 42·00 2·75
130 1s. chocolate (large holes) (6.5.97) . . . . 25·00 3·00
a. Imperf vert (horiz pair) £225
131 1s. sepia (large holes) (22.5.00) . . . . 25·00 3·00
a. Imperf between (vert pair) £250
132 **3** 2s. carmine (15.2.77) . . . . 38·00 5·00
a. Imperf between (horiz pair) . . . . † £650
b. Imperf (pair)
133 2s. rose-carmine (1885) . . . . 42·00 6·50
134 2s. rose-carmine (*large holes*) (6.12.98) . . . . 30·00 6·50

The perforation with larger, clean-cut holes resulted from the fitting of new pins to the machine.

(b) P 10.

135 **1** 6d. Prussian blue (11.11.79) . . . . £110 15·00
136 6d. bright blue (1879) . . . . £130 15·00
136*a* 1s. reddish lake-brown £300

(c) P 10 × 11½–12½, 11½–12½ × 10, or compound.

137 **3** 4d. violet-slate (21.5.79) . . . . £110 15·00
138 4d. dull purple (4.10.79) . . . . 45·00 2·75
139 **1** 6d. Prussian blue (29.12.77) . . . . 65·00 2·50
140 6d. bright blue . . . . 85·00 5·50
141 6d. bright ultramarine . . . . 55·00 2·00
142 1s. reddish lake-brown (9.2.85) . . . . 90·00 9·50
143 1s. dull brown (29.6.86) . . . . £120 11·00
144 **3** 2s. carmine (27.12.77) . . . . 60·00 6·00
145 2s. rose-carmine (1887) . . . . 55·00 5·50
a. Imperf between (horiz pair) . . . . † £750

10 11 12

1901–02. Wmk Crown SA (wide). W **10**. P 11½–12½ (large holes).

146 **4** 9d. claret (1.2.02) . . . . 16·00 16·00
147 **1** 1s. dark brown (12.6.01) . . . . 22·00 12·00
148 1s. dark reddish brown (1902) . . . . 24·00 13·00
a. Imperf horiz (vert pair) £1200
149 1s. red-brown (aniline) (18.7.02) . . . . 22·00 15·00
150 **3** 2s. crimson (29.8.01) . . . . 30·00 15·00
151 2s. carmine . . . . 25·00 11·00

(Plates and electrotypes by D.L.R. Printed in Adelaide)

1868–76. W **10**.

(a) Rouletted.

152 **12** 2d. deep brick-red (8.68) . . . . 70·00 3·75
153 2d. pale orange-red (5.10.68) . . . . 65·00 2·75
a. Printed on both sides . . . . † £375
b. Imperf between (horiz pair) . . . . † £550
c. Imperf horiz (vert pair) . . . . † £850

(b) P 11½–12½.

154 **11** 1d. blue-green (10.1.75) . . . . 80·00 15·00
155 **12** 2d. pale orange-red (5.5.69) £900 £200

(c) P 11½–12½ × roulette.

156 **12** 2d. pale orange-red (20.8.69) . . . . — £140

(d) P 10 × roulette.

157 **12** 2d. pale orange-red (7.5.70) . . . . £250 27·00

(e) P 10.

158 **11** 1d. blue-green (4.75) . . . . 35·00 4·75
159 **12** 2d. brick-red (4.70) . . . . 18·00 1·00
160 2d. orange-red (1.7.70) . . . . 11·00 1·00
a. Printed on both sides . . . . † £300

(f) P 10 × 11½–12½, 11½–12½ × 10, or compound.

161 **11** 1d. blue-green (27.8.75) . . . . 70·00 17·00
162 **12** 2d. brick-red (19.1.71) . . . . £450 10·00
163 2d. orange-red (3.2.71) . . . . £120 12·00
a. Imperf (8.76) £1000 £1000

1869. Wmk Large Star W **2**.

(a) Rouletted.

164 **12** 2d. orange-red (13.3.69) . . . . 70·00 15·00

(b) P 11½–12½ × roulette.

165 **12** 2d. orange-red (1.8.69) . . . . — 95·00

(c) P 11½–12½.

165*a* **12** 2d. orange-red (7.69) . . . . — £850

1871 (15 July). Wmk V and Crown, W **7**. P 10.

166 **12** 2d. brick-red . . . . 70·00 19·00

13

HALF-
PENNY

(14)

1876–1904. Wmk Crown SA (close). W **13**.

(a) P 10 (1876–85).

167 **11** 1d. blue-green (9.2.76) . . . . 11·00 30
a. *Yellowish green* (11.78) . . . . 13·00 30
b. *Deep green* (11.79) . . . . 13·00 30
ba. Imperf between (horiz pair)
bb. Printed double . . . . † —
168 **12** 2d. orange-red (8.76) . . . . 11·00 30
a. *Dull brick-red* (21.5.77) . . . . 12·00 30
b. *Blood-red* (31.10.79) . . . . £225 3·25
c. *Pale red* (4.85) . . . . 10·00 30

(b) P 10 × 11½–12½, 11½–12½ × 10 or compound (1877–80).

169 **11** 1d. deep green (11.2.80) . . . . 35·00 4·00
a. *Blue-green* (2.3.80) . . . . 20·00 3·00
170 **12** 2d. orange-red (4.9.77) . . . . £130 4·00
a. *Dull brick-red* (6.80) . . . . £130 4·00

(c) P 11½–12½ (1877–84).

171 **11** 1d. blue-green (2.84) . . . . — £130
172 **12** 2d. orange-red (14.9.77) . . . . — £130
a. *Blood-red* (1.4.80) . . . . — £130

(d) P 15 (1893).

173 **11** 1d. green (8.5.93) . . . . 9·00 80
174 **12** 2d. pale orange (9.2.93) . . . . 10·00 50
a. *Orange-red* . . . . 10·00 50
b. Imperf between (vert pair) £325

(e) P 13 (1895–1903).

175 **11** 1d. pale green (11.1.95) . . . . 7·50 20
a. *Green* . . . . 7·50 20
b. Imperf between (vert pair)
176 1d. rosine (8.8.99) . . . . 4·00 20
a. *Scarlet* (23.12.03) . . . . 4·25 30
b. *Deep red* . . . . 4·00 30
177 **12** 2d. pale orange (19.1.95) . . . . 5·00 10
a. *Orange-red* (9.5.95) . . . . 8·00 10
178 2d. bright violet (10.10.99) . . . . 4·00 10

(f) P 12 × 11½ (comb) (1904).

179 **11** 1d. rosine (2.2.04) . . . . 7·00 50
a. *Scarlet* (25.7.04) . . . . 6·00 20
180 **12** 2d. bright violet (11.10.04) . . . . 6·00 70

Examples of the 1d. pale green with thicker lettering come from a worn plate.

1882 (1 Jan). *No. 167 surch with T* **14**.

181 **11** ½d.on 1d. blue-green . . . . 11·00 7·00

15 16

17 18

1883–99. W **13** (sideways on ½d.).

(a) P 10 (1883–95).

182 **15** ½d. chocolate (1.3.83) . . . . 4·50 1·00
a. Imperf between (horiz pair) . . . . † £750
b. *Red-brown* (4.4.89) . . . . 4·25 1·00
c. *Brown* (1895) . . . . 4·00 1·00
183 **16** 3d. sage-green (12.86) . . . . 13·00 2·00
a. *Olive-green* (6.6.90) . . . . 12·00 2·25
b. *Deep green* (12.4.93) . . . . 8·50 2·00
s. Optd "Specimen" . . . . 30·00
184 **17** 4d. pale violet (3.90) . . . . 15·00 2·25
a. *Aniline violet* (3.1.93) . . . . 16·00 2·50
s. Optd "Specimen" . . . . 35·00
185 **18** 6d. pale blue (4.87) . . . . 13·00 2·00
a. *Blue* (5.5.87) . . . . 15·00 80
s. Optd "Specimen" . . . . 30·00

(b) P 10 × 11½–12½, 11½–12½ × 10 or compound (1891).

186 **15** ½d. red-brown (25.9.91) . . . . 9·00 3·75
a. Imperf between (horiz pair) £140

(c) P 11½–12½ (1890).

187 **15** ½d. red-brown (12.10.90) . . . . 11·00 2·25

(d) P 15 (1893–94).

188 **15** ½d. pale brown (1.93) . . . . 4·25 1·00
a. *Deep brown* . . . . 4·25 1·00
b. Imperf between (horiz pair) £140
c. Perf 12½ between (pair) . . . . £180 42·00
189 **17** 4d. purple (1.1.94) . . . . 20·00 3·00
a. *Slate-violet* . . . . 20·00 3·00
190 **18** 6d. blue (20.11.93) . . . . 35·00 3·50

(e) P 13 (1895–99).

191 **15** ½d. pale brown (9.95) . . . . 2·75 30
a. *Deep brown* (19.3.97) . . . . 3·50 30
192 **16** 3d. pale olive-green (26.7.97) . . . . 7·00 1·75
a. *Deep olive-green* (27.11.99) . . . . 5·00 1·75
193 **17** 4d. violet (21.1.96) . . . . 6·00 50
194 **18** 6d. pale blue (3.96) . . . . 7·00 1·50
a. *Blue* . . . . 7·00 1·50

REPRINTS. In 1884, and in later years, reprints on paper wmkd Crown SA, W **10**, were made of Nos. 1, 2, 3, 4, 12, 13, 14, 15, 19, 24, 27, 28, 32, 33, 34, 35, 36, 37, 38, 40, 43, 44, 49a, 53, 65, 67, 67 with surcharge in red, 70, 71, 72, 73, 78, 79, 81, 83, 86, 90, 118, 119, 120, 121, 122, 155, 158, 159, 164, 181, 182. They are overprinted "REPRINT".

In 1889 examples of the reprints for Nos. 1/3, 12, 15, 19, 27, 32/8, 44, 67, 67 surcharged in red, 70/1, 73, 83, 86, 118, 121/2, 158/9, 164 and 181/2, together with No. 141 overprinted "Specimen", were supplied to the U.P.U. for distribution.

19

2½d.

(20)

(21)

(Plates and electrotypes by D.L.R. Printed in Adelaide)

1886 (20 Dec)–**96**. *T* **19** *(inscr* "POSTAGE & REVENUE"*)*. W **13**. Parts of two or more wmks, on each stamp, sometimes sideways. P 10.

195 2s.6d. mauve . . . . 45·00 8·5
a. Perf 11½–12½. *Dull violet* . . . . 35·00 6·5
bb. *Bright aniline violet* . . . . 38·00 8·5
196 5s. rose-pink . . . . 60·00 15·0
a. Perf 11½–12½ . . . . 45·00 15·0
ab. *Rose-carmine* . . . . 45·00 17·0
197 10s. green . . . . £130 45·0
a. Perf 11½–12½ . . . . £110 42·0
198 15s. brownish yellow £350 £27
a. Perf 11½–12½ £375 £16
199 £1 blue £275 £12
a. Perf 11½–12½ £225 £1
200 £2 Venetian red £1000 £35
a. Perf 11½–12½ £950 £32
201 50s. dull pink £1500 £45
a. Perf 11½–12½ £1400 £40
202 £3 sage green £1600 £45
a. Perf 11½–12½ £1500 £40
203 £4 lemon £3500
a. Perf 11½–12½ £3000 £70
204 £5 grey £3000
a. Perf 11½–12½ £3000
205 £5 brown (P 11½–12½) (1896) £2250 £75

206 £10 bronze £3500 £950
a. Perf 11½–12½ £2750 £850
207 £15 silver £8500
a. Perf 11½–12½ £7500 £1300
208 £20 claret £10000
a. Perf 11½–12½ £9000 £1600
195s/208s Optd "Specimen" *Set of* 14 . . . . £650

Variations exist in the length of the words and shape of the letters of the value inscription.

The 2s.6d. dull violet, 5s. rose-pink, 10s., £1 and £5 brown exist perf 11½–12½ with either large or small holes; the 2s.6d. aniline, 5s. rose-carmine, 15s., £2 and 50s. with large holes only and the remainder only with small holes.

Stamps perforated 11½–12½ small holes, are, generally speaking, rather rarer than those with the 1895 (large holes) gauge.

Stamps perf 10 were issued on 20 Dec 1886. Stamps perf 11½–12½ (small holes) are known with earliest dates covering the period from June 1890 to Feb 1896. Earliest dates of stamps with large holes range from July 1896 to May 1902.

1891 (1 Jan)–**93**. *T* **17/18** *surch with T* **20/1**. W **13**.

(a) P 10.

229 **17** 2½d.on 4d. pale green (Br.) . . . . 7·50 2·50
a. Fraction bar omitted . . . . 95·00 75·00
b. Deep green . . . . 8·00 1·75
ba. Fraction bar omitted . . . . 95·00 70·00
bb. "2" and "½" closer together . . . . 25·00 18·00
bc. Imperf between (horiz pair)
bd. Imperf between (vert pair) . . . . † £1000
s. Optd "Specimen" . . . . 30·00
230 **18** 5d.on 6d. pale brn (C.) . . . . 16·00 4·75
a. Deep brown . . . . 16·00 4·50
b. No stop after "5D" £160
s. Optd "Specimen" . . . . 30·00

(b) P 10 × 11½–12½ or 11½–12½ × 10.

231 **17** 2½d.on 4d. pale green (Br.) . . . . 21·00 3·50
a. Deep green . . . . 21·00 3·50

(c) P 11½–12½.

232 **17** 2½d.on 4d. deep green . . . . 32·00 45·00

(d) P 15.

233 **17** 2½d.on 4d. green (14.10.93) . . . . 21·00 2·75
a. Fraction bar omitted
b. "2" and "½d." closer . . . . 60·00 22·00

22 Red Kangaroo

23

24 G.P.O., Adelaide

(Des M. Tannenberg, plates by D.L.R.)

1894 (1 Mar)–**1906**. W **13**.

(a) P 15.

234 **22** 2½d. violet-blue . . . . 22·00 2·25
235 **23** 5d. brown-purple . . . . 24·00 3·00
234s/5s Optd "Specimen" *Set of* 2 . . . . 60·00

(b) P 13.

236 **22** 2½d. violet-blue (11.2.95) . . . . 17·00 70
237 2½d. indigo (25.3.98) . . . . 5·00 1·50
238 **23** 5d. Brown-purple (1.96) . . . . 6·50 80
a. Purple . . . . 6·50 70

(c) P 12 × 11½ (comb).

239 **22** 2½d. indigo (4.7.06) . . . . 7·50 2·25
240 **23** 5d. dull purple (1.05) . . . . 12·00 2·00

(Typo D.L.R.)

1899 (27 Dec)–**1905**. W **13**.

(a) P 13.

241 **24** ½d. yellow-green . . . . 1·50 50

(b) P 12 × 11½ (comb).

242 **24** ½d. yellow-green (7.05) . . . . 2·75 1·00

25

The measurements given indicate the length of the value inscription in the bottom label. The dates are those of the earliest known postmarks.

1902–04. *As T* **19**, *but top tablet as T* **25** *(thin* "POSTAGE"*)*. W **13**.

(a) P 11½–12½.

268 3d. olive-green (18½ mm) (1.8.02) . . . . 6·00 2·00
a. Wmk sideways . . . . † £1400
269 4d. red-orange (17 mm) (29.11.02) . . . . 9·50 2·00
270 6d. blue-green (16–16½ mm) (29.11.02) . . . . 6·00 2·00
271 8d. ultramarine (19 mm) (25.4.02) . . . . 8·00 7·00
272 8d. ultramarine (16½ mm) (22.3.04) . . . . 9·00 7·00
a. "EIGNT" (R.2/9) £1200 £2250
273 9d. rosy lake (19.9.02) . . . . 8·00 4·00
a. Imperf between (vert pair) £550
b. Imperf between (horiz pair)
274 10d. dull yellow (29.11.02) . . . . 12·00 8·00
275 1s. brown (18.8.02) . . . . 15·00 4·25
a. Imperf between (horiz pair)
b. Imperf between (vert pair) £750
c. "POSTAGE" and value in red-brown £850 £850
276 2s.6d. pale violet (19.9.02) . . . . 40·00 20·00
a. Bright violet (2.2.03) . . . . 23·00 12·00
277 5s. rose (17.10.02) . . . . 60·00 40·00
278 10s. green (1.11.02) . . . . £110 65·00
279 £1 blue (1.11.02) £250 £140

(b) P 12.

280 3d. olive-green (20 mm) (15.4.04) . . . . 11·00 2·50
a. "POSTAGE" omitted; value below "AUSTRALIA" £1200
281 4d. orange-red (17½–18 mm) (18.2.03) . . . . 9·50 2·25
282 6d. blue-green (15 mm) (14.11.03) . . . . 19·00 4·75
283 9d. rosy lake (2.12.03) . . . . 55·00 10·00

PRINTER. Stamp printing in Adelaide ceased in 1909 when the Printer of Stamps, J. B. Cooke, was appointed head of the Commonwealth Stamp Printing Branch in Melbourne. From 9 March 1909 further printings of current South Australia stamps were made in Melbourne.

26

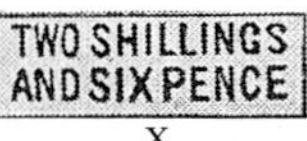

V X

In Type X the letters in the bottom line are slightly larger than in Type V, especially the "A", "S" and "P".

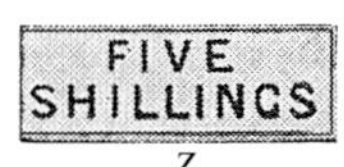

Y Z

In Type Z the letters "S" and "G" are more open than in Type Y. Nos. 196/a and 277 are similar to Type Y with all letters thick and regular and the last "S" has the top curve rounded instead of being slightly flattened.

1904–11. *As T* **19**, *but top tablet as T* **26** *(thick* "POSTAGE"*)*. W **13**. P 12.

284 6d. blue-green (27.4.04) . . . . 12·00 3·00
a. Imperf between (vert pair) £1000
285 8d. bright ultramarine (4.7.05) . . . . 9·00 7·00
a. Value closer (15¼ mm) . . . . 26·00
b. Dull ultramarine (2.4.08) . . . . 19·00 4·50
ba. Ditto. Value closer (15¼ mm) . . . . 50·00
286 9d. rosy lake (17–17¼ mm) (18.7.04) . . . . 12·00 4·50
a. Value 16½–16¾ mm (2.06) . . . . 28·00 6·50
b. Brown-lake. Perf 12½ small holes (6.6.11) . . . . 13·00
287 10d. dull yellow (8.07) . . . . 14·00 12·00
a. Imperf between (horiz pair) £750 £700
b. Imperf between (vert pair) £700
288 1s. brown (12.4.04) . . . . 17·00 3·00
a. Imperf between (vert pair) £475
b. Imperf between (horiz pair) £550
289 2s.6d. bright violet (V.) (14.7.05) . . . . 50·00 15·00
a. Dull violet (X) (8.06) . . . . 50·00 15·00
290 5s. rose-scarlet (Y) (8.04) . . . . 48·00 29·00
a. Scarlet (Z) (8.06) . . . . 48·00 29·00
b. Pale rose. Perf 12½ (small holes) (Z) (7.10) . . . . 65·00 38·00
291 10s. green (26.8.08) £110 £130
292 £1 blue (29.12.04) £200 £120
a. Perf 12½ (small holes) (7.10) £150 £110

The "value closer" variety on the 8d. occurs six times in the sheet of 60. The value normally measures 16½ mm but in the variety it is 15¼ mm.

The 9d., 5s. and £1, perf 12½ (small holes), are late printings made in 1910–11 to use up the Crown SA paper.

No. 286*b* has the value as Type C of the 9d. on Crown over A paper.

27

1905–11. W **27**. P 12 × 11½ (new comb machine).

293 **24** ½d. pale green (4.07) . . . . 5·00 80
a. Yellow-green . . . . 5·00 80
294 **11** 1d. rosine (2.12.05) . . . . 4·50 10
a. Scarlet (4.11) . . . . 4·00 1·00
295 **12** 2d. bright violet (2.2.06) . . . . 8·00 10
aa. Imperf three sides (horiz pair) £1000
a. Mauve (4.08) . . . . 4·50 10
296 **22** 2½d. indigo-blue (14.9.10) . . . . 9·00 6·00
297 **23** 5d. brown-purple (11.3.08) . . . . 13·00 3·50

No. 295aa is perforated at foot.

Three types of the 9d., perf 12½, distinguishable by the distance between "NINE" and "PENCE".

A. Distance 1¾ mm. B. Distance 2¼ mm. C. Distance 2½ mm.

1906–12. *T* **19** *(*"POSTAGE" *thick as T* **26***)*. W **27**. P 12 or 12½ (small holes).

298 3d. sage-green (19 mm) (26.6.06) . . . . 7·00 2·50
a. Imperf between (horiz pair) . . . . † £1000
b. Perf 12½. *Sage-green* (17 mm) (9.12.09) . . . . 7·00 2·50
c. Perf 12½. *Deep olive* (20 mm) (7.10) . . . . 42·00 10·00
d. Perf 12½. *Yellow-olive* (14 mm) (16.12.11) . . . . 12·00 11·00
da. Perf 12½. *Bright olive-green* (19–19¾ mm) (5.12) . . . . 12·00 13·00
e. Perf 11 (17 mm) (1910) £800 £550
299 4d. orange-red (10.9.06) . . . . 10·00 2·25
a. Orange . . . . 10·00 2·25
b. Perf 12½. *Orange* . . . . 10·00 3·75
300 6d. blue-green (1.9.06) . . . . 8·00 2·25
a. Perf 12½ (21.4.10) . . . . 7·50 3·50
ab. Perf 12½. Imperf between (vert pair) £650 £550
301 8d. bright ultramarine (P 12½) (8.09) . . . . 10·00 11·00
a. Value closer (8.09) . . . . 42·00 38·00
302 9d. brown-lake (3.2.06) . . . . 10·00 3·00
a. Imperf between (vert pair) £550
aa. Imperf between (horiz pair) £700
b. Deep lake (9.5.08) . . . . 42·00 6·50
c. Perf 12½. *Lake* (A) (5.9.09) . . . . 11·00 4·25
d. Perf 12½. *Lake* (B) ((7.09) . . . . 20·00 4·50
e. Perf 12½. *Brown-lake* . . . . 20·00 6·50
ea. Perf 12½. *Deep lake*. Thin paper (C) . . . . 20·00 5·50
f. Perf 11 (1909) . . . . — £1100
303 1s. brown (30.5.06) . . . . 12·00 4·50
a. Imperf between (horiz pair) £650
b. Perf 12½ (10.3.10) . . . . 10·00 4·75
304 2s.6d. bright violet (X) (10.6.09) . . . . 50·00 12·00
a. Perf 12½. *Pale violet* (X) (6.10) . . . . 50·00 15·00
ab. Perf 12½. *Deep purple* (X) (15.11.12) . . . . 50·00 35·00
305 5s. bright rose (P 12½) (Z) (24.4.11) . . . . 65·00

The "value closer" variety of the 8d. occurred 11 times in the sheet of 60 in the later printing only. On No. 301 the value measures 16½ mm while on No. 301a it is 15¼ mm.

The 1s. brown, perf compound of 11½ and 12½, formerly listed is now omitted, as it must have been perforated by the 12 machine, which in places varied from 11½ to 13. The 4d. has also been reported with a similar perforation.

STAMP BOOKLETS

There are very few surviving examples of Nos. SB1/4. Listings are provided for those believed to have been issued with prices quoted for those known still to exist.

1904 (1 Jan)–**09**. *Black on red cover as No. SB1 of New South Wales. Stapled.*

SB1 £1 booklet containing two hundred and forty 1d. in four blocks of 30 and two blocks of 60
a. Red on pink cover (1909)
b. Blue on pink cover £10000

1904 (1 Jan). *Black on grey cover as No. SB1. Stapled.*

SB2 £1 booklet containing one hundred and twenty 2d. in four blocks of 30

1910 (May). *Black on cream cover as No. SB3 of New South Wales. Stapled.*

SB3 2s. booklet containing eleven ½d. (No. 262A), either in block of 6 plus block of 5 or block of 11, and eighteen 1d. (No. 264A), either in three blocks of 6 or block of 6 plus block of 12

Unsold stock of No. SB3 was uprated with one additional ½d. in May 1911.

1911 (Aug). *Red on pink cover as No. SB3. Stapled.*

SB4 2s. Booklet containing twelve 12d. (No. 262A), either in two blocks of 6 or block of 12 and eighteen 1d. (No. 264A) , either in three blocks of 6 or block of 6 plus block of 12 . . . . £4000

OFFICIAL STAMPS

A. Departmentals

Following suspected abuses involving stamps supplied for official use it was decided by the South Australian authorities that such supplies were to be overprinted with a letter, or letters, indicating the department of the administration to which the stamps had been invoiced.

The system was introduced on 1 April 1868 using overprints struck in red. Later in the same year the colour of the overprints was amended blue, and, during the latter months of 1869, to black.

In 1874 the Postmaster-General recommended that this somewhat cumbersome system be replaced by a general series of "O.S." overprints with the result that the separate accounting for the Departmentals ceased on 30 June of that year. Existing stocks continued to be used, however, and it is believed that much of the residue was passed to the Government Printer to pay postage on copies of the *Government Gazette*.

We are now able to provide a check list of these most interesting issues based on the definitive work. *The Departmental Stamps of South Australia* by A. R. Butler, FRPSL, RDP, published by the Royal Philatelic Society, London in 1978.

No attempt has been made to assign the various overprints to the catalogue numbers of the basic stamps, but each is clearly identified by both watermark and perforation. the colours are similar to those of the contemporary postage stamps, but there can be shade variations. Errors of overprint are recorded in footnotes, but not errors occurring on the basic stamps used.

Most departmental overprints are considered to be scarce to rare in used condition, with unused examples, used multiples and covers being regarded as considerable rarities.

Forgeries of a few items do exist, but most can be readily identified by comparison with genuine examples. A number of forged overprints on stamps not used for the genuine issues also occur.

A. (Architect)

Optd in red with stop. W **2**. 2d. (Roul), 4d. (P 11½–12½), 6d. (Roul), 1s. (Roul)
Optd in red without stop W **2**. Roul. 1d., 2d., 6d., 1s.
Optd in black.*(a)* W **2**. 4d. (P 10 × 11½–12½), 6d. (P 11½–12½), 2s. (Roul)
(b) W **10**. 2d. D.L.R. (Roul), 2d. D.L.R. (P 10)

A.G. (Attorney-General)

Optd in red. W **2**. Roul. 1d., 2d., 6d., 1s.
Optd in blue. *(a)* W **2**. Roul. 6d.
(b) W **10**. Roul. 2d. D.L.R.
Optd in black. *(a)* W **2**. 1d (P 11½–12½ × Roul), 4d. (P 11½–12½), 4d.(P 10), 6d. (P 11½–12½ × Roul), 6d. (P 11½–12½), 1s. (P 11½–12½ × Roul), 1s. (P 11½–12½) 1s. (P 10)
(b) W **10**. 2d. D.L.R. (Roul), 2d. D.L.R. (P 10)

A.O. (Audit Office)

Optd in red. W **2**. 2d. (Roul), 4d. (P 11½–12½), 6d. (Roul)
Optd in blue. *(a)* W **2**. P 11½–12½. 1d., 6d.
(b) W **10**. Roul. 2d. D.L.R.
Optd in black. *(a)* W **2**. 1d. (P 11½–12½), 1d. (P 10), 2d. D.L.R. (Roul), 4d.(P 11½–12½) 4d. (P 10), 4d. (P 10 × 11½–12½), 6d. (Roul), 6d. (P 11½–12½), 1s. (P 11½–12½), 1s. (P 11½–12½ × Roul)
(b) W **7**. P 10. 4d.
(c) W **10**. 2d. D.L.R. (Roul), 2d. D.L.R. (P 10)

B.D. (Barracks Department)

Optd in red. W **2**. Roul. 2d., 6d., 1s.

B.G. (Botanic Garden)

Optd in black. (*a*) W **2**. 1d. (P 11½–12½ × R), 1d. (P 11½–12½), 1d.(P 10 × 11½–12½), 2d. D.L.R. (Roul), 6d. (Roul), 6d. (P 11½–12½ × Roul, 6d.(P 11½–12½), 1s. (P 11½–12½ × Roul), 1s. (P 11½–12½), 1s. (P 10), 1s. (P 10 × 11½–12½)
(*b*) W **7**. P 10, 2d. D.L.R.
(*c*) W **10**. 2d. D.L.R. (Roul), 2d. D.L.R. (P 10)
The 6d. (W **2**. Roul) is known without stamp after "B".

B.M. (Bench of Magistrates)

Optd in red. W **2**. Roul. 2d.
Optd in black. W **10**. Roul. 2d. D.L.R.

C. (Customs)

Optd in red. W **2**. 1d. (Roul), 2d. (Roul), 4d. (P 11½–12½), 6d. (Roul), 1s. (Roul)
Optd in blue (*a*) W **2**. Roul. 1d., 4d., 6d., 1s., 2s.
(*b*) W **10**. Roul. 2d. D.L.R.
Optd in black. (*a*) W **2** 1d. (Roul), 1d. (P 10), 1d. (P 10 × 11½–12½), 4d.(P 11½–12½), 4d. (P 10), 4d. (P 10 × 11½–12½), 6d. (Roul), 6d.(P 11½–12½), 6d. (P 10), 1s. (P 11½–12½ × Roul), 1s. (P 11½–12½), 2s. (Roul)
(*b*) W **7**. P 10. 2d. D.L.R.
(*c*) W **10**. 2d. D.L.R. (Roul), 2d. D.L.R. (P 10 × Roul), 2d. D.L.R. (P 10), 2d. D.L.R. (P 10 × 11½–12½)
The 2d. (W **10**. (Roul) with black overprint is known showing the error "G" for "C".

C.D. (Convict Department)

Optd in red. W **2**. 2d. (Roul), 4d. (P 11½–12½), 6d. (Roul), 1s. (Roul)
Optd in black. (*a*) W **2**. 1d. (P 11½–12½ × Roul), 2d. D.L.R. (Roul), 4d.(P 11½–12½), 6d. (Roul), 6d. (P 11½–12½ × Roul, 1s. (P 11½–12½ × Roul)
(*b*) W **10**. 2d. D.L.R. (Roul), 2d. D.L.R. (P 11½–12½), 2d. D.L.R.(P 11½–12½ × Roul)

C.L. (Crown Lands)

Optd in red. W **2**. 2d. (Roul), 4d. (P 11½–12½), 6d. (Roul), 1s. (Roul)
Optd in blue. (*a*) W **2**. Roul. 4d., 6d.
(*b*) W **10**. Roul. 2d. D.L.R.
Optd in black. (*a*) W **2**. 2d. D.L.R. (Roul), 4d. (P 11½–12½), 4d. (P 10), 4d.(P 10 × 11½–12½), 6d. (Roul), 6d. (P 11½–12½), 1s. (P 11½–12½ × Roul), 2s.(Roul), 2s. (P 11½–12½)
(*b*) W **7**. P 10. 2d. D.L.R., 4d.
(*c*) W **10**. 2d. D.L.R. (Roul), 2d. D.L.R. (P 10), 2d. D.L.R. (P 10 × 11½–12½)
The 2s. (W **2**. P 11½–12½) with black overprint is known showing the stop omitted after "L".

C.O. (Commissariat Office)

Optd in red. W **2**. (Roul), 4d. (P 11½–12½) 6d. (Roul), 1s. (Roul)
Optd in black. (*a*) W **2**. 4d. (P 10), 4d. (P 10 × 11½–12½), 6d. (P 11½–12½), 1s.(P 11½–12½), 2s. (Roul), 2s. (P 11½–12½)
(*b*) W **10**. 2d. D.L.R. (Roul), 2d. D.L.R. (P 10)
The 6d. (W **2**. Roul) with red overprint is known showing the error "O" for "C", and the 2s. (W **2**. P 11½–12½) with black overprint with the stop omitted after "O".

C.P. (Commissioner of Police)

Optd in red. W **2**. 2d. (Roul). 4d. (P 11½–12½), 6d. (Roul)

C.S. (Chief Secretary)

Optd in red. W **2**. 2d. (Roul), 4d. (P 11½–12½), 6d. (Roul), 1s. (Roul)
Optd in blue.(*a*) W **2**. Roul. 4d., 6d.
(*b*) W **10**. Roul. 2d. D.L.R.
Optd in black. (*a*) W **2**. 2d. D.L.R. (Roul), 4d. (Roul), 4d. (P 11½–12½ × Roul), 4d.(P 11½–12½), 4d. (P 10), 4d. (P 10 × 11½–12½), 6d. (P 11½–12½ × Roul), 6d.(P 11½–12½), 6d. (P 10), 6d. (P 10 × 11½–12½), 1s. (P 11½–12½ × Roul), 1s.(P 11½–12½), 1s. (P 10), 1s. (P 10 × 11½–12½), 2s. (P 10 × 11½–12½)
(*b*) W **7**. P 10. 2d.
(*c*) W **10**. 2d. D.L.R. (Roul), 2d. D.L.R. (P 10)
The 6d. and 1s. (W **2**. Roul) with red overprint are known showing the error "G" for "C".

C.Sgn. (Colonial Surgeon)

Optd in red. W **2**. 2d. (Roul), 4d. (P 11½–12½), 6d. (Roul)
Optd in black. (*a*) W **2**. 2d. D.L.R. (Roul), 4d. (P 10), 4d. (P 10 × 11½–12½), 6d.(Roul), 6d. (P 11½–12½ × Roul) 6d. (P 11½–12½)
(*b*) W **10**. 2d. D.L.R. (Roul), 2d. D.L.R. (P 11½–12½ × Roul), 2d. (P 10 × Roul), 2d. D.L.R. (P 10)
Two types of overprint exist on the 2d. D.L.R., the second type having block capitals instead of the serifed type used for the other values.

D.B. (Destitute Board)

Optd in red. W **2**. 1d. (Roul), 2d. (Roul), 4d. (P 11½–12½), 6d. (Roul), 1s. (Roul)
Optd in blue. (*a*) W **2**. 2d. D.L.R. (Roul), 4d. (P 11½–12½), 6d. (Roul)
(*b*) W **10**. Roul. 2d. D.L.R.
Optd in black. (*a*) W **2**. 1d. (P 11½–12½), 4d. (P 11½–12½), 4d. (P 10), 6d. (P 10 × 11½–12½) 1s (P 10)
(*b*) W **10**. 2d. D.L.R. (Roul), 2d. D.L.R. (P 11½–12½), 2d. D.L.R. (P 10), 2d. D.L.R. (P 10 × 11½–12½)
The 2d. D.L.R. (W **10**. P 10) with black overprint is known showing the stop omitted after "D".

D.R. (Deeds Registration)

Optd in red. W **2**. Roul, 2d., 6d.

E. (Engineer)

Optd in red. W **2**. 2d. (Roul), 4d. (P 11½–12½), 6d. (Roul), 1s. (Roul)
Optd in blue. (*a*) W **2**. Roul. 1s.
(*b*) W **10**. Roul. 2d. D.L.R.
Optd in black. (*a*) W **2**. 4d. (P 11½–12½), 4d. (P 10), 4d. (P 10 × 11½–12½), 6d.(P 11½–12½), 1s. (P 11½–12½ × Roul), 1s. (P 11½–12½), 1s. (P 10 × 11½–12½)
(*b*) W **7**. P 10. 4d.
(*c*) W **10**. P 10. 2d. D.L.R.

E.B. (Education Board)

Optd in red. W **2**. 2d. (Roul), 4d. (P 11½–12½), 6d. (Roul)
Optd in blue. (*a*) W **2**. Roul. 4d., 6d.
(*b*) W **10**. Roul. 2d. D.L.R.
Optd in black. (*a*) W **2**. 2d. D.L.R. (Roul), 4d (Roul), 4d. (P 11½–12½), 4d. (P 10), 6d. (P 11½–12½ × Roul), 6d. (P 11½ × 12½)
(*b*) W **7**. P 10. 2d. D.L.R.
(*c*) W **10**. 2d. D.L.R. (Roul), 2d. D.L.R. (P 10), 2d. D.L.R. (P 10 × 11½–12½)

G.F. (Gold Fields)

Optd in black. (*a*) W **2**. Roul. 6d.
(*b*) W **10**. 2d. D.L.R. (P 10 × Roul), 2d. D.L.R. (P 10)

G.P. (Government Printer)

Optd in red. W **2**. Roul. 1d., 2d., 6d., 1s.
Optd in blue. (*a*) W **2**. Roul. 1d., 6d., 1s., 2s.
(*b*) W **10**. Roul. 2d. D.L.R.
Optd in black. (*a*) W **2**. 1d. (Roul), 1d. (P 11½–12½ × Roul), 1d. (P 11½–12½) 1d.(P 10) 1d. (P 10 × 11½–12½), 6d. (P 11½–12½ × Roul), 1s. (P 10 × 11½–12½), 2s. (Roul), 2s. (P 11½–12½) 2s. (P 10 × 11½–12½)
(*b*) W **10**. 2d. D.L.R. (Roul), 2d. D.L.R.(P 10)
The 1d. and 1s. (W **2**. Roul) with red overprint are known showing "C.P." instead of "G.P.".

G.S. (Government Storekeeper)

Optd in red. W **2**. Roul. 2d.

G.T. (Goolwa Tramway)

Optd in red. W **2**. 1d. (Roul), 2d. (Roul), 4d. (P 11½–12½), 6d. (Roul), 1s. (Roul)
Optd in black. (*a*) W **2**. 2d. D.L.R. (Roul), 4d. (P 11½–12½)
(*b*) W **10**. Roul. 2d. D.L.R.
The 2d. and 6d. (both W **2**. Roul) with red overprint are known showing the stop omitted after "T". The 6d, and 1s. (W **2**. Roul) with red overprint are known showing "C.T.", instead of "G.T.".

H. (Hospitals)

Optd in black. (*a*) W **2**. P 10 × 11½–12½. 4d.
(*b*) W **7**. P 10. 2d. D.L.R.
(*c*) W **10**. 2d. D.L.R. (P 10), 2d. D.L.R. (P 10 × 11½–12½)

H.A. (House of Assembly)

Optd in red. W **2**. 1d. (Roul), 2d. (Roul), 4d. (P 11½–12½), 6d. (Roul), 1s. (Roul)
Optd in black. (*a*) W **2**. 1d. (P 11½–12½), 1d. (P 10) 1d. (P 10 × 11½–12½), 4d.(P 11½–12½), 4d. (P 10) 6d. (Roul), 6d. (P 11½–12½) 1s. (P 11½–12½ × Roul), 1s. (P 11½–12½)
(*b*) W **10**. 2d. D.L.R. (Roul), 2d. D.L.R. (P 10)

I.A. (Immigration Agent)

Optd in red. W **2**. 1d. (Roul), 2d. (Roul), 4d. (P 11½–12½), 6d. (Roul)

I.E. (Intestate Estates)

Optd in black. W **10**. P 10. 2d. D.L.R.

I.S. (Inspector of Sheep)

Optd in red. W **2**. Roul. 2d., 6d.
Optd in blue. W **2**. P 11½–12½. 6d.
Optd in black. (*a*) W **2**. 2d. D.L.R. (Roul), 6d. (P 11½–12½ × Roul)
(*b*) W **10**. 2d. D.L.R. (Roul). 2d. D.L.R. (P 10)

L.A. (Lunatic Asylum)

Optd in red. W **2**. 1d. (Roul), 2d. (Roul), 4d. (P 11½–12½), 6d. (Roul), 1s. (Roul)
Optd in black. (*a*) W **2**. 4d. (P 11½–12½), 4d. (P 10), 4d. (P 10 × 11½–12½), 6d.(P 11½–12½), 1s. (P 11½–12½), 2s. (Roul)
(*b*) W **10**. 2d. D.L.R. (Roul), 2d. D.L.R. (P 10)

L.C. (Legislative Council)

Optd in red. W **2**. Roul. 2d., 6d.
Optd in black. (*a*) W **2**. Roul. 6d.
(*b*) W **10**. 2d. D.L.R. (Roul), 2d. D.L.R. (P 10 × Roul)
The 2d. and 6d. (both W **2**. Roul) with red overprint are known showing the stop omitted after "C".

L.L. (Legislative Librarian)

Optd in red. W **2**. 2d. (Roul), 4d. (P 11½–12½), 6d. (Roul)
Optd in black. (*a*) W **2**. P 11½–12½. 6d.
(*b*) W **10**. P 10. 2d. D.L.R.
The 2d. and 6d. (both W **2**. Roul) with red overprint are known showing the stop omitted from between the two letters.

L.T. (Land Titles)

Optd in red. W **2**. 2d. (Roul), 4d. (P 11½–12½), 6d. (Roul), 1s. (Roul)
Optd in blue. W **10**. Roul. 2d. D.L.R.
Optd in black. (*a*) W **2**. 4d. (P 11½–12½), 4d. (P 10), 4d. (P 10 × 11½–12½), 6d.(P 11½–12½ × Roul), 6d. (P 11½–12½), 6d. (P 10), 6d. (P 10 × 11½–12½)
(*b*) W **7**. P 10. 2d. D.L.R.
(*c*) W **10**. 2d. D.L.R. (Roul), 2d. D.L.R. (P 10)
The 2d. and 6d. (both W **2**. Roul) with red overprint are known showing the stop omitted after "T".

M. (Military)

Optd in red. W **2**. Roul. 2d., 6d., 1s.
Optd in black. W **2**. 6d. (P 11½–12½ × Roul), 1s. (P 11½–12½ × Roul), 2s. (Roul)

M.B. (Marine Board)

Optd in red. W **2**. 1d. (Roul), 2d. (Roul), 4d. (Roul), 4d. (P 11½–12½), 6d. (Roul), 1s. (Roul)
Optd in black. (*a*) W **2**. 1d. (Roul), 1d. (P 11½–12½), 2d. D.L.R. (Roul), 4d. (P 11½–12½ × Roul), 4d. (P 11½–12½), 4d. (P 10), 4d. (P 10 × 11½–12½), 6d. (Roul), 6d. (P 11½–12½), 6d. (P 10), 6d. (P 10 × 11½–12½), 1s. (P 11½–12½ × Roul), 1s. (P 11½–12½) 1s. (P 10), 1s. (P 10 × 11½–12½)
(*b*) W **7**. P 10. 4d.
(*c*) W **10**. Roul. 2d. D.L.R.

M.R. (Manager of Railways)

Optd in red. W **2**. Roul. 2d., 6d.
Optd in black. (*a*) W **2**. 1d. (P 11½–12½), 1d. (P 10), 2d. D.L.R. (Roul), 4d. (Roul), 4d. (P 11½–12½), 6d. (P 11½–12½ × Roul), 1s. (P 11½–12½ × Roul), 2s.(P 11½–12½ 1, 2s. (P 10 × 11½–12½)
(*b*) W **10**. 2d. D.L.R. (Roul), 2d. D.L.R. (P 10), 2d. D.L.R. (P 10 × 11½–12½)

M.R.G. (Main Roads Gambierton)

Optd in red without stops. W **2**. Roul. 2d., 6d.
Optd in blue without stops. W **10**. Roul. 2d. D.L.R.
Optd in black without stops. W **10**. 2d. D.L.R. (Roul), 2d. D.L.R (Roul 10)
Optd in black with stops. W **10**. 2d. D.L.R. (Roul), 2d. D.L.R (Roul 10)
The 2d. D.L.R. (W **10**. P 10) with black overprint is known showing the stops omitted after "M" and "R".

N.T. (Northern Territory)

Optd in black (*a*) W **2**. P 11½–12½. 1d., 3d. on 4d., 6d., 1s.
(*b*) W **10**. 2d. D.L.R. (Roul), 2d. D.L.R. (P 10)

O.A. (Official Assignee)

Optd in red. W **2**. 2d. (Roul), 4d. (P 11½–12½)
Optd in blue. W **10**. Roul. 2d. D.L.R.
Optd in black. (*a*) W **2**. P 10. 4d.
(*b*) W **7**. P 10. 2d. D.L.R.
(*c*) W **10**. 2d. D.L.R. (Roul), 2d. D.L.R. (P 10 × roul), 2d D.L.R. (P 10)

P. (Police)

Optd in blue. (*a*) W **2**. Roul. 6d.
(*b*) W **10**. Roul. 2d. D.L.R.
Optd in black. (*a*) W **2**. 6d. (P 11½–12½ × Roul), 6d. (P 11½–12½), 6d. (P 10)
(*b*) W **7**. P 10. 2d. D.L.R.
(*c*) W **10**. 2d. D.L.R. (Roul), 2d. D.L.R. (P 11½–12½), 2d. D.L.R.(P 11½–12½ × Roul), 2d. D.L.R. (P 10 × Roul), 2d. D.L.R. (P 10), 2d. D.L.R.(P 10 × 11½–12½)

P.A. (Protector of Aborigines)

Optd in red. W **2**. Roul. 2d., 6d.
Optd in black. (*a*) W **2**. P. 2d. D.L.R., 6d.
(*b*) W **10**. 2d. D.L.R. (Roul), 2d. D.L.R. (P 10)

P.O. (Post Office)

Optd in red. W **2**. Roul. 1d., 2d., 6d., 1s.
Optd in blue. (*a*) W **2**. Roul. 2d.
(*b*) W **10**. Roul. 2d. D.L.R.
Optd in black. (*a*) W **2**. 1d. (P 10 × 11½–12½), 2d. D.L.R. (Roul), 2d. D.L.R. (P 11½–12½ × Roul), 4d. (P 11½–12½), 6d. (Roul), 6d. (P 11½ × 12½), 1s. (P 11½–12½ × Roul, 1s. (P 11½ × 12½) 1s. (P 11½–12½), 1s. (P 10) 1s. (P 10 × 11½–12½)
(*b*) W **10**. 2d. D.L.R. (Roul), 2d. (P 11½–12½ × Roul), 2d. D.L.R. (P 10 × Roul), 2d. D.L.R. (P 10)
The 4d. (W **2**. P 11½–12½) with black overprint is known showing the stop omitted after "O".

P.S. (Private Secretary)

Optd in red. W **2**. 1d. (Roul), 2d. (Roul), 4d. (P 11½–12½), 6d. (Roul), 1s. (Roul)
Optd in black. (*a*) W **2**. 1d. (P 11½–12½ × Roul), 1d. (P 11½–12½), 1d. (P 10), 2d.(Roul), 3d. (in black) on 4d. (P 11½–12½), 3d. (in red) on 4d. (P 10), 3d. (in black) on 4d. (P 10), 4d. (P 11½–12½), 4d. (P 10), 4d. (P 10 × 11½–12½) 6d.(Roul), 6d. (P 11½–12½ × Roul), 6d. (P 11½–12½), 6d. (P 10), 9d. (Roul), 9d.(P 11½–12½) 10d. on 9d. (P 10), 10d. on 9d. (P 10 × 11½–12½), 1s. (P 11½–12½ × Roul)
(*b*) W **7**. P 10. 2d. D.L.R.
(*c*) W **10**. 2d. D.L.R. (Roul), 2d. D.L.R. (P 10)

P.W. (Public Works)

Optd in red without stop after "W". W **2**. Roul. 2d., 6d., 1s.
Optd in black. (*a*) W **2**. 2d. D.L.R. (Roul), 4d. (P 10), 6d. (Roul), 6d.(P 11½–12½), 1s. (P 11½–12½ × Roul)
(*b*) W **10**. 2d. D.L.R. (Roul), 2d. D.L.R. (P 10)

R.B. (Road Board)

Optd in red. W **2**. 1d. (Roul), 2d. (Roul), 4d. (P 11½–12½), 6d. (Roul), 1s. (Roul)
Optd in blue without stops. W **10**. Roul. 2d D.L.R
Optd in black.(*a*) W **2**. 1d. (P 11½–12½ × Roul), 1d. (P 10), 4d. (Roul), 4d. (P 10), 6d. (P 10), 2s. (Roul)
(*b*) W **7**. P 10. 2d. D.L.R.
(*c*) W **10**. 2d. D.L.R. (Roul), 2d. (D.L.R.) (P 10 × Roul), 2d. D.L.R. (P 10)

The 6d. (W **2**. Roul) with red overprint is known showing the stop omitted after "B".

R.G. (Registrar-General)

Optd in red. W **2**. Roul. 2d., 6d., 1s.
Optd in blue. (*a*) W **2**. P 11½–12½ × Roul. 6d.
(*b*) W **10**. 2d. D.L.R. (Roul), 2d. D.L.R. (P 11½–12½ × Roul)
Optd in black. (*a*) W **2**. 2d. D.L.R. (Roul), 6d. (P 10), 6d. (P 10 × 11½–12½), 1s.(P 11½–12½ x Roul), 1s. (P 10)
(*b*) W **7**. P 10. 2d. D.L.R.
(*c*) W **10**. 2d. D.L.R. (Roul), 2d. D.L.R. (P 10 × Roul), 2d. D.L.R. (P 10), 2d. D.L.R. (P 10 × 11½–12½)

The 2d. (W **2**. Roul) with red overprint is known showing "C" for "G".

S. (Sheriff)

Optd in red. W **2**. Roul. 2d., 6d.
Optd in blue. W **10**. Roul. 2d. D.L.R.
Optd in black. (*a*) W **2**. 6d. (Roul), 6d. (P 11½–12½ × Roul), 6d. (P 11½–12½), 6d.(P 10)
(*b*) W **10**. 2d. D.L.R. (Roul), 2d. D.L.R. (P 10 × Roul), 2d. D.L.R. (P 10)

S.C. (Supreme Court)

Optd in red. W **2**. Roul. 2d. 6d.
Optd in black. W **10**. P 10. 2d. D.L.R.

S.G. (Surveyor-General)

Optd in red. W **2**. 2d. (Roul), 4d. (P 11½–12½), 6d. (Roul)
Optd in blue. (*a*) W **2**. Roul. 4d.
(*b*) W **10**. Roul. 2d. D.L.R.
Optd in black. (*a*) W **2**. 2d. D.L.R. (Roul), 4d. (P 11½–12½), 4d. (P 10) 4d.(P 10 × 11½–12½), 6d. (P 11½–12½ × Roul), 6d. (P 11½–12½), 6d. (P 10), 6d.(P 10 × 11½–12½)
(*b*) W **7**. P 10. 2d. D.L.R.
(*c*) W **10**. 2d. D.L.R. (Roul), 2d. D.L.R. (P 11½–12½), 2d. D.L.R. (P 10 × Roul), 2d. D.L R (P 10)

The 2d. (W **7** and W **10**. P 10) with black overprint are known showing "C" for "G".

S.M. (Stipendiary Magistrate)

Optd in red. W **2**. Roul. 1d., 2d., 4d., 6d., 1s.
Optd in blue. (*a*) W **2**. Roul. 2d., 4d., 6d.
(*b*) W **10**. Roul. 2d. D.L.R.
Optd in black. (*a*) W **2**. 1d. (P 11½–12½), 1d. (P 10), 2d. D.L.R. (Roul), 4d. (Roul), 4d. (P 11½–12½ × Roul), 4d. (P 11½–12½), 4d. (P 10), 4d. (P 10 × 11½–12½), 6d. (P 11½–12½ × Roul), 6d. (P 11½–12½), 6d. (P 10), 6d. (P 10 × 11½–12½), 1s. (P 11½–12½ × Roul)
(*b*) W **7**. P 10. 2d. D.L.R.
(*c*) W **10**. 2d. D.L.R. (Roul), 2d. D.L.R. (P 11½–12½), 2d. D.L.R. (P 10 × Roul) 2d. D.L.R. (P 10), 2d D.L.R. (P 10 × 11½–12½)

The 2d. and 4d. (both W **2**. Roul) with red overprint are known showing the stop omitted after "M".

S.T. (Superintendent of Telegraphs)

Optd in red. W **2**. Roul. 2d., 6d.
Optd in blue. W **10**. Roul. 2d. D.L.R.
Optd in black. (*a*) W **2**. Roul. 2d. D.L.R., 6d.
(*b*) W **7**. P 10. 2d. D.L.R.
(*c*) W **10**. 2d. D.L.R. (Roul), 2d. D.L.R. (P 10 × Roul), 2d. D.L.R. (P 10)

The 2d. and 6d. (both W **2**. Roul) with red overprint are known showing the stop omitted after "T".

T. (Treasury)

Optd in red. W **2**. 1d. (Roul), 2d. (Roul), 4d. (P 11½–12½ × Roul), 6d. (Roul), 1s.(Roul)
Optd in blue. (*a*) W **2**. Roul. 1d., 4d., 6d.
(*b*) W **10**. Roul. 2d. D.L.R.
Optd in black. (*a*) W **2**. 1d. (P 10), 2d. D.L.R. (Roul), 4d. (Roul), 4d.(P 11½–12½), 4d. (P 10), 6d. (Roul), 6d. (P 11½–12½), 1s. (P 11½–12½ × Roul), 1s. (P 10 × 11½–12½), 2s. (Roul), 2s. (P 11½–12½), 2s. (P 10 × 11½–12½)
(*b*) W **7**. P 10. 2d. D.L.R.
(*c*) W **10**. 2d. D.L.R. (Roul), 2d. D.L.R. (P 10)

T.R. (Titles Registration)

Optd in black. (*a*) W **2**. 4d. (P 11½–12½), 4d. (P 10 × 11½–12½), 6d.(P 11½–12½), 1s. (P 11½–12½)
(*b*) W **10**. P 10. 2d. D.L.R.

V. (Volunteers)

Optd in black. (*a*) W **2**. 4d. (P 10 × 11½–12½), 6d. (P 11½–12½), 1s.(P 11½–12½)
(*b*) W **10**. P 10. 2d. D.L.R.
(*c*) W **10**. 2d. D.L.R. (Roul), 2d. D.L.R. (P 10 × Roul), 2d. D.L.R. (P 10)

The 2d. (W **10**. P 10 × Roul) overprinted in black is only known showing the stop omitted after "V".

VA. (Valuator of Runs)

Optd in black without stop after "V". (*a*) W **2**. Roul. 4d.
(*b*) W **10**. P 10. 2d. D.L.R.

VN. (Vaccination)

Optd in black without stop after "V". W **2**. 4d. (P 10), 4d. (P 10 × 11½–12½)

W. (Waterworks)

Optd in red. W **2**. Roul. 2d.
Optd in black. W **10**. 2d. D.L.R. (Roul), 2d. D.L.R. (P 10)

The 2d. (W **2**. Roul) with red overprint is known showing the stop omitted after "W".

B. General

O.S. (O 1) **O.S.** (O 2)

1874–77. *Optd with Type* O **1**. W **2**.

		(*a*) P 10.		
O1	**3**	4d. dull purple (18.2.74)	£1100	£300
		(*b*) P 11½–12½ × 10.		
O2	**1**	1d. green (2.1.74)	—	£250
O3	**3**	4d. dull violet (12.2.75)	65·00	5·00
O4	**1**	6d. Prussian blue (20.10.75)	75·00	9·00
O4*a*	**3**	2s. rose-pink		
O5		2s. carmine (3.12.76)	—	£100
		(*c*) P 11½–12½.		
O 6	**1**	1d. deep yellow-green (30.1.74)	£1200	£150
		a. Printed on both sides	—	£650
O 7	**3**	3d.on 4d. ultramarine (26.6.77)	£2250	£1000
		a. No stop after "S"	—	£1500
O 8		4d. dull violet (13.7.74)	50·00	6·50
		a. No stop after "S"	—	40·00
O 9	**1**	6d. bright blue (31.8.75)	90·00	13·00
		a. "O.S." double	—	£100
O10		6d. Prussian blue (27.3.74)	80·00	7·50
		a. No stop after "S"	—	45·00
O11	**4**	9d. red-purple (22.3.76)	£1100	£550
		a. No stop after "S"	£1600	£850
O12	**1**	1s. red-brown (5.8.74)	70·00	6·00
		a. "O.S." double	—	£100
		b. No stop after "S"	£160	45·00
O13	**3**	2s. crimson-carmine (13.7.75)	£130	20·00
		a. No stop after "S"	—	75·00
		b. No stops	—	90·00
		c. Stops at top of letters		

1876–85. *Optd with Type* O **1**. W **8**.

		(*a*) P 10.		
O14	**1**	6d. bright blue (1879)	80·00	13·00
		(*b*) P 10 × 11½–12½, 11½–12½ × 10, or compound.		
O15	**3**	4d. violet-slate (24.1.78)	70·00	6·50
O16		4d. plum (29.11.81)	38·00	2·75
O17		4d. deep mauve	38·00	2·50
		a. No stop after "S"	£120	30·00
		b. No stop after "O"		
		c. "O.S." double		
		d. "O.S." inverted	—	£130
O18	**1**	6d. bright blue (1877)	65·00	4·75
		a. "O.S." inverted		
		b. No stop after "O"		
O19		6d. bright ultramarine (27.3.85)	60·00	4·50
		a. "O.S." inverted		
		b. "O.S." double		
		c. "O.S." double, one inverted	—	£275
		d. No stop after "S"	—	40·00
		e. No stops after "O" & "S"		
O20		1s. red-brown (27.3.83)	55·00	7·00
		a. "O.S." inverted		
		b. No stop after "O"		
		c. No stop after "S"	—	45·00
O21	**3**	2s. carmine (16.3.81)	£100	8·00
		a. "O.S." inverted	—	£170
		b. No stop after "S"	—	60·00
		(*c*) P 11½–12½.		
O22	**3**	3d.on 4d. ultramarine	£2250	
O23		4d. violet-slate (14.3.76)	£140	11·00
O24		4d. deep mauve (19.8.79)	55·00	4·00
		a. "O.S." inverted		
		b. "O.S." double, one inverted		
		c. No stop after "S"	—	35·00
O25	**1**	6d. Prussian blue (6.77)	65·00	7·00
		a. "O.S." double	—	75·00
		b. "O.S." inverted		
O26	**4**	8d.on 9d. brown (9.11.76)	£1600	£750
		a. "O.S." double	£2250	
		b. "O" only	—	£1000
O26*c*		9d. purple	£3000	
O27	**1**	1s. red-brown (12.2.78)	35·00	8·50
		a. "O.S." inverted	£225	£110
		b. No stop after "S"	£190	45·00
O28		1s. lake-brown (8.11.83)	38·00	3·50
O29	**3**	2s. rose-carmine (12.8.85)	£100	8·50
		a. "O.S." double	—	£100
		b. "O.S." inverted	—	£110
		c. No stop after "S"	—	45·00

1891–1903. *Optd with Type* O **2**.

		(*a*) W **8**. P 11½–12½.		
O30	**1**	1s. lake-brown (18.4.91)	50·00	10·00
O31		1s. Vandyke brown	60·00	7·00
O32		1s. dull brown (2.7.96)	38·00	5·50
		a. No stop after "S"	—	60·00
O33		1s. sepia (large holes) (4.1.02)	30·00	5·50
		a. "O.S." double		
		b. No stop after "S"		
O34	**3**	2s. carmine (26.6.00)	85·00	15·00
		a. No stop after "S"		
		(*b*) W **8**. P 10 × 11½–12½.		
O35	**3**	2s. rose-carmine (9.11.95)	70·00	10·00
		a. No stop after "S"	£140	
		b. "O.S." double		
		(*c*) W **10**. P 11½–12½.		
O36	**1**	1s. dull brown (1902)	55·00	12·00

1874–76. *Optd with Type* O **1**. W **10**.

		(*a*) P 10.		
O37	**11**	1d. blue-green (30.9.75)	85·00	20·00
		a. "O.S." inverted		
		b. No stop after "S"		
O38	**12**	2d. orange-red (18.2.74)	19·00	2·50
		a. No stop after "S"	—	26·00
		b. "O.S." double		
		(*b*) P 10 × 11½–12½, 11½–12½ × 10, or compound.		
O39	**11**	1d. blue-green (16.9.75)		
		a. No stop after "S"		
O40	**12**	2d. orange-red (27.9.76)	—	9·00
		(*c*) P 11½–12½.		
O41	**11**	1d. blue-green (13.8.75)	—	24·00
		a. "O.S." inverted		
		b. No stop after "S"		
O42	**12**	2d. orange-red (20.5.74)	—	90·00

1876–80. *Optd with Type* O **1**. W **13**.

		(*a*) P 10.		
O43	**11**	1d. blue-green (2.10.76)	13·00	1·00
		a. "O.S." inverted	—	45·00
		b. "O.S." double	65·00	40·00
		c. "O.S." double, one inverted		
		d. No stops	—	25·00
		e. No stop after "O"		
		f. No stop after "S"	—	12·00
		g. Deep green	16·00	1·00
		ga. "O.S." double	—	45·00
O44	**12**	2d. orange-red (21.9.77)	8·00	1·00
		a. "O.S." inverted	—	20·00
		b. "O.S." double	75·00	35·00
		c. "O.S." double, one inverted		
		d. "O.S." double, both inverted	—	£110
		e. No stops	—	50·00
		f. No stop after "O"	—	16·00
		g. No stop after "S"		
		h. Dull brick-red	35·00	1·00
		(*b*) P 10 × 11½–12½, 11½–12½ × 10 or compound.		
O45	**11**	1d. deep green (14.8.80)	—	28·00
		a. "O.S." double		
O46	**12**	2d. orange-red (6.4.78)	55·00	10·00
		a. "O.S." inverted	—	£110
		b. No stop after "S"	—	50·00
		(*c*) P 11½–12½.		
O47	**12**	2d. orange-red (15.7.80)	—	70·00

1882 (20 Feb). *No. 181 optd with Type* O **1**.

O48	**11**	½d.on 1d. blue-green	60·00	15·00
		a. "O.S." inverted		

1888 (15 Nov)–**91**. *Nos. 184 and 185a optd with Type* O **1**. P 10.

O49	**17**	4d. pale violet (24.1.91)	65·00	5·00
O50	**18**	6d. blue	23·00	1·25
		a. "O.S." double		
		b. No stop after "S"		

1891. *Nos. 229b and 231a/2 optd with Type* O **1**.

		(*a*) P 10.		
O51	**17**	2½d.on 4d. deep green (Br.) (1 Aug)	65·00	9·50
		a. "2" and "½" closer together	—	45·00
		b. "O.S." inverted		
		c. "O.S." double		
		d. "OS." omitted (in vert pair with normal)		
		e. No stop after "S"		
		(*b*) P 10 × 11½–12½ or 11½–12½ × 10.		
O52	**17**	2½d.on 4d. deep green (Br.) (1 Oct)	70·00	15·00
		(*c*) P 11½–12½.		
O53	**17**	2½d.on 4d. deep green (Br.) (1 June)	£120	60·00

1891–96. *Optd with Type* O **2**. W **13**.

		(*a*) P 10.		
O54	**11**	1d. deep green (22.4.91)	21·00	2·00
		a. "OS." double	65·00	35·00
		b. "O.S." double, one inverted		
		c. No stop after "S"	40·00	10·00
		d. Blackish blue opt	£200	4·00
O55	**12**	2d. orange-red (22.4.91)	21·00	1·50
		a. "O.S." double		
		b. "O.S." double, both inverted		
		c. No stop after "S"	—	12·00
		(*b*) P 15.		
O56	**11**	1d. green (8.9.94)	11·00	1·25
		a. "O.S." double		
		b. No stop after "S"		
O57	**12**	2d. orange-red (16.6.94)	11·00	50
		a. "O.S." double	—	26·00
		b. "O.S." inverted	—	19·00
		(*c*) P 13.		
O58	**11**	1d. green (20.5.95)	20·00	60
		a. No stop after "S"	60·00	10·00
O59	**12**	2d. orange-red (11.2.96)	20·00	50
		a. "O.S." double	95·00	
		b. No stop after "S"	55·00	10·00

1891–99. *Optd with Type* O **2**. W **13** (sideways on ½d.).

(a) P 10.

O60 **15** ½d. brown (2.5.94) . . . 18·00 5·00
a. No stop after "S" . . . 50·00 29·00
O61 **17** 4d. pale violet (13.2.91) . . . 50·00 3·50
a. "O.S." double
b. "S." omitted . . . — 65·00
c. No stop after "S"
d. Aniline violet (31.8.93) . . . 50·00 4·00
da. "O.S." double
dc. No stop after "S"
O62 **18** 6d. blue (4.4.93) . . . 20·00 2·50
a. No stop after "S"
b. Blackish blue opt

(b) P 10 × 11½–12½.

O63 **15** ½d. brown (26.3.95) . . . 15·00 7·00

(c) P 11½–12½.

O64 **15** ½d. red-brown (13.6.91) . . . 40·00 10·00

(d) P 15.

O65 **15** ½d. pale brown (8.6.95) . . . 27·00 8·50
O66 **17** 4d. slate-violet (4.4.95) . . . 65·00 4·50
a. "O.S." double . . . £170 35·00
O67 **18** 6d. blue (20.9.93) . . . 27·00 3·50

(e) P 13.

O68 **15** ½d. deep brown (17.5.98) . . . 16·00 6·00
a. Opt triple, twice sideways . . . £170
O69 **17** 4d. violet (12.96) . . . 65·00 3·00
a. "O.S." double . . . £140 35·00
b. No stop after "S" . . . £140 26·00
O70 **18** 6d. blue (13.9.99) . . . 29·00 2·00
a. No stop after "S" . . . 90·00 55·00

1891–95. *Nos.* 229*b*, 230*a and* 231*a optd with Type* O **2**.

(a) P 10.

O71 **17** 2½d.on 4d. deep green (Br.) (18.8.94) . . . 38·00 12·00
a. Fraction bar omitted
b. "2" and "½" closer together . . . 90·00 35·00
c. "O.S." inverted . . . £170
d. No stop after "S" . . . — 45·00
O72 **18** 5d.on 6d. deep brown (C.) (2.12.91) . . . 45·00 17·00
a. No stop after "5D" . . . £200
b. No stop after "S" . . . £110 45·00

(b) P 10 × 11½–12½.

O73 **17** 2½d.on 4d. deep green (Br.) (17.9.95) . . . — 55·00
a. "O.S." double

1897–1901. *Nos.* 235/6 *and* 238*a optd with Type* O **2**.

(a) P 15.

O74 **23** 5d. brown-purple (29.3.01) . . . 65·00 11·00

(b) P 13

O75 **22** 2½d. violet-blue (5.7.97) . . . 50·00 7·00
a. No stop after "s" . . . — 32·00
O76 **23** 5d. purple (29.9.01) . . . 65·00 13·00
a. No stop after "S"

O. S.

(O 3)

1899–1901. *Optd with Type* O **3**. W **13**. P 13.

O80 **24** ½d. yellow-green (12.2.00) . . . 15·00 6·00
a. "O.S." inverted . . . 60·00
b. No stop after "S" . . . 38·00
O81 **11** 1d. rosine (22.9.99) . . . 13·00 1·60
a. "O.S." inverted . . . 50·00 35·00
b. "O.S." double . . . † £200
c. No stop after "S" . . . 42·00 16·00
O82 **12** 2d. bright violet (1.6.00) . . . 15·00 80
a. "O.S." inverted . . . 45·00 24·00
b. "O.S." double
c. No stop after "S" . . . 35·00
O83 **22** 2½d. indigo (2.10.01) . . . 55·00 19·00
a. "O.S." inverted . . . — 70·00
b. No stop after "S" . . . £160
O84 **17** 4d. violet (18.11.00) . . . 50·00 5·00
a. "O.S." inverted . . . £180
b. No stop after "S" . . . £140
O85 **18** 6d. blue (8.10.00) . . . 21·00 5·00
a. No stop after "S" . . . 60·00

1891 (May). *Optd as Type* O **3** *but wider*. W **13**. P 10.

O86 **19** 2s.6d. pale violet . . . £3250 £2750
O87 5s. pale rose . . . £3250 £2750

Only one sheet (60) of each of these stamps was printed.

The use of stamps overprinted "O S" was made invalid by the Posts and Telegraph Act of 1 November 1902.

South Australia became part of the Commonwealth of Australia on 1 January 1901.

TASMANIA

PRICES FOR STAMPS ON COVER

Nos.	1/4	*from* × 6
Nos.	5/12	*from* × 5
Nos.	14/24	*from* × 3
Nos.	25/56	*from* × 5
Nos.	57/77	*from* × 6
Nos.	78/9	—
Nos.	80/90	*from* × 3
No.	91	—
Nos.	92/109	*from* × 3
No.	110	—
Nos.	111/23	*from* × 3
Nos.	124/6	—
Nos.	127/34	*from* × 5
Nos.	135/55	*from* × 4
Nos.	156/8	*from* × 20
Nos.	159/66	*from* × 10
Nos.	167/9	*from* × 15
Nos.	170/4	*from* × 6
Nos.	216/22	*from* × 15
Nos.	223/5	—
Nos.	226/7	*from* × 15
Nos.	229/36	*from* × 20
Nos.	237/57	*from* × 10
No.	258	—
Nos.	259/62	*from* × 10
Nos.	F1/25	—
Nos.	F26/9	*from* × 15
Nos.	F30/9	—

SPECIMEN OVERPRINTS. Those listed are from U.P.U. distributions between 1892 and 1904. Further "Specimen" overprints exist, but these were used for other purposes.

1

2

3

(Eng C.W. Coard. Recess H. and C. Best at the *Courier* newspaper, Hobart)

1853 (1 Nov). *Twenty-four varieties in four rows of six each.* No wmk. Imperf.

(a) Medium soft yellowish paper with all lines clear and distinct.

1 **1** 1d. pale blue . . . £4000 £1000
2 1d. blue . . . £4000 £1000

(b) Thin hard white paper with lines of the engraving blurred and worn.

3 **1** 1d. pale blue . . . £3750 £900
4 1d. blue . . . £3750 £900

1853 (1 Nov)–**54**. No wmk. Imperf. *In each plate there are twenty-four varieties in four rows of six each.*

(a) Plate I. Finely engraved. All lines in network and background thin, clear, and well defined. (1853).

(i) First state of the plate, brilliant colours.

5 **2** 4d. bright red-orange . . . £3000 £700
a. Double impression
6 4d. bright brownish orange . . . — £850

(ii) Second state of plate, with blurred lines and worn condition of the central background.

7 **2** 4d. red-orange . . . £2250 £450
8 4d. orange . . . £2000 £425
9 4d. pale orange . . . — £425

(b) Plate II. Coarse engraving, lines in network and background thicker and blurred (Dec. 1854).

10 **2** 4d. orange . . . £2000 £400
a. Double print, one albino
11 4d. dull orange . . . £2000 £350
12 4d. yellowish orange . . . £2000 £350

In the 4d. Plate I, the outer frame-line is thin all round. In Plate II it is, by comparison with other parts, thicker in the lower left angle.

The 4d. is known on vertically laid paper from proof sheets. Examples from Plate I have the lines close together and those from Plate II wide apart (Price £5000 *unused*).

In 1879 reprints were made of the 1d. in blue and the 4d., Plate I, in brownish yellow, on thin, tough, white wove paper, and perforated 11½. In 1887, a reprint from the other plate of the 4d. was made was made in reddish brown and black, and in 1889 of the 1d. in blue and in black, and of the 4d. (both plates) in yellow and in black on white card, imperforate. As these three plates were defaced after the stamps had been superseded, all these reprints show two, or three thick strokes across the Queen's head.

All three plates were destroyed in July 1950.

PERKINS BACON "CANCELLED". For notes on these handstamps, showing"CANCELLED" between horizontal bars forming an oval, see Catalogue Introduction.

(Eng W. Humphrys, after water-colour sketch by E. Corbould. Recess P.B.)

1855 (17 Aug–16 Sept). Wmk Large Star. W w **1**. Imperf.

14 **3** 1d. carmine (16.9) (H/S "CANCELLED" in oval £6500) . . . £4500 £800
15 2d. deep green (16.9) . . . £2000 £500
16 2d. green (16.9) (H/S "CANCELLED" in oval £7500) . . . £2000 £450
17 4d. deep blue . . . £1500 95·00
18 4d. blue (H/S "CANCELLED" in oval £5500) . . . £1500 £110

Proofs of the 1d. and 4d. on thick paper, *without watermark*, are sometimes offered as the issued stamps. The 6d. dull lilac on this watermark was prepared, but not issued. Examples exist from a creased proof sheet (*Price* £750 *unused*).

(Recess H. and C. Best, Hobart, from P.B. plates)

1856 (Apr)–**57**. No wmk. Imperf.

(a) Thin white paper.

19 **3** 1d. pale brick-red (4.56) . . . £5000 £550
20 2d. dull emerald-green (1.57) . . . £6000 £850
21 4d. deep blue (5.57) . . . £700 £100
22 4d. blue (5.57) . . . £600 £100
23 4d. pale blue (5.57) . . . — £140

(b) Pelure paper.

24 **3** 1d. deep red-brown (11.56) . . . £3500 £650

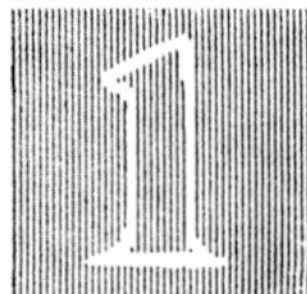

4

7

8

(Recess H. Best (August 1857–May 1859), J. Davies (August 1859–March 1862), J. Birchall (March 1863), M. Hood (October 1863–April 1864), Govt Printer (from July 1864), all from P.B. plates)

1857 (Aug)–**69**. Wmk double-lined numerals "1", "2" or "4" as W **4** on appropriate value. Imperf.

25 **3** 1d. deep red-brown . . . £475 32·00
26 1d. pale red-brown . . . £325 24·00
27 1d. brick-red (1863) . . . £160 22·00
28 1d. dull vermilion (1865) . . . 95·00 22·00
29 1d. carmine (1867) . . . £100 22·00
a. Double print . . . — £140
b. Error. Wmkd "2" (1869)
30 2d. dull emerald-green . . . — 95·00
31 2d. green . . . — 45·00
a. double print . . . — £170
32 2d. yellow-green . . . £350 85·00
33 2d. deep green (1858) . . . £300 55·00
34 2d. slate-green (1860) . . . £180 70·00
35 4d. deep blue . . . — 75·00
a. Double print . . . — £170
36 4d. pale blue . . . £140 20·00
37 4d. blue . . . £140 22·00
a. Double print . . . — £170
38 4d. bright blue . . . £140 22·00
a. Printed on both sides . . . †
b. Double print . . . — £140
39 4d. cobalt-blue . . . — 70·00

Printings before July 1864 were all carried out at the *Courier* printing works which changed hands several times during this period.

CANCELLATIONS. Beware of early Tasmanian stamps with pen-cancellations cleaned off and faked postmarks applied.

(Recess P.B.)

1858. Wmk double-lined numerals "6" or "12" as W **4**. Imperf.

40 **7** 6d. dull lilac (H/S "CANCELLED" in oval £7500) . . . £650 80·00
41 **8** 1s. verm (shades) (H/S "CANCELLED" in oval £6000) . . . £500 70·00

(Recess J. Davies (March 1860), J. Birchall (April 1863), Govt Printer (from February 1865), all from P.B. plates)

1860 (Mar)–**67**. Wmk double-lined "6" as W **4**. Imperf.

44 **7** 6d. dull slate-grey . . . £300 60·00
45 6d. grey . . . — 65·00
46 6d. grey-violet (4.63) . . . £200 60·00
a. Double print . . . — £27[illegible]
47 6d. dull cobalt (2.65) . . . £450 95·0[illegible]
48 6d. slate-violet (2.65) . . . £325 50·0[illegible]
49 6d. reddish mauve (4.67) . . . £700 £15[illegible]

In 1871 reprints were made of the 6d. (in mauve) and the 1s. on white wove paper, and perforated 11½. They are found with or without "REPRINT". In 1889 they were again reprinted on white card, imperforate. These later impressions are also found overprinted "REPRINT" and perforated 11½.

PERFORATED ISSUES. From 1 October 1857 the Tasmania Post Office only supplied purchasers requiring five or more complete sheets of stamps. The public obtained their requirements, at face value, from licensed stamp vendors, who obtained their stocks at discount from the Post Office.

From 1863 onwards a number of the stamp vendors applied their own roulettes or perforations. The Hobart firm of J. Walch & Sons achieved this so successfully that they were given an official contract in July 1869 to perforate sheets for the Post Office. The Government did not obtain a perforating machine until late in 1871.

1863–71. Double-lined numeral watermarks. Various unofficial roulettes and perforations.

(a) By J. Walch & Sons, Hobart.

(i) Roulette about 8, often imperf × roul (1863–68).

50 **3** 1d. brick-red . . . — £20[illegible]
51 1d. carmine . . . £375 £13[illegible]
52 2d. yellow-green . . . — £55[illegible]
53 2d. slate green
54 4d. pale blue . . . — £18[illegible]
55 **7** 6d. dull lilac . . . — £22[illegible]
56 **8** 1s. vermilion . . . — £65[illegible]

(ii) P 10 (1864–69).

57 **3** 1d. brick-red . . . 70·00 26·[illegible]
58 1d. dull vermilion . . . 70·00 26·[illegible]
a. Double print . . . †
59 1d. carmine . . . 60·00 24·0[illegible]
60 2d. yellow-green . . . £375 £10[illegible]
61 2d. slate-green . . . £400 £17[illegible]
62 4d. pale blue . . . £130 13·0[illegible]
63 4d. blue . . . £130 13·[illegible]
a. Double print . . . — £13[illegible]
64 **7** 6d. grey-violet . . . £200 18·[illegible]
65 6d. dull cobalt . . . £300 70·[illegible]
66 6d. slate-violet . . . — 25·[illegible]
67 6d. reddish mauve . . . £400 80·[illegible]
68 **8** 1s. vermilion . . . £150 24·[illegible]
a. Imperf vert (horiz pair)

(iii) P 12 (1865–71—from July 1869 under contract to the Post Office).

69 **3** 1d. dull vermilion . . . 65·00
a. Double print . . . †
70 1d. carmine . . . 50·00 10·[illegible]
a. Error. Wmkd "2" (*pen cancel* £100) . . . — £13[illegible]
71 2d. yellow-green . . . £180 55·[illegible]
72 4d. deep blue . . . £100 16·[illegible]
73 4d. blue . . . £100 18·[illegible]
74 4d. cobalt-blue . . . — 42·[illegible]

7 6d. slate-violet . . . £170 24·00
a. Imperf between (vert pair)
6d. reddish mauve . . . 85·00 38·00
a. Imperf between (vert or horiz pair) (*pen cancel* £200)
8 1s. vermilion . . . £160 38·00
a. Double print . . . — £170
b. Imperf between (horiz pair) (*pen cancel* £200)

(iv) Perf compound 10 × 12 (1865–69).

3 1d. carmine . . . £1600
4d. blue . . . — £1200

(b) P 12½ by R. Harris, Launceston (1864–68).

3 1d. brick-red . . . 75·00 30·00
1d. dull vermilion . . . 70·00 24·00
1d. carmine . . . 40·00 11·00
2d. yellow-green . . . £350 £110
2d. slate-green . . . £300 £140
4d. blue . . . £170 45·00
4d. bright blue . . . £170 45·00
7 6d. dull cobalt . . . £350 90·00
6d. slate-violet . . . £250 50·00
6d. reddish mauve . . . £425 £120
8 1s. vermilion . . . £300 95·00

(c) Imperf × oblique roulette 11½ at Oatlands (1866).

3 4d. blue . . . — £500
7 6d. dull cobalt . . . † —

(d) Oblique roulette 10–10½, possibly at Deloraine (1867).

3 1d. brick-red . . . — £425
1d. carmine . . . £1200 £350
2d. yellow-green . . . — £550
4d. bright blue . . . — £500
7 6d. grey-violet . . . — £800

(e) Oblique roulette 14–15, probably at Cleveland (1867–69).

7 3 1d. brick-red . . . — £475
8 1d. dull vermilion . . . — £475
9 1d. carmine . . . — £475
0 2d. yellow-green . . . — £600
1 4d. pale blue . . . — £450
2 7 6d. grey-violet . . . — £750
3 8 1s. vermilion . . . — £900

(f) Pin-perf 5½ to 9½ at Longford (1867).

4 3 1d. carmine . . . £450 £110
5 2d. yellow-green
6 4d. bright blue . . . — £225
7 7 6d. grey-violet . . . — £200
8 6d. reddish mauve . . . — £550
9 8 1s. vermilion

(g) Pin-perf 12 at Oatlands (1867).

0 3 4d. blue

(h) Pin-perf 13½ to 14½ (1867).

1 3 1d. brick-red . . . — £275
2 1d. dull vermilion . . . — £275
3 1d. carmine
4 2d. yellow-green . . . — £400
5 4d. pale blue . . . — £225
6 7 6d. grey-violet . . . — £500
7 8 1s. vermilion

(j) Serrated perf 19 at Hobart (1868–69).

8 3 1d. carmine (*pen-cancel* £9) . . . £350 £130
9 2d. yellow-green . . . — £350
0 4d. deep blue . . . £850 £120
1 4d. cobalt-blue . . . — £120
2 7 6d. slate-violet . . . — £500
3 8 1s. vermilion

(k) Roul 4½, possibly at Macquarie River (1868).

4 3 4d. blue
5 7 6d. reddish mauve
6 8 1s. vermilion

An example of the 1d. carmine is known peforated 10 on three les and serrated 19 on the fourth.

For stamps perforated 11½ or 12 by the Post Office see Nos. 134a/ .

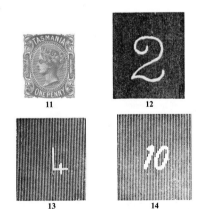

11

12

13

14

(Typo Govt Printer, Hobart, from plates made by D.L.R.)

70 (1 Nov)–**71**. Wmk single-lined numerals W **12** (2d.), **13** (1d., 4d.) or **14** (1d., 10d.).

(a) P 12 by J. Walch & Sons.

27 **11** 1d. rose-red (wmk "10") . . . 42·00 10·00
a. Imperf (pair) . . . £550 £550
b. Deep rose-red . . . 55·00 8·00
28 1d. rose-red (wmk "4") (3.71) . . . 55·00 14·00
a. Imperf (pair) . . . — £500
29 2d. yellow-green . . . 70·00 6·50
a. Imperf (pair)
b. Blue-green . . . 75·00 6·50
30 4d. blue . . . £700 £400
131 10d. black . . . 24·00 25·00
a. Imperf (pair) . . . £250

(b) P 11½ by the Post Office (1871).

132 **11** 1d. rose-red (wmk "10") . . . £1000
133 2d. yellow-green . . . £120 7·00
a. Blue-green . . . 65·00 4·50
ab. Double print
134 10d. black . . . 27·00 25·00

The above were printed on paper obtained from New South Wales.

See also Nos. 144/55, 156/8, 159/66, 170/4, 226/7, 242 and 255/6.

(Recess P.B.)

1871. Wmk double-lined numeral "**12**". P 11½ by the Post Office.

134*a* **7** 1s. vermilion

(Recess Govt Printer, Hobart)

1871–91. Double-lined numeral watermarks as W **4**. Perforated by the Post Office.

(a) P 11½.

135 **7** 6d. dull lilac . . . 95·00 22·00
136 6d. lilac . . . 90·00 22·00
a. Imperf between (pair) . . . — £600
137 6d. deep slate-lilac (3.75) . . . 90·00 22·00
a. Imperf (pair) . . . — £550
138 6d. bright violet (5.78) . . . 90·00 32·00
a. Double print . . . — £130
b. Imperf between (horiz pair) . . . £1100
139 6d. dull reddish lilac (10.79) . . . 85·00 40·00
140 **8** 1s. brown-red (1.73) . . . £110 45·00
a. Imperf between (horiz pair)
141 1s. orange-red (3.75) . . . £100 45·00
141*a* 1s. orange (5.78)

(b) P 12.

142 **7** 6d. reddish purple (1884) . . . 90·00 20·00
a. Imperf between (horiz pair) . . . £650
143 6d. dull claret (7.91) . . . 26·00 13·00

The perforation machine used on Nos. 142/3 was previously owned by J. Walch and Sons and passed to the ownership of the Government in 1884. It may have been used to perforate leftover sheets of previous printings.

15

16

"Wedge" flaw (Right pane R. 10/6)

(Typo Govt Printer, Hobart, from plates made by D.L.R.)

1871 (25 Mar)–**78**. W **15**.

(a) P 11½.

144 **11** 1d. rose (5.71) . . . 7·00 1·00
a. Imperf (pair) (*pen cancel* £35) . . . — £650
b. Bright rose . . . 7·00 1·00
c. Carmine . . . 8·50 1·00
d. Pink . . . 9·50 2·25
e. Vermilion (4.75) . . . £250 75·00
f. Wedge flaw . . . £150 30·00
145 2d. deep green (11.72) . . . 26·00 1·00
a. Blue-green . . . 29·00 1·00
b. Yellow-green (12.75) . . . £150 2·50
146 3d. pale red-brown . . . 45·00 3·75
a. Imperf (pair) . . . £250
b. Imperf horiz (vert pair) . . . £1100
c. Deep red-brown . . . 45·00 4·25
ca. Purple-brown (1.78) . . . 45·00 3·75
d. Imperf (pair) . . . — £550
da. Brownish purple . . . 45·00 3·75
147 4d. pale yellow (8.8.76) . . . 60·00 18·00
a. Ochre (7.78) . . . 60·00 9·00
b. Buff . . . 50·00 9·50
148 9d. blue (2.10.71) . . . 16·00 6·50
a. Imperf (pair) . . . £200
b. Double print
149 5s. purple (*pen cancel* £3.75) . . . £190 60·00
a. Imperf (pair)
b. Mauve . . . £170 60·00

(b) P 12.

150 **11** 1d. rose . . . 80·00 7·50
a. Carmine . . . 85·00 9·00
b. Wedge flaw . . . — 60·00
151 2d. green . . . £500 £130
a. Imperf (pair) . . . — £750
152 3d. red-brown . . . 80·00 16·00
a. Deep red-brown . . . 80·00 16·00
153 4d. buff . . . £250 17·00
154 9d. pale blue . . . 28·00
a. Imperf between (horiz pair) . . . £1000
155 5s. purple . . . £325
a. Mauve . . . £225

(Type D.L.R.)

1878 (28 Oct). W **16**. P 14.

156 **11** 1d. carmine . . . 3·50 75
a. Rose-carmine . . . 3·50 75
b. Scarlet . . . 3·50 75
157 2d. pale green . . . 4·25 75
a. Green . . . 4·25 75
158 8d. dull purple-brown . . . 14·00 4·75

Plate scratch (Left pane R. 10/1)

(Typo Govt Printer, Hobart (some printings of 1d. in 1891 by *Mercury* Press) from plates made by Victoria Govt Printer, Melbourne (½d.) or D.L.R. (others)).

1880 (Apr)–**91**. W **16** (sideways on 1d.).

(a) P 11½.

159 **11** ½d. orange (8.3.89) . . . 3·00 2·75
a. Deep orange . . . 3·00 2·75
160 1d. dull red (14.2.89) . . . 5·50 2·25
a. Vermilion-red . . . 5·50 2·25
b. Wedge flaw . . . 50·00 20·00
161 3d. red-brown . . . 13·00 3·50
a. Imperf (pair) . . . £180
162 4d. deep yellow (1.83) . . . 35·00 13·00
a. Chrome-yellow . . . 35·00 14·00
b. Olive-yellow . . . £110 22·00
c. Buff . . . 30·00 9·50

(b) P 12.

163 **11** ½d. orange . . . 2·00 3·50
a. Deep orange . . . 1·90 3·50
ab. Wmk sideways
164 1d. pink (1891) . . . 19·00 4·25
a. Imperf (pair) . . . £160 £180
b. Rosine . . . 12·00 2·75
c. Dull rosine . . . 15·00 3·75
ca. Imperf (pair) . . . £150
d. Wedge flaw . . . 85·00 25·00
165 3d. red-brown . . . 8·00 4·00
a. Imperf between (horiz pair) . . . £700
b. Plate scratch . . . 65·00 35·00
166 4d. deep yellow . . . 70·00 14·00
a. Chrome-yellow . . . 85·00 13·00
ab. Printed both sides . . . £600

SPECIMEN AND PRESENTATION REPRINTS OF TYPE 11. In 1871 the 1d., 2d., 3d., 4d. blue, 9d., 10d. and 5s. were reprinted on soft white wove paper to be followed, in 1879, by the 4d. yellow and 8d. on rough white wove. Both these reprintings were perforated 11½. In 1886 it was decided to overprint remaining stocks with the word "REPRINT".

In 1889 Tasmania commenced sending sample stamps to the U.P.U. in Berne and a further printing of the 4d. blue was made, imperforate, on white card. This, together with the 5s. in mauve on white card, both perforated 11½and overprinted "REPRINT", were included in presentation sets supplied to members of the states' legislatures in 1901.

Halfpenny
(17)

d. 2½
(18) (2¼ mm between "d", and "2")

d. 2½
(19) (3½ mm between "d" and "2")

1889 (1 Jan). *No. 156b surch locally with T* **17**.

167 **11** ½d.on 1d. scarlet . . . 9·50 14·00
a. "al" in "Half" printed sideways (R. 1/2) . . . £1000 £800

No. 167a occurred in a second printing and was later corrected.

A reprint on white card, perforated 11½ or imperforate, overprinted "REPRINT" was produced in 1901.

1891 (1 Jan–June). *Surch locally. W* **16**.

(a) With T **18**. P 11½.

168 **11** 2½d.on 9d. pale blue . . . 9·00 4·25
a. Surch double, one inverted . . . £400 £450
b. Deep blue (May) . . . 9·00 4·75

(b) With T **19**. P 12.

169 **11** 2½d.on 9d. pale blue (June)
a. Blue surch . . . 5·00 3·50

A reprint, using a third setting, perforated 11½ and overprinted "REPRINT" was produced in 1901.

(Typo Govt Printer, Hobart)

1891 (Apr–Aug). W **15**.

(a) P 11½.

170 **11** ½d. orange . . . 28·00 13·00
a. Brown-orange . . . 23·00 12·00
171 1d. rosine . . . 16·00 6·50
a. Wedge flaw . . . £110 40·00

(b) P 12.

172 **11** ½d. orange . . . 22·00 17·00
a. Imperf (pair) . . . £130
173 1d. dull rosine . . . 21·00 14·00
a. Rosine . . . 35·00 18·00
b. Wedge flaw . . . £130 75·00
174 4d. bistre (Aug) . . . 16·00 11·00

20

21

21a

(Typo D.L.R.)

1892 (12 Feb)–**99**. W **16**. P 14.

No.	Type	Description	Unused	Used
216	**20**	½d. orange and mauve (11.92)	1·50	80
217	**21**	2½d. purple	2·50	1·25
218	**20**	5d. pale blue and brown	5·50	2·25
219		6d. violet and black (11.92)	8·00	2·75
220	**21a**	10d. purple-lake and deep green (30.1.99)	9·00	10·00
221	**20**	1s. rose and green (11.92)	8·00	2·50
222		2s.6d. brown and blue (11.92)	22·00	15·00
223		5s. lilac and red (3.2.97)	48·00	18·00
224		10s. mauve and brown (11.92)	90·00	60·00
225		£1 green and yellow (2.97)	£300	£250
216/25 *Set of* 10			£450	£325
216s/25s Optd "Specimen" *Set of* 10			£325	

See also Nos. 243 and 257/8.

(Typo Govt Printer, Hobart)

1896. W **16**. P 12.

No.	Type	Description	Unused	Used
226	**11**	4d. pale bistre	12·00	6·50
227		9d. pale blue	8·00	2·75
		a. Blue	8·50	3·25

22 Lake Marion

23 Mount Wellington

24 Hobart

25 Tasman's Arch

26 Spring River, Port Davey

27 Russell Falls

28 Mount Gould, Lake St. Clair

29 Dilston Fall

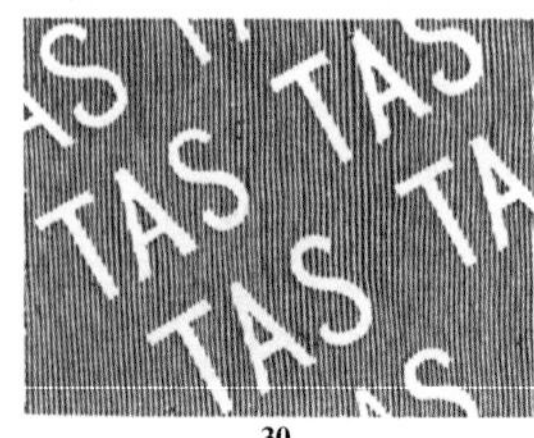
30

(Eng L. Phillips. Recess D.L.R.)

1899 (Dec)–**1900**. W **30**. P 14.

No.	Type	Description	Unused	Used
229	**22**	½d. deep green (31.3.00)	8·50	6·00
230	**23**	1d. bright lake (13.12.99)*	5·50	1·50
231	**24**	2d. deep violet (15.12.99)*	14·00	1·75
232	**25**	2½d. indigo (1900)	16·00	3·75
233	**26**	3d. sepia (1900)	10·00	4·50
234	**27**	4d. deep orange-buff (1900)	17·00	5·50
235	**28**	5d. bright blue (31.3.00)	23·00	10·00
236	**29**	6d. lake (31.3.00)	24·00	18·00
229/36 *Set of* 8			£110	45·00
229s/36s Optd "Specimen" *Set of* 8			£350	

*Earliest known postmark dates.

See also Nos. 237/9, 240/1, 245/8, 249/54, 259 and 261/2.

DIFFERENCES BETWEEN LITHOGRAPHED AND TYPOGRAPHED PRINTINGS OF TYPES 22/9

Lithographed	Typographed
General appearance fine.	*Comparatively crude and coarse appearance.*
½d. All "V over Crown" wmk.	All "Crown over A" wmk.
1d. The shading on the path on the right bank of the river consists of very fine dots. In printings from worn stones the dots hardly show.	The shading on the path is coarser, consisting of large dots and small patches of colour.
The shading on the white mountain is fine (or almost absent in many stamps).	The shading on the mountain is coarse, and clearly defined.
2d. Three rows of windows in large building on shore, at extreme left, against inner frame.	Two rows of windows.
3d. Clouds very white.	Clouds dark.
Stars in corner ornaments have long points.	Stars have short points.
Shading of corner ornaments is defined by a coloured outer line.	Shading of ornaments terminates against white background.
4d. Lithographed only.	—
6d. No coloured dots at base of waterfall.	Coloured dots at base of waterfall.
Outer frame of value tablets is formed by outer line of design.	Thick line of colour between value tablets and outer line. Small break in inner frame below second "A" of "TASMANIA".

(Litho, using transfers from D.L.R. plates, Victoria Government Printing Office, Melbourne)

1902 (Jan)–**04**. Wmk V over Crown, W w **10** (sideways on ½d., 2d.). P 12½.

No.	Type	Description	Unused	Used
237	**22**	½d. green (2.03)	3·50	1·50
		a. Wmk upright		
		b. Perf 11	4·75	5·50
		c. Perf comp of 12½ and 11	70·00	45·00
		d. Perf comp of 12½ and 12	£250	
		s. Optd "Specimen"	65·00	
238	**23**	1d. carmine-red	7·50	1·25
239	**24**	2d. deep reddish violet	6·50	70
		a. Perf 11	6·50	4·00
		b. Perf comp of 12½ and 11	75·00	45·00
		c. Wmk upright (2.04)	—	10·00
		d. Deep rose-lilac (4.05)	13·00	20
		da. Perf 11	9·00	1·75
		db. Perf comp of 12½ and 11		
		s. Optd "Specimen"	65·00	

As the V and Crown paper was originally prepared for stamps of smaller size, portions of two or more watermarks appear on each stamp.

We only list the main groups of shades in this and the following issues. There are variations of shade in all values, particularly in the 2d. where there is a wide range, also in the 1d. in some issues.

(Typo, using electrotyped plates, Victoria Govt Ptg Office, Melbourne)

1902 (Oct)–**04**. Wmk V over Crown, W w **10**. P 12½.

No.	Type	Description	Unused	Used
240	**23**	1d. pale red (wmk sideways)	12·00	1·50
		a. Perf 11	27·00	3·25
		b. Perf comp of 12½ and 11	£190	48·00
		c. Wmk upright (1.03)	27·00	7·50
		ca. Perf 11	35·00	8·50
		d. Rose-red (wmk upright) (4.03)	7·00	2·00
		da. Perf 11	18·00	2·00
		db. Perf comp of 12½ and 11	£190	48·00
		ds. Optd "Specimen"	65·00	
241		1d. scarlet (wmk upright) (9.03)	5·00	1·25
		a. Perf 11	7·50	1·75
		b. Perf comp of 12½ and 11		
		c. Rose-scarlet (1904)	4·50	1·25
		ca. Perf 11	5·00	1·75
		cb. Perf comp of 12½ and 11	70·00	20·00

The 1d. scarlet of September 1903 was from new electrotyped plates which show less intense shading.

(Typo Victoria Govt Ptg Office, Melbourne)

1903 (Apr–Dec). Wmk V over Crown, W w **10**. P 12½.

No.	Type	Description	Unused	Used
242	**11**	9d. blue (Apr)	8·00	3·50
		a. Perf 11	8·00	8·00
		b. Perf comp of 12½ and 11	£450	£450
		c. Wmk sideways	65·00	22·00
		d. Pale blue	10·00	6·00
		e. Bright blue	10·00	6·50
		f. Ultramarine	£350	
		g. Indigo	£130	
243	**20**	1s. rose and green (Dec)	15·00	4·75
		a. Perf 11	38·00	
242s/3s Optd "Specimen" *Set of* 2			£130	

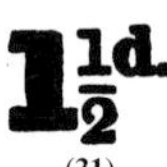
(31)

ONE PENNY
(32)

1904 (29 Dec). *No. 218 surch with T* **31**.

No.	Type	Description	Unused	Used
244	**20**	1½d.on 5d. pale blue and brown	1·25	70
		s. Optd "Specimen"	38·00	

Stamps with inverted surcharge or without surcharge *se-tenant* with stamps with normal surcharge were obtained irregularly and were not issued for postal use.

PRINTER. The Victoria Govt Ptg Office became the Commonwealth Stamp Printing Branch in March 1909.

(Litho, using transfers from D.L.R. plates, Victoria Govt Ptg Office, Melbourne)

1905 (Sep)–**12**. Wmk Crown over A, W w **11** (sideways on horiz stamps). P 12½.

No.	Type	Description	Unused	Used
245	**24**	2d. deep purple	6·00	3
		a. Perf 11	19·00	7
		b. Perf comp of 12½ and 11	20·00	3·7
		c. Perf comp of 12½ and 12	—	70·0
		d. Perf comp of 11 and 12	£140	
		e. Slate-lilac (1906)	7·00	
		ea. Perf 11	25·00	7
		eb. Perf comp of 12½ and 11		
		ed. Perf comp of 11 and 12		
		f. Reddish lilac (1907)	16·00	1·5
		fa. Perf 11		
		fb. Perf comp of 12½ and 11	80·00	
246	**26**	3d. brown (5.06)	8·50	3·7
		a. Perf 11	15·00	9·0
		b. Perf comp of 12½ and 11	90·00	
247	**27**	4d. pale yellow-brown (3.07)	13·00	3·7
		a. Perf 11	22·00	7·0
		b. Orange-buff (5.09)	18·00	3·7
		ba. Perf 11	23·00	12·0
		bb. Perf comp of 12½ and 11	£190	
		c. Brown-ochre (wmk sideways). Perf 11 (6.11)	24·00	35·0
		d. Orange-yellow (3.12)	15·00	18·0
		da. Perf 11	32·00	35·0
		db. Perf comp of 12½ and 11	£190	
248	**29**	6d. lake (7.08)	40·00	6·0
		a. Perf 11	48·00	6·0
		b. Perf comp of 12½ and 11	£180	£19

Stamps with perf compound of 12½ and 12 or 11 and 12 are found on sheets which were sent from Melbourne incompletely perforated along the outside edge of the pane or sheet. The missing perforations were applied in Hobart using a line machine measuring 12 (11.8 is the exact gauge). This perforation can only occur on one side of a stamp.

(Typo, using electrotyped plates, Victoria Govt Ptg Office, Melbourne).

1905 (Aug)–**11**. Wmk Crown over A, W w **11** (sideways on hori designs). P 12½.

No.	Type	Description	Unused	Used
249	**22**	½d. yellow-green (10.12.08)	1·75	4
		a. Perf 11	1·50	4
		b. Perf comp of 12½ and 11	40·00	14·0
		c. Perf comp of 11 and 12	£110	
		d. Wmk upright (1909)	9·50	3·0
		da. Perf 11		
250	**23**	1d. rose-red	1·75	2
		a. Perf 11	4·00	2
		b. Perf comp of 12½ and 11	4·50	2·7
		c. Perf comp of 12½ and 12	70·00	8·0
		d. Perf comp of 11 and 12	85·00	32·0
		e. Wmk sideways (1908)	9·50	1·7
		ea. Perf 11	—	2·0
		f. Imperf (pair)	£250	
250*g*		1d. carmine-red (3.10)	5·50	1·7
		ga. Perf 11	7·50	2·0
		gb. Perf comp of 12½ and 11	9·00	5·0
		gc. Perf comp of 12½ and 12	75·00	
		gd. Perf comp of 11 and 12	90·00	
		ge. Imperf (pair)	£275	
		h. Carmine-vermilion (1911)	11·00	4·0
		ha. Perf 11	14·00	4·2
		hb. Perf comp of 12½ and 11		
		hc. Perf comp of 12½ and 12		
		hd. Perf comp of 11 and 12		
251	**24**	2d. plum (8.07)	9·00	2
		a. Wmk upright	15·00	2·
		b. Perf 11	2·75	2
		ba. Wmk upright (12.07)	15·00	2·
		c. Perf comp of 12½ and 11	23·00	8·
		d. Perf comp of 12½ and 12	£170	60·0
		e. Perf comp of 11 and 12	£110	45·0
		f. Bright reddish violet (1910)	5·00	2·0
		fa. Perf 11	5·00	1·
		fb. Perf comp of 12½ and 11	26·00	
253	**26**	3d. brown (3.09)	8·00	4·
		a. Wmk upright		
		b. Perf 11	14·00	5·
		c. Perf comp of 12½ and 11	£160	
254	**29**	6d. carmine-lake (12.10)	17·00	24·
		a. Perf 11	20·00	32·
		b. Perf comp of 12½ and 11	£200	
		c. Dull carmine-red (3.11)	22·00	29·
		ca. Wmk upright	35·00	
		cb. Perf 11	25·00	35·
		cc. Perf comp of 12½ and 11	£180	

The note after No. 248 re perfs compound with perf 12 also applies here.

Nos. 250/f were printed from the same plates as Nos. 241/cb. Nos. 250g/hd are from a further pair of new plates and the images are sharper.

(Typo Victoria Govt Printing Office, Melbourne).

1906–13. Wmk Crown over A, W w **11**. P 12½.

No.	Type	Description	Unused	Used
255	**11**	8d. purple-brown (1907)	18·00	7·
		a. Perf 11	15·00	4·
256		9d. blue (1907)	7·00	4·
		a. Perf 11	7·00	4·
		b. Perf comp of 12½ and 11 (1909)	60·00	
		c. Perf comp of 12½ and 12 (1909)	£170	
		d. Perf comp of 11 and 12	£250	
257	**20**	1s. rose and green (1907)	13·00	4·
		a. Perf 11 (1907)	24·00	16·
		b. Perf comp of 12½ and 11	23·00	
		c. Perf comp of 12½ and 12	£100	
258		10s. mauve and brown (1906)	£140	£1
		a. Perf 11	£225	
		b. Perf comp of 12½ and 12	£300	

The note after No. 248 re perfs compound with perf 12, also applies here.

(Typo, using stereotyped plates, Commonwealth Stamp Ptg Branch, Melbourne)

1911 (Jan). Wmk Crown over A, W w **11** (sideways). P 12½.

259	**24**	2d. bright violet	7·00	3·50
		a. Wmk upright	22·00	4·00
		b. Perf 11	7·00	3·50
		c. Perf comp of 12½ and 11	65·00	22·00
		d. Perf comp of 12½ and 12	£200	

Stamps from this stereotyped plate differ from No. 251 in the width of the design (33 to 33¼ mm, against just over 32 mm), in the taller, bolder letters of "TASMANIA", in the slope of the mountain in the left background, which is clearly outlined in white, and in the outer vertical frame-line at left, which appears "wavy". Compare Nos. 260, etc, which are always from this plate.

1912 (Oct). No. 259 *surch with T* **32**. P 12½.

260	**24**	1d.on 2d. bright violet (R.)	1·00	80
		a. Perf 11	1·50	80
		b. Perf comp of 12½ and 11	£110	£110

(Typo, using electrotyped plates, Commonwealth Stamp Ptg Branch, Melbourne).

1912 (Dec). *Thin paper, white gum (as Victoria, 1912).* W w **11** (sideways on 3d.). P 12½.

261	**23**	1d. carmine-vermilion	17·00	10·00
		a. Perf 11	17·00	10·00
		b. Perf comp of 12½ and 11		
262	**26**	3d. brown	50·00	60·00

STAMP BOOKLETS

There are very few surviving examples of Nos. SB1/4. Listings are provided for those believed to have been issued with prices quoted for those known to still exist.

1904 (1 Jan)–**09**. *Black on red cover as* No. SB1 *of New South Wales. Stapled.*

SB1 £1 booklet containing two hundred and forty 1d. in twelve blocks of 20 (5 × 4)
a. Red on pink cover (1909)
b. Blue on pink cover

1904 (1 Jan). *Black on grey cover* No. SB1. *Stapled.*

SB2 £1 booklet containing two hundred and twenty 2d. in four blocks of 30

1910 (1 May). *Black on white cover as No.* SB3. *of New South Wales. Stapled.*

SB3 2s. booklet containing eleven ½d. (No. 249), either in block of 6 plus block of 5 or block of 11, and eighteen 1d. (No. 250), either in three blocks of 6 or block of 6 plus block of 12 . . . £3500

Unsold stock No. SB3 was uprated with one additional ½d. in May 1911.

1911 (Aug). *Red on pink cover as* No. SB3. *Stapled.*

SB4 2s. booklet containing twelve ½d. (No. 249), either in two blocks of 6 or block of 12, and eighteen 1d. (No. 250), either in three blocks of 6 or block of 6 plus block of 12 . . . £2750

POSTAL FISCAL STAMPS

VALIDITY. Nos. F1/29 were authorised for postal purposes on 1 November 1882.

CLEANED STAMPS. Beware of postal fiscal stamps with pen-cancellations removed.

F 1 F 2

F 3 F 4

(Recess Alfred Bock, Hobart)

1863–**80**. Wmk double-lined "1". W **4**.

(a) Imperf.

F1	F 1	3d. green (1.65)	£140	85·00
F2	F 2	2s.6d. carmine (11.63)	£140	85·00
		2s.6d. lake (5.80)		
F3	F 3	5s. brown (1.64)	£325	£275
		5s. sage-green (1880)	£170	£120
F4	F 4	10s. orange (1.64)	£475	£275
		10s. salmon (5.80)	£325	£275

(b) P 10.

F8	F 1	3d. green	80·00	42·00
F9	F 2	2s.6d. carmine	85·00	
F10	F 3	5s. brown	£140	
F11	F 4	10s. orange	£100	

(c) P 12.

F12	F 1	3d. green	80·00	55·00
F13	F 2	2s.6d. carmine	80·00	65·00
F14	F 3	5s. brown	£150	
F15		5s. sage-green	75·00	55·00
F16	F 4	10s. orange	95·00	75·00
F17		10s. salmon	75·00	55·00

(d) P 12½.

F18	F 1	3d. green	£150	
F19	F 2	2s.6d. carmine	£140	
F20	F 3	5s. brown	£200	
F21	F 4	10s. orange-brown	£140	

(e) P 11½.

F22	F 1	3d. green		
F23	F 2	2s.6d. lake	80·00	70·00
F24	F 3	5s. sage-green	75·00	55·00
F25	F 4	10s. salmon	£120	85·00

See also No. F30.

In 1879, the 3d., 2s.6d., 5s. (brown), and 10s. (orange) were reprinted on thin, tough, white paper, and are found with or without "REPRINT". In 1889 another reprint was made on white card, imperforate and perforated 12. These are also found with or without "REPRINT".

F 5 Duck-billed Platypus

REVENUE

(F 6)

(Typo D.L.R.)

1880 (19 Apr). W **16** (sideways). P 14.

F26	F 5	1d. slate	19·00	6·00
F27		3d. chestnut	19·00	3·50
F28		6d. mauve	80·00	2·25
F29		1s. rose-pink	£100	12·00
		a. Perf comp of 14 and 11		

All values are known imperf, but not used.

Reprints are known of the 1d. in deep blue and the 6d. in lilac. The former is on yellowish white, the latter on white card. Both values also exist on wove paper, perf 12, with the word "REPRINT".

1888. W **16**. P 12.

F30	F 2	2s.6d. lake	35·00	26·00
		a. Imperf between (horiz pair)	£650	

1900 (15 Nov). *Optd with Type* F **6**.

(a) On Types F **2** *and* F **4**.

F32	F 2	2s.6d. lake (No. F30)	£225	
		a. "REVFNUE"	£325	
		b. Opt inverted	£450	
		c. Imperf	£275	
F33	F 4	10s. salmon (No. F17)		
		a. "REVFNUE"		

(b) On Nos. F27 *and* F29.

F34	F 5	3d. chestnut	23·00	23·00
		a. Double opt, one vertical	85·00	£120
F35		1s. rose-pink		

(c) On stamps as Nos. F26/9, *but typo locally*. W **16**. P 12.

F36	F 5	1d. blue	20·00	
		a. Imperf between (horiz pair)	£300	
		b. "REVENUE" inverted	£100	
		c. "REVENUE" double	£160	
		d. Pale blue	19·00	
F37		6d. mauve	55·00	
		a. Double print	£250	
F38		1s. pink	85·00	

(d) On No. 225.

F39	**20**	£1 green and yellow	£140	£120
		a. Opt double, one vertical	£275	£275

It was not intended that stamps overprinted with Type F **6** should be used for postal purposes, but an ambiguity in regulations permitted such usage until all postal fiscal stamps were invalidated for postal purposes on 30 November 1900.

Printings of some of the above with different watermarks, together with a 2d. as Nos. F36/8, did not appear until after the stamps had become invalid for postal purposes.

Tasmania became part of the Commonwealth of Australia on 1 January 1901.

VICTORIA

PRICES FOR STAMPS ON COVER

Nos.	1/17	*from* × 2
Nos.	18/22	*from* × 4
Nos.	23/4	*from* × 2
No.	25	*from* × 3
Nos.	26/32	*from* × 2
No.	33	*from* × 6
No.	34	*from* × 8
Nos.	35/9	*from* × 4
No.	40	*from* × 3
Nos.	41/53	*from* × 2
No.	54	*from* × 3
No.	55	—
No.	56	*from* × 4
Nos.	57/72	*from* × 2
No.	73	*from* × 3
Nos.	74/80	*from* × 2
No.	81	*from* × 3
Nos.	82/7	*from* × 4
Nos.	88/200	*from* × 3
Nos.	201/6	*from* × 5
Nos.	207/8	*from* × 10
Nos.	209/14	*from* × 5
Nos.	215/19	—
Nos.	220/6	*from* × 20
Nos.	227/33	—
Nos.	234/7	*from* × 20
Nos.	238/52	—
Nos.	253/6	*from* × 20
No.	257	*from* × 10
No.	258	*from* × 20
No.	259	*from* × 10
Nos.	260/4	—
Nos.	265/6	*from* × 20
Nos.	267/73	*from* × 10
Nos.	274/91	—
Nos.	292/304	*from* × 10
Nos.	305/9	*from* × 5
Nos.	310/23	*from* × 10
Nos.	324/8	—
No.	329	*from* × 12
Nos.	330/50	*from* × 8
Nos.	351/2	—
Nos.	353/4	*from* × 4
No.	355	*from* × 10
Nos.	356/73	*from* × 15
Nos.	374/5	*from* × 3
Nos.	376/98	*from* × 10
Nos.	399/400	—
Nos.	401/6	*from* × 10
Nos.	407/15	—
Nos.	416/30	*from* × 10
Nos.	431/2	—
Nos.	433/43	*from* × 4
Nos.	444/53	—
Nos.	454/5	*from* × 10
Nos.	456/63	*from* × 6
No.	464	—
Nos.	D1/8	*from* × 30
Nos.	D9/10	—
Nos.	D11/37	*from* × 30

During the expansion of the Australian settlements in the fourth decade of the nineteenth century the growing population of the Port Phillip District in the south of New South Wales led to a movement for its creation as a separate colony. This aspiration received the approval of the British Government in 1849, but the colony of Victoria, as it was to be called, was not to be created until 1 July 1851.

In the meantime the New South Wales Legislative Council voted for the introduction of postal reforms, including the use of postage stamps, from 1 January 1850, and this act was also to apply to the Port Phillip District where stamps inscribed "VICTORIA" would predate the creation of that colony by eighteen months.

Until the end of 1859 the stamps of Victoria, with the exception of Nos. 40 and 73, were produced by local contractors working under the supervision of the colonial administration.

SPECIMEN OVERPRINTS. Those listed are from U.P.U. distributions in 1892 and 1897. Further "Specimen" overprints exist, but these were used for other purposes.

HAM PRINTINGS. The first contractor was Thomas Ham of Melbourne. He was responsible for the initial printings of the "Half-Length" 1d., 2d. and 3d., together with the replacement "Queen on Throne" 2d. The first printings were produced from small sheets of 30 (5 × 6) laid down directly from the engraved die which showed a single example of each value. Subsequent printings, of which No. 4*a* was the first, were in sheets of 120 (two panes of 60) laid down using intermediate stones of various sizes. Impressions from the first printings were fine and clear, but the quality deteriorated when intermediate stones were used.

1 Queen Victoria ("Half Length")

(Lithographed by Thomas Ham, Melbourne)

1850 (3 Jan)–**53**. Imperf.

1d. Thin line at top

2d. Fine border and background

3d. White area to left of orb

(a) Original state of dies: 1d. (tops of letters of "VICTORIA" *reach to top of stamp); 2d. (fine border and background); 3d. (thicker white outline around left of orb, central band of orb does not protrude at left). No frame-lines on dies.*

1	**1**	1d. orange-vermilion	£16000	£2000
		a. Orange-brown	†	£1000
		b. Dull chocolate-brown	£6000	£1200
2		2d. lilac-mauve (*shades*) (Stone A)	£4000	£600
3		2d. brown-lilac (*shades*) (Stone B)	£3000	£325
		a. Grey-lilac	—	£325
4		3d. bright blue (*shades*)	£2500	£375
		a. Blue (*shades*)	£2500	£225
		ab. Retouched (between Queen's head and right border) (No. 11 in transfer group) (8 varieties)	—	£350
		ac. Retouched (under "V") (No. 10 in transfer group)	£6000	£350

With the exception of No. 4*a* the above were printed from small stones of 30 (5 × 6) laid down directly from the engraved die which showed a single example of each value. There were two stones of the 2d. and one for each of the other values. No. 4*a* is the second printing of the 3d. for which the sheet size was increased to 120, the printing stone being constructed from an intermediate stone of 15 (5 × 3).

1d. Thick line at top

2d. Coarse background

3d. White area small and band protuding to left of orb

(b) Second state of dies: 1d. (more colour over top of letters of "VICTORIA"*); 2d. (fine border as (a) but with coarse background); 3d. (thinner white outline around left of orb, central band of orb protrudes at left).*

5 **1** 1d. red-brown (*shades*) (2.50) £4000 £350
a. Pale dull red-brown £3000 £350
6 2d. grey-lilac (*shades*) (1.50) £1300 £120
a. Dull grey £1300 £130
7 3d. blue (*shades*) (6.51) £1200 £130
a. Retouched (22 varieties) *from* £2000 £275

Pritnted in sheets of 120 (10 × 12) with the printing stones constructed from intermediate stones of 30 (5 × 6) for the 1d. and 2d. or 10 (5 × 2) for the 3d. It is believed that the use of the smaller intermediate stone for the latter resulted in the many retouches.

Frame-lines added

(c) Third state of dies: As in (b) but with frame-lines added, very close up, on all four sides.

8 **1** 1d. dull orange-vermilion (11.50) £1700 £475
a. Dull red (shades) £1400 £140
9 1d. deep red-brown (5.51) . . . . — £550
a. Brownish red (shades) £800 £130
b. Dull rose (shades) £800 £130
10 2d. grey (*shades*) (8.50) £950 £150
a. Olive-grey (shades) £1200 £150
11 3d. blue (*shades*) (12.52) . . . . £450 60·00
a. Deep blue (shades) . . . . £600 60·00
b. Pale greenish blue (shades) £750 £120

Printed in sheets of 120 (12 × 10) produced from intermediate stones of 30 (6 × 5) for No. 8 and 12 (6 × 2) for the others.

White veil

(d) As (c) but altered to give, for the 1d. and 3d., the so-called "white veils", and for the 2d., the effect of vertical drapes to the veil.

12 **1** 1d. reddish brown (6.51) £850 £120
a. Bright pinky red (shades) £600 £120
13 2d. drab (1.51) £1200 £130
a. Grey-drab £1200 £130
b. Lilac-drab . . . . — £130
c. Red-lilac . . . . — £600
d. Void lower left corner . . . . — £2750
14 3d. blue (*shades*) (1.53) . . . . £450 55·00
a. Deep blue (shades) . . . . £450 55·00
b. Greenish blue (shades) . . . . £600 60·00
c. Retouched (9 varieties) £850 £140

Printed in sheets of 120 (12 × 10) produced from intermediate stones of 12 (6 × 2) on which the details of the veil were amended as described above.

The "void corner" error occurred on the printing stone. It is believed that only four examples still exist.

2d. Coarse border and background

(e) Fourth state of 2d. die only: Coarse border and background. Veil details as in original die.

15 **1** 2d. red-lilac (*shades*) (5.50) £700 £225
a. Lilac £700 £225
b. Grey . . . . — £325
c. Dull brownish lilac £550 £120
d. Retouched lower label—value omitted . . . . *from* — £5500
e. Other retouches (17 varieties) . . . . *from* £1200 £275

Printed in sheets of 120 (12 × 10) produced from an intermediate stone of 30 (6 × 5).

(f) 2d. as (e), but with veils altered to give effect of vertical drapes.

16 **1** 2d. lilac-grey (1.51) £850 £130
a. Deep grey £1000 £130
b. Brown-lilac (shades) . . . . £750 70·00
17 2d. cinnamon (*shades*) (2.51) £650 £120
a. Drab (shades) . . . . £700 70·00
b. Pale dull brown (shades) . . . . . . £800 80·00
c. Greenish grey . . . . £650 70·00
d. Olive-drab (shades) £750 £140
e. Buff . . . . † £160

Printed in sheets of 120 (12 × 10) produced from two successive intermediate stones of 30 (6 × 5) on which the details of the veil were amended as described above.

This was the final printing of the 2d. "Half Length" as the die for this value had been damaged. A replacement 2d. design was ordered from Thomas Ham.

For the later printings of the 1d. and 3d. in this design see Nos. 23/4, 26/31, 48/9 and 78/9.

2 Queen on Throne

3

(Recess-printed by Thomas Ham)

1852 (27 Dec). *Imperf.*

18 **2** 2d. reddish brown . . . . £190 22·00
a. Chestnut . . . . — £120
b. Purple-brown . . . . £275 22·00

Printed in sheets of 50 (10 × 5) from a hand-engraved plate of the same size. Each stamp in the sheet had individual corner letters made-up of various combinations, none of which contained the letter "J".

Reprints were made in 1891 using the original plate, on paper wmk V over Crown, both imperf and perf 12½.

For later printings of this design see Nos. 19/22 and 36/9.

CAMPBELL & CO PRINTINGS. In May 1853 the Victoria postal authorities placed an order for 1d. and 6d. stamps in the "Queen on Throne" design with Perkins, Bacon in London. These would not arrive for some time, however, and supplies of Ham's printings were rapidly becoming exhausted. Local tenders were, therefore, solicited for further supplies of the 1d. and 3d. "Half Lengths" and the 2d. "Queen on Throne". That received from J. S. Campbell& Co was accepted. The stamps were produced by lithography, using transfers from either the "Half Length" engraved die or the 2d. "Queen on Throne"engraved plate of 50. Stamps from the Campbell & Co printings can be distinguished from later printings in lithography by the good quality paper used.

(Lithographed by J. S. Campbell & Co, Melbourne, using transfers taken from Ham's engraved plate)

1854 (Jan–Jul). *Good quality white or toned paper.* Imperf.

(a) Clear impressions with details around back of throne generally complete.

19 **2** 2d. brownish purple . . . . £180 28·00
a. Grey-brown . . . . £275 28·00
b. Purple-black . . . . — 28·00
c. Dull lilac-brown (toned paper only) . . £325 42·00

(b) Poor impressions with details around back of throne not fully defined.

20 **2** 2d. violet-black (2.54) . . . . £275 28·00
a. Grey-black . . . . £375 28·00
b. Grey-lilac . . . . £275 28·00
c. Dull brown (on toned) . . . . £275 28·00
ca. Substituted transfer (in pair) . . . . — £2000

(c) Weak impressions with background generally white without details. Toned paper only.

21 **2** 2d. grey-purple (7.54) . . . . £150 24·00
a. Purple-black . . . . £150 24·00

(d) Printings using an intermediate stone. Impression flat and blurred. Background details usually complete. Toned paper only.

22 **2** 2d. grey-drab (*shades*) (5.54) . . . . . . £250 24·00
a. Black . . . . — £110

Nos. 19/21 were produced using transfers taken directly from the original Ham engraved plate. It is believed that the different strengths of the impressions were caused by the amount of pressure exerted when the transfers were taken. The stamps were printed in sheets of 100 (2 panes 10 × 5). On one stone a block of four at bottom left, lettered "FL GM" over "QV RW", was damaged and the stone was repaired by using a block of four substituted transfers. These were lettered "VZ WA" over "FL GM". No. 20ca covers any one of these substituted transfers in pair with normal. As horizontal pairs these are lettered "WA HN" or "GM SX" and as vertical "VZ" over "VZ" or "WA" over "WA".

For No. 22 an intermediate stone was used to produce a printing stone of 300 (6 panes 10 × 5). The insertion of a further stage into the process caused the blurred appearance of stamps from this printing. No. 22*a* is believed to come from proof sheets issued to post offices for normal use. Examples are usually cancelled with Barred Oval 108 and Barred Numerals 1 and 2.

(Lithographed by J.S. Campbell & Co, Melbourne)

1854 (Feb–June). *Good quality wove paper.* Imperf.

23 **1** 1d. orange-red (*shades*) £550 £120
a. Rose £2250 £300
24 3d. blue (*shades*) (6.54) . . . . £550 38·00
a. Retouched under "C" of "VICTORIA" . . . . — £130

The 1d. was produced in sheets of 192 (two panes of 96 (12 × 8)) and the 3d. in sheets of 320 (two panes of 160 (18 × 9)). Both printing stones were constructed from transfers taken from intermediate stones of 24 (6 × 4). The spacing between stamps is far wider than on the Ham printings. The 3d. panes of 160 were constructed using six complete transfers of 24 and three of 6 with the final impression in the bottom two rows removed.

The 1d. Campbell printings have the frame lines almost completely absent due to lack of pressure when taking transfers.

The 3d. retouch, No. 24a, occurs on R. 3/5 of the intermediat stone.

CAMPBELL AND FERGUSSON PRINTINGS. Increased posta rates in early 1854 led to a requirement for a 1s. value and in Apr a contract for this stamp was awarded to Campbell and Fergusso (the new corporate style of J. S. Campbell & Co). Further contract to print the 1d. and 3d. "Half Lengths" and the 2d. "Queen o Throne" followed. All were produced by lithography with the tw "Half Lengths" using transfers from the original engraved die an the 2d. "Queen on Throne" transfers from Ham's original engrave plate.

All Campbell and Fergusson printings were on paper of a poore quality than that used for the earlier contract.

(Lithographed by Campbell & Fergusson)

1854 (6 Jul). *Poorer quality paper.* Imperf.

25 **3** 1s. blue (*shades*) . . . . £700 23·0
a. Greenish blue . . . . £800 23·0
b. Indigo-blue . . . . — £12

No. 25 was produced in sheets of 100 (8 × 12 with an additiona stamp appearing at the end of rows 6 to 9). The printing stones use each contained four such sheets. They were constructed from a intermediate stone of 40 (8 × 5) taken from a single engraved di Each pane of 100 showed two complete transfers of 40, one of 2 and one of a vertical strip of 4.

For this stamp rouletted or perforated see Nos. 54 and 81.

(Lithographed by Campbell & Fergusson)

1854 (Jul)–**57**. *Poorer quality paper.* Imperf.

26 **1** 1d. brown (*shades*) £550 £10
a. Brick-red (shades) . . . . £650 80·0
b. Dull red (shades) . . . . £700 80·0
27 1d. *Orange-brown (shades)* (8.55) £450 £1
a. Dull rose-red (shades) . . . . £450 65·0
b. Bright rose-pink £550 £1
c. Retouched (6 varieties) £1500 £40
28 1d. pink (*shades*) (2.55) . . . . £425 38·0
a. Rose (shades) . . . . £425 38·0
b. Lilac-rose (shades) . . . . £475 38·0
c. Dull brown-red (shades) . . . . . . — £1
d. Retouched (8 varieties) £800 £32
29 3d. bright blue (*shades*) (7.57) . . . . . £475 55·0
a. Greenish blue (shades) . . . . £425 45·0
b. Retouch under "C" of "VICTORIA" . . . . — £1
30 3d. *Prussian blue (shades)* (11.56) . . . . £550 75·0
a. Milky blue £1000 £12
b. Retouch under "C" of "VICTORIA" . . . . — £2
31 3d. steel-blue (*shades*) (heavier impression) (5.55) . . . . — 50·
a. Greenish blue (shades) . . . . £400 38·
b. Blue (shades) . . . . £400 38·
c. Deep blue (shades) . . . . £400 38·
d. Indigo (shades) . . . . — 42·

The 1d. was produced in sheets of 400 (2 panes 20 × 1 constructed from transfers originating from the J. S. Campbell Co intermediate stone. Each pane contained six complete transfe of 24, three of 12, two of 8 and one of 4.

The 3d. was produced in sheets of 320 (2 panes of 160) (No. 2 200 (No. 30) or 400 (2 panes of 200) (No. 31.) The stone for No. was constructed from transfers taken from the J. S. Campb intermediate stone with the retouch on R. 3/5 still present. The pan of 160 contained six transfers of 24 and three of 6 with the la impression in both rows 8 and 9 removed. Quality of impression generally poor. The stone for No. 30, once again taken from t Campbell intermediate stone, was laid down in the sar combination of transfers as the 1d. value. Impressions from it we however, so poor that transfers from a new intermediate stone we used for No. 31. Impressions from this stone, on which the par of 200 were in a similar layout to the 1d. were much further apa than those on the stones used to produce Nos. 29/30.

The Campbell and Fergusson printings of the "Half Lengths" a listed in the order in which they were printed.

CALVERT PRINTINGS. Contracts for the provision of oth values required by the postal rate changes in 1853 were placed w Samuel Calvert of Melbourne who used typography as the printi process. Calvert continued to print, and later roulette, stamps the Victoria Post Office until March 1858 when it was discover that he had placed some of the stock in pawn.

4

5

6

(Typographed from woodblocks by Samuel Calvert)

1854 (1 Sep)–**55**. Imperf.

32 **4** 6d. reddish brown (13.9.54) £300 38
a. Dull orange £180 18
b. Orange-yellow £180 19
33 **5** 6d. ("TOO LATE") lilac and green (1.1.55) £1000 £1
34 **6** 1s. ("REGISTERED") rose-pink and blue (1.12.54) £1200 £1
35 **4** 2s. dull bluish green/*pale yellow* £1400 £1

No. 33 was provided to pay the additional fee on letters pos after the normal closure of the mails. This service was only availa in the larger towns; examples are usually postmarked Castlema Geelong or Melbourne. The service was withdrawn on 30 June 1 and remaining stocks of the "TOO LATE" stamps were used normal postal purposes.

No. 34 was issued to pay the registration fee and was so u until 5 January 1858 after which remaining stocks were used normal postage.

These four values were produced from individually-engra boxwood woodblocks. The 6d. was in sheets of 100 printed by impressions from two plates of 25. The 2s. was in sheets of 50 fr a single plate of 25. The bicoloured "TOO LATE" "REGISTERED" stamps are unusual in that Calvert used common woodblock "key" plate of 25 for both values combi with "duty" plates made up from metal stereos. Both values w originally in sheets of 50, but the "REGISTERED" later appea in sheets of 100 for which a second "key" plate of 25 was utilis

For these stamps rouletted or perforated see Nos. 53, 55/8, 60/1 and 82.

(Lithographed by Campbell & Fergusson)

1855 (Mar)–**56**. *Poorer quality paper.* Imperf.

(a) Printings from stones which were not over-used; background around top of throne generally full and detail good.

36 **2** 2d. lilac (*shades*) (7.55) . . . £150 24·00
 a. Purple (shades) . . . £150 24·00
 b. "TVO" for "TWO" . . . £5000 £850

(b) Early printings from stones which were over-used. Similar characteristics to those above, though detail is not quite so full. Distinctive shades.

37 **2** 2d. brown . . . — 70·00
 a. Brown-purple . . . £180 24·00
 b. Warm purple . . . — 24·00
 c. Rose-lilac . . . — 24·00
 d. Substituted transfer (pair) . . . — £600

(c) Later printings from the same stones used for No. 37 *when in a worn condition. Impressions heavy, coarse and overcoloured; details blurred; generally white background around top of throne.*

38 **2** 2d. dull lilac-mauve (1856) . . . £180 27·00
 a. Dull mauve . . . £180 27·00
 b. Grey-violet . . . — 27·00
 c. Red-lilac . . . — 28·00
 d. Substituted transfer (pair) . . . — £600

(d) Printings from a stone giving blotchy and unpleasing results, with poor definition. Mainly shows in extra colour patches found on most stamps.

39 **2** 2d. dull purple (7.55) . . . — 45·00
 a. Dull grey-lilac . . . £190 45·00
 b. On thick card paper . . . — £550

The Campbell and Fergusson 2d. "Queen on Throne" printings were in sheets of 200 (4 panes 10 × 5) constructed from transfers taken from the original Ham engraved plate.

Four separate stones were used. On Stone A a creased transfer running through R. 4/8, 4/9 and 5/8 caused the "TVO" variety on the stamp from the bottom row of one pane. On Stone C the impression in the first vertical row of one pane were found to be so faulty that they were replaced by substituted transfers taken from elsewhere on the sheet causing abnormal horizontal pairs lettered "UY BF", "TX MQ", "DI WA", "SW GM" and "CH RW". The vertical pairs from the substituted transfers are lettered "UY" over "TX" and "DI" over "SW".

PERKINS BACON "CANCELLED". For notes on these handstamps, showing "CANCELLED" between horizontal bars forming an oval, see Catalogue Introduction.

7 Queen on Throne

8 "Emblems"

(Recess Perkins, Bacon & Co, London)

1856 (23 Oct). Wmk Large Star. Imperf.

40 **7** 1d. yellow-green (H/S "CANCELLED" in oval £5500) . . . £140 22·00

Supplies of this stamp, and the accompanying 6d. which was only issued rouletted (see No. 73), arrived in the colony at the end of 1854, but the 1d. was not placed on sale until almost two years later.

No. 40 was reprinted from the original plate in 1891. Examples, in either dull yellow-green or bright blue-green, are imperforate and on V over Crown watermarked paper.

(Typographed from electrotypes by Calvert)

1857 (26 Jan–6 Sept). Imperf.

(*a*) Wmk Large Star, W w **1**.

41 **8** 1d. yellow-green (18 Feb) . . . 95·00 15·00
 a. Deep green . . . £110 28·00
 b. Printed on both sides . . . † £1100
42 4d. vermilion . . . £250 10·00
 a. Brown-vermilion . . . £225 9·00
 b. Printed on both sides . . . † £1100
43 4d. dull red (20 July) . . . £160 7·50
44 4d. dull rose (6 Sept) . . . £225 7·50

(b) No wmk. Good quality medium wove paper.

45 **8** 2d. pale lilac (25 May) . . . £225 11·00
 a. Grey-lilac . . . £225 11·00

Nos. 41/5 were produced in sheets of 120, arranged as four panes of 30 (6 × 5) (1d. and 4d.) or twelve panes of 10 (2 × 5) (2d.), using electrotypes taken from a single engraved die of each value. The setting of the 4d. was rearranged before the printing of Nos. 43/4.

Only two examples of No. 41b and No. 42b have been recorded.

For this printing rouletted or perforated see Nos. 46/7, 50/2, 59, 74 and 77.

ROULETTES AND PERFORATIONS. In August 1857 a rouletting machine was provided at the G.P.O., Melbourne, to enable the counter clerks to separate stamp stocks before sale to the public. This machine produced roulettes of 7½–9 in one direction across six rows at a time. There was also a single wheel device which gauged 7–7½. Both were in use between the earliest known date of 12 August and the end of 1857.

Calvert was granted a separate contract in October 1857 to roulette the stamps he printed, but only Nos. 57/61 had been produced when it was found, in April 1858, that he had pawned a quantity of the sheets. His contracts were terminated and his successor, F. W. Robinson, used a roulette machine of a different gauge before switching to a gauge 12 perforating machine in January 1859.

1857 (12 Aug–Sept). Rouletted 7–9 by counter clerks at G.P.O., Melbourne.

46 **8** 1d. yellow-green (No. 41) . . . £350 75·00
47 2d. pale lilac (No. 45) . . . — 30·00
 a. Grey-lilac . . . — 30·00
48 **1** 3d. blue (*shades*) (No. 24) . . . — £190
 a. Retouch under "C" of "VICTORIA" . . .
49 3d. bright blue (*shades*) (No. 29) . . . — £200
 a. Greenish blue (shades) . . . £1000 £180
 b. Retouch under "C" of "VICTORIA" . . .
50 **8** 4d. vermilion (No. 42) . . . — £100
51 4d. dull red (No. 43) . . . — 38·00
52 4d. dull rose (No. 44) (Sept) . . . — 26·00
53 **4** 6d. reddish brown (No. 32) . . . — 55·00
 a. Dull orange . . . — 35·00
 b. Orange-yellow . . . — 45·00
54 **3** 1s. blue (*shades*) (No. 25) . . . — 90·00
 a. Greenish blue . . . — 90·00
55 **6** 1s. ("REGISTERED") rose-pink and blue (No.34) . . . £4000 £225
56 **4** 2s. dull bluish green/*pale yellow* (No. 35) . . . £3750 £375

With the exception of the 1s., Nos. 54/a, these stamps are normally found rouletted on one or two sides only.

1857 (Oct). Rouletted by Calvert.

(a) Rouletted 7–9 on all four sides and with finer points than No. 53b.

57 **4** 6d. orange-yellow (No. 32*b*) . . . — 60·00

(*b*) Serpentine roulette 10–10½.

58 **4** 6d. orange-yellow (No. 32b) . . . — 75·00

(*c*) Serrated 18–19.

59 **8** 2d. grey-lilac (No. 45*a*) . . . £600 £400
60 **4** 6d. orange-yellow (No. 32*b*) . . . — 80·00

(*d*) Compound of serrated 18–19 and serpentine 10–10½.

61 **4** 6d. orange-yellow (No. 32*b*) . . . — £120

No. 59 was not covered by the contract given to Calvert, but it is believed to be a test run for the rouletting machine. No. 61 always shows serrated 18–19 on three sides and the serpentine roulette at the top or bottom of the stamp.

(Typo from electrotypes by Calvert)

1858 (14 Jan–Apr). *Good quality white wove paper.* No wmk.

(*a*) Rouletted 7–9 on all four sides.

62 **8** 1d. pale emerald . . . £300 20·00
 a. Emerald-green . . . £300 20·00
63 4d. rose-pink (18 Jan) . . . £200 6·00
 a. Bright rose . . . £200 6·00
 b. Reddish pink . . . — 11·00
 c. Imperf horiz (vert pair) . . . † £450

(*b*) Imperf (Apr).

64 **8** 1d. pale emerald . . . £190 11·00
 a. Emerald-green . . . — 14·00
65 4d. rose-pink . . . £250 23·00
 a. Bright rose . . . — 23·00
 b. Reddish pink . . . — 30·00

Nos. 62/5 were produced in sheets of 120, arranged as four panes of 30 (6 × 5).

The Royal Collection contains a used horizontal pair of the 4d. showing the vertical roulettes omitted.

The majority of Nos. 64/5 were issued in April after Calvert's contracts had been terminated, although there is some evidence that imperforate sheets of the 4d., at least, were issued earlier.

For the 1d. of this issue perforated see No. 75.

ROBINSON PRINTINGS. Calvert's contracts were cancelled in April 1858 and the work was then placed with F. W. Robinson, who had unsuccessfully tendered in 1856. The same electrotypes were used, but a perforating machine was introduced from January 1859. Robinson continued to print and perforate stamps under contract until the end of 1859 when the Victoria Post Office purchased his equipment to set up a Stamp Printing Branch and appointed him Printer of Postage Stamps.

(Typo from electrotypes by Robinson)

1858 (May–Dec).

(*a*) Imperf.

(*i*) *Coarse quality wove paper.*

66 **8** 4d. dull rose (*oily ink*) . . . — 60·00

(*ii*) *Smooth vertically-laid paper.*

67 **8** 4d. dull rose (*oily ink*) . . . — 35·00
 a. Dull rose-red . . . — 35·00
68 4d. dull rose-red (*normal ink*) (20 May) . . . £400 19·00

(*b*) Rouletted 5½–6½.

(*i*) *Smooth-laid paper.*

69 **8** 2d. brown-lilac (*shades*) (*horiz laid*) (June) . . . £120 8·00
 a. Vert laid paper (21 Sept) . . . £200 10·00
70 2d. violet (*horiz laid*) (27 Nov) . . . £150 6·00
 a. Dull violet . . . £180 18·00
71 4d. pale dull rose (*vert laid*) (1 June) . . . £150 3·75
 a. Horiz laid paper . . . † £850
 b. Dull rose-red . . . £120 3·75
 c. Rose-red . . . £120 3·50
 ca. Serrated 19 . . . † £475

(*ii*) *Good quality wove paper.*

72 **8** 1d. yellow-green (24 Dec) . . . £275 24·00

Nos. 66/72 were produced in sheets of 120, arranged as four panes of 30 (6 × 5).

For stamps of this issue perforated see Nos. 76 and 80.

(Recess Perkins, Bacon & Co, London)

1858 (1 Nov). Wmk Large Star, W w **1**. Rouletted 5½–6½.

73 **7** 6d. bright blue . . . £150 14·00
 a. Light blue . . . £200 25·00

No. 73 was received from London at the same time as the 1d., No. 40, but was kept in store until November 1858 when the stock was rouletted by Robinson. When issued the gum was in a poor state.

Imperforate examples exist from Perkins Bacon remainders. Examples are known handstamped "CANCELLED" in oval of bars. *Price* £5500.

Imperforate reprints, in shades of indigo, were made from the original plate in 1891 on V over Crown watermarked paper.

1859 (Jan–May). P 12 by Robinson.

74 **8** 1d. yellow-green (No. 41) . . . — £275
75 1d. emerald-green (No. 64*a*) . . . — £275
 a. Imperf between (horiz pair) . . .
76 1d. yellow-green (as No. 72) (11 Jan) . . . £180 14·00
 a. Imperf horiz (vert pair) . . . — £300
 b. Thin, glazed ("Bordeaux") paper . . . † £150
77 2d. pale lilac (No. 45) . . . — £250
 a. Grey-lilac . . . — £250
78 **1** 3d. blue (shades) (No. 24) (2 Feb) . . . £750 £110
 a. Retouch under "C" of "VICTORIA" . . . — £350
79 3d. greenish blue (*shades*) (No.29*a*) . . . † £350
 a. Retouch under "C" of "VICTORIA" . . . † £1000
80 **8** 4d. dull rose-red (No. 68) . . . — £300
81 **3** 1s. blue (*shades*) (No. 25) (4 Feb) . . . £130 15·00
 a. Greenish blue . . . £150 12·00
 b. Indigo-blue . . . — 30·00
82 **4** 2s. dull bluish green/*pale yellow* (No. 35) (May) . . . £275 35·00

The 1s. was reprinted in 1891 using transfers taken from the original die. These reprints were on V over Crown watermarked paper and perforated 12½.

For perforated 6d. black and 2s. blue both as Type **4** see Nos. 102 and 129/30.

(Typo from electrotypes by Robinson)

1859 (17 May–23 Dec). P 12.

(*a*) *Good quality wove paper.*

83 **8** 4d. dull rose . . . £150 4·00
 a. Roul 5½–6½ . . . † £800

(*b*) *Poorer quality wove paper.*

84 **8** 1d. dull green (July) . . . £120 11·00
 a. Green (11 Nov) . . . £120 11·00
85 4d. rose-carmine (16 July) . . . £150 5·00
 a. *Rose-pink* (*thick paper*) (30 Nov) . . . — 10·00

(*c*) *Horizontally laid paper with the lines wide apart.*

86 **8** 1d. dull green (18 July) . . .
 a. Laid lines close together . . . — 22·00
 b. Green (shades) (Oct) . . . £130 12·00
87 4d. rose-pink (*shades*) (23 Dec) . . . £120 7·50
 a. Laid lines close together . . . — 10·00

STAMP PRINTING BRANCH. On 1 January 1860 F. W. Robinson was appointed Printer of Postage Stamps and his equipment purchased by the Post Office to establish the Stamp Printing Branch. All later Victoria issues were printed by the Branch which became part of the Victoria Government Printing Office in December 1885. In 1909 the Commonwealth Stamp Printing Office under J. B. Cooke was established in Melbourne and produced stamps for both the states and Commonwealth until 1918.

9

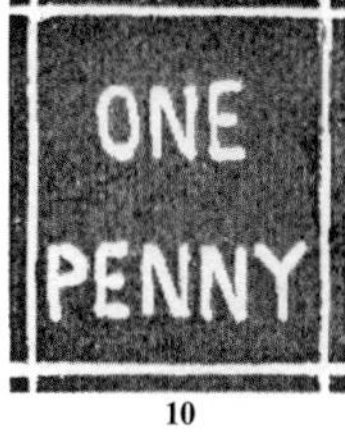

10

11

(Des and eng F. Grosse. Typo from electrotypes)

1860 (31 Jan)–**66**. P 12.

(*a*) No wmk.

88 **9** 3d. deep blue (*horiz laid paper*) . . . £300 35·00
 a. Light blue . . .
89 4d. rose-pink (*thin glazed Bordeaux paper*) (21.4.60) . . . — 12·00
 a. Rose . . . £275 15·00
 ab. Thick coarse paper (7.60) . . . £275 12·00

(b) On paper made by T. H. Saunders of London wmkd with the appropriate value in words as W **10**.

90 **9** 3d. pale blue (1.61) . . . £120 7·00
 a. Bright blue (10.61) . . . £120 8·50
 b. Blue (4.63) . . . £130 6·00
 c. Deep blue (4.64) . . . £130 6·00
 d. "TRREE" for "THREE" in wmk . . . — £425
91 3d. maroon (13.2.66) . . . £110 25·00
 a. Perf 13 . . . £130 28·00
92 4d. rose-pink (1.8.60) . . . — 7·50
 a. Rose-red . . . 80·00 3·75
 b. Rose-carmine . . . — 8·50
 c. Dull rose . . . 80·00 3·75
 d. Printed on "FIVE SHILLINGS" diagonal wmk paper (11.9.62) . . . £1500 20·00
93 6d. orange (25.10.60) . . . £3500 £225
94 6d. black (20.8.61) . . . £110 5·50
 a. Grey-black . . . £110 5·50

(c) On paper made by De La Rue wmkd with the appropriate value as a single-lined numeral as W **11**.

95 **9** 4d. dull rose-pink (9.10.62) . . . 90·00 5·00
 a. Dull rose . . . 95·00 5·50
 b. Rose-red . . . — 5·00
 c. Roul 8 (28.7.63) . . . — £250
 d. Imperf (31.7.63) . . . — 75·00
 e. Perf 13 × 12 . . .

All three values were produced in sheets of 120, initially as four panes of 30 (6 × 5). Printings of the 3d. from 1864 were in a changed format of six panes of 20 (4 × 5).

The "TRREE" watermark error comes from early printings of No. 90 on R. 10/7.

Two examples of the 4d. on Saunders paper are known bisected in 1863, but such use was unauthorised.

Nos. 95c/e were issued during July and August 1863 when the normal perforating machine had broken down.

Reprints, from new plates, were made of the 3d. and 4d. in 1891 on "V over Crown" paper and perforated 12½.

1860 (Apr)–**63**. P 12.

(a) No wmk.

96	**8**	1d. bright green (*horiz laid paper*)		
97		1d. bright green (*thin, glazed Bordeaux paper*) (25.5.60)	—	32·00

(b) On paper made by T. H. Saunders of London wmkd with the appropriate value in words as W **10**.

98	**8**	1d. pale yellowish green (8.7.60)	65·00	4·50
		a. Yellow-green	75·00	4·75
		b. Error. Wmkd "FOUR PENCE"	†	£5000
99		2d. brown-lilac (7.7.61)	—	26·00
100		2d. bluish slate (8.61)	£100	5·50
		a. Greyish lilac (9.61)	£110	5·50
		b. Slate-grey (1.62)	—	5·50
		c. Printed on "THREE PENCE" wmkd paper. *Pale slate* (27.12.62)	£110	12·00
		ca. Bluish grey (2.63)	£120	15·00

*(c) On paper made by De La Rue wmkd single-lined "*2*",* W **11**.

101	**8**	2d. dull reddish lilac (24.4.63)	£160	9·00
		a. Grey-lilac (10.63)	£150	14·00
		ab. Error. Wmkd "6"	†	£4000
		b. Grey-violet (11.63)	£100	11·00
		c. Slate (12.63)	£150	20·00

Only two examples of No. 98b have been recorded, one of which is in the Royal Collection.

1861 (22 Jun). *On paper made by T. H. Saunders of London wmkd "SIX PENCE" as* W **10**. P 12.

102	**4**	6d. black	£160	42·00

No. 102 was produced as an emergency measure after the decision had been taken to change the colour of the current 6d. from orange (No. 93) to black (No. 94). During the changeover the old Calvert "woodblock" plates were pressed into service to provide two months' supply.

12

13

(Des, eng and electrotyped De Gruchy & Leigh, Melbourne. Typo)

1861 (1 Oct)–**64**. P 12.

(a) On paper made by T. H. Saunders of London. Wmk "ONE PENNY" as W **10**.

103	**12**	1d. pale green	80·00	7·50
		a. Olive-green	—	8·50

(b) On paper made by De La Rue. Wmk single-lined "1" as W **11**.

104	**12**	1d. olive-green (1.2.63)	60·00	10·00
		a. Pale green (9.63)	60·00	5·50
		b. Apple-green (4.64)	60·00	5·50

(c) On paper supplied to Tasmania by Perkins, Bacon. Wmk double-lined "1", W **4** *of Tasmania.*

105	**12**	1d. yellow-green (10.12.63)	£110	8·50
		a. Dull green	—	8·50
		b. Imperf between (pair)	†	—

All printings were in sheets of 120 containing four panes of 30 (6 × 5).

Reprints from new plates were made in 1891 on paper watermarked "V over Crown" and perforated 12½.

(Frame die eng F. Grosse. Typo from electrotypes)

1862 (26 Apr)–**64**. *Centre vignette cut from T* **9** *with a new frame as T* **13**.

(a) On paper made by T. H. Saunders of London. Wmk "SIX PENCE" as W **10**. P 12.

106	**13**	6d. grey	85·00	6·50
		a. Grey-black	85·00	8·00
		b. Jet-black	90·00	9·00

(b) On paper made by De La Rue. Wmk single-lined "6" as W **11**.

107	**13**	6d. grey (p 12) (18.6.63)	75·00	4·75
		a. Jet-black	—	6·00
		b. Grey-black	75·00	5·00
		c. Perf 13. *Jet-black*	85·00	6·00
		ca. Grey-black	85·00	6·00

Printings before August 1863 were in sheets of 120 containing four panes of 30 (6 × 5). For subsequent printings of No. 107 the format was changed to six panes of 20 (4 × 5).

Reprints from new plates were made in 1891 on paper watermarked "V over Crown" and perforated 12½.

SINGLE-LINED NUMERAL WATERMARK PAPERS. The first consignment of this paper, showing watermarks as W **11**, arrived in Victoria during October 1862. Five further consignments followed, all but the last supplied by De La Rue.

The complexity of the scheme for different watermarks for each value, together with the time required to obtain further supplies from Great Britain, resulted in the emergency use of paper obtained from Tasmania and of the wrong numeral watermark on certain printings.

The final order for this paper was placed, in error with the firm of T. H. Saunders of London. Although the actual watermarks are the same (the dandy rolls were the property of the Victoria Government and supplied to each firm in turn) there are considerable differences between the two types of paper. That manufactured by Saunders is of a more even quality and is smoother, thicker, less brittle and less white than the De La Rue type.

De La Rue supplied white paper watermarked "1", "2", "4", "6" and "8", blue paper watermarked "1" and green paper watermarked "2".

The Saunders consignment of October 1865 contained white paper watermarked"1", "4" and "6", blue paper watermarked "1", green paper watermarked"2" and pink paper watermarked "10".

It is helpful for comparison purposes to note that all white paper watermarked"2" or "8" can only be De La Rue and all pink paper watermarked "10"can only be Saunders.

14

15

16

17

18

(Des and eng F. Grosse. Typo from electrotypes)

1863–**74**. *"Laureated" series.*

(a) On paper made by De La Rue wmkd with the appropriate value in single-lined numerals as W **11**.

108	**14**	1d. pale green (P 12) (9.9.64)	75·00	7·50
		a. Perf 12½ × 12 (9.64)		
		b. Perf 13 (10.10.64)	70·00	4·50
		c. Bluish green (P 13)	65·00	3·75
		ca. Printed double	†	£750
		d. Green (P 12) (7.65)	70·00	3·75
		da. Perf 13	65·00	4·00
		e. Deep green (P 12) (12.65)	85·00	4·00
		ea. Perf 13	—	4·00
		eb. Perf 12 × 13	—	8·00
		f. Bright yellow-green (P 13)	—	16·00
109		2d. violet (P 12) (1.4.64)	70·00	7·00
		a. Dull violet (P 12) (10.64)	75·00	7·00
		ab. Perf 12½ × 12		
		ac. Perf 12½		
		ad. Perf 13	75·00	5·50
		b. Dull lilac (P 13) (4.65)	60·00	5·50
		ba. Perf 12 (7.66)	—	9·00
		bb. Perf 12 × 13 (7.66)	—	10·00
		c. Reddish mauve (P 13) (11.65)	65·00	7·50
		d. Rose-lilac (P 13) (1.66)	60·00	7·00
		da. Perf 12 × 13 or 13 × 12	60·00	7·00
		e. Grey (P 12) (7.66)	90·00	8·50
		ea. Perf 13	60·00	3·75
110		4d. deep rose (P 12) (11.9.63)	£120	4·00
		a. Printed double	†	£750
		b. Rose-pink (P 12) (9.63)	90·00	2·50
		c. Pink (P 12) (7.5.64)	90·00	2·50
		ca. Error. Wmkd single-lined "8"	†	£5500
		cb. Perf 12½ × 12 (9.64)		
		d. Dull rose (P 13) (10.64)	80·00	2·50
		e. Dull rose-red (P 13)	80·00	2·50
		ea. Perf 12 (8.65)	£130	75·00
111	**16**	6d. blue (P 12) (13.2.66)	48·00	5·50
		a. Perf 13	48·00	3·00
		b. Perf 12 × 13	45·00	3·25
112	**14**	8d. orange (P 13) (22.2.65)	£350	55·00
113	**17**	1s. blue/*blue* (P 13) (10.4.65)	£110	3·75
		a. Perf 12 × 13 (4.66)	£110	3·75
		ab. Imperf between (vert pair)	†	£2500
		b. Bright blue/blue (P 13) (6.67)	90·00	3·25
		c. Indigo-blue/blue (P 13) (3.68)	—	3·25
		d. Dull blue/blue (P 12) (6.74)	—	3·50

(b) Emergency printings on Perkins, Bacon paper borrowed from Tasmania. Wmk double-lined "4" as W **4** of Tasmania.

114	**14**	4d. deep rose (P 12) (7.1.64)	£120	4·50
		a. Pale rose (P 12)	—	4·00
		b. Dull reddish rose (P 13) (11.8.65)	£120	4·25
		ba. Perf 12	—	4·25
		bb. Perf 12 × 13	—	13·00
		c. Red (P 13) (4.12.65)	£130	4·25

(c) Emergency printings on De La Rue paper as W **11**, *but showing incorrect single-lined numeral.* P 13.

115	**14**	1d. brt yellow-grn (wmkd "8") (27.12.66)	£130	15·00
116		1d. brt yellow-green (wmkd "6") (6.67)	—	24·00
117		2d. grey (wmkd "8") (18.1.67)	£120	5·00
118	**15**	3d. lilac (wmkd "8") (29.9.66)	£120	26·00
119	**16**	10d. grey (wmkd "8") (21.10.65)	£500	£110
		a. Grey-black	£500	£120

(d) On paper made by T. H. Saunders wmkd with the appropriate value in single-lined numerals as W **11**.

120	**14**	1d. deep yellow-green (P 12 × 13) (1.66)	£120	10·00
		a. Perf 13 (3.66)	65·00	4·25
		b. Perf 12 (7.66)	—	11·00
121		4d. rose-red (P 13) (12.12.65)	75·00	3·25
		a. Perf 12 × 13 or 13 × 12 (2.66)	£110	6·50
		b. Perf 12 (4.66)	—	6·50
122	**16**	6d. blue (P 13) (28.5.66)	42·00	1·50
		a. Perf 12	48·00	3·75
		b. Perf 12 × 13	42·00	2·00
		ba. Imperf between (horiz pair)	†	£1200
123		10d. dull purple/*pink* (P 13) (22.3.66)	90·00	5·00
		a. Perf 12 × 13	£130	6·50
		b. Blackish brown/pink (P 13) (12.69)	95·00	5·50
		c. Purple-brown/pink (P 13) (11.70)		
124	**17**	1s. bright blue/*blue* (P 13) (5.12.70)	60·00	2·50
		a. Pale dull blue/blue (P 12) (1.73)	£130	3·50
		ab. Perf 13	—	8·50
		b. Indigo-blue/blue (P 12) (9.73)	—	5·50
		ba. Perf 13	60·00	3·75

(e) Emergency printings on Saunders paper as W **11**, *but showing incorrect single-lined numeral.* P 13.

125	**14**	1d. brt yellow-green (wmkd "4") (6.3.67)	95·00	13·00
126		1d. brt yellow-green (wmkd "6") (6.67)	£140	20·00
127		2d. grey (wmkd "4") (21.2.67)	95·00	5·00
128		2d. grey (wmkd "6") (13.5.67)	£160	6·0

The 1d., 2d., 4d. and 8d. were originally produced in sheets of 120 containing eight panes of 15 (3 × 5). The 3d. and 6d. were in sheets of 120 (12 × 10) and the 1d. (from February 1866), 2d. (from July 1866) and 4d. (from April 1866) subsequently changed to this format. The 10d. was in sheets of 120 containing twenty panes of 6 (2 × 3). The 1s. was originally in sheets of 60 containing three panes of 20 (4 × 5), but this changed to 120 (12 × 10) in April 1866.

Only single examples are thought to exist of Nos. 110a, 110ca 113ab, and 122ba and two of No. 108ca.

For later emergency printings on these papers see Nos. 153/66.

(Typo from composite woodblock and electrotype plate)

(a) On De La Rue paper. Wmk single-lined "2" as W **11**.

129	**4**	2s. light blue/*green* (P 13) (22.11.64)	£160	6·5
		a. Dark blue/green (P 12) (9.65)	£180	12·0
		ab. Perf 13 (6.66)	£160	7·0
		b. Blue/green (P 13) (6.68)	£150	4·7
		c. Greenish blue/green (P 13) (7.73)	£150	6·5
		ca. Perf 12	£170	7·5
		d. Deep greenish blue/green (P 12½)	£150	6·0

(b) On Saunders paper. Wmk single-lined "2" as W **11**.

130	**4**	2s. dark blue/*green* (P 13) (23.11.67)	£170	7·0
		a. Blue/green (P 13) (10.71)	£170	6·5
		ab. Perf 12 (8.74)	£190	7·5
		c. Deep greenish blue/green (P 12½) (7.80)	£150	5·5

Nos. 129/30 were produced in sheets of 30 containing two panes of 15 (3 × 5). The plate contained eighteen of the original woodblock impressions and twelve electrotypes taken from them.

19

20

V OVER CROWN WATERMARKS. The changeover from the numeral watermarks to a general type to be used for all values was first suggested at the end of 1865, but the first supplies did not reach Melbourne until April 1867. Five different versions were used before the V over Crown watermark was superseded by the Commonwealth type in 1905. The five versions are listed as follows

Type **19**	De La Rue paper supplied 1867 to 1882. Shows four points at the top of the crown with the left and right ornaments diamond-shaped
Type **33**	De La Rue paper supplied 1882 to 1895 No points at the top of the crown with the left and right ornament oval-shaped
Type **82**	Waterlow paper supplied 1896 to 1899. Wide base to crown
Type **85**	Waterlow paper used for postal issues 1899 to 1905. Wide top to crown
Type **104**	James Spicer and Sons paper used for postal issues August and September 1912. Narrow crown

(Type from electrotypes)

1867–**81**. Wmk. V over Crown. W **19**.

(a) P 13.

131	**14**	1d. bright yellow-green (10.8.67)	65·00	3·
		a. Bright olive-green (1.69)	95·00	19·
		b. Yellow-green (4.69)	65·00	3·
		c. Dull green (3.70)	65·00	3·
		d. Pale green (10.70)	60·00	3·
		e. Grass-green (1871)	60·00	3·
		f. Bluish green (*shades*) (7.72)	60·00	3·
		g. Green (*shades*) (9.72)	60·00	3·
132		2d. slate-grey (*shades*) (26.8.67)	70·00	3·
		a. Grey-lilac (29.1.68)	70·00	5·
		b. Lilac (26.8.68)	50·00	3·
		c. Dull mauve (*shades*) (10.68)	50·00	3·
		d. Lilac-grey (1.69)	—	3·
		e. Lilac-rose (2.69)	55·00	3·
		f. Mauve (4.69)	70·00	3·
		g. Red-lilac (5.69)	55·00	3·
		h. Dull lilac (6.69)	55·00	2·
		i. Silver-grey (9.69)	£110	7·
133	**15**	3d. lilac (28.8.67)	£200	32·
		a. Grey-lilac (6.68)	£225	35·
134		3d. yellow-orange (12.6.69)	27·00	3·
		a. Dull orange (6.70)	25·00	3·
		b. Orange (3.73)	—	3·
		c. Bright orange (3.73)	29·00	3·
		d. Orange-brown (*glazed paper*) (10.78)	28·00	8·
135	**14**	4d. dull rose (28.11.67)	75·00	5·
		a. Wmk sideways	†	65·
		b. Aniline red (*shades*) (21.4.69)	—	7·
		c. Rose-pink (11.69)	—	5·
		d. Rose (*shades*) (8.71)	70·00	3·
		e. Dull rose (*glazed paper*) (5.3.79)	70·00	3·
		f. Dull rose-red (*glazed paper*) (11.79)	—	4·
		g. Bright lilac-rose (*aniline*) (*glazed paper*) (2.80)	80·00	3·
		h. Rosine (*aniline*) (*glazed paper*) (9.80)	£200	5·
136	**16**	6d. deep blue (15.1.68)	—	3·

a. Blue (21.12.68) . . . . 29·00 1·75
b. Indigo-blue (10.69) . . . . . . 29·00 1·75
c. Prussian blue (9.72) . . . . . . 27·00 1·75
d. Indigo (4.73) . . . . 29·00 2·00
e. Dull blue (*worn plate*) (3.74) . . . — 1·75
f. Dull ultramarine (2.12.75) . . . . 38·00 1·75
g. Light Prussian blue (12.75) . . . 55·00 1·75
h. Dull violet-blue (7.77) . . . . . — 7·50
i. Blue (*glazed paper*) (6.78) . . . . 42·00 1·75
j. Dull milky-blue (*glazed paper*) (9.79) . . . . 38·00 1·75
k. Prussian blue (*glazed paper*) (4.80) . . . . — 1·75
l. Light blue (*glazed paper*) (4.81) . . 42·00 1·75
m. Deep blue (*glazed paper*) (10.81) . . 38·00 1·75

137 **14** 8d. lilac-brown/*pink* (24.1.77) . . . . 80·00 5·50
a. Purple-brown/pink (2.78) . . . . 80·00 5·50
b. Chocolate/pink (8.78) . . . . . 85·00 6·00
ba. Compound perf 13 × 12 . . . . . † £325
c. Red-brown/pink (12.78) . . . . . 80·00 5·00

138 **17** 1s. light blue/*blue* (11.5.75) . . . . £100 7·50

139 **18** 5s. blue/*yellow* (26.12.67) £1700 £300
a. Wmk reversed . . . . — £500

140 5s. indigo-blue and carmine (I) (8.10.68) . . . . £225 24·00
a. Blue and carmine (4.69) . . . . £190 15·00
b. Pale bright blue and carmine (*glazed paper*) (24.7.77) . . . . — 20·00
c. Grey-blue and carmine (*glazed paper*) (4.78) . . . . £180 17·00
d. Wmk sideways. *Deep lavender-blue and carmine* (4.6.80) . . . . . . £180 20·00

141 5s. bright blue and red (II) (*glazed paper*) (12.5.81) . . . . £160 16·00
a. Indigo-blue and red (*glazed paper*) . . . . — 21·00

(*b*) P 12.

142 **14** 1d. pale green (10.71) . . . . . . 70·00 3·25
a. Grass-green (1871) . . . . . . 60·00 3·25
b. Bluish green (*shades*) (7.72) . . . — 3·25
c. Green (*shades*) (9.72) . . . . . 60·00 3·00

143 **15** 3d. dull orange (5.72) . . . . . . 25·00 2·25
a. Orange (3.73) . . . . — 2·10
b. Bright orange (3.73) . . . . . . — 2·50
c. Dull orange-yellow (*glazed paper*) (12.80) . . . .

144 **14** 4d. rose (*shades*) (8.71) . . . . . . 70·00 3·00
a. Compound perf 12 × 13 . . . . . — £400
b. Dull rose (*glazed paper*) (3.79) . . — 3·00
c. Dull rose-red (*glazed paper*) (11.79) . . . . — 3·00
d. Bright lilac-rose (*aniline*) (*glazed paper*) (2.80) . . . . — 7·50
e. Rosine (*aniline*) (*glazed paper*) (9.80) . . . . 80·00 5·50

45 **16** 6d. deep blue (2.2.72) . . . . . .
a. Prussian blue (9.72) . . . . . . 29·00 2·25
b. Indigo (4.73) . . . . 38·00 2·50
c. Dull blue (worn plate) . . . . .
d. Blue (*glazed paper*) (6.78) . . . . — 2·25
e. Dull milky-blue (*glazed paper*) . . — 2·25
f. Light blue (*glazed paper*) (4.81) . . — 3·25

46 **14** 8d. red-brn/*pink* (*glazed paper*) (11.80) . . . . 75·00 7·00

47 **17** 1s. light blue/*blue* (5.75) . . . . . — 7·50

48 **18** 5s. bright blue and red (II) (*glazed paper*) (5.81) . . . . £160 13·00
a. Indigo-blue and red . . . . . . £250 17·00

(*c*) P 12½.

49 **15** 3d. dull orange-yellow (*glazed paper*) (12.80) . . . . 38·00 4·25

50 **14** 4d. rosine (*aniline*) (*glazed paper*) (9.80) . . . .

51 **16** 6d. Prussian blue (*glazed paper*) (4.80) . . . .
a. Light blue (*glazed paper*) (4.81) . .
b. Deep blue (*glazed paper*) (10.81) . . 38·00 2·75

52 **14** 8d. lilac-brown/*pink* (8.77) . . . . . 75·00 7·00
a. *Red-brown/pink* (*glazed paper*) (11.80) . . . . † £500

The same electrotypes as the previous issues were used for this eries with the exception of the 5s. which was a new value. The 1d., d., 3d., 4d., 6d. and 1s. plates were arranged to print sheets of 120 12 × 10) and the 8d. conformed to this when reintroduced in 1877. New plates for the 1d. (1868), 2d. (1869) and 6d. (1875) were onstructed by Robinson's successor, J. P. Atkinson, using the nproved facilities then available.

Atkinson was also responsible for the printing of the 5s. value. 'he original printings in blue on yellow paper were produced in heets of 25, or possibly 50, using a vertical strip of five electrotypes.)ue to its size the 5s. did not exactly fit the watermarked paper and,) avoid a preprinted sheet number, a proportion of the printing vas made on the back of the paper creating the reversed watermark ariety, No. 139a. These varieties occur in the first printing only as tkinson created a plate of 25 for the second printing in March 868. Printings of the 5s. bicoloured to April 1880 were made from lectrotypes taken from the monocoloured plate. These showed a lue line beneath the crown (Type I). In early 1881 this plate was ound to be too worn for further use and a new die was made from 'hich a plate of 100 was constructed. Stamps from this plate are ithout the blue line beneath the crown(Type II).

'ERFORATIONS. Various perforating machines were in use uring this period. The use of line machines gauging 12 ceased round 1883. Of the line machines gauging 13 two were converted) comb types in 1873 and were eventually replaced by the 12½ auge line and comb machines first used in 1876.

(Typo from electrotypes)

867–70. *Emergency printings on various papers due to shortages of V over Crown paper.* P 13.

ι) Perkins, Bacon paper borrowed from Tasmania. Wmkd double-lined numerals as W **4** of Tasmania.

53 **14** 1d. pale yellowish green (wmkd "1") (24.9.67) . . . . 65·00 3·50
a. Deep yellow-green (10.67) . . . . 65·00 3·50

54 1d. pale yellow-green (wmkd "4") (27.5.68) . . . . £1400 90·00

155 2d. grey-lilac (wmkd "4") (3.2.68) . . £110 4·25
a. Slate (4.68) . . . . £110 3·50
b. Mauve (7.68) . . . . — 4·50
c. Imperf (pair) . . . . † £3250

156 2d. mauve (wmkd "1") (30.6.68) . . . £110 5·50

157 **15** 3d. grey-lilac (wmkd "1") (8.68) . . . £150 48·00

158 **14** 4d. dull rose-red (wmkd "4") (5.68) . . £110 5·00

159 **16** 6d. blue (wmkd "4") (20.6.68) . . . . £150 15·00
a. Indigo-blue . . . . — 17·00

160 6d. blue (wmkd "1") (28.7.68) . . . . 55·00 4·25

161 6d. dull blue (wmkd "2") (1870) . . . † £2250

(*b*) *Saunders paper.* Wmkd in words as W **10**.

162 **14** 1d. pale yellow-green (wmkd "SIX PENCE") (23.3.68) . . . . £500 26·00

163 2d. slate-grey (wmkd "SIX PENCE") (6.68) . . . . † £4250

164 **16** 6d. blue (wmkd "SIX PENCE") (20.5.68) . . . . £375 20·00
a. Indigo-blue . . . . — 24·00

165 6d. dull blue (wmkd "THREE PENCE") (6.12.69) . . . . £200 7·50
a. Deep blue . . . . — 8·50

166 6d. dull blue (wmkd "FOUR PENCE") (21.5.70) . . . . £375 25·00
a. Deep blue . . . . — 26·00

(*c*) V over Crown, W **19**, *coloured paper.*

167 **14** 2d. mauve/*lilac* (7.68) . . . . 65·00 6·50
a. *Lilac/lilac* . . . . 65·00 6·00

(*d*) *Saunders single-lined numeral "4" as W* **11**.

168 **16** 6d. dull blue (21.5.70) . . . . † £1600

The supply of paper was so short during 1868 that many odds and ends were utilised. Nos. 161 (five known), 163 (one known) and 168 (ten known)are the rarest of these emergency printings.

(Printed in Melbourne from a double electrotyped plate of 240 supplied by D.L.R.)

1870 (28 Jan)–**73**. Wmk V over Crown. W **19**.

169 **20** 2d. brown-lilac (P 13) . . . . . . 65·00 1·50
a. Dull lilac-mauve (9.70) . . . . . 55·00 1·00
b. Mauve (*worn plate*) (3.73) . . . . 55·00 1·25

170 2d. dull lilac-mauve (p 12) (28.7.71) . . 60·00 2·50
a. Mauve (*worn plate*) (3.73) . . . . 60·00 2·25

9 9

NINEPENCE

(**21**)

1871 (22 Apr). No. 123*c surch with T* **21** *in blue.*

171 **16** 9d.on 10d. purple-brown/*pink* . . . . £325 10·00
a. Blackish brown/pink . . . . . . £400 12·00
b. Surch double . . . . † £1100

22 23 24 25 26 27

(Des and eng W. Bell. Typo from electrotyped plates)

1873 (25 Mar)–**74**. *Saunders paper.* Wmk single-lined "10" as W **11**.

172 **25** 9d. pale brown/*pink* (P 13) . . . . . 70·00 13·00
a. Red-brown/pink (7.74) . . . . . 65·00 13·00

173 9d. pale brown/*pink* (P 12) . . . . . 75·00 14·00

½ ½

HALF

(**28**)

1873 (25 Jun). No. 131g *surch with T* **28** *in red.*

174 **14** ½d.on 1d. green (P 13) . . . . . . 50·00 12·00
a. Grass-green . . . . 55·00 12·00
b. Short "1" at right (R. 1/3) . . . . — 70·00

175 ½d.on 1d. green (P 12) . . . . . . 70·00 14·00
a. Grass-green . . . . 70·00 14·00
b. Short "1" at right (R. 1/3) . . . . — 75·00

Die I

Die II

Two Dies of 2d.:

Die I. Single-lined outer oval
Die II. Double-lined outer oval

(Des and eng W. Bell. Typo from electrotyped plates)

1873–87. Wmk V over Crown, W **19** (sideways on ½d.).

(*a*) P 13.

176 **22** ½d. rose-red (10.2.74) . . . . . . 11·00 1·00
a. Lilac-rose (1874) . . . . 12·00 1·50
b. Rosine (*shades*) (*glazed paper*) (12.80) . . . . 9·50 1·00
c. Pale red (*glazed paper*) (1882) . . 11·00 1·00
d. Mixed perf 13 and 12 . . . . . . † £375

177 **23** 1d. *dull bluish green* (14.12.75) . . . 24·00 1·75
a. Green (*shades*) (1877) . . . . . 24·00 1·75
b. Yellow-green (*glazed paper*) . . . 24·00 1·50

178 **24** 2d. deep lilac-mauve (I) (1.10.73) . . . 35·00 65
a. Dull violet-mauve . . . . 35·00 65
b. Dull mauve . . . . 35·00 65
c. Pale mauve (*worn plate*) (*glazed paper*) (1.79) . . . . 35·00 80
d. Mixed perf 13 and 12 . . . . . £350 £250

179 2d. lilac-mauve (II) (*glazed paper*) (17.12.78) . . . . 32·00 65
a. Grey-mauve (1.80) . . . . — 70
b. Pale mauve (6.80) . . . . 42·00 70
c. Vert pair, lower stamp imperf horiz . . . . † £1600

180 **26** 1s. indigo-blue/*blue* (16.8.76) . . . . 65·00 3·50
a. Wmk sideways . . . . † £750
b. Deep blue/blue (7.77) . . . . . . 70·00 3·50
c. Pale blue/blue (3.80) . . . . . . 75·00 3·50
d. Bright blue/blue (9.80) . . . . . 80·00 7·50
e. Bright blue/blue (*glazed paper*) (21.11.83) . . . . 80·00 5·00
f. Pale blue/blue (*glazed paper*) . . .
g. Mixed perf 13 and 12 . . . . . . † —

(*b*) P 12.

181 **22** ½d. rose-red (1874) . . . . 11·00 2·25
a. Lilac-rose (1874) . . . . 11·00 2·25
b. Rosine (*shades*) (*glazed paper*) . . 11·00 2·00
c. Pale red (*glazed paper*) (1882) . . 11·00 2·25

182 **23** 1d. dull bluish green (1875) . . . . . 28·00 2·50
a. Green (*shades*) (1877) . . . . . 27·00 6·00
b. Yellow-green (*glazed paper*) . . . — 3·50

183 **24** 2d. deep lilac-mauve (I) (1873) . . . . — 4·25
a. Dull violet-mauve . . . . — 4·25
b. Dull mauve . . . . 42·00 2·25
c. Pale mauve (*worn plate*) (*glazed paper*) (1879) . . . . — 2·50

184 2d. lilac-mauve (II) (*glazed paper*) (1878) . . . . 45·00 1·75
a. Grey-mauve (*glazed paper*) (1880) . . . . — 1·75
b. Pale mauve (*glazed paper*) (1880) . . . . — 3·00

185 **25** 9d. lilac-brown/*pink* (1.12.75) . . . . £110 13·00

186 **26** 1s. deep blue/*blue* (1880) . . . . . . — 7·50
a. Bright blue/blue (1880) . . . . . — 7·50

(*c*) P 12½.

187 **22** ½d. rosine (*shades*) (*glazed paper*) (1880) . . . .
a. Pale red (*glazed paper*) (1882) . .

188 **23** 1d. yellow-green (*glazed paper*) (1880) . . . .

189 **24** 2d. grey-mauve (II) (*glazed paper*) (1880) . . . .
a. Pale mauve (1880) . . . .

190 **27** 2s. deep blue/*green* (*glazed paper*) (8.7.81) . . . . £120 18·00
a. Light blue/green (*glazed paper*) (4.83) . . . .
ab. Wmk sideways . . . . £130 22·00
b. Ultramarine/green (*glazed paper*) (6.84) . . . . — 28·00
ba. Wmk sideways . . . . — 50·00

8d 8d

EIGHTPENCE

(**29**)

1876 (1 Jul). No. 185 *surch with T* **29**.

191 **25** 8d.on 9d. lilac-brown/*pink* . . . . . £190 15·00
a. "F.IGHTPENCE" . . . . — £250

No. 191a was caused by a broken "E" and it occurred once in each sheet of 120.

1877. *Saunders paper.* Wmk "10" as W **11**.

192 **14** 8d. lilac-brown/*pink* (P 13) . . . . . — £500
a. Purple-brown/pink (2.78) . . . . £100 9·50
b. Chocolate/pink (8.78) . . . . . † £600
c. Red-brown/pink (8.79) . . . . . 85·00 5·00

193 8d. red-brown/*pink* (P 12) (8.79) . . . £200 14·00

194 8d. red-brown/*pink* (P 12½) (8.79) . . . — 50·00

Nos. 192/4 occur amongst the V over Crown printings, the two types of pink paper having become mixed.

1878. *Emergency printings on coloured papers.* Wmk V over Crown, W **19** (sideways on ½d.). P 13.

195 **22** ½d. rose-red/*pink* (1.3.78) . . . . . 32·00 21·00

196 **23** 1d. yellow-green/*yellow* (5.3.78) . . . . 85·00 15·00

197 1d. yellow-green/*drab* (5.4.78) . . . . £120 50·00

198 **24** 2d. dull violet-mauve/*lilac* (21.2.78) . . — £650

199 2d. dull violet-mauve/*green* (23.2.78) . . . . £160 20·00

200 2d. dull violet-mauve/*brown* (21.3.78) . . . . £150 20·00

There was a shortage of white V over Crown, W **19**, watermarked paper in the early months of 1878 and various coloured papers were used for printings of the ½d., 1d. and 2d. values until fresh stocks of white paper were received.

30

31

32

(Des and eng C. Naish. Typo from electrotyped plates)

1880 (3 Nov)–**84**. Wmk V over Crown. W **19**.

No.	Type	Description	Unused	Used
201	**30**	1d. green (P 12½) (2.84)	90·00	12·00
202	**31**	2d. sepia (P 12½)	26·00	60
		a. Sepia-brown (2.81)	24·00	60
		b. Brown (*aniline*) (5.81)	27·00	60
		c. Dull black-brown (10.81)	—	60
		d. Dull grey-brown (3.82)	23·00	60
203		2d. sepia (P 13)		
		a. Mixed perf 13 and 12	†	£600
204		2d. sepia (P 12)	—	75·00
		a. Sepia-brown (2.81)	—	75·00
		b. Brown (*aniline*) (5.81)	—	75·00
205		2d. mauve (*worn plate*) (P 12½) (2.84)	—	7·00
206	**32**	4d. rose-carmine (P 12½) (10.81)	55·00	5·00
		a. Rosine (7.82)	55·00	4·50

Nos. 201 and 205 are subsequent printings of stamps first produced on watermark W **33**.

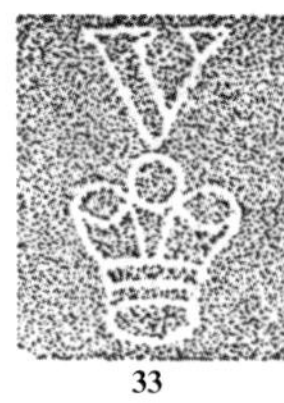
33

1882–84. Wmk V over Crown W **33** (sideways on ½d.). P 12½.

No.	Type	Description	Unused	Used
207	**22**	½d. rosine (3.83)	14·00	4·50
		a. Perf 12	—	19·00
208	**23**	1d. yellow-green (9.82)	24·00	2·25
		a. Perf 12		
209	**30**	1d. yellow-green (29.10.83)	24·00	1·75
		a. Green (1.84)	22·00	1·75
		b. Pale green (5.84)	22·00	1·50
210	**31**	2d. dull grey-brown (15.8.82)	23·00	1·00
		a. Chocolate (3.83)	23·00	1·00
		ab. Perf 12	†	£325
211		2d. mauve (20.12.83)	17·00	1·00
		a. Worn plate (2.84)	18·00	1·00
		b. Perf 12	†	£750
		c. Mixed perf 12 and 12½	†	£750
212	**15**	3d. yellow-orange (13.4.83)	40·00	10·00
		a. Dull brownish orange	45·00	12·00
213	**32**	4d. rose-red (3.83)	50·00	8·00
214	**16**	6d. dull violet-blue (10.11.82)	26·00	1·50
		a. Indigo-blue (11.83)	26·00	1·50
		b. Light ultramarine (8.84)	26·00	1·50

Reprints were made in 1891 of the "Laureated" 1d., 2d., 3d. (in yellow), 4d., 6d., 8d. (in orange-yellow), 10d. (in greenish slate) and 5s. (in blue and red), of the Bell ½d., 1d., 2d. (Die II), 9d. and 1s. and of the Naish 2d. (in brown), 4d. (in pale red) and 2s. With the exception of the Bell 9d., which was watermarked W **19**, all were watermarked W **33** and perforated 12½. Some were from new plates.

THE POST OFFICE ACT OF 1883. Following official concern as to the number of different series of adhesive stamps, both fiscal and postal, used in Victoria it was decided that the system should be unified to the extent that the postage stamps, Stamp Statute fiscals and Stamp Duty fiscals should be replaced by a single series valid for all three purposes. As the Stamp Duty series contained the largest number of values it was adopted as the basis of the new range.

The regulations for the changeover were detailed in the Post Office Act of 1883 which came into force on 1 January 1884. From that date all existing Stamp Statute (first produced in 1871) and Stamp Duty (first produced in 1879) issues became valid for postal purposes, and the previous postage stamps could be used for fiscal fees.

Until matters could be organised printings of some of the existing postage values continued and these will be found included in the listings above.

Printing of the Stamp Statute series was discontinued in early 1884.

The existing Stamp Duty range was initially supplemented by postage stamps overprinted "STAMP DUTY" for those values where the available fiscal design was considered to be too large to be easily used on mail. These overprints were replaced by smaller designs inscribed "STAMP DUTY".

Stamp Statute and Stamp Duty values which became valid for postal purposes on 1 January 1884 have previously been listed in this catalogue as Postal Fiscals. Under the circumstances this distinction appears somewhat arbitrary and all such stamps are now shown in the main listing. Used prices quoted are for examples with postal cancellations. In some instances prices are also provided for fiscally used and these are marked "F.C.".

34

35

36

37

(Des and dies eng J. Turner (3d., 2s.6d.), W. Bell (others). Typo from electrotypes)

1884 (1 Jan*). *Stamp Statute series. Vert designs as T* **34/6**, *and others showing Queen Victoria, and T* **37**. P 13.

(a) Wmk single-lined numerals according to face value, as W **11**, (sideways). *Paper manufactured by T. H. Saunders unless otherwise stated.*

No.	Description	Unused	Used
215	1s. blue/*blue*	70·00	22·00
	a. Perf 12	85·00	28·00
216	2s. blue/*green* (*D.L.R. paper*)	£110	70·00
	a. Perf 12	£110	70·00
217	2s. deep blue/*green*	£110	
	a. Perf 12	—	70·00
	b. Wmk upright		
218	10s. brown-olive/*pink*		
219	10s. red-brown/*pink*	£850	£200
	a. Wmk upright Perf 12		

(b) Wmk V over Crown W **19** (sideways). P 13.

No.	Description	Unused	Used
220	1d. pale green	40·00	32·00
	a. Green (wmk upright) (P 12½)	75·00	55·00
221	3d. mauve	£550	£300
222	4d. rose	£450	£225
	a. Wmk upright	£550	
223	6d. blue	65·00	22·00
	a. Ultramarine	55·00	19·00
	ab. Perf 12	65·00	20·00
224	1s. blue/*blue*	65·00	22·00
	a. Perf 12	70·00	26·00
	b. Ultramarine/blue (P 12½)	—	42·00
	ba. Perf 12	—	30·00
	c. Deep blue/blue (P 12½)	65·00	22·00
	ca. Perf 12	70·00	22·00
225	2s. blue/*green*	£100	65·00
	a. Perf 12	£100	
	b. Deep blue/blue-green (*glazed paper*)	£100	70·00
	ba. Perf 12	£100	75·00
226	2s.6d. orange	—	£120
	a. Perf 12		
	b. Yellow (*glazed paper*)	£300	
	ba. Perf 12	£300	£120
	c. Orange-yellow (*glazed paper*) (P 12½)	—	£130
	ca. Perf 12		
227	5s. blue/*yellow*	£275	70·00
	a. Perf 12	£275	
	b. Wmk upright		
	ba. Perf 12		
	c. Ultram/lemon (*glazed paper*) (P 12½)	£275	70·00
	ca. Wmk upright		
228	10s. brown/*pink*	£850	£200
	a. Purple-brown/pink	£850	£200
	ab. Perf 12		
229	£1 slate-violet/*yellow*	£600	£160
	a. Wmk upright		
	b. Mauve/yellow		
	ba. Perf 12	£600	£160
	bb. Perf 12½	£600	£160
230	£5 black and yellow-green	£3250	£750
	a. Perf 12		
	b. Wmk upright. Perf 12½	£3250	£750

(c) Wmk V over Crown (sideways) W **33**.

No.	Description	Unused	Used
231	1d. yellowish green (P 12½)	55·00	55·00
232	2s.6d. pale orange-yellow (P 12)	£275	£120
233	£5 black & yellow-grn (wmk upright) (P 12)	—	£750

(**38**)

1884 (1 Jan*). *No.* 220 *surch with T* **38** *in red.*

No.	Description	Unused	Used
234	½d.on 1d. pale green	55·00	55·00

*The dates quoted are those on which the stamps became valid for postal purposes. The ½d., 1d., 4d., 6d., 1s., 5s. and £1 were issued for fiscal purposes on 26 April 1871. The 10s. was added to the series in June 1871, the £5 in September 1871, the 2s.6d. in July 1876 and the 3d. in October 1879.

All values of the Stamp Statute series were reprinted in 1891 on paper watermarked W **19** (5s., 10s., £1) or W **33** (others). The £5 was pulled from the original plate, but the others were produced from new electrotypes taken from the original dies.

39 40 41

42 43 44

45 46 47

48 49 50

51 52 53

54

55

56

57

58

59

60

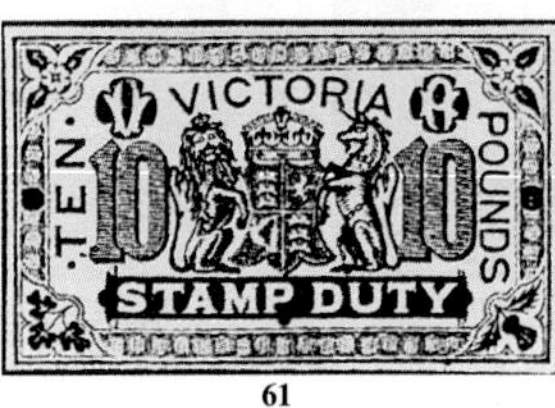

61

(Des H. Samson and F. Oxenbould (T **39**), C. Jackson and L. Lang (all others except T **40**). Dies eng C. Jackson, J. Turner, J. Whipple, A. Williams and other employees of Sands & MacDougall. T **40** die eng C. Naish)

384 (1 Jan*)–**96**. *Existing Stamp Duty series.*

(a) Litho. Wmk V over Crown. W **19** (sideways). P 13.

35	**39**	1d. blue-green	65·00	21·00
		a. Perf 12	65·00	21·00
		b. Perf 12½		
36	**43**	1s.6d. rosine	£170	23·00
		a. Perf 12	—	29·00
		b. Perf 12½		
37	**45**	3s. purple/*blue*	£400	40·00
		a. Perf 12	£475	48·00
		b. Perf 12½		
38	**46**	4s. orange-red	90·00	18·00
		a. Perf 12	90·00	18·00
		b. Perf 12½		
39	**48**	6s. apple-green	£275	32·00
		a. Perf 12½		
40	**49**	10s. brown/*rose* (*glazed paper*)	£425	80·00
		a. Perf 12		
		b. Perf 12½		
		c. Wmk upright		
		cb. Perf 12½		
:1	**50**	15s. mauve	£1100	£180
:2	**51**	£1 red-orange	£425	75·00
		a. Perf 12½	£425	75·00
:3	**52**	£15s. dull rose (wmk upright)	£1100	£200
:4	**53**	£110s. deep grey-olive	£1100	£130
		a. Wmk upright	—	£160
5	–	35s. grey-violet (wmk upright) (F.C. £180)	£4500	
6	**54**	£2 blue	—	£110
7	**55**	45s. dull brown-lilac	£2250	£170
8	**56**	£5 rose-red (wmk upright) (F.C. £55)	£2250	£400
9	**57**	£6 blue/*pink* (wmk upright) (*glazed paper*) (F.C. £110)	—	£600
0	**58**	£7 violet/*blue* (wmk upright) (F.C. £110)	—	£600
1	**59**	£8 brownish red/*yellow* (wmk upright) (*glazed paper*) (F.C. £110)	—	£750
2	**60**	£9 yellow-green/*green* (wmk upright) (*glazed paper*) (F.C. £110)	—	£750

(b) Typo from electrotypes.

(i) Wmk V over Crown. W **19** (sideways). P 13.

3	**39**	1d. yellowish green	48·00	21·00
		a. Perf 12	48·00	21·00
		b. Perf 12½		
4	**40**	1d. pale bistre	17·00	3·50
		a. Perf 12	17·00	4·25
		b. Perf 12½		
5	**41**	6d. dull blue	65·00	10·00
		a. Perf 12	70·00	18·00
		b. Perf 12½		
6	**42**	1s. deep blue/*blue*	75·00	5·50
		a. Perf 12	75·00	7·00
		b. Perf 12½		
		c. Brt blue/blue (*glazed paper*) (P 12½)	75·00	6·50
		ca. Perf 12	—	7·00
		d. Ultramarine/blue (*glazed paper*) (P 12½) (11.84)	£120	7·00
7		1s. chalky blue/*lemon* (*glazed paper*) (P 12½) (3.3.85)	90·00	24·00
3	**44**	2s. deep blue/*green* (*glazed paper*)	£150	22·00
		a. Perf 12	—	24·00
		b. Perf 12½	—	26·00
		c. Indigo/green	£130	26·00
		ca. Perf 12	£170	27·00
		cb. Perf 12½		
9	**45**	3s. mar/*bl* (*glazed paper*) (P 12½) (8.8.84)	£325	32·00
)	**47**	5s. claret/*yellow* (*glazed paper*)	50·00	6·00
		a. Perf 12	65·00	12·00
		b. Perf 12½		
		c. Pale claret/yellow (P 12½)	50·00	13·00
		ca. Perf 12	70·00	13·00
		d. Reddish purple/lemon (P 12½) (6.87)	45·00	12·00
		e. Brown-red/yellow (P 12½) (5.93)	75·00	29·00
	49	10s. *chocolate/rose* (*glazed paper*)	—	80·00
		a. Perf 12		
		b. Perf 12½		
		c. Wmk upright		
2	**51**	£1 yellow-orange/*yellow* (P 12)	£600	75·00
		a. Orange/yellow (P 12½) (8.84)	£550	55·00
		b. Reddish orange/yellow (P 12½) (9.88)	£350	55·00

263	**54**	£2 deep blue (P 12)	—	£110
264	**61**	£10 dull mauve (P 12)		
		a. Deep red-lilac (P 12)	£2500	£150

(ii) Wmk V over Crown W **33** (sideways). P 12½.

265	**40**	1d. ochre	27·00	4·75
		a. Perf 12	27·00	4·75
266	**41**	6d. ultramarine	75·00	8·50
		a. Perf 12	75·00	8·50
267	**43**	1s.6d. pink (1.85)	£140	26·00
		a. Bright rose-carmine (4.86)	£160	23·00
268	**45**	3s. drab (20.10.85)	75·00	16·00
		a. Olive-drab (1.93)	70·00	16·00
269	**46**	4s. red-orange (5.86)	80·00	15·00
		a. Yellow-orange (12.94)		
		ab. Wmk upright	£100	13·00
270	**47**	5s. rosine (8.5.96)	75·00	19·00
271	**48**	6s. pea-green (12.11.91)	£110	40·00
		a. Apple-green (wmk upright)	£180	38·00
272	**49**	10s. dull bluish green (10.85)	£180	38·00
		a. Grey-green (5.86)	£140	29·00
273	**50**	15s. purple-brown (12.85)	£650	80·00
		a. Brown (wmk upright) (5.95)	£650	85·00
274	**52**	£15s. pink (wmk upright) (6.8.90)	£1100	90·00
275	**53**	£110s. pale olive (6.88)	£800	80·00
276	**54**	£2 bright blue	—	80·00
		a. Blue (7.88)	£800	80·00
277	**55**	45s. lilac (15.8.90)	£2500	£100
278	**56**	£5 rose-pink (P 12)	—	£375
		a. Pink (P 12½)	—	£475
279	**61**	£10 mauve (3.84)	£2500	£110
		a. Lilac (6.85)	—	£120

*This is the date on which the stamps became valid for postal use. The 1d., 6d., 1s., 1s.6d., 2s., 3s., 4s., 5s., 10s., 15s., £1, £1 10s., £2, £5 and £10 were issued for fiscal purposes on 18 December 1879 with the £1 5s., 35s., 45s.,£6 and £9 added to the range later the same month and the 6s., £7 and £8 in January 1880.

Used prices for the £1 5s., £1 10s., £2 (No. 276a), 45s. and £10 watermarked W **33** are for examples from the cancelled-to-order sets sold to collectors by the Victoria postal authorities between September 1900 and 30 June 1902.

Similar Stamp Duty designs were prepared for 7s., 8s., 9s., 11s., 12s., 13s., 14s., 16s., 17s., 18s., and 19s., but were never issued.

The two different 1d. designs were reprinted in 1891 on W **33** paper.

For these designs with later watermarks see Nos. 345/50 and 369/71.

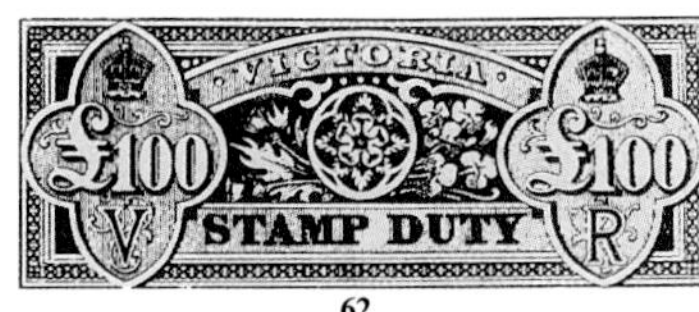

62

(Des C. Jackson and L. Lang. Dies eng C. Jackson)

1884 (1 Jan*)–**00**. *High value Stamp Duty series.*

(a) Recess-printed direct from the die.

(i) Wmk V over Crown W **19** (sideways). P 12½.

280	**62**	£25 yellow-green (F.C. £65)		
		a. Wmk upright		
		b. Perf 13		
		c. Deep green (F.C. £65)		
		ca. Wmk upright		
281		£50 bright mauve (F.C. £95)		
		a. Wmk upright		
		b. Perf 13		
282		£100 crimson-lake (F.C. £130)		
		a. Wmk upright		
		b. Perf 13		

(ii) Wmk V over Crown W **33** (sideways). P 12½.

283	**62**	£25 yellow-green		
		a. Perf 12		
		b. Deep green (1.85) (F.C. £65)	—	£500
		c. Bright blue-green (10.90) (F.C £65)		
		ca. Wmk upright		
284		£50 dull lilac-mauve (wmk upright) (F.C. £95)		
		a. Black-violet (10.90) (F.C £75)	—	£500
		ab. Wmk upright		
285	**62**	£100 crimson (F.C. £140)		
		a. Wmk upright		
		b. Perf 12 (F.C. £140)		
		c. Aniline crimson (wmk upright) (2.85) (F.C. £140)	—	£650
		d. Scarlet-red (5.95)	—	£650
		da. Wmk upright	—	£475

(b) Litho. Wmk V over Crown W **33** (sideways). P 12½.

286	**62**	£25 dull yellowish green (1.86) (F.C.£50)		
		a. Wmk upright (11.87)		
		b. Dull blue-green (9.88) (F.C £50)		
		ba. Wmk upright		
287		£50 dull purple (1.86) (F.C. £70)		
		a. Wmk upright		
		b. Bright violet (11.89) (F.C. £70)		
		ba. Wmk upright		
288		£100 rosine (1.86) (F.C. £110)		
		a. Wmk upright		

(c) Typo from electrotyped plates. Wmk V over Crown. W **33**. P 12½.

289	**62**	£25 dull blue-green (12.97)	—	£130
290		£50 bright mauve (10.97)	—	£200
291		£100 pink-red (10.19.00)	—	£275

*This is the date on which the stamps became valid for postal use. All three values were issued for fiscal purposes on 18 December 1879.

Used prices for Nos. 283*b*, 284*a*, 285*c*/*d* and 289/91 are for examples from the cancelled-to-order sets described beneath No. 279*a*. "F.C." indicates that the price quoted is for a stamp with a fiscal cancellation.

For the £25 and £50 with watermark W **82** see Nos. 351/2.

63

(Des and die eng C. Naish. Typo from electrotyped plates)

1884 (23 Apr)–**92**. *New design inscr* "STAMP DUTY". Wmk V over Crown, W **33** (sideways). P 12½.

292	**63**	2s.6d. brown-orange	85·00	14·00
		a. Yellow (8.85)	80·00	11·00
		b. Lemon-yellow (2.92)	80·00	11·00

For this design on later watermarks see Nos. 344 and 370.

64 65 66

67 68

(Des and dies eng C. Naish. Typo from electrotyped plates)

1885 (1 Jan)–**95**. *New designs inscr* "STAMP DUTY". P 12½.

(a) W **19**.

293	**68**	8d. rose/*pink*	26·00	6·50
		a. Rose-red/pink (2.88)	28·00	6·50
294	**66**	1s. deep dull blue/*lemon* (11.85)	75·00	8·50
		a. Dull blue/yellow (6.86)	75·00	9·00
295	**68**	2s. olive/*bluish green* (12.85)	60·00	3·00

(b) W **33**.

296	**64**	½d. pale rosine	8·00	1·00
		a. Deep rosine (7.85)	11·00	1·25
		b. Salmon (9.85)	11·00	1·25
297	**65**	1d. yellowish green (1.85)	11·00	1·00
		a. Dull pea-green (2.85)	16·00	1·75
298	**66**	2d. lilac	10·00	30
		a. Mauve (1886)	10·00	30
		b. Rosy-mauve (1886)	12·00	50
299	**65**	3d. yellowish brown	14·00	1·00
		a. Pale ochre (9.86)	10·00	1·00
		b. Bistre-yellow (9.92)	10·00	1·00
300	**67**	4d. magenta	48·00	3·00
		a. Bright mauve-rose (12.86)	50·00	3·50
		b. Error. *Lilac* (12.86)	£3250	£700
301	**65**	6d. chalky blue (1.85)	65·00	2·50
		a. Bright blue (3.85)	42·00	2·10
		b. Cobalt (7.85)	42·00	2·10
302	**68**	8d. bright scarlet/*pink* (3.95)	30·00	9·00
303		2s. olive-green/*pale green* (1.90)	29·00	5·00
304		2s. apple-green (12.8.95)	25·00	50·00
		a. Blue-green (29.10.95)	18·00	9·50

The plates for the 1d., 6d., 1s. and 2s. were derived from the dies of the 2d. (1s.), 3d. (1d. and 6d.) and 8d. (2s.). In each instance lead moulds of six impressions were taken from the original die and the face values altered by hand creating six slightly different versions.

Two states of the 2d. die exist with the second showing a break in the top frame line near the right-hand corner. This damaged die was used for seven impressions on Plate 1 and all 120 on Plate 2.

No. 300b occurred during the December 1886 printing of the 4d. when about fifty sheets were printed in the colour of the 2d. by mistake. The sheets were issued to Melbourne post offices and used examples are known postmarked between 21 December 1886 and 4 March 1887. Nine unused are also believed to exist.

Reprints of the ½d., 1d., 2d., 4d., 6d. and 1s. values were made in 1891 from the existing plates. The 1s. was watermarked W **19** and the remainder W **33**.

For some of these values used with later watermarks see Nos. 336, 343, 361 and 369.

(69)

1885 (Feb–Nov). *Optd with T* **69**. P 12½.

(a) W **19**.

305	**15**	3d. dull orge-yell (*glazed paper*) (B.) (Nov)	—	£130
306	**26**	1s. pale blue/*blue* (*glazed paper*) (P 13)	95·00	20·00
		a. Deep blue/*blue*	—	22·00
		b. Blue opt (F.C. £14)	£1200	£600
307	**27**	2s. ultramarine/*grn* (*glazed paper*) (Mar)	90·00	18·00
		a. Wmk sideways	£100	22·00

(b) W **33**.

308	**15**	3d. yellow-orange (B.) (Nov)	60·00	24·00
		a. Dull brownish orange (B.)	65·00	26·00
309	**32**	4d. rose-red (B.) (Nov)	55·00	35·00

Unauthorised reprints of the 4d. and 1s., both with blue overprints and watermarked W **33**, were made during 1895–96. The 4d. reprint, which is in pale red, also exists without the overprint.

70 71 72 73 74 75 76 77 78 79 80

(Des S. Reading (1d.) (No. 313), M. Tannenberg (2½d., 5d.), C. Naish (1s.6d.), P. Astley (others). Dies eng C. Naish (2d., 4d. (both existing dies with lines added behind Queen's head) and 1s.6d.), S. Reading (originally as an employee of Fergusson & Mitchell) (others). Typo from electrotyped plates)

1886 (26 Jul)–**96**. W **33** (sideways on ½d., 1s., £5, £7 to £9). P 12½.

310	**70**	½d. lilac-grey (28.8.86)	21·00	5·00
		a. *Grey-black*	—	35·00
311		½d. pink (15.2.87)	10·00	50
		a. *Rosine* (*aniline*) (1889)	6·50	30
		b. *Rose-red* (1891)	6·50	30
		c. *Vermilion* (1896)	7·00	35
312	**71**	1d. green	8·00	65
		a. *Yellow-green* (1887)	8·00	65
313	**72**	1d. dull chestnut (1.1.90)	8·50	50
		a. *Deep red-brown* (1890)	8·50	50
		b. *Orange-brown* (1890)	8·50	30
		c. *Brown-red* (1890)	8·50	30
		d. *Yellow-brown* (1891)	8·50	30
		e. *Bright yellow-orange*	50·00	12·00
		f. *Brownish orange* (1894)	5·50	30
314	**73**	2d. pale lilac (17.12.86)	9·00	20
		a. *Pale mauve* (1887)	10·00	20
		b. *Deep lilac* (1888, 1892)	7·00	20
		c. *Purple* (1894)	4·00	25
		d. *Violet* (1895)	4·00	20
		e. Imperf	—	£750
315	**74**	2½d. red-brown/*lemon* (1.1.91)	19·00	3·00
		a. *Brown-red/yellow* (1892)	15·00	80
		b. *Red/yellow* (1893)	12·00	70
316	**75**	4d. rose-red (1.4.87)	17·00	1·00
		a. *Red* (1893)	11·00	90
317	**76**	5d. purple-brown (1.1.91)	9·00	1·75
		a. *Pale reddish brown* (1893)	7·50	1·75
318	**77**	6d. bright ultramarine (27.8.86)	18·00	1·25
		a. *Pale ultramarine* (1887)	17·00	50
		b. *Dull blue* (1891)	16·00	50
319	**25**	9d. apple-green (18.10.92)	25·00	9·00
320		9d. carmine-rose (15.10.95)	27·00	7·50
		a. *Rosine* (*aniline*) (1896)	32·00	7·50
321	**78**	1s. dull purple-brown (14.3.87)	55·00	2·00
		a. *Lake* (1890)	42·00	2·50
		b. *Carmine-lake* (1892)	21·00	1·25
		c. *Brownish red* (1896)	22·00	1·60
322	**79**	1s.6d. pale blue (9.88)	£140	70·00
323		1s.6d. orange (19.9.89)	18·00	7·00
		a. *Red-orange* (1893)	18·00	6·50
324	**80**	£5 pale blue and maroon (7.2.88)†	£1800	90·00
325		£6 yellow and pale blue (1.10.87)†	£2000	£120
326		£7 rosine and black (17.10.89)†	£2250	£130
327		£8 mauve & brown-orange (2.8.90)†	£2500	£160
328		£9 apple-green and rosine (21.8.88)†	£2750	£170

†The used prices provided for these stamps are for cancelled-to-order examples.

Unauthorised reprints of the ½d. lilac-grey and 1s.6d. pale blue were made in 1894–95 on W **33** paper and perforated 12½. These differ in shade from the originals and have rougher perforations. It should be noted that the original printing of No. 322 does not occur with inverted watermark, but the reprint does.

A single example of No. 314e is known postmarked "737" (Foster). A second, postmarked "249" (Mortlake), was reported in 1892. It is known that an imperforate sheet was sold at Mortlake P.O. in 1890. Other examples are believed to be clandestine.

Later printings of the £5 to £9 values, as No. 324/8 but on W **85** paper perforated 12½ or 11, were not valid for postal use (*Price from £275 each, unused*).

A £10 value as Type **80** was prepared, but not issued.

1891 (17 Jun). W **19**. P 12½.

329	**72**	1d. orange-brown/*pink*	5·50	2·25

No. 329 was an emergency printing during a shortage of white W **33** paper.

81

82

(Die eng A. Williams (1½d.). Typo from electrotyped plates).

1896 (11 Jun)–**99**. W **82** (sideways on ½d., 1½d., 1s., 2s.6d. to 15s.). P 12½.

330	**70**	½d. light scarlet (1.7.96)	3·75	60
		a. *Carmine-rose* (1897)	4·00	60
		b. *Dp carmine-red* (*coarse impression*) (1899)	—	2·00
		c. Wmk upright	†	60·00
331		½d. emerald (1.8.99)	13·00	2·75
		a. Wmk upright		
332	**72**	1d. brown-red (13.6.96)	5·50	10
		a. *Brownish orange* (1897)	5·50	10
		b. Wmk sideways		
333	**81**	1½d. apple-green (7.10.97)	3·00	3·25
334	**73**	2d. violet	8·00	10
		a. Wmk sideways	†	75·00
335	**74**	2½d. blue (1.8.99)	8·00	6·00
336	**65**	3d. ochre (11.96)	7·50	65
		a. *Buff* (1898)	7·00	65
		b. Wmk sideways		
337	**75**	4d. red (6.97)	13·00	2·25
338	**76**	5d. red-brown (7.97)	15·00	1·00
339	**77**	6d. dull blue (9.96)	13·00	65
340	**25**	9d. rosine (8.96)	27·00	3·25
		a. *Rose-carmine* (1898)	—	3·25
		b. *Dull rose* (1898)	24·00	3·25
		c. Wmk sideways		
341	**78**	1s. brownish red (3.97)	15·00	2·00
		a. Wmk upright		
342	**79**	1s.6d. brown-orange (8.98)	38·00	19·00
343	**68**	2s. blue-green (4.97)	35·00	6·50
344	**63**	2s.6d. yellow (9.96)	90·00	13·00
		a. Wmk upright (1898)	£100	13·00
345	**45**	3s. olive-drab (12.96)	55·00	18·00
		a. Wmk upright (1898)	55·00	18·00
346	**46**	4s. orange (9.97)	80·00	11·00
347	**47**	5s. rosine (2.97)	80·00	12·00
		a. *Rose-carmine* (1897)	80·00	12·00
		b. Wmk upright. *Rosine* (1899)	80·00	13·00
348	**48**	6s. pale yellow-green (4.99)†	85·00	23·00
349	**49**	10s. grey-green (4.97)	£140	18·00
		a. *Blue-green* (1898)	£140	18·00
350	**50**	15s. brown (4.97)†	£400	50·00
351	**62**	£25 dull bluish green (1897)†	—	£130
352		£50 dull purple (1897)†	—	£170

†The used prices provided for these stamps are for cancelled-to-order examples.

83

84

(Des M. Tannenberg. Dies eng A. Mitchelhill. Typo from electrotyped plates)

1897 (22 Oct). *Hospital Charity Fund.* W **82** (sideways). P 12½.

353	**83**	1d.(1s.) blue	18·00	18·00
354	**84**	2½d. (2s.6d) red-brown	85·00	70·00
353s/4s		Optd "Specimen" *Set of* 2	£140	

These stamps were sold at 1s. and 2s.6d., but only had postal validity for 1d. and 2½d. with the difference going to the Fund.

1899 (1 Aug). W **33** (sideways). P 12½.

355	**81**	1½d. brown-red/*yellow*	3·00	1·75

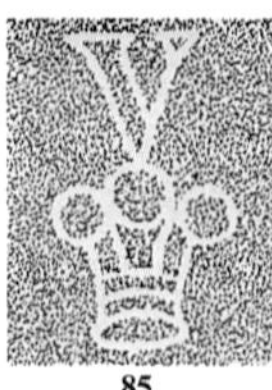

85

1899 (1 Aug)–**1901**. W **85** (sideways on ½d., 1s. and 2s.6d. to 10s.). P 12½.

356	**70**	½d. emerald (12.99)	4·75	40
		a. *Deep blue-green*	5·00	40
		b. Wmk upright	—	10·00
357	**72**	1d. rose-red	7·00	15
		a. *Rosine* (1900)	4·50	10
		b. Wmk sideways		
358		1d. olive (6.6.01)	5·50	4·00
359	**73**	2d. violet	11·00	10
		a. Wmk sideways	†	—
360	**74**	2½d. blue (10.99)	14·00	1·50
361	**65**	3d. bistre-yellow (9.99)	7·00	2·00
		a. Wmk sideways		
362		3d. slate-green (20.6.01)	21·00	9·50
363	**75**	4d. rose-red (12.99)	8·00	2·00
364	**76**	5d. red-brown (10.99)	16·00	2·00
365	**77**	6d. dull ultramarine (1.00)	9·50	1·75
366	**25**	9d. rose-red (9.99)	17·00	1·7
		a. Wmk sideways		
367	**78**	1s. brown-red (5.00)	18·00	2·5
368	**79**	1s.6d. orange (2.00)	19·00	13·0
369	**68**	2s. blue-green (6.00)	20·00	8·0
370	**63**	2s.6d. yellow (1.00)	£300	18·0
371	**45**	3s. pale olive (4.00)†	£130	22·0
372	**47**	5s. rose-red (4.00)	£100	22·0
373	**49**	10s. green (3.00)†	£150	22·0

†The used prices provided for these stamps are for cancelled-to order examples.

From 1 July 1901 stamps inscribed "STAMP DUTY" could onl be used for fiscal purposes.

86 Victoria Cross

87 Australian Troops in South Africa

(Des Sands and MacDougall (1d.), J. Sutherland (2d.). Dies eng S. Reading. Typo from electrotyped plates).

1900 (22 May). *Empire Patriotic Fund.* W **85** (sideways). P 12½.

374	**86**	1d. (1s.) olive-brown	75·00	45·0
375	**87**	2d. (2s.) emerald-green	£150	£15

These stamps were sold at 1s. and 2s., but only had postal validi for 1d. and 2d. with the difference going to the Fund.

FEDERATION. The six Australian colonies were federated as th Commonwealth of Australia on 1 January 1901. Under the term of the Post and Telegraph Act their postal services we amalgamated on 1 March 1901, but other clauses to safeguard th financial position of the individual States provided them with a larg degree of independence until 13 October 1910 when issues of eac state could be used throughout Australia. Postage stamps for th Commonwealth of Australia did not appear until January 1913.

It was agreed in 1901 that stamp printing should be centralis at Melbourne under J. B. Cooke of South Australia who w appointed Commonwealth Stamp Printer. By 1909 t Commonwealth Stamp Printing Branch in Melbourne w producing stamps for Papua, South Australia, Tasmania a Western Australia in addition to those of Victoria.

On federation it was decided to separate postal and fiscal stam issues so Victoria needed urgent replacements for the current Stam Duty series which reverted to fiscal use only on 30 June 1901.

1901 (29 Jan). *Re-use of previous designs without* "POSTAGE" *ins* W **82** (2s.) or W **85** (others) (sideways on ½d.). P 12 × 12½.

376	**22**	½d. bluish green	2·00	1·
		a. "VICTCRIA" (R. 7/19)	35·00	25·
377	**31**	2d. reddish violet	8·00	1·
378	**15**	3d. dull orange	15·00	2·
379	**32**	4d. bistre-yellow	25·00	14·
380	**16**	6d. emerald	9·00	7·
381	**26**	1s. yellow	45·00	38·
382	**27**	2s. blue/*pink*	42·00	23·
383	**18**	5s. pale red and deep blue	48·00	40·

88 89 90 91 92

93

94

95

96

97 98 99

100

101

102

I II III

Three die states of ½d.:

I. Outer vertical line of colour to left of "V" continuous except for a break opposite the top of "V". Triangles either end of "VICTORIA" are more or less solid colour.

II. Die re-engraved. Three breaks in outer line of colour left of "V". White lines added to left triangle.

III. Die re-engraved. As II, but equivalent triangle at right also contains white lines.

I

II

III

I and II

III

hree die states of 1d.:

. Thick lines fill top of oval above Queen's head.

I. Die re-engraved. Lines thinner, showing white space between.

II. Die re-engraved. As II, but with bottom left value table recut to show full point separated from both "1" and the circular frame.

wo die states of 2d.:

. Frame line complete at top right corner. Bottom right corner comes to a point.

I. Break in right frame line just below the top corner. Bottom right corner is blunted.

vo types of 1s.:

. "POSTAGE" 6 mm long (produced by a hand punch applied twice to each impression on the previous 1s. electrotyped plate. Slight variations in position occur).

. "POSTAGE" 7 mm long (produced from new electrotyped plates incorporating the "POSTAGE" inscriptions).

(Eng S. Reading after photo by W. Stuart (£1, £2))

01 (29 Jan)–**10**. *Previous issues with* "POSTAGE" *added and new designs (£1, £2).* W **85** (sideways on ½d., 1½., £1, £2).

(a) P 12 × 12½.

4	**88**	½d. blue-green (I) (26.6.01)	3·00	60
		a. Wmk upright (1903)	3·25	60
		b. Die state II (6.04)	4·25	60
		ba. Wmk upright	4·25	6·50
5	**89**	1d. rose (I)	6·50	20
		a. Dull red (12.02)	6·00	20
		ab. Wmk sideways	†	75·00
		b. Die state II (4.01)	2·25	15
		ba. Dull red (12.02)	1·75	15
		bb. Wmk sideways		
		c. Die state III. *Pale rose-red*	3·00	70
		ca. Wmk sideways	60·00	60·00
6	**90**	1½d. maroon/*yellow* (9.7.01)	9·00	5·00
		a. Wmk upright. *Brn-red/yell* (9.01)	2·10	55
		b. Dull red-brown/yellow (1906)	2·10	55
		ba. *On yellow-buff back* (1908)	3·75	1·00
7	**91**	2d. lilac (I) (26.6.01)	9·50	30
		a. Die state II	28·00	1·50
		b. Reddish violet (1902)	9·50	30
		ba. Die state II	28·00	1·50
		c. Bright purple (II) (1905)	7·00	30
		d. Rosy mauve (II) (1905)		
		e. Wmk sideways		
8	**92**	2½d. dull blue	9·50	35
		a. Deep blue (1902)	11·00	35
		b. Wmk sideways		
389	**93**	3d. dull orange-brown (5.7.01)	8·00	1·25
		a. Chestnut (1901)	7·50	55
		b. Yellowish brown (1903)	7·50	55
		ba. Wmk sideways	11·00	18·00
390	**94**	4d. bistre-yellow (26.6.01)	5·50	65
		a. Brownish bistre (1905)	9·00	70
391	**95**	5d. reddish brown	9·50	40
		a. Purple-brown (1903)	9·00	40
392	**96**	6d. emerald (5.7.01)	12·00	90
		a. Dull green (1904)	14·00	1·00
393	**97**	9d. dull rose-red (5.7.01)	15·00	2·50
		a. Wmk sideways (1901)	27·00	7·50
		b. Pale red (1901)	15·00	1·25
		c. Dull brownish red (1905)	19·00	2·50
394	**98**	1s. yellow-orange (A) (5.7.01)	16·00	1·75
		a. Yellow (1902)	18·00	1·75
		b. Type B (4.03)	19·00	3·00
		ba. Orange (1904)	18·00	2·50
		bb. Wmk sideways (1905)	32·00	12·00
395	**99**	2s. blue/*rose* (5.7.01)	22·00	2·00
		a. Wmk sideways	†	£850

(b) P 12½.

396	**88**	½d. blue-green (III) (6.05)	8·00	60
397	**92**	2½d. dull blue (1901)	£550	£550
		a. Wmk sideways	†	£850
398	**100**	5s. rose-red and pale blue (5.7.01)	60·00	15·00
		a. Scarlet and deep blue	70·00	13·00
		b. Rosine and blue (12.04)	70·00	13·00
399	**101**	£1 carmine-rose (18.11.01)	£250	£120
400	**102**	£2 deep blue (2.6.02)	£500	£300

(c) P 11.

401	**88**	½d. blue-green (I) (9.02)	7·00	3·25
		a. Wmk upright (1903)	3·25	1·50
		b. Die state II (6.04)	6·50	1·50
		c. Die state III (6.05)	8·00	1·75
402	**89**	1d. dull red (I) (12.02)	55·00	40·00
		a. Die state II	45·00	18·00
		ab. Pale red (*aniline*) (3.03)	7·50	2·25
		ac. Pale rose (*aniline*) (1904)	28·00	4·00
		b. Die state III. *Pale rose-red* (7.05)	45·00	25·00
403	**90**	1½d. dull red-brown/*yellow* (1910)	65·00	65·00
404	**91**	2d. bright purple (II) (1905)	£550	£225
		a. Rosy mauve (II) (1905)	†	£180
405	**93**	3d. yellowish brown (1903)	5·50	6·50
		a. Wmk sideways	15·00	24·00
406	**96**	6d. emerald (2.03)	12·00	18·00
		a. Dull green (1905)	£550	£225
407	**101**	£1 rose (5.05)	£350	£150
408	**102**	£2 deep blue (1905)	£1400	£1000

(d) Compound or mixed perf 12½ and 11.

409	**88**	½d. blue-green (I) (1901)	30·00	11·00
		a. Wmk upright (1903)	—	11·00
		b. Die state II (1904)	27·00	24·00
		ba. Wmk upright	42·00	
410	**89**	1d. dull red (I) (1902)	—	£250
		a. Die state II	£500	£190
411	**90**	1½d. maroon/*yellow* (1903)	£600	£300
412	**91**	2d. reddish violet (I) (1903)	†	£400
413	**93**	3d. dull orange-brown (1902)	—	£750
414	**96**	6d. emerald (1903)	†	£700
415	**100**	5s. rosine and blue (12.04)	£1400	

Examples of the 1d. Die state II perforated 12½ exist with two black lines printed across the face of the stamp. These were prepared in connection with stamp-vending machine trials.

1905–13. Wmk Crown over A, W w **11** (sideways on ½d., £1, £2).

(a) P 12 × 12½.

416	**88**	½d. blue-green (shades) (III) (21.10.05)	2·50	30
		a. Wmk upright. Thin, ready gummed paper (6.12)	3·75	5·50
417	**89**	1d. rose-red (III) (16.7.05)	1·50	10
		a. Pale rose (1907)	1·25	10
		b. Rose-carmine (1911)	3·50	1·40
		ba. Wmk sideways	14·00	6·00
		c. Thin, ready gummed paper (10.12)	4·50	2·00
418	**91**	2d. dull mauve (II) (13.9.05)	6·00	30
		a. Lilac (1906)	6·00	25
		b. Reddish violet (1907)	6·00	25
		c. Bright mauve (1910)	5·50	1·00
		ca. Thin, ready gummed paper (8.12)	28·00	6·00
419	**92**	2½d. blue (10.08)	3·00	40
		a. Indigo (1909)	6·50	1·00
420	**93**	3d. orange-brown (11.11.05)	8·00	1·25
		a. Yellow-orange (1908)	8·00	1·25
		b. Dull orange-buff (1909)	8·00	1·25
		c. Ochre (1912)	8·00	4·50
421	**94**	4d. yellow-bistre (15.1.06)	7·00	65
		a. Olive-bistre (1908)	7·00	65
		b. Yellow-olive (1912)	7·00	3·25
422	**95**	5d. chocolate (14.8.06)	7·00	2·25
		a. Dull reddish brown (1908)	7·00	2·25
		b. Wmk sideways	†	£500
		c. Thin, ready gummed paper (19.10.12)	13·00	13·00
423	**96**	6d. dull green (25.10.05)	13·00	80
		a. Dull yellow-green (1907)	13·00	80
		b. Emerald (1909)	13·00	1·10
		c. Yellowish green (1911)	13·00	2·75
		d. Emerald. Thin, ready gummed paper (11.12)	21·00	20·00
424	**97**	9d. brown-red (11.12.05)	14·00	2·50
		a. Orange-brown (1906)	14·00	2·25
		b. Red-brown (1908)	15·00	2·25
		c. Pale dull rose (1909)	15·00	3·50
		d. Rose-carmine (1910)	9·50	1·25
		e. Wmk sideways		
425	**98**	1s. orange (B) (13.2.06)	8·00	2·00
		a. Yellow-orange (1906)	11·00	2·00
		b. Yellow (1908)	13·00	2·00
		ba. Thin, ready gummed paper (11.12)	28·00	22·00
		c. Pale orange. Thin, ready gummed paper (1913)	28·00	24·00

(b) P 12½.

426	**88**	½d. blue-green (shades) (III) (1905)	2·25	1·00
		a. Wmk upright (1909)	15·00	3·50
		b. Thin, ready gummed paper (1912)	5·00	
		ba. Wmk upright	4·00	6·00
427	**89**	1d. rose-red (III) (1905)	4·50	60
		a. Rose-carmine (1911)	6·50	2·50
428	**92**	2½d. indigo (1909)	14·00	2·50
429	**96**	6d. yellowish green (1911)	20·00	10·00
430	**100**	5s. rose-red and ultramarine (12.07)	70·00	15·00
		a. Rose-red and blue (1911)	80·00	20·00
		ab. Wmk sideways	85·00	23·00
431	**101**	£1 salmon (12.2.07)	£250	£130
		a. Dull rose (1910)	£250	£130
		ab. Wmk upright (1911)	£300	£150
432	**102**	£2 dull blue (18.7.06)	£550	£375

(c) P 11.

433	**88**	½d. blue-green (shades) (III) (1905)	1·60	30
		a. Wmk upright. Thin, ready gummed paper (1912)	15·00	20·00
434	**89**	1d. rose-red (III) (1905)	4·00	1·25
		a. Pale rose (1907)	4·00	1·25
		b. Rose-carmine (1911)	7·00	3·75
		ba. Wmk sideways	11·00	8·50
		c. Thin, ready gummed paper (10.12)	8·00	4·75
435	**91**	2d. lilac (II) (1906)	†	£250
		a. Reddish violet (1907)	65·00	17·00
		b. Bright mauve (1910)	26·00	11·00
436	**92**	2½d. blue (1908)	60·00	14·00
		a. Indigo (1909)	12·00	8·50
437	**93**	3d. orange-brown (1905)	10·00	11·00
		a. Yellow-orange (1908)	†	£130
		b. Dull orange-buff (1909)	15·00	19·00
		c. Ochre (1912)	8·00	7·50
		d. Wmk sideways		
438	**94**	4d. yellow-bistre (1906)	9·00	17·00
		a. Olive-bistre (1909)		
		b. Yellow-olive (1912)	8·50	17·00
439	**95**	5d. chocolate (1906)	†	£700
		a. Dull reddish brown (1908)	†	£700
440	**96**	6d. emerald (1909)	10·00	17·00
		a. Yellowish green (1911)	15·00	21·00
441	**97**	9d. rose-carmine (1910)	†	£600
442	**98**	1s. yellow-orange (B) (1906)	†	£250
		a. Orange (1910)	£600	
443	**100**	5s. rose-red and ultramarine (12.07)	70·00	9·50
444	**101**	£1 salmon (12.2.07)	£375	£130
445	**102**	£2 dull blue (1.07)	£800	£425

(d) Compound or mixed perfs of 12½ and 11, 12 × 12½ or 11.

446	**88**	½d. blue-green (*shades*) (III) (1905)	19·00	16·00
		a. Wmk upright. Thin, ready gummed paper (1912)	£110	80·00
447	**89**	1d. rose-red (III) (1905)	45·00	45·00
		a. Pale rose (1907)	—	55·00
		b. Rose-carmine (1911)	—	55·00
448	**91**	2d. reddish violet (II) (1907)	£450	£300
449	**93**	3d. orange-brown (1905)	†	£375
		a. Ochre (1912)	£375	
450	**94**	4d. bistre (1908)	†	£475
451	**96**	6d. emerald (1909)	—	£550
		a. Yellowish green (1911)	†	£375
452	**97**	9d. orange-brown (1906)	†	£650
		a. Red-brown (1908)	†	£650
453	**98**	1s. yellow-orange (1906)	£900	

(e) Rotary comb perf 11½ × 12¼.

454	**89**	1d. pale rose (III) (2.10)	6·50	1·75
		a. Rose-carmine (1911)		
		b. Wmk sideways		
		c. Thin, ready gummed paper (7.12)	3·25	4·00
		d. Rose-red. Thin, ready gummed (10.12)	3·25	4·00
455	**91**	2d. lilac (II) (1910)	13·00	1·50

The original Crown over A watermark paper used by Victoria was of medium thickness and had toned gum applied after printing. Stocks of this paper lasted until 1912 when further supplies were ordered from a new papermakers, Cowan and Sons. This paper was much thinner and was supplied with white gum already applied. The first delivery arrived in June 1912 and a second in September of the same year.

The rotary comb perforating machine gauging 11½ × 12¼ was transferred from South Australia in 1909 when J. B. Cooke moved to Melbourne.

Examples of the 1d. perforated 12½ or 11 exist with two black lines across the face of the stamp. These were prepared in connection with stamp-vending machine trials.

ONE PENNY

(103)

104

1912 (29 Jun). No. 455 *surch with T* **103** *in red.*

456	**91**	1d.on 2d. lilac (II)	70	50

1912 (1 Aug). W **104**.

(a) P 12 × 12½.

457 **89** 1d. rose-carmine (III) . . . 2·75 3·50
a. Wmk sideways . . . 50·00
458 **91** 2d. reddish violet (II) (Sept) . . . 3·00 4·25
a. Lilac . . . 5·50 7·00
459 **97** 9d. rose-carmine . . . 16·00 18·00

(b) P 12½.

460 **88** ½d. bluish green (III) . . . 3·00 4·50

(c) P 11.

461 **88** ½d. bluish green (III) . . . 20·00 20·00
462 **89** 1d. rose-carmine (III) . . . 28·00 15·00
a. Wmk sideways . . .
463 **97** 9d. rose-carmine . . . 21·00 26·00

(d) Compound or mixed perfs 12½ and 11.

464 **97** 9d. rose-carmine . . . † £650

Nos. 457/64 were emergency printings caused by the non-arrival of stocks of the Cowan thin, ready gummed Crown over A watermarked paper. Paper watermarked W **104** had been introduced in 1911 and was normally used for Victoria fiscal stamps. This watermark can be easily distinguished from the previous W **85** by its narrow crown.

STAMP BOOKLETS

There are very few surviving examples of Nos. SB1/4. Listings are provided for those believed to have been issued with prices quoted for those known to still exist.

1904 (Mar)–**09**. *Black on red cover as* No. SB1 *of New South Wales. Stapled.*

SB1 £1 booklet containing two hundred and forty 1d. in four blocks of 30 and two blocks of 60 . . .
a. Red on pink cover (1909) . . . £16000
b. Blue on pink cover . . . £14000

1904 (Mar). *Black on grey cover as* No. SB1. *Stapled.*

SB2 £1 booklet containing one hundred and twenty 2d. in four blocks of 30 . . .

1910 (May). *Black on white cover as* No. SB3 *of New South Wales. Stapled.*

SB3 2s. booklet containing eleven ½d. (No. 426), either in block of 6 plus block of 5 or block of 11, and eighteen 1d. (No.427), either in three blocks of 6 or block of 6 plus block of 12 . . . £3250
a. Black on pale green cover . . . £3250

Unsold stock of No. SB3 was uprated with one additional ½d. in May 1911.

1911 (1 Aug). *Red on pink cover as* No. SB3. *Stapled.*

SB4 2s. Booklet containing twelve ½d. (No.426), either in two blocks of 6 or block of 12, and eighteen 1d. (No.427), either in three blocks of 6 or block of 6 plus block of 12 . . . £2500

POSTAGE DUE STAMPS

D 1

(Dies eng A. Williams (values) and J. McWilliams (frame). Typo)

1890 (12 Oct)–**94**. Wmk V over Crown, W 33. P 12 × 12½.

D 1 **D 1** ½d. dull blue and brown-lake (24.12.90) . . . 4·50 3·25
a. Dull blue and deep claret . . . 2·75 3·50
D 2 1d. dull blue and brown-lake . . . 6·00 1·40
a. Dull blue and brownish red (1.93) . . . 8·50 1·50
D 3 2d. dull blue and brown-lake . . . 10·00 1·75
a. Dull blue and brownish red (3.93) . . . 12·00 1·00
D 4 4d. dull blue and brown-lake . . . 13·00 2·00
a. Dull blue and pale claret (5.94) . . . 15·00 6·00
D 5 5d. dull blue and brown-lake . . . 13·00 2·00
D 6 6d. dull blue and brown-lake . . . 14·00 3·00
D 7 10d. dull blue and brown-lake . . . 75·00 45·00
D 8 1s. dull blue and brown-lake . . . 48·00 6·50
D 9 2s. dull blue and brown-lake . . . £110 50·00
D10 5s. dull blue and brown-lake . . . £160 90·00
D1/10 *Set of* 10 . . . £400 £170
D1as/10s Optd "Specimen" *Set of* 10 . . . £300

A used example of the 6d. showing compound perforation of 12 × 12½ and 11 exists in the Royal Collection.

1895 (17 Jan)–**96**. *Colours changed.* Wmk V over Crown. P 12 × 12½.

D11 **D 1** ½d. rosine and bluish green . . . 4·50 1·60
a. Pale scarlet and yellow-green (3.96) . . . 3·75 1·50
D12 1d. rosine and bluish green . . . 4·00 1·25
a. Pale scarlet and yellow-green (3.96) . . . 5·00 1·25
D13 2d. rosine and bluish green . . . 8·00 1·50
a. Pale scarlet and yellow-green (3.96) . . . 8·50 1·25
D14 4d. rosine and bluish green . . . 9·50 1·50
a. Pale scarlet and yellow-green (3.96) . . . 9·50 1·75
D15 5d. rosine and bluish green . . . 11·00 11·00
a. Pale scarlet and yellow-green (3.96) . . . 11·00 7·00
D16 6d. rosine and bluish green . . . 10·00 5·50
D17 10d. rosine and bluish green . . . 20·00 10·00
D18 1s. rosine and bluish green . . . 16·00 3·25
D19 2s. pale red & yellowish green (28.3.95) . . . 60·00 20·00
D20 5s. pale red & yellowish green (28.3.95) . . . £100 40·00
D11/20 *Set of* 10 . . . £225 80·00

1897 (1 July)–**99**. Wmk V over Crown. W **82**. P 12 × 12½.

D21 **D 1** 1d. pale scarlet and yellow-green . . . 7·00 1·25
a. Dull red and bluish green (8.99) . . . 9·00 1·25
D22 2d. pale scarlet and yellow-green . . . 9·50 1·25
a. Dull red and bluish green (6.99) . . . 10·00 1·00
D23 4d. pale scarlet and yellow-green . . . 18·00 2·25
a. Dull red and bluish green (8.99) . . . 20·00 2·00
D24 5d. pale scarlet and yellow-green . . . 18·00 3·75
D25 6d. pale scarlet and yellow-green . . . 9·00 4·00
D21/5 *Set of* 5 . . . 55·00 11·00

1900 (1 Jun)–**04**. Wmk V over Crown. W **85**. P 12 × 12½.

D26 **D 1** ½d. rose-red and pale green . . . 8·00 5·00
a. Pale red and deep green (8.01) . . . 4·50 4·75
b. Scarlet and deep green (1.03) . . . — 25·00
c. Aniline rosine and green (6.04) . . . 7·50 8·00
D27 1d. rose-red and pale green . . . 9·00 80
a. Pale red and deep green (9.01) . . . 8·50 35
b. Scarlet and deep green (2.02) . . . 9·50 70
c. Aniline rosine and green (9.03) . . . 9·00 1·25
D28 2d. rose-red and pale green (7.00) . . . 11·00 1·50
a. Pale red and deep green (9.01) . . . 11·00 1·50
b. Scarlet and deep green (2.02) . . . 11·00 85
c. Aniline rosine and green (9.03) . . . 11·00 1·50
D29 4d. rose-red and pale green (5.01) . . . 21·00 5·50
a. Pale red and deep green (9.01) . . . 20·00 2·50
b. Scarlet and deep green (6.03) . . . 20·00 3·25
c. Aniline rosine and green (6.04) . . . 21·00 3·75
D30 5d. scarlet and deep green (1.03) . . . 17·00 7·00
D31 1s. scarlet and deep green (3.02) . . . 19·00 6·50
D32 2s. scarlet and deep green (1.03) . . . £110 65·00
D33 5s. scarlet and deep green (1.03) . . . £130 65·00
D26/33 *Set of* 8 . . . £275 £130

1905 (Dec)–**09**. Wmk Crown over A, W w **11**. P 12 × 12½.

D34 **D 1** ½d. aniline rosine and pale green (1.06) . . . 11·00 11·00
a. Scarlet & pale yellow-green (7.07) . . . 5·00 6·00
b. Dull scarlet and pea-green (3.09) . . . 6·50 7·00
ba. Compound perf 12 × 12½ and 11 . . . £350 £225
D35 1d. aniline rosine and pale green . . . 45·00 6·00
a. Scarlet & pale yellow-green (5.06) . . . 6·50 2·50
b. Dull scarlet and pea-green (1.07) . . . 10·00 2·50
D36 2d. aniline scarlet & dp yell-grn (5.06) . . . 14·00 2·75
a. Dull scarlet and pea-green (11.07) . . . 10·00 2·50
D37 4d. dull scarlet and pea-green (1908) . . . 18·00 10·00
D34/7 *Set of* 4 . . . 35·00 19·00

A printing of the 5d. in dull scarlet and pea-green on this paper was prepared in 1907–08, but not put into use. A few examples have survived, either mint or cancelled-to-order from presentation sets (*Price* £1200 *mint*, £900 *cancelled-to-order*).

WESTERN AUSTRALIA

PRICES FOR STAMPS ON COVER

Nos.	1/6	*from* × 6
Nos.	15/32	*from* × 4
Nos.	33/46	*from* × 5
Nos.	49/51	*from* × 6
Nos.	52/62	*from* × 10
Nos.	63/*a*	*from* × 8
No.	67	*from* × 6
Nos.	68/92*a*	*from* × 10
Nos.	94/102	*from* × 40
Nos.	103/5	*from* × 8
Nos.	107/10*a*	*from* × 12
Nos.	111*a*/*b*	—
Nos.	112/16	*from* × 25
Nos.	117/25	*from* × 10
Nos.	126/8	—
Nos.	129/34	*from* × 8
Nos.	135/6	—
Nos.	138/48	*from* × 12
Nos.	151/63	*from* × 5
Nos.	168/9	*from* × 20
Nos.	170/1	*from* × 4
Nos.	172/3	*from* × 40
Nos.	F11/22	*from* × 10
Nos.	T1/2	—

SPECIMEN OVERPRINTS. Those listed are from U.P.U. distributions between 1889 and 1892. Further "Specimen" overprints exist, but those were used for other purposes.

1 2 3 4

GUM. The 1854 and 1857–59 issues are hardly ever seen with gum so the unused prices quoted are for examples without gum.

(Eng W. Humphrys. Recess P.B.)

1854 (1 Aug). W **4** (sideways).

(a) Imperf.

1 **1** 1d. black . . . £800 £19

(b) Rouletted 7½ to 14 and compound.

2 **1** 1d. black . . . £1600 £45

In addition to the supplies received from London a further printing, using the original plate and watermarked paper from Perkins, Bacon, was made in the colony before the date of issue.

The 1d. is also known pin-perforated.

(Litho H. Samson (later A. Hillman), Government Lithographer)

1854 (1 Aug)–**55**. W **4** (sideways).

(a) Imperf.

3 **2** 4d. pale blue . . . £275 £17
a. Blue . . . £275 £17
b. Deep dull blue . . . £1400 £65
c. Slate-blue (1855) . . . £1800 £80
d. "T" of "POSTAGE" shaved off to a point at foot (R. 7/5, 7/10, 7/15, 7/20) . . . £900 £70
e. Top of letters of "AUSTRALIA" cut off so that they are barely 1 mm high . . . † £90
f. "PEICE" instead of "PENCE" . . . † £90
g. "CE" of "Pence" close together . . . † £110
h. Frame inverted (R. 8/1, 8/6, 8/11, 8/16) . . . † £650
i. Tilted border (R. 7/4, 7/9, 7/14, 7/19) . . . £1100 £8
j. "WEST" in squeezed-down letters and "F" of "FOUR" with pointed foot (R. 2/17) . . . £1200 £9
k. "ESTERN" in squeezed-down letters and "U" of "FOUR" squeezed up (R. 3/17) . . . £2000 £15
l. Small "S" in "POSTAGE" (R. 4/17) . . . £1200 £9
m. "EN" of "PENCE" shorter (R. 6/4) . . . £1000 £8
n. "N" of "PENCE" tilted to right with thin first downstroke (R. 6/16) . . . £1000 £8
o. Swan and water above "ENCE" damaged (R. 6/20) . . . £1000 £8
p. "F" of "FOUR" slanting to left (R. 7/17) . . . £1000 £8
q. "WESTERN" in squeezed-down letters only 1½ mm high (R. 8/17) . . . £1300 £9
r. "P" of "PENCE" with small head (R. 9/15) . . . £1000 £8
s. "RALIA" in squeezed-down letters only 1½ mm high (R. 9/16) . . . £1200 £8
t. "PE" of "PENCE" close together (R. 10/15) . . . £1000 £8
u. "N" of "PENCE" narrow (R. 10/16) . . . £1000 £8
v. Part of right cross-stroke and downstroke of "T" of "POSTAGE" cut off (R. 11/15) . . . £1000 £8
w. "A" in "POSTAGE" with thin right limb (R. 11/16) . . . £1000 £8
x. Coloured line above "AGE" of "POSTAGE" (R. 8/6) . . . £1100 £8
y. No outer line above "GE" of "POSTAGE" and coloured line under "FOU" of "FOUR" (R. 8/11) . . . £1200 £9
4 **3** 1s. salmon . . . — £22
a. Deep red-brown . . . £1300 £6
b. Grey-brown (1.55) . . . £500 £3
c. Pale brown (10.55) . . . £375 £3

(b) Rouletted 7½ to 14 and compound.

5 **2** 4d. pale blue . . . £1200 £4
a. Blue . . . — £4
b. Slate-blue (1855) . . . — £14
6 **3** 1s. grey-brown (1.55) . . . £2500 £8
a. Pale brown (10.55) . . . £2250 £7

The 1s. is also known pin-perforated.

The 4d. value was prepared from the Perkins, Bacon 1d. plate. block of 60(5 × 12) was taken as a transfer from this plate, frames painted out and then individually replaced by transfers tak from a single impression master plate of the frame. Four transf were then taken from this completed intermediate stone to constr the printing stone of 240 impressions. This first printing stone w used by H. Samson to print the initial supplies in July 1854.

The intermediate stone had carried several transfer errors, most prominent of which was the "T" of "POSTAGE" sliced foot, which appeared on four positions of the printing st (No. 3d.)

The original printing stone also contained three scarce crea transfers, whose exact positions in the sheet have yet to established (Nos. 3e/g.)These were corrected during the f printing.

Further supplies were required in January 1855 and A. Hillm Samson's successor, found, after printing three further sheets fr the first printing stone, that two of the impressions on intermediate stone were defective giving one inverted and one til frame (Nos. 3h/i). was then prepared on which the four positions the inverted frame were individually corrected.

None of the creased transfers from the first printing stone app on the second, which exhibits its own range of similar varie (Nos. 3j/w).

For the third printing in October 1855 the impressions show the inverted frame were replaced on the printing stone with fr individual transfers of the frame. On two of the positions traces the original frame transfer remained visible (Nos. 3x/y).

The same stone was used for a further printing in December 1 and it is believed that the slate-blue shade occurred from one of 1855 printings.

The above varieties, with the exception of Nos. 3e/g, also oc on the rouletted stamps.

The 1s. value was produced in much the same way, based o transfer from the Perkins, Bacon 1d. plate.

5

(Litho A. Hillman, Government Lithographer)

1857 (7 Aug)–**59**. W **4** (sideways).

		(a) Imperf.		
15	**5**	2d. brown-black/*red* (26.2.58)	£2250	£550
		a. Printed both sides	£2750	£800
16		2d. brown-black/*Indian red* (26.2.58)	£2500	£800
		a. Printed both sides	£2750	£850
17		6d. golden bronze	£8000	£1500
18		6d. black-bronze	£3500	£650
19		6d. grey-black (1859)	£3500	£550
		(b) Rouletted 7½ to 14 and compound.		
20	**5**	2d. brown-black/*red*	£5500	£1300
		a. Printed both sides	—	£1600
21		2d. brown-black/*Indian red*	—	£1400
22		6d. black-bronze	£5000	£900
23		6d. grey-black	—	£950

The 2d. and 6d. are known pin-perforated.

Prices quoted for Nos. 15/23 are for "cut-square" examples. Collectors are warned against "cut-round" copies with corners added.

(Recess in the colony from P.B. plates)

1860 (11 Aug)–**64**. W **4** (sideways).

		(a) Imperf.		
24	**1**	2d. pale orange	75·00	70·00
25		2d. orange-vermilion	75·00	70·00
		a. Wmk upright		
25*b*		2d. deep vermilion	£1000	£650
26		4d. blue (21.6.64)	£250	£1600
		a. Wmk upright	£250	
27		4d. deep blue	£250	£1700
28		6d. sage-green (27.7.61)	£1400	£400
28*a*		6d. deep sage-green	—	£550
		(b) Rouletted 7½ to 14.		
29	**1**	2d. pale orange	£450	£190
30		2d. orange-vermilion	£500	£200
31		4d. deep blue	£3250	
32		6d. sage-green	£2750	£600

PERKINS BACON "CANCELLED". For notes on these handstamps, showing "CANCELLED" between horizontal bars forming an oval, see Catalogue Introduction.

(Recess P.B.)

1861. W **4** (sideways).

		(a) Intermediate perf 14–16.		
33	**1**	1d. rose	£400	£120
34		2d. blue	£150	40·00
35		4d. vermilion	£700	£1700
36		6d. purple-brown	£450	85·00
37		1s. yellow-green	£550	£160
		(b) P 14 at Somerset House.		
38	**1**	1d. rose	£200	55·00
39		2d. blue	90·00	35·00
40		4d. vermilion	£225	£160
		(c) Perf clean-cut 14–16.		
41	**1**	2d. blue	75·00	24·00
		a. Imperf between (pair)		
42		6d. purple-brown	£250	48·00
43		1s. yellow-green	£425	70·00
		a. Wmk upright	—	70·00
		(d) P 14–16 very rough (July).		
44	**1**	1d. rose-carmine (H/S "CANCELLED" in oval £9000)	£225	45·00
45		6d. purple/*blued* (H/S "CANCELLED" in oval £8000)	£1600	£350
46		1s. deep green (H/S "CANCELLED" in oval £6500)	£1300	£300

Perkins, Bacon experienced considerable problems with their perforating machine during the production of these stamps.

The initial printing showed intermediate perforation 14–16. Further supplies were then sent, in late December 1860, to Somerset House to be perforated on their comb 14 machine. The Inland Revenue Board were only able to process the three lower values, although the 6d. purple-brown and 1s. yellow-green are known from this perforation overprinted "SPECIMEN".

The Perkins, Bacon machine was repaired the following month and the 6d., 1s. and a further supply of the 2d. were perforated on it to give a clean-cut 14-16 gauge.

A final printing was produced in July 1861, but by this time the machine had deteriorated so that it produced a very rough 14–16.

(Recess D.L.R. from P.B. plates)

1863 (16 Dec)–**64**. No wmk. P 13.

49	**1**	1d. carmine-rose	65·00	3·50
50		1d. lake	65·00	3·50
51		6d. deep lilac (15.4.64)	£130	38·00
51*a*		6d. dull violet (15.4.64)	£190	45·00

Both values exist on thin and on thick papers, the former being the scarcer.

Both grades of paper show a marginal sheet watermark, "T H SAUNDERS 1860" in double-lined large and small capitals, but parts of this watermark rarely occur on the stamps.

(Recess D.L.R. from P.B. plates)

1864 (27 Dec)–**79**. Wmk Crown CC (sideways* on 1d.). P 12½.

52	**1**	1d. bistre	60·00	5·00
		w. Wmk Crown to right of CC	60·00	5·00
53		1d. yellow-ochre (16.10.74)	75·00	7·50
		w. Wmk Crown to right of CC	75·00	7·50
54		2d. chrome-yellow (18.1.65)	65·00	2·25
55		2d. yellow	65·00	2·25
		a. Wmk sideways (5.79)	—	18·00
		aw. Wmk Crown to right of CC	—	18·00
		b. Error. Mauve (1879)	£6500	£5500
		x. Wmk reversed	65·00	2·25
56		4d. carmine (18.1.65)	75·00	4·50
		a. Doubly printed	£6000	
		w. Wmk inverted	—	24·00
57		6d. violet (18.1.65)	90·00	6·00
		a. Doubly printed	†	£8000
		b. Wmk sideways	—	£200
		x. Wmk reversed	—	6·00
58		6d. indigo-violet	£350	32·00
		x. Wmk reversed	—	32·00
59		6d. lilac (1872)	£170	6·00
60		6d. mauve (12.5.75)	£160	6·00
		x. Wmk reversed	—	6·00
61		1s. bright green (18.1.65)	£120	12·00
		s. Handstamped "Specimen"	£100	
62		1s. sage-green (10.68)	£300	26·00

*The normal sideways watermark shows Crown to left of CC, *as seen from the back of the stamp.*

Beware of fakes of No. 55b made by altering the value tablet of No. 60.

7

ONE PENNY
(8)

(Typo D.L.R)

1871 (29 Oct)–**73**. Wmk Crown CC (sideways). P 14.

63	**7**	3d. pale brown	38·00	4·50
		a. Cinnamon (1873)	38·00	4·00
		s. Handstamped "Specimen"	85·00	

1874 (10 Dec). No. 55 *surch with T* **8** *by Govt Printer.*

67	**1**	1d.on 2d. yellow (G.)	£350	55·00
		a. Pair, one without surch		
		b. Surch triple	†	£3000
		c. "O" of "ONE" omitted		

Forged surcharges of T **8** are known on stamps wmk Crown CC perf 14, and on Crown CA, perf 12 and 14.

(Recess D.L.R. from P.B. plates)

1876–81. Wmk Crown CC (sideways*). P 14.

68	**1**	1d. ochre	60·00	2·75
		w. Wmk Crown to right of CC	60·00	2·75
69		1d. bistre (1878)	95·00	3·75
70		1d. yellow-ochre (1879)	65·00	1·75
71		2d. chrome-yellow	60·00	1·25
		a. Wmk upright (1877)	85·00	2·25
74		4d. carmine (1881)	£400	90·00
75		6d. lilac (1877)	£120	3·25
		a. Wmk upright (1879)	£500	15·00
		bw. Wmk Crown to right of CC	—	3·25
75*c*		6d. reddish lilac (1879)	£120	5·50

*The normal sideways watermark shows Crown to left of CC, *as seen from the back of the stamp.*

(Recess D.L.R. from P.B. plates)

1882 (Mar)–**85**. Wmk Crown CA (sideways*).

		(a) P 14.		
76	**1**	1d. yellow-ochre	22·00	1·50
		w. Wmk Crown to right of CA	22·00	1·50
		x. Wmk sideways reversed		
77		2d. chrome-yellow	26·00	1·25
		a. Wmk upright	†	—
78		4d. carmine (8.82)	£100	6·50
		a. Wmk upright (1885)	—	75·00
		w. Wmk Crown to right of CA	—	6·50
79		6d. reddish lilac (1882)	85·00	3·00
80		6d. lilac (1884)	85·00	4·00
		s. Handstamped "Specimen"	90·00	
		w. Wmk Crown to right of CA	—	5·00
		y. Wmk sideways inverted and reversed	—	25·00
		(b) P 12 × 14.		
81	**1**	1d. yellow-ochre (2.83)	£1500	£150
		(c) P 12.		
82	**1**	1d. yellow-ochre (2.83)	70·00	4·00
83		2d. chrome-yellow (6.83)	95·00	4·00
		a. Imperf between (pair)		
84		4d. carmine (5.83)	£160	30·00
		w. Wmk Crown to right of CA	—	30·00
85		6d. lilac (6.83)	£300	29·00
		w. Wmk Crown to right of CA	—	29·00

*The normal sideways watermark shows Crown to left of CA, *as seen from the back of the stamp.*

(Typo D.L.R.)

1882 (July)–**95**. Wmk Crown CA (sideways). P 14.

86	**7**	3d. pale brown	16·00	2·00
87		3d. red-brown (12.95)	8·50	2·00

The 3d. stamps in other colours, watermark Crown CA and perforated 12, are colour trials dating from 1883.

½ (9) **1d.** (10) **1d.** (11)

1884 (19 Feb). *Surch with T* **9**, *in red, by Govt Printer.*

89	**1**	½d.on 1d. yellow-ochre (No.76)	15·00	22·00
		a. Thin bar	80·00	95·00
90		½d.on 1d. yellow-ochre (No.82)	9·50	17·00

Inverted or double surcharges are forgeries made in London about 1886.

The "Thin bar" varieties occur on R. 12/3, R. 12/8, R. 12/13 and R. 12/18, and show the bar only 0.2 mm thick.

1885 (May). Nos. 63/*a surch, in green, by Govt Printer.*

		(a) Thick "1" with slanting top, T **10** *(Horizontal Rows 1/5).*		
91		1d.on 3d. pale brown	60·00	13·00
		a. Cinnamon	48·00	12·00
		b. Vert pair. Nos. 91/2	£200	
		(b) Thin "1" with straight top, T **11** *(Horizontal Row 6).*		
92		1d.on 3d. pale brown	£160	35·00
		a. Cinnamon	£130	35·00

12

13

14

15

(Typo D.L.R.)

1885 (May)–**93**. Wmk Crown CA (sideways). P 14.

94	**12**	½d. yellow-green	3·50	60
94*a*		½d. green	3·50	60
95	**13**	1d. carmine (2.90)	19·00	40
96	**14**	2d. bluish grey (6.90)	26·00	1·00
96*a*		2d. grey	25·00	1·00
97	**15**	2½d. deep blue (1.5.92)	11·00	1·25
97*a*		2½d. blue	10·00	1·25
98		4d. chestnut (7.90)	10·00	1·00
99		5d. bistre (1.5.92)	9·00	3·25
100		6d. bright violet (1.93)	15·00	1·25
101		1s. pale olive-green (4.90)	28·00	4·50
102		1s. olive-green	18·00	4·25
94s/101s (ex 1d., 6d.) Handstamped (Nos. 96, 98, 101) or optd "Specimen" *Set of* 6			£275	

(Recess D.L.R. from P.B. plates)

1888 (Mar–Apr). Wmk Crown CA (sideways). P 14.

103	**1**	1d. carmine-pink	17·00	3·00
104		2d. grey	48·00	1·25
105		4d. red-brown (April)	75·00	20·00
103s/5s H/S "Specimen" *Set of* 3			£160	

ONE PENNY (16) **Half-penny** (17)

1893 (Feb). *Surch with T* **16**, *in green, by Govt Printer.*

107	**7**	1d.on 3d. pale brown (No. 63)	12·00	3·25
108		1d.on 3d. cinnamon (No. 63*a*)	12·00	3·25
		a. Double surcharge	£950	
109		1d.on 3d. pale brown (No. 86)	45·00	4·50

1895 (21 Nov). *Surch with T* **17** *by Govt Printer.*

		(a) In green.		
110	**7**	½d.on 3d. pale brown (No. 63)	7·50	23·00
110*a*		½d.on 3d. cinnamon (No. 63*a*)	5·50	22·00
		b. Surcharge double	£750	
		(b) In red and in green.		
111*a*	**7**	½d.on 3d. cinnamon (No.63*a*)	80·00	£190
111*b*		½d.on 3d. red-brown (No.87)	60·00	£130

Green was the adopted surcharge colour but a trial had earlier been made in red on stamps watermarked Crown CC. As they proved unsatisfactory they were given another surcharge in green. The trial stamps were inadvertently issued and, to prevent speculation, a further printing of the duplicated surcharge was made, but on both papers, Crown CC (No. 111*a*) and Crown CA (No. 111*b*).

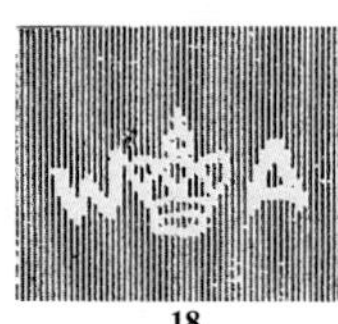

18

19

20

21

(Typo D.L.R.)

1898 (Dec)–**1907**. Wmk W Crown A, W **18**. P 14.

112	**13**	1d. carmine	5·00	10
113	**14**	2d. bright yellow (1.99)	15·00	1·75
114	**19**	2½d. blue (1.01)	8·50	50
115	**20**	6d. bright violet (10.06)	24·00	1·50
116	**21**	1s. olive-green (4.07)	27·00	3·50

22

23

24

25 26 27
28 29 30

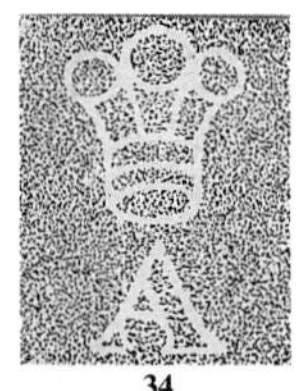
31

32

33

(Typo Victoria Govt Printer, Melbourne, Commonwealth Stamp Ptg Branch from March 1909)

1902 (Oct)–**12**. Wmk V and Crown, W **33** (sideways on horiz designs).

(a) P 12½ or 12½ × 12 (horiz), 12 × 12½ (vert).
117 **22** 1d. carmine-rose (1.03) 12·00 40
a. Wmk upright (10.02) 16·00 50
118 **23** 2d. yellow (4.1.03) 12·00 2·50
a. Wmk upright (1903) 25·00 2·75
119 **24** 4d. chestnut (4.03) 13·00 2·00
a. Wmk upright £225
120 **15** 5d. bistre (4.9.05) 70·00 55·00
121 **25** 8d. apple-green (3.03) 18·00 2·50
122 **26** 9d. yellow-orange (5.03) 27·00 8·00
a. Wmk upright (11.03) 55·00 25·00
123 **27** 10d. red (3.03) 30·00 6·50
124 **28** 2s. bright red/*yellow* 80·00 21·00
a. Wmk sideways £180 16·00
b. Orange/yellow (7.06) 42·00 9·00
c. Brown-red/yellow (5.11) 42·00 9·00
125 **29** 2s.6d. deep blue/*rose* 42·00 8·00
126 **30** 5s. emerald-green 70·00 23·00
127 **31** 10s. deep mauve £160 70·00
a. Bright purple (1910) £450 £250
128 **32** £1 orange-brown (1.11.02) £300 £160
a. Orange (10.7.09) £600 £300

(b) P 11.
129 **22** 1d. carmine-rose £160 18·00
a. Wmk upright
130 **23** 2d. yellow £200 20·00
a. Wmk upright † £300
131 **24** 4d. chestnut £650 £225
132 **15** 5d. bistre 48·00 48·00
133 **26** 9d. yellow-orange 85·00 80·00
134 **28** 2s. bright red/*yellow* £170 £110
a. Orange/yellow £300 £140

(c) Perf compound of 12½ or 12 and 11.
135 **22** 1d. carmine-rose £600 £350
136 **23** 2d. yellow £750 £450
137 **24** 4d. chestnut

Type **22** is similar to Type **13** but larger.

34 35

1905–12. Wmk Crown and A, W **34** (sideways).

(a) P 12½ or 12½ × 12 (horiz), 12 × 12½ (vert).
138 **12** ½d. green (6.10) 4·25 4·75
139 **22** 1d. rose-pink (10.05) 8·50 60
a. Wmk upright (1.06) 8·50 60
b. Carmine (1909) 11·00 60
c. Carmine-red (1912) 11·00 7·00
140 **23** 2d. yellow (15.11.05) 6·50 1·75
a. Wmk upright (4.10)
141 **7** 3d. brown (2.06) 18·00 1·75
142 **24** 4d. bistre-brown (12.06) 19·00 5·50
a. Pale chestnut (1908) 19·00 5·00
b. Bright brown-red (14.10.10) 10·00 2·50
143 **15** 5d. pale olive-bistre (8.05) 15·00 7·50
a. Olive-green (1.09) 15·00 7·50
b. Pale greenish yellow (5.12) 55·00 75·00
144 **25** 8d. apple-green (22.4.12) 18·00 40·00
145 **26** 9d. orange (11.5.06) 25·00 4·25
a. Red-orange (6.10) 40·00 4·25
b. Wmk upright (7.12) 40·00 24·00
146 **27** 10d. rose-orange (16.2.10) 22·00 16·00
148 **30** 5s. emerald-grn (wmk upright) (9.07) £110 85·00

(b) P 11.
150 **12** ½d. green
151 **22** 1d. rose-pink 26·00 9·50
a. Carmine-red 35·00 8·50
b. Wmk upright 45·00 15·00
152 **23** 2d. yellow 32·00 16·00
153 **7** 3d. brown 15·00 4·00
154 **24** 4d. yellow-brown £600 £200
a. Pale chestnut — £275
155 **15** 5d. pale olive-bistre 28·00 10·00
a. Olive-green 16·00 12·00
157 **26** 9d. orange £100 £110
a. Red-orange — 90·00
b. Wmk upright (1912) † £600

(c) Perf compound of 12½ or 12 and 11.
161 **22** 1d. rose-pink (wmk upright) £500 £250
162 **23** 2d. yellow £425 £225
163 **7** 3d. brown £600 £375
164 **26** 9d. red-orange

1912 (Mar). Wmk Crown and A W **35** (sideways). P 11½ × 12.
168 **20** 6d. bright violet 11·00 8·00
169 **21** 1s. sage-green 26·00 12·00
a. Perf 12½ (single line) — £650

1912 (7 Aug). *Thin paper and white gum (as Victoria)*. W **34** (sideways).
170 **7** 3d. brown (P 12½) 50·00 50·00
a. Wmk upright 50·00 50·00
171 3d. brown (P 11)
a. Wmk upright

ONE PENNY

(**36**)

1912 (6 Nov). Nos. 140 *and* 162 *surch with T* **36** *in Melbourne*.

(a) P 12½ or 12 × 12½.
172 **23** 1d.on 2d. yellow 1·00 1·00
a. Wmk upright 3·75 6·50

(b) Perf compound of 12½ and 11.
173 **23** 1d.on 2d. yellow £425

STAMP BOOKLETS

There are very few surviving examples of Nos. SB1/4. Listings are provided for those believed to have been issued with prices quoted for those known to still exist.

1904 (1 Jan)–**09**. *Black on red cover as* No. SB1 *of New South Wales. Stapled.*
SB1 £1 booklet containing two hundred and forty 1d. in four blocks of 30 and two blocks of 60
a. Red on pink cover (1909) £15000
b. blue on pink cover

1904 (1 Jan). *Black on grey cover as* No. SB1. *Stapled.*
SB2 £1 Booklet containing one hundred and twenty 2d. in four blocks of 30

1910 (May). *Black on cream cover as* No. SB3 *of New South Wales. Stapled.*
SB3 2s. booklet containing eleven ½d. (No. 138), either in block of 6 plus block of 5 or block of 11, and eighteen 1d. (No. 139) either in three blocks of 6 or block of 6 plus block of 12 £4000

Unsold stock of No. SB3 was uprated with one additional ½d. in May 1911.

1911 (1 Aug). *Red on pink cover as* No. SB3. *Stapled.*
SB4 2s. Booklet containing twelve ½d. (No. 138), either in two blocks of 6 or block of 12, and eighteen 1d. (No. 139), either in three blocks of 6 or block of 6 plus block of 12 £3500

POSTAL FISCAL STAMPS

By the Post and Telegraph Act of 5 September 1893 the current issue of fiscal stamps up to and including the 1s. value, Nos. F11/15, was authorised for postal use.

These stamps had been initially supplied, for fiscal purposes, in February 1882 and had been preceded by a series of "I R" surcharges and overprints on postage stamps which were in use for a period of about six months. Examples of these 1881–82 provisionals can be found postally used under the terms of the 1893 Act but, as they had not been current for fiscal purposes for over eleven years, we no longer list them.

F 3

(Typo D.L.R.)

1893 (5 Sep). *Definitive fiscal stamps of Feb 1882.* Wmk CA over Crown. P 14.
F11 F 3 1d. dull purple 12·00 2·25
F12 2d. dull purple £130 45·00
F13 3d. dull purple 48·00 3·25
F14 6d. dull purple 55·00 4·50
F15 1s. dull purple 95·00 9·00

The 1s. value is as Type F 3 but with rectangular outer frame and circular frame surrounding swan.

Higher values in this series were not validated by the Act for postal use.

Two varieties of watermark exist on these stamps. Initial supplies showed an indistinct watermark with the base of the "A" 4 mm wide. From 1896 the paper used showed a clearer watermark on which the base of the "A" was 5 mm wide.

1897. Wmk W Crown A, W **18**. P 14.
F19 F 3 1d. dull purple 9·50 2·25
F20 3d. dull purple 40·00 3·25
F21 6d. dull purple 40·00 3·50
F22 1s. dull purple 90·00 11·00

The above were invalidated for postal purposes from 1 January 1901.

TELEGRAPH STAMPS USED FOR POSTAGE

The 1d. Telegraph stamps were authorised for postal purposes from 25 October 1886.

T 1

1886 (25 Oct). Wmk Crown CC.
T1 T 1 1d. bistre (P 12½) 35·00 4·50
T2 1d. bistre (P 14) 35·00 5·00

Copies of a similar 6d. value are known postally used, but such use was unauthorised.

OFFICIAL STAMPS

Stamps of the various issues from 1854–85 are found with a circular hole punched out, the earlier size being about 3 mm. in diameter and the later 4 mm. These were used on official correspondence by the Commissariat and Convict Department, branches of the Imperial administration separate from the colonial government. This system of punching ceased by 1886. Subsequently many stamps between Nos. 94 and 148 may be found punctured,"PWD", "WA" or "OS".

Western Australia became part of the Commonwealth of Australia on 1 January 1901.

COMMONWEALTH OF AUSTRALIA

On 1 March 1901 control of the postal service passed to the federal administration although it was not until 13 October 1910 that the issues of the various states became valid for use throughout Australia. Postal rates were standardised on 1 May 1911.

The first national postage due stamps appeared in July 1902, but it was not until January 1913 that postage stamps inscribed "AUSTRALIA"were issued.

PRICES FOR STAMPS ON COVER TO 1945		
Nos.	1/19	*from* × 4
Nos.	20/3	*from* × 2
Nos.	24/30	*from* × 4
Nos.	35/47*f*	*from* × 3
Nos.	51/5*a*	*from* × 4
Nos.	55*b*/75	*from* × 3
Nos.	76/84	*from* × 4
Nos.	85/104	*from* × 3
Nos.	105/6	*from* × 4
Nos.	107/15	*from* × 3
No.	116	*from* × 5
Nos.	117/20	*from* × 4
Nos.	121/39*a*	*from* × 2
Nos.	140/*a*	*from* × 5
Nos.	141/4	*from* × 3
No.	146	*from* × 6
Nos.	147/53	*from* × 3
Nos.	153*a*/*b*	*from* × 2
Nos.	154/63	*from* × 3
Nos.	164/211	*from* × 2
Nos.	D1/118	*from* × 8
Nos.	O123/36	*from* × 5

PRINTERS. Except where otherwise stated, all Commonwealt stamps to No. 581 were printed under Government authority a Melbourne. Until 1918 there were two establishments (both of th Treasury Dept)—the Note Printing Branch and the Stamp Printin Branch. The former printed T **3** and **4**.

In 1918 the Stamp Printing Branch was closed and all stamp were printed by the Note Printing Branch. In 1926 control wa transferred from the Treasury to the Commonwealth Bank c Australia, and on 14 January 1960 the branch was attached to th newly established Reserve Bank of Australia.

Until 1942 stamps bore in the sheet margin the initials or name of successive managers and from 1942 to March 1952 th imprint"Printed by the Authority of the Government of th Commonwealth of Australia". After November 1952 (or Nos D129/31 for Postage Dues)imprints were discontinued.

SPECIMEN OVERPRINTS. These come from Specimen sets, firs made available to the public on 15 December 1913. In these sets th lower values were cancelled-to-order, but stamps with a face valu of 7s.6d. or 75c. were overprinted "Specimen" in different type These overprints are listed as they could be purchased from th Australian Post Office.

It is, however, believed that examples of No. 11 overprinted"Specimen" were distributed by the U.P.U. in 192 Supplies of the 1902 and 1902–04 postage due stamps overprinte "Specimen" were supplied to the U.P.U. by some of the states.

1

2

Die I

Die II

Dies of Type 1 (mono-coloured values only):—

Die I. Break in inner frame line at lower left level with top of words of value.
Die II. Die repaired showing no break.

Die I was only used for the ½d., 1d., 2d. and 3d. Several plates were produced for each except the 3d. When the second plate of the 3d. was being prepared the damage became aggravated after making 105 out of the 120 units when the die was returned for repair. This gave rise to the *se-tenant* pairs showing the two states of the die.

Die II was used until 1945 and deteriorated progressively with damage to the frame lines and rounding of the corners.

Specialists recognise seven states of this die, but we only list the two most major of the later versions.

Die IIA. This state is as Die II, but, in addition, shows a break in the inner left-hand frame line, 9 mm from the top of the design (occurs on 1d., 2d. and 6d.).

Die IIB. As Die IIA, but now also showing break in outer frame line above "ST", and (not illustrated) an incomplete corner to the inner frame line at top right (occurs on 3d., 6d., 9d., 1s. and £1 (No. 75)).

(Des B. Young. Eng S. Reading. Typo J. B. Cooke)

1913 (2 Jan)–**14**. W **2**. P 12.
1 **1** ½d. green (Die I) (14.1.13) . . . 6·00 3·50
a. Printed on the gummed side . . . £2000
bw. Wmk inverted . . . 35·00 10·00
c. Wmk sideways . . . † £8000
cw. Wmk sideways inverted . . . † £10000
2 1d. red (Die I) . . . 8·50 1·00
a. Wmk sideways . . . £850 £180
aw. Wmk sideways inverted . . . £900 £200
b. Carmine . . . 8·50 1·00
cw. Wmk inverted . . . 30·00 5·00
d. Die II Red (16.1.13) . . . 9·00 1·00
da. Wmk sideways . . . £900 £200
daw. Wmk sideways inverted . . . £950 £225
db. Carmine . . . 8·50 1·00
dw. Wmk inverted . . . 30·00 5·00
e. Die IIA. *Red* (4.14) . . . 15·00 1·25
eb. Carmine . . . 15·00 1·25
ew. Wmk inverted . . . 50·00 8·00
3 2d. grey (Die I) (15.1.13) . . . 30·00 4·50
w. Wmk inverted . . . 55·00 11·00
4 2½d. indigo (Die II) (27.1.13) . . . 29·00 13·00
5 3d. olive (Die I) (28.1.13) . . . 48·00 8·50
a. imperf three sides (horiz pair) . . . £24000
b. in pair with Die II . . . £500 £200
c. Yellow-olive . . . 48·00 9·50
ca. In pair with Die II . . . £500 £250
dw. Wmk inverted . . . £120 35·00
e. Die II *Olive* . . . £170 55·00
ea. Yellow-olive . . . £170 55·00
ew. Wmk inverted . . . £400 £140
6 4d. orange (Die II) (19.2.13) . . . 50·00 22·00
a. Orange-yellow . . . £200 50·00
8 5d. chestnut (Die II) (18.1.13) . . . 42·00 32·00
9 6d. ultramarine (Die II) (18.1.13) . . . 48·00 20·00
a. Retouched "E" . . . £1800 £650
b. Die IIA (substituted cliche) (11.13) . . . £1600 £600
w. Wmk inverted . . . £275 £100
10 9d. violet (Die II) (1.2.13) . . . 45·00 24·00
11 1s. emerald (Die II) (25.1.13) . . . 50·00 17·00
a. Blue-green . . . 50·00 17·00
w. Wmk inverted . . . £350 65·00
12 2s. brown (Die II) (28.1.13) . . . £160 75·00
13 5s. grey and yellow (Die II) (20.3.13) . . . £300 £160
14 10s. grey and pink (Die II) (20.3.13) . . . £650 £500
15 £1 brown and ultram (Die II) (20.3.13) . . . £1200 £1300
16 £2 black and rose (Die II) (8.4.13) . . . £2750 £1800
1/16 *Set of* 15 . . . £5000 £3500
14s/16s Optd "Specimen" *Set of* 3 . . . £600

The watermark on Nos. 1c, 2a and 2da shows the Crown pointing to the left and on Nos. 1cw, 2aw and 2daw pointing to the right, *as seen from the back of the stamp.* Two examples of 1c and one example of 1cw are known, all used.

The 3d. was printed from two plates, one of which contained 105 stamps as Die I and 15 as Die II. The other plate contained Die I stamps only.

No. 5a. shows the stamp perforated at foot only. Examples are known from the top or bottom rows of different sheets.

No. 9a shows a badly distorted second "E" in "PENCE", which is unmistakable. It occurs on the upper plate right pane R. 10/6 and was replaced by a substitute cliché in Die IIA (No. 9b) in the November 1913 printing.

See also Nos. 24/30 (W **5**), 35/45*b* (W **6**), 73/5 (W **6**, new colours), 107/14(W **7**), 132/8 (W **15**), 212 (2s. re-engraved).

3

4 Laughing Kookaburra

(Des R. A. Harrison. Eng and recess T. S. Harrison)

1913 (9 Dec)–**14**. No wmk. P 11.
17 **3** 1d. red . . . 2·50 4·50
a. Imperf between (horiz pair) . . . £2500
b. Imperf horiz (vert pair) . . . £1600
c. Pale rose-red . . . 7·00 12·00
ca. Imperf between (vert pair) . . . £1800
cb. Imperf between (horiz pair) . . . £2500
19 **4** 6d. claret (26.8.14) . . . 65·00 38·00

All printings from Plate 1 of the 1d. were in the shade of No. 17*c*. This plate shows many retouches.

5

5a

1d. Die II

Dot before "1" (Plate 3 right pane R. 4/3)

"Secret mark" (Plate 4 left pane R. 1/1)

Flaw under neck (Plate 4 left pane R. 7/1)

"RA" joined (Plate 4 left pane R. 10/6)

1d. Die II. The flaw distinguishing the so-called Die II, a white upward spur to the right of the base of the "1" in the left value tablet, is now known to be due to a defective roller-die. It occurred on all stamps in the second and third vertical rows of upper left plate, right pane. Each of the twenty defective impressions differs slightly; a typical example is illustrated above.

(Dies eng P.B. Typo J. B. Cooke until May 1918, then T. S. Harrison)

1914 (17 Jul)–**20**. W **5**. P 14¼ × 14 (comb).
20 **5a** ½d. bright green (22.2.15) . . . 3·75 1·00
a. Perf 14¼ (line) (12.15) . . . £3500 £350
b. Green (1916) . . . 3·75 1·00
c. Yellow-green (1916) . . . 23·00 10·00
d. Thin "1" in fraction at right (Pl 5 rt pane R. 8/1) . . . £9000 £2500
w. Wmk inverted . . . 13·00 4·00
21 1d. carmine-red (*shades*) (Die I) (P 14¼ (line)) . . . 25·00 4·00
a. Die II . . . £4500 £600
bw. Wmk inverted . . . † £2000
c. Perf 14¼ × 14 (comb) . . . 7·00 60
ca. Rusted cliché (Pl 2 rt pane R. 6/4 and 5) (9.16) . . . £5500 £325
cb. Substituted cliché (Pl 2 rt pane R. 6/5) (2.18) . . . £850 60·00
cc. Pale carmine (*shades*) (1917) . . . 10·00 60
cd. Rose-red (1917) . . . 11·00 2·50
ce. Carmine-pink (1918) . . . £100 10·00
cf. Carmine (*aniline*) (1920) . . . 16·00 3·25
cg. Dot before "1" . . . 40·00 6·00
ch. "Secret mark" . . . 40·00 6·00
ci. Flaw under neck . . . 40·00 6·00
cj. "RA" joined . . . 40·00 6·00
cw. Wmk inverted . . . 12·00 2·00
d. Die II *Carmine-red* (*shades*) . . . £300 6·00
db. Substituted cliché (Pl 2 right pane R. 6/4) (2.18) . . . £850 60·00
dc. Pale carmine (*shades*) . . . £350 7·00
dw. Wmk inverted . . . £450 16·00
22 4d. orange (6.1.15) . . . 27·00 2·50
a. Yellow-orange (1915) . . . 27·00 3·25
b. Lemon-yellow (3.16) . . . 70·00 14·00
c. Pale orange-yellow (1.17) . . . 75·00 11·00
d. Dull orange (1920) . . . 42·00 3·25
e. Line through "FOUR PENCE" (Pl 2 right pane R. 2/6) (*all shades*) . . . *From* £300 90·00
w. Wmk inverted . . . 40·00 12·00
23 5d. brown (*p* 14¼ (line)) (22.2.15) . . . 25·00 4·00
aw. Wmk inverted . . . £225 65·00
b. Perf 14¼ × 14 (comb) . . . 18·00 2·00
ba. Yellow-brown (1920) . . . 25·00 2·75
bw. Wmk inverted . . . £120 45·00

The variety No. 20d was caused by the engraving of a new fraction in a defective electro in 1918.

No. 21ca was caused by rusting on two positions of the steel plate 2 and shows as white patches on the back of the King's neck and on, and beside, the top of the right frame (right pane R. 6/4) and on the left frame, wattles, head and ears of kangaroo (right pane R. 6/5). These were noticed in December 1916 when the damaged impressions were removed and replaced by a pair of copper electros (Die II for R. 6/4 and Die I for R. 6/5), showing rounded corners and some frame damage, the former also showing a white spot under tail of emu. In time the tops of the crown quickly wore away.

Most of Nos. 20/3 were perforated 14 by a comb machine (exact gauge 14.25 × 14), but printings of the ½d. in December 1915, of the 1d. in July and August 1914 and of the 5d. until June 1917 were perforated by a line machine measuring 14.2.

See also Nos. 47/fa (W **5**, rough paper), 48/52 (W **6**a), 53/*ba* (1d. Die III), 56/66*b* and 76/81 (W **5**, new colours), 82 (W **6**a), 83/4 (no wmk), 85/104(W **7**), 124/31 (W **15**).

(Typo J. B. Cooke)

1915 (15 Jan–Aug). W **5**. P 12.
24 **1** 2d. grey (Die I) . . . 55·00 12·00
w. Wmk inverted . . . † £2000
25 2½d. indigo (Die II) (July) . . . 60·00 30·00
26 6d. ultramarine (Die II) (April) . . . £130 22·00
a. Bright blue . . . £200 50·00
b. Die IIA. *Ultramarine* (substituted cliché) (Upper plate rt pane R. 10/6) . . . £1800 £550
ba. Bright blue . . . £2250 £750
w. Wmk inverted . . . † £3000
27 9d. violet (Die II) (9 July) . . . £150 40·00
w. Wmk inverted . . . £1600 £800
28 1s. blue-green (Die II) (Apr) . . . £140 24·00
29 2s. brown (Die II) (March) . . . £425 90·00
30 5s. grey and yellow (Die II) (12 Feb) . . . £600 £275
a. Yellow portion doubly printed . . . £10000 £2500
w. Wmk inverted . . . £650 £325
24/30 *Set of* 7 . . . £1400 £450

6

6a

Nos. 38da and 73a (Upper plate left pane R. 1/6)

(Typo J. B. Cooke (to May 1918), T. S. Harrison to February 1926), A. J. Mullett (to June 1927) and thereafter J. Ash).

1915 (8 Oct)–**28**. W **6** (narrow Crown). P 12.
35 **1** 2d. grey (Die I) (11.15) . . . 27·00 6·50
a. In pair with Die IIA* . . . £2250 £850
bw. Wmk inverted . . . 35·00 11·00
c. Silver-grey (*shiny paper*) . . . 28·00 10·00
d. Die IIA. *Silver-grey* (*shiny paper*) (3.18) . . . 42·00 12·00
daw. Wmk inverted . . . † £4500
dba. Grey (1920) . . . 45·00 12·00
36 2½d. deep blue (Die II) (9.17) . . . 23·00 10·00
aw. Wmk inverted . . . 55·00 22·00
b. Deep indigo (1919) . . . 29·00 8·50
ba. "1" of fraction omitted (Lower plate left pane R. 6/3) . . . £20000 £5500
37 3d. yellow-olive (Die I) . . . 28·00 4·50
a. In pair with Die II . . . £200 95·00
b. Olive-green (1917) . . . 30·00 4·50
ba. In pair with Die II . . . £200 95·00
cw. Wmk inverted . . . 50·00 11·00
d. Die II *Yellow-olive* . . . 80·00 27·00
da. Olive-green . . . 85·00 27·00
dw. Wmk inverted . . . £190 80·00
e. Die IIB. *Light olive* (1.23) . . . 40·00 12·00

38 6d. ultramarine (Die II) (15.12.15) . . 55·00 7·50
a. Die IIA (substituted cliché) (Upper plate rt pane R. 10/6) £1400 £450
b. Dull blue (6.18) . . . . 65·00 11·00
ba. Die IIA (substituted cliché) £1500 £500
cw. Wmk inverted . . . . £150 40·00
d. Die IIB. *Brt ultramarine* (23.7.21) . . . . 55·00 8·50
da. Leg of kangaroo broken £2250 £500
dw. Wmk inverted . . . . — 45·00
39 9d. violet (Die II) (29.7.16) . . . . . . 38·00 10·00
aw. Wmk inverted . . . . £110 35·00
b. Die IIB. *Violet* (16.4.19) . . . . . 40·00 8·00
bw. Wmk inverted . . . . 95·00 28·00
40 1s. blue-green (Die II) (6.16) . . . . . . 35·00 3·75
aw. Wmk inverted . . . . £100 28·00
b. Die IIB (9.12.20) . . . . 42·00 3·50
ba. Wmk sideways (13.12.27) . . . . . 60·00 £140
bw. Wmk inverted . . . . £100 28·00
41 2s. brown (Die II) (6.16) . . . . £180 13·00
a. Imperf three sides (horiz pair) . . . £30000
b. Red-brown (aniline) . . . . £450 90·00
w. Wmk inverted £450 £160
42 5s. grey and yellow (Die II) (4.18) . . £180 75·00
a. Grey and orange (1920) . . . . . . £200 85·00
b. Grey and deep yellow . . . . . . £190 80·00
ba. Wmk sideways . . . . † £12000
c. Grey and pale yellow . . . . £180 75·00
w. Wmk inverted £500 £200
43 10s. grey and pink (Die II) (5.2.17) . . £425 £250
a. Grey and bright aniline pink (10.18) £375 £180
ab. Wmk sideways £13000 £6000
aw. Wmk inverted £1200 £450
b. Grey and pale aniline pink (1922) . £450 £200
44 £1 chocolate & dull blue (Die II) (7.16) £1700 £900
a. Chestnut and bright blue (6.17) . . £1800 £950
aa. Frame printed double, one albino . . . .
ab. Wmk sideways £22000 £11000
aw. Wmk inverted £2250 £1300
b. Bistre-brown and bright blue (7.19) £1800 £1000
45 £2 black and rose (Die II) (12.19) . . £2500 £1700
a. Grey and crimson (1921) £2250 £1600
b. Purple-black and pale rose (6.24) . . £1900 £1200
35/45*b* *Set of* 11 . . . . £4000 £2000
43s/5s Optd "Specimen" *Set of* 3 . . . . . . £500

*The Die IIA of No. 35a is a substituted cliché introduced to replace a cracked plate which occurred on R. 10/1 of the upper plate left pane. The Die IIA characteristics are more pronounced in this cliché than on the sheet stamps from this die. The break at left, for instance, extends to the outer, in addition to the inner, frame line.

One plate of the 3d. contained mixed Die I and Die II stamps as described.

All values were printed by both Cooke and Harrison, and the 9d., 1s. and 5s. were also printed by Mullett and Ash.

The watermark on No. 42ba shows the Crown pointing to the left *as seen from the back of the stamp*. One example is known.

1916 (Nov)–**18**. *Rough, unsurfaced paper, locally gummed.* W **5**. P 14.

47 **5a** 1d. scarlet (Die I) . . . . 18·00 2·50
a. Deep red (1917) . . . . 18·00 2·50
b. Rose-red (1918) . . . . 28·00 2·75
ba. Substituted cliché (Pl 2 rt pane R. 6/5) . . . . £800 60·00
c. Rosine (1918) . . . . £130 13·00
ca. Substituted cliché (Pl 2 rt pane R. 6/5) £1300 £200
d. Dot before "1" . . . . 55·00 10·00
e. Secret mark . . . . 55·00 10·00
f. Flaw under neck . . . . 55·00 10·00
g. "RA" joined . . . . 55·00 10·00
hw. Wmk inverted . . . . 40·00 4·75
i. Die II *Rose-red* (1918) . . . . . . £275 23·00
ia. Substituted cliché (Pl 2 rt pane R. 6/4) . . . . £800 60·00
iw. Wmk inverted . . . . £400 35·00
j. Die II *Rosine* (1918) . . . . £400 65·00
ja. Substituted cliché (Pl 2 rt pane R. 6/4) £1300 £200

All examples of the 5d. on this paper were perforated "OS" and will be found listed as No. O60.

(Typo J. B. Cooke to May 1918 thereafter T. S. Harrison)

1918 (4 Jan)–**20**. W *6a* (Mult). P 14.

48 **5a** ½d. green (*shades*) . . . . 5·00 2·50
a. Thin 1 in fraction at right (Pl 5 rt pane R. 8/1) . . . . £100 75·00
b. Wmk sideways . . . . † £10000
bw. Wmk sideways inverted . . . . . † £10000
w. Wmk inverted . . . . 19·00 10·00
49 1d. carmine-pink (Die I) (23.1.18) . . £120 70·00
aw. Wmk inverted . . . . † £3000
b. Deep red (1918) £2000 £1000
c. Dot before "1" £450 £200
d. Secret mark £450 £200
e. Flaw under neck £450 £200
f. "RA" joined £450 £200
50 1d. carmine (10.12.19) . . . . 35·00 8·00
aw. Wmk inverted £600 £750
b. Deep red (aniline) (1920) £325 £120
c. Dot before "1" . . . . £110 50·00
d. Secret mark . . . . £110 50·00
e. Flaw under neck . . . . £110 50·00
f. "RA" joined . . . . £110 50·00
51 1½d. black-brown (30.1.19) . . . . . . 5·00 3·25
a. Very thin paper (2.19) . . . . . . 20·00 13·00
w. Wmk inverted . . . . 20·00 9·50
52 1½d. red-brown (4.19) . . . . 12·00 2·25
a. Chocolate (1920) . . . . 11·00 2·25
w. Wmk inverted . . . . 40·00 11·00

No. 48 was printed by Cooke and Harrison, Nos. 49/*b* by Cooke only and Nos. 50/2*a* by Harrison only. Nos. 49/*b* have rather yellowish gum, that of No. 50 being pure white.

The watermark on No. 48b shows the Crown pointing to the left and on No. 48bw pointing to the right, *as seen from the back of the stamp*. One example of each is known.

1d. Die III

1d. Die III. In 1917 a printing (in sheets of 120) was made on paper originally prepared for printing War Savings Stamps, with watermark T **5**. A special plate was made for this printing, differing in detail from those previously used. The shading round the head is even; the solid background of the words "ONE PENNY" is bounded at each end by a white vertical line; and there is a horizontal white line cutting the vertical shading lines at left on the King's neck.

(Typo J. B. Cooke)

1918 (15 Jul). *Printed from a new Die III plate on white unsurfaced paper, locally gummed.* W **5**. P 14.

53 **5a** 1d. rose-red . . . . 60·00 28·00
a. Rose-carmine . . . . 60·00 30·00
w. Wmk inverted . . . . 90·00 45·00

(Typo T. S. Harrison or A. J. Mullett (1s. 4d. from March 1926))

1918 (9 Nov)–**23**. W **5** P 14.

56 **5a** ½d. orange (9.11.23) . . . . 2·50 2·75
w. Wmk inverted . . . . 6·00 7·00
57 1d. violet (*shades*) (12.2.22) . . . . . 6·00 1·50
a. Imperf three sides (horiz pair) . . £20000
b. Red-violet . . . . 8·00 2·25
c. Dot before "1" . . . . 30·00 10·00
d. Secret mark . . . . 30·00 10·00
e. Flaw under neck . . . . 30·00 10·00
f. "RA" joined . . . . 30·00 10·00
58 1½d. black-brown . . . . 8·50 1·50
w. Wmk inverted . . . . 16·00 3·75
59 1½d. deep red-brown (4.19) . . . . . . 6·50 70
a. Chocolate (1920) . . . . 6·50 60
w. Wmk inverted . . . . 17·00 4·75
60 1½d. bright red-brown (20.1.22) . . . . 15·00 3·75
61 1½d. green (7.3.23) . . . . 4·00 80
a. Coarse unsurfaced paper (1923) . . £130 55·00
w. Wmk inverted . . . . † £3500
62 2d. brown-orange (9.20) . . . . 15·00 1·00
a. Dull orange (1921) . . . . 18·00 1·00
w. Wmk inverted . . . . † £3000
63 2d. bright rose-scarlet (19.1.22) . . . . 9·00 1·50
a. Dull rose-scarlet . . . . 9·00 1·50
w. Wmk inverted £4500
64 4d. violet (21.6.21) . . . . 13·00 15·00
a. Line through "FOUR PENCE" (Pl 2 rt pane R. 2/6) £12000 £3000
b. "FOUR PENCE" in thinner letters (Pl 2 rt pane R. 2/6) £425 £250
65 4d. ultramarine (*shades*) (23.3.22) . . . 48·00 8·50
a. "FOUR PENCE" in thinner letters (Pl 2 rt pane R. 2/6) £400 £150
b. Pale milky blue . . . . 75·00 13·00
w. Wmk inverted . . . . 75·00 £100
66 1s. 4d. pale blue (2.12.20) . . . . . . 55·00 25·00
a. Dull greenish blue . . . . 60·00 24·00
b. Deep turquoise (1922) £1500 £850
56/66 *Set of* 11 . . . . £160 50·00

In addition to a number of mint pairs from two sheets purchased at Gumeracha, South Australia, with the bottom row imperforate on three sides, a single used example of No. 57 imperforate on three sides is known.

No. 61a was printed on a batch of coarse unsurfaced paper during 1923. Examples may be indentified by a mesh effect in the paper, with mint stamps having a yellowish gum.

The 4d. ultramarine was originally printed from the Cooke plates but the plates were worn in mid-1923 and Harrison prepared a new pair of plates. Stamps from these plates can only be distinguished by the minor flaws which are peculiar to them.

The variety of Nos. 64 and 65 with "FOUR PENCE" thinner, was caused by the correction of the line through "FOUR PENCE" flaw early in the printing of No. 64.

(Typo T. S. Harrison (to February 1926), A. J. Mullett (to June 1927), thereafter J. Ash)

1923 (6 Dec)–**24**. W **6**. P 12.

73 **1** 6d. chestnut (Die IIB) . . . . 24·00 1·75
a. Leg of kangaroo broken (Upper plate lt pane R. 1/6) . . . . 75·00 £110
w. Wmk inverted . . . . † £4500
74 2s. maroon (Die II) (1.5.24) . . . . . . 55·00 26·00
w. Wmk inverted £300 £150
75 £1 grey (Die IIB) (1.5.24) £400 £225
s. Optd "Specimen" . . . . 75·00

The 6d. and 2s. were printed by all three printers, but the £1 only by Harrison.

No. 73a was corrected during the Ash printing.

(Typo T. S. Harrison (to February 1926), thereafter A. J. Mullett)

1924 (1 May–18 Aug). P 14.

(*a*) W **5**.

76 **5a** 1d. sage-green . . . . 3·00 1·50
a. Dot before "1" . . . . 25·00 8·00
b. Secret mark . . . . 25·00 8·00
c. Flaw under neck . . . . 25·00 8·00
d. "RA" joined . . . . 25·00 8·00
w. Wmk inverted . . . . 12·00 6·00
77 1½d. scarlet (*shades*) . . . . 2·25 40
a. Very thin paper . . . . 40·00 20·00
b. "HALEPENCE" (Pl 22 left pane R. 4/4) . . . . 30·00 23·00
c. "RAL" of AUSTRALIA" thin (Pl 22 Left pane R. 5/4) . . . . 30·00 23·00
d. Curved "1" and thin fraction at left (Pl 24 rt pane R. 7/5) . . . . 30·00 23·00
w. Wmk inverted . . . . 32·00 10·00
78 2d. red-brown . . . . 20·00 7·00
a. Bright red-brown . . . . 26·00 8·00
w. Wmk inverted . . . . † £4500
79 3d. dull ultramarine . . . . 26·00 2·00
a. Imperf three sides (horiz pair) . . £6000
80 4d. olive-yellow . . . . 29·00 5·50
a. Olive-green . . . . 29·00 6·00
w. Wmk inverted . . . . † £2500
81 4½d. violet . . . . 23·00 3·50

(*b*) W **6a**.

82 **5a** 1d. sage-green (20 May) . . . . 8·50 8·50
a. Dot before "1" . . . . 45·00 50·00
b. Secret mark . . . . 45·00 50·00
c. Flaw under neck . . . . 45·00 50·00
d. "RA" joined . . . . 45·00 50·00
w. Wmk inverted . . . . † £3000

(*c*) No wmk.

83 **5a** 1d. sage-green (18 August) . . . . . 5·50 9·50
a. Dot before "1" . . . . 30·00 50·00
b. Secret mark . . . . 30·00 50·00
c. Flaw under neck . . . . 30·00 50·00
d. "RA" joined . . . . 30·00 50·00
84 1½d. scarlet (14 August) . . . . 12·00 9·50
76/84 *Set of* 9 . . . . £110 42·00

Nos. 78/*a* and 82/4 were printed by Harrison only but the remainder were printed by both Harrison and Mullett.

In the semi-transparent paper of Nos. 54a and 77a the watermark is almost indistinguishable.

Nos. 77b, 77c and 77d are typical examples of retouching of which there are many others in these issues. In No. 77c the letters "RAL" differ markedly from the normal. There is a white stroke cutting the oval frame-line above the"L", and the right-hand outer line of the Crown does not cut the white frame-line above the "A".

It is believed that No. 79a occurs on the bottom row of at least four sheets purchased from post offices in Victoria during 1926.

7

I

II

New Dies

1d. For differences see note above No. 20.
1½d. From new steel plates made from a new die. Nos. 87*a* and 96*a* are the Ash printings, the ink of which is shiny.
2d. Die I. Height of frame 25.6 mm. Left-hand frame-line thick and uneven behind Kangaroo. Pearls in Crown vary in size.
Die II. Height of frame 25.6 mm. Left-hand frame-line thin and even. Pearls in Crown are all the same size.
Die III. Height 25.1 mm; lettering and figures of value bolder than Die I.
3d. Die II has bolder letters and figures than Die I, as illustrated above.
5d. Die II has a bolder figure "5" with flat top compared with Die I of the earlier issues.

(Typo A. J. Mullett or J. Ash (from June 1927))

1926–**30**. W **7**.

(*a*) P 14.

85 **5a** ½d. orange (10.3.27) . . . . 6·00 7·50
w. Wmk inverted . . . . 65·00 45·00
86 1d. sage-green (23.10.26) . . . . . . 3·25 1·00
a. Dot before "1" . . . . 45·00 15·00
b. Secret mark . . . . 45·00 15·00
c. Flaw under neck . . . . 65·00 25·00
d. "RA" joined . . . . 65·00 25·00
w. Wmk inverted . . . . 16·00 4·75
87 1½d. scarlet (5.11.26) . . . . 7·50 2·00
a. Golden scarlet (1927) . . . . . . 12·00 2·50
w. Wmk inverted . . . . 14·00 4·50
89 2d. red-brown (Die I) (17.8.27) . . . . 28·00 40·00
90 3d. dull ultramarine (12.26) . . . . . 24·00 5·00
w. Wmk inverted . . . . † £3000
91 4d. yellow-olive (17.1.28) . . . . . . 48·00 40·00
92 4½d. violet (26.10.27) . . . . 18·00 3·75
93 1s. 4d. pale greenish blue (6.9.27) . . . 90·00 80·00
w. Wmk inverted . . . . † £5000
85/93 *Set of* 8 . . . . £200 £160

(*b*) P 13½ × 12½.

94 **5a** ½d. orange (21.11.28) . . . . 2·25 1·40
95 1d. sage-green (Die I) (23.12.26) . . . 2·25 70
aa. Dot before "1" . . . . 75·00 35·00
ab. Secret mark . . . . 85·00 40·00
ac. Flaw under neck . . . . 85·00 40·00
ad. "RA" joined . . . . 85·00 40·00
aw. Wmk inverted . . . . 11·00 4·50
b. Die II (6.28) . . . . 50·00 80·00
bw. Wmk inverted £500 £450
96 1½d. scarlet (14.1.27) . . . . 2·25 1·00
a. Golden scarlet (1927) . . . . . . 2·25 1·00
w. Wmk inverted . . . . 12·00 2·50
97 1½d. red-brown (16.9.30) . . . . 5·50 5·50
98 2d. red-brown (Die II) (28.4.28) . . . 8·00 9·00

99 2d. golden scarlet (Die II) (2.8.30) . . . . 12·00 2·25
a. Die III (9.9.30) . . . . 9·00 85
ab. No wmk £850 £1600
ac. Tête-bêche (pair) £100000
aw. Wmk inverted (*from booklets*) . . 9·00 1·40
100 3d. dull ultramarine (Die I) (28.2.28) . . . . 38·00 6·50
aw. Wmk inverted £130 £325
b. Die II *Deep ultramarine* (28.9.29) . . . . 24·00 1·40
bw. Wmk inverted . . . . † £3000
102 4d. yellow-olive (19.4.29) . . . . 23·00 3·25
w. Wmk inverted . . . . † £3000
103 4½d. violet (11.28) . . . . 48·00 24·00
103*a* 5d. orange-brown Die II (27.8.30) . . . . 24·00 7·00
104 1s. 4d. turquoise (30.9.28) . . . . 80·00 26·00
w. Wmk inverted . . . . † £5500
94/104 *Set of* 11 . . . . £190 70·00

Owing to defective manufacture, part of the sheet of the 2d. (Die III), discovered in July 1931, escaped unwatermarked; while the watermark in other parts of the same sheet was faint or normal.

Only one example of No. 99ac is known.

8 Parliament House, Canberra

9 "DH66" Biplane and Pastoral Scene

(Des R. A. Harrison. Die eng J. A. C. Harrison (Waterlow, London). Plates and printing by A. J. Mullett)

1927 (9 May). *Opening of Parliament House, Canberra.* No wmk. P 11.
105 **8** 1½d. brownish lake 50 50
a. Imperf between (vert pair) £2500
b. Imperf between (horiz pair) £3500 £3500

(Eng H. W. Bell. Recess J. Ash)

1928 (29 Oct–2 Nov). *4th National Stamp Exhibition, Melbourne. As T* **4**. No wmk. P 11.
106 3d. blue (2 Nov) . . . . 4·25 5·00
MS106*a* 65 × 70 mm. No. 106 × 4 . . . . £110 £200
ab. Imperf (pane of four) £40000

No. **MS**106*a* comes from special sheets of 60 stamps divided into 15 blocks of 4 (5 × 3) and separated by wide gutters perforated down the middle, printed and sold at the Exhibition.

(Typo J. Ash)

1929 (Feb)–**30**. W **7**. P 12.
107 **1** 6d. chestnut (Die IIB) (25.9.29) . . . . 23·00 4·50
108 9d. violet (Die IIB) . . . . 30·00 17·00
a. Die II (substituted cliché) . . . .
109 1s. blue-green (Die IIB) (12.6.29) . . . . 38·00 6·00
w. Wmk inverted . . . . † £3500
110 2s. maroon (Die II) (3.29) . . . . 45·00 15·00
111 5s. grey and yellow (Die II) (30.11.29) . . . . £190 80·00
112 10s. grey and pink (Die II) £325 £425
114 £2 black and rose (Die II) (11.30) . . £2250 £500
107/14 *Set of* 7 . . . . £2500 £950
112s/14s Optd "Specimen" *Set of* 2 . . . . £325

No. 108a comes from six substituted clichés taken from plate 2 (Die II) and inserted in plate 4 (Die IIB) at positions left pane R. 1/3-4, 2/3-4 and 8/6 and right pane R. 2/1. This substitution took place towards the end of the previous printings on W **6**. The variety can also be found on stamps with W **15**, see Nos. 133a/b.

(Des R. A. Harrison and H. Herbert. Eng A. Taylor. Recess J. Ash)

1929 (20 May). *Air.* No wmk. P 11.
115 **9** 3d. green (*shades*) . . . . 8·00 4·00

Variations of up to ¾mm in the design size of No. 115 are due to paper shrinkage on the printings produced by the "wet" process. The last printing, in 1935, was printed by the "dry" method.

10 Black Swan

11 "Capt. Charles Sturt" (J. H. Crossland)

(Des G. Pitt Morrison. Eng F. D. Manley. Recess J. Ash)

1929 (28 Sep). *Centenary of Western Australia.* No wmk. P 11.
116 **10** 1½d. dull scarlet . . . . 1·25 1·60
a. Re-entry ("T" of "AUSTRALIA" clearly double) (Pl 2 R. 7/4) . . . 55·00 60·00

(Des R. A. Harrison. Eng F. D. Manley. Recess J. Ash)

1930 (2 Jun). *Centenary of Exploration of River Murray by Capt. Sturt.* No wmk. P 11.
117 **11** 1½d. scarlet . . . . 1·00 1·00
118 3d. blue . . . . 3·25 6·50

No. 117 with manuscript surcharge of "2d. paid P M L H I" was issued by the Postmaster of Lord Howe Island during a shortage of 2d. stamps between 23 August and 17 October 1930 (*Price £600 un. or used*). A few copies of the 1½d. value No. 96*a* were also endorsed (*Price £1200 un. or used*). These provisionals are not recognized by the Australian postal authorities.

TWO

PENCE

(**12**)

13 Fokker F. VIIa/3m *Southern* Cross above Hemispheres

1930 (28 Jul–2 Aug). *T* **5a** *surch as T* **12**. W **7**. P 13½ × 12½.
119 2d.on 1½d. golden scarlet . . . . 1·50 1·00
120 5d.on 4½d. violet (2 Aug) . . . . 6·00 9·50

No. 120 is from a redrawn die in which the words "FOURPENCE HALFPENNY" are noticeably thicker than in the original die and the figure "4" has square instead of tapering serifs. The redrawn die also shows thin white lines to the left and right of the tablet carrying "FOURPENCE HALFPENNY".

Stamps from the redrawn die without the surcharge were printed, but not issued thus. Some stamps, *cancelled to order*, were included in sets supplied by the post office. A few mint copies, which escaped the cancellation were found and some may have been used postally (*Price £2250 unused, £45 used c.t.o.*).

(Des and eng F. D. Manley. Recess John Ash)

1931 (19 Mar). *Kingsford Smith's Flights.* No wmk. P 11.

(*a*) *Postage.*
121 **13** 2d. rose-red . . . . 1·00 1·00
122 3d. blue . . . . 4·50 5·00

(*b*) *Air. Inscr* "AIR MAIL SERVICE" *at sides.*
123 **13** 6d. violet . . . . 5·50 13·00
a. Re-entry ("FO" and "LD" double) (Pl 1 R. 5/5) . . . . 50·00 80·00
121/3 *Set of* 3 . . . . 10·00 17·00

15

17 Superb Lyrebird

(Typo John Ash).

1931–36. W **15**.

(*a*) P 13½ × 12½.
124 **5a** ½d. orange (2.33) . . . . 4·75 6·00
125 1d. green (Die I) (10.31) . . . . 1·75 20
w. Wmk inverted . . . . 16·00 3·50
x. Wmk reversed £400 £275
y. Wmk inverted and reversed . . . £700 £450
126 1½d. red-brown (10.36) . . . . 6·00 10·00
127 2d. golden scarlet (Die III) (18.12.31) . . . . 1·75 10
w. Wmk inverted (from booklets) . . 2·25 50
128 3d. ultramarine (Die II) (30.9.32) . . 18·00 1·25
w. Wmk inverted £3000 £3000
129 4d. yellow-olive (2.33) . . . . 18·00 1·25
w. Wmk inverted . . . . † £3000
130 5d. orange-brown (Die II) (25.2.32) . . . . 15·00 20
w. Wmk inverted . . . . † £3000
131 1s. 4d. turquoise (18.8.32) . . . . 50·00 3·50
w. Wmk inverted . . . . † £3500
124/31 *Set of* 8 . . . . £100 20·00

(*b*) P 12.
132 **1** 6d. chestnut (Die IIB) (20.4.32) . . . . 22·00 27·00
133 9d. violet (Die IIB) (20.4.32) . . . . 28·00 1·25
a. Die II (substituted cliché) . . . .
ab. In pair with Die IIB . . . .
134 2s. maroon (Die II) (6.8.35) . . . . 5·00 60
135 5s. grey and yellow (Die II) (12.32) . . £120 12·00
136 10s. grey and pink (Die II) (31.7.32) . . £250 £100
137 £1 grey (Die IIB) (11.35) £450 £160
138 £2 black and rose (Die II) (6.34) . . . £1900 £350
132/8 *Set of* 7 . . . . £2500 £600
136s/8s Optd "Specimen" *Set of* 3 . . . . 75·00

Stamps as No. 127, but without watermark and perforated 11, are forgeries made in 1932 to defraud the P.O. (*Price* £300, *unused*).

For re-engraved type of No. 134, see No. 212.

For 133a/ab see note below No 114.

(Des and eng F. D. Manley. Recess John Ash)

1931 (4 Nov). *Air Stamp. As T* **13** *but inscr* "AIR MAIL SERVICE" *in bottom tablet.* No wmk. P 11.
139 6d. sepia . . . . 13·00 12·00

1931 (17 Nov). *Air.* No. 139 *optd with Type* **O 4**.
139*a* 6d. sepia . . . . 35·00 55·00

This stamp was not restricted to official use but was on general sale to the public.

(Des and eng F. D. Manley. Recess John Ash)

1932 (15 Feb). No wmk. P 11.
140 **17** 1s. green . . . . 42·00 2·00
a. Yellow-green . . . . 48·00 2·75

18 Sydney Harbour Bridge

19 Laughing Kookaburra

(Des R. A. Harrison. Eng F. D. Manley. Printed John Ash)

1932 (14 Mar). *Opening of Sydney Harbour Bridge.*

(*a*) *Recess.* No wmk. P 11.
141 **18** 2d. scarlet . . . . 2·25 3·25
142 3d. blue . . . . 4·50 7·00
143 5s. blue-green £375 £180

(*b*) *Typo.* W **15**. P 10½.
144 **18** 2d. scarlet . . . . 2·00 1·40
141/4 *Set of* 4 . . . . £375 £180

Stamps as No. 144 without wmk and perf 11 are forgeries made in 1932 to defraud the P.O. (*Price* £500, *unused*).

(Des and eng F. D. Manley. Recess John Ash)

1932 (1 June). W **15**. P 13½ × 12½.
146 **19** 6d. red-brown . . . . 25·00 55
w. Wmk inverted . . . . † £1100

20 Melbourne and R. Yarra

21 Merino Ram

(Des and eng F. D. Manley. Recess John Ash)

1934 (2 Jul–Aug). *Centenary of Victoria.* W **15**. P 10½.
147 **20** 2d. orange-vermilion . . . . 2·50 1·75
a. Perf 11½ (Aug) . . . . 6·00 1·50
148 3d. blue . . . . 4·00 5·50
a. Perf 11½ (Aug) . . . . 4·00 8·00
149 1s. black . . . . 50·00 20·00
a. Perf 11½ (Aug) . . . . 55·00 22·00
147/9 *Set of* 3 . . . . 50·00 25·00
147a/9a *Set of* 3 . . . . 60·00 28·00

Stamps were originally issued perforated 10½, but the gauge was subsequently changed to 11½ in August 1934 due to difficulties in separating stamps in the first perforation.

(Des and eng F. D. Manley. Recess John Ash)

1934 (1–26 Nov). *Death Centenary of Capt. John Macarthur (founder of Australian sheep farming)* W **15**. P 11½.
150 **21** 2d. carmine-red (A) . . . . 4·50 1·50
150*a* 2d. carmine-red (B) (26 Nov) . . . . 25·00 3·25
151 3d. blue . . . . 10·00 12·00
152 9d. bright purple . . . . 27·00 45·00
150/2 *Set of* 3 . . . . 38·00 50·00

Type A of the 2d. shows shading on the hill in the background varying from light to dark (as illustrated). Type B has the shading almost uniformly dark.

22 Hermes

23 Cenotaph, Whitehall

(Des F. D. Manley. Eng E. Broad and F. D. Manley. Recess John Ash until April 1940; W. C. G. McCracken thereafter)

1934 (1 Dec)–**48**.

(*a*) No wmk. P 11.
153 **22** 1s.6d. dull purple . . . . 35·00 1·00

(*b*) W **15**. *Chalk-surfaced paper.* P 13½ × 14.
153*a* **22** 1s.6d. dull purple (22.10.37) . . . . 9·00 45
b. Thin rough ordinary paper (12.2.48) . . . . 2·00 1·40

(Des B Cottier; adapted and eng F. D. Manley. Recess John Ash)

1935 (18 Mar). *20th Anniv of Gallipoli Landing.* W **15**. P 13½ × 12½ or 11 (1s.).
154 **23** 2d. scarlet . . . . 1·50 30
155 1s. black (chalk-surfaced) . . . . 42·00 38·00

The 1s. perforated 13½ × 12½ is a plate proof (*Price* £1500, *unused*).

24 King George V on "Anzac"

25 Amphitrite and Telephone Cable

(Des and eng F. D. Manley. Recess John Ash)

1935 (2 May). *Silver Jubilee. Chalk-surfaced paper.* W **15** (sideways). P 11½.
156 **24** 2d. scarlet . . . . 1·50 30
157 3d. blue . . . . 5·00 8·00
158 2s. bright violet . . . . 27·00 42·00
156/8 *Set of* 3 . . . . 30·00 45·00

(Des and eng F. D. Manley. Recess John Ash)

1936 (1 Apr). *Opening of Submarine Telephone Link to Tasmania.* W **15**. P 11½.
159 **25** 2d. scarlet 75 50
160 3d. blue . . . . 2·75 2·75

26 Site of Adelaide, 1836; Old Gum Tree, Glenelg; King William St, Adelaide

(Des and eng F. D. Manley. Recess John Ash)

1936 (3 Aug). *Centenary of South Australia.* W **15**. P 11½.

161	**26**	2d. carmine	1·25	40
162		3d. blue	4·00	3·50
163		1s. green	10·00	8·50
161/3 *Set of* 3			14·00	11·00

27 Wallaroo **28** Queen Elizabeth **28a** Queen Elizabeth

29 **30** King George VI **30a**

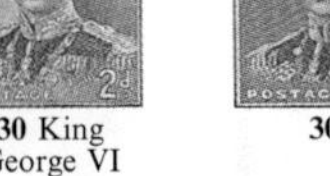

31 King George VI **32** Koala **33** Merino Ram

34 Laughing Kookaburra **35** Platypus **36** Superb Lyrebird

38 Queen Elizabeth **39** King George VI

40 King George VI and Queen Elizabeth

Dies of 3d.:

Die I Die Ia Die II

Die I. The letters "TA" of "POSTAGE" at right are joined by a white flaw; the outline of the chin consists of separate strokes.

No. 168a is a preliminary printing made with unsuitable ink and may be detected by the absence of finer details; the King's face appears whitish and the wattles are blank. The greater part of this printing was distributed to the Press with advance notices of the issue.

Die Ia. As Die I, but "T" and "A" have been clearly separated by individual retouches made on the plates.

Die II A completely new die. "T" and "A" are separate and a continuous line has been added to the chin. The outline of the cheek extends to about 1 mm above the lobe of the King's right ear.

Die III. Differs from Dies I and II in the King's left eyebrow which is shaded downwards from left to right instead of from right to left.

Line to Kangaroo's ear (Right pane R. 6/8)

Medal flaw (Right pane R. 2/5)

(Des R. A. Harrison (T **28/30**), F. D. Manley (T **27**, **31/6**), H. Barr (T **38/9**), H. Barr and F. D. Manley (T **40**). Eng F. D. Manley and T. C. Duffell (T **34**), T. C. Duffell (revised lettering for **T28***a*, **30***a*), F. D. Manley (others). All recess with John Ash, W. C. G. McCracken or "By Authority ..." imprints)

1937–49. *Chalk-surfaced paper (3d.* (No. 168)*, 5s., 10s., £1).* W **15** (sideways on 5d., 9d., 5s. and 10s.).

(a) P 13½ × 14 (vert designs) or 14 × 13½ (horiz).

164	**27**	½d. orange (3.10.38)	2·50	50
165	**28**	1d. emerald-green (10.5.37)	70	40
166	**29**	1½d. maroon (20.4.38)	9·00	4·00
167	**30**	2d. scarlet (10.5.37)	70	30
168	**31**	3d. blue (Die I) (2.8.37)	60·00	14·00
		a. "White wattles" (from 1st ptg)	£120	70·00
		b. Die Ia	£140	7·00
		c. Die II (3.38)	60·00	4·25
		ca. Bright blue (ordinary thin paper) (20.12.38)	60·00	3·25
170	**32**	4d. green (1.2.38)	11·00	1·75
171	**33**	5d. purple (1.12.38)	1·50	60
172	**34**	6d. purple-brown (2.8.37)	20·00	1·25
173	**35**	9d. chocolate (1.9.38)	4·50	1·25
174	**36**	1s. grey-green (2.8.37)	48·00	2·25
175	**31**	1s.4d. pale magenta (3.10.38)	2·00	2·00
		a. Deep magenta (1943)	3·25	2·25
		(b) P 13½.		
176	**38**	5s. claret (1.4.38)	16·00	2·00
		a. Thin rough ordinary paper (4.2.48)	3·75	2·50
177	**39**	10s. dull purple (1.4.38)	38·00	14·00
		a. Thin rough ordinary paper (11.48)	42·00	32·00
		s. Optd "Specimen"	30·00	
178	**40**	£1 bl-slate (1.11.38)	55·00	30·00
		a. Thin rough ordinary paper (4.4.49)	55·00	60·00
		s. Optd "Specimen"	£425	
164/78 *Set of* 14			£225	55·00

(c) P 15 × 14 (vert designs) or 14 × 15 (horiz) (1d. and 2d. redrawn with background evenly shaded and lettering strengthened).

179	**27**	½d. orange (28.1.42)	55	10
		a. Line to kangaroo's ear	15·00	
		b. Coil pair (1942)	17·00	22·00
		ba. Coil block of four (1943)	£450	
180	**28a**	1d. emerald-green (1.8.38)	3·00	30
181		1d. maroon (10.12.41)	1·50	30
		a. Coil pair (1942)	14·00	22·00
182	**29**	1½d. maroon (21.11.41)	4·75	8·50
183		1½d. emerald-green (10.12.41)	1·00	1·50
184	**30a**	2d. scarlet (11.7.38)	3·00	10
		a. Coil pair (10.41)	£325	£375
		b. Medal flaw	£140	
		w. Wmk inverted (*from booklets*)	6·50	60
185		2d. bright purple (10.12.41)	50	1·50
		a. Coil pair (1942)	42·00	60·00
		b. Medal flaw	48·00	
		w. Wmk inverted (*from coils*)	£120	50·00
186	**31**	3d. bright blue (Die III) (11.40)	45·00	3·25
187		3d. purple-brown (Die III) (10.12.41)	40	10
188	**32**	4d. green (10.42)	1·00	10
		w. Wmk inverted	†	£1100
189	**33**	5d. purple (17.12.45)	50	1·50
190	**34**	6d. red-brown (6.42)	2·25	10
		a. Purple-brown (1944)	1·75	10
191	**35**	9d. chocolate (12.9.43)	1·00	20
192	**36**	1s. grey-green (29.3.41)	1·25	10
		w. Wmk inverted	£1300	£900
179/92 *Set of* 14			60·00	15·00

For unwmkd issue, see Nos. 228/30*d*.

Thin paper. Nos. 176a, 177a, 178a. In these varieties the watermark is more clearly visible on the back and the design is much less sharp. On early printings of No. 176a the paper appears tinted.

SPECIAL COIL PERFORATION. This special perforation of large and small holes on the narrow sides of the stamps was introduced after 1939 for stamps issued in coils and was intended to facilitate separation. Where they exist they are listed as "Coil pairs".

The following with "special coil" perforation were placed on sale in *sheets*:Nos. 179, 205, 222a (1952), 228, 230, 237, 262 (1953), 309, 311, and 314. These are listed as "Coil blocks of four".

Coils with "normal" perforations also exist for Nos. 180 and 184.

41 "Governor Phillip at Sydney Cove" (J. Alcott)

"Tail" flaw (Left pane R. 7/1. Later retouched)

(Des and eng E. Broad and F. D. Manley. Recess J. Ash)

1937 (1 Oct). *150th Anniv of Foundation of New South Wales.* W **15**. P 13½ × 14.

193	**41**	2d. scarlet	2·25	30
		a. "Tail" flaw	£350	85·00
194		3d. bright blue	6·00	2·25
195		9d. purple	16·00	10·00
193/5 *Set of* 3			22·00	11·00

42 A.I.F. and Nurse

(Des and eng F. D. Manley from drawing by Virgil Reilly. Recess W. C. G. McCracken)

1940 (15 Jul). *Australian Imperial Forces.* W **15** (sideways). P 14 × 13½.

196	**42**	1d. green	1·75	2·25
197		2d. scarlet	1·75	1·00
198		3d. blue	12·00	9·00
199		6d. brown-purple	22·00	16·00
196/9 *Set of* 4			35·00	25·00

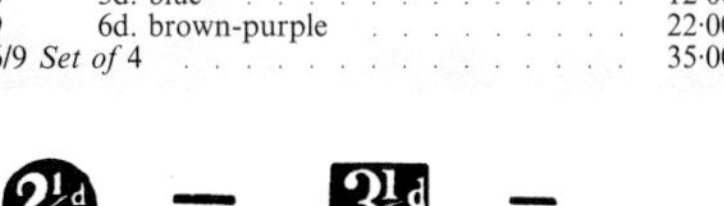

(**43**) (**44**) (**45**)

(Opts designed by F. D. Manley)

1941 (10 Dec). Nos. 184, 186 *and* 171 *surch with T* **43/5**.

200	**30a**	2½d.on 2d. scarlet (V.)	75	70
		a. Pair, one without surcharge	£6000	
		b. Medal flaw	£150	
201	**31**	3½d.on 3d. bright blue (Y. on Black)	1·00	2·00
202	**33**	5½d.on 5d. purple (V.)	4·00	5·00
200/2 *Set of* 3			5·25	7·00

Nos. 200/2 were prepared in connection with the imposition of a ½d. "war tax" increase on most postage rates.

One sheet of the 2½d. on 2d. was discovered showing the surcharge omitted on R. 1/4 and R. 1/5.

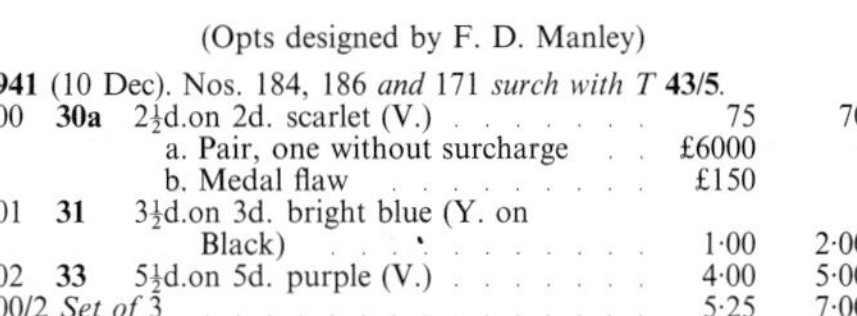

46 Queen Elizabeth **46a** Queen Elizabeth **47** King George VI

48 King George VI **49** King George VI **50** Emu

(Des F. D. Manley. Eng F. D. Manley and T. C. Duffell (T **46***/a*) or F. D. Manley (others))

1942–50. *Recess.* W **15**. P 15 × 14.

203	**46**	1d. brown-purple (2.1.43)	1·25	10
		a. Coil pair (1944)	22·00	30·00
204	**46a**	1½d. green (1.12.42)	1·25	10
205	**47**	2d. bright purple (4.12.44)	65	1·25
		b. Coil pair (1.49)	90·00	£110
		ba. Coil block of four (5.50)	£1000	
206	**48**	2½d. scarlet (7.1.42)	40	10
		a. Imperf (pair)*	£3500	
		w. Wmk inverted (*from booklets*)	4·50	70
207	**49**	3½d. bright blue (3.42)	70	50
		a. Deep blue	1·25	50
208	**50**	5½d. slate-blue (12.2.42)	1·00	10
203/8 *Set of* 6			4·75	1·75

*No. 206a comes in horizontal pair with the right-hand stamp completely imperforate and the left-hand stamp imperforate at right only.

Coils with normal perforations exist for 1d.

For stamps as Nos. 204/5 but without watermark see Nos. 229/30.

The following items are understood to have been the subject of unauthorised leakages from the Commonwealth Note and Stamp Printing Branch and are therefore not listed by us.

It is certain that none of this material was distributed to post offices for issue to the public.

Imperforate all round. 1d. Princess Elizabeth; 1½d. Queen; 2½d. King;4d. Koala; 6d. Kookaburra; 9d. Platypus; 1s. Lyrebird (small) (also imperf three sides); 1s.6d. Air Mail (Type **22**); 2½d. Mitchell; 2½d. Newcastle(also imperf three sides or imperf vertically).

Also 2½d. Peace, unwatermarked; 2½d. King, *tête-bêche*; 3½d. Newcastle, in dull ultramarine; 2½d. King on "toned" paper.

52 Duke and Duchess of Gloucester

(Des F. D. Manley. Eng F. D. Manley and T. C. Duffell. Recess)

1945 (19 Feb). *Arrival of Duke and Duchess of Gloucester in Australia.* W **15**. P 14½.

209	**52**	2½d. lake	10	10
210		3½d. ultramarine	15	80
211		5½d. indigo	20	80
209/11		*Set of* 3	40	1·50

A

B

945 (24 Dec). *Kangaroo type, as* No. 134, *but re-engraved as* B. W **15**. P 12.

12	**1**	2s. maroon	2·25	4·75
		w. Wmk inverted	†	£4500

No. 134 has two background lines between the value circle and TWO SHILLINGS"; No. 212 has only one line in this position. here are also differences in the shape of the letters.

53 Star and Wreath

56 Sir Thomas Mitchell and Queensland

(Des F. D. Manley (2½d.), F. D. Manley and G. Lissenden (3½d.), G. Lissenden (5½d.). Eng F. D. Manley. Recess)

946 (18 Feb). *Victory Commemoration. T* **53** *and similar designs.* W **15** (sideways on 5½d.). P 14½.

13		2½d. scarlet	10	10
14		3½d. blue	30	1·00
15		5½d. green	35	65
13/15		*Set of* 3	70	1·50

Designs: *Horiz*—3½d. Flag and dove. *Vert*—5½d. Angel.

These designs were re-issued in 1995 with face values in decimal urrency.

Des F. D. Manley. Eng F. D. Manley and T. C. Duffell. Recess)

946 (14 Oct). *Centenary of Mitchell's Exploration of Central Queensland.* W **15**. P 14½.

16	**56**	2½d. scarlet	10	10
17		3½d. blue	40	1·25
18		1s. grey-olive	40	50
16/18		*Set of* 3	80	1·60

57 Lt. John Shortland R.N.

58 Steel Foundry

59 Coal Carrier Cranes

)es and eng G. Lissenden (5½d.), F. D. Manley (others). Recess)

47 (8 Sep). *150th Anniv of City of Newcastle, New South Wales.* W **15** (sideways on 3½d.). P 14½ or 15 × 14 (2½d.).

9	**57**	2½d. lake	10	10
0	**58**	3½d. blue	40	1·00
1	**59**	5½d. green	40	55
9/21		*Set of* 3	80	1·50

60 Queen Elizabeth II when Princess

(Des R. A. Harrison. Eng. F. D. Manley. Recess)

1947 (20 Nov)–**52**. *Marriage of Princess Elizabeth.* P 14 × 15.

(a) W **15** (sideways).

222	**60**	1d. purple	15	30

(b) No wmk.

222*a*	**60**	1d. purple (8.48)	10	10
		b. Coil pair (1.50)	2·25	5·00
		c. Coil block of four (9.52)	4·75	

61 Hereford Bull

61a Hermes and Globe

62 Aboriginal Art

62a Commonwealth Coat of Arms

(Des G. Sellheim (T **62**), F.D. Manley (others). Eng G. Lissenden (T **62**), F. D. Manley (1s.3d., 1s.6d., 5s.), F. D. Manley and R. J. Becker (10s., £1, £2). Recess)

1948 (16 Feb)–**56**. W **15** (sideways).

(a) P 14½.

223	**61**	1s.3d. brown-purple	1·75	1·10
223*a*	**61a**	1s.6d. blackish brown (1.9.49)	70	10
224	**62**	2s. chocolate	2·00	10

(b) P 14½ × 13½.

224*a*	**62a**	5s. claret (11.4.49)	2·75	20
		ab. Thin paper (1951)	32·00	21·00
224*b*		10s. purple (3.10.49)	14·00	85
224*c*		£1 blue (28.11.49)	30·00	3·50
224*d*		£2 green (16.1.50)	80·00	14·00
223/24*d*		*Set of* 7	£120	17·00
224bs/ds		Optd "Specimen" *Set of* 3	£140	

(c) No wmk. P 14½.

224*e*	**61a**	1s.6d. blackish brown (2.12.56)	11·00	1·50
224*f*	**62**	2s. chocolate (27.6.56)	11·00	60

No. 224ab is an emergency printing on white Harrison paper instead of the toned paper used for No. 224a.

No. 224b exists with watermark inverted and overprinted "SPECIMEN".

63 William J. Farrer

64 F. von Mueller

65 Boy Scout

(Des and eng F. D. Manley. Recess)

1948 (12 Jul). *William J. Farrer (wheat research) Commemoration.* W **15**. P 15 × 14.

225	**63**	2½d. scarlet	20	10

(Des and eng F. D. Manley. Recess)

1948 (13 Sep). *Sir Ferdinand von Mueller (botanist) Commemoration.* W **15**. P 15 × 14.

226	**64**	2½d. lake	20	10

(Des and eng F. D. Manley. Recess)

1948 (15 Nov). *Pan-Pacific Scout Jamboree, Wonga Park.* W **15** (sideways). P 14 × 15.

227	**65**	2½d. lake	20	10

See also No. 254.

Sky retouch (normally unshaded near hill) (Rt pane R.6/8) (No. 228a retouched in 1951)

"Green mist" retouch. A large area to the left of the bird's feathers is recut. (upper plate left pane R.9/3)

1948–56. No wmk. P 15 × 14 or 14 × 15 (9d.).

228	**27**	½d. orange (15.9.49)	20	10
		a. Line to kangaroo's ear	15·00	
		b. Sky retouch	26·00	
		c. Coil pair (1950)	75	2·50
		ca. Line to kangaroo's ear	45·00	
		cb. Sky retouch (in pair)	£130	
		d. Coil block of four (1953)	2·75	
229	**46a**	1½d. green (17.8.49)	1·25	1·25
230	**47**	2d. bright purple (20.12.48)	80	1·75
		aa. Coil pair	3·00	6·50
230*a*	**32**	4d. green (18.8.56)	2·00	1·75
230*b*	**34**	6d. purple-brown (18.8.56)	5·50	80
230*c*	**35**	9d. chocolate (13.12.56)	22·00	3·25
230*d*	**36**	1s. grey-green (13.12.56)	4·00	1·00
		da. "Green mist" retouch	£1100	
228/30*d*		*Set of* 7	32·00	8·75

66 "Henry Lawson" (Sir Lionel Lindsay)

67 Mounted Postman and Convair CV 240 Aircraft

(Des F. D. Manley. Eng. E. R. M. Jones. Recess)

1949 (17 Jun). *Henry Lawson (poet) Commemoration.* P 15 × 14.

231	**66**	2½d. maroon	20	10

(Des Sir Daryl Lindsay and F. D. Manley. Eng F. D. Manley. Recess)

1949 (10 Oct). *75th Anniv of Founding of U.P.U.* P 15 × 14.

232	**67**	3½d. ultramarine	30	60

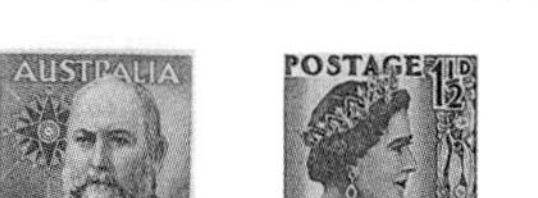

68 John, Lord Forrest of Bunbury

69 Queen Elizabeth

70 King George VI

(Des and eng F. D. Manley. Recess)

1949 (28 Nov). *John, Lord Forrest of Bunbury (explorer and politician) Commemoration.* W **15**. P 15 × 14.

233	**68**	2½d. lake	20	10

(Des and eng F. D. Manley. Recess)

1950 (12 Apr)–**52**.

(a) W **15**. P 15 × 14.

234	**70**	2½d. scarlet (12.4.50)	10	10
235		3d. scarlet (28.2.51)	15	25
		aa. Coil pair (4.51)	17·00	28·00

(b) No wmk.

236	**69**	1½d. green (19.6.50)	40	40
237		2d. yellow-green (28.3.51)	15	10
		a. Coil pair	6·00	9·00
		b. Coil block of four (11.52)	12·00	
237*c*	**70**	2½d. purple-brown (23.5.51)	15	35
237*d*		3d. grey-green (14.11.51)	15	10
		da. Coil pair (12.51)	24·00	30·00
234/7*d*		*Set of* 6	1·00	1·00

On 14 October 1951 No. 235 was placed on sale in sheets of 144 originally intended for use in stamp booklets. These sheets contain 3 panes of 48 (16 × 3) with horizontal gutter margin between.

71 Aborigine

72 Reproduction of First Stamps of New South Wales

73 Reproduction of First Stamps of Victoria

(Des and eng F. D. Manley. Recess)

1950 (14 Aug). W **15**. P 15 × 14.

238	**71**	8½d. brown	15	60

For T **71** in a larger size, see Nos. 253/*b*.

(Des and eng G. Lissenden (T **72**), E. R. M. Jones (T **73**). Recess)

1950 (27 Sep). *Centenary of First Adhesive Postage Stamps in Australia.* P 15 × 14.

239 **72** 2½d. maroon . . . 25 10
a. Horiz pair. Nos. 239/40 . . . 50 70
240 **73** 2½d. maroon . . . 25 10

Nos. 239/40 were printed alternately in vertical columns throughout the sheet.

74 Sir Edmund Barton

75 Sir Henry Parkes

76 "Opening First Federal Parliament" (T. Roberts)

77 Federal Parliament House, Canberra

(Des and eng F. D. Manley. Recess)

1951 (1 May). *50th Anniv of Commonwealth of Australia.* P 15 × 14.

241 **74** 3d. lake . . . 40 10
a. Horiz pair. Nos. 241/2 . . . 2·00 2·50
242 **75** 3d. lake . . . 40 10
243 **76** 5½d. blue . . . 20 2·25
244 **77** 1s.6d. purple-brown . . . 35 50
241/4 *Set of* 4 . . . 2·25 2·75

Nos. 241/2 were printed alternately in vertical columns throughout the sheet.

78 E. H. Hargraves

79 C. J. Latrobe

(Des and eng F. D. Manley. Recess)

1951 (2 Jul). *Centenaries of Discovery of Gold in Australia and of Responsible Government in Victoria.* P 15 × 14.

245 **78** 3d. maroon . . . 30 10
a. Horiz pair. Nos. 245/6 . . . 1·00 1·75
246 **79** 3d. maroon . . . 30 10

Nos. 245/6 were printed alternately in vertical columns throughout the sheet.

80

81 King George VI

82

(Des E. R. M. Jones (7½d.), F. D. Manley (others) Eng. F. D. Manley. Recess)

1951–52. W **15** (sideways on 1s.0½d.). P 14½ (1s.0½d.) or 15 × 14 (others).

247 **80** 3½d. brown-purple (28.11.51) . . . 10 10
a. Imperf between (horiz pair) . . . £7500
248 4½d. scarlet (20.2.52) . . . 15 1·25
249 6½d. brown (20.2.52) . . . 15 70
250 6½d. emerald-green (9.4.52) . . . 10 25
251 **81** 7½d. blue (31.10.51) . . . 15 80
a. Imperf three sides (vert pair) . . . £9500
252 **82** 1s.0½d. indigo (19.3.52) . . . 60 60
247/52 *Set of* 6 . . . 1·10 3·25

No. 251a occurs on the left-hand vertical row of one sheet.

(Des F. D. Manley. Eng E. R. M. Jones. Recess)

1952 (19 Mar)–**65**. P 14½.

(a) W **15** (sideways*).

253 2s.6d. deep brown . . . 1·50 70
aw. Wmk Crown to left of C of A . . . † £850

(b) No wmk.

253*b* 2s.6d. deep brown (30.1.57) . . . 4·00 75
ba. Sepia (10.65) . . . 13·00 13·00

Design:—2s.6d. As T **71** but larger (21 × 25½ mm).

*The normal sideways watermark on No. 253 shows Crown to right of C of A, *as seen from the back of the stamp.*

No. 253*ba* was an emergency printing and can easily be distinguished from No. 253*b* as it is on white Harrison paper, No. 253*b* being on toned paper.

(Des and eng F. D. Manley. Recess)

1952 (19 Nov). *Pan-Pacific Scout Jamboree, Greystanes. As T* **65**, *but inscr* "1952–53". W **15** (sideways). P 14 × 15.

254 3½d. brown-lake . . . 20 10

STAMP BOOKLETS

Illustrations of booklet covers are reduced to ½ size, *unless otherwise stated.*

All booklets from 1913 to 1949 were stapled.

1913 (17 Jan). *Red on pink cover* (SB1) *or blue on pink cover with map of Australia on front and picture of State G.P.O. on back* (SB2).

SB1 2s. booklet containing twelve ½d. and eighteen 1d. (Nos. 1/2) in blocks of 6 . . . £1300
SB2 £1 booklet containing two hundred and forty 1d. (No. 2) in blocks of 30 . . . £13000

1914 (6 Oct)–**18**. *Red on pink cover* (Nos. SB2*a*/3), *black on red cover* (No. SB4) *or blue on pink cover with map of Australia on front and picture of State G.P.O. on back* (No. SB5).

SB2*a* 2s. booklet containing twelve ½d. and eighteen 1d. (Nos. 1, 21c) in blocks of 6 . . . £2000
SB3 2s. booklet containing twelve ½d. and eighteen 1d. (Nos. 20, 21c) in blocks of 6 (1915) . . . £2000
SB4 2s. booklet containing twenty-four 1d. (No. 21c) in blocks of 6 (10.5.17) . . . £2500
a. Black on green cover . . . £2500
b. Red on green cover . . . £2500
SB5 £1 booklet containing two hundred and forty 1d. (No. 21c) in blocks of 30 . . . £13000
a. Back cover without G.P.O. picture (1918)

Records show that a £1 booklet containing one hundred and twenty 2d. stamps was issued in very limited quantities during 1914. No examples are known to have survived.

1919 (Jan–Apr). *Black on pink* (Nos. SB6/7) *or black on green* (*Nos. SB8/9c*) *covers.*

SB6 2s.3d. booklet containing eighteen 1½d. (No. 58) in blocks of 6 . . . £2000
a. Black on green cover . . . £2000
SB7 2s.3d. booklet containing eighteen 1½d. (No. 51) in blocks of 6 . . . £1800
a. Black on green cover . . . £1800
SB8 2s.3d. booklet containing eighteen 1½d. (No. 59) in blocks of 6 (Apr) . . . £1800
a. Black on pink cover . . . £1800
SB9 2s.3d. booklet containing eighteen 1½d. (No. 52) in blocks of 6 (Apr) . . . £1800
a. Black on pink cover
b. Black on blue cover . . . £1800
SB9*c* £1 booklet containing one hundred and sixty 1½d. (No. 51) in blocks of 20 . . . £15000
SB9*d* £1 booklet containing one hundred and sixty 1½d. (No. 52) in blocks of 20 (Apr) . . . £13000

1920 (Dec)–**22**. *Black on blue* (Nos. SB10, SB12), *black on white* (No. SB11) *or black on brown* (No. SB14) *covers.*

SB10 2s. booklet containing twelve 2d. (No. 62) in blocks of 6 . . . £2250
a. Black on pink cover . . . £2250
b. Black on orange cover (3.22) . . . £2750
SB11 2s. booklet containing twelve 2d. (No. 63) in blocks of 6 (3.22) . . . £2250
a. Black on orange cover (7.22) . . . £2750
b. Black on pink cover . . . £2250
c. Brown on buff cover . . . £2250
d. Black on pink cover . . . £2250
SB12 £1 booklet containing one hundred and twenty 2d. (No. 62) in blocks of 15 (1.21) . . . £13000
a. Black on pink cover
SB13 £1 booklet containing ninety 2d. and fifteen 4d. (Nos. 63, 65) in blocks of 15 (3.22)
SB14 £1 booklet containing one hundred and twenty 2d. (No. 63) in blocks of 15 (8.22) . . . £13000

1923 (Oct)–**24**. *Black on rose* (No. SB15), *or green on pale green* (Nos. SB16/18) *covers.*

SB15 2s.3d. booklet containing eighteen 1½d. (No. 61) in blocks of 6 . . . £1600
a. Black on pale green cover . . . £1600
b. Green on pale green cover . . . £1600
SB16 2s.3d. booklet containing eighteen 1½d. (No. 77) in blocks of 6 (5.24) . . . £1600
SB17 £1 booklet containing one hundred and sixty 1½d. (No. 61) in blocks of 20 (3.24) . . . £11000
SB18 £1 booklet containing one hundred and sixty 1½d. (No. 77) in blocks of 20 (5.24) . . . £11000

1927 (Jan–June). *Green on pale green covers.*

SB19 2s.3d. booklet containing eighteen 1½d. (No. 87) in blocks of 6 . . . £950
SB20 2s.3d. booklet containing eighteen 1½d. (No. 96) in blocks of 6 . . . £950
SB21 £1 booklet containing one hundred and sixty 1½d.(No. 96) in blocks of 20 (June) . . . £9000

1927 (9 May). *Opening of Parliament House, Canberra. Green on pale green cover with picture of H.M.S.* Renown *on back (2s.).*

SB22 2s. booklet containing sixteen 1½d. (No. 105) in blocks of 8 . . . 80·00
SB22*a* 10s. booklet containing eighty 1½d. (No. 105) in blocks of 8

Surviving examples of No. SB22*a* are without front cover and have a blank back cover.

1928 (Nov). *Green on pale green cover.*

SB23 2s.3d. booklet containing eighteen 1½d. (No. 96a or 96w) in blocks of 6 . . . £350

1930 (July)–**35**. *Air. Black on blue cover inscr* "AIR MAIL. SAVES TIME" *and biplane.*

SB24 3s. booklet containing twelve 3d. (No. 115) in blocks of 4 plus two panes of air mail labels . . . £700
a. Cover inscr "USE THE AIR MAIL" and monoplane (5.35) . . . £1400
b. Black on pale green cover inscr "USE THE AIR MAIL" (5.35) . . . £950

1930 (9 Sep)–**33**. *Green on pale green covers inscr* "USE THE AIR MAIL" *on the back (2s).*

SB25 2s. booklet containing twelve 2d. (No. 99a or 99aw) in blocks of 6 . . . £300
SB25*a* 2s. booklet containing twelve 2d. (No. 127 or 127w) in blocks of 6 (1.32) . . . £300
ab. Cover with parcel rates on back (1933) . . . £400
SB26 £1 booklet containing one hundred and twenty 2d. (No. 99) in blocks of 20 . . . £6000
SB26*a* £1 booklet containing one hundred and twenty 2d. (No. 99a) in blocks of 20 . . . £6000

1934 (June). *Black on cream cover inscr* "Address your mail fully..." *on front.*

SB26*b* 2s. booklet containing twelve 2d. (No. 127 or 127w) in blocks of 6 . . . £475

1935–38. *Black on green cover with Commonwealth Savings Bank advertisement on front inscr* "WHEREVER THERE IS A MONEY ORDER POST OFFICE".

SB26*c* 2s. booklet containing twelve 2d. (No. 127 or 127w) in blocks of 6 . . . £350
ca. Front cover inscr "IN MOST MONEY ORDER OFFICES" (1936) . . . £325
cb. Ditto with waxed interleaves (1938) . . . £375

1938 (Dec). *Black on green cover as* No. SB26*c*. *Postal rates on interleaves.*

SB27 2s. booklet containing twelve 2d. (No. 184 or 184w) in blocks of 6 . . . £37
a. With waxed interleaves. Postal rates on back cover . . . £47
b. Black on buff cover . . . £47

1942 (Aug). *Black on buff cover, size 73 × 47½ mm. Postal rates on interleaves.*

SB28 2s.6d. booklet containing twelve 2½d. (No. 206 or 206w) in blocks of 6, upright within the booklet . . . £11
a. With waxed interleaves. Postal rates on back cover . . . £20

1949 (Sept). *Black on buff cover, size 79½ × 42½ mm including figure of Hermes.*

SB29 2s.6d. booklet containing twelve 2½d. (No. 206) in blocks of 6, sideways within the booklet . . . 80·0

B 1

1952 (24 June). *Vermilion and deep blue on green cover as Type B* **1**.

SB30 3s.6d. booklet containing twelve 3½d. (No. 247) in blocks of 6 . . . 17·0
a. With waxed interleaves . . . 90·0

POSTAGE DUE STAMPS

POSTAGE DUE PRINTERS. Nos. D1/62 were typographed at the New South Wales Government Printing Office, Sydney. They were not used in Victoria.

D 1

D 2

D 3

Type D **1** adapted from plates of New South Wales Type D No letters at foot.

1902 (1 Jul). *Chalk-surfaced paper.* Wmk Type D **2** (inverted on 1d 3d. and 4d.).

(a) P 11½, 12.

D1 D **1** ½d. emerald-green *or* dull green . . . 3·25 4·
D2 1d. emerald-green . . . 12·00 7·
w. Wmk upright . . . 30·00 20·
D3 2d. emerald-green . . . 35·00 8·
D4 3d. emerald-green . . . 30·00 21·
w. Wmk upright . . . 35·00 25·
D5 4d. emerald-green . . . 42·00 12·
w. Wmk upright . . . 50·00 22·
D6 6d. emerald-green . . . 55·00 9·
w. Wmk inverted . . . 55·00 9·
D7 8d. emerald-green *or* dull green . . . 95·00 75·
D8 5s. emerald-green *or* dull green . . . £180 70·
D1/8 *Set of* 8 . . . £400 £1
D1s/7s Opt "Specimen" *Set of* 7 . . . £275

(b) P 11½, 12, compound with 11.

D 9 D **1** 1d. emerald-green . . . £250 £1
w. Wmk upright . . . £275 £1
D10 2d. emerald-green . . . £350 £1
w. Wmk inverted . . . £375 £1

(c) P 11.

D12 D **1** 1d. emerald-green (*wmk upright*) . . . £1100 £4

Stamps may be found showing portions of the margin watermark "NEW SOUTH WALES POSTAGE".

1902 (July)–**04**. *Type* D **3** *(with space at foot filled in). Chalk-surfaced paper.* Wmk Type D **2** (inverted on 3d., 4d., 6d., 8d. a 5s.).

(a) P 11½, 12.

D13 D **3** 1d. emerald-green (10.02) . . . £180 95·
D14 2d. emerald-green (3.03) . . . — £1
D15 3d. emerald-green (3.03) . . . £225 80·
D17 5d. emerald-green . . . 48·00 9·
D18 10d. emerald-green *or* dull green . . . 75·00 17
D19 1s. emerald-green . . . 55·00 12
D20 2s. emerald-green . . . £100 18

(b) P 11½, 12, compound with 11.

D22 D **3** ½d. emerald-green *or* dull green (3.04) . . . 8·00 7·
w. Wmk inverted . . . 9·00 7·

D23 1d. emerald-green *or* dull grn (10.02) 7·50 2·75
w. Wmk inverted 7·50 2·75
D24 2d. emerald-green *or* dull green (3.03) 22·00 2·75
w. Wmk inverted 22·00 2·75
D25 3d. emerald-green *or* dull green (3.03) 65·00 14·00
w. Wmk upright 85·00 26·00
D26 4d. emerald-green *or* dull green (5.03) 55·00 9·00
w. Wmk upright 55·00 11·00
D27 5d. emerald-green 55·00 20·00
D28 6d. emerald-green (3.04) 55·00 10·00
D29 8d. emerald-green (3.04) £120 50·00
D30 10d. emerald-green *or* dull green 95·00 18·00
D31 1s. emerald-green 85·00 18·00
D32 2s. emerald-green £130 27·00
D33 5s. emerald-green *or* dull green (5.03) £190 22·00

(c) P 11.
D34 D 3 ½d. emerald-green *or* dull green (wmk inverted) (3.04) £250 £160
D35 1d. emerald-green *or* dull green (10.02) 80·00 25·00
w. Wmk inverted 95·00 35·00
D36 2d. emerald-green (3.03) £120 27·00
w. Wmk inverted £120 27·00
D37 3d. emerald-green *or* dull green (3.03) 65·00 35·00
w. Wmk upright 65·00 35·00
D38 4d. emerald-green *or* dull green (5.03) £140 50·00
w. Wmk upright £140 50·00
D39 5d. emerald-green £200 45·00
D40 6d. emerald-green (3.04) 85·00 16·00
D41 1s. emerald-green £250 38·00
D42 5s. emerald-green (5.03) £600 £110
D43 10s. dull green (10.03) £1600 £1400
D44 20s. dull green (10.03) £3500 £2250
D13/44 *Set of* 14 £5500 £3500
D13s/44s *Set of* 14 £850
The 10s. and 20s. values were only issued in South Wales.

D 4

D 6

906 (Jan)–08. *Chalk-surfaced paper.* Wmk Type D 4.

(a) P 11½, 12, compound with 11.
D45 D 3 ½d. green (1.07) 9·50 9·50
w. Wmk inverted 9·50 9·50
D46 1d. green 14·00 3·25
w. Wmk inverted 14·00 3·25
D47 2d. green 32·00 4·75
w. Wmk inverted 32·00 4·75
D48 3d. green (7.08) £500 £250
D49 4d. green (4.07) 60·00 22·00
w. Wmk inverted 60·00 22·00
D50 6d. green (3.08) £180 23·00
w. Wmk inverted £180 23·00
D45/50 *Set of* 6 £700 £275

(b) P 11.
D51 D 3 1d. dull green £1300 £500
aw. Wmk inverted — £500
D51*b* 2d. green † £1200
D52 4d. dull green (4.07) £1900 £1000
No. D51*b* is only known pen-cancelled.
Shades exist.

907 (July–Sept). *Chalk-surfaced paper.* Wmk Type w **11** (Crown over double lined A) (inverted on ½d.). P 11½ × 11.
D53 D 3 ½d. dull green 25·00 60·00
w. Wmk upright 40·00 80·00
D54 1d. dull green (August) 65·00 40·00
w. Wmk inverted 65·00 40·00
D55 2d. dull green (Sept) £110 90·00
w. Wmk inverted £130 90·00
D56 4d. dull green (Sept) £170 85·00
w. Wmk inverted £170 85·00
y. Wmk inverted and reversed £350
D57 6d. dull green (Sept) £200 £110
w. Wmk inverted — £200
D53/7 *Set of* 5 £500 £350

908 (Sept)–09. *Stroke after figure of value. Chalk-surfaced paper.* Wmk Type D 4 (inverted on 10s.).

(a) P 11½ × 11.
D58 D 6 1s. dull green (1909) 75·00 8·50
D59 5s. dull green £225 48·00

(b) P 11.
D60 D 6 2s. dull green (1909) £900 £2000
D61 10s. dull green (1909) £2250 £3000
D62 20s. dull green (1909) £5500 £8000
D58/62 *Set of* 5 £8000 £12000
Nos. D61/2 were only issued in New South Wales.

D 7

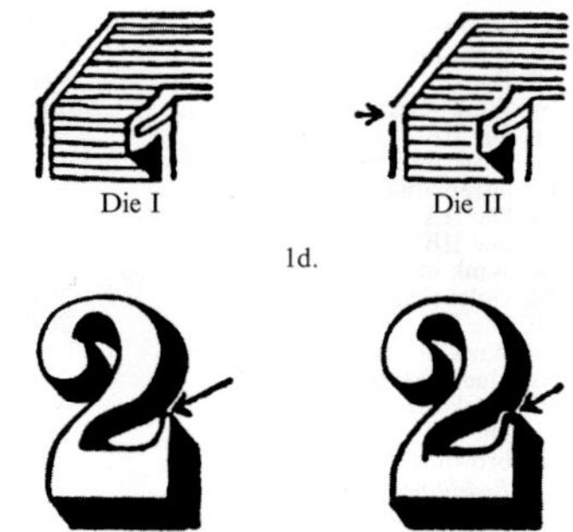

1d.

Die I Die II

2d.

(Typo J. B. Cooke, Melbourne)

1909 (1 Jul)–**10**. Wmk Crown over A, Type w **11**.

(a) P 12 × 12½ (comb).
D63 D 7 ½d. rosine and yellow-green (8.09) 14·00 26·00
D64 1d. rosine and yellow-green (I) 14·00 4·00
b. Die II (7.10) 19·00 1·75
D65 2d. rosine and yellow-green (I) 26·00 3·50
a. Die II (8.10) 25·00 1·75
D66 3d. rosine and yellow-green (9.09) 27·00 13·00
D67 4d. rosine and yellow-green (8.09) 25·00 5·00
D68 6d. rosine and yellow-green (8.09) 27·00 4·00
D69 1s. rosine and yellow-green (8.09) 30·00 3·25
D70 2s. rosine and yellow-green (8.09) 70·00 11·00
D71 5s. rosine and yellow-green (10.09) 90·00 13·00
D72 10s. rosine and yellow-green (11.09) £250 £150
D73 £1 rosine and yellow-green (11.09) £475 £275
D63/73 *Set of* 11 £900 £450

(b) P 11.
D74 D 7 1d. rose and yellow-green (II) £1600 £650
D74*a* 2d. rose and yellow-green (II) £8000 £3000
D75 6d. rose and yellow-green £8500 £4000
Only one unused example, without gum, and another pen-cancelled are known of No. D74*a*.
The 1d. of this printing is distinguishable from No. D78 by the colours, the green being very yellow and the rose having less of a carmine tone. The paper is thicker and slightly toned, that of No D78 being pure white; the gum is thick and yellowish, No. D78 having thin white gum.
All later issues of the 1d. and 2d. are Die II.

(Typo J.B. Cooke (later ptgs by T.S. Harrison))

1912 (Dec)–**23**. *Thin paper. White gum.* W w **11**.

(a) P 12½ (line).
D76 D 7 ½d. scarlet and pale yellow-green (7.13) 23·00 26·00
w. Wmk inverted 38·00 32·00

(b) P 11.
D77 D 7 ½d. rosine & brt apple-green (10.14) 11·00 17·00
a. Wmk sideways 6·50 7·50
D78 1d. rosine & brt apple-green (8.14) 7·50 2·00
a. Wmk sideways 12·00 2·00
w. Wmk inverted 42·00 16·00

(c) P 14.
D79 D 7 ½d. rosine & brt apple-green (11.14) 80·00 £100
a. Carmine & apple-green (Harrison) (1919) 9·00 16·00
D80 1d. rosine & brt apple-green (9.14) 55·00 12·00
a. Scarlet & pale yellow-green (2.18) 20·00 5·00
aw. Wmk inverted † £300
b. Carmine & apple-green (Harrison) (1919) 12·00 3·75
D81 2d. scarlet & pale yellow-green (1.18) 17·00 8·00
a. Carmine & apple-green (Harrison) (10.18) 18·00 3·75
D82 3d. rosine and apple-green (5.16) 75·00 32·00
a. Wmk sideways £3250 £2000
D83 4d. carmine & apple-green (Harrison) (5.21) 90·00 55·00
b. Carmine & pale yellow-grn 65·00 50·00
ba. Wmk sideways £600 £350
D85 1s. scarlet & pale yellow-green (6.23) 25·00 13·00
D86 10s. scarlet & pale yellow-green (5.21) £900
D87 £1 scarlet & pale yellow-green (5.21) £750 £1000

(d) Perf 14 compound with 11.
D88 D 7 1d. carmine and apple-green £4000
D76/88 *Set of* 8 £1700

(Typo T. S. Harrison (to Feb 1926), A. J. Mullett (to June 1927) and J. Ash (thereafter))

1922 (1 May)–**30**. W **6**.

(a) P 14.
D91 D 7 ½d. carmine & yellow-green (17.5.23) 2·50 6·50
D92 1d. carmine and yellow-green 4·00 1·00
D93 1½d. carmine and yellow-green (3.25) 1·50 9·00
D94 2d. carmine & yellow-green (3.3.22) 3·50 2·25
D95 3d. carmine and yellow-green 9·50 3·50
D96 4d. carmine & yellow-green (7.2.22) 35·00 14·00
D97 6d. carmine and yellow-green (8.22) 26·00 13·00

(b) P 11.
D98 D 7 4d. carmine and yellow-green (22.9.30) 6·50 4·50
D91/8 *Set of* 8 75·00 45·00
All values perforated 14 were printed by Harrison and all but the 1d. by Mullett and Ash. The 4d. perforated 11 was produced by J. Ash. There is a wide variation of shades in this issue.

(Typo J. Ash)

1931 (Oct)–**36**. W **15**.

(a) P 14.
D100 D 7 1d. carmine and yellow-green (10.31) 7·00 11·00
a. Imperf between (horiz pair) † £8500
D102 2d. carmine & yellow-grn (19.10.31) 7·00 11·00

(b) P 11.
D105 D 7 ½d. carmine and yellow-green (4.34) 12·00 14·00
D106 1d. carmine & yellow-grn (21.11.32) 7·50 2·00
D107 2d. carmine & yellow-green (1933) 9·00 60
D108 3d. carmine and yellow-green (5.36) 70·00 70·00
D109 4d. carmine & yellow-green (23.5.34) 6·50 2·75
D110 6d. carmine and yellow-green (4.36) £325 £300
D111 1s. carmine and yellow-green (8.34) 48·00 35·00
D105/11 *Set of* 7 £425 £375

D 8

D 9

A

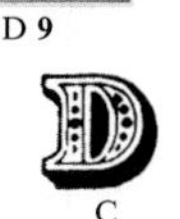
B C

Type A. Solid rectangle inside "D" (ptgs of ½d., 1d., 2d., 4d. and 6d. from 1909 to 1945)
Type B. Shaded area inside "D" (ptgs of 3d. from 1909 to 1945)
Type C. Solid segment of circle inside "D" (ptgs of all values below 1s. from 1946)

D

E

Type D. Six lines of shading above numeral and four below (ptgs of 1s. from 1909 to 1945)
Type E. Larger "1" with only three background lines above; hyphen more upright (ptgs of 1s. from 1946 to 1953)

(Frame recess. Value typo J. Ash to 1940, then W. C. G. McCracken)).

1938 (1 Jul). W **15**. P 14½ × 14.
D112 D 8 ½d. carmine and green (A) (Sept) 3·00 2·75
D113 1d. carmine and green (A) 10·00 60
D114 2d. carmine and green (A) 13·00 1·50
D115 3d. carmine and green (B) (Aug) 32·00 15·00
D116 4d. carmine and green (A) (Aug) 13·00 60
D117 6d. carmine and green (A) (Aug) 70·00 42·00
D118 1s. carmine and green (D) (Aug) 50·00 12·00
D112/18 *Set of* 7 £170 65·00
Shades exist.

1946–57. *Redrawn as Type C and E (1s).* W **15**. P 14½ × 14.
D119 D 9 ½d. carmine and green (9.56) 1·25 3·25
D120 1d. carmine and green (17.6.46) 1·25 80
w. Wmk inverted
D121 2d. carmine and green (9.46) 4·50 1·25
D122 3d. carmine and green (6.8.46) 6·00 1·25
D123 4d. carmine and green (30.7.52) 9·00 2·25
D124 5d. carmine and green (16.12.48) 12·00 3·50
D125 6d. carmine and green (9.47) 11·00 2·00
D126 7d. carmine and green (26.8.53) 4·25 8·50
D127 8d. carmine and green (24.4.57) 10·00 26·00
D128 1s. carmine and green (9.47) 18·00 1·75
D119/28 *Set of* 10 65·00 45·00
There are many shades in this issue.

OFFICIAL STAMPS

From 1902 the departments of the Commonwealth government were issued with stamps of the various Australian States perforated "OS" to denote official use. These were replaced in 1913 by Commonwealth of Australia issues with similar perforated initials as listed below.

During the same period the administrations of the Australian States used their own stamps and those of the Commonwealth perforated with other initials for the same purpose. These States issues are outside the scope of this catalogue.

Most shades listed under the postage issues also exist perforated "OS". Only those which are worth more than the basic colours are included below.

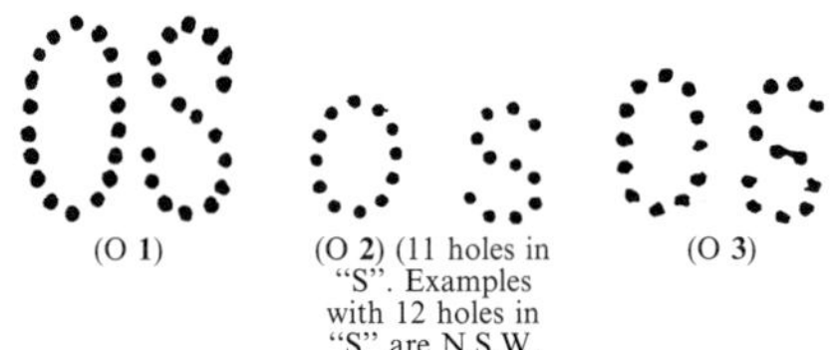

(O 1) (O 2) (11 holes in "S". Examples with 12 holes in "S" are N.S.W. state issues) (O 3)

1913 (Jan–Apr). *Nos. 1/16 punctured as Type* O **1**. W **2**. P 12.

No.	Type	Description	Unused	Used
O 1	**1**	½d. green (Die I)	15·00	8·50
		w. Wmk inverted	†	70·00
O 2		1d. red (Die I)	14·00	3·00
		cw. Wmk inverted	70·00	7·00
		d. Die II	18·00	5·00
		da. Wmk sideways	†	£400
		dw. Wmk inverted	70·00	7·00
O 3		2d. grey (Die I)	27·00	11·00
O 4		2½d. indigo (Die II)	£250	£110
O 5		3d. olive (Die I)	90·00	40·00
		ca. In pair with Die II	£650	
		dw. Wmk inverted	£100	45·00
		e. Die II	£275	70·00
		ew. Wmk inverted	£350	80·00
O 6		4d. orange (Die II)	£140	19·00
		a. Orange-yellow	£200	80·00
O 7		5d. chestnut (Die II)	£120	28·00
O 8		6d. ultramarine (Die II)	90·00	17·00
		w. Wmk inverted	£200	70·00
O 9		9d. violet (Die II)	£110	42·00
		w. Wmk inverted	†	£2750
O10		1s. emerald (Die II)	£140	25·00
		w. Wmk inverted	£425	£130
O11		2s. brown (Die II)	£250	£110
		a. Double print	†	£1500
O12		5s. grey and yellow	£600	£350
O13		10s. grey and pink	£1800	£1100
O14		£1 brown and ultramarine	£2750	£2000
O15		£2 black and rose	£5000	£3000
O1/15 *Set of* 15			£10000	£6000

1914. *Nos. 1/16 punctured as Type* O **2**. W **2**. P 12.

No.	Type	Description	Unused	Used
O16	**1**	½d. green (Die I)	12·00	9·00
		w. Wmk inverted	†	42·00
O17		1d. red (Die I)	14·00	5·50
		d. Die II	22·00	3·00
		e. Die IIA	16·00	2·25
O18		2d. grey (Die I)	50·00	4·50
		w. Wmk inverted	80·00	12·00
O19		2½d. indigo (Die II)	£250	£100
O20		3d. olive (Die I)	70·00	6·00
		dw. Wmk inverted		
		e. Die II	£180	45·00
		ew. Wmk inverted	£275	70·00
O21		4d. orange (Die II)	£150	70·00
		a. Orange-yellow	£200	90·00
O22		5d. chestnut (Die II)	£120	42·00
O23		6d. ultramarine (Die II)	75·00	12·00
		w. Wmk inverted	£180	65·00
O24		9d. violet (Die II)	75·00	23·00
O25		1s. emerald (Die II)	80·00	20·00
O26		2s. brown (Die II)	£200	85·00
O27		5s. grey and yellow	£950	£500
O28		10s. grey and pink	£2000	£1200
O29		£1 brown and ultramarine	£3250	£2000
O30		£2 black and rose	£5500	£3250
O16/30 *Set of* 15			£11000	£6500

1915. *Nos. 24 and 26/30 punctured as Type* O **2**. W **5**. P 12.

No.	Type	Description	Unused	Used
O31	**1**	2d. grey (Die I)	80·00	11·00
O33		6d. ultramarine (Die II)	£130	15·00
		b. Die IIA	£1400	£400
O34		9d. violet (Die II)	£180	65·00
O35		1s. blue-green (Die II)	£180	40·00
O36		2s. brown (Die II)	£550	95·00
O37		5s. grey and yellow	£700	£130
		a. Yellow portion doubly printed	†	£2250
		w. Wmk inverted	£800	£160

1914–21. *Nos. 20/3 punctured as Type* O **2**. W **5**. P 14¼ × 14 (comb).

No.	Type	Description	Unused	Used
O38	**5a**	½d. bright green	10·00	2·75
		a. Perf 14¼ (line)	†	—
		w. Wmk inverted	16·00	6·50
O39		1d. carmine-red (I) (No. 21c)	11·00	80
		gw. Wmk inverted	17·00	2·50
		h. Die II	£300	14·00
O41		4d. orange	40·00	3·50
		a. Yellow-orange	55·00	7·50
		b. Pale orange-yellow	95·00	15·00
		c. Lemon-yellow	£225	48·00
		w. Wmk inverted	50·00	17·00
O42		5d. brown (P 14¼ (line))	50·00	3·25
		aw. Wmk inverted	£140	45·00
		b. Printed on the gummed side (wmk inverted)	£1500	
		c. Perf 14¼ × 14 (comb)	50·00	3·25
		cw. Wmk inverted	£120	30·00

1915–28. *Nos. 35/45 punctured as Type* O **2**. W **6**. P 12.

No.	Type	Description	Unused	Used
O43	**1**	2d. grey (Die I)	19·00	5·00
		bw. Wmk inverted	23·00	7·50
		d. Die IIA	30·00	15·00
		da. Printed double	†	—
O44		2½d. deep blue (Die II)	48·00	12·00
		w. Wmk inverted	†	24·00
O45		3d. yellow-olive (Die I)	24·00	4·25
		cw. Wmk inverted	28·00	7·50
		d. Die II	90·00	42·00
		dw. Wmk inverted	£130	60·00
		e. Die IIB	24·00	14·00
		ew. Wmk inverted	38·00	16·00
O46		6d. ultramarine (Die II)	35·00	5·00
		a. Die IIA	£1100	£350
		d. Die IIB	48·00	14·00
		dw. Wmk inverted	65·00	19·00
O47		9d. violet (Die II)	26·00	12·00
		b. Die IIB	26·00	12·00
		bw. Wmk inverted	†	17·00
O48		1s. blue-green (Die II)	23·00	2·50
		aw. Wmk inverted	60·00	15·00
		b. Die IIB	23·00	3·50
O49		2s. brown (Die II)	£110	15·00
		b. Red-brown (aniline)	£300	60·00
		w. Wmk inverted	£375	£180
O50		5s. grey and yellow	£170	45·00
		w. Wmk inverted	£400	£170
O51		10s. grey and pink	£400	60·00
O52		£1 chocolate and dull blue	£2000	£1200
		ab. Wmk sideways. *Chestnut & brt blue*	†	£8000
		aw. Wmk inverted	£2500	£1700
O53		£2 black and rose	£2000	£850
O43/53 *Set of* 11			£4250	£2000

1916–20. *Nos. 47f and 5d. as No. 23 punctured as Type* O **2**. *Rough paper*. W **5**. P 14.

No.	Type	Description	Unused	Used
O54	**5a**	1d. scarlet (Die I)	21·00	6·00
		a. Deep red	21·00	6·00
		b. Rose-red	21·00	6·00
		c. Rosine	60·00	12·00
		dw. Wmk inverted	25·00	8·00
		e. Die II. *Rose-red*	£225	14·00
		f. Die II. *Rosine*	£425	40·00
		fw. Wmk inverted		
O60		5d. bright chestnut (9.20)	£1400	£120

All examples of the 5d. on this paper were perforated "OS".

1918–20. *Nos. 48/52 punctured as Type* O **2**. W **6***a*. P 14.

No.	Type	Description	Unused	Used
O61	**5a**	½d. green	15·00	2·00
		w. Wmk inverted	20·00	9·00
O62		1d. carmine-pink (I)	†	—
O63		1d. carmine (I)	£100	38·00
O64		1½d. black-brown	18·00	2·50
		a. Very thin paper	55·00	22·00
		w. Wmk inverted	48·00	10·00
O65		1½d. red-brown	22·00	2·25
		w. Wmk inverted	40·00	9·00
O61/5 *Set of* 4			£120	40·00

1918–23. *Nos. 56/9 and 61/6 punctured as Type* O **2**. W **5**. P 14.

No.	Type	Description	Unused	Used
O66	**5a**	½d. orange	16·00	10·00
O67		1d. violet	23·00	13·00
		w. Wmk inverted	†	£4500
O68		1½d. black-brown	25·00	2·75
		w. Wmk inverted	38·00	7·00
O69		1½d. deep red-brown	21·00	2·00
		aw. Wmk inverted	35·00	7·00
O69*b*		1½d. bright red-brown	†	—
O70		1½d. green	14·00	1·25
O71		2d. brown-orange	13·00	1·25
		w. Wmk inverted	£150	40·00
O72		2d. bright rose-scarlet	17·00	4·00
		w. Wmk inverted	£150	40·00
O73		4d. violet	42·00	13·00
O74		4d. ultramarine	60·00	11·00
O75		1s.4d. pale blue	50·00	17·00
		b. Deep turquoise	£1000	£650
O66/75 *Set of* 10			£250	65·00

1923–24. *Nos. 73/5 punctured as Type* O **2**. W **6**. P 12.

No.	Type	Description	Unused	Used
O76	**1**	6d. chestnut (Die IIB)	22·00	2·50
O77		2s. maroon (Die II)	55·00	12·00
O78		£1 grey (Die IIB)	£650	£350
O76/8 *Set of* 3			£700	£350

1924. *Nos. 76/84 punctured as Type* O **2**. P 14.

(a) W **5**.

No.	Type	Description	Unused	Used
O79	**5a**	1d. sage-green	7·50	2·25
O80		1½d. scarlet	6·50	60
		w. Wmk inverted	60·00	10·00
		wa. Printed on the gummed side	£225	
O81		2d. red-brown	20·00	15·00
		a. Bright red-brown	35·00	21·00
O82		3d. dull ultramarine	32·00	6·00
O83		4d. olive-yellow	40·00	6·00
O84		4½d. violet	70·00	12·00
		w. Wmk inverted	†	£3250

(b) W **6***a*.

No.	Type	Description	Unused	Used
O85	**5a**	1d. sage-green	15·00	15·00

(c) No wmk.

No.	Type	Description	Unused	Used
O86		1d. sage-green	70·00	65·00
O87		1½d. scarlet	75·00	65·00
O79/87 *Set of* 9			£300	£170

1926–30. *Nos. 85/104 punctured as Type* O **2**. W **7**.

(a) P 14.

No.	Type	Description	Unused	Used
O88	**5a**	½d. orange	£170	75·00
O89		1d. sage-green	10·00	1·25
O90		1½d. scarlet	21·00	2·00
		a. Golden scarlet	23·00	4·50
		w. Wmk inverted	23·00	3·50
O92		2d. red-brown (Die I)	£120	40·00
O93		3d. dull ultramarine	60·00	13·00
		w. Wmk inverted	60·00	13·00
O94		4d. yellow-olive	£130	38·00
O95		4½d. violet	£130	35·00
O96		1s.4d. pale greenish blue	£300	£120
O88/96 *Set of* 8			£850	£300

(b) P 13½ × 12½.

No.	Type	Description	Unused	Used
O 97	**5a**	½d. orange	4·00	1·25
O 98		1d. sage-green (Die I)	4·00	1·25
		b. Die II	95·00	£120
O100		1½d. scarlet	7·50	2·00
		a. Golden scarlet	4·75	2·25
		w. Wmk inverted	6·50	2·75
O102		1½d. red-brown	16·00	3·75
O103		2d. red-brown (Die II)	26·00	14·00
O104		2d. golden scarlet (Die II)	16·00	3·75
		a. Die III	13·00	2·75
		aw. Wmk inverted	20·00	7·00
O106		3d. dull ultramarine (Die I)	28·00	5·00
		aw. Wmk inverted	40·00	20·00
		b. Die II. *Deep ultramarine*	14·00	1·50
		bw. Wmk inverted	£4500	£2750
O108		4d. yellow-olive	22·00	3·75
O109		4½d. violet	£100	£100
O110		5d. orange-brown (Die II)	50·00	7·00
O111		1s.4d. turquoise	£225	24·00
O97/111 *Set of* 11			£425	£140

1927 (9 May). *Opening of Parliament House, Canberra. No. 105 punctured as Type* O **3**.

No.	Type	Description	Unused	Used
O112	**8**	1½d. brownish lake	15·00	7·50

1928 (29 Oct). *National Stamp Exhibition, Melbourne. No. 106 punctured as Type* O **2**.

No.	Type	Description	Unused	Used
O113		3d. blue	13·00	9·00

1929–30. *Nos. 107/14 punctured as Type* O **2**. W **7**. P 12.

No.	Type	Description	Unused	Used
O114	**1**	6d. chestnut (Die IIB)	23·00	4·00
O115		9d. violet (Die IIB)	42·00	5·50
O116		1s. blue-green (Die IIB)	23·00	4·00
O117		2s. maroon (Die II)	65·00	8·00
O118		5s. grey and yellow	£200	40·00
O118*a*		10s. grey and pink	£1700	
O118*b*		£2 black and rose	£3250	

1929 (20 May). *Air. No. 115 punctured as Type* O **3**.

No.	Type	Description	Unused	Used
O119	**9**	3d. green	23·00	12·00

1929 (28 Sep). *Centenary of Western Australia. No. 116 punctured as Type* O **3**.

No.	Type	Description	Unused	Used
O120	**10**	1½d. dull scarlet	15·00	10·00

1930 (2 Jun). *Centenary of Exploration of River Murray by Capt Sturt. Nos. 117/18 punctured as Type* O **2**.

No.	Type	Description	Unused	Used
O121	**11**	1½d. scarlet	10·00	7·00
O122		3d. blue	14·00	8·00

OS

(O **4**)

1931 (4 May). *Nos. 121/2 optd with Type* O **4**.

No.	Type	Description	Unused	Used
O123	**13**	2d. rose-red	55·00	18·0
O124		3d. blue	£200	32·0

For No. 139 overprinted with Type O **4**, see No. 139*a*.

1932 (Feb)–**33**. *Optd as Type* O **4**.

(a) W **7**.

(i) P 13½ × 12½.

No.	Type	Description	Unused	Used
O125	**5a**	2d. golden scarlet (Die III)	10·00	1·5
		a. Opt inverted	†	£450
		w. Wmk inverted	£2000	£150
O126		4d. yellow-olive (3.32)	16·00	3·7

(ii) P 12.

No.	Type	Description	Unused	Used
O127	**1**	6d. chestnut (3.32)	45·00	50·0

(b) W **15**.

(i) P 13½ × 12½.

No.	Type	Description	Unused	Used
O128	**5a**	½d. orange (11.7.32)	4·75	1·5
		a. Opt inverted	£5000	£300
O129		1d. green (3.32)	3·25	4
		w. Wmk inverted	£400	£20
		x. Wmk reversed	£650	£30
O130		2d. golden scarlet (Die III)	9·00	5
		a. Opt inverted	†	£475
O131		3d. ultramarine (Die II) (2.33)	7·50	4·0
O132		5d. orange-brown (7.32)	35·00	27·0

(ii) P 12.

No.	Type	Description	Unused	Used
O133	**1**	6d. chestnut (9.32)	22·00	20·0
		a. Opt inverted	†	£1000

(c) Recess. No wmk. P 11.

No.	Type	Description	Unused	Used
O134	**18**	2d. scarlet (3.32)	5·00	2·0
O135		3d. blue (3.32)	14·00	5·0
O136	**17**	1s. green (3.32)	40·00	27·0

No. O128a and probably the other inverted overprints we caused by the insertion of a stamp upside down into sheets repair before surcharging.

Issue of overprinted official stamps ceased in February 1933 and thereafter mail from the federal administration was carried free.

BRITISH COMMONWEALTH OCCUPATION FORCE (JAPAN)

Nos. J1/7 were used by the Australian forces occupying Japan after the Second World War. Initially their military post office supplied unoverprinted Australian stamps, but it was decided to introduce the overprinted issue to prevent currency speculation.

B.C.O.F.
JAPAN
1946

(**1**)

B.C.O.F.
JAPAN
1946

(**2**)

1946 — O.F. AN — O.F. AN

Wrong fount "6" (left pane R. 9/4) — Normal — Narrow "N" (right pane R. 1/8)

1946 (11 Oct)–**48**. *Stamps of Australia optd as T1 (1d., 3d.,) or T2 (others) at Hiroshima Printing Co, Japan.*

J1 **27** ½d. orange (No. 179) 3·75 6·00
a. Wrong fount "6" 90·00 £110
b. Narrow "N" 90·00 £110
c. Stop after "JAPAN" (right pane R.5/5) 90·00 £110
J2 **46** 1d. brown-purple (No. 203) 3·00 3·00
a. Blue-black overprint 55·00 95·00
J3 **31** 3d. purple-brown (No. 187) 2·50 2·50
a. Opt double £600
J4 **34** 6d. purple-brown (No. 189*a*) (8.5.47) 16·00 11·00
a. Wrong fount "6" £200 £180
b. Stop after "JAPAN" (right pane R. 5/5) £200 £180
c. Narrow "N" £200 £180
J5 **36** 1s. grey-green (No. 191) (8.5.47) 16·00 13·00
a. Wrong fount "6" £250 £200
b. Stop after "JAPAN" (right pane R. 5/5) £250 £200
c. Narrow "N" £250 £200
J6 **1** 2s. maroon (No. 212) (8.5.47) 42·00 50·00
J7 **38** 5s. claret (No. 176) (8.5.47) 95·00 £130
a. Thin rough paper (No. 176a) 80·00 £130
J1/7 *Set of* 7 £140 £190

The ½d., 1d. and 3d. values were first issued on 11 October 1946, and withdrawn two days later, but were re-issued together with the other values on 8 May 1947.

The following values with T **2** in the colours given were from proof sheets which, however, were used for postage: ½d. (red) 1d. (red or black) and 3d. (gold, red or black). (*Prices for black opts* £100, *each, and for red or gold from* £300 each, *all un*).

The use of B.C.O.F. stamps ceased on 12 February 1949.

NAURU

Stamps of MARSHALL ISLANDS were used in Nauru from the opening of the German Colonial Post Office on 14 July 1908 until 8 September 1914.

Following the occupation by Australian forces on 6 November 1914 the "N.W. PACIFIC ISLANDS" overprints on Australia (see NEW GUINEA) were used from 2 January 1915.

PRICES FOR STAMPS ON COVER TO 1945

Nos.	1/12	*from* × 10
Nos.	13/16	*from* × 4
Nos.	17/25	—
Nos.	26/39	*from* × 6
Nos.	40/3	*from* × 10
Nos.	44/7	*from* × 15

BRITISH MANDATE

NAURU (1) — NAURU (2) — NAURU (3)

916 (2 Sept)–**23**. *Stamps of Great Britain (1912–22) over-printed at Somerset House.*

(a) With T **1** *(12½ mm long) at foot.*

1 ½d. yellow-green 2·25 7·50
a. "NAUP.U" £375
b. Double opt, one albino 60·00
2 1d. bright scarlet 1·75 6·00
a. "NAUP.U" £650
2*b* 1d. carmine-red 12·00
bb. Double opt, one albino £225
3 1½d. red-brown (1923) 55·00 80·00
4 2d. orange (Die I) 2·00 13·00
a. "NAUP.U" £375 £500
b. Double opt, one albino £110
c. Triple opt, two albino
y. Wmk inverted and reversed £110
5 2d. orange (Die II) (1923) 70·00 £100
6 2½d. blue 2·75 7·00
a. "NAUP.U" £425 £550
b. Double opt, one albino £225
7 3d. bluish violet 2·00 4·00
a. "NAUP.U" £450 £600
b. Double opt, one albino £275
8 4d. slate-green 2·00 8·50
a. "NAUP.U" £600 £800
b. Double opt, one albino £225
9 5d. yellow-brown 2·25 9·50
a. "NAUP.U" £1000
b. Double opt, one albino £150
0 6d. purple (*chalk-surfaced paper*) 4·00 10·00
a. "NAUP.U" £900
b. Double opt, one albino £275
1 9d. agate 8·50 23·00
a. Double opt, one albino £275
2 1s. bistre-brown 7·00 19·00
a. Double opt, one albino £325
s. Optd "Specimen" £130
/12 *Set of* 11 80·00 £170

(b) With T **2** *(13½ mm long) at centre (1923).*

3 ½d. green 4·50 42·00
4 1d. scarlet 19·00 32·00
5 1½d. red-brown 24·00 42·00
a. Double opt, one albino £160
6 2d. orange (Die II) 30·00 60·00
3/16 *Set of* 4 70·00 £160

The "NAUP.U" errors occur on R.6/2 from Control I 16 only. he ink used on this batch of overprints was shiny jet-black.

There is a constant variety consisting of short left stroke to "N" which occurs at R. 1/8 on Nos. 1, 2, 2*b*, 4 (£30 *each*); 3 (£175); 5 (£200); 6, 7 (£40 *each*); 8, 9, 10 (£60 *each*); 11, 12 (£85 *each*). All unused prices.

(c) With T **3**.

(i) Waterlow printing.

17 5s. rose-carmine £2250 £1600
s. Optd "Specimen" £1500
18 10s. indigo-blue (R.) £7000 £4750
a. Double opt, one albino £8000 £7000
s. Optd "Specimen" £1000

(ii) De La Rue printing.

19 2s.6d. sepia-brown (*shades*) £600 £700
a. Double opt, one albino £1300
b. Treble opt, two albino £1400
s. Optd "Specimen" £275
20 2s.6d. yellow-brown (*shades*) 65·00 £100
21 2s.6d. brown (*shades*) 70·00 95·00
a. Re-entry (R. 2/1)
22 5s. bright carmine (*shades*) £100 £140
a. Treble opt, two albino £650
s. Optd "Specimen" £250
23 10s. pale blue (R.) £250 £325
a. Treble opt (Blk.+R.+albino) £2250
b. Double opt, one albino £900
23*c* 10s. deep bright blue (R.) £500 £550

(iii) Bradbury, Wilkinson printing (1919).

24 2s.6d. chocolate-brown 85·00 £130
b. Double opt, one albino £375
25 2s.6d. pale brown 75·00 £110
a. Double opt, one albino £350

The initial printing of the 2s.6d. to 10s. values, made in Sept 1915 but not known to have been issued before 2 Sept 1916, comprised 1½ sheets each of the 2s.6d. (No. 19) and 10s. (No. 18) and 3 sheets of the 5s. (No. 17), as well as the supply of "Specimens", where the 5s. value was mostly from the De La Rue printing (No. 22).

The original supply of the 2s.6d. value (No. 19) included distinct shade variants, covered by "sepia-brown (*shades*)". The "Specimens" are mostly in a deeper shade than the issued stamp. One half-sheet of 20 was quite deep, and only appears to exist cancelled "SE 2 16", apart from a mint block of 4 in the Royal Collection. The full sheet of 40 was in a slightly paler shade and included 12 double, one albino and 8 treble, two albino varieties. A few sheets in sepia-brown shades were also included in later supplies of the 2s.6d. value, but these were mostly in shades of yellow-brown (No. 20) and brown (No. 21).

Examples of most values between Nos. 1 and 25 are known showing a forged P.O. Pleasant Island postmark dated "NO 2 21".

AUSTRALIAN MANDATE

4 *Century* (freighter)

(Des R. A. Harrison. Eng T. S. Harrison. Recess Note Printing Branch of the Treasury, Melbourne and from 1926 by the Commonwealth Bank of Australia)

1924–48. No wmk. P 11.

A. Rough surfaced, greyish paper (1924–34).

26A **4** ½d. chestnut 1·75 2·75
27A 1d. green 3·50 2·75
28A 1½d. scarlet 4·00 4·00
29A 2d. orange 4·00 11·00
30A 2½d. slate-blue 6·00 25·00
c. *Greenish blue* (1934) 8·00 17·00
31A 3d. pale blue 4·00 13·00
32A 4d. olive-green 7·50 18·00
33A 5d. brown 4·25 7·00
34A 6d. dull violet 4·75 12·00
35A 9d. olive-brown 9·50 19·00
36A 1s. brown-lake 6·50 13·00
37A 2s.6d. grey-green 28·00 50·00
38A 5s. claret 50·00 £100
39A 10s. yellow £130 £180
26A/39A *Set of* 14 £225 £400

B. Shiny surfaced, white paper (1937–48).

26B **4** ½d. chestnut 6·50 13·00
c. Perf 14 (1947) 1·40 10·00
27B 1d. green 2·50 3·00
28B 1½d. scarlet 1·00 1·50
29B 2d. orange 2·25 8·00
30dB 2½d. dull blue (1948) 3·00 4·00
da. Imperf between (vert pair) £5500 £5500
db. Imperf between (horiz pair) £5500 £5500
31cB 3d. greenish grey (1947) 3·50 13·00
32B 4d. olive-green 4·25 13·00
33B 5d. brown 4·00 4·00
34B 6d. dull violet 4·00 5·00
35B 9d. olive-brown 7·50 21·00
36B 1s. brown-lake 6·50 2·75
37B 2s.6d. grey-green 28·00 35·00
38B 5s. claret 38·00 50·00
39B 10s. yellow 95·00 £120
26B/39B *Set of* 14 £180 £250

HIS MAJESTY'S JUBILEE. 1910 - 1935 (5) — **6**

1935 (12 July). *Silver Jubilee. T* **4** *(shiny surfaced, white paper) optd with T* **5**.

40 1½d. scarlet 75 80
41 2d. orange 1·50 4·25
42 2½d. dull blue 1·50 1·50
43 1s. brown-lake 5·00 3·50
40/3 *Set of* 4 8·00 9·00

(Recess John Ash, Melbourne)

1937 (10 May). *Coronation*. P 11.

44 **6** 1½d. scarlet 45 1·75
45 2d. orange 45 2·75
46 2½d. blue 45 1·75
47 1s. purple 65 1·75
44/7 *Set of* 4 1·75 7·25

Japanese forces invaded Nauru on 26 August 1942 and virtually all the inhabitants were removed to Truk in the Caroline Islands.

The Australian army liberated Nauru on 13 September 1945. After an initial period without stamps Australian issues were supplied during October 1945 and were used from Nauru until further supplies of Nos. 26/39 became available. The deportees did not return until early in 1946.

NEW GUINEA

Stamps of Germany and later of GERMAN NEW GUINEA were used in New Guinea from 1888 until 1914.

During the interim period between the "G.R.I." surcharges and the "N.W. PACIFIC ISLANDS" overprints, stamps of AUSTRALIA perforated "OS" were utilised.

PRICES FOR STAMPS ON COVER

Nos.	1/30	*from* × 3
Nos.	31/2	—
Nos.	33/49	*from* × 3
Nos.	50/9	*from* × 2
Nos.	60/2	—
Nos.	63/4	*from* × 2
Nos.	64*c*/*q*	—
Nos.	65/81	*from* × 5
Nos.	83/5	—
Nos.	86/97	*from* × 5
No.	99	—
Nos.	100/16	*from* × 4
Nos.	117/18	—
Nos.	119/24	*from* × 4
Nos.	125/203	*from* × 2
Nos.	204/5	—
Nos.	206/11	*from* × 8
Nos.	212/25	*from* × 2
Nos.	O1/33	*from* × 8

AUSTRALIAN OCCUPATION

Stamps of German New Guinea surcharged

G.R.I. 2d. (1) — G.R.I. 1s. (2) — 1 (3)

SETTINGS. The "G.R.I" issues of New Guinea were surcharged on a small hand press which could only accommodate one horizontal row of stamps at a time. In addition to complete sheets the surcharges were also applied to multiples and individual stamps which were first lightly affixed to plain paper backing sheets. Such backing sheets could contain a mixture of denominations, some of which required different surcharges.

Specialists recognise twelve settings of the low value surcharges (1d. to 8d.):

Setting 1 (Nos. 1/4 7/11) shows the bottom of the "R" 6 mm from the top of the "d"

Setting 2 (Nos. 16/19, 22/6) shows the bottom of the "R" 5 mm from the top of the "d"

Setting 3 was used for the Official stamps (Nos. O1/2)

Setting 4, which included the 2½d. value for the first time, and Setting 5 showed individual stamps with either 6 mm or 5 mm spacing.

These five settings were for rows of ten stamps, but the remaining seven, used on odd stamps handed in for surcharging, were applied as strips of five only. One has, so far, not been reconstructed, but of the remainder three show the 6 mm spacing, two the 5 mm and one both.

On the shilling values the surcharges were applied as horizontal rows of four and the various settings divide into two groups, one with 3½ to 4½ mm between the bottom of the "R" and the top of numeral, and the second with 5½ mm between the "R" and numeral. The first group includes the very rare initial setting on which the space is 4 to 4½ mm.

G.R.I, 2d. "1" for "I" (Setting 1) — G.R.I. 1d. Short "1" (Setting 1) — G.R.I. 1s. Large "S" (Setting 1)

1914 (17 Oct)–**15**. *Stamps of 1901 surch.*

(a) As T **1**. *"G.R.I." and value 6 mm apart.*

1 1d.on 3pf. brown £400 £450
a. "1" for "I" £950
b. Short "1" £950
c. "1" with straight top serif (Setting 6) £950
d. "I" for "1" (Setting 12) £1200
2 1d.on 5pf. green 45·00 65·00
a. "1" for "I" £200 £275
b. Short "1" £200 £275
c. "1" with straight top serif (Settings 6 and 9) £325 £375
3 2d.on 10pf. carmine 50·00 80·00
a. "1" for "I" £250 £325
4 2d.on 20pf. ultramarine 50·00 60·00
a. "1" for "I" £225 £275
e. Surch double, one "G.R.I." albino £2500
f. Surch inverted £5500
5 2½d.on 10pf. carmine (27.2.15) 65·00 £140
a. Fraction bar omitted (Setting 9) £1200 £1300

6 2½d.on 20pf. ultramarine (27.2.15) . . . . . 75·00 £150
a. Fraction bar omitted (Setting 9) . . .
7 3d.on 25pf. black and red/*yellow* £190 £275
a. "1" for "I" £700 £800
8 3d.on 30pf. black and orange/*buff* £250 £300
a. "1" for "I" £750
e. Surch double £5000 £4750
9 4d.on 40pf. black and carmine £250 £325
a. "1" for "I" £850
e. Surch double £1200 £1700
f. Surch inverted £5500
10 5d.on 50pf. black and purple/*buff* £450 £700
a. "1" for "I" £1300 £1600
e. Surch double £5500
11 8d.on 80pf. black and carmine/*rose* £650 £900
a. "1" for "I" £1800 £2250
d. No stop after "d" £2250
e. Error. Surch "G.R.I. 4d." £4500

(b) As T **2**. *"G.R.I." and value 3½ to 4 mm apart.*

12 1s.on 1m. carmine £1600 £2250
a. Large "s" £4750 £4750
13 2s.on 2m. blue £1700 £2500
a. Large "s" £4500 £6000
c. Error. Surch "G.R.I. 5s." £16000
d. Error. Surch "G.R.I. 2d." corrected by handstamped "S" £16000
14 3s.on 3m. violet-black £3250 £4250
a. Large "s" £6000
b. No stop after "I" (Setting 3) £6500 £6500
15 5s.on 5m. carmine and black £7000 £8500
a. Large "s" £14000
b. No stop after "I" (Setting 3) £9500 £12000
c. Error. Surch "G.R.I. 1s." £22000

G.R.I.

3d.

Thick "3" (Setting 2)

G.R.I.

5d.

Thin "5" (Setting 2)

1914 (16 Dec)–**15**. *Stamps of 1901 surch.*

(a) As T **1**. *"G.R.I." and value 5 mm apart.*

16 1d.on 3pf. brown . . . . 45·00 55·00
a. "I" for "1" (Setting 11) £425
b. Short "1" (Setting 2) £200
c. "1" with straight top serif (Settings 2 and 6) . . . . 75·00 90·00
e. Surch double £475 £700
f. Surch double, one inverted £2000
g. Surch inverted £1200 £1600
h. Error. Surch "G.R.I. 4d." £5000
17 1d.on 5pf. green . . . . 18·00 30·00
b. Short "1" (Setting 2) £110 £160
c. "1" with straight top serif (Setting 2) . . . . 35·00 60·00
e. "d" inverted . . . . † £1000
f. "1d" inverted . . . . † £3500
g. "G.R.I." without stops or spaces . . . £3500
ga. "G.R.I." without stops, but with normal spaces . . . . — £3500
h. "G.I.R." instead of "G.R.I." £4750 £5000
i. Surch double £1300
18 2d.on 10pf. carmine . . . . 24·00 40·00
e. No stop after "d" (Setting 2) £130 £180
f. Stop before, instead of after, "G" (Settings 4 and 5) £3500
g. Surch double £5500 £5500
h. Surch double, one inverted . . . . . . — £3500
i. In vert pair with No. 20 . . . . . . £13000
j. In horiz pair with No. 20 . . . . . . £13000
k. Error. Surch ".GR.I. 1d." £4000 £3500
l. Error. Surch "G.I.R. 3d." £5000
19 2d.on 20pf. ultramarine . . . . 28·00 45·00
e. No stop after "d" (Setting 2) . . . . . 95·00 £130
f. No stop after "I" (Setting 11) £800
g. "R" inverted (Settings 4 and 5) . . . . — £3500
h. Surch double £1000 £1700
i. Surch double, one inverted £1600 £1900
j. Surch inverted £3500 £4000
k. Albino surch (in horiz pair with normal) £9500
l. In vert pair with No. 21 . . . . £8500 £10000
m. Error. Surch "G.R.I. 1d." £5500 £5500
20 2½d.on 10pf. carmine (27.2.15) £160 £250
21 2½d.on 20pf. ultramarine (27.2.15) £1500 £1800
a. Error. Surch "G.R.I. 3d." (in vert pair with normal) £21000
22 3d.on 25pf. black and red/*yellow* £110 £150
e. Thick "3" £500
f. Surch double £4000 £4750
g. Surch inverted £4000 £4750
h. Surch omitted (in horiz pair with normal) £9500
i. Error. Surch "G.R.I. 1d." £9000
23 3d.on 30pf. black and orange/*buff* . . . . 90·00 £130
e. No stop after "d" (Setting 2) £550
f. Thick "3" £475
g. Surch double £1200 £1700
h. Surch double, one inverted £1500 £1900
i. Surch double, both inverted £4000 £4750
j. Surch inverted £3500
k. Albino surch £6000
l. Surch omitted (in vert pair with normal) £5000
m. Error. Surch "G.R.I. 1d." £4000 £5000
24 4d.on 40pf. black and carmine £100 £160
e. Surch double £1000
f. Surch double, one inverted £1900
g. Surch double, both inverted £4500
h. Surch inverted £2500
i. Error. Surch "G.R.I. 1d." £2500
ia. Surch "G.R.I. 1d." inverted £4500
j. Error. Surch "G.R.I. 3d." double £7500
k. No stop after "I" (Setting 11) £1900
25 5d.on 50pf. black and purple/*buff* £160 £190
e. Thin "5" £750 £1300
f. Surch double £1500
g. Surch double, one inverted £3500 £4750
h. Surch double, both inverted £4000 £4750
i. Surch inverted £2500
j. Error. Surch "G.I.R. 3d." £8000
26 8d.on 80pf. black and carmine/*rose* £325 £400
e. Surch double £2750 £3250
f. Surch double, one inverted £2750 £3250
g. Surch triple £3000 £3500
h. Surch inverted £4500 £5000
i. Error. Surch "G.R.I. 3d." £8500

(b) As T **2**. *"G.R.I." and value 5½ mm apart.*

27 1s.on 1m. carmine £2750 £3750
a. No stop after "I" (Setting 7) £5000
28 2s.on 2m. blue £2750 £4250
a. No stop after "I" (Setting 7) £5000
29 3s.on 3m. violet-black £4750 £7500
a. "G.R.I." double £15000
30 5s.on 5m. carmine and black £18000 £20000

1915 (1 Jan). *Nos. 18 and 19 further surch with T* **3**.
31 1d. on 2d. on 10pf. £14000 £14000
32 1d. on 2d. on 20pf. £13000 £8500

German New Guinea Registration Labels surcharged

4

4a

G.R.I.

3d.

Sans serif "G" and different "3"

1915 (Jan). *Registration Labels surch "G.R.I. 3d." in settings of five or ten and used for postage. Each black and red on buff. Inscr "(Deutsch Neuguinea)" spelt in various ways as indicated.* P 14 (No. 43) or 11½ (others).

I. With name of town in sans-serif letters as T **4**.

33 **Rabaul** "(Deutsch Neuguinea)" £180 £200
a. "G.R.I. 3d." double £2000 £2750
b. No bracket before "Deutsch" £700 £900
ba. No bracket and surch double £5000
d. "(Deutsch-Neuguinea)" £250 £375
da. "G.R.I. 3d." double £5000 £5000
db. No stop after "I" £650
dc. "G.R.I. 3d" inverted £5000
dd. No bracket before "Deutsch" £1000 £1400
de. No bracket after "Neuguinea" £1000 £1400
34 **Deulon** "(Deutsch Neuguinea)" £12000
35 **Friedrich-Wilhelmshafen** "(Deutsch Neuguinea)" £170 £450
a. No stop after "d" £325
b. "G" omitted £2750
c. Sans-serif "G" £5500
d. Sans-serif "G" and different "3" £4750
e. Surch inverted . . . . † £5000
f. "(Deutsch-Neuguinea)" £180 £450
fa. No stop after "d" £375
36 **Herbertshohe** "(Deutsch Neuguinea)" . . £190 £500
a. No stop after "d" £400
b. No stop after "I" £700
c. "G" omitted £3000
d. Surch omitted (in horiz pair with normal) £7000
e. "(Deutsch Neu-Guinea)" £350 £600
37 **Kawieng** "(Deutsch-Neuguinea)" £600
a. No bracket after "Neuguinea" £2500
b. "Deutsch Neu-Guinea" £250 £475
ba. No stop after "d" £425
bb. "G.R.I." double £2500
be. "3d." double £2500
bd. "G" omitted £3500
38 **Kieta** "(Deutsch-Neuguinea)" £350 £600
a. No bracket before "Deutsch" £1200 £1800
b. No stop after "d" £650
c. Surch omitted (right hand stamp of horiz pair) £5500
e. No stop after "I" £950
f. "G" omitted £3250
39 **Manus** "(Deutsch Neuguinea)" £200 £550
a. "G.R.I. 3d." double £3000
b. No bracket before "Deutsch" £900 £1400
40 **Stephansort** "(Deutsch Neu-Guinea)" . . † £1800
a. No stop after "d" . . . . † £3750

II. With name of town in letters with serifs as T **4a**.

41 **Friedrich Wilhelmshafen** "(Deutsch-Neuguinea)" £160 £425
b. No stop after "d" £325 £700
c. No stop after "I" £650 £1000
d. No bracket before "Deutsch" £1000 £1500
e. No bracket after "Neuguinea" £1000 £1500
42 **Kawieng** "(Deutsch Neuguinea)" £150 £400
a. No stop after "d" £375
b. No stop after "I" . . . .
43 **Manus** "(Deutsch-Neuguinea)" £2000 £3000
a. No stop after "I" £3500 £3500

Examples of Nos. 33db, 36b, 38e, 41c and 43a also show the stop after "R" either very faint or missing completely.

Stamps of Marshall Islands surcharged

SETTINGS. The initial supply of Marshall Islands stamps, obtained from Nauru, was surcharged with Setting 2 (5 mm between "R" and "d") on the penny values and with the 3½ to 4 setting on the shilling stamps.

Small quantities subsequently handed in were surcharged, often on the same backing sheet as German New Guinea values, with Settings 6, 7 or 12 (all 6 mm between "R" and "d") for the penny values and with a 5½ mm setting for the shilling stamps.

1914 (16 Dec). *Stamps of 1901 surch.*

(a) As T **1**. *"G.R.I." and value 5 mm apart.*

50 1d.on 3pf. brown . . . . 50·00 85·00
c. "1" with straight top serif (Setting 2) . . £110 £180
d. ".G.R.I." and "1" with straight top serif (Settings 4 and 5) . . . . † £4500
e. Surch inverted £2750
51 1d.on 5pf. green . . . . 50·00 55·00
c. "1" with straight top serif (Settings 2 and 11) £100 £120
d. "I" for "1" (Setting 11) £700
e. "1" and "d" spaced £275 £300
f. Surch double £1200 £1800
g. Surch inverted £1400
52 2d.on 10pf. carmine . . . . 17·00 26·00
e. No stop after "G" (Setting 2) £550
f. Surch double £1100 £1800
g. Surch double, one inverted £1400 £1800
h. Surch inverted £2250
i. Surch sideways £4250
53 2d.on 20pf. ultramarine . . . . 18·00 30·00
e. No stop after "d" (Setting 2) . . . . . 48·00 80·00
g. Surch double £1400 £1900
h. Surch double, one inverted £3000 £3250
i. Surch inverted £3750 £3750
54 3d.on 25pf. black and red/*yellow* £275 £375
e. No stop after "d" (Settings 2 and 11) . . £500 £700
f. Thick "3" £750
g. Surch double £1400 £1900
h. Surch double, one inverted £1400
i. Surch inverted £3750
55 3d.on 30pf. black and orange/*buff* £300 £400
e. No stop after "d" (Setting 2) £550 £700
f. Thick "3" £800
g. Surch inverted £2500 £3000
h. Surch double £2250
56 4d.on 40pf. black and carmine . . . . . . £100 £13[illegible]
e. No stop after "d" (Setting 2) . . . . . £250 £40[illegible]
f. "d" omitted (Setting 2) . . . . † £375[illegible]
g. Surch double . . . . £2500 £300[illegible]
h. Surch triple £4500
i. Surch inverted £3250
j. Error. Surch "G.R.I. 1d." £6500
k. Error. Surch "G.R.I. 3d." £6500
57 5d.on 50pf. black and purple/*buff* . . . . £140 £18[illegible]
e. Thin "5" £2500
f. "d" omitted (Setting 2) £1400
g. Surch double £4000
h. Surch inverted £4500
58 8d.on 80pf. black and carmine/*rose* . . . . £400 £50[illegible]
e. Surch double £3000
f. Surch double, both inverted . . . . . £4000 £450[illegible]
g. Surch triple £4750
h. Surch inverted £3750

(b) As T **2**. *"G.R.I." and value 3½–4 mm apart.*

59 1s.on 1m. carmine . . . . £1900 £325[illegible]
b. No stop after "I" . . . . £3500 £475[illegible]
e. Surch double £12000
60 2s.on 2m. blue . . . . £1200 £225[illegible]
b. No stop after "I" . . . . £2500 £375[illegible]
e. Surch double £12000
f. Surch double, one inverted . . . . . . £11000 £1100[illegible]
61 3s.on 3m. violet-black . . . . £3500 £500[illegible]
b. No stop after "I" £4750
e. Surch double . . . . £13000 £1600[illegible]
62 5s.on 5m. carmine and black . . . . . . £7000 £900[illegible]
e. Surch double, one inverted . . . . . . † £2000

1915 (Jan). *Nos. 52 and 53 further surch with T* **3**.
63 1d.on 2d. on 10pf. carmine . . . . £140 £17[illegible]
a. "1" double £8000
b. "1" inverted . . . . £8500 £850[illegible]
c. Small "1" £350
64 1d.on 2d. on 20pf. ultramarine . . . . . . £3000 £225[illegible]
a. On No. 53e . . . . £5000 £300[illegible]
b. "1" inverted . . . . £9000 £900[illegible]

The surcharged "1" on No. 63c is just over 4 mm tall. Type **3** i[illegible] 6 mm tall.

1915. *Stamps of 1901 surch.*

(a) As T **1**. *"G.R.I." and value 6 mm apart.*

64*c* 1d.on 3pf. brown £1000
cc. "1" with straight top serif (Setting 6) . . . .
cd. "I" for "1" (Setting 12) £1400
ce. Surch inverted £4500
64*d* 1d.on 5pf. green £1000
dc. "1" with straight top serif (Setting 6) £1400
dd. "I" for "1" (Setting 12) £1400
de. Surch inverted £4500
df. Surch double £4500
64*e* 2d.on 10pf. carmine £1500
ea. Surch sideways £5000
64*f* 2d.on 20pf. ultramarine £1300
fe. Surch inverted £4500
64*g* 2½d.on 10pf. carmine £7500
64*h* 2½d.on 20pf. ultramarine £11000
64*i* 3d.on 25pf. black and red/*yellow* £1700
64*j* 3d.on 30pf. black and orange/*buff* £1700
je. Error. Surch "G.R.I. 1d." £6000
64*k* 4d.on 40pf. black and carmine £1700
ke. Surch double £4750
kf. Surch inverted £4750
64*l* 5d.on 50pf. black and purple/*buff* £1500
le. Surch double £4750
64*m* 8d.on 80pf. black and carmine/*rose* £2250
me. Surch inverted £5500

(b) As T **2**. *"G.R.I." and value 5½ mm apart.*

64*n* 1s.on 1m. carmine £6500
na. Large "s" (Setting 5) £8000
nb. No stop after "I" (Setting 7) £8000
64*o* 2s.on 2m. blue £5000
as. Large "s" (Setting 5) £7500
as. Surch double, one inverted £20000
64*p* 3s.on 3m. violet-black £10000
pa. Large "s" (Setting 5) £14000
ph. No stop after "I" (Setting 7) £14000
pe. Surch inverted £20000
64*q* 5s.on 5m. carmine and black £18000
qa. Large "s" (Setting 5) £21000

Stamps of Australia overprinted

N. W. PACIFIC ISLANDS.	N. W. PACIFIC ISLANDS.	N. W. PACIFIC ISLANDS.
(a)	(b)	(c)

(6)

1915–16. *Stamps of Australia optd in black as T* **6** *(a), (b) or (c).*

(i) T **5***a.* W **5** of Australia.P 14¼ × 14 (4 Jan–15 Mar 1915).

65 ½d. green . . . 2·75 8·00
a. Bright green . . . 3·00 9·50
aw. Wmk inverted . . . 70·00
67 1d. pale rose (Die I) (4.1) . . . 7·00 6·50
a. Dull red . . . 7·00 6·50
b. Carmine-red . . . 7·00 6·50
ba. Substituted cliché (Pl 2 rt pane R. 6/5) . . . £1200 £750
bb. Dot before "1" . . .
bc. "Secret mark" . . .
bd. Flaw under neck . . .
be. "RA" joined . . .
c. Die II. *Carmine-red* . . . £100 £140
ca. Substituted cliché (Pl 2 rt pane R. 6/4) . . . £1200 £750
70 4d. yellow-orange . . . 4·00 15·00
a. Pale orange-yellow . . . 17·00 30·00
b. Chrome-yellow . . . £250 £275
c. Line through "FOUR PENCE" (Pl 2 rt pane R. 2/6) *(all shades) from* . . . £350 £550
72 5d. brown (P 14¼ (line)) . . . 2·25 16·00

(ii) T **1**. W **2** of Australia. P 12 (4 Jan 1915–March 1916).

73 2d. grey (Die I) . . . 18·00 50·00
74 2½d. indigo (Die II) (4.1.15) . . . 2·75 16·00
76 3d. yellow-olive (Die I) . . . 20·00 50·00
a. Die II . . . £300 £400
ab. In pair with Die I . . . £500 £700
c. Greenish olive . . . £190 £275
ca. Die II . . . £1300
ch. In pair with Die I . . . £2250
78 6d. ultramarine (Die II) . . . 65·00 75·00
a. Retouched "E" . . . £5000 £5500
w. Wmk inverted . . . £100 £130
79 9d. violet (Die II) . . . 48·00 55·00
81 1s. green (Die II) . . . 50·00 55·00
83 5s. grey and yellow (Die II) (3.16) . . . £850 £1300
84 10s. grey and pink (Die II) (12.15) . . . £110 £160
85 £1 brown and ultramarine (Die II) (12.15) . . . £425 £600

(iii) T **1**. W **5** of Australia. P 12 (Oct 1915–July 1916).

86 2d. grey (Die I) . . . 17·00 21·00
87 2½d. indigo (Die II) (7.16) . . . £11000 £11000
88 6d. ultramarine (Die II) . . . 10·00 12·00
89 9d. violet (Die II) (12.16) . . . 16·00 21·00
90 1s. emerald (Die II) (12.15) . . . 11·00 24·00
91 2s. brown (Die II) (12.15) . . . 90·00 £110
92 5s. grey and yellow (Die II) (12.15) . . . 70·00 £100

(iv) T **1**. W **6** of Australia. P 12 (Dec 1915–1916).

94 2d. grey (Die I) . . . 5·50 15·00
a. In pair with Die IIA . . . £500
96 3d. yellow-olive (Die I) . . . 5·50 11·00
a. Die II . . . 75·00 £120
ab. In pair with Die I . . . £160
97 2s. brown (Die II) (8.16) . . . 30·00 45·00
w. Wmk inverted . . . 30·00 70·00
99 £1 chocolate and dull blue (Die II) (8.16) . . . £250 £400

Dates for Nos. 67 and 74 are issue dates at Rabaul. The stamps were in use from 2 January 1915 on Nauru. All other dates are those of despatch. Nos. 65/6, 68/73, 76/81 were despatched on 15 March 1915.

For Die IIA of 2d. see note below Australia No. 45.

SETTINGS. Type **6** exists in three slightly different versions, illustrated above as (*a*), (*b*), and (*c*). These differ in the letters "S" of "ISLANDS" as follows:

(*a*) Both "SS" normal.
(*b*) First "S" with small head and large tail and second "S" normal.
(*c*) Both "SS" with small head and large tail.

Type **11**, which also shows the examples of "S" as the normal version, can be identified from Type **6** (*a*) by the relative position of the second and third lines of the overprint. On Type **6** (*a*) the "P" of "PACIFIC" is exactly over the first "S" of "ISLANDS". On Type **11** the "F" appears over the space between "I" and "S".

It has been established, by the study of minor variations, that there are actually six settings of the "N.W. PACIFIC ISLANDS" overprint, including that represented by T **11**, but the following are the different arrangements of Type **6** (*a*), (*b*), and (*c*) which occur.

A. Horizontal rows 1 and 2 all Type (*a*). Row 3 all Type (*b*). Rows 4 and 5 all Type (*c*).

B. (½d. green only). As A, except that the types in the bottom row run (*c*) (*c*) (*c*) (*c*) (*b*) (*c*).

C. As A, but bottom row now shows types (*a*) (*c*) (*c*) (*c*) (*b*) (*c*).

Horizontal strips and pairs showing varieties (*a*) and (*c*), or (*b*) and (*c*) *se-tenant* are scarce.

The earliest printing of the 1d. and 2½d. values was made on sheets with margin attached on two sides, the later printings being on sheets from which the margins had been removed. In this printing the vertical distances between the overprints are less than in later printings, so that in the lower horizontal rows of the sheet the overprint is near the top of the stamp.

The settings used on King George stamps and on the Kangaroo type are similar, but the latter stamps being smaller the overprints are closer together in the vertical rows.

PURPLE OVERPRINTS. We no longer differentiate between purple and black overprints in the above series. In our opinion the two colours are nowadays insufficiently distinct to warrant separation.

PRICES. The prices quoted for Nos. 65 to 101 apply to stamps with opts Types **6** (*a*) or **6** (*c*). Stamps with opt Type **6** (*b*) are worth 25 per cent premium. Vertical strips of three, showing (*a*), (*b*) and (*c*), are worth from four times the prices quoted for singles as Types **6** (*a*) or **6** (*c*).

One Penny	N. W. PACIFIC ISLANDS.
(10)	(11)

1918 (23 May). *Nos.* 72 *and* 81 *surch locally with T* **10**.

100 1d.on 5d. brown . . . 90·00 80·00
101 1d.on 1s. green . . . 90·00 75·00

Types **6** (*a*), (*b*), (*c*) occur on these stamps also.

1918–23. *Stamps of Australia optd with T* **11** ("P" *of* "PACIFIC" *over space between* "I" *and* "S" *of* "ISLANDS").

(i) T **5***a.* W **5** of Australia. P 14¼ × 14.

102 ½d. green . . . 1·50 3·50
103 1d. carmine-red (Die I) . . . 3·25 1·60
a. Substituted cliché (Pl 2 rt pane R. 6/5) . . . £650 £375
ab. Dot before "1" . . .
ac. "Secret mark" . . .
ad. Flaw under neck . . .
ae. "RA" joined . . .
b. Die II . . . £110 48·00
ba. Substituted cliché (Pl 2 rt pane R. 6/4) . . . £650 £375
104 4d. yellow-orange (1919) . . . 3·25 16·00
a. Line through "FOUR PENCE" (Pl 2 rt pane R. 2/6) . . . £800 £1200
105 5d. brown (1919) . . . 2·50 12·00

(ii) T **1**. W **6** of Australia. P 12.

106 2d. grey (Die I) (1919) . . . 7·00 20·00
a. Die II . . . 11·00 40·00
107 2½d. indigo (Die II) (1919) . . . 3·25 16·00
a. "1" of "½" omitted . . . £5500 £7000
b. Blue (1920) . . . 7·00 27·00
109 3d. greenish olive (Die I) (1919) . . . 23·00 26·00
a. Die II . . . 50·00 60·00
ab. In pair with Die I . . . £350 £400
b. Light olive (Die IIB) (1923) . . . 24·00 32·00
110 6d. ultramarine (Die II) (1919) . . . 4·50 14·00
a. Greyish ultramarine (1922) . . . 42·00 65·00
112 9d. violet (Die IIB) (1919) . . . 8·50 40·00
113 1s. emerald (Die II) . . . 6·50 30·00
a. Pale blue-green . . . 14·00 30·00
115 2s. brown (Die II) (1919) . . . 21·00 38·00
116 5s. grey and yellow (Die II) (1919) . . . 60·00 65·00
117 10s. grey and bright pink (Die II) (1919) . . . £150 £200
118 £1 bistre-brown & grey-bl (Die II) (1922) . . . £2750 £4000

(iii) T **5***a.* W **6***a.* of Australia (Mult Crown A). P 14.

119 ½d. green (1919) . . . 1·00 3·50
w. Wmk inverted . . . 42·00

(iv) T **5***a.* W **5** of Australia. *Colour changes and new value.*

120 1d. violet (*shades*) (1922) . . . 1·75 6·50
a. Dot before "1" . . .
b. "Secret mark" . . .
c. Flaw under neck . . .
d. "RA" joined . . .
121 2d. orange (1921) . . . 6·00 2·75
122 2d. rose-scarlet (1922) . . . 9·00 3·75
123 4d. violet (1922) . . . 20·00 40·00
a. "FOUR PENCE" in thinner letters (Pl 2 rt pane R. 2/6) . . . £650 £1000
124 4d. ultramarine (1922) . . . 11·00 60·00
a. "FOUR PENCE" in thinner letters (Pl 2 rt pane R. 2/6) . . . £750
120/4 *Set of* 5 . . . 42·00 £100

Type **11** differs from Type **6** (*a*) in the position of the "P" of "PACIFIC", which is further to the left in Type **11**.

For 1d. rosine Dies I and II on rough unsurfaced paper see Nos. O16/b.

MANDATED TERRITORY OF NEW GUINEA

A civil administration for the Mandated Territory of New Guinea was established on 9 May 1921.

PRINTERS. See note at the beginning of Australia.

12 Native Village

(**13**)

(Des R. Harrison. Eng T. Harrison. Recess Note Printing Branch, Treasury, Melbourne, from 1926 Note Ptg Branch, Commonwealth Bank of Australia, Melbourne)

1925 (23 Jan)–**28**. P 11.

125 **12** ½d. orange . . . 2·50 7·00
126 1d. green . . . 2·50 5·50
126*a* 1½d. orange-vermilion (1926) . . . 3·25 2·75
127 2d. claret . . . 2·50 4·50
128 3d. blue . . . 4·50 4·00
129 4d. olive-green . . . 13·00 21·00
130 6d. dull yellow-brown . . . 20·00 48·00
a. Olive-bistre (1927) . . . 6·00 48·00
b. Pale yellow-bistre (1928) . . . 4·50 48·00
131 9d. dull purple (*to* violet) . . . 13·00 45·00
132 1s. dull blue-green (6.4.25) . . . 15·00 27·00
133 2s. brown-lake (6.4.25) . . . 30·00 48·00
134 5s. olive-bistre (6.4.25) . . . 48·00 65·00
135 10s. dull rose (6.4.25) . . . £100 £180
136 £1 dull olive-green (6.4.25) . . . £190 £300
125/36 *Set of* 13 . . . £375 £600

1931 (8 June). *Air. Optd with T* **13**. P 11.

137 **12** ½d. orange . . . 1·50 6·50
138 1d. green . . . 1·60 5·00
139 1½d. orange-vermilion . . . 1·25 5·00
140 2d. claret . . . 1·25 7·00
141 3d. blue . . . 1·75 13·00
142 4d. olive-green . . . 1·25 9·00
143 6d. pale yellow-bistre . . . 1·75 14·00
144 9d. violet . . . 3·00 17·00
145 1s. dull blue-green . . . 3·00 17·00
146 2s. brown-lake . . . 7·00 42·00
147 5s. olive-bistre . . . 20·00 65·00
148 10s. bright pink . . . 75·00 £100
149 £1 olive-grey . . . £140 £250
137/49 *Set of* 13 . . . £225 £500

14 Raggiana Bird of Paradise (Dates either side of value)

(**15**)

(Recess John Ash, Melbourne)

1931 (2 Aug). *Tenth Anniv of Australian Administration. T* **14** *(with dates).* P 11.

150 **14** 1d. green . . . 4·00 1·50
151 1½d. vermilion . . . 5·00 10·00
152 2d. claret . . . 5·00 2·25
153 3d. blue . . . 5·00 4·75
154 4d. olive-green . . . 6·50 20·00
155 5d. deep blue-green . . . 5·00 20·00
156 6d. bistre-brown . . . 5·00 19·00
157 9d. violet . . . 8·50 19·00
158 1s. pale blue-green . . . 6·00 15·00
159 2s. brown-lake . . . 10·00 30·00
160 5s. olive-brown . . . 42·00 55·00
161 10s. bright pink . . . 85·00 £130
162 £1 olive-grey . . . £190 £250
150/62 *Set of* 13 . . . £325 £500

1931 (2 Aug). *Air. Optd with T* **15**.

163 **14** ½d. orange . . . 3·25 3·25
164 1d. green . . . 4·00 4·75
165 1½d. vermilion . . . 3·75 10·00
166 2d. claret . . . 3·75 3·00
167 3d. blue . . . 6·00 6·50
168 4d. olive-green . . . 6·00 6·00
169 5d. deep blue-green . . . 6·00 11·00
170 6d. bistre-brown . . . 7·00 26·00
171 9d. violet . . . 8·00 15·00
172 1s. pale blue-green . . . 7·50 15·00
173 2s. dull lake . . . 16·00 48·00
174 5s. olive-brown . . . 42·00 70·00
175 10s. bright pink . . . 60·00 £120
176 £1 olive-grey . . . £110 £250
163/76 *Set of* 14 . . . £250 £500

1932 (30 June)–**34**. *T* **14** *(redrawn without dates).* P 11.

177 1d. green . . . 2·00 20
178 1½d. claret . . . 2·00 11·00
179 2d. vermilion . . . 2·00 20
179*a* 2½d. green (14.9.34) . . . 6·50 21·00
180 3d. blue . . . 2·50 80
180*a* 3½d. aniline carmine (14.9.34) . . . 13·00 11·00
181 4d. olive-green . . . 2·50 6·00
182 5d. deep blue-green . . . 2·50 70
183 6d. bistre-brown . . . 4·00 3·25
184 9d. violet . . . 9·50 22·00
185 1s. blue-green . . . 4·50 10·00
186 2s. dull lake . . . 4·00 17·00
187 5s. olive . . . 27·00 45·00
188 10s. pink . . . 48·00 70·00
189 £1 olive-grey . . . 95·00 £100
177/89 *Set of* 15 . . . £200 £275

1932 (30 June)–**34**. *Air. T* **14** *(redrawn without dates), optd with T* **15**. P 11.

190 ½d. orange . . . 60 1·50
191 1d. green . . . 1·25 1·50
192 1½d. claret . . . 1·75 7·50
193 2d. vermilion . . . 1·75 30
193*a* 2½d. green (14.9.34) . . . 6·00 2·50
194 3d. blue . . . 3·25 3·00
194*a* 3½d. aniline carmine (14.9.34) . . . 4·50 3·25
195 4d. olive-green . . . 4·50 10·00
196 5d. deep blue-green . . . 7·00 7·50
197 6d. bistre-brown . . . 4·50 15·00
198 9d. violet . . . 6·00 9·00
199 1s. pale blue-green . . . 6·00 9·00
200 2s. dull lake . . . 10·00 48·00
201 5s. olive-brown . . . 48·00 55·00
202 10s. pink . . . 80·00 80·00
203 £1 olive-grey . . . 75·00 55·00
190/203 *Set of* 16 . . . £225 £275

The ½d. orange redrawn without dates exists without overprint, but it is believed that this was not issued (*Price* £100 *un*).

16 Bulolo Goldfields

(Recess John Ash, Melbourne)

1935 (1 May). *Air.* P 11.

204 **16** £2 bright violet . . . £225 £130
205 £5 emerald-green . . . £550 £400

(17)

18

1935 (27 June). *Silver Jubilee. As Nos. 177 and 179, but shiny paper. Optd with T* **17**.

206	1d. green	75	50
207	2d. vermilion	1·75	50

(Recess John Ash, Melbourne)

1937 (18 May). *Coronation.* P 11.

208 **18**	2d. scarlet	50	75
209	3d. blue	50	1·50
210	5d. green	50	1·50
	a. Re-entry (design completely duplicated) (Pl 2a R. 5/2)	60·00	90·00
211	1s. purple	50	75
208/11 *Set of* 4		1·75	4·00

(Recess John Ash, Melbourne)

1939 (1 Mar). *Air. Inscr* "AIRMAIL POSTAGE" *at foot.* P 11.

212 **16**	½d. orange	3·75	7·00
213	1d. green	3·25	4·50
214	1½d. claret	4·00	9·50
215	2d. vermilion	8·00	3·50
216	3d. blue	13·00	18·00
217	4d. yellow-olive	14·00	8·50
218	5d. deep green	12·00	3·75
219	6d. bistre-brown	25·00	18·00
220	9d. violet	25·00	24·00
221	1s. pale blue-green	25·00	19·00
222	2s. dull lake	65·00	48·00
223	5s. olive-brown	£130	95·00
224	10s. pink	£375	£250
225	£1 olive-green	£100	£110
212/25 *Set of* 14		£700	£550

OFFICIAL STAMPS

O. S.
G.R.I.
1d. (O 1) **O S** (O 2) **O S** (O 3)

1915 (27 Feb). *Stamps of 1901 surch as Type* **O1**. "G.R.I." *and value 3½ mm apart.*

O1	1d.on 3pf. brown	26·00	75·00
	a. "1" and "d" spaced	75·00	£170
	b. Surch double	£2250	
O2	1d.on 5pf. green	80·00	£140
	a. "1" and "d" spaced	£160	£300

1919–23. *Stamps of Australia optd with T* **11** *and punctured* "O S" *(8 × 15½ mm with eleven holes in the perforated "S").*

(i) T **5a**. *of Australia.* W **5**. P 14¼ × 14.

O3	1d. carmine-red (Die I)	£100	22·00
	b. Die II	—	£225
O4	4d. yellow-orange	£110	45·00
	a. Line through "FOUR PENCE" (Pl 2 rt pane R. 2/6)		
O5	5d. brown (1921)	£160	45·00

(ii) T **1** *of Australia.* W **6**. P 12.

O 6	2d. grey (Die I)	£160	32·00
O 7	2½d. indigo (Die II)	£275	£160
	b. Blue	£375	£160
O 8	3d. greenish olive (Die I) (1921)	£325	65·00
O 9	6d. ultramarine (Die II) (1921)	£325	£110
	a. Greyish ultramarine	£275	£120
O10	9d. violet (Die IIB) (1921)	85·00	65·00
O11	1s. emerald (Die II) (1921)	£160	80·00
	a. Pale blue-green	£225	80·00
O12	2s. brown (Die II) (1922)	£130	80·00
O13	5s. grey and yellow (Die II) (1922)	—	£275
O14	10s. grey and bright pink (Die II) (1921)		

(iii) T **5a** *of Australia.* W **5**. *Rough unsurfaced paper, locally gummed.* P 14.

O16	1d. rosine (Die I) (1920)	£425	£130
	b. Die II	£1200	£425

(iv) T **5a** *of Australia.* W **5**. *Colour changes and new value.* P 14.

O17	1d. violet (*shades*) (1923)	£160	22·00
O18	2d. orange (1921)	65·00	22·00
O19	2d. rose-scarlet (1923)	£160	17·00
O20	4d. violet (1921)	£110	55·00
	a. "FOUR PENCE" in thinner letters (Pl 2 rt pane R. 2/6)		
O21	4d. ultramarine (1922)	£140	65·00

Dates quoted for Nos. O3/21 are those of despatch from Australia. The earliest postmark date recorded is 2 April 1919 on No. O3. Their continued use on mail from government departments after the establishment of the civil administration is confirmed by a notice in the official *New Guinea Gazette* of 1 August 1921.

Australian postal archives indicate that nine sheets of the £1 Type **1** perforated "O S" were sent to New Guinea in September 1921. There is a pane of 30 of this stamp in the Royal Collection, but as no other examples are known it may not have been issued for postal purposes.

1925 (6 Apr)–**31**. *Optd with Type* O**2**. P 11.

O22 **12**	1d. green	1·00	4·50
O23	1½d. orange-vermilion (1931)	5·50	17·00
O24	2d. claret	1·75	3·75
O25	3d. blue	3·50	7·50
O26	4d. olive-green	4·50	8·50
O27	6d. olive-bistre	20·00	35·00
	a. Pale yellow-bistre (1931)	7·00	35·00
O28	9d. violet	4·00	35·00
O29	1s. dull blue-green	5·50	35·00
O30	2s. brown-lake	28·00	60·00
O22/30 *Set of* 9		55·00	£180

1931 (2 Aug). *Optd with Type* O**3**. P 11.

O31 **14**	1d. green	6·00	13·00
O32	1½d. vermilion	7·00	12·00
O33	2d. claret	10·00	7·00
O34	3d. blue	6·50	6·00
O35	4d. olive-green	5·50	8·50
O36	5d. deep blue-green	10·00	12·00
O37	6d. bistre-brown	14·00	17·00
O38	9d. violet	16·00	28·00
O39	1s. pale blue-green	16·00	28·00
O40	2s. brown-lake	40·00	70·00
O41	5s. olive-brown	£100	£170
O31/41 *Set of* 11		£200	£350

1932 (30 June)–**34**. *T* **14** *(redrawn without dates), optd with Type* O**3**. P 11.

O42	1d. green	7·00	8·00
O43	1½d. claret	8·00	12·00
O44	2d. vermilion	8·00	3·25
O45	2½d. green (14.9.34)	3·25	6·00
O46	3d. blue	8·00	25·00
O47	3½d. aniline carmine (14.9.34)	3·25	9·00
O48	4d. olive-green	8·00	19·00
O49	5d. deep blue-green	7·00	19·00
O50	6d. bistre-brown	13·00	42·00
O51	9d. violet	12·00	42·00
O52	1s. pale blue-green	15·00	29·00
O53	2s. dull lake	35·00	75·00
O54	5s. olive-brown	£120	£170
O42/54 *Set of* 13		£200	£400

Civil Administration in New Guinea was suspended in 1942, following the Japanese invasion.

Various New Guinea stamps exist overprinted with an anchor and three Japanese characters in a style similar to the Japanese Naval Control Area overprints found on the stamps of Netherlands Indies. These overprints on New Guinea are bogus. Two different versions are known, one produced in Japan during 1947 and the other in Australia during the late 1980s.

On resumption, after the Japanese defeat in 1945, Australian stamps were used until the appearance of the issue for the combined territories of Papua & New Guinea.

NORFOLK ISLAND

Norfolk Island, first settled in 1788 from New South Wales, was transferred to Tasmania on 29 September 1844. It became a separate settlement on 1 November 1856 under the control of the Governor of New South Wales. The island was declared an Australian Territory on 1 July 1914. Unlike the other External Territories it retains an independent postal administration.

A Post Office was opened on Norfolk Island in 1832. The stamps of TASMANIA were used on Norfolk Island from July 1854 until May 1855, such use being identified by the "72" numeral cancellation. Stamps of NEW SOUTH WALES were first used on the island in 1877, but were not regularly available until 1898. The first "NORFOLK ISLAND" cancellation was supplied in 1892, but not used until 1898. Stamps of AUSTRALIA were in use from 1913 to 1947.

1 Ball Bay

(Des and eng F. Manley. Recess Note Printing Branch, Reserve Bank of Australia)

1947 (10 June)–**59**. *Toned paper.* P 14.

1 **1**	½d. orange	85	60
	a. White paper (11.56)	1·10	5·50
2	1d. bright violet	50	60
	a. White paper (8.57)	5·00	16·00
3	1½d. emerald-green	50	70
	a. White paper (11.56)	7·50	21·00
4	2d. reddish violet	55	40
	a. White paper (11.56)	90·00	£130
5	2½d. scarlet	80	30
6	3d. chestnut	70	70
6*a*	3d. emerald-green (*white paper*) (6.7.59)	14·00	7·50
7	4d. claret	1·75	40
8	5½d. indigo	70	30
9	6d. purple-brown	70	30
10	9d. magenta	1·25	40
11	1s. grey-green	70	40
12	2s. yellow-bistre	1·00	1·00
12*a*	2s. deep blue (*white paper*) (6.7.59)	20·00	8·00
1/12*a* *Set of* 14		40·00	19·00

Stamps as Type **1**, some in different colours, perforated 11 were prepared in 1940 but never issued. Examples exist from sheets stolen prior to the destruction of these stocks.

PAPUA (BRITISH NEW GUINEA)

Stamps of QUEENSLAND were used in British New Guinea (Papua) from at least 1885 onwards. Post Offices were opened at Daru (1894), Kulumadau (Woodlarks) (1899), Nivani (1899), Port Moresby (1885), Samarai (1888), Sudest (1899) and Tamata (1899). Stamps were usually cancelled "N.G." (at Port Moresby from 1885) or "BNG" (without stops at Samarai or with stops at the other offices) from 1888. Queensland stamps were replaced in Papua by the issue of 1901.

PRICES FOR STAMPS ON COVER

Nos.	1/7	*from* × 15
No.	8	—
Nos.	9/15	*from* × 20
No.	16	—
Nos.	17/27	*from* × 6
No.	28	—
Nos.	39/45*a*	*from* × 5
Nos.	47/71	*from* × 8
Nos.	72/4	—
Nos.	75/92a	*from* × 8
Nos.	93/103	*from* × 6
Nos.	104/5	—
Nos.	106/11	*from* × 10
Nos.	112/14	*from* × 6
No.	115	—
Nos.	116/28	*from* × 5
Nos.	130/53	*from* × 4
Nos.	154/7	*from* × 12
Nos.	158/67	*from* × 4
No.	168	*from* × 3
Nos.	O1/54	*from* × 10
Nos.	O55/66*a*	*from* × 7

1 Lakatoi (trading canoe) with Hanuabada Village in Background

2 (Horizontal)

Deformed "d" at left (R. 4/3)

(Recess D.L.R.)

1901 (1 July)–**05**. Wmk Mult Rosettes, W **2**. P 14.

A. Wmk horizontal. Thick paper. Line perf.

1 **1**	½d. black and yellow-green	10·00	18·0
	a. Thin paper	£170	£14
2	1d. black and carmine	8·00	10·0
3	2d. black and violet	11·00	7·0
4	2½d. black and ultramarine	18·00	10·0
	a. Thin paper	£225	£16
	ab. Black and dull blue	£500	£35
5	4d. black and sepia	48·00	35·0
	a. Deformed "d" at left	£250	£20
6	6d. black and myrtle-green	45·00	35·0
7	1s. black and orange	60·00	65·0
8	2s.6d. black and brown (1.1.05)	£550	£50

B. Wmk vertical. Medium to thick paper. Line or comb perf.

9 **1**	½d. black and yellow-green	8·50	3·7
	a. Thin paper (*comb perf*) (1905)	14·00	23·0
10	1d. black and carmine	3·50	2·0
11	2d. black and violet	9·50	4·0
	a. Thin paper (*comb perf*) (1905)	50·00	16·0
12	2½d. black and ultramarine (*shades*)	13·00	12·0
13	4d. black and sepia	32·00	50·0
	a. Deformed "d" at left	£200	£27
	b. Thin paper (*comb perf*) (1905)	£190	
	ba. Deformed "d" at left	£900	
14	6d. black and myrtle-green	48·00	75·0
	a. Thin paper (*comb perf*) (1905)	£600	
15	1s. black and orange	55·00	85·0
	a. Thin paper (*comb perf*) (1905)	£550	
16	2s.6d. black and brown (1905)	£3000	£225
	a. Thin paper (*comb perf*)	£500	£100
1/16 *Set of* 8		£600	£60

The paper used for Nos. 1/8 is white, of consistent thickness an rather opaque. The thin paper used for the horizontal watermar printings is of variable thickness, readily distinguishable from th thick paper by its greater transparency and by the gum which is thi and smooth.

Nos. 9/16 were initially printed on the same thick paper as th stamps with horizontal watermark and were line perforated. Valu from ½d. to 2½d. were subsequently printed on medium paper o which the watermark was more visible. These were comb perforate The thin paper with vertical watermark, produced in 1905, is muc more transparent and has smooth gum. Printings were made on th paper for all values except the 2½d., but only the ½d. and 2d. we issued in Papua although used examples of the 2s.6d. are als known. The entire printing of the 1d. on thin paper with vertic watermark was used for subsequent overprints.

The sheets of the ½d., 2d. and 2½d. show a variety known a "white leaves" on R. 4/5, while the 2d. and 2½d. (both R. 6/2) an the ½d. and 1s. (both R. 6/3) show what is known as the "unshade leaves" variety.

Papua. (3) **Papua.** (4)

1906–07. *I. Optd with T* **3** *(large opt), at Port Moresby (8 N 1906).*

A. Wmk horizontal. Thick paper. Line perf.

17 **1**	4d. black and sepia	£190	£1
	a. Deformed "d" at left	£600	£5
18	6d. black and myrtle-green	42·00	48·(
19	1s. black and orange	20·00	38·(

20 2s.6d. black and brown £140 £150

B. Wmk vertical. Thin paper (½d., 1d., 2d.) or medium to thick paper (others). Comb perf (½d. to 2½d.) or line perf (others).

21 1 ½d. black and yellow-green . . . . . . 4·75 20·00
22 1d. black and carmine . . . . 13·00 18·00
23 2d. black and violet . . . . 5·00 3·00
24 2½d. black and ultramarine . . . . . . 3·75 15·00
25 4d. black and sepia £170 £130
a. Deformed "d" at left £550
26 6d. black and myrtle-green . . . . . . 28·00 55·00
27 1s. black and orange £1200 £900
28 2s.6d. black and brown £7500 £6500
17/28 *Set of* 8 . . . . £325 £375

II. Optd with T 4 (small opt), at Brisbane (May–June 1907).

A. Wmk horizontal. Thick paper. Line perf.

34 1 ½d. black and yellow-green . . . . . .
a. Thin paper . . . . 60·00 80·00
35 2½d. black and ultramarine . . . . . .
a. Thin paper . . . . 38·00 60·00
ac. *Black and dull blue* £140 £150
36 1s. black and orange £160 £225
37 2s.6d. black and brown . . . . . . 32·00 50·00
a. Opt reading downwards £4000
c. Opt double (horiz) . . . . † £3000
d. Opt triple (horiz) . . . . † £2500

B. Wmk vertical. Thin paper (½d., 1d., 2d., 4d., 6d.) or medium to thick paper (2½d., 1s., 2s.6d.). Line or comb perf (2½d.), line perf (1s., 2s.6d.) or comb perf (others).

38 1 ½d. black and yellow-green . . . . . . 9·00 10·00
a. Opt double £1800
39 1d. black and carmine . . . . 3·50 5·00
a. Opt reading upwards £2250 £1300
40 2d. black and violet . . . . 4·50 2·25
a. Opt double £1800
41 2½d. black and ultramarine . . . . . . 8·50 18·00
42 4d. black and sepia . . . . 27·00 50·00
a. Deformed "d" at left £170 £275
43 6d. black and myrtle-green . . . . . . 29·00 42·00
a. Opt double £2750 £4500
44 1s. black and orange . . . . 60·00 75·00
b. Thin paper (*comb perf*) . . . . . . 27·00 40·00
ba. Opt double, one diagonal £7000 £4500
45 2s. black and brown £6000 £4500
a. Thin paper (*comb perf*) . . . . . . 38·00 48·00
34/45 (*cheapest*) *Set of* 8 . . . . £120 £190

In the setting of this overprint Nos. 10,16, and 21 have the "p" of "Papua" with a defective foot or inverted "d" for "p", and in No. 17 the "pua" of "Papua" is a shade lower than the first "a".

No. 37a comes from a single sheet on which the overprints were sideways. Examples exist showing one, two or four complete or partial overprints.

PRINTERS. All the following issues were printed at Melbourne by the Stamp Ptg Branch (to 1928) or Note Ptg Branch.

WATERMARK VARIETIES. When printing the lithographed issues, Nos. 47/83, little attention was paid to the position of the watermark. Nos. 47, 49/58 and 75/83 all come either upright or inverted while Nos. 48 and 59/71 all occur with watermark sideways to left or right. Nos. 51/2 are known with watermark reversed and others may well exist.

5 Large "PAPUA"

B

C

Three types of the 2s.6d.:—

A. Thin top to "2" and small ball. Thin "6" and small ball. Thick uneven stroke.

B. Thin top to 2" and large, well shaped ball. Thin "6" and large ball. Very thick uneven stroke.

C. Thick top to "2" and large, badly shaped ball. Thick "6" and uneven ball. Thin even line.

Type A is not illustrated as the stamp is distinguishable by perf and watermark.

The litho stones were prepared from the engraved plates of the 1901 issue, value for value except the 2s.6d. for which the original plate was mislaid. No. 48 containing Type A was prepared from the original ½d. plate with the value inserted on the stone and later a fresh stone was prepared from the 1d. plate and this contained Type B. Finally, the original plate of the 2s.6d. was found and a third stone was prepared from this, and issued in 1911. These stamps show Type C.

6 Small "PAPUA"

(Litho Stamp Ptg Branch, Melbourne, from transfers taken from original engraved plates)

1907–10. *A. Large* "PAPUA". Wmk Crown over A, W w **11**.

(a) Wmk upright. P 11.

47 5 ½d. black and yellow-green (11.07) . . . 1·50 3·50

(b) Wmk sideways. P 11.

48 5 2s.6d. black and chocolate (A) (12.09) 48·00 60·00
a. "POSTAGIE" at left (R.1/5) £550 £650

B. Small "PAPUA" I. Wmk upright.

(a) P 11 (1907–8).

49 6 1d. black and rose (6.08) . . . . 4·75 5·00
50 2d. black and purple (10.08) . . . . . 9·50 4·50
51 2½d. black and bright ultramarine
(7.08) . . . . 19·00 27·00
a. *Black and pale ultramarine* . . . . 5·50 6·50
52 4d. black and sepia (20.11.07) . . . . . 4·25 11·00
a. Deformed "d" at left . . . . . . 30·00 50·00
53 6d. black and myrtle-green (4.08) . . . 11·00 16·00
54 1s. black and orange (10.08) . . . . . 23·00 20·00

(b) P 12½ (1907–9).

55 6 2d. black and purple (10.08) . . . . . 22·00 6·50
56 2½d. black and bright ultramarine
(7.08) £120 £130
b. *Black and pale ultramarine* . . . . 48·00 75·00
57 4d. black and sepia (20.11.07) . . . . . 8·00 8·00
a. Deformed "d" at left . . . . . . 50·00 50·00
58 1s. black and orange (1.09) . . . . . 60·00 85·00

II. Wmk sideways.

(a) P 11 (1909–10).

59 6 ½d. black and yellow-green (12.09) . . . 2·25 2·75
a. *Black and deep green* (1910) . . . 28·00 42·00
60 1d. black and carmine (1.10) . . . . . 9·00 8·00
61 2d. black and purple (1.10) . . . . . 11·00 9·00
62 2½d. black and dull blue (1.10) . . . . 4·25 20·00
63 4d. black and sepia (1.10) . . . . . . 4·75 9·00
a. Deformed "d" at left . . . . . . 30·00 48·00
64 6d. black and myrtle-green (11.09) . . . 10·00 18·00
65 1s. black and orange (3.10) . . . . . 45·00 60·00

(b) P 12½ (1909–10).

66 6 ½d. black and yellow-green (12.09) . . . 1·60 3·75
a. *Black and deep green* (1910) . . . 30·00 38·00
67 1d. black and carmine (12.09) . . . . 6·50 12·00
68 2d. black and purple (1.10) . . . . . 3·50 5·50
69 2½d. black and dull blue (1.10) . . . . 9·00 40·00
70 6d. black and myrtle-green (11.09) . . . £3000 £4000
71 1s. black and orange (3.10) . . . . . 13·00 40·00

(c) Perf compound of 11 and 12½.

72 6 ½d. black and yellow-green £2250 £2250
73 2d. black and purple £850

(d) Mixed perfs 11 and 12½.

74 6 4d. black and sepia £7500

Compound perforations on the 4d. are fakes.

The only known examples of No. 74 come from the top row of a sheet perforated 11 and with an additional line perf 12½ in the top margin.

(Litho Stamp Ptg Branch, Melbourne, by J. B. Cooke, from new stones made by fresh transfers)

1910 (Sept)–**11**. *Large "PAPUA".* W w **11** (upright). P 12½.

75 5 ½d. black and green (12.10) . . . . . 3·50 11·00
76 1d. black and carmine . . . . 9·00 8·50
77 2d. black & dull purple (*shades*)
(12.10) . . . . 4·50 5·00
a. "C" for "O" in "POSTAGE"
(R. 4/3) . . . . 65·00 65·00
78 2½d. black and blue-violet (10.10) . . . 4·75 17·00
79 4d. black and sepia (10.10) . . . . . 4·75 10·00
a. Deformed "d" at left . . . . . . 24·00 50·00
80 6d. black and myrtle-green . . . . . . 7·50 7·50
81 1s. black and deep orange (12.10) . . . 5·50 19·00
82 2s.6d. black and brown (B) . . . . . . 35·00 45·00
83 2s.6d. black and brown (C) (1911) . . 42·00 55·00
75/82 *Set of* 8 . . . . 65·00 £110

A variety showing a white line or "rift" in clouds occurs on R. 5/3 in Nos. 49/74 and the "white leaves" variety mentioned below No. 16 occurs on the 2d. and 2½d. values in both issues. They are worth about three times the normal price.

8

ONE PENNY
(9)

(Eng S. Reading. Typo J. B. Cooke)

1911–15. *Printed in one colour.* W **8** (sideways*).

(a) P 12½ (1911–12).

84 6 ½d. yellow-green . . . . 1·25 3·75
a. *Green* . . . . 50 2·25
w. Wmk Crown to right of A . . . . 10·00
85*a* 1d. rose-pink 70 75
w. Wmk Crown to right of A . . . . 20·00 20·00
86 2d. bright mauve 70 75
w. Wmk Crown to right of A . . . . 60·00 40·00
87 2½d. bright ultramarine . . . . 4·75 8·50
a. *Dull ultramarine* . . . . 5·50 8·50
aw. Wmk Crown to right of A . . . . 50·00
88 4d. pale olive-green . . . . 2·25 11·00
w. Wmk Crown to right of A . . . . — 40·00
89 6d. orange-brown . . . . 3·75 5·00
w. Wmk Crown to right of A . . . . 75·00
90*a* 1s. yellow . . . . 9·00 15·00
w. Wmk Crown to right of A . . . . 75·00
91 2s.6d. rose-carmine . . . . 32·00 38·00
w. Wmk Crown to right of A £170
84/91 *Set of* 8 . . . . 48·00 70·00

(b) P 14.

92 6 1d. rose-pink (6.15) . . . . 22·00 6·00
a. *Pale scarlet* . . . . 6·50 2·00
w. Wmk Crown to right of A . . . . — 40·00

*The normal sideways watermark shows Crown to left of A, *as seen from the back of the stamp.*

(Typo J. B. Cooke (1916–18), T. S. Harrison (1918–26), A. J. Mullett (No. 95*b* only) (1926–27), or John Ash (1927–31))

1916 (Aug)–**31**. *Printed in two colours.* W **8** (sideways*). P 14.

93 6 ½d. myrtle and apple green (Harrison
and Ash) (1919) . . . . 80 1·00
a. *Myrtle and pale olive-green*
(1927) . . . . 1·75 2·25
w. Wmk Crown to right of A . . . . 5·00 6·00
94 1d. black and carmine-red . . . . . . 1·40 1·25
a. *Grey-black and red* (1918) . . . . 1·60 1·25
aw. Wmk Crown to right of A . . . . 3·25 50
b. *Intense black and red* (Harrison)
(*wmk Crown to right of A*)
(1926) . . . . 2·50 2·50
95 1½d. pale grey-blue (*shades*) & brn
(1925) . . . . 1·50 80
aw. Wmk Crown to right of A . . . . 15·00 5·00
b. *Cobalt and light brown* (Mullett)
(*wmk Crown to right of A*)
(1927) . . . . 6·00 3·25
c. *Bright blue and bright brown*
(1929) . . . . 2·75 2·00
d. "POSTACE" at right (R.1/1) (all
printings) . . . . *From* 32·00 32·00
96 2d. brown-purple & brown-lake
(1919) . . . . 1·75 75
a. *Deep brown-purple and lake*
(1931) . . . . 25·00 1·75
aw. Wmk Crown to right of A . . . . 30·00 2·00
b. *Brown-purple and claret* (1931) . . 2·00 75
97 2½d. myrtle and ultramarine (1919) . . 4·75 12·00
98 3d. black and bright blue-green
(12.16) . . . . 1·75 1·75
a. Error. Black and deep greenish
Prussian blue† £500 £500
b. *Sepia-black & brt bl-grn*
(Harrison) . . . . 22·00 19·00
c. *Black and blue-green* (1927) . . . 4·50 8·00
99 4d. brown and orange (1919) . . . . . 2·50 5·00
a. *Light brown and orange* (1927) . . 9·00 16·00
aw. Wmk Crown to right of A . . . . 8·00 15·00
100 5d. bluish slate and pale brown
(1931) . . . . 4·25 16·00
101 6d. dull and pale purple (*wmk Crown
to right of A*) (1919) . . . . 3·25 9·50
aw. Wmk Crown to left of A . . . . 12·00
b. *Dull purple and red-purple* (*wmk
Crown to left of A*) (1927) . . . . 13·00 16·00
c. "POSTACE" at left (R. 6/2) (all
printings) . . . . *From* 70·00 £100
102 1s. sepia and olive (1919) . . . . . 3·50 7·00
a. *Brown and yellow-olive* (1927) . . 6·50 14·00
103 2s.6d. maroon and pale pink
(1919) . . . . 20·00 40·00
a. *Maroon & brt pink* (*shades*)
(1927) . . . . 19·00 50·00
104 5s. black and deep green (12.16) . . . 45·00 48·00
105 10s. green and pale ultramarine
(1925) £140 £160
93/105 *Set of* 13 . . . . £200 £275

*The normal sideways watermark shows Crown to left of A, *as seen from the back of the stamp.*

†Beware of similar shades produced by removal of yellow pigment. No 98a is a colour trial, prepared by Cooke, of which, it is believed, five sheets were sold in error.

The printers of various shades can be determined by their dates of issue. The Ash printings are on whiter paper.

For 9d. and 1s.3d. values, see Nos. 127/8.

1917 (Oct). *Nos. 84, 86/9 and 91 surch with T* **9** *by Govt Ptg Office, Melbourne.*

106 6 1d.on ½d. yellow-green . . . . 1·50 1·60
a. *Green* . . . . 1·00 1·25
w. Wmk Crown to right of A . . . . 4·25 4·50
107 1d.on 2d. bright mauve . . . . . . 12·00 15·00
108 1d.on 2½d. ultramarine . . . . . . 1·25 3·75
109 1d.on 4d. pale olive-green . . . . . 1·75 4·50
w. Wmk Crown to right of A . . . . — 40·00
110 1d.on 6d. orange-brown . . . . . . 8·00 17·00
111 1d.on 2s.6d. rose-carmine . . . . . . 1·50 6·00
106/11 *Set of* 6 . . . . 23·00 42·00

AIR MAIL
(10)

(11)

1929 (Oct)–**30**. *Air. Optd with T* **10** *by Govt Printer, Port Moresby.*

(a) Cooke printing. Yellowish paper.

112 6 3d. black and bright blue-green . . . . 1·25 12·00
a. Opt omitted in vert pair with
normal £3500

(b) Harrison printing. Yellowish paper.

113 6 3d. sepia-black and bright blue-green 50·00 65·00

(c) Ash printing. White paper.

114 6 3d. black and blue-green . . . . . . 1·00 7·00
a. Opt omitted (in horiz pair with
normal) £4000
b. Ditto, but vert pair £3500
c. Opt vertical, on back £3250
d. Opts *tête-bêche* (vert pair) £3500

1930 (15 Sept). *Air. Optd with T* **11**, *in carmine by Govt Printer, Port Moresby.*

(a) Harrison printings. Yellowish paper.

115 6 3d. sepia-black and bright blue-green £1600 £2750
116 6d. dull and pale purple . . . . . . 3·00 16·00
a. "POSTACE" at left (R. 6/2) . . . 65·00 £110
117 1s. sepia and olive . . . . 8·00 23·00
a. Opt inverted £5500

(b) Ash printings. White paper.

118 6 3d. black and blue-green . . . . . . 1·00 6·00
119 6d. dull purple and red-purple . . . . 7·00 10·00
a. "POSTACE" at left (R. 6/2) . . . 70·00 £100
120 1s. brown and yellow-olive . . . . . 4·25 15·00
118/20 *Set of* 3 . . . . 11·00 28·00

The rare Harrison printing with this overprint, No. 115, should not be confused with examples of the Ash printing, No. 118, which have been climatically toned.

5d.

TWO PENCE (12)   **FIVE PENCE** (13)

1931 (1 Jan). *Surch with T* **12** *by Govt Printer, Port Moresby.*

(a) Mullett printing.
121 **6** 2d.on 1½d. cobalt and light brown . . . 12·00 24·00
a. "POSTACE" at right (R. 1/1) . . . £140 £225

(b) Ash printing.
122 **6** 2d.on 1½d. bright blue and bright brown . . . 1·00 2·00
a. POSTACE" at right (R. 1/1) . . . 25·00 42·00

1931. *Surch as T* **13** *by Govt Printer, Port Moresby.*

(a) Cooke printing.
123 **6** 1s.3d. on 5s. black and deep green . . 4·25 9·00

(b) Harrison printing. Yellowish paper.
124 **6** 9d.on 2s.6d. maroon and pale pink (Dec) . . . 6·00 22·00

(c) Ash printings. White paper.
125 **6** 5d.on 1s. brown and yellow-olive (26.7) . . . 1·00 1·75
126 9d.on 2s.6d. maroon and bright pink 5·50 8·50

(Typo J. Ash)

1932. W **15** of Australia (Mult "C of A"). P 11.
127 **5** 9d. lilac and violet . . . 4·50 32·00
128 1s.3d. lilac and pale greenish blue . . . 7·50 32·00
127s/8s Optd "Specimen" *Set of* 2 . . . £450

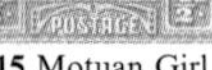
15 Motuan Girl

18 Raggiana Bird of Paradise

20 Native Mother and Child

22 Papuan Motherhood

(Des F. E. Williams (2s., £1 and frames of other values), E. Whitehouse (2d., 4d., 6d., 1s., and 10s.); remaining centres from photos by Messrs F. E. Williams and Gibson. Recess J. Ash (all values) and W. C. G. McCracken (½d., 1d., 2d., 4d.))

1932 (14 Nov)–**40**. *T* **15**, **18**, **20**, **22** *and similar designs.* No wmk. P 11.
130 ½d. black and orange . . . 1·50 3·25
a. Black and buff (McCracken) (1940) . . 13·00 22·00
131 1d. black and green . . . 1·75 60
132 1½d. black and lake . . . 1·50 8·00
133 2d. red . . . 11·00 30
134 3d. black and blue . . . 3·25 6·50
135 4d. olive-green . . . 5·50 9·50
136 5d. black and slate-green . . . 3·00 3·00
137 6d. bistre-brown . . . 7·50 5·50
138 9d. black and violet . . . 10·00 21·00
139 1s. dull blue-green . . . 4·00 8·50
140 1s.3d. black and dull purple . . . 15·00 26·00
141 2s. black and slate-green . . . 15·00 24·00
142 2s.6d. black and rose-mauve . . . 25·00 38·00
143 5s. black and olive-brown . . . 55·00 55·00
144 10s. violet . . . 85·00 85·00
145 £1 black and olive-grey . . . £180 £150
130/145 *Set of* 16 . . . £375 £375

Designs: *Vert* (*as T***15**)—1d. A Chieftain's son; 1½d. Treehouses; 3d. Papuan dandy 5d. Masked dancer; 9d. Papuan shooting fish; 1s.3d. Lakatoi; 2s. Papuan art; 2s.6d. Pottery making; 5s. Native policeman; £1 Delta house. (*As T***18**)—1s. *Dubu*—or ceremonial platform. *Horiz* (*as T***20**)—10s. Lighting a fire.

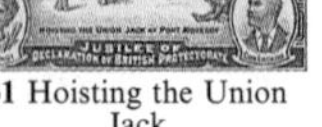
31 Hoisting the Union Jack

32 Scene on H.M.S. *Nelson*

(Recess J. Ash)

1934 (6 Nov). *50th Anniv of Declaration of British Protectorate.* P 11.
146 **31** 1d. green . . . 1·00 3·50
147 **32** 2d. scarlet . . . 1·75 3·00
148 **31** 3d. blue . . . 1·75 3·00
149 **32** 5d. purple . . . 11·00 15·00
146/9 *Set of* 4 . . . 14·00 22·00

HIS MAJESTY'S JUBILEE.
1910 1935
(33)

HIS MAJESTY'S
JUBILEE.
1910 — 1935
(34)

MAJESTY'S
Normal

MAJESTY'S
"Accent" flaw (R.5/4)

1935 (9 July). *Silver Jubilee. Nos. 131, 133/4 and 136 optd with T* **33** *or* **34** *(2d.).*
150 1d. black and green . . . 75 3·00
a. "Accent" flaw . . . 27·00 50·00
151 2d. scarlet . . . 2·00 3·00
152 3d. black and blue . . . 1·75 3·00
a. "Accent" flaw . . . 45·00 70·00
153 5d. black and slate-green . . . 2·50 3·00
a. "Accent" flaw . . . 60·00 80·00
150/3 *Set of* 4 . . . 6·25 11·00

35

36 Port Moresby

(Recess J. Ash)

1937 (14 May). *Coronation.* P 11.
154 **35** 1d. green . . . 45 15
155 2d. scarlet . . . 45 1·00
156 3d. blue . . . 45 1·00
157 5d. purple . . . 45 1·60
154/7 *Set of* 4 . . . 1·60 3·25

Some covers franked with these stamps and posted on 2 June 1937 were postmarked 2 April 1937 in error.

(Recess J. Ash)

1938 (6 Sept). *Air. 50th Anniv of Declaration of British Possession.* P 11.
158 **36** 2d. rose-red . . . 3·00 2·25
159 3d. bright blue . . . 3·00 2·25
160 5d. green . . . 3·00 3·25
161 8d. brown-lake . . . 6·00 14·00
162 1s. mauve . . . 19·00 15·00
158/62 *Set of* 5 . . . 30·00 32·00

37 Natives poling Rafts

(Recess J. Ash)

1939 (6 Sept). *Air.* P 11.
163 **37** 2d. rose-red . . . 3·00 4·00
164 3d. bright blue . . . 3·00 8·00
165 5d. green . . . 3·00 1·75
166 8d. brown-lake . . . 8·00 2·75
167 1s. mauve . . . 10·00 7·50

(Recess W. C. G. McCracken)

1941 (2 Jan). *Air.* P 11½.
168 **37** 1s.6d. olive-green . . . 30·00 35·00
163/168 *Set of* 6 . . . 50·00 55·00

OFFICIAL STAMPS

1908 (Oct). *Punctured "OS".*
O1 **1** 2s.6d. black and brown (No. 37) . . . £600 35·00
O2 2s.6d. black and brown (No. 45) . . . £2500 £2250
a. Thin paper (No. 45a) . . . £700 £550

1908 (Dec)–**10**. *Nos. 49/71 punctured* "OS".

I. Wmk upright.

(a) P 11.
O4 **6** 1d. black and rose . . . 15·00 6·00
O5 2d. black and purple . . . 24·00 4·50
O6 2½d. black and bright ultramarine . . . 32·00 30·00
a. Black and pale ultramarine . . . 16·00 4·25
O7 4d. black and sepia . . . 16·00 4·50
a. Deformed "d" at left . . . 85·00 25·00
O8 6d. black and myrtle-green . . . 50·00 24·00
O9 1s. black and orange . . . 50·00 18·00
O4/9 *Set of* 6 . . . £150 55·00

(b) P 12½.
O10 **6** 2d. black and purple . . . 40·00 9·50
O11 2½d. black and bright ultramarine . . . £130 85·00
b. Black and pale ultramarine . . . 75·00 60·00
O12 4d. black and sepia . . . 40·00 9·00
a. Deformed "d" at left . . . £150 55·00
O13 1s. black and orange . . . £120 55·00
O10/13 *Set of* 4 . . . £250 £120

II. Wmk sideways.

(a) P 11.
O14 **6** ½d. black and yellow-green . . . 18·00 4·50
a. Black and deep green . . . 50·00 30·00
O15 1d. black and carmine . . . 40·00 12·00
O16 2d. black and purple . . . 14·00 2·00
O17 2½d. black and dull blue . . . 24·00 5·00
O18 4d. black and sepia . . . 19·00 10·00
a. Deformed "d" at left . . . 95·00 50·00
O19 **6** 6d. black and myrtle-green . . . 35·00 5·00
O20 1s. black and orange . . . £120 42·00
O14/20 *Set of* 7 . . . £250 70·00

(b) P 12½.
O21 **6** ½d. black and yellow-green . . . 13·00 1·50
a. Black and deep green . . . 50·00 30·00
O22 1d. black and carmine . . . 35·00 4·00
O23 2d. black and purple . . . 22·00 3·00
O24 2½d. black and dull blue . . . 45·00 14·00
O25 6d. black and myrtle-green . . . — £1100
O26 1s. black and orange . . . 42·00 15·00

1910. *Nos. 47/8 punctured "OS".*
O27 **5** ½d. black & yellow-green (wmk upright) . . . 16·00 13·00
O28 2s.6d. black & chocolate (wmk sideways) . . . £110 85·00

1910–11. *Nos. 75/83 punctured* "OS".
O29 **5** ½d. black and green . . . 17·00 8·00
O30 1d. black and carmine . . . 40·00 7·00
O31 2d. black and dull purple . . . 15·00 8·50
a. "C" for "O" in "POSTAGE" . . . £150 75·00
O32 2½d. black and blue-violet . . . 23·00 6·50
O33 4d. black and sepia . . . 27·00 6·00
a. Deformed "d" at left . . . £120 35·00
O34 6d. black and myrtle-green . . . 27·00 6·00
O35 1s. black and deep orange . . . 40·00 9·00
O36 2s.6d. black and brown (B) . . . 80·00 30·00
O37 2s.6d. black and brown (C) . . . 95·00 65·00
O29/36 *Set of* 8 . . . £225 70·00

1911–12. *Nos. 84/91 punctured* "OS".
O38 **6** ½d. yellow-green . . . 9·00 2·0
O39 1d. rose-pink . . . 13·00 1·2
O40 2d. bright mauve . . . 13·00 1·2
w. Wmk Crown to right of A . . . — 22·0
O41 2½d. bright ultramarine . . . 17·00 7·5
O42 4d. pale olive-green . . . 22·00 15·0
O43 6d. orange-brown . . . 20·00 6·0
O44 1s. yellow . . . 30·00 11·0
O45 2s.6d. rose-carmine . . . 65·00 70·0
O38/45 *Set of* 8 . . . £170 £10

1930. *Nos. 93/6a and 98c/103 punctured* "OS".
O46 **6** ½d. myrtle and apple green . . . 7·00 12·0
O47 1d. intense black and red . . . 14·00 3·2
O48 1½d. bright blue and bright brown . . . 9·00 12·0
a. "POSTACE" at right . . . 85·00 £10
O49 2d. deep brown-purple and lake . . . 21·00 30·0
O50 3d. black and blue-green . . . 48·00 65·0
O51 4d. light brown and orange . . . 27·00 29·0
O52 6d. dull purple and pale purple . . . 15·00 28·0
a. "POSTACE" at left . . . £150 £19
O53 1s. brown and yellow-olive . . . 30·00 50·0
O54 2s.6d. maroon and pale pink . . . 80·00 £11
O46/54 *Set of* 9 . . . £225 £30

O S
(O 1)

(Typo T. S. Harrison (1d. and 2s.6d.) and J. Ash)

1931 (29 July)–**32**. *Optd with Type* **O1**. W **8** or W **15** of Australi (9d., 1s.3d.). P 14 or 11 (9d., 1s.3d.).
O55 **6** ½d. myrtle and apple-green . . . 2·00 4·7
O56 1d. grey black and red . . .
a. Intense black and red . . . 4·00 8·0
O57 1½d. bright blue and bright brown . . . 1·60 12·
a. "POSTACE" at right . . . 45·00 £12
O58 2d. brown-purple and claret . . . 3·75 9·
O59 3d. black and blue-green . . . 2·50 22·
O60 4d. light brown and orange (No. 99aw) . . . 2·50 18·
O61 5d. bluish slate and pale brown . . . 6·00 38·
O62 6d. dull purple and red-purple . . . 4·00 8·
a. "POSTACE" at left . . . 85·00 £1
O63 9d. lilac and violet (1932) . . . 30·00 48·
O64 1s. brown and yellow-olive . . . 9·00 30·
O65 1s.3d. lilac & pale greenish blue (1932) . . . 30·00 48·
O66 2s.6d. maroon & pale pink (Harrison) . . . 40·00 85·
a. Maroon and bright pink (Ash) . . . 40·00 85·
O55/66 *Set of* 12 . . . £120 £3

Civil Administration in Papua was suspended in 1942. C resumption, after the Japanese defeat in 1945, Australian stam were used until the appearance of the issue of the combin territories of Papua & New Guinea.

Baghdad
***see* Iraq**

Bahamas

The British Post Office at Nassau was established during the early days of the West Indies packet system, and was certainly operating by 1733. The first known local postmark dates from 1802.

The crowned-circle handstamp No. CC1 was issued in 1846 and was generally replaced, for the public mails, by various stamps of Great Britain in 1858.

Local mail deliveries were rudimentary until 1859 when Nos. 1/2 were issued by the colonial authorities for interisland mails. Examples used for this purpose are usually cancelled in manuscript or with a "27" postmark. The "local" 1d. stamp became valid for overseas mails in May, 1860, when the colonial authorities took over this service from the British G.P.O.

For illustrations of the handstamp and postmark types see BRITISH POST OFFICES ABROAD notes, following GREAT BRITAIN.

NASSAU

CROWNED-CIRCLE HANDSTAMPS

CC1 CC **2** BAHAMAS (Nassau) (18.5.1846) (R.) *Price on cover* £2250

No. CC1 was later struck in black and used as an Offical Paid mark between July 1899 and September 1935. Handstamps as Types CC **1** and CC **3** (only three known) struck in black were used for the same purpose from 1933 until 1953; but it is believed that these were never employed during the pre-stamp period. *Price on cover from* £50.

Stamps of GREAT BRITAIN *cancelled* "A 05" *as Type* **2**.

1858–60.

Z1 1d. rose-red (1857), perf 14 . . . £1800
Z2 2d. blue (1858) (Plate Nos. 7, 8) . . . £1300
Z3 4d. rose (1857) . . . £450
Z4 6d. lilac (1856) . . . £350
Z5 1s. green (1856) . . . £2250

PRICES FOR STAMPS ON COVER TO 1945		
No.	1	*from* × 8
No.	2	—
Nos.	3/6	*from* × 8
No.	7	—
Nos.	8/11	*from* × 10
Nos.	12/15	*from* × 4
Nos.	16/19*a*	*from* × 6
Nos.	20/5	*from* × 15
Nos.	26/8	*from* × 4
No.	29	—
Nos.	30/2	*from* × 15
No.	33	*from* × 30
Nos.	35/7	*from* × 6
Nos.	38/9	*from* × 10
No.	39*b*	*from* × 30
No.	40	*from* × 50
No.	41	*from* × 6
No.	42	*from* × 15
No.	43	*from* × 5
Nos.	44/*a*	*from* × 10
No.	45	*from* × 40
Nos.	47/57	*from* × 4
Nos.	58/89	*from* × 2
Nos.	90/130	*from* × 3
Nos.	131/2	*from* × 10
Nos.	141/5	*from* × 4
Nos.	146/8	*from* × 6
Nos.	149/57	*from* × 3
Nos.	158/60	*from* × 4
No.	161	*from* × 8
Nos.	162/75	*from* × 5
Nos.	S1/3	*from* × 20

CROWN COLONY

1

2

3

(Eng and recess P.B.)

1859 (10 June)–**60**. No wmk. Imperf.

(a) Thick, opaque paper.

1 **1** 1d. reddish lake (*shades*) . . . £4500 £2250

(b) Thin paper.

2 **1** 1d. dull lake (4.60) . . . 55·00 £1500

No. 1, the printing on thick opaque paper, is very rare in unused condition. Unused remainders, on medium to thick, but slightly transparent, paper are worth about £250.

Collectors are warned against false postmarks upon the remainder stamps of 1d., imperf, on thin paper.

1860 (Oct). No wmk. Clean-cut perf 14 to 16.

3 **1** 1d. lake (H/S "CANCELLED" in oval £6500) . . . £4000 £700

For notes on "CANCELLED" examples see Catalogue Introduction. Examples with this handstamp on No. 3 are imperforate horizontally.

1861 (June)–**62**. No wmk.

(a) Rough perf 14 to 16.

4 **1** 1d. lake . . . £750 £300
5 **2** 4d. dull rose (Dec, 1861) . . . £1400 £375
   a. Imperf between (pair) . . . £25000
6 6d. grey-lilac (Dec, 1861) . . . £3500 £550
   a. Pale dull lilac . . . £3000 £500

(b) P 11 to 12½ (1862).

7 **1** 1d. lake . . . £2250

No. 7 was a perforation trial on a new machine at Perkins, Bacon. It was not sent out to the Colony and is also known part perforated.

(Recess D.L.R.)

1862. No wmk.*

(a) P 11½, 12.

8 **1** 1d. carmine-lake . . . £1000 £170
9 1d. lake . . . £1300 £200
10 **2** 4d. dull rose . . . £3250 £400
11 6d. lavender-grey . . . £9500 £500

(b) P 11½, 12, compound with 11.

12 **1** 1d. carmine-lake . . . £2000 £850
13 1d. lake . . . £2250 £950
14 **2** 4d. dull rose . . . £16000 £1800
15 6d. lavender-grey . . . £17000 £1800

(c) P 13.

16 **1** 1d. lake . . . £900 £160
17 1d. brown-lake . . . £750 £130
18 **2** 4d. dull rose . . . £2750 £375
19 6d. lavender-grey . . . £3250 £475
   a. Lilac . . . £2750 £450

*Stamps exist with part of papermaker's sheet wmk ("T. H. SAUNDERS" and date).

1863–77. Wmk Crown CC.

(a) P 12½.

20 **1** 1d. brown-lake . . . 90·00 55·00
   w. Wmk inverted . . . £140 90·00
   x. Wmk reversed
21 1d. carmine-lake . . . £100 60·00
   w. Wmk inverted . . . £140 80·00
   x. Wmk reversed . . . £110 60·00
22 1d. carmine-lake (aniline) . . . £110 65·00
   w. Wmk inverted . . . £160
   x. Wmk reversed
23 1d. rose-red . . . 60·00 40·00
   w. Wmk inverted . . . £100
   x. Wmk reversed . . . 60·00 40·00
24 1d. red . . . 60·00 40·00
   w. Wmk inverted
   x. Wmk reversed . . . — 40·00
25 1d. vermilion . . . 65·00 40·00
   w. Wmk inverted . . . £100 70·00
   x. Wmk reversed . . . 65·00 40·00
   y. Wmk inverted and reversed . . . £150
26 **2** 4d. bright rose . . . £275 60·00
   w. Wmk inverted . . . — £180
   x. Wmk reversed
27 4d. dull rose . . . £400 60·00
   w. Wmk inverted . . . — £180
   x. Wmk reversed . . . £375 60·00
   y. Wmk inverted and reversed . . . £850
28 4d. brownish rose (*wmk reversed*) . . . £450 80·00
   w. Wmk inverted
29 6d. rose-lilac . . . — £2250
   w. Wmk inverted . . . £6500
30 6d. lilac (*shades*) . . . £375 70·00
   w. Wmk inverted . . . — £180
   x. Wmk reversed
31 6d. deep violet . . . £160 60·00
   w. Wmk inverted . . . — £180
   x. Wmk reversed . . . £180 65·00
   y. Wmk inverted and reversed
32 6d. violet (aniline) . . . £250 90·00
   x. Wmk reversed . . . £250 95·00

(b) P 14.

33 **1** 1d. scarlet-vermilion (1877) . . . 50·00 15·00
   x. Wmk reversed . . . 60·00 22·00
34 1d. scarlet (or scarlet-vermilion) (aniline) . . . £1000
   x. Wmk reversed
35 **2** 4d. bright rose (1876) . . . £375 40·00
   w. Wmk inverted . . . — £180
36 4d. dull rose . . . £1500 40·00
   w. Wmk inverted
37 4d. rose-lake . . . £425 40·00

No. 29 is believed to be the shade of the first printing only and should not be confused with other lilac shades of the 6d.

No. 34 is not known postally used, although manuscript fiscal cancellations on this shade do exist.

(Typo D.L.R.)

1863–80. Wmk Crown CC.

(a) P 12½.

38 **3** 1s. green (1865) . . . £2500 £300

(b) P 14.

39 **3** 1s. deep green . . . £200 35·00
   aw. Wmk inverted
   b. Green . . . £120 25·00
   ba. Thick paper (1880) . . . 8·00 7·00
   bw. Wmk inverted (thick paper) . . . — £150

1882 (Mar). Wmk Crown CA.

(a) P 12.

40 **1** 1d. scarlet-vermilion . . . 48·00 12·00
   x. Wmk reversed . . . — 55·00
41 **2** 4d. rose . . . £550 45·00

(b) P 14.

42 **1** 1d. scarlet-vermilion . . . £425 60·00
   x. Wmk reversed
43 **2** 4d. rose . . . £800 60·00
   x. Wmk reversed . . . £850 60·00

1882 (Mar)–**98**. Wmk Crown CA. P 14.

44 **3** 1s. green . . . 35·00 14·00
44*a* 1s. blue-green (1898) . . . 35·00 24·00

(**4**)

5

1883. *No. 31 surch with T* **4**.

45 **2** 4d.on 6d. deep violet . . . £550 £400
   a. Surch inverted . . . £14000 £8500
   x. Wmk reversed . . . £600 £450

Type **4** was applied by handstamp and occurs in various positions.

Caution is needed in buying Nos. 45/x.

Sloping "2" (R. 10/6)   Malformed "E"

(Typo D.L.R.)

1884–90. Wmk Crown CA. P 14.

47 **5** 1d. pale rose . . . 70·00 12·00
48 1d. carmine-rose . . . 7·00 2·50
49 1d. bright carmine (aniline) . . . 2·75 6·50
50 2½d. dull blue (1888) . . . 70·00 17·00
51 2½d. blue . . . 42·00 7·50
   a. Sloping "2" . . . £400 £120
52 2½d. ultramarine . . . 9·50 2·25
   a. Sloping "2" . . . £140 70·00
   s. Optd "Specimen" . . . 65·00
   w. Wmk inverted . . . £150 75·00
53 4d. deep yellow . . . 9·50 4·00
54 6d. mauve (1890) . . . 6·00 26·00
   a. Malformed "E" (R. 6/6) . . . £180 £325
   s. Optd "Specimen" . . . 65·00
56 5s. sage-green . . . 65·00 75·00
57 £1 Venetian red . . . £275 £225
47/57 *Set of* 6 . . . £325 £300

Examples of Nos. 54/7 are known showing a forged Bahamas postmark dated "AU 29 94".

6 Queen's Staircase, Nassau

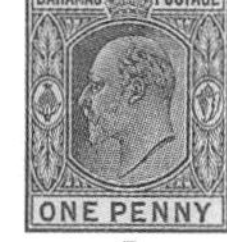

7

8

(Recess D.L.R.)

1901 (23 Sept)–**03**. Wmk Crown CC. P 14.

58 **6** 1d. black and red . . . 8·50 3·00
   w. Wmk inverted . . . 90·00 90·00
59 5d. black and orange (1.03) . . . 8·50 48·00
   y. Wmk inverted and reversed . . . £110 £160
60 2s. black and blue (1.03) . . . 27·00 50·00
61 3s. black and green (1.03) . . . 38·00 60·00
   w. Wmk inverted
   y. Wmk inverted and reversed . . . £110 £120
58/61 *Set of* 4 . . . 75·00 £140
58s/61s Optd "Specimen" *Set of* 4 . . . £130

For stamps in this design, but with Mult Crown CA or Mult Script CA watermarks see Nos. 75/80 and 111/14.

(Typo D.L.R.)

1902 (18 Dec)–**10**. Wmk Crown CA. P 14.

62 **7** 1d. carmine . . . 1·50 2·50
63 2½d. ultramarine . . . 6·50 1·25
   a. Sloping "2" . . . £250 £120
64 4d. orange . . . 15·00 60·00
65 4d. deep yellow (3.10) . . . 23·00 70·00
66 6d. brown . . . 3·50 20·00
   a. Malformed "E" (R. 6/6) . . . £150 £225
67 1s. grey-black and carmine . . . 20·00 50·00
68 1s. brownish grey and carmine (6.07) . . . 22·00 50·00
69 5s. dull purple and blue . . . 65·00 80·00
70 £1 green and black . . . £250 £325
62/70 *Set of* 7 . . . £325 £475
62s/70s Optd "Specimen" *Set of* 7 . . . £275

Examples of most values are known showing a forged Nassau postmark dated "2 MAR 10".

1906 (Apr)–**11**. Wmk Mult Crown CA. P 14.

71 **7** ½d. pale green (5.06) . . . 5·00 3·00
   s. Optd "Specimen" . . . 55·00
72 1d. carmine-rose . . . 25·00 1·25
73 2½d. ultramarine (4.07) . . . 25·00 26·00
   a. Sloping "2" . . . £350 £400
   w. Wmk inverted . . . £120 £120
74 6d. bistre-brown (8.11) . . . 17·00 48·00
   a. Malformed "E" (R. 6/6) . . . £275 £475
71/4 *Set of* 4 . . . 65·00 70·00

1911 (Feb)–**19**. Wmk Mult Crown CA. P 14.

75 **6** 1d. black and red . . . 17·00 2·75
   a. Grey-black and scarlet (1916) . . . 4·75 2·50
   b. Grey-black & deep carmine-red (1919) . . . 7·50 6·00
76 3d. purple/*yellow* (*thin paper*) (18.5.17) . . . 4·75 28·00
   a. Reddish purl/buff (*thick paper*) (1.19) . . . 5·50 4·50
   s. Optd "Specimen" . . . 38·00
   x. Wmk reversed . . . † £275
77 3d. black and brown (23.3.19) . . . 2·00 2·25
   s. Optd "Specimen" . . . 38·00
   w. Wmk inverted

No.	Type	Description	Unused	Used
78		5d. black and mauve (18.5.17)	2·75	5·50
		s. Optd "Specimen"	38·00	
79		2s. black and blue (11.16)	29·00	55·00
		w. Wmk inverted		
80		3s. black and green (8.17)	60·00	55·00
		w. Wmk inverted	£150	£150
		y. Wmk inverted and reversed	£120	£120
75/80 *Set of* 6			90·00	£110

(Typo D.L.R.)

1912–19. Wmk Mult Crown CA. *Chalk-surfaced paper (1s. to £1).* P 14.

No.	Type	Description	Unused	Used
81	**8**	½d. green	80	8·50
		a. Yellow-green	2·50	13·00
82		1d. carmine (aniline)	3·50	30
		a. Deep rose	8·00	2·25
		b. Rose	11·00	2·75
		w. Wmk inverted	£150	80·00
83		2d. grey (1919)	2·25	3·00
84		2½d. ultramarine	4·75	26·00
		a. Deep dull blue	14·00	35·00
85		4d. orange-yellow	5·50	20·00
		a. Yellow	2·50	14·00
86		6d. bistre-brown	1·75	4·25
		a. Malformed "E" (R. 6/6)	95·00	£140
87		1s. grey-black and carmine	1·75	9·00
		a. Jet-black and carmine	14·00	22·00
88		5s. dull purple and blue	40·00	70·00
		a. Pale dull purple and deep blue	50·00	75·00
89		£1 dull green and black	£160	£300
		a. Green and black	£200	£325
81/9 *Set of* 9			£190	£375
81s/9s Optd "Specimen" *Set of* 9			£300	

1.1.17. (9) **WAR TAX** (10)

1917 (18 May). *No. 75b optd with T* **9** *in red by D.L.R.*

No.	Type	Description	Unused	Used
90	**6**	1d. grey-black and deep carmine-red	40	2·00
		a. Long stroke to "7" (R. 4/6)	40·00	75·00
		s. Optd "Specimen"	65·00	

It was originally intended to issue No. 90 on 1 January 1917, but the stamps were not received in the Bahamas until May. Half the proceeds from their sale were donated to the British Red Cross Society.

1918 (21 Feb–10 July). *Nos. 75/6, 81/2 and 87 optd at Nassau with T* **10**.

No.	Type	Description	Unused	Used
91	**8**	½d. green	9·00	42·00
		a. Opt double		
		b. Opt inverted		
92		1d. carmine (aniline)	1·00	50
		a. Opt double		
		b. Opt inverted		
		w. Wmk inverted	£225	
		x. Wmk reversed	£225	
93	**6**	1d. black and red (10 July)	3·50	4·50
		a. Opt double, one inverted	£850	
		b. Opt double	£1700	£1800
		c. Opt inverted	£1500	£1600
		x. Wmk reversed	£180	
94		3d. purple/*yellow* (*thin paper*)	2·25	2·25
		a. Opt double	£1600	£1700
		b. Opt inverted	£1100	£1200
95	**8**	1s. grey-black and carmine	95·00	£140
		a. Opt double		
91/5 *Set of* 5			£100	£170

No. 93 was only on sale for ten days.

WAR TAX (11) **WAR TAX** (12) **WAR CHARITY 3.6.18.** (13)

1918 (1 June–20 July). *Optd by D.L.R. in London with T* **11** *or* **12** *(3d).*

No.	Type	Description	Unused	Used
96	**8**	½d. green	1·75	1·75
		w. Wmk inverted		
		x. Wmk reversed		
97		1d. carmine	1·00	35
		a. Wmk sideways	£350	
		w. Wmk inverted		
		y. Wmk inverted and reversed	£275	
98	**6**	3d. purple/*yellow* (20 July)	1·00	1·50
		w. Wmk inverted	85·00	
		x. Wmk reversed		
99	**8**	1s. grey-black and carmine (R.)	9·00	2·75
96/9 *Set of* 4			11·50	5·75
96s/9s Optd "Specimen" *Set of* 4			£130	

1919 (21 Mar). *No. 77 optd with T* **12** *by D.L.R.*

No.	Type	Description	Unused	Used
100	**6**	3d. black and brown	50	4·00
		a. "C" and "A" missing from wmk	£1200	
		s. Optd "Specimen"	50·00	
		w. Wmk inverted	50·00	

No. 100a shows the "C" omitted from one impression and the "A" missing from the next one to the right (as seen from the front of the stamp). The "C" is badly distorted in the second watermark.

1919 (1 Jan). *No. 75b optd with T* **13** *by D.L.R.*

No.	Type	Description	Unused	Used
101	**6**	1d. grey-black and deep carmine-red (R.)	30	2·50
		a. Opt double	£1700	
		s. Optd "Specimen"	55·00	
		w. Wmk inverted	60·00	
		x. Wmk reversed	60·00	
		y. Wmk inverted and reversed	85·00	

The date is that originally fixed for the issue of the stamp. The year 1918 was also the bicentenary of the appointment of the first Royal governor.

WAR TAX (14) **WAR TAX** (15)

1919 (14 July).

(a) Optd with T **14** *by D.L.R.*

No.	Type	Description	Unused	Used
102	**8**	½d. green (R.)	30	1·25
103		1d. carmine	1·50	1·50
104	–	1s. grey-black and carmine (R.)	18·00	32·00

(b) No. 77 optd with T **15**.

No.	Type	Description	Unused	Used
105	**6**	3d. black and brown	75	8·00
		w. Wmk inverted	50·00	
		x. Wmk reversed	65·00	
		y. Wmk inverted and reversed	70·00	
102/5 *Set of* 4			18·00	38·00
102s/5s *Set of* 4			£130	

16

17 Great Seal of the Bahamas.

(Recess D.L.R.)

1920 (1 Mar). *Peace Celebration.* Wmk Mult Crown CA (sideways*). P 14.

No.	Type	Description	Unused	Used
106	**16**	½d. green	1·00	5·50
		x. Wmk sideways reversed	£275	£275
107		1d. carmine	2·75	1·00
		x. Wmk sideways reversed	£375	
		y. Wmk Crown to right of CA and reversed	£375	
108		2d. slate-grey	2·75	7·50
		a. "C" of "CA" missing from Wmk	£800	
109		3d. deep brown	2·75	9·00
		w. Wmk Crown to right of CA	£200	
110		1s. deep myrtle-green	12·00	35·00
		a. Substituted crown in Wmk	£1200	
		x. Wmk sideways reversed	£500	
106/10 *Set of* 5			19·00	50·00
106s/10s Optd "Specimen" *Set of* 5			£160	

*The normal sideways watermark shows Crown to left of CA, *as seen from the back of the stamp.*

For illustration of the substituted watermark crown see Catalogue Introduction.

1921 (29 Mar)–**29**. Wmk Script CA. P 14.

No.	Type	Description	Unused	Used
111	**6**	1d. grey and rose-red	1·00	1·75
112		5d. black and purple (8.29)	3·75	45·00
113		2s. black and blue (11.22)	19·00	22·00
114		3s. black and green (9.24)	48·00	65·00
111/14 *Set of* 4			65·00	£120
111s/14s Optd or Perf (5d.) "Specimen" *Set of* 4			£170	

Examples of all values are known showing a forged Nassau postmark dated "2 MAR 10".

Elongated "E" (left pane R. 9/6)

1921 (8 Sept)–**37**. Wmk Mult Script CA. *Chalk-surfaced paper (3d., 1s., 5s., £1).* P 14.

No.	Type	Description	Unused	Used
115	**8**	½d. green (1924)	50	40
		a. Elongated "E"	40·00	
116		1d. carmine	1·00	15
117		1½d. brown-red (1934)	5·00	1·00
118		2d. grey (1927)	1·25	2·75
119		2½d. ultramarine (1922)	1·00	2·75
120		3d. purple/*pale yellow* (1931)	6·50	16·00
		a. Purple/orange-yellow (1937)	7·50	17·00
121		4d. orange-yellow (1924)	1·50	5·00
122		6d. bistre-brown (1922)	70	1·25
		a. Malformed "E" (R.6/6)	90·00	£130
123		1s. black and carmine (1926)	2·75	5·50
124		5s. dull purple and blue (1924)	35·00	65·00
125		£1 green and black (1926)	£170	£325
115/25 *Set of* 11			£200	£375
115s/25s Optd or Perf (1½d., 3d.) "Specimen" *Set of* 11			£400	

(Recess B.W.)

1930 (2 Jan). *Tercentenary of Colony.* Wmk Mult Script CA. P 12.

No.	Type	Description	Unused	Used
126	**17**	1d. black and scarlet	2·00	2·75
127		3d. black and deep brown	4·00	15·00
128		5d. black and deep purple	4·00	15·00
129		2s. black and deep blue	18·00	48·00
130		3s. black and green	42·00	85·00
126/30 *Set of* 5			60·00	£150
126s/30s Perf "Specimen" *Set of* 5			£150	

18

(Recess B.W.)

1931 (14 July)–**46**. Wmk Mult Script CA. P 12.

No.	Type	Description	Unused	Used
131	**18**	2s. slate-purple and deep ultramarine	22·00	28·00
		a. Slate-purple and indigo (9.42)	80·00	40·0
		b. Brownish black and indigo (13.4.43)	8·00	3·7
		c. Brownish black and steel-blue (6.44)	13·00	1·7
132		3s. slate-purple and myrtle-green	28·00	26·0
		a. Brownish black and green (13.4.43)	8·00	2·5
		b. Brownish blk & myrtle-grn (1.10.46)	8·00	4·0
131s/2s Perf "Specimen" *Set of* 2			75·00	

Most of the stamps from the September 1942 printing (No. 131 and further stocks of the 3s. similar to No. 132) were used for the 1942 "LANDFALL" overprints.

1935 (6 May). *Silver Jubilee. As Nos. 91/4 of Antigua.* P 13½ × 14.

No.	Description	Unused	Used
141	1½d. deep blue and carmine	1·00	3·0
	h. Dot by flagstaff	85·00	
	i. Dash by turret	£140	
142	2½d. brown and deep blue	5·00	9·0
	f. Diagonal line by turret	£120	
	g. Dot to left of chapel	£180	
143	6d. light blue and olive-green	7·00	13·0
	g. Dot to left of chapel	£200	
	h. Dot by flagstaff	£225	
144	1s. slate and purple	7·00	10·0
	h. Dot by flagstaff	£225	
141/4 *Set of* 4		18·00	32·0
141s/4s Perf "Specimen" *Set of* 4		95·00	

For illustrations of plate varieties see Omnibus section following Zanzibar.

19 Greater Flamingos in flight

20 King George VI

(Recess Waterlow)

1935 (22 May). Wmk Mult Script CA. P 12½.

No.	Type	Description	Unused	Used
145	**19**	8d. ultramarine and scarlet	6·00	3·2
		s. Perf "Specimen"	45·00	

1937 (12 May). *Coronation. As Nos. 95/7 of Antigua, but printed by D.L.R.* P 14.

No.	Description	Unused	Used
146	½d. green	15	1
147	1½d. yellow-brown	30	1·1
148	2½d. bright blue	50	1·1
146/8 *Set of* 3		85	2·1
146s/8s Perf "Specimen" *Set of* 3		70·00	

Accent flaw (right pane R. 1/5) (1938 ptg only)

Short "T" in "TWO" (right pane R. 3/6) (Retouched on No. 152*c*, although bottom of letter is still pointed)

(Typo D.L.R.)

1938 (11 Mar)–**52**. Wmk Mult Script CA. *Chalk-surfaced paper (1s. to £1).* P 14.

No.	Type	Description	Unused	Used
149	**20**	½d. green	1·00	1·2
		a. Elongated "E"	90·00	
		b. Accent flaw	£140	
		c. Bluish green (11.9.42)	1·75	2·2
		ca. Elongated "E"	£120	
		d. Myrtle-green (11.12.46)	6·50	6·
		da. Elongated "E"	£250	
149*e*		½d. brown-purple (18.2.52)	1·00	2·
		ea. Error. Crown missing	£7500	
		eb. Error. St Edward's Crown	£3250	
		ec. Elongated "E"	£110	
150		1d. carmine	8·50	3·
150*a*		1d. olive-grey (17.9.41)	3·25	3·
		ab. Pale slate (11.9.42)	60	
151		1½d. red-brown (19.4.38)	1·50	1·
		a. Pale red-brown (19.4.48)	6·50	2·
152		2d. pale slate (19.4.38)	18·00	4·
		a. Short "T"	£650	
152*b*		2d. scarlet (17.9.41)	1·00	
		ba. Short "T"	95·00	
		bb. "TWO PENCE" printed double	†	£70
		bc. Dull rose-red (19.4.48)	3·25	3·
152*c*		2d. green (1.5.51)	1·00	
153		2½d. ultramarine	3·25	1·
153*a*		2½d. violet (1.7.43)	1·25	1·
		ab. "2½ PENNY" printed double	£3250	
154		3d. violet (19.4.38)	16·00	3·
154*a*		3d. blue (4.43)	60	1·
		ab. Bright ultramarine (19.4.48)	4·25	4·
154*b*		3d. scarlet (1.2.52)	60	3·
154*c*		10d. yellow-orange (18.11.46)	2·50	

155 1s. grey-black and carmine (*thick paper*) (15.9.38) . . . 23·00 6·00
a. Brownish grey and scarlet (4.42) . . . £350 65·00
b. Ordinary paper. *Black and carmine* (9.42) . . . 22·00 7·00
c. Ordinary paper. *Grey-black and bright crimson* (6.3.44) . . . 12·00 75
d. Pale brownish grey and crimson (19.4.48) . . . 14·00 1·50
156 5s. lilac & blue (*thick paper*) (19.4.38) . . . £170 £100
a. Reddish lilac and blue (4.42) . . . £1500 £500
b. Ordinary paper. *Purple & bl* (9.42) . . . 28·00 18·00
c. Ordinary paper. *Dull mauve and deep blue* (11.46) . . . 90·00 55·00
d. Brown-purple & dp brt bl (19.4.48) . . . 35·00 11·00
e. Red-purple & dp bright blue (8.51) . . . 24·00 15·00
157 £1 deep grey-green and black (*thick paper*) (15.9.38) . . . £250 £140
a. Ordinary paper. *Blue-green and black* (13.4.43) . . . 60·00 50·00
b. Ordinary paper. *Grey-green and black* (3.44) . . . £130 80·00
149/57a *Set of* 17 . . . £140 75·00
149s/57s Perf "Specimen" *Set of* 14 . . . £475

Nos. 149/50*a* exist in coils, constructed from normal sheets.

No. 149eb occurs on a row in the watermark in which the crowns and letters "CA" alternate.

The thick chalk-surfaced paper, used for the initial printing of the 1s., 5s. and £1, was usually toned and had streaky gum. The April 1942 printing for the 1s. and 5s., which was mostly used for the 'LANDFALL' overprints, was on thin, white chalk-surfaced paper with clear gum. Printings of the three values between September 1942 and November 1946 were on a thick, smooth, opaque ordinary paper.

21 Sea Garden, Nassau

22 Fort Charlotte

23 Greater Flamingos in flight

3d.
(24)

(Recess Waterlow)

1938 (1 July). Wmk Mult Script CA. P 12½.
158 **21** 4d. light blue and red-orange . . . 1·00 1·00
159 **22** 6d. olive-green and light blue . . . 60 1·00
160 **23** 8d. ultramarine and scarlet . . . 6·75 2·25
158/60 *Set of* 3 . . . 7·50 3·75
158s/60s Perf "Specimen" *Set of* 3 . . . £110

1940 (28 Nov). *No. 153 surcharged with T* **24** *by The Nassau Guardian.*
161 **20** 3d. on 2½d. blue . . . 1·50 1·75

1492
LANDFALL
OF
COLUMBUS
1942
(25)

"RENCE" flaw (Right pane R. 9/3. Later corrected.

1942 (12 Oct). *450th Anniv of Landing of Columbus in New World. Optd as T* **25** *by The Nassau Guardian.*
162 **20** ½d. bluish green . . . 30 60
a. Elongated "E" . . . 50·00
b. Opt double . . . £1100
163 1d. pale slate . . . 30 60
164 1½d. red-brown . . . 40 60
165 2d. scarlet . . . 50 65
a. Short "T" . . . 90·00
166 2½d. ultramarine . . . 50 65
167 3d. ultramarine . . . 30 65
a. "RENCE" flaw . . . £140
168 **21** 4d. light blue and red-orange . . . 40 90
a. "COIUMBUS" (R. 5/2) . . . £650 £750
169 **22** 6d. olive-green and light blue . . . 40 1·75
a. "COIUMBUS" (R. 5/2) . . . £650 £800
170 **23** 8d. ultramarine and scarlet . . . 1·50 70
a. "COIUMBUS" (R. 5/2) . . . £5000 £2500
171 **20** 1s. brownish grey and scarlet . . . 6·50 4·00
a. Ordinary paper. *Black and carmine* . . . 7·00 6·00
b. Ordinary paper. *Grey-black and bright crimson* . . . 11·00 6·50
172 **18** 2s. slate-purple and indigo . . . 15·00 19·00
a. Brownish black and indigo . . . 8·00 10·00
b. Brownish black and steel-blue . . . 26·00 26·00
c. Stop after "COLUMBUS" (R. 2/12) . . . £3000
173 3s. slate-purple and myrtle-green . . . 7·00 6·50
a. Brownish black and green . . . 40·00 32·00
b. Stop after "COLUMBUS" (R. 2/12) . . . £2000
174 **20** 5s. reddish lilac and blue . . . 42·00 17·00
a. Ordinary paper. *Purple and blue* . . . 20·00 14·00
175 £1 deep grey-green & blk (*thick paper*) . . . 80·00 70·00
a. Ordinary paper. *Grey-green & black* . . . 30·00 25·00
162/75a *Set of* 14 . . . 65·00 60·00
162s/75s Perf "Specimen" *Set of* 14 . . . £450

These stamps replaced the definitive series for a period of six months. Initially stocks of existing printings were used, but when further supplies were required for overprinting a number of new printings were produced, some of which, including the new colour of the 3d., did not appear without overprint until much later.

1946 (11 Nov). *Victory. As Nos. 110/11 of Antigua.*
176 1½d. brown . . . 10 60
177 3d. blue . . . 10 60
176s/7s Perf "Specimen" *Set of* 2 . . . 60·00

26 Infant Welfare Clinic

(Recess C.B.N.)

1948 (11 Oct). *Tercentenary of Settlement of Island of Eleuthera. T* **26** *and similar horiz designs. P* 12.
178 ½d. orange . . . 30 1·00
179 1d. sage-green . . . 30 35
180 1½d. yellow . . . 30 80
181 2d. scarlet . . . 30 40
182 2½d. brown-lake . . . 70 75
183 3d. ultramarine . . . 2·50 85
184 4d. black . . . 60 70
185 6d. emerald-green . . . 2·25 80
186 8d. violet . . . 1·00 70
187 10d. carmine . . . 1·00 35
188 1s. sepia . . . 2·00 50
189 2s. magenta . . . 4·00 8·50
190 3s. blue . . . 8·50 8·50
191 5s. mauve . . . 13·00 4·50
192 10s. grey . . . 10·00 10·00
193 £1 vermilion . . . 9·50 15·00
178/93 *Set of* 16 . . . 50·00 48·00

Designs:—1d. Agriculture (combine harvester); 1½d. Sisal; 2d. Straw work; 2½d. Dairy farm; 3d. Fishing fleet; 4d. Hatchet Bay, Eleuthera; 6d. Tuna fishing; 8d. Paradise Beach; 10d. Modern hotels; 1s. Yacht racing; 2s. Water sports (skiing); 3s. Shipbuilding; 5s. Transportation; 10s. Salt production, Inagua, £1, Parliament Buildings.

1948 (1 Dec). *Royal Silver Wedding. As Nos. 112/13 of Antigua.*
194 1½d. red-brown . . . 20 25
195 £1 slate-green . . . 32·00 32·00

1949 (10 Oct). *75th Anniv of Universal Postal Union. As Nos. 114/17 of Antigua.*
196 2½d. violet . . . 35 50
197 3d. deep blue . . . 2·25 2·75
198 6d. greenish blue . . . 55 2·50
199 1s. carmine . . . 55 75
196/9 *Set of* 4 . . . 3·25 6·00

STAMP BOOKLETS

1938. *Black on pink cover with map and* "BAHAMAS ISLES OF JUNE" *on reverse. Stapled.*
SB1 2s. booklet containing twelve 1d. (No. 150) in blocks of 6 and eight 1½d. (No. 151) in folded block of 8 . . . £9000

SPECIAL DELIVERY STAMPS

SPECIAL
DELIVERY
(S 1)

1916 (1 May). *No. 59 optd with Type* S **1** *by The Nassau Guardian.*
S1 **6** 5d. black and orange . . . 6·00 38·00
a. Opt double . . . £800 £1200
b. Opt double, one inverted . . . £950 £1300
c. Opt inverted . . . £1300 £1400
d. Pair, one without opt . . . £20000 £30000
x. Wmk reversed . . .

There were three printings from similar settings of 30, and each sheet had to pass through the press twice. The first printing of 600 was on sale from 1 May 1916 in Canada at Ottawa, Toronto, Westmount (Montreal) and Winnipeg; and under an agreement with the Canadian P.O. were used in combination with Canadian stamps and were cancelled in Canada. The second printing (number unknown) was made about the beginning of December 1916, and the third of 6000, issued probably on 1 March 1917, were on sale only in the Bahamas. These printings caused the revocation, in mid-December 1916, of the agreement by Canada, which no longer accepted the stamps as payment of the special delivery fee and left them to be cancelled in the Bahamas.

It is not possible to identify the printings of the normal stamps without plating both the basic stamp and the overprint, though, in general, the word "SPECIAL" is further to the right in relation to "DELIVERY" in the third printing than in the first or second. Our prices for No. S1 are for the third printing and any stamps which can be positively identified as being from the first or second printings would be worth about eight times as much unused, and any on cover are very rare. All the errors appear to be from the third printing.

SPECIAL
DELIVERY
(S 2)

SPECIAL
DELIVERY
(S 3)

1917 (2 July). *As No. 59, but Wmk Mult Crown CA. Optd with Type* S **2** *by D.L.R.*
S2 **6** 5d. black and orange . . . 50 7·50
s. Optd "Specimen" . . . 65·00

1918. *No. 78 optd with Type* S **3** *by D.L.R.*
S3 **6** 5d. black and mauve (R.) . . . 30 2·75
s. Optd "Specimen" . . . 65·00

Nos. S2/3 were only on sale in the Bahamas.

Bahawalpur
see after Pakistan

Bahrain

An independent shaikhdom, with an Indian postal administration from 1884. A British postal administration operated from 1 April 1948 to 31 December 1965.

The first, and for 62 years the only, post office in Bahrain opened at the capital, Manama, on 1 August 1884 as a sub-office of the Indian Post Office at Bushire (Iran), both being part of the Bombay Postal Circle.

Unoverprinted postage stamps of India were supplied to the new office, continuing on sale there until 1933.

Z 1

Z 2

Stamps of INDIA *cancelled with Type* Z **1** (*this was normally struck elsewhere on the envelope with the stamps obliterated with "B" enclosed in a circular background of horizontal bars*) (1884–86)

1882–90. *Queen Victoria* (Nos. 84/101).
Z1 ½a. deep blue-green . . . £200
Z2 2a. pale blue . . . £200

Stamps of INDIA *cancelled with Type* Z **2** (*squared-circle*) (1886–1909)

1882–90. *Queen Victoria* (Nos. 84/101).
Z 5 ½a. deep blue-green . . . 7·00
Z 5*a* ½a. blue-green . . . 8·00
Z 6 1a. brown-purple . . . 9·00
Z 6*a* 1a. plum . . . 9·00
Z 7 1a.6p. sepia . . . 25·00
Z 8 2a. pale blue . . . 14·00
Z 8*a* 2a. blue . . . 14·00
Z 9 3a. orange . . . 25·00
Z 9*a* 3a. brown-orange . . . 12·00
Z10 4a. olive-green . . . 25·00
Z11 8a. dull mauve . . . 30·00

1891. *Surch on Queen Victoria* (No. 102).
Z12 2½a. on 4a.6p. yellow-green . . . 15·00

1892–97. *Queen Victoria* (Nos. 103/6).
Z13 2a.6p. yellow-green . . . 9·00
Z14 1r. green and aniline carmine . . . 35·00

1900–02. *Queen Victoria* (Nos. 112/18).
Z15 ½a. pale yellow-green . . . 12·00
Z15*a* ½a. yellow-green . . . 12·00
Z16 1a. carmine . . . 12·00
Z17 2½a. ultramarine . . . 22·00

OFFICIAL STAMPS

1883–99. *Queen Victoria* (Nos. O37*a*/48).
Z18 ½a. blue-green . . . 30·00
Z19 1a. brown-purple . . . 35·00

Z 3

Z 4

Stamps of INDIA *cancelled with Type* Z **3** (*single circle, principally intended for use as a backstamp*) (1897–1920)

1882–90. *Queen Victoria* (Nos. 84/101).
Z21 ½a. blue-green . . . 15·00
Z22 3a. brown-orange . . . 20·00

1892–97. *Queen Victoria* (Nos. 103/6).
Z23 1r. green and aniline carmine . . . 40·00

1899. *Queen Victoria* (No. 111).
Z24 3p. aniline carmine . . . 15·00

1900–02. *Queen Victoria* (Nos. 112/18).
Z25 ½a. pale yellow-green . . . 15·00
Z25*a* ½a. yellow-green . . . 15·00
Z26 1a. carmine . . . 15·00

Z27	2a.6p. ultramarine	25·00

1902–11. *King Edward VII* (Nos. 119/47).

Z28	½a. green	15·00
Z29	2a. mauve	15·00
Z30	2a.6p. ultramarine	12·00

1906–07. *King Edward VII* (Nos. 149/50).

Z31	½a. green	8·00
Z32	1a. carmine	10·00

1911–22. *King George V*. Wmk Star (Nos. 151/91).

Z33	3p. grey	12·00
Z34	½a. light green	8·00
Z35	2a. purple	17·00
Z36	2a.6p. ultramarine (No. 171)	20·00

Stamps of INDIA *cancelled with Type* Z 4 (*double circle with date band and black lines in centre*) (1902–24)

1876. *Queen Victoria* (Nos. 80/2).

Z40	6a. pale brown	35·00

1882–90. *Queen Victoria* (Nos. 84/101).

Z41	3a. brown-orange	20·00
Z42	4a. olive-green	25·00
Z43	8a. dull mauve	25·00
Z44	12a. purple/*red*	50·00

1895. *Queen Victoria* (Nos. 107/9).

Z45	2r. carmine and yellow-brown	£150
Z46	5r. ultramarine and violet	£180

1899. *Queen Victoria* (No. 111).

Z47	3p. aniline carmine	7·00

1900–02. *Queen Victoria* (Nos. 112/18).

Z48	½a. pale yellow-green	9·00
Z48*a*	½a. yellow-green	9·00
Z49	1a. carmine	11·00
Z50	2a. pale violet	28·00
Z51	2a.6p. ultramarine	25·00

1902–11. *King Edward VII* (Nos. 119/47).

Z52	3p. grey	7·00
Z52*a*	3p. slate-grey	8·00
Z53	½a. yellow-green	4·50
Z53*a*	½a. green	4·50
Z54	1a. carmine	5·50
Z55	2a. violet	12·00
Z55*a*	2a. mauve	12·00
Z56	2a.6p. ultramarine	7·00
Z57	3a. orange-brown	15·00
Z58	4a. olive	18·00
Z59	6a. olive-bistre	30·00
Z60	8a. purple	35·00
Z61	2r. rose-red and yellow-brown	£100

1905. *Surcharged on King Edward VII* (No. 148).

Z62	¼a. on ½a. green	15·00

1906–07. *King Edward VII* (Nos. 149/50).

Z63	½a. green	6·00
Z64	1a. carmine	7·00

1911–22. *King George V*. Wmk Star (Nos. 151/91).

Z65	3p. grey	10·00
Z66	½a. light green	4·50
Z67	1a. carmine	7·00
Z67*a*	1a. rose-carmine	7·00
Z68	1½a. chocolate (Type A)	20·00
Z69	2a. purple	12·00
Z70	2a.6p. ultramarine (No. 171)	9·00
Z71	3a. orange	15·00
Z72	6a. yellow-bistre	25·00

1922–26. *King George V*. Wmk Star (Nos. 197/200).

Z73	1a. chocolate	12·00

OFFICIAL STAMPS

1902–09. *King Edward VII* (Nos. O54/65).

Z74	2a. mauve	30·00

1906. *King Edward VII* (Nos. O66/7).

Z75	1a. carmine	30·00

Z 5

1911–22. *King George V*. Wmk Star (Nos. 151/91).

Z79	3p. grey	12·00
Z80	½a. light green	8·00
Z80*a*	½a. emerald	9·00
Z81	1a. aniline carmine	10·00
Z81*a*	1a. pale rose-carmine	11·00
Z82	1½a. chocolate (Type A)	25·00
Z83	2a. purple	15·00
Z83*a*	2a. reddish purple	15·00
Z83*b*	2a. bright reddish violet	18·00
Z84	2a.6p. ultramarine (No. 171)	12·00
Z85	3a. orange	20·00
Z86	6a. yellow-bistre	30·00
Z87	1r. brown and green (*shades*)	40·00

1922–26. *King George V*. Wmk Star (Nos. 197/200).

Z88	1a. chocolate	15·00
Z89	3a. ultramarine	25·00

1926–33. *King George V*. Wmk Multiple Star (Nos. 201/19).

Z 90	3p. slate	7·00
Z 91	½a. green	7·00
Z 92	1a. chocolate	6·00
Z 93	2a. bright purple (No. 205)	25·00
Z 94	2a. purple (No. 206)	12·00
Z 95	3a. ultramarine	20·00
Z 95*a*	3a. blue	20·00
Z 96	4a. sage-green (No. 211)	15·00
Z 97	8a. reddish purple	20·00
Z 98	1r. chocolate and green	25·00
Z 99	2r. carmine and orange	40·00
Z100	5r. ultramarine and purple	60·00

The 1a. is known with inverted watermark.

1929. *Air* (Nos. 220/5).

Z101	2a. deep blue-green	15·00
Z102	3a. blue	15·00
Z103	4a. olive-green	20·00
Z104	6a. bistre	25·00

1931. *Inauguration of New Delhi* (Nos. 226/31).

Z105	¼a. olive-green and orange-brown	25·00
Z106	1a. mauve and chocolate	15·00

Nos. Z101/6 and Z136/41 come with watermark sideways to left or right.

OFFICIAL STAMPS

1902–09. *King Edward VII* (Nos. O54/65).

Z107	2a. mauve	30·00

1912–13. *King George V*. Wmk Star (Nos. O73/96).

Z108	½a. light green	20·00
Z109	1a. rose-carmine	20·00
Z110	2a. reddish purple	25·00

Z 6

Stamps of INDIA *cancelled with Type* Z 6 (*double circle with black arc in lower segment*) (1924–33)

1911–22. *King George V*. Wmk Star (Nos. 151/91).

Z115	3p. grey	10·00
Z116	½a. light green	7·00
Z117	1a. aniline carmine	8·00
Z118	2a. purple	12·00
Z119	6a. yellow-bistre	17·00

1922–26. *King George V*. Wmk Star (Nos. 197/200).

Z120	1a. chocolate	8·00
Z121	3a. ultramarine	15·00

1926–33. *King George V*. Wmk Multiple Star (Nos. 201/19).

Z122	3p. slate	4·50
Z123	½a. green	4·50
Z124	1a. chocolate	4·50
Z124*a*	*Tête-Bêche* (pair)	
Z125	1½a. rose-carmine	18·00
Z126	2a. bright purple (No. 205)	18·00
Z127	2a. purple (No. 206)	7·00
Z128	3a. blue	8·00
Z130	4a. sage-green (No. 211)	10·00
Z131	8a. reddish purple	14·00

The ½a. and 1a. are known with watermark inverted.

1929. *Air* (Nos. 220/5).

Z132	2a. deep blue-green	9·00
Z133	3a. blue	9·00
Z134	4a. olive-green	12·00
Z135	6a. bistre	15·00

1931. *Inauguration of New Delhi* (Nos. 226/31).

Z136	¼a. violet and green	14·00
Z137	2a. green and blue	18·00

Nos. Z132/5 and Z136/7 exist with watermark showing stars pointing left or right.

1932–36. *King George V*. Wmk Multiple Star (Nos. 232/9).

Z138	1a. chocolate	8·00
Z139	1a.3p. mauve	8·00
Z140	2a. vermilion	12·00
Z141	3a. carmine	15·00

PRICES FOR STAMPS ON COVER TO 1945

Nos. 1/14	*from* × 5
Nos. 15/19	*from* × 6
Nos. 20/37	*from* × 2
Nos. 38/50	*from* × 6

(Currency. 12 pies = 1 anna; 16 annas = 1 rupee)

BAHRAIN (1) BAHRAIN (2)

Stamps of India overprinted with T 1 *or T* 2 *(rupee values)*.

1933 (10 Aug)–**37**. *King George V*. Wmk Mult Star, T **69**.

1	**55**	3p. slate (11.33)	3·50	45
2	**56**	½a. green	7·50	3·25
		w. Wmk inverted	38·00	21·00
3	**80**	9p. deep green (*litho*)	3·75	2·25
		a. Typo ptg (1937)	10·00	11·00
4	**57**	1a. chocolate	7·00	2·50
		w. Wmk inverted	24·00	8·00
5	**82**	1a.3p. mauve	6·50	1·75
		w. Wmk inverted	7·50	1·75
6	**70**	2a. vermilion	10·00	15·00
		w. Wmk inverted	13·00	16·00
7	**62**	3a. blue	19·00	50·00
8	**83**	3a.6p. ultramarine	3·75	30
		w. Wmk inverted	10·00	60
9	**71**	4a. sage-green	18·00	50·00
10	**65**	8a. reddish purple	6·00	30
		w. Wmk inverted	†	60·00
11	**66**	12a. claret	7·50	1·25
		w. Wmk inverted	†	55·00
12	**67**	1r. chocolate and green	16·00	7·50
13		2r. carmine and orange	28·00	35·00
14		5r. ultramarine and purple	£130	£140
		w. Wmk inverted	95·00	£130
1/14w		*Set of* 14	£200	£275

1934–37. *King George V*. Wmk Mult Star. T **69**.

15	**79**	½a. green (1935)	4·50	1·2
		w. Wmk inverted	8·50	1·0
16	**81**	1a. chocolate	10·00	40
		w. Wmk inverted (from booklets)	25·00	35·0
17	**59**	2a. vermilion (1935)	42·00	7·5
17*a*		2a. vermilion (*small die*) (1937)	65·00	2
18	**62**	3a. carmine	4·75	5
19	**63**	4a. sage-green (1935)	5·00	4
15/19		*Set of* 6	£120	9·0

1938–41. *King George VI*.

20	**91**	3p. slate (5.38)	12·00	4·0
21		½a. red-brown (5.38)	7·00	1
22		9p. green (5.38)	7·00	6·5
23		1a. carmine (5.38)	7·00	1
24	**92**	2a. vermilion (1939)	5·00	2·0
26	–	3a. yellow-green (1941)	12·00	5·5
27	–	3a.6p. bright blue (7.38)	6·00	3·5
28	–	4a. brown (1941)	£130	70·0
30	–	8a. slate-violet (1940)	£160	35·0
31	–	12a. lake (1940)	£110	45·0
32	**93**	1r. grey and red-brown (1940)	3·50	1·7
33		2r. purple and brown (1940)	13·00	6·5
34		5r. green and blue (1940)	15·00	13·0
35		10r. purple and claret (1941)	65·00	35·0
36		15r. brown and green (1941)	£110	£12
		w. Wmk inverted	50·00	55·0
37		25r. slate-violet and purple (1941)	£100	85·0
20/37		*Set of* 16	£650	£32

1942–45. *King George VI on white background.*

38	**100a**	3p. slate	2·50	1·5
39		½a. purple	4·25	2·0
40		9p. green	13·00	16·0
41		1a. carmine	4·50	6
42	**101**	1a.3p. bistre	8·50	18·0
43		1½a. dull violet	5·00	5·5
44		2a. vermilion	6·00	1·5
45		3a. bright violet	18·00	5·5
46		3½a. bright blue	4·75	18·0
47	**102**	4a. brown	3·00	1·5
48		6a. turquoise-green	14·00	9·0
49		8a. slate-violet	4·50	3·0
50		12a. lake	7·50	4·2
38/50		*Set of* 13	85·00	75·0

Unoverprinted India Victory stamps, Nos. 278/81, were placed o sale in Bahrain during January 1946.

Although the stamps of Pakistan were never placed on sale i Bahrain examples of the 1947 "PAKISTAN" overprints on Ind can be found cancelled in Bahrain from air mail originating Dubai or Sharjah.

Stamps of Great Britain surcharged

For similar surcharges without the name of the country, se BRITISH POSTAL AGENCIES IN EASTERN ARABIA.

BAHRAIN 1 ANNA (3) BAHRAIN 5 RUPEES (4)

1948 (1 Apr)–**49**. *Surch as T* **3**, **4** *(2r. and 5r.) or similar surch wi bars at foot (10r.).*

51	**128**	½a.on ½d. pale green	50	1·
52		1a.on 1d. pale scarlet	50	1·
53		1½a.on 1½d. pale red-brown	50	2·
54		2a.on 2d. pale orange	50	
55		2½a.on 2½d. light ultramarine	50	3·
56		3a.on 3d. pale violet	50	
57	**129**	6a.on 6d. purple	50	
58	**130**	1r.on 1s. bistre-brown	1·25	
59	**131**	2r.on 2s.6d. yellow-green	5·50	4·

60 5r.on 5s. red . . . 5·50 4·75
60*a* **132** 10r.on 10s. ultramarine (4.7.49) . . . 70·00 48·00
51/60a *Set of* 11 . . . 75·00 60·00

BAHRAIN 2½ ANNAS
(5)

BAHRAIN 15 RUPEES
(6)

1948 (26 Apr). *Silver Wedding, surch as T* **5** *or* **6**.
61 **137** 2½a.on 2½d. ultramarine . . . 1·00 1·00
62 **138** 15r.on £1 blue . . . 30·00 48·00

1948 (29 July). *Olympic Games, surch as T* **5**, *but in one line (6a.) or two lines (others); the 1r. also has a square of dots as T* **7**.
63 **139** 2½a.on 2½d. ultramarine . . . 1·00 3·25
a. Surch double . . . £1000 £1700
54 **140** 3a.on 3d. violet . . . 1·00 3·00
65 **141** 6a.on 6d. bright purple . . . 1·50 3·00
56 **142** 1r.on 1s. brown . . . 2·00 3·00
53/6 *Set of* 4 . . . 5·00 11·00

Fifteen used examples of No. 63a are known, of which thirteen, ncluding a block of 4, were postmarked at Experimental P.O. K-121 Muharraq), one on cover from F.P.O. 756 (Shaibah) on 25 October 1948 and one apparently cancelled-to-order at Bahrain on 10 October 1949.

BAHRAIN
3 ANNAS

(7)

1949 (10 Oct). *75th Anniv of U.P.U., surch as T* **7**, *in one line (2½a.) or in two lines (others).*
57 **143** 2½a.on 2½d. ultramarine . . . 40 2·25
58 **144** 3a.on 3d. violet . . . 60 2·75
59 **145** 6a.on 6d. bright purple . . . 50 3·00
70 **146** 1r.on 1s. brown . . . 1·25 2·00
57/70 *Set of* 4 . . . 2·50 9·00

BAHRAIN 2 RUPEES
(7a)

BAHRAIN 2 RUPEES
Type II

BAHRAIN
Extra bar (R. 6/1)

Three Types of 2r.:
Type I. As Type **7a** showing "2" level with "RUPEES" and "BAHRAIN" sharp.
Type II. "2" raised. "BAHRAIN" worn. 15 mm between "BAHRAIN" and "2 RUPEES".
Type III. As Type II, but 16 mm between "BAHRAIN" and "2 RUPEES". Value is set more to the left of "BAHRAIN".

950 (2 Oct)–**55**. *Surch as T* **3** *or* **7a** *(rupee values).*
1 **128** ½a.on ½d. pale orange (3.5.51) . . . 2·50 2·25
2 1a.on 1d. light ultramarine (3.5.51) . . . 3·00 20
3 1½a.on 1½d. pale green (3.5.51) . . . 3·00 13·00
4 2a.on 2d. pale red-brown (3.5.51) . . . 1·50 30
5 2½a.on 2½d. pale scarlet (3.5.51) . . . 3·00 13·00
6 **129** 4a.on 4d. light ultramarine . . . 3·00 1·50
7 **147** 2r.on 2s.6d. yellow-green (3.5.51) . . . 24·00 8·50
a. Surch Type II (1953) . . . 75·00 35·00
b. Surch Type III (1955) . . . £800 90·00
ba. "I" inverted and raised (R. 2/1) . . . £3000 £650
8 **148** 5r.on 5s. red (3.5.51) . . . 13·00 3·75
a. Extra bar . . . £325
9 **149** 10r.on 10s. ultramarine (3.5.51) . . . 29·00 7·50
1/79 *Set of* 9 . . . 75·00 45·00

STAMP BOOKLETS

934. *Red and black on tan cover. Mysore Sandal Soap advertisement on front.*
B1 16a. booklet containing sixteen 1a. (Nos. 16 and/or 16w) in blocks of 4 . . . £1100

Bangkok
see British Post Office in Siam

Barbados

Regular mails between Barbados and Great Britain were established at an early date in the island's development and it is believed that the British Mail Packet Agency at Bridgetown was opened in 1688 as part of the considerable expansion of the Packet Service in that year.

From 1 August 1851 the colonial authorities were responsible for the internal post system, but the British G.P.O. did not relinquish control of the overseas post until 1858.

For illustrations of the handstamp types see BRITISH POST OFFICES ABROAD notes, following GREAT BRITAIN.

CROWNED-CIRCLE HANDSTAMPS

CC1 CC **1** BARBADOES (3.10.1849) (R.)
Price on cover £450

Combination covers exist with the local postage paid by a Barbados 1d. stamp and the overseas fee by an example of No. CC1.

During shortages of ½d. stamps in 1893 (17 February to 15 March) and of the ½d. in 1896 (23 January to 4 May) No. CC1 was utilised, struck in black, on local mail. *Price on cover from* £90.

PRICES FOR STAMPS ON COVER TO 1945	
Nos. 1/35	*from* × 5
Nos. 43/63	*from* × 4
Nos. 64/6	*from* × 10
Nos. 67/83	*from* × 5
Nos. 86/8	*from* × 3
Nos. 89/103	*from* × 4
No. 104	*from* × 20
Nos. 105/15	*from* × 4
Nos. 116/24	*from* × 8
Nos. 125/33	*from* × 5
Nos. 135/44	*from* × 4
Nos. 145/52	*from* × 6
No. 153	*from* × 8
Nos. 158/62	*from* × 5
Nos. 163/9	*from* × 3
Nos. 170/96	*from* × 4
Nos. 197/8	*from* × 10
Nos. 199/212	*from* × 6
Nos. 213/39	*from* × 3
No. 240	*from* × 10
Nos. 241/4	*from* × 5
Nos. 245/7	*from* × 6
Nos. 248/56*a*	*from* × 4
Nos. 257/61	*from* × 5
Nos. D1/3	*from* × 25

PERKINS BACON "CANCELLED". For notes on these handstamps, showing "CANCELLED" between horizontal bars forming an oval, see Catalogue Introduction.

CROWN COLONY

1 Britannia

2 Britannia

(Recess Perkins, Bacon & Co)

1852 (15 April)–**55**. *Paper blued.* No wmk. Imperf.
1 **1** (½d.) yellow-green . . . — £700
2 (½d.) deep green . . . 95·00 £325
3 (1d.) blue . . . 38·00 £190
4 (1d.) deep blue . . . 25·00 70·00
4*a* (2d.) greyish slate . . . £250 £1200
b. Bisected (1d.) (on cover) (1854) . . . † £7000
5 (4d.) brownish red (1855) . . . 90·00 £275

The bisect, No. 4b was authorised for use between 4 August and 21 September 1854 during a shortage of 1d. stamps.

Nos. 5*a*/*b* were never sent to Barbados and come from the Perkins Bacon remainders sold in the 1880's.

Apart from the shade, which is distinctly paler, No. 4*a* can be distinguished from No. 5*b* by the smooth even gum, the gum of No. 5*b* being yellow and patchy, giving a mottled appearance to the back of the stamp. No. 5*a* also has the latter gum.

Prepared for use but not issued.

5a **1** (No value), slate-blue (*shades*) . . . 22·00
5b (No value), deep slate . . . £200

1855–58. *White paper.* No wmk. Imperf.
7 **1** (½d.) yellow-green (1857) . . . £475 £110
8 (½d.) green (1858) . . . £130 £200
9 (1d.) pale blue . . . 90·00 70·00
10 (1d.) deep blue (H/S "CANCELLED" in oval £6000) . . . 32·00 60·00

1858 (10 Nov). No wmk. Imperf.
11 **2** 6d. pale rose-red . . . £700 £120
11*a* 6d. deep rose-red . . . £700 £180
12 1s. brown-black . . . £250 £110
12*a* 1s. black . . . £225 75·00

BISECTS. The various 1d. bisects recorded between Nos. 14a and 73a were principally used for the ½d. inland rate, covering newspapers from 1854 onwards.

Prices for Nos. 24a, 52a, 66a and 73a are for examples on dated piece, undated pieces being worth considerably less. Nos. 14a, 15a and 19a are only known on undated piece and the prices for these bisects are for items in this condition.

1860. No wmk.
(a) Pin-perf 14.
13 **1** (½d.) yellow-green . . . £1800 £425
14 (1d.) pale blue . . . £1700 £150
a. Bisected (½d.) (on piece) . . . † £1000
15 (1d.) deep blue . . . £1700 £170
a. Bisected (½d.) (on piece) . . . † £1000
(b) Pin-perf 12½.
16 **1** (½d.) yellow-green . . . £7000 £650
16*a* (1d.) blue . . . — £1400
(c) Pin-perf 14 × 12½.
16*b* **1** (½d.) yellow-green . . . — £7000

1861. No wmk. Clean-cut perf 14 to 16.
17 **1** (½d.) deep green (H/S "CANCELLED" in oval £6000) . . . £100 9·50
18 (1d.) pale blue . . . £650 60·00
19 (1d.) blue . . . £750 65·00
a. Bisected (½d.) (on piece) . . . † £750

1861–70. No wmk.
(a) Rough perf 14 to 16.
20 **1** (½d.) deep green . . . 21·00 22·00
21 (½d.) green . . . 16·00 13·00
21*a* (½d.) blue-green . . . 55·00 75·00
b. Imperf (pair) . . . £550
22 (½d.) grass-green . . . 27·00 22·00
a. Imperf (pair) . . . £650
23 (1d.) blue (1861) . . . 45·00 2·25
a. Imperf (pair) . . . £550
24 (1d.) deep blue . . . 35·00 3·50
a. Bisected diag (½d.) (on piece) (1863) . . . † £600
25 (4d.) dull rose-red (1861) . . . 85·00 40·00
a. Imperf (pair) . . . £750
26 (4d.) dull brown-red (1865) . . . £130 50·00
a. Imperf (pair) . . . £1000
27 (4d.) lake-rose (1868) . . . £110 75·00
a. Imperf (pair) . . . £1100
28 (4d.) dull vermilion (1869) . . . £250 80·00
a. Imperf (pair) . . . £1000
29 **2** 6d. rose-red (1861) (Handstamped "CANCELLED" in oval £6000) . . . £275 13·00
30 6d. orange-red (1864) . . . 95·00 20·00
31 6d. bright orange-vermilion (1868) . . . 85·00 21·00
32 6d. dull orange-vermilion (1870) . . . 95·00 16·00
a. Imperf (pair) . . . £500
33 6d. orange (1870) . . . £110 30·00
34 1s. brown-black (1863) . . . 65·00 5·50
a. Error. Blue . . . £13000
35 1s. black (1866) . . . 55·00 7·00
a. Imperf between (horiz pair) . . . £6000
(b) Prepared for use, but not issued. P 11 to 12.
36 **1** (½d.) grass-green . . . £8000
37 (1d.) blue . . . £2000

The bisect, No. 24a, was first authorised for use in April 1863 and further examples have been reported up to January 1869 during shortages of ½d. stamps.

No. 34a was an error on the part of the printer who supplied the first requisition of the 1s. value in the colour of the 1d. The 1s. blue stamps were never placed on sale, but the Barbados Colonial Secretary circulated some samples which were defaced by a manuscript corner-to-corner cross. A number of these samples subsequently had the cross removed.

Nos. 36/7 were never sent to Barbados and come from the Perkins Bacon remainders. It is believed that the imperforate pairs came from the same source.

1870. Wmk Large Star, Type w **1**. Rough perf 14 to 16.
43 **1** (½d.) green . . . £110 6·50
a. Imperf (pair) . . . £950
43*b* (½d.) yellow-green . . . £150 42·00
44 (1d.) blue . . . £1500 50·00
a. Blue paper . . . £3000 95·00
45 (4d.) dull vermilion . . . £900 £100
46 **2** 6d. orange-vermilion . . . £800 60·00
47 1s. black . . . £350 18·00

1871. Wmk Small Star, Type w **2**. Rough perf 14 to 16.
48 **1** (1d.) blue . . . £130 2·00
49 (4d.) dull rose-red . . . £950 35·00
50 **2** 6d. orange-vermilion . . . £550 14·00
51 1s. black . . . £160 8·50

1872. Wmk Small Star, Type w **2**.
(a) Clean-cut perf 14½ to 15½.
52 **1** (1d.) blue . . . £250 2·00
a. Bisected diag (½d.) (on piece) . . . † £1000
53 **2** 6d. orange-vermilion . . . £800 65·00
54 1s. black . . . £140 8·50
(b) P 11 to 13 × 14½ to 15½.
56 **1** (½d.) green . . . £275 40·00
57 (4d.) dull vermilion . . . £650 95·00

1873. Wmk Large Star, Type w **1**.
(a) Clean-cut perf 14½ to 15½.
58 **1** (½d.) green . . . £275 15·00
59 (4d.) dull rose-red . . . £950 £170
60 **2** 6d. orange-vermilion . . . £700 65·00
a. Imperf between (horiz pair) . . . £5500
b. Imperf (pair) . . . 80·00
61 1s. black . . . £140 11·00
a. Imperf between (horiz pair) . . . £5000
(b) Prepared for use, but not issued. P 11 to 12.
62 **2** 6d. orange-vermilion . . . £5000

Only eight mint examples, in two strips of four, are known of No. 62.

Two used singles of No. 60b have been seen.

1873 (June). Wmk Small Star, Type w **2** (sideways = two points upwards). P 14.
63 **2** 3d. brown-purple . . . £325 £110

3

1873 (June). Wmk Small Star, Type w **2** (sideways). P 15½ × 15.
64 **3** 5s. dull rose £950 £300
s. Handstamped "Specimen" £300

1874 (May)–**75**. Wmk Large Star, Type w **1**.
(a) Perf 14.
65 **2** ½d. deep green 30·00 6·50
66 1d. deep blue 80·00 2·25
a. Bisected (½d.) (on piece) (5.75) † £750
(b) Clean-cut perf 14½ to 15½.
66*a* **2** 1d. deep blue † £8000
b. Imperf (pair)

(Recess D.L.R)

1875–80. Wmk Crown CC (sideways* on 6d., 1s.).
(a) P 12½.
67 **2** ½d. bright green 48·00 4·25
x. Wmk reversed — 10·00
68 4d. deep red £225 11·00
w. Wmk inverted £325 30·00
x. Wmk reversed £225 13·00
69 6d. bright yellow (aniline) £950 90·00
70 6d. chrome-yellow £600 70·00
a. Wmk upright † £1800
w. Wmk Crown to right of CC — 75·00
x. Wmk sideways reversed
71 1s. violet (aniline) £500 3·50
x. Wmk sideways reversed £500 3·00
y. Wmk sideways inverted and reversed — 10·00
(b) P 14.
72 **2** ½d. bright green (1876) 11·00 50
s. Handstamped "Specimen" in red 90·00
sa. Handstamped "Specimen" in black £120
w. Wmk inverted — 13·00
x. Wmk reversed 11·00 75
73 1d. dull blue 60·00 80
a. Bisected (½d.) (on piece) (3.77) † £400
s. Handstamped "Specimen" in red 90·00
sa. Handstamped "Specimen" in black £120
w. Wmk inverted
x. Wmk reversed
74 1d. grey-blue 60·00 65
a. Wmk sideways † £850
w. Wmk inverted £100 20·00
x. Wmk reversed 75·00 90
y. Wmk inverted and reversed — 32·00
75 3d. mauve-lilac (1878) £110 6·50
s. Handstamped "Specimen" in black £120
w. Wmk inverted † 75·00
76 4d. red (1878) £110 8·50
s. Handstamped "Specimen" in black £120
x. Wmk reversed
77 4d. carmine £170 2·00
w. Wmk inverted † 50·00
x. Wmk reversed
78 4d. crimson-lake £500 2·50
79 6d. chrome-yellow (1876) £120 1·25
s. Handstamped "Specimen" in black £120
w. Wmk Crown to right of CC £130 2·00
x. Wmk sideways reversed — 2·00
80 6d. yellow £325 6·50
w. Wmk Crown to right of CC — 10·00
81 1s. purple (1876) £140 3·50
s. Handstamped "Specimen" in red £120
w. Wmk Crown to right of CC £130 3·50
x. Wmk sideways reversed
82 1s. violet (aniline) £3500 35·00
w. Wmk Crown to right of CC — 35·00
x. Wmk sideways reversed
83 1s. dull mauve £425 3·25
a. Bisected (6d.) (on piece) (1.80) † —
x. Wmk sideways reversed — 10·00
(c) P 14 × 12½.
84 **2** 4d. red £5500

*The normal sideways watermark shows Crown to left of CC, *as seen from the back of the stamp.*

Only two examples, both used, of No. 70a have been reported.

Nos. 72sa/3sa were from postal stationery and are without gum.

Very few examples of No. 84 have been found unused and only one used specimen is known.

1D. (3a) 1D. (3b) 1D. (3c)

1878 (28 Mar). *No. 64 surch by West Indian Press with T* **3***a/c sideways twice on each stamp and then divided vertically by 11½ to 13 perforations. The lower label, showing the original face value, was removed before use.*

(a) With T **3a.** *Large numeral "1", 7 mm high with curved serif, and large letter "D", 2¾ mm high.*
86 **3** 1d.on half 5s. dull rose £4250 £650
a. No stop after "D" £13000 £1700
b. Unsevered pair (both No. 86) £17000 £2000
c. Ditto, Nos. 86 and 87 — £3750
ca. Pair without dividing perf † £25000
d. Ditto, Nos. 86 and 88 £25000 £6000
(b) With T **3b.** *As last, but numeral with straight serif.*
87 **3** 1d.on half 5s. dull rose £5000 £800
a. Unsevered pair † £2750
(c) With T **3c.** *Smaller numeral "1", 6 mm high and smaller "D", 2½ mm high.*
88 **3** 1d.on half 5s. dull rose £6500 £900
a. Unsevered pair £20000 £3750

All types of the surcharge are found reading upwards as well as downwards, and there are minor varieties of the type.

4

HALF-PENNY
(5)

(Typo D.L.R)

1882 (28 Aug)–**86**. Wmk Crown CA. P 14.
89 **4** ½d. dull green (1882) 16·00 1·50
w. Wmk inverted
90 ½d. green 16·00 1·50
91 1d. rose (1882) 60·00 2·25
a. Bisected (½d.) (on cover) † £1200
w. Wmk inverted
92 1d. carmine 19·00 1·00
93 2½d. ultramarine (1882) 90·00 1·50
w. Wmk inverted — £100
94 2½d. deep blue £100 1·50
95 3d. deep purple (1885) £100 30·00
96 3d. reddish purple 4·25 17·00
97 4d. grey (1882) £250 3·25
98 4d. pale brown (1885) 10·00 3·00
w. Wmk inverted — 75·00
x. Wmk reversed † £120
y. Wmk inverted and reversed † £225
99 4d. deep brown 5·00 1·50
100 6d. olive-black (1886) 75·00 42·00
102 1s. chestnut (1886) 27·00 21·00
103 5s. bistre (1886) £150 £190
89/103 *Set of* 9 £550 £250
95s/103s (ex 4d. grey) Optd "Specimen" *Set of* 5 £400

1892 (July). *No. 99 surch with T* **5** *by West Indian Press.*
104 **4** ½d.on 4d. deep brown 2·25 4·50
a. No hyphen 10·00 20·00
b. Surch double (R.+Bk.) £650 £850
ba. Surch double (R.+Bk.) both without hyphen £1800 £2000
c. Surch double, one albino
d. Surch "PENNY HALF" £350 £200

Nos. 104b/ba come from a sheet with a trial surcharge in red which was subsequently surcharged again in black and put back into stock.

No. 104c is known in a horizontal pair with the left hand stamp showing the first two letters of the second impression inked. The right hand stamp shows a complete albino surcharge.

6 Seal of Colony

BARBADOS VICTORIA:R:I 1837 1897 ONE PENNY
7

(Typo D.L.R.)

1892 (July)–**1903**. Wmk Crown CA. P 14.
105 **6** ¼d. slate-grey and carmine (5.5.96) 2·50 10
w. Wmk inverted
106 ½d. dull green 2·50 10
w. Wmk inverted — 75·00
107 1d. carmine 4·75 10
108 2d. slate-black and orange (5.99) 8·00 75
109 2½d. ultramarine 17·00 20
110 5d. grey-olive 7·00 4·50
111 6d. mauve and carmine 16·00 2·00
112 8d. orange and ultramarine 4·00 22·00
113 10d. dull blue-green and carmine 8·00 6·50
114 2s.6d. blue-black and orange 48·00 48·00
w. Wmk inverted £110 £120
115 2s.6d. violet and green (29.5.03) 85·00 £160
105/15 *Set of* 11 £180 £225
105s/15s Optd "Specimen" *Set of* 11 £200

See also Nos. 135/44 and 163/9.

(Typo D.L.R.)

1897 (16 Nov)–**98**. *Diamond Jubilee.* T **7**. Wmk Crown CC. P 14.
(a) White paper.
116 ¼d. grey and carmine 4·00 60
117 ½d. dull green 4·00 60
118 1d. rose 4·00 60
119 2½d. ultramarine 7·50 85
w. Wmk inverted
120 5d. olive-brown 18·00 16·00
121 6d. mauve and carmine 24·00 22·00
122 8d. orange and ultramarine 9·50 24·00
123 10d. blue-green and carmine 48·00 55·00
124 2s.6d. blue-black and orange 70·00 55·00
w. Wmk inverted
116/24 *Set of* 9 £170 £150
116s/24s Optd "Specimen" *Set of* 9 £160
(b) Paper blued.
125 ¼d. grey and carmine 28·00 30·00
126 ½d. dull green 29·00 30·00
127 1d. carmine 38·00 40·00
128 2½d. ultramarine 40·00 45·00
129 5d. olive-brown £225 £250
130 6d. mauve and carmine £130 £140
131 8d. orange and ultramarine £140 £150
132 10d. dull green and carmine £190 £225
133 2s.6d. blue-black and orange £120 £130

1905. Wmk Mult Crown CA. P 14.
135 **6** ¼d. slate-grey and carmine 8·50 2·75
136 ½d. dull green 17·00 10
137 1d. carmine 17·00 10
139 2½d. blue 18·00 15
141 6d. mauve and carmine 15·00 16·00
142 8d. orange and ultramarine 45·00 90·00
144 2s.6d. violet and green 45·00 £100
135/144 *Set of* 7 £150 £190

See also Nos. 163/9.

8 Nelson Monument

(Des Mrs. G. Goodman. Recess D.L.R.)

1906 (1 Mar). *Nelson Centenary.* Wmk Crown CC. P 14.
145 **8** ¼d. black and grey 8·50 1·7
w. Wmk inverted 35·00 38·0
146 ½d. black and pale green 9·50 1
w. Wmk inverted
x. Wmk reversed † 65·0
147 1d. black and red 12·00 1
w. Wmk inverted 50·00
x. Wmk reversed † 65·0
148 2d. black and yellow 1·75 4·5
149 2½d. black and bright blue 3·75 1·2
w. Wmk inverted
150 6d. black and mauve 18·00 25·0
151 1s. black and rose 21·00 50·0
145/51 *Set of* 7 65·00 75·0
145s/51s Optd "Specimen" *Set of* 7 £160

Two sets may be made of the above: one on thick, opaque creamy white paper; the other on thin, rather transparent, bluis white paper.

See also Nos. 158/62*a*.

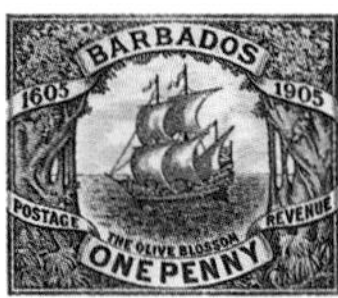

9 *Olive Blossom*, 1605

Kingston Relief Fund. 1d.
(10)

(Des Lady Carter. Recess D.L.R.)

1906 (15 Aug). *Tercentenary of Annexation.* Wmk Multiple Crow CA (sideways). P 14.
152 **9** 1d. black, blue and green 10·00 2
s. Optd "Specimen" 65·00

1907 (25 Jan–25 Feb). *Kingston Relief Fund. No. 108 surch with T* **1** *by T. E. King & Co., Barbados.*
153 **6** 1d.on 2d. slate-black and orange (R.) 2·75 6·5
a. Surch inverted (25.2.07) 1·75 6·5
b. Surch double £800 £85
c. Surch double, both inverted £800
d. Surch *tête-bêche* (pair) £1000
e. No stop after "1d." 45·00 75·0
ea. Do., surch inverted (25.2.07) 40·00 90·0
eb. Do., surch double — £140
f. Vert pair, one normal, one surch double — £95

The above stamp was sold for 2d. of which 1d. was retained f the postal revenue, and the other 1d. given to a fund for the reli of the sufferers by the earthquake in Jamaica.

An entire printing as No. 153a was created after a sheet inverted surcharges was found in the initial supply.

1907 (6 July). *Nelson Centenary.* Wmk Mult Crown CA. P 14.
158 **8** ¼d. black and grey 5·00 5·
161 2d. black and yellow 25·00 27·
162 2½d. black and bright blue 8·00 24·
a. Black and indigo £700 £8
158/62 *Set of* 3 35·00 50·

1909 (July)–**10**. Wmk Mult Crown CA. P 14.
163 **6** ¼d. brown 8·00
164 ½d. blue-green 20·00 1·
165 1d. red 19·00
166 2d. greyish slate (8.10) 7·50 11·
167 2½d. bright blue (1910) 48·00 8·
168 6d. dull and bright purple (1910) 10·00 16·
169 1s. black/*green* (8.10) 10·00 14·
163/9 *Set of* 7 £110 45·
163s/9s (ex ¼d., 2½d.) Optd "Specimen" *Set of* 5 £130

11

12

13

(Typo D.L.R.)

1912 (23 July)–**16**. Wmk Mult Crown CA. P 14.

170 **11** ½d. brown . . . 1·50 1·50
a. *Pale brown* (1916) . . . 1·50 2·50
aw. Wmk inverted
171 ½d. green . . . 3·75 10
a. Wmk sideways . . . † —
172 1d. red (13.8.12) . . . 9·00 10
a. *Scarlet* (1915) . . . 25·00 3·25
173 2d. greyish slate (13.8.12) . . . 3·00 14·00
174 2½d. bright blue (13.8.12) . . . 1·50 50
175 **12** 3d. purple/*yellow* (13.8.12) . . . 1·50 14·00
176 4d. red and black/*yellow* (13.8.12) . . . 1·75 18·00
177 6d. purple and dull purple (13.8.12) . . . 12·00 12·00
178 **13** 1s. black/*green* (13.8.12) . . . 8·50 14·00
179 2s. blue and purple/*blue* (13.8.12) . . . 42·00 48·00
180 3s. violet and green (13.8.12) . . . 90·00 £100
170/80 *Set of* 11 . . . £160 £200
170s/80s Optd "Specimen" *Set of* 11 . . . £150

14

WAR TAX
(15)

(Recess D.L.R.)

916 (16 June)–**19**. Wmk Mult Crown CA. P 14.

81 **14** ¼d. deep brown . . . 75 40
a. *Chestnut-brown* (9.17) . . . 1·50 35
b. *Sepia-brown* (4.18) . . . 3·75 2·75
w. Wmk inverted . . . 17·00 18·00
y. Wmk inverted and reversed . . . 38·00
82 ½d. green . . . 1·10 15
a. *Deep green* (9.17) . . . 1·60 15
b. *Pale green* (4.18) . . . 2·25 80
w. Wmk inverted . . . 30·00
y. Wmk inverted and reversed
83 1d. deep red . . . 17·00 6·00
a. *Bright carmine-red* (4.17) . . . 2·50 15
b. *Pale carmine-red* (9.17) . . . 6·00 65
w. Wmk inverted . . . 30·00
x. Wmk reversed
y. Wmk inverted and reversed . . . 30·00
84 2d. grey . . . 4·75 22·00
a. *Grey-black* (9.19) . . . 35·00 70·00
y. Wmk inverted and reversed
85 2½d. deep ultramarine . . . 3·50 2·50
a. *Royal blue* (11.17) . . . 3·50 2·50
w. Wmk inverted
y. Wmk inverted and reversed . . . 38·00 38·00
86 3d. purple/*yellow* (thin paper) . . . 2·50 7·00
a. *Dp purple/yell* (thick paper) (9.19) . . . 28·00 42·00
87 4d. red/*yellow* . . . 1·00 14·00
88 6d. purple . . . 4·00 4·50
89 1s. black/*green* . . . 7·00 11·00
90 2s. purple/*blue* . . . 16·00 7·50
y. Wmk inverted and reversed . . . 65·00
91 3s. deep violet . . . 50·00 £130
w. Wmk inverted
y. Wmk inverted and reversed
81/91 *Set of* 11 . . . 85·00 £180
81s/91s "Specimen" *Set of* 11 . . . £190

Dates quoted for shades are those of despatch from Great Britain.
Examples of the ½d. and 1d. values can be found perforated either line or by comb machines.
See also Nos. 199/200*a*.

917 (10 Oct)–**18**. *War Tax. Optd in London with T* **15**.

97 **11** 1d. bright red . . . 50 15
s. Optd "Specimen" . . . 55·00
w. Wmk inverted . . . — £100
98 1d. pale red (*thicker bluish paper*) (4.18) . . . 3·50 50

918 (18 Feb)–**20**. *Colours changed.* Wmk Mult Crown CA. P 14.

99 **14** 4d. black and red . . . 80 3·75
x. Wmk reversed . . . £140
00 3s. green and deep violet . . . 20·00 70·00
a. *Green and bright violet* (1920) . . . £250 £375
99s/200s Optd "Specimen" *Set of* 2 . . . £130

The centres of these are from a new die having no circular border ne.

16 Winged Victory from the Louvre

17 Victory from Victoria Memorial, London

(Recess D.L.R.)

1920 (9 Sept)–**21**. *Victory.* P 14.

(*a*) Wmk Mult Crown CA (sideways* on T **17**).

201 **16** ¼d. black and bistre-brown . . . 30 70
a. "C" of "CA" missing from wmk . . . £250
c. Substituted crown in wmk . . . £300
w. Wmk inverted
x. Wmk reversed . . . 35·00
y. Wmk inverted and reversed . . . 42·00
202 ½d. black and bright yellow-green . . . 1·00 15
a. "C" of "CA" missing from wmk . . . £275 £225
b. "A" of "CA" missing from wmk . . . £275
c. Substituted crown in wmk . . . £375
w. Wmk inverted . . . — 90·00
x. Wmk reversed . . . 90·00
y. Wmk inverted and reversed . . . 90·00 90·00
203 1d. black and vermilion . . . 4·00 10
a. "A" of "CA" missing from wmk . . . † £325
c. Substituted crown in wmk . . . † £325
w. Wmk inverted . . . 38·00 40·00
y. Wmk inverted and reversed
204 2d. black and grey . . . 2·25 8·00
a. "C" of "CA" missing from wmk . . . £325
205 2½d. indigo and ultramarine . . . 2·75 18·00
a. "C" of "CA" missing from wmk . . . £350
w. Wmk inverted . . . — 90·00
y. Wmk inverted and reversed . . . 90·00 £100
206 3d. black and purple . . . 3·00 6·50
w. Wmk inverted . . . 30·00 38·00
207 4d. black and blue-green . . . 3·25 7·00
208 6d. black and brown-orange . . . 3·75 15·00
w. Wmk inverted . . . 60·00 90·00
wa. "C" of "CA" missing from wmk . . . £950
209 **17** 1s. black and bright green . . . 10·00 29·00
a. "C" of "CA" missing from wmk . . . £800
w. Wmk Crown to left of CA
x. Wmk sideways reversed . . . £110
y. Wmk sideways inverted and reversed . . . £120
210 2s. black and brown . . . 28·00 42·00
w. Wmk Crown to left of CA . . . 65·00 90·00
x. Wmk sideways reversed . . . £110
y. Wmk sideways inverted and reversed
211 3s. black and dull orange . . . 32·00 50·00
a. "C" of "CA" missing from wmk . . . £750
w. Wmk Crown to left of CA . . . 75·00
x. Wmk sideways reversed
y. Wmk sideways inverted and reversed

(*b*) Wmk Mult Script CA.

212 **16** 1d. black and vermilion (22.8.21) . . . 17·00 30
201/12 *Set of* 12 . . . 95·00 £160
201s/12s Optd "Specimen" *Set of* 12 . . . £225

*The normal sideways watermark on Nos. 209/11 shows Crown to right of CA, *as seen from the back of the stamp.*
For illustration of the substituted watermark crown see Catalogue Introduction.

18

19

(Recess D.L.R.)

1921 (14 Nov)–**24**. P 14.

(*a*) Wmk Mult Crown CA.

213 **18** 3d. purple/*pale yellow* . . . 2·00 6·50
a. "A" of "CA" missing from wmk
x. Wmk reversed . . . † £140
214 4d. red/*pale yellow* . . . 1·75 15·00
215 1s. black/*emerald* . . . 5·50 14·00
w. Wmk inverted

(*b*) Wmk Mult Script CA.

217 **18** ¼d. brown . . . 25 10
x. Wmk reversed . . . 28·00
y. Wmk inverted and reversed . . . 40·00
219 ½d. green . . . 1·50 10
220 1d. red . . . 80 10
aw. Wmk inverted . . . 24·00 30·00
ax. Wmk reversed
ay. Wmk inverted and reversed
b. *Bright rose-carmine* . . . 6·50 1·00
bw. Wmk inverted . . . 24·00
221 2d. grey . . . 1·75 20
y. Wmk inverted and reversed
222 2½d. ultramarine . . . 1·50 8·00
225 6d. reddish purple . . . 3·50 5·50
226 1s. black/*emerald* (18.9.24) . . . 48·00 £100
227 2s. purple/*blue* . . . 10·00 19·00
228 3s. deep violet . . . 14·00 60·00
y. Wmk inverted and reversed
213/28 *Set of* 12 . . . 75·00 £200
213s/28s Optd "Specimen" *Set of* 12 . . . £170

1925 (1 Apr)–**35**. Wmk Mult Script CA. P 14.

229 **19** ¼d. brown . . . 25 10
230 ½d. green . . . 50 10
a. Perf 13½ × 12½ (2.32) . . . 6·50 10
231 1d. scarlet . . . 50 10
a. Perf 13½ × 12½ (2.32) . . . 6·00 50
231*b* 1½d. orange (1933) . . . 14·00 3·25
ba. Perf 13½ × 12½ (15.8.32) . . . 2·00 1·00
232 2d. grey . . . 50 3·25
233 2½d. blue . . . 50 80
a. *Bright ultramarine* (1933) . . . 16·00 2·00
ab. Perf 13½ × 12½ (2.32) . . . 6·50 4·00
234 3d. purple/*pale yellow* . . . 1·00 45
a. *Reddish purple/yellow* (1935) . . . 6·00 6·00
235 4d. red/*pale yellow* . . . 75 1·00
236 6d. purple . . . 1·00 90
237 1s. black/*emerald* . . . 2·00 6·50
a. Perf 13½ × 12½ (8.32) . . . 50·00 30·00
b. *Brownish black/bright yellow-green* (1934) . . . 4·50 10·00
238 2s. purple/*blue* . . . 7·00 6·50
238*a* 2s.6d. carmine/*blue* (1.9.32) . . . 22·00 28·00
239 3s. deep violet . . . 11·00 13·00
229/39 *Set of* 13 . . . 42·00 55·00
229s/39s Optd or Perf (1½d., 2s.6d.) "Specimen" *Set of* 13 . . . £180

Nos. 230/1 exist in coils constructed from normal sheets.

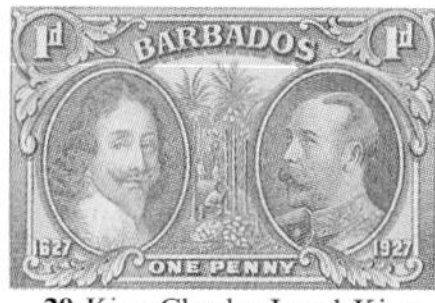

20 King Charles I and King George V

21 Badge of the Colony

(Recess B.W.)

1927 (17 Feb). *Tercentenary of Settlement of Barbados.* Wmk Mult Script CA. P 12½.

240 **20** 1d. carmine . . . 1·00 75
s. Optd "Specimen" . . . 45·00

1935 (6 May). *Silver Jubilee. As Nos. 91/4 of Antigua, but ptd by Waterlow.* P 11 × 12.

241 1d. deep blue and scarlet . . . 50 20
j. Damaged turret . . . £130
242 1½d. ultramarine and grey . . . 3·75 6·00
j. Damaged turret . . . £170
243 2½d. brown and deep blue . . . 2·25 4·00
m. "Bird" by turret . . . £190
244 1s. slate and purple . . . 17·00 18·00
l. Kite and horizontal log . . . £325
241/4 *Set of* 4 . . . 21·00 25·00
241s/4s Perf "Specimen" *Set of* 4 . . . 85·00

For illustrations of plate varieties see Omnibus section following Zanzibar.

1937 (14 May). *Coronation. As Nos. 95/7 of Antigua, but printed by D.L.R.* P 14.

245 1d. scarlet . . . 30 15
246 1½d. yellow-brown . . . 40 65
247 2½d. bright blue . . . 70 75
245/7 *Set of* 3 . . . 1·25 1·40
245s/7s Pair "Specimen" *Set of* 3 . . . 60·00

Recut line (R. 10/6)

Extra frame line (R. 11/9)

Mark on central ornament (R. 1/3, 2/3, 3/3)

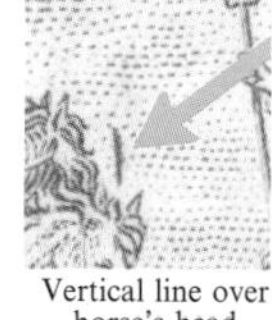
Vertical line over horse's head (R. 4/10) (corrected on Dec 1947 ptg)

"Flying mane" (R. 4/1) (corrected on Dec 1947 ptg)

Curved line at top right (R. 7/8) (corrected on Dec 1947 ptg)

Cracked plate (extends to top right ornament) (R. 6/10))

(Recess D.L.R.)

1938 (3 Jan)–**47**. Wmk Mult Script CA. P 13½ × 13.

No.	Type	Description	Unused	Used
248	**21**	½d. green	6·00	15
		a. Recut line	£120	40·00
		b. Perf 14 (8.42)	70·00	1·25
		ba. Recut line	£350	75·00
248*c*		½d. yellow-bistre (16.10.42)	15	30
		ca. "A" of "CA" missing from wmk	£1100	
		cb. Recut line	21·00	25·00
249		1d. scarlet (12.40)	£275	4·00
		a. Perf 14 (3.1.38)	16·00	10
249*b*		1d. blue-green (1943)	4·50	80
		c. Perf 14 (16.10.42)	15	10
		ca. "A" of "CA" missing from wmk	£1100	
250		1½d. orange	15	40
		a. "A" of "CA" missing from wmk	£1100	
		b. Perf 14 (11.41)	4·75	65
250*c*		2d. claret (3.6.41)	50	2·50
		ca. Extra frame line	40·00	70·00
250*d*		2d. carmine (20.9.43)	20	70
		da. Extra frame line	27·00	38·00
		db. "A" of "CA" missing from wmk	†	—
		e. Perf 14 (11.9.44)	60	1·75
		ea. Extra frame line	30·00	55·00
251		2½d. ultramarine	50	60
		a. Mark on central ornament	40·00	40·00
		b. Blue (17.2.44)	1·75	4·50
		ba. "A" of "CA" missing from wmk	£1000	
		bb. Mark on central ornament	55·00	70·00
252		3d. brown	20	2·25
		a. Vertical line over horse's head	75·00	£120
		b. Perf 14 (4.41)	20	60
		ba. Vertical line over horse's head	75·00	90·00
252*c*		3d. blue (1.4.47)	20	1·75
		ca. Vertical line over horse's head	75·00	£100
253		4d. black	20	10
		a. Flying mane	95·00	60·00
		b. Curved line at top right	80·00	50·00
		c. Cracked plate	80·00	50·00
		d. Perf 14 (11.9.44)	20	4·50
		da. Flying mane	95·00	£140
		db. Curved line at top right	80·00	£120
		dc. Cracked plate	80·00	£120
254		6d. violet	80	40
254*a*		8d. magenta (9.12.46)	55	2·00
255		1s. olive-green	16·00	2·50
		a. Deep brown-olive (19.11.45)	1·00	10
256		2s.6d. purple	7·00	1·50
256*a*		5s. indigo (3.6.41)	3·25	7·00
		ab. "A" of "CA" missing from wmk	£1600	
248/56*a*		*Set of* 16	32·00	15·00
248s/56as		Perf "Specimen" *Set of* 16	£225	

No. 249a was perforated by two machines, one gauging 13.8 × 14.1 line (1938), the other 14.1 comb (October 1940).

Nos. 248/*c* and 249/*c* exist in coils constructed from normal sheets.

22 Kings Charles I, George VI, Assembly Chamber and Mace

(Recess D.L.R.)

1939 (27 June). *Tercentenary of General Assembly.* Wmk Mult Script CA. P 13½ × 14.

No.	Type	Description	Unused	Used
257	**22**	½d. green	2·75	1·00
258		1d. scarlet	2·75	35
259		1½d. orange	2·75	60
260		2½d. bright ultramarine	2·75	4·50
261		3d. brown	2·75	3·00
257/61		*Set of* 5	12·00	8·50
257s/61s		Perf "Specimen" *Set of* 5	£150	

Two flags on tug (R. 5/2)

1946 (18 Sept). *Victory. As Nos. 110/11 of Antigua.*

No.	Description	Unused	Used
262	1½d. red-orange	15	15
	a. Two flags on tug	23·00	
263	3d. brown	15	15
262s/3s	Perf "Specimen" *Set of* 2	55·00	

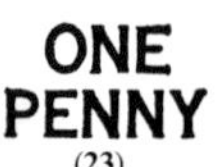

ONE PENNY

(23)

Short "Y" (R. 6/2)

Broken "E" (R. 7/4and 11/4)

(Surch by Barbados Advocate Co)

1947 (21 Apr). *Surch with T* **23**.

(a) P 14.

No.	Type	Description	Unused	Used
264	**21**	1d.on 2d. carmine (No. 250*e*)	1·75	2·50
		a. Extra frame line	70·00	80·00
		b. Short "Y"	70·00	80·00
		c. Broken "E"	38·00	42·00

(b) P 13½ × 13.

No.	Type	Description	Unused	Used
264*d*	**21**	1d.on 2d. carmine (No. 250*d*)	3·00	5·00
		da. Extra frame line	£170	£200
		db. Short "Y"	£170	£200
		dc. Broken "E"	£100	£130

The relationship of the two words in the surcharge differs on each position of the sheet.

1948 (24 Nov). *Royal Silver Wedding. As Nos. 112/13 of Antigua.*

No.	Description	Unused	Used
265	1½d. orange	30	10
266	5s. indigo	10·00	8·00

1949 (10 Oct). *75th Anniv of Universal Postal Union. As Nos. 114/17 of Antigua.*

No.	Description	Unused	Used
267	1½d. red-orange	30	75
268	3d. deep blue	2·00	2·50
269	4d. grey	35	2·50
270	1s. olive	35	60
267/70	*Set of* 4	2·75	5·75

(New Currency. 100 cents = 1 West Indian, later Barbados, dollar)

24 Dover Fort

27 Statue of Nelson

(Recess B.W.)

1950 (1 May). *T* **24**, **27** *and similar designs.* Wmk Mult Script CA. P 11 × 11½ (*horiz*), 13½ (*vert*).

No.	Description	Unused	Used
271	1c. indigo	30	2·75
272	2c. emerald-green	15	2·00
273	3c. reddish brown and blue-green	1·25	3·00
274	4c. carmine	15	40
275	6c. light blue	15	2·25
276	8c. bright blue and purple-brown	1·25	2·50
277	12c. greenish blue and brown-olive	1·00	1·00
278	24c. scarlet and black	1·00	50
279	48c. violet	8·50	6·50
280	60c. green and claret	9·50	9·00
281	$1.20, carmine and olive-green	9·50	4·00
282	$2.40, black	17·00	18·00
271/282	*Set of* 12	45·00	45·00

Designs: *Horiz*—2c. Sugar cane breeding; 3c. Public buildings; 6c. Casting net; 8c. *Frances W. Smith* (schooner); 12c. Four-winged Flyingfish; 24c. Old Main Guard Garrison; 60c. Careenage; $2.40, Seal of Barbados. *Vert*—18c. St. Michael's Cathedral; $1.20, Map of Barbados and wireless mast.

1951 (16 Feb). *Inauguration of B.W.I. University College. As Nos. 118/19 of Antigua.*

No.	Description	Unused	Used
283	3c. brown and blue-green	30	30
284	12c. blue-green and brown-olive	55	2·00

36 King George VI and Stamp of 1852

(Recess Waterlow)

1952 (15 Apr). *Barbados Stamp Centenary.* Wmk Mult Script CA. P 13½.

No.	Type	Description	Unused	Used
285	**36**	3c. green and slate-green	25	40
286		4c. blue and carmine	25	1·00
287		12c. slate-green and bright green	30	1·00
288		24c. red-brown and brownish black	30	55
285/8		*Set of* 4	1·00	2·75

STAMP BOOKLETS

1906 (Feb).
SB1 2s.½d. booklet containing twenty-four 1d. (No. 137) in blocks of 6

1909. *Black on red cover. Stapled.*
SB1*a* 1s.6d. booklet containing eighteen 1d. (No. 165) in blocks of 6

1913 (June). *Black on red cover. Stapled.*
SB2 2s. booklet containing twelve ½d. and eighteen 1d. (Nos. 171/2) in blocks of 6 . . . £2000

1916 (16 June). *Black on red cover. Stapled.*
SB3 2s. booklet containing twelve ½d. and eighteen 1d. (Nos. 182/3) in pairs . . . £1000

1920 (Sept). *Black on red cover. Stapled.*
SB4 2s. booklet containing twelve ½d. and eighteen 1d. (Nos. 202/3) in pairs

1932 (12 Nov). *Black on pale green cover. Austin Cars and Post Office Guide advertisements on front. Stapled.*
SB5 2s. booklet containing ½d. and 1d. (Nos. 230a, 231a) each in block of 10 and 1½d. (No. 231ba) in block of 6 . . . £1500

1933 (4 Dec). *Black on pale green cover. Advocate Co. Ltd. advertisement on front. Stapled.*
SB6 2s. booklet containing ½d. and 1d. (Nos. 230/1) each in block of 10 and 1½d. (No. 231*b*) in block of 6 . . . £1800

1938 (3 Jan). *Black on light blue cover. Advocate Co. Ltd. advertisement on front. Stapled.*
SB7 2s. booklet containing ½d. and 1d. (Nos. 248, 249a) each in block of 10 and 1½d. (No. 250) in block of 6 . . . £2000

POSTAGE DUE STAMPS

D 1

(Typo D.L.R.)

1934 (2 Jan)–**47**. Wmk Mult Script CA. P 14.

No.	Type	Description	Unused	Used
D1	**D 1**	½d. green (10.2.35)	1·25	8·5
D2		1d. black	1·25	1·2
		a. Bisected (½d.) (on cover)	†	£120
D3		3d. carmine (13.3.47)	20·00	20·0
D1/3		*Set of* 3	20·00	27·0
D1s/3s		Perf "Specimen" *Set of* 3	75·00	

The bisected 1d. was officially authorised for use between Marc 1934 and February 1935. Some specimens had the value "½d." written across the half stamp in red or black ink (*Price on cove* £1400).

(Typo D.L.R.)

1950 (8 Dec)–**53**. *Values in cents.* Wmk Mult Script CA. *Ordinar paper.* P 14.

No.	Type	Description	Unused	Used
D4	**D 1**	1c. green	3·75	26·0
		a. Chalk-surfaced paper. *Deep green* (29.11.51)	30	3·0
		ab. Error. Crown missing, W **9***a*	£400	
		ac. Error. St. Edward's Crown, W **9***b*	£225	
D5		2c. black	7·00	14·0
		a. Chalk-surfaced paper (20.1.53)	1·00	6·0
		ac. Error. St. Edward's Crown, W **9***b*	£400	
D6		6c. carmine	16·00	17·0
		a. Chalk-surfaced paper (20.1.53)	1·00	8·5
		ab. Error. Crown missing, W **9***a*	£200	
		ac. Error. St. Edward's Crown, W **9***b*	£160	
D4/6		*Set of* 3	24·00	50·0
D4a/6a		*Set of* 3	2·10	16·0

The 1c. has no dot below "c".

Barbuda

(*see after* Antigua)

Basutoland

Stamps of CAPE OF GOOD HOPE were used in Basutolar from about 1876, initially cancelled by upright oval with frame number type postmarks of that colony. Cancellation numbe known to have been used in Basutoland are 133 (Quthing), 15 (Mafeteng), 210 (Mohaleshoek), 277 (Morija), 281 (Maseru), 3 (Thlotse Heights) and 688 (Teyateyaneng).

From 1910 until 1933 the stamps of SOUTH AFRICA were use. Stamps of the Union provinces are also known used Basutoland during the early years of this period and can also found cancelled-to-order during 1932–33.

The following post offices and postal agencies existed Basutoland before December 1933. Stamps of Cape of Good Ho or South Africa with recognisable postmarks from them are wor a premium. For a few of the smaller offices or agencies there a as yet, no actual examples recorded. Dates given are those genera accepted as the year in which the office was first opened.

Bokong (1931)	Motsekuoa (1915)
Butha Buthe (1907)	Mount Morosi (1918)
Jonathan's (1927)	Mphotos (1914)
Khabos (1927)	Peka (1908)
Khetisas (1930)	Phamong (1932)
Khukhune (1933)	Pitseng (1921)
Kolonyama (1914)	Qachasnek (1895)
Kueneng (1914)	Qalo (1923?)
Leribe (1890)	Quthing (1882)
Mafeteng (1874)	Rankakalas (1933)
Majara (1912)	Roma Mission (1913)
Makhoa (1932)	Sebapala (1930)
Makoalis (1927)	Seforong (1924)
Mamathes (1919)	Sehlabathebe (1921)
Mapoteng (1925)	Sekake (1931)

Marakabeis (1932)	Teyateyaneng (1886)
Maseru (1872)	Thaba Bosigo (1913)
Maseru Rail (1915?)	Thabana Morena (1922)
Mashai (1929)	Thabaneng (1914)
Matsaile (1930)	Thaba Tseka (1929)
Mekading (1914)	Thlotse Heights (1872)
Mofokas (1915)	Tsepo (1923)
Mohaleshoek (1873)	Tsoelike (1927)
Mokhotlong (1921)	Tsoloane (1918)
Morija (1884)	

For further details of the postal history of Basutoland see *The Cancellations and Postal Markings of Basutoland/Lesotho* by A. H. Scott, published by Collectors Mail Auctions (Pty) Ltd, Cape Town, from which the above has been, with permission, extracted.

PRICES FOR STAMPS ON COVER TO 1945	
Nos. 1/19	*from* × 5
Nos. 11/14	*from* × 6
Nos. 15/17	*from* × 10
Nos. 18/28	*from* × 6
Nos. 29/31	*from* × 10
Nos. O1/4	*from* × 4
Nos. D1/2	*from* × 25

CROWN COLONY

1 King George V, Nile Crocodile and Mountains

(Recess Waterlow)

1933 (1 Dec). Wmk Mult Script CA. P 12½.

1	**1**	½d. emerald	1·00	1·75
2		1d. scarlet	75	1·25
3		2d. bright purple	1·00	80
4		3d. bright blue	75	1·25
5		4d. grey	2·00	7·00
6		6d. orange-yellow	2·25	1·75
7		1s. red-orange	2·25	4·50
8		2s.6d. sepia	21·00	45·00
9		5s. violet	50·00	70·00
10		10s. olive-green	£130	£140
1/10 *Set of* 10			£190	£250
1s/10s Perf "Specimen" *Set of* 10			£275	

1935 (4 May). *Silver Jubilee. As Nos. 91/4 of Antigua.* P 13½ × 14.

11	1d. deep blue and carmine	55	1·00
	f. Diagonal line by turret	80·00	
12	2d. ultramarine and grey	65	1·25
	f. Diagonal line by turret	70·00	£110
	g. Dot to left of chapel	£110	
13	3d. brown and deep blue	3·75	4·25
	g. Dot to left of chapel	£170	
	h. Dot by flagstaff	£170	
	i. Dash by turret	£190	
14	6d. slate and purple	3·75	4·25
	g. Dot to left of chapel	£190	
	h. Dot by flagstaff	£190	
	i. Dash by turret	£190	
11/14 *Set of* 4		8·00	9·75
11s/14s Perf "Specimen" *Set of* 4		90·00	

For illustrations of plate varieties see Omnibus section following Zanzibar.

1937 (12 May). *Coronation. As Nos. 95/7 of Antigua, but printed by D.L.R.* P 14.

15	1d. scarlet	35	1·00
16	2d. bright purple	50	1·00
17	3d. bright blue	60	1·00
15/17 *Set of* 3		1·25	2·75
15s/17s Perf "Specimen" *Set of* 3		65·00	

2 King George VI, Nile Crocodile and Mountains

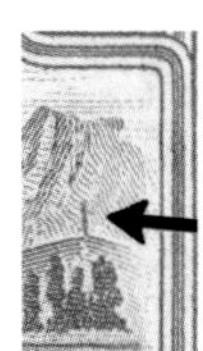

Tower flaw (R. 2/4)

(Recess Waterlow)

938 (1 Apr). Wmk Mult Script CA. P 12½.

8	**2**	½d. green	30	1·25
9		1d. scarlet	50	70
		a. Tower flaw	£110	
0		1½d. light blue	40	50
1		2d. bright purple	30	60
2		3d. bright blue	30	1·25
3		4d. grey	1·50	3·50
4		6d. orange-yellow	60	1·50
5		1s. red-orange	60	1·00
6		2s.6d. sepia	9·00	8·50
7		5s. violet	24·00	9·50
8		10s. olive-green	24·00	17·00
8/28 *Set of* 11			55·00	40·00
8s/28s Perf "Specimen" *Set of* 11			£225	

Basutoland

(3)

1945 (3 Dec). *Victory. Stamps of South Africa, optd with T* **3**, *inscr alternately in English and Afrikaans.*

			Un. pair	*Used pair*	*Used single*
29	**55**	1d. brown and carmine	40	60	10
30	**56**	2d. slate-blue and violet	40	50	10
31	**57**	3d. deep blue and blue	40	70	15
29/31 *Set of* 3			1·10	1·75	30

4 King George VI

5 King George VI and Queen Elizabeth

6 Queen Elizabeth II as Princess, and Princess Margaret

7 The Royal Family

(Recess Waterlow)

1947 (17 Feb). *Royal Visit.* Wmk Mult Script CA. P 12½.

32	**4**	1d. scarlet	10	10
33	**5**	2d. green	10	10
34	**6**	3d. ultramarine	10	10
35	**7**	1s. mauve	15	10
32/5 *Set of* 4			40	30
32s/5s Perf "Specimen" *Set of* 4			85·00	

1948 (1 Dec). *Royal Silver Wedding. As Nos. 112/13 of Antigua.*

36	1½d. ultramarine	20	10
37	10s. grey-olive	30·00	27·00

1949 (10 Oct). *75th Anniv of Universal Postal Union. As Nos. 114/17 of Antigua.*

38	1½d. blue	20	1·50
39	3d. deep blue	1·75	2·00
40	6d. orange	1·00	2·50
41	1s. red-brown	50	1·25
38/41 *Set of* 4		3·00	6·50

OFFICIAL STAMPS

OFFICIAL

(O 1)

1934 (4 May). *Nos. 1/3 and 6 optd with Type* O **1**.

O1	**1**	½d. emerald	£4000	£3500
O2		1d. scarlet	£1600	£1000
O3		2d. bright purple	£1000	£550
O4		6d. orange-yellow	£11000	£4750
O1/4 *Set of* 4			£16000	£9000

Collectors are advised to buy these stamps only from reliable sources. They were not sold to the public.

POSTAGE DUE STAMPS

D 1

Normal

Large "d." (R. 9/6, 10/6)

(Typo D.L.R.)

1933 (1 Dec)–**52**. *Ordinary paper.* Wmk Mult Script CA. P 14.

D1	**D 1**	1d. carmine	1·75	8·00
		a. Scarlet (1938)	35·00	42·00
		b. Chalk-surfaced paper. *Deep carmine* (24.10.51)	1·50	2·25
		ba. Error. Crown missing, W **9***a*	£150	
		bb. Error. St. Edward's Crown, W **9***b*	75·00	
D2		2d. violet	7·50	16·00
		a. Chalk-surfaced paper (6.11.52)	30	12·00
		ab. Error. Crown missing, W **9***a*	£160	
		ac. Error. St. Edward's Crown, W **9***b*	80·00	
		ad. Large "d"	6·00	
D1s/2s Perf "Specimen" *Set of* 2			42·00	

Batum

Batum, the outlet port on the Black Sea for the Russian Transcaucasian oilfields, was occupied by the Turks on 15 April 1918.

Under the terms of the armistice signed at Mudros on 30 October 1918 the Turks were to withdraw and be replaced by an Allied occupation of Batum, the Baku oilfields and the connecting Transcaucasia Railway. British forces arrived off Batum in early December and the oblast, or district, was declared a British military governorship on 25 December 1918. The Turkish withdrawal was complete five days later.

The provision of a civilian postal service was initially the responsibility of the Batum Town Council. Some form of mail service was in operation by February 1919 with the postage prepaid in cash. Letters are known showing a framed oblong handstamp, in Russian, to this effect. The Town Council was responsible for the production of the first issue, Nos. 1/6, but shortly after these stamps were placed on sale a strike by Council employees against the British military governor led to the postal service being placed under British Army control.

SURCHARGES. Types **2** and **4/8** were all applied by handstamp. Most values from No. 19 onwards are known showing the surcharge inverted, surcharge double or in pairs with surcharge *tête-bêche*.

BRITISH OCCUPATION

(Currency. 100 kopeks = 1 rouble)

PRICES FOR STAMPS ON COVER		
Nos.	1/6	*from* × 60
Nos.	7/10	*from* × 15
Nos.	11/28	*from* × 60
Nos.	19/20	*from* × 15
Nos.	21/44	—
Nos.	45/53	*from* × 200

1 Aloe Tree

БАТУМ. ОБ.

Руб 10 Руб

(2)

1919 (4 Apr). *Litho.* Imperf.

1	**1**	5k. green	6·50	13·00
2		10k. ultramarine	6·50	13·00
3		50k. yellow	2·75	4·00
4		1r. chocolate	4·25	4·25
5		3r. violet	9·50	15·00
6		5r. brown	10·00	22·00
1/6 *Set of* 6			35·00	65·00

Nos. 1/6 were printed in sheets of 198 (18 × 11).

1919 (13 Apr). *Russian stamps (Arms types) handstamped with T* **2**.

7	10r.on 1k. orange (imperf)	48·00	60·00
8	10r.on 3k. carmine-red (imperf)	20·00	25·00
9	10r.on 5k. brown-lilac (perf)	£375	£375
10	10r.on 10 on 7k. deep blue (perf)	£325	£325

A similar handstamped surcharge, showing the capital letters without serifs, is bogus.

BRITISH OCCUPATION

(3)

1919 (10 Nov). *Colours changed and new values. Optd with T* **3**.

11	**1**	5k. yellow-green	13·00	12·00
12		10k. bright blue	13·00	12·00
13		25k. orange-yellow	13·00	12·00
14		1r. pale blue	3·75	11·00
15		2r. pink	1·00	4·00
16		3r. bright violet	1·00	4·00
17		5r. brown	1·25	4·00
		a. "CCUPATION" (R. 5/1)	£400	
18		7r. brownish red	4·25	7·00
11/18 *Set of* 8			45·00	60·00

Nos. 11/18 were printed in sheets of 432 (18 × 24).

(4)

БАТУМЪ
BRITISH
P.15 P.
OCCUPATION
О БЛ.

(5)

1919 (27 Nov)–**20**. *Russian stamps (Arms types) handstamped with T* **4** *or* **5**. Imperf.

19	10r. on 3k. carmine-red	16·00	20·00
20	15r. on 1k. orange	50·00	60·00
	a. Red surch	42·00	48·00
	b. Violet surch (10.3.20)	55·00	65·00

Nos. 20a/b have the handstamp in soluble ink.

1920 (12 Jan). *Russian stamps (Arms types) handstamped as T* **4**.

(a) Imperf.

21	50r. on 1k. orange	£375	£400
22	50r. on 2k. yellow-green (R.)	£475	£600

(b) Perf.

23	50r. on 2k. yellow-green	£475	£500
24	50r. on 3k. carmine-red	£950	£1000
25	50r. on 4k. red	£700	£750

26 50r. on 5k. brown-lilac £425 £475
27 50r. on 10k. deep blue (R.) £1200 £1300
28 50r. on 15k. blue and red-brown £475 £550

(6)

1920 (30 Jan–21 Feb). *Russian stamps (Arms types) handstamped as T* **6**.

(a) Perf.

29 25r. on 5k. brown-lilac (21 Feb) . . . . . . 40·00 42·00
a. Blue surch . . . . 40·00 42·00
30 25r. on 10 on 7k. blue (21 Feb) £110 £120
a. Blue surch . . . . 65·00 70·00
31 25r. on 20 on 14k. dp carmine & bl (21 Feb) . . . . 70·00 75·00
a. Blue surch . . . . 65·00 70·00
32 25r. on 25k. deep violet & lt green (21 Feb) £110 £120
a. Blue surch . . . . 90·00 95·00
33 25r. on 50k. green and copper-red (21 Feb) . . . . 65·00 70·00
a. Blue surch . . . . 70·00 75·00
34 50r. on 2k. yellow-green . . . . 95·00 £100
35 50r. on 3k. carmine-red . . . . 95·00 £100
36 50r. on 4k. red . . . . 85·00 90·00
37 50r. on 5k. brown-lilac . . . . 65·00 70·00

(b) Imperf.

38 50r. on 2k. yellow-green £300 £375
39 50r. on 3k. carmine-red £375 £450
40 50r. on 5k. brown-lilac £1100 £1200

1920 (10 Mar). *Romanov issue, as T* **25** *of Russia, handstamped with T* **6**.
41 50r. on 4k. rose-carmine (B.) . . . . 55·00 70·00

РУБ 25 ЛЕЙ

25 РУБ. 25

(7)

R.50R.
BRITISH
OCCUPATION
РУБ.

(8)

1920 (1 Apr). *Nos. 3, 11 and 13 handstamped with T* **7** *(Nos. 42/3) or* **8** *(No. 44).*
42 25r. on 5k. yellow-green . . . . 29·00 30·00
a. Blue surch . . . . 40·00 40·00
43 25r. on 25k. orange-yellow . . . . 23·00 24·00
a. Blue surch . . . . 95·00 95·00
44 50r. on 50k. yellow . . . . 18·00 22·00
a. "50" cut . . . . 14·00 15·00
b. Blue surch . . . . 90·00 90·00
ba. "50" cut £160 £160

Nos. 44a and 44ba show the figures broken by intentional file cuts applied as a protection against forgery. The "5" is cut at the base and on the right side of the loop. The "0" is chipped at top and foot, and has both vertical lines severed.

1920 (19 June). *Colours changed and new values. Optd with T* **3**. Imperf.
45 **1** 1r. chestnut . . . . 1·00 8·00
a. "BPITISH" . . . . 55·00
46 2r. pale blue . . . . 1·00 8·00
a. "BPITISH" . . . . 65·00
47 3r. pink . . . . 1·25 8·00
a. "BPITISH" . . . . 65·00
48 5r. black-brown . . . . 1·00 8·00
a. "BPITISH" . . . . 65·00
49 7r. yellow . . . . 1·00 8·00
a. "BPITISH" . . . . 65·00
50 10r. myrtle-green . . . . 1·00 8·00
a. "BPITISH" . . . . 65·00
51 15r. violet . . . . 1·50 9·50
a. "BPITISH" £140
52 25r. scarlet . . . . 1·10 9·00
a. "BPITISH" £120
53 50r. deep blue . . . . 1·50 12·00
a. "BPITISH" £200
45/53 *Set of* 9 . . . . 9·25 70·00

Nos. 45/53 were printed in sheets of 308 (22×14). The "BPITISH" error occurs on R. 1/19 of the overprint.

POSTCARD STAMPS

When Nos. 7/10 were issued on 13 April 1919 a similar 35k. surcharge was applied to stocks of various Russian postcards held by the post office. The majority of these had stamp impressions printed directly on to the card, but there were also a few cards, originally intended for overseas mail, on which Russia 4k. stamps had been affixed.

PRICES. Those in the left-hand column are for unused examples on complete postcard; those on the right for used examples off card. Examples used on postcard are worth more.

1919 (13 Apr). *Russian stamps handstamped as T* **2**.
P1 35k.on 4k. red (Arms type) £2750 £3250
P2 35k.on 4k. carmine-red (Romanov issue) . . £7500 £8500

Batum was handed over to the National Republic of Georgia on 7 July 1920.

Bechuanaland

Before the 1880s the only Europeans in the area which became Bechuanaland were scattered hunters and traders, together with the missionaries who were established at Kuruman as early as 1816.

Tribal conflicts in the early years of the decade led to the intervention of Boers from the Transvaal who established the independent republics of Goshen and Stellaland.

STELLALAND

The Boer republic of Stellaland was proclaimed towards the end of 1882. A postal service was organised from the capital, Vryburg, and stamps were ordered from a firm in Cape Town. These were only valid within the republic. Until June 1885 mail to other parts of South Africa was sent through Christiana, in the Transvaal, and was franked with both Stellaland and Transvaal stamps.

No date stamps or obliterators were used by the Stellaland Post Office. Stamps were pen-cancelled with the initials of a postal official and the date.

PRICES FOR STAMPS ON COVER

The issues of Stellaland are very rare on cover.

1 Arms of the Republic

(Litho by Van der Sandt, de Villiers & Co., Cape Town)

1884 (29 Feb). P 12.
1 **1** 1d. red £180 £325
a. Imperf between (horiz pair) £3750
b. Imperf between (vert pair) £3750
2 3d. orange . . . . 22·00 £325
a. Imperf between (horiz pair) £700
b. Imperf between (vert pair) £1300
c. Imperf vert (horiz pair) £900
3 4d. olive-grey . . . . 21·00 £350
a. Imperf between (horiz pair) £650
b. Imperf between (vert pair) £1500
4 6d. lilac-mauve . . . . 22·00 £350
a. Imperf between (horiz pair) £1000
b. Imperf between (vert pair) £1300
5 1s. green . . . . 45·00 £600

In 1884 the British Government, following appeals from local chiefs for protection, decided to annex both Goshen and Stellaland. A force under Sir Charles Warren from the Cape reached Vryburg on 7 February 1885 and continued to Mafeking, the principal town of Goshen.

On 30 September 1885 Stellaland and other territory to the south of the Molopo River was constituted the Crown Colony of British Bechuanaland. A protectorate was also proclaimed over a vast tract of land to the north of the Molopo.

Stellaland stamps continued to be used until 2 December 1885 with external mail, franked with Stellaland and Cape of Good Hope stamps, postmarked at Barkly West and Kimberley in Griqualand West.

1885 (Oct). *Handstamped* "Twee" *sideways in violet-lake.*
6 **1** 2d. on 4d. olive-grey £3500

On 2 December 1885 Cape of Good Hope stamps overprinted "British Bechuanaland" were placed on sale at the Vryburg post office.

BRITISH BECHUANALAND

CROWN COLONY

PRICES FOR STAMPS ON COVER		
Nos.	1/8	*from* × 12
No.	9	*from* × 80
Nos.	10/21	*from* × 8
Nos.	22/8	*from* × 10
No.	29	*from* × 10
No.	30	*from* × 10
Nos.	31/2	*from* × 12
Nos.	33/7	*from* × 20
Nos.	38/9	*from* × 25

British
Bechuanaland
(1)

BRITISH
BECHUANALAND
(2)

1885 (2 Dec)–**87**. *Stamps of Cape of Good Hope ("Hope" seated) optd with T* **1**, *by W. A. Richards & Sons, Cape Town.*

(a) Wmk Crown CC (No. 3) or Crown CA (others).
1 ½d. grey-black (No. 40a) (R.) . . . . 14·00 22·00
a. Opt in lake £3250 £3250
b. Opt double (Lake+Black) £650
2 3d. pale claret (No. 43) . . . . 35·00 45·00
a. No dot to 1st "i" of "British" £350
3 4d. dull blue (No. 30) (12.86?) . . . . . . 55·00 65·00

(b) Wmk Anchor (Cape of Good Hope. Type **13**).
4 ½d. grey-black (No. 48*a*) (3.87) . . . . . . 7·00 12·00
a. Error. "ritish" £2000
b. Opt double £3000
5 1d. rose-red (No. 49) . . . . 10·00 9·00
a. Error. "ritish" £2750 £2250
b. No dot to 1st "i" of "British" £150 £150
c. Opt double . . . . † £1900
6 2d. pale bistre (No. 50) . . . . 35·00 8·00
a. Error. "ritish" £5000 £3500
b. No dot to 1st "i" of "British" £350 £150
c. Opt double . . . . † £1800
7 6d. reddish purple (No. 52) . . . . £100 38·00
a. No dot to 1st "i" of "British" £1000 £500
8 1s. green (No. 53) (11.86?) £250 £150
a. Error. "ritish" £15000 £11000

Nos. 1/8 were overprinted from settings of 120. The missing "B" errors are believed to have occurred on one position for one of these settings only. The 'No dot to 1st "i"' variety occurs on R. 10/3 of the left pane.

Overprints with stop after "Bechuanaland" are forged.

1887 (1 Nov). *No. 197 of Great Britain optd with T* **2**, *by D.L.R.*
9 ½d. vermilion . . . . 1·25 1·25
a. Opt double £2250
s. Handstamped "Specimen" . . . . 85·00

3

4

5

(Typo D.L.R.)

1887 (1 Nov).

(a) Wmk Orb (Great Britain Type **48**). P 14.
10 **3** 1d. lilac and black . . . . 15·00 1·7
11 2d. lilac and black . . . . 70·00 1·7
a. Pale dull lilac and black . . . . 55·00 23·0
12 3d. lilac and black . . . . 3·50 5·5
a. Pale reddish lilac and black . . . . . 60·00 18·0
13 4d. lilac and black . . . . 45·00 2·2
14 6d. lilac and black . . . . 55·00 2·5

(b) Wmk Script "V R" (sideways, reading up). P 13½.
15 **4** 1s. green and black . . . . 29·00 5·5
16 2s. green and black . . . . 50·00 35·0
17 2s.6d. green and black . . . . 60·00 60·0
18 5s. green and black . . . . 90·00 £15
19 10s. green and black £180 £35

(c) Two Orbs (sideways). P 14×13½.
20 **5** £1 lilac and black £800 £70
21 £5 lilac and black £3000 £150
10s/21s H/S "Specimen" *Set of* 12 . . . . . . £900

Nos. 10/21 were produced by overprinting a series o "Unappropriated Die" designs originally produced by the Board o Inland Revenue for use as Great Britain fiscal stamps.

Several values are known on blued paper. No. 11*a* is the firs printing of the 2d. (on safety paper?) and has a faded appearance.

When purchasing Nos. 20/21 in used condition beware of copie with fiscal cancellations cleaned off and bearing forged postmarks.

For No. 15 surcharged "£5" see No. F2.

1d.
(6)

1s.
(7)

One
Half-
Penny
(8)

1888 (7 Aug). *Nos. 10/11 and 13/15 surch as T* **6** *or* **7** *by P. Townshend & Co, Vryburg.*
22 **3** 1d. on 1d. lilac and black . . . . 7·50 6·5
23 2d. on 2d. lilac and black (R.) . . . . . 23·00 3·0
a. Pale dull lilac and black (No. 11a) . . 90·00 48·0
b. Curved foot to "2" £225 £15
c. Surch in green . . . . † £350
25 4d. on 4d. lilac and black (R.) £250 £35
26 6d. on 6d. lilac and black . . . . £100 10·0
a. Surch in blue . . . . † £1100
28 **4** 1s. on 1s. green and black . . . . £150 80·0

Nos. 23c and 26a are from two sheets of surcharge tria subsequently put into stock and used at Vryburg (2d.) or Mafekin (6d.) during 1888-89.

1888 (Dec). *No. 12a surch with T* **8**, *by P. Townshend & Co, Vryburg*
29 **3** ½d. on 3d. pale reddish lilac and black £150 £16
a. Broken "f" in "Half" £5500

No. 29 was produced from a setting of 60 (12×5).

No. 29a shows the letter "f" almost completely missing and occu on R. 5/11 of the setting. Five examples are known, one being i the Royal Collection.

Errors of spelling on this surcharge are bogus.

British Bechuanaland. (9) | British Bechuanaland. (10) | BRITISH BECHUANALAND (11)

1889 (Jan). *No. 48a of Cape of Good Hope* (wmk Anchor) *optd with T* **9**, *by P. Townshend & Co, Vryburg.*

30 ½d. grey-black (G.) . . . . . . 3·25 24·00
 b. Opt double, one inverted £1200
 c. Opt double, one vertical £550
 ca. *Se-tenant* with stamp without opt . . . £3500
 e. "British" omitted £3000

No. 30 was produced using a setting of 30 (6 × 5). No. 30e occurred on R. 5/1 of the setting on some sheets only. At least one pane was printed with the overprint misplaced upwards on the top half so that "British" was omitted from all stamps in row 5.

n n
Normal "n" Inverted "u"

1891 (Nov). *Nos. 49/50 of Cape of Good Hope* (wmk Anchor), *optd with T* **10**, *reading upwards.*

31 1d. rose-red . . . . 10·00 8·00
 a. Horiz pair, one without opt . . . £3000
 b. "British" omitted . . . . . — £1500
 c. "Bechuanaland" omitted £1500
 d. Inverted "u" for 2nd "n" . . . .
32 2d. pale bistre . . . . 3·25 2·25
 a. No stop after "Bechuanaland" . . . £275 £325
 b. Inverted "u" for 2nd "n" . . . .
31s/2s H/S "Specimen" *Set of* 2 . . . . £130

The overprint on Nos. 31 and 32 was of 120 impressions in two panes of 60 (6 × 10). That on No. 32 was applied both by a stereo plate and by a forme made up from loose type. No. 31 was overprinted only with the latter. No. 32a is from the stereo overprinting (left pane, R. 3/3), 31d and 32b are from the typeset overprinting (left pane, R. 10/4).

See also Nos. 38 and 39.

1891 (1 Dec)–**1904**. *Nos. 172, 200, 205, 208 and 211 of Great Britain optd with T* **11**, *by D.L.R.*

33 1d. lilac . . . . 6·00 1·50
34 2d. grey-green and carmine . . . . 10·00 4·00
35 4d. green and purple-brown . . . . 2·50 50
 a. Bisected (2d.) (on cover) (11.99) . . . † £2250
36 6d. purple/*rose-red* . . . . . 3·50 2·00
37 1s. dull green (7.94) . . . . . 13·00 16·00
 a. Bisected (6d.) (on cover) (12.04) . . . † —
33/7 *Set of* 5 . . . . 32·00 22·00
33s/6s H/S "Specimen" *Set of* 4 . . . . £170

No. 35a was used at Palapye Station and No. 37a at Kanye, both in the Protectorate.

1893 (Dec)–**95**. *As Nos. 31/2, but T* **10** *reads downwards.*

38 1d. rose-red . . . . 2·25 2·25
 a. Pair, one without opt . . . .
 b. "British" omitted £2000
 c. Optd "Bechuanaland. British" . . . £1000 £1100
 d. Inverted "u" for 2nd "n" £100 £110
 e. No dots to "i" of "British" . . . £100 £110
 f. Opt reading up, no dots to "i" of "British" £1600
39 2d. pale bistre (15.3.95) . . . . 4·75 2·25
 a. Opt double £1200 £650
 b. "British" omitted £600 £500
 c. "Bechuanaland" omitted . . . . — £500
 d. Optd "Bechuanaland. British" . . . £400 £225
 e. Inverted "u" for 2nd "n" £120 £120
 f. No dots to "i" of "British" . . . £120 £120
 g. Opt reading up, no dots to "i" of "British" . . . .

The same typeset overprint was used for Nos. 38 and 39 as had been employed for Nos. 31 and 32 but applied the other way up; the inverted "u" thus falling on the right pane, R. 1/3. The no dots to "i" variety only occurs on this printing (right pane, R. 1/4). Some sheets of both values were overprinted the wrong way up, resulting in Nos. 38f. and 39g.

On 16 November 1895 British Bechuanaland was annexed to the Cape of Good Hope and ceased to have its own stamps, but they remained in use in the Protectorate until superseded in 1897. The Postmaster-General of Cape Colony had assumed control of the Bechuanaland postal service on 1 April 1893 and the Cape, and subsequently the South African, postal authorities continued to be responsible for the postal affairs of the Bechuanaland Protectorate until 1963.

BECHUANALAND PROTECTORATE

PRICES FOR STAMPS ON COVER TO 1945	
Nos. 40/51	*from* × 10
Nos. 52/71	*from* × 6
Nos. 72/82	*from* × 5
Nos. 83/98	*from* × 4
Nos. 99/110	*from* × 6
Nos. 111/17	*from* × 10
Nos. 118/28	*from* × 4
Nos. 129/31	*from* × 10
Nos. D1/3	*from* × 50
Nos. D4/6	*from* × 60
No. F1	*from* × 5
No. F2	—
No. F3	*from* × 5

This large area north of the Molopo River was proclaimed a British Protectorate on 30 September 1885 at the request of the native chiefs.

A postal service using runners was inaugurated on 9 August 1888 and Nos. 40 to 55 were issued as a temporary measure with the object of assessing the cost of this service

Protectorate (12) 15½ mm | Protectorate 1d (13)

1888 (7 Aug). *No. 9 optd with T* **12** *and Nos. 10/19 surch or optd only as T* **13** *by P. Townshend & Co. Vryburg.*

40 – ½d. vermilion . . . . . . 3·75 27·00
 a. "Protectorate" double £325
 s. Handstamped "Specimen" . . . . 85·00
41 3 1d. on 1d. lilac and black . . . . 8·00 14·00
 a. Small figure "1" (R. 5/4, 7/2, 10/2) £400 £450
 b. Space between "1" and "d" (R. 10/9) £500
42 2d. on 2d. lilac and black . . . . 25·00 17·00
 b. Curved foot to "2" £650 £450
43 3d. on 3d. pale reddish lilac and black £130 £180
44 4d. on 4d. lilac and black £325 £325
 a. Small figure "4" £3500 £3500
45 6d. on 6d. lilac and black . . . . 70·00 40·00
46 4 1s. green and black . . . . . 85·00 50·00
 a. First "o" omitted £4250 £3000
 s. Handstamped "Specimen" £110
47 2s. green and black £600 £900
 a. First "o" omitted £10000
48 2s.6d. green and black £550 £800
 a. First "o" omitted £9000
49 5s. green and black £1200 £2000
 a. First "o" omitted £14000
50 10s. green and black £3750 £5500
 a. First "o" omitted £21000

Nos. 40/5 were produced from a basic setting of 120 (12 × 10) on which a faulty first "o" in "Protectorate" occurred on R. 5/12. For Nos. 46/50 the setting was reduced to 84 (12 × 7) and on many sheets the first "o" on R. 5/12 failed to print.

The normal space between "1" and "d" measures 1mm. On No. 41b it is 1.7mm.

See also Nos. 54/5.

1888 (Dec). *No. 25 optd with T* **12** *by P. Townshend & Co, Vryburg.*

51 3 4d. on 4d. lilac and black . . . . 75·00 35·00

Bechuanaland Protectorate. (14) | Protectorate Fourpence (15)

1889 (Jan). *No. 48a of Cape of Good Hope* (wmk Anchor), *optd with T* **14** *by P. Townshend & Co., Vryburg.*

52 ½d. grey-black (G.) . . . . . . 2·75 40·00
 a. Opt double £450 £650
 ab. Ditto, one reading "Protectorate Bechuanaland" £900
 b. "Bechuanaland" omitted £1300
 c. Optd "Protectorate Bechuanaland" . . . £600 £700

1889 (1 Aug). *No. 9 surch with T* **15** *by P. Townshend & Co., Vryburg.*

53 4d. on ½d. vermilion . . . . . 22·00 3·50
 a. "rpence" omitted (R. 9/2) . . . . † £6000
 b. "ourpence" omitted (R. 9/2) . . . £10000
 c. Surch (T **15**) inverted . . . . † £4000
 cb. Ditto. "ourpence" omitted . . . . † £11000
 s. Handstamped "Specimen" £130

Examples of No. 53c are postmarked "679" (Tati).

Protectorate (16) 15 mm | Protectorate (17)

1890. *No. 9 optd.*

54 16 ½d. vermilion £150 £160
 a. Type **16** inverted . . . . . 75·00 95·00
 b. Type **16** double £100 £150
 c. Type **16** double and inverted . . . £600 £600
 d. Optd "Portectorate" inverted . . . £6500
 w. Wmk inverted . . . . . .
55 17 ½d. vermilion £170 £300
 a. Type **17** double £1200
 b. Optd "Protectorrte" . . . . .
 c. Optd "Protectorrte" double . . . £12000

These were trial printings made in 1888 which were subsequently issued.

In June 1890 the Bechuanaland Protectorate and the Colony of British Bechuanaland came under one postal administration and the stamps of British Bechuanaland were used in the Protectorate until 1897.

BRITISH BECHUANALAND (18) | BECHUANALAND PROTECTORATE (19)

1897. *No. 61 of Cape of Good Hope* (wmk Anchor), *optd as T* **18**.

(a) Lines 13 mm apart, bottom line 16 mm long, by Taylor & Marshall, Cape Town.

56 ½d. yellow-green (July?) . . . . . 2·50 10·00

(b) Lines 13½ mm apart bottom line 15 mm long, by P. Townshend & Co, Vryburg.

57 ½d. yellow-green (April) . . . . . 19·00 75·00
 a. Opt double, one albino inverted . . . £200

(c) Lines 10½ mm apart, bottom line 15 mm long, by W. A. Richards & Sons, Cape Govt Printers.

58 ½d. yellow-green (July?) . . . . . 8·00 45·00

Although issued only in the Protectorate, the above were presumably overprinted "BRITISH BECHUANALAND" because stamps bearing this inscription were in use there at the time.

1897 (Oct)–**1902**. *Nos. 172, 197, 200, 202, 205 and 208 of Great Britain (Queen Victoria) optd with T* **19** *by D.L.R.*

59 ½d. vermilion . . . . 1·00 2·25
60 ½d. blue-green (25.2.02) . . . . . 1·40 3·50
61 1d. lilac . . . . 4·00 75
62 2d. grey-green and carmine . . . . 3·25 3·50
63 3d. purple/*yellow* (12.97) . . . . . 5·50 8·50
64 4d. green and purple-brown . . . . 15·00 12·00
65 6d. purple/*rose-red* . . . . . . 23·00 11·00
59/65 *Set of* 7 . . . . 48·00 38·00
59s/65s Optd or H/S (No. 60s) "Specimen" *Set of* 7 . . . . £225

BECHUANALAND (20) | PROTECTORATE | BECHUANALAND PROTECTORATE (21)

1904 (29 Nov)–**13**. *Nos. 216, 218/19, 230 and 313/14 (Somerset House ptgs) of Great Britain (King Edward VII) optd with T* **20**, *by D.L.R.*

66 ½d. blue-green (3.06) . . . . . 2·00 2·00
67 ½d. yellowish green (11.08) . . . . 3·75 3·50
68 1d. scarlet (4.05) . . . . . . 7·50 30
 s. Optd "Specimen" . . . . . 60·00
69 2½d. ultramarine . . . . . . 7·50 5·00
 a. Stop after "P" in "PROTECTORATE" £950 £1200
70 1s. deep green and scarlet (10.12) . . . 35·00 £130
 a. Opt double, one albino £200
71 1s. green and carmine (1913) . . . . 40·00 £120
 s. Optd "Specimen" . . . . . 95·00

No. 69a occurs on R. 5/9 of the lower pane.

1912 (Sept)–**14**. *No. 342 of Great Britain (King George V,* wmk Crown*) optd with T* **20**.

72 1d. scarlet . . . . 2·00 60
 a. No cross on crown . . . . . £150 75·00
 b. *Aniline scarlet* (No. 343) (1914) . . . £140 80·00

1913 (1 July)–**24**. *Stamps of Great Britain (King George V) optd.*

(a) Nos. 351, 357, 362, 367, 370/1, 376, 379, 385 and 395 (wmk Simple Cypher, *T* **100**) *optd with T* **20**.

73 ½d. green (*shades*) . . . . . . 1·25 1·75
74 1d. scarlet (*shades*) (4.15) . . . . 2·75 75
 a. *Carmine-red* (1922) . . . . . 26·00 2·50
75 1½d. red-brown (12.20) . . . . . 3·00 3·00
76 2d. reddish orange (Die I) . . . . 4·00 4·25
 a. *Orange* (Die I) (1921) . . . . 16·00 4·50
 aw. Wmk inverted . . . . . .
77 2d. orange (Die II) (1924) . . . . 35·00 5·00
78 2½d. cobalt-blue . . . . 3·50 20·00
 a. *Blue* (1915) . . . . . . 8·00 23·00
79 3d. bluish violet . . . . . . 6·00 12·00
80 4d. grey-green . . . . 6·50 20·00
81 6d. reddish purple (*shades*) . . . . 7·00 16·00
 a. Opt double, one albino . . . .
82 1s. bistre . . . . 9·50 20·00
 a. *Bistre-brown* (1923) . . . . . 25·00 32·00
 s. Optd "Specimen" . . . . . 75·00
73/82 *Set of* 9 . . . . 40·00 85·00

(b) With T **21**.

(i) *Waterlow printings (Nos. 399 and 401)* (1914–15).

83 2s.6d. deep sepia-brown (1.15) £120 £250
 a. Re-entry (R. 2/1) £1000 £1500
 b. Opt double, one albino £275
84 5s. rose-carmine (1914) £160 £375
 a. Opt double, one albino £375
83s/4s Optd "Specimen" *Set of* 2 . . . . £275

(ii) *D.L.R. printings (Nos. 407/8 and 409)* (1916–19).

85 2s.6d. pale brown (7.16) £110 £250
 a. Re-entry (R. 2/1) £1100 £1500
86 2s.6d. sepia (1917) £130 £225
 a. Opt treble, two albino . . . .
 b. Re-entry (R. 2/1) £1100
87 5s. bright carmine (8.19) £300 £425
 a. Opt double, one albino £450

(iii) *B.W. printings (Nos. 414 and 416)* (1920–23).

88 2s.6d. chocolate-brown (7.23) . . . . 85·00 £160
 a. Major re-entry (R. 1/2) £1900
 b. Opt double, one albino £550
 c. Opt treble, two albino £500
89 5s. rose-red (7.20) £110 £275
 a. Opt treble, two albino £375
 b. Opt double, one albino . . . .

Examples of Nos. 83/9 are known showing a forged Lobatsi postmark dated "6 MAY 35" or "6 MAY 39".

1925 (July)–**27**. *Nos. 418/19, 421, 423/4, 426/a and 429 of Great Britain* (wmk Block Cypher, *T* **111**) *optd with T* **20**.

91 ½d. green (1927) . . . . . . 1·50 1·75
92 1d. scarlet (8.25) . . . . . . 2·00 70
 w. Wmk inverted . . . . . .
93 2d. orange (Die II) . . . . . . 1·75 1·00

94 3d. violet (10.26) . . . 4·75 18·00
a. Opt double, one albino . . . £200
w. Wmk inverted . . . £200
95 4d. grey-green (10.26) . . . 4·75 35·00
a. Printed on the gummed side . . .
96 6d. reddish purple (*chalk-surfaced paper*) (12.25) . . . 35·00 65·00
97 6d. purple (*ordinary paper*) (1926) . . . 48·00 48·00
98 1s. bistre-brown (10.26) . . . 9·00 24·00
w. Wmk inverted . . . £325 £300
91/8 *Set of* 8 . . . 95·00 £170

No. 94w. also shows the variety, opt double, one albino.

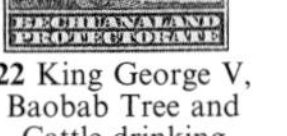

22 King George V, Baobab Tree and Cattle drinking

23 King George VI, Baobab Tree and Cattle drinking

(Des from photo by Resident Commissioner, Ngamiland, Recess Waterlow)

1932 (12 Dec). Wmk Mult Script CA. P 12½.
99 **22** ½d. green . . . 1·00 30
a. Imperf between (horiz pair) . . . £16000
100 1d. scarlet . . . 1·00 25
101 2d. brown . . . 1·00 30
102 3d. ultramarine . . . 1·00 2·25
103 4d. orange . . . 1·25 5·50
104 6d. purple . . . 2·50 4·00
105 1s. black and olive-green . . . 3·00 7·00
106 2s. black and orange . . . 24·00 45·00
107 2s.6d. black and scarlet . . . 19·00 30·00
108 3s. black and purple . . . 35·00 42·00
109 5s. black and ultramarine . . . 65·00 75·00
110 10s. black and brown . . . £120 £130
99/110 *Set of* 12 . . . £250 £300
99s/110s Perf "Specimen" *Set of* 12 . . . £275

Examples of most values are known showing a forged Lobatsi postmark dated "6 MAY 35" or "6 MAY 39".

1935 (4 May). *Silver Jubilee. As Nos. 91/4 of Antigua but ptd by B.W.* P 11 × 12.
111 1d. deep blue and scarlet . . . 30 3·25
a. Extra flagstaff . . . £250
b. Short extra flagstaff . . . £325
c. Lightning conductor . . . £300
d. Flagstaff on right-hand turret . . . £300
e. Double flagstaff . . . £300
112 2d. ultramarine and grey-black . . . 1·00 3·25
a. Extra flagstaff . . . £100 £150
b. Short extra flagstaff . . . £110
c. Lightning conductor . . . 95·00
113 3d. brown and deep blue . . . 2·50 3·50
a. Extra flagstaff . . . £140
b. Short extra flagstaff . . . £150
c. Lightning conductor . . . £130
114 6d. slate and purple . . . 4·00 3·50
a. Extra flagstaff . . . £130
b. Short extra flagstaff . . . £130
c. Lightning conductor . . . £130
111/14 *Set of* 4 . . . 7·00 12·00
111s/14s Perf "Specimen" *Set of* 4 . . . 90·00

For illustrations of plate varieties see Omnibus section following Zanzibar.

1937 (12 May). *Coronation. As Nos. 95/7 of Antigua, but printed by D.L.R.* P 14.
115 1d. scarlet . . . 45 40
116 2d. yellow-brown . . . 60 1·00
117 3d. bright blue . . . 60 1·25
115/17 *Set of* 3 . . . 1·50 2·40
115s/17s Perf "Specimen" *Set of* 3 . . . 65·00

(Recess Waterlow)

1938 (1 Apr)–**52**. Wmk Mult Script CA. P 12½.
118 **23** ½d. green . . . 2·00 2·50
a. Light yellowish green (1941) . . . 7·00 7·00
b. Yellowish green (4.43) . . . 5·00 4·00
c. Deep green (4.49) . . . 3·25 9·00
119 1d. scarlet . . . 75 50
120 1½d. dull blue . . . 9·00 2·00
a. Light blue (4.43) . . . 1·00 1·00
121 2d. chocolate-brown . . . 75 50
122 3d. deep ultramarine . . . 1·00 2·50
123 4d. orange . . . 2·00 3·50
124 6d. reddish purple . . . 4·75 3·00
a. Purple (1944) . . . 4·00 2·50
ab. "A" of "CA" missing from wmk . . . † —
125 1s. black and brown-olive . . . 4·00 5·00
a. Grey-black & olive-green (21.5.52) . . . 15·00 22·00
126 2s.6d. black and scarlet . . . 14·00 14·00
127 5s. black and deep ultramarine . . . 30·00 17·00
a. Grey-black & dp ultram (10.46) . . . 75·00 50·00
128 10s. black and red-brown . . . 14·00 21·00
118/28 *Set of* 11 . . . 65·00 60·00
118s/28s Pert "Specimen" *Set of* 11 . . . £225

Bechuanaland
(24)

1945 (3 Dec). *Victory. Stamps of South Africa optd with T* **24**. *Inscr alternately in English and Afrikaans.*

			Un. pair	Used pair	Used single
129	**55**	1d. brown and carmine	50	1·00	10
130	**56**	2d. slate-blue and violet	50	1·25	10
131	**57**	3d. deep blue and blue	50	1·25	10
		a. Opt omitted (in vert pair with normal)	£8000		
129/31 *Set of* 3			1·40	3·25	25

No. 131a comes from a sheet on which the overprint was displaced downwards so that it is omitted from stamps in the top row and shown on the sheet margin at foot.

(Recess Waterlow)

1947 (17 Feb). *Royal Visit. As Nos. 32/5 of Basutoland.* Wmk Mult Script CA. P 12½.
132 1d. scarlet . . . 10 10
133 2d. green . . . 10 10
134 3d. ultramarine . . . 10 10
135 1s. mauve . . . 10 10
132/5 *Set of* 4 . . . 35 30
132s/5s Perf "Specimen" *Set of* 4 . . . 85·00

1948 (1 Dec). *Royal Silver Wedding. As Nos. 112/13 of Antigua.*
136 1½d. ultramarine . . . 30 10
137 10s. black . . . 27·00 35·00

1949 (10 Oct). *75th Anniv of Universal Postal Union. As Nos. 114/17 of Antigua.*
138 1½d. blue . . . 30 1·25
139 3d. deep blue . . . 1·25 2·50
140 6d. magenta . . . 45 1·50
141 1s. olive . . . 45 1·50
138/41 *Set of* 4 . . . 2·25 6·00

POSTAGE DUE STAMPS

BECHUANALAND
(D 1)

PROTECTORATE
(D 2)

BECHUANALAND PROTECTORATE

1926 (1 Jan). *Nos. D9/10 and D13 of Great Britain, optd with Types D* **1** *or D* **2** *(2d.).*
D1 ½d. emerald (wmk sideways - inverted) . . . 4·50 85·00
D2 1d. carmine . . . 4·50 50·00
D3 2d. agate . . . 6·00 85·00
D1/3 *Set of* 3 . . . 13·50 £200

D 3

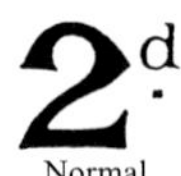
Normal

Large "d" (R. 9/6, 10/6)

Serif on "d" (R. 1/6)

(Typo D.L.R.)

1932 (12 Dec)–**58**. *Ordinary paper.* Wmk Mult Script CA. P 14.
D4 **D 3** ½d. sage-green . . . 6·00 42·00
D5 1d. carmine . . . 7·00 9·00
a. Chalk-surfaced paper (27.11.58) . . . 1·50 18·00
D6 2d. violet . . . 9·00 48·00
a. Large "d" . . . £100
b. Serif on "d" . . . £150
c. Chalk-surfaced paper (27.11.58) . . . 1·75 20·00
ca. Large "d" . . . 32·00
cb. Serif on "d" . . . 45·00
D4/6b *Set of* 3 . . . 8·50 65·00
D4s/6s Perf "Specimen" *Set of* 3 . . . 70·00

No. D6a first occurred on the 1947 printing.

POSTAL FISCAL STAMPS

The following stamps issued for fiscal purposes were each allowed to be used for postal purposes for a short time. No. F2 was used by the public because the word "POSTAGE" had not been obliterated and No. F3 because the overprint did not include the words "Revenue only" as did the contemporary fiscal overprints for Basutoland and Swaziland.

Bechuanaland Protectorate
(F 1)

£5
(F 2)

Bechuanaland Protectorate.
(F 3)

1910 (July). *No. 266a of Transvaal optd with Type* F **1** *by Transvaal Govt Ptg Wks, Pretoria.*
F1 6d. black and brown-orange (Bl-Blk) . . . £160 £325

No. F1 was supplied to Assistant Commissioners in January 1907 for revenue purposes. The "POSTAGE" inscription was not obliterated, however, and the stamp is known postally used for a period of a year from July 1910.

1918. *No. 15 surch with Type* F **2** *at top.*
F2 **4** £5 on 1s. green and black (F.C. £650) £11000

1921. *No. 4b of South Africa optd with Type* F **3**, *in varying positions.*
F3 1d. scarlet . . . 42·00 £130
a. Opt double, one albino . . . £160

Bermuda

The first internal postal system for Bermuda was organised by Joseph Stockdale, the proprietor of the *Bermuda Gazette*, in January 1784. This service competed with that of the colonial post office, set up in May 1812, until 1818.

Control of the overseas postal services passed to the British G.P.O. in 1818. The internal delivery system was discontinued between 1821 and 1830. The overseas posts became a colonial responsibility in September 1859.

For illustrations of the handstamp types see BRITISH POST OFFICES ABROAD notes, following GREAT BRITAIN.

CROWNED-CIRCLE HANDSTAMPS

CC1 CC **1** ST. GEORGES BERMUDA (R.) (1.8.1845) . . . *Price on cover* £7000
CC2 IRELAND ISLE BERMUDA (R.) (1.8.1845) . . . *Price on cover* £7000
CC3 HAMILTON BERMUDA (R.) (13.11.1846) . . . *Price on cover* £3750

For Nos. CC1 and CC3 used as adhesive Postmasters' Stamps see Nos. O7 and O6.

PRICES FOR STAMPS ON COVER TO 1845	
Nos. 1/11	*from* × 5
Nos. 12/17	*from* × 10
Nos. 19/29*a*	*from* × 8
Nos. 30/a	*from* × 10
Nos. 31/4	*from* × 4
Nos. 34*a*/55	*from* × 3
Nos. 56/8	*from* × 10
Nos. 59/76	*from* × 4
Nos. 76*a*/93	*from* × 3
Nos. 94/7	*from* × 4
Nos. 98/106	*from* × 3
Nos. 107/15	*from* × 4
Nos. 116/21	*from* × 5
No. 122	*from* × 20

COLONY

O 1

O 2

1848–61. *Postmasters' Stamps. Adhesives prepared and issued by the postmasters at Hamilton and St. Georges. Dated as given in brackets.*

(a) By W. B. Perot at Hamilton.
O1 O **1** 1d. black/*bluish grey* (1848) . . . — £11000
O2 1d. black/*bluish grey* (1849) . . . — £12000
O3 1d. red/*thick white* (1853) . . . — £9000
O4 1d. red/*bluish wove* (1854) . . . — £27500
O5 1d. red/*bluish wove* (1856) . . . — £17000
O6 O **2** (1d.) carmine-red/*bluish laid* (1861) . . . — £7500

(b) By J. H. Thies at St. Georges. As Type O **2** *but inscr* "ST. GEORGES".
O7 – (1d.) carmine-red/*buff* (1860) . . . † £6500

Stamps of Type O **1** bear manuscript value and signature, the dates being those shown on the eleven known examples. The stamps are distributed between the dates as follows: 1848 three examples, 1849 two examples, 1853 three examples, 1854 two examples, 185[illegible] one example.

It is believed that the franking value of Nos. O6/7 was 1d., although this is not shown on the actual stamps. Four examples are known of this type used from Hamilton, from March 1861 (and one unused), and five used from St. Georges between July 1860 and January 1863, both issues being cancelled by pen.

Prices shown reflect our estimation of value based on known copies. For instance of the two copies known of No. O4, one is [illegible] the Royal collection and the other is on entire.

It is possible that a fourth postmaster's provisional was used by Robert Ward at Hamilton in late 1862 when two examples of Type O **2** on laid paper are known cancelled by blue crayon.

1

2

3

4

5

(Typo D.L.R.)

1865–1903. Wmk Crown CC.

(a) P 14.

No.	Type	Description	Unused	Used
1	1	1d. rose-red (25.9.65)	90·00	1·25
		a. Imperf	£26000	£15000
		w. Wmk inverted	£300	£110
2		1d. pale rose	£120	7·00
		w. Wmk inverted	£325	£130
3	2	2d. dull blue (14.3.66)	£375	24·00
		w. Wmk inverted	—	£325
4		2d. bright blue (1877)	£400	17·00
		w. Wmk inverted	—	£325
5	3	3d. yellow-buff (10.3.73)	£475	65·00
		aw. Wmk inverted	£1000	£180
		ax. Wmk reversed		
5*b*		3d. orange (1875)	£1800	£150
6	4	6d. dull purple (25.9.65)	£950	75·00
		w. Wmk inverted	—	£750
7		6d. dull mauve (2.7.74)	23·00	12·00
		w. Wmk inverted	95·00	£110
8	5	1s. green (25.9.65)	£275	55·00
		w. Wmk inverted	£550	£250

(b) P 14 × 12½.

No.	Type	Description	Unused	Used
10	3	3d. yellow-buff (12.81)	£170	60·00
10*a*	4	6d. bright mauve (1903)	13·00	22·00
		aw. Wmk inverted	£550	
11	5	1s. green (11.93)	11·00	£120
		a. Imperf between (vert strip of 3)	£12000	
		w. Wmk inverted		

No. 11a occurs from Rows 8, 9, and 10 of four panes, possibly from a single sheet. Some of the stamps have become partially separated. One *used* vertical pair is known (*Price* £12000).

Although they arrived in Bermuda in March 1880, stamps perforated 14 × 12½ were not issued until the dates given above.

THREE PENCE (6) THREE PENCE (6a)

THREE PENCE (7) One Penny. (8)

1874 (12 Mar–19 May). *Nos. 1 and 8 surch diagonally.*

(a) With T **6** *("P" and "R" different type).*

No.	Type	Description	Unused	Used
12	1	3d. on 1d. rose-red	£16000	
13	5	3d. on 1s. green	£2500	£850

(b) With T **6a** *("P" same type as "R").*

No.	Type	Description	Unused	Used
13*b*	5	3d. on 1s. green	£2000	£800

(c) With T **7** *(19 May).*

No.	Type	Description	Unused	Used
14	5	3d. on 1s. green	£1500	£650

The 3d. on 1d. was a trial surcharge which was not regularly issued, though a few specimens were postally used before 1879. Nos. 13, 13*b* and 14, being handstamped, are found with double or partial double surcharges.

(Surch by Queens Printer, Donald McPhee Lee)

1875 (March–May). *Surch with T* **8**.

No.	Type	Description	Unused	Used
15	2	1d.on 2d. (No. 3) (23 Apr)	£700	£375
		a. No stop after "Penny"	£14000	£8500
16	3	1d.on 3d. (No. 5) (8 May)	£450	£350
17	5	1d.on 1s. (No. 8) (11 Mar)	£500	£250
		a. Surch inverted	†	£23000
		b. No stop after "Penny"	£16000	£11000

It is emphasised that the prices quoted for Nos. 12/17 are for fine examples. The many stamps from these provisional issues which are in inferior condition are worth much less.

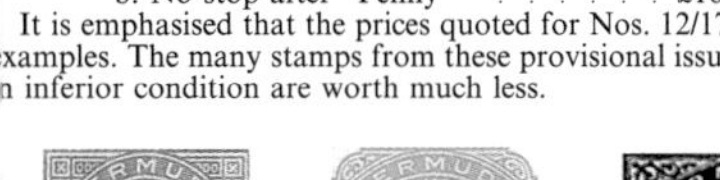

9

10

11

(Typo D.L.R.)

1880 (25 Mar). Wmk Crown CC. P 14.

No.	Type	Description	Unused	Used
19	9	½d. stone	2·75	4·25
		w. Wmk inverted	85·00	£150
		y. Wmk inverted and reversed		
20	10	4d. orange-red	17·00	1·75
		w. Wmk inverted		
		x. Wmk reversed		

(Typo D.L.R.)

1883–1904. Wmk Crown CA. P 14.

No.	Type	Description	Unused	Used
21	9	½d. dull green (10.92)	3·25	3·00
21*a*		½d. deep grey-green (1893)	2·50	80
22	1	1d. dull rose (12.83)	£160	4·25
		w. Wmk inverted	—	£180
23		1d. rose-red	80·00	3·25
		w. Wmk inverted	—	£180
24		1d. carmine-rose (3.86)	50·00	70
24*a*		1d. aniline carmine (1889)	9·00	20
		aw. Wmk inverted	£180	£110
25	2	2d. blue (12.86)	55·00	4·00
26		2d. aniline purple (7.93)	14·00	3·75
26*a*		2d. brown purple (1898)	3·50	1·50
27	11	2½d. deep ultramarine (10.11.84)	14·00	2·75
		aw. Wmk inverted	£350	£130
27*b*		2½d. pale ultramarine	5·50	40
		bw. Wmk inverted	—	£120

No.	Type	Description	Unused	Used
28	3	3d. grey (20.1.86)	22·00	6·50
28*a*	10	4d. orange-brown (18.1.04)	30·00	50·00
		ax. Wmk reversed	£375	
29	5	1s. yellow-brown (1893)	16·00	17·00
		ax. Wmk reversed	—	£500
29*b*		1s. olive-brown	13·00	16·00
		bx. Wmk reversed		
21/9b *Set of* 8			£130	70·00
21s, 26s & 29s Optd "Specimen" *Set of* 3			£375	

1893 PROVISIONAL POSTCARD. Following the reduction of the overseas postcard rate to 1d. in 1893 existing stocks of postal stationery postcards, including some from the September 1880 issue franked with Nos. 19 and 22, were surcharged "One Penny". This surcharge was applied by the *Royal Gazette* press. It is generally believed that an individual in the Post Office acquired all the examples showing Nos. 19 and 22, but provisional postcards are known used to Europe or locally. *Price from* £550 *unused*, £1400 *used.*

ONE FARTHING

(12)

13 Dry Dock

14

1901. *As Nos. 29/a but colour changed, surch with T* **12** *by D.L.R.*

No.	Type	Description	Unused	Used
30	5	¼d.on 1s. dull grey (11.1.01)	2·00	50
		as. Optd "Specimen"	75·00	
30*b*		¼d.on 1s. bluish grey (18.3.01)	2·25	85
		ba. "F" in "FARTHING" inserted by handstamp	£6000	£7000

Eight examples of No. 30ba are known, six unused (one being in the Royal Collection) and two used (one on postcard). It would appear that the "F" in position one of an unspecified horizontal row was damaged and an additional impression of the letter was then inserted by a separate handstamp.

(Typo D.L.R.)

1902 (Nov)–**03**. Wmk Crown CA. P 14.

No.	Type	Description	Unused	Used
31	13	½d. black and green (12.03)	12·00	2·25
32		1d. brown and carmine	8·00	10
33		3d. magenta and sage-green (9.03)	3·00	2·00
31/3 *Set of* 3			21·00	3·75
31s/3s Optd "Specimen" *Set of* 3			£140	

1906–10. Wmk Mult Crown CA. P 14.

No.	Type	Description	Unused	Used
34	13	¼d. brown and violet (9.08)	1·75	1·50
35		½d. black and green (12.06)	19·00	65
36		½d. green (3.09)	14·00	2·75
37		1d. brown and carmine (4.06)	27·00	20
		w. Wmk inverted	£400	£250
38		1d. red (5.08)	19·00	10
39		2d. grey and orange (10.07)	7·50	11·00
40		2½d. brown and ultramarine (12.06)	16·00	7·00
41		2½d. blue (14.2.10)	12·00	6·50
42		4d. blue and chocolate (11.09)	3·00	16·00
34/42 *Set of* 9			£110	40·00
34s, 36s, 38s/42s Optd "Specimen" *Set of* 7			£350	

(Recess D.L.R.)

1910–25. Wmk Mult Crown CA. P 14.

No.	Type	Description	Unused	Used
44	14	¼d. brown (26.3.12)	1·75	2·50
		a. Pale brown	60	1·50
45		½d. green (4.6.10)	1·50	25
		a. Deep green (1918)	7·50	1·25
		w. Wmk inverted		
		x. Wmk reversed	£375	£275
		y. Wmk inverted and reversed		
46		1d. red (I) (15.10.10)	15·00	30
		a. Rose-red (1916)	20·00	30
		b. Carmine (12.19)	55·00	8·00
		w. Wmk inverted	£475	£450
		x. Wmk reversed		
		y. Wmk inverted and reversed	£375	
47		2d. grey (1.13)	3·00	10·00
		x. Wmk reversed		
48		2½d. blue (27.3.12)	3·50	60
		w. Wmk inverted		
		x. Wmk reversed	—	£300
		y. Wmk inverted and reversed	£225	£150
49		3d. purple/*yellow* (1.13)	2·00	6·00
49*a*		4d. red/*yellow* (1.9.19)	6·00	12·00
50		6d. purple (26.3.12)	16·00	20·00
		a. Pale claret (2.6.24)	11·00	8·00
51		1s. black/*green* (26.3.12)	4·25	4·00
		a. Jet black/olive (1925)	4·75	15·00
44/51 *Set of* 9			42·00	38·00
44s/51s *Set of* 9			£400	

Nos. 44 to 51*a* are comb-perforated 13.8 × 14 or 14. No. 45 exists also line-perforated 14 probably from the printing dispatched to Bermuda on 13 March 1911.

See also Nos. 76*b*/87*a*.

15

HIGH VALUE KEY TYPES. The reign of King Edward VII saw the appearance of the first in a new series of "key type" designs, initially for Nyasaland, to be used for high value denominations where a smaller design was felt to be inappropriate. The system was extended during the reign of King George V, using the portrait as Bermuda Type **15**, to cover Bermuda, Ceylon, Leeward Islands, Malaya — Straits Settlements, Malta and Nyasaland. A number of these territories continued to use the key type concept for high value King George VI stamps and one, Leeward Islands, for stamps of Queen Elizabeth II.

In each instance the King George V issues were printed in sheets of 60 (12 × 5) on various coloured papers. The system utilised a common "head" plate used with individual "duty" plates which printed the territory name and face value.

Many of the major plate flaws on the King George V head plate occur in different states, having been repaired and then damaged once again, perhaps on several occasions. Later printings of R. 1/12 show additional damage to the crown and upper scrolls. The prices quoted in the listings are for examples approximately as illustrated.

Break in scroll (R. 1/12)

Broken crown and scroll (R. 2/12)

Nick in top right scroll (R. 3/12) (Some printings from 1920 onwards show attempts at repair)

Break through scroll (R. 1/9. Ptgs from June 1929. Some show attempts at repair)

Break in lines below left scroll (R. 4/9. Ptgs from May 1920)

Damaged leaf at bottom right (R. 5/6. Ptgs from April 1918)

Gash in fruit and leaf (R. 5/12. Ptgs from November 1928)

(Typo D.L.R)

918 (1 Apr)–**22**. Wmk Mult Crown CA. *Chalk-surfaced paper*. P 14.

No.	Type	Description	Unused	Used
1*b*	**15**	2s. purple and blue/*blue* (19.6.20)	18·00	50·00
		ba. Break in scroll	£250	
		bb. Broken crown and scroll	£200	
		be. Break in lines below left scroll	£225	
		bf. Damaged leaf at bottom right	£200	
		bx. Wmk reversed	£1700	£2250
2		2s.6d. black and red/*blue*	29·00	80·00
		a. Break in scroll	£300	
2*b*		4s. black and carmine (19.6.20)	60·00	£160
		ba. Break in scroll	£275	
		bb. Broken crown and scroll	£275	£450
		bc. Nick in top right scroll	£275	
		be. Break in lines below left scroll	£300	
		bf. Damaged leaf at bottom right	£275	
3		5s. deep green and deep red/*yellow*	60·00	£120
		a. Break in scroll	£400	
		c. Nick in top right scroll	£400	
		d. Green and carmine-red/pale yellow (1920)	48·00	£100
		da. Break in scroll	£350	£475
		db. Broken crown and scroll	£350	£475
		de. Break in lines below left scroll	£375	
		df. Damaged leaf at bottom right	£350	
		dw. Wmk inverted	£350	
		dx. Wmk reversed	£2500	
		dy. Wmk inverted and reversed	£2500	
4		10s. green and carmine/*pale bluish green*	£180	£350
		a. Break in scroll	£650	
		c. Green and red/pale bluish green (10.22)	£250	£400
		ca. Break in scroll	£750	
		cb. Broken crown and scroll	£750	
		ce. Break in lines below left scroll	£800	
		cf. Damaged leaf at bottom right	£750	
		cw. Wmk inverted		
5		£1 purple and black/*red*	£325	£550
		a. Break in scroll	£850	
		b. Broken crown and scroll	£1000	
		c. Nick in top right scroll	£1000	
		d. Break through scroll	£1700	
		e. Break in lines below left scroll	£1100	
		f. Damaged leaf at bottom right	£1000	
		g. Gash in fruit and leaf	£1700	
		w. Wmk inverted	£1600	
b/5 Set of 6			£600	£1100
bs/5s Optd "Specimen" Set of 6			£800	

Beware of cleaned copies of the 10s. with faked postmarks.
Examples of Nos. 51*b*/5 are known showing a forged Hamilton ouble ring postmark dated "22 JAN 13".
See also Nos. 88/93.

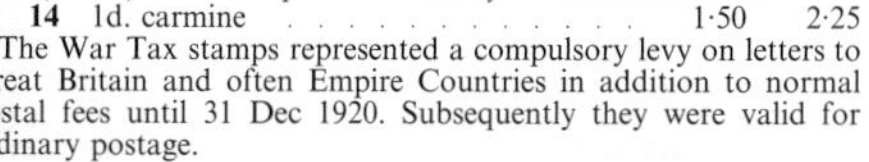

(16) (17)

18 (4 May). *Nos. 46 and 46a optd with T* **16** *by the Bermuda Press.*

No.	Type	Description	Unused	Used
5	**14**	1d. red	50	1·00
		a. Rose-red	50	1·25
		ay. Wmk inverted and reversed		

20 (5 Feb). *No. 46b optd with T* **17** *by the Bermuda Press.*

No.	Type	Description	Unused	Used
	14	1d. carmine	1·50	2·25

The War Tax stamps represented a compulsory levy on letters to reat Britain and often Empire Countries in addition to normal ostal fees until 31 Dec 1920. Subsequently they were valid for dinary postage.

18 19

(Des by the Governor (Gen. Sir James Willcocks). Typo D.L.R.)

1920 (11 Nov)–**21**. *Tercentenary of Representative Institutions (1st issue). Chalk-surfaced paper (3d. to 1s.).* P 14.

(a) Wmk Mult Crown CA (sideways*) (19.1.21).

No.	Type	Description	Unused	Used
59	**18**	¼d. brown	3·25	19·00
		a. "C" of "CA" missing from wmk	£500	
		b. "A" of "CA" missing from wmk	£500	
		w. Wmk Crown to right of CA	£180	
		x. Wmk sideways reversed	£200	
60		½d. green	3·50	10·00
		a. "C" of "CA" missing from wmk	£750	
		w. Wmk Crown to right of CA	£275	
		x. Wmk sideways reversed	£225	
		y. Wmk sideways inverted and reversed		
61		2d. grey	13·00	42·00
		a. "C" of "CA" missing from wmk	£750	
		w. Wmk Crown to right of CA	£375	
		y. Wmk sideways inverted and reversed	£425	
62		3d. dull and deep purple/*pale yellow*	12·00	40·00
		w. Wmk Crown to right of CA		
		x. Wmk sideways reversed		
63		4d. black and red/*pale yellow*	12·00	35·00
		a. "C" of "CA" missing from wmk	£1100	
64		1s. black/*blue-green*	16·00	48·00

(b) Wmk Mult Script CA (sideways).

No.	Type	Description	Unused	Used
65	**18**	1d. carmine	3·75	30
66		2½d. bright blue	14·00	13·00
67		6d. dull and bright purple (19.1.21)	26·00	75·00
59/67 *Set of 9*			90·00	£250
59s/67s Optd "Specimen" *Set of 9*			£350	

*The normal sideways watermark shows Crown to left of CA, *as seen from the back of the stamp.*

(Des H. J. Dale. Recess D.L.R.)

1921 (12 May). *Tercentenary of Representative Institutions (2nd issue).* P 14.

(a) Wmk Mult Crown CA (sideways*).

No.	Type	Description	Unused	Used
68	**19**	2d. slate-grey	6·00	28·00
		a. "C" of "CA" missing from wmk	—	£600
		w. Wmk Crown to left of CA	£450	
69		2½d. bright ultramarine	9·00	3·00
		a. "C" of "CA" missing from wmk	£800	
		b. "A" of "CA" missing from wmk	£800	
		x. Wmk sideways reversed	—	£400
70		3d. purple/*pale yellow*	5·50	16·00
71		4d. red/*pale yellow*	16·00	21·00
		x. Wmk sideways reversed	£225	
72		6d. purple	12·00	50·00
		a. "C" of "CA" missing from wmk	£950	
		b. "A" of "CA" missing from wmk	£1000	
		c. Substituted crown in wmk	†	£1500
73		1s. black/*green*	23·00	50·00

(b) Wmk Mult Script CA (sideways*).

No.	Type	Description	Unused	Used
74	**19**	¼d. brown	1·50	3·75
		w. Wmk Crown to left of CA		
		x. Wmk sideways reversed		
75		½d. green	2·75	6·00
		w. Wmk Crown to left of CA	£150	£170
		y. Wmk sideways inverted and reversed	£300	
		ys. Optd "Specimen"	£100	
76		1d. deep carmine	2·50	35
		a. "C" of "CA" missing from wmk		
		w. Wmk Crown to left of CA	—	£375
		y. Wmk sideways inverted and reversed	£750	
68/76 *Set of 9*			65·00	£160
68s/76s Optd "Specimen" *Set of 9*			£325	

*The normal sideways watermark shows Crown to right of CA, *as seen from the back of the stamp.*

For illustration of the substituted watermark crown see Catalogue Introduction.

Examples of most values of Nos. 59/76 are known showing part strikes of the forged Hamilton postmark mentioned below Nos. 51*b*/5.

I II III

Three Types of the 1d.

I. Scroll at top left very weak and figure "1" has pointed serifs.
II. Scroll weak. "1" has square serifs and "1d" is heavy.
III. Redrawn. Scroll is completed by a strong line and "1" is thinner with long square serifs.

I II

Two Types of the 2½d.

I. Short, thick figures, especially of the "1", small "d".
II. Figures taller and thinner, "d" larger.

1922–34. Wmk Mult Script CA. P 14.

No.	Type	Description	Unused	Used
76*b*	**14**	¼d. brown (7.28)	1·50	3·00
77		½d. green (11.22)	1·50	15
		w. Wmk inverted		
		x. Wmk reversed		
78		1d. scarlet (I) (11.22)	17·00	60
		a. Carmine (7.24)	18·00	60
		bx. Wmk reversed		
78*c*		1d. carmine (II) (12.25)	40·00	6·00
		cx. Wmk reversed		
		d. Scarlet (8.27)	11·00	80
79		1d. scarlet (III) (10.28)	12·00	30
		a. Carmine-lake (1934)	25·00	2·25
79*b*		1½d. red-brown (27.3.34)	9·00	35
80		2d. grey (12.23)	1·50	1·50
		x. Wmk reversed	65·00	
81		2½d. pale sage-green (12.22)	2·25	1·50
		a. Deep sage-green (1924)	1·75	1·50
		aw. Wmk inverted		
		ax. Wmk reversed		
		ay. Wmk inverted and reversed		
82		2½d. ultramarine (I) (1.12.26)	2·50	50
		aw. Wmk inverted	£140	
82*b*		2½d. ultramarine (II) (3.32)	1·75	70
83		3d. ultramarine (12.24)	16·00	26·00
		w. Wmk inverted	£120	
84		3d. purple/*yellow* (10.26)	4·00	1·00
85		4d. red/*yellow* (8.24)	2·00	1·00
		x. Wmk reversed		
86		6d. purple (8.24)	1·00	80
87		1s. black/*emerald* (10.27)	4·75	9·00
		a. Brownish black/yellow-green (1934)	35·00	50·00
76*b*/87 *Set of 12*			50·00	40·00
76*b*s/87s Optd or Perf (1½d.) "Specimen" *Set of 12*			£500	

Both comb and line perforations occur on Nos. 76*b*/87*a*.

Detailed gauges are as follows:

13.7 × 13.9 comb	—	Nos. 77, 78/*a*, 80, 81/*a*, 83, 84, 85, 86, 87
13.75 line	—	Nos. 76*b*, 77, 78*c*/*d*, 79/*a*, 79*b*, 80, 82, 82*b*, 84, 85, 86, 87/*a*
13.75 × 14 line	—	Nos. 77, 78*c*/*d*, 79*b*, 80, 82*b*, 86, 87*a*
14 × 13.75 line	—	Nos. 79/*a*
14 line	—	Nos. 81/*a*

Breaks in scrolls at right (R. 1/3. Ptgs of 12s.6d. from July 1932)

1924–32. Wmk Mult Script CA. *Chalk-surfaced paper.* P 14.

No.	Type	Description	Unused	Used
88	**15**	2s. purple and bright blue/*pale blue* (1.9.27)	45·00	70·00
		a. Break in scroll	£225	
		b. Broken crown and scroll	£225	
		e. Break in lines below left scroll	£250	
		f. Damaged leaf at bottom right	£225	
		g. Purple and blue/grey-blue (1931)	55·00	80·00
		ga. Break in scroll	£275	
		gb. Broken crown and scroll	£275	
		gd. Break through scroll	£325	
		ge. Break in lines below left scroll	£325	
		gf. Damaged leaf at bottom right	£275	
		gg. Gash in fruit and leaf	£275	
89		2s.6d. black and carmine/*pale blue* (4.27)	60·00	£100
		a. Break in scroll	£275	
		b. Broken crown and scroll	£275	
		e. Break in lines below left scroll	£325	
		f. Damaged leaf at bottom right	£275	
		g. Black and red/blue to deep blue (6.29)	70·00	£110
		ga. Break in scroll	£325	
		gb. Broken crown and scroll	£325	
		gd. Break through scroll	£375	
		ge. Break in lines below left scroll	£375	
		gf. Damaged leaf at bottom right	£325	
		gg. Gash in fruit and leaf	£325	
		h. Grey-black and pale orange-vermilion/grey-blue (3.30)	£2750	£2750
		ha. Break in scroll	£4500	
		hb. Broken crown and scroll	£4500	
		hd. Break through scroll	£4500	
		he. Break in lines below left scroll	£4500	
		hf. Damaged leaf at bottom right	£4500	
		hg. Gash in fruit and leaf	£4500	
		i. Black and carmine-red/deep grey-blue (8.30)	90·00	£120
		ia. Break in scroll	£450	
		ib. Broken crown and scroll	£450	

id. Break through scroll £500
ie. Break in lines below left scroll . . £500
if. Damaged leaf at bottom right . . £450
ig. Gash in fruit and leaf £450
j. *Black and scarlet-vermilion/dp bl* (9.31) . . . . 85·00 £120
ja. Break in scroll £425
jb. Broken crown and scroll £425
jc. Nick in top right scroll £475
jd. Break through scroll £475
je. Break in lines below left scroll . . £475
jf. Damaged leaf at bottom right . . £425
jg. Gash in fruit and leaf £425
k. *Black & brt orange-vermilion/deep blue* (8.32) £3000 £2750
kb. Broken crown and scroll £4750
kd. Break through scroll £4750
ke. Break in lines below left scroll . . £4750
kf. Damaged leaf at bottom right . . £4750
kg. Gash in fruit and leaf £4750

92 10s. green and red/*pale emerald* (12.24) £130 £250
a. Break in scroll £600
b. Broken crown and scroll £500
e. Break in lines below left scroll . . £600
f. Damaged leaf at bottom right . . £500
g. *Green and red/deep emerald* (1930) £140 £275
ga. Break in scroll £600
gb. Broken crown and scroll £550
gc. Nick in top right scroll £600
gd. Break through scroll £600
ge. Break in lines below left scroll . . £600
gf. Damaged leaf at bottom right . . £550
gg. Gash in fruit and leaf £550

93 12s.6d. grey and orange (8.32) £250 £350
a. Break in scroll £700 £850
b. Broken crown and scroll £750 £900
c. Nick in top right scroll £750
d. Break through scroll £850
e. Break in lines below left scroll . . £850
f. Damaged leaf at bottom right . . £750
g. Gash in fruit and leaf £750
h. Break in scrolls at right £850
i. Error. Ordinary paper . . . .

88/93 *Set of* 4 . . . . £425 £700
88s/93s Optd or Perf (12s.6d) "Specimen" *Set of* 4 . . . . £500

The true No. 89*h* is the only stamp on grey-blue paper, other deeper orange-vermilion shades exist on different papers. No. 89k was despatched to Bermuda in July/August 1932, but is not known used before 1937.

Beware of fiscally used 2s.6d. 10s. and 12s.6d. stamps cleaned and bearing faked postmarks. Large quantities were used for a "head tax" levied on travellers leaving the country.

For 12s.6d. design inscribed "Revenue" at both sides see No. F1 under POSTAL FISCAL.

1935 (6 May). *Silver Jubilee. As Nos. 91/4 of Antigua, but ptd by Waterlow.* P 11 × 12.

94 1d. deep blue and scarlet 45 60
j. Damaged turret £170
m. "Bird" by turret £110 £120
95 1½d. ultramarine and grey . . . . 70 2·25
m. "Bird" by turret £120
96 2½d. brown and deep blue . . . . 1·40 1·25
m. "Bird" by turret £170 £170
97 1s. slate and purple . . . . 15·00 25·00
k. Kite and vertical log £170 £225
l. Kite and horizontal log £325
94/7 *Set of* 4 . . . . 16·00 26·00
94s/7s Perf "Specimen" *Set of* 4 . . . . £170

For illustrations of plate varieties see Omnibus section following Zanzibar.

20 Red Hole, Paget

21 South Shore

22 *Lucie* (yacht)

23 Grape Bay, Paget Parish

24 Point House, Warwick Parish

25 Gardener's Cottage, Par-la-Ville, Hamilton

(Recess B.W.)

1936 (14 Apr)–**47**. *T* 12. Wmk Mult Script CA (sideways on horiz designs).

98 **20** ½d. bright green 10 10
99 **21** 1d. black and scarlet 30 30
100 1½d. black and chocolate . . . . 1·00 50
101 **22** 2d. black and pale blue . . . . 5·00 1·50
102 **23** 2½d. light and deep blue . . . . 1·00 25
103 **24** 3d. black and scarlet . . . . 2·75 1·40
104 **25** 6d. carmine-lake and violet 80 10
a. Claret and dull violet (6.47) . . . . 3·50 1·50
105 **23** 1s. green . . . . 5·00 9·50
106 **20** 1s.6d. brown 50 10
98/106 *Set of* 9 . . . . 15·00 12·00
98s/106s Perf "Specimen" *Set of* 9 . . . . £250

All are line-perf 11.9, except printings of the 6d. from July 1951 onwards, which are comb-perf 11.9 × 11.75.

1937 (14 May). *Coronation. As Nos. 95/7 of Antigua, but printed by D.L.R.* P 14.

107 1d. scarlet 50 80
108 1½d. yellow-brown . . . . 60 1·50
109 2½d. bright blue . . . . 70 1·50
107/9 *Set of* 3 . . . . 1·60 3·50
107s/9s Perf "Specimen" *Set of* 3 . . . . £130

26 Ships in Hamilton Harbour

27 St. David's Lighthouse

28 White-tailed Tropic Bird, Arms of Bermuda and Native Flower

29 King George VI

(Des Miss Higginbotham (T **28**). Recess B.W.)

1938 (20 Jan)–**52**. *T* **22**, *T* **23** *(but with portrait of King George VI) and T* **26** *to* **28**. Wmk Mult Script CA. P 12.

110 **26** 1d. black and red (*a*) (*b*) 85 20
111 1½d. deep blue and purple-brown (*a*) (*b*) . . . . 7·00 1·50
a. Blue and brown (*a*) (3.43) . . . . 7·00 3·25
b. lt blue & purple-brn (*a*) (*b*) (9.45) . . . . 2·25 70
ba. "A" of "CA" missing from wmk £1500
112 **22** 2d. light blue and sepia (*a*) . . . . 45·00 8·50
112*a* 2d. ultramarine and scarlet (*a*) (*b*) (8.11.40) . . . . 1·50 1·00
113 **23** 2½d. light and deep blue (*a*) . . . . 11·00 1·25
113*a* 2½d. lt blue & sepia-black (*a*) (18.12.41) . . . . 3·00 2·00
b. Pale blue & sepia-black (*a*) (3.43) . . . . 2·75 2·00
c. Bright blue and deep sepia-black (*b*) (23.9.52) . . . . 5·00 5·50
114 **27** 3d. black and rose-red (*a*) . . . . 18·00 3·00
114*a* 3d. black & deep blue (*a*) (*b*) (16.7.41) . . . . 1·75 40
114*b* **28** 7½d. black, blue & brt grn (*a*) (18.12.41) . . . . 7·00 2·75
c. Black, blue & yellow-grn (*a*) (3.43) . . . . 5·50 2·75
115 **23** 1s. green (*a*) (*b*) . . . . 2·00 50
a. Bluish green (*b*) (20.6.52) . . . . 6·50 6·50

Perforations. Two different perforating machines were used on the various printings of these stamps: (*a*) the original 11.9 line perforation; (*b*) 11.9 × 11.75 comb perforation, introduced in July 1950. These perforations occur as indicated above.

Shading omitted from top right scroll (R. 1/1. March 1943 ptgs of 2s. and £1)

Lower right scroll with broken tail (R. 2/10. Line perforated printings only)

Broken top right scroll (R. 5/11. Line perforated ptgs only. A retouched state of the flaw is visible in later ptgs up to March 1943)

Broken lower right scroll (R. 5/12. Occurs on printings made between May 1941 and March 1943)

Gash in chin (R. 2/5. Ptgs between May 1941 and March 1943)

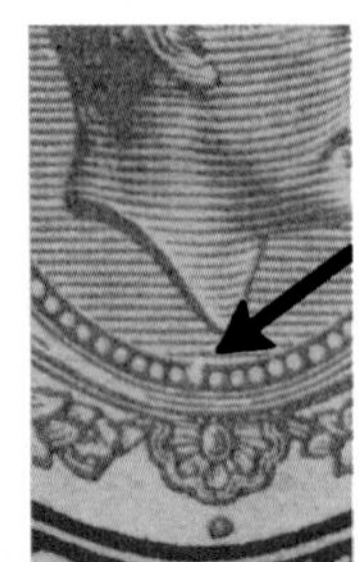
Missing pearl (R. 5/1, Nov 1945 ptg of 5s. only)

"ER" joined (R. 1/2. Occurs in its complete state on 1938 ptg only. Subsequent ptgs show it incomplete)

Damaged left value tablet (R. 1/11. Part of 1951 ptg only)

(Typo D.L.R.)

1938 (20 Jan)–**53**. *T* **29**. Wmk Mult Crown CA (£1) or Mult Script CA (others). *Chalk-surfaced paper*. P 14 (comb).

116 2s. deep purple and ultramarine/*grey-blue* . . . . £110 11·
a. Deep reddish purple and ultram/grey-blue (21.11.40)* . . . . £350 25·
b. Perf 14¼ line. *Deep purple and ultram/grey-blue* (14.11.41)* . . . . £300 85·
bc. Lower right scroll with broken tail . . £2000 £7
bd. Broken top right scroll £1400 £5
be. Broken lower right scroll £1400 £5
bf. Gash in chin £1500 £6
c. Ordinary paper. *Pur & bl/dp bl* (7.6.42) . . . . 8·00 1·
ce. Broken lower right scroll . . . . £225 85·
cf. Gash in chin . . . . £250 90·
d. Ordinary paper. *Purple and deep blue/pale blue* (5.3.43) . . . . 12·00 1·
db. Shading omitted from top right scroll £1200 £6
de. Broken lower right scroll £600 £3
df. Gash in chin £650 £3
e. Perf 13. Ordinary paper. *Dull purple and blue/pale blue* (15.2.50) . . . . 17·00 15·
f. Perf 13. Ordinary paper. *Reddish purple and blue/pale blue* (10.10.50) . . 8·50 17·
117 2s.6d. black and red/*grey-blue* . . . . 70·00 9·
a. Perf 14¼ line. *Black and red/grey-blue* (21.2.42)* £550 £1
ac. Lower right scroll with broken tail . . £2250 £8
ad. Broken top right scroll £1600 £6
ae. Broken lower right scroll £1600 £6
af. Gash in chin £1700 £7
b. Ordinary paper. *Black and red/pale blue* (5.3.43) . . . . 19·00 6·
be. Broken lower right scroll £600 £2
bf. Gash in chin £650 £3
c. Perf 13. Ordinary paper. *Black and orange-red/pale blue* (10.10.50) . . . . 20·00 11·
d. Perf 13. Ordinary paper. *Black and red/ pale blue* (18.6.52) . . . . 16·00 12·
118 5s. green and red/*yellow* . . . . £140 27·
a. Pale green & red/yellow (14.3.39)* . . £300 70·
b. Perf 14¼ line. *Dull yellow-green and red/yellow* (5.1.43)* . . . . £250 30·
bc. Lower right scroll with broken tail . . £1500 £5
bd. Broken top right scroll £900 £3
be. Broken lower right scroll £900 £3
bf. Gash in chin £950 £3
c. Ordinary paper. *Dull yellow-green & carmine-red/pale yellow* (5.42)* £650 £1
ce. Broken lower right scroll £4000 £11
cf. Gash in chin £4000 £11

d. Ordinary paper. *Pale bluish green and carmine-red/pale yellow* (5.3.43) . . . . £100 50·00
de. Broken lower right scroll £800 £450
df. Gash in chin £800 £450
e. Ordinary paper. *Green and red/pale yellow* (11.45)* . . . . 50·00 20·00
ea. Missing pearl £750
f. Perf 13. Ordinary paper. *Yellow-green and red/pale yellow* (15.2.50) . . . . . 25·00 20·00
g. Perf 13. *Green and scarlet/yellow (chalk-surfaced)* (10.10.50) . . . . . . 40·00 50·00

119 10s. green and deep lake/*pale emerald* . . . £450 £325
a. Bluish green & deep red/green (8.39)* £225 £130
b. Perf 14¼ line. Ordinary paper. *Yellow green and carmine/green* (1942)* . . . £475 £120
bc. Lower right scroll with broken tail . . £2250 £950
bd. Broken top right scroll £1500 £700
be. Broken lower right scroll £1500 £700
bf. Gash in chin £1600 £750
c. Ordinary paper. *Yellowish green and deep carmine-red/green* (5.3.43) . . . . 70·00 60·00
ce. Broken lower right scroll £2250
cf. Gash in chin £2250
d. Ordinary paper. *Deep green and dull red/green (emerald back)* (11.12.46) . . 80·00 60·00
e. Perf 13. Ordinary paper. *Green and vermilion/green* (19.9.51) . . . . . . 38·00 42·00
f. Perf 13. Ordinary paper. *Green and dull red/green* (16.4.53) . . . . . . 35·00 48·00

20 12s.6d. deep grey and brownish orange . . £500 £425
a. Grey and brownish orange (shades) . . £190 65·00
b. Grey and pale orange (9.11.40)* . . . 95·00 50·00
c. Ordinary paper (2.3.44)* . . . . . . £110 65·00
ce. Broken lower right scroll £1900 £2000
cf. Gash in chin £1900
d. Ordinary paper. *Grey and yell*† (17.9.47)* £650 £475
e. Perf 13. *Grey and pale orange (chalk surfaced)* (10.10.50) . . . . 95·00 75·00

21 £1 purple and black/*red* £275 £100
a. "ER" joined £750 £500
b. Pale purple & black/pale red (13.5.43)* . . . . 80·00 60·00
bb. Shading omitted from top right scroll £2250
be. Broken lower right scroll £1400 £950
bf. Gash in chin £1400 £950
c. Dp reddish pur and blk/pale red (5.3.43)* . . . . 60·00 60·00
ce. Broken lower right scroll £1300
cf. Gash in chin £1300
d. Perf 13. *Violet & black/scarlet* (7.12.51) . . . . 50·00 75·00
da. Damaged left value tablet £2250
e. Perf 13. *Brt violet & blk/scar* (10.12.52) £160 £170

10/21d *Set of* 16 . . . . £275 £180
10s/21s Perf "Specimen" *Set of* 16 . . . . . . £1600

Following extensive damage to their printing works on 9 December 1940 much of De La Rue's work was transferred to other firms operating under their supervision. It is understood that Williams Lea & Co produced those new printings ordered for the Bermuda high value stamps during 1941. The first batch of these printings showed the emergency use, by Williams Lea, of a 14¼ line perforating machine (exact gauge 14.15) instead of the comb perforation (exact gauge 13.9 × 13.8).

Dates marked * are those of earliest known use.

In No. 116c the coloured surfacing of the paper is mottled with white specks sometimes accompanied by very close horizontal lines. In Nos. 116d, 117b and 118c/d the surfacing is the same colour as the back, sometimes applied in widely spaced horizontal lines giving the appearance of laid paper.

†No. 120d is the so-called "lemon" shade.

HALF PENNY

X X

30

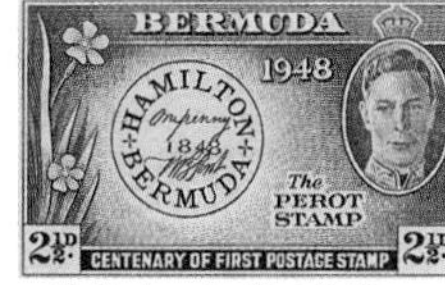

31 Postmaster Perot's Stamp

1940 (20 Dec). *No. 110 surch with T* **30** *by Royal Gazette, Hamilton.*
22 **26** ½d. on 1d. black and red (*shades*) . . . 40 1·00

The spacing between "PENNY" and "X" varies from 12½ mm to 14 mm.

1946 (6 Nov). *Victory. As Nos. 110/11 of Antigua.*
23 1½d. brown 15 15
24 3d. blue 15 15
23s/4s Perf "Specimen" *Set of* 2 . . . . 90·00

1948 (1 Dec). *Royal Silver Wedding. As Nos. 112/13 of Antigua.*
25 1½d. red-brown 30 50
26 £1 carmine . . . . 40·00 48·00

(Recess B.W.)

1949 (11 Apr). *Centenary of Postmaster Perot's Stamp.* Wmk Mult Script CA. P 13½.
27 **31** 2½d. blue and brown 15 25
28 3d. black and blue 15 15
29 6d. violet and green 15 15
27/9 *Set of* 3 . . . . 40 50

1949 (10 Oct). *75th Anniv of Universal Postal Union. As Nos. 114/17 of Antigua.*
30 2½d. blue-black . . . . 30 1·25
31 3d. deep blue . . . . 1·40 1·25
32 6d. purple 40 75
33 1s. blue-green . . . . 40 1·25
30/3 *Set of* 4 . . . . 2·25 4·00

STAMP BOOKLETS

1948 (5 Apr–10 May). *Pink (No. SB1), or light blue (No. SB2) covers. Stapled.*
SB1 5s. booklet containing six 1d., 1½d., 2d., 2½d. and 3d. (Nos. 110, 111*b*, 112*a*, 113*b*, 114*a*) in blocks of 6 (10 May) £140
SB2 10s.6d. booklet containing six 3d. and eighteen 6d. (Nos. 114*a*, 104) in blocks of 6 with twelve air mail labels £150

POSTAL FISCAL

1937 (1 Feb). *As T* **15**, *but inscr "REVENUE" at each side.* Wmk Mult Script CA. *Chalk-surfaced paper.* P 14
F1 12s.6d. grey and orange £1000 £1200
a. Break in scroll (R. 1/12) £3000 £5000
b. Broken crown and scroll (R. 2/12) £3000
d. Break through scroll (R. 1/9) . . . £2500
e. Break in lines below left scroll . . . £2500
f. Damaged leaf at bottom right . . . £2500
g. Gash in fruit and leaf £2500
h. Breaks in scrolls at right (R. 1/3) . . £3000

No. F1 was issued for fiscal purposes towards the end of 1936. Its use as a postage stamp was authorised from 1 February to April 1937. The used price quoted above is for examples postmarked during this period. Later in the same year postmarks with other dates were obtained by favour.

For illustration of No. F1a/h see above Nos. 51*b* and 88.

British Central Africa *see* Nyasaland Protectorate

British Columbia and Vancouver Island *see* Canada

British Commonwealth Occupation Force *see after* Australia

British East Africa *see* Kenya, Uganda and Tanganyika

British Forces in Egypt *see* Egypt

British Guiana

The postal service from what was to become British Guiana dates from 1796, being placed on a more regular basis after the final British occupation.

An inland postal system was organised in 1850, using the adhesive stamps of British Guiana, but, until 1 May 1860, overseas mails continued to be the province of the British G.P.O. The stamps of Great Britain were supplied for use on such letters from 11 May 1858 and examples of their use in combination with British Guiana issues have been recorded.

For illustration of the handstamp and postmark type see BRITISH POST OFFICES ABROAD notes, following GREAT BRITAIN.

CROWNED-CIRCLED HANDSTAMPS

The provision of a handstamp, probably as Type CC **1**, inscribed "DEMERARA", is recorded in the G.P.O. proof book under 1 March 1856. No examples have been reported. A further handstamp, as Type CC **6**, recorded in the proof book on 17 February 1866, is known used as a cancellation in at least two instances, *circa* 1868.

GEORGETOWN (DEMERARA)

Stamps of GREAT BRITAIN *cancelled* "A 03" *as Type* **2**.

1856–60.
Z1 1d. rose-red (1857), *perf* 14 . . . . £325
Z2 4d. rose (1857) £160
Z3 6d. lilac (1856) £120
a. Azure paper . . . .
Z4 1s. green (1856) £1400

NEW AMSTERDAM (BERBICE)

Stamps of GREAT BRITAIN *cancelled* "A 04" *as Type* **2**.

1858–60.
Z5 1d. rose-red (1857), *perf* 14 . . . . £800
Z6 2d. blue (1858) (Plate Nos. 7, 8) £850
Z7 4d. rose (1857) £375
Z8 6d. lilac (1856) £250
Z9 1s. green (1856) £1600

PRICES FOR STAMPS ON COVER TO 1945		
Nos.	1/21	*from* × 3
No.	23	†
Nos.	24/7	*from* × 3
Nos.	29/115	*from* × 5
Nos.	116/24	*from* × 8
Nos.	126/36	*from* × 7
Nos.	137/59	*from* × 8
Nos.	162/5	*from* × 10
Nos.	170/4	*from* × 8
Nos.	175/89	*from* × 10
No.	192	*from* × 30
Nos.	193/210	*from* × 5
Nos.	213/15	*from* × 8
Nos.	216/21	*from* × 5
Nos.	222/4	*from* × 10
Nos.	233/50	*from* × 4
No.	251	—
Nos.	252/7	*from* × 4
Nos.	259/82	*from* × 5
Nos.	283/7	*from* × 8
Nos.	288/300	*from* × 5
Nos.	301/4	*from* × 6
Nos.	305/7	*from* × 8
Nos.	308/19	*from* × 5
Nos.	D1/4	*from* × 15
Nos.	O1/12	*from* × 15

CROWN COLONY

(Currency. 100 cents = 1 dollar)

1

2

(Set up and printed at the office of the *Royal Gazette*, Georgetown, British Guiana)

1850 (1 July)–**51**. *Type-set. Black impression.*

(a) Medium wove paper. Prices are for—I. *Cut square.* II. *Cut round.*

			I *Used*	II *Used*
1	**1**	2c. *rose* (1.3.51)	—	£70000
2		4c. *orange*	£32000	£5000
3		4c. *lemon-yellow* (1851)	£48000	£6000
4		8c. *green*	£18000	£3750
5		12c. *blue*	£6500	£2500
6		12c. *indigo*	£11000	£3250
7		12c. *pale blue* (1851)	£10000	£3500
		a. "2" of "12" with straight foot	—	£8000
		b. "1" of "12" omitted	†	£40000

(b) Pelure paper (1851).

8 **1** 4c. *pale yellow* £60000 £7000

These stamps were usually initialled by the postmaster, or the Post Office clerks, before they were issued. The initials are—E. T. E. D(alton), E. D. W(ight), J. B. S(mith), H. A. K(illikelley), and W. H. L(ortimer). There are several types of each value and it has been suggested that the setting contained one horizontal row of four slightly different impressions.

Ten examples of No. 1 have been recorded, including three pairs on separate covers.

(Litho Waterlow)

1852 (1 Jan). *Surface-coloured paper.* Imperf.

			Un	*Used*
9	**2**	1c. black/*magenta*	£8500	£4250
10		4c. black/*deep blue*	£11000	£6000

There are two types of each value.

Reprints on thicker paper, and perf 12½, were made in 1865 (*Price* £17 *either value*).

Such reprints with the perforations removed are sometimes offered as genuine originals.

CONDITION. Prices for Nos. 9 to 21 are for fine copies. Poor to medium specimens can be supplied when in stock at much lower rates.

3

4

5

(Dies eng and stamps litho Waterlow)

1853–59. Imperf.

(a) Original printing.

11	**3**	1c. vermilion	£3000	£1000

This 1c. in *reddish brown* is probably a proof (*Price* £650).

A B C D

A. "O" large and 1 mm from left corner.
B. "O" small and ¾ mm from left corner.
C. "O" small and ¾ mm from left corner. "NT" widely spaced.
D. "ONE" close together, "O" 1¼ mm from left corner.

(b) Fresh lithographic transfers from the 4c. with varying labels of value. White line above value (1857–59).

12	**3**	1c. dull red (A)	£3000	£1100
13		1c. brownish red (A)	£6500	£1500
14		1c. dull red (B)	£3500	£1200
15		1c. brownish red (B)	£7000	£1600
16		1c. dull red (C)	£4500	£1500
16*a*		1c. brownish red (C)	—	£1800
17		1c. dull red (D)	£13000	£5500

1853–55. Imperf.

18	**4**	4c. deep blue	£2000	£650
		a. Retouched	£3000	£900
19		4c. blue (1854)	£1300	£450
		a. Retouched	£2000	£600
20		4c. pale blue (1855)	£950	£375
		a. Retouched	£1500	£550

The 4c. value was produced from transfers from the original 1c., with the bottom inscription removed, teamed with a new face value. The join often shows as a white line or traces of it above the label of value and lower corner figures. In some stamps on the sheet this line is missing, owing to having been retouched, and in these cases a line of colour usually appears in its place.

The 1c. and 4c. stamps were printed in 1865 from fresh transfers of five varieties. These are on thin paper and perf 12½ (*Price* £14 *each unused*).

1860 (May). *Figures in corners framed.* Imperf

21	**5**	4c. blue	£3750	£500

6

(Type-set and printed at the *Official Gazette* by Baum and Dallas, Georgetown)

1856.

(a) Surface-coloured paper.

23	**6**	1c. black/*magenta*	†	—
24		4c. black/*magenta* (Jan)	†	£6500
25		4c. black/*rose-carmine* (Aug)	£22000	£9000
26		4c. black/*blue* (Sept)	†	£45000

(b) Paper coloured through.

27	**6**	4c. black/*deep blue* (Aug)	†	£65000

Since only one example of No. 23 is known, no market price can be given. This celebrated stamp frequently termed "the world's rarest", was last on the market in 1980. It is initialled by E. D. Wight and postmarked at Demerara on 4 April 1856.

These stamps, like those of the first issue, were initialled before being issued; the initials are—E.T.E.D (alton), E.D.W. (ight), C.A.W (atson), and W.H.L (ortimer). C.A.W. only appears on stamps postmarked between 14 March and 4 April and also 16–20 May. E.T.E.D. is only known on stamps between 1–5 July and on 1 August. All examples on the rose-carmine or blue papers show E.D.W.

Stamps as Type **6** were printed in sheets of 4 (2 × 2) each stamp differing slightly in the position of the inscriptions. There is evidence that the setting was re-arranged at some point before August, *possibly* to accommodate the production of the 1c.

PAPERMAKERS' WATERMARKS. Seven different papermakers' watermarks were used in the period 1860 to 1875 and stamps bearing portions of these are worth a premium.

7

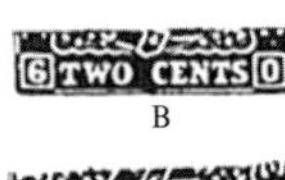
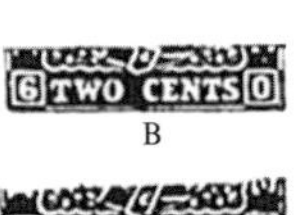
A B C D

E F

(Dies eng and litho Waterlow)

1860 (July)–**63**. *Tablets of value as illustrated. Thick paper.* P 12.

29	**7**	1c. pale rose	£1400	£200
30		2c. deep orange (8.60)	£200	45·00
31		2c. pale orange	£225	48·00
32		4c. deep blue (8.60)	£450	80·00
33		4c. blue	£300	55·00
34		8c. brownish rose	£475	90·00
35		8c. pink	£400	65·00
36		12c. lilac	£475	42·00
37		12c. grey-lilac	£400	40·00
38		24c. deep green (6.63)	£1300	£110
39		24c. green	£1000	65·00

The 1c. was reprinted in 1865 on *thin* paper, P 12½–13, and in a different shade. *Price* £15.

The 12c. in both shades is frequently found surcharged with a large "5d" in *red*; this is to denote the proportion of postage repayable by the colony to Great Britain for overseas letters.

1861 (3 Aug*). *Colour changed. Thick paper.* P 12.

40	**7**	1c. reddish brown	£325	95·00

*Earliest known postmark date.

1862–65.

(a) Thin paper. P 12.

41	**7**	1c. brown	£475	£190
42		1c. black (1863)	95·00	50·00
43		2c. orange	90·00	45·00
44		4c. blue	£110	40·00
45		4c. pale blue	95·00	29·00
46		8c. pink (1863)	£130	60·00
47		12c. dull purple (1863)	£160	26·00
48		12c. purple	£180	29·00
49		12c. lilac	£190	38·00
50		24c. green	£850	90·00

(b) Thin paper. P 12½–13 (1863).

51	**7**	1c. black	60·00	19·00
52		2c. orange	75·00	19·00
53		4c. blue	75·00	17·00
54		8c. pink	£225	80·00
55		12c. brownish lilac	£550	£110
56		24c. green	£600	65·00

Copies are found on *pelure* paper.

(c) Medium paper. P 12½–13.

57	**7**	1c. black (1864)	48·00	38·00
58		2c. deep orange (1864)	65·00	24·00
59		2c. orange	70·00	22·00
60		4c. greyish blue (1864)	80·00	18·00
61		4c. blue	95·00	25·00
62		8c. pink (1864)	£150	60·00
63		12c. brownish lilac (1865)	£475	£100
64		24c. green (1864)	£180	50·00
65		24c. deep green	£300	75·00

(d) Medium paper. P 10 (No. 1865).

65*a*	**7**	12c. grey-lilac	£500	80·00

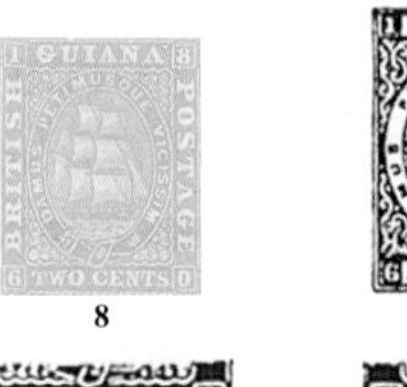
8 9

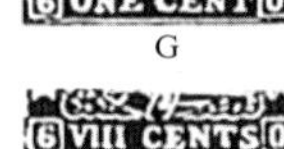
G

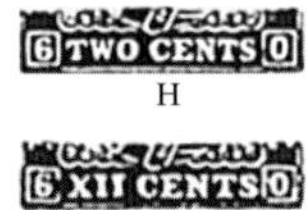
H I K

New transfers for the 1c., 2c., 8c., and 12c. with the spaces between values and the word "CENTS" about 1 mm.

1863–76. *Medium paper*

(a) P 12½–13 (1863–68).

66	**8**	1c. black (1866)	45·00	25·00
67		2c. orange-red (1865)	50·00	6·00
68		2c. orange	50·00	6·00
69	**9**	6c. blue (1865)	£120	55·00
70		6c. greenish blue	£130	60·00
71		6c. deep blue	£190	65·00
72		6c. milky blue	£120	55·00
73	**8**	8c. pink (1868)	£225	19·00
74		8c. carmine	£250	21·00
75		12c. grey-lilac (1867)	£450	30·00
76		12c. brownish purple	£550	40·00
77	**9**	24c. green (*perf* 12)	£250	20·00
78		24c. yellow-green (*perf* 12)	£160	10·00
79		24c. yellow-green (*perf* 12½–13)	£160	10·00
80		24c. green (*perf* 12½–13) (1864)	£160	10·00
81		24c. blue-green (*perf* 12½–13)	£190	20·00
82		48c. pale red	£250	55·00
83		48c. deep red	£275	55·00
84		48c. carmine-rose	£300	55·00

The 4c. corresponding to this issue can only be distinguished from that of the previous issue by minor plating flaws.

There is a variety of the 6c. with stop before "VICISSIM".

Varieties of most of the values of issues of 1863–64 and 1866 are to be found on both very thin and thick papers.

(b) P 10 (1866–71).

85	**8**	1c. black (1869)	11·00	4·50
86		1c. grey-black	13·00	11·00
87		2c. orange (1868)	27·00	3·50
88		2c. reddish orange	38·00	4·75
89		4c. slate-blue	90·00	13·00
90		4c. blue	85·00	7·50
		a. Bisected (on cover)	†	£5500
		b. Ditto. Imperf (on cover)	†	—
91		4c. pale blue	80·00	9·50
92	**9**	6c. milky blue (1867)	£130	32·00
93		6c. ultramarine	£140	55·00
94		6c. dull blue	£130	35·00
95	**8**	8c. pink (5.71)	£130	25·00
96		8c. brownish pink	£150	27·00
96*a*		8c. carmine	£225	35·00
97		12c. pale lilac (1867)	£225	16·00
98		12c. grey-lilac	£170	15·00
99		12c. brownish grey	£170	17·00
100		12c. lilac	£170	17·00
101	**9**	24c. deep green	£250	9·50
102		24c. bluish green	£225	8·00
103		24c. yellow-green	£180	7·50
104		48c. crimson (1867)	£325	28·00
		s. Handstamped "Specimen"	£250	
		as. Perf "Specimen"	£200	
105		48c. red	£325	24·00

(c) P 15 (1875–76).

106	**8**	1c. black	48·00	7·50
107		2c. orange-red	£130	8·50
108		2c. orange	£130	8·50
109		4c. bright blue	£225	95·00
111	**9**	6c. ultramarine	£650	85·00
112	**8**	8c. deep rose (1876)	£225	80·0
113		12c. lilac	£550	60·0
114	**9**	24c. yellow-green	£600	35·0
115		24c. deep green	£950	65·0

There is a variety of the 48c. with stop after "P" in "PETIMUSQUE".

Imperforate stamps of this and of the previous issue are considered to be proofs, although examples of the 24c. imperforate from the 1869–73 period are known commercially used.

PRICES for stamps of the 1862 issue are for good average copies. Copies with roulettes on all sides very seldom occur and do not exist in marginal positions.

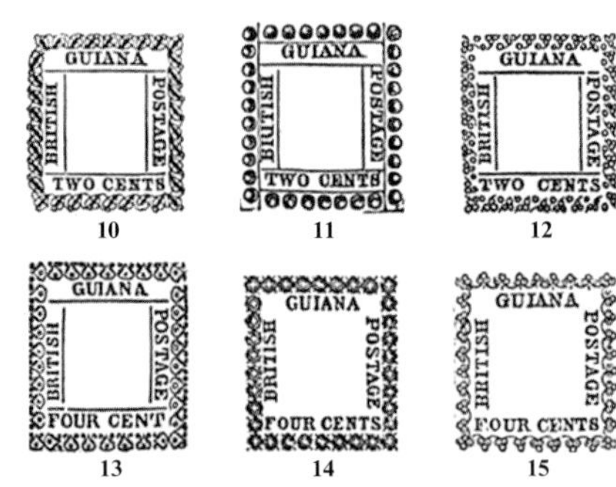
10 11 12 13 14 15

(Type-set and printed at the Office of the *Royal Gazette*, Georgetown)

1862 (Sept). *Black on coloured paper. Roul 6.*

116	**10**	1c. *rose*	£2750	£47
		a. Unsigned	£350	
		b. Wrong ornament (as T **13**) at left (R. 1/1)	—	£80
		c. "1" for "I" in "BRITISH" (R. 1/5)	—	£80
117	**11**	1c. *rose*	£3500	£65
		a. Unsigned	£400	
		b. Narrow "T" in "CENTS" (R. 3/1)	—	£8
		c. Wrong ornament (as T **15**) at top (R. 3/3)	—	£8
		d. "1" for "I" in "BRITISH" and italic "S" in "POSTAGE" (R. 3/5)	—	£8
118	**12**	1c. *rose*	£5000	£8
		a. Unsigned	£650	
		b. "1" for "I" in "GUIANA" (R. 4/4)	—	£8
		c. Wrong ornament (as T **15**) at left (R. 4/5)	—	£8
		d. "C" for "O" in "POSTAGE" (R. 4/6)	—	£8
119	**10**	2c. *yellow*	£2750	£3
		a. Unsigned	£1200	
		b. Wrong ornament (as T **13**) at left (R. 1/1)	—	£5
		c. "1" for "I" in "BRITISH" (R. 1/5)	—	£5
120	**11**	2c. *yellow*	£3500	£4
		a. Unsigned	£1300	
		b. "C" for "O" in "TWO" and narrow "T" in "CENTS" (R. 3/1)	—	£5
		c. Wrong ornament (as T **15**) at top (R. 3/3)	—	£5
		d. Italic "S" in "CENTS" (R. 3/4)	—	£5
		e. "1" for "I" in "BRITISH" and italic "S" in "POSTAGE" (R. 3/5)	—	£5
		f. Italic "T" in "TWO" (R. 3/6)	—	£5
121	**12**	2c. *yellow*	£5000	£6
		a. Unsigned	£1600	
		b. "1" for "I" in "GUIANA" (R. 4/4)	—	£6
		c. Wrong ornament (as T **15**) at left (R. 4/5)	—	£6
		d. "C" for "O" in "POSTAGE" (R. 4/6)	—	£6
122	**13**	4c. *blue*	£3000	£6
		a. Unsigned	£650	
		b. Wrong ornament (as T **15**) at left (R. 1/6)	£4000	£9
		c. Wrong ornament (as T **15**) at top and italic "S" in "CENTS" (R. 2/2)	—	£9
		d. Ornament omitted at right (R. 2/4)	—	£9

23 14 4c. *blue* . . . £3750 £800
a. Unsigned . . . £700
b. With inner frame lines (as in T **10**/**13**) (R. 2/5–6) . . . £5000 £1300
ba. "1" for "I" in "BRITISH" (R. 2/5) . . . £5000 £1300
c. "1" for "I" in "BRITISH" and "GUIANA" (R. 4/1) . . . — £950
24 15 4c. *blue* . . . £3750 £800
a. Unsigned . . . £750
b. Wrong ornament (as T **12**) at foot (R. 3/1) . . . — £950
c. Italic "S" in "CENTS" (R. 3/2) . . . — £950
d. Italic "S" in "BRITISH" (R. 3/3) . . . — £950

Stamps were initialled across the centre before use by the Acting Receiver-General, Robert Mather. Black was used on the 1c., red for the 2c. and an ink which appears white for the 4c.

The three values of this provisional were each printed in sheets of 24 (6×4). The 1c. and 2c. were produced from the same setting of the border ornaments which contained 12 examples as Type **10** (Rows 1 and 2), 8 as Type **11** (R. 3/1 to R. 4/2) and 4 as Type **12** (R. 4/3-6).

The setting of the 4c. contained 10 examples as Type **13** (R. 1/1 to R. 2/4), 8 as Type **14** (R. 2/5–6 and Row 4) and 6 as Type **15** (Row 3).

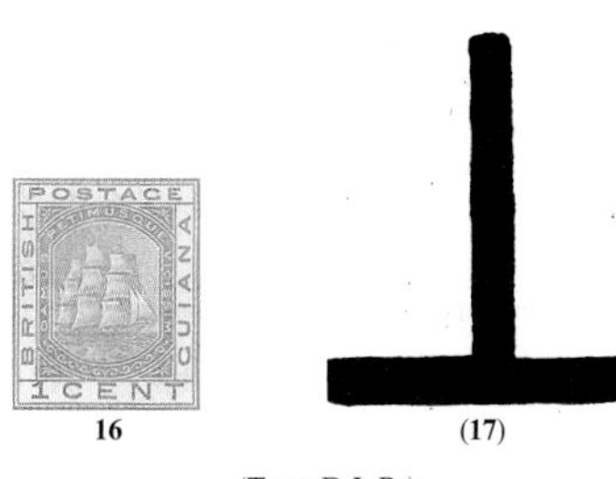

16 **(17)**

(Typo D.L.R.)

1876 (1 July)–**79**. Wmk Crown CC.

(a) P 14.

126 16 1c. slate . . . 2·75 1·40
127 2c. orange . . . 50·00 1·75
w. Wmk inverted . . .
128 4c. blue . . . £120 9·00
129 6c. brown . . . 75·00 7·00
130 8c. rose . . . £110 75
w. Wmk inverted . . .
131 12c. pale violet . . . 50·00 1·25
w. Wmk inverted . . .
132 24c. emerald-green . . . 60·00 3·00
w. Wmk inverted . . .
133 48c. red-brown . . . £120 28·00
134 96c. olive-bistre . . . £475 £250
126/34 *Set of* 9 . . . £950 £250
126s/32s, 134s Handstamped "Specimen" *Set of* 8 . . . £700
131sa/2sa Perf "Specimen" *Set of* 2 . . . £200

(b) P 12½ (1877).

135 16 4c. blue . . . £1200 £200

(c) Perf compound of 14×12½ (1879).

136 16 1c. slate . . . — £200

1878. *Provisionals. Various stamps with old values ruled through with thick bars, in black ink, the bars varying in depth of colour.*

(a) With two horiz bars (17 Apr).

137 16 (1c.) on 6c. brown . . . 38·00 £110

(b) Official stamps with horiz bars across "OFFICIAL" *(end Aug).*

138 8 1c. black . . . £225 75·00
139 16 1c. slate . . . £170 60·00
140 2c. orange . . . £325 65·00

(c) With horiz and vert bars as T **17** *(6 Nov).*

141 9 (1c.)on 6c. ultramarine (93) . . . £170 75·00
142 16 (1c.)on 6c. brown . . . £300 £100
a. Optd with vert bar only . . . † £4500

(d) Official stamps with bars across "OFFICIAL" *(23 Nov).*

(i) With two horiz bars and one vert.

144 16 (1c.) on 4c. blue . . . £300 £100
145 (1c.) on 6c. brown . . . £400 £100
146 8 (2c.) on 8c. rose . . . £1900 £275

(ii) With one horiz bar and one vert.

147 16 (1c.) on 4c. blue . . . † £2500
148 (2c.) on 8c. rose . . . £375 £110

1 **2** **2**
(18) **(19)** **(20)**

1881 (21 Dec). *No. 134 with old value ruled through with bar in black ink and surch.*

149 18 1c.on 96c. olive-bistre . . . 3·50 6·00
a. Bar in red . . .
b. Bar omitted . . .
150 19 2c.on 96c. olive-bistre . . . 5·00 11·00
a. Bar in red . . .
b. Bar omitted . . .
151 20 2c.on 96c. olive-bistre . . . 50·00 95·00
a. Bar in red . . .

In the setting of 60 Type **19** occurs on the first five vertical rows and Type **20** on the sixth.

1 **2** **2**
(21) **(23)** **(24)**

1881 (28 Dec). *Various stamps with old value ruled with bar and surch.*

(a) On No. 105.

152 21 1c.on 48c. red . . . 45·00 5·00
a. Bar omitted . . . — £600

(b) On Official stamps (including unissued 48c. optd with Type O **2**).

153 21 1on 12c. brownish purple (O4) . . . £120 70·00
154 1on 48c. red-brown . . . £150 95·00
155 23 2on 12c. pale violet (O11) . . . 75·00 28·00
a. Pair. Nos. 155/6 . . . £1100 £1200
b. Surch double . . . £800 £425
c. Surch double (T **23** + **24**) . . . £3000
d. Extra bar through "OFFICIAL"
156 24 2on 12c. pale violet (O11) . . . £475 £325
157 23 2on 24c. emerald-green (O12) . . . 85·00 45·00
a. Pair. Nos. 157/8 . . . £1300 £1400
b. Surch double . . . £1100
158 24 2on 24c. emerald-green (O12) . . . £600 £600
159 19 2on 24c. green (O5) . . . £275 £140

On Nos. 149/59 the bar is found in various thicknesses ranging from 1 to 4 mm.

It is believed that the same composite surcharge setting of 60 (6×10) was used for Nos. 155/6 and 157/8. Type **24** occurs on R. 7/2, 4-6 and R. 8/1.

26 **27**

(Type-set, Baldwin & Co. Georgetown)

1882 (9 Jan). *Black impression.* P 12. *Perforated with the word* "SPECIMEN" *diagonally.*

162 26 1c. *magenta* . . . 45·00 28·00
a. Imperf between (horiz pair) . . . † —
b. Without "SPECIMEN" . . . £600 £375
c. "1" with foot . . . 95·00 65·00
163 2c. *yellow* . . . 80·00 50·00
a. Without "SPECIMEN" . . . £500 £425
b. Small "2" . . . 80·00 50·00
164 27 1c. *magenta* . . . 45·00 28·00
a. Without "SPECIMEN" . . . £600 £375
b. "1" with foot . . . 95·00 65·00
c. Imperf between (horiz pair) . . . † £4750
165 2c. *yellow* . . . 75·00 48·00
a. Bisected diagonally (1c.) (on cover) . . .
b. Without "SPECIMEN" . . . £500 £425
c. Small "2" . . . £120 85·00

These stamps were perforated "SPECIMEN" as a precaution against fraud. Stamps are known with "SPECIMEN" double.

The 1c. and 2c. stamps were printed in separate sheets; but utilising the same clichés, these being altered according to the face value required. Two settings were used, common to both values:—

1st setting. Four rows of three, T **26** being Nos. 5, 6, 7, 8, 11 and 12, and T **27** the remainder.

From this setting there were two printings of the 2c., but only one of the 1c.

2nd setting. Six rows of two, T **26** being Nos. 3, 7, 8, 9, 11 and 12, and T **27** the remainder.

There were two printings of each value from this setting.

Se-tenant pairs are worth about 20% more.

The "1" with foot occurs on T **27** on No. 9 in the first setting and on T **26** on No. 7 in the first printing only of the second setting.

The small "2" appears on T **26** in the first setting on Nos. 6, 7 8 and 12 in the first printing and on Nos. 7, 8 and 12 only in the second printing: in the second setting it comes on Nos. 3, 9 and 12 in the first printing and on Nos. 9, 11 and 12 in the second printing. On T **27** the variety occurs in the first setting on No. 9 of the second printing only and in the second setting on No. 10 in both printings.

(Typo D.L.R.)

1882. Wmk Crown C.A. P 14.

170 16 1c. slate (27 Jan) . . . 8·50 30
171 2c. orange (27 Jan) . . . 23·00 15
a. Value doubly printed . . . † £5000
x. Wmk reversed . . .
172 4c. blue . . . 90·00 5·00
173 6c. brown . . . 5·00 6·50
w. Wmk inverted . . .
174 8c. rose . . . 90·00 40
x. Wmk reversed . . .
170/4 *Set of* 5 . . . £190 11·00
170s/4s Perf "Specimen" *Set of* 5 . . . £300

INLAND

2 CENTS
REVENUE
(28)

4 CENTS **4 CENTS**
(a) Two types of "4" *(b)*

6 **6**
(c) Two types of "6" *(d)*

1888–89. *T* **16** *(without value in lower label) optd "INLAND REVENUE", and surch with value as T* **28**, *by D.L.R.* Wmk Crown CA. P 14.

175 1c. dull purple (8.89) . . . 1·25 20
176 2c. dull purple (25.5.89) . . . 1·25 40
177 3c. dull purple . . . 1·00 20
178 4c. dull purple *(a)* . . . 9·00 30
a. Larger figure "4" *(b)* . . . 20·00 6·00
179 6c. dull purple *(c)* . . . 9·00 3·75
a. Figure 6 with straight top *(d)* . . . 19·00 4·25
180 8c. dull purple (8.89) . . . 1·50 30
181 10c. dull purple . . . 6·00 2·50
182 20c. dull purple . . . 20·00 12·00
183 40c. dull purple . . . 22·00 21·00
184 72c. dull purple (1.10.88) . . . 42·00 55·00
185 $1 green (1.10.88) . . . £425 £500
186 $2 green (1.10.88) . . . £200 £250
187 $3 green (1.10.88) . . . £140 £180
188 $4 green *(a)* (1.10.88) . . . £450 £600
a. Larger figure "4" *(b)* . . . £1400 £1700
189 $5 green (1.10.88) . . . £275 £300
175/89 *Set of* 15 . . . £1400 £1700

Nos. 175/89 were surcharged in settings of 60 (6×10). No. 178a occurs on all stamps in the third vertical row, No. 179a in the fourth and sixth vertical rows and No. 188a in the second vertical row.

INLAND

2
(29) **30**

(31)

1889 (6 June). *No. 176 surch with T* **29** *in red by Official Gazette.*

192 "2" on 2c. dull purple . . . 2·00 15

The varieties with figure "2" *inverted* or *double* were made privately by a postal employee in Demerara.

1889 (Sept). Wmk Crown CA. P 14.

193 30 1c. dull purple and slate-grey . . . 3·50 1·75
194 2c. dull purple and orange . . . 2·25 10
w. Wmk inverted . . .
195 4c. dull purple and ultramarine . . . 4·50 2·00
196 4c. dull purple and cobalt . . . 21·00 2·25
197 6c. dull purple and brown . . . 35·00 16·00
198 6c. dull purple and maroon . . . 7·00 12·00
199 8c. dull purple and rose . . . 12·00 1·50
w. Wmk inverted . . . — 70·00
200 12c. dull purple and bright purple . . . 18·00 2·25
200*a* 12c. dull purple and mauve . . . 8·50 2·25
201 24c. dull purple and green . . . 6·00 2·50
202 48c. dull purple and orange-red . . . 16·00 9·00
x. Wmk reversed . . .
203 72c. dull purple and red-brown . . . 28·00 38·00
204 72c. dull purple and yellow-brown . . . 65·00 75·00
205 96c. dull purple and carmine . . . 65·00 70·00
x. Wmk reversed . . .
206 96c. dull purple and cosine . . . 75·00 80·00
193/205 *Set of* 10 . . . £140 £120
193s/205s Optd "Specimen" *Set of* 10 . . . £140

1890 (15 July). *Stamps of 1888-89 surch locally "One Cent", in red, as in T* **31**.

207 1c.on $1 (No. 185) . . . 1·25 35
a. Surch double . . . £160 £100
208 1c.on $2 (No. 186) . . . 2·00 60
a. Surch double . . . 75·00
209 1c.on $3 (No. 187) . . . 2·00 1·25
a. Surch double . . . 95·00
210 1c.on $4 (No. 188) . . . 2·00 7·00
a. Surch double . . . 85·00
b. Larger figure "4" *(b)* . . . 12·00 28·00
207/10 *Set of* 4 . . . 6·50 8·50

1890–91. *Colours changed.* Wmk Crown CA. P 14

213 30 1c. sea-green (12.90) . . . 75 10
214 5c. ultramarine (1.91) . . . 2·75 10
215 8c. dull purple and greenish black (10.90) . . . 2·75 1·10
213/15 *Set of* 3 . . . 5·50 1·10
213s/15s Optd "Specimen" *Set of* 3 . . . 60·00

32 Mount Roraima

33 Kaieteur Falls

(Recess D.L.R.)

1898 (18 July). *Queen Victoria's Jubilee.* Wmk Crown CC (sideways* on T **32**). P 14.

216 32 1c. blue-black and carmine-red . . . 5·00 75
w. Wmk Crown to left of CC . . . 6·00 1·00
x. Wmk sideways reversed . . .
y. Wmk sideways inverted and reversed . . .
217 33 2c. brown and indigo . . . 25·00 2·50
a. Imperf between (horiz pair) . . . £6000
x. Wmk reversed . . . — £110
218 2c. brown and blue . . . 27·00 2·50
219 32 5c. deep green and sepia . . . 48·00 3·75
a. Imperf between (horiz pair) . . .
w. Wmk Crown to left of CC . . . 45·00 3·50
220 33 10c. blue-black and brown-red . . . 25·00 20·00
221 32 15c. red-brown and blue . . . 30·00 16·00
216/21 *Set of* 5 . . . £120 38·00
216s/21s Optd "Specimen" *Set of* 5 . . . £110

*The normal sideways watermark on Type **32** shows Crown to right of CC, *as seen from the back of the stamp.*

A second plate was later used for the 1c. on which the lines of shading on the mountains in the background are strengthened, and those along the ridge show distinct from each other, whereas, in the original, they are more or less blurred. In the second plate the shading of the sky is less pronounced.

TWO CENTS.
(34)

Shaved "E"

35

(Surch at Printing Office of the *Daily Chronicle*, Georgetown)

1899 (24 Feb–15 June). *Surch with T* **34**.
222 **32** 2c.on 5c. (No. 219) (15 June) . . . . 3·25 2·00
a. No stop after "CENTS" . . . . £110 75·00
b. Comma after "CENTS" (R. 7/2) . . . . 60·00
c. "CINTS" (R. 4/1) £120
d. Shaved "E" (R. 6/2) . . . . 38·00
w. Wmk Crown to left of CC . . . . 3·75 2·25
223 **33** 2c.on 10c. (No. 220) . . . . 2·25 2·25
a. No stop after "CENTS" (R. 5/5 or 2/9) . . . . 20·00 50·00
b. "GENTS" for "CENTS" (R. 5/7) . . . . 50·00 70·00
c. Surch inverted £475 £550
ca. Surch inverted and stop omitted £3500
d. Shaved "E" (R. 4/2 or 3/8) . . . . 26·00
x. Wmk reversed £100
224 **32** 2c.on 15c. (No. 221) . . . . 1·50 1·25
a. No stop after "CENTS" (R. 9/2) . . . . 65·00 65·00
b. Surch double £700 £850
ba. Surch double, one without stop
d. Surch inverted £475 £650
da. Surch inverted and stop omitted
f. Shaved "E" (R. 6/2) . . . . 32·00
222/4 *Set of* 3 . . . . 6·25 5·00

No. 222c was caused by damage to the first "E" of "CENTS" which developed during surcharging. The listing is for an example with only the upright stroke of the letter visible.

There were two settings of No. 223 with the no stop and shaved "E" varieties occurring on R. 5/5 and R. 4/2 of the first and on R. 2/9 and R. 3/8 of the second.

No. 224b occurred on the first five vertical columns of one sheet, the surcharges on the right hand vertical column being normal.

Only two examples of No. 224ba are known.

There is only one known example of No. 224da.

1900–03. Wmk Crown CA. P 14.
233 **30** 1c. grey-green (1902) . . . . 1·75 3·25
234 2c. dull purple and carmine . . . . 3·25 30
235 2c. dull purple and black/*red* (1901) . . . . 1·25 10
w. Wmk inverted . . . . — 70·00
236 6c. grey-black and ultramarine (1902) . . . . 6·50 11·00
237 48c. grey and purple-brown (1901) . . . . 50·00 35·00
a. Brownish grey and brown . . . . 29·00 28·00
238 60c. green and rosine (1903) . . . . 60·00 £180
233/8 *Set of* 6 . . . . 90·00 £200
233s/8s Optd "Specimen" *Set of* 6 . . . . 95·00

No. 233 is a reissue of No. 213 in non-fugitive ink.

1905–07. Wmk Multiple Crown CA. *Ordinary paper (1c. to 60c.) or chalk-surfaced paper (72, 96c.)*.
240 **30** 1c. grey-green . . . . 4·25 30
aw. Wmk inverted
b. Chalk-surfaced paper . . . . 4·50 30
241 2c. purple and black/*red* . . . . 9·50 10
a. Chalk-surfaced paper . . . . 3·50 10
242 4c. dull purple and ultramarine . . . . 8·00 14·00
a. Chalk-surfaced paper . . . . 6·00 12·00
243 5c. dull purple and blue/*blue* (1.5.05) . . . . 11·00 11·00
a. Chalk-surfaced paper . . . . 3·50 6·50
s. Optd "Specimen" . . . . 20·00
244 6c. grey-black and ultramarine . . . . 16·00 45·00
a. Chalk-surfaced paper . . . . 15·00 42·00
aw. Wmk inverted
245 12c. dull and bright purple . . . . 22·00 32·00
a. Chalk-surfaced paper . . . . 22·00 42·00
246 24c. dull purple and green (1906) . . . . 11·00 10·00
a. Chalk-surfaced paper . . . . 3·75 4·50
247 48c. grey and purple-brown . . . . 25·00 29·00
a. Chalk-surfaced paper . . . . 14·00 20·00
248 60c. green and rosine . . . . 25·00 85·00
a. Chalk-surfaced paper . . . . 14·00 85·00
249 72c. purple and orange-brown (1907) . . . . 32·00 65·00
250 96c. black & vermilion/*yellow* (20.11.05) . . . . 35·00 45·00
s. Optd "Specimen" . . . . 30·00
240/50 *Set of* 11 . . . . £140 £275

1905. *Optd* "POSTAGE AND REVENUE". Wmk Multiple Crown CA. *Chalk-surfaced paper*. P 14.
251 **35** $2.40, green and violet £160 £275
s. Optd "Specimen" . . . . 75·00

1907–10. *Colours changed*. Wmk Mult Crown CA. P 14
252 **30** 1c. blue-green . . . . 15·00 2·75
253 2c. rose-red . . . . 16·00 10
a. Redrawn (1910) . . . . 8·50 10
254 4c. brown and purple . . . . 2·25 60
255 5c. ultramarine . . . . 14·00 2·50
256 6c. grey and black . . . . 13·00 7·00
257 12c. orange and mauve . . . . 4·00 4·00
252/7 *Set of* 6 . . . . 50·00 15·00
253s/7s Optd "Specimen" *Set of* 5 . . . . 75·00

In No. 253a the flag at the main truck is close to the mast, whereas in the original type it appears to be flying loose from halyards. There are two background lines above the value "2 CENTS" instead of three and the "S" is further away from the end of the tablet.

37

War
Tax
(38)

(Typo D.L.R.)

1913–21. Wmk Mult Crown CA. *Chalk-surfaced paper (4c. and 48c. to 96c.)*. P 14.
259 **37** 1c. yellow-green . . . . 2·50 80
a. Blue-green (1917) . . . . 1·50 25
260 2c. carmine . . . . 1·25 10
a. Scarlet (1916) . . . . 3·00 10
b. Wmk sideways . . . . † £1800
261 4c. brown and bright purple (1914) . . . . 5·50 25
aw. Wmk inverted
b. Deep brown and purple . . . . 3·75 25
262 5c. bright blue . . . . 1·75 1·00
263 6c. grey and black . . . . 2·75 1·25
264 12c. orange and violet . . . . 1·25 1·00
265 24c. dull purple and green (1915) . . . . 3·25 4·00
266 48c. grey and purple-brown (1914) . . . . 22·00 17·00
267 60c. green and rosine (1915) . . . . 15·00 50·00
268 72c. purple and orange-brown (1915) . . . . 42·00 75·00
269 96c. black and vermilion/*yellow* (1915) . . . . 30·00 60·00
a. White back (1913) . . . . 19·00 48·00
b. On lemon (1916) . . . . 19·00 48·00
bs. Optd "Specimen" . . . . 30·00
c. On pale yellow (1921) . . . . 20·00 60·00
cs. Optd "Specimen" . . . . 30·00
259/69a *Set of* 11 . . . . £110 £180
259s/69as Optd "Specimen" *Set of* 11 . . . . £130

Examples of Nos. 267/9c are known with part strikes of forged postmarks of Grove dated "29 OCT 1909" and of Georgetown dated "30 OCT 1909".

1918 (4 Jan). *No. 260a optd with T* **38**, *by D.L.R.*
271 **37** 2c. scarlet . . . . 1·25 15

The relative position of the words "WAR" and "TAX" vary considerably in the sheet.

1921–27. Wmk Mult Script CA. *Chalk-surfaced paper (24c. to 96c.)*. P 14.
272 **37** 1c. green (1922) . . . . 4·75 30
273 2c. rose-carmine . . . . 4·25 20
w. Wmk inverted . . . . † £130
274 2c. bright violet (1923) . . . . 2·50 10
275 4c. brown and bright purple (1922) . . . . 4·75 10
276 6c. bright blue (1922) . . . . 3·00 30
277 12c. orange and violet (1922) . . . . 2·75 1·50
278 24c. dull purple and green . . . . 2·00 4·50
279 48c. black and purple (1926) . . . . 9·50 3·50
280 60c. green and rosine (1926) . . . . 10·00 48·00
281 72c. dull purple & orange-brown (1923) . . . . 23·00 65·00
282 96c. black and red/*yellow* (1927) . . . . 20·00 45·00
272/82 *Set of* 11 . . . . 75·00 £150
272s/82s Optd "Specimen" *Set of* 11 . . . . £160

39 Ploughing a Rice Field

40 Indian shooting Fish

(Recess Waterlow)

1931 (21 July). *Centenary of County Union T* **39/40** *and similar designs*. Wmk Mult Script CA. P 12½.
283 1c. emerald-green . . . . 2·50 1·25
284 2c. brown . . . . 2·00 10
285 4c. carmine . . . . 1·75 45
286 6c. blue . . . . 2·25 2·75
287 $1 violet . . . . 24·00 48·00
283/7 *Set of* 5 . . . . 29·00 48·00
283s/7s Perf "Specimen" *Set of* 5 . . . . 75·00

Designs: *Vert*—4c., $1 Kaieteur Falls. *Horiz*—6c. Public buildings, Georgetown.

43 Ploughing a Rice Field

44 Gold Mining

(Recess Waterlow)

1934 (1 Oct)–**51**. *T* **40** *(without dates at top of frame)*, **43/4** *and similar designs*. Wmk Mult Script CA (sideways on horiz designs). P 12½.
288 **43** 1c. green 60 80
289 **40** 2c. red-brown . . . . 1·50 70
290 **44** 3c. scarlet 30 10
aa. Wmk error. Crown missing £2250 £1700
a. Perf 12½ × 13½ (30.12.43) 60 80
b. Perf 13 × 14 (28.4.49) 60 10
291 – 4c. slate-violet . . . . 2·00 1·75
a. Imperf between (vert pair) . . . . † £16000
b. Imperf horiz (vert pair) £7000 £7500
292 – 6c. deep ultramarine . . . . 2·75 3·7
293 – 12c. red-orange 20 2
a. Perf 14 × 13 (16.4.51) . . . . 50 1·0
294 – 24c. purple . . . . 3·50 7·0
295 – 48c. black . . . . 7·00 8·5
296 – 50c. green . . . . 10·00 17·0
297 – 60c. red-brown . . . . 26·00 27·0
298 – 72c. purple . . . . 1·25 2·2
299 – 96c. black . . . . 20·00 30·0
300 – $1 bright violet . . . . 32·00 30·0
288/300 *Set of* 13 . . . . 95·00 £11
288s/300s Perf "Specimen" *Set of* 13 . . . . £150

Designs: *Vert*—4c., 50c. Kaieteur Falls (as No. 285, but with date omitted); 96c. Sir Walter Raleigh and his son. *Horiz*—6c. Shooting logs over falls; 12c. Stabroek Market; 24c. Sugar cane in punts; 48c Forest road; 60c. Victoria Regia Lilies; 72c. Mount Roraima; $ Botanical Gardens.

Examples of Nos. 295/300 are known with forged Georgetow postmarks dated "24 JY 31" or "6 MY 35".

1935 (6 May). *Silver Jubilee. As Nos. 91/4 of Antigua.*
301 2c. ultramarine and grey 20 1
f. Diagonal line by turret . . . . 30·00
h. Dot by flagstaff . . . . 70·00
302 6c. brown and deep blue . . . . 1·00 2·0
f. Diagonal line by turret . . . . 65·00
g. Dot to left of chapel . . . . 95·00
h. Dot by flagstaff . . . . 95·00
303 12c. green and indigo . . . . 4·25 8·0
f. Diagonal line by turret . . . . 95·00
h. Dot by flagstaff £160
i. Dash by turret £160
304 24c. slate and purple . . . . 6·00 8·0
h. Dot by flagstaff £190
i. Dash by turret £190
301/4 *Set of* 4 . . . . 10·50 16·0
301s/4s *Set of* 4 . . . . 85·00

For illustrations of plate varieties see Omnibus section followin Zanzibar.

1937 (12 May). *Coronation. As Nos. 95/7 of Antigua, but ptd b D.L.R.* P 14.
305 2c. yellow-brown 15
306 4c. grey-black 50 4
307 6c. bright blue . . . . 60 1·2
305/7 *Set of* 3 . . . . 1·10 1·6
305s/7s Perf "Specimen" *Set of* 3 . . . . 65·00

53 South America

54 Victoria Regia Lilies

(Recess Waterlow)

1938 (1 Feb)–**52**. *As earlier types but with portrait of King George as in T* **53/4**. Wmk Mult Script CA. P 12½
308 **43** 1c. yellow-green . . . . 17·00
a. Green (1940) 30
ab. Perf 14 × 13 (1949) 30
309 – 2c. slate-violet 60
a. Perf 13 × 14 (28.4.49) 30
310 **53** 4c. scarlet and black 70
a. Imperf horiz (vert pair) £16000 £120
b. Perf 13 × 14 (1952) 50
311 **40** 6c. deep ultramarine 40
a. Perf 13 × 14 (24.10.49) 50
312 – 24c. blue-green . . . . 26·00 10·
a. Wmk sideways . . . . 1·25
313 – 36c. bright violet (7.3.38) . . . . 2·00
a. Perf 13 × 14 (13.12.51) . . . . 3·00
314 – 48c. orange 60
a. Perf 14 × 13 (8.5.51*) . . . . 1·50 1·
315 – 60c. red-brown . . . . 13·00 4·
316 – 96c. purple . . . . 2·75 2·
a. Perf 12½ × 13½ (1944) . . . . 6·00 8·
b. Perf 13 × 14 (8.2.51) . . . . 2·75 6·
317 – $1 bright violet . . . . 13·00
a. Perf 14 × 13 (1951) £350 £4
318 – $2 purple (11.6.45) . . . . 5·50 16·
a. Perf 14 × 13 (9.8.50) . . . . 11·00 15·
319 **54** $3 red-brown (2.7.45) . . . . 27·00 25
a. Bright red-brown (12.46) . . . . 28·00 28
b. Perf 14 × 13. *Red-brown* (29.10.52) . . . . 26·00 45·
308a/19 *Set of* 12 . . . . 60·00 42·
308s/19s Perf "Specimen" *Set of* 12 . . . . £225

Designs: *Vert*—2c., 36c. Kaieteur Falls; 96c. Sir Walter Rale and his son. *Horiz*—24c. Sugar cane in punts; 48c. Forest road; 6 Shooting logs over falls; $1 Botanical Gardens; $2 Mount Rorair

*Earliest known postmark date.

1946 (1 Oct). *Victory. As Nos. 110/11 of Antigua.*
320 3c. carmine 10
321 6c. blue 30
320s/1s Perf "Specimen" *Set of* 2 . . . . 55·00

1948 (20 Dec). *Royal Silver Wedding. As Nos. 112/13 of Antig but $3 in recess.*
322 3c. scarlet 10
323 $3 red-brown . . . . 14·00 23

1949 (10 Oct). *75th Anniv of Universal Postal Union. As Nos. 114 of Antigua.*
324 4c. carmine 10
325 6c. deep blue . . . . 1·50 1
326 12c. orange 15
327 24c. blue-green 15
324/7 *Set of* 4 . . . . 1·60 2

1951 (16 Feb). *University College of B.W.I. As Nos. 118/19 of Antigua.*
328 3c. black and carmine . . . 30 30
329 6c. black and blue . . . 30 60

STAMP BOOKLETS

1909 (14 June). *Black on pink cover without face value. Stapled.*
SB1 49c. booklet containing twelve 1c. and eighteen 2c. (Nos. 252/3) in blocks of 6 . . .

1923. *Black on pink cover without face value. Stapled.*
SB2 30c. booklet containing six 1c. and twelve 2c. (Nos. 272, 274) in blocks of 6 . . .

1923. *Black on pink without face value. Stapled.*
SB3 48c. booklet containing twelve 1c. and eighteen 2c. (Nos. 272, 274) in blocks of 6 . . . £1300
a. With face value on front cover . . .

1923. *Black on red cover without face value. Stapled.*
SB4 72c. booklet containing twelve 1c., six 2c. and twelve 4c. (Nos. 272, 274/5) in blocks of 6 . . . £1700

1934. *Black on orange cover. Stitched.*
SB5 24c. booklet containing eight 1c. and eight 2c. (Nos. 288/9) in blocks of 4 . . .

1934. *Black on orange cover. Stitched.*
SB6 36c. booklet containing four 1c., eight 2c. and four 4c. (Nos. 288/9, 291) in blocks of 4 . . .

1938. *Black on orange cover. Stitched.*
SB7 36c. booklet containing four 1c., eight 2c. and four 4c. (Nos. 308/10) in blocks of 4 . . . £300

1944. *Black on orange cover. Stitched.*
SB8 24c. booklet containing eight 1c. and eight 2c. (Nos. 308/9) in blocks of 4 . . . £180

1945–49. *Black on red cover. Stitched.*
SB9 24c. booklet containing 1c., 2c. and 3c. (Nos. 290, 308, 309), each in block of 4 . . .
a. Containing Nos. 290, 308*a*, 309 . . . 65·00
b. Containing Nos. 290, 308*a*, 309a . . . 65·00
c. Containing Nos. 290a, 308*a*, 309 . . . 65·00
d. Containing Nos. 290b, 308*a*, 309 . . . 65·00
e. Containing Nos. 290b, 308*a*, 309a . . . 65·00
f. Containing Nos. 290b, 308*a*, 309a . . . 65·00

POSTAGE DUE STAMPS

D 1

(Typo D.L.R.)

1940 (Mar)–**55**. Wmk Mult Script CA. *Chalk-surfaced paper (4c.).* P 14.
D1 D 1 1c. green . . . 6·00 7·00
a. Chalk-surfaced paper. Deep green, (30.4.52) . . . 1·50 13·00
ab. W **9***a* (Crown missing) . . . £275
ac. W **9***b* (St. Edward's Crown) . . . £110
D2 2c. black . . . 23·00 2·00
a. Chalk-surfaced paper (30.4.52) . . . 1·75 3·75
ab. W **9***a* (Crown missing) . . . £200
ac. W **9***b* (St. Edward's Crown) . . . 95·00
D3 4c. bright blue (1.5.52) . . . 30 9·50
a. W **9***a* (Crown missing) . . . £180
b. W **9***b* (St. Edward's Crown) . . . 95·00
D4 12c. scarlet . . . 30·00 4·50
a. Chalk-surfaced paper (19.7.55) . . . 16·00 26·00
D1a/4a *Set of* 4 . . . 18·00 48·00
D1s, D2s and D4s Perf "Specimen" *Set of* 3 . . . 60·00

OFFICIAL STAMPS

OFFICIAL (O 1) OFFICIAL (O 1a) OFFICIAL (O 2)

1875. *Optd with Type* O **1** *(1c.) or* O **1a** *(others) by litho.* P 10.
O1 **8** 1c. black (R.) . . . 55·00 18·00
a. Imperf between (horiz pair) . . . † £10000
O2 2c. orange . . . £180 14·00
O3 8c. rose . . . £325 £120
O4 **7** 12c. brownish purple . . . £2250 £500
O5 **9** 24c. green . . . £1100 £225

Two types of the word "OFFICIAL" are found on each value. On the 1c. the word is either 16 or 17 mm long. On the other values the chief difference is in the shape and position of the letter "o" in "OFFICIAL". In one case the "o" is upright, in the other it slants to the left.

1877. *Optd with Type* O **2** *by typo.* Wmk Crown CC. P 14.
O6 **16** 1c. slate . . . £250 65·00
a. Imperf between (vert pair) . . . † £15000
O7 2c. orange . . . £120 15·00
O8 4c. blue . . . 85·00 20·00
O9 6c. brown . . . £5500 £600
O10 8c. rose . . . £2000 £450

Prepared for use, but not issued.

O11 **16** 12c. pale violet . . . £1400
O12 24c. green . . . £1500

The "OFFICIAL" overprints have been extensively forged.

The use of Official stamps was discontinued in June 1878, but was resumed in June 1981.

British Honduras

It is recorded that the first local post office was established by the inhabitants in 1809, but Belize did not become a regular packet port of call until December 1829. The post office came under the control of the British G.P.O. in April 1844 and the stamps of Great Britain were supplied for use on overseas mail from May 1858.

The colonial authorities took over the postal service on 1 April 1860, the Great Britain stamps being withdrawn at the end of the month. There was no inland postal service until 1862.

For illustrations of the handstamp and postmark types see BRITISH POST OFFICES ABROAD notes, following GREAT BRITAIN.

BELIZE

CROWNED-CIRCLE HANDSTAMPS

CC1 CC **1b** BELIZE (R.) (13.11.1841) *Price on cover* £4000

Stamps of GREAT BRITAIN *cancelled* "A 06" *as Type* **2**.

1858–60.
Z1 1d. rose-red (1857), *perf* 14 . . . £900
Z2 4d. rose (1857) . . . £375
Z3 6d. lilac (1856) . . . £375
Z4 1s. green (1856) . . . £1600

PRICES FOR STAMPS ON COVER TO 1945	
Nos. 1/4	*from* × 20
Nos. 5/16	*from* × 25
Nos. 17/22	*from* × 20
Nos. 23/6	*from* × 10
Nos. 27/30	*from* × 15
Nos. 35/42	*from* × 20
Nos. 43/4	*from* × 30
Nos. 49/50	*from* × 25
Nos. 51/69	*from* × 15
Nos. 80/100	*from* × 6
Nos. 101/10	*from* × 5
Nos. 111/20	*from* × 15
Nos. 121/2	*from* × 8
No. 123	*from* × 10
Nos. 124/37	*from* × 6
Nos. 138/42	*from* × 10
Nos. 143/9	*from* × 8
Nos. 150/61	*from* × 5
Nos. D1/3	*from* × 30

CROWN COLONY

1

(Typo D.L.R.)

1865 (1 Dec). No wmk. P 14.
1 **1** 1d. pale blue . . . 60·00 55·00
a. Imperf between (pair) . . .
2 1d. blue . . . 70·00 60·00
3 6d. rose . . . £300 £150
4 1s. green . . . £325 £120
a. In horiz pair with 6d. . . . £19000
b. In vert pair with 1d. . . . £26000

In the first printing all three values were printed in the same sheet separated by horizontal and vertical gutter margins. The sheet comprised two panes of 60 of the 1d. at the top with a pane of 60 of the 1s. at bottom left and another of 6d. at bottom right. Copies of 1d. *se-tenant* with the 6d. are not known. There were two later printings of the 1d. but they were in sheets without the 6d. and 1s.

1872–79. Wmk Crown CC.

(a) P 12½.
5 **1** 1d. pale blue . . . 75·00 17·00
w. Wmk inverted . . . £190
y. Wmk inverted and reversed . . .
6 1d. deep blue (1874) . . . 85·00 17·00
7 3d. red-brown . . . £130 75·00
8 3d. chocolate (1874) . . . £150 90·00
9 6d. rose . . . £275 40·00
9*a* 6d. bright rose-carmine (1874) . . . £475 50·00
10 1s. green . . . £400 28·00
10*a* 1s. deep green (1874) . . . £375 22·00
b. Imperf between (horiz pair) . . . † £14000
w. Wmk inverted . . .

(b) P 14 (1877–79).
11 **1** 1d. pale blue (1878) . . . 70·00 16·00
12 1d. blue . . . 65·00 10·00
a. Imperf between (horiz pair) . . . £5500
13 3d. chestnut . . . £130 17·00
14 4d. mauve (1879) . . . £180 8·50
x. Wmk reversed . . .
15 6d. rose (1878) . . . £375 £180
w. Wmk inverted . . . — £350
16 1s. green . . . £225 11·00
a. Imperf between (pair) . . .

1882–87. Wmk Crown CA. P 14.
17 **1** 1d. blue (4.84) . . . 45·00 13·00
18 1d. rose (1884) . . . 23·00 13·00
a. Bisected (½d.) (on cover) . . .
s. Optd "Specimen" . . . £200
19 1d. carmine (1887) . . . 50·00 18·00
20 4d. mauve (7.82) . . . 75·00 4·75
w. Wmk inverted . . . — £100
21 6d. yellow (1885) . . . £275 £200
22 1s. grey (1.87) . . . £250 £160
s. Optd "Specimen" . . . 75·00

(New Currency. 100 cents = 1 British Honduras dollar)

2 CENTS (2) TWO (3) 2 CENTS (4)

1888 (1 Jan). *Stamps of 1872–79 (*wmk Crown CC*), surch locally as T* **2**.

(a) P 12½.
23 **1** 2c.on 6d. rose . . . £225 £150
24 3c.on 3d. chocolate . . . £13000 £5000

(b) P 14.
25 **1** 2c.on 6d. rose . . . £140 £120
a. Surch double . . . £2000
b. Bisected (1c.) (on cover) . . . † £225
c. Slanting "2" with curved foot . . . £1400
w. Wmk inverted . . . — £350
26 3c.on 3d. chestnut . . . 85·00 85·00

There are very dangerous forgeries of these surcharges.

1888. *Stamps of 1882–87 (*wmk Crown CA*), surch locally as T* **2**, P 14.
27 **1** 2c.on 1d. rose . . . 8·50 22·00
a. Surch inverted . . . £2500 £2250
b. Surch double . . . £900 £900
c. Bisected (1c.) (on cover) . . . † £180
28 10c.on 4d. mauve . . . 50·00 16·00
29 20c.on 6d. yellow . . . 27·00 35·00
30 50c.on 1s. grey . . . £375 £500
a. Error. "5" for "50" . . . £9500

Various settings were used for the surcharges on Nos. 23/30, the most common of which was of 36 (6 × 6) impressions. For No. 29 this setting was so applied that an albino surcharge occurs in the margin above each stamp in the first horizontal row.

The same setting was subsequently amended, by altering the "2" to "1", to surcharge the 4d. value. As this was in sheets of 30 it was only necessary to alter the values on the bottom five rows of the setting. Albino surcharges once again occur in the top margin of the sheet, but, as the type in the first horizontal row remained unaltered, these read "20 CENTS" rather than the "10 CENTS" on the actual stamps.

1888 (Mar). *No. 30 further surch locally with T* **3**.
35 **1** "TWO" on 50c. on 1s. grey (R.) . . . 50·00 95·00
a. Bisected (1c.) (on cover) . . . † £200
b. Surch in black . . . £11000 £9000
c. Surch double (R.+Blk.) . . . £11000 £9000

1888 (July)–**91**. *Surch in London as T* **4**. Wmk Crown CA. P 14.
36 **1** 1c.on 1d. dull green (?12.91) . . . 80 1·50
37 2c.on 1d. carmine . . . 60 2·25
a. Bisected (1c.) (on cover) . . . † 90·00
w. Wmk inverted . . .
38 3c.on 3d. red-brown . . . 3·25 1·40
39 6c.on 3d. ultramarine (?4.91) . . . 2·75 16·00
40 10c.on 4d. mauve . . . 12·00 50
a. Surch double . . . £2250
41 20c.on 6d. yellow (2.89) . . . 12·00 14·00
42 50c.on 1s. grey (11.88) . . . 29·00 85·00
36/42 *Set of* 7 . . . 55·00 £110
36s/42s Optd "Specimen" *Set of* 7 . . . £350

(5)

FIVE (6) 15 (7)

1891. *Stamps of 1888–9 surch locally.*

(a) With T **5** *(May).*
43 **1** 6c.on 10c. on 4d. mauve (R.) . . . 1·50 2·00
a. "6" and bar inverted . . . £450 £450
b. "6" only inverted . . . — £3250
44 6c.on 10c. on 4d. mauve (Blk.) . . . 1·25 1·50
a. "6" and bar inverted . . . £3000 £800
b. "6" only inverted . . . † £3250

Of variety (b) only six copies of each can exist, as one of each of these errors came in the first six sheets, and the mistake was then corrected. Of variety (a) more copies exist.

Essays are known with "SIX" in place of "6" both with and without bars (*price* £100 *and* £450 *respectively*). Although not issued we mention them, as three contemporary covers franked with them are known.

(b) With T **6/7** *(23 Oct).*
49 **1** 5c.on 3c. on 3d. red-brown . . . 1·25 1·40
a. Wide space between "I" and "V" . . . 55·00 70·00
b. "FIVE" and bar double . . . £325 £350
50 15c.on 6c. on 3d. ultramarine (R.) . . . 13·00 27·00
a. Surch double . . .

8

9

10

11

(Typo D.L.R.)

1891 (July)–**1901**. Wmk Crown CA. P 14.
51 **8** 1c. dull green (4.95) . . . 2·50 1·25
a. Malformed "S" . . . £200 £120
w. Wmk inverted
52 2c. carmine-rose . . . 2·50 20
a. Malformed "S" . . . £200 80·00
b. Repaired "S" . . . £180 80·00
53 3c. brown . . . 6·50 4·00
w. Wmk inverted . . . £150
54 5c. ultramarine (4.95) . . . 12·00 75
a. Malformed "S" . . . £400 £150
55 **11** 5c. grey-black & ultram/*blue* (10.00) 16·00 2·50
56 **8** 6c. ultramarine . . . 6·50 2·00
57 **9** 10c. mauve and green (4.95) . . . 10·00 8·50
58 **10** 10c. dull purple and green (1901) . . . 11·00 7·50
59 **9** 12c. pale mauve and green . . . 23·00 7·00
a. Violet and green . . . 2·50 2·00
60 24c. yellow and blue . . . 5·50 14·00
a. Orange and blue . . . 30·00 55·00
61 25c. red-brown and green (4.95) . . . 75·00 £130
62 **10** 50c. green and carmine (3.98) . . . 24·00 60·00
63 **11** $1 green and carmine (12.99) . . . 70·00 £130
64 $2 green and ultramarine (12.99) . . . £100 £160
65 $5 green and black (12.99) . . . £275 £350
51/65 *Set of* 15 . . . £550 £800
51s/65s Optd "Specimen" *Set of* 15 . . . £350

For illustrations of Nos. 51a, 52a/b and 54a see above Gambia No. 37.

Most values are known with a forged Belize postmark dated "OC 23 09".

1899 (1 July). *Optd* "REVENUE" *12 mm long.*
66 **8** 5c. ultramarine . . . 13·00 2·50
a. "BEVENUE" . . . £100 £110
b. Malformed "S" at right . . . £400 £300
c. Repaired "S" at right . . . £400
d. Opt 11 mm long . . . 23·00 8·00
67 **9** 10c. mauve and green . . . 5·00 16·00
a. "BEVENUE" . . . £200 £300
b. "REVENU" . . . £475
c. Opt 11 mm long . . . 19·00 45·00
cb. "REVENU" . . . £600 £700
68 25c. red-brown and green . . . 2·75 35·00
a. "BEVENUE" . . . £120 £300
b. "REVE UE"
c. Repaired "S" at right . . . £550
d. Opt 11 mm long . . . 4·00 50·00
69 **1** 50c.on 1s. grey . . . £160 £300
a. "BEVENUE" . . . £3250
c. Opt 11 mm long . . . £275 £400

Two minor varieties, a small "U" and a tall, narrow "U" are found in the word "REVENUE".

The overprint setting of 60 (6 × 10) contained 43 examples of the 12 mm size and 17 of the 11 mm. The smaller size overprints occur on R. 8/1, R. 8/3 to 6 and on all positions in Rows 9 and 10.

The "BEVENUE" error appears on R. 6/4 and, it is believed, "REVE UE" comes from R. 6/6. Both occur on parts of the printing only. The missing "E" developed during the overprinting and damage to this letter can be observed on at least eight positions in the setting.

14

15

(Typo D.L.R.)

1902 (10 Oct)–**04**. Wmk Crown CA. P 14.
80 **14** 1c. grey-green and green (28.4.04) . . . 1·25 23·00
81 2c. purple and black/*red* (18.3.03) . . . 75 25
w. Wmk inverted . . . — 70·00
82 5c. grey-black and blue/*blue* . . . 7·00 30
w. Wmk inverted
83 **15** 20c. dull and bright purple (28.4.04) . . . 6·00 17·00
80/3 *Set of* 4 . . . 13·50 35·00
80s/3s Optd "Specimen" *Set of* 4 . . . 55·00

1904 (Dec)–**07**. Wmk Mult Crown CA. *Ordinary paper (1, 2c.) or chalk-surfaced paper (others)*. P 14.
84 **14** 1c. grey-green and green (8.05) . . . 10·00 12·00
a. Chalk-surfaced paper (1906) . . . 1·00 2·25
85 2c. purple and black/*red* . . . 2·75 30
a. Chalk-surfaced paper (1906) . . . 75 20
86 5c. grey-black and blue/*blue* (5.2.06) . . . 1·75 20
87 **15** 10c. dull purple & emerald-green (20.9.07) . . . 5·00 11·00
89 25c. dull purple and orange (20.9.07) . . . 7·00 48·00
90 50c. grey-green and carmine (20.9.07) . . . 15·00 70·00
91 **14** $1 grey-green and carmine (20.9.07) . . . 55·00 75·00
92 $2 grey-green and blue (20 9 07) . . . 95·00 £150
93 $5 grey-green and black (20.9.07) . . . £250 £275
84/93 *Set of* 9 . . . £375 £550
87s/93s *Set of* 6 . . . £225

Examples of most values are known showing a forged Belize postmark dated "OC 23 09".

1908 (7 Dec)–**11**. *Colours changed.* Wmk Mult Crown CA. *Chalk-surfaced paper (25c.)*. P 14.
95 **14** 1c. blue-green (1.7.10) . . . 11·00 30
96 2c. carmine . . . 12·00 10
w. Wmk inverted
97 5c. ultramarine (1.6.09) . . . 1·75 10
100 **15** 25c. black/*green* (14.10.11) . . . 3·00 45·00
95/100 *Set of* 4 . . . 25·00 45·00
96s/100s Optd "Specimen" *Set of* 3 . . . 70·00

16

17

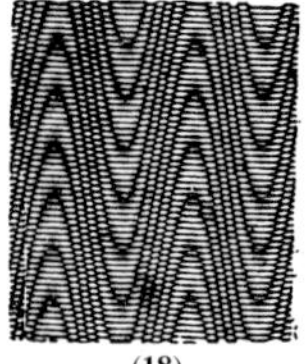
(18)

1913–21. Wmk Mult Crown CA. *Chalk-surfaced paper (10c. to $5)*. P 14.
101 **16** 1c. blue-green . . . 3·75 1·50
a. Yellow-green (13.3.17) . . . 6·50 2·25
w. Wmk inverted
102 2c. red . . . 3·50 1·00
a. Bright scarlet (1915) . . . 6·00 1·00
b. Dull scarlet (8.17) . . . 3·00 1·50
c. Red/bluish . . . 12·00 8·00
w. Wmk inverted
103 3c. orange (16.4.17) . . . 80 20
104 5c. bright blue . . . 2·00 85
105 **17** 10c. dull purple and yellow-green . . . 3·00 6·50
a. Dull purple and bright green (1917) . . . 14·00 25·00
106 25c. black/*green* . . . 1·25 12·00
a. On blue-green, olive back (8.17) . . . 5·00 11·00
b. On emerald back (1921) . . . 1·75 27·00
107 50c. purple and blue/*blue* . . . 12·00 15·00
108 **16** $1 black and carmine . . . 19·00 50·00
109 $2 purple and green . . . 65·00 80·00
110 $5 purple and black/*red* . . . £200 £250
101/10 *Set of* 10 . . . £275 £375
101s/10s Optd "Specimen" *Set of* 10 . . . £225

1915–16. *Optd with T* **18**, *in violet.*
111 **16** 1c. green (30.12.15) . . . 3·00 17·00
a. Yellow-green (6.6.16) . . . 50 13·00
112 2c. scarlet (3.11.15) . . . 3·50 50
113 5c. bright blue (29.7.15) . . . 30 6·00
111s/13s Optd "Specimen" *Set of* 3 . . . £100

These stamps were shipped early in the 1914–18 war, and were thus overprinted, so that if seized by the enemy, they could be distinguished and rendered invalid.

WAR
(19)

WAR
(20)

21

1916 (23 Aug). *No. 111 optd locally with T* **19**.
114 **16** 1c. green . . . 10 1·25
a. Opt inverted . . . £200 £250

1917–18. *Nos. 101 and 103 optd with T* **19**.
116 **16** 1c. blue-green (6.17) . . . 1·50 3·50
aw. Wmk inverted . . . £200
ax. Wmk reversed . . . £200
b. Yellow-green (3.3.17) . . . 20 1·75
118 3c. orange (12.3.18) . . . 3·75 5·00
a. Opt double . . . £325

1918. *Nos. 101 and 103 optd with T* **20**.
119 **16** 1c. blue-green (25.4.18) . . . 10 30
a. Yellow-green . . . 3·50 4·50
120 3c. orange (9.18) . . . 70 1·75
y. Wmk inverted and reversed . . . £200
119s/20s Optd "Specimen" *Set of* 2 . . . £100

(Recess D.L.R.)

1921 (28 Apr). *Peace Commemoration.* Wmk Mult Crown CA (sideways). P 14.
121 **21** 2c. rose-red . . . 3·25 50
a. "C" of "CA" missing from wmk . . . £300
s. Optd "Specimen" . . . 45·00

1921 (26 Nov). Wmk Mult Script CA. P 14.
122 **16** 1c. green . . . 3·50 12·00
s. Optd "Specimen" . . . 45·00

1922 (4 Jan). *As T* **21** *but with words* "PEACE" *omitted.* Wmk Mult Script CA (sideways). P 14.
123 4c. slate . . . 7·50 50
s. Optd "Specimen" . . . 45·00

22

BELIZE
RELIEF FUND
PLUS
3 CENTS
(23)

(Typo D.L.R.)

1922 (1 Aug)–**33**. *Ordinary paper (1c. to 5c.) or chalk-surfaced paper (others)*. P 14.

(a) Wmk Mult Crown CA.
124 **22** 25c. black/*emerald* . . . 6·50 40·00
125 $5 purple and black/*red* (1.10.24) . . . £200 £225

(b) Wmk Mult Script CA.
126 **22** 1c. green (2.1.29) . . . 6·00 6·50
127 2c. brown (1.3.23) . . . 1·50 1·50
128 2c. rose-carmine (10.12.26) . . . 2·50 1·50
129 3c. orange (1933) . . . 17·00 4·0
130 4c. grey (1.10.29) . . . 8·00 85
131 5c. ultramarine . . . 1·50 55
a. Milky blue (1923) . . . 4·75 3·75
132 10c. dull purple and sage-green (1.12.22) . . . 1·25 30
133 25c. black/*emerald* (1.10.24) . . . 1·25 8·50
134 50c. purple and blue/*blue* (1.11.23) . . . 4·75 16·00
136 $1 black and scarlet (2.1.25) . . . 8·00 23·00
137 $2 yellow-green and bright purple . . . 32·00 80·00
124/37 *Set of* 13 . . . £250 £350
124s/37s Optd or Perf (1c., 3c., 4c.) "Specimen" *Set of* 13 . . . £250

1932 (2 May). *Belize Relief Fund. Surch as T* **23**. Wmk Mult Script CA. P 14.
138 **22** 1c.+1c. green . . . 80 8·0
139 2c.+2c. rose-carmine . . . 85 8·0
140 3c.+3c. orange . . . 95 19·0
141 4c.+4c. grey (R.) . . . 11·00 22·0
142 5c.+5c. ultramarine . . . 6·50 14·0
138/42 *Set of* 5 . . . 18·00 65·0
138s/42s Perf "Specimen" *Set of* 5 . . . £110

1935 (6 May). *Silver Jubilee. As Nos. 91/4 of Antigua, but ptd by B.W. & Co.* P 11 × 12.
143 3c. ultramarine and grey-black . . . 2·00 5
a. Extra flagstaff . . . 55·00 75·0
b. Short extra flagstaff . . . 80·00
c. Lightning conductor . . . 60·00
d. Flagstaff on right-hand turret . . . £120
144 4c. green and indigo . . . 2·00 3·5
a. Extra flagstaff . . . £180
c. Lightning conductor . . . £190
d. Flagstaff on right-hand turret . . . £200
e. Double flagstaff . . . £225
145 5c. brown and deep blue . . . 2·00 1·5
146 25c. slate and purple . . . 4·00 4·0
a. Extra flagstaff . . . £250
b. Short extra flagstaff . . . £325
c. Lightning conductor . . . £250
d. Flagstaff on right-hand turret . . . £300
e. Double flagstaff . . . £325
143/6 *Set of* 4 . . . 9·00 8·5
143s/6s Perf "Specimen" *Set of* 4 . . . 85·00

For illustrations of plate varieties see Omnibus section following Zanzibar.

1937 (12 May). *Coronation. As Nos. 95/7 of Antigua, but printed by D.L.R.* P 14.
147 3c. orange . . . 30
148 4c. grey-black . . . 70
149 5c. bright blue . . . 80 1·9
147/9 *Set of* 3 . . . 1·60 2·2
147s/9s "Specimen" *Set of* 3 . . . 60·00

24 Maya Figures

25 Chicle Tapping

(Recess B.W.)

1938 (10 Jan)–**47**. *T* **24/5** *and similar designs.* Wmk Mult Script CA (sideways on horizontal stamps). P $11\frac{1}{2} \times 11$ (horiz designs) or $11 \times 11\frac{1}{2}$ (vert designs).
150 1c. bright magenta and green (14.2.38) . . . 10 1·
151 2c. black and scarlet (14.2.38) . . . 20 1·
a. Perf 12 (1947) . . . 2·50 1·
152 3c. purple and brown . . . 50
153 4c. black and green . . . 50
154 5c. mauve and dull blue . . . 1·50
155 10c. green and reddish brown (14.2.38) . . . 1·50
156 15c. brown and light blue (14.2.38) . . . 3·25
157 25c. blue and green (14.2.38) . . . 3·00 1·
158 50c. black and purple (14.2.38) . . . 12·00 3·
159 $1 scarlet and olive (28.2.38) . . . 22·00 10·
160 $2 deep blue and maroon (28.2.38) . . . 29·00 17·
161 $5 scarlet and brown (28.2.38) . . . 32·00 25·
150/61 *Set of* 12 . . . 90·00 55·
150s/61s Perf "Specimen" *Set of* 12 . . . £200

Designs: *Vert*—3c. Cohune palm; $1 Court House, Belize; Mahogany felling; $5 Arms of Colony. *Horiz*—4c. Local produc 5c. Grapefruit; 10c. Mahogany logs in river; 15c. Sergeant's Ca 25c. Dorey; 50c. Chicle industry.

1946 (9 Sept). *Victory. As Nos. 110/11 of Antigua.*
162 3c. brown . . . 10
163 5c. blue . . . 10
162s/3s Perf "Specimen" *Set of* 2 . . . 60·00

1948 (1 Oct). *Royal Silver Wedding. As Nos. 112/13 of Antigua.*
164 4c. green . . . 15
165 $5 brown . . . 17·00 45·

36 Island of St. George's Cay

37 H.M.S. *Merlin*

(Recess Waterlow)

1949 (10 Jan). *150th Anniv of Battle of St. George's Cay.* Wmk Mult Script CA. P 12½.

166	**36**	1c. ultramarine and green	10	1·00
167		3c. blue and yellow-brown	10	1·50
168		4c. olive and violet	10	1·00
169	**37**	5c. brown and deep blue	1·00	40
170		10c. green and red-brown	1·00	30
171		15c. emerald and ultramarine	1·00	30
166/71		*Set of* 6	2·75	4·00

1949 (10 Oct). *75th Anniv of U.P.U. As Nos. 114/17 of Antigua.*

172	4c. blue-green	30	30
173	5c. deep blue	1·50	50
174	10c. red-brown	40	3·00
175	25c. blue	35	50
172/5	*Set of* 4	2·25	3·75

1951 (16 Feb). *Inauguration of B.W.I. University College. As Nos. 118/19 of Antigua.*

176	3c. reddish violet and brown	45	1·50
177	10c. green and brown	45	30

STAMP BOOKLETS

1920. *Black on pink cover inscr "British Honduras–100–Two Cent Stamps". Stapled.*
SB1 $2 booklet containing one hundred 2c. (No. 102*b*) in blocks of 10 (5 × 2)

1920. *Grey-blue cover inscr "British Honduras–100–Three Cent Stamps". Stapled.*
SB2 $3 booklet containing one hundred 3c. (No. 103) in blocks of 10 (5 × 2)

1923. *Black on pink cover inscr "British Honduras–100–Two Cent Stamps". Stapled.*
SB3 $2 booklet containing one hundred 2c. brown (No. 127) in blocks of 10 (5 × 2)

1927. *Black on pink cover inscr "British Honduras–100–Two Cent Stamps". Stapled.*
SB4 $2 booklet containing one hundred 2c. rose-carmine (No. 128) in blocks of 10 (5 × 2)

POSTAGE DUE STAMPS

D 1

(Typo D.L.R.)

1923–64. Wmk Mult Script CA. *Ordinary paper.* P 14.

D1	**D 1**	1c. black	2·25	13·00
		a. Chalk-surfaced paper (25.9.56)	50	21·00
		b. White uncoated paper (9.4.64)	14·00	27·00
D2		2c. black	2·25	7·50
		a. Chalk-surfaced paper (25.9.56)	50	19·00
D3		4c. black	1·25	6·00
		a. Missing top serif on "C" (R. 6/6)	21·00	
		b. Chalk-surfaced paper (25.9.56)	90	15·00
		ba. Missing top serif on "C" (R. 6/6)	20·00	
		w. Wmk inverted	£190	
D1/3		*Set of* 3	5·25	24·00
D1a/3b		*Set of* 3	1·75	50·00
D1s/3s		Optd "Specimen" *Set of* 3	60·00	

The early ordinary paper printings were yellowish and quite distinct from No. D1b.

Stamps in this design, but with different watermark, were issued between 1965 and 1972.

British Levant

The term "British Levant" is used by stamp collectors to describe the issues made by various British Post Offices within the former Turkish Empire.

Arrangements for the first such service were included amongst the terms of a commercial treaty between the two countries in 1832, but the system did not start operations until September 1857 when a post office for civilian use was opened in Constantinople, replacing the Army Post Office which had existed there since June 1854.

Eventually the number of British Post Offices grew to five:

Beyrout (Beirut, Lebanon). Opened 1873, closed 30 September 1914.

Constantinople (Istanbul). Opened 1 September 1857, closed 30 September 1914, re-opened 4 February 1919, finally closed 27 September 1923.

Salonica (Thessalonika, Greece). Opened 1 May 1900, closed October 1914. The city was captured by Greek troops on 7 November 1912 and incorporated into Greece by the Treaty of London (July 1913).

Smyrna (Izmir). Opened 1872, closed 30 September 1914, re-opened 1 March 1919, finally closed September 1922. Between 15 May 1919 and 8 September 1922 the city was under Greek occupation.

Stamboul (a sub-office of Constantinople). Opened 1 April 1884, closed 25 August 1896, re-opened 10 February 1908, finally closed 30 September 1914.

Stamps from the two British Post Offices in Egypt still technically part of the Turkish Empire, are listed under EGYPT.

A. BRITISH POST OFFICES IN TURKISH EMPIRE, 1857–1914

For illustrations of the postmark types see BRITISH POST OFFICES ABROAD notes, following GREAT BRITAIN.

From 1 August 1885 letter and registered charges were prepaid with surcharged stamps (No. 1 onwards). Until 14 August 1905 postcards and parcels continued to be franked with unoverprinted Great Britain stamps. Only a limited range of values were stocked for this purpose and these are listed. Other values exist with Levant postmarks, but these stamps did not originate from the local post offices.

After 15 August 1905 the post offices were supplied with Great Britain stamps overprinted "LEVANT". Subsequent examples of unoverprinted stamps with Levant postmarks are omitted from the listing. The use of such stamps during 1919–22 at Constantinople and Smyrna is, however, covered by a later note.

BEYROUT (BEIRUT)

Between 1873 and 1876 much of the mail from the British Post Office in Beyrout sent to European addresses was forwarded through the French or Italian Post Offices at Alexandria. Such covers show Great Britain stamps used in combination with those of French or Italian P.O's in the Turkish Empire.

Stamps of GREAT BRITAIN *cancelled* "G 06" *or circular postmark as in Types* **8**, **18** or **20**.

1873.

Z 1	½d. rose-red (1870–79) Plate Nos. 12, 13, 14, 19, 20.	*From*	38·00
Z 2	1d. rose-red (1864–79) Plate Nos. 107, 118, 130, 140, 145, 148, 155, 157, 162, 167, 177, 179, 180, 184, 185, 186, 187, 195, 198, 200, 203, 204, 211, 213, 215, 218, 220, 222.	*From*	16·00
Z 3	1½d. lake-red (1870–74) (Plate 3)		£250
Z 4	2d. blue (1858–69) Plate Nos. 13, 14, 15.	*From*	21·00
Z 5	2½d. rosy mauve (1875) (*blued paper*) Plate No. 1.		75·00
Z 6	2½d. rosy mauve (1875–76) Plate Nos. 1, 2, 3.	*From*	32·00
Z 7	2½d. rosy mauve (1876–79) Plate Nos. 3, 4, 5, 6, 7, 8, 9, 10, 11, 12, 13, 14, 15, 16, 17.	*From*	25·00
Z 8	2½d. blue (1880) Plate Nos. 17, 18, 19, 20.	*From*	15·00
Z 9	2½d. blue (1881) Plate Nos. 21, 22, 23.	*From*	11·00
Z10	3d. rose (1867–73) (Plate No. 10)		
Z11	3d. rose (1873–76) Plate Nos. 12, 15, 16, 18, 19, 20.		40·00
Z12	3d. rose (1881) (Plate Nos. 20, 21)		
Z13	4d. vermilion (1865–73) Plate Nos. 11, 12, 13, 14.	*From*	38·00
Z14	4d. vermilion (1876) (Plate No. 15)		£180
Z15	4d. sage-green (1877) Plate Nos. 15, 16.		£120
Z16	4d. grey-brown (1880) wmk Large Garter (Plate No. 17)		
Z17	4d. grey-brown (1880) wmk Crown Plate Nos. 17, 18.		48·00
Z18	6d. mauve (1870) (Plate Nos. 8, 9)		
Z19	6d. buff (1872–73) Plate Nos. 11, 12.	*From*	85·00
Z20	6d. chestnut (1872) (Plate No. 11)		42·00
Z21	6d. grey (1873) (Plate No. 12)		
Z22	6d. grey (1874–80) Plate Nos. 13, 14, 15, 16, 17.	*From*	30·00
Z23	8d. orange (1876)		£350
Z24	10d. red-brown (1867)		£160
Z25	1s. green (1867–73) Plate Nos. 6, 7.		30·00
Z26	1s. green (1873–77) Plate Nos. 8, 9, 10, 12, 13.	*From*	42·00
Z27	1s. orange-brown (1880) (Plate No. 13)		
Z28	1s. orange-brown (1881) Plate Nos. 13, 14.		55·00
Z29	2s. blue (1867)		£150
Z30	5s. rose (1867) (Plate Nos. 1, 2)	*From*	£600

1880.

Z31	½d. deep green	9·50
Z32	½d. pale green	11·00
Z33	1d. Venetian red	13·00
Z34	1½d. Venetian red	16·00
Z35	2d. pale rose	45·00
Z36	2d. deep rose	45·00
Z37	5d. indigo	75·00

1881.

Z38	1d. lilac (14 *dots*)	
Z39	1d. lilac (16 *dots*)	6·00

1884.

Z40	½d. slate-blue	12·00
Z41	1½d. lilac	75·00
Z42	2d. lilac	65·00
Z43	2½d. lilac	11·00
Z44	4d. dull green	£170
Z45	5d. dull green	£110
Z46	1s. dull green	£250

1887–92.

Z47	½d. vermilion	6·00
Z54	6d. purple/*rose-red*	21·00
Z55	1s. dull green	£130

1900.

Z56	½d. blue-green	9·00
Z57	1s. green and carmine	£170

1902–04. *De La Rue ptgs.*

Z58	½d. blue-green	4·75
Z59	½d. yellowish green	5·00
Z60	1d. scarlet	4·25
Z64	1s. dull green and carmine	29·00

CONSTANTINOPLE

Stamps of GREAT BRITAIN *cancelled* "C" *or circular postmark as in Types* **1**, **10**, **18** or **19**.

1857.

Z 68	½d. rose-red (1870–79) Plate Nos. 5, 6, 10, 11, 12, 13, 14, 15, 20.	*From*	24·00
Z 69	1d. red-brown (1854), Die I, wmk Small Crown, perf 16		
Z 70	1d. red-brown (1855), Die II, wmk Small Crown, perf 14		
Z 71	1d. red-brown, (1855), Die II, wmk Large Crown, perf 14		19·00
Z 72	1d. rose-red (1857)		7·00
Z 73	1d. rose-red (1861) Alphabet IV		
Z 74	1d. rose-red (1864–79) Plate Nos. 71, 72, 73, 74, 76, 78, 79, 80, 81, 83, 85, 87, 89, 90, 92, 93, 94, 95, 96, 97, 99, 101, 102, 105, 106, 108, 109, 110, 113, 116, 118, 119, 120, 121, 122, 123, 124, 125, 127, 129, 130, 131, 134, 135, 136, 137, 138, 140, 141, 143, 144, 145, 146, 147, 148, 149, 150, 151, 152, 155, 156, 157, 158, 159, 160, 161, 162, 163, 164, 165, 166, 167, 170, 171, 172, 173, 174, 175, 176, 177, 178, 179, 180, 181, 183, 184, 186, 187, 188, 189, 190, 191, 192, 193, 194, 195, 196, 197, 198, 200, 201, 203, 204, 205, 206, 207, 208, 210, 212, 214, 215, 216, 220, 222, 224.	*From*	8·00
Z 75	1½d. rose-red (1870) (Plate 1)		£200
Z 76	2d. blue (1855), wmk Large Crown, perf 14. (Plate Nos. 5, 6)		
Z 77	2d. blue (1858–69) Plate Nos. 7, 8, 9, 12, 13, 14, 15.	*From*	12·00
Z 78	2½d. rosy mauve (1875–76) (*blued paper*) (Plate Nos. 1, 2)	*From*	55·00
Z 79	2½d. rosy mauve (1875–76) Plate Nos. 1, 2, 3.	*From*	30·00
Z 80	2½d. rosy mauve (*Error of Lettering*)		
Z 81	2½d. rosy mauve (1876–79) Plate Nos. 3 to 17.	*From*	23·00
Z 82	2½d. blue (1880–81) Plate Nos. 17, 18, 19, 20.	*From*	11·00
Z 83	2½d. blue (1881) (Plate Nos. 21, 22, 23)		7·50
Z 84	3d. carmine-rose (1862) (Plate No. 2)		£130
Z 85	3d. rose (1865) (Plate No. 4)		75·00
Z 86	3d. rose (1867–73) (Plate Nos. 4 to 10)		70·00
Z 87	3d. rose (1873–76) Plate Nos. 11, 12, 15, 16, 17, 18, 19.		21·00
Z 88	3d. rose (1881) (Plate No. 21)		
Z 89	3d.on 3d. lilac (1883) (Plate No. 21)		
Z 90	4d. rose (1857)		45·00
	a. *Rose-carmine*		
Z 91	4d. red (1862) (Plate Nos. 3, 4)	*From*	38·00
Z 92	4d. vermilion (1865–73) Plate Nos. 7 to 14.	*From*	26·00
Z 93	4d. vermilion (1876) (Plate No. 15)		£150
Z 94	4d. sage-green (1877) Plate Nos. 15, 16.		90·00
Z 95	4d. grey-brown (1880) wmk Large Garter (Plate No. 17)		
Z 96	4d. grey-brown (1880) wmk Crown (Plate Nos. 17, 18)	*From*	35·00
Z 97	6d. lilac (1856)		60·00
Z 98	6d. lilac (1862) (Plate Nos. 3, 4)	*From*	38·00
Z 99	6d. lilac (1865–67) Plate Nos. 5, 6.		35·00
Z100	6d. lilac (1867) (Plate No. 6)		40·00
Z101	6d. violet (1867–70) Plate Nos. 6, 8, 9.	*From*	32·00
Z102	6d. buff (1872–73) Plate Nos. 11, 12.		50·00
Z103	6d. chestnut (1872) (Plate No. 11)		30·00
Z104	6d. grey (1873) (Plate No. 12)		75·00
Z105	6d. grey (1874–76) Plate Nos. 13, 14, 15, 16.	*From*	24·00
Z106	6d. grey (1881–82) (Plate Nos. 17, 18)		26·00
Z107	6d.on 6d. lilac (1883)		70·00
	a. Dots slanting (Letters MI or SJ)		£110
Z108	8d. orange (1876)		£325
Z109	10d. red-brown (1867), wmk Emblems		£14000
Z110	10d. red-brown (1867)		£160
Z111	1s. green (1856)		£110
Z112	1s. green (1862)		60·00
Z113	1s. green (1862) ("K" *variety*)		
Z114	1s. green (1862) (*thick paper*)		

Z115 1s. green (1865) (Plate No. 4) 65·00
Z116 1s. green (1867–73) *From* 16·00
Plate Nos. 4, 5, 6, 7.
Z117 1s. green (1873–77) *From* 27·00
Plate Nos. 8, 9, 10, 11, 12, 13.
Z118 1s. orange-brown (1880) (Plate No. 13) £180
Z119 1s. orange-brown (1881) *From* 45·00
Plate Nos. 13, 14.
Z120 2s. blue (1867) 90·00
Z121 5s. rose (1867–74) *From* £250
Plate Nos. 1, 2.
Z122 5s. rose (1882) (*white paper*) £850
Z123 5s. rose (1882) (*blued paper*) £1000

1880.
Z124 ½d. deep green 6·50
Z125 ½d. pale green 7·50
Z126 1d. Venetian red 7·50
Z127 2d. pale rose 38·00
Z128 2d. deep rose 38·00
Z129 5d. indigo

1881.
Z130 1d. lilac (14 *dots*)
Z131 1d. lilac (16 *dots*) 2·50

1883–84.
Z132 ½d. slate-blue 6·50
Z133 1½d. lilac
Z134 2d. lilac 55·00
Z135 2½d. lilac 7·00
Z136 3d. lilac
Z137 4d. dull green
Z138 5d. dull green 90·00
Z139 6d. dull green
Z140 9d. dull green
Z141 1s. dull green £190
Z142 2s.6d. lilac (*blued paper*) £500
Z143 2s.6d. lilac (*white paper*) 80·00
Z144 5s. rose (*blued paper*)
Z145 5s. rose (*white paper*)

1887–92.
Z146 ½d. vermilion 2·50
Z154 6d. purple/*rose-red* 10·00
Z157 1s. dull green 75·00

1900.
Z158 ½d. blue-green 4·00
Z159 1s. green and carmine £140

1902–04. *De La Rue ptgs.*
Z160 ½d. blue-green 3·00
Z161 ½d. yellowish green 3·50
Z162 1d. scarlet 2·50
Z169 6d. purple 11·00
Z172 1s. green and carmine 18·00
Z173 2s.6d. lilac
Z174 5s. carmine

POSTAL FISCALS

Z175 1d. purple (wmk Anchor) (1868)
Z176 1d. purple (wmk Orb) (1881) £600

SALONICA

Stamps of GREAT BRITAIN *cancelled with circular postmark as in Type* **18** *or double-circle datestamp.*

1900.
Z202 ½d. vermilion (1887) 17·00
Z203 ½d. blue-green (1900) 19·00
Z204 1d. lilac (1881) 19·00
Z205 6d. purple/red (1887) 25·00
Z206 1s. green and carmine (1900) £160
Z207 5s. rose (white paper) (1883) £800

1902.
Z208 ½d. blue-green 23·00
Z209 ½d. yellow-green 17·00
Z209*a* 1d. scarlet 17·00
Z209*c* 1s. green and carmine 42·00

SMYRNA (IZMIR)

Stamps of GREAT BRITAIN *cancelled* "F 87" *or circular postmark as in Type* **8**, **16** *or* **18**.

1872.
Z210 ½d. rose-red (1870–79) *From* 28·00
Plates 11, 12, 13, 14, 15.
Z211 1d. rose-red (1864–79) *From* 13·00
Plate Nos. 120, 124, 134, 137, 138, 139, 140, 142, 143, 145, 146, 148, 149, 150, 151, 152, 153, 155, 156, 157, 158, 159, 160, 161, 162, 163, 164, 166, 167, 168, 169, 170, 171, 172, 173, 174, 175, 176, 177, 178, 183, 184, 185, 186, 187, 188, 191, 193, 195, 196, 198, 200, 201, 204, 210, 212, 215, 217, 218.
Z212 1½d. lake-red (1870–74) (Plate Nos. 1, 3) *From* £225
Z213 2d. blue (1858) wmk Large Crown, perf 16
Z214 2d. blue (1858–69) *From* 16·00
Plate Nos. 13, 14, 15.
Z215 2½d. rosy mauve (1875) (*blued paper*) 60·00
Plate No. 1.
Z216 2½d. rosy mauve (1875–76) *From* 27·00
Plate Nos. 1, 2, 3.
Z217 2½d. rosy mauve (*Error of lettering*)
Z218 2½d. rosy mauve (1876–79) *From* 22·00
Plate Nos. 3, 4, 5, 6, 7, 8, 9, 10, 11, 12, 13, 14, 15, 16, 17.
Z219 2½d. blue (1880) *From* 11·00
Plate Nos. 17, 18,19, 20.
Z220 2½d. blue (1881) 9·00
Plate Nos. 21, 22, 23.
Z221 3d. rose (1867–73) 35·00
Plate Nos. 5, 7, 9, 10.
Z222 3d. rose (1873–76) (Plate No. 14)
Z223 4d. vermilion (1865–73) 26·00
Plate Nos. 12, 13, 14.
Z224 4d. vermilion (1876) (Plate No. 15) £150
Z225 4d. sage-green (1877) 90·00
Plate Nos. 15, 16.
Z226 4d. grey-brown (1880) wmk Large Garter (Plate No. 17)
Z227 4d. grey-brown (1880) wmk Crown (Plate Nos. 17, 18) *From* 32·00
Z228 6d. buff (1872–73) *From* 70·00
Plate Nos. 11, 12.
Z229 6d. chestnut (1872) (Plate No. 11)
Z230 6d. grey (1873) (Plate No. 12) 75·00
Z231 6d. grey (1874–80) *From* 26·00
Plate Nos. 13, 14, 15, 16, 17.
Z232 6d. grey (1881–82) (Plate Nos. 17, 18) 50·00
Z233 6d.on 6d. lilac (1883) 85·00
Z234 8d. orange (1876)
Z235 9d. straw (1867) £225
Z236 10d. red-brown (1867) £130
Z237 1s. green (1867–73) (Plate Nos. 6, 7)
Z238 1s. green (1873–77) *From* 30·00
Plate Nos. 8, 9, 10, 11, 12, 13.
Z239 1s. orange-brown (1880) (Plate No. 13) £160
Z240 1s. orange-brown (1881) (Plate Nos. 13, 14) 42·00
Z241 5s. rose (1867–74) (Plate No. 2)

1880.
Z242 ½d. deep green 7·00
Z243 ½d. pale green 8·00
Z244 1d. Venetian red 12·00
Z245 1½d. Venetian red 80·00
Z246 2d. pale rose 32·00
Z247 2d. deep rose 32·00
Z248 5d. indigo 50·00

1881.
Z249 1d. lilac (16 *dots*) 4·50

1884.
Z250 ½d. slate-blue 9·50
Z251 2d. lilac 60·00
Z252 2½d. lilac 10·00
Z253 4d. dull green
Z254 5d. dull green £100
Z255 1s. dull green £225

1887.
Z256 ½d. vermilion 4·75
Z263 6d. purple/*rose-red* 16·00
Z264 1s. dull green £110

1900.
Z265 ½d. blue-green 7·00
Z266 1s. green and carmine

1902–04. *De La Rue ptgs.*
Z267 ½d. blue-green 4·50
Z268 ½d. yellowish green 5·00
Z269 1d. scarlet 4·00
Z276 6d. purple 13·00
Z279 1s. green and carmine 24·00
Z280 2s.6d. purple
Z281 5s. carmine

STAMBOUL (CONSTANTINOPLE)

Stamps of GREAT BRITAIN *cancelled* "S" *as Type* **10**, *or circular postmarks inscribed either* "BRITISH POST OFFICE CONSTANTINOPLE S" *or* "BRITISH POST OFFICE STAMBOUL" *as Type* **18**.

1884.
Z296 ½d. slate-blue 18·00
Z297 1d. lilac 9·00
Z298 2d. lilac
Z299 2½d. lilac 11·00
Z300 5d. dull green £100

1887–92.
Z306 ½d. vermilion 9·00
Z314 6d. purple/*rose-red* 26·00
Z317 1s. dull green

The "S" cancellation was in use from 1885 to 1891 and the "Stamboul" mark from 1892 to 1896, when the office was closed, and from its reopening in 1908 to 1914. The "CONSTANTINOPLE S" handstamp was normally used as a back stamp, but can be found cancelling stamps in the period 1885 to 1892.

PRICES FOR STAMPS ON COVER	
Nos. 1/3a	*from* × 8
Nos. 4/6*a*	*from* × 5
Nos. 7/40	*from* × 3
Nos. L1/10	*from* × 6
Nos. L11/17	*from* × 3

I. TURKISH CURRENCY

(40 paras = 1 piastre)

Following the depreciation of the Turkish piastre against sterling in 1884 it was decided to issue stamps surcharged in Turkish currency to avoid speculation. During the early period unsurcharged stamps of Great Britain remained on sale from the British Post Offices at the current rate of exchange until replaced by "LEVANT" overprints.

80 PARAS (1) **4 PIASTRES** (2) **12 PIASTRES** (3)

PRINTERS. Nos. 1/24 were surcharged or overprinted by De La Rue, *unless otherwise stated.*

Stamps of Great Britain (Queen Victoria) surch as T 1 to 3

1885 (1 Aug)–**88**.
1 **64** 40pa.on 2½d. lilac 95·00 1·25
2 **62** 80pa.on 5d. green £180 9·50
3 **58** 12pi.on 2s.6d. lilac/*bluish* £350 £225
a. On white paper (4.88) 45·00 22·00

Nos. 3, 11 and 33 were surcharged from a horizontal setting of eight clichés of which three showed a small final 'S'.

1887 (June)–**96**.
4 **74** 40pa.on 2½d. purple/*blue* 3·75 10
a. Surch double £1900 £2500
5 **78** 80pa.on 5d. purple and blue (7.90) 15·00 30
a. Small "0" in "80" £180 85·00
w. Wmk inverted † £550
6 **81** 4pi.on 10d. dull purple & carm (10.10.96) 42·00 8·00
a. Dull purple and deep bright carmine 42·00 11·00
b. Large, wide "4" (R. 1/2, 1/4) £180 65·00

No. 5a first appeared on the June 1895 printing when the size of the surcharge plate was increased from 60 to 120. On the Victorian stamp the variety comes on R. 4/1 and 4/7. The same setting was used for the first printing of the Edward VII surcharge, but here the sheet size was further increased to 240 so that No. 9a occurs on R. 4/1, 4/7, 14/1 and 14/7.

1893 (25 Feb). *Roughly handstamped at Constantinople, as T* **1**.
7 **71** 40pa.on ½d. vermilion £425 £100

This provisional was in use for five days only at the Constantinople and Stamboul offices. As fraudulent copies were made with the original handstamp, and can be found "used" on piece cancelled by fraudulent use of the usual canceller, this stamp should only be purchased from undoubted sources.

The handstamp became damaged during use so that by 1 March the top of the "S" was broken. Used examples dated 25 or 26 February showing the broken "S" *must* be fraudulent. It is also known with genuine handstamp inverted (*Price* £850 *unused*, £325 *used*).

1902–05. *Stamps of King Edward VII surch as T* **1** *to* **3**.
8 **86** 40pa.on 2½d. ultramarine (3.02) 14·00 1[illegible]
a. Pale ultramarine 15·00 1[illegible]
ab. Surch double † £225[illegible]
9 **89** 80pa.on 5d. dull purple & ultram (5.6.02) 7·00 2·5[illegible]
a. Small "0" in "80" £225 £19[illegible]
10 **92** 4pi.on 10d. dull purple & carmine (6.9.02) 11·00 4·0[illegible]
a. No cross on crown £110 90·0[illegible]
b. Chalk-surfaced paper 6·00 10·0[illegible]
ba. Chalk-surfaced paper. No cross on crown 85·00 £10[illegible]
11 **94** 12pi.on 2s.6d. lilac (29.8.03) 35·00 35·0[illegible]
a. Chalk-surfaced paper. *Pale dull purple* 70·00 75·0[illegible]
b. Chalk-surfaced paper. *Dull purple* 38·00 35·0[illegible]
12 **95** 24pi.on 5s. bright carmine (15.8.05) 32·00 40·0[illegible]
8/12 *Set of* 5 85·00 70·0[illegible]
9s/11s Optd "Specimen" *Set of* 3 £150

No. 9a only occurs on the first printing of 80pa. on 5d.

1 PIASTRE
(4)

1905–08. *Surch in* "PIASTRES" *instead of* "PARAS" *as T* **4** *and* **2**
13 **86** 1pi.on 2½d. ultramarine (17.4.06) 14·00 1[illegible]
a. Surch double † £140
w. Wmk inverted £750 £75[illegible]
14 **89** 2pi.on 5d. dull purple & ultram (11.11.05) 28·00 2·5[illegible]
a. Chalk-surfaced paper (1.08) 24·00 2·5[illegible]
ab. Slate-purple and ultramarine 28·00 7·0[illegible]

1 Piastre (5) **1 PIASTRE 10 PARAS** (6)

1906 (2 July). *Issued at Beyrout. No. L4 surch with T* **5** *by America[illegible] Press, Beyrout.*
15 **85** 1pi.on 2d. grey-green and carmine £1300 £60[illegible]

1909 (16 Nov–Dec). *Stamps of King Eaward VII surch as T [illegible] (30pa.)* **6**, *and* **2** *(5 pi). Ordinary paper (No. 19) or chalk-surface[illegible] paper (others)*
16 **84** 30pa.on 1½d. pale dull purple and green 10·00 1·2[illegible]
a. Surch double, one albino
17 **87** 1pi.10pa. on 3d. dull purple/*orange-yell* 12·00 35·[illegible]
18 **88** 1pi.30pa. on 4d. green & chocolate-brn 5·00 17·[illegible]
19 1pi.30pa. on 4d. pale orange (16.12.09) 17·00 60·[illegible]
20 **83** 2pi.20pa. on 6d. dull purple 19·00 60·[illegible]
21 **93** 5pi.on 1s. dull green and carmine 4·25 9·[illegible]
s. Optd "Specimen" 60·00
16/21 *Set of* 6 60·00 £1[illegible]

1¾ PIASTRE (7) **4** Normal "4" **4** Pointed "4"

1910 (24 Jan). *Stamps of King Edward VII surch as T* **7**. *Chal[illegible] surfaced paper (Nos. 22 and 24).*
22 **87** 1¼pi.on 3d. dull purple/*orange-yellow* 50 1·[illegible]
23 **88** 1¾pi.on 4d. pale orange 50 [illegible]
a. Orange-red 5·50 6·[illegible]
b. Thin, pointed "4" in fraction 5·50 26·[illegible]
24 **83** 2½pi.on 6d. dull purple 1·40 [illegible]
22/4 *Set of* 3 2·25 2·[illegible]

No. 23b occurs in the first and seventh vertical rows of the she[illegible] The variety also occurs on No. 38, but not on No. 38b.

1 PIASTRE (8) **1 PIASTRE** (9)

TYPE DIFFERENCES. In T **4** the letters are tall and narrow and the space enclosed by the upper part of the "A" is small.

In T **8** the opening of the "A" is similar but the letters are shorter and broader, the "P" and the "E" being particularly noticeable.

In T **9** the letters are short and broad, but the "A" is thin and open.

1911–13. *Stamps of King Edward VII, Harrison or Somerset House ptgs, surch at Somerset House.*

No.	Type	Description	Unused	Used
		(a) Surch with T **4** *(20 July).*		
25	**86**	1pi.on 2½d. bright blue (perf 14)	15·00	9·00
		a. Surch double, one albino	£200	
26		1pi.on 2½d. bright blue (perf 15 × 14) (14.10.11)	15·00	2·50
		a. Dull blue	15·00	2·00
		(b) Surch with T **8**.		
27	**86**	1pi.on 2½d. bright blue (perf 15 × 14) (3.12)	12·00	2·50
		a. Dull blue	21·00	3·25
		(c) Surch with T **9** *(7.12).*		
28	**86**	1pi.on 2½d. bright blue (perf 15 × 14)	65·00	60
		a. Dull blue	65·00	60
		(d) Surch with T **1** *to* **3** *(1911–13).*		
29	**84**	30pa.on 1½d. reddish purple and bright green (22.8.11)	6·50	55
		a. Slate-purple and green	10·00	2·25
		b. Surch double, one albino	50·00	
30	**89**	2pi.on 5d. dull reddish purple and bright blue (13.5.12)	12·00	1·50
		a. Deep dull reddish purple and bright blue	14·00	2·25
31	**92**	4pi.on 10d. dull purple & scarlet (26.6.12)	30·00	13·00
		a. Dull reddish purple & aniline pink	£250	85·00
		b. Dull reddish purple and carmine	12·00	11·00
		c. No cross on crown		
32	**93**	5pi.on 1s. green and carmine (1913)	23·00	5·50
		a. Surch double, one albino	£200	
33	**94**	12pi.on 2s.6d. dull reddish pur (3.2.12)	50·00	38·00
		a. Dull greyish purple	50·00	38·00
34	**95**	24pi.on 5s. carmine (1913)	55·00	75·00
		a. Surch double, one albino	£225	
29/34 *Set of* 6			£140	£110

1913 (Apr)–**14**. *Stamps of King George V,* wmk Royal Cypher, *surch as T* **1** *(30pa.),* **9** *(1pi.)* **7** *or* **2** *(4 and 5pi.).*

No.	Type	Description	Unused	Used
35	**105**	30pa.on 1½d. red-brown (4.13)	3·50	14·00
		a. Surch double, one albino	£100	
36	**104**	1pi.on 2½d. cobalt-blue (6.13)	6·50	10
		a. Bright blue	5·00	15
37	**106**	1¼pi.on 3d. dull reddish violet (9.13)	4·75	4·25
		a. Violet	6·00	6·00
		b. Surch double, one albino	£300	
38		1¾pi.on 4d. deep grey-green (7.13)	3·00	6·00
		a. Thin, pointed "4" in fraction	45·00	80·00
		b. Grey-green	4·50	5·00
39	**108**	4pi.on 10d. turquoise-blue (12.13)	7·50	19·00
40		5pi.on 1s. bistre-brown (1.14)	40·00	60·00
35/40 *Set of* 6			55·00	90·00

II. BRITISH CURRENCY

Stamps overprinted "LEVANT" were for use on parcels, with the ½d. and 1d. principally used for printed paper and post cards. They replaced unoverprinted Great Britain stamps, Nos. Z58/64, Z160/74, Z208/9*c* and Z267/81, which had previously been used for these purposes.

From October 1907 the three lowest values were also used for certain other amended postal rates until Nos. 16/21 were introduced.

LEVANT

(L 1)

1905 (15 Aug)–**12**. *Stamps of King Edward VII optd with Type* L **1**.

No.	Type	Description	Unused	Used
		(a) De La Rue ptgs.		
L1	**83**	½d. pale yellowish green	8·50	15
		a. Yellowish green	8·50	15
L2		1d. scarlet	7·00	15
		a. Bright scarlet	7·00	90
L3	**84**	1½d. dull purple and green	5·00	1·75
		a. Chalk-surfaced paper. *Pale dull purple and green*	13·00	3·00
L4	**85**	2d. grey-green and carmine-red	6·50	26·00
		a. Chalk-surfaced paper. *Pale grey-green and carmine-red*	3·00	7·00
		ab. Dull blue-green and carmine	3·00	8·00
L5	**86**	2½d. ultramarine	8·50	20·00
L6	**87**	3d. dull purple/*orange-yellow*	6·00	12·00
L7	**88**	4d. green and grey-brown	8·50	42·00
		a. Green and chocolate-brown	17·00	45·00
L8	**89**	5d. dull purple and ultramarine	16·00	29·00
L9	**83**	6d. pale dull purple	12·00	25·00
L10	**93**	1s. dull green and carmine	35·00	50·00
		a. Chalk-surfaced paper	35·00	50·00
L1/10 *Set of* 10			95·00	£170
		(b) Harrison ptgs optd at Somerset House.		
L11	**83**	½d. dull yellow-green (*p.* 14) (2.12)	26·00	24·00
		a. Dull green	26·00	24·00
		b. Deep dull green	32·00	28·00

On 28 December 1909 all values, except for the ½d. and 1d. were withdrawn from sale. A further consignment of the 2d, No. L4*ab*, probably ordered in error was however, received, and, as there was no requirement for this value, sold mainly to collectors. Subsequently dated cancellations on the withdrawn values are philatelic, being worth much less than the used prices quoted.

ANT

Distorted "N" (R. 2/10, 12/10)

1911–13. *Stamps of King George V optd with Type* L **1** *at Somerset House.*

No.	Type	Description	Unused	Used
		(a) Die A. Wmk Crown.		
L12	**98**	½d. green (No. 322) (12.9.11)	1·50	1·50
		a. Distorted "N"	28·00	
L13	**99**	1d. carmine-red (No. 327) (1.1.12)	50	5·50
		a. No cross on crown	£150	
		b. Opt double, one albino	£100	
		c. Distorted "N"	18·00	
		(b) Redrawn types. Wmk Crown.		
L14	**101**	½d. green (No. 339) (19.3.12)	75	20
		a. Yellow-green	1·75	65
		b. Distorted "N"	17·00	
L15	**102**	1d. bright scarlet (No. 341) (24.2.12)	75	1·60
		a. Scarlet (No. 342)	2·00	1·60
		b. Opt triple, two albino	42·00	
		c. Distorted "N"	17·00	
		(c) New types. Wmk Royal Cypher (7.13).		
L16	**105**	½d. green (No. 351)	30	1·00
		a. Yellow-green	1·25	2·00
		b. Distorted "N"	15·00	
L17	**104**	1d. scarlet (No. 357)	30	4·75
		a. Vermilion	8·00	9·50
		b. Distorted "N"	15·00	

Similar overprints were issued when the British Post Offices reopened in 1919, and are listed below.

B. BRITISH POST OFFICES IN CONSTANTINOPLE AND SMYRNA, 1919–1923

CONSTANTINOPLE

Following the occupation of Constantinople by Allied forces a British Military Post Office was opened for civilian use on 4 February 1919. During the period of its existence stamps of Great Britain with face values to 10s. were available and such use can be identified by the following cancellations:

"FIELD POST OFFICE H12" (4 February 1919 to 18 March 1919)

"ARMY POST OFFICE Y" (20 March 1919 to June 1920)

"ARMY POST OFFICE S.X.3" (March 1919 to April 1920)

"British A.P.O. CONSTANTINOPLE" (July 1919 to July 1920).

Of these four marks the first two types were also used for military mail.

The office reverted to civilian control on 29 July 1920, Nos. 41/50 and L18/24 being intended for its use.

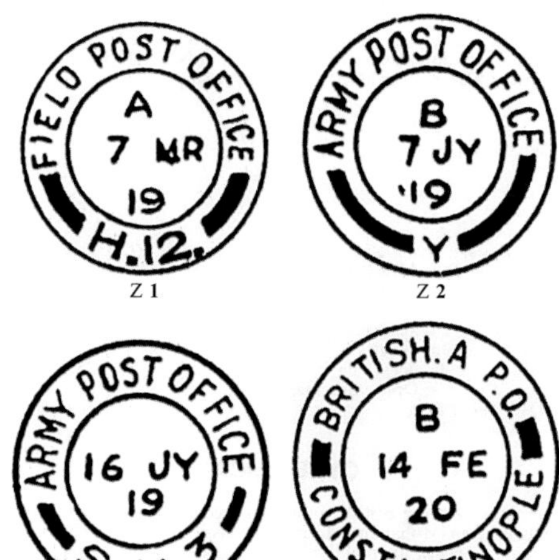

Z 1 Z 2 Z 3 Z 4

1919–20. *Used at the Army Post Office. Stamps of* GREAT BRITAIN *cancelled with Types* Z **1**, Z **2**, Z **3**, Z **4**.

No.	Description	Used
Z176	½d. green	2·00
Z177	1d. scarlet	2·00
Z178	1½d. brown	3·25
Z179	2d. orange (Die I)	2·50
Z180	2½d. blue	4·00
Z181	4d. grey-green	8·50
Z182	6d. purple	4·50
Z183	9d. agate	22·00
Z184	1s. bistre	5·50
Z185	2s.6d. brown	32·00
Z186	5s. rose-red	50·00
Z187	10s. dull grey-blue	90·00

1920–21. *Used at the Civilian Post Office. Stamps of* GREAT BRITAIN *cancelled with Type* **18** *or double-circle datestamp.*

No.	Description	Used
Z188	½d. green	2·00
Z189	1d. scarlet	2·00
Z190	1½d. brown	3·25
Z191	2d. orange (Die I)	2·50
Z192	2½d. blue	4·00
Z193	3d. violet	6·50
Z194	4d. grey-green	8·50
Z195	5d. brown	13·00
Z196	6d. purple	4·50
Z197	10d. turquoise-blue	22·00
Z198	1s. bistre	5·50
Z199	2s.6d. brown	32·00
Z200	5s. rose-red	50·00
Z201	10s. dull grey-blue	90·00

PRICES FOR STAMPS ON COVER	
Nos. 41/50	*from* × 2
Nos. L18/24	*from* × 5

Stamps of Great Britain surch at Somerset House

I. TURKISH CURRENCY

1½ PIASTRES (10) **15 PIASTRES** (11)

18¾

Short hyphen bar (R. 4/12, 14/12.)

1921 (Aug). *Stamps of King George V,* wmk Royal Cypher, *surch as T* **1** *(30pa.),* **10** *and* **11** *(15 and 18¾pi.).*

No.	Type	Description	Unused	Used
41	**105**	30pa.on ½d. green	75	12·00
		a. Yellow-green	3·25	14·00
42	**104**	1½pi.on 1d. bright scarlet	1·50	1·25
		a. Vermilion	8·00	3·50
		b. Scarlet-vermilion	7·00	4·00
43		3¾pi.on 2½d. blue	1·25	25
		a. Dull Prussian blue	28·00	2·75
44	**106**	4½pi.on 3d. violet	2·00	3·75
		a. Bluish violet	2·50	3·00
45	**107**	7½pi.on 5d. brown	50	10
		a. Yellow-brown	2·00	20
46	**108**	15pi.on 10d. turquoise-blue	70	15
47		18¾pi.on 1s. bistre-brown	4·25	4·25
		a. Short hyphen bar	55·00	
		b. Olive-bistre	6·00	4·75
		ba. Short hyphen bar	70·00	

45 PIASTRES (12) **45** Joined figures (second stamp in each horiz row)

1921. *Stamps of King George V (Bradbury, Wilkinson printing) surch as T* **12**.

No.	Type	Description	Unused	Used
48	**109**	45pi.on 2s.6d. chocolate-brown	20·00	45·00
		a. Joined figures	35·00	65·00
		b. Olive-brown	50·00	60·00
		ba. Joined figures	70·00	85·00
49		90pi.on 5s. rose-red	25·00	30·00
		a. Surch double, one albino	£225	
50		180pi.on 10s. dull grey-blue	45·00	40·00
		a. Surch double, one albino	£225	
41/50 *Set of* 10			90·00	£120
47s/50s Optd "Specimen" *Set of* 4			£275	

II. BRITISH CURRENCY

1921. *Stamps of King George V optd as Type* L **1**.

No.	Type	Description	Unused	Used
L18	**106**	2d. reddish orange (Die I)	1·25	29·00
		a. Bright orange	2·25	29·00
L19		3d. bluish violet	7·50	10·00
L20		4d. grey-green	5·00	14·00
L21	**107**	5d. yellow-brown	12·00	28·00
L22		6d. dull purple (*chalk-surfaced paper*)	24·00	42·00
		a. Reddish purple	26·00	8·50
L23	**108**	1s. bistre-brown	13·00	8·50
		a. Olive-bistre	13·00	8·50
		s. Optd "Specimen"	65·00	
L24	**109**	2s.6d. chocolate-brown	38·00	90·00
		a. Olive-brown	65·00	£120
		s. Optd "Specimen"	£140	
L18/24 *Set of* 7			85·00	£170

On No. L24 the letters of the overprint are shorter, being only 3 mm high.

Nos. 41/50 and L18/24 were used at the Constantinople office only.

SMYRNA

When the office re-opened on 1 March 1919 existing stocks of surcharged or overprinted issues were utilised until they were exhausted in mid-1920. During this period examples of Nos. 24, 29*a*, 30*a*, 33*b*/7, 39/40, L4*b*, L14/17 are known with commercial postmarks. These stamps were supplemented and finally replaced in mid-1920 by ordinary stamps of Great Britain.

Stamps of GREAT BRITAIN *cancelled with circular postmark as Type* **18** *or with* "REGISTERED" *oval.*

No.	Description	Used
Z282	½d. green	2·50
Z283	1d. scarlet	2·50
Z284	1½d. brown	3·50
Z285	2d. orange (Die I)	3·00
Z286	2d. orange (Die II)	26·00
Z287	2½d. blue (*shades*)	5·00
Z288	2½d. dull Prussian blue	£400
Z289	4d. grey-green	11·00
Z290	6d. purple	8·00
Z291	10d. turquoise-blue	29·00
Z292	1s. bistre	8·50
Z293	2s.6d. brown	60·00
Z294	5s. rose-red	85·00
Z295	10s. dull grey-blue	£140

C. BRITISH FIELD OFFICE IN SALONICA

These overprints were originally prepared for use by a civilian post office to be set up on Mt. Athos, Northern Greece. When the project was abandoned they were placed on sale at the Army Field Office in Salonica.

PRICES FOR STAMPS ON COVER
Nos. S1/8 *from* × 6

Levant

(S 1)

1916 (end Feb–9 Mar). *Stamps of Gt. Britain, optd with Type* S **1** *by Army Printing Office, Salonica.*

No.	Type	Description	Unused	Used
S1	**105**	½d. green	42·00	£200
		a. Opt double	£2000	£2750
		b. Vert pair, one without opt	£1000	£1400
S2	**104**	1d. scarlet	42·00	£190
		a. Opt double	£1400	£1700
S3	**106**	2d. reddish orange (Die I)	£140	£350
S4		3d. bluish violet	£100	£350
S5		4d. grey-green	£140	£350
S6	**107**	6d. reddish pur (*chalk-surfaced paper*)	80·00	£300
		a. Vert pair, one without opt	£1200	£1600
S7	**108**	9d. agate	£300	£550
		a. Opt double	£8500	£6500
S8		1s. bistre-brown	£250	£475
S1/8 *Set of* 8			£950	£2500

There are numerous forgeries of this overprint.

All values can be found with an additional albino overprint, inverted on the gummed side.

British New Guinea *see* New Guinea *after* Australia

British Occupation of Iraq *see* Iraq

British Occupation of Italian Colonies

PRICES FOR STAMPS ON COVER TO 1945
Nos. M1/21 *from* × 4
Nos. MD1/5 *from* × 10
Nos. S1/9 *from* × 4

The above prices refer to covers from the territories concerned, not examples used in Great Britain.

MIDDLE EAST FORCES

For use in territory occupied by British Forces in Eritrea (1942), Italian Somaliland (from 13 April 1942), Cyrenaica (1943), Tripolitania (1943), and some of the Dodecanese Islands (1945).

PRICES. Our prices for used stamps with "M.E.F." overprints are for specimens with identifiable postmarks of the territories in which they were issued. These stamps were also used in the United Kingdom with official sanction, from the summer of 1950 onwards, and with U.K. postmarks are worth considerably less.

PRINTERS. Considerable research has been undertaken to discover the origins of Nos. M1/10. It is now suggested that Nos. M1/5, previously assigned to Harrison and Sons, were produced by the Army Printing Services, Cairo, and that the smaller printing, Nos. M6/10, previously identified as the work of the Army Printing Services, Cairo, was from an unidentified printer within the Middle East Forces area.

M.E.F. **M.E.F.**

(M **1**)Opt. 14 mm long. Regular lettering and upright oblong stops.

(M **2**)Opt. 13½ mm long. Regularlettering and square stops.

M.E.F.

(M **2a**)Opt. 13½ mm long. Rough lettering and round stops.

(Illustrations twice actual size)

M.E.F.

Sliced "M" (R. 6/10)

1942 (2 Mar). *Stamps of Great Britain optd.* W **127**. P 15 × 14.

(a) With Type M **1**.

No.	Type	Description	Unused	Used
M 1	**128**	1d. scarlet (No. 463)	1·50	2·25
		a. Sliced "M"	70·00	80·00
M 2		2d. orange (No. 465)	75	3·25
		a. Sliced "M"	45·00	
M 3		2½d. ultramarine (No. 466)	70	1·00
		a. Sliced "M"	45·00	
M 4		3d. violet (No. 467)	60	20
M 5	**129**	5d. brown	60	20
		a. Sliced "M"	45·00	48·00

(b) With Type M **2**.

No.	Type	Description	Unused	Used
M 6	**128**	1d. scarlet (No. 463)	55·00	13·00
		a. Optd with Type M **2a**	45·00	9·00
		b. Nos. M6/a *se-tenant* vert	£200	85·00
M 7		2d. orange (No. 465)	75·00	95·00
		a. Optd with Type M **2a**	65·00	85·00
		b. Nos. M7/a *se-tenant* vert	£325	£300
M 8		2½d. ultramarine (No. 466)	50·00	7·50
		a. Optd with Type M **2a**	45·00	5·50
		b. Nos. M8/a *se-tenant* vert	£190	60·00
M 9		3d. violet (No. 467)	£120	35·00
		a. Optd with Type M **2a**	£110	32·00
		ab. Opt double	†	£2250
		b. Nos. M9/a *se-tenant* vert	£450	£180
M10	**129**	5d. brown	£400	90·00
		a. Optd with Type M **2a**	£375	80·00
		b. Nos. M10/a *se-tenant* vert	£1200	£600

See note after No. M21.

Nos. M6/10 were issued in panes of 60 (6 × 10), rows 2, 3, and 7 being overprinted with Type M **2** and the other seven rows with Type M **2***a*.

M.E.F.

(M **3**) Optd 13½ mm long. Regular lettering and upright oblong stops.

(Illustration twice actual size)

1943 (1 Jan)–**47**. *Stamps of Great Britain optd with Type* M **3** *by Harrison & Sons.* W **127**, P 15 × 14 (1d. to 1s.); W **133**, P 14 (others).

No.	Type	Description	Unused	Used
M11	**128**	1d. pale scarlet (No. 486)	1·50	10
M12		2d. pale orange (No. 488)	1·50	1·25
M13		2½d. light ultramarine (No. 489)	50	10
M14		3d. pale violet (No. 490)	1·50	10
M15	**129**	5d. brown	3·25	10
M16		6d. purple	40	10
M17	**130**	9d. deep olive-green	85	10
M18		1s. bistre-brown	50	10
M19	**131**	2s.6d. yellow-green	7·00	1·00
M20		5s. red (1947)	13·00	17·00
M21	**132**	10s. ultramarine (1947)	15·00	10·00
M11/21 *Set of* 11			40·00	27·00
M18s/21s Optd "Specimen" *Set of* 4			£550	

The overprint on No. M15 should not be confused with the other overprints on the 5d. value. It can be distinguished from No. M5 by the ½ mm difference in length; and from No. M10 by the more intense colour, thicker lettering and larger stops.

POSTAGE DUE STAMPS

M.E.F.

(MD **1**)

1942. *Postage Due stamps of Great Britain Nos. D27/30 and D33 optd with Type* MD **1**, *in blue-black.*

No.	Type	Description	Unused	Used
MD1	D **1**	½d. emerald	30	12·00
MD2		1d. carmine	30	1·75
MD3		2d. agate	1·25	1·25
MD4		3d. violet	50	4·25
MD5		1s. deep blue	3·75	12·00
		s. Optd "Specimen"	£160	
MD1/5 *Set of* 5			5·50	28·00

CYRENAICA

In June 1949 the British authorities recognised the leader of the Senussi, Amir Mohammed Idris Al-Senussi, as Amir of Cyrenaica with autonomy in internal affairs.

(Currency. 10 millièmes = 1 piastre, 100 piastres = 1 Egyptian pound)

24 Mounted Warrior

25 Mounted Warrior

(Recess Waterlow)

1950 (16 Jan). P 12½.

No.	Type	Description	Unused	Used
136	**24**	1m. brown	1·75	3·50
137		2m. carmine	2·00	3·50
138		3m. orange-yellow	2·00	3·50
139		4m. blue-green	2·00	3·50
140		5m. grey-black	2·00	2·50
141		8m. orange	2·00	2·00
142		10m. violet	2·00	1·50
143		12m. scarlet	2·00	1·50
144		20m. blue	2·00	1·50
145	**25**	50m. ultramarine and purple-brown	3·25	3·50
146		100m. carmine and black	8·50	9·00
147		200m. violet and deep blue	12·00	25·00
148		500m. orange-yellow and green	42·00	65·00
136/148 *Set of* 13			75·00	£110

POSTAGE DUE STAMPS

D **26**

(Recess Waterlow)

1950 (16 Jan). P 12½.

No.	Type	Description	Unused	Used
D149	D **26**	2m. brown	45·00	95·00
D150		4m. blue-green	45·00	95·00
D151		8m. scarlet	45·00	£100
D152		10m. orange	45·00	£100
D153		20m. orange-yellow	45·00	£110
D154		40m. blue	45·00	£140
D155		100m. grey-brown	45·00	£150
D149/155 *Set of* 7			£275	£700

On 24 December 1951 Cyrenaica united with Tripolitania, Fezzan and Ghadames to form the independent Kingdom of Libya, whose issues are listed in Part 13 (*Africa since Independence F—M*) of this catalogue.

ERITREA

From early 1950 examples of Nos. E1/32 exist precancelled in manuscript by a black or blue horizontal line for use by British troops on concession rate mail.

BRITISH MILITARY ADMINISTRATION

(Currency. 100 cents = 1 shilling)

B. M. A.
ERITREA
10
CENTS

(E **1**)

B. M. A.
ERITREA
5 SHILLINGS

(E **2**)

SH. 50 Normal

SH .50 Misplaced Stop

1948–49. *Stamps of Great Britain surch as Types* E **1** *or* E **2**.

No.	Type	Description	Unused	Used
E 1	**128**	5c.on ½d. pale green	70	65
E 2		10c.on 1d. pale scarlet	1·00	2·50
E 3		20c.on 2d. pale orange	50	2·25
E 4		25c.on 2½d. light ultramarine	70	60
E 5		30c.on 3d. pale violet	1·25	4·50
E 6	**129**	40c.on 5d. brown	50	4·25
E 7		50c.on 6d. purple	50	1·00
E 7*a*	**130**	65c.on 8d. bright carmine (1.2.49)	7·00	2·00
E 8		75c.on 9d. deep olive-green	70	75
E 9		1s.on 1s. bistre-brown	70	50
E10	**131**	2s.50c. on 2s.6d. yellow-green	8·00	10·00
		a. Misplaced stop (R. 4/7)	£100	£130
E11		5s.on 5s. red	8·00	16·00
E12	**132**	10s.on 10s. ultramarine	22·00	22·00
E1/12 *Set of* 13			45·00	60·00

BRITISH ADMINISTRATION

1950 (6 Feb). *As Nos. E1/12, but surch* "B.A. ERITREA" *and new values instead of* "B.M.A." *etc.*

No.	Type	Description	Unused	Used
E13	**128**	5c.on ½d. pale green	1·25	8·0
E14		10c.on 1d. pale scarlet	30	3·0
E15		20c.on 2d. pale orange	30	8
E16		25c.on 2½d. light ultramarine	30	6
E17		30c.on 3d. pale violet	30	2·2
E18	**129**	40c.on 5d. brown	50	1·7
E19		50c.on 6d. purple	30	2
E20	**130**	65c.on 8d. bright carmine	2·25	1·5
E21		75c.on 9d. deep olive-green	30	2
E22		1s.on 1s. bistre-brown	30	1
E23	**131**	2s.50c. on 2s.6d. yellow-green	7·00	4·7
E24		5s.on 5s. red	7·00	12·0
E25	**132**	10s.on 10s. ultramarine	60·00	55·0
E13/25 *Set of* 13			70·00	80·0

1951 (28 May*). *Nos. 503/4, 506/7 and 509/11 of Great Britain surc* "B.A. ERITREA" *and new values.*

No.	Type	Description	Unused	Used
E26	**128**	5c.on ½d. pale orange	30	7
E27		10c.on 1d. light ultramarine	30	7
E28		20c.on 2d. pale red-brown	30	3
E29		25c.on 2½d. pale scarlet	30	3
E30	**147**	2s.50c. on 2s.6d. yellow-green	10·00	23·0
E31	**148**	5s.on 5s. red	21·00	23·0
E32		10s.on 10s. ultramarine	22·00	23·0
E26/32 *Set of* 7			48·00	65·0

*This is the local release date. The stamps were placed on sale i London on 3 May.

POSTAGE DUE STAMPS

B. M. A.
ERITREA
10 CENTS

(ED **1**)

1948. *Postage Due stamps of Great Britain Nos. D27/30 and D3 surch as Type* ED **1**.

No.	Type	Description	Unused	Used
ED1	D **1**	5c.on ½d. emerald	9·50	22·0
ED2		10c.on 1d. carmine	9·50	24·0
		a. No stop after "B"	£120	

ED3 20c.on 2d. agate . . . 7·00 16·00
a. No stop after "A" . . . 60·00
b. No stop after "B" (R. 1/9) . . £130
ED4 30c.on 3d. violet . . . 9·50 16·00
ED5 1s.on 1s. deep blue . . . 17·00 30·00
ED1/5 *Set of* 5 . . . 48·00 95·00

1950 (6 Feb). *As Nos. ED1/5, but surch* "B.A. ERITREA" *and new values instead of* "B.M.A." *etc.*
ED 6 **D 1** 5c.on ½d. emerald . . . 11·00 48·00
ED 7 10c.on 1d. carmine . . . 10·00 15·00
a. "C" of "CENTS" omitted . . £1900
ab. "C" omitted and vertical oblong for "E" of "CENTS" . . . £3500
ED 8 20c.on 2d. agate . . . 11·00 14·00
ED 9 30c.on 3d. violet . . . 13·00 22·00
w. Wmk sideways-inverted* . . . — 55·00
ED10 1s.on 1s. deep blue . . . 15·00 23·00
a. Stop after "A" omitted (R. 2/13) . . . £325
ED6/10 *Set of* 5 . . . 55·00 £110

No. ED7a, and probably No. ED7ab, occurred on R. 7/17, but the error was quickly corrected.

*No. ED9w shows the Crowns pointing to the left, *as seen from the back of the stamp.*

Stamps of Ethiopia were used in Eritrea after 15 September 1952 following federation with Ethiopia.

SOMALIA

BRITISH OCCUPATION

E.A.F.

(S 1 "East Africa Forces")

1943 (15 Jan)–**46**. *Stamps of Great Britain optd with Type* S **1**, *in blue.*
S1 **128** 1d. pale scarlet . . . 60 60
S2 2d. pale orange . . . 1·50 1·25
S3 2½d. light ultramarine . . . 50 3·50
S4 3d. pale violet . . . 80 15
S5 **129** 5d. brown . . . 1·00 40
S6 6d. purple . . . 50 1·25
S7 **130** 9d. deep olive-green . . . 1·00 2·25
S8 1s. bistre-brown . . . 2·25 15
S9 **131** 2s.6d. yellow-green (1946) . . . 10·00 6·50
S1/9 *Set of* 9 . . . 16·00 14·50
S8s/9s Optd "Specimen" *Set of* 2 . . . £275

The note *re* used prices above Type M 1 of Middle East Forces also applies to the above issue.

BRITISH MILITARY ADMINISTRATION

(Currency. 100 cents = 1 shilling)

1948 (27 May). *Stamps of Great Britain surch* "B.M.A./SOMALIA" *and new values, as Types* E **1** *and* E **2** *of Eritrea.*
S10 **128** 5c.on ½d. pale green . . . 1·25 1·75
S11 15c.on 1½d. pale red-brown . . . 1·75 15·00
S12 20c.on 2d. pale orange . . . 3·00 4·25
S13 25c.on 2½d. light ultramarine . . . 2·25 4·50
S14 30c.on 3d. pale violet . . . 2·25 9·00
S15 **129** 40c.on 5d. brown . . . 1·25 20
S16 50c.on 6d. purple . . . 50 2·00
S17 **130** 75c.on 9d. deep olive-green . . . 2·00 18·00
S18 1s.on 1s. bistre-brown . . . 1·25 20
S19 **131** 2s.50c. on 2s.6d. yellow-green . . . 4·25 25·00
a. Misplaced stop (R. 4/7) . . . 90·00 £250
S20 5s.on 5s. red . . . 9·50 40·00
S10/20 *Set of* 11 . . . 26·00 £110

For illustration of No. S19a, see previous column above No. E1 of Eritrea.

BRITISH ADMINISTRATION

1950 (2 Jan). *As Nos. S10/20, but surch* "B.A./SOMALIA" *and new values, instead of* "B.M.A." *etc.*
S21 **128** 5c.on ½d. pale green . . . 20 3·00
S22 15c.on 1½d. pale red-brown . . . 75 17·00
S23 20c.on 2d. pale orange . . . 75 7·50
S24 25c.on 2½d. light ultramarine . . . 50 7·50
S25 30c.on 3d. pale violet . . . 1·25 4·50
S26 **129** 40c.on 5d. brown . . . 55 1·00
S27 50c.on 6d. purple . . . 50 1·00
S28 **130** 75c.on 9d. deep olive-green . . . 2·00 7·00
S29 1s.on 1s. bistre-brown . . . 60 1·50
S30 **131** 2s.50c. on 2s.6d. yellow-green . . . 4·00 24·00
S31 5s.on 5s. red . . . 11·00 30·00
S21/31 *Set of* 11 . . . 20·00 95·00

Somalia reverted to Italian Administration on 1 April 1950 later becoming independent. Later issues will be found listed in Part 8 (Italy and Switzerland) of this catalogue.

TRIPOLITANIA

BRITISH MILITARY ADMINISTRATION

(Currency. 100 centesimi = 1 Military Administration lira)

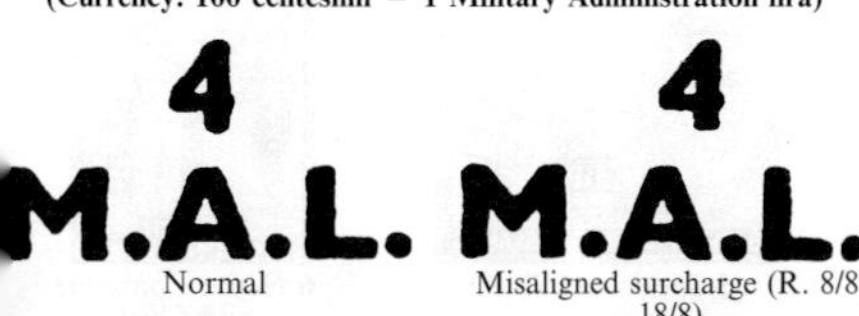

Normal — Misaligned surcharge (R. 8/8, 18/8)

1948 (1 July). *Stamps of Great Britain surch* "B.M.A./TRIPOLITANIA" *and new values, as Types* E **1** *and* E **2** *of Eritrea, but expressed in M(ilitary) A(dministration) L(ire).*
T 1 **128** 1l.on ½d. pale green . . . 90 1·50
T 2 2l.on 1d. pale scarlet . . . 30 15
T 3 3l.on 1½d. pale red-brown . . . 30 50
a. Misaligned surch . . . 30·00 45·00
T 4 4l.on 2d. pale orange . . . 30 70
a. Misaligned surch . . . 30·00 55·00
T 5 5l.on 2½d. light ultramarine . . . 30 20
T 6 6l.on 3d. pale violet . . . 30 40
T 7 **129** 10l.on 5d. brown . . . 30 15
T 8 12l.on 6d. purple . . . 30 20
T 9 **130** 18l.on 9d. deep olive-green . . . 80 65
T10 24l.on 1s. bistre-brown . . . 70 1·50
T11 **131** 60l.on 2s.6d. yellow-green . . . 3·50 8·50
T12 120l.on 5s. red . . . 15·00 19·00
T13 **132** 240l.on 10s. ultramarine . . . 22·00 95·00
T1/13 *Set of* 13 . . . 40·00 £110

BRITISH ADMINISTRATION

1950 (6 Feb). *As Nos. T1/13, but surch* "B.A. TRIPOLITANIA" *and new values, instead of* "B.M.A." *etc.*
T14 **128** 1l.on ½d. pale green . . . 2·75 12·00
T15 2l.on 1d. pale scarlet . . . 2·50 40
T16 3l.on 1½d. pale red-brown . . . 1·00 12·00
a. Misaligned surch . . . 45·00 £150
T17 4l.on 2d. pale orange . . . 1·00 4·50
a. Misaligned surch . . . 45·00 £100
T18 5l.on 2½d. light ultramarine . . . 70 70
T19 6l.on 3d. pale violet . . . 1·75 3·25
T20 **129** 10l.on 5d. brown . . . 50 4·00
T21 12l.on 6d. purple . . . 2·00 50
T22 **130** 18l.on 9d. deep olive-green . . . 2·25 2·50
T23 24l.on 1s. bistre-brown . . . 2·50 3·75
T24 **131** 60l.on 2s.6d. yellow-green . . . 6·50 12·00
T25 120l.on 5s. red . . . 20·00 22·00
T26 **132** 240l.on 10s. ultramarine . . . 35·00 65·00
T14/26 *Set of* 13 . . . 70·00 £130

1951 (3 May). *Nos. 503/7 and 509/11 of Great Britain surch* "B.A. TRIPOLITANIA" *and new values.*
T27 **128** 1l.on ½d. pale orange . . . 20 6·00
T28 2l.on 1d. light ultramarine . . . 20 1·00
T29 3l.on 1½d. pale green . . . 30 8·00
T30 4l.on 2d. pale red-brown . . . 20 1·25
T31 5l.on 2½d. pale scarlet . . . 30 7·50
T32 **147** 60l.on 2s.6d. yellow-green . . . 5·50 22·00
T33 **148** 120l.on 5s. red . . . 9·00 27·00
T34 **149** 240l.on 10s. ultramarine . . . 38·00 50·00
T27/34 *Set of* 8 . . . 48·00 £110

POSTAGE DUE STAMPS

1948. *Postage Due stamps of Great Britain Nos. D27/30 and D33 surch* "B.M.A./TRIPOLITANIA" *and new values, as* Type ED **1** of Eritrea, but expressed in M(ilitary) A(dministration) L(ire).
TD1 **D 1** 1l.on ½d. emerald . . . 5·50 50·00
a. No stop after "A" . . . 65·00
TD2 2l.on 1d. carmine . . . 2·50 32·00
a. No stop after "A" . . . 42·00
b. No stop after "M" (R. 1/17) . . . 95·00
TD3 4l.on 2d. agate . . . 7·50 32·00
a. No stop after "A" . . . £130
b. No stop after "M" . . . £170
TD4 6l.on 3d. violet . . . 7·50 21·00
TD5 24l.on 1s. deep blue . . . 28·00 £100
TD1/5 *Set of* 5 . . . 45·00 £200

1950 (6 Feb). *As Nos. TD1/5, but surch* "B.A. TRIPOLITANIA" *and new values, instead of* "B.M.A." *etc.*
TD 6 **D 1** 1l.on ½d. emerald . . . 12·00 80·00
a. No stop after "B" . . . £140
TD 7 2l.on 1d. carmine . . . 2·75 27·00
a. No stop after "B" . . . 70·00
TD 8 4l.on 2d. agate . . . 4·00 35·00
a. No stop after "B" . . . 80·00
TD 9 6l.on 3d. violet . . . 18·00 60·00
a. No stop after "B" . . . £200
w. Wmk sideways-inverted* . . . 55·00
TD10 24l.on 1s. deep blue . . . 48·00 £140
a. No stop after "A" . . . £425
b. No stop after "B" . . . £425
TD6/10 *Set of* 5 . . . 75·00 £300

*No. TD9w shows the Crowns pointing to the left, *as seen from the back of the stamp.*

Tripolitania became part of the independent kingdom of Libya on 24 December 1951.

British P.Os in Crete

BRITISH ADMINISTRATION OF CANDIA PROVINCE (HERAKLEION)

Crete, formerly part of the Turkish Empire, was made autonomous, under Turkish suzerainty, in November 1898 with British, French, Italian and Russian troops stationed in separate zones to keep the peace.

Overseas mail franked with Nos. B1/5 was forwarded through the Austrian post office at Canea, being additionally franked with stamps of the Austro-Hungarian Post Offices in the Turkish Empire.

(Currency. 40 pares = 1 piastre)

PRICES FOR STAMPS ON COVER		
No. B1	*from* × 10	
Nos. B2/5	—	

B 1

B 2

1898 (25 Nov). *Handstruck locally.* Imperf.
B1 **B 1** 20pa. bright violet . . . £425 £225

1898 (3 Dec). *Litho by M. Grundmann, Athens.* P 11½.
B2 **B 2** 10pa. blue . . . 8·00 19·00
a. Imperf (pair) . . . £250
B3 20pa. green . . . 14·00 17·00
a. Imperf (pair) . . . £250

1899. P 11½.
B4 **B 2** 10pa. brown . . . 8·50 26·00
a. Imperf (pair) . . . £250
B5 20pa. rose . . . 19·00 15·00
a. Imperf (pair) . . . £250

The British postal service closed at the end of 1899.

British P.O. in Siam

(Bangkok)

An overseas postal service for foreign residents was operated by the British Consulate at Bangkok from 1858. Mail was despatched by steamer to Singapore and from 1876 onwards was increasingly franked with Straits Settlements stamps. These were initially cancelled on arrival at Singapore, but later an oval postmark inscribed "BRITISH CONSULATE BANGKOK" was used. In 1883 a circular "BANGKOK" datestamp was introduced for use with Nos. 1/23. Both cancellations can also be found used on Hong Kong stamps between 1881 and 1885.

(Currency. 100 cents = 1 Straits dollar)

Stamps of Straits Settlements (see Malaysia) cancelled with oval postmark inscribed "BRITISH CONSULATE BANGKOK" *around Royal Arms.*

1882. Wmk Crown CC (Nos. 11/15, 33 and 35).
Z1 2c. brown . . . £375
Z2 4c. rose . . . £375
Z3 6c. dull lilac . . . £425
Z4 8c. orange-yellow . . . £375
Z5 10c.on 30c. claret (thin "0") (No. 33) . . . £1000
Z6 10c.on 30c. claret (thick "10") (No. 34) . . . £1000
Z7 10c.on 30c. claret (thin "1", thick "0") (No. 35) . . . £1100
Z8 12c. blue . . . £475

Subsequent Straits Settlements values to 8c. watermarked Crown CA are known used at Bangkok in 1883 and 1884. During this period the stamps overprinted "B" were on sale at the British Post Office.

PRICES FOR STAMPS ON COVER
The issues of the British Post Offices in Siam are worth from × 100 the prices quoted for used stamps when on cover.

B

(1)

1882 (May)–**85**. *Stamps of Straits Settlements optd with T* **1**.

(a) On No. 9 of 1867.
1 32c. on 2a. yellow (1885) . . . £35000

(b) On Nos. 11/13, 14a, 15/17 and 19 of 1867–72 and Nos. 48/9 of 1882. Wmk Crown CC.
2 2c. brown . . . £3000 £1500
3 4c. rose . . . £2500 £1300
a. Opt double . . . — £7500
4 5c. purple-brown . . . £300 £325
5 6c. lilac . . . £225 £120
6 8c. orange . . . £2000 £225
7 10c. slate . . . £375 £150
8 12c. blue . . . £950 £475
9 24c. green . . . £700 £150
10 30c. claret . . . £30000 £20000
11 96c. grey . . . £7500 £3000

(c) On Nos. 59/60 of April 1883.
12 2c. on 32c. pale red (*Wide* "S") . . . £2500 £2500
13 2c. on 32c. pale red (*Wide* "E") . . . £3000 £3000

(d) On Nos. 50/3 of 1882 and Nos. 63/7 of 1883–84. Wmk *Crown CA.*
14 2c. brown . . . £475 £350
15 2c. pale rose (1883) . . . 55·00 45·00
a. Opt inverted . . . — £9500
b. Opt double . . . £2750 £2750
c. Opt treble . . . £10000
16 4c. rose (1883) . . . £550 £325
17 4c. pale brown (1883) . . . 75·00 70·00
a. Opt double . . . £3500
b. Broken oval . . . £1100 £1100
18 5c. blue (1884) . . . £250 £170
19 6c. lilac (1884) . . . £180 £110
20 8c. orange (1883) . . . £160 65·00
a. Opt inverted . . . £17000 £10000
21 10c. slate (1883) . . . £160 85·00
22 12c. brown-purple (1883) . . . £275 £150
23 24c. yellow-green (1884?) . . . £4750 £2750

The prices quoted for the overprint double errors, Nos. 3a, 15b and 17a, are for stamps showing two clear impressions of the overprint. Examples showing partial doubling, on these and other values, are worth a small premium over the price quoted for normal stamps.

No. 17b shows the edge of the central oval broken above the "O" of "POSTAGE". It occurs on R. 10/5 of the lower right pane.

The use of these stamps ceased on 30 June 1885. Siam joined the Universal Postal Union on 1 July 1885.

British Postal Agencies in Eastern Arabia

Certain Arab States in Eastern Arabia, whilst remaining independent, had British postal administrations replacing Bahrain, and subsequently Indian, post offices at Dubai and Muscat.

Bahrain and Kuwait (from 1948) and Qatar (from 1957) used British stamps overprinted and surcharged in local currency. Abu Dhabi (from 1964) and Trucial States (from 1961 and used only in Dubai) had definitive issues made under the auspices of the British Agencies.

In addition, British stamps were surcharged with value only for use in Muscat and certain other states. They were formerly listed under Muscat as they were first put on sale there, but in view of their more extended use, the list has been transferred here, retaining the same numbering.

The stamps were used in Muscat from 1 April 1948 to 29 April 1966; in Dubai from 1 April 1948 to 6 January 1961; in Qatar: Doha from August 1950, Umm Said from February 1956, to 31 March 1957; and in Abu Dhabi from 30 March 1963 (Das Island from December 1960) to 29 March 1964.

Nos. 21/2 were placed on sale in Kuwait Post Offices in April and May 1951 and from February to November 1953 due to shortages of stamps with "KUWAIT" overprint. Isolated examples of other values can be found commercially used from Bahrain or Kuwait.

(Currency. 12 pies = 1 anna; 16 annas = 1 rupee)

Stamps of Great Britain surcharged

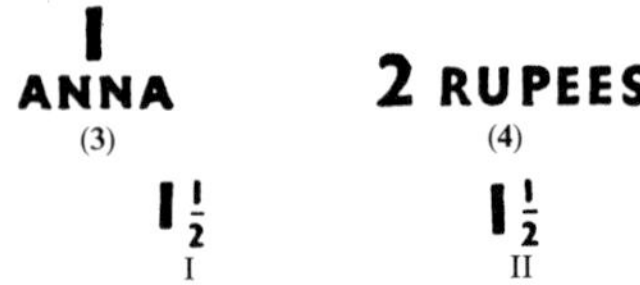

(3) (4)

1½ I 1½ II

Two types of 1½a. surcharge:

I. "1" 3¼ mm high and aligns with top of "2" in "½" (Rows 1 to 10).

II. "1" 3½ mm high with foot of figure below top of "2" (Rows 11 to 20).

1948 (1 Apr). *Surch with T* **3** *(½a. to 1r.) or* **4** *(2r.).*

No.	Type	Description	Unused	Used
16	**128**	½a.on ½d. pale green	2·75	7·00
17		1a.on 1d. pale scarlet	3·00	30
18		1½a.on 1½d. pale red-brown (I)	9·00	2·75
		a. Type II	9·00	2·75
		b. Vert pair. Nos. 18/a	50·00	
19		2a.on 2d. pale orange	2·00	3·25
20		2½a.on 2½d. light ultramarine	3·50	6·00
21		3a.on 3d. pale violet	3·50	10
22	**129**	6a.on 6d. purple	4·00	10
23	**130**	1r.on 1s. bistre-brown	4·50	50
24	**131**	2r.on 2s.6d. yellow-green	10·00	38·00
16/24 *Set of* 9			38·00	50·00

One example of No. 22 is known with the surcharge almost completely omitted from position R. 20/2 in the sheet.

(5) (6)

1948 (26 Apr). *Royal Silver Wedding. Nos. 493/4 surch with T* **5** *or* **6**.

No.	Type	Description	Unused	Used
25	**137**	2½a.on 2½d. ultramarine	2·00	2·75
26	**138**	15r.on £1 blue	23·00	35·00

1948 (29 July). *Olympic Games. Nos. 495/8 surch with new values in* "ANNAS" *or* "1 RUPEE", *as T* **5/6**, *but in one line on 2½a. (vert) or 6a. and 1r. (horiz) and grills obliterating former values of all except 2½a.*

No.	Type	Description	Unused	Used
27	**139**	2½a.on 2½d. ultramarine	35	2·50
28	**140**	3a.on 3d. violet	45	2·50
29	**141**	6a.on 6d. bright purple	45	2·75
30	**142**	1r.on 1s. brown	1·25	2·75
		a. Surch double	£900	
27/30 *Set of* 4			2·25	9·50

1949 (10 Oct). *75th Anniv of Universal Postal Union. Nos. 499/502 surch with new values in* "ANNAS" *or* "1 RUPEE" *as T* **3/4**, *but all in one line, with grills obliterating former values.*

No.	Type	Description	Unused	Used
31	**143**	2½a.on 2½d. ultramarine	50	3·00
32	**144**	3a.on 3d. violet	60	3·00
33	**145**	6a.on 6d. bright purple	60	2·75
34	**146**	1r.on 1s. brown	2·00	3·50
31/4 *Set of* 4			3·25	11·00

2 RUPEES (6a)   2 RUPEES (6b)

Type **6a**. "2" and "RUPEES" level and in line with lower of the two bars.

Type **6b**. "2" raised in relation to "RUPEES" and whole surcharge below the lower bar.

1950 (2 Oct)–**55**. *Nos. 503/8 surch as T* **3** *and No. 509 with T* **6a**.

No.	Type	Description	Unused	Used
35	**128**	½a.on ½d. pale orange (3.5.51)	70	9·00
36		1a.on 1d. light ultramarine (3.5.51)	30	7·50
37		1½a.on 1½d. pale green (I) (3.5.51)	9·00	24·00
		a. Type II	9·00	24·00
		b. Vert pair. Nos. 37/a	50·00	
38		2a.on 2d. pale red-brown (3.5.51)	30	8·50
39		2½a.on 2½d. pale scarlet (3.5.51)	30	16·00
40	**129**	4a.on 4d. light ultramarine	30	3·50
41	**147**	2r.on 2s.6d. yellow-green (3.5.51)	28·00	7·00
		a. Surch with Type *6b* (1955)	£170	65·00
35/41 *Set of* 7			35·00	65·00

British Solomon Islands

The first British Resident Commissioner, Charles Woodford, was appointed in 1896 and an administrative centre established at Tulagi.

Mail was initially sent unstamped by sealed bag to Sydney where New South Wales stamps were applied and cancelled. Later the Resident Commissioner kept a stock of New South Wales stamps which were still not cancelled until arrival at Sydney. From April 1906 Mr. Woodford used a vertical oblong "BRITISH SOLOMON ISLANDS PAID" handstamp in place of New South Wales stamps which were then added to many of the covers by the postal authorities in Sydney.

PRICES FOR STAMPS ON COVER TO 1945

Nos.	1/7	*from* × 12
Nos.	8/17	*from* × 25
Nos.	18/36	*from* × 6
Nos.	37/8	—
Nos.	39/51	*from* × 6
No.	52	—
Nos.	53/6	*from* × 2
Nos.	57/9	*from* × 6
Nos.	60/72	*from* × 2
Nos.	D1/8	*from* × 5

BRITISH PROTECTORATE

1

2

(Des C. M. Woodford. Litho W. E. Smith & Co. Sydney)

1907 (14 Feb). No wmk. P 11.

No.	Type	Description	Unused	Used
1	**1**	½d. ultramarine	9·00	14·00
2		1d. rose-carmine	23·00	25·00
3		2d. indigo	30·00	30·00
		a. Imperf between (horiz pair)	£12000	
4		2½d. orange-yellow	32·00	42·00
		a. Imperf between (vert pair)	£4750	
		b. Imperf between (horiz pair)	£6500	£4750
5		5d. emerald-green	55·00	65·00
6		6d. chocolate	50·00	60·00
		a. Imperf between (vert pair)	£4000	
7		1s. bright purple	70·00	75·00
1/7 *Set of* 7			£250	£275

Nos. 1/7 did not become valid for international postage until early September 1907. Overseas covers before that date show additional New South Wales values.

Three types exist of the ½d. and 2½d., and six each of the other values, differing in minor details.

Forgeries of Nos. 1/7 show different perforations and have the boat paddle touching the shore. Genuine stamps show a gap between the paddle and the shore.

(Recess D.L.R.)

1908 (1 Nov)–**11**. Wmk Mult Crown CA (sideways). P 14.

No.	Type	Description	Unused	Used
8	**2**	½d. green	1·50	1·00
9		1d. red	1·25	1·00
10		2d. greyish slate	1·25	1·00
11		2½d. ultramarine	3·75	2·00
11*a*		4d. red/*yellow* (6.3.11)	3·25	11·00
12		5d. olive	9·00	6·00
13		6d. claret	10·00	6·50
14		1s. black/*green*	8·50	6·00
15		2s. purple/*blue* (7.3.10)	40·00	55·00
16		2s.6d. red/*blue* (7.3.10)	48·00	70·00
17		5s. green/*yellow* (7.3.10)	75·00	£100
8/17 *Set of* 11			£180	£225
8s/17s Optd "Specimen" *Set of* 11			£250	

The ½d. and 1d. were issued in 1913 on rather thinner paper and with brownish gum.

3

4

(T **3** and **4**. Typo D.L.R.)

1913. *Inscribed* "POSTAGE POSTAGE". Wmk Mult Crown CA. P 14.

No.	Type	Description	Unused	Used
18	**3**	½d. green (1.4)	80	3·50
19		1d. red (1.4)	1·25	14·00
20		3d. purple/*yellow* (27.2)	80	4·00
		a. On orange-buff	8·00	24·00
21		11d. dull purple and scarlet (27.2)	3·00	12·00
18/21 *Set of* 4			5·25	30·00
18s/21s Optd "Specimen" *Set of* 4			70·00	

1914 (Mar)–**23**. *Inscribed* "POSTAGE REVENUE". *Chalk-surfaced paper (3d. to £1).* Wmk Mult Crown CA. P 14.

No.	Type	Description	Unused	Used
22	**4**	½d. green	80	12·00
23		½d. yellow-green (1917)	4·50	18·00
24		1d. carmine-red	1·50	1·25
25		1d. scarlet (1917)	4·75	6·50
26		2d. grey (7.14)	3·00	9·00
27		2½d. ultramarine (7.14)	2·00	5·00
28		3d. purple/*pale yellow* (3.23)	20·00	85·00
29		4d. black and red/*yellow* (7.14)	2·00	2·50
30		5d. dull purple and olive-green (7.14)	20·00	30·00
31		5d. brown-purple and olive-green (7.14)	20·00	30·00
32		6d. dull and bright purple (7.14)	6·00	14·00
33		1s. black/*green* (7.14)	4·75	7·0
		a. On blue-green, olive back (1923)	7·50	24·0
34		2s. purple and blue/*blue* (7.14)	7·00	10·0
35		2s.6d. black and red/*blue* (7.14)	9·50	20·0
36		5s. green and red/*yellow* (7.14)	30·00	48·0
		a. On orange-buff (1920)	48·00	70·0
37		10s. green and red/*green* (7.14)	80·00	70·0
38		£1 purple and black/*red* (7.14)	£225	£120
22/38 *Set of* 14			£350	£400
22s/38s Optd "Specimen" *Set of* 14			£400	

Variations in the coloured papers are mostly due to climate and do not indicate separate printings.

1922–31. *Chalk-surfaced paper (4d. and 5d. to 10s).* Wmk Mul Script CA. P 14.

No.	Type	Description	Unused	Used
39	**4**	½d. green (10.22)	30	3·5
40		1d. scarlet (4.23)	11·00	11·0
41		1d. dull violet (2.27)	1·00	7·5
42	**3**	1½d. bright scarlet (7.24)	2·25	6
43	**4**	2d. slate-grey (4.23)	4·50	15·0
44		3d. pale ultramarine (11.23)	70	4·5
45		4d. black and red/*yellow* (7.27)	3·50	23·0
45*a*		4½d. red-brown (1931)	3·00	20·0
46		5d. dull purple and olive-green (12.27)	3·00	27·0
47		6d. dull and bright purple (12.27)	3·75	27·0
48		1s. black/*emerald* (12.27)	2·75	12·0
49		2s. purple and blue/*blue* (2.27)	8·00	38·0
50		2s.6d. black and red/*blue* (12.27)	7·50	42·0
51		5s. green and red/*pale yellow* (12.27)	26·00	55·0
52		10s. green and red/*emerald* (1.25)	90·00	95·0
39/52 *Set of* 15			£150	£32
39s/52s Optd or Perf (4½d.) "Specimen" *Set of* 16			£325	

1935 (6 May). *Silver Jubilee. As Nos. 91/4 of Antigua.* P 13½ × 14.

No.	Description	Unused	Used
53	1½d. deep blue and carmine	1·00	1·0
	f. Diagonal line by turret	50·00	
	h. Dot by flagstaff	90·00	
54	3d. brown and deep blue	3·00	6·0
	f. Diagonal line by turret	90·00	£13
	h. Dot by flagstaff	£170	
55	6d. light blue and olive-green	9·00	12·0
	a. Frame printed double, one albino		
	b. Frame printed triple, two albino	£1200	
	h. Dot by flagstaff	£250	
	i. Dash by turret	£250	
56	1s. slate and purple	7·50	10·0
	a. Frame printed double, one albino	£1500	
	f. Diagonal line by turret	£180	
	h. Dot by flagstaff	£250	
	i. Dash by turret	£250	
53/6 *Set of* 4		18·00	26·0
53s/6s Perf "Specimen" *Set of* 4		95·00	

The second albino impression on No. 55b is sometimes almc co-incidental with the inked impression of the frame.

For illustrations of plate varieties see Omnibus section followir Zanzibar.

1937 (13 May). *Coronation. As Nos. 95/7 of Antigua.* P 11 × 11½.

No.	Description	Unused	Used
57	1d. violet	30	1·
58	1½d. carmine	30	
59	3d. blue	50	
57/9 *Set of* 3		1·00	1·
57s/9s Perf "Specimen" *Set of* 3		70·00	

5 Spears and Shield

6 Native Constable and Chief

7 Canoe House

8 Roviana Canoe

(Recess D.L.R. (2d., 3d., 2s. and 2s.6d.), Waterlow (others))

1939 (1 Feb)–**51**. *T* **5/8** *and similar designs.* Wmk Mult Script CA. P 13½ (2d., 3d., 2s. and 2s.6d.) or 12½ (others).

60	½d. blue and blue-green	15	1·00
61	1d. brown and deep violet	30	1·50
62	1½d. blue-green and carmine	70	1·25
63	2d. orange-brown and black	80	1·50
	a. Perf 12 (7.11.51)	30	1·50
64	2½d. magenta and sage-green	2·75	2·25
	a. Imperf horiz (vert pair)	£9500	
65	3d. black and ultramarine	1·25	1·50
	a. Perf 12 (29.11.51)	1·50	2·50
66	4½d. green and chocolate	4·00	13·00
67	6d. deep violet and reddish purple	75	1·00
68	1s. green and black	1·25	1·00
69	2s. black and orange	7·00	5·50
70	2s.6d. black and violet	28·00	4·50
71	5s. emerald-green and scarlet	32·00	11·00
72	10s. sage-green and magenta (27.4.42)	4·00	8·50
60/72	*Set of* 13	75·00	48·00
60s/72s	Perf "Specimen" *Set of* 13	£325	

Designs: *Horiz* (*as T* **8**)—1½d. Artificial Island, Malaita; 1s. Breadfruit; 5s. Malaita canoe. (As T **7**)—3d. Roviana canoes; 2s. Tinakula volcano; 2s.6d. Bismarck Scrub Fowl. *Vert* (*as T* **6**)—4½d., 10s. Native house, Reef Islands; 6d. Coconut plantation.

Examples of No. 64a from the first two rows of the only known sheet are perforated between stamp and top margin.

1946 (15 Oct). *Victory. As Nos. 110/11 of Antigua.*

73	1½d. carmine	15	1·00
74	3d. blue	15	10
73s/4s	Perf "Specimen" *Set of* 2	60·00	

Pocket handkerchief flaw (R. 1/6)

949 (14 Mar). *Royal Silver Wedding. As Nos. 112/13 of Antigua.*

75	2d. black	50	50
	a. Pocket handkerchief flaw	27·00	
76	10s. magenta	10·00	8·00

949 (10 Oct). *75th Anniv of U.P.U. As Nos. 114/17 of Antigua.*

77	2d. red-brown	50	1·00
78	3d. deep blue	2·25	1·50
79	5d. deep blue-green	50	1·75
80	1s. blue-black	50	1·50
77/80	*Set of* 4	3·25	5·25

POSTAGE DUE STAMPS

D 1

(Typo B.W.)

940 (1 Sept). Wmk Mult Script CA. P 12.

D1	D 1	1d. emerald-green	6·50	7·00
D2		2d. scarlet	7·00	7·00
D3		3d. brown	7·00	11·00
D4		4d. blue	11·00	11·00
D5		5d. grey-green	12·00	21·00
D6		6d. purple	12·00	15·00
D7		1s. violet	14·00	26·00
D8		1s.6d. turquoise-green	29·00	48·00
D1/8		*Set of* 8	85·00	£130
D1s/8s		Perf "Specimen" *Set of* 8	£150	

Brunei

Sultan Hashim Jalil-ul-alam Akamudin, 1885–1906

Currency. 100 cents = 1 Straits, later Malayan and Brunei, dollar)

For many years the status of the 1895 issue remained uncertain to such an extent that the 1906 provisionals on Labuan were taken to be the first issue of Brunei.

The 1895 "Star and Crescent" design stamps were, from their first appearance, considered bogus or, at best, as an issue made purely for philatelic purposes. Research into the background of the events surrounding the set led to the publication, in 1933, of the original agreement between Sultan Hashim and J. C. Robertson, dated 20 August 1894, which made clear that the stamps fulfilled a genuine postal purpose. Although Robertson and his partners intended to exploit the philatelic sales for their own benefit, the agreement testifies, as does other evidence, to the use of the stamps by the Sultan for his postal service. As Brunei did not, at that time, belong to any local or international postal union, the stamps were only valid within the state or on mail to Labuan or Sarawak. Items for further afield required franking with Labuan stamps in addition. Although most covers surviving are addressed to Robertson's associates, enough commercial covers and cards exist to show that there was, indeed, a postal service.

PRICES FOR STAMPS ON COVER TO 1945

Nos.	1/10 are rare used on cover.	
Nos.	11/22	*from* × 30
Nos.	23/33	*from* × 25
Nos.	34/50	*from* × 10
Nos.	51/9	*from* × 12
Nos.	60/78	*from* × 8

The Sarawak Government maintained a post office at the coal mining centre of Brooketon, and the stamps of SARAWAK were used there from 1893 until the office was handed over to Brunei in February 1907.

1 Star and Local Scene

(Litho in Glasgow)

1895 (22 July). P 13–13½.

1	**1**	½c. brown	3·25	20·00
2		1c. brown-lake	3·25	15·00
3		2c. black	4·00	15·00
4		3c. deep blue	3·75	14·00
5		5c. deep blue-green	6·50	16·00
6		8c. plum	6·50	28·00
7		10c. orange-red	8·00	28·00
		a. Imperf (pair)	£1400	
8		25c. turquoise-green	65·00	80·00
9		50c. yellow-green	18·00	95·00
10		$1 yellow-olive	20·00	£110
1/10		*Set of* 10	£120	£375

BRUNEI. BRUNEI.

BRUNEI. (2) TWO CENTS. (3) 25 CENTS. (4)

Line through "B" (R. 5/10)

(Optd by Govt Printer, Singapore)

1906 (1 Oct). *Nos. 117/26 of Labuan (see North Borneo), optd with T* **2**, *or surch as T* **3** *or* **4** *(25c.), in red.* P 13½ or 14 (1c.).

11	1c. black and purple	30·00	55·00
	a. Error. Opt in black	£1800	£2500
	b. Line through "B"	£400	
	c. Perf 13½–14, comp 12–13	£120	
12	2c.on 3c. black and sepia	2·75	10·00
	a. "BRUNEI" double	£3750	£2500
	b. "TWO CENTS" double	£6000	
	c. Line through "B"	£130	
13	2c.on 8c. black and vermilion	27·00	80·00
	a. "TWO CENTS" double	£9000	
	b. "TWO CENTS" omitted (in vert pair with normal)	£10000	
	c. Line through "B"	£375	
14	3c. black and sepia	29·00	85·00
	a. Line through "B"	£375	
15	4c.on 12c. black and yellow	4·00	5·00
	a. Line through "B"	£140	
16	5c.on 16c. green and brown	45·00	75·00
	a. Line through "B"	£425	
17	8c. black and vermilion	9·50	32·00
	a. Line through "B"	£225	
18	10c.on 16c. green and brown	6·50	22·00
	a. Line through "B"	£190	
19	25c.on 16c. green and brown	£100	£120
	a. Line through "B"	£800	
20	30c.on 16c. green and brown	£100	£120
	a. Line through "B"	£800	
21	50c.on 16c. green and brown	£100	£120
	a. Line through "B"	£800	
22	$1on 8c. black and vermilion	£100	£120
	a. Line through "B"	£800	
11/22	*Set of* 12	£475	£750

Only one sheet of the 1c. received the black overprint.

The surcharges were applied in settings of 50. Nos. 13a/b occur from one sheet on which the surcharge from the second impression of the setting was misplaced to give two surcharges on row five and none on row ten.

Examples of all values are known showing a forged Brunei postmark dated "13 JUL".

Sultan Mohamed Jemal-ul-Alam, 1906–1924

PRINTERS. All Brunei stamps from Nos. 23 to 113 were recess-printed by De La Rue.

5 View on Brunei River

1907 (26 Feb)–**10**. Wmk Mult Crown CA. P 14.

23	**5**	1c. grey-black and pale green	2·25	11·00
		x. Wmk reversed	15·00	
24		2c. grey-black and scarlet	2·50	4·50
		x. Wmk reversed	32·00	
25		3c. grey-black and chocolate	10·00	22·00
		x. Wmk reversed	35·00	
26		4c. grey-black and mauve	7·50	10·00
		a. Grey-black and reddish purple (1909)	70·00	60·00
		w. Wmk inverted		
		x. Wmk reversed	60·00	
27		5c. grey-black and blue	50·00	90·00
		x. Wmk reversed	90·00	
		y. Wmk inverted and reversed	£200	
28		8c. grey-black and orange	7·50	23·00
29		10c. grey-black and deep green	4·50	6·00
30		25c. pale blue and ochre-brown	32·00	48·00
31		30c. violet and black	23·00	22·00
32		50c. green and deep brown	15·00	22·00
33		$1 red and grey	60·00	90·00
23/33		*Set of* 11	£190	£300
23s/33s		Optd "Specimen" *Set of* 11	£275	

I

II

I	Double plate. Lowest line of shading on water is dotted.
II	Single plate. Dotted line of shading removed.

Stamps printed in two colours are as I.

1908 (12 June)–**22**. *Colours changed. Double or single plates.* Wmk Mult Crown CA. P 14.

34	**5**	1c. green (I)	80	2·25
35		1c. green (II) (1911)	60	2·00
		a. "A" missing from wmk	£200	
		b. "C" missing from wmk	£200	
36		2c. black and brown (5.4.11)	3·25	1·25
		w. Wmk inverted	65·00	
37		3c. scarlet (I)	4·00	1·25
		a. Substituted crown in wmk	£500	
38		3c. scarlet (II) (1916)	90·00	38·00
39		4c. claret (II) (17.4.12)	3·50	75
40		5c. black and orange (1916)	7·00	7·00
41		8c. blue and indigo-blue (10.08)	7·00	11·00
42		10c. purple/*yellow* (II) (11.12)	2·00	1·75
		a. On pale yellow (1922)	1·25	4·00
		as. Optd "Specimen"	48·00	
		w. Wmk inverted	£120	
		x. Wmk reversed	85·00	
		y. Wmk inverted and reversed	—	£275
43		25c. deep lilac (II) (30.5.12)	4·00	17·00
		a. Deep dull purple (1920)	12·00	17·00
44		30c. purple and orange-yellow (18.3.12)	9·00	12·00
45		50c. black/*green* (II) (1912)	27·00	65·00
		a. On blue-green (1920)	8·50	35·00
46		$1 black and red/*blue* (18.3.12)	21·00	48·00
47		$5 carmine/*green* (I) (1910)	£130	£200
48		$25 black/*red* (I) (1910)	£550	£950
34/47		*Set of* 12	£180	£300
34s/48s		Optd "Specimen" *Set of* 13	£550	

The used price for No. 48 is for a cancelled-by-favour example, dated before December 1941; there being no actual postal rate for which this value could be used. Examples dated after 1945 are worth much less.

For illustration of the substituted watermark crown see Catalogue Introduction.

Retouch Normal

MALAYA-
BORNEO
EXHIBITION,
1922.
(6)

RETOUCHES. We list the very distinctive 5c. Retouch (top left value tablet, R. 1/8), but there are others of interest, notably in the clouds.

1916. *Colours changed. Single plates.* Wmk Mult Crown CA. P 14.

No.	Type	Description	Unused	Used
49	5	5c. orange	16·00	18·00
		a. "5c." retouch	£450	£450
50		8c. ultramarine	6·00	25·00
49s/50s		Optd "Specimen" *Set of* 2	£110	

MALAYA-BORNEO EXHIBITION OVERPRINTS. These were produced from a setting of 30 examples, applied twice to overprint the complete sheet of 60 stamps. Three prominent overprint flaws exist, each occurring on all the stamps in two vertical rows of the sheet.

H I	**E X**	**N E**
Short "I" (all stamps in 2nd and 8th vertical rows)	Broken "E" (all stamps in 4th and 10th vertical rows)	Broken "N" (all stamps in 6th and 12th vertical rows)

(Optd by Govt Printer, Singapore)

1922 (31 Mar). *Optd with T* **6**, *in black.*

No.	Type	Description	Unused	Used
51	5	1c. green (II)	4·25	27·00
		a. Short "I"	7·00	42·00
		b. Broken "E"	7·00	42·00
		c. Broken "N"	7·00	42·00
52		2c. black and brown	4·50	32·00
		a. Short "I"	10·00	48·00
		b. Broken "E"	10·00	48·00
		c. Broken "N"	10·00	48·00
53		3c. scarlet (II)	6·00	42·00
		a. Short "I"	12·00	60·00
		b. Broken "E"	12·00	60·00
		c. Broken "N"	12·00	60·00
54		4c. claret (II)	9·00	50·00
		a. Short "I"	14·00	75·00
		b. Broken "E"	14·00	75·00
		c. Broken "N"	14·00	75·00
55		5c. orange (II)	13·00	55·00
		a. "5c." retouch (and short "I")	£375	£750
		b. Short "I"	19·00	85·00
		c. Broken "E"	19·00	85·00
		d. Broken "N"	19·00	85·00
56		10c. purple/*yellow* (II)	6·50	55·00
		a. Short "I"	14·00	85·00
		b. Broken "E"	14·00	85·00
		c. Broken "N"	14·00	85·00
57		25c. deep dull purple (II)	14·00	80·00
		a. Short "I"	30·00	£130
		b. Broken "E"	30·00	£130
		c. Broken "N"	30·00	£130
		x. Wmk reversed		
58		50c. black/*blue-green* (II)	45·00	£150
		a. Short "I"	80·00	£225
		b. Broken "E"	80·00	£225
		c. Broken "N"	80·00	£225
59		$1 black and red/*blue*	70·00	£190
		a. Short "I"	£120	£275
		b. Broken "E"	£120	£275
		c. Broken "N"	£120	£275
51/9		*Set of* 9	£150	£600

Examples of all values are known showing a forged Brunei postmark dated "13 JUL".

Sultan Ahmed Tajudin Akhazul Khairi Wadin, 1924–1950

7 Native houses, Water Village

1924 (Feb)–**37**. *Printed from single plates as Type* **II**, *except* 30c. *and* $1 *as Type* **I**. Wmk Mult Script CA. P 14.

No.	Type	Description	Unused	Used
60	5	1c. black (9.26)	1·00	75
		a. "A" of "CA" missing from wmk	£750	
61		2c. brown (3.24)	90	7·00
62		2c. green (3.33)	2·00	1·00
63		3c. green (3.24)	80	6·50
64		4c. maroon (3.24)	1·50	1·25
65		4c. orange (1929)	2·00	1·00
66		5c. orange-yellow* (3.24)	5·00	1·50
		a. "5c." retouch	£200	£130
67		5c. grey (1931)	15·00	12·00
		a. "5c." retouch	£475	£425
68		5c. chocolate (1933)	13·00	70
		a. "5c." retouch	£250	55·00
69	7	6c. intense black** (3.24)	14·00	10·00
		x. Wmk reversed		
70		6c. scarlet (1931)	3·75	11·00
71	5	8c. ultramarine (9.27)	6·00	5·00
72		8c. grey-black (1933)	13·00	75
73		10c. purple/*yellow* (3.37)	14·00	27·00
74	7	12c. blue	4·50	9·00
		a. Pale greenish blue (1927)	£130	£200
75	5	25c. slate-purple (1931)	8·00	13·00
76		30c. purple and orange-yellow (1931)	12·00	16·00
77		50c. black/*emerald* (1931)	8·00	15·00
78		$1 black and red/*blue* (1931)	24·00	75·00
60/78		*Set of* 19	£130	£190
60s/78s		(*ex* 10c.) Optd (Nos. 60/1, 63/4, 66, 69, 71, 74) or Perf "Specimen" *Set of* 18	£375	

*For 5 c, orange, see No. 82. No. 66 is a "Wet" printing and No. 82 a "Dry".

**For 6c. black, see No. 83. Apart from the difference in shade there is a variation in size, No. 69 being 37¾ mm long and No. 83 39 mm.

The 2c. orange and 3c. blue-green in Type **5**, and the 6c. greenish grey, 8c. red and 15c. ultramarine in Type **7** were not issued without the Japanese Occupation overprint, although unoverprinted examples exist. It is believed that these 1941 printings were produced and possibly perforated, by other firms in Great Britain following bomb damage to the De La Rue works at the end of 1940 (*Price for set of* 5, *£475 un*).

During the life of this issue De La Rue changed the method of production from a "Wet" to a "Dry" process. Initially the stamps were printed on ungummed paper which was dampened before being put on the press. Once the paper had dried, and contracted in the process, the gum was then applied. "Dry" printings, introduced around 1934, were on pre-gummed paper. The contraction of the "Wet" printings was considerable and usually involves a difference of between 0.5 mm and 1 mm when compared with the larger "Dry" printings. The following stamps occur from both "Wet" and "Dry" versions: 1c., 2c. green, 4c. orange, 5c. chocolate, 6c. scarlet, 8c. grey-black, 10c. and 25c.

Stamps of this issue can be found either line or comb perforated.

Brunei was occupied by the Japanese Army in January 1942 and remained under Japanese administration until liberated by the 9th Australian Division in June 1945.

After the cessation of hostilities with the Japanese postal services were re-introduced by the British Military Administration. Post offices under B.M.A. control were opened at Brunei Town and Kuala Belait on 17 December 1945 where B.M.A. overprints on the stamps of NORTH BORNEO and SARAWAK were used until the reappearance of Brunei issues on 2 January 1947.

Redrawn clouds (R. 1/1 of No. 80*ab* only)

1947 (2 Jan)–**51**. *Colours changed and new values.* Wmk Mult Script CA. P 14.

No.	Type	Description	Unused	Used
79	5	1c. chocolate	50	2·00
		a. "A" of "CA" missing from wmk	£1100	
80		2c. grey	60	4·25
		a. Perf 14½ × 13½ (25.9.50)	2·00	4·50
		ab. Black (27.6.51)	2·00	6·50
		ac. Redrawn clouds	65·00	
81	7	3c. green	1·00	5·50
82	5	5c. orange*	80	1·25
		a. "5c." retouch	55·00	75·00
		b. Perf 14½ × 13½ (25.9.50)	4·00	13·00
		c. Ditto "5c." retouch	£120	£190
83	7	6c. black*	1·00	4·25
84	5	8c. scarlet	40	1·00
		a. Perf 13 (25.1.51)	55	8·50
85		10c. violet	70	30
		a. Perf 14½ × 13½ (25.9.50)	2·00	5·50
86		15c. ultramarine	1·50	70
87		25c. deep claret	2·25	1·00
		a. Perf 14½ × 13½ (25.1.51)	1·75	8·00
88		30c. black and orange	1·75	1·00
		a. Perf 14½ × 13½ (25.1.51)	1·75	11·00
89		50c. black	3·25	80
		a. Perf 13 (25.9.50)	1·75	15·00
90		$1 black and scarlet	8·00	75
91		$5 green and red-orange (2.2.48)	16·00	17·00
92		$10 black and purple (2.2.48)	65·00	30·00
79/92		*Set of* 14	90·00	60·00
79s/92s		Perf "Specimen" *Set of* 14	£225	

*See also Nos. 66 and 69.

The 1, 2, 3, 5, 6, 10 and 25c. values utilised the plates of the pre-war issue and were line perforated until the introduction of the 14½ × 13½ comb machine for some values in 1950–51. The 8, 15, 50c., $1, $5 and $10 were from new plates with the sheets comb perforated. The 30c. was initially a pre-war plate, but it is believed that a new plate was introduced in 1951.

8 Sultan Ahmed Tajudin and Water Village

1949 (22 Sept). *Sultan's Silver Jubilee.* Wmk Mult Script CA. P 13.

No.	Type	Description	Unused	Used
93	8	8c. black and carmine	85	1·25
94		25c. urple and red-orange	85	1·60
95		50c. black and blue	85	1·60
93/5		*Set of* 3	2·25	4·00

1949 (10 Oct). *75th Anniv of Universal Postal Union. As Nos. 114/17 of Antigua.*

No.	Type	Description	Unused	Used
96		8c. carmine	1·00	1·25
97		15c. deep blue	3·50	1·50
98		25c. magenta	1·00	1·50
99		50c. blue-black	1·00	1·25
96/9		*Set of* 4	6·00	5·00

JAPANESE OCCUPATION OF BRUNEI

Japanese forces landed in Northern Borneo on 15 December 1941 and the whole of Brunei had been occupied by 6 January 1942.

Brunei, North Borneo, Sarawak and, after a short period, Labuan, were administered as a single territory by the Japanese. Until September-October 1942, previous stamp issues, without overprint, continued to be used in conjunction with existing postmarks. From the Autumn of 1942 onwards unoverprinted stamps of Japan were made available and examples can be found used from the area for much of the remainder of the War. Japanese Occupation issues for Brunei, North Borneo and Sarawak were equally valid throughout the combined territory but not, in practice, equally available.

PRICES FOR STAMPS ON COVER	
Nos. J1/16	*from* × 8
Nos. J17/20	—

(**1**) ("Imperial Japanese Government")

(**2**) ("Imperial Japanese Postal Service $3")

1942 (Oct)–**44**. *Stamps of Brunei handstamped with T* **1** *in violet to blue.* Wmk Mult Script CA (except Nos. J18/19, Mult Crown CA). P 14.

No.	Type	Description	Unused	Used
J 1	5	1c. black	7·00	23·00
		a. Red opt	70·00	90·00
J 2		2c. green	50·00	£110
J 3		2c. orange (1943)	4·00	9·00
J 4		3c. blue-green	28·00	75·00
		a. Opt omitted (in pair with normal)	£1900	
J 5		4c. orange	3·00	13·00
J 6		5c. chocolate	3·00	13·00
		a. "5c." retouch	£150	£375
J 7	7	6c. greenish grey (P 14 × 11½) (1944)	40·00	£225
J 8		6c. scarlet	£550	£550
J 9	5	8c. grey-black	£650	£850
J10	7	8c. red	4·50	12·00
		a. Opt omitted (in pair with normal)	£1500	
J11	5	10c. purple/*yellow*	8·50	26·00
J12	7	12c. blue	26·00	26·00
		a. Red opt	£200	£300
J13		15c. ultramarine (1944)	15·00	26·00
J14	5	25c. slate-purple	25·00	50·00
		a. Red opt	£325	£400
J15		30c. purple and orange-yellow	95·00	£18[illegible]
J16		50c. black/*emerald*	38·00	60·00
		a. Red opt	£350	
J17		$1 black and red/*blue* (1944)	55·00	70·00
		a. Red opt	—	£750
J18		$5 carmine/*green* (1944)	£850	£1900
J19		$25 black/*red* (1944)	£900	£1900

The overprint varies in shade from violet to blue, and being handstamped, exists inverted, double, double one inverted and treble.

Nos. J3, J4, J7, J10 and J13 were not issued without the overprint (See footnote below Brunei No. 78).

1944 (11 May). *No.* J1 *surch with T* **2** *in orange-red.*

No.	Type	Description	Unused	Used
J20	5	$3on 1c. black	£6000	£550[illegible]
		a. Surch on No. 60 of Brunei	£7500	

Three separate handstamps were used to apply Type **2**, one for the top line, one for the bottom and the third for the two central characters.

Burma

(Currency. 12 pies = 1 anna; 16 annas = 1 rupee)

Stamps of India were used in Burma from 1854 and, after 185[illegible] individual examples can be identified by the use of the concentr[illegible] octagonal postmarks of the Bengal Postal Circle of which th[illegible] following were supplied to Burmese post offices:

Type A No. B 156 (Rangoon)

Type B No. B5 (Akyab)

B5	Akyab	B146	Pegu
B12*	Bassein	B150	Prome
B22	Nga Thine Khyoung	B156*	Rangoon
B56	Amherst	B159	Sandoway
B108	Kyouk Phyoo	B165	Sarawah (*to* 1860)
B111	Meeaday	B165	Henzada (*from* 1861)
B112	Mengyee	B171	Shoay Gyeen
B127	Moulmein	B173	Sittang
B128	Mergui	B179	Thayetmyo
B129	Tavoy	B181	Toungoo
B133	Myanoung	B227	Port Blair
B136	Namayan		

*Exists in black or blue. Remainder in black only.

Akyab, Moulmein and Rangoon used postmarks as both Type A and Type B, Port Blair as Type B only and the remainder as Type A only.

From 1860 various types of duplex cancellations were introduced and Burmese examples can be identified when sufficient of the left-hand portion is visible on the stamp. Such marks were issued for the following offices:

Akyab	Rangoon
Bassein	Rangoon C.R.H. (Cantonment Receiving House)
Mandalay	Thayetmyo
Moulmein	Toungoo
Port Blair	
Prome	

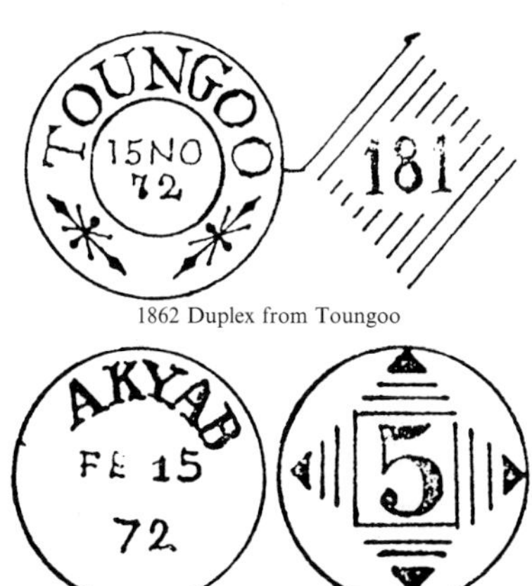

1862 Duplex from Toungoo

1865 Duplex from Akyab

During 1875, a further series of duplex marks was introduced in which the right-hand portion of the cancellation included the office code number, prefixed by the letter "R" for Rangoon:

R–1	Rangoon	R–9	Myanoung
R–1/1	Rangoon Cantonment	R–10	Port Blair
R–2	Akyab	1/R–10	Nancowry
R–3	Bassein	R–11	Prome
R–4	Henzada	R–12	Sandoway
R–5	Kyouk Phyoo	R–13	Shwegyeen
R–6	Mandalay	R–14	Tavoy
R–7	Mergui	R–15	Thayetmyo
R–8	Moulmein	R–16	Tounghoo
1/R–8	Amherst		

1875 type from Rangoon

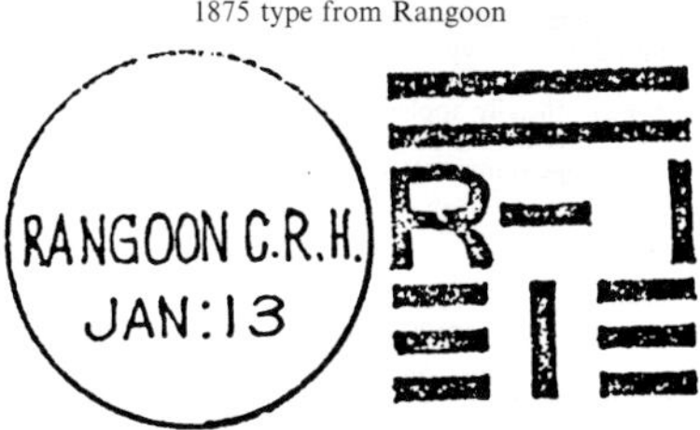

1875 type from Rangoon Cantonment Receiving House

From 1886 the whole of Burma was united under the Crown and the post offices were supplied with circular date stamps giving the name of the town.

Most Indian stamps, both postage and official, issued during the period were supplied to post offices in Burma. None of the imperforates printed by De La Rue have been seen however, and from the later issues the following have not been recorded with Burma postmarks:

Nos. 39a, 66a, 68, 85a, 92a, 110a/b, 148a, 155a, 165, 192a/c, 195a/b, O15, O38, O40b, O50a/b, O76a, O101a, O102, O103/a, O104/5 and O142.

The value of most India stamps used in Burma coincides proportionately with the used prices quoted for India, but some, especially the provisional surcharges, are extremely rare with Burmese postmarks. Stamps of the face value of 2 r. and above from the reigns of Victoria and Edward VII are more common with telegraph cancellations than with those of the postal service.

PRICES FOR STAMPS ON COVER TO 1945		
Nos.	1/18	*from* × 6
Nos.	18*a*/33	*from* × 4
No.	34	*from* × 5
Nos.	35/50	*from* × 8
Nos.	O1/27	*from* × 15

BRITISH ADMINISTRATION

From 1 January 1886 Burma was a province of the Indian Empire but was separated from India and came under direct British administration on 1 April 1937.

BURMA (1) **BURMA** (1a)

1937 (1 Apr). *Stamps of India. (King George V inscr "*INDIA POSTAGE*") optd with T* **1** *or* **1a** *(rupee values).* W **69**. P 14.

No.		Description	Unused	Used
1		3p. slate	60	10
		w. Wmk inverted	1·75	60
2		½a. green	1·00	10
		w. Wmk inverted	2·00	60
3		9p. deep green (*typo*)	1·00	10
		w. Wmk inverted	1·75	60
4		1a. chocolate	1·00	10
		w. Wmk inverted	1·75	60
5		2a. vermilion (*small die*)	75	10
6		2½a. orange	60	10
		w. Wmk inverted	1·75	60
7		3a. carmine	1·00	30
		w. Wmk inverted	3·50	1·25
8		3½a. deep blue	2·00	10
		aw. Wmk inverted	2·75	30
		b. Dull blue	8·50	6·00
		bw. Wmk inverted	6·00	4·00
9		4a. sage-green	1·00	10
		w. Wmk inverted	—	35·00
10		6a. bistre	75	35
		w. Wmk inverted	—	35·00
11		8a. reddish purple	1·50	10
12		12a. claret	4·25	1·25
		w. Wmk inverted	11·00	2·00
13		1r. chocolate and green	24·00	3·00
14		2r. carmine and orange	28·00	11·00
		w. Wmk inverted	40·00	14·00
15		5r. ultramarine and purple	38·00	18·00
16		10r. green and scarlet	90·00	60·00
		w. Wmk inverted	†	—
17		15r. blue and olive (wmk inverted)	£325	£120
18		25r. orange and blue	£650	£300
		w. Wmk inverted	£650	£300
1/18		*Set of* 18	£1000	£450

The opt is at top on all values except the 3a.

The 1a. has been seen used from Yenangyaung on 22 Mar 1937.

2 King George VI and "Chinthes"

3 King George VI and "Nagas"

4 *Karaweik* (royal barge)

8 King George VI and Peacock

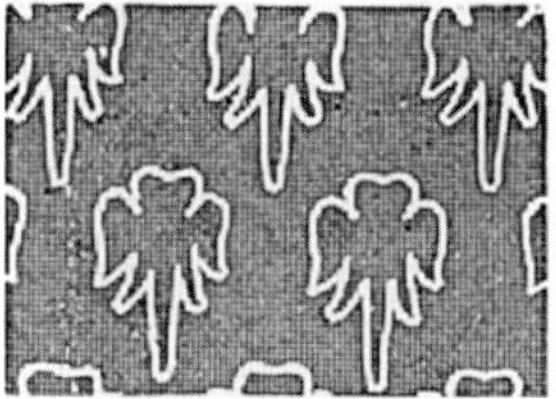

10 Elephants' Heads

Extra trees flaw (R. 11/8)

(Des Maung Kyi (2a.6p.), Maung Hline (3a.), Maung Ohn Pe (3a.6p.) and N. K. D. Naigamwalla (8a.). Litho Security Ptg Press, Nasik)

1938 (15 Nov)–**40**. *T* **2/4**, **8** *and similar designs.* W **10**. P 14 (vert) or 13½ × 13 (horiz).

No.	Type	Description	Unused	Used
18*a*	2	1p. red-orange (1.8.40)	3·00	1·00
19		3p. bright violet	20	1·00
20		6p. bright blue	20	10
21		9p. yellow-green	1·00	1·00
22	3	1a. purple-brown	20	10
23		1½a. turquoise-green	20	1·25
24		2a. carmine	45	10
25	4	2a.6p. claret	14·00	1·50
26	–	3a. dull violet	14·00	2·25
27	–	3a.6p. light blue and blue	1·25	4·50
		a. Extra trees flaw	55·00	
28	3	4a. greenish blue	60	10
29	–	8a. myrtle-green	5·00	30
30	8	1r. purple and blue	5·00	20
31		2r. brown and purple	16·00	1·75
32	–	5r. violet and scarlet	48·00	25·00
33	–	10r. brown and myrtle	55·00	50·00
18*a*/33		*Set of* 16	£150	80·00

Designs: *Horiz* (*as* T **4**)—3a. Burma teak; 3a.6p. Burma rice; 8a. River Irrawaddy. *Vert* (*as* T **8**)—5r., 10r. King George VI and "Nats".

The 1a. exists lithographed or typographed, the latter having a "Jubilee" line in the sheet margin.

COMMEMORATION
POSTAGE STAMP
6th MAY 1840

(11)

1940 (6 May). *Centenary of First Adhesive Postage Stamps. No. 25 surch with T* **11**.

No.	Type	Description	Unused	Used
34	4	1a. on 2a.6p. claret	4·00	2·00

For stamps issued in 1942–45 see under Japanese Occupation.

CHIN HILLS DISTRICT. This area, in the far north-west of the country, remained in British hands when the Japanese overran Burma in May 1942.

During the period July to December 1942 the local officials were authorised to produce provisional stamps and the letters "OHMS" are known overprinted by typewriter on Nos. 3, 20, 22/4, 28/9 and 31 of Burma or handstamped, in violet, on Nos. 25, 27 and 29. The two types can also occur together or in combination with a handstamped "SERVICE".

From early in 1943 ordinary postage stamps of India were used from the Chin Hills post offices of Falam, Haka, Fort White and Tiddim, this expedient continuing until the fall of Falam to the Japanese on 7 November 1943.

The provisional stamps should only be collected on Official cover where dates and the sender's handwriting can be authenticated.

BRITISH MILITARY ADMINISTRATION

Preparations for the liberation of Burma commenced in February 1943 when the Civil Affairs Service (Burma) (CAS(B)) was set up at Delhi as part of the proposed military administration structure. One of the specific tasks assigned to CAS(B) was the operation of a postal service for the civilian population.

Operations against the Japanese intensified during the second half of 1944. The port of Akyab in the Arakan was reoccupied in January 1945. The 14th Army took Mandalay on 29 March and Rangoon was liberated from the sea on 3 May.

Postal services for the civilian population started in Akyab on 13 April 1945, while post offices in the Magwe Division around Meiktila were operating from 4 March. Mandalay post offices opened on 8 June and those in Rangoon on 16 June, but the full network was only completed in December 1945, just before the military administration was wound up.

MILY ADMN (12) **MILY ADMN** (13)

1945 (from 11 Apr). *Nos. 18a to 33 optd with T* **12** *(small stamps) or* **13** *(others) by Security Printing Press, Nasik.*

No.	Type	Description	Unused	Used
35	2	1p. red-orange	10	10
		a. Opt omitted (in pair with normal)	£1600	
36		3p. bright violet	10	75
37		6p. bright blue	10	30
38		9p. yellow-green	30	75
39	3	1a. purple-brown (16.6)	10	10
40		1½a. turquoise-green (16.6)	10	15
41		2a. carmine	10	15
42	4	2a.6p. claret	2·00	1·00
43	–	3a. dull violet	1·50	20
44	–	3a.6p. light blue and blue	10	70
		a. Extra trees flaw	26·00	
45	3	4a. greenish blue	10	60
46	–	8a. myrtle-green	10	70
47	8	1r. purple and blue	40	50
48		2r. brown and purple	40	1·25
49	–	5r. violet and scarlet	40	1·25
50	–	10r. brown and myrtle	40	1·25
35/50		*Set of* 16	4·75	8·50

Only the typographed version of the 1a., No. 22, received this overprint.

The missing overprints on the 1p. occur on the stamps from the bottom row of one sheet. A further block with two examples of the variety caused by a paper fold also exists.

The exact dates of issue for Nos. 35/50 are difficult to establish.

The initial stock of overprints is known to have reached CAS(B) headquarters, Imphal, at the beginning of April 1945. Postal directives issued on 11 April refer to the use of the overprints in Akyab and in the Magwe Division where surcharged pre-war postal stationery envelopes had previously been in use. The 6p., 1a., 1½a. and 2a.values were placed on sale at Mandalay on 8 June and the 1a. and 2a. at Rangoon on 16 June. It has been suggested that only a limited service was initially available in Rangoon. All values were on sale by 9 August 1945.

BRITISH CIVIL ADMINISTRATION

1946 (1 Jan). *As Nos. 19/33, but colours changed.*

No.	Type	Description	Unused	Used
51	2	3p. brown	10	2·00
52		6p. deep violet	10	30
53		9p. green	15	2·50
54	3	1a. blue	15	20
55		1½a. orange	15	10
56		2a. claret	15	40
57	4	2a.6p. greenish blue	2·75	4·00
57*a*	–	3a. blue-violet	6·50	4·00
57*b*	–	3a.6p. black and ultramarine	50	2·00
		ba. Extra trees flaw	55·00	
58	3	4a. purple	50	30
59	–	8a. maroon	1·75	3·00
60	8	1r. violet and maroon	1·25	1·00
61		2r. brown and orange	6·00	3·75
62	–	5r. green and brown	6·00	17·00
63		10r. claret and violet	8·50	21·00
51/63		*Set of* 15	30·00	55·00

No. 54 was printed in typography only.

14 Burman

(Des A. G. I. McGeogh. Litho Nasik)

1946 (2 May). *Victory. T* **14** *and similar vert designs.* W **10** (sideways). P 13.

64	9p. turquoise-green	20	20
65	1½a. violet	20	10
66	2a. carmine	20	10
67	3a.6p. ultramarine	50	20
64/7 *Set of* 4		1·00	50

Designs:—1½a. Burmese woman; 2a. Chinthe; 3a.6p. Elephant.

INTERIM BURMESE GOVERNMENT

ကြားဖြတ် အစိုးရ။ — ားဖြတ်ကြ အစိုးရ။ — တ်ကြားဖြ အစိုးရ။

(**18** *Trans.* "Interim Government") **18***a* **18***b*

Type **18***a* shows the first character transposed to the end of the top line (R. 6/15).

Type **18***b* shows the last two characters transposed to the front of the top line (R. 14/14).

Some sheets of the 3p. show both errors corrected by a handstamp as Type **18**.

1947 (1 Oct). *Stamps of 1946 optd with T* **18** *(small stamps) or larger opt (others).*

68	**2**	3p. brown	70	70
		a. Opt Type **18***a*	42·00	
		ab. Corrected by handstamp as Type **18**		
		b. Opt Type **18***b*	42·00	
		ba. Corrected by handstamp as Type **18**		
69		6p. deep violet	10	30
		a. Opt Type **18***a*	23·00	
70		9p. green	10	30
		a. Opt inverted	21·00	25·00
71	**3**	1a. blue	10	30
		a. Vert pair, one with opt omitted		
72		1½a. orange	1·00	10
73		2a. claret	30	15
		a. Horiz pair, one with opt omitted		
		b. Opt Type **18***a*	35·00	
74	**4**	2a.6p. greenish blue	1·75	1·00
75	–	3a. blue-violet	2·50	1·75
76	–	3a.6p. black and ultramarine	50	2·00
		a. Extra trees flaw	50·00	
77	**3**	4a. purple	1·75	30
78	–	8a. maroon	1·75	1·75
79	**8**	1r. violet and maroon	4·50	1·00
80		2r. brown and orange	4·50	4·00
81	–	5r. green and brown	4·50	4·50
82	–	10r. claret and violet	3·25	4·50
68/82 *Set of* 15			24·00	20·00

The 3p., 6p., 2a., 2a.6p., 3a.6p. and 1r. are also known with overprint inverted.

OFFICIAL STAMPS

BURMA SERVICE (O 1)

BURMA SERVICE (O 1a)

1937 (Apr–June). *Stamps of India. (King George V inscr* "INDIA POSTAGE"*) optd with Type* O **1** *or* O **1a** *(rupee values).* W **69**. P 14.

O 1	3p. slate	2·00	10
	w. Wmk inverted	—	17·00
O 2	½a. green	9·00	10
	w. Wmk inverted	†	—
O 3	9p. deep green	5·00	30
O 4	1a. chocolate	5·00	10
O 5	2a. vermilion (*small die*)	9·50	35
	w. Wmk inverted	—	17·00
O 6	2½a. orange	5·00	2·00
O 7	4a. sage-green	5·00	10
O 8	6a. bistre	4·25	8·00
O 9	8a. reddish purple (1.4.37)	4·00	1·00
O10	12a. claret (1.4.37)	4·00	6·00
O11	1r. chocolate and green (1.4.37)	15·00	4·25
O12	2r. carmine and orange	35·00	40·00
	w. Wmk inverted	40·00	45·00
O13	5r. ultramarine and purple	95·00	50·00
O14	10r. green and scarlet	£275	£130
O1/14 *Set of* 14		£425	£225

For the above issue the stamps were either overprinted "BURMA" and "SERVICE" at one operation or had the two words applied separately. Research has yet to establish if all values exist with both forms of overprinting.

SERVICE (O 2)

SERVICE (O 3)

1939. *Nos. 19/24 and 28 optd with Type* O **2** *(typo) and Nos. 25 and 29/33 optd with Type* O **3** *(litho).*

O15	**2**	3p. bright violet	15	20
O16		6p. bright blue	15	20
O17		9p. yellow-green	4·00	3·75
O18	**3**	1a. purple-brown	15	15
O19		1½a. turquoise-green	3·50	1·75
O20		2a. carmine	1·25	20
O21	**4**	2a.6p. claret	16·00	14·00
O22	**3**	4a. greenish blue	4·50	50
O23	—	8a. myrtle-green	15·00	4·00
O24	**8**	1r. purple and blue	16·00	5·50
O25		2r. brown and purple	30·00	15·00
O26	—	5r. violet and scarlet	25·00	29·00
O27	—	10r. brown and myrtle	£130	38·00
O15/27 *Set of* 13			£225	£100

Both versions of the 1a. value exist with this overprint.

1946. *British Civil Administration. Nos. 51/6 and 58 optd with Type* O **2** *(typo) and Nos. 57 and 59/63 optd with Type* O **3** *(litho).*

O28	**2**	3p. brown	2·00	3·50
O29		6p. deep violet	2·00	2·25
O30		9p. green	50	3·25
O31	**3**	1a. blue	20	2·00
O32		1½a. orange	20	20
O33		2a. claret	20	2·00
O34	**4**	2a.6p. greenish blue	1·75	6·50
O35	**3**	4a. purple	20	70
O36	–	8a. maroon	3·25	3·50
O37	**8**	1r. violet and maroon	60	4·25
O38		2r. brown and orange	7·50	45·00
O39	–	5r. green and brown	9·00	50·00
O40	–	10r. claret and violet	17·00	60·00
O28/40 *Set of* 13			40·00	£160

1947. *Interim Burmese Government. Nos. O28/40 optd with T* **18** *(small stamps) or larger opt (others).*

O41	**2**	3p. brown	30	40
O42		6p. deep violet	2·00	10
O43		9p. green	3·00	90
O44	**3**	1a. blue	3·00	80
O45		1½a. orange	6·00	30
O46		2a. claret	3·25	15
O47	**4**	2a.6p. greenish blue	27·00	12·00
O48	**3**	4a. purple	13·00	40
O49	–	8a. maroon	12·00	4·00
O50	**8**	1r. violet and maroon	14·00	2·25
O51		2r. brown and orange	14·00	20·00
O52	–	5r. green and brown	14·00	20·00
O53	–	10r. claret and violet	14·00	30·00
O41/53 *Set of* 13			£110	80·00

Later stamp issues will be found listed in Part 21 (*South-East Asia*) of this catalogue.

JAPANESE OCCUPATION OF BURMA

PRICES FOR STAMPS ON COVER

Nos.	J1/44	—
Nos.	J45/6	*from* × 6
Nos.	J47/56	*from* × 8
No.	J56*g*	—
Nos.	J57/72	*from* × 6
Nos.	J73/5	*from* × 25
No.	J76	*from* × 8
No.	J77	*from* × 20
Nos.	J78/81	*from* × 25
Nos.	J82/4	*from* × 10
Nos.	J85/7	*from* × 40
No.	J88	*from* × 12
Nos.	J89/97	*from* × 30
Nos.	J98/104	*from* × 50
Nos.	J105/111	*from* × 30

BURMA INDEPENDENCE ARMY ADMINISTRATION

The Burma Independence Army, formed by Aung San in 1941, took control of the Delta area of the Irrawaddy in May 1942. They reopened a postal service in the area and were authorised by the Japanese to overprint local stocks of stamps with the Burmese emblem of a peacock.

Postage and Official stamps with the peacock overprints or handstamps were used for ordinary postal purposes with the probable exception of No. J44.

DISTINGUISHING FEATURES. Type **1**. Body and head of Peacock always clearly outlined by broad uncoloured band. There are four slightly different sub-types of overprint Type **1**.

Type **2**. Peacock with slender neck and more delicately detailed tail. Clear spur on leg at right. Heavy fist-shaped blob of ink below and parallel to beak and neck.

Type **4**. No basic curve. Each feather separately outlined. Straight, short legs.

Type **5**. Much fine detail in wings and tail in clearly printed overprints. Thin, long legs ending in claws which, with the basic arc, enclose clear white spaces in well printed copies. Blob of colour below beak shows shaded detail and never has the heavy fist-like appearance of this portion in Type **2**.

Two sub-types may be distinguished in Type **5**, the basic arc of one having a chord of 14–15 mm and the other 12½–13 mm.

Type **6**. Similar to Type **5**, but with arc deeply curved and reaching nearly to the top of the wings. Single diagonal line parallel to neck below beak.

Collectors are warned against forgeries of these overprints, often in the wrong colours or on the wrong values.

(1)

(2)

(3)

1942 (May). *Stamps of Burma overprinted with the national device o[f] a Peacock.*

I. Overprinted at Myaungmya.

A. With Type **1** *in black.*

On Postage Stamps of King George V.

J 1		9p. deep green (No. 3)	£110	
J 2		3½a. deep blue (No. 8)	55·00	

On Official Stamp of King George V.

J 3		6a. bistre (No. O8)	75·00	

On Postage Stamps of King George VI.

J 4	**2**	9p. yellow-green	£150	
J 5	**3**	1a. purple-brown	£550	
J 6		4a. greenish blue (opt black on red)	£160	
		a. Triple opt, black on double red	£425	

On Official Stamps of King George VI.

J 7	**2**	3p. bright violet	26·00	85·0
J 8		6p. bright blue	18·00	60·0
J 9	**3**	1a. purple-brown	18·00	50·0
J 9*a*		1½a. turquoise-green	£650	
J10		2a. carmine	24·00	95·0
J11		4a. greenish blue	24·00	75·0

The overprint on No. J6 was apparently first done in red in erro[r] and then corrected in black. Some stamps have the black overprin[t] so accurately superimposed that the red hardly shows. These ar[e] rare.

Nos. J5 and J9 exist with the Peacock overprint on both th[e] typographed and the litho printings of the original stamps.

B. With Types **2** *or* **3** *(rupee values), in black.*

On Postage Stamps of King George VI.

J12	**2**	3p. bright violet	18·00	70·0
J13		6p. bright blue	50·00	£10
J14		9p. yellow-green	21·00	65·0
J15	**3**	1a. purple-brown	14·00	60·0
J16		2a. carmine	21·00	80·0
J17		4a. greenish blue	40·00	£10
		a. Opt double		
		b. Opt inverted	£650	
		c. Opt double, one inverted	£425	
		d. Opt double, both inverted	£650	
J18		1r. purple and blue	£275	
J19		2r. brown and purple	£160	

The Myaungmya overprints (including No. J44) are usuall[y] clearly printed.

(4)

(5)

(6)

Type **5** generally shows the details of the peacock much le[ss] clearly and, due to heavy inking, or careless impression, sometim[es] appears as almost solid colour.

Type **6** was officially applied only to postal stationery. Howeve[r] the handstamp remained in the possession of a postal official wh[o] used it on postage stamps after the war. These stamps are no long[er] listed.

II. Handstamped (at Pyapon?) with T **4**, *in black (so-call[ed] experimental type).*

On Postage Stamps of King George VI.

J19*a*	**2**	6p. bright blue	85·00	
J19*b*	**3**	1a. purple-brown	£100	£2
J20		2a. carmine	£130	£3
J21		4a. greenish blue	£700	£7

Unused specimens of Nos. J20/1 are usually in poor condition.

III. Overprinted at Henzada with T **5** *in blue, or blue-black.*

On Postage Stamps of King George V.

J22		3p. slate (No. 1)	3·50	20·
		a. Opt double	10·00	50·
J23		9p. deep green (No. 3)	24·00	65·
		a. Opt double	80·00	
J24		2a. vermilion (No. 5)	£100	£1

On Postage Stamps of King George VI.

J25	**2**	1p. red-orange	£200	£3
J26		3p. bright violet	38·00	75·
J27		6p. bright blue	25·00	50·
		a. Opt double	£100	£1
		b. Clear opt, on back and front	£275	
J28		9p. yellow-green	£850	
J29	**3**	1a. purple-brown	9·00	40·
		a. Opt inverted	£700	
J30		1½a. turquoise-green	21·00	65·
		a. Opt omitted (in pair with normal)	£1900	
J31		2a. carmine	21·00	65·
		a. Opt double	£700	
J32		4a. greenish blue	42·00	95·
		a. Opt double	£250	
		b. Opt inverted	£1200	

On Official Stamps of King George VI.

J33	**2**	3p. bright violet	£130	£2
J34		6p. bright blue	£140	£2
J35	**3**	1½a. turquoise-green	£170	£3
J35*a*		2a. carmine	£350	£4
J36		4a. greenish blue	£1000	

(6a) ("Yon Thon" = "Office use")

V. Official Stamp of King George VI optd at Myaungmya with Type **6a** *in black.*

J44 7 8a. myrtle-green . . . . 90·00

No. J44 was probably for official use.

There are two types of T **6a**, one with base of peacock 8 mm long and the other with base about 5 mm long. The neck and other details also vary. The two types are found *se-tenant* in the sheet. Stocks of the peacock types were withdrawn when the Japanese Directorate-General took control of the postal services in the Delta in August 1942.

JAPANESE ARMY ADMINISTRATION

7

8 Farmer

1942 (1 June). *Impressed by hand. Thick yellowish paper. No gum.* P 12 × 11.

J45 7 (1a.) red . . . . 38·00 65·00

This device was the personal seal of Yano Sitza, the Japanese official in charge of the Posts and Telegraphs department of the Japanese Army Administration. It was impressed on paper already perforated by a line machine. Some stamps show part of the papermaker's watermark, either "ABSORBO DUPLICATOR" or "ELEPHANT BRAND", each with an elephant.

Other impressions of this seal on different papers, and showing signs of wear, were not valid for postal purposes.

(Des T. Kato. Typo *Rangoon Gazette* Press)

1942 (15 June). *Value in annas.* P 11 or 11 × 11½. *Laid bâtonné paper. No gum.*

J46 8 1a. scarlet . . . . 17·00 17·00

Some stamps show part of the papermaker's watermark, either "ELEPHANT BRAND" or "TITAGHUR SUPERFINE", each with an elephant.

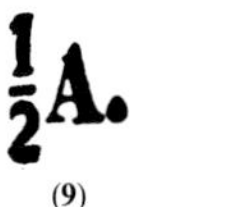

(9)

1R.

(10)

1942 (22 Sept). *(a) Nos. 314/17, 320/2, 325, 327 and 396 of Japan surch as T* **9/10**.

J47 9 ½a.on 1s. chestnut (Rice harvesting) . . 28·00 35·00
a. Surch inverted £100 £100
b. Surch double, one inverted £150

J48 ½a.on 2s. bright scarlet (General Nogi) . . . . 35·00 38·00
a. Surch inverted . . . . 90·00 95·00
b. Surch double, one inverted £150

J49 ¾a.on 3s. green (Power station) . . . 60·00 65·00
a. Surch inverted £120 £120
b. Surch double, one inverted . . . . — £160

J50 1a.on 5s. claret (Admiral Togo) . . . 50·00 48·00
a. Surch inverted £170 £170
b. Surch double, one inverted £190 £190
c. Surch omitted (in pair with normal) . . . . — £250

J51 3a.on 7s. green (Diamond Mts) . . . 90·00 £100
a. Surch inverted £170

J52 4a.on 4s. emerald (Togo) . . . . . 48·00 50·00
a. Surch inverted £170

J53 8a.on 8s. violet (Meiji Shrine) . . . £150 £150
a. Surch inverted £225 £225
b. Surch double, one inverted £350
c. Surch in red £225 £250
d. Red surch inverted £350
e. Surch double (black and red) . . . £600

J54 10 1r.on 10s. deep carmine (Yomei Gate) . . . . 19·00 25·00
a. Surch inverted . . . . 80·00 90·00
b. Surch double . . . . 80·00 £100
c. Surch double (black and red) . . . £400 £400
d. Surch omitted (in pair with normal) £225 £225
e. Surch omitted (in pair with inverted surch) £325

J55 2r.on 20s. ultramarine (Mt Fuji) . . . 50·00 50·00
a. Surch inverted £110 £110
b. Surch double, one inverted £130
c. Surch omitted (in pair with normal black surch) £160 £160
d. Surch in red . . . . 50·00 50·00
e. Red surch inverted £110 £110
f. Red surch double £110 £110
g. Surch omitted (in pair with normal red surch) £200 £200
ga. Surch omitted (in pair with double red surch) . . . .
h. Surch double (black and red) . . . £350

J56 9 5r.on 30s. turquoise (Torii Shrine) . . 12·00 27·00
a. Surch inverted . . . . 85·00
b. Surch double £110
c. Surch double, one inverted £150
d. Surch omitted (in pair with normal surch) £190 £190
e. Surch omitted (in pair with inverted black surch) £275
f. Surch in red . . . . 26·00 32·00
fa. Red surch inverted . . . . 90·00 90·00
fb. J56a and J56fa *se-tenant* £425 £425
fc. Surch omitted (in pair with normal red surch) £190 £190

(b) No. 386 of Japan commemorating the fall of Singapore similarly surch.

J56*g* 9 4a.on 4+2s. green and red £150 £160
h. Surch omitted (in pair with normal) £500
ha. Surch omitted (in pair with inverted surch) £550
i. Surch inverted £350

(New Currency. 100 cents = 1 rupee)

15C.

(11)

15C.

(12)

15C.

(13)

1942 (15 Oct). *Previous issues, with "anna" surcharges obliterated, handstamped with new value in cents, as T* **11** *and* **12** *(No. J57 handstamped with new value only).*

(a) On No. J46.

J57 5c.on 1a. scarlet . . . . 14·00 18·00
a. Surch omitted (in pair with normal) . . £1200

(b) On Nos. J47/53.

J58 1c.on ½a. on 1s. chestnut . . . . 50·00 50·00
a. "1 c." omitted (in pair with normal) £500
b. "¼ a." inverted £250

J59 2c.on ½a. on 2s. bright scarlet . . . . . 48·00 50·00

J60 3c.on ¾a. on 3s. green . . . . 50·00 50·00
a. Surch in blue £180

J61 5c.on 1a. on 5s. claret . . . . 65·00 65·00

J62 10c.on 3a. on 7s. green £110 £100

J63 15c.on 4a. on 4s. emerald . . . . 38·00 40·00

J64 20c.on 8a. on 8s. violet £475 £425
a. Surch on No. J53c (surch in red) . . . £275 £150

The "anna" surcharges were obliterated by any means available, in some cases by a bar or bars, and in others by the butt of a pencil dipped in ink. In the case of the fractional surcharges, the letter "A" and one figure of the fraction, were sometimes barred out, leaving the remainder of the fraction to represent the new value, e.g. the "1" of "½" deleted to create the 2c. surcharge or the "4" of "¾" to create the 3c. surcharge.

1942. *Nos. 314/17, 320/1 and 396 of Japan surcharged in cents only as T* **13**.

J65 1c.on 1s. chestnut (Rice harvesting) . . . 24·00 20·00
a. Surch inverted £110 £110

J66 2c.on 2s. brt scarlet (General Nogi) . . . 48·00 32·00

J67 3c.on 3s. green (Power station) . . . . 60·00 50·00
a. Pair, with and without surch . . . . — £250
b. Surch inverted £120
c. Surch in blue . . . . 85·00 95·00
d. Surch in blue inverted £200 £225

J68 5c.on 5s. claret (Admiral Togo) . . . . 65·00 48·00
a. Pair, with and without surch £300
b. Surch in violet £130 £150
ba. Surch inverted . . . . — £225

J69 10c.on 7s. green (Diamond Mts) . . . . 80·00 60·00

J70 15c.on 4s. emerald (Togo) . . . . 18·00 21·00
a. Surch inverted £120 £130
b. Pair, with and without surch . . . . — £225

J71 20c.on 8s. violet (Meiji Shrine) . . . . . £160 85·00
a. Surch double £300

Nos. J67c and J68b were issued for use in the Shan States.

BURMESE GOVERNMENT

On 1 November 1942 the Japanese Army Administration handed over the control of the postal department to the Burmese Government. On 1 August 1943 Burma was declared by the Japanese to be independent.

14 Burma State Crest

15 Farmer

(Des U Tun Tin and Maung Tin from drawing by U Ba Than. Typo Rangoon)

1943 (15 Feb). *No gum.* P 11.

J72 14 5c. scarlet . . . . 19·00 23·00
a. Imperf . . . . 20·00 23·00
ab. Printed on both sides . . . . . . 85·00

No. J72 was usually sold affixed to envelopes, particularly those with the embossed 1a. King George VI stamp, which it covered. Unused specimens off cover are not often seen and blocks are rare.

1943. *Typo. No gum.* P 11½.

J73 15 1c. orange (22 March) . . . . 3·00 4·50
a. Brown-orange . . . . 2·25 4·75

J74 2c. yellow-green (24 March) . . . . 60 1·00
a. "3" for "2" in face value (R. 2/10) £170
b. Blue-green . . . . 9·50

J75 3c. light blue (25 March) . . . . . . 3·00 1·00
a. On laid paper . . . . 19·00 28·00
b. Imperf between (horiz pair) . . . . — £275

J76 5c. carmine (small "c") (17 March) . . . . 18·00 12·00

J77 5c. carmine (large "C") . . . . . . 3·00 4·00
a. Imperf (pair) £110
b. "G" for "C" (R. 2/6) £170

J78 10c. grey-brown (25 March) . . . . . 6·00 4·50
a. Imperf (pair) £110
b. Imperf between (horiz pair) . . . . — £275

J79 15c. magenta (26 March) . . . . . . 30 2·00
a. Imperf between (vert strip of 3)
b. On laid paper . . . . 6·00 18·00
ba. Inverted "C" in value (R. 2/3) . . £140

J80 20c. grey-lilac (29 March) . . . . . . 30 1·00

J81 30c. deep blue-green (29 March) . . . 30 1·25

The 1c., 2c. and 3c. have large "C" in value as illustrated. The 10c. and higher values have small "c". Nos. J73/81 had the face values inserted individually into the plate used for No. J46 with the original face value removed. There were a number of printings for each value, often showing differences such as missing stops, various founts of figures or "c", etc., in the value tablets.

The face value error, No. J74a, was later corrected.

Some sheets of No. J75a show a sheet watermark of Britannia seated within a crowned oval spread across fifteen stamps in each sheet. This paper was manufactured by T. Edmonds and the other half of the sheet carried the watermark inscription "FOOLSCAP LEDGER". No stamps have been reported showing letters from this inscription, but a block of 25 is known on laid paper showing a different sheet watermark "HERTFORDSHIRE LEDGER MADE IN ENGLAND". Examples showing parts of these sheet watermarks are rare.

No. J79a shows the horizontal perforations omitted between rows 3/4 and 4/5.

There are marked varieties of shade in this issue.

16 Soldier carving word "Independence"

17 Rejoicing Peasant

18 Boy with National Flag

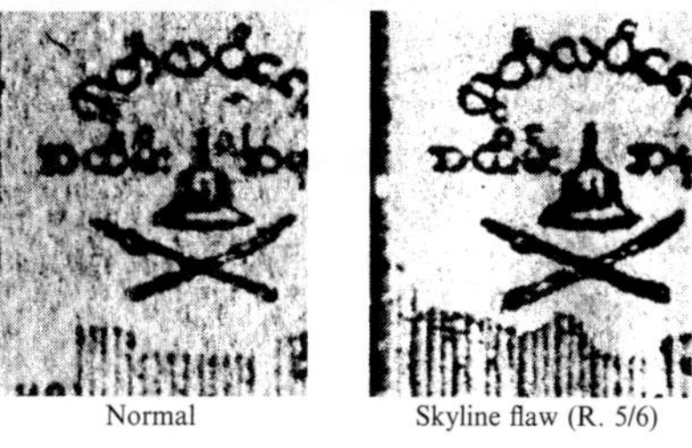

Normal

Skyline flaw (R. 5/6)

(Des Maung Ba Thit (**16**), Naung Ohn Maung (**17**), and Maung Soi Yi (**18**). Typo State Press, Rangoon)

1943 (1 Aug). *Independence Day.*

(a) P 11.

J82 16 1c. orange . . . . 9·50 15·00
J83 17 3c. light blue . . . . 10·00 16·00
J84 18 5c. carmine . . . . 18·00 8·50
a. Skyline flaw . . . . 80·00
J82/4 *Set of* 3 . . . . 35·00 35·00

(b) Rouletted.

J85 16 1c. orange . . . . 1·25 1·75
b. Perf × roul £100 £100
c. Imperf (pair) . . . . 45·00 55·00
J86 17 3c. light blue . . . . 2·50 2·50
b. Perf × roul . . . . 90·00 90·00
c. Imperf (pair) . . . . 45·00 55·00
J87 18 5c. carmine . . . . 2·00 2·50
a. Horiz roulette omitted (vert pair) . . . .
b. Perf × roul . . . . 60·00 60·00
c. Imperf (pair) . . . . 45·00 55·00
d. Skyline flaw . . . . 13·00
J85/7 *Set of* 3 . . . . 5·25 6·00

The stamps perf × rouletted may have one, two or three sides perforated.

The rouletted stamps often appear to be roughly perforated owing to failure to make clean cuts. These apparent perforations are very small and quite unlike the large, clean holes of the stamps perforated 11.

A few imperforate sets, mounted on a special card folder and cancelled with the commemorative postmark were presented to officials. These are rare.

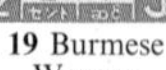
19 Burmese Woman

20 Elephant carrying Log

21 Watch Tower, Mandalay

(Litho G. Kolff & Co, Batavia)

1943 (1 Oct). P 12½.

J88	**19**	1c. red-orange	20·00	15·00
J89		2c. yellow-green	50	2·00
J90		3c. deep violet	50	2·25
		a. Bright violet	1·75	3·75
J91	**20**	5c. carmine	65	60
J92		10c. blue	1·75	1·10
J93		15c. red-orange	1·00	3·00
J94		20c. yellow-green	1·00	1·75
J95		30c. olive-brown	1·00	2·00
J96	**21**	1r. red-orange	30	2·00
J97		2r. bright violet	30	2·25
J88/97		*Set of* 10	25·00	29·00

22 Bullock Cart

23 Shan Woman

၂၀ ဆင့်။

(**24** "Burma State" and value)

(Litho G. Kolff & Co, Batavia)

1943 (1 Oct). *Issue for Shan States.* P 12½.

J98	**22**	1c. olive-brown	28·00	35·00
J99		2c. yellow-green	28·00	35·00
J100		3c. bright violet	4·00	10·00
J101		5c. ultramarine	2·00	5·50
J102	**23**	10c. blue	14·00	17·00
J103		20c. carmine	30·00	17·00
J104		30c. olive-brown	19·00	48·00
J98/104		*Set of* 7	£110	£150

The Shan States, except for the frontier area around Keng Tung which was ceded to Thailand on 20 August 1943, were placed under the administration of the Burmese Government on 24 December 1943, and these stamps were later overprinted as T **24** for use throughout Burma.

1944 (1 Nov). *Optd as T* **24** *(the lower characters differ for each value).*

J105	**22**	1c. olive-brown	3·50	6·00
J106		2c. yellow-green	50	2·75
		a. Opt inverted	£400	£650
J107		3c. bright violet	2·25	7·00
J108		5c. ultramarine	1·00	1·50
J109	**23**	10c. blue	3·25	2·00
J110		20c. carmine	50	1·50
J111		30c. olive-brown	50	1·75
J105/11		*Set of* 7	10·00	20·00

Bushire

BRITISH OCCUPATION

(Currency. 20 chahis = 1 kran; 10 kran = 1 toman)

Bushire, a seaport town of Persia, was occupied by the British on 8 August 1915. The Persian postal authorities resumed control on 18 October 1915. British forces returned to Bushire during 1916, but mail from this period was carried by Indian Army F.P.O. No. 319.

PRICES FOR STAMPS ON COVER		
Nos.	1/29	*from* × 5

Types of Iran (Persia) overprinted

57

66

67

68

BUSHIRE
Under British
Occupation.
(1)

1915 (15 Aug). *Nos. 361/3, 365, 367/70, 372, 374/6 and 378/9 of Iran optd with T* **1** *at the British Residency.*

1	**57**	1ch. orange and green	42·00	45·00
		a. No stop	£120	£130
2		2ch. sepia and carmine	42·00	40·00
		a. No stop	£120	£120
3		3ch. green and grey	50·00	60·00
		a. No stop	£150	£170
4		5ch. carmine and brown	£300	£300
5		6ch. brown-lake and green	40·00	28·00
		a. No stop	£120	£100
6		9ch. indigo-lilac and brown	40·00	45·00
		a. No stop	£130	£140
		b. Opt double		
7		10ch. brown and carmine	42·00	45·00
		a. No stop	£140	£150
8		12ch. blue and green	55·00	55·00
		a. No stop	£160	£170
9		24ch. green and purple	90·00	60·00
		a. No stop	£250	£180
10		1kr. carmine and blue	85·00	32·00
		a. Double overprint	£6500	
		b. No stop	£225	£110
11		2kr. claret and green	£225	£170
		a. No stop	£750	£450
12		3kr. black and lilac	£180	£190
		a. No stop	£600	£600
13		5kr. blue and red	£130	£110
		a. No stop	£450	£400
14		10kr. rose and bistre-brown	£110	£100
		a. No stop	£425	£375

Nos. 1/3 and 5/14 were overprinted in horizontal strips of 10 and No. 4 in horizontal strips of 5. Eight different settings are recognized with the "No stop" variety occurring on stamp 9 from four settings with 3 mm between "Under" and "British" and on stamp 10 from one setting where the gap is 2 mm.

1915 (Sept). *Nos. 426/40 and 441 of Iran optd with T* **1**.

15	**66**	1ch. deep blue and carmine	£375	£350
16		2ch. carmine and deep blue	£6500	£7000
17		3ch. deep green	£450	£425
18		5ch. vermilion	£5500	£5500
19		6ch. carmine and green	£4500	£4500
20		9ch. deep violet and brown	£650	£650
21		10ch. brown and deep green	£950	£950
22		12ch. ultramarine	£1200	£1200
23		24ch. sepia and brown	£450	£425
24	**67**	1kr. black, brown and silver	£450	£475
25		2kr. carmine, slate and silver	£425	£450
26		3kr. sepia, dull lilac and silver	£550	£550
27		5kr. slate, sepia and silver	£500	£550
		a. Opt inverted	—	£13000
28	**68**	1t. black, violet and gold	£450	£500
29		3t. red, crimson and gold	£3250	£3250

Nos. 15/29 were overprinted in strips of 5.

Examples of overprint Type **1** on Iran No. 414, 1ch. on 5ch. (previously No. 30), are now believed to be forged.

Cameroon

Allied operations against the German protectorate of Kamerun commenced in September 1914 and were completed in 18 February 1916. The territory was divided, under an Anglo-French agreement, on 31 March 1916, with the British administering the area in the west along the Nigerian border. League of Nations mandates were issued for the two sections of Cameroon, which were converted into United Nations trusteeships in 1946.

Supplies of Kamerun stamps were found on the German steamer *Professor Woermann*, captured at Freetown, and these were surcharged, probably in Sierra Leone, and issued by the Cameroons Expeditionary Force at Duala in July 1915.

A French post office opened in Duala on 10 November 1915 using stamps of Gabon overprinted "Corps Expeditionnaire Franco Anglais Cameroun". Although under the overall control of the British combined force commander, this office remained part of the French postal system.

PRICES FOR STAMPS ON COVER
The stamps of British Occupation of Cameroons are rare used on cover.

CAMEROONS EXPEDITIONARY FORCE

A

B

C.E.F. 1d. (1)

C.E.F. 1s. (2)

SETTINGS. Nos. B1/3 were surcharged from a setting of 100 (10 × 10) with the face value changed for the 1d.

Nos. B4 and B6/9 were surcharged from a common setting of 5 (5 × 10) with the face value amended.

No. B5 was surcharged from a setting of 10 in a vertical stri repeated across the sheet. The figures of the surcharge on this ar in a different style from the remainder of the pence stamps.

Nos. B10/13 were surcharged from a common setting of 20 (4 × 5) with the face value amended.

Different fount "d" (R. 1/10, 6/9, 10/10)

"1" with thin serifs (R. 5/1)

Large "3" (R. 3/5, 3/10)

Short "4" (R. 10/2, 10/7)

"s" inverted (R. 3/4)

"s" broken at top (R. 3/1)

1915 (12 July). *Stamps of German Kamerun. Types* A *and* B, *surc as T* **1** *(Nos. B1/9) or* **2** *(Nos. B10/13) in black or blue.*

B1	A	½d.on 3pf. (No. K7) (B.)	13·00	32·0
		a. Different fount "d"	£130	£27
B2		½d.on 5pf. (No. K21 wmk lozenges) (B.)	3·25	9·5
		a. Different fount "d"	35·00	90·0
		b. Surch double	†	£85
		ba. Surch double, one albino	£190	
B3		1d.on 10pf. (No. K22 wmk lozenges) (B.)	1·25	9·5
		a. "1" with thin serifs	13·00	65·0
		b. Surch double	£275	
		ba. Surch double, one albino	90·00	
		c. "1d." only double	£1800	
		d. Surch triple, two albino	£200	
		e. Surch in black	14·00	55·0
		ea. "1" with thin serifs	£160	
B4		2d.on 20pf. (No. K23 wmk lozenges)	3·50	21·0
		a. Surch double, one albino	£190	
B5		2½d.on 25pf. (No. K11)	12·00	48·0
		a. Surch double	£7000	
		ab. Surch double, one albino		
B6		3d.on 30pf. (No. K12)	12·00	48·0
		a. Large "3"	£750	
		b. Surch triple, two albino	£225	
B7		4d.on 40pf. (No. K13)	12·00	48·0
		a. Short "4"	£600	£90
		b. Surch triple, two albino	£200	
		c. Surch quadruple, three albino	£1600	
B8		6d.on 50pf. (No. K4)	12·00	48·0
		a. Surch double, one albino	£180	
B9		8d.on 80pf. (No. K15)	12·00	48·0
		a. Surch triple, two albino	£1000	
B10	B	1s.on 1m. (No. K16)	£160	£70
		a. "s" inverted	£800	£250
B11		2s.on 2m. (No. K17)	£160	£7
		a. "s" inverted	£800	£25
		b. Surch double, one albino	£1400	
B12	B	3s.on 3m. (No. K18)	£160	£70
		a. "s" inverted	£800	£250
		b. "s" broken at top	£550	
		c. Surch double	£7500	
		ca. Surch triple, two albino	£1400	
B13		5s.on 5m. (No. K25a wmk lozenges)	£190	£7
		a. "s" inverted	£900	£27
		b. "s" broken at top	£650	
B1/13		*Set of* 13	£650	£27

The 1d. on 10pf. was previously listed with "C.E.F." omitte This was due to misplacement, so that all stamps (except for a pa in the Royal Collection) from the bottom row show traces of t overprint on the top perforations.

Examples of all values exist showing a forged Duala, Kamer postmark dated "11 10 15". Another forged cancel dated "16 15" is also known. This can be identified by the lack of a serif the index letter "b".

The stamps of Nigeria were subsequently used in Briti Cameroons and the area was administered as part of Nigeria fro February 1924.

For issues of Cameroon under French administration see *Part (France)*.

Canada

Separate stamp issues appeared for British Columbia and Vancouver Island, Canada, New Brunswick, Newfoundland, No Scotia and Prince Edward Island before these colonies joined the Dominion of Canada.

BRITISH COLUMBIA & VANCOUVER ISLAN

Vancouver Island was organised as a Crown Colony in 1849 a the mainland territory was proclaimed a separate colony as Briti Columbia in 1858. The two colonies combined, as British Columb on 19 November 1866.

PRICES FOR STAMPS ON COVER

Nos.	2/3	*from* × 6
Nos.	11/12	*from* × 2
Nos.	13/14	*from* × 6
Nos.	21/2	*from* × 10
Nos.	23/7	*from* × 6
Nos.	28/9	*from* × 10
No.	30	—
No.	31	*from* × 10
Nos.	32/3	—

1

(Typo D.L.R.)

860. No wmk. P 14.

1	2½d. deep reddish rose	£350	£180
	2½d. pale reddish rose	£350	£180

When Vancouver Island adopted the dollar currency in 1862 the ½d. was sold at 5c. From 18 May until 1 November 1865 examples Nos. 2/3 were used to prepay mail from Vancouver Island to ritish Columbia at the price of 15 cents a pair.

From 20 June 1864 to 1 November 1865, the 2½d. was sold in ritish Columbia for 3d. and was subsequently used for the same urpose during a shortage of 3d. stamps in 1867.

Imperforate plate proofs exist in pale dull red (*Price* £2750 *un*)

VANCOUVER ISLAND

(New Currency. 100 cents = 1 dollar)

2

3

(Typo D.L.R.)

65 (19 Sept). Wmk Crown CC.

(a) Imperf (1866).

	2	5c. rose	£20000	£8000
	3	10c. blue	£1500	£850

(b) P 14.

	2	5c. rose	£275	£150
		w. Wmk inverted	£1200	
		x. Wmk reversed	†	£600
	3	10c. blue	£225	£140
		w. Wmk inverted	£800	£600

Medium or poor copies of Nos. 11 and 12 can be supplied at uch lower prices, when in stock.

After the two colonies combined Nos. 13/14 were also used in itish Columbia.

BRITISH COLUMBIA

4

(Typo D.L.R.)

65 (1 Nov)–**67**. Wmk Crown CC. P 14.

4	3d. deep blue	85·00	65·00
	3d. pale blue (19.7.67)	80·00	65·00
	w. Wmk inverted	£300	£190

British Columbia changed to the dollar currency on 1 January 66. Remaining stocks of No. 21 and the supply of No. 22, when inally arrived, were sold at 12½c. a pair.

(New Currency. 100 cents = 1 dollar)

TWO CENTS (5) **5.CENTS.5** (6)

68–**71**. *T* **4** *in various colours. Surch as T* **5** *or* **6**. Wmk Crown CC.

(a) P 12½ (3.69).

5c. red (Bk.)	£800	£750
10c. lake (B.)	£600	£475
25c. yellow (V.)	£425	£425
50c. mauve (R.)	£475	£425
$1 green (G.)	£850	£900

(b) P 14.

2c. brown (Bk.) (1.68)	£130	£130
5c. pale red (Bk.) (5.69)	£160	£130
10c. lake (B.)	£850	
25c. yellow (V.) (21.7.69)	£160	£130
50c. mauve (R.) (23.2.71)	£450	£900
w. Wmk inverted	£700	
$1 green (G.)	£750	

Nos. 30 and 33 were not issued.

British Columbia joined the Dominion of Canada on 20 July 71.

COLONY OF CANADA

The first British post offices in what was to become the colony of Canada were opened at Quebec, Montreal and Trois Rivières during, 1763. These, and subsequent, offices remained part of the British G.P.O. system until 6 April 1851.

The two provinces of Upper Canada (Ontario) and Lower Canada (Quebec) were united in 1840.

For illustration of the handstamp types see BRITISH POST OFFICES ABROAD notes, following GREAT BRITAIN.

NEW CARLISLE, GASPÉ

POSTMASTER'S PROVISIONAL ENVELOPE

1

1851 (7 April).

1 **1** 3d. black

Only one example is known, addressed to Toronto, with the impression cancelled by the signature of the postmaster, R. W. Kelly.

QUEBEC

CROWNED-CIRCLE HANDSTAMPS

CC1 CC **1b** QUEBEC L.C. (R.) (13.1.1842)
Price on cover £150

PRICES FOR STAMPS ON COVER

Nos.	1/23	*from* × 2
Nos.	25/8	*from* × 3
Nos.	29/43*a*	*from* × 3
Nos.	44/5	*from* × 8

1 American Beaver (Designed by Sir Sandford Fleming)

2 Prince Albert

3

Major re-entry: Line though "EE PEN" (Upper pane R. 5/7)

(T **1/6**. Eng and recess Rawdon, Wright, Hatch and Edson, New York)

1851. *Laid paper.* Imperf.

1	**1**	3d. red (23 April)	£11000	£700
1*a*		3d. orange-vermilion	£11000	£700
		b. Major re-entry	—	£1800
2	**2**	6d. slate-violet (15 May)	£17000	£950
3		6d. brown-purple	£18000	£1200
		a. Bisected (3d.) on cover	†	£22000
4	**3**	12d. black (14 June)	£75000	£40000

There are several re-entries on the plate of the 3d. in addition to the major re-entry listed. All re-entries occur in this stamp on all papers.

Forgeries of the 3d. are known without the full stop after "PENCE". They also omit the foliage in the corners, as do similar forgeries of the 6d.

4

5

6 Jacques Cartier

1852–**57**. Imperf.

A. *Handmade wove paper, varying in thickness (1852–56).*

5	**1**	3d. red	£1200	£160
		a. Bisected (1½d.) on cover (1856)	†	£24000
6		3d. deep red	£1300	£170
7		3d. scarlet-vermilion	£1600	£170
8		3d. brown-red	£1300	£170
		a. Bisected (1½d.) on cover (1856)	†	£24000
		b. Major re-entry (*all shades*) *from*	£3000	£650
9	**2**	6d. slate-violet	£14000	£950
		a. Bisected (3d.) on cover	†	£13000
10		6d. greenish grey	£14000	£950
11		6d. brownish grey	£15000	£1100
12	**5**	7½d. yellow-green (*shades*) (2.6.57)	£7000	£1500
13	**6**	10d. bright blue (1.55)	£7000	£1200
14		10d. dull blue	£6500	£1100
15		10d. blue *to* deep blue	£7000	£1200
		a. Major re-entry (*all shades*) from	—	£2000
16	**3**	12d. black	—	£55000

B. *Machine-made medium to thick wove paper of a more even hard texture with more visible mesh. Clearer impressions (1857).*

17	**4**	½d. deep rose (1.8.57)	£800	£450
18	**1**	3d. red	£1700	£450
		a. Bisected (1½d.) on cover	†	£22000
		b. Major re-entry	—	£1300
19	**2**	6d. grey-lilac	£17000	£2000
20	**6**	10d. blue *to* deep blue	£7000	£2000
		a. Major re-entry	£11000	£2500

C. *Thin soft horizontally ribbed paper (1857).*

21	**4**	½d. deep rose	£6000	£1700
		a. Vertically ribbed paper	£6500	£2500
22	**1**	3d. red	£3000	£400
		a. Major re-entry	—	£1200

D. *Very thick soft wove paper (1857).*

23	**2**	6d. reddish purple	£16000	£2500
		a. Bisected (3d.) on cover	†	£20000

Bisected examples of the 3d. value were used to make up the 7½d. Canadian Packet rate to England from May 1856 until the introduction of the 7½d. value on 2 June 1857.

The 7½d. and 10d. values can be found in wide and narrow versions. These differences are due to shrinkage of the paper, which was wetted before printing and then contracted unevenly during drying. The width of these stamps varies between 17 and 18 mm.

The listed major re-entry on the 10d. occurs on R.3/5 and shows strong doubling of the top frame line and the left-hand "8d. stg." with a line through the lower parts of "ANAD" and "ENCE". Smaller re-entries occur on all values.

Examples of the 12d. on wove paper come from a proof sheet used for postal purposes by the postal authorities.

The 3d. is known perforated 14 and also *percé en scie* 13. Both are contemporary, but were unofficial.

1858–**59**. P 11¾.

A. *Machine-made medium to thick wove paper with a more even hard texture.*

25	**4**	½d. deep rose (12.58)	£1900	£600
		a. Lilac-rose	£2000	£650
26	**1**	3d. red (1.59)	£2500	£300
		a. Major re-entry	—	£1100
27	**2**	6d. brownish grey (1.59)	£7500	£2500
		a. Slate-violet	£7500	£2250

B. *Thin soft horizontally ribbed paper.*

27*b*	**4**	½d. deep rose-red	—	£3250
28	**1**	3d. red	—	£1200
		a. Major re-entry		

(New Currency. 100 cents = 1 dollar)

7

8 American Beaver

9 Prince Albert

10

11 Jacques Cartier

(Recess A.B.N. Co)

(On 1 May 1858, Messrs. Rawdon, Wright, Hatch and Edson joined with eight other firms to form "The American Bank Note Co" and the "imprint" on sheets of the following stamps has the new title of the firm with "New York" added.)

1859 (1 July). P 12.

29	**7**	1c. pale rose (to rose-red)	£225	28·00
30		1c. deep rose (to carmine-rose)	£300	48·00
		a. Imperf (pair)	£2750	
		b. Imperf × perf		
31	**8**	5c. pale red	£250	11·00
32		5c. deep red	£250	11·00
		a. Re-entry* (R.3/8)	£2500	£450
		b. Imperf (pair)	£7500	
		c. Bisected (2½c.) with 10c. on cover	†	£4250
33	**9**	10c. black-brown	£6500	£1300
		a. Bisected (5c.), on cover	†	£6000
33*b*		10c. deep red-purple	£2500	£500
		ba. Bisected (5c.), on cover	†	£4000
34		10c. purple (*shades*)	£850	45·00
		a. Bisected (5c.), on cover	†	£4000
35		10c. brownish purple	£750	45·00
36		10c. brown (to pale)	£750	45·00
		a. Bisected (5c.), on cover	†	£4750
37		10c. dull violet	£850	50·00
38		10c. bright red-purple	£800	45·00
		a. Imperf (pair)	£7000	
39	**10**	12½c. deep yellow-green	£700	42·00
40		12½c. pale yellow-green	£650	42·00
41		12½c. blue-green	£800	50·00
		a. Imperf (pair)	£3000	
		b. Imperf between (vert pair)		
42	**11**	17c. deep blue	£850	60·00
		a. Imperf (pair)	£3250	
43		17c. slate-blue	£1000	90·00
43*a*	**4**	17c. indigo	£900	65·00

*The price of No. 32a is for the very marked re-entry showing oval frame line doubled above "CANADA". Slighter re-entries are worth from £30 upwards in used condition.

As there were numerous P.O. Dept. orders for the 10c., 12½c. and 17c. and some of these were executed by more than one separate printing, with no special care to ensure uniformity of colour, there is a wide range of shade, especially in the 10c., and some shades recur at intervals after periods during which other shades predominated. The colour-names given in the above list therefore represent groups only.

It has been proved by leading Canadian specialists that the perforations may be an aid to the approximate dating of a particular stamp, the gauge used measuring 11¾ × 11¾ from mid-July 1859 to mid-1863, 12 × 11¾ from March 1863 to mid-1865 and 12 × 12 from April 1865 to 1868. Exceptionally, in the 5c. value many sheets were perforated 12 × 12 between May and October, 1862, whilst the last printings of the 12½c. and 17c. perf 11¾ × 11¾ were in July 1863, the perf 12 × 11¾ starting towards the end of 1863.

12

(Recess A.B.N. Co)

1864 (1 Aug). P 12.

44	**12**	2c. rose-red	£425	£150
45		2c. bright rose	£425	£150
		a. Imperf (pair)	£1600	

The Colony of Canada became part of the Dominion of Canada on 1 July 1867.

NEW BRUNSWICK

New Brunswick, previously part of Nova Scotia, became a separate colony in June 1784. The colony became responsible for its postal service on 6 July 1851.

PRICES FOR STAMPS ON COVER		
Nos.	1/4	*from* × 2
Nos.	5/6	*from* × 3
Nos.	7/9	*from* × 10
Nos.	10/12	*from* × 30
No.	13	—
Nos.	14/17	*from* × 2
No.	18	*from* × 5
No.	19	*from* × 100

1 Royal Crown and Heraldic Flowers of the United Kingdom

(Recess P.B.)

1851 (5 Sept). *Blue paper.* Imperf.

1	**1**	3d. bright red	£2000	£350
2		3d. dull red	£2000	£325
		a. Bisected (1½d.) (on cover)	†	£2750
2*b*		6d. mustard-yellow	£6000	£1500
3		6d. yellow	£4500	£800
4		6d. olive-yellow	£4500	£700
		a. Bisected (3d.) (on cover)	†	£3000
		b. Quartered (1½d.) (on cover)	†	£38000
5		1s. reddish mauve	£13000	£4000
6		1s. dull mauve	£14000	£4500
		a. Bisected (6d.) (on cover)	†	£22000
		b. Quartered (3d.) (on cover)	†	£30000

Reprints of all three values were made in 1890 on thin, hard, white paper. The 3d. is bright orange, the 6d. and 1s. violet-black.

Nos. 2a and 4b were to make up the 7½d. rate to Great Britain, introduced on 1 August 1854.

(New Currency. 100 cents = 1 dollar)

2 Locomotive

3

3a Charles Connell

4

5

6 Paddle-steamer *Washington*

7 King Edward VII when Prince of Wales

(Recess A.B.N. Co)

1860 (15 May)–**63**. No wmk. P 12.

7	**2**	1c. brown-purple	55·00	40·00
8		1c. purple	38·00	38·00
9		1c. dull claret	38·00	38·00
		a. Imperf vert (horiz pair)	£550	
10	**3**	2c. orange (1863)	19·00	19·00
11		2c. orange-yellow	23·00	19·00
12		2c. deep orange	24·00	19·00
		a. Imperf horiz (vert pair)	£450	
13	**3a**	5c. brown	£4500	
14	**4**	5c. yellow-green	17·00	13·00
15		5c. deep green	17·00	13·00
16		5c. sap-green (deep yellowish green)	£300	40·00
17	**5**	10c. red	38·00	40·00
		a. Bisected (5c.) (on cover) (1860)	†	£600
18	**6**	12½c. indigo	50·00	40·00
19	**7**	17c. black	38·00	48·00

Beware of forged cancellations.

No. 13 was not issued due to objections to the design showing Charles Connell, the Postmaster-General. Most of the printing was destroyed.

New Brunswick joined the Dominion of Canada on 1 July 1867 and its stamps were withdrawn in March of the following year.

NEWFOUNDLAND

Newfoundland became a self-governing colony in 1855 and a Dominion in 1917. In 1934 the adverse financial situation led to the suspension of the constitution.

The first local postmaster, at St. John's, was appointed in 1805, the overseas mails being routed via Halifax, Nova Scotia. A regular packet service was established between these two ports in 1840, the British G.P.O. assuming control of the overseas mails at the same time.

The responsibility for the overseas postal service reverted to the colonial administration on 1 July 1851.

For illustrations of the handstamp types see BRITISH POST OFFICES ABROAD notes, following GREAT BRITAIN.

ST. JOHN'S

CROWNED-CIRCLE HANDSTAMPS

CC1 CC **1a** ST. JOHN'S NEWFOUNDLAND (R.) (27.6.1846) . . . . . . *Price on cover* £900

PRICES FOR STAMPS ON COVER TO 1945		
No.	1	*from* × 30
Nos.	2/4	*from* × 3
No.	5	*from* × 20
No.	6	*from* × 10
No.	7	*from* × 3
No.	8	*from* × 30
No.	9	*from* × 8
No.	10	—
No.	11	*from* × 8
No.	12	*from* × 3
Nos.	13/14	*from* × 20
Nos.	15/17	—
Nos.	18/20	*from* × 20
No.	21	*from* × 15
Nos.	22/3	—
No.	25	*from* × 30
No.	26	*from* × 5
No.	27	*from* × 8
No.	28	*from* × 3
Nos.	29/30	*from* × 10
No.	31	*from* × 30
No.	32	*from* × 8
No.	33	*from* × 5
No.	33*a*	—
Nos.	34/9	*from* × 8
Nos.	40/1	*from* × 5
Nos.	42/3	*from* × 30
Nos.	44/8	*from* × 8
No.	49	*from* × 50
Nos.	50/3	*from* × 10
No.	54	*from* × 4
Nos.	55/8*b*	*from* × 10
No.	59	*from* × 100
No.	59*a*	*from* × 10
Nos.	60/1	*from* × 4
Nos.	62/5	*from* × 8
Nos.	65*a*/79	*from* × 3
Nos.	83/90	*from* × 10
Nos.	91/3	*from* × 2
No.	94	*from* × 50
Nos.	95/141	*from* × 3
Nos.	142/*a*	*from* × 1½
No.	143	*from* × 8
Nos.	144/8*f*	*from* × 2
Nos.	149/62	*from* × 3
No.	163	—
Nos.	164/78	*from* × 2
Nos.	179/90	*from* × 3
No.	191	—
Nos.	192/220	*from* × 2
No.	221	—
Nos.	222/9	*from* × 3
Nos.	230/4	*from* × 2
No.	235	—
Nos.	236/91	*from* × 2
Nos.	D1/6	*from* × 10

1

2

4

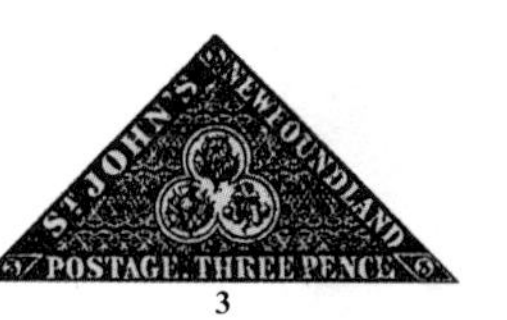

3

5

Royal Crown and Heraldic flowers of the United Kingdom

(Recess P.B.)

1857 (1 Jan)–**64**. *Thick, machine-made paper with a distinct mesh.* No wmk. Imperf.

1	**1**	1d. brown-purple	£100	£170
		a. Bisected (½d.) (1864) (on cover)	†	£13000
2	**2**	2d. scarlet-vermilion (15 Feb)	£10000	£4750
3	**3**	3d. yellowish green	£750	£425
4	**4**	4d. scarlet-vermilion	£6500	£2500
5	**1**	5d. brown-purple	£180	£375
6	**4**	6d. scarlet-vermilion	£13000	£3250
7	**5**	6½d. scarlet-vermilion	£2250	£2750
8	**4**	8d. scarlet-vermilion	£250	£450
		a. Bisected (4d.) (1859) (on cover)	†	£4250
9	**2**	1s. scarlet-vermilion	£14000	£5000
		a. Bisected (6d.) (1860) (on cover)	†	£13000

The 6d. and 8d. differ from the 4d. in many details, as does also the 1s. from the 2d.

PERKINS BACON "CANCELLED". For notes on these handstamps, showing "CANCELLED" between horizontal bars forming an oval, see Catalogue Introduction.

1860 (15 Aug–Dec). *Medium, hand-made paper without mesh.* Imperf.

10	**2**	2d. orange-vermilion	£325	£47
11	**3**	3d. grn *to* dp grn* (H/S "CANCELLED" in oval £6000)	75·00	£15
12	**4**	4d. orange-verm (H/S "CANCELLED" in oval £9000)	£2500	£85
		a. Bisected (2d.) (12.60) (on cover)	†	£1400
13	**1**	5d. Venetian red (H/S "CANCELLED" in oval £8000)	90·00	£32
14	**4**	6d. orange-vermilion	£3000	£60
15	**2**	1s. orange-verm (H/S "CANCELLED" in oval £13000)	£20000	£850
		a. Bisected (6d.) (12.60) (on cover)	†	£4000

*No. 11 includes stamps from the July and November 186 printings which are very difficult to distinguish.

The 1s. on horizontally or vertically *laid* paper is now considere to be a proof (*Price* £11000).

Stamps of this and the following issue may be found with part c the paper-maker's watermark "STACEY WISE 1858".

BISECTS. Collectors are warned against buying bisected stamps c these issues without a reliable guarantee.

1862–64. *New colours. Hand-made paper without mesh.* Imperf.

16	**1**	1d. chocolate-brown	£180	£32
		a. Red-brown	£4250	
17	**2**	2d. rose-lake	£180	£42
18	**4**	4d. rose-lake (H/S "CANCELLED" in oval £7500)	32·00	95·0
		a. Bisected (2d.) (1864) (on cover)	†	–
19	**1**	5d. chocolate-brown	70·00	£32
		a. Red-brown	55·00	£20
20	**4**	6d. rose-lake (H/S "CANCELLED" in oval £7500)	23·00	£10
		a. Bisected (3d.) (1863) (on cover)	†	£900
21	**5**	6½d. rose-lake (H/S "CANCELLED" in oval £6500)	75·00	£45
22	**4**	8d. rose-lake	85·00	£60
23	**2**	1s. rose-lake (H/S "CANCELLED" in oval £6500)	40·00	£30
		a. Bisected (6d.) (1863) (on cover)	†	£140

Nos. 16/23 come from printings made in July (2d., 4d., 6d., 6½d and 1s. only) or November 1861 (all values). The paper used wa from the same manufacturer as that for Nos. 11/15, but was of mo variable thickness and texture, ranging from a relatively so medium paper, which can be quite opaque, to a thin har transparent paper. The rose-lake stamps also show a considerab variation in shade ranging from pale to deep. The extensi remainders of this issue were predominately in pale shades on th hard paper, but it is not possible to distinguish between stamps fro the two printings with any certainty. Deep shades of the 2d., 4c 6d., 6½d. and 1s. on soft opaque paper do, however, command considerable premium.

Beware of buying used specimens of the stamps which are wor much less in unused condition, as many unused stamps have be provided with faked postmarks. A guarantee should be obtained

(New Currency. 100 cents = 1 dollar)

6 Atlantic Cod

7 Common Seal on Ice-floe

8 Prince Consort

9 Queen Victoria

10 Schooner

11 Queen Victoria

(Recess A.B.N. Co, New York)

865 (15 Nov)–**71**. P 12.

(a) Thin yellowish paper.

5	**6**	2c. yellowish green	£120	50·00
		a. Bisected (1c.) (on cover) (1870)	†	£4250
6	**7**	5c. brown	£500	£170
		a. Bisected (2½c.) (on cover)		
7	**8**	10c. black	£300	80·00
		a. Bisected (5c.) (on cover) (1869)	†	£3250
8	**9**	12c. red-brown	£425	£150
		a. Bisected (6c.) (on cover)	†	£3250
9	**10**	13c. orange-yellow	£100	80·00
0	**11**	24c. blue	35·00	38·00

(b) Medium white paper.

1	**6**	2c. bluish green (*to* deep) (1870)	80·00	35·00
2	**8**	10c. black (1871)	£190	40·00
3	**9**	12c. chestnut (1870)	48·00	48·00
3*a*	**11**	24c. blue (1870?)	£1200	£450

The inland postage rate was reduced to 3c. on 8 May, 1870. Until e 3c. value became available examples of No. 25 were bisected to ovide 1c. stamps.

12 King Edward VIIwhen Prince of Wales

14 Queen Victoria

I

II

In Type II the white oval frame line is unbroken by the scroll ntaining the words "ONE CENT", the letters "N.F." are smaller d closer to the scroll, and there are other minor differences.

(Recess National Bank Note Co, New York)

68 (Nov). P 12.

12	1c. dull purple (I)	55·00	50·00

(Recess A.B.N. Co)

68 (Nov)–**73**. P 12.

12	1c. brown-purple (II) (5.71)	90·00	60·00
14	3c. vermilion (7.70)	£250	£100
	3c. blue (1.4.73)	£275	20·00
7	5c. black	£250	£110
14	6c. rose (7.70)	8·50	19·00

76–79. Rouletted.

12	1c. lake-purple (II) (1877)	90·00	48·00
6	2c. bluish green (1879)	£130	45·00
14	3c. blue (1877)	£275	4·25
7	5c. blue	£180	3·50
	a. Imperf (pair)		

15 King Edward VII when Prince of Wales

16 Atlantic Cod

17

18 Common Seal on Ice-floe

(Recess British American Bank Note Co, Montreal)

1880–82. P 12.

44	**15**	1c. dull grey-brown	29·00	9·50
		a. Dull brown	27·00	9·50
		b. Red-brown	30·00	14·00
46	**16**	2c. yellow-green (1882)	50·00	24·00
47	**17**	3c. pale dull blue	85·00	6·00
		a. Bright blue	80·00	3·75
48	**18**	5c. pale dull blue	£225	9·00

19 Newfoundland Dog

20 Atlantic Brigantine

21 Queen Victoria

(Recess British American Bank Note Co, Montreal)

1887 (15 Feb)–**88**. *New colours and values.* P 12.

49	**19**	½c. rose-red	12·00	7·50
50	**15**	1c. blue-green (1.88)	11·00	7·50
		a. Green	6·00	3·25
		b. Yellow-green	11·00	9·00
51	**16**	2c. orange-vermilion (1.88)	17·00	5·00
52	**17**	3c. deep brown (1.88)	65·00	1·50
53	**18**	5c. deep blue (1.88)	£100	4·75
54	**20**	10c. black (1.88)	55·00	55·00
49/54 *Set of* 6			£225	70·00

For reissues of 1880/8 stamps in similar colours, see Nos. 62/5*a*.

(Recess B.A.B.N.)

1890 (Nov). P 12.

55	**21**	3c. deep slate	29·00	2·00
		a. Imperf (pair)		
56		3c. slate-grey (*to* grey)	30·00	2·00
		a. Imperf horiz (vert pair)	£400	
57		3c. slate-violet	40·00	4·00
58		3c. grey-lilac	40·00	2·00
58*a*		3c. brown-grey	40·00	6·00
58*b*		3c. purple-grey	42·00	6·00

There is a very wide range of shades in this stamp, and those given only cover the main groups.

Stamps on pink paper are from a consignment recovered from the sea and which were affected by the salt water.

(Recess British American Bank Note Co, Montreal)

1894 (Aug–Dec). *Changes of colour.* P 12.

59	**19**	½c. black (11.94)	9·50	5·00
59*a*	**18**	5c. bright blue (12.94)	70·00	3·75
60	**14**	6c. crimson-lake (12.94)	17·00	16·00
61	**9**	12c. deep brown	55·00	60·00

The 6c. is printed from the old American Bank Note Company's plates.

1896 (Jan)–**98**. *Reissues.* P 12.

62	**19**	½c. orange-vermilion	48·00	55·00
63	**15**	1c. deep brown	70·00	55·00
63*a*		1c. deep green (1898)	18·00	13·00
64	**16**	2c. green	£100	60·00
65	**17**	3c. deep blue	80·00	19·00
65*a*		3c. chocolate-brown	90·00	85·00
62/5*a* *Set of* 6			£375	£250

The above were *reissued* for postal purposes. The colours were generally brighter than those of the original stamps.

22 Queen Victoria

23 John Cabot

24 Cape Bonavista

25 Caribou hunting

26 Mining

27 Logging

28 Fishing

29 *Matthew* (Cabot)

30 Willow Grouse

31 Group of Grey Seals

32 Salmon-fishing

33 Seal of the Colony

34 Iceberg off St. John's

35 Henry VII

(Des R. O. Smith. Recess A.B.N. Co)

1897 (24 June). *400th Anniv of Discovery of Newfoundland and 60th year of Queen Victoria's reign.* P 12.

66	**22**	1c. green	2·50	6·50
67	**23**	2c. bright rose	2·25	2·75
		a. Bisected (1c.) on cover	†	£275
68	**24**	3c. bright blue	3·50	1·00
		a. Bisected (1½c.) on cover	†	£275
69	**25**	4c. olive-green	9·50	4·00
70	**26**	5c. violet	13·00	3·00
71	**27**	6c. red-brown	9·50	3·25
		a. Bisected (3c.) on cover	†	£275
72	**28**	8c. orange	21·00	9·00
73	**29**	10c. sepia	42·00	7·50
74	**30**	12c. deep blue	35·00	6·50
75	**31**	15c. bright scarlet	20·00	18·00
76	**32**	24c. dull violet-blue	25·00	21·00
77	**33**	30c. slate-blue	48·00	70·00
78	**34**	35c. red	60·00	60·00
79	**35**	60c. black	17·00	13·00
66/79 *Set of* 14			£275	£200

The 60c. surcharged "TWO—2—CENTS" in three lines is an essay made in December 1918 (*Price* £350).

ONE CENT

(36)

ONE CENT

(37)

ONE CENT

(38)

1897 (19 Oct). *T* **21** *surch with T* **36/8** *by* Royal Gazette, *St. Johns, on stamps of various shades.*

80	**36**	1c.on 3c. grey-purple	50·00	22·00
		a. Surch double, one diagonal	£1100	
		d. Vert pair, one without lower bar and "ONE CENT"	£3500	
81	**37**	1c.on 3c. grey-purple	£110	90·00
82	**38**	1c.on 3c. grey-purple	£500	£400

Nos. 80/2 occur in the same setting of 50 (10 × 5) applied twice to each sheet. Type **36** appeared in the first four horizontal rows, Type **37** on R. 5/1–8 and Type **38** on R. 5/9 and 10.

Trial surcharges in red or red and black were not issued. (*Price*: Type **36***in red* £800, *in red and black* £800: Type **37***in red* £2250, *in red and black* £2500: Type **38***in red* £5500, *in red and black* £6500).

These surcharges exist on stamps of various shades, but those on brown-grey are clandestine forgeries, having been produced by one of the printers at the *Royal Gazette*.

39 Prince Edward later Duke of Windsor

40 Queen Victoria

41 King E-dward VIIwhen Prince of Wales

42 Queen Alexandra when Princess of Wales

43 Queen Mary when Duchess of York

44 King George V when Duke of York

(Recess A.B.N. Co)

1897 (4 Dec)–**1918**. P 12.

83 **39** ½c. olive (8.98) . . . 2·25 1·50
 a. Imperf (pair) . . . £400
84 **40** 1c. carmine . . . 3·25 3·50
85 1c. blue-green (6.98) . . . 12·00 20
 a. Yellow-green . . . 9·00 20
 b. Imperf horiz (vert pair) . . . £190
86 **41** 2c. orange . . . 4·00 4·50
 a. Imperf (pair) . . . — £325
87 2c. scarlet (6.98) . . . 16·00 40
 a. Imperf (pair) . . . £250 £250
 b. Imperf between (pair) . . . £350
88 **42** 3c. orange (6.98) . . . 20·00 30
 a. Imperf horiz (vert pair) . . . £325
 b. Imperf (pair) . . . £250 £250
 c. Red-orange/bluish (6.18) . . . 32·00 2·75
89 **43** 4c. violet (21.10.01) . . . 25·00 4·50
 a. Imperf (pair) . . . £425
90 **44** 5c. blue (6.99) . . . 42·00 3·00
83/90 *Set of* 8 . . . £110 16·00

No. 88*c* was an emergency war-time printing made by the American Bank Note Co from the old plate, pending receipt of the then current 3c. from England.

The imperforate errors of this issue are found used, but only as philatelic "by favour" items. It is possible that No. 86a only exists in this condition.

45 Map of Newfoundland

(Recess A.B.N. Co)

1908 (31 Aug). P 12.

94 **45** 2c. lake . . . 27·00 1·00

46 King James I

47 Arms of Colonisation Co

48 John Guy

49 *Endeavour* (immigrant ship), 1610

50 Cupids

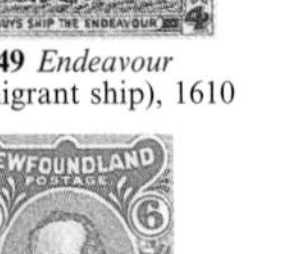
51 Sir Francis Bacon

52 View of Mosquito

53 Logging Camp, Red Indian Lake

54 Paper Mills, Grand Falls

55 King Edward VII

56 King George V

6c. (A) "Z" in "COLONIZATION" reversed. (B) "Z" correct.

(Litho Whitehead, Morris & Co Ltd)

1910 (15 Aug).

(a) P 12.

95 **46** 1c. green . . . 8·50 2·50
 a. "NFWFOUNDLAND" (Right pane R. 5/1) . . . 60·00 90·00
 b. "JAMRS" (Right pane R. 5/2) . . . 60·00 90·00
 c. Imperf between (horiz pair) . . . £300 £325
96 **47** 2c. rose-carmine . . . 15·00 2·00
97 **48** 3c. olive . . . 6·00 16·00
98 **49** 4c. violet . . . 15·00 14·00
99 **50** 5c. bright blue . . . 27·00 8·50
100 **51** 6c. claret (A) . . . 45·00 £150
100*a* 6c. claret (B) . . . 23·00 85·00
101 **52** 8c. bistre-brown . . . 50·00 95·00
102 **53** 9c. olive-green . . . 42·00 80·00
103 **54** 10c. purple-slate . . . 55·00 £100
104 **55** 12c. pale red-brown . . . 55·00 80·00
 a. Imperf (pair) . . . £325
105 **56** 15c. black . . . 65·00 £100
95/105 *Set of* 11 . . . £325 £500

(b) P 12 × 14.

106 **46** 1c. green . . . 4·50 8·00
 a. "NFWFOUNDLAND" . . . 55·00 £130
 b. "JAMRS" . . . 55·00 £130
 c. Imperf between (horiz pair) . . . £550 £600
107 **47** 2c. rose-carmine . . . 5·00 40
 a. Imperf between (horiz pair) . . . £550
108 **50** 5c. bright blue (P 14 × 12) . . . 8·00 2·75

(c) P 12 × 11.

109 **46** 1c. green . . . 1·75 30
 a. Imperf between (horiz pair) . . . £275
 b. Imperf between (vert pair) . . . £325
 c. "NFWFOUNDLAND" . . . 24·00 50·00
 e. "JAMRS" . . . 24·00 50·00

(d) P 12 × 11½.

110 **47** 2c. rose-carmine . . . £225 £200

(Dies eng Macdonald & Sons. Recess A. Alexander & Sons, Ltd)

1911 (7 Feb). *As T* **51** *to* **56**, *but recess printed.* P 14.

111 6c. claret (B) . . . 18·00 45·00
112 8c. yellow-brown . . . 48·00 70·00
 a. Imperf between (horiz pair) . . . £550
 b. Imperf (pair) . . . £300
113 9c. sage-green . . . 45·00 £110
 a. Imperf between (horiz pair) . . . £500
114 10c. purple-black . . . 90·00 £120
 a. Imperf between (horiz pair) . . . £475
 b. Imperf (pair) . . . £250
115 12c. red-brown . . . 60·00 60·00
116 15c. slate-green . . . 65·00 £110
111/16 *Set of* 6 . . . £275 £450

The 9c. and 15c. exist with papermaker's watermark "E. TOWGOOD FINE".

57 Queen Mary

58 King George V

59 Duke of Windsor when Prince of Wales

60 King George VI when Prince Albert

61 Princess Mary, the Princess Royal

62 Prince Henry, Duke of Gloucester

63 Prince George, Duke of Kent

64 Prince John

65 Queen Alexandra

66 Duke of Connaught

67 Seal of Newfoundland

(1c. to 5c., 10c. eng and recess D.L.R.; others eng Macdonald & Co, recess A. Alexander & Sons)

1911 (19 June)–**16**. *Coronation.* P 13½ × 14 (comb) (1c. to 5c., 10c.) or 14 (line) (others).

117 **57** 1c. yellow-green . . . 9·00 30
 a. Blue-green (1915) . . . 10·00 30
118 **58** 2c. carmine . . . 4·50 20
 a. Rose-red (blurred impression). Perf 14 (1916) . . . 9·00 55
119 **59** 3c. red-brown . . . 21·00 32·00
120 **60** 4c. purple . . . 19·00 26·00
121 **61** 5c. ultramarine . . . 7·00 1·50
122 **62** 6c. slate-grey . . . 13·00 25·00
123 **63** 8c. aniline blue . . . 55·00 75·0
 a. Greenish blue . . . 70·00 90·0
124 **64** 9c. violet-blue . . . 19·00 45·0
125 **65** 10c. deep green . . . 29·00 40·0
126 **66** 12c. plum . . . 25·00 45·0
127 **67** 15c. lake . . . 20·00 45·0
117/27 *Set of* 11 . . . £200 £30

The 2c. rose-red, No. 118*a* is a poor war-time printing by Alexander & Sons.

Although No. 123 has a typical aniline appearance it is believed that the shade results from the thinning of non-aniline ink.

68 Reindeer

FIRST TRANS-ATLANTIC AIR POST April, 1919.
(69)

(Des J. H. Noonan. Recess D.L.R.)

1919 (2 Jan). *Newfoundland Contingent, 1914–1918.* P 14.

130 **68** 1c. green *(a) (b)* . . . 3·75 2
131 2c. scarlet *(a) (b)* . . . 3·75 8
 a. Carmine-red (b) . . . 13·00 4
132 3c. brown *(a) (b)* . . . 7·00 2
 a. Red-brown (b) . . . 9·00 3
133 4c. mauve *(a)* . . . 7·50 7
 a. Purple (b) . . . 13·00 3
134 5c. ultramarine *(a) (b)* . . . 9·00 1·2
135 6c. slate-grey *(a)* . . . 7·00 40·0
136 8c. bright magenta *(a)* . . . 11·00 45·0
137 10c. deep grey-green *(a)* . . . 7·00 4·2
138 12c. orange *(a)* . . . 18·00 60·0
139 15c. indigo *(a)* . . . 15·00 60·0
 a. Prussian blue (a) . . . 85·00 £1
140 24c. bistre-brown *(a)* . . . 22·00 28·0
141 36c. sage-green *(a)* . . . 15·00 29·0
130/41 *Set of* 12 . . . £110 £2

Each value bears with "Trail of the Caribou" the name of different action: 1c. Suvla Bay; 3c. Gueudecourt; 4c. Beaumo Hamel; 6c. Monchy; 10c. Steenbeck; 15c. Langemarck; 24 Cambrai; 36c. Combles; 2c., 5c., 8c., and 12c. inscribed "Roy Naval Reserve-Ubique".

Perforations. Two perforating heads were used: *(a)* com 14 × 13.9; *(b)* line 14.1 × 14.1.

1919 (12 Apr). *Air. No. 132 optd with T* **69**, *by Robinson & Co Lt at the offices of the "Daily News".*

142 **68** 3c. brown . . . £15000 £80

These stamps franked correspondence carried b Lieut. H. Hawker on his Atlantic flight. 18 were damaged an destroyed, 95 used on letters, 11 given as presentation copies, an the remaining 76 were sold in aid of the Marine Disasters Fund.

1919 (19 April). *Nos. 132 optd in MS.* "Aerial Atlantic Mail. J.A.R

142*a* **68** 3c. brown . . . — £200

This provisional was made by W. C. Campbell, the Secretary the Postal Department, and the initials are those of t Postmaster, J. A. Robinson, for use on correspondence intended be carried on the abortive Morgan-Raynham Trans-Atlantic fligh The mail was eventually delivered by sea.

In addition to the 25 to 30 used examples, one unused, no gu copy of No. 142*a* is known.

Single examples of a similar overprint on the 2c., (No. 131) a 5c. (No. 134) are known used on cover, the former with unoverprinted example of the same value.

Trans-Atlantic AIR POST, 1919. ONE DOLLAR.
(70)

THREE CENTS
(71)

1919 (9 June). *Air. No. 75 surch with T* **70** *by* Royal Gazet *St. John's.*

143 **31** $1on 15c. bright scarlet . . . £110 £1
 a. No comma after "AIR POST" . . . £140 £1
 b. As Var a and no stop after "1919" . . . £350 £4
 c. As Var a and "A" of "AIR" under "a" of "Trans" . . . £350 £4

These stamps were issued for use on the mail carried on the fi successful flight across the Atlantic by Capt. J. Alcock a Lieut. A. Brown, and on other projected Trans-Atlantic fligh (Alcock flown cover, *Price* £3000).

The surcharge was applied in a setting of which 16 were norm 7 as No. 143a, 1 as No. 143b and 1 as No. 143c.

1920 (Sept). *Nos. 75 and 77/8 surch as T* **71**, *by* Royal Gazette *(with only one bar, at top of stamp).*

A. *Bars of surch 10½ mm apart.* B. *Bars 13½ mm apart.*

144 **33** 2c.on 30c. slate-blue (24 Sept) . . . 4·50 19
 a. Surch inverted . . . £550 £6
145 **31** 3c.on 15c. bright scarlet (A) (13 Sept) . . . £180 £
 a. Surch inverted . . . £1400
146 3c.on 15c. bright scarlet (B) (13 Sept) . . . 21·00 17
147 **34** 3c.on 35c. red (15 Sept) . . . 8·50 13
 a. Surch inverted . . . £1100
 b. Lower bar omitted . . . £130 £
 c. "THREE" omitted . . . £1200

Our prices for Nos. 147b and 147c are for stamps with lower or "THREE" entirely missing. The bar may be found in all sta of incompleteness and stamps showing broken bar are not of m value.

On the other hand, stamps showing either only the top or bott of the letters "THREE" are scarce, though not as rare as No. 14

The 6c. T **27** surcharged "THREE CENTS", in red or black an essay (*Price* £500). The 2c. on 30c. with red surcharge is a col trial (*Price* £650).

AIR MAIL to Halifax, N.S. 1921.

(72)

1921 (16 Nov). *Air. No. 78 optd with T* **72** *by* Royal Gazette.

I. *2¾ mm between* "AIR" *and* "MAIL".

148	**34**	35c. red	£100	90·00
		a. No stop after "1921"	90·00	80·00
		b. No stop and first "1" of "1921" below "f" of "Halifax"	£200	£180
		c. As No. 148, inverted	£4500	
		d. As No. 148a, inverted	£4000	
		e. As No. 148b, inverted	£9000	

II. *1½ mm between* "AIR" *and* "MAIL".

148*f*	**34**	35c. red	£110	£100
		g. No stop after "1921"	£130	£120
		h. No stop and first "1" of "1921" below "f" of "Halifax"	£200	£180
		i. As No. 148f, inverted	£5000	
		k. As No. 148g, inverted	£6500	
		l. As No. 148h, inverted	£9000	

Type **72** was applied as a setting of 25 which contained ten stamps as No. 148a, seven as No. 148, four as No. 148*f*, two as No. 148*g*, one as No. 148b and one as No. 148h.

73 Twin Hills, Tor's Cove

74 South-West Arm, Trinity

75 Statue of the Fighting Newfoundlander St. John's

(Recess D.L.R.)

1923 (9 July)–**26**. *T* **73/5** *and similar designs.* P 14 (comb or line).

149	1c. green	1·75	20
150	2c. carmine	1·00	10
	a. Imperf (pair)	£170	
151	3c. brown	1·50	10
152	4c. deep purple	1·00	30
153	5c. ultramarine	2·50	1·75
154	6c. slate	4·50	8·50
155	8c. purple	6·00	3·50
156	9c. slate-green	18·00	29·00
157	10c. violet	6·50	3·50
	a. Purple	8·00	2·75
158	11c. sage-green	3·75	17·00
159	12c. lake	3·25	10·00
160	15c. Prussian blue	3·25	19·00
161	20c. chestnut (28.4.24)	10·00	12·00
162	24c. sepia (22.4.24)	45·00	75·00
149/62 *Set of* 14		95·00	£160

Designs: *Horiz* (*as T***73**)—6c. Upper Steadies, Humber River; 11c. Shell Bird Island; 20c. Placentia. (*As T***74**)—8c. Quidi Vidi, near St. John's; 9c. Caribou crossing lake; 12c. Mount Moriah, Bay of Islands. *Vert* (*as T***75**)—4c. Humber River, 5c. Coast at Trinity; 10c. Humber River Canyon; 15c. Humber River near Little Rapids; 24c. Topsail Falls.

Perforations. Three perforating heads were used: comb 13.8 × 14 (all values); line 13.7 and 14, and combinations of these two (for all except 6, 8, 9 and 11c.).

Air Mail DE PINEDO 1927

(87)

1927 (18 May). *Air. No. 79 optd with T* **87**, *by Robinson & Co, Ltd.*

163	**35**	60c. black (R.)	£28000	£7500

For the mail carried by De Pinedo to Europe 300 stamps were overprinted, 230 used on correspondence, 66 presented to De Pinedo, Government Officials, etc., and 4 damaged and destroyed. Stamps without overprint were also used.

88 Newfoundland and Labrador

89 S.S. *Caribou*

90 King George Vand Queen Mary

91 Duke of Windsor when Prince of Wales

92 Express Train

93 Newfoundland Hotel, St. John's

94 Heart's Content

95 Cabot Tower, St. John's

96 War Memorial, St. John's

97 G.P.O., St. John's

98 Vickers "Vimy" Aircraft

99 Parliament House, St. John's

100 Grand Falls, Labrador

(Recess D.L.R.)

1928 (3 Jan)–**29**. *Publicity issue.* P 14 (1c.) 13½ × 13 (2, 3, 5, 6, 10, 14, 20c.), 13 × 13½ (4c.) (all comb), or 14–13½* (line) (others).

164	**88**	1c. deep green	2·25	1·25
165	**89**	2c. carmine	3·25	50
166	**90**	3c. brown	5·00	1·25
		a. Perf 14–13½ (line)	2·25	1·25
167	**91**	4c. mauve	7·50	2·75
		a. Rose-purple (1929)	8·00	7·50
168	**92**	5c. slate-grey	13·00	5·50
		a. Perf 14–13½ (line)	26·00	7·50
169	**93**	6c. ultramarine	4·50	24·00
		a. Perf 14–13½ (line)	10·00	24·00
170	**94**	8c. red-brown	3·75	28·00
171	**95**	9c. deep green	2·00	15·00
172	**96**	10c. deep violet	17·00	16·00
		a. Perf 14–13½ (line)	6·00	19·00
173	**97**	12c. carmine-lake	2·00	21·00
174	**95**	14c. brown-purple (8.28)	13·00	12·00
		a. Perf 14–13½ (line)	6·00	8·50
175	**98**	15c. deep blue	3·75	28·00
176	**99**	20c. grey-black	17·00	16·00
		a. Perf 14–13½ (line)	2·75	7·00
177	**97**	28c. deep green (12.28)	28·00	48·00
178	**100**	30c. sepia	6·00	17·00
164/78 (*cheapest*) *Set of* 15			80·00	£200

*Exact gauges for the various perforations are: 14 comb = 14 × 13.9; 13½ × 13 comb = 13.5 × 12.75; 14–13½ line = 14–13.75.

See also Nos. 179/87 and 198/208.

D 1c. P

D 2c. P

D 3c. P

D 4c. P

D 5c. P

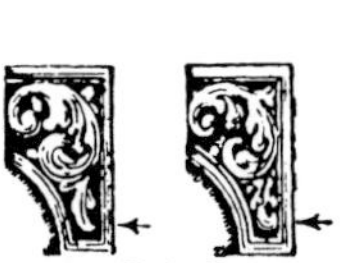
D 6c. P

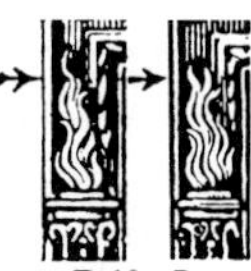
D 10c. P

D 15c. P

D 20c. P

D. De La Rue printing

P. Perkins, Bacon printing

1929 (10 Aug)–**31**. *Perkins, Bacon printing. Former types re-engraved.* No wmk. P 14 (comb) (1c.), 13½ (comb) (2, 6c.), 14–13½ (line) (20c.) or 13½ × 14 (comb) (others)*.

179	**88**	1c. green (26.9.29)	3·50	30
		a. Perf 14–13½ (line)	3·50	30
		b. Imperf between (vert pair)	£140	
		c. Imperf (pair)	£130	
180	**89**	2c. scarlet	1·75	40
		a. Imperf (pair)	£120	
		b. Perf 14–13½ (line)	3·25	1·00
181	**90**	3c. red-brown	1·00	20
		a. Imperf (pair)	£120	
182	**91**	4c. reddish purple (26.8.29)	2·75	80
		a. Imperf (pair)	£130	
183	**92**	5c. deep grey-green (14.9.29)	7·00	3·25
184	**93**	6c. ultramarine (8.11.29)	8·00	15·00
		a. Perf 14–13½ (line)	2·25	17·00
185	**96**	10c. violet (5.10.29)	4·25	3·50
186	**98**	15c. blue (1.30)	17·00	80·00
187	**99**	20c. black (1.1.31)	55·00	55·00
179/87 *Set of* 9			85·00	£140

*Exact gauges for the various perforations are: 14 comb = 14 × 13.9; 13½ comb = 13.6 × 13.5; 14–13½ line = 14–13.75; 13½ × 14 comb = 13.6 × 13.8.

THREE CENTS

(101)

Trans-Atlantic AIR MAIL By B. M. "Columbia" September 1930 Fifty Cents

(102)

(Surch by Messrs D. R. Thistle, St. John's)

1929 (23 Aug). *No. 154 surch with T* **101**.

188	3c.on 6c. slate (R.)	1·00	5·50
	a. Surch inverted	£600	£900
	b. Surch in black	£700	

1930 (25 Sept). *Air. No. 141 surch with T* **102** *by Messrs D. R. Thistle.*

191	**68**	50c. on 36c. sage-green	£5500	£4500

103 Aeroplane and Dog-team

104 Vickers-Vimy Biplane and early Sailing Packet

105 Routes of historic Transatlantic Flights

106

(Des A. B. Perlin. Recess P.B.)

1931. *Air*. P 14.

(a) Without wmk (2.1.31).

192 **103** 15c. chocolate . . . 7·50 14·00
a. Imperf between (horiz or vert pair) . . . £750
b. Imperf (pair) . . . £450
193 **104** 50c. green . . . 32·00 55·00
a. Imperf between (horiz or vert pair) . . . £800 £900
b. Imperf (pair) . . . £600
194 **105** $1 deep blue . . . 50·00 95·00
a. Imperf between (horiz or vert pair) . . . £800
b. Imperf (pair) . . . £650
192/4 *Set of* 3 . . . 80·00 £150

(b) Wmk W **106**, (sideways*) (13.3.31).

195 **103** 15c. chocolate . . . 6·50 20·00
a. Pair, with and without wmk . . . 30·00
b. Imperf between (horiz or vert pair) . . . £650
ba. Ditto, one without wmk (vert pair) . . . £1000
c. Imperf (pair) . . . £450
d. Wmk Cross (pair) . . . £100
196 **104** 50c. green . . . 29·00 65·00
a. Imperf between (horiz or vert pair) . . . £750
b. Imperf (pair)
c. Pair, with and without wmk . . . £250
197 **105** $1 deep blue . . . 80·00 £140
a. Imperf between (horiz or vert pair) . . . £750
b. Imperf horiz (vert pair) . . . £600
c. Pair, with and without wmk . . . £450
d. Imperf (pair) . . . £500
195/7 *Set of* 3 . . . £100 £200

"WITH AND WITHOUT WMK" PAIRS listed in the issues from No. 195a onwards must have one stamp *completely* without any trace of watermark.

1931 (25 March–July). *Perkins, Bacon printing (re-engraved types)*. W **106** (sideways on 1c., 4c., 30c.). P 13½ (1c.) or 13½ × 14 (others), both comb*.

198 **88** 1c. green (7.31) . . . 8·50 3·00
a. Imperf between (horiz pair) . . . £500
199 **89** 2c. scarlet (7.31) . . . 6·00 4·25
w. Wmk inverted . . . 40·00
200 **90** 3c. red-brown (7.31) . . . 2·00 2·75
w. Wmk inverted . . . 40·00
201 **91** 4c. reddish purple (7.31) . . . 2·00 1·25
202 **92** 5c. deep grey-green (7.31) . . . 7·00 12·00
203 **93** 6c. ultramarine . . . 8·00 25·00
w. Wmk inverted . . . 45·00
204 **94** 8c. chestnut (1.4.31) . . . 26·00 32·00
w. Wmk inverted . . . 55·00
205 **96** 10c. violet (1.4.31) . . . 14·00 12·00
206 **98** 15c. blue (1.7.31) . . . 21·00 60·00
207 **99** 20c. black (1.7.31) . . . 60·00 18·00
208 **100** 30c. sepia (1.7.31) . . . 28·00 45·00
198/208 *Set of* 11 . . . £160 £190

*Exact gauges for the two perforations are: 13½ = 13.6 × 13.5; 13½ × 14 = 13.6 × 13.8.

107 Atlantic Cod

108 King George V

109 Queen Mary

110 Duke of Windsor when Prince of Wales

111 Caribou

112 Queen Elizabeth II when Princess

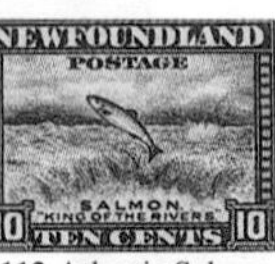
113 Atlantic Salmon

114 Newfoundland Dog

115 Harp Seal

116 Cape Race

117 Sealing Fleet

118 Fishing Fleet

(Recess P.B.)

1932 (2 Jan). W **106** (sideways* on vert designs). P 13½ (comb).

209 **107** 1c. green . . . 2·75 30
a. Imperf (pair) . . . £110
b. Perf 13 (line) . . . 17·00 27·00
ba. Imperf between (vert pair) . . . £110
w. Wmk top of shield to right . . . 40·00
210 **108** 2c. carmine . . . 1·50 20
a. Imperf (pair) . . . £130
c. Perf 13 (line) . . . 11·00 22·00
w. Wmk top of shield to right . . . 40·00
211 **109** 3c. orange-brown . . . 1·50 20
a. Imperf (pair) . . . 80·00
c. Perf 13 (line) . . . 16·00 28·00
ca. Imperf between (vert pair) . . . £250
d. Perf 14 (line). Small holes . . . 19·00 24·00
da. Imperf between (vert pair) . . . £180
w. Wmk top of shield to right . . . 40·00
212 **110** 4c. bright violet . . . 6·00 2·00
w. Wmk top of shield to right
213 **111** 5c. maroon . . . 5·00 1·75
a. Imperf (pair) . . . £160
w. Wmk top of shield to right
214 **112** 6c. light blue . . . 4·00 14·00
215 **113** 10c. black-brown . . . 70 65
a. Imperf (pair) . . . 65·00
w. Wmk inverted . . . 10·00
216 **114** 14c. black . . . 4·25 5·50
a. Imperf (pair) . . . £130
217 **115** 15c. claret . . . 1·25 2·00
a. Imperf (pair) . . . £160
b. Perf 14 (line) . . . 8·00 10·00
218 **116** 20c. green . . . 1·00 1·00
a. Imperf (pair) . . . £130
b. Perf 14 (line) . . . 80·00 80·00
w. Wmk inverted . . . 20·00
219 **117** 25c. slate . . . 2·00 2·25
a. Imperf (pair) . . . £150
b. Perf 14 (line) . . . 40·00 55·00
ba. Imperf between (vert pair) . . . £350
220 **118** 30c. ultramarine . . . 38·00 35·00
a. Imperf (pair) . . . £375
b. Imperf between (vert pair) . . . £750
c. Perf 14 (line) . . . £275
209/20 *Set of* 12 . . . 60·00 60·00

*The normal sideways watermark shows the top of the shield to left, *as seen from the back of the stamp*.

Nos. 209b, 210c and 211c were only issued in stamp booklets.

For similar stamps in different perforations see Nos. 222/8c and 276/89.

TRANS-ATLANTIC
WEST TO EAST
Per Dornier DO-X
May, 1932.
One Dollar and Fifty Cents

(**119**)

1932 (19 May). *Air. No. 197 surch as T* **119**, *by Messrs. D. R. Thistle*. P 14.

221 **105** $1.50 on $1 deep blue (R.) . . . £200 £225
a. Surch inverted . . . £10000

120 Queen Mother, when Duchess of York

121 Corner Brook Paper Mills

122 Loading Iron Ore, Bell Island

(Recess P.B.)

1932 (15 Aug)–**38**. W **106** (sideways* on vert designs). P 13½ (comb).

222 **107** 1c. grey . . . 2·00 10
a. Imperf (pair) . . . 42·00
c. Perf 14 (line) . . . 6·50 11·00
d. Perf 14 (line). Small holes . . . 15·00 27·00
e. Pair, with and without wmk . . . 40·00
w. Wmk top of shield to right . . . 50·00
223 **108** 2c. green . . . 1·25 10
a. Imperf (pair) . . . 35·00
c. Perf 14 (line) . . . 8·00 11·00
ca. Imperf between (horiz pair) . . . £275
d. Perf 14 (line). Small holes . . . 19·00 28·00
e. Pair, with and without wmk . . . 45·00
w. Wmk top of shield to right . . . 35·00
224 **110** 4c. carmine (21.7.34) . . . 3·00 40
a. Imperf (pair) . . . 55·00
b. Perf 14 (line) . . . 4·25 6·00
ba. Imperf between (horiz or vert pair) . . . £130
w. Wmk top of shield to right . . . 50·00
225 **111** 5c. violet (Die I) . . . 2·00 1·75
a. Imperf (pair) . . . 60·00
b. Perf 14 (line). Small holes . . . 25·00 26·00
c. Die II . . . 70 30
ca. Imperf (pair) . . . 65·00
cb. Perf 14 (line) . . . 22·00 22·00
cbw. Wmk top of shield to right . . . 40·00
cc. Imperf between (horiz pair) . . . £200
cd. Pair, with and without wmk . . . £120
226 **120** 7c. red-brown . . . 2·75 3·75
b. Perf 14 (line) . . . £140
ba. Imperf between (horiz pair) . . . £450
c. Imperf (pair) . . . £160
w. Wmk top of shield to right
227 **121** 8c. brownish red . . . 3·25 2·00
a. Imperf (pair) . . . 90·00
w. Wmk inverted
228 **122** 24c. bright blue . . . 1·00 3·25
a. Imperf (pair) . . . £250
b. Doubly printed . . . £900
w. Wmk inverted . . . 25·00
228*c* **118** 48c. red-brown (1.1.38) . . . 7·50 10·00
ca. Imperf (pair) . . . 95·00
222/8*c* *Set of* 8 . . . 19·00 17·00

*The normal sideways watermark shows the top of the shield to left, *as seen from the back of the stamp*.

No. 223. Two dies exist of the 2c. Die I was used for No. 210 and both dies for No. 223. The differences, though numerous, are very slight.

No. 225. There are also two dies of the 5c., Die I only being used for No. 213 and both dies for the violet stamp. In Die II the antler pointing to the "T" of "POSTAGE" is taller than the one pointing to the "S" and the individual hairs on the underside of the caribou's tail are distinct.

For similar stamps in a slightly larger size and perforated 12½ or 13½ (5c.) see Nos. 276/89.

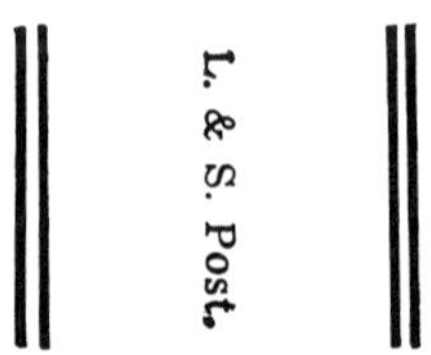

(**123**) "L.&S."—Land and Sea

1933 (9 Feb). *No. 195 optd with T* **123** *for ordinary postal use, by Messrs D. R. Thistle*. W **106** (sideways). P 14.

229 **103** 15c. chocolate . . . 3·75 12·0
a. Pair, one without wmk . . . 24·00
b. Opt reading up . . . £2250
c. Vertical pair, one without opt . . . £4250

124 Put to Flight

125 Land of Heart's Delight

(Des J. Scott. Recess P.B.)

1933 (9 June). *Air. T* **124/5** *and similar horiz designs*. W **10** (sideways). P 14 (5, 30, 75c.) or 11½ (10, 60c.).

230 5c. red-brown . . . 18·00 18·0
a. Imperf (pair) . . . £160
b. Imperf between (horiz or vert pair) . . . £1000
231 10c. orange-yellow . . . 14·00 32·0
a. Imperf (pair) . . . £130
232 30c. light blue . . . 32·00 45·0
a. Imperf (pair) . . . £400
233 60c. green . . . 50·00 £1
a. Imperf (pair) . . . £450
234 75c. yellow-brown . . . 50·00 £1
a. Imperf (pair) . . . £400
b. Imperf between (horiz or vert pair) . . . £2500
230/4 *Set of* 5 . . . £150 £2

Designs:—30c. Spotting the herd; 60c. News from home; 75 Labrador.

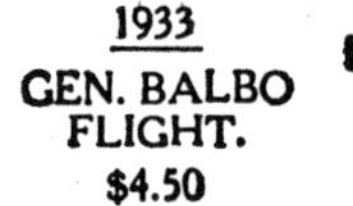

(**129**)

(Surch by Robinson & Co, St. John's)

1933 (24 July). *Air. Balbo Transatlantic Mass Formation Fligh No. 234 surch with T* **129**. W **106**. P 14.

235 $4.50 on 75c. yellow-brown . . . £275 £3
a. Surch inverted . . . £50000
b. Surch on 10c. (No. 231) . . . £50000

No. 235a. When this error was discovered the stamps we ordered to be officially destroyed but four copies which had be torn were recovered and skilfully repaired. In addition, fo undamaged examples exist and the price quoted is for one of the

130 Sir Humphrey Gilbert

131 Compton Castle, Devon

132 Gilbert Coat of Arms

(Recess P.B.)

1933 (3 Aug). *350th Anniv of the Annexation by Sir Humph Gilbert. T* **130/2** *and similar designs*. W **106** (sideways* on v designs). P 13½ (comb†).

236 1c. slate . . . 1·00 1
a. Imperf (pair) . . . 48·00
237 2c. green . . . 1·50
a. Imperf (pair) . . . 48·00
b. Doubly printed . . . £325
238 3c. chestnut . . . 2·25 1

239 4c. carmine 80 50
a. Imperf (pair) 45·00
240 5c. violet 2·00 80
241 7c. greenish blue 14·00 17·00
a. Perf 14 (line) 11·00 40·00
242 8c. vermilion 8·00 15·00
a. Brownish red £300
b. Bisected (4c.) (on cover) † £400
243 9c. ultramarine 7·00 14·00
a. Imperf (pair) £225
b. Perf 14 (line) 55·00 70·00
244 10c. brown-lake 4·00 10·00
a. Imperf (pair) £275
b. Perf 14 (line) 70·00 75·00
245 14c. grey-black 15·00 30·00
a. Perf 14 (line) 18·00 48·00
246 15c. claret 13·00 26·00
w. Wmk top of shield to right 7·50 21·00
247 20c. grey-green 14·00 19·00
a. Perf 14 (line) 24·00 40·00
w. Wmk inverted 45·00
248 24c. maroon 15·00 23·00
a. Imperf (pair) £110
b. Perf 14 (line) 25·00 42·00
w. Wmk top of shield to right 35·00
249 32c. olive-black 7·50 50·00
a. Perf 14 (line) 22·00 70·00
w. Wmk top of shield to right 20·00
236/49 *Set of* 14 80·00 £180

Designs: *Horiz*—4c. Eton College; 7c. Gilbert commissioned by Elizabeth I; 8c. Fleet leaving Plymouth, 1583; 9c. Arrival at St. John's; 10c. Annexation, 5 August 1583; 20c. Map of Newfoundland, 1626. *Vert*—5c. Anchor token; 14c. Royal Arms; 15c. Gilbert in the *Squirrel*; 24c. Queen Elizabeth I. 32c. Gilbert's statue at Truro.

*The normal sideways watermark shows the top of the shield to left, *as seen from the back of the stamp.*

†Exact gauges for the two perforations are: 13½ comb = 13.4; 14 line = 13.8.

1935 (6 May). *Silver Jubilee. As Nos. 91/4 of Antigua, but ptd by B.W.* P 11 × 12.
250 **133** 4c. rosine 1·00 1·75
251 5c. bright violet 1·25 2·50
252 7c. blue 1·75 7·00
253 24c. olive-green 5·00 12·00
250/3 *Set of* 4 8·00 21·00
250s/3s Perf "Specimen" *Set of* 4 £130

1937 (12 May). *Coronation Issue. As Nos. 95/7 of Antigua, but name and value uncoloured on coloured background.* P 11 × 11½.
254 **134** 2c. green 1·00 3·00
255 4c. carmine 1·60 3·50
256 5c. purple 3·00 4·00
254/6 *Set of* 3 5·00 9·50
254s/6s Perf "Specimen" *Set of* 3 85·00

144 Atlantic Cod

Die I

Die II

No. 258. In Die II the shading of the King's face is heavier and dots have been added down the ridge of the nose. The top frame line is thicker and more uniform.

Fish-hook flaw (R. 1/7 or 3/3)

Re-entry to right of design (inscr oval, tree and value) (R. 4/8)

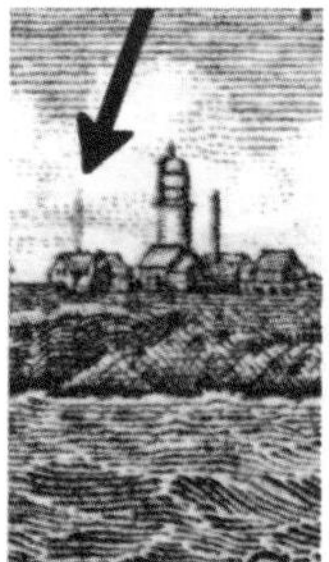
Extra chimney (R. 6/5)

(Recess P.B.)

1937 (12 May). *Additional Coronation Issue. T* **144** *and similar horiz designs.* W **106**. P 14 (line)*.
257 1c. grey 3·00 30
a. Pair, with and without wmk 24·00
b. Fish-hook flaw 26·00
c. Perf 13½ (line) 3·50 50
ca. Pair, with and without wmk 28·00
cb. Fish-hook flaw 30·00
d. Perf 13 (comb) 28·00 50·00
da. Pair, with and without wmk
db. Fish-hook flaw £170
258 3c. orange-brown (I) 11·00 3·50
a. Pair, with and without wmk 70·00
b. Imperf between (horiz pair)
c. Perf 13½ (line) 10·00 5·00
ca. Pair, with and without wmk
cb. Imperf between (vert pair) £400
d. Perf 13 (comb) 6·50 3·75
e. Die II (P 14, *line*) 6·00 3·50
ea. Pair, with and without wmk £100
ec. Perf 13½ (line) 6·00 4·50
eca. Pair, with and without wmk £120
ecb. Imperf between (vert pair) £500
ed. Perf 13 (comb) 7·00 3·25
eda. Pair, with and without wmk £110
259 7c. bright ultramarine 2·50 1·25
a. Pair, with and without wmk
b. Re-entry at right 55·00
c. Perf 13½ (line) 3·00 1·75
ca. Pair, with and without wmk
cb. Re-entry at right 60·00
d. Perf 13 (comb) £350 £450
db. Re-entry at right £1400
260 8c. scarlet 2·00 3·50
a. Pair, with and without wmk 65·00
b. Imperf between (horiz or vert pair) £650
c. Imperf (pair) £350
d. Perf 13½ (line) 2·50 4·25
da. Pair, with and without wmk 70·00
db. Imperf between (vert pair)
e. Perf 13 (comb) 7·00 12·00
261 10c. blackish brown 4·50 8·50
a. Pair, with and without wmk 85·00
b. Perf 13½ (line) 4·50 10·00
ba. Pair, with and without wmk 70·00
c. Perf 13 (comb) 3·25 12·00
cw. Wmk inverted 75·00
262 14c. black 1·40 2·75
a. Pair, with and without wmk 60·00
b. Perf 13½ (line) 1·75 4·00
ba. Pair, with and without wmk 60·00
c. Perf 13 (comb) £12000 £6500
263 15c. claret 12·00 4·25
a. Pair, with and without wmk 75·00
bw. Wmk inverted 75·00
c. Perf 13½ (line) 11·00 5·00
ca. Pair, with and without wmk 70·00
cb. Imperf between (vert pair) £475
d. Perf 13 (comb) 22·00 25·00
da. Pair, with and without wmk £120
264 20c. green 3·00 10·00
a. Pair, with and without wmk
c. Extra chimney 48·00
dw. Wmk inverted 85·00
e. Perf 13½ (line) 3·00 11·00
ea. Pair, with and without wmk £140
eb. Imperf between (vert pair) £750
ec. Extra chimney 55·00
f. Perf 13 (comb) 2·50 9·00
fc. Extra chimney 48·00
265 24c. light blue 2·50 2·75
a. Pair, with and without wmk £150
c. Perf 13½ (line) 2·50 3·00
ca. Pair, with and without wmk £150
cb. Imperf between (vert pair) £800
d. Perf 13 (comb) 27·00 27·00
266 25c. slate 2·75 2·25
a. Pair, with and without wmk £130
b. Perf 13½ (line) 2·75 3·50
ba. Pair, with and without wmk £130
c. Perf 13 (comb) 29·00 60·00
267 48c. slate-purple 8·50 6·00
a. Pair, with and without wmk £180
c. Perf 13½ (line) 9·00 7·50
ca. Pair, with and without wmk £180
cb. Imperf between (vert pair) £750
d. Perf 13 (comb) 35·00 75·00
257/67 *Set of* 11 40·00 40·00

Designs:—3c. Map of Newfoundland; 7c. Reindeer; 8c. Corner Brook paper mills; 10c. Atlantic Salmon; 14c. Newfoundland dog; 15c. Harp Seal; 20c. Cape Race; 24c. Bell Island; 25c. Sealing fleet; 48c. The Banks fishing fleet.

The line perforations measure 14.1 (14) or 13.7 (13½). The comb perforation measures 13.3 × 13.2. One example of the 7c. has been reported perforated 13½ × 14.

The paper used had the watermarks spaced for smaller format stamps. In consequence, the individual watermarks are out of alignment so that stamps from the second vertical row were sometimes without watermark.

155 King George VI **156** Queen Mother

(Recess P.B.)

1938 (12 May). *T* **155/6** *and similar vert designs.* W **106** (sideways). P 13½ (comb).
268 2c. green 2·50 1·00
a. Pair, with and without wmk £140
b. Imperf (pair) 85·00
269 3c. carmine 1·00 1·00
a. Perf 14 (line) £425 £300
b. Pair, with and without wmk £190
c. Imperf (pair) 85·00
270 4c. light blue 2·25 60
a. Pair, with and without wmk 90·00
b. Imperf (pair) 80·00
w. Wmk inverted 65·00
271 7c. deep ultramarine 1·00 4·75
a. Imperf (pair) £130
268/71 *Set of* 4 6·00 6·50

Designs:—4c. Queen Elizabeth II as princess; 7c. Queen Mary.
For similar designs, perf 12½, see Nos. 277/81.

159 King George VI and Queen Elizabeth

(Recess B.W.)

1939 (17 June). *Royal Visit.* No wmk. P 13½.
272 **159** 5c. deep ultramarine 3·25 1·00

2
▲ CENTS 
(**160**)

1939 (20 Nov). *No. 272 surch as T* **160**, *at St. John's.*
273 **159** 2c. on 5c. deep ultramarine (Br.) 2·50 50
274 4c. on 5c. deep ultramarine (C.) 2·00 1·00

161 Grenfell on the *Strathcona* (after painting by Gribble)

162 Memorial University College

(Recess C.B.N.)

1941 (1 Dec). *50th Anniv of Sir Wilfred Grenfell's Labrador Mission.* P 12.
275 **161** 5c. blue 30 1·00

Damaged "A" (R. 5/9)

(Recess Waterlow)

1941–44. W **106** (sideways* on vert designs). P 12½ (line).
276 **107** 1c. grey 20 1·00
277 **155** 2c. green 30 75
w. Wmk top of shield to right 35·00
278 **156** 3c. carmine 30 30
a. Pair, with and without wmk 80·00
b. Damaged "A" 50·00 32·00
w. Wmk top of shield to right 35·00
279 – 4c. blue (As No. 270) 2·25 40
a. Pair, with and without wmk £150
w. Wmk top of shield to right 35·00
280 **111** 5c. violet (Die I) (P 13½ *comb*) £110
a. Perf 12½ (line) (6.42) 2·75 70
ab. Pair, with and without wmk £130
ac. Printed double £400
ad. Imperf vert (horiz pair) £400
b. Imperf (pair) £140
281 – 7c. deep ultramarine (As No. 271) 6·00 14·00
a. Pair, with and without wmk £160
282 **121** 8c. rose-red 2·00 2·75
a. Pair, with and without wmk £150
283 **113** 10c. black-brown 1·75 2·25
284 **114** 14c. black 5·50 7·00
285 **115** 15c. claret 5·50 8·50
286 **116** 20c. green 5·50 6·00
287 **122** 24c. blue 3·25 17·00
w. Wmk top of shield to right 55·00
288 **117** 25c. slate 8·50 11·00
289 **118** 48c. red-brown (1944) 4·00 7·00
276/89 *Set of* 14 42·00 70·00

*The normal sideways watermark shows the top of the shield to left, *as seen from the back of the stamp*.

Nos. 276/89 are redrawn versions of previous designs with slightly larger dimensions; the 5c. for example, measures 21 mm in width as opposed to the 20.4 mm of the Perkins Bacon printings.

No. 280. For Die I see note relating to No. 225.

(Recess C.B.N.)

1943 (1 Jan). P 12.

290	**162**	30c. carmine	1·00	2·75

163 St. John's

TWO CENTS
(164)

(Recess C.B.N.)

1943 (1 June). *Air.* P 12.

291	**163**	7c. ultramarine	50	1·00

1946 (21 Mar). *No. 290 surch locally with T* **164**.

292	**162**	2c. on 30c. carmine	30	1·00

165 Queen Elizabeth II when Princess

166 Cabot off Cape Bonavista

(Recess Waterlow)

1947 (21 Apr). *Princess Elizabeth's 21st Birthday.* W **106** (sideways). P 12½.

293	**165**	4c. light blue	30	1·00
		a. Imperf vert (horiz pair)	£350	

(Recess Waterlow)

1947 (24 June). *450th Anniv of Cabot's Discovery of Newfoundland.* W **106** (sideways). P 12½.

294	**166**	5c. mauve	20	1·00
		a. Imperf between (horiz pair)	£1500	

STAMP BOOKLETS

1926. *Black on pink cover with Ayre and Sons advertisement on front. Stapled.*

SB1 40c. booklet containing eight 1c. and sixteen 2c. (Nos. 149/50) in blocks of 8 . . . £1200

B 1

1932 (2 Jan). *Black on buff cover as Type* **B 1**. *Stapled.*

SB2 40c. booklet containing four 1c., twelve 2c. and four 3c. (Nos. 209b, 210c, 211c) in blocks of 4 . . . £350
a. Contents as No. SB2, but containing Nos. 209b, 210 and 211c . . . £425
b. Contents as No. SB2, but containing Nos. 222d, 223d and 211d . . . £400

B 2

1932. *Black on cream cover as Type* **B 2**. *Stapled.*

SB3 40c. booklet containing four 1c., twelve 2c. and four 3c. (Nos. 222, 223, 211) in blocks of 4 . . . £350

POSTAGE DUE STAMPS

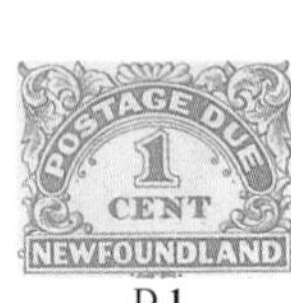

D 1

D 6ac

(Litho John Dickinson & Co, Ltd)

1939 (1 May)–**49**. P 10.

D1	**D 1**	1c. green	2·25	9·50
		a. Perf 11 (1949)	3·25	12·00
D2		2c. vermilion	13·00	7·50
		a. Perf 11 × 9 (1946)	14·00	20·00
D3		3c. ultramarine	5·00	23·00
		a. Perf 11 × 9 (1949)	13·00	42·00
		b. Perf 9	£700	
D4		4c. orange	9·00	17·00
		a. Perf 11 × 9 (May 1948)	12·00	55·00
D5		5c. brown	5·50	26·00
D6		10c. violet	7·00	18·00
		a. Perf 11 (W **106**) (1949)	22·00	85·00
		ab. Ditto. Imperf between (vert pair)	£800	
		ac. "POSTAGE LUE" (R. 3/3 or 3/8)	£130	£350
D1/6 *Set of* 6			38·00	90·00

Newfoundland joined the Dominion of Canada on 31 March 1949.

NOVA SCOTIA

Organised postal services in Nova Scotia date from April 1754 when the first of a series of Deputy Postmasters was appointed, under the authority of the British G.P.O. This arrangement continued until 6 July 1851 when the colony assumed responsibility for its postal affairs.

For illustrations of the handstamp types see BRITISH POST OFFICES ABROAD notes, following GREAT BRITAIN.

AMHERST

CROWNED-CIRCLE HANDSTAMPS

CC1 CC 1 AMHERST. N.S.(R) (25.2.1845) *Price on cover* £1000

ST. MARGARETS BAY

CROWNED-CIRCLE HANDSTAMPS

CC2 CC 1 ST. MARGARETS BAY. N.S.(R) (30.6.1845) *Price on cover* £9500

Nos. CC1/2 were later used during temporary shortages of stamps, struck in red or black.

PRICES FOR STAMPS ON COVER		
No.	1	*from* × 5
Nos.	2/4	*from* × 2
Nos.	5/8	*from* × 4
Nos.	9/10	*from* × 10
Nos.	11/13	*from* × 2
Nos.	14/15	—
No.	16	*from* × 4
Nos.	17/19	*from* × 10
Nos.	20/5	*from* × 2
No.	26	*from* × 50
Nos.	27/8	*from* × 4
No.	29	*from* × 10

1

2

Crown and Heraldic Flowers of United Kingdom and Mayflower of Nova Scotia.

(Recess P.B.)

1851 (1 Sept)–**57**. *Bluish paper.* Imperf.

1	**1**	1d. red-brown (12.5.53)	£2000	£400
		a. Bisected (½d.) (on cover)	†	£55000
2	**2**	3d. deep blue	£1000	£160
		a. Bisected (1½d.) (on cover)	†	£2500
3		3d. bright blue	£900	£120
		a. Bisected (1½d.) (on cover)	†	£2500
4		3d. pale blue (1857)	£750	£140
		a. Bisected (1½d.) (on cover)	†	£2500
5		6d. yellow-green	£4000	£450
		a. Bisected (3d.) (on cover)	†	£3250
6		6d. deep green (1857)	£10000	£750
		a. Bisected (3d.) (on cover)	†	£5500
		b. Quartered (1½d.) (on cover)	†	£40000
7		1s. cold violet	£19000	£5000
		a. Bisected (6d.) (on cover)	†	£48000
		b. Quartered (3d.) (on cover)	†	£65000
7*c*		1s. deep purple (1851)	£15000	£3750
		d. Watermarked	£20000	£5000
8		1s. purple (1857)	£14000	£2750
		a. Bisected (6d.) (on cover)	†	£38000

The watermark on No. 7d consists of the whole or part of a letter from the name "T. H. SAUNDERS" (the papermakers).

The stamps formerly catalogued on almost white paper are probably some from which the bluish paper has been discharged.

Reprints of all four values were made in 1890 on thin, hard, white paper. The 1d. is brown, the 3d. blue, the 6d. deep green, and the 1s. violet-black.

The 3d. bisects, which were authorised on 19 October 1854, are usually found used to make up the 7½d. rate.

(New Currency. 100 cents = 1 dollar)

3

4

5

(Recess American Bank Note Co, New York)

1863. P 12.

(a) Yellowish paper.

9	**3**	1c. jet black	3·50	13·0
		a. Bisected (½c.) (on cover)	†	£1000
10		1c. grey-black	3·50	13·0
11		2c. grey-purple	11·00	15·0
11*a*		2c. purple	17·00	14·0
12		5c. blue	£375	17·0
13		5c. deep blue	£375	17·0
14	**4**	8½c. deep green	3·25	42·0
15		8½c. yellow-green	3·25	42·0
16		10c. scarlet	16·00	26·0
17	**5**	12½c. black	28·00	26·0
17*a*		12½c. greyish black	—	26·0

(b) White paper.

18	**3**	1c. black	3·25	14·0
		a. Imperf vert (horiz pair)	£150	
19		1c. grey	3·25	14·0
20		2c. dull purple	3·50	14·0
21		2c. purple	3·50	14·0
22		2c. grey-purple	3·50	14·0
		a. Bisected (1c.) (on cover)	†	£450
23		2c. slate-purple	3·50	12·0
24		5c. blue	£400	19·0
25		5c. deep blue	£400	19·0
26	**4**	8½c. deep green	17·00	40·0
27		10c. scarlet	6·00	25·0
28		10c. vermilion	4·00	25·0
		a. Bisected (5c.) (on cover)	†	£75
29	**5**	12½c. black	50·00	30·0

Nova Scotia joined the Dominion of Canada on 1 July 1867.

PRINCE EDWARD ISLAND

Prince Edward Island, previously administered as part of Nova Scotia, became a separate colony in 1769.

PRICES FOR STAMPS ON COVER		
Nos.	1/4	*from* × 3
No.	5	—
No.	6	*from* × 5
Nos.	7/8	*from* × 10
Nos.	9/11	*from* × 8
Nos.	12/18	*from* × 6
Nos.	19/20	*from* × 10
Nos.	21/6	*from* × 4
Nos.	27/31	*from* × 8
Nos.	32/3	*from* × 40
Nos.	34/7	*from* × 8
No.	38	*from* × 30
Nos.	39/41	*from* × 20
No.	42	*from* × 50
Nos.	43/7	*from* × 8

1 2 3 4 5 6

Two Dies of 2d.:

Die I. Left-hand frame and circle merge at centre left (all stamps in the sheet of 60 (10 × 6) except R. 2/5)

Die II. Left-hand frame and circle separate at centre left (R. 2/5). There is also a break in the top frame line.

(Typo Charles Whiting, London)

1861 (1 Jan). *Yellowish toned paper.*

(a) P 9.

1	**1**	2d. rose (I)	£275	£1
		a. Imperf between (horiz pair)	£5000	
		b. Imperf horiz (vert pair)		
		c. Bisected (1d.) (on cover)	†	£40
		d. Die II		
2		2d. rose-carmine (I)	£300	£1
		a. Die II		
3	**2**	3d. blue	£600	£2
		a. Bisected (1½d.) (on cover)	†	£35
		b. Double print	£1700	
4	**3**	6d. yellow-green	£850	£3

(b) Rouletted.

5	**1**	2d. rose (I)	†	£50

The 2d. and 3d., perf 9, were authorised to be bisected and us for half their normal value.

1862–69. *Yellowish toned paper.*

(a) P 11 (1862) or 11¼ (1869).

6	4	1d. brown-orange	42·00	75·00
6*a*		2d. rose (I) (1869)	†	£500
7	6	9d. bluish lilac (29.3.62)	85·00	65·00
8		9d. dull mauve	85·00	65·00

(b) P 11½–12 *(1863-69).*

9	4	1d. yellow-orange (1863)	29·00	42·00
		a. Bisected (½d.) (on cover)	†	£2500
		b. Imperf between (horiz pair)	£375	
10		1d. orange-buff	30·00	42·00
11		1d. yellow	32·00	42·00
12	1	2d. rose (I) (1863)	11·00	10·00
		a. Imperf vert (horiz pair)		
		b. Bisected (1d.) (on cover)	†	£2000
		c. Die II	80·00	80·00
13		2d. deep rose (I)	12·00	13·00
		a. Die II	85·00	90·00
14	2	3d. blue (1863)	19·00	20·00
		a. Imperf horiz (vert pair)		
		b. Bisected (1½d.) (on cover)		
15		3d. deep blue	19·00	19·00
16	5	4d. black (1869)	20·00	26·00
		a. Imperf vert (horiz pair)	£250	
		b. Bisected (2d.) (on cover)	†	£1800
		c. Imperf between (horiz strip of 3)	£325	
17	3	6d. yellow-green (15.12.66)	£100	90·00
		a. Bisected (3d.) (on cover)	†	£3500
18		6d. blue-green (1868)	90·00	95·00
19	6	9d. lilac (1863)	75·00	75·00
20		9d. reddish mauve (1863)	75·00	75·00
		a. Imperf vert (horiz pair)	£500	
		b. Bisected (4½d.) (on cover)	†	£3000

A new perforator, gauging exactly 11¼, was introduced in 1869. Apart from No. 6a, it was used in compound with the perf 11½–12 machine.

(c) Perf compound of 11 or 11¼ (1869) and 11½–12.

21	4	1d. yellow-orange	£200	85·00
22	1	2d. rose (I)	£180	70·00
		a. Die II		
23	2	3d. blue	£225	70·00
24	5	4d. black	£300	£250
25	3	6d. yellow-green	£275	£275
26	6	9d. reddish mauve	£325	£275

1870. *Coarse, wove bluish white paper.* P 11½–12.

27	1	2d. rose (I)	12·00	12·00
		a. Die II	85·00	95·00
28		2d. rose-pink (I)	6·50	9·50
		a. Die II	65·00	75·00
		b. "TWC" (R. 6/4)	70·00	80·00
		c. Imperf between (horiz pair)	£150	
		d. Imperf horiz (vert pair)	£150	
29	2	3d. pale blue	10·00	13·00
30		3d. blue	10·00	13·00
		a. Imperf between (horiz pair)	£300	
31	5	4d. black	4·75	27·00
		a. Imperf between (horiz pair)	£140	
		b. Bisected (2d.) (on cover)	†	£1800

(New Currency. 100 cents = 1 dollar)

7

(Recess British-American Bank Note Co., Montreal and Ottawa)

1870 (1 June). P 12.

32	7	4½d. (3d. stg), yellow-brown	45·00	60·00
33		4½d. (3d. stg), deep brown	48·00	65·00

8 9 10 11 12 13

(Typo Charles Whiting, London)

1872 (1 Jan).

(a) P 11½–12.

34	8	1c. orange	4·75	18·00
35		1c. yellow-orange	4·75	15·00
36		1c. brown-orange	5·50	18·00
37	10	3c. rose	16·00	25·00
		a. Stop between "PRINCE. EDWARD"	45·00	60·00
		b. Bisected (1½c.) (on cover)		
		c. Imperf horiz (vert pair)	£425	

(b) Perf 12 to 12¼ large holes.

38	9	2c. blue	16·00	38·00
		a. Bisected (1c.) (on cover)	†	£3000
39	11	4c. yellow-green	5·00	20·00
40		4c. deep green	6·00	18·00
		a. Bisected (2c.) (on cover)	†	£3000
41	12	6c. black	4·50	19·00
		a. Bisected (3c.) (on cover)	†	£1600
		b. Imperf between (horiz pair)	£250	
		c. Imperf vert (horiz pair)		
42	13	12c. reddish mauve	4·25	32·00

(c) P 12½–13, smaller holes.

43	8	1c. orange	14·00	
44		1c. brown-orange	5·50	18·00
45	10	3c. rose	16·00	28·00
		a. Stop between "PRINCE. EDWARD"	55·00	75·00
45*b*	12	6c. black	—	£250

(d) Perf compound of *(a)* and *(c)* 11½–12 × 12½–13.

46	8	1c. orange	40·00	45·00
47	10	3c. rose	45·00	48·00
		a. Stop between "PRINCE. EDWARD"	£200	£225

Prince Edward Island joined the Dominion of Canada on 1 July 1873.

DOMINION OF CANADA

On 1 July 1867, Canada, Nova Scotia and New Brunswick were united to form the Dominion of Canada.

The provinces of Manitoba (1870), British Columbia (1871), Prince Edward Island (1873), Alberta (1905), Saskatchewan (1905), and Newfoundland (1949) were subsequently added, as were the Northwest Territories (1870) and Yukon Territory (1898).

PRICES FOR STAMPS ON COVER TO 1945	
Nos. 46/67	*from* × 2
Nos. 68/71	*from* × 10
Nos. 72/89	*from* × 3
Nos. 90/100	*from* × 2
Nos. 101/2	*from* × 5
Nos. 103/11	*from* × 3
Nos. 115/20	*from* × 6
Nos. 121/49	*from* × 3
Nos. 150/65	*from* × 2
Nos. 166/72	*from* × 3
Nos. 173/87	*from* × 5
Nos. 188/95	*from* × 2
Nos. 196/215	*from* × 3
Nos. 219/224*b*	*from* × 4
Nos. 225/45	*from* × 2
Nos. 246/55	*from* × 8
Nos. 256/310	*from* × 2
No. 312	*from* × 20
No. 313	*from* × 10
Nos. 315/18	*from* × 2
Nos. 319/28	*from* × 3
Nos. 329/40	*from* × 2
Nos. 341/400	*from* × 1
Nos. R1/11	*from* × 5
Nos. S1/3	*from* × 8
No. S4	*from* × 6
No. S5	*from* × 5
Nos. S6/11	*from* × 3
Nos. S12/14	*from* × 5
Nos. D1/8	*from* × 4
Nos. D9/13	*from* × 5
Nos. D14/24	*from* × 4

13

14

15

Large types

PRINTERS. Nos. 46/120 were recess-printed by the British American Bank Note Co at Ottawa or Montreal.

1868 (1 Apr)–**90**. *As T* **13/15** *(various frames).*

I. *Ottawa printings.* P 12.

(a) Thin rather transparent crisp paper.

46	13	½c. black (1.4.68)	80·00	70·00
47	14	1c. red-brown (1.4.68)	£375	60·00
48		2c. grass-green (1.4.68)	£400	45·00
49		3c. red-brown (1.4.68)	£700	25·00
50		6c. blackish brown (1.4.68)	£1000	£170
51		12½c. bright blue (1.4.68)	£650	£130
52		15c. deep reddish purple	£900	£180

In these first printings the impression is generally blurred and the lines of the background are less clearly defined than in later printings.

(b) Medium to stout wove paper (1868–71).

53	13	½c. black	60·00	50·00
54		½c. grey-black	60·00	50·00
		a. Imperf between (pair)		
		b. Watermarked	£12000	£6000
55	14	1c. red-brown	£300	40·00
		a. Laid paper	£7000	£1600
		b. Watermarked (1868)	£1900	£200
56		1c. deep orange (Jan, 1869)	£800	80·00
56*a*		1c. orange-yellow (May (?), 1869)	£650	60·00
56*b*		1c. pale orange-yellow	£750	75·00
		ba. Imperf		
57		2c. deep green	£350	30·00
57*a*		2c. pale emerald-green (1871)	£450	48·00
		ab. Bisected (1c. with 2c. to make 3c. rate) on cover	†	£4500
		ac. Laid paper	†	£60000
57*d*		2c. bluish green	£375	30·00
		da. Watermarked (1868)	£1600	£225
58		3c. brown-red	£700	16·00
		a. Laid paper	£6000	£300
		b. Watermarked (1868)	£2500	£170
59		6c. blackish brown (*to* chocolate)	£700	42·00
		a. Watermarked (1868)	£3250	£600
59*b*		6c. yellow-brown (1870)	£700	38·00
		ba. Bisected (3c.), on cover	†	£2250
60		12½c. bright blue	£500	40·00
		a. Imperf horiz (vert pair)	†	£11000
		b. Watermarked (1868)	£1800	£250
60*c*		12½c. pale dull blue (milky)	£500	45·00
61		15c. deep reddish purple	£500	60·00
61*a*		15c. pale reddish purple	£450	60·00
		ab. Watermarked (1868)	—	£1200
61*b*		15c. dull violet-grey	£225	30·00
		ba. Watermarked (1868)	£3000	£500
61*c*		15c. dull grey-purple	£300	30·00

The official date of issue was 1 April 1868. Scattered examples of most values can be found used in the second half of March.

The watermark on the stout paper stamps consists of the words "E & G BOTHWELL CLUTHA MILLS," in large double-lined capitals which can be found upright, inverted or reversed. Portions of one or two letters only may be found on these stamps, which occur in the early printings of 1868.

The paper may, in most cases, be easily divided if the stamps are laid face downwards and carefully compared. The thin hard paper is more or less transparent and shows the design through the stamp; the thicker paper is softer to the feel and more opaque.

Of the 2c. laid paper No. 57ac two examples only are known.

II. *Montreal printings. Medium to stout wove paper.*

(a) P 11½ × 12 or 11¾ × 12.

62	13	½c. black (1873)	70·00	70·00
63	15	5c. olive-green (1.10.75)	£700	65·00
		a. Perf 12	£3500	£800
64	14	15c. dull grey-purple (1874)	£750	£160
65		15c. lilac-grey (3.77)	£900	£160
		a. Script watermark	£7500	£1800
		b. "BOTHWELL" watermark	†	£750
66		15c. slate	£900	£300

(b) P 12.

67	14	15c. clear deep violet (1879)	£2250	£500
68		15c. deep slate (1881)	£150	29·00
69		15c. slaty blue (1887)	£150	29·00
70		15c. slate-purple (*shades*) (7.88–92)	65·00	17·00

No. 63a gauges 12 or above on all four sides.

The watermark on No. 65a is part of "Alex.Pirie & Sons" which appeared as script letters once per sheet in a small batch of the paper used for the 1877 printing. For a description of the sheet watermark on No. 65b, see note after No. 61*c*.

Several used examples of the 12½c. have been reported perforated 11½ × 12 or 11¾ × 12.

The last printing of the 15c. slate-purple, No. 70, took place at Ottawa.

III. *Ottawa printings. Thinnish paper of poor quality, often toned grey or yellowish.* P 12.

71	14	15c. slate-violet (*shades*) (5.90)	65·00	20·00
		a. Imperf (pair). *Brown-purple*	£1100	

Examples of No. 71 are generally found with yellowish streaky gum.

21 *Small type*

Strand of hair

Straw in hair

1870–88. *As T* **21** *(various frames). Ottawa (1870–73) and Montreal printings.* P 12 (or slightly under).

Papers	*(a)*	1870–80.	*Medium to stout wove.*
	(b)	1870–72.	*Thin, soft, very white.*
	(c)	1878–97.	*Thinner and poorer quality.*

72	21	1c. bright orange (*a, b*) (2.1870–73)	£150	23·00
		a. Thick soft paper (1871)	£425	£120
73		1c. orange-yellow (*a*) (1876–79)	60·00	2·50
74		1c. pale dull yellow (*a*) (1877–79)	38·00	1·75
75		1c. bright yellow (*a, c*) (1878–97)	26·00	1·00
		a. Imperf (pair) (*c*)	£350	
		b. Bisected (½c.) (on *Railway News*)	†	£3500
		c. Printed both sides	£1600	
		d. Strand of hair	—	50·00
76		1c. lemon-yellow (*c*) (1880)	90·00	16·00
77		2c. dp green (*a, b*) (1872–73 & 1876–78)	85·00	2·00

78		2c. grass-green (c) (1878–88)	48·00	1·00
		a. Imperf (pair)	£400	
		b. Bisected (1c. with 2c. to make 3c. rate) on cover	†	£1600
79		3c. Indian red (a) (1.70)	£900	50·00
		a. Perf 12½ (2.70)	£4750	£500
80		3c. pale rose-red (a) (9.70)	£300	8·50
81		3c. deep rose-red (a, b) (1870–73)	£325	9·00
		a. Thick soft paper (1.71)	—	£150
82		3c. dull red (a, c) (1876–88)	70·00	2·00
83		3c. orange-red (*shades*) (a, c) (1876–88)	50·00	1·50
84		3c. rose-carm (c) (10.88.–4.89)	£350	11·00
85		5c. olive-green (a, c) (2.76–88)	£225	8·00
		a. Straw in hair	—	£100
86		6c. yellowish brown (a, b, c) (1872–73 and 1876–90)	£190	12·00
		a. Bisected (3c.) on cover	†	£1600
		b. Perf 12 × 11½ (1873)	†	—
87		10c. pale lilac-magenta (a) (1876–?)	£500	50·00
88		10c. deep lilac-magenta (a, c) (3.76–88)	£475	60·00
89		10c. lilac-pink (3.88)	£275	30·00

Nos. 75 and 78 were printed in the same shades during the second Ottawa period. Nos. 75a and 78a date from *circa* 1894–95.

There are four variants of the Strand of Hair, with the strand in the same position but varying in length. R. 2/13 and R. 3/16 have been identified. The illustration shows the "Long Strand".

Examples of paper (a) can often be found showing traces of ribbing, especially on the 2c. value.

No. 79a was issued in New Brunswick and Nova Scotia.

One used copy of the 10c. perf 12½ has been reported.

1873–79. *Montreal printings. Medium to stout wove paper.* P 11½ × 12 or 11¾ × 12.

90	21	1c. bright orange	£200	35·00
91		1c. orange-yellow (1873–79)	£170	13·00
92		1c. pale dull yellow (1877–79)	£160	18·00
93		1c. lemon-yellow (1879)	£200	18·00
94		2c. deep green (1873–78)	£250	20·00
95		3c. dull red (1875–79)	£250	18·00
96		3c. orange-red (1873–79)	£250	18·00
97		5c. olive-green (1.2.76–79)	£425	28·00
98		6c. yellowish brown (1873–79)	£425	38·00
99		10c. very pale lilac magenta (1874)	£950	£250
100		10c. deep lilac-magenta (1876–79)	£650	£200

27

5c. on 6c. re-entry (R. 3/4)

1882–97. *Montreal (to March 1889) and Ottawa printings. Thinnish paper of poor quality.* P 12.

101	27	½c. black (7.82–97)	11·00	7·00
102		½c. grey-black	11·00	7·00
		ab. Imperf (pair) (1891–93?)	£450	
		ac. Imperf between (pair)	£750	

1889–97. *Ottawa printings. Thinnish paper of poor quality, often toned grey or yellowish.* P 12.

103	21	2c. dull sea-green	48·00	1·25
104		2c. blue-green (7.89–91)	38·00	1·75
105		3c. bright vermilion (4.89–97)	32·00	80
		a. Imperf (pair) (1891–93?)	£350	
106		5c. brownish grey (5.89)	65·00	1·75
		a. Imperf (pair) (1891–93)	£425	
107		6c. deep chestnut (10.90)	32·00	8·50
		a. "5c." re-entry*	£2500	£1300
		b. Imperf (pair) (1891–93?)	£450	
108		6c. pale chestnut	40·00	8·50
109		10c. salmon-pink	£275	£110
110		10c. carmine-pink (4.90)	£170	24·00
		a. Imperf (pair) (1891–93?)	£500	
111		10c. brownish red (1894?)	£170	24·00
		a. Imperf (pair)	£450	

On No. 107a the top portion of the 5c. design cuts across "CANADA POSTAGE", the white circle surrounding the head, and can be seen on the top of the head itself. Lesser re-entries are visble on R. 2/10 and R. 3/1.

The 1c. showed no change in the Ottawa printings, so is not included. The 2c. reverted to its previous grass-green shade in 1891.

The 3c. is known bisected and used as a ½ stamp for the 2c. "drop letter" rate at Halifax in 1892.

28

29

(Recess B.A.B.N.)

1893 (17 Feb). P 12.

115	28	20c. vermilion	£160	42·00
		a. Imperf (pair)	£1200	
116		50c. blue	£225	24·00
		a. Imperf (*Prussian blue*) (pair)	£1300	

1893 (1 Aug). P 12.

117	29	8c. pale bluish grey	90·00	4·50
		a. Imperf (pair)	£500	
118		8c. bluish slate	£100	4·50
119		8c. slate-purple	90·00	4·50
120		8c. blackish purple	80·00	4·50
		a. Imperf (pair)	£600	

PRINTERS. The following stamps to No. 287 were recess-printed by the American Bank Note Co, Ottawa, which in 1923 became the Canadian Bank Note Co.

30

(Des L. Pereira and F. Brownell)

1897 (19 June). *Jubilee issue.* P 12.

121	30	½c. black	48·00	48·00
122		1c. orange	10·00	4·50
123		1c. orange-yellow	10·00	4·50
		a. Bisected (½c.) (on *Railway News*)	†	£3000
124		2c. green	16·00	9·00
125		2c. deep green	16·00	9·00
126		3c. carmine	12·00	2·25
127		5c. slate-blue	40·00	14·00
128		5c. deep blue	40·00	14·00
129		6c. brown	85·00	85·00
130		8c. slate-violet	32·00	29·00
131		10c. purple	50·00	42·00
132		15c. slate	85·00	85·00
133		20c. vermilion	85·00	85·00
134		50c. pale ultramarine	£130	95·00
135		50c. bright ultramarine	£130	£100
136		$1 lake	£425	£425
137		$2 deep violet	£700	£350
138		$3 bistre	£850	£700
139		$4 violet	£800	£600
140		$5 olive-green	£800	£600
121/40 *Set of* 16			£3500	£2750
133s/40s Handstamped "Specimen" *Set of* 7			£1800	

No. 123a was used on issues of the *Railway News* of 5, 6 and 8 November 1897 and must be on a large part of the original newspaper with New Glasgow postmark.

31

32

(From photograph by W. & D. Downey, London)

1897–98. P 12.

141	31	½c. grey-black (9.11.97)	6·00	4·75
142		½c. black	7·50	5·00
		a. Imperf (pair)	£400	
143		1c. blue-green (12.97)	18·00	90
		a. Imperf (pair)	£400	
144		2c. violet (12.97)	18·00	1·50
		a. Imperf (pair)	£400	
145		3c. carmine (1.98)	25·00	50
		a. Imperf (pair)	£750	
146		5c. deep blue/*bluish* (12.97)	60·00	2·75
		a. Imperf (pair)	£400	
147		6c. brown (12.97)	60·00	23·00
		a. Imperf (pair)	£750	
148		8c. orange (12.97)	75·00	7·00
		a. Imperf (pair)	£425	
149		10c. brownish purple (1.98)	£130	55·00
		a. Imperf (pair)	£450	
141/9 *Set of* 8			£350	80·00

BOOKLET PANES. Most definitive booklets issued from 1900 onwards had either the two horizontal sides or all three outer edges imperforate. Stamps from the panes show one side or two adjacent sides imperforate.

Two types of the 2c.

Die Ia. Frame consists of four fine lines.
Die Ib. Frame has one thick line between two fine lines.

The die was retouched in 1900 for Plates 11 and 12, producing weak vertical frame lines and then retouched again in 1902 for Plates 15 to 20 resulting in much thicker frame lines. No. 155*b* covers both states of the retouching.

1898–1902. P 12.

150	32	½c. black (9.98)	3·25	1·10
		a. Imperf (pair)	£400	
151		1c. blue-green (6.98)	23·00	40
152		1c. deep green/*toned paper*	24·00	80
		a. Imperf (pair)	£750	
153		2c. dull purple (Die Ia) (9.98)	23·00	30
		a. Thick paper (6.99)	90·00	10·00
154		2c. violet (Die Ia)	22·00	30
154*a*		2c. reddish purple (Die Ia)	42·00	1·00
155		2c. rose-carmine (Die Ia) (20.8.99)	30·00	30
		a. Imperf (pair)	£325	
155*b*		2c. rose-carmine (Die Ib) (1900)	42·00	65
		ba. Booklet pane of 6 (11.6.00)	£750	
156		3c. rose-carmine (6.98)	48·00	1·00
157		5c. slate-blue/*bluish*	95·00	2·00
		a. Imperf (pair)	£800	
158		5c. Prussian blue/*bluish*	£100	2·00
159		6c. brown (9.98)	85·00	50·00
		a. Imperf (pair)	£700	
160		7c. greenish yellow (23.12.02)	55·00	14·00
161		8c. orange-yellow (10.98)	£110	27·00
162		8c. brownish orange	£100	27·00
		a. Imperf (pair)	£700	
163		10c. pale brownish purple (11.98)	£160	14·00
164		10c. deep brownish purple	£160	14·00
		a. Imperf (pair)	£700	
165		20c. olive-green (29.12.00)	£300	48·00
150/65 *Set of* 11			£800	£140

The 7c. and 20c. also exist imperforate, but unlike the values listed in this condition, they have no gum. (*Price*, 7c. £350, 20c. £1400 *pair, un*).

33

(Des R. Weir Crouch, G. Hahn, A. H. Howard and R. Holmes. Eng C. Skinner. Design recess, colours added by typo)

1898 (7 Dec). *Imperial Penny Postage. Design in black. British possessions in red. Oceans in colours given.* P 12.

166	33	2c. lavender	29·00	5·50
167		2c. greenish blue	25·00	5·00
168		2c. blue	25·00	4·75
		a. Imperf (pair)	£350	

Forgeries of Type **33** are without horizontal lines across the continents and have a forged Montreal postmark of 24.12.98.

1899 (4 Jan). *Provisionals used at Port Hood, Nova Scotia. No. 156 divided vertically and handstamped.*

169	32	"1" in blue, on ½ of 3c.	—	£3500
170		"2" in violet, on ½ of 3c.	—	£3000

Nos. 169/70 were prepared by the local postmaster during a shortage of 2c. stamps caused by a change in postage rates.

2 CENTS

(34)

35 King Edward VII

1899. *Surch with T* **34**, *by Public Printing Office.*

171	31	2c.on 3c. carmine (8 Aug)	13·00	8·00
		a. Surch inverted	£275	
172	32	2c.on 3c. rose-carmine (28 July)	17·00	4·25
		a. Surch inverted	£275	

(Des King George V when Prince of Wales and J. A. Tilleard)

1903 (1 July)–**12**. P 12.

173	35	1c. pale green	23·00	50
174		1c. deep green	21·00	50
175		1c. green	21·00	50
176		2c. rose-carmine	20·00	50
		a. Booklet pane of 6	£750	
177		2c. pale rose-carmine	20·00	50
		a. Imperf (pair) (18.7.09)	28·00	32·00
178		5c. blue/*bluish*	70·00	2·50
179		5c. indigo/*bluish*	70·00	2·75
180		7c. yellow-olive	55·00	2·75
181		7c. greenish bistre	65·00	2·75
181*a*		7c. straw (1.12)	£110	38·00
182		10c. brown-lilac	£110	12·00
183		10c. pale dull purple	£110	12·00
184		10c. dull purple	£110	12·00
185		20c. pale olive-green (27.9.04)	£200	23·00
186		20c. deep olive-green	£225	23·00
		s. Handstamped "Specimen"	75·00	
187		50c. deep violet (19.11.08)	£350	85·00
173/87 *Set of* 7			£700	£110

The 1c., 5c., 7c. and 10c. exist imperforate but are believed to be proofs. (*Prices per pair*, 1c. £400, 5c. £600. 7c. £400, 10c. £600).

IMPERFORATE AND PART-PERFORATED SHEETS. Prior to 1946 many Canadian issues exist imperforate, or with other perforation varieties, in the colours of the issued stamps and, usually, with gum. In the years before 1927 such examples are believed to come from imprimatur sheets, removed from the Canadian Post Office archives. From 1927 until 1946 it is known that the printers involved in the production of the various issues submitted several imperforate plate proof sheets of each stamp to the Post Office authorities for approval. Some of these sheets or part sheets were retained for record purposes, but the remainder found their way on to the philatelic market.

Part-perforated sheets also occur from 1927–29 issues.

From 1908 until 1946 we now only list and price such varieties of this type which are known to be genuine errors, sold from post offices. Where other imperforate or similar varieties are known they are recorded in footnotes.

It is possible, and in some cases probable, that some imperforate varieties listed before 1908 may have also been removed from the archives as mentioned above, but it is far harder to be explicit over the status of this earlier material.

36 King George V and Queen Mary when Prince and Princess of Wales

37 Jacques Cartier and Samuel Champlain

(Des Machado)

1908 (16 July). *Quebec Tercentenary. T* **36/7** *and similar horiz designs.* P 12.

188		½c. sepia	3·50	3·50
189		1c. blue-green	13·00	2·75

190 2c. carmine 18·00 1·00
191 5c. indigo 45·00 20·00
192 7c. olive-green 50·00 40·00
193 10c. violet 55·00 45·00
194 15c. brown-orange 80·00 70·00
195 20c. dull brown £110 90·00
188/95 *Set of* 8 £350 £250

Designs:—2c. King Edward VII and Queen Alexandra; 5c. Champlain's House in Quebec; 7c. Generals Montcalm and Wolfe; 10c. Quebec in 1700; 15c. Champlain's departure for the West; 20c. Cartier's arrival before Quebec.

Some values exist on both toned and white papers.

Nos. 188/95 exist imperforate. (*Price* £375, *un, for each pair*).

WET AND DRY PRINTINGS. Until the end of December 1922 all Canadian stamps were produced by the "wet" method of recess-printing in which the paper was dampened before printing, dried and then gummed.

In late December 1922 the Canadian Bank Note Co. began to use the "dry" process in which the paper was gummed before printing. Late printings of the 3c. brown were the first stamps to be produced by this method, but the changeover was not completed until January 1926.

"Dry" printings have a sharper appearance and can often be found with a degree of embossing showing on the reverse. Stamps from "wet" printings shrink during drying and are narrower than "dry" examples. In many cases the difference can be as great as 0.5 mm. On some early booklet panes the difference is in the vertical, rather than the horizontal, measurement.

On Nos. 196/215 all values only exist from "wet" printings, except the 3c., 20c. and 50c. which come from both types of printing.

44

1911–22. P 12.

96 **44** 1c. yellow-green (22.12.11) 5·50 50
a. With fine horiz lines across stamp 35·00 8·50
97 1c. bluish green 5·50 50
a. Booklet pane of 6 (1.5.13) 50·00
98 1c. deep bluish green 6·00 50
99 1c. deep yellow-green 6·00 65
a. Booklet pane of 6 18·00
00 2c. rose-red (15.12.11) 5·00 50
01 2c. deep rose-red 5·00 50
a. Booklet pane of 6 (1.12) 32·00
02 2c. pale rose-red 5·00 50
a. With fine horiz lines across stamp 25·00 12·00
03 2c. carmine 6·00 50
04 3c. brown (6.8.18) 6·00 50
05 3c. deep brown 5·00 50
a. Booklet pane of 4+2 labels (2.22) 50·00
05*b* 5c. deep blue (17.1.12) 60·00 75
06 5c. indigo 90·00 3·50
06*a* 5c. grey-blue 85·00 2·25
06*b* 7c. straw (12.1.12) 75·00 13·00
07 7c. pale sage-green (1914) £200 32·00
08 7c. olive-yellow (1915) 20·00 3·00
09 7c. yellow-ochre (1916) 20·00 3·00
10 10c. brownish purple (12.1.12) 90·00 2·75
11 10c. reddish purple £100 3·75
12 20c. olive-green (23.1.12) 29·00 1·50
13 20c. olive 29·00 1·75
14 50c. grey-black (26.1.12) £100 8·00
15 50c. sepia 48·00 3·75
96/215 *Set of* 8 £225 11·00

The 20c. and 50c. values exist imperforate (*Price* £1300 *un, for ach pair*).

912 (1 Nov)–**21**. *For use in coil-machines.*

(a) P 12 × imperf.

16 **44** 1c. yellow-green (1914) 3·50 10·00
17 1c. blue-green 13·00 23·00
a. Two large holes at top and bottom (vert pair) (7.18) 75·00 90·00
18 2c. deep rose-red (1914) 25·00 18·00
18*a* 3c. brown (1921) 3·50 6·00

No. 217a has two large holes about 3½ mm in diameter in the top nd bottom margins. They were for experimental use in a vending achine at Toronto in July 1918 and were only in use for two days.

The 1c. and 2c. also exist with two small "V" shaped holes about 5 mm apart at top which are gripper marks due to modifications ade in vending machines in 1917.

(b) Imperf × perf 8.

19 **44** 1c. yellow-green (9.12) 13·00 5·00
20 1c. blue-green 16·00 5·00
a. With fine horiz lines across stamp 55·00
21 2c. carmine (9.12) 11·00 1·50
22 2c. rose-red 12·00 2·25
23 2c. scarlet 32·00 5·00
24 3c. brown (8.18) 5·00 2·00

(c) P 8 × imperf.

24a **44** 1c. blue-green (15.2.13) 60·00 48·00
24b 2c. carmine (15.2.13) 60·00 48·00

The stamps imperf × perf 8 were sold in coils over the counter; ose perf 8 × imperf were on sale in automatic machines. Varieties owing perf 12 on 2 or 3 adjacent sides and 1 or 2 sides imperf are om booklets, or the margins of sheets.

(45)

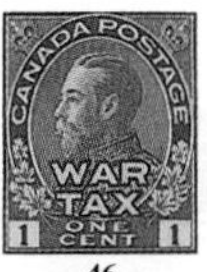

46

47

1915 (12 Feb). *Optd with T* **45**.

225 **44** 5c. blue £110 £200
226 20c. olive-green 55·00 £100
227 50c. sepia (R.) £110 £160
225/7 *Set of* 3 £250 £425

These stamps were intended for tax purposes, but owing to ambiguity in an official circular dated 16 April 1915, it was for a time believed that their use for postal purposes was authorised. The position was clarified by a further circular on 20 May 1916 which made clear that Nos. 225/7 were for fiscal use only.

1915. P 12.

228 **46** 1c. green (15.4.15) 8·00 50
229 2c. carmine-red (16.4.15) 13·00 70
230 2c. rose-carmine 14·00 3·00

Die I

Die II

In Die I there is a long horizontal coloured line under the foot of the "T", and a solid bar of colour runs upwards from the "1" to the "T".

In Die II this solid bar of colour is absent, and there is a short horizontal line under the left side of the "T", with two short vertical dashes and a number of dots under the right-hand side.

1916 (1 Jan). P 12.

231 **47** 2c.+1c. rose-red (Die I) 26·00 1·25
232 2c.+1c. bright carmine (Die I) 26·00 1·25
233 2c.+1c. scarlet (Die I) 22·00 1·25

1916 (Feb). Imperf × perf 8 (coils).

234 **47** 2c.+1c. rose-red (Die I) 55·00 12·00

1916 (July). P 12 × 8.

235 **47** 2c.+1c. carmine-red (Die I) 18·00 45·00
236 2c.+1c. bright rose-red (Die I) 18·00 45·00

1916 (Aug). P 12.

237 **47** 2c.+1c. carmine-red (Die II) £100 18·00

1916 (Aug). *Colour changed.*

(a) P 12.

238 **47** 2c.+ 1c. brown (Die I) £180 20·00
239 2c.+ 1c. yellow-brown (Die II) 4·00 50
a. Imperf (pair) £900
240 2c.+ 1c. deep brown (Die II) 11·00 50

(b) Imperf × perf 8.

241 **47** 2c.+ 1c. brown (Die I) £100 7·50
a. Pair, 241 and 243 £350
243 2c.+ 1c. deep brown (Die II) 40·00 3·50

No. 239a, which is a genuine error, should not be confused with ungummed proofs of the Die I stamp, No. 238 (*Price per pair*, £140).

This value also exists p 12 × imperf or imperf × p 12, but was not issued with these perforations (*Price, in either instance*, £300, *un, per pair*).

48 Quebec Conference, 1864, from painting "The Fathers of Confederation", by Robert Harris

1917 (15 Sept). *50th Anniv of Confederation.* P 12.

244 **48** 3c. bistre-brown 18·00 1·75
245 3c. deep brown 20·00 2·00

No. 244 exists imperforate (*Price per pair*, £325 *un*).

Die I (top). Space between top of "N" and oval frame line and space between "CENT" and lower frame line.

Die II (bottom). "ONE CENT" appears larger so that "N" touches oval and "CENT" almost touches frame line. There are other differences but this is the most obvious one.

Die I (top). The lowest of the three horizontal lines of shading below the medals does not touch the three heavy diagonal lines; three complete white spaces over both "E's" of "THREE"; long centre bar to figures "3". Vertical spandrel lines fine.

Die II (bottom). The lowest horizontal line of shading touches the first of the three diagonal lines; two and a half spaces over first "E" and spaces over second "E" partly filled by stem of maple leaf; short centre bar to figures "3". Vertical spandrel lines thick. There are numerous other minor differences.

WET AND DRY PRINTINGS. See notes above No. 196.

On Nos. 246/63 all listed items occur from both "wet" and "dry" printings except Nos. 246aa/ab, 248aa, 256, 259, 260 and 262 which come "wet" only, and Nos. 246a, 248/a, 252/4*a*, 256b and 263 which are "dry" only.

1922–31. *As T* **44**.

(a) P 12.

246 **44** 1c. chrome-yellow (Die I) (7.6.22) 2·50 60
aa. Booklet pane of 4+2 labels (7.22) 55·00
ab. Booklet pane of 6 (12.22) 29·00
a. Die II (1925) 5·50 30
247 2c. deep green (6.6.22) 2·25 10
aa. Booklet pane of 4+2 labels (7.22) 38·00
ab. Booklet pane of 6 (12.22) £275
b. Thin paper (9.24) 3·00 4·50
248 3c. carmine (Die I) (18.12.23) 3·75 10
aa. Booklet pane of 4+2 labels (12.23) 32·00
a. Die II (11.24) 21·00 80
249 4c. olive-yellow (7.7.22) 8·00 3·50
a. Yellow-ochre 8·00 3·50
250 5c. violet (2.2.22) 5·00 1·75
a. Thin paper (9.24) 5·00 8·00
b. Reddish violet (1925) 7·00 2·00
251 7c. red-brown (12.12.24) 12·00 7·00
a. Thin paper £130 30·00
252 8c. blue (1.9.25) 19·00 10·00
253 10c. blue (20.2.22) 20·00 3·25
254 10c. bistre-brown (1.8.25) 18·00 3·00
a. Yellow-brown 18·00 3·00
255 $1 brown-orange (22.7.23) 50·00 8·00
246/55 *Set of* 10 £130 32·00

The $1 differs from T **44** in that the value tablets are oval.

Nos. 249/55 exist imperforate (*Prices per un pair* 4c. *to* 8c. £1000 *each*, 10c. £1100, $1 £1300).

(b) Imperf × perf 8.

256 **44** 1c. chrome-yellow (Die I) (1922) 4·00 5·50
a. Imperf horiz (vert pair) (1924) £160
b. Die II (1925) 4·50 7·00
c. Do. Imperf horiz (vert pair) (1927) 11·00 27·00
257 2c. deep green (26.7.22) 9·00 2·25
b. Imperf horiz (vert pair) (1927) 12·00 27·00
258 3c. carmine (Die I) (9.4.24) 60·00 10·00
a. Imperf horiz (vert pair) (1924) £250
b. Die II (1925) 80·00 25·00
256/8 *Set of* 3 65·00 16·00

Nos. 256a, 256c, 257b and 258a come from coil printings sold in sheet form. Those issued in 1924 were from "wet" printings and those in 1927 from "dry". A "wet" printing of No. 257b, issued in 1924, also exists (*Price* £160 *mint*), but cannot be identified from that issued in 1927 except by the differences between "wet" and "dry" stamps.

(c) Imperf (pairs).

259 **44** 1c. chrome-yellow (Die I) (6.10.24) 50·00 70·00
260 2c. deep green (6.10.24) 50·00 70·00
261 3c. carmine (Die I) (31.12.23)† 28·00 42·00

(d) P 12 × imperf.

262 **44** 2c. deep green (9.24) 65·00 65·00

(e) P 12 × 8.

263 **44** 3c. carmine (Die II) (24.6.31) 2·50 3·25

†Earliest known postmark.

Nos. 259 to 261 were on sale only at the Philatelic Branch, P.O. Dept, Ottawa.

No. 263 was produced by adding horizontal perforations to unused sheet stock of No. 258b. The stamps were then issued in 1931 pending the delivery of No. 293.

2 CENTS
(49)

2
CENTS
(50)

1926. *No. 248 surch.*

(a) With T **49**, *by the Govt Printing Bureau.*

264 **44** 2c.on 3c. carmine (12.10.26) 42·00 50·00
a. Pair, one without surch £325
b. On Die II £375

(b) With T **50**, *by the Canadian Bank Note Co.*

265 **44** 2c.on 3c. carmine (4.11.26) 16·00 21·00
a. Surch double (partly treble) £200

51 Sir J. A. Macdonald

52 "The Fathers of Confederation"

53 Parliament Buildings, Ottawa

54 Sir W. Laurier

55 Canada, Map 1867–1927

1927 (29 June). *60th Anniv of Confederation.* P 12.

I. *Commemorative Issue. Inscr* "1867–1927 CANADA CONFEDERATION".

266	**51**	1c. orange	2·50	1·50
267	**52**	2c. green	2·25	30
268	**53**	3c. carmine	7·00	5·00
269	**54**	5c. violet	3·50	3·50
270	**55**	12c. blue	24·00	5·00
266/70 *Set of* 5			35·00	14·00

Nos. 266/70 exist imperforate, imperf × perf or perf × imperf (*Prices from* £70, *un, per pair*).

57 Sir W. Laurier and Sir J. A. Macdonald

56 Darcy McGee

58 R. Baldwin and L. H. Lafontaine

II. *Historical Issue.*

271	**56**	5c. violet	3·00	2·50
272	**57**	12c. green	16·00	4·50
273	**58**	20c. carmine	17·00	12·00
271/3 *Set of* 3			32·00	17·00

Nos. 271/3 exist imperforate, imperf × perf or perf × imperf (*Prices from* £70, *un, per pair*).

59

(Des H. Schwartz)

1928 (21 Sept). *Air.* P 12.

274	**59**	5c. olive-brown	6·00	3·50

No. 274 exists imperforate, imperf × perf or perf × imperf (*Price per pair*, £150, *un*).

60 King George V

61 Mt Hurd and Indian Totem Poles

62 Quebec Bridge

63 Harvesting with Horses

64 *Bluenose* (fishing schooner)

65 Parliament Buildings, Ottawa

1928–29.

(a) P 12.

275	**60**	1c. orange (25.10.28)	2·75	60
		a. Booklet pane of 6	18·00	
276		2c. green (16.10.28)	1·25	20
		a. Booklet pane of 6	18·00	
277		3c. lake (12.12.28)	17·00	15·00
278		4c. olive-bistre (16.8.29)	13·00	6·50
279		5c. violet (12.12.28)	6·50	3·50
		a. Booklet pane of 6 (6.1.29)	95·00	
280		8c. blue (21.12.28)	7·50	4·75
281	**61**	10c. green (5.12.28)	8·50	1·25
282	**62**	12c. grey-black (8.1.29)	22·00	10·00
283	**63**	20c. lake (8.1.29)	27·00	12·00
284	**64**	50c. blue (8.1.29)	£100	38·00
285	**65**	$1 olive-green (8.1.29)	£110	65·00
		a. Brown-olive	£225	£100
275/85 *Set of* 11			£275	£140

(b) Imperf × perf 8 (5.11.28).

286	**60**	1c. orange	13·00	22·00
287		2c. green	13·00	4·50

Slight differences in the size of many Canadian stamps, due to paper shrinkage, are to be found.

Nos. 275/85 exist imperforate, imperf × perf or perf × imperf (*Prices per unused pair*, 1c. to 8c., *from* £70, 10c. to 20c., *from* £120, 50c. and $1, *from* £400). *Tête-bêche* horizontal pairs of the 1c., 2c. and 5c. are also known from uncut booklet sheets (*Prices per pair*, £275, *un*).

PRINTERS. The following stamps to No. 334 were recess-printed by the British American Bank Note Co, Ottawa.

66

67 Parliamentary Library, Ottawa

68 The Old Citadel, Quebec

69 Harvesting with Tractor

70 Acadian Memorial Church and Statue of "Evangeline", Grand Pre, Nova Scotia

71 Mt Edith Cavell, Canadian Rockies

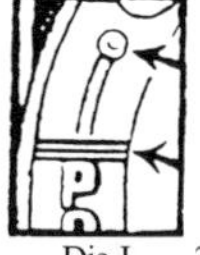

Die I 1c. Die II Die I 2c. Die II

1c. Die I. Three thick coloured lines and one thin between "P" and ornament, at right. Curved line in ball-ornament short.

Die II. Four thick lines. Curved line longer.

2c. Die I. Three thick coloured lines between "P" and ornament, at left. Short line in ball.

Die II. Four thick lines. Curved line longer.

1930–31.

(a) P 11.

288	**66**	1c. orange (I) (17.7.30)	1·75	1·00
289		1c. green (I) (6.12.30)	1·50	10
		b. Booklet pane of 6 (21.7.31)	25·00	
		d. Die II (8.31)	1·25	10
		da. Imperf (pair)	£1000	
		db. Booklet pane of 4+2 labels (13.11.31)	80·00	
290		2c. green (I) (6.6.30)	1·75	10
		a. Booklet pane of 6 (17.6.30)	35·00	
291		2c. scarlet (I) (17.11.30)	70	1·25
		a. Booklet pane of 6 (17.11.30)	23·00	
		b. Die II	90	10
292		2c. deep brown (I) (4.7.31)	1·50	3·50
		a. Booklet pane of 6 (23.7.31)	35·00	
		b. Die II (4.7.31)	1·25	10
		ba. Booklet pane of 4+2 labels (13.11.31)	£110	
293		3c. scarlet (13.7.31)	90	10
		a. Booklet pane of 4+2 labels	35·00	
294		4c. yellow-bistre (5.11.30)	6·50	4·50
295		5c. violet (18.6.30)	2·75	4·50
296		5c. deep slate-blue (13.11.30)	5·50	20
		a. Dull blue	16·00	65
297		8c. blue (13.8.30)	11·00	16·00
298		8c. red-orange (5.11.30)	7·50	5·50
299	**67**	10c. olive-green (15.9.30)	15·00	1·00
		a. Imperf (pair)	£900	
300	**68**	12c. grey-black (4.12.30)	14·00	5·50
301	**69**	20c. red (4.12.30)	22·00	1·00
302	**70**	50c. blue (4.12.30)	80·00	17·00
303	**71**	$1 olive-green (4.12.30)	95·00	23·00
288/303 *Set of* 16			£225	70·00

(b) Imperf × perf $8\frac{1}{2}$.

304	**66**	1c. orange (I) (14.7.30)	11·00	15·00
305		1c. green (I) (4.2.31)	6·00	7·00
306		2c. green (I) (27.6.30)	4·00	5·00
307		2c. scarlet (I) (19.11.30)	4·50	5·50
308		2c. deep brown (I) (4.7.31)	9·00	1·50
309		3c. scarlet (13.7.31)	14·00	1·50
304/9 *Set of* 6			42·00	32·00

Nos. 300/3 exist imperforate (*Prices per unused pair*, 12c. £600, 20c. £600, 50c. £600, $1 £800).

Some low values in the above and subsequent issues have been printed by both Rotary and "Flat plate" processes. The former can be distinguished by the gum, which has a striped appearance.

For 13c. bright violet, T **68**, see No. 325.

72 Mercury and Western Hemisphere

73 Sir Georges Etienne Cartier

(Des H. Schwartz)

1930 (4 Dec). *Air.* P 11.

310	**72**	5c. deep brown	19·00	18·0

1931 (30 Sept). P 11.

312	**73**	10c. olive-green	6·00	2

No. 312 exists imperforate (*Price per pair*, £400, *un*).

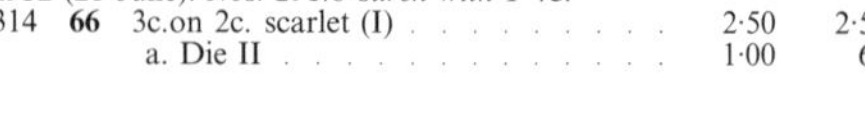

(74) (75)

1932 (22 Feb). *Air. No. 274 surch with T* **74**.

313	**59**	6c. on 5c. olive-brown	3·00	2·5

Examples of this stamp with surcharge inverted, surcharge double, surcharge triple or surcharge omitted in pair with normal are not now believed to have been regularly issued. Such "errors" have also been forged and collectors are warned against forged examples, some of which bear unauthorized markings which purport to be the guarantee of Stanley Gibbons Ltd.

1932 (21 June). *Nos. 291/b surch with T* **75**.

314	**66**	3c.on 2c. scarlet (I)	2·50	2·5
		a. Die II	1·00	6

76 King George V

77 Duke of Windsor when Prince of Wales

78 Allegory of British Empire

6 6
OTTAWA CONFERENCE
1932

(79)

1932 (12 July). *Ottawa Conference.* P 11.

(a) Postage stamps.

315	**76**	3c. scarlet	70	
316	**77**	5c. blue	9·00	5·
317	**78**	13c. green	9·50	6·

(b) Air. No. 310 surch with T **79**.

318	**72**	6c. on 5c. deep brown (B.)	10·00	12·
315/18 *Set of* 4			26·00	21·

80 King George V

"3" level Die I

"3" raised Die II

1932 (1 Dec)–**33**.

(a) P 11.

319 **80** 1c. green . . . 60 10
a. Booklet pane of 6 (28.12.33) . . . 15·00
b. Booklet pane of 4+2 labels (19.9.33) . . . 80·00
320 2c. sepia . . . 70 10
a. Booklet pane of 6 (7.9.33) . . . 15·00
b. Booklet pane of 4+2 labels (19.9.33) . . . 80·00
321 3c. scarlet (Die I) . . . 1·00 10
a. Booklet pane of 4+2 labels (22.8.33) . . . 48·00
b. Die II (29.11.32) . . . 85 10
ba. Booklet pane of 4+2 labels (19.9.33) . . . 35·00
322 4c. yellow-brown . . . 35·00 9·00
323 5c. blue . . . 10·00 10
a. Imperf vert (horiz pair) . . . £1100
324 8c. red-orange . . . 23·00 4·25
325 **68** 13c. bright violet . . . 38·00 2·25
319/25 *Set of* 7 . . . 95·00 14·00

A plate block of four from Plate I exists printed in varnish ink.

Nos. 319/25 exist imperforate (*Prices per unused pair*, 1c. to 8c. £170, 13c. £500).

(b) Imperf × perf $8\frac{1}{2}$ (1933).

326 **80** 1c. green . . . 13·00 3·50
327 2c. sepia . . . 19·00 2·50
328 3c. scarlet (Die II) . . . 12·00 1·50
326/8 *Set of* 3 . . . 40·00 6·75

81 Parliament Buildings, Ottawa

1933 (18 May). *U.P.U. Congress Preliminary Meeting.* P 11.

329 **81** 5c. blue . . . 6·00 3·00

No. 329 exists imperforate (*Price per pair* £500, *un*).

WORLD'S GRAIN EXHIBITION & CONFERENCE

REGINA 1933

(**82**)

1933 (24 July). *World's Grain Exhibition and Conference, Regina. No. 301 optd with T* **82** *in blue.*

330 **69** 20c. red . . . 16·00 7·00

No. 330 exists imperforate (*Price per pair* £500, *un*).

83 S.S. *Royal William* (after S. Skillett)

84 Jacques Cartier approaching Land

1933 (17 Aug). *Centenary of First Trans-Atlantic Steamboat Crossing.* P 11.

331 **83** 5c. blue . . . 9·50 3·00

No. 331 exists imperforate (*Price per pair* £500, *un*).

1934 (1 July). *Fourth Centenary of Discovery of Canada.* P 11.

332 **84** 3c. blue . . . 2·50 1·50

No. 332 exists imperforate (*Price per pair* £500, *un*).

85 U.E.L. Statue, Hamilton

86 Seal of New Brunswick

1934 (1 July). *150th Anniv of Arrival of United Empire Loyalists.* P 11.

333 **85** 10c. olive-green . . . 8·50 5·00

No. 333 exists imperforate (*Price per pair* £800, *un*).

1934 (16 Aug). *150th Anniv of Province of New Brunswick.* P 11.

334 **86** 2c. red-brown . . . 1·50 2·25

No. 334 exists imperforate (*Price per pair* £450, *un*).

PRINTERS. The following stamps were recess-printed (except where otherwise stated) by the Canadian Bank Note Co, Ottawa, until No. 616.

87 Queen Elizabeth II when Princess

89 King George V and Queen Mary

1935 (4 May). *Silver Jubilee. T* **87**, **89** *and similar designs.* P 12.

335 1c. green . . . 55 70
336 2c. brown . . . 60 70
337 3c. carmine-red . . . 1·75 70
338 5c. blue . . . 5·50 6·50
339 10c. green . . . 3·25 4·25
340 13c. blue . . . 6·50 6·50
335/40 *Set of* 6 . . . 16·00 17·00

Designs: *Vert (as T***87**)—2c. King George VI when Duke of York; 5c. King Edward VIII when Prince of Wales. *Horiz (as T* **89**)—10c. Windsor Castle; 13c. Royal Yacht *Britannia.*

Nos. 335/40 exist imperforate (*Price* £200, *un, for each pair*).

93 King George V

94 Royal Canadian Mounted Policeman

99 Daedalus

1935 (1 June–5 Nov). *T* **93/4**, **99** *and similar designs.*

(a) Postage. (i) P 12.

341 **93** 1c. green . . . 1·50 10
a. Booklet pane of 6 (19.8.35) . . . 22·00
b. Booklet pane of 4+2 labels (22.7.35) . . . 55·00
342 2c. brown . . . 1·50 10
a. Booklet pane of 6 (16.11.35) . . . 26·00
b. Booklet pane of 4+2 labels (22.7.35) . . . 55·00
343 3c. scarlet . . . 1·50 10
a. Booklet pane of 4+2 labels . . . 30·00
b. Printed on the gummed side . . . £225
344 4c. yellow . . . 3·25 1·75
345 5c. blue . . . 3·00 10
a. Imperf vert (horiz pair) . . . £200
346 8c. orange . . . 3·75 3·50
347 **94** 10c. carmine . . . 6·50 50
348 – 13c. purple . . . 7·00 65
349 – 20c. olive-green . . . 17·00 70
350 – 50c. deep violet . . . 25·00 4·75
351 – $1 bright blue . . . 40·00 11·00
341/51 *Set of* 11 . . . £100 20·00

(ii) *Coil stamps.* Imperf × perf 8.

352 **93** 1c. green (5.11.35) . . . 13·00 5·50
353 2c. brown (14.10.35) . . . 9·50 4·25
354 3c. scarlet (20.7.35) . . . 9·00 1·75
352/4 *Set of* 3 . . . 28·00 10·50

(b) Air. P 12.

355 **99** 6c. red-brown . . . 3·00 1·00
a. Imperf vert (horiz pair) . . . £5000

Designs: *Horiz (as* **794**)—13c. Confederation Conference, Charlottetown, 1864; 20c. Niagara Falls; 50c. Parliament Buildings, Victoria, British Columbia; $1 Champlain Monument, Quebec.

Nos. 341/51 (*Prices per pair*, 1c. *to* 8c. *each* £130, 10c. *to* $1 *each* £250, *un*) and 355 (*Price per pair* £475, *un*) exist imperforate.

100 King George VI and Queen Elizabeth

1937 (10 May). *Coronation.* P 12.

356 **100** 3c. carmine . . . 1·25 65

No. 356 exists imperforate (*Price per pair* £500, *un*).

101 King George VI

102 Memorial Chamber, Parliament Buildings, Ottawa

107 Fairchild 45-80 Sekani Seaplane over *Distributor* on River Mackenzie

(T **101**. Photograph by Bertram Park)

1937–38. *T* **101/2**, **107** *and similar designs.*

(a) Postage. (i) P 12.

357 **101** 1c. green (1.4.37) . . . 1·50 10
a. Booklet pane of 4+2 labels (14.4.37) . . . 28·00
b. Booklet pane of 6 (18.5.37) . . . 3·50
358 2c. brown (1.4.37) . . . 1·75 10
a. Booklet pane of 4+2 labels (14.4.37) . . . 55·00
b. Booklet pane of 6 (3.5.38) . . . 11·00
359 3c. scarlet (1.4.37) . . . 1·75 10
a. Booklet pane of 4+2 labels (14.4.37) . . . 4·25
360 4c. yellow (10.5.37) . . . 4·00 1·75
361 5c. blue (10.5.37) . . . 4·00 10
362 8c. orange (10.5.37) . . . 3·75 1·75
363 **102** 10c. rose-carmine (15.6.38) . . . 5·00 10
a. Red . . . 5·00 10
364 – 13c. blue (15.11.38) . . . 16·00 1·25
365 – 20c. red-brown (15.6.38) . . . 22·00 1·00
366 – 50c. green (15.6.38) . . . 45·00 9·00
367 – $1 violet (15.6.38) . . . 60·00 9·50
a. Imperf horiz (vert pair) . . . £3000
357/67 *Set of* 11 . . . £150 22·00

Nos. 357/67 exist imperforate (*Prices per pair* 1c. to 8c. *each* £190, 10c. to 50c. *each* £300, $1 £400 *un*).

(ii) *Coil stamps.* Imperf × perf 8.

368 **101** 1c. green (15.6.37) . . . 3·50 2·50
369 2c. brown (18.6.37) . . . 3·50 3·50
370 3c. scarlet (15.4.37) . . . 19·00 75
368/70 *Set of* 3 . . . 23·00 6·00

(b) Air. P 12.

371 **107** 6c. blue (15.6.38) . . . 11·00 80

Designs: *Horiz (as T***107**)—13c. Entrance to Halifax Harbour; 20c. Fort Garry Gate, Winnipeg; 50c. Entrance, Vancouver Harbour; $1 Chateau de Ramezay, Montreal.

No. 371 exists imperforate (*Price per pair* £425, *un*).

108 Queen Elizabeth II when Princess and Princess Margaret

109 National War Memorial

110 King George VI and Queen Elizabeth

1939 (15 May). *Royal Visit.* P 12.

372 **108** 1c. black and green . . . 1·75 10
373 **109** 2c. black and brown . . . 80 60
374 **110** 3c. black and carmine . . . 80 10
372/4 *Set of* 3 . . . 3·00 70

Nos. 372/4 exist imperforate (*Price* £375, *un, for each pair*).

111 King George VI in Naval uniform

112 King George VI in Military uniform

113 King George VI in Air Force uniform

114 Grain Elevator

116 Parliament Buildings

117 Ram Tank

121 Air Training Camp

1942 (1 July)–**48**. *War Effort. T* **111/14**, **116/17**, **121** *and similar designs.*

(a) Postage. (i) P 12.

375 **111** 1c. green . . . 1·50 10
a. Booklet pane of 4+2 labels (12.9.42) . . . 25·00
b. Booklet pane of 6 (24.11.42) . . 2·50
376 **112** 2c. brown . . . 1·75 10
a. Booklet pane of 4+2 labels (12.9.42) . . . 30·00
b. Booklet pane of 6 (6.10.42) . . 18·00
377 **113** 3c. carmine-lake . . . 1·25 60
a. Booklet pane of 4+2 labels (20.8.42) . . . 4·25
378 3c. purple (30.6.43) . . . 90 10
a. Booklet pane of 4+2 labels (28.8.43) . . . 6·00
b. Booklet pane of 6 (24.11.47) . . 13·00
379 **114** 4c. slate . . . 5·50 1·00
380 **112** 4c. carmine-lake (9.4.43) . . . 70 10
a. Booklet pane of 6 (3.5.43) . . . 3·50
381 **111** 5c. blue . . . 3·00 10
382 – 8c. red-brown . . . 5·50 75
383 **116** 10c. brown . . . 6·50 10
384 **117** 13c. dull green . . . 7·00 7·00
385 14c. dull green (16.4.43) . . . 18·00 1·00
386 – 20c. chocolate . . . 14·00 35
387 – 50c. violet . . . 26·00 3·50
388 – $1 blue . . . 42·00 6·00
375/88 *Set of* 14 . . . £120 18·00

Nos. 375/88 exist imperforate (*Prices per pair* 1c. to 8c. *each* £200, 10c. to 20c. *each* £300, 50c. and $1 *each* £400, *un*).

(ii) *Coil stamps.* Imperf × perf 8.

389 **111** 1c. green (9.2.43) . . . 1·00 1·50
390 **112** 2c. brown (24.11.42) . . . 2·25 2·00
391 **113** 3c. carmine-lake (23.9.42) . . . 2·00 6·00
392 3c. purple (19.8.43) . . . 7·50 3·75
393 **112** 4c. carmine-lake (13.5.43) . . . 6·00 1·50
389/93 *Set of* 5 . . . 17·00 13·00

(iii) *Booklet stamps.* Imperf × perf 12 (1.9.43).

394 **111** 1c. green . . . 3·25 1·25
a. Booklet pane of 3 . . . 9·00
395 **113** 3c. purple . . . 3·25 1·50
a. Booklet pane of 3 . . . 9·00
396 **112** 4c. carmine-lake . . . 3·25 1·75
a. Booklet pane of 3 . . . 9·00
394/6 *Set of* 3 . . . 9·00 4·00

Nos. 394/6 are from booklets in which the stamps are in strips of three, imperforate at top and bottom and right-hand end.

(iv) *Coil stamps.* Imperf × perf 9½.

397 **111** 1c. green (13.7.48) . . . 3·00 4·00
397*a* **112** 2c. brown (1.10.48) . . . 7·50 19·00
398 **113** 3c. purple (2.7.48) . . . 4·75 6·00
398*a* **112** 4c. carmine-lake (22.7.48) . . . 7·00 3·50
397/8*a* *Set of* 4 . . . 20·00 29·00

(b) Air. P 12.

399 **121** 6c. blue (1.7.42) . . . 21·00 6·00
400 7c. blue (16.4.43) . . . 3·25 10

Designs: *Horiz* (*as T***114**)—8c. Farm scene. (*As T* **117**)—20c. Launching of corvette H.M.C.S. *La Malbaie*, Sorel; 50c. Munitions factory; $1 H.M.S. *Cossack* (destroyer).

Nos. 399/400 exist imperforate (*Price* £475, *un, for each pair*).

122 Ontario Farm Scene

129 Alexander Graham Bell and "Fame"

1946 (16 Sept)–**47**. *Peace Re-conversion. T* **122** *and similar horiz designs.* P 12.

(a) Postage.

401 8c. brown . . . 1·25 2·00
402 10c. olive-green . . . 1·75 10
403 14c. sepia . . . 4·00 1·25
404 20c. slate . . . 3·00 10
405 50c. green . . . 16·00 3·25
406 $1 purple . . . 25·00 3·25

(b) Air.

407 7c. blue . . . 4·50 10
a. Booklet pane of 4 (24.11.47) . . . 9·00
401/7 *Set of* 7 . . . 50·00 9·00

Designs:—7c. Canada Geese in flight 10c. Great Bear Lake; 14c. St. Maurice River Power Station; 20c. Combine Harvester; 50c. Lumbering in British Columbia; $1 *Abegweit* (train ferry), Prince Edward Is.

1947 (3 Mar). *Birth Centenary of Bell (inventor of telephone).* P 12.
408 **129** 4c. blue . . . 15 10

130 "Canadian Citizenship"

131 Queen Elizabeth II when Princess

1947 (1 July). *Advent of Canadian Citizenship and Eightieth Anniv of Confederation.* P 12.
409 **130** 4c. blue . . . 10 10

(From photograph by Dorothy Wilding)

1948 (16 Feb). *Princess Elizabeth's Marriage.* P 12.
410 **131** 4c. blue . . . 10 10

132 Queen Victoria, Parliament Building, Ottawa, and King George VI

133 Cabot's Ship *Matthew*

1948 (1 Oct). *One Hundred Years of Responsible Government.* P 12.
411 **132** 4c. grey . . . 10 10

1949 (1 Apr). *Entry of Newfoundland into Canadian Confederation.* P 12.
412 **133** 4c. green . . . 30 10

134 "Founding of Halifax, 1749" (C. W. Jefferys)

1949 (21 June). *Bicentenary of Halifax, Nova Scotia.* P 12.
413 **134** 4c. violet . . . 30 10

135 **136** **137**

138 King George VI **139** King George VI

(From photographs by Dorothy Wilding)

1949 (15 Nov)–**51**.

(i) P 12.

414 **135** 1c. green . . . 10 10
415 **136** 2c. sepia . . . 1·00 35
415*a* 2c. olive-green (25.7.51) . . . 75 10
416 **137** 3c. purple . . . 30 10
a. Booklet pane of 4+2 labels (12.4.50) . . . 2·25
417 **138** 4c. carmine-lake . . . 20 10
a. Booklet pane of 6 (5.5.50) . . . 27·00
417*b* 4c. vermilion (2.6.51) . . . 50 10
ba. Booklet pane of 6 . . . 6·00
418 **139** 5c. blue . . . 2·00 10
414/18 *Set of* 7 . . . 4·25 50

(ii) Imperf × perf 9½ (coil stamps).

419 **135** 1c. green (18.5.50) . . . 1·75 1·00
420 **136** 2c. sepia (18.5.50) . . . 7·50 6·00
420*a* 2c. olive-green (9.10.51) . . . 1·75 2·50
421 **137** 3c. purple (18.5.50) . . . 2·25 2·75
422 **138** 4c. carmine-lake (20.4.50) . . . 14·00 9·00
422*a* 4c. vermilion (27.11.51) . . . 2·75 2·75
419/22*a* *Set of* 6 . . . 27·00 22·00

(iii) Imperf × perf 12 (booklets).

422*b* **135** 1c. green (18.5.50) . . . 50 1·75
ba. Booklet pane of 3 . . . 1·50
423 **137** 3c. purple (18.5.50) . . . 1·25 1·00
a. Booklet pane of 3 . . . 3·75
423*b* **138** 4c. carmine-lake (18.5.50) . . . 15·00 8·00
ba. Booklet pane of 3 . . . 45·00
423*c* 4c. vermilion (25.10.51) . . . 7·50 7·00
ca. Booklet pane of 3 . . . 22·00
422*b*/3*c* *Set of* 4 . . . 22·00 16·00

These booklet panes are imperforate at top, bottom and right-hand end.

140 King George VI

141 Oil Wells in Alberta

(From photograph by Dorothy Wilding)

1950 (19 Jan). *As T* **135/9** *but without* "POSTES POSTAGE", *as T* **140**.

(i) P 12.

424 1c. green . . . 10 50
425 2c. sepia . . . 10 1·75
426 3c. purple . . . 10 65
427 4c. carmine-lake . . . 10 20
428 5c. blue . . . 30 1·25
424/8 *Set of* 5 . . . 60 3·75

(ii) Imperf × perf 9½ (coil stamps).

429 1c. green . . . 30 1·00
430 3c. purple . . . 80 1·50

1950 (1 Mar). P 12.
431 **141** 50c. green . . . 6·00 1·00

142 Drying Furs

143 Fisherman

1950 (2 Oct). P 12.
432 **142** 10c. brown-purple . . . 2·00 10

1951 (1 Feb). P 12.
433 **143** $1 ultramarine . . . 38·00 5·00

144 Sir R. L. Borden

145 W. L. Mackenzie King

1951 (25 June). *Prime Ministers (1st issue).* P 12.
434 **144** 3c. blue-green . . . 10 5[illegible]
435 **145** 4c. rose-carmine . . . 10 1[illegible]

See also Nos. 444/5, 475/6 and 483/4.

146 Mail Trains, 1851 and 1951

147 SS. *City of Toronto* and SS. *Prince George*

148 Mail Coach and DC-4M North Star

149 Reproduction of 3d., 1851

1951 (24 Sept). *Canadian Stamp Centenary.* P 12.
436 **146** 4c. black . . . 35 [illegible]
437 **147** 5c. violet . . . 65 1·7[illegible]
438 **148** 7c. blue . . . 35 1·0[illegible]
439 **149** 15c. scarlet . . . 1·40 [illegible]
436/9 *Set of* 4 . . . 2·50 2·7[illegible]

150 Queen Elizabeth II when Princess and Duke of Edinburgh

1951 (26 Oct). *Royal Visit.* P 12.
440 **150** 4c. violet . . . 10 [illegible]

STAMP BOOKLETS

Booklet Nos. SB1/48 are stapled.

All booklets up to and including No. SB41 contain pan[illegible] consisting of two rows of three (3 × 2).

B 1

1900 (11 June). *Red on pink cover. Two panes of six 2c. (No. 155b[illegible]*
SB1 25c. booklet. Cover as Type B **1** with English text . . . £17[illegible]

1903 (1 July). *Red on pink cover. Two panes of six 2c. (No. 176a[illegible]*
SB2 25c. booklet. Cover as Type B **1** with English text . . . £18[illegible]

1912 (Jan)–**16**. *Red on pink cover. Two panes of six 2c. (No. 201a).*
SB3 25c. booklet. Cover as Type **B 1** with English text . . . 60·00
a. Cover handstamped "NOTICE Change in Postal Rates For New Rates See Postmaster" . . . 60·00
b. French text (4.16) . . . £100
ba. Cover handstamped "AVIS Changement des tarifs Postaux Pour les nouveaux tarifs consulter le maitre de poste" . . . £100

1913 (1 May)–**16**. *Green on pale green cover. Four panes of six 1c. (No. 197a).*
SB4 25c. booklet. Cover as Type **B 1** with English text . . . £350
a. Containing pane No. 199a . . . 65·00
ab. Cover handstamped "NOTICE Change in Postal Rates For New Rates See Postmaster" . . . 65·00
b. French text (28.4.16) . . . £500
ba. Containing pane No. 199a . . . £130
bb. Cover handstamped "AVIS Changement des tarifs Postaux Pour les nouveaux tarifs consulter le maitre de poste" . . . £275

1922 (Mar). *Black on brown cover. Two panes of four 3c. and 2 labels (No. 205a).*
SB5 25c. booklet. Cover as Type **B 1** with English text . . . £300
a. French text . . . £600

1922 (July–Dec). *Black on blue cover. Panes of four 1c., 2c. and 3c. (Nos. 246aa, 247aa, 205a) and 2 labels.*
SB6 25c. booklet. Cover as Type **B 1** with English text . . . £300
a. French text (Dec) . . . £475

1922 (Dec). *Black on orange cover. Four panes of six 1c. (No. 246ab).*
SB7 25c. booklet. Cover as Type **B 1** with English text . . . £100
a. French text . . . £130

1922 (Dec). *Black on green cover. Two panes of six 2c. (No. 247ab).*
SB8 25c. booklet. Cover as Type **B 1** with English text . . . £600
a. French text . . . £700

1923 (Dec). *Black on blue cover. Panes of four 1c., 2c. and 3c. (Nos. 246aa, 247aa, 248aa) and 2 labels.*
SB9 25c. booklet. Cover as Type **B 1** with English text . . . £200
a. French text . . . £325

1923 (Dec)–**24**. *Black on brown cover. Two panes of four 3c. (No. 248aa) and 2 labels.*
SB10 25c. booklet. Cover as Type **B 1** with English text . . . £180
a. French text (5.24) . . . £275

B 2

1928 (16 Oct). *Black on green cover. Two panes of six 2c. (No. 276a).*
SB11 25c. booklet. Cover as Type **B 2** with English text . . . 55·00
a. French text . . . 75·00

1928 (25 Oct). *Black on orange cover. Four panes of six 1c. (No. 275a).*
SB12 25c. booklet. Cover as Type **B 2** with English text . . . £100
a. French text . . . £190

1929 (6 Jan). *Plain manilla cover. Three panes of six 1c., two panes of six 2c. and one pane of six 5c. (Nos. 275a, 276a, 279a).*
SB13 72c. booklet. Plain cover . . . £300
a. With "Philatelic Div., Fin. Br. P.O. Dept., Ottawa" circular cachet on front cover . . . £800
b. With "1928" in the centre of the circular cachet . . . £900

1930 (17 June). *Black on green cover. Two panes of six 2c. (No. 290a).*
SB14 25c. booklet. Cover as Type **B 2** with English text . . . 80·00
a. French text . . . £110

1930 (17 Nov). *Black on red cover. Two panes of six 2c. (No. 291a).*
SB15 25c. booklet. Cover as Type **B 2** with English text . . . 55·00
a. French text . . . 75·00

1931 (13 July). *Black on red cover. Two panes of four 3c. (No. 293a) and 2 labels.*
SB16 25c. booklet. Cover as Type **B 2** with English text . . . 80·00
a. French text . . . £110

1931 (21 July). *Black on green cover. Four panes of six 1c. (No. 289b).*
SB17 25c. booklet. Cover as Type **B 2** with English text . . . £120
a. French text . . . £160

1931 (23 July). *Black on brown cover. Two panes of six 2c. (No. 292a).*
SB18 25c. booklet. Cover as Type **B 2** with English text . . . 80·00
a. French text . . . £110

1931 (13 Nov). *Black on blue cover. Panes of four 1c., 2c. and 3c. (Nos. 289db, 292ba, 293a) and 2 labels.*
SB19 25c. booklet. Cover as Type **B 2** with English text . . . £250
a. French text . . . £350

1933 (22 Aug–13 Nov). *Black on red cover. Two panes of four 3c. (No. 321a) and 2 labels.*
SB20 25c. booklet. Cover as Type **B 2** with English text (13 Nov) . . . 85·00
a. French text (22 Aug) . . . £160

1933 (7 Sept). *Black on brown cover. Two panes of six 2c. (No. 320a).*
SB21 25c. booklet. Cover as Type **B 2** with English text . . . 60·00
a. French text . . . £100

1933 (19 Sept–5 Dec). *Black on blue cover. Panes of four 1c., 2c. and 3c. (Nos. 319b, 320b, 321ba) and 2 labels.*
SB22 25c. booklet. Cover as Type **B 2** with English text . . . £200
a. French text (5 Dec) . . . £300

1933 (28 Dec)–**34**. *Black on green cover. Four panes of six 1c. (No. 319a).*
SB23 25c. booklet. Cover as Type **B 2** with English text . . . 85·00
a. French text (26.3.34) . . . £120

B 3

1935 (1 June–8 Aug). *Red on white cover. Two panes of four 3c. (No. 343a) and 2 labels.*
SB24 25c. booklet. Cover as Type **B 3** with English text (8 Aug) . . . 55·00
a. French text (1 June) . . . 70·00

1935 (22 July–1 Sept). *Blue on white cover. Panes of four 1c., 2c. and 3c. (Nos. 341b, 342b, 343a) and 2 labels.*
SB25 25c. booklet. Cover as Type **B 3** with English text . . . £140
a. French text (1 Sept) . . . £180

1935 (19 Aug–18 Oct). *Green on white cover. Four panes of six 1c. (No. 341a).*
SB26 25c. booklet. Cover as Type **B 3** with English text . . . 90·00
a. French text (18 Oct) . . . £130

1935 (16–18 Mar). *Brown on white cover. Two panes of six 2c. (No. 342a).*
SB27 25c. booklet. Cover as Type **B 3** with English text . . . 70·00
a. French text (18 Mar) . . . £120

B 4

1937 (14 Apr)–**38**. *Blue and white cover. Panes of four 1c., 2c. and 3c. (Nos. 357a, 358a, 359a) and 2 labels.*
SB28 25c. booklet. Cover as Type **B 3** with English text . . . 85·00
a. French text (4.1.38) . . . £130
SB29 25c. booklet. Cover as Type **B 4** with English text 57 mm wide . . . 70·00
a. English text 63 mm wide . . . £110
b. French text 57 mm wide (4.1.38) . . . 90·00
ba. French text 63 mm wide . . . £170

1937 (23–27 Apr). *Red and white cover. Two panes of four 3c. (No. 359a) and 2 labels.*
SB30 25c. booklet. Cover as Type **B 3** with English text (27 Apr) . . . 24·00
a. French text (23 Apr) . . . 50·00
SB31 25c. booklet. Cover as Type **B 4** with English text 57 mm wide (27 Apr) . . . 10·00
a. English text 63 mm wide . . . 48·00
b. French text 57 mm wide (23 Apr) . . . 13·00
ba. French text 63 mm wide . . . £170

1937 (18 May)–**38**. *Green and white cover. Four panes of six 1c. (No. 357b).*
SB32 25c. booklet. Cover as Type **B 3** with English text . . . 40·00
a. French text (14.10.38) . . . 60·00
SB33 25c. booklet. Cover as Type **B 4** with English text 57 mm wide . . . 22·00
a. English text 63 mm wide . . . 60·00
b. French text 57 mm wide (14.10.38) . . . 18·00
ba. French text 63 mm wide . . . £150

1938 (3 May)–**39**. *Brown and white cover. Two panes of six 2c. (No. 358b).*
SB34 25c. booklet. Cover as Type **B 3** with English text . . . 55·00
a. French text (3.3.39) . . . 75·00
SB35 25c. booklet. Cover as Type **B 4** with English text 57 mm wide . . . 23·00
a. English text 63 mm wide . . . 70·00
b. French text 57 mm wide . . . 42·00
ba. French text 63 mm wide . . . £100

1942 (20–29 Aug). *Red and white cover. Two panes of four 3c. (No. 377a) and 2 labels.*
SB36 25c. booklet. Cover as Type **B 4** with English text . . . 8·50
a. French text (29 Aug) . . . 12·00

1942 (12–14 Sept). *Violet and white cover. Panes of four 1c., 2c. and 3c. (Nos. 375a, 376a, 377a), each with 2 labels.*
SB37 25c. booklet. Cover as Type **B 4** with English text (14 Sept) . . . 48·00
a. French text (12 Sept) . . . 90·00

1942 (6 Oct)–**43**. *Brown and white cover. Two panes of six 2c. (No. 376b).*
SB38 25c. booklet. Cover as Type **B 4** with English text . . . 48·00
a. French text (6.4.43) . . . 70·00

1942 (24 Nov)–**46**. *Green and white cover. Four panes of six 1c. (No. 375b).*
SB39 25c. booklet. Cover as Type **B 4** with English text . . . 11·00
a. French text (16.2.43) . . . 17·00
b. Bilingual text (8.1.46) . . . 25·00

1943 (3 May)–**46**. *Orange and white cover. One pane of six 4c. (No. 380a).*
SB40 25c. booklet. Cover as Type **B 4** with English text . . . 4·00
a. French text (12.5.43) . . . 15·00
b. Bilingual text (8.1.46) . . . 18·00

1943 (28 Aug)–**46**. *Purple and white cover. Two panes of four 3c. (No. 378a) and 2 labels.*
SB41 25c. booklet. Cover as Type **B 4** with English text . . . 10·00
a. French text (7.9.43) . . . 28·00
b. Bilingual text (8.1.46) . . . 22·00

B 5

1943 (1 Sept)–**46**. *Black and white cover. Panes of three 1c., 3c. and 4c. (Nos. 394a, 395a, 396a) (3 × 1).*
SB42 25c. booklet. Cover as Type **B 5** with English text . . . 30·00
a. French text (18.9.43) . . . 40·00
c. Bilingual text (23.1.46) . . . 38·00

B 6

1947 (24 Nov). *Brown on orange cover. Panes of six 3c. and 4c. (3 × 2) and two panes of four 7c. (2 × 2) (Nos. 378b, 380a, 407a).*
SB43 $1 booklet. Cover as Type **B 6** with English text . . . 25·00
a. French text . . . 40·00

1950 (12 Apr–18 May). *Purple and white cover. Two panes of four 3c. (No. 416a) and 2 labels (3 × 2).*
SB44 25c. booklet. Cover as Type **B 4** with English text . . . 5·00
a. Bilingual text (18 May) . . . 5·00

1950 (5–10 May). *Orange and white cover. One pane of six 4c. (No. 417a) (3 × 2).*
SB45 25c. booklet, Cover as Type **B 4** with English text . . . 35·00
a. Stitched . . . 60·00
b. Bilingual text (10 May) . . . 40·00

1950 (18 May). *Black and white cover. Panes of three 1c., 3c. and 4c. (Nos. 422ba, 423a, 423ba) (3 × 1).*
SB46 25c. booklet. Cover as Type **B 5** with English text . . . 50·00
a. Bilingual text . . . 55·00

1951 (2 June). *Orange and white cover. One pane of six 4c. (No. 417ba) (3 × 2).*

SB47	25c. booklet. Cover as Type B **4** with English text	6·00	
	a. Stitched	12·00	
	b. Bilingual text	12·00	

1951 (25 Oct)–**52**. *Black and white cover. Panes of three 1c., 3c. and 4c. (Nos. 422ba, 423a, 423ca) (3 × 1).*

SB48	25c. booklet. Cover as Type B **5** with English text	32·00	
	a. Bilingual text (9.7.52)	38·00	

REGISTRATION STAMPS

R **1**

(Eng and recess-printed British-American Bank Note Co, Montreal and Ottawa)

1875 (15 Nov)–**92**. *White wove paper.*

(a) P 12 (or slightly under).

R1	R **1**	2c. orange	60·00	1·00
R2		2c. orange-red (1889)	70·00	6·00
R3		2c. vermilion	75·00	7·50
		a. Imperf (pair)	†	£2500
R4		2c. rose-carmine (1888)	£150	55·00
R5		5c. yellow-green (1878)	£100	1·50
R6		5c. deep green	80·00	1·25
		a. Imperf (pair)	£650	
R7		5c. blue-green (1888)	90·00	1·50
R7*a*		5c. dull sea-green (1892)	£130	3·25
R8		8c. bright blue	£325	£225
R9		8c. dull blue	£300	£200

(b) P 12 × $11\frac{1}{2}$ or 12 × $11\frac{3}{4}$.

R10	R **1**	2c. orange	£300	60·00
R11		5c. green (*shades*)	£750	£150

SPECIAL DELIVERY STAMPS

PRINTERS. The following Special Delivery and Postage Due Stamps were recess-printed by the American Bank Note Co (to 1928), the British American Bank Note Co (to 1934), and the Canadian Bank Note Co (1935 onwards).

S **1**

1898–**1920**. P 12.

S1	S **1**	10c. blue-green (28.6.98)	80·00	8·00
S2		10c. deep green (12.13)	48·00	7·00
S3		10c. yellowish green (8.20)	55·00	7·00

The differences between Types I and II (figures "10" with and without shading) formerly illustrated were due to wear of the plate. There was only one die.

S **2**

S **3** Mail-carrying, 1867 and 1927

1922 (21 Aug). P 12.

S4	S **2**	20c. carmine-red	35·00	6·50

No. S4 exists in two slightly different sizes due to the use of "wet" or "dry" printing processes. See note below No. 195.

1927 (29 June). *60th Anniversary of Confederation.* P 12.

S5	S **3**	20c. orange	11·00	10·00

No. S5 exists imperforate, imperf × perf or perf × imperf (*Price, in each instance,* £140 *per pair, un*).

S **4**

1930 (2 Sept). P 11.

S6	S **4**	20c. brown-red	42·00	7·00

1932 (24 Dec). *Type as* S **4**, *but inscr* "CENTS" *in place of* "TWENTY CENTS". P 11.

S7		20c. brown-red	45·00	15·00

No. S7 exists imperforate (*Price per pair* £425, *un*).

S **5** Allegory of Progress

(Des A. Foringer)

1935 (1 June). P 12.

S8	S **5**	20c. scarlet	3·50	2·75

No. S8 exists imperforate (*Price per pair* £450, *un*).

S **6** Canadian Coat of Arms

1938–**39**. P 12.

S9	S **6**	10c. green (1.4.39)	20·00	3·50
S10		20c. scarlet (15.6.38)	40·00	26·00

Nos. S9/10 exist imperforate (*Price* £475, *un, for each pair*).

≡10 10≡

(S **7**)

1939 (1 Mar). *Surch with Type* S **7**.

S11	S **6**	10c. on 20c. scarlet	10·00	10·00

S **8** Coat of Arms and Flags

S **9** Lockheed L.18 Lodestar

1942 (1 July)–**43**. *War Effort.* P 12.

(a) Postage.

S12	S **8**	10c. green	7·00	30

(b) Air.

S13	S **9**	16c. ultramarine	6·00	45
S14		17c. ultramarine (1.4.43)	4·50	55

Nos. S12/14 exist imperforate (*Prices per un pair* 10c. £450, 16c. £500, 17c. £500).

S **10** Arms of Canada and Peace Symbols

S **11** Canadair DC-4M North Star

1946 (16 Sept–5 Dec). P 12.

(a) Postage.

S15	S **10**	10c. green	3·50	30

(b) Air. (i) Circumflex accent in "EXPRS".

S16	S **11**	17c. ultramarine	4·50	5·00

(ii) Grave accent in "EXPRS".

S17	S **11**	17c. ultramarine (5.12.46)	6·00	5·00

POSTAGE DUE STAMPS

PRINTERS. See note under "Special Delivery Stamps".

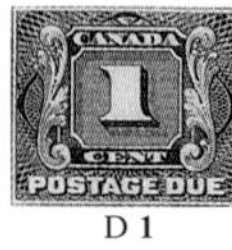

D **1**

D **2**

1906 (1 July)–**28**. P 12.

D1	D **1**	1c. dull violet	9·00	2·75
D2		1c. red-violet (1916)	10·00	3·75
		a. Thin paper (10.24)	15·00	20·00
D3		2c. dull violet	20·00	1·00
D4		2c. red-violet (1917)	21·00	1·25
		a. Thin paper (10.24)	29·00	20·00
D5		4c. violet (3.7.28)	45·00	50·00
D6		5c. dull violet	26·00	3·50
D7		5c. red-violet (1917)	26·00	3·50
		a. Thin paper (10.24)	17·00	28·00
D8		10c. violet (3.7.28)	32·00	19·00
D1/8 *Set of* 5			£110	65·00

The 1c., 2c. and 5c. values exist imperforate (*Price* £325 *for each un pair*).

Printings up to October 1924 used the "wet" method, those from mid 1925 onwards the "dry". For details of the differences between these two methods, see above No. 196.

1930–**32**. P 11.

D 9	D **2**	1c. bright violet (14.7.30)	8·50	11·00
D10		2c. bright violet (21.8.30)	7·50	1·90
D11		4c. bright violet (14.10.30)	15·00	6·50
D12		5c. bright violet (12.12.31)	16·00	28·00
D13		10c. bright violet (24.8.32)	65·00	27·00
D9/13 *Set of* 5			£100	65·00

Nos. D9/11 and D13 exist imperforate, No. D13 also exists imperf × perf (*Price for vertical pair* £650, *un*).

D **3**

D **4**

1933–**34**. P 11.

D14	D **3**	1c. violet (5.5.34)	9·50	14·0
D15		2c. violet (20.12.33)	7·50	4·5
D16		4c. violet (12.12.33)	12·00	15·0
D17		10c. violet (20.12.33)	24·00	32·0
D14/17 *Set of* 4			48·00	60·0

No. D14 exists imperforate (*Price per pair* £350, *un*).

1935–**65**. P 12.

D18	D **4**	1c. violet (14.10.35)	80	1
D19		2c. violet (9.9.35)	2·00	1
D20		3c. violet (4.65)	5·00	5·0
D21		4c. violet (2.7.35)	1·50	1
D22		5c. violet (12.48)	3·75	2·0
D23		6c. violet (1957)	2·00	3·0
D24		10c. violet (16.9.35)	70	1
D18/24 *Set of* 7			14·00	9·0

The 1c., 2c., 4c. and 10c. exist imperforate (*Price* £170 *for eac un pair*).

OFFICIAL STAMPS

Stamps perforated "O H M S" were introduced in May 1923 fo use by the Receiver General's department in Ottawa and by th Assistant Receiver Generals' offices in provincial cities. From 1 Ju 1939 this use was extended to all departments of the federa government and such stamps continued to be produced unt replaced by the "O.H.M.S." overprinted issue of 1949.

The perforated initials can appear either upright, inverted c sideways on individual stamps. The prices quoted are for th cheapest version. Stamps perforated with Type O **1** are only price used. Only isolated examples are known mint and these are ver rare.

A number of forged examples of the perforated "O.H.M.S." ar known, in particular of Type O **1**. Many of these forged perforate initials were applied to stamps which had already been used and th can aid their detection. Genuine examples, postmarked after th perforated initials were applied, often show the cancellation in bleeding into the holes.

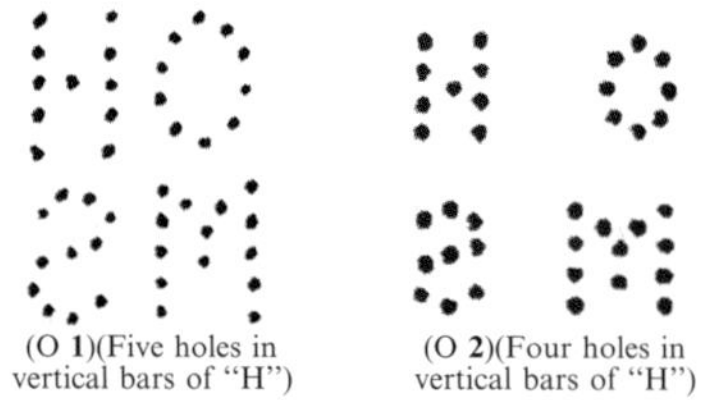

(O **1**)(Five holes in vertical bars of "H") (O **2**)(Four holes in vertical bars of "H")

1923 (May). *Nos. 196/215 punctured as Type* O **1**.

O1	**44**	1c. yellow-green	—	20·
O2		2c. carmine	—	18·
O3		3c. deep brown	—	16·
O4		5c. deep blue	—	20·
O5		7c. yellow-ochre	—	35·
O6		10c. reddish purple	—	35·
O7		20c. olive	—	22·
O8		50c. sepia	—	35·
O1/8 *Set of* 8			—	£1

1923 (May). *50th Anniv of Confederation. No. 244 punctured Type* O **1**.

O9	**48**	3c. bistre-brown	—	£1

1923 (May)–**31**. *Nos. 246/55 and 263 punctured as Type* O **1**.

(a) P 12.

O10	**44**	1c. chrome-yellow (Die I)	—	18·
		a. Die II (1925)	—	18·
O11		2c. deep green	—	13·
O12		3c. carmine (Die I) (12.23)	—	13·
		a. Die II (1924)	—	16·
O13		4c. olive-yellow	—	18·
O14		5c. violet	—	18·
		a. Thin paper (1924)	—	22·
O15		7c. red-brown (1924)	—	27·
O16		8c. blue (1925)	—	32·
O17		10c. blue	—	22·

O18 10c. bistre-brown (1925) — 13·00
O19 $1 brown-orange (7.23) — 55·00
O10/19 *Set of* 10 — £200

(b) P 12 × 8.
O20 **44** 3c. carmine (Die II) (1931) — 42·00

1927 (29 June). *60th Anniv of Confederation. Nos. 266/73 punctured as Type* O **1**.

(a) Commemorative issue.
O21 **51** 1c. orange — 18·00
O22 **52** 2c. green — 25·00
O23 **53** 3c. carmine — 35·00
O24 **54** 5c. violet — 23·00
O25 **55** 12c. blue — £140
O21/5 *Set of* 5 — £225

(b) Historical issue.
O26 **56** 5c. violet — 18·00
O27 **57** 12c. green — £110
O28 **58** 20c. carmine — 70·00
O26/8 *Set of* 3 — £180

1928 (21 Sept). *Air. No. 274 punctured as Type* O **1**.
O29 **59** 5c. olive-brown — 90·00

1928–29. *Nos. 275/85 punctured as Type* O **1**.
O30 **60** 1c. orange — 23·00
O31 2c. green — 15·00
O32 3c. lake — 40·00
O33 4c. olive-bistre — 48·00
O34 5c. violet — 16·00
O35 8c. blue — 45·00
O36 **61** 10c. green — 13·00
O37 **62** 12c. grey-black — £120
O38 **63** 20c. lake — 38·00
O39 **64** 50c. blue — £140
O40 **65** $1 olive-green — £120
O30/40 *Set of* 11 — £550

930–31. *Nos. 288/97 and 300/5 punctured as Type* O **1**.
O41 **66** 1c. orange (Die I) — 23·00
O42 1c. green (Die I) — 13·00
a. Die II — 11·00
O43 2c. green (Die I) — 35·00
O44 2c. scarlet (Die I) — 18·00
a. Die II — 16·00
O45 2c. deep brown (Die I) — 22·00
a. Die II — 18·00
O46 3c. scarlet — 13·00
O47 4c. yellow-bistre — 42·00
O48 5c. violet — 29·00
O49 5c. deep slate-blue — 23·00
O50 8c. blue — 55·00
O51 8c. red-orange — 40·00
O52 **67** 10c. olive-green — 18·00
O53 **68** 12c. grey-black — 75·00
O54 **69** 20c. red — 38·00
O55 **70** 50c. blue — 55·00
O56 **71** $1 olive-green — £130
O41/56 *Set of* 15 — £500

930 (4 Dec). *Air. No. 310 punctured as Type* O **1**.
O57 **72** 5c. deep brown — £140

931 (30 Sept). *No. 312 punctured as Type* O **1**.
O58 **73** 10c. olive-green — 18·00

932 (22 Feb). *Air. No. 313 punctured as Type* O **1**.
O59 **59** 6c. on 5c. olive-brown — 95·00

932 (21 June). *Nos. 314/a punctured as Type* O **1**.
O60 **66** 3c.on 2c. scarlet (Die I) — 30·00
a. Die II — 23·00

932 (12 July). *Ottawa Conference. Nos. 315/18 punctured as Type* O **1**.

(a) Postage.
61 **76** 3c. scarlet — 15·00
62 **77** 5c. blue — 27·00
63 **78** 13c. green — £160

(b) Air.
64 **72** 6c. on 5c. deep brown — £120
61/4 *Set of* 4 — £300

932–33. *Nos. 319/25 punctured as Type* O **1**.
65 **80** 1c. green — 13·00
66 2c. sepia — 13·00
67 3c. scarlet — 13·00
68 4c. yellow-brown — 45·00
69 5c. blue — 20·00
70 8c. red-orange — 45·00
71 **68** 13c. bright violet — 45·00
65/71 *Set of* 7 — £180

933 (18 May). *U.P.U. Congress Preliminary Meeting. No. 329 punctured as Type* O **1**.
72 **81** 5c. blue — 38·00

933 (24 July). *World's Grain Exhibition and Conference, Regina. No. 330 punctured as Type* O **1**.
73 **69** 20c. red — 45·00

933 (17 Aug). *Centenary of First Trans-Atlantic Steamboat Crossing. No. 331 punctured as Type* O **1**.
74 **83** 5c. blue — 40·00

934 (1 July). *Fourth Centenary of Discovery of Canada. No. 332 punctured as Type* O **1**.
75 **84** 3c. blue — 45·00

934 (1 July). *150th Anniv of Arrival of United Empire Loyalists. No. 333 punctured as Type* O **1**.
76 **85** 10c. olive-green — 48·00

1934 (16 Aug). *150th Anniv of Province of New Brunswick. No. 334 punctured as Type* O **1**.
O77 **86** 2c. red-brown — 60·00

1935 (4 May). *Silver Jubilee. Nos. 335/40 punctured as Type* O **1**.
O78 **87** 1c. green — 25·00
O79 – 2c. brown — 32·00
O80 **89** 3c. carmine-red — 40·00
O81 – 5c. blue — 38·00
O82 – 10c. green — £110
O83 – 13c. blue — £110
O78/83 *Set of* 6 — £325

1935. *Nos. 341/51 and 355 punctured as Type* O **1**.

(a) Postage.
O84 **93** 1c. green — 15·00
O85 2c. brown — 28·00
O86 3c. scarlet — 25·00
O87 4c. yellow — 45·00
O88 5c. blue — 25·00
O89 8c. orange — 45·00
O90 **94** 10c. carmine — 35·00
O91 – 13c. purple — 45·00
O92 – 20c. olive-green — 48·00
O93 – 50c. deep violet — 35·00
O94 – $1 bright blue — 95·00

(b) Air.
O95 **99** 6c. red-brown — 75·00
O84/95 *Set of* 12 — £475

1937 (10 May). *Coronation. No. 356 punctured as Type* O **1**.
O96 **100** 3c. carmine — 40·00

1937–38. *Nos. 357/67, 370 and 371 punctured as Type* O **1**.

(a) Postage.
O 97 **101** 1c. green — 2·50
O 98 2c. brown — 2·75
O 99 3c. scarlet — 2·50
O100 4c. yellow — 8·00
O101 5c. blue — 6·50
O102 8c. orange — 13·00
O103 **102** 10c. rose-carmine — 20·00
a. Red — 23·00
O104 – 13c. blue — 28·00
O105 – 20c. red-brown — 28·00
O106 – 50c. green — 65·00
O107 – $1 violet — 95·00
O97/107 *Set of* 11 — £250

(b) Coil stamp.
O108 **101** 3c. scarlet — 65·00

(c) Air.
O109 **107** 6c. blue — 28·00

1939 (15 May). *Royal Visit. Nos. 372/4 punctured as Type* O **1**.
O110 **108** 1c. black and green — 32·00
O111 **109** 2c. black and brown — 42·00
O112 **110** 3c. black and carmine — 32·00
O110/12 *Set of* 3 — 95·00

1939 (1 July). *Air. No. 274 punctured as Type* O **2**.
O113 **59** 5c. olive-brown 21·00 14·00

1939 (1 July). *Nos. 347/50 and 355 punctured as Type* O **2**.

(a) Postage.
O114 **94** 10c. carmine 55·00 38·00
O115 – 13c. purple 60·00 38·00
O116 – 20c. olive-green 75·00 48·00
O117 – 50c. deep violet 60·00 38·00

(b) Air.
O118 **99** 6c. red-brown 50·00 42·00
O114/18 *Set of* 5 £275 £180

1939 (1 July). *Coronation. No. 356 punctured as Type* O **2**.
O119 **100** 3c. carmine 70·00 45·00

1939 (1 July). *Nos. 357/67, 369/70 and 371 punctured as Type* O **2**.

(a) Postage.
O120 **101** 1c. green 1·50 10
O121 2c. brown 2·25 10
O122 3c. scarlet 2·50 10
O123 4c. yellow 5·00 2·25
O124 5c. blue 3·50 20
O125 8c. orange 13·00 4·25
O126 **102** 10c. rose-carmine 60·00 3·25
a. Red 9·00 30
O127 – 13c. blue 15·00 1·50
O128 – 20c. red-brown 35·00 2·00
O129 – 50c. green 48·00 8·00
O130 – $1 violet £110 30·00
O120/30 *Set of* 11 £225 42·00

(b) Coil stamps.
O131 **101** 2c. brown 70·00 48·00
O132 3c. scarlet 70·00 48·00

(c) Air.
O133 **107** 6c. blue 3·00 80

1939 (1 July). *Royal Visit. Nos. 372/4 punctured as Type* O **2**.
O134 **108** 1c. black and green 80·00 38·00
O135 **109** 2c. black and brown 80·00 38·00
O136 **110** 3c. black and carmine 80·00 38·00
O134/6 *Set of* 3 £225 £100

1942–43. *War Effort. Nos. 375/88 and 399/400 punctured as Type* O **2**.

(a) Postage.
O137 **111** 1c. green 40 10
O138 **112** 2c. brown 50 10
O139 **113** 3c. carmine-lake 1·10 50
O140 3c. purple 60 10
O141 **114** 4c. slate 3·75 1·00
O142 **112** 4c. carmine-lake 55 10
O143 **111** 5c. blue 1·25 15
O144 – 8c. red-brown 7·50 2·00
O145 **116** 10c. brown 4·50 20
O146 **117** 13c. dull green 7·50 6·50
O147 14c. dull green 9·00 85
O148 – 20c. chocolate 13·00 70
O149 – 50c. violet 38·00 5·50
O150 – $1 blue 90·00 25·00

(b) Air.
O151 **121** 6c. blue 4·00 2·50
O152 7c. blue 3·50 25
O137/52 *Set of* 16 £160 40·00

1946. *Peace Re-conversion. Nos. 401/7 punctured as Type* O **2**.

(a) Postage.
O153 **122** 8c. brown 14·00 3·50
O154 – 10c. olive-green 3·25 15
O155 – 14c. sepia 5·00 65
O156 – 20c. slate 5·50 50
O157 – 50c. green 25·00 5·00
O158 – $1 purple 60·00 15·00

(b) Air.
O159 – 7c. blue 3·00 50
O153/9 *Set of* 7 £100 23·00

1949. *Nos. 415 and 416 punctured as Type* O **2**.
O160 **136** 2c. sepia 1·25 1·25
O161 **137** 3c. purple 1·25 1·25

O.H.M.S.
(O 3)

1949. *Nos. 375/6, 378, 380 and 402/7 optd as Type* O **3** *by typography.*

(a) Postage.
O162 **111** 1c. green 2·00 2·50
a. Missing stop after "S" £180 60·00
O163 **112** 2c. brown 12·00 12·00
a. Missing stop after "S" £160 90·00
O164 **113** 3c. purple 1·25 2·00
O165 **112** 4c. carmine-lake 2·25 2·00
O166 – 10c. olive-green 4·00 15
a. Missing stop after "S" 85·00 35·00
O167 – 14c. sepia 4·50 3·00
a. Missing stop after "S" £110 60·00
O168 – 20c. slate 12·00 60
a. Missing stop after "S" £160 50·00
O169 – 50c. green £160 £120
a. Missing stop after "S" £950 £600
O170 – $1 purple 45·00 48·00
a. Missing stop after "S" £1800

(b) Air.
O171 – 7c. blue 24·00 7·00
a. Missing stop after "S" £140 70·00
O162/71 *Set of* 10 £225 £140

Forgeries exist of this overprint. Genuine examples are 2.3 × 15 mm and show the tops of all letters aligned, as are the stops.
Only a few sheets of the $1 showed the variety, No. O170a.

MISSING STOP VARIETIES. These occur on R. 6/2 of the lower left pane (Nos. O162a, O163a and O176a) or R. 10/2 of the lower left pane (O166a, O167a, O168a, O169a, O170a and O171a). No. O176a also occurs on R. 8/8 of the upper left pane in addition to R. 6/2 of the lower left pane.

1949–50. *Nos. 414/15, 416/17, 418 and 431 optd as Type* O **3** *by typography.*
O172 **135** 1c. green 1·75 1·00
O173 **136** 2c. sepia 3·00 1·50
O174 **137** 3c. purple 2·25 1·00
O175 **138** 4c. carmine-lake 2·25 15
O176 **139** 5c. blue (1949) 4·00 2·00
a. Missing stop after "S" 85·00 38·00
O177 **141** 50c. green (1950) 32·00 28·00
O172/7 *Set of* 6 40·00 30·00

G (O 4) **G** (O 5)

Variations in thickness are known in Type O **4** these are due to wear and subsequent cleaning of the plate. All are produced by typography. Examples showing the "G" applied by lithography are forgeries.

1950 (2 Oct)–**52**. *Nos. 402/4, 406/7, 414/18 and 431 optd with Type* O **4** *(1 to 5c.) or* O **5** *(7c. to $1).*

(a) Postage.
O178 **135** 1c. green 1·25 10
O179 **136** 2c. sepia 2·50 2·75
O180 2c. olive-green (11.51) 1·75 10
O181 **137** 3c. purple 2·00 10
O182 **138** 4c. carmine-lake 2·00 60
O183 4c. vermilion (1.5.52) 2·50 30
O184 **139** 5c. blue 3·00 1·00
O185 – 10c. olive-green 3·00 10
O186 – 14c. sepia 14·00 5·00
O187 – 20c. slate 25·00 30
O188 **141** 50c. green 13·00 13·00
O189 – $1 purple 70·00 70·00

(b) Air.
O190 – 7c. blue 24·00 14·00
O178/90 *Set of* 13 £150 95·00

1950–51. *Nos. 432/3 optd with Type* O **5**.
O191 **142** 10c. brown-purple 3·75 10
a. Opt omitted in pair with normal £450 £350
O192 **143** $1 ultramarine (1.2.51) 60·00 70·00

OFFICIAL SPECIAL DELIVERY STAMPS

1923 (May). *Nos. S3/4 punctured as Type* O **1**.
OS1 **S 1** 10c. yellowish green — 85·00
OS2 **S 2** 20c. carmine-red — 70·00

1927 (29 June). *60th Anniv of Confederation. No. S5 punctured as Type* O **1**.
OS3 **S 3** 20c. orange . . . . — 80·00

1930 (2 Sept). *Inscr* "TWENTY CENTS" *at foot. No. S6 punctured as Type* O **1**.
OS4 **S 4** 20c. brown-red . . . . — 65·00

1932 (24 Dec). *Inscr* "CENTS" *at foot. No. S7 punctured as Type* O **1**.
OS5 **S 4** 20c. brown-red . . . . — 65·00

1935 (1 June). *No. S8 punctured as Type* O **1**.
OS6 **S 5** 20c. scarlet . . . . — 65·00

1938–39. *Nos. S9/10 punctured as Type* O **1**.
OS7 **S 6** 10c. green . . . . — 42·00
OS8 20c. scarlet . . . . — 65·00

1939 (1 Mar). *No. S11 punctured as Type* O **1**.
OS9 **S 6** 10c. on 20c. scarlet . . . . — 65·00

1939 (1 July). *Inscr* "CENTS" *at foot. No. S7 punctured as Type* O **2**.
OS10 S 4 20c. brown-red . . . . £160 85·00

1939 (1 July). *No. S8 punctured as Type* O **2**.
OS11 **S 5** 20c. scarlet . . . . 90·00 42·00

1939 (1 July). *No. S9 punctured as Type* O **2**.
OS12 **S 6** 10c. green . . . . 7·00 5·00

1939 (1 July). *No. S11 punctured as Type* O **2**.
OS13 **S 6** 10c. on 20c. scarlet . . . . £110 55·00

1942–43. *Nos. S12/14 punctured as Type* O **2**.

(a) Postage.

OS14 **S 8** 10c. green . . . . 9·00 6·50

(b) Air.

OS15 **S 9** 16c. ultramarine . . . . 17·00 13·00
OS16 17c. ultramarine . . . . 10·00 8·00

1946–47. *Nos. S15/17 punctured as Type* O **2**.

(a) Postage.

OS17 **S 10** 10c. green . . . . 6·50 4·50

(b) Air.

OS18 **S 11** 17c. ultramarine (circumflex accent) . . . . 30·00 23·00
OS19 17c. ultramarine (grave accent) . . 60·00 60·00

1950. *No. S15 optd as Type* O **3**, *but larger.*
OS20 **S 10** 10c. green . . . . 17·00 24·00

1950 (2 Oct). *No. S15 optd as Type* O **4**, *but larger.*
OS21 **S 10** 10c. green . . . . 26·00 29·00

The use of official stamps was discontinued on 31 December 1963.

Cape of Good Hope *see* South Africa

Cayman Islands

The first post office was opened at Georgetown in April 1889. The stamps of Jamaica with the following cancellations were used until 19 February 1901. At some stage, probably around 1891, a supply of the Jamaica 1889 1d., No. 27, was overprinted "CAYMAN ISLANDS", but these stamps were never issued. Two surviving examples are known, one unused and the other cancelled at Richmond in Jamaica.

Types of Jamaica

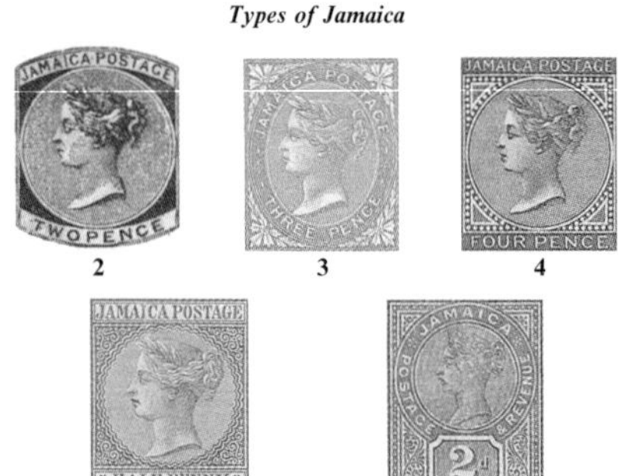

2 3 4 8 11

13

PRICES OF NOS. Z1/27. These are for a single stamp showing a clear impression of the postmark. Nos. Z1, 2, 6/8, 11/13, 18, 22 and Z25 are known used on cover and these are worth considerably more.

GEORGETOWN, GRAND CAYMAN

Z 1

Z 2 Z 3

Stamps of JAMAICA *cancelled with Type* Z **1** *in purple.*

1889–94.
Z1 **8** ½d. yellow-green (No. 16) £500
Z2 **11** 1d. purple and mauve (No. 27) £500
Z2*a* **2** 2d. slate (No. 20*a*) £4500
Z3 **11** 2d. green (No. 28) £900
Z4 2½d. dull purple and blue (No. 29) £1100
Z5 **4** 4d. red-orange (No. 22) £2750

Stamps of JAMAICA *cancelled with Type* Z **2** *in purple or black.*

1895–98.
Z6 **8** ½d. yellow-green (No. 16) £600
Z7 **11** 1d. purple and mauve (No. 27) £475
Z8 2½d. dull purple and blue (No. 29) £800
Z9 **3** 3d. sage-green (No 21) £3500

Stamps of JAMAICA *cancelled with Type* Z **3**

1898–1901.
Z10 **8** ½d. yellow-green (No. 16) £475
a. Green (No. 16*a*) £475
Z11 **11** 1d. purple and mauve (No. 27) £475
Z12 **13** 1d. red (No. 31) (1900) £500
Z13 **11** 2½d. dull purple and blue (No. 29) £700

OFFICIAL STAMPS

Stamps of JAMAICA *cancelled with Type* Z **1** *in purple.*

1890–94.
Z14 **8** ½d. green (No. O1) (*opt 17–17½ mm long*) . . . £1200
Z15 ½d. green (No. O3) (*opt 16 mm long*) (1893) . . £2750
Z16 **11** 1d. rose (No. O4) £1200
Z17 2d. grey (No. O5) £3500

Stamps of JAMAICA *cancelled with Type* Z **2** *in purple or black.*

1895–98.
Z18 **8** ½d. green (No. O3) £2250
Z19 **11** 1d. rose (No. O4) £3750
Z20 2d. grey (No. O5) £3750

STAKE BAY, CAYMAN BRAC

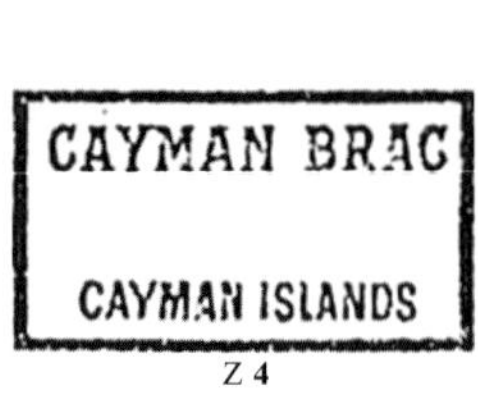

Z 4 Z 5

Stamps of JAMAICA *cancelled with Type* Z **4**.

1898–1900.
Z21 **8** ½d. yellow-green (No. 16) £3000
Z22 **11** 1d. purple and mauve (No. 27) £3250
Z23 2d. green (No. 28) £4000
Z24 2½d. dull purple and blue (No. 29) £3250

Stamps of JAMAICA *cancelled with Type* Z **5**.

1900–01.
Z25 **8** ½d. yellow-green (No. 16) £3250
Z26 **11** 1d. purple and mauve (No. 27) £3000
Z27 **13** 1d. red (No. 31) £3000
Z28 **11** 2½d. dull purple and blue (No. 29) £2500

PRICES FOR STAMPS ON COVER TO 1945	
Nos. 1/2	*from* × 25
Nos. 3/12	*from* × 5
Nos. 13/16	*from* × 4
Nos. 17/19	*from* × 12
Nos. 25/34	*from* × 5
Nos. 35/52*b*	*from* × 4
Nos. 53/67	*from* × 5
Nos. 69/83	*from* × 4
Nos. 84/95	*from* × 6
Nos. 96/9	*from* × 5
Nos. 100/11	*from* × 4
Nos. 112/14	*from* × 6
Nos. 115/26	*from* × 2

DEPENDENCY OF JAMAICA

1 2 3

(T **1/3**, **8/9** and **12/13** typo D.L.R.)

1900 (1 Nov). Wmk Crown CA. P 14.
1 **1** ½d. deep green . . . . 9·00 19·0
a. Pale green . . . . 4·50 15·0
2 1d. rose-carmine . . . . 4·50 2·2
a. Pale carmine . . . . 13·00 12·0
1s/2s Optd "Specimen" *Set of* 2 . . . . £130

(Dented frame under "A" (R. 1/6 of left pane) (The variety is believed to have occurred at some point between 9 January and 9 April 1902 and is then present on all subsequent printings of the "POSTAGE POSTAGE" design)

1902 (1 Jan)–**03**. Wmk Crown CA. P 14.
3 **2** ½d. green (15.9.02) . . . . 4·50 25·0
a. Dented frame £120
4 1d. carmine (6.3.03) . . . . 10·00 9·0
a. Dented frame £170 £20
5 2½d. bright blue . . . . 10·00 12·0
a. Dented frame £180
6 6d. brown . . . . 29·00 60·0
a. Dented frame £325
7 **3** 1s. orange . . . . 60·00 £11
a. Dented frame £450 £70
3/7 *Set of* 5 . . . . £100 £19
3s/7s Optd "Specimen" *Set of* 5 . . . . £200

1905 (Feb–Oct). Wmk Mult Crown CA. P 14.
8 **2** ½d. green . . . . 7·00 8·5
a. Dented frame £120 £18
9 1d. carmine (18 Oct) . . . . 14·00 17·0
a. Dented frame £250 £32
10 2½d. bright blue . . . . 7·00 3·2
a. Dented frame £140 £16
11 6d. brown . . . . 16·00 38·
a. Dented frame £275 £4
12 **3** 1s. orange . . . . 32·00 48·
a. Dented frame £350
8/12 *Set of* 5 . . . . 65·00 £1

1907 (13 Mar). Wmk Mult Crown CA. P 14.
13 **3** 4d. brown and blue . . . . 32·00 60·
a. Dented frame £325 £5
14 **2** 6d. olive and rose . . . . 32·00 70·
a. Dented frame £325 £5
15 **3** 1s. violet and green . . . . 55·00 80·
a. Dented frame £400
16 5s. salmon and green £180 £3
a. Dented frame £1300 £17
13/16 *Set of* 4 . . . . £275 £4
13s/16s Optd "Specimen" *Set of* 4 . . . . . . £200

One Halfpenny. (4) ½D (5) 1D (6)

1907 (30 Aug). *No. 9 surch at Govt Printing Office, Kingston, wi*
T **4**.
17 **2** ½d. on 1d. carmine . . . . 42·00 70·
a. Dented frame £400 £6

1907 (Nov). *No. 16 handstamped at Georgetown P.O. with T* **5** *or*
18 **3** ½d. on 5s. salmon and green (26 Nov) £250 £3
a. Surch inverted £30000
b. Surch double £9500 £95
c. Surch double, one inverted . . . . .
d. Surch omitted (in pair with normal) £45000
e. Dented frame £1300
19 1d. on 5s. salmon and green (23 Nov) £250 £3
a. Surch double £14000
b. Surch inverted £48000
c. Dented frame £1300 £17

The ½d. on 5s. may be found with the figures "1" or "2" omitted, owing to defective handstamping.

8

9

2½D
(10)

1907 (27 Dec)–09. *Chalk-surfaced paper (3d. to 10s.).* P 14.

(a) Wmk Mult Crown CA.

25 8 ½d. green . . . 2·50 4·00
26 1d. carmine . . . 1·50 75
27 2½d. ultramarine (30.3.08) . . . 3·50 3·50
28 9 3d. purple/*yellow* (30.3.08) . . . 3·25 6·50
29 4d. black and red/*yellow* (30.3.08) . . . 50·00 70·00
30 8 6d. dull and bright purple (2.10.08) . . 10·00 35·00
a. Dull purple and violet-purple . . . 32·00 55·00
31 9 1s. black/*green* (5.4.09) . . . 7·50 22·00
32 5s. green and red/*yellow* (30.3.08) . . . 38·00 60·00

(b) Wmk Crown CA (30.3.08).

33 9 1s. black/*green* . . . 60·00 85·00
34 8 10s. green and red/*green* . . . £160 £225
25/34 *Set of* 10 . . . £300 £450
25s/30s, 32s/4s Optd "Specimen" *Set of* 9 . . . £325

1908 (12 Feb). *No. 13 handstamped locally with T* **10**.
35 3 2½d. on 4d. brown and blue . . . £1500 £2500
a. Surch double . . . £30000 £18000
b. Dented frame . . . £9000

No. 35 should only be purchased when accompanied by an expert committee's certificate or similar form of guarantee.

MANUSCRIPT PROVISIONALS. During May and June 1908 supplies of ½d. and 1d. stamps became exhausted, and the payment of postage was indicated by the postmistress, Miss Gwendolyn Parsons, using a manuscript endorsement. Such endorsements were in use from 12 May to 1 June.

Price on cover
MP1 "(Postage Paid G.A.P.)" (12 May to 1 June) . . . £3250
MP1*a* "(Postage Paid G.A.P.)" ½ or 1d. (23 May) . . . £4750

In October of the same year there was a further shortage of ½d. stamps and the manuscript endorsements were again applied by either the new Postmaster, William Graham McCausland or by Miss Parsons who remained as his assistant.

MP2 "Pd ¼d/W.G. McC" (4 to 27 October) . . . £250
MP2*a* "¼d Pd./W.G. McC" (14 October) . . . £1200
MP3 "Paid" (7 October) . . . £6500
MP4 "Pd ¼d" (8 October) . . . £5500
MP5 "Paid ¼d/ GAP. asst." (15 October) . . . £5500

No. MP2 exists in different inks and formats.

Manuscript endorsement for the 2½d. rate is also known, but this is thought to have been done by oversight.

A 1d. surcharge on 4d. (No. 29), issued in mid-May, was intended as a revenue stamp and was never authorised for postal use (*price* £225 *un.*). Used examples were either cancelled by favour or passed through the post in error. Exists with surcharge inverted (*price* £1600 *un.*), surcharge double (*price* £2500 *un.*) or surcharge double, both inverted (*price* £2500 *un.*).

11

12

13

1908 (30 June)–09. Wmk Mult Crown CA. *Litho.* P 14.
38 11 ¼d. brown . . . 2·00 50
a. Grey-brown (2.09) . . . 3·00 1·00
s. Optd "Specimen" . . . 85·00

1912 (24 Apr)–20. *Die I.* Wmk Mult Crown CA. *Chalk-surfaced paper (3d. to 10s.).* P 14.
13 ¼d. brown (10.2.13) . . . 1·00 40
12 ½d. green . . . 2·75 5·00
w. Wmk inverted . . . † £275
1d. red (25.2.13) . . . 3·25 2·50
13 2d. pale grey . . . 1·00 10·00
12 2½d. bright blue (26.8.14) . . . 7·00 11·00
a. Deep bright blue (9.11.17) . . . 18·00 25·00
13 3d. purple/*yellow* (26.11.14) . . . 15·00 40·00
a. White back (19.11.13) . . . 3·50 8·00
b. On lemon (12.3.18) . . . 2·50 18·00
bs. Optd "Specimen" . . . 65·00
c. On orange-buff (1920) . . . 10·00 30·00
d. On buff (1920) . . .
e. On pale yellow (1920) . . . 3·50 30·00
4d. black and red/*yellow* (25.2.13) . . . 1·00 10·00
12 6d. dull and bright purple (25.2.13) . . 3·75 7·50
13 1s. black/*green* (15.5.16) . . . 3·50 26·00
as. Optd "Specimen" . . . 65·00
b. White back (19.11.13) . . . 3·50 3·50
2s. purple and bright blue/*blue* . . . 12·00 48·00
3s. green and violet . . . 19·00 65·00
5s. green and red/*yellow* (26.8.14) . . 75·00 £160
12 10s. deep green and red/*green* (26.11.14) . . . £120 £200
as. Optd "Specimen" . . . 95·00
b. White back (19.11.13) . . . 85·00 £150
c. On blue-green, olive back (5.10.18) . . . £100 £190
/52*b Set of* 13 . . . £200 £425
s/4s, 45as, 46s/7s, 48*b*s, 49s/51s, 52*b*s Optd "Specimen" *Set of* 13 . . . £375

WAR STAMP. 1½d (14)

WAR STAMP. 1½d (15)

1½d Straight serif (Left-hand pane R. 10/2)

1917 (26 Feb). *T* **12** *surch with T* **14** *or* **15** *at Kingston, Jamaica.*
53 14 1½d. on 2½d. deep blue . . . 9·00 11·00
a. No fraction bar . . . £120 £170
b. Missing stop after "STAMP" (R. 1/4) . . . £400
54 15 1½d. on 2½d. deep blue . . . 1·75 6·00
a. No fraction bar . . . 70·00 £120
b. Straight serif . . . 80·00 £150

On No. 53 "WAR STAMP" and "1½d." were applied separately.

WAR STAMP 1½d (16)

WAR STAMP 1½d (17)

WAR STAMP 1½d. (18)

1917 (4 Sept). *T* **12** *surch with T* **16** *or* **17** *by D.L.R.*
55 16 1½d. on 2½d. deep blue . . . £700 £1900
56 17 1½d. on 2½d. deep blue . . . 30 60
s. Optd "Specimen" . . . £120
x. Wmk reversed . . . 90·00

De La Rue replaced surcharge Type **16** by Type **17** after only a few sheets as it did not adequately obliterate the original face value. A small quantity, said to be 3½ sheets, of Type **16** was included in the consignment in error.

1919–20. *T* **12** *and* **13** *(2½d. special printing), optd only, or surch in addition at Kingston (No. 58) or by D.L.R. (others).*
57 16 ½d. green (4.2.19) . . . 60 2·50
a. Short opt (right pane R. 10/1) . . 24·00
58 18 1½d. on 2d. grey (10.3.20) . . . 1·50 7·00
59 17 1½d. on 2½d. orange (4.12.19) . . . 80 1·25
57s, 59s Optd "Specimen" *Set of* 2 . . . £100

The ½d. stamps on *buff* paper, and later consignments of the 2d. T **13** on *pinkish*, derived their colour from the paper in which they were packed for despatch from England.

No. 57a shows the overprint 2 mm high instead of 2½ mm.

A further surcharge as No. 58, but in red, was prepared in Jamaica during April 1920, but these were not issued.

19

20 King William IV and King George V

1921 (4 Apr)–26. P 14.

(a) Wmk Mult Crown CA.

60 19 3d. purple/*orange-buff* . . . 1·50 8·00
aw. Wmk inverted . . . £120 £170
ay. Wmk inverted and reversed . . . 85·00 £130
b. purple/pale yellow . . . 45·00 60·00
bw. Wmk inverted
62 4d. red/*yellow* (1.4.22) . . . 1·00 4·00
63 1s. black/*green* . . . 1·25 9·50
x. Wmk reversed
64 5s. yellow-green/*pale yellow* . . . 16·00 70·00
a. Deep green/pale yellow . . . 80·00 £120
b. blue-green/pale yellow . . . 85·00 £140
c. Deep green/orange-buff (19.11.21) . . . £120 £190
67 10s. carmine/*green* (19.11.21) . . . 60·00 £110
60/7 *Set of* 5 . . . 70·00 £180
60s/7s Optd "Specimen" *Set of* 5 . . . £200

(b) Wmk Mult Script CA.

69 19 ¼d. yellow-brown (1.4.22) . . . 50 1·50
y. Wmk inverted and reversed . . . £225
70 ½d. pale grey-green (1.4.22) . . . 50 30
w. Wmk inverted
y. Wmk inverted and reversed
71 1d. deep carmine-red (1.4.22) . . . 1·40 85
72 1½d. orange-brown . . . 1·75 30
73 2d. slate-grey (1.4.22) . . . 1·75 4·00
74 2½d. bright blue (1.4.22) . . . 50 50
x. Wmk reversed . . . £250
75 3d. purple/*yellow* (29.6.23) . . . 1·00 4·00
y. Wmk inverted and reversed . . . £250
76 4½d. sage-green (29.6.23) . . . 2·25 3·00
77 6d. claret (1.4.22) . . . 5·50 32·00
a. Deep claret . . . 19·00 40·00
79 1s. black/*green* (15.5.25) . . . 9·50 32·00
80 2s. violet/*blue* (1.4.22) . . . 14·00 24·00
81 3s. violet (1.4.22) . . . 23·00 16·00
82 5s. green/*yellow* (15.2.25) . . . 24·00 45·00
83 10s. carmine/*green* (5.9.26) . . . 60·00 85·00
69/83 *Set of* 14 . . . £130 £225
69s/83s Optd "Specimen" *Set of* 14 . . . £350

An example of the 4d, No. 62, is known with the 'C' missing from the watermark in the top sheet margin.

"A.S.R." PROVISIONAL. On the night of 9/10 November 1932 the Cayman Brac Post Office at Stake Bay, and its contents, was destroyed by a hurricane. Pending the arrival of replacement stamp stocks and cancellation the Postmaster, Mr A. S. Rutty, initialled covers to indicate that postage had been paid. Those destined for overseas addresses additionally received a "Postage Paid" machine postmark in red when they passed through Kingston, Jamaica.

Price on cover
MP6 Endorsed "A.S.R." in manuscript . . . £5500
MP7 Endorsed "A.S.R." in manuscript and "Postage Paid" machine postmark in red . . . £8000

These emergency arrangements lasted until 19 December.

(Recess Waterlow)

1932 (5 Dec). *Centenary of the "Assembly of Justices and Vestry".* Wmk Mult Script CA. P 12½.
84 20 ¼d. brown . . . 1·50 1·00
a. "A" of "CA" missing from wmk . . . £1100 £1100
85 ½d. green . . . 2·75 8·00
a. "A" of "CA" reversed in wmk . . £1300
86 1d. scarlet . . . 2·75 8·00
87 1½d. red-orange . . . 2·75 2·75
a. "A" of "CA" missing from wmk
88 2d. grey . . . 2·75 3·50
89 2½d. ultramarine . . . 2·75 1·50
90 3d. olive-green . . . 3·25 5·00
91 6d. purple . . . 9·50 23·00
92 1s. black and brown . . . 17·00 32·00
93 2s. black and ultramarine . . . 45·00 75·00
94 5s. black and green . . . 85·00 £120
95 10s. black and scarlet . . . £250 £350
84/95 *Set of* 12 . . . £375 £550
84s/95s Perf "Specimen" *Set of* 12 . . . £500

The design of Nos. 92/5 differs slightly from Type **20**.

No. 85a shows one "A" of the watermark reversed so that its head points to right when seen from the back. It is believed that this stamp may also exist with "A" missing.

Examples of all values are known showing a forged George Town postmark dated "DE 31 1932".

21 Cayman Islands

24 Queen or Pink Conch Shells

(Recess Waterlow)

1935 (1 May)–36. *T* **21**, **24** *and similar designs.* Wmk Mult Script CA. P 12½.
96 21 ¼d. black and brown . . . 50 1·00
97 – ½d. ultramarine & yellow-green (1.1.36) . . . 1·00 1·00
98 – 1d. ultramarine and scarlet . . . 4·00 2·25
99 24 1½d. black and orange . . . 1·50 1·75
100 – 2d. ultramarine and purple . . . 3·75 1·10
101 – 2½d. blue and black (1.1.36) . . . 3·25 1·25
102 21 3d. black and olive-green . . . 2·50 3·00
103 – 6d. bright purple and black (1.1.36) . . . 8·50 4·00
104 – 1s. ultramarine and orange (1.1.36) . . . 6·00 6·50
105 – 2s. ultramarine and black . . . 45·00 35·00
106 – 5s. green and black . . . 50·00 50·00
107 24 10s. black and scarlet . . . 70·00 90·00
96/107 *Set of* 12 . . . £170 £180
96s/107s Perf "Specimen" *Set of* 12 . . . £275

Designs: *Horiz*—½d., 2d., 1s. Cat boat; 1d., 2s. Red-footed Booby; 2½d., 6d., 5s. Hawksbill Turtles.

Examples of all values are known showing a forged George Town postmark dated "AU 23 1936".

1935 (6 May). *Silver Jubilee. As Nos. 91/4 of Antigua*
108 ½d. black and green . . . 15 1·00
f. Diagonal line by turret . . . 35·00
h. Dot by flagstaff . . . 55·00
i. Dash by turret . . . 70·00
109 2½d. brown and deep blue . . . 1·00 1·00
110 6d. light blue and olive-green . . . 1·00 4·00
h. Dot by flagstaff . . . £160
i. Dash by turret . . . £160
111 1s. slate and purple . . . 7·00 7·00
h. Dot by flagstaff . . . £275
i. Dash by turret . . . £300
108/11 *Set of* 4 . . . 8·25 11·50
108s/11s Perf "Specimen" *Set of* 4 . . . £120

For illustrations of plate varieties see Omnibus section following Zanzibar.

1937 (13 May). *Coronation Issue. As Nos. 95/7 of Antigua.* P 11×11½.
112 ½d. green . . . 30 1·60
113 1d. carmine . . . 50 20
114 2½d. blue . . . 95 40
112/14 *Set of* 3 . . . 1·60 2·00
112s/14s *Set of* 3 . . . 90·00

26 Beach View

27 Dolphin (fish) (*Coryphaena hippurus*)

(Recess D.L.R. (½d., 2d., 6d., 1s., 10s.), Waterlow (others))

1938 (5 May)–48. *T* **26/7** *and similar designs.* Wmk Mult Script CA (sideways on ¼d., 1d., 1½d., 2½d., 3d., 2s., 5s.). Various perfs.
115 26 ¼d. red-orange (P 12½) . . . 70 55
a. Perf 13½×12½ (16.7.43) . . . 10 65

116	**27**	½d. green (P 13 × 11½)	1·00	55
		a. Perf 14 (16.7.43)	1·25	1·40
		ab. "A" of "CA" missing from wmk	£1100	
117	–	1d. scarlet (P 12½)	30	75
118	**26**	1½d. black (P 12½)	30	10
119	–	2d. violet (P 11½ × 13)	3·00	40
		a. Perf 14 (16.7.43)	60	30
120	–	2½d. bright blue (P 12½)	40	20
120*a*	–	2½d. orange (P 12½) (25.8.47)	2·50	50
121	–	3d. orange (P 12½)	40	15
121*a*	–	3d. bright blue (P 12½) (25.8.47)	3·00	30
122	–	6d. olive-green (P 11½ × 13)	11·00	4·00
		a. Perf 14 (16.7.43)	3·00	1·25
		b. Brownish ol (P 11½ × 13) (8.7.47)	3·00	1·50
123	**27**	1s. red-brown (P 13 × 11½)	6·50	1·50
		a. Perf 14 (16.7.43)	4·50	2·00
		ab. "A" of "CA" missing from wmk	£1200	
124	**26**	2s. yellow-green (*shades*) (P 12½)	48·00	14·00
		a. Deep green (16.7.43)	25·00	9·00
125	–	5s. carmine-lake (P 12½)	32·00	15·00
		a. Crimson (1948)	70·00	22·00
126	–	10s. chocolate (P 11½ × 13)	23·00	9·00
		a. Perf 14 (16.7.43)	23·00	9·00
		aw. Wmk inverted		
115/26a *Set of* 14			85·00	35·00
115s/26s Perf "Specimen" *Set of* 14			£350	

Designs: *Horiz* (*as T* **26**)—1d., 3d. Cayman Islands map; 2½d., 5s. *Rembro* (schooner). *Vert* (*as* T **27**)—2d., 6d., 10s. Hawksbill Turtles.

Stop after "1946" (Plate B1 R. 2/1)

1946 (26 Aug). *Victory. As Nos. 110/11 of Antigua.*

127	1½d. black	20	10
128	3d. orange-yellow	20	10
	a. Stop after "1946"	20·00	
127s/8s Perf "Specimen" *Set of* 2		80·00	

1948 (29 Nov). *Royal Silver Wedding. As Nos. 112/13 of Antigua.*

129	½d. green	10	20
130	10s. violet-blue	15·00	16·00

1949 (10 Oct). *75th Anniv of Universal Postal Union. As Nos. 114/17 of Antigua.*

131	2½d. orange	30	1·00
132	3d. deep blue	1·50	2·25
133	6d. olive	60	2·25
134	1s. red-brown	60	50
131/4 *Set of* 4		2·75	5·50

31 Cat Boat

32 Coconut Grove, Cayman Brac

(Recess B.W.)

1950 (2 Oct). *T* **31/2** *and similar horiz designs.* Wmk Mult Script CA. P 11½ × 11.

135	¼d. bright blue and pale scarlet	15	60
136	½d. reddish violet and emerald-green	15	1·25
137	1d. olive-green and deep blue	60	75
138	1½d. green and brown	30	75
139	2d. reddish violet and rose-carmine	1·25	1·50
140	2½d. turquoise and black	1·25	60
141	3d. bright green and light blue	1·40	1·50
142	6d. red-brown and blue	2·00	1·25
143	9d. scarlet and grey-green	7·00	2·00
144	1s. brown and orange	3·25	2·75
145	2s. violet and reddish purple	8·50	9·50
146	5s. olive-green and violet	13·00	7·00
147	10s. black and scarlet	18·00	15·00
135/47 *Set of* 13		50·00	40·00

Designs:—1d. Green Turtle; 1½d. Thatch rope industry; 2d. Cayman seamen; 2½d. Map of Cayman Islands; 3d. Parrotfish; 6d. Bluff, Cayman Brac; 9d. Georgetown harbour; 1s. Turtle in "crawl"; 2s. *Ziroma* (schooner); 5s. Boat-building; 10s. Government Offices, Grand Cayman.

Ceylon

PRICES FOR STAMPS ON COVER TO 1945

No.	1	*from* × 5
Nos.	2/12	*from* × 4
Nos.	16/17	*from* × 5
Nos.	18/59	*from* × 8
Nos.	60/2	*from* × 15
Nos.	63/72	*from* × 8
Nos.	121/38	*from* × 6
Nos.	139/41	†
Nos.	142/3	*from* × 10
Nos.	146/51	*from* × 6
Nos.	151a/2	†
Nos.	153/93	*from* × 8
Nos.	195/201	*from* × 12
Nos.	202/43	*from* × 6
Nos.	245/9	*from* × 4
Nos.	250/5	*from* × 5
Nos.	256/64	*from* × 4
Nos.	265/76	*from* × 3
Nos.	277/88	*from* × 4
Nos.	289/300	*from* × 8
Nos.	301/18	*from* × 2
Nos.	319/23	—
Nos.	330/7b	*from* × 4
Nos.	338/56	*from* × 2
Nos.	357/60	—
Nos.	361/2	*from* × 5
Nos.	363/7	*from* × 3
Nos.	368/78	*from* × 2
Nos.	379/82	*from* × 4
Nos.	383/5	*from* × 3
Nos.	386/97	*from* × 2
Nos.	398/9	*from* × 8
Nos.	O1/17	*from* × 30

CROWN COLONY

PRICES. The prices of the imperf stamps of Ceylon vary greatly according to condition. The following prices are for fine copies with four margins.

Poor to medium specimens can be supplied at much lower prices.

1

2

3

NOTE. Beware of stamps of Type **2** which are often offered with corners added.

(Recess P.B.)

1857 (1 Apr). *Blued paper.* Wmk Star W w **1**. Imperf.

1	**1**	6d. purple-brown	£7500	£450

Collectors should beware of proofs with faked watermark, often offered as originals.

PERKINS BACON "CANCELLED". For notes on these handstamps, showing "CANCELLED" between horizontal bars forming an oval, see Catalogue Introduction.

1857 (2 July)–**59**. Wmk Star, W w **1**. *White paper.*

(a) Imperf.

2	**1**	1d. deep turquoise-blue (24.8.57)	£650	29·00
		a. Blue	£750	48·00
		b. Blued paper	—	£200
3		2d. green (*shades*) (24.8.57)	£150	55·00
		a. Yellowish green	£500	90·00
4	**2**	4d. dull rose (23.4.59)	£50000	£4500
5	**1**	5d. chestnut	£1500	£150
6		6d. purple-brown (1859)	£1800	£140
		a. Brown	£6000	£475
		b. Deep brown	£7000	£1000
		c. Light brown	—	£900
7	**2**	8d. brown (23.4.59)	£22000	£1500
8		9d. purple-brown (23.4.59)	£32000	£900
9	**3**	10d. dull vermilion	£800	£300
10		1s. slate-violet	£4500	£200
11	**2**	1s.9d. green (H/S "CANCELLED" in oval £6500)	£750	£800
		a. Yellow-green	£4000	£3000
12		2s. dull blue (23.4.59)	£5500	£1200

(b) Unofficial perf 7½ (1s.9d.) or roul (others).

13	**1**	1d. blue	£5500	
14		2d. green	£2500	£1200
15	**2**	1s.9d. green	£6500	

Nos. 13/15 were privately produced, probably by commercial firms for their own convenience.

The 10d. also exists with "CANCELLED" in oval, but no examples are believed to be in private hands.

4

(Typo D.L.R.)

1857 (Oct)–**64**. No wmk. *Glazed paper.*

(a) Imperf.

16	**4**	½d. reddish lilac (*blued paper*)	£3250	£475
17		½d. dull mauve (1858)	£170	£190
		a. Private roul	£5500	

(b) P 12½.

18	**4**	½d. dull mauve (1864)	£200	£170

(Recess P.B.)

1861–64. Wmk Star, W w **1**.

(a) Clean-cut and intermediate perf 14 to 15½.

19	**1**	1d. light blue	£950	£180
		a. Dull blue (H/S "CANCELLED" in oval £6500)	£150	12·00
20		2d. green (*shades*)	£160	28·0
		a. Imperf between (vert pair)	†	—
		b. Yellowish green (H/S "CANCELLED" in oval £6500)	£170	24·00
21	**2**	4d. dull rose (H/S "CANCELLED" in oval £6500)	£2000	£300
22	**1**	5d. chestnut (H/S "CANCELLED" in oval £4500)	80·00	8·0
23		6d. brown (H/S "CANCELLED" in oval £7000)	£2000	£11
		a. Bistre-brown	—	£18
24	**2**	8d. brown (H/S "CANCELLED" in oval £6000)	£1900	£50
25		9d. purple-brown	£5500	£22
26	**3**	1s. slate-violet (H/S "CANCELLED" in oval £6500)	95·00	13·0
27	**2**	2s. dull blue	£2750	£65

(b) Rough perf 14 to 15½.

28	**1**	1d. dull blue	£120	7·0
		a. Blued paper	£500	20·0
29		2d. green	£400	80·0
30	**2**	4d. rose-red	£400	80·0
		a. Deep rose-red	£425	90·0
31	**1**	6d. deep brown	£850	£10
		a. Light brown	£1400	£14
		b. Olive-sepia	£750	90·0
32	**2**	8d. brown	£1400	£55
		a. Yellow-brown	£1400	£35
33		9d. deep brown (H/S "CANCELLED" in oval £5000)	75·00	65·0
		a. Light brown	£800	95·0
		b. Olive-sepia	£500	60·0
34	**3**	10d. dull vermilion	£225	22·0
		a. Imperf vert (horiz pair)	†	–
35		1s. slate-violet	£225	15·0
36	**2**	1s.9d. light green (*prepared for use, but not issued*)	£650	
37		2s. dull blue (H/S "CANCELLED" in oval £6000)	£600	£14
		a. Deep dull blue	£850	£17

(c) P 12½ by D.L.R.

38	**3**	10d. dull vermilion (9.64)	£225	16·0

The line machine used for Nos. 19/37 produced perforations of variable quality due to wear, poor cleaning and faulty servicing, but it is generally accepted that the clean-cut and intermediate versions occurred on stamps perforated up to March 1861 and the rough variety when the machine was used after that date.

(Recess D.L.R.)

1862. No wmk. *Smooth paper.*

(a) P 13.

39	**1**	1d. dull blue	£120	6·0
40		5d. lake-brown	£1400	£1
41		6d. brown	£160	25·0
		a. Deep brown	£140	23·0
42	**2**	9d. brown	£1200	95·0
43	**3**	1s. slate-purple	£1600	80·0

(b) P 11½, 12.

44	**1**	1d. dull blue	£1200	£1
		a. Imperf between (horiz pair)	†	£100

Nos. 39/44 were printed on paper showing a papermaker's watermark of "T H SAUNDERS 1862", parts of which can be found on individual stamps. Examples are rare and command a premium.

The 1s. is known imperforate, but was not issued in this condition.

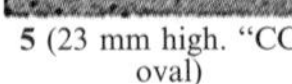

5 (23 mm high. "CC" oval)

6 (21½ mm high. "CC" round and smaller)

(Typo (½d.) or recess (others) D.L.R.)

1863–65. W **5**. *Paper medium thin and slightly soft.*

(a) P 11½, 12.

45	**1**	1d. deep blue	£2500	£3
		x. Wmk reversed	£3250	£4

(b) P 13.

46	**1**	6d. sepia	£1500	£1
		x. Wmk reversed	—	£1
		y. Wmk inverted and reversed	£2000	£3
47	**2**	9d. sepia	£3750	£7

(c) P 12½.

48	**4**	½d. dull mauve (1864)	40·00	30
		aw. Wmk inverted	£170	55
		b. Reddish lilac	50·00	38
		c. Mauve	30·00	30

No.	Type	Description	Unused	Used
49	1	1d. deep blue	£110	5·00
		a. Imperf		
		w. Wmk inverted	†	32·00
		x. Wmk reversed	£120	5·50
		y. Wmk inverted and reversed	†	40·00
50		2d. grey-green (1864)	70·00	10·00
		a. Imperf		
		bw. Wmk inverted	£190	45·00
		by. Wmk inverted and reversed	†	90·00
		c. Bottle-green	†	£3500
		d. Yellowish green	£7500	£400
		dx. Wmk reversed	†	£750
		e. Emerald (wmk reversed)	£130	95·00
		ew. Wmk inverted	£375	£225
51		2d. ochre (*wmk reversed*) (1866)	£225	£225
		w. Wmk inverted	£475	£475
		y. Wmk inverted and reversed	£400	£375
52	2	4d. rose-carmine (1865)	£550	£140
		ax. Wmk reversed	£700	
		b. Rose	£375	80·00
		bx. Wmk reversed	£425	£100
53	1	5d. red-brown (*shades*) (1865)	£170	60·00
		w. Wmk inverted	†	£150
		x. Wmk reversed	£200	50·00
54		5d. grey-olive (1866)	£1800	£350
		ax. Wmk reversed	£1500	£300
		b. Yellow-olive	£750	£225
		bx. Wmk reversed	£750	£225
55		6d. sepia	£140	4·00
		aw. Wmk inverted	†	60·00
		b. Reddish brown	£170	12·00
		c. Blackish brown	£140	9·00
		ca. Double print	†	£2750
		cw. Wmk inverted	†	48·00
		cx. Wmk reversed	£180	38·00
		cy. Wmk inverted and reversed	†	£100
56	2	8d. reddish brown (*shades*) (1864)	90·00	45·00
		x. Wmk reversed	£130	65·00
		y. Wmk inverted and reversed	£250	85·00
57		9d. sepia	£300	42·00
		x. Wmk reversed	£475	75·00
58	3	10d. vermilion (1866)	£1700	60·00
		ax. Wmk reversed	†	£130
		b. Orange-red	£4000	£400
		bx. Wmk reversed	†	£500
59	2	2s. steel-blue (*shades*) (1864)	£250	30·00
		x. Wmk reversed	†	85·00
		y. Wmk inverted and reversed	£475	£160

Watermarks as Type **5** were arranged in four panes, each of 60, with the words "CROWN COLONIES" between the panes. Parts of this marginal watermark often appear on the stamps.

The ½d. dull mauve, 2d. ochre and 5d. grey-olive with this watermark also exist imperforate, but are not known used. The 6d. sepia and 2s. steel-blue also exist imperforate on wove paper without watermark.

One used example of the 2d. grey-green is known showing private roulettes added to an imperforate stamp (*Price* £2750).

7 8

(Typo D.L.R.)

1866–68. Wmk Crown CC.

(a) P 12½.

No.	Type	Description	Unused	Used
60	7	3d. rose	£180	80·00

(b) P 14.

No.	Type	Description	Unused	Used
61	8	1d. blue (*shades*) (1868)	20·00	8·00
		w. Wmk inverted	†	95·00
62	7	3d. carmine-rose (1867)	70·00	40·00
		a. Bright rose	75·00	45·00

Nos. 60/1 exist imperforate.

(Recess D.L.R.)

1867–70. W **6**. *Specially produced hand-made paper*. P 12½.

No.	Type	Description	Unused	Used
63	1	1d. dull blue	£150	10·00
		aw. Wmk inverted	£350	80·00
		ax. Wmk reversed	£150	10·00
		b. Deep blue	£140	8·00
		bw. Wmk inverted	—	85·00
		bx. Wmk reversed	£200	30·00
64		2d. ochre	£110	10·00
		ax. Wmk reversed	—	32·00
		b. Bistre	50·00	7·00
		bw. Wmk inverted	£100	
		c. Olive-bistre	£150	20·00
		cw. Wmk inverted	£150	
		d. Yellow	85·00	5·00
		dx. Wmk reversed	55·00	20·00
65	2	4d. rose	£200	55·00
		ax. Wmk reversed	£180	45·00
		b. Rose-carmine	55·00	15·00
		bw. Wmk inverted	†	75·00
		bx. Wmk reversed	55·00	15·00
		by. Wmk inverted and reversed	£350	£110
66	1	5d. yellow-olive	85·00	13·00
		ax. Wmk reversed	75·00	17·00
		ay. Wmk inverted and reversed		
		b. Olive-green	£100	13·00
		c. Bronze-green	32·00	45·00
		6d. deep brown (1869)	75·00	10·00
		a. Blackish brown	95·00	8·50
		aw. Wmk inverted	†	90·00
		ax. Wmk reversed	£130	16·00
		b. Red-brown	32·00	35·00
	2	8d. chocolate	60·00	55·00
		ax. Wmk reversed	—	85·00
		b. Lake-brown	£130	75·00
		bx. Wmk reversed	—	90·00
		9d. bistre-brown (12.68)	£425	30·00
		ax. Wmk reversed	£350	25·00
		b. Blackish brown	45·00	6·00
70	3	10d. dull vermilion (*wmk reversed*)	£3000	£140
		ay. Wmk inverted and reversed	†	£225
		b. Red-orange	48·00	12·00
		bx. Wmk reversed	—	9·50
		by. Wmk inverted and reversed	£400	
		c. Orange	80·00	9·50
71		1s. reddish lilac (1870)	£275	27·00
		ax. Wmk reversed	£400	50·00
		b. Reddish violet	90·00	7·00
		bw. Wmk inverted	†	£110
		bx. Wmk reversed	£200	42·00
72	2	2s. steel-blue	£180	18·00
		ax. Wmk reversed	†	40·00
		b. Deep blue	£120	12·00
		bx. Wmk reversed	£150	18·00

Watermarks as Type **6** were arranged in one pane of 240 (12 × 20) with the words "CROWN COLONIES" twice in each side margin.

Unused examples of the 1d. dull blue, 1d. deep blue, 5d. yellow-olive, 6d. deep brown, 9d. blackish brown and 10d. red orange with this watermark exist imperforate.

PRINTERS. All stamps from No. 121 to 367 were typographed by De La Rue & Co. Ltd, London.

(New Currency. 100 cents = 1 rupee)

9 10 11
12 13 14
15 16 17
18 19

1872–80. Wmk Crown CC.

(a) P 14.

No.	Type	Description	Unused	Used
121	9	2c. pale brown (*shades*)	16·00	2·50
		w. Wmk inverted	90·00	45·00
122	10	4c. grey	35·00	1·50
		w. Wmk inverted	—	48·00
123		4c. rosy-mauve (1880)	55·00	1·50
124	11	8c. orange-yellow	40·00	5·50
		a. Yellow	28·00	6·00
		w. Wmk inverted	†	£110
126	12	16c. pale violet	85·00	2·75
		w. Wmk inverted	†	£110
127	13	24c. green	55·00	2·00
		w. Wmk inverted	†	£110
128	14	32c. slate (1877)	£150	15·00
		w. Wmk inverted	£375	£110
129	15	36c. blue	£150	18·00
		x. Wmk reversed	£300	75·00
130	16	48c. rose	75·00	5·50
		w. Wmk inverted	—	42·00
131	17	64c. red-brown (1877)	£275	65·00
132	18	96c. drab	£200	26·00
		w. Wmk inverted	†	£140
121/32		*Set of* 11	£1000	£110

(b) P 14 × 12½.

No.	Type	Description	Unused	Used
133	9	2c. brown	£350	65·00
134	10	4c. grey	£1400	26·00
135	11	8c. orange-yellow	£375	45·00
		w. Wmk inverted	†	£180

(c) P 12½.

No.	Type	Description	Unused	Used
136	9	2c. brown	£2500	£170
137	10	4c. grey	£1400	£250

(d) P 12½ × 14.

No.	Type	Description	Unused	Used
138	19	2r.50 dull-rose (1879)	£475	£300

(e) Prepared for use and sent out to Ceylon, but not issued unsurcharged.

No.	Type	Description	Unused	Used
139	14	32c. slate (P 14 × 12½)	£900	
140	17	64c. red-brown (P 14 × 12½)	£1100	
141	19	2r.50 dull rose (P 12½)	£1500	

FORGERIES.—Beware of forged overprint and surcharge varieties on Victorian issues.

SIXTEEN

16

CENTS

(20)

1882 (Oct). *Nos. 127 and 131 surch as T* **20** *by Govt Printer.*

No.	Type	Description	Unused	Used
142	13	16c.on 24c. green	24·00	6·50
		a. Surch inverted		
143	17	20c.on 64c. red-brown	9·50	5·00
		a. Surch double	†	£1100

1883–98. Wmk Crown CA.

(a) P 14.

No.	Type	Description	Unused	Used
146	9	2c. pale brown	55·00	1·75
147		2c. dull green (1884)	2·50	15
		s. Optd "Specimen"	£300	
		w. Wmk inverted	£130	50·00
148	10	4c. rosy mauve	3·00	30
149		4c. rose (1884)	3·75	11·00
		s. Optd "Specimen"	£300	
150	11	8c. orange	4·25	8·00
		a. Yellow (1898)	3·50	7·00
151	12	16c. pale violet	£1500	£150

(b) Trial perforation. P 12.

No.	Type	Description	Unused	Used
151*a*	9	2c. dull green	£3000	
151*b*	10	4c. rose	£3000	
151*c*	13	24c. brown-purple	£3250	

(c) Prepared for use and sent out to Ceylon, but not issued unsurcharged. P 14.

No.	Type	Description	Unused	Used
152	13	24c. brown-purple	£1100	
		s. Optd "Specimen"	£500	

Although delivered in 1884 it is believed that the 4c. rose, No. 149, was not used until the early 1890s.

See also Nos. 246, 256 and 258 for the 2c. and 4c. in different colours.

Postage &

FIVE
CENTS

Revenue

(21)

TEN
CENTS

(22)

Twenty
Cents

(23)

One Rupee
Twelve
Cents

(24)

1885 (1 Jan–Mar). *T* **10/19** *surch locally as T* **21/24**.

I. Wmk Crown CC.

(a) P 14.

No.	Type	Description	Unused	Used
153	21	5c.on 16c. pale violet	†	£2750
154		5c.on 24c. green	£2750	£100
155		5c.on 32c. slate	55·00	15·00
		a. Surch inverted	†	£1300
		b. Dark grey	£130	32·00
156		5c.on 36c. blue	£250	10·00
		a. Surch inverted	†	£1800
		x. Wmk reversed	†	75·00
157		5c.on 48c. rose	£1100	55·00
158		5c.on 64c. red-brown	95·00	6·00
		a. Surch double	†	£1000
159		5c.on 96c. drab	£450	65·00
161	22	10c.on 16c. pale violet	£5000	£2000
162		10c.on 24c. green	£425	£110
163		10c.on 36c. blue	£375	£170
164		10c.on 64c. red-brown	£400	£150
165		20c.on 24c. green	55·00	18·00
166	23	20c.on 32c. slate	60·00	55·00
		a. Dark grey	65·00	45·00
		aw. Wmk inverted	£160	
167		25c.on 32c. slate	15·00	4·50
		a. Dark grey	26·00	8·00
168		28c.on 48c. rose	38·00	6·00
		a. Surch double	†	£1200
169	22	30c.on 36c. blue	14·00	9·00
		x. Wmk reversed	11·00	8·50
		xa. Surch inverted	£200	£100
170		56c.on 96c. drab	24·00	18·00

(b) P 14 × 12½.

No.	Type	Description	Unused	Used
172	21	5c.on 32c. slate	£650	50·00
173		5c.on 64c. red-brown	£600	40·00
174	22	10c.on 64c. red-brown	60·00	95·00
		a. Imperf between (vert pair)	£3000	
175	24	1r.12 on 2r.50 dull rose (P 12½)	£475	95·00
176		1r.12 on 2r.50 dull rose (P 12½ × 14)	95·00	42·00

II. Wmk Crown CA. P 14.

No.	Type	Description	Unused	Used
178	21	5c.on 4c. rose (3.85)	20·00	3·50
		a. Surch inverted	†	£300
179		5c.on 8c. orange-yellow	70·00	7·00
		a. Surch double	†	£1500
		b. Surch inverted	†	£2000
180		5c.on 16c. pale violet	95·00	11·00
		a. Surch inverted	†	£190
182		5c.on 24c. brown-purple	—	£500
184	22	10c.on 16c. pale violet	£5000	£1100
185		10c.on 24c. brown-purple	13·00	6·00
186		15c.on 16c. pale violet	11·00	7·50

The 5c. on 4c. rosy mauve and 5c. on 24c. green, both watermarked Crown CA, previously catalogued are now considered to be forgeries.

REVENUE AND POSTAGE

5 CENTS (25) 10 CENTS (26) 1 R. 12 C. (27)

1885. *T* **11/15**, **18** *and* **19** *surch with T* **25/7** *by D.L.R.* P 14.

(a) Wmk Crown CA.

187 **25** 5c.on 8c. lilac 16·00 1·40
w. Wmk inverted † 70·00
x. Wmk reversed † £160
188 **26** 10c.on 24c. brown-purple 9·50 6·50
189 15c.on 16c. orange-yellow 55·00 9·00
190 28c.on 32c. slate 23·00 2·50
191 30c.on 36c. olive-green 28·00 14·00
192 56c.on 96c. drab 50·00 14·00

(b) Wmk Crown CC (sideways).

193 **27** 1r.12 on 2r.50 dull rose 38·00 85·00
187/93 *Set of* 7 £200 £110
187s/93s Optd "Specimen" *Set of* 7 £800

28

29

1886. Wmk Crown CA. P 14.

195 **28** 5c. dull purple 2·25 10
w. Wmk inverted — 80·00
196 **29** 15c. sage-green 5·00 1·25
w. Wmk inverted † £130
197 15c. olive-green 5·50 1·25
198 25c. yellow-brown 3·75 1·00
a. Value in yellow £100 70·00
199 28c. slate 18·00 1·40
195s, 197s/9s Optd "Specimen" *Set of* 4 £250

Six plates were used for the 5c., No. 195, between 1885 and 1901, each being replaced by its successor as it became worn. Examples from the worn plates show thicker lines in the background and masses of solid colour under the chin, in front of the throat, at the back of the neck and at the base.

30

1887. Wmk Crown CC (sideways). *White or blued paper.* P 14.

201 **30** 1r.12 dull rose 22·00 20·00
a. Wmk upright 42·00 60·00
aw. Wmk inverted † £160
s. Optd "Specimen" £110

TWO CENTS (31) Two (32) 2 Cents (33)

Two Cents (34) 2 Cents (35)

1888–90. *Nos. 148/9 surch with T* **31/5**.

202 **31** 2c.on 4c. rosy mauve 1·40 80
a. Surch inverted 20·00 19·00
b. Surch double, one inverted — £200
203 2c.on 4c. rose 2·25 30
a. Surch inverted 13·00 14·00
b. Surch double — £225
204 **32** 2(c).on 4c. rosy mauve 75 30
a. Surch inverted 28·00 30·00
b. Surch double 65·00 65·00
c. Surch double, one inverted 60·00 55·00
205 2(c).on 4c. rose 5·00 20
a. Surch inverted £225
b. Surch double 70·00 75·00
c. Surch double, one inverted 75·00 80·00
206 **33** 2c.on 4c. rosy mauve 65·00 28·00
a. Surch inverted £100 38·00
b. Surch double, one inverted £130
207 2c.on 4c. rose 2·25 75
a. Surch inverted 12·00 8·50
b. Surch double £130 £110
c. Surch double, one inverted 8·00 10·00
w. Wmk inverted £100
208 **34** 2c.on 4c. rosy mauve 45·00 19·00
a. Surch inverted £130 30·00
209 2c.on 4c. rose 2·50 1·10
a. Surch inverted 12·00 5·50
b. Surch double 95·00 95·00
c. Surch double, one inverted 12·00 6·00
210 **35** 2c.on 4c. rosy mauve 45·00 27·00
a. Surch inverted 70·00 40·00
b. Surch double, one inverted 85·00 85·00
c. Surch double — £225
d. "s" of "Cents" inverted (R. 3/5) — £400
e. As d. Whole surch inverted
211 2c.on 4c. rose 10·00 1·00
a. Surch inverted 17·00 5·50
b. Surch double 85·00 85·00
c. Surch double, one inverted 19·00 8·50
d. "s" of "Cents" inverted (R. 3/5) — £180
x. Wmk reversed † 95·00
209s, 211s Optd "Specimen" *Set of* 2 60·00

The 4c. rose and the 4c. rosy mauve are found surcharged "Postal Commission 3 (or "Three") Cents". They denote the extra commission charged by the Post Office on postal orders which had not been cashed within three months of the date of issue. For a short time the Post Office did not object to the use of these stamps on letters.

POSTAGE Five Cents REVENUE (36) FIFTEEN CENTS (37)

1890. *No. 197 surch with T* **36**.

233 5c.on 15c. olive-green 2·50 2·00
a. Surch inverted 45·00 48·00
b. Surch double £100 £120
c. "Flve" for "Five" (R. 1/1) £100 80·00
d. Variety as c, inverted — £1000
e. "REVENUE" omitted £160 £140
f. Inverted "s" in "Cents" 60·00 70·00
g. Variety as f, and whole surch inverted £1100
h. "REVENUE" omitted and inverted "s" in "Cents" £900
i. "POSTAGE" spaced between "T" and "A" (R. 1/5) 65·00 70·00
j. Variety as i, and whole surch inverted — £850
s. Optd "Specimen" 30·00

1891. *Nos. 198/9 surch with T* **37**.

239 **29** 15c.on 25c. yellow-brown 11·00 12·00
240 15c.on 28c. slate 14·00 8·50

3 Cents (38)

39

1892. *Nos. 148/9 and 199 surch with T* **38**.

241 **10** 3c.on 4c. rosy mauve 1·00 3·25
242 3c.on 4c. rose 3·75 7·00
s. Optd "Specimen" 35·00
w. Wmk inverted £100
ws. Optd "Specimen" 75·00
243 **29** 3c.on 28c. slate 4·00 3·50
a. Surch double £120
241/3 *Set of* 3 8·00 12·00

1893–99. Wmk Crown CA. P 14.

245 **39** 3c. terracotta and blue-green 3·25 45
246 **10** 4c. carmine-rose (1898) 7·50 8·00
247 **29** 30c. bright mauve and chestnut 4·25 2·00
a. Bright violet and chestnut 5·00 2·50
249 **19** 2r.50 purple/red (1899) 28·00 48·00
245/9 *Set of* 4 38·00 55·00
245s, 247s/9s Optd "Specimen" *Set of* 3 60·00

Six Cents (40) 2 R. 25 C. (41)

1898 (Dec)–**99**.

(a) No. 196 surch with T **40**.

250 **29** 6c.on 15c. sage-green 70 75

(b) As No. 138, but colour changed and perf 14, surch as T **41** *(1899).*

254 **19** 1r.50 on 2r.50 slate 20·00 45·00
w. Wmk inverted £120 £170
255 2r.25 on 2r.50 yellow 35·00 80·00
250s/5s Optd "Specimen" *Set of* 3 70·00

43

1899–1900. Wmk Crown CA (1r.50, 2r.25 wmk Crown CC). P 14.

256 **9** 2c. pale orange-brown 2·50 30
257 **39** 3c. deep green 2·50 55
258 **10** 4c. yellow 3·00 2·75
259 **29** 6c. rose and black 1·50 45
260 **39** 12c. sage-green and rose (1900) 4·00 7·00
261 **29** 15c. blue 5·50 1·25
262 **39** 75c. black and red-brown 4·75 6·00
263 **43** 1r.50 rose 19·00 35·00
264 2r.25 dull blue 30·00 35·00
256/64 *Set of* 9 65·00 80·00
256s/64s Optd "Specimen" *Set of* 9 £180

44

45

46

47

48

1903 (29 May)–**05**. Wmk Crown CA. P 14.

265 **44** 2c. red-brown (21.7.03) 2·00 2
266 **45** 3c. green (11.6.03) 2·00 1·0
267 4c. orange-yellow and blue 2·00 3·5
268 **46** 5c. dull purple (2.7.03) 1·50 6
269 **47** 6c. carmine (5.11.03) 9·50 1·5
w. Wmk inverted 65·00
270 **45** 12c. sage-green and rosine (13.8.03) 5·00 9·5
271 **48** 15c. blue (2.7.03) 6·50 3·0
272 25c. bistre (11.8.03) 4·00 8·0
273 30c. dull violet and green 3·25 4·0
274 **45** 75c. dull blue and orange (31.3.05) 3·00 18·0
275 **48** 1r.50 greyish slate (7.4.04) 65·00 55·0
276 2r.25 brown and green (12.4.04) 65·00 50·0
265/76 *Set of* 12 £150 £14
265s/76s Optd "Specimen" *Set of* 12 £150

1904 (13 Sept)–**05**. Wmk Mult Crown CA. *Ordinary paper.* P 14.

277 **44** 2c. red-brown (17.11.04) 1·50 1
278 **45** 3c. green (17.11.04) 1·50 1
279 4c. orange and ultramarine 2·00 1·5
280 **46** 5c. dull purple (29.11.04) 2·25 1·2
a. Chalk-surfaced paper (5.10.05) 4·00 7
281 **47** 6c. carmine (11.10.04) 1·50 1
282 **45** 12c. sage-green and rosine (29.9.04) 1·50 1·7
283 **48** 15c. blue (1.12.04) 2·00 6
284 25c. bistre (5.1.05) 6·00 3·7
285 30c. violet and green (7.9.05) 2·50 3·0
286 **45** 75c. dull blue and orange (25.5.05) 5·25 8·0
287 **48** 1r.50 grey (5.1.05) 25·00 10·0
288 2r.25 brown and green (22.12.04) 22·00 29·0
277/88 *Set of* 12 65·00 50·0

50

51

1908. Wmk Mult Crown CA. P 14.

289 **50** 5c. deep purple (26 May) 2·50 1
290 5c. dull purple 3·75
291 **51** 6c. carmine (6 June) 1·25 1
289s, 291s Optd "Specimen" *Set of* 2 65·00

1910 (1 Aug)–**11**. Wmk Mult Crown CA. P 14.

292 **44** 2c. brown-orange (20.5.11) 1·50
293 **48** 3c. green (5.7.11) 1·00
294 10c. sage-green and maroon 2·50 2·
295 25c. grey 2·50 1·
296 50c. chocolate 4·00 7·
297 1r. purple/*yellow* 7·50 10·
298 2r. red/*yellow* 15·00 27·
299 5r. black/*green* 38·00 65·
300 10r. black/*red* 85·00 £1
292/300 *Set of* 9 £140 £2
292s/300s Optd "Specimen" *Set of* 9 £190

Examples of Nos. 298/300 are known showing a forged Colomb registered postmark dated '27.1.10'.

52

53

(A)

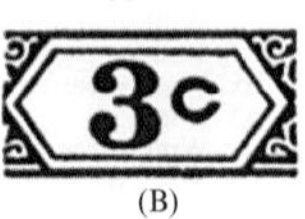
(B)

Most values in Type **52** were produced by two printi operations, using "Key" and "Duty" plates. Differences in the tv Dies of the Key plate are described in the introduction to tl catalogue.

In the Ceylon series, however, the 1c. and 5c. values, togetl with later printings of the 3c. and 6c., were printed from spec plates at one operation. These plates can be identified by the lar "C" in the value tablet (see illustration A). Examples of these valu from Key and Duty plates printing have value tablet illustration B. The 3c. and 5c. stamps from the single plates *resem* Die I, and the 1c. and 6c. Die II, although in the latter case t inner top corners of the side panels are square and not curved.

1912–25. Wmk Mult Crown CA. *Chalk-surfaced paper (30c. 100r.).* P 14.

(a) Printed from single plates. Value tablet as A.

301 **52** 1c. brown (1919) 1·00
w. Wmk inverted 20·00

302 3c. blue-green (1919) 2·50 45
w. Wmk inverted 20·00 30·00
y. Wmk inverted and reversed 24·00 40·00
303 5c. purple 7·00 2·75
a. Wmk sideways (Crown to right of CA) £400
x. Wmk reversed † £110
y. Wmk inverted and reversed 80·00
304 5c. bright magenta 1·00 60
w. Wmk inverted — 80·00
305 6c. pale scarlet (1919) 8·50 85
a. Wmk sideways (Crown to left of CA) 38·00 75·00
w. Wmk inverted 27·00 40·00
306 6c. carmine 15·00 1·25
a. Wmk sideways (Crown to right of CA) 48·00
y. Wmk inverted and reversed 28·00

(b) Printed from Key and Duty plates. Die I. 3c. and 6c. have value tablet as B.

307 52 2c. brown-orange 40 30
a. Deep orange-brown 30 20
308 3c. yellow-green 6·50 2·25
a. Deep green (1917) 4·50 1·10
309 6c. scarlet (*shades*) 1·10 50
a. Wmk sideways † —
310 10c. sage-green 3·00 1·75
a. Deep sage-green (1917) 5·00 2·50
w. Wmk inverted £100
311 15c. deep bright blue 2·50 1·25
a. Ultramarine (1918) 1·75 1·25
aw. Wmk inverted 24·00
312 25c. orange and blue 6·50 4·50
a. Yellow and blue (1917) 1·75 1·75
aw. Wmk inverted £100 £100
313 30c. blue-green and violet 4·00 3·25
a. Yellow-green and violet (1915) 7·00 4·00
ab. Wmk sideways (Crown to right of CA) 26·00
abw. Wmk Crown to left of CA 28·00
aw. Wmk inverted 42·00
314 50c. black and scarlet 1·25 1·75
w. Wmk inverted 18·00
315 1r. purple/*yellow* 3·25 3·50
a. White back (1913) 3·00 4·75
as. Optd "Specimen" 50·00
b. On lemon (1915) 4·25 8·00
bs. Optd "Specimen" 45·00
c. On orange-buff (1918) 26·00 35·00
cw. Wmk inverted 65·00
d. On pale yellow (1922) 4·50 10·00
ds. Optd "Specimen" 42·00
316 2r. black and red/*yellow* 3·25 11·00
a. White back (1913) 2·75 12·00
as. Optd "Specimen" 50·00
b. On lemon (1915) 23·00 27·00
bs. Optd "Specimen" 40·00
c. On orange-buff (1919) 40·00 42·00
cw. Wmk inverted 60·00
d. On pale yellow (1921) 40·00 40·00
17 5r. black/*green* 17·00 28·00
a. White back (1914) 19·00 32·00
as. Optd "Specimen" 48·00
b. On blue-grn (olive back) (1917) 16·00 35·00
bs. Optd "Specimen" 55·00
bw. Wmk inverted 65·00 80·00
c. Die II. *On emerald back* (1923) 45·00 95·00
cs. Optd "Specimen" 60·00
18 10r. purple and black/*red* 60·00 80·00
aw. Wmk inverted £150
b. Die II (1923) 75·00 £130
bw. Wmk inverted £300
19 20r. black and red/*blue* £120 £130
20 53 50r. dull purple £350
a. Break in scroll £700
b. Broken crown and scroll £700
f. Damaged leaf at bottom right £700
s. Optd "Specimen" £140
21 100r. grey-black £1400
a. Break in scroll £2500
b. Broken crown and scroll £2500
f. Damaged leaf at bottom right £2500
s. Optd "Specimen" £275
w. Wmk inverted £3000
22 500r. dull green £4500
a. Break in scroll £7500
b. Broken crown and scroll £7500
f. Damaged leaf at bottom right
s. Optd "Specimen" £450
23 1000r. purple/*red* (1925) £16000
b. Broken crown and scroll £21000
e. Break in lines below left scroll
f. Damaged leaf at bottom right
s. Optd "Specimen" £850
)1/18 *Set of* 14 90·00 £120
)1s/19s Optd "Specimen" *Set of* 15 £375

For illustrations of the varieties on Nos. 320/3 see above No. 51*b* of Bermuda.

The 2c. and 5c. exist in coils, constructed from normal sheets, used in stamp-affixing machines introduced in 1915.

Sideways watermark varieties are described as seen *from the back of the stamp.*

The "substituted crown" watermark variety is known on the sheet margin of the 1c., No. 301.

WAR STAMP
(54)

WAR STAMP ONE CENT
(55)

1918 (18 Nov)–**19**.

(a) Optd with T **54** *by Govt Printer, Colombo.*

330 52 2c. brown-orange 20 40
a. Opt inverted 35·00 40·00
b. Opt double 26·00 30·00
c. Opt omitted in pair with opt inverted £375
331 3c. blue-green (No. 302) (1919) 1·75 40
332 3c. deep green (No. 308*a*) 20 50
a. Opt double 60·00 65·00
333 5c. purple 50 30
a. Opt double 32·00 38·00
w. Wmk inverted 80·00
334 5c. bright magenta 2·25 2·25
a. Opt inverted 35·00 40·00
b. Opt double 26·00 35·00

(b) Surch with T **55**.

335 52 1c.on 5c. purple 50 40
y. Wmk inverted and reversed 80·00
336 1c.on 5c. bright magenta 1·25 20
330s, 332s/3s, 335s Optd "Specimen" *Set of* 4 £100

Collectors are warned against forgeries of the errors in the "WAR STAMP" overprints.

1918. *Surch as T* **55**, *but without "*WAR STAMP*"*.

337 52 1c.on 5c. purple 15 25
a. Surch double £140
bs. Optd "Specimen" 35·00
337*c* 1c.on 5c. bright magenta 2·00 2·75

1921–32. Wmk Mult Script CA. *Chalk-surfaced paper (30c. to 100r.)* P 14.

(a) Printed from single plates. Value tablet as A.

338 52 1c. brown (1927) 75 35
339 3c. green (5.5.22) 2·75 75
w. Wmk inverted 19·00 30·00
340 3c. slate-grey (1923) 75 20
a. Wmk sideways £1000
w. Wmk inverted 23·00
341 5c. purple (1927) 50 15
342 6c. carmine-red (3.8.21) 2·00 75
w. Wmk inverted 20·00 30·00
y. Wmk inverted and reversed 35·00
343 6c. bright violet (1922) 1·00 15
w. Wmk inverted 23·00
y. Wmk inverted and reversed 35·00

(b) Printed from Key and Duty plates.

344 52 2c. brown-orange (Die II) (1927) 60 25
345 9c. red/*pale yellow* (Die II) (1926) 80 30
346 10c. sage-green (Die I) (16.9.21) 1·40 40
aw. Wmk inverted 28·00
ay. Wmk inverted and reversed 22·00 35·00
b. Die II (1924) 1·75 60
c. Vert gutter pair. Die I and Die II. Nos. 346 and 346b £250
347 12c. rose-scarlet (Die I) (1925) 4·50 5·50
a. Die II 1·00 2·25
as. Optd "Specimen" 80·00
b. Vert gutter pair. Die I and Die II. Nos. 347/a £120
348 15c. ultramarine (Die I) (30.5.22) 3·25 9·50
349 15c. green/*pale yellow* (Die I) (1923) 1·50 1·25
a. Die II (1924) 1·50 1·00
aw. Wmk inverted 23·00
b. Vert gutter pair. Die I and Die II. Nos. 349/a £225
350 20c. bright blue (Die I) (1922) 3·50 6·00
aw. Wmk inverted 45·00
b. Die II (1924) 3·50 45
c. Vert gutter pair. Die I and Die II. Nos. 350 and 350b £225
351 25c. yellow and blue (Die I) (17.10.21) 1·60 1·90
aw. Wmk inverted 60·00
b. Die II (1924) 3·00 1·25
c. Vert gutter pair. Die I and Die II. Nos. 351/b £150
352 30c. yellow-green & vio (Die I) (15.3.22) 1·60 2·75
a. Die II (1924) 3·00 1·25
b. Vert gutter pair. Die I and Die II. Nos. 352/a £425
353 50c. black and scarlet (Die II) (1922) 1·60 80
a. Die I (1932) 55·00 75·00
354 1r. purple/*pale yellow* (Die I) (1923) 15·00 26·00
a. Die II (1925) 16·00 24·00
b. Vert gutter pair. Die I and Die II. Nos. 354/a £325
355 2r. black & red/*pale yell* (Die II) (1923) 7·00 7·50
356 5r. black/*emerald* (Die II) (1924) 28·00 50·00
357 20r. black and red/*blue* (Die II) (1924) £140 £180
358 53 50r. dull purple (1924) £400 £700
a. Break in scroll £700
b. Broken crown and scroll £700
e. Break in lines below left scroll £700
f. Damaged leaf at bottom right £700
g. Gash in fruit and leaf £700
s. Optd "Specimen" £150
359 100r. grey-black (1924) £1500
a. Break in scroll £2500
b. Broken crown and scroll £2500
e. Break in lines below left scroll £2500
f. Damaged leaf at bottom right £2500
s. Optd "Specimen" £325
360 100r. dull purple and blue (24.10.27) £1300
a. Break in scroll £2000
b. Broken crown and scroll £2000
e. Break in lines below left scroll £2000
f. Damaged leaf at bottom right £2000
g. Gash in fruit and leaf £2000
s. Optd "Specimen" £325
338/56 *Set of* 19 60·00 85·00
338s/57s Optd "Specimen" *Set of* 20 £475

The 2c. to 30c. and 1r. values produced from Key and Duty plates were printed in sheets of 240 using two plates one above the other. Nos. 346c, 347b, 349b, 350c, 351b, 353b and 354b come from printings in 1924 and 1925 which combined Key Plate 7 (Die I) with Key Plate 12 (Die II).

No. 353a, from Key Plate 23, was a mistake; the "retired" Die I being issued in error when it became necessary to replace Key Plate 21.

For illustrations of the varieties on Nos. 358/60 see above No. 51*b* of Bermuda.

2 Cents.
(56)

57

(Surch at Ceylon Govt Printing Works)

1926 (27 Nov). *Surch as T* **56**.

361 52 2c.on 3c. slate-grey 80 1·00
a. Surch double 70·00
b. Bar omitted 75·00 85·00
362 5c.on 6c. bright violet 50 40
361s/2s Optd "Specimen" *Set of* 2 55·00

No. 361b comes from the bottom horizontal row of the sheet which was often partially obscured by the selvedge during surcharging.

1927 (27 Nov)–**29**. Wmk Mult Script CA. *Chalk-surfaced paper.* P 14.

363 57 1r. dull and bright purple (1928) 2·50 1·25
364 2r. green and carmine (1929) 3·75 2·75
365 5r. green and dull purple (1928) 14·00 20·00
366 10r. green and brown-orange 35·00 80·00
367 20r. dull purple and blue £100 £180
363/7 *Set of* 5 £140 £250
363s/7s Optd "Specimen" *Set of* 5 £150

No. 364. Collectors are warned against faked 2r. stamps, showing what purports to be a double centre.

58 Tapping Rubber

60 Adam's Peak

(Recess D.L.R. (2, 3, 20, 50c.), B.W. (others))

1935 (1 May)–**36**. *T* **58**, **60** *and similar designs.* Wmk Mult Script CA (sideways on 10, 15, 25, 30c. and 1r.). Various perfs.

368 2c. black and carmine (P 12 × 13) 30 40
a. Perf 14 9·00 40
369 3c. blk & ol-green (P 13 × 12) (1.10.35) 35 40
a. Perf 14 27·00 35
370 6c. black & blue (P 11 × 11½) (1.1.36) 30 30
371 9c. green & orange (P 11 × 11½) (1.1.36) 1·00 65
372 10c. black & purple (P 11½ × 11) (1.6.35) 1·25 2·25
373 15c. red-brown and green (P 11½ × 11) 1·00 50
374 20c. black & grey-blue (P 12 × 13) (1.1.36) 1·75 2·50
375 25c. deep blue & chocolate (P 11½ × 11) 1·40 1·25
376 30c. carm & green (P 11½ × 11) (1.8.35) 2·25 2·75
377 50c. black and mauve (P 14) (1.1.36) 8·50 1·75
378 1r. vio-bl & chocolate (P 11½ × 11) (1.7.35) 18·00 16·00
368/78 *Set of* 11 32·00 26·00
368s/78s Perf "Specimen" *Set of* 11 £160

Designs: *Vert*—6c. Colombo Harbour; 9c. Pluking tea; 20c. Coconut Palms. *Horiz*—10c. Hill paddy (rice); 15c. River scene; 25c. Temple of the Tooth, Kandy; 30c. Ancient irrgation tank; 50c. Wild elephants; 1r. Trincomalee.

1935 (6 May). *Silver Jubilee. As Nos.* 91/4 *of Antigua.* P 13½ × 14.

379 6c. ultramarine and grey 65 30
f. Diagonal line by turret 60·00 30·00
g. Dot to left of chapel 85·00 45·00
h. Dot by flagstaff 85·00 45·00
i. Dash by turret 90·00 50·00
380 9c. green and indigo 70 1·25
f. Diagonal line by turret 80·00
g. Dot to left of chapel £100
h. Dot by flagstaff £110
381 20c. brown and deep blue 4·25 2·75
f. Diagonal line by turret £180
g. Dot to left of chapel £275 £170
382 50c. slate and purple 5·25 9·00
f. Diagonal line by turret £275 £325
h. Dot by flagstaff £325 £350
379/82 *Set of* 4 9·75 12·00
379s/82s Perf "Specimen" *Set of* 4 £100

For illustrations of plate varieties, see Omnibus section following Zanzibar.

1937 (12 May). *Coronation. As Nos. 95/7 of Antigua.* P 11 × 11½.

No.		Description	Unused	Used
383		6c. carmine	65	15
384		9c. green	2·50	3·50
385		20c. blue	3·50	3·00
383/5		*Set of* 3	6·00	6·00
383s/5s		Perf "Specimen" *Set of* 3	80·00	

69 Tapping Rubber

70 Sigiriya (Lion Rock)

71 Ancient Guard-stone, Anuradhapura

72 King George VI

Apostrophe flaw (Frame Pl IA R. 6/6) (ptg of 1 Jan 1943 only)

(Recess B.W. (6, 10, 15, 20, 25, 30c., 1r., 2r. (both)), D.L.R (others) T **72** typo D.L.R.)

1938–49. *T* **69/72** *and designs as 1935–36, but with portrait of King George VI instead of King George V,* "POSTAGE & REVENUE" *omitted and some redrawn.* Wmk Mult Script CA (sideways on 10, 15, 25, 30c. and 1r.). *Chalk-surfaced paper (5r.).* P 11 × 11½ (6, 20c., 2r. (both)), 11½ × 11 (10, 15, 25, 30c., 1r.), 11½ × 13 (2c.), 13 × 11½ (3, 50c.), 13½ (5c.) or 14 (5r.).

No.	Type	Description	Unused	Used
386	**69**	2c. black and carmine (25.4.38)	13·00	1·75
		a. Perf 13½ × 13 (1938)	£120	1·75
		b. Perf 13½ (25.4.38)	2·00	10
		c. Perf 11 × 11½ (17.2.44)	65	85
		cw. Wmk inverted	—	£600
		d. Perf 12 (22.4.49)	2·00	3·50
387	**60**	3c. black and deep blue-green (21.3.38)	10·00	80
		a. Perf 13 × 13½ (1938)	£250	9·00
		b. Perf 13½ (21.3.38)	4·00	10
		c. Perf 14 (line) (7.41)	£120	1·00
		d. Perf 11½ × 11 (14.5.42)	80	10
		da. "A" of "CA" missing from wmk	£850	£850
		dw. Wmk inverted	†	—
		e. Perf 12 (14.1.46)	65	85
387*f*	–	5c. sage-green & orange (1.1.43)	30	10
		fa. Apostrophe flaw	60·00	35·00
		g. Perf 12 (1947)	1·75	30
388	–	6c. black and blue (1.1.38)	30	10
389	**70**	10c. black and light blue (1.2.38)	2·25	10
		a. Wmk upright (1.6.44)	2·50	50
390	–	15c. green and red-brown (1.1.38)	2·00	10
		a. Wmk upright (23.7.45)	2·75	60
391	–	20c. black and grey-blue (15.1.38)	3·25	10
392	–	25c. deep blue and chocolate (15.1.38)	5·00	30
		a. Wmk upright (1944)	4·25	10
393	–	30c. carmine and green (1.2.38)	11·00	2·00
		a. Wmk upright (16.4.45)	12·00	3·25
394	–	50c. black and mauve (25.4.38)	£160	42·00
		a. Perf 13 × 13½ (25.4.38)	£350	2·75
		b. Perf 13½ (25.4.38)	19·00	30
		c. Perf 14 (line) (4.42)	£100	27·00
		d. Perf 11½ × 11 (14.5.42)	4·25	3·50
		e. Perf 12 (14.1.46)	4·00	20
395	–	1r. blue-violet and chocolate (1.2.38)	16·00	1·25
		a. Wmk upright (1944)	18·00	2·25
396	**71**	2r. black and carmine (1.2.38)	13·00	2·50
		a. "A" of "CA" missing from wmk		
396*b*		2r. black and violet (15.3.47)	2·00	1·60
397	**72**	5r. green and purple (1.7.38)	38·00	4·50
		a. Ordinary paper. *Green and pale purple* (19.2.43)	14·00	3·50
386/97a		(*cheapest*) *Set of* 14	65·00	10·00
386s/97s		Perf "Specimen" *Set of* 14	£325	

Designs: *Vert*—5c. Coconut palms; 6c. Colombo Harbour; 20c. Plucking tea. *Horiz*—15c. River scene; 25c. Temple of the Tooth, Kandy; 30c. Ancient irrigation tank; 50c. Wild elephants; 1r. Trincomalee.

Printings of the 2c., 3c. and 50c. perforated 11 × 11½ or 11½ × 11 were produced by Bradbury, Wilkinson after the De La Rue works had been bombed in December 1940.

3 CENTS
(73)

3 CENTS
(74)

1940–41. *Nos. 388 and 391 surch by Govt Ptg Office, Colombo.*

No.	Type	Description	Unused	Used
398	**73**	3c.on 6c. black and blue (10.5.41)	25	10
399	**74**	3c.on 20c. black and grey-blue (5.11.40)	2·50	1·50

1946 (10 Dec). *Victory. As Nos. 110/11 of Antigua.*

No.		Description	Unused	Used
400		6c. blue	10	20
401		15c. brown	10	80
400s/1s		Perf "Specimen" *Set of* 2	60·00	

75 Parliament Building

76 Adam's Peak

(Des R. Tenison and M. S. V. Rodrigo. Recess B.W.)

1947 (25 Nov). *Inauguration of New Constitution. T* **75/6** *and similar designs.* Wmk Mult Script CA. P 11 × 12 (horiz) or 12 × 11 (vert).

No.		Description	Unused	Used
402		6c. black and blue	10	15
403		10c. black, orange and carmine	15	20
404		15c. green and purple	15	80
405		25c. ochre and emerald-green	15	50
402/5		*Set of* 4	50	1·50
402s/5s		Perf "Specimen" *Set of* 4	85·00	

Designs: *Horiz*—15c. Temple of the Tooth. *Vert*—25c. Anuradhapura.

DOMINION

79 Lion Flag of Dominion

80 D. S. Senanayake

81 Lotus Flowers and Sinhalese Letters "Sri"

(Recess (flag typo) B.W.)

1949 (4 Feb–5 Apr). *First Anniv of Independence.*

(*a*) Wmk Mult Script CA (sideways on 4c.). P 12½ × 12 (4c.) or 12 × 12½ (5c.).

No.	Type	Description	Unused	Used
406	**79**	4c. yellow, carmine and brown	15	20
407	**80**	5c. brown and green	10	10

(*b*) W **81** (sideways on 15c.). P 13 × 12½ (15c.) or 12 × 12½ (25c.) (5 April).

No.	Type	Description	Unused	Used
408	**79**	15c. yellow, carmine and vermilion	30	15
409	**80**	25c. brown and blue	15	65
406/9		*Set of* 4	50	1·00

The 15c. is larger, measuring 28 × 12 mm.

82 Globe and Forms of Transport

83

84

(Recess U.L.R.)

1949 (10 Oct). *75th Anniv of Universal Postal Union.* W **81**. P (25c.) or 12 (others).

No.	Type	Description	Unused	Used
410	**82**	5c. brown and bluish green	75	
411	**83**	15c. black and carmine	1·10	2·
412	**84**	25c. black and ultramarine	1·10	1·
410/12		*Set of* 3	2·75	3·(

85 Kandyan Dancer

88 Sigiriya (Lion Rock)

89 Octagon Library, Temple of the Tooth

90 Ruins at Madirigiriya

(Recess B.W.)

1950 (4 Feb). *T* **85**, **88/90** *and similar designs.* W **81**. P 11 × 1 (75c.), 11½ × 11 (1r.), 12 × 12½ (others).

No.		Description	Unused	Used
413		4c. purple and scarlet	10	
414		5c. green	10	
415		15c. blue-green and violet	1·50	
416		30c. carmine and yellow	30	
417		75c. ultramarine and orange	4·75	
418		1r. deep blue and brown	1·75	
413/18		*Set of* 6	7·50	1·

Designs: *Vert* (*as T* **88**)—5c. Kiri Vehera, Polonnaruwa; 15 Vesak Orchid.

For these values with redrawn inscriptions see Nos. 450/1, 45 456, 460 and 462.

91 Sambars, Ruhuna National Park

92 Ancient Guard-stone, Anuradhapura

96 Star Orchid

97 Rubber Plantation

99 Tea Plantation

I. No. 424 II. No. 424a (Dot added)

(Photo Courvoisier)

1951 (1 Aug)–**54**. *T* **91/2**, **96/7**, **99** *and similar designs.* No wm P 11½.

No.		Description	Unused	Used
419		2c. brown and blue-green (15.5.54)	10	1·
420		3c. black and slate-violet (15.5.54)	10	1·
421		6c. brown-black & yellow-green (15.5.54)	10	
422		10c. green and blue-grey	1·00	
423		25c. orange-brown & bright blue (15.3.54)	10	
424		35c. red and deep green (I) (1.2.52)	1·50	1·
		a. Type II (1954)	6·00	
425		40c. deep brown (15.5.54)	5·00	1·
426		50c. indigo and slate-grey (15.3.54)	30	
427		85c. black and deep blue-green (15.5.54)	50	
428		2r. blue and deep brown (15.5.54)	6·50	1·
429		5r. brown and orange (15.3.54)	4·75	1·
430		10r. red-brown and buff (15.3.54)	38·00	11·
419/30		*Set of* 12	50·00	17·

Designs: *Vert* (*as T* **91**)—6c. Harvesting rice; 10c. Coconut tre 25c. Sigiriya fresco. (*As T* **99**)—5r. Bas-relief, Anuradhapura; 1 Harvesting rice. *Horiz* (*as T* **97**)—50c. Outrigger canoe; (*as T* **99**) 2r. River Gal Dam.

Nos. 413/30 (except 422) were reissued in 1958–62, redrawn w 'CEYLON' much smaller and other inscriptions in Sinhalese.

STAMPS BOOKLETS

1905 (Oct). *Black on grey (No. SB1) or black on buff (No. SB1a) covers. Stapled.*
SB1 1r.21, booklet containing twenty-four 5c. (No. 280) in blocks of 12
SB1*a* 1r.45, booklet containing twenty-four 6c. (No. 281) in blocks of 6 . . . £4000

1908. *Black on grey cover. Advertisement on back cover. Stapled.*
SB2 1r.20, booklet containing twenty-four 5c. (No. 289) in blocks of 12

1912. *Black on grey cover. Advertisement on back cover, Stapled.*
SB2*a* 1r.20, booklet containing twenty-four 5c. (No. 304) in blocks of 12

1919. *Black on orange covers. Telegraph details on back cover. Stapled.*
SB3 1r.44, booklet containing twenty-four 6c. (No. 311) in blocks of 6
a. Black on grey cover. Advertisement on back cover
SB4 1r.44, booklet containing twenty-four 3c. and twelve 6c. (Nos. 310/11) in blocks of 6
a. Advertisement on back cover

1922. *Black on green covers. "Fiat" advertisement on back cover. Stapled.*
SB5 1r.44, booklet containing twenty-four 6c. (No. 356) in blocks of 6
SB6 1r.46, booklet containing twenty-four 3c. and twelve 6c. (Nos. 355/6) in blocks of 6
a. Black on orange cover. "Colombo Jewelry Store" advertisement on back cover

1926. *Black on green covers. Kennedy & Co. (No. SB7) or Fiat (No. SB8) advertisements on back cover. Stapled.*
SB7 2r.06, booklet containing twelve 3c., 5c. on 6c. and 9c. (Nos. 355, 362 and 357) in blocks of 6 . . . £2750
SB8 2r.16, booklet containing twenty-four 9c. (No. 357) in blocks of 6

1932. *Black on green covers. Stapled.*
SB 9 1r.80, booklet containing thirty 6c. (No. 356) in blocks of 6 and pane of three airmail labels . . . £1100
SB10 2r.70, booklet containing thirty 9c. (No. 357) in blocks of 6 and pane of three airmail labels

1935 (May). *Silver Jubilee of King George V. Black on light blue (No. SB11) or light green (No. SB12) covers. Stapled.*
SB11 1r.80, booklet containing thirty 6c. (No. 379) in blocks of 6 . . . £1200
SB12 2r.70, booklet containing thirty 9c. (No. 380) in blocks of 6 . . . £1500

1935 (Dec)–**36**. *Black on blue (No. SB13) or green (No. SB14) covers. Stapled.*
SB13 1r.80, booklet containing thirty 6c. (No. 370) in blocks of 6 and pane of four airmail labels . . £750
a. Stamps in blocks of 10 . . . £750
SB14 2r.70, booklet containing thirty 9c. (No. 371) in blocks of 6 and pane of four airmail labels . . £850
a. Stamps in blocks of 10 (1936) . . . £850

1937 (Apr–June). *Coronation of King George VI. Black on blue (No. SB15) or olive-green (No. SB16) covers. Stapled.*
SB15 1r.80, booklet containing thirty 6c. (No. 383) in blocks of 10 and pane of four airmail labels (June) . . . £900
SB16 2r.70, booklet containing thirty 9c. (No. 384) in blocks of 10 and pane of four airmail labels . . . £950

1938. *Black on blue (No. SB17) or grey (No. SB18) covers. Stapled.*
SB17 1r.80, booklet containing thirty 6c. (No. 388) in blocks of 10 and pane of four airmail labels . . . £1100
SB18 3r. booklet containing fifteen 20c. (No. 391) in blocks of 5 or 10 and pane of four airmail labels . . . £1100

1941. *Black on pink cover, with contents amended in manuscript. Stapled.*
SB19 1r.80, booklet containing sixty 3c. on 6c. (No. 398) in blocks of 10
a. Black on blue cover

1951 (5 Dec). *Black on buff cover. Stitched.*
SB20 1r. booklet containing twenty 5c. (No. 414) in blocks of four and pane of airmail labels . . . 12·00
a. Containing two blocks of ten 5c. stamps and no airmail labels . . . 45·00

1952 (21 Jan). *Black on green cover. Stitched.*
SB21 6r. booklet containing eight 75c. (No. 417) in blocks of 4 and two panes of four airmail labels . . . 18·00

OFFICIAL STAMPS

1869. Issues of 1867–68 overprinted "SERVICE" in block letters. Although these stamps were prepared for use and sent out to the colony, they were never issued.

Prices:
/601«s12)

Until 1 October 1895 all Official mail was carried free. After that date postage was paid on Official letters to the general public, on certain interdepartmental mail and on all packets over 1lb in weight. Nos. O1/17 were provided for this purpose.

On Service
(O 3)

1895. *Optd with Type* **O 3** *by the Govt Printer, Colombo.*

O1	**9**	2c. green (No. 147)	8·50	45
		w. Wmk inverted	†	—
O2	**39**	3c. terracotta and blue-green (No. 245)	10·00	80
O3	**28**	5c. dull purple (No. 195)	3·50	30
O4	**29**	15c. sage-green (No. 196)	12·00	50
O5		25c. yellow-brown (No. 198)	10·00	1·75
O6		30c. bright mauve and chestnut (No. 247)	13·00	60
O7	**30**	1r.12 dull rose (*wmk sideways*) (No. 201)	75·00	55·00
		a. Opt double, one albino	£250	
		b. Wmk upright	90·00	70·00
O1/7 *Set of* 7			£110	55·00

1899 (June)–**1900**. *Nos. 256/7 and 261/2 optd with Type* **O 3**.

O 8	**9**	2c. pale orange-brown (3.00)	7·00	60
O 9	**39**	3c. deep green (9.00)	8·00	2·25
O10	**29**	15c. blue (9.00)	16·00	60
O11	**39**	75c. black and red-brown (R.)	5·50	6·50
O8/11 *Set of* 4			32·00	8·75

1903 (26 Nov)–**04**. *Nos. 265/6, 268 and 271/3 optd with Type* **O 3**.

O12	**44**	2c. red-brown (4.1.04)	13·00	1·00
O13	**45**	3c. green	7·50	2·00
O14	**46**	5c. dull purple	19·00	1·50
O15	**48**	15c. blue	28·00	2·50
O16		25c. bistre (15.7.04)	22·00	18·00
O17		30c. dull violet and green (14.3.04)	12·00	1·50
O12/17 *Set of* 6			90·00	24·00

Stamps overprinted "On Service" were withdrawn on 1 October 1904.

POSTAL FISCALS

1952 (1 Dec). *As T* **72** *but inscr* "REVENUE" *at sides. Chalk-surfaced paper.*
F1 10r. dull green and yellow-orange . . . 65·00 29·00

This revenue stamp was on sale for postal use from 1 December 1952 until 14 March 1954.

Cook Islands
***see after* New Zealand**

Cyprus

Cyprus was part of the Turkish Ottoman Empire from 1571.

The first records of an organised postal service date from 1871 when a post office was opened at Nicosia (Lefkosa) under the jurisdiction of the Damascus Head Post Office. Various stamps of Turkey from the 1868 issue onwards are known used from this office, cancelled "KIBRIS", in Arabic, within a double-lined oblong. Manuscript cancellations have also been reported. The records report the opening of a further office at Larnaca (Tuzla) in 1873, but no cancellation for this office has been identified.

To provide an overseas postal service the Austrian Empire opened a post office in Larnaca during 1845. Stamps of the Austrian Post Offices in the Turkish Empire were placed on sale there from 1 June 1864 and were cancelled with an unframed straight-line mark or circular date stamp. This Austrian post office closed on 6 August 1878.

BRITISH ADMINISTRATION

Following the convention with Turkey, Great Britain assumed the administration of Cyprus on 11 July 1878 and the first post office, as part of the British G.P.O. system, was opened at Larnaca on 27 July 1878. Further offices at Famagusta, Kyrenia, Limassol, Nicosia and Paphos followed in September 1878.

The stamps of Great Britain were supplied to the various offices as they opened and continued to be used until the Cyprus Administration assumed responsibility for the postal service on 1 April 1880. With the exception of "969" (Nicosia) similar numeral cancellations had previously been used at offices in Great Britain.

Numeral postmarks for Headquarters Camp, Nicosia ("D48") and Polymedia (Polemidhia) Camp, Limassol ("D47") were supplied by the G.P.O. in London during January 1881. These cancellations had three bars above and three bars below the numeral. Similar marks, but with four bars above and below, had previously been used in London on newspapers and bulk mail.

Although both three bar cancellations subsequently occur on Cyprus issues only, isolated examples have been found on loose Great Britain stamps and there are no known covers or pieces which confirm such usage in Cyprus.

For illustrations of the postmark types see BRITISH POST OFFICES ABROAD notes, following GREAT BRITAIN.

FAMAGUSTA

Stamps of GREAT BRITAIN *cancelled* "982" *as Type* **9**.

1878–80.

Z1	½d. rose-red (1870–79) (Plate Nos. 11, 13)	£700
Z2	1d. rose-red (1864–79) Plate Nos. 145, 174, 181, 193, 202, 204, 206, 215, 217.	£475
Z3	2d. blue (1858–69) (Plate Nos. 13, 14, 15)	£950
Z4	2½d. rosy mauve (1876) (Plate Nos. 13, 16)	£1100
Z5	6d. grey (1874–80) (Plate No. 15)	
Z6	1s. green (1873–77) (Plate No. 12)	£1900

KYRENIA

Stamps of GREAT BRITAIN *cancelled* "974" *as Type* **9**.

1878–80.

Z 8	½d. rose-red (1870–79) (Plate No. 13)	
Z 9	1d. rose-red (1864–79) *From* Plate Nos. 168, 171, 193, 196, 206, 207, 209, 220.	£550
Z10	2d. blue (1858–69) (Plate Nos. 13, 15) *From*	£850
Z11	2½d. rosy mauve (1876–79) *From*	£1000
Z12	4d. sage-green (1877) (Plate No. 16)	
Z13	6d. grey (1874–80) (Plate No. 16)	

LARNACA

Stamps of GREAT BRITAIN *cancelled* "942" *as Type* **9**.

1878–80.

Z14	½d. rose-red (1870–79) *From* Plate Nos. 11, 12, 13, 14, 15, 19, 20.	£250
Z15	1d. rose-red (1864–79) *From* Plate Nos. 129, 131, 146, 154, 170, 171, 174, 175, 176, 177, 178, 179, 181, 182, 183, 184, 187, 188, 190, 191, 192, 193, 194, 195, 196, 197, 198, 199, 200, 201, 202, 203, 204, 205, 206, 207, 208, 209, 210, 212, 213, 214, 215, 216, 217, 218, 220, 221, 222, 225.	£170
Z16	1½d. lake-red (1870) (Plate No. 3)	£1700
Z17	2d. blue (1858–69) (Plate Nos. 9, 13, 14, 15)	£225
Z18	2½d. rosy mauve (1876–79) *From* Plate Nos. 4, 5, 6, 8, 9, 10, 11, 12, 13, 14, 15, 16, 17.	60·00
Z19	2½d. blue (1880) (Plate Nos. 17, 18)	£500
Z21	4d. sage-green (1877) (Plate Nos. 15, 16)	£550
Z22	6d. grey (1874–76) (Plate Nos. 15, 16, 17)	£500
Z23	6d. pale buff (1872–73) (Plate No. 11)	£1900
Z24	8d. orange (1876)	£4500
Z25	1s. green (1873–77) (Plate Nos. 12, 13)	£900
Z27	5s. rose (1874) (Plate No. 2)	£4500

LIMASSOL

Stamps of GREAT BRITAIN *cancelled* "975" *as Type* **9**.

1878–80.

Z28	½d. rose-red (1870–79) (Plate Nos. 11, 13, 15, 19)	£450
Z29	1d. rose-red (1864–79) *From* Plate Nos. 159, 160, 171, 173, 174, 177, 179, 184, 187, 190, 193, 195, 196, 197, 198, 200, 202, 206, 207, 208, 209, 210, 213, 215, 216, 218, 220, 221, 222, 225.	£275
Z30	1½d. lake-red (1870–74) (Plate No. 3)	£1800
Z31	2d. blue (1858–69) (Plate Nos. 14, 15) *From*	£400
Z32	2½d. rosy-mauve (1876–80) *From* Plate Nos. 11, 12, 13, 14, 15, 16.	£170
Z33	2½d. blue (1880) (Plate No. 17)	£1200
Z34	4d. sage-green (Plate No. 16)	£700

NICOSIA

Stamps of GREAT BRITAIN *cancelled* "969" *as Type* **9**.

1878–80.

Z35	½d. rose-red (1870–79) Plate Nos. 12, 13, 14, 15, 20.	£450
Z36	1d. rose-red (1864–79) *From* Plate Nos. 170, 171, 174, 189, 190, 192, 193, 195, 196, 198, 200, 202, 203, 205, 206, 207, 210, 212, 214, 215, 218, 221, 222, 225.	£275
Z37	2d. blue (1858–69) (Plate Nos. 14, 15)	£450
Z38	2½d. rosy mauve (1876–79) *From* Plate Nos. 10, 11, 12, 13, 14, 15, 16.	£170
Z42	4d. sage-green (1877) (Plate No. 16)	£800
Z43	6d. grey (1873) (Plate No. 16)	£800

PAPHOS

Stamps of GREAT BRITAIN *cancelled* "981" *as Type* **9**.

1878–80.

Z44	½d. rose-red (1870–79) (Plate Nos. 13, 15)	
Z45	1d. rose-red (1864–79) *From* Plate Nos. 196, 201, 202, 204, 206, 213, 217.	£500
Z46	2d. blue (1858–69) (Plate No. 15)	£850
Z47	2½d. rosy mauve (1876–79) *From* Plate Nos. 13, 14, 15, 16.	£500

PRICES FOR STAMPS ON COVER TO 1945

No.	1	*from* × 10
No.	2	*from* × 50
No.	3	*from* × 100
No.	4	*from* × 8
Nos.	5/6	—
Nos.	7/10	*from* × 15
Nos.	11/15	*from* × 5
No.	16	—
Nos.	16*a*/24	*from* × 10
No.	25	*from* × 40
No.	26	—
No.	27	*from* × 10
No.	28	—
No.	29	*from* × 30
Nos.	31/5*a*	*from* × 10
Nos.	36/7	—
Nos.	40/9	*from* × 8
Nos.	50/71	*from* × 5
Nos.	74/99	*from* × 4
Nos.	100/2	—

Nos.	103/17	*from* × 4
No.	117*a*	—
Nos.	118/31	*from* × 5
No.	132	—
Nos.	133/43	*from* × 5
Nos.	144/7	*from* × 6
Nos.	148/63	*from* × 5

PERFORATION. Nos. 1/122 are perf 14.

Stamps of Great Britain overprinted

CYPRUS (1) **CYPRUS** (2)

(Optd by D.L.R.)

1880 (1 April).
1 **1** ½d. rose . . . £110 £100
a. Opt double (Plate 15) . . . † £13000

Plate No.	*Un.*	*Used.*	*Plate No.*	*Un.*	*Used.*
12.	£180	£250	19.	£5000	£700
15.	£110	£100			

2 **2** 1d. red . . . 11·00 38·00
a. Opt double (Plate 208) . . . £15000
aa. Opt double (Plate 218) . . . £4250
b. Vert pair, top stamp without opt (Plate 208) . . . £18000

174.	£1200	£1200	208.	95·00	55·00
181.	£350	£170	215.	11·00	50·00
184.	£12000	£2250	216.	16·00	38·00
193.	£700	†	217.	12·00	50·00
196.	£600	†	218.	18·00	55·00
201.	12·00	50·00	220.	£350	£375
205.	55·00	50·00			

3 **2** 2½d. rosy mauve . . . 2·25 8·50
a. Large thin "C" (Plate 14) (BK, JK) . . . 45·00 £170
b. Large thin "C" (Plate 15) (BK, JK) . . . 75·00 £400
w. Wmk inverted (Plate 15) . . . £325

14.	2·25	8·50	15.	3·50	24·00

4 **2** 4d. sage-green (Plate 16) . . . £120 £200
5 6d. grey (Plate 16) . . . £500 £650
6 1s. green (Plate 13) . . . £650 £450
No. 3 has been reported from Plate 9.

HALF-PENNY (3) 18 mm **HALF-PENNY** (4) 16 or 16½ mm

HALF-PENNY (5) 13 mm **30 PARAS** (6)

(Optd by Govt Ptg Office, Nicosia)

1881 (Feb–June). *No. 2 surch.*
7 **3** ½d.on 1d. red (Feb) . . . 70·00 85·00
a. "HALFPENN" (BG, LG) (*all plates*) . . . *From* £1800 £1800

Plate No.	*Un.*	*Used.*	*Plate No.*	*Un.*	*Used.*
174.	£150	£300	215.	£650	£700
181.	£150	£170	216.	70·00	85·00
201.	90·00	£120	217.	£800	£700
205.	70·00	85·00	218.	£450	£550
208.	£160	£275	220.	£250	£325

8 **4** ½d.on 1d. red (Apr) . . . £120 £160
a. Surch double (Plates 201 and 216) . . . £2750 £2500

201.	£120	£160	218.	—	£10000
216.	£350	£400			

9 **5** ½d.on 1d. red (1 June) . . . 45·00 65·00
aa. Surch double (Plate 205) . . . £700
ab. Surch double (Plate 215) . . . £450 £600
b. Surch treble (Plate 205) . . . £3500
ba. Surch treble (Plate 215) . . . £700
bc. Surch treble (Plate 218) . . . £3500
c. Surch quadruple (Plate 205) . . . £4250
ca. Surch quadruple (Plate 215) . . . £4250

205.	£250	—	217.	£130	80·00
215.	45·00	65·00	218.	70·00	95·00

The surcharge on No. 8 was handstamped; the others were applied by lithography.

(New Currency: 40 paras = 1 piastre, 180 piastres = £1)

1881 (June). *No. 2 surch with T* **6** *by lithography.*
10 **6** 30paras on 1d. red . . . £100 80·00
a. Surch double, one invtd (Plate 216) . . . £3500
aa. Surch double, one invtd (Plate 220) . . . £1300 £1000

201.	£120	90·00	217.	£170	£170
216.	£100	80·00	220.	£150	£160

7

"US" damaged at foot (R. 5/5 of both panes)

(Typo D.L.R)

1881 (1 July). *Die I.* Wmk Crown CC.
11 **7** ½pi. emerald-green . . . £180 45·00
w. Wmk inverted . . . £550 £325
12 1pi. rose . . . £375 32·00
13 2pi. blue . . . £450 32·00
w. Wmk inverted . . . — £550
14 4pi. pale olive-green . . . £900 £275
15 6pi. olive-grey . . . £1500 £425
Stamps of Queen Victoria initialled "J.A.B." or overprinted "POSTAL SURCHARGE" with or without the same initials were employed for accounting purposes between the Chief Post Office and sub-offices, the initials are those of the then Postmaster, Mr. J. A. Bulmer.

1882 (May)–**88**. *Die I**. Wmk Crown CA.
16 **7** ½pi. emerald-green (5.82) . . . £5000 £425
a. Dull green (4.83) . . . 16·00 1·50
ab. Top left triangle detached . . . — £200
17 30pa. pale mauve (7.6.82) . . . 60·00 20·00
a. Top left triangle detached . . . £850 £475
b. Damaged "US" . . . £650 £325
18 1pi. rose (3.83) . . . 90·00 2·00
a. Top left triangle detached . . . — £225
19 2pi. blue (4.83) . . . £120 2·00
a. Top left triangle detached . . . — £225
20 4pi. deep olive-green (10.83) . . . £500 32·00
a. Pale olive-green . . . £350 25·00
ab. Top left triangle detached . . . — £550
21 6pi. olive-grey (7.82) . . . 48·00 17·00
a. Top left triangle detached . . . — £425
22 12pi. orange-brown (1966) . . . £180 35·00
a. Top left triangle detached . . . — £700
s. Optd "Specimen" . . . £800
16a/22 *Set of* 7 . . . £800 90·00
*For description and illustrations of Dies I and II see Introduction.
For illustration of "top left triangle detached" variety see above No. 21 of Antigua.
See also Nos. 31/7.

½ (8) **½** **30 PARAS** (9) Spur on "1" (position 3 in setting)

(Surch litho by Govt Ptg Office, Nicosia)

1882. *Surch with T* **8**/**9**.

(a) Wmk crown CC.
23 ½on ½pi. emerald-green (6.82) . . . £600 75·00
c. Spur on "1" . . . £800 £110
w. Wmk inverted
24 30pa.on 1pi. rose (22.5.82) . . . £1500 £110

(b) Wmk Crown CA.
25 **7** ½on ½pi. emerald-green (27.5.82) . . . £140 6·50
a. Surch double . . . † £2750
b. "½" inserted by hand . . . † —
c. Spur on "1" . . . £200 12·00
Nos. 23 and 25 were surcharged by a setting of 6 arranged as a horizontal row.
No. 25b shows an additional handstamped "½" applied to examples on which the surcharge was so misplaced as to almost omit one of the original "½s."

1/2 **1/2** (10)

11

Varieties of numerals:

1 Normal 1 Large 1 Small

2 Normal 2 Large

1886 (Apr). *Surch with T* **10** *(fractions approx 6 mm apart) in typography.*

(a) Wmk Crown CC.
26 **7** ½on ½pi. emerald-green . . . £17000

(b) Wmk Crown CA.
27 **7** ½on ½pi. emerald-green . . . £225 70·00
a. Large "2" at right . . . £2250 £750

1886 (May–June). *Surch with T* **10** *(fractions approx 8 mm apart) in typography.*

(a) Wmk Crown CC.
28 **7** ½on ½pi. emerald-green . . . £7500 £425
a. Large "1" at left . . . — £1700
b. Small "1" at right . . . £14000 £2250
c. Large "2" at left . . . — £2250
d. Large "2" at right . . . † £2250

(b) Wmk Crown CA.
29 **7** ½on ½pi. emerald-green (June) . . . £350 9·50
a. Large "1" at left . . . £2500 £225
b. Small "1" at right . . . £2750 £275
c. Large "2" at left . . . £2750 £300
d. Large "2" at right . . . £2750 £300
Nos. 28/9 were surcharged in a setting of 60. The large "1" at left and large "2" at right both occur in the fourth vertical row, the large "2" at left in the fifth vertical row and the small "1" at right in the top horizontal row.
A third type of this surcharge is known with the fractions spaced approximately 10 mm apart on CA paper with postmarks from August 1886. This may be due to the shifting of type.

1892–94. *Die II.* Wmk Crown CA.
31 **7** ½pi. dull green . . . 5·00 7[illegible]
32 30pa. mauve . . . 5·00 5·0[illegible]
a. Damaged "US" . . . £160 £16[illegible]
33 1pi. carmine . . . 11·00 2·0[illegible]
34 2pi. ultramarine . . . 14·00 1·7[illegible]
35 4pi. olive-green . . . 50·00 29·0[illegible]
a. Pale olive-green . . . 18·00 24·0[illegible]
36 6pi. olive-grey (1894) . . . £160 £55[illegible]
37 12pi. orange brown (1893) . . . £130 £32[illegible]
31/7 *Set of* 7 . . . £300 £80[illegible]

1894 (14 Aug)–**96**. *Colours changed and new values. Die II.* Wmk Crown CA.
40 **7** ½pi. green and carmine (1896) . . . 4·00 1·2[illegible]
w. Wmk inverted
41 30pa. bright mauve and green (1896) . . . 2·00 1·2[illegible]
a. Damaged "US" . . . £120 £10[illegible]
42 1pi. carmine and blue (1896) . . . 6·00 1·2[illegible]
43 2pi. blue and purple (1896) . . . 7·00 1·2[illegible]
44 4pi. sage-green and purple (1896) . . . 15·00 5·0[illegible]
45 6pi. sepia and green (1896) . . . 12·00 16·0[illegible]
46 9pi. brown and carmine . . . 15·00 18·0[illegible]
47 12pi. orange-brown and black (1896) . . . 17·00 55·0[illegible]
48 18pi. greyish slate and brown . . . 48·00 48·0[illegible]
49 45pi. grey-purple and blue . . . 90·00 £13[illegible]
40/9 *Set of* 10 . . . £190 £25[illegible]
40s/9s Optd "Specimen" *Set of* 10 . . . £325

LIMASSOL FLOOD HANDSTAMP. Following a flood o[n] 14 November 1894, which destroyed the local stamp stocks, th[e] postmaster of Limassol produced a temporary handstamp showin[g] "½C.P." which was applied to local letters with the usual c.d.s.

(Typo D.L.R.)

1902–04. Wmk Crown CA.
50 **11** ½pi. green and carmine (12.02) . . . 4·00 1·2[illegible]
w. Wmk inverted . . . 75·00 48·0[illegible]
51 30pa. violet and green (2.03) . . . 8·00 2·7[illegible]
a. Mauve and green . . . 16·00 6·5[illegible]
b. Damaged "US" . . . £225 £11[illegible]
52 1pi. carmine and blue (9.03) . . . 17·00 3·0[illegible]
53 2pi. blue and purple (2.03) . . . 55·00 10·0[illegible]
54 4pi. olive-green and purple (9.03) . . . 28·00 19·0[illegible]
55 6pi. sepia and green (9.03) . . . 40·00 £12[illegible]
56 9pi. brown and carmine (5.04) . . . £100 £20[illegible]
57 12pi. chestnut and black (4.03) . . . 13·00 55·0[illegible]
58 18pi. black and brown (5.04) . . . 80·00 £15[illegible]
59 45pi. dull purple and ultramarine (10.03) . . . £200 £50[illegible]
50/9*Set of* 10 . . . £500 £95[illegible]
50sw/9s Optd "Specimen" *Set of* 10 . . . £450
The ½pi "SPECIMEN" is only known with watermark inverted.

Broken top left triangle (Left pane R. 7/5)

1904–10. Wmk Mult Crown CA.
60 **11** 5pa. bistre and black (14.1.08) . . . 1·00 [illegible]
a. Broken top left triangle . . . 50·00 50·[illegible]
w. Wmk inverted . . . £850
61 10pa. orange and green (12.06) . . . 3·00 [illegible]
aw. Wmk inverted . . . — 80·[illegible]
b. Yellow and green . . . 38·00 5·[illegible]
bw. Wmk inverted . . . — 90·[illegible]
c. Broken top left triangle . . . 70·00 45·[illegible]
62 ½pi. green and carmine (1.7.04) . . . 4·50 [illegible]
a. Broken top left triangle . . . 90·00 32·[illegible]
w. Wmk inverted . . . 95·00 65·[illegible]
63 30pa. purple and green (1.7.04) . . . 14·00 1·[illegible]
a. Violet and green (1910) . . . 16·00 2·[illegible]
b. Broken top left triangle . . . £170 65·[illegible]
c. Damaged "US" . . . £170 60·[illegible]
w. Wmk inverted . . . † £7[illegible]
64 1pi. carmine and blue (11.04) . . . 5·00 1·[illegible]
a. Broken top left triangle . . . £100 55·[illegible]
65 2pi. blue and purple (11.04) . . . 6·00 1·[illegible]
a. Broken top left triangle . . . £140 75·[illegible]
66 4pi. olive-green and purple (2.05) . . . 11·00 8·[illegible]
a. Broken top left triangle . . . £190 £1[illegible]
67 6pi. sepia and green (17.7.04) . . . 14·00 15·[illegible]
a. Broken top left triangle . . . £200
68 9pi. brown and carmine (30.5.04) . . . 30·00 8·[illegible]
a. Yellow-brown and carmine . . . 28·00 22·[illegible]
aw. Wmk inverted . . . £130 80·[illegible]
b. Broken top left triangle . . . £325 £2[illegible]

69 12pi. chestnut and black (4.06) . . . . 25·00 40·00
a. Broken top left triangle £325
70 18pi. black and brown (16.6.04) . . . 30·00 11·00
a. Broken top left triangle £400 £250
71 45pi. dull purple & ultram (15.6.04) . . 75·00 £140
a. Broken top left triangle. £700
60/71 *Set of* 12 . . . . £200 £200
60s/1s Optd "Specimen" *Set of* 2 . . . . £130

12

13

Broken bottom left triangle (Right pane R. 10/6)

(Typo D.L.R.)

1912 (July)–**15**. Wmk Mult Crown CA.
74 **12** 10pa. orange and green (11.12) . . . . 3·25 2·50
a. Wmk sideways . . . . † £2250
b. *Orange-yellow & brt green* (8.15) . . . . 2·25 1·25
ba. Broken bottom left triangle . . . 70·00 48·00
75 ½pi. green and carmine . . . . . . 1·75 20
a. *Yellow-green and carmine* . . . 7·50 1·90
ab. Broken bottom left triangle . . . 85·00 55·00
w. Wmk inverted . . . . † £850
76 30pa. violet and green (3.13) . . . . . 2·50 60
a. Broken bottom left triangle . . . 70·00 42·00
w. Wmk inverted . . . .
77 1pi. rose-red and blue (9.12) . . . . 4·00 1·75
a. *Carmine and blue* (1.15?) . . . . 13·00 4·25
ab. Broken bottom left triangle . . . £140 65·00
78 2pi. blue and purple (7.13) . . . . . 6·50 2·00
a. Broken bottom left triangle . . . £110 55·00
79 4pi. olive-green and purple . . . . . 4·25 4·75
a. Broken bottom left triangle . . . 85·00 95·00
80 6pi. sepia and green . . . . 3·50 8·50
a. Broken bottom left triangle . . . 85·00
81 9pi. brown and carmine (3.15) . . . . 24·00 26·00
a. *Yellow-brown and carmine* . . . . 27·00 29·00
b. Broken bottom left triangle . . . £300
82 12pi. chestnut and black (7.13) . . . . 15·00 35·00
b. Broken bottom left triangle . . . £190
83 18pi. black and brown (3.15) . . . . . 26·00 30·00
a. Broken bottom left triangle . . . £275
84 45pi. dull purple and ultramarine (3.15) . . . . 80·00 £120
a. Broken bottom left triangle . . . £550
74/84 *Set of* 11 . . . . £150 £200
74s/84s Optd "Specimen" *Set of* 11 . . . . . . £400

1921–23.

(a) Wmk Mult Script CA.
85 **12** 10pa. orange and green . . . . 6·00 7·50
a. Broken bottom left triangle . . . £100 £110
86 10pa. grey and yellow (1923) . . . . 12·00 6·50
a. Broken bottom left triangle . . . £160 £130
87 30pa. violet and green . . . . 2·50 40
a. Broken bottom left triangle . . . 75·00 38·00
w. Wmk inverted . . . .
y. Wmk inverted and reversed . . . † £750
88 30pa. green (1923) . . . . 7·00 40
a. Broken bottom left triangle . . . £120 38·00
89 1pi. carmine and blue . . . . 17·00 27·00
a. Broken bottom left triangle . . . £180
90 1pi. violet and red (1922) . . . . . . 3·00 4·00
a. Broken bottom left triangle . . . 80·00 90·00
91 1½pi. yellow and black (1922) . . . . 5·00 4·75
a. Broken bottom left triangle . . . £100 £100
92 2pi. blue and purple . . . . 20·00 13·00
a. Broken bottom left triangle . . . £225 £160
93 2pi. carmine and blue (1922) . . . . . 9·50 22·00
a. Broken bottom left triangle . . . £160
94 2¾pi. blue and purple (1922) . . . . . 7·00 9·00
a. Broken bottom left triangle . . . £150 £160
95 4pi. olive-green and purple . . . . . 12·00 17·00
a. Broken bottom left triangle . . . £170
w. Wmk inverted . . . . † £750
96 6pi. sepia and green (1923) . . . . . 16·00 65·00
a. Broken bottom left triangle . . . £190
97 9pi. brown and carmine (1922) . . . . 27·00 70·00
a. *Yellow-brown and carmine* . . . . 80·00 £120
b. Broken bottom left triangle . . . £325
98 18pi. black and brown (1923) . . . . . 60·00 £130
a. Broken bottom left triangle . . . £425
99 45pi. dull purple & ultramarine (1923) £170 £250
a. Broken bottom left triangle . . . £850
85/99 *Set of* 15 . . . . £325 £550
85s/99s Optd "Specimen" *Set of* 15 . . . . . . £500

(b) Wmk Mult Crown CA (1923).
100 **12** 10s. green and red/*pale yellow* . . . £375 £750
a. Broken bottom left triangle . . . £1800
101 £1 purple and black/*red* £1000 £1800
a. Broken bottom left triangle . . . £3500 £6000
100s/1s Optd "Specimen" *Set of* 2 . . . . £500
Examples of Nos. 96/101 are known showing a forged Limassol postmark dated "14 MR 25".

1924–28. *Chalk-surfaced paper.*

(a) Wmk Mult Crown CA.
102 **13** £1 purple and black/*red* £300 £700

(b) Wmk Mult Script CA.
103 **13** ¼pi. grey and chestnut . . . . 1·00 15
w. Wmk inverted . . . . † £850
104 ½pi. black . . . . 2·75 9·00
105 ¾pi. green . . . . 2·25 1·00
106 1pi. purple and chestnut . . . . . . 2·00 70
107 1½pi. orange and black . . . . 2·00 7·50
108 2pi. carmine and green . . . . 2·25 13·00
109 2¾pi. bright blue and purple . . . . . 3·25 3·00
110 4pi. sage-green and purple . . . . . 3·25 2·75
111 4½pi. black and orange/*emerald* . . . 3·50 3·50
112 6pi. olive-brown and green . . . . . 3·75 5·50
113 9pi. brown and purple . . . . 6·00 4·50
114 12pi. chestnut and black . . . . . . 9·00 55·00
115 18pi. black and orange . . . . 20·00 5·00
116 45pi. purple and blue . . . . 38·00 38·00
117 90pi. green and red/*yellow* . . . . . 90·00 £180
117*a* £5 black/*yellow* (1928) £2750 £6000
as. Optd "Specimen" £900
Examples of No. 102 are known showing a forged Limassol postmark dated "14 MR 25" and of No. 117*a* showing a forged Registered Nicosia postmark dated "6 MAY 35".

CROWN COLONY

1925. Wmk Mult Script CA. *Chalk-surfaced paper (½, ¾ and 2pi.)*
118 **13** ½pi. green . . . . 2·25 1·00
119 ¾pi. brownish black . . . . 2·00 10
120 1½pi. scarlet . . . . 2·50 30
121 2pi. yellow and black . . . . 6·00 3·25
122 2½pi. bright blue . . . . 3·00 30
102/22 (*ex* £5) *Set of* 21 . . . . £450 £850
102s/22s (*ex* £5) Optd "Specimen" *Set of* 21 . . . £650
In the above set the fraction bar in the value is horizontal. In Nos. 91, 94, 107 and 109 it is diagonal.

14 Silver Coin of Amathus, 6th-cent B.C.

16 Map of Cyprus

(Recess B.W.)

1928 (1 Feb). *50th Anniv of British Rule. T* **14**, **16** *and similar designs.* Wmk Mult Script CA. P 12.
123 ¾pi. deep dull purple . . . . 2·75 1·00
124 1pi. black and greenish blue . . . . . 3·00 1·50
125 1½pi. scarlet . . . . 4·50 2·00
126 2½pi. light blue . . . . 3·50 2·25
127 4pi. deep brown . . . . 5·50 6·00
128 6pi. blue . . . . 7·50 21·00
129 9pi. maroon . . . . 7·50 11·00
130 18pi. black and brown . . . . 18·00 18·00
131 45pi. violet and blue . . . . 40·00 48·00
132 £1 blue and bistre-brown £200 £300
123/32 *Set of* 10 . . . . £250 £375
123s/32s Optd "Specimen" *Set of* 10 . . . . . . £550
Designs: *Vert*—1pi. Zeno (philosopher); 2½pi. Discovery of body of St. Barnabas; 4pi. Cloister, Abbey of Bella Paise; 9pi. Tekke of Umm Haram; 18pi. Statue of Richard I, Westminster; 45pi. St. Nicholas Cathedral, Famagusta (now Lala Mustafa Pasha Mosque); £1 King George V. *Horiz*—6pi. Badge of Cyprus.

24 Ruins of Vouni Palace

25 Small Marble Forum, Salamis

30 St. Sophia Cathedral, Nicosia (now Selimiye Mosque)

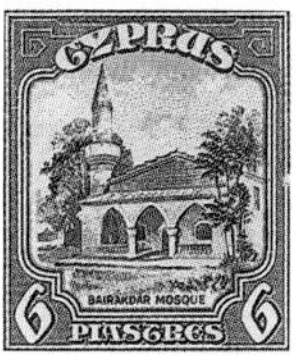

31 Bayraktar Mosque, Nicosia

(Recess Waterlow)

1934 (1 Dec). *T* **24/5**, **30/1** *and similar designs.* Wmk Mult Script CA (sideways on ½pi., 1½pi., 2½pi., 4½pi., 6pi., 9pi. and 18pi.). P 12½.
133 ¼pi. ultramarine and orange-brown . . . 1·00 50
a. Imperf between (vert pair) £23000 £16000
134 ½pi. green . . . . 1·25 1·00
a. Imperf between (vert pair) £11000 £12000
135 ¾pi. black and violet . . . . 1·50 10
a. Imperf between (vert pair) £25000
136 1pi. black and red-brown . . . . 1·00 80
a. Imperf between (vert pair) £13000 £13000
b. Imperf between (horiz pair) £10000
137 1½pi. carmine . . . . 2·00 55
138 2½pi. ultramarine . . . . 2·00 1·75
139 4½pi. black and crimson . . . . 3·00 3·75
140 6pi. black and blue . . . . 9·00 12·00
141 9pi. sepia and violet . . . . 7·00 4·75
142 18pi. black and olive-green . . . . 40·00 29·00
143 45pi. green and black . . . . 65·00 50·00
133/43 *Set of* 11 . . . . £120 95·00
133s/43s Perf "Specimen" *Set of* 11 . . . . . . £325
Designs: *Horiz.*—¾pi. Church of St. Barnabas and St. Hilarion, Peristerona; 1pi. Roman theatre, Soli; 1½pi. Kyrenia Harbour; 2½pi. Kolossi Castle; 45pi. Forest scene, Troodos. *Vert*—9pi. Queen's Window, St. Hilarion Castle; 18pi. Buyuk Khan, Nicosia.

1935 (6 May). *Silver Jubilee. As Nos. 91/4 of Antigua, but ptd by Waterlow & Sons.* P 11 × 12.
144 ¾pi. ultramarine and grey . . . . 1·75 40
145 1½pi. deep blue and scarlet . . . . . . 3·75 2·50
l. Kite and horizontal log £225
146 2½pi. brown and deep blue . . . . . . 3·75 1·50
147 9pi. slate and purple . . . . 14·00 14·00
144/7 *Set of* 4 . . . . 21·00 17·00
144s/7s Perf "Specimen" *Set of* 4 . . . . £150
For illustration of plate variety see Omnibus section following Zanzibar.

1937 (12 May). *Coronation. As Nos. 95/7 of Antigua.* P 11 × 11½.
148 ¾pi. grey 60 40
149 1½pi. carmine 90 80
150 2½pi. blue . . . . 2·00 1·25
148/50 *Set of* 3 . . . . 3·25 2·25
148s/50s Perf "Specimen" *Set of* 3 . . . . £120

35 Vouni Palace

36 Map of Cyprus

37 Othello's Tower, Famagusta

38 King George VI

(Recess Waterlow)

1938 (12 May)–**51**. *T* **35** *to* **38** *and other designs as 1934, but with portrait of King George VI.* Wmk Mult Script CA. P 12½.
151 **35** ¼pi. ultramarine and orange-brown 20 20
152 **25** ½pi. green 50 10
152*a* – ½pi. violet (2.7.51) . . . . 2·25 20
153 – ¾pi. black and violet . . . . 15·00 50
154 – 1pi. orange . . . . 1·00 10
a. Perf 13½ × 12½ (5.44) . . . . . £450 27·00
155 – 1½pi. carmine . . . . 5·50 1·50
155*a* – 1½pi. violet (15.3.43) 50 30
155*ab* – 1½pi. green (2.7.51) . . . . 2·75 50
155*b* – 2pi. black and carmine (2.2.42) . . 70 10
c. Perf 12½ × 13½ (10.44) . . . . 2·50 7·50
156 – 2½pi. ultramarine . . . . 26·00 2·50
156*a* – 3pi. ultramarine (2.2.42) . . . . . 2·00 15
156*b* – 4pi. ultramarine (2.7.51) . . . . . 3·00 30
157 **36** 4½pi. grey . . . . 1·00 10
158 **31** 6pi. black and blue . . . . 1·50 1·00
159 **37** 9pi. black and purple . . . . 2·50 20
160 – 18pi. black and olive-green . . . . 7·00 85
a. Black and sage-green (19.8.47) . . . . 9·00 1·50
161 – 45pi. green and black . . . . 20·00 2·50
162 **38** 90pi. mauve and black . . . . 23·00 5·00
163 £1 scarlet and indigo . . . . . . 50·00 24·00
151/63 *Set of* 19 . . . . £150 35·00
151s/63s Perf "Specimen" *Set of* 16 . . . . . . £400
Designs: *Horiz*—¾pi., 2pi. Peristerona Church; 1pi. Soli Theatre; 1½pi. Kyrenia Harbour; 2½pi., 3pi., 4pi. Kolossi Castle; 45pi. Forest scene. *Vert*—18pi. Buyuk Khan, Nicosia.

Dot between "1" and "½" in right-hand value tablet (Pl B1 R. 9/1)

1946 (21 Oct). *Victory. As Nos. 110/11 of Antigua.*
164 1½pi. deep violet 15 10
a. Dot between "1" and "½" . . . . . 23·00
165 3pi. blue 15 15
164s/5s Perf "Specimen" *Set of* 2 . . . . £100

Extra decoration (R. 3/5)

1948 (20 Dec). *Royal Silver Wedding. As Nos. 112/13 of Antigua.*
166 1½pi. violet 50 20
a. Extra decoration . . . . . 38·00
167 £1 indigo . . . . . 42·00 50·00

1949 (10 Oct). *75th Anniv of Universal Postal Union. As Nos. 114/17 of Antigua but inscr "CYPRUS" (recess).*
168 1½pi. violet 40 70
169 2pi. carmine-red . . . . . 1·50 1·50
170 3pi. deep blue . . . . . 70 1·00
171 9pi. purple . . . . . 70 2·00
168/71 *Set of* 4 . . . . . 3·00 4·75

Cyrenaica *see* British Occupation of Italian Colonies

Dominica

CROWN COLONY

A British packet agency was operating on Dominica from about 1778, the date of the earliest known use of a postal marking. This was replaced by a branch office of the British G.P.O. which opened at Roseau on 8 May 1858. The stamps of Great Britain were used from that date until 1 May 1860, after which the colonial authorities assumed responsibility for the postal service. Until the introduction of Nos. 1/3 in 1874 No. CC1 and later handstamps were utilised.

For illustrations of handstamp and postmark types see BRITISH POST OFFICES ABROAD notes, following GREAT BRITAIN.

ROSEAU

CROWNED/CIRCLE HANDSTAMPS

CC1 CC **1** DOMINICA (Black or R.) (17.5.1845)
Price on cover £500

No. CC1 is also known struck in black on various adhesive stamps as late as 1883.

Stamps of GREAT BRITAIN *cancelled* "A 07" *as Type* **2**.

1858–1860.
Z1 1d. rose-red (1857), *perf* 14 . . . . . £275
Z2 2d. blue (1858) (Plate No. 7) £750
Z3 4d. rose (1857) £325
Z4 6d. lilac (1856) £300
Z5 1s. green £1400

PRICES FOR STAMPS ON COVER TO 1945

Nos.	1/3	*from* × 25
No.	4	*from* × 40
No.	5	*from* × 100
No.	6	*from* × 40
Nos.	7/8	*from* × 100
No.	9	*from* × 40
Nos.	10/12	*from* × 15
Nos.	13/15	*from* × 100
No.	17	*from* × 50
Nos.	18/a	—
No.	19	*from* × 40
Nos.	20/5	*from* × 30
No.	26	—
Nos.	27/90	*from* × 5
No.	91	—
Nos.	92/8	*from* × 10
Nos.	99/109	*from* × 3
Nos.	R1/3	*from* × 15
No.	R4	*from* × 50
No.	R6	*from* × 3

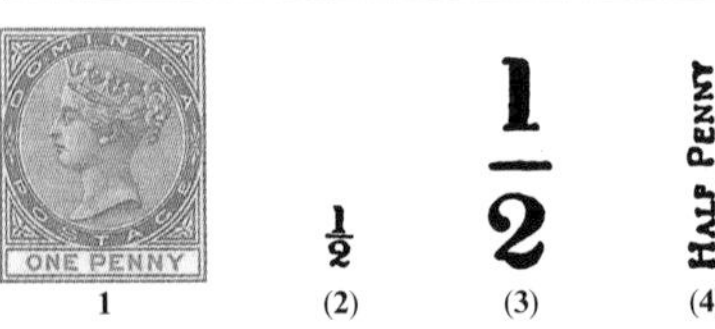
1 (2) (3) (4)

(Typo D.L.R.)

1874 (4 May). Wmk Crown CC. P 12½.
1 **1** 1d. lilac . . . . . £150 48·00
2 6d. green £550 £100
3 1s. dull magenta . . . . . £325 70·00

NCE NCE
Normal Malformed "CE" (R. 10/6)

1877–79. Wmk Crown CC. P 14.
4 **1** ½d. olive-yellow (1879) . . . . . 13·00 50·00
5 1d. lilac . . . . . 6·00 2·00
a. Bisected vert or diag (½d.) (on cover or card) . . . . . † £1800
w. Wmk inverted . . . . . 70·00
6 2½d. red-brown (1879) . . . . . £225 29·00
w. Wmk inverted . . . . . † £150
7 4d. blue (1879) . . . . . £110 2·50
a. Malformed "CE" in "PENCE" . . . £1500 £200
8 6d. green . . . . . £150 20·00
9 1s. magenta . . . . . £120 50·00

1882 (25 Nov)–**83**. *No. 5 bisected vertically and surch.*
10 **2** ½(d.), in *black*, on half 1d. . . . . £180 42·00
a. Surch inverted £1000 £800
b. Surcharges *tête-bêche* (pair) £1700
11 **3** ½(d.), in *red*, on half 1d. (12.82) . . . . 30·00 17·00
a. Surch inverted £1000 £475
c. Surch double £1600 £650
12 **4** ½d. in *black*, on half 1d. (3.83) . . . . 65·00 20·00
b. Surch double £800

Type **4** is found reading up or down.

1883–86. Wmk Crown CA. P 14.
13 **1** ½d. olive-yellow . . . . . 3·25 10·00
14 1d. lilac (1886) . . . . . 28·00 12·00
a. Bisected (½d.) (on cover) . . . . . † £1900
15 2½d. red-brown (1884) . . . . . £140 2·00
w. Wmk inverted £325

Half Penny (5) One Penny (6)

1886 (1 Mar). *Nos. 8 and 9 surch locally.*
17 **5** ½d.on 6d. green . . . . . 4·25 3·75
18 **6** 1d.on 6d. green £21000 £10000
a. Thick bar (approx 1 mm) . . . . . † £16000
19 1d.on 1s. magenta . . . . . 14·00 17·00
a. Surch double £5500 £3000

It is believed that only two sheets of the 1d. on 6d. were surcharged. On one of these sheets the six stamps in the top row showed the thick bar variety, No. 18a.

1886–90. Wmk Crown CA. P 14.
20 **1** ½d. dull green . . . . . 1·50 5·50
22 1d. rose (1887) . . . . . 16·00 17·00
a. Deep carmine (1889) . . . . . 2·75 6·50
b. Bisected (½d.) (on cover) . . . . . † £1800
w. Wmk inverted £130
23 2½d. ultramarine (1888) . . . . . 3·75 5·00
24 4d. grey . . . . . 3·25 5·00
a. Malformed "CE" in "PENCE" . . £160 £225
25 6d. orange (1888) . . . . . 9·00 48·00
26 1s. dull magenta (1890) £160 £275
20/6 *Set of* 6 . . . . . £160 £300
20s/5s Optd "Specimen" *Set of* 5 . . . . . £225

The stamps of Dominica were superseded by the general issue for Leeward Islands on 31 October 1890, but the sets following were in concurrent use with the stamps inscribed "LEEWARD ISLANDS" until 31 December 1939, when the island came under the administration of the Windward Islands.

9 "Roseau from the Sea" (Lt. Caddy)

10

(T **9** to **11** typo D.L.R.)

1903 (1 Sept)–**07**. Wmk Crown CC (sideways* on T **9**). *Ordinary paper.* P 14.
27 **9** ½d. green and grey-green . . . . . 4·00 2·50
a. Chalk-surfaced paper (1906) . . . 14·00 18·00
28 1d. grey and red . . . . . 8·00 75
a. Chalk-surfaced paper (1906) . . . 29·00 6·00
29 2d. green and brown . . . . . 2·50 4·50
a. Chalk-surfaced paper (1906) . . . 26·00 38·00
30 2½d. grey and bright blue . . . . . 5·00 4·00
a. Chalk-surfaced paper (3.9.07) . . . 21·00 50·00
31 3d. dull purple and grey-black . . . . . 8·00 3·25
a. Chalk-surfaced paper (1906) . . . 38·00 30·00
32 6d. grey and chestnut . . . . . 4·50 18·00
33 1s. magenta and grey-green . . . . . 27·00 42·00
a. Chalk-surfaced paper (1906) . . . 75·00 £150
34 2s. grey-black and purple . . . . . 26·00 29·00
35 2s.6d. grey-green and maize . . . . . 18·00 75·00
36 **10** 5s. black and brown . . . . . 90·00 £140
27/36 *Set of* 10 . . . . . £170 £275
27s/36s Optd "Specimen" *Set of* 10 . . . . . £130

*The normal sideways watermark shows Crown to right of CC, *as seen from the back of the stamp.*

1907–08. Wmk Mult Crown CA (sideways* on T **9**). *Chalk-surfaced paper.* P 14.
37 **9** ½d. green . . . . . 3·50 3·25
38 1d. grey and red . . . . . 2·00 40
39 2d. green and brown . . . . . 5·50 16·00
40 2½d. grey and bright blue . . . . . 4·50 21·00
41 3d. dull purple and grey-black . . . . . 4·00 14·00
42 6d. black and chestnut . . . . . 50·00 85·00
43 1s. magenta and grey-green (1908) . . . 3·75 55·00
44 2s. grey-black and purple (1908) . . . 22·00 32·00
45 2s.6d. grey-green and maize (1908) . . . 22·00 60·00
46 **10** 5s. black and brown (1908) . . . . . 60·00 60·00
37/46 *Set of* 10 . . . . . £160 £300

*The normal sideways watermark shows Crown to right of CA, *as seen from the back of the stamp.*

Examples of Nos. 27/36 and 37/46 are known showing a forged Gen. Post Office Dominica postmark dated "JU 1 11".

11

WAR TAX ONE HALFPENNY (12)

1908–21. Wmk Mult Crown CA (sideways* on T **9**). *Chalk-surfaced paper (3d., 6d., 1s.).* P 14.
47 **9** ½d. blue-green . . . . . 3·00 3·75
aw. Wmk Crown to left of CA . . . 2·50 2·75
ay. Wmk sideways inverted and reversed . . . . .
b. Dp green (wmk Crown to left of CA) . . . . . 3·50 2·25
48 1d. carmine-red . . . . . 3·00 30
aw. Wmk Crown to left of CA . . . 3·50 40
b. Scarlet (1916) . . . . . 1·50 40
bw. Wmk Crown to left of CA . . . 1·00 50
49 2d. grey (1909) . . . . . 4·00 12·00
aw. Wmk Crown to left of CA . . . 3·50 16·00
b. Slate (wmk Crown to left of CA) (1918) . . . . . 3·50 12·00
50 2½d. blue . . . . . 8·50 6·00
aw. Wmk Crown to left of CA . . . — 9·00
b. Bright blue (1918) . . . . . 5·00 9·00
bw. Wmk Crown to left of CA . . . 6·00 13·00
51 3d. purple/*yellow* (1909) . . . . . 3·00 4·25
a. Ordinary paper (wmk Crown to left of CA) (1912) . . . . . 3·00 4·50
ab. *On pale yellow* (1920) . . . . . 8·50 15·00
52 6d. dull and bright purple (1909) . . . 10·00 15·00
a. Ordinary paper. *Dull purple* (wmk Crown to left of CA) (1915) . . . 3·50 18·00
53 1s. black/*green* (1910) . . . . . 3·00 2·75
a. Ordinary paper (wmk Crown to left of CA) (1912) . . . . . 3·00 4·00
as. Optd "Specimen" in red . . . . 65·00
53*b* 2s. purple and deep blue/*blue* (wmk Crown to left of CA) (1919) . . . 25·00 85·00
53*c* 2s.6d. black and red/*blue* (wmk Crown to left of CA) (1921) . . . 25·00 90·00
54 **11** 5s. red and green/*yellow* (1914) . . . 55·00 80·00
47/54 *Set of* 10 . . . . . £110 £27[illegible]
48s/54s Optd "Specimen" (1s. optd in blk) *Set of* 9 . . . . . £180

The watermark orientation differs according to the printings. Unless otherwise stated the watermark shows the Crown to right of CA *as seen from the back of the stamp.*

1916 (Sept). *No. 47b surch with T* **12** *by De La Rue.*
55 **9** ½d.on ½d. deep green (R.) . . . . . 75 7[illegible]
a. Small "O" in "ONE" . . . . . 6·50 7·5[illegible]

No. 55a occurs on ten stamps within each sheet of 60.

1918 (18 Mar). *No. 47b optd with T* **12** *locally, from D.L.R. plat[e] but with* "ONE HALF-PENNY" *blanked out.*
56 **9** ½d. deep green (Blk.) . . . . . 2·75 6·[illegible]
w. Wmk Crown to right of CA . . . .

The blanking out of the surcharge was not completely successf[ul] so that it almost always appears as an albino to a greater or less[er] extent.

WAR TAX (14)

1918 (1 June)–**19**. *Nos. 47b and 51a optd with T* **14** *by De La Ru[e].*
57 **9** ½d. deep green . . . . . 15 [illegible]
w. Wmk Crown to right of CA . . . . 50·00
x. Wmk reversed . . . . .
58 3d. purple/*yellow* (R.) (1919) . . . . . 1·50 4·[illegible]

WAR TAX =1½D.= (15)

1½D. Short Fraction Bar (R. 6/4)

1919. *As No. 50aw, but colour changed, surch with T* **15** *by De L[a] Rue.*
59 **9** 1½d.on 2½d. orange (R.) . . . . . 15 [illegible]
a. Short fraction bar . . . . . 8·00 35·[illegible]
b. "C" and "A" missing from wmk . .

No. 59b shows the "C" omitted from one impression with t[he] "A" missing from the next one to the left (as seen from the back [of] the stamp). The "C" is badly distorted in the second watermark.

1920 (1 June). *As No. 59, but without* "WAR TAX".
60 **9** 1½d.on 2½d. orange (Blk.) . . . . . 2·50 4·[illegible]
a. Short fraction bar . . . . . 55·00 70·[illegible]
b. "A" of "CA" missing from wmk
55s/60s Optd "Specimen" *Set of* 6 . . . . . £170

1921–22. Wmk Mult Script CA (sideways*). *Chalk-surfaced pap[er] (6d.).* P 14.
62 **9** ½d. blue-green . . . . . 2·50 15·[illegible]
63 1d. carmine-red . . . . . 2·00 3·[illegible]
w. Wmk Crown to right of CA . . . . — 13·[illegible]
64 1½d. orange . . . . . 3·00 11·[illegible]
65 2d. grey . . . . . 2·75 3·[illegible]
66 2½d. bright blue . . . . . 2·00 8·[illegible]
67 6d. purple . . . . . 2·50 38·[illegible]
69 2s. purple and blue/*blue* (1922) . . . . 32·00 90·[illegible]
70 2s.6d. black and red/*blue* . . . . . 32·00 95·[illegible]
62/70 *Set of* 8 . . . . . 70·00 £2[illegible]
62s/70s Optd "Specimen" *Set of* 8 . . . . . £140

*The normal sideways watermark shows Crown to left of CA, *seen from the back of the stamp.*

The 1½d. has figures of value, in the lower corner and [in] ornamentation below words of value.

16

(Typo D.L.R.)

923 (1 Mar)–**33**. *Chalk-surfaced paper.* P 14.

(a) Wmk Mult Script CA (sideways*).

71 **16** ½d. black and green 1·75 60
72 1d. black and bright violet 2·00 1·75
73 1d. black and scarlet (1933) 9·00 1·00
74 1½d. black and scarlet 2·75 65
75 1½d. black and red-brown (1933) 9·00 70
76 2d. black and grey 1·75 50
77 2½d. black and orange-yellow 1·50 9·00
78 2½d. black and ultramarine (1927) 4·25 2·00
79 3d. black and ultramarine 1·50 12·00
30 3d. black and red/*yellow* (1927) 1·50 1·00
31 4d. black and brown 2·50 5·50
32 6d. black and bright magenta 3·50 7·00
33 1s. black/*emerald* 2·25 2·75
34 2s. black and blue/*blue* 10·00 19·00
35 2s.6d. black and red/*blue* 18·00 19·00
36 3s. black and purple/*yellow* (1927) 3·25 12·00
37 4s. black and red/*emerald* 11·00 22·00
38 5s. black and green/*yellow* (1927) 22·00 48·00

(b) Wmk Mult Crown CA (sideways*).

9 **16** 3s. black and purple/*yellow* 4·00 65·00
0 5s. black and green/*yellow* 9·00 50·00
1 £1 black and purple/*red* £225 £350
1/91 *Set of* 21 £325 £550
1s/91s Optd or Perf (Nos. 73s, 75s) "Specimen" *Set of* 21 £350

*The normal sideways watermark shows Crown to left of CA, *as seen from the back of the stamp.*

Examples of most values are known showing a forged G.P.O. Dominica postmark dated "MY 19 27".

935 (6 May). *Silver Jubilee. As Nos. 91/4 of Antigua.*

2 1d. deep blue and carmine 75 20
f. Diagonal line by turret 38·00
h. Dot by flagstaff 60·00
3 1½d. ultramarine and grey 1·75 1·25
f. Diagonal line by turret 55·00
h. Dot by flagstaff 85·00
4 2½d. brown and deep blue 1·75 2·50
5 1s. slate and purple 1·75 4·00
h. Dot by flagstaff £140
i. Dash by turret £140
2/5 *Set of* 4 5·50 7·00
2s/5s Perf "Specimen" *Set of* 4 85·00

For illustrations of plate varieties see Omnibus section following Zanzibar.

937 (12 May). *Coronation. As Nos. 95/7 of Antigua.* P 11 × 11½.

5 1d. carmine 40 10
7 1½d. yellow-brown 40 10
3 2½d. blue 60 1·50
5/8 *Set of* 3 1·25 1·50
5s/8s Perf "Specimen" *Set of* 3 65·00

17 Fresh Water Lake **18** Layou River

(Recess Waterlow)

938 (15 Aug)–**47**. *T* **17/18** *and similar horiz designs.* Wmk Mult Script CA. P 12½.

99 **17** ½d. brown and green 10 15
00 **18** 1d. grey and scarlet 20 20
01 – 1½d. green and purple 30 70
02 – 2d. carmine and grey-black 50 1·25
03 – 2½d. purple and bright blue 4·00 1·75
a. purple & bright ultramarine (8.42) 20 1·25
04 **18** 3d. olive-green and brown 30 50
04*a* – 3½d. ultramarine and purple (15.10.47) 2·00 2·00
05 **17** 6d. emerald-green and violet 1·75 1·50
05*a* 7d. green and yellow-brown (15.10.47) 2·00 1·50
06 – 1s. violet and olive-green 3·25 1·50
06*a* **18** 2s. slate and purple (15.10.47) 6·00 8·00
07 **17** 2s.6d. black and vermilion 12·00 4·75
08 **18** 5s. light blue and sepia 7·50 8·00
08*a* – 10s. black and brown-orange (15.10.47) 12·00 15·00
9/108*a* *Set of* 14 42·00 42·00

Designs:—1½d., 2½d., 3½d. Picking limes; 2d., 1s., 10s. Boiling Lake.

21 King George VI

(Photo Harrison)

40 (15 Apr)–**42**. Wmk Mult Script CA. *Chalk-surfaced paper.* P 15 × 14.

9 **21** ½d. chocolate 1·00 15
a. Ordinary paper (1942) 10 10
s/109s Perf "Specimen" *Set of* 15 £250

1946 (14 Oct). *Victory. As Nos. 110/11 of Antigua.*

110 1d. carmine 20 10
111 3½d. blue 20 10
110s/11s Perf "Specimen" *Set of* 2 55·00

1948 (1 Dec). *Royal Silver Wedding. As Nos. 112/13 of Antigua.*

112 1d. scarlet 15 10
113 10s. red-brown 12·00 23·00

(New Currency. 100 cents = 1 B.W.I., later East Caribbean dollar)

1949 (10 Oct). *75th Anniv of Universal Postal Union. As Nos. 114/17 of Antigua.*

114 5c. blue 20 15
115 6c. brown 1·25 2·25
116 12c. purple 45 1·25
a. "A" of "CA" missing from wmk — £500
117 24c. olive 30 30
114/17 *Set of* 4 2·00 3·50

1951 (16 Feb). *Inauguration of B.W.I. University College. As Nos. 118/19 of Antigua.*

118 3c. yellow-green and reddish violet 50 1·10
119 12c. deep green and carmine 75 30

22 King George VI

23 Drying Cocoa

(Photo Harrison (½c.). Recess B.W. (others))

1951 (1 July). *T* **22** *and designs as T* **23**. Wmk Mult Script CA. *Chalk-surfaced paper (½c.),* P 15 × 14 (½c.), 13½ × 13 ($2.40), 13 × 13½ (others).

120 ½c. chocolate 10 30
121 1c. black and vermilion 10 30
b. "A" of "CA" missing from wmk £500
c. "JA" for "CA" in wmk £500
122 2c. red-brown and deep green 10 30
a. "C" of "CA" missing from wmk £600
b. "A" of "CA" missing from wmk £600
c. "JA" for "CA" in wmk — £600
123 3c. green and reddish violet 15 1·75
a. "C" of "CA" missing from wmk
c. "JA" for "CA" in wmk £500
124 4c. brown-orange and sepia 70 1·75
a. "C" of "CA" missing from wmk £600
b. "A" of "CA" missing from wmk £600
125 5c. black and carmine 85 30
a. "C" of "CA" missing from wmk £800
b. "A" of "CA" missing from wmk £800
c. "JA" for "CA" in wmk
126 6c. olive and chestnut 90 30
a. "C" of "CA" missing from wmk
b. "A" of "CA" missing from wmk £1000
127 8c. blue-green and blue 90 70
b. "A" of "CA" missing from wmk
128 12c. black and bright green 60 1·25
a. "C" of "CA" missing from wmk £1200
129 14c. blue and violet 95 1·75
a. "C" of "CA" missing from wmk £1200
b. "A" of "CA" missing from wmk † —
c. "JA" for "CA" in wmk £1000
130 24c. reddish violet and rose-carmine 75 30
a. "C" of "CA" missing from wmk £1200
131 48c. bright green and red-orange 3·75 8·00
a. "C" of "CA" missing from wmk £1200
b. "A" of "CA" missing from wmk £1200
c. "JA" for "CA" in wmk
132 60c. carmine and black 3·75 6·00
c. "JA" for "CA" in wmk £800
133 $1.20, emerald and black 4·50 6·00
a. "C" of "CA" missing from wmk £1400
b. "A" of "CA" missing from wmk £1400
134 $2.40, orange and black 23·00 38·00
120/34 *Set of* 15 32·00 60·00

Designs: *Horiz*—2c., 60c. Making Carib baskets; 3c., 48c. Lime plantation; 4c. Picking oranges; 5c. Bananas; 6c. Botanical Gardens; 8c. Drying vanilla beans; 12c., $1.20, Fresh Water Lake; 14c. Layou River; 24c. Boiling Lake. *Vert*—$2.40, Picking oranges.

Examples of Nos. 121b, 122b, 124b, 125b, 126b, 129b, 131b and 133b show traces of the *left leg* of the "A", *as seen from the back of the stamp.*

Nos. 121c, 122c, 123c, 125c, 129c, 131c and 132c may represent an attempt to repair the missing "C" variety.

NEW
CONSTITUTION
1951
(34)

1951 (15 Oct). *New Constitution. Nos. 123, 125, 127 and 129 optd with T* **34** *by B.W.*

135 3c. green and reddish violet 15 70
a. "C" of "CA" missing from wmk £600 £650
136 5c. black and carmine 15 1·00
a. "JA" for "CA" in wmk £700
137 8c. blue-green and blue (R.) 15 15
a. "JA" for "CA" in wmk
138 14c. blue and violet (R.) 65 20
b. "A" of "CA" missing from wmk £900
135/8 *Set of* 4 1·00 1·90

POSTAL FISCALS

REVENUE (R 1) **Revenue** (R 2)

1879–88. *Optd with Type* R **1** *by De La Rue.* P 14.

(a) Wmk Crown CC.

R1 **1** 1d. lilac 80·00 8·00
a. Bisected vert (½d.) on cover † —
R2 6d. green 3·00 24·00
w. Wmk inverted £120
R3 1s. magenta 9·00 16·00
111/3 *Set of* 3 85·00 42·00

(b) Wmk Crown CA.

R4 **1** 1d. lilac (1888) 4·75 4·25

1888. *Optd with Type* R **2** *locally.* Wmk Crown CA.

R6 **1** 1d. rose £250 70·00

East Africa (G.E.A.) *see* Tanganyika

East Africa and Uganda Protectorates *see* Kenya, Uganda and Tanganyika

Egypt

TURKISH SUZERAINTY

In 1517 Sultan Selim I added Egypt to the Ottoman Empire, and it stayed more or less under Turkish rule until 1805, when Mohammed Ali became governor. He established a dynasty of governors owing nominal allegiance to the Sultan of Turkey until 1914.

Khedive Ismail

18 January 1863–26 June 1879

He obtained the honorific title of Khedive (viceroy) from the Sultan in 1867.

The operations of British Consular Post Offices in Egypt date from August 1839 when the first packet agency, at Alexandria, was opened. Further agencies at Suez (1 January 1847) and Cairo (1856) followed. Alexandria became a post office on 17 March 1858 with Cairo following on 23 February 1859 and Suez on 1 January 1861.

Great Britain stamps were issued to Alexandria in March 1858 and to the other two offices in August/September 1859. "B O1" cancellations as Type **2** were issued to both Alexandria and Cairo. Cancellations with this number as Types **8**, **12** and **15** were only used at Alexandria.

Before 1 July 1873 combination covers showing Great Britain stamps and the first issue of Egypt exist with the latter paying the internal postage to the British Post Office at Alexandria.

The Cairo office closed on 30 June 1873 and the other two on 30 March 1878. Suez continued to function as a transit office for a number of years.

Stamps issued after 1877 can be found with the Egyptian cancellation "Port Said", but these are on letters posted from British ships.

For cancellations used during the 1882 and 1885 campaigns, see BRITISH FORCES IN EGYPT at the end of the listing.

For illustrations of the handstamp and postmark types see BRITISH POST OFFICES ABROAD notes following GREAT BRITAIN.

ALEXANDRIA

CROWNED-CIRCLE HANDSTAMPS

CC1 CC **1b** ALEXANDRIA (R.) (13.5.1843) *Price on cover* £2750

Stamps of GREAT BRITAIN *cancelled* "B 01" *as in Types* **2** *(also used at Cairo),* **8**, **12** or **15**.

1858 (Mar)–**78**.

Z 1 ½d. rose-red (1870–79) *From* 19·00
Plate Nos. 5, 6, 8, 10, 13, 14, 15, 19, 20.
Z 2 1d. rose-red (1857) 7·00
Z 3 1d. rose-red (1861) (Alph IV)
Z 4 1d. rose-red (1864–79) *From* 9·50
Plate Nos. 71, 72, 73, 74, 76, 78, 79, 80, 81, 82, 83, 84, 85, 86, 87, 88, 89, 90, 91, 92, 93, 94, 95, 96, 97, 98, 99, 101, 102, 103, 104, 106, 107, 108, 109, 110, 111, 112, 113, 114, 115, 117, 118, 119, 120, 121, 122, 123, 124, 125, 127, 129, 130, 131, 133, 134, 136, 137, 138, 139, 140, 142, 143, 144, 145, 146, 147, 148, 149, 150, 152, 154, 156, 157, 158, 159, 160, 162, 163, 165, 168, 169, 170, 171, 172, 174, 175, 177, 179, 180, 181, 182, 183, 185, 188, 190, 198, 200, 203, 206, 210, 220.

Z 5 2d. blue (1858–69) . . . . From 9·50
Plate Nos. 7, 8, 9, 13, 14, 15.
Z 6 2½d. rosy mauve (1875) (blued *paper*) . . From 60·00
Plate Nos. 1, 2.
Z 7 2½d. rosy mauve (1875–6) (Plate Nos. 1, 2, 3) . . . 29·00
Z 8 2½d. rosy mauve (*Error of Lettering*) £1300
Z 9 2½d. rosy mauve (1876–79) . . . . . . From 25·00
Plate Nos. 3, 4, 5, 6, 7, 8, 9.
Z10 3d. carmine-rose (1862) £120
Z11 3d. rose (1865) (Plate No. 4) . . . . 60·00
Z12 3d. rose (1867–73) . . . . From 23·00
Plate Nos. 4, 5, 6, 7, 8, 9.
Z13 3d. rose (1873–76) . . . . From 21·00
Plate Nos. 11, 12, 14, 15, 16, 18, 19.
Z15 4d. rose (1857) . . . . 42·00
Z16 4d. red (1862) (Plate Nos. 3, 4) . . . . From 42·00
Z17 4d. vermilion (1865–73) . . . . 23·00
Plate Nos. 7, 8, 9, 10, 11, 12, 13, 14
Z18 4d. vermilion (1876) (Plate No. 15) £160
Z19 4d. sage-green (1877) (Plate No. 15) £110
Z20 6d. lilac (1856) . . . . 48·00
Z21 6d. lilac (1862) (Plate Nos. 3, 4) . . . From 42·00
Z22 6d. lilac (1865–67) (Plate Nos. 5, 6) . . . From 32·00
Z23 6d. lilac (1867) (Plate No. 6) . . . . 42·00
Z24 6d. violet (1867–70) (Plate Nos. 6, 8, 9) From 30·00
a. Imperf (Plate No. 8) £1200
Z25 6d. buff (1872–73) (Plate Nos. 11, 12) . . From 55·00
Z26 6d. chestnut (1872) (Plate No. 11) . . . . . . 27·00
Z27 6d. grey (1873) (Plate No. 12) . . . . 80·00
Z28 6d. grey (1874–76) (Plate Nos. 13, 14, 15) . . . . From 23·00
Z29 9d. straw (1862) £150
Z30 9d. bistre (1862) . . . .
Z31 9d. straw (1865) . . . .
Z32 9d. straw (1867) . . . .
Z33 10d. red-brown (1867) £130
Z34 1s. green (1856) £120
Z35 1s. green (1862) . . . . 75·00
Z36 1s. green (1862) ("K" *variety*) . . . .
Z37 1s. green (1865) (Plate No. 4) . . . . 35·00
Z38 1s. green (1867–73) (Plate Nos. 4, 5, 6, 7) . . . . From 15·00
Z39 1s. green (1873–77) . . . . From 27·00
Plate Nos. 8, 9, 10, 11, 12, 13.
Z40 2s. blue (1867) £100
Z41 5s. rose (1867–74) (Plate Nos. 1, 2) . . . From £250

CAIRO

CROWNED-CIRCLE HANDSTAMPS

CC2 CC **6** CAIRO (R. or Blk.) (23.3.1859)
Price on cover £3750

Cancellation "B 01" as Type **2** (also issued at Alexandria) was used to cancel mail franked with Great Britain stamps between April 1859 and June 1873.

SUEZ

CROWNED-CIRCLE HANDSTAMPS

CC3 CC **1** SUEZ (B. or Black) (16.7.1847)
Price on cover £4250

Stamps of GREAT BRTAIN *cancelled* "B 02" *as in Types* **2** *and* **8**, *or with circular date stamp as Type* **5**.

1859 (Aug)–**78**.
Z42 ½d. rose-red (1870–79) . . . . 28·00
Plate Nos. 6, 10, 11, 12, 13, 14.
Z43 1d. rose-red (1857) . . . . 9·00
Z44 1d. rose-red (1864–79) . . . . . . From 11·00
Plate Nos. 73, 74, 78, 79, 80, 81, 83, 84, 86, 87, 90, 91, 93, 94, 96, 97, 100, 101, 106, 107, 108, 110, 113, 118, 119, 120, 121, 122, 123, 124, 125, 129, 130, 131, 134, 136, 137, 138, 140, 142, 143, 144, 145, 147, 148, 149, 150, 151, 152, 153, 154, 156, 158, 159, 160, 161, 162, 163, 164, 165, 166, 167, 168, 170, 174, 176, 177, 178, 179, 180, 181, 182, 184, 185, 186, 187, 189, 190, 205.
Z45 2d. blue (1858–69) . . . . From 14·00
Plate Nos. 8, 9, 13, 14, 15.
Z46 2½d. rosy mauve (1875) (blued *paper*) . . From 60·00
Plate Nos. 1, 2, 3.
Z47 2½d. rosy mauve (1875–76) . . . . . . From 32·00
Plate Nos. 1, 2, 3.
Z48 2½d. rosy mauve (*Error of Lettering*) £1300
Z49 2½d. rosy mauve (1876–79) . . . . . . From 24·00
Plate Nos. 3, 4, 5, 6, 7, 8, 9, 10.
Z50 3d. carmine-rose (1862) £130
Z51 3d. rose (1865) (Plate No. 4) . . . . 70·00
Z52 3d. rose (1867–73) (Plate Nos. 5, 6, 7, 8, 10) . . .
Z53 3d. rose (1873–76) (Plate Nos. 12, 16) . . From 24·00
Z54 4d. rose (1857) . . . . 50·00
Z55 4d. red (1862) (Plate Nos. 3, 4) . . . . From 45·00
Z56 4d. vermilion (1865–73) . . . . . . From 27·00
Plate Nos. 7, 8, 9, 10, 11, 12, 13, 14.
Z57 4d. vermilion (1876) (Plate No. 15) . . . . . .
Z58 4d. sage-green (1877) (Plate No. 15) £120
Z59 6d. lilac (1856) . . . . 48·00
Z60 6d. lilac (1862) (Plate Nos. 3, 4) . . . From 42·00
Z61 6d. lilac (1865–67) (Plate Nos. 5, 6) . . . From 35·00
Z62 6d. lilac (1867) (Plate No. 6) . . . . 45·00
Z63 6d. violet (1867–70) (Plate Nos. 6, 8, 9) From 35·00
Z64 6d. buff (1872–73) (Plate Nos. 11, 12) . . From 60·00
Z65 6d. pale chestnut (Plate No.12) (1872) £2250
Z66 6d. chestnut (1872) (Plate No. 11) . . . . . . 30·00
Z67 6d. grey (1873) (Plate No. 12) . . . . 90·00
Z68 6d. grey (1874–76) . . . . From 25·00
Plate Nos, 13, 14, 15, 16.
Z69 8d. orange (1876) . . . .
Z70 9d. straw (1862) £160
a. Thick paper . . . .
Z71 9d. bistre (1862) . . . .
Z72 9d. straw (1867) . . . .
Z73 10d. red-brown (1867) £175
Z74 1s. green (1856) £140
Z75 1s. green (1862) . . . . 80·00
Z76 1s. green (1862) ("K" *variety*) . . . .
Z77 1s. green (1865) (Plate No. 4) . . . . 45·00
Z78 1s. green (1867–73) (Plate Nos. 4, 5, 6, 7) . . . . From 18·00
Z79 1s. green (1873–77) . . . . From 27·00
Plate Nos. 8, 9, 10, 11, 12.
Z80 2s. blue (1867) £150
Z81 5s. rose (1867–74) (Plate Nos. 1, 2) . . . From £275

PRICES FOR STAMPS ON COVER

Nos.	1/41	*from* × 8
Nos.	42/3	*from* × 30
Nos.	44/83	*from* × 5
Nos.	84/97	*from* × 2
Nos.	D57/70	*from* × 12
Nos.	D71/86	*from* × 5
Nos.	D84/103	*from* × 2
Nos.	O64/87	*from* × 5
Nos.	O88/101	*from* × 2

(Currency: 40 paras = 1 piastre)

1

2

(3)

(Typo (1pi) or litho (others) Pellas Brothers, Genoa. Inscr (T **3**) applied typo (1, 2pi.) or litho (others))

1866 (1 Jan). *Various designs as T* **1** *with black inscriptions as T* **3**. *The lowest group of characters indicates the value. 1pi.* no wmk, others W **2** (inverted). P 12½.
1 5pa. grey . . . . 42·00 27·00
a. Greenish grey . . . . 42·00 27·00
b. Imperf (pair) £180
c. Imperf between (pair) £300
d. Perf 12½ × 13 and compound . . . . 50·00 48·00
e. Perf 13 . . . . £250 £300
w. Wmk upright £250 £200
2 10pa. brown . . . . 55·00 29·00
a. Imperf (pair) £160
b. Imperf between (pair) £350
c. Perf 12½ × 13 and compound . . . . 80·00 48·00
d. Perf 12½ × 15 . . . . £250 £275
e. Perf 13 . . . . £170 £190
w. Wmk upright . . . . 65·00 29·00
3 20pa. pale blue . . . . 70·00 30·00
a. Greenish blue . . . . 70·00 30·00
b. Imperf (pair) £240
c. Imperf between (pair) £400
d. Perf 12½ × 13 and compound . . . . £100 80·00
e. Perf 13 . . . . £425 £250
w. Wmk upright . . . . 70·00 29·00
4 1pi. claret . . . . 60·00 4·75
a. Imperf (pair) £100
b. Imperf between (pair) £400
c. Perf 12½ × 13 and compound . . . . 90·00 20·00
d. Perf 13 . . . . £300 £190
5 2pi. yellow . . . . 90·00 42·00
a. Orange-yellow . . . . 90·00 42·00
b. Imperf (pair) . . . .
c. Imperf between (pair) £350 £350
d. Bisected diag (1pi.) (on cover) . . . . † £2250
e. Perf 12½ × 13 and compound . . . . £120 48·00
f. Perf 12½ × 15 . . . . £130
w. Wmk upright . . . . 90·00 42·00
6 5pi. rose £250 £170
a. Imperf (pair) . . . .
b. Imperf between (pair) £1000
c. Perf 12½ × 13 and compound £275
d. Error. Inscr 10pi., perf 12½ × 15 . . . £900 £750
da. Imperf £500
w. Wmk upright £250 £170
7 10pi. slate £275 £250
a. Imperf (pair) . . . .
b. Imperf between (pair) £2000
c. Perf 12½ × 13 and compound £425 £425
d. Perf 13 . . . . £1600
w. Wmk upright £275 £250

The 2pi. bisected was authorised for use between 16 and 31 July 1867 at Alexandria or Cairo.

Stamps perforated 12½, 12½ × 13 and compound, and 13 occur in the same sheets with the 13 gauge usually used on the top, left-hand, right-hand or bottom rows. Each sheet of 200 contained one stamp perforated 13 all round, two 13 on three sides, one 13 on two adjacent sides, eighteen 13 × 12½, eight 12½ × 13, eight 13 on one side and eighteen 13 at top or bottom. So many sheets were received imperforate or part-perforated that some stock was passed to V. Penasson of Alexandria who applied the 12½ × 15 gauge.

The two halves of each background differ in minor details of the ornamentation. All values can be found with either half at the top.

Proofs of all values exist on smooth paper, without watermark. Beware of forgeries.

All values also exist with the watermark reversed (*same price as upright*) or inverted and reversed (*same price as inverted*).

4

5

6

(Des F. Hoff. Litho V. Penasson, Alexandria)

1867 (1 Aug)–**71**. W **6** (*impressed on reverse*). P 15 × 12½.
11 **4** 5pa. orange-yellow . . . . 27·00 8·0
a. Imperf (pair) . . . .
b. Imperf between (horiz pair) . . . £170
w. Wmk inverted £250 £20
12 10pa. dull lilac . . . . 75·00 9·0
b. Bright mauve (7.69) . . . . . . 55·00 9·0
ba. Bisected diag (5pa.) (on piece) (17.11.71) . . . . † £75
w. Wmk inverted £300 £20
13 20pa. deep blue-green . . . . £100 13·0
a. Pale blue-green . . . . £100 13·0
b. Yellowish green (7.69) . . . . . £110 12·0
w. Wmk inverted £350 £20
14 **5** 1pi. dull rose-red *to* rose . . . . . 14·00 1·0
a. Lake . . . . £120 32·0
b. Imperf (pair) £100
c. Imperf between (horiz pair) . . . £170
d. Bisected diag (20pa.) (on piece) . . † £75
e. Rouletted . . . . 55·00
w. Wmk inverted . . . . 50·00 30·0
15 2pi. bright blue . . . . £110 16·0
a. Pale blue . . . . £110 16·0
b. Imperf (pair) . . . .
c. Imperf between (pair) £425
d. Bisected diag (1pi.) (on cover) . . . † —
e. Perf 12½ £225
w. Wmk inverted £400 £30
16 5pi. brown £300 £18
w. Wmk inverted £500 £30

Each value was engraved four times, the resulting blocks bein used to form sheets of 200. There are therefore four types showin minor variations for each value.

No. 12ba was used on newspapers from Alexandria betwee 17 November 1871 and 20 January 1872.

Stamps printed both sides, both imperf and perf, come fror printer's waste. The 1pi. rose without watermark is a proof.

7

8 (Side panels transposed and inverted)

8*a* (I)

8*a* (II)

WATERMARK 8*a*. There are two types of this watermark whic as they are not always easy to distinguish, we do not list separatel Type II is slightly wider and less deep and the crescent is flatter tha in Type I. The width measurement for Type I is generally abo 14 mm and for Type II about 15 mm, but there is some variatic within the sheets for both types.

Nos. 26/43, 45/7*a*, 49/*a*, 50/1 and 57 come with Type I on Nos. 44*a*, 48/*a*, 52, 54*b*, 73/7 and 78 exist with both types watermark (but No. 83 and official overprints on these stamps st require research); our prices are generally for Type II. Oth watermarked issues between 1888 and 1907 have Type watermarks only.

1872 (1 Jan)–**75**. *T* **7** *(the so-called "Penasson" printing*). Thi opaque paper.* W **8*a***. P 12½ × 13½.

A. LITHOGRAPHED.

26 **7** 20pa. blue (*shades*) . . . . £120 50·
a. Imperf (pair) . . . .
b. Imperf between (pair) . . . . . . — £20
c. Perf 13½ . . . . £200 55·
w. Wmk inverted . . . . £200 75·
27 1pi. red (*shades*) . . . . £225 10·
a. Perf 13½ . . . . £500 23·
w. Wmk inverted . . . . £600 30·

B. TYPOGRAPHED.

28 **7** 5pa. brown (*shades*) . . . . 7·00 4·
a. Perf 13½ . . . . 24·00 9·
w. Wmk inverted . . . . £100 60·
29 10pa. mauve . . . . 6·00 3·
a. Perf 13½ . . . . 6·00 3·
w. Wmk inverted . . . . 40·00 25·
30 20pa. blue (*shades*) . . . . 55·00 3·
a. Perf 13½ . . . . 80·00 20·
w. Wmk inverted . . . . 50·00 30·
31 1pi. rose-red . . . . 50·00 1·
a. Bisected (20pa.) (on piece with No. 31) (7.75) . . . . † £6
b. Perf 13½ . . . . 80·00 3·
w. Wmk inverted . . . . 38·00 25·
32 2pi. chrome-yellow . . . . 85·00 4·
a. Bisected (1pi.) (on piece) (7.74) . . — £6
b. Perf 13½ . . . . 18·00 4·
w. Wmk inverted . . . .
33 2½pi. violet . . . . 80·00 16
a. Perf 13½ £700 £1
w. Wmk inverted . . . . 90·00 30
34 5pi. yellow-green . . . . £180 32·
a. *Tête-bêche* (pair) . . . .
b. Perf 13½ . . . . £275 55·
w. Wmk inverted . . . . £200 90·

*It is now accepted that stamps in both processes were printed by the Goverment Printing Works at Bûlaq, Cairo, although Penasson may have been involved in the production of the dies.

The lithographed and typographed stamps each show the characteristic differences between these two processes:—

The typographed stamps show the coloured lines of the design impressed into the paper and an accumulation of ink along the margins of the lines.

The lithographed stamps are essentially flat in appearance, without the heaping of the ink. Many of the 20pa. show evidence of retouching, particularly of the outer frame lines.

The 1p. bisected was used at Gedda, on 5 July 1875, or Scio, and the 2pi. vertically bisected at Gallipolli or Scio.

See also footnote below No. 41

1874 (Nov)–**75**. *Typo from new stereos at Bûlaq, on thinner paper.* W **8**a. P 12½.

35 **8** 5pa. brown (3.75) . . . 8·50 3·75
a. *Tête-bêche* (vert pair) . . . 35·00 35·00
b. *Tête-bêche* (horiz pair) . . . £275 £300
c. Imperf (pair)
d. Imperf between (pair) . . . £100 £120
ew. Wmk inverted . . . 8·50 3·75
f. Perf 13½ × 12½ . . . 14·00 3·75
fa. *Tête-bêche* (vert pair) . . . 60·00 60·00
fb. *Tête-bêche* (horiz pair) . . . £325 £350
fw. Wmk inverted . . . 14·00 3·75
36 **7** 10pa. grey-lilac (*shades*) (8.75) . . . 8·50 2·75
a. *Tête-bêche* (vert pair) . . . £140 £160
b. *Tête-bêche* (horiz pair)
c. Imperf (pair)
dw. Wmk inverted
e. Perf 13½ × 12½ . . . 20·00 3·25
ea. *Tête-bêche* (vert pair) . . . £140 £160
eb. *Tête-bêche* (horiz pair)
ew. Wmk inverted . . . 20·00 3·50
37 20pa. grey-blue (*shades*) (2.75) . . . 90·00 3·00
b. Bisected diag (10pa.) (on cover) . . . † —
cw. Wmk inverted
d. Perf 13½ × 12½ . . . 9·00 2·50
da. Imperf between (pair) . . . £300
38 1pi. red (*shades*) (4.75) . . . 7·50 65
a. *Tête-bêche* (vert pair) . . . 90·00 90·00
b. *Tête-bêche* (horiz pair) . . . £300 £300
c. Imperf (pair)
d. Imperf between (pair) . . . — 80·00
ew. Wmk inverted . . . 9·50 1·50
f. Perf 13½ × 12½ . . . 70·00 1·25
fa. *Tête-bêche* (vert pair) . . . £350 £350
fb. *Tête-bêche* (horiz pair)
fw. Wmk inverted . . . 80·00 7·50
39 2pi. yellow (12.74) . . . 75·00 3·00
a. *Tête-bêche* (pair) . . . £400 £400
bw. Wmk inverted . . . 90·00 7·50
c. Perf 13½ × 12½ . . . 5·50 6·00
ca. *Tête-bêche* (pair) . . . £400 £400
cb. Bisected diag (1pi.) (on cover) (4.75) . . . † £2500
cw. Wmk inverted . . . 7·50 6·50
d. Perf 12½ × 13½ . . . 65·00 15·00
da. *Tête-bêche* (pair) . . . £850
dw. Wmk inverted . . . 80·00 18·00
40 2½pi. violet . . . 8·50 5·00
a. *Tête-bêche* (pair) . . . £350
bw. Wmk inverted . . . 12·00 7·50
c. perf 12½ × 13½ . . . 55·00 19·00
ca. *Tête-bêche* (pair) . . . £1000 90·00
cw. Wmk inverted . . . 50·00 25·00
41 5pi. green . . . 55·00 19·00
a. Imperf (pair) . . . † —
bw. Wmk inverted . . . £100 50·00
c. Perf 12½ × 13½ . . . £300 £275

The 2pi. bisected was used at Gedda and are all postmarked 3 April.

The 1872 printings have a thick line of colour in the top margin of the sheet and the other margins are all plain, an exception being the 5pa., which on the majority of the sheets has the line at the right-hand side of the sheet. The 1874–75 printings have a wide fancy border all round every sheet.

The 1872 printings are on thick opaque paper, with the impressions sharp and clear. The 1874–75 printings are on thinner paper, often semi-transparent and oily in appearance, and having the impressions very blurred and badly printed. These are only general distinctions and there are a number of exceptions.

The majority of the 1874–75 stamps have blind or defective perforations, while the 1872 stamps have clean-cut perfs.

The two printings of the 5pa. to 1pi. values can be identified by their perforation gauges, which are always different; the 5pa. also differs in the side panels (Types **7** and **8**). Only the perf 12½ × 13½ varieties of the three higher values may need to be distinguished. As well as the general points noted above the following features are also helpful:

2pi. In the 1872 issue the left-hand Arabic character in the top inscription is one complete shape, resembling an inverted "V" with a horizontal line on top. In the 1874 issue the character has three separate components, a line with two dots below.

2½ pi. There is a distinct thinning of the frame line in the top right-hand corner of the 1872 issue. This sometimes takes the form of a short white line within the frame.

5pi. In the 1872 issue the top frame line is split for its entire length; in the 1874 issue the line is solid for all or most of its length. The 1872 printing always has a white dot above the "P" of "PIASTRE"; this dot appears on only a few positions of the 1874 printing.

There seem to be many different compositions of the sheets containing the *tête-bêche* varieties, settings being known with 1, 3, and 10 inverted stamps in various sheets. Sheets of the 5pa. are known with 9 of the 20 horizontal rows inverted, giving vertical *tête-bêche* pairs; four stamps were inverted within their row giving four horizontal *tête-bêche* pairs.

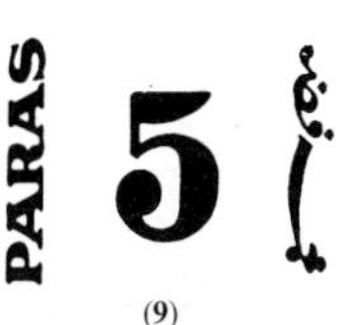
(9)

1878 (Dec). *No. 40 surch as T* **9** *at Bûlaq.* P 12½.

42 **7** 5pa.on 2½pi. violet . . . 6·00 6·00
a. Surch inverted . . . 70·00 70·00
b. *Tête-bêche* (pair) . . . £3500
dw. Wmk inverted . . . 7·50 7·50
e. Perf 12½ × 13½ . . . 6·50 8·00
ea. Surch inverted . . . £140 £140
eb. *Tête-bêche* (pair)
ew. Wmk inverted . . . 8·00 10·00
43 10pa.on 2½ pi. violet . . . 11·00 10·00
a. Surch inverted . . . 75·00 75·00
b. *Tête-bêche* (pair) . . . £1500
dw. Wmk inverted . . . 15·00 15·00
e. Perf 12½ × 13½ . . . 15·00 15·00
ea. Surch inverted . . . £110 £110
eb. *Tête-bêche* (pair) . . . £1500
ew. Wmk inverted . . . 25·00 25·00

10 11 12
13 14 15

(Typo De La Rue)

1879 (1 Apr). *Ordinary paper.* W **8**a (*inverted on* 10*pa.*). P 14.

44 **10** 5pa. deep brown . . . 2·00 30
a. Pale brown . . . 2·00 30
w. Wmk inverted . . . £120 £100
45 **11** 10pa. reddish lilac . . . 50·00 3·00
46 **12** 20pa. pale blue . . . 60·00 1·75
w. Wmk inverted . . . 90·00 15·00
47 **13** 1pi. rose . . . 26·00 20
a. Pale rose . . . 26·00 20
w. Wmk inverted . . . 60·00 10·00
48 **14** 2pi. orange . . . 30·00 50
a. Orange-yellow . . . 28·00 80
w. Wmk inverted . . . 35·00 2·00
49 **15** 5pi. green . . . 55·00 11·00
a. Blue-green . . . 55·00 10·00
w. Wmk inverted . . . 50·00 11·00

See also Nos. 50/6.

Khedive Tewfik

26 June 1879–7 January 1892

British troops were landed in Egypt in 1882 to secure the Suez Canal against a nationalist movement led by Arab Pasha. Arabi was defeated at Tel-el-Kebir and British troops remained in Egypt until 1954. A British resident and consul-general advised the Khedive. Holders of this post were Sir Evelyn Baring (Lord Cromer), 1883–1907; Sir Eldon Gorst, 1907–11; and Lord Kitchener, 1911–14.

1881–**1902**. *Colours changed. Ordinary paper.* W **8**a (*inverted on* No. 50). P 14.

50 **11** 10pa. claret (1.81) . . . 50·00 7·00
51 10pa. bluish grey (25.1.82) . . . 9·00 1·75
w. Wmk inverted . . . 40·00 3·00
52 10pa. green (15.12.84) . . . 1·75 1·00
w. Wmk inverted . . . 20·00 3·00
53 **12** 20pa. rose-carmine (15.12.84) . . . 14·00 55
a. Bright rose . . . 14·00 50
w. Wmk inverted . . . 35·00 7·00
54 **13** 1pi. blue (15.12.84) . . . 5·50 20
a. Deep ultramarine . . . 6·50 20
b. Pale ultramarine . . . 4·50 20
cw. Wmk inverted . . . 26·00 10·00
d. Chalk-surfaced paper. *Ultramarine* (1902) . . . 2·50 10
da. Blue . . . 2·50 10
dw. Wmk inverted . . . 75·00 40·00
55 **14** 2pi. orange-brown (1.8.93) . . . 12·00 30
aw. Wmk inverted . . . 80·00 40·00
b. Chalk-surfaced paper (1902) . . . 12·00 10
ba. Orange . . . 23·00 1·00
bw. Wmk inverted . . . — 30·00
56 **15** 5pi. pale grey (15.12.84) . . . 13·00 50
a. Slate . . . 11·00 50
bw. Wmk inverted
c. Chalk-surfaced paper. *Slate-grey* (1902) . . . 16·00 15

(17)

1884 (1 Feb). *Surch with T* **17** *at Bûlaq.*

57 **15** 20pa.on 5pi. green . . . 7·00 1·25
a. Surch inverted . . . 65·00 60·00
w. Wmk inverted . . . 50·00 30·00

(New Currency: 1000 milliemes = 100 piastres = £1 Egyptian)

18 19 20

21

22

1888 (1 Jan)–**1909**. *Ordinary paper.* W **8**a. P 14.

58 **18** 1m. pale brown . . . 2·00 10
a. Deep brown . . . 2·50 10
bw. Wmk inverted . . . 25·00 4·00
c. Chalk-surfaced paper. *Pale brown* (1902) . . . 2·25 10
ca. Deep brown . . . 2·25 10
cw. Wmk inverted . . . 40·00 5·00
59 **19** 2m. blue-green . . . 1·25 10
a. Green . . . 1·25 10
bw. Wmk inverted . . . 40·00 5·00
c. Chalk-surfaced paper. *Green* (1902) . . . 1·00 10
cw. Wmk inverted . . . 40·00 5·00
60 **20** 3m. maroon (1.1.92) . . . 3·00 1·00
61 3m. yellow (1.8.93) . . . 4·50 50
a. Orange-yellow . . . 3·75 15
bw. Wmk inverted . . . 45·00 15·00
c. Chalk-surfaced paper. *Orange-yellow* (1902) . . . 2·25 10
cw. Wmk inverted . . . 75·00 30·00
62 **21** 4m. verm (*chalk-surfaced paper*) (1906) . . . 3·00 10
a. Bisected (2m.) (on cover) (11.09) . . . † —
63 5m. rose-carmine . . . 3·25 10
a. Bright rose . . . 3·25 10
b. Aniline rose . . . 4·25 10
cw. Wmk inverted
d. Chalk-surfaced paper. *Rose* (1902) . . . 2·25 10
da. Deep aniline rose . . . 4·00 20
64 **22** 10p. mauve (1.1.89) . . . 15·00 80
a. Aniline mauve . . . 18·00 80
bw. Wmk inverted
c. Chalk-surfaced paper. *Mauve* (1902) . . . 22·00 50

No. 62a was used at Gizira in conjunction with the 1m. value and the Official, No. O64.

No. 63d exists in coils constructed from normal sheets.

Kedive Abbas Hilmi

7 January 1892–19 December 1914

A set of three values, in a common design showing Cleopatra and a Nile boat, was prepared in 1895 for the Nile Winter Fête, but not issued. Examples survive from the De La Rue archives.

29 Nile Feluccas

30 Cleopatra from Temple of Dendera

31 Ras-el-Tin Palace, Alexandria

35 Archway of Ptolemy III, Karnak

37 Rock Temple of Abu Simbel

(Typo D.L.R.)

1914 (8 Jan). W **8**a. P 13½ × 14 (1m. to 10m.) or 14 (20m. to 200m.).

73 **29** 1m. sepia . . . 1·25 40
74 **30** 2m. green . . . 2·00 20
w. Wmk inverted
75 **31** 3m. yellow-orange . . . 1·50 35
a. Double impression
w. Wmk inverted . . . — 3·00
76 – 4m. vermilion . . . 2·75 65
w. Wmk inverted . . . — 1·75
77 – 5m. lake . . . 3·00 10
a. Wmk sideways star to right* (booklets) . . . 10·00 22·00
aw. Wmk sideways star to left . . . 10·00 22·00
w. Wmk inverted . . . 15·00 10·00
78 – 10m. dull blue . . . 4·25 10
w. Wmk inverted . . . — 15·00
79 **35** 20m. olive . . . 6·50 30
w. Wmk inverted . . . — 6·00
80 – 50m. purple . . . 13·00 40
w. Wmk inverted . . . — 50·00
81 **37** 100m. slate . . . 13·00 60
82 – 200m. maroon . . . 26·00 3·50
73/82 *Set of* 10 . . . 65·00 6·00

Designs: *As T* **29**—4m. Pyramids at Giza; 5m. Sphinx; 10m. Colossi of Amenophis III at Thebes. *As T* **35**—50c. Cairo Citadel; 200m. Aswân Dam.

*The normal sideways watermark shows the star to the right of the crescent, *as seen from the back of the stamp.*

All the above exist imperforate, but imperforate stamps without watermark are proofs.

See also Nos. 84/95.

BRITISH PROTECTORATE

On 18 December 1914, after war with Turkey had begun, Egypt was declared to be a British protectorate. Abbas Hilmi was deposed, and his uncle, Hussein Kamil, was proclaimed Sultan of Egypt.

Sultan Hussain Kamil

19 December 1914–9 October 1917

(39)

1915 (15 Oct). *No. 75 surch with T* **39**, *at Blâq.*
83 **31** 2m.on 3m. yellow-orange . . . . . . 55 2·00
a. Surch inverted £200 £200
b. Surch double, one albino £120
w. Wmk inverted . . . .

Sultan Ahmed Fuad

9 October 1917–15 March 1922

40 (A) (B)

41 Statue of Rameses II, Luxor **42**

(Typo Harrison)

1921–22. *As Nos. 73/82 and new designs (15m.).* W **40**. P 14 (20, 50, 100m.) or 13½ × 14 (others).
84 **29** 1m. sepia (A) . . . . 1·50 2·00
a. Two dots omitted (B) (R. 10/10) . . . . . 35·00 45·00
w. Wmk inverted . . . . 10·00 7·50
85 **30** 2m. green . . . . 4·00 3·75
a. Imperf between (pair) . . . .
w. Wmk inverted . . . . 15·00 10·00
86 2m. vermilion (1922) . . . . . . 3·50 65
w. Wmk inverted . . . . 15·00 10·00
87 **31** 3m. yellow-orange . . . . . . 4·50 2·00
w. Wmk inverted . . . . 16·00 10·00
88 – 4m. green (1922) . . . . . . 5·00 6·50
w. Wmk inverted . . . . — 10·00
89 – 5m. lake (1.21) . . . . 4·00 10
a. Imperf between (pair) . . . .
w. Wmk inverted . . . . 15·00 10·00
90 – 5m. pink (11.21) . . . . 4·00 10
w. Wmk inverted . . . . 15·00 10·00
91 – 10m. dull blue . . . . 4·00 20
w. Wmk inverted . . . . — 10·00
92 – 10m. lake (9.22) . . . . 1·75 30
w. Wmk inverted . . . . — 10·00
93 **41** 15m. indigo (3.22) . . . . . . 4·00 15
w. Wmk inverted . . . . — 8·00
94 **42** 15m. indigo . . . . 22·00 3·00
w. Wmk inverted . . . . 24·00 10·00
95 **35** 20m. olive . . . . 9·50 30
w. Wmk inverted . . . . 20·00 10·00
96 – 50m. purple . . . . 10·00 1·25
w. Wink inverted . . . . 18·00 12·00
97 **37** 100m. slate (1922) . . . . . . 70·00 7·50
84/97 *Set of* 13 . . . . £110 21·00

Type **42** was printed first; but because the Arabic inscription at right was felt to be unsuitable the stamps were withheld and the corrected Type **41** printed and issued. Type **42** was released later.

STAMP BOOKLETS

1903 (1 Jan). *Black on pink cover inscr* "Egyptian Post Office" *in English and French. Stapled.*
SB1 121m. booklet containing twenty-four 5m. (No. 63c) in blocks of 6 . . . . £2000
Price reduced to 120m. from 1 July 1911.

1903 (1 July). *Black on blue cover inscr* "Egyptian Post Office" *in English and French. Stapled.*
SB2 73m. booklet containing twenty-four 3m. (No. 61ab) in blocks of 6 . . . .

1911 (1 July). *Black on pink cover inscr* "Egyptian Post Office" *in English and Arabic. Stapled.*
SB3 120m. Contents as No. SB1 . . . . £2000

1914 (8 Jan). *Black on pink cover inscr* "Egyptian Post Office" *in English and Arabic. Stapled.*
SB4 125m. booklet containing twenty-four 5m. (No. 77a) in blocks of 6 . . . .

1919 (1 Jan). *Black on pink cover inscr* "Egyptian Post Office" *in English and Arabic. Stapled.*
SB5 120m. Contents as No. SB4 . . . . £1200

1921 (12 June). *Deep blue on pink cover inscr* "POST OFFICE" *in English and Arabic. Stapled.*
SB6 120m. booklet containing twenty-four 5m. (No. 89) in blocks of 6 . . . .
a. Stitched £1000

1921 (Nov). *Deep blue or pink cover inscr* "POST OFFICE" *in English and Arabic. Stapled.*
SB7 120m. booklet containing twenty-four 5m. (No. 90) in blocks of 6 . . . . £750

POSTAGE DUE STAMPS

D **16** D **23** D **24**

(Des L. Barkhausen. Litho V. Penasson, Alexandria)

1884 (1 Jan). W **6** (*impressed on reverse*). P 10½.
D57 D **16** 10pa. red . . . . 45·00 9·00
a. Imperf (Pair) . . . . . .
b. Imperf between (pair) . . . £110
w. Wmk inverted . . . . . . 75·00 15·00
D58 20pa. red . . . . £110 28·00
w. Wmk inverted . . . . . . £190 40·00
D59 1pi. red . . . . £130 45·00
w. Wmk inverted £200 £100
D60 2pi. red . . . . £225 10·00
w. Wmk inverted . . . . . . £325 20·00
D61 5pi. red . . . . 14·00 42·00
w. Wmk inverted . . . . . . 32·00 48·00

1886 (1 Aug)–**87**. No wmk. P 10½.
D62 D **16** 10pa. rose-red (1887) . . . . . . 55·00 11·00
a. Imperf between (pair) . . . 90·00
D63 20pa. rose-red . . . . £225 40·00
a. Imperf between (pair) . . .
D64 1pi. rose-red . . . . 30·00 8·00
a. Imperf between (pair) . . . £120 £120
D65 2pi. rose-red . . . . 30·00 3·75
a. Imperf between (pair) . . . £120

Specialists distinguish four types of each value in both these issues.

(Litho V. Penasson, Alexandria)

1888 (1 Jan). No wmk. P 11½.
D66 D **23** 2m. green . . . . 13·00 20·00
a. Imperf between (pair) . . . £170 £170
D67 5m. rose-carmine . . . . . . 32·00 20·00
D68 1p. blue . . . . £130 35·00
a. Imperf between (pair) . . . £170
D69 2p. orange . . . . £150 12·00
D70 5p. grey £200 £180
a. With stop after left-hand "PIASTRES" £275 £225

Specialists distinguish four types of each value. No. D70a occurs on all examples of one of these types in the sheet except that on R. 2/1.

Beware of forgeries of the 5p.

(Typo De La Rue)

1889 (Apr)–**1907**. *Ordinary paper.* W **8***a*. P 14.
D71 D **24** 2m. green . . . . 7·00 50
a. Bisected (1m.) (on cover with unbisected 2m.) (2.98) . . . . † £250
bw. Wmk inverted . . . . . . 8·00 50
c. Chalk-surfaced paper (1906) . . . . 14·00 50
D72 4m. maroon . . . . 2·25 50
aw. Wmk inverted . . . . . . 4·00 1·00
b. Chalk-surfaced paper (1906) . . . . 2·75 50
D73 1p. ultramarine . . . . . . 5·50 50
aw. Wmk inverted . . . . . . 7·50 50
b. Chalk-surfaced paper (1906) . . . . 6·50 50
D74 2p. orange . . . . 5·50 70
a. Bisected diagonally (1p.) (on cover) . . . . † —
bw. Wmk inverted . . . . . . 5·00 70
c. Chalk-surfaced paper (1907) . . . . 5·00 70

No. D71a was authorised for use on Egyptian Army letters from the Sudan campaign which were only charged 3m. postage due.

See also Nos. 84/6 for stamps with watermark sideways.

3 Millièmes

(D **26**) (D **27**)

Type D **26**

The Arabic figure at right is less than 2 mm from the next character, which consists of a straight stroke only.

Type D **27**

The distance is 3 mm and the straight character has a comma-like character above it. There are other minor differences.

1898 (7 May)–**1907**. *No.* D74 *surch at Blâq. Ordinary paper.*

(a) With Type D **26**.
D75 D **24** 3m.on 2p. orange . . . . . . 1·25 4·00
a. Surch inverted . . . . . . 60·00 75·00
b. Pair, one without surch . . .
c. Arabic "2" for "3" . . . . .
d. Arabic "3" over "2" £100

No. D75c occurred in the first printing on positions 10, 20, 30, 40, 50 and 60 of the pane of 60 (the Arabic figure is the right-hand character of the second line—see illustration on page xvii). In the second printing the correct figure was printed on top to form No. D75d The error was corrected in subsequent printings.

(b) With Type D **27** *(11.04).*
D76 D **24** 3m.on 2p. orange . . . . . . 3·75 13·00
a. Surch inverted . . . . . . 50·00 60·00
b. Surch double £200
c. Chalk-surfaced paper (1907) . . . .

1914–15. *As Nos. D71/3 but* wmk sideways*.
D84 D **24** 2m. bright green (1915) . . . . 12·00 3·75
w. Wmk star to left of crescent 19·00 13·00
D85 4m. maroon . . . . 12·00 14·00
w. Wmk star to left of crescent 23·00
D86 1p. dull ultramarine . . . . . . 22·00 9·50
w. Wmk star to left of crescent 16·00 11·00

*The normal sideways watermark shows star to right of crescent *as seen from the back of the stamp.*

D **43** D **44**

(Typo Harrison)

1921 (Apr)–**22**. *Chalk-surfaced paper.* W **40** (sideways*). P 14 × 13½
D 98 D **43** 2m. green . . . . 2·75 4·0
w. Wmk stars below crescents . . . . 9·00 4·0
D 99 2m. scarlet (1922) . . . . . . 1·00 1·5
w. Wmk stars below crescents . . . . 7·50 4·0
D100 4m. scarlet . . . . 5·00 14·0
D101 4m. green (1922) . . . . . . 4·00 1·0
w. Wmk stars below crescents . . . . 12·00 5·0
D102 D **44** 10m. deep slate-blue (11.21) . . . 6·50 18·0
D103 10m. lake (1922) . . . . 5·50 7
w. Wmk stars below crescents . . . . 10·00 4·0
D98/103 *Set of* 6 . . . . 22·00 35·0

*The normal sideways watermark shows the stars above th crescents.

OFFICIAL STAMPS

O.H.H.S. أميري

"O.H.H.S."

O **25** (O **28**) (O **29**)

(Typo De La Rue)

1893 (1 Jan)–**1914**. *Ordinary paper.* W **8***a*. P 14.
O64 O **25** (–) chestnut . . . . 2·50
a. Chalk-surfaced paper (1903)
bw. Wmk inverted . . . . . .
c. Wmk sideways star to right. Chalk-surfaced paper (1914) 10·00 9·
cw. Wmk sideways star to left . .

From January 1907 No. O64 was used on most official mail to addresses within Egypt. In 1907 it was replaced by Nos. O73/8, but the use of No. O64 for unregistered official mail to Egyptian addresses was resumed on 1 January 1909.

After No. O64c was withdrawn in 1915 the remaining stock was surcharged 1p., 2p., 3p. or 5p. for fiscal use.

1907 (1 Feb–Aug). *Nos. 54da, 56c, 58c, 59c, 61c and 63d optd wi Type* O **28** *by De La Rue.*
O73 **18** 1m. pale brown . . . . 1·75
O74 **19** 2m. green . . . . 4·00
a. Opt double . . . .
O75 **20** 3m. orange-yellow . . . . . . 2·75 1·
O76 **21** 5m. rose . . . . 5·00
O77 **13** 1p. blue . . . . 2·00
O78 **15** 5p. slate-grey (Aug) . . . . . 16·00 3·
O73/8 *Set of* 6 . . . . 28·00 4·

Nos. O73/8 were used on all official mail from February 19 until 1 January 1909 after which their use was restricted to registere items and those sent to addresses overseas.

1913 (Nov). *No. 63d optd at Blâq.*

(a) With Type O **29**.
O79 **21** 5m. rose . . . . — £3
a. Opt inverted . . . .

(b) As Type O **29** *but without inverted commas.*
O80 **21** 5m. rose . . . . 7·00
a. No stop after "S" (R. 11/10) . . 55·00 16·
b. Opt inverted . . . . £200 75·

O.H.H.S. اميرى O.H.H.S. أميرى O.H.H.S. أميرى

(O **38**) (O **39**) (O **43**)

1914 (Dec)–**15**. *Stamps of 1902–6 and 1914 optd with Type* O **38** *Blâq.*
O83 **29** 1m. sepia (1.15) . . . . . . 1·50 3·
a. No stop after "S" (R. 10/10) . . 12·00 25·
O84 **19** 2m. green (3.15) . . . . . . 3·75 6·
a. No stop after "S" . . . . . 14·00 23·
b. Opt inverted . . . . 35·00 35·
c. Opt double £325
O85 **31** 3m. yellow-orange (3.15) . . . . 2·00 3·
a. No stop after "S" (R. 10/10) . . 14·00 25·

O86	21	4m. vermilion (12.14)	4·25	2·00
		a. Opt inverted	£190	£140
		b. Pair, one without opt		
O87	–	5m. lake (1.15)	4·00	1·00
		a. No stop after "S" (R. 10/10)	15·00	22·00
O83/7		*Set of* 5	14·00	15·00

No. O84a occurs on three positions from the first printing and on two different positions from the second.

1915 (Oct). *Nos. 59ab, 62 and 77 optd lithographically with Type* O **39** *at Blâq.*

O88	19	2m. green	2·00	4·00
		a. Opt inverted	20·00	20·00
		b. Opt double	25·00	
O89	21	4m. vermilion	5·50	6·50
O90	–	5m. lake	6·50	1·25
		a. Pair, one without opt	£275	

1922. *Nos. 84, etc optd lithographically with Type* O **43** *at Blâq.*

O 98	29	1m. sepia (A) (28.6)	3·50	10·00
		a. Two dots omitted (B)	£200	
		w. Wmk inverted		
O 99	30	2m. vermilion (16.6)	7·50	16·00
O100	31	3m. yellow-orange (28.6)	65·00	£130
O101	–	5m. pink (13.3)	17·00	4·25

Egypt was declared to be an independent kingdom on 15 March 1922, and Sultan Ahmed Fuad became king.

Later stamp issues will be found listed in Part 19 (*Middle East*) of this catalogue.

EGYPTIAN POST OFFICES ABROAD

From 1865 Egypt operated various post offices in foreign countries. No special stamps were issued for these offices and use in them of unoverprinted Egyptian stamps can only be identified by the cancellation. Stamps with such cancellations are worth more than the used prices quoted in the Egypt listings.

Such offices operated in the following countries. An * indicates that details will be found under that heading elsewhere in the catalogue.

ETHIOPIA

A B

C D

MASSAWA. *Open Nov* 1867 *to* 5 Dec 1885. *Postmark types* A (*also without* REGIE), B, C, D. *An Arabic seal type is also known on stampless covers.*

SENHIT (near Keren). *Open* 1878 *to* April 1885. *Only one cover, cancelled* "Mouderie Senhit" *in* 1879, *is known, together with one showing possible hand-drawn cancellation.*

A post office is also recorded at Harar in 1878, but no postal marking has so far been reported

SOMALILAND*

Unoverprinted stamps of Egypt used from 1876 until 1884.

SUDAN*

Unoverprinted stamps of Egypt used from 1867 until 1897.

TURKISH EMPIRE

E F

G H

I J

K L

M N

O

The offices are listed according to the spelling on the cancellation. The present-day name (if different) and country are given in brackets.

ALESSANDRETTA (Iskenderun, Turkey). *Open* 14 July 1870 *to* Feb 1872. *Postmark types* E, I.

BAIROUT (Beirut, Lebanon). *Open* 14 July 1870 *to* Feb 1872. *Postmark types* E, J.

CAVALA (Kavala, Greece). *Open* 14 July 1870 *to* Feb 1872. *Postmark type* E.

COSTANTINOPOLI (Istanbul, Turkey). *Open* 13 June 1865 *to* 30 June 1881. *Postmark types* E, F, O.

DARDANELLI (Canakkle, Turkey). *Open* 10 June 1868 *to* 30 June 1881. *Postmark types* H, K.

DJEDDAH, *see* GEDDA.

GALIPOLI (Gelibolu, Turkey). *Open* 10 June 1868 *to* 30 June 1881. *Postmark types* E, L.

GEDDA, DJEDDAH (Jeddah, Saudi Arabia). *Open* 8 June 1865 *to* 30 June 1881. *Postmark types* F, G (*also with year replacing solid half-circle*), O (*all spelt* GEDDA), D (*spelt* DJEDDAH).

JAFFA (Jaffa, Israel). *Open* 14 July 1870 *to* Feb 1872. *Postmark type* E.

LAGOS (Port Logo, Greece). *Open* 14 July 1870 *to* Feb 1872. *Postmark type* E.

LATAKIA (Syria). *Open* 14 July 1870 *to* Feb 1872. *Postmark type* E.

LEROS (Aegean Is). *Open* July 1873 *to* January 1874 *and* May *to* October 1874. *Postmark type* E.

MERSINA (Mersin, Turkey). *Open* 14 July 1870 *to* Feb 1872. *Postmark type* E.

METELINO (Lesbos, Greece). *Open* 14 July 1870 *to* 30 June 1881. *Postmark types* E, M.

RODI (Rhodes, Greece). *Open* 13 Aug 1872 *to* 30 June 1881. *Postmark type* E.

SALONNICCHI (Thessaloniki, Greece). *Open* 14 July 1870 *to* Feb 1872. *Postmark type* E.

SCIO (Chios, Aegean Is.). *Open* 14 July 1870 *to* 30 June 1881. *Postmark types* E, N.

SMIRNE (Izmir, Turkey). *Open* 14 Nov 1865 *to* 30 June 1881. *Postmark types* E (*also without* "V. R."), F.

TENEDOS (Bozcaada, Turkey). *Open* 14 July 1870 *to* March 1871. *Postmark type* E.

TRIPOLI (Lebanon). *Open* 14 July 1870 *to* Feb 1872. *Postmark type* E.

VOLO (Volos, Greece). *Open* 14 July 1870 *to* Feb 1872. *Postmark type* E.

BRITISH FORCES IN EGYPT

Following the rise of a nationalist movment led by Arabi Pasha, and serious disturbances in Alexandria, British troops landed at Ismalia in August 1882 and defeated the nationalists at Tel-el-Kebir on 13 September. A British Army Post Office detachment landed at Alexandria on 21 August and provided a postal service for the troops, using Great Britain stamps, from various locations until it was withdrawn on 7 October

During the Gordon Relief Expedition of 1884–85 a postal detachment was sent to Suakin on the Red Sea. This operated between 25 March and 30 May 1885 using Great Britain stamps.

ZA 1

Stamps of GREAT BRITAIN *cancelled with Type* ZA **1**.

1882 (Aug–Oct).

ZA1	½d. rose-red (Plate No. 20)	
ZA2	½d. green (1880)	£300
ZA3	1d. Venetian red (1880)	
ZA4	1d. lilac (1881)	£175
ZA5	2½d. blue (1881) (Plate Nos. 21, 22, 23)	£100

1885. *Used at Suakin.*

ZA6	½d. slate-blue (1884)	
ZA7	1d. lilac (1881)	£300
ZA8	2½d. lilac (1884)	£225
ZA9	5d. dull green (1884)	£500

From 1 November 1932 to 29 February 1936 members of the British Forces in Egypt and their families were allowed to send letters to the British Isles at reduced rates. Special seals, which were on sale in booklets at N.A.A.F.I. Institutes and Canteens, were used instead of Egyptian stamps. These seals were stuck on the back of the envelopes, letters bearing the seals being franked on the front with a hand-stamp inscribed "EGYPT POSTAGE PREPAID" in a double circle surmounted by a crown.

PRICES FOR STAMPS ON COVER		
Nos.	A1/9	*from* × 5
No.	A10	*from* × 2
No.	A11	*from* × 5
No.	A12	*from* × 100
No.	A13	*from* × 20
No.	A14	*from* × 100
No.	A15	*from* × 20

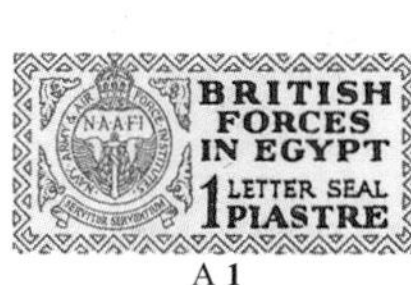

A 1 A 2

(Des Lt-Col. C. Fraser. Typo Hanbury, Tomsett & Co. Ltd, London)

1932 (1 Nov)–**33**. P 11.

(a) Inscr "POSTAL SEAL".

A1	A 1	1p. deep blue and red	90·00	3·50

(b) Inscr "LETTER SEAL".

A2	A 1	1p. deep blue and red (8.33)	28·00	85

(Des Sgt. W. F. Lait. Litho Walker & Co, Amalgamated Press, Cairo)

1932 (26 Nov)–**35**. *Christmas Seals.* P 11½.

A3	A 2	3m. black/*azure*	48·00	70·00
A4		3m. brown-lake (13.11.33)	7·50	50·00
A5		3m. deep blue (17.11.34)	7·00	26·00
A6		3m. vermilion (23.11.35)	1·25	35·00
		a. Pale vermilion (19.12.35)	7·50	20·00

A 3

(Des Miss Waugh. Photo Harrison)

1934 (1 June)–**35**.

(a) P 14½ x 14.

A7	A 3	1p. carmine	35·00	85
A8		1p. green (5.12.34)	4·00	4·00

(b) P 13½ × 14.

A9	A 3	1p. carmine (24.4.35)	2·25	3·00

JUBILEE COMMEMORATION 1935

(A 4)

1935 (6 May). *Silver Jubilee. As No. A9, but colour changed and optd with Type* A **4**, *in red.*

A10	A **3**	1p. ultramarine	£225	£180

Xmas 1935
3 Milliemes

(A 5)

1935 (16 Dec). *Provisional Christmas Seal. No. A9 surch with Type* A **5**.

A11	A **3**	3m.on 1p. carmine	16·00	70·00

The seals and letter stamps were replaced by the following Army Post stamps issued by the Egyptian Postal Administration. No. A9 was accepted for postage until 15 March 1936.

A **6** King Fuad I

A **7** King Farouk

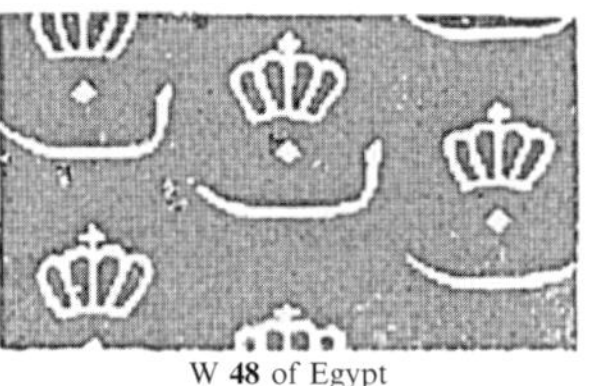
W **48** of Egypt

(Types A **6**/A **7**. Photo Survey Dept, Cairo)

1936. W **48** of Egypt. P 13½ × 14.

A12	A **6**	3m. green (1.12.36)	1·00	1·00
A13		10m. carmine (1.3.36)	3·75	10
		w. Wmk inverted		

1939 (16 Dec). W **48** of Egypt. P 13 × 13½.

A14	A **7**	3m. green	3·25	5·00
A15		10m. carmine	4·75	10
		w. Wmk inverted		

These stamps were withdrawn in April 1941 but the concession, without the use of special stamps, continued until October 1951 when the postal agreement was abrogated.

SUEZ CANAL COMPANY

PRICES FOR STAMPS ON COVER	
Nos. 1/4	*from* × 20

100 Centimes = 1 Franc

On 30 November 1855 a concession to construct the Suez Canal was granted to Ferdinand de Lesseps and the Compagnie Universelle du Canal Maritime de Suez was formed. Work began in April 1859 and the canal was opened on 17 November 1869. In November 1875 the Khedive sold his shares in the company to the British Government, which then became the largest shareholder.

The company transported mail free of charge between Port Said and Suez from 1859 to 1867, when it was decided that payment should be made for the service and postage stamps were introduced in July 1868. Letters for destinations beyond Port Said or Suez required additional franking with Egyptian or French stamps.

The imposition of charges for the service was not welcomed by the public and in August the Egyptian Government agreed to take it over.

1

(Litho Chezaud, Aine & Tavernier, Paris)

1868 (8 July). Imperf.

1	**1**	1c. black	£250	£1000
2		5c. green	85·00	£500
3		20c. blue	75·00	£500
4		40c. pink	£130	£750

Shades of all values exist.

Stamps can be found showing parts of the papermaker's watermark "LA+-F" (La Croix Frères).

These stamps were withdrawn from sale on 16 August 1868 and demonetised on 31 August.

Many forgeries exist, unused and cancelled. The vast majority of these forgeries show vertical lines, instead of cross-hatching, between "POSTES" and the central oval. It is believed that other forgeries, which do show cross-hatching, originate from the plate of the 40c. value which is missing from the company's archives. These are, however, on thin, brittle paper with smooth shiny gum.

Falkland Islands

PRICES FOR STAMPS ON COVER TO 1945		
No.	1	*from* × 100
No.	2	*from* × 50
Nos.	3/4	*from* × 10
No.	5	—
Nos.	6/10	*from* × 30
Nos.	11/12	*from* × 15
Nos.	13/17	*from* × 10
Nos.	17*b*/*c*	*from* × 100
Nos.	18/21	*from* × 10
Nos.	22/*b*	*from* × 30
Nos.	23/4	*from* × 100
Nos.	25/6	*from* × 30
No.	27	*from* × 20
No.	28	*from* × 40
No.	29	*from* × 5
Nos.	30/*b*	*from* × 50
No.	30*c*	*from* × 15
No.	31	*from* × 5
Nos.	32/8	*from* × 15
Nos.	41/2	—
Nos.	43/8	*from* × 12
Nos.	49/50	—
Nos.	60/5	*from* × 10
Nos.	66/9	—
Nos.	70/1	*from* × 10
Nos.	72/*b*	—
Nos.	73/9	*from* × 4
No.	80	—
No.	115	*from* × 2
Nos.	116/19	*from* × 20
Nos.	120/2	*from* × 6
Nos.	123/6	—
Nos.	127/34	*from* × 5
Nos.	135/8	—
Nos.	139/45	*from* × 50
Nos.	146/63	*from* × 5

CROWN COLONY

1

2

1869–76. *The Franks.*

FR1	**1**	In black, *on cover*	£6500
FR2	**2**	In red, *on cover* (1876)	£12000

On *piece*, No. FR1 on white or coloured paper £100; No. FR2 on white £160.

The first recorded use of No. FR1 is on a cover to London datestamped 4 January 1869. The use of these franks ceased when the first stamps were issued.

3

½d.
(4)

In the ½d., 2d., 2½d. and 9d. the figures of value in the lower corners are replaced by small rosettes and the words of value are in colour.

NOTE. Nos. 1, 2, 3, 4, 8, 10, 11 and 12 exist with one or two sides imperf from the margin of the sheets.

(Recess B.W.)

1878–79. No wmk. P 14, 14½.

1	**3**	1d. claret (19.6.78)	£650	£375
2		4d. grey-black (Sept 1879)	£1100	£150
		a. On wmkd paper	£2750	£500
3		6d. blue-green (19.6.78)	75·00	65·00
4		1s. bistre-brown (1878)	60·00	65·00

No. 2a shows portions of the papermaker's watermark—"R. TURNER, CHAFFORD MILLS"—in ornate double-lined capitals.

NOTES. The dates shown for Nos. 5/12 and 15/38 are those on which the printer delivered the various printings to the Crown Agents. Several months could elapse before the stamps went on sale in the Colony, depending on the availability of shipping.

The plates used for these stamps did not fit the paper so that the watermark appears in all sorts of positions on the stamp. Well centred examples are scarce. Examples can also be found showing parts of the marginal watermarks, either CROWN AGENTS horizontally in letters 12 mm high or "CROWN AGENTS FOR THE COLONIES" vertically in 7 mm letters. Both are in double-lined capitals.

1882 (22 Nov). Wmk Crown CA (upright). P 14, 14½.

5	**3**	1d. dull claret	£325	£150
		a. Imperf vert (horiz pair)	£45000	
		x. Wmk reversed	£800	
		y. Wmk inverted and reversed	£500	£300
6		4d. grey-black	£350	80·00
		w. Wmk inverted	£550	£200

1885 (23 Mar)–**91**. Wmk Crown CA (sideways*). P 14, 14½.

7	**3**	1d. pale claret	65·00	48·00
		w. Wmk Crown to right of CA	85·00	60·00
		x. Wmk sideways reversed	£225	£110
		y. Wmk Crown to right of CA and reversed	£170	£110
8		1d. brownish claret (3.10.87)	90·00	45·00
		a. Bisected (on cover) (1.1891)	†	£2250
		w. Wmk Crown to right of CA	£100	45·00
		x. Wmk sideways reversed	£180	£100
		y. Wmk Crown to right of CA and reversed	£180	£140
9		4d. pale grey-black	£600	60·00
		w. Wmk Crown to right of CA	£600	70·0
		x. Wmk sideways reversed	£650	£17
		y. Wmk Crown to right of CA and reversed	£650	£13
10		4d. grey-black (3.10.87)	£375	42·0
		w. Wmk Crown to right of CA	£375	42·0
		x. Wmk sideways reversed	£750	£10
		y. Wmk Crown to right of CA and reversed	£600	70·0

*The normal sideways watermark shows Crown to left of CA, *as seen from the back of the stamp.*

For No. 8a see note below No. 14.

1889 (26 Sept)–**91**. Wmk Crown CA (upright). P 14, 14½.

11	**3**	1d. red-brown (21.5.91)	£180	75·0
		a. Bisected (on cover) (7.91)	†	£250
		x. Wmk reversed	£400	£19
12		4d. olive grey-black	£130	50·0
		w. Wmk inverted	£550	£30
		x. Wmk reversed	£375	£15

For No. 11a see note below No. 14.

1891 (Jan–11 July). *Nos. 8 and 11 bisected diagonally and each ha handstamped with T* **4**.

13	**3**	½d.on half of 1d. brownish claret (No. 8)	£550	£30
		a. Unsevered pair	£2500	£100
		b. Unsevered pair *se-tenant* with unsurcharged whole stamp	£17000	
		c. Bisect *se-tenant* with unsurcharged whole stamp	†	£150
14		½d.on half of 1d. red-brown (No. 11) (11 July)	£650	£27
		a. Unsevered pair	£3250	£140
		b. Bisect *se-tenant* with unsurcharged whole stamp	†	£140

1891 PROVISIONALS. In 1891 the postage to the Unite Kingdom and Colonies was reduced from 4d. to 2½d. per half ounc As no ½d. or 2½d. stamps were available the bisection of the 1d. wa authorised from 1 January 1891. This authorisation was withdraw on 11 January 1892, although bisects were accepted for postage unt July of that year. The ½d. and 2½d. stamps were placed on sale fror 10 September 1891.

Cork Cancel used in 1891

The Type **4** surcharge was not used regularly; unsurcharge bisects being employed far more frequently. Genuine bisects shou be cancelled with the cork cancel illustrated above. The use of ar other postmark, including a different cork cancel or an "F.I obliterator, requires date evidence linked to known mail ship sailin to prove authenticity.

After 10 September 1891 the post office supplied "posthumous examples of the surcharged bisects to collectors. These were witho postal validity and differ from Type **4** by showing a large full sto long fraction bar or curly tail to "2". Some of the posthumo surcharges were applied to No. 18 which was not used for tl original bisects. Examples are also known showing the surchar double, inverted or sideways.

1891 (10 Sept)–**1902**. Wmk Crown CA (upright). P 14, 14½.

15	**3**	½d. blue-green (10 Sept–Nov 1891)	21·00	26·
		x. Wmk reversed	£300	£2
		y. Wmk inverted and reversed	£325	£3
16		½d. green (20.5.92)	16·00	15·
		ax. Wmk reversed	£140	£1
		ay. Wmk inverted and reversed	£275	£2
		b. Deep dull green (15.4.96)	40·00	30·
17		½d. deep yellow-green (1894–95)	17·00	21·
		ay. Wmk inverted and reversed	£140	£1
		b. Yellow-green (19.6.99)	2·00	3·
		c. Dull yellowish green (13.1.1902)	5·50	4·
		cx. Wmk reversed	£300	£3
18		1d. orange red-brown (14.10.91)	75·00	60·
		a. Brown	£100	60·
		w. Wmk inverted	£750	£3
		x. Wmk reversed	£180	£1
19		1d. reddish chestnut (20.4.92)	42·00	42·
20		1d. orange-brn (wmk reversed) (18.1.94)	50·00	45·
21		1d. claret (23.7.94)	£100	80·
		x. Wmk reversed	75·00	50·
22		1d. Venetian red (pale to deep) (1895–96)	19·00	17·
		ax. Wmk reversed	10·00	12·
		b. Venetian claret (1898?)	30·00	13·
23		1d. pale red (19.6.99)	5·50	2·
		x. Wmk reversed	£275	£2
24		1d. orange-red (13.1.1902)	11·00	4·

2d. purple (pale to deep) (1895–98) 6·50 12·00
x. Wmk reversed £350 £375
2d. reddish purple (15.4.96) 5·00 11·00
2½d. pale chalky ultramarine (10.9.91) £140 42·00
2½d. dull blue (19.11.91) £150 22·00
x. Wmk reversed £300 £250
2½d. Prussian blue (18.1.94) £225 £130
2½d. ultramarine (1894–96) 26·00 11·00
ax. Wmk reversed 50·00 14·00
ay. Wmk inverted and reversed £550
b. Pale ultramarine (10.6.98) 30·00 14·00
bx. Wmk reversed £110 75·00
c. Deep ultramarine (18.9.1901) 35·00 35·00
cx. Wmk reversed £250 £250
4d. brownish black (wmk reversed) (18.1.94) £700 £325
4d. olive-black (11.5.95) 10·00 21·00
6d. orange-yellow (19.11.91) £170 £140
x. Wmk reversed 55·00 42·00
6d. yellow (15.4.96) 30·00 42·00
9d. pale reddish orange (15.11.95) 35·00 55·00
x. Wmk reversed £275 £325
y. Wmk inverted and reversed £425 £425
9d. salmon (15.4.96) 42·00 55·00
x. Wmk reversed £275 £325
1s. grey-brown (15.11.95) 50·00 55·00
x. Wmk reversed £150 £160
1s. yellow-brown (15.4.96) 48·00 48·00
x. Wmk reversed £150 £160
/38 *Set of* 8 £150 £170
, 26s, 28s, 33s, 35s Optd "Specimen" *Set of* £600

The ½d. and 2½d. were first placed on sale in the Falkland Islands 10 September 1891. Such stamps came from the August 1891 nting. The stock of the May printings sent to the Falkland Islands s lost at sea.

The 2½d. ultramarine printing can sometimes be found in a violet ade, but the reason for this is unknown.

5

6

(Recess B.W.)

98 (5 Oct). Wmk Crown CC. P 14, 14½.
5 2s.6d. deep blue £225 £250
6 5s. red £190 £225
/2s Optd "Specimen" *Set of* 2 £450

7

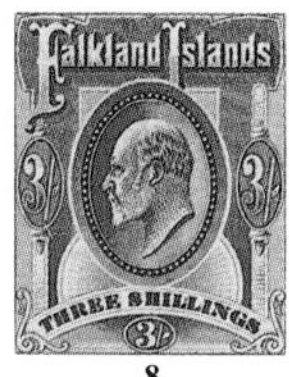
8

(Recess D.L.R.)

04 (16 July)–**12**. Wmk Mult Crown CA. P 14.
7 ½d. yellow-green 4·25 1·50
aw. Wmk inverted £250 £160
ax. Wmk reversed £650
b. Pale yellow-green (on thick paper) (6.08) 15·00 9·00
bw. Wmk inverted
c. Deep yellow-green (7.11) 10·00 3·00
1d. vermilion 11·00 1·50
aw. Wmk inverted £250 £170
ax. Wmk reversed £350 £300
b. Wmk sideways (7.06) 1·00 2·50
c. Thick paper (1908) 17·00 1·75
cw. Wmk inverted £350 £300
cx. Wmk reversed £425 £300
d. Dull coppery red (on thick paper) (3.08) £200 35·00
dx. Wmk reversed £650 £350
e. Orange-vermilion (7.11) 17·00 2·75
ex. Wmk reversed £350 £350
2d. purple (27.12.04) 16·00 26·00
ax. Wmk reversed £120 £120
b. Reddish purple (13.1.12) £225 £275
2½d. ultramarine (*shades*) 29·00 7·50
aw. Wmk inverted £225 £160
ay. Wmk inverted and reversed — £500
b. Deep blue (13.1.12) £250 £150
6d. orange (27.12.04) 38·00 48·00
1s. brown (27.12.04) 40·00 32·00
8 3s. green £160 £140
aw. Wmk inverted £1400 £1100
b. Deep green (4.07) £130 £120
bx. Wmk reversed £1400 £1000
5s. red (27.12.04) £190 £150
'50 *Set of* 8 £400 £350
/50s Optd "Specimen" *Set of* 8 £550

Examples of Nos. 41/50 and earlier issues are known with a ged Falkland Islands postmark dated "OCT 15 10".

For details of South Georgia underprint, South Georgia provisional handstamps and Port Foster handstamp see under FALKLAND ISLANDS DEPENDENCIES.

9

10

(Des B. MacKennal. Eng J. A. C. Harrison. Recess D.L.R.)

1912 (3 July)–**20**. Wmk Mult Crown CA. P 13¾ × 14 (comb) (½d. to 1s.) or 14 (line) (3s. to £1).
60 9 ½d. yellow-green 2·75 3·50
a. Perf 14 (line). *Dp yell-green* (1914) 18·00 35·00
b. Perf 14 (line). *Deep olive* (1918) 24·00 £110
c. Deep olive (4.19) 3·50 35·00
ca. Printed both sides † £5500
d. Dull yellowish green (on thick greyish paper) (1920) 4·50 32·00
61 1d. orange-red 5·00 2·50
a. Perf 14 (line). *Orange-vermilion* (1914, 1916) 27·00 2·50
b. Perf 14 (line). *Vermilion* (1918) † £750
c. Orange-vermilion (4.19) 3·75 3·00
d. Orange-vermilion (on thick greyish paper) (1920) 7·00 2·00
dx. Wmk reversed £160
62 2d. maroon 25·00 23·00
a. Perf 14 (line). *Dp reddish pur* (1914) £130 £100
b. Perf 14 (line). *Maroon* (4.18) £140 £100
c. Deep reddish purple (4.19) 7·00 16·00
63 2½d. deep bright blue 19·00 24·00
a. Perf 14 (line). *Dp bright blue* (1914) 28·00 35·00
b. Perf 14 (line). *Deep blue* (1916, 4.18) 29·00 40·00
c. Deep blue (4.19) 7·00 17·00
64 6d. yellow-orange (6.7.12) 14·00 20·00
aw. Wmk inverted £425 £375
b. Brown-orange (4.19) 14·00 42·00
65 1s. light bistre-brown (6.7.12) 32·00 30·00
a. Pale bistre-brown (4.19) 60·00 £110
b. Brown (on thick greyish paper) (1920) 32·00 £140
66 10 3s. slate-green 85·00 80·00
67 5s. deep rose-red 95·00 £100
a. Reddish maroon (1914) £200 £200
b. Maroon (1916) 80·00 £110
bx. Wmk reversed £2750 £1600
68 10s. red/*green* (11.2.14) £160 £250
69 £1 black/*red* (11.2.14) £425 £500
60/9 (*inc* 67*b*) *Set of* 11 £800 £1000
60s/9s (*inc both* 67*s and* 67*as*) Optd "Specimen" *Set of* 11 £1500

The exact measurement of the comb perforation used for Type **9** is 13.7 × 13.9. The line perforation, used for the 1914, 1916 and 1918 printings and for all the high values in Type **10**, measured 14.1 × 14.1.

It was previously believed that all examples of the 1d. in vermilion with the line perforation were overprinted to form No. 71, but it has now been established that some unoverprinted sheets of No. 61b were used during 1919.

Many of the sheets showed stamps from the left-hand side in a lighter shade than those from the right. It is believed that this was due to the weight of the impression. Such differences are particularly noticeable on the 2½d. 1916 and 1918 printings where the lighter shades, approaching milky blue in appearance, are scarce.

All 1919 printings show weak impressions of the background either side of the head caused by the poor paper quality.

Examples of all values are known with forged postmarks, including one of Falkland Islands dated "5 SP 19" and another of South Shetlands dated "20 MR 27".

WAR STAMP
(11)

2½D
(12)

1918 (22 Oct*)–**20**. *Optd by Govt Printing Press, Stanley, with T* **11**.
70 9 ½d. deep olive (line perf) (No. 60b) 1·00 11·00
a. Yellow-green (No. 60) (4.19) 17·00 £500
ab. Albino opt £1400
b. Deep olive (comb perf) (No. 60c) (4.19) 50 6·50
c. *Dull yellowish green* (on thick greyish paper) (No. 60*d*) (5.20) 8·00 70·00
cx. Wmk reversed £200
71 1d. vermilion (line perf) (No. 61b) 2·00 18·00
a. Opt double, one albino £400
b. Orange-verm (line perf) (No. 61a) (4.19) 17·00 †
c. Orange-verm (comb perf) (No. 61*c*) (4.19) 50 3·75
ca. Opt double £1900
cx. Wmk reversed £400
d. Orange-vermilion (on thick greyish paper) (No. 61*d*) (5.20) 90·00 £180
72 1s. light bistre-brown (No. 65) 35·00 80·00
a. Pale bistre-brown (No. 65*a*) (4.19) 4·00 48·00
ab. Opt double, one albino £1400
ac. Opt omitted (in pair with normal) £7500
b. Brown (on thick greyish paper) (No. 65*b*) (5.20) 5·50 45·00
ba. Opt double, one albino £1400
bw. Wmk inverted £190 £275
bx. Wmk reversed £850

*Earliest known postal use. Cancellations dated 8 October were applied much later.

There were five printings of the "WAR STAMP" overprint, but all, except that in May 1920, used the same setting. Composition of the five printings was as follows:
October 1918. Nos. 70, 71 and 72
January 1919. Nos. 70, 71 and 72
April 1919. Nos. 70/*b*, 71*b*/*c* and 72*a*
October 1919. Nos. 70*b*, 71*c* and 72*a*
May 1920. Nos. 70*c*, 71*d* and 72*b*.

It is believed that the entire stock of No. 70*a* was sold to stamp dealers. Only a handful of used examples are known which may have subsequently been returned to the colony for cancellation.

No. 71ca exists in a block of 12 (6 × 2) from the bottom of a sheet on which the first stamp in the bottom row shows a single overprint, but the remainder have overprint double.

Examples of Nos. 70/2 are known with a forged Falkland Islands postmark dated "5 SP 19".

1921–**28**. Wmk Mult Script CA. P 14.
73 9 ½d. yellowish green 3·00 4·00
a. Green (1925) 3·00 4·00
74 1d. dull vermilion (1924) 5·00 1·25
aw. Wmk inverted † £1500
ay. Wmk inverted and reversed £300
b. Orange-vermilion (*shades*) (1925) 5·50 1·25
75 2d. deep brown-purple (8.23) 15·00 7·00
aw. Wmk inverted — £1300
ax. Wmk reversed £1400
b. Purple-brown (1927) 18·00 25·00
c. Reddish maroon (1.28) 8·00 24·00
cy. Wmk inverted and reversed
76 2½d. deep blue 22·00 16·00
a. Indigo (28.4.27) 16·00 20·00
b. Deep steel-blue (1.28) 6·50 16·00
c. Prussian blue (10.28) £300 £450
77 2½d. deep purple/*pale yellow* (8.23) 4·50 35·00
a. Pale purple/*pale yellow* (1925) 4·50 35·00
ay. Wmk inverted and reversed £350
78 6d. yellow-orange (1925) 8·00 38·00
w. Wmk inverted £225
x. Wmk reversed £1200
79 1s. deep ochre 16·00 48·00
80 10 3s. slate-green (8.23) 80·00 £160
73/80 *Set of* 8 £120 £275
73s/80s (*inc both* 76s *and* 76*as*) Optd "Specimen" *Set of* 9 £700

Dates quoted above are those of despatch from Great Britain.

No. 76*c* only occurred in part of the October 1928 printing. The remainder were in the deep steel-blue shade of the January 1928 despatch, No. 76*b*.

1928 (7 Feb). *No. 75b surch with T* **12**.
115 9 2½d.on 2d. purple-brown £850 £850
a. Surch double £32000

No. 115 was produced on South Georgia during a shortage of 2½d. stamps. The provisional was withdrawn on 22 February 1928.

13 Fin Whale and Gentoo Penguins

14

(Recess P.B.)

1929 (2 Sept)–**36**. P 14 (comb).
(a) Wmk Mult Script CA.
116 13 ½d. green 1·25 3·00
a. Line perf (1936) 4·00 8·00
117 1d. scarlet 3·75 80
a. Line perf. *Deep red* (1936) 7·00 14·00
118 2d. grey 2·75 2·75
119 2½d. blue 2·75 2·25
120 14 4d. orange (*line perf*) (18.2.32) 16·00 13·00
a. Deep orange (1936) 40·00 48·00
121 13 6d. purple 16·00 13·00
a. Line perf. *Reddish purple* (1936) 42·00 25·00
122 1s. black/*emerald* 22·00 35·00
a. Line perf. *On bright emerald* (1936) 23·00 27·00
123 2s.6d. carmine/*blue* 48·00 48·00
124 5s. green/*yellow* 75·00 90·00
125 10s. carmine/*emerald* £140 £180
(b) Wmk Mult Crown CA.
126 13 £1 black/*red* £300 £375
116/26 *Set of* 11 £550 £650
116s/26s Perf "Specimen" *Set of* 11 £1000

Two kinds of perforation exist:
A. Comb perf 13.9:—original values of 1929.
B. Line perf 13.9, 14.2 or compound (small holes)—4d. and 1936 printings of ½d., 1d., 6d. and 1s. On some sheets the last vertical row of perforations shows larger holes.

Examples of most values are known with forged postmarks, including one of Port Stanley dated "14 JY 31" and another of South Georgia dated "AU 30 31".

15 Romney Marsh Ram

26 King George V

Thick serif to "1" at left (R. 1/3, first printing only)

(Des (except 6d.) by G. Roberts. Eng and recess B.W.)

1933 (2 Jan–Apr). *Centenary of British Administration. T* **15**, **26** *and similar designs.* Wmk Mult Script CA. P 12.

No.	Description	Unused	Used
127	½d. black and green	1·75	6·50
128	1d. black and scarlet	3·50	2·25
	a. Thick serif to 1 at left	£150	£110
129	1½d. black and blue	14·00	17·00
130	2d. black and brown	10·00	22·00
131	3d. black and violet	15·00	18·00
132	4d. black and orange	16·00	16·00
133	6d. black and slate	50·00	60·00
134	1s. black and olive-green	45·00	70·00
135	2s.6d. black and violet	£170	£190
136	5s. black and yellow	£550	£750
	a. Black and yellow-orange (Apr)	£1500	£1700
137	10s. black and chestnut	£600	£850
138	£1 black and carmine	£1600	£2000
127/38	*Set of* 12	£2750	£3750
127s/38s	Perf "Specimen" *Set of* 12	£2500	

Designs: *Horiz*—1d. Iceberg; 1½d. Whale-catcher *Bransfield*; 2d. Port Louis; 3d. Map of Falkland Islands; 4d. South Georgia; 6d. Fin Whale; 1s. Government House, Stanley. *Vert*—2s.6d. Battle Memorial; 5s. King Penguin; 10s. Coat of Arms.

Examples of all values are known with forged Port Stanley postmarks dated "6 JA 33". Some values have also been seen with part strikes of the forged Falkland Islands postmark mentioned below Nos. 60/9 and 70/2.

(Des H. Fleury. Recess B.W.)

1935 (7 May). *Silver Jubilee. As Nos. 91/4 of Antigua, but printed by B.W.* P 11 × 12.

No.	Description	Unused	Used
139	1d. deep blue and scarlet	3·25	40
	b. Short extra flagstaff	£450	£325
	d. Flagstaff on right-hand turret	£300	£200
	e. Double flagstaff	£300	£225
140	2½d. brown and deep blue	10·00	1·75
	b. Short extra flagstaff	£1200	£750
	d. Flagstaff on right-hand turret	£300	£200
	e. Double flagstaff	£450	£300
	l. Re-entry on value tablet (R. 8/1)	£200	£110
141	4d. green and indigo	11·00	4·50
	b. Short extra flagstaff	£650	£400
	d. Flagstaff on right-hand turret	£425	£300
	e. Double flagstaff	£475	£350
142	1s. slate and purple	8·00	3·50
	a. Extra flagstaff	£3000	£2250
	b. Short extra flagstaff	£650	£350
	c. Lightning conductor	£1800	£900
	d. Flagstaff on right-hand turret	£700	£400
	e. Double flagstaff	£750	£425
139/42	*Set of* 4	29·00	9·00
139s/42s	Perf "Specimen" *Set of* 4	£375	

For illustrations of plate varieties see Omnibus section following Zanzibar

1937 (12 May). *Coronation. As Nos. 95/7 of Antigua.* P 11 × 11½.

No.	Description	Unused	Used
143	½d. green	30	10
144	1d. carmine	50	45
145	2½d. blue	1·00	1·00
143/5	*Set of* 3	1·60	1·40
143s/5s	Perf "Specimen" *Set of* 3	£250	

27 Whales' Jaw Bones

(Des G. Roberts (Nos. 146, 148/9, 158 and 160/3), K. Lellman (No. 159). Recess B.W.)

1938 (3 Jan)–**50**. *Horiz designs as T* **27**. Wmk Mult Script CA. P 12.

No.	Description	Unused	Used
146	½d. black and green (*shades*)	30	75
147	1d. black and carmine	32·00	80
	a. Black and scarlet	3·75	85
148	1d. black and violet (14.7.41)	2·50	1·75
	a. Black and purple-violet (1.43)	7·50	2·00
149	2d. black and deep violet	1·25	50
150	2d. black and carmine-red (14.7.41)	1·00	2·25
	a. Black and red (1.43)	2·75	1·00
151	2½d. black and bright blue	1·25	30
152	2½d. black and blue (15.6.49)	6·50	7·00
153	3d. black and blue (14.7.41)	6·50	2·50
	a. Black and deep blue (1.43)	11·00	2·50
154	4d. black and purple	3·00	65
155	6d. black and brown	2·50	1·50
156	6d. black (15.6.49)	6·00	4·25
157	9d. black and grey-blue	20·00	1·40
158	1s. pale blue	75·00	18·00
	a. Deep blue (1941)	19·00	3·00
159	1s.3d. black and carmine-red (11.12.46)	2·50	1·40
160	2s.6d. slate	55·00	12·00
161	5s. bright blue and pale brown	£120	70·00
	b. Indigo and yellow-brown (1942)	£700	90·00
	c. Blue and buff-brown (9.2.50)	£170	£250
162	10s. black and orange-brown	£100	35·00
	a. black and orange (1942?)	£250	35·00
	b. black and red-orange (1949)	70·00	£200
	c. black and deep reddish orange (1950)	£250	£250
163	£1 black and violet	£130	50·00
146/63	*Set of* 18	£400	£170
146s/51s, 153s/5s, 157s/63s	Perf "Specimen" *Set of* 16	£1300	

Designs:—Nos. 147 and 150, Black-necked Swan; 148/9, Battle Memorial; 151 and 153, Flock of sheep; 152 and 154, Magellan Goose; 155/6, *Discovery II* (polar supply vessel); 157, *William Scoresby* (research ship); 158, Mount Sugar Top; 159, Turkey Vultures; 160, Gentoo Penguins; 161, Southern Sealion; 162, Deception Island; 163, Arms of Falkland Islands.

Examples of values issued before 1946 are known with forged Port Stanley postmarks dated "14 JY 41" and "28 JY 43".

1946 (7 Oct). *Victory. As Nos. 110/11 of Antigua.* P 13½–14.

No.	Description	Unused	Used
164	1d. dull violet	30	35
165	3d. blue	45	35
164s/5s	Perf "Specimen" *Set of* 2	£200	

1948 (1 Nov). *Royal Silver Wedding. As Nos. 112/13 of Antigua.*

No.	Description	Unused	Used
166	2½d. ultramarine	2·00	1·00
167	£1 mauve	90·00	55·00

1949 (10 Oct). *75th Anniv of Universal Postal Union. As Nos. 114/17 of Antigua.*

No.	Description	Unused	Used
168	1d. violet	1·50	75
169	3d. deep blue	5·00	2·00
170	1s.3d. deep blue-green	3·00	2·25
171	2s. blue	3·00	7·50
168/71	*Set of* 4	11·00	11·00

39 Sheep

43 Arms of the Colony

(Des from sketches by V. Spencer. Recess Waterlow)

1952 (2 Jan). *T* **39**, **43** *and similar designs.* Wmk Mult Script CA. P 13 × 13½ (vert) or 13½ × 13 (horiz).

No.	Description	Unused	Used
172	½d. green	1·00	70
173	1d. scarlet	2·25	40
174	2d. violet	4·25	2·50
175	2½d. black and light ultramarine	1·00	50
176	3d. deep ultramarine	1·75	1·00
177	4d. reddish purple	8·00	1·50
178	6d. bistre-brown	12·00	1·00
179	9d. orange-yellow	9·00	2·00
180	1s. black	24·00	80
181	1s.3d. orange	15·00	5·00
182	2s.6d. olive-green	20·00	11·00
183	5s. purple	13·00	9·00
184	10s. grey	26·00	11·00
185	£1 black	26·00	17·00
172/185	*Set of* 14	£150	55·00

Designs: *Horiz*—1d. *Fitzroy* (supply ship); 2d. Magellan Goose; 2½d. Map of Falkland Islands; 4d. Auster Autocrat aircraft; 6d. *John Biscoe I* (research ship); 9d. View of the Two Sisters; 1s.3d. Kelp goose and gander; 10s. Southern Sealion and South American Fur Seal; £1 Hulk of *Great Britain*. *Vert*—1s. Gentoo Penguins; 2s.6d. Sheep-shearing; 5s. Battle Memorial.

FALKLAND ISLANDS DEPENDENCIES

PRICES FOR STAMPS ON COVER TO 1945	
Nos. A1/D8	*from* × 20

A. GRAHAM LAND

For use at Port Lockroy (established 1 February 1944) and Hope Bay (established 12 February 1945) bases.

Falkland Islands definitive stamps with face values of 1s.3d. and above were valid for use from Graham Land in conjunction with Nos. A1/8 and subsequently Nos. G1/16.

Stamps of FALKLAND ISLANDS *cancelled at Port Lockroy or Hope Bay with Graham Land circular datestamps between* 12 February 1944 *and* 31 January 1954.

1938–50. *King George VI (Nos. 159/63).*

No.	Description	Price
Z1	1s.3d. black and carmine-red	£100
Z2	2s.6d. slate	48·00
Z3	5s. indigo and yellow-brown	£140
Z4	10s. black and orange	60·00
Z5	£1 black and violet	80·00

1952. *King George VI (Nos. 181/5)*

No.	Description	Price
Z 6	1s.3d. orange	85·00
Z 7	2s.6d. olive-green	95·00
Z 8	5s. purple	£110
Z 9	10s. grey	£120
Z10	£1 black	£130

GRAHAM LAND

DEPENDENCY OF

(A 1)

1944 (12 Feb)–**45**. *Falkland Islands Nos. 146, 148, 150, 153/5, 157 and 158a optd with Type A* **1**, *in red, by B.W.*

No.	Description	Unused	Used
A1	½d. black and green	30	1·75
	a. Blue-black and green	£800	£450
A2	1d. black and violet	30	1·00
A3	2d. black and carmine-red	50	1·00
A4	3d. black and blue	50	1·00
A5	4d. black and purple	2·00	1·75
A6	6d. black and brown	16·00	2·25
	a. Blue-black and brown (24.9.45)	16·00	
A7	9d. black and grey-blue	1·00	1·25
A8	1s. deep blue	1·00	1·25
A1/8	*Set of* 8	19·00	10·00
A1s/8s	Perf "Specimen" *Set of* 8	£425	

B. SOUTH GEORGIA

The stamps of Falkland Islands were used at the Grytviken whaling station on South Georgia from 3 December 1909.

Mr. J. Innes Wilson, the Stipendary Magistrate whose duties included those of postmaster, was issued with a stock of stamps, values ½d. to 5s., together with an example of the current "FALKLAND ISLANDS" circular datestamp. This was used to cancel the stamps, but, as it gave no indication that mail had originated at South Georgia, a straight-line handstamp inscribed "SOUTH GEORGIA", or subsequently "South Georgia", was also supplied. It was intended that this should be struck directly on to each letter or card below the stamp, but it can sometimes be found struck across the stamp instead.

The use of the "South Georgia" handstamp continued after the introduction of the "SOUTH GEORGIA" circular datestamp in June 1910 apparently for philatelic purposes, but no example has been reported used after June 1912.

SOUTH GEORGIA.

Z 1

South Georgia.

Z 2

No.	Description	On piece	On cover/card
ZU1	Example of Type Z **1** used in conjunction with "FALKLAND ISLANDS" postmark (22 Dec 1909 to 30 March 1910) *Price from*	£1300	£4750
ZU2	Example of Type Z **2** used in conjunction with "FALKLAND ISLANDS" postmark (May 1910) *Price from*	£900	£3750
ZU3	Example of Type Z **2** used in conjunction with "SOUTH GEORGIA" postmark (June 1910 to June 1912) *Price from*	£250	£900

Stamps of FALKLAND ISLANDS *cancelled at Grytviken with South Georgia circular datestamps between* June 1910 *and* 31 January 1954.

1891–1902. *Queen Victoria (Nos. 32, 36 and 38)*

No.	Description	Price
Z11	4d. olive-black	£190
Z12	9d. salmon	£190
Z13	1s. yellow-brown	£200

1904–12. *King Edward VII (Nos. 43/50).*

No.	Description	Price
Z14	½d. green	16·00
Z15	1d. vermilion	16·00
	d. Dull coppery red (on thick paper)	45·00
Z16	2d. purple	65·00
	b. Reddish purple	£300
Z17	2½d. ultramarine	23·00
	b. Deep blue	£190
Z18	6d. orange	£130
Z19	1s. brown	£130
Z20	3s. green	£275
Z21	5s. red	£325

SOUTH GEORGIA PROVISIONAL HANDSTAMPS. During October 1911 the arrival of the German South Polar Expedition at Grytviken, South Georgia, resulted in the local supply of stamps becoming exhausted. The Acting Magistrate, Mr. E. B. Binnie, who was also responsible for the postal facilities, produced a handstamp reading "Paid at (or At) SOUTH GEORGIA" which, together with a manuscript indication of the postage paid and his signature, was used on mail from 18 October 1911 to January 1912. Further examples, signed by John Innes Wilson, are known from February 1912, but these may be philatelic.

No.	Description	Price
PH1	"Paid 1 at SOUTH GEORGIA EBB" *Price on cover*	£
PH1*a*	"Paid 1 At SOUTH GEORGIA EBB" (16 Dec) *Price on cover*	£
PH2	"Paid 2½ at SOUTH GEORGIA EBB" *Price on cover*	£
PH2*a*	"Paid 2½ At SOUTH GEORGIA EBB" (16 Dec) *Price on cover*	£

1912–23. *King George V.* Wmk Mult Crown CA (Nos. 60/9).

No.	Description	Price
Z22	½d. green	17·00
	a. Perf 14 (line). *Deep yellow-green*	35·00
	d. Dull yellowish green (on thick greyish paper)	40·00
Z23	1d. orange-red	11·00
	a. Perf 14 (line). *Orange-vermilion*	11·00
	d. Orange-vermilion	11·00
Z24	2d. maroon	45·00
Z25	2½d. deep bright blue	32·00
	c. Deep blue	30·00
Z26	6d. yellow-orange	55·00
	b. Brown-orange	60·00
	ba. Bisected (diag) (3d.) (on cover) (3.23)	£12000
Z27	1s. bistre-brown	£110
	a. Pale bistre-brown	£140
	b. Brown (on thick greyish paper)	£170
Z28	3s. slate-green	£170
Z29	5s. deep rose-red	£200
	a. Reddish maroon	£300
	b. Maroon	£275
Z30	10s. red/*green*	£375
Z31	£1 black/*red*	£550

1918–20. "WAR STAMP" *ovpts (Nos. 70/2).*

No.	Description	Price
Z32	½d. deep olive	18·00
Z33	1d. vermilion	18·00
Z34	1s. light bistre-brown	95·00

1921–28. *King George V.* Wmk Mult Script CA (Nos. 73/80).
Z35 ½d. yellowish green . . . 5·50
Z36 1d. dull vermilion . . . 4·50
Z37 2d. deep brown-purple . . . 26·00
Z38 2½d. deep blue . . . 23·00
 a. Bisected (diag) (1d.) (on cover) (3.23) . . . £7500
 b. Prussian blue . . . £450
Z39 2½d. deep purple/*pale yellow* . . . 50·00
Z40 6d. yellow-orange . . . 50·00
Z41 1s. deep ochre . . . 60·00
Z42 3s. slate-green . . . £190

1928 PROVISIONAL. For listing of the 2½d. on 2d. surcharge issued at Grytviken on 7 February 1928 see No. 115 of Falkland Islands.

1929–36. *King George V. Whale and Penguins design (Nos. 116/26).*
Z43 ½d. green . . . 6·00
Z44 1d. scarlet . . . 4·50
Z45 2d. grey . . . 12·00
Z46 2½d. blue . . . 5·00
Z47 4d. orange . . . 23·00
Z48 6d. purple . . . 32·00
Z49 1s. black/*emerald* . . . 42·00
Z50 2s.6d. carmine/*blue* . . . 90·00
Z51 5s. green/*yellow* . . . £140
Z52 10s. carmine/*emerald* . . . £275
Z53 £1 black/*red* . . . £550

Examples of most values are known with forged postmarks dated 'Au 30' in 1928, 1930 and 1931.

1933. *Centenary of British Administration (Nos. 127/38).*
Z54 ½d. black and green . . . 8·50
Z55 1d. black and scarlet . . . 4·50
Z56 1½d. black and blue . . . 22·00
Z57 2d. black and brown . . . 26·00
Z58 3d. black and violet . . . 23·00
Z59 4d. black and orange . . . 21·00
Z60 6d. black and slate . . . 75·00
Z61 1s. black and olive-green . . . 85·00
Z62 2s.6d. black and violet . . . £250
Z63 5s. black and yellow . . . £850
 a. Black and yellow-orange . . . £1800
Z64 10s. black and chestnut . . . £1000
Z65 £1 black and carmine . . . £2500

1935. *Silver Jubilee (Nos. 139/42).*
Z66 1d. deep blue and scarlet . . . 4·00
Z67 2½d. brown and deep blue . . . 5·00
Z68 4d. green and indigo . . . 6·00
Z69 1s. slate and purple . . . 6·00

1937. *Coronation (Nos. 143/5).*
Z70 ½d. green . . . 2·50
Z71 1d. carmine . . . 2·50
Z72 2½d. blue . . . 2·50

1938–50. *King George VI (Nos. 146/63).*
Z73 ½d. black and green . . . 4·00
Z74 1d. black and carmine . . . 6·50
 a. Black and scarlet . . . 3·00
Z75 1d. black and violet . . . 6·00
Z76 2d. black and deep violet . . . 7·50
Z77 2d. black and carmine-red . . . 8·50
Z78 2½d. black and bright blue (No. 151) . . . 3·00
Z79 3d. black and blue . . . 9·00
Z80 4d. black and purple . . . 7·50
Z81 6d. black and brown . . . 9·50
Z82 9d. black and grey-blue . . . 13·00
Z83 1s. pale blue . . . 35·00
 a. Deep blue . . . 35·00
Z84 1s.3d. black and carmine-red . . . 48·00
Z85 2s.6d. slate . . . 32·00
Z86 5s. bright blue and pale brown . . . £130
 a. Indigo and yellow-brown . . . £140
 b. Blue and buff-brown . . . £300
Z87 10s. black and orange . . . 60·00
Z88 £1 black and violet . . . 80·00

Falkland Islands definitive stamps with values of 1s.3d. and above continued to be valid from South Georgia after the introduction of Nos. B1/8 and subsequently Nos. G1/16. Forged South Georgia postmarks exist dated "30 MR 49".

1952. *King George VI (Nos. 181/5).*
Z89 1s.3d. orange . . . 48·00
Z90 2s.6d. olive-green . . . 85·00
Z91 5s. purple . . . 95·00
Z92 10s. grey . . . £110
Z93 £1 black . . . £120

1944 (24 Feb)–**45.** *Falkland Islands Nos. 146, 148, 150, 153/5, 157 and 158a optd* "SOUTH GEORGIA/DEPENDENCY OF", *in red, as Type A* **1** *of Graham Land.*
B1 ½d. black and green . . . 30 1·75
 a. Wmk sideways . . . £3000
B2 1d. black and violet . . . 30 1·00
B3 2d. black and carmine-red . . . 50 1·00
B4 3d. black and blue . . . 50 1·00
B5 4d. black and purple . . . 2·00 1·75
B6 6d. black and brown . . . 16·00 2·25
 a. Blue-black and brown (24.9.45) . . . 16·00
B7 9d. black and grey-blue . . . 1·00 1·25
B8 1s. deep blue . . . 1·00 1·25
B1/8 *Set of* 8 . . . 19·00 10·00
B1s/8s Perf "Specimen" *Set of* 8 . . . £425

C. SOUTH ORKNEYS

Used from the *Fitzroy* in February 1944 and at Laurie Island (established January 1946).

Falkland Islands definitive stamps with face values of 1s.3d. and above were valid for use from the South Orkneys in conjunction with Nos. C1/8 and subsequently Nos. G1/16.

Stamps of FALKLAND ISLANDS *cancelled on the* Fitzroy, *at Laurie Island or at Signy Island with South Orkneys circular datestamps between* 21 February 1944 *and* 31 January 1954.

1938–50. *King George VI (Nos. 160/3).*
Z95 2s.6d. slate . . . 48·00
Z96 5s. indigo and yellow-brown . . . £140
Z97 10s. black and orange . . . 60·00
Z98 £1 black and violet . . . 80·00

1952. *King George VI (Nos. 181/5).*
Z 99 1s.3d. orange . . . 85·00
Z100 2s.6d. olive-green . . . 95·00
Z101 5s. purple . . . £110
Z102 10s. grey . . . £120
Z103 £1 black . . . £130

1944 (21 Feb)–**45.** *Falkland Islands Nos. 146, 148, 150, 153/5, 157 and 158a optd* "SOUTH ORKNEYS/DEPENDENCY OF", *in red, as Type A* **1** *of Graham Land.*
C1 ½d. black and green . . . 30 1·75
C2 1d. black and violet . . . 30 1·00
 w. Wmk inverted . . . £3750
C3 2d. black and carmine-red . . . 50 1·00
C4 3d. black and blue . . . 50 1·00
C5 4d. black and purple . . . 2·00 1·75
C6 6d. black and brown . . . 16·00 2·25
 a. Blue-black and brown (24.9.45) . . . 16·00
C7 9d. black and grey-blue . . . 1·00 1·25
C8 1s. deep blue . . . 1·00 1·25
C1/8 *Set of* 8 . . . 19·00 10·00
C1s/8s Perf "Specimen" *Set of* 8 . . . £425

D. SOUTH SHETLANDS

Postal facilities were first provided at the Port Foster whaling station on Deception Island for the 1912–13 whaling season and were available each year between November and the following April until March 1931.

No postmark was provided for the 1912–13 season and the local postmaster was instructed to cancel stamps on cover with a straight-line "PORT FOSTER" handstamp. Most letters so cancelled subsequently received a "FALKLAND ISLANDS" circular postmark dated between 19 and 28 March 1913. It is known that only low value stamps were available at Port Foster. Higher values, often with other "FALKLAND ISLANDS" postmark dates, were, it is believed, subsequently "made to order".

Stamps of FALKLAND ISLANDS *cancelled at Port Foster, Deception Island with part of* "PORT FOSTER" *straightline handstamp.*

1904–12. *King Edward VII (Nos. 43c, 44e).*
Z104 ½d. deep yellow-green . . . £1300
Z105 1d. orange-vermilion . . . £1300

1912. *King George V.* Wmk Mult Crown CA (Nos. 60/1).
Z106 ½d. yellow-green . . . £1300
Z107 1d. orange-red . . . £1300

Stamps of FALKLAND ISLANDS *cancelled at Port Foster with part of oval* "DECEPTION ISLAND SOUTH SHETLANDS" *postmark in black or violet between* 1914 *and* 1927.

1904–12. *King Edward VII (No. 43c).*
Z108 ½d. deep yellow-green . . . £300

1912–20. *King George V.* Wmk Mult Crown CA (Nos. 60/9).
Z110 ½d. yellow-green . . . 95·00
Z111 1d. orange-red . . . 95·00
Z112 2d. maroon . . . £130
Z113 2½d. deep bright blue . . . £130
Z114 6d. yellow-orange . . . £160
Z115 1s. light bistre-brown . . . £180
Z116 3s. slate-green . . . £400
Z117 5s. deep rose-red . . . £450
Z118 10s. red/*green* . . . £600
Z119 £1 black/*red* . . . £800

1918–20. "WAR STAMP" *ovpts (Nos. 70/2).*
Z120 ½d. deep olive . . . £130
Z121 1d. vermilion . . . £130
Z122 1s. light bistre-brown . . . £275

1921–28. *King George V.* Wmk Mult Script CA (Nos. 73/80).
Z123 ½d. yellowish green . . . £130
Z126 2½d. deep blue . . . £160
Z129 1s. deep ochre . . . £180

Stamps of FALKLAND ISLANDS *cancelled at Port Foster with* "SOUTH SHETLANDS" *circular datestamp between* 1923 *and* March 1931.

1912–20. *King George V.* Wmk Mult Crown CA (Nos. 60/9).
Z129*a* ½d. dull yellowish green (on thick greyish paper) . . . 80·00
Z130 1d. orange-vermilion . . . 65·00
Z131 2d. deep reddish purple . . . 75·00
Z132 2½d. deep bright blue
 c. Deep blue
Z133 6d. brown-orange . . . £100
Z134 1s. bistre-brown
Z135 3s. slate-green . . . £225
Z136 5s. maroon . . . £275
Z137 10s. red/*green* . . . £425
Z138 £1 black/*red* . . . £750

Examples of all values are known with forged postmarks dated "20 MR 27".

1918–20. "WAR STAMP" *ovpts (Nos. 70/2).*
Z139 1d. vermilion
Z140 1s. light bistre-brown

1921–28. *King George V.* Wmk Mult Script CA (Nos. 73/80).
Z141 ½d. yellowish green . . . 42·00
Z142 1d. dull vermilion . . . 42·00
Z143 2d. deep brown-purple . . . 65·00
Z144 2½d. deep blue . . . 55·00
 a. Prussian blue
Z145 2½d. deep purple/*pale yellow* . . . 85·00
Z146 6d. yellow-orange . . . 75·00
Z147 1s. deep ochre . . . 75·00
Z148 3s. slate-green . . . £250

1929. *King George V. Whale and Penguins design (Nos. 116/26).*
Z149 ½d. green . . . 65·00
Z150 1d. scarlet . . . 65·00
Z151 2d. grey . . . 85·00
Z152 2½d. blue . . . 75·00
Z153 6d. purple . . . 95·00
Z154 1s. black/*emerald* . . . 95·00
Z155 2s.6d. carmine/*blue* . . . £150
Z156 5s. green/*yellow* . . . £170
Z157 10s. carmine/*emerald* . . . £375
Z158 £1 black/*red* . . . £700

The whaling station at Port Foster was abandoned at the end of the 1930–31 season.

It was reoccupied as a Falkland Islands Dependencies Survey base on 3 February 1944.

Falkland Islands definitive stamps with face values of 1s.3d. and above were valid for use from the South Shetlands in conjunction with Nos. D1/8 and subsequently Nos. G1/16.

Stamps of FALKLAND ISLANDS *cancelled at Port Foster or Admiralty Bay with South Shetlands circular datestamps between* 5 February 1944 *and* 31 January 1954.

1938–50. *King George VI (Nos. 160/3).*
Z159 2s.6d. slate . . . 48·00
Z160 5s. indigo and yellow-brown . . . £140
Z161 10s. black and orange . . . 60·00
Z162 £1 black and violet . . . 80·00

1952. *King George VI (Nos. 181/5).*
Z163 1s.3d. orange . . . 85·00
Z164 2s.6d. olive-green . . . 95·00
Z165 5s. purple . . . £110
Z166 10s. grey . . . £120
Z167 £1 black . . . £130

1944 (5 Feb)–**45.** *Falkland Islands Nos. 146, 148, 150, 153/5, 157 and 158a optd* "SOUTH SHETLANDS/DEPENDENCY OF", *in red, as Type A* **1** *of Graham Land.*
D1 ½d. black and green . . . 30 1·75
D2 1d. black and violet . . . 30 1·00
D3 2d. black and carmine-red . . . 50 1·00
D4 3d. black and blue . . . 50 1·00
D5 4d. black and purple . . . 2·00 1·75
D6 6d. black and brown . . . 16·00 2·25
 a. Blue-black and brown (24.9.45) . . . 16·00
D7 9d. black and grey-blue . . . 1·00 1·25
D8 1s. deep blue . . . 1·00 1·25
D1/8 *Set of* 8 . . . 19·00 10·00
D1s/8s Perf "Specimen" *Set of* 8 . . . £425

From 12 July 1946 to 16 July 1963, Graham Land, South Georgia, South Orkneys and South Shetlands used FALKLAND ISLANDS DEPENDENCIES stamps.

E. FALKLAND ISLANDS DEPENDENCIES

For use at the following bases:
Admiralty Bay (South Shetlands) (*opened* January 1948, *closed* January 1961)
Argentine Islands (Graham Land) (*opened* 1947)
Deception Island (South Shetlands)
Grytviken (South Georgia)
Hope Bay (Graham Land) (*closed* 4 February 1949, *opened* February 1952)
Laurie Island (South Orkneys) (*closed* 1947)
Port Lockroy (Graham Land) (*closed* 16 January 1962)
Signy Island (South Orkneys) (*opened* 1946)
Stonington Island (Graham Land) (*opened* 1946, *closed* 1950, *opened* 1958, *closed* 1959, *opened* 1960)

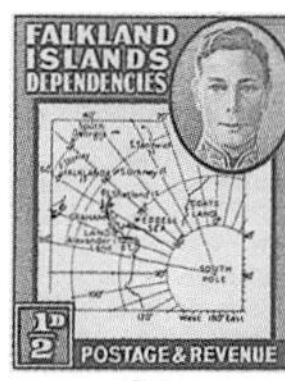

G 1

Extra island (Plate 1 R. 3/9)

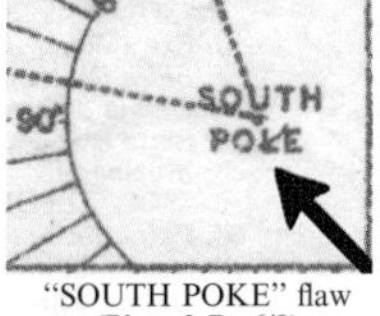

"SOUTH POKE" flaw (Plate 2 R. 6/8)

Missing "I" in "S. Shetland Is." (Plate 1 R. 1/2)

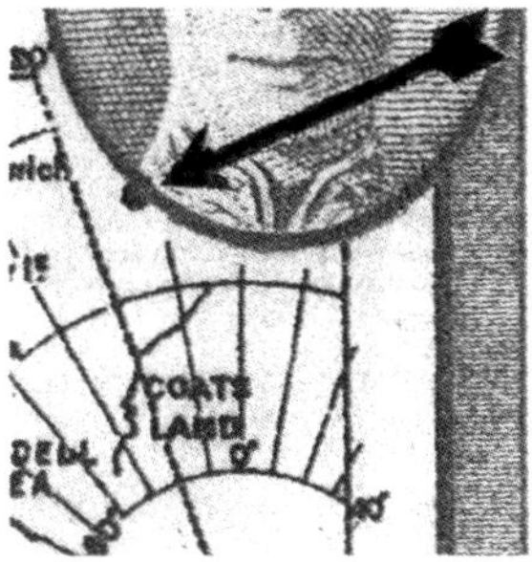

Extra dot by oval (Plate 1 R. 4/6)

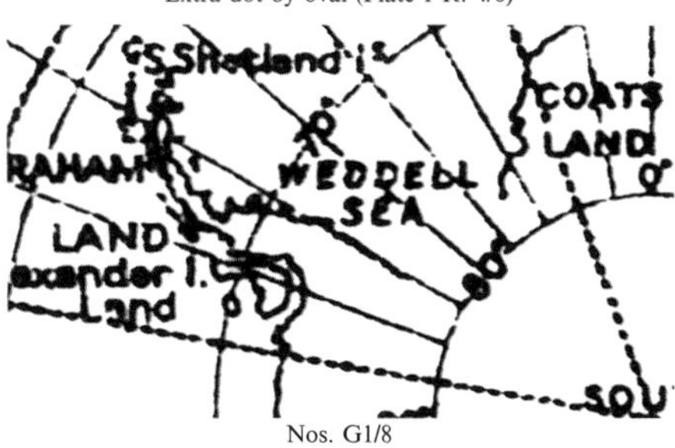

Nos. G1/8

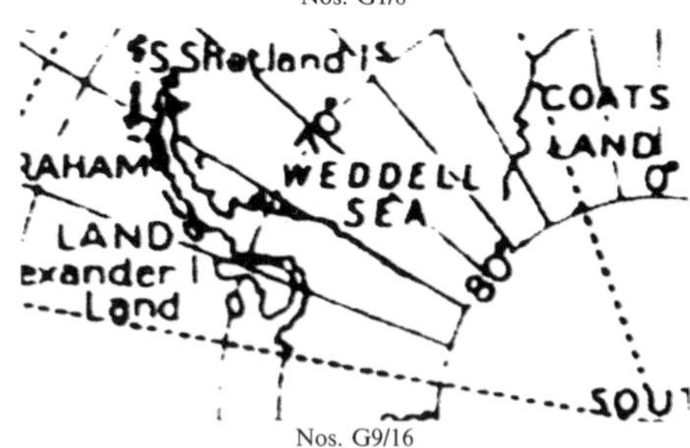

Nos. G9/16

On Nos. G9 to G16 the map is redrawn; the "o°" meridian does not pass through the "S" of "COATS", the "n" of "Alexander" is not joined to the "L" of "Land" below, and the loops of letters "s" and "t" are generally more open.

(Map litho, frame recess D.L.R.)

1946 (12 July*)–**49**. Wmk Mult Script CA (sideways). P 12.

(a) Map thick and coarse.

G1 **G 1** ½d. black and green . . . 1·00 3·00
a. Gap in 80th parallel . . . 3·00 5·00
aa. Extra island . . . 90·00 £120
b. Missing "I" . . . 90·00 £120
c. "SOUTH POKE" . . . 90·00 £120
d. Extra dot by oval . . . 90·00 £120
G2 1d. black and violet . . . 1·25 1·75
a. Gap in 80th parallel . . . 3·50 4·25
aa. Extra island . . . 85·00 £100
b. Missing "I" . . . 85·00 £100
d. Extra dot by oval . . . 85·00 £100
G3 2d. black and carmine . . . 1·25 2·50
a. Gap in 80th parallel . . . 3·50 4·75
aa. Extra island . . . 95·00 £120
b. Missing "I" . . . 95·00 £120
d. Extra dot by oval . . . 95·00 £120
G4 3d. black and blue . . . 1·25 4·75
a. Gap in 80th parallel . . . 3·50 7·00
aa. Extra island . . . £100 £140
b. Missing "I" . . . £100 £140
d. Extra dot by oval . . . £100 £140
G5 4d. black and claret . . . 2·25 4·75
a. Gap in 80th parallel . . . 6·00 8·50
c. "SOUTH POKE" . . . £130 £160
G6 6d. black and orange . . . 3·25 4·75
a. Gap in 80th parallel . . . 7·00 9·00
aa. Extra island . . . £140 £170
b. Missing "I" . . . £140 £170
c. "SOUTH POKE" . . . £140 £170
d. Extra dot by oval . . . £140 £170
e. Black and ochre . . . 50·00 95·00
ea. Gap in 80th parallel . . . 85·00 £140
eaa. Extra island . . . £325
eb. Missing "I" . . . £325
ec. "SOUTH POKE" . . . £325
ed. Extra dot by oval . . . £325
G7 9d. black and brown . . . 2·00 3·75
a. Gap in 80th parallel . . . 5·50 7·50
c. "SOUTH POKE" . . . £120 £140
G8 1s. black and purple . . . 2·00 4·25
a. Gap in 80th parallel . . . 5·50 8·50
c. "SOUTH POKE" . . . £120 £150
G1/8 *Set of* 8 . . . 13·00 27·00
G1s/8s Perf "Specimen" *Set of* 8 . . . £550

(b) Map thin and clear (16.2.48).

G 9 **G 1** ½d. black and green . . . 2·25 12·00
a. Recess frame printed double, one albino and inverted . . . £1200
G10 1d. black and violet . . . 1·50 15·00
G11 2d. black and carmine . . . 2·75 21·00
G11*a* 2½d. black and deep blue (6.3.49) . . . 6·50 6·00
G12 3d. black and blue . . . 2·75 4·50
G13 4d. black and claret . . . 17·00 24·00
G14 6d. black and orange . . . 24·00 8·00
G15 9d. black and brown . . . 24·00 8·00
G16 1s. black and purple . . . 24·00 8·00
G9/16 *Set of* 9 . . . 95·00 95·00

*This is the date of issue for South Georgia. Nos. G1/8 were released in London on 11 February.

The gap in the 80th parallel occurs six times in each sheet of all values in positions R. 1/4, 1/9, 3/4, 3/9, 5/4 and 5/9.

A constant variety, dot on "T" of "SOUTH", occurs on R. 5/2, 5/4, 5/6, 5/8 and 5/10 of all values of the "thin map" set with the exception of the 2½d.

1946 (4 Oct*). *Victory. As Nos. 110/11 of Antigua.*
G17 1d. deep violet . . . 50 30
G18 3d. blue . . . 75 30
G17s/18s Perf "Specimen" *Set of* 2 . . . £150

*This is the date of issue for South Georgia. The stamps were placed on sale from the South Orkneys on 17 January 1947, from the South Shetlands on 30 January 1947 and from Graham Land on 10 February 1947.

1948 (6 Dec). *Royal Silver Wedding. As Nos. 112/13 of Antigua, but 1s. in recess.*
G19 2½d. ultramarine . . . 1·75 2·00
G20 1s. violet-blue . . . 1·75 2·25

1949 (10 Oct). *75th Anniv of U.P.U. As Nos. 114/17 of Antigua.*
G21 1d. violet . . . 1·00 2·00
G22 2d. carmine-red . . . 5·00 3·25
G23 3d. deep blue . . . 3·25 1·25
G24 6d. red-orange . . . 4·00 3·00
G21/4 *Set of* 4 . . . 12·00 8·50

Fiji

PRICES FOR STAMPS ON COVER TO 1945

Nos.	1/9	*from* × 6
Nos.	10/34	*from* × 5
Nos.	35/59	*from* × 8
Nos.	60/3	—
Nos.	64/9	*from* × 20
Nos.	70/5	*from* × 5
Nos.	76/103	*from* × 8
Nos.	104/14	*from* × 5
Nos.	115/24	*from* × 4
Nos.	125/37	*from* × 3
Nos.	138/241	*from* × 4
Nos.	242/5	*from* × 3
Nos.	246/8	*from* × 8
Nos.	249/66*b*	*from* × 2
No.	267	*from* × 8
Nos.	D1/5*c*	*from* × 4
Nos.	D6/10	*from* × 20
Nos.	D11/18	*from* × 15

King Cakobau 1852–Oct 1874

Christian missionaries reached Fiji in 1835 and early letters are known to and from their mission stations, sent via Sydney, Hobart or Auckland.

In 1852 Cakobau, the chief of the island of Bau, declared himself King of Fiji and converted to Christianity two years later. Internal problems and difficulties with the American government led the king to offer to cede Fiji to Great Britain. The offer was refused, but resulted in the appointment of a British Consul in 1858. A Consular Post Office operated from September 1858 until 1872 and franked mail with New South Wales stamps from 1863.

The destruction of plantations in the Confederacy during the American Civil War led to an increased demand for Fijian cotton and this upsurge in commercial activity encouraged *The Fiji Times* newspaper on Levuka to establish a postal service on 1 November 1870.

1

(Type-set and printed at the office of *The Fiji Times*, Levuka, Ovalau, Fiji)

1870 (1 Nov)–**71**. *Rouletted in the printing.*

(a) Quadrillé paper.

1 **1** 1d. black/*rose* . . . £3250 £3500
2 3d. black/*rose* . . . £3500 £3500
3 6d. black/*rose* . . . £2000 £2000
4 1s. black/*rose* . . . £1500 £1800

(b) Laid bâtonné paper (1871).

5 **1** 1d. black/*rose* . . . £900 £1800
a. Vert strip of 4. Nos. 5, 7/9 . . . £35000
6 3d. black/*rose* . . . £1500 £2750
7 6d. black/*rose* . . . £1100 £1800
8 9d. black/*rose* . . . £2250 £3000
a. Comma after "EXPRESS" (R. 4/4) . . . £3000
9 1s. black/*rose* . . . £1200 £1400

Nos. 1/4 were printed *se-tenant* as a sheet of 24 (6 × 4) with the 6d. stamps in the first horizontal row, the 1s. in the second, the 1d. in the third and the 3d. in the fourth. Nos. 5/9 were produced from the same plate on which three of the 3d. impressions had been replaced with three 9d. values.

The issued stamps showed the vertical frame lines continuous from top to bottom of the sheet with the horizontal rules broken and not touching the verticals. Used examples are cancelled in manuscript or by the star cancellation used at Bau.

There are no reprints of these stamps, but the 1d., 3d., 6d. and 1s. are known in the correct type on *yellow wove* paper and are believed to be proofs.

There are also three different sets of imitations made by the proprietors of *The Fiji Times* to meet the demands of collectors:—

The first was produced in 1876 on *white wove* or *vertically laic* paper, rouletted on dotted lines and arranged in sheets of 40 (5 rows of 8) comprising 1d., 3d., 6d., 9d. and 1s.; the horizontal frame lines are continuous and the vertical ones broken.

The second was produced before 1888 on *thick rosy mauve wove* paper, rouletted on dotted lines and arranged in sheets of 30 (5 rows of 6) comprising 1s., 9d., 6d., 3d. and 1d.; the vertical frame lines are continuous and the horizontal ones broken.

The third only came to light in the 1960s and is rare, only one complete sheet being recorded, which has since been destroyed. The sheet arrangement is the same as Nos. 1/4, which suggests that this was the first imitation to be produced. It is on *off-white wove* paper rouletted on closely dotted or solid lines, with vertical frame line continuous and the horizontal ones broken, as in the originals. These differ from the proofs mentioned above in that the lettering is slightly larger and the figures also differ.

King Cakobau established a formal government in June 1871 and stamps for the royal post office were ordered from Sydney. These arrived in October 1871 and the postal service was placed on a firm basis by the First Postal Act in December of that year. Under its terms *The Fiji Times* service closed on 17 January 1872 and the British Consular Post Office followed six months later.

2

3

Two
Cents
(4)

(Eng and electrotyped by A. L. Jackson. Typo Govt Printing Office, Sydney)

1871 (Oct). *Wove paper.* Wmk "FIJI POSTAGE" in small sans seri capitals across the middle row of stamps in the sheet. P 12½.
10 **2** 1d. blue . . . 50·00 £12
11 3d. pale yellow-green . . . £110 £35
12 **3** 6d. rose . . . £140 £30

The 3d. differs from T **2** in having a white circle containing squar dots surrounding the centre.

All three values are known *imperf*, but were not issued in tha condition.

See notes after No. 33b.

1872 (13 Jan). *Surch as T* **4**, *in local currency, by Govt Ptg Offic Sydney.*
13 **2** 2c.on 1d. pale blue . . . 50·00 65·0
a. Deep blue . . . 35·00 50·0
14 6c.on 3d. yellow-green . . . 70·00 70·0
15 **3** 12c.on 6d. carmine-rose . . . 95·00 80·0

CROWN COLONY

King Cakobau renewed his offer to cede Fiji to Great Britain ar this took place on 12 October 1874.

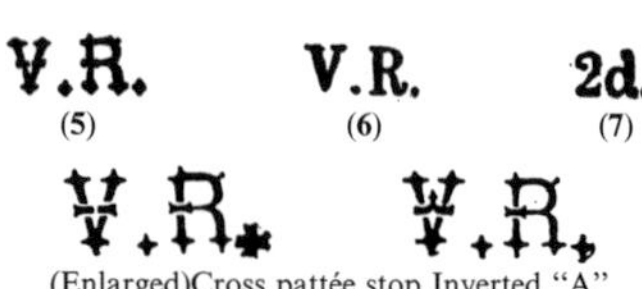

(5) (6) (7)

(Enlarged)Cross pattée stop Inverted "A"

Cross pattée stop after "R" (R. 3/6).
Round raised stop after "V" (R. 3/8)
Round raised stops after "V" and "R" (R. 3/9).
Inverted "A" for "V" (R. 3/10).
No stop after "R" (R. 2/3 on T **5**, R. 5/3 on T **6**).
Large stop after "R" (R. 5/10).

(Optd at *Polynesian Gazette* Office, Levuka)

1874 (21 Oct). *Nos. 13/15 optd.*

(a) With T **5**.

16	2	2c.on 1d. blue	£900	£250
		a. No stop after "R"	£2250	£1000
		b. Cross pattée stop after "R"	£2250	£1000
		c. Round raised stop after "V"	£2250	£1000
		d. Round raised stops after "V" and "R"	£2250	£1000
		e. Inverted "A" for "V"	£2250	£1000
		f. Vert pair. Nos. 16 and 19	£5000	
17		6c.on 3d. green	£1500	£650
		a. No stop after "R"	£3750	£1600
		b. Cross pattée stop after "R"	£3750	£1600
		c. Round raised stop after "V"	£3750	£1600
		d. Round raised stops after "V" and "R"	£3750	£1600
		e. Inverted "A" for "V"	£3750	£1600
		f. Vert pair. Nos. 17 and 20	£7000	
18	3	12c.on 6d. rose	£650	£200
		a. No stop after "R"	£2000	£1000
		b. Cross pattée stop after "R"	£2000	£1000
		c. Round raised stop after "V"	£2000	£1000
		d. Round raised stops after "V" and "R"	£2000	£1000
		e. Inverted "A" for "V"	£2000	£1000
		f. Opt inverted	—	£4500
		g. Vert pair. Nos. 18 and 21	£4000	

(b) With T **6**.

19	2	2c.on 1d. blue	£1000	£275
		a. No stop after "R"	£2250	£1000
		f. Large stop after "R"	—	£1000
20		6c.on 3d. green	£1900	£900
		a. No stop after "R"	£3750	£1600
21	3	12c.on 6d. rose	£800	£225
		a. No stop after "R"	£2000	£1000
		b. Opt inverted	£5000	

Nos. 16/21 were produced in sheets of 50 (10 × 5) of which the top three rows were overprinted with Type **5** and the lower two with Type **6**.

1875. *Stamps of 1874 surch at Polynesian Gazette Office, Levuka, with T* **7**.

(a) In red (May).

22	2	2d.on 6c. on 3d. green (No. 17)	£550	£180
		a. No stop after "R"	£1600	£650
		b. Cross pattée stop after "R"	£1600	£650
		c. Round raised stop after "V"	£1600	£650
		d. Round raised stops after "V" and "R"	£1600	£650
		e. Inverted "A" for "V"	£1600	£650
		f. No stop after "2d" (R. 1/2)	£1600	£650
		g. Vert pair. Nos. 22/3	£3000	
23		2d.on 6c. on 3d. green (No. 20)	£700	£275
		a. No stop after "R"	£1600	£650
		b. Stop between "2" and "d" (R. 5/7)	£1600	£650

(b) In black (30 Sept).

24	2	2d.on 6c. on 3d. green (No. 17)	£1500	£450
		a. No stop after "R"	£3250	£1200
		b. Cross pattée stop after "R"	£3250	£1200
		c. Round raised stop after "V"	£3250	£1200
		d. Round raised stops after "V" and "R"	£3250	£1200
		e. Inverted "A" for "V"	£3250	£1200
		f. No stop after "2d" (R. 1/2)	£3250	£1200
		g. "V.R." double		
		h. Vert pair. Nos. 24/5	£6500	
25		2d.on 6c. on 3d. green (No. 20)	£1900	£650
		a. No stop after "R"	£3250	£1200
		b. Stop between "2" and "d" (R. 5/7)	£3250	£1200
		c. "V.R." double	£3750	£3500

1875 (20 Nov). *No. 15 surch at Polynesian Gazette Office, Levuka, with T* **7** *and "V.R." at one operation.*

(a) "V.R." T **5**.

26	3	2d.on 12c. on 6d. rose	£1900	£800
		a. No stop after "R"	—	£2000
		b. Round raised stop after "R"	—	£1300
		c. Inverted "A" for "V" (R. 1/3, 2/8, 4/4)	£2500	£1100
		d. Do. and round raised stop after "V" (R. 3/3, 3/6, 3/8, 3/10)	£2250	£950
		e. As "a" and round raised stops after "R" and "V" (R. 3/2, 3/9)	£2750	£1200
		f. Surch double	—	£3750
		g. Vert pair. Nos. 26/7	£7000	

(b) "V.R." T **6**.

27	3	2d.on 12c. on 6d. rose	£2000	£850
		a. Surch double	—	£4000

The setting used for Nos. 26/7 was similar to that of Nos. 16/21, but the fourth stamp in the fourth row had a Type **5** "V.R." instead of a Type **6**.

The position of No. 26b is not known.

(8)

Two Pence

(9)

(Typo Govt Printing Office, Sydney, from plates of 1871)

1876–77. *On paper previously lithographed "VR" as T* **8**, *the 3d. surch with T* **9**. P 12½.

(a) Wove paper (31.1.76).

28	2	1d. grey-blue	50·00	50·00
		a. Dull blue	50·00	50·00
		b. Doubly printed	£550	
		c. Void corner (R. 2/1)	£550	£325
		d. Imperf vert (horiz pair)	£850	
29		2d.on 3d. pale green	48·00	55·00
		a. Deep green	45·00	55·00
30	3	6d. pale rose	65·00	65·00
		a. Dull rose	50·00	55·00
		b. Carmine-rose	55·00	55·00
		c. Doubly printed	£2500	

(b) Laid paper (5.1.77).

31	2	1d. blue	18·00	29·00
		a. Deep blue	19·00	29·00
		b. Void corner (R. 2/1)	£300	£250
		c. Imperf vert (horiz pair)	£700	
32		2d.on 3d. yellow-green	60·00	70·00
		a. Deep yellow-green	60·00	70·00
		b. Imperf between (pair)	£850	
		c. Perf 10	£350	
		ca. Imperf vert (horiz pair)	£950	
		d. Perf 11	£300	
33	3	6d. rose	50·00	28·00
		a. Carmine-rose	50·00	35·00
		b. Imperf vert (horiz pair)	£700	

The 3d. *green* is known without the surcharge T **9** on wove paper and also without the surcharge and the monogram. In this latter condition it can only be distinguished from No. 11 by its colour, which is a fuller, deeper yellow-green.

Stamps on both wove and laid paper *imperf* are from printer's trial or waste sheets and were not issued.

All values are known on laid paper without the monogram "VR" and the 3d. stamp also without the surcharge but these are also believed to be from printer's trial sheets which were never issued for postal purposes. Being on laid paper they are easily distinguishable from Nos. 10/12.

1877 (12 Oct). *Optd with T* **8** *and surch as T* **9**. *Laid paper.* P 12½.

34	2	4d.on 3d. mauve	85·00	25·00
		a. Imperf vert (horiz pair)	£850	

10

11

A Four Pence

B Four Pence

Type A: Length 12½ mm

Type B: Length 14 mm

Note also the different shape of the two "e"s.

(Typo from new plates made from original dies of 1871 with "CR" altered to "VR" at Govt Printing Office, Sydney. 2d. and 4d. made from old 3d. die.)

1878–99. *Surcharges as T* **9** *or as Types A or B for 4d. value. Wove paper with paper-maker's name "T. H. SAUNDERS" or "SANDERSON" in double-lined capitals extending over seven stamps in each full sheet.*

(a) P 12½ (1878–80).

35	10	1d. pale ultramarine (19.2.79)	9·00	9·00
		a. Ultramarine	12·00	9·00
36		2d.on 3d. green (17.10.78)	6·00	20·00
37		2d. yellow-green (1.9.79)	18·00	10·00
		a. Blue-green	30·00	14·00
		b. Error. Ultramarine	£25000	
38	11	6d. rose (30.7.80)	£100	22·00

(b) P 10 (1881–90).

39	10	1d. dull blue (11.5.82)	55·00	3·00
		a. Ultramarine	18·00	2·75
		b. Cambridge blue (12.7.83)	50·00	4·25
40		2d. yellow-green (20.10.81)	15·00	1·00
		a. Blue-green	25·00	5·00
41		4d.on 1d. mauve (29.1.90)	42·00	30·00
42		4d.on 2d. pale mauve (A) (23.5.83)	75·00	12·00
		a. Dull purple	75·00	12·00
43		4d.on 2d. dull purple (B) (7.11.88)	—	£140
44		4d. mauve (13.9.90)	60·00	
		a. Deep purple	60·00	60·00
45	11	6d. pale rose (11.3.85)	70·00	19·00
		a. Bright rose	18·00	18·00

(c) P 10 × 12½ (1881–82).

46	10	1d. ultramarine (11.5.82)	£100	32·00
47		2d. green (20.10.81)	£160	60·00
48	11	6d. rose (20.10.81)	£350	55·00
		a. Pale rose	£350	55·00

(d) P 12½ × 10 (1888–90).

49	10	1d. ultramarine (1890)	—	£300
49*a*		2d. green (1888)		
49*b*		4d.on 2d. dull purple (A)	†	—

(e) P 10 × 11¾ (3.9.86).

50	10	1d. dull blue	70·00	13·00
		a. Ultramarine		
51		2d. yellow-green	65·00	8·50

(f) P 11¾ × 10 (1886–88).

51*a*	10	1d. dull blue (7.11.88)	£225	42·00
		ab. Ultramarine		
51*b*		2d. yellow-green (3.9.86)	—	£500
52	11	6d. rose (1887)	†	£750

(g) P 11 × 10 (1892–93).

53	10	1d. ultramarine (18.8.92)	14·00	11·00
54		4d. pale mauve (18.8.92)	11·00	12·00
55	11	6d. pale rose (14.2.93)	8·50	19·00
		a. Rose	15·00	23·00

(h) P 11 (1897–99).

56	10	4d. mauve (14.7.96)	12·00	8·50
57	11	6d. dull rose (14.7.96)	26·00	42·00
		a. Printed both sides (12.99)	£1100	£900
		b. Bright rose	45·00	50·00

(i) P 11 × 11¾ (1896)*.

58	10	4d. deep purple (14.7.96)	35·00	
		a. Bright purple	8·50	6·50
59	11	6d. rose (23.7.96)	32·00	
		a. Bright rose	8·00	3·75

(j) Imperf (pairs) (1882–90).

60	10	1d. ultramarine		
61		2d. yellow-green		
62		4d.on 2d. pale mauve		
63	11	6d. rose	—	£1300

*Under this heading are included stamps from several perforating machines with a gauge varying between 11.6 and 12.

No. 37b was printed in the colour of the 1d. in error. Only four examples have been reported, one of which was subsequently destroyed.

In the absence of detailed information on dates of issue printing dates are quoted for Nos. 35/63 and 76/103.

12

13

(Eng A. L. Jackson. Typo Govt Printing Office, Sydney)

1881–99. Paper-maker's name wmkd as previous issue.

(a) P 10 (19.10.81).

64	12	1s. pale brown	85·00	20·00
		a. Deep brown	85·00	22·00

(b) P 11 × 10 (1894).

65	12	1s. pale brown	45·00	45·00

(c) P 11 (1897).

66	12	1s. pale brown	40·00	14·00

(d) P 11 × 11¾ (5.99).

67	12	1s. pale brown	35·00	9·00
		a. Brown	35·00	9·00
		b. Deep brown	45·00	45·00

(e) P 11¾ × 11 (3.97).

68	12	1s. brown	55·00	50·00

Dates given of earliest known use.

Forgeries exist.

(Centre typo, frame litho Govt Printing Office, Sydney)

1882 (23 May). Toned paper wmkd with paper-maker's name "Cowan" in old English outline type once in each sheet. P 10.

69	13	5s. dull red and black	55·00	28·00

An unknown quantity of the 1s. and 264 sheets (13,200 stamps) of the 5s. were cancelled by the Fiji Post Office and sold as remainders. A number of different "SUVA" remainder cancellations have been recorded between "15 DEC 00" and "21 DE 1902".

An electrotyped plate was also produced for the frame of the 5s.. This printing was not used for postal purposes but examples were included among the remainders, all cancelled "15 DEC 00". The electrotyped printing is on paper watermarked "NEW SOUTH WALES GOVERNMENT" in double-line capitals and differs in a number of respects from the original, most notably in the circular frame surrounding the Queen's head, which is notably thicker than the litho printing. Examples are rare.

2½d. (14) **2 ½d.** (15)

Types **14** (fraction bar 1 mm from "2") and **15** (fraction bar 2 mm from "2") are from the same setting of 50 (10 × 5) with Type **15** occurring on R. 1/2, 2/2, 3/2 and 4/2.

(Stamps typo in Sydney and surch at Govt Printing Office, Suva)

1891 (1 Jan). *T* **10** *surch.* P 10.
70 **14** 2½d.on 2d. green . . . . . 45·00 48·00
71 **15** 2½d.on 2d. green £130 £140

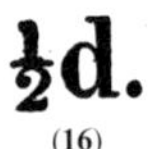
(**16**)

5d (**17**)

FIVE PENCE (**18**) 2 mm spacing

FIVE PENCE (**19**) 3 mm spacing

1892 (1 Mar)–**93**. P 10.

(a) Surch on T **10**.
72 **16** ½d.on 1d. dull blue . . . . . 50·00 75·00
a. Ultramarine . . . . . 45·00 70·00
73 **17** 5d.on 4d. deep purple (25.7.92) . . . . 50·00 70·00
a. Dull purple . . . . . 50·00 70·00

(b) Surch on T **11**.
74 **18** 5d.on 6d. brownish rose (30.11.92) . . 55·00 65·00
a. Bright rose . . . . . 55·00 60·00
b. Perf 10 × 12½ . . . . .
75 **19** 5d.on 6d. rose (4.1.93) . . . . . 70·00 80·00
a. Deep rose . . . . . 60·00 70·00
b. Brownish rose . . . . . 60·00

20

21 Native Canoe

22

(Typo in Sydney)

1891–1902. Wmk in sheet, either "SANDERSON" or "NEW SOUTH WALES GOVERNMENT" in outline capitals.

(a) P 10 (1891–94).
76 **20** ½d. slate-grey (26.4.92) . . . . . 4·50 4·25
77 **21** 1d. black (19.9.94) . . . . . 11·00 4·25
78 2d. pale green (19.9.94) . . . . . 95·00 11·00
79 **22** 2½d. chocolate (8.6.91) . . . . . 40·00 16·00
80 **21** 5d. ultramarine (14.2.93) . . . . . 80·00 55·00

(b) P 11 × 10 (1892–93).
81 **20** ½d. slate-grey (20.10.93) . . . . . 6·00 17·00
82 **21** 1d. black (14.2.93) . . . . . 7·00 3·75
83 2d. green (14.2.93) . . . . . 15·00 5·00
84 **22** 2½d. chocolate (17.8.92) . . . . . 20·00 24·00
a. Brown . . . . . 9·00 9·00
b. Yellowish brown . . . . .
85 **21** 5d. ultramarine (14.2.93) . . . . . 13·00 7·50

(c) P 11 (1893–96).
86 **20** ½d. slate-grey (2.6.96) . . . . . 3·00 6·00
a. Greenish slate . . . . . 2·50 6·00
87 **21** 1d. black (31.10.95) . . . . . 4·75 4·75
88 1d. pale mauve (2.6.96) . . . . . 6·00 1·00
a. Rosy mauve . . . . . 7·00 1·00
89 2d. dull green (17.3.94) . . . . . 6·00 80
a. Emerald-green . . . . . 7·00 2·00
90 **22** 2½d. brown (31.10.95) . . . . . 23·00 9·00
a. Yellowish brown . . . . . 14·00 19·00
91 **21** 5d. ultramarine (14.2.93) £150

(d) P 10 × 11¾ (1893–94).
92 **20** ½d. greenish slate £1000
93 **21** 1d. black (20.7.93) . . . . . 17·00 5·50
94 2d. dull green (19.9.94) £600 £375

(e) P 11¾ × 10 (19.9.94).
94*a* **20** ½d. greenish slate . . . . . — £1000

(f) P 11¾ (1894–98).
95 **20** ½d. greenish slate (19.9.94) . . . . . 2·75 9·00
a. Grey . . . . . 32·00
96 **21** 1d. black (19.9.94) . . . . . £200 30·00
97 1d. rosy mauve (4.5.98) . . . . . 5·50 7·50
98 2d. dull green (19.9.94) . . . . . 90·00 38·00

(g) P 11 × 11¾ (1895–97).
99 **20** ½d. greenish slate (8.10.97) . . . . . 1·00 3·25
100 **21** 1d. black (31.10.95) £3000 £1500
101 1d. rosy mauve (14.7.96) . . . . . 5·50 80
a. Pale rosy mauve . . . . . 4·50 2·00
102 2d. dull green (26.7.97) . . . . . 35·00 4·00
103 **22** 2½d. brown (26.7.97) . . . . . 11·00 17·00
a. Yellow-brown . . . . . 5·00 5·00

(h) P 11¾ × 11 (1897–98).
103*b* **20** ½d. greenish slate (8.10.97) . . . . . 4·00 7·50
103*c* **21** 1d. rosy mauve (10.2.97) . . . . . 11·00 5·00
103*d* 2d. dull green (4.5.98) (*shades*) £200 £100

The 2½d. brown is known doubly printed, but only occurs in the remainders and with the special obliteration (*Price* £120 *cancelled-to-order*). It was never issued for postal use.

23

24

(Typo D.L.R.)

1903 (1 Feb). Wmk Crown CA. P 14.
104 **23** ½d. green and pale green . . . . . 2·25 2·00
105 1d. dull purple and black/*red* . . . . 13·00 55
106 **24** 2d. dull purple and orange . . . . 3·75 1·25
107 **23** 2½d. dull purple and blue/*blue* . . . . 14·00 3·50
108 3d. dull purple and purple . . . . 1·50 4·00
109 **24** 4d. dull purple and black . . . . 1·50 2·50
110 **23** 5d. dull purple and green . . . . 1·50 2·75
111 **24** 6d. dull purple and carmine . . . . 1·50 1·75
112 **23** 1s. green and carmine . . . . 11·00 65·00
113 **24** 5s. green and black . . . . 55·00 £140
114 **23** £1 grey-black and ultramarine . . . £300 £375
104/14 *Set of* 11 . . . . . £375 £550
104s/14s Optd "Specimen" *Set of* 11 . . . . . £300

1904–09. Wmk Mult Crown CA. *Chalk-surfaced paper (1s.)*. P 14.
115 **23** ½d. green and pale green . . . . . 15·00 3·00
116 1d. purple and black/*red* . . . . . 27·00 10
117 1s. green and carmine (1909) . . . . 28·00 40·00
115/17 *Set of* 3 . . . . . 60·00 40·00

1906–12. *Colours changed.* Wmk Mult Crown CA. *Chalk surfaced paper (6d. to £1)*. P 14.
118 **23** ½d. green (1908) . . . . . 11·00 3·25
119 1d. red (1906) . . . . . 9·50 10
w. Wmk inverted . . . . . † —
120 2½d. bright blue (1910) . . . . . 6·50 7·50
121 **24** 6d. dull purple (1910) . . . . . 13·00 28·00
122 **23** 1s. black/*green* (1911) . . . . . 4·25 10·00
123 **24** 5s. green and red/*yellow* (1911) . . . . 55·00 60·00
124 **23** £1 purple and black/*red* (1912) . . . £300 £275
118/24 *Set of* 7 . . . . . £350 £350
119s/24s Optd "Specimen" *Set of* 6 . . . . . £325

Nos. 112/14, 117 and 120/4 are known with a forged registered postmark of Suva dated "10 DEC 1909".

25

26

WAR STAMP
(**27**)

(Typo D.L.R.)

1912 (Oct)–**23**. *Die I.* Wmk Mult Crown CA. *Chalk-surfaced paper (5d. to £1)*. P 14.
125 **26** ¼d. brown (1.4.16) . . . . . 2·50 30
a. Deep brown (1917) . . . . . 1·50 40
y. Wmk inverted and reversed . . .
126 **25** ½d. green . . . . . 1·50 1·00
a. Yellow-green (1916) . . . . . 8·50 8·50
b. Blue-green (1917) . . . . . 1·25 50
w. Wmk inverted £100
y. Wmk inverted and reversed . . . £100
127 1d. carmine . . . . . 2·00 10
a. Bright scarlet (1916) . . . . . 2·00 75
ax. Wmk reversed . . . . . † —
b. Deep rose (1916) . . . . . 9·50 2·00
bw. Wmk inverted . . . . . † —
128 **26** 2d. greyish slate (5.14) . . . . . 1·75 10
a. Wmk sideways . . . . .
b. "C" of "CA" missing from wmk . . . . . † —
129 **25** 2½d. bright blue (5.14) . . . . . 3·00 3·50
130 3d. purple/*yellow* (5.14) . . . . . 4·25 5·50
a. Wmk sideways £350 £450
b. On lemon (1915) . . . . . 2·00 8·50
c. On pale yellow (1921) . . . . . 1·75 14·00
ca. "A" of "CA" missing from wmk . . . . .
cw. Wmk inverted . . . . .
d. Die II. *On pale yellow* (1922) . . . 2·50 24·00
131 **26** 4d. black and red/*yellow* (5.14) . . . 23·00 20·00
a. On lemon . . . . . 3·00 16·00
b. On orange-buff (1920) . . . . . 50·00 65·00
c. On pale yellow (1921) . . . . . 6·50 14·00
cw. Wmk inverted £400
d. Die II. *On pale yellow* (1922) . . . 3·00 25·00
ds. Optd "Specimen" . . . . . 40·00
132 **25** 5d. dull purple and olive-green (5.14) . . . . . 4·75 11·00
133 **26** 6d. dull and bright purple (5.14) . . . 2·00 5·50
134 **25** 1s. black/*green* (10.13) . . . . . 1·25 14·00
a. White back (4.14) . . . . . 1·00 11·00
b. On blue-green, olive back (1916) . . . . . 3·75 10·00
c. On emerald back (1921) . . . . . 5·50 40·00
cs. Optd Specimen" . . . . . 45·00
d. Die II. *On emerald back* (1922) . . . 2·75 24·00
135 **26** 2s.6d. black and red/*blue* (19.1.16) . . . 32·00 30·00
136 5s. green and red/*yellow* . . . . . 32·00 40·00
137 **25** £1 purple and black/*red* (5.14) . . . £250 £275
a. Die II (1923) £250 £275
125/37 *Set of* 13 . . . . . £300 £350
125s/37s Optd "Specimen" *Set of* 13 . . . . . £425

1915 (1 Dec)–**19**. *Optd with T* **27** *by Govt Printer, Suva.*
138 **25** ½d. green . . . . .
a. Yellow-green (1916) . . . . . 75 4·50
b. Blue-green (1917) . . . . . 75 2·75
c. Opt inverted £600
d. Opt double . . . . .
139 1d. carmine . . . . . 27·00 23·00
a. Bright scarlet . . . . . 1·75 75
ab. Horiz pair, one without opt . . . £5500
c. Opt inverted £700
d. Deep rose (1919) . . . . . 2·75 2·25
138s/9s H/S "Specimen" *Set of* 2 . . . . . £120

No. 139ab occurred on one pane of 120 only, the overprint being so misplaced that all the stamps of the last vertical row escaped it entirely.

Nos. 140/227 are no longer used.

1922–29. *Die II.* Wmk Mult Script CA. *Chalk-surfaced paper (1s. to 5s.)*. P 14.
228 **26** ¼d. deep brown (1923) . . . . . 2·50 24·00
229 **25** ½d. green (1923) . . . . . 75 2·00
w. Wmk inverted . . . . .
230 1d. carmine-red . . . . . 2·50 1·00
231 1d. violet (6.1.27) . . . . . 1·25 10
232 **26** 1½d. scarlet (6.1.27) . . . . . 4·00 1·75
233 2d. grey . . . . . 1·25 10
a. Face value omitted £18000
234 **25** 3d. bright blue (1924) . . . . . 2·75 1·00
235 **26** 4d. black and red/*lemon* (1924) . . . 5·00 7·00
a. On pale yellow (1929) . . . . . 45·00 24·00
236 **25** 5d. dull purple and sage-green (1927) . . . . . 1·50 2·00
237 **26** 6d. dull and bright purple . . . . . 2·00 1·25
238 **25** 1s. black/*emerald* (1924) . . . . . 4·75 6·00
w. Wmk inverted . . . . .
239 **26** 2s. purple and blue/*blue* (6.1.27) . . . 25·00 60·0
240 2s.6d. black and red/*blue* (1925) . . . 11·00 32·0
241 5s. green and red/*pale yellow* (1926) . . . . . 32·00 65·0
228/41 *Set of* 14 . . . . . 85·00 £18
228s/41s Optd "Specimen" *Set of* 14 . . . . . £300

The 2d. imperforate with watermark Type **10** of Ireland cam from a trial printing and was not issued.

Only one example of No. 233a is known. It was caused by a obstruction during the printing of the duty plate.

1935 (6 May). *Silver Jubilee. As Nos. 91/4 of Antigua.*
242 1½d. deep blue and carmine . . . . . 80 7·0
a. Deep blue and aniline red . . . . . 9·00 22·0
b. Frame printed double, one albino . . £1000
f. Diagonal line by turret . . . . . 50·00
h. Dot by flagstaff £110
i. Dash by turret £110
243 2d. ultramarine and grey . . . . . 1·50 3
f. Diagonal line by turret . . . . . 70·00
g. Dot to left of chapel £150
244 3d. brown and deep blue . . . . . 2·50 3·0
f. Diagonal line by turret £100
h. Dot by flagstaff £190
i. Dash by turret £190
245 1s. slate and purple . . . . . 4·50 6·0
a. Frame printed double, one albino . . £1500
f. Diagonal line by turret £160
h. Dot by flagstaff £275
242/5 *Set of* 4 . . . . . 8·50 15·0
242s/5s Perf "Specimen" *Set of* 4 . . . . . £100

For illustrations of plate varieties see Omnibus section followin Zanzibar.

1937 (12 May). *Coronation. As Nos. 95/7 of Antigua.* P 11 × 11½.
246 1d. purple . . . . . 60 1·0
247 2d. grey-black . . . . . 60 1·7
248 3d. Prussian blue . . . . . 60 1·7
246/8 *Set of* 3 . . . . . 1·60 4·0
246s/8s Perf "Specimen" *Set of* 3 . . . . . 70·00

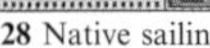
28 Native sailing Canoe

29 Native Village

30 Camakua (canoe)

31 Map of Fiji Islands

Two Dies of Type **30**:

Die I Die II Empty Canoe Native in Canoe

Two Dies of Type **31**:

Die I Die II Without "180°" With "180°"

Extra palm frond (R. 5/8)

Extra line (R. 2/1)

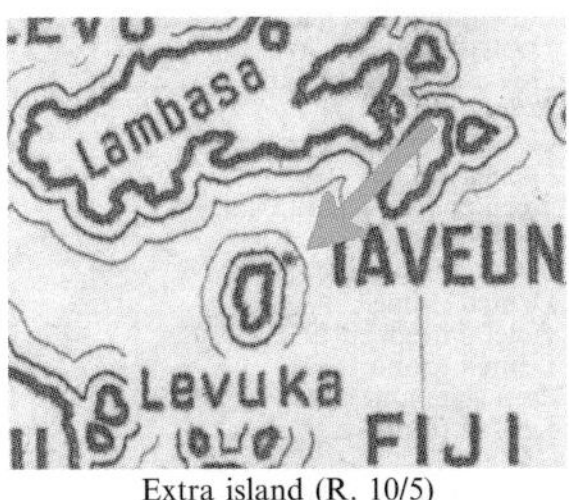

Extra island (R. 10/5)

Spur on arms medallion (Pl 2 R. 4/2) (ptg of 26 Nov 1945)

Des V. E. Ousey (½d., 1s., 2s.6d.), Miss C. D. Lovejoy (1d., 1½d., 5d.), Miss I. Stinson (3d., 5s.) and A. V. Guy (2d. (Nos. 253/4), 2½d., 6d., 2s.). Recess De La Rue (½d., 1½d., 2d., (Nos. 253/5a), 2½d., 6d., 8d., 1s.5d., 1s.6d.), Waterlow (others))

938 (5 Apr)–**55**. *T* **28/31** *and similar designs.* Wmk Mult Script CA. Various perfs.

49	**28**	½d. green (P 13½)	20	75
		a. Perf 14 (5.41)	20·00	3·50
		b. Perf 12 (8.48)	1·00	3·00
		ba. Extra palm frond	55·00	
50	**29**	1d. brown and blue (P 12½)	50	20
51	**30**	1½d. carmine (Die I) (P 13½)	15·00	35
52		1½d. carmine (Die II) (P 13½) (1.10.40)	1·40	3·00
		a. Deep carmine (10.42)	4·00	1·25
		b. Perf 14 (6.42)	18·00	19·00
		c. Perf 12 (21.7.49)	1·00	1·25
53	**31**	2d. brown and green (Die I) (P 13½)	38·00	40
		a. Extra line	£325	65·00
54		2d. brown and green (Die II) (P 13½) (1.10.40)	16·00	16·00
55	–	2d. green & mag (P 13½) (19.5.42)	40	60
		a. Perf 12 (27.5.46)	55	70
56	**31**	2½d. brown & grn (Die II) (P 14) (6.1.42)	60	1·00
		a. Extra island	28·00	
		b. Perf 13½ (6.1.42)	70	80
		ba. Extra island	30·00	
		c. Perf 12 (19.1.48)	1·00	50
		ca. Extra island	32·00	
57	–	3d. blue (P 12½)	1·00	30
		a. Spur on arms medallion	£200	£120
58	–	5d. blue and scarlet (P 12½)	42·00	10·00
59	–	5d. yell-green & scar (P 12½) (1.10.40)	20	30
50	**31**	6d. black (Die I) (P 13 × 12)	60·00	12·00
51		6d. black (Die II) (P 13½) (1.10.40)	3·00	2·25
		a. Violet-black (1.44)	25·00	28·00
		b. Perf 12. *Black* (5.6.47)	1·50	1·50
1*c*	–	8d. carmine (P 14) (15.11.48)	1·00	2·25
		d. Perf 13 (7.6.50)	70	2·75
2	–	1s. black and yellow (P 12½)	75	70
3	–	1s.5d. black & carm (P 14) (13.6.40)	20	10
3*a*	–	1s.6d. ultramarine (P 14) (1.8.50)	3·50	2·75
		b. Perf 13 (16.2.55)	1·25	15·00
4	–	2s. violet and orange (P 12½)	2·50	40
5	–	2s.6d. green and brown (P 12½)	2·75	1·50
6	–	5s. green and purple (P 12½)	2·75	1·75
6*a*	–	10s. orange & emer (P 12½) (13.3.50)	35·00	40·00
6*b*	–	£1 ultram & carm (P 12½) (13.3.50)	48·00	50·00
9/66*b Set of* 22			£250	£120
9s/66s (*excl* 8d. *and* 1s.6d.) Perf "Specimen" *t of* 18			£450	

Designs: *Horiz* (*as T* **30**)—2d. (Nos. 255/a) Government Offices. *s T* **29**)—3d. Canoe and arms of Fiji; 8d., 1s.5d., 1s.6d. Arms of ji; 2s. Suva Harbour; 2s.6d. River scene; 5s. Chief's hut. *Vert* (*as* **29**)—5d. Sugar cane; 1s. Spearing fish by torchlight; 10s. Paww tree; £1 Police bugler.

2½d.

(42)

1941 (10 Feb). *No. 254 surch with T* **42** *by Govt Printer, Suva.*

267	**31**	2½d.on 2d. brown and green	2·00	20

1946 (17 Aug). *Victory. As Nos. 110/11 of Antigua.*

268	2½d. green	10	1·00
	a. Printed double, one albino	£300	
269	3d. blue	10	10
268s/9s	Perf "Specimen" *Set of* 2	70·00	

1948 (17 Dec). *Royal Silver Wedding. As Nos. 112/13 of Antigua.*

270	2½d. green	40	1·25
271	5s. violet-blue	14·00	7·50

1949 (10 Oct). *75th Anniv of U.P.U. As Nos. 114/17 of Antigua.*

272	2d. bright reddish purple	30	40
273	3d. deep blue	2·00	2·50
274	8d. carmine-red	30	2·50
275	1s.6d. blue	35	1·00
272/5	*Set of* 4	2·75	5·75

43 Children Bathing

44 Rugby Football

(Recess B.W.)

1951 (17 Sept). *Health Stamps.* Wmk Mult Script CA. P 13½.

276	**43**	1d.+1d. brown	10	70
277	**44**	2d.+1d. green	30	70

STAMP BOOKLETS

1909. *Black and red cover. Stapled.*

SB1 2s. booklet containing eleven ½d. (No. 118) in blocks of 5 and 6, and eighteen 1d. (No. 119) in blocks of 6 . . . £2750

1914. *Black on red cover. Stapled.*

SB2 2s. booklet containing eleven ½d. (No. 126) in blocks of 5 and 6, and eighteen 1d. (No. 127) in blocks of 6 . . . £2250

1939 (10 Mar)–**40**. *Black on deep green covers. No advertising pages. Stapled.*

SB3 3s. booklet containing eight ½d. and eight 1d. (Nos. 249/50) in blocks of 8 and twelve 2d. (No. 253) in blocks of 6 . . . £1000
a. Including four advertising pages (black on pale greenish buff cover) (1940) . . . £850

SB4 5s.9d. booklet containing ten ½d. and ten 1d. (Nos. 249/50) in blocks of 10 and twenty-seven 2d. (No. 253) in blocks of 9 . . . £3750
a. Including four advertising pages (black on pink cover) (1940) . . . £3250

Nos. SB3/4 were produced locally and Nos. SB3a/4a by De La Rue.

POSTAGE DUE STAMPS

D 1

D 2

(Typo Govt Printer, Suva)

1917 (1 Jan). *Thick yellowish white laid paper. No gum.* P 11.

D1	**D 1**	½d. black	£800	£400
		a. Se-tenant strip of 8: 1d.(× 3)+½d.+4d.+3d.(× 3)	£13000	
D2		1d. black	£350	85·00
D3		2d. black	£300	70·00
D4		3d. black	£350	80·00
D5		4d. black	£800	£400

Nos. D1/2 and D4/5 were printed, *se-tenant*, in sheets of 96 (8 × 12) with each horizontal row containing three 1d., one ½d., one 4d. and three 3d. in that order. Only thirty-one such sheets were issued. The 2d. was printed separately in sheets of 84 (7 × 12). On all these sheets marginal copies were imperforate on the outer edge.

1917 (21 April)–**18**. *Narrower setting, value in ½d. as Type D* **2**.

D5*a*	½d. black	£475	£275
D5*b*	1d. black	£275	£120
D5*c*	2d. black (5.4.18)	£900	£600

1d. and 2d. stamps must have wide margins (3½ to 4mm) on the vertical sides to be Nos. D2 or D3. Stamps with narrow margins of approximately the same width on all four sides are Nos. D5*b* or D5*c*.

Nos. D5*a*/*c* were printed in separate sheets of 84 (7 × 12). The marginal copies are perforated on all sides.

D 3

D 4

(Typo D.L.R.)

1918 (1 June). Wmk Mult Crown CA. P 14.

D 6	**D 3**	½d. black	3·00	20·00
D 7		1d. black	3·50	5·00
D 8		2d. black	3·25	7·50
D 9		3d. black	3·25	48·00
D10		4d. black	6·00	27·00
D6/10 *Set of* 5			17·00	95·00
D6s/10s Optd "Specimen" *Set of* 5			£150	

D9 exists with watermark sideways (Crown to right of CA *as seen from the back of the stamp*) and overprinted "SPECIMEN". (*Price*, £500).

No postage due stamps were in use between 31 August 1931 and 3 July 1940.

(Typo Waterlow)

1940 (3 July). Wmk Mult Script CA. P 12½.

D11	**D 4**	1d. emerald-green	7·00	60·00
D12		2d. emerald-green	9·00	60·00
D13		3d. emerald-green	13·00	65·00
D14		4d. emerald-green	15·00	70·00
D15		5d. emerald-green	17·00	70·00
D16		6d. emerald-green	19·00	75·00
D17		1s. carmine-lake	22·00	£100
D18		1s.6d. carmine-lake	23·00	£150
D11/18 *Set of* 8			£110	£600
D11s/18s Perf "Specimen" *Set of* 8			£180	

All values are known with forged postmarks, including one of Levuka dated "8 APR 41" and others of Suva dated "12 AUG 42", "14 AU 42" or "20 MR 45".

The use of postage due stamps was discontinued on 30 April 1946.

Gambia

PRICES FOR STAMPS ON COVER TO 1945		
Nos.	1/4	*from* × 25
Nos.	5/8	*from* × 20
Nos.	10/20	*from* × 25
Nos.	21/31	*from* × 50
Nos.	32/6	*from* × 20
Nos.	37/44	*from* × 10
Nos.	45/68	*from* × 8
Nos.	69/70	*from* × 25
Nos.	72/85	*from* × 8
Nos.	86/142	*from* × 5
Nos.	143/6	*from* × 6
Nos.	147/9	*from* × 8
Nos.	150/61	*from* × 3

WEST AFRICAN SETTLEMENT

British traders were active in the River Gambia area from the beginning of the 17th century, but it was not until 1808 that it was officially recognised as a Settlement. Administration passed from the merchants to the Governor of Freetown (Sierra Leone) in 1821 and in 1843 Gambia became a separate colony with a Protectorate declared over the banks of the river for 300 miles inland in 1857. A period of colonial retrenchment in 1865 saw a return to Settlement status under Sierra Leone, but Gambia once again became a Crown Colony in 1888.

There was no government postal service before 1858.

PRICES. The prices of Nos. 1 to 8 are for fine copies, with good margins and embossing. Brilliant or poor copies can be supplied at prices consistent with their condition.

DOUBLE EMBOSSING. The majority of the stamps of T **1** with so-called "double embossing" are merely specimens in which the printing and embossing do not register accurately and have no special value. We no longer list "twice embossed" or "twice embossed, once inverted" varieties as they are considered to be outside the scope of this catalogue.

1

(Typo and embossed by D.L.R.)

1869 (18 Mar)–**72**. No wmk. Imperf.

1	**1**	4d. brown	£500	£190
2		4d. pale brown (1871)	£450	£200
3		6d. deep blue	£475	£200
3*a*		6d. blue	£550	£170
4		6d. pale blue (17.2.72)	£2250	£1000

Our prices for the 6d. pale blue, No. 4, are for stamps which are pale by comparison with specimens of the "deep blue" and "blue" colour groups listed under Nos. 3 and 3*a*. The date given is the earliest known postmark. An exceptionally pale shade is recognized by specialists and this is rare.

1874 (Aug). Wmk Crown CC. Imperf.

5	**1**	4d. brown	£375	£190
		w. Wmk inverted	£500	£275
		x. Wmk reversed	£500	£275
		y. Wmk inverted and reversed	£600	£325

6 4d. pale brown £400 £200
7 6d. deep blue £325 £200
w. Wmk inverted £425 £275
x. Wmk reversed £475 £300
y. Wmk inverted and reversed £475 £300
8 6d. blue £325 £190
a. Sloping label £600 £350
b. Wmk sideways † —
w. Wmk inverted £425 £275

SLOPING LABEL VARIETY. Traces of this flaw first occur in the 6d. imperforate on R. 1/1 and R. 1/5. In the perforated printings the variety on R. 1/5 is much more pronounced and appears as illustrated above. Our listings are these examples from R.1/5, less noticeable varieties of this type from R. 1/1, which slope from right to left, being worth less. These varieties continued to appear until the introduction of a new 6d. plate in 1893, used for No. 34.

1880–81. Wmk Crown CC. P 14*.

A. Wmk sideways†.

10A 1 ½d. orange £275 £225
w. Wmk Crown to left of CC
12A 1d. maroon £425 £350
w. Wmk Crown to left of CC
y. Wmk sideways inverted and reversed
13A 2d. rose £130 65·00
w. Wmk Crown to left of CC
14A 3d. bright ultramarine £425 £375
w. Wmk Crown to left of CC
15A 4d. brown £425 60·00
w. Wmk Crown to left of CC £400 55·00
16A 4d. pale brown £400 55·00
w. Wmk Crown to left of CC £375 50·00
17A 6d. deep blue £180 85·00
c. Sloping label £450 £225
18A 6d. blue £180 85·00
c. Sloping label £450 £225
w. Wmk Crown to left of CC
19A 1s. green £375 £250
20A 1s. deep green £375 £250
w. Wmk Crown to left of CC £500 —
10A/20A *Set of* 7 £2000 £1200

B. Wmk upright.

10B 1 ½d. orange 8·00 14·00
11B ½d. dull orange 8·00 14·00
w. Wmk inverted 55·00
x. Wmk reversed 45·00
12B 1d. maroon 4·50 6·00
w. Wmk inverted £100 £100
13B 2d. rose 25·00 11·00
w. Wmk inverted † £250
14B 3d. bright ultramarine 65·00 32·00
14cB 3d. pale dull ultramarine 50·00 26·00
w. Wmk inverted 65·00 40·00
15B 4d. brown £190 14·00
w. Wmk inverted † £170
16B 4d. pale brown £190 15·00
17B 6d. deep blue 85·00 45·00
c. Sloping label £225 £150
18B 6d. blue 85·00 45·00
c. Sloping label £225 £150
19B 1s. green £225 £130
w. Wmk inverted † £375
20B 1s. deep green £225 £130
10B/20B *Set of* 7 £500 £225

*There were three different printings of these stamps. The original supply, sent in June 1880 and covering all seven values, had watermark sideways and was perforated by a line machine. In October of the same year a further printing of the lowest five values had the watermark changed to upright, but was still with line perforation. The final printing, sent May 1881 and containing all values, also had watermark upright, but was perforated on a comb machine.

†The normal sideways watermark shows Crown to right of CC, *as seen from the back of the stamp.*

1886–93. Wmk Crown CA (sideways*). P 14.

21 1 ½d. myrtle-green (1887) 2·75 2·25
w. Wmk Crown to right of CA 32·00
x. Wmk sideways reversed 45·00
22 ½d. grey-green 3·25 3·25
22*b* 1d. maroon † £15000
23 1d. crimson (1887) 5·50 7·50
23*a* 1d. aniline crimson 6·50 9·00
23*b* 1d. pale carmine 6·00 9·00
24 2d. orange (1887) 10·00 5·00
25 2d. deep orange 1·60 8·00
26 2½d. ultramarine (1887) 3·75 2·00
27 2½d. deep bright blue 3·00 1·25
w. Wmk Crown to right of CA £100
28 3d. slate-grey (1886) 6·00 14·00
29 3d. grey 4·50 15·00
30 4d. brown (1887) 6·00 2·00
31 4d. deep brown 6·00 2·00
a. Wmk upright † £1500
w. Wmk Crown to right of CA 70·00 70·00
32 6d. yellowish olive-green (1886) 75·00 30·00
a. Sloping label £180 75·00
bw. Wmk Crown to right of CA £160
32*d* 6d. olive-green (1887) 60·00 55·00
da. Sloping label £160 £140
33 6d. bronze-green (1889) 27·00 55·00
a. Sloping label 60·00 £100
bw. Wmk Crown to right of CA £160
33*c* 6d. deep bronze-green (1889) 28·00 55·00
ca. Sloping label 60·00 £100
34 6d. slate-green (1893) 11·00 45·00
35 1s. violet (1887) 3·25 16·00
36 1s. deep violet 5·00 19·00
36*b* 1s. aniline violet £1100
21/36 *Set of* 8 35·00 70·00
21s/4s, 32cs Optd "Specimen" *Set of* 4 £400

*The normal sideways watermark shows Crown to left of CA, *as seen from the back of the stamp.*

The above were printed in panes of 15 on paper intended for larger panes. Hence the watermark is sometimes misplaced or omitted and letters from "CROWN AGENTS FOR THE COLONIES" from the margin may appear on the stamps.

The ½d., 2d., 3d., 4d., 6d. (No. 32) and 1s. with watermark Crown CA are known imperforate (*price from* £1100, *unused*).

Only three examples, all used, are recorded of the 1d. maroon, No. 22*b*.

The previously listed 3d. "pearl-grey" shade has been deleted as it is impossible to distinguish from other 3d. shades when it occurs on a single stamp. Sheets from this late printing can be identified by three coloured dots in the left sheet margin and one in the right, this being the reverse of the normal arrangement.

Only three used examples are known of the 4d. with upright watermark, No. 31a.

CROWN COLONY

2

Normal

Malformed "S"

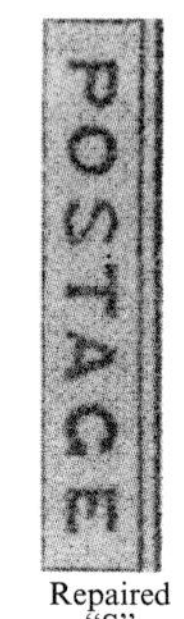

Repaired "S"

The Malformed "S" occurs on R. 7/3 of the left pane from Key Plate 2. This was used to print the initial supply of all values. Printings of the ½d., 1d. and 2½d. despatched on 24 September 1898 had the "S" repaired as shown above. Subsequent printings of the ½d., 1d. and 3d. were from Key Plate 3.

(Typo D.L.R.)

1898 (2 May)–**1902**. Wmk Crown CA. P 14.

37 2 ½d. dull green (*shades*) 2·75 1·75
a. Malformed "S" £250
b. Repaired "S" £275 £225
38 1d. carmine (*shades*) 1·50 75
a. Malformed "S" £250
b. Repaired "S" £275 £275
39 2d. orange and mauve 6·00 3·50
a. Malformed "S" £300 £300
40 2½d. ultramarine 1·75 2·50
a. Malformed "S" £250
b. Repaired "S" £300
41 3d. reddish purple and blue 23·00 12·00
a. Malformed "S" £375
b. Deep purple and ultramarine (1902) 90·00 £100
42 4d. brown and blue 9·00 30·00
a. Malformed "S" £325
43 6d. olive-green and carmine 10·00 27·00
a. Malformed "S" £350
44 1s. violet and green 29·00 65·00
a. Malformed "S" £475
37/44 *Set of* 8 75·00 £130
37s/44s Optd "Specimen" *Set of* 8 £160

3

4

Dented frame (R. 1/6 of left pane)

1902 (13 Mar)–**05**. Wmk Crown CA. P 14.

45 3 ½d. green (19.4.02) 3·00 2·50
a. Dented frame 80·00 85·00
46 1d. carmine 4·00 1·00
a. Dented frame 90·00 70·00
47 2d. orange and mauve (14.6.02) 3·25 2·00
a. Dented frame £120 £110
48 2½d. ultramarine (14.6.02) 29·00 18·00
a. Dented frame £300 £225
49 3d. purple and ultramarine (19.4.02) 12·00 3·50
a. Dented frame £200 £150
50 4d. brown and ultramarine (14.6.02) 3·25 24·00
a. Dented frame £160
51 6d. pale sage-green & carmine (14.6.02) 4·50 12·00
a. Dented frame £170
52 1s. violet and green (14.6.02) 42·00 80·00
a. Dented frame £400
53 4 1s.6d. green and carmine/*yellow* (6.4.05) 7·00 18·00
a. Dented frame £225
54 2s. deep slate and orange (14.6.02) 48·00 60·00
a. Dented frame £400
55 2s.6d. purple and brown/*yellow* (6.4.05) 15·00 60·00
a. Dented frame £300
56 3s. carmine and green/*yellow* (6.4.05) 20·00 60·00
a. Dented frame £300
45/56 *Set of* 12 £170 £300
45s/56s Optd "Specimen" *Set of* 12 £190

1904 (Aug)–**06**. Wmk Mult Crown CA. P 14.

57 3 ½d. green (9.05) 4·50 3(
a. Dented frame £100 75·0(
58 1d. carmine 4·50 1!
a. Dented frame £110 60·0(
59 2d. orange and mauve (23.2.06) 12·00 2·2!
a. Dented frame £200 £12(
60 2½d. bright blue (8.05) 6·00 4·7!
a. Bright blue and ultramarine 14·00 25·0(
b. Dented frame £140 £14(
61 3d. purple and ultramarine (9.05) 7·50 2·0(
a. Dented frame £150 £12(
62 4d. brown and ultramarine (23.2.06) 18·00 40·0(
a. Dented frame £250
63 4 5d. grey and black (6.4.05) 14·00 19·0(
a. Dented frame £225
64 3 6d. olive-green and carmine (23.2.06) 18·00 55·0(
a. Dented frame £250
65 4 7½d. green and carmine (6.4.05) 11·00 38·0(
a. Dented frame £180
66 10d. olive and carmine (6.4.05) 21·00 30·0(
a. Dented frame £275
67 3 1s. violet and green (9.05) 22·00 48·0
a. Dented frame £275
68 4 2s. deep slate and orange (7.05) 70·00 90·0
a. Dented frame £425
57/68 *Set of* 12 £190 £30
63s, 65s/6s Optd "Specimen" *Set of* 3 70·00

See also Nos. 72/85.

HALF PENNY

(5)

ONE PENNY

(6)

1906 (10 Apr). *Nos. 55 and 56 surch with T* **5** *or* **6** *by Govt Printe*
69 ½d.on 2s.6d. purple and brown/*yellow* 50·00 60·0
a. Dented frame £450
70 1d.on 3s. carmine and green/*yellow* 55·00 30·0
a. Surch double £1800 £50(
b. Dented frame £500

No. 69 was surcharged in a setting of 30 (6 × 5), the spacin between the words and the bars being 5 mm on rows 1, 2 and and 4 mm on rows 3 and 4. Constant varieties occur on R. 2/ (broken "E") and R. 5/1 (dropped "Y") of the setting.

No. 70 was surcharged in a setting of 60 (6 × 10) and a simila dropped "Y" variety occurs on R. 6/3 and R. 8/4, the latter conjunction with a dropped "E".

Both values were withdrawn on 24 April when fresh supplies ½d. and 1d. definitives were received from London.

1909 (1 Oct). *Colours changed.* Wmk Mult Crown CA. P 14.

72 3 ½d. blue-green 4·00 3·
a. Dented frame 90·00 £1(
73 1d. red 7·00
a. Dented frame £130 75·(
74 2d. greyish slate 1·60 11·(
a. Dented frame £120
75 3d. purple/yellow 3·50 1·(
a. Purple/lemon-yellow 5·50 1·
b. Dented frame £130 £1
76 4d. black and red/*yellow* 1·25
a. Dented frame £130 £1
77 4 5d. orange and purple 1·50 1·
a. Dented frame £140 £1
78 3 6d. dull and bright purple 2·25 2·
a. Dented frame £150 £1
79 4 7½d. brown and blue 2·50 2·
a. Dented frame £150 £1
80 10d. pale sage-green and carmine 2·50 7·
a. Dented frame £160
81 3 1s. black/*green* 3·25 17·(
a. Dented frame £160
82 4 1s.6d. violet and green 14·00 60·
a. Dented frame £250
83 2s. purple and bright blue/*blue* 14·00 20·
a. Dented frame £250
84 2s.6d. black and red/*blue* 21·00 20·
a. Dented frame £300
85 3s. yellow and green 23·00 48·
a. Dented frame £300
72/85 *Set of* 14 90·00 £1
73s/85s Optd "Specimen" *Set of* 13 £250

Most values between Nos. 45 and 85 are known with forg postmarks. These include circular types of Bathurst, dated "JA 97", and Macarthy Island, dated "FE 17 10", and an oval register Gambia postmark dated "22 JU 10".

7

8

Split "A" (R. 8/3 of left pane) (ptgs to 1918)

(Type D.L.R)

1912 (1 Sept)–**22**. Wmk Mult Crown CA. *Chalk-surfaced paper (5s.)* P 14.

86 **7** ½d. deep green . . . 1·75 1·50
a. Green . . . 2·50 1·50
b. Pale green (1916) . . . 3·50 3·25
c. Split "A" . . . 75·00
87 1d. red . . . 2·50 80
a. Rose-red . . . 2·25 30
b. Scarlet (1916) . . . 3·75 90
c. Split "A" . . . 85·00
88 **8** 1½d. olive-green and blue-green . . . 50 30
a. Split "A" . . . 85·00
89 **7** 2d. greyish slate . . . 50 2·75
a. Split "A" . . . 85·00
90 2½d. deep bright blue . . . 4·00 3·00
a. Bright blue . . . 4·50 2·50
b. Split "A" . . . £140
91 3d. purple/*yellow* . . . 50 30
a. On lemon (1917) . . . 14·00 18·00
b. On orange-buff (1920) . . . 10·00 8·50
c. On pale yellow . . . 1·25 1·00
d. Split "A" . . . £110
92 4d. black and red/*yellow* . . . 1·00 10·00
a. On lemon (1917) . . . 2·50 7·50
b. On orange-buff (1920) . . . 8·00 11·00
c. On pale yellow . . . 1·50 7·50
d. Split "A" . . . £120
w. Wmk inverted . . . £110
93 **8** 5d. orange and purple . . . 1·00 2·00
a. Split "A" . . . £130
94 **7** 6d. dull and bright purple . . . 1·00 2·50
a. Split "A" . . . £130
95 **8** 7½d. brown and blue . . . 1·25 6·50
a. Split "A" . . . £180
96 10d. pale sage-green and carmine . . . 2·00 17·00
a. Deep sage-green and carmine . . . 2·00 15·00
b. Split "A . . . £200
97 **7** 1s. black/*green* . . . 2·00 1·00
a. On emerald back (1921) . . . 1·00 20·00
b. Split "A" . . . £150
98 **8** 1s.6d. violet and green . . . 11·00 10·00
a. Split "A" . . . £375
99 2s. purple and blue/*blue* . . . 3·50 6·00
a. Split "A" . . . £350
00 2s.6d. black and red/*blue* . . . 3·25 14·00
a. Split "A" . . . £350
01 3s. yellow and green . . . 8·50 27·00
a. Split "A" . . . £475
02 5s. green and red/*pale yellow* (1922) . . . 80·00 £130
6/102 *Set of* 17 . . . £110 £200
6s/102s Optd "Specimen" *Set of* 17 . . . £325

921–22. Wmk Mult Script CA. *Chalk-surfaced paper (4s.)*. P 14.

08 **7** ½d. dull green . . . 30 17·00
x. Wmk reversed . . . 95·00
09 1d. carmine-red . . . 1·00 5·00
x. Wmk reversed . . . 90·00 90·00
10 **8** 1½d. olive-green and blue-green . . . 1·25 13·00
11 **7** 2d. grey . . . 1·00 2·25
x. Wmk reversed . . . 80·00
12 2½d. bright blue . . . 50 6·00
13 **8** 5d. orange and purple . . . 1·75 16·00
x. Wmk reversed . . . 42·00
14 **7** 6d. dull and bright purple . . . 1·75 17·00
x. Wmk reversed . . . 22·00
15 **8** 7½d. brown and blue . . . 2·00 30·00
x. Wmk reversed . . . 22·00
16 10d. pale sage-green and carmine . . . 7·00 15·00
x. Wmk reversed . . . 50·00
17 4s. black and red (1922) . . . 75·00 £130
w. Wmk inverted . . . 70·00 £150
08/17 *Set of* 10 . . . 80·00 £225
08s/17s Optd "Specimen" *Set of* 10 . . . £200

Forged postmarks of the types mentioned below No. 85 have also een seen on various values between No. 86 and 117. Collectors ould beware of partial strikes which do not show the year date.

9

10

(Recess D.L.R.)

22 (1 Sept)–**29**. *Portrait and shield in black.* P 14*.

(a) Wmk Mult Crown CA.

8 **9** 4d. red/*yellow* (*a*) . . . 2·50 3·00
9 7½d. purple/*yellow* (*a*) . . . 3·25 6·50
0 **10** 1s. purple/*yellow* (*a*) . . . 9·00 23·00
w. Wmk inverted . . . 90·00 £130
1 5s. *green/yellow* (*c*) . . . 40·00 £120
w. Wmk inverted
8/21 *Set of* 4 . . . 50·00 £140
8s/21s Optd or H/S (5s.) "Specimen" *Set of* . . . £140

(b) Wmk Mult Script CA.

2 **9** ½d. green (*abd*) . . . 55 55
3 ½d. deep green (*bd*) (1925) . . . 4·00 1·25
4 1d. brown (*abd*) . . . 80 20
5 1½d. bright rose-scarlet (*abd*) . . . 80 20
6 2d. grey (*ab*) . . . 1·00 3·25
7 2½d. orange-yellow (*b*) . . . 1·00 11·00
w. Wmk inverted . . . 90·00
8 3d. bright blue (*abd*) . . . 1·00 20
9 4d. red/*yellow* (*bd*) (1.3.27) . . . 5·50 19·00
0 5d. sage-green (*a*) . . . 2·00 10·00
1 6d. claret (*ad*) . . . 1·25 30
2 7½d. purple/*yellow* (*ab*) (1927) . . . 7·00 55·00
3 10d. blue (*a*) . . . 4·50 18·00
4 **10** 1s. purple/*yellow* (*aef*) (9.24) . . . 2·50 1·25
a. Blackish purple/yell-buff (*c*) (1929) . . . 42·00 45·00
5 1s.6d. blue (*af*) . . . 11·00 14·00

136 2s. purple/*blue* (*ac*) . . . 4·00 4·25
137 2s.6d. deep green (*a*) . . . 4·50 9·50
138 3s. bright aniline violet (*a*) . . . 12·00 48·00
139 3s. slate-purple (*c*) (1928) . . . £180 £350
140 4s. brown (*ace*) . . . 5·50 16·00
141 5s. green/yellow (*acf*) (9.26) . . . 12·00 38·00
142 10s. sage-green (*ce*) . . . 70·00 £100
122/42 *Set of* 19 . . . £130 £300
122s/42s Optd "Specimen" *Set of* 19 . . . £400

Perforations. A number of different perforating machines were used for the various printings of these stamps and the following varieties are known: (*a*) the original 14 line perforation; (*b*) 14 × 13.8 comb perforation used for Type **9**; (*c*) 13.8 × 13.7 comb perforation used for Type **10**; (*d*) 13.7 line perforation used for Type **9**; (*e*) 14 × 13.8 compound line perforation used for Type **10**; (*f*) 13.8 × 14 compound line perforation used for Type **10**. The occurrence of these perforations on the individual values is indicated by the letters shown after the colour descriptions above.

No. 139 has been faked, but note that this stamp is comb perf 13.8 × 13.7 whereas No. 138 is line perf 14 exactly. There are also shades of the slate-purple.

Most values of the above issue are known with a forged oval registered Gambia postmark dated "22 JU 10", often with the year date not shown. Collectors should exercise particular caution in buying used examples of No. 139.

1935 (6 May). *Silver Jubilee. As Nos. 91/4 of Antigua, but printed by B.W.* P 11 × 12.

143 1½d. deep blue and scarlet . . . 50 60
a. Extra flagstaff . . . £250
b. Short extra flagstaff . . . £170
c. Lightning conductor . . . £325
d. Flagstaff on right-hand turret . . . £225
e. Double flagstaff . . . £225
144 3d. brown and deep blue . . . 55 70
a. Extra flagstaff . . . £170
b. Short extra flagstaff . . . £160
c. Lightning conductor . . . £160
145 6d. light blue and olive-green . . . 1·00 3·50
a. Extra flagstaff . . . £150
b. Short extra flagstaff . . . £180
c. Lightning conductor . . . £170
d. Flagstaff on right-hand turret . . . £375
146 1s. slate and purple . . . 4·00 7·50
a. Extra flagstaff . . . £200
b. Short extra flagstaff . . . £275
c. Lightning conductor . . . £225
d. Flagstaff on right-hand turret . . . £450
143/6 *Set of* 4 . . . 5·50 11·00
143s/6s Perf "Specimen" *Set of* 4 . . . 95·00

For illustrations of plate varieties see Omnibus section following Zanzibar.

Sheets from the second printing of the 6d. and 1s. in November 1935 had the extra flagstaff partially erased with a sharp point.

1937 (12 May). *Coronation. As Nos. 95/7 of Antigua.* P 11 × 11½

147 1d. yellow-brown . . . 30 70
148 1½d. carmine . . . 30 35
149 3d. blue . . . 55 1·00
147/9 *Set of* 3 . . . 1·00 1·90
147s/9s Perf "Specimen" *Set of* 3 . . . 70·00

11 Elephant (from Colony Badge)

(Recess B.W.)

1938 (1 Apr)–**46**. Wmk Mult Script CA. P 12.

150 **11** ½d. black and emerald-green . . . 15 70
151 1d. purple and brown . . . 20 50
152 1½d. brown-lake and bright carmine . . . £150 12·00
a. Brown-lake and scarlet . . . 3·25 2·25
b. Brown-lake and vermilion . . . 30 2·00
152*c* 1½d. blue and black (2.1.45) . . . 30 1·50
153 2d. blue and black . . . 6·00 3·25
153*a* 2d. lake and scarlet (1.10.43) . . . 60 2·25
154 3d. light blue and grey-blue . . . 30 10
154*a* 5d. sage-green & purple-brn (13.3.41) . . . 50 50
155 6d. olive-green and claret . . . 1·50 35
156 1s. slate-blue and violet . . . 2·00 10
156*a* 1s.3d. chocolate & lt blue (28.11.46) . . . 3·00 2·50
157 2s. carmine and blue . . . 4·50 3·25
158 2s.6d. sepia and dull green . . . 12·00 2·50
159 4s. vermilion and purple . . . 21·00 2·50
160 5s. blue and vermilion . . . 21·00 4·00
161 10s. orange and black . . . 21·00 7·00
150/61 *Set of* 16 . . . 85·00 28·00
150s/61s Perf "Specimen" *Set of* 16 . . . £325

1946 (6 Aug). *Victory. As Nos. 110/11 of Antigua.*

162 1½d. black . . . 10 10
163 3d. blue . . . 10 20
162s/3s Perf "Specimen" *Set of* 2 . . . 60·00

1948 (24 Dec). *Royal Silver Wedding. As Nos. 112/13 of Antigua.*

164 1½d. black . . . 25 10
165 £1 mauve . . . 13·00 14·00

1949 (10 Oct). *75th Anniv of Universal Postal Union. As Nos. 114/17 of Antigua.*

166 1½d. blue-black . . . 30 1·25
167 3d. deep blue . . . 1·25 1·75
168 6d. magenta . . . 50 1·00
169 1s. violet . . . 35 40
166/9 *Set of* 4 . . . 2·25 4·00

Gibraltar

CROWN COLONY

Early details of postal arrangements in Gibraltar are hard to establish, although it is known that postal facilities were provided by the Civil Secretary's Office from 1749. Gibraltar became a packet port in July 1806, although the Civil Secretary's office continued to be responsible for other mail. The two services were amalgamated on 1 January 1857 as a Branch Office of the British G.P.O., the control of the postal services not reverting to Gibraltar until 1 January 1886.

Spanish stamps could be used at Gibraltar from their introduction in 1850 and, indeed, such franking was required on letters weighing over ½ oz. sent to Spain after 1 July 1854. From 1 July 1856 until 1 January 1876 all mail to Spain required postage to be prepaid by Spanish stamps and these issues were supplied by the Gibraltar postal authorities, acting as a Spanish Postal Agent. The mail forwarded under this system was cancelled at San Roque with a horizontal barred oval, later replaced by a cartwheel type mark showing numeral 63. From 1857 combination covers showing the 2d. ship mail fee paid in British stamps and the inland postage by Spanish issues exist.

Stamps of Great Britain were issued for use in Gibraltar from 3 September 1857 (earliest recorded cover is dated 7 September 1857) to the end of 1885.

The initial supply contained 1d., 4d. and 6d. values. No supplies of the 2d. or 1s. were sent until the consignment of October 1857. No other values were supplied until early 1862.

For illustrations of the postmark types see BRITISH POST OFFICES ABROAD notes following GREAT BRITAIN.

Stamps of GREAT BRITAIN cancelled "G" as Type **1** *(3 Sept 1857 to 19 Feb 1859)*

Z 1 1d. red-brown (1854) Die I, *wmk* Small Crown, *perf* 16 . . . £350
Z 2 1d. red-brown (1855), Die II, *wmk* Small Crown, *perf* 16 . . . £600
Z 3 1d. red-brown (1855), Die II, *wmk* Small Crown *perf* 14 . . . £300
Z 4 1d. red-brown (1855), Die II, *wmk* Large Crown, *perf* 14 . . . 80·00
Z 5 1d. rose-red (1857), Die II, *wmk* Large Crown, *perf* 14 . . . 22·00
Z 6 2d. blue (1855), *wmk* Small Crown, *perf* 14 . . . £400
Z 7 2d. blue (1855–58), *wmk* Large Crown, *perf* 16 . . . £325
Z 8 2d. blue (1855), *wmk* Large Crown, *perf* 14 . . . *From* 60·00
Plate Nos. 5, 6.
Z 9 2d. blue (1858) (Plate No. 7) . . . £250
Z10 4d. rose (1857) . . . 55·00
a. Thick glazed paper
Z11 6d. lilac (1856) . . . 40·00
Z12 6d. lilac (1856) (blued *paper*) . . . £750
Z13 1s. green (1856) . . . £110
a. Thick paper
Z14 1s. green (1856) (blued *paper*) . . . £1300

Stamps of GREAT BRITAIN cancelled "A 26" as in Types **2**, **5**, **11** *or* **14** *(20 Feb 1859 to 31 Dec 1885).*

Z15 ½d. rose-red (1870–79) . . . *From* 28·00
Plate Nos. 4, 5, 6, 8, 10, 11, 12, 13, 14, 15, 19, 20.
Z16 1d. red-brown (1841), *imperf* . . . £1300
Z17 1d. red-brown (1855), *wmk* Large Crown, *perf* 14 . . . £170
Z18 1d. rose-red (1857), *wmk* Large Crown, *perf* 14 . . . 13·00
Z19 1d. rose-red (1864–79) . . . *From* 21·00
Plate Nos. 71, 72, 73, 74 ,76, 78, 79, 80, 81, 82, 83, 84, 85, 86, 87, 88, 89, 90, 91, 92, 93, 94, 95, 96, 97, 98, 99, 100, 101, 102, 103, 104, 105, 106, 107, 108, 109, 110, 111, 112, 113, 114, 115, 116, 117, 118, 119, 120, 121, 122, 123, 124, 125, 127, 129, 130, 131, 132, 133, 134, 135, 136, 137, 138, 139, 140, 141, 142, 143, 144, 145, 146, 147, 148, 149, 150, 151, 152, 153, 154, 155, 156, 157, 158, 159, 160, 161, 162, 163, 164, 165, 166, 167, 168, 169, 170, 171, 172, 173, 174, 175, 176, 177, 178, 179, 180, 181, 182, 183, 184, 185, 186, 187, 188, 189, 190, 191, 192, 193, 194, 195, 196, 197, 198, 199, 200, 201, 202, 203, 204, 205, 206, 207, 208, 209, 210, 211, 212, 213, 214, 215, 216, 217, 218, 219, 220, 221, 222, 223, 224, 225.
Z20 1½d. lake-red (1870) (Plate No. 3) . . . £450
Z21 2d. blue (1855), *wmk* Large Crown, *perf* 14. . . . £130
Plate No. 6.
Z22 2d. blue (1858–69) . . . *From* 20·00
Plate Nos. 7, 8, 9, 12, 13, 14, 15.
Z23 2½d. rosy mauve (1875) (blued *paper*) . . . *From* £100
Plate Nos. 1, 2, 3.
Z24 2½d. rosy mauve (1875–76) . . . *From* 28·00
Plate Nos. 1, 2, 3.
Z25 2½d. rosy mauve (*Error of Lettering*) . . . £1800
Z26 2½d. rosy mauve (1876–79) . . . *From* 21·00
Plate Nos. 3, 4, 5, 6, 7, 8, 9, 10, 11, 12, 13, 14, 15, 16, 17.
Z27 2½d. blue (1880–81) . . . *From* 13·00
Plate Nos. 17, 18, 19, 20.
Z28 2½d. blue (1881) (Plate Nos. 21, 22, 23) . . . *From* 10·00
Z29 3d. carmine-rose (1862) . . . £170
Z30 3d. rose (1865) (Plate No. 4) . . . 60·00
Z31 3d. rose (1867–73) . . . *From* 40·00
Plate Nos. 4, 5, 6, 7, 8, 9, 10.
Z32 3d. rose (1873–76) . . . *From* 48·00
Plate Nos. 11, 12, 14, 15, 16, 17, 18, 19, 20.
Z33 3d. rose (1881) (Plate Nos. 20, 21)
Z34 3d. lilac (1883) (3d. *on* 3d.) . . . £130
Z35 4d. rose (1857) . . . 60·00
Z36 4d. red (1862) (Plate Nos. 3, 4) . . . *From* 48·00
Z37 4d. vermilion (1865–73) . . . *From* 30·00
Plate Nos. 7, 8, 9, 10, 11, 12, 13, 14.
Z38 4d. vermilion (1876) (Plate No. 15) . . . £250
Z39 4d. sage-green (1877) (Plate Nos. 15, 16) . . . £110
Z40 4d. grey-brown (1880) *wmk* Large Garter . . . £225
Plate No. 17.

Z41 4d. grey-brown (1880) *wmk* Crown . . . *From* 50·00
Plate Nos. 17, 18.
Z42 6d. lilac (1856) . . . 42·00
Z43 6d. lilac (1862) (Plate Nos. 3, 4) . . . *From* 38·00
Z44 6d. lilac (1865–67) (Plate Nos. 5, 6) . . . *From* 32·00
Z45 6d. lilac (1867) (Plate No. 6) . . . 45·00
Z46 6d. violet (1867–70) (Plate Nos. 6, 8, 9) *From* 32·00
Z47 6d. buff (1872–73) (Plate Nos. 11, 12) . . *From* £150
Z48 6d. chestnut (1872) (Plate No. 11) . . . 32·00
Z49 6d. grey (1873) (Plate No. 12) . . . 95·00
Z50 6d. grey (1874–80) . . . *From* 30·00
Plate Nos. 13, 14, 15, 16, 17.
Z51 6d. grey (1881) (Plate Nos. 17, 18) . . . £200
Z52 6d. lilac (1883) (6d. *on* 6d.) . . . 95·00
Z53 8d. orange (1876) . . . £425
Z54 9d. bistre (1862) . . . £250
Z55 9d. straw (1862) . . . £600
Z56 9d. straw (1865) . . . £550
Z57 9d. straw (1867) . . . £180
Z58 10d. red-brown (1867) . . . £150
Z59 1s. green (1856) . . . £100
Z60 1s. green (1862) . . . 70·00
Z61 1s. green (1862) ("K" *variety*) . . . £2000
Z62 1s. green (1865) (Plate No. 4) . . . 60·00
Z63 1s. green (1867–73) (Plate Nos. 4, 5, 6, 7) . . . *From* 26·00
Z64 1s. green (1873–77) . . . *From* 65·00
Plate Nos. 8, 9, 10, 11, 12, 13.
Z65 1s. orange-brown (1880) (Plate No. 13) . . . £300
Z66 1s. orange-brown (1881) . . . *From* 90·00
Plate Nos. 13, 14.
Z67 2s. blue (1867) . . . £200
Z68 5s. rose (1867) (Plate No. 1) . . . £700

1880.
Z69 ½d. deep green . . . 25·00
Z70 ½d. pale green . . . 25·00
Z71 1d. Venetian red . . . 24·00
Z72 1½d. Venetian red . . . £225
Z73 2d. pale rose . . . 70·00
Z74 2d. deep rose . . . 70·00
Z75 5d. indigo . . . £120

1881.
Z76 1d. lilac (14 *dots*) . . . 28·00
Z77 1d. lilac (16 *dots*) . . . 9·50

1884.
Z78 ½d. slate-blue . . . 23·00
Z79 2d. lilac . . . 85·00
Z80 2½d. lilac . . . 16·00
Z81 3d. lilac . . .
Z82 4d. dull green . . . £160
Z83 6d. dull green . . .

POSTAL FISCAL

Z83*a* 1d. purple (Die 4) (1878) *wmk* Small Anchor . . . £650
Z84 1d. purple (1881), *wmk* Orb . . . £1100

PRICES FOR STAMPS ON COVER TO 1945

Nos.	1/2	*from* × 25
No.	3	*from* × 10
No.	4	*from* × 25
Nos.	5/6	*from* × 8
Nos.	7/33	*from* × 6
Nos.	39/45	*from* × 5
Nos.	46/109	*from* × 3
Nos.	110/13	*from* × 4
Nos.	114/17	*from* × 3
Nos.	118/20	*from* × 5
Nos.	121/31	*from* × 3

GIBRALTAR
(1)

1886 (1 Jan). *Contemporary types of Bermuda optd with T* **1** *by D.L.R.* Wmk Crown CA. P 14.
1 **9** ½d. dull green . . . 13·00 7·00
2 **1** 1d. rose-red . . . 50·00 4·25
3 **2** 2d. purple-brown . . . £100 75·00
w. Wmk inverted . . .
4 **11** 2½d. ultramarine . . . £140 3·25
a. Optd in blue-black . . . £500 £150
w. Wmk inverted . . . — £375
5 **10** 4d. orange-brown . . . £130 85·00
6 **4** 6d. deep lilac . . . £200 £180
7 **5** 1s. yellow-brown . . . £425 £350
1/7 *Set of* 7 . . . £950 £650
1s/3s, 4as/7s Optd "Specimen" *Set of* 7 . . . £3250

PRINTER. All Gibraltar stamps to No. 109 were typographed by De La Rue & Co, Ltd.

2

3

4 5

1886 (Nov)–**87**. Wmk Crown CA. P 14.
8 **2** ½d. dull green (1.87) . . . 9·50 3·75
9 **3** 1d. rose (2.87) . . . 42·00 4·25
10 **4** 2d. brown-purple (12.86) . . . 30·00 19·00
w. Wmk inverted . . . £400
11 **5** 2½d. blue . . . 80·00 2·75
w. Wmk inverted . . . £225 65·00
12 **4** 4d. orange-brown (16.4.87) . . . 75·00 75·00
13 6d. lilac (16.4.87) . . . £100 £100
14 1s. bistre (2.87) . . . £190 £180
w. Wmk inverted . . .
8/14 *Set of* 7 . . . £475 £350
8s/14s Optd "Specimen" *Set of* 7 . . . £500

Examples of Nos. 3, 6/7 and 14 are known showing a forged Gibraltar postmark dated "JU-13 87".

See also Nos. 39/45.

5 CENTIMOS
(6)

5
"5" with short foot (all stamps in 1st, 5th and 6th vertical columns (5c. on ½d.) or all stamps in 2nd vertical column (25c. on 2d., 25c. on 2½d., 50c. on 6d. and 75c. on 1s.)

1889 (1 Aug). *Surch as T* **6**.
15 **2** 5c.on ½d. green . . . 6·00 19·00
a. "5" with short foot . . . 6·00 19·00
16 **3** 10c.on 1d. rose . . . 12·00 9·50
17 **4** 25c.on 2d. brown-purple . . . 4·75 7·00
a. "5" with short foot . . . 10·00 13·00
ab. Small "I" (R. 6/2) . . . £100 £150
b. Broken "N" (R. 10/5) . . . £100 £150
18 **5** 25c.on 2½d. bright blue . . . 20·00 2·25
a. "5" with short foot . . . 35·00 5·00
ab. Small "I" (R. 6/2) . . . £325 £100
b. Broken "N" (R. 10/5) . . . £325 £100
19 **4** 40c.on 4d. orange-brown . . . 50·00 70·00
20 50c.on 6d. bright lilac . . . 55·00 70·00
a. "5" with short foot . . . 90·00 £110
21 75c.on 1s. bistre . . . 55·00 65·00
a. "5" with short foot . . . 90·00 £100
15/21 *Set of* 7 . . . £180 £200
15s/21s Optd "Specimen" *Set of* 7 . . . £350

10c., 40c. and 50c. values from this issue and that of 1889–96 are known bisected and used for half their value from various post offices in Morocco (*price on cover from* £500). These bisects were never authorised by the Gibraltar Post Office.

Broken "M" (Pl 2 R. 4/5)

7

Flat top to "C" (Pl 2 R. 4/4)

1889 (8 Oct*)–**96**. *Issue in Spanish currency.* Wmk Crown CA. P 14.
22 **7** 5c. green . . . 4·50 80
a. Broken "M" . . . £130 65·00
w. Wmk inverted . . . £225 £170
23 10c. carmine . . . 4·50 50
b. Value omitted . . . £5000
24 20c. olive-green and brown (2.1.96) . . . 42·00 18·00
w. Wmk inverted . . . £275
25 20c. olive-green (8.7.96) . . . 11·00 70·00
a. Flat top to "C" . . . £180
26 25c. ultramarine . . . 18·00 70
a. Deep ultramarine . . . 28·00 80
27 40c. orange-brown . . . 3·75 2·75
28 50c. bright lilac (1890) . . . 3·25 2·00
29 75c. olive-green (1890) . . . 32·00 32·00
30 1p. bistre (11.89) . . . 75·00 20·00
31 1p. bistre and ultramarine (6.95) . . . 4·75 5·00
32 2p. black and carmine (2.1.96) . . . 10·00 30·00
33 5p. slate-grey (12.89) . . . 42·00 £100
22/33 *Set of* 12 . . . £225 £250
22s/4s, 26s/33s Optd "Specimen" *Set of* 11 . . . £375
*Earliest recorded postmark date.

1898 (1 Oct). *Reissue in Sterling currency.* Wmk Crown CA. P 14.
39 **2** ½d. grey-green . . . 6·00 1·75
w. Wmk inverted . . .
40 **3** 1d. carmine . . . 6·50 50
w. Wmk inverted . . . † £1100
41 **4** 2d. brown-purple and ultramarine . . . 22·00 1·75
42 **5** 2½d. bright ultramarine . . . 30·00 50
w. Wmk inverted . . . £225 75·00
43 **4** 4d. orange-brown and green . . . 18·00 6·50
a. "FOUR PENCE" trimmed at top (Pl 2 R. 8/4) . . . £425
44 6d. violet and red . . . 42·00 20·00
45 1s. bistre and carmine . . . 38·00 16·00
w. Wmk inverted . . .
39/45 *Set of* 7 . . . £140 42·00
39s/45s Optd "Specimen" *Set of* 7 . . . £275

No. 39 is greyer than No. 8, No. 40 brighter and deeper than No. 9 and No. 42 much brighter than No. 11.

8

9

½ ½
Normal Large "2" 2½d.

This occurs on R. 10/1 in each pane of 60. The diagonal stroke is also longer.

1903 (1 May). Wmk Crown CA. P 14.
46 **8** ½d. grey-green and green . . . 10·00 9·5
47 1d. dull purple/*red* . . . 30·00 6
48 2d. grey-green and carmine . . . 19·00 25·0
49 2½d. dull purple and black/*blue* . . . 4·75 6
a. Large "2" in "½" . . . £225 £12
50 6d. dull purple and violet . . . 16·00 21·0
51 1s. black and carmine . . . 28·00 35·0
52 **9** 2s. green and blue . . . £130 £18
53 4s. dull purple and green . . . 80·00 £14
54 8s. dull purple and black/*blue* . . . £110 £14
55 £1 dull purple and black/*red* . . . £500 £60
46/55 *Set of* 10 . . . £800 £100
46s/55s Optd "Specimen" *Set of* 10 . . . £500

1904–08. Wmk Mult Crown CA. *Ordinary paper (½d. to 2d. and 6d. to 2s.) or chalk-surfaced paper (others).* P 14.
56 **8** ½d. dull and bright green (4.4.04*) . . . 11·00 2·5
a. Chalk-surfaced paper (10.05) . . . 12·00 7·0
57 1d. dull purple/*red* (6.9.04*) . . . 10·00 5
a. Bisected (½d.) (on card) . . . † £130
bw. Wmk inverted . . .
c. Chalk-surfaced paper (16.9.05) . . . 5·00 8
58 2d. grey-green and carmine (9.1.05) . . . 14·00 5·
a. Chalk-surfaced paper (2.07) . . . 8·50 5·
59 2½d. purple and black/*blue* (4.5.07) . . . 35·00 90·
a. Large "2" in "½" . . . £500 £85
60 6d. dull purple and violet (19.4.06) . . . 35·00 22·
a. Chalk-surfaced paper (4.08) . . . 30·00 11·
61 1s. black and carmine (13.10.05) . . . 48·00 13·
a. Chalk-surfaced paper (4.06) . . . 50·00 13·
62 **9** 2s. green and blue (2.2.05) . . . 75·00 95·
a. Chalk-surfaced paper (10.07) . . . 80·00 85·
63 4s. deep purple and green (6.08) . . . £225 £27
64 £1 deep purple and black/*red* (15.3.08) . . . £500 £55
56/64 *Set of* 9 . . . £800 £90
*Earliest known date of use.

1906 (Oct)–**12**. *Colours changed.* Wmk Mult Crown CA. *Chalk-surfaced paper (6d. to 8s.).* P 14.
66 **8** ½d. blue-green (1907) . . . 4·00 1·
x. Wmk reversed . . . † £10
67 1d. carmine . . . 5·50
a. Wmk sideways . . . — £35
w. Wmk inverted . . . † £5
68 2d. greyish slate (5.10) . . . 8·00 11·
69 2½d. ultramarine (6.07) . . . 5·00 1·
a. Large "2" in "½" . . . £225 £1
70 6d. dull and bright purple (18.3.12) . . . £140 £3
71 1s. black/*green* (1910) . . . 23·00 21·
72 **9** 2s. purple and bright blue/*blue* (4.10) . . . 50·00 48·
73 4s. black and carmine (4.10) . . . £110 £1
x. Wmk reversed . . . £1400 £15
74 8s. purple and green (1911) . . . £190 £1
66/74 *Set of* 9 . . . £475 £7
67s/74s Optd "Specimen" *Set of* 8 . . . £600

Examples of Nos. 55, 64 and 73/4 are known showing a forged oval registered postmark dated "6 OC 10".

10

11

HALEPENN
"HALEPENNY" (Pl 1 R. 7/3. Occurs on ptgs from 1917)

1912 (17 July)–**24**. Wmk Mult Crown CA. *Ordinary paper (½d. to 2½d) or chalk-surfaced paper (others)*. P 14.
76 **10** ½d. blue-green 3·25 70
 a. Yellow-green (4.17) 4·75 1·75
 b. "HALEPENNY" £140 £110
 w. Wmk inverted † £850
 x. Wmk reversed † £1100
77 1d. carmine-red 3·50 75
 a. Scarlet (6.16) 3·50 1·25
 ay. Wmk inverted and reversed
78 2d. greyish slate 9·50 1·50
79 2½d. deep bright blue 6·50 2·00
 a. Large "2" in "½" £190 £120
 b. Pale ultramarine (1917) 7·00 2·00
 ba. Large "2" in "½" £275 £120
80 6d. dull purple and mauve 9·00 15·00
81 1s. black/*green* 9·00 3·25
 a. Ordinary paper (8.18) £550
 b. On blue-green, olive back (1919) 12·00 26·00
 c. On emerald surface (12.23) 25·00 65·00
 d. On emerald back (3.24) 19·00 90·00
 ds. Optd "Specimen" 75·00
82 **11** 2s. dull purple and blue/*blue* 26·00 3·50
83 4s. black and carmine 32·00 55·00
84 8s. dull purple and green 80·00 95·00
85 £1 dull purple and black/*red* £130 £200
76/85 *Set of* 10 £275 £325
76s/85s Optd "Specimen" *Set of* 10 £475

WAR TAX
(12)

1918 (15 Apr). *Optd with T* **12** *by Beanland, Malin & Co, Gibraltar.*
86 **10** ½d. green 1·00 1·75
 a. Opt double £800
 b. "HALEPENNY"
 w. Wmk inverted £425
 y. Wmk inverted and reversed £400
Two printings of this overprint exist, the second being in slightly heavier type on a deeper shade of green.

3 PENCE (I) THREE PENCE (II)

1921–27. Wmk Mult Script CA. *Chalk-surfaced paper (6d. to 8s.)*. P 14.
89 **10** ½d. green (25.4.27) 1·50 1·50
90 1d. carmine-red (2.21) 1·75 1·00
91 1½d. chestnut (1.12.22) 1·75 55
 a. Pale chestnut (7.24) 1·75 30
 w. Wmk inverted † £650
93 2d. grey (17.2.21) 1·25 1·25
94 2½d. bright blue (2.21) 20·00 35·00
 a. Large "2" in "½" £425 £500
95 3d. bright blue (I) (1.1.22) 3·00 4·25
 a. Ultramarine 2·50 1·50
97 6d. dull purple and mauve (1.23) 6·00 3·75
 a. Bright purple & magenta (22.7.26) 1·60 3·50
98 1s. black/*emerald* (20.6.24) 10·00 17·00
99 **11** 2s. grey-purple and blue/*blue* (20.6.24) 19·00 70·00
 a. Reddish purple and blue/blue (1925) 7·00 42·00
100 4s. black and carmine (20.6.24) 65·00 £110
101 8s. dull purple and green (20.6.24) £200 £375
89/101 *Set of* 11 £275 £500
89s/101s Optd "Specimen" *Set of* 11 £550
The ½d. exists in coils, constructed from normal sheets, first issued in 1937.

1925 (15 Oct)–**32**. *New values and colours changed.* Wmk Mult Script CA. *Chalk-surfaced paper*. P 14.
102 **10** 1s. sage-green and black (8.1.29) 14·00 23·00
 a. Olive and black (1932) 14·00 12·00
103 **11** 2s. red-brown and black (8.1.29) 9·50 30·00
104 2s.6d. green and black 9·50 18·00
105 5s. carmine and black 15·00 50·00
106 10s. deep ultramarine and black 32·00 70·00
107 £1 red-orange and black (16.11.27) £140 £180
108 £5 violet and black (16.11.27) £1300 £4000
 s. Optd "Specimen" £700
102/7 *Set of* 6 £200 £325
102s/7s Optd or Perf (1s., 2s.) "Specimen" *Set of* 6 £400
Examples of Nos. 83/5, 99/101 and 102/8 are known showing forged oval registered postmarks dated "24 JA 25" or "6 MY 35".

1930 (11 Apr). *T* **10** *inscribed "THREE PENCE"*. Wmk Mult Script CA. P 14.
109 3d. ultramarine (II) 7·50 2·00
 s. Perf "Specimen" 70·00

13 The Rock of Gibraltar

(Des Capt. H. St. C. Garrood. Recess D.L.R.)

1931–33. Wmk Mult Script CA. P 14.
110 **13** 1d. scarlet (1.7.31) 2·50 2·50
 a. Perf 13½ × 14 16·00 6·00
111 1½d. red-brown (1.7.31) 1·75 2·25
 a. Perf 13½ × 14 13·00 4·00
112 2d. pale grey (1.11.32) 6·50 1·75
 a. Perf 13½ × 14 15·00 2·50
113 3d. blue (1.6.33) 5·50 3·00
 a. Perf 13½ × 14 24·00 32·00
110/13 *Set of* 4 15·00 8·50
110a/13a *Set of* 4 60·00 40·00
110s/13s Perf "Specimen" *Set of* 4 £170
Figures of value take the place of both corner ornaments at the base of the 2d. and 3d.

1935 (6 May). *Silver Jubilee. As Nos. 91/4 of Antigua but ptd by B.W.* P 11 × 12.
114 2d. ultramarine and grey-black 1·60 2·50
 a. Extra flagstaff 65·00 85·00
 b. Short extra flagstaff £110 £130
 c. Lightning conductor 70·00 85·00
 d. Flagstaff on right-hand turret £170 £180
 e. Double flagstaff £170 £180
115 3d. brown and deep blue 3·25 3·50
 a. Extra flagstaff £300 £325
 b. Short extra flagstaff £250 £275
 c. Lightning conductor £275 £300
116 6d. green and indigo 9·50 12·00
 a. Extra flagstaff £225 £275
 b. Short extra flagstaff £375 £375
 c. Lightning conductor £225 £275
117 1s. slate and purple 10·00 10·00
 a. Extra flagstaff £200 £200
 b. Short extra flagstaff £350 £350
 c. Lightning conductor £225 £225
114/17 *Set of* 4 21·00 25·00
114s/17s Perf "Specimen" *Set of* 4 £180
For illustrations of plate varieties see Omnibus section following Zanzibar.

1937 (12 May). *Coronation. As Nos. 95/7 of Antigua.* P 11 × 11½.
118 ½d. green 25 30
119 2d. grey-black 1·50 3·00
120 3d. blue 2·75 3·00
118/20 *Set of* 3 4·00 5·50
118s/20s Perf "Specimen" *Set of* 3 £100

14 King George VI

15 Rock of Gibraltar

16 The Rock (North Side)

Ape on rock R. 1/5

Broken second "R" in "GIBRALTAR" (Frame Pl 2 R. 9/4)

(Des Captain H. St. C. Garrood. Recess D.L.R.)

1938 (25 Feb)–**51**. *Designs as T* **14/16**. *Mult Script CA.*
121 ½d. deep green (P 13½ × 14) 10 40
122 1d. yellow-brown (P 14) 26·00 2·25
 a. Perf 13½ (1940) 27·00 2·25
 ab. Perf 13½. Wmk sideways (1940) 6·50 7·00
 b. Perf 13. Wmk sideways. *Red-brown* (1942) 50 60
 c. Perf 13. Wmk sideways. *Deep brown* (1944) 1·50 3·50
 d. Perf 13. *Red-brown* (1949) 2·50 1·50
123 1½d. carmine (P 14) 35·00 75
 a. Perf 13½ £250 35·00
123*b* 1½d. slate-violet (P 13) (1.1.43) 50 1·50
124 2d. grey (P 14) 26·00 40
 aa. Ape on rock £250 40·00
 a. Perf 13½ (1940) 2·00 35
 ab. Perf 13½. Wmk sideways (1940) £600 42·00
 b. Perf 13. Wmk sideways (1943) 75 1·25
 ba. "A" of "CA" missing from wmk £1200
124*c* 2d. carm (P 13) (*wmk sideways*) (15.7.44) 50 60
125 3d. light blue (P 13½) 22·00 1·00
 a. Perf 14 £130 5·00
 b. Perf 13 (1942) 50 30
 ba. Greenish blue (2.51) 3·50 2·50
125*c* 5d. red-orange (P 13) (1.10.47) 1·00 1·25
126 6d. carm & grey-violet (P 13½) (16.3.38) 48·00 3·00
 a. Perf 14 £120 1·25
 b. Perf 13 (1942) 4·25 1·75
 c. Perf 13. *Scarlet and grey-violet* (1945) 5·00 3·75
127 1s. black and green (P 14) (16.3.38) 42·00 23·00
 a. Perf 13½ 70·00 7·00
 b. Perf 13 (1942) 3·25 4·25
 ba. Broken "R" £225
128 2s. black and brown (P 14) (16.3.38) 65·00 25·00
 a. Perf 13½ £120 32·00
 b. Perf 13 (1942) 5·00 6·50
 ba. Broken "R" £275
129 5s. black and carmine (P 14) (16.3.38) 95·00 £160
 a. Perf 13½ 38·00 17·00
 b. Perf 13 (1944) 17·00 17·00
 ba. Broken "R" £375
130 10s. black and blue (P 14) (16.3.38) 65·00 £120
 a. Perf 13 (1943) 38·00 25·00
 ab. Broken "R" £500
131 £1 orange (P 13½ × 14) (16.3.38) 38·00 45·00
121/31 Set of 14 £130 85·00
121s/31s Perf "Specimen" *Set of* 14 £600
Designs:—½d., £1, Type **14**. *Horiz as T* **15/16**—1d., 1½d. (*both*), Type **15**; 2d. (*both*), Type **16**; 3d., 5d. Europa Point; 6d. Moorish Castle; 1s. Southport Gate; 2s. Eliott Memorial; 5s. Government House; 10s. Catalan Bay.

The ½d., 1d. and both colours of the 2d. exist in coils constructed from normal sheets. These were originally joined vertically, but, because of technical problems, the 1d. and 2d. grey were subsequently issued in horizontal coils. The 2d. carmine only exists in the horizontal version.
Examples of Nos. 129/31 are known showing forged oval registered postmarks dated "6 OC 43", "18 OC 43", "3 MR 44" and "4 AU 44."

1946 (12 Oct). *Victory. As Nos. 110/11 of Antigua.*
132 ½d. green 10 75
133 3d. ultramarine 40 1·00
132s/3s Perf "Specimen" *Set of* 2 85·00

1948 (1 Dec). *Royal Silver Wedding. As Nos. 112/13 of Antigua.*
134 ½d. green 1·00 1·75
135 £1 brown-orange 50·00 70·00

1949 (10 Oct). *75th Anniv of Universal Postal Union. As Nos. 114/17 of Antigua.*
136 2d. carmine 1·00 1·25
137 3d. deep blue 2·00 1·50
138 6d. purple 1·25 2·00
139 1s. blue-green 1·00 3·25
136/9 *Set of* 4 4·75 7·25

NEW CONSTITUTION 1950
(23)

1950 (1 Aug). *Inauguration of Legislative Council. Nos. 124c, 125ba, 126b and 127b optd as T* **23**.
140 **16** 2d. carmine 30 1·50
141 – 3d. greenish blue 65 1·00
142 – 6d. carmine and grey-violet 75 2·00
 a. Opt double £850 £1000
143 – 1s. black and green (R.) 75 2·00
 a. Broken "R" 65·00
140/3 *Set of* 4 2·25 6·00
On stamps from the lower part of the sheet of No. 142a the two impressions are almost coincident.

STAMP BOOKLETS

1906 (Oct). *Black on red cover. Stapled.*
SB1 2s.½d. booklet containing twenty-four ½d. and twelve 1d. (Nos. 56a, 67) in blocks of 6

1912 (17 July). *Black on red cover with Edwardian cypher. Stapled.*
SB2 2s.½d. booklet containing twenty-four ½d. and twelve 1d. (Nos. 76/7) in blocks of 6

Gilbert and Ellice Islands

No organised postal service existed in the Gilbert and Ellice Islands before the introduction of stamp issues in January 1911. A New Zealand Postal Agency was, however, provided on Fanning Island, one of the Line Islands, primarily for the use of the staff of the Pacific Cable Board cable station which was established in 1902. The agency opened on 29 November 1902 and continued to operate until replaced by a Protectorate post office on 14 February 1939. The cable station closed on 16 January 1964. Fanning Island is now known as Tabuaeran.

Z 1

The following NEW ZEALAND *stamps are known postmarked on Fanning Island with Type* Z **1** (*in use from November* 1902 *until November* 1936. *The earliest known cover is postmarked* 20 *December* 1902.

1882–1900 Q.V. (P 11) ½d., 1d., 2d. (*Nos.* 236/8)
1898 Pictorials (*no wmk*) 1d., 2d. (*Nos.* 247/8)
1900 Pictorials (*W* **38**) ½d. 1½d., 2d. (*Nos.* 273, 275b, 276)
1901 1d. "Universal" (*W* **38**) (*No.* 278)
1902 1d. "Universal" (*no wmk*) (*No.* 295)
1902 ½d. Pictorial (*W* **43**) (*No.* 302b)
1902–09 Pictorials (*W* **43**) 2d., 2½d., 3d., 6d., 8d., 9d., 1s., 2s., 5s. (*Nos.* 309, 312/13, 315, 319/20, 326, 328/9)
1907–08 Pictorials (*W* **43**) 4d. (*No.* 379)
1908 1d. "Universal" (*De La Rue paper*) 1d. (*No.* 386)
1909–12 King Edward VII (*typo*) ½d. (*No.* 387)
1909–16 King Edward VII (*recess*) 2d., 3d., 4d., 5d., 6d., 8d., 1s. (*Nos.* 388/91, 393/6, 398)
1909–26 1d. "Universal" (*W* **43**) 1d. (*Nos.* 405, 410)
1915–30 King George V (*recess*) 1½d., 2d. bright violet, 2½d., 3d., 4d. bright violet, 4½d., 6d., 7½d., 9d., 1s. (*Nos.* 416/17, 419/20, 422/3, 425/6, 429/30)
1915–34 King George V (*typo*) ½d., 1½d. (all 3), 2d., 3d. (*Nos.* 435/40, 446, 448, 449)
1915 "WAR STAMP" opt ½d. (*No.* 452)
1920 Victory 1d., 1½d. (*Nos.* 454/5)
1922 2d. on ½d. (*No.* 459)
1923–25 Penny Postage 1d. (*No.* 460)
1926–34 Admiral design 1d. (*No.* 468)
1935–36 Pictorials ½d., 2d., 4d., 8d., 1s. (*Nos.* 556, 559, 562, 565, 567)

1935 Silver Jubilee ½d., 1d., 6d. (*Nos.* 573/5)
1936 Anzac 1d. + 1d. (*No.* 592)

Z 2

The following NEW ZEALAND *stamps are known postmarked on Fanning Island with Type* Z **2** (*in use from* 7 *December* 1936 *to* 13 *February* 1939):

1935–36 Pictorials (*W* **43**) 1d (*No.* 557)
1936–39 Pictorials (*W* **98**) ½d., 1d., 1½d. (*Nos.* 577/9)
1936 Chambers of Commerce Congress ½d. (*No.* 593)
1936 Health 1d.+1d. (*No.* 598)
1937 Coronation 1d., 2½d., 6d. (*Nos.* 599/601)
1938–39 King George VI ½d., 1d., 1½d. (*Nos.* 603, 605, 607)

The schooner which carried the mail from Fanning Island also called at Washington Island, another of the Line group. Problems arose, however, as the authorities insisted that mail from Washington must first pass through the Fanning Island Postal Agency before being forwarded which resulted in considerable delays. Matters were resolved by the opening of a New Zealand Postal Agency on Washington Island which operated from 1 February 1921 until the copra plantations were closed in early 1923. The postal agency was re-established on 15 May 1924, but finally closed on 30 March 1934. Covers from this second period occur with incorrectly dated postmarks. Manuscript markings on New Zealand Nos. 578, 599/600 and 692 are unofficial and were applied during the resettlement of the island between 1937 and 1948. Washington Island is now known as Teraina.

Z 3

The following NEW ZEALAND stamps are known postmarked on Washington Island with Type **Z 3**:

1909–16 King Edward VII 5d., 8d. (*Nos.* 402, 404*b*)
1915–30 King George V (*recess*) 6d., 7½d., 8d., 9d., 1s. (*Nos.* 425/7, 429/30)
1915–34 King George V (*typo*) ½d., 1½d., 2d., 3d. (*Nos.* 435, 438/9, 449)
1915 "WAR STAMP" opt ½d (*No.* 452)
1920 Victory 1d., 1½d., 6d. (*Nos.* 454/5, 457)
1922 2d. on ½d. (*No.* 459)
1926–34 Admiral design 1d. (*No.* 468)

The above information is based on a special survey undertaken by members of the Kiribati & Tuvalu Philatelic Society and the Pacific Islands Study Circle, co-ordinated by Mr. Michael Shaw.

PRICES FOR STAMPS ON COVER TO 1945		
Nos.	1/7	*from* × 5
Nos.	8/11	*from* × 10
Nos.	12/23	*from* × 6
No.	24	—
No.	26	*from* × 15
Nos.	27/30	*from* × 6
No.	35	—
Nos.	36/9	*from* × 4
Nos.	40/2	*from* × 12
Nos.	43/54	*from* × 4
Nos.	D1/8	*from* × 5

BRITISH PROTECTORATE

GILBERT& ELLICE

PROTECTORATE

(1)

2 Pandanus Pine

1911 (1 Jan). *Stamps of Fiji optd with T* **1**. Wmk Mult Crown CA. *Chalk-surfaced paper* (*5d. to 1s.*).
1 **23** ½d. green . . . 4·75 45·00
2 1d. red . . . 45·00 28·00
3 **24** 2d. grey . . . 8·50 15·00
4 **23** 2½d. ultramarine . . . 12·00 29·00
5 5d. purple and olive-green . . . 45·00 75·00
6 **24** 6d. dull and bright purple . . . 20·00 45·00
7 **23** 1s. black/*green* (R.) . . . 20·00 60·00
1/7 *Set of* 7 . . . £130 £275
1s/7s Optd "Specimen" *Set of* 7 . . . £275
The 2d. to 6d. are on special printings which were not issued without overprint.
Examples of Nos. 1/7 are known showing a forged Ocean Island postmark dated "JY 15 11".

(Recess D.L.R.)

1911 (Mar). Wmk Mult Crown CA. P 14.
8 **2** ½d. green . . . 4·75 15·00
9 1d. carmine . . . 2·00 7·00
w. Wmk inverted . . . £325
10 2d. grey . . . 1·50 7·00
11 2½d. blue . . . 5·00 11·00
8/11 *Set of* 4 . . . 11·50 35·00
8s/11s Optd "Specimen" *Set of* 4 . . . £140

3

WAR TAX

(5)

(Typo D.L.R.)

1912 (May)–**24**. *Die I* (*½d. to 5s.*) *or Die II* (*£1*). Wmk Mult Crown CA. *Chalk-surfaced paper* (*3d. to £1*). P 14.
12 **3** ½d. green (7.12) . . . 50 4·50
a. Yellow-green (1914) . . . 4·50 11·00
13 1d. carmine (12.12) . . . 2·25 5·50
a. Scarlet (1915) . . . 3·75 11·00
14 2d. greyish slate (1.16) . . . 15·00 26·00
15 2½d. bright blue (1.16) . . . 1·75 11·00
16 3d. purple/*yellow* (1918) . . . 2·50 8·50
17 4d. black and red/*yellow* (10.12) . . . 75 7·00
18 5d. dull purple and sage-green . . . 1·75 7·00
19 6d. dull and bright purple . . . 1·25 7·50
20 1s. black/*green* . . . 1·25 5·50
21 2s. purple and blue/*blue* (10.12) . . . 14·00 30·00
22 2s.6d. black and red/*blue* (10.12) . . . 16·00 25·00
23 5s. green and red/*yellow* (10.12) . . . 32·00 60·00
24 £1 purple and black/*red* (Die II) (3.24) . . . £550 £1400
12/24 Set of 13 . . . £600 £1400
12s/24s Optd "Specimen" Set of 13 . . . £600

CROWN COLONY

1918 (June). *Optd with T* **5**.
26 **3** 1d. red . . . 50 6·50
s. Optd "Specimen" . . . 60·00

1922–**27**. *Die II.* Wmk Mult Script CA. *Chalk-surfaced paper* (*10s.*). P 14.
27 **3** ½d. green (1923) . . . 3·25 3·25
28 1d. violet (1927) . . . 4·50 5·00
29 1½d. scarlet (1924) . . . 4·50 2·00
30 2d. slate-grey . . . 7·00 26·00
35 10s. green and red/*emerald* (3.24) . . . £150 £350
27s/35s Optd "Specimen" *Set of* 5 . . . £275
Examples of most values between Nos. 12 and 35 are known showing part strikes of the forged postmark mentioned below Nos. 1/7. Collectors should exercise particular caution when buying used examples of Nos. 24 and 35.

1935 (6 May). *Silver Jubilee. As Nos.* 91/4 *of Antigua, but ptd by B.W.* P 11 × 12.
36 1d. ultramarine and grey-black . . . 2·25 9·00
d. Flagstaff on right-hand turret . . . £180
e. Double flagstaff . . . £275
37 1½d. deep blue and scarlet . . . 1·75 3·75
d. Flagstaff on right-hand turret . . . £180
e. Double flagstaff . . . £275
38 3d. brown and deep blue . . . 5·50 12·00
d. Flagstaff on right-hand turret . . . £275
e. Double flagstaff . . . £325
39 1s. slate and purple . . . 20·00 20·00
d. Flagstaff on right-hand turret . . . £400
e. Double flagstaff . . . £450 £475
36/9 *Set of* 4 . . . 26·00 40·00
36s/9s Perf "Specimen" *Set of* 4 . . . £120
For illustrations of plate varieties see Omnibus section following Zanzibar.

1937 (12 May). *Coronation. As Nos.* 95/7 *of Antigua, but ptd by D.L.R.* P 14.
40 1d. violet . . . 35 65
41 1½d. scarlet . . . 35 65
42 3d. bright blue . . . 40 70
40/2 *Set of* 3 . . . 1·00 1·75
40s/2s Perf "Specimen" *Set of* 3 . . . 85·00

6 Great Frigate Bird

7 Pandanus Pine

8 Canoe crossing Reef

(Recess B.W. (½d., 2d., 2s.6d.), Waterlow (1d., 5d., 6d., 2s., 5s.), D.L.R. (1½d., 2½d., 3d., 1s.))

1939 (14 Jan)–**55**. *T* **6**/**8** *and similar horiz designs.* Wmk Mult Script CA (sideways on ½d., 2d. and 2s.6d.). P 11½ × 11 (½d., 2d., 2s.6d.), 12½ (1d., 5d., 6d., 2s., 5s.) or 13½ (1½d., 2½d., 3d., 1s.).
43 ½d. indigo and deep bluish green . . . 60 1·00
a. "A" of "CA" missing from wmk
44 1d. emerald and plum . . . 30 1·50
45 1½d. brownish black and bright carmine . . . 30 1·25
46 2d. red-brown and grey-black . . . 75 1·00
47 2½d. brownish black and deep olive . . . 40 7
a. Brownish black & olive-green (12.5.43) . . . 4·00 4·2
48 3d. brownish black and ultramarine . . . 45 1·0
a. Perf 12. *Black and bright blue* (24.8.55) . . . 50 2·2
49 5d. deep ultramarine and sepia . . . 4·25 1·5
a. Ultramarine and sepia (12.5.43) . . . 5·00 6·5
b. Ultramarine & blackish brn (20.10.44) . . . 4·25 5·0
50 6d. olive-green and deep violet . . . 50 6
51 1s. brownish black and turquoise-green . . . 14·00 2·2
a. Brownish black & turquoise-bl (12.5.43) . . . 5·50 3·2
ab. Perf 12 (8.5.51) . . . 2·75 15·0
52 2s. deep ultramarine and orange-red . . . 10·00 10·0
53 2s.6d. deep blue and emerald . . . 10·00 11·0
54 5s. deep rose-red and royal blue . . . 13·00 14·0
43/54 *Set of* 12 . . . 38·00 40·0
43s/54s Perf "Specimen" *Set of* 12 . . . £275
Designs: *As T* **6**—2d. Canoe and boat-house; 2s.6d. Gilber Islands canoe. *As T* **7**—5d. Ellice Islands canoe; 6d. Coconut palms 2s. H.M.C.S. *Nimanoa*; 5s. Coat of arms. *As T* **8**—2½d. Nativ house; 3d. Seascape; 1s. Cantilever jetty, Ocean Island.

1946 (16 Dec). *Victory. As Nos.* 110/11 *of Antigua.*
55 1d. purple . . . 15 4
56 3d. blue . . . 15 4
55s/6s Perf "Specimen" *Set of* 2 . . . 70·00

1949 (29 Aug). *Royal Silver Wedding. As Nos.* 112/13 *of Antigua.*
57 1d. violet . . . 40 5
58 £1 scarlet . . . 12·00 19·0

1949 (10 Oct). *75th Anniv of U.P.U. As Nos.* 114/17 *of Antigua.*
59 1d. purple . . . 40 1·0
60 2d. grey-black . . . 2·00 2·5
61 3d. deep blue . . . 50 2·2
62 1s. blue . . . 50 2·0
59/62 *Set of* 4 . . . 3·00 7·0

POSTAGE DUE STAMPS

D 1

(Typo B.W.)

1940 (Aug). Wmk Mult Script CA. P 12.
D1 **D 1** 1d. emerald-green . . . 9·00 23·0
D2 2d. scarlet . . . 9·50 23·0
D3 3d. brown . . . 14·00 24·0
D4 4d. blue . . . 16·00 30·0
D5 5d. grey-green . . . 21·00 30·0
D6 6d. purple . . . 21·00 30·0
D7 1s. violet . . . 23·00 42·0
D8 1s.6d. turquoise-green . . . 45·00 85·0
D1/8 *Set of* 8 . . . £140 £2
D1s/8s Perf "Specimen" *Set of* 8 . . . £170
Examples of all values are known showing a forged Post Offic Ocean Island postmark dated "16 DE 46".

Gold Coast

Gold Coast originally consisted of coastal forts, owned by t Royal African Company, trading with the interior. In 1821, due raids by the Ashanti king, the British Government took over t forts, together with some of the hinterland, and the Gold Coast w placed under the Governor of Sierra Leone.

The administration was handed back to a merchantile compar in 1828, but the forts returned to British Government rule in 184 The colony was reconstituted by Royal Charter on 24 July 187 and at that time also included the settlement at Lagos which becar a separate colony in January 1886.

Following the end of the final Ashanti War the whole of t territory was annexed in September 1901.

A postal service was established at Cape Coast Castle in 185 There is no record of British stamps being officially issued in t Colony before 1875, apart from those used on board the ships the West African Squadron, but examples do, however, ex cancelled by Gold Coast postmarks.

CROWN COLONY

PRICES FOR STAMPS ON COVER TO 1945		
Nos.	1/3	*from* × 15
Nos.	4/8	*from* × 20
Nos.	9/10	*from* × 10
Nos.	11/20	*from* × 25
Nos.	22/5	—
Nos.	26/34	*from* × 10
Nos.	35/6	*from* × 20
Nos.	38/69	*from* × 6
Nos.	70/98	*from* × 3
Nos.	100/2	—
Nos.	103/12	*from* × 5
Nos.	113/16	*from* × 3
Nos.	117/19	*from* × 4
Nos.	120/32	*from* × 3
No.	D1	*from* × 6
No.	D2	*from* × 20
Nos.	D3/4	*from* × 12

1

ONE
PENNY.

(2)

(Typo D.L.R.)

1875 (1 July). Wmk Crown CC. P 12½.
1 1 1d. blue . . . . £450 80·00
2 4d. magenta £425 £120
3 6d. orange . . . . £650 65·00

1876–84. Wmk Crown CC. P 14.
4 1 ½d. olive-yellow (1879) . . . . 65·00 23·00
5 1d. blue . . . . 20·00 6·50
a. Bisected (½d.) (on cover) (1884) . . † £3250
w. Wmk inverted £275 £130
6 2d. green (1879) . . . . 85·00 9·00
a. Bisected (1d.) (on cover) (1884) . . † £2750
b. Quartered (½d.) (on cover) (1884) . . † £4500
7 4d. magenta . . . . £180 6·00
a. Bisected (2d.) (on cover) (1884) . . † £5000
b. Quartered (1d.) (on cover) (1884) . . † £7000
w. Wmk inverted £475
8 6d. orange . . . . £130 18·00
a. Bisected (3d.) (on cover) (1884) . . † £6500
b. Sixth (1d.) (on cover) (1884) . . † £8000

During 1884 some values were in short supply and the use of bisects and other divided stamps is known as follows:
No. 5a. Used as part of 2½d. rate from Accra and Quittah
No. 6a. Used as 1d. rate from Addah, Cape Coast Castle, Quittah, Salt Pond, Secondee and Winnebah
No. 6b. Used as part of 2½d. rate from Cape Coast Castle
No. 7a. Used as 2d. or as part of 2½d. rate from Quittah
No. 7b. Used as 1d. rate from Appam, Axim, Cape Coast, Castle and Winnebah
No. 8a. Used as 3d. rate from Secondee
No. 8b. Used as 1d. rate from Cape Coast Castle and Winnebah.

Examples of bisects used on piece are worth about 10% of the price quoted for those on cover.

The 4d., No. 7, is known surcharged "1 d". This was previously listed as No. 8c, but there are now serious doubts as to its authenticity. The three examples reported of this stamp all show *different* surcharges!

1883. Wmk Crown CA. P 14.
9 1 ½d. olive-yellow (January) . . . . £180 65·00
10 1d. blue (May) . . . . £850 70·00

PENNY

Short "P" and distorted "E" (Pl 1 R. 5/6)
("P" repaired for Pl 2)

1884 (Aug)–**91**. Wmk Crown CA. P 14.
11 1 ½d. green . . . . 3·25 1·00
a. Dull green . . . . 3·00 80
w. Wmk inverted £130 £130
12 1d. rose-carmine . . . . 3·75 50
a. Carmine . . . . 3·75 50
b. Bisected (½d.) (on cover) . . † £3750
c. Short "P" and distorted "E" . . £120
13 2d. grey . . . . 12·00 3·75
aw. Wmk inverted £180 £180
b. Slate . . . . 3·75 50
c. Bisected (1d.) (on cover) . . † £4250
d. Quartered (½d.) (on cover) . . † —
14 2½d. ultramarine and orange (13.3.91) . . 4·25 70
15 3d. olive-yellow (9.89) . . . . 10·00 4·50
a. Olive . . . . 10·00 4·50
16 4d. deep mauve (3.85) . . . . 10·00 1·50
a. Rosy mauve . . . . 11·00 3·00
17 6d. orange (1.89) . . . . 10·00 5·00
a. Orange-brown . . . . 10·00 5·00
b. Bisected (3d.) (on cover) . . † —
18 1s. violet (1888) . . . . 32·00 12·00
a. Bright mauve . . . . 5·50 1·25
19 2s. yellow-brown (1888) . . . . 80·00 35·00
a. Deep brown . . . . 45·00 15·00
11/19a *Set of* 9 . . . . 85·00 26·00
14s/15s, 18s/19s Optd "Specimen" *Set of* 4 . . £150

During 1884 to 1886 and in 1889 some values were in short supply and the use of bisects and other divided stamps is known as follows:
No. 12b. Used as part of 2½d. rate from Cape Coast Castle
No. 13c. Used as 1d. or as part of 2d. rate from Cape Coast Castle, Chamah, Dixcove and Elmina
No. 13d. Used as part of 2½d. rate from Cape Coast Castle
No. 17b. Used as 3d. from Appam

1889 (Mar). *No. 17 surch with T* **2**.
20 1 1d.on 6d. orange . . . . £110 48·00
a. Surch double . . . . † £3250

In some sheets examples may be found with the bar and "PENNY" spaced 8 mm, the normal spacing being 7 mm.

USED HIGH VALUES. Until the introduction of airmail in 1929 there was no postal use for values over 10s. Post Offices did, however, apply postal cancellations to high value stamps required for telegram fees.

3

4

1889 (Sept)–**94**. Wmk Crown CA. P 14.
22 3 5s. dull mauve and blue . . . . 65·00 15·00
23 10s. dull mauve and red . . . . 75·00 15·00
a. Dull mauve and carmine £600 £200
24 20s. green and red £3250
25 20s. dull mauve and black/*red* (4.94) . . £160 35·00
w. Wmk inverted . . . . £250 85·00
22a/5s Optd "Specimen" *Set of* 4 . . . . £400

No. 24 was withdrawn from sale in April 1893 when a large part of the stock was stolen. No 20s. stamps were available until the arrival of the replacement printing a year later.

1898 (May)–**1902**. Wmk Crown CA. P 14.
26 3 ½d. dull mauve and green . . . . 2·50 1·00
27 1d. dull mauve and rose . . . . 2·75 50
aw. Wmk inverted . . . . — £100
27*b* 4 2d. dull mauve and orange-red (1902) . . . . 48·00 £140
28 3 2½d. dull mauve and ultramarine . . 5·00 5·00
29 4 3d. dull mauve and orange . . . . 5·00 1·50
30 6d. dull mauve and violet . . . . 5·50 1·50
31 3 1s. green and black (1899) . . . . 10·00 16·00
32 2s. green and carmine . . . . 13·00 18·00
33 5s. green and mauve (1900) . . . . 50·00 29·00
34 10s. green and brown (1900) . . . . £140 50·00
26/34 *Set of* 10 . . . . £250 £225
26s/34s Optd "Specimen" *Set of* 10 . . . . £180

1901 (6 Oct). *Nos. 28 and 30 surch with T* **2**.
35 1d.on 2½d. dull mauve and ultramarine . . 3·25 4·00
a. "ONE" omitted £1000
36 1d.on 6d. dull mauve and violet . . . . 3·25 3·50
a. "ONE" omitted £275 £550

6

7

8

1902. Wmk Crown CA. P 14.
38 6 ½d. dull purple and green (Aug) . . . . 1·50 40
39 1d. dull purple and carmine (May) . . 1·50 15
w. Wmk inverted . . . . — 75·00
40 7 2d. dull purple and orange-red (Apr) . . 22·00 7·00
w. Wmk inverted
41 6 2½d. dull purple and ultramarine (Aug) . . . . 4·50 9·00
42 7 3d. dull purple and orange (Aug) . . 3·00 1·50
43 6d. dull purple and violet (Aug) . . 3·75 1·50
w. Wmk inverted . . . . — 95·00
44 6 1s. green and black (Aug) . . . . 14·00 3·25
45 2s. green and carmine (Aug) . . . . 15·00 18·00
46 5s. green and mauve (Aug) . . . . 40·00 90·00
47 10s. green and brown (Aug) . . . . 55·00 £130
48 20s. purple and black/*red* (Aug) . . £130 £180
38/48 *Set of* 11 . . . . £250 £400
38s/48s Optd "Specimen" *Set of* 11 . . . . £200

Examples of Nos. 45/8 are known showing a forged Accra postmark dated "25 MAR 1902".

1904–06. Wmk Mult Crown CA. *Ordinary paper (½d. to 6d.) or chalk-surfaced paper (2s.6d.)*.
49 6 ½d. dull purple and green (3.06) . . 2·50 7·00
50 1d. dull purple and carmine (10.04) . . 8·50 30
a. Chalk-surfaced paper (5.06) . . 9·50 2·00
w. Wmk inverted
51 7 2d. dull purple and orange-red (11.04) . . . . 5·00 50
a. Chalk-surfaced paper (8.06) . . 25·00 2·25
52 6 2½d. dull purple and ultramarine (6.06) . . . . 48·00 48·00
53 7 3d. dull purple and orange (8.05) . . 60·00 6·00
a. Chalk-surfaced paper (4.06) . . 16·00 60
54 6d. dull purple and violet (3.06) . . 65·00 2·50
a. Chalk-surfaced paper (9.06) . . 40·00 1·50
57 2s.6d. green and yellow (3.06) . . 28·00 £110
s. Optd Specimen" . . . . 45·00
49/57 *Set of* 7 . . . . £130 £150

1907–13. Wmk Mult Crown CA. *Ordinary paper (½d. to 2½d. and 2s.) or chalk-surfaced paper (3d. to 1s., 2s.6d., 5s.)*. P 14.
59 6 ½d. dull green (5.07) . . . . 3·50 30
a. Blue-green (1909) . . . . 7·50 1·50
60 1d. red (2.07) . . . . 7·00 40
61 7 2d. greyish slate (4.09) . . . . 2·25 40
62 6 2½d. blue (4.07) . . . . 7·50 2·00
w. Wmk inverted
63 7 3d. purple/*yellow* (16.4.09) . . . . 8·00 55
64 6d. dull and deep purple (12.08) . . 17·00 55
a. Dull and bright purple (1911) . . 3·75 3·50
65 6 1s. black/*green* (10.09) . . . . 12·00 50
66 2s. purple and blue/*blue* (1910) . . 8·00 16·00
a. Chalk-surfaced paper (1912) . . 18·00 16·00
67 7 2s.6d. black and red/*blue* (1911) . . 28·00 90·00
68 6 5s. green and red/*yellow* (1913) . . 55·00 £180
59/68 *Set of* 10 . . . . £120 £275
59s/68s Optd "Specimen" *Set of* 10 . . . . £250

A 10s. green and red on green, and a 20s. purple and black on red, both Type **6**, were prepared for use but not issued. Both exist overprinted "SPECIMEN" (*Price for* 10s. *in this condition*, £300). An example of the 10s. exists without "SPECIMEN" overprint.

(Typo D.L.R.)

1908 (Nov). Wmk Mult Crown CA. P 14.
69 8 1d. red . . . . 3·00 10
a. Wmk sideways . . . . † £1600
s. Optd "Specimen" . . . . 45·00

9

10

11

(Typo D.L.R.)

1913–21. *Die I*. Wmk Mult Crown CA. *Chalk-surfaced paper (3d. to 20s.)*. P 14.
70 9 ½d. green . . . . 2·00 1·00
a. Yellow-green (1916) . . . . 2·75 1·25
72 10 1d. red . . . . 1·25 10
a. Scarlet (1917) . . . . 1·50 50
74 11 2d. grey . . . . 3·50 2·50
a. Slate-grey (1920) . . . . 8·00 8·00
w. Wmk inverted . . . . † £180
76 9 2½d. bright blue . . . . 5·50 1·00
a. "A" of "CA" missing from wmk £400
x. Wmk reversed . . . . † £180
77 11 3d. purple/*yellow* (8.15) . . . . 2·00 80
as. Optd "Specimen" . . . . 32·00
aw. Wmk inverted . . . . — 95·00
b. White back (9.13) . . . . 1·00 40
c. On orange-buff (1919) . . . . 5·50 7·00
cw. Wmk inverted
d. On buff (1920)
e. Die II. *On pale yellow* (1921) . . 38·00 5·00
ew. Wmk inverted . . . . † £225
78 6d. dull and bright purple . . . . 2·75 2·25
79 9 1s. black/*green* . . . . 2·50 1·25
a. Wmk sideways
bw. Wmk inverted
c. On blue-green, olive back (1916) . . 5·50 75
cs. Optd "Specimen" . . . . 42·00
cw. Wmk inverted
d. On emerald back (1920) . . . . 2·00 2·00
ds. Optd "Specimen" . . . . 38·00
e. Die II. *On emerald back* (1921) . . 1·50 50
es. Optd "Specimen" . . . . 42·00
ew. Wmk inverted
80 2s. purple and blue/*blue* . . . . 8·50 3·00
aw. Wmk inverted . . . . — £190
b. Die II (1921) . . . . £150 65·00
81 11 2s.6d. black and red/*blue* . . . . 5·00 13·00
a. Die II (1921) . . . . 22·00 42·00
82 9 5s. green and red/*yellow* (1916) . . 12·00 50·00
as. Optd "Specimen" . . . . 45·00
b. White back (10.13) . . . . 10·00 50·00
c. On orange-buff (1919) . . . . 75·00 80·00
d. On buff (1920)
e. On pale yellow (1921) £100 £130
f. Die II. *On pale yellow* (1921) . . 30·00 £130
fw. Wmk inverted £190
83 10s. green and red/*green* . . . . 48·00 85·00
a. On blue-green, olive back (1916) . . 18·00 65·00
b. On emerald back (1921) . . . . 30·00 £130
84 20s. purple and black/*red* . . . . £120 80·00
70/84 *Set of* 12 . . . . £160 £200
70s/6s, 77bs, 78s/81s, 82bs/4s Optd "Specimen" *Set of* 12 . . . . £250

The 10s. and 20s. were withdrawn locally from September 1920 and, in common with other Gold Coast stamps, were not available to stamp dealers from the Crown Agents in London.

WAR TAX

ONE PENNY

(12)

13 King George V and Christiansborg Castle

1918 (17 June). *Surch with T* **12**.
85 10 1d.on 1d. red . . . . 1·75 50
s. Optd "Specimen" . . . . 50·00

1921–24. *Die I (15s., £2) or Die II (others)*. Wmk Mult Script CA. *Chalk-surfaced paper (6d. to £2)*. P 14.
86 9 ½d. green 80 50
87 10 1d. chocolate-brown (1922) 70 10
88 11 1½d. red (1922) . . . . 1·75 10
89 2d. grey . . . . 1·75 30
90 9 2½d. yellow-orange (1922) . . . . 75 9·00
91 11 3d. bright blue (1922) . . . . 1·75 60
94 6d. dull and bright purple . . . . 2·00 3·00
95 9 1s. black/*emerald* (1924) . . . . 2·75 3·25
96 2s. purple and blue/*blue* (1923) . . 3·00 3·25
97 11 2s.6d. black and red/*blue* (1924) . . 7·00 24·00
98 9 5s. green and red/*pale yellow* (1924) . . . . 12·00 50·00
100 11 15s. dull purple and green (Die I) . . £130 £325
a. Die II (1924) £110 £325
as. Optd "Specimen" £100
102 £2 green and orange (Die I) £375 £900
86/100a *Set of* 12 . . . . £130 £375
86s/102s Optd "Specimen" *Set of* 13 . . . . £400

The Duty plate for the 1½d., 15s. and £2 has the words "GOLD COAST" in distinctly larger letters.

Examples of Nos. 100/a and 102 are known showing parts of forged Accra postmarks. These are dated "3 MAY 44" and "8 MAY 44", but are invariably positioned so that the year date is not shown.

(Des W. Palmer. Photo Harrison)

1928 (1 Aug). Wmk Mult Script CA. P 13½ × 15.
103 13 ½d. blue-green 70 40
104 1d. red-brown 70 10
105 1½d. scarlet . . . . 1·25 1·50
106 2d. slate . . . . 1·25 20
107 2½d. orange-yellow . . . . 1·50 3·50
108 3d. bright blue . . . . 1·25 40
109 6d. black and purple . . . . 1·50 40

110 1s. black and red-orange . . . 3·00 75
111 2s. black and bright violet . . . 20·00 4·75
112 5s. carmine and sage-green . . . 50·00 45·00
103/12 *Set of* 10 . . . 75·00 50·00
103s/12s Optd "Specimen" *Set of* 10 . . . £200

1935 (6 May). *Silver Jubilee. As Nos. 91/4 of Antigua, but printed by B.W.* P 11 × 12.
113 1d. ultramarine and grey-black . . . 60 50
a. Extra flagstaff . . . £120 £100
b. Short extra flagstaff . . . £150
c. Lightning conductor . . . £110
d. Flagstaff on right-hand turret . . . £190
114 3d. brown and deep blue . . . 3·00 6·00
a. Extra flagstaff . . . £130
c. Lightning conductor . . . £150
115 6d. green and indigo . . . 7·00 14·00
a. Extra flagstaff . . . £160 £190
b. Short extra flagstaff . . . £275
c. Lightning conductor . . . £180
d. Flagstaff on right-hand turret . . . £350
116 1s. slate and purple . . . 4·75 18·00
a. Extra flagstaff . . . £170
b. Short extra flagstaff . . . £225
c. Lightning conductor . . . £190
113/16 *Set of* 4 . . . 14·00 35·00
113s/16s Perf "Specimen" *Set of* 4 . . . 95·00
For illustrations of plate varieties see Omnibus section following Zanzibar.

1937 (12 May). *Coronation. As Nos. 95/7 of Antigua.* P 11 × 11½.
117 1d. buff . . . 1·25 2·25
118 2d. slate . . . 1·25 4·00
119 3d. blue . . . 1·50 2·00
117/19 *Set of* 3 . . . 3·50 7·50
117s/19s Perf "Specimen" *Set of* 3 . . . 65·00

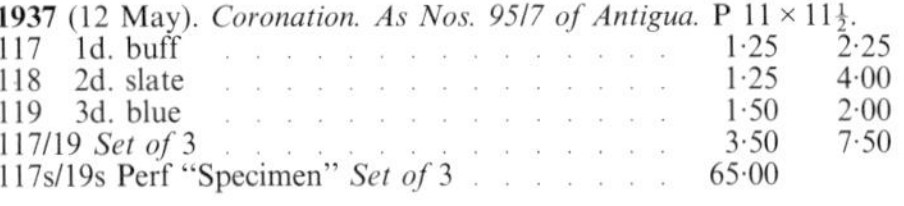

14

15 King George VI and Christiansborg Castle, Accra

(Recess B.W.)

1938 (1 Apr)–**44**. Wmk Mult Script CA. P 11½ × 12 (1s.3d., 10s.) or 12 (others).
120 **14** ½d. green . . . 3·50 1·75
a. Perf 12 × 11½ (1940) . . . 40 50
121 1d. red-brown . . . 4·00 30
a. Perf 12 × 11½ (1939) . . . 40 10
122 1½d. scarlet . . . 6·00 2·75
a. Perf 12 × 11½ (1940) . . . 40 50
123 2d. slate . . . 6·00 1·50
a. Perf 12 × 11½ (1940) . . . 40 10
124 3d. blue . . . 4·50 1·00
a. Perf 12 × 11½ (1940) . . . 40 35
125 4d. magenta . . . 5·50 3·00
a. Perf 12 × 11½ (1942) . . . 80 1·25
126 6d. purple . . . 7·00 50
a. Perf 12 × 11½ (1939) . . . 80 20
127 9d. orange . . . 5·50 1·75
a. Perf 12 × 11½ (1944) . . . 1·25 55
128 **15** 1s. black and olive-green . . . 10·00 2·25
a. Perf 11½ × 12 (1940) . . . 1·50 65
129 1s.3d. brown & turquoise-bl (12.4.41) . . . 2·00 50
130 2s. blue and violet . . . 27·00 17·00
a. Perf 11½ × 12 (1940) . . . 5·00 13·00
131 5s. olive-green & carmine . . . 50·00 21·00
a. Perf 11½ × 12 (1940) . . . 10·00 16·00
132 10s. black and violet (7.40) . . . 7·00 23·00
120a/32 *Set of* 13 . . . 27·00 50·00
120s/32s Perf "Specimen" *Set of* 13 . . . £225
All values except 1s.3d. and 10s. exist in two perforations: (*a*) Line-perforated 12, from early printings; (*b*) Comb-perforated 12 × 11.8 (vertical design) or 11.8 × 12 (horiz design) from later printings. The 1s.3d. and 10s. only exist comb-perforated 11.8 × 12.
The ½d. and 1d. values exist in coils constructed from normal sheets.

1946 (14 Oct). *Victory. As Nos. 110/11 of Antigua.* P 13½ × 14.
133 2d. slate-violet . . . 14·00 2·75
a. Perf 13½ . . . 10 10
134 4d. claret . . . 2·00 3·50
a. Perf 13½ . . . 1·50 2·75
133s/4s Perf "Specimen" *Set of* 2 . . . 65·00

16 Northern Territories Mounted Constabulary

17 Christiansborg Castle

(Des B. A. Johnston (1½d.), M. Ziorkley and B. A. Abban (2d.), P.O. draughtsman (2½d.), C. Gomez (1s.), M. Ziorkley (10s.); others from photographs. Recess B.W.)

1948 (1 July). *T* **16/17** *and similar designs.* Wmk Mult Script CA. P 12 × 11½ (vert) or 11½ × 12 (horiz).
135 ½d. emerald-green . . . 20 30
136 1d. blue . . . 15 15
137 1½d. scarlet . . . 1·25 70
138 2d. purple-brown . . . 55 10
139 2½d. yellow-brown and scarlet . . . 2·00 3·50
140 3d. light blue . . . 4·00 50
141 4d. magenta . . . 3·50 2·00
142 6d. black and orange . . . 30 30
143 1s. black and vermilion . . . 60 30
144 2s. sage-green and magenta . . . 3·25 2·00
145 5s. purple and black . . . 26·00 6·00
146 10s. black and sage-green . . . 8·00 6·00
135/46 *Set of* 12 . . . 45·00 19·00
135s/46s Perf "Specimen" *Set of* 12 . . . £250
Designs: *Horiz*—1½d. Emblem of Joint Provincial Council; 2½d. Map showing position of Gold Coast; 3d. Nsuta manganese mine; 4d. Lake Bosumtwi; 1s. Breaking cocoa pods; 2s. Gold Coast Regt Trooping the Colour; 5s. Surfboats. *Vert*—2d. Talking drums; 6d. Cocoa farmer; 10s. Forest.
Nos. 135/6 exist in coils constructed from normal sheets.

1948 (20 Dec). *Royal Silver Wedding. As Nos. 112/13 of Antigua.*
147 1½d. scarlet . . . 30 30
148 10s. grey-olive . . . 17·00 23·00

1949 (10 Oct). *75th Anniv of U.P.U. As Nos. 114/17 of Antigua.*
149 2d. red-brown . . . 25 20
a. "A" of "CA" missing from wmk
150 2½d. orange . . . 1·50 3·50
151 3d. deep blue . . . 35 1·50
152 1s. blue-green . . . 35 30
149/52 *Set of* 4 . . . 2·25 5·00
As on other examples of this variety No. 149a shows traces of the left leg of the "A".

POSTAGE DUE STAMPS

D 1

(Typo D.L.R.)

1923 (6 Mar). *Yellowish toned paper.* Wmk Mult Script CA. P 14.
D1 D **1** ½d. black . . . 15·00 £110
D2 1d. black . . . 75 1·25
D3 2d. black . . . 13·00 5·50
D4 3d. black . . . 22·00 3·50
D1/4 *Set of* 4 . . . 45·00 £110
D1s/4s Optd "Specimen" *Set of* 4 . . . 75·00
A bottom marginal strip of six of No. D2 is known showing the "A" of "CA" omitted from the watermark in the margin below the third vertical column.

3d — Normal
3d — Lower serif at left of "3" missing (R. 9/1)

1/- — Row 4 (No. D8)
1/- — Row 5 (No. D8c)

The degree of inclination of the stroke on the 1s. value varies for each vertical row of the sheet: Rows 1, 2 and 6 104°, Row 3 108°, Row 4 107° and Row 5 (No. D8c) 100°.

1951–52. Wmk Mult Script CA. *Chalk-surfaced paper.* P 14.
D5 D **1** 2d. black (13.12.51) . . . 3·50 22·00
a. Error. Crown missing, W **9***a* . . . £700
b. Error. St. Edward's Crown, W **9***b* . . . £375
c. Large "d" (R. 9/6, 10/6) . . . 25·00
d. Serif on "d" (R. 1/6) . . . 42·00
D6 3d. black (13.12.51) . . . 2·50 20·00
a. Error. Crown missing, W **9***a* . . . £700
b. Error. St. Edward's Crown, W **9***b* . . . £375
c. Missing serif . . . 38·00
D7 6d. black (1.10.52) . . . 1·75 8·00
a. Error. Crown missing, W **9***a* . . . £900
b. Error. St. Edward's Crown, W **9***b* . . . £650
D8 1s. black (1.10.52) . . . 1·75 65·00
b. Error. St. Edward's Crown, W **9***b* . . . £800
c. Upright stroke . . . 12·00
D5/8 *Set of* 4 . . . 8·50 £100
For illustration of Nos. D5c/d see Nos. D4/6 of Bechuanaland.

Grenada

The earliest recorded postmark of the British administration of Grenada dates from 1784, and, although details of the early period are somewhat sparse, it would appear that the island's postal service was operated at a branch of the British G.P.O. In addition to a Packet Agency at St. George's, the capital, there was a further agency at Carriacou, in the Grenadines, which operated for a few years from 15 September 1847.

Stamps of Great Britain were supplied to the St. George's office from April 1858 until the colony assumed responsibility for the postal service on 1 May 1860. Following the take-over the crowned-circle handstamp, No. CC2, was again used until the Grenada adhesives were issued in 1861.

There was no internal postal service before 1861.

For illustrations of the handstamp and postmark types see BRITISH POST OFFICES ABROAD notes, following GREAT BRITAIN.

CARRIACOU

CROWNED-CIRCLE HANDSTAMPS

A crowned-circle handstamp for Carriacou is recorded in the G.P.O. proof book but no example has been reported used from Grenada.

ST. GEORGE'S

CROWNED-CIRCLE HANDSTAMPS

CC2 CC **1** GRENADA (R.) (24.10.1850) *Price on cover* . . . £1200

Stamps of GREAT BRITAIN *cancelled* "A 15" *as Type* **2**.

1858–60.
Z1 1d. rose-red (1857), *perf* 14 . . . £425
Z2 2d. blue (1858) (Plate No. 7) . . . £1000
Z3 4d. rose (1857) . . . £275
Z4 6d. lilac (1856) . . . £120
Z5 1s. green (1856) . . . £1000

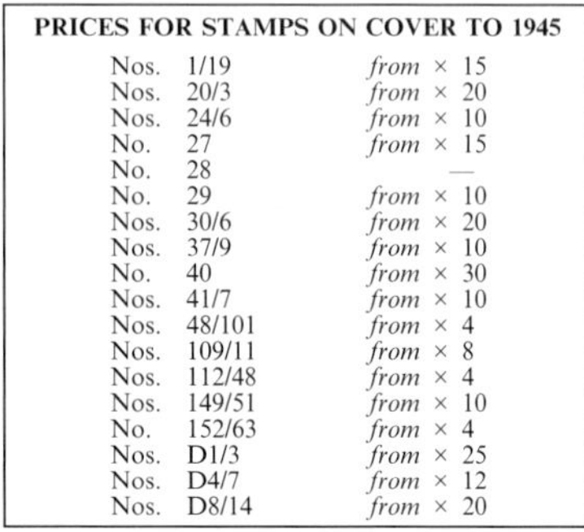

PRICES FOR STAMPS ON COVER TO 1945

Nos.	1/19	*from* × 15
Nos.	20/3	*from* × 20
Nos.	24/6	*from* × 10
No.	27	*from* × 15
No.	28	—
No.	29	*from* × 10
Nos.	30/6	*from* × 20
Nos.	37/9	*from* × 10
No.	40	*from* × 30
Nos.	41/7	*from* × 10
Nos.	48/101	*from* × 4
Nos.	109/11	*from* × 8
Nos.	112/48	*from* × 4
Nos.	149/51	*from* × 10
No.	152/63	*from* × 4
Nos.	D1/3	*from* × 25
Nos.	D4/7	*from* × 12
Nos.	D8/14	*from* × 20

CROWN COLONY

PRINTERS. Types **1** and **5** recess-printed by Perkins, Bacon and Co.

PERKINS BACON "CANCELLED". For notes on these handstamps, showing "CANCELLED" between horizontal bars forming an oval, see Catalogue Introduction.

1

2 Small Star

(Eng C. Jeens)

1861 (3 June)–**62**. No wmk. *Wove paper.*
(*a*) Rough perf 14 to 16.
1 **1** 1d. bluish green . . . £4500 £3[illegible]
2 1d. green (5.62) . . . 50·00 42·[illegible]
a. Imperf between (horiz pair)
3 6d. rose (*shades*) (H/S "CANCELLED" in oval £8000) . . . £900 90·[illegible]
(*b*) Perf 11 to 12½.
3*a* **1** 6d. lake-red (6.62) . . . £750
The 1d. bluish green also exists handstamped "CANCELLED" in oval, but the only known example is in the Royal Collection.
No. 3*a* is only known unused, and may be the result of perforating machine trials undertaken by Perkins, Bacon. It has also been seen on horizontally laid paper (*Price* £1200).

SIDEWAYS WATERMARK. W **2/3** when sideways show two points of star downwards.

1863–71. W **2** (Small Star). Rough perf 14 to 16.
4 **1** 1d. green (3.64) . . . 75·00 12·[illegible]
a. Wmk sideways . . . — 24·[illegible]
5 1d. yellowish green . . . £100 26·[illegible]
6 6d. rose (*shades*) (5.63) . . . £600 13·[illegible]
a. Wmk sideways . . . — 60·[illegible]
7 6d. orange-red (*shades*) (5.66) . . . £650 12·[illegible]
8 6d. dull rose-red (*wmk sideways*) . . . £3500 £2[illegible]
9 6d. vermilion (5.71) . . . £750 12·[illegible]
a. Double impression . . . — £20[illegible]

1873 (Jan). W **2** (Small Star, sideways). Clean-cut perf 15.
10 **1** 1d. deep green . . . 85·00 38·[illegible]
a. Bisected diag (on cover) . . . † £90[illegible]
b. Imperf between (pair) . . . — £60[illegible]
No. 10a, and later bisected 1d. values, were authorised until 18[illegible] to pay the island newspaper rate (½d.) or the newspaper rate to Great Britain (1½d.). Examples also exist on covers to France.

3 Large Star

4 Broad-pointed Star

1873 (Sept)–**74**. W **3** (Large Star). Intermediate perf 15.
11 **1** 1d. blue-green (*wmk sideways*) (2.74) . . 75·00 19·00
a. Double impression . . . .
b. Bisected diag (on cover) . . . . . . † £9000
12 6d. orange-vermilion . . . . £600 26·00

5

POSTAGE
ONE SHILLING
(6)

NOTE. The early ½d., 2½d., 4d. and 1s. postage stamps were made by surcharging the undenominated Type **5** design.

The surcharges were from two founts of type—one about 1½ mm high, the other 2 mm high—so there are short and tall letters on the same stamp; also the spacing varies considerably, so that the length of the words varies.

Examples of Type **5** with surcharges, but without the "POSTAGE" inscription, are revenue stamps.

1875 (July). *Surch with T* **6**. W **3**. P 14.
13 **5** 1s. deep mauve (B.) . . . . £650 11·00
a. "SHLLIING" . . . . † £700
b. "NE SHILLING" . . . . † £2500
c. Inverted "S" in "POSTAGE" £3500 £500
d. "OSTAGE" £5000 £2000

1875 (Dec). W **3** (Large Star, upright).
14 **1** 1d. green to yellow-green (P 14) . . . . 75·00 7·50
a. Bisected diag (on cover) . . . . . . † £9000
15 1d. green (P 15) £8000 £2250

No. 14 was perforated at Somerset House. 40 sheets of No. 15 were perforated by Perkins, Bacon to replace spoilages and to complete the order.

1878 (Aug). W **2** (Small Star, sideways). Intermediate perf 15.
16 **1** 1d. green . . . . £225 38·00
b. Bisected diag (on cover) . . . . . . † £9000
17 6d. deep vermilion . . . . £800 35·00
a. Double impression . . . . — £2000

1879 (Dec). W **2** (Small Star, upright). Rough perf 15.
18 **1** 1d. pale green (*thin paper*) . . . . . . £300 26·00
a. Double impression . . . .
b. Bisected diag (on cover) . . . . . . † —

1881 (Apr). W **2** (Small Star, sideways). Rough perf 14½.
19 **1** 1d. green . . . . £150 8·50
a. Bisected diag (on cover) . . . . . . † £9000

POSTAGE POSTAGE POSTAGE

HALF-PENNY (7) TWO PENCE HALF-PENNY (8) FOUR PENCE (9)

1881 (Apr). *Surch with T* **7/9**. P 14½.

(*a*) W **3** (Large Star, sideways on ½d.)
20 **5** ½d. pale mauve . . . . 30·00 10·00
21 ½d. deep mauve . . . . 11·00 5·50
a. Imperf (pair) £300
ab. Ditto. "OSTAGE" (R. 9/4) £4250
b. Surch double £300
c. "OSTAGE" (R. 9/4) £190 £130
d. No hyphen £190 £130
e. "ALF-PENNY" £3500
f. Wmk upright £300 £140
g. Ditto. "OSTAGE" (R. 9/4) £1700 £750
22 2½d. rose-lake . . . . 60·00 7·00
a. Imperf (pair) £500
b. Imperf between (horiz pair) £3750
c. No stop . . . . £250 75·00
d. "PENCF" (R. 8/12) £450 £180
23 4d. blue . . . . £100 8·00
a. Wmk sideways . . . . † £500
b. Inverted "S" in "POSTAGE" . . .

(*b*) W **4** (Broad-pointed Star).
24 **5** 2½d. rose-lake . . . . £160 50·00
a. No stop £550 £200
b. "PENCF" (R. 8/12) £750 £275
25 2½d. claret £425 £120
a. No stop £1100 £500
b. "PENCF" (R. 8/12) £1600 £700
25*c* 2½d. deep claret £650 £225
d. No stop £2250 £900
e. "PENCF" (R. 8/12) £2750 £1100
26 4d. blue £250 £180

Examples of the "F" for "E" error on the 2½d. value should not be confused with a somewhat similar broken "E" variety. The latter is always without the stop and shows other damage to the "E". The authentic error always occurs with the full stop shown.

The "no stop" variety occurs on R. 3/4, R. 6/2, R. 8/3 and R. 9/7.

ONE PENNY (10) POSTAGE. (11) POSTAGE POSTAGE (12)

1883 (Jan). *Revenue stamps (T* **5** *with green surcharge as in T* **10***) optd for postage.* W **2** (Small Star). P 14½.

(*a*) *Optd horizontally with T* **11**.
27 **5** 1d. orange . . . . £325 55·00
a. "POSTAGE" inverted £2750 £2250
b. "POSTAGE" double £1400 £1100
c. Inverted "S" in "POSTAGE" . . . £1000 £600
d. Bisected diag (on cover) . . . . . . † £3000

(*b*) *Optd diagonally with T* **11** *twice on each stamp, the stamp being cut and each half used as ½d.*
28 **5** Half of 1d. orange £650 £225
a. Unsevered pair £4250 £1200
b. "POSTAGE" inverted . . . . — £1200

(*c*) *Optd with T* **12**, *the stamps divided diagonally and each half used as ½d.*
29 **5** Half of 1d. orange £275 £110
a. Unsevered pair £1500 £450

Nos. 27/9 exist with wmk either upright or sideways.

1d. Revenue stamps with "POSTAGE" added in black manuscript were used at Gouyave during February and March 1883 (*Price* £4000, *used*). Similar manuscript overprints, in red were also used at Grenville in June 1883 and in black or red at Sauteurs in September 1886 (*Price from* £6000, *used*).

13 d. 1 POSTAGE. (14) 15

(Typo D.L.R.)

1883. Wmk Crown CA. P 14.
30 **13** ½d. dull green (February) . . . . . . 1·25 1·00
a. *Tête-bêche* (vert pair) . . . . . . 4·25 15·00
31 1d. carmine (February) . . . . 70·00 3·25
a. *Tête-bêche* (vert pair) £225 £250
32 2½d. ultramarine (May) . . . . 7·00 1·00
a. *Tête-bêche* (vert pair) . . . . . . 26·00 50·00
33 4d. greyish slate (May) . . . . 5·50 1·75
a. *Tête-bêche* (vert pair) . . . . . . 18·00 55·00
34 6d. mauve (May) . . . . 3·25 4·00
a. *Tête-bêche* (vert pair) . . . . . . 18·00 55·00
35 8d. grey-brown (February) . . . . . . 9·00 12·00
a. *Tête-bêche* (vert pair) . . . . . . 32·00 75·00
36 1s. pale violet (April) . . . . £120 55·00
a. *Tête-bêche* (vert pair) £1300 £1600
30/36 *Set of* 7 . . . . £190 70·00

Types **13** and **15** were printed in rows *tête-bêche* in the sheets, so that 50% of the stamps have inverted watermarks.

1886 (1 Oct–Dec). *Revenue stamps (T* **5** *with green surch as T* **10**), *surch with T 14.* P 14.

(*a*) Wmk Large Star, *T* **3**.
37 **5** 1d.on 1½d. orange . . . . 42·00 30·00
a. Surch inverted £300 £300
b. Surch double £500 £300
c. "THRFE" £250 £225
d. "PFNCE" £250 £225
e. "HALH" £250 £225
f. Bisected diag (on cover) . . . . . . † £1900
38 1d.on 1s. orange (December) . . . . . 38·00 30·00
a. "POSTAGE" (no stop) £400
b. "SHILLNG" £450 £375
c. Wide space (3½ mm) between "ONE" and "SHILLING" £325 £250
d. Bisected diag (on cover) . . . . . . † £2000

(*b*) Wmk Small Star, *T* **2**.
39 **5** 1d.on 4d. orange (November) . . . . . £160 90·00

1887 (Jan). Wmk Crown CA. P 14.
40 **15** 1d. carmine . . . . 1·50 1·25
a. *Tête-bêche* (vert pair) . . . . . . 3·00 19·00
s. Optd "Specimen" . . . . 50·00

Due to the sheet formation 50% of the stamps have inverted watermarks.

4d. POSTAGE (16) HALF PENNY POSTAGE (17)

1888 (31 Mar)–**91**. *Revenue stamps (T* **5** *with green surch as T* **10***) further surcharged.* W **2**. P 14½, and No. 35.

I. *Surch with T* **16**.

(*a*) *4 mm between value and "POSTAGE".*
41 **5** 4d.on 2s. orange . . . . 38·00 18·00
a. Upright "d" (R. 5/6) £750 £400
b. Wide space (2¼ mm) between "TWO" and "SHILLINGS" £275 £150
c. First "S" in "SHILLINGS" inverted £475 £325
d. Imperf between (horiz pair) £5000

(*b*) *5 mm between value and "POSTAGE".*
42 **5** 4d.on 2s. orange . . . . 70·00 30·00
a. Wide space £325 £225
b. "S" inverted £650 £550

II. *Surch as T* **17** (*December 1889*).
43 **5** ½d.on 2s. orange . . . . 12·00 20·00
a. Surch double £300 £325
b. Wide space £110 £130
c. "S" inverted £275 £300

POSTAGE d. AND 1 REVENUE (18) POSTAGE AND REVENUE 1d. (19) 2½d. (20)

III. *Surch with T* **18** (*December 1890*).
44 **5** 1d.on 2s. orange . . . . 80·00 75·00
a. Surch inverted £750
b. Wide space £325 £325
c. "S" inverted £700 £650

IV. *Surch with T* **19** (*January 1891*).
45 **5** 1d.on 2s. orange . . . . 60·00 55·00
a. No stop after "1d" (R. 3/8) £375
b. Wide space £250 £250
c. "S" inverted £500 £500
46 **13** 1d.on 8d. grey-brown . . . . 10·00 13·00
a. *Tête-bêche* (vert pair) . . . . . . 40·00 60·00
b. Surch inverted £325 £275
c. No stop after "1d" (R. 6/5) £250 £250

V. *Surch with T* **20** (*December 1891*).
47 **13** 2½d.on 8d. grey-brown . . . . 8·00 11·00
a. *Tête-bêche* (vert pair) . . . . . . 40·00 60·00
b. Surch inverted . . . .
c. Surch double £850 £800
d. Surch double, one inverted £550 £500
e. Surch treble . . . . — £900
f. Surch treble, two inverted . . . . — £850
s. Optd "Specimen" . . . . 65·00

The surcharges, Types **16/19**, were applied to half sheets as a setting of 60 (12 × 5).

The wide space between "TWO" and "SHILLINGS" occurs on R. 1/4 and 10/3 of the original 2s. Revenue stamp which was printed in sheets of 120 (12 × 10).

Type **18** was a two-step surcharge comprising "1d./Revenue", followed by "POSTAGE/AND". An example of No. 44 is known with the "POSTAGE" omitted due to faulty registration and the word applied by hand in a slightly different type style.

There are two varieties of fraction in Type **20**, which each occur 30 times in the setting; in one the "1" has horizontal serif and the "2" commences in a ball; in the other the "1" has sloping serif and the "2" is without ball.

See also D4/7.

21 22 **23** Flagship of Columbus. (Columbus named Grenada "La Concepcion")

(Typo D.L.R.)

1895 (6 Sept)–**99**. Wmk Crown CA. P 14.
48 **22** ½d. mauve and green (9.99) . . . . . 2·50 1·75
49 **21** 1d. mauve and carmine (5.96) . . . . 4·50 75
50 2d. mauve and brown (9.99) . . . . . 40·00 32·00
x. Wmk reversed . . . . — £180
51 2½d. mauve and ultramarine . . . . . 5·50 1·50
52 **22** 3d. mauve and orange . . . . 6·50 16·00
53 **21** 6d. mauve and green . . . . 12·00 30·00
54 **22** 8d. mauve and black . . . . 12·00 45·00
55 1s. green and orange . . . . 19·00 40·00
48/55 *Set of* 8 . . . . 90·00 £150
48s/55s Optd "Specimen" *Set of* 8 . . . . . £150

(Recess D.L.R.)

1898 (15 Aug). *400th Anniv of Discovery of Grenada by Columbus.* Wmk Crown CC. P 14
56 **23** 2½d. ultramarine . . . . 14·00 6·00
a. Bluish paper . . . . 32·00 40·00
s. Optd "Specimen" . . . . 85·00

24 25

(Typo D.L.R.)

1902. Wmk Crown CA. P 14.
57 **24** ½d. dull purple and green . . . . . . 3·25 1·25
58 **25** 1d. dull purple and carmine . . . . . 4·50 30
59 2d. dull purple and brown . . . . . 3·00 10·00
60 2½d. dull purple and ultramarine . . . 3·50 2·75
61 **24** 3d. dull purple and orange . . . . . 3·75 9·00
62 **25** 6d. dull purple and green . . . . . 2·50 17·00
63 **24** 1s. green and orange . . . . 4·00 27·00
64 2s. green and ultramarine . . . . . 21·00 55·00
65 **25** 5s. green and carmine . . . . 42·00 60·00
66 **24** 10s. green and purple £120 £250
57/66 *Set of* 10 . . . . £180 £375
57s/66s Optd "Specimen" *Set of* 10 . . . . £190

1904–06. Wmk Mult Crown CA. *Ordinary paper.* P 14.
67 **24** ½d. purple and green (1905) . . . . . 17·00 26·00
68 **25** 1d. purple and carmine . . . . 9·00 2·50
69 2d. purple and brown (1905) . . . . 55·00 £110
70 2½d. purple and ultramarine (1905) . . 55·00 65·00
71 **24** 3d. purple and orange (1905) . . . . 2·75 7·00
a. Chalk-surfaced paper . . . . . . 2·75 8·50

72 **25** 6d. purple and green (1906) 5·50 15·00
a. Chalk-surfaced paper 8·50 22·00
73 **24** 1s. green and orange (1905) 6·00 26·00
74 2s. green and ultramarine (1906) 50·00 70·00
a. Chalk-surfaced paper 28·00 75·00
75 **25** 5s. green and carmine (1906) 65·00 95·00
76 **24** 10s. green and purple (1906) £150 £250
67/76 *Set of* 10 £350 £600

Examples of most values between Nos. 57 and 76 are known showing a forged G.P.O. Grenada B.W.I. postmark dated "OC 6 09".

26 Badge of the Colony **27** Badge of the Colony

(Recess D.L.R.)

1906. Wmk Mult Crown CA. P 14.
77 **26** ½d. green 4·50 30
78 1d. carmine 6·50 10
y. Wmk inverted and reversed
79 2d. orange 3·00 3·00
80 2½d. blue 6·00 1·75
a. Ultramarine 9·00 3·50

(Typo D.L.R.)

1908. Wmk Crown CA. *Chalk-surfaced paper.* P 14.
82 **27** 1s. black/*green* 28·00 60·00
83 10s. green and red/*green* 90·00 £180

1908–11. Wmk Mult Crown CA. *Chalk-surfaced paper.* P 14.
84 **27** 3d. dull purple/*yellow* 4·75 1·75
85 6d. dull purple and purple 20·00 23·00
86 1s. black/*green* (1911) 7·00 4·50
87 2s. blue and purple/*blue* 19·00 12·00
88 5s. green and red/*yellow* 60·00 70·00
77/88 *Set of* 11 £225 £325
77s/80s, 82s/5s, 87s/8s Optd "Specimen" *Set of* 10 £200

Examples of Nos. 82/8 are known showing a forged G.P.O. Grenada B.W.I. postmark dated "OC 6 09".

28 WAR TAX **(29)** WAR TAX **(30)**

(Typo D.L.R.)

1913 (3 Jan)–**22**. Wmk Mult Crown CA. *Chalk-surfaced paper (3d. to 10s.).* P 14.
89 **28** ½d. yellow-green 1·00 1·60
90 ½d. green 1·00 1·00
91 1d. red 2·25 30
92 1d. scarlet (1916) 4·25 1·00
w. Wmk inverted
93 2d. orange 1·75 30
94 2½d. bright blue 1·75 3·50
95 2½d. dull blue (1920) 4·75 5·50
96 3d. purple/*yellow* 65 85
a. White back (3.14) 65 1·50
as. Optd "Specimen" 32·00
b. On lemon (1917) 4·00 9·00
c. On pale yellow (1921) 6·00 28·00
97 6d. dull and bright purple 1·50 9·00
98 1s. black/*green* 1·00 10·00
a. White back (3.14) 1·25 7·50
as. Optd "Specimen" 35·00
b. On blue-green, olive back (1917) 48·00 80·00
c. On emerald surface 1·50 14·00
d. On emerald back (6.22) 1·00 13·00
ds. Optd "Specimen" 35·00
dw. Wmk inverted 80·00
99 2s. purple and blue/*blue* 6·50 12·00
100 5s. green and red/*yellow* 17·00 60·00
a. On pale yellow (1921) 25·00 75·00
as. Optd "Specimen" 48·00
101 10s. green and red/*green* 55·00 90·00
a. On emerald back (6.22) 55·00 £160
as. Optd "Specimen" 60·00
89/101 *Set of* 10 80·00 £170
89s/101s Optd "Specimen" (1s. optd in red) *Set of* 10 £180
98sa 1s. optd in black 35·00

1916 (1 June). *Optd with T* **29** *by Govt Press, St. George's.*
109 **28** 1d. red (*shades*) 2·25 1·75
a. Opt inverted £275
b. Triangle for "A" in "TAX" 55·00 70·00
s. Handstamped "Specimen" 50·00

A small "A" in "WAR", 2 mm high is found on Nos. 29, 38 and 48 of the setting of 60 and a very small "A" in "TAX", 1½ mm high, on No. 11. Value about twice normal. The normal "A" is 2¼ mm high.

No. 109b is on No. 56 of the setting.

1916 (1 Sept)–**18**. *Optd with T* **30** *in London.*
111 **28** 1d. scarlet 30 20
a. Carmine-red/bluish (5.18) 3·25 1·50
s. Optd "Specimen" 40·00
w. Wmk inverted £120

1921–32. Wmk Mult Script CA. *Chalk-surfaced paper (3d. (No. 122) to 10s.)* P 14.
112 **28** ½d. green 1·25 30
113 1d. carmine-red 80 75
114 1d. brown (1923) 1·50 30
115 1½d. rose-red (6.22) 1·50 1·50
116 2d. orange 1·25 30
117 2d. grey (1926) 2·50 2·75
117*a* 2½d. dull blue 4·50 3·50
118 2½d. grey (6.22) 1·00 9·00
119 2½d. bright blue (1926) 4·50 3·75
120 2½d. ultramarine (1931) 4·50 8·50
120*a* 2½d. chalky blue and blue (1932) 50·00 50·00
121 3d. bright blue (6.22) 1·25 11·00
122 3d. purple/*yellow* (1926) 3·00 5·00
123 4d. black and red/*yellow* (1926) 1·00 3·75
124 5d. dull purple & sage-green (27.12.22) 1·50 4·25
125 6d. dull and bright purple 1·25 19·00
126 6d. black and carmine (1926) 2·25 2·50
127 9d. dull purple and black (27.12.22) 2·25 9·50
128 1s. black/*emerald* (1923) 2·50 45·00
129 1s. chestnut (1926) 3·00 10·00
130 2s. purple and blue/*black* (1922) 6·00 17·00
131 2s.6d. black and carmine/*blue* (1929) 7·00 20·00
132 3s. green and violet (27.12.22) 6·00 27·00
133 5s. green and red/*pale yellow* (1923) 12·00 35·00
134 10s. green and red/*emerald* (1923) 50·00 £130
112/19, 121/34 *Set of* 22 £110 £325
112s/34s Optd or Perf (2s.6d.) "Specimen" *Set of* 23 £375

Some values of Nos. 89/101 and 112/34 have been seen with part strikes of the forged postmark mentioned after Nos. 67/76 and 77/88.

31 Grand Anse Beach **32** Badge of the Colony

33 Grand Etang **34** St. George's

(Recess Waterlow)

1934 (23 Oct)–**36**. Wmk Mult Script CA (sideways on T **32**). P 12½.
135 **31** ½d. green 15 1·25
a. Perf 12½ × 13½ (1936) 4·50 45·00
136 **32** 1d. black and sepia 1·00 3·00
a. Perf 13½ × 12½ (1936) 60 35
137 **33** 1½d. black and scarlet 4·75 3·25
a. Perf 12½ × 13½ (1936) 1·25 55
138 **32** 2d. black and orange 1·00 75
139 **34** 2½d. blue 50 50
140 **32** 3d. black and olive-green 1·00 2·75
141 6d. black and purple 2·00 1·75
142 1s. black and brown 2·00 4·00
143 2s.6d. black and ultramarine 8·00 28·00
144 5s. black and violet 38·00 50·00
135/44 *Set of* 10 50·00 80·00
135s/44s Perf "Specimen" *Set of* 10 £160

1935 (6 May). *Silver Jubilee. As Nos. 91/4 of Antigua but ptd by Waterlow.* P 11 × 12.
145 ½d. black and green 80 1·25
k. Kite and vertical log 45·00
l. Kite and horizontal log 60·00
146 1d. ultramarine and grey 80 1·75
l. Kite and horizontal log 65·00
147 1½d. deep blue and scarlet 80 2·25
l. Kite and horizontal log 85·00
148 1s. slate and purple 6·50 19·00
l. Kite and horizontal log £190
145/8 *Set of* 4 8·00 22·00
145s/8s Perf "Specimen" *Set of* 4 80·00

For illustrations of plate varieties see Omnibus section following Zanzibar.

1937 (12 May). *Coronation. As Nos. 95/7 of Antigua.* P 11 × 11½.
149 1d. violet 40 1·00
150 1½d. carmine 40 40
151 2½d. blue 80 1·00
149/51 *Set of* 3 1·40 2·00
149s/51s Perf "Specimen" *Set of* 3 60·00

35 King George VI

(Photo Harrison)

1937 (12 July)–**50**. Wmk Mult Script CA. *Chalk-surfaced paper.* P 15 × 14.
152 **35** ½d. brown 1·40 20
a. Ordinary paper (11.42) 30 80
b. Ordinary paper. *Chocolate* (1.45) 20 80
c. Chalk-surfaced paper. *Chocolate* (8.50) 50 3·25

The ordinary paper is thick, smooth and opaque.

36 Grand Anse Beach **40** Badge of the Colony

Line on sail (Centre Pl 3 R. 1/1. Later partially retouched)

Colon flaw (R. 5/6. Corrected on ptg of Nov 1950)

(Recess D.L.R. (10s.), Waterlow (others))

1938 (16 Mar)–**50**. *As T* **31/4** *(but portrait of King George VI as in T* **36***) and T* **40**. Wmk Mult Script CA (sideways on T **32**) P 12½ or 12 × 13 (10s.).
153 **36** ½d. yellow-green 5·50 1·2
a. Blue-green (10.9.43) 60 1·2
b. Perf 12½ × 13½ (1938) 6·00 8
ba. Blue-green 6·50 5·0
154 **32** 1d. black and sepia 1·00 2
a. Perf 13½ × 12½ (1938) 50 5
ab. Line on sail 70·00
155 **33** 1½d. black and scarlet 50 8
a. Perf 12½ × 13½ (1938) 2·25 3
156 **32** 2d. black and orange 30 5
a. Perf 13½ × 12½ (1938) 2·50 8
ab. Line on sail 85·00
157 **34** 2½d. bright blue 30 3
a. Perf 12½ × 13½ (?March 1950) £4500 £20
158 **32** 3d. black and olive-green 14·00 1·4
a. Perf 13½ × 12½ (16.3.38) 6·00 1·0
ab. Black and brown-olive (1942) 30 8
ac. Line on sail 65·00
b. Perf 12½. *Black & brn-ol* (16.8.50) 30 1·9
ba. Colon flaw 65·00
159 6d. black and purple 1·25 4
a. Perf 13½ × 12½ (1942) 2·25 5
160 1s. black and brown 2·25 4
a. Perf 13½ × 12½ (1941) 4·00 1·7
161 2s. black and ultramarine 19·00 1·7
a. Perf 13½ × 12½ (1941) 23·00 1·5
162 5s. black and violet 3·75 2·0
a. Perf 13½ × 12½ (1947) 2·75 5·5
163 **40** 10s. steel blue and carmine (*narrow*) (P 12 × 13) 55·00 9·0
a. Perf 14. *Steel blue and bright carmine (narrow)* £180 45·0
b. Perf 14. *Slate-blue and bright carmine (narrow)* (1943) £190 £11
c. Perf 12. *Slate-blue and bright carmine (narrow)* (1943) £500 £130
d. Perf 14. *Slate-blue and carmine lake (wide)* (1944) £100 8·0
e. Perf 14. *Blue-black and carmine (narrow)* (1943) 30·00 8·5
f. Perf 14. *Blue-black and bright carmine (wide)* (1947) 25·00 25·0
152/63e *Set of* 12 45·00 13·0
152s/63s Perf "Specimen" *Set of* 12 £225

In the earlier printings of the 10s. the paper was dampened befor printing and the subsequent shrinkage produced narrow frames 2 to 23¾ mm wide. Later printings were made on dry paper producin wide frames 24¼ mm wide.

No. 163a is one of the earlier printings, line perf 13.8 × 14.1. Lat printings of the 10s. are line perf 14.1.

Nos. 163b/c show a blurred centre caused by the use of a wor plate.

Nos. 163a and 163b may be found with gum more or less yello due to local climatic conditions.

Examples of No. 163c are known showing forged St. George postmarks dated "21 AU 42", "21 AU 43" or "2 OC 43".

1946 (25 Sept). *Victory. As Nos. 110/11 of Antigua.*
164 1½d. carmine 10
165 3½d. blue 10
164s/5s Perf "Specimen" *Set of* 2 60·00

1948 (27 Oct). *Royal Silver Wedding. As Nos. 112/13 of Antigua.*
166 1½d. scarlet 15
167 10s. slate-green 12·00 17·

(New Currency. 100 cents = 1 West Indian, later Eastern Caribbean, dollar)

1949 (10 Oct). *75th Anniv of Universal Postal Union. As Nos. 114/ of Antigua.*
168 5c. ultramarine 15
169 6c. olive 1·50 2·
170 12c. magenta 15
171 24c. red-brown 15
168/71 *Set of* 4 1·75 2·

41 King George VI — 42 Badge of the Colony — 43 Badge of the Colony

(Recess B.W. (T **41**), D.L.R. (others))

951 (8 Jan). Wmk Mult Script CA. P 11½ (T **41**), 11½ × 12½ (T **42**), and 11½ × 13 (T **43**).

72 **41** ½c. black and red-brown . . . . . 15 1·60
73 1c. black and emerald-green . . . 15 25
74 2c. black and brown 15 50
75 3c. black and rose-carmine 15 10
76 4c. black and orange 35 40
77 5c. black and violet 20 10
78 6c. black and olive 30 60
79 7c. black and light blue . . . . . 1·75 10
80 12c. black and purple . . . . 2·25 30
81 **42** 25c. black and sepia . . . . 2·25 80
82 50c. black and blue . . . . 6·50 40
83 $1.50, black and yellow-orange . . . 7·50 7·00
84 **43** $2.50, slate-blue and carmine . . . . 5·50 5·50
72/184 *Set of* 13 . . . . 24·00 15·00

951 (16 Feb). *Inauguration of B.W.I. University College. As Nos. 118/19 of Antigua.*

85 3c. black and carmine . . . . 45 1·00
86 6c. black and olive 45 40

NEW CONSTITUTION

1951

(44)

951 (21 Sept). *New Constitution. Nos. 175/7 and 180 optd with T* **44** *by B.W.*

87 **41** 3c. black and rose-carmine 15 60
88 4c. black and orange 15 60
89 5c. black and violet (R.) 15 70
90 12c. black and purple 15 70
87/90 *Set of* 4 . . . . 55 2·40

POSTAGE DUE STAMPS

D 1

1d.

SURCHARGE POSTAGE

(D 2)

(Typo D.L.R.)

892 (18 Apr).

(a) Type D **1**. Wmk Crown CA. P14.

1 **D 1** 1d. blue-black . . . . 25·00 1·50
2 2d. blue-black . . . . £160 1·50
3 3d. blue-black . . . . £160 2·50
1/3 *Set of* 3 . . . . £325 5·00

(b) Nos. 34 and 35 surch locoally as Type D **2**.

4 **13** 1d.on 6d. mauve (10.92) . . . . . . 80·00 1·25
a. *Tête-bêche* (vert pair) £1200 £800
b. Surch double . . . . — £160
5 1d.on 8d. grey-brown (8.92) . . . . . £750 3·25
a. *Tête-bêche* (vert pair) £3500 £1400
6 2d.on 6d. mauve (10.92) . . . . . . £150 2·50
a. *Tête-bêche* (vert pair) £1700 £1100
7 2d.on 8d. grey-brown (8.92) . . . . . £1500 10·00
a. *Tête-bêche* (vert pair) £5000 £3000

Nos. D4/7 were in use from August to November 1892. As pplies of Nos. D1/3 were available from April or May of that year would not appear that they were intended for postage due irposes. There was a shortage of 1d. postage stamps in July and ugust, but this was alleviated by Nos. 44/5 which were still ailable. The provisionals *may* have been intended for postal irposes, but the vast majority appear to have been used ilatelically.

06 (July)–**11**. Wmk Mult Crown CA. P 14.

8 **D 1** 1d. blue-black (1911) . . . . 3·50 7·50
9 2d. blue-black . . . . 11·00 1·75
10 3d. blue-black (9.06) . . . . 13·00 6·00
8/10 *Set of* 3 . . . . 25·00 13·50

21 (Dec)–**22**. *As Type* D **1**, *but inscr* "POSTAGE DUE". Wmk Mult Script CA. P 14.

11 1d. black . . . . 1·25 1·00
12 1½d. black (15.12.22) . . . . 8·50 21·00
13 2d. black . . . . 2·00 1·75
14 3d. black . . . . 2·00 4·50
11/14 *Set of* 4 . . . . 12·00 25·00
11s/14s Optd "Specimen" *Set of* 4 . . . . . . 80·00

52 (1 Mar). *As Type* D **1**, *but inscr* "POSTAGE DUE". *Value in cents.* Wmk Mult Script CA. *Chalk-surfaced paper.* P 14.

15 2c. black . . . . 30 7·00
a. Error. Crown missing. W **9***a* £110
b. Error. St. Edward Crown. W **9***b* . . . 50·00
16 4c. black . . . . 30 13·00
a. Error. Crown missing. W **9***a* £110
b. Error. St. Edward Crown. W **9***b* . . . 50·00

D17 6c. black . . . . 45 12·00
a. Error. Crown missing. W **9***a* £170
b. Error. St. Edward Crown. W **9***b* . . . 95·00
D18 8c. black . . . . 75 12·00
a. Error. Crown missing. W **9***a* £325
b. Error. St. Edward Crown. W **9***b* . . . £180
D15/18 *Set of* 4 . . . . 1·60 40·00

Griqualand West *see* South Africa

Heligoland

Stamps of HAMBURG (see Part 7 (*Germany*) of this catalogue) were used in Heligoland until 16 April 1867. The Free City of Hamburg ran the Heligoland postal service between 1796 and 1 June 1866. Its stamps continued in use on the island until replaced by Heligoland issues.

PRICES FOR STAMPS ON COVER
Nos. 1/19 *from* × 3

PRINTERS. All the stamps of Heligoland were typographed at the Imperial Printing Works, Berlin.

REPRINTS. Many of the stamps of Heligoland were subsequently reprinted at Berlin (between 1875 and 1885), Leipzig (1888) and Hamburg (1892 and 1895). Of these only the Berlin productions are difficult to distinguish from the originals so separate notes are provided for the individual values. Leipzig reprints can be identified by their highly surfaced paper and those from Hamburg by their 14 perforation. All of these reprints are worth much less than the original stamps priced below.

There was, in addition, a small reprinting of Nos. 13/19, made by the German government in 1890 for exchange purposes, but examples of this printing are far scarcer than the original stamps.

Forgeries, printed by lithography instead of typography, also exist for Nos. 1/4, 6 and 8 perforated 12½ or 13. Forged cancellations can also be found on originals and, on occasion, genuine postmarks on reprints.

1

(Currency. 16 schillings = 1 mark)

Three Dies of Embossed Head for Types **1** and **2**:

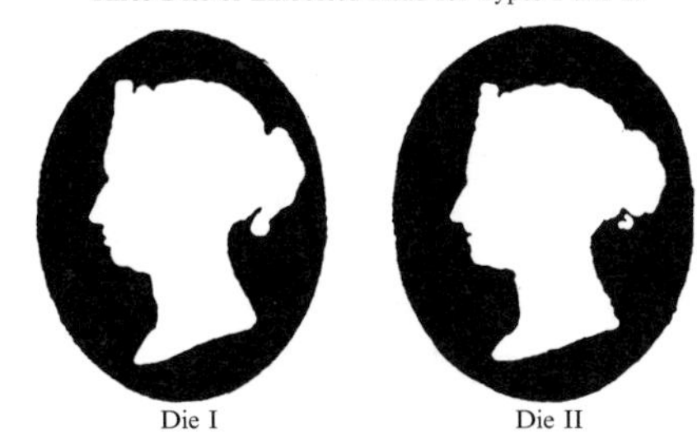

Die I — Die II

Die III

Die I. Blob instead of curl beneath the chignon. Outline of two jewels at top of diadem.
Die II. Curl under chignon. One jewel at top of diadem.
Die III. Shorter curl under chignon. Two jewels at top of diadem.

(Des Wedding. Die eng E. Schilling)

1867 (Mar)–**68**. *Head Die I embossed in colourless relief. Roul.*

1 **1** ½sch. blue-green and rose £300 £800
a. Head Die II (7.68) £700 £1100
2 1sch. rose and blue-green (21.3.67) . . . £160 £180
3 2sch. rose and grass-green (21.3.67) . . . 11·00 55·00
4 6sch. green and rose . . . . 13·00 £250

For Nos. 1/4 the second colour given is that of the spandrels on the ½ and 1sch., and of the spandrels and central background for the 2 and 6sch.

All four values exist from the Berlin, Leipzig and Hamburg reprintings. The following points are helpful in identifying originals from Berlin reprints; for Leipzig and Hamburg reprints see general note above:

½sch. – Reprints are all in yellowish green and show Head Die II
1sch. – All reprints are Head Die III
2sch. – Berlin reprints are in dull rose with a deeper blue-green
6sch. – Originals show white specks in green. Berlin reprints have a more solid bluish green

1869 (Apr)–**73**. *Head embossed in colourless relief.* P 13½ × 14½.

5 **1** ¼sch. rose and green (background) (I) (*quadrillé paper*) (8.73) . . . . . . 26·00 £1500
a. Error. Green and rose (background) (9.73) £110 £3000
b. *Deep rose and pale green* (background) (11.73) . . . . . . 85·00 £1500
6 ½sch. blue-green and rose (II) £190 £200
a. *Yellow green and rose* (7.71) . . . £140 £190
b. Quadrille paper (6.73) . . . . . . 95·00 £150
7 ¾sch. green and rose (I) (*quadrillé paper*) (12.73) . . . . 29·00 £1100
8 1sch. rose and yellow-green (III) (7.71) £140 £180
a. Quadrillé paper. *Rose and pale blue-green* (6.73) £120 £180
9 1½sch. grn & rose (I) (*quadrillé paper*) (9.73) . . . . 65·00 £250

For Nos. 5/9 the second colour given is that of the spandrels on the ½ and 1sch., of the central background on the ¼ and 1½sch., and of the central background, side labels and side marginal lines of the ¾sch.

No. 5a was a printing of the ¼sch. made in the colour combination of the 1½sch. by mistake.

A further printing of the ½sch. (head die I) in deep rose-red and yellowish green (background), on non-*quadrillé* paper, was made in December 1874, but not issued (*Price* £15, *unused*).

All five values exist from the Berlin, Leipzig and Hamburg reprintings. The following points are helpful in identifying originals from Berlin reprints; for Leipzig and Hamburg reprints see general note above:

¼sch. – All Berlin and some Hamburg reprints are Head Die II
½sch. – Berlin reprints on thinner paper with solid colour in the spandrels
¾sch. – Berlin reprints on thinner, non-quadrille paper
1sch. – Berlin reprints are on thinner paper or show many breaks in the rose line beneath "SCHILLING" at the top of the design or in the line above it at the foot
1½sch. – All Berlin and some Hamburg reprints are Head Die II

Berlin, Leipzig and Hamburg reprints also exist of the 2 and 6sch., but these values do not come as perforated originals.

(New Currency. 100 pfennig = 1 mark)

2

3

4

5

(Des H. Gätke. Die eng E. Schilling (T **2**), A. Schiffner (others))

1875 (Feb)–**90**. *Head Die II on T* **2** *embossed in colourless relief.* P 13½ × 14½.

10 **2** 1pf. (½d.) deep green and rose . . . . 11·00 £500
11 2pf. (½d.) deep rose and deep green . . 11·00 £600
12 **3** 3pf. (⅜d.) pale green, red and yellow (6.76) £225 £1100
a. *Green, red and orange* (6.77) . . . £160 £850
13 **2** 5pf. (¾d.) deep yellow-green and rose 11·00 19·00
a. *Deep green and rose* (6.90) . . . . 15·00 42·00
14 10pf. (1½d.) deep rose and deep green . . 32·00 22·00
a. *Scarlet and pale blue-green* (5.87) . . . . 11·00 22·00
15 **3** 20pf. (2½d.) rose, green and yellow (6.76) £200 £120
a. *Rose-carmine, dp green & orge* (4.80) . . . . £150 50·00
b. *Dull red, pale green and lemon* (7.88) . . . . 14·00 29·00
c. *Aniline verm, brt grn & lemon* (6.90) . . . . 12·00 50·00
16 **2** 25pf. (3d.) deep green and rose . . . . 13·00 28·00
17 50pf. (6d.) rose and green . . . . . . 20·00 35·00
18 **4** 1m. (1s.) deep green, scarlet & black (8.79) £140 £200
a. Perf 11½ £1000
b. *Deep green, aniline rose & black* (5.89) £140 £200
19 **5** 5m. (5s.) deep green, aniline rose, black and yellow (8.79) £150 £950
a. Perf 11½ £1000
ab. Imperf between (horiz pair) £3750

For stamps as Type **2** the first colour is that of the central background and the second that of the frame. On the 3pf. the first colour is of the frame and the top band of the shield, the second is the centre band and the third the shield border. The 20pf. is similar, but has the centre band in the same colour as the frame and the upper band on the shield in the second colour.

The 1, 2 and 3pf. exist from the Berlin, Leipzig and Hamburg reprintings. There were no such reprints for the other values. The following points are helpful in identifying originals from Berlin reprints; for Leipzig and Hamburg reprints see general note above:

1pf. – Berlin printings show a peculiar shade of pink
2pf. – All reprints are much lighter in shade than the deep rose and deep green of the originals
3pf. – Berlin reprints either show the band around the shield in brownish orange, or have this feature in deep yellow with the other two colours lighter

Heligoland was ceded to Germany on 9 August 1890.

Hong Kong

CROWN COLONY

Hong Kong island was formally ceded to Great Britain on 26 January 1841. The Hong Kong Post Office was established in October 1841, when much of the business previously transacted through the Macao postal agency was transferred to the island. The first cancellation is known from April 1842, but local control of the posts was short-lived as the Hong Kong Office became a branch of the British G.P.O. on 15 April 1843.

The colonial authorities resumed control of the postal service on 1 May 1860 although the previously established postal agencies in the Chinese Treaty Ports remained part of the British G.P.O. system until 1 May 1868.

For illustrations of the handstamp types see BRITISH POST OFFICES ABROAD notes following GREAT BRITAIN.

CROWNED-CIRCLE HANDSTAMPS

CC1 **CC 1b** HONG KONG (R.) (17.10.1843)
Price on cover £650
CC2 **CC 1** HONG KONG (R.) (21.8.1844)
Price on cover £900
CC3 **CC 3** HONG KONG (R.) (16.6.1852)
Price on cover £400

We no longer list the Great Britain stamps with obliteration "B 62" within oval. The Government notification dated 29 November 1862 stated that only the Hong Kong stamps to be issued on 8 December would be available for postage and the stamps formerly listed were all issued in Great Britain later than the date of the notice.

(Currency. 100 cents = 1 Hong Kong dollar)

PRICES FOR STAMPS ON COVER TO 1945	
Nos. 1/27	*from* × 6
Nos. 28/36	*from* × 4
Nos. 37/9	*from* × 5
Nos. 40/4	*from* × 4
Nos. 45/8	*from* × 10
Nos. 49/50	*from* × 4
No. 51	*from* × 15
Nos. 52/61	*from* × 5
Nos. 62/99	*from* × 4
Nos. 100/32	*from* × 3
Nos. 133/6	*from* × 2
Nos. 137/9	*from* × 4
Nos. 140/68	*from* × 2
Nos. D1/12	*from* × 8
Nos. F1/11	*from* × 4
No. F12	*from* × 3
Nos. P1/3	*from* × 2

PRINTERS. All definitive issues up to 1962 were typographed by De La Rue and Co., *except for some printings between* 1941 *and* 1945.

1

2

3

1862 (8 Dec)–**63**. No wmk. P 14.
1 **1** 2c. brown £400 90·00
a. Deep brown (1863) £550 £110
2 8c. yellow-buff £700 70·00
3 12c. pale greenish blue £550 55·00
4 **3** 18c. lilac £600 50·00
5 24c. green £1000 £100
6 48c. rose £2750 £325
7 96c. brownish grey £3750 £425

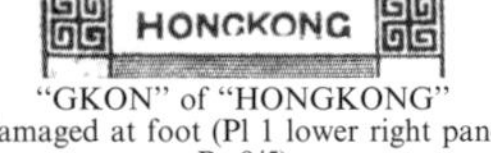

"GKON" of "HONGKONG" damaged at foot (Pl 1 lower right pane R. 9/5)

1863 (Aug)–**71**. Wmk Crown CC. P 14.
8 **1** 2c. deep brown (11.64) £275 27·00
a. Brown £120 7·00
b. Pale yellowish brown £140 11·00
w. Wmk inverted £475 70·00
y. Wmk inverted and reversed † £600
x. Wmk reversed — £120
9 **2** 4c. grey £130 14·00
ay. Wmk inverted and reversed † £600
b. Slate £110 6·00
bw. Wmk inverted £375 70·00
c. Deep slate £150 11·00
d. Greenish grey £300 48·00
dw. Wmk inverted † £325
e. Bluish slate £450 22·00
ew. Wmk inverted £1000 £130
f. Perf 12½. *Slate* (8.70) £12000 £275
fw. Wmk inverted — £700
10 6c. lilac £400 12·00
a. Mauve £500 13·00
w. Wmk inverted £950 70·00
x. Wmk reversed £1200 90·00
11 **1** 8c. pale dull orange (10.64) £500 9·50
a. Brownish orange £450 11·00
b. Bright orange £400 11·00
w. Wmk inverted £950 85·00
x. Wmk reversed £1000 £120
12 12c. pale greenish blue (4.65) £950 32·00
a. Pale blue 28·00 5·50
b. Deep blue £225 12·00
w. Wmk inverted — 75·00
x. Wmk reversed — 80·00
13 **3** 18c. lilac (1866) £7000 £300
w. Wmk inverted † £850
x. Wmk reversed £18000 £1100
y. Wmk inverted and reversed † £1800
14 24c. green (10.64) £500 8·50
a. Pale green £600 15·00
b. Deep green £850 28·00
w. Wmk inverted £2000 90·00
x. Wmk reversed £1800 £110
15 **2** 30c. vermilion £800 14·00
a. Orange-vermilion £700 15·00
b. "GKON" of "HONGKONG" damaged at foot — £900
w. Wmk inverted £2000 95·00
x. Wmk reversed — £120
16 30c. mauve (14.8.71) £225 5·50
a. "GKON" of "HONGKONG" damaged at foot — £375
w. Wmk inverted £950 80·00
x. Wmk reversed — £120
17 48c. pale rose (1.65) £1000 48·00
a. Rose-carmine £850 26·00
w. Wmk inverted £1900 £110
x. Wmk reversed — £160
18 96c. olive-bistre (1.65) £38000 £650
w. Wmk inverted † £1800
19 96c. brownish grey (1865) £1300 55·00
a. Brownish black £1500 45·00
w. Wmk inverted £1800 £160
y. Wmk inverted and reversed † £1400

There is a wide range of shades in this issue, of which we can only indicate the main groups.

No. 12 is the same shade as No. 3 without wmk, the impression having a waxy appearance.

A single used example of the 48c. in a bright claret shade is known. No other stamps in this shade, either mint or used, have been discovered.

See also Nos. 22 and 28/31.

16 cents. (4) **28 cents.** (5) **5 cents.** (6) **10 cents.** (7)

ts. No. 20b

1876 (Aug)–**77**. *Nos.* 13 *and* 16 *surch with T* **4** *or* **5** *by Noronha and Sons, Hong Kong.*
20 **3** 16c.on 18c. lilac (1.4.77) £2250 £150
a. Space between "n" and "t" £7000 £850
b. Space between "s" and stop £7000 £850
w. Wmk inverted £5000 £800
21 **2** 28c.on 30c. mauve £1300 50·00
a. "GKON" of "HONGKONG" damaged at foot — £650

1877 (Aug). *New value.* Wmk Crown CC. P 14.
22 **3** 16c. yellow £1800 65·00
w. Wmk inverted £3250 £300

1880 (1 Mar–Sept). *Surch with T* **6** *or* **7** *by Noronha and Sons.*
23 **1** 5c.on 8c. brt orange (No. 11*b*) (Sept) £950 £100
a. Surch inverted † £16000
b. Surch double † £17000
24 **3** 5c.on 18c. lilac (No. 13) £900 60·00
x. Wmk reversed £1800 £950
25 **1** 10c.on 12c. pale blue (No. 12*a*) £950 55·00
a. Blue £1300 85·00
26 **3** 10c.on 16c. yellow (No. 22) (May) £4250 £150
a. Surch inverted † £75000
b. Surch double † £75000
w. Wmk inverted † £1400
27 10c.on 24c. green (No. 14) (June) £1400 85·00
w. Wmk inverted † £450

Two examples of No. 26*b* are known, both used in Shanghai.

1880 (Mar–Dec). *Colours changed and new values.* Wmk Crown CC. P 14.
28 **1** 2c. dull rose £150 22·00
a. Rose £160 23·00
29 **2** 5c. blue (Dec) £450 40·00
w. Wmk inverted — £150
30 10c. mauve (Nov) £550 14·00
w. Wmk inverted — £130
31 **3** 48c. brown £1200 90·00

1882 (May)–**96**. Wmk Crown CA. P 14.
32 **1** 2c. rose-lake (7.82) £160 26·00
a. Rose-pink £200 32·00
ab. Perf 12 £70000 £70000
w. Wmk inverted — £110
33 2c. carmine (1884) 35·00 1·5
a. Aniline carmine 38·00 1·5
w. Wmk inverted — 85·0
34 **2** 4c. slate-grey (1.4.96) 12·00 1·2
w. Wmk inverted — 85·0
35 5c. pale blue 26·00 8
a. Blue 27·00 8
aw. Wmk inverted £275 75·0
x. Wmk reversed — £18
36 10c. dull mauve (8.82) £650 13·0
w. Wmk inverted — £14
37 10c. deep blue-green (1884) £1800 38·0
a. Green (2.84) £130 1·2
aw. Wmk inverted
38 10c. purple/*red* (1.1.91) 23·00 1·2
w. Wmk inverted £375 80·0
x. Wmk reversed £650 95·0
y. Wmk inverted and reversed
39 30c. yellowish green (1.1.91) £130 38·0
a. Grey-green 80·00 20·0
38s, 39as Optd "Specimen" *Set of* 2 £400

Examples of No. 39 should not be confused with washed or fade[d] stamps from the grey-green shade which tend to turn to a ver[y] yellow-green when dampened.

For other stamps with this watermark, but in colours changed t[o] the U.P.U. scheme see Nos. 56/61.

20 CENTS (8) **50 CENTS** (9) **1 DOLLAR** (10)

1885 (Sept). *As Nos. 15, 19 and 31, but* wmkd Crown CA, *surc[h] with T* **8** *to* **10** *by De La Rue.*
40 **2** 20c.on 30c. orange-red £100 5·5
a. Surch double
w. Wmk inverted £800 £25
41 **3** 50c.on 48c. yellowish brown £375 30·0
w. Wmk inverted — £20
42 $1on 96c. grey-olive £700 65·0
40s/2s Optd "Specimen" *Set of* 3 £1100

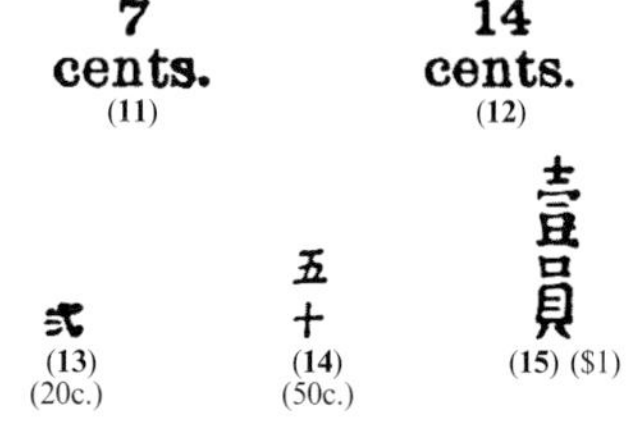

(11) (12) (13) (20c.) (14) (50c.) (15) ($1)

1891 (1 Jan–Mar).

(a) Nos. 16 and 37 surch with T **11** *or* **12** *by Noronha and Son[s], Hong Kong.*
43 **2** 7c.on 10c. green 70·00 8·
a. Antique "t" in "cents" (R. 1/1) £600 £1
b. Surch double £6000 £13
44 14c.on 30c. mauve (Feb) £160 60·
a. Antique "t" in "cents" (R. 1/1) £2750 £9
b. "GKON" of "HONGKONG" damaged at foot — £12

(b) As Nos. 40/2 (surch with T **8** *to* **10** *by De La Rue), but colou[rs] changed.*
45 **2** 20c.on 30c. yellowish green (No. 39) £170 £1
a. Grey-green (No. 39*a*) £110 £1
46 **3** 50c.on 48c. dull purple £250 £2
47 $1on 96c. purple/*red* £750 £3
45as/7s Optd "Specimen" *Set of* 3 £850

(c) Nos. 45/7 with further surch, T **13/15**, *in Chinese characte[rs], handstamped locally (Mar).*
48 **2** 20c.on 30c. yellowish green 55·00 8·
a. Grey-green 32·00 7·
b. Surch double £25000
49 **3** 50c.on 48c. dull purple 75·00 5·
50 $1on 96c. purple/*red* £425 22·
w. Wmk inverted

The true antique "t" variety (Nos. 43a and 44a) should not [be] confused with a small "t" showing a short foot. In the antique "[t]" the crossbar is accurately bisected by the vertical stroke, which [is] thicker at the top. The lower curve bends towards the right a[nd] does not turn upwards to the same extent as on the normal.

The handstamped surcharges on Nos. 48/50 were applied over t[he] original Chinese face values. The single character for "2" w[as] intended to convert "30c." to "20c.". There were six sligh[tly] different versions of the "2" handstamp and three for the "50c."

The errors of the Chinese surcharges previously listed on t[he] above issue and also on Nos. 52 and 55 are now omitted as bei[ng] outside the scope of the catalogue. While some without dou[bt] possess philatelic merit, it is impossible to distinguish between t[he] genuine errors and the clandestine copies made to order with t[he] original chops. No. 55c is retained as this represents a distinc[tly] different chop which was used for the last part of the printing.

1841 Hong Kong JUBILEE 1891 (16) **10 CENTS** (17) 拾 (18) 拾 (19)

1891 (22 Jan). *50th Anniversary of Colony. Optd with T* **16** *[by] Noronha and Sons, Hong Kong.*
51 **1** 2c. carmine (No. 33) £450 £1
a. Short "J" in "JUBILEE" (R. 1/6) £700 £
b. Short "U" in "JUBILEE" (R. 1/1) £700 £
c. Broken "1" in "1891" (R. 2/1) £850 £2
d. Tall narrow "K" in "Kong" (R. 1/3) £1200 £4
e. Opt double £16000 £12
f. Space between "O" and "N" of "Hong" (R. 1/5) £1600 £7

Most of the supply of No. 51, which was only on sale for three days, was overprinted from a setting of 12 (6 × 2) applied five times to complete each sheet. There were six printings from this setting, but a second setting, possibly of 30 or 60, was used for the seventh. Positions quoted are from the setting of twelve. Most varieties only occur in some printings and many less marked overprint flaws also exist.

The prices quoted for No. 51e are for examples on which the two impressions are distinctly separated. Examples on which the two impressions are almost coincidental are worth considerably less.

1898 (1 Apr). Wmk Crown CA. P 14.

*(a) Surch with T **10** by D.L.R. and handstamped Chinese characters as T **15**.*

52 **3** $1on 96c. black . . . £160 27·00
a. Grey-black . . . £150 27·00

*(b) Surch with T **10** only.*

53 **3** $1on 96c. black . . . £3250 £4000
a. Grey-black . . . £2750 £3750
as. Optd "Specimen" . . . £600

1898 (1 Apr).

*(a) Surch with T **17** by Noronha and Sons, Hong Kong.*

54 **2** 10c.on 30c. grey-green (No. 39*a*) . . . £550 £1000
a. Figures "10" widely spaced (1½ mm) . . . £3750
b. Surch double

Type **17** was applied in a horizontal setting of 12, No. 54a appearing on position 12 for the early printings only.

*(b) As No. 54, but with handstamped Chinese characters, T **18**, in addition.*

55 **2** 10c.on 30c. grey-green (No. 39*a*) . . . 48·00 70·00
a. Yellowish green . . . 80·00 £110
b. Figures "10" widely spaced (1½ mm) . . . £700 £900
c. Chinese character large (Type **19**) . . . £900 £1000
ca. Ditto. Figures "10" widely spaced . . . £6500
d. Surch Type **17** double
s. Handstamped "Specimen" . . . £140

1900 (Aug)–**01**. Wmk Crown CA. P 14.

56 **1** 2c. dull green . . . 27·00 85
w. Wmk inverted . . . £150 75·00
57 **2** 4c. carmine (1901) . . . 19·00 85
w. Wmk inverted . . . † —
58 5c. yellow . . . 22·00 6·50
w. Wmk inverted . . . — £325
59 10c. ultramarine . . . 50·00 1·75
w. Wmk inverted . . . — 95·00
60 **1** 12c. blue (1901) . . . 40·00 55·00
61 **2** 30c. brown (1901) . . . 40·00 22·00
56/61 *Set of* 6 . . . £180 80·00
56s/9s, 61s Optd "Specimen" *Set of* 5 . . . £550

20

21

22

23

1903 (Jan–July). Wmk Crown CA. P 14.

62 **20** 1c. dull purple and brown . . . 2·00 50
63 2c. dull green (July) . . . 9·50 1·50
w. Wmk inverted
64 **21** 4c. purple/*red* (July) . . . 12·00 40
65 5c. dull green and brown-orange (July) . . . 11·00 9·00
66 8c. slate and violet (12 Feb) . . . 10·00 1·25
67 **20** 10c. purple and blue/*blue* (July) . . . 38·00 1·50
68 **23** 12c. green and purple/*yellow* (12 Feb) . . . 8·50 4·25
69 20c. slate and chestnut (June) . . . 45·00 3·25
70 **22** 30c. dull green and black (21 May) . . . 48·00 20·00
71 **23** 50c. dull green and magenta (June) . . . 38·00 38·00
72 **20** $1 purple and sage-green (June) . . . 80·00 22·00
73 **23** $2 slate and scarlet (July) . . . £250 £250
74 **22** $3 slate and dull blue (July) . . . £300 £325
75 **23** $5 purple and blue-green (June) . . . £450 £475
76 **22** $10 slate and orange/*blue* (July) . . . £1000 £425
w. Wmk inverted . . . † —
62/76 *Set of* 15 . . . £2000 £1400
62s/76s Optd "Specimen" *Set of* 15 . . . £1500

No. 63w is known used at Shanghai.

1904 (4 Oct)–**06**. Wmk Mult Crown CA. *Chalk-surfaced paper (8, 12c., $3, $5) or ordinary paper (others).* P 14.

77 **20** 2c. dull green . . . 7·50 1·25
a. Chalk-surfaced paper (1906) . . . 11·00 3·25
aw. Wmk inverted . . . † £800
78 **21** 4c. purple/*red* . . . 16·00 40
a. Chalk-surfaced paper (1906) . . . 9·00 75
79 5c. dull green and brown-orange . . . 26·00 8·00
a. Chalk-surfaced paper (1906) . . . 15·00 5·00
aw. Wmk inverted
80 8c. slate and violet (1906) . . . 11·00 2·00
81 **20** 10c. purple and blue/*blue* (3.05) . . . 18·00 1·25
82 **23** 12c. green and purple/*yellow* (1906) . . . 13·00 5·50
83 20c. slate and chestnut . . . 35·00 2·25
a. Chalk-surfaced paper (1906) . . . 30·00 2·25
w. Wmk inverted . . . † £400
84 **22** 30c. dull green and black . . . 38·00 21·00
a. Chalk-surfaced paper (1906) . . . 45·00 18·00
85 **23** 50c. green and magenta . . . 65·00 9·00
a. Chalk-surfaced paper (1906) . . . 65·00 12·00

86 **20** $1 purple and sage-green . . . £110 24·00
a. Chalk-surfaced paper (1906) . . . £110 24·00
87 **23** $2 slate and scarlet . . . £225 £110
a. Chalk-surfaced paper (1905) . . . £200 95·00
88 **22** $3 slate and dull blue (1905) . . . £225 £190
89 **23** $5 purple and blue-green (1905) . . . £400 £350
90 **22** $10 slate and orange/*blue* (5.05) . . . £1600 £1100
aw. Wmk inverted . . . † —
b. Chalk-surfaced paper (1906) . . . £1700 £950
77/90 *Set of* 14 . . . £2500 £1500

No. 77aw is known used at Shanghai in October 1908.

1907–11. *Colours changed and new value.* Wmk Mult Crown CA. *Chalk-surfaced paper (6c. and 20c. to $2).* P 14.

91 **20** 1c. brown (9.10) . . . 4·25 1·00
x. Wmk reversed . . . † £1100
92 2c. deep green . . . 22·00 1·75
a. Green . . . 22·00 1·50
w. Wmk inverted . . . £1100 £750
93 **21** 4c. carmine-red . . . 8·00 40
94 **22** 6c. orange-vermilion and purple (10.07) . . . 23·00 4·50
95 **20** 10c. bright ultramarine . . . 24·00 40
96 **23** 20c. purple and sage-green (3.11) . . . 45·00 42·00
97 **22** 30c. purple and orange-yellow (3.11) . . . 50·00 25·00
98 **23** 50c. black/*green* (3.11) . . . 40·00 15·00
99 $2 carmine-red and black (1910) . . . £275 £275
91/9 *Set of* 9 . . . £450 £325
91s, 93s/9s Optd "Specimen" *Set of* 8 . . . £900

No. 91x was used at Canton during December 1912 and No. 92w at Shanghai during 1908.

24

25

26

27

28

(A) (B)

In Type A of the 25c. the upper Chinese character in the left-hand label has a short vertical stroke crossing it at the foot. In Type B this stroke is absent.

1912 (9 Nov)–**21**. Wmk Mult Crown CA. *Chalk-surfaced paper (12c. to $10).* P 14.

100 **24** 1c. brown . . . 2·50 55
a. Black-brown . . . 4·00 2·00
b. Crown broken at right (R. 9/2) . . . £225 £160
101 2c. deep green . . . 7·00 30
a. Green . . . 7·00 30
w. Wmk inverted . . . † —
y. Wmk inverted and reversed . . . † —
102 **25** 4c. carmine-red . . . 4·50 30
a. Scarlet (1914) . . . 17·00 1·75
103 **26** 6c. yellow-orange . . . 4·25 1·00
a. Brown-orange . . . 5·00 1·75
w. Wmk inverted . . . £650 £650
104 **25** 8c. grey . . . 23·00 5·00
a. Slate (1914) . . . 35·00 5·00
105 **24** 10c. ultramarine . . . 35·00 30
a. Deep bright ultramarine . . . 24·00 30
106 **27** 12c. purple/*yellow* . . . 5·50 7·00
a. White back (1914) . . . 7·00 13·00
as. Optd "Specimen" . . . 90·00
107 20c. purple and sage-green . . . 6·00 1·00
108 25c. purple & magenta (Type A) (1.14) . . . 19·00 22·00
109 25c. purple & magenta (Type B) (8.19) . . . £150 55·00
110 **26** 30c. purple and orange yellow . . . 30·00 7·50
a. Purple and orange . . . 18·00 6·00
w. Wmk inverted
111 **27** 50c. black/*blue-green* . . . 15·00 1·50
a. White back (5.14) . . . 14·00 4·25
as. Optd "Specimen" . . . £150
b. On blue-green, olive back (1917) . . . £1200 30·00
c. On emerald surface (9.19) . . . 23·00 8·00
d. On emerald back (7.12.21) . . . 23·00 6·50
ds. Optd "Specimen" . . . £160
w. Wmk inverted . . . £1500
112 **24** $1 purple and blue/*blue* . . . 42·00 3·50
w. Wmk inverted . . . £150 £100
113 **27** $2 carmine-red and grey-black . . . £130 50·00
114 **26** $3 green and purple . . . £190 80·00
115 **27** $5 green and red/*green* . . . £600 £375
a. White back (5.14) . . . £550 £300
as. Optd "Specimen" . . . £300
b. On blue-green, olive back (1917) . . . £1000 £300
bs. Optd "Specimen" . . . £325
bw. Wmk inverted . . . £3000
116 **26** $10 purple and black/*red* . . . £600 85·00
100/16 *Set of* 17 . . . £1700 £550
100s/16s Optd "Specimen" *Set of* 17 . . . £1800

No. 100b occurred on R. 9/2 of the lower right pane before being retouched.

Broken flower at top right (Upper left pane R. 1/3)

1921 (Jan)–**37**. Wmk Mult Script CA. *Chalk-surfaced paper (12c. to $5).* P 14.

117 **24** 1c. brown . . . 1·00 40
118 2c. blue-green . . . 2·50 50
a. Yellow-green (1932) . . . 7·50 1·00
bw. Wmk inverted . . . 70·00
118*c* 2c. grey (14.4.37) . . . 18·00 7·50
119 **26** 3c. grey (8.10.31) . . . 6·00 1·00
120 4c. carmine-rose . . . 3·50 70
a. Carmine-red (1932) . . . 3·00 30
b. Top of lower Chinese characters at right broken off (R. 9/4) . . . 90·00 70·00
121 5c. violet (16.10.31) . . . 8·50 30
122 8c. grey . . . 12·00 35·00
123 8c. orange (7.12.21) . . . 4·00 1·50
w. Wmk inverted . . . £850
124 **24** 10c. bright ultramarine . . . 4·25 30
aw. Wmk inverted . . . £140
124*b* **27** 12c. purple/*yellow* (3.4.33) . . . 15·00 2·00
125 20c. purple and sage-green (7.12.21) . . . 4·75 30
126 **28** 25c. purple and magenta (B) (7.12.21) . . . 4·50 70
a. Broken flower . . . 38·00 42·00
w. Wmk inverted . . . † £200
127 **26** 30c. purple & chrome-yellow (7.12.21) . . . 10·00 1·50
a. Purple and orange-yellow . . . 26·00 7·00
w. Wmk inverted . . . £160
128 **27** 50c. black/*emerald* (1924) . . . 13·00 30
129 **24** $1 purple and blue/*blue* (7.12.21) . . . 32·00 50
130 **27** $2 carmine-red & grey-black (7.12.21) . . . £110 6·00
131 **26** $3 green and dull purple (1926) . . . £170 60·00
132 **27** $5 green and red/*emerald* (1925) . . . £475 70·00
117/32 *Set of* 18 . . . £800 £170
117s/32s Optd or Perf (2c. grey, 3, 5, 12c.) "Specimen" *Set of* 18 . . . £1700

No. 120b occurs on R. 9/4 of the lower left pane.

1935 (6 May). *Silver Jubilee. As Nos. 91/4 of Antigua, but ptd by B.W.* P 11 × 12.

133 3c. ultramarine and grey-black . . . 4·00 3·50
c. Lightning conductor . . . £350 £225
134 5c. green and indigo . . . 8·50 3·50
a. Extra flagstaff . . . £325 £275
b. Short extra flagstaff . . . £400
c. Lightning conductor . . . £350
d. Flagstaff on right-hand turret . . . £400 £250
135 10c. brown and deep blue . . . 20·00 1·75
136 20c. slate and purple . . . 38·00 8·00
b. Short extra flagstaff . . . £800 £325
d. Flagstaff on right-hand turret . . . £750 £325
e. Double flagstaff . . . £750 £325
133/6 *Set of* 4 . . . 60·00 15·00
133s/6s Perf "Specimen" *Set of* 4 . . . £375

For illustrations of plate varieties see Omnibus section following Zanzibar.

1937 (12 May). *Coronation. As Nos. 95/7 of Antigua.* P 11 × 11½.

137 4c. green . . . 4·50 4·00
138 15c. carmine . . . 10·00 3·25
139 25c. blue . . . 13·00 2·75
137/9 *Set of* 3 . . . 25·00 9·00
137s/9s Perf "Specimen" *Set of* 3 . . . £200

29 King George VI

Short right leg to "R" (Right pane R. 7/3, left pane R. 3/1)

1938–52. Wmk Mult Script CA. *Chalk-surfaced paper (80c., $1 (No. 155), $2 (No. 157), $5 (No. 159), $10 (No. 161)).* P 14.

140 **29** 1c. brown (24.5.38) . . . 1·75 2·00
a. Pale brown (4.2.52) . . . 2·25 6·00
141 2c. grey (5.4.38) . . . 2·00 30
a. Perf 14½ × 14 (28.9.45) . . . 1·75 5·00
142 4c. orange (5.4.38) . . . 4·50 1·25
a. Perf 14½ × 14 (28.9.45) . . . 4·50 3·25
143 5c. green (24.5.38) . . . 1·25 20
a. Perf 14½ × 14 (28.9.45) . . . 2·50 5·00
144 8c. red-brown (1.11.41) . . . 1·75 2·50
a. Imperf (pair) . . . £25000
145 10c. bright violet (13.4.38) . . . 50·00 75
a. Perf 14½ × 14. *Dull violet* (28.9.45) . . . 9·50 20
b. Dull reddish violet (9.4.46) . . . 6·00 70
c. Reddish lilac (9.4.47) . . . 16·00 20
146 15c. scarlet (13.4.38) . . . 2·00 30
147 20c. black (1.2.46) . . . 1·25 30
148 20c. scarlet-vermilion (1.4.48) . . . 7·00 40
a. Rose-red (25.4.51) . . . 16·00 5·50
149 25c. bright blue (5.4.38) . . . 29·00 1·75
150 25c. pale yellow-olive (9.4.46) . . . 4·75 1·75
151 30c. yellow-olive (13.4.48) . . . £150 2·00
a. Perf 14½ × 14. *Yellowish olive* (28.9.45) . . . 24·00 8·50
152 30c. blue (9.4.46) . . . 7·00 20

3 50c. purple (13.4.38) . . . . 55·00 70
a. Perf 14½ × 14. *Dp mag* (28.9.45) . . . . 30·00 1·10
ab. Printed both sides, inverted on reverse £1500
b. Reddish purple (9.4.46) . . . . . 16·00 1·75
c. Chalk-surfaced paper. *Brt purple* (9.4.47) . . . . 9·00 20
4 80c. carmine (2.2.48) . . . . 5·00 95
5 $1 dull lilac and blue (*chalk-surfaced paper*) (27.4.38) . . . . 8·00 3·00
a. Short right leg to "R" £110
b. Ordinary paper. *Pale reddish lilac and blue* (28.9.45) . . . . 13·00 9·00
ba. Short right leg to "R" £150
5 $1 red-orange and green (9.4.46) . . 18·00 30
a. Short right leg to "R" £170
b. Chalk-surfaced paper (21.6.48) . . 48·00 2·50
ba. Short right leg to "R" £300
c. Chalk-surfaced paper. *Yellow orange and green* (6.11.52) . . . . 80·00 15·00
ca. Short right leg to "R" £425
7 $2 red-orange and green (24.5.38) . . 70·00 17·00
3 $2 reddish violet and scarlet (9.4.46) . . . . 30·00 3·25
a. Chalk-surfaced paper (9.4.47) . . 35·00 1·00
) $5 dull lilac and scarlet (2.6.38) . . . 60·00 50·00
) $5 green and violet (9.4.46) . . . . 80·00 7·50
a. Yellowish green and violet (9.4.46) . . . . £190 18·00
ab. Chalk-surfaced paper (9.4.47) . . £110 3·25
1 $10 green and violet (2.6.38) . . . . £500 90·00
2 $10 bright lilac and blue (9.4.46) . . . £140 29·00
a. Chalk-surfaced paper. *Reddish violet and blue* (9.4.47) . . . . . £180 18·00
)/62 *Set of* 23 . . . . £900 £180
)s/62s Perf "Specimen" *Set of* 23 . . . . . . £2250

Following bomb damage to the De La Rue works on the night 29 December 1940 various emergency arrangements were made complete current requisitions for Hong Kong stamps:

Nos. 141a, 143a, 145a, 151a and 153a (all printings perforated ½ × 14 except the 4c.) were printed and perforated by Bradbury, ilkinson & Co. Ltd. using De La Rue plates. These stamps are rough-surfaced paper.

Nos. 142a and 144 were printed by Harrison & Sons in sheets of) (12 × 10) instead of the normal 120 two panes (6 × 10).

Printings of the $1 and $2 values were made by Williams, Lea & . using De La Rue plates.

With the exception of the 8c. it is believed that none of these intings were issued in Hong Kong before its occupation by the panese on 25 December 1941, although examples could be tained in London from late 1941. The issue dates quoted are those which the stamps were eventually released in Hong Kong lowing liberation in 1945.

Nos. 160/*a* were separate printings released in Hong Kong on the me day.

No. 144a. One imperforate sheet was found and most of the mps were sold singly to the public at a branch P.O. and used for stage.

30 Street Scene

31 *Empress of Japan* (liner) and Junk

(Des W. E. Jones. Recess B.W.)

41 (26 Feb). *Centenary of British Occupation. T* **30/1** *and similar designs.* Wmk Mult Script CA (sideways on horiz designs). P 13½ × 13 (2c. and 25c.) or 13 × 13½ (others).
3 2c. orange and chocolate . . . . 5·00 2·00
4 4c. bright purple and carmine . . . . . 5·00 3·00
5 5c. black and green . . . . 3·00 50
6 15c. black and scarlet . . . . 6·00 1·75
7 25c. chocolate and blue . . . . 13·00 5·00
8 $1 blue and orange . . . . 48·00 7·50
3/8 *Set of* 6 . . . . 70·00 18·00
3s/8s Perf "Specimen" *Set of* 6 . . . . . . £400

Designs: *Horiz*—5c. The University; 15c. The Harbour; $1 *Falcon* ipper) and Short S.23 Empire "C" Class flying boat. *Vert*—25c. ie Hong Kong Bank.

Hong Kong was under Japanese occupation from 25 December 41 until 30 August 1945. The Japanese post offices in the colony ere closed from 31 August and mail was carried free, marked with chets reading "HONG KONG/1945/POSTAGE PAID". Military ministration lasted until 1 May 1946. Hong Kong stamps were -introduced on 28 September 1945.

36 King George VI and Phoenix

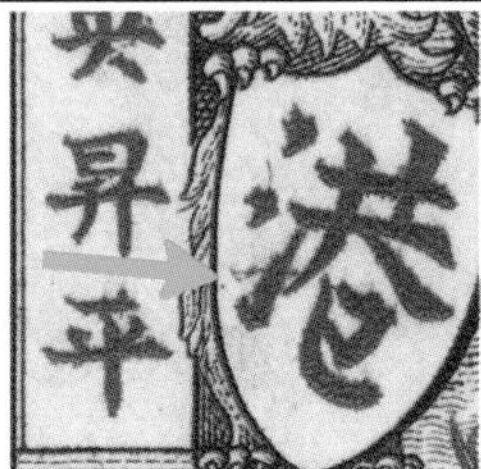

Extra stroke (R. 1/2)

(Des W. E. Jones. Recess D.L.R.)

1946 (29 Aug). *Victory.* Wmk Mult Script CA. P 13.
169 **36** 30c. blue and red (*shades*) . . . . . . 2·75 1·75
a. Extra stroke . . . . 65·00 55·00
170 $1 brown and red . . . . 3·50 75
a. Extra stroke . . . . 85·00 45·00
169s/70s Perf "Specimen" *Set of* 2 . . . . £170

Spur on "N" of "KONG" (R. 2/9)

1948 (22 Dec). *Royal Silver Wedding. As Nos. 112/13 of Antigua.*
171 10c. violet . . . . 3·00 1·00
a. Spur on "N" . . . . 60·00 45·00
172 $10 carmine . . . . £275 85·00

1949 (10 Oct). *75th Anniv of Universal Postal Union. As Nos. 114/17 of Antigua.*
173 10c. violet . . . . 4·50 1·00
174 20c. carmine-red . . . . 17·00 3·00
175 30c. deep blue . . . . 15·00 2·75
176 80c. bright reddish purple . . . . 35·00 9·50
173/6 *Set of* 4 . . . . 65·00 14·50

STAMP BOOKLETS

BOOKLET CONTENTS. In Nos. SB1/4 and SB6/7 the 1c. and 2c. were normally each in blocks of 12 or two blocks of 6 and the 4c. in blocks of 12 and 4 or two blocks of 8, all having been taken from normal sheets. No. SB5 had both the 2c. and 4c. in blocks of 12 and 4 or as two blocks of 8. Other content formats exist.

1904 (1 Jan). *Black on white cover showing contents and postage rates with "K & W LD" imprint on front. Stapled.*
SB1 $1 booklet containing tweleve 1c. (No. 62), twelve 2c. (No. 56) and sixteen 4c. (No. 57) . . . .
a. 4c. No. 64 (King Edward VII) instead of No. 57 (Q.V.) £5000

1905–06. *Black on white cover showing contents and postage rates with "Hongkong Printing Press" imprint on front. Metal fastener.*
SB2 $1 booklet containing twelve 1c., twelve 2c. and sixteen 4c. (Nos. 62/4) £4000
a. 2c. and 4c. (Nos. 77/8) (MCA ordinary paper) instead of Nos. 63/4 (CA) (1906) . . . . . .
b. 2c. and 4c. (Nos. 77a/8a) (MCA chalk-surfaced paper) instead of Nos. 77/8 (MCA ordinary paper) (1906) . . . .

Some examples of No. SB2 show the reference to Australia on the front cover deleted in manuscript. No. SB2a has the rate information reset to omit "EXCEPT AUSTRALIA".

1907 (Dec). *Black on white cover showing contents and postage rates for both Hong Kong and Agencies in China with "Hongkong Printing Press" imprint. Metal fastener.*
SB3 $1 booklet containing twelve 1c. (No. 62), twelve 2c. (No. 92) and sixteen 4c. (No. 93) . . . .
a. Stapled £3250

1910 (May)–**11**. *Black on white cover showing contents, but no postage rates, with "Hongkong Printing Press" imprint on front. Stapled.*
SB4 $1 booklet containing twelve 1c. (No. 62), twelve 2c. (No. 92) and sixteen 4c. (No. 93) . . . . .
a. 1c. No. 91 (MCA) instead of No. 62 (CA) (9.11) £3250

1912 (Apr). *Black on cream cover showing contents, but no postage rates, with "Hongkong Printing Press" imprint on front. Stapled.*
SB5 $1 booklet containing four 1c., sixteen 2c. and sixteen 4c. (Nos. 91/3) £4000

1913 (Feb). *Black on cream cover showing contents, but no postage rates, with "Hongkong Printing Press" imprint on front. Stapled.*
SB6 $1 booklet containing twelve 1c., twelve 2c. and sixteen 4c. (Nos. 100/2) (MCA wmk) £3000

1922–24. *Black on cream cover showing contents, but no postage rates, with "Hongkong Printing Press" imprint on front. Stapled.*
SB7 $1 booklet containing twelve 1c., twelve 2c. and sixteen 4c. (Nos. 117/18, 120) (Script wmk) . . £3250
a. With Ye Olde Printers Ltd imprint (1924) . . .

POSTAGE DUE STAMPS

PRINTERS. Nos. D1/12 were typographed by De La Rue & Co.

D 1 Post-office Scales

1923 (Dec)–**56**. Wmk Mult Script CA. Ordinary paper. P 14.
D1 D 1 1c. brown . . . . 2·50 65
a. Wmk sideways (1931) . . . . . 1·50 3·25
ab. Chalk-surfaced paper (21.3.56) . . . . 30 1·00
D2 2c. green . . . . 23·00 6·00
a. Wmk sideways (1928) . . . . . 11·00 5·00
D3 4c. scarlet . . . . 40·00 7·00
a. Wmk sideways (1928) . . . . . 27·00 7·00
D4 6c. yellow . . . . 27·00 13·00
a. Wmk sideways (1931) . . . . . 70·00 35·00
D5 10c. bright ultramarine . . . . . . 24·00 8·50
a. Wmk sideways (1934) . . . . . 95·00 16·00
D1/5 *Set of* 5 . . . . £100 30·00
D1a/5a *Set of* 5 . . . . £180 55·00
D1s/5s Optd "Specimen" *Set of* 5 . . . . £300

1938 (Feb)–**63**. Wmk Mult Script CA (sideways). Ordinary paper. P 14.
D6 D 1 2c. grey . . . . 13·00 9·00
a. Chalk-surfaced paper (21.3.56) . . . . 1·10 10·00
D7 4c. orange . . . . 18·00 6·50
a. Chalk-surfaced paper. *Orange-yellow* (23.5.61) . . . . 2·50 10·00
D8 6c. scarlet . . . . 9·50 5·50
D9 8c. chestnut (26.2.46) . . . . . . 5·50 32·00
D10 10c. violet . . . . 35·00 50
a. Chalk-surfaced paper (17.9.63) . . . . 16·00 12·00
D11 20c. black (26.2.46) . . . . 13·00 3·00
D12 50c. blue (7.47) . . . . 55·00 15·00
D6a/12 *Set of* 7 . . . . 90·00 65·00
D6s/12s Perf "Specimen" *Set of* 7 . . . . £350

POSTCARD STAMPS

Stamps specially surcharged for use on Postcards.

PRICES. Those in the left-hand column are for unused examples on complete postcards; those on the right for used examples off card. Examples used on postcards are worth more.

3 CENTS (P 1) **THREE** (P 2)

1879 (1 Apr). *Nos. 22 and 13 surch as Type* **P 1** *by Noronha & Sons.*
P1 **3** 3c. on 16c. yellow (No. 22) £350 £400
P2 5c. on 18c. lilac (No. 13) £325 £425

1879 (Nov). *No. P2 handstamped with Type* **P 2**.
P3 **3** 3c. on 5c. on 18c. lilac £7000 £7500

POSTAL FISCAL STAMPS

I. Stamps inscribed "STAMP DUTY"

NOTE. The dated circular "HONG KONG" cancellation with "PAID ALL" in lower segment was used for fiscal purposes, in black, from 1877. Previously it appears in red on mail to the U.S.A., but is usually not used as a cancellation.

F 1

F 2

F 3

1874–1902. Wmk Crown CC.

(*a*) P 15½ × 15.
F1 **F 1** $2 Olive-green . . . . £350 55·00
F2 **F 2** $3 dull violet . . . . £325 40·00
b. Bluish paper . . . .
F3 **F 3** $10 rose-carmine £7500 £700

(*b*) P 14.
F4 **F 1** $2 dull bluish green (10.97) £400 £250
F5 **F 2** $3 dull mauve (3.02) £550 £425
a. Bluish paper £1500
F6 **F 3** $10 grey-green £11000 £11000
Optd "Specimen" *Set of* 2 . . . . £450

Nos. F1/3 and F7 exist on various papers, ranging from thin to thick.

All three of the values perforated 15½ × 15 were authorised for postal use in 1874. The $10 rose-carmine was withdrawn from such use in 1880, the $2 in September 1897 and the $3 in 1902.

The $2 and $3 perforated 14 were available for postal purposes until July 1903. The $10 in grey-green was issued for fiscal purposes in 1884 and is known with postal cancellations.

12
CENTS.
(F 4)

(F 5)

1880. *No. F3 surch with type* F **4** *by Noronha and Sons, Hong Kong.*
F7 F **3** 12c. on $10 rose-carmine £800 £300

1890 (24 Dec). Wmk Crown CA. P 14.
F8 F **5** 2c. dull purple . . . . 90·00 20·00
w. Wmk inverted . . . .
No. F8 was authorised for postal use between 24 and 31 December 1890.

(F 6)

ONE
DOLLAR
(F 7)

(F 8)

1891 (1 Jan). *Surch with Type* F **6** *by D.L.R.* Wmk Crown CA. P 14.
F9 F **3** $5on $10 Purple/*red* £300 £100
s. Optd "Specimen" £200
No. F9 was in use for postal purposes until June 1903.

1897 (Sept). *Surch with Type* F **7** *by Noronha and Sons, Hong Kong, and with the value in Chinese characters subsequently applied twice by handstamp as T* **15**.
F10 F **1** $1on $2 olive-green (No. F1) £200 £110
a. Both Chinese handstamps omitted £3500 £2500
F11 $1on $2 dull bluish green (No. F4) £225 £130
a. Both Chinese handstamps omitted £1800 £1500
b. Diagonal Chinese handstamp omitted £11000
c. Vertical Chinese handstamp omitted . . . .
s. Handstamped "Specimen" . . . £140

1938 (11 Jan). Wmk Mult script CA. P 14.
F12 F **8** 5c. green . . . . 65·00 11·00
No. F12 was authorised for postal use between 11 and 20 January 1938 due to a shortage of 5c., No 121.
Forged cancellations are known on this stamp inscribed "VICTORIA 9.AM 11 JA 38 HONG KONG" without side bars between the rings.

II. Stamps overprinted "S.O." (Stamp Office) or "S.D." (Stamp Duty)

S. O. S. D.

(S 1) (S 2)

1891 (1 Jan). *Optd with Types* S **1** *or* S **2**.
S1 S **1** 2c. carmine (No. 33) £900 £350
S2 S **2** 2c. carmine (No. 33) £400 £180
a. Opt inverted . . . . † £5000
S3 S **3** 10c. Purple/*red* (No. 38) £1600 £400
Examples of No. S1 exist the "O" amended to "D" in manuscript.

Other fiscal stamps are found apparently postally used, but there is no evidence that this use was authorised.

JAPANESE OCCUPATION OF HONG KONG

Hong Kong surrendered to the Japanese on 25 December 1941. The postal service was not resumed until 22 January 1942 when the G.P.O. and Kowloon Central Office re-opened.

Japanese postmarks used in Hong Kong can be identified by the unique combination of horizontal lines in the central circle and three stars in the lower segment of the outer circle. Dates shown on such postmarks are in the sequence Year/Month/Day with the first shown as a Japanese regnal year number so that Showa 17 = 1942 and so on.

Initially six current Japanese definitives, 1, 2, 3, 4, 10 and 30s. (Nos. 297, 315/17, 322 and 327) were on sale, but the range gradually expanded to cover all values between ½s. and 10y. with Nos. 313/14, 318, 325, 328/31, 391, 395/6, 398/9 and 405 of Japan also available from Hong Kong post offices during the occupation. Philatelic covers exist showing other Japanese stamps, but these were not available from the local post offices. Supply of these Japanese stamps was often interrupted and, during the period between 28 July 1942 and 21 April 1943, circular "Postage Paid" handstamps were sometimes used. A substantial increase in postage rates on 16 April 1945 led to the issue of the local surcharges, Nos. J1/3.

PRICES FOR STAMPS ON COVER	
Nos. J1/3	*from* × 7

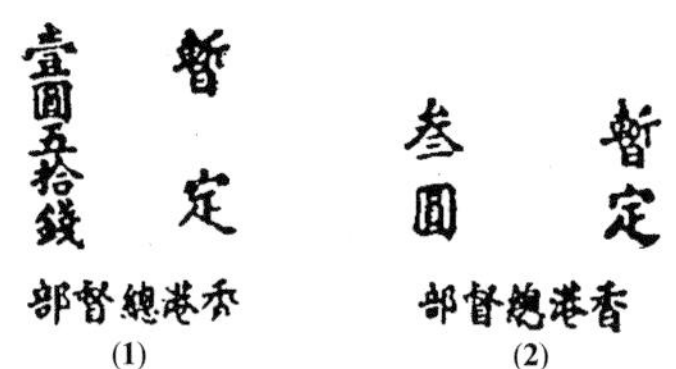
(1) (2)

1945 (16 Apr). *Stamps of Japan surch with T* **1** *(No. J1) or as T* **2**.
J1 1.50 yen on 1s. brown . . . . 30·00 27·00
J2 3yen on 2s. scarlet . . . . 12·00 21·00
J3 5yen on 5s. claret £900 £150
Designs (18½ × 22 mm):—1s. Girl Worker; 2s. Gen. Nogi; 5s. Admiral Togo.
No. J3 has four characters of value similarly arranged but differing from T **2**.

BRITISH POST OFFICES IN CHINA

Under the terms of the 1842 Treaty of Nanking China granted Great Britain and its citizens commercial privileges in five Treaty Ports, Amoy, Canton, Foochow, Ningpo and Shanghai. British Consuls were appointed to each Port and their offices, as was usual during this period, collected and distributed mail for the British community. This system was formally recognised by a Hong Kong Government notice published on 16 April 1844. Mail from the consular offices was postmarked when it passed through Hong Kong.

The number of Chinese Treaty Ports was increased to sixteen by the ratification of the Treaty of Peking in 1860 with British postal facilities being eventually extended to the Ports of Chefoo, Hankow, Kiungchow (Hoihow), Swatow, Tainan (Anping) and Tientsin.

As postal business expanded the consular agencies were converted into packet agencies or post offices which passed under the direct control of the Hong Kong postal authorities on 1 May 1868.

In May 1898 the British Government leased the territory of Wei Hai Wei from China for use as a naval station to counter the Russian presence at Port Arthur.

The opening of the Trans-Siberia Railway and the extension of Imperial Penny Postage to the Treaty Port agencies resulted in them becoming a financial burden on the colonial post office. Control of the agencies reverted to the G.P.O., London, on 1 January 1911.

The pre-adhesive postal markings of the various agencies are a fascinating, but complex, subject. Full details can be found in *Hong Kong & the Treaty Ports of China & Japan* by F. W. Webb (reprinted edition J. Bendon, Limassol, 1992) and in various publications of the Hong Kong Study Circle.

From 15 October 1864 the use of Hong Kong stamps on mail from the Treaty Ports became compulsory, although such stamps were, initially, not cancelled (with the exception of Amoy) until they reached Hong Kong where the "B62" killer was applied. Cancellation of mail at the actual Ports commenced during 1866 at Shanghai and Ningpo, spreading to all the agencies during the next ten years. Shanghai had previously used a c.d.s. on adhesives during 1863 and again in 1865–66.

The main types of cancellation used between 1866 and 1930 are illustrated below. The illustrations show the style of each postmark and no attempt has been made to cover differences in type letters or figures, arrangement, diameter or colour.

Until 1885 the vertical and horizontal killers were used to obliterate the actual stamps with an impression of one of the circular date stamps shown elsewhere on the cover. Many of the early postmarks were also used as backstamps or transit marks and, in the notes which follow, references to use are for the first appearance of the mark, not necessarily its first use as an obliterator.

Illustrations in this section are taken from *Hong Kong & the Treaty Ports of China & Japan* by F. W. Webb and are reproduced with the permission of the Royal Philatelic Society, London.

Details of the stamps known used from each post office are taken, with permission, from *British Post Offices in the Far East* by Edward B. Proud, published by Proud-Bailey Co. Ltd.

Postmark Types

Type **A**Vertical killer

Type **B** Horizontal killer

Type **C**Name horizontal

Type **D**Name curved

Type **E**Double circle Name at top

Type **F**Double circle Name at foot

Type **G**Single circle Name at top

PRICES. The prices quoted in this section are for fine used stam which show a clear impression of a substantial part of t cancellation.

AMOY

One of the five original Treaty Ports, opened to British trade the Treaty of Nanking in 1842. A consular postal agency w established in 1844 which expanded in 1876 into two separa offices, one on the off-shore island of Ku Lang Seu and the oth in Amoy itself.

Amoy "PAID" (*supplied* 1858) *used* 1859–67
Type **A** ("A1") (*supplied* 1866) *used at Ku Lang Seu* 1869–8
Type **D** (*supplied* 1866) *used* 1867–1922
Type **B** ("D27") (*supplied* 1876) *used at Amoy* 1876–84
Type **C** *used* 1876–94
Type **F** (*supplied* 1913) *used* 1916–22

Stamps of HONG KONG *cancelled at Amoy between* 1864 *and* 19 *with postmarks detailed above.*

1862. No wmk (Nos. 1/7).
Z1 2c. brown £1
Z2 8c. yellow-buff £1
Z3 12c. pale greenish blue £1
Z4 18c. lilac £1
Z5 24c. green £1
Z6 48c. rose . . . .
Z7 96c. brownish grey £6

1863–71. Wmk Crown CC (Nos. 8/19).
Z8 2c. brown . . . . 35·
Z9 4c. grey . . . . 38·
a. Perf 12½ . . . .
Z10 6c. lilac . . . . 55·
Z11 8c. orange . . . . 45·
Z12 12c. blue . . . . 20·
Z13 18c. lilac £7
Z14 24c. green . . . . 50·
Z15 30c. vermilion . . . . 80·
Z16 30c. mauve . . . . 15·
Z17 48c. rose . . . . 50·
Z18 96c. olive-bistre £15
Z19 96c. brownish grey £2

1876–77. (Nos. 20/1).
Z20 16c. on 18c. lilac £3
Z21 28c. on 30c. mauve £1

1877. Wmk Crown CC (No. 22).
Z22 16c. yellow £1

1880. (Nos. 23/7).
Z23 5c.on 8c. orange £1
Z24 5c.on 18c. lilac £1
Z25 10c.on 12c. blue £1
Z26 10c.on 16c. yellow £2
Z27 10c.on 24c. green £1

1880. Wmk Crown CC (Nos. 28/31).
Z28 2c. rose . . . . 45·
Z29 5c. blue . . . . 70·
Z30 10c. mauve . . . . 60·
Z31 48c. brown £1

1882–96. Wmk Crown CA (Nos. 32/9).
Z31*a* 2c. rose-lake . . . .
Z32 2c. carmine . . . . 4·
Z33 4c. slate-grey . . . . 10·
Z34 5c. blue . . . . 4·
Z35 10c. dull mauve . . . . 32·
Z36 10c. green . . . . 4·
Z37 10c. purple/*red* . . . . 4·
Z38 30c. green . . . . 30·

1885. (Nos. 40/2).
Z39 20c.on 30c. orange-red . . . . 12·
Z40 50c.on 48c. yellowish brown . . . . . . 55·
Z41 $1on 96c. grey-olive . . . . 90·

1891. (Nos. 43/50).
Z42 7c.on 10c. green . . . . 21·
Z43 14c.on 30c. mauve . . . . 90·
Z44 20c.on 30c. green . . . . 14·
Z45 50c.on 48c. dull purple . . . . 16·
Z46 $1on 96c. purple/*red* . . . . 40·

1891. *50th Anniv of Colony* (No. 51).
Z47 2c. carmine £8

8. (No. 52).
$1 on 96c. black 50·00

8. (No. 55).
10c. on 30c. green £200

0–01. Wmk Crown CA (Nos. 56/61).
2c. dull green 4·00
4c. carmine 2·75
5c. yellow 16·00
10c. ultramarine 4·50
12c. blue £120
30c. brown 60·00

3. Wmk Crown CA (Nos. 62/76).
1c. dull purple and brown 4·25
2c. dull green 4·00
4c. purple/*red* 2·50
5c. dull green and brown-orange 18·00
8c. slate and violet 6·50
10c. purple and blue/*blue* 3·75
12c. green and purple/*yellow* 12·00
20c. slate and chestnut 9·00
30c. dull green and black 42·00
50c. dull green and magenta 65·00
$2 slate and scarlet £350
$3 slate and dull blue £500

4–06. Wmk Mult Crown CA (Nos. 77/90).
2c. dull green 3·75
4c. purple/*red* 2·50
5c. dull green and brown-orange 14·00
8c. slate and violet 9·00
10c. purple and blue/*blue* 3·75
12c. green and purple/*yellow* 16·00
20c. slate and chestnut 8·50
30c. dull green and black 28·00
50c. green and magenta 25·00
$1 purple and sage-green 65·00
$2 slate and scarlet £275
$5 purple and blue-green £450

7–11. Wmk Mult Crown CA (Nos. 91/9).
1c. brown 4·25
2c. green 3·75
4c. carmine-red 2·50
6c. orange-vermilion and purple 14·00
10c. bright ultramarine 3·50
20c. purple and sage-green 55·00
30c. purple and orange-yellow 50·00
50c. black/*green*

2–15. Wmk Crown CA (Nos. 100/16).
1c. brown 5·00
2c. green 4·75
4c. red 2·50
6c. orange 4·25
8c. grey 19·00
10c. ultramarine 3·75
12c. purple/*yellow* 20·00
0 20c. purple and sage-green 6·50
2 30c. purple and orange-yellow 16·00
3 50c. black/*green* 10·00
4 $1 purple and blue/*blue* 22·00
5 $3 green and purple £130

POSTCARD STAMPS

9. (Nos. P1/2).
06 3c. on 16c. yellow £550
07 5c. on 18c. lilac £600

POSTAL FISCAL STAMPS

4–1902. Wmk Crown CC. P $15\frac{1}{2} \times 15$ (Nos. F1/3)
09 $2 olive-green £130
10 $3 dull violet £130

1. (No. F9).
16 $5 on $10 purple/*red* £250

7. (No. F10).
18 $1 on $2 olive-green

ANPING

nping is the port for Tainan, on the island of Formosa, opened British trade in 1860. A British Vice-consulate operated in the t and mail is known postmarked there between 1889 and 1895. mosa passed under Japanese control in 1895 and British Treaty t rights then lapsed.

ype **D** *used* 1889–95

ps of HONG KONG *cancelled at Anping between* 1889 *and* 1895 *ith postmark detailed above.*

2–91. Wmk Crown CA (Nos. 32/9).
0 2c. carmine £750
1 5c. blue £600
3 10c. green £750
4 10c. purple/*red* £900

5. (Nos. 40/2).
6 20c. on 30c. orange-red £750
7 50c. on 48c. yellowish brown £1100

CANTON

British postal service was organised in Canton from 1834, but closed when the foreign communities were evacuated in August 9. The city was one of the original Treaty Ports and a consular ncy was opened there in 1844. The consulate closed during the s of December 1856, being replaced by a temporary postal ncy at Whampoa, further down the river. When British forces ched Canton a further temporary agency was set up on 23 March 9, but both closed in July 1863 when the consulate was re-blished.

Type **A** ("C1") (*supplied* 1866) *used* 1875–84
Type **C** (*supplied* 1866) *used* 1870–1901
Type **D** *used* 1890–1922

Stamps of HONG KONG *cancelled at Canton between* 1870 *and* 1916 *with postmarks detailed above.*

1862. No wmk (Nos. 1/7).
Z135 18c. lilac £110

1863–71. Wmk Crown CC (Nos. 8/19).
Z136 2c. brown 38·00
Z137 4c. grey 40·00
Z138 6c. lilac 48·00
Z139 8c. orange 42·00
Z140 12c. blue 20·00
Z142 24c. green 60·00
Z143 30c. vermilion
Z144 30c. mauve 19·00
Z145 48c. rose 80·00
Z147 96c. brownish grey £110

1876–77. (Nos. 20/1).
Z148 16c. on 18c. lilac £300
Z149 28c. on 30c. mauve £120

1877. Wmk Crown CC (No. 22).
Z150 16c. yellow £150

1880. (Nos. 23/7).
Z151 5c.on 8c. orange £170
Z152 5c.on 18c. lilac £130
Z153 10c.on 12c. blue £120
Z154 10c.on 16c. yellow £275
Z155 10c.on 24c. green £160

1880. Wmk Crown CC (Nos. 28/31).
Z156 2c. rose 40·00
Z157 5c. blue 55·00
Z158 10c. mauve 48·00

1882–96. Wmk Crown CA (Nos. 32/9).
Z159 2c. rose-lake 35·00
Z160 2c. carmine 2·75
Z161 4c. slate-grey 11·00
Z162 5c. blue 4·50
Z163 10c. dull mauve 24·00
Z164 10c. green 8·50
Z165 10c. purple/*red* 4·25
Z166 30c. green 32·00

1886. (Nos. 40/2).
Z167 20c.on 30c. orange-red 12·00
Z168 50c.on 48c. yellowish brown 55·00
Z169 $1on 96c. grey-olive 95·00

1891. (Nos. 43/50).
Z170 7c.on 10c. green 21·00
Z171 14c.on 30c. mauve £100
Z171*a* 20c.on 30c. green (No. 45) £225
Z172 20c.on 30c. green (No. 48) 17·00
Z173 50c.on 48c. dull purple 19·00
Z174 $1on 96c. purple/*red* 50·00

1891. *50th Anniv of Colony* (No. 51).
Z175 2c. carmine £800

1898. (No. 52).
Z176 $1 on 96c. black £110

1898. (No. 55).
Z177 10c. on 30c. grey-green £150

1900–01. Wmk Crown CA (Nos. 56/61)
Z178 2c. dull green 3·75
Z179 4c. carmine 3·50
Z180 5c. yellow 26·00
Z181 10c. ultramarine 3·50
Z182 12c. blue 85·00
Z183 30c. brown 55·00

1903. Wmk Crown CA (Nos. 62/76).
Z184 1c. dull purple and brown 4·00
Z185 2c. dull Green Green 4·00
Z186 4c. purple/*red* 2·75
Z187 5c. dull green and brown-orange 18·00
Z188 8c. slate and violet 8·00
Z189 10c. purple and blue/*blue* 4·00
Z190 12c. green and purple/*yellow* 13·00
Z191 20c. slate and chestnut 7·50
Z192 30c. dull green and black 40·00

1904–06. Wmk Mult Crown CA (Nos. 77/90).
Z199 2c. dull green 3·75
Z200 4c. purple/*red* 2·75
Z201 5c. dull green and brown-orange 17·00
Z202 8c. slate and violet 12·00
Z203 10c. purple and blue/*blue* 3·75
Z204 12c. green and purple/*yellow* 19·00
Z205 20c. slate and chestnut 10·00
Z206 30c. dull green and black 28·00
Z207 50c. green and magenta 30·00
Z208 $1 purple and sage-green 50·00
Z209 $2 slate and scarlet £400
Z210 $3 slate and dull blue £475
Z212 $10 slate and orange/*blue* £1300

1907–11. Wmk Mult Crown CA (Nos. 91/9).
Z213 1c. brown 4·00
Z214 2c. green 4·00
Z215 4c. carmine-red 2·75
Z216 6c. orange-vermilion and purple 15·00
Z217 10c. bright ultramarine 3·50
Z218 20c. purple and sage-green 60·00
Z219 30c. purple and orange-yellow 45·00
Z220 50c. black/*green* 38·00

1912–15. Wmk Mult Crown CA (Nos. 100/16).
Z222 1c. brown 4·00
Z223 2c. green 3·25
Z224 4c. red 2·25
Z225 6c. orange 4·00
Z226 8c. grey 17·00
Z227 10c. ultramarine 3·75
Z228 12c. purple/*yellow* 15·00
Z229 20c. purple and sage-green 5·50
Z231 30c. purple and orange-yellow 16·00
Z232 50c. black/*green* 5·50
Z235 $3 green and purple £140

POSTCARD STAMPS

1879. (Nos. P1/2).
ZP236 3c.on 16c. yellow £500
ZP237 5c.on 18c. lilac £600

POSTAL FISCAL STAMPS

1874–1902. Wmk Crown CC. P $15\frac{1}{2} \times 15$ (Nos. F1/3)
ZF238 $2 olive-green £160

1891. (No. F9).
ZF246 $5 on $10 purple/*red* £325

1897. (No. F10).
ZF247 $1 on $2 olive-green

CHEFOO

Chefoo was opened to British trade in 1860. Although a consulate was established in 1863 no organised postal agency was provided until 1 January 1903 when one was opened at the premises of Curtis Brothers, a commercial firm.

Type **E** (*supplied* 1902) *used* 1903–20
Type **D** (*supplied* 1907) *used* 1907–13
Type **F** *used* 1916–22

Stamps of HONG KONG *cancelled at Chefoo between* 1903 *and* 1916 *with postmarks detailed above.*

1882–96. Wmk Crown CA (Nos. 32/9).
Z249 5c. blue 28·00

1891. (Nos. 43/50).
Z250 20c. on 30c. grey-green (No. 48*a*) 42·00

1898. (No. 52).
Z251 $1 on 96c. black 85·00

1900–01. Wmk Crown CA (Nos. 56/61).
Z252 2c. dull green 26·00
Z253 4c. carmine 25·00
Z254 5c. yellow 50·00
Z255 10c. ultramarine 26·00
Z257 30c. brown £100

1903. Wmk Crown CA (Nos. 62/76).
Z258 1c. dull purple and brown 9·50
Z259 2c. dull green 8·50
Z260 4c. purple/*red* 8·00
Z261 5c. dull green and brown-orange 21·00
Z262 8c. slate and violet 17·00
Z263 10c. purple and blue/*blue* 9·50
Z264 12c. green and purple/*yellow* 26·00
Z268 $1 purple and sage-green

1904–06. Wmk Mult Crown CA (Nos. 77/90).
Z273 2c. dull green 8·50
Z274 4c. purple/*red* 7·00
Z275 5c. dull green and brown-orange 15·00
Z276 8c. slate and violet 16·00
Z277 10c. purple and blue/*blue* 8·50
Z278 12c. green and purple/*yellow* 24·00
Z279 20c. slate and chestnut 19·00
Z280 30c. dull green and black 45·00
Z281 50c. green and magenta 48·00
Z282 $1 purple and sage-green 80·00
Z283 $2 slate and scarlet £190
Z284 $3 slate and dull blue £375
Z285 $5 purple and blue-green

1907–11. Wmk Mult Crown CA (Nos. 91/9).
Z287 1c. brown 9·50
Z288 2c. green 9·00
Z289 4c. carmine-red 8·00
Z290 6c. orange-vermilion and purple 23·00
Z291 10c. bright ultramarine 8·50
Z292 20c. purple and sage-green 65·00
Z293 30c. purple and orange-yellow 48·00
Z295 $2 carmine-red and black

1912–15. Wmk Mult Crown CA (Nos. 100/16).
Z296 1c. brown 7·50
Z297 2c. green 7·00
Z298 4c. red 5·50
Z299 6c. orange 12·00
Z300 8c. grey 25·00
Z301 10c. ultramarine 7·00
Z302 12c. purple/*yellow* 24·00
Z303 20c. purple and sage-green 10·00
Z305 30c. purple and orange-yellow 14·00
Z306 50c. black/*green* 8·50
Z307 $1 purple and blue/*blue* 12·00
Z308 $2 carmine-red and grey-black 75·00
Z309 $3 green and purple £110
Z310 $5 green and red/*green* £450
Z311 $10 purple and black/*red* £275

FOOCHOW

Foochow, originally known as Foochowfoo, was one of the original Treaty Ports opened to British trade in 1842. A British consulate and postal agency was established in June 1844.

Type **A** ("F1") (*supplied* 1866) *used* 1873–84
Type **D** (inscr "FOOCHOWFOO") (*supplied* 1866) *used* 1867–1905
Type **D** (inscr "FOOCHOW") (*supplied* 1894) *used* 1894-1917
Type **E** (inscr "B.P.O.") *used* 1906–10
Type **F** *used* 1915–22

Stamps of HONG KONG *cancelled at Foochow between* 1867 *and* 1916 *with postmarks detailed above.*

1882. No wmk (Nos. 1/7).
Z312 18c. lilac £130

1863–71. Wmk Crown CC (Nos. 8/19).
Z313 2c. brown 35·00
Z314 4c. grey 35·00
Z315 6c. lilac 45·00
Z316 8c. orange 45·00
Z317 12c. blue 17·00
Z318 18c. lilac £700
Z319 24c. green 70·00
Z320 30c. vermilion
Z321 30c. mauve 14·00
Z322 48c. rose 85·00
Z324 96c. brownish grey £300

1876–77. (Nos. 20/1).
Z325 16c.on 18c. lilac £325
Z326 28c.on 30c. mauve £150

1877. Wmk Crown CC (No. 22).
Z327 16c. yellow £130

1880. (Nos. 23/7).
Z328 5c.on 8c. orange £350
Z329 5c.on 18c. lilac £130
Z330 10c.on 12c. blue £130
Z331 10c.on 16c. yellow
Z332 10c.on 24c. green £170

1880. Wmk Crown CC (Nos. 28/31).
Z333 2c. rose 35·00
Z334 5c. blue 65·00
Z335 10c. mauve 42·00
Z336 48c. brown £160

1882–96. Wmk Crown CA (Nos. 32/9).
Z336*a* 2c. rose-lake 35·00
Z337 2c. carmine 2·50
Z338 4c. slate-grey 7·00
Z339 5c. blue 3·25
Z340 10c. dull mauve 26·00
Z341 10c. green 11·00
Z342 10c. purple/*red* 4·00
Z343 30c. green 35·00

1885. (Nos. 40/2).
Z344 20c.on 30c. orange-red 14·00
Z345 50c.on 48c. yellowish brown 48·00
Z346 $1on 96c. grey-olive 85·00

1891. (Nos. 43/50).
Z347 7c.on 10c. green
Z348 14c.on 30c. mauve 90·00
Z348*a* 20c.on 30c. green (No. 45) £200
Z349 20c.on 30c. green (No. 48) 20·00
Z350 50c.on 48c. dull purple 23·00
Z351 $1on 96c. purple/*red* 50·00

1898. (No. 52).
Z353 $1on 96c. black 70·00

1898. (No. 55).
Z354 10c.on 30c. green £190

1900–01. Wmk Crown CA (Nos. 56/61).
Z355 2c. dull green 3·75
Z356 4c. carmine 4·25
Z357 5c. yellow 16·00
Z358 10c. ultramarine 3·75
Z360 30c. brown 60·00

1903. Wmk Crown CA (Nos. 62/76).
Z361 1c. dull purple and brown 4·25
Z362 2c. dull green 3·75
Z363 4c. purple/*red* 2·50
Z364 5c. dull green and brown-orange 18·00
Z365 8c. slate and violet 9·50
Z366 10c. purple and blue/*blue* 4·00
Z367 12c. green and purple/*yellow* 14·00
Z368 20c. slate and chestnut 9·50
Z369 30c. dull green and black 35·00
Z370 50c. dull green and magenta 50·00

1904–06. Wmk Mult Crown CA (Nos. 77/90).
Z376 2c. dull green 3·75
Z377 4c. purple/*red* 2·50
Z378 5c. dull green and brown-orange 12·00
Z379 8c. slate and violet 8·50
Z380 10c. purple and blue/*blue* 4·00
Z381 12c. green and purple/*yellow* 17·00
Z382 20c. slate and chestnut 8·50
Z383 30c. dull green and black 30·00
Z384 50c. green and magenta 27·00
Z385 $1 purple and sage-green 48·00

1907–11. Wmk Mult Crown CA (Nos. 91/9).
Z390 1c. brown 3·50
Z391 2c. green 3·50
Z392 4c. carmine-red 2·50
Z393 6c. orange-vermilion and purple 14·00
Z394 10c. bright ultramarine 3·25
Z395 20c. purple and sage-green 60·00
Z396 30c. purple and orange-yellow 45·00
Z397 50c. black/*green* 32·00

1912–15. Wmk Mult Crown CA (Nos. 100/16).
Z399 1c. brown 4·25
Z400 2c. green 3·75
Z401 4c. red 2·50
Z402 6c. orange 9·00
Z403 8c. grey 18·00
Z404 10c. ultramarine 3·75
Z406 20c. purple and sage-green 5·50
Z407 25c. purple and magenta (Type A)
Z408 30c. purple and orange-yellow 11·00

POSTCARD STAMPS

1874–1902. (Nos. P1/2).
ZP413 3c. on 16c. yellow £600

POSTAL FISCAL STAMPS

1874–1902. Wmk Crown CC. P $15\frac{1}{2} \times 15$ (Nos. F1/3).
ZF415 $2 olive-green £130
ZF416 $3 dull violet £110

HANKOW

Hankow, on the Yangtse River 600 miles from the sea, became a Treaty Port in 1860. A British consulate opened the following year, but no organised British postal agency was established until 1872.

Type **D** (*supplied* 1874) *used* 1874–1916
Type **B** ("D29") (*supplied* 1876) *used* 1878–83
Type **F** *used* 1916–22

Stamps of HONG KONG *cancelled at Hankow between* 1874 *and* 1916 *with postmarks detailed above.*

1862. No wmk (Nos. 1/7).
Z426 18c. lilac £170

1863–71. Wmk Crown CC (Nos. 8/19).
Z427 2c. brown 80·00
Z428 4c. grey 80·00
Z429 6c. lilac 95·00
Z430 8c. orange 90·00
Z431 12c. blue 30·00
Z432 18c. lilac £750
Z433 24c. green £100
Z435 30c. mauve £100
Z436 48c. rose £140
Z438 96c. brownish grey

1876–77. (Nos. 20/1).
Z439 16c.on 18c. lilac £350
Z440 28c.on 30c. mauve £170

1877. Wmk Crown CC (No. 22).
Z441 16c. yellow £225

1880. (Nos. 23/7).
Z442 5c.on 8c. orange £180
Z443 5c.on 18c. lilac £150
Z444 10c.on 12c. blue £160
Z445 10c.on 16c. yellow £325
Z446 10c.on 24c. green £180

1880. Wmk Crown CC (Nos. 28/31).
Z447 2c. rose 60·00
Z448 5c. blue 70·00
Z449 10c. mauve 75·00
Z450 48c. brown £225

1882–96. Wmk Crown CA (Nos. 32/9).
Z451 2c. carmine 7·00
Z452 4c. slate-grey 15·00
Z453 5c. blue 7·50
Z454 10c. dull mauve 55·00
Z455 10c. green 9·00
Z456 10c. purple/*red* 8·00
Z457 30c. green 42·00

1885. (Nos. 40/2).
Z458 20c.on 30c. orange-red 25·00
Z459 50c.on 48c. yellowish brown 60·00
Z460 $1on 96c. grey-olive £110

1891. (Nos. 43/50).
Z461 7c.on 10c. green 26·00
Z462 14c.on 30c. mauve £110
Z463 20c.on 30c. green 18·00
Z464 50c.on 48c. dull purple 18·00
Z465 $1on 96c. purple/*red* 50·00

1898. (No. 52).
Z467 $1on 96c. black 70·00

1898. (No. 55).
Z468 10c.on 30c. green £200

1900–01. Wmk Crown CA (Nos. 56/61).
Z469 2c. dull green 4·50
Z470 4c. carmine 4·75
Z471 5c. yellow 20·00
Z472 10c. ultramarine 6·00
Z473 12c. blue £100
Z474 30c. brown 60·00

1903. Wmk Crown CA (Nos. 62/76).
Z475 1c. dull purple and brown 4·75
Z476 2c. dull green 4·50
Z477 4c. purple/*red* 3·75
Z478 5c. dull green and brown-orange 17·00
Z479 8c. slate and violet 13·0
Z480 10c. purple and blue/*blue* 4·2
Z481 12c. green and purple/*yellow* 16·0
Z482 20c. slate and chestnut 11·0
Z483 30c. dull green and black 35·0
Z484 50c. dull green and magenta 60·0
Z485 $1 purple and sage-green 48·0

1904–06. Wmk Mult Crown CA (Nos. 77/90).
Z490 2c. dull green 4·2
Z491 4c. purple/*red* 3·7
Z492 5c. dull green and brown-orange 15·0
Z493 8c. slate and violet 8·5
Z494 10c. purple and blue/*blue* 4·2
Z495 12c. green and purple/*yellow* 17·0
Z496 20c. slate and chestnut 14·0
Z497 30c. dull green and black 30·0
Z498 50c. green and magenta 24·0
Z499 $1 purple and sage-green 48·0
Z500 $2 slate and scarlet £30
Z502 $5 purple and blue-green £55
Z503 $10 slate and orange/*blue* £140

1907–11. Wmk Mult Crown CA (Nos. 91/9).
Z504 1c. brown 4·5
Z505 2c. green 4·0
Z506 4c. carmine-red 2·7
Z507 6c. orange-vermilion and purple 17·0
Z508 10c. bright ultramarine 4·2
Z509 20c. purple and sage-green 65·0
Z510 30c. purple and orange-yellow 50·0

1912–15. Wmk Mult Crown CA (Nos. 100/16).
Z513 1c. brown 5·0
Z514 2c. green 4·
Z515 4c. red 3·
Z516 6c. orange 8·
Z518 10c. ultramarine 4·
Z520 20c. purple and sage-green 10·
Z522 30c. purple and orange-yellow 17·
Z523 50c. black/*green* 11·
Z527 $5 green and red/*green* £4

POSTCARD STAMPS

1879. (Nos. P1/2).
ZP528 3c.on 16c. yellow £8

POSTAL FISCAL STAMPS

1874–1902. Wmk Crown CC.

(a) P $15\frac{1}{2} \times 15$ (Nos. F1/3).
ZF529 $2 olive-green £1

(b) P 14 (Nos. F4/6).
ZF532 $2 dull bluish green

1897. (No. F11).
ZF533 $1on $2 dull bluish green £4

KIUNGCHOW (HOIHOW)

Kiungchow, a city on the island of Hainan, and its port Hoihow was added to the Treaty Port system in 1860. A consul postal agency was opened at Kiungchow in 1876, being transferr to Hoihow in 1878. A second agency was opened at Kiungchow 1879.

Type **B** ("D28") (*supplied* 1876) *used* 1879–83
Type **D** (inscr "KIUNG-CHOW") (*supplied* 1878) *used* 1879–81

"REGISTERED KIUNG-CHOW" with "REGISTERED" removed (*originally supplied* 1876) *used* 1883–85
Type **D** (inscr "HOIHOW") *used* 1885–1922

Stamps of HONG KONG *cancelled at Kiungchow (Hoihow) betw* 1879 *and* 1916 *with postmarks detailed above.*

1863–71. Wmk Crown CC (Nos. 8/19).
Z540 2c. brown £7
Z541 4c. grey £5
Z542 6c. lilac £9
Z543 8c. orange £6
Z544 12c. blue £5
Z546 24c. green £8
Z547 30c. vermilion
Z548 30c. mauve £3
Z549 48c. rose £12
Z551 96c. brownish grey £13

1876–77. (Nos. 20/1).
Z552 16c. on 18c. lilac £1
Z553 28c. on 30c. mauve £1

1877. (No. 22).
Z554 16c. yellow £1

1880. (Nos. 23/7).
Z555 5c.on 8c. orange £
Z556 5c.on 18c. lilac £
Z557 10c.on 12c. blue £
Z558 10c.on 16c. yellow £1
Z559 10c.on 24c. green

1880. Wmk Crown CC (Nos. 28/31).
Z561 5c. blue . . . £550
Z562 10c. mauve . . . £700

1882–96. Wmk Crown CA (Nos. 32/9).
Z564 2c. carmine . . . 42·00
Z565 4c. slate-grey . . . 55·00
Z566 5c. blue . . . 42·00
Z567 10c. dull mauve . . . £475
Z568 10c. green . . . 50·00
Z569 10c. purple/*red* . . . 42·00
Z570 30c. green . . . 85·00

1886. (Nos. 40/2).
Z571 20c.on 30c. orange-red . . . 90·00
Z572 50c.on 48c. yellowish brown . . . 95·00
Z573 $1on 96c. grey-olive . . . £160

1891. (Nos. 43/50).
Z574 7c. on 10c. green . . . £150
Z576 20c. on 30c. green . . . 42·00
Z577 50c. on 48c. dull purple . . . 55·00
Z578 $1 on 96c. purple/*red* . . . £110

1891. *50th Anniv of Colony* (No. 51).
Z579 2c. carmine . . . £1500

1898. (No. 52).
Z580 $1 on 96c. black . . . £200

1898. (No. 55).
Z581 10c. on 30c. green . . . £425

1900–01. Wmk Crown CA (Nos. 56/61).
Z582 2c. dull green . . . 60·00
Z583 4c. carmine . . . 29·00
Z584 5c. yellow . . . 65·00
Z585 10c. ultramarine . . . 32·00
Z587 30c. brown . . . £140

903. Wmk Crown CA (Nos. 62/76).
Z588 1c. dull purple and brown . . . 21·00
Z589 2c. dull green . . . 21·00
Z590 4c. purple/*red* . . . 16·00
Z591 5c. dull green and brown-orange . . . 38·00
Z592 8c. slate and violet . . . 35·00
Z593 10c. purple and blue/*blue* . . . 19·00
Z594 12c. green and purple/*yellow* . . . 42·00
Z597 50c. dull green & magenta
Z598 $1 purple and sage-green . . . £225
Z599 $2 slate and scarlet . . . £650

904. Wmk Mult Crown CA (Nos. 77/90).
603 2c. dull green . . . 20·00
604 4c. purple/*red* . . . 16·00
605 5c. dull green and brown-orange . . . 38·00
606 8c. slate and violet . . . 24·00
607 10c. purple and blue/*blue* . . . 18·00
608 12c. green and purple/*yellow* . . . 40·00
609 20c. slate and chestnut . . . 48·00
610 30c. dull green and black . . . 65·00
612 $1 purple and sage-green . . . £325

907–11. Wmk Mult Crown CA (Nos. 91/9).
617 1c. brown . . . 20·00
618 2c. green . . . 19·00
619 4c. carmine-red . . . 16·00
620 6c. orange-vermilion and purple . . . 40·00
621 10c. bright ultramarine . . . 18·00
622 20c. purple and sage-green . . . 70·00

912–15. Wmk Mult Crown CA (Nos. 100/16).
625 1c. brown . . . 18·00
626 2c. green . . . 17·00
627 4c. red . . . 16·00
628 6c. orange . . . 24·00
629 8c. grey
630 10c. ultramarine . . . 16·00
631 12c. purple/*yellow* . . . 40·00
632 20c. purple and sage-green . . . 32·00
633 25c. purple and magenta (Type A) . . . 70·00
635 50c. black/*green* . . . 48·00
636 $1 purple and blue/*blue* . . . 50·00

POSTAL FISCAL STAMPS

874–1902. Wmk Crown CC.

(a) P 15½ × 15 (Nos. F1/3).
F641 $2 olive-green . . . £180

(b) P 14 (Nos. F4/6).
F644 $2 dull bluish green . . . £375

97. (Nos. F10/11).
F650 $1 on $2 olive-green . . . £350

NINGPO

Ningpo was one of the 1842 Treaty Ports and a consular postal ency was established there in 1844.

Type **A** ("N1") (*supplied* 1866) *used* 1870–82
Type **C** (*supplied* 1866) *used* 1870–99
Type **D** *used* 1899–1922

mps of HONG KONG *cancelled at Ningpo between* 1866 *and* 1916 *with postmarks detailed above.*

62. No wmk (Nos. 1/7).
552 18c. lilac . . . £350

63–71. Wmk Crown CC (Nos. 8/19).
553 2c. brown . . . £180
554 4c. grey . . . £180
a. Perf 12½
555 6c. lilac . . . £225

Z656 8c. orange . . . £180
Z657 12c. blue . . . £110
Z658 18c. lilac
Z659 24c. green . . . £200
Z660 30c. vermilion . . . £225
Z661 30c. mauve . . . 95·00
Z662 48c. rose . . . £300
Z663. 96c. olive-bistre
Z664 96c. brownish grey . . . £375

1876–77. (Nos. 20/1).
Z665 16c. on 18c. lilac . . . £425
Z666 28c. on 30c. mauve . . . £225

1877. Wmk Crown CC (No. 22).
Z667 16c. yellow . . . £250

1880. (Nos. 23/7).
Z668 5c.on 8c. orange . . . £275
Z669 5c.on 18c. lilac . . . £225
Z670 10c.on 12c. blue . . . £250
Z672 10c.on 24c. green . . . £275

1880. Wmk Crown CC (Nos. 28/31).
Z674 5c. blue . . . £130
Z675 10c. mauve . . . £130
Z676 48c. brown . . . £475

1882–96. Wmk Crown CA (Nos. 32/9).
Z677 2c. carmine . . . 35·00
Z678 4c. slate-grey . . . 55·00
Z679 5c. blue . . . 35·00
Z680 10c. dull mauve . . . £130
Z681 10c. green . . . 38·00
Z682 10c. purple/*red* . . . 38·00
Z683 30c. green . . . 75·00

1885. (Nos. 40/2).
Z685 50c. on 48c. yellowish brown . . . 90·00

1891. (Nos. 43/50).
Z686 7c.on 10c. green . . . 45·00
Z687 14c.on 30c. mauve
Z688 20c.on 30c. green . . . 30·00
Z689 50c.on 48c. dull purple . . . 50·00
Z690 $1on 96c. purple/*red* . . . 90·00

1898. (No. 52).
Z692 $1 on 96c. black . . . £100

1898. (No. 55).
Z693 10c. on 30c. green . . . £250

1900–01. Wmk Crown CA (Nos. 56/61).
Z694 2c. dull green . . . 20·00
Z695 4c. carmine . . . 19·00
Z697 10c. ultramarine . . . 20·00

1903. Wmk Crown CA (Nos. 62/76).
Z700 1c. dull purple and brown . . . 19·00
Z701 2c. dull green . . . 19·00
Z702 4c. purple/*red* . . . 14·00
Z703 5c. dull green and brown-orange . . . 35·00
Z704 8c. slate and violet . . . 22·00
Z705 10c. purple and blue/*blue* . . . 16·00
Z706 12c. green and purple/*yellow* . . . 42·00
Z709 50c. dull green and magenta . . . 70·00

1904–06. Wmk Mult Crown CA (Nos. 77/90).
Z715 2c. dull green . . . 18·00
Z716 4c. purple/*red* . . . 16·00
Z718 8c. slate and violet . . . 32·00
Z720 12c. green and purple/*yellow* . . . 42·00
Z721 20c. slate and chestnut . . . 42·00
Z722 30c. dull green and black . . . 55·00
Z724 $1 purple and sage-green . . . 75·00

1907–11. Wmk Mult Crown CA (Nos. 91/9).
Z729 1c. brown . . . 15·00
Z730 2c. green . . . 15·00
Z731 4c. carmine-red . . . 13·00
Z733 10c. bright ultramarine . . . 15·00
Z734 20c. purple and sage-green . . . 75·00
Z735 30c. purple and orange-yellow . . . 65·00

1912–15. Wmk Mult Crown CA (Nos. 100/16).
Z738 1c. brown . . . 16·00
Z739 2c. green . . . 15·00
Z740 4c. red . . . 14·00
Z742 8c. grey . . . 42·00
Z743 10c. ultramarine . . . 15·00
Z745 20c. purple and sage-green
Z747 30c. purple and orange-yellow
Z749 $1 purple and blue/*blue* . . . 45·00

POSTCARD STAMPS

1879. (Nos. P1/2).
ZP751 3c. on 16c. yellow . . . £900

POSTAL FISCAL STAMPS

1874–1902. Wmk Crown CC. P 15½ × 15 (Nos. F1/3).
ZF754 $2 olive-green . . . £225

1881. (No. F7).
ZF760 12c. on $10 rose-carmine

1897. (No. F10).
ZF763 $1 on $2 olive-green

SHANGHAI

Shanghai was one of the original Treaty Ports of 1842 and a packet agency was opened at the British consulate in April 1844. It moved to a separate premises in 1861 and was upgraded to a Post Office in September 1867.

British military post offices operated in Shanghai from 1927 until 1940.

Type **D** (inscr "SHANGHAE" (*supplied* 1861) *used* 1861–99

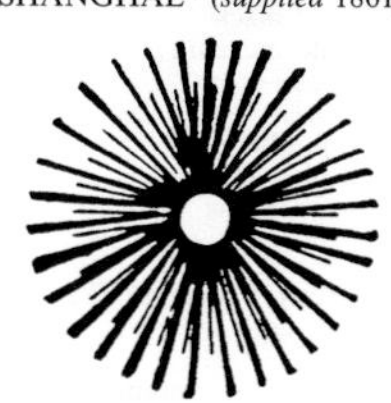

Sunburst *used* 1864–65
Type **A** ("S1") (*supplied* 1866) *used* 1866–85
Type **D** (inscr "SHANGHAI) (*supplied* 1885) *used* 1886-1906
Type **G** (inscr "B.R.O." at foot) (*supplied* 1904) *used* 1904–21
Type **G** (inscr "Br.P.O." at foot) (*supplied* 1907) *used* 1907–22
Type **E** (figures "I" to "VIII" at foot) *used* 1912–22

Stamps of HONG KONG *cancelled at Shanghai between* 1863 *and* 1916 *with postmarks detailed above.*

1862. No wmk (Nos. 1/7).
Z765 2c. brown . . . 95·00
Z766 8c. yellow-buff . . . £120
Z767 12c. pale greenish blue . . . 85·00
Z768 18c. lilac . . . 75·00
Z769 24c. green . . . £140
Z770 48c. rose . . . £425
Z771 96c. brownish grey . . . £550

1863–71. Wmk Crown CC (Nos. 8/19).
Z772 2c. brown . . . 9·00
Z773 4c. grey . . . 7·50
a. Perf 12½ . . . £275
Z774 6c. lilac . . . 15·00
Z775 8c. orange . . . 13·00
Z776 12c. blue . . . 7·50
Z777 18c. lilac . . . £350
Z778 24c. green . . . 12·00
Z779 30c. vermilion . . . 18·00
Z780 30c. mauve . . . 6·50
Z781 48c. rose . . . 30·00
Z782 96c. olive-bistre . . . £850
Z783 96c. brownish grey . . . 48·00

1876–77. (Nos. 20/1).
Z784 16c. on 18c. lilac . . . £170
Z785 28c. on 30c. mauve . . . 55·00

1877. Wmk Crown CC (No. 22).
Z786 16c. yellow . . . 70·00

1880. (Nos. 23/7).
Z787 5c.on 8c. orange . . . £100
Z788 5c.on 18c. lilac . . . 60·00
Z789 10c.on 12c. blue . . . 55·00
Z790 10c.on 16c. yellow . . . £170
Z791 10c.on 24c. green . . . 85·00

1880. Wmk Crown CC (Nos. 28/31).
Z792 2c. rose . . . 23·00
Z793 5c. blue . . . 42·00
Z794 10c. mauve . . . 17·00
Z795 48c. brown . . . £100

1882–96. Wmk Crown CA (Nos. 32/9).
Z795*a* 2c. rose-lake . . . 28·00
Z796 2c. carmine . . . 1·25
Z797 4c. slate-grey . . . 2·25
Z798 5c. blue . . . 1·10
Z799 10c. dull mauve . . . 15·00
Z800 10c. green . . . 1·50
Z801 10c. purple/*red* . . . 1·40
Z802 30c. green . . . 22·00

1885. (Nos. 40/2).
Z803 20c. on 30c. orange-red . . . 7·00
Z804 50c. on 48c. yellowish brown . . . 38·00
Z805 $1 on 96c. grey-olive . . . 75·00

1891. (Nos. 43/50).
Z806 7c.on 10c. green . . . 12·00
Z807 14c.on 30c. mauve . . . 65·00
Z807*a* 50c.on 48c. dull purple (No. 46) . . . £300
Z807*b* $1on 96c. purple/*red* (No. 47) . . . £400
Z808 20c.on 30c. green . . . 7·50
Z809 50c.on 48c. dull purple (No. 49) . . . 7·00
Z810 $1on 96c. purple/*red* (No. 50) . . . 25·00

1898. (No. 52).
Z812 $1 on 96c. black . . . 32·00

1898. (No. 55).
Z813 10c. on 30c. green . . . 85·00

1900–01. Wmk Crown CA (Nos. 56/61).
Z814 2c. dull green . . . 1·10
Z815 4c. carmine . . . 1·10
Z816 5c. yellow . . . 7·50
Z817 10c. ultramarine . . . 2·25
Z818 12c. blue . . . 70·00
Z819 30c. brown . . . 29·00

1903. Wmk Crown CA (Nos. 62/76).

Z820	1c. dull purple and brown	75
Z821	2c. dull green	1·75
Z822	4c. purple/*red*	60
Z823	5c. dull green and brown-orange	11·00
Z824	8c. slate and violet	2·25
Z825	10c. purple and blue/*blue*	1·75
Z826	12c. green and purple/*yellow*	6·00
Z827	20c. slate and chestnut	4·25
Z828	30c. dull green and black	28·00
Z829	50c. dull green and magenta	42·00
Z830	$1 purple and sage-green	29·00
Z831	$2 slate and scarlet	£275
Z832	$3 slate and dull blue	£400
Z833	$5 purple and blue-green	£500
Z834	$10 slate and orange/*blue*	£550

1904–06. Wmk Mult Crown CA (Nos. 77/90).

Z835	2c. dull green	1·75
Z836	4c. purple/*red*	60
Z837	5c. dull green and brown-orange	7·50
Z838	8c. slate and violet	2·75
Z839	10c. purple and blue/*blue*	1·75
Z840	12c. green and purple/*yellow*	8·00
Z841	20c. slate and chestnut	2·75
Z842	30c. dull green and black	24·00
Z843	50c. green and magenta	12·00
Z844	$1 purple and sage-green	27·00
Z845	$2 slate and scarlet	£110
Z846	$3 slate and dull blue	£250
Z847	$5 purple and blue-green	£400
Z848	$10 slate and orange/*blue*	£1000

1907–11. Wmk Mult Crown CA (Nos. 91/9).

Z849	1c. brown	1·50
Z850	2c. green	1·90
Z851	4c. carmine-red	60
Z852	6c. orange-vermilion and purple	5·00
Z853	10c. bright ultramarine	60
Z854	20c. purple and sage-green	48·00
Z855	30c. purple and orange-yellow	28·00
Z856	50c. black/*green*	20·00
Z857	$2 carmine-red and black	£325

1912–15. Wmk Mult Crown CA (Nos. 100/16).

Z858	1c. brown	1·00
Z859	2c. green	60
Z860	4c. red	45
Z861	6c. orange	1·50
Z862	8c. grey	8·50
Z863	10c. ultramarine	50
Z864	12c. purple/*yellow*	8·50
Z865	20c. purple and sage-green	1·40
Z867	30c. purple and orange-yellow	8·00
Z868	50c. black/*green*	3·00
Z869	$1 purple and blue/*blue*	4·25

POSTCARD STAMPS

1879. (Nos. P1/2).

ZP871	3c. on 16c. yellow	£400
ZP872	5c. on 18c. lilac	£425

POSTAL FISCAL STAMPS

1874–1902. Wmk Crown CC.

(a) P 15½ × 15 (Nos. F1/5).

ZF874	$2 olive-green	60·00
ZF875	$3 dull violet	42·00
ZF876	$10 rose-carmine	£700

(b) P 14.

ZF877	$2 dull bluish green	£275
ZF878	$3 dull mauve	£450

1881. (No. F7).

ZF880	12c. on $10 rose-carmine	£300

1891. (No. F9).

ZF882	$5 on $10 purple/*red*	£130

1897. (No. F10/11).

ZF883	$1 on $2 olive-green	£170
ZF884	$1 on $2 dull bluish green	£250

SWATOW

Swatow became a Treaty Port in 1860 and a consular packet agency was opened in the area made available for foreign firms during the following year. In 1867 the original agency was transferred to the Chinese city on the other side of the Han river, but a second agency was subsequently opened in the foreign concession during 1883.

Type **A** ("S2") (*supplied* 1866) *used* 1875–85
Type **C** (*supplied* 1866) *used* 1866–90
Type **D** (*supplied* 1883) *used* 1884–1922
Type **F** *used* 1916–22

Stamps of HONG KONG *cancelled at Swatow between* 1866 *and* 1916 *with postmarks detailed above.*

1862. No wmk (Nos. 1/7).

Z885	18c. lilac	£200

1863–71. Wmk Crown CC (Nos. 8/19).

Z886	2c. brown	£100
Z887	4c. grey	£100
	a. Perf 12½	
Z888	6c. lilac	£375
Z889	8c. orange	£100
Z890	12c. blue	42·00
Z891	18c. lilac	£750
Z892	24c. green	£120
Z893	30c. vermilion	
Z894	30c. mauve	42·00
Z895	48c. rose	£130
Z897	96c. brownish grey	£600

1876–77. (Nos. 20/1).

Z898	16c.on 18c. lilac	£425
Z899	28c.on 30c. mauve	£190

1877. Wmk Crown CC (No. 22).

Z900	16c. yellow	£425

1880. (Nos. 23/7).

Z901	5c.on 8c. orange	£190
Z902	5c.on 18c. lilac	£170
Z903	10c.on 12c. blue	£180
Z904	10c.on 16c. yellow	£350
Z905	10c.on 24c. green	£250

1880. Wmk Crown CC (Nos. 28/31).

Z906	2c. rose	85·00
Z907	5c. blue	90·00
Z908	10c. mauve	£100

1882–96. Wmk Crown CA (Nos. 32/9).

Z910	2c. carmine	6·00
Z911	4c. slate-grey	18·00
Z912	5c. blue	6·50
Z913	10c. dull mauve	70·00
Z914	10c. green	8·00
Z915	10c. purple/*red*	6·00
Z916	30c. green	40·00

1885. (Nos. 40/2).

Z917	20c. on 30c. orange-red	12·00

1891. (Nos. 43/50).

Z919	7c.on 10c. green	20·00
Z920	14c.on 30c. mauve	95·00
Z920*a*	50c.on 48c. dull purple (No. 46)	£325
Z921	$1on 96c. purple/*red* (No. 47)	£475
Z922	20c.on 30c. green	19·00
Z923	50c.on 48c. dull purple (No. 49)	20·00
Z924	$1on 96c. purple/*red* (No. 50)	42·00

1891. *50th Anniv of Colony* (No. 51).

Z925	2c. carmine	£850

1898. (No. 52).

Z926	$1 on 96c. black	60·00

1898. (No. 55).

Z927	10c. on 30c. green	£180

1900–01. Wmk Crown CA (Nos. 56/61).

Z928	2c. dull green	6·00
Z929	4c. carmine	4·75
Z930	5c. yellow	17·00
Z931	10c. ultramarine	5·00
Z933	30c. brown	42·00

1903. Wmk Crown CA (Nos. 62/76).

Z934	1c. dull purple and brown	5·00
Z935	2c. dull green	5·00
Z936	4c. purple/*red*	3·75
Z937	5c. dull green and brown-orange	15·00
Z938	8c. slate and violet	9·00
Z939	10c. purple and blue/*blue*	5·00
Z940	12c. green and purple/*yellow*	13·00
Z941	20c. slate and chestnut	7·50
Z942	30c. dull green and black	35·00
Z944	$1 purple and sage-green	55·00

1904–06. Wmk Mult Crown CA (Nos. 77/90).

Z949	2c. dull green	5·00
Z950	4c. purple/*red*	4·00
Z951	5c. dull green and brown-orange	15·00
Z952	8c. slate and violet	9·00
Z953	10c. purple and blue/*blue*	4·75
Z954	12c. green and purple/*yellow*	13·00
Z955	20c. slate and chestnut	9·00
Z956	30c. dull green and black	32·00
Z957	50c. green and magenta	24·00
Z958	$1 purple and sage-green	50·00
Z959	$2 slate and scarlet	£180
Z962	$10 slate and orange/*blue*	£1200

1907–11. Wmk Mult Crown CA (Nos. 91/9).

Z963	1c. brown	6·00
Z964	2c. green	6·00
Z965	4c. carmine-red	4·00
Z966	6c. orange-vermilion and purple	11·00
Z967	10c. bright ultramarine	4·50
Z969	30c. purple and orange-yellow	45·00
Z970	50c. black/*green*	30·00

1912–15. Wmk Mult Crown CA (Nos. 100/16).

Z972	1c. brown	4·50
Z973	2c. green	4·00
Z974	4c. red	3·50
Z975	6c. orange	6·00
Z976	8c. grey	18·00
Z977	10c. ultramarine	3·50
Z978	12c. purple/*yellow*	12·00
Z979	20c. purple and sage-green	4·75
Z980	25c. purple and magenta (Type A)	38·00
Z981	30c. purple and orange-yellow	17·00
Z982	50c. black/*green*	9·00
Z983	$1 purple and blue/*blue*	16·00

POSTCARD STAMPS

1879. (Nos. P1/2).

ZP986	3c. on 16c. yellow	£850

POSTAL FISCAL STAMPS

1874–1902. Wmk Crown CC.

(a) P 15½ × 15 (Nos. F1/3).

ZF988	$2 olive-green	£10
ZF989	$3 dull violet	90·0

(b) P 14.

ZF991	$2 dull bluish green	£35

TIENTSIN

Tientsin became a Treaty Port in 1860. A British consulate was established in 1861, but no formal postal agency was organised there until 1882. It was not, however, very successful and was closed during 1890. The British Post Office reopened on 1 October 1906 under the management of the Chinese Engineering and Mining Company.

British military post offices operated in Tientsin from 1927 until 1940.

Type **E** *used* 1906–13
Type **G** (*supplied* 1907) *used* 1907–22

Stamps of HONG KONG *cancelled at Tientsin between* 1906*and* 1916 *with postmarks detailed above.*

1903. Wmk Crown CA (Nos. 62/76).

Z998	1c. dull purple and brown	10·0
Z999	5c. dull green and brown-orange	24·0
Z1000	8c. slate and violet	9·5
Z1000*a*	12c. green and purple/*yellow*	27·0

1904–06. Wmk Mult Crown CA (Nos. 77/90).

Z1001	2c. dull green	4·7
Z1002	4c. purple/*red*	3·7
Z1003	5c. dull green and brown-orange	13·0
Z1004	8c. slate and violet	10·0
Z1005	10c. purple and blue/*blue*	4·5
Z1006	12c. green and purple/*yellow*	16·0
Z1007	20c. slate and chestnut	10·0
Z1008	30c. dull green and black	30·0
Z1009	50c. green and magenta	24·0
Z1010	$1 purple and sage-green	40·0
Z1011	$2 slate and scarlet	£17
Z1012	$3 slate and dull blue	£45
Z1013	$5 purple and blue-green	£55
Z1014	$10 slate and orange/*blue*	£160

1907–11. Wmk Mult Crown CA (Nos. 91/9).

Z1015	1c. brown	5·0
Z1016	2c. green	4·0
Z1017	4c. carmine-red	3·2
Z1018	6c. orange-vermilion and purple	15·0
Z1019	10c. bright ultramarine	4·0
Z1020	20c. purple and sage-green	65·
Z1021	30c. purple and orange-yellow	50·
Z1022	50c. black/*green*	40·
Z1023	$2 carmine-red and black	£42

1912–15. Wmk Mult Crown CA (Nos. 100/16).

Z1024	1c. brown	4·
Z1025	2c. green	4·
Z1026	4c. red	3·
Z1027	6c. orange	6·
Z1028	8c. grey	24·
Z1029	10c. ultramarine	4·
Z1031	20c. purple and sage-green	7·
Z1033	30c. purple and orange-yellow	13·
Z1034	50c. black/*green*	8·
Z1035	$1 purple and blue/*blue*	10·
Z1037	$3 green and purple	£1

WEI HAI WEI

The territory of Wei Hai Wei was leased from the Chinese by the British Government from 24 May 1898 having been previous occupied by the Japanese. At that time there were no organised postal services from the area, although a private local post did operate between the port and Chefoo from 8 December 1898 un 15 March 1899. A Chinese Imperial post office opened in March 1899 to be followed by a British postal agency on the offshore island of Liu Kung Tau on 1 September 1899. A second British agency opened at Port Edward on 1 April 1904.

Liu Kung Tau oval *used* 1899–1901
Type **D** (inscr "LIU KUNG TAU") (*supplied* 1899) *used* 1901–30

Stamps of HONG KONG *cancelled at Liu Kung Tau between* 18 *and* 1916 *with postmarks detailed above.*

1863–71. Wmk Crown CC (Nos. 8/19).

Z1039	12c. pale blue	

1882–96. Wmk Crown CA (Nos. 32/9).

Z1040	2c. carmine	40
Z1041	4c. slate-grey	55
Z1042	5c. blue	40
Z1043	10c. purple/*red*	25
Z1044	30c. green	48

1891. (Nos. 48/50).
Z1045 20c. on 30c. green 32·00
Z1046 50c. on 48c. dull purple 32·00

1898. (No. 52).
Z1047 $1 on 96c. black 70·00

1900–01. Wmk Crown CA (Nos. 56/61).
Z1049 2c. dull green 6·00
Z1050 4c. carmine 6·00
Z1051 5c. yellow 20·00
Z1052 10c. ultramarine 6·50
Z1053 12c. blue 90·00
Z1054 30c. brown 55·00

1903. Wmk Crown CA (Nos. 62/76).
Z1055 1c. dull purple and brown 5·50
Z1056 2c. dull green 5·00
Z1057 4c. purple/*red* 4·50
Z1058 5c. dull green and brown-orange 15·00
Z1059 8c. slate and violet 11·00
Z1060 10c. purple and blue/*blue* 7·50
Z1061 12c. green and purple/*yellow* 22·00
Z1062 20c. slate and chestnut 11·00
Z1063 30c. dull green and black 35·00
Z1064 50c. dull green and magenta 65·00
Z1065 $1 purple and sage-green 50·00

1904–06. Wmk Mult Crown CA (Nos. 77/90).
Z1070 2c. dull green 5·00
Z1071 4c. purple/*red* 4·50
Z1073 8c. slate and violet 9·50
Z1076 20c. slate and chestnut
Z1078 50c. green and magenta 45·00

1907–11. Wmk Mult Crown CA (Nos. 91/9).
Z1084 1c. brown 5·50
Z1085 2c. green 5·50
Z1086 4c. carmine-red 4·25
Z1088 10c. bright ultramarine 4·75
Z1089 20c. purple and sage-green 65·00
Z1090 30c. purple and orange-yellow 50·00
Z1091 50c. black/*green* 45·00

1912–15. Wmk Mult Crown CA (Nos. 100/16).
Z1093 1c. brown 6·50
Z1094 2c. green 4·50
Z1095 4c. red 4·00
Z1096 6c. orange 8·50
Z1097 8c. grey 23·00
Z1098 10c. ultramarine 4·75
Z1104 $1 purple and blue/*blue* 22·00

POSTAL FISCAL STAMPS

1874–1902. Wmk Crown CC. P 14 (Nos. F4/6).
Z1106 $2 dull bluish green £750

PORT EDWARD
13 JUL 1904
WEI-HAI-WEI

Port Edward rectangle used 1904–08
Type **D** (inscr "WEI-HAI-WEI" at top and "PORT EDWARD" at foot) (*supplied* 1907) *used* 1907–30

Stamps of HONG KONG *cancelled at Port Edward between* 1904 *and* 1916 *with postmarks detailed above.*

1900–01. Wmk Crown CA (Nos. 56/61).
Z1109 2c. dull green 55·00
Z1110 10c. ultramarine 65·00

1903. Wmk Crown CA (Nos. 62/76).
Z1111 1c. dull purple and brown 20·00
Z1112 2c. dull green 20·00
Z1113 4c. purple/*red* 18·00
Z1114 5c. dull green and brown-orange 27·00
Z1115 8c. slate and violet 27·00
Z1116 10c. purple and blue/*blue* 21·00
Z1117 12c. green and purple/*yellow* 35·00
Z1118 20c. slate and chestnut 50·00
Z1119 30c. dull green and black 50·00
Z1120 50c. dull green and magenta 60·00
Z1121 $1 purple and sage-green 55·00

1904–06. Wmk Mult Crown CA (Nos. 77/90).
Z1126 2c. dull green 11·00
Z1127 4c. purple/*red* 10·00
Z1128 5c. dull green and brown-orange 17·00
Z1129 8c. slate and violet 12·00
Z1132 20c. slate and chestnut 50·00
Z1133 30c. dull green and black 45·00
Z1134 50c. green and magenta 48·00

1907–11. Wmk Mult Crown CA (Nos. 91/9).
Z1140 1c. brown 11·00
Z1141 2c. green 11·00
Z1142 4c. carmine-red 7·50
Z1143 6c. orange-vermilion and purple
Z1144 10c. bright ultramarine 8·50

1912–15. Wmk Mult Crown CA (Nos. 100/16).
Z1151 1c. brown 9·50
Z1152 2c. green 7·00
Z1153 4c. red 4·25
Z1155 8c. grey 20·00
Z1156 10c. ultramarine 4·75
Z1158 20c. purple and sage-green 13·00

Z1161 50c. black/*green* 15·00
Z1162 $1 purple and blue/*blue* 16·00

PRICES FOR STAMPS ON COVER		
Nos. 1/14	*from* × 50	
Nos. 15/17	—	
Nos. 18/28	*from* × 30	

The overprinted stamps Nos. 1/17 were introduced on 1 January 1917 to prevent currency speculation in the Treaty Ports. They were used in the then-existing agencies of Amoy, Canton, Chefoo, Foochow, Hankow, Hoihow, Ningpo,. Shanghai, Swatow, Tientsin and were also supplied to the British naval base of Wei Hai Wei.

CHINA

(1)

1917 (1 Jan)–**21**. *Stamps of Hong Kong, 1912–21 (*wmk Mult Crown CA*), optd with T* **1**, *at Somerset House.*
1 1c. brown 4·00 1·50
a. Black-brown 3·50 2·50
b. Crown broken at right £325 £375
c. Wmk sideways † £2500
w. Wmk inverted † £1000
2 2c. green 6·00 30
3 4c. carmine-red 4·75 30
4 6c. orange 4·75 60
5 8c. slate 11·00 1·25
6 10c. ultramarine 11·00 30
y. Wmk inverted and reversed † £400
7 12c. purple/*yellow* 10·00 4·00
8 20c. purple and sage-green 11·00 60
9 25c. purple and magenta (A) 8·00 15·00
11 30c. purple and orange-yellow 30·00 5·00
12 50c. black/*blue-green* (*olive back*) 60·00 1·50
a. Emerald surface (1917?) 42·00 8·50
b. On emerald back (1919) 32·00 5·50
c. On white back (1920) £350 70·00
13 $1 reddish purple and bright blue/*blue* 65·00 2·50
a. Grey-purple and blue/blue (1921) 65·00 7·00
14 $2 carmine-red and grey-black £200 50·00
15 $3 green and purple £500 £180
16 $5 green and red/*blue-green* (*olive back*) £350 £250
17 $10 purple and black/*red* £850 £475
1/17 *Set of* 16 £1900 £900
12s/17s H/S "Specimen" *Set of* 6 £2000

1922 (Mar)–**27**. As last, but wmk Mult Script CA.
18 1c. brown 2·00 3·50
19 2c. green 3·00 2·25
w. Wmk inverted £160
20 4c. carmine-rose 5·00 2·00
a. Lower Chinese character at right broken at top £190 £160
21 6c. orange-yellow 4·25 4·25
22 8c. grey 7·00 14·00
23 10c. bright ultramarine. 8·00 3·25
w. Wmk inverted £150
24 20c. purple and sage-green 13·00 5·00
25 25c. purple and magenta (B) 21·00 65·00
a. Broken flower £475
26 50c. black/*emerald* (1927) 55·00 £170
s. Handstamped "Specimen" £250
27 $1 purple and blue/*blue* 70·00 55·00
28 $2 carmine-red and grey-black £200 £250
18/28 *Set of* 11 £350 £500

STAMP BOOKLETS

1917. *Black on red cover inscribed "*BRITISH POST OFFICE AGENCIES IN CHINA*". Stapled.*
SB1 $1 booklet containing eight 2c., six 4c. and six 10c. (Nos. 2/3, 6) £4500

1922. *Cover as No. SB1. Stapled.*
SB2 $1 booklet containing eight 2c., six 4c., and six 10c. (Nos. 19/20, 23) £4250

The British P.O.'s in the Treaty Ports closed by agreement with the Chinese on 30 November 1922, but the above over- printed issues continued in use at the Wei Hai Wei offices until they in turn closed on 30 September 1930. Under the terms of the Convention signed with China the Royal Navy continued to use the base at Wei Hai Wei until the mid-1930s.

BRITISH POST OFFICES IN JAPAN

Under the terms of the Anglo-Japanese Treaty of Yedo, signed on 26 August 1858, five Japanese ports were opened to British trade. British consulates were established at Decima (Nagasaki), Kanagawa (Yokohama), Hiogo (Kobe) and Hakodadi (Hakodate).The postage stamps of Hong Kong became available at the Yokohama and Nagasaki consulates during October 1864 and at Hiogo in 1869, although cancellation of mail did not commence until 1866 at Yokohama and Nagasaki or 1876 at Hiogo. Japan became a member of the U.P.U. on 1 June 1877 and all of the British Postal Agencies were closed by the end of 1879.

For illustrations of postmark types see BRITISH POST OFFICES IN CHINA.

HAKODATE

A British consular office existed at Hakodate, but it was never issued with a c.d.s. obliterator or Hong Kong stamps. No British covers are recorded from this consulate prior to opening of the Japanese Post Office.

HIOGO

The Port of Hiogo (Kobe) was first opened to foreigners on 1 January 1868. The British Consular mail service at Hiogo commenced during 1869 to serve the foreigners at Hiogo, Kobe and Osaka. The cities of Hiogo and Kobe later merged to become the single city of Kobe. The consular office at Hiogo closed on 30 November 1879.

Type **B** ("D30") (*supplied* 1876) *used* 1876–79
Type **D** (*supplied* 1876) *used* 1876–79

Stamps of HONG KONG *cancelled at Hiogo between* 1876 *and* 1879 *with postmarks detailed above.*

1863–71. Wmk Crown CC (Nos. 8/19).
Z1 2c. brown £4250
Z2 4c. grey £3250
Z3 6c. lilac £3750
Z4 8c. orange £3500
Z5 12c. blue £4250
Z6 18c. lilac
Z7 24c. green £3250
Z8 30c. vermilion
Z9 30c. mauve £4250
Z10 48c. rose £5500
Z12 96c. brownish grey £5500

1877. (Nos. 20/1).
Z13 16c. on 18c. lilac

1877. Wmk Crown CC (No. 22).
Z15 16c. yellow £4500

NAGASAKI

The British Consulate opened in Nagasaki on 14 June 1859, but, with few British residents at the port, the consular staff found it inconvenient to carry out postal duties so that few Nagasaki c.d.s. or "N2" cancellations exist. The postal service was terminated on 30 September 1879.

Type **A** ("N2") (*supplied* 1866) *used* 1876–79
Type **D** (*supplied* 1866) *used* 1876–79

Stamps of HONG KONG *cancelled at Nagasaki between* 1876 *and* 1879 *with postmarks detailed above.*

1862. No wmk (Nos. 1/8).
Z15*a* 18c. lilac £1700

1863–71. Wmk Crown CC (Nos. 8/19).
Z16 2c. brown £1400
Z17 4c. grey £1200
Z18 6c. lilac £1200
Z19 8c. orange £1200
Z20 12c. blue £1300
Z21 18c. lilac £2250
Z22 24c. green £1700
Z24 30c. mauve £1500
Z25 48c. rose £2250
Z27 96c. brownish grey

1876–77. (Nos. 20/1).
Z28 16c. on 18c. lilac £1800
Z29 28c. on 30c. mauve £1300

1877. Wmk Crown CC (No. 22).
Z30 16c. yellow £1500

YOKOHAMA

The British Consulate opened in Kanagawa on 21 July 1859, but was relocated to Yokohama where it provided postal services from 1 July 1860 until a separate Post Office was established in July 1867. The British Post Office in Yokohama closed on 31 December 1879.

Type **A** ("Yl") (*supplied* 1866) *used* 1867–79
Type **D** (*supplied* 1866) *used* 1866–79

Stamps of HONG KONG *cancelled at Yokohama between* 1866 *and* 1879 *with postmarks detailed above.*

1862. No wmk (Nos. 1/8).
Z30*a* 8c. yellow-buff £200
Z31 18c. lilac 95·00

1863–71. Wmk Crown CC (Nos. 8/19).
Z32 2c. brown 19·00
Z33 4c. grey 20·00
a. Perf 12½ £550
Z34 6c. lilac 25·00
Z35 8c. orange 25·00
Z36 12c. blue 19·00
Z37 18c. lilac £600
Z38 24c. green 21·00
Z39 30c. vermilion 40·00
Z40 30c. mauve 19·00
Z41 48c. rose 45·00
Z42 96c. olive-bistre £3500
Z43 96c. brownish grey 60·00

1876–77. (Nos. 20/1).
Z44 16c. on 18c. lilac £275
Z45 28c. on 30c. mauve 80·00

1877. Wmk Crown CC (No. 22).
Z46 16c. yellow £110

POSTAL FISCAL STAMPS

1874. Wmk Crown CC. P 15½ × 15 (Nos. F1/3).
ZF47 $2 olive-green £100
ZF48 $3 dull violet 95·00
ZF49 $10 rose-carmine £1300

India

PRICES FOR STAMPS ON COVER TO 1945

Nos.	S1/3	*from* × 2
No.	1	†
Nos.	2/26	*from* × 3
Nos.	27/30	—
Nos.	31/4	*from* × 8
Nos.	35/49	*from* × 3
No.	50	†
Nos.	51/3	*from* × 4
Nos.	54/65	*from* × 2
Nos.	66/8	*from* × 5
Nos.	69/74	*from* × 3
Nos.	73/277	*from* × 2
Nos.	O1/14	*from* × 6
Nos.	O15/18	—
No.	O19	*from* × 5
Nos.	O20/30*a*	*from* × 10
No.	O30*b*	†
Nos.	O31/133	*from* × 6
Nos.	O135/150	*from* × 2

(Currency. 12 pies = 1 anna; 16 annas = 1 rupee)

ISSUE FOR SIND PROVINCE

1

1852 (1 July). "Scinde Dawk." *Embossed.*

S1 **1** ½a. white . . . £4500 £800
S2 ½a. blue . . . £12000 £3500
S3 ½a. scarlet . . . £70000 £8000

These stamps were issued under the authority of Sir Bartle Frere, Commissioner in Sind.

No. S3 is on sealing wax (usually cracked). Perfect copies are very rare.

It is believed that examples in red were issued first followed, in turn, by those in white and blue. The latter, which shows an extra ring round the circumference, may have been produced by De La Rue. The Scinde Dawks were withdrawn in October 1854.

EAST INDIA COMPANY ADMINISTRATION

2 (*Much reduced*)

3

The ½a., 1a. and 4a. were lithographed in Calcutta at the office of the Surveyor-General. The die was engraved by Mr. Maniruddin (spelling uncertain). *Ungummed* paper watermarked as T **2** (the "No. 4" paper) with the Arms of the East India Co in the sheet. The watermark is sideways on the ½a. and 1a., and upright on the 4a. where the paper was trimmed so that only the central portion showing the oval and the arms was used. Imperforate.

1854 (1 April).

1 **3** ½a. vermilion . . . £800
a. Deep vermilion . . . £1200

This stamp, with 9½ arches in the side border, was prepared for use and a supply was sent to Bombay, but was not officially issued.

The vermilion shade is normally found on toned paper and the deep vermilion on white.

ILLUSTRATIONS. Types **4/8** are shown twice actual size.

4

1854 (1 Oct)–**55**. *Die I.*

2 **4** ½a. blue . . . 55·00 15·00
a. Printed on both sides . . . † £8000
b. Printed double . . . † £6000
3 ½a. pale blue . . . 85·00 20·00
4 ½a. deep blue . . . 70·00 20·00
5 ½a. indigo . . . £250 65·00

We give the official date of validity. Stamps were on sale to the public from mid September. Actual usage at Toungoo, Burma, is known from mid August.

These stamps were printed between 5 May and 29 July 1854 (Printing 30 millions).

4a

Die II.

6 **4a** ½a. blue . . . 50·00 75·00
7 ½a. indigo . . . 60·00 85·00

The bulk were printed between 1 and 12 August 1854, with some extra sheets on or before 2 November (Printing about 2 millions).

5

Die III (1855).

8 **5** ½a. pale blue . . . £750 38·00
8*a* ½a. blue . . . £700 35·00
9 ½a. greenish blue . . . £1500 £160
10 ½a. deep blue . . . £950 70·00

These stamps were printed between 3 July and 25 August 1855 (Printing about 4¾ millions).

THE THREE DIES OF THE ½ ANNA

DIE I. *Chignon shading* mostly solid blobs of colour. *Corner ornaments*, solid blue stars with long points, always conspicuous. *Band below diadem* always heavily shaded. *Diadem and jewels*. The middle and right-hand jewels usually show a clearly defined cross. *Outer frame lines*. Stamps with white or faintly shaded chignons and weak frame lines are usually Die I (worn state).

DIE II. *Chignon* normally shows much less shading. A strong line of colour separates hair and chignon. *Corner ornaments*. The right blue star is characteristic (see illustration) but tends to disappear. It never obliterates the white cross. *Band below diadem*. As Die I but heavier, sometimes solid. *Diadem and jewels*. As Die I but usually fainter. *Outer frame lines*. Always strong and conspicuous.

DIE III. *Chignon shading* shows numerous fine lines, often blurred. *Corner ornaments* have a small hollow blue star with short points, which tends to disappear as in Die II. *Band below diadem*, shows light shading or hardly any shading. *Diadem and jewels*. Jewels usually marked with a solid squat star. The ornaments between the stars appear in the shape of a characteristic white "w". *Frame lines* variable.

The above notes give the general characteristics of the three Dies, but there are a few exceptions due to retouching, etc.

6 (*See note below No.* 14)

Die I.

11 **6** 1a. deep red . . . £375 48·0
12 1a. red . . . £225 35·0

Printing of these stamps commenced on 26 July 1854, an continued into August (Printing, see note below No. 14).

7

Die II: With more lines in the chignon than in Die I, and with whit curved line where chignon joins head.*

13 **7** 1a. deep red . . . £150 50·0
14 1a. dull red . . . 45·00 38·

*Very worn printings of Die II may be found with chignon near as white as in Die I.

In stamps of Die I, however, the small blob of red projecting fro the hair into the chignon is always visible.

These stamps were printed in August and September 1854 (Tot printing, Dies I and II together, about 7¾ millions).

8

Die III. With pointed bust (1855).

15 **8** 1a. red . . . £900 £1
16 1a. dull red . . . £1400 £1

These stamps were printed between 7 July and 25 August 18 (Printing, about 1½ millions).

9

NOTE. Our catalogue prices for Four Annas stamps are for cut-square specimens, with clear margins and in good condition. Cut-to-shape copies are worth from 3% to 20% of these prices according to condition.

Four Dies of the Head:—

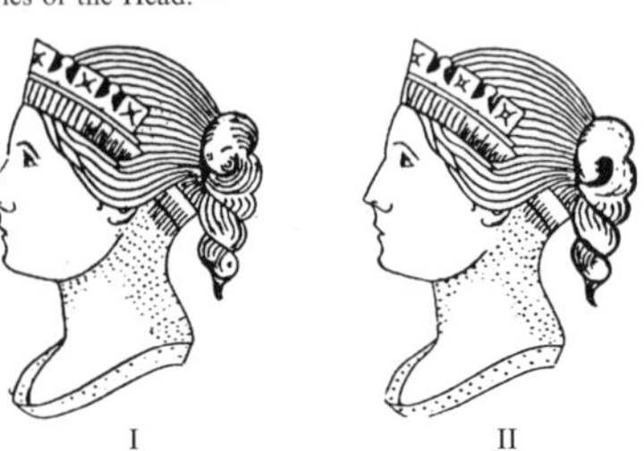

DIE I. Band of diadem and chignon strongly shaded.

IE II. Lines in band of diadem worn. Few lines in the upper part of the chignon, which, however, shows a strong drawn comma-like mark.

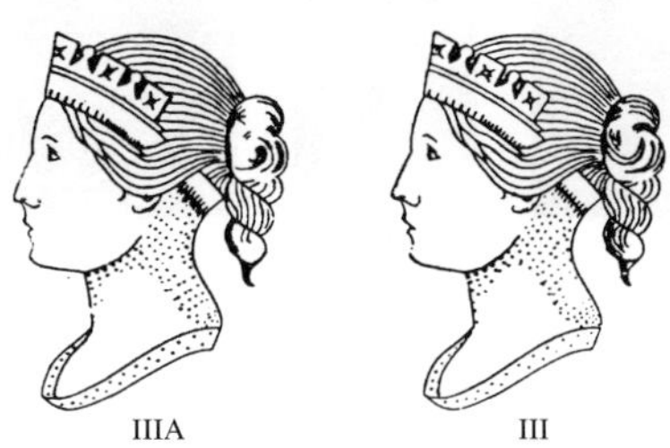

IIIA III

IE IIIA. Upper part of chignon partly redrawn, showing two short, curved vertical lines in the NE corner. "Comma" has disappeared.

IE III. Upper part of chignon completely redrawn, but band of diadem shows only a few short lines.

wo Dies of the Frame:—

ie I. Outer frame lines weak. Very small dots of colour, or none at all, in the "R" and "A's". The white lines to the right of "INDIA" are separated, by a line of colour, from the inner white circle.

e II. Outer frame lines strengthened. Dots in the "R" and "A's" strong. White lines to right of "INDIA" break into inner white circle.

(Des Capt. H. Thuillier)

54 (15 Oct)–55. W 2 upright, central portion only. Imperf.

Printing. Head Die I. Frame Die I. Stamps widely spaced and separated by blue wavy line.

		Un	Used	Us pr
9	4a. indigo and red	£4250	£500	£1800
	4a. blue and pale red	£4250	£425	£1600
	a. Head inverted	†£27000/£85000		†

This printing was made between 13 and 28 Oct 1854 (Printing, ,040).

Twenty-seven confirmed examples of No. 18a are now known, y three of which are cut-square. The range of prices quoted ects the difference in value between a sound cut-to-shape stamp d the finest example known.

Printing. Head Die II. Frame Die I. Stamps widely spaced and separated by blue wavy line.

9	4a. blue and red	£4000	£275	£1000
	a. Blue (head) printed double	†	£6000	†
	4a. indigo and deep red	£4000	£325	£1200

This printing was made between 1 and 13 Dec 1854 (Printing, ,960).

No. 19a is only known used cut-to-shape.

Printing. Head Dies II, IIIA and III. Frame Dies I and II. mps, often in bright shades, widely spaced and separated by wavy line (1855).

9	4a. blue and red (*shades*) (Head III, Frame I)	£9000	£1100	£3500
	a. Head II, Frame I	—	£1600	£5000
	b. Head IIIA, Frame I	—	£1600	£4750
	c. Head III, Frame II	—	—	£9500

This printing was made between 10 March and 2 April 1855 (Printing, 138,960).

4th Printing. Head Die III. Frame Die II. Stamps closely spaced 2 to 2½ mm without separating line (1855).

22	9	4a. deep blue and red	£2750	£275	£850
23		4a. blue and red	£2500	£225	£750
		a. Blue (head) printed double	†	£4500	†
24		4a. pale blue and pale red	£2750	£300	£900

This printing was made between 3 April and 9 May 1855 (Printing, 540,960).

No. 23a is only known used cut-to-shape.

5th Printing. Head Die III. Frame Die II. Stamps spaced 4 to 6 mm without separating line (1855).

25	9	4a. blue and rose-red	£4500	£400	£1600
26		4a. deep blue and red	£4500	£400	£1600

This printing was made between 4 Oct and 3 Nov 1855 (Printing, 380,064).

Serrated perf about 18, or pin-perf.

27	½a. blue (Die I)	†	£4000	—
28	1a. red (Die I)	†	£2250	—
29	1a. red (Die II)	†	£2000	—
30	4a. blue and red (Die II)	†	£9000	—

This is believed to be an unofficial perforation. Most of the known specimens bear Madras circle postmarks (C122 to C126), but some are known with Bombay postmarks. Beware of fakes.

BISECTS. The bisected stamps for issues between 1854 and 1860 were used exclusively in the Straits Settlements during shortages of certain values. Prices quoted are for those with Singapore "B 172" cancellations. Penang marks are considerably rarer.

10

11

(Plate made at Mint, Calcutta. Typo Stamp Office)

1854 (4 Oct). Sheet wmk sideways, as W **2** but with "No. 3" at top left. Imperf.

31	**10**	2a. green (*shades*)	85·00	24·00
		a. Bisected (1a.) (1857) (on cover)		†£120000
34		2a. emerald-green	£1000	

The 2a. was also printed on paper with a sideways sheet watermark incorporating the words "STAMP OFFICE. One Ana" in double-ring circle, etc. (*Price* £475 *unused*, £375 *used*).

Apart from the rare emerald-green shade, there is a range of shades of No. 31 varying from bluish to yellowish green.

Many stamps show traces of lines external to the design shown in our illustration. Stamps with this frame on all four sides are scarce.

Many reprints of the ½, 1, 2, and 4a. exist.

PRINTERS. All Indian stamps from No. 35 to 200 were typographed by De La Rue & Co.

1855 (1 Oct). *Blue glazed paper.* No wmk. P 14.

35	**11**	4a. black	£450	15·00
		a. Imperf (pair)	£3000	£3000
		b. Bisected (2a.) (1859) (on cover)	†	£7500
36		8a. carmine (Die I)	£425	13·00
		a. Imperf (pair)	£1800	
		b. Bisected (4a.) (1859) (on cover)	†	£50000

The first supply of the 4a. was on white paper, but it is difficult to distinguish it from No. 45.

In the 8a. the paper varies from deep blue to almost white.

For difference between Die I and Die II in the 8a., see illustrations above No. 73.

1856–64. *Paper yellowish to white.* No wmk. P 14.

37	**11**	½a. blue (Die I)	60·00	3·25
		a. Imperf (pair)	£325	£950
38		½a. pale blue (Die I)	55·00	1·50
39		1a. brown	50·00	2·25
		a. Imperf between (vert pair)		
		b. Imperf (pair)	£750	£1300
		c. Bisected (½a.) (1859) (on cover)	†	£55000
40		1a. deep brown	70·00	3·50
41		2a. dull pink (1860)	£450	28·00
		a. Imperf (pair)	£1700	
42		2a. yellow-buff (1859)	£225	28·00
		a. Imperf (pair)	£1000	£1800
43		2a. yellow (1863)	£325	30·00
44		2a. orange (1858)	£425	30·00
		a. Imperf (pair)		
45		4a. black	£250	8·50
		a. Bisected diagonally (2a.) (1859) (on cover)	†	£20000
		b. Imperf (pair)	£1800	£1800
46		4a. grey-black	£200	4·75
47		4a. green (1864)	£950	35·00
48		8a. carmine (Die I)	£275	20·00
49		8a. pale carmine (Die I)	£325	20·00
		a. Bisected (4a.) (1859) (on cover)	†	£50000

Prepared for use, but not officially issued.

50	**11**	2a. yellow-green	£700	£800
		a. Imperf (pair)	£1700	

This stamp is known with trial obliterations, and a few are known postally used. It also exists *imperf*, but is not known used thus.

For difference between Die I and Die II in the ½a., see illustrations above No. 73.

CROWN COLONY

On the 1 November 1858, Her Majesty Queen Victoria assumed the government of the territories in India "heretofore administered in trust by the Honourable East India Company".

12

13

1860 (9 May). No wmk. P 14.

51	**12**	8p. purple/*bluish*	£200	85·00
52		8p. purple/*white*	40·00	4·50
		a. Bisected diagonally (4p.) (1862) (on cover)	†	£55000
		b. Imperf (pair)	£2000	£3000
53		8p. mauve	55·00	6·50

1865. *Paper yellowish to white.* W **13**. P 14.

54	**11**	½a. blue (Die I)	11·00	50
		a. Imperf	†	£800
		w. Wmk inverted	—	18·00
55		½a. pale blue (Die I)	11·00	50
56	**12**	8p. purple	8·50	9·50
		w. Wmk inverted	30·00	
57		8p. mauve	11·00	9·50
58	**11**	1a. pale brown	6·00	70
59		1a. deep brown	5·00	60
		w. Wmk inverted	48·00	24·00
60		1a. chocolate	9·00	80
61		2a. yellow	85·00	4·50
62		2a. orange	45·00	1·75
		a. Imperf (pair)	†	£3000
63		2a. brown-orange	21·00	2·00
		w. Wmk inverted	55·00	30·00
64		4a. green	£325	21·00
		w. Wmk inverted	†	90·00
65		8a. carmine (Die I)	£1100	75·00
		w. Wmk inverted	£1600	£170

The 8p. mauve, No. 57, is found variously surcharged "NINE" or "NINE PIE" by local postmasters, to indicate that it was being sold for 9 pies, as was the case during 1874. Such surcharges were made without Government sanction. (*Price, from* £400 *unused*).

The stamps of India, wmk Elephant's Head, surcharged with a crown and value in "cents", were used in the Straits Settlements.

14

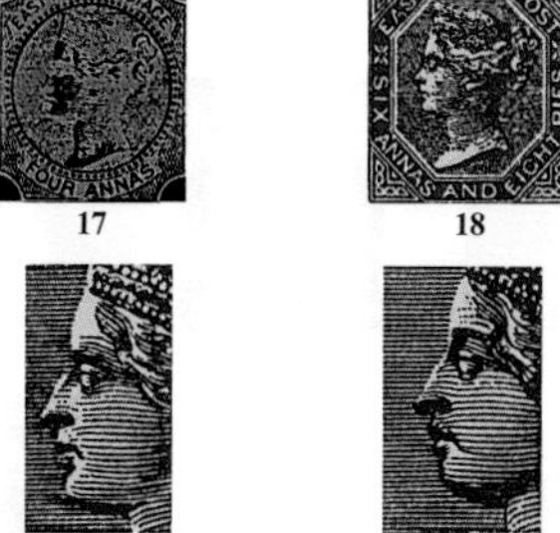

(15) (16)

1866 (28 June). *Fiscal stamps as T* **14** *optd.* Wmk Crown over "INDIA". P 14 (at sides only).

(a) As T **15**.

66	6a. purple (G.)	£600	£110
	a. Overprint inverted	†	£9000

There are 20 different types of this overprint.

(b) With T **16**.

68	6a. purple (G.)	£1100	£140

17 18

Die I Die II

Two Dies of 4a.:—

Die I.—Mouth closed, line from corner of mouth downwards only. Pointed chin.

Die II.—Mouth slightly open; lips, chin, and throat defined by line of colour. Rounded chin.

1866 (1 Aug)–**78**. W **13**. P 14.

69	**17**	4a. green (Die I)	65·00	3·25
70		4a. deep green (Die I)	70·00	3·25
71		4a. blue-green (Die II) (1878)	20·00	2·25
72	**18**	6a.8p. slate (4.67)	40·00	20·00
		a. Imperf (pair)	£1700	

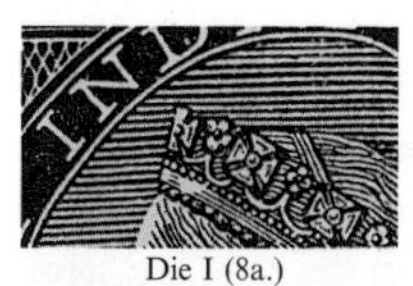

Die I (8a.)

Die I (½a.)

Die II (8a.)

Die II (½a.)

1868 (1 Jan). *Die II. Profile redrawn and different diadem.* W **13**. P 14.

No.	Type	Description	Unused	Used
73	**11**	8a. rose (Die II)	29·00	5·50
		w. Wmk inverted	45·00	
74		8a. pale rose (Die II)	29·00	5·50

1873. *Die II. Features, especially the mouth, more firmly drawn.* W **13**. P 14.

No.	Type	Description	Unused	Used
75	**11**	½a. deep blue (Die II)	4·25	50
76		½a. blue (Die II)	4·25	50
		w. Wmk inverted	42·00	
		y. Wmk inverted and reversed	†	70·00

19

20

1874 (18 July–1 Sept). W **13**. P 14.

No.	Type	Description	Unused	Used
77	**19**	9p. bright mauve (18.7.74)	14·00	14·00
78		9p. pale mauve	14·00	14·00
79	**20**	1r. slate (1.9.74)	40·00	24·00

21

22

1876 (19 Aug). W **13**. P 14.

No.	Type	Description	Unused	Used
80	**21**	6a. olive-bistre	6·50	2·50
		w. Wmk inverted	60·00	
81		6a. pale brown	5·50	1·50
82	**22**	12a. Venetian red	8·00	20·00

EMPIRE

Queen Victoria assumed the title of Empress of India in 1877, and the inscription on the stamps was altered from "EAST INDIA" to "INDIA".

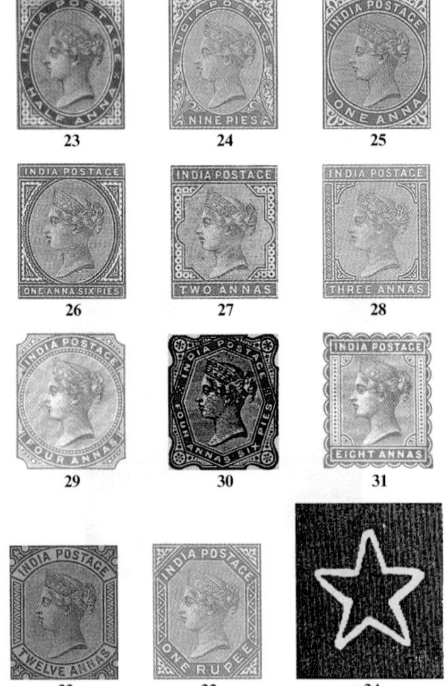
23 24 25 26 27 28 29 30 31 32 33 34

1882 (1 Jan)–**90**. W **34**. P 14.

No.	Type	Description	Unused	Used
84	**23**	½a. deep blue-green (1883)	3·75	10
		w. Wmk inverted		
85		½a. blue-green	3·75	10
		a. Double impression	£400	£500
		w. Wmk inverted	—	65·00
86	**24**	9p. rose (1883)	1·00	1·90
87		9p. aniline carmine	1·00	1·90
		w. Wmk inverted	—	65·00
88	**25**	1a. brown-purple (1883)	3·75	30
89		1a. plum	3·75	30
		w. Wmk inverted	—	65·00
90	**26**	1a.6p. sepia	1·00	1·25
91	**27**	2a. pale blue (1883)	3·75	30
92		2a. blue	3·75	30
		a. Double impression	£850	£1100
93	**28**	3a. orange	14·00	6·00
94		3a. brown-orange (1890)	8·00	1·00
		w. Wmk inverted	—	75·00
95	**29**	4a. olive-green (6.85)	14·00	1·00
96		4a. slate-green	14·00	1·00
		w. Wmk inverted	—	55·00
97	**30**	4a.6p. yellow-green (1.5.86)	18·00	4·50
98	**31**	8a. dull mauve (1883)	23·00	2·00
99		8a. magenta	22·00	2·00
100	**32**	12a. purple/*red* (1.4.88)	7·00	3·25
		w. Wmk inverted	—	75·00
101	**33**	1r. slate (1883)	15·00	5·00
		w. Wmk inverted	—	65·00
84/101 *Set of* 11			90·00	18·00
97s, 100s Handstamped "Specimen" *Set of* 2			75·00	

No. 92a is from a sheet of 2a. stamps with a very marked double impression issued in Karachi in early 1898.

2½ As.
(35)

36

37

1891 (1 Jan). *No. 97 surch with T* **35** *by Govt Press, Calcutta.*

No.	Type	Description	Unused	Used
102	**30**	2½a.on 4½a. yellow-green	3·00	60
		a. Surch double, one albino		

There are several varieties in this surcharge due to variations in the relative positions of the letters and figures.

1892 (Jan)–**97**. W **34**. P 14.

No.	Type	Description	Unused	Used
103	**36**	2a.6p. yellow-green	2·50	40
104		2a.6p. pale blue-green (1897)	3·25	80
105	**37**	1r. green and rose	22·00	5·50
106		1r. green and aniline carmine	10·00	2·00

38

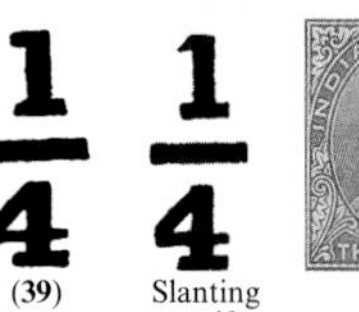
(39) Slanting serif (Lower pane R. 1/1)

40

USED HIGH VALUES. It is necessary to emphasise that used prices quoted for the following and all later high value stamps are for postally used copies.

(Head of Queen from portrait by von Angeli)

1895 (1 Sept). W **34**. P 14.

No.	Type	Description	Unused	Used
107	**38**	2r. carmine and yellow-brown	35·00	11·00
107*a*		2r. carmine and brown	40·00	13·00
108		3r. brown and green	27·00	10·00
109		5r. ultramarine and violet	38·00	25·00
107/9 *Set of* 3			90·00	40·00

1898 (1 Oct). *No. 85 surch with T* **39** *by Govt Press, Calcutta.*

No.	Type	Description	Unused	Used
110	**23**	¼a.on ½a. blue-green	10	50
		a. Surch double	£180	
		b. Double impression of stamp	£200	
		c. Slanting serif on "1"	20·00	

1899. W **34**. P 14.

No.	Type	Description	Unused	Used
111	**40**	3p. aniline carmine	40	10

1900 (1 Oct)–**12**. W **34**. P 14.

No.	Type	Description	Unused	Used
112	**40**	3p. grey	75	1·00
113	**23**	½a. pale yellow-green	1·60	45
114		½a. yellow-green	2·00	45
115	**25**	1a. carmine	1·75	20
116	**27**	2a. pale violet	3·25	1·90
117		2a. mauve (1902)	7·50	2·50
118	**36**	2a.6p. ultramarine	3·25	4·00
112/18 *Set of* 5			9·50	6·75

41 42 43

44 45 46

47 48 49

50

51

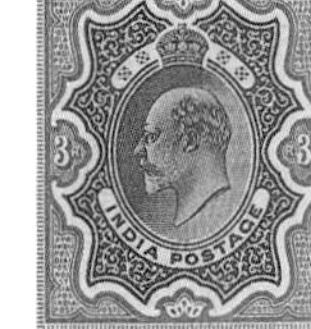
52

1902 (9 Aug)–**11**. W **34**. P 14.

No.	Type	Description	Unused	Used
119	**41**	3p. grey	1·00	1
120		3p. slate-grey (1904)	1·00	1
121	**42**	½a. yellow-green	1·50	2
122		½a. green	1·50	2
123	**43**	1a. carmine	1·50	1
124	**44**	2a. violet (13.5.03)	4·00	4
125		2a. mauve	3·25	1
126	**45**	2a.6p. ultramarine (1902)	4·75	6
		w. Wmk inverted	†	£15
127	**46**	3a. orange-brown (1902)	4·75	6
128	**47**	4a. olive (20.4.03)	3·00	6
129		4a. pale olive	3·50	6
130		4a. olive-brown	9·00	3·0
131	**48**	6a. olive-bistre (6.8.03)	12·00	4·7
132		6a. maize	10·00	4·5
133	**49**	8a. purple (*shades*) (8.5.03)	8·50	1·0
134		8a. claret (1910)	12·00	1·0
135	**50**	12a. purple/*red* (1903)	8·50	2·0
136	**51**	1r. green and carmine (1903)	6·50	7
137		1r. green and scarlet (1911)	35·00	2·5
138	**52**	2r. rose-red and yellow-brown (1903)	38·00	4·0
139		2r. carmine and yellow-brown	38·00	4·0
		w. Wmk inverted	†	£18
140		3r. brown and green (1904)	25·00	19·0
141		3r. red-brown and green (1911)	35·00	22·0
142		5r. ultramarine and violet (1904)	55·00	35·0
143		5r. ultramarine and deep lilac (1911)	£100	48·0
144		10r. green and carmine (1909)	£100	28·
146		15r. blue and olive-brown (1909)	£130	42·
147		25r. brownish orange and blue (1909)	£750	£8
119/47 *Set of* 17			£1000	£8

No. 147 can often be found with telegraph cancellation; these ca be supplied at one third of the price given above.

1905 (2 Feb). *No. 122 surch with T* **39**.

No.	Type	Description	Unused	Used
148	**42**	¼ on½a. green	55	
		a. Surch inverted	—	£8

It is doubtful if No. 148a exists unused with genuine surcharge

53

54

1906 (6 Dec)–**07**. W **34**. P 14.

No.	Type	Description	Unused	Used
149	**53**	½a. green	3·00	
150	**54**	1a. carmine (7.1.07)	1·75	

55 58 * 61 64

56

57

59 60

62

63

65

66

67

"Rs" flaw in right value tablet (R. 1/4)

T **58**. Two types of the 1½a.; (A) As illustrated. (B) Inscribed As". "ONE AND A HALF ANNAS".

1 (1 Dec)–**22**. W **34**. P 14.

	55	3p. grey (1912)	1·40	20
		w. Wmk inverted		
		3p. pale grey	1·50	20
		3p. bluish grey (1922)	2·00	50
		w. Wmk inverted	12·00	
		3p. slate	1·50	20
		a. "Rs" flaw	14·00	
b		3p. violet-grey	2·50	50
	56	½a. light green (1912)	1·50	15
		½a. emerald	1·90	15
		w. Wmk inverted	†	32·00
		½a. bright green	1·90	15
	57	1a. rose-carmine	2·50	20
		1a. carmine	2·50	20
		1a. aniline carmine	2·25	15
		1a. pale rose-carmine (*chalk-surfaced paper*) (1918)	2·75	40
	58	1½a. chocolate (Type A) (1919)	3·00	30
		1½a. grey-brown (Type A)	7·50	2·50
		1½a. chocolate (Type B) (1921)	3·25	4·00
		w. Wmk inverted	9·00	
	59	2a. purple	3·25	40
		2a. reddish purple	5·00	30
		2a. deep mauve	4·25	40
		w. Wmk inverted	19·00	
		2a. bright reddish violet	5·50	50
	60	2a.6p. ultramarine (1912)	2·75	3·00
	61	2a.6p. ultramarine (1913)	2·75	20
	62	3a. orange	4·00	20
		3a. dull orange	6·50	45
	63	4a. deep olive (1912)	6·00	50
		4a. olive-green	6·00	50
		w. Wmk inverted	19·00	
	64	6a. yellow-bistre (1912)	4·00	1·25
		6a. brown-ochre	4·00	1·00
	65	8a. deep magenta (1912)	6·00	1·40
		8a. deep mauve	11·00	1·10
		w. Wmk inverted	50·00	
		8a. bright mauve	30·00	6·00
		8a. purple	14·00	1·50
	66	12a. carmine-lake (1912)	6·00	2·25
		12a. claret	15·00	2·50
	67	1r. red-brown and deep blue-green (1913)	15·00	2·00
		w. Wmk inverted	42·00	
		1r. brown and green (*shades*)	19·00	1·50
a		1r. orange-brown and deep turquoise-green	32·00	3·25
		2r. carmine and brown (1913)	21·00	1·75
		w. Wmk inverted	60·00	
		5r. ultramarine and violet (1913)	48·00	6·50
		10r. green and scarlet (1913)	70·00	12·00
		15r. blue and olive (1913)	90·00	24·00
		25r. orange and blue (1913)	£160	35·00
/91 *Set of* 19			£400	85·00

Examples of the ½a. printed double are now believed to be forgeries.

RGERIES.—Collectors are warned against forgeries of all the r surcharges of India, and particularly the errors.

NINE

PIES

(68)

21. *T* **57** *surch with T* **68**.

	9p.on 1a. rose-carmine	85	30
	a. Error. "NINE NINE"	75·00	£130
	b. Error. "PIES PIES"	75·00	£130
	c. Surch double	£150	£180
	w. Wmk inverted	†	55·00
	9p.on 1a. carmine-pink	1·75	60
	9p.on 1a. aniline carmine	8·00	3·00

n the initial setting of the surcharge No. 192a occurred on 2/13–16 of the fourth pane and No. 192b on R. 4/13-16 of the rd. For the second setting No. 192a was corrected. Examples of . 192b still occur but on R. 2/13-16 of the third pane. Later ntings showed this corrected also.

22. *T* **56** *surch with T* **39**.

	¼a.on ½a. bright green	50	35
	a. Surch inverted	9·00	
	b. Surch omitted (in horiz pair with normal)	£200	
	c. Slanting serif on "1"		
	w. Wmk inverted		
	¼a.on ½a. emerald	2·00	65
	w. Wmk inverted		

22–26. W **34**. P 14.

	57	1a. chocolate	75	10
		w. Wmk inverted	20·00	
	58	1½a. rose-carmine (Type B) (1926)	3·00	30
	61	2a.6p. orange (1926)	5·00	2·75
	62	3a. ultramarine (1923)	12·00	60
/200 *Set of* 4			18·00	3·25

69

70

71

PRINTERS. The following issues of postage and contemporary official stamps were all printed by the Security Printing Press, Nasik, *unless otherwise stated.*

1926–33. *Typo.* W **69**. P 14.

201	**55**	3p. slate	30	10
		w. Wmk inverted	1·40	30
202	**56**	½a. green	1·25	10
		w. Wmk inverted	2·00	30
203	**57**	1a. chocolate	50	10
		a. *Tête-bêche* (pair) (1932)	1·25	10·00
		w. Wmk inverted	50	10
204	**58**	1½a. rose-carmine (Type B) (1929)	2·00	10
		w. Wmk inverted	2·25	30
205	**59**	2a. bright purple	7·00	8·00
		a. Stop under "s" in right value tablet (R. 4/16)	90·00	
		w. Wmk inverted	†	32·00
206	**70**	2a. purple	1·40	10
		a. *Tête-bêche* (pair) (1933)	9·00	38·00
		w. Wmk inverted	1·60	30
207	**61**	2a.6p. orange (1929)	1·75	10
		w. Wmk inverted	1·75	40
208	**62**	3a. ultramarine	8·50	1·00
209		3a. blue (1928)	8·50	10
		w. Wmk inverted	8·50	75
210	**63**	4a. pale sage-green	1·50	10
		w. Wmk inverted	—	7·00
211	**71**	4a. sage-green	6·00	10
		w. Wmk inverted	12·00	50
212	**65**	8a. reddish purple	4·00	10
		w. Wmk inverted	6·00	40
213	**66**	12a. claret	5·00	30
		w. Wmk inverted	7·00	80
214	**67**	1r. chocolate and green	5·00	45
		a. Chocolate (head) omitted	£3500	
		w. Wmk inverted	9·00	75
215		2r. carmine and orange	12·00	80
		w. Wmk inverted	12·00	1·50
216		5r. ultramarine and purple	24·00	1·25
		w. Wmk inverted	42·00	2·00
217		10r. green and scarlet (1927)	48·00	3·00
		w. Wmk inverted	90·00	5·00
218		15r. blue and olive (1928)	40·00	30·00
		w. Wmk inverted	24·00	30·00
219		25r. orange and blue (1928)	95·00	35·00
		w. Wmk inverted	£130	45·00
201/19 *Set of* 18			£225	70·00

Examples of the ½a. printed double are believed to be forgeries.

72 De Havilland D.H. 66 Hercules

Missing tree-top (R. 11/6of 8a.)

Reversed serif on second "I" of "INDIA"

(Des R. Grant. Litho)

1929 (22 Oct). *Air.* W **69** (sideways*). P 14.

220	**72**	2a. deep blue-green	2·75	65
		w. Wmk stars pointing left	1·75	75
221		3a. blue	1·00	2·00
		w. Wmk stars pointing left	2·00	2·25
222		4a. olive-green	2·25	1·25
		w. Wmk stars pointing left	3·00	1·25
223		6a. bistre	2·25	1·00
		w. Wmk stars pointing left	2·50	1·00
224		8a. purple	2·75	1·00
		a. Missing tree-top	£110	65·00
		b. Reversed serif	£190	£100
		w. Wmk stars pointing left	3·25	1·00
225		12a. rose-red	12·00	6·00
		w. Wmk stars pointing left	12·00	6·00
220/5 *Set of* 6			20·00	10·50

*The normal sideways watermark shows the stars pointing right, *as seen from the back of the stamp.*

73 Purana Qila

(Des H. W. Barr. Litho)

1931 (9 Feb). *Inauguration of New Delhi. T* **73** *and similar horiz designs.* W **69** (sideways*). P 13½ × 14.

226	¼a. olive-green and orange-brown	2·00	3·50
	a. "F" for "P" in "PURANA"	£100	£110
	w. Wmk stars pointing left	1·75	3·50
227	½a. violet and green	1·25	40
	w. Wmk stars pointing left	2·00	40
228	1a. mauve and chocolate	1·25	20
	w. Wmk stars pointing left	2·50	25
229	2a. green and blue	1·50	2·75
	w. Wmk stars pointing left	2·00	1·25
230	3a. chocolate and carmine	3·75	2·50
	w. Wmk stars pointing left	2·50	2·50
231	1r. violet and green	9·50	26·00
	w. Wmk stars pointing left	8·00	26·00
226/31 *Set of* 6		14·50	30·00

Designs:—½a. War Memorial Arch; 1a. Council House; 2a. The Viceroy's House; 3a. Government of India Secretariat; 1r. Dominion Columns and the Secretariat.

*The normal sideways watermark shows the stars pointing to the right, *as seen from the back of the stamp.*

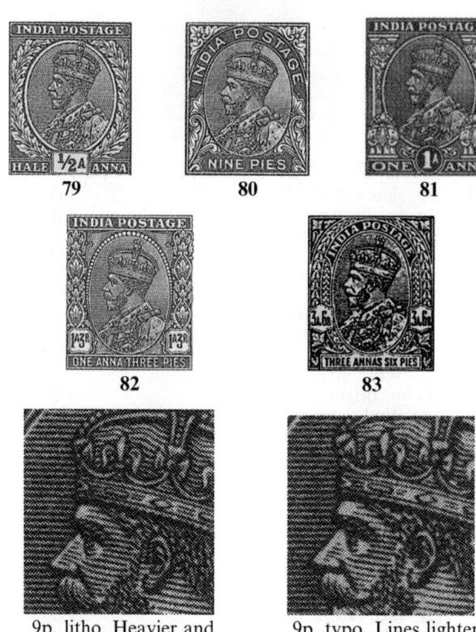
79 80 81

82 83

9p. litho. Heavier and longer lines on face. King's nose often shows 6 horizontal lines and always has lowest line long and thin

9p. typo. Lines lighter and shorter. Always 5 lines on King's nose with the lowest short and thick

(T **82/3** des T. I. Archer. 9p. litho or typo; 1a.3p, 3a.6p. litho; others typo)

1932–36. W **69**. P 14.

232	**79**	½a. green (1934)	4·00	10
		w. Wmk inverted	—	75
233	**80**	9p. deep green (*litho*) (22.4.32)	1·75	10
		aw. Wmk inverted	2·50	70
233*b*		9p. deep green (*typo*) (27.8.34)	2·00	10
234	**81**	1a. chocolate (1934)	4·50	10
		w. Wmk inverted	—	70
235	**82**	1a.3p. mauve (22.4.32)	60	10
		w. Wmk inverted	60	30
236	**70**	2a. vermilion	9·50	4·00
		aw. Wmk inverted	10·00	6·50
236*b*	**59**	2a. vermilion (1934)	3·75	50
		bw. Wmk inverted	—	15·00
236*c*		2a. vermilion (*small die*) (1936)	4·75	30
		cw. Wmk inverted	—	6·50
237	**62**	3a. carmine	6·00	10
		w. Wmk inverted	—	1·50
238	**83**	3a.6p. ultramarine (22.4.32)	4·00	20
		w. Wmk inverted	4·00	30
239	**64**	6a. bistre (1935)	7·00	1·50
		w. Wmk inverted	—	13·00
232/9 *Set of* 9			35·00	5·50

No. 236*b* measures 19 × 22.6 mm and No. 236*c* 18.4 × 21.8 mm.

84 Gateway of India, Bombay

"Bird" flaw (R. 9/3)

1935 (6 May). *Silver Jubilee. T* **84** *and similar horiz designs. Litho.* W **69** (sideways*). P 13½ × 14.

240	½a. black and yellow-green	85	20
	w. Wmk stars pointing left	75	15
241	9p. black and grey-green	50	20
	w. Wmk stars pointing left	50	30
242	1a. black and brown	1·25	20
	w. Wmk stars pointing left	60	10
243	1¼a. black and bright violet	50	10
	w. Wmk stars pointing left	90	15
244	2½a. black and orange	2·50	1·60
	w. Wmk stars pointing left	1·75	1·00
245	3½a. black and dull ultramarine	3·75	4·00
	a. "Bird" flaw	£130	90·00
	w. Wmk stars pointing left	4·25	4·00
246	8a. black and purple	3·50	3·25
	w. Wmk stars pointing left	5·50	3·75
240/6 *Set of* 7		10·00	8·00

Designs:—9p. Victoria Memorial, Calcutta; 1a. Rameswaram Temple, Madras; 1¼a. Jain Temple, Calcutta; 2½a. Taj Mahal, Agra; 3½a. Golden Temple, Amritsar; 8a. Pagoda in Mandalay.

*The normal sideways watermark shows the stars pointing to the right, *as seen from the back of the stamp.*

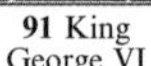

91 King George VI

92 Dak Runner

93 King George VI

1937 (23 Aug)–**40**. *Typo* W **69**. P $13\frac{1}{2} \times 14$ or $14 \times 13\frac{1}{2}$ (T **93**).

No.	Type	Description	Unused	Used
247	**91**	3p. slate (15.12.37)	1·00	10
248		$\frac{1}{2}$a. red-brown (15.12.37)	4·00	10
		w. Wmk inverted		
249		9p. green	8·00	20
		w. Wmk inverted		
250		1a. carmine	1·25	10
		a. *Tête-bêche* (vert pair) (1940)	2·50	1·75
		w. Wmk inverted (from booklets)	1·50	1·50
251	**92**	2a. vermilion (15.12.37)	4·75	30
		w. Wmk inverted		
252	–	2a.6p. bright violet (15.12.37)	1·25	20
		w. Wmk inverted		
253	–	3a. yellow-green (15.12.37)	6·00	30
		w. Wmk inverted		
254	–	3a.6p. bright blue (15.12.37)	3·25	50
		w. Wmk inverted		
255	–	4a. brown (15.12.37)	13·00	20
		w. Wmk inverted	—	20·00
256	–	6a. turquoise-green (15.12.37)	14·00	80
257	–	8a. slate-violet (15.12.37)	7·50	50
		w. Wmk inverted		
258	–	12a. lake (15.12.37)	18·00	1·10
		w. Wmk inverted		
259	**93**	1r. grey and red-brown (15.12.37)	1·25	15
		w. Wmk inverted		
260		2r. purple and brown (15.12.37)	4·25	30
		w. Wmk inverted	25·00	
261		5r. green and blue (15.12.37)	22·00	50
		w. Wmk inverted	45·00	
262		10r. purple and claret (15.12.37)	17·00	80
		w. Wmk inverted	†	50·00
263		15r. brown and green (15.12.37)	70·00	60·00
		w. Wmk inverted	£110	90·00
264		25r. slate-violet and purple (15.12.37)	£100	18·00
		w. Wmk inverted	—	£100
247/64		*Set of* 18	£250	75·00

Designs: *Horiz as T* **92**—2a.6p. Dak bullock cart; 3a. Dak tonga; 3a.6p. Dak camel; 4a. Mail train; 6a. *Strathnaver* (liner); 8a. Post truck; 12a. Armstrong Whitworth AW.27 Ensign I mail plane (small head).

No. 250a comes from surplus booklet sheets issued as normal stock following the rise in postal rates.

100a King George VI

101 King George VI

102 King George VI

103 Armstrong Whitworth A.W.27 Ensign I Mail Plane (large head)

(T **100a**/**102** des T. I. Archer. Typo ($1\frac{1}{2}$a. on 3a. litho also))

1940–43. W **69**. P $13\frac{1}{2} \times 14$.

No.	Type	Description	Unused	Used
265	**100a**	3p. slate	30	10
		w. Wmk inverted	15·00	
266		$\frac{1}{2}$a. purple (1.10.42)	1·00	10
		w. Wmk inverted	—	12·00
267		9p. green	1·00	10
		w. Wmk inverted	—	15·00
268		1a. carmine (1.4.43)	1·00	10
		w. Wmk inverted		
269	**101**	1a.3p. yellow-brown	1·00	10
		aw. Wmk inverted		
269*b*		$1\frac{1}{2}$a. dull violet (9.42)	1·25	10
		bw. Wmk inverted		
270		2a. vermilion	1·50	10
		w. Wmk inverted		
271		3a. bright violet (1942)	3·25	10
		w. Wmk inverted	—	10·00
272		$3\frac{1}{2}$a. bright blue	1·00	50
		w. Wmk inverted		
273	**102**	4a. brown	1·00	10
		w. Wmk inverted		
274		6a. turquoise-green	3·50	10
		w. Wmk inverted	†	32·00
275		8a. slate-violet	1·50	30
		w. Wmk inverted		
276		12a. lake	3·50	60
277	**103**	14a. purple (15.10.40)	18·00	1·40
265/77		*Set of* 14	35·00	2·50

The $1\frac{1}{2}$a. and 3a. were at first printed by lithography and were of finer execution and without Jubilee lines in the sheet margins. The two values exist with watermark inverted from both processes.

105 "Victory" and King George VI

3 PIES
(**106**)

1946 (2 Jan). *Victory. Litho.* W **69**. P 13.

No.	Type	Description	Unused	Used
278	**105**	9p. yellow-green (8.2.46)	50	1·00
279		$1\frac{1}{2}$a. dull violet	30	30
		w. Wmk inverted	—	20·00
280		$3\frac{1}{2}$a. bright blue	85	75
281		12a. claret (8.2.46)	1·50	1·00
278/81		*Set of* 4	2·75	2·75

1946 (8 Aug). *Surch with T* **106**.

No.	Type	Description	Unused	Used
282	**101**	3p. on 1a.3p. yellow-brown	10	15

DOMINION

301 Asokan Capital (Inscr reads "Long Live India")

302 Indian National Flag

303 Douglas DC-4

(Des T. I. Archer. Litho)

1947 (21 Nov–15 Dec). *Independence.* W **69**. P $14 \times 13\frac{1}{2}$ ($1\frac{1}{2}$a.) or $13\frac{1}{2} \times 14$ (others).

No.	Type	Description	Unused	Used
301	**301**	$1\frac{1}{2}$a. grey-green (15 Dec)	15	10
302	**302**	$3\frac{1}{2}$a. orange-red, blue and green	1·00	2·00
		w. Wmk inverted	8·50	8·50
303	**303**	12a. ultramarine (15 Dec)	1·50	2·50
301/3		*Set of* 3	2·40	4·00

304 Lockheed Constellation

(Des T. I. Archer. Litho)

1948 (29 May). *Air. Inauguration of India–U.K. Air Service.* W **69**. P $13\frac{1}{2} \times 14$.

No.	Type	Description	Unused	Used
304	**304**	12a. black and ultramarine	1·25	3·00

305 Mahatma Gandhi

306 Mahatma Gandhi

(Photo Courvoisier)

1948 (15 Aug). *First Anniv of Independence.* P $11\frac{1}{2}$.

No.	Type	Description	Unused	Used
305	**305**	$1\frac{1}{2}$a. brown	2·50	60
306		$3\frac{1}{2}$a. violet	4·25	2·50
307		12a. grey-green	6·00	1·50
308	**306**	10r. purple-brown and lake	45·00	40·00
305/8		*Set of* 4	50·00	40·00

307 Ajanta Panel

308 Konarak Horse

309 Trimurti

310 Bodhisattva

311 Nataraja

312 Sanchi Stupa, East Gate

313 Bodh Gaya Temple

314 Bhuvanesvara

315 Gol Gumbad, Bijapur

316 Kandarya Mahadeva Temple

317 Golden Temple, Amritsar

318 Victory Tower, Chittorgarh

319 Red Fort, Delhi

320 Taj Mahal, Agra

321 Qutb Minar, Delhi

322 Satrunjaya Temple, Palitana

(Des T. I. Archer and I. M. Das. Typo (low values), litho (rup[ee] values))

1949 (15 Aug). W **69** (sideways* on 6p., 1r. and 10r.). P 14 (3p. [to] 2a.), $13\frac{1}{2}$ (3a. to 12a.), $14 \times 13\frac{1}{2}$ (1r. and 10r.), $13\frac{1}{2} \times 14$ (2r. a[nd] 5r.), 13 (15r.).

No.	Type	Description	Unused	Used
309	**307**	3p. slate-violet	15	
		w. Wmk inverted		
310	**308**	6p. purple-brown	25	
		w. Wmk star pointing right	4·00	1
311	**309**	9p. yellow-green	40	
312	**310**	1a. turquoise	60	
		w. Wmk inverted		
313	**311**	2a. carmine	80	
		w. Wmk inverted	15·00	1
314	**312**	3a. brown-orange	1·50	
315	**313**	$3\frac{1}{2}$a. bright blue	1·50	3
316	**314**	4a. lake	4·00	
		w. Wmk inverted	18·00	1
317	**315**	6a. violet	1·50	
		w. Wmk inverted	3·00	
318	**316**	8a. turquoise-green	1·50	
		w. Wmk inverted	—	50
319	**317**	12a. dull blue	1·50	
		w. Wmk inverted	9·50	1
320	**318**	1r. dull violet and green	9·00	
		w. Wmk star pointing left	25·00	1
321	**319**	2r. claret and violet	10·00	
		w. Wmk inverted	40·00	1
322	**320**	5r. blue-green and red-brown	28·00	1
		w. Wmk inverted	65·00	2
323	**321**	10r. purple-brown and deep blue	48·00	7
		a. Purple-brown and blue	95·00	4
		aw. Wmk star pointing left	£150	
324	**322**	15r. brown and claret	16·00	19
309/24		*Set of* 16	£110	26

*The normal sideways watermark has the star pointing to the [...] on the 6p. value and to the right on the 1r. and 10r. (323*a*) w[hen] *seen from the back of the stamp.*

For T **310** with statue reversed see No. 333.

323 Globe and Asokan Capital

949 (10 Oct). *75th Anniv of U.P.U. Litho.* W **69**. P 13.
25 **323** 9p. green . . . . . 1·00 2·75
26 2a. rose . . . . . 1·00 2·50
27 3½a. bright blue . . . . . 1·50 2·50
28 12a. brown-purple . . . . . 2·00 2·50
25/8 *Set of* 4 . . . . . 5·00 9·25

REPUBLIC

324 Rejoicing Crowds

328 As T **310**, but statue reversed

(Des D. J. Keymer & Co. Litho)

950 (26 Jan). *Inauguration of Republic. T* **324** *and similar designs.* W **69** (sideways on 3½a.). P 13.
29 2a. scarlet . . . . . 1·25 50
w. Wmk inverted . . . . . 19·00 2·25
30 3½a. ultramarine . . . . . 1·75 3·00
31 4a. violet . . . . . 1·75 1·00
32 12a. maroon . . . . . 3·50 2·25
w. Wmk inverted . . . . . 21·00 6·00
29/32 *Set of* 4 . . . . . 7·50 6·00
Designs: *Vert*—3½a. Quill, ink-well and verse. *Horiz*—4a. Ear of orn and plough; 12a. Spinning-wheel and cloth.

950 (15 July)–**51**. *Typo.* W **69**. P 14 (1a.), 13½ (others).
33 **328** 1a. turquoise . . . . . 3·50 10
aw. Wmk inverted . . . . .
33*b* **313** 2½a. lake (30.4.51) . . . . . 3·00 3·25
33*c* **314** 4a. bright blue (30.4.51) . . . . . 6·00 10
33/*c* *Set of* 3 . . . . . 11·00 3·25

329 *Stegodon ganesa*

330 Torch

51 (13 Jan). *Centenary of Geological Survey of India. Litho.* W **69**. P 13.
4 **329** 2a. black and claret . . . . . 2·00 1·00

51 (4 Mar). *First Asian Games, New Delhi. Litho.* W **69** (sideways). P 14.
5 **330** 2a. reddish purple & brn-orge . . . 1·00 65
6 12a. chocolate and light blue . . . . 4·00 1·75

STAMP BOOKLETS

04. *Black on green (No. SB1) or black on pink (No. SB2) covers. Stapled.*
1 12½a. booklet containing twenty-four ½a. (No. 121) in blocks of 6 . . . . . £900
2 12½a. booklet containing twelve 1a. (No. 123) in blocks of 6 . . . . . £900

06–11. *Black on green (No. SB3), black on pink (No. SB4) or black on green and pink (No. SB5) match book type covers inscr* "Post Office of India" *and royal cypher of King Edward VII. Stapled.*
3 1r. booklet containing thirty-two ½a. (No. 149) in blocks of 4 . . . . . £475
a. Without "Post Office of India" inscr £425
b. Ditto and showing royal cypher of King George V (1911) £400
4 1r. booklet containing sixteen 1a. (No. 150) in blocks of 4 (1907) £425
a. Without "Post Office of India" inscr £375
b. Ditto and showing royal cypher of King George V (1911) £400
5 1r. booklet containing sixteen ½a. and eight 1a. (Nos. 149/50) in blocks of 4 (1907) £950
a. Without "Post Office of India" inscr £850
b. Ditto and showing royal cypher of King George V (1911) £800

12–22. *Black on green (Nos. SB6/7, SB12), black on pink (No. SB8), black on green and pink (No. SB9), black on purple (No. SB10) or black on blue (No. SB11) match book type covers with foreign postage rates on back. Stapled.*
6 1r. booklet containing sixty-four 3p. (No. 152) in blocks of 4 (blank back cover) £500
7 1r. booklet containing thirty-two ½a. (No. 155) in blocks of 4 . . . . . £190
a. Blank back cover £190
b. Advertisement contractor's notice on back cover £275
c. Advertisement on back (1922) £275

SB 8 1r. booklet containing sixteen 1a. (No. 159) in blocks of 4 . . . . . £150
a. Blank back cover £150
b. Advertisements on front flap and back cover (1922) £180
SB 9 1r. booklet containing sixteen ½a. and eight 1a. (Nos. 155, 159) in blocks of 4 (blank back cover) £140
a. Advertisement on back £150
SB10 1r.8a. booklet containing sixteen 1½a. (No. 163) in blocks of 4 (1919) £350
a. Blank back cover (1921) £350
SB11 2r. booklet containing sixteen 2a. (No. 169) in blocks of 4 (blank back cover) (1921) £425
a. Black on purple cover with postage rates on back (1922) £425
SB12 2r. booklet containing sixteen 2a. (No. 166) in blocks of 4 (1922) £425
a. Black on purple cover £425

1921. *Black on buff match book type cover. Stapled.*
SB13 1r.2a. booklet containing twenty-four 9p. on 1a. (No. 192) in blocks of 4 . . . . . £110

1922. *Black on brown (No. SB14) or black on green and pink (No. SB15) match book type covers with foreign postage rates on back. Stapled.*
SB14 1r. booklet containing sixteen 1a. (No. 197) in blocks of 4 . . . . . £225
a. Advertisement on back £225
b. Advertisements on front flap and back cover . . . . .
c. Black on lilac cover with blank back £225
ca. Advertisements on front flap and back cover £300
d. Black on pink cover with blank back £275
SB15 1r. booklet containing sixteen ½a. and eight 1a. (Nos. 155, 197) in blocks of 4 (blank back cover) £450

1926–28. *Black on brown (No. SB16) or black on purple (No. SB17) match book type covers with foreign postage rates on back. Stapled.*
SB16 1r. booklet containing sixteen 1a. (No. 203) in blocks of 4 . . . . . 90·00
SB17 2r. booklet containing sixteen 2a. (No. 205) in blocks of 4 . . . . . £300
a. Containing No. 206 (1928) £350

1929. *Black on brown (No. SB18) or black on purple (No. SB19) separate leaf covers. Stitched.*
SB18 1r. booklet containing sixteen 1a. (No. 203) in blocks of 4 (blank back cover) . . . . . 90·00
a. Advertisement contractor's notice on back cover . . . . . 90·00
b. Advertisements on front flap and back cover £110
c. Advertisement on back cover £110
SB19 2r. booklet containing sixteen 2a. (No. 205) in blocks of 4 (foreign postage rates on back cover) £325
a. Advertisement contractor's notice on back cover £325
b. Containing No. 206 (foreign postage rates on back cover) £375
ba. Advertisement contractor's notice on back cover £375

1932. *Black on brown cover. Stitched.*
SB20 1r.4a. booklet containing sixteen 1¼a. (No. 235) in blocks of 4 . . . . . £300

1934. *Black on buff cover. Stitched.*
SB21 1r. booklet containing sixteen 1a. (No. 234) in blocks of 4 . . . . . £160

1937. *Black on red cover. Stamps with wmk upright or inverted. Stitched.*
SB22 1r. booklet containing sixteen 1a. (No. 250) in blocks of 4 . . . . . £225

OFFICIAL STAMPS

Stamps overprinted "POSTAL SERVICE" or "I.P.N." were not used as postage stamps, and are therefore omitted.

Service.
(O 1)

(Optd by the Military Orphanage Press, Calcutta)

1866 (1 Aug)–**72**. *Optd with Type* O **1**. P 14.

(a) No wmk.
O 1 **11** ½a. blue . . . . . — £250
O 2 ½a. pale blue £1000 £130
a. Opt inverted . . . . .
O 3 1a. brown . . . . . — £160
O 4 1a. deep brown . . . . . — £130
O 5 8a. carmine . . . . . 21·00 50·00

(b) Wmk Elephant's Head, T **13**.
O 6 **11** ½a. blue . . . . . £225 22·00
w. Wmk inverted . . . . . † £130
O 7 ½a. pale blue . . . . . £225 12·00
a. Opt inverted . . . . .
b. No dot on "i" (No. 50 on pane) . . . . . — £250
c. No stop (No. 77 on pane) . . . . — £200
O 8 **12** 8p. purple (1.72) . . . . . 20·00 50·00
a. No dot on "i" £225 £300
b. No stop £225
O 9 **11** 1a. brown . . . . . £200 15·00
O10 1a. deep brown . . . . . £200 38·00
a. No dot on "i" . . . . . — £425
b. No stop . . . . . — £350
O11 2a. orange . . . . . £170 80·00
O12 2a. yellow . . . . . £170 80·00
a. Opt inverted . . . . .
b. Imperf . . . . .
w. Wmk inverted £250
y. Wmk inverted and reversed . . . † £300

O13 4a. green . . . . . £190 75·00
a. Opt inverted . . . . .
O14 **17** 4a. green (Die I) £950 £250
A variety with wide and more open capital "S" occurs six times in sheets of all values except No. O8. Price four times the normal.
Reprints exist of Nos. O6, O9 and O14; the latter is Die II instead of Die I.
Reprints of the overprint have also been made, in different setting, on the 8 pies, purple, no watermark.

O 2

O 6

O 3

O 4

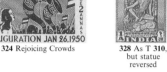

(No. O15 surch at Calcutta, others optd at Madras)

1866 (Oct). *Fiscal stamps, Nos. O15/18 with top and bottom inscrs removed, surch or optd.* Wmk Crown over "INDIA".

(a) Surch as in Type O **2**. *Thick blue glazed paper.* Imperf × perf 14.
O15 O **2** 2a. purple £275 £225

(b) Optd "SERVICE POSTAGE" *in two lines as in Types* O **3/4** *and similar type.* Imperf × perf 14.
O16 O **3** 2a. purple (G.) £800 £400
O17 O **4** 4a. purple (G.) £3250 £1100
O18 – 8a. purple (G.) £3750 £3750
a. Optd on complete stamp (inscr "FOREIGN BILL") . . . . . † £9500

(c) Optd "SERVICE POSTAGE" *in semi-circle.* Wmk Large Crown. P 15½ × 15.
O19 O **6** ½a. mauve/*lilac* (G.) . . . . . £400 85·00
a. Opt double £2750
So-called reprints of Nos. O15 to O18 are known, but in these the surcharge differs entirely in the spacing, etc., of the words; they are more properly described as Government imitations. The imitations of No. O15 have surcharge in *black* or in *green*. No. O19 exists with reprinted overprint which has a full stop after "POSTAGE".

PRINTERS. The following stamps up to No. O108 were overprinted by De La Rue and thereafter Official stamps were printed or overprinted by the Security Printing Press at Nasik.

Service. (O 7)

On H. M. S. (O 8)

On H. M. S. (O 9)

1867–73. *Optd with Type* O **7**. Wmk Elephant's Head, T **13**. P 14.
O20 **11** ½a. blue (Die I) . . . . . 35·00 50
w. Wmk inverted . . . . . † 80·00
O21 ½a. pale blue (Die I) . . . . . 42·00 2·00
O22 ½a. blue (Die II) (1873) . . . . . £150 70·00
O23 1a. brown . . . . . 40·00 50
w. Wmk inverted . . . . . † 95·00
O24 1a. deep brown . . . . . 42·00 2·25
O25 1a. chocolate . . . . . 48·00 2·25
O26 2a. yellow . . . . . 22·00 2·50
O27 2a. orange . . . . . 5·00 2·25
O28 **17** 4a. pale green (Die I) . . . . . 16·00 2·00
O29 4a. green (Die I) . . . . . 3·00 1·50
O30 **11** 8a. rose (Die II) (1868) . . . . . 3·25 1·50
O30*a* 8a. pale rose (Die II) . . . . . 3·25 1·50
aw. Wmk inverted . . . . . 35·00 24·00

Prepared for use, but not issued.
O30*b* **18** 6a.8p. slate £275

1874–82. *Optd with Type* O **8**.

(a) In black.
O31 **11** ½a. blue (Die II) . . . . . 11·00 20
O32 1a. brown . . . . . 16·00 20
O33 2a. yellow . . . . . 55·00 32·00
O33*a* 2a. orange . . . . . 45·00 21·00
O34 **17** 4a. green (Die I) . . . . . 16·00 3·00
O35 **11** 8a. rose (Die II) . . . . . 7·50 5·00

(b) Optd in blue-black.
O36 **11** ½a. blue (Die II) (1877) . . . . . £300 42·00
O37 1a. brown (1882) £500 £120

1883–99. Wmk Star, T **34**. *Optd with Type* O **9**. P 14.
O37*a* **40** 3p. aniline carmine (1899) 20 10
O38 **23** ½a. deep blue-green . . . . . 1·75 10
a. Opt double . . . . . † £1100
O39 ½a. blue-green . . . . . 1·50 10

No.	Type	Description	Unused	Used
O40	**25**	1a. brown-purple	2·75	50
		a. Opt inverted	£350	£450
		aw. Wmk inverted	†	£550
		b. Opt double	†	£1200
		c. Opt omitted (in horiz pair with normal)	£1500	
O41		1a. plum	75	10
O42	**27**	2a. pale blue	6·00	60
O43		2a. blue	7·00	60
O44	**29**	4a. olive-green	18·00	50
O44*a*		4a. slate-green	18·00	50
O45	**31**	8a. dull mauve	19·00	1·25
O46		8a. magenta	9·00	50
O47	**37**	1r. green and rose (1892)	45·00	4·50
O48		1r. green and carmine (1892)	15·00	40
O37*a*/48 *Set of* 7			45·00	2·00

1900. *Colours changed. Optd with Type* O **9**.

No.	Type	Description	Unused	Used
O49	**23**	½a. pale yellow-green	2·00	90
O49*a*		½a. yellow-green	3·50	50
		ab. Opt double	£900	
O50	**25**	1a. carmine	3·00	10
		a. Opt inverted	†	£1300
		b. Opt double	†	£1400
O51	**27**	2a. pale violet	35·00	1·50
O52		2a. mauve	42·00	50
O49/52 *Set of* 3			35·00	1·00

1902–09. *Stamps of King Edward VII optd with Type* O **9**.

No.	Type	Description	Unused	Used
O54	**41**	3p. grey (1903)	2·50	75
O55		3p. slate-grey (1905)	2·50	75
		a. No stop after "M" (R. 6/10)	£180	£120
O56	**42**	½a. green	1·25	30
O57	**43**	1a. carmine	1·00	10
O58	**44**	2a. violet	4·50	40
O59		2a. mauve	3·25	10
O60	**47**	4a. olive	12·00	30
O61		4a. pale olive	12·00	30
O62	**48**	6a. olive-bistre (1909)	1·50	15
O63	**49**	8a. purple (*shades*)	6·00	1·00
O64		8a. claret	8·00	85
O65	**51**	1r. green and carmine (1905)	4·00	80
O54/65 *Set of* 8			28·00	3·00

1906. *New types. Optd with Type* O **9**.

No.	Type	Description	Unused	Used
O66	**53**	½a. green	1·25	10
		a. No stop after "M" (R. 6/10)	£110	50·00
O67	**54**	1a. carmine	2·00	10
		a. No stop after "M" (R. 6/10)	£170	80·00
		b. Opt albino (in pair with normal)	£1000	

On

H. S.

M.

(O9*a*)

1909. *Optd with Type* O **9a**.

No.	Type	Description	Unused	Used
O68	**52**	2r. carmine and yellow-brown	8·50	1·50
O68*a*		2r. rose-red and yellow-brown	8·50	1·50
O69		5r. ultramarine and violet	14·00	1·50
O70		10r. green and carmine	28·00	15·00
O70*a*		10r. green and scarlet	65·00	7·00
O71		15r. blue and olive-brown	60·00	40·00
O72		25r. brownish orange and blue	£140	60·00
O68/72 *Set of* 5			£225	£100

NINE

SERVICE (O **10**) (14 mm) SERVICE (O **11**) (21½ mm) PIES (O **12**)

1912–13. *Stamps of King George V (wmk Single Star, T* **34**) *optd with Type* O **10** *or* O **11** *(rupee values).*

No.	Type	Description	Unused	Used
O73	**55**	3p. grey	40	10
O73*a*		3p. pale grey	30	10
O74		3p. bluish grey	75	10
		a. Opt omitted (in pair with normal)		
O75		3p. slate	50	30
		a. "Rs" Flaw		
O75*b*		3p. violet-grey	3·25	30
O76	**56**	½a. light green	50	10
O77		½a. emerald	50	15
O78		½a. bright-green	50	15
		a. Opt double	£100	
O80	**57**	1a. rose-carmine	1·00	10
O81		1a. carmine	1·60	10
O82		1a. aniline carmine	1·60	10
		a. Opt double	†	£900
O83	**59**	2a. purple	75	30
O83*a*		2a. reddish purple	75	25
O84		2a. deep mauve	75	30
O84*a*		2a. bright reddish violet	2·50	25
O85	**63**	4a. deep olive	1·00	10
O86		4a. olive-green	1·00	10
O87	**64**	6a. yellow-bistre	1·50	2·50
O88		6a. brown-ochre	3·50	4·25
O89	**65**	8a. deep magenta	2·50	1·25
O89*a*		8a. deep mauve	2·50	1·25
O90		8a. bright mauve	17·00	3·25
O91	**67**	1r. red-brown and deep blue-grn (1913)	3·25	1·75
O91*a*		1r. brown and green	2·50	1·40
O92		2r. rose-carmine & brown (1913)	3·75	6·00
O93		5r. ultramarine and violet (1913)	16·00	22·00
O94		10r. green and scarlet (1913)	50·00	50·00
O95		15r. blue and olive (1913)	90·00	£100
O96		25r. orange and blue (1913)	£200	£160
O73/96 *Set of* 13			£325	£300

1921. *No. O80 surch with Type* O **12**.

No.	Type	Description	Unused	Used
O97	**57**	9p. on 1a. rose-carmine	1·25	75

1922. *No. 197 optd with Type* O **10**.

No.	Type	Description	Unused	Used
O98	**57**	1a. chocolate	1·75	10

ONE
RUPEE

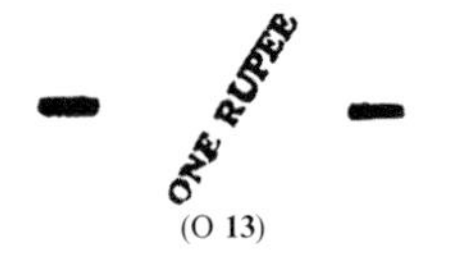

(O **13**) (O **14**)

1925. *Official stamps surcharged.*

(a) Issue of 1909, as Type O **13**.

No.	Type	Description	Unused	Used
O 99	**52**	1r. on 15r. blue and olive	4·25	4·00
O100		1r. on 25r. chestnut and blue	20·00	70·00
O101		2r. on 10r. green and scarlet	3·75	4·25
O101*a*		2r. on 10r. green and carmine	£200	50·00

(b) Issue of 1912 with Type O **14**.

No.	Type	Description	Unused	Used
O102	**67**	1r.on 15r. blue and olive	19·00	75·00
O103		1r.on 25r. orange and blue	5·50	11·00
		a. Surch inverted	£700	

(c) Issue of 1912, as Type O **13**.

No.	Type	Description	Unused	Used
O104	**67**	2r. on 10r. green and scarlet	£800	

Examples of the above showing other surcharge errors are believed to be of clandestine origin.

SERVICE

ONE ANNA (O **15**)

ONE ANNA (O **16**)

1926. *No. O62 surch with Type* O **15**.

No.	Type	Description	Unused	Used
O105	**48**	1a. on 6a. olive-bistre	30	30

1926. *Postage stamps of 1911–22 (wmk Single Star), surch as Type* O **16**.

No.	Type	Description	Unused	Used
O106	**58**	1a.on 1½a. chocolate (A)	20	10
O107		1a.on 1½a. chocolate (B)	2·50	4·50
		a. Error. On 1a. chocolate (197)	£160	
O108	**61**	1a.on 2a.6p. ultramarine	60	80

The surcharge on No. O108 has no bars at top.

Examples of Nos. O106/7 with inverted or double surcharges are believed to be of clandestine origin.

SERVICE (O **17**) (13½ mm) SERVICE (O **18**) (19½ mm)

1926–31. *Stamps of King George V (wmk Multiple Star, T* **69**) *optd with Types* O **17** *or* O **18** *(rupee values).*

No.	Type	Description	Unused	Used
O109	**55**	3p. slate (1.10.29)	15	10
		w. Wmk inverted	2·00	60
O110	**56**	½a. green (1931)	7·50	60
		w. Wmk inverted	—	1·75
O111	**57**	1a. chocolate	15	10
		w. Wmk inverted	2·00	60
O112	**70**	2a. purple	30	10
		w. Wmk inverted	1·75	50
O113	**71**	4a. sage-green	50	20
		w. Wmk inverted	2·25	80
O115	**65**	8a. reddish purple	1·25	10
		w. Wmk inverted	80	30
O116	**66**	12a. claret (1927)	70	2·50
		w. Wmk inverted	—	3·75
O117	**67**	1r. chocolate and green (1930)	3·50	1·00
		w. Wmk inverted	3·25	2·25
O118		2r. carmine and orange (1930)	8·00	8·50
		w. Wmk inverted	—	14·00
O120		10r. green and scarlet (1931)	75·00	48·00
O109/20 *Set of* 10			85·00	55·00

1930. *As No. O111, but optd as Type* O **10** *(14 mm).*

No.	Type	Description	Unused	Used
O125	**57**	1a. chocolate	—	5·00
		w. Wmk inverted	90·00	5·50

1932–36. *Stamps of King George V (wmk Mult Star, T* **69**) *optd with Type* O **17**.

No.	Type	Description	Unused	Used
O126	**79**	½a. green (1935)	1·00	10
O127	**80**	9p. deep green (*litho*)	30	15
		aw. Wmk inverted		
O127*b*		9p. deep green (*typo*)	1·50	15
O127*c*	**81**	1a. chocolate (1936)	2·50	10
		cw. Wmk inverted	4·00	60
O128	**82**	1a.3p. mauve	30	10
		w. Wmk inverted	60	40
O129	**70**	2a. vermilion	1·00	2·50
		w. Wmk inverted		
O130	**59**	2a. vermilion (1935)	2·75	1·25
O130*a*		2a. verm (*small die*) (1936)	1·25	10
		aw. Wmk inverted		
O131	**61**	2a.6p. orange (22.4.32)	50	10
		w. Wmk inverted	2·00	90
O132	**63**	4a. sage-green (1935)	1·50	10
		w. Wmk inverted		
O133	**64**	6a. bistre (1936)	21·00	10·00
O126/33 *Set of* 9			26·00	11·00

1937–39. *Stamps of King George VI optd as Types* O **17** *or* O **1**[8] *(rupee values).*

No.	Type	Description	Unused	Used
O135	**91**	½a. red-brown (1938)	17·00	7
O136		9p. green (1937)	19·00	8
O137		1a. carmine (1937)	3·50	1
O138	**93**	1r. grey and red-brown (5.38)	50	5
O139		2r. purple and brown (5.38)	1·75	2·5
		w. Wmk inverted	—	25·0
O140		5r. green and blue (10.38)	3·50	6·5
		w. Wmk inverted		
O141		10r. purple and claret (1939)	14·00	6·5
O135/41 *Set of* 7			55·00	16·0

(O **19**)

O **20**

1939 (May). *Stamp of King George V, surch with Type* O **19**.

No.	Type	Description	Unused	Used
O142	**82**	1a.on 1¼a. mauve	12·00	2
		w. Wmk inverted		

(Des T. I. Archer)

1939 (1 June)–**42**. *Typo.* W **69**. P 14.

No.	Type	Description	Unused	Used
O143	O **20**	3p. slate	50	1
O144		½a. red-brown	5·00	1
O144*a*		½a. purple (1942)	30	1
O145		9p. green	30	
O146		1a. carmine	30	
O146*a*		1a.3p. yellow-brown (1941)	3·25	
		aw. Wmk inverted		
O146*b*		1½a. dull violet (1942)	65	
		bw. Wmk inverted		
O147		2a. vermilion	60	
		w. Wmk inverted		
O148		2½a. bright violet	60	1·
O149		4a. brown	60	
O150		8a. slate-violet	90	
O143/50 *Set of* 11			11·50	1·7

1948 (15 Aug). *First Anniv of Independence. Nos. 305/8 optd* [as] *Type* O **17**.

No.	Type	Description	Unused	Used
O150*a*	**305**	1½a. brown	42·00	32·
O150*b*		3½a. violet	£750	£4
O150*c*		12a. grey-green	£2000	£18
O150*d*	**306**	10r. purple-brown and lake	£12000	

Nos. O150*a/d* were only issued to the Governor-Genera[l's] Secretariat.

O **21** Asokan Capital

O **22**

(Des T.I. Archer)

1950 (2 Jan)–**51**. *Typo (*O **21***) or litho (*O **22***).* W **69**. P 14.

No.	Type	Description	Unused	Used
O151	O **21**	3p. slate-violet (1.7.50)	15	
O152		6p. purple-brown (1.7.50)	30	
O153		9p. green (1.7.50)	1·25	
O154		1a. turquoise (1.7.50)	1·25	
O155		2a. carmine (1.7.50)	1·75	
		w. Wmk inverted		
O156		3a. red-orange (1.7.50)	4·00	2·
O157		4a. lake (1.7.50)	5·50	
O158		4a. ultramarine (1.10.51)	50	
O159		6a. bright violet (1.7.50)	4·00	
O160		8a. red-brown (1.7.50)	2·00	
		w. Wmk inverted	14·00	
O161	O **22**	1r. violet	3·00	
		w. Wmk inverted		
O162		2r. rose-carmine	1·00	
O163		5r. bluish green	2·00	2
O164		10r. reddish brown	3·00	20
O151/64 *Set of* 14			27·00	23

INDIA USED ABROAD

In the years following 1858 the influence of the Indian Emp[ire], political, military and economic, extended beyond its borders i[nto] neighbouring states, the Arabian Gulf, East Africa and the Far Ea[st]. Such influence often led to the establishment of Indian civil p[ost] offices in the countries concerned where unoverprinted stamps [of] India were used.

Such offices operated in the following countries. An * indica[tes] that details will be found under that heading elsewhere in [the] catalogue.

ADEN*

Unoverprinted stamps of India used from 1854 until 1937.

BAHRAIN*

Unoverprinted stamps of India used from 1884 until 1933.

BRITISH EAST AFRICA (KENYA, UGANDA AND TANGANYIKA)*

Unoverprinted stamps of India used during August [and] September 1890.

FRENCH INDIAN SETTLEMENTS

The first Indian post office, at Chandernagore, was open in 1784 o be followed by offices in the other four Settlements. By an greement with the French, dating from 1814, these offices handled nail destined for British India, Great Britain, the British Empire nd most other foreign destinations except France and the French olonies. In later years the system was expanded by a number of ub-offices and it continued to operate until the French territories vere absorbed into India on 2 May 1950 (Chandernagore) or November 1954.

Chandernagore. Opened 1784. Used numeral cancellations "B86" or "86".
  Sub-offices:
    Gondalpara (opened 1906)
    Lakhiganj (opened 1909)
    Temata (opened 1891)
Karikal. Opened 1794. Used numeral cancellations in "C147", "147" or "6/M-21".
  Sub-offices:
    Ambagarattur (opened 1904)
    Kottuchari (opened 1901)
    Nedungaon (opened 1903)
    Puraiyar Road (opened 1901)
    Settur (opened 1905)
    Tirumalrayapatnam (opened 1875) – used numeral cancellation "6/M-21/1")
    Tiramilur (opened 1898)
Mahe. Opened 1795. Used numeral cancellations "C192" or "9/M-14".
Pondicherry. Opened 1787. Used numeral cancellations "C111", "111" (also used elsewhere), "6/M-19" (also used elsewhere) or "6/M-20".
  Sub-offices:
    Ariyankuppam (opened 1904)
    Bahoor (opened 1885)
    Mudaliarpet (opened 1897)
    Muthialpet (opened 1885)
    Pondicherry Bazaar (opened 1902)
    Pondicherry Railway Station (opened 1895)
    Olugarai (opened 1907)
    Vallinur (opened 1875) – used numeral cancellation "M-19/1"
    Yanam. Opened 1876. Used numeral cancellation "5/M-4".

IRAN

The British East India Company was active in the Arabian Gulf om the early years of the 17th century with their first factory rading centre) being established at Jask in 1619. After 1853 this mmercial presence was converted into a political arm of the dian Government culminating in the appointment of a Political esident to Bushire in 1862.

The first Indian post office in Iran (Persia) opened at Bushire on May 1864 with monthly mail services operating to the Resident ere and to the British Legation at Tehran. Further offices in the her Gulf ports followed, but, unless otherwise stated below, all ere closed on 1 April 1923.

Abadan. Opened 1917.
Ahwaz. Opened March 1915.
Bandar Abbas. Opened 1 April 1867. Used numeral cancellations "258", "22" or "I/K-5".
Bushire. Opened I May 1864. Used numeral cancellations "308", "26" (also used elsewhere) or "K-5".
Chabbar. Opened 20 August 1913.
Duzdab. Opened 1922. Closed 1927?
Henjam. Opened 21 June 1913.
Jask. Opened 1 September 1880.
Kuh-Malik-Siah-Ziarat. Opened January 1906. Closed 1924.
Linga. Opened 1 April 1867. Used numeral cancellations "21" or "2/K-5".
Moidan-i-Naphtan. Opened 1917.
Mirjawa. Opened January 1921. Closed 1930.
Mohammera. Opened 19 July 1892.

IRAQ*

Unoverprinted stamps of India used from 1868 until 1918.

KUWAIT*

Unoverprinted stamps of India used from 1904 until 1923.

MALAYA (STRAITS SETTLEMENTS)*

Unoverprinted stamps of India used from 1854 until 1867.

MUSCAT*

Unoverprinted stamps of India used from 1864 until 1947.

NEPAL

A post office was opened in the British Residency at Kathmandu 1816 following the end of the Gurkha War. Stamps of India were ed from 1854, initially with "B137", "137" or "C-37" numeral ncellations. The Residency Post Office continued to provide the erseas mail service after Nepal introduced its own issues in 1881. n 1920 the Residency Post Office became the British Legation st Office. On the independence of India in 1947 the service was nsferred to the Indian Embassy and continued to function until 55.

PORTUGUESE INDIA

A British post office was open in Damaun by 1823 and Indian mps were used there until November 1883, some with "13" and B-19" numeral cancellations.

No other British post offices were opened in the Portuguese ritories, but from 1854 Indian stamps were sold by the local post ces. Between 1871 and 1877 mail intended for, or passing ough, British India required combined franking of India and rtuguese India issues. After 1877 the two postal administrations epted the validity of each other's stamps.

SOMALILAND PROTECTORATE*

Unoverprinted stamps of India used from 1887 until 1903.

TIBET

The first Indian post office in Tibet accompanied the Tibetan Frontier Commission in 1903. The Younghusband Military Expedition to Lhasa in the following year operated a number of Field Post Offices which were replaced by civil post offices at Gartok (opened 23 September 1906), Gyantse (opened March 1905), Pharijong (opened 1905) and Yatung (opened 1905). All Indian post offices in Tibet closed on 1 April 1955 except Gartok which, it is believed, did not operate after 1943. A temporary post office, C-622, operated at Gyantse between July 1954 and August 1955 following a flood disaster.

TRUCIAL STATES

Unoverprinted stamps of India used at Dubai from 19 August 1909 until 1947.

ZANZIBAR

Unoverprinted stamps of India used from 1875 until 1895.

CHINA EXPEDITIONARY FORCE

Following the outbreak of the Boxer Rising in North China the Peking Legations were besieged by the rebels in June 1900. An international force, including an Indian Army division, was assembled for their relief. The Legations were relieved on 14 August 1900, but operations against the Boxers continued in North China with Allied garrisons at key cities and along the Peking–Tientsin–Shanhaikwan railway. The last Indian Army battalion, and accompanying Field Post Offices, did not leave North China until 1 November 1923.

Field Post Offices accompanied the Indian troops and commenced operations on 23 July 1900 using unoverprinted Indian postage and official stamps. The unoverprinted postage issues were replaced in mid-August by stamps overprinted "C.E.F." to prevent currency speculation. The use of unoverprinted official stamps continued as they were not valid for public postage.

PRICES FOR STAMPS ON COVER	
Nos. C1/10	*from* × 15
No. C10*c*	†
Nos. C11/22	*from* × 8
Nos. C23/34	*from* × 20

C. E. F.
(C 1)

Stamps of India overprinted with Type* C 1, *in black

1900 (16 Aug). *Stamps of Queen Victoria.*

C 1	**40**	3p. carmine	40	1·25
		a. No stop after "C" (R. 1/2)		
		b. No stop after "F"	£140	
		c. Opt double, one albino		
C 2	**23**	½a. blue-green	75	30
		a. Opt double		
		b. No stop after "F"	£140	
C 3	**25**	1a. plum	4·25	1·50
		a. No stop after "F"	£190	
C 4	**27**	2a. pale blue	3·00	9·00
		a. No stop after "F"	£190	
C 5	**36**	2a.6p. green	2·75	13·00
		a. No stop after "F"	£275	
C 6	**28**	3a. orange	2·75	16·00
		a. Opt double, one albino	£120	
		b. No stop after "F"	£275	
C 7	**29**	4a. olive-green	2·75	7·50
		a. Opt double, one albino	£120	
		b. No stop after "F"	£275	
C 8	**31**	8a. magenta	2·75	18·00
		a. No stop after "F"	£325	
		b. Opt double, one albino	£120	
C 9	**32**	12a. purple/*red*	16·00	16·00
		a. Opt double, one albino	£160	
		b. No stop after "F"	£400	
C10	**37**	1r. green and carmine	22·00	23·00
		a. No stop after "F"	£400	£400
		b. Opt double, one albino	£180	
C1/10 *Set of* 10			50·00	95·00

Prepared, but not issued.

C10*c*	**26**	1a.6p. sepia	£200	

The missing stop after "F" variety occurs in the ninth row of the upper pane.

1904 (27 Feb).

C11	**25**	1a. carmine	30·00	8·00

1905 (16 Sept)–**11**. *Stamps of King Edward VII.*

C12	**41**	3p. grey (4.11)	5·00	6·50
		a. Opt double, one albino	£120	
		b. Opt triple, one albino	£375	
		c. Slate-grey	4·75	6·50
C13	**43**	1a. carmine	7·50	70
		a. Opt double, one albino	£100	
C14	**44**	2a. mauve (11.3.11)	14·00	2·50
		a. Opt double, one albino	£130	
C15	**45**	2a.6p. ultramarine (11.3.11)	3·25	5·00
C16	**46**	3a. orange-brown (11.3.11)	3·75	4·00
C17	**47**	4a. olive-green (11.3.11)	8·50	13·00
C18	**49**	8a. claret (11.3.11)	8·00	7·50
		a. Purple	60·00	55·00
C19	**50**	12a. purple/*red* (1909)	11·00	19·00
		a. No stop after "E"	£475	
C20	**51**	1r. green and carmine (11.3.11)	14·00	28·00
C12/20 *Set of* 9			65·00	75·00

1908 (Dec)–**09**. "POSTAGE & REVENUE".

C21	**53**	½a. green (No. 149) (29.9.09)	1·75	1·50
		a. Opt double, one albino	£110	
C22	**54**	1a. carmine (No. 150)	2·50	30
		a. Opt double, one albino	£150	

1914 (5 May)–**22**. *Stamps of King George V.* Wmk Star.

C23	**55**	3p. grey (7.10.14)	5·50	27·00
		a. Opt double, one albino	£275	
C24	**56**	½a. light green	4·00	6·00
C25	**57**	1a. aniline carmine	5·00	4·00
C26	**58**	1½a. chocolate (Type A) (9.3.21)	25·00	80·00
		a. Opt double, one albino	£170	
C27	**59**	2a. purple (11.19)	18·00	70·00
		a. Opt triple	£425	
		b. Deep mauve	20·00	75·00
C28	**61**	2a.6p. bright blue (2.19)	13·00	26·00
C29	**62**	3a. orange (5.22)	27·00	£225
C30	**63**	4a. olive-green (5.22)	24·00	£170
C32	**65**	8a. deep mauve (12.21)	25·00	£350
C33	**66**	12a. carmine-lake (8.20)	24·00	£120
C34	**67**	1r. brown and green (10.21)	65·00	£325
C23/34 *Set of* 11			£200	£1200

Most dates quoted for Nos. C23/34 are those of the earliest recorded postmarks.

On No. C27a two of the overprints are only lightly inked.

BRITISH RAILWAY ADMINISTRATION

As a vital communications link the North China Railway (Peking–Tientsin–Shanhaikwan) was captured by Russian forces during operations against the Boxers. Control of the line was subsequently, in February 1901, assigned to the China Expeditionary Force and a British Railway Administration was set up to run it. By international agreement the line was to provide postal services for the other national contingents and also, to a lesser extent, for the civilian population. Travelling post offices were introduced and, on 20 April 1901, a late letter service for which an additional fee of 5c. was charged.

Type **32** of China

B.R.A.
5
Five Cents
(BR **35**)

1901 (20 Apr). *No. 108 of China surch with Type* BR **35**.

BR133	**32**	5c.on ½c. brown (Bk.)	£325	£100
		a. Surch inverted	£8000	£2500
		b. Surch in green	£275	£140
		ba. Imperf between (horiz pair)	†	£16000

No. BR133 was used for the collection of the 5c. late letter fee and was affixed to correspondence by a postal official at the railway station. It was cancelled with a violet circular postmark showing "RAILWAY POST OFFICE" at top and the name of the station (PEKING, TIENTSIN, TONGKU, TONGSHAN or SHANHAIKWAN) at foot. With the exception of official mail it could only be used in combination with Indian stamps overprinted "C.E.F.", stamps from the other allied contingents or of the Chinese Imperial Post (*Price used on cover*: No. BR133 *from* £250. No. BR133b *from* £300).

It is suggested that stamps overprinted in black were used at Tientsin and Tongku with those in green being available at Peking, Tongshan and Shanhaikwan.

The late fee charge was abolished on 20 May 1901 and No. BR133 was then withdrawn. The British Railway Administration continued to run the line, and its travelling post offices, until it was returned to its private owners in September 1902.

INDIAN EXPEDITIONARY FORCES 1914–21

Nos. E1/13 were for use of Indian forces sent overseas during the First World War and its aftermath. Examples were first used in France during September 1914. Other areas where the stamps were used included East Africa, Mesopotamia and Turkey. "I.E.F." overprints ceased to be valid for postage on 15 October 1921.

PRICES FOR STAMPS ON COVER	
Nos. E1/13	*from* × 10

I. E. F.
(E 1)

1914 (Sept). *Stamps of India (King George V) optd with Type* E **1**.

E 1	**55**	3p. grey	15	30
		a. No stop after "F"	23·00	28·00
		b. No stop after "E"	£110	£110
		c. Opt double	42·00	35·00
E 2	**56**	½a. light green	50	30
		a. No stop after "F"	75·00	75·00
		b. Opt double	£140	£275
E 3	**57**	1a. aniline carmine	1·25	30
		a. No stop after "F"	32·00	38·00
E 4		1a. carmine	4·25	4·25
E 5	**59**	2a. purple	1·25	30
		a. No stop after "F"	55·00	70·00
		b. No stop after "E"	£250	£275
E 6	**61**	2a.6p. ultramarine	1·50	3·50
		a. No stop after "F"	£170	£180
E 7	**62**	3a. orange	1·00	1·50
		a. No stop after "F"	£160	£170
E 8	**63**	4a. olive-green	1·00	1·50
		a. No stop after "F"	£250	£275
E 9	**65**	8a. deep magenta	1·25	2·50
		a. No stop after "F"	£250	£275
E10		8a. deep mauve	11·00	15·00
E11	**66**	12a. carmine-lake	2·25	6·00
		a. No stop after "F"	£300	£300
		b. Opt double, one albino	55·00	
E12		12a. claret		

No.	Type	Description	Unused	Used
E13	**67**	1r. red-brown and deep blue-green	2·50	4·00
		a. Opt double, one albino	£100	
		b. Brown and green	3·50	5·00
E1/13 *Set of* 10			11·50	18·00

The "no stop after F" variety occurred on R. 4/12 of the upper pane, in one printing.

INDIAN NATIONAL ARMY

The following are stated to have been used in the Japanese occupied areas of India during the drive on Imphal. Issued by the Indian National Army.

Genuine examples are inscribed "PROVISIONAL GOVERNMENT OF FREE INDIA". Forgeries also exist inscribed "PROVISIONAL GOVT. OF FREE INDIA".

Typo in Rangoon. No gum. Perf 11½ or imperf. 1p. violet, 1p. maroon, 1a. green. *Price from £55 each unused.*

Ten stamps, sharing six different designs, inscribed "AZAD HIND", were produced in Germany during the Second World War, but did no postal duty.

JAPANESE OCCUPATION OF THE ANDAMAN AND NICOBAR ISLANDS

The Andaman Islands in the Bay of Bengal were occupied on the 23 March 1942 and the Nicobar Islands in July 1942. Civil administration was resumed in October 1945.

The following Indian stamps were surcharged with large figures preceded by a decimal point:—

Postage stamps—.3 on ½a. (No. 248), .5 on 1a. (No. 250), .10 on 2a. (No. 236*b*), .30 on 6a. (No. 274).

Official stamps—.10 on 1a.3p. (No. O146*a*), .20 on 3p. (No. O143), .20 in red on 3p. (No. O143).

Prices from £400 *each unused.*

INDIAN CONVENTION STATES

The following issues resulted from a series of postal conventions agreed between the Imperial Government and the state administrations of Patiala (1 October 1884), Gwalior, Jind and Nabha (1 July 1885), and Chamba and Faridkot (1 January 1887).

Under the terms of these conventions the British Indian Post Office supplied overprinted British India issues to the state administrations which, in turn, had to conform to a number of conditions covering the issue of stamps, rates of postage and the exchange of mail.

Such overprinted issues were valid for postage within the state of issue, to other "Convention States" and to destinations in British India.

Stamps of Chamba, Gwalior, Jind, Nabha and Patiala ceased to be valid for postage on 1 January 1951, when they were replaced by those of the Republic of India, valid from 1 April 1950.

RULERS OF INDIAN CONVENTION AND FEUDATORY STATES. Details of the rulers of the various states during the period when stamps were issued are now provided in a somewhat simplified form which omits reference to minor titles. Dates quoted are of the various reigns, extended to 1971 when the titles of the surviving rulers of the former princely states were abolished by the Indian Government.

During the absorption of the Convention and Feudatory States there was often an interim period during which the administration was handed over. In some instances it is only possible to quote the end of this interim period as the point of transfer.

Stamps of India overprinted

In the Queen Victoria issues we omit varieties due to broken type, including the numerous small "A" varieties which may have come about through damaged type. We do, however, list the small "G", small "R" and tall "R" in "GWALIOR" as these were definitely the result of the use of type of the wrong size.

Variations in the length of the words due to unequal spacing when setting are also omitted.

CHAMBA

PRICES FOR STAMPS ON COVER	
Nos. 1/27	*from* × 20
Nos. 28/120	*from* × 12
Nos. O1/86	*from* × 25

Raja Sham Singh, 1873–1904

CHAMBA STATE (1) — CHAMBA (2)

1887 (1 Jan)–**95**. *Queen Victoria. Optd with T* **1**.

No.	Type	Description	Unused	Used
1	**23**	½a. blue-green	40	50
		a. "CHMABA"	£325	£425
		b. "8TATE"	£650	
		c. Opt double	£600	
2	**25**	1a. brown-purple	1·25	1·50
		a. "CHMABA"	£475	£550
		b. "8TATE"	£1200	
3		1a. plum	2·00	1·50
4	**26**	1a.6p. sepia (1895)	1·50	10·00
5	**27**	2a. dull blue	1·75	2·00
		b. "CHMABA"	£1800	£2000
		c. "8TATE"	£1800	
6		2a. ultramarine	1·10	1·40
7	**36**	2a.6p. green (1895)	29·00	80·00
8	**28**	3a. orange (1887)	7·00	18·00
9		3a. brown-orange (1891)	1·50	4·25
		a. "CHMABA"	£4500	£4750
		b. Opt inverted		
10	**29**	4a. olive-green	3·75	7·50
		a. "CHMABA"	£1400	£1600
		b. "8TATE"	£3000	
11		4a. slate-green	4·25	5·50
		a. Opt double, one albino	65·00	
12	**21**	6a. olive-bistre (1890)	3·50	15·00
		a. Opt treble, two albino	90·00	
13		6a. bistre-brown	13·00	15·00
14	**31**	8a. dull mauve (1887)	6·50	8·00
		a. "CHMABA"	£3750	£3750
15		8a. magenta (1895)	6·00	15·00
16	**32**	12a. purple/*red* (1890)	5·50	12·00
		a. "CHMABA"	£6500	
		b. First "T" in "STATE" inverted	£6500	
		c. Opt double, one albino	38·00	
17	**33**	1r. slate (1887)	38·00	£110
		a. "CHMABA"	£10000	
18	**37**	1r. green and carmine (1895)	7·00	13·00
		a. Opt double one albino	50·00	
19	**38**	2r. carmine and yellow-brown (1895)	85·00	£300
20		3r. brown and green (1895)	90·00	£250
21		5r. ultramarine and violet (1895)	£100	£425
		a. Opt double, one albino	£180	
1/21 *Set of* 15			£350	£1100

1900–04. *Colours changed.*

No.	Type	Description	Unused	Used
22	**40**	3p. carmine	30	50
		a. Opt double, one albino	38·00	
23		3p. grey (1904)	30	1·60
		a. Opt inverted	75·00	
24	**23**	½a. pale yellow-green (1902)	1·25	2·50
25		½a. yellow-green (1903)	40	1·00
26	**25**	1a. carmine (1902)	30	30
27	**27**	2a. pale violet (1903)	7·50	24·00
22/7 *Set of* 5			8·00	25·00

Raja Bhuri Singh, 1904–1919

1903–05. *King Edward VII. Optd with T* **1**.

No.	Type	Description	Unused	Used
28	**41**	3p. pale grey	15	1·00
29		3p. slate-grey (1905)	25	1·00
30	**42**	½a. green	30	25
31	**43**	1a. carmine	1·25	40
32	**44**	2a. pale violet (1904)	1·40	2·75
33		2a. mauve	1·25	2·50
34	**46**	3a. orange-brown (1905)	3·00	4·00
		a. Opt double, one albino	38·00	
35	**47**	4a. olive (1904)	4·25	15·00
36	**48**	6a. olive-bistre (1905)	3·50	18·00
		a. Opt double, one albino	38·00	
37	**49**	8a. purple (*shades*) (1904)	4·25	17·00
38		8a. claret	8·50	22·00
39	**50**	12a. purple/*red* (1905)	6·00	23·00
		a. Opt double, one albino	38·00	
40	**51**	1r. green and carmine (1904)	6·50	20·00
		a. Opt double, one albino	48·00	
28/40 *Set of* 10			27·00	90·00

1907. *Nos. 149/50 of India optd with T* **1**.

No.	Type	Description	Unused	Used
41	**53**	½a. green	1·25	3·00
		a. Opt double, one albino	35·00	
42	**54**	1a. carmine	1·40	3·00

1913. *King George V optd with T* **1**.

No.	Type	Description	Unused	Used
43	**55**	3p. grey	20	60
		a. Pale grey	60	
		b. Bluish grey	70	
44	**56**	½a. light green	35	65
		a. Emerald	70	1·00
		b. Bright green	85	
		w. Wmk inverted		
45	**57**	1a. rose-carmine	5·50	7·00
		a. Aniline carmine	1·00	2·75
		ab. Opt double, one albino	35·00	
47	**59**	2a. purple	2·50	8·00
		a. Reddish purple	3·00	8·00
		b. Deep mauve	4·00	
		c. Bright reddish violet	6·00	
48	**62**	3a. orange	2·75	6·50
		a. Dull orange	—	5·50
49	**63**	4a. olive	2·50	3·75
50	**64**	6a. yellow-bistre	2·75	4·50
		a. Brown-ochre	3·50	4·25
51	**65**	8a. deep magenta	3·75	11·00
		a. Deep mauve	4·25	10·00
		b. Bright mauve	7·00	
		c. Purple	7·00	
52	**66**	12a. carmine-lake	3·50	10·00
		a. Claret	7·00	11·00
53	**67**	1r. red-brown and deep blue-green	13·00	23·00
		a. Opt double, one albino	35·00	
		b. Brown and green	13·00	23·00
		c. Orange-brown and deep turquoise-green	17·00	
43/53 *Set of* 10			29·00	60·00

Raja Ram Singh, 1919–1935

1921. *No. 192 of India optd with T* **2**.

No.	Type	Description	Unused	Used
54	**57**	9p. on 1a. rose-carmine	1·00	17·00

1923–27. *Optd with T* **1**. *New values, etc.*

No.	Type	Description	Unused	Used
55	**57**	1a. chocolate	2·00	3·75
56	**58**	1½a. chocolate (Type A)	22·00	£100
57		1½a. chocolate (Type B) (1924)	1·40	4·75
58		1½a. rose-carmine (Type B) (1927)	75	17·00
59	**61**	2a.6p. ultramarine	60	3·00
60		2a.6p. orange (1927)	1·60	15·00
61	**62**	3a. ultramarine (1924)	2·75	18·00
55/61 *Set of* 7			28·00	£140

Nos. 58 and 60 with inverted overprint are of clandestine origin.

CHAMBA STATE (3) — CHAMBA STATE (4)

1927–37. *King George V (Nasik printing, wmk Mult Star). Optd a[t] Nasik with T* **3** *or* **4** *(1r.)*

No.	Type	Description	Unused	Used
62	**55**	3p. slate (1928)	10	1·1
		w. Wmk inverted	3·25	
63	**56**	½a. green (1928)	20	1·6
		w. Wmk inverted	1·50	
64	**80**	9p. deep green (*litho*) (1932)	2·50	13·0
64*a*		9p. deep green (*typo*)	7·00	15·0
65	**57**	1a. chocolate	1·60	7
		w. Wmk inverted	3·50	1·1
66	**82**	1a.3p. mauve (1932)	1·10	4·7
		w. Wmk inverted	3·50	4·7
67	**58**	1½a. rose-carmine (B) (1932)	5·00	5·5
		w. Wmk inverted	5·00	5·5
68	**70**	2a. purple (1928)	1·40	2·2
69	**61**	2a.6p. orange (1932)	1·75	14·0
		w. Wmk inverted	1·75	15·0
70	**62**	3a. bright blue (1928)	1·00	16·0
71	**71**	4a. sage-green (1928)	1·00	4·5
72	**64**	6a. bistre (*wmk inverted*) (1937)	26·00	£15
73	**65**	8a. reddish purple (1928)	1·40	9·0
		w. Wmk inverted	1·25	7·5
74	**66**	12a. claret (1928)	1·40	11·0
75	**67**	1r. chocolate and green (1928)	6·00	22·0
		w. Wmk inverted	9·00	22·0
62/75 *Set of* 14			45·00	£22

Raja Lakshman Singh, 1935–1971

1935–36. *New types and colours. Optd with T* **3**.

No.	Type	Description	Unused	Used
76	**79**	½a. green	1·10	8·0
77	**81**	1a. chocolate	1·50	
78	**59**	2a. vermilion (No. 236*b*)	1·00	21·0
79		2a. vermilion (*small die*, *No.* 236*c*)	£100	£1
80	**62**	3a. carmine	2·00	9·0
81	**63**	4a. sage-green (1936)	3·25	13·
76/81 *Set of* 6			£100	£14

CHAMBA STATE (5) — CHAMBA (6) — CHAMBA (7)

1938. *King George VI. Nos. 247/64 optd with T* **3** *(3p. to 1a.), T[*5*] (2a. to 12a.) or T* **4** *(rupee values).*

No.	Type	Description	Unused	Used
82	**91**	3p. slate	7·00	12·
83		½a. red-brown	1·00	7·
84		9p. green	7·50	27·
85		1a. carmine	1·00	2·
86	**92**	2a. vermilion	5·00	9·
87	–	2a.6p. bright violet	5·50	22·
88	–	3a. yellow-green	6·00	22·
89	–	3a.6p. bright blue	6·00	23·
90	–	4a. brown	18·00	19·
91	–	6a. turquoise-green	18·00	50·
92	–	8a. slate-violet	18·00	48·
93	–	12a. lake	12·00	48·
94	**93**	1r. grey and red-brown	27·00	55·
95		2r. purple and brown	48·00	£2
96		5r. green and blue	80·00	£3
97		10r. purple and claret	£130	£5
98		15r. brown and green	£160	£8
99		25r. slate-violet and purple	£225	£8
82/99 *Set of* 18			£700	£27

1942–47. *Optd with T* **6** *(to 12a.),* "CHAMBA" *only, as in T (14a.) or T* **7** *(rupee values).*

(a) Stamps of 1937. W **69** (inverted on 15r.).

No.	Type	Description	Unused	Used
100	**91**	½a. red-brown	35·00	25·
101		1a. carmine	45·00	32·
102	**93**	1r. grey and red-brown	20·00	50·
103		2r. purple and brown	24·00	£2
104		5r. green and blue	45·00	£2
105		10r. purple and claret	65·00	£4
106		15r. brown and green	£150	£6
		w. Wmk upright	—	£8
107		25r. slate-violet and purple	£140	£6
100/7 *Set of* 8			£450	£20

(b) Stamps of 1940–43.

No.	Type	Description	Unused	Used
108	**100a**	3p. slate	70	4
109		½a. purple (1943)	70	4
110		9p. green	1·00	13
111		1a. carmine (1943)	1·00	3
112	**101**	1½a. dull violet (1943)	1·00	8
113		2a. vermilion (1943)	5·00	9
114		3a. bright violet	15·00	32
115		3½a. bright blue	8·00	32
116	**102**	4a. brown	10·00	10
117		6a. turquoise-green	13·00	35
118		8a. slate-violet	13·00	42
119		12a. lake	19·00	55
120	**103**	14a. purple (1947)	11·00	3
108/120 *Set of* 13			90·00	£2

The 3a. exists printed by lithography or typography.

OFFICIAL STAMPS

SERVICE

CHAMBA STATE (O 1)

1887 (1 Jan)–**98**. *Queen Victoria. Optd with Type* O **1**.

No.	Type	Description	Unused	Used
O 1	**23**	½a. blue-green	30	
		a. "CHMABA"	£190	£
		b. "SERV CE"		
		c. "8TATE"	£650	
		d. Thin seriffed "I" in "SERVICE"	£130	

No.	Type	Description	Unused	Used
O 2	25	1a. brown-purple	1·50	70
		a. "CHMABA"	£375	£350
		b. "SERV CE"	£2500	
		c. "8TATE"	£1500	
		d. "SERVICE" double	£1300	£1000
		e. "SERVICE" double, one albino	48·00	
O 3		1a. plum	1·25	10
		a. Thin seriffed "I" in "SERVICE"	£160	
O 4	27	2a. dull blue	1·90	1·25
		a. "CHMABA"	£1000	£1300
O 5		2a. ultramarine (1887)	1·50	1·50
		a. Thin seriffed "I" in "SERVICE"	£250	
O 6	28	3a. orange (1890)		
O 7		3a. brown-orange (1891)	2·00	9·50
		a. "CHMABA"	£2500	£2750
		b. Thin seriffed "I" in "SERVICE"		
		c. Opt double, one albino		
O 8	29	4a. olive-green	2·50	4·50
		a. "CHMABA"	£1000	£1300
		b. "SERV CE"	£3000	
		c. "8TATE"	£3000	
O 9		4a. slate-green	1·50	7·50
		a. Thin seriffed "I" in "SERVICE"		
O10	21	6a. olive-bistre (1890)	4·25	10·00
		a. "SERVICE" double, one albino	48·00	
O11		6a. bistre-brown		
O12	31	8a. dull mauve (1887)	3·25	6·00
		a. "CHMABA"	£4750	£4750
O13		8a. magenta (1895)	2·00	1·75
		a. Thin seriffed "I" in "SERVICE"	£475	
O14	32	12a. purple/*red* (1890)	7·50	38·00
		a. "CHMABA"	£6000	
		b. First "T" in "STATE" inverted	£6000	
		c. Thin seriffed "I" in "SERVICE"		
		d. "SERVICE" double, one albino	48·00	
		e. "CHAMBA STATE" double, one albino		
O15	33	1r. slate (1890)	13·00	£110
		a. "CHMABA"	£4500	
O16	37	1r. green and carmine (1898)	6·00	32·00
		a. Thin seriffed "I" in "SERVICE"		
O1/16		*Set of* 10	35·00	£180

Printings up to and including that of December 1895 had the "SERVICE" overprint applied to sheets of stamps already overprinted with Type 1. From the printing of September 1898 onwards both "SERVICE" and "CHAMBA STATE" were overprinted at the same time. Nos. O6, O8 and O12 only exist using the first method, and No. O16 was only printed using the second.

The thin seriffed "I" in "SERVICE" variety occurred on R. 19/12 of the September 1898 printing only.

1902–04. *Colours changed. Optd as Type* O **1**.

No.	Type	Description	Unused	Used
O17	40	3p. grey (1904)	40	50
O18	23	½a. pale yellow-green	45	3·00
O19		½a. yellow-green	3·25	1·75
O20	25	1a. carmine	70	40
O21	27	2a. pale violet (1903)	9·00	27·00
O17/21		*Set of* 4	9·50	27·00

1903–05. *King Edward VII. Stamps of India optd as Type* O **1**.

No.	Type	Description	Unused	Used
O22	41	3p. pale grey	30	15
		a. Opt double, one albino	32·00	
O23		3p. slate-grey (1905)	30	65
O24	42	½a. yellow-green	25	10
O25	43	1a. carmine	75	30
O26	44	2a. pale violet (1904)	2·25	1·00
O27		2a. mauve	1·25	70
O28	47	4a. olive (1905)	3·50	16·00
O29	49	8a. purple (1905)	5·00	15·00
O30		8a. claret	8·00	21·00
		a. Opt double, one albino	38·00	
O31	51	1r. green and carmine (1905)	1·75	10·00
O22/31		*Set of* 7	11·50	38·00

The 2a. mauve King Edward VII, overprinted "On H.M.S.", was discovered in Calcutta, but was not sent to Chamba, and is an unissued variety (*Price un.* £35).

1907. *Nos. 149/50 of India, optd with Type* O **1**.

No.	Type	Description	Unused	Used
O32	53	½a. green	40	75
		a. Opt inverted	£4000	£4000
		b. Opt double, one albino	32·00	
O33	54	1a. carmine	2·25	1·50

The inverted overprint, No. O32*a*, was due to an inverted cliché on R. 20/1 which was corrected after a few sheets had been printed.

1913–23. *King George V Official stamps (wmk Single Star) optd with T* **1**.

No.	Type	Description	Unused	Used
O34	55	3p. grey	20	40
		a. Pale grey	40	50
		b. Bluish grey	40	50
		c. Slate	30	75
O36	56	½a. light green	10	15
		a. Emerald	1·40	30
		b. Bright green	1·60	30
O38	57	1a. aniline carmine	10	10
		a. Rose-carmine	4·50	50
O40	59	2a. purple (1914)	1·10	12·00
		a. Reddish purple	6·00	
		b. Bright reddish violet(1923)	6·00	12·00
O41	63	4a. olive	1·10	15·00
O42	65	8a. deep magenta	1·75	16·00
		a. Deep mauve	3·25	16·00
O43	67	1r. red-brown and deep blue-green (1914)	4·25	25·00
		a. Opt double, one albino	35·00	
		b. Brown and green	6·00	27·00
O34/43		*Set of* 7	7·75	60·00

No. O36 with inverted overprint and No. O38*a* with double or inverted overprint (on gummed side) are of clandestine origin.

1914. *King George V. Optd with Type* O **1**.

No.	Type	Description	Unused	Used
O44	59	2a. purple	15·00	
O45	63	4a. olive	12·00	

1921. *No. O97 of India optd with T* **2** *at top.*

No.	Type	Description	Unused	Used
O46	57	9p. on 1a. rose-carmine	15	6·00

1925. *As 1913–14. New colour.*

No.	Type	Description	Unused	Used
O47	57	1a. chocolate	2·50	50

CHAMBA STATE SERVICE (O 2)

CHAMBA STATE SERVICE (O 3)

1927–39. *King George V (Nasik printing, wmk Mult Star), optd at Nasik with Type* O **2** *or* O **3** *(rupee values).*

No.	Type	Description	Unused	Used
O48	55	3p. slate (1928)	50	30
		w. Wmk inverted	—	1·00
O49	56	½a. green (1928)	35	15
O50	80	9p. deep green (1932)	2·50	8·50
O51	57	1a. chocolate	20	10
		w. Wmk inverted	—	60
O52	82	1a.3p. mauve (1932)	5·00	60
		w. Wmk inverted		
O53	70	2a. purple (1928)	1·40	60
O54	71	4a. sage-green (1928)	1·10	1·75
O55	65	8a. reddish purple (1930)	4·50	8·00
		w. Wmk inverted	6·00	
O56	66	12a. claret (1928)	2·75	20·00
		w. Wmk inverted	10·00	
O57	67	1r. chocolate and green (1930)	12·00	35·00
O58		2r. carmine and orange (1939)	21·00	£180
O59		5r. ultramarine and purple (1939)	42·00	£250
O60		10r. green and scarlet (1939)	60·00	£250
O48/60		*Set of* 13	£140	£650

1935–39. *New types and colours. Optd with Type* O **2**.

No.	Type	Description	Unused	Used
O61	79	½a. green	3·50	50
O62	81	1a. chocolate	2·50	45
O63	59	2a. vermilion	3·75	1·00
O64		2a. vermilion (*small die*) (1939)	5·00	15·00
O65	63	4a. sage-green (1936)	6·00	5·00
O61/5		*Set of* 5	19·00	20·00

1938–40. *King George VI. Optd with Type* O **2** *or* O **3** *(rupee values).*

No.	Type	Description	Unused	Used
O66	91	9p. green	13·00	48·00
O67		1a. carmine	12·00	3·00
O68	93	1r. grey and red-brown (1940?)	£250	£700
O69		2r. purple and brown (1939)	40·00	£325
O70		5r. green and blue (1939)	60·00	£400
O71		10r. purple and claret (1939)	90·00	£700
O66/71		*Set of* 6	£425	£2000

CHAMBA SERVICE (O 4)

1940–43.

(a) Official stamps optd with T **6**.

No.	Type	Description	Unused	Used
O72	O 20	3p. slate	70	80
O73		½a. red-brown	15·00	2·25
O74		½a. purple (1943)	70	2·50
O75		9p. green	5·00	8·00
		w. Wmk inverted	16·00	12·00
O76		1a. carmine (1941)	70	2·00
O77		1a.3p. yellow-brown (1941)	55·00	16·00
O78		1½a. dull violet (1943)	5·50	6·50
O79		2a. vermilion	5·50	6·00
O80		2½a. bright violet (1941)	2·50	19·00
O81		4a. brown	5·50	10·00
O82		8a. slate-violet	13·00	50·00
		w. Wmk inverted	12·00	50·00

(b) Postage stamps optd with Type O **4**.

No.	Type	Description	Unused	Used
O83	93	1r. grey and red-brown (1942)	20·00	£170
O84		2r. purple and brown (1942)	35·00	£225
O85		5r. green and blue (1942)	65·00	£350
O86		10r. purple and claret (1942)	80·00	£600
O72/86		*Set of* 15	£275	£1300

Chamba became part of Himachal Pradesh on 15 April 1948.

FARIDKOT

For earlier issues, see under INDIAN FEUDATORY STATES

PRICES FOR STAMPS ON COVER	
Nos. 1/17	*from* × 30
Nos. O1/15	*from* × 40

Raja Bikram Singh, 1874–1898

FARIDKOT STATE (1)

1887 (1 Jan)–**1900**. *Queen Victoria. Optd with T* **1**.

No.	Type	Description	Unused	Used
1	23	½a. deep green	1·50	1·25
		a. "ARIDKOT"		
		b. "FAR DKOT"	—	£1400
		c. Opt double, one albino	42·00	
2	25	1a. brown-purple	1·50	2·25
3		1a. plum	1·75	1·50
4	27	2a. blue	3·00	5·00
5		2a. deep blue	3·50	6·00
6	28	3a. orange	6·00	9·50
7		3a. brown-orange (1893)	3·00	4·00
8	29	4a. olive-green	7·00	14·00
		a. "ARIDKOT"	£1200	
9		4a. slate-green	7·00	20·00
10	21	6a. olive-bistre	28·00	50·00
		a. "ARIDKOT"	£1600	
		b. Opt double, one albino	42·00	
11		6a. bistre-brown	2·00	14·00
12	31	8a. dull mauve	11·00	35·00
		a. "ARIDKOT"	£2500	
13		8a. magenta	16·00	£110
		a. Opt double, one albino	35·00	
14	32	12a. purple/*red* (1900)	38·00	£375
15	33	1r. slate	42·00	£350
		a. "ARIDKOT"	£2500	
16	37	1r. green and carmine (1893)	32·00	90·00
		a. Opt double, one albino	60·00	
1/16		*Set of* 10	£130	£800

The ½a., 1a., 2a., 3a., 4a., 8a. and 1r. (No. 16) are known with broken "O" (looking like a "C") in "FARIDKOT".

Raja Balbir Singh, 1898–1906

1900. *Optd with T* **1**.

No.	Type	Description	Unused	Used
17	40	3p. carmine	1·50	40·00

OFFICIAL STAMPS

SERVICE FARIDKOT STATE (O 1)

1887 (1 Jan)–**98**. *Queen Victoria. Optd with Type* O **1**.

No.	Type	Description	Unused	Used
O 1	23	½a. deep green	50	60
		a. "SERV CE"	£1600	
		b. "FAR DKOT"		
		c. Thin seriffed "I" in "SERVICE"	£180	
		d. "FARIDKOT STATE" double, one albino	38·00	
O 2	25	1a. brown-purple	1·00	1·50
		a. Thin seriffed "I" in "SERVICE"	£190	
		b. Opt double, one albino	45·00	
O 3		1a. plum	1·25	1·50
		a. "SERV CE"	£2250	
O 4	27	2a. dull blue	2·00	8·50
		a. "SERV CE"	£2250	
O 5		2a. deep blue	1·60	12·00
O 6	28	3a. orange	6·00	8·00
		a. "SERVICE" double, one albino		
O 7		3a. brown-orange (12.98)	2·00	30·00
		a. Thin seriffed "I" in "SERVICE"	£475	
O 8	29	4a. olive-green	4·75	22·00
		a. "SERV CE"	£2250	
		b. "ARIDKOT"		
		c. "SERVICE" treble, two albino	75·00	
O 9		4a. slate-green	10·00	38·00
		a. "SERVICE" double, one albino	35·00	
O10	21	6a. olive-bistre	28·00	80·00
		a. "ARIDKOT"	£1300	
		b. "SERVIC"	£2250	
		c. "SERVICE" double, one albino	48·00	
		d. "FARIDKOT STATE" double, one albino	48·00	
O11		6a. bistre-brown	20·00	25·00
O12	31	8a. dull mauve	6·50	26·00
		a. "SERV CE"	£2500	
O13		8a. magenta	15·00	£110
O14	33	1r. slate	48·00	£180
		a. "SERVICE" double, one albino	75·00	
O15	37	1r. green and carmine (12.98)	80·00	£500
		a. Thin seriffed "I" in "SERVICE"		
O1/15		*Set of* 9	£150	£700

The ½a., 1a., 2a., 3a., 4a., 8a. and 1r. (No. O15) are known with the broken "O".

Printings up to and including that of November 1895 had the "SERVICE" overprint applied to sheets already overprinted with Type **1**. From December 1898 onwards "SERVICE" and "FARIDKOT STATE" were overprinted at one operation to provide fresh supplies of Nos. O1/3, O7 and O15.

The thin seriffed "I" variety occurs on the December 1898 overprinting only.

This State ceased to use overprinted stamps after 31 March 1901.

GWALIOR

PRICES FOR STAMPS ON COVER	
Nos. 1/3	*from* × 10
Nos. 4/11	—
Nos. 12/66	*from* × 5
Nos. 67/128	*from* × 4
Nos. 129/37	*from* × 5
Nos. O1/94	*from* × 12

OVERPRINTS. From 1885 to 1926 these were applied by the Government of India Central Printing Press, Calcutta, and from 1927 at the Security Press, Nasik, *unless otherwise stated.*

Maharaja Jayaji Rao Sindhia, 1843–1886

गवालियर

GWALIOR (1)

GWALIOR गवालियर (2)

GWALIOR — Small "G"   GWALIOR — Small "R"

GWALIOR — Tall "R" (original state)   GWALIOR — Tall "R" (damaged state)

OVERPRINT VARIETIES OF TYPE 2.

Small "G" — Occurs on R. 7/11 from June 1900 printing of ½, 1, 2, 3, 4a. and 3p. (No. 38), and on R. 3/1 of a left pane from May 1901 printing of 2, 3 and 5r.

Small "R" — Occurs on R. 9/3 from June 1900 printing of 3p. to 4a. and on R. 2/3 from May 1901 printing of 2, 3 and 5r.

Tall "R" — Occurs on R. 20/2 from printings between June 1900 and May 1907. The top of the letter is damaged on printings from February 1903 onwards.

1885 (1 July)–**97**. *Queen Victoria*. I. *Optd with T* **1**.

(a) Space between two lines of overprint 13 mm. Hindi inscription 13 to 14 mm long (May 1885).

1 **23** ½a. blue-green . . . £110 23·00
2 **25** 1a. brown-purple . . . 75·00 27·00
3 **27** 2a. dull blue . . . 65·00 13·00
1/3 *Set of* 3 . . . £225 55·00

A variety exists of the ½a. in which the space between the two lines of overprint is only 9½ mm but this is probably from a proof sheet.

(b) Space between two lines of overprint 15 mm on 4a. and 6a. and 16 to 17 mm on other values (June 1885). Hindi inscription 13 to 14 mm long.

4 **23** ½a. blue-green . . . 45·00
a. Opt double, one albino . . . 65·00
b. Hindi inscr 15 to 15½ mm long . . . £100
ba. Opt double, one albino . . . £150
c. Pair. Nos. 4/4b . . . £550
5 **25** 1a. brown-purple . . . 50·00
a. Opt double, one albino . . . 60·00
b. Hindi inscr 15 to 15½ mm long . . . £100
ba. Opt double, one albino . . . £120
c. Pair. Nos. 5/5b . . . £550
6 **26** 1a.6p. sepia . . . 70·00
b. Hindi inscr 15 to 15½ mm long . . . £180
c. Pair. Nos. 6/6b . . . £650
7 **27** 2a. dull blue . . . 50·00
b. Hindi inscr 15 to 15½ mm long . . . £110
c. Pair. Nos. 7/7b . . . £400
8 **17** 4a. green . . . 75·00
b. Hindi inscr 15 to 15½ mm long . . . £160
c. Pair. Nos. 8/8b . . . £700
9 **21** 6a. olive-bistre . . . 75·00
a. Opt double, one albino . . . 80·00
b. Hindi inscr 15 to 15½ mm long . . . £180
ba. Opt double, one albino . . . £190
c. Pair. Nos. 9/9b . . . £700
10 **31** 8a. dull mauve . . . 70·00
b. Hindi inscr 15 to 15½ mm long . . . £160
c. Pair. Nos. 10/10b . . . £700
11 **33** 1r. slate . . . 70·00
b. Hindi inscr 15 to 15½ mm long . . . £160
c. Pair. Nos. 11/11b . . . £700
4/11 *Set of* 8 . . . £450
4b/11b *Set of* 8 . . . £1000

The two types of overprint on these stamps occur in the same settings, with about a quarter of the stamps in each sheet showing the long inscription. Nos. 4/7 and 10/11 were overprinted in sheets of 240 and Nos. 8/9 in half-sheets of 160.

II. *Optd with T* **2**. *Hindi inscription 13 to 14 mm long.*

(a) In red (Sept 1885).

12 **23** ½a. blue-green . . . 85 20
b. Hindi inscr 15 to 15½ mm long . . . 1·40 55
c. Pair. Nos. 12/12b . . . 12·00 14·00
13 **27** 2a. dull blue . . . 13·00 14·00
b. Hindi inscr 15 to 15½ mm long . . . 30·00 32·00
c. Pair. Nos. 13/13b . . . £350 £375
14 **17** 4a. green . . . 21·00 12·00
b. Hindi inscr 15 to 15½ mm long . . . £180 95·00
c. Pair. Nos. 14/14b . . . £600
15 **33** 1r. slate . . . 7·50 20·00
aw. Wmk inverted . . . 16·00 30·00
b. Hindi inscr 15 to 15½ mm long . . . 32·00 70·00
bw. Wmk inverted . . . 48·00 95·00
c. Pair. Nos. 15/15b . . . 70·00 £120
cw. Wmk inverted . . . 90·00
12/15 *Set of* 4 . . . 38·00 42·00
12b/15b *Set of* 4 . . . £200 £180

No. 14 was overprinted in half-sheets of 160, about 40 stamps having the Hindi inscription 15 to 15½ mm long. The remaining three values were from a setting of 240 containing 166 13 to 14 mm long and 74 15 to 15½ mm long.

Reprints have been made of Nos. 12 to 15, but the majority of the specimens have the word "REPRINT" overprinted upon them.

(b) In black (1885–97).

16 **23** ½a. blue-green (1889) . . . 1·40 1·50
a. Opt double
b. Opt double, one albino . . . 21·00
c. Hindi inscr 15 to 15½ mm long . . . 35 10
ca. Opt double . . . † £500
cb. Opt double, one albino . . . 70·00
cc. "GWALICR" . . . 85·00 £100
cd. Small "G" . . . 65·00 48·00
ce. Small "R" . . . 75·00
cf. Tall "R" . . . 75·00 75·00
d. Pair. Nos. 16/16c . . . 50·00 55·00
17 **24** 9p. carmine (1891) . . . 30·00 50·00
a. Opt double, one albino . . . 55·00
c. Hindi inscr 15 to 15½ mm long . . . 55·00 75·00
ca. Opt double, one albino . . . 85·00
d. Pair. Nos. 17/17c . . . £250
18 **25** 1a. brown-purple . . . 1·00 20
c. Hindi inscr 15 to 15½ mm long . . . 2·50 35
d. Pair. Nos. 18/18c . . . 14·00 15·00
19 1a. plum (*Hindi inscr 15 to 15½ mm long*) . . . 2·25 10
a. Small "G" . . . 75·00 55·00
b. Small "R" . . . 80·00
c. Tall "R" . . . 95·00
20 **26** 1a.6p. sepia . . . 85 1·00
c. Hindi Inscr 15 to 15½ mm long . . . 1·40 50
d. Pair. Nos. 20/20c . . . 14·00 17·00
21 **27** 2a. dull blue . . . 5·50 80
c. Hindi inscr 15 to 15½ mm long . . . 1·25 10
ca. "R" omitted . . . £475 £475
d. Pair. Nos. 21/21c . . . £140
22 2a. deep blue . . . 8·50 1·75
c. Hindi inscr 15 to 15½ mm long . . . 2·50 35
ca. Small "G" . . . £150 £140
cb. Small "R" . . . £200
cc. Tall "R" . . . £225 £225
d. Pair. Nos. 22/22c . . . £160
23 **36** 2a.6p. yellow-green (*Hindi inscr 15 to 15½ mm long*) (1896) . . . 6·00 17·00
a. "GWALICR" . . . £550
24 **28** 3a. orange . . . 6·00 11·00
a. Opt double, one albino . . . 48·00
c. Hindi inscr 15 to 15½ mm long . . . 55·00 38·00
ca. Opt double, one albino
d. Pair. Nos. 24/24c . . . £250
25 3a. brown-orange . . . 26·00 4·50
c. Hindi inscr 15 to 15½ mm long . . . 2·00 15
ca. Opt double, one albino . . . 38·00
cb. Small "G" . . . £250 £250
cc. Small "R" . . . £550
cd. Tall "R" . . . £200 £200
d. Pair. Nos. 25/25c . . . £200
26 **29** 4a. olive-green (1889) . . . 6·00 1·00
c. Hindi inscr 15 to 15½ mm long . . . 10·00 3·25
d. Pair. Nos. 26/26c . . . £120
27 4a. slate-green . . . 7·00 1·75
c. Hindi inscr 15 to 15½ mm long . . . 3·00 70
ca. Opt double, one albino . . . 60·00
cb. Small "G" . . . £475 £300
cc. Small "R" . . . £475
cd. Tall "R" . . . £350 £325
d. Pair. Nos. 27/27c . . . 38·00
28 **21** 6a. olive-bistre . . . 6·50 13·00
c. Hindi inscr 15 to 15½ mm long . . . 3·00 13·00
d. Pair. Nos. 28/28c . . . 55·00
29 6a. bistre-brown . . . 2·00 7·00
c. Hindi inscr 15 to 15½ mm long . . . 3·25 9·50
d. Pair. Nos. 29/29c . . . 23·00
30 **31** 8a. dull mauve . . . 10·00 35·00
c. Hindi inscr 15 to 15½ mm long . . . 3·75 85
d. Pair. Nos. 30/30c . . . £300
31 8a. magenta (*Hindi inscr 15 to 15½ mm long*) (1897) . . . 6·50 7·50
32 **32** 12a. purple/*red* (1891) . . . 3·25 8·00
c. Hindi inscr 15 to 15½ mm long . . . 3·25 65
ca. Pair, one without opt . . . £3250
cb. Tall "R" . . . £950 £700
d. Pair. Nos. 32/32c . . . 80·00
33 **33** 1r. slate (1889) . . . £100 £375
c. Hindi inscr 15 to 15½ mm long . . . 2·75 1·50
d. Pair. Nos. 33/33c . . . £450
34 **37** 1r. green and carmine (*Hindi inscr 15 to 15½ mm long*) (1896) . . . 3·75 3·25
a. Opt double, one albino . . . 75·00
b. "GWALICR" . . . £750 £900
35 **38** 2r. carmine and yellow-brown (*Hindi inscr 15 to 15½ mm long*) (1896) . . . 5·50 3·00
a. Small "G" . . . £300 £180
b. Small "R" . . . £325 £200
c. Opt double, one albino . . . 75·00
36 3r. brown and green (*Hindi inscr 15 to 15½ mm long*) (1896) . . . 7·50 3·50
a. Small "G" . . . £325 £190
b. Small "R" . . . £350 £225
37 5r. ultramarine and violet (*Hindi inscr 15 to 15½ mm long*) (1896) . . . 14·00 6·50
a. Small "G" . . . £350 £225
b. Small "R" . . . £400 £250
16/37 *Set of* 16 . . . 75·00 85·00

Printings to 1891 continued to use the setting showing both types, but subsequently a new setting containing the larger overprint only was used.

The ½a., 1a., 2a. and 3a. exist with space between "I" and "O" of "GWALIOR".

The "GWALICR" error occurs on R. 1/5 in the May 1896 printing only.

Maharaja Madhav Rao Sindhia, 1886–1925

1899–1911.

(a) Optd with T **2** *(B).*

38 **40** 3p. carmine . . . 30 20
a. Opt inverted . . . £850 £475
b. Small "G" . . . 55·00 55·00
d. Small "R" . . . 65·00
e. Tall "R" . . . 48·00
f. Opt double, one albino . . . 38·00
39 3p. grey (1904) . . . 6·50 60·00
e. Tall "R" . . . £250
f. Opt double, one albino . . . 55·00
40 **23** ½a. pale yellow-green (1901) . . . 50 1·10
e. Tall "R" . . . 90·00
f. Opt double, one albino . . . 23·00
40*g* ½a. yellow-green (1903) . . . 3·00 1·50
ge. Tall "R" . . . £130
41 **25** 1a. carmine (1901) . . . 1·00 35
e. Tall "R" . . . 95·00
f. Opt double, one albino . . . 42·00
42 **27** 2a. pale violet (1903) . . . 1·40 4·25
e. Tall "R" . . . £140
43 **36** 2a.6p. ultramarine (1903) . . . 1·10 5·00
e. Tall "R" . . . £190
38/43 *Set of* 6 . . . 9·75 65·00

(b) Optd as T **2**, *but* "GWALIOR" *13 mm long. Opt spaced 2¾ mm.*

44 **38** 3r. brown and green (1911) . . . £180 £180
45 5r. ultramarine and violet (1910) . . . 60·00 55·00
a. Opt double, one albino . . . 90·00

1903–11. *King Edward VII. Optd as T* **2**.

A. "GWALIOR" *14 mm long. Overprint spaced 1¾ mm (1903–06).*

46A **41** 3p. pale grey . . . 70 20
e. Tall "R" . . . 35·00 38·00
f. Slate-grey (1905) . . . 1·10 30
fe. Tall "R" . . . 40·00 42·00
48A **42** ½a. green . . . 20 10
e. Tall "R" . . . 32·00 38·00
49A **43** 1a. carmine . . . 20 10
e. Tall "R" . . . 38·00 42·00
f. Opt double, one albino . . . 35·00
50A **44** 2a. pale violet (1904) . . . 1·25 70
e. Tall "R" . . . 90·00
f. Mauve . . . 1·90 20
fe. Tall "R" . . . £110 £100
52A **45** 2a.6p. ultramarine (1904) . . . 19·00 70·00
e. Tall "R" . . . £850
53A **46** 3a. orange-brown (1904) . . . 1·50 35
e. Tall "R" . . . £130 £120
54A **47** 4a. olive . . . 1·50 40
e. Tall "R" . . . £180 £150
f. Pale olive . . . 8·00 2·00
fe. Tall "R" . . . £300
56A **48** 6a. olive-bistre (1904) . . . 2·75 2·75
e. Tall "R" . . . £850
57A **49** 8a. purple (*shades*) (1905) . . . 3·25 1·40
e. Tall "R" . . . £350 £250
59A **50** 12a. purple/*red* (1905) . . . 3·00 16·00
e. Tall "R" . . . £850
60A **51** 1r. green and carmine (1905) . . . 2·50 1·75
e. Tall "R" . . . £750 £750
61A **52** 2r. carmine and yellow-brown (1906) . . . 30·00 42·00
a. Opt double, one albino . . . 50·00
46A/61A *Set of* 12 . . . 60·00 £120

B. "GWALIOR" *13 mm long. Overprint spaced 2¾ mm (1908–11).*

46B **41** 3p. pale grey . . . 2·00 1[illegible]
f. Slate-grey . . . 2·50 4[illegible]
49B **43** 1a. carmine . . . 3·00 9[illegible]
50fB 2a. mauve . . . 2·50 1[illegible]
52B **45** 2a.6p. ultramarine . . . 1·25 7·5[illegible]
53B **46** 3a. orange-brown . . . 3·00 2[illegible]
54fB 4a. pale olive . . . 3·75 6[illegible]
56B **48** 6a. olive-bistre . . . 4·50 1·2[illegible]
57B **49** 8a. purple (*shades*) . . . 7·00 1·5[illegible]
f. Claret . . . 16·00 2·2[illegible]
fa. Opt double, one albino . . . 48·00
59B **50** 12a. purple/*red* . . . 3·75 3·2[illegible]
f. Opt double, one albino . . . 60·00
60B **51** 1r. green and carmine . . . 4·50 1·1[illegible]
61B **52** 2r. carmine and yellow-brown . . . 9·00 11·0[illegible]
a. Opt double, one albino . . . 48·00
62B 3r. brown and green (1910) . . . 26·00 45·0[illegible]
a. Red-brown and green . . . 60·00 70·0[illegible]
63B 5r. ultramarine and violet (1911) . . . 19·00 27·0[illegible]
46B/63B *Set of* 13 . . . 80·00 85·0[illegible]

1907–08. *Nos. 149 and 150 of India optd as T* **2**.

(a) "GWALIOR" *14 mm long. Overprint spaced 1¾ mm.*

64 **53** ½a. green . . . 10 7[illegible]
e. Tall "R" . . . 50·00 80·0[illegible]

(b) "GWALIOR" *13 mm long. Overprint spaced 2¾ mm (1908).*

65 **53** ½a. green . . . 80 [illegible]
66 **54** 1a. carmine . . . 1·50 [illegible]

1912–14. *King George V. Optd as T* **2**.

67 **55** 3p. grey . . . 10 [illegible]
a. Opt double . . . † £8[illegible]
b. Pale grey . . . 30 [illegible]
c. Bluish grey . . . — [illegible]
d. Slate . . . 50 [illegible]
da. "Rs" flaw . . . 30·00 35·[illegible]
68 **56** ½a. light green . . . 20 [illegible]
a. Emerald . . . 60 [illegible]
b. Bright green . . . 60 [illegible]
ba. Opt inverted . . . † £3[illegible]
69 **57** 1a. aniline carmine . . . 25 [illegible]
a. Opt double . . . 25·00
70 **59** 2a. purple . . . 60 [illegible]
a. Reddish purple . . . 70 [illegible]
aw. Wmk inverted . . . † 75·[illegible]
b. Deep mauve . . . 1·40 [illegible]
c. Bright reddish violet . . . 1·40 [illegible]
71 **62** 3a. orange . . . 50 [illegible]
a. Dull orange . . . 60 [illegible]
72 **63** 4a. olive (1913) . . . 60 [illegible]
73 **64** 6a. yellow-bistre . . . 1·00 1·[illegible]
a. Brown-ochre . . . 1·00 1·[illegible]
74 **65** 8a. deep magenta (1913) . . . 1·10 [illegible]
a. Deep mauve . . . 2·25 [illegible]
b. Bright mauve . . . 6·00 1·[illegible]
75 **66** 12a. carmine-lake (1914) . . . 1·25 2·[illegible]
a. Claret . . . — 3·[illegible]
76 **67** 1r. red-brown and deep blue-green (1913) . . . 6·50 [illegible]
a. Opt double, one albino . . . 20·00
b. Brown and green . . . 5·50 [illegible]
ba. Opt double . . . £650
c. Orange-brown and deep turquoise-green . . . — 1·[illegible]
77 2r. carmine-rose and brown (1913) . . . 4·50 4·[illegible]
a. Opt double, one albino . . . 50·00
78 5r. ultramarine and violet (1913) . . . 20·00 6·[illegible]
a. Opt double, one albino . . . 70·00
67/78 *Set of* 12 . . . 32·00 14·[illegible]

GWALIOR

(3)

1921. *No. 192 of India optd with T* **3**.

79 **57** 9p. on 1a. rose-carmine . . . 10

No. 79 with inverted overprint is of clandestine origin.

1923–27. *Optd as T* **2**. *New colours and values.*

80 **57** 1a. chocolate . . . 70
a. Opt double, one albino . . . 38·00
81 **58** 1½a. chocolate (B) (1925) . . . 1·50
82 1½a. rose-carmine (B) (1927) . . . 20
83 **61** 2a.6p. ultramarine (1925) . . . 1·75 1·[illegible]
84 2a.6p. orange (1927) . . . 35
85 **62** 3a. ultramarine (1924) . . . 1·50
80/5 *Set of* 6 . . . 5·50 3·[illegible]

No. 82 with inverted overprint is of clandestine origin.

Maharaja George Jivaji Rao Sindhia, 1925–1961

GWALIOR गवालियर (4)

GWALIOR गवालियर (5)

1928–36. *King George V (Nasik printing, wmk Mult Star), optd at Nasik with T* **4** *or* **5** *(rupee values).*

86 **55** 3p. slate (1932) 75 15
w. Wmk inverted 1·00 1·00
87 **56** ½a. green (1930) 1·50 10
w. Wmk inverted
88 **80** 9p. deep green (*litho*) (1932) 1·75 20
aw. Wmk inverted 2·50 80
88*b* 9p. deep green (*typo*) 2·75 50
89 **57** 1a. chocolate 75 10
w. Wmk inverted — 1·00
90 **82** 1a.3p. mauve (1936) 50 15
91 **70** 2a. purple 75 30
w. Wmk inverted 75 30
92 **62** 3a. bright blue 1·00 40
93 **71** 4a. sage-green 1·25 1·00
w. Wmk inverted 1·75 2·25
94 **65** 8a. reddish purple (*wmk inverted*) 1·25 1·10
95 **66** 12a. claret 1·50 3·00
96 **67** 1r. chocolate and green 2·00 3·00
w. Wmk inverted 4·00 3·00
97 2r. carmine and orange 8·00 4·50
w. Wmk inverted 7·00 4·00
98 5r. ultramarine and purple (*wmk inverted*) (1929) 17·00 24·00
99 10r. green and scarlet (1930) 50·00 38·00
00 15r. blue & olive (*wmk inverted*) (1930) 80·00 60·00
.01 25r. orange and blue (1930) £170 £140
36/101 *Set of* 16 £300 £250

935–36. *New types and colours. Optd with T* **4**.

.02 **79** ½a. green (1936) 50 20
w. Wmk inverted 3·75 2·50
03 **81** 1a. chocolate 20 10
04 **59** 2a. vermilion (1936) 1·75 2·50
02/4 *Set of* 3 2·25 2·50

938–48. *King George VI. Nos. 247/50, 253, 255/6 and 259/64 optd with T* **4** *or* **5** *(rupee values).*

05 **91** 3p. slate 6·50 10
06 ½a. red-brown 7·00 10
07 9p. green (1939) 40·00 3·25
08 1a. carmine 6·50 15
09 – 3a. yellow-green (1939) 17·00 3·75
10 – 4a. brown 42·00 2·50
11 – 6a. turquoise-green (1939) 3·00 8·50
12 **93** 1r. grey and red-brown (1942) 8·00 1·50
13 2r. purple and brown (1948) 40·00 9·00
14 5r. green and blue (1948) 30·00 32·00
15 10r. purple and claret (1948) 30·00 40·00
16 15r. brown and green (1948) 90·00 £160
17 25r. slate-violet and purple (1948) 80·00 £120
05/117 *Set of* 13 £350 £325

942–45. *King George VI. Optd with T* **4**.

18 **100a** 3p. slate 45 10
w. Wmk inverted — 16·00
19 ½a. purple (1943) 45 10
20 9p. green 45 10
21 1a. carmine (1943) 40 10
a. Opt double — £150
22 **101** 1½a. dull violet 6·00 20
23 2a. vermilion 65 20
24 3a. bright violet 13·00 1·00
a. Opt double — £150
25 **102** 4a. brown 1·75 20
26 6a. turquoise-green (1945) 14·00 23·00
27 8a. slate-violet (1944) 2·75 2·75
28 12a. lake (1943) 4·50 20·00
18/28 *Set of* 11 40·00 42·00

The 1½a. and 3a. exist printed by lithography or typography.

GWALIOR गवालियर (6)

949 (Apr). *King George VI. Optd with T* **6** *at the Alizah Printing Press, Gwalior.*

29 **100a** 3p. slate 1·40 50
30 ½a. purple 75 50
31 1a. carmine 75 60
32 **101** 2a. vermilion 19·00 2·00
33 3a. bright violet 45·00 25·00
34 **102** 4a. brown 4·50 2·75
35 6a. turquoise-green 42·00 48·00
36 8a. slate-violet 90·00 45·00
37 12a. lake £350 £130
29/37 *Set of* 9 £500 £225

OFFICIAL STAMPS

गवालियर सरविस (O 1)

गवालियर सरविस (O 2)

1895–96. *Queen Victoria. Optd with Type* O **1**.

O 1 **23** ½a. blue-green 30 10
a. Hindi characters transposed 26·00 28·00
b. 4th Hindi character omitted £450 40·00
c. Opt double † £900
O 2 **25** 1a. brown-purple 8·50 1·10
O 3 1a. plum 1·00 10
a. Hindi characters transposed 40·00 42·00
b. 4th Hindi character omitted — 65·00
O 4 **27** 2a. dull blue 2·00 40
O 5 2a. deep blue 1·40 40
a. Hindi characters transposed 60·00 80·00
b. 4th Hindi character omitted 80·00 £100
O 6 **29** 4a. olive-green 2·25 75
a. Hindi characters transposed £550 £500
b. 4th Hindi character omitted £2250 £1300
O 7 4a. slate-green 1·75 1·00
a. Hindi characters transposed £300
O 8 **31** 8a. dull mauve 2·75 1·90
a. Opt double, one albino 35·00
O 9 8a. magenta 2·00 1·40
a. Hindi characters transposed £1300 £1400
b. 4th Hindi character omitted
O10 **37** 1r. green and carmine (1896) 5·50 3·00
a. Hindi characters transposed £2500
O1/10 *Set of* 6 10·50 5·25

In the errors listed above it is the last two Hindi characters that are transposed, so that the word reads "Sersiv". The error occurs on R. 19/1 in the sheet from the early printings up to May 1896.

1901–04. *Colours changed.*

O23 **40** 3p. carmine (1902) 50 20
O24 3p. grey (1904) 1·50 2·25
O25 **23** ½a. pale yellow-green 4·00 15
O26 ½a. yellow-green 50 10
O27 **25** 1a. carmine 4·25 10
O28 **27** 2a. pale violet (1903) 85 1·50
O23/8 *Set of* 5 7·00 3·75

1903–08. *King Edward VII. Optd as Type* O **1**.

(a) Overprint spaced 10 mm (1903–5).

O29 **41** 3p. pale grey 60 10
a. Slate-grey (1905) 60 10
O31 **42** ½a. green 2·50 10
O32 **43** 1a. carmine 1·00 10
O33 **44** 2a. pale violet (1905) 2·00 50
a. Mauve 1·50 30
O35 **47** 4a. olive (1905) 14·00 1·25
a. Opt double, one albino 50·00
O36 **49** 8a. purple (1905) 4·50 70
a. Claret 14·00 4·25
ab. Opt double, one albino 40·00
O38 **51** 1r. green and carmine (1905) 2·75 1·75
O29/38 *Set of* 7 25·00 3·75

(b) Overprint spaced 8 mm (1907–8).

O39 **41** 3p. pale grey 4·25 15
a. Slate-grey 6·50 1·10
O41 **42** ½a. green 2·50 15
O42 **43** 1a. carmine 1·00 10
O43 **44** 2a. mauve 13·00 75
O44 **47** 4a. olive 3·00 1·00
O45 **49** 8a. purple 3·50 3·75
O46 **51** 1r. green and carmine (1908) 32·00 11·00
O39/46 *Set of* 7 55·00 15·00

1907–08. *Nos. 149 and 150 of India optd as Type* O **1**.

(a) Overprint spaced 10 mm (1908).

O47 **53** ½a. green 6·50 10
O48 **54** 1a. carmine 5·00 15
a. Opt double, one albino 35·00

(b) Overprint spaced 8 mm (1907).

O49 **53** ½a. green 1·25 15
O50 **54** 1a. carmine 55·00 3·00

1913–23. *King George V. Optd with Type* O **1**.

O51 **55** 3p. grey 20 10
a. Pale grey 20 10
b. Bluish grey — 30
c. Slate 20 10
ca. "Rs" flaw 65·00
O52 **56** ½a. light green 20 10
b. Emerald — 10
ba. Opt double £110 £160
c. Bright green 20 10
O53 **57** 1a. rose-carmine 8·50 50
a. Aniline carmine 30 10
ab. Opt double 65·00
O54 1a. chocolate (1923) 2·75 15
O55 **59** 2a. purple 70 50
a. Reddish purple 1·25 20
b. Deep mauve 2·00
c. Bright reddish violet 1·40 30
O56 **63** 4a. olive 60 90
O57 **65** 8a. deep magenta 1·00 1·60
a. Deep mauve 1·10 1·00
b. Bright mauve 2·25
O58 **67** 1r. red-brown and deep blue-green 24·00 20·00
a. Opt double, one albino 60·00
b. Brown and green 20·00 17·00
c. Orange-brown and deep turquoise-green 24·00 20·00
O51/8 *Set of* 8 23·00 18·00

1921. *No. O97 of India optd with T* **3**.

O59 **57** 9p. on 1a. rose-carmine 10 30

1927–35. *King George V (Nasik printing, wmk Mult Star), optd at Nasik as Type* O **1** *(but top line measures 13 mm instead of 14 mm) or with Type* O **2** *(rupee values).*

O61 **55** 3p. slate 30 10
w. Wmk inverted 10 50
O62 **56** ½a. green 10 15
w. Wmk inverted 2·50
O63 **80** 9p. deep green (1932) 10 15
O64 **57** 1a. chocolate 10 10
w. Wmk inverted 1·40 50
O65 **82** 1a.3p. mauve (1933) 50 15
w. Wmk inverted 3·25
O66 **70** 2a. purple 20 15
w. Wmk inverted 2·50
O67 **71** 4a. sage-green 60 30
w. Wmk inverted — 1·60
O68 **65** 8a. reddish purple (1928) 50 1·00
w. Wmk inverted 2·50 1·50
O69 **67** 1r. chocolate and green 1·00 1·75
w. Wmk inverted 1·90 3·00
O70 2r. carmine and orange (1935) 11·00 12·00
O71 5r. ultramarine and purple (1932) 16·00 £150
w. Wmk inverted 17·00
O72 10r. green and scarlet (1932) £120 £350
O61/72 *Set of* 12 £140 £475

1936–37. *New types. Optd as Type* O **1** *(13 mm).*

O73 **79** ½a. green 15 15
w. Wmk inverted — 3·50
O74 **81** 1a. chocolate 15 15
O75 **59** 2a. vermilion 20 40
O76 2a. vermilion (*small die*) 2·25 1·10
O77 **63** 4a. sage-green (1937) 60 75
O73/7 *Set of* 5 3·00 2·25

1938. *King George VI. Optd as Type* O **1** *(13 mm).*

O78 **91** ½a. red-brown 6·50 30
O79 1a. carmine 1·10 20

गवालियर (O 3)

1A 1A (O 4)

1940–42. *Official stamps optd with Type* O **3**.

O80 O **20** 3p. slate 50 10
O81 ½a. red-brown 3·25 25
O82 ½a. purple (1942) 50 10
O83 9p. green (1942) 70 60
O84 1a. carmine 2·25 10
O85 1a.3p. yellow-brown (1942) 38·00 1·75
w. Wmk inverted — 18·00
O86 1½a. dull violet (1942) 1·00 30
O87 2a. vermilion 1·00 30
O88 4a. brown (1942) 1·25 2·25
O89 8a. slate-violet (1942) 3·50 7·50
O80/9 *Set of* 10 48·00 12·00

1941. *Stamp of 1932 (King George V) optd with Type* O **1** *and surch with Type* O **4**.

O90 **82** 1a.on 1a.3p. mauve 23·00 2·75
w. Wmk inverted 30·00 6·50

1942–47. *King George VI. Optd with Type* O **2**.

O91 **93** 1r. grey and red-brown 10·00 16·00
O92 2r. purple and brown 18·00 75·00
O93 5r. green and blue (1943) 30·00 £450
O94 10r. purple and claret (1947) 80·00 £900
O91/4 *Set of* 4 £120 £1300

Gwalior became part of Madhya Bharat by 1 July 1948.

JIND

For earlier issues, see under INDIAN FEUDATORY STATES

PRICES FOR STAMPS ON COVER	
Nos. 1/4	*from* × 20
Nos. 5/16	—
Nos. 17/40	*from* × 15
Nos. 41/149	*from* × 8
Nos. O1/86	*from* × 15

Raja Raghubir Singh, 1864–1887

JHIND STATE (1)

JEEND STATE (2)

JHIND STATE (3)

1885 (1 July). *Queen Victoria. Optd with T* **1**.

1 **23** ½a. blue-green 3·00 3·75
a. Opt inverted 85·00 £100
2 **25** 1a. brown-purple 30·00 40·00
a. Opt inverted £750 £800
3 **27** 2a. dull blue 13·00 16·00
a. Opt inverted £550 £600
4 **17** 4a. green 55·00 75·00
5 **31** 8a. dull mauve £425
a. Opt inverted £9000
6 **33** 1r. slate £450
a. Opt inverted £10000
1/6 *Set of* 6 £900

The overprint inverted errors occurred on R. 10/8 in the setting of 120, although it is believed that one pane of the ½a. had the overprint inverted on the entire pane. Examples of inverted overprints on the ½a., 1a. and 2a. with the lines much less curved are thought to come from a trial printing.

All six values exist with reprinted overprint. This has the words "JHIND" and "STATE" 8 and 9 mm in length respectively, whereas in the originals the words are 9 and 9½ mm.

1885. *Optd with T* **2**.

7 **23** ½a. blue-green (R.) £100
8 **25** 1a. brown-purple £100
9 **27** 2a. dull blue (R.) £100
10 **17** 4a. green (R.) £140
a. Opt double, one albino £180
11 **31** 8a. dull mauve £160
12 **33** 1r. slate (R.) £170
7/12 *Set of* 6 £700

1886. *Optd with T* **3**, *in red.*

13 **23** ½a. blue-green 28·00
a. "JEIND" for "JHIND" £950

14 **27** 2a. dull blue . . . 29·00
a. "JEIND" for "JHIND" . . . £1200
b. Opt double, one albino . . . 65·00
15 **17** 4a. green . . . 48·00
a. Opt double, one albino . . . 55·00
b. Opt treble, two albino . . . 80·00
16 **33** 1r. slate . . . 55·00
a. "JEIND" for "JHIND" . . . £1700
13/16 *Set of* 4 . . . £140
Examples of No. 14a usually show an additional albino "SERVICE" overprint as Type O **16**.

1886–99. *Optd with T* **3**.
17 **23** ½a. blue-green . . . 70 10
a. Opt inverted . . . £200
18 **25** 1a. brown-purple . . . 1·25 20
a. "JEIND" for "JHIND" . . . £475
b. Opt double, one albino . . . 38·00
19 1a. plum (1899) . . . 3·00 1·00
20 **26** 1a.6p. sepia (1896) . . . 1·50 2·75
a. Opt double, one albino . . . 42·00
21 **27** 2a. dull blue . . . 1·75 40
22 2a. ultramarine . . . 1·50 60
a. Opt double, one albino . . . 42·00
23 **28** 3a. brown-orange (1891) . . . 1·75 60
24 **29** 4a. olive-green . . . 2·75 2·00
25 4a. slate-green . . . 3·75 3·00
26 **21** 6a. olive-bistre (1891) . . . 6·50 17·00
a. Opt double, one albino . . . 38·00
27 6a. bistre-brown . . . 2·00 10·00
28 **31** 8a. dull mauve . . . 5·00 15·00
a. "JEIND" for "JHIND" . . . £1600
29 8a. magenta (1897) . . . 7·50 23·00
a. Opt double, one albino . . . 38·00
30 **32** 12a. purple/*red* (1896) . . . 5·00 21·00
a. Opt double, one albino . . . 38·00
31 **33** 1r. slate . . . 10·00 42·00
32 **37** 1r. green and carmine (1897) . . . 8·50 48·00
33 **38** 2r. carmine and yellow-brown (1896) . . . £250 £750
34 3r. brown and green (1896) . . . £450 £750
35 5r. ultramarine and violet (1896) . . . £475 £750
17/35 *Set of* 14 . . . £1100 £2000
Varieties exist in which the word "JHIND" measures 10½ mm and 9¾ mm instead of 10 mm. Such varieties are to be found on Nos. 17, 18, 21, 24, 28 and 31.

Raja (Maharaja from 1911) Ranbir Singh, 1887–1959

1900–04. *Colours changed.*
36 **40** 3p. carmine . . . 1·10 1·00
37 3p. grey (1904) . . . 30 3·00
38 **23** ½a. pale yellow-green (1902) . . . 3·25 5·00
39 ½a. yellow-green (1903) . . . 7·50 10·00
40 **25** 1a. carmine (1902) . . . 40 5·00
a. Opt double, one albino . . . 32·00
36/40 *Set of* 4 . . . 4·50 12·50

1903–09. *King Edward VII. Optd with T* **3**.
41 **41** 3p. pale grey . . . 25 10
a. Opt double, one albino . . . 17·00
42 3p. slate-grey (1905) . . . 35 55
43 **42** ½a. green . . . 1·00 1·50
44 **43** 1a. carmine . . . 2·25 1·40
45 **44** 2a. pale violet . . . 2·25 2·25
46 2a. mauve (1906) . . . 2·00 80
a. Opt double, one albino . . . 32·00
47 **45** 2a.6p. ultramarine (1909) . . . 50 5·00
a. Opt double, one albino . . . 25·00
48 **46** 3a. orange-brown . . . 1·00 40
a. Opt double . . . £110 £200
49 **47** 4a. olive . . . 6·50 9·50
a. Opt double, one albino . . . 45·00
50 4a. pale olive . . . 6·50 9·00
51 **48** 6a. bistre (1905) . . . 6·50 18·00
a. Opt double, one albino . . . 38·00
52 **49** 8a. purple (*shades*) . . . 2·50 19·00
53 8a. claret . . . 13·00 27·00
54 **50** 12a. purple/*red* (1905) . . . 2·50 12·00
55 **51** 1r. green and carmine (1905) . . . 2·75 16·00
a. Opt double, one albino . . . 48·00
41/55 *Set of* 11 . . . 25·00 75·00

1907–09. *Nos. 149/50 of India optd with T* **3**.
56 **53** ½a. green . . . 20 20
57 **54** 1a. carmine (1909) . . . 50 70

1913. *King George V. Optd with T* **3**.
58 **55** 3p. grey . . . 10 1·75
59 **56** ½a. light green . . . 10 75
60 **57** 1a. aniline carmine . . . 10 45
61 **59** 2a. purple . . . 15 4·00
62 **62** 3a. orange . . . 1·50 10·00
63 **64** 6a. yellow-bistre . . . 6·00 24·00
58/63 *Set of* 6 . . . 7·25 38·00

JIND STATE (4) JIND STATE (5) JIND STATE (6)

1914–27. *King George V. Optd with T* **4**.
64 **55** 3p. grey . . . 75 35
a. Pale grey . . . 75 20
b. Bluish grey . . . 1·40 30
c. Slate . . . 1·40
65 **56** ½a. light green . . . 1·90 15
a. Emerald . . . — 50
b. Bright green . . . 2·00 30
66 **57** 1a. aniline carmine . . . 1·25 15
67 **58** 1½a. chocolate (Type A) (1922) . . . 1·75 4·25
a. Type B (1924) . . . 35 1·50
69 **59** 2a. purple . . . 2·50 50
a. Reddish purple . . . 6·00 75
b. Bright reddish violet (1922) . . . 6·00 75
70 **61** 2a.6p. ultramarine (1922) . . . 35 4·00
71 **62** 3a. orange . . . 50 3·00
72 **63** 4a. olive . . . 1·60 8·00
73 **64** 6a. yellow-bistre . . . 2·75 15·00
a. Brown-ochre . . . 2·25 13·00
74 **65** 8a. deep magenta . . . 3·75 10·00
a. Deep mauve (1925) . . . 7·00 9·00
b. Bright mauve (1918) . . . — 17·00
75 **66** 12a. carmine-lake . . . 3·00 14·00
76 **67** 1r. red-brown and deep blue-green . . . 8·00 17·00
a. Opt double, one albino . . . 32·00
b. Brown and green . . . 12·00
77 2r. carmine and yellow-brown (1927) . . . 5·50 £110
78 5r. ultramarine and violet (1927) . . . 38·00 £200
64/78 *Set of* 15 . . . 65·00 £350
No. 71 with inverted overprint is of clandestine origin.

1922. *No. 192 of India optd "JIND" in block capitals.*
79 **57** 9p. on 1a. rose-carmine . . . 1·25 13·00

1924–27. *Optd with T* **4**. *New colours.*
80 **57** 1a. chocolate . . . 4·25 1·90
81 **58** 1½a. rose-carmine (Type B) (1927) . . . 20 1·50
82 **61** 2a.6p. orange (1927) . . . 50 6·00
83 **62** 3a. bright blue (1925) . . . 1·75 4·00
80/3 *Set of* 4 . . . 6·00 12·00
Nos. 81/2 with inverted overprint are of clandestine origin.

1927–37. *King George V (Nasik printing, wmk Mult Star), optd at Nasik with T* **5** *or* **6** *(rupee values).*
84 **55** 3p. slate . . . 10 10
w. Wmk inverted . . . 2·25
85 **56** ½a. green (1929) . . . 10 35
86 **80** 9p. deep green (1932) . . . 1·40 40
87 **57** 1a. chocolate (1928) . . . 15 10
w. Wmk inverted . . . — 1·60
88 **82** 1a.3p. mauve (1932) . . . 25 30
89 **58** 1½a. rose-carmine (Type B) (1930) . . . 60 2·50
w. Wmk inverted . . . 1·10 2·50
90 **70** 2a. purple (1928) . . . 2·00 40
w. Wmk inverted . . . 2·00 40
91 **61** 2a.6p. orange (1930) . . . 1·00
w. Wmk inverted . . . 1·00 9·00
92 **62** 3a. bright blue (1930) . . . 3·75 12·00
w. Wmk inverted . . . 9·00
93 **83** 3a.6p. ultramarine (1937) . . . 3·00 20·00
w. Wmk inverted . . . 60 16·00
94 **71** 4a. sage-green (1928) . . . 4·25 3·00
w. Wmk inverted . . . 1·50 2·50
95 **64** 6a. bistre (1937) . . . 65 17·00
w. Wmk inverted . . . 4·50
96 **65** 8a. reddish purple (1930) . . . 3·75 2·00
w. Wmk inverted . . . 3·75
97 **66** 12a. claret (1930)
w. Wmk inverted . . . 5·00 18·00
98 **67** 1r. chocolate and green (1930) . . . 3·75 4·50
w. Wmk inverted
99 2r. carmine and orange (1930) . . . 32·00 £120
w. Wmk inverted . . . 19·00
100 5r. ultramarine and purple (1928) . . . 12·00 38·00
w. Wmk inverted . . . 40·00
101 10r. green and carmine (1928) . . . 13·00 18·00
102 15r. blue & olive (*wmk inverted*) (1929) . . . 75·00 £500
103 25r. orange and blue (1929) . . . £110 £650
84/103 *Set of* 20 . . . £225 £1300

1934. *New types and colours. Optd with T* **5**.
104 **79** ½a. green . . . 30 25
105 **81** 1a. chocolate . . . 1·50 30
w. Wmk inverted . . . — 3·50
106 **59** 2a. vermilion . . . 1·75 60
107 **62** 3a. carmine . . . 2·50 40
108 **63** 4a. sage-green . . . 3·00 1·25
104/8 *Set of* 5 . . . 8·00 2·50

1937–38. *King George VI. Nos. 247/64 optd with T* **5** *or T* **6** *(rupee values).*
109 **91** 3p. slate . . . 11·00 1·75
110 ½a. red-brown . . . 75 3·25
111 9p. green (1937) . . . 75 3·00
112 1a. carmine (1937) . . . 75 60
113 **92** 2a. vermilion . . . 1·75 15·00
114 – 2a.6p. bright violet . . . 1·25 17·00
115 – 3a. yellow-green . . . 6·00 14·00
116 – 3a.6p. bright blue . . . 3·00 17·00
117 – 4a. brown . . . 9·00 15·00
118 – 6a. turquoise-green . . . 5·50 21·00
119 – 8a. slate-violet . . . 4·50 19·00
120 – 12a. lake . . . 2·75 23·00
121 **93** 1r. grey and red-brown . . . 12·00 32·00
122 2r. purple and brown . . . 15·00 95·00
123 5r. green and blue . . . 25·00 75·00
124 10r. purple and claret . . . 45·00 70·00
125 15r. brown and green . . . £110 £700
126 25r. slate-violet and purple . . . £450 £750
109/26 *Set of* 18 . . . £650 £1700

JIND
(7)

1941–43. *King George VI. Optd with T* **7**.

(a) Stamps of 1937. W **69** (inverted on 15r.).
127 **91** 3p. slate . . . 14·00 17·00
128 ½a. red-brown . . . 1·00 1·25
129 9p. green . . . 12·00 14·00
130 1a. carmine . . . 1·00 4·25
131 **93** 1r. grey and red-brown . . . 8·00 23·00
132 2r. purple and brown . . . 17·00 28·00
133 5r. green and blue . . . 40·00 85·00
134 10r. purple and claret . . . 55·00 80·00
135 15r. brown and green . . . £130 £140
136 25r. slate-violet and purple . . . 60·00 £350
127/36 *Set of* 10 . . . £300 £650

(b) Stamps of 1940–43.
137 **100a** 3p. slate (1942) . . . 50 75
138 ½a. purple (1943) . . . 50 1·40
139 9p. green (1942) . . . 60 3·25
140 1a. carmine (1942) . . . 65 1·25
141 **101** 1a.3p. yellow-brown . . . 1·00 3·75
142 1½a. dull violet (1942) . . . 8·00 4·00
143 2a. vermilion . . . 1·75 3·50
144 3a. bright violet (1942) . . . 21·00 4·25
145 3½a. bright blue . . . 9·00 8·00
146 **102** 4a. brown . . . 4·75 4·00
147 6a. turquoise-green . . . 5·50 13·00
148 8a. slate-violet . . . 2·75 11·00
149 12a. lake . . . 14·00 14·00
137/149 *Set of* 13 . . . 65·00 65·00
The 1½a. and 3a. exist printed by lithography or typography.

OFFICIAL STAMPS

SERVICE

SERVICE (O 14) SERVICE (O 15) JHIND STATE (O 16)

1885 (1 July). *Queen Victoria. Nos. 1/3 of Jind optd with Type* O **14**.
O1 **23** ½a. blue green . . . 90 3[illegible]
a. Opt Type **1** inverted . . . 95·00 60·0[illegible]
O2 **25** 1a. brown-purple . . . 60 1[illegible]
a. Opt Type **1** inverted . . . 12·00 7·5[illegible]
O3 **27** 2a. dull blue . . . 35·00 42·0[illegible]
a. Opt Type **1** inverted . . . £1000
The three values have had the overprint reprinted in the same way as the ordinary stamps of 1885. See note after No. 6.

1885. *Nos. 7/9 of Jind optd with Type* O **15**.
O7 **23** ½a. blue-green (R.) . . . 90·00
a. "JEEND STATE" double, one albino . . . £130
O8 **25** 1a. brown-purple . . . 75·00
O9 **27** 2a. dull blue (R.) . . . 85·00
O7/9 *Set of* 3 . . . £225

1886. *Optd with Type* O **16**, *in red.*
O10 **23** ½a. blue-green . . . 16·00
a. "ERVICE" . . . £3000
b. "JEIND" . . . £650
c. "JHIND STATE" double, one albino . . . 60·00
O11 **27** 2a. dull blue . . . 25·00
a. "ERVICE" . . . £1800
b. "JEIND" . . . £950
c. "SERVICE" double, one albino . . . 42·00
d. "JHIND STATE" double, one albino . . . 42·00

1886–1902. *Optd with Type* O **16**.
O12 **23** ½a. blue-green . . . 1·00 1[illegible]
a. "JHIND STATE" double, one albino . . . 38·00
O13 **25** 1a. brown-purple . . . 21·00
a. "ERVICE
b. "JEIND" . . . £450
c. "SERVICE" double, one albino . . . 25·00
O14 1a. plum (1902) . . . 9·50 [illegible]
O15 **27** 2a. dull blue . . . 2·50 [illegible]
a. "SERVICE" double, one albino . . . 38·00
b. "SERVICE" treble, two albino . . . 42·00
O16 2a. ultramarine . . . 1·00 [illegible]
a. "JHIND STATE" double, one albino . . . 42·00
O17 **29** 4a. olive-green (1892) . . . 2·00 1·[illegible]
a. "JHIND STATE" double, one albino . . . 35·00
O18 4a. slate-green . . . 2·00 1·[illegible]
O19 **31** 8a. dull mauve (1892) . . . 4·00 3·[illegible]
O20 8a. magenta (1897) . . . 3·75 6·[illegible]
a. "JHIND STATE" double, one albino . . . 38·00
O21 **37** 1r. green and carmine (1896) . . . 6·00 38·[illegible]
a. "SERVICE" double, one albino . . . 48·00
b. "JHIND STATE" treble, two albino . . . 65·00
O12/21 *Set of* 6 . . . 21·00 40·[illegible]
Varieties mentioned in note after No. 35 exist on Nos. O12, O1[illegible] O17 and O20.
Printings up to and including that of October 1897 had t[illegible] "SERVICE overprint. Type O **15**, applied to sheets alrea[illegible] overprinted with Type **3**. From the printing of December 18[illegible] onwards "SERVICE" and "JHIND STATE" were overprinted [illegible] one operation, as Type O **16**, to provide fresh supplies of Nos. O1[illegible] O14 and O21.

1902. *Colour changed. Optd with Type* O **16**.
O22 **23** ½a. yellow-green . . . 1·75
a. "V" of "SERVICE" omitted . . . £110 60·[illegible]
No. O22a normally shows a tiny trace of the "V" remainin[illegible] Examples showing the letter completely missing are worth mu[illegible] more.

1903–06. *King Edward VII stamps of India optd with Type* O **16**.
O23 **41** 3p. pale grey . . . 40
O24 3p. slate-grey (1906) . . . 40
O25 **42** ½a. green . . . 2·25
a. "HIND" . . . £2250 £2[illegible]
b. Opt double, one albino . . . 28·00
c. "SERV CE" . . . † £2[illegible]
O26 **43** 1a. carmine . . . 1·75
a. "HIND" . . . — £2[illegible]
b. Opt double, one albino . . . 30·00
O27 **44** 2a. pale violet . . . 1·75
O28 2a. mauve . . . 90
O29 **47** 4a. olive . . . 90
a. Opt double, one albino . . . 40·00
O30 **49** 8a. purple (*shades*) . . . 7·50 5·[illegible]
O31 8a. claret . . . 4·25 1·[illegible]
O32 **51** 1r. green and carmine (1906) . . . 2·50 2·[illegible]
O23/32 *Set of* 7 . . . 11·50 4·[illegible]
The "HIND" error Nos. O25a and O26a occurred on o[illegible] position in the bottom row of the sheet.

1907. *Nos. 149/50 of India optd with Type* O **16**.

O33 **53** ½a. green . . . 50 10
O34 **54** 1a. carmine . . . 75 10

1914–27. *King George V. Official stamps of India optd with T* **4**.

O35 **55** 3p. grey . . . 10 10
a. "JIND STATE" double, one albino . . . 38·00
b. Pale grey . . . 10 10
c. Bluish grey . . . — 30
O36 **56** ½a. light green . . . 10 10
a. Emerald . . . 1·10 30
b. Bright green . . . 30 10
O37 **57** 1a. aniline carmine . . . 60 10
a. Pale rose-carmine . . . 1·50 10
O39 **59** 2a. purple . . . 25 30
a. Reddish purple . . . — 15
b. Deep mauve . . . 1·25 30
O40 **63** 4a. olive . . . 85 15
O41 **64** 6a. brown-ochre (1926) . . . 1·25 2·25
O42 **65** 8a. deep magenta . . . 70 1·00
a. Deep mauve . . . 1·40 1·50
O43 **67** 1r. red-brown and deep blue-green . . . 1·50 1·75
a. "JIND STATE" double, one albino . . . 38·00
b. Brown and green . . . 6·00
O44 2r. carmine and yellow-brown (1927) . . . 14·00 65·00
O45 5r. ultramarine and violet (1927) . . . 19·00 £180
O35/45 *Set of* 10 . . . 35·00 £225

No. O40 with double overprint is of clandestine origin.

1924. *As 1914–27. New colour.*

O46 **57** 1a. chocolate . . . 60 10

JIND STATE SERVICE (O 17) — JIND STATE SERVICE (O 18) — JIND SERVICE (O 19)

1927–37. *King George V (Nasik printing, wmk Mult Star), optd with Types* O **17** *or* O **18** *(rupee values).*

O47 **55** 3p. slate (1928) . . . 10 20
O48 **56** ½a. green (1929) . . . 10 90
O49 **80** 9p. deep green (*litho*) (1932) . . . 60 15
O49*a* 9p. deep green (*typo*) . . . — 75
O50 **57** 1a. chocolate . . . 10 10
w. Wmk inverted . . . 85
O51 **82** 1a.3p. mauve (1932) . . . 40 15
w. Wmk inverted . . . 1·40 70
O52 **70** 2a. purple (1929) . . . 25 15
O53 **61** 2a.6p. orange (1937) . . . 90 19·00
O54 **71** 4a. sage-green (1929) . . . 35 25
w. Wmk inverted . . . 1·40 1·00
O55 **64** 6a. bistre (1937) . . . 1·75
w. Wmk inverted . . . 3·00 14·00
O56 **65** 8a. reddish purple (1929) . . . — 1·75
w. Wmk inverted . . . 60 1·75
O57 **66** 12a. claret (1928) . . . 1·60 14·00
O58 **67** 1r. chocolate and green (1928) . . . 3·75 3·75
O59 2r. carmine and orange (1930) . . . 40·00 32·00
w. Wmk inverted . . . 32·00
O60 5r. ultramarine and purple (1929) . . . 13·00 £190
O61 10r. green and carmine (1928) . . . 32·00 £110
w. Wmk inverted . . . 42·00
O47/61 *Set of* 15 . . . 80·00 £350

1934. *Optd with Type* O **17**.

O62 **79** ½a. green . . . 20 15
O63 **81** 1a. chocolate . . . 20 15
O64 **59** 2a. vermilion . . . 30 15
w. Wmk inverted . . . 70 1·50
O65 **63** 4a. sage-green . . . 4·50 30
O62/5 *Set of* 4 . . . 4·75 65

1937–40. *King George VI. Optd with Types* O **17** *or* O **18** *(rupee values).*

O66 **91** ½a. red-brown (1938) . . . 50·00 30
O67 9p. green . . . 85 9·50
O68 1a. carmine . . . 55 30
O69 **93** 1r. grey and red-brown (1940) . . . 27·00 45·00
O70 2r. purple and brown (1940) . . . 42·00 £180
O71 5r. green and blue (1940) . . . 70·00 £325
O72 10r. purple and claret (1940) . . . £250 £900
O66/72 *Set of* 7 . . . £400 £1300

1939–43.

(a) Official stamps optd with T **7**.

O73 O **20** 3p. slate . . . 50 1·10
O74 ½a. red-brown . . . 1·50 70
O75 ½a. purple (1943) . . . 60 30
O76 9p. green . . . 2·25 9·50
O77 1a. carmine . . . 3·00 15
O78 1½a. dull violet (1942) . . . 8·00 1·25
O79 2a. vermilion . . . 4·50 30
w. Wmk inverted . . . 9·50 2·75
O80 2½a. bright violet . . . 3·50 8·00
O81 4a. brown . . . 6·00 3·00
O82 8a. slate-violet . . . 6·00 5·00

(b) Postage stamps optd with Type O **19**.

O83 **93** 1r. grey and red-brown (1942) . . . 18·00 45·00
O84 2r. purple and brown (1942) . . . 32·00 £130
O85 5r. green and blue (1942) . . . 70·00 £325
O86 10r. purple and claret (1942) . . . £140 £425
O73/86 *Set of* 14 . . . £250 £850

Jind was absorbed into the Patiala and East Punjab States Union by 20 August 1948.

NABHA

PRICES FOR STAMPS ON COVER	
Nos. 1/3	*from* × 15
Nos. 4/6	—
Nos. 10/36	*from* × 12
Nos. 37/117	*from* × 7
Nos. O1/68	*from* × 15

Raja Hira Singh, 1871–1911.

NABHA STATE (1) — NABHA STATE (2)

1885 (1 July). *Queen Victoria. Optd with T* **1**.

1 **23** ½a. blue-green . . . 3·50 4·50
2 **25** 1a. brown-purple . . . 42·00 £150
3 **27** 2a. dull blue . . . 17·00 45·00
4 **17** 4a. green . . . 75·00 £190
5 **31** 8a. dull mauve . . . £300
6 **33** 1r. slate . . . £325
1/6 *Set of* 6 . . . £700

All six values have had the overprint reprinted. On the reprints the words "NABHA" and "STATE" both measure 9¼ mm in length, whereas on the originals these words measure 11 and 10 mm respectively. The varieties with overprint double come from the reprints.

1885 (Nov)–**1900**. *Optd with T* **2**.

(a) In red.

10 **23** ½a. blue-green . . . 60 60
11 **27** 2a. dull blue . . . 2·50 2·00
a. Opt double, one albino . . . 48·00
12 **17** 4a. green . . . 35·00 £170
13 **33** 1r. slate . . . £110 £225
a. Opt double, one albino . . . £140
10/13 *Set of* 4 . . . £130 £350

(b) In black (Nov 1885–97).

14 **23** ½a. blue-green (1888) . . . 50 10
15 **24** 9p. carmine (1892) . . . 1·50 3·00
16 **25** 1a. brown-purple . . . 2·00 90
17 1a. plum . . . 1·75 80
18 **26** 1a.6p. sepia (1891) . . . 1·50 3·00
a. "ABHA" for "NABHA" . . . £300
19 **27** 2a. dull blue (1888) . . . 2·50 1·75
20 2a. ultramarine . . . 2·00 1·50
21 **28** 3a. orange (1889) . . . 7·00 17·00
a. Opt double, one albino . . . 32·00
22 3a. brown-orange . . . 3·00 2·00
23 **29** 4a. olive-green (1888) . . . 5·00 2·25
24 4a. slate-green . . . 5·00 2·25
25 **21** 6a. olive-bistre (1889) . . . 5·50 12·00
26 6a. bistre-brown . . . 2·50 3·00
27 **31** 8a. dull mauve . . . 2·50 2·00
a. Opt double, one albino . . . 38·00
28 **32** 12a. purple/*red* (1889) . . . 3·50 4·00
a. Opt double, one albino . . . 35·00
29 **33** 1r. slate (1888) . . . 11·00 45·00
30 **37** 1r. green and carmine (1893) . . . 10·00 4·25
a. "N BHA" for "NABHA"
b. Opt double, one albino . . . 48·00
31 **38** 2r. carmine and yellow-brown (1897) . . . £110 £225
a. Opt double, one albino . . . £190
32 3r. brown and green (1897) . . . £110 £300
33 5r. ultramarine and violet (1897) . . . £110 £425
14/33 *Set of* 15 . . . £325 £900

(c) New value. In black (Nov 1900).

36 **40** 3p. carmine . . . 30 20

1903–09. *King Edward VII. Optd with T* **2**.

37 **41** 3p. pale grey . . . 75 15
a. "NAB STA" for "NABHA STATE" . . . £850
b. Opt double, one albino . . . 23·00
37*c* 3p. slate-grey (1906) . . . 75 15
38 **42** ½a. green . . . 1·00 60
a. "NABH" for "NABHA" . . . £1000
39 **43** 1a. carmine . . . 1·60 70
40 **44** 2a. pale violet . . . 1·50 2·50
40*a* 2a. mauve . . . 2·75 35
40*b* **45** 2a.6p. ultramarine (1909) . . . 18·00 85·00
ba. Opt double, one albino . . . 32·00
41 **46** 3a. orange-brown . . . 1·00 40
a. Opt double, one albino . . . 42·00
42 **47** 4a. olive . . . 2·50 1·75
43 **48** 6a. olive-bistre . . . 2·50 15·00
a. Opt double, one albino . . . 27·00
44 **49** 8a. purple . . . 9·00 20·00
44*a* 8a. claret . . . 11·00 21·00
45 **50** 12a. purple/*red* . . . 3·50 20·00
46 **51** 1r. green and carmine . . . 9·00 12·00
37/46 *Set of* 11 . . . 45·00 £140

1907. *Nos. 149/50 of India optd with T* **2**.

47 **53** ½a. green . . . 1·50 1·25
48 **54** 1a. carmine . . . 1·00 70

Maharaja Ripudaman (Gurcharan) Singh, 1911–1928.

1913. *King George V. Optd with T* **2**.

49 **55** 3p. grey . . . 30 35
a. Pale grey . . . 25 20
b. Bluish grey . . . 1·00 30
c. Slate . . . 1·00
50 **56** ½a. light green . . . 35 15
a. Emerald . . . 1·25 50
b. Bright green . . . 50 20
51 **57** 1a. aniline carmine . . . 1·00 10
52 **59** 2a. purple . . . 60 60
a. Reddish purple . . . 1·00 50
b. Deep mauve . . . 1·25 50
53 **62** 3a. orange . . . 50 35
a. Dull orange . . . 85 50
54 **63** 4a. olive . . . 65 1·25
55 **64** 6a. yellow-bistre . . . 85 4·75
a. Brown-ochre . . . 1·00 5·00
56 **65** 8a. deep magenta . . . 3·50 4·00
a. Deep mauve . . . 3·00 3·25
b. Bright mauve . . . 4·50
57 **66** 12a. carmine-lake . . . 1·90 20·00
58 **67** 1r. red-brown and deep blue-green . . . 8·00 4·50
a. Opt double, one albino . . . 42·00
b. Brown and green . . . 12·00 3·75
c. Orange-brown and deep turquoise-green . . . 14·00
49/58 *Set of* 10 . . . 15·00 32·00

1924. *As 1913. New colour.*

59 **57** 1a. chocolate . . . 4·75 2·50

No. 59 with inverted or double overprint is of clandestine origin.

NABHA STATE (3) — NABHA STATE (4)

1927–36. *King George V (Nasik printing, wmk Mult Star), optd as T* **3** *or* **4** *(rupee values).*

60 **55** 3p. slate (1932) . . . 1·40 15
w. Wmk inverted . . . 2·75 1·40
61 **56** ½a. green (1928) . . . 70 20
61*a* **80** 9p. deep green (*litho*) (1934) . . . 10·00 10·00
61*b* 9p. deep green (*typo*) . . . 2·25 1·10
62 **57** 1a. chocolate . . . 1·50 15
w. Wmk inverted
63 **82** 1a.3p. mauve (1936) . . . 1·75 5·50
w. Wmk inverted . . . 75
64 **70** 2a. purple (1932) . . . 2·50 35
65 **61** 2a.6p. orange (1932) . . . 80 8·00
66 **62** 3a. bright blue (1930) . . . 2·75 1·10
67 **71** 4a. sage-green (1932) . . . 3·00 1·75
71 **67** 2r. carmine and orange (1932) . . . 26·00 95·00
72 5r. ultramarine and purple (*wmk inverted*) (1932) . . . 70·00 £275
60/72 *Set of* 11 . . . £100 £350

Maharaja Partab Singh, 1928–1971

1936–37. *New types and colours. Optd as T* **3**.

73 **79** ½a. green . . . 50 40
74 **81** 1a. chocolate . . . 45 30
75 **62** 3a. carmine (1937) . . . 4·00 13·00
76 **63** 4a. sage-green (1937) . . . 4·25 3·50
73/6 *Set of* 4 . . . 8·25 15·00

NABHA STATE (5) — NABHA (6)

1938. *King George VI. Nos. 247/64 optd as T* **3** *(3p. to 1a.), T* **5** *(2a. to 12a.) or T* **4** *(rupee values).* W **69** (inverted on 15r.).

77 **91** 3p. slate . . . 7·00 70
78 ½a. red-brown . . . 6·00 1·00
79 9p. green . . . 19·00 4·00
80 1a. carmine . . . 2·75 70
81 **92** 2a. vermilion . . . 1·25 6·00
82 – 2a.6p. bright violet . . . 1·25 9·00
83 – 3a. yellow-green . . . 1·40 5·00
84 – 3a.6p. bright blue . . . 1·40 19·00
85 – 4a. brown . . . 7·00 7·00
86 – 6a. turquoise-green . . . 3·00 20·00
87 – 8a. slate-violet . . . 2·25 20·00
88 – 12a. lake . . . 2·50 20·00
89 **93** 1r. grey and red-brown . . . 11·00 26·00
90 2r. purple and brown . . . 25·00 90·00
91 5r. green and blue . . . 35·00 £170
92 10r. purple and claret . . . 55·00 £350
93 15r. brown and green . . . £170 £650
94 25r. slate-violet and purple . . . £140 £650
w. Wmk inverted . . . £250 £750
77/94 *Set of* 18 . . . £425 £1800

1941–45. *King George VI. Optd with T* **6**.

(a) Stamps of 1937.

95 **91** 3p. slate (1942) . . . 32·00 4·00
96 ½a. red-brown (1942) . . . 75·00 5·00
97 9p. green (1942) . . . 11·00 13·00
98 1a. carmine (1942) . . . 11·00 2·75
95/8 *Set of* 4 . . . £120 22·00

(b) Stamps of 1940–43.

105 **100a** 3p. slate (1942) . . . 1·00 1·00
106 ½a. purple (1943) . . . 3·00 1·10
107 9p. green (1942) . . . 2·50 1·10
108 1a. carmine (1945) . . . 1·00 3·25
109 **101** 1a.3p. yellow-brown . . . 1·00 2·75
110 1½a. dull violet (1942) . . . 2·00 2·00
111 2a. vermilion (1943) . . . 1·10 4·00
112 3a. bright violet (1943) . . . 5·00 3·75
113 3½a. bright blue (1944) . . . 15·00 48·00
114 **102** 4a. brown . . . 1·75 1·00
115 6a. turquoise-green (1943) . . . 10·00 45·00
116 8a. slate-violet (1943) . . . 9·00 35·00
117 12a. lake (1943) . . . 6·00 48·00
105/17 *Set of* 13 . . . 50·00 £170

The 1½a. exists printed by lithography or typography.

OFFICIAL STAMPS

SERVICE

SERVICE (O 8) — NABHA STATE (O 9)

1885 (1 July). *Nos. 1/3 of Nabha optd with Type* O **8**.

O1 **23** ½a. blue-green . . . 3·25 1·00
O2 **25** 1a. brown-purple . . . 60 20
a. Opt Type O **8** double . . . † £1400
O3 **27** 2a. dull blue . . . 70·00 £130
O1/3 *Set of* 3 . . . 70·00 £130

The three values have had the overprint reprinted in the same way as the ordinary stamps of 1885.

1885 (Nov)–**97**. *Optd with Type* O **9**.

No.	Type	Description	Unused	Used
		(a) In red.		
O 4	**23**	½a. blue-green	6·50	4·00
O 5	**27**	2a. deep blue	1·25	55
		(b) In black (Nov 1885–97).		
O 6	**23**	½a. blue-green (1888)	40	10
		a. "SERVICE." with stop	£120	2·25
		b. "S ATE" for "STATE		
		c. "SERVICE" double, one albino	32·00	
O 7	**25**	1a. brown-purple	1·25	60
O 8		1a. plum	1·25	25
		a. "SERVICE." with stop	7·00	75
		ab. "SERVICE." with stop, and "NABHA STATE" double	†	£250
O 9	**27**	2a. dull blue (1888)	2·25	1·00
O10		2a. ultramarine	2·75	1·40
O11	**28**	3a. orange (1889)	24·00	75·00
O12		3a. brown-orange	24·00	75·00
		a. "NABHA STATE" double, one albino	48·00	
O13	**29**	4a. olive-green (1888)	3·00	1·25
O14		4a. slate-green	3·00	1·25
O15	**21**	6a. olive-bistre (1889)	18·00	28·00
		a. "SERVICE" double, one albino	38·00	
O16		6a. bistre-brown	£650	
O17	**31**	8a. dull mauve (1889)	2·75	1·00
O18	**32**	12a. purple/*red* (1889)	6·50	18·00
		a. SERVICE" double, one albino	38·00	
		b. "NABHA STATE double, one albino	35·00	
O19	**33**	1r. slate (1889)	35·00	£250
O20	**37**	1r. green and carmine (1.97)	30·00	75·00
O6/20 *Set of* 10			£110	£400

Printings up to and including that of August 1895 had the "SERVICE" overprint applied to sheets of stamps already overprinted with Type **2**. From the printing of January 1897 onwards the two parts of the overprint were applied at one operation. This method was only used for printings of the ½a., 1a. and 1r. (O20).

1903–06. *King Edward VII stamps of India optd with Type* O **9**.

No.	Type	Description	Unused	Used
O24	**41**	3p. pale grey (1906)	5·00	20·00
O25		3p. slate-grey (1906)	1·40	13·00
		a. Opt double, one albino	30·00	
O26	**42**	½a. green	80	35
O27	**43**	1a. carmine	70	10
O28	**44**	2a. pale violet	2·25	1·00
O29		2a. mauve	1·75	40
		a. Opt double, one albino	38·00	
O30	**47**	4a. olive	1·60	50
O32	**49**	8a. purple (*shades*)	1·40	1·50
		a. Opt double, one albino	28·00	
O33		8a. claret	8·50	3·75
O34	**51**	1r. green and carmine	1·60	2·25
O24/34 *Set of* 7			8·50	16·00

1907. *Nos. 149/50 of India optd with Type* O **9**.

No.	Type	Description	Unused	Used
O35	**53**	½a. green	75	50
		a. Opt double, one albino	18·00	
O36	**54**	1a. carmine	75	30
		a. Opt double, one albino	30·00	

1913. *King George V. Optd with Type* O **9**.

No.	Type	Description	Unused	Used
O37	**63**	4a. olive	10·00	55·00
O38	**67**	1r. red-brown and deep blue-green	55·00	£400
		a. Opt double, one albino	£100	

1913. *Official stamps of India optd with T* **2**.

No.	Type	Description	Unused	Used
O39	**55**	3p. grey	85	9·50
		a. Pale grey	70	7·50
		b. Bluish grey	85	7·50
		c. Slate	60	7·50
O40	**56**	½a. light green	40	15
		a. Emerald	75	10
		b. Bright green	50	15
O41	**57**	1a. aniline carmine	30	10
O42	**59**	2a. purple	50	50
		a. Reddish purple	1·25	20
		b. Deep mauve	1·25	20
		c. Bright reddish violet		
O43	**63**	4a. olive	50	50
O44	**65**	8a. deep magenta	1·00	1·50
		a. Deep mauve	2·25	
		b. Bright mauve	2·75	
O46	**67**	1r. red-brown & deep blue-green	4·25	2·75
		a. Brown and green	6·00	2·75
O39/46 *Set of* 7			6·75	11·00

NABHA STATE SERVICE
(O 10)

NABHA SERVICE
(O 11)

1932–42?. *King George V (Nasik printing, wmk Mult Star), optd at Nasik with Type* O **10**.

No.	Type	Description	Unused	Used
O47	**55**	3p. slate	10	15
O48	**81**	1a. chocolate (1935)	15	15
O49	**63**	4a. sage-green (1942?)	21·00	2·50
O50	**65**	8a. reddish purple (1937)	1·00	2·00
O47/50 *Set of* 4			21·00	4·25

1938. *King George VI. Optd as Type* O **10**.

No.	Type	Description	Unused	Used
O53	**91**	9p. green	3·50	3·75
O54		1a. carmine	15·00	90

1940–43.

No.	Type	Description	Unused	Used
		(a) Official stamps optd with T **6**.		
O55	O **20**	3p. slate (1942)	80	1·10
O56		½a. red-brown (1942)	90	30
O57		½a. purple (1943)	3·50	80
O58		9p. green	1·25	20
O59		1a. carmine (1942)	60	20
O61		1½a. dull violet (1942)	70	40
O62		2a. vermilion (1942)	2·00	1·10
		w. Wmk inverted	3·50	1·60
O64		4a. brown (1942)	3·50	3·00
O65		8a. slate-violet (1942)	5·50	17·00
		(b) Postage stamps optd with Type O **11**.		
O66	**93**	1r. grey and red-brown (1942)	8·50	35·00
O67		2r. purple and brown (1942)	27·00	£160
O68		5r. green and blue (1942)	£170	£500
O55/68 *Set of* 12			£200	£650

Nabha was absorbed into the Patiala and East Punjab States Union by 20 August 1948.

PATIALA

PRICES FOR STAMPS ON COVER	
Nos. 1/6	*from* × 10
Nos. 7/34	*from* × 6
Nos. 35/45	*from* × 8
Nos. 46/115	*from* × 4
Nos. O1/84	*from* × 15

Maharaja Rajindra Singh, 1876–1900

PUTTIALLA STATE
(1)

STATE
(2)

PUTTIALLA STATE
(2)

PATIALA STATE
(3)

1884 (1 Oct). *Queen Victoria. Optd with T* **1**, *in red.*

No.	Type	Description	Unused	Used
1	**23**	½a. blue-green	3·75	3·75
		a. Opt double, one sideways	£2250	£650
		b. Opt double, one albino	65·00	
2	**25**	1a. brown-purple	48·00	55·00
		a. Opt double		
		b. Optd in red and in black	£650	
3	**27**	2a. dull blue	12·00	12·00
4	**17**	4a. green	70·00	75·00
5	**31**	8a. dull mauve	£350	£850
		a. Opt inverted	£7500	
		b. Optd in red and in black	95·00	£350
		ba. Ditto. Opts inverted	£4750	
		c. Opt double, one albino	£425	
6	**33**	1r. slate	£130	£475
1/6 *Set of* 6			£550	£1300

Nos. 5a and 5ba each occur once in the setting of 120. The 8a. value also exists with a trial overprint (showing the words more curved) reading downwards (*Price £500 unused*), which should not be confused with No. 5a.

1885. *Optd with T* **2**.

No.	Type	Description	Unused	Used
		(a) In red.		
7	**23**	½a. blue-green	2·25	30
		a. "AUTTIALLA"	15·00	24·00
		b. "STATE" only		
		c. Wide spacing between lines	6·00	6·00
8	**27**	2a. dull blue	4·00	1·75
		a. "AUTTIALLA"	32·00	
		b. Wide spacing between lines	21·00	21·00
		ba. Ditto "AUTTIALLA"	£475	
9	**17**	4a. green	3·25	3·00
		a. Optd in red and in black	£200	
		b. Wide spacing between lines	£350	
		c. Opt double, one albino	40·00	
10	**33**	1r. slate	10·00	65·00
		a. "AUTTIALLA"	£425	
		b. Wide spacing between lines	£350	
		(b) In black.		
11	**25**	1a. brown-purple	60	30
		a. Optd in red and in black	8·50	70·00
		b. "AUTTIALLA"	70·00	
		ba. Ditto. Optd in red and in black	£1400	
		c. Opt double	£225	£250
		d. Wide spacing between lines	£225	
12	**31**	8a. dull mauve	16·00	38·00
		a. "AUTTIALLA"	£350	
		b. Opt double, one albino	70·00	
		c. Wide spacing between lines	£350	
7/12 *Set of* 6			32·00	£100

The ½, 2 and 4a. (T **29**), and 1r. (all overprinted in black), are proofs.

All six values exist with reprinted overprints, and the error "AUTTIALLA STATE" has been reprinted in complete sheets on all values and in addition in black on the ½, 2, 4a. and 1r. Nearly all these however, are found with the word "REPRINT" overprinted upon them. On the genuine "AUTTIALLA" errors, which occur on R. 9/12 in the setting of 120, the word "STATE" is 8½ mm long; on the reprints only 7¾ mm.

Nos. 7c, 8b, 9b, 10b, 11d and 12c show 1¼ mm spacing between the two lines of overprint. The normal spacing is ¾ mm.

Nos. 7/8 and 10/12 exist with error "PUTTILLA", but their status is uncertain (*Price, from £500, unused*).

1891–96. *Optd with T* **3**.

No.	Type	Description	Unused	Used
13	**23**	½a. blue-green (1892)	40	10
14	**24**	9p. carmine	1·00	1·75
15	**25**	1a. brown-purple	1·40	30
16		1a. plum	1·75	80
		a. "PATIALA" omitted	£180	£375
		b. "PA" omitted		
		c. "PATIA" omitted		
		d. "PATIAL" omitted		
17	**26**	1a.6p. sepia	1·25	1·00
18	**27**	2a. dull blue (1896)	1·25	30
19		2a. ultramarine	1·60	75
20	**28**	3a. brown-orange	1·90	60
21	**29**	4a. olive-green (1896)	2·00	60
		a. "PATIALA" omitted	£450	£225
22		4a. slate-green	2·25	60
23	**21**	6a. bistre-brown	2·50	11·00
24		6a. olive-bistre	2·75	17·00
		a. Opt double, one albino	48·00	
25	**31**	8a. dull mauve		
26		8a. magenta (1896)	2·00	11·00
27	**32**	12a. purple/*red*	2·00	12·00
28	**37**	1r. green and carmine (1896)	4·25	42·00
29	**38**	2r. carmine and yellow-brown (1895)	£110	£650
30		3r. brown and green (1895)	£150	£700
		a. Opt double, one albino	£200	
		b. Opt treble, two albino	£170	
31		5r. ultramarine and violet (1895)	£200	£750
13/31 *Set of* 14			£425	£2000

The errors on the 1a. plum and 4a. olive-green occur on R. 19/1 in the December 1898 printing. Nos. 16b/d are early stages of the error before the entire word was omitted.

1899–1902. *Colours changed and new value. Optd with T* **3**.

No.	Type	Description	Unused	Used
32	**40**	3p. carmine (1899)	30	15
		a. Pair, one without opt	£3250	
		b. Opt double, one albino	38·00	
33	**23**	½a. pale yellow-green	90	30
34	**25**	1a. carmine	2·50	90
32/4 *Set of* 3			3·25	1·25

Maharaja Bhupindra Singh, 1900–1938

1903–06. *King Edward VII. Optd with T* **3**.

No.	Type	Description	Unused	Used
35	**41**	3p. pale grey	40	10
		a. Additional albino opt of Jind Type **3**	£225	
		b. "S" in "STATE" sideways (R. 20/1)	£900	£900
36		3p. slate-grey (1906)	40	10
37	**42**	½a. green	1·10	15
38	**43**	1a. carmine	50	10
		a. Horiz pair, one without opt	£900	
39	**44**	2a. pale violet	1·25	65
		a. Mauve	8·00	1·00
40	**46**	3a. orange-brown	1·25	35
41	**47**	4a. olive (1905)	2·75	1·25
42	**48**	6a. olive-bistre (1905)	3·25	7·50
43	**49**	8a. purple (1906)	3·50	1·60
44	**50**	12a. purple/*red* (1906)	6·00	21·00
45	**51**	1r. green and carmine (1905)	3·25	3·75
35/45 *Set of* 10			21·00	32·00

1912. *Nos. 149/50 of India optd with T* **3**.

No.	Type	Description	Unused	Used
46	**53**	½a. green	40	2[illegible]
47	**54**	1a. carmine	1·75	9[illegible]

1912–26. *King George V. Optd with T* **3**.

No.	Type	Description	Unused	Used
48	**55**	3p. grey	25	1[illegible]
		a. Pale grey	60	1[illegible]
		b. Bluish grey	1·40	
		c. Slate	1·40	3[illegible]
		ca. "Rs" flaw	28·00	
49	**56**	½a. light green	70	2[illegible]
		a. Emerald	1·00	3[illegible]
		b. Bright green	70	3[illegible]
50	**57**	1a. aniline carmine	1·40	2[illegible]
51	**58**	1½a. chocolate (Type A) (1922)	30	5[illegible]
52	**59**	2a. purple	85	7[illegible]
		a. Reddish purple	1·50	
		b. Deep mauve	1·50	
		c. Bright reddish violet	1·50	
53	**62**	3a. orange	2·00	8[illegible]
54	**63**	4a. olive	3·00	2·5[illegible]
55	**64**	6a. yellow-bistre	1·25	3·2[illegible]
		a. Brown-ochre (1921)	3·75	4·5[illegible]
56	**65**	8a. deep magenta	2·75	1·5[illegible]
		a. Purple (1921)	4·25	2·2[illegible]
57	**66**	12a. carmine-lake	3·50	8·0[illegible]
58	**67**	1r. red-brown and deep blue-green	6·00	11·0[illegible]
		a. Opt double, one albino	35·00	
		b. Brown and green (1924)	8·50	
59		2r. carmine & yell-brn (1926)	13·00	£14[illegible]
60		5r. ultramarine and violet (1926)	27·00	£15[illegible]

1923–26. *As 1912–26. New colours.*

No.	Type	Description	Unused	Used
61	**57**	1a. chocolate	2·75	4[illegible]
62	**62**	3a. ultramarine (1926)	3·25	7·0[illegible]
48/62 *Set of* 15			60·00	£30[illegible]

PATIALA STATE
(4)

PATIALA STATE
(5)

1928–34. *King George V (Nasik printing, wmk Mult Star) optd [illegible] Nasik with T* **4** *or* **5** *(rupee values).*

No.	Type	Description	Unused	Used
63	**55**	3p. slate (1932)	1·75	1[illegible]
		w. Wmk inverted	2·75	1·1[illegible]
64	**56**	½a. green	25	[illegible]
		w. Wmk inverted	2·00	1·[illegible]
65	**80**	9p. deep green (*litho*) (1934)	1·50	7[illegible]
65*a*		9p. deep green (*typo*)	1·75	3[illegible]
66	**57**	1a. chocolate	75	2[illegible]
		w. Wmk inverted	3·00	1·0[illegible]
67	**82**	1a.3p. mauve (1932)	3·00	1[illegible]
		w. Wmk inverted	3·50	1·2[illegible]
68	**70**	2a. purple	1·75	4[illegible]
		w. Wmk inverted	2·75	
69	**61**	2a.6p. orange (1934)	4·50	1·5[illegible]
		w. Wmk inverted	3·00	
70	**62**	3a. bright blue (1929)	2·75	1·5[illegible]
71	**71**	4a. sage-green	3·75	1·1[illegible]
		w. Wmk inverted	6·00	
72	**65**	8a. reddish purple (1933)	5·00	2·5[illegible]
73	**67**	1r. chocolate and green (1929)	7·00	7·5[illegible]
		w. Wmk inverted	—	11·0[illegible]
74		2r. carmine and orange	21·00	
		w. Wmk inverted	10·00	50·[illegible]
63/74 *Set of* 12			35·00	60·[illegible]

1935–37. *Optd with T* **4**.

No.	Type	Description	Unused	Used
75	**79**	½a. blue-green (1937)	85	[illegible]
76	**81**	1a. chocolate (1936)	1·10	[illegible]
77	**59**	2a. vermilion (No. 236*b*) (1936)	40	1·[illegible]
78	**62**	3a. carmine	8·00	5·[illegible]
		w. Wmk inverted	5·50	7·[illegible]
79	**63**	4a. sage-green	1·75	2·[illegible]
75/9 *Set of* 5			8·50	8·[illegible]

PATIALA STATE
(6)

PATIALA
(7)

PATIALA
(8)

1937–38. *King George VI. Nos. 247/64 optd with T* **4** *(3p. to 1a.), T* **6** *(2a. to 12a.), or T* **5** *(rupee values).*

80 **91** 3p. slate . . . 30·00 35
81 ½a. red-brown . . . 10·00 50
82 9p. green (1937) . . . 4·00 1·00
83 1a. carmine (1937) . . . 2·75 20
84 **92** 2a. vermilion . . . 1·50 7·50
85 – 2a.6p. bright violet . . . 4·50 16·00
86 – 3a. yellow-green . . . 4·00 7·00
87 – 3a.6p. bright blue . . . 5·50 20·00
88 – 4a. brown . . . 22·00 13·00
89 – 6a. turquoise-green . . . 21·00 45·00
90 – 8a. slate-violet . . . 22·00 32·00
91 – 12a. lake . . . 22·00 50·00
92 **93** 1r. grey and red-brown . . . 22·00 38·00
93 2r. purple and brown . . . 24·00 85·00
94 5r. green and blue . . . 30·00 £180
95 10r. purple and claret . . . 45·00 £300
96 15r. brown and green . . . 95·00 £475
97 25r. slate-violet and purple . . . £120 £500
80/97 *Set of* 18 . . . £425 £1600

Maharaja Yadavindra Singh, 1938–1971

1941–46. *King George VI. Optd with T* **7** *or* **8** *(rupee value).*

(a) Stamps of 1937.

98 **91** 3p. slate . . . 10·00 1·75
99 ½a. red-brown . . . 6·50 1·25
100 9p. green . . . £200 5·00
w. Wmk inverted
101 1a. carmine . . . 22·00 1·50
102 **93** 1r. grey and red-brown (1946) . . . 12·00 80·00
98/102 *Set of* 5 . . . £225 85·00

(b) Stamps of 1940–43.

103 **100a** 3p. slate (1942) . . . 3·00 15
104 ½a. purple (1943) . . . 3·00 15
a. Pair, one without opt . . . £5000
105 9p. green (1942) . . . 1·00 15
a. Vert pair, one without opt . . . £2750
106 1a. carmine (1944) . . . 1·00 10
107 **101** 1a.3p. yellow-brown . . . 1·60 2·75
108 1½a. violet (1942) . . . 12·00 2·75
109 2a. vermilion (1944) . . . 9·00 35
110 3a. bright violet (1944) . . . 8·00 2·00
111 3½a. bright blue (1944) . . . 19·00 28·00
112 **102** 4a. brown (1944) . . . 8·00 2·75
113 6a. turquoise-green (1944) . . . 3·25 21·00
114 8a. slate-violet (1944) . . . 3·00 11·00
115 12a. lake (1945) . . . 13·00 65·00
103/15 *Set of* 13 . . . 75·00 £120

The 1½a. exists printed by lithography or typography.

OFFICIAL STAMPS

SERVICE (O 2) **SERVICE** (O 3)

1884 (1 Oct). *Nos. 1/3 of Patiala optd with Type* O **2**, *in black.*

O1 **23** ½a. blue-green . . . 11·00 30
O2 **25** 1a. brown-purple . . . 90 10
a. Opt Type **1** inverted . . . £1600 £275
b. Opt Type **1** double . . . † £110
c. "SERVICE" double . . . £1600 £550
d. "SERVICE" inverted . . . † £1600
w. Wmk inverted . . . † £275
O3 **27** 2a. dull blue . . . £4250 £120

Essays of No. O3 exist on which "STATE" measures 10 mm long (normal 9 mm) and the words of the Type **1** overprint are more curved. These are rare (*Price* £900 *unused*).

1885–90.

(a) No. 7 of Patiala optd with Type O **2**, *in black.*

O4 **23** ½a. blue-green . . . 75 20
a. "SERVICE" double . . . † £600
b. "AUTTIALLA" . . . 60·00 16·00
ba. "AUTTIALLA", and "SERVICE" double . . . † £4500

(b) No. 11 of Patiala optd with Type O **2**, *in black.*

O5 **25** 1a. brown purple . . . 60 10
a. "SERVICE" double . . . £1500
b. "SERVICE" double, one inverted . . . † £550
c. "AUTTIALLA" . . . £600 45·00
d. "PUTTIALLA STATE" double . . . † £1100

(c) As No. 7 of Patiala, but optd in black, and No. 8, optd with Type O **3**.

O6 **23** ½a. blue-green (Bk.) (1890) . . . 1·50 10
O7 **27** 2a. dull blue (R.) . . . 60 20
a. "SERVICE" double, one inverted . . . 30·00 £180

Stamps as Nos. O4/5, but with Type O **3** (in red on the ½a.), were prepared for use but not issued, although some were erroneously overprinted "REPRINT". No. O7 with overprint in black is a proof. The ½a "AUTTIALLA" has been reprinted in complete sheets, and can be found with "AUTTIALLA" double.

No. O7 exists with error "PUTTILLA", but its status is uncertain.

SERVICE

PATIALA STATE (O 4) **PATIALA STATE SERVICE** (O 5) **PATIALA STATE SERVICE** (O 6)

1891 (Nov)–**1900**. *Optd with Type* O **4**, *in black.*

O8 **23** ½a. blue-green (9.95) . . . 40 10
a. "SERVICE" inverted . . . 55·00
b. "SERV CE" . . . £900
c. "STA E" . . . £500 £450
O9 **25** 1a. plum (10.1900) . . . 4·50 10
a. "SERVICE" inverted . . . 60·00

O10 **27** 2a. dull blue (12.98) . . . 4·00 1·50
a. Deep blue . . . 3·25 1·75
b. "SERVICE" inverted . . . 60·00 £180
c. Thin seriffed "I" in "SERVICE" . . . £180
O12 **28** 3a. brown-orange . . . 1·00 2·25
a. "SERV CE"
O13 **29** 4a. olive-green . . . 1·00 70
a. Slate-green (9.95) . . . 1·00 30
b. "SERV CE"
O15 **21** 6a. bistre-brown . . . 1·40 35
a. Olive-bistre . . . £1200
O16 **31** 8a. dull mauve . . . 2·25 1·00
a. Magenta (12.98) . . . 2·25 1·25
b. "SERV CE" . . . £3250
c. Thin seriffed "I" in "SERVICE" . . . £375
O18 **32** 12a. purple/*red* . . . 1·00 50
a. "SERV CE" . . . £4500
O19 **33** 1r. slate . . . 1·40 65
a. "SERV CE"
O8/19 *Set of* 9 . . . 14·50 6·00

Stamps from the first printing of November 1891 (Nos. O12/13, O15/16, O18/19) had the "SERVICE" overprint, as Type O **3**, applied to sheets already overprinted with Type **3**. Subsequent printings of Nos. O8/10*a*, O13*a* and O16*a* had both overprints applied at one operation as shown on Type O **4**.

The errors with "SERVICE" inverted occur from a trial printing, in two operations, during 1894, which was probably not issued. Some of the "SERV CE" varieties may also come from the same trial printing.

1902 (Jan)–**03**. *Optd with Type* O **4**.

O20 **25** 1a. carmine . . . 50 10
O21 **37** 1r. green and carmine (5.03) . . . 5·50 9·00

1903–10. *King Edward VII stamps of India optd with Type* O **4**.

O22 **41** 3p. pale grey . . . 30 10
a. Slate-grey (1909) . . . 40 15
O24 **42** ½a. green . . . 40 10
O25 **43** 1a. carmine . . . 60 10
O26 **44** 2a. pale violet (1905) . . . 60 25
a. Mauve . . . 50 10
O28 **46** 3a. orange-brown . . . 3·25 2·50
O29 **47** 4a. olive (1905) . . . 1·50 20
a. Opt double, one albino . . . 48·00
O30 **49** 8a. purple (*shades*) . . . 1·25 75
a. Claret (1910) . . . 3·75 1·75
O32 **51** 1r. green and carmine (1906) . . . 1·50 80
O22/32 *Set of* 8 . . . 8·50 4·25

1907. *Nos. 149/50 of India optd with Type* O **4**.

O33 **53** ½a. green . . . 50 20
O34 **54** 1a. carmine . . . 50 10

1913–26. *King George V. Official stamps of India optd with T* **3**.

O35 **55** 3p. grey . . . 10 20
a. Pale grey . . . 30 30
b. Slate (1926) . . . 30 30
O36 **56** ½a. light green . . . 10 10
a. Emerald . . . 1·60 50
b. Bright green . . . 50 30
O37 **57** 1a. aniline carmine . . . 10 10
O38 1a. chocolate (1925) . . . 7·00 1·00
O39 **59** 2a. purple . . . 60 40
a. Reddish purple . . . — 1·00
b. Deep mauve . . . 1·00 35
O40 **63** 4a. olive . . . 50 30
O41 **64** 6a. brown-ochre (1926) . . . 1·50 2·25
O42 **65** 8a. deep magenta . . . 55 70
O43 **67** 1r. red-brown and deep blue-green . . . 1·40 1·40
O44 2r. carmine and yellow-brown (1926) . . . 16·00 42·00
O45 5r. ultramarine and violet (1926) . . . 9·00 20·00
O35/45 *Set of* 11 . . . 32·00 60·00

1927–36. *King George V (Nasik printing, wmk Mult Star), optd at Nasik with Type* O **5** *or Type* O **6** *(rupee values).*

O47 **55** 3p. slate . . . 10 10
a. Blue opt . . . 1·50 1·25
w. Wmk inverted . . . 2·50 1·10
O48 **56** ½a. green (1932) . . . 85 55
w. Wmk inverted . . . — 3·00
O49 **57** 1a. chocolate . . . 15 10
w. Wmk inverted . . . 1·25 50
O50 **82** 1a.3p. mauve (1932) . . . 40 10
w. Wmk inverted . . . 3·25 20
O51 **70** 2a. purple . . . 20 30
w. Wmk inverted
O52 2a. vermilion (1933) . . . 30 35
O53 **61** 2a.6p. orange (1933) . . . 2·25 35
w. Wmk inverted . . . 60 80
O54 **71** 4a. sage-green (1935) . . . 50 30
w. Wmk inverted . . . 2·50 1·40
O55 **65** 8a. reddish purple (1929) . . . 1·00 65
w. Wmk inverted . . . 1·00 80
O56 **67** 1r. chocolate and green (1929) . . . 4·50 2·50
w. Wmk inverted . . . 2·75 2·75
O57 2r. carmine and orange (1936) . . . 10·00 35·00
O47/57 *Set of* 11 . . . 15·00 35·00

1935–39. *New types. Optd with Type* O **5**.

O58 **79** ½a. green (1936) . . . 10 10
O59 **81** 1a. chocolate (1936) . . . 30 30
O60 **59** 2a. vermilion . . . 15 30
O61 2a. vermilion (*small die*) (1939) . . . 16·00 3·50
O62 **63** 4a. sage-green (1936) . . . 2·00 85
O58/62 *Set of* 5 . . . 17·00 4·50

1937–39. *King George VI. Optd with Type* O **5** *or* O **6** *(rupee values).*

O63 **91** ½a. red-brown (1938) . . . 75 20
O64 9p. green (1938) . . . 13·00 55·00
O65 1a. carmine . . . 75 30
O66 **93** 1r. grey and red-brown (1939) . . . 1·00 5·50
O67 2r. purple and brown (1939) . . . 4·50 5·00
O68 5r. green and blue (1939) . . . 15·00 50·00
O63/8 *Set of* 6 . . . 32·00 £100

1A——1A (O 7) 1A SERVICE 1A (O 8) PATIALA SERVICE (O 9)

1939–40. *Stamp of 1932 (King George V).*

(a) Optd with Types O **5** *and* O **7**.

O69 **82** 1a.on 1a.3p. mauve . . . 9·00 2·25
w. Wmk inverted . . . 9·00 2·75

(b) Optd with T **4** *and* O **8**.

O70 **82** 1a.on 1a.3p. mauve (1940) . . . 8·00 2·50
w. Wmk inverted . . . 8·00 3·00

"SERVICE" measures 9¼ mm on No. O69 but only 8¾ mm on O70.

1939–44.

(a) Official stamps optd with T **7**.

O71 **O 20** 3p. slate (1940) . . . 1·25 10
O72 ½a. red-brown . . . 4·75 10
w. Wmk inverted . . . — 12·00
O73 ½a. purple (1942) . . . 50 10
O74 9p. green . . . 50 40
w. Wmk inverted
O75 1a. carmine . . . 2·50 10
O76 1a.3p. yellow-brown (1941) . . . 1·00 25
O77 1½a. dull violet (1944) . . . 5·00 90
O78 2a. vermilion (1940) . . . 8·00 30
w. Wmk inverted . . . 12·00
O79 2½a. bright violet (1940) . . . 2·75 75
O80 4a. brown (1943) . . . 1·50 2·25
O81 8a. slate-violet (1944) . . . 3·00 5·50

(b) Postage stamps optd with Type O **9**.

O82 **93** 1r. grey and red-brown (1943) . . . 5·00 9·00
O83 2r. purple and brown (1944) . . . 12·00 55·00
O84 5r. green and blue (1944) . . . 20·00 75·00
O71/84 *Set of* 14 . . . 60·00 £130

Patiala became part of the Patiala and East Punjab States Union by 20 August 1948.

INDIAN FEUDATORY STATES

These stamps were only valid for use within their respective states, *unless otherwise indicated.*

Postage stamps of the Indian States, current at that date, were replaced by those of the Republic of India on 1 April 1950.

Unless otherwise stated, all became obsolete on 1 May 1950 (with the exception of the "Anchal" stamps of Travancore-Cochin which remained current until 1 July 1951 or Sept 1951 for the Official issues).

ALWAR

PRICES FOR STAMPS ON COVER		
Nos. 1/2		*from* × 25
No. 3		*from* × 50
No. 4		—
No. 5		*from* × 50

Maharao Raja (Maharaja from 1889) Mangal Singh, 1874–1892.

1 (¼a.).

1877. *Litho. Rouletted.*

1 **1** ¼a. steel blue . . . 13·00 7·00
a. Bright greenish blue . . . 7·50 7·00
b. Ultramarine . . . 4·00 1·00
c. Grey-blue (shades) . . . 3·50 1·00
2 1a. pale yellowish brown . . . 7·50 4·50
a. Brown (shades) . . . 2·75 1·25
b. Chocolate . . . 9·00 8·00
c. Pale reddish brown . . . 2·25 1·25

Maharaja Jai Singh, 1892–1937

1899–1901. *Redrawn.* P 12.

(a) Wide margins between stamps.

3 **1** ¼a. slate-blue . . . 7·00 2·75
a. Imperf between (horiz pair) . . . £300 £375
b. Imperf between (vert pair) . . . £600 £650
4 ¼a. emerald-green . . . £550

(b) Narrower margins (1901).

5 **1** ¼a. emerald-green . . . 3·75 2·50
a. Imperf between (horiz pair) . . . £200 £250
b. Imperf between (vert pair) . . . £200 £250
c. Imperf horiz (vert pair) . . . £225
d. Imperf (pair) . . . £275
e. Pale yellow-green . . . 5·50 2·75
ea. Imperf (pair) . . . £475
eb. Imperf between (horiz pair) . . . † £475

In the redrawn type only the bottom outer frameline is thick, whereas in the original 1877 issue the left-hand frameline is also thick, as shown in Type **1**.

The stamps of Alwar became obsolete on 1 July 1902.

BAHAWALPUR
See after **PAKISTAN**

BAMRA

PRICES FOR STAMPS ON COVER	
Nos. 1/6	—
Nos. 8/40	*from* × 25

Raja Sudhal Deo, 1869–1903

GUM. The stamps of Bamra were issued without gum.

1 (¼a.) 1a 2 (½a.)

3 (1a.) 4 (2a.) 5 (4a.)

6 (8a.)

(illustrations actual size)

(Typo Jagannata Ballabh Press, Deogarh)

1888. Imperf.
1 **1** ¼a. black/*yellow* . . . £375
a. "g" inverted (R. 5/1) . . . £4000
b. Last native character inverted . . . £4000
c. Last native character as Type **1a** . . . £4000
2 **2** ½a. black/*rose* . . . 75·00
a. "g" inverted (R. 5/1) . . . £1500
3 **3** 1a. black/*blue* . . . 50·00
a. "g" inverted (R. 5/1) . . . £1300
b. Scroll inverted (R. 8/4) . . . £1100
4 **4** 2a. black/*green* . . . 75·00 £275
a. "a" omitted (R. 8/3) . . . £1500
b. Scroll inverted (R. 8/4) . . . £1300
5 **5** 4a. black/*yellow* . . . 65·00 £275
a. "a" omitted (R. 8/3) . . . £1400
b. Scroll inverted (R. 8/4) . . . £1200
6 **6** 8a. black/*rose* . . . 40·00
a. "a" omitted (R. 8/3) . . . £1200
b. Horiz pair, one printed on back . . . £600
c. Scroll inverted (R. 8/4) . . . £1000

These stamps were all printed from the same plate of 96 stamps, 12 × 8, but for some values only part of the plate was used. There are 96 varieties of the ½, 4 and 8a., 72 of the 1a., 80 of the 2a. and not less than 88 of the ¼a.

The scroll ornament can be found pointing to either the right or the left.

There are two forms of the third native character. In the first five horizontal rows it is as in T **1** and in the last three rows as in T **4**.

These stamps have been reprinted: the ¼a. and ½a. in blocks of 8 varieties (all showing scroll pointing to right), and all the values in blocks of 20 varieties (all showing scroll pointing to left). On the reprints the fourth character is of a quite different shape.

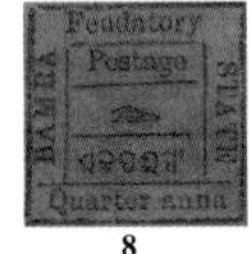

8

1890 (July)–**93**. *Black on coloured paper. Nos. 24/5 and 39/40 show face value as "One Rupee".*

(a) "Postage" with capital "P".
8 **8** ¼a. on *rose-lilac* . . . 4·00 5·00
a. "Eeudatory" (R. 2/4) . . . 18·00 27·00
b. "Quatrer" (R. 1/3) . . . 18·00 27·00
c. Inverted "e" in "Postage" (R. 2/3) . . . 18·00 27·00
9 ¼a. on *bright rose* . . . 1·90 2·75
10 ¼a. on *reddish purple* . . . 1·90 2·50
a. First "a" in "anna" inverted (R. 3/3) . . . 40·00 45·00
b. "AMRA" inverted (R. 4/4) . . . 55·00 55·00
c. "M" and second "A" in "BAMRA" inverted (R. 4/4) . . . 75·00 75·00
11 ½a. on *dull green* . . . 2·50 2·75
a. "Eeudatory" (R. 2/4) . . . 48·00 60·00
12 ½a. on *blue-green* . . . 4·25 4·00
13 1a. on *bistre-yellow* . . . 4·25 3·00
a. "Eeudatory" (R. 2/4) . . . £100 £110
14 1a. on *orange-yellow* . . . 38·00 38·00
a. "annas" for "anna" . . . £140 £140
15 2a. on *rose-lilac* . . . 16·00 28·00
a. "Eeudatory" (R. 2/4) . . . £150 £200
16 2a. on *bright rose* . . . 4·00 4·50
17 2a. on *dull rose* . . . 10·00 7·00
18 4a. on *rose-lilac* . . . £600 £750
a. "Eeudatory" (R. 2/4) . . . £3750
19 4a. on *dull rose* . . . 8·50 5·50
a. "Eeudatory" (R. 2/4) . . . £900 £900
b. "BAMBA" (R. 2/1) . . . £900 £900
20 4a. on *bright rose* . . . 6·00 8·00
20*a* 4a. on *deep pink* . . . 14·00 12·00
21 8a. on *rose-lilac* . . . 20·00 50·00
a. "Foudatory" and "Postagc" (R. 1/2) . . . £180 £275
b. "BAMBA" (R. 2/1) . . . £180 £275
22 8a. on *bright rose* . . . 13·00 16·00
23 8a. on *dull rose* . . . 24·00 14·00
24 1r. on *rose-lilac* . . . 48·00 85·00
a. "Eeudatory" (R. 2/4) . . . £425 £500
b. "BAMBA" (R. 2/1) . . . £350 £400
c. "Postagc" (R. 1/2) . . . £350 £400
25 1r. on *bright rose* . . . 17·00 20·00
a. Small "r" in "rupee" . . . £180 £180

(b) "postage" with small "p" (1891–93).
26 **8** ¼a. on *bright rose* . . . 1·90 2·75
27 ¼a. on *reddish purple* . . . 1·90 2·50
28 ½a. on *dull green* . . . 3·50 3·50
a. First "a" in "anna" inverted (R. 3/3) . . . 30·00 32·00
29 ½a. on *blue-green* . . . 4·25 4·00
a. First "a" in "anna" inverted (R. 3/3) . . . 32·00 32·00
30 1a. on *bistre-yellow* . . . 3·75 3·00
31 1a. on *orange-yellow* . . . 38·00 38·00
32 2a. on *bright rose* . . . 4·25 4·50
33 2a. on *dull rose* . . . 10·00 7·00
34 4a. on *dull rose* . . . 10·00 5·50
35 4a. on *bright rose* . . . 6·50 8·50
35*a* 4a. on *deep pink* . . . 17·00 14·00
36 8a. on *rose-lilac* . . . 45·00 85·00
37 8a. on *bright rose* . . . 16·00 18·00
38 8a. on *dull rose* . . . 24·00 14·00
39 1r. on *rose-lilac* . . . 70·00 £120
40 1r. on *bright rose* . . . 22·00 22·00
a. Small "r" in "rupee" . . . £225 £225
b. Small "r" in "rupee" and native characters in the order 2, 3, 1, 4, 5 (R. 4/4) . . . £1400 £1400

There are 10 settings of Type **8**. The first setting (of 20 (4 × 5)) has capital "P" throughout. The remaining settings (of 16 (4 × 4)) have capital "P" and small "p" mixed.

For the first setting the 8a. and 1r. values were printed within the same block, the ten left-hand stamps being 8a. values and the ten right-hand stamps 1r.

The various stamps were distributed between the settings as follows:
Setting I—Nos. 8/c, 11/a, 13/a, 15/a, 18/19a, 21, 24/a
Setting II—Nos. 19, 19b, 21/b, 24, 24b/c, 34, 36, 39
Setting III—Nos. 9, 11, 13, 16, 26, 28, 30, 32
Setting IV—Nos. 20, 22, 25, 35, 37, 40
Setting V—Nos. 10, 10b/c, 20*a*, 27, 35*a*
Setting VI—Nos. 11, 12, 28, 28a, 29/a
Setting VII—Nos. 10/a, 12, 17, 19, 23, 25a, 27, 29, 33/4, 38, 40a/b
Setting VIII—Nos.17, 33
Setting IX—Nos. 10/a, 12, 14/a, 17, 19, 23, 27, 29, 31, 33/4, 38
Setting X—Nos. 19, 34

There are 4 sizes of the central ornament, which represents an elephant's trunk holding a stick:—(*a*) 4 mm long; (*b*) 5 mm; (*c*) 6¼ mm; (*d*) 11 mm. These ornaments are found pointing to right or left, either upright or inverted.

Ornaments (*a*) are found in all settings; (*b*) in all settings from Settings III to X; (*c*) in Settings I and II; and (*d*) only in Setting I.

The stamps of Bamra have been obsolete since 1 January 1895.

BARWANI

PRICES FOR STAMPS ON COVER	
Nos. 1/43	*from* × 3

PROCESS. All Barwani stamps are typographed from clichés, and are in sheets of 4, *unless otherwise indicated.*

Issues to about 1930 were printed by the Barwani State Printing Press, and subsequently by the *Times of India* Press, Bombay.

GUM. Nos. 1/31 were issued without gum.

BOOKLET PANES. Those stamps which were printed in sheets of 4 were issued in stamp booklets, binding holes appearing in the side margin.

Rana Ranjit Singh, 1894–1930

1

2

3

1921 (Mar?). *Clear impression. Medium wove paper.* P 7 all round.
1 **1** ¼a. blue-green (dull *to* deep) . . . £130 £325
2 ½a. dull blue . . . £225 £475
a. Imperf (pair) . . . — £1400
No. 1 also exists perforated on two sides only.

1921 (June?). *Blurred impression. Soft wove paper.* P 7 on two or three sides.
3 **1** ¼a. green (*shades*) . . . 20·00 95·00
4 ½a. ultramarine (dull *to* pale) . . . 17·00 £140

NOTE. As the small sheets of Barwani stamps were often not perforated all round, many of the earlier stamps are perforated on two or three sides only. Owing to the elementary method of printing, the colours vary greatly in depth, even within a single sheet.

1921. *Clear impression. Vertically laid bâtonné paper.* Imperf.
5 **1** ¼a. green (*shades*) . . . 20·00 65·00
6 ½a. green (*shades*) . . . 4·50
a. Perf 11 at top or bottom only . . . 3·50
It is suggested that No. 5 may be an error due to printing from the wrong plate.

1922?. *Clear impression. Thickish glazed wove paper.* P 7 on two or three sides.
7 **1** ½a. dull blue . . . 85·00

1922. *Smooth, soft medium wove paper.* P 7 on two or three sides.

(a) Clear impression.
8 **1** ¼a. deep grey-blue . . . 42·00 90·00

(b) Poor impression.
9 **1** ¼a. steel blue . . . 17·00
Examples of No. 9 exist with perforations on all four sides.

1922. P 11 on two or three sides.

(a) Thick, glazed white wove paper.
10 **2** 1a. vermilion (*shades*) . . . 2·25 19·00
a. Imperf between (vert pair) . . . £225
b. Doubly printed . . . £800
11 2a. purple (*to* violet) . . . 2·25 22·00
a. Doubly printed . . . £275
b. Imperf between (horiz pair) . . . £180 £300
c. Imperf between (vert pair) . . . £180

(b) Thick, toned wove paper.
12 **2** 2a. purple . . . 15·00 48·00

1922. *Poor impression. Thin, poor wove paper.* Pin-perf 8½ on two or three sides.
13 **1** ¼a. grey (*to* grey-blue) . . . 1·60 40·00
a. Imperf (pair) . . . £300
b. Imperf between (vert pair) . . . £130

1923. *Thin, smooth, unglazed wove paper.* P 11 on two or three sides.
14 **1** ½a. green (pale *to* deep) . . . 1·25 19·00
a. Imperf between (vert pair) . . . £450
15 **2** 1a. brown-red . . . £2500 £3000

1923. *Poor impression. Thick, soft wove paper.* P 7.
16 **1** ½a. green (pale *to* deep) . . . 25·00
No. 16 also exists perforated on two or three sides.

1923 (Mar?). *Poor quality wove paper.* P 7 on two or three sides.
17 **1** ¼a. black . . . 75·00 £275
a. Imperf between (horiz pair) . . . £1800

1923 (May?). *Horizontally laid bâtonné paper.* P 12.
18 **1** ¼a. rose (*shades*) . . . 1·75 12·00
a. Imperf between (vert pair) . . . £400
ab. Imperf between (horiz pair) . . . £800
b. Pin perf 6 . . . £130 65·00
c. Perf compound of 12 and 6 . . . 48·00 65·00
d. Perf 7 . . . £475 £550
da. On wove paper . . . £1700
No. 18 was issued in sheets of 12 (3 panes of 4) and was printed on paper showing a sheet watermark of Britannia and a double lined inscription. No. 18d was only issued in booklet panes of 4.

1925. *Vertically laid bâtonné paper.* P 11.
19 **1** ¼a. blue (pale *to* deep) . . . 1·00 11·00
a. *Tête-bêche* (horiz pair) . . . £2000
No. 19 was issued in sheets of 8 and was printed on paper wit a sheet watermark of a shell and an inscription "SHELL" in double lined capitals.

1927. *Very poor impression. Thin, brittle wove paper.* P 7.
20 **1** ¼a. milky blue (*shades*) . . . 9·00 30·0
21 ½a. yellow-green (*shades*) . . . 10·00 55·0
a. Imperf between (horiz pair) . . . £900
22 **3** 4a. orange-brown . . . 75·00 £35
a. Imperf between (horiz pair) . . . £1400
20/2 *Set of* 3 . . . 85·00 £40

1927. *Thick wove paper.* Sewing machine perf 6-10.
23 **3** 4a. yellow-brown . . . 90·00
a. Imperf between (horiz pair) . . . £1900
b. Perf 7 . . . 20·00 £19
c. Orange-brown . . . £110 £37

1928–32?. *Thick glazed paper.*

(a) P 7.
24 **1** ¼a. deep bright blue . . . 11·00
25 ½a. bright yellow-green . . . 22·00

(b) P 10½ *(rough) (Nov 1928).*
26 **1** ¼a. ultramarine . . . 4·50
a. *Tête-bêche* (horiz pair) . . . 10·00
b. Horiz pair, one stamp printed on reverse . . . £1200
27 ½a. apple-green . . . 4·75
a. *Tête-bêche* (vert pair) . . . 9·00

(c) P 11 *(clean-cut) (1929–32?).*
28 **1** ¼a. bright blue . . . 2·25 11·0
a. Indigo . . . 1·75 11·0
ab. Imperf between (horiz pair) . . . 75·00
ac. Imperf between (horiz strip of 4) . . . £350
b. Deep dull blue . . . 1·50 11·0
ba. Imperf between (vert pair) . . . £250
c. Ultramarine . . . 2·00 12·0
29 ½a. myrtle-green . . . 2·75 12·0
a. Imperf between (horiz pair) . . . £200
b. Turquoise-green . . . 3·50 14·0
ba. Imperf between (vert pair) . . . £450 £50
30 **2** 1a. rose-carmine (1931) . . . 12·00 35·0
a. Imperf between (vert pair) . . . † £140
31 **3** 4a. salmon (*to* orange) (1931) . . . 65·00 £17
a. Imperf between (horiz pair) . . . £1700
28/31 *Set of* 4 . . . 75·00 £2

No. 26 was printed in sheets of 8 (4 × 2) with the two centre pa *tête-bêche* while No. 27, in similar sheets, had the two horizont rows *tête-bêche*. Both sheets are always found with one long si imperforate.

Nos. 28/31 were printed in sheets of 8, the two lower valu existing either 4 × 2 or 2 × 4 and the two higher values 4 × 2 onl No *tête-bêche* pairs were included in these printings. It is believ that a small printing of No. 31 was produced in sheets of 4, b details are uncertain.

Rana Devi Singh, 1930–1971

4 Rana Devi Singh

5 Rana Devi Singh

932 (Oct)–47. *Medium to thick wove paper.*

A. Close setting *(2½–4½ mm).* P 11, 12 or compound *(1932–41).*

32A 4 ¼a. slate 1·75 19·00
33A ½a. blue-green 2·75 19·00
34A 1a. brown 3·00 18·00
a. Imperf between (horiz pair) £1400
35A 2a. purple *(shades)* 3·50 32·00
6A 4a. olive-green 6·00 35·00
32A/6A *Set of* 5 15·00 £110

B. Wide setting *(6–7 mm).* P 11 *(1945–47).*

2B 4 ¼a. slate 4·25 25·00
3B ½a. blue-green 4·00 19·00
4B 1a. brown 9·00 19·00
b. Chocolate. Perf 8½ (1947) 12·50 42·00
5aB 2a. rose-carmine £200 £450
6B 4a. olive-green 22·00 40·00

The measurements given in the heading indicate the vertical pacing between impressions. There are eight settings of this nteresting issue: four "Close" where the overall stamp dimensions rom centre to centre of perfs vary in width from 21½ to 23 mm and n height from 25 to 27½ mm; three "Wide", width 23–23½ mm and eight 29–30 mm and one "Medium" (26½ × 31 mm) (No. 34B*b* nly).

933–47. P 11.

. *Close setting (3–4½ mm). Thick, cream-surfaced wove paper (1933 and 1941 (No. 38Aa).*

7A 1 ¼a. black 3·75 55·00
8A ½a. blue-green 10·00 27·00
a. Yellowish green (1941) 9·00 24·00
9A 2 1a. brown *(shades)* 17·00 25·00
2A 3 4a. sage-green 30·00 80·00

Wide setting (7–10 mm). Medium to thick wove paper (1939–47).

7B 1 ¼a. black (1945) 3·75 29·00
8aB ½a. yellowish green (1945) 4·50 30·00
9B 2 1a. brown *(shades)* 11·00 24·00
a. Perf 8½ (5 mm) (1947) 11·00 40·00
B 2a. bright purple 80·00 £225
B 2a. rose-carmine (1945) 24·00 95·00
2B 3 4a. sage-green (1941) 28·00 55·00
a. Pale sage-green (1939) 13·00 40·00

There were two "Close" settings (over-all stamp size 25 × 29 mm) nd five "Wide" settings with over-all sizes 26½–31½ × 31–36½ mm. here was also one "Medium" setting (26½ × 31 mm) but this was onfined to the 1a. perf 8½, No. 39a.

938. P 11.

3 5 1a. brown 30·00 55·00

Stamps printed in red with designs similar to Types **3** and **5** were tended for fiscal use.

STAMP BOOKLETS

Nos. 1/17, 18d/da and 20/5 are believed to have been issued in wn or stapled booklets, usually containing thirty-two examples of e value in blocks of 4. All these early booklets had plain covers, ten in shades of brown. Few complete booklets have survived om this period.

Nos. 32/47, produced by the *Times of India* Press in a series of ne printings between 1932 and 1947, were only issued in booklet rm. Booklets from the 1932, 1933, 1937 and 1939 printings had ain card or paper covers in various colours, usually containing ght blocks of 4, except for the 1933 printing, which contained venty blocks of 4. Booklets from the 1945 printing had plain white ssue covers from the same stock as the interleaving. All these oklets were stapled at left.

The following booklets, from a printing in 1941, and a series of ree printings in 1947, had printed covers, produced by a ndstamp in the case of Nos. SB14/15.

41. *Buff, green (No. SB3) or blue (No. SB7) card covers inscribed* "BARWANI STATE POSTAGE STAMPS", *booklet value in brackets and number and value of stamps thus "(Rs 4) 32 2 Annas". Panes of 4 with margin at left only. Stapled.*

(a) Booklets 59 × 55 mm.

31 8a. booklet containing thirty-two ¼a. (No. 32A) £700
32 1r. booklet containing thirty-two ½a. (No. 33A) £800
33 2r. booklet containing thirty-two 1a. (No. 34A) £900
34 4r. booklet containing thirty-two 2a. (No. 35A) £375
35 8r. booklet containing thirty-two 4a. (No. 36A) £500

(b) Booklets 63 × 60 mm (No. SB6) or 73 × 72 mm (No. SB7).

6 1r. booklet containing thirty-two ½a. (No. 38A*a*) £850
37 8r. booklet containing thirty-two 4a. (No. 42B) £1100

47. *Grey tissue covers inscribed "32 STAMPS VALUE ...." Panes of 4 with margins all round. Stapled at left.*

(a) Booklets 70 × 95 mm.

8 1r. booklet containing thirty-two ½a. (No. 33B) £600
9 2r. booklet containing thirty-two 1a. (No. 34B) £950
10 8r. booklet containing thirty-two 4a. (No. 36B) £1000

(b) Booklets 76 × 95 mm.

11 8a. booklet containing thirty-two ¼a. (No. 37B) £850
12 4r. booklet containing thirty-two 2a. (No. 41B) £900
13 8r. booklet containing thirty-two 4a. (No. 42B*a*) £475

47. *Buff paper covers with violet handstamp inscribed* "32 STAMPS VALUE Rs 2/-". *Panes of 4 with margins all round, Sewn with twine at left.*

14 2r. booklets (71 × 69 *mm*) containing thirty-two 1a. (No. 34B*b*) £450
15 2r. booklet (71 × 73 *mm*) containing thirty-two 1a. (No. 39B*a*) £400

47. *Grey tissue covers inscribed* "32 STAMPS VALUE As 8". *Panes of 4 with margins all round. Stapled at left.*

16 8a. booklet (70 × 75 *mm*) containing thirty-two ½a. (No. 32B) £200
17 8a. booklet (85 × 75 *mm*) containing thirty-two ¼a. (No. 37B) £250

Barwani became part of Madhya Bharat by 1 July 1948.

BHOPAL

PRICES FOR STAMPS ON COVER	
Nos. 1/100	*from* × 10
Nos. O301/57	*from* × 15

The correct English inscription on these stamps is "H.H. NAWAB SHAH JAHAN BEGAM". In the case of Nos. 22 and 23 the normal stamps are spelt "BEGAN" and specimens with "BEGAM" are "errors".

As the stamps were printed from lithographic stones on which each unit was drawn separately by hand, numerous errors of spelling occurred. These are constant on all sheets and are listed. Some of our illustrations inadvertently include errors of spelling.

ILLUSTRATIONS. Types **1/3*a*** and **6/12*a*** are shown actual size.

EMBOSSING. Nos. 1/99 were only valid for postage when embossed with the device, in Urdu, of the ruling Begam. On T **1/3** and **6** to **12*a***. this was intended to fill the central part of the design. Almost all varieties can be found with the embossing inverted or sideways, as well as upright.

Shah Jahan

Sultan Johan

(actual size)

The various basic types were often in concurrent use but for greater convenience the following list is arranged according to types instead of being in strict chronological order.

GUM. Nos. 1/99 were issued without gum.

Nawab Shah Jahan Begam, 16 November 1868–15 June 1901

1 (¼a.)

1872. *Litho.*

(a) Double frame. Sheets of 20 (5 × 4).

1 1 ¼a. black £475 £375
a. "BFGAM" (R. 3/1) £1400 £1200
b. "BEGAN" (R. 2/2, R. 4/4) £800 £700
c. "EGAM" (R. 4/5) £1400 £1200
2 ½a. red 17·00 38·00
a. "BFGAM" (R. 3/1) 60·00 £130
b. "BEGAN" (R. 2/2, R. 4/4) 42·00 85·00
c. "EGAM" (R. 4/5) 60·00 £130

2 (½a.)

(b) Single frame. Sheets of 20 (4 × 5).

3 2 ¼a. black † £4750
4 ½a. red 30·00 55·00
a. "NWAB" (R. 2/2) £140 £225

3 (¼a.)

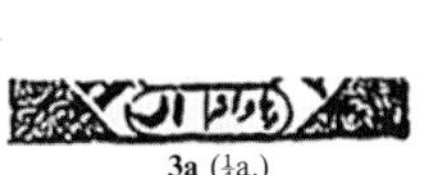
3a (¼a.)

1878 (1 Jan). *All lettered "EEGAM" for "BEGAM". Sheets of 20 (4 × 5).*

(a) Plate 1. Frame lines extend horiz and vert between stamps throughout sheet.

5 3 ¼a. black 7·00 12·00

(b) Plate 2. Frame lines normal.

5*a* 3a ¼a. black 7·00 14·00

Apart from the frame line difference between Types **3** and **3*a*** the stamps can also be distinguished by the differences in the value tablets, notably the thin vertical line in the centre in Type **3*a*** compared with the slightly diagonal and heavier line in Type **3**.

4 (¼a.)

5 (½a.)

1878 (June?)–**79**. *Value in parenthesis (Nos. 6/7). Sheets of 32 (4 × 8).* Imperf.

6 4 ¼a. green (1879) 12·00 20·00
7 ¼a. green *(perf)* (1879) 9·00 14·00
8 5 ½a. red 6·00 12·00
a. "JAHN" (R. 5/2) 28·00
b. "NWAB" (R. 3/2, R. 4/2) 18·00
c. "EEGAM" (R. 1/3) 28·00
9 ½a. brown 24·00 38·00
a. "JAHN" (R. 5/2) £130 £170
b. "NWAB" (R. 3/2, R. 4/2) 80·00 £110
c. "EEGAM" (R. 1/3) £130 £170

The ½a. shows the "N" of "NAWAB" reversed on R. 6/4 and the "N" of "JAHAN" reversed on R. 1/2–4 and R. 2/2-4.

1880. *T* **5** *redrawn; value not in parenthesis. Sheets of 32 (4 × 8).*

(a) Imperf.

10 ¼a. blue-green 7·50
a. "NAWA" (R. 2/2–4) 24·00
b. "CHAH" (R. 8/3) 65·00
11 ½a. brown-red 16·00 19·00

(b) Perf.

12 ¼a. blue-green 9·00
a. "NAWA" (R. 2/2–4) 35·00
b. "CHAH" (R. 8/3) 90·00
13 ½a. brown-red 14·00

The ¼a. shows the "N" of "NAWAB" reversed on R. 8/4.

Nos. 12/13 sometimes come with gum.

1884. *T* **5** *again redrawn. Sheets of 32 (4 × 8), some with value in parenthesis, others not.* Perf.

14 ¼a. greenish blue 4·50 12·00
a. "ANAWAB" (R. 8/1–4) 13·00

In this plate there is a slanting dash under and to left of the letters "JA" of "JAHAN," instead of a character like a large comma, as on all previous varieties of this design. With the exception of R. 1/1 all stamps in the sheet show "N" of "JAHAN" reversed.

1895. *T* **5** *again redrawn. Sheets of 8 (2 × 4). Laid paper.*

15 ¼a. red *(imperf)* 5·50 2·50
16 ¼a. red *(perf)* — £650

In these cases where the same design has been redrawn several times, and each time in a number of varieties of type, it is not easy to distinguish the various issues. Nos. 6 and 7 may be distinguished from Nos. 10 and 12 by the presence or absence of the parenthesis marks (); 8, 9 and 11 differ principally in colour; 8 and 15 are very much alike, but differ in the value as well as in paper.

6 (1a.)

1881. *Sheets of 24 (4 × 6).* Imperf.

17 6 ¼a. black 5·00 17·00
a. "NWAB" (R. 6/2–4) 13·00
18 ½a. red 4·50 11·00
a. "NWAB" (R. 6/2–4) 10·00
19 1a. brown 4·00 13·00
a. "NWAB" (R. 6/2–4) 8·00
20 2a. blue 2·50 13·00
a. "NWAB" (R. 6/2–4) 5·00
21 4a. buff 15·00 48·00
a. "NWAB" (R. 6/2–4) 42·00
17/21 *Set of* 5 28·00 90·00

In this issue all values were produced from the same drawing, and therefore show exactly the same varieties of type. The value at foot in this and all the following issues is given in only one form.

7 (½a.)

1886. *Similar to T* **6** *but normally lettered (incorrectly) "BEGAN"; larger lettering. Sheets of 32 (4 × 8).*

(a) Imperf.

22 7 ½a. pale red 2·25 9·00
a. "BEGAM" (R. 2/1) 10·00
b. "NWAB" (R. 3/4) 10·00

(b) Perf.

23 7 ½a. pale red £550
a. "BEGAM" (R. 2/1) £900
b. "NWAB" (R. 3/4) £900

8 (4a.)

1886. *T* **8**. *T* **6** *redrawn. Sheets of 24 (4 × 6). The "M" of "BEGAM" is an inverted "W". The width of the stamps is rather greater than the height.*

(a) Wove paper. Imperf.

24 **8** 4a. yellow . . . £800
a. "EEGAM" (R. 2/3–4, R. 3/3–4, R. 4/2, R. 4/4, R. 6/1) . . . £950

(b) Laid paper.

25 **8** 4a. yellow (*imperf*) . . . 8·50 27·00
a. "EEGAM" (R. 2/3–4, R. 3/3–4, R. 4/2, R. 4/4, R. 6/1) . . . 12·00
26 4a. yellow (*perf*) . . . 3·50 16·00
a. "EEGAM" (R. 2/3–4, R. 3/3–1, R. 4/2, R. 4/4, R. 6/1) . . . 5·50 22·00

1889. *T* **6** *again redrawn. Sheets of 32 (4 × 8) lettered "BEGAN".*

27 ¼a. black (*perf*) . . . 1·25 4·25
a. "EEGAN" (R. 7/3) . . . 12·00 24·00
b. Imperf between (horiz pair) . . . £225
28 ¼a. black (*imperf*) . . . 1·25 4·00
a. "EEGAN" (R. 7/3) . . . 14·00 24·00

9 (¼a.)

1889–90. *T* **9**. *T* **6** *again redrawn. Sheets of 24 (4 × 6), all with "M" like an inverted "W". Wove paper.*

(a) Imperf.

29 **9** ¼a. black . . . 2·00 1·50
30 1a. brown . . . 1·75 4·00
a. "EEGAM" (R. 2/3) . . . 12·00 22·00
b. "BBGAM" (R. 3/1) . . . 12·00 22·00
31 2a. blue . . . 1·50 1·75
a. "BBEGAM" (R. 1/2) . . . 7·50 12·00
b. "NAWAH" (R. 4/2) . . . 7·50 12·00
32 4a. orange-yellow . . . 2·00 3·25
29/32 *Set of* 4 . . . 6·50 9·50

(b) Perf.

33 **9** ¼a. black . . . 2·25 3·25
a. Imperf between (horiz pair) . . . £250
34 1a. brown . . . 4·00 5·50
a. "EEGAM" (R. 2/3) . . . 22·00 30·00
b. "BBGAM" (R. 3/1) . . . 22·00 30·00
35 2a. blue . . . 1·75 2·50
a. "BBEGAM" (R. 1/2) . . . 8·00 15·00
b. "NAWAH" (R. 4/2) . . . 8·00 15·00
36 4a. orange-yellow . . . 2·50 6·00
33/6 *Set of* 4 . . . 9·50 15·50

Nos. 32 and 36 are nearly square, in many cases rather larger in height than in width.

1891. *As last, but sheets of 32 (4 × 8).*

37 **9** ½a. red (*imperf*) . . . 1·60 3·25
38 ½a. red (*perf*) . . . 1·25 4·25

1894–98. *T* **6** *again redrawn.*

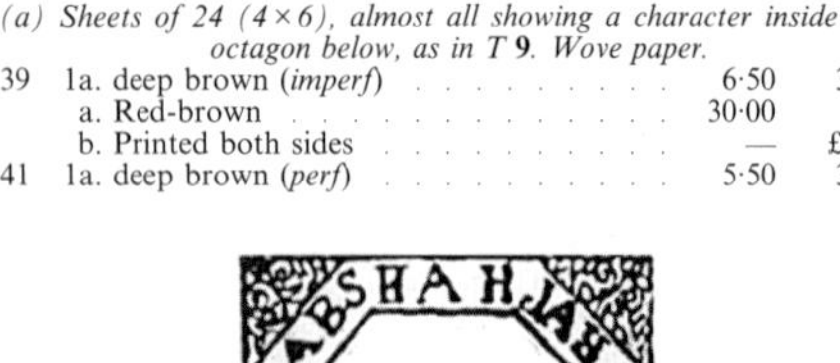

(a) Sheets of 24 (4 × 6), almost all showing a character inside the octagon below, as in T **9**. *Wove paper.*

39 1a. deep brown (*imperf*) . . . 6·50 3·50
a. Red-brown . . . 30·00
b. Printed both sides . . . — £450
41 1a. deep brown (*perf*) . . . 5·50 3·50

10 (1a.)

(b) As Nos. 39/41, but printed from a new stone showing the lines blurred and shaky. Wove paper. Imperf (1898).

42 **10** 1a. purple-brown . . . 2·75 3·75
a. "NAWAH" (R. 4/1) . . . 15·00 21·00
43 1a. purple-brown/*buff* . . . 2·75 3·75
a. "NAWAH" (R. 4/1) . . . 15·00 21·00
b. Printed on both sides . . .

The above are known without embossing.

11 (¼a.)

1895. *Sheets of 8 (2 × 4), lettered "EEGAM". White laid paper.*

44 **11** ¼a. black (*imperf*) . . . 3·00 2·50
a. "A" inserted (R. 4/2) . . . 7·50 6·00
45 ¼a. black (*perf*) . . . 85·00 38·00
a. "NAW B" (R. 4/2) . . . £275 £150

On the perf stamp the second "A" in "NAWAB" was missing on R. 4/2 in the setting. This letter was later inserted for the imperf printing varying progressively from small to large.

12 (½a.)

1895. *Narrow label at bottom. Sheets of 8 (2 × 4), lettered "W W" for "H H". Laid paper.*

46 **12** ½a. black (*imperf*) . . . 1·00 1·50

12a

1896. *Sheets of 8 (2 × 4). Laid paper.*

47 **12a** ½a. red (*imperf*) . . . 1·75 1·75

No. 47 is a combination of Types **1** and **6**, having the double outer frame to the octagon and the value in one form only.

13 (¼a.)

14 (¼a.)

1884. *Sheets of 32 (4 × 8).* Perf.

48 **13** ¼a. blue-green . . . £130 £160
a. "JAN" (R. 2/1–2, R. 3/1, R. 3/3–4, R. 4/1–3, R. 5/1–3) . . . £130 £160
b. "BEGM" (R. 2/3–4) . . . £350 £400
c. "NWAB" and "JAN" (R. 3/2) . . . £600
ca. "NWAB" and "JN" (R. 5/4) . . . £600
d. "SHAHAN" (R. 4/4) . . . £600
e. "JAHA" (R. 6/2–4) . . . £275

1896. *T* **14**, *double-lined frame round each stamp. Sheets of 6 (2 × 3), lettered "JAN". Laid paper.*

49 **14** ¼a. bright green (*imperf*) . . . 4·50 12·00

15 (¼a.)

16 (½a.)

1884. *Sheets of 32 (4 × 8). Laid paper.*

50 **15** ¼a. blue-green (*imperf*) . . . £120 £140
a. "NWAB" (R. 1/1) . . . £325
b. "SAH" (R. 1/4) . . . £325
c. "NAWA" and "JANAN" (R. 3/2) . . . £325
51 ¼a. blue-green (*perf*) . . . 80 3·50
a. "NWAB" (R. 1/1) . . . 3·50
b. "SAH" (R. 1/4) . . . 3·50
c. "NAWA" and "JANAN" (R. 3/2) . . . 3·50
d. Imperf between (vert pair) . . . £225
52 ½a. black (*imperf*) . . . 1·75 2·00
a. "NWAB" (R. 1/1) . . . 8·50 9·50
b. "SAH" (R. 1/4) . . . 8·50 9·50
c. "NAWA" and "JANAN" (R. 3/2) . . . 8·50 9·50
53 ½a. black (*perf*) . . . 65 2·75
a. "NWAB" (R. 1/1) . . . 3·00 6·00
b. "SAH" (R. 1/4) . . . 3·00 6·00
c. "NAWA" and "JANAN" (R. 3/2) . . . 3·00 6·00

The ½a. of this issue is in *blue-green*, or *greenish blue*. Both values were printed from the same stone, the value alone being altered. There are therefore the same varieties of each. These are the only stamps of this design on laid paper.

Both values show the "N" of "NAWAB" reversed on R. 1/1–4, R. 2/1–4, R. 3/1–4 and the "N" of "JAHAN" reversed on R. 1/1–4, R. 2/1–7, R. 3/4.

1886. *T* **15** *redrawn. Sheets of 32 (4 × 8). Wove paper.*

54 ¼a. green (*imperf*) . . . 45 2·75
a. "NAWA" (R. 6/3–4) . . . 1·50 4·75
b. "NWAB" (R. 1/1) . . . 2·50 7·00
c. "NWABA" (R. 7/4) . . . 2·50 7·00
d. "NAWAA" (R. 6/2) . . . 2·50 7·00
e. "BEGAAM" and "NWABA" (R. 7/3) . . . 2·50 7·00
55 ¼a. green (*perf*) . . . 2·50 3·50
a. "NAWA" (R. 6/3–4) . . . 7·50
b. "NWAB" (R. 1/1) . . . 11·00
c. "NWABA" (R. 7/4) . . . 11·00
d. "NAWAA" (R. 6/2) . . . 11·00
e. "BEGAAM" and "NWABA" (R. 7/3) . . . 11·00
f. Imperf between (horiz pair) . . . £140
56 ½a. red (*imperf*) . . . 55 1·2
a. "SAH" (R. 1/4) . . . 3·50 5·0
b. "NAWABA" (R. 6/3–4) . . . 2·75 4·0

The ¼a. varies from *yellow-green* to *deep green*.

All examples of the ¼a. value show the "N" of "NAWAB reversed. On the same value the "N" of "JAHAN" is reversed o all positions except R. 3/2, R. 4/1, R. 4/3. On the ½a. both "N"s ar always reversed.

1888. *T* **15** *again redrawn. Sheets of 32 (4 × 8), letters in upper angle smaller. "N" of "NAWAB" correct. Wove paper.*

57 ¼a. deep green (*imperf*) . . . 70 1·6
a. "SAH" (R. 6/2) . . . 3·75 5·5
b. "NAWA" (R. 4/4) . . . 3·75 5·5
58 ¼a. deep green (*perf*) . . . 1·50 2·2
a. "SAH" (R. 6/2) . . . 5·50 6·5
b. "NAWA" (R. 4/4) . . . 5·50 6·5
c. Imperf between (vert pair) . . . £190

Nos. 50 to 58 have the dash under the letter "JA" as in No. 14

1891. *T* **15** *again redrawn. Sheets of 32 (4 × 8), lettered "NWAB. Wove paper.*

(a) Imperf.

59 ½a. red . . . 1·60 1·0
a. "SAH" (R. 2/4) . . . 4·75

(b) P 3 to 4½, or about 7.

60 ½a. red . . . 60 1·5
a. "SAH" (R. 2/4) . . . 4·50

Nos. 59 and 60 have the comma under "JA". The "N" "JAHAN" is reversed on R. 1/1–3, R. 2/1–2.

1894. *T* **15** *again redrawn; letters in corners larger than in 1888, val in very small characters. Sheets of 32 (4 × 8), all with "G" in lef hand lower corner. Wove paper.*

61 ¼a. green (*imperf*) . . . 1·00 1·0
a. "NAWAH" (R. 4/4) . . . 5·50 6·0
b. Value in brackets (R. 1/1) . . . 5·50 6·0
62 ¼a. green (*perf*) . . . 2·50 1·7
a. "NAWAH" (R. 4/4) . . . 10·00 9·
b. Value in brackets (R. 1/1) . . . 10·00 9·

Nos. 61 and 62 have neither the dash nor the comma under "JA

1898. *T* **16**; *oval narrower, stops after "H.H.", space aft "NAWAB". The line down the centre is under the first "H" "SHAH" or between "HA" instead of being under the second "H or between "AH". Sheets of 32 (4 × 8). Wove paper.* Imperf.

63 **16** ¼a. bright green . . . 55
a. "SHAN" (R. 1/1) . . . 3·00 3·
64 ¼a. pale green . . . 60
a. "SHAN" (R. 1/1) . . . 3·00 3·
65 ¼a. black . . . 30
a. "SHAN" (R. 1/1) . . . 3·00 3·

1899. *T* **15** *redrawn. Sheets of 32 (4 × 8), the first "A" of "NAWA always absent. Numerous defective and malformed letters. Wo paper.* Imperf.

66 ½a. black . . . 3·75 4·
a. "NWASBAHJANNI" (R. 2/4) . . . 18·00 21·
b. "SBAH" (R. 3/3, R. 4/3–4, R.5/1–2, R. 6/4) . . . 8·50 11·
c. "SBAN" (R. 8/2) . . . 18·00 21·
d. "NWIB" (R. 3/2) . . . 18·00 21·
e. "BEIAM" (R. 4/4) . . . 18·00 21·
f. "SHH" (R. 6/3) . . . 18·00 21·
g. "SBAH" and "BBGAM" (R. 3/4) . . . 18·00 21·
h. "BBGAM" (R. 1/3) . . . 18·00 21·

17 (8a.)

18 (¼a.)

1890. *T* **17**. *Sheets of 10 (2 × 5). Single-line frame to each stamp.*

(a) Wove paper.

67 **17** 8a. slate-green (*imperf*) . . . 45·00 80·
a. "HAH" (R. 3/1, R. 4/1, R. 5/1) . . . 60·00 £1
b. "JABAN" (R. 2/2) . . . 60·00
68 8a. slate-green (*perf*) . . . 45·00 80
a. "HAH" (R. 3/1, R. 4/1, R. 5/1) . . . 60·00
b. "JABAN" (R. 2/2) . . . 60·00

(b) Thin laid paper.

69 **17** 8a. green-black (*imperf*) . . . 55·00 £1
a. "HAH" (R. 3/1, R. 4/1, R. 5/1) . . . 70·00
b. "JABAN" (R. 2/2) . . . 70·00
70 8a. green-black (*perf*) . . . 55·00 £1
a. "HAH" (R. 3/1, R. 4/1, R. 5/1) . . . 75·00 £1
b. "JABAN" (R. 2/2) . . . 75·00

The "N" of "NAWAB" is reversed on R. 5/2 and the "N" of "JAHAN" on R. 1/1–2, R. 2/2, R. 3/2, R. 4/2 and R. 5/2.

893. *T* **17** *redrawn. No frame to each stamp, but a frame to the sheet. Sheets of 10 (2 × 5).*

(a) Wove paper.

1 8a. green-black (*imperf*) . . . 20·00 20·00
2 8a. green-black (*perf*) . . . 25·00 32·00

(b) Thin laid paper. Imperf.

3 8a. green-black . . . £160 £180

898. *Printed from a new stone. Lettering irregular. Sheets of 10 (2 × 5). Wove paper.* Imperf.

4 8a. green-black . . . 38·00 48·00
a. Reversed "E" in "BEGAM" (R. 1/2, R. 3/2) . . . 75·00 85·00
5 8a. black . . . 35·00 48·00
a. Reversed "E" in "BEGAM" (R. 1/2, R. 3/2) . . . 75·00 85·00

896–1901. *Sheets of 32 (4 × 8).*

(a) Wove paper. Imperf.

6 **18** ¼a. black . . . 1·00 1·00

(b) Printed from a new stone, lines shaky (1899).

7 **18** ¼a. black . . . 2·25 2·25

(c) The same, on thick wove paper (1901).

8 **18** ¼a. black . . . £500 £500

Nawab Sultan Jahan Begam, 16 June 1901–17 May 1926

19 (¼a.)

20

02. *T* **19**. *With the octagonal embossed device of the previous issues. Sheets of 16 (4 × 4) ¼a. or 8 (2 × 4) others. Thin, yellowish wove paper.* Imperf.

19 ¼a. rose . . . 4·25 7·00
¼a. rose-red . . . 2·50 4·25
½a. black . . . 3·00 5·00
a. Printed both sides . . . £550 £550
1a. brown . . . 5·00 13·00
1a. red-brown . . . 4·00 11·00
2a. blue . . . 6·00 11·00
4a. orange . . . 55·00 85·00
4a. yellow . . . 35·00 70·00
8a. lilac . . . 85·00 £150
1r. rose . . . £200 £300
/88 *Set of 7* . . . £300 £500

03. *With a circular embossed device. Sheets of 16 (4 × 4) ¼a. (two plates) or 8 (2 × 4) (others). Wove paper.*

19 ¼a. rose-red . . . 1·10 4·00
a. Laid paper . . . 80 6·00
¼a. red . . . 80 3·75
a. Laid paper . . . 30 4·75
½a. black . . . 85 4·50
a. Laid paper . . . 85 6·50
1a. brown . . . 1·75 5·50
a. Laid paper . . . 85·00
1a. red-brown . . . 5·00
a. Laid paper
2a. blue . . . 5·00 20·00
a. Laid paper . . . £150 £170
4a. orange (*laid paper*) . . . £225 £225
4a. yellow . . . 16·00 42·00
a. Laid paper . . . £110 £100
8a. lilac . . . 42·00 £110
a. Laid paper . . . £1300
1r. rose . . . 65·00 £150
a. Laid paper . . . £1100
/98 *Set of 7* . . . £120 £300

03. *No. 71 optd with initial of the new Begam, either 6 or 11 mm long, in red.*

8a. green-black . . . £100 £100
a. Opt inverted . . . £250 £250

Some of the previous stamps remained on sale (and probably in use) after the issue of the series of 1902, and some of these were afterwards put on sale with the new form of embossing; fresh plates were made of some of the old designs, in imitation of the earlier issues, and impressions from these were also sold with the new embossed device. We no longer list these doubtful items.

(Recess Perkins, Bacon & Co)

08. P 13½.

20 1a. green . . . 3·75 3·75
a. Printed both sides . . . £100
b. Imperf (pair)

The ordinary postage stamps of Bhopal became obsolete on 1 July 1908.

OFFICIAL STAMPS

SERVICE (O 1) **SERVICE** (O 2)

(Recess and optd Perkins, Bacon)

1908–11. *As T* **20**, *but inscribed* "H.H. BEGUM'S SERVICE" *at left.* No wmk. P 13 to 14. Overprinted.

(a) With Type O **1**.

O301 ½a. yellow-green . . . 2·25 10
a. Imperf (pair) . . . £120
b. Pair, one without overprint . . . £475
c. Opt double, one inverted . . . £110
ca. Ditto. Imperf (pair) . . . £140
d. Opt inverted . . . £140 £140
e. Imperf between (horiz pair) . . . £600
O302 1a. carmine-red . . . 4·25 35
a. Opt inverted . . . 85·00 85·00
b. Imperf (pair) . . . 95·00
c. Red . . . 5·00 10
O303 2a. ultramarine . . . 24·00 10
a. Imperf (pair) . . . 55·00
O304 4a. brown (1911) . . . 11·00 40
O301/4 *Set of 4* . . . 38·00 60

(b) With Type O **2**.

O305 ½a. yellow-green . . . 5·50 60
O306 1a. carmine-red . . . 8·00 90
O307 2a. ultramarine . . . 3·50 50
a. Opt inverted . . . 25·00
O308 4a. brown (1911) . . . 70·00 1·10
a. Opt inverted . . . 20·00 70·00
b. Opt double . . . 95·00
c. Imperf (pair) . . . 80·00
d. Imperf (pair) and opt inverted . . . 80·00
O305/8 *Set of 4* . . . 80·00 2·75

The two overprints differ in the shape of the letters, noticeably in the "R".

Nawab Mohammad Hamidullah. Khan
17 May 1928 to transfer of administration to India, 1 June 1949

SERVICE

(O 3)

(O 4)

(Des T. I. Archer. Litho Indian Govt Ptg Wks, Nasik)

1930 (1 July)–**31**. *Type* O **4** *(25½ × 30½ mm) optd with Type* O **3**. P 14.

O309 O **4** ½a. sage-green (1931) . . . 9·00 1·40
O310 1a. carmine-red . . . 10·00 15
O311 2a. ultramarine . . . 9·50 45
O312 4a. chocolate . . . 9·00 90
O309/12 *Set of 4* . . . 35·00 2·50

The ½a., 2a. and 4a. are inscribed "POSTAGE" at left.

(Litho Perkins, Bacon)

1932–34. *As Type* O **4** *(21 × 25 mm), but inscr "POSTAGE" at left. Optd with Type* O **1**.

(a) "BHOPAL STATE" at right. P 13.

O313 ¼a. orange . . . 2·50 50
a. Perf 11½ (1933) . . . 5·50 20
b. Perf 14 (1934) . . . 11·00 30
c. Perf 13½ (1934) . . . 12·00 30
ca. Vert pair, one without opt . . . £110

(b) "BHOPAL GOVT" at right. P 13½.

O314 ½a. yellow-green . . . 5·50 10
O315 1a. carmine-red . . . 9·00 15
a. Vert pair, one without opt . . . £200
O316 2a. ultramarine . . . 9·00 45
O317 4a. chocolate . . . 7·50 1·00
a. Perf 14 (1934) . . . 15·00 40
O313/17 *Set of 5* . . . 30·00 1·10

No. O317 is comb-perforated and No. O317a line-perforated.

¼A (O 5) THREE PIES (O 6) ONE ANNA (O 7)

1935–36. *Nos. O314, O316 and O317 surch as Types* O **5** *to* O **7**.

O318 O **5** ¼a.on ½a. yellow-green (R.) . . . 24·00 14·00
a. Surch inverted . . . £160 75·00
b. Vert pair. Nos. O318/19 . . . 40·00 22·00
ba. Ditto. Surch inverted . . . £350 £160
O319 O **6** 3p.on ½a. yellow-green (R.) . . . 3·00 3·50
a. "THEEE PIES" (R. 7/10) . . . 65·00 48·00
b. "THRFE" for "THREE" (R. 10/6) . . . 65·00 48·00
c. Surch inverted . . . 70·00 38·00
O320 O **5** ¼a.on 2a. ultramarine (R.) . . . 26·00 17·00
a. Surch inverted . . . £160 65·00
b. Vert pair. Nos. O320/1 . . . 40·00 24·00
ba. Ditto. Surch inverted . . . £350 £150
O321 O **6** 3p.on 2a. ultramarine (R.) . . . 4·50 3·75
a. Surch inverted . . . 70·00 38·00
b. "THEEE PIES" (R. 7/10) . . . 70·00 45·00
ba. Ditto. Surch inverted . . . £475 £400
c. "THRFE" for "THREE" (R. 10/6) . . . 70·00 45·00
ca. Ditto. Surch inverted . . . £475 £400
O322 O **5** ¼a.on 4a. chocolate (R.) . . . £800 £275
a. Vert pair. Nos. O322 and O324 . . . £1200 £450
O323 ¼a.on 4a. chocolate (No. O317a) (Blk.) (25.5.36) . . . 65·00 23·00
a. Vert pair. Nos. O323 and O325 . . . 95·00 45·00
O324 O **6** 3p.on 4a. chocolate (R.) . . . £100 50·00
a. "THEEE PIES" (R. 7/10) . . . £500 £400
c. "THRFE" for "THREE" (R. 10/6) . . . £500 £400
O325 3p.on 4a. chocolate (No. O317a) (Blk.) (25.5.36) . . . 2·50 3·25
a. "THRER" for "THREE" (R. 8/2) . . . £325 £190
b. "FHREE" for "THREE" (R. 3/10, R. 10/1) . . . £350 £250
c. "PISE" for "PIES" (R. 10/10) . . . £500 £375
d. "PIFS" for "PIES" (R. 7/9) . . . £300 £190
O326 O **7** 1a.on ½a. yellow-green (V.) . . . 3·75 1·50
a. Surch inverted . . . 65·00 40·00
b. First "N" in "ANNA" inverted (R. 4/5) . . . 85·00 50·00
ba. Ditto. Surch inverted . . . £475 £375
O327 1a.on 2a. ultramarine (R.) . . . 2·25 1·75
a. Surch inverted . . . 75·00 38·00
b. First "N" in "ANNA" inverted (R. 4/5) . . . 65·00 50·00
ba. Ditto. Surch inverted . . . £475 £375
O327*d* 1a.on 2a. ultramarine (V.) . . . 42·00 42·00
da. Surch inverted . . . 85·00 85·00
db. First "N" in "ANNA" inverted (R. 4/5) . . . £450 £450
dc. Ditto. Surch inverted . . . £800 £800
O328 1a.on 2a. ultram (Blk.) (25.5.36) . . . 70 1·40
a. "ANNO" . . . £1300
O329 1a.on 4a. chocolate (B.) . . . 4·75 5·00
a. First "N" in "ANNA" inverted (R. 4/5) . . . 85·00 70·00
b. Perf 14 . . . 9·00 4·50
ba. Ditto. First "N" in "ANNA" inverted (R. 4/5) . . . £180 90·00

Nos. O318 to O325 are arranged in composite sheets of 100 (10 × 10). The two upper horizontal rows of each value are surcharged as Type O **5** and the next five rows as Type O **6**. The remaining three rows are also surcharged as Type O **6** but in a slightly narrower setting.

The surcharge on No. O323 differs from Type O **5** in the shape of the figures and letter.

O 8

(Des T. I. Archer. Litho Indian Govt Ptg Wks, Nasik (No. O330). Typo Bhopal Govt Ptg Wks (others))

1935–39. *As Type O* **8**.

(a) Litho. Inscr "BHOPAL GOVT POSTAGE". Optd "SERVICE" (13½ mm). P 13½.

O330 1a.3p. blue and claret . . . 3·50 75

(b) Typo. Inscr "BHOPAL STATE POSTAGE". Optd "SERVICE" (11 mm). P 12.

O331 1a.6p. blue and claret (1937) . . . 2·25 75
a. Imperf between (pair) . . . £160 £170
b. Opt omitted . . . £140 £100
c. Opt double, one inverted . . . £375 £375
d. Imperf (pair) . . . † £140
e. Blue printing double . . . † £130
O332 1a.6p. claret (1939) . . . 5·50 1·25
a. Imperf between (pair) . . . £160 £170
b. Opt omitted . . . — £325
c. Opt double, one inverted . . . — £325
d. Opt double . . . — £325

PRINTERS. From No. O333 all issues were printed by the Bhopal Govt Ptg Wks in typography.

O 9

O 10 Taj Mahal and Be-Nazir Palaces

1936 (July)–**38.** *Optd "SERVICE".* P 12.

O333 O **9** ¼a. orange (Br.) . . . 90 40
a. Imperf between (vert pair) . . . £140
ab. Imperf between (horiz pair) . . . † £275
b. Opt inverted . . . £325 £225
c. Black opt . . . 8·50 75
ca. Opt inverted . . . † £300
cb. Opt double . . . † £250
O334 ¼a. yellow (Br.) (1938) . . . 3·00 1·10
O335 1a. scarlet . . . 1·50 10
a. Imperf between (horiz pair) . . . £120 £110
b. Imperf between (vert pair) . . . † £225
c. Imperf between (block of four) . . . £325 £325
d. Imperf vert (horiz pair) . . . † £130

1936–49. *As Type* O **10** *(various palaces).* P 12.

(a) Optd "SERVICE" (13½ mm).

O336 ½a. purple-brown and yellow-green . . . 70 70
a. Imperf between (vert pair) . . . † £170
ab. Imperf between (horiz pair) . . . † £170
b. Opt double . . . £250 £160
c. Frame double . . . £120 15·00
d. Purple-brown and green (1938) . . . 70 40

(b) Optd "SERVICE" (11 mm).

O337 2a. brown and blue (1937) . . . 2·00 75
a. Imperf between (vert pair) . . . † £250
ab. Imperf between (horiz pair) . . . † £180
b. Opt inverted . . . £275 £275
c. Opt omitted . . . £350
d. Pair, one without opt . . . £475
e. As d. but opt inverted . . . £750

O338 2a. green and violet (1938) . . . 8·50 30
a. Imperf between (vert pair) . . . † £180
b. Imperf between (vert strip of 3) . . . £120 £140
c. Frame double . . . † £200
d. Centre double . . . † £225
O339 4a. blue and brown (1937) . . . 3·50 50
a. Imperf between (horiz pair) . . . † £475
b. Opt omitted . . . † £225
c. Opt double . . . † £140
d. Centre double . . . † £300
e. Blue and reddish brown (1938) . . . 3·25 55
ea. Frame double . . . † £200
O340 8a. bright purple and blue (1938) . . . 4·75 1·75
a. Imperf between (vert pair) . . . † £325
b. Opt omitted . . . † £130
c. Opt double . . . † £140
d. Imperf vert (horiz pair) and opt omitted . . . † £225
e. Imperf (pair) and opt omitted . . . † £225
O341 1r. blue and reddish purple (Br.) (1938) . . . 18·00 7·00
a. Imperf horiz (vert pair) . . . † £1100
b. Opt in black (1942) . . . 16·00 4·50
ba. Light blue and bright purple . . . 38·00 28·00
bb. Laid paper . . . £550 £600
O336/41 *Set of* 6 . . . 32·00 7·50

(c) Optd "SERVICE" (11½ mm) with serifs.

O342 1r. dull blue and bright purple (Blk.) (1949) . . . 42·00 75·00
a. "SREVICE" for "SERVICE" (R. 6/6) . . . £130 £190
b. "SERVICE" omitted . . . £700

(d) Optd "SERVICE" (13½ mm) with serifs.

O343 8a. bright purple and blue (1949) . . . 75·00 £100
a. "SERAICE" for "SERVICE" (R. 6/5) . . . £350 £450
b. Fig "1" for "I" in "SERVICE" (R. 7/1) . . . £350 £450

The ½a. is inscr "BHOPAL GOVT" below the arms, other values have "BHOPAL STATE".

Designs:—(37½ × 22½ *mm*) ½a. The Moti Mahal; 2a. The Moti Masjid. (39 × 24 *mm*)—8a. Ahmadabad Palace. (45½ × 27½ *mm*)—1r. Rait Ghat.

O **11** Tiger

O **13** The Moti Mahal

1940. *As Type* O **11** *(animals)*. P 12.
O344 ¼a. bright blue . . . 3·75 1·40
O345 1a. bright purple (Spotted Deer) . . . 20·00 2·00

1941. *As Type* O **8** *but coloured centre inscr "SERVICE"; bottom frame inscr* "BHOPAL STATE POSTAGE". P 12.
O346 1a.3p. emerald-green . . . 1·50 1·50
a. Imperf between (pair) . . . £425 £425

1944–17. *As Type* O **13** *(various palaces)*. P 12.
O347 ½a. green . . . 90 90
a. Imperf (pair) . . . † 80·00
b. Imperf between (vert pair) . . . † £150
c. Doubly printed . . . † £120
O348 2a. violet . . . 8·00 3·25
a. Imperf (pair) . . . † 80·00
c. Bright purple (1945) . . . 2·25 3·25
d. Mauve (1947) . . . 11·00 15·00
e. Error. Chocolate (imperf) . . . £180 £180
O349 4a. chocolate . . . 5·00 1·75
a. Imperf (pair) . . . † 95·00
b. Imperf vert (horiz pair) . . . † £190
c. Doubly printed . . . † £140
O347/9 *Set of* 3 . . . 7·25 5·50

Design inscr "BHOPAL STATE":—2a. The Moti Masjid; 4a. Be-Nazir Palaces.

O **14** Arms of Bhopal — 2 As. (O **15**) — 2 As. (O **16**)

1944–49. P 12.
O350 O **14** 3p. bright blue . . . 65 65
a. Imperf between (vert pair) . . . £100 £110
b. Imperf between (horiz pair) . . . † £200
c. Stamp doubly printed . . . 45·00
O351 9p. chestnut (*shades*) (1945) . . . 8·50 3·00
a. Imperf (pair) . . . † £160
b. Orange-brown . . . 2·00 3·25
O352 1a. purple (1945) . . . 4·25 1·40
a. Imperf horiz (vert pair) . . . † £325
b. Violet (1946) . . . 7·50 2·75
O353 1½a. claret (1945) . . . 1·25 75
a. Imperf between (horiz pair) . . . † £300
b. Imperf between (vert pair) . . .
O354 3a. yellow . . . 9·50 11·00
a. Imperf (pair) . . . † £160
b. Imperf horiz (vert pair) . . . † £225
c. Imperf vert (horiz pair) . . .
d. Orange-brown (1949) . . . 90·00 90·00
O355 6a. carmine (1945) . . . 14·00 40·00
a. Imperf (pair) . . . † £190
b. Imperf horiz (vert pair) . . . † £225
c. Imperf vert (horiz pair) . . . † £225
O350/5 *Set of* 6 . . . 30·00 50·00

1949 (July). *Surch with Type* O **15**. P 12.
O356 O **14** 2a.on 1½a. claret . . . 2·50 6·50
a. Stop omitted . . . 12·00 24·00
b. Imperf (pair) . . . £190 £225
ba. Stop omitted (pair) . . . £475 £550
c. "2" omitted (in pair with normal) . . . £700

The "stop omitted" variety occurs on positions 60 and 69 in the sheet of 81.

1949. *Surch with Type* O **16**. Imperf.
O357 O **14** 2a.on 1½a. claret . . . £700 £700
a. Perf 12 . . . £700 £700

Three different types of "2" occur in the setting of Type O **16**.

BHOR

PRICES FOR STAMPS ON COVER	
Nos. 1/2	*from* × 40
No. 3	*from* × 6

GUM. The stamps of Bhor were issued without gum.

Pandit Shankar Rao, 1871–1922

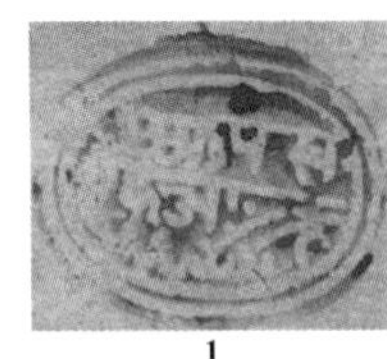
1

2

1879. *Handstamped. Very thick to thin native paper.* Imperf.
1 **1** ½a. carmine (*shades*) . . . 2·75 4·25
a. *Tête-bêche* (pair) . . . £600
2 **2** 1a. carmine (*shades*) . . . 4·75 6·50

3

1901. *Typo. Wove paper.* Imperf.
3 **3** ½a. red . . . 12·50 35·00

BIJAWAR

PRICES FOR STAMPS ON COVER
The stamps of Bijawar are very rare used on cover.

Maharaja Sarwant Singh, 1899–1941

1

2

(Typo Lakshmi Art Ptg Works, Bombay)

1935 (1 July)–**36**.

(a) P 11.

1 **1** 3p. brown . . . 5·50 4·00
a. Imperf (pair) . . . 7·00
b. Imperf between (vert pair) . . . 85·00
c. Imperf horiz (vert pair) . . . 50·00
2 6p. carmine . . . 5·00 4·50
a. Imperf (pair) . . . 85·00
b. Imperf between (vert pair) . . . 80·00
c. Imperf between (horiz pair) . . . 85·00 £120
d. Imperf horiz (vert pair) . . . 85·00
3 9p. violet . . . 6·50 4·25
a. Imperf (pair) . . . £140
b. Imperf between (vert pair) . . . 90·00
c. Imperf between (horiz pair) . . . 80·00
d. Imperf horiz (vert pair) . . . 85·00
4 1a. blue . . . 7·00 4·75
a. Imperf (pair) . . . 85·00
b. Imperf between (vert pair) . . . 85·00
c. Imperf between (horiz pair) . . . £140
d. Imperf horiz (vert pair) . . . 85·00
e. Imperf vert (horiz strip of 3) . . . £160
5 2a. deep green . . . 7·00 4·75
a. Imperf (pair) . . . £100
b. Imperf horiz (vert pair) . . . 11·00
c. Imperf between (vert pair) . . . 35·00
d. Imperf between (horiz pair) . . . 50·00 80·00
1/5 *Set of* 5 . . . 28·00 19·00

(b) Roul 7 (1936).

6 **1** 3p. brown . . . 4·50 4·00
a. Printed on gummed side . . . £450
7 6p. carmine . . . 5·50 19·00
8 9p. violet . . . 5·50 85·00
9 1a. blue . . . 8·00 90·00
10 2a. deep green . . . 9·50 95·00
6/10 *Set of* 5 . . . 30·00 £250

1937 (May). *Typo.* P 9.
11 **2** 4a. orange . . . 11·00 70·00
a. Imperf between (vert pair) . . . £140
b. Imperf (pair) . . . £200
12 6a. lemon . . . 12·00 70·0
a. Imperf between (vert pair) . . . £140
b. Imperf (pair) . . . £200
13 8a. emerald-green . . . 13·00 85·0
a. Imperf (pair) . . . £225
14 12a. greenish blue . . . 13·00 85·0
a. Imperf (pair) . . . £250
15 1r. bright violet . . . 32·00 £13
a. "1 Rs" for "1 R" (R. 1/2) . . . 48·00 £30
b. Imperf (pair) . . . £300
ba. "1 Rs" for "1 R" (R. 1/2) . . . £850
11/15 *Set of* 5 . . . 75·00 £40

The stamps of Bijawar were withdrawn in 1941.

BUNDI

PRICES FOR STAMPS ON COVER	
No. 1	*from* × 2
No. 2	*from* × 4
Nos. 3/53	*from* × 10
Nos. 54/63	*from* × 5
Nos. 64/78	*from* × 2
Nos. 79/92	*from* × 10
Nos. O1/52	*from* × 15
Nos. O53/9	*from* × 20

GUM. Nos. 1/17 were issued without gum.

ILLUSTRATIONS. Types **1/10** and the tablet inscriptions fo Type 11 are shown actual size.

In Nos. 1 to 17 characters denoting the value are below th dagger, except in Nos. 2a, 11 and 17.

All Bundi stamps until 1914 are imperforate.

Maharao Raja Raghubir Singh, 1889–1927

1

1894 (May). *Each stamp with a distinct frame and the stamps n connected by the framing lines. Three vertical lines on dagger. La or wove paper.*
1 **1** ½a. slate-grey . . . £6000 £16
a. Last two letters of value below the rest . . . † £37

2 (Block of four stamps)

1894 (Dec). *Stamps joined together, with no space between them. T vertical lines on dagger. Thin wove paper.*
2 **2** ½a. slate-grey . . . 35·00 38
a. Value at top, name below . . . £180 £2
b. Right upper ornament omitted . . . £1500 £15
c. Last two letters of value below the rest . . . £1100 £1
d. Left lower ornament omitted . . . £1500 £15

3

1896 (Nov). *Dagger shorter, lines thicker. Stamps separate. L paper.*
3 **3** ½a. slate-grey . . . 4·00 8
a. Last two letters of value below the rest . . . £300 £

4 (1 anna)

5 (2 annas)

6 (2 annas)

897–98. *No shading in centre of blade of dagger. The stamps have spaces between them, but are connected by the framing lines, both vertically and horizontally. Laid paper.*

Blade of dagger comparatively narrow, and either triangular, as in T **4** *and* **6**, *or with the left-hand corner not touching the bar behind it, as in T* **5** *(1897–98).*

4	**4**	1a. Indian red	9·50	21·00
5	**5**	1a. red	8·50	13·00
6		2a. green	13·00	18·00
7	**6**	2a. yellow-green	10·00	22·00
8	**5**	4a. green	50·00	75·00
9		8a. Indian red	85·00	£190
0		1r. yellow/*blue*	£225	£400
/10 *Set of 5*			£350	£650

7

. *Blade varying in shape, but as a rule not touching the bar; value ove and name below the dagger, instead of the reverse (Jan 1898).*

1	**7**	4a. emerald-green	32·00	
		a. Yellow-green	21·00	50·00

8 (½ anna)

9 (8 annas)

. *Blade wider and (except on the ½ a.) almost diamond shaped; it nearly always touches the bar (1898–1900).*

	8	½a. slate-grey (5.2.98)	3·75	3·75
	9	1a. Indian red (7.98)	2·75	2·75
		2a. pale green (9.11.98)	8·00	12·00
		a. First two characters of value (= two) omitted	£1200	£1200
		8a. Indian red (7.98)	9·50	13·00
		1r. yellow/*blue* (7.98)	25·00	42·00
		a. On wove paper	12·00	21·00
/16a *Set of 5*			32·00	48·00

10

IV. *Inscriptions as on No. 11; point of dagger to left (9.11.98).*

10	4a. green	21·00	26·00
	a. Yellow-green	12·00	17·00

All the above stamps are lithographed in large sheets, containing many varieties of type as there are stamps in the sheets.

11 Raja protecting Sacred Cows

Type **11** was produced from separate clichés printed as a block of four. The same clichés were used for all values, but not necessarily in the same order within the block. The Devanagri inscriptions, "RAJ BUNDI" at top and the face value at bottom, were inserted into the basic clichés as required so that various differences exist within the 58 settings which have been identified.

The denominations may be identified from the following illustrations. The ½a., 3a. and rupee values can be easily distinguished by their colours.

Bottom tablets:—

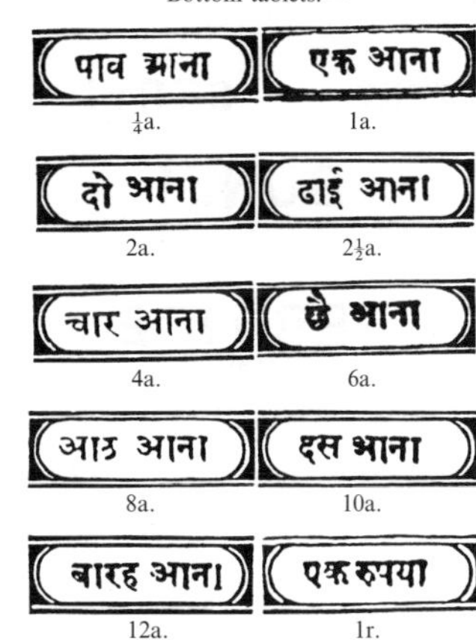

¼a. 1a. 2a. 2½a. 4a. 6a. 8a. 10a. 12a. 1r.

The nine versions of the inscriptions are as follows:

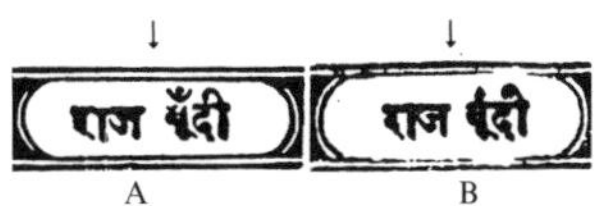

A B

Top tablet

Type A. Top tablet has inscription in two separate words with a curved line over the first character in the second. The second word has three characters.
Bottom tablet has short line above the first character in the second word.

Type B. Top tablet as Type A, but without the curved line over the first character in the second word.
Bottom tablet as Type A.

C

Type C. Top tablet as Type B, but with large loop beneath the first character in the second word. This loop is usually joined to the main character, but is sometimes detached as in the illustration.
Bottom tablet as Type A.

D E

Top tablet Bottom tablet

Type D. Top tablet in thinner lettering with the inscription shown as one word of six characters. The fourth character has a curved line above it, as in Type A, and a loop beneath, as in Type C.
Bottom tablet as Type A, but thinner letters.

Type E. Top tablet as Type C.
Bottom tablet shows a redrawn first character to the second word. This has the line at top extending over the entire character.

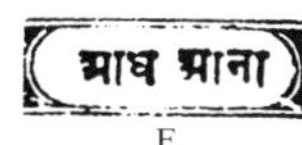

F

Bottom tablet

Type F. Top tablet as Type B.
Bottom tablet as Type E, but first character in second word differs.

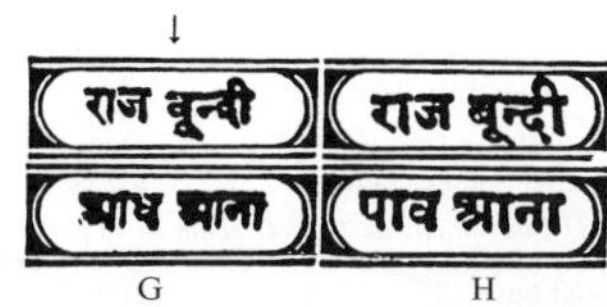

G H

Type G. Top tablet as Type C, but without dot over first character in second word. There are now four characters in the second word.
Bottom tablet as Type E.

Type H. Top tablet as Type G, but with characters larger and bolder.
Bottom tablet as Type E, but with characters larger and bolder.

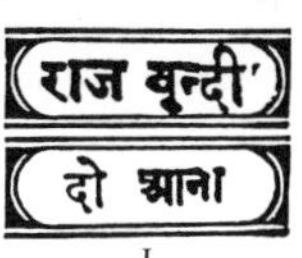

I

Type I. Top tablet as Type H.
Bottom tablet as Type E.

Some settings contained more than one inscription type within the block of four so that *se-tenant* examples are known of Type B with Type C (¼, 1, 2, 4, 8, 10 and 12a.), Type C with Type E (¼, ½ and 4a.) and Type E with Type F (½ and 4a.). Type F only exists from this mixed setting.

1914 (Oct)–**41**. *T* **11**. *Typo. Ungummed paper except for Nos. 73/8.*

I. *Rouletted in colour.*

(a) Inscriptions as Type A. Thin wove paper (1916–23).

18	½a. black	2·50	10·00
19	1a. vermilion	4·50	20·00
20	2a. emerald	4·50	32·00
	a. Deep green (coarse ptg on medium wove paper) (1923)	3·50	9·00
21	2½a. chrome-yellow (*shades*) (1917)	7·50	32·00
	a. Printed both sides	£1000	
22	3a. chestnut (1917)	20·00	35·00
23	4a. yellow-green	20·00	
24	6a. cobalt (1917)	20·00	90·00
25	1r. reddish violet (1917)	23·00	95·00

A special printing of the 1a. took place in late 1917 in connection with the "OUR DAY" Red Cross Society Fund. This had the "RAJ BUNDI" inscription in the bottom tablet with the face value below it. The top tablet carried four Devanagri characters for "OUR DAY". No evidence has been found to suggest that this 1a. stamp was used for postal purposes (*Price*, £180 *unused*).

(b) Inscriptions as Type B. Thin wove or pelure paper (1914–23).

25*a*	¼a. cobalt (1916)	3·25	20·00
	ab. Stamp doubly printed	£375	
26	¼a. ultramarine (*shades*) (1917)	1·90	4·25
	a. Indigo (1923)	3·50	8·00
	b. Error. Black (1923)		
27	½a. black	2·75	6·00
28	1a. vermilion (1915)	3·25	10·00
	a. Carmine (1923)	9·00	11·00
	b. Red (*shades*) (1923)	5·00	11·00
29	2a. emerald (*shades*) (1915)	6·50	18·00
30	2½a. olive-yellow (1917)	6·00	23·00
31	3a. chestnut (1917)	6·00	35·00
32	4a. apple-green (1915)	3·50	38·00
32*a*	4a. olive-yellow (1917)	£140	£160
33	6a. pale ultramarine (*shades*) (1917)	13·00	85·00
	a. Deep ultramarine (1917)	7·00	£100
34	8a. orange (1915)	7·50	90·00
35	10a. olive-sepia (1917)	£225	£500
	a. Yellow-brown	£300	
36	12a. sage-green (1917)	£550	
36*a*	1r. lilac (*shades*) (1915)	25·00	

(c) Inscriptions as Type C. Thin to medium wove paper (1917–41).

37	¼a. ultramarine (*shades*) (1923)	6·50	7·50
	a. Indigo (1923)	6·50	9·00
	b. Error. Black (1923)		
	c. Cobalt (medium wove paper) (1937)	19·00	19·00
38	½a. black	1·50	4·50
39	1a. orange-red	17·00	22·00
	a. Carmine (1923)	15·00	20·00
	b. *Deep red (medium wove paper)* (1936)	19·00	19·00
40	2a. emerald	9·00	23·00
	a. Sage-green	7·50	23·00
41	4a. yellow-green (*shades*)	48·00	£100
	a. Olive-yellow	£100	£150
	b. Bright apple-green (medium wove paper) (1936)	£425	£250
42	8a. reddish orange	9·00	55·00
43	10a. brown-olive	16·00	85·00
	a. Olive-sepia	38·00	£120
	b. Yellow-brown	75·00	
44	12a. sage-green	13·00	85·00
45	1r. lilac	25·00	£130
46	2r. red-brown and black	70·00	£225
	a. Chocolate and black (medium wove paper) (1936)	60·00	£275
47	3r. blue and red-brown	£100	£275
	a. Grey-blue and chocolate (medium wove paper) (1941)	£100	
	ab. Chocolate (inscriptions) inverted	£10000	
48	4r. emerald and scarlet	£200	£350
49	5r. scarlet and emerald	£225	£375

(d) Inscriptions as Type D. Thin wove paper (1918?).

50	2½a. buff (*shades*)	13·00	45·00
51	3a. red-brown	23·00	26·00
	a. Semi-circle and dot omitted from 4th character	38·00	42·00
52	10a. bistre	30·00	95·00
	a. 4th character turned to left instead of downwards	48·00	
53	12a. grey-olive	38·00	£100
	a. 4th character turned to left instead of downwards	65·00	
	b. Blackish green	55·00	
	ba. 4th character turned to left instead of downwards	85·00	

(e) Inscriptions as Type E.

(i) Medium wove paper (1930–37).

54	¼a. deep slate	18·00	23·00
54*a*	¼a. indigo (*thin wove paper*) (1935)	18·00	23·00
	b. Cobalt (1937)	18·00	17·00

55	½a. black	13·00	13·00
56	1a. carmine-red	23·00	29·00
57	3a. chocolate (*shades*) (1936)	11·00	32·00
58	4a. yellow-olive (1935)	£550	£200
	a. Bright apple-green (1936)	£500	£200
	ab. No tail to 4th character	£750	£350

(ii) Very thick wove paper (1930–32).

59	¼a. indigo (1932)	20·00	25·00
60	½a. black	85·00	90·00
61	1a. bright scarlet (1931)	20·00	23·00
	a. Carmine-red	75·00	85·00

(iii) Thin horizontally laid paper (1935).

62	¼a. indigo	4·50	19·00
63	1a. scarlet-vermilion	9·50	25·00

Nos. 62 and 63 exist in *tête-bêche* blocks of four on the same or opposite sides of the paper.

(f) Inscriptions as Type F. Medium wove paper (1935).

63*a*	½a. black	80·00	
63*b*	4a. yellow-olive	£900	£500

(g) Inscriptions as Type G.

(i) Horizontally laid paper (1935).

64	½a. black	85·00	85·00
	a. Vert laid paper	80·00	80·00
65	1a. scarlet	70·00	50·00
66	4a. bright green	20·00	40·00

(ii) Medium wove paper (1936).

66*a*	½a. black	4·00	25·00
66*b*	4a. yellow-green	£1000	£500

(h) Inscriptions as Type H. Medium wove paper (1935–41).

67	¼a. ultramarine	1·75	7·00
68	½a. black (1938)	75·00	75·00
69	1a. deep red	7·50	35·00
	a. Rosine (1938)	17·00	38·00
70	4a. emerald (1938)	18·00	27·00
71	4r. yellow-green and vermilion (1941)	£180	
72	5r. vermilion and yellow-green (1941)	£250	

No. 70 shows the currency spelt as "ANE" with the last letter missing and an accent over the Devanagri "N".

II. P 11.

(a) Inscriptions as Type H. Medium wove paper with gum (1939–41).

73	¼a. ultramarine	25·00	38·00
	a. Greenish blue (1941)	1·75	48·00
74	½a. black	32·00	32·00
75	1a. scarlet-vermilion (1940)	£120	60·00
	a. Rose (1940)	12·00	50·00
76	2a. yellow-green (1941)	16·00	75·00

(b) Inscriptions as Type I. Medium wove paper with gum (1940).

77	½a. black	£130	£100
78	2a. bright apple-green	50·00	50·00

FISCAL USE. Collectors are warned that the low values of the later settings of Type **11** were extensively used for fiscal purposes. Stamps which have been fraudulently cleaned of pen-cancels, regummed or provided with forged postmarks are frequently met with. Particular care should be exercised with examples of Nos. 58/*a*, 64/5, 68/70, 74/5*a* and 77.

Maharao Raja Ishwari Singh, 1927–1945

20

1941–44. *Typo.* P 11.

79	**20**	3p. bright blue	2·00	3·50
80		6p. deep blue	3·50	6·00
81		1a. orange-red	4·50	7·50
82		2a. chestnut	6·50	15·00
		a. Deep brown (*no gum*) (1944)	14·00	17·00
83		4a. bright green	12·00	42·00
84		8a. dull green	15·00	£150
85		1r. deep blue	38·00	£225
79/85 *Set of* 7			75·00	£400

The first printing only of Nos. 79/85 is usually with gum; all further printings, including No. 82*a*, are without gum.

Maharao Raja Bahadur Singh, 1945–1971

21 Maharao Raja Bahadur Singh

22 Bundi

(Typo *Times of India* Press, Bombay)

1947. P 11.

86	**21**	¼a. blue-green	1·90	30·00
87		½a. violet	1·90	28·00
88		1a. yellow-green	1·90	27·00
89	–	2a. vermilion	1·90	55·00
90	–	4a. orange	1·90	80·00
91	**22**	8a. ultramarine	2·50	
92		1r. chocolate	15·00	
86/92 *Set of* 7			24·00	

On the 2 and 4a. the Maharao is in Indian dress.

OFFICIAL STAMPS

PRICES. Prices for Nos. O1/52 are for unused examples. Used stamps are generally worth a small premium over the prices quoted.

बूंदी BUNDI

सरविस (O 1) SERVICE (O 2)

BUNDI

SERVICE (O 3)

1915–41. *T* **11** *handstamped as Types* O **1/3**. *Ungummed paper except Nos. O47/52.*

A. *Optd with Type* O **1**. B. *Optd with Type* O **2**. C. *Optd with Type* O **3**.

I. *Rouletted in colour*

(a) Inscriptions as Type A. Thin wove paper.

		A	B	C
O 1	½a. black	£300	†	†
	a. Red opt	£275	†	†
O 1*b*	2a. emerald	3·00	£275	†
	ba. Deep green (coarse ptg on medium wove paper)	6·50	14·00	£225
	bb. Red opt	13·00	15·00	†
O 2	2½a. chrome-yellow (*shades*)	3·00	16·00	£225
	a. Red opt	£160	£190	†
O 3	3a. chestnut	3·00	21·00	†
	a. Green opt	£160	†	†
	b. Red opt	£200	£200	†
O 4	6a. cobalt	24·00	26·00	£275
	a. Red opt	£250	£275	£300
O 5	1r. reddish violet	48·00	42·00	†
	a. Red opt	£325	£350	†

(b) Inscriptions as Type B. Thin wove or pelure paper.

		A	B	C
O 6	¼a. ultramarine (*shades*)	1·60	1·75	7·50
	a. Red opt	1·25	4·00	£170
O 7	½a. black	8·00	6·00	32·00
	a. Red opt	4·25	11·00	£170
O 8	1a. vermilion	4·00	†	†
	a. Red opt	—	†	†
	b. Carmine	24·00	12·00	70·00
	c. Red (*shades*)	—	7·00	—
O 9	2a. emerald (*shades*)	29·00	38·00	†
	a. Red opt	—	£120	†
O 9*b*	3a. chestnut (R.)	—	†	†
O10	4a. apple-green	12·00	65·00	£225
	a. Red opt	£275	†	†
O10*b*	4a. olive-yellow	£250	£275	†
	ba. Red opt	—	£475	†
O11	6a. pale ultramarine (*shades*)	13·00	£225	†
	a. Red opt	£275	£275	†
	b. Deep ultramarine	55·00	75·00	†
	ba. Red opt	£190	£170	†
O12	8a. orange	45·00	60·00	£350
	a. Red opt	£300	†	†
O13	10a. olive-sepia	£180	£250	£500
	a. Red opt	£600	£650	£800
O14	12a. sage-green	£140	£425	£550
	a. Red opt	†	†	£800
O14*b*	1r. lilac	£300	†	†

(c) Inscriptions as Type C. Thin to medium wove paper.

		A	B	C
O15	¼a. ultramarine (*shades*)	3·00	4·00	18·00
	a. Red opt	1·00	5·00	£275
	b. Green opt	3·75	42·00	†
	c. Cobalt (*medium wove paper*)	50·00	50·00	£300
	ca. Red opt	38·00	16·00	£110
O16	½a. black	8·00	3·00	12·00
	a. Red opt	75	8·00	£180
	b. Green opt	3·00	†	†
O17	1a. orange-red	1·25	—	†
	a. Carmine	23·00	8·00	18·00
	b. Deep red (*medium wove paper*)	32·00	42·00	80·00
	ba. Red opt	†	£140	†
O18	2a. emerald	5·00	16·00	65·00
	a. Red opt	†	£100	†
	b. Sage-green	9·50	13·00	75·00
O19	4a. yellow-green (*shades*)	9·50	70·00	†
	b. Red opt	—	†	†
	c. Olive-yellow	£120	£110	†
	ca. Red opt	£350	£350	†
O20	8a. reddish orange	15·00	26·00	£250
	a. Red opt	£250	£375	†
O21	10a. brown-olive	50·00	80·00	£400
	a. Red opt	£400	£400	£450
O22	12a. sage-green	42·00	95·00	£450
	a. Red opt	£500	†	£500
O23	1r. lilac	£120	†	†
	a. Red opt	£350	†	†
O24	2r. red-brown and black	£375	£180	†
	a. Red opt	†	£900	†
	b. Green opt	£900		
	c. Chocolate and black (*medium wove paper*)	£650	£650	†
O25	3r. blue and red-brown	£350	£200	†
	a. Red opt	£850	†	†
	b. Grey-blue & chocolate (*medium wove paper*)	£900	£900	†
	ba. Red opt	£950	†	†
O26	4r. emerald and scarlet	£300	£300	†
O27	5r. scarlet and emerald	£325	£325	†

(d) Inscriptions as Type D. Thin wove paper.

		A	B	C
O28	2½a. buff (*shades*)	15·00	18·00	†
	b. Red opt	£190	—	†
O29	3a. red-brown	32·00	24·00	
	a. Variety as No. 51a	50·00	45·00	
	b. Red opt	†	£350	
O30	10a. bistre	42·00	80·00	£45
	a. Variety as No. 52a	70·00	£130	£65
	b. Red opt	£400	£500	
O31	12a. grey-olive	60·00	90·00	£37
	a. Variety as No. 53a	90·00	£150	£55
	b. Red opt	£400	£475	
	ba. Variety as No. 53a	£500	†	

(e) Inscriptions as Type E.

(i) Medium wove paper.

		A	B	C
O32	¼a. deep slate	30·00	15·00	
	a. Red opt	27·00	38·00	
O32*b*	¼a. indigo (*thin wove paper*)	32·00	38·00	
	ba. Red opt	32·00	35·00	
	bb. Green opt	80·00	85·00	
	c. Cobalt	55·00	55·00	£30
	ca. Red opt	35·00	30·00	£11
O33	½a. black	38·00	12·00	
	a. Red opt	22·00	10·00	
	b. Green opt	£275	£190	
O34	1a. carmine-red	32·00	32·00	£25
O35	3a. chocolate (*shades*)	£180	£120	£22
	a. Red opt	£450	£450	
O35*b*	4a. yellow-olive	†	£500	
	ba. Bright apple-green	£850	†	

(ii) Very thick wove paper.

		A	B	C
O36	¼a. indigo	9·00	12·00	
	a. Red opt	23·00	48·00	
	b. Green opt	90·00	†	
O37	½a. black	£110	£120	
O38	1a. bright scarlet	13·00	15·00	£25
	a. Carmine-red	£110	75·00	

(iii) Thin horizontally laid paper.

		A	B	C
O39	¼a. indigo	75·00	85·00	
	a. Red opt	5·00	8·00	£19
O40	1a. scarlet-vermilion	40·00	25·00	
	a. Red opt	£300	£325	

Nos. O39/40a exist in *tête-bêche* blocks of four on the same c opposite sides of the paper.

(f) Inscriptions as Type F. Medium wove paper.

		A	B	C
O40*b*	½a. black	—	£400	
	ba. Red opt	£325	£400	
O40*c*	4a. yellow-olive	†	£700	

(g) Inscriptions as Type G.

(i) Horizontally laid paper.

		A	B	C
O41	½a. black (red opt)	£130	£130	
	a. Vert laid paper	£150	£150	
	ab. Red opt	£190	60·00	£3
O42	4a. bright green	£200	£190	
	a. Red opt	£250	£350	

(ii) Medium wove paper.

		A	B	C
O42*b*	½a. black	£225	£225	
	ba. Red opt	£325	£325	

(h) Inscriptions as Type H. Medium wove paper.

		A	B	C
O43	¼a. ultramarine	25·00	75·00	
	a. Red opt	£170	£300	
O44	½a. black	75·00	£120	
	a. Red opt	60·00	†	£4
O45	1a. rosine	£180	£160	£4
O46	4a. emerald	£160	£180	£4
	a. Red opt	£400	†	£4

II. P 11.

(a) Inscriptions as Type H. Medium wove paper with gum.

		A	B	C
O47	¼a. ultramarine	45·00	60·00	£1
	a. Red opt	70·00	80·00	
	b. Greenish blue	70·00	70·00	£1
	c. Ditto. Red opt	£190	†	
O48	½a. black	45·00	60·00	£3
	a. Red opt	90·00	£275	£1
O49	1a. scarlet-vermilion	£200	£250	£4
	a. Stamp doubly printed	†	†	£8
	b. Rose	£130	£120	£3
O50	2a. yellow-green	£400	£180	£2

(b) Inscriptions as Type I. Medium wove paper with gum.

		A	B	C
O51	½a. black	£120	£250	£4
	a. Red opt	£350	£425	
O52	2a. bright apple-green	£400	£400	£7

Until 1941 it was the general practice to carry official mail f but some of the above undoubtedly exist postally used.

1941. *Nos. 79 to 85 optd "SERVICE".*

O53	**20**	3p. bright blue (R.)	5·50	12
O54		6p. deep blue (R.)	13·00	12
O55		1a. orange-red	13·00	8
O56		2a. brown	12·00	9
O57		4a. bright green	35·00	80
O58		8a. dull green	£140	£4
O59		1r. deep blue (R.)	£160	£4
O53/9 *Set of* 7			£350	£9

Two different types of "R" occur in the "SERVICE" overpri On five positions in the sheet of 12 the "R" shows a larger lo and a pointed diagonal leg.

Bundi became part of the Rajasthan Union by 15 April 1948.

BUSSAHIR (BASHAHR)

PRICES FOR STAMPS ON COVER

Nos.	1/21	*from* × 8
Nos.	22/23	*from* × 2
Nos.	24/43	*from* × 8

Raja Shamsher Singh, 1850–1914

1

2

3

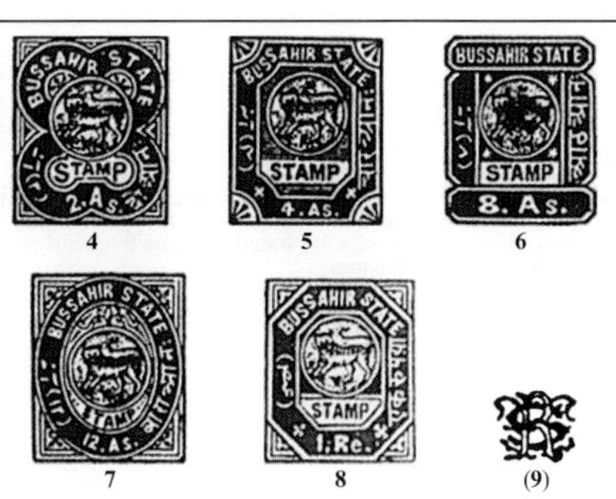

4 5 6 7 8 (9)

The initials are those of the Tika Raghunath Singh, son of the then Raja, who was the organiser and former director of the State Post Office.

(Litho at the Bussahir Press by Maulvi Karam Bakhsh, Rampur)

1895 (20 June). *Laid paper. Optd with T* **9** *in pale greenish blue (B.), rose (R.), mauve (M.) or lake (L.). With or without gum.*

(a) Imperf.

1 **1** ¼a. pink (M.) (1.9.95) . . . £1400
a. Monogram in rose . . . £1900
2 ½a. grey (R.) . . . £400
a. Monogram in mauve
3 1a. vermilion (M.) . . . £160
4 2a. orange-yellow (M.) . . . 55·00 £160
a. Monogram in rose . . . £100 £170
b. Monogram in lake . . . 70·00
c. Monogram in blue . . . £180
5 4a. slate-violet (M.) . . . 95·00
a. Monogram in rose . . . £130
b. Monogram in lake . . . £120
c. Without monogram . . . £275
6 8a. red-brown (M.) . . . 95·00 £180
a. Monogram in blue . . . £130
b. Monogram in rose . . . £160
c. Monogram in lake
d. Without monogram . . . £200
e. Thick paper . . . £120
7 12a. green (L.) . . . £225
a. Monogram in mauve
8 1r. ultramarine (R.) . . . 90·00
a. Monogram in mauve . . . £160
b. Monogram in lake . . . £130
c. Without monogram . . . £275

(b) Perf with a sewing machine; gauge and size of holes varying between 7 and 11½.

9 **1** ¼a. pink (B.) . . . 50·00 85·00
a. Monogram in mauve . . . — £140
b. Without monogram . . . £275 £120
10 **2** ½a. grey (R.) . . . 20·00 £100
a. Without monogram . . . £550
11 **3** 1a. vermilion (M.) . . . 21·00 80·00
a. Without monogram
12 **4** 2a. orange-yellow (B.) . . . 30·00 85·00
a. Monogram in rose
b. Monogram in mauve . . . 95·00
c. Without monogram . . . — £180
13 **5** 4a. slate-violet (B.) . . . 21·00 85·00
a. Monogram in rose . . . 29·00 £110
b. Monogram in mauve . . . 42·00
c. Without monogram . . . 40·00
14 **6** 8a. red-brown (M.) . . . 22·00 95·00
a. Monogram in blue . . . 50·00 £140
b. Monogram in rose . . . 80·00
c. Without monogram . . . £100
15 **7** 12a. green (R.) . . . 65·00 £110
a. Monogram in mauve . . . £120
b. Monogram in lake . . . £110
c. Without monogram . . . £170
16 **8** 1r. ultramarine (R.) . . . 38·00 £100
a. Monogram in mauve . . . 95·00
b. Without monogram . . . £225 £325
9/16 *Set of* 8 . . . £225 £650

1899. *As 1895, but pin-perf or rouletted.*

17 **3** 1a. vermilion (M.) . . . £170 £190
18 **4** 2a. orange-yellow (M.) . . . 50·00 £130
a. Monogram in lake . . . 60·00
b. Monogram in rose . . . 80·00
c. Monogram in blue . . . £120
d. Without monogram . . . £325
19 **5** 4a. slate-violet (L.) . . . £225
a. Monogram in blue
b. Monogram in rose . . . £300
c. Monogram in mauve . . . £300
20 **7** 12a. green (R.) . . . £400 £450
21 **8** 1r. ultramarine (R.) . . . £400

Nos. 1 to 21 were in sheets of 24. They seem to have been overprinted and perforated as required. Those first issued for use were perforated, but they were subsequently supplied imperf, both to collectors and for use. Nos. 17 to 21 were some of the last supplies. No rule seems to have been observed as to the colour of the overprinted monogram; pale blue, rose and mauve were used from the first. The pale blue varies to greenish blue or blue-green, and appears quite green on the yellow stamps. The lake is possibly a mixture of the mauve and the rose—it is a quite distinct colour and apparently later than the others. Specimens without overprint are either remainders left in the Treasury or copies that have escaped accidentally; they have been found sticking to the backs of others that bore the overprint.

Varieties may also be found doubly overprinted, in two different colours.

10

11 12

T **11**. Lines of shading above and at bottom left and right of shield.
T **12**. White dots above shield and ornaments in bottom corners.

13

14

15

16

(Printed at the Bussahir Press by Maulvi Karam Bakhsh)

1896–97. *Wove paper. Optd with monogram "R.S.", T* **9**, *in rose. Recess singly from line-engraved dies. With or without gum.* Various perfs.

22 **10** ¼a. deep violet (1897) . . . — £800
23 **11** ½a. grey-blue . . . £600 £225
23*a* ½a. deep blue (1897) . . . — £325

No. 23 exists sewing-machine perf about 10 and also perf 14½–16. Nos. 22 and 23*a* are pin-perf.

1896–1900. *As Nos. 22/3, but lithographed in sheets of various sizes. No gum.*

(a) Imperf.

24 **10** ¼a. slate-violet (R.) . . . 6·00
a. Monogram in mauve . . . 8·00
b. Monogram in blue . . . 10·00
c. Monogram in lake . . . 17·00
25 **11** ½a. blue (*shades*) (R.) . . . 7·00 15·00
a. Monogram in mauve . . . 7·50 15·00
b. Monogram in lake . . . 8·00
c. Without monogram
d. Laid paper (B.) . . . £100
da. Monogram in lake
26 **13** 1a. olive (*shades*) (R.) . . . 14·00 32·00
a. Monogram in mauve . . . 35·00
b. Monogram in lake . . . 35·00

(b) Pin-perf or rouletted.

27 **10** ¼a. slate-violet (R.) . . . 17·00 15·00
a. Monogram in lake . . . 21·00 18·00
b. Monogram in mauve . . . — 27·00
28 **11** ½a. blue (*shades*) (R.) . . . 11·00 27·00
a. Monogram in mauve . . . 15·00 28·00
b. Monogram in lake . . . 28·00 38·00
c. Monogram in blue . . . £110
d. Laid paper (M.)
29 **13** 1a. olive (*shades*) (R.) . . . 20·00
a. Monogram in mauve . . . 45·00 45·00
b. Monogram in lake . . . 45·00 45·00
30 **14** 2a. orange-yellow (B.) . . . £500 £550

Originally printings of the ¼a. and ½a. were in sheets of 8 (stone I), but this was subsequently increased to 24 (4 × 6). The 1a. and 2a. were always in sheets of 4.

Nos. 25d/da were printed from stone I and care is needed to distinguish this laid paper printing from some of the reprints on similar paper. Stamps from stone I are without marginal lines and are very clear impressions; reprints from stone IV have thick marginal lines and, in those shades similar to No. 25, show indistinct impressions.

1900–01. *¼a., 1a, colours changed; ½a. redrawn type; 2a. with dash before "STATE" and characters in lower left label; 4a. new value. No gum.*

(a) Imperf.

31 **10** ¼a. vermilion (M.) . . . 4·00 8·50
a. Monogram in blue . . . 4·25 8·50
b. Without monogram
31*c* **12** ½a. blue (M.) . . . 9·00 22·00
ca. Monogram in rose . . . 27·00
cb. Without monogram . . . 45·00
32 **13** 1a. vermilion (M.) . . . 4·00 12·00
a. Monogram in blue . . . 6·00 8·50
b. Monogram in lake
c. Without monogram . . . 40·00
33 **15** 2a. ochre (M.) (9.00) . . . 40·00 80·00
34 2a. yellow (M.) (11.00) . . . 40·00
a. Monogram in blue . . . 40·00 85·00
b. Without monogram . . . 65·00
35 2a. orange (B.) (1.01) . . . 45·00 80·00
a. Monogram in mauve . . . 45·00 75·00
b. Without monogram . . . 50·00
36 **16** 4a. claret (R.) . . . 42·00 95·00
a. Monogram in mauve . . . 55·00 £110
b. Monogram in blue . . . 75·00 £120
c. Without monogram . . . 29·00

(b) Pin-perf or rouletted.

37 **10** ¼a. vermilion (M.) . . . 3·50 8·50
a. Monogram in blue . . . 4·25
b. Without monogram
37*c* **12** ½a. blue (M.) . . . 40·00 55·00
38 **13** 1a. vermilion (M.) . . . 5·00 12·00
a. Monogram in blue . . . 8·00 9·50
39 1a. brown-red (M.) (3.01) . . . — £190
40 **15** 2a. ochre (M.) (9.00) . . . 48·00
a. Monogram in blue
41 2a. yellow (M.) (11.00) . . . 38·00 65·00
a. Monogram in rose . . . 55·00 85·00
b. Monogram in blue . . . 65·00 95·00
42 2a. orange (M.) (1.01) . . . 48·00 60·00
a. Monogram in blue . . . 70·00 75·00
b. Without monogram . . . — £180
43 **16** 4a. claret (R.) . . . 50·00
a. Monogram in blue . . . 60·00 £130
b. Monogram in mauve . . . 85·00

The ¼a., ½a. and 1a. are in sheets of 24; the 2a. in sheets of 50 differing throughout in the dash and the characters added at lower left; the 4a. in sheets of 28.

(17)

The stamps formerly catalogued with large overprint "R.N.S." (T **17**) are now believed never to have been issued for use.

Remainders are also found with overprint "P.S.", the initials of Padam Singh who succeeded Raghunath Singh in the direction of the Post Office, and with the original monogram "R.S." in a damaged state, giving it the appearance of a double-lined "R."

The stamps of Bussahir have been obsolete since 1 April 1901. Numerous remainders were sold after this date, and all values were later reprinted in the colours of the originals, or in fancy colours, from the original stones, or from new ones. Printings were also made from new types, similar to those of the second issue of the 8a., 12a. and 1r. values, in sheets of 8.

Reprints are frequently found on laid paper.

Collectors are warned against obliterated copies bearing the Rampur postmark with date "19 MA 1900." Many thousand remainders and reprints were thus obliterated for export after the closing of the State Post Office.

CHARKHARI

PRICES FOR STAMPS ON COVER	
Nos. 1/4	*from* × 2
Nos. 5/26	*from* × 20
Nos. 27/44	*from* × 3
Nos. 45/53	*from* × 100
Nos. 54/5	*from* × 5
No. 56	*from* × 2

Maharaja Malkhan Singh, 1880–1908

1

¼ ½ 1 2 4
¼ ½ 1 2 4

The top row shows the figures of value used in the stamps of 1894–97, and the bottom row those for the 1904 issue. In the 4a. the figure slopes slightly to the right in the first issue, and to the left in the second.

1894. *Typo from a single die. No gum.* Imperf.

1 **1** ¼ anna, rose . . . £1100 £700
2 1 annas, dull green . . . £1600 £2250
3 2 annas, dull green . . . £2000
4 4 annas, dull green . . . £1200

Nos. 1/2 are known pin-perforated.

1897. *Inscr "ANNA". No gum.* Imperf.

5 **1** ¼a. magenta . . . 48·00 60·00
a. Purple . . . 3·25 3·25
b. Violet . . . 3·00 3·00
6 ½a. purple . . . 2·75 3·75
a. Violet . . . 2·50 3·00
7 1a. blue-green . . . 4·75 7·50
a. Turquoise-blue . . . 4·00 4·75
b. Indigo . . . 13·00 20·00
c. Figure of value inverted . . . £1100
8 2a. blue-green . . . 8·00 15·00
a. Turquoise-blue . . . 7·00 8·00
b. Indigo . . . 15·00 23·00
9 4a. blue-green . . . 9·50 17·00
a. Turquoise-blue . . . 6·00 10·00
b. Indigo . . . 25·00 40·00
ba. Figure of value sideways . . . £1100
5/9 *Set of* 5 . . . 20·00 25·00

Minor varieties may be found with the first "A" in "ANNA" not printed.

All values are known on various coloured papers, but these are proofs or trial impressions.

1904. *Numerals changed as illustrated above. No gum.*

10 **1** ¼a. violet . . . 1·75 2·50
11 ½a. violet . . . 3·25 3·50
12 1a. green . . . 5·00 13·00
13 2a. green . . . 26·00 26·00
14 4a. green . . . 17·00 30·00
10/14 *Set of* 5 . . . 48·00 70·00

Stamps of this issue can be found showing part of the papermaker's watermark. "Mercantile Script Extra Strong John Haddon & Co.".

Maharaja Jujhar Singh, 1908–1914

2 (Right-hand sword over left)

Type I

POSTAGE STAMP

Type II

Type I. "P" of "POSTAGE" in same size as other letters. "E" small with long upper and lower arms. White dot often appears on one or both of the sword hilts.
Type II. "P" larger than the other letters. "E" large with short upper and lower arms. No dots occur on the hilts.

1909–19. *Litho in Calcutta. Wove paper.* P 11.

(a) Type I.

15 **2** 1p. chestnut . . . 40·00 45·00
a. Pale chestnut . . . 3·75 38·00
b. Orange-brown . . . 3·75 38·00
16 1p. turquoise-blue . . . 60 45
a. Imperf between (horiz pair) . . . £160
b. Greenish blue (1911) . . . 90 1·00
c. Pale turquoise-green . . . 1·50 70
17 ½a. vermilion . . . 2·00 1·00
a. Imperf (pair) . . . £750
b. Deep rose-red . . . 90 1·25
18 1a. sage-green . . . 2·25 2·25
a. Yellow-olive . . . 1·90 1·60
19 2a. grey-blue . . . 3·00 3·25
a. Dull violet-blue . . . 3·00 3·50
20 4a. deep green . . . 3·75 4·75
21 8a. brown-red . . . 7·50 17·00
22 1r. pale chestnut . . . 13·00 35·00
15*a*/22 *Set of* 8 . . . 30·00 90·00

(b) Type II.

24 **2** 1p. turquoise-blue . . . 3·50 3·75
25 ½a. vermilion . . . 1·60 1·60
b. Deep rose-red . . . 4·75 4·75
26 1a. yellow-olive (1919) . . . 3·00 3·00
a. Sage-green . . . 1·75 1·60
24/6 *Set of* 3 . . . 6·25 6·25

No. 15, from the original printing, shows an upstroke to the "1", not present on other brown printings of this value.
See also Nos. 31/44.

3 "I" below Swords. Right sword overlaps left. Double frame lines.

4 "JI" below Swords. Left sword overlaps right. Single frame line.

1912–17. *Handstamped. Wove paper. No gum.* Imperf.

27 **3** 1p. violet . . . £500 80·00
a. Dull purple . . . — 90·00
28 **4** 1p. violet (1917) . . . 7·00 5·00
a. Dull purple . . . 15·00 5·50
b. *Tête-bêche* (pair) . . . 75·00 75·00
c. Laid paper . . . — £400
d. Pair, one stamp sideways . . . — £120

Maharaja Ganga Singh, 1914–1920

Maharaja Arimardan Singh, 1920–1942

5 (actual size 63 × 25 mm)

6 (Left-hand sword over right)

1921. *Handstamped. No gum.*

(a) Wove paper. Imperf.

29 **5** 1a. violet . . . 70·00 80·00
a. Dull purple . . . 90·00 95·00

(b) Laid paper. P 11.

30 **5** 1a. violet . . . 65·00 £120
a. Imperf . . . £160 £170

(Typo State Ptg Press, Charkhari)

1930–45. *Wove paper. No gum.* Imperf.

31 **6** 1p. deep blue . . . 35 14·00
a. Vert pair, top ptd inverted on back, bottom normal upright . . . 13·00
b. *Tête-bêche* (vert pair) . . . £275
c. Perf 11 × imperf (horiz pair) (1939) . . . 55·00 55·00
d. Bluish slate . . . 22·00
e. Laid paper (1944) . . . — £325
32 1p. dull *to* light green (*pelure*) (1943) . . . 55·00 £170
33 1p. violet (1943) . . . 17·00 £120
a. *Tête-bêche* (vert pair) . . . 50·00
34 ½a. deep olive . . . 1·50 14·00
35 ½a. red-brown (1940) . . . 5·50 22·00
a. *Tête-bêche* (vert pair) . . . £425
36 ½a. black (*pelure*) (1943) . . . 60·00 £150
37 ½a. red (*shades*) (1943) . . . 19·00 35·00
a. *Tête-bêche* (vert pair) . . . 40·00
b. Laid paper (1944) . . . — £275
38 ½a. grey-brown . . . 65·00 80·00
39 1a. green . . . 1·00 14·00
a. Emerald (1938) . . . 40·00 60·00
40 1a. chocolate (1940) . . . 8·50 22·00
a. *Tête-bêche* (vert pair) . . . 75·00
b. Lake-brown . . . — 48·00
41 1a. red (1940) . . . 95·00 55·00
a. Carmine . . . — 55·00
b. Laid paper (1944) . . . — £300
42 2a. light blue . . . 1·25 16·00
a. *Tête-bêche* (vert pair) . . . 9·50
43 2a. greenish grey (1941?) . . . 48·00 60·00
a. *Tête-bêche* (vert pair) . . . 90·00
b. Laid paper (1944) . . . — £325
c. Greyish green . . . 80·00 £150
43*d* 2a. yellow-green (1945) . . . — £650
44 4a. carmine . . . 3·00 19·00
a. *Tête-bêche* (vert pair) . . . 14·00

There are two different versions of No. 37a, one with the stamps *tête-bêche* base to base and the other showing them top to top.

7 Goverdhan Temple

½ As.

(8)

(Typo Batliboi Litho Works, Bombay)

1931 (25 June). *T* **7** *and similar designs.* P 11, 11½, 12 or compound.

45 ½a. blue-green . . . 1·40 10
a. Imperf between (horiz pair) . . . 35·00 11·00
b. Imperf between (vert pair) . . . 35·00 35·00
c. Imperf horiz (vert pair) . . . 35·00
46 1a. blackish brown . . . 1·40 10
a. Imperf between (horiz pair) . . . 11·00 8·00
b. Imperf between (vert pair) . . . 12·00 8·00
c. Imperf horiz (vert pair) . . . 12·00
47 2a. violet . . . 1·10 10
a. Imperf between (horiz pair) . . . 30·00 25·00
b. Imperf between (vert pair) . . . 30·00 25·00
c. Imperf horiz (vert pair) . . . 22·00
d. Doubly printed . . . 9·00
48 4a. olive-green . . . 1·10 15
a. Imperf between (vert pair) . . . 60·00 60·00
49 8a. magenta . . . 1·40 10
a. Imperf between (horiz pair) . . . 40·00 25·00
b. Imperf between (vert pair) . . . 40·00 40·00
c. Imperf horiz (vert pair) . . . 40·00 13·00
50 1r. green and rose . . . 2·00 20
a. Imperf between (vert pair) . . . £100 £100
b. Green (centre) omitted . . . — £140
c. Imperf horiz (vert pair) . . . £120
51 2r. red and brown . . . 3·50 25
a. Imperf horiz (vert pair) . . . 95·00 15·00
52 3r. chocolate and blue-green . . . 11·00 40
a. Imperf between (horiz pair) . . . — £160
b. *Tête-bêche* (pair) . . . £190 20·00
c. Chocolate (centre) omitted . . . 21·00
53 5r. turquoise and purple . . . 8·50 50
a. Imperf between (horiz pair) . . . £160
b. Centre inverted . . . 65·00 30·00
c. Centre doubly printed . . . — 80·00
45/53 *Set of* 9 . . . 28·00 1·60

Designs:—½a. The Lake; 1a. Imlia Palace, 2a. Industrial School; 4a. Bird's-eye view of City; 8a. The Fort; 1r. Guest House. 2r. Palace Gate; 3r. Temples at Rainpur.

This issue was the subject of speculative manipulation, large stocks being thrown on the market cancelled-to-order at very low prices and unused at less than face value. The issue was an authorized one but was eventually withdrawn by the State authorities.

1939 (1 Dec)–**40**. *Nos. 21/2 surch as T* **8**.

54 **2** ½a.on 8a. brown-red (1940) . . . 28·00 £120
a. No space between "½" and "As" . . . 32·00 £120
b. Surch inverted . . . £275 £375
c. "1" of "½" inverted . . . £275
55 1a.on 1r. chestnut (1940) . . . 90·00 £350
a. Surch inverted . . . £300
56 "1ANNA" on 1r. chestnut . . . £650 £650

Maharaja Jaiendra Singh, 1942–1971

Charkhari became part of Vindhya Pradesh by 1 May 1948.

COCHIN

(6 puttans = 5 annas. 12 pies = 1 anna; 16 annas = 1 rupee)

Stamps of Cochin were also valid on mail posted to Travancore.

PRICES FOR STAMPS ON COVER		
Nos. 1/3	*from* × 30	
Nos. 4/5	*from* × 10	
Nos. 6/6*b*	*from* × 3	
Nos. 7/9	*from* × 20	
Nos. 11/22	*from* × 15	
Nos. 26/128	*from* × 8	
Nos. O1/105	*from* × 15	

Raja Kerala Varma I, 1888–1895

1

2

(Dies eng P. Orr & Sons, Madras; typo Cochin Govt, Ernakulam)

1892 (13 Apr). *No wmk, or wmk large Umbrella in the sheet.* P 12.

1 **1** ½ put. buff . . . 2·50 3·00
a. Orange-buff . . . 2·75 2·75
b. Yellow . . . 2·75 3·25
c. Imperf (pair)
2 1 put. purple . . . 2·75 2·00
a. Imperf between (vert pair) . . . † £2250
3 **2** 2 put. deep violet . . . 2·00 2·25
1/3 *Set of* 3 . . . 6·50 6·25

1893. *Laid paper.* P 12.

4 **1** ½ put. orange-buff . . . £475 £13(
a. Orange . . . — £13(
b. Yellow . . . — £13(

WATERMARKS. Prior to the 1911–23 issue, printed by Perkins Bacon & Co, little attention was paid to the position of th[e] watermark. Inverted and sideways watermarks are frequently found in the 1898 and 1902–03 issues.

1894. *Wmk small Umbrella on each stamp.* P 12.

5 **1** ½ put. buff . . . 4·50 3·5(
a. Orange . . . 1·60 1·5(
ab. Imperf (pair)
b. Yellow . . . 3·75 1·0(
6 1 put. purple . . . 6·00 5·5(
7 **2** 2 put. deep violet . . . 3·50 3·7[5]
a. Imperf (pair)
b. Doubly printed . . . † £120[0]
c. Printed both sides . . . £1500
d. *Tête-bêche* (pair) . . . £3250
5/7 *Set of* 3 . . . 10·00 9·2[5]

The paper watermarked with a small umbrella is more transparent than that of the previous issue. The wmk is not easy to distinguish.
The 1 put. in deep violet was a special printing for fiscal use only.

Raja Rama Varma I, 1895–1914

1896 (End). *Similar to T* **1**, *but 28 × 33 mm.* P 12.

(a) Wmk Arms and inscription in sheet.

8 1 put. violet . . . 80·00 80·0[0]

(b) Wmk Conch Shell to each stamp.

9 1 put. deep violet . . . 19·00 32·0[0]

Nos. 8/9 were intended for fiscal use, but are also known used fo[r] postal purposes.

3

4

5

6

1898. *Thin yellowish paper. Wmk small Umbrella on each stam[p]. With or without gum.* P 12.

11 **3** 3 pies, blue . . . 1·40 1·[ ]
a. Imperf between (horiz pair) . . . £500
b. Imperf between (vert pair) . . . £600
c. Doubly printed . . . £600
12 **4** ½ put. green . . . 1·50 [9]
a. Imperf between (horiz pair) . . . £1000
b. Stamp sideways (in pair)
13 **5** 1 put. pink . . . 3·50 1·[ ]
a. *Tête-bêche* (pair) . . . £2750 £20[ ]
b. Laid paper . . . † £16[ ]
ba. Laid paper. *Tête-bêche* (pair) . . . † £65[ ]
c. Red . . . 2·50 1·[ ]
d. Carmine-red . . . 3·50 1·[ ]
14 **6** 2 put. deep violet . . . 3·00 2·[ ]
a. Imperf between (vert pair) . . . £500
b. Imperf between (vert strip of 3) . . . £650
11/14 *Set of* 4 . . . 7·50 5·[ ]

1902–03. *Thick white paper. Wmk small Umbrella on each stam[p]. With or without gum.* P 12.

16 **3** 3 pies, blue . . . 80
a. Doubly printed . . . — £2[ ]
b. Imperf between (horiz pair) . . . † £6[ ]
17 **4** ½ put. green . . . 1·10
a. Stamp sideways (in pair) . . . £750 £7[ ]
b. Doubly printed . . . — £2[ ]
c. Imperf between (horiz pair) . . . † £10[ ]
18 **5** 1 put. pink (1903) . . . 1·75
a. *Tête-bêche* (pair) . . . † £30[ ]
19 **6** 2 put. deep violet . . . 2·50
a. Doubly printed . . . £800 £3[ ]
16/19 *Set of* 4 . . . 5·50 1·[ ]

(7) (7a)

(7b)

1909. *T* **3** *(Paper and perf of 1903), surch with T* **7**. *Wmk is alwa[ys] sideways. No gum.*

22 **3** 2 on3 pies, rosy mauve . . . 15
a. Surch Type **7** inverted . . . 85·00 85
b. Surch Type **7***a* . . . £600 £3[ ]
c. Surch Type **7***b*
d. Stamps *tête-bêche* . . . £130 £1[ ]
e. Stamps and surchs *tête-bêche* . . . £170 £1[ ]

Varieties a, d and e were caused by the inversion of one sta[mp] (No. 7) in the plate and the consequent inversion of [the] corresponding surcharge to correct the error.

Types **7***a* and **7***b* were applied by handstamp to correct [the] omission of the surcharge on R. 3/2 in different settings. Oth[er] sheets show a handstamped version of Type **7**.

8 Raja Rama Varma I

8a

(Recess Perkins, Bacon & Co)

1911–13. *Currency in pies and annas.* W **8a**. P 14.

No.	Type	Description	Unused	Used
26	**8**	2p. brown	30	10
		a. Imperf (pair)		
27		3p. blue	90	10
		a. Perf 14 × 12½	27·00	2·50
		w. Wmk inverted	—	65·00
28		4p. green	1·50	10
		aw. Wmk inverted	—	£110
28*b*		4p. apple-green	2·50	40
		bw. Wmk inverted		
29		9p. carmine	1·10	10
		a. Wmk sideways		
30		1a. brown-orange	2·75	10
31		1½a. purple	5·50	45
32		2a. grey (1913)	7·50	40
33		3a. vermilion (1913)	35·00	35·00
26/33 *Set of* 8			48·00	35·00

No. 27a is line perforated. Nos. 27 and 33 exist perforated 14 either from comb or line machines. The other values only come from the comb machine.

Raja (Maharaja from 1921) Rama Varma II, 1914–1932

9 Raja Rama Varma II

10 Raja Rama Varma II

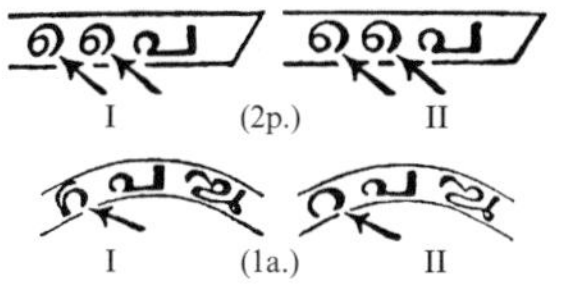
I (2p.) II

I (1a.) II

(Recess Perkins, Bacon & Co)

1916–30. W **8a**. P 13½ to 14.

No.	Type	Description	Unused	Used
35	**10**	2p. brown (Die I) (*a*) (*b*) (*c*)	6·00	10
		a. Imperf (pair)	£550	
		b. Die II (*b*) (*c*) (1930)	1·60	10
36		4p. green (*a*) (*b*)	1·00	10
37		6p. red-brown (*a*) (*b*) (*c*) (1922)	2·50	10
		w. Wmk inverted	—	90·00
38		8p. sepia (*b*) (1923)	1·50	10
39		9p. carmine (*a*)	16·00	25
40		10p. blue (*b*) (1923)	3·50	10
41	**9**	1a. orange (Die I) (*a*)	13·00	1·75
		a. Die II (*a*) (*b*) (1922)	8·50	30
42	**10**	1½a. purple (*b*) (1923)	2·25	20
43		2a. grey (*a*) (*b*) (*d*)	4·25	10
44		2¼a. yellow-green (*a*) (*d*) (1922)	4·25	3·25
45		3a. vermilion (*a*) (*b*)	11·00	35
35/45 *Set of* 11			50·00	4·50

Four different perforating heads were used for this issue: (*a*) comb 13.9; (*b*) comb 13.6; (*c*) line 13.8; (*d*) line 14.2. Values on which each perforation occur are shown above. Stamps with perforation (*a*) are on hand-made paper, while the other perforations are on softer machine-made paper with a horizontal mesh.

2

2 2

Two pies (11) Two pies (12) Two pies (13)

2 2

Two Pies (14) Two Pies (15)

1922–29. *T* **8** *(P 14), surch with T* **11/15**.

No.	Type	Description	Unused	Used
46	**11**	2p.on 3p. blue	40	30
		a. Surch double	£325	£325
47	**12**	2p.on 3p. blue	2·50	90
		a. Surch double	£550	
		b. "Pies" for "pies" (R. 4/8)	42·00	20·00
		ba. Surch double		
		c. Perf 12½ at foot		
48	**13**	2p.on 3p. blue (6.24)	4·25	35
		a. "Pies" for "pies" (R. 4/8)	50·00	16·00
		b. Perf 14 × 12½	14·00	16·00
		ba. Ditto. "Pies" for "pies" (R. 4/8)	£225	£250
49	**14**	2p.on 3p. blue (1929)	7·00	7·00
		a. Surch double	£325	
		b. Surch with Type **15**	65·00	£100
		ba. Ditto. Surch double	£1400	

There are four settings of these overprints. The first (July 1922) consisted of 39 stamps with Type **11**, and 9 with Type **12**, and in Type **11** the centre of the "2" is above the "o" of "Two". In the second setting (May 1924) there were 36 of Type **11** and 12 of Type **12**, and the centre of the figure is above the space between "Two" and "Pies". The third setting (June 1924) consists of stamps with Type **13** only.

The fourth setting (1929) was also in sheets of 48. No. 49b being the first stamp in the fourth row.

No. 47c is from the bottom row of a sheet and was re-perforated 12½ line at foot as the bottom line of 14 perforations were too far from the design.

ONE ANNA ഒരു അണ

ANCHAL & REVENUE (16)

Three Pies ൩ 3

മൂന്നു പൈ (17)

1928. *Surch with T* **16**.

No.	Type	Description	Unused	Used
50	**10**	1a.on 2¼a. yellow-green (*a*)	5·00	12·00
		a. "REVENUF" for "REVENUE"	50·00	80·00
		b. Surch double		

1932–33. *Surch as T* **17**. W **8a**. P 13½.

No.	Type	Description	Unused	Used
51	**10**	3p.on 4p. green (*b*)	1·10	90
		a. "r" in "Three" inverted	†	£300
52		3p.on 8p. sepia (*b*)	1·50	2·50
53		9p.on 10p. blue (*b*)	1·50	3·00
51/3 *Set of* 3			3·75	5·75

Maharaja Rama Varma III, 1932–1941

18 Maharaja Rama Varma III

(Recess Perkins, Bacon & Co)

1933–38. *T* **18** *(but frame and inscription of 1a. as T* **9***).* W **8a**. P 13 × 13½.

No.	Type	Description	Unused	Used
54	**18**	2p. brown (1936)	60	30
55		4p. green	60	10
56		6p. red-brown	70	10
57	–	1a. brown-orange	70	10
58	**18**	1a.8p. carmine	3·00	4·75
59		2a. grey (1938)	4·50	1·00
60		2¼a. yellow-green	1·50	15
61		3a. vermilion (1938)	5·00	1·60
62		3a.4p. violet	1·50	1·40
63		6a.8p. sepia	1·75	11·00
64		10a. blue	3·00	13·00
54/64 *Set of* 11			20·00	30·00

For stamps in this design, but lithographed, see Nos. 67/71.

1934. *Surcharged as T* **14**. W **8a**. P 13½.

No.	Type	Description	Unused	Used
65	**10**	6p.on 8p. sepia (R.) (*b*)	75	60
66		6p.on 10p. blue (R.) (*b*)	1·75	2·00

"DOUBLE PRINTS". The errors previously listed under this description are now identified as blanket offsets, a type of variety outside the scope of this catalogue. Examples occur on issues from 1938 onwards.

SPACING OF OVERPRINTS AND SURCHARGES. The typeset overprints and surcharges issued from 1939 onwards show considerable differences in spacing. Except for specialists, however, these differences have little significance as they occur within the same settings and do not represent separate printings.

(Litho The Associated Printers, Madras)

1938. W **8a**. P 11.

No.	Type	Description	Unused	Used
67	**18**	2p. brown	1·00	40
		aw. Wmk inverted	£140	75·00
		b. Perf 13 × 13½	5·50	60
68		4p. green	1·00	25
		aw. Wmk inverted		
		b. Perf 13 × 13½	8·00	16·00
69		6p. red-brown	2·25	10
		aw. Wmk inverted	†	—
		b. Perf 13 × 13½	†	£2500
70		1a. brown-orange	65·00	80·00
		aw. Wmk inverted		
		b. Perf 13 × 13½	85·00	£100
71		2¼a. sage-green	6·00	15
		a. Perf 13 × 13½	13·00	5·50
67/71 *Set of* 5			65·00	80·00

Most examples of Nos. 70/b were used fiscally. Collectors are warned against examples which have been cleaned and regummed or provided with forged postmarks.

ANCHAL (19) ANCHAL (19a) THREE PIES (20)

SURCHARGED ONE ANNA THREE PIES (21) ANCHAL

ANCHAL NINE PIES (22) ANCHAL

NINE PIES (23) SURCHARGED NINE PIES (24)

1939 (Jan). *Nos. 57 and 70 optd with T* **19a**.

No.	Type	Description	Unused	Used
72	**18**	1a. brown-orange (*recess*) (T **19**)	3·00	1·00
		w. Wmk inverted	†	£120
73		1a. brown-orange (*litho*) (T **19**)	£250	1·00
		aw. Wmk inverted	†	—
		b. Perf 13 × 13½	—	£275
74		1a. brown-orange (*litho*) (T **19a**)	75	1·60
		a. Perf 13 × 13½	11·00	50

In 1939 it was decided that there would be separate 1a. stamps for revenue and postal purposes. The "ANCHAL" overprints were applied to stamps intended for postal purposes.

1942–44. *T* **18** *variously optd or surch.*

I. *Recess-printed stamp. No. 58.*

No.	Description	Unused	Used
75	3p.on 1a.8p. carmine (T **20**)	£160	80·00
76	3p.on 1a.8p. carmine (T **21**)	4·00	8·50
77	6p.on 1a.8p. carmine (T **20**)	3·25	20·00
78	1a.3p. on 1a.8p. carmine (T **21**)	1·00	30

II. *Lithographed stamps. Nos. 68, 70 and 70b.*

No.	Description	Unused	Used
79	3p.on 4p. (T **21**)	6·00	4·00
	a. Perf 13 × 13½	14·00	4·00
80	6p.on 1a. (T **22**)	£325	£225
	a. "SIX PIES" double	†	£900
81	6p.on 1a. (T **23**)	£225	£180
	a. Perf 13 × 13½	£110	60·00
82	9p.on 1a. (T **22**)	£120	£120
83	9p.on 1a. (T **23**) (P 13 × 13½)	£250	38·00
84	9p.on 1a. (T **24**) (P 13 × 13½)	18·00	5·50

Maharaja Kerala Varma II, 1941–1943

26 Maharaja Kerala Varma II

27 (The actual measurement of this wmk is 6¼ × 3⅝ in.)

(Litho The Associated Printers, Madras)

1943. *Frame of 1a. inscr "ANCHAL & REVENUE".* P 13 × 13½.

(*a*) W **8a**.

No.	Type	Description	Unused	Used
85	**26**	2p. grey-brown	2·00	2·75
		a. Perf 11	†	£1800
85*b*		4p. green	£650	£275
85*c*		1a. brown-orange	90·00	£110
85/*c* *Set of* 3			£700	£350

(*b*) W **27**.

No.	Type	Description	Unused	Used
86	**26**	2p. grey-brown	25·00	2·75
		a. Perf 11	†	£2500
87		4p. green	7·00	20·00
		a. Perf 11	3·00	4·00
88		6p. red-brown	2·00	10
		a. Perf 11	8·00	1·40
89		9p. ultramarine (P 11)	32·00	1·00
		a. Imperf between (horiz pair)	£1600	
90		1a. brown-orange	£200	£170
		a. Perf 11	22·00	45·00
91		2¼a. yellow-green	22·00	2·25
		a. Perf 11	28·00	8·50

Part of W **27** appears on many stamps in each sheet, while others are entirely without wmk.

Although inscribed "ANCHAL (= Postage) & REVENUE" most examples of Nos. 85*c* and 90/*a* were used fiscally. Collectors are warned against examples which have been cleaned and regummed or provided with forged postmarks.

Maharaja Ravi Varma, 1943–1946

1943. *T* **26** *variously optd or surch.* P 13 × 13½.

(a) W **8a**.

92 3p.on 4p. (T **21**) . . . 70·00 18·00
92*a* 9p.on 1a. (T **23**) . . . 5·00 2·75
92*b* 9p.on 1a. (T **24**) . . . 5·50 2·50
92*c* 1a.3p. on 1a. (T **21**) . . . † £3000

(b) W **27**.

93 2p.on 6p. (T **20**) . . . 75 3·25
a. Perf 11 . . . 85 2·75
94 3p.on 4p. (T **20**) (P 11) . . . 3·25 10
95 3p.on 4p. (T **21**) . . . 4·50 10
96 3p.on 6p. (T **20**) . . . 85 20
a. Perf 11 . . . 85 85
97 4p.on 6p. (T **20**) . . . 3·75 10·00

No. 92*c* is believed to be an error; a sheet of No. 85*b*, having been included in a stock of No. O52 intended to become No. O66.

28 Maharaja Ravi Varma

29 Maharaja Ravi Varma

I

II

(Litho The Associated Printers, Madras)

1944–48. W **27** *No gum.*

(a) Type I. P 11.

98 **28** 9p. ultramarine (1944) . . . 12·00 2·50

(b) Type II. P 13.

98*a* **28** 9p. ultramarine (1946) . . . 10·00 15·00
ab. Perf 13 × 13½ . . . 38·00 3·25
99 1a.3p. magenta (1948) . . . 6·00 8·50
a. Perf 13 × 13½ . . . £200 45·00
100 1a.9p. ultramarine (*shades*) (1948) . . 8·00 13·00
98*a*/100 *Set of* 3 . . . 22·00 22·00

Nos. 98*a*/100 are line-perforated, Nos. 98ab and 99a comb-perforated.

Maharaja Kerala Varma III, 1946–48

(Litho The Associated Printers, Madras)

1946–48. *Frame of 1a. inscr "*ANCHAL & REVENUE*".* W **27**. *No gum (except for stamps perf 11).* P 13.

101 **29** 2p. chocolate . . . 1·75 10
a. Imperf horiz (vert pair) . . . £1700 £1700
c. Perf 11 . . . 8·00 60
d. Perf 11 × 13 . . . £375 £140
102 3p. carmine . . . 50 15
103 4p. grey-green . . . £1900 80·00
104 6p. red-brown (1947) . . . 20·00 4·00
a. Perf 11 . . . £160 4·00
105 9p. ultramarine . . . 50 10
a. Imperf between (horiz pair) . . . † £1600
106 1a. orange (1948) . . . 6·50 27·00
a. Perf 11 . . . £500
107 2a. black . . . £100 8·00
a. Perf 11 . . . £130 6·50
108 3a. vermilion . . . 65·00 75
101/8 *Set of* 8 . . . £2000 £100

Although inscribed "ANCHAL (= Postage) & REVENUE" most examples of No. 106 were used fiscally.

The 1a.3p. magenta, 1a.9p. ultramarine and 2¼a. yellow-green in Type **29** subsequently appeared surcharged or overprinted for official use. Examples of the 1a.3p. magenta exist without overprint, but may have not been issued in this state (*Price* £200 *unused*).

30 Maharaja Kerala Varma III

Die I

Die II

Two dies of 2p.:

Die I. Back of headdress almost touches value tablet. Narrow strip of tunic visible below collar.

Die II. Back of headdress further away from tablet. Wider strip of tunic visible below collar.

Die I

Die II

Two dies of 3a.4p.

Die I. frame around head broken by value tablets. Two white lines below value inscription.

Die II. continuous frame around head. Single white line below value inscription.

Tail to turban flaw (R. 1/7)

(Litho The Associated Printers, Madras)

1948–50. W **27** (upright or inverted). P 11.

109 **30** 2p. grey-brown (I) . . . 1·75 15
a. Imperf vert (horiz pair) . . . † £1600
b. Die II . . . — 1·50
110 3p. carmine . . . 75 15
a. Imperf between (vert pair) . . . — £1300
111 4p. green . . . 14·00 2·25
a. Imperf vert (horiz pair) . . . £275 £325
112 6p. chestnut . . . 14·00 25
a. Imperf vert (horiz pair) . . . £800
113 9p. ultramarine . . . 2·50 25
114 2a. black . . . 50·00 1·25
115 3a. orange-red . . . 60·00 85
a. Imperf vert (horiz pair) . . . £2000
116 3a.4p. violet (1950) . . . 70·00 £350
a. Tail to turban flaw . . . £250 £600
b. Die II . . .
109/16 *Set of* 8 . . . £190 £350

Maharaja Rama Varma IV, 1948–1964

31 Chinese Nets

32 Dutch Palace

(Litho The Associated Printers, Madras)

1949. W **27**. P 11.

117 **31** 2a. black . . . 4·00 6·50
a. Imperf vert (horiz pair) . . . £425
118 **32** 2¼a. green . . . 2·75 6·50
a. Imperf vert (horiz pair) . . . £425

A used example of a 2¼a. value in a slightly different design exists showing a larger portrait of the ruler, the conch shell at upper right pointing to the right and with shading below "DUTCH PALACE". This may have come from a proof sheet subsequently used for postal purposes.

SIX PIES

ആറു പൈ

(33)

പൈ

Normal

പൈ

Error

Due to similarities between two Malayalam characters some values of the 1948 provisional issue exist with an error in the second word of the Malayalam surcharge. On Nos. 119, 122 and O103 this occurs twice in the setting of 48. No. 125 shows four examples and No. O104b one. Most instances are as illustrated above, but in two instances on the setting for No. 125 the error occurs on the second character.

1949. *Surch as T* **33**.

(i) On 1944–48 issue. P 13.

119 **28** 6p.on 1a.3p. magenta . . . 4·25 4·0
a. Incorrect character . . . 30·00 28·0
120 1a.on 1a.9p. ultramarine (R.) . . . 1·25 1·4

(ii) On 1946–48 issue.

121 **29** 3p.on 9p. ultramarine . . . 8·50 19·0
122 6p.on 1a. 3p. magenta . . . 14·00 13·0
a. Surch double . . . † £47
b. Incorrect character . . . 85·00 80·0
123 1a.on 1a. 9p. ultramarine (R.) . . . 3·00 2·0
a. Surch in black . . . † £225
b. Black surch with smaller native characters 7½ mm instead of 10 mm long . . . † £325

(iii) On 1948–50 issue.

124 **30** 3p.on 9p. ultramarine . . . 1·75 1·7
a. Larger native characters 20 mm instead of 16½ mm long . . . 2·50 5
ab. Imperf between (vert pair) . . . † £140
b. Surch double . . . £425
c. Surch both sides . . . £350
125 3p.on 9p. ultramarine (R.) . . . 3·75 2·7
a. Incorrect character . . . 24·00 18·0
126 6p.on 9p. ultramarine (R.) . . . 1·50 4
119/26 *Set of* 8 . . . 35·00 38·0

The 9p. ultramarine (T **29**) with 6p. surcharge (T **33**) in red wa prepared for use but not issued (*Price* £200 *unused*)

1949. *Surch as T* **20**. W **27**. P 13.

127 **29** 6p.on 1a. orange . . . 55·00 £12
128 9p.on 1a. orange . . . 80·00 £12

OFFICIAL STAMPS

On C G S

(O 1)

ON C G S

(O **2** Small "ON")

ON C G S

(O **3** "G" without serif)

1913. *Optd with Type* O **1** *(3p.) or* O **2** *(others).*

O1 **8** 3p. blue (R.) . . . £120 1
a. Black opt . . . † £10
b. Inverted "S" . . . — 48·
c. Opt double . . . † £5
O2 4p. green (*wmk sideways*) . . . 8·50
a. Opt inverted . . . — £2
O3 9p. carmine . . . 95·00
a. Wmk sideways . . . 15·00
w. Wmk inverted . . . † 85·
O4 1½a. purple . . . 38·00
a. Opt double . . . — £5
O5 2a. grey . . . 13·00
O6 3a. vermilion . . . 48·00
O7 6a. violet . . . 45·00 2·
O8 12a. ultramarine . . . 38·00 6·
O9 1½r. deep green . . . 35·00 60·
O1/9 *Set of* 9 . . . £325 65·

1919–33. *Optd as Type* O **3**.

O10 **10** 4p. green (*a*) (*b*) . . . 3·75
a. Opt double . . . — £4
O11 6p. red-brown (*a*) (*b*) (1922) . . . 8·00
a. Opt double . . . — £3
w. Wmk inverted . . . †
O12 8p. sepia (*b*) (1923) . . . 11·00
O13 9p. carmine (*a*) (*b*) . . . 50·00
O14 10p. blue (*b*) (1923) . . . 12·00
a. Opt double . . . † £5
O15 1½a. purple (*a*) (*b*) (1921) . . . 5·50
a. Opt double . . . † £5
O16 2a. grey (*b*) (1923) . . . 40·00
O17 2¼a. yellow-green (*a*) (*b*) (1922) . . . 12·00
a. Opt double . . . † £3
O18 3a. vermilion (*a*) (*b*) (*c*) . . . 16·00
a. Opt inverted . . . † £3
O19 6a. violet (*a*) (*b*) (1924) . . . 35·00
O19*a* 12a. ultramarine (*a*) (*b*) (1929) . . . 15·00 4·
O19*b* 1½r. deep green (*a*) (*b*) (1933) . . . 23·00 £1
O10/19*b* *Set of* 12 . . . £200 £1

All values exist showing a straight-backed "C" variety on R. 4/1.

8 Eight pies

(O **4** 27½ mm high)

ON C G S

(O **5** Straight back to "C")

ON C G S

(O **6** Circular "O"; "N" without serifs)

1923 (Jan)–**24**. *T* **8** *and* **10** *surch with Type* O **4**.

O20 8p.on 9p. carmine (No. O3) . . . £350 1
a. "Pies" for "pies" (R. 4/8) . . . £900 55·
b. Wmk sideways . . . £130
ba. "Pies" for "pies" (R. 4/8) . . . £375 18
e. Surch double . . . † £3
O21 8p.on 9p. carm (*a*) (*b*) (No. O13) (11.24) . . . 70·00
a. "Pies" for "pies" (R. 4/8) . . . £190 12
b. Surch double . . . † £2
c. Opt Type O **3** double . . . † £2

Varieties with smaller "i" or "t" in "Eight" and small "i" in "Pies" are also known from a number of positions in the setting.

1925 (Apr). *T* **10** *surch as Type* O **4**.
O22 10p.on 9p. carmine (*b*) (No. O13) 70·00 70
b. Surch double † £300
c. Surch 25 mm high (*a*) £180 90
ca. Surch double † £325

1929. *T* **8** *surch as Type* O **4**.
O23 10p.on 9p. carmine (No. O3a) £900 11·00
a. Surch double † £425
b. Wmk upright — 55·00

1929–31. *Optd with Type* O **5**.
O24 **10** 4p. green (*b*) (1931) 22·00 1·40
a. Inverted "S" £160 14·00
O25 6p. red-brown (*b*) (*c*) (*d*) (1930) 13·00 10
a. Inverted "S" 90·00 4·25
O26 8p. sepia (*b*) (1930) 7·00 10
a. Inverted "S" 60·00 4·75
O27 10p. blue (*b*) 6·00 10
a. Inverted "S" 55·00 5·00
O28 2a. grey (*b*) (1930) 30·00 15
a. Inverted "S" £160 7·50
O29 3a. vermilion (*b*) (1930) 8·00 15
a. Inverted "S" 85·00 8·00
O30 6a. violet (*b*) (*d*) (1930) 80·00 3·00
a. Inverted "S" £475 85·00
O24/30 *Set of* 7 £150 4·25

1933. *Nos. O26/7 surch as T* **14**, *in red*.
O32 **10** 6p.on 8p. sepia (*b*) 2·25 10
a. Inverted "S" 20·00 4·25
O33 6p.on 10p. blue (*b*) 4·00 10
a. Inverted "S" 40·00 3·75

The inverted "S" varieties occur on R. 2/1 of one setting of this overprint only.

1933–38. *Recess-printed stamps of 1933–38 optd.*

(*a*) *With Type* O **5**.
O34 **18** 4p. green 2·50 10
O35 6p. red-brown (1934) 2·50 10
O36 1a. brown-orange 13·00 10
O37 1a.8p. carmine 1·50 30
O38 2a. grey 13·00 10
O39 2¼a. yellow-green 4·00 10
O40 3a. vermilion 42·00 10
O41 3a.4p. violet 1·50 15
O42 6a.8p. sepia 1·50 20
O43 10a. blue 1·50 70
O34/43 *Set of* 10 75·00 1·75

(*b*) *With Type* O **6** (*typo*).
O44 **18** 1a. brown-orange (1937) 38·00 60
O45 2a. grey-black (1938) 21·00 1·75
O46 3a. vermilion (1938) 11·00 1·75
O44/6 *Set of* 3 65·00 3·75

ON C G S (O 7 Curved back to "c") — ON C G S (O 8)

ON C G S (O 9 Circular "O"; N with serifs) — ON C G S (O 10 Oval "O") — ON C G S (O 11)

1938–44. *Lithographed stamps of 1938.* W **8***a*, optd.

(*a*) *With Type* O **7** *or* O **8** (*1a*). P 11.
O47 **18** 4p. green 26·00 2·25
a. Inverted "S" 32·00 2·25
b. Perf 13 × 13½ 21·00 2·50
O48 6p. red-brown 24·00 40
a. Inverted "S" 28·00 50
O49 1a. brown-orange £250 2·50
O50 2a. grey-black 18·00 90
a. Inverted "S" 19·00 1·00

(*b*) *With Type* O **9** (*litho*) *or* O **10** (*6p.*).
O51 **18** 6p. red-brown (P 13 × 13½) 10·00 3·25
O52 1a. brown-orange 1·00 10
O53 3a. vermilion 3·00 1·10

(*c*) *With Type* O **11**.
O53*a* **18** 6p. red-brown £750 £350

The inverted "S" varieties, Nos. O47a, O48a and O50a, occur 21 times in the setting of 48.

1942–43. *Unissued stamps optd with Type* O **10**. *Litho.* W **27**. P 11.
O54 **18** 4p. green 65·00 15·00
a. Perf 13 × 13½ 2·25 70
O55 6p. red-brown £110 11·00
a. Perf 13 × 13½ 20·00 90
ab. Optd both sides † £130
O56 1a. brown-orange 12·00 5·00
a. Perf 13 × 13½ 1·60 4·25
ab. Optd both sides † £130
O56*b* 2a. grey-black (1943) 55·00 80
ba. Opt omitted † £1200
O56*c* 2¼a. sage-green (1943) £1100 6·00
O56*d* 3a. vermilion (1943) 17·00 5·00

1943. *Official stamps variously surch with T* **20** *or* **21**.

(*i*) *On 1½a. purple of 1919–33.*
O57 **10** 9p.on 1½a. (*b*) (T **20**) £425 23·00

(*ii*) *On recess printed 1a.8p. carmine of 1933–44 (Type* O **5** *opt).*
O58 3p.on 1a.8p. (T **21**) 5·50 1·75
O59 9p.on 1a.8p. (T **20**) £100 26·00
O60 1a.9p. on 1a.8p. (T **20**) 2·50 1·75
O61 1a.9p. on 1a.8p. (T **21**) 80 30

(*iii*) *On lithographed stamps of 1938–44. P 11.* (*a*) W **8***a*.
O62 **18** 3p.on 4p. (Types O **7** and **20**) (P 13 × 13½) 22·00 7·50
a. Surch double £350 £160
O63 3p.on 4p. (Types O **7** and **21**) (P 13 × 13½) £110 48·00
O64 3p.on 1a. (Types O **9** and **20**) 2·00 3·25
O65 9p.on 1a. (Types O **9** and **20**) £200 45·00
O66 1a.3p. on 1a. (Types O **9** and **21**) £275 90·00

(*b*) W **27**.
O67 **18** 3p.on 4p. (Types O **10** and **20**) (P 13 × 13½) 80·00 45·00
O67*a* 3p.on 4p. (Types O **10** and **21**) (P 13 × 13½) £650
O67*b* 3p.on 1a. (Types O **10** and **20**) £120 65·00
ba. Perf 13 × 13½ 90·00 65·00

1944. *Optd with Type* O **10**. W **27**. P 13 × 13½.
O68 **26** 4p. green 26·00 4·50
a. Perf 11 £130 5·50
b. Perf 13 £350 65·00
O69 6p. red-brown 1·75 10
a. Opt double — 65·00
b. Perf 11 70 10
ba. Opt double — 65·00
c. Perf 13 7·00 2·25
O70 1a. brown-orange £2000 48·00
O71 2a. black 4·75 60
O72 2¼a. yellow-green 3·00 1·00
a. Optd both sides † £120
O73 3a. vermilion 7·00 80
a. Perf 11 7·50 40

Stamps perforated 13 × 13½ are from a comb machine; those perforated 13 from a line perforator.

1944. *Optd with Type* O **10** *and variously surch as Types* **20** *and* **21**. W **27**.
O74 **26** 3p.on 4p. (T **20**) 2·75 10
a. Perf 11 7·00 60
ab. Optd Type O **10** on both sides † £130
O75 3p.on 4p. (T **21**) 4·50 30
a. Perf 11 £375 £160
O76 3p.on 1a. (T **20**) 19·00 4·50
O77 9p.on 6p. (T **20**) 8·00 2·50
a. Stamp printed both sides † £350
O78 9p.on 6p. (T **21**) 3·50 30
O79 1a.3p. on 1a. (T **20**) 7·50 1·60
O80 1a.3p. on 1a. (T **21**) 3·25 10
O74/80 *Set of* 7 45·00 8·50

1946–47. *Stamps of 1944–48 (Head Type II) optd with Type* O **10**. P 13.
O81 **28** 9p. ultramarine 2·75 10
a. Stamp printed both sides † £450
b. Perf 13 × 13½ 4·25 10
O82 1a.3p. magenta (1947) 1·60 20
a. Opt double 19·00 12·00
b. Optd on both sides
ba. Optd both sides, opt double and inverted on reverse 50·00
O83 1a.9p. ultramarine (1947) 40 1·00
a. Opt double
b. Pair, one without opt † £1300
O81/3 *Set of* 3 4·25 1·10

1947–48. *Stamps of 1946–48 and unissued values optd with Type* O **2**. P 13.
O84 **29** 3p. carmine 1·00 10
a. Stamp printed both sides † £475
O85 4p. grey-green 27·00 5·50
O86 6p. red-brown 8·00 80
O87 9p. ultramarine 75 10
O88 1a.3p. magenta 2·75 70
O89 1a.9p. ultramarine 3·25 40
O90 2a. black 13·00 3·00
O91 2¼a. yellow-green 21·00 3·25
O84/91 *Set of* 8 70·00 12·50

1948–49. *Stamps of 1948–50 and unissued values optd with Type* O **7**.
O92 **30** 3p. carmine 1·25 15
a. "C" for "G" in opt 13·00 3·00
O93 4p. green 1·25 30
a. Imperf between (horiz pair) † £1300
b. Imperf between (vert pair) † £1300
c. Optd on both sides 70·00 70·00
d. "C" for "G" in opt 13·00 4·75
O94 6p. chestnut 2·50 10
a. Imperf between (vert pair) † £1400
b. "C" for "G" in opt 23·00 3·00
O95 9p. ultramarine 2·50 10
a. "C" for "G" in opt 20·00 3·75
O96 2a. black 2·00 15
a. "C" for "G" in opt 18·00 4·25
O97 2¼a. yellow-green 2·75 5·50
a. "C" for "G" in opt 25·00 42·00
O98 3a. orange-red 1·10 50
a. "C" for "G" in opt 17·00 9·00
O99 3a.4p. violet (I) 38·00 35·00
a. "C" for "G" in opt £275 £300
b. Tail to turban flaw £250
c. Die II 60·00 50·00
O92/9 *Set of* 8 45·00 38·00

The "C" for "G" variety occurs on R. 1/4. Nos. O92/9, O103/4 and O104b also exist with a flat back to "G" which occurs twice in each sheet on R. 1/5 and R. 2/8.

No. O93 exists with watermark sideways, but can usually only be identified when in multiples.

1949. *Official stamps surch as T* **33**.

(*i*) *On 1944 issue.*
O100 **28** 1a.on 1a.9p. ultramarine (R.) 60 60

(*ii*) *On 1948 issue.*
O101 **29** 1a.on 1a.9p. ultramarine (R.) 21·00 14·00

(*iii*) *On 1949 issue.*
O103 **30** 6p.on 3p. carmine 1·00 60
a. Imperf between (vert pair) † £900
b. Surch double † £275
c. "C" for "G" in opt 12·00 10·00
d. Incorrect character 12·00 10·00
O104 9p.on 4p. green (18 *mm long*) 75 2·25
a. Imperf between (horiz pair) £650 £750
b. Larger native characters, 22 mm long 1·10 80
ba. Ditto. Imperf between (horiz pair) £650 £650
bb. Incorrect character 18·00 13·00
c. "C" for "G" in opt 15·00 24·00
ca. Ditto. Larger native characters, 22 mm long 18·00 14·00
O100/4 *Set of* 4 21·00 14·00

No. O104 exists with watermark sideways, but can usually only be identified when in multiples.

1949. *No. 124a, but with lines of surch 17½ mm apart, optd "SERVICE".*
O105 **30** 3p.on 9p. ultramarine 60 70
a. Imperf between (horiz pair) † £1500

From 1 July 1949 Cochin formed part of the new state of Travancore-Cochin. Existing stocks of Cochin issues continued to be used in conjunction with stamps of Travancore surcharged in Indian currency.

DHAR

PRICES FOR STAMPS ON COVER	
Nos. 1/4	*from* × 50
No. 5	*from* × 30
No. 6	—
Nos. 7/9	*from* × 50
No. 10	—

Raja (Maharaja from 1877) Anand Rao Puar III, 1857–1898

1

2

अर्धा बलड. No. 1c — अर्धा लबड. No. 1d — आर्धा डबल. No. 2

1897–1900. *Type-set. Colour-fugitive paper. With oval hand-stamp in black. No gum.* Imperf.
1 **1** ½p. black/*red* (three characters at bottom left) 2·50 2·75
a. Handstamp omitted £250
b. Line below upper inscription (R. 2/2) 55·00 55·00
c. Character transposed (R. 2/3) 23·00 23·00
d. Character transposed (R. 2/5) 55·00
2 ½p. black/*red* (four characters at bottom left) 2·50 3·00
a. Handstamp omitted £180
3 ¼a. black/*orange* 2·75 3·75
a. Handstamp omitted £225
4 ½a. black/*magenta* 4·00 4·75
a. Handstamp omitted £225 £190
b. Line below upper inscription (R. 2/2) £100 £110
5 1a. black/*green* 8·00 13·00
a. Handstamp omitted £400
b. Printed both sides £750
c. Line below upper inscription (R. 2/2) £180 £190
6 2a. black/*yellow* 26·00 42·00
e. Top right corner ornament transposed with one from top of frame (R. 2/5) £100 £130
1/6 *Set of* 6 42·00 60·00

Nos. 1/6 were each issued in sheets of 10 (5 × 2), but may, on the evidence of a single sheet of the ½ price value, have been printed in sheets of 20 containing two of the issued sheets *tête-bêche*.

Research has identified individual characteristics for stamps printed from each position in the sheet.

The same research suggests that the type remained assembled during the entire period of production, being amended as necessary to provide the different values. Seven main settings have been identified with changes sometimes occurring during their use which form sub-settings.

The distribution of stamps between the main settings was as follows:
Setting I—½p.
Setting II—¼a., 1a.
Setting III—1a.
Setting IV—½p., ½a., 1a.
Setting V—½p.
Setting VI—½p. (No. 2). ¼a.
Setting VII—2a.

The listed constant errors all occurred during Setting IV.

In No. 1c the three characters forming the second word in the lower inscription are transposed to the order (2) (3) (1) and in No. 1d to the order (3) (2) (1).

On Nos. 1b, 4b and 5c the line which normally appears above the upper inscription is transposed so that it appears below the characters.

All values show many other constant varieties including mistakes in the corner and border ornaments, and also both constant and non-constant missing lines, dots and characters.

Examples of complete forgeries and faked varieties on genuine stamps exist.

Raja (Maharaja from 1918) Udaji Rao Puar II, 1898–1926

(Typo at Bombay)

1898–1900. P 11 *to* 12.
7 **2** ½a. carmine . . . 3·75 6·00
a. Imperf (pair) . . . 38·00
b. Deep rose . . . 3·25 5·50
8 1a. claret . . . 3·50 7·00
9 1a. reddish violet . . . 4·00 13·00
a. Imperf between (horiz pair) . . . £400
b. Imperf (pair) . . . £100
10 2a. deep green . . . 6·50 22·00
7/10 *Set of* 4 . . . 15·50 42·00

The stamps of Dhar have been obsolete since 31 March 1901.

DUNGARPUR

PRICES FOR STAMPS ON COVER	
Nos. 1/15	*from* × 2

Maharawal Lakshman Singh, 1918–1971

1 State Arms

(Litho Shri Lakshman Bijaya Printing Press, Dungarpur)

1933–47. P 11.
1 **1** ¼a. bistre-yellow . . . — £170
2 ¼a. rose (1935) . . . — £500
3 ¼a. red-brown (1937) . . . — £325
4 1a. pale turquoise-blue . . . — £140
5 1a. rose (1938) . . . — £1600
6 1a.3p. deep reddish violet (1935) . . . — £200
7 2a. deep dull green (1947) . . . — £300
8 4a. rose-red (1934) . . . — £500

Nos. 2 and 5 are known in a *se-tenant* strip of 3, the centre stamp being the 1a. value.

2 3 4

Maharawal Lakshman Singh

Three dies of ½a. (*shown actual size*):

Die I. Size 21 × 25½ mm. Large portrait (head 5 mm and turban 7½ mm wide), correctly aligned (sheets of 12 and left-hand stamps in subsequent blocks of four *se-tenant* horizontally with Die II)

Die II. Size 20 × 24½ mm. Large portrait (head 4¾ mm and turban 7 mm wide), but with less detail at foot and with distinct tilt to left (right-hand stamps in sheets of four horizontally *se-tenant* with Die I)

Die III. Size 21 × 25½ mm. Small portrait (head 4½ mm and turban 6½ mm wide) (sheets of 4)

(Typo L. V. Indap & Co, Bombay)

1939–46. *T* **2** *(various frames) and* **3/4**. Various perfs.
9 **2** ¼a. orange (P 12, 11, 10½ *or* 10) . . . £850 70·00
10 ½a. verm (Die I) (P 12, 11 *or* 10½) (1940) . . . £250 50·00
a. Die II (P 10½) (1944) . . . £250 65·00
ab. Horiz pair. Die I and Die II . . . £550 £160
b. Die III (P 10) (1945) . . . £325 50·00
c. Imperf between (vert pair) . . . † £2500
11 1a. deep blue (P 12, 11, 10½ *or* 10) . . . £250 45·00
12 **3** 1a.3p. brt mauve (P 10½ *or* 10) (1944) . . . £850 £190
13 **4** 1½a. deep violet (P 10) (1946) . . . £900 £190
14 **2** 2a. brt green (P 12, *pin* perf 11½) (1943) . . . £1100 £375
15 4a. brown (P 12, 10½ *or* 10) (1940) . . . £850 £160

Stamps perforated 12, 11 and 10½ were printed in sheets of 12 (4 × 3) which were imperforate along the top, bottom and, sometimes, at right so that examples exist with one or two adjacent sides imperforate. Stamps perforated 10 were printed in sheets of 4 either imperforate at top, bottom and right-hand side or fully perforated.

Dungarpur became part of Rajasthan by 15 April 1948.

DUTTIA (DATIA)

PRICES FOR STAMPS ON COVER	
Nos. 1/15	—
Nos. 16/40	*from* × 20

All the stamps of Duttia were impressed with a circular handstamp (as a rule in *blue*) before issue.

This handstamp shows the figure of Ganesh in the centre, surrounded by an inscription in Devanagari reading "DATIYA STET POSTAJ 1893". Stamps could not be used for postage without this control mark.

PROCESS. Nos. 1/15 were type-set and printed singly. Nos. 16/40 were typo from plates comprising 8 or more clichés.

GUM. The stamps of Duttia (*except* No. 250 were issued without gum.

Maharaja Bhawani Singh, 1857–1907

Rectangular labels each showing a double hand-drawn frame (in black for the 1a. and in red for the others), face value in black and the Ganesh handstamp are known on thin cream (½a.), rose (1a.), orange (2a.) or pale yellow (4a.) paper. These are considered by some specialists to be the first stamps of Duttia, possibly issued during 1893, but the evidence for this is inconclusive.

1 (2a.)

2 (½a.) Ganesh

3 (4a.)

1894?. *Rosettes in lower corners. Control handstamp in blue.* Imperf.
1 **1** ½a. black/*green* . . . £9000
2 2a. grey-blue/*yellow* . . . £2500
a. Handstamp in black . . . £2500

Only two examples of No. 1 have been reported. In both instances the Devanagari inscription was originally 8a., but was amended in manuscript to ½a.

1896. *Control handstamp in blue.* Imperf.
3 **2** 1a. red . . . £2500 £3000
a. Handstamp in black . . . £2500 £3000

1896. *Control handstamp in blue.* Imperf.
4 **3** ¼a. black/*orange* . . . £3250
a. Without handstamp . . . £2000
5 ½a. black/*blue-green* . . . £4750
a. Without handstamp . . . £2000
6 2a. black/*yellow* . . . £1900
a. Without handstamp . . . £10000
7 4a. black/*rose* . . . £1300
a. Without handstamp . . . £10000

Two types of centre:

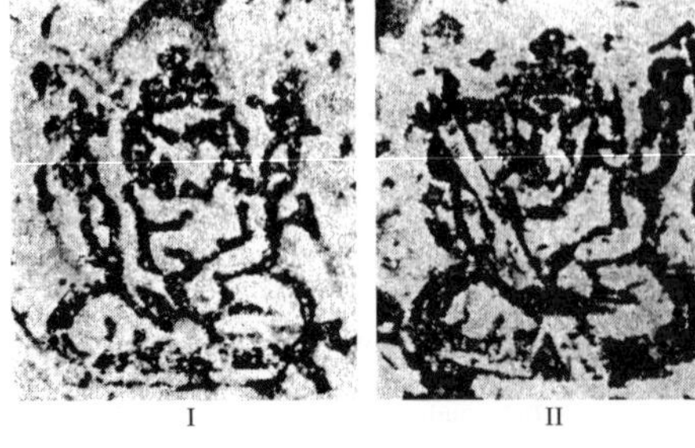

I II

Type I. Small Ganesh. Height 13 mm. Width of statue 11 mm. Width of pedestal 8 mm.

Type II. Large Ganesh. Height 13½ mm. Width of statue 11½ mm. Width of pedestal 11½ mm. "Flag" in god's right hand; "angle" above left. All stamps also show dot at top right corner.

1897–98. Imperf.
8 **2** ½a. black/*green* (I) (value in one group) . . . 50·00
a. *Tête-bêche* (horiz pair) . . . £1000
b. Value in two groups . . . 20·00 £20(
ba. *Tête-bêche* (vert pair) . . . £1000
bb. Type II (1898) . . . 22·00
9 1a. black/*white* (I) . . . 80·00 £25(
a. *Tête-bêche* (horiz pair) . . . £1000
b. Laid paper . . . 18·00
ba. *Tête-bêche* (vert pair) . . . £900
c. Type II (1898) . . . 90·00
ca. Laid paper . . . 22·00
10 2a. black/*yellow* (I) . . . 26·00 £22
a. *On lemon* . . . 35·00
b. Type II (1898) . . . 32·00 £27
11 4a. black/*rose* (I) . . . 22·00 £18(
a. *Tête-bêche* (horiz pair) . . . £250
b. *Tête-bêche* (vert pair) . . . £150
c. Doubly printed . . . £2000
d. Type II (1898) . . . 25·00

A used example of the 4a. is known showing black roulettes a foot.

4 (½a.) 5 (2a.)

1897. *Name spelt "DATIA."* Imperf.
12 **4** ½a. black/*green* . . . 75·00 £45
13 1a. black/*white* . . . £150
14 2a. black/*yellow* . . . 90·00
a. *Tête-bêche* (vert pair) . . . £3500
15 4a. black/*rose* . . . 85·00
a. *Tête-bêche* (vert pair) . . . £3500
12/15 *Set of* 4 . . . £350

1899–1906.

(a) Rouletted in colour or in black, horizontally and at end of rows
16 **5** ¼a. vermilion . . . 3·25
a. Rose-red . . . 2·50
b. Pale rose . . . 2·25
c. Lake . . . 3·75 17·0
d. Carmine . . . 3·75
e. Brownish red . . . 8·00
ea. *Tête-bêche* (pair) . . . £3000
17 ½a. black/*blue-green* . . . 2·75 17·0
a. On deep green . . . 5·00
b. On yellow-green (pelure) . . . 4·75 18·0
c. On dull green (1906) . . . 2·75
18 1a. black/*white* . . . 2·75 17·0
19 2a. black/*lemon-yellow* . . . 8·00
a. On orange-yellow . . . 10·00
b. On buff-yellow . . . 2·50 19·0
ba. Handstamp in black . . . 10·00
bb. Without handstamp . . . £225
c. On pale yellow (1906) . . . 2·75 19·0
20 4a. black/*deep rose* . . . 3·25 18·0
a. *Tête-bêche* (pair)
b. Handstamp in black . . . 14·00
c. Without handstamp . . . £190

(b) Rouletted in colour between horizontal rows, but imperf at to and bottom and at ends of rows.
20*d* **5** ¼a. brownish red . . . 35·00
21 1a. black/*white* . . . 14·00 40·(
a. Without handstamp . . . £475

One setting of 16 (8 × 2) of the ¼a. value (No. 16*e*) showed a inverted cliché at R. 1/2.

1904–05. *Without rouletting.*
22 **5** ¼a. red . . . 3·75 26·
a. Without handstamp . . . £325
23 ½a. black/*green* . . . 15·00
24 1a. black (1905) . . . 12·00 30·(

Maharaja Govind Singh, 1907–1955

1911. P 13½. *Stamps very wide apart.*
25 **5** ¼a. carmine . . . 6·50 42·
a. Imperf horiz (vert pair) . . . £225
b. Imperf between (horiz pair) . . . £250
c. Stamps closer together (with gum) . . . 7·00 30·
d. As c. Imperf vert (horiz pair) . . . £110
25*e* 1a. black . . . £750

No. 25*e* was mainly used for fiscal purposes (*Price on piece*, £7 but one example has been seen used on a registered postcard.

1912?. *Printed close together.*

(a) Coloured roulette × imperf.
26 **5** ½a. black/*green* . . . 7·00 32·

(b) Printed wide apart. P 13½ × *coloured roulette* (¼*a.*) 13½ × imperf (½*a.*).
27 **5** ¼a. carmine . . . 5·50 32·
a. Without handstamp . . . £225
28 ½a. black/*dull green* . . . 12·00 38·

1916. *Colours changed. Control handstamp in blue (Nos. 29/33) black (No. 34).* Imperf.
29 **5** ¼a. deep blue . . . 5·50 21·
30 ½a. green . . . 5·50 23·
a. Without handstamp . . . † £7
31 1a. purple . . . 5·00 24·
a. *Tête-bêche* (vert pair) . . . 24·00
ab. Without handstamp . . . £700
32 2a. brown . . . 15·00 28·
33 2a. lilac . . . 5·50 27·
a. Handstamp in black . . . 25·00
b. Without handstamp . . . £150
34 4a. Venetian red (date?) . . . 75·00
a. Without handstamp . . . £550

1918. *Colours changed.*

(a) Imperf.

35 **5** ¼a. blue 3·50 15·00
36 1a. pink 3·00 17·00
a. Handstamp in black 7·00
b. Without handstamp £160

(b) P 11½.

37 **5** ¼a. black 4·50 21·00

1920. *Rouletted.*

38 **5** ¼a. blue 2·50 11·00
a. Roul × perf 7 35·00 35·00
b. Imperf between (vert pair) £500
c. Without handstamp £120
d. Handstamp in black 7·00
39 ½a. pink 3·25 16·00
a. Roul × perf 7 £170
b. Without handstamp £160

1920. Rough perf about 7.

40 **5** ½a. dull red 13·00 32·00
a. Handstamp in black 38·00
b. Without handstamp £180

The stamps of Duttia have been obsolete since 1 April 1921.

FARIDKOT

PRICES FOR STAMPS ON COVER

Nos.	N1/4	*from* × 10
Nos.	N5/6	*from* × 50
Nos.	N7/8	—

GUM. The stamps of Faridkot (Nos. N1/8) were issued without gum.

Raja Bikram Singh, 1874–1898

N **1** (1 folus = ¼a.)

N **2** (1 paisa = ¼a.)

N **3**

1879–86. *Rough, handstamped impression.* Imperf.

(a) Native thick laid paper.

N1 N **1** 1f. ultramarine 35·00 40·00
N2 N **2** 1p. ultramarine £110 £120

(b) Ordinary laid paper.

N3 N **1** 1f. ultramarine 14·00 16·00
N4 N **2** 1p. ultramarine 65·00 85·00

(c) Wove paper, thick to thinnish.

N5 N **1** 1f. ultramarine 2·00 3·50
a. *Tête-bêche* (pair) £250
N6 N **2** 1p. ultramarine 3·50 8·50
a. Pair, one stamp sideways £1100

(d) Thin wove whity brown paper.

N7 N **2** 1p. ultramarine 28·00 30·00

Faridkot signed a postal convention with the Imperial Government which led to the provision of India issues overprinted "FARIDKOT STATE" from 1 January 1887. These are listed in the Convention States section.

Although the previous issues were no longer valid for postal purposes the state authorities continued to sell them to collectors for many years after 1887. Initially remaining stocks of Nos. N1/7 were on offer, but these were soon supplemented by Type N **1** handstamped in other colours, examples of a ½a., handstamped in various colours, which had originally been prepared in 1877 and by a replacement 1p, as Type N **3**, (*Price* £1.25 *unused, tête-bêche pair*, £200, *unused*) which had not done postal duty before the convention came into force. The sale of such items was clearly an important source of revenue as the 1f. as Type N **1**, yet another version of the 1p. and the ½a. subsequently appeared printed in sheets by lithography for sale to stamp collectors.

HYDERABAD

PRICES FOR STAMPS ON COVER

Nos.	1/3	*from* × 10
Nos.	4/12	—
Nos.	13/60	*from* × 5
Nos.	O1/53	*from* × 10

The official title of the State in English was The Dominions of the Nizam and in Urdu "Sarkar-i-Asafia" (State of the successors of Asaf). This Urdu inscription appears in many of the designs.

Nawab Mir Mahbub Ali Khan Asaf Jah VI, 1869–1911

1

2

(Eng Mr. Rapkin. Plates by Nissen & Parker, London. Recess Mint, Hyderabad)

1869 (8 Sept). P 11½.

1 **1** 1a. olive-green 15·00 7·00
a. Imperf between (horiz pair) £130
b. Imperf horiz (vert pair) £450 £110
c. Imperf (pair) £350 £350
d. Imperf vert (horiz pair) † £275

Reprints in the colour of the issue, and also in fancy colours, were made in 1880 on white wove paper, perforated 12½. Fakes of No. 1c are known created by the removal of the outer perforations from examples of Nos. 1a/b.

1870 (16 May). *Locally engraved; 240 varieties of each value; wove paper. Recess.* P 11½.

2 **2** ½a. brown 4·00 4·25
3 2a. sage-green 48·00 42·00

Stamps exist showing traces of lines in the paper, but they do not appear to be printed on true laid paper.

Reprints of both values were made in 1880 on white wove paper, perforated 12½: the ½a. in grey-brown, yellow-brown, sea-green, dull blue and carmine and the 2a. in bright green and in blue-green.

3

A Normal

2a.

B Variety

In A the coloured lines surrounding each of the four labels join a coloured circle round their inner edge, in B this circle is missing.

C

3a.

D

C. Normal

D. Character ˆ omitted

Left side of central inscription omitted (Pl 4 R. 2/11)

Dot at top of central inscription omitted

Second dot in bottom label omitted

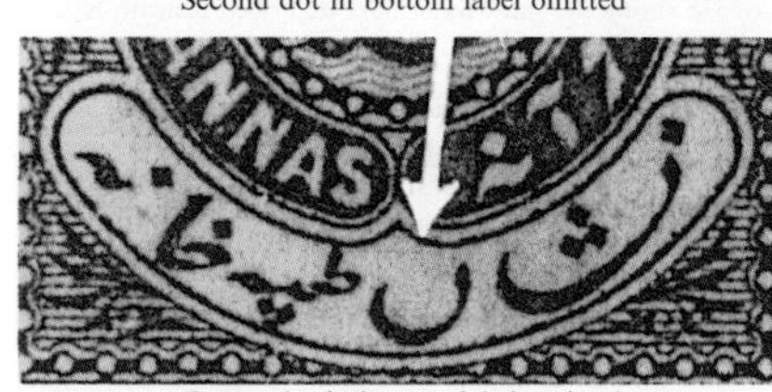
Centre dot in bottom label omitted

(Plates by Bradbury, Wilkinson & Co. Recess Mint, Hyderabad)

1871–1909.

(a) No wmk.

(i) Rough perf 11½.

4 **3** ½a. red-brown 18·00 20·00
a. Dot at top of central inscription omitted £150
5 1a. purple-brown £110 £120
a. Imperf horiz (vert pair) † £1500
b. Dot at top of central inscription omitted £750 £750
6 2a. green (A) £900
7 3a. ochre-brown 35·00 45·00
8 4a. slate £140 £150
9 8a. deep brown
10 12a. dull blue £300

(ii) Pin perf 8-9.

11 **3** ½a. red-brown — £400
12 1a. drab £350 £170

(iii) P 12½.

13 **3** ½a. orange-brown 1·90 10
a. Imperf vert (horiz pair) † 85·00
ab. Imperf horiz (vert pair) † £600
b. Orange 2·25 10
c. Red-brown 1·90 10
d. Brick-red 1·90 10
da. Imperf vert (horiz pair) † 85·00
db. Doubly printed £450 £160
e. Rose-red 2·00 20
ea. Doubly printed † £200
f. Error. Magenta 48·00 8·00
g. Left side of central inscription omitted £225 70·00
h. Dot at top of central inscription omitted 50·00 2·50
14 1a. purple-brown 5·50 5·50
a. Doubly printed £450
b. Drab 1·00 15
ba. Imperf (pair) — £300
bb. Doubly printed £200
c. Grey-black 1·60 10
ca. Imperf (pair) † £750
d. Black (1909) 1·60 10
da. Doubly printed £450 £250
db. Imperf vert (horiz pair) † £700
dc. Imperf horiz (vert pair) † £700
e. Dot at top of central inscription omitted — £130
f. Second dot in bottom label omitted 90·00 38·00
15 2a. green (A) 2·75 15
a. Deep green (A) 3·00 40
b. Blue-green (A) 2·75 40
ba. Blue-green (B) £180 65·00
c. Pale green (A) 2·75 15
ca. Pale green (B) £180 75·00
d. Sage-green (A) (1909) 2·75 35
da. Sage-green (B) £130 45·00
e. Dot at top of central inscription omitted £275 £100
f. Centre dot in bottom panel omitted £130 42·00
16 3a. ochre-brown (C) 2·00 1·25
a. Character omitted (D) £170 70·00
b. Chestnut (C) 1·60 1·00
ba. Character omitted (D) £120 55·00
17 4a. slate 5·50 2·50
a. Imperf horiz (vert pair) £700 £700
b. Greenish grey 3·75 2·25
ba. Imperf vert (horiz pair) £1100
c. Olive-green 4·00 1·50
18 8a. deep brown 2·00 3·00
a. Imperf vert (horiz pair) £750
19 12a. pale ultramarine 3·25 6·00
a. Grey-green 3·50 3·75
13/19 *Set of* 7 15·00 8·75

(b) W **7**. P 12½.

19*b* **3** 1a. black (1909) £100 12·00
19*c* 2a. sage-green (A) (1909) — 95·00
19*d* 12a. bluish grey (1909?) £950

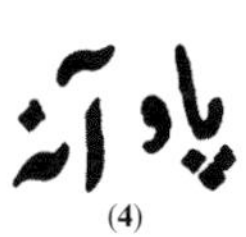
(**4**)

5

1898. *Surch with T* **4**. P 12½.

20 **3** ¼a.on ½a. orange-brown 50 85
a. Surch inverted 32·00 22·00
b. Pair, one without surcharge £475
c. Left side of central inscription omitted £140

(Des Khusrat Ullah. Recess Mint, Hyderabad)

1900 (20 Sept). P 12½.

21 **5** ¼a. deep blue 4·75 3·25
a. Pale blue 4·75 3·25

6

7

(Plates by Allan G. Wyon, London. Recess Mint, Hyderabad)

1905 (7 Aug). W **7**. P 12½.

No.	Type	Description	Unused	Used
22	**6**	¼a. dull blue	1·50	45
		a. Imperf (pair)	30·00	85·00
		b. Dull ultramarine	5·00	80
		ba. Perf 11 × 12½	27·00	24·00
		c. Pale blue-green	21·00	2·50
23		½a. orange	5·00	35
		a. Perf 11		
		b. Vermilion	2·75	25
		ba. Imperf (pair)	28·00	85·00
		c. Yellow	75·00	16·00

1908–11. W **7**. P 12½.

No.	Type	Description	Unused	Used
24	**6**	¼a. grey	60	10
		a. Imperf between (horiz pair)	£275	£275
		b. Imperf between (vert pair)	†	£275
		c. Perf 11½, 12	2·00	35
		d. Perf 11	60·00	20·00
25		½a. green	2·75	10
		a. Imperf between (vert pair)	£250	
		b. Perf 11½, 12	4·25	10
		c. Perf 13½	95·00	35·00
		d. Pale green	2·75	20
		da. Perf 11½, 12	4·25	10
		e. Blue-green	5·00	90
26		1a. carmine	2·00	10
		a. Perf 11½, 12	5·00	70
		b. Perf 11	27·00	8·50
		c. Double impression (P 12½ × 11)		
27		2a. lilac	1·50	40
		a. Perf 11½, 12	3·50	1·10
		b. Perf 11	2·50	55
		c. Perf 13½	1·40	15
		ca. Imperf between (horiz pair)	†	£400
		cb. Rose-lilac	1·25	10
28		3a. brown-orange (1909)	1·40	50
		a. Perf 11½, 12	8·00	2·00
		b. Perf 11	1·25	60
		c. Perf 13½	1·60	30
29		4a. olive-green (1909)	1·50	65
		a. Perf 11½, 12	6·50	4·25
		b. Perf 11	30·00	9·50
		ba. Imperf between (pair)	£550	£550
		c. Perf 13½	1·00	30
30		8a. purple (1911)	3·00	4·50
		a. Perf 11½, 12		
		b. Perf 11	1·75	3·50
		c. Perf 13½	1·10	60
31		12a. blue-green (1911)	95·00	60·00
		a. Perf 11½, 12	14·00	18·00
		b. Perf 11		
		c. Perf 13½	4·50	2·50
24/31c		*Set of* 8	13·00	3·75

The above perforations also exist compound.

Nawab Mir Osman Ali Khan Asaf Jah VII, 1911–1967

1912. *New plates engraved by Bradbury, Wilkinson & Co.* W **7**. P 12½.

No.	Type	Description	Unused	Used
32	**6**	¼a. grey-black	1·40	10
		a. Imperf horiz (vert pair)	†	£250
		b. Perf 11½, 12	70	35
		c. Perf 11	90	15
		ca. Imperf between (horiz pair)	†	£250
		cb. Imperf between (vert pair)	†	£250
		d. Perf 13½	60	10
33		¼a. brown-purple (*shades*) (P 13½)	90	10
		a. Imperf horiz (vert pair)	†	£250
34		½a. deep green	75	10
		a. Imperf between (pair)	†	£275
		b. Imperf (pair). Laid paper	90·00	70·00
		c. Perf 11½, 12	6·50	55
		d. Perf 11	8·00	10
		e. Perf 13½		

The above perforations also exist compound.

In Wyon's ¼a. stamp the fraction of value is closer to the end of the label than in the B.W. issue. In the Wyon ¼a. and ½a. the value in English and the label below are further apart than in the B.W.

Wyon's ¼a. measures 19½ × 20 mm and the ½a. 19½ × 20½ mm; both stamps from the Bradbury plates measure 19¾ × 21½ mm.

8 Symbols

9

1915. *Inscr* "Post & Receipt". W **7**. P 13½.

No.	Type	Description	Unused	Used
35	**8**	½a. green	80	10
		a. Imperf between (pair)	65·00	70·00
		b. Emerald-green	3·00	20
		c. Perf 12½	6·50	35
		ca. Imperf between (pair)		
		d. Perf 11	60	10
		da. Imperf between (pair)	†	£200
		db. Imperf vert (horiz pair)	†	£200
		e. Imperf (pair)	£140	90·00
36		1a. carmine	1·50	10
		a. Imperf between (pair)	£190	
		b. Scarlet	1·25	10
		ba. Imperf between (horiz pair)	†	£200
		bb. Imperf between (vert pair)	†	£200
		bc. Imperf vert (horiz pair)	†	£200
		c. Perf 12½	16·00	85
		ca. Imperf between (pair)		
		cc. Scarlet		
		d. Perf 11	1·10	20
		da. Scarlet	—	21·00
		e. Imperf (pair)	£180	£180

The above perforations also exist compound.

For ½a. claret, see No. 58.

1927 (1 Feb). As W **7**, but larger and sideways. P 13½.

No.	Type	Description	Unused	Used
37	**9**	1r. yellow	9·00	11·00

10 (4 pies)

11 (8 pies)

1930 (6 May). *Surch as T* **10** *and* **11**. W **7**. P 13½.

No.	Type	Description	Unused	Used
38	**6**	4p.on ¼a. grey-black (R.)	65·00	18·00
		a. Perf 11	†	£200
		b. Perf 12½	†	80·00
		c. Perf 11½, 12	†	£450
39		4p.on ¼a. brown-purple (R.)	25	10
		a. Imperf between (pair)	£450	£450
		b. Surch double	†	£190
		c. Perf 11	†	£425
		d. Black surch	£425	£425
40	**8**	8p.on ½a. green (R.)	25	10
		a. Imperf between (horiz pair)	†	£200
		b. Perf 11	£275	£140
		c. Perf 12½	†	£275

12 Symbols

13 The Char Minar

14 Bidar College

(Plates by De La Rue. Recess Stamps Office, Hyderabad)

1931 (12 Nov)–**47**. *T* **12** *to* **14** *(and similar types)*. W **7**. *Wove paper.* P 13½.

No.	Type	Description	Unused	Used
41	**12**	4p. black	30	10
		a. Laid paper (1947)	2·50	5·00
		b. Imperf (pair)	48·00	80·00
42		8p. green	50	10
		a. Imperf between (vert pair)	—	£600
		b. Imperf (pair)	60·00	95·00
		c. Laid paper (1947)	3·00	4·50
43	**13**	1a. brown (*shades*)	50	10
		a. Imperf between (horiz pair)	—	£550
		b. Perf 11	†	£750
44	–	2a. violet (*shades*)	2·50	10
		a. Imperf (pair)	£130	£190
45	–	4a. ultramarine	1·40	70
		a. Imperf (pair)	£140	£250
46	–	8a. orange	5·00	3·50
		a. Yellow-orange (1944)	65·00	30·00
47	**14**	12a. scarlet	5·00	11·00
48	–	1r. yellow	4·75	4·25
41/8		*Set of* 8	18·00	18·00

Designs (as T **14**): *Horiz*—2a. High Court of Justice; 4a. Osman Sagar Reservoir. *Vert*—8a. Entrance to Ajanta Caves; 1r. Victory Tower, Daulatabad.

Nos. 41a and 42c have a large sheet watermark "THE NIZAM's GOVERNMENT HYDERABAD DECCAN" and arms within a circle, but this does not appear on all stamps.

15 Unani General Hospital

16 Family Reunion

(Litho Indian Security Printing Press, Nasik)

1937 (13 Feb). *Various horiz designs as T* **15**, *inscr* "H.E.H. THE NIZAM'S SILVER JUBILEE". P 14.

No.	Type	Description	Unused	Used
49		4p. slate and violet	60	1·50
50		8p. slate and brown	90	1·50
51		1a. slate and orange-yellow	1·25	1·25
52		2a. slate and green	1·50	4·25
49/52		*Set of* 4	3·75	7·50

Designs:—8p. Osmania General Hospital; 1a. Osmania University; 2a. Osmania Jubilee Hall.

(Des T. I. Archer. Typo)

1945 (6 Dec). *Victory.* W **7** (very faint). *Wove paper.* P 13½.

No.	Type	Description	Unused	Used
53	**16**	1a. blue	10	10
		a. Imperf between (vert pair)	£500	
		b. Laid paper	70	70

No. 53b shows the sheet watermark described beneath Nos. 41/8.

17 Town Hall

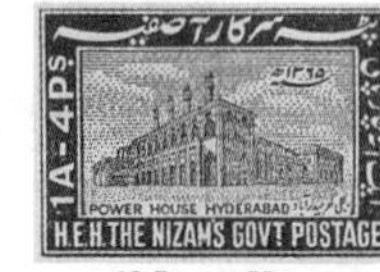

18 Power House, Hyderabad

(Des. T. I. Archer. Litho Government Press)

1947 (17 Feb). *Reformed Legislature.* P 13½.

No.	Type	Description	Unused	Used
54	**17**	1a. black	1·40	1·60
		a. Imperf between (pair)	—	£750

(Des T. I. Archer. Typo)

1947–49. *As T* **18** *(inscr* "H. E. H. THE NIZAM'S GOVT. POSTAGE"*)*. W **7**. P 13½.

No.	Type	Description	Unused	Used
55		1a.4p. green	1·10	1·75
56		3a. greenish blue	1·75	3·25
		a. Bluish green	2·25	3·50
57		6a. sepia	4·00	14·00
		a. Red-brown (1949)	18·00	29·00
		ab. Imperf (pair)	£120	
55/7		*Set of* 3	6·25	17·00

Designs:—3a. Kaktyai Arch, Warangal Fort; 6a. Golkunda Fort

1947. *As 1915 issue but colour changed.* P 13½.

No.	Type	Description	Unused	Used
58	**8**	½a. claret	1·90	75
		a. Imperf between (horizontal pair)	—	£275
		b. Imperf between (vert pair)	—	£500

An Independence commemorative set of four, 4p., 8p., 1a. and 2a., was prepared in 1948, but not issued.

1948. *As T* **12** *("POSTAGE" at foot). Recess.* W **7**. P 13½.

No.	Type	Description	Unused	Used
59		6p. claret	7·50	6·50

Following intervention by the forces of the Dominion of India during September 1948 the Hyderabad postal system was taken over by the Dominion authorities, operating as an agency of the India Post Office.

1949. *T* **12** *("POSTAGE" at top). Litho.* W **7**. P 13½.

No.	Type	Description	Unused	Used
60	**12**	2p. bistre-brown	1·40	2·5
		a. Imperf between (horizontal pair)	†	£70
		b. Imperf (pair)	£150	£47

No. 60 was produced from a transfer taken from a plate of the 4p., No. 41, with each impression amended individually.

OFFICIAL STAMPS

Official stamps became valid for postage within India from 1910.

(O 1) (O 1a) (O 2)

1873.

I. *Handstamped as Type* O **1** *in red.*

No.	Type	Description	Unused	Used
O1	**1**	1a. olive-green	75·00	22·0
		a. Black opt	—	£25
O2	**2**	½a. brown	—	£55
		a. Black opt	—	£47
O3		2a. sage-green	—	£47
		a. Black opt	—	£16

At least ten different handstamps as Type O **1** were used to produce Nos. O1/17. These differ in the size, shape and spacing of the characters. The prices quoted are for the cheapest versions where more than one is known to exist on a particular stamp.

Imitations of these overprints on genuine stamps and on reprints are found horizontally or vertically in various shades of red, magenta and in black.

II. *T* **3** *handstamped as Type* O **1** *in red.*

(a) Rough perf 11½.

No.	Type	Description	Unused	Used
O4		½a. red-brown		
		a. Black opt	—	£6
O5		1a. purple-brown	—	£9
		a. Black opt	£130	£1
O6		2a. green (A)		
		a. Black opt	—	£9
O7		4a. slate	—	£10
		a. Black opt		
O8		8a. deep brown		
		a. Black opt	£1000	£9
O8*b*		12a. dull blue	—	£10

(b) Pin perf 8–9.

No.	Type	Description	Unused	Used
O8*c*		1a. drab (*black opt*)	7·00	85·
		ca. Second dot in bottom label omitted	£150	

(c) P 12½.

No.	Type	Description	Unused	Used
O 9		½a. red-brown	12·00	4·
		a. Black opt	8·00	3·
		ab. Left side of central inscription omitted	—	£1
		ac. Dot at top of central inscription omitted	—	48·
O11		1a. purple-brown	90·00	65·
		a. Black opt	—	26·
O12		1a. drab	17·00	18·
		a. Black opt	2·00	1·
		ab. Second dot in bottom label omitted	90·00	90·
O13		2a. green (*to* deep) (A)	32·00	28·
		a. Black opt	3·75	4·
		ab. Inner circle missing (B)	£225	
		ac. Centre dot in bottom label omitted	£120	£1
O14		3a. ochre-brown	£120	£1
		a. Black opt	30·00	24·
O15		4a. slate	55·00	35·
		a. Black opt	15·00	15·
O16		8a. deep brown	60·00	£1
		a. Imperf vert (horiz pair)	£650	
		b. Black opt	40·00	32·
O17		12a. blue	90·00	£1
		a. Black opt	45·00	70·

The use of Official Stamps (Sarkari) was discontinued in 18[illegible] but was resumed in 1909, when the current stamps were over-printed from a new die.

1909–11. *Optd with Type* O **1***a*.

(a) On Type **3**. P 12½.

No.	Type	Description	Unused	Used
O18		½a. orange-brown	85·00	4
		a. Opt inverted	†	£4

O19 1a. black . . . 75·00 30
a. Second dot in bottom label omitted . . . — 6·00
O20 2a. sage-green (A) . . . 80·00 40
a. Optd on No. 15da (B) . . . — 10·00
b. Stamp doubly printed . . . † £150
c. Centre dot in bottom label omitted . . . — 8·00
d. Opt double . . . † £200
O20*e* 3a. ochre-brown . . . 4·50 1·75
ea. Character omitted (D) . . . — £350
O20*f* 4a. olive-green . . . £350 4·50
fa. Perf 11½, 12 . . . — £300
O20*g* 8a. deep brown . . . — 35·00
O20*h* 12a. grey-green . . . — 70·00

(*b*) *On Type* **6** (*Wyon ptgs*). P 12½.

O21 ½a. orange . . . — 2·00
a. Vermilion . . . £110 15
ab. Opt inverted . . . † £350
ac. Imperf horiz (vert pair) . . . † £350
O22 ½a. green . . . 17·00 10
a. Pale green . . . 17·00 10
b. Opt inverted . . . † 70·00
c. Imperf between (vert pair) . . . † £250
d. Imperf between (horiz pair) . . . † £225
e. Stamp doubly printed . . . † £130
f. Perf 11½, 12 . . . 15·00 30
fa. Pale green . . . 15·00 30
fb. Opt inverted . . . † 70·00
g. Perf 11
ga. Pale green
h. Perf 13½ . . . — 70·00
O23 1a. carmine . . . 48·00 15
a. Opt double . . . £190
b. Perf 11½, 12 . . . 60·00 30
ba. Stamp doubly printed . . . — £130
c. Perf 11 . . . — 5·50
O24 2a. lilac . . . 50·00 40
a. Perf 11½, 12 . . . 90·00 4·50
b. Perf 11 . . . £400
O25 3a. brown-orange . . . £120 11·00
b. Perf 11½, 12 . . . £190 23·00
ba. Opt inverted . . . † £170
c. Perf 11 . . . £400 40·00
d. Perf 13½ . . . — 75·00
O26 4a. olive-green (1911) . . . 26·00 40
a. Perf 11½, 12 . . . 90·00 3·25
b. Perf 11 . . . — 17·00
O27 8a. purple (1911) . . . 13·00 2·25
a. Perf 11½, 12 . . . 95·00 7·00
b. Perf 11 . . . £400 £110
O28 12a. blue-green (1911) . . . 9·00 2·00
a. Imperf between (horiz pair) . . . † £850
b. Perf 11½, 12 . . . 26·00 3·00
c. Perf 11 . . . † £400

(*c*) *On Type* **6** (*Bradbury Wilkinson ptgs*). P 11.

O28*d* **6** ½a. deep green . . . £425

1911–12. *Optd with Type* O **2**.

(*a*) *Type* **6** (*Wyon printings*). P 13½ (8a, 12a.) or 12½ (others).

O29 ½a. grey . . . 50·00 1·00
a. Perf 11½, 12 . . . 22·00 50
ab. Imperf between (vert pair) . . . † £300
b. Perf 11 . . . 85·00 35·00
c. Perf 13½
O30 ½a. pale green . . . 38·00 1·50
a. Perf 11½, 12 . . . — 30
b. Perf 13½
O31 1a. carmine . . . 1·10 15
a. Opt inverted . . . — 38·00
b. Imperf horiz (vert pair) . . . † £300
c. Perf 11½, 12 . . . 5·50 15
d. Perf 11 . . . 1·00 15
e. Perf 13½
O32 2a. lilac . . . 6·50 1·25
a. Perf 11½, 12 . . . 21·00 2·75
b. Perf 11 . . . 1·40 50
c. Perf 13½ . . . 5·50 10
ca. Imperf between (horiz pair) . . . † £400
cb. Rose-lilac . . . 1·75 10
O33 3a. brown-orange . . . 19·00 3·25
a. Opt inverted . . . † 75·00
b. Perf 11½, 12 . . . 12·00 2·50
ba. Opt inverted . . . † 80·00
c. Perf 11 . . . 29·00 3·25
ca. Opt inverted . . . † 75·00
d. Perf 13½ . . . 18·00 60
da. Opt inverted . . . † 65·00
O34 4a. olive-green . . . 14·00 2·00
a. Opt inverted . . . — 75·00
b. Perf 11½, 12 . . . 4·50 2·75
ba. Opt inverted . . . — 80·00
c. Perf 11 . . . 3·00 1·40
d. Perf 13½ . . . 2·75 15
da. Opt inverted . . . † 75·00
O35 8a. purple . . . 4·50 20
a. Perf 11½, 12
b. Perf 11 . . . £325 42·00
c. Perf 12½ . . . — £375
O36 12a. blue-green . . . 16·00 1·25
a. Perf 11½, 12
b. Perf 11
c. Perf 12½

(*b*) *Type* **6** (*Bradbury, Wilkinson printings*). P 12½.

O37 ½a. grey-black . . . 3·25 50
a. Opt inverted . . . † 60·00
b. Pair, one without opt
c. Imperf between (vert pair) . . . † £225
d. Perf 11½, 12 . . . 7·50 1·40
da. Opt inverted . . . † 60·00
db. Pair, one without opt
e. Perf 11 . . . 1·25 40
ea. Opt sideways . . . † 60·00
f. Perf 13½ . . . 3·25 10
fa. Opt inverted . . . † 65·00
fb. Pair, one without opt . . . † £130
fc. Imperf between (horiz pair) . . . † £200
O38 ½a. brown-purple (*shades*) (P 13½) . . . 2·50 10
a. Imperf horiz (vert pair) . . . † £225
b. Imperf between (horiz pair) . . . † £250
c. Perf 11
O39 ½a. deep green . . . 3·25 15
a. Opt inverted . . . — 24·00
b. Perf 11½, 12 . . . 8·50 1·60
ba. Pair, one without opt . . . † £130
c. Perf 11 . . . 2·75 15
ca. Opt inverted . . . — 27·00
cb. Imperf horiz (vert pair) . . . † £250
d. Perf 13½ . . . 2·25 10
da. Imperf between (horiz pair) . . . † £190
db. Imperf between (vert pair) . . . † £250
dc. Yellow-green . . . — 60

1917–20. *T* **8** *optd with Type* O **2**. P 13½.

O40 ½a. green . . . 2·25 10
a. Opt inverted . . . † 21·00
b. Pair, one without opt . . . † 95·00
c. Imperf between (horiz pair) . . . † £140
ca. Imperf vert (horiz pair) . . . † £150
d. Imperf between (vert pair) . . . † £200
e. Emerald-green . . . 3·25 40
f. Perf 12½ . . . — 3·75
g. Perf 11 . . . 7·00 30
ga. Opt inverted . . . † 23·00
gb. Pair, one without opt
O41 1a. carmine . . . 3·50 10
a. Opt inverted . . . † 26·00
b. Opt double . . . † 80·00
c. Imperf horiz (vert pair) . . . † £200
d. Stamp printed double
e. Scarlet (1920) . . . 1·50 10
ea. Stamp printed double . . . † £150
eb. Imperf between (horiz pair) . . . † £250
ec. Imperf between (vert pair) . . . † £180
ed. Imperf horiz (vert pair) . . . † £200
ee. Opt inverted . . . † £100
f. Perf 12½ . . . — 3·50
g. Perf 11 . . . 10·00 15
ga. Opt inverted . . . † 17·00
gb. Scarlet (1920) . . . — 23·00

1930–34. *T* **6** *and* **8** *optd as Type* O **2** *and surch at top of stamp, in red, as T* **10** *or* **11**.

O42 4p.on ½a. grey-black (O37*f*) (1934) . . . £300 17·00
O43 4p.on ½a. brown-purple (O38) . . . 1·25 10
b. Imperf between (horiz pair) . . . † £200
c. Imperf between (vert pair) . . . † £190
d. Imperf horiz (vert pair) . . . † £190
e. Red surch double . . . † 85·00
f. Black opt double . . . † £180
g. Perf 11 . . . † £475
h. Stamp doubly printed . . . † £180
O44 8p.on ½a. green (O40) . . . 90 10
c. Imperf between (horiz pair) . . . † £180
ca. Imperf between (vert pair) . . . † £200
d. Red surch double . . . † 85·00
e. Stamp doubly printed . . . † £170
f. Black opt double . . . † £180
O45 8p.on ½a. yellow-green (O39*db*) . . . 35·00 45·00

For Nos. O42/5 the red surcharge was intended to appear on the upper part of the stamp, above the official overprint, Type O **2**, but surcharge and overprint are not infrequently found superimposed on one another.

1934–44. *Nos. 41/8 optd with Type* O **2**.

O46 4p. black . . . 1·60 10
a. Imperf (pair) . . . 70·00
b. Imperf between (vert pair) . . . £600 £550
c. Imperf between (horiz pair) . . . — £550
O47 8p. green . . . 80 10
a. Opt inverted . . . † £150
b. Imperf between (horiz pair) . . . — £550
c. Opt double . . . † £120
d. Imperf (pair) . . . £130 £160
O48 1a. brown . . . 1·10 10
a. Imperf between (vert pair) . . . £450 £425
b. Imperf between (horiz pair) . . . — £425
c. Imperf (pair) . . . £140 £180
d. Opt double . . . — £160
O49 2a. violet . . . 5·50 10
a. Imperf vert (horiz pair) . . . † £950
O50 4a. ultramarine . . . 2·25 20
a. Opt double . . . † £400
b. Imperf between (vert pair) . . . † £1100
O51 8a. orange (1935) . . . 10·00 60
a. Yellow-orange (1944) . . . — 38·00
O52 12a. scarlet (1935) . . . 8·00 1·75
O53 1r. yellow (1935) . . . 17·00 2·25
O46/53 *Set of* 8 . . . 42·00 4·50

1947. *No. 58 optd with Type* O **2**.

O54 ½a. claret . . . 9·00 7·00

1949. *No. 60 optd with Type* O **2**.

O55 **12** 2p. bistre-brown . . . 7·00 9·00

1950. *No. 59 optd with Type* O **2**.

O56 6p. claret . . . 10·00 21·00

IDAR

PRICES FOR STAMPS ON COVER	
Nos. 1/2*b*	*from* × 2
Nos. 3/6	*from* × 3
Nos. F1/5	*from* × 2

Maharaja Himmat Singh, 1931–1960

1 Maharaja Himmat Singh

2 Maharaja Himmat Singh

(Typo M. N. Kothari & Sons, Bombay)

1932 (1 Oct)–**43**. P 11.

(*a*) *White panels.*

1 **1** ½a. light green . . . — 32·00
a. Pale yellow-green (*thick paper*) (1939) . . . 17·00 21·00
b. Emerald (1941) . . . 16·00 21·00
ba. Imperf between (pair) . . . £1200
c. Yellow-green (1943) . . . 14·00 20·00
ca. Imperf between (horiz pair) . . . £1100

(*b*) *Coloured panels.*

2 **1** ½a. pale yellow-green (*thick paper*) (1939) . . . 30·00 27·00
a. Emerald (1941) . . . 21·00 23·00
b. Yellow-green (1943) . . . 13·00 22·00

In No. 2 the whole design is composed of half-tone dots. In No. 1 the dots are confined to the oval portrait.

(Typo P. G. Mehta & Co, Hitmatnagar)

1944 (21 Oct). P 12.

3 **2** ½a. blue-green . . . 3·25 65·00
a. Imperf between (vert pair) . . . £250
b. Yellow-green . . . 3·00 65·00
ba. Imperf between (vert pair) . . . 12·00
4 1a. violet . . . 3·25 55·00
a. Imperf (pair) . . . £200
b. Imperf vert (horiz pair) . . . £225
5 2a. blue . . . 3·50 90·00
a. Imperf between (vert pair) . . . 75·00
b. Imperf between (horiz pair) . . . £200
6 4a. vermilion . . . 3·75 95·00
a. Doubly printed . . . £700
3/6 *Set of* 4 . . . 12·00 £275

Nos. 1 to 6 are from booklet panes of 4 stamps, producing single stamps with one or two adjacent sides imperf.

The 4a. violet is believed to be a colour trial (*Price* £300, *unused*).

POSTAL FISCAL STAMPS

F 1

F 2

1936 (?). *Typo*. P 11½ *on two or three sides.*

F1 F **1** 1a. reddish lilac and bright green . . . — £550

1940 (?)–**45**. *Typo*. P 12 *on two or three sides.*

F2 – 1a. violet . . . — £130
a. Perf 11 . . . 80·00 £130
F3 F **2** 1a. violet (1943) . . . — £130
F4 1¼a.on 1a. violet . . . £120 £275
F5 1¼a. yellow-green (1945) . . . 16·00
a. Imperf between (vert pair) . . . 38·00
b. Blue-green (1945) . . . 65·00 £130

No. F2 shows the portrait as Type **1**. Used prices are for examples with postal cancellations. No. F4 shows a handstamped surcharge in Gujerati.

Idar became part of Bombay Province on 10 June 1948.

INDORE

(HOLKAR STATE)

PRICES FOR STAMPS ON COVER	
Nos. 1/15	*from* × 20
Nos. 16/43	*from* × 6
Nos. S1/7	*from* × 40

Maharaja Tukoji Rao Holkar II, 1843–1886

1 Maharaja Tukoji Rao Holkar II

(Litho Waterlow & Sons)

1886 (6 Jan). P 15.

(*a*) *Thick white paper.*

1 **1** ½a. bright mauve . . . 9·50 10·00

(*b*) *Thin white or yellowish paper.*

2 **1** ½a. pale mauve . . . 2·75 1·75
a. Dull mauve . . . 3·00 2·00

Maharaja Shivaji Rao Holkar, 1886–1903

2 Type I

2a Type II

TYPES 2 AND 2a. In addition to the difference in the topline character (marked by arrow), the two Types can be distinguished by the difference in the angles of the 6-pointed stars and the appearance of the lettering. In Type I the top characters are smaller and more cramped than the bottom; in Type II both are in the same style and similarly spaced.

1889 (Sept). *Handstamped. No gum.* Imperf.

No.	Type	Description	Unused	Used
3	**2**	½a. black/*pink*	35·00	35·00
4	**2a**	½a. black/*pink*	3·00	3·75
		a. *Tête-bêche* (pair)	£190	

3 Maharaja Shivaji Rao Holkar

4 Maharaja Tukoji Holkar III

5 Maharaja Tukoji Holkar III

(Recess Waterlow)

1889–92. *Medium wove paper.* P 14 *to* 15.

No.	Type	Description	Unused	Used
5	**3**	¼a. orange (9.2.92)	1·25	80
		a. Imperf between (horiz pair)	†	£550
		b. Very thick wove paper	2·00	1·00
		c. Yellow	1·75	1·00
6		½a. dull violet	1·75	60
		a. Brown-purple	1·50	15
		b. Imperf between (vert pair)	£500	
7		1a. green (7.2.92)	1·75	90
		a. Imperf between (vert pair)	£800	
		b. Very thick wove paper	75·00	
8		2a. vermilion (7.2.92)	4·75	1·50
		a. Very thick wove paper	6·00	3·50
5/8 *Set of* 4			8·25	3·00

Maharaja Tukoji Rao Holkar III, 1903–1926

(Recess Perkins, Bacon & Co)

1904–20. P 13½, 14.

No.	Type	Description	Unused	Used
9	**4**	¼a. orange	50	10
10	**5**	½a. lake (1909)	8·50	10
		a. Brown-lake (shades)	10·00	15
		b. Imperf (pair)	19·00	
11		1a. green	1·75	10
		a. Imperf (pair)	£120	
		b. Perf 12½ (1920)	†	£100
12		2a. brown	11·00	75
		a. Imperf (pair)	75·00	
13		3a. violet	18·00	7·00
14		4a. ultramarine	14·00	2·75
		a. Dull blue	5·00	1·25
9/14*a* *Set of* 6			40·00	8·25

पाव आना.
(6)

7 Maharaja Yeshwant Rao Holkar II

1905 (June). *No. 6a surch "QUARTER ANNA" in Devanagari, as T* **6**.

No.	Type	Description	Unused	Used
15	**3**	¼a. on ½a. brown-purple	5·00	20·00

On 1 March 1908 the Indore State postal service was amalgamated with the Indian Imperial system. Under the terms of the agreement stamps showing the Maharaja would still be used for official mail sent to addresses within the state. Initially Nos. 9/14 were used for this purpose, the "SERVICE" overprints, Nos. S1/7, being withdrawn.

Maharaja Yeshwant Rao Holkar II, 1926–1961

(Recess Perkins, Bacon & Co)

1927–37. P 13 *to* 14.

No.	Type	Description	Unused	Used
16	**7**	¼a. orange (*a*) (*d*) (*e*)	40	20
17		½a. claret (*a*) (*d*) (*e*)	1·25	10
18		1a. green (*a*) (*d*) (*e*)	2·25	10
19		1¼a. green (*c*) (*d*) (1933)	2·50	50
20		2a. sepia (*a*)	5·00	1·75
21		2a. bluish green (*d*) (1936)	13·00	1·40
		a. Imperf (pair)	25·00	£140
22		3a. deep violet (*a*)	1·75	9·00
23		3a. Prussian blue (*d*) (1935?)	17·00	
		a. Imperf (pair)	30·00	£350
24		3½a. violet (*d*) (1934)	7·00	10·00
		a. Imperf (pair)	50·00	£350
25		4a. ultramarine (*a*)	4·00	4·00
26		4a. yellow-brown (*d*) (1937)	27·00	1·60
		a. Imperf (pair)	30·00	£250
27		8a. slate-grey (*a*)	5·50	4·50
28		8a. red-orange (*d*) (1937)	21·00	20·00
29		12a. carmine (*d*) (1934)	5·00	10·00
30	–	1r. black and light blue (*b*)	8·00	14·00
31	–	2r. black and carmine (*b*)	42·00	45·00
32	–	5r. black & brown-orange (*b*)	75·00	80·00

Nos. 30/32 are as Type **7**, but larger, size 23 × 28 mm.

Five different perforating heads were used for this issue: (*a*) comb 13.6; (*b*) comb 13.9; (*c*) line 13.2; (*d*) line 13.8; (*e*) line 14.2. Values on which each perforation occur are indicated above.

Nos. 21a, 23a, 24a and 26a were specifically ordered by the state government in 1933 and are known used for postage *circa* 1938–42. A plate proof of the 1r. in green and carmine is also known postally used (*Price of pair £35 unused, £375 used*).

Nos. 16/19 and 28/32 also exist as imperforate plate proofs, but these were never sent to India.

QUARTER ANNA
(8)

9

1940 (1 Aug). *Surch in words as T* **8** *by Times of India Press, Bombay.*

No.	Type	Description	Unused	Used
33	**7**	¼a.on 5r. black and brown-orange (*b*)	13·00	1·50
		a. Surch double (Blk.+G.)	†	£400
34		½a.on 2r. black and carmine (*b*)	18·00	2·50
35		1a.on 1¼a. green (*c*) (*d*) (*e*)	18·00	70
		b. Surch inverted (*d*)	90·00	
		c. Surch double (*c*)	£350	
33/5 *Set of* 3			45·00	4·25

(Typo "Times of India" Press, Bombay)

1940–46. P 11.

No.	Type	Description	Unused	Used
36	**9**	¼a. red-orange	2·00	10
37		½a. claret (1941)	2·50	10
38		1a. green (1941)	9·00	10
39		1¼a. yellow-green (1941)	14·00	1·25
		a. Imperf (pair)	£200	
40		2a. turquoise-blue (1941)	11·00	1·00
41		4a. yellow-brown (1946)	12·00	11·00
		Larger size (23 × 28 mm).		
42		2r. black and carmine (1943)	11·00	£140
43		5r. black and yellow-orange (1943)	11·00	£180
36/43 *Set of* 8			65·00	£300

OFFICIAL STAMPS

SERVICE
(S 1)

SERVICE
(S 2)

1904–06.

No.	Type	Description	Unused	Used
		(a) Optd with Type S **1**.		
S1	**4**	¼a. orange (1906)	30	80
S2	**5**	½a. lake	25	10
		a. Opt inverted	20·00	35·00
		b. Opt double	18·00	
		c. Imperf (pair)	65·00	
		d. Brown-lake	25	10
		da. Opt inverted	18·00	
		e. Pair, one without opt	£450	
S3		1a. green	15	20
S4		2a. brown (1905)	30	30
		a. Vert pair, one without opt	£700	
S5		3a. violet (1906)	2·00	2·75
		a. Imperf (pair)	£325	
S6		4a. ultramarine (1905)	4·00	1·50
		(b) Optd with Type S **2**.		
S7	**5**	½a. lake	10	90
		a. Opt double	£400	
S1/7 *Set of* 7			6·50	6·00

Types S **1** and S **2** differ chiefly in the shape of the letter "R".

Indore became part of Madhya Bharat by 1 July 1948.

JAIPUR

PRICES FOR STAMPS ON COVER	
No. 1	*from* × 3
No. 2	*from* × 2
Nos. 3/5	*from* × 10
Nos. 6/70	*from* × 4
Nos. 71/80	*from* × 6
Nos. O1/34	*from* × 8

Maharaja Sawai Madho Singh II, 1880–1922

1

1a

2

Chariot of the Sun God, Surya

Type **1** – Value at sides in small letters and characters. "HALF ANNA", shown as one word except for R. 1/1 and 1/3, measuring between 13½ and 15 mm. Sheets of 12 (4 × 3) with stamps 2 to 2½ mm apart.

Type **1a** – Value in large letters and characters. "HALF ANNA", always with a gap between the two words, measuring between 14½ and 15½ mm. Sheets of 24 (4 × 6) with stamps 3 to 4 mm apart.

Type **2** – Value in large letters and characters. "HALF ANNA" measuring 16 to 17 mm. Both side inscriptions start below the inner frame line. Sheets of 24 (4 × 6) with stamps 1½ to 2 mm apart.

(Litho Durbar Press, Jaipur)

1904 (14 July). Roughly perf 14.

No.	Type	Description	Unused	Used
1	**1**	½a. pale blue	£110	£15
		a. Ultramarine	£150	£18
		b. Imperf, *ultramarine*	£350	
2	**1a**	½a. grey-blue	£1500	£20
		a. Imperf	£350	£55
		b. Ultramarine	—	£32
3	**2**	½a. pale blue	2·75	5·5
		a. Deep blue	3·00	5·5
		b. Ultramarine	3·25	5·5
		c. Imperf	£350	£35
4	**1**	1a. dull red	4·50	13·0
		a. Scarlet	4·50	13·0
5		2a. pale green	4·25	13·0
		a. Emerald-green	4·50	

Nos. 1b, 2a and 3c are on gummed paper. Imperforate plate proofs also exist for Nos. 1/5, but these are ungummed.

3 Chariot of the Sun God, Surya

(Recess Perkins, Bacon & Co)

1904. P 12.

No.	Type	Description	Unused	Used
6	**3**	½a. blue	5·00	7·5
		a. Perf 12½	24·00	17·0
		b. Perf comp of 12 and 12½	15·00	17·0
7		1a. brown-red	50·00	50·0
		a. Perf 12½	£120	£12
		b. Perf comp of 12 and 12½	£120	£12
		c. Carmine	2·25	4·5
		ca. Imperf between (vert pair)	£475	£65
		cb. Perf comp of 12 and 12½	10·00	16·0
8		2a. deep green	6·50	13·0
		a. Perf 12½	£150	£10
		b. Perf comp of 12 and 12½	25·00	35·0

Nos. 6b, 7b, 7cb and 8b occur on the bottom two rows of shee otherwise perforated 12.

1905–08. Wmk "JAs WRIGLEY & SON Ld. 219" "SPECIA POSTAGE PAPER LONDON" or "PERKINS BACON & C Ld LONDON" in sheet. P 13½

No.	Type	Description	Unused	Used
9	**3**	¼a. olive-yellow (1906)	75	8
10		½a. blue (1906)	2·50	2·5
		a. Indigo	1·25	
11		1a. brown-red (1906)	5·50	4·
		a. Bright red (1908)	2·75	
12		2a. deep green (1906)	1·75	7
13		4a. chestnut	6·00	2·0
14		8a. bright violet	3·00	2·7
15		1r. orange-yellow	18·00	18·
		a. Yellow	20·00	16·
		b. Yellow-ochre	22·00	27·
9/15 *Set of* 7			30·00	21·

4 Chariot of the Sun God, Surya

३ आना
(5)

(Typo Jaipur State Press)

1911. *Thin wove paper. No gum.* Imperf.

No.	Type	Description	Unused	Used
16	**4**	¼a. green	2·00	2·
		a. Printed double	6·50	
		ab. Ditto, one inverted		
		b. "¼" inverted in right upper corner (R. 1/2)	5·00	
		c. No stop after "STATE" (R. 3/1)	5·00	
17		¼a. greenish yellow	30	
		a. Printed double	2·00	
		b. "¼" inverted in right upper corner (R. 1/2)	1·50	
		c. No stop after "STATE" (R. 3/1)	1·50	
18		½a. ultramarine	30	
		a. Printed double	2·00	
		b. No stop after "STATE" (R. 3/1)	75	
		c. Large "J" in "JAIPUR" (R. 1/2)	75	
		d. "⅓" for "½" at lower left (R. 3/1)	1·50	
		e. "1½a." at lower right (R. 3/2)	1·50	
19		½a. grey-blue	2·25	2·
		a. No stop after "STATE" (R. 3/1)	3·50	
		b. Large "J" in "JAIPUR" (R. 1/2)	3·50	
		c. "⅓" for "½" at lower left (R. 3/1)	4·00	
		d. "1½a." at lower right (R. 3/2)	4·50	
20		1a. rose-red	50	
		a. Printed double	£190	
21		2a. greyish green	2·75	5·
		a. Deep green	2·00	6·
		ab. Printed double	£200	

Issued in sheets of 6 (2 × 3). There are three recognised settin Nos. 18d/e and 19c/d come from Setting B, and Nos. 16b/c, 17b 18b/c and 19a/b from Setting C.

One sheet of the ¼a. is known in blue.

(Typo Jaipur State Press)

1912–22. Paper-maker's wmk "DORLING & CO. LONDON" in sheet. P 11.
22 3 ¼a. pale olive-yellow 40 1·10
a. Imperf horiz (vert pair) £200 £200
b. Imperf vert (horiz pair) — £160
23 ¼a. olive 50 1·40
a. Imperf between (horiz pair) £190
b. Imperf vert (horiz pair) £200
c. Imperf horiz (vert pair) £200
d. *Tête-bêche* (pair) £400
24 ¼a. bistre 30 1·40
a. Imperf between (horiz pair) £190
b. Imperf between (vert pair) † £275
c. Imperf horiz (vert pair) † £275
d. Doubly printed † £550
25 ½a. pale ultramarine 1·25 85
a. Imperf vert (horiz pair) † £450
b. Blue 1·25 60
ba. Imperf between (horiz pair) £350
26 1a. carmine (1918) 4·25 4·25
a. Imperf between (vert pair) † £650
b. Imperf horiz (vert pair) † £650
27 1a. rose-red 3·50 8·50
a. Imperf between (vert pair) £650
28 1a. scarlet (1922) 3·00 2·50
a. Imperf between (vert pair) £700 £700
29 2a. green (1918) 3·50 3·75
30 4a. chocolate 4·50 7·50
31 4a. pale brown 5·00 8·50
a. Imperf vert (horiz pair) £475
22/31 *Set of* 5 11·50 14·00

Maharaja Sawai Man Singh II 1922–1970

926. *Surch with T* **5**.
2 3 3a.on 8a. bright violet (R.) 1·50 2·50
a. Surch inverted £170 £140
3 3a.on 1r. yellow (R.) 2·25 4·75
a. Surch inverted £450 £170
c. Yellow-ochre 7·50 9·50

928. *As 1913–18 issue*. Wmk "DORLING & CO. LONDON" (½a., 1a., 2a.) or "OVERLAND BANK" (all values) in sheet. *No gum*. P 12.
4 3 ½a. ultramarine 3·00 4·00
a. Perf comp of 12 and 11 14·00 8·00
5 1a. rose-red 25·00 17·00
a. Imperf between (vert pair) £500
6 1a. scarlet 40·00 12·00
a. Perf comp of 12 and 11 55·00 25·00
7 2a. green 80·00 27·00
a. Perf comp of 12 and 11 £190 60·00
8 8a. bright violet
9 1r. orange-vermilion £300 £425

The "OVERLAND BANK" paper has a coarser texture. The ½a. nd 2a. values also exist on this paper perforated 11, but such amps are difficult to distinguish from examples of Nos. 25 and 29.

6 Chariot of the Sun God, Surya

7 Maharaja Sawai Man Singh II

8 Sowar in Armour

(Des T. I. Archer. Litho Indian Security Printing Press, Nasik)

931 (14 Mar). *Investiture of Maharaja. T* **6/8** *and similar designs*. No wmk. P 14.
¼a. black and deep lake 2·00 2·00
½a. black and violet 40 10
1a. black and blue 7·00 7·50
2a. black and buff 6·00 7·50
2½a. black and carmine 30·00 50·00
3a. black and myrtle 14·00 40·00
4a. black and olive-green 14·00 50·00
6a. black and deep blue 6·00 45·00
8a. black and chocolate 14·00 75·00
1r. black and pale olive 30·00 £225
2r. black and yellow-green 28·00 £275
5r. black and purple 42·00 £300
/51 *Set of* 12 £170 £950

Designs: *Vert*—1a. Elephant and state banner; 2½a. Common eafowl; 8a. Sireh-Deorhi Gate. *Horiz*—3a. Bullock carriage; 4a. ephant carriage; 6a. Albert Museum; 1r. Chandra Mahal; 2r. mber Palace; 5r. Maharajas Jai Singh and Man Singh.

Eighteen of these sets were issued for presentation purposes with special overprint "INVESTITURE-MARCH 14,1931" in red *rice for set of* 12 £3250 *unused*, £4250 *used*).

10 Maharaja Sawai Man Singh II

One Rupee
(**11**)

(Des T. I. Archer. Litho Indian Security Printing Press, Nasik)

1932–46. P 14.

(*a*) *Inscr "*POSTAGE & REVENUE*"*.
52 **10** 1a. black and blue 1·75 85
53 2a. black and buff 2·75 1·75
54 4a. black and grey-green 4·00 8·00
55 8a. black and chocolate 5·50 11·00
56 1r. black and yellow-bistre 21·00 90·00
57 2r. black and yellow-green 80·00 £375
52/7 *Set of* 6 £100 £450

(*b*) *Inscr "*POSTAGE*"*.
58 **7** ¼a. black and brown-lake 40 20
59 ¾a. black and brown-red (1943?) 6·50 3·25
60 1a. black and blue (1943?) 8·00 2·75
61 2a. black and buff (1943?) 7·00 3·50
62 2½a. black and carmine 3·25 2·25
63 3a. black and green 2·50 50
64 4a. black and grey-green (1943?) 30·00 £110
65 6a. black and deep blue 3·75 24·00
a. Black and pale blue (1946) 8·50 60·00
66 8a. black and chocolate (1946) 20·00 95·00
67 1r. black and yellow-bistre (1946) 20·00 £140
58/67 *Set of* 10 90·00 £350

1936. *Nos. 57 and 51 surch with T* **11**.
68 **10** 1r. on 2r. black and yellow-green (R.) 8·50 85·00
69 – 1r. on 5r. black and purple 8·50 70·00

पाव आना
(**12**)

13 Maharaja and Amber Palace

1938 (Dec). *No. 41 surch "QUARTER ANNA" in Devanagari, T* **12**.
70 **7** ¼a. on ½a. black and violet (R.) 12·00 15·00

(Recess D.L.R.)

1947 (Dec)–**48**. *Silver Jubilee of Maharajas Accession to Throne. Various designs as T* **13**. P 13½ × 14.
71 ¼a. red-brown and green (5.48) 1·25 3·75
72 ½a. green and violet 40 3·50
73 ¾a. black and lake (5.48) 1·25 4·25
74 1a. red-brown and ultramarine 75 3·50
75 2a. violet and scarlet 75 3·75
76 3a. green and black (5.48) 1·40 4·75
77 4a. ultramarine and brown 60 3·50
78 8a. vermilion and brown 70 4·50
79 1r. purple and green (5.48) 2·00 30·00
71/9 *Set of* 9 8·25 55·00

Designs:—¼a. Palace Gate; ¾a. Map of Jaipur; 1a. Observatory; 2a. Wind Palace; 3a. Coat of Arms; 4a. Amber Fort Gate; 8a. Chariot of the Sun; 1r. Maharaja's portrait between State flags.

3 PIES
(**14**)

1947 (1 Dec). *No. 41 surch with T* **14**.
80 **7** 3p.on ½a. black and violet (R.) 15·00 24·00
a. "PIE" for "PIES" 45·00 85·00
b. Bars at left vertical 60·00 90·00
c. Surch inverted 42·00 35·00
d. Surch inverted and "PIE" for "PIES" £180 £170
e. Surch double, one inverted 60·00 48·00
f. As variety e, but inverted surch showing "PIE" for "PIES" £375 £350

There were three settings of Type **14**, each applied to quarter sheets of 30 (6 × 5). No. 80a occurs in two of these settings on R. 5/5 and one of these settings also shows No. 80b on R. 6/1.

OFFICIAL STAMPS

SERVICE (O 1) SERVICE (O 2)

1928 (13 Nov)–**31**. *T* **3** *typographed. No gum (except for Nos. O6/a)*. P 11, 12, or compound. Wmk "DORLING & CO. LONDON" (4a.) or "OVERLAND BANK" (others).

(*a*) *Optd with Type* O **1**.
O1 ¼a. olive 1·25 2·00
a. Bistre 1·75 1·75
O2 ½a. pale ultramarine (Blk.) 75 20
a. Imperf between (horiz pair) £300 £300
b. Imperf between (vert pair) † £600
c. Opt inverted † £350
d. Opt double (R. and Blk.) † £425
O3 ½a. pale ultramarine (R.) (13.10.30) 2·50 25
a. Imperf horiz (vert pair) £600
b. Stamp doubly printed † £425
O3*c* 1a. rose-red 80 25
d. Imperf between (horiz pair) † £600
O4 1a. scarlet 1·25 50
a. Opt inverted £700 £700
b. Imperf between (horiz pair) † £650
O5 2a. green 75 40
a. Imperf between (vert pair) † £750
b. Imperf between (horiz pair) £750 £750
O6 4a. pale brown (with gum) 4·25 1·75
a. Chocolate (with gum) 2·00 1·75
O7 8a. bright violet (R.) (13.10.30) 17·00 55·00
O8 1r. orange-vermilion 35·00 £275

(*b*) *Optd with Type* O **2**.
O 9 ½a. ultramarine (Blk.) (11.2.31) £180 15
a. Imperf vert (horiz pair) † £700
O10 ½a. ultramarine (R.) (15.10.30) £180 15
a. Imperf between (vert pair) † £700
O11 8a. bright violet (11.2.31) £400 £190
O12 1r. orange-vermilion (11.2.31) £400 £275

SERVICE (O 3) आध आना (O 4)

1931–37. *Nos. 41/3 and 46 optd at Nasik with Type* O **3**, *in red*.
O13 **7** ½a. black and violet 30 10
O14 – 1a. black and blue £225 2·00
O15 **8** 2a. black and buff (1936) 2·75 5·50
O16 – 4a. black and olive-green (1937) 35·00 28·00
O13/16 *Set of* 4 £250 32·00

1932. *No. O5 surch with Type* O **4**.
O17 **3** ½a. on 2a. green £150 1·50

1932–37. *Nos. 52/6 optd at Nasik with Type* O **3**, *in red*.
O18 **10** 1a. black and blue 3·25 15
O19 2a. black and buff 3·75 15
O20 4a. black and grey-green (1937) £275 7·50
O21 8a. black and chocolate 7·50 1·10
O22 1r. black and yellow-bistre 20·00 21·00
O18/22 *Set of* 5 £275 27·00

1936–46. *Stamps of 1932–46, inscr "*POSTAGE*"*.
(*a*) *Optd at Nasik with Type* O **3**, *in red*.
O23 **7** ¼a. black and brown-lake (1936) 40 10
O24 ¾a. black and brown-red (1944) 1·50 50
O25 1a. black and blue (1941?) 4·00 30
O26 2a. black and buff (date?) 4·00 2·25
O27 2½a. black and carmine (1946) 9·00 90·00
O28 4a. black and grey-green (1942) 4·00 4·50
O29 8a. black and chocolate (1943) 4·00 6·50
O30 1r. black and yellow-bistre (date?) 40·00
O23/9 *Set of* 7 25·00 95·00
(*b*) *Optd locally as Type* O **2** *(16 mm long), in black*.
O31 **7** ½a. black and red-brown (1936) 80·00 65·00

9 PIES
(O 5)

1947. *No. O25 surch with Type* O **5**, *in red*.
O32 **7** 9p. on 1a. black and blue 3·75 3·00

1947 (Dec). *No. O13 surch as T* **14**, *but "3 PIES" placed higher*.
O33 **7** 3p.on ½a. black and violet (R.) 4·75 12·00
a. Surch double, one inverted 40·00 40·00
ab. "PIE" for "PIES" in inverted surcharge £225 £250
c. Surch inverted — £1400

1948 (Dec). *No. O13 surch "THREE-QUARTER ANNA" in Devanagari, as T* **12**, *but with two bars on each side*.
O34 **7** ¾a.on ½a. black and violet (R.) 15·00 16·00
a. Surch double £1300 £1300

There are three different types of surcharge in the setting of 30, which vary in one or other of the Devanagari characters.

Jaipur became part of Rajasthan by 7 April 1949.

JAMMU AND KASHMIR

PRICES FOR STAMPS ON COVER

Nos.	1/73	*from* × 3
Nos.	74/84	*from* × 2
No.	85	—
Nos.	86/9	*from* × 2
Nos.	90/101	*from* × 10
Nos.	101*b*/23	*from* × 5
Nos.	124/36	*from* × 10
Nos.	138/9	*from* × 100
Nos.	140/61*a*	*from* × 15
Nos.	162/8	*from* × 5
No.	O1	*from* × 2
Nos.	O2/4	*from* × 4
No.	O5	—
Nos.	O6/14	*from* × 30
Nos.	O15/18	—

ILLUSTRATIONS. Designs of Jammu and Kashmir are illustrated actual size.

Maharaja Ranhir Singh, 1857–1885

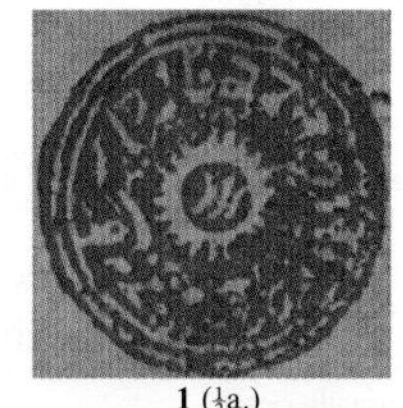
1 (½a.)

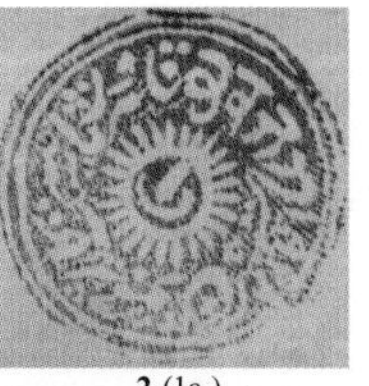
2 (1a.)

3 (4a.)

Characters denoting the value (on the circular stamps only) are approximately as shown in the central circles of the stamps illustrated above.

These characters were taken from Punjabi merchants' notation and were not familiar to most of the inhabitants of the state. Type **1** was certainly the ½ anna value, but there has long been controversy over the correct face values of Types **2** and **3**.

The study of surviving material suggests that, to some extent, this confusion involved contemporary post office officials. Although covers posted at Jammu, where the stamps were in use for twelve years, show Type **2** used as the 1a. value and Type **3** as the 4a., those originating from Srinagar (Kashmir) during 1866–68 show both Types **2** and **3** used as 1a. stamps.

In the following listing we have followed contemporary usage at Jammu and this reflects the prevailing opinion amongst modern authorities.

GUM. The stamps of Jammu and Kashmir were issued without gum.

PRICES. Prices for the circular stamps, Nos. 1/49, are for cut-square examples. Cut-to-shape examples are worth from 10% to 20% of these prices, according to condition.

A. *Handstamped in watercolours*

1866 (23 Mar). *Native paper, thick to thin, usually having the appearance of laid paper and tinted grey or brown. For Jammu and Kashmir.*

1	**1**	½a. grey-black	£170	85·00
2		½a. ultramarine	£2500	£2500
3	**2**	1a. royal blue	£600	£400
3*a*		1a. ultramarine	£400	90·00
4		1a. grey-black	£1400	£1200
5	**3**	4a. royal blue		
5*a*		4a. ultramarine	£750	£375

No. 4 may be an error of colour. It is only known used in Kashmir.

1867–76. *Reissued for use in Jammu only.*

6	**3**	4a. grey-black	£1500	
7		4a. indigo	£1700	£950
8		4a. red (1869)	70·00	£110
9		4a. orange-red (1872)	£170	£250
10		4a. orange (1872)		
11		4a. carmine-red (1876)	£800	

1874–76. *Special Printings.*

12	**1**	½a. red	80·00	£275
12*a*		½a. orange-red	£600	£650
13	**2**	1a. red	£160	£250
13*a*		1a. orange-red	£600	£650
13*b*		1a. orange	£750	
14	**1**	½a. deep black	19·00	£150
		a. *Tête-bêche* (pair)	£425	
15	**2**	1a. deep black	£250	
16	**3**	4a. deep black	£225	
17	**1**	½a. bright blue (1876)	£300	£375
18	**2**	1a. bright blue (1876)	£100	£300
19	**3**	4a. bright blue (1876)	£170	
20	**1**	½a. emerald-green	85·00	£225
21	**2**	1a. emerald-green	90·00	£225
22	**3**	4a. emerald-green	£200	£375
23	**1**	½a. yellow	£550	£750
24	**2**	1a. yellow	£750	
25	**3**	4a. yellow	£425	
25*a*		4a. deep blue-black (1876)	£1200	£700

These special printings were available for use, but little used.

B. *Handstamped in oil colours. Heavy blurred prints*

1877 (June)–**78**.

(a) Native paper.

26	**1**	½a. red	30·00	50·00
27	**2**	1a. red	35·00	£160
28	**3**	4a. red	£225	£425
29	**1**	½a. black	28·00	50·00
32		½a. slate-blue	£130	£200
34	**2**	1a. slate-blue	26·00	£225
35	**1**	½a. sage-green	£110	
36	**2**	1a. sage-green	£120	
37	**3**	4a. sage-green	£120	

(b) European laid paper, medium to thick.

38	**1**	½a. red	—	£800
39	**3**	4a. red	£350	£375
41	**1**	½a. black	24·00	50·00
		a. Printed both sides	£700	
		b. *Tête-bêche* (pair)	£350	
44		½a. slate-blue	40·00	£225
45	**2**	1a. slate-blue	50·00	£325
46	**3**	4a. slate-blue	£700	£700
47		4a. sage-green	£1100	
48	**1**	½a. yellow	£120	

(c) Thick yellowish wove paper.

49	**1**	½a. red (1878)	—	£800

Forgeries exist of the ½a. and 1a. in types which were at one time supposed to be authentic.

Reprints and imitations (of which some of each were found in the official remainder stock) exist in a great variety of fancy colours, both on native paper, usually thinner and smoother than that of the originals, and on various thin European *wove* papers, on which the originals were never printed.

The imitations, which do not agree in type with the above illustrations, are also to be found on *laid* paper.

All the reprints, etc. are in oil colours or printer's ink. The originals in oil colour are usually blurred, particularly when on native paper. The reprints, etc. are usually clear.

FOR USE IN JAMMU

½a. ½a.

1a. **4** ½a.

T **4** to **11** have a star at the top of the oval band; the characters denoting the value are in the upper part of the inner oval. All are dated 1923, corresponding with A.D. 1866.

T **4**. *Printed in blocks of four, three varieties of ½ anna and one of 1 anna.*

1867 (Sept). *In watercolour on native paper.*

52	½a. grey-black	£750	£250
53	1a. grey-black	£2000	£900
54	½a. indigo	£325	£225
55	1a. indigo	£650	£325
56	½a. deep ultramarine	£225	£150
57	1a. deep ultramarine	£600	£325
58	½a. deep violet-blue	£160	85·00
59	1a. deep violet-blue	£600	£325

1868 (May)–**72**. *In watercolour on native paper.*

60	½a. red (*shades*)	6·50	3·25
61	1a. red (*shades*)	15·00	9·50
62	½a. orange-red	£190	65·00
63	1a. orange-red	£650	£250
64	½a. orange (1872)	£100	£110
65	1a. orange (1872)	£1900	£1200

1874–76. *Special printings; in watercolour on native paper.*

66	½a. bright blue (1876)	£1200	£300
67	1a. bright blue (1876)	£375	£400
68	½a. emerald-green	£1500	£900
69	1a. emerald-green	£2500	£1500
69*a*	½a. jet-black	£130	£160
69*b*	1a. jet-black	£1500	£1300

1877 (June)–**78**. *In oil colour.*

(a) Native paper.

70	½a. red	9·00	6·50
71	1a. red	28·00	21·00
72	½a. brown-red (1878)	—	35·00
73	1a. brown-red (1878)	—	£110
74	½a. black	†	£800
75	1a. black	†	£1800
76	½a. deep blue-black	†	£1300
77	1a. deep blue-black	†	£3500

(b) Laid paper (medium or thick).

78	½a. red	—	£800

(c) Thick wove paper.

79	½a. red	†	£375
80	1a. red		

(d) Thin laid, bâtonné paper.

84	½a. red	†	£1200
85	1a. red	£3500	

The circular and rectangular stamps listed under the heading "Special Printings' did not supersede those in *red*, which was the normal colour for Jammu down to 1878. It is not known for what reason other colours were used during that period, but these stamps were printed in 1874 or 1875 and were certainly put into use. The rectangular stamps were again printed in *black* (jet-black, as against the greyish black of the 1867 printings) at that time, and impressions of the two periods can also be distinguished by the obliterations, which until 1868 were in *magenta* and after that in *black*.

There are reprints of these, in *oil* colour, *brown-red* and *bright blue*, on native paper; they are very clearly printed, which is not the case with the originals in *oil* colour.

4a

1877 (Sept). *Provisional. Seal obliterator of Jammu handstamped in red watercolour on pieces of native paper, and used as a ½ anna stamp.*

86	**4a**	(½a.) rose-red	—	£1100

FOR USE IN KASHMIR

5

1866 (Sept(?)). *Printed from a single die. Native laid paper.*

87	**5**	½a. black	£2500	£375

Forgeries of this stamp are commonly found, copied from ar illustration in *Le Timbre-Poste*.

6 (½a.)

7 (1a.)

1867 (Apr). *Native laid paper.*

88	**6**	½a. black	£1100	£16
89	**7**	1a. black	£1900	£42

Printed in sheets of 25 (5 × 5), the four top rows being ½a. an the bottom row 1a.

8 (¼a.)

9 (2a.)

10 (4a.)

11 (8a.)

1867–77. *Native laid paper.*

90	**8**	¼a. black	2·75	3·2
91	**6**	½a. ultramarine (6.67)	3·00	1·2
		a. Bisected (¼a.) (on cover) (1877)	†	£50(
92		½a. violet-blue (1870)	5·50	3·(
93	**7**	1a. ultramarine (6.67)	£3250	£13(
94		1a. orange (7.67)	10·00	8·
95		1a. brown-orange (1868)	10·00	8·
96		1a. orange-vermilion (1876)	14·00	9·
97	**9**	2a. yellow	13·00	15·
98		2a. buff	20·00	16·(
99	**10**	4a. emerald-green	32·00	32·(
		a. *Tête-bêche* (pair)	£950	
100		4a. sage-green	£275	£1
100*a*		4a. myrtle-green	£600	£6(
101	**11**	8a. red (1868)	35·00	32·(
		a. *Tête-bêche* (pair)	£1000	

Of the above, the ½a. and 1a. were printed from the same pla of 25 as Nos. 88/9, the ¼a. and 2a. from a new plate of 10 (5 × 2 the top row being ¼a. and the lower 2a., and the 4a. and 8a. fro single dies. Varieties at one time catalogued upon European pape were apparently never put into circulation, though some of the were printed while these stamps were still in use.

Nos. 86 to 101 are in watercolour.

No. 91a was used at Srinagar, in conjunction with an India ½a and was cancelled "KASHMIR 5/L-6".

FOR USE IN JAMMU AND KASHMIR

In the following issues there are 15 varieties on the sheets of t ⅛a., ¼a. and ½a.; 20 varieties of the 1a. and 2a. and 8 varieties of t 4a. and 8a. The value is in the lower part of the central oval.

12 (¼a.)

13 (½a.)

14 (1a.) 15 (2a.)

16 (4a.) 17 (8a.)

8 (May)–79. *Provisional printings.*

I. *Ordinary white laid paper, of varying thickness.*

(a) Rough perf 10 to 12 (i) or 13 to 16 (ii).

b	**12**	¼a. red (i)		
	13	½a. red (i)	12·00	14·00
	14	1a. red (i)	£1000	
	13	½a. slate-violet (i)	70·00	50·00
a	**14**	1a. violet (ii)		
b	**15**	2a. violet (i)	£1400	

(b) Imperf.

	13	½a. slate-violet (*shades*)	14·00	12·00
	14	1a. slate-purple	22·00	23·00
		1a. mauve	35·00	32·00
	15	2a. violet	23·00	23·00
		2a. bright mauve	32·00	29·00
		2a. slate-blue	48·00	48·00
		2a. dull blue	90·00	90·00
	12	¼a. red	19·00	16·00
	13	½a. red	8·00	8·50
	14	1a. red	7·50	9·00
	15	2a. red	75·00	75·00
	16	4a. red	£180	£160

II. *Medium wove paper.*

(a) Rough perf 10 to 12.

	13	½a. red	—	£225

(b) Imperf.

b	**12**	¼a. red		
	13	½a. red	14·00	7·50
	14	1a. red	12·00	8·50
	15	2a. red	65·00	

III. *Thick wove paper.* Imperf.

	13	½a. red	25·00	48·00
	14	1a. red	42·00	19·00
	15	2a. red	17·00	20·00

)f the above stamps those in red were intended for use in Jammu
 those in shades of violet and blue for use in Kashmir.

'9. *Definitive issue. Thin wove paper, fine to coarse.*

(a) Rough perf 10 to 12.

	13	½a. red	£275	£180

(b) Imperf.

	12	¼a. red	3·00	3·50
	13	½a. red	75	75
		a. Bisected (¼a.) on postcard	†	£3250
	14	1a. red	2·50	3·00
	15	2a. red	3·25	4·25
	16	4a. red	8·50	8·50
	17	8a. red	9·00	9·50

:he plates were transferred from Jammu to Srinagar in early 1881
en further printings in red and all orange stamps were produced.

0 (Mar). *Provisional printing in watercolour on thin bâtonné aper.* Imperf.

a	**12**	¼a. ultramarine	£800	£500

1–83. *As Nos. 124 to 130. Colour changed.*

(a) Rough perf 10 to 12.

b	**13**	½a. orange		

(b) Imperf.

	12	¼a. orange	8·50	12·00
	13	½a. orange	20·00	14·00
	14	1a. orange	20·00	11·00
		a. Bisected (½a.) (on cover)	†	£3500
	15	2a. orange	15·00	11·00
	16	4a. orange	35·00	45·00
	17	8a. orange	60·00	65·00

Nos. 126a and 133a were used at Leh between April and July 3.

Nos. 125/30 and 132/6 were re-issued between 1890 and 1894 and d concurrently with the stamps which follow. Such re-issues can identified by the "three circle" cancellations, introduced in cember 1890.

18 (⅛a.)

3–94. *New colours. Thin wove papers, toned, coarse to fine, or fine white (1889).* Imperf.

	18	⅛a. yellow-brown	1·10	1·60
		⅛a. yellow	1·10	1·60
140	**12**	¼a. sepia	1·00	65
141		¼a. brown	1·00	65
		a. Double impression	£1100	
142		¼a. pale brown	1·00	65
		a. Error. Green	60·00	
143	**13**	½a. dull blue	6·00	
144		½a. bright blue	45·00	
145		½a. vermilion	1·10	60
146		½a. rose	1·25	85
147		½a. orange-red	1·10	60
148	**14**	1a. greenish grey	85	85
149		1a. bright green	1·10	1·10
		a. Double impression		
150		1a. dull green	85	85
151		1a. blue-green	1·50	
152	**15**	2a. red/*yellow*	2·00	1·10
153		2a. red/*yellow-green*	3·00	3·25
154		2a. red/*deep green*	14·00	14·00
155	**16**	4a. deep green	3·25	4·00
156		4a. green	3·50	3·25
157		4a. pale green	3·50	3·25
158		4a. sage-green	3·75	
159	**17**	8a. pale blue	7·00	8·50
159*a*		8a. deep blue	10·00	12·00
160		8a. bright blue	9·00	11·00
161		8a. indigo-blue	11·00	13·00
161*a*		8a. slate-lilac	10·00	18·00

Well-executed forgeries of the ¼a. to 8a. have come from India, mostly postmarked; they may be detected by the type, which does not agree with any variety on the genuine sheets, and also, in the low values, by the margins being filled in with colour, all but a thin white frame round the stamp. The forgeries of the 8a. are in sheets of eight like the originals.

Other forgeries of nearly all values also exist, showing all varieties of type. All values are on thin, coarse wove paper.

In February 1890, a forgery, in watercolour, of the ½a. orange on thin wove or on thin laid paper appeared, and many have been found genuinely used during 1890 and 1891 (*Price* £3).

Nos. 143 and 144 were never issued.

Examples of the ¼a. brown, ½a. orange-red and 1a. green on wove paper exist with clean-cut perf 12.

There is a reference in the Jammu and Kashmir State Administration Report covering 1890–91 to the re-introduction of perforating and the machine-gumming of paper at the Jammu printing works.

The few known examples, the ¼a. being only recorded used, the others unused or used, would appear to date from this period, but there is, as yet, no direct confirmation as to their status.

Maharaja Partap Singh, 1885–1925

1887–94. *Thin creamy laid paper.* Imperf.

162	**18**	⅛a. yellow	48·00	55·00
163	**12**	¼a. brown	9·00	6·50
164	**13**	½a. brown-red (March 1887)	—	65·00
165		½a. orange-red	8·00	5·00
166	**14**	1a. grey-green	£100	£100
168	**17**	8a. blue (*Printed in watercolour*)	£150	£150
		a. On wove paper	£100	£100

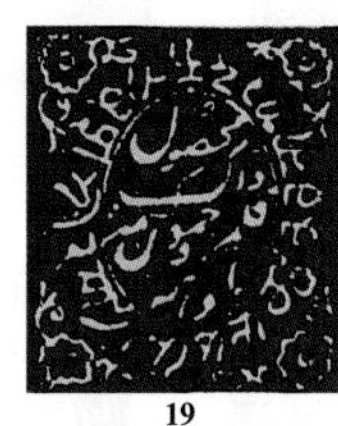

19

T **19** represents a ¼a. stamp, which exists in sheets of twelve varieties, in *red* and *black* on thin wove and laid papers, also in *red* on native paper, but which does not appear ever to have been issued for use. It was first seen in 1886.

The ¼a. *brown* and the 4a. *green* both exist on ordinary white laid paper and the ½a. *red* on native paper. None of these are known to have been in use.

OFFICIAL STAMPS

1878.

I. *White laid paper.*

(a) Rough perf 10 to 12.

O1	**13**	½a. black	—	£1500

(b) Imperf.

O2	**13**	½a. black	95·00	90·00
O3	**14**	1a. black	65·00	65·00
O4	**15**	2a. black	55·00	55·00

II. *Medium wove paper.* Imperf.

O5	**14**	1a. black	£275	

1880–94. *Thin wove papers, toned, coarse to fine, or fine white (1889).* Imperf.

O 6	**12**	¼a. black	1·00	1·25
		a. Double print	£200	
O 7	**13**	½a. black	15	40
		a. Printed both sides	£425	
O 8	**14**	1a. black	20	70
O 9	**15**	2a. black	30	45
O10	**16**	4a. black	60	1·10
O11	**17**	8a. black	1·75	1·10

1887–94. *Thin creamy laid paper.* Imperf.

O12	**12**	¼a. black	6·50	6·50
O13	**13**	½a. black	3·75	4·00
O14	**14**	1a. black	2·00	2·75
O15	**15**	2a. black	13·00	
O16	**16**	4a. black	50·00	55·00
O17	**17**	8a. black	28·00	45·00

1889. *Stout white wove paper.* Imperf.

O18	**12**	¼a. black	£180	£110

The stamps of Jammu and Kashmir have been obsolete since 1 November 1894.

JASDAN

PRICES FOR STAMPS ON COVER	
Nos. 1/2	*from* × 2
No. 3	*from* × 3
Nos. 4/6	*from* × 4

Darbar Ala Khachar, 1919–1971

1 Sun

(Typo L. V. Indap & Co, Bombay)

1942 (15 Mar)–**47**. *Stamps from booklet panes.* Various perfs.

1	**1**	1a. deep myrtle-green (P 10½)	£800	£500
2		1a. light green (P 12)	£475	£475
3		1a. light green (P 10½) (1943)	£130	£160
4		1a. pale yellow-green (P 8½–9) (1946)	16·00	£130
5		1a. dull yellow-green (P 10) (1945)	24·00	£150
6		1a. bluish green (P 8½–9) (1947)	19·00	£130

Nos. 1/4 were issued in panes of four with the stamps imperforate on one or two sides; Nos. 5/6 were in panes of eight perforated all round.

A 1a. rose with the arms of Jasdan in the centre is a fiscal stamp.

Jasdan was merged with the United State of Kathiawar (later Saurashtra) by 15 April 1948.

JHALAWAR

PRICES FOR STAMPS ON COVER	
Nos. 1/2	*from* × 25

Maharaj Rana Zalim Singh, 1875–1896

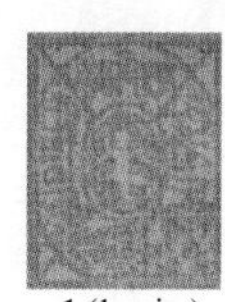

1 (1 paisa)

2 (¼ anna)

(Figure of an Apsara, "RHEMBA", a dancing nymph of the Hindu Paradise)

1886–90. *Typo in horizontal strips of 12. Laid paper. No gum.*

1	**1**	1p. yellow-green	4·25	11·00
		a. Blue-green	95·00	42·00
2	**2**	¼a. green (*shades*)	1·10	2·25

The stamps formerly listed as on wove paper are from sheets on laid paper, with the laid paper lines almost invisible.

The Maharaj Rana was deposed in 1896 and much of the state's territory transferred to Kotah on 1 January 1899.

Raj (Maharaj from 1918) Rana Rhawani Singh, 1899–1929

The stamps of Jhalawar have been obsolete since 1 November 1900.

JIND

PRICES FOR STAMPS ON COVER	
Nos. J1/34	*from* × 100

ILLUSTRATIONS. Designs of Jind are illustrated actual size.

Raja Raghubir Singh, 1864–1887

J 1 (½a.)

J 2 (1a.)

J 3 (2a.)

J 4 (4a.)

J 5 (8a.)

(Litho Jind State Rajah's Press, Sungroor)

1874. *Thin yellowish paper.* Imperf.

J1	**J 1**	½a. blue	6·00	3·25
		a. No frame to value. (Retouched all over) (R. 4/7)	£300	£160
J2	**J 2**	1a. rosy mauve	7·00	6·50
J3	**J 3**	2a. yellow	1·00	3·75
J4		2a. brown-buff	£180	£100
J5	**J 4**	4a. green	20·00	6·00
J6	**J 5**	8a. dull purple	£500	£140
J6*a*		8a. bluish violet	£180	80·00
J7		8a. slate-blue	£150	70·00

Nos. J1/7 were produced from two sets of stones. Those from the first set had rather blurred impressions, but those from the second are clearer with a conspicuous white frame around the value. Nos. J4 and J6*a*/13 were only printed from the second set.

1876. *Bluish laid card-paper. No gum.* Imperf.

J8	**J 1**	½a. blue	75	3·75
J9	**J 2**	1a. purple	1·50	8·50
J10	**J 3**	2a. brown	3·00	11·00
J11	**J 4**	4a. green	2·25	11·00
J11*a*	**J 5**	8a. bluish violet	8·00	20·00
J12		8a. slate-blue	7·00	10·00
J13		8a. steel-blue	9·00	15·00

Stocks of the ½a. (No. J8) and 2a. (No. J4) were perforated 12 in 1885 for use as fiscal stamps.

J 6 (¼a.)

J 7 (½a.)

J 8 (1a.)

J 9 (2a.)

J 10 (4a.)

J 11 (8a.)

(Litho Jind State Rajah's Press, Sungroor)

1882–85. *Types J* **6** *to J* **11**. *No gum.*

A. Imperf *(1882–4).*

(a) Thin yellowish wove paper.

J15	¼a. buff (*shades*)	30	1·50
J16	¼a. red-brown	30	1·25
	a. Doubly printed	42·00	
J17	½a. lemon	1·25	1·75
J18	½a. buff	1·90	1·50
J19	½a. brown-buff	80	60
J20	1a. brown (*shades*)	1·75	3·25
J21	2a. blue	1·75	8·00
J22	2a. deep blue	2·50	1·00
J23	4a. sage-green	1·50	90
J24	4a. blue-green	1·75	3·00
J25	8a. red	5·50	4·50

(b) Various thick laid papers.

J26	¼a. brown-buff	1·25	
J27	½a. lemon	1·25	
J28	½a. brown-buff		
J29	1a. brown	1·25	2·50
J30	2a. blue	18·00	21·00
J31	8a. red	2·50	10·00

(c) Thick white wove paper.

J32	¼a. brown-buff	14·00	
J33	½a. brown-buff	28·00	
J34	1a. brown	4·25	
J35	8a. red	4·75	9·00

B. Perf 12 *(1885).*

(a) Thin yellowish wove paper.

J36	¼a. buff (*shades*)	75	2·75
	a. Doubly printed	85·00	
J37	¼a. red-brown	3·50	
J38	½a. lemon	£130	£130
J39	½a. buff	60	3·75
J40	½a. brown-buff	3·00	4·75
J41	1a. brown (*shades*)	2·50	4·75
J42	2a. blue	3·50	9·00
J43	2a. deep blue	2·75	6·00
J44	4a. sage-green	5·00	10·00
J45	4a. blue-green	2·00	
	a. Imperf vert (horiz pair)	£500	
J46	8a. red	9·50	

(b) Various thick laid papers.

J47	½a. brown-buff	6·50	
J48	½a. lemon	£100	22·00
J49	1a. brown	1·50	
J50	2a. blue	20·00	24·00
J51	8a. red	2·50	8·50

(c) Thick white wove paper.

J52	1a. brown		
J53	8a. red	9·50	

The perforated stamps ceased to be used for postal purposes in July 1885, but were used as fiscals to at least the mid-1920s. Other varieties exist, but they must either be fiscals or reprints, and it is not quite certain that all those listed above were issued as early as 1885.

Jind became a Convention State and from 1 July 1885 used overprinted Indian stamps.

KISHANGARH

PRICES FOR STAMPS ON COVER		
Nos. 1/3		—
Nos. 4/91	*from* × 8	
Nos. O1/32	*from* × 30	

GUM. The stamps of Kishangarh were issued without gum, *except for* Nos. 42/50 and O17/24.

Maharaja Sardul Singh, 1879–1900

1

1899–1900. *Medium wove paper. Typo from a plate of 8 (4 × 2).*

1	**1**	1a. green (*imperf*)	22·00	55·00
2		1a. green (*pin-perf*) (1900)	70·00	

1900. *Thin white wove paper. Printed from a single die.* Imperf.

3	**1**	1a. blue	£400	

ILLUSTRATIONS. Types **2** to **10a** are shown actual size.

2 (¼a.)

3 (½a.)

4 (1a.)

5 (2a.) Maharaja Sardul Singh

6 (4a.)

7 (1r.)

8 (2r.)

9 (5r.)

1899 (Sept)**–1901**. *Thin white wove paper.*

(a) Imperf.

4	**2**	¼a. green (1900)	£500	£700
5		¼a. carmine	6·50	
		a. Rose-pink	1·00	2·00
6		¼a. magenta	5·00	5·00
		a. Doubly printed	85·00	
7	**3**	½a. lilac (1900)	£130	£225
8		½a. red (1899)	£2000	£110
9		½a. green (1899)	28·00	32·0
10		½a. pale yellow-olive	42·00	42·0
11		½a. slate-blue (1900)	38·00	38·0
		b. Deep blue	6·50	7·5
		c. Light blue	1·60	1·7
		ca. Pair, one stamp sideways	£1000	
12	**4**	1a. slate	4·50	5·0
		a. Laid paper	45·00	
12*b*		1a. pink	60·00	£17
13		1a. mauve	6·00	5·5
		a. Laid paper	32·00	
14		1a. brown-lilac	1·10	1·0
		a. Laid paper	28·00	
15	**5**	2a. dull orange	4·50	4·5
		a. Laid paper	£475	£42
16	**6**	4a. chocolate	6·00	
		a. Lake-brown	6·00	9·0
		b. Chestnut	6·00	9·0
		c. Laid paper (*shades*)	70·00	70·0
17	**7**	1r. dull green	18·00	30·0
18		1r. brown-lilac	20·00	25·0
19	**8**	2r. brown-red	75·00	£10
		a. Laid paper	60·00	
20	**9**	5r. mauve	70·00	80·0
		a. Laid paper	70·00	

(b) Pin-perf 12½ or 14 *(from Nov 1899).*

21	**2**	¼a. green	£200	£37
		a. Imperf between (pair)	£1000	
22		¼a. carmine	4·50	6·0
		a. Rose-pink	25	4
		ab. *Tête-bêche* (horiz pair)	£850	
		ac. Doubly printed	£100	
		b. Rose		
23		¼a. magenta	5·00	7·0
		a. Bright purple		
		ab. Doubly printed		
24	**3**	½a. green	18·00	23·0
		a. Imperf between (pair)	£160	
25		½a. pale yellow-olive	13·00	16·0
		a. Imperf vert (horiz pair)	£160	
		b. Imperf between (horiz pair)	†	£35
26		½a. deep blue	1·90	3·2
		a. Light blue	85	5
		ab. Doubly printed	£110	£11
27	**4**	1a. slate	4·75	3·2
		a. Laid paper	40·00	20·0
27*b*		1a. pink	70·00	£19
28		1a. mauve	85	1·6
		a. Laid paper	38·00	13·0
29		1a. brown-lilac	75	1·0
		a. Laid paper	35·00	13·0
30	**5**	2a. dull orange	4·00	5·0
		a. Laid paper	£600	
31	**6**	4a. chocolate	2·00	5·5
		a. Lake-brown	2·50	5·5
		b. Chestnut	3·50	6·
		c. Laid paper (*shades*)	55·00	50·
32	**7**	1r. dull green	10·00	15·
		a. Laid paper	80·00	
33		1r. pale olive-yellow	£700	
34	**8**	2r. brown-red	32·00	48·
		a. Laid paper	40·00	
35	**9**	5r. mauve	32·00	48·
		a. Laid paper	60·00	

All the above, both imperf and pin-perf, were printed singl sometimes on paper with spaces marked in pencil. They exist vertical *tête-bêche* pairs imperf between from the centre of the shee *Prices from 3 × normal, unused.* No. 22ab is an error.

FISCAL STAMPS. Many of the following issues were produced different colours for fiscal purposes. Such usage is indicated by th initials "M.C.", punched hole or violet Stamp Office handstamp.

Maharaja Madan Singh, 1900–1926

10 (¼a.)

10a (1r.)

1901. *Toned wove paper.* Pin-perf.

36	**10**	¼a. dull pink	8·00	6·
37	**4**	1a. violet	40·00	27·
38	**10a**	1r. dull green	14·00	16·
36/8		*Set of* 3	55·00	45·

Nos. 36/8 were printed in sheets of 24. Sheets of the 1r. we always torn to remove R. 5/4 where the cliché is believed to ha been defective.

The 1a. (No. 37) differs from T **4** in having an inscription native characters below the words "ONE ANNA".

11 (½a.)

12 Maharaja Sardul Singh

1903. *Litho. Thick white wove glazed paper.* Imperf.

39	**11**	½a. pink	10·00	3
		a. Printed both sides	†	£11
40	**12**	2a. dull yellow	3·00	6

12a (8a.)

4. *Printed singly. Thin paper.* Pin-perf.
12a 8a. grey 5·00 7·50
a. *Tête-bêche* (vert pair) 26·00
b. Doubly printed £120

13 Maharaja Madan Singh

14 Maharaja Madan Singh

(Recess Perkins, Bacon & Co)

4–10. *With gum.* P 12½.
13 ¼a. carmine 45 65
a. Perf 13½ (1910) 65 55
b. Perf 12×12½ 95·00
½a. chestnut 1·75 85
a. Perf 13½ (1906) 75 30
1a. blue 4·25 2·75
a. Perf 13½ (1906) 1·75 1·75
2a. orange-yellow 15·00 7·00
a. Perf 13½ (1907) 18·00 15·00
4a. brown 19·00 18·00
a. Perf 13½ (1907) 14·00 16·00
b. Perf 12 60·00 48·00
8a. violet (1905) 8·00 20·00
1r. green 24·00 35·00
2r. olive-yellow 25·00 £140
5r. purple-brown 23·00 £170
50 *Set of* 9 £100 £325
tamps in other colours, all perforated 13½, were produced by kins Bacon as business samples.

2. *Printed from half-tone blocks. No ornaments to left and right f value in English; large ornaments on either side of value in Hindi. mall stop after "STATE".*

(a) Thin wove paper. Rouletted.
14 2a. deep violet ("TWO ANNA") 3·50 8·00
a. *Tête-bêche* (vert pair) 9·00 30·00
b. Imperf (pair) £375
No. 51 is printed in four rows, each inverted in respect to that ve and below it.

(b) Thick white chalk-surfaced paper. Imperf.
14 2a. lilac ("TWO ANNA") £1400 £650

Thick white chalk-surfaced paper. Rouletted in colour (Medallion only in half-tone).
14 ¼a. ultramarine 16·00 16·00

3. *No ornaments on either side of value in English. Small rnaments in bottom label. With stop after "STATE". Thick white halk-surfaced paper. Rouletted.*
14 2a. purple ("TWO ANNAS") 2·50 5·00

15

पाव आना
No. 59e. This occurs on R. 3/3on one setting only

2 TWO ANNAS 2
No. 60. Small figures

2 TWO ANNAS 2
No. 60b. Large figures

(Typo Diamond Soap Works, Kishangarh)

3 (Aug). *Thick surfaced paper. Half-tone centre. Type-set nscriptions. Rouletted. Inscr* "KISHANGARH".
15 ¼a. pale blue 30 90
a. Imperf (pair) 7·00
b. Roul×imperf (horiz pair) 25·00
ba. Imperf between (horiz pair) 42·00
c. "QUARTER" (R. 4/4) 5·00 7·00
ca. As last, imperf (pair) 28·00
cb. As last, roul×imperf 55·00
d. "KISHANGAHR" (R. 2/3) 5·00 7·00
da. As last, imperf (pair) 28·00
db. As last, roul×imperf 55·00
dc. As last, imperf between (horiz pair) 85·00
e. Character omitted 7·00 7·00
ea. As last, imperf (pair) 32·00
2a. purple 7·00 18·00
a. KISHANGAHR" (R. 2/3) 50·00 90·00
b. Large figures "2" 32·00 55·00

3–16. *Stamps printed far apart, horizontally and vertically, therwise as No. 54, except as noted below.*
14 ¼a. blue 20 45
½a. green (1915) 20 1·00
a. Printed both sides £200
b. Imperf (pair) £150 £150
c. *Emerald-green* (1916) 1·75 4·00

65 1a. red 1·00 2·50
a. Without stop* 1·40 4·75
ab. Imperf (pair) £180
66 2a. purple ("TWO ANNAS") (1915) 6·00 7·00
67 4a. bright blue 6·00 8·00
68 8a. brown 7·00 38·00
69 1r. mauve 16·00 £110
a. Imperf (pair) £275
70 2r. deep green 90·00 £275
71 5r. brown 40·00 £375
63/71 *Set of* 9 £150 £750

*For this issue, ornaments were added on either side of the English value (except in the ¼a.) and the inscription in the right label was without stop, except in the case of No. 65.

In Nos. 70 and 71 the value is expressed as "RUPIES" instead of "RUPEES".

Initial printings of the ¼a., 1a. and 4a. were in sheets of 20 containing two panes of 10 separated by a central gutter margin. Stamps from these sheets measure 20×25½ mm and have heavier screening dots on the perforation margins than on the designs. Subsequent printings of these stamps, and of other values in the set, were from single pane sheets of 20 on which the designs measured 19½×23¾ mm and with the screening dots uniform across the sheet.

Maharaja Yagyanarayan Singh, 1926–1939

16 Maharaja Yagyanarayan Singh

17 Maharaja Yagyanarayan Singh

1928–36. *Thick surfaced paper. Typo.* Pin-perf.
72 16 ¼a. light blue 80 2·00
73 ½a. yellow-green 2·75 1·75
a. *Deep green* 3·00 3·00
ab. Imperf (pair) 90·00 90·00
ac. Imperf between (vert or horiz pair) £110 £110
74 17 1a. carmine 75 1·50
a. Imperf (pair) £170 £110
75 2a. purple 3·00 8·50
75*a* 2a. magenta (1936) 6·00 12·00
ab. Imperf (pair) £275
76 16 4a. chestnut 1·50 1·75
a. Imperf (pair)
77 8a. violet 3·50 26·00
78 1r. light green 15·00 55·00
79 2r. lemon-yellow (1929) 28·00 £180
80 5r. claret (1929) 35·00 £200
a. Imperf (pair) £110
72/80 *Set of* 9 80·00 £425

The 4a. to 5r. are slightly larger than, but otherwise similar to, the ¼a. and ½a. The 8a. has a dotted background covering the whole design.

Maharaja Samar Singh, 1939–1971

1943–47. *As last, but thick, soft, unsurfaced paper. Poor impression. Typo.* Pin-perf.
81 16 ¼a. pale dull blue (1945) 4·25 9·50
a. Imperf (pair) 35·00
82 ¼a. greenish blue (1947) 2·00 8·00
a. Imperf (pair) 28·00
83 ½a. deep green (1944) 1·00 2·25
a. Imperf (pair) 25·00 25·00
b. Imperf between (vert or horiz pair) 45·00
84 ½a. yellow-green (1946) 5·50 8·00
a. Imperf (pair) 30·00 30·00
b. Imperf between (vert or horiz pair) 45·00
85 17 1a. carmine-red (1944) 7·50 3·00
a. Double print £300
b. Imperf (pair) 35·00 35·00
c. Imperf between (vert or horiz pair) 45·00
d. *Red-orange* (1947) 70·00 30·00
da. Imperf (pair) £120 90·00
86 2a. bright magenta 9·00 13·00
a. Imperf (pair) 70·00 75·00
87 2a. maroon (1947) 80·00 16·00
a. Imperf (pair) 48·00 50·00
b. Imperf between (vert or horiz pair) £100
88 16 4a. brown (1944) 25·00 17·00
a. Imperf (pair)
89 8a. violet (1945) 48·00 £130
90 1r. green (1945) 50·00 £140
a. Imperf (pair) £180 £300
90*b* 2r. yellow (date?)
ba. Imperf (pair) £475
91 5r. claret (1945) £550 £600
a. Imperf (pair) £325

OFFICIAL STAMPS

ON
K S
D
(O 1)

1918. *Handstamped with Type* O 1.

(a) Stamps of 1899–1901.

(i) Imperf.
O 1 2 ¼a. green — £160
O 2 ½a. rose-pink — 6·00
a. Pair, one without opt — 75·00
O 3 4 1a. mauve — 55·00
O 3*a* 1a. brown-lilac 45·00 5·50
ab. Pair, one without opt £180 75·00
O 4 6 4a. chocolate — £100

(ii) Pin-perf.
O 5 2 ¼a. green — £120
O 6 ½a. rose-pink 2·25 60
a. Pair, one without opt 85·00 40·00
b. Stamp doubly printed 90·00 60·00
O 7 3 ¼a. light blue £150 38·00
O 8 4 1a. mauve 42·00 1·50
a. Pair, one without opt † £100
O 9 1a. brown-lilac 40·00 1·50
O10 5 2a. dull orange — £130
O11 6 4a. chocolate 50·00 16·00
a. Pair, one without opt — 85·00
O12 7 1r. dull green £150 £100
O13 8 2r. brown-red — £800
O14 9 5r. mauve — £1600

(b) Stamp of 1901.
O14*a* 10a 1r. dull green — £700

(c) Stamps of 1903 and 1904.
O15 12 2a. dull yellow 70·00 5·00
a. Stamp printed both sides † £750
b. Red opt £375 £200
O16 12a 8a. grey 75·00 22·00
a. Red opt — £200

(d) Stamps of 1904–5. P 13½ (¼a. to 4a.) or 12½ (others).
O17 13 ¼a. carmine — £275
O18 ½a. chestnut 75 35
a. Pair, one without opt — 50·00
O19 1a. blue 7·50 4·00
a. Red opt 23·00 7·00
b. Pair, one without opt — 70·00
O20 2a. orange-yellow — £850
O21 4a. brown 55·00 18·00
a. Red opt 70·00 35·00
O22 8a. violet £325 £190
a. Red opt — £200
O23 1r. green £650 £600
a. Red opt — £550
O24 5r. purple-brown

(e) Stamps of 1913.
O25 15 ¼a. pale blue 6·00
a. Imperf (pair) 85·00
b. Roul×imperf (horiz pair) £140
c. "QUARTER" 22·00
ca. As last, imperf (pair) £130
d. "KISHNGAHR" 22·00
da. As last, imperf (pair) £130
e. Character omitted 22·00
ea. As last, imperf (pair) £130
O26 14 2a. purple (No. 54) — 95·00
a. Red opt £140 20·00
O27 15 2a. purple £450 £475
a. "KISHANGAHR" £800
b. Large figures "2" £600 £650

(f) Stamps of 1913–16.
O28 14 ¼a. blue 60 50
a. Red opt 2·00 1·75
O29 ½a. green 90 75
a. Pair, one without opt — 65·00
b. Red opt 3·50 1·60
ba. Pair, one without opt — £130
O30 1a. red 10·00 5·00
a. Without stop (No. 65a) 1·00 1·00
ab. Pair, one without opt £120
ac. Red opt £130 80·00
O31 2a. purple 6·00 4·00
a. Red opt £130 65·00
b. Pair, one without opt — 70·00
O32 4a. bright blue 21·00 15·00
a. Red opt — 30·00
O33 8a. brown £110 40·00
a. Red opt — 85·00
O34 1r. mauve £325 £325
O35 2r. deep green
O36 5r. brown £1500

This overprint is found inverted as often as it is upright; and many other "errors" exist.

Kishangarh became part of Rajasthan by 15 April 1948.

LAS BELA

PRICES FOR STAMPS ON COVER	
Nos. 1/12	*from* × 8

Mir Kamal Khan, 1896–1926

1

2

(Litho Thacker & Co, Bombay)

1897–98. *Thick paper.* P 11½.
1 1 ½a. black on *white* 22·00 15·00

1898–1900. P 11½.
2 1 ½a. black on *greyish blue* (1898) 15·00 8·50
3 ½a. black on *greenish grey* (1899) 13·00 7·50
a. "BFLA" for "BELA" £160
b. Imperf between (horiz strip of 3)

4 ½a. black on *thin white surfaced paper* (1899) . . . . 25·00 40·00
5 ½a. black on *slate* (1900) . . . . 26·00 40·00
a. Imperf between (horiz pair) £850

1901–02. P 11½.
6 **1** ½a. black on *pale grey* . . . . 12·00 8·50
a. "BFLA" for "BELA" £130 £170
7 ½a. black on *pale green* (1902) . . . . 20·00 22·00
8 **2** 1a. black on *orange* . . . . 17·00 19·00

There are at least 14 settings of the above ½a. stamps, the sheets varying from 16 to 30 stamps.

No. 6a occurred on R. 3/2 of the July 1901 printing in sheets of 16 (4 × 4).

1904 (Feb–Nov). *Stamps printed wider apart.* P 11½.
11 **1** ½a. black on *pale blue* . . . . 12·00 7·00
a. Imperf between (pair) £700
b. Imperf between (horiz strip of 3) . . £950
c. Perf 12½ (Nov) . . . . 16·00 9·50
12 ½a. black on *pale green* . . . . 12·00 7·00
c. Perf 12½ (Nov) . . . . 16·00 9·50

There are five plates of the above two stamps, each consisting of 18 (3 × 6) varieties.

All the coloured papers of the ½a. show coloured fibres, similar to those in granite paper.

The stamps of Las Bela have been obsolete since 1 April 1907.

MORVI

PRICES FOR STAMPS ON COVER
Nos. 1/17 *from* × 6
Nos. 18/19 *from* × 3

Thakur (Maharaja from 1926) Lakhdirji, 1922–48

1 Maharaja Lakhdirji

2 Maharaja Lakhdirji

3 Maharaja Lakhdirji

1931 (1 April). *Typo.* P 12.

(a) Printed in blocks of four. Stamps 10 mm apart (Nos. 1/2) or 6¾ mm apart (No. 3). Perf on two or three sides.
1 **1** 3p. deep red . . . . 3·00 15·00
2 ½a. blue . . . . 25·00 38·00
3 2a. yellow-brown . . . . 90·00
1/3 *Set of* 3 . . . . £110

(b) Printed in two blocks of four. Stamps 5½ mm apart. Perf on four sides.
4 **1** 3p. bright scarlet . . . . 6·00 20·00
a. Error. Dull blue . . . . 4·25 20·00
b. Ditto. Double print £600
c. Ditto. Printed on gummed side . . . £600
5 ½a. dull blue . . . . 2·50 13·00
a. Chalk-surfaced paper . . . . 2·75 13·00
6 1a. brown-red . . . . 3·25 23·00
7 2a. yellow-brown . . . . 4·00 32·00
4/7 *Set of* 4 . . . . 14·00 80·00

Nos. 1/3 were supplied to post offices in panes of four sewn into bundles with interleaving.

1932–33. *Horizontal background lines wider apart and portrait smaller than in T* **1**. *Typo.* P 11.
8 **2** 3p. carmine-rose (*shades*) . . . . 3·50 10·00
9 6p. green . . . . 5·50 13·00
a. Imperf between (horiz pair) £1800
b. Emerald-green . . . . 4·00 10·00
10 1a. ultramarine (*to deep*) . . . . 3·25 10·00
a. Imperf between (vert pair) £1400
11 2a. bright violet (1933) . . . . 10·00 30·00
a. Imperf between (vert pair) £1400
8/11 *Set of* 4 . . . . 19·00 55·00

1934. *Typo. London ptg.* P 14.
12 **3** 3p. carmine . . . . 2·25 2·50
13 6p. emerald-green . . . . 1·00 5·00
14 1a. purple-brown . . . . 1·10 10·00
a. Imperf between (horiz pair) . . . . † £1300
15 2a. bright violet . . . . 2·50 21·00
12/15 *Set of* 4 . . . . 6·25 35·00

1935–48. *Typo. Morvi Press ptg.* Rough perf 11.
16 **3** 3p. scarlet (*shades*) . . . . 1·25 3·25
a. Imperf between (horiz pair) £1300
17 6p. grey-green . . . . 75 2·50
a. Emerald-green . . . . 7·00 26·00
b. Yellow-green . . . . 7·00
18 1a. brown . . . . 12·00 14·00
a. Pale yellow-brown . . . . 16·00 26·00
b. Chocolate . . . . 23·00 32·00
19 2a. dull violet (*to deep*) . . . . 2·50 16·00
16/19 *Set of* 4 . . . . 15·00 32·00

Nos. 17*a*, 18*a* and 18*b* were issued between 1944 and 1948.

Maharaja Mahendra Singh, 1948–1957

Morvi was merged with the United State of Kathiawar (later Saurashtra) by 15 April 1948.

NANDGAON

PRICES FOR STAMPS ON COVER
The stamps of Nandgaon are very rare used on cover.

GUM. The stamps of Nandgaon were issued without gum.

Raja Mahant Balram Das, 1883–1897

1

2 (½ a.)

(Litho at Poona)

1891. Imperf.
1 **1** ½a. blue . . . . 5·00 £150
a. Dull blue . . . . 5·50
2 2a. rose . . . . 22·00 £450

The few covers in existence franked with Nos. 1/2 have undated manuscript cancellations, but other forms are known on loose examples.

The state was under Imperial administration from January 1888 to November 1891 and it is possible that Nos. 1/2 may have appeared in late 1887.

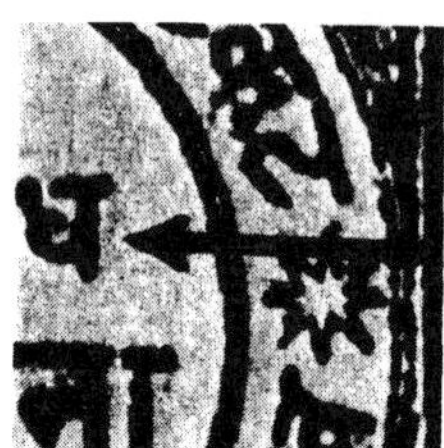
Last character in top line omitted

(Typo Balram Press, Raj-Nandgaon)

1893 (1 Jan)–**94**. *Printed in sheets of 16 (4 × 4).* Imperf.

(a) Stamps printed wide apart (8 to 10 mm) without wavy lines between them. Thin, toned wove paper.
3 **2** ½a. dull *to* deep green . . . . 11·00 75·00
4 2a. red . . . . 9·50 75·00
b. Dull rose . . . . 9·50 75·00

(b) Stamps printed closer together (4 to 7 mm) with wavy lines between them. Thin, white wove paper (1894).
5 **2** ½a. green . . . . 23·00 60·00
a. Last character in top line omitted (R. 4/3) . . . . 90·00
6 1a. rose . . . . 48·00 £110
ba. Laid paper £200

There were three settings of Type **2** with a number of separate printings made from the third:
Setting I - Nos. 3, 4, 4a, 4*b*, O2
Setting II - Nos. 5, 5b, 6, 6a, 6b
Setting III - Nos. 5, 6ba, O3, O3*a*, O4, O4a, O5 and subsequent reprints.

The same clichés were used for all values with the face value inscriptions changed. These exist in two different sizes with both occurring on the ½a., the small on the 1a. and the large on the 2a. except for No. O5 which has the small type.

The ordinary postage stamps of Nandgaon became obsolete on 1 July 1894.

OFFICIAL STAMPS

(O **1**)("M.B.D." = Mahant Balram Das)

1893. *Handstamped with ruler's initials in oval. Type O* **1**, *in purple.*
O1 **1** ½a. blue £350
O2 2a. rose £750

1894. *Handstamped with Type O* **1** *in purple.*

(a) Stamps printed wide apart (8 to 10 mm) without wavy lines between them. Thin, toned wove paper.
O2*a* **2** ½a. dull green £500
O3 2a. red . . . . 24·00 £120

(b) Stamps printed closer together (4 to 7 mm) with wavy lines between them. Thin, white wove paper.
O4 **2** ½a. yellow-green . . . . 5·50 9·50
a. Sage-green . . . . 7·00
O5 1a. rose (*shades*) . . . . 8·50 32·00
a. Thin laid paper . . . . 10·00 80·00
O6 2a. rose (*shades*) . . . . 8·00 20·00

Further printings took place in 1895 after the Official stamps were withdrawn from postal use on 31 December 1894. These were all on thin, white wove paper with the ½a. and 2a. in slightly different shades and the 1a. in brown or ultramarine.

There is a forgery of the handstamp, Type O **1**, which shows 8 mm between the two ornaments below the initials instead of the normal 4 mm.

NAWANAGAR

PRICES FOR STAMPS ON COVER
No. 1 *from* × 20
No. 2 *from* × 8
Nos. 3/4 *from* × 2
No. 5 —
Nos. 6/12 —
Nos. 13/15 *from* × 100
Nos. 16/18 —

GUM. The stamps of Nawanagar were issued without gum.

Jam Vibhaji 1882–1895

1 (1 docra)

2 (2 docra)

3 (3 docra)

1877. *Typo in sheets of 32 (4 × 8 or 8 × 4). Laid paper.*

(a) Imperf.
1 **1** 1doc. blue (*shades*) 50 2
a. *Tête-bêche* (pair) £1000
b. Doubly printed . . . . 85·00

(b) Perf 12½ (line).
2 **1** 1doc. slate-blue . . . . 70·00 £
a. Perf 11 (harrow) . . . . 75·00
ab. *Tête-bêche* (pair) £1300

The inverted clichés which cause the *tête-bêche* pairs come f different settings and occur on R. 3/2 (No. 1a) or R. 4/4 (No. of sheets of 32 (4 × 8).

1877. *T* **2** *and* **3**. *Type-set in black. Wove paper. Thick horizontal vertical frame lines. Stamp 19 mm wide.*
3 1doc. *deep mauve* . . . . £3000 £
a. Stamp 14½-15 mm wide . . . . † £
b. Stamp 16 mm wide . . . . † £
4 2doc. *green* £3000 £1
5 3doc. *yellow* £3000 £1

1880. *As last, but thin frame lines, as illustrated. Stamp 15 to 18 wide.*
6 1doc. *deep mauve* . . . . 3·00
a. On rose . . . . 3·00
ab. Stamp 14 mm wide . . . . 3·00
7 1doc. *magenta* (*stamp* 14 *mm wide*) . . . . 3·00
8 2doc. *yellow-green* . . . . 3·75 1
a. On blue-green . . . . 7·00
b. Error. Yellow £325
c. Stamp 14 mm wide . . . . 3·75
ca. On blue-green . . . . 8·50
9 3doc. *orange-yellow* . . . . 9·50
a. On yellow . . . . 4·25 1
ab. On laid paper . . . . 90·00
b. Stamp 14 mm wide. *On yellow* . . . . 5·00 1
ba. On laid paper . . . . 42·00

There are several different settings of each value of this serie

No. 8b occurs in the sheet of the 3 doc. value from one set only.

4 (1 docra)

1893. *Typo in sheets of 36.* P 12.

(a) Thick paper.
10 **4** 1doc. black . . . . 2·75
a. Imperf (pair) £500
11 3doc. orange . . . . 3·00

(b) Thick laid paper.
12 **4** 1doc. black £550

(c) Thin wove paper.
13 **4** 1doc. black *to* grey . . . . 1·25
a. Imperf between (pair) £450
b. Imperf (pair) £425
c. Imperf horiz (vert pair) £600
d. Imperf between (horiz strip of 6) £1200
14 2doc. green . . . . 1·40
a. Imperf (pair) £475
b. Imperf between (vert pair) £500
15 3doc. orange-yellow . . . . 1·50
a. Imperf between (pair) £500
b. Orange . . . . 1·40
ba. Imperf (pair) £475
bb. Imperf vert (horiz pair) £500
bc. Imperf between (horiz pair) £500

(d) Thin, soft wove paper.
16 **4** 1doc. black
17 2doc. deep green . . . . 3·00
18 3doc. brown-orange . . . . 4·00

Cancellations for postal purposes were intaglio seals, applie black. Other forms of cancellation were only used on remainde

The stamps of Nawanagar became obsolete on 1 January 18

NEPAL

Nepal being an independent state, its stamps will be found li in Part 21 (*South-East Asia*) of this catalogue.

ORCHHA

PRICES FOR STAMPS ON COVER	
Nos. 1/2	—
Nos. 3/7	*from* × 8
Nos. 8/30	*from* × 50
Nos. 31/45	*from* × 4

A set of four stamps, ½a. red, 1a. violet, 2a. yellow and 4a. deep lue-green, in a design similar to T **2**, was prepared in 1897 with tate authority but not put into use. These exist both imperforate nd pin-perforated. (*Price for set of* 4, £16 *unused or c.t.o.*)

Maharaja Partab Singh, 1874–1930

1

2

(T **1/2** litho Shri Pratap Prabhakar)

913. *Background to arms unshaded, Very blurred impression. Wove paper. No gum.* Imperf.

1	½a. green		32·00	90·00
	1a. red		20·00	£160

914–35. *Background shaded with short horizontal lines. Clearer impression. Wove paper. No gum.* Imperf.

2	½a. bright ultramarine	1·75	4·00
	a. Grey-blue	40	3·75
	b. Deep blue	1·60	3·50
	ba. Laid paper	£600	
	½a. green (*shades*)	55	4·75
	a. Dull green	1·50	5·00
	b. Apple-green	2·25	4·50
	1a. scarlet	2·50	7·00
	a. Laid paper	—	£400
	b. Indian red	1·75	10·00
	c. Carmine	2·50	5·50
	ca. Laid paper (1935)	£200	£250
	2a. red-brown (1916)	4·50	23·00
	a. Light brown	11·00	23·00
	b. Chestnut	19·00	24·00
	4a. ochre (1917)	10·00	32·00
	a. Yellow-orange	8·00	32·00
	b. Yellow	8·50	29·00
7 *Set of* 5		13·50	60·00

There are two sizes of T **2** in the setting of 8 (4 × 2). In each value amps from the upper row are slightly taller than those from the wer.

Maharaja Vir Singh II, 1930–1956

3 Maharaja Vir Singh II

4 Maharaja Vir Singh II

(Typo Lakshmi Art Ptg Wks, Bombay)

35 (1 Apr). *Thick, chalk-surfaced wove paper.* P 9½, 10, 10 × 9½, 11, 11 × 9½, 11½, 11½ × 11, 11½ × 12, 12 *or* 12 × 11.

3	¼a. purple and slate	1·60	3·00
	a. Imperf between (vert pair)		
	b. Ordinary paper	50	2·50
	ba. Imperf between (vert pair)	11·00	
	bb. Imperf vert (horiz pair)	65·00	
	bc. Imperf horiz (vert pair)	65·00	
	½a. olive-grey and emerald	50	1·75
	a. Imperf (pair)	75·00	
	¾a. magenta and deep myrtle-green	50	1·75
	a. Imperf (pair)	75·00	
	1a. myrtle-green and purple-brown	50	1·75
	a. Imperf (pair)	65·00	75·00
	b. Imperf horiz (vert pair)		
	c. Imperf vert (horiz pair)		
	1¼a. slate and mauve	45	1·75
	a. Imperf (pair)	75·00	£250
	b. Imperf between (horiz pair)	75·00	
	c. Frame doubly printed	75·00	
	1½a. brown and scarlet	45	1·75
	a. Imperf between (vert pair)	75·00	
	b. Imperf between (horiz pair)	75·00	
	2a. blue and red-orange	45	1·75
	a. Imperf (pair)	13·00	
	b. Imperf between (horiz pair)	75·00	
	2½a. olive-brown and dull orange	65	1·90
	a. Imperf (pair)	13·00	
	b. Imperf between (horiz pair)	75·00	
	3a. bright blue and magenta	65	1·90
	a. Imperf between (horiz pair)	75·00	£110
	b. Imperf (pair)	75·00	
	4a. deep reddish purple and sage-green	65	3·75
	a. Imperf (pair)	9·00	
	b. Imperf between (vert pair)	75·00	
	c. Imperf vert (horiz pair)	75·00	
	6a. black and pale ochre	70	3·75
	a. Imperf (pair)	9·00	

19		8a. brown and purple	2·25	4·75
		a. Imperf (pair)	9·00	
		b. Imperf between (vert pair)	85·00	
20		12a. bright emerald and bright purple	1·00	4·75
		a. Imperf (pair)	9·00	
		b. Imperf between (vert pair)	85·00	
21		12a. pale greenish blue and bright purple	26·00	65·00
22		1r. chocolate and myrtle-green	80	5·50
		a. Imperf (pair)	9·50	
		b. Imperf between (horiz pair)	75·00	
23	4	1r. chocolate and myrtle-green	8·00	20·00
		a. Imperf (pair)	85·00	
		b. Imperf between (horiz pair)	£100	
24	3	2r. purple-brown and bistre-yellow	2·75	14·00
		a. Imperf (pair)	9·50	
25		3r. black and greenish blue	1·50	14·00
		a. Imperf (pair)	9·50	
26		4r. black and brown	2·75	16·00
		a. Imperf (pair)	9·50	
27		5r. bright blue and plum	3·00	17·00
		a. Imperf (pair)	9·50	
28		10r. bronze-green and cerise	7·00	24·00
		a. Imperf (pair)	13·00	
		b. Imperf between (horiz pair)	95·00	
29		15r. black and bronze-green	12·00	55·00
		a. Imperf (pair)	13·00	
30		25r. red-orange and blue	16·00	65·00
		a. Imperf (pair)	16·00	
8/20, 22/30 *Set of* 22			55·00	£225

Values to 5r. except the 1a., are inscribed "POSTAGE", and the remaining values "POSTAGE & REVENUE".

The central portrait of Type **3** is taken from a half-tone block and consists of large square dots. The portrait of Type **4** has a background of lines.

Owing to a lack of proper State control considerable quantities of these stamps circulated at below face value and the issue was subsequently withdrawn, supplies being exchanged for the 1939–42 issue. We are, however, now satisfied that the lower values at least did genuine postal duty until 1939.

Used prices are for stamps cancelled-to-order, postally used examples being worth considerably more.

5 Maharaja Vir Singh II

6 Maharaja Vir Singh II

(Litho Indian Security Printing Press, Nasik)

1939–42?. P 13½ × 14 (T **5**) *or* 14 × 13½ (T **6**).

31	5	¼a. chocolate	3·75	65·00
32		½a. yellow-green	3·75	50·00
33		¾a. bright blue	4·25	85·00
34		1a. scarlet	3·75	17·00
35		1¼a. blue	3·75	85·00
36		1½a. mauve	4·00	£100
37		2a. vermilion	3·75	65·00
38		2½a. turquoise-green	4·25	£180
39		3a. slate-violet	5·50	95·00
40		4a. slate	7·00	25·00
41		8a. magenta	11·00	£180
42	6	1r. grey-green	19·00	
43		2r. bright violet	40·00	£475
44		5r. yellow-orange	£120	
45		10r. turquoise-green (1942)	£450	
46		15r. slate-lilac (date ?)	£9000	
47		25r. claret (date ?)	£6500	

Orchha became part of Vindhya Pradesh by 1 May 1948.

POONCH

PRICES FOR STAMPS ON COVER	
No. 1	*from* × 3
Nos. 1*a*/2	*from* × 2
Nos. 3/63	*from* × 10
Nos. O1/10	*from* × 30

Poonch was ruled by a junior branch of the Jammu and Kashmir princely family and by treaty, was subject to the "advice and consent" of the Maharaja of that state.

The Poonch postal service operated an office at Kahuta in the Punjab which acted as the office of exchange between the state post and that of British India.

GUM. The stamps of Poonch were issued without gum, except for some examples of Nos. 7/10.

The stamps of Poonch are all imperforate, and handstamped in watercolours.

ILLUSTRATIONS. Designs of Poonch are illustrated actual size.

Raja Moti Singh, 1852–1892

1

2

1876. *T* **1** *(22 × 21 mm). Central face value in circle and five rosettes in outer frame. Yellowish white, wove paper.*

1	6p. red	£10000	£130

1877. *As T* **1** *(19 × 17 mm). Central face value in oval and two rosettes in outer frame. Same paper.*

1*a*	½a. red	£11000	£4000

1879. *T* **2** *(21 × 19 mm). Central face value in oval and one rosette in outer frame. Same paper.*

2	½a. red	—	£4000

3 (½a.)

4 (1a.)

5 (2a.)

6 (4a.)

1880. *Yellowish white, wove paper.*

3	3	½a. red	38·00	16·00
4	4	1a. red	90·00	50·00
5	5	2a. red	£160	£100
6	6	4a. red	£170	£120

1884. *Toned wove bâtonné paper.*

7	3	½a. red	4·25	4·25
8	4	1a. red	19·00	
9	5	2a. red	18·00	21·00
10	6	4a. red	35·00	35·00

These are sometimes found gummed.

7 (1 pice)

1884–87. *Various papers.*

(a) White laid bâtonné or ribbed bâtonné.

No.	Type	Description	Unused	Used
11	**7**	1p. red	18·00	20·00
		a. Pair, one stamp sideways	£200	
12	**3**	½a. red	2·50	3·25
		a. *Tête-bêche* (pair)	£2250	
13	**4**	1a. red	3·25	
		a. Pair, one stamp sideways	£1100	
14	**5**	2a. red	8·00	9·50
15	**6**	4a. red	10·00	

(b) Thick white laid paper.

No.	Type	Description	Unused	Used
22	**7**	1p. red	55·00	
23	**3**	½a. red	65·00	
24	**4**	1a. red	70·00	
25	**5**	2a. red	70·00	
26	**6**	4a. red	85·00	

(c) Yellow wove bâtonné.

No.	Type	Description	Unused	Used
27	**7**	1p. red	3·50	3·50
		a. Pair, one stamp sideways	35·00	
28	**3**	½a. red	4·00	5·00
29	**4**	1a. red	40·00	
30	**5**	2a. red	7·50	9·50
31	**6**	4a. red	4·00	4·25

(d) Orange-buff wove bâtonné.

No.	Type	Description	Unused	Used
32	**7**	1p. red	2·50	3·00
		a. Pair, one stamp sideways	25·00	30·00
		b. *Tête-bêche* (pair)	40·00	
33	**3**	½a. red	22·00	
34	**5**	2a. red	80·00	
35	**6**	4a. red	19·00	

(e) Yellow laid paper.

No.	Type	Description	Unused	Used
36	**7**	1p. red	2·00	3·25
		a. Pair, one stamp sideways	18·00	
		b. *Tête-bêche* (pair)	26·00	
37	**3**	½a. red	3·25	
38	**4**	1a. red	40·00	
39	**5**	2a. red	48·00	48·00
40	**6**	4a. red	38·00	

(f) Yellow laid bâtonné.

No.	Type	Description	Unused	Used
41	**7**	1p. red	10·00	8·00

(g) Buff laid or ribbed bâtonné paper thicker than (d).

No.	Type	Description	Unused	Used
42	**4**	1a. red	60·00	
43	**6**	4a. red	65·00	

(h) Blue-green laid paper (1887).

No.	Type	Description	Unused	Used
44	**3**	½a. red	35·00	
45	**4**	1a. red	2·75	4·50
46	**5**	2a. red	30·00	
47	**6**	4a. red	55·00	

(i) Yellow-green laid paper.

No.	Type	Description	Unused	Used
48	**3**	½a. red		

(j) Blue-green wove bâtonné.

No.	Type	Description	Unused	Used
49	**7**	1p. red	40·00	38·00
49*a*	**3**	½a. red	£1000	
50	**4**	1a. red	2·00	3·25

(k) Lavender wove bâtonné.

No.	Type	Description	Unused	Used
51	**4**	1a. red	70·00	
52	**5**	2a. red	2·25	3·25
		a. Pair, one stamp sideways	£2250	

(l) Blue wove bâtonné.

No.	Type	Description	Unused	Used
53	**7**	1p. red	2·50	2·25
		a. Pair, one stamp sideways	25·00	35·00
		b. *Tête-bêche* (pair)	38·00	
54	**4**	1a. red	£350	

(m) Various coloured papers.

No.	Type	Description	Unused	Used
55	**7**	1p. red/*grey-blue laid*	8·00	4·50
56		1p. red/*lilac laid*	45·00	48·00
		a. Pair, one stamp sideways	£300	£300
		b. *Tête-bêche* (pair)	£275	

1888. *Printed in aniline rose on various papers.*

No.	Type	Description	Unused	Used
57	**7**	1p. on *blue wove bâtonné*	4·50	
		a. *Tête-bêche* (pair)	75·00	
58		1p. on *buff laid*	13·00	
		a. *Tête-bêche* (pair)	£110	
59	**3**	½a. on *white laid*	20·00	
60	**4**	1a. on *green laid*	14·00	16·00
61		1a. on *green wove bâtonné*	8·50	8·50
62	**5**	2a. on *lavender wove bâtonné*	7·50	7·50
63	**6**	4a. on *yellow laid*	14·00	16·00
		a. Pair, one stamp sideways	£700	
		b. *Tête-bêche* (pair)	£700	

OFFICIAL STAMPS

Raja Baldeo Singh, 1892–1918

1887.

(a) White laid batonné paper.

No.	Type	Description	Unused	Used
O 1	**7**	1p. black	2·25	2·50
		a. Pair, one stamp sideways	13·00	16·00
		b. *Tête-bêche* (pair)	16·00	
O 2	**3**	½a. black	2·75	3·50
O 3	**4**	1a. black	2·50	2·75
O 4	**5**	2a. black	3·75	3·75
O 5	**6**	4a. black	6·00	9·50

(b) White or toned wove bâtonné paper.

No.	Type	Description	Unused	Used
O 6	**7**	1p. black	2·25	
		a. Pair, one stamp sideways	27·00	
		b. *Tête-bêche* (pair)	38·00	
O 7	**3**	½a. black	2·75	3·25
		a. Pair, one stamp sideways	£1600	
O 8	**4**	1a. black	15·00	14·00
O 9	**5**	2a. black	6·50	6·50
O10	**6**	4a. black	10·00	

RAJASTHAN

Rajasthan was formed in 1948–49 from a number of States in Rajputana; these included Bundi, Jaipur and Kishangarh, whose posts continued to function more or less separately until ordered by the Indian Government to close on 1 April 1950.

PRICES FOR STAMPS ON COVER	
Nos. 1/7	*from* × 15
Nos. 8/10	—
Nos. 11/12	*from* × 5
Nos. 13/14	—
Nos. 15/25	*from* × 4
Nos. 26/42	*from* × 3
No. 43	*from* × 5
Nos. 44/60	*from* × 3
No. 61	*from* × 5
Nos. 62/5	—

BUNDI

सं॰ रा॰
सरकार

(1)

1948–49. *Nos. 86/92 of Bundi. (a) Handstamped with T* **1**.

A. *In black.* B. *In violet.* C. *In blue.*

No.	Description	A	B	C
1	¼a. blue-green	5·50	5·50	29·00
	a. Pair, one without opt	£275	†	†
2	½a. violet	5·00	4·00	35·00
	a. Pair, one without opt	£300	£275	†
3	1a. yellow-green	4·75	12·00	38·00
	a. Pair, one without opt	†	£275	†
4	2a. vermilion	10·00	25·00	—
5	4a. orange	38·00	28·00	90·00
6	8a. ultramarine	5·50	8·00	60·00
7	1r. chocolate	—	£190	75·00

The above prices are for unused, used stamps being worth about six times the unused prices. Most of these handstamps are known, sideways, inverted or double.

(b) Machine-printed as T **1** *in black.*

No.	Description	Unused	Used
8	¼a. blue-green		
9	½a. violet		
10	1a. yellow-green		
11	2a. vermilion	6·00	70·00
	a. Opt inverted	£250	
12	4a. orange	3·00	70·00
	a. Opt double	£225	
13	8a. ultramarine	20·00	
	a. Opt inverted	£500	
	b. Opt double	£375	
14	1r. chocolate	7·50	

JAIPUR

राजस्थान

RAJASTHAN

(2)

1950 (26 Jan). *T* **7** *of Jaipur optd with T* **2**.

No.	Description	Unused	Used
15	¼a. black and brown-lake (No. 58) (B.)	5·50	17·00
16	½a. black and violet (No. 41) (R.)	4·00	18·00
17	¾a. black and brown-red (No. 59) (Blue-blk.)	8·00	21·00
	a. Opt in pale blue	14·00	35·00
18	1a. black and blue (No. 60) (R.)	4·50	38·00
19	2a. black and buff (No. 61) (R.)	8·00	48·00
20	2½a. black and carmine (No. 62) (B.)	8·50	24·00
21	3a. black and green (No. 63) (R.)	9·50	55·00
22	4a. black and grey-green (No. 64) (R.)	9·00	65·00
23	6a. black and pale blue (No. 65*a*) (R.)	9·50	90·00
24	8a. black and chocolate (No. 66) (R.)	15·00	£130
25	1r. black and yellow-bistre (No. 67) (R.)	18·00	£180
15/25	*Set of* 11	90·00	£600

KISHANGARH

1948 (Oct)–**49**. *Various stamps of Kishangarh handstamped with T* **1** *in red.*

(a) On stamps of 1899–1901.

No.	Type	Description	Unused	Used
26		¼a. rose-pink (No. 5*a*) (B.)	£190	
26*a*		¼a. rose-pink (No. 22*a*)	—	£180
27		½a. deep blue (No. 26)	£350	
29		1a. brown-lilac (No. 29)	14·00	38·00
		b. Imperf (pair)	40·00	80·00
		c. Violet handstamp	—	£300
		d. Black handstamp	—	£350
30		4a. chocolate (No. 31)	70·00	90·00
		a. Violet handstamp	—	£425
31		1r. dull green (No. 32)	£225	£250
31*a*		2r. brown-red (No. 34)	£300	
32		5r. mauve (No. 35)	£275	£275

(b) On stamps of 1904–10.

No.	Type	Description	Unused	Used
33	**13**	½a. chestnut	—	£130
33*a*		1a. blue	—	£170
34		4a. brown	13·00	
		a. Blue handstamp	£200	
35	**12a**	8a. grey	90·00	£140
36	**13**	8a. violet	11·00	
37		1r. green	12·00	
38		2r. olive-yellow	19·00	
39		5r. purple-brown	26·00	
		a. Blue handstamp	£375	

(c) On stamps of 1912–16.

No.	Type	Description	Unused	Used
40	**14**	½a. green (No. 64)	—	£180
41		1a. red	—	£180
42		2a. deep violet (No. 51)	£350	
43		2a. purple (No. 66)	3·00	7·50
44		4a. bright blue	—	£425
45		8a. brown	5·00	
		a. Pair, one without handstamp	£350	
46		1r. mauve	10·00	
47		2r. deep green	10·00	
48		5r. brown	£325	

(d) On stamps of 1928–36.

No.	Type	Description	Unused	Used
49	**16**	½a. yellow-green	£120	
49*a*		2a. magenta	—	£32
50		4a. chestnut	£180	
51		8a. violet	6·00	50·0
		a. Pair, one without handstamp	£325	
52		1r. light green	21·00	
53		2r. lemon-yellow	16·00	
54		5r. claret	16·00	

(e) On stamps of 1943–47.

No.	Type	Description	Unused	Used
55	**16**	¼a. pale dull blue	85·00	85·0
56		¼a. greenish blue	42·00	42·0
		a. Imperf (pair)	£190	
57		½a. deep green	28·00	30·0
		a. Violet handstamp	—	£17
57*b*		½a. yellow-green	38·00	40·0
		ba. Imperf (pair)	£190	
		bb. Blue handstamp	—	£16
58	**17**	1a. carmine-red	50·00	50·0
		a. Violet handstamp	—	£19
58*b*		1a. orange-red (*imperf*)	£130	
		ba. Blue handstamp	£140	
59		2a. bright magenta	£140	£14
60		2a. maroon (*imperf*)	£160	
61	**16**	4a. brown	2·50	7·5
62		8a. violet	15·00	50·0
63		1r. green	6·50	
64		2r. yellow	90·00	
65		5r. claret	50·00	

A 1a. value in deep violet-blue was issued for revenue purposes but is known postally used (*Price* £70 *used*).

RAJPIPLA

PRICES FOR STAMPS ON COVER	
No. 1	*from* × 30
Nos. 2/3	—

Maharana Ganbhir Singh, 1860–1897

The Rajpipla state post was opened to the public sometime in th late 1870s. Adhesive stamps were preceded by postal stationer lettersheets which were first reported in 1879.

1 (1 pice) **2** (2a.) **3** (4a.)

1880. *Litho. With or without gum (1p.) or no gum (others).* P 1 (1p.) or 12½.

No.	Type	Description	Unused	Used
1	**1**	1p. blue (1 June)	3·00	30·
2	**2**	2a. green	25·00	85·
		a. Imperf between (pair)	£550	£5
3	**3**	4a. red	13·00	55·
1/3		*Set of* 3	38·00	£1

No. 1 was produced in sheets of 64 (8 × 8) and the higher valu in sheets of 20 (5 × 4).

These stamps became obsolete in 1886 when the Imperial post service absorbed the Rajpipla state post.

SHAHPURA

PRICES FOR STAMPS ON COVER	
Nos. 1/4	*from* × 2
No. F1	*from* × 2

DATES. Those quoted are of first known use.

Rajadhiraj Nahar Singh, 1870–1932

RAJ SHAHPURA Postage 1 pice
1

RAJ SHAHPURA 1 pice
2

1914–17. *Typo.*

No.	Type	Description	Unused	Used
1	**1**	1p. carmine/*bluish grey* (P 11)	—	£5
2		1p. carmine/*drab* (*imperf*) (1917)	—	£8

Some examples of No. 1 are imperforate on one side or on tv adjacent sides.

1920–28. *Typo.* Imperf.

No.	Type	Description	Unused	Used
3	**2**	1p. carmine/*drab* (1928)	—	£11
4		1a. black/*pink*	—	£13

POSTAL FISCAL

Rajadhiraj Umaid Singh, 1932–1947

Rajadhiraj Sudarshan Deo, 1947–1971

F 1

1932–47. *Typo.* P 11, 11½ or 12.

No.	Type	Description	Unused	Used
F1	**F 1**	1a. red (*shades*)	70·00	£2
		a. Pin-perf 7 (1947)		

Nos. F1/a were used for both fiscal and postal purposes. nuscript cancellations must be assumed to be fiscal, unless on er showing other evidence of postal use. The design was first ed for fiscal purposes in 1898.

hahpura became part of Rajasthan by 15 April 1948.

SIRMOOR

PRICES FOR STAMPS ON COVER
The stamps of Sirmoor are very rare used on cover.

Raja Shamsher Parkash, 1886–1898

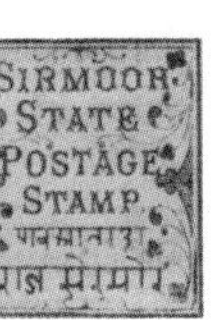

1 (1 pice)

2

3 Raja Shamsher Parkash

8 (June)–**80**. *Litho*. P 11½.

1	1	1p. pale green	12·00	£250
		1p. blue (on *laid* paper) (1880)	4·00	£150
		a. Imperf between (pair)	£325	
		b. Imperf (pair)	£325	

(Litho at Calcutta)

2. *Thick wove paper*. P 11½.

	2	1p. yellow-green	85	90
		a. Imperf between (vert pair)	70·00	
		b. Deep green	75	75
		ba. Imperf between (vert pair)	70·00	70·00
		1p. blue	80	80
		a. Imperf between (vert pair)	60·00	60·00
		b. Imperf between (horiz pair)	60·00	60·00
		c. Imperf vert (horiz pair)	60·00	
		d. Imperf (pair)	75·00	

These were originally made as reprints, about 1891, to supply lectors, but there being very little demand for them they were put o use. The design was copied (including the perforations) from illustration in a dealer's catalogue.

A

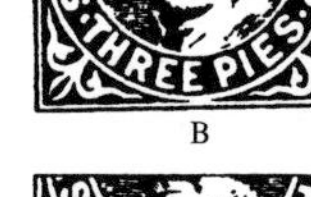

B

C

D

There were seven printings of stamps as Type **3**, all in sheets of (10 × 7) and made up from groups of transfers which can be ced through minor varieties.

Printings I to V and VII of the 3p. and 6p. are as Types A and both with large white dots evenly spaced between the ends of the per and lower inscriptions).

Printing VI is as Type B (small white dots and less space) and pe D (large white dots unevenly positioned between the criptions).

(Litho Waterlow)

85–96. P 14 to 15.

	3	3p. chocolate (A)	55	30
		a. Brown (B) (1896)	30	35
		3p. orange (A) (1888)	1·50	20
		a. Type B (1896)	30	20
		ab. Imperf (pair)	£550	
		6p. blue-green (C)	4·25	3·00
		a. Green (C) (1888)	95	50
		b. Bright green (C) (1891)	60·00	60·00
		c. Deep green (C) (1894)	60	35
		d. Yellowish green (D) (1896)	40	1·50
		1a. bright blue	2·50	3·00
		a. Dull blue (1891)	7·00	4·50
		b. Steel-blue (1891)	85·00	85·00
		c. Grey-blue (1894)	2·25	1·00
		d. Slate-blue (1896)	50	2·00
		2a. pink	4·25	11·00
		a. Carmine (1894)	3·50	3·00
		b. Rose-red (1896)	3·25	4·00

Composition of the various printings was as follows:

Printing I	—	Nos. 5, 7, 8 and 9
Printing II	—	Nos. 6 and 7*a*
Printing III	—	Nos. 6, 7*b* and 8*a*
Printing IV	—	Nos. 5, 6, 7*a*, and 8*b*
Printing V	—	Nos. 6, 7*c*, 8*c* and 9*a*
Printing VI	—	Nos. 5*a*, 6a, 7*d*, 8*d* and 9*b*
Printing VII	—	Only exists overprinted "On S. S. S." (Nos. 78/81).

4 Indian Elephant

5 Raja Shamsher Parkash

(Recess Waterlow & Sons)

1894–99. P 12 to 15 and compounds.

22	4	3p. orange-brown	2·50	30
23		6p. green	75	30
		a. Imperf between (vert pair)	£1500	
24		1a. blue	4·00	1·60
25		2a. rose	2·50	1·00
26		3a. yellow-green	19·00	35·00
27		4a. deep green	11·00	19·00
28		8a. deep blue	15·00	24·00
29		1r. vermilion	30·00	55·00
22/9		*Set of* 8	75·00	£120

Raja Surindra Bikram Parkash, 1898–1911

(Recess Waterlow & Sons)

1899. P 13 to 15.

30	5	3a. yellow-green	2·50	22·00
31		4a. deep green	3·50	17·00
32		8a. deep blue	5·50	13·00
33		1r. vermilion	9·00	40·00
30/3		*Set of* 4	18·00	85·00

OFFICIAL STAMPS

NOTE. The varieties occurring in the machine-printed "On S.S.S." overprints may, of course, also be found in the inverted and double overprints, and many of them are known thus.

Roman figures denote printings of the basic stamps (Nos. 7/21). Where more than one printing was overprinted the prices quoted are for the commonest.

I. MACHINE-PRINTED

On
S. S.
S.
(11)

1890. *Optd with T* **11**.

(a) In black.

50	3	6p. green (C)	£950	£950
		a. Stop before first "S"		
51		2a. pink	55·00	£150
		a. Stop before first "S"	£140	

(b) In red.

52	3	6p. green (C)	19·00	2·50
		a. Stop before first "S"	55·00	25·00
53		1a. bright blue	45·00	13·00
		a. Stop before first "S"	£120	60·00
		b. Opt inverted	£1100	£600

(c) Doubly optd in red and in black.

53*c*	3	6p. green (C)	£950	£950
		ca. Stop before first "S"	£2250	£2250

Nos. 50, 52 and 53*c* are from Printing II and the remainder from Printing I.

On
S. S.
S.
(12)

On
S. S.
S.
(13)

1891. *Optd with T* **12**.

(a) In black.

54	3	3p. orange (A)	2·50	35·00
		a. Opt inverted	£425	
55		6p. green (C)	1·50	1·50
		a. Opt double	£170	
		b. No stop after lower "S"	22·00	22·00
		c. Raised stop before lower "S"	£150	£110
56		1a. bright blue	£325	£400
57		2a. pink	14·00	55·00

(b) In red.

58	3	6p. green (C)	27·00	3·00
		a. Opt inverted	£200	£170
		b. Opt double	£200	£180
59		1a. bright blue	22·00	28·00
		a. Opt inverted	†	£500
		b. Opt double	†	£500
		c. No stop after lower "S"	£170	£180

(c) In black and red.

59*d*	3	6p. green (C)	£1000	

Nos. 54/5, 58 and 59*d* are from Printing II and the others from Printing I.

1892–97. *Optd with T* **13**.

(a) In black.

60	3	3p. orange (A)	60	50
		a. Type B	3·00	60
		b. Opt inverted	£225	
		c. First "S" inverted and stop raised	5·00	5·00
		d. No stop after lower "S"	5·00	5·00
		e. Raised stop after second "S"	35·00	16·00
		f. Vertical pair, Types **12** and **13**	£130	
61		6p. green (C)	6·00	1·40
		a. Deep green (C)	1·60	50
		b. First "S" inverted and stop raised	35·00	15·00
		c. Raised stop after second "S"	35·00	13·00
		d. No stop after lower "S"	45·00	18·00
		e. Opt double	£550	
62		1a. steel-blue		
		a. Grey-blue	9·00	1·00
		b. Opt double	£375	
		c. First "S" inverted and stop raised	35·00	10·00
		d. No stop after lower "S"	£150	55·00
		e. Raised stop after second "S"	60·00	12·00
63		2a. pink	11·00	17·00
		a. Carmine	7·00	7·00
		b. Opt inverted	£750	£750
		c. First "S" inverted and stop raised	35·00	35·00
		d. No stop after lower "S"	35·00	35·00
		e. Raised stop after second "S"	£150	£150

(b) In red.

64	3	6p. green (C)	4·00	50
		a. Bright green (C)	8·50	1·00
		b. Opt inverted	£120	95·00
		c. First "S" inverted and stop raised	21·00	5·00
		d. Vertical pair, Types **12** and **13**	£130	£130
65		1a. bright blue	16·00	3·25
		a. Steel-blue	11·00	1·00
		b. Opt inverted	£250	£180
		c. Opt double	£300	
		d. First "S" inverted and stop raised	35·00	8·00
		e. No stop after lower "S"	35·00	8·00

(c) Doubly overprinted in black and red.

65*f*	3	6p. bright green (C)	—	£950
		fa. Green (C). Red opt inverted	†	£1400

The printings used for this issue were as follows:

Printing I	—	Nos. 63 and 65
Printing II	—	Nos. 60, 64 and 65*fa*
Printing III	—	Nos. 60, 64*a* and 65*f*
Printing IV	—	Nos. 61, 62, 64 and 65*a*
Printing V	—	Nos. 60, 61*a*, 62*a* and 63*a*
Printing VI	—	No. 60a

There are seven settings of this overprint, the first of which was a composite setting of 20 (10 × 2), with examples of Type **12** in the upper row. The inverted "S" and the missing stop occur in the 3rd and 6th settings with the latter also including the raised stop after second "S".

On
S. S.
S.
(14)

On
S. S.
S.
(15)

1896–97. *Optd as T* **14**.

66	3	3p. orange (B) (1897)	10·00	1·25
		a. Comma after first "S"	48·00	30·00
		b. Opt inverted		
		c. Opt double	†	£550
67		6p. deep green (C)	5·50	60
		a. Yellowish green (D)	—	2·75
		b. Comma after first "S"	45·00	18·00
		c. Comma after lower "S"	£160	20·00
		d. "S" at right inverted	£160	42·00
68		1a. grey-blue	7·00	1·25
		a. Comma after first "S"	60·00	22·00
		b. Comma after lower "S"	£180	24·00
		c. "S" at right inverted	—	45·00
69		2a. carmine (1897)	17·00	14·00
		a. Comma after first "S"	£120	£120

Nos. 66 and 67*a* are from Printing VI and the remainder from Printing V.

There are four settings of this overprint, (1) 23 mm high, includes the comma after lower "S"; (2) and (3) 25 mm high, with variety, comma after first "S"; (4) 25 mm high, with variety, "S" at right inverted.

1898 (Nov). *Optd with T* **15**.

70	3	6p. deep green (C)	£180	8·00
		a. Yellowish green (D)	£170	6·50
		b. Small "S" at right	£300	25·00
		c. Comma after lower "S"	—	50·00
		d. Lower "S" inverted and stop raised	—	50·00
71		1a. grey-blue	£190	15·00
		a. Small "S" at right	£325	40·00
		b. Small "S" without stop	—	£180

No. 70*a* is from Printing VI and the others Printing V.

There are two settings of this overprint. Nos. 70b and 71a/b occur in the first setting, and Nos. 70c/d in the second setting.

On
S. S.
S.
(16)

On
S. S.
S.
(17)

1899 (July). *Optd with T* **16**.
72 **3** 3p. orange (B) . . . . £250 6·50
73 6p. deep green (C) . . . . — 21·00
No. 72 is from Printing VI and No. 73 from Printing V.

1899 (Dec)–**1900**. *Optd as T* **17**.
74 **3** 3p. orange (B) . . . . — 7·00
a. Raised stop after lower "S" . . . . † 60·00
b. Comma after first "S" . . . . † £200
c. No stop after first "S" . . . . † £120
75 6p. deep green (C) . . . . — 6·50
a. Yellowish green (D) . . . . † 7·50
b. Raised stop after lower "S" . . . . † 60·00
c. Comma after first "S" . . . . † £190
76 1a. bright blue . . . . † £150
a. Grey-blue . . . . † 9·00
b. Slate-blue . . . . — 11·00
c. Raised stop after lower "S" . . . . † 90·00
d. Comma after first "S" . . . . † £225
e. No stop after first "S" . . . . † £130
77 2a. carmine . . . . — £120
a. Raised stop after lower "S" . . . . † £450

There are two settings of this overprint: (1) 22 mm high, with raised stop variety; (2) 23 mm high, with "comma" and "no stop" varieties.

The printings used for this issue were as follows:
Printing I — No. 76
Printing V — Nos. 75, 76*a* and 77
Printing VI — Nos. 74, 75*a* and 76*b*

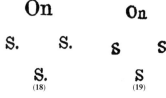

On S. S. S. (18) — On S S S (19)

(Optd by Waterlow & Sons)

1900. *Optd with T* **18**.
78 **3** 3p. orange . . . . 3·00 7·00
79 6p. green 50 45
80 1a. blue 35 60
81 2a. carmine . . . . 3·25 60·00
Nos. 78/81 were from Printing VII which was not issued without the overprint.

II. HANDSTAMPED

The words "On" and each letter "S" struck separately (except for Type **22** which was applied at one operation).

1894. *Handstamped with T* **19**.
(a) In black.
82 **3** 3p. orange (A) . . . . 3·00 3·75
a. "On" only . . . . 65·00
83 6p. green (C) . . . . 5·00 6·00
a. Deep green (C) . . . . 10·00 13·00
b. "On" only . . . . 65·00 65·00
84 1a. bright blue . . . . 48·00 38·00
a. Dull blue . . . . 17·00 18·00
b. Steel-blue
c. Grey-blue . . . . 17·00 16·00
d. "On" only . . . . — 90·00
85 2a. carmine . . . . 18·00 18·00
a. "On" only £100
(b) In red.
86 **3** 6p. green (C) £110 £120
86*a* 1a. grey-blue £375 £375

The printings used for this issue were as follows:
Printing I — No. 84
Printing III — No. 84*a*
Printing IV — Nos. 83, 84*b* and 86
Printing V — Nos. 82, 83*a*, 84*c*, 85 and 86*a*

1896. *Handstamped with letters similar to those of T* **13**, *with stops, but irregular.*
87 **3** 3p. orange (A) . . . . 80·00 65·00
a. Type B
88 6p. green (C)
a. Deep green (C) . . . . 70·00 60·00
b. "On" omitted £140
88*c* 1a. grey-blue . . . . 95·00 95·00
89 2a. carmine £180

Printings used for this issue were as follows:
Printing II — No. 88
Printing III — No. 87
Printing IV — No. 88
Printing V — Nos. 87, 88*a*, 88*c* and 89
Printing VI — No. 87*a*

1897. *Handstamped with letters similar to those of T* **14**, *with stops, but irregular.*
90 **3** 3p. orange (B) . . . . 9·00 18·00
91 6p. deep green (C) . . . . 55·00 65·00
a. "On" only . . . . — £100
92 1a. grey-blue £275 £275
a. "On" only . . . . — £100
93 2a. carmine £110 £110
No. 90 was from Printing VI and the remainder from Printing V.

1897. *Handstamped with letters similar to those of T* **16**, *with stops, but irregular.*
93*a* **3** 6p. deep green (C) £150 £120
No. 93a is from Printing V.

ON S S S (20) — On S S S (21)

1896.
(a) Handstamped with T **20**.
94 **3** 3p. orange (A) . . . . 60·00 65·00
95 2a. carmine . . . . 65·00 70·00
(b) Handstamped with T **21**.
96 **3** 3p. orange (A) £150 £160
97 6p. bright green (C)
98 1a. bright blue £250
a. Dull blue
98*b* 2a. carmine £275
No. 98 comes from Printing 1, No. 98*a* from Printing III, No. 97 possibly from Printing IV and the remainder from Printing V.

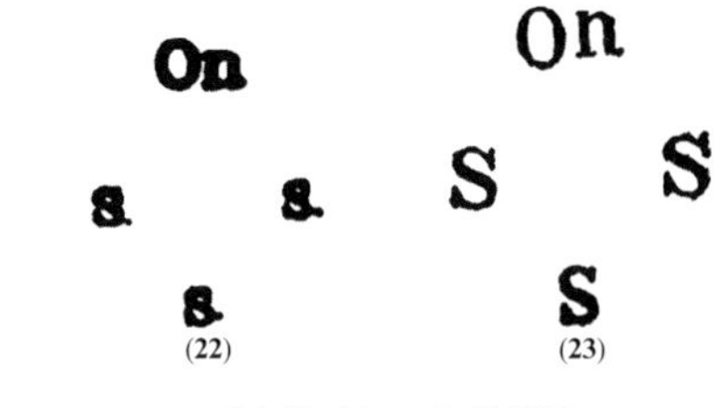
(22) (23)

(c) Handstamped with T **22**.
99 **3** 3p. orange (B) £120
100 6p. deep green £180
101 1a. grey-blue £225
101*a* 2a. carmine £350
No. 99 is from Printing VI and the others from Printing V.

1899. *Handstamped with T* **23**.
102 **3** 3p. orange (A) . . . . — £160
a. Type B . . . . 21·00 7·00
103 6p. green (C)
a. Deep green (C) . . . . 24·00 16·00
b. Yellowish green (D) . . . . 15·00 16·00
104 1a. bright blue . . . . — £110
a. Grey-blue . . . . 45·00 40·00
105 2a. pink
a. Carmine . . . . 48·00 24·00
b. Rose-red . . . . 60·00 40·00
c. "On" only . . . . — £130

Printings used for this issue were as follows:
Printing I — Nos. 104 and 105
Printing IV — Nos. 102 and 103
Printing V — Nos. 102, 103*a*, 104*a* and 105*a*
Printing VI — Nos. 102a, 103*b* and 105*b*

On S S S (24)

1901 (?). *Handstamped with T* **24**.
105*d* **3** 6p. yellowish green (D) . . . . — £375
From Printing VI.

III. MIXED MACHINE-PRINTED AND HANDSTAMPED

1896.
(i) Handstamped "On" as in T **19**, *and machine-printed opt T* **13** *complete.*
106 **3** 6p. green (C) . . . . — £475
(ii) Handstamped opt as T **14**, *and machine-printed opt T* **13** *complete.*
107 **3** 6p. deep green (C)
No.106 is from Printing IV and No. 107 from Printing V.
Various other types of these handstamps are known to exist, but in the absence of evidence of their authenticity we do not list them. It is stated that stamps of T **4** were never officially overprinted.

The stamps of Sirmoor have been obsolete since 1 April 1902.

SORUTH

PRICES FOR STAMPS ON COVER

Nos.	1/2	*from* × 5
Nos.	4/4*a*	—
Nos.	5/8	*from* × 1
No.	8*a*	*from* × 3
No.	9	*from* × 1
Nos.	10/11	*from* × 5
No.	11*e*	*from* × 1
No.	12	*from* × 4
No.	13	*from* × 5
Nos.	14/15	*from* × 3
Nos.	16/24	*from* × 20
Nos.	33/6	*from* × 50
Nos.	37/8	*from* × 10
No.	40/1	*from* × 50
Nos.	42/57	*from* × 10
Nos.	O1/13	*from* × 20
No.	58	*from* × 15
No.	59	*from* × 6
No.	60	*from* × 10
No.	61	*from* × 6
Nos.	O14/22	*from* × 10

The name "Saurashtra", corrupted to "Sorath" or "Soruth", was originally used for all the territory later known as Kathiawar. Strictly speaking the name should have been applied only to a portion of Kathiawar including the state of Junagadh. As collectors have known these issues under the heading of "Soruth" for so long, we retain the name.

GUM. Nos. 1/47 of Soruth were issued without gum.

JUNAGADH

Nawab Mahabat Khan II, 1851–1882

(Currency 40 dokras or 16 annas = 1 koree)

1 (= "Saurashtra Post 1864–65")

1864 (Nov). *Handstamped in water-colour.* Imperf.
1 **1** (1a.) black/*azure to grey* (laid) . . . . £650 65·0
2 (1a.) black/*azure to grey* (wove) . . . . — £16
4 (1a.) black/*cream* (laid) . . . . † £130
4*a* (1a.) black/*cream* (wove) . . . . — £75

ILLUSTRATIONS. Types **2** to **11** are shown actual size.

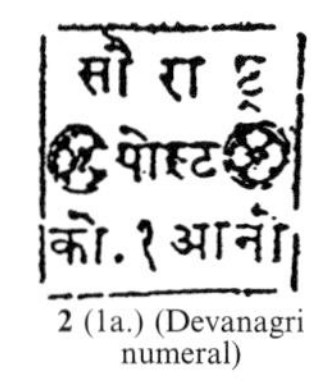
2 (1a.) (Devanagri numeral)

3 (1a.) (Gujarati numeral)

4 (4a.) (Devanagri numeral)

5 (4a.) (Gujarati numeral)

Differences in first character of bottom line on Nos. 8/*a*:

Type A "u" (error) — Type B "ka" (correct)

(Typeset Nitiprakash Ptg Press, Junagadh)

1868 (June)–**75**. *Designs as T* **2** *to* **5**. Imperf.
A. Inscriptions in Gujarati characters. Wove paper.
5 1a. black/*yellowish* . . . . † £80
B. Inscriptions in Devanagri characters (as in the illustrations).
I Accents over first letters in top and bottom lines. Wove paper.
6 1a. red/*green* . . . . † £25
7 1a. red/*blue* . . . . † £25
7*a* 1a. red/*yellow* . . . . † £40
8 1a. black/*pink* (first character in bottom line as Type A) . . . . † £11
8*a* 1a. black/*pink* (first character in bottom line as Type B) £850 £1
9 2a. black/*yellow* (1869) . . . . † £40
II. Accents over second letters in top and bottom lines.
(a) Wove paper.
10 **2** 1a. black/*pink* (1869) . . . . £450 60·
a. Printed both sides . . . . †
b. First two characters in last word of bottom line omitted (R. 4/1) . . . . — £6
(b) Laid paper.
11 **2** 1a. black/*azure* (1870) . . . . 70·00 8·
a. Final character in both top and bottom lines omitted (R. 1/1) . . . . — £1
b. First two characters in last word of bottom line omitted (R. 4/1) . . . . — £1
c. Doubly printed . . . . † £7
d. *Se-tenant* pair. Nos. 11/12 . . . . £325 £1
11*e* 1a. black/*white* . . . . † £35
12 **3** 1a. black/*azure* (1870) . . . . £180 18·
a. Printed both sides . . . . † £8
b. Final character in bottom line omitted (R. 1/1) £475 £1
c. Accent omitted from last word in bottom line (R. 5/2, 5/4) . . . . — 90·
d. Large numeral (R. 4/1) £600 £1
e. First character in middle line omitted (R. 2/4) . . . . — £3
f. Central two characters in middle line omitted (R. 2/4) . . . . — £4
13 1a. red/*white* (1875) . . . . 18·00 19·
a. First two characters in bottom line omitted (R. 5/1) . . . . 90·00 £1

14 5 4a. black/*white* £200 £375
a. First two characters in last word of bottom line omitted (R. 4/1) . . . £950
b. Final character in bottom line omitted (R. 5/2) £1900
15 4 4a. black/*white* £110 £180
a. Final character in bottom line omitted (R. 1/1) £475

The settings of Nos. 5/7 are unknown.
Nos. 10/15, and probably Nos. 8/9, were printed in sheets of 20 (4 × 5). The same type was used throughout, but changes occurred as the loose type was amended.
Specialists now recognise four main settings for the 1a., one of which was amended for the 2a. and another for the 4a. There are sub-settings within some of these groups:

1a. Setting I (pink wove paper) (No. 8)
Setting II (pink wove paper) (No. 8*a*)
Setting III (pink wove paper) (No. 10)
Setting IV (Devanagri numerals only) (pink wove paper) (Nos. 10/b)
Setting IVA (Devanagri numerals only) (azure vertical laid paper) (Nos. 11, 11b)
Setting IVB (Devanagri and Gujarati numerals mixed) (azure horizontal laid paper) (Nos. 11/a, 11d, 12)
Setting IVC (Devanagri and Gujarati numerals mixed) (azure or white vertical laid paper) (Nos. 11, 11c/d, 11*e*, 12/b 12e/f)
Setting IVD (Devanagri and Gujarati numerals mixed) (azure vertical laid paper) (Nos. 11, 11d, 12, 12d)
Setting IVE (Gujarati numerals only) (white vertical laid paper) (Nos. 13/a)
2a. Setting I (probably derived from 1a. Setting II) (yellow wove paper) (No. 9)
4a. Setting IA (Gujarati numerals only) (white vertical laid paper) (Nos. 14/a)
Setting IB (Devanagri numerals only) (white horizontal laid paper) (No. 15)
Setting IC (Devanagri numerals only) (white vertical laid paper) (Nos. 15/a)
Setting ID (only Gujarati numerals so far identified) (white vertical laid paper) (Nos. 14, 14b)

Settings IVA/D of the 1a. were subsequently adapted to form settings IA/D of the 4a.
The two known examples of No. 8 both come from the top row of the sheet. Marginal inscriptions indicate that No. 8*a* is from a separate setting.
Official imitations, consisting of 1a. carmine-red on white wove and white laid, 1a. black on blue wove, 4a. black on white wove, 4a. black on blue wove, 4a. red on white laid—all imperforate; 1a. carmine-red on white laid, 1a. black on blue wove, 4a. black on white laid and blue wove—all perforated 12, were made in 1890. Entire sheets of originals have 20 stamps (4 × 5), the imitations only 4 or 16.

6

7

(Typo Nitiprakash Ptg Press, Junagadh)

1878 (16 Jan)–86. *Laid paper with the lines wide apart.* Imperf
16 6 1a. green 75 30
a. Printed both sides £475 £500
b. Laid lines close together (1886) . . . 75 30
17 7 4a. vermilion . . . . . 2·25 1·60
a. Printed both sides £550
b. Scarlet/bluish . . . . 3·25 2·75
18 4a. brown . . . . . 11·00

Nawab Bahadur Khan III, 1882–1892

1886. P 12. *(a) On toned laid paper with the lines close together.*
19 6 1a. green 40 15
a. Imperf vert (horiz pair) £110
b. Imperf between (vert pair) . . . † £275
c. Imperf horiz (vert pair) . . . † £275
d. Doubly printed . . . . † £425
e. Error. Blue £600 £600
f. On bluish white laid paper . . . 3·00 4·00
fa. Imperf between (vert pair) . . . £170 £190
fb. Imperf vert (horiz pair) . . . £170
g. Emerald-green . . . . 2·75 1·50
20 7 4a. red . . . . . 1·50 75
a. On bluish white laid paper . . . 9·00 14·00
ab. Printed both sides . . . £325
b. Carmine . . . . 3·25 2·50
4a. brown . . . . . 8·50

(b) Wove paper.
6 1a. green . . . . . 2·25 75
a. Imperf (pair) . . . . 65·00 85·00
b. Error. Blue . . . . — £600
c. Imperf horiz (vert pair) . . . £130
7 4a. red . . . . . 3·75 9·00
a. Imperf (pair) £170 £200
b. Imperf between (horiz pair) . . . £300
c. Imperf vert (horiz pair) . . . £300
4a. brown . . . . . 14·00

There is a very wide range of colours in both values. The laid paper, on which imperforate printings continued to appear until 1912, is found both vertical and horizontal.
The 1a. was originally issued in sheets of 15 (5 × 3), but later appeared in sheets of 20 (5 × 4) with marginal inscriptions. Stamps were sometimes printed in double sheets showing two impressions of the plate printed *tête-bêche* on the same or opposite sides of the paper.
The 4a. was in horizontal strips of 5. No. 20 exists as a sheet of 10 (5 × 2), with two impressions of the plate printed *tête-bêche*, and No. 23 in a similar sized sheet but with both impressions upright.

Nawab Rasul Khan 1892–1911
Nawab Mahabat Khan III, 1911–1959

(Indian currency)

Three pies. ત્રણ પાઈ. (8)

One anna. એક આનો. (9)

1913 (1 Jan). *Surch in Indian currency with T* **8** *or* **9**. P 12.

(a) On toned wove paper.
33 6 3p.on 1a. emerald-green 15 20
a. Imperf (pair) £350
b. Imperf between (horiz pair) . . . £325
c. Imperf vert (horiz pair) . . . £325
d. Doubly printed £200
34 7 1a.on 4a. red . . . . . 2·00 5·50
a. Imperf (pair) £600
b. Capital "A" in "Anna" . . . 6·00
c. Surch inverted £700
d. Imperf between (horiz pair) . . .

(b) On white wove paper.
35 6 3p.on 1a. emerald-green 15 20
a. Imperf between vert (pair) . . . £450
b. Surch inverted . . . . 35·00 20·00
c. Surch double . . . . † —
36 7 1a.on 4a. carmine . . . . 1·75 5·50
a. Imperf (pair) . . . .
b. Surch both sides £750
c. Capital "A" in "Anna" . . . 13·00

(c) On white laid paper.
37 6 3p.on 1a. emerald-green . . . . 75·00 30·00
a. Imperf (pair) . . . . — £425
b. Larger English surch (21 mm long with capital "p" in "Pies") inverted . . . . † £1700
38 7 1a.on 4a. red . . . . . 7·50 45·00
a. Capital "A" in "Anna" . . . £275
b. Surch inverted £700
c. Surch double £700
d. Surch double, one inverted . . . £700

The 1a. surcharge with capital "A" in "Anna" comes from a separate setting.

10

11

(Dies eng Thacker & Co, Bombay. Typo Junagadh State Press)

1914 (1 Sept). *New plates. T* **6/7** *redrawn as T* **10/11**. *Wove paper.* P 12.
40 10 3p. green 85 35
a. Imperf (pair) . . . . 6·50 20·00
b. Imperf vert (horiz pair) . . . 80·00
c. Laid paper . . . . 3·00 1·50
ca. Imperf (pair) . . . . 16·00 30·00
d. Error. Red (imperf) . . . . † £1900
41 11 1a. red . . . . . 1·00 1·60
a. Imperf (pair) . . . . 20·00 75·00
b. Imperf horiz (vert pair) . . . £425
c. Laid paper £250 £110

12 Nawab Mahabat Khan III

13 Nawab Mahabat Khan III

(Dies eng Popatlal Bhimji Pandya. Typo Junagadh State Press)

1923 (1 Sept). *Blurred impression. Laid paper.* Pin-perf 12.
42 12 1a. red . . . . . 3·00 8·00
Sheets of 16 stamps (8 × 2).
This setting was later printed on wove paper, but single examples cannot readily be distinguished from No. 46b.

ત્રણ પાઇ (14)

ત્રણ પાઈ (14a)

1923 (1 Sept). *Surch with T* **14**.
43 12 3p.on 1a. red . . . . . 4·00 7·00
a. Surch with T **14***a* . . . . 4·75 12·00
Four stamps in the setting have surch. T **14***a*, i.e. with top of last character curved to right.

1923 (Oct). *Blurred impression. Wove paper.* Pin-perf 12, small holes.
44 13 3p. mauve 35 45
Sheets of 16 (4 × 4).

1924. *Clear impression. Wove paper.* P 12, large holes.
45 13 3p. mauve (1.24) . . . . 1·75 35
46 12 1a. red (4.24) . . . . 6·50 7·00
a. Imperf (pair) . . . . 50·00
b. Pin perf . . . . 3·50 3·75

The first plate of the 3p., which printed No. 44, produced unsatisfactory impressions, so it was replaced by a second plate, producing two panes of 16 (4 × 4), from which No. 45 comes. Sheets printed from the first plate had very large margins.
The 1a. is also from a new plate, giving a clearer impression. Sheets of 16 stamps (4 × 4).

1929. *Clear impressions. Laid paper.* P 12, large holes.
47 13 3p. mauve . . . . . 4·75 3·75
a. Imperf (pair) . . . . 3·25 30·00
b. Perf 11 . . . . . 9·50 7·50
ba. Imperf between (horiz pair) . . . 3·00 25·00
Sheets of two panes of 16 (4 × 4).
The laid paper shows several sheet watermarks.
No. 47ba was intentional to create a 6p. franking required by a rate change in October 1929.

15 Junagadh City

16 Gir Lion

17 Nawab Mahabat Khan III

18 Kathi Horse

(Des Amir Sheikh Mahamadbhai. Litho Indian Security Printing Press, Nasik)

1929 (1 Oct). *Inscr "POSTAGE".* P 14.
49 15 3p. black and blackish green . . . 90 10
50 16 ½a. black and deep blue . . . 5·50 10
51 17 1a. black and carmine . . . 5·00 1·00
52 18 2a. black and dull orange . . . 12·00 1·90
a. Grey and dull yellow . . . 27·00 1·90
53 15 3a. black and carmine . . . 5·00 8·50
54 16 4a. black and purple . . . 13·00 23·00
55 18 8a. black and yellow-green . . . 10·00 22·00
56 17 1r. black and pale blue . . . 7·00 23·00
49/56 *Set of* 8 . . . . . 50·00 70·00

1935 (1 Jan). *As T* **17**, *but inscr* "POSTAGE AND REVENUE". P 14.
57 17 1a. black and carmine . . . . 6·00 1·00

OFFICIAL STAMPS

SARKARI
(O 1)

1929 (1 Oct). *Optd with Type* O **1**, *in vermilion, at Nasik.*
O1 15 3p. black and blackish green . . . 1·25 15
a. Red opt . . . . 1·00 10
O2 16 ½a. black and deep blue . . . 2·50 10
a. Red opt . . . . 3·50 40
O3 17 1a. black and carmine (No. 51) . . 3·25 35
a. Red opt . . . . 2·25 15
O4 18 2a. black and dull orange . . . 2·50 1·00
a. Grey and dull yellow . . . 19·00 60
b. Red opt . . . . 24·00 2·75
O5 15 3a. black and carmine . . . 75 30
a. Red opt . . . . 16·00 1·50
O6 16 4a. black and purple . . . 3·00 45
a. Red opt . . . . 20·00 2·50
O7 18 8a. black and yellow-green . . . 3·00 2·50
O8 17 1r. black and pale blue . . . 2·50 18·00
O1/8 *Set of* 8 . . . . . 16·00 20·00

SARKARI
(O 2)

SARKARI
(O 3)

1932 (Jan)–**35**. *Optd with Type* O **2**, *in red, at Junagadh State Press.*
O 9 15 3a. black and carmine . . . 21·00 17·00
a. Optd with Type O **3** (1.35) . . 85·00 7·00
O10 16 4a. black and purple . . . 27·00 16·00
O11 18 8a. black and yellow-green . . . 30·00 18·00
O12 17 1r. black and pale blue . . . 25·00 80·00
a. Optd with Type O **3** (1.35) . . £130 £120
O9/12 *Set of* 4 . . . . . 90·00 £115

1938. *No. 57 optd with Type* O **1**, *in vermilion.*
O13 17 1a. black and carmine . . . 15·00 2·25
a. Brown-red opt . . . . 12·00 1·50

The state was occupied by Indian troops on 9 November 1947 following the flight of the Nawab to Pakistan.

UNITED STATE OF SAURASHTRA

The administration of Junagadh state was assumed by the Government of India on 9 November 1947. An Executive Council took office on 1 June 1948.
Under the new Constitution of India the United State of Saurashtra was formed on 15 February 1948, comprising 221 former states and estates of Kathiawar, including Jasdan, Morvi, Nawanagar and Wadhwan, but excluding Junagadh. A referendum was held by the Executive Council of Junagadh which then joined the United State on 20 January 1949. It is believed that the following issues were only used in Junagadh.
The following issues were surcharged at the Junagadh State Press.

POSTAGE & REVENUE

ONE ANNA
(19)

Postage & Revenue

ONE ANNA
(20)

1949. *Stamps of 1929 surch.*

(a) With T **19** *in red.*

58 **16** 1a.on ½a. black and deep blue (5.49) . . 9·50 4·75
a. Surch double . . . . † £450
b. "AFNA" for "ANNA" and inverted "N" in "REVENUE" £2000
c. Larger first "A" in "ANNA" (R. 2/5) . . . . 80·00 60·00

(b) With T **20** *in green.*

59 **18** 1a.on 2a. grey and dull yellow (2.49) 12·00 22·00
a. "evenue" omitted . . . . . . — £550

No. 58b may have occurred on R. 2/5 with No. 58c being caused by its correction.

A number of other varieties occur on No. 58, including: small "V" in "REVENUE" (R. 2/3); small "N" in "REVENUE" (R. 2/4, 3/4); small "E" in "POSTAGE" (R. 3/2); thick "A" in "POSTAGE" (R. 4/4); inverted "N" in "REVENUE" and small second "A" in "ANNA" (R. 4/5); small "O" in "ONE" (R. 5/1); small "V" and "U" in "REVENUE" (R. 6/3); small "N" in "ONE" (R. 7/2).

In No. 59 no stop after "ANNA" is known on R. 1/4, 4/2, 7/4 and 8/3 and small "N" in "ONE" on R. 2/4.

21

(Typo Waterlow)

1949 (Sept). *Court Fee stamps of Bhavnagar state optd "SAURASHTRA" and further optd "U.S.S. REVENUE & POSTAGE" as in T* **21**, *in black.* P 11.

60 **21** 1a. purple . . . . 10·00 9·50
a. "POSTAGE" omitted (R. 1/2) . . . £275 £190
b. Opt double £250 £300

The Court Fee stamps were in sheets of 80 (8 × 10) and were overprinted in a setting of 40 applied twice to each sheet.

Minor varieties include small "S" in "POSTAGE" (R. 2/1 of the setting); small "N" in "REVENUE" (R. 2/7); small "U" in "REVENUE" (R. 3/2); small "V" in "REVENUE" (R. 3/8, 5/5); and small O" in "POSTAGE" (R. 4/7).

Various missing stop varieties also occur.

POSTAGE & REVENUE
ONE ANNA
(22)

1950 (2 Mar). *Stamp of 1929 surch with T* **22**.

61 **15** 1a.on 3p. black and blackish green . . 40·00 55·00
a. "P" of "POSTAGE" omitted (R. 8/1) £500 £600
b. "O" of "ONE" omitted (R. 6/1) . . £750

Other minor varieties include small second "A" in "ANNA" (R. 1/2); small "S" in "POSTAGE" with small "V" in "REVENUE" (R. 3/4, 6/1) and small "V" in "REVENUE" (R. 2/3, 3/1).

OFFICIAL STAMPS

1948 (July–Dec). *Nos. O4/O7 surch "ONE ANNA" (2¼ mm high) by Junagadh State Press.*

O14 **18** 1a.on 2a. grey & dull yellow (B.) . . £7500 25·00
O15 **15** 1a.on 3a. black and carmine (Aug) £2000 60·00
a. Surch double . . . . † £2500
O16 **16** 1a.on 4a. black and purple (Dec) . . £325 50·00
a. "ANNE" for "ANNA" (R. 5/4) £2250 £375
b. "ANNN" for "ANNA" (R. 7/5) £2250 £375
O17 **18** 1a.on 8a. black & yellow-green (Dec) . . . . £300 40·00
a. "ANNE" for "ANNA" (R. 5/4) £2250 £275
b. "ANNN" for "ANNA" (R. 7/5) £2250 £275

Numerous minor varieties of fount occur in this surcharge.

1948 (Nov). *Handstamped "ONE ANNA" (4 mm high).*

O18 **17** 1a.on 1r. (No. O8) . . . . £1500 40·00
O19 1a.on 1r. (No. O12) . . . . £600 42·00
a. Optd on No. O12a . . . . . . — 70·00

A used copy of No. O12 is known surcharged in black as on Nos. O14/17. This may have come from a proof sheet.

1949 (Jan). *Postage stamps optd with Type O* **2**, *in red.*

O20 **15** 3p. black and blackish green . . . . £250 12·00
O21 **16** ½a. black and deep blue . . . . . . £550 12·00
O22 **18** 1a.on 2a. grey and dull yellow (No. 59) . . . . 75·00 23·00

Various wrong fount letters occur in the above surcharges.

MANUSCRIPT OVERPRINTS. Nos. 49, 50, 57, 58, 59 and 60 are known with manuscript overprints reading "Service" or "SARKARI" (in English or Gujerati script), usually in red. Such provisionals were used at Gadhda and Una between June and December 1949 (*Price from* £100 *each, used on piece*).

The United State of Saurashtra postal service was incorporated into that of India on 30 March 1950.

TRAVANCORE

PRICES FOR STAMPS ON COVER	
Nos. 1/77	*from* × 10
Nos. O1/108	*from* × 15

(16 cash = 1 chuckram; 28 chuckrams = 1 rupee)

"Anchel" or "Anchal" = Post Office Department.

The stamps of Travancore were valid on mail posted to Cochin.

PRINTERS. All stamps of Travancore were printed by the Stamp Manufactory, Trivandrum, *unless otherwise stated.*

PRINTING METHODS. The dies were engraved on brass from which electrotypes were made and locked together in a forme for printing the stamps. As individual electrotypes became worn they were replaced by new ones and their positions in the forme were sometimes changed. This makes it difficult to plate the early issues. From 1901 plates were made which are characterised by a frame (or "Jubilee" line) round the margins of the sheets.

Up to the 6 cash of 1910 the dies were engraved by Dharmalingham Asari.

SHADES. We list only the main groups of shades but there are many others in view of the large number of printings and the use of fugitive inks. Sometimes shade variation is noticeable within the same sheet.

Maharaja Rama Varma X, 1885–1924

1 Conch or Chank Shell

1888 (16 Oct). *As T* **1**, *but each value differs slightly. Laid paper.* P 12.

1 **1** 1ch. ultramarine (*shades*) . . . . 4·25 3·50
2 2ch. red . . . . 4·00 9·50
3 4ch. green . . . . 17·00 14·00
1/3 *Set of* 3 . . . . 23·00 24·00

The paper bears a large sheet watermark showing a large conch shell surmounted by "GOVERNMENT" in large outline letters, in an arch with "OF TRAVANCORE" at foot in a straight line. Many stamps in the sheet are without watermark.

These stamps on laid paper in abnormal colours are proofs.

2

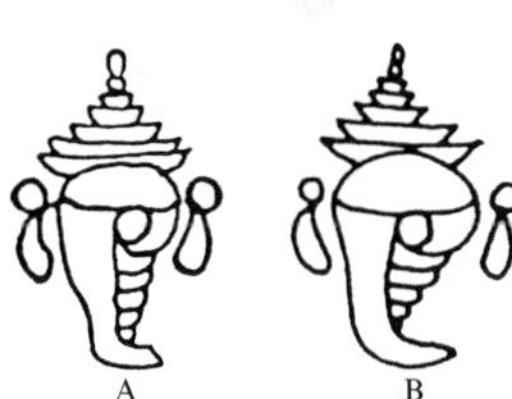
A B C

Three forms of watermark Type **2**.
(*as seen from the back of the stamp*)

WATERMARKS AND PAPERS.

Type A appeared upright on early printings of the 1, 2 and 4ch. values on odd-sized sheets which did not fit the number of shells. Later it was always sideways with 15 mm between the shells on standard-sized sheets of 84 (14 × 6) containing 60 shells (10 × 6). It therefore never appears centred on the stamps and it occurs on hand-made papers only.

Type B is similar in shape but can easily be distinguished as it is invariably upright, with 11 mm between the shells, and is well centred on the stamps. It also occurs only on handmade papers. It was introduced in 1904 and from 1914, when Type A was brought back into use, it was employed concurrently until 1924.

Type C is quite different in shape and occurs on machine-made papers. There are two versions. The first, in use from 1924 to 1939, has 84 shells 11 mm apart and is always upright and well centred. The second, introduced in 1929 and believed not to have been used after 1930, has 60 shells (12 × 5) 15 mm apart and is invariably badly centred so that some stamps in the sheet are without watermark. This second version is normally found upright, but a few sideways watermark varieties are known and listed as Nos. 35g, 37c, O31j and O32i. We do not distinguish between the two versions of Type C in the lists, but stamps known to exist in the second version are indicated in footnotes. The machine-made paper is generally smoother and of more even texture.

NO WATERMARK VARIETIES. Some of these were formerly listed but we have now decided to omit them as they do not occur in full sheets. They arise in the following circumstances: (*a*) on sheets with wmk A; (*b*) on sheets with the wide-spaced form of wmk C and (*c*) on late printings of the pictorial issues of 1939–46. They are best collected in pairs, with and without watermark.

DATES OF ISSUE. In the absence of more definite information the dates voted usually refer to the first reported date of new printings on different watermarks but many were not noted at the time and the dates of these are indicated by a query. Dated postmarks on single stamps are difficult to find.

3 4 5
6 7 8

1889–1904. *Wove paper.* Wmk A (upright or sideways). P 1 (sometimes rough).

4 **1** ½ch. slate-lilac (1894) . . . . 2·25 5
a. Doubly printed . . . . † £22
b. Reddish lilac 60 2
ba. Imperf between (vert pair) £225 £22
bb. Doubly printed . . . . † £22
c. Purple (1899) . . . . 1·25 2
ca. Doubly printed . . . . † £22
d. Dull purple (1904) . . . . . . 1·50 2
5 **5** ¾ch. black (14.3.01) . . . . 3·00 1·C
6 **1** 1ch. ultramarine . . . . 1·50 1
a. *Tête-bêche* (pair) £2000 £20C
b. Doubly printed . . . . † £35
c. Imperf vert (horiz pair) . . . . . † £37
d. Imperf between (vert pair) . . . . † £37
e. Pale ultramarine (1892) . . . . . 2·75 2
f. Violet-blue (1901) . . . . 3·50 4
7 2ch. salmon (1890) . . . . 4·00 1·C
a. Rose (1891) . . . . 3·50 3
ab. Imperf (pair) . . . . † £4C
b. Pale pink (1899) . . . . 3·00 3
ba. Imperf between (vert pair) £150
bb. Doubly printed £200
c. Red (1904) . . . . 3·00
ca. Imperf between (horiz pair) £300 £3C
8 4ch. green . . . . 3·25 7
a. Yellow-green (1901) . . . . . . 2·50 5
b. Dull green (1904) . . . . 6·50 1·(
ba. Doubly printed . . . . † £3

Nos. 6, 6*d*, 7 and 8 occur with the watermark upright ar sideways. No. 7*a* is known only with the watermark upright. Th remainder exist only with the watermark sideways.

The sheet sizes were as follows:

½ch. 56 (14 × 4) except for No. 4*d* which was 84 (14 × 6), initia without border, later with border.

¾ch. 84 (14 × 6) with border.

1ch. No. 6, 80 (10 × 8) and later 84 (14 × 6) without border ar then with border; No. 6*d*, 96 (16 × 6); No. 6*e*, 84 (14 × 6) wi border.

2ch. No. 7, 80 (10 × 8); No. 7*a*, 70 (10 × 7); Nos, 7*b*, 7*c*, (10 × 6).

4ch. No. 8, 60 (10 × 6); Nos. 8*a*/*b*, 84 (14 × 6) with border.

After 1904 all stamps in Types **3** to **8** were in standard-sized shee of 84 (14 × 6) with border.

For later printings watermarked Type A, see Nos. 23/30.

1904–20. Wmk B, upright (centred). P 12, sometimes rough.

9 **3** 4ca. pink (11.08) 30
a. Imperf between (vert pair) £200 £2
10 **1** 6ca. chestnut (2.10) 30
a. Imperf between (horiz pair) . . . † £2
11 ½ch. reddish lilac . . . . 1·10
a. Reddish violet (6.10) . . . . . . 1·00
b. Lilac . . . . 1·25
c. "CHUCRRAM" (R. 5/6) . . . . . 5·50 3·
d. Imperf horiz (vert pair) . . . . . † £1
12 **4** 10ca. pink (1920) . . . . 28·00 5·
13 **5** ¾ch. black . . . . 1·50
14 **1** 1ch. bright blue . . . .
a. Blue . . . . 3·50
b. Deep blue . . . . 3·50
c. Indigo (8.10) 75
d. Chalky blue (1912) . . . . . . 4·00
15 1¼ch. claret (*shades*) (10.14) 55
a. Imperf between (horiz pair) . . . £250 £2
16 2ch. salmon . . . . 18·00 6·
a. Red (8.10) 60
17 **6** 3ch. violet (11.3.11) . . . . 2·75
a. Imperf between (vert pair) £200 £2
b. Imperf between (vert strip of 3) . . † £2
18 **1** 4ch. dull green . . . . 11·00 3·
a. Slate-green . . . . 2·25
19 **7** 7ch. claret (1916) . . . . 2·00
a. Error. Carmine-red . . . . . . — 50
20 **8** 14ch. orange-yellow (1916) . . . . . 2·75 1·
a. Imperf vert (horiz strip of 3) . . . £450

(9)

1 C
(10)

5. *Surch as T* **9**. Wmk B.

1 ¼on ½ch. reddish lilac 40 30
a. Reddish violet 40 20
b. Lilac 60 30
c. "CHUCRRAM" (R. 5/6) 3·50 3·25
d. Surch inverted 48·00 30·00
⅜on ½ch. reddish lilac 20 35
a. Reddish violet 20 35
b. Lilac 20 35
c. "CHUCRRAM" (R. 5/6) 3·25 3·50
d. Surch inverted — 42·00
e. Surch double
f. "8" omitted — 40·00

4–22. Reversion to wmk A (sideways). P 12 (sometimes rough).

3 4ca. pink (1915) 8·00 60
4 5ca. olive-bistre (30.10.21) 80 20
a. Imperf between (horiz pair) 45·00 50·00
b. Imperf between (horiz strip of 3) 90·00 95·00
c. "TRAVANCOPE" — 8·00
1 6ca. orange-brown (2.15) 5·50 40
½ch. reddish violet (12.14) 2·75 40
a. "CHUCRRAM" (R. 5/6) 10·00 3·75
b. Imperf between (horiz pair) £170
4 10ca. pink (26.10.21) 40 10
1 1ch. grey-blue (5.22) 10·00 2·25
a. Deep blue 10·00 2·25
1¼ch. claret (12.19) 11·00 35
a. Imperf between (horiz pair) † £275
6 3ch. reddish lilac (8.22) 12·00 1·50

1 (Mar). *Surch as T* **10**. Wmk A (sideways).

3 1c.on 4ca. pink 15 20
a. Surch inverted 20·00 9·50
b. On wmk B (upright)
1 5c.on 1ch. grey-blue (R.) 1·00 10
a. Deep blue 1·00 10
b. Stamp printed both sides
c. Imperf between (vert pair) † £200
d. Surch inverted 13·00 8·50
e. Surch double 50·00 38·00
f. On wmk B (upright). *Deep blue* 23·00 20·00
fa. Surch inverted † £160

BINO OVERPRINT VARIETIES. Stamps with overprint ıble, one albino are frequently found in the provisional and cial issues of Travancore, and are only worth a small premium r the normal prices.

Maharaja Bala Rama Varma XI, 1924–1971

4–39. Wmk C. *Machine-made paper*. P 12.

4 5ca. olive-bistre (18.6.25) 11·00 2·75
a. Imperf between (horiz pair) £150
b. "TRAVANCOPE" — 13·00
5ca. chocolate (1930) 2·75 20
a. Imperf between (horiz pair) 38·00
b. Imperf between (vert pair) † £150
1 6ca. brown-red (3.24) 4·25 10
a. Imperf between (horiz pair) 23·00 25·00
b. Imperf between (vert pair) £100 £100
c. Printed both sides 50·00
d. Perf 12½ 4·25 50
e. Perf comp of 12 and 12½ 6·00 4·00
f. Perf 12½ × 11 — 90·00
g. Wmk sideways — 18·00
½ch. reddish violet (date?) 4·25 4·25
a. "CHUCRRAM" (R. 5/6) 32·00
4 10ca. pink (8.24) 2·25 10
a. Imperf between (horiz pair) 75·00 75·00
b. Imperf between (vert pair) 23·00 26·00
c. Wmk sideways (16.9.28) — 7·50
5 ¾ch. black (4.10.32) 9·00 50
¾ch. mauve (16.11.32) 35 10
a. Imperf between (horiz pair) † £150
b. Perf 12½ (8.37) 9·50 70
ba. Imperf between (horiz pair) £140
c. Perf comp of 12 and 12½ 15·00 6·00
ca. Imperf between (horiz pair) £170
¾ch. reddish violet (1939) 3·50 70
a. Perf 12½ 4·75 50
b. Perf comp 12 and 12½ 7·50 2·25
c. Perf 11 — 90·00
d. Perf comp of 12 and 11 — 90·00
1 1ch. slate-blue (8.26) 2·75 30
a. Indigo 4·25 20
b. Imperf between (horiz pair) † £200
c. Imperf between (vert pair) † £200
d. Perf 12½ 10·00 1·10
1½ch. rose (1932) 2·75 10
a. Imperf between (horiz strip of 3) £180
b. Perf 12½ 22·00 2·75
c. Perf comp of 12 and 12½ — 32·00
2ch. carmine-red (4.6.29) 3·00 30
6 3ch. violet (4.25) 6·50 15
a. Imperf between (vert pair) 90·00 90·00
b. Perf 12½ — 11·00
c. Perf comp of 12 and 12½ — 30·00
1 4ch. grey-green (5.4.34) 5·00 45
7 7ch. claret (1925) 9·50 1·75
a. Doubly printed † £375
b. Carmine-red (date?) 65·00 55·00
c. Brown-purple (1932) 16·00 4·50
ca. Perf 12½ 8·50 15·00
cb. Perf comb of 12 and 12½ 7·50 15·00
8 14ch. orange-yellow (date?) 40·00
da. Perf 12½ £180

It is believed that the 12½ perforation and the perf 12 and 12½ npound were introduced in 1937 and that the 11 perforation ne later, probably in 1939.

The 5ca. chocolate, 6ca., 10ca. and 3ch. also exist on the despaced watermark (60 shells to the sheet of 84).

11 Sri Padmanabha Shrine

12 State Chariot

13 Maharaja Bala Rama Varma XI

(Des M. R. Madhawan Unnithan. Plates by Calcutta Chromotype Co. Typo Stamp Manufactory, Trivandrum)

1931 (6 Nov). *Coronation. Cream or white paper.* Wmk C. P 11½, 12.

47 **11** 6ca. black and green 1·60 1·60
a. Imperf between (horiz pair) £180 £200
48 **12** 10ca. black and ultramarine 1·25 70
a. Imperf between (vert pair) † £400
49 **13** 3ch. black and purple 2·75 2·75
47/9 *Set of* 3 5·00 4·50

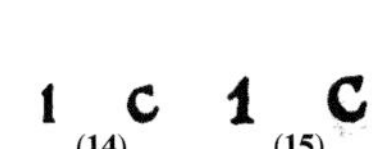

1 c (**14**) 1 C (**15**)

16 Maharaja Bala Rama Varma XI and Subramania Shrine

1932 (14 Jan).

(i) Surch as T **14**.

(a) Wmk A (sideways).

50 **1** 1c.on 1¼ch. claret 15 50
a. Imperf between (horiz pair) £100
b. Surch inverted 4·25 7·50
c. Surch double 30·00 30·00
d. Pair, one without surch 95·00 £110
e. "c" omitted 45·00 45·00
51 2c.on 1¼ch. claret 15 20
a. Surch inverted 4·25 7·00
b. Surch double 28·00
c. Surch double, one inverted 60·00
d. Surch treble 65·00
e. Surch treble, one inverted 70·00 70·00
f. Pair, one without surch £100 £110
g. "2" omitted 45·00 45·00
h. "c" omitted 45·00 45·00
i. Imperf between (horiz pair) £100
j. Imperf between (vert pair) £110

(b) Wmk B (upright).

52 **1** 1c.on 1¼ch. claret 75 1·00
a. Surch inverted 20·00
b. Surch double 38·00
53 2c.on 1¼ch. claret 6·50 6·50
a. Imperf between (horiz pair) £120

(c) Wmk C.

54 **1** 1c.on 1¼ch. claret 14·00 18·00
a. Surch inverted 55·00 60·00
55 2c.on 1¼ch. claret 26·00 18·00

(ii) Surch as T **10**. Wmk B.

56 **1** 2c. on 1¼ch. claret 4·00 14·00

1932 (5 Mar). *Surch as T* **15**. Wmk C.

57 **4** 1c.on 5ca. chocolate 15 15
a. Imperf between (horiz pair) £110
b. Surch inverted 7·50 10·00
c. Surch inverted on back only 70·00
d. Pair, one without surch 95·00
e. "1" omitted 38·00
f. "C" omitted — 38·00
g. "TRAVANCOPE" 8·50
58 1c.on 5ca. slate-purple 1·25 20
a. Surch inverted † £200
b. "1" inverted 75·00 75·00
59 2c.on 10ca. pink 15 15
a. Imperf between (horiz pair) £110
b. Surch inverted 5·00 8·00
c. Surch double 21·00 23·00
d. Surch double, one inverted 65·00 65·00
e. Surch double, both inverted 45·00

No. 58 was not issued without the surcharge.

(Plates by Indian Security Printing Press, Nasik. Typo Stamp Manufactory, Trivandrum)

1937 (29 Mar). *Temple Entry Proclamation. T* **16** *and similar horiz designs.* Wmk C. P 12.

60 6ca. carmine 1·40 1·25
a. Imperf between (horiz strip of 3) £450
b. Perf 12½ 1·60 1·50
c. Compound perf 30·00 30·00
61 12ca. bright blue 2·50 30
a. Perf 12½ 3·00 70
ab. Imperf between (vert pair) £425
b. Compound perf 48·00
62 1½ch. yellow-green 1·50 1·40
a. Imperf between (vert pair) £350
b. Perf 12½ 24·00 6·50
c. Compound perf
63 3ch. violet 3·25 2·25
a. Perf 12½ 4·75 2·75
60/3 *Set of* 4 7·75 4·75

Designs:—Maharaja's portrait and temples—12ca. Sri Padmanabha; 1½ ch. Mahadeva; 3ch. Kanyakumari.

COMPOUND PERFS. This term covers stamps perf compound of 12½ and 11, 12 and 11 or 12 and 12½, and where two or more combinations exist the prices are for the commonest. Such compounds can occur on values which do not exist, perf 12 all round.

17 Lake Ashtamudi

18 Maharaja Bala Rama Varma XI

(Des Nilakantha Pellai. Plates by Indian Security Printing Press, Nasik. Typo Stamp Manufactory, Trivandrum)

1939 (9 Nov). *Maharaja's 27th Birthday. T* **17**/**18** *and similar designs.* Wmk C. P 12½.

64 1ch. yellow-green 4·50 10
a. Imperf between (horiz pair) 22·00
b. Perf 11 9·00 10
ba. Imperf between (vert pair) 38·00 45·00
bb. Imperf between (vert strip of 3) 21·00 38·00
c. Perf 12 19·00 1·40
ca. Imperf between (horiz pair) 20·00
cb. Imperf between (vert pair) 40·00
d. Compound perf 22·00 2·50
da. Imperf between (vert pair) £110
65 1½ch. scarlet 3·25 3·00
a. Doubly printed £275
b. Imperf between (horiz pair) 29·00
c. Imperf between (vert pair) 23·00
d. Perf 11 3·75 19·00
da. Imperf horiz (vert pair) 8·00
e. Perf 12 29·00 4·00
f. Perf 13½ 15·00 55·00
g. Compound perf 42·00 5·50
h. Imperf (pair) 30·00
66 2ch. orange 5·00 1·40
a. Perf 11 17·00 50
b. Perf 12 90·00 4·00
c. Compound perf 90·00 5·50
67 3ch. brown 6·00 10
a. Doubly printed — £130
b. Imperf between (horiz pair) 38·00 50·00
c. Perf 11 19·00 30
ca. Doubly printed 42·00 55·00
d. Perf 12 32·00 3·00
da. Imperf between (vert pair) £120 £130
e. Compound perf 30·00 1·00
68 4ch. red 5·50 40
a. Perf 11 32·00 50
b. Perf 12 28·00 6·50
c. Compound perf £150 £110
69 7ch. pale blue 9·00 16·00
a. Perf 11 75·00 27·00
ab. Blue 70·00 26·00
b. Compound perf 90·00 32·00
70 14ch. turquoise-green 7·00 50·00
a. Perf 11 10·00 90·00
64/70 *Set of* 7 35·00 65·00

Designs: *Vert as T***18**—1½ch., 3ch. Portraits of Maharaja in different frames. *Horiz as T***17**—4ch. Sri Padmanabha Shrine; 7ch. Cape Comorin; 14ch. Pachipari Reservoir.

19 Maharaja and Aruvikara Falls

2 CASH (**20**)

(Des Nilakantha Pellai. Plates by Indian Security Printing Press, Nasik. Typo Stamp Manufactory, Trivandrum)

1941 (20 Oct). *Maharaja's 29th Birthday. T* **19** *and similar horiz design.* Wmk C. P 12½.

71 6ca. blackish violet 6·50 10
a. Perf 11 6·50 10
ab. Imperf between (vert pair) 20·00
ac. Imperf horiz (vert pair) 40·00 55·00
b. Perf 12 21·00 1·25
ba. Imperf between (horiz pair) 24·00
bb. Imperf between (vert pair) 42·00
bc. Imperf between (vert strip of 3) 22·00
c. Compound perf 6·50 80
72 ¾ch. brown 7·00 20
a. Perf 11 8·50 20
ab. Imperf between (horiz pair) £140
ac. Imperf between (vert pair) 30·00 42·00
ad. Imperf between (vert strip of 3) 26·00
ae. Block of four imperf between (horiz and vert) £180
b. Perf 12 48·00 8·50
c. Compound perf 11·00 1·10

Design:—¾ch. Maharaja and Marthanda Varma Bridge, Alwaye.

1943 (17 Sept). *Nos. 65, 71 (colour changed) and 72 surch as T* **20**. P 12½.
73 2ca.on 1½ch. scarlet . . . 1·40 80
a. Imperf between (vert pair) . . . 40·00
b. "2" omitted . . . £250 £250
c. "CA" omitted . . . £375
d. "ASH" omitted . . . £375
e. Perf 11 . . . 40 20
ea. "CA" omitted . . . £375
f. Compound perf . . . 60 90
fa. Imperf between (vert pair) . . . £130
fb. "2" omitted . . . £275
74 4ca.on ¾ch. brown . . . 3·75 1·40
a. Perf 11 . . . 4·00 30
b. Perf 12 . . . — £120
c. Compound perf . . . 4·50 1·00
75 8ca.on 6ca. scarlet . . . 4·50 10
a. Perf 11 . . . 3·50 10
ab. Imperf between (horiz pair) . . . 35·00
b. Perf 12 . . . — 70·00
c. Compound perf . . . 14·00 7·00
73/5 *Set of* 3 . . . 7·00 55

21 Maharaja Bala Rama Varma XI

SPECIAL
(**22**)

(Des Nilakantha Pellai. Plates by Indian Security Printing Press, Nasik. Typo Stamp Manufactory, Trivandrum)

1946 (24 Oct). *Maharaja's 34th Birthday*. Wmk C. P 12½.
76 **21** 8ca. carmine . . . 24·00 3·50
a. Perf 11 . . . 65 1·40
b. Perf 12 . . . 32·00 2·50
ba. Imperf between (horiz pair) . . . 32·00 48·00
bb. Imperf between (horiz strip of 3) . . . 50·00
c. Compound perf

1946. *No. O103 revalidated for ordinary postage with opt T* **22**, *in orange*. P 12½.
77 **19** 6ca. blackish violet . . . 6·00 2·50
a. Perf 11 . . . 32·00 6·00
b. Compound perf . . . 6·00 5·50

OFFICIAL STAMPS

GUM. Soon after 1911 the Official stamps were issued without gum. Thus only the initial printings of the 1, 2, 3 and 4ch. values were gummed. As Nos. O38/9, O41/2 and O95 were overprinted on stamps intended for normal postage these, also, have gum.

PRINTINGS. Sometimes special printings of postage stamps were made specifically for overprinting for Official use, thus accounting for Official stamps appearing with watermarks or in shades not listed in the postage issues.

SETTINGS. These are based on the study of complete sheets of 84, and the measurements given are those of the majority of stamps on the sheet. Examples are known showing different measurements as each overprint was set individually in loose type, but these are not included in the listings.

On S. S (O **1**)
On S S (O **2**)
Rounded "O"

1911 (16 Aug)–**30**. *Contemporary stamps optd with Type* O **1** *(13 mm wide)*. P 12, sometimes rough.

(a) Wmk B (upright) *(16.8.11-21)*.
O 1 **3** 4ca. pink (1916) . . . 20 10
a. Opt inverted . . . † 75·00
b. Opt double . . . £100 80·00
c. "S S" inverted . . . 32·00 16·00
d. Imperf (pair) . . . £225 £225
e. Stamp doubly printed . . . † £225
f. Left "S" inverted . . . — 16·00
O 2 **1** 6ca. chestnut (date ?) . . . 35·00 35·00
O 3 ½ch. reddish lilac (R.) (1919) . . . 1·00 35
a. "CHUCRRAM" (R. 5/6) . . . 9·50 4·50
O 4 **4** 10ca. pink (1921) . . . 17·00 3·00
a. "O" inverted . . . 48·00 9·00
b. Left "S" inverted . . . 48·00 9·00
c. Right "S" inverted . . . 48·00 9·00
d. Opt inverted . . . † £100
O 5 **1** 1ch. chalky blue (R.) . . . 65 10
a. Imperf between (vert pair) . . . † £170
b. Opt inverted . . . 7·00 4·25
c. Opt double . . . 60·00 50·00
d. "nO" for "On" . . . 75·00 75·00
e. "O" inverted . . . 7·00 2·00
f. Left "S" inverted . . . 7·50 2·25
g. Right "S" inverted . . . 8·00 2·50
h. "S S" inverted . . . — 45·00
O 6 2ch. red . . . 35 10
a. Opt inverted . . . 8·00 8·00
b. "O" inverted . . . 8·00 1·25
c. Left "S" inverted . . . 8·00 1·25
d. Right "S" inverted . . . 9·00 2·00
O 7 2ch. red (B.) (date ?) . . . — 95·00
O 8 **6** 3ch. violet . . . 35 10
a. Imperf between (vert pair) . . . £170 £170
b. Imperf vert (horiz pair) . . . £150
c. Opt inverted . . . 10·00 10·00
d. Opt double . . . 80·00 65·00
e. Right "S" inverted . . . 4·75 1·00
f. Right "S" omitted . . . £100 £100
g. Left "S" omitted . . . £100 £100
O 9 3ch. violet (B.) (date ?) . . . £140 70·00
O10 **1** 4ch. slate-green . . . 55 10
a. Imperf between (horiz pair) . . . — £225
b. Opt inverted . . . 45·00 13·00
c. Opt double . . . £100 85·00
d. "O" inverted . . . 10·00 2·40
e. Left "S" inverted . . . 11·00 3·25
f. Right "S" inverted . . . 12·00 3·75
g. Left "S" omitted . . . £100 £100
O11 4ch. slate-green (B.) (1921) . . . — 55·00
a. "O" inverted . . . — £130
b. Left "S" inverted . . . — £130
c. Right "S" inverted . . . — £130

(b) Wmk A (sideways) *(1919–25)*.
O12 **3** 4ca. pink . . . 3·75 15
a. Imperf (pair) . . . £275 £275
b. Opt inverted . . . 60·00 17·00
c. "O" inverted . . . 32·00 8·50
d. Left "S" inverted . . . 38·00 10·00
e. Right "S" inverted . . . 38·00 11·00
O13 4ca. pink (B.) (1921) . . . 45·00 75
a. "O" inverted . . . — 22·00
O14 **4** 5ca. olive-bistre (1921) . . . 60 10
a. Opt inverted . . . 12·00 9·00
b. "O" inverted . . . 5·00 1·50
c. Left "S" inverted . . . 5·50 1·50
d. Right "S" inverted . . . 5·50 1·50
O15 **1** 6ca. orange-brown (1921) . . . 30 10
a. Imperf between (vert pair) . . . † £180
b. Opt inverted . . . 11·00 8·50
c. Opt double . . . 65·00 65·00
d. "O" inverted . . . 6·00 1·60
e. Left "S" inverted . . . 6·50 1·60
f. Right "S" inverted . . . 7·00 1·60
O16 6ca. orange-brown (B.) (1921) . . . 10·00 1·50
a. Opt inverted . . . £100 £100
b. "O" inverted . . . 45·00 14·00
c. Left "S" inverted . . . 45·00 14·00
d. Right "S" inverted . . . 45·00 14·00
O17 ½ch. reddish violet (R.) (date?) . . . 1·75 25
a. *Reddish lilac* (date?) . . . 1·75 25
b. Imperf between (horiz pair) . . . £140 £130
c. Imperf between (vert pair) . . . 60·00 65·00
d. Stamp doubly printed . . . 48·00
e. Opt inverted . . . 10·00 3·25
f. Opt double, both inverted . . . £130
g. "CHUCRRAM" (R. 5/6) . . . 9·00 3·25
h. "On" omitted . . . — £120
i. Right "S" inverted . . . — 27·00
j. Right "S" omitted . . . — £120
O18 **4** 10ca. pink (3.21) . . . 65 10
a. *Scarlet* (1925?) . . . — 10·00
b. Opt inverted . . . — 18·00
c. Opt double . . . 85·00 70·00
d. "O" inverted . . . 9·00 2·75
e. Left "S" inverted . . . 7·50 2·00
f. Right "S" inverted . . . 9·00 2·75
g. Imperf between (horiz pair) . . . — £140
O19 10ca. pink (B.) (date?) . . . 70·00 19·00
a. Opt inverted . . . — 80·00
b. "O" inverted . . . — 50·00
O20 **1** 1ch. grey-blue (R.) (date?) . . . 4·50 60
a. *Deep blue* . . . 4·50 80
b. "O" inverted . . . 35·00 8·00
c. Left "S" inverted . . . 38·00 9·50
d. "On" omitted
e. Opt inverted . . . † 60·00
O21 1¼ch. claret (12.19) . . . 40 10
a. Stamp doubly printed . . . — £250
b. Opt inverted . . . 9·00 8·00
c. Opt double . . . 45·00
d. "O" inverted . . . 11·00 2·00
e. Left "S" inverted . . . 14·00 3·50
f. Right "S" inverted . . . 14·00 3·75
g. Error. Carmine . . . 50·00
O22 1¼ch. claret (B.) (1921) . . . — 65·00
a. "O" inverted . . . — £140
b. Left "S" inverted . . . — £140
c. Right "S" inverted . . . — £140

(c) Wmk C *(1925–30)*.
O23 **4** 5ca. olive-bistre (1926) . . . 40 40
a. Imperf between (horiz pair) . . . £180 £180
b. Opt inverted . . . 19·00 16·00
c. "O" inverted (R. 1/7) . . . 5·00 3·00
d. Left "S" inverted (R. 6/1, 6/8) . . . 4·50 2·50
e. Right "S" inverted (R. 6/7) . . . 5·00 3·00
O23*f* 5ca. chocolate (1930) . . . 50·00
fa. Opt inverted . . . — £110
O24 10ca. pink (1926) . . . 3·75 15
a. Imperf between (vert pair) . . . — £170
b. Opt inverted . . . 65·00 65·00
c. "O" inverted (R. 1/7) . . . 24·00 3·00
d. Left "S" inverted (R. 6/1, 6/8) . . . 20·00 2·50
e. Right "S" inverted (R. 6/7) . . . 24·00 3·00
f. Stamp doubly printed
g. Opt double . . . † £100
O25 **1** 1¼ch. claret (1926) . . . 15·00 40
a. "O" inverted (R. 1/7) . . . 50·00 6·00
b. Left "S" inverted (R. 6/1, 6/8) . . . 45·00 5·00
c. Right "S" inverted (R. 6/7) . . . 50·00 6·00
d. Opt double . . . † £100
O26 **7** 7ch. claret . . . 1·50 30
a. "O" inverted (R. 1/7) . . . 16·00 4·00
b. Left "S" inverted (R. 6/1, 6/8) . . . 14·00 3·50
c. Right "S" inverted (R. 6/7) . . . 16·00 4·00
d. Error. Carmine-red . . . 60·00
O27 **8** 14ch. orange-yellow . . . 2·25 40
a. "O" inverted (R. 1/7) . . . 16·00 4·00
b. Left "S" inverted (R. 6/1, 6/8) . . . 14·00 3·00
c. Right "S" inverted (R. 6/7) . . . 16·00 3·75

1926–30. *Contemporary stamps optd with Type* O **2** *(16½ mm wi*
Wmk C. P 12.
O28 **4** 5ca. olive-bistre . . . 3·50
a. Right "S" inverted . . . 18·00
b. Left "S" inverted . . . 21·00
O29 5ca. chocolate (1930) . . . 25
a. Imperf between (vert pair) . . . † £
b. Opt inverted . . . 19·00
c. "O" inverted . . . 3·75
d. Left "S" inverted . . . 3·75
O30 **1** 6ca. brown-red (date?) . . . 4·75
a. "O" inverted . . . 21·00
b. Left "S" inverted . . . 24·00
c. Opt double . . . † £
O31 **4** 10ca. pink . . . 30
a. Imperf between (horiz pair) . . . 65·00 6
b. Imperf between (vert pair) . . . 50·00 5
c. Imperf vert (horiz strip of 3) . . . † £
d. Opt inverted . . . 9·00
e. "Ou" for "On" . . . 45·00 4
f. "O" inverted . . . 4·50
g. Left "S" inverted . . . 4·00
h. Right "S" inverted . . . 4·00
i. Left "S" omitted . . . 42·00 4
j. Wmk sideways . . . 21·00
O32 **1** 1¼ch. claret (*shades*) . . . 1·60
a. Imperf between (horiz pair) . . . 85·00 9
b. Imperf between (vert pair) . . . £100 £
c. Opt inverted . . . 22·00 2
d. "O" inverted . . . 19·00
e. Left "S" inverted . . . 19·00
f. Right "S" inverted . . . 19·00
g. Left "S" omitted . . . £120 £
h. Right "S" omitted . . . £120 £
i. Wmk sideways . . . —
ia. Imperf between (vert pair) . . . £120
O33 **6** 3ch. violet . . . 9·00
a. Opt inverted . . . † £
b. "O" inverted . . . 45·00 1
c. "O" omitted . . . 95·00 8
d. "Ou" for "On" . . . £130 £
e. Left "S" inverted . . . — 3
O34 **7** 7ch. claret (date?) . . . £110
O35 **8** 14ch. orange-yellow . . . 42·00
a. Imperf between (vert pair) . . . £450
b. "O" inverted . . . £100

The 5ca. olive-bistre, 3ch. and 7ch. exist only with the nor watermark spaced 11 mm; the 5ca. chocolate and 14ch. exist o with the wide 15 mm spacing; the 6ca., 10ca. and 1¼ch. exist in b forms.

On S S (O **3**)
On S S (O **4**) Italic "S S"
On S S (O **5**)

1930. Wmk C. P 12.

(a) Optd with Type O **3**.
O36 **4** 10ca. pink . . . £200 £
O37 **1** 1¼ch. carmine-rose . . . 4·00 3

(b) Optd with Type O **4**.
O38 **5** ¾ch. black (R.) . . . 35
a. Left "S" omitted . . . 85·00 85
b. Right "S" omitted . . . 85·00
c. Large roman "S" at left . . . — 90

(c) Optd with Type O **5**.
O39 **5** ¾ch. black (R.) . . . 35
a. Opt inverted . . . † £
b. "n" omitted . . . 95·00 95
O40 **1** 4ch. slate-green (R.) . . . 29·00 14

On S S (O **6**)
On S S (O **7**) Oval "O"
On S S (O **8**)

1930–39?. *Contemporary stamps overprinted*. P 12.

(a) With Type O **6** *(16 mm high)*.

(i) Wmk A.
O41 **3** 4ca. pink . . . 25·00 50
a. Large right "S" as Type O **2**(R. 6/14) . . . £110 £

(ii) Wmk B.
O42 **3** 4ca. pink . . . 20·00 55
a. Large right "S" as Type O **2**(R. 6/14) . . . £100 £

(iii) Wmk C.
O43 **1** 6ca. brown-red (1932) . . . 35
a. Opt inverted . . . 20·00
b. Opt double . . . 45·00 45
c. "O" inverted (R. 5/11-12) . . . 8·00 5
O44 **4** 10ca. pink . . . 2·50 1
O45 **5** ¾ch. mauve (1933) . . . 3·75
a. Imperf between (horiz pair) . . . 95·00 70
b. Imperf between (horiz strip of 3) . . . † £
c. Imperf between (vert pair) . . . † £
d. Stamp doubly printed . . . † £
e. Perf 12½ . . . 7·00
f. Perf comp of 12 and 12½ . . . 17·00 2
g. Right "S" inverted . . . — 25
O46 **1** 1¼ch. carmine-rose . . . 12·00 1
a. Opt double . . . £110 85
b. Large right "S" as Type O **2**(R. 6/14) . . . £110 55
O47 4ch. grey-green . . . 1·75 5

O48 4ch. grey-green (R.) (27.10.30) 70 20
a. Imperf between (horiz pair) £120 £120
b. Opt double 25·00 25·00
c. "O" inverted 32·00 20·00
d. Large right "S" as Type O **2**(R. 6/14) 45·00 30·00
e. Imperf between (vert pair) £120
O49 **8** 14ch. orange-yellow (1931) 8·50 1·75
a. Imperf between (vert pair) † £150

For the 1½ch. and 3ch., and for Nos. O43 and O48/9 but perf 12½, see Nos. O66/70 (new setting combining Types O **6** and O **8**).

(b) With Type O **7** *(14 mm high).* Wmk C.

O50 **3** 4ca. pink 12·00 32·00
a. "O" inverted 45·00 80·00
O51 **4** 5ca. chocolate (1932) 21·00 9·00
a. Opt inverted 65·00 65·00
O52 **1** 6ca. brown-red 20 10
a. Imperf between (vert pair) 55·00 55·00
b. Opt inverted 26·00
c. Opt double † 65·00
d. "nO" for "On" £120 £120
e. Right "S" inverted 22·00 16·00
f. Left "S" omitted — 80·00
g. Large "n" as Type O **5** (R. 1/1, 1/14) 20·00 12·00
h. Large italic left "S" as Type O **5** 22·00 13·00
i. Perf 12½ — 9·00
j. Perf compound of 12 and 12½ — 21·00
O53 ¼ch. reddish violet (1932) 40 15
a. "CHUCRRAM" (R. 5/6) 8·50 5·50
b. "Ou" for "On" 60·00 60·00
c. Left "S" omitted — £110
d. "O" of "On" omitted £160
O54 ¼ch. reddish violet (R.) (1935) 20 10
a. Imperf between (vert pair) £120 £120
b. "CHUCRRAM" (R. 5/6) 3·50 3·00
c. Left "S" inverted 24·00 22·00
O55 **4** 10ca. pink (date ?) 3·75 2·25
a. Imperf between (horiz pair) 12·00 20·00
b. Imperf between (vert pair) 10·00 19·00
c. "O" inverted 35·00 22·00
d. Right "S" inverted 35·00 22·00
O56 **5** ¾ch. mauve (1933?) 30 15
a. Imperf between (vert pair) † £130
b. "Ou" for "On" 65·00 65·00
c. "O" inverted 24·00 21·00
d. Right "S" inverted — 21·00
e. Opt double † £120
f. Perf comp of 12 and 12½ 27·00 18·00
O57 **1** 1ch. deep blue (R.) (1935) 1·75 40
a. Slate-blue 1·00 25
b. Imperf between (horiz pair) £110 £110
c. Imperf between (vert pair) 27·00 38·00
d. Perf 12½ 8·00 3·75
e. Perf comp of 12 and 12½ 21·00 7·50
O58 1¼ch. claret 1·25 1·40
O59 1½ch. rose (1933) 40 10
a. Imperf between (vert pair) † £140
b. Opt double 70·00 70·00
c. "O" inverted 4·50 2·50
e. Large "n" as Type O **5** (R. 1/1, 1/14) 50·00 23·00
f. Large italic left "S" as Type O **5** 55·00 23·00
g. Left "S" inverted — 24·00
h. Perf 12½ — 11·00
i. Perf comp of 12 and 12½ — 22·00
ia. Stamp doubly printed — £180
O60 **6** 3ch. reddish violet (1933) 1·25 60
a. "O" inverted 21·00 9·00
b. Opt double † 95·00
O61 3ch. violet (R.) (1934) 70 10
a. Imperf between (horiz pair) 85·00 45·00
b. Imperf between (vert pair) 65·00 42·00
c. Opt inverted † 50·00
d. "O" inverted 20·00 13·00
e. Perf 12½ — 2·50
ea. Imperf between (vert pair) † £170
f. Perf comp of 12 and 12½ — 12·00
fa. Imperf between (horiz pair) † £170
g. "Ou" for "On" — 80·00
O62 **1** 4ch. grey-green (1934) — £250
O63 4ch. grey-green (R.) (1935?) 1·00 20
a. "Ou" for "On" (R. 1/1) 60·00 45·00
O64 **7** 7ch. claret (*shades*) 1·25 30
a. Imperf between (vert pair) 28·00 38·00
b. "O" inverted 45·00 20·00
c. Left "S" inverted 48·00 24·00
d. Perf 12½ — 8·00
e. Perf comp of 12 and 12½ — 8·00
ea. Imperf between (vert pair) † £100
eb. Imperf between (vert strip of 3) £140 £140
O65 **8** 14ch. orange (1933) 1·75 40
a. Imperf between (horiz pair) 35·00 48·00
b. Imperf between (vert pair) £140
c. Opt inverted £350 £350

(c) New setting combining Type O **8** *(18 mm high) in top row with Type* O **6** *(16 mm high) for remainder.* Wmk C *(dates?).*

A. Type O **8**.

O66A **1** 6ca. brown-red 7·50 3·75
a. Perf 12½ 7·50 3·75
O67A 1½ch. rose 42·00 6·00
a. Perf 12½ 48·00 8·50
O68A **6** 3ch. violet (R.) 55·00 8·50
a. Perf 12½ 70·00 22·00
b. Perf comp of 12 and 12½ 95·00 25·00
O69A **1** 4ch. grey-green (R.) 48·00 24·00
a. Perf 12½ 55·00 22·00
O70A **8** 14ch. orange-yellow 50·00 16·00
a. Perf 12½ 55·00 17·00

B. Type O **6**.

O66Ba **1** 6ca. brown-red (P 12½) 3·25 90
ab. Imperf between (vert pair) £100 £100
ac. "O" inverted 17·00 8·50
g. Perf comp of 12 and 12½ — 18·00
O67B 1½ch. rose 11·00 35
a. Perf 12½ 16·00 50
ab. "O" inverted 50·00 18·00
c. Perf comp of 12 and 12½ — 22·00
O68B **6** 3ch. violet (R.) 11·00 1·00
a. Perf 12½ 19·00 1·00
b. Perf comp of 12 and 12½ 28·00 6·50
O69Ba **1** 4ch. grey-green (R.) (P 12½) 7·50 3·00
ab. Imperf between (horiz pair) † £180
ac. "O" inverted 80·00 35·00
O70Ba **8** 14ch. orange-yellow (P 12½) 14·00 1·00

Nos. O66/70A/B in vertical *se-tenant* pairs are very scarce. As with the postage issues it is believed that the 12½ and compound perforations were issued between 1937 and 1939.

1 ch

8 c (O 9)

1 ch Wrong fount "1 c" (R. 6/7)

1932. *Official stamps surch as T* **14** *or with Type* O **9**. P 12.

(a) With opt Type O **1**.

(i) Wmk A *(sideways).*

O71 **4** 6c.on 5ca. olive-bistre 50·00 22·00
a. "O" inverted £160 70·00
b. Left "S" inverted £150 65·00
c. Right "S" inverted £160 70·00

(ii) Wmk C.

O72 **4** 6c.on 5ca. olive-bistre 25·00 9·50
a. "O" inverted 65·00 22·00
b. Left "S" inverted 60·00 20·00
c. Right "S" inverted 65·00 22·00
O73 12c.on 10ca. pink £130

(b) With opt Type O **2**. Wmk C.

O74 **4** 6c.on 5ca. olive-bistre 1·60 1·40
a. Opt and surch inverted 48·00
b. Surch inverted 65·00
c. Left "S" inverted 14·00 5·50
d. Right "S" inverted 14·00 5·50
e. "6" omitted — 75·00
O75 6c.on 5ca. chocolate 20 25
a. Surch inverted 9·00 9·50
b. Surch double £100
c. Surch double, one inverted 95·00
d. "O" inverted 4·25 4·25
e. Left "S" inverted 4·25 4·25
f. Pair, one without surch £250
O76 12c.on 10ca. pink 1·50 75
a. Opt inverted 13·00 14·00
b. Surch inverted 7·00 7·00
c. Opt and surch inverted 35·00 35·00
d. Pair, one without surch £300
e. "O" inverted 7·00 3·50
f. Left "S" inverted 7·00 3·50
g. "Ou" for "On" 85·00 85·00
h. Right "S" inverted 7·00 3·50
i. "c" omitted (R. 6/1) 55·00 55·00
O77 **1** 1ch.8c. on 1¼ch. claret 2·25 1·00
a. Surch inverted † 85·00
b. "O" inverted 10·00 4·25
c. Left "S" inverted 10·00 4·25
d. Right "S" inverted 10·00 4·25
e. Wrong fount "1 c" 24·00 18·00

(c) With opt Type O **3**. Wmk C.

O78 **4** 12c.on 10ca. pink † £350
O79 **1** 1ch.8c. on 1¼ch. carmine-rose 55·00 35·00
a. "n" omitted £200
b. Wrong fount "1 c" £190 £140

(d) With opt Type O **6**. Wmk C.

O80 **4** 12c.on 10ca. pink 95·00 25·00
O81 **1** 1ch.8c. on 1¼ch. carmine-rose £100 20·00
a. Wrong fount "1 c" £275 80·00
b. "h" omitted
c. Brown-red — 21·00

(e) With opt Type O **7**. Wmk C.

O82 **4** 6c.on 5ca. chocolate 20 30
a. Opt inverted 75·00 75·00
b. Surch inverted 11·00 12·00
c. Right "S" omitted £100 £100
d. Two quads for right "S" £450
e. Right "S" inverted 26·00
O83 12c.on 10ca. pink 20 15
a. Opt inverted 7·50 8·50
b. Surch inverted 6·00 7·00
c. Opt and surch inverted 35·00 35·00
d. Opt double † 85·00
e. "O" inverted 16·00 16·00
f. Right "S" inverted 17·00 17·00
g. "On" omitted — 95·00
h. "n" omitted — 95·00
i. "c" omitted (R. 6/1) 32·00 32·00
j. Surch double † 90·00
O84 **1** 1ch.8c. on 1¼ch. claret 35 25
a. Imperf between (vert pair) † £275
b. Opt omitted † £450
c. Surch inverted 14·00 15·00
d. Surch double 65·00
e. "O" inverted 4·50 2·75
f. Wrong fount "1 c" 18·00 15·00

SERVICE (O **10**)13 mm ("R" with curved tail)

SERVICE (O-**11**)13½ mm("R" with straight tail)

SERVICE 8 CASH (O **12**)

1939–41. *Nos. 35 and 40 with type-set opt, Type* O **10**. P 12½.

O85 **1** 6ca. brown-red (1941) 80 30
a. Perf 11 1·40 75
b. Perf 12 70 30
c. Compound perf 70 1·10
O86 **5** ¾ch. reddish violet £110 60·00
a. Perf 12 23·00 1·40
b. Compound perf £100 60·00

1939 (9 Nov). *Maharaja's 27th Birthday. Nos. 64/70 with type-set opt, Type* O **10**. P 12½.

O87 1ch. yellow-green 5·00 25
O88 1½ch. scarlet 5·50 75
a. "SESVICE" 85·00 26·00
b. Perf 12 40·00 7·50
ba. "SESVICE" — £130
bb. Imperf between (horiz pair) † £170
c. Compound perf 13·00 2·00
O89 2ch. orange 5·50 5·50
a. "SESVICE" 95·00 £110
b. Compound perf 90·00 90·00
O90 3ch. brown 4·25 20
a. "SESVICE" 75·00 21·00
b. Perf 12 23·00 45
ba. "SESVICE" £200 42·00
c. Compound perf 9·50 3·50
O91 4ch. red 11·00 4·00
O92 7ch. pale blue 12·00 2·75
O93 14ch. turquoise-green 15·00 4·00
O87/93 *Set of 7* 50·00 15·50

1940 ((?))–**45**. *Nos. 40a and 42b optd with Type* O **11** *from stereos.* P 12½.

O94 **5** ¾ch. reddish violet 13·00 20
a. Imperf between (horiz pair) £130 £140
b. Perf 11 60·00 1·10
c. Perf 12 21·00 20
d. Compound perf 45·00 75
O95 **1** 1½ch. rose (1945) 13·00 8·00
a. Perf 12 4·50 1·00
b. Compound perf 22·00 12·00

1941 (?)–**42**. *Nos. 64/70 optd with Type* O **11** *from stereos.* P 12½.

O 96 1ch. yellow-green 1·00 10
a. Imperf between (vert pair) 48·00 50·00
b. Opt inverted † 40·00
c. Opt double 22·00
d. Perf 11 75 10
da. Imperf between (vert pair) 32·00
db. Opt double £110 £110
e. Perf 12 3·00 50
ea. Imperf between (vert pair) 90·00 90·00
eb. Stamp doubly printed £130
ec. Opt inverted † £110
ed. Opt double 23·00 28·00
f. Compound perf 7·50 1·00
fa. Imperf between (vert pair) † £150
O 97 1½ch. scarlet 3·75 10
a. Imperf between (horiz pair) 55·00
b. Perf 11 1·75 15
ba. Imperf between (vert pair) £110 £110
bb. Imperf between (vert strip of 3) 80·00
bc. Imperf between (horiz pair) † £120
c. Perf 12 6·00 50
ca. Imperf between (vert strip of 3) £150
d. Compound perf 3·00 30
e. Imperf (pair) 26·00
O 98 2ch. orange 1·75 30
a. Perf 11 8·50 1·40
ab. Imperf between (vert pair)
b. Perf 12 90·00 90·00
ba. Imperf between (vert pair) £375 £375
c. Compound perf 90·00 90·00
O 99 3ch. brown 1·25 10
a. Imperf between (vert pair)
b. Perf 11 2·75 10
c. Perf 12 5·00 1·75
ca. Imperf between (vert pair) £300 £300
d. Compound perf 18·00 75
O100 4ch. red 2·75 75
a. Perf 11 3·50 45
b. Perf 12 17·00 4·25
c. Compound perf 60·00 21·00
O101 7ch. pale blue 7·50 35
a. Perf 11 5·50 4·25
b. Perf 12 22·00 8·50
c. Compound perf 18·00 4·50
d. Blue (P 11) 11·00 5·50
da. Perf 12 8·50 5·50
db. Compound perf 25·00 17·00
O102 14ch. turquoise-green 13·00 70
a. Perf 11 13·00 1·50
b. Perf 12 9·50 2·40
c. Compound perf 65·00 7·50
O96/102 *Set of 7* 20·00 1·90

1942. *Maharaja's 29th Birthday. Nos 71/2 optd with Type* O **11**. P 12½.

O103 6ca. blackish violet 40 50
a. Perf 11 70 1·00
b. Perf 12 60·00 6·50
c. Compound perf 1·50 1·00
O104 ¾ch. brown 4·50 10
a. Imperf between (vert pair) † £350
b. Perf 11 7·00 10
c. Perf 12 60·00 2·25
d. Compound perf 9·00 85

1943. *Surch with Type* O **12**. P 12½.

O105 **19** 8ca.on 6ca. scarlet 2·50 20
a. Perf 11 1·25 10
ab. Surch inverted † £900
b. Compound perf 7·00 1·25

1943–45. *Nos. 73/4 optd with Type* O **11**. P 12½.

O106 2ca.on 1½ch. scarlet 50 60
a. Perf 11 50 15
ab. Pair, one without surch £275
b. Compound perf 70 1·00
ba. "2" omitted £300 £300
c. Perf 12
O107 4ca.on ¾ch. brown (1945) 3·25 30
a. Perf 11 2·00 20
b. Compound perf 1·75 1·10

1946. *Maharaja's 34th Birthday. Optd with Type* O **11**. P 11.
O108 **21** 8ca. carmine . . . 2·25 70
a. Imperf between (horiz pair) . . 38·00
ab. Imperf between (vert pair) . . † £160
b. Opt double . . † £225
c. Perf 12½ . . 3·50 1·10
ca. Stamp doubly printed . . 30·00
d. Perf 12 . . 3·50 1·40
da. Stamp doubly printed . . 42·00

From 1 July 1949 Travancore formed part of the new State of Travancore-Cochin and stamps of Travancore surcharged in Indian currency were used.

TRAVANCORE-COCHIN

On 1 July 1949 the United State of Travancore and Cochin was formed ("U.S.T.C.") and the name was changed to State of Travancore-Cochin ("T.C.") by the new constitution of India on 26 January 1950.

PRICES FOR STAMPS ON COVER	
Nos. 1/13	*from* × 8
Nos. O1/17	*from* × 15

NO WATERMARK VARIETIES. These were formerly listed but we have now decided to omit them as they do not occur in full sheets. They are best collected in pairs, with and without watermarks.

COMPOUND PERFS. The notes above Type **17** of Travancore also apply here.

VALIDITY OF STAMPS. From 6 June 1950 the stamps of Travancore-Cochin were valid on mail from both Indian and state post offices to destinations in India and abroad.

ONE ANNA
ഒരണ
(**1**)2p. on 6ca.

രണ്ടു പൈസ — Normal

രണ്ടു പൈസ — 1st character of 2nd group as 1st character of 1st group (Rt pane R. 14/2)

1949 (1 July). *Stamps of Travancore surch in "PIES" or "ANNAS" as T* **1**. P 12½.
1 **19** 2p.on 6ca. blackish violet (R.) . . 2·75 1·40
a. Surch inverted . . 38·00
b. Character error . . £140 90·00
c. "O" inverted (Rt pane R. 13/1) . . 35·00 16·00
d. Perf 11 . . 1·75 30
da. Imperf between (vert pair) . . £160 £160
db. Pair, one without surch . . £100
dc. Character error . . £130 85·00
dd. "O" inverted (Rt pane R. 13/1) . . 35·00 17·00
e. Perf 12 . . 40 20
ea. Imperf between (horiz pair) . . 60·00
eb. Imperf between (vert pair) . . 5·50 15·00
ec. Surch inverted . . 95·00
ed. Character error . . £130 85·00
ee. Imperf between (vert strip of 3) . . 35·00
ef. Block of four imperf between (horiz and vert) . . 60·00
eg. "O" inverted (Rt pane R. 13/1) . . 30·00 16·00
eh. Imperf between (horiz strip of 3) . . 60·00
f. Perf 14 . . † £475
g. Imperf (pair) . . 8·50
ga. Character error . . £250
h. Compound perf . . — 35·00
2 **21** 4p.on 8ca. carmine . . 1·25 30
a. Surch inverted . . 45·00
b. "S" inverted (Rt pane R. 3/7) . . 85·00 42·00
c. Perf 11 . . 2·25 30
ca. Imperf between (vert pair) . . £160 £160
cb. Surch inverted . . 95·00
cc. Pair, one without surch . . £120
cd. "FOUP" for "FOUR" . . £160 £100
ce. "S" inverted (Rt pane R. 3/7) . . 85·00 42·00
d. Perf 12 . . 85 30
da. Imperf between (vert pair) . . 18·00
db. Pair, one without surch . . £110
dc. "FOUP" for "FOUR" . . £110 85·00
dd. "S" inverted (Rt pane R. 3/7) . . 90·00 48·00
de. Surch inverted . . £120
e. Imperf (pair) . . 70·00
f. Compound perf . . — 35·00
g. Perf 13½ . . † £500
3 **17** ½a.on 1ch. yellow-green . . 3·50 30
a. "NANA" for "ANNA" (Lt pane R. 3/3) . . £130 85·00
b. Inverted "H" in "HALF" . . — 95·00
c. Imperf between (vert pair) . . † £140
d. Perf 11 . . 2·50 20
da. Imperf between (vert pair) . . 28·00
db. Surch inverted . . † £180
dc. "NANA" for "ANNA" (Lt pane R. 3/3) . . £170 £100
dd. Inverted "H" in "HALF" . . — 95·00
e. Perf 12 . . 65 40
ea. Imperf between (horiz pair) . . 50·00 55·00
eb. Imperf between (vert pair) . . 5·50 13·00
ec. Surch inverted . . 5·00
ed. "NANA" for "ANNA" (Lt pane R. 3/3) . . £200 £120
ee. Block of four imperf between (horiz and vert) . . 48·00
f. Perf 14 . . † £400
g. Imperf (pair) . . 9·00 19·00
h. Compound perf . . — 32·00
4 **18** 1a.on 2ch. orange . . 3·50 30
a. Perf 11 . . 55 30
ab. Surch double . . 50·00
b. Perf 12 . . 3·50 50
ba. Imperf between (horiz pair) . . 7·50
bb. Imperf between (vert pair) . . 4·25 11·00
bc. Block of four imperf between (horiz and vert) . . 50·00
c. Perf 13½ . . £160 2·00
d. Imperf (pair) . . 8·50
e. Compound perf . . 38·00 23·00
5 – 2a.on 4ch. red (68) . . 3·25 60
a. Surch inverted . . † £250
b. "O" inverted . . 40·00 16·00
c. Perf 11 . . 3·25 60
ca. "O" inverted . . — 18·00
d. Perf 12 . . 2·75 55
da. "O" inverted . . 45·00 18·00
e. Compound perf . . 45·00 26·00
6 **18** 3a.on 7ch. pale blue (69) . . 11·00 4·75
a. Perf 11 . . 5·00 3·00
ab. Blue . . 55·00 4·50
ac. "3" omitted . . † £550
b. Perf 12 . . 11·00 2·75
c. Compound perf . . — 65·00
ca. Blue . . — 85·00
7 – 6a.on 14ch. turquoise-green (70) . . 15·00 27·00
a. Accent omitted from native surch (Rt pane R. 13/4) . . £250 £275
b. Perf 11 . . 13·00 22·00
ba. Accent omitted from native surch (Rt pane R. 13/4) . . £250 £275
c. Perf 12 . . 15·00 23·00
ca. Accent omitted from native surch (Rt pane R. 13/4) . . £275 £300
d. Compound perf . . 32·00 38·00
da. Accent omitted from native surch (Rt pane R. 13/4) . . £375
e. Imperf (pair)
1/7 *Set of 7* . . 21·00 24·00

There are two settings of the ½a. surcharge. In one the first native character is under the second downstroke of the "H" and in the other it is under the first downstroke of the "A" of "HALF". They occur on stamps perf 12½, 11 and 12 equally commonly and also on the Official stamps.

U. S. T. C. (**2**) **T.-C.** (**3**) **SIX PIES** (**4**)

1949. *No. 106 of Cochin optd with T* **2**.
8 **29** 1a. orange . . 4·75 55·00
a. No stop after "S" (R. 1/6) . . 75·00
b. Raised stop after "T" (R. 4/1) . . 75·00

1950 (1 Apr). *No. 106 of Cochin optd with T* **3**.
9 **29** 1a. orange . . 6·00 50·00
a. No stop after "T" . . 50·00 £225
b. Opt inverted . . £200
ba. No stop after "T" . . £1500

The no stop variety occurs on No. 5 in the sheet and again on No. 8 in conjunction with a short hyphen

1950 (1 Apr). *No. 9 surch as T* **4**.
10 **29** 6p.on 1a. orange . . 3·50 45·00
a. No stop after "T" (R. 1/5) . . 19·00
b. Error. Surch on No. 8 . . 15·00
ba. No stop after "S" . . £200
bb. Raised stop after "T" . . £200
11 9p.on 1a. orange . . 3·00 40·00
a. No stop after "T" (R. 1/5) . . 17·00
b. Error. Surch on No. 8 . . £160
ba. No stop after "S" . . £600
bb. Raised stop after "T" . . £600

5 Conch or Chank Shell

6 Palm Trees

(Litho Indian Security Printing Press, Nasik)

1950 (24 Oct). W **69** of India. P 14.
12 **5** 2p. rose-carmine . . 2·50 2·50
13 **6** 4p. ultramarine . . 3·25 15·00

The ordinary issues of Travancore-Cochin became obsolete on 1 July 1951.

OFFICIAL STAMPS

VALIDITY. Travancore-Cochin official stamps were valid for use throughout India from 30 September 1950.

SERVICE (O **1**) **SERVICE** (O **2**)

1949 (1 July)–**51**. *Stamps of Travancore surch with value as T* **1** *and optd "SERVICE". No gum.* P 12½.

(a) With Type O **1**.

(i) Wmk C of Travancore.
O1 **19** 2p.on 6ca. blackish violet (R.) . . 1·40 50
a. Imperf between (vert pair) . . £160 £160
b. Character error (Rt pane R. 14/2) . . 38·00 26·00
c. "O" inverted . . 23·00 12·00
d. Pair, one without surch . . £150
e. Perf 11 . . 90 20
ea. Imperf between (vert pair) . . £160 £160
eb. Character error (Rt pane R. 14/2) . . 42·00 32·0
ec. "O" inverted . . 23·00 12·0
f. Perf 12 . . 40 4
fa. Imperf between (horiz pair) . . 8·50 18·0
fb. Imperf between (vert pair) . . 6·00
fc. Character error (Rt pane R. 14/2) . . 38·00 28·0
fd. "O" inverted . . 23·00
fe. Block of four imperf between (horiz and vert) . . 27·00
g. Imperf (pair) . . 8·50 19·0
ga. Character error (Rt pane R. 14/2) . . £225
h. Compound perf . . 60·00
O2 **21** 4p.on 8ca. carmine . . 3·00 8
a. "FOUB" for "FOUR" (Lt pane R. 2/3) . . £180 £11
b. Perf 11 . . 3·00 3
ba. "FOUB" for "FOUR" (Lt pane R. 2/3) . . 95·00 32·0
c. Perf 12 . . 3·00 5
ca. "FOUB" for "FOUR" (Lt pane R. 2/3) . . £110 55·0
d. Compound perf . . 18·00 17·0
O3 **17** ½a.on 1ch. yellow-green . . 50 2
a. Pair, one without surch . . 80·00
b. Surch inverted . . 26·00
c. "NANA" for "ANNA" (Lt pane R. 3/3) . . £200 70·0
d. Perf 11 . . 1·00 2
da. Pair, one without surch . . £140
db. Surch inverted . . 55·00
dc. "NANA" for "ANNA" (Lt pane R. 3/3) . . £200 85·0
e. Perf 12 . . 9·50 2·0
ea. "NANA" for "ANNA" (Lt pane R. 3/3) . . £375 £15
eb. Pair, one without surch . . £100
ec. Surch inverted on back only . . £250
f. Compound perf . . — 22·0
O4 **18** 1a.on 2ch. orange . . 18·00 5·5
a. Surch inverted . . 90·00
b. Pair, one without surch . . £550
c. Perf 11 . . 16·00 7·5
ca. Pair, one without surch . . £600
O5 – 2a.on 4ch. red (68) . . 1·50 8
b. Perf 11 . . 5·00 6
ba. Surch inverted . . £700
bb. "O" inverted . . — 38·0
c. Perf 12 . . 5·50 4·5
ca. "O" inverted . . — 70·0
cb. Pair, one without surch . . £250
d. Compound perf . . — 30·0
e. Imperf (pair) . . 12·00
O6 – 3a.on 7ch. pale blue (69) . . 5·50 2·0
a. Imperf between (vert pair) . . 19·00
b. Blue . . 40·00 7·0
c. Perf 11 . . 3·00 1·0
ca. Blue . . 40·00 6·5
d. Perf 12 . . 3·50 4·5
da. Imperf between (horiz pair) . . 18·00
db. Imperf between (vert pair) . . 8·50
dc. Block of four imperf between (horiz and vert) . . 40·00
dd. Blue . . 40·00 5·0
e. Imperf (pair) . . 11·00
O7 – 6a.on 14ch. turquoise-green (70) . . 15·00 8·5
a. Imperf between (vert pair) . . 30·00
b. Perf 11 . . 13·00 8·0
c. Perf 12 . . 45·00 8·5
ca. Imperf between (horiz pair) . . 27·00
cb. Imperf between (vert pair) . . 32·00
cc. Block of four imperf between (horiz and vert) . . 60·00
d. Imperf (pair) . . 14·00
O1/7 *Set of 7* . . 32·00 14·

(ii) W **27** of Cochin.
O8 **19** 2p.on 6ca. blackish violet (R.) . . 30 1·
a. Type O 1 double . . 18·00
b. Perf 11 . . 50 1·
c. Perf 12 . . 70 1·
O9 – 2a.on 4ch. red (68) . . 1·90 1·
a. Perf 11 . . 60
ab. Imperf between (vert pair) . . £225 £2
b. Compound perf . . 50·00 30·

(b) With Type O **2**.

(i) Wmk C of Travancore.
O10 **21** 4p.on 8ca. carmine . . 50
a. "FOUB" for "FOUR" (Lt pane R. 2/3) . . £100 38·
b. 2nd "E" of "SERVICE" in wrong fount . . £110 48·
c. "S" in "PIES" inverted . . — 50·
d. Imperf between (vert pair) . . † £1
e. Perf 11 . . 30
ea. Imperf between (horiz pair) . . 4·50
eb. Imperf between (vert pair) . . 32·00
ec. "FOUB" for "FOUR" (Lt pane R. 2/3) . . 95·00 32·
ed. 2nd "E" of "SERVICE" in wrong fount . . £110 55·
ee. "S" in "PIES" inverted . . — 70·
ef. Block of four imperf between (horiz and vert) . . 35·00
f. Perf 12 . . 30
fa. Imperf between (horiz pair) . . 6·00
fb. Imperf between (vert pair) . . 2·00
fc. Block of four imperf between (horiz and vert) . . 14·00 25
fd. "FOUB" for "FOUR" (Lt pane R. 2/3) . . £110 40
ff. 2nd "E" of "SERVICE" in wrong fount . . £110 48
fg. "FOUK" for "FOUR" . . † £4
fh. Imperf between (vert strip of 3) . . 50·00
g. Perf 13½ . . 4·00 1
h. Compound perf . . 8·00 8
i. Imperf (pair) . . 6·00
ia. 2nd "E" of "SERVICE" in wrong fount . . £170
O11 **17** ½a.on 1ch. yellow-green . . 70

a. "AANA" for "ANNA" (Rt pane R. 13/1) £170 60·00
b. Perf 11 30 20
ba. Imperf between (horiz pair) 70·00 70·00
bb. Imperf between (vert pair) 9·50
bc. Block of four imperf between (horiz and vert) 60·00
bd. "AANA" for "ANNA" (Rt pane R. 13/1) 75·00 40·00
c. Perf 12 85 15
ca. Imperf between (horiz pair) 3·50
cb. Imperf between (vert pair) 3·50 10·00
cc. "AANA" for "ANNA" (Rt pane R. 13/1) 95·00 55·00
cd. Block of four imperf between (horiz and vert) 24·00
d. Compound perf 22·00 16·00
da. "AANA" for "ANNA" (Rt pane R. 13/1) — £180
e. Imperf (pair) 7·00 16·00

12 18 1a.on 2ch. orange 40 30
a. Imperf between (vert pair) † £150
ab. Imperf between (horiz pair) † £150
b. Perf 11 3·25 50
ba. Imperf between (horiz pair) 7·50 18·00
bb. Imperf between (vert pair) 90·00 90·00
c. Perf 12 40 20
ca. Imperf between (horiz pair) 7·00
cb. Imperf between (vert pair) 3·75 12·00
cc. Block of four imperf between (horiz and vert) 21·00
d. Compound perf 26·00 18·00
e. Imperf (pair) 15·00

13 – 2a.on 4ch. red (68) 3·50 80
a. "O" inverted (Lt pane R. 14/3) 80·00 40·00
b. Perf 11 1·50 1·10
ba. "O" inverted (Lt pane R. 14/3) 70·00 40·00
c. Perf 12 9·00 1·10
ca. Imperf between (vert pair) £130 £140
cb. "O" inverted (Lt pane R. 14/3) £130 40·00
cc. Pair, one without surch † £750
d. Compound perf 23·00 13·00

14 – 3a.on 7ch. pale blue (69) 7·00 1·10
a. "S" inverted in "SERVICE" (Lt pane R. 6/3) 75·00 32·00
b. First "E" inverted (Lt pane R. 7/4) £170 £130
c. "C" inverted (Lt pane R.4/1 and 5/1) 90·00 75·00
d. Second "E" inverted (Lt pane R. 3/2) £160 £120
e. Perf 11 1·50 1·10
ea. "S" inverted in "SERVICE" (Lt pane R. 6/3) 50·00 32·00
f. Perf 12 3·75 1·60
fa. "S" inverted in "SERVICE" (Lt pane R. 6/3) £130 80·00
g. Compound perf — 45·00
h. Imperf (pair) 45·00

15 – 6a.on 14ch. turquoise-green (70) 1·50 3·75
a. Accent omitted from native surch 16·00 13·00
b. "S" inverted in "SERVICE" (Lt pane R. 11/4) 75·00 42·00
c. Perf 11 12·00 3·50
ca. Accent omitted from native surch 60·00 22·00
cb. "S" inverted in "SERVICE" (Lt pane R. 11/4) £130 50·00
d. Perf 12 42·00 4·50
da. Accent omitted from native surch £130 30·00
db. "S" inverted in "SERVICE" (Lt pane R. 11/4) £275 65·00
e. Compound perf 75·00 75·00

10/15 *Set of* 6 5·00 5·50

(ii) W **27** of Cochin.

16 **17** ½a.on 1ch. yellow-green 2·00 65
a. Perf 11 40 40
b. Perf 12 18·00 9·50
c. Compound perf 11·00 3·00

7 **18** 1a.on 2ch. orange 1·40 75
a. Perf 11 50 40
b. Perf 12 12·00 4·00
c. Perf 13½ 2·00 1·00
d. Compound perf 5·00 3·00

Nos. O2, O10, O12 and O17 have the value at top in English and bottom in native characters with "SERVICE" in between. All ers have "SERVICE" below the surcharge.

Type O 2 was overprinted at one operation with the surcharges.

Nos. O10b, O10ed, O10ff and O10ia, show the second "E" of ERVICE" with serifs matching those on the surcharge. The riety occurred on Right pane R. 10/6 and R. 11/6, but was soon rrected.

The "accent omitted" varieties on No. O15 occur on Left pane 5/1 and Right pane R. 1/4, 12/4, 14/1 and 13/4.

The Official stamps became obsolete in September 1951.

WADHWAN

PRICES FOR STAMPS ON COVER	
No. 1	*from* × 30
No. 2	—
Nos. 3/6	*from* × 30

Thakur Bal Singh, 1885–1910

1

(Litho Thacker & Co, Bombay)

1888–94.

(a) Thin toned wove paper.

1 **1** ¼pice, black (I, III) (P 12½ *large holes*) 17·00 60·00
a. Imperf between (vert pair) (I)
b. Pin-perf 6½ irregular (I) 95·00
c. Compound of 12½ and pin-perf 6½ (I) £170
2 ¼pice, black (II) (P 12½ *irregular small holes*) 42·00

(b) Medium toned wove paper.

3 **1** ¼pice, black (III) (P 12½) 11·00 45·00
4 ¼pice, black (V) (P 12) 9·00 12·00

(c) Thick off-white or toned wove paper.

5 **1** ¼pice, black (IV, VI) (P 12) (7.92) 7·50 8·50
a. Perf compound of 12 and 11 (IV) 19·00 48·00
6 ¼pice, black (VII) (*fine impression*) (P 12) (1894) 7·50 21·00

Sheets from the Stone IV printing had at least one horizontal line of perforations gauging 11, normally between the bottom two rows of the sheet.

These stamps were lithographed from seven different stones taken from a single die. Brief details of the individual stones are as follows:

Stone I – No. 1. Sheet size not known, but possibly 28 (4 × 7). Sheet margins imperforate
Stone II – No. 2. Sheets of 42 (7 × 6) with imperforate margins
Stone III – Nos. 1 (thin paper) and 3 (medium paper). Sheets of 40 (4 × 10) with imperforate margins
Stone IV – Nos. 5/a. Sheets of 32 (4 × 8) with imperforate margins at top and right
Stone V – No. 4. Sheets of 20 (4 × 5) with imperforate margins at top, right and bottom
Stone VI – No. 5. Sheets of 30 (5 × 6) with all margins perforated
Stone VII – No. 6. Sheets of 32 (4 × 8) with all margins perforated. Much finer impression than the other stones

Stamps from stones I and II come with or without the dot before "STATE". Those from the later stones always show the dot. The shading on the pennant above the shield can also be used in stone identification. Stamps from stones I to III show heavy shading on the pennant, but this is less evident on stone IV and reduced further to a short line or dot on stones V to VII. There is a ")" hairline after "HALF" on the majority of stamps from Stone III.

The stamps of Wadhwan became obsolete on 1 January 1895.

Ionian Islands

The British occupation of the Ionian Islands was completed in 1814 and the archipelago was placed under the protection of Great Britain by the Treaty of Paris of 9 November 1815. The United States of the Ionian Islands were given local self-government, which included responsibility for the postal services. Crowned-circle handstamps were, however, supplied in 1844, although it is believed these were intended for use on prepaid mail to foreign destinations.

Examples of the Great Britain 1855 1d. red-brown stamp are known used at Corfu, cancelled as No. CC2, but it is believed that these originate from mail sent by the British garrison.

For illustrations of the handstamp types see BRITISH POST OFFICES ABROAD notes, following GREAT BRITAIN.

CEPHALONIA

CROWNED-CIRCLE HANDSTAMPS

CC1 **CC 1** CEPHALONIA (19.4.1844) *Price on cover* £1000

CORFU

CROWNED-CIRCLE HANDSTAMPS

CC2 **CC 1** CORFU (19.4.1844) *Price on cover* £500
CC3 **CC 1** CORFU (G. or B.) (1844) *Price on cover* —

ZANTE

CROWNED-CIRCLE HANDSTAMPS

CC4 **CC 1** ZANTE (G. or B.) (19.4.1844) *Price on cover* £1000

Nos. CC1/2 were later, circa 1860/1, struck in green (Cephalonia) or red (Corfu).

It is believed that examples of No. CC4 in black are from an unauthorised use of this handstamp which is now on display in the local museum. A similar handstamp, but without "PAID AT" was introduced in 1861.

PRICES FOR STAMPS ON COVER	
Nos. 1/3	*from* × 10

PERKINS BACON "CANCELLED". For notes on these handstamps, showing "CANCELLED" between horizontal bars forming an oval, see Catalogue Introduction.

1

(Eng C. Jeens. Recess Perkins, Bacon & Co)

1859 (15 June). Imperf.

1 **1** (½d.) orge (no wmk) (H/S "CANCELLED" in oval £5500) 80·00 £500
2 (1d.) blue (wmk "2") (H/S "CANCELLED" in oval £5500) 20·00 £180
3 (2d.) carm (wmk "1") (H/S "CANCELLED" in oval £5500) 15·00 £180

On 30 May 1864, the islands were ceded to Greece, and these stamps became obsolete.

Great care should be exercised in buying used stamps, on or off cover, as forged postmarks are plentiful.

Iraq

Indian post offices were opened at Baghdad and Basra, then part of the Turkish Empire, on 1 January 1868. Unoverprinted stamps of India were used, Baghdad being allocated numeral cancellations "356", "18" and "K-6", and Basra (also spelt Bussorah, Busreh, Busrah, Busra) "357", "19" and "1/K-6".

Both offices closed on 30 September 1914, but Basra re-opened in December 1914 when Indian stamps overprinted "I.E.F." were used.

(Currency. 16 annas = 1 rupee)

I. ISSUES FOR BAGHDAD

PRICES FOR STAMPS ON COVER	
Nos. 1/25	*from* × 6

BRITISH OCCUPATION

British and Indian troops occupied the port of Basra on 22 November 1914 to protect the oil pipeline. They then advanced up the rivers, and after a hard campaign, took Baghdad from the Turks on 11 March 1917.

IN BRITISH BAGHDAD OCCUPATION 2 Ans
(1)

1917 (1 Sept). *Stamps of Turkey, surch as T* **1** *in three operations.*

(a) Pictorial designs of 1914. T **32**, *etc., and* **31**.

1 **32** ½a.on 2pa. claret (Obelisk) £120 £140
a. "IN BRITISH" omitted £6000
2 **34** ½a.on 5pa. dull purple (Leander's Tower) 85·00 90·00
a. Value omitted £5500
3 **36** ½a.on 10pa. green (Lighthouse garden) £550 £650
4 **31** ½a.on 10pa. green (Mosque of Selim) £950 £1100
5 **37** 1a.on 20pa. red (Castle) £375 £400
a. "BAGHDAD" double £1300
6 **38** 2a.on 1pi. bright blue (Mosque) £150 £180

(b) As (a), but overprinted with small five-pointed Star.

7 **37** 1a.on 20pa. red (B.) £200 £250
a. "OCCUPATION" omitted £4750
b. "BAGHDAD" double £1300
8 **38** 2a.on 1pi. bright blue (R.) £3000 £3500

(c) Postal Jubilee stamps (Old G.P.O.). P 12½.

9 **60** ½a.on 10pa. carmine £400 £425
a. Perf 13½ £800 £850
10 1a.on 20pa. blue £3500
a. Value omitted £7000
b. Perf 13½ £850 £1000
11 2a.on 1pi. black and violet £180 £190
a. "BAGHDAD" omitted £4750
b. Perf 13½ 85·00 95·00
ba. "IN BRITISH" twice † £6000

(d) T **30** *(G.P.O., Constantinople) with opt T* **26**.

12 **30** 2a.on 1pi. ultramarine £350 £475
a. "IN BRITISH" omitted £6500

No. 11ba shows "BAGHDAD" superimposed on a second impression of "IN BRITISH" at the top of the stamp. The only known example is on cover.

(e) Stamps optd with six-pointed Star and Arabic date "1331" within Crescent. T **53** *(except No. 16, which has five-pointed Star and Arabic "1332", T* **57**).

13 **30** ½a.on 10pa. green (R.) 85·00 90·00
14 1a.on 20pa. rose £350 £375
a. Value omitted £3750 £3750
b. Optd with T **26** (Arabic letter "B") also £4500 £4500
15 **23** 1a.on 20pa. rose (No. 554a) £400 £425
a. Value omitted £6500
16 **21** 1a.on 20pa. carmine (No. 732) £3250 £4000
17 **30** 2a.on 1pi. ultramarine (R.) 95·00 £110
a. "BAGHDAD" omitted † —
18 **21** 2a.on 1pi. dull blue (No. 543) (R.) £160 £170
a. "OCCUPATION" omitted £6500

(f) Stamps with similar opt, but date between Star and Crescent (Nos. 19 and 22, T **54**; *others T* **55** *five-pointed Star).*

19 **23** ½a.on 10pa. grey-green (No. 609a) (R.) £100 £110
a. "OCCUPATION" omitted £5000
20 **60** ½a.on 10pa. carmine (P 12½) (B.) £150 £160
a. Perf 13½ £325 £350
21 **30** 1a.on 20pa. rose £100 £120
22 **28** 1a.on 20pa. rose (Plate II) (No. 617) £375 £425
23 **15** 1a.on 10pa. on 20pa. claret (No. 630) £170 £170
a. "OCCUPATION" omitted £5500 £5500

24	30	2a.on 1pi. ultramarine (R.)	£160	£170
		a. "OCCUPATION" omitted	£5500	
		b. "BAGHDAD" omitted	£5500	
25	28	2a.on 1pi. ultramarine (Pl. II) (No. 645)	£1300	£1500

The last group () have the Crescent obliterated by hand in violet-black ink, as this included the inscription, "Tax for the relief of children of martyrs".

II. ISSUES FOR MOSUL

PRICES FOR STAMPS ON COVER	
Nos. 1/8	*from* × 40

BRITISH OCCUPATION

A British and Indian force occupied Mosul on 1 November 1918. As the status of the vilayet was disputed stocks of "IRAQ IN BRITISH OCCUPATION" surcharges were withdrawn in early 1919 and replaced by Nos. 1/8.

POSTAGE

I.E.F. 'D'

1 Anna (1)   **4** I   **4** II

Two types of tougra in central design:
(a) Large "tougra" or sign-manual of El Ghazi 7 mm high.
(b) Smaller "tougra" of Sultan Rechad 5½ mm high.

Two types of 4a. surcharge:
I. Normal "4". Apostrophes on D 3½ mm apart.
II. Small "4" Apostrophes on D 4½ mm apart.

1919 (28 Jan). *Turkish Fiscal stamps surch as T* **1** *by Govt Press, Baghdad.* P 11½ (½a.), 12 (1a.), or 12½ (others).

1	½a.on 1pi. green and red	2·25	1·90
2	1a.on 20pa. black/*red* (*a*)	1·40	1·75
	a. Imperf between (horiz pair)	£600	
	b. Surch double	£500	
	c. "A" of "Anna" omitted	£200	
3	1a.on 20pa. black/*red* (*b*)	4·00	3·00
	b. Surch double	£600	
4	2½a.on 1pi. mauve and yellow (*b*)	1·50	1·50
	a. No bar to fraction (R. 2/4)	32·00	45·00
	b. Surch double	£700	
5	3a.on 20pa. green (*a*)	1·60	4·00
6	3a.on 20pa. green and orange (*b*)	35·00	55·00
7	4a.on 1pi. deep violet (*a*) (I)	3·00	3·50
	a. "4" omitted	£1400	
	c. Surch double	£850	
7*d*	4a.on 1pi. deep violet (*a*) (II)	9·50	13·00
	da. Surch double, one with "4" omitted	£2250	
8	8a.on 10pa. lake (*a*)	4·00	5·00
	a. Surch inverted	£650	£750
	b. Surch double	£550	£650
	c. No apostrophe after "D" (R. 1/5)	26·00	38·00
	d. Surch inverted. No apostrophe after "D"		
	e. "na" of "Anna" omitted	£250	
	f. Error. 8a. on 1pi. deep violet	£1800	

No. 4a occurs on some sheets only. No. 8c comes from the first setting only.

Nos. 1/8 were replaced by "IRAQ IN BRITISH OCCUPATION" surcharges during 1921.

In December 1925 the League of Nations awarded the vilayet of Mosul to Iraq.

III. ISSUES FOR IRAQ

PRICES FOR STAMPS ON COVER	
Nos. 1/18	*from* × 4
Nos. 41/154	*from* × 2
Nos. O19/171	*from* × 2

BRITISH OCCUPATION

IN BRITISH **IRAQ** **1An.** **OCCUPATION**
(1)

A

B

1918 (1 Sept)–**21**. *Turkish pictorial issue of 1914, surch as T* **1** *by Bradbury Wilkinson.* P 12.

(*a*) No wmk. *Tougra as A (1 Sept 1918–20).*

1	34	½a.on 5pa. dull purple	50	1·00
2	36	½a.on 10pa. green	70	20
3	37	1a.on 20pa. red	50	10
4	34	1½a.on 5pa. dull purple (1920)	4·25	50
5	38	2½a.on 1pi. bright blue	1·25	1·40
		a. Surch inverted	£3750	
6	39	3a.on 1½pi. grey and rose	1·25	25
		a. Surch double (Bk. + R.)	£1600	£2250
7	40	4a.on 1¾pi. red-brown and grey	1·50	25
		a. Centre inverted	†	£16000
8	41	6a.on 2pi. black and green	1·60	1·25
		a. Centre omitted		
9	42	8a.on 2½pi. green and orange	1·25	60
		a. Surch inverted	†	£9500
10	43	12a.on 5pi. deep lilac	1·75	4·00
11	44	1r.on 10pi. red-brown	2·25	1·40
12	45	2r.on 25pi. yellow-green	7·50	2·50
13	46	5r.on 50pi. rose	20·00	21·00
14	47	10r.on 100pi. indigo	50·00	17·00
1/14 *Set of* 14			85·00	45·00
1s/14s (ex 1½a. on 5pa.) Perf "Specimen" *Set of* 13			£275	

(*b*) No wmk. *Tougra as B (one device instead of two) (1921).*

15	44	1r. on 10pi. red-brown	£100	24·00

(*c*) Wmk Mult Script CA (sideways on ½a., 1½a.) *(1921).*

16	36	½a. on 10pa. green	1·50	2·00
17	34	1½a. on 5pa. dull purple	1·50	1·00
18	45	2r. on 25pi. yellow-green	13·00	11·00
16/18 *Set of* 3			14·50	12·50
16s/18s Optd "Specimen" *Set of* 3			60·00	

Designs: *Horiz*—5pa. Leander's Tower; 10pa. Lighthouse-garden, Stamboul; 20pa. Castle of Europe; 1pi. Mosque of Sultan Ahmed; 1½ pi. Martyrs of Liberty Monument; 1¾pi. Fountains of Suleiman; 2pi. Cruiser *Hamidiye*; 2½ pi. Candilli, Bosphorus; 5pi. Former Ministry of War; 10pi. Sweet Waters of Europe; 25pi. Suleiman Mosque; 50pi. Bosphorus at Rumeli Hisar; 100pi. Sultan Ahmed's Fountain.

The original settings of Nos. 1/18 showed the surcharge 27 mm wide, except for the 2½a. (24 mm), 4a. (26½ mm), 6a. (32 mm), 8a. (30½ mm), 12a. (33 mm), 1r. (31½ mm), 2r. (30 mm) and 5r. (32 mm). The 6a., 8a. and 5r. also exist from a subsequent setting on which the surcharge was 27½ mm wide.

Nos. 2, 3, 5, 6 and 7/9 are known bisected and used on philatelic covers. All such covers have Makinah or F.P.O. 339 cancellations.

During January 1923 an outbreak of cholera in Baghdad led to the temporary use for postal purposes of the above issue overprinted "REVENUE".

LEAGUE OF NATIONS MANDATE

On 25 April 1920 the Supreme Council of the Allies assigned to the United Kingdom a mandate under the League of Nations to administer Iraq.

The Emir Faisal, King of Syria in 1920, was proclaimed King of Iraq on 23 August 1921.

King Faisal I

23 August 1921–8 September 1933

2 Sunni Mosque, Muadhdham

3 Winged Cherub

4 Allegory of Date Palm

(Des Miss Edith Cheesman (½a., 1a., 4a., 6a., 8a., 2r., 5r., 10r.), Mrs. C. Garbett (Miss M. Maynard) (others). Typo (1r.) or recess (others) Bradbury, Wilkinson)

1923 (1 June)–**25**. *T* **2/4** *and similar designs.* Wmk Mult Script CA (sideways on 2a., 3a., 4a., 8a., 5r.). P 12.

41	2	½a. olive-green	1·00	10
42	–	1a. brown	2·25	10
43	3	1½a. lake	1·00	10
44	–	2a. orange-buff	1·00	15
45	–	3a. grey-blue (1923)	1·00	15
46	–	4a. violet	2·75	30
		w. Wmk crown to left of CA	†	£100
47	–	6a. greenish blue	1·00	30
48	–	8a. olive-bistre	3·00	30
49	4	1r. brown and blue-green	5·00	1·50
50	2	2r. black	14·00	7·00
51		2r. olive-bistre (1925)	40·00	3·25
52	–	5r. orange	27·00	13·00
53	–	10r. lake	32·00	20·00
41/53 *Set of* 13			£120	40·00
41s/53s Optd "Specimen" *Set of* 13			£250	

Designs: *Horiz* (*as T* **2**)—1a. Gufas on the Tigris. (30 × 24 *mm*)—2a. Bull From Babylonian wall-sculpture, 6a., 10r. Shiah Mosque, Kadhimain. (34 × 24 *mm*)—3a. Arch of Ctesiphon. *Vert* (*as T* **3**)—4a., 8a., 5r. Tribal Standard, Dulaim Camel Corps.

The normal sideways watermark on Nos. 44, 45, 46, 48 and 52 shows the crown to right of CA, *as seen from the back of the stamp.*

With the exception of Nos. 49 and 50, later printings of these stamps and of No. 78 are on a thinner paper.

10

11 King Faisal I

12

(Recess Bradbury, Wilkinson)

1927 (1 Apr). Wmk Mult Script CA. P 12.

78	10	1r. red-brown	7·00	50
		s. Optd "Specimen"	32·00	

See note below No. 53.

(Recess Bradbury Wilkinson)

1931 (17 Feb). Wmk Mult Script CA (sideways on 1r. to 25r.). P 12

80	11	½a. green	1·50	3
81		1a. red-brown	1·50	3
82		1½a. scarlet	1·50	5
83		2a. orange	1·25	1
84		3a. blue	1·25	2
85		4a. slate-purple	1·25	2·0
86		6a. greenish blue	1·50	8
87		8a. deep green	1·50	2·5
88	12	1r. chocolate	3·50	2·0
89		2r. yellow-brown	5·50	4·7
90		5r. orange	19·00	32·0
91		10r. scarlet	65·00	85·0
92	10	25r. violet	£500	£65
80/91 *Set of* 12			90·00	£12
80s/92s Perf "Specimen" *Set of* 13			£500	

(New Currency. 1000 fils = 1 dinar)

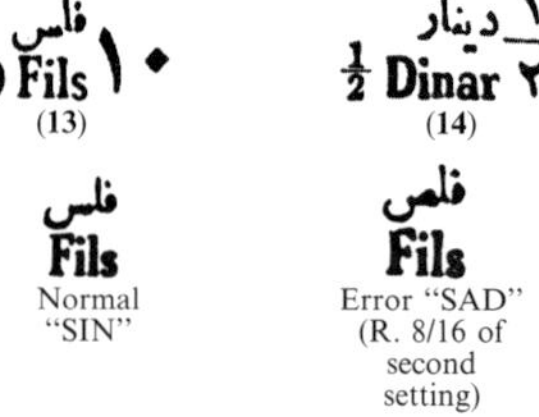

(13)   (14)
Normal "SIN"   Error "SAD" (R. 8/16 of second setting)

(Surcharged at Govt Ptg Wks, Baghdad)

1932 (1 Apr). *Nos. 80/92 and 46 surch in "Fils" or "Dinar" as T* **1**[3] *or* **14**.

106	11	2f.on ½a. green (R.)	50	
107		3f.on ½a. green	50	
		a. Surch double	£140	
		b. Surch inverted	£140	
		c. Arabic letter "SAD" instead of "SIN"	22·00	22·0
108		4f.on 1a. red-brown (G.)	2·25	2
109		5f.on 1a. red-brown	75	
		a. Inverted Arabic "5" (R. 8/11)	30·00	35·0
		b. Surch inverted	£250	
110		8f.on 1½a. scarlet	50	
		a. Surch inverted	£140	
111		10f.on 2a. orange	50	
		a. Inverted Arabic "1" (R. 8/13)	20·00	20·0
		b. No space between "10" and "Fils"	50	
112		15f.on 3a. blue	1·50	1·
113		20f.on 4a. slate-purple	1·75	1·
		a. Surch inverted	£250	
114	–	25f.on 4a. violet (No. 46)	2·75	4·
		a. "Flis" for "Fils" (R. 2/1, 10/8, 10/15)	£300	£3
		b. Inverted Arabic "5" (R. 10/7, 10/14)	£375	£4
		c. Vars a and b in *se-tenant* pair	£800	
		d. Error 20f. on 4a. violet (R. 10/1, 10/9)	£1300	
115	11	30f.on 6a. greenish blue	2·25	
		a. Error 80f. on 6a. greenish blue	£1100	
116		40f.on 8a. deep green	2·50	4·
117	12	75f.on 1r. chocolate	2·00	4·
		a. Inverted Arabic "5"	35·00	50·
118		100f.on 2r. yellow-brown	5·50	4·
119		200f.on 5r. orange	14·00	24·
120		½d.on 10r. scarlet	50·00	75·
		a. No bar in English "½"	£700	£8
		b. Scarlet-vermilion	55·00	90·
121	10	1d.on 25r. violet	£100	£1
106/121 *Set of* 16			£170	£2

Nos. 106/13 and 115/16 were in sheets of 160 (16 × 10) No. 1 sheets of 150 (15 × 10) and Nos. 117/21 sheets of 100 (10 × 10). The were three settings of the surcharge for the 3f. and two settings the 5, 10, 25, 40, 100 and 200f. Nos. 109a and 111a come from t first setting and Nos. 107c, 111b and 114a/b come from the secor

No. 109a can be easily identified as it shows the point of Arabic numeral at the foot of the surcharge.

All 10f. stamps from the second setting are as No. 111b exce for R. 4/7–8 and 15–16 where the spacing is the same as for the fi setting (Type **13**).

No. 114d shows "20" instead of "25". Many examples of t error were removed from the sheets before issue. The Arabic va "25" was unaltered.

No. 115a shows the error in the English face value only.

No. 117a occurs on R. 1/2, 1/7 and a third position in the f vertical row not yet identified.

No. 120a occurs on R. 10/1, one position in the first horizor row and another in the second.

No. 120b was a special printing of No. 91 which does not ex unsurcharged.

15

1932 (9 May). *T* **10** *to* **12**, *but with values altered to "FILS" "DINAR" as in T* **15**. Wmk Mult Script CA (sideways on 50f. 1d.). P 12.

138	11	2f. ultramarine	50
139		3f. green	50
140		4f. brown-purple	50
141		5f. grey-green	50
142		8f. scarlet	1·50
143		10f. yellow	1·50
144		15f. blue	1·50
145		20f. orange	1·75
146		25f. mauve	1·75
147		30f. bronze-green	2·25
148		40f. violet	1·50

49 **12** 50f. brown . . . 1·50 20
50 75f. dull ultramarine . . . 3·00 2·75
51 100f. deep green . . . 4·50 70
52 200f. scarlet . . . 13·00 3·25
53 **10** ½d. deep blue . . . 40·00 35·00
54 1d. claret . . . 80·00 80·00
38/54 *Set of* 17 . . . £140 £110
38s/54s Perf "Specimen" *Set of* 17 . . . £200

OFFICIAL STAMPS

ON STATE SERVICE
(O 2)

920 (16 May)–**23**. *As Nos. 1/18, but surch includes additional wording "ON STATE SERVICE" as Type* O **2** *in black.*

(a) No wmk. *Tougra as A.*
)19 **36** ¼a.on 10pa. blue-green . . . 6·50 1·75
)20 **37** 1a.on 20pa. red . . . 2·00 60
)21 **34** 1½a.on 5pa. purple-brown . . . 16·00 2·50
)22 **38** 2½a.on 1pi. blue . . . 2·25 2·50
)23 **39** 3a.on 1½pi. black and rose . . . 17·00 80
)24 **40** 4a.on 1¾pi. red-brown and grey-blue . . . 18·00 3·00
)25 **41** 6a.on 2pi. black and green . . . 17·00 4·75
)26 **42** 8a.on 2½pi. yellow-green & orge-brn . . . 15·00 3·00
)27 **43** 12a.on 5pi. purple . . . 10·00 7·00
28 **44** 1r.on 10pi. red-brown . . . 15·00 7·00
)29 **45** 2r.on 25pi. olive-green . . . 20·00 11·00
)30 **46** 5r.on 50pi. rose-carmine . . . 35·00 28·00
)31 **47** 10r.on 100pi. slate-blue . . . 50·00 75·00
)19/31 *Set of* 13 . . . £200 £130

(b) No wmk. Tougra as B (No. 15) (1922).
32 **44** 1r.on 10pi. red-brown . . . 25·00 7·00

(c) Wmk Mult Script CA (sideways on ½a. to 8a.) (1921–23).
33 **36** ½a.on 10pa. green . . . 1·00 1·00
34 **37** 1a.on 20pa. red . . . 3·50 1·00
35 **34** 1½a.on 5pa. purple-brown . . . 2·75 65
36 **40** 4a.on 1¾pi. red-brown and grey-blue . . . 2·00 1·60
37 **41** 6a.on 2pi. black and green (10.3.23) . . . 16·00 90·00
38 **42** 8a.on 2½pi. yellow-green & orge-brn . . . 3·25 2·00
39 **43** 12a.on 5pi. purple (10.3.23) . . . 18·00 65·00
40 **45** 2r.on 25pi. olive-green (10.3.23) . . . 50·00 85·00
33/40 *Set of* 8 . . . 85·00 £225
33s/40s Optd "Specimen" *Set of* 8 . . . £140

Nos. O25/6, O30 and O37/8 only exist from the setting with the urcharge 27½ mm wide.

ON STATE SERVICE
(O 6)

ON STATE SERVICE
(O 7)

23. *Optd with Types* O **6** *(horiz designs) or* O **7** *(vert designs).*
54 **2** ½a. olive-green . . . 1·50 1·00
55 – 1a. brown . . . 1·75 20
56 **3** 1½a. lake . . . 1·75 1·75
57 – 2a. orange-buff . . . 2·00 40
58 – 3a. grey-blue . . . 2·50 1·00
59 – 4a. violet . . . 4·25 1·00
60 – 6a. greenish blue . . . 3·75 1·25
61 – 8a. olive-bistre . . . 4·00 2·50
62 **4** 1r. brown and blue-green . . . 7·50 1·75
63 **2** 2r. black (R.) . . . 20·00 8·50
64 – 5r. orange . . . 48·00 30·00
65 – 10r. lake . . . 70·00 48·00
54/65 *Set of* 12 . . . £150 85·00
54s/65s Optd "Specimen" *Set of* 12 . . . £225

ON STATE SERVICE
(O 8)

ON STATE SERVICE
(O 9)

24–25. *Optd with Types* O **8** *(horiz designs) or* O **9** *(vert designs).*
56 **2** ½a. olive-green . . . 1·25 10
57 – 1a. brown . . . 1·00 10
58 **3** 1½a. lake . . . 1·00 30
59 – 2a. orange-buff . . . 1·50 10
70 – 3a. grey-blue . . . 2·00 10
71 – 4a. violet . . . 4·00 30
72 – 6a. greenish blue . . . 1·75 20
73 – 8a. olive-bistre . . . 3·75 35
74 **4** 1r. brown and blue-green . . . 9·50 1·50
75 **2** 2r. olive-bistre (1925) . . . 35·00 3·75
76 – 5r. orange . . . 50·00 42·00
77 – 10r. lake . . . 75·00 42·00
66/77 *Set of* 12 . . . £170 80·00
66s/77s Optd "Specimen" *Set of* 12 . . . £225

27 (1 Apr). *Optd with Type* O **9**.
79 **10** 1r. red-brown . . . 6·00 1·75
s. Optd "Specimen" . . . 32·00

ON STATE SERVICE

ON STATE SERVICE
(O 12)

(O 13)

1931. *Optd.*

(a) As Type O **12**.
O 93 **11** ½a. green . . . 65 2·75
O 94 1a. red-brown . . . 80 10
O 95 1½a. scarlet . . . 4·50 21·00
O 96 2a. orange . . . 80 10
O 97 3a. blue . . . 85 1·25
O 98 4a. slate-purple . . . 1·00 1·50
O 99 6a. greenish blue . . . 4·50 19·00
O100 8a. deep green . . . 4·75 19·00

(b) As Type O **13**, *horizontally.*
O101 **12** 1r. chocolate . . . 14·00 18·00
O102 2r. yellow-brown . . . 22·00 65·00
O103 5r. orange . . . 42·00 £120
O104 10r. scarlet . . . 80·00 £190

(c) As Type O **13**, *vertically upwards.*
O105 **10** 25r. violet . . . £550 £700
O93/104 *Set of* 12 . . . £160 £400
O93s/105s Perf "Specimen" *Set of* 13 . . . £500

1932 (1 Apr). *Official issues of 1924–25 and 1931 surch in "FILS" or "DINAR", as T* **13** *or* **14**.
O122 **11** 3f.on ½a. green . . . 3·50 3·50
a. Pair, one without surch . . . £275
O123 4f.on 1a. red-brown (G.) . . . 2·50 10
O124 5f.on 1a. red-brown . . . 2·50 10
a. Inverted Arabic "5" (R. 8/11) . . . 45·00 30·00
O125 **3** 8f.on 1½a. lake (No. O68) . . . 5·50 50
O126 **11** 10f.on 2a. orange . . . 3·00 10
a. Inverted Arabic "1" (R. 8/13) . . . 38·00 27·00
b. "10" omitted . . . † £1500
c. No space between "10" and "Fils" . . . 3·00 10
O127 15f.on 3a. blue . . . 4·25 2·50
O128 20f.on 4a. slate-purple . . . 4·25 2·50
O129 25f.on 4a. slate-purple . . . 4·50 2·00
O130 – 30f.on 6a. greenish blue (No. O72) . . . 4·75 1·75
O131 **11** 40f.on 8a. deep green . . . 4·00 3·50
a. "Flis" for "Fils" (R. 7/5, 7/13) . . . £250 £325
O132 **12** 50f.on 1r. chocolate . . . 5·50 3·50
a. Inverted Arabic "5" (R. 1/2) . . . 80·00 85·00
O133 75f.on 1r. chocolate . . . 6·00 6·00
a. Inverted Arabic "5" . . . 50·00 60·00
O134 **2** 100f.on 2r. olive-bistre (surch at top) . . . 18·00 3·50
a. Surch at foot . . . 20·00 12·00
O135 – 200f.on 5r. orange (No. O76) . . . 23·00 23·00
O136 – ½d.on 10r. lake (No. O77) . . . 65·00 85·00
a. No bar in English "½" (R. 2/10) . . . £750 £850
O137 **10** 1d.on 25r. violet . . . £120 £190
O122/37 *Set of* 16 . . . £250 £300

Nos. O122/4, O126/9 and O131 were in sheets of 160 (16 × 10), Nos. O130, O134 and O136 150 (10 × 15), No. O135 150 (15 × 10) and Nos. O125, O132/3 and O137 in sheets of 100 (10 × 10). There was a second setting of the surcharge for the 3f. (equivalent to the third postage setting), 10f. to 25f., 40f. to 100f. and 1d. Nos. O126c, O131a and O134a come from the second setting.

All 100f. stamps from the second setting are as No. O134a.

For notes on other varieties see below No. 121.

1932 (9 May). *Optd.*

(a) As Type O **12**.
O155 **11** 2f. ultramarine . . . 1·50 10
O156 3f. green . . . 1·50 10
O157 4f. brown-purple . . . 1·50 10
O158 5f. grey-green . . . 1·50 10
O159 8f. scarlet . . . 1·50 10
O160 10f. yellow . . . 2·25 10
O161 15f. blue . . . 2·50 10
O162 20f. orange . . . 2·50 15
O163 25f. mauve . . . 2·50 15
O164 30f. bronze-green . . . 3·50 20
O165 40f. violet . . . 4·50 30

(b) As Type O **13**, *horizontally.*
O166 **12** 50f. brown . . . 3·25 20
O167 75f. dull ultramarine . . . 2·50 1·00
O168 100f. deep green . . . 11·00 2·00
O169 200f. scarlet . . . 20·00 6·50

(c) As Type O **13**, *vertically upwards.*
O170 **10** ½d. deep blue . . . 12·00 24·00
O171 1d. claret . . . 60·00 90·00
O155/71 *Set of* 17 . . . £120 £110
O155s/71s Perf "Specimen" *Set of* 17 . . . £300

The British Mandate was given up on 3 October 1932 and Iraq became an independent kingdom. Later issues will be found listed in Part 19 (*Middle East*) of this catalogue.

Ireland (Republic)

All the issues of Ireland are listed together here, in this section of the Gibbons Catalogue, purely as a matter of convenience to collectors.

PRICES FOR STAMPS ON COVER TO 1945		
Nos.	1/15	*from* × 5
Nos.	17/21	*from* × 3
Nos.	26/9a	*from* × 5
Nos.	30/43	*from* × 4
Nos.	44/6	—
Nos.	47/63	*from* × 5
Nos.	64/6	*from* × 3
Nos.	67/70	*from* × 6
Nos.	71/82	*from* × 2
Nos.	83/8	*from* × 3
Nos.	89/98	*from* × 2
Nos.	99/104	*from* × 3
Nos.	105/37	*from* × 2
Nos.	D1/4	*from* × 7
Nos.	D5/14	*from* × 6

PROVISIONAL GOVERNMENT

16 January—6 December 1922

Stamps of Great Britain overprinted. T 104/8, W 100; T 109, W 110

Rialtas Sealadac na hÉireann 1922
(1)

Rialtas Sealadac na hÉireann 1922.
(2)

Rialtas Sealadac na hÉireann 1922
(3)

("Provisional Government of Ireland, 1922")

1922 (17 Feb–July). *T* **104** *to* **108** *(W* **100***) and* **109** *of Great Britain overprinted in black.*

(a) With T **1**, *by Dollard Printing House Ltd. Optd in black*.*
1 **105** ½d. green . . . 1·50 40
a. Opt inverted . . . £450 £600
2 **104** 1d. scarlet . . . 1·50 35
a. Opt inverted . . . £275 £325
b. Opt double, both inverted, one albino . . . £350
c. Opt double . . . † —
w. Wmk inverted . . . £170
3 1d. carmine-red . . . 3·75 70
4 2½d. bright blue . . . 2·00 5·50
a. Red opt (1 Apr) . . . 1·25 3·75
5 **106** 3d. bluish violet . . . 4·25 4·00
6 4d. grey-green . . . 4·00 12·00
a. Red opt (1 Apr) . . . 8·50 15·00
b. Carmine opt (July) . . . 40·00 65·00
7 **107** 5d. yellow-brown . . . 4·25 8·50
x. Wmk reversed . . . — £250
8 **108** 9d. agate . . . 11·00 22·00
a. Opt double, one albino
b. Red opt (1 Apr) . . . 14·00 18·00
c. Carmine opt (July) . . . 80·00 85·00
9 10d. turquoise-blue . . . 8·50 45·00
1/9 *Set of* 8 . . . 32·00 80·00

*All values except 2½d. and 4d. are known with greyish black overprint, but these are difficult to distinguish.

The carmine overprints on the 4d. and 9d. may have been produced by Alex Thom & Co. Ltd. There was a further overprinting of the 2½d. at the same time, but this is difficult to distinguish.

The ½d. with red overprint is a trial or proof printing (*Price* £160).

Bogus inverted *T* **1** overprints exist on the 2d., 4d., 9d and 1s. values.

(b) With T **2**, *by Alex Thom & Co Ltd.*
10 **105** 1½d. red-brown . . . 1·75 1·25
a. Error. ""PENCF" . . . £375 £300
w. Wmk inverted . . . — £140
x. Wmk reversed . . . — £140
12 **106** 2d. orange (Die I) . . . 3·25 50
a. Opt inverted . . . £190 £275
w. Wmk inverted . . . — £120
x. Wmk reversed . . . — £140
13 2d. orange (Die II) . . . 3·00 50
a. Opt inverted . . . £325 £425
w. Wmk inverted . . . — £140
14 **107** 6d. reddish pur (*chalk-surfaced paper*) . . . 13·00 16·00
15 **108** 1s. bistre-brown . . . 13·00 9·50
10/15 *Set of* 5 . . . 30·00 25·00

Varieties occur throughout the *T* **2** overprint in the relative positions of the lines of the overprint, the "R" of "Rialtas" being over either the "Se" or "S" of "Sealadac" or intermediately.

(c) With T **3** *by Dollard Printing House Ltd.*
17 **109** 2s.6d. chocolate-brown . . . 40·00 75·00
18 2s.6d. reddish brown . . . 60·00 85·00
19 5s. rose-red . . . 65·00 £140
21 10s. dull grey-blue . . . £120 £275
17/21 *Set of* 3 . . . £200 £450

1922 (19 June–Aug). *Optd as T* **2**, *in black, by Harrison & Sons, for use in horiz and vert coils.*
26 **105** ½d. green . . . 2·25 13·00
27 **104** 1d. scarlet . . . 2·75 6·50
28 **105** 1½d. red-brown (21.6) . . . 4·00 38·00
29 **106** 2d. bright orange (Die I) . . . 18·00 35·00
29*a* 2d. bright orange (Die II) (August) . . . 19·00 29·00
ay. Wmk inverted and reversed . . . — £250
26/9a *Set of* 5 . . . 40·00 £110

The Harrison overprint measures 15 × 17 mm (maximum) against the 14½ × 16 mm of *T* **2** (Thom printing) and is a much bolder black than the latter, while the individual letters are taller, the "i" of "Rialtas" being specially outstanding as it extends below the foot of the "R".

The "R" of "Rialtas" is always over the "Se" of "Sealadac".

1922. *Optd by Thom.*

(a) As T **2** *but bolder, in dull to shiny blue-black or red (June–Nov).*
30 **105** ½d. green . . . 2·75 80
31 **104** 1d. scarlet . . . 2·00 50
a. "Q" for "O" (No. 357ab) . . . £1200 £1100
b. Reversed "Q" for "O" (No. 357ac) . . . £350 £250
32 **105** 1½d. red-brown . . . 3·50 3·50
33 **106** 2d. orange (Die I) . . . 18·00 1·50

34 2d. orange (Die II) . . . 2·75 50
y. Wmk inverted and reversed . . . £140 £140
35 **104** 2½d. blue (R.) . . . 6·00 21·00
36 **106** 3d. violet . . . 3·00 2·00
y. Wmk inverted and reversed . . . 85·00 85·00
37 4d. grey-green (R.) . . . 3·25 6·00
38 **107** 5d. yellow-brown . . . 4·75 9·50
39 6d. reddish pur (*chalk-surfaced paper*) . . . 8·00 3·25
w. Wmk inverted . . . 85·00 60·00
40 **108** 9d. agate (R.) . . . 13·00 17·00
41 9d. olive-green (R.) . . . 5·00 38·00
42 10d. turquoise-blue . . . 26·00 60·00
43 1s. bistre-brown . . . 9·00 12·00
30/43 *Set of* 14 . . . 95·00 £150

Both 2d. stamps exist with the overprint inverted but there remains some doubt as to whether they were issued.

These Thom printings are distinguishable from the Harrison printings by the size of the overprint, and from the previous Thom printings by the intensity and colour of the overprint, the latter being best seen when the stamp is looked through with a strong light behind it.

(b) As with T **3**, *but bolder, in shiny blue-black (Oct–Dec).*
44 **109** 2s.6d. chocolate-brown . . . £190 £250
45 5s. rose-red . . . £190 £275
46 10s. dull grey-blue . . . £900 £1100
44/6 *Set of* 3 . . . £1100 £1500

The above differ from Nos. 17/21 not only in the bolder impression and colour of the ink but also in the "h" and "e" of "heireann" which are closer together and horizontally aligned.

Rialtas Sealadaċ na hÉireann 1922.
(4)

Saorstát Éireann 1922
(5 Wide date)("Irish Free State 1922")

1922 (21 Nov–Dec). *Optd by Thom with T* **4** *(wider setting) in shiny blue-black.*
47 **105** ½d. green . . . 1·00 1·75
a. Opt in jet-black . . . £100 90·00
48 **104** 1d. scarlet . . . 4·75 2·50
49 **105** 1½d. red-brown (4 December) . . . 3·00 12·00
50 **106** 2d. orange (Die II) . . . 9·00 7·00
51 **108** 1s. olive-bistre (4 December) . . . 45·00 60·00
47/51 *Set of* 5 . . . 55·00 75·00

The overprint *T* **4** measures 15¾ × 16 mm (maximum).

IRISH FREE STATE

6 December 1922—29 December 1937

1922 (Dec)–**23**.

(a) Optd by Thom with T **5**, *in dull to shiny blue-black or red.*
52 **105** ½d. green . . . 1·25 30
a. No accent in "Saorstat" . . . £1200 £1000
b. Accent inserted by hand . . . 90·00 £110
53 **104** 1d. scarlet . . . 1·25 50
aa. No accent in "Saorstat" . . . £8000 £6000
a. No accent and final "t" missing . . . £7000 £5000
b. Accent inserted by hand . . . £140 £170
c. Accent and "t" inserted . . . £225 £275
d. Reversed "Q" for "O" (No. 357ac) . . . £300 £250
54 **105** 1½d. red-brown . . . 3·50 8·50
55 **106** 2d. orange (Die II) . . . 1·50 1·00
56 **104** 2½d. bright blue (R.) (6.1.23) . . . 6·50 8·00
a. No accent . . . £150 £190
57 **106** 3d. bluish violet (6.1.23) . . . 3·75 11·00
a. No accent . . . £300 £325
58 4d. grey-green (R.) (16.1.23) . . . 3·25 7·50
a. No accent . . . £160 £190
59 **107** 5d. yellow-brown . . . 3·50 4·75
60 6d. reddish pur (*chalk-surfaced paper*) . . . 2·00 2·00
a. Accent inserted by hand . . . £800 £800
y. Wmk inverted and reversed . . . 70·00 40·00
61 **108** 9d. olive-green (R.) . . . 3·25 5·50
a. No accent . . . £250 £275
62 10d. turquoise-blue . . . 16·00 60·00
63 1s. bistre-brown . . . 7·00 11·00
a. No accent . . . £6500 £7500
b. Accent inserted by hand . . . £700 £750
64 **109** 2s.6d. chocolate-brown . . . 35·00 55·00
a. Major Re-entry . . . £950 £1100
b. No accent . . . £400 £450
c. Accent reversed . . . £475 £550
65 5s. rose-red . . . 70·00 £140
a. No accent . . . £500 £600
b. Accent reversed . . . £650 £700
66 10s. dull grey-blue . . . £160 £325
a. No accent . . . £2500 £3000
b. Accent reversed . . . £3250 £4000
52/66 *Set of* 15 . . . £275 £550

The accents inserted by hand are in dull black. The reversed accents are grave (thus "à") instead of acute ("á"). A variety with "S" of "Saorstat" directly over "é" of "éireann", instead of to left, may be found in all values except the 2½d. and 4d. In the 2s. 6d., 5s. and 10s. it is very slightly to the left in the "S" over "é" variety, bringing the "á" of "Saorstat" directly above the last "n" of "éireann".

(b) Optd with T **5**, *in dull or shiny blue-black, by Harrison, for use in horiz or vert coils (7.3.23).*
67 ½d. green . . . 1·75 11·00
a. Long "1" in "1922" . . . 20·00 50·00
y. Wmk inverted and reversed
68 1d. scarlet . . . 4·00 11·00
a. Long "1" in "1922" . . . 75·00 £140
69 1½d. red-brown . . . 6·00 45·00
a. Long "1" in "1922" . . . 85·00 £225
70 2d. orange (Die II) . . . 7·00 11·00
a. Long "1" in "1922" . . . 32·00 50·00
w. Wmk inverted . . . — £170
67/70 *Set of* 4 . . . 17·00 70·00

In the Harrison overprint the characters are rather bolder than those of the Thom overprint, and the foot of the "1" of "1922" is usually rounded instead of square. The long "1" in "1922" has a serif at foot. The second "e" of "eireann" appears to be slightly raised.

PRINTERS. The following and all subsequent issues to No. 148 were printed at the Government Printing Works, Dublin, *unless otherwise stated.*

6 "Sword of Light"

7 Map of Ireland

8 Arms of Ireland

9 Celtic Cross

10

(Des J. J. O'Reilly, *T* **6**; J. Ingram, *T* **7**; Miss M. Girling, *T* **8**; and Miss L. Williams, *T* **9**. Typo. Plates made by Royal Mint, London)

1922 (6 Dec)–**34**. W**10**. P 15 × 14.
71 **6** ½d. bright green (20.4.23) . . . 1·00 90
a. Imperf × perf 14, Wmk sideways (11.34) . . . 20·00 45·00
w. Wmk inverted . . . 32·00 15·00
72 **7** 1d. carmine (23.2.23) . . . 1·00 10
aw. Wmk inverted
b. Perf 15 × imperf (single perf) (1933) . . . 85·00 £160
c. Perf 15 × imperf (7.34) . . . 12·00 42·00
cw. Wmk inverted
d. Booklet pane. Three stamps plus three printed labels (21.8.31) . . . £250
dw. Wmk inverted
73 1½d. claret (2.2.23) . . . 1·60 2·50
w. Wmk inverted
74 2d. grey-green (6.12.22) . . . 1·50 10
a. Imperf × perf 14, Wmk sideways (11.34) . . . 38·00 70·00
b. Perf 15 × imperf (1934) . . . £9000 £1500
w. Wmk inverted . . . 22·00 5·00
y. Wmk inverted and reversed . . . 32·00 7·00
75 **8** 2½d. red-brown (7.9.23) . . . 4·00 4·25
w. Wmk inverted . . . 55·00 8·00
76 **9** 3d. ultramarine (16.3.23) . . . 2·00 75
w. Wmk inverted . . . 70·00 12·00
77 **8** 4d. slate-blue (28.9.23) . . . 2·00 3·25
w. Wmk inverted . . . 80·00 25·00
78 **6** 5d. deep violet (11.5.23) . . . 8·00 9·50
w. Wmk inverted
79 6d. claret (21.12.23) . . . 4·50 3·50
w. Wmk inverted . . . £120 25·00
80 **8** 9d. deep violet (26.10.23) . . . 13·00 8·00
w. Wmk inverted
81 **9** 10d. brown (11.5.23) . . . 9·00 18·00
w. Wmk inverted
82 **6** 1s light blue (15.6.23) . . . 17·00 5·50
w. Wmk inverted
71/82 *Set of* 12 . . . 55·00 50·00

No. 72b is imperf vertically except for a single perf at each top corner. It was issued for use in automatic machines.

See also Nos. 111/22.

Saorstát Éireann 1922
(**11** Narrow Date)

12 Daniel O'Connell

1925 (Aug)–**28**. *T* **109** *of Great Britain (Bradbury, Wilkinson printing) optd at the Government Printing Works, Dublin or by Harrison and Sons.*

(a) With T **11** *in black or grey-black (25.8.25).*
83 2s. 6d.chocolate-brown . . . 40·00 90·00
a. Wide and narrow date (pair) (1927) . . . £250
84 5s. rose-red . . . 60·00 £140
a. Wide and narrow date (pair) (1927) . . . £425
85 10s. dull grey-blue . . . £130 £325
a. Wide and narrow date (pair) (1927) . . . £1100
83/5 *Set of* 3 . . . £200 £500

The varieties with wide and narrow date *se-tenant* are from what is known as the "composite setting," in which some stamps showed the wide date, as *T* **5**, while in others the figures were close together, as in *T* **11**.

Single specimens of this printing with wide date may be distinguished from Nos. 64 to 66 by the colour of the ink, which is black or grey-black in the composite setting and blue-black in the Thom printing.

The type of the "composite" overprint usually shows distinct sign of wear.

(b) As T **5** *(wide date) in black (1927–28).*
86 2s.6d. chocolate-brown (9.12.27) . . . 45·00 50·0
a. Circumflex accent over "a" . . . £250 £30
b. No accent over "a" . . . £400 £42
c. Flat accent on "a" . . . £350 £40
87 5s. rose-red (2.28) . . . 65·00 90·0
a. Circumflex accent over "a" . . . £375 £42
c. Flat accent on "a" . . . £450 £50
88 10s. dull grey-blue (15.2.28) . . . £150 £19
a. Circumflex accent over "a" . . . £900 £110
c. Flat accent on "a" . . . £1000 £120
86/8 *Set of* 3 . . . £225 £30

This printing can be distinguished from the Thom overprints in dull black, by the clear, heavy impression (in deep black) which often shows in relief on the back of the stamp.

The variety showing a circumflex accent over the "a" occurred on R. 9/2. The overprint in this position finally deteriorated to such an extent that some examples of the 2s.6d. were without accent (No. 86b). A new cliché was then introduced with the accent virtually flat and which also showed damage to the "a" and the crossbar of the "t".

(Des L. Whelan. Typo)

1929 (22 June). *Catholic Emancipation Centenary.* W **10**. P 15 × 14
89 **12** 2d. grey-green . . . 50 4
90 3d. blue . . . 4·00 8·5
91 9d. bright violet . . . 4·00 4·0
89/91 *Set of* 3 . . . 7·50 11·5

13 Shannon Barrage

14 Reaper

(Des E. L. Lawrenson. Typo)

1930 (15 Oct). *Completion of Shannon Hydro-Electric Scheme.* W 1 P 15 × 14.
92 **13** 2d. agate . . . 1·00

(*T* **14** and **15** des G. Atkinson. Typo)

1931 (12 June). *Bicentenary of the Royal Dublin Society.* W 1 P 15 × 14.
93 **14** 2d. blue . . . 65

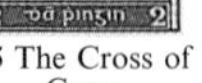
15 The Cross of Cong

16 Adoration of the Cross

17 Hurler

1932 (12 May). *International Eucharistic Congress.* W **10**. P 15 × 1
94 **15** 2d. grey-green . . . 1·25
w. Wmk inverted
95 3d. blue . . . 2·25 5·

(*T* **16** to **19** des R. J. King. Typo)

1933 (18 Sept). *"Holy Year".* W **10**. P 15 × 14.
96 **16** 2d. grey-green . . . 1·25
97 3d. blue . . . 2·50 2·

1934 (27 July). *Golden Jubilee of the Gaelic Athletic Association.* **10**. P 15 × 14.
98 **17** 2d. green . . . 1·00

1935 (Mar–July). *T* **109** *of Great Britain (Waterlow printings) op as T* **5** *(wide date), at the Government Printing Works, Dublin.*
99 **109** 2s.6d. chocolate (No. 450) . . . 45·00 55·
a. Flat accent on "a" (R. 9/2) . . . £275 £2
100 5s. bright rose-red (No. 451) . . . 80·00 85·
a. Flat accent on "a" (R. 9/2) . . . £350 £3
101 10s. indigo (No. 452) . . . £275 £2
a. Flat accent on "a" (R. 9/2) . . . £950 £8
99/101 *Set of* 3 . . . £350 £3

18 St. Patrick

19 Ireland and New Constitution

1937 (8 Sept). W **10**. P 14 × 15.
102 **18** 2s.6d. emerald-green . . . £140 65
w. Wmk inverted . . . £600 £2
103 5s. maroon . . . £180 £1
w. Wmk inverted . . . £500 £2
104 10s. deep blue . . . £140 55
w. Wmk inverted
102/4 *Set of* 3 . . . £425 £2

See also Nos. 123/5.

EIRE

29 December 1937–17 April 1949

1937 (29 Dec). *Constitution Day.* W **10**. P 15×14.
105 **19** 2d. claret . . . . 1·00 20
w. Wmk inverted . . . . — £190
06 3d. blue . . . . 4·00 3·75
For similar stamps see Nos. 176/7.

20 Father Mathew

(Des S. Keating. Typo)

1938 (1 July). *Centenary of Temperance Crusade.* W **10**. P 15×14.
07 **20** 2d. agate . . . . 1·50 40
w. Wmk inverted . . . .
08 3d. blue . . . . 10·00 6·50

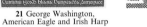

21 George Washington, American Eagle and Irish Harp

22

(Des G. Atkinson. Typo)

1939 (1 Mar). *150th Anniv of U.S. Constitution and Installation of First U.S. President.* W **10**. P 15×14.
09 **21** 2d. scarlet . . . . 1·75 1·00
10 3d. blue . . . . 3·25 4·50

IZE OF WATERMARK. *T* **22** can be found in various sizes from bout 8 to 10 mm high. This is due to the use of two different dandy olls supplied by different firms and to the effects of paper shrinkage nd other factors such as pressure and machine speed.

White line above left value tablet joining horizontal line to ornament (R. 3/7)

940–68. *Typo.* W **22**. P 15×14 or 14×15 (2s. 6d. to 10s.).
1 **6** ½d. bright green (24.11.40) . . . . 2·00 40
w. Wmk inverted . . . . 50·00 7·50
2 **7** 1d. carmine (26.10.40) 30 10
aw. Wmk inverted . . . . 2·00 30
b. From coils. Perf 14 × imperf (9.40) . . . . 60·00 65·00
c. From coils. Perf 15 × imperf (20.3.46) . . . . 40·00 18·00
cw. Wmk inverted . . . . 40·00 18·00
d. Booklet pane. Three stamps plus three printed labels £1700
dw. Wmk inverted . . . .
3 1½d. claret (1.40) . . . . 14·00 30
w. Wmk inverted . . . . 40·00 8·50
4 2d. grey-green (1.40) 30 10
w Wmk inverted . . . . 2·50 1·00
5 **8** 2½d. red-brown (3.41) . . . . 9·50 15
w. Wmk inverted . . . . 20·00 4·25
6 **9** 3d. blue(12.40) 70 10
w. Wmk inverted . . . . 3·75 70
7 **8** 4d. slate-blue (12.40) 55 10
w. Wmk inverted . . . . 16·00 3·00
8 **6** 5d. deep violet (7.40) 65 10
w. Wmk inverted . . . . 30·00 1·50
9 6d. claret (3.42) . . . . 2·25 50
aw. Wmk inverted . . . . 23·00 3·25
b. Chalk-surfaced paper (1967) . . 1·25 20
bw. Wmk inverted . . . . 13·00 2·50
9c 8d. scarlet (12.9.49) 80 80
cw. Wmk inverted . . . . 35·00 12·00
0 **8** 9d. deep violet (7.40) . . . . 1·50 80
w. Wmk inverted . . . . 10·00 2·00
1 **9** 10d. brown (7.40) 60 80
aw. Wmk inverted . . . . 11·00 4·00
1b 11d. rose (12.9.49) . . . . 1·50 2·25
2 **6** 1s. light blue (6.40) . . . . 65·00 17·00
w. Wmk inverted £700 £160
3 **18** 2s.6d. emerald-green (10.2.43) . . . 40·00 1·25
aw. Wmk inverted . . . . 95·00 23·00
b. Chalk-surfaced paper (1967) . . 1·50 2·50
bw. Wmk inverted . . . . 30·00 4·25
4 5s. maroon (15.12.42) . . . . 40·00 3·00
a. Line flaw . . . .
bw. Wmk inverted . . . . £180 40·00
c. Chalk-surfaced paper (1968?) . . 13·00 4·25
ca. Purple . . . . 6·00 8·50
cb. Line flaw . . . . 95·00
cw. Wmk inverted . . . . 35·00 9·50
5 10s. deep blue (7.45) . . . . 60·00 7·00
aw. Wmk inverted . . . . £200 80·00
b. Chalk-surfaced paper (1968) . . 19·00 12·00
ba. Blue . . . . 7·00 16·00
bw. Wmk inverted . . . . £140 65·00
1/25 *Set of* 17 . . . . £100 30·00
There is a wide range of shades and also variation in paper used this issue.
See also Nos. 227/8.

1941
i gcuimne
aiséirge
1916

(**23** Trans "In memory of the rising of 1916")

24 Volunteer and G.P.O., Dublin

1941 (12 Apr). *25th Anniv of Easter Rising (1916). Provisional issue. T* **7** *and* **9** *(2d. in new colour), optd with T* **23**.
126 **7** 2d. orange (G.) . . . . 1·00 50
127 **9** 3d. blue (V.) . . . . 24·00 10·00

(Des V. Brown. Typo)

1941 (27 Oct). *25th Anniv of Easter Rising (1916). Definitive issue.* W **22**. P 15×14.
128 **24** 2½d. blue-black . . . . 1·75 70

25 Dr. Douglas Hyde

26 Sir William Rowan Hamilton

27 Bro. Michael O'Clery

(Des S. O'Sullivan. Typo)

1943 (31 July). *50th Anniv of Founding of Gaelic League.* W **22**. P 15×14.
129 **25** ½d. green 40 30
130 2½d. claret . . . . 1·50 10

(Des S. O'Sullivan from a bust by Hogan. Typo)

1943 (13 Nov). *Centenary of Announcement of Discovery of Quaternions.* W **22**. P 15×14.
131 **26** ½d. green 40 50
w. Wmk inverted . . . .
132 2½d. brown . . . . 1·75 10

(Des R. J. King. Typo)

1944 (30 June). *Tercentenary of Death of Michael O'Clery. (Commemorating the "Annals of the Four Masters".* W **22** (sideways*). P 14×15.
133 **27** ½d. emerald-green 10 10
w. Wmk facing right 55 20
134 1s. red-brown 70 10
w. Wmk facing right . . . . 3·00 65
*The normal sideways watermark shows the top of the e facing left, *as seen from the back of the stamp.*
Although issued as commemoratives these two stamps were kept in use as part of the current issue, replacing Nos. 111 and 122.

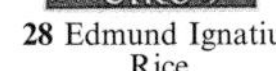

28 Edmund Ignatius Rice

29 "Youth Sowing Seeds of Freedom"

(Des S. O'Sullivan. Typo)

1944 (29 Aug). *Death Centenary of Edmund Rice (founder of Irish Christian Brothers).* W **22**. P 15×14.
135 **28** 2½d. slate . . . . 1·25 45
w. Wmk inverted . . . .

(Des R. J. King. Typo)

1945 (15 Sept). *Centenary of Death of Thomas Davis (founder of Young Ireland Movement).* W **22**. P 15×14.
136 **29** 2½d. blue . . . . 1·00 35
w. Wmk inverted . . . . — £140
137 6d. claret . . . . 6·00 4·00

30 "Country and Homestead"

(Des R. J. King. Typo)

1946 (16 Sept). *Birth Centenaries of Davitt and Parnell (land reformers).* W **22**. P 15×14.
138 **30** 2½d. scarlet . . . . 2·00 25
139 3d. blue . . . . 2·75 3·75

31 Angel Victor over Rock of Cashel

(Des R. J. King. Recess Waterlow (1d. to 1s.3d. until 1961), D. L. R. (8d., 1s.3d. from 1961 and 1s.5d.))

1948 (7 Apr)–**65**. *Air. T* **31** *and similar horiz designs.* W **22**. P 15 (1s. 5d.) or 15×4 (others).
140 **31** 1d. chocolate (4.4.49) . . . . 1·50 3·75
141 3d. blue . . . . 3·00 2·25
142 6d. magenta . . . . 80 1·50
aw. Wmk inverted . . . .
142*b* 8d. lake-brown (13.12.54) . . . . . 6·50 7·50
143 1s. green (4.4.49) . . . . 1·00 1·50
143*a* 1s.3d. red-orange (13.12.54) . . . . 8·00 1·25
aw. Wmk inverted £550 £250
143*b* 1s.5d. deep ultramarine (1.4.65) . . 2·75 1·00
140/3*b Set of* 7 . . . . 21·00 17·00
Design:—3d, 8d. Lough Derg; 6d. Croagh Patrick; 1s. Glendalough

35 Theobald Wolfe Tone

(Des K. Uhlemann. Typo)

1948 (19 Nov). *150th Anniv of Insurrection.* W **22**. P 15×14.
144 **35** 2½d. reddish purple . . . . 1·00 10
w. Wmk inverted . . . .
145 3d. violet . . . . 3·25 3·25

REPUBLIC OF IRELAND

18 April 1949

36 Leinster House and Arms of Provinces

37 J. C. Mangan

(Des Muriel Brandt. Typo)

1949 (21 Nov). *International Recognition of Republic.* W **22**. P 15×14.
146 **36** 2½d. reddish brown . . . . 1·50 10
147 3d. bright blue . . . . 6·00 4·25

(Des R. J. King. Typo)

1949 (5 Dec). *Death Centenary of James Clarence Mangan (poet).* W **22**. P 15×14.
148 **37** 1d. green . . . . 1·50 25
w. Wmk inverted . . . .

38 Statue of St. Peter, Rome

(Recess Waterlow & Sons)

1950 (11 Sept). *Holy Year.* W **22**. P 12½.
149 **38** 2½d. violet . . . . 1·00 40
150 3d. blue . . . . 8·00 11·00
151 9d. brown . . . . 8·00 11·00
149/51 *Set of* 3 . . . . 15·00 20·00

STAMP BOOKLETS

Nos. SB1 to SB24 are stitched. Subsequent booklets have their panes attached by the selvedge, *unless otherwise stated.*

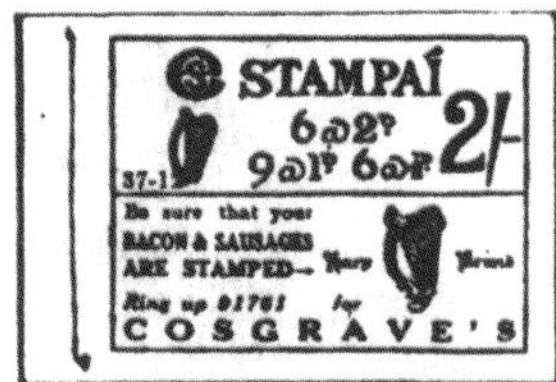

B 1 Harp and Monogram

B 2 Harp and "EIRE"

1931 (21 Aug)–**40**. *Black on red cover as Type* **B 1**.
SB1 2s. booklet containing six ½d., six 2d. (Nos. 71, 74), each in block of 6, and nine 1d. (No. 72) in block of 6 and pane of 3 stamps and 3 labels (No. 72d or 72dw) . . . . *From* £2000
Edition Nos.:—31–1, 31–2, 32–3, 33–4, 33–5, 34–6, 34–7, 35–8, 35–9, 36–10, 36–11, 37–12, 37–13, 37–14, 15–38, 16–38, 17–38
a. Cover as Type **B 2**
Edition Nos.:–18–39, 19–39, 20–39, 21–40, 22–40

1940. *Black on red cover as Type* **B 2**.

SB2	2s. booklet containing six ½d., six 2d. (Nos. 71, 74), each in block of 6, and nine 1d. (No. 72) in block of 6 and pane of 3 stamps and 3 labels (No. 112d or 112dw)	£7000
	Edition No.:—22–40	

1940. *Black on red cover as Type* **B 2**.

SB3	2s. booklet containing six ½d., six 2d. (Nos. 111, 114), each in block of 6, and nine 1d. (No. 112) in block of 6 and pane of 3 stamps and 3 labels (No. 112d or 112dw)	£7000
	Edition No.:—23–40	

1941–44. *Black on red cover as Type* **B 2**.

SB4	2s. booklet containing twelve ½d., six 1d. and six 2d. (Nos. 111/12, 114) in blocks of 6	£800
	Edition Nos.:—24–41, 25–42, 26–44	

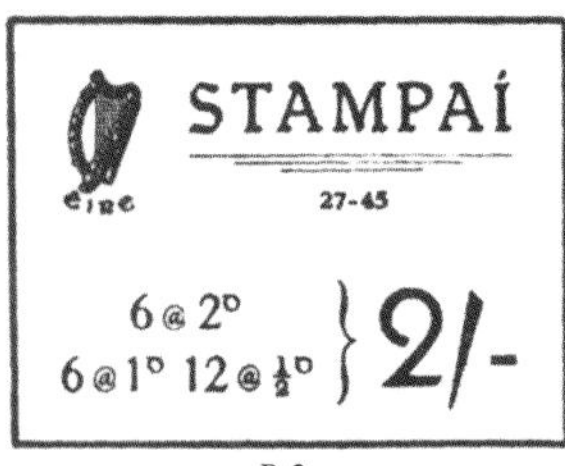

B 3

1945. *Black on red cover as Type* **B 3**.

SB5	2s. booklet containing twelve ½d., six 1d. and six 2d. (Nos. 111/12, 114) in blocks of 6	£700
	Edition No.:—27–45	

1946. *Black on buff cover as Type* **B 2**.

SB6	2s. booklet containing twelve ½d., six 1d. and six 2d. (Nos. 111/12, 114) in blocks of 6	£500
	Edition No.:—28–46	

1946–47. *Black on buff cover as Type* **B 2**.

SB7	2s. booklet containing twelve ½d, six 1d. and six 2d. (Nos. 133, 112, 114) in blocks of 6 *From*	£250
	Edition Nos.:—29–46, 30–47	

B 4 Harp only

1948–50. *Black on red cover as Type* **B 4**.

SB8	2s.6d. booklet containing six ½d., twelve 1d. and six 2½d. (Nos. 133, 112, 115) in blocks of 6	£140
	Edition Nos.:—31–48, 32–49, 33–50	

1951–53. *Black on buff cover as Type* **B 4**.

SB9	2s.6d. booklet containing six ½d., twelve 1d. and six 2½d. (Nos. 133, 112, 115) in blocks of 6	50·00
	Edition Nos.:—34–51, 35–52, 36–53	

POSTAGE DUE STAMPS

From 1922 to 1925 Great Britain postage due stamps in both script and block watermarks were used without overprint.

D 1

(Des Ruby McConnell. Typo Govt Printing Works, Dublin)

1925 (20 Feb). W **10**. P 14 × 15.

D1	D 1	½d. emerald-green	12·00	16·00
D2		1d. carmine	15·00	3·00
		a. Wmk sideways	£700	£300
		w. Wmk inverted	£350	30·00
D3		2d. deep green	35·00	5·50
		a. Wmk sideways	50·00	17·00
		w. Wmk inverted	85·00	25·00
D4		6d. plum	6·00	7·50
D1/4 *Set of* 4			60·00	29·00

1940–70. W **22**. P 14 × 15.

D 5	D 1	½d. emerald-green (1942)	35·00	23·00
		w. Wmk inverted	£350	£170
D 6		1d. carmine (1941)	1·50	70
		w. Wmk inverted	65·00	7·50
D 7		1½d. vermilion (1953)	2·25	6·50
		w. Wmk inverted	17·00	24·00
D 8		2d. deep green (1940)	2·75	70
		w. Wmk inverted	24·00	7·50
D 9		3d. blue (10.11.52)	2·50	2·75
		w. Wmk inverted	7·00	5·00
D10		5d. blue-violet (3.3.43)	4·50	3·00
		w. Wmk inverted	6·50	7·00
D11		6d. plum (21.3.60)	3·75	2·00
		a. Wmk sideways (1968)	1·00	1·00
D12		8d. orange (30.10.62)	8·50	9·00
		w. Wmk inverted	17·00	19·00
D13		10d. bright purple (27.1.65)	8·50	7·50
D14		1s. apple-green (10.2.69)	6·00	9·50
		a. Wmk sideways (1970)	75·00	8·50
D5/14 *Set of* 10			65·00	55·00

Jamaica

Records show that the first local Postmaster for Jamaica on a regular basis was appointed as early as 1671, although a reasonably organised service did not evolve until 1687–8. In the early years of the 18th century overseas mail was carried by the British packets, but between 1704 and 1711 this service was run on a commercial basis by Edmund Dummer. Following the collapse of the Dummer scheme Jamaica was virtually without a Post Office until 1720 and it was not until 1755 that overseas mail was again carried by British packets.

Stamps of Great Britain were used in Jamaica from 8 May 1858, initially on overseas mail only, but their use was extended to mail sent to Jamaican addresses from 1 February 1859. The island assumed responsibility for the postal service on 1 August 1860 and the use of Great Britain stamps then ceased.

KINGSTON

Z 1

Stamps of GREAT BRITAIN *cancelled "A 01" as Type* Z **1**.

1858–60.

Z1	1d. rose-red (1857), *perf* 16	£275
Z2	1d. rose-red (1857), *perf* 14	38·00
Z4	4d. rose-carmine *or* rose (1857)	38·00
Z5	6d. lilac (1856)	38·00
Z6	1s. green (1856)	£130

Z 2

Stamps of GREAT BRITAIN *cancelled "A 01" as Type* Z **2**.

1859–60.

Z 7	1d. rose-red (1857), *perf* 14	£180
Z 9	4d. rose-carmine *or* rose (1857)	40·00
Z10	6d. lilac (1856)	40·00
Z11	1s. green (1856)	£325

Z 3

Stamps of GREAT BRITAIN *cancelled "A 01" as Type* Z **3**.

1859–60.

Z12	1d. rose-red (1857), *perf* 14	£225
Z14	4d. rose-carmine *or* rose (1857)	£130
	a. Thick glazed paper	£400
Z15	6d. lilac (1856)	£130
Z16	1s. green (1856)	

Cancellation "A 01" was later used by the London, Foreign Branch Office.

OTHER JAMAICA POST OFFICES

British stamps were issued to several District post offices between 8 May 1858 and 1 March 1859 (i.e. before the Obliterators A 27—A 78 were issued). These can only be distinguished (off the cover) when they have the Town's date-stamp on them. They are worth about three times the price of those with an obliteration number.

Stamps of GREAT BRITAIN *cancelled "A 27" to "A 78" as Type* Z **1**

1859–60.

"A 27". ALEXANDRIA

Z17	1d. rose-red (1857), *perf* 14	£450
Z17*a*	2d. blue (1855) Large Crown, *perf* 14 (Plate 6)	£500
Z18	4d. rose (1857)	£170
Z19	6d. lilac (1856)	£40

"A 28". ANNOTTO BAY

Z20	1d. rose-red (1857), *perf* 14	£32
Z21	4d. rose (1857)	80·0
Z22	6d. lilac (1856)	£25

"A 29". BATH

Z23	1d. rose-red (1857), *perf* 14	£13
Z24	4d. rose (1857)	90·0
Z25	6d. lilac (1856)	£42

"A 30". BLACK RIVER

Z26	1d. rose-red (1857), *perf* 14	£13
Z27	4d. rose (1857)	60·0
Z28	6d. lilac (1856)	£13

"A31". BROWN'S TOWN

Z29	1d. rose-red (1857), *perf* 14	£17
Z30	4d. rose (1857)	£17
Z31	6d. lilac (1856)	£17

"A 32". BUFF BAY

Z32	1d. rose-red (1857), *perf* 14	£13
Z33	4d. rose (1857)	£16
Z34	6d. lilac (1856)	£13

"A 33". CHAPELTON

Z35	1d. rose-red (1857), *perf* 14	£17
Z36	4d. rose (1857)	£11
Z37	6d. lilac (1856)	£17

"A34". CLAREMONT

Z38	1d. rose-red (1857), *perf* 14	£32
Z39	4d. rose (1857)	£16
Z40	6d. lilac (1856)	£32

"A35". CLARENDON

Z41	1d. rose-red (1857), *perf* 14	£27
Z42	4d. rose (1857)	£11
Z43	6d. lilac (1856)	£17

"A 36". DRY HARBOUR

Z44	1d. rose-red (1857), *perf* 14	£40
Z45	4d. rose (1857)	£32
Z46	6d. lilac (1856)	£27

"A 37". DUNCANS

Z47	1d. rose-red (1857), *perf* 14	
Z48	4d. rose (1857)	£40
Z49	6d. lilac (1856)	£27

"A 38". EWARTON

A 38 was allocated to EWARTON but this office was close towards the end of 1858 before the postmark arrived. A 38 was r issued to Falmouth in 1862.

"A 39". FALMOUTH

Z53	1d. rose-red (1857), *perf* 14	90·
Z54	4d. rose (1857)	50·
Z55	6d. lilac (1856)	65·
Z56	1s. green (1856)	£6

"A40". FLINT RIVER

Z57	1d. rose-red (1857), *perf* 14	£1
Z58	4d. rose (1857)	£1
Z59	6d. lilac (1856)	£1
Z60	1s. green (1856)	£6

"A 41". GAYLE

Z61	1d. rose-red (1857), *perf* 14	£4
Z62	4d. rose (1857)	£1
Z63	6d. lilac (1856)	£1
Z64	1s. green (1856)	£3

"A 42". GOLDEN SPRING

Z65	1d. rose-red (1857), *perf* 14	£1
Z66	4d. rose (1857)	£1
Z67	6d. lilac (1856)	£4
Z68	1s. green (1856)	£6

"A 43". GORDON TOWN

Z69	1d. rose-red (1857), *perf* 14	
Z70	4d. rose (1857)	
Z71	6d. lilac (1856)	£4

"A 44". GOSHEN

Z72	1d. rose-red (1857), *perf* 14	£1
Z73	4d. rose (1857)	£1
Z74	6d. lilac (1856)	60·

"A 45". GRANGE HILL

Z75	1d. rose-red (1857), *perf* 14	£1
Z76	4d. rose (1857)	50·
Z77	6d. lilac (1856)	65·
Z77*a*	1s. green (1856)	£4

"A 46". GREEN ISLAND

Z78	1d. rose-red (1857), *perf* 14	£3
Z79	4d. rose (1857)	£1
Z80	6d. lilac (1856)	£2
Z81	1s. green (1856)	£6

"A 47". HIGHGATE

Z82	1d. rose-red (1857), *perf* 14	£1
Z83	4d. rose (1857)	£1
Z84	6d. lilac (1856)	£1

"A 48". HOPE BAY

Z85	1d. rose-red (1857), *perf* 14	£4
Z86	4d. rose (1857)	£1
Z87	6d. lilac (1856)	£4

"A 49". LILLIPUT

Z88	1d. rose-red (1857), *perf* 14	£1
Z89	4d. rose (1857)	£1
Z90	6d. lilac (1856)	80

"A 50". LITTLE RIVER

A 50 was allocated for use at LITTLE RIVER but this office v closed late in 1858, before the obliterator could be issued. Issued Malvern in 1862.

"A 51". LUCEA

Z91	1d. rose-red (1857), *perf* 14	£250
Z92	4d. rose (1857)	60·00
Z93	6d. lilac (1856)	£160

"A 52". MANCHIONEAL

Z94	1d. rose-red (1857), *perf* 14	£325
Z95	4d. rose (1857)	£170
Z96	6d. lilac (1856)	

"A 53". MANDEVILLE

Z97	1d. rose-red (1857), *perf* 14	£170
Z98	4d. rose (1857)	60·00
Z99	6d. lilac (1856)	£150

"A 54". MAY HILL

Z100	1d. rose-red (1857), *perf* 14	90·00
Z101	4d. rose (1857)	85·00
Z102	6d. lilac (1856)	60·00

"A 55". MILE GULLY

Z103	1d. rose-red (1857), *perf* 14	£275
Z104	4d. rose (1857)	£160
Z105	6d. lilac (1856)	£160

"A 56". MONEAGUE

Z106	1d. rose-red (1857), *perf* 14	£160
Z107	4d. rose (1857)	£200
Z108	6d. lilac (1856)	£425

"A 57". MONTEGO BAY

Z109	1d. rose-red (1857), *perf* 14	£170
Z110	4d. rose (1857)	50·00
Z111	6d. lilac (1856)	60·00
Z112	1s. green (1856)	£600

"A 58". MONTPELIER

113	1d. rose-red (1857), *perf* 14	
114	4d. rose (1857)	
115	6d. lilac (1856)	£700

"A 59". MORANT BAY

116	1d. rose-red (1857), *perf* 14	£325
117	4d. rose (1857)	60·00
118	6d. lilac (1856)	65·00

"A 60". OCHO RIOS

119	1d. rose-red (1857), *perf* 14	
120	4d. rose (1857)	85·00
121	6d. lilac (1856)	£150

"A 61". OLD HARBOUR

122	1d. rose-red (1857), *perf* 14	£160
123	4d. rose (1857)	£120
124	6d. lilac (1856)	£120

"A 62". PLANTAIN GARDEN RIVER

125	1d. rose-red (1857), *perf* 14	£120
126	4d. rose (1857)	85·00
127	6d. lilac (1856)	£120

"A 63". PEAR TREE GROVE

No genuine specimen of A 63 has been found on a British stamp.

"A 64". PORT ANTONIO

131	1d. rose-red (1857), *perf* 14	£400
132	4d. rose (1857)	£250
133	6d. lilac (1856)	£250

"A 65". PORT MORANT

134	1d. rose-red (1857), *perf* 14	£250
135	4d. rose (1857)	90·00
136	6d. lilac (1856)	£250

"A 66". PORT MARIA

137	1d. rose-red (1857), *perf* 14	£160
138	4d. rose (1857)	65·00
139	6d. lilac (1856)	£250

"A 67". PORT ROYAL

140	1d. rose-red (1857), *perf* 14	£325
140*a*	2d. blue (1858) (plate 9)	
141	4d. rose (1857)	£325
142	6d. lilac (1856)	£325

"A 68". PORUS

143	1d. rose-red (1857), *perf* 14	£160
144	4d. rose (1857)	80·00
145	6d. lilac (1856)	£325

"A 69". RAMBLE

146	1d. rose-red (1857), *perf* 14	£160
147	4d. rose (1857)	£160
	a. Thick glazed paper	£400
149	6d. lilac (1856)	£250

"A 70". RIO BUENO

150	1d. rose-red (1857), *perf* 14	
151	4d. rose (1857)	£150
152	6d. lilac (1856)	95·00

"A 71". RODNEY HALL

153	1d. rose-red (1857), *perf* 14	£130
154	4d. rose (1857)	90·00
155	6d. lilac (1856)	£120

"A 72". ST. DAVID

156	1d. rose-red (1857), *perf* 14	£160
157	4d. rose (1857)	£325
158	6d. lilac (1856)	

"A 73". ST. ANN'S BAY

159	1d. rose-red (1857), *perf* 14	£160
160	4d. rose (1857)	85·00
161	6d. lilac (1856)	£160

"A 74". SALT GUT

162	1d. rose-red (1857), *perf* 14	£150
163	4d. rose (1857)	
164	6d. lilac (1856)	£160

"A 75". SAVANNAH-LA-MAR

165	1d. rose-red (1857), *perf* 14	90·00
166	4d. rose (1857)	55·00
167	6d. lilac (1856)	£160
168	1s. green (1856)	£500

"A 76". SPANISH TOWN

169	1d. rose-red (1857), *perf* 14	£100
170	4d. rose (1857)	50·00
171	6d. lilac (1856)	90·00
Z172	1s. green (1856)	£375

"A 77". STEWART TOWN

Z173	1d. rose-red (1857), *perf* 14	£425
Z174	4d. rose (1857)	£275
Z175	6d. lilac (1856)	£160

"A 78". VERE

Z176	1d. rose-red (1857), *perf* 14	£250
Z177	4d. rose (1857)	80·00
Z178	6d. lilac (1856)	55·00
Z179	1s. green (1856)	£600

PRICES FOR STAMPS ON COVER

Nos.	1/6	*from* × 4
Nos.	7/15	*from* × 6
Nos.	16/26	*from* × 8
Nos.	27/9	*from* × 6
No.	30	*from* × 5
Nos.	31/2	*from* × 15
Nos.	33/6	*from* × 5
Nos.	37/56	*from* × 3
No.	57	*from* × 4
Nos.	58/67	*from* × 3
Nos.	68/77	*from* × 6
Nos.	78/89	*from* × 3
Nos.	90/103	*from* × 4
Nos.	104/7	*from* × 5
Nos.	108/17	*from* × 3
Nos.	118/20	*from* × 5
Nos.	121/33*a*	*from* × 4
Nos.	134/40	*from* × 8
Nos.	F1/9	*from* × 3
Nos.	O1/5	*from* × 3

CROWN COLONY

PRINTERS. Until 1923, all the stamps of Jamaica were typographed by De La Rue & Co, Ltd, London, *unless otherwise stated.*

The official dates of issue are given, where known, but where definite information is not available the dates are those of earliest known use, etc.

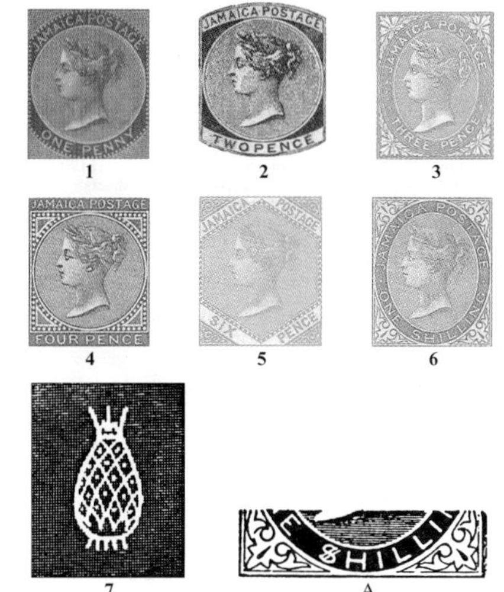

1 2 3 4 5 6 7 A

1860 (23 Nov)–**70**. W **7**. P 14.

1	**1**	1d. pale blue	60·00	15·00
		a. Pale greenish blue	65·00	19·00
		b. Blue	50·00	12·00
		c. Deep blue (1865)	95·00	28·00
		d. Bisected (½d.) (20.11.61) (on cover)	†	£650
		w. Wmk inverted	£100	40·00
2	**2**	2d. rose	£190	50·00
		a. Deep rose	£120	50·00
		w. Wmk inverted	—	60·00
3	**3**	3d. green (10.9.63)	£130	25·00
		w. Wmk inverted	£160	40·00
4	**4**	4d. brown-orange	£200	45·00
		a. Red-orange	£200	22·00
		w. Wmk inverted		
5	**5**	6d. dull lilac	£180	19·00
		a. Grey-purple	£275	32·00
		b. Deep purple (1870)	£800	45·00
		w. Wmk inverted	—	75·00
6	**6**	1s. yellow-brown	£450	24·00
		a. Purple-brown (1862)	£550	23·00
		b. Dull brown (1868)	£180	27·00
		c. "$" for "S" in "SHILLING" (A)	£1800	£600
		w. Wmk inverted	—	50·00

The diagonal bisection of the 1d. was authorised by a P.O. notice dated 20 November 1861 to pay the ½d. rate for newspapers or book post. Specimens are only of value when on original envelope or wrapper. The authority was withdrawn as from 1 December 1872. Fakes are frequently met with. Other bisections were unauthorised.

The so-called "dollar variety" of the 1s. occurs once in each sheet of stamps in all shades and in later colours, etc, on the second stamp in the second row of the left upper pane. The prices quoted above are for the dull brown shade, the prices for the other shades being proportionate to their normal value.

All values except the 3d. are known imperf, mint only.

There are two types of watermark in the 3d. and 1s., one being short and squat and the other elongated.

8

9

10

1870–83. Wmk Crown CC.

(a) P 14.

7	**8**	½d. claret (29.10.72)	14·00	3·50
		a. Deep claret (1883)	16·00	5·50
		w. Wmk inverted	—	29·00
8	**1**	1d. blue (4.73)	55·00	75
		a. Deep blue	60·00	1·50
		w. Wmk inverted	£120	24·00
9	**2**	2d. rose (4.70)	60·00	70
		a. Deep rose	75·00	1·00
		w. Wmk inverted	85·00	24·00
10	**3**	3d. green (1.3.70)	95·00	8·50
		w. Wmk inverted	—	55·00
11	**4**	4d. brown-orange (1872)	£170	11·00
		a. Red-orange (1883)	£350	6·00
		w. Wmk inverted	—	48·00
12	**5**	6d. mauve (10.3.71)	60·00	5·50
		w. Wmk inverted	—	38·00
13	**6**	1s. dull brown (*to* deep) (23.2.73)	25·00	8·50
		a. "$" for "S" in "SHILLING" (A)	£1200	£600
		w. Wmk inverted	—	55·00

(b) P 12½.

14	**9**	2s. Venetian red (27.8.75)	40·00	17·00
		w. Wmk inverted	60·00	70·00
15	**10**	5s. lilac (27.8.75)	90·00	£140
		w. Wmk inverted	£120	£190
7/15		*Set of* 9	£550	£170

The ½d., 1d., 4d., 2s. and 5s. are known imperforate.

1883–97. Wmk Crown CA. P 14.

16	**8**	½d. yellow-green (2.85)	2·75	1·00
		a. Green	1·00	10
		w. Wmk inverted	—	24·00
		x. Wmk reversed	—	38·00
17	**1**	1d. blue (1884)	£300	4·50
18		1d. rose (*to* deep) (3.3.85)	55·00	85
		a. Carmine (1886)	32·00	60
		w. Wmk inverted	—	38·00
19	**2**	2d. rose (*to* deep) (17.3.84)	£200	4·00
		w. Wmk inverted	—	48·00
20		2d. grey (1885)	90·00	3·50
		a. Slate (1886)	70·00	50
		w. Wmk inverted	—	24·00
21	**3**	3d. sage-green (11.86)	4·00	1·00
		a. Pale olive-green	2·50	1·25
22	**4**	4d. red-orange* (9.3.83)	£350	22·00
		aw. Wmk inverted		
		b. Red-brown (*shades*) (1885)	2·00	35
		bw. Wmk inverted	60·00	24·00
23	**5**	6d. deep yellow (4.10.90)	22·00	7·00
		a. Orange-yellow	4·00	3·50
24	**6**	1s. brown (*to* deep) (3.97)	5·00	6·00
		a. "$" for "S" in "SHILLING" (A)	£800	£450
		b. Chocolate	15·00	12·00
25	**9**	2s. Venetian red (2.97)	27·00	20·00
26	**10**	5s. lilac (2.97)	48·00	70·00
16/26		*Set of* 11	£600	£100
		16s, 18s, 20s/3s Optd "Specimen" *Set of* 6	£475	

*No. 22 is the same colour as No. 11a.

The 1d. carmine, 2d. slate, and 2s. are known imperf. All values to the 6d. inclusive are known perf 12. These are proofs.

11

TWO PENCE
HALF-PENNY

(12)

1889 (8 Mar)–**91**. *Value tablet in second colour.* Wmk Crown CA. P 14.

27	**11**	1d. purple and mauve	3·50	20
		w. Wmk inverted	—	24·00
28		2d. green	20·00	3·50
		a. Deep green (*brown gum*)	5·50	6·00
		aw. Wmk inverted	65·00	
29		2½d. dull purple and blue (25.2.91)	5·00	50
		w. Wmk inverted	65·00	
27/9		*Set of* 3	12·50	3·75
		27s/9s Optd "Specimen" *Set of* 3	£100	

A very wide range of shades may be found in the 1d. The headplate was printed in many shades of purple, and the dutyplate in various shades of mauve and purple and also in carmine, etc. There are fewer shades for the other values and they are not so pronounced.

1890 (4 June)–**91**. *No. 22b surch with T* **12** *by C. Vendyres, Kingston.*

30	**4**	2½d.on 4d. red-brown	27·00	8·50
		a. Spacing between lines of surch 1½ mm (2.91)	32·00	17·00
		b. Surch double	£325	£225
		c. "PFNNY" for "PENNY"	75·00	65·00
		ca. Ditto and broken "K" for "Y"	£130	£110
		w. Wmk inverted	70·00	35·00

This provisional was issued pending receipt of No. 29 which is listed above for convenience of reference.

Three settings exist. (1) Ten varieties arranged in a single vertical row and repeated six times in the pane. (2) Twelve varieties, in two horizontal rows of six, repeated five times, alternate rows show 1 and 1½ mm spacing between lines of surcharge. (3) Three varieties, arranged horizontally and repeated twenty times. All these settings can be reconstructed by examination of the spacing and relative position of the words of the surcharge and of the broken letters, etc, which are numerous.

A variety reading "PFNNK", with the "K" unbroken, is a forgery.

Surcharges misplaced either horizontally or vertically are met with, the normal position being central at the foot of the stamp with "HALF-PENNY" covering the old value.

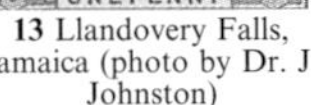
13 Llandovery Falls, Jamaica (photo by Dr. J. Johnston)

14 Arms of Jamaica

(Recess D.L.R.)

1900 (1 May)–**01**. Wmk Crown CC (sideways*). P 14.
31 **13** 1d. red 3·00 20
w. Wmk Crown to left of CC 3·25 50
x. Wmk reversed — 38·00
y. Wmk sideways inverted and reversed
32 1d. slate-black and red (25.9.01) 3·00 20
a. Blued paper £110 £100
b. Imperf between (vert pair) £7500
w. Wmk Crown to left of CC 11·00 10·00
x. Wmk reversed — 38·00
y. Wmk sideways inverted and reversed
31s/2s Optd "Specimen" *Set of* 2 £130

*The normal sideways wmk shows Crown to right of CC, *as seen from the back of the stamp.*

Many shades exist of both centre and frame of the bi-coloured 1d. which was, of course, printed from two plates and the design shows minor differences from that of the 1d. red which was printed from a single plate.

(Typo D.L.R.)

1903 (16 Nov)–**04**. Wmk Crown CA. P 14.
33 **14** ½d. grey and dull green 1·50 30
a. "SER.ET" for "SERVIET" 40·00 45·00
w. Wmk inverted 30·00 30·00
34 1d. grey and carmine (24.2.04) 1·75 10
a. "SER.ET" for "SERVIET" 32·00 35·00
35 2½d. grey and ultramarine 3·00 30
a. "SER.ET" for "SERVIET" 60·00 75·00
36 5d. grey and yellow (1.3.04) 15·00 23·00
a. "SER.ET" for "SERVIET" £650 £850
w. Wmk inverted 80·00
33/6 *Set of* 4 19·00 23·00
33s/6s Optd "Specimen" *Set of* 4 75·00

The "SER.ET" variety occurs on R. 4/2 of the left upper pane. It was corrected by De La Rue in July 1905.

The centres of the above and later bi-coloured stamps in the Arms type vary in colour from grey to grey-black.

15 Arms type redrawn

16 Arms type redrawn

1905–11. Wmk Mult Crown CA. P 14.

(a) Arms types. Chalk-surfaced paper.
37 **14** ½d. grey and dull green (20.11.05) 4·50 20
a. "SER.ET" for "SERVIET" 26·00 40·00
w. Wmk inverted
38 **15** ½d. yell-grn (*ordinary paper*) (8.11.06) 8·50 50
aw. Wmk inverted † £100
b. Dull green 3·75 20
c. Deep green 4·50 20
39 **14** 1d. grey and carmine (20.11.05) 18·00 50
w. Wmk inverted — 85·00
40 **16** 1d. carmine (*ordinary paper*) (1.10.06) 1·50 10
w. Wmk inverted 32·00
41 **14** 2½d. grey and ultramarine (12.11.07) 3·00 3·75
42 2½d. pale ultramarine (*ordinary paper*) (21.9.10) 2·50 1·25
a. Deep ultramarine 2·50 1·75
43 5d. grey and orange-yellow (24.4.07) 60·00 65·00
a. "SER.ET" for "SERVIET" £850 £1100
44 6d. dull and bright purple (18.8.11) 13·00 12·00
45 5s. grey and violet (11.05) 42·00 35·00
37/45 *Set of* 9 £130 £100
38s, 40s, 42s, 44s/5s Optd "Specimen" *Set of* 5 £140

See note below No. 36 concerning grey centres.

(b) Queen Victoria types. Ordinary paper.
46 **3** 3d. olive-green (3.8.05) 6·00 3·75
a. Sage-green (1907) 5·00 3·00
47 3d. purple/*yellow* (10.3.10) 4·50 3·50
a. Chalk-surfaced paper. *Pale purple/yellow* (11.7.10) 2·00 1·50
aw. Wmk inverted 42·00 45·00
48 **4** 4d. red-brown (6.6.08) 70·00 65·00
49 4d. black/*yellow* (*chalk-surfaced paper*) (21.9.10) 7·50 40·00
50 4d. red/*yellow* (3.10.11) 1·50 8·00
51 **5** 6d. dull orange (27.6.06) 15·00 25·00
a. Golden yellow (9.09) 25·00 48·00
52 6d. lilac (19.11.09) 27·00 40·00
a. Chalk-surfaced paper. *Purple* (7.10) 10·00 17·00
53 **6** 1s. brown (11.06) 19·00 27·00
a. Deep brown 27·00 40·00
b. "$" for "S" in "SHILLING" (A) £1000 £1100
54 1s. black/*green* (*chalk-surfaced paper*) (21.9.10) 4·25 8·50
a. "$" for "S" in "SHILLING" (A) £900 £1100
55 **9** 2s. Venetian red (11.08) £100 £150
56 2s. pur/*bl* (*chalk-surfaced paper*) (21.9.10) 6·50 3·50
46/56 *Set of* 11 £200 £300
47s, 49s, 50s, 52s, 54s/56s Optd "Specimen" *Set of* 6 £170

No. 38 exists in coils constructed from normal sheets.

17

18

(T **17/18** typo D.L.R.)

1911 (3 Feb). Wmk Mult Crown CA. P 14.
57 **17** 2d. grey 3·00 13·00
s. Optd "Specimen" 35·00

1912–20. Wmk Mult Crown CA. *Chalk-surfaced paper (3d. to 5s.)*. P 14.
58 **18** 1d. carmine-red (5.12.12) 1·50 10
a. Scarlet (1916) 1·75 70
59 1½d. brown-orange (13.7.16) 1·00 60
a. Yellow-orange 13·00 1·00
b. Wmk sideways † £1500
60 2d. grey (2.8.12) 2·00 1·75
a. Slate-grey 1·25 3·00
61 2½d. blue (13.2.13) 1·50 15
a. Deep bright blue 65 1·00
62 3d. purple/*yellow* (6.3.12) 50 45
a. White back (2.4.13) 55 40
b. On lemon (25.9.16) 3·75 1·50
bs. Optd "Specimen" 32·00
w. Wmk inverted
63 4d. black and red/*yellow* (4.4.13) 50 3·50
a. White back (7.5.14) 75 4·00
b. On lemon (1916) 23·00 19·00
bs. Optd "Specimen" 32·00
c. On pale yellow (1919) 22·00 15·00
64 6d. dull and bright purple (14.11.12) 4·50 9·00
a. Dull purple and bright mauve (1915) 75 1·00
b. Dull purple & bright magenta (1920) 3·50 2·25
65 1s. black/*green* (2.8.12) 2·25 2·00
a. White back (4.1.15) 1·00 4·75
b. On blue-green, olive back (1920) 2·25 5·50
66 2s. purple and bright blue/*blue* (10.1.19) 13·00 25·00
67 5s. green and red/*yellow* (5.9.19) 60·00 90·00
a. On pale yellow (1920) 60·00 90·00
b. On orange-buff (1920) £120 £160
58/67 *Set of* 10 70·00 £110
58s/67s Optd "Specimen" *Set of* 10 £190

No. 58 exists in coils constructed from normal sheets.

The paper of No. 67 is a bright yellow and the gum rough and dull. No. 67*a* is on practically the normal creamy "pale yellow" paper, and the gum is smooth and shiny. The paper of No. 67*b* approaches the "coffee" colour of the true "orange-buff", and the colours of both head and frame are paler, the latter being of a carmine tone.

For the ½d. and 6d. with Script wmk see Nos. 89*a*/90.

RED CROSS LABELS. A voluntary organization, the Jamaica War Stamp League later the Jamaica Patriotic Stamp League, was founded in November 1915 by Mr. Lewis Ashenheim, a Kingston solicitor. The aims of the League were to support the British Red Cross, collect funds for the purchase of aircraft for the Royal Flying Corps and the relief of Polish Jews.

One fund-raising method used was the sale, from 1 December 1915, of ½d. charity labels. These labels, which were available from post offices, depicted a bi-plane above a cross and were printed in red by Dennison Manufacturing Company, Framingham, U.S.A., the stamps being perforated 12 except for those along the edges of the sheet which have one side imperforate.

From 22 December 1915 supplies of the labels were overprinted "JAMAICA" in red, the colour of this overprint being changed to black from 15 January 1916. Copies sold from 11 March 1916 carried an additional "Half-Penny" surcharge, also in black.

Such labels had no postal validity when used by the general public, but, by special order of the Governor, were accepted for the payment of postage on the League's official mail. To obtain this concession the envelopes were to be inscribed "Red Cross Business" or "Jamaica Patriotic Stamp League" and the labels used endorsed with Mr. Ashenheim's signature. Such covers are rare.

WAR STAMP.
(19)

WAR
STAMP.
(20)

WAR
STAMP.
(21)

(T **19/21** optd Govt Printing Office, Kingston)

1916 (1 Apr–Sept). *Optd with T* **19**.
68 **15** ½d. yellow-green 10 35
a. No stop after "STAMP" (R. 18/2) 10·00 24·00
b. Opt double £100 £120
c. Opt inverted 90·00 £110
d. Space between "W" and "A" (R. 20/1) 11·00 24·00
e. Blue-green 10 60
ea. No stop after "STAMP" (R. 3/11 or 11/1) 11·00 24·00
eb. Space between "W" and "A" (R. 20/1) 14·00 28·00
w. Wmk inverted
69 **18** 3d. purple/*yellow* (white back) 12·00 27·00
a. On lemon (6.16) 1·00 17·00
ab. No stop after "STAMP" (R. 8/6 or 9/6) 23·00 75·00
b. On pale yellow (9.16) 9·00 25·00

Minor varieties: ½d. (i) Small "P"; (ii) "WARISTAMP" (raised quad between words); (iii) Two stops after "STAMP". 3d. "WARISTAMP". There were several settings of the overprint used for each value. Where two positions are quoted for a variety these did not occur on the same sheet.

NOTE. The above and succeeding stamps with "WAR STAMP" overprint were issued for payment of a special war tax on letters and postcards or on parcels. Ordinary unoverprinted stamps could also be used for this purpose.

1916 (Sept–Dec). *Optd with T* **20**.
70 **15** ½d. blue-green (*shades*) (2.10.16) 10 3
a. No stop after "STAMP" (R. 5/7) 11·00 32·0
b. Opt omitted (in pair with normal) £3500 £325
c. "R" inserted by hand (R. 11/10) £1000 £90
w. Wmk inverted 38·00
71 **18** 1½d. orange (1.9.16) 10 1
aa. Wmk sideways † £170
a. No stop after "STAMP" (R. 4/12, 8/6, 10/10, 11/1, 18/12, 19/12) 5·00 7·5
b. "S" in "STAMP" omitted (R. 6/12) (Dec) £130 £14
c. "S" inserted by hand £300
d. "R" in "WAR" omitted (R. 1/10) £1500 £140
e. "R" inserted by hand £850 £75
f. Inverted "d" for "P" £200 £16
w. Wmk inverted 16·00 16·0
72 3d. purple/*lemon* (2.10.16) 1·50 1·0
aa. Opt inverted £300
a. No stop after "STAMP" (R. 5/7) 30·00 55·0
b. "S" in "STAMP" omitted (R. 6/12) (Dec) £475 £45
c. "S" inserted by hand £180 £18
e. On yellow (12.16) 6·50 9·0
ea. "S" in "STAMP" omitted (R. 6/12) £600 £55
eb. "S" inserted by hand £350 £27

Nos. 70c, 71c, 71e, 72c and 72eb show the missing "R" or "S" inserted by handstamp. The 3d. is known with this "S" handstamp inverted or double.

Minor varieties, such as raised quads, small stop, double stop, spaced letters and letters of different sizes, also exist in the overprint. The setting was altered several times.

1917 (March). *Optd with T* **21**.
73 **15** ½d. blue-green (*shades*) (25.3.17) 50 3
a. No stop after "STAMP" (R. 2/5, 8/11, 8/12) 8·50 21·0
b. Stop inserted and "P" impressed a second time (R. 7/6) £200
c. Optd on back only £180
d. Opt inverted 12·00 35·0
74 **18** 1½d. orange (3.3.17) 20
aa. Wmk sideways † £150
a. No stop after "STAMP" (R. 2/5, 8/11, 8/12) 3·00 18·
b. Stop inserted and "P" impressed a second time (R. 7/6) £250
c. Opt double 80·00 85·
d. Opt inverted 80·00 75·
e. "WAP STAMP" (R. 6/2)
w. Wmk inverted 16·00 21·
75 3d. purple/*yellow* (3.3.17) 50 1·4
a. No stop after "STAMP" (R. 2/5, 8/11, 8/12) 15·00 35·
b. Stop inserted and "P" impressed a second time (R. 7/6) £225
c. Opt inverted £140
d. Opt sideways (reading up) £325
da. Opt omitted (in horiz pair with No. 75d) £2500

No. 75da shows the left-hand stamp as No. 75d and the right hand stamp without overprint.

There are numerous minor varieties in this overprint with the setting being altered several times.

WAR STAMP
(22)

1919 (4 Oct)–**20**. *Optd with T* **22** *in red by D.L.R.*
76 **15** ½d. green 20
77 **18** 3d. purple/*yellow* 4·00 3·
a. Pale purple/buff (3.1.20) 3·00 1·
b. Deep purple/buff (1920) 7·00 6·
76s/7s Optd "Specimen" *Set of* 2 70·00

We list the most distinct variations in the 3d. The buff tone of the paper varies considerably in depth.

23 Jamaica Exhibition, 1891

24 Arawak Woman preparing Cassava

25 War Contingent embarking, 1915

26 King's House, Spanish Town

Re-entry. Nos. 80a, 93a

The greater part of the design is re-entered, the hull showing in very solid colour and the people appear very blurred. There are also minor re-entries on stamps above (R. 7/4 and 6/4).

27 Return of War Contingent, 1919

A B

28 Landing of Columbus, 1494

29 Cathedral, Spanish Town

34

(Typo (½d., 1d.), recess (others) D.L.R.)

1919–21. *T* **23/29**, **34** *and similar vert designs.* Wmk Mult Crown CA (sideways* on 1d., 1½d. and 10s.). *Chalk-surfaced paper (½d., 1d.).* P 14.

	23	½d. green and olive-green (12.11.20)	1·00	1·00
		w. Wmk inverted		
		x. Wmk reversed		
		y. Wmk inverted and reversed		
	24	1d. carmine and orange (3.10.21)	1·75	1·75
		w. Wmk Crown to left of CA		
	25	1½d. green (*shades*) (4.7.19)	40	1·00
		a. Major re-entry (R. 8/4)	65·00	
		b. "C" of "CA" missing from wmk	†	£225
		c. "A" of "CA" missing from wmk	†	—
		w. Wmk Crown to left of CA	20·00	
		y. Wmk sideways inverted and reversed	—	35·00
	26	2d. indigo and green (18.2.21)	1·00	4·00
		w. Wmk inverted	35·00	
		y. Wmk inverted and reversed	35·00	
	27	2½d. deep blue and blue (A) (18.2.21)	13·00	3·00
		a. Blue-black and deep blue	1·50	1·75
		b. "C" of "CA" missing from wmk	—	£200
		c. "A" of "CA" missing from wmk	£200	
		w. Wmk inverted	25·00	
		x. Wmk reversed	30·00	
		y. Wmk inverted and reversed	30·00	
	28	3d. myrtle-green and blue (8.4.21)	1·50	2·50
		w. Wmk inverted	30·00	32·00
	29	4d. brown and deep green (21.1.21)	2·50	9·00
		w. Wmk inverted		
		x. Wmk reversed		
	–	1s. orange-yell & red-orge (10.12.20)	3·75	5·50
		a. Frame inverted	£20000	£14000
		b. "C" of "CA" missing from wmk	£300	
		c. "A" of "CA" missing from wmk		
		w. Wmk inverted		
		x. Wmk reversed		
	–	2s. light blue and brown (10.12.20)	13·00	26·00
		b. "C" of "CA" missing from wmk	£600	
		c. "A" of "CA" missing from wmk		
		w. Wmk inverted	32·00	40·00
		x. Wmk reversed		
		y. Wmk inverted and reversed		
	–	3s. violet-blue and orange (10.12.20)	20·00	85·00
88	–	5s. blue and yellow-orange (15.4.21)	55·00	80·00
		a. Blue and pale dull orange	48·00	75·00
		w. Wmk inverted		
		x. Wmk reversed		
89	–	10s. myrtle-green (6.5.20)	75·00	£150
78/89 *Set of* 12			£150	£325
78s/89s Optd "Specimen" *Set of* 12			£250	

Designs: *Vert*—1s. Statue of Queen Victoria, Kingston; 2s. Admiral Rodney Memorial Spanish Town; 3s. Sir Charles Metcalfe Statue, Kingston; 5s. Jamaican scenery.

*The normal sideways wmk on Nos. 79/80 shows Crown to right of CA, *as seen from the back of the stamp.*

The 2½d. of the above series showed the Union Jack at left, incorrectly, as indicated in illustration A. In the issue on paper with Script wmk the design was corrected (Illustration B).

An example of No. 80 has been reported with the "A" inverted to the left of and above its normal position.

The "C" omitted variety has been reported on an example of No. 88 overprinted "Specimen".

A 6d. stamp showing the reading of the Declaration of Freedom from Slavery in 1836 was prepared and sent out in April 1921, but for political reasons was not issued and the stock was destroyed. Copies overprinted "Specimen" are known on both the Mult CA and Script CA papers, and are worth £700 each. The Mult CA "Specimen" exists with watermark reversed (*Price*, £900). Price without "Specimen" on Script CA £17000.

"Bow" flaw (R.18/12)

1921 (21 Oct)–**27**. Wmk Mult Script CA. *Chalk-surfaced paper (6d.).* P 14.

89*a*	**18**	½d. green (3.11.27)	1·75	10
		ab. Bow flaw	50·00	25·00
		as. Optd "Specimen"	45·00	
90		6d. dull purple and bright magenta	8·50	4·00
		s. Optd "Specimen"	40·00	

35 "POSTAGE & REVENUE" added

36 "Port Royal in 1853" (A. Duperly)

(Printing as before; the 6d. recess-printed)

1921–29. *As Nos. 78/89.* Wmk Mult Script CA (sideways* on 1d. and 1½d.). *Chalk-surfaced paper (½d., 1d.).* P 14.

91	**23**	½d. green and olive-green (5.2.22)	50	50
		a. Green and deep olive-green	30	50
		w. Wmk inverted	26·00	26·00
92	**35**	1d. carmine and orange (5.12.22)	1·50	10
		w. Wmk Crown to right of CA	15·00	15·00
		x. Wmk reversed	—	38·00
93	**25**	1½d. green (*shades*) (2.2.21)	1·00	45
		a. Major re-entry (R. 8/4)	65·00	
		w. Wmk Crown to left of CA	—	20·00
		x. Wmk reversed	21·00	21·00
		y. Wmk sideways inverted and reversed	—	42·00
94	**26**	2d. indigo and green (4.11.21)	6·50	80
		a. Indigo and grey-green (1925)	9·00	1·00
		w. Wmk inverted	†	—
95	**27**	2½d. deep blue and blue (B) (4.11.21)	5·50	1·75
		a. Dull blue and blue (B)	6·00	60
		w. Wmk inverted	25·00	25·00
		x. Wmk reversed		
		y. Wmk inverted and reversed		
96	**28**	3d. myrtle-green and blue (6.3.22)	2·50	70
		a. Green and pale blue	1·25	15
		w. Wmk inverted		
		x. Wmk reversed		
97	**29**	4d. brown and deep green (5.12.21)	1·00	30
		a. Chocolate and dull green	1·00	30
		w. Wmk inverted	26·00	
		x. Wmk reversed	35·00	
98	**36**	6d. black and blue (5.12.22)	12·00	2·00
		a. Grey and dull blue	12·00	1·50
99	–	1s. orange and red-orange (4.11.21)	1·75	80
		a. Orange-yellow and brown-orange	1·75	65
		w. Wmk inverted		
		x. Wmk reversed	—	£100
100	–	2s. light blue and brown (5.2.22)	3·25	65
		w. Wmk inverted	30·00	30·00
101	–	3s. violet-blue and orange (23.8.21)	11·00	9·00
102	–	5s. blue and yellow-brown (8.11.23)	28·00	25·00
		a. Blue and pale dull orange	55·00	65·00
		b. Blue and yellow-orange (1927)	26·00	23·00
		c. Blue and pale bistre-brown (1929)	27·00	22·00
		w. Wmk inverted	—	£140
		x. Wmk reversed		
103	**34**	10s. myrtle-green (3.22)	50·00	70·00
91/103 *Set of* 13			£110	95·00
91s/103s Optd "Specimen" *Set of* 13			£250	

*The normal sideways wmk shows Crown to left of CA on No. 92 or Crown to right of CA on No. 93, *both as seen from the back of the stamp.*

The frame of No. 102*a* is the same colour as that of No. 88*a*.

The designs of all values of the pictorial series, with the exception of the 5s. and 10s. (which originated with the Governor, Sir Leslie Probyn), were selected by Mr. F. C. Cundall, F.S.A. The 1d. and 5s. were drawn by Miss Cundall, the 3d. by Mrs. Cundall, and the 10s. by De La Rue & Co. The 6d. is from a lithograph. The other designs are from photographs, the frames of all being the work of Miss Cundall and Miss Wood.

37

38

39

(Centres from photos by Miss V. F. Taylor. Frames des F. C. Cundall, F.S.A., and drawn by Miss Cundall. Recess B.W.)

1923 (1 Nov). *Child Welfare.* Wmk Mult Script CA. P 12.

104	**37**	½d.+½d. black and green	60	5·50
105	**38**	1d.+½d. black and scarlet	1·75	10·00
106	**39**	2½d.+½d. black and blue	8·50	18·00
104/6 *Set of* 3			9·50	30·00
104s/6s Optd "Specimen" *Set of* 3			£120	

Sold at a premium of ½d. for the Child Welfare League, these stamps were on sale annually from 1 November to 31 January, until 31 January 1927, when their sale ceased, the remainders being destroyed on 21 February 1927.

40

41

42

Die I

Die II

(Recess D.L.R.)

1929–32. Wmk Mult Script CA. P 14.

108	**40**	1d. scarlet (Die I) (15.3.29)	2·50	20
		a. Die II (1932)	5·00	10
109	**41**	1½d. chocolate (18.1.29)	2·00	15
110	**42**	9d. maroon (5.3.29)	3·25	1·00
108/10 *Set of* 3			7·00	1·10
108s/10s Perf "Specimen" *Set of* 3			75·00	

In Die I the shading below JAMAICA is formed of thickened parallel lines, and in Die II of diagonal cross-hatching.

43 Coco Palms at Don Christopher's Cove

44 Wag Water River, St. Andrew

45 Priestman's River, Portland

(Dies eng and recess Waterlow)

1932. Wmk Mult Script CA (sideways on 2d. and 2½d.). P 12½.

111	**43**	2d. black and green (4.11.32)	14·00	2·75
		a. Imperf between (vert pair)	£5500	
112	**44**	2½d. turquoise-blue & ultram (5.3.32)	3·25	1·50
		a. Imperf between (vert pair)	£11000	£11000
113	**45**	6d. grey-black and purple (4.2.32)	13·00	1·75
111/13 *Set of* 3			27·00	5·50
111s/13s Perf "Specimen" *Set of* 3			80·00	

1935 (6 May). *Silver Jubilee. As Nos. 91/4 of Antigua, but ptd by B.W.* P 11 × 12.

114	1d. deep blue and scarlet	40	15
	b. Short extra flagstaff	£850	
	d. Flagstaff on right-hand turret	85·00	
	e. Double flagstaff	85·00	

115 1½d. ultramarine and grey-black . . . . . 60 1·50
a. Extra flagstaff . . . . 80·00 £110
b. Short extra flagstaff . . . . 95·00
c. Lightning conductor . . . . 85·00
116 6d. green and indigo . . . . 6·00 15·00
a. Extra flagstaff £180 £225
b. Short extra flagstaff £200
c. Lightning conductor £170
117 1s. slate and purple . . . . 5·00 8·00
a. Extra flagstaff £250 £300
b. Short extra flagstaff £300
c. Lightning conductor £200
114/17 *Set of* 4 . . . . 11·00 22·00
114s/17s Perf "Specimen" *Set of* 4 . . . . . . 85·00

For illustrations of plate varieties see Omnibus section following Zanzibar.

1937 (12 May). *Coronation. As Nos. 95/7 of Antigua, but printed by D.L.R.* P 14.
118 1d. scarlet 30 15
119 1½d. grey-black 65 30
120 2½d. bright blue . . . . 1·00 70
118/20 *Set of* 3 . . . . 1·75 1·00
118s/20s Perf "Specimen" *Set of* 3 . . . . . . 65·00

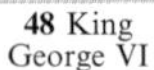

48 King George VI

49 Coco Palms at Don Christopher's Cove

50 Bananas

51 Citrus Grove

52 Kingston Harbour

53 Sugar Industry

54 Bamboo Walk

55 King George VI

56 Tobacco Growing and Cigar Making

Repaired chimney (Centre plate 1 R. 11/1)

(Recess D.L.R. (T **48**, 5s. and 10s.), Waterlow (others))

1938 (10 Oct)–**52**. *T* **48/56** *and as Nos. 88, 112/13, but with inset portrait of King George VI, as in T* **49**. Wmk Mult Script CA. P 13½ × 14 (½d., 1d., 1½d.), 14 (5s., 10s.) or 12½ (others).
121 **48** ½d. blue-green (10.10.38) . . . . . 1·75 10
a. Wmk sideways . . . . † £4000
121*b* ½d. orange (25.10.51) . . . . . . 1·00 30
122 1d. scarlet . . . . 1·25 10
122*a* 1d. blue-green (25.10.51) . . . . . 1·50 10
123 1½d. brown . . . . 1·25 10
124 **49** 2d. grey and green (10.12.38) . . . 1·25 80
a. Perf 13 × 13½ (1939) . . . . . . 2·75 50
ab. "C" of "CA" missing from wmk £750
b. Perf 12½ × 13 (1951) . . . . . . 1·25 10
125 **44** 2½d. greenish blue & ultram (10.12.38) . . . . 3·00 1·75
126 **50** 3d. ultramarine and green (10.12.38) . . . . 75 1·50
a. "A" of "CA" missing from wmk £750
126*b* 3d. greenish blue and ultram (15.8.49) . . . . 1·25 1·25
126*c* 3d. green and scarlet (1.7.52) . . . 2·75 30
127 **51** 4d. brown and green (10.12.38) . . 50 10
128 **45** 6d. grey and purple (10.12.38) . . . 4·50 30
a. Perf 13½ × 13 (10.10.50) . . . . 2·25 10
129 **52** 9d. lake (10.12.38) 50 50
a. "A" of "CA" missing from wmk . . . .
130 **53** 1s. green and purple-brown (10.12.38) . . . . 6·00 20
a. Repaired chimney £500 £100
131 **54** 2s. blue and chocolate (10.12.38) . . 22·00 1·00
132 – 5s. slate-blue & yellow-orge (10.12.38) . . . . 14·00 3·75
a. Perf 14, line (1941) £3250 £190
b. Perf 13 (24.10.49) . . . . 7·00 3·00
ba. Blue and orange (10.10.50) . . . 7·50 3·00
133 **55** 10s. myrtle-green (10.12.38) . . . . 11·00 9·00
aa. Perf 13 (10.10.50) . . . . 11·00 7·00
133*a* **56** £1 chocolate and violet (15.8.49) . . 28·00 26·00
121/33*a Set of* 18 . . . . 80·00 38·00
121s/33s Perf "Specimen" *Set of* 13 . . . . . £200

No. 130a occurred in conjunction with Frame plate 2 on printings between 1942 and 1951.

No. 132a shows the emergency use of a line perforation machine, giving an irregular gauge of 14–14.15, after the De La Rue works were damaged in December 1940. The normal comb measures 13.8 × 13.7.

Nos. 121 and 122 exist in coils constructed from normal sheets.

SELF-GOVERNMENT

57 Courthouse, Falmouth

58 King Charles II and King George VI

59 Institute of Jamaica

(Recess Waterlow)

1945 (20 Aug)–**46**. *New Constitution. T* **57/9** *and similar designs.* Wmk Mult Script CA. P 12½.
134 **57** 1½d. sepia 20 30
a. Perf 12½ × 13 (1946) . . . . . 4·75 50
135 **58** 2d. green . . . . 9·50 90
a. Perf 12½ × 13 (1945) 30 50
136 **59** 3d. ultramarine 20 50
a. Perf 13 (1946) . . . . 1·90 2·75
137 – 4½d. slate 30 30
a. Perf 13 (1946) . . . . 2·50 2·25
138 – 2s. red-brown 30 50
139 – 5s. indigo . . . . 1·25 1·00
140 **59** 10s. green . . . . 85 2·25
134/40 *Set of* 7 . . . . 3·00 4·75
134s/40s Perf "Specimen" *Set of* 7 . . . . . . £140

Designs: *Vert* (as *T* **57**)—2s. "Labour and Learning". *Horiz* (as *T* **59**)—4½d. House of Assembly; 5s. Scroll, flag and King George VI.

1946 (14 Oct). *Victory. As Nos. 110/11 of Antigua.* P 13½ × 14.
141 1½d. purple-brown . . . . 2·50 10
a. Perf 13½ . . . . 30 1·75
142 3d. blue . . . . 3·25 2·25
a. Perf 13½ . . . . 30 4·75
141s/2s Perf "Specimen" *Set of* 2 . . . . . . 55·00

1948 (1 Dec). *Royal Silver Wedding. As Nos. 112/13 of Antigua.*
143 1½d. red-brown (P 14 × 15) 30 10
144 £1 scarlet (P 11½ × 11) . . . . 25·00 48·00

1949 (10 Oct). *75th Anniv of Universal Postal Union. As Nos. 114/17 of Antigua.*
145 1½d. red-brown (P 13½–14) 20 15
146 2d. deep blue-green (P 11 × 11½) . . . . 1·25 2·25
147 3d. deep blue (P 11 × 11½) . . . . . . 35 1·25
148 6d. purple (P 13½–14) . . . . 40 2·50
145/8 *Set of* 4 . . . . 2·00 5·50

(Recess Waterlow)

1951 (16 Feb). *Inauguration of B.W.I. University College. As Nos. 118/19 of Antigua.* P 14 × 14½.
149 2d. black and red-brown 30 30
150 6d. grey-black and purple 35 30

69 Scout Badge and Map of Caribbean

70 Scout Badge and Map of Jamaica

(Litho B.W.)

1952 (5 Mar). *First Caribbean Scout Jamboree.* Wmk Mult Scrip CA. P 13½ × 13 (2d.) or 13 × 13½ (6d.).
151 **69** 2d. blue, apple-green and black . . . 15 1C
152 **70** 6d. yellow-green, carmine-red and black 30 5C

STAMP BOOKLETS

1912. *Black on red covers. Stapled.*
SB1 2s. booklet containing twenty-four 1d. (No. 40) in blocks of 6 (9 Mar) . . . .
SB2 2s. booklet containing twelve ½d. and eighteen 1d. (Nos. 38, 58), each in blocks of 6 (5 Dec) . . . £130

1923 (Dec). *Black on red cover. Stapled.*
SB3 2s. booklet containing twelve ½d. (No. 91) in blocks of 4 and eighteen 1d. (No. 92) in blocks of 6 . . . . £85

1928 (5 Sept). *Black on red cover. Stapled.*
SB5 1s.6d. booklet containing twelve ½d. and 1d. (Nos. 89*a*, 92), each in blocks of 6 . . . .

1929 (July)–**32**. *Black on red cover. Stapled.*
SB6 2s. booklet containing six ½d., twelve 1d. and six 1½d. (Nos. 89*a*, 108/9) in blocks of 6 . . . . . £100
a. With 1d. Die II (No. 108a) (1932) . . . . . .

1930–33. *Black on red cover. Stapled.*
SB7 2s. booklet containing twelve ½d. and eighteen 1d. (Nos. 89*a*, 108), each in blocks of 6 . .
a. With 1d. Die II (No. 108a) (1933) . . . £750

1935. *Silver Jubilee. Black on pink cover. Stapled.*
SB8 2s. booklet containing twenty-four 1d. (No. 114) in blocks of 6 . . . . £120
a. In blocks of 4 . . . . £170

1938–40. *Black on green cover inscr "JAMAICA POSTAG STAMPS" in one line. Inland Postage Rates on interleaf. Staple*
SB9 2s. booklet containing twelve ½d. and eighteen 1d. (Nos. 121/2), each in blocks of 6 (inland letter rate 1d. per oz) £37
a. Inland letter rate 1½d. for first 2 oz (1940) . . .

1942–47. *Black on blue cover inscr "JAMAICA POSTAG STAMPS" in three lines. Inland Postage Rates on inside fro cover. Stapled.*
SB10 2s. booklet containing twelve ½d. and eighteen 1d. (Nos. 121/2), each in blocks of 6 (Inland letter rate 1½d. for first 2 oz) £2
a. Black on yellow cover (1947) £1

1946. *New Constitution. Black on blue cover. Stapled.*
SB12 2s. booklet containing sixteen 1½d. (No. 134a) in blocks of 4 . . . . £2

1952. *Black on yellow cover. Stapled.*
SB13 2s. booklet containing twelve ½d and eighteen 1d. (Nos. 121*b*, 122*a*), each in blocks of 6 . . . . 25·

POSTAL FISCALS

Revenue stamps were authorised for postal use by Post Offi notice of 12 October 1887.

F 1

(Typo D.L.R.)

1865–73. P 14.

(a) Wmk Pineapple (T 7).
F1 F **1** 1d. rose (1865) . . . . 75·00 95·
a. Imperf (pair) £400

(b) Wmk Crown CC.
F2 F **1** 1d. rose (1871) . . . . 55·00 55·

(c) Wmk CA over Crown (Type w **7** sideways, covering tv stamps).
F3 F **1** 1d. rose (1873) . . . . 21·00 7·
a. Imperf . . . .

F 2

F 3

(Typo D.L.R.)

1855–74. *(Issued). Glazed paper.* P 14.

(a) No wmk.

F4 F 2 1½d. blue/*blue* (1857) . . . 45·00 45·00
a. Imperf (1855)
b. Blue on white . . . 50·00 55·00
F5 3d. purple/*blue* (1857) . . . 45·00 50·00
a. Imperf (1855)
b. Purple on lilac (1857) . . . 45·00 50·00
ba. Imperf (1855)
c. Purple on white (1857) . . . 50·00 50·00

(b) Wmk Crown CC.

F6 F 2 3d. purple/*lilac* (1874) . . . 16·00 17·00

All the above stamps *imperf* are exceedingly rare postally used.

1858 (1 Jan). *(Issued).* No wmk. P 15½ × 15.

F7 F 3 1s. rose/*bluish* . . . 70·00 75·00
F8 5s. lilac/*bluish* . . . £325 £375
F9 10s. green/*bluish* . . . £400 £450

Telegraph stamps were also used postally, but no authority was given for such use.

OFFICIAL STAMPS

OFFICIAL (O 1) **OFFICIAL** (O 2)

1890 (1 Apr)–**91**. *No. 16a optd with Type* O **1** *by C. Vendryes, Kingston.*

(a) "OFFICIAL" 17 to 17½ mm long.

O1 **8** ½d. green . . . 9·00 1·25
a. "O" omitted . . . £475
b. One "I" omitted
c. Both "I"s omitted . . . £550 £550
d. "L" omitted . . . £600 £600
e. Opt inverted . . . 70·00 75·00
f. Opt double . . . 70·00 75·00
g. Opt double, one inverted . . . £350 £350
h. Opt double, one vertical . . . £550
j. Pair, overprints *tête-bêche*

(b) "OFFICIAL" 15 to 16 mm long.

O2 **8** ½d. green (3.91) . . . 26·00 23·00
a. Opt double . . . £500

There were five settings of the locally-overprinted Officials. No. O1 occurred from settings I (2 × 10), II (3 × 6), IV and V (horizontal row of 6 each). No. O2 came from setting III (2 × 6). There are numerous minor varieties, due to broken type, etc. (*e.g.* a broken "E" used for "F").

Stamps with the 17–17½ mm opt were reissued in 1894 during a temporary shortage of No. O3.

1890 (1 Apr)–**91**. *Optd with Type* O **2** *by D.L.R.* Wmk Crown CA. P 14.

O3 **8** ½d. green (1891) . . . 9·00 75
O4 **11** 1d. rose . . . 4·75 1·00
O5 2d. grey . . . 11·00 1·00
O3/5 *Set of* 3 . . . 22·00 2·50
O3s/5s Optd "Specimen" *Set of* 3 . . . £100

Nos. O4/5 were not issued without overprint.

The use of Official stamps ceased from 1 January 1898.

Kenya, Uganda and Tanganyika

BRITISH EAST AFRICA

The area which became British East Africa had been part of the domain of the Zanzibari Sultans since 1794. In 1887 the administration of the province was granted to the British East Africa Association, incorporated as the Imperial British East Africa Company the following year.

Company post offices were established at Lamu and Mombasa in May 1890, British mails having been previously sent via the Indian post office on Zanzibar, opened in 1875.

A German postal agency opened at Lamu on 22 November 1888 and continued to operate until 31 March 1891, using German stamps. These can be identified by the "LAMU/OSTAFRIKA" cancellations and are listed under German East Africa in our Part 7 (*Germany*) catalogue.

PRICES FOR STAMPS ON COVER

Nos.	1/3	*from* × 10
Nos.	4/19	*from* × 30
Nos.	20/6	*from* × 3
Nos.	27/8	*from* × 8
Nos.	29/30	*from* × 20
No.	31	*from* × 10
No.	32	—
Nos.	33/47	*from* × 10
No.	48	*from* × 15
Nos.	49/64	*from* × 12
Nos.	65/79	*from* × 15
Nos.	80/91	*from* × 8
Nos.	92/6	*from* × 12
Nos.	97/9	—

(Currency. 16 annas = 1 rupee)

BRITISH EAST AFRICA COMPANY ADMINISTRATION

BRITISH EAST AFRICA COMPANY HALF ANNA (1)

BRITISH EAST AFRICA COMPANY 1 ANNA (2)

(Surch D.L.R.)

1890 (23 May). *Stamps of Great Britain (Queen Victoria) surch as T* **1** *or T* **2** *(1a. and 4a.).*

1 ½a.on 1d. deep purple (No. 173) . . . £275 £200
2 1a.on 2d. grey-green and carmine (No. 200) . . . £475 £275
3 4a.on 5d. dull purple and blue (No. 207*a*) . . . £500 £300

A copy of the ½a. with the short crossbar of "F" in "HALF" omitted exists in the Royal Collection but is the only known example.

The second stamp of each horizontal row of the 4a. on 5d. had the "BRITISH" shifted to the left, placing the "B" directly over the "S" of "EAST". In the normal overprint the "B" is over "ST" as shown in Type (**2**).

Following the exhaustion of stocks of Nos. 1/3, stamps of India were used at Mombasa (and occasionally at Lamu) from late July 1890 until the arrival of Nos. 4/19. The following listing is for stamps clearly cancelled with the MOMBASA 21 mm circular date stamp (code "C"). Examples with LAMU circular date stamp are worth much more. Indian stamps used after October 1890, including other values, came from ship mail.

Stamps of INDIA 1882–90 (Nos. 84/101) cancelled at Mombasa between July and October 1890.

Z1 ½a. blue-green . . . £450
Z2 1a. brown-purple . . . £400
Z3 1a.6p. sepia . . . £650
Z4 2a. blue . . . £750
Z5 3a. orange . . . £750
Z6 4a.6p. yellow-green . . . £225
Z7 8a. dull mauve . . . £400
Z8 1r. slate . . . £750

3

4

5 ANNAS. (5)

(Litho B.W.)

1890 (14 Oct)–**95**. P 14.

4 **3** ½a. dull brown . . . 3·25 6·00
a. Imperf (pair) . . . £1300 £550
b. Deep brown (21.10.93) . . . 70 4·75
ba. Imperf (pair) . . . £900 £375
bb. Imperf between (horiz pair) . . . £1600 £650
bc. Imperf between (vert pair) . . . £950 £500
c. Pale brown (16.1.95) . . . 1·00 8·50
5 1a. blue-green . . . 4·75 6·00
aa. "ANL" (broken "D") (R. 6/5) . . . £700 £700
a. Imperf (pair) . . . £2500 £650
ab. "ANL" (broken "D") (R. 6/5) . . . £12000
b. Deep blue-green (16.1.95) . . . 75
ba. Imperf (pair)
6 2a. vermilion . . . 2·75 4·25
a. Imperf (pair) . . . £1800 £700
7 **3** 2½a. black/*yellow-buff* (9.91) . . . 95·00 25·00
a. Imperf between (horiz pair) . . . £4250
b. Black/pale buff (9.92) . . . 95·00 9·00
c. Black/bright yellow (21.10.93) . . . 4·50 5·00
cb. Imperf (pair) . . . £1000 £400
cc. Imperf between (horiz pair) . . . £1400 £450
cd. Imperf between (vert pair) . . . £1400 £600
8 3a. black/*dull red* (30.3.91) . . . 12·00 13·00
a. Black/bright red (21.10.93) . . . 2·00 6·50
ab. Imperf (pair) . . . £950 £400
ac. Imperf between (horiz pair) . . . £900 £425
ad. Imperf between (vert pair) . . . £700 £375
9 4a. yellow-brown . . . 2·50 6·50
a. Imperf (pair) . . . £2000 £950
10 4a. grey (*imperf*) . . . £1200 £1400
11 4½a. dull violet (30.3.91) . . . 35·00 15·00
a. Brown-purple (21.10.93) . . . 2·50 17·00
ab. Imperf (pair) . . . £1500 £450
ac. Imperf between (horiz pair) . . . £1400 £950
ad. Imperf between (vert pair) . . . £1000 £500
12 8a. blue . . . 5·50 9·50
a. Imperf (pair) . . . £3500 £850
13 8a. grey . . . £275 £225
14 1r. carmine . . . 6·00 9·00
a. Imperf (pair) . . . £8000 £900
15 1r. grey . . . £225 £225
16 **4** 2r. brick-red . . . 14·00 29·00
17 3r. slate-purple . . . 8·50 42·00
18 4r. ultramarine . . . 12·00 42·00
19 5r. grey-green . . . 30·00 70·00
4/9, 11/19 *Set of* 15 . . . £500 £500

For the 5a. and 7½a. see Nos. 29/30.

The dates quoted for these stamps are of the earliest recorded use of the various consignments based on known shipping movements. It is possible that the initial supply may have been placed on sale before 14 October 1890, as an example of the ½a. exists postmarked on 13 October, at Mombasa.

The paper of Nos. 7, 7*b*, 7*c*, 8 and 8*a* is coloured on the surface only.

Printings of 1890/92 are on thin paper having the outer margins of the sheets imperf and bearing sheet watermark "PURE LINEN WOVE BANK" and "W. C. S. & Co." in a monogram, the trademark of the makers, Messrs. William Collins, Sons & Co.

1893/94 printings are on thicker coarser paper with outer margins perforated through the selvedge and without watermark. Single specimens cannot always be distinguished by lack of watermark alone. Exceptions are the 1893 printings of the 2½a. and 3a. which were on Wiggins Teape paper showing a sheet watermark of "1011" in figures 1 centimetre high.

Nos. 7 (coloured through) and 16/19 on thick unwatermarked paper are from a special printing made for presentation purposes.

The printings of the 4a., 8a. and 1r. values in grey were intended for fiscal purposes, but in the event, were made available for postal use.

Forgeries of the 4a., 8a., 1r. grey and 2 to 5r. exist. The latter are common and can be distinguished by the scroll above "LIGHT" where there are five vertical lines of shading in the forgeries and seven in the genuine stamps. Forged cancellations exist on the commoner stamps. Beware of "imperf" stamps made by trimming margins of stamps from marginal rows.

1891. *Mombasa Provisionals.*

(a) New value handstamped in dull violet, with original face value obliterated and initials added in black manuscript.

20 **3** "½Anna" on 2a. verm ("A.D.") (January) . . . £4750 £850
a. "½ Anna" double . . . † £6000
b. Original face value not obliterated . . . † £1800
21 "1Anna" on 4a. brn ("A.B.") (February) . . . £8500 £1900

(b) Manuscript value and initials in black.

22 **3** "½Anna" on 2a. verm ("A.D.") (original face value not obliterated) (January) . . . † £2500
a. Error. "½ Annas" ("A.D.")
23 "½Anna" on 2a. vermilion ("A.B.") (February) . . . £4500 £850
a. Error. "½ Annas" ("A.B.") . . . † £1000
24 "½Anna" on 3a. black/*dull red* ("A.B.") (May) . . . £7000 £2000
25 "1Anna" on 3a. black/*dull red* ("V.H.M.") (June) . . . £7000 £1200
26 "1Anna" on 4a. brown ("A.B.") (March) . . . £4250 £1500

A.D. = Andrew Dick, Chief Accountant.
A.B. = Archibald Brown, Cashier of the Company.
VH.M. = Victor H. Mackenzie, Bank Manager.

(Surch B.W.)

1894 (1 Nov). *Surch as T* **5**.

27 **3** 5a.on 8a. blue . . . 65·00 85·00
28 7½a.on 1r. carmine . . . 65·00 85·00
27s/8s Handstamped "Specimen" *Set of* 2 . . . 90·00

Forgeries exist.

1895 (16 Jan). No wmk. P 14.

29 **3** 5a. black/*grey-blue* . . . 1·25 10·00
30 7½a. black . . . 1·25 16·00
29s/30s Handstamped "Specimen" *Set of* 2 . . . 75·00

The date quoted is that of earliest known use of stamps from this consignment.

These two stamps have "LD" after "COMPANY" in the inscription.

The paper of No. 29 is coloured on the surface only.

1895 (Feb). *No. 8 surch with manuscript value and initials ("T.E.C.R."). Original face value obliterated in manuscript.*

31 **3** "½anna" on 3a. black/*dull red* (19.2) . . . £425 50·00
32 "1anna" on 3a. black/*dull red* (22.2) . . . £5500 £2500

T.E.C.R. = T.E.C. Remington, Postmaster at Mombasa.

Similar manuscript surcharges on the black/*bright red* shade (No. 8*a*) are believed to be forgeries.

The Company experienced considerable financial problems during 1894 with the result that the British Government agreed to assume the administration of the territory, as a protectorate, on 1 July 1895.

IMPERIAL ADMINISTRATION

BRITISH EAST AFRICA (6)

$2\frac{1}{2}$ (7)

(Handstamped at Mombasa)

1895 (9 July). *Handstamped with T* **6**.

33 **3** ½a. deep brown . . . 75·00 23·00
a. Pale brown . . . £110 42·00
b. Dull brown . . . † £2000
c. Double . . . £450 £425
d. Inverted . . . £4750
34 1a. blue-green . . . £150 £110
a. Double . . . £475 £450
b. "ANL" (broken "D") (R. 6/5) . . . £2250
35 2a. vermilion . . . £180 95·00
a. Double . . . £650 £475
36 2½a. black/*bright yellow* . . . £180 55·00
a. Double . . . £650 £425
37 3a. black/*dull red* . . . 80·00 50·00
38 4a. yellow-brown . . . 50·00 35·00
a. Double . . . £475 £450
39 4½a. dull violet . . . £200 £100
a. Double . . . £700 £550
b. Brown-purple . . . £1200 £950
ba. Double . . . £2750 £2000
40 5a. black/*grey-blue* . . . £225 £140
a. Double . . . £900 £800
b. Inverted . . . † £3500
41 7½a. black . . . £120 80·00
a. Double . . . £650 £550
42 8a. blue . . . 95·00 75·00
a. Double . . . £600 £600
b. Inverted . . . £4750

43 1r. carmine . . . 55·00 50·00
a. Double . . . £550 £550
44 **4** 2r. brick-red . . . £450 £250
45 3r. slate-purple . . . £225 £120
a. Double . . . £850 £850
b. Inverted
46 4r. ultramarine . . . £190 £160
a. Double . . . £800 £800
47 5r. grey-green . . . £425 £250
a. Double . . . £1300 £1300
33/47 *Set of* 15 . . . £2250 £1400

Forgeries exist.

The ½a. stamps used for this issue were mainly from the 1893–94 printings on thicker paper, but two used examples are known on the 1890–92 thin paper printing with sheet watermark (No. 4).

1895 (29 Sept). *No. 39 surch with T* **7** *by The Zanzibar Gazette.*
48 **3** 2½a.on 4½a. dull violet (R.) . . . £160 75·00
a. Opt (*T* **6**) double . . . £900 £850

British East Africa
(8)

British East Africa
(9)

SETTING OF TYPE 8. This consisted of 120 impressions in 10 horizontal rows of 12 stamps. This matched the size of the pane for all the Indian issues to 1r. with the exception of the 6a. The sheets of this value contained four panes, each 8 × 10, which meant that the outer vertical margins also received the overprint.

The setting of Type **9** is not known.

Although only the one setting was used for the low values it is known that some of the overprint errors occurred, or were corrected, during the course of the various printings.

(Overprinted at the offices of *The Zanzibar Gazette*)

1895 (27 Oct)–**96**. *Stamps of India (Queen Victoria) optd with* T **8** or **9** (2r. to 5r.). W **13** (Elephant Head) (6a.) or W **34** (Large Star) (others) of India.
49 ½a. blue-green (No. 85) (8.11.95) . . . 6·50 5·50
a. "Britlsh" for "British" . . . £5500 £5000
b. "Br1tish" for "British" (R. 10/12) . . . £375
c. "Afr1ca" for "Africa" (R. 1/11) . . . £400
d. Opt double, one albino . . . £225
50 1a. plum (No. 89) (8.11.95) . . . 5·50 6·00
a. "Britlsh" for "British" . . . £6500 £3500
b. "Br1tish" for "British" (R. 10/12) . . . £425
c. "Afr1ca" for "Africa" (R. 1/11) . . . £450
51 1a.6p. sepia (No. 90) (23.11.95) . . . 4·00 4·00
a. "Br1tish" for "British" (R. 10/12) . . . £475
b. "Afr1ca" for "Africa" (R. 1/11) . . . £500
52 2a. blue (No. 92) (8.11.95) . . . 5·50 3·00
a. "Britlsh" for "British" . . . £6500 £6500
b. "Br1tish" for "British" (R. 10/12) . . . £375 £250
c. "Afr1ca" for "Africa" (R. 1/11) . . . £400 £275
53 2a.6p. yellow-green (No. 103) . . . 7·00 2·50
a. "Biitish" for "British" . . . £7500
b. "Bpitish" for "British" . . . £7500
c. "Britlsh" for "British" . . . † £3750
d. "Eas" for "East" (R. 2/12) . . . £1100 £1400
e. "Br1tish" for "British" (R. 10/12) . . . £500 £275
f. "Afr1ca" for "Africa" (R. 1/11) . . . £550 £300
54 3a. brown-orange (No. 94) (18.12.95) . . . 10·00 11·00
a. "Br1tish" for "British (R. 10/12) . . . £500 £500
b. "Afr1ca" for "Africa" (R. 1/11) . . . £550
55 4a. olive-green (No. 95) (18.12.95) . . . 32·00 28·00
a. Slate-green . . . 28·00 24·00
b. "Br1tish" for "British" (R. 10/12) . . . £650 £500
c. "Afr1ca" for "Africa" (R. 1/11) . . . £700 £550
56 6a. pale brown (No. 81) (18.12.95) . . . 35·00 50·00
a. "Br1tish" for "British" (R. 10/8) . . . £1200
b. "Afr1ca" for "Africa" (R. 1/7) . . . £1200
c. "E st" for "East" . . . † —
d. Opt double, one albino . . . £750
57 8a. dull mauve (No. 98) (18.12.95) . . . 85·00 70·00
a. "Br1tish" for "British" (R. 10/12) . . . £1400
b. "Afr1ca" for "Africa" (R. 1/11) . . . £1400
c. Magenta (1896) . . . 28·00 50·00
ca. "Br1tish" for "British" (R. 10/12) . . . £750 £650
cb. "Afr1ca" for "Africa" (R. 1/11) . . . £800 £700
cc. Inverted "a" for "t" of "East" (R. 2/12) . . . † £12000
58 12a. purple/*red* (No. 100) (18.12.95) . . . 22·00 32·00
a. "Br1tish" for "British" (R. 10/12) . . . £700 £700
b. "Afr1ca" for "Africa" (R. 1/11) . . . £750
59 1r. slate (No. 101) (18.12.95) . . . 90·00 65·00
a. "Br1tish" for "British" (R. 10/12) . . . £1600
b. "Afr1ca" for "Africa" (R. 1/11) . . . £1600
60 1r. green & aniline carm (No. 106) (1896) . . . 45·00 £120
a. Inverted "a" for "t" of "East" (R. 2/12) . . . £8000
b. "Br1tish" for "British" (R. 10/12) . . . £1100
c. "Afr1ca" for "Africa" (R. 1/11) . . . £1100
d. Opt double, one sideways . . . £425 £850
e. Opt double, one albino . . . £550
61 2r. carm & yellow-brn (No. 107) (18.12.95) . . . 90·00 £150
a. "B" handstamped . . . £5500 £5500
62 3r. brown and green (No. 108) (18.12.95) . . . £100 £150
a. "B" handstamped . . . £5500 £5500
b. Opt double, one albino . . . £1200
63 5r. ultramarine & vio (No. 109) (18.12.95) . . . £120 £160
a. Opt double . . . £1900
b. "B" handstamped . . . £5000 £5000
c. Opt double, one albino . . . £1200
49/63 *Set of* 15 . . . £550 £750

The relative horizontal positions of the three lines of the overprint vary considerably but the distance vertically between the lines of the overprint is constant.

In both the "Br1tish" and "Afr1ca" errors the figure one is in a smaller type size.

There are other varieties, such as inverted "s" in "British", wide and narrow "B", and inverted "V" for "A" in "Africa" (R.1/1 and R.6/7).

During the overprinting of Nos. 61/3 the "B" of "British" sometimes failed to print so that only traces of the letter appeared. It was replaced by a handstamped "B" which is often out of alignment with the rest of the overprint. The handstamp is known double.

The 2, 3 and 5r., normally overprinted in larger type than the lower values, are also known with a smaller overprint, for use as specimen stamps for the U.P.U. These were not issued for postal purposes (*Price* £450 *un per set*). The lower values were reprinted at the same time using similar type to the original overprint.

Forgeries exist.

2½
(10)

11

1895 (20 Dec). *No. 51 surch locally with T* **10** *in bright red.*
64 2½on 1½a. sepia . . . 90·00 42·00
a. Inverted "1" in fraction (R. 5/7, 10/7) . . . £900 £600
b. "Br1tish" for "British" (R. 10/12) . . . £1300
c. "Afr1ca" for "Africa" (R. 1/11) . . . £1300

The setting of Type **10** was in 5 horizontal rows of 12 stamps, repeated twice for each pane.

No. 51 also exists surcharged with *T* **12**, **13** and **14** in brown-red. These stamps were sent to the Postal Union authorities at Berne, but were never issued to the public (*Price unused*: *T* **12** £85, *T* **13** £190, *T* **14** £140).

(Recess D.L.R.)

1896 (26 May)–**1901**. Wmk Crown CA. P 14.
65 **11** ½a. yellow-green . . . 2·25 80
x. wmk reversed . . . † —
66 1a. carmine-rose . . . 6·00 40
a. Bright rose-red . . . 5·50 40
b. Rosine (1901) . . . 22·00 4·00
w. Wmk inverted . . . £120 £120
x. Wmk reversed . . . £170 £150
67 2a. chocolate . . . 4·50 4·25
x. Wmk reversed . . . † £170
68 2½a. deep blue . . . 8·00 1·75
a. Violet-blue . . . 14·00 2·50
b. Inverted "S" in "ANNAS" (R. 1/1) . . . £120 55·00
x. Wmk reversed . . . £170 £150
69 3a. grey . . . 3·75 7·00
x. Wmk reversed . . . £120 £120
70 4a. deep green . . . 6·00 3·50
71 4½a. orange-yellow . . . 8·00 16·00
72 5a. yellow-bistre . . . 7·50 4·25
73 7½a. mauve . . . 5·00 22·00
74 8a. grey-olive . . . 4·50 5·50
75 1r. pale dull blue . . . 55·00 23·00
a. Ultramarine . . . 75·00 65·00
76 2r. orange . . . 65·00 25·00
77 3r. deep violet . . . 65·00 30·00
78 4r. carmine-lake . . . 55·00 70·00
79 5r. sepia . . . 55·00 40·00
a. Thin "U" in "RUPEES" (R. 3/2) . . . £1300 £1300
x. Wmk reversed . . . † £375
65/79 *Set of* 15 . . . £325 £225
65s/79s Optd "Specimen" *Set of* 15 . . . £275

Examples of some values exist apparently without watermark due to the paper being misplaced on the press.

(Overprinted at the offices of *The Zanzibar Gazette*)

1897 (2 Jan). *Nos. 156/7, 159 and 165/7 of Zanzibar optd with T* **8**. Wmk Single Rosette.
80 ½a. yellow-green and red . . . 55·00 45·00
81 1a. indigo and red . . . 95·00 90·00
82 2a. red-brown and red . . . 38·00 21·00
83 4½a. orange and red . . . 50·00 30·00
a. No right serif to left-hand "4" . . . £700
b. No fraction bar at right . . . £700 £450
84 5a. bistre and red . . . 55·00 35·00
a. "Bri" for "British" . . . £1500 £1500
85 7½a. mauve and red . . . 50·00 35·00
a. "Bri" for "British" . . . £1600
b. Optd on front and back
80/5 *Set of* 6 . . . £300 £225

Nos. 84a and 85a appear to have occurred when the type was obscured during part of the overprinting.

The above six stamps exist with an overprint similar to *T* **8** but normally showing a stop after "Africa". These overprints (in red on the 1a.) were made officially to supply the U.P.U. (*Price* £300 *un per set*). However, the stop does not always show. Pieces are known showing overprints with and without stop *se-tenant* (including the red overprint on the 1a.).

Stamps of Zanzibar, wmk "Multiple Rosettes" and overprinted with *T* **8** are forgeries.

2½
(12)

2½
(13)

2½
(14)

SETTING OF TYPES 12/14. The setting of 60 (6 × 10) contained 26 examples of Type **12**, 10 of Type **13** and 24 of Type **14**.

1897 (2 Jan). *Nos. 157 and 162 of Zanzibar optd with T* **8** *and further surch locally, in red.*
86 **12** 2½on 1a. indigo and red . . . £110 65·00
b. Opt Type **8** double . . . £5500
87 **13** 2½on 1a. indigo and red . . . £250 £100
88 **14** 2½on 1a. indigo and red . . . £130 75·00
a. Opt Type **8** double . . . £6000
89 **12** 2½on 3a. grey and red . . . £110 55·00
90 **13** 2½on 3a. grey and red . . . £250 95·00
91 **14** 2½on 3a. grey and red . . . £130 60·00
86/91 *Set of* 6 . . . £900 £400

Both the notes after No. 85 also apply here.

A special printing for U.P.U. requirements was made with the 2½ surcharge on the 1a. and 3a. stamps overprinted as *T* **8** but *with stop* after "Africa". It also included a "2" over "1" error in *T* **14**.

15

(Recess D.L.R.)

1897 (Nov)–**1903**. Wmk Crown CC. P 14.
92 **15** 1r. grey-blue . . . 75·00 32·0
a. Dull blue (1901) . . . 65·00 32·0
b. Bright ultramarine (1903) . . . £300 £20
93 2r. orange . . . 85·00 85·0
94 3r. deep violet . . . £100 £12
95 4r. carmine . . . £325 £37
x. Wmk reversed . . . £450 £45
y. Wmk inverted and reversed . . . £800
96 5r. deep sepia . . . £250 £32
97 10r. yellow-bistre . . . £325 £35
s. Optd "Specimen" . . . 65·00
x. Wmk reversed . . . £600
98 20r. pale green . . . £700 £150
a. Optd "Specimen" . . . £125
99 50r. mauve . . . £1600
s. Optd "Specimen" . . . £250
x. Wmk reversed . . . £1800 £600
xs. Optd "Specimen" . . . £275
92s/6s Optd "Specimen" *Set of* 5 . . . £180

On 1 April 1901 the postal administrations of British East Afric and Uganda were merged. Subsequent issues were inscribed "EAS AFRICA AND UGANDA PROTECTORATES".

EAST AFRICA AND UGANDA PROTECTORATES

For earlier issues see BRITISH EAST AFRICA and UGANDA. For the issues of the Mandated Territory of Tanganyika and th war-time issues that preceded them, see TANGANYIKA.

PRICES FOR STAMPS ON COVER TO 1945	
Nos. 1/43	*from* × 3
Nos. 44/75	*from* × 2
Nos. 76/95	*from* × 3
Nos. 96/105	—
Nos. 110/23	*from* × 2
Nos. 124/7	*from* × 3
Nos. 128/30	*from* × 5
Nos. 131/54	*from* × 3
Nos. D1/12	*from* × 8

PRINTERS. All the stamps issued between 1903 and 1927 we typographed by De La Rue & Co. Ltd, London.

USED HIGH VALUES. Beware of cleaned fiscally cancelled copi with faked postmarks.

1

2

1903 (24 July)–**04**. P 14.

(*a*) Wmk Crown CA.
1 **1** ½a. green (16.2.04) . . . 4·00 12·
2 1a. grey and red . . . 1·75 1·
3 2a. dull and bright purple (24.7.03) . . . 8·50 2·
w. Wmk inverted . . . £120 £1
4 2½a. blue . . . 12·00 48·
5 3a. brown-purple and green . . . 17·00 55·
6 4a. grey-green and black . . . 11·00 22·
7 5a. grey and orange-brown . . . 18·00 48·
8 8a. grey and pale blue . . . 21·00 40·

(*b*) Wmk Crown CC. *Ordinary paper.*
9 **2** 1r. green . . . 16·00 55·
a. Chalk-surfaced paper . . . 50·00 90·
10 2r. dull and bright purple . . . 70·00 80·
11 3r. grey-green and black . . . 90·00 £1
12 4r. grey and emerald-green . . . 95·00 £1
13 5r. grey and red . . . £100 £1
14 10r. grey and ultramarine . . . £190 £3
a. Chalk-surfaced paper . . . £275 £3
w. Wmk inverted . . . £425
15 20r. grey and stone . . . £550 £11
s. Optd "Specimen" . . . £120
16 50r. grey and red-brown . . . £1400 £25
s. Optd "Specimen" . . . £250
w. Wmk inverted . . . £2500
1/13 *Set of* 13 . . . £425 £7
1s/14s Optd "Specimen" *Set of* 14 . . . £275

1904–07. Wmk Mult Crown CA. *Ordinary paper (½a. to 8a.) chalk-surfaced paper (1r. to 50r.).*
17 **1** ½a. grey-green . . . 8·50 3·
a. Chalk-surfaced paper . . . 7·50 3·
18 1a. grey and red . . . 3·75
a. Chalk-surfaced paper . . . 8·00 1·
19 2a. dull and bright purple . . . 3·25 2·
a. Chalk-surfaced paper . . . 2·75 2·
20 2½a. blue . . . 8·00 30·
21 2½a. ultramarine and blue . . . 7·50 17·
22 3a. brown-purple and green . . . 3·75 32·
a. Chalk-surfaced paper . . . 3·75 28·
23 4a. grey-green and black . . . 7·50 18·
a. Chalk-surfaced paper . . . 7·50 18·

24		5a. grey and orange-brown	8·00	15·00
		a. Chalk-surfaced paper	6·50	28·00
25		8a. grey and pale blue	7·00	8·50
		a. Chalk-surfaced paper	7·00	19·00
26	**2**	1r. green (1907)	27·00	60·00
		w. Wmk inverted	†	£325
27		2r. dull and bright purple (1906)	38·00	55·00
28		3r. grey-green and black (1907)	55·00	£100
29		4r. grey and emerald-green (1907)	75·00	£140
		w. Wmk inverted	£300	
30		5r. grey and red (1907)	85·00	£110
31		10r. grey and ultramarine (1907)	£160	£190
		w. Wmk inverted	£400	£450
32		20r. grey and stone (1907)	£550	£950
33		50r. grey and red-brown (1907)	£1500	£2750
7/30 *Set of* 13			£275	£500

(New Currency. 100 cents = 1 rupee)

1907–08. Wmk Mult Crown CA. *Chalk-surfaced paper (10, 12, 25, 50, 75c.).* P 14.

4	**1**	1c. brown	2·50	15
5		3c. grey-green	12·00	70
		a. Blue-green	14·00	2·75
6		6c. red	2·75	10
7		10c. lilac and pale olive	9·00	8·50
8		12c. dull and bright purple	10·00	2·75
9		15c. bright blue	20·00	8·50
0		25c. grey-green and black	8·50	7·00
1		50c. grey-green and orange-brown	12·00	12·00
2		75c. grey and pale blue (1908)	4·50	32·00
4/42 *Set of* 9			75·00	65·00
4s/42s Optd "Specimen" *Set of* 9			£170	

Original

Redrawn

910. *T* **1** *redrawn. Printed from a single plate.* Wmk Mult Crown CA. P 14.

3		6c. red	12·00	30

In the redrawn type a fine white line has been cut around the alue tablets and above the name tablet separating the latter from ne leaves above, EAST AFRICA AND UGANDA is in shorter nd thicker letters and PROTECTORATES in taller letters than in o. 36

3

4

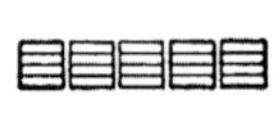

4
cents
(5)

912–21. Wmk Mult Crown CA. *Chalk-surfaced paper (25c. to 500r.).* P 14.

	3	1c. black	30	1·75
		3c. green	2·00	60
		a. Deep blue-green (1917)	4·50	1·50
		w. Wmk inverted	†	—
		6c. red	70	60
		a. Scarlet (1917)	14·00	2·50
		10c. yellow-orange	2·00	50
		a. Orange (1921)	10·00	2·75
		12c. slate-grey	2·75	50
		15c. bright blue	2·75	80
		25c. black and red/*yellow*	50	1·25
		a. White back (5.14)	50	4·50
		as. Optd "Specimen"	35·00	
		b. On lemon (1916)	11·00	11·00
		bs. Optd "Specimen"	35·00	
		c. On orange-buff (1921)	45·00	17·00
		d. On pale yellow (1921)	10·00	5·00
		50c. black and lilac	1·50	1·25
		75c. black/*green*	1·50	17·00
		a. White back (5.14)	1·00	16·00
		as. Optd "Specimen"	35·00	
		b. On blue-green, olive back	6·00	7·50
		bs. Optd "Specimen"	35·00	
		c. On emerald, olive back (1919)	42·00	£150
		d. On emerald back (1921)	11·00	50·00
	4	1r. black/*green*	1·75	4·25
		a. On emerald back (1919)	5·00	50·00
		2r. red and black/*blue*	20·00	38·00
		w. Wmk inverted	£170	
		3r. violet and green	20·00	85·00
		4r. red and green/*yellow*	45·00	£100
		a. On pale yellow	£100	£170
		5r. blue and dull purple	48·00	£140
		10r. red and green/*green*	£110	£180
		20r. black and purple/*red*	£300	£300
		20r. purple and blue/*blue* (1918)	£350	£400
		50r. dull rose-red and dull greyish green	£550	£600
		a. Carmine and green	£650	£700
		s. Optd "Specimen"	£140	
		100r. purple and black/*red*	£4250	£2250
		s. Optd "Specimen"	£275	
		500r. green and red/*green*	£16000	
		s. Optd "Specimen"	£550	
/58 *Set of* 15			£225	£500
s/60s Optd "Specimen" *Set of* 17			£550	

For values in this series overprinted "G.E.A." (German East rica) see Tanganyika Nos. 45/62.

19 (7 Apr). *No. 46a surch with T* **5** *by the Swift Press, Nairobi.*

	3	4c.on 6c. scarlet (*shades*)	1·25	15
		a. Bars omitted	40·00	70·00
		b. Surch double	£120	£200
		c. Surch inverted	£275	£375
		d. Pair, one without surch	£1300	£1500
		e. Surch on back	£400	
		s. Handstamped "Specimen"	60·00	

1921–22. Wmk Mult Script CA. *Chalk-surfaced paper (50c. to 50r.).* P 14.

65	**3**	1c. black	70	1·75
		w. Wmk inverted	£250	£250
66		3c. green	6·00	7·00
		a. Blue-green	15·00	10·00
67		6c. carmine-red	4·50	9·00
68		10c. orange (12.21)	8·50	1·25
69		12c. slate-grey	5·00	£110
70		15c. bright blue	8·00	16·00
71		50c. black and dull purple	14·00	£110
72	**4**	2r. red and black/*blue*	70·00	£180
73		3r. violet and green	£120	£225
74		5r. blue and dull purple	£150	£250
75		50r. carmine and green	£1900	£4000
		s. Optd "Specimen"	£300	
65/74 *Set of* 10			£350	£800
65s/74s Optd "Specimen" *Set of* 10			£300	

For values in this series overprinted "G.E.A." see Tanganyika Nos. 63/73.

KENYA AND UGANDA

(New Currency. 100 cents = 1 East Africa shilling)

On 23 July 1920, Kenya became a Crown Colony with the exception of the coastal strip, previously part of the Sultan of Zanzibar's territories, which remained a protectorate.

The northern province of Jubaland was ceded to Italy on 29 June 1925 and later incorporated into Italian Somaliland.

6

7

1922 (1 Nov)–**27**. Wmk Mult Script CA. P 14.

(*a*) Wmk upright. *Ordinary paper.*

76	**6**	1c. pale brown	1·00	3·00
		a. Deep brown (1923)	1·50	3·50
		ax. Wmk reversed	£150	
77		5c. dull violet	3·50	75
		a. Bright violet	6·50	1·50
78		5c. green (1927)	2·00	50
79		10c. green	1·50	30
		w. Wmk inverted		
80		10c. black (5.27)	4·00	20
81		12c. jet-black	7·50	35·00
		a. Grey-black	4·25	26·00
82		15c. rose-carmine	1·25	10
83		20c. dull orange-yellow	3·25	10
		a. Bright orange	4·25	10
84		30c. ultramarine	2·00	50
85		50c. grey	2·50	10
86		75c. olive	4·50	9·00

(*b*) Wmk sideways*. *Chalk-surfaced paper.*

87	**7**	1s. green	4·00	2·50
88		2s. dull purple	8·00	9·00
		w. Wmk Crown to right of CA	†	—
89		2s.50, brown (1.10.25)	18·00	75·00
90		3s. brownish grey	17·00	6·50
		a. Jet-black	40·00	32·00
91		4s. grey (1.10.25)	21·00	80·00
92		5s. carmine-red	22·00	22·00
93		7s.50, orange-yellow (1.10.25)	70·00	£150
94		10s. bright blue	48·00	48·00
		w. Wmk Crown to right of CA		
95		£1 black and orange	£150	£225
96		£2 green and purple (1.10.25)	£650	£1000
		s. Optd "Specimen"	£140	
97		£3 purple and yellow (1.10.25)	£850	
		s. Optd "Specimen"	£140	
98		£4 black and magenta (1.10.25)	£1700	
		s. Optd "Specimen"	£170	
99		£5 black and blue	£1800	
		s. Optd "Specimen"	£200	
		w. Wmk Crown to right of CA	£2250	
100		£10 black and green	£8000	
		s. Optd "Specimen"	£275	
101		£20 red and green (1.10.25)	£16000	
		s. Optd "Specimen"	£400	
102		£25 black and red	£19000	
		s. Optd "Specimen"	£425	
103		£50 black and brown	£26000	
		s. Optd "Specimen"	£500	
104		£75 purple and grey (1.10.25)	£65000	
		s. Optd "Specimen"	£700	
105		£100 red and black (1.10.25)	£65000	
		s. Optd "Specimen"	£750	
76/95 *Set of* 20			£350	£600
76s/95s Optd "Specimen" *Set of* 20			£450	

*The normal sideways watermark shows Crown to left of CA, *as seen from the back of the stamp.*

KENYA, UGANDA AND TANGANYIKA

The postal administrations of Kenya, Tanganyika and Uganda were amalgamated on 1 January 1933. On the independence of the three territories the combined administration became the East African Posts and Telecommunications Corporation.

8 South African Crowned Cranes

9 Dhow on Lake Victoria

10 Lion

11 Kilimanjaro

12 Nile Railway Bridge, Ripon Falls

13 Mt. Kenya

14 Lake Naivasha

I II

(Des 1c., 20c., 10s., R. C. Luck, 10c., £1, A. Ross, 15c., 2s., G. Gill Holmes, 30c., 5s., R. N. Ambasana, 65c., L. R. Cutts. *T* **10** typo, remainder recess D.L.R.).

1935 (1 May)–**37**. Wmk Mult Script CA. *Chalk-surfaced paper (10c., £1).* P 12 × 13 (**10**), 14 (**9** and **14**) and **13** (remainder).

110	**8**	1c. black and red-brown	1·00	1·50
111	**9**	5c. black and green (I)	1·75	60
		a. Rope joined to sail (II) (1937)	20·00	4·75
		b. Perf 13 × 12 (I) (1936)	£3500	£550
		ba. Rope joined to sail (II) (1937)	£600	£170
112	**10**	10c. black and yellow	3·50	60
113	**11**	15c. black and scarlet	2·00	10
		a. Frame double, one albino	†	—
114	**8**	20c. black and orange	3·00	20
115	**12**	30c. black and blue	2·00	1·00
116	**9**	50c. bright purple and black (I)	1·75	10
117	**13**	65c. black and brown	2·75	2·00
118	**14**	1s. black and green	1·50	75
		a. Perf 13 × 12 (1936)	£1200	£120
119	**11**	2s. lake and purple	5·00	4·00
120	**14**	3s. blue and black	6·50	15·00
		a. Perf 13 × 12 (1936)	£1900	
121	**12**	5s. black and carmine	17·00	27·00
122	**8**	10s. purple and blue	65·00	85·00
123	**10**	£1 black and red	£150	£180
110/23 *Set of* 14			£225	£275
110s/23s Perf "Specimen" *Set of* 14			£275	

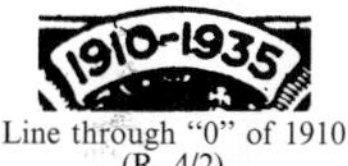

Line through "0" of 1910 (R. 4/2)

1935 (6 May). *Silver Jubilee. As Nos. 91/4 of Antigua.* P $13\frac{1}{2}$ × 14.

124	20c. light blue and olive-green	60	10
	f. Diagonal line by turret	75·00	32·00
	g. Dot to left of chapel	£120	60·00
	h. Dot by flagstaff	£120	60·00
	i. Dash by turret	£130	60·00
125	30c. brown and deep blue	2·50	3·50
	f. Diagonal line by turret	£130	£150
	g. Dot to left of chapel	£200	
	h. Dot by flagstaff	£200	
	i. Dash by turret	£200	
126	65c. green and indigo	1·75	2·75
	f. Diagonal line by turret	£130	
	g. Dot to left of chapel	£200	
127	1s. slate and purple	2·00	2·50
	f. Diagonal line by turret	£140	
	g. Dot to left of chapel	£225	
	h. Dot by flagstaff	£225	
	i. Line through "0" of 1910	£110	£130
124/7 *Set of* 4		6·00	8·00
124s/7s Perf "Specimen" *Set of* 4		£120	

For illustrations of the other plate varieties see Omnibus section following Zanzibar.

Broken leaf (R. 6/1)

1937 (12 May). *Coronation. As Nos, 95/7 of Antigua, but printed by D.L.R.*

128	5c. green	20	10
129	20c. orange	40	30
	a. Broken leaf	40·00	
130	30c. bright blue	60	1·50
128/30 *Set of* 3		1·10	1·75
128s/30s Perf "Specimen" *Set of* 3		75·00	

15 Dhow on Lake Victoria

Damaged left-hand value tablet (Frame Pl 2–2, with Centre Pl 4A or 4B, R. 9/6)

Retouched value tablet (Frame Pl 2–2, with Centre Pls 4B, 5, 6 or 7, R. 9/6)

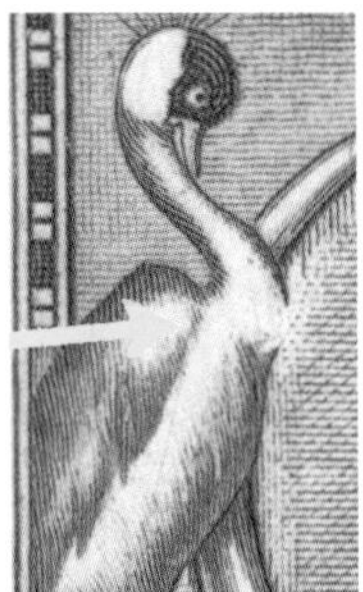
Break in bird's breast (Frame Pl 2–2, with Centre Pls 4A or 4B, R. 2/5)

Sky retouch (Pl 7A R. 10/6)

Damage on mountain (Pl 7B R. 6/7. August 1948 ptg. Retouched in June 1949 for 10c. and 1s.)

Mountain retouch (Pl 7B, R. 5/10 and 6/7. Ptgs from June 1949 onwards)

With dot

Dot removed

In the 50c. printing of 14 June 1950 using Frame-plate 3, the dot was removed by retouching on all but five stamps (R. 5/2, 6/1, 7/2, 7/4 and 9/1). In addition, other stamps show traces of the dot where the retouching was not completely effective.

PERFORATIONS. In this issue, to aid identification, the perforations are indicated to the nearest quarter.

(*T* **10** typo, others recess D.L.R.)

1938 (11 Apr)–**54**. *As T* **8** *to* **14** *(but with portrait of King George VI in place of King George V, as in T* **15**). Wmk Mult Script CA. *Chalk-surfaced paper (£1)*.

131 **8** 1c. black & red-brown (P 13¼) (2.5.38) . . . 2·00 85
a. Perf 13¼ × 13¾. *Black & chocolate-brown* (1942) . . . 30 50
ab. "A" of "CA" missing from wmk . . . £400
ac. Damaged value tablet . . . 90·00
ad. Retouched value tablet . . . 45·00 65·00
ae. Break in bird's breast . . . 85·00
af. Black & dp chocolate-brn (10.6.46) . . . 2·25 2·25
ag. Ditto. Retouched tablet . . . 50·00 70·00
ah. Black and red-brown (26.9.51) . . . 3·50 2·75
132 **15** 5c. black and green (II) (P 13 × 11¾) . . . 4·00 50
133 5c. reddish brown & orange (P 13 × 11¾) (1.6.49) . . . 50 3·00
a. Perf 13 × 12½ (14.6.50) . . . 1·75 3·00
134 **14** 10c. red-brn & orge (P 13 × 11¾) (2.5.38) . . . 2·00 10
aw. Wmk inverted
b. Perf 14 (22.4.41) . . . £120 6·50
135 10c. black and green (P 13 × 11¾) (1.6.49) . . . 30 85
a. Mountain retouch . . . 75·00 70·00
b. Sky retouch
c. Perf 13 × 12½ (14.6.50) . . . 1·75 10
136 10c. brown and grey (P 13 × 12½) (1.4.52) . . . 1·00 55
137 **11** 15c. black and rose-red (P 13¼) (2.5.38) . . . 18·00 55
a. Perf 13¾ × 13¼ (2.43) . . . 4·75 3·75
ab. "A" of "CA" missing from wmk
138 15c. black & green (P 13¾ × 13¼) (1.4.52) . . . 2·00 4·00
139 **8** 20c. black and orange (P 13¼) (2.5.38) . . . 38·00 30
a. Perf 14 (19.5.41) . . . 55·00 1·75
b. Perf 13¼ × 13¾ (25.2.42) . . . 6·50 10
ba. Deep black and deep orange (8.51) . . . 15·00 1·50
bw. Wmk inverted . . . † —
140 **15** 25c. blk & carm-red (P 13 × 12½) (1.4.52) . . . 1·25 2·25
141 **12** 30c. black & dull vio-bl (P 13¼) (2.5.38) . . . 50·00 40
a. Perf 14 (3.7.41) . . . £140 11·00
b. Perf 13¼ × 13¾ (10.5.42) . . . 2·75 10
142 30c. dull purple and brown (P 13¼ × 13¾) (1.4.52) . . . 1·50 40
143 **8** 40c. black & blue (P 13¼ × 13¾) (1.4.52) . . . 1·75 3·25
144 **15** 50c. purple & blk (II) (P 13 × 11¾) (2.5.38) . . . 17·00 1·00
a. Rope not joined to sail (I) (R. 2/5) . . . £225 £225
b. Dull claret and black (29.7.47) . . . 50·00 7·00
c. Brown purple and black (4.48) . . . 50·00 6·50
d. Reddish purple and black (28.4.49) . . . 32·00 3·75
e. Ditto. Perf 13 × 12½ (10.49) . . . 7·00 55
ea. Dot removed (14.6.50) . . . 18·00 55
eb. Ditto. In pair with normal . . . £325 £120
ew. Wmk inverted . . . † £3250
145 **14** 1s. black & yellowish brn (P 13 × 11¾) (2.5.38) . . . 21·00 30
a. Black and brown (9.42) . . . 11·00 30
ab. Damage on mountain . . . — £350
ac. Mountain retouch . . . £950 £200
aw. Wmk inverted . . . † £2250
b. Perf 13 × 12½ (10.49) . . . 11·00 60
ba. Deep black and brown (clearer impression) (14.6.50) . . . 20·00 2·25
146 **11** 2s. lake-brn & brn-pur (P 13¼) (2.5.38) . . . £110 2·00
a. Perf 14 (1941) . . . 70·00 11·00
b. Perf 13¾ × 13¼ (24.2.44) . . . 19·00 30
147 **14** 3s. dull ultramarine & blk (P 13 × 11¾) (2.5.38) . . . 35·00 3·50
a. Deep violet-blue and black (29.4.47) . . . 48·00 8·50
ab. Damage on mountain . . . £1500
ac. Perf 13 × 12½ (14.6.50) . . . 25·00 3·00
148 **12** 5s. black and carmine (P 13¼) (2.5.38) . . . £130 16·00
a. Perf 14 (1941) . . . 35·00 2·00
b. Perf 13¼ × 13¾ (24.2.44) . . . 25·00 1·25
149 **8** 10s. purple and blue (P 13¼) (2.5.38) . . . £120 21·00
a. Perf 14. *Reddish purple & bl* (1941) . . . 32·00 17·00
b. Perf 13¼ × 13¾ (24.2.44) . . . 40·00 3·75
150 **10** £1 black and red (P 11¾ × 13) (12.10.38) . . . £300 £120
a. Perf 14 (1941) . . . 23·00 15·00
ab. Ordinary paper (24.2.44) . . . 23·00 16·00
b. Perf 12½ (21.1.54) . . . 13·00 29·00
131/50a (*cheapest*) *Set of* 20 . . . £150 35·00
131s/50s Perf "Specimen" *Set of* 13 . . . £500

No. 131ab occurs once in some sheets, always in the sixth vertical row.

The first printing of the 50c. utilised the King George V centre plate on which each impression had been individually corrected to show the rope joined to sail. R. 2/5 was missed, however, and this continued to show Type I until replaced by a further printing from a new plate in September 1938.

Stamps perf 14, together with Nos. 131a, 137a, 139b, 141b, 146b, 148b and 149b, are the result of air raid damage to the De La Rue works which destroyed the normal perforators. Dates quoted for these stamps represent earliest known postmarks.

10c
KENYA
TANGANYIKA
UGANDA
(**16**)

A screw head in the surcharging forme appears as a crescent moon (R. 20/4)

1941 (1 July)–**42**. *Pictorial Stamps of South Africa variously surch as T* **16** *by Government Printer, Pretoria. Inscr alternately in English and Afrikaans.*

		Unused pair	*Used pair*	*Used single*
151	5c.on 1d. grey & carmine (No. 56)	1·00	1·75	15
152	10c.on 3d. ultramarine (No. 59)	2·50	8·00	30
153	20c.on 6d. green & verm (No. 61a)	2·50	3·00	2(
154	70c.on 1s. brown and chalky blue (No. 62) (20.4.42)	15·00	4·75	4:
	a. Crescent moon flaw	65·00		
151/4	*Set of* 4	19·00	16·00	1·0(
151s/4s	Handstamped "Specimen" *Set of* 4	£200		

1946 (11 Nov). *Victory. As Nos. 110/11 of Antigua.*
155 20c. red-orange . . . 30 1(
156 30c. blue . . . 30 6:
155s/6s Perf "Specimen" *Set of* 2 . . . 60·00

Examples of Nos. 155/6 were prereleased at Lindi on 15 Octobe 1946.

1948 (1 Dec). *Royal Silver Wedding. As Nos. 112/13 of Antigua.*
157 20c. orange . . . 15 1
158 £1 scarlet . . . 35·00 50·0

1949 (10 Oct). *75th Anniv of Universal Postal Union. As Nos. 114/1 of Antigua.*
159 20c. red-orange . . . 15 1
160 30c. deep blue . . . 1·75 1·5
161 50c. grey . . . 45 2
162 1s. red-brown . . . 50 4
159/62 *Set of* 4 . . . 2·50 2·0

17 Lake Naivasha

(Recess D.L.R.)

1952 (1 Feb). *Visit of Princess Elizabeth and Duke of Edinburg* Wmk Mult Script CA. P 13 × 12½.
163 **17** 10c. black and green . . . 10 1·:
164 1s. black and brown . . . 20 2·(

STAMP BOOKLETS

1912–17. *Black on pink cover. Letter rate given as 6 cents per o Stapled.*
SB1 1r.80, booklet containing twelve 3c. and twenty four 6c. (Nos. 45/6), each in blocks of 6 . . . £12(
a. Letter rate 6 cents per ½oz. Contains Nos. 45*a*/6*a*
SB2 2r. booklet containing six 3c. and thirty 6c. (Nos. 45/6), each in blocks of 6 . . . £12

1938. *Black on pink cover. Stapled.*
SB3 3s.40, booklet containing twelve 15c. and eight 20c. (Nos. 137, 139), each in blocks of 4 . . . £2

1950–52. *Blue on yellow cover. Stapled.*
SB4 1s. booklet containing four 5c. and eight 10c. (Nos. 133a, 135c), each in blocks of 4 . . . £1
a. Contents as SB4, but 10c. changed to No. 136. Stitched (1952) . . . 38·

POSTAGE DUE STAMPS

D 1

D 2

(Typo Waterlow)

1928 (Sept)–**33**. Wmk Mult Script CA. P 15 × 14.
D1 **D 1** 5c. violet . . . 2·50
D2 10c. vermilion . . . 2·50
D3 20c. yellow-green . . . 2·50 3
D4 30c. brown (1931) . . . 17·00 14
D5 40c. dull blue . . . 6·50 14
D6 1s. grey-green (1933) . . . 65·00 £
D1/6 *Set of* 6 . . . 85·00 £
D1s/6s Optd or Perf (30c., 1s.) "Specimen" *Set of* 6 . . . £180

(Typo D.L.R.)

1935 (1 May)–**60**. Wmk Mult Script CA. P 14.
D 7 **D 2** 5c. violet . . . 2·75 1
D 8 10c. scarlet . . . 30
D 9 20c. green . . . 40
D10 30c. brown . . . 1·25
a. Bistre-brown (19.7.60) . . . 3·00 8
D11 40c. ultramarine . . . 1·50 3
D12 1s. grey . . . 19·00 19
D7/12 *Set of* 6 . . . 22·00 23
D7s/12s Perf "Specimen" *Set of* 6 . . . £130

Kuwait

Kuwait, an independent Arab shaikhdom since 1756, placed itself ınder British protection in 1899 to counter the spread of Ottoman nfluence in the Arabian Gulf.

The first, somewhat limited, postal service, via Bushire, commenced with the appointment of a Political Agent to Kuwait in August 1904. Because of diplomatic problems this system continued ıntil 21 January 1915 when a regular Indian post office was established.

Limited supplies of Indian stamps were used by the Political Agency postal service, but these became available to the general public from 21 January 1915. Stamps seen postally used from Kuwait before 1923 are usually ½a., 1a., 1r. or 5r. values, with the occasional Official issue. Much more common are values to 15r., both postage and Official, used telegraphically.

Before 1910 the name of the shaikhdom was spelt "KOWEIT" nd this spelling appears on various circular postmarks used etween 1915 and 1923. The more modern version of the name was rst used for a postal cancellation in 1923.

1915 "KOWEIT"

1923 "KUWAIT"

On 1 August 1921 responsibility for the Kuwait postal service assed to the Iraq Post Office.

PRICES FOR STAMPS ON COVER TO 1945	
Nos. 1/15	*from* × 5
Nos. 16/29	*from* × 3
Nos. 31/51	*from* × 2
Nos. 52/63	*from* × 4
Nos. O1/27	*from* × 10

SED HIGH VALUES. It is necessary to emphasize that used rices quoted for high value stamps are for postally used examples.

(Currency. 16 annas = 1 rupee)

KUWAIT (1) KUWAIT (2)

23 (1 Apr)–**24**. *Stamps of India (King George V), optd with T* **1** *or* **2** *(rupee values, 15½ mm) by Indian Govt Ptg Wks.* W **34** (Large Star) of India. P 14.

½a. emerald (No. 156) 3·50 6·00
a. Opt double £200
b. Vert pair, one without opt £500
c. Light green
1a. chocolate (No. 197) 2·75 3·25
a. Opt double £300
b. Opt omitted (lower stamp of vert pair) £850
1½a. chocolate (A) ("ANNA") (No. 163) 2·25 4·25
2a. bright reddish violet (No. 169) 3·75 4·00
a. Reddish purple 5·50
2a.6p. ultramarine (No. 171) 2·75 8·00
3a. dull orange (No. 173) 4·25 20·00
3a. ultramarine (No. 200) (1924) 9·00 2·75
4a. deep olive (No. 174) 8·00 24·00
a. Olive-green
6a. brown-ochre (No. 178) 8·50 13·00
8a. purple (No. 182) 8·00 32·00
12a. carmine-lake (No. 183) 14·00 42·00
a. Claret 14·00 42·00
1r. brown and green (No. 186) 21·00 32·00
a. Orange-brown & deep turquoise-green 23·00 35·00
2r. carmine and brown (No. 187) 40·00 90·00
5r. ultramarine and violet (No. 188) 80·00 £200
10r. green and scarlet (No. 189) £130 £450
15 *Set of* 15 £300 £750

Essays of the overprint using the obsolete spelling "KOWEIT" ere prepared in 1923 and can be found on the original 14 values the postage stamps and on the 13 stamps of the Official series. *rice per set of 27 unused £20000)*.

Nos. 1/4 and 6/7 are all known with inverted overprint and the erprint is also known on examples of India No. 165 ("ANNAS"). is doubtful if such errors were actually sold at the Kuwait Post ffice, although some are known on registered or ordinary covers.

KUWAIT (3) KUWAIT (4)

1929–37. *Stamps of India (King George V, Nasik printing), optd with T* **3** *or* **4** *(rupee values)*. W **69** (Mult Stars) of India. P 14.

16 ½a. green (No. 202) 3·25 1·40
aw. Wmk inverted 3·25 2·50
16*b* ½a. green (No. 232) (1934) 4·50 1·40
bw. Wmk inverted — 11·00
17 1a. chocolate (No. 203) 7·00 1·75
aw. Wmk inverted 14·00 5·50
17*b* 1a. chocolate (No. 234) (1934) 5·50 1·25
18 2a. purple (No. 206) 3·25 1·25
19 2a. vermilion (No. 236) 20·00 85·00
aw. Wmk inverted 20·00 90·00
19*b* 2a. vermilion (No. 236*b*) (1934) 16·00 6·50
19*c* 2a. vermilion (*small die*) (No. 236c) (1937) 4·50 2·50
20 3a. blue (No. 209) 2·75 1·75
21 3a. carmine (No. 237) 5·50 4·25
22 4a. sage-green (*wmk inverted*) (No. 211w) 25·00 80·00
22*a* 4a. pale sage-green (No. 210) (1934) 6·50 14·00
22*b* 6a. bistre (No. 239) (1937) 22·00 55·00
23 8a. reddish purple (No. 212) 19·00 13·00
w. Wmk inverted 9·00 22·00
24 12a. claret (*wmk inverted*) (No. 213w) (1933) 22·00 40·00
w. Wmk upright — 60·00
25 1r. chocolate and green (No. 214) 45·00 27·00
a. Extended "T" £350
w. Wmk inverted 10·00
26 2r. carm & orge (*wmk inverted*) (No. 215w) 10·00 65·00
a. Extended "T" £350 £700
w. Wmk upright — £150
27 5r. ultramarine and purple (No. 216) (1937) 80·00 £200
a. Extended "T" £500
28 10r. green and scarlet (No. 217) (1934) £170 £375
a. Extended "T" £950
29 15r. bl & ol (*wmk inverted*) (No. 218w) (1937) £500 £750
a. Extended "T" £1600
16/29 *Set of* 20 £850 £1500

The "T" of "KUWAIT" shows a ¾ mm downward extension on R. 3/2, lower left pane.

Nos. 16, 17, 18/19 and 22 are inscribed "INDIA POSTAGE & REVENUE". The remainder are inscribed "INDIA POSTAGE".

No. 19*b* measures 19 × 22.6 mm and No. 19*c* 18.4 × 21.8 mm.

Examples of most values are known showing a forged Kuwait postmark dated "11 NOV 37".

1933 (1 Feb)–**34**. *Air. Nos. 220/3 of India optd as T* **2** *(16½ mm.)*.

31 2a. deep blue-green 14·00 27·00
w. Wmk stars to right 14·00 27·00
32 3a. blue 3·00 2·50
w. Wmk stars to right 3·00 3·25
33 4a. olive-green 85·00 £170
34 6a. bistre (2.34) 3·50 4·50
w. Wmk stars to right 3·50 4·50
31/4 *Set of* 4 90·00 £180

The normal sideways watermark on Nos. 31/4 shows stars pointing to left, *as seen from the back of the stamp*.

The 3a. value exists with a most pronounced lithography double print. *Price* £850 *un.*, £650 *used*. Examples of this and other stamps with slight double prints are of little additional value.

1939. *Nos. 248, 250/1, 253, 255/63 of India (King George VI) optd with T* **3** *or* **4** *(rupee values)*.

36 ½a. red-brown 7·00 1·75
38 1a. carmine 7·00 1·50
39 2a. vermilion 7·00 2·50
41 3a. yellow-green 7·00 2·00
43 4a. brown 38·00 18·00
44 6a. turquoise-green 25·00 8·50
45 8a. slate-violet 28·00 32·00
46 12a. lake 20·00 60·00
47 1r. grey and red-brown 12·00 3·25
a. Extended "T" £325 £250
b. Opt triple, one inverted
48 2r. purple and brown 3·75 16·00
a. Extended "T" £300 £350
49 5r. green and blue 13·00 19·00
a. Extended "T" £450
50 10r. purple and claret 60·00 75·00
a. Opt double £350
b. Extended "T" £650
51 15r. brown and green £150 £200
a. Extended "T" £900
w. Wmk inverted 85·00 £160
36/51w *Set of* 13 £275 £350

On later printings the extended "T" variety was corrected in two stages.

Examples of most values are known showing a forged Kuwait postmark dated "17 NOV 39".

> Following the rebellion in Iraq, control of the Kuwait postal service was assumed by the Indian authorities on 24 May 1941.
>
> Unoverprinted stamps of INDIA were used in Kuwait between 1941 and 1945.

1945. *Nos. 265/8 and 269a of India (King George VI, on white background) optd with T* **3**.

52 3p. slate 2·25 3·50
53 ½a. purple 1·75 3·00
54 9p. green 3·75 9·00
55 1a. carmine 1·50 2·25
56 1½a. dull violet 4·25 8·50
57 2a. vermilion 4·25 3·25
58 3a. bright violet 5·50 5·50
59 3½a. bright blue 4·25 8·50
60 4a. brown 5·50 3·00
60*a* 6a. turquoise-green 14·00 9·00
61 8a. slate-violet 7·00 4·25
62 12a. lake 8·50 4·25
63 14a. purple 15·00 18·00
52/63 *Set of* 13 70·00 75·00

Following a short period of Pakistani control, from August 1947 the Kuwait postal service passed to British administration on 1 April 1948.

KUWAIT 1 ANNA (5) KUWAIT 5 RUPEES (6)

NOTE. From 1948 onwards, for stamps with similar surcharges, but without name of country, see British Postal Agencies in Eastern Arabia.

1948 (1 Apr)–**49**. *Nos. 470, 475 476a/7 478a and 485/90 of Great Britain (King George VI), surch as T* **5** *or* **6** *(rupee values)*.

64 ½a.on ½d. pale green 1·50 1·75
65 1a.on 1d. pale scarlet 1·50 1·75
66 1½a.on 1½d. pale red-brown 2·00 1·50
67 2a.on 2d. pale orange 1·50 1·50
68 2½a.on 2½d. light ultramarine 2·00 1·00
69 3a.on 3d. pale violet 1·50 70
a. Pair, one surch albino
70 6a.on 6d. purple 1·50 75
71 1r.on 1s. bistre-brown 3·50 1·75
72 2r.on 2s. 6d. yellow-green 3·75 4·50
73 5r.on 5s. red 5·50 4·50
73*a* 10r.on 10s. ultramarine (4.7.49) 38·00 6·00
64/73*a* *Set of* 11 55·00 23·00

KUWAIT 2½ ANNAS (7) KUWAIT 15 RUPEES (8)

1948 (1 May). *Royal Silver Wedding. Nos. 493/4 of Great Britain surch with T* **7** *or* **8**.

74 2½a.on 2½d. ultramarine 2·00 2·00
75 15r.on £1 blue 30·00 30·00
a. Short bars (R. 3/4) £130

No. 75a has the bars cancelling the original face value 3 mm long instead of the 3½ mm of the normal surcharge.

1948 (29 July). *Olympic Games. Nos. 495/8 of Great Britain surch as T* **7**, *but in one line (6a.) or two lines (others)*.

76 2½a.on 2½d. ultramarine 1·00 2·25
77 3a.on 3d. violet 1·00 2·25
78 6a.on 6d. bright purple 1·25 2·25
79 1r.on 1s. brown 1·25 2·25
76/9 *Set of* 4 4·00 8·00

1949 (10 Oct). *75th Anniv of U.P.U. Nos. 499/502 of Great Britain surch "KUWAIT" and new values*.

80 2½a.on 2½d. ultramarine 1·00 2·25
81 3a.on 3d. violet 1·00 3·00
82 6a.on 6d. bright purple 1·00 3·00
83 1r.on 1s. brown 1·00 1·25
80/3 *Set of* 4 3·50 8·50

KUWAIT 2 RUPEES Type I — KUWAIT 2 RUPEES Type II

(8*a*)

KUWAIT 10 RUPEES Type I

KUWAIT 10 RUPEES Type II

(8*b*)

2r. Type I Type-set surcharge. "2" level with "RUPEES". Surcharge sharp.
Type II. Plate-printed surcharge. "2" raised. Surcharge worn.
10r. Type I. Type-set surcharge. "1" and "O" spaced. Surcharge sharp and clean.
Type II. Plate-printed surcharge. "1" and "O" closer together. Surcharge appears heavy and worn, see especially "A", "R" and "P".

KUWAIT Extra bar in centre (R. 7/2) — KUWAIT Extra bar at top (R. 2/2)

1950 (2 Oct)–**54**. *Nos. 503/11 of Great Britain (King George VI) surch us T***5** *or* **8***a*/*b* *(rupee values)*.

84 ½a.on ½d. pale orange (3.5.51) 2·00 1·50
85 1a.on 1d. light ultramarine (3.5.51) 2·00 1·60
86 1½a.on 1½d. pale green (3.5.51) 2·00 2·25
87 2a.on 2d. pale red-brown (3.5.51) 2·00 1·50

88 2¼a.on 2½d. pale scarlet (3.5.51) . . . . . . 2·00 2·75
89 4a.on 4d. light ultramarine . . . . . . 1·75 1·50
90 2r.on 2s. 6d. yellow-green (I) (3.5.51) . . . 15·00 4·75
a. Extra bar in centre £500 £375
b. Type II surch (1954) . . . . . . £180 50·00
91 5r.on 5s. red (3.5.51) . . . . . . 22·00 5·00
a. Extra bar at top £375 £275
92 10r.on 10s. ultramarine (I) (3.5.51) . . . . 30·00 8·00
a. Type II surch (1952) . . . . . . £225 55·00
84/92 *Set of* 9 . . . . . . 70·00 26·00

No. 92a is known with surch spaced 10 mm apart instead of 9 mm.

OFFICIAL STAMPS

KUWAIT SERVICE (O 1)
KUWAIT SERVICE (O 2)

1923–24. *Stamps of India (King George V), optd with Type O* **1** *or O* **2** *(rupee values, 15½–16 mm)*. W **34** (Large Star) of India. P 14.

O 1 ½a. light green (No. 155) . . . . . . 2·25 26·00
a. Opt double, one albino . . . . . . 85·00
O 2 1a. chocolate (No. 197) . . . . . . 3·00 15·00
a. Opt double, one albino . . . . . . 80·00
O 3 1½a. chocolate (A) (No. 163) . . . . . . 3·50 38·00
O 4 2a. bright reddish violet (No. 169) . . . 5·50 27·00
a. Reddish purple . . . . . . 8·00
O 5 2a.6p. ultramarine (No. 171) . . . . . . 4·50 65·00
O 6 3a. dull orange (No. 173) . . . . . . 3·50 65·00
O 7 3a. ultramarine (No. 200) (1924) . . . . 5·00 55·00
O 8 4a. olive-green (No. 175) . . . . . . 3·50 60·00
O 9 8a. purple (No. 182) . . . . . . 6·00 90·00
O10 1r. brown and green (No. 186) . . . . 18·00 £150
a. Orange-brown & deep turquoise-green . . . . . . 22·00
b. Opt double, one albino £110
O11 2r. carmine and brown (No. 187) . . . 18·00 £200
O12 5r. ultramarine and violet (No. 188) . . . 75·00 £400
a. Opt double, one albino £150
O13 10r. green and scarlet (No. 189) 120 £350
O14 15r. blue and olive (No. 190) £180 £475
O1/14 *Set of* 14 . . . . . . £400 £1800

1929–33. *Nos. 203, 206, 209 and 211/18w of India (King George V, Nasik printing) optd as Types O* **1** *(spaced 10 mm) or O2 (14½ mm × 19–20 mm wide)*. W **69** (Mult Stars) of India. P 14.

O16 1a. chocolate . . . . . .
w. Wmk inverted . . . . . . 4·00 26·00
O17 2a. purple . . . . . . 55·00 £170
O19 3a. blue . . . . . . 4·50 40·00
O20 4a. sage-green . . . . . . 4·25 70·00
w. Wmk inverted . . . . . .
O21 8a. reddish purple . . . . . . 5·00 90·00
w. Wmk inverted . . . . . . 6·50
O22 12a. claret . . . . . . 26·00 £170
w. Wmk inverted . . . . . . 42·00
O23 1r. chocolate and green . . . . . . 4·00 £180
O24 2r. carmine and orange (*wmk inverted*) . . . 7·00 £275
O25 5r. ultramarine & purple (*wmk inverted*) . . . . . . 26·00 £400
O26 10r. green and scarlet . . . . . . 50·00 £600
O27 15r. blue and olive (*wmk inverted*) £120 £1100
O16w/27 *Set of* 11 . . . . . . £275 £2750

Labuan
see North Borneo

Lagos
see Nigeria

Leeward Islands

The Federal Colony of the Leeward Islands was constituted in 1871 formalising links between Antigua, British Virgin Islands, Dominica, Montserrat and St. Kitts-Nevis which stretched back to the 1670s. Issues for the individual islands were superseded by those inscribed "LEEWARD ISLANDS", but were in concurrent use with them from 1903. Dominica was transferred to the Windward Islands on 31 December 1939.

PRICES FOR STAMPS ON COVER TO 1945		
Nos.	1/8	*from* × 10
Nos.	9/16	*from* × 12
Nos.	17/19	*from* × 8
Nos.	20/8	*from* × 5
Nos.	29/35	*from* × 4
Nos.	36/45	*from* × 5
Nos.	46/57	*from* × 4
Nos.	58/87	*from* × 5
Nos.	88/91	*from* × 6
Nos.	92/4	*from* × 10
Nos.	95/114	*from* × 5

PRINTERS. All the stamps of Leeward Islands were typographed by De La Rue & Co, Ltd, London, *except where otherwise stated*.

1

2

1890 (31 Oct). *Name and value in second colour.* Wmk Crown CA. P 14.

1 **1** ½d. dull mauve and green . . . . . . 3·50 1·25
2 1d. dull mauve and rose . . . . . . 3·75 20
3 2½d. dull mauve and blue . . . . . . 4·75 20
w. Wmk inverted £300 £180
4 4d. dull mauve and orange . . . . . . 4·50 8·00
5 6d. dull mauve and brown . . . . . . 11·00 12·00
6 7d. dull mauve and slate . . . . . . 4·50 11·00
7 **2** 1s. green and carmine . . . . . . 19·00 50·00
8 5s. green and blue £120 £250
1/8 *Set of* 8 . . . . . . £150 £300
1s/8s Optd "Specimen" *Set of* 8 . . . . . . £200

The colours of this issue are fugitive.

(3)

One Penny
(4)

One Penny
(5)

1897 (22 July). *Queen. Victoria's Diamond Jubilee. Handstamped with T* **3**.

9 **1** ½d. dull mauve and green . . . . . . 4·00 13·00
a. Opt double £1200
10 1d. dull mauve and rose . . . . . . 4·50 13·00
a. Opt double £1000
b. Opt triple £3250
11 2½d. dull mauve and blue . . . . . . 4·75 13·00
a. Opt double £1200
12 4d. dull mauve and orange . . . . . . 35·00 70·00
a. Opt double £1200
13 6d. dull mauve and brown . . . . . . 48·00 90·00
a. Opt double £1400
14 7d. dull mauve and slate . . . . . . 48·00 90·00
a. Opt double £1400
15 **2** 1s. green and carmine £120 £190
a. Opt double £1800
16 5s. green and blue £450 £750
a. Opt double £5000
9/16 *Set of* 8 . . . . . . £600 £1100

Beware of forgeries.

1902 (11 Aug). *Nos. 4/6 surch locally.*

17 **4** 1d.on 4d. dull mauve and orange . . . 3·00 5·00
a. Pair, one with tall narrow "O" in "One" . . . . . . 35·00 70·00
b. Surch double . . . . . .
18 1d.on 6d. dull mauve and brown . . . . 4·00 11·00
a. Pair, one with tall narrow "O" in "One" . . . . . . 50·00 £120
19 **5** 1d.on 7d. dull mauve and slate . . . . 3·50 7·00
17/19 *Set of* 3 . . . . . . 9·50 21·00

The tall narrow "O" variety occurred on R. 1/1, 5/3, 5/5 and 7/4.

6

7

8

LEEWARD ISLANDS

Wide "A" (R. 6/1 of both panes. Replaced in 1912)

LEEWARD ISLANDS

Dropped "R" (R.1/1 of both panes from Pl 2 (1st ptg only))

1902 (1 Sept–Oct). Wmk Crown CA. P 14.

20 **6** ½d. dull purple and green . . . . . . 5·50 1·00
21 1d. dull purple and carmine . . . . . . 7·00 20
22 **7** 2d. dull purple and ochre (Oct) . . . . 2·75 4·25
23 **6** 2½d. dull purple and ultramarine . . . . 5·50 2·25
a. Wide "A" in "LEEWARD" £225 £150
24 **7** 3d. dull purple and black (Oct) . . . . 4·50 7·50
25 **6** 6d. dull purple and brown . . . . . . 2·50 8·00
26 **8** 1s. green and carmine . . . . . . 3·50 19·00
a. Dropped "R" in "LEEWARD" . . . £325 £500
27 **7** 2s.6d. green and black (Oct) . . . . . . 27·00 70·00
28 **8** 5s. green and blue . . . . . . 48·00 75·00
20/8 *Set of* 9 . . . . . . 95·00 £170
20s/8s Optd "Specimen" *Set of* 9 . . . . . . £140

1905 (Apr)–**08**. Wmk Mult Crown CA. *Ordinary paper (½d., 3d.) or chalk-surfaced paper (others).*

29 **6** ½d. dull purple and green (2.06) . . . . 3·50 2·0
a. Chalk-surfaced paper (25.7.08) . . . 20·00 12·0
30 1d. dull purple and carmine (29.8.06) . . 8·50 8
31 **7** 2d. dull purple and ochre (25.7.08) . . . 5·00 14·0
32 **6** 2½d. dull purple and ultramarine (23.7.06) . . . . . . 60·00 32·0
a. Wide "A" in "LEEWARD" £550 £32
33 **7** 3d. dull purple and black . . . . . . 12·00 40·0
a. Chalk-surfaced paper (18.4.08) . . . 40·00 75·0
34 **6** 6d. dull purple and brown (15.7.08) . . . 40·00 70·0
35 **8** 1s. green and carmine (15.7.08) . . . . 42·00 £10
29/35 *Set of* 7 . . . . . . £150 £22

1907 (14 Apr)–**11**. Wmk Mult Crown CA. *Chalk-surfaced paper (3d. to 5s.).* P 14.

36 **7** ¼d. brown (7.8.09) . . . . . . 2·75 1·7
37 **6** ½d. dull green . . . . . . 3·50 1·2
38 1d. bright red (7.07) . . . . . . 10·00 8
a. Rose-carmine (1910) . . . . . . 38·00 3·5
39 **7** 2d. grey (3.8.11) . . . . . . 3·50 7·5
40 **6** 2½d. bright blue (5.07) . . . . . . 7·00 4·2
a. Wide "A" in "LEEWARD" £225 £18
41 **7** 3d. purple/*yellow* (28.10.10) . . . . . . 3·50 7·5
42 **6** 6d. dull and bright purple (3.8.11) . . . 8·50 7·0
43 **8** 1s. black/*green* (3.8.11) . . . . . . 5·50 21·0
44 **7** 2s. 6d. black and red/*blue* (15.9.11) . . . 40·00 48·0
45 **8** 5s. green and red/*yellow* (21.11.10) . . . 42·00 65·0
36/45 *Set of* 10 . . . . . . £110 £15
36s/45s Optd "Specimen" *Set of* 10 . . . . . . £200

10

11

12

13

1912 (23 Oct)–**22**. *Die I (¼d. to 3d., 6d., 1s., 2s.6d. 5s.) or Die (4d., 2s.).* Wmk Mult Crown CA. *Chalk-surfaced paper (3d. 5s.).* P 14.

46 **10** ¼d. brown . . . . . . 1·75 1·
a. Pale brown . . . . . . 3·50 2·
47 **11** ½d. yellow-green (12.12) . . . . . . 5·50 2·
a. Deep green (1916) . . . . . . 5·00 1·
48 1d. red . . . . . . 5·00 1·
a. Bright scarlet (8.15) . . . . . . 6·50 1·
49 **10** 2d. slate-grey (9.1.13) . . . . . . 4·00 5·
50 **11** 2½d. bright blue . . . . . . 3·25 7·
a. Deep bright blue (1914) . . . . . . 3·75 4·
51 **10** 3d. purple/*yellow* (9.1.13) . . . . . . 1·75 10·
a. White back (11.13) . . . . . . 65·00 £1
as. Optd "Specimen" . . . . . . 42·00
b. On lemon (11.14) . . . . . . 5·00 16·
c. On buff (1920) . . . . . . 35·00 50·
cs. Optd "Specimen" . . . . . . 42·00
d. On orange-buff (1920) . . . . . . 3·75 13·
dw. Wmk inverted £275
52 4d. blk & red/*pale yell* (Die 11) (12.5.22) . . . . . . 3·75 22·
53 **11** 6d. dull and bright purple (9.1.13) . . . 3·00 8·
54 **12** 1s. black/*green* (9.1.13) . . . . . . 3·00 8·
a. *White back* (11.13) . . . . . . 50·00 38·
as. Optd "Specimen" . . . . . . 45·00
b. On blue-green, olive back (1917) . . . 9·00 8·
bs. Optd "Specimen" . . . . . . 48·00
55 **10** 2s. purple & blue/*blue* (Die II) (12.5.22) . . . . . . 8·50 55·
56 2s.6d. black and red/*blue* (11.13) . . . 12·00 38·
57 **12** 5s. green and red/*yellow* (9.14) . . . . 50·00 95·
a. White back (11.13) . . . . . . 42·00 80·
as. Optd "Specimen" . . . . . . 50·00
b. On lemon (1915) . . . . . . 26·00 70·
c. On orange-buff (1920) . . . . . . 95·00 £1
46/57*b* *Set of* 12 . . . . . . 70·00 £2
46s/57s Optd "Specimen" *Set of* 12 . . . . . . £275

Nos. 51a, 54a and 57 were only on sale from Montserrat.

"D I" shaved at foot 1d. R. 7/3 of left pane (all ptgs between Sept 1947 and July 1949. 1s. R. 9/6 of right pane (all ptgs between 1932 and 1938)

1921 (Oct)–**32**. Wmk Mult Script CA or Mult Crown CA (£ *Chalk-surfaced paper (3d. to £1)*.P 14.

(a) Die II (1921–29).

58 **10** ¼d. brown (1.4.22) . . . . . . 2·25 1
59 **11** ½d. blue-green . . . . . . 1·00
60 1d. carmine-red . . . . . . 2·25
61 1d. bright violet (21.8.22) . . . . . . 2·25 1
62 1d. bright scarlet (1929) . . . . . . 7·50 2
63 **10** 1½d. carmine-red (10.9.26) . . . . . . 3·25 2
64 1½d. red-brown (1929) . . . . . . 1·25
65 2d. slate-grey (6.22) . . . . . . 2·00
w Wmk inverted . . . . . . † £
x. Wmk reversed . . . . . .
66 **11** 2½d. orange-yellow (22.9.23) . . . . . . 6·50 50
67 2½d. bright blue (1.3.27) . . . . . . 3·50 1

8 10 3d. light ultramarine (22.9.23) 4·75 26·00
a. *Deep ultramarine* (1925) 50·00 50·00
9 3d. purple/*yellow* (1.7.27) 1·50 6·50
0 4d. black and red/*pale yellow* (2.24) 3·00 21·00
1 5d. dull purple and olive-green (12.5.22) 2·50 4·25
2 11 6d. dull and bright purple (17.7.23) 10·00 27·00
3 12 1s. black/*emerald* (17.7.23) 6·50 8·00
4 10 2s. purple and blue/*blue* (12.5.22) 16·00 42·00
a. *Red-purple and blue/blue* (1926) 7·50 48·00
aw. Wmk inverted £250
5 2s.6d. black and red/*blue* (17.7.23) 6·50 23·00
6 3s. bright green and violet (12.5.22) 12·00 25·00
7 4s. black and red (12.5.22) 12·00 42·00
8 12 5s. green and red/*pale yellow* (17.7.23) 38·00 70·00
9 13 10s. green and red/*green* (1928) 55·00 85·00
a. Break in scroll £170
b. Broken crown and scroll £170
e. Break in lines below left scroll £170
f. Damaged leaf at bottom right £170
0 £1 purple and black/*red* (1928) £225 £250
a. Break in scroll £375
b. Broken crown and scroll £375
e. Break in lines below left scroll £375
f. Damaged leaf at bottom right £375
8/80 *Set of* 22 £350 £600
8s/80s Optd or Perf (£1) "Specimen" *Set of* 3 £550

(b) Reversion to Die I (Plate 23) (1931–32).

1 10 ¼d. brown 6·00 16·00
2 11 ½d. blue-green 27·00 32·00
3 1d. bright scarlet 25·00 50
4 10 1½d. red-brown 4·25 2·75
5 11 2½d. bright blue 7·00 3·50
6 6d. dull and bright purple 19·00 80·00
7 12 1s. black/*emerald* 50·00 75·00
a. "D I" flaw £400
b. "A" of "CA" missing from wmk — £2000
1/7 *Set of* 7 £120 £190

No. 60 may not have been used locally before January 1923.

No. 68*a* was issued in St. Kitts-Nevis.

Nos. 59, 62 and 82/3 exist in coils, constructed from normal heets. No. 82 was only issued in this form.

For illustrations of varieties on Nos. 79/80 see above No. 51*b* of armuda.

Nos. 81/7 result from the use, in error, of Die I which had eviously been "retired" in late 1920, to produce Plate 23.

35 (6 May). *Silver Jubilee. As Nos. 91/4 of Antigua, but printed by Waterlow.* P 11 × 12.
1d. deep blue and scarlet 1·60 1·50
1½d. ultramarine and grey 2·25 70
2½d. brown and deep blue 2·25 3·50
1s. slate and purple 9·00 18·00
k. Kite and vertical log £275
l. Kite and horizontal log £300
/91 *Set of* 4 13·50 21·00
s/91s Perf "Specimen" *Set of* 4 90·00

For illustrations of plate varieties see Omnibus section following anzibar.

37 (12 May). *Coronation. As Nos. 95/7 of Antigua, but printed by D.L.R.*
1d. scarlet 70 20
1½d. buff 70 40
2½d. bright blue 80 1·00
/4 *Set of* 3 2·00 1·40
s/4s Perf "Specimen". *Set of* 3 70·00

14

15

(Die A) (Die B)

In Die B the figure "1" has a broader top and more projecting if.

"ISLANDS" flaw (R. 1/2 of right pane) (Pl. 2 ptgs from November 1942 until corrected in July 1949)

Broken second "E" in "LEEWARD" (R. 4/1 of right pane) (Pl. 3 ptgs from August 1942 until corrected in June 1949) (A similar variety occurs on 5s.)

Broken top right scroll (R. 5/11) (1942 ptg of 10s. only. Corrected on £1 value from same period)

Broken lower right scroll (R. 5/12. 1942 ptgs only)

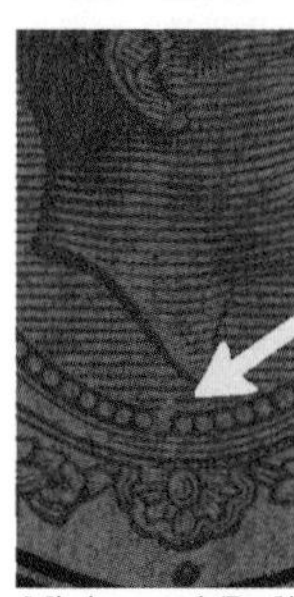

Missing pearl (R. 5/1. 1944 ptgs only)

Gash in chin (R. 2/5. 1942 ptgs only)

1938 (25 Nov)–**51**. *T* **14** *(and similar type, but shaded value tablet, ½d., 1d., 2½d., 6d.) and* **15** *(10s., £1). Chalk-surfaced paper (3d. to £1).* P 14.

(a) Wmk Mult Script CA.

95 ¼d. brown 60 1·50
a. Chalk-surfaced paper. *Dp brn* (13.6.49) 30 1·75
96 ½d. emerald 70 70
a. "ISLANDS" flaw 60·00
97 ½d. slate-grey (*chalk-surfaced paper*) (1.7.49) 75 1·50
98 1d. scarlet (Die A) 9·50 2·50
99 1d. scarlet (*shades*) (Die B) (1940) 2·25 1·75
a. "D I" flaw (9.47) £180
b. Carmine (9.42) 1·50 6·50
c. Red (13.9.48) 6·00 3·25
ca. "D I" flaw £180
100 1d. bl-grn (*chalk-surfaced paper*) (1.7.49) 55 15
a. "D I" flaw £140
101 1½d. chestnut 1·00 50
102 1½d. yellow-orange and black (*chalk-surfaced paper*) (1.7.49) 85 40
103 2d. olive-grey 3·00 1·25
a. Slate-grey (11.42) 5·50 3·00
104 2d. scarlet (*chalk-surfaced paper*) (1.7.49) 1·40 1·25
105 2½d. bright blue 15·00 2·50
a. Light bright blue (11.42) 80 1·25
106 2½d. black and purple (*chalk-surfaced paper*) (1.7.49) 55 15
107 3d. orange 35·00 2·75
a. Ordinary paper. *Pale orange* (11.42) 50 85
108 3d. bright blue (1.7.49) 65 15
109 6d. deep dull purple and bright purple 23·00 5·50
a. Ordinary paper (8.42) 6·50 2·25
ab. Broken "E" £300
b. Purple and deep magenta (29.9.47) 7·50 3·50
ba. Broken "E" £300 £250
110 1s. black/*emerald* 16·00 2·00
a. "D I" flaw £425
b. Ordinary paper (3.42) 4·25 1·00
ba. Grey and black/emerald (8.42) 18·00 4·00
bb. Black and grey/emerald (11.42) £130 12·00
111 2s. reddish purple and blue/*blue* 21·00 2·50
a. Ordinary paper (3.42) 10·00 2·00
ab. Deep purple and blue/blue (29.9.47) 11·00 2·50
112 5s. green and red/*yellow* 48·00 16·00
a. Broken "E" (R. 3/4 of left pane) £700 £600
b. Ordinary paper (12.43) 32·00 15·00
ba. Broken "E" (R. 3/4 of left pane) £600
c. Bright green and red/yellow (24.10.51) 55·00 50·00
113 10s. bluish green and deep red/*green* £200 £130
a. Ordinary paper. *Pale green and dull red/green* (26.6.44*) £550 £300
ad. Broken top right scroll £3250
ae. Broken lower right scroll £3250 £3250
af. Gash in chin £3250 £3250
b. Ordinary paper. *Green and red/green* (22.2.45*) £150 70·00
c. Ordinary paper. *Deep green and deep vermilion/green* (15.10.47*) £120 75·00
ca. Missing pearl £1300

(b) Wmk Mult Crown CA

114 £1 brown-purple and black/*red* £325 £275
a. Purple and black/carmine (21.9.42*) 85·00 45·00
ae. Broken lower right scroll £1200 £650
af. Gash in chin £1200 £650
b. Brown-purple & black/salmon (5.2.45*) 35·00 24·00
ba. Missing pearl £1100 £750
c. Perf 13. *Violet & black/scarlet* (4.1.52*) 32·00 38·00
ca. Wmk sideways £3000
cw. Wmk inverted £2500
95/114*b* *Set of* 19 £190 £110
95s/114s Perf "Specimen" *Set of* 13 £500

*Dates quoted for Nos. 113a/14c are earliest known postmark dates. Nos. 113a and 114a were despatched to the Leeward Islands in March 1942, Nos. 113b and 114*b* in December 1943, No. 113*c* in June 1944 and No. 114c on 13 December 1951.

Nos. 96, 98/9 and 99b exist in coils constructed from normal sheets.

Printings of the 10s. in March 1942 (No. 113*a*) and of the £1 in February and October 1942 (No. 114*a*) were made by Williams Lea & Co. Ltd. following bomb damage to the De La Rue works in 1940.

For illustrations of Nos. 99a, 99ca, 100a and 110a see above No. 58.

1946 (1 Nov). *Victory. As Nos. 110/11 of Antigua.*
115 1½d. brown 15 50
116 3d. red-orange 15 50
115s/16s Perf "Specimen" *Set of* 2 65·00

1949 (2 Jan). *Royal Silver Wedding. As Nos. 112/13 of Antigua.*
117 2½d. ultramarine 10 10
118 5s. green 4·25 3·25

1949 (10 Oct). *75th Anniv of Universal Postal Union. As Nos. 114/17 of Antigua.*
119 2½d. blue-black 15 1·75
120 3d. deep blue 2·00 1·75
121 6d. magenta 15 1·75
122 1s. blue-green 15 1·75
119/22 *Set of* 4 2·25 6·25

(New Currency. 100 cents = 1 B.W.I. dollar)

1951 (16 Feb). *Inauguration of B.W.I. University College. As Nos. 118/19 of Antigua.*
123 3c. orange and black 30 1·00
124 12c. rose-carmine and reddish violet 70 1·00

Long Island

PRICES FOR STAMPS ON COVER

Most covers from Long Island are philatelic, but these are worth from × 2 (Nos. 1/3) or from × 5 (Nos. 4/36).

The Turkish island of Chustan (or Keustan) in the Gulf of Smyrna was occupied by the Royal Navy during April 1916 and renamed Long Island.

The following stamps were provided by the Civil Administrator, Lieut-Cmdr H. Pirie-Gordon, for the postal service inaugurated on 7 May 1916.

USED STAMPS. Stamps of Long Island were cancelled by hand-drawn circular date stamps in blue crayon for the Northend post office ("N") or in red crayon for Nikola post office ("S").

QUANTITIES ISSUED. The figures quoted do not include the remainders subsequently recorded as having been destroyed.

(1)

G.R.I.
LONG ISLAND
Postage &
Revenue
ONE PENNY

2

1916 (7 May). *Turkish fiscal stamps surch by typewriter as in T* **1**. No wmk. P 12.
1 ½d.on 20pa. green and buff (new value in red, remainder of surch in black) . . . £2500 £4250
2 1d.on 10pa. carmine and buff £2750 £4250
3 2½d.on 1pi. violet and buff (R.) £2500 £4250
Quantities issued: ½d. 25; 1d.20; 2½d. 25.

1916 (7 May). *Typewritten as T* **2** *in various colours of ribbon and carbon. Each stamp initialled by the Civil Administrator. No gum.* Imperf.

(a) On pale green paper with horizontal grey lines. No wmk. *Sheets of 12 (4 × 3) or 16 (4 × 4) with stamps initialled in red ink.*
4 ½d. black £1200 £950
a. "GRI" double £2000
b. "7" for "&" £3250
5 ½d. blue £950
a. "G.R.I." double £2000
b. "7" for "&" £3250
6 ½d. mauve £425 £500
a. "G.R.I." double £1100
b. "7" for "&" £2500
Quantity issued: 140 in all.

(b) On thin horiz laid paper with sheet wmk of "Silver Linen" in double-lined letters. Sheets of 20 (4 × 5) or 16 (some ptgs of 1s.) with stamps initialled in red ink.
7 ½d. black £450 £600
a. "postage" for "Postage" £2250
b. "7" for "&" £2250
8 ½d. blue £700 £750
b. "7" for "&" £2250
9 ½d. mauve £225 £300
a. "postage" for "Postage" £1100
b. "7" for "&" £1400
10 1d. black £170 £325
a. "7" for "&" £1300
b. "Rvevue" for "Revenue" £1300
g. "Postagg" for "Postage" £2000
11 1d. blue £250 £400
a. "7" for "&" £2000
c. "postage" for "Postage" £2000
e. "G.R?I?" for "G.R.I." £2000
f. "ONR" for "ONE" £1100
12 1d. mauve £130 £250
a. "7" for "&" £1500
b. "Rvevue" for "Revenue" £2000
c. "postage" for "Postage" £2000
e. "G.R?I?" for "G.R.I." . . . . † £2000
f. "ONR" for "ONE" £850 £1100
g. "Postagg" for "Postage" £1400
13 1d. red £160 £275
a. "7" for "&" £1400
c. "postage" for "Postage" £2000
f. "ONR" for "ONE" £1100 £1200
14 2½d. black £950
15 2½d. blue £950 £1200
16 2½d. mauve £2000 £1300
17 6d. black (inscr "SIX PENCE") £1300 £1700
a. "SIXPENCE" (one word) £2500
b. Without red ink initials . . . . . . † £2000
19 6d. mauve (inscr "SIX PENCE") £450 £950
a. "SIXPENCE" (one word) £1800
20 1s. black £130 £350
a. "ISLANA" for "ISLAND" £2000
b. "Postge" for "Postage" £1100 £1600
c. "Rebenue" for "Revenue" £2000
21 1s. blue £1200
22 1s. mauve £120 £425
a. "ISLANA" for "ISLAND" £1500
b. "Postge" for "Postage" £2000
c. "Rebenue" for "Revenue" £2000
Quantities issued (all colours); ½d. 237; 1d. 881; 2½d. 80; 6d. 89; 1s. 383.

(c) On thin wove paper. No wmk. *Sheets of 24 with stamps initialled in indelible pencil.*
23 ½d. black £350 £440
25 ½d. mauve £700
26 1d. black £400 £500
27 1d. red £5500 £1000
30 2d. black £190 £475
b. Error. 1d. and 2d. *se-tenant* £4750
c. Initialled in red ink £1000 £1100
31 2d. mauve £190 £325
a. Error. 1d. and 2d. *se-tenant* £4500
32 2½d. black £425 £550
33 2½d. blue £1300
34 2½d. mauve £1100 £1100
35 6d. black £200 £475
a. "Rvenne &" for "Revenue" £2000
b. Error. 2d. and 6d. *se-tenant*, also "ISLND" for "ISLAND" £4750 £4750
c. "PENCC" £1700
36 6d. blue £850
a. "Rvenne &" for "Revenue" £2500
b. Error. 2d. and 6d. *se-tenant*, also "ISLND" for "ISLAND" £5000
c. "PENCC" £2000
Quantities issued (all colours); ½d. 114; 1d. 120; 2d. 249; 2½d. 115; 6d.200.

TOP SHEETS AND CARBONS. It is believed that the production sequence of the typewritten stamps was as follows:
½d. on pale green (Nos. 4/6)
Two black top sheets of 12 (4 × 3) and one of 16 (4 × 4)
Two blue carbon sheets of 12 (4 × 3) and one of 16 (4 × 4)
Five mauve carbon sheets of 12, two from one top sheet and three from the other
Varieties: "7" for "&" occurs on an unknown position from one of the sheets of 12 and "G.R.I." double occurs on R. 3/2-4 of the other
½d. on laid paper (Nos. 7/9) in sheets of 20 (4 × 5)
Three black top sheets
Three blue carbon sheets
Eight mauve carbon sheets, two or three from each top sheet
Varieties: "postage" occurs on R. 3/2 of one top sheet and "7" for "&" on R. 4/2 of another
1d. on laid paper (Nos. 10/13) in sheets of 20 (4 × 5)
Eleven red top sheets
Fifteen black carbon sheets, three each from five of the top sheets
Six blue carbon sheets, one each from six of the top sheets
Twenty-two mauve carbon sheets, probably two from each top sheet
Varieties: "7" for "&" on R. 3/3, "postage" on R. 3/3, "Rvevue" on R. 1/3 and "Postagg" on R. 2/4, all from different top sheets. The position of "G.R?I?" is not known. "ONR" occurs from three different top sheets on R. 5/1, R. 5/2 & 4 or R. 4/1 and 5/2
2½d. on laid paper (Nos. 14/16) in sheets of 20 (4 × 5)
One black top sheet
One blue carbon sheet
Two mauve carbon sheets
6d. on laid paper (Nos. 17/19) in sheets of 20 (4 × 5)
One black top sheet
One blue carbon sheet*
Three mauve carbon sheets
Variety: "SIXPENCE" occurs on R. 1/2-3
1s. on laid paper (Nos. 20/2)
Five black top sheets, four of 20 (4 × 5) and one of 16 (4 × 4)
Nine black carbon sheets three each from two of the top sheets of 20 and three from the top sheet of 16
Two blue carbon sheets, one each fom two of the top sheets of 20
Twelve mauve carbon sheets, nine from various top sheets of 20 and three from the top sheet of 16
Varieties: "ISLANA" occurs on R. 1/2 of one of the sheets of 20 and "Postge" on R. 1/3 of the sheet of 16. "Rebenue" comes from one of the other sheets of 20
½d. on wove paper (Nos. 23/5) in sheets of 24 (4 × 6)
One black top sheet
Three black carbon sheets
One blue carbon sheet*
One mauve carbon sheet
1d. on wove paper (Nos. 26/7) in sheets of 24 (4 × 6)
One red top sheet
Three black carbon sheets
One blue carbon sheet*
One mauve carbon sheet*
2d. on wove paper (Nos. 30/1) in sheets of 24 (4 × 6)
Two black top sheets
Six black carbon sheets, three from each top sheet. One initialled in red ink
Four mauve carbon sheets, two from each top sheet
Variety: the "1d." error occurs on R. 5/2 from one top sheet
2½d. on wove paper (Nos. 32/4) in sheets of 24 (4 × 6)
One black top sheet
Three black carbon sheets
One blue carbon sheet
One mauve carbon sheet
6d. on wove paper (Nos. 35/6) in sheets of 24 (4 × 6)
Two black top sheets
Six black carbon sheets, three from each top sheet
Two blue carbon sheets, one from each top sheet
Varieties: the "2d." error occurs on R. 5/3 from one top sheet which also showed "PENCC" on R. 3/2, and "Rvenne &" on R. 4/1 of the other

*These carbons are described in written records, but their existence has yet to be confirmed by actual examples.

Madagascar

PRICES FOR STAMPS ON COVER		
Nos.	1/47	—
Nos.	50/6	*from* × 75
Nos.	57/62	*from* × 30

BRITISH CONSULAR MAIL

After May 1883 mail from the British community at Antananarivo, the capital, was sent by runner to the British Consulate at Tamatave for forwarding via the French Post Office.

In March of the following year the British Vice-Consul at Antananarivo, Mr. W. C. Pickersgill, reorganised this service and issued stamps for use on both local and overseas mail. Such stamps were only gummed at one of the top corners. This was to facilitate their removal from overseas mail where they were replaced by Mauritius stamps (at Port Louis) or by French issues (at the Vice-Consulate) for transmission via Tamatave and Reunion. Local mail usually had the stamps removed also, being marked with a "PAID" or a Vice-Consular handstamp, although a few covers have survived intact.

CONDITION. Due to the type of paper used, stamps of the British Consular Mail are usually found with slight faults, especially thins. Our prices are for average examples, really fine stamps being worth a premium.

USED STAMPS. Postmarks are not usually found on these issues. Cancellations usually take the form of a manuscript line or cross in crayon, ink or pencil or as five parallel horizontal bars in black or red, approximately 15 mm long. Examples of Nos. 1/3, 5/8 and 11 showing a red diagonal line are believed to be cancelled-to-order.

1

2

1884 (Mar). *Typo locally. Rouletted vertically in colour. No gur except on one upper corner. With circular consular handstan reading* "BRITISH VICE-CONSULATE ANTANANARIVC *around Royal arms in black.*

(a) Inscr "LETTER".
1 **1** 6d. (½ oz) magenta £400 £42
a. Violet handstamp £1900
2 1s. (1 oz) magenta . . . . £375 £4(
3 1s.6d. (1½oz) magenta £425
4 2s. (2 oz) magenta £600 £6

(b) Inscr "POSTAL PACKET".
5 **1** 1d. (1 oz) magenta £425 £3
a. Without handstamp £4500 £45
6 2d. (2 oz) magenta £275 £2
7 3d. (3 oz) magenta £300 £2
8 4d. (1 oz amended in ms to "4 oz") magenta £700 £6
a. Without manuscript amendment . . . £3500 £35
ab. Violet handstamp £1200
ac. Without handstamp £4250 £42

Nos. 1/8 were printed in horizontal strips of four, each str containing two impressions of the setting. Each strip usua contained two stamps with normal stops after "B.C.M." and tv with a hollow stop after "B" (1d., 2d., 3d., 4d., 6d. and 2s.) or af "M" (1s. and 1s.6d.), although the 2d. has also been seen with hollow stop after "M" and the 6d. with hollow stops after both " and "C".

Several values are known with the handstamp either inverted double.

1886. *Manuscript provisionals.*

(a) No. 2 with "SHILLING" *erased and* "PENNY" *written abc in red ink.*
9 **1** 1d.on 1s. (1 oz) magenta . . . .

(b) No. 2 surch "4½d." *and* "W.C.P." *in red ink with a line throu the original value.*
10 **1** 4½d.on 1s. (1 oz) magenta . . . .

1886. *As No. 1, but colour changed. Handstamped with circu* "BRITISH VICE-CONSULATE ANTANANARIVO" *in bla*
11 **1** 6d. (½ oz) rose-red £650 £5

1886. *As No. 8, but handstamped* "BRITISH CONSULAR MA ANTANANARIVO" *in black.*
12 **1** 4d. (1 oz) magenta £1600
a. Violet handstamp £4250

1886. *Typo locally.* "POSTAGE" *and value in words printed in bla Rouletted vertically in colour. No gum, except on one upper corr*

I. "POSTAGE" *29½ mm long. Stops after* "POSTAGE" *and val*

(a) Handstamped "BRITISH VICE-CONSULA *ANTANANARIVO" in black.*
14 **2** 1d. rose . . . . £100 £
a. Violet handstamp £275
15 1½d. rose . . . . £1300 £1(
a. Violet handstamp . . . . £900 £
16 2d. rose £140
a. Violet handstamp £275
17 3d. rose £1300 £9
a. Violet handstamp . . . . £350 £
18 4½d. rose . . . . £900 £
a. Violet handstamp . . . . £475 £
19 8d. rose £2250 £2
a. Violet handstamp £1100 £1

0 9d. rose . . . £2750 £2500
a. Violet handstamp . . . £950

b) *Handstamped "BRITISH CONSULAR MAIL ANTANANARIVO" in black.*

1 2 1d. rose . . . 75·00
2 1½d. rose . . . 80·00
3 2d. rose . . . £100
4 3d. rose . . . 95·00 £140
a. Handstamp in red . . . † £9000
5 4½d. rose . . . 95·00 £130
a. Handstamp in red . . . † £5000
6 8d. rose . . . £120
a. Handstamp in violet . . . £1300
7 9d. rose . . . £130 £180
a. Without handstamp . . . £3000
b. Handstamp in violet . . . £250

I. "POSTAGE" *29½ mm long. No stops after* "POSTAGE" *or value.*

a) *Handstamped "BRITISH VICE-CONSULATE ANTANANARIVO" in violet.*

8 2 1d. rose . . . £900
9 1½d. rose . . . £1700
) 3d. rose . . . £1000
4½d. rose . . . £1500
2 6d. rose . . . £1200

b) *Handstamped "BRITISH CONSULAR MAIL ANTANANARIVO" in black.*

3 1d. rose . . . 75·00 £120
a. Without handstamp . . . £2250
b. Violet handstamp . . . 95·00
4 1½d. rose . . . 75·00 £110
a. Without handstamp . . . £2250
b. Violet handstamp . . . £150
5 2d. rose . . . 70·00 £110
b. Violet handstamp . . . £160
5 3d. rose . . . 80·00 £120
a. Without handstamp . . . £3250
b. Violet handstamp . . . £140
7 4½d. rose . . . 80·00 £120
a. Without handstamp . . . £3500
b. Violet handstamp . . . £140
3 6d. rose . . . 80·00 £120
a. Without handstamp . . . £3500
b. Violet handstamp . . . £325

I. "POSTAGE" *24½ mm long. No stop after* "POSTAGE", *but stop after value.*

) *Handstamped "BRITISH VICE-CONSULATE ANTANANARIVO" in violet.*

2 4d. rose . . . £400
8d. rose . . . £500
a 1s. rose
1s.6d. rose . . . £3750
2s. rose . . . £2250
a. Handstamp in black

) *Handstamped "BRITISH CONSULAR MAIL ANTANANARIVO" in black.*

4d. rose . . . £180
a. Without handstamp . . . £2500
b. Violet handstamp . . . £400
8d. rose . . . £650
a. Without handstamp . . . £2750
b. Violet handstamp . . . £550
1s. rose . . . £450
a. Without handstamp . . . £3000
b. Violet handstamp . . . £1200
1s.6d. rose . . . £550
a. Without handstamp . . . £3000
b. Violet handstamp . . . £1300
2s. rose . . . £600
a. Without handstamp . . . £3250
b. Violet handstamp . . . £1500

The above were also printed in horizontal strips of four.

The stamps of the British Consular Mail were suppressed in 1887, t the postal service continued with the charges paid in cash.

BRITISH INLAND MAIL

In January 1895 the Malagasy government agreed that a ndicate of British merchants at Antananarivo, including the Vice-nsul, should operate an inland postal service during the war with ance. Mail was sent by runner to the port of Vatomandry and warded via Durban where Natal stamps were added.

Nos. 50/62 were cancelled with dated circular postmarks inscribed RITISH MAIL".

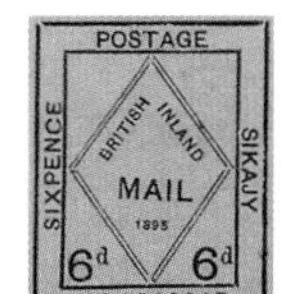

4

5 Malagasy Runners

(Typeset London Missionary Society Press, Antananarivo)

)5 (1 Jan). *Rouletted in black.*

(a) Thick laid paper.

4 4d. black . . . 28·00 14·00
a. "FUOR" for "FOUR" (R. 3/2) . . . — £900

(b) In black on coloured wove paper.

4 1d. *blue-grey* . . . 28·00 13·00
6d. *pale yellow* . . . 28·00 13·00
8d. *salmon* . . . 28·00 13·00
1s. *fawn* . . . 40·00 13·00
2s. *bright rose* . . . 50·00 18·00
a. Italic "2" at left (R. 1/2) . . . £140 60·00
4s. *grey* . . . 65·00 13·00
6 *Set of 7* . . . £250 85·00

There are six types of each value, printed in blocks of 6 (2×3) arated by gutters, four times on each sheet; the upper and lower cks being *tête-bêche*.

(Typo John Haddon & Co, London)

1895 (Mar). *The inscription in the lower label varies for each value.* P 12.

57 5 2d. blue . . . 6·00 48·00
a. Imperf between (horiz pair) . . . £400
58 4d. rose . . . 6·50 48·00
a. Imperf between (horiz pair) . . . £250
b. Imperf between (vert pair) . . . £275
c. Imperf vert (horiz pair) . . . £275
59 6d. green . . . 6·50 48·00
a. Imperf between (horiz pair) . . . £550
60 1s. slate-blue . . . 6·50 60·00
a. Imperf between (horiz pair) . . . £425
61 2s. chocolate . . . 15·00 80·00
a. Imperf between (horiz pair) . . . £450
62 4s. bright purple . . . 26·00 £110
a. Imperf between (horiz pair) . . . £1500
57/62 *Set of 6* . . . 60·00 £350

This post was suppressed when the French entered Antananarivo on 30 September 1895.

Malaya

The Federation of Malaya was formed on 1 February 1948 by the former Straits Settlements of Malacca and Penang, the four Federated Malay States and the five Unfederated States. It did not, however, issue any stamps until it became an independent member of the Commonwealth in 1957.

The philatelic history of the component parts of the federation is most complex.

The method adopted is to show the general issues for the area first, before dealing with the issues for the individual States. The section is divided as follows:

I. STRAITS SETTLEMENTS
II. FEDERATED MALAY STATES
III. MALAYAN POSTAL UNION
IV. MALAYA (BRITISH MILITARY ADMINISTRATION)
V. MALAYAN STATES—Johore, Kedah, Kelantan, Malacca, Negri Sembilan (with Sungei Ujong), Pahang, Penang, Perak, Perlis, Selangor, Trengganu
VI. SIAMESE POSTS IN NORTHERN MALAYA 1887–1909
VII. JAPANESE OCCUPATION OF MALAYA 1942–45
VIII. THAI OCCUPATION OF MALAYA 1943–45

I. STRAITS SETTLEMENTS

The three original Settlements, Malacca, Penang (with Province Wellesley) and Singapore (with Christmas Island), were formed into a Crown Colony on 1 April 1867. The Cocos (Keeling) Islands were transferred to Straits Settlements on 7 February 1886. Labuan was attached to the Colony in 1896, becoming the fourth Settlement in 1906, but was transferred to North Borneo in 1946.

The first known prestamp cover with postal markings from Penang (Prince of Wales Island) is dated March 1806 and from Malacca, under British civil administration, February 1841. The civil post office at Singapore opened on 1 February 1823.

The stamps of India were used at all three post offices from late in 1854 until the Straits Settlements became a separate colony on 1 September 1867.

The Indian stamps were initially cancelled by dumb obliterators and their use in the Straits Settlements can only be identified from complete covers. In 1856 cancellations of the standard Indian octagonal type were issued, numbered "B 109" for Malacca, "B 147" for Penang and "B 172" for Singapore.

CURRENCY. Before 1867 official accounts of the East India Company administration for the Straits Settlements were kept in rupees, although the vast majority of commercial transactions used Spanish American silver dollars, supplies of which reached Malaya via the Philippines.

This confusing situation was rapidly amended when the Straits Settlements became a Crown Colony on 1 April 1867 and Spanish American dollars were declared to be the only legal currency. In 1874 American trade dollars and Japanese yen were also accepted, but in 1890 recognition of the Spanish American dollars was restricted to those from the Mexican mints. A shortage of silver coinage led to the introduction of silver British trade dollars in 1895 which also circulated in Hong Kong and Labuan.

Dollar banknotes first appeared in 1899, but Mexican dollars were not finally replaced until the issue of silver Straits Settlements dollars in 1903, the gold value of which was set at 2s.4d. in January 1906.

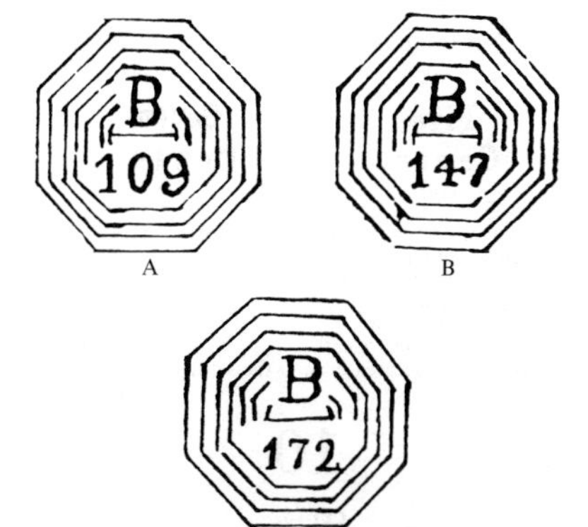

A B C

The Penang and Singapore octagonals were replaced by a duplex type, consisting of a double-ringed datestamp and a diamond-shaped obliterator containing the office number, in 1863 and 1865 respectively.

D

E

PRICES. Catalogue prices in this section are for stamps with clearly legible, if partial, examples of the postmarks.

EAST INDIA COMPANY ADMINISTRATION

MALACCA

Stamps of INDIA *cancelled with Type* A.

1854. *(Nos. 2/34).*
Z1 ½a. blue (Die I) . . . £1200
Z2 1a. red (Die I) . . . £950
Z3 1a. dull red (Die II) . . . £1000
Z4 2a. green . . . £1400
Z4*a* 4a. blue and pale red (Head Die I) (*cut-to-shape*) . . . £1500
Z5 4a. blue and red (Head Die II) (*cut-to-shape*) . . . £1500
Z5*a* 4a. blue and red (Head Die III) (*cut-to-shape*) . . . £1500

1855. *(Nos. 35/6).*
Z6 8a. carmine (Die I)/*blue glazed* . . . £400

1856–64. *(Nos. 37/49).*
Z 7 ½a. pale blue (Die I) . . . £250
Z 8 1a. brown . . . £170
Z 8*a* 2a. dull pink . . . £275
Z 9 2a. yellow-buff . . . £180
Z10 2a. yellow . . . £190
Z11 4a. green . . . £375
Z12 8a. carmine (Die I) . . . £250

1860. *(Nos. 51/3).*
Z13 8p. purple/*bluish* . . . £700
Z14 8p. purple/*white* . . . £325

1865. *(Nos. 54/65).*
Z15 4a. green . . . £375

PENANG

Stamps of INDIA *cancelled with Type* B.

1854. *(Nos. 2/34).*
Z20 ½a. blue (Die I) . . . £375
Z21 1a. red (Die I) . . . £160
Z22 2a. green . . . £225
Z23 4a. blue and pale red (Head Die I) . . . £1400
Z24 4a. blue and red (Head Die II) . . . £1400
Z25 4a. blue and red (Head Die III) . . . £950

1855. *(Nos. 35/6).*
Z26 4a. black/*blue glazed* . . . 80·00
Z27 8a. carmine (Die I)/*blue glazed* . . . 70·00
a. Bisected (4a.) (1860) (on cover) . . . £55000

1856–64. *(Nos. 37/49).*
Z28 ½a. pale blue (Die I) . . . 75·00
Z29 1a. brown . . . 45·00
Z30 2a. dull pink . . . 65·00
Z31 2a. yellow-buff . . . 60·00
Z32 2a. yellow . . . 60·00
Z33 2a. orange . . . 60·00
Z34 4a. black . . . 45·00
Z35 8a. carmine (Die I) . . . 55·00

1860. *(Nos. 51/3).*
Z36 8p. purple/*white* . . . £130

Stamps of INDIA *cancelled with Type* D.

1854. *(Nos. 2/34).*
Z38 1a. red (Die I) . . . £2500

1856–64. *(Nos. 37/49).*
Z39 ½a. pale blue (Die I) . . . £170
Z40 1a. brown . . . 45·00
Z41 2a. yellow . . . 55·00
Z42 4a. black . . . 48·00
Z43 4a. green . . . £140
Z44 8a. carmine (Die I) . . . 50·00

1860. *(Nos. 51/3).*
Z45 8p. purple/*white* . . . 80·00
Z46 8p. mauve . . . 80·00

1865. *(Nos. 54/65).*
Z47 8p. purple
Z48 1a. deep brown 45·00
Z49 2a. yellow 55·00
Z50 4a. green £150
Z51 8a. carmine (Die I)

1866–67. *(Nos. 69/72).*
Z52 4a. green (Die 1) £150

SINGAPORE

Stamps of INDIA *cancelled with Type* C.

1854. *(Nos. 2/34).*
Z60 ½a. blue (Die I) £170
Z61 1a. red (Die I) £100
Z62 1a. dull red (Die II) £140
Z63 1a. red (Die III) £1100
Z64 2a. green 80·00
a. Bisected (1a.) (1857) (on cover) £120000
Z65 4a. blue and pale red (Head Die I) £1100
Z66 4a. blue and red (Head Die II) £1200
Z67 4a. blue and red (Head Die III) £750

1855. *(Nos. 35/6).*
Z68 4a. black/*blue glazed* 38·00
a. Bisected (2a.) (1859) (on cover) £7500
Z69 8a. carmine/*blue glazed* 40·00
a. Bisected (4a.) (1859) (on cover) £50000

1856–66. *(Nos. 37/49).*
Z70 ½a. pale blue (Die I) 38·00
Z71 1a. brown 24·00
a. Bisected (½a.) (1859) (on cover) £55000
Z72 2a. dull pink 42·00
Z73 2a. yellow-buff 35·00
Z74 2a. yellow 38·00
Z75 2a. orange 42·00
Z76 4a. black 24·00
a. Bisected (2a.) (1859) (on cover) £20000
Z77 4a. green £110
Z78 8a. carmine (Die I) 32·00
a. Bisected (4a.) (1866) (on cover) £50000

1860–61. *(Nos. 51/3).*
Z79 8p. purple/*bluish* £500
Z80 8p. purple/*white* 65·00
a. Bisected diagonally (4p.) (1861) (on cover) £55000
Z81 8p. mauve 70·00

1865. *(Nos. 54/65).*
Z82 ½a. blue (Die I) 45·00
Z83 8p. purple £110
Z84 1a. deep brown 35·00
Z85 2a. yellow 40·00
Z86 2a. orange 40·00
Z87 4a. green £110
Z88 8a. carmine (Die I) £275

1866–67. *(Nos. 69/72).*
Z89 4a. green (Die I) £120
Z90 6a.8p. slate £250

OFFICIAL STAMPS

1866–67. *(Nos. O6/14).*
Z91 ½a. pale blue £350
Z92 2a. yellow £475

Stamps of INDIA *cancelled with Type* E.

1856–64. *(Nos. 37/49).*
Z100 1a. brown £250
Z101 2a. yellow £325
Z102 4a. black £325
Z103 8a. carmine (Die I) £325

1860. *(Nos. 51/3).*
Z104 8p. purple/*white* £350

1865. *(Nos. 54/65).*
Z105 2a. yellow £300
Z106 2a. orange £300
Z107 4a. green £375

PRICES FOR STAMPS ON COVER

Nos.	1/9	*from* × 15
No.	10	—
Nos.	11/19	*from* × 8
Nos.	20/1	*from* × 20
Nos.	22/39	*from* × 10
Nos.	41/6	*from* × 20
No.	47	—
Nos.	48/9	*from* × 10
Nos.	50/62	*from* × 20
Nos.	63/71	*from* × 15
No.	72	—
Nos.	73/8	*from* × 20
No.	80	*from* × 30
Nos.	82/5	*from* × 10
Nos.	86/7	*from* × 20
Nos.	88/94	*from* × 15
Nos.	95/105	*from* × 8
Nos.	106/9	*from* × 20
Nos.	110/21	*from* × 6
No.	122	—
Nos.	123/6	*from* × 5
Nos.	127/38	*from* × 4
Nos.	139/40	—
Nos.	141/51	*from* × 15
Nos.	152/67	*from* × 4
Nos.	168/9	—
Nos.	193/212	*from* × 3
Nos.	213/15	—
Nos.	216/17	*from* × 10
Nos.	218/40*a*	*from* × 3
Nos.	240*b*/*d*	—
Nos.	241/55	*from* × 15
Nos.	256/9	*from* × 4
Nos.	260/98	*from* × 3
Nos.	D1/6	*from* × 20

PRINTERS. All Straits Settlements issues were printed in typography by De La Rue & Co, Ltd, London, *unless otherwise stated.*

USED PRICES. The prices quoted for Nos. 1/9 are for fine used examples. Those showing parts of commercial "chops" are worth less.

CROWN COLONY

(Currency. 100 cents = 1 Spanish American dollar)

THREE-HALF-CENTS
(1)

32 CENTS
(2)

1867 (1 Sept). *Nos. 54, 59, 61, 69 and 73 of India surch as T* **1** *or* **2** *(24c., 32c.) by De La Rue.* W **13** (Elephant's head) of India. P 14.
1 1½c.on ½a. blue (Die I) (R.) 85·00 £200
2 2c.on 1a. deep brown (R.) £120 80·00
3 3c.on 1a. deep brown (B.) £120 85·00
4 4c.on 1a. deep brown (Bk.) £225 £250
5 6c.on 2a. yellow (P.) £550 £225
6 8c.on 2a. yellow (G.) £180 42·00
7 12c.on 4a. green (R.) £900 £300
a. Surch double £2000
8 24c.on 8a. rose (Die II) (B.) £400 80·00
9 32c.on 2a. yellow (Bk.) £325 90·00

The 32c. was re-issued for postal use in 1884.
No. 7a. is only known unused.

1869. (?) *No. 1 with* "THREE HALF" *deleted and* "2" *written above, in black manuscript.*
10 2on 1½c. on ½a. blue £9500 £4500

This stamp has been known from very early days and was apparently used at Penang, but nothing is known of its history.

5

6

7

8

9

1867 (Dec)–**72**. *Ornaments in corners differ for each value.* Wmk Crown CC. P 14.
11 **5** 2c. brown (6.68) 27·00 4·25
a. Yellow-brown 28·00 4·25
b. Deep brown 80·00 11·00
w. Wmk inverted
12 4c. rose (7.68) 45·00 7·00
a. Deep rose 60·00 9·50
w. Wmk inverted £130
13 6c. dull lilac (1.68) 80·00 15·00
a. Bright lilac 85·00 15·00
w. Wmk inverted † £160
14 **6** 8c. orange-yellow £140 9·00
a. Orange £140 10·00
w. Wmk inverted £275 £100
15 12c. blue £100 6·50
a. Ultramarine £110 9·00
w. Wmk inverted £300
16 **7** 24c. blue-green £110 5·00
a. Yellow-green £225 21·00
w. Wmk inverted
17 **8** 30c. claret (12.72) £200 11·00
w. Wmk inverted
18 **9** 32c. pale red £450 65·00
w. Wmk inverted † £200
19 96c. grey £275 42·00
a. Perf 12½ (6.71) £2000 £225

Five Cents.
(10)

Seven Cents.
(11)

1879 (May). *Nos. 14a and 18 surch with T* **10** *and* **11**.
20 **6** 5c.on 8c. orange 90·00 £140
a. No stop after "Cents" £750 £800
b. "F i" spaced £800 £850
21 **9** 7c.on 32c. pale red £110 £140
a. No stop after "Cents" £1000 £1100

The no stop error occured once in the setting.

10 cents.
(12)

10 (*a*) 10 (*b*) 10 (*c*) 10 (*d*)
10 (*e*) 10 (*f*) 10 (*g*) 10 (*h*)
10 (*i*) 10 (*j*) 10 (*jj*) 10 (*k*) 10 (*l*)

(*a*) "1" thin curved serif and thin foot, "0" narrow.
(*b*) "1" thick curved serif and thick foot: "0" broad. Both numerals heavy.
(*c*) "1" as (*a*); "0" as (*b*).
(*d*) "1" as (*a*) but thicker; "0" as (*a*).
(*e*) As (*a*) but sides of "0" thicker.
(*f*) "1" as (*d*); "0" as (*e*).
(*g*) As (*a*) but "0" narrower.
(*h*) "1" thin, curved serif and thick foot; "0" as (*g*).
(*i*) "1" as (*b*); "0" as (*a*).
(*j*) "1" as (*d*); "0" as (*g*) but raised.
(*jj*) "1" as (*a*) but shorter, and with shorter serif and thicker foot; "0" as (*g*) but level with "1".
(*k*) "1" as (*jj*); "0" as (*a*).
(*l*) "1" straight serif; "0" as (*g*).

1880 (Mar). *No. 17 surch with T* **12** *(showing numerals (a) to (jj)).*
22 10c.on 30c. claret (*a*) £325 75·00
23 10c.on 30c. claret (*b*) £300 70·00
24 10c.on 30c. claret (*c*) £4250 £650
25 10c.on 30c. claret (*d*) £1900 £225
26 10c.on 30c. claret (*e*) £8000 £1300
27 10c.on 30c. claret (*f*) £8000 £1300
28 10c.on 30c. claret (*g*) £2750 £450
29 10c.on 30c. claret (*h*) £8000 £1300
30 10c.on 30c. claret (*i*) £8000 £1300
31 10c.on 30c. claret (*j*) £8000 £1300
32 10c.on 30c. claret (*jj*) £8000 £1300

Nos. 22/32 come from the same setting of 60 (6 × 10) containing twenty examples of No. 22 (R. 1/1-2, 1/4, 1/6, 2/1-6, 3/1, 3/3, 3/5, 4/1, 4/3-4, 10/1, 10/3-5), twenty-two of No. 23 (R. 4/6, 5/1-6, 6/1-6, 7/1, 8/2-4, 9/1-5), six of No. 25 (R. 1/5, 3/2, 3/4, 4/2, 4/5, 10/2), four of No. 28 (R. 7/2-5), two of No. 24 (R. 9/6, 10/6) and one each of Nos. 26 (R. 3/6), 27 (R. 1/3), 29 (R. 7/6), 30 (R. 8/1), 31 (R. 8/6) and 32 (R. 8/5).

No. 23 is known with large stop after "cents" and also with stop low.

1880 (Apr). *No. 17 surch as T* **12**, *but without "cents.", showing numerals (a) to (c), (g) to (i), (k) and (l).*
33 10on 30c. claret (*a*) £160 50·0
w. Wmk inverted † £16
34 10on 30c. claret (*b*) £170 50·0
w. Wmk inverted † £16
35 10on 30c. claret (*c*) £500 £11
w. Wmk inverted † £35
36 10on 30c. claret (*g*) £1300 £32
aw. Wmk inverted † £70
36*b* 10on 30c. claret (*h*) † —
37 10on 30c. claret (*i*) £3500 £85
38 10on 30c. claret (*k*) £3500 £85
39 10on 30c. claret (*l*) £3500 £85

Nos. 33/9 were surcharged from an amended setting of 60 (6 × 10) of which 59 positions have been identified. Of those known No. 33 occurs on twenty-four (R. 6/1-6, 7/1-6, 8/1-6, 9/1-2, 9/6, 10/1-3), No. 34 on twenty-one (R. 1/2-6, 2/1-6, 3/1-6, 4/3-5, 5/6), No. 35 on eight (R. 1/1, 4/2, 4/6, 5/1-5), No. 36 on three (R. 9/3-5) and Nos. 37 (R. 10/6), 38 (R. 10/4) and 39 (R. 10/5) on one each. R. 4/1 remains unidentified.

The existence of No. 36*b*, known as a single example from the 6th vertical column, and a stamp in the Royal Collection with "1" as (*b*) and "0" as (*g*) suggests that there may have been another setting.

5 cents.
(13)

5 cents.
(14)

5 cents.
(15)

1880 (Aug). *No. 14a surch with T* **13** *to* **15**.
41 **13** 5c.on 8c. orange £120 £15
42 **14** 5c.on 8c. orange £110 £14
43 **15** 5c.on 8c. orange £400 £47

Surcharged in a setting of 60 (6 × 10) with *T* **13** on rows one to four, *T* **14** on rows five to nine and *T* **15** on row ten.

10 cents.
(16)

5 cents.
(17)

1880–81. *Nos. 13, 15/a and 17 surch with T* **16**.
44 10c.on 6c. lilac (11.81) 60·00 6·0
a. Surch double — £190
45 10c.on 12c. ultramarine (1.81) 65·00 16·0
a. Blue 48·00 9·0
46 10c.on 30c. claret (12.80) £375 85·0

A second printing of the 10c. on 6c. has the surcharge heavier and the "10" usually more to the left or right of "cents".

1882 (Jan). *No. 12 surch with T* **17**.
47 5c.on 4c. rose £250 £27

18

19

1882 (Jan). Wmk Crown CC. P 14.
48 **18** 5c. purple-brown . . . . 80·00 90·00
49 **19** 10c. slate . . . . £375 65·00
s. Optd "Specimen" £375

1882. Wmk Crown CA. P 14.
50 **5** 2c. brown (Aug) . . . . £225 40·00
51 4c. rose (April) . . . . £110 5·50
52 **6** 8c. orange (Sept) . . . . 3·00 1·00
w. Wmk inverted . . . .
53 **19** 10c. slate (Oct) . . . . 5·00 1·25
w. Wmk inverted . . . .
For the 4c. in deep carmine see No. 98.

TWO CENTS — **20a** "S" wide
TWO CENTS — **20b** "E" and "S" wide
TWO CENTS — **20c** "N" wide
TWO CENTS — **20d** All letters narrow
TWO CENTS — **20e** "EN" and "S" wide
TWO CENTS — **20f** "E" wide

883 (Apr). *Nos. 52 and 18 surch with T* **20a/f.**
4 **20a** 2c.on 8c. orange £190 £100
5 **20b** 2c.on 8c. orange £190 £100
6 **20c** 2c.on 8c. orange £190 £100
7 **20d** 2c.on 8c. orange . . . . £110 70·00
a. Surch double £2500 £1000
8 **20e** 2c.on 8c. orange £850 £400
9 **20a** 2c.on 32c. pale red £600 £170
0 **20f** 2c.on 32c. pale red £750 £200
a. Surch double . . . .

The 8c. was surcharged using one of two triplet settings, either 54 55 + 56 or 57 + 57 + 57, applied to rows 2 to 10. A single andstamp, either No. 57 or No. 58, was then used to complete row . The 32c. was surcharged in the same way with a triplet of 59 + 0 + 59 and a single handstamp as No. 60.

2 Cents. (21) — 4 Cents (22) — 8 Cents (23)

883 (June–July). *Nos. 51 and 15 surch with T* **21**.
1 2c.on 4c. rose . . . . 75·00 85·00
a. "s" of "Cents" inverted £1200 £1300
2 2c.on 12c. blue (July) £250 £130
a. "s" of "Cents" inverted £3500 £1800
The inverted "S" error occurred once in the setting of 60.

Broken oval above "O" of "POSTAGE" (Lower right pane R. 10/5)

883 (July)–**91**. Wmk Crown CA. P 14.
5 2c. pale rose . . . . 35·00 3·50
a. Bright rose (1889) . . . . 6·50 85
4c. pale brown . . . . 24·00 1·25
a. Broken oval . . . . £225 48·00
b. Deep brown . . . . 35·00 3·25
ba. Broken oval . . . . £350 80·00
w. Wmk inverted . . . . £110 75·00
18 5c. blue (8.83) . . . . 12·00 1·00
w. Wmk inverted . . . . † £180
5 6c. lilac (11.84) . . . . 25·00 9·50
a. Violet . . . . 2·00 3·50
aw. Wmk inverted . . . .
6 12c. brown-purple . . . . 65·00 11·00
7 24c. yellow-green (2.84) . . . . 70·00 6·50
a. Blue-green . . . . 4·25 3·75
8 30c. claret (9.91) . . . . 9·00 10·00
w. Wmk inverted . . . . 85·00 70·00
9 32c. orange-vermilion (1.87) . . . . 7·00 2·50
w. Wmk inverted . . . . 55·00 55·00
96c. olive-grey (7.88) . . . . 75·00 48·00
a/71 *Set of* 9 . . . . £180 70·00
s/5s, 67s Optd "Specimen" *Set of* 4 . . . . £800
Most examples of the 4c. in shades of olive-bistre are thought to colour changelings.
For the 4c. in deep carmine and 12c. in claret see Nos. 98 and 2.

84 (Feb–Aug). *Nos. 65, 15 and 67 surch with T* **22** *or* **23**.
18 4c.on 5c. blue (Aug) £3000 £3750
4c.on 5c. blue (R.) (Aug) . . . . £110 95·00
6 8c.on 12c. blue £425 £120
w. Wmk inverted . . . . † £400

75 8c.on 12c. brown-purple (Aug) £300 £120
a. Inverted "8" . . . . † —
b. "s" of "Cents" low (R. 5/1) £2000 £1000

1884 (Aug). *No. 65 surch with T* **20d/f.**
76 **20d** 2c.on 5c. blue £120 £130
77 **20e** 2c.on 5c. blue £120 £130
a. Pair, with and without surch . . . .
b. Surch double . . . .
78 **20f** 2c.on 5c. blue £120 £130
Surcharged as a triplet, 77 + 76 + 78. On No. 76 "TS" are dropped below the line.

8 (24) — 3 CENTS (25) — THREE CENTS (26)

1884 (Sept). *No. 75 additionally surch with large numeral as T* **24** *in red.*
80 **6** 8on 8c. on 12c. dull purple £225 £250
a. Surch *T* **24** double £4500
b. Surch *T* **23** in blue £6500
c. "s" of "Cents" low £1600 £1800
Examples as No. 75, but with Type **23** in blue, were further surcharged in error.
A similar "4" surcharge in red on No. 73 exists from a trial printing of which seven examples are known, all used on an official's correspondence (*Price* £21000 *used*).

1885. *No. 65 and T* **9** *in new colour,* wmk Crown CA, *surch with T* **25** *or* **26**.
82 **25** 3c.on 5c. blue (Sept) £120 £225
a. Surch double £2250
83 **26** 3c.on 32c. pale magenta (Dec) . . . . 3·25 3·75
a. Deep magenta . . . . 1·25 1·00
s. Optd "Specimen" £200
The surcharge on No. 82 was applied locally by a triplet setting. No. 83 was surcharged by De La Rue in complete panes.

3 cents (27) — 2 Cents (28)

1886 (Apr). *No. 48 surch with T* **27**.
84 **18** 3c.on 5c. purple-brown £190 £200
The surcharge on No. 84 was applied by a triplet setting.

1887 (July). *No. 65 surch with T* **28**.
85 **18** 2c.on 5c. blue . . . . 23·00 65·00
a. "C" of "Cents" omitted . . . . — £2750
b. Surch double £1100 £1000
The surcharge on No. 85 was applied by a triplet setting.

10 CENTS (29) — THIRTY CENTS (30)

1891 (Nov). *Nos. 68 and 70 surch with T* **29** *and* **30**.
86 **7** 10c.on 24c. yellow-green . . . . 3·00 1·25
a. Narrow "0" in "10" (R. 4/6) . . . . 28·00 30·00
w. Wmk inverted . . . . 50·00 55·00
87 **9** 30c.on 32c. orange-vermilion . . . . 7·50 3·50
w. Wmk inverted . . . .
The "R" of "THIRTY" and "N" of "CENTS" are found wide or narrow and in all possible combinations.

ONE CENT (31) — ONE CENT (32)

1892. *Stamps of 1882–91* (wmk Crown CA) *surch with* T **31**.
88 1c.on 2c. bright rose (Mar) . . . . 2·00 3·75
89 1c.on 4c. brown (Apr) . . . . 5·00 5·50
a. Surch double £1200
b. Broken oval £100 £110
w. Wmk inverted . . . .
90 1c.on 6c. lilac (Feb) . . . . 1·40 5·00
a. Surch double, one inverted £1300 £1200
w. Wmk inverted . . . .
91 1c.on 8c. orange (Jan) . . . . 1·00 1·25
92 1c.on 12c. brown-purple (Mar) . . . . 5·00 9·00
88/92 *Set of* 5 . . . . 13·00 22·00
The three settings used for Nos. 88/92 contained various combinations of the following varieties: "ON" of "ONE" and "N" of "CENT" wide; "O" wide, "N" of "ONE" narrow and "N" of "CENT" wide "O" narrow and both letters "N" wide; "ON" narrow, and "N" of "CENT" wide "O" wide and both letters "N" narrow; "ON" wide and "N" of "CENT" narrow; "ON" and "N" of "CENT" narrow; "O" narrow "N" of "ONE" wide and "N" of "CENT" narrow. Antique "N" and "E" letters also occur.

1892–94. *Colours changed.* Wmk Crown CA. P 14. *Surch with T* **32** *and* **26** *by De La Rue.*
93 **6** 1c.on 8c. green (3.92) . . . . 1·00 1·50
94 **9** 3c.on 32c. carmine-rose (6.94) . . . . 2·25 70
a. Surch omitted £3750
93s/4s Optd "Specimen" *Set of* 2 . . . . £120
No. 94a comes from a sheet found at Singapore on which all stamps in the upper left pane had the surcharge omitted. Five vertical inter-panneau pairs still exist with the surcharge omitted on the upper stamps (*Price* £27000 *unused*). The only used example of the error is on cover.

33

34

4 cents. (35)

1892 (Mar)–**99**. Wmk Crown CA. P 14.
95 **33** 1c. green (9.92) . . . . 3·50 70
a. Malformed "S" £300 £120
b. Repaired "S" £275 £110
96 3c. carmine-rose (2.95) . . . . 11·00 40
a. Malformed "S" £400 £130
97 3c. brown (3.99) . . . . 6·00 60
a. Repaired "S" £350 £130
b. Yellow-brown . . . . 4·50 60
98 **5** 4c. deep carmine (7.99) . . . . 4·75 1·25
a. Broken oval . . . . £120 65·00
99 **18** 5c. brown (6.94) . . . . 5·00 1·00
100 5c. magenta (7.99) . . . . 2·25 2·00
101 **6** 8c. ultramarine (6.94) . . . . 4·50 50
a. Bright blue . . . . 7·00 80
102 12c. claret (3.94) . . . . 11·00 8·50
103 **33** 25c. purple-brown and green . . . . 24·00 6·50
a. Malformed "S" £650 £325
b. Repaired "S" £600 £300
c. Dull purple and green . . . . 23·00 6·00
104 50c. olive-green and carmine . . . . 20·00 2·50
a. Repaired "S" £650 £275
105 **34** $5 orange and carmine (10.98) £325 £250
a. Repaired "S" £2750 £2750
95/105 *Set of* 11 . . . . £375 £250
95s/101s, 103s/5s Optd "Specimen" *Set of* 10 . . . . £475

1898 (26 Dec). *T* **18** *and* **6** *surch with T* **35** *at Singapore.*
106 4c.on 5c. brown (No. 99) . . . . 2·75 4·75
107 4c.on 5c. blue (No. 65) . . . . 3·75 13·00
a. Surch double . . . . — £1300
108 4c.on 8c. ultramarine (No. 101) . . . . 1·40 2·75
a. Surch double £1000 £900
b. Bright blue (No. 101*a*) . . . . 1·00 1·00
106/8*b Set of* 3 . . . . 6·75 17·00
Nos. 107 and 108*b* exist with stop spaced 1½ mm from the "S" (R. 10/6).

FOUR CENTS (36)

37

38

1899 (Mar). *T* **18** (wmk Crown CA. P 14), *surch with T* **36** *by De La Rue.*
109 4c.on 5c. carmine 75 30
a. Surch omitted £27000
s. Optd "Specimen" . . . . 45·00
x. Wmk reversed . . . . 75·00
No. 109a is only known unused.

1902 (Apr)–**03**. Wmk Crown CA. P 14.
110 **37** 1c. grey-green (7.02) . . . . 2·75 3·00
a. Pale green . . . . 4·50 3·25
111 3c. dull purple and orange . . . . 3·50 20
w. Wmk inverted . . . . — £200
112 4c. purple/*red* (9.02) . . . . 4·75 30
113 **38** 5c. dull purple (8.02) . . . . 5·50 85
114 8c. purple/*blue* . . . . 4·00 20
115 10c. purple and black/*yellow* (9.02) . . . . 25·00 1·50
116 **37** 25c. dull purple and green (8.02) . . . . 12·00 6·00
117 **38** 30c. grey and carmine (7.02) . . . . 18·00 8·00
118 **37** 50c. deep green and carmine (9.02) . . . . 20·00 20·00
a. Dull green and carmine . . . . 23·00 23·00
119 **38** $1 dull green and black (9.02) . . . . 22·00 65·00
120 **37** $2 dull purple and black (9.02) . . . . 70·00 70·00
121 **38** $5 dull green & brown-orange (10.02) £190 £160
122 **37** $100 purple and green/*yellow* (3.03) £9500
s. Optd "Specimen" £400
110/21 *Set of* 12 . . . . £325 £300
110s/21s Optd "Specimen" *Set of* 12 . . . . £350

(Currency 100 cents = 1 Straits, later Malayan, dollar)

39

40

41

42

(Des N. Trotter and W. Egerton)

1903 (Dec)–**04**. Wmk Crown CA. P 14.
123 **39** 1c. grey-green . . . . 1·75 8·00
124 **40** 3c. dull purple (1.04) . . . . 11·00 4·50
125 **41** 4c. purple/*red* (4.04) . . . . 4·75 30
126 **42** 8c. purple/*blue* (7.04) . . . . 48·00 1·25
123/6 *Set of* 4 . . . . 60·00 12·50
123s/6s Optd "Specimen" *Set of* 4 . . . . £150

1904 (Aug)–**10**. Wmk Multiple Crown CA. *Ordinary paper (1c. to $1 and $5) or chalk-surfaced paper ($2, $25, $100)*. P 14.

127 **39** 1c. deep green (9.04) 2·75 10
a. Chalk-surfaced paper (12.05) 9·50 1·50
w. Wmk inverted 90·00 55·00
128 **40** 3c. dull purple 2·25 30
a. Chalk-surfaced paper (8.06) 9·50 1·50
aw. Wmk inverted 90·00 65·00
b. Plum (2.08) 7·50 1·75
129 **41** 4c. purple/*red* (6.05) 10·00 75
a. Chalk-surfaced paper (10.05) 10·00 1·25
aw. Wmk inverted 60·00 50·00
130 **38** 5c. dull purple (12.06) 11·00 2·25
a. Chalk-surfaced paper (12.06) 14·00 8·00
131 **42** 8c. purple/*blue* (8.05) 28·00 1·50
a. Chalk-surfaced paper (12.05) 23·00 2·75
132 **38** 10c. purple and black/*yellow* (8.05) 8·00 80
a. Chalk-surfaced paper (11.05) 12·00 3·00
133 **37** 25c. dull purple and green (1.05) 32·00 23·00
a. Chalk-surfaced paper (11.05) 40·00 23·00
134 **38** 30c. grey and carmine (3.05) 48·00 2·50
a. Chalk-surfaced paper (3.06) 50·00 2·75
135 **37** 50c. dull green and carmine (10.05) 55·00 15·00
a. Chalk-surfaced paper (11.06) 29·00 15·00
136 **38** $1 dull green and black (3.05) 55·00 22·00
a. Chalk-surfaced paper (3.06) 45·00 18·00
137 **37** $2 dull purple and black (10.05) £100 90·00
138 **38** $5 dull green & brown-orange (10.05) £200 £160
a. Chalk-surfaced paper (1.08) £190 £140
139 **37** $25 grey-green and black (7.06) £1500 £1500
s. Optd "Specimen" £225
140 $100 purple and green/*yellow* (6.10) £11000
127/38 *Set of* 12 £450 £250

STRAITS
SETTLEMENTS.
(43)

Straits Settlements.
(44)

STRAITS
SETTLEMENTS.

FOUR CENTS.
(45)

1906 (20 Dec)–**07**. *T* **18** *of Labuan (Nos. 117 etc.) optd with T* **43** *or* **44** *(10c.) or additionally surch with T* **45**, *in black (No. 145) claret (No. 151) or brown-red (others) at Singapore*. P 13½–14.

141 1c. black and purple (P 14½–15) 60·00 £170
a. Perf 14 £275 £400
b. Line through "B" £550
142 2c. black and green £300 £375
a. Perf 14½–15 £170 £300
b. Perf 13½–14 comp 12–13 £1100 £1100
c. Line through "B" £900
143 3c. black and sepia (1.07) 20·00 85·00
a. Line through "B" £300
144 4c.on 12c. black and yellow 2·50 6·00
a. No stop after "CENTS" (R. 1/8, 6/8) £350
b. Line through "B" £150
145 4c.on 16c. green and brown (Blk.) 4·50 8·00
a. "STRAITS SETTLEMENTS" in both brown-red and black £650 £700
b. Ditto. In vert pair with normal £4750
c. Line through "B" £160
146 4c.on 18c. black and pale brown 2·75 6·50
a. No stop after "CENTS" (R. 1/8, 6/8) £275
b. "FOUR CENTS" and bar double £7500
c. "FOUR CENTS" and bar 1½ mm below normal position (pair with normal) £1300
d. Line through "B" £150
147 8c. black and vermilion 3·00 8·00
a. Line through "B" £150
148 10c. brown and slate 7·50 7·50
a. No stop after "Settlements" (R. 1/4, 6/4) £325
b. Line through "B" £200
149 25c. green and greenish blue (1.07) 16·00 38·00
a. Perf 14½–15 90·00 £130
b. Perf 13½–14 comp 14½–15 £350
c. Line through "B" £300
150 50c. dull purple and lilac (1.07) 16·00 70·00
a. Line through "B" £350
151 $1 claret and orange (Claret) (1.07) 45·00 £110
a. Perf 14½–15 £550
b. Line through "B" £550
141/51 *Set of* 11 £300 £700

Nos. 141/51 were overprinted by a setting of 50 (10 × 5) applied twice to the sheets of 100. The "FOUR CENTS" surcharges were applied separately by a similar setting.

No. 145a shows impressions of Type **43** in both brown-red and black. It is known from one complete sheet and the top half of another.

No. 146b occurred on row 5 from one sheet only. No. 146c occurred on R. 4/10 and 9/10 of the first printing.

The line through "B" flaw occurs on R. 5/10 of the basic stamp. For illustration see Labuan.

46

47

1906 (Sept)–**12**. Wmk Mult Crown CA. *Ordinary paper (1c. to 10c.) or chalk-surfaced paper (21c. to $500)*. P 14.

152 **39** 1c. blue-green (3.10) 23·00 1·10
153 **40** 3c. red (6.08) 3·25 10
154 **41** 4c. red (7.07) 5·50 2·50
155 4c. dull purple (2.08) 5·50 10
a. Chalk-surfaced paper (1.12) 11·00 2·50
as. Optd "Specimen" 75·00
156 4c. claret (9.11) 2·00 80
157 **38** 5c. orange (4.09) 2·75 2·50
158 **42** 8c. blue 3·50 60
159 **38** 10c. purple/*yellow* (7.08) 7·50 1·00
a. Chalk-surfaced paper (5.12) 16·00 8·00
160 **46** 21c. dull purple and claret (11.10) 6·50 38·00
161 **37** 25c. dull and bright purple (7.09) 14·00 8·00
162 **38** 30c. purple and orange-yellow (11.09) 40·00 4·25
163 **46** 45c. black/*green* (11.10) 2·50 4·00
164 **37** 50c. black/*green* (4.10) 5·00 5·00
165 **38** $1 black and red/*blue* (10.10) 15·00 5·50
166 **37** $2 green and red/*yellow* (12.09) 24·00 24·00
167 **38** $5 green and red/*green* (11.09) £120 75·00
w. Wmk inverted £900
168 **47** $25 purple and blue/*blue* (5.11) £1400 £1100
s. Optd "Specimen" £325
169 $500 purple and orange (5.10) £80000
s. Optd "Specimen" £1200
152/67 *Set of* 16 £225 £160
153s/67s Optd "Specimen" *Set of* 15 £650

Beware of dangerous forgeries of No. 169.

48 49 50 51 52 53

54

1912–**23**. *$25, $100 and $500 as T* **47**, *but with head of King George V. Die I (5, 10, 25, 30, 50c., $1, $2, $5)*. Wmk Mult Crown CA. *Ordinary paper (Nos. 193/6, 198/201, 203) or chalk-surfaced paper (others)*. P 14.

193 **48** 1c. green (9.12) 6·50 1·25
a. Pale green (1.14) 7·00 1·25
b. Blue-green (1917) 7·00 1·75
bw. Wmk inverted † £250
194 1c. black (2.19) 1·50 1·00
w. Wmk inverted † £250
195 **52** 2c. green (10.19) 1·00 50
196 **49** 3c. red (2.13) 2·75 1·25
a. Scarlet (2.17) 2·25 10
y. Wmk inverted and reversed £250
197 **50** 4c. dull purple (3.13) 1·50 60
a. Wmk sideways † £1500
w. Wmk inverted † £250
198 4c. rose-scarlet (2.19) 1·75 15
aw. Wmk inverted † £250
b. Carmine 1·75 20
199 **51** 5c. orange (8.12) 1·75 50
a. Yellow-orange 2·75 1·00
200 **52** 6c. dull claret (3.20) 1·75 50
a. Deep claret 6·00 2·75
aw. Wmk inverted £250
201 8c. ultramarine (3.13) 2·00 80
w. Wmk inverted † £250
202 **51** 10c. purple/*yellow* (9.12) 1·50 1·00
aw. Wmk inverted † £275
b. White back (1913) 1·50 1·10
bs. Optd "Specimen" 48·00
c. On lemon (1916) 16·00 1·25
cs. Optd "Specimen" 70·00
d. Wmk sideways † £2750
203 10c. deep bright blue (1918) 6·00 40
a. Bright blue (1919) 4·00 50
204 **53** 21c. dull and bright purple (11.13) 5·00 9·50
205 **54** 25c. dull purple and mauve (7.14) 12·00 9·00
aw. Wmk inverted £100 £120
b. Dull purple and violet (1919) 65·00 11·00
207 **51** 30c. dull purple and orange (12.14) 8·00 2·25
208 **53** 45c. black/*green* (*white back*) (12.14) 6·50 18·00
a. On blue-green, olive back (7.18) 3·25 20·00
as. Optd "Specimen" 55·00
b. On emerald back (6.22) 3·25 13·00
209 **54** 50c. black/*green* (7.14) 5·50 3·00
a. On blue-green, olive back (1918) 18·00 7·50
b. On emerald back (1921) 12·00 9·50
c. Die II. *On emerald back* (1922) 3·00 4·00
cs. Optd "Specimen" 55·00
210 **51** $1 black and red/*blue* (10.14) 9·00 8·50
w. Wmk inverted £120 £130
211 **54** $2 grn & red/*yell, white back* (1914) 8·50 42·00
a. Green and red/yellow (1915) 10·00 42·00
as. Optd "Specimen" 55·00
b. On orange-buff (1921) 55·00 70·00
c. On pale yellow (1921) 60·00 80·00
212 **51** $5 grn & red/*grn, white back* (11.13) 80·00 42·00
a. Green and red/green (1915) 80·00 65·00
as. Optd "Specimen" 75·00
b. On blue-green, olive back (1918) £150 90·00
bw. Wmk inverted
c. On emerald back (1920) £180 £100
d. Die II. *On emerald back* (1923) £100 70·00
ds. Optd "Specimen" 90·00
213 – $25 purple and blue/*blue* £1200 £425
a. Break in scroll £2000
b. Broken crown and scroll £2000
e. Break in lines below scroll £2000
f. Damaged leaf at bottom right £2000
s. Optd "Specimen" £250
214 – $100 black and carmine/*blue* (8.12) £5000
a. Break in scroll £7500
b. Broken crown and scroll £7500
e. Break in lines below scroll
f. Damaged leaf at bottom right
s. Optd "Specimen" £500
215 – $500 purple and orange-brown (8.12) £40000
a. Break in scroll £48000
b. Broken crown and scroll £48000
f. Damaged leaf at bottom right
s. Optd "Specimen" £1300
193/212 *Set of* 19 £140 £120
193s/212s Optd "Specimen" *Set of* 19 £650

The 6c. is similar to *T* **52**, but the head is in a beaded oval as in *T* **53**. The 2c., 6c. (and 12c. below) have figures of value on a circular ground while in the 8c. this is of oval shape.

For illustrations of the varieties on Nos. 213/15 see above No. 51*b* of Bermuda.

RED CROSS

2c.
(55)

MALAYA-
BORNEO
EXHIBITION.
(56)

1917 (1 May). *Surch with T* **55**.

216 **49** 2c.on 3c. scarlet 2·25 26·00
a. No stop (R. 2/3) £325 £600
217 **50** 2c.on 4c. dull purple 3·25 26·00
a. No stop (R. 2/3) £350 £600

Nos. 216a and 217a occur in the first setting only.

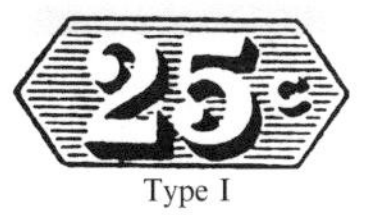
Type I

Type II

The duty plate for the 25c. value was replaced in 1926. In Type II the solid shading forming the back of the figure 2 extends to the top of the curve; the upturned end of the foot of the 2 is short; two background lines above figure 5; c close to 5; STRAITS SETTLEMENTS in taller letters.

1921–**33**. Wmk Mult Script CA. *Ordinary paper (1c. to 6c., 10c. (No. 230), 12c.) or chalk-surfaced paper (others)*. P 14.

218 **48** 1c. black (3.22) 50 10
219 **52** 2c. green (5.21) 50 10
w. Wmk inverted 30·00
x. Wmk reversed † —
y. Wmk inverted and reversed
220 2c. brown (12.25) 7·00 2·50
221 **49** 3c. green (9.23) 1·50 80
w. Wmk inverted 30·00
222 **50** 4c. carmine-red (9.21) 2·00 4·50
223 4c. bright violet (8.24) 60 10
w. Wmk inverted 30·00
224 4c. orange (8.29) 1·00 10
225 **51** 5c. orange (Die I) (5.21) 1·50 15
a. Wmk sideways † £2250
bw. Wmk inverted 30·00
bx. Wmk reversed † —
c. Die II (1922) 2·25 1·25
226 5c. brown (Die II) (1932) 2·75 10
a. Die I (1933) 5·00 10
227 **52** 6c. dull claret (10.22) 2·00 15
w. Wmk inverted 30·00 38·00
228 6c. rose-pink (2.25) 20·00 9·50
229 6c. scarlet (1.27) 2·50 10
230 **51** 10c. bright blue (Die I) (1921) 1·75 2·75
w. Wmk inverted 30·00
231 10c. purple/*pale yellow* (Die I) (1923) 2·50 7·00
a. Die II (11.26) 2·00 30
b. Purple/brt yellow (Die II) (1932) 9·50 2·25
ba. Die I (1933) 6·00 10
232 **52** 12c. bright blue (1.22) 1·00 20
w. Wmk inverted 30·00
233 **53** 21c. dull and bright purple (2.23) 6·00 48·00
234 **54** 25c. dull purple and mauve (Die I, Type I) (1921) 28·00 70·00
a. Die II, Type I (1923) 15·00 3·75
b. Die II, Type II (1927) 5·00 1·75
235 **51** 30c. dull purple & orange (Die I) (1921) 23·00 38·00
a. Die II (1922) 2·00 1·25
236 **53** 35c. dull purple & orange-yellow (8.22) 12·00 6·00
a. Dull purple and orange 3·50 5·50
237 35c. scarlet and purple (4.31) 10·00 7·00
238 **54** 50c. black/*emerald* (9.25) 1·75 40
239 **51** $1 black and red/*blue* (Die II) (1921) 6·00 65
240 **54** $2 grn & red/*pale yell* (Die II) (1923) 10·00 8·00
240*a* **51** $5 green and red/*green* (Die II) (1926) 90·00 32·00

240*b* – $25 purple and blue/*blue* (5.23) £700 £120
ba. Break in scroll £1300
bb. Broken crown and scroll £1300
be. Break through lines below left scroll
bf. Damaged leaf at bottom right
bs. Optd "Specimen" £200
240*c* – $100 black and carmine/*blue* (5.23) £4000 £1600
ca. Break in scroll £5500
cb. Broken crown and scroll £5500
ce. Break through lines below left scroll
cf. Damaged leaf at bottom right
cs. Optd "Specimen" £425
240*d* – $500 purple and orange-brown (4.23) £32000
da. Break in scroll £38000
db. Broken crown and scroll £40000
de. Break through lines below left scroll
df. Damaged leaf at bottom right
ds. Optd "Specimen" £1200
218/40*a* *Set of* 24 £160 £110
218s/40as (*ex* 6c. rose-pink) Optd or Perf
Nos. 224s, 226s, 237s) "Specimen" *Set of* 23 £650

Nos. 240*b*/*d* are as Type **47**, but with portrait of George V.

The 2c. green was reissued in 1927, and exists with "Specimen" overprint 15.5 × 1.75 mm instead of the 14.5 × 2.5 mm of the original issue (*Price*, £65).

An 8c. in carmine was prepared but not issued (Optd "Specimen" £400).

The paper of Nos. 231*b*/ba is the normal *pale yellow* at the back, but with a bright yellow surface.

In 1926 new Key and Duty plates were made of 100 (10 × 10) instead of the usual 60 (6 × 10).

For illustrations of the varieties on Nos. 240*b*/*d* see above No. 51*b* of Bermuda.

SETTINGS OF TYPE 56. Nos. 241/55 were produced using a typeset block of 12 (6 × 2) overprints from which ten stereos were taken to provide a forme for the complete sheet of 120. Two such formes were prepared of which the second was only used for a limited number of Straits Settlements sheets in addition to the Kedah and Trengganu issues.

Several constant varieties occur on the original typeset block of 12 and so appear ten times on sheets printed from both Settings I and II. These include:

Oval last "O" in "BORNEO" (R. 1/3 of typeset block of 12)
Raised stop after "EXHIBITION" (R. 2/2 of typeset block of 12)
Small second "A" in "MALAYA" (R. 2/6 of typeset block of 12).

The two formes also produced constant varieties in each setting which include:

Setting I
No hyphen (Left pane. R. 7/1 or 9/2)
No stop (Left and right panes. Either on R. 10/4 (right pane) or, for some sheets, on other stamps from even numbered horizontal rows in the 4th vertical column (both panes))
Third "I" in "EXHIBITION" omitted (R. 8/5, 10/5 (left pane)). This must have occurred very late in the use of this setting and is only found on the 5c. and 10c.

Setting II
No stop (Left pane. R. 1/5)
"EXH.BITION" (Left pane. Stamps from even numbered horizontal rows in the 3rd vertical column)

1922 (Apr). *Malaya-Borneo Exhibition, Singapore. Optd with T* **56**.

(*a*) Wmk Mult Crown CA (*Nos. 195, 198/9, 201, 205, 208a, 210, 211b and 212b*).

241 **52** 2c. green 28·00 75·00
b. Oval last "O" in "BORNEO" 55·00 £120
c. Raised stop after "EXHIBITION" 55·00 £120
d. Small second "A" in "MALAYA" 55·00 £120
e. No hyphen £170
f. No stop 65·00 £130
242 **50** 4c. rose-scarlet 7·50 23·00
b. Oval last "O" in "BORNEO" 16·00 42·00
c. Raised stop after "EXHIBITION" 16·00 42·00
d. Small second "A" in "MALAYA" 16·00 42·00
e. No hyphen 60·00
f. No stop 20·00 48·00
h. "EXH.BITION" 60·00
243 **51** 5c. orange 5·00 19·00
b. Oval last "O" in "BORNEO" 11·00 35·00
c. Raised stop after "EXHIBITION" 11·00 35·00
d. Small second "A" in "MALAYA" 11·00 35·00
e. No hyphen 40·00
f. No stop 13·00 40·00
h. "EXH.BITION" 40·00
244 **52** 8c. ultramarine 1·75 7·50
b. Oval last "O" in "BORNEO" 4·75 14·00
c. Raised stop after "EXHIBITION" 4·75 14·00
d. Small second "A" in "MALAYA" 4·75 14·00
e. No hyphen 28·00
f. No stop 5·50 16·00
h. "EXH.BITION" 28·00
245 **54** 25c. dull purple and mauve 3·25 32·00
b. Oval last "O" in "BORNEO" 8·50 55·00
c. Raised stop after "EXHIBITION" 8·50 55·00
d. Small second "A" in "MALAYA" 8·50 55·00
e. No hyphen 38·00
f. No stop 9·50 65·00
h. "EXH.BITION" 38·00
246 **53** 45c. black/*blue-green* (*olive back*) 3·00 28·00
b. Oval last "O" in "BORNEO" 8·00 48·00
c. Raised stop after "EXHIBITION" 8·00 48·00
d. Small second "A" in "MALAYA" 8·00 48·00
e. No hyphen 35·00
f. No stop 9·00 55·00
247 **51** $1 black and red/*blue* £200 £750
b. Oval last "O" in "BORNEO" £350
c. Raised stop after "EXHIBITION" £350
d. Small second "A" in "MALAYA" £350
e. No hyphen
f. No stop £375
248 **54** $2 green and red/*orange-buff* 26·00 £120
a. *On pale yellow* (No. 211c) 65·00 £160
b. Oval last "O" in "BORNEO" 48·00 £200
c. Raised stop after "EXHIBITION" 48·00 £200
d. Small second "A" in "MALAYA" 48·00 £200
e. No hyphen £160
f. No stop 55·00 £225
h. "EXH.BITION"
249 **51** $5 green & red/*blue-green* (*olive-back*) £225 £425
b. Oval last "O" in "BORNEO" £325
c. Raised stop after "EXHIBITION" £325
d. Small second "A" in "MALAYA" £325
e. No hyphen £1000
f. No stop £350

(*b*) Wmk Mult Script CA (*Nos. 218/19, 222, 225b, 230 and 239*).

250 **48** 1c. black 3·00 13·00
b. Oval last "O" in "BORNEO" 7·00 21·00
c. Raised stop after "EXHIBITION" 7·00 21·00
d. Small second "A" in "MALAYA" 7·00 21·00
e. No hyphen 35·00
f. No stop 8·50 24·00
h. "EXH.BITION" 35·00
251 **52** 2c. green 2·50 14·00
b. Oval last "O" in "BORNEO" 5·50 23·00
c. Raised stop after "EXHIBITION" 5·50 23·00
d. Small second "A" in "MALAYA" 5·50 23·00
e. No hyphen 28·00
f. No stop 6·50 25·00
h. "EXH.BITION" 28·00
252 **50** 4c. carmine-red 3·50 29·00
b. Oval last "O" in "BORNEO" 8·00 55·00
c. Raised stop after "EXHIBITION" 8·00 55·00
d. Small second "A" in "MALAYA" 8·00 55·00
e. No hyphen 35·00
f. No stop 9·00 60·00
253 **51** 5c. orange (Die II) 2·75 40·00
b. Oval last "O" in "BORNEO" 7·00 70·00
c. Raised stop after "EXHIBITION" 7·00 70·00
d. Small second "A" in "MALAYA" 7·00 70·00
e. No hyphen 35·00
f. No stop 8·50 80·00
g. Third "I" in "EXHIBITION" omitted £1400
254 10c. bright blue 2·25 26·00
b. Oval last "O" in "BORNEO" 6·00 48·00
c. Raised stop after "EXHIBITION" 6·00 48·00
d. Small second "A" in "MALAYA" 6·00 48·00
e. No hyphen 28·00
f. No stop 7·00 55·00
g. Third "I" in "EXHIBITION" omitted £800
255 $1 black and red/*blue* (Die II) 20·00 £130
b. Oval last "O" in "BORNEO" 42·00 £225
c. Raised stop after "EXHIBITION" 42·00 £225
d. Small second "A" in "MALAYA" 42·00 £225
e. No hyphen
f. No stop 48·00 £250
h. "EXH.BITION"
242/55 *Set of* 11 £275 £750

Examples of most values are known with part strikes of a forged Singapore postmark dated "AU 1 1910".

1935 (6 May). *Silver Jubilee. As Nos. 91/4 of Antigua. but ptd by Waterlow & Sons.* P 11 × 12.

256 5c. ultramarine and grey 3·00 30
257 8c. green and indigo 3·00 3·25
258 12c. brown and deep blue 3·00 4·00
j. Damaged turret £300
259 25c. slate and purple 3·25 5·00
256/9 *Set of* 4 11·00 11·50
256s/9s Perf "Specimen" *Set of* 4 £160

For illustration of plate variety see Omnibus section following Zanzibar.

57 58

1936 (1 Jan)–**37**. *Chalk-surfaced paper.* Wmk Mult Script CA. P 14.

260 **57** 1c. black (1.1.37) 1·00 20
261 2c. green (1.2.36) 1·25 70
262 4c. orange (15.6.36) 2·25 70
263 5c. brown (1.8.36) 1·00 30
264 6c. scarlet (1.2.36) 1·25 1·10
265 8c. grey 1·75 70
266 10c. dull purple (1.7.36) 2·00 60
267 12c. bright ultramarine (1.9.36) 2·00 2·50
268 25c. dull purple and scarlet (1.2.36) 1·25 50
269 30c. dull purple and orange 1·25 3·25
270 40c. scarlet and dull purple 1·25 2·50
271 50c. black/*emerald* (1.9.36) 4·50 1·25
272 $1 black and red/*blue* (1.7.36) 19·00 1·75
273 $2 green and scarlet (1.4.36) 42·00 10·00
274 $5 green and red/*emerald* (1.1.37) 95·00 10·00
260/74 *Set of* 15 £160 32·00
260s/74s Perf "Specimen" *Set of* 15 £300

1937 (12 May). *Coronation. As Nos. 95/7 of Antigua, but printed by D. L. R.*

275 4c. orange 30 10
276 8c. grey-black 70 10
277 12c. bright blue 1·50 60
275/7 *Set of* 3 2·25 65
275s/7s Perf "Specimen" *Set of* 3 £100

1937–41. *Chalk-surfaced paper.* Wmk Mult Script CA. P 14 or 15 × 14 (15c.).

(*a*) *Die I* (*printed at two operations*).

278 **58** 1c. black (1.1.38) 6·00 10
279 2c. green (6.12.37) 18·00 20
280 4c. orange (1.1.38) 17·00 20
281 5c. brown (19.11.37) 20·00 30
282 6c. scarlet (10.1.38) 11·00 50
283 8c. grey (26.1.38) 38·00 10
284 10c. dull purple (8.11.37) 8·00 10
285 12c. ultramarine (10.1.38) 8·00 50
286 25c. dull purple and scarlet (11.12.37) 42·00 1·10
287 30c. dull purple and orange (1.12.37) 23·00 2·00
288 40c. scarlet and dull purple (20.12.37) 11·00 2·25
289 50c. black/*emerald* (26.1.38) 11·00 10
290 $1 black and red/*blue* (26.1.38) 15·00 20
291 $2 green and scarlet (26.1.38) 32·00 6·00
292 $5 green and red/*emerald* (26.1.38) 25·00 3·50

(*b*) *Die II* (*printed at one operation*).

293 **58** 2c. green (28.12.38) 50·00 40
294 2c. orange (6.10.41) 2·00 11·00
295 3c. green (*ordinary paper*) (5.9.41) 4·50 4·00
296 4c. orange (29.10.38) 75·00 10
297 5c. brown (18.2.39) 28·00 10
298 15c. ultram (*ordinary paper*) (6.10.41) 6·00 10·00
278/98 *Set of* 18 £275 35·00
278s/92s 294s/5s, 298s Perf "Specimen" *Set of* 18 £400

Die I. Lines of background outside central oval touch the oval and the foliage of the palm tree is usually joined to the oval frame. The downward-pointing palm frond, opposite the King's eye, has two points.

Die II. Lines of background are separated from the oval by a white line and the foliage of the palm trees does not touch the outer frame. The palm frond has only one point.

Nos. 295 and 298 were printed by Harrison and Sons following bomb damage to the De La Rue works on 29 December 1940.

The 6c. grey, 8c. scarlet and $5 purple and orange were only issued with the BMA overprint, but the 8c. without overprint is known although in this state it was never issued (*Price* £14).

STAMP BOOKLETS

1914–19. *Black on blue (No. SB1) or grey (No. SB1b) covers, Stapled.*

SB1 $1 booklet containing twenty-five 4c. dull purple (No. 197) in two blocks of 12 and one single
a. Containing 4c. rose-scarlet (No. 198) (1919)
SB1*b* $1 booklet containing four 1c., sixteen 3c. and twelve 4c. (Nos. 193, 196/7) in blocks of four

1921. *Black on blue cover. Stapled.*

SB2 $1 booklet containing twenty-five 4c. (No. 222) in two blocks of 12 and one single
a. Contents as SB2, but four blocks of 6 and one single

1922. *Black on red cover. Stapled.*

SB3 $1 booklet containing 5c. (No. 225) in block of 8 and 6c. (No. 227) in block of 10 £1400

1925–29. *Black on red cover. Stapled.*

SB4 $1.20 booklet containing thirty 4c. bright violet (No. 223) in blocks of 10 £2500
a. Containing 4c. orange (No. 224) (1929) £2750

1927. *Black on grey (No. SB5), green (No. SB6) or blue (No. SB7) covers. Stapled.*

SB5 $1 booklet containing 4c. and 6c. (Nos. 223, 229) in blocks of 10 £1800
SB6 $1.20 booklet containing twenty 6c. (No. 229) in blocks of 10 £1800
SB7 $1.20 booklet containing 2c., 4c. and 6c. (Nos. 219, 223, 229) in blocks of 10 £2750

1933. *Black on buff cover. Stapled.*

SB8 $1 booklet containing twenty 5c. (No. 226a) in blocks of 10

1936. *Stapled.*

SB9 $1 booklet containing twenty 5c. (No. 263) in blocks of 10
SB10 $1.30 booklet containing 5c. and 8c. (Nos. 263, 265) in blocks of 10

1938. *Black on buff (No. SB11) or black on green (No. SB12) covers. Stapled.*
SB11 $1 booklet containing twenty 5c. (No. 281) in blocks of 10 . . . £1800
SB12 $1.30 booklet containing 5c. and 8c. (Nos. 281, 283) in blocks of 10 and pane of airmail labels . . . £2000

POSTAGE DUE STAMPS

D 1

1924 (1 Jan)–**26**. Wmk Mult Script CA. P 14.

D1 **D 1**	1c. violet	5·00	6·50
D2	2c. black	3·25	1·25
D3	4c. green (5.26)	2·00	4·75
D4	8c. scarlet	4·50	55
D5	10c. orange	6·00	85
D6	12c. bright blue	7·00	65
D1/6 *Set of* 6		25·00	13·00
D1s/6s *Set of* 6		£250	

For later issues of Postage Due stamps, see MALAYAN POSTAL UNION.

The Straits Settlements were occupied by the Japanese in 1942. After the Second World War the stamps of MALAYA (BRITISH MILITARY ADMINISTRATION) were used. In 1946 Singapore became a separate Crown Colony and Labuan was transferred to North Borneo. Separate stamps were issued for Malacca and Penang, which both joined the Malayan Federation on 1 February 1948.

II. FEDERATED MALAY STATES

On 1 July 1896, the States of Negri Sembilan, Pahang, Perak and Selangor were organised on a federal basis to be known as the Federated Malay States. For the time being each State continued with individual issues, but stamps for the use of the Federation replaced these in 1900.

PRICES FOR STAMPS ON COVER	
Nos. 1/13	*from* × 12
No. 14	—
Nos. 15/22	*from* × 10
Nos. 23/5	*from* × 3
No. 26	—
Nos. 27/50	*from* × 6
No. 51	—
Nos. 52/81	*from* × 5
No. 82	—
Nos. D1/6	*from* × 10

PRINTERS. All issues of the Federated Malay States were printed in typography by De La Rue & Co, Ltd, London, *unless otherwise stated.*

FEDERATED MALAY STATES (1) FEDERATED MALAY STATES (2)

1900. *Optd with* T **1** *(cent values) or* **2** *(dollar values).*

(a) Stamps of Negri Sembilan (T 3).

1	1c. dull purple and green	3·00	7·00
2	2c. dull purple and brown	29·00	65·00
3	3c. dull purple and black	2·50	4·00
4	5c. dull purple and olive-yellow	70·00	£170
5	10c. dull purple and orange	7·00	27·00
6	20c. green and olive	85·00	£100
7	25c. green and carmine	£225	£350
8	50c. green and black	90·00	£130
1/8 *Set of* 8		£450	£750
1s/8s Optd "Specimen" *Set of* 8		£180	

(b) Stamps of Perak (T 44 and 45).

9	5c. dull purple and olive-yellow	15·00	55·00
10	10c. dull purple and orange	70·00	65·00
11	$1 green and pale green	£170	£225
	w. Wmk inverted	£800	
12	$2 green and carmine	£140	£225
13	$5 green and ultramarine	£350	£500
14	$25 green and orange	£7500	
	s. Optd "Specimen"	£325	
11s/13s Optd "Specimen" *Set of* 3		£140	

The Negri Sembilan 3c. dull purple and black does not exist without overprint Type **1**.

The stamps of STRAITS SETTLEMENTS were used in Federated Malay States from 16 July 1900 until replaced by the 1900–1 issue.

3

4

1900–01. P 14.

(a) T 3. Wmk Crown CA, sideways (1901).

15	1c. black and green	6·50	6·50
	a. Grey and green	3·25	1·00
	b. Grey-brown and green	9·50	30
16	3c. black and brown	9·00	3·75
	a. Grey and brown	5·50	35
	b. Grey-brown and brown	4·25	20
17	4c. black and carmine	16·00	6·00
	a. Grey and carmine	6·50	3·75
	b. Grey-brown and carmine	22·00	2·25
18	5c. green and carmine/*yellow*	2·25	3·00
19	8c. black and ultramarine	42·00	16·00
	a. Grey and ultramarine	20·00	5·50
	b. Grey-brown and ultramarine	27·00	3·75
20	10c. black and claret	£100	32·00
	a. Grey and claret	75·00	7·50
	b. Black and purple	£130	30·00
	c. Grey and purple	80·00	10·00
	d. Grey-brown and purple	85·00	7·00
21	20c. mauve and black	17·00	10·00
22	50c. black and orange-brown	£150	£130
	a. Grey and orange-brown	£100	50·00
	b. Grey-brown and orange-brown	90·00	42·00
15/22 *Set of* 8		£200	60·00
15s/22s Optd "Specimen" *Set of* 8		£180	

Later printings in 1903–4 show the two upper lines of shading in the background at the corner nearest to the "S" of "STATE" blurred and running into one another, whereas in earlier printings these lines are distinct. Two plates were used for printing the central design of *T* **3**. In Plate 1 the lines of background are regular throughout, but in Plate 2 they are lighter around the head and back of the tiger. The 5c. was the only value with single wmk to be printed from Plate 2. Stamps with multiple wmk were printed for a short time from Plate 1, and show the two blurred lines of background near "S" of "STATE," but the majority of these stamps were printed from Plate 2 and later plates.

(b) T 4. Wmk Crown CC (1900).

23	$1 green and pale green	£110	£120
24	$2 green and carmine	£120	£130
25	$5 green and bright ultramarine	£225	£250
	a. Green and pale ultramarine	£225	£225
26	$25 green and orange	£2000	£1100
	s. Optd "Specimen"	£225	
23s/5s Optd "Specimen" *Set of* 3		£140	

Two dies for 1c. green and 4c. scarlet

Die I. "Head" and duty plates. Thick frame line below "MALAY" and in the 1c. the "c" is thin whilst in the 4c. it is thick.

Die II. Single working plate. Thin frame line below "MALAY" and in the 1c. the "c" is thicker whilst in the 4c. it is thinner.

1904 (Aug)–**22**. *T* **3** *and T* **4** *(dollar values).* Wmk Mult Crown CA (sideways* on *T* **3**). *Ordinary paper (1c. to 50c.) or chalk-surfaced paper ($1 to $25).*

27	1c. grey and green (8.04)	70·00	8·50
	a. Grey-brown and green	35·00	70
28	1c. green (Die I) (8.7.06)	13·00	30
29	1c. green (Die II) (1908)	4·75	20
	a. Yellow-green	18·00	1·75
	aw. Wmk Crown to right of CA	42·00	9·00
	b. Blue-green	23·00	1·75
30	1c. deep brown (21.1.19)	2·25	90
	w. Wmk Crown to right of CA		
31	2c. green (18.2.19)	2·50	30
	w. Wmk Crown to right of CA	42·00	11·00
32	3c. grey and brown (10.04)	60·00	1·00
	a. Grey-brown and brown (12.05)	40·00	1·75
	ab. Chalk-surfaced paper	40·00	2·75
33	3c. brown (11.7.06)	7·50	15
34	3c. carmine (2.2.09)	3·00	10
	aw. Wmk Crown to right of CA	6·50	40
	b. Scarlet (1.17)	15·00	50
	bw. Wmk Crown to right of CA	24·00	4·25
35	3c. grey (29.10.18)	2·00	20
	w. Wmk Crown to right of CA	38·00	11·00
36	4c. grey and scarlet (8.04)	42·00	3·50
	a. Chalk-surfaced paper. *Grey and rose*	17·00	2·00
	b. Grey-brown and scarlet	35·00	3·25
	c. Black and scarlet	22·00	2·50
	d. Black and rose	5·00	80
	dw. Wmk Crown to right of CA	8·00	80
	e. Black and deep rose (aniline) (1909)	50·00	5·00
	f. Jet black and rose (1914)	24·00	2·25
37	4c. scarlet (Die I) (11.2.19)	3·50	4·75
38	4c. scarlet (Die II) (15.4.19)	1·75	15
	aw. Wmk Crown to right of CA	42·00	5·00
	b. Wmk upright (2.22)	—	£375
39	5c. green and carmine/*yellow* (5.06)	8·50	1·75
	aw. Wmk Crown to right of CA	55·00	18·00
	b. Chalk-surfaced paper	26·00	4·50
	c. Deep green and carmine/yellow	10·00	2·25
	d. On orange-buff (1921)	14·00	6·00
	e. On pale yellow (4.22)	10·00	4·50
40	6c. orange (11.2.19)	2·50	3·00
41	8c. grey and ultramarine (2.05)	70·00	19·00
	aw. Wmk Crown to right of CA		
	b. Grey-brown and ultramarine (12.05)	19·00	4·25
	ba. Chalk-surfaced paper	55·00	13·00
	bb. Wmk upright (3.07)	8·00	4·75
42	8c. ultramarine (8.3.10)	13·00	1·00
	aw. Wmk Crown to right of CA	70·00	25·00
	b. Deep blue (1918)	16·00	1·25
43	10c. grey-brown and claret (8.04)	70·00	6·00
	a. Chalk-surfaced paper (1905)	85·00	8·50
	b. Black and claret	24·00	65
	bw. Wmk Crown to right of CA	40·00	1·50
	c. Grey-brown and purple (1905)	70·00	3·25
	d. Black and purple	24·00	2·75
	dy. Wmk Crown to right of CA and reversed	†	£200
	e. Jet-black and bright purple (1914)	80·00	5·00
44	10c. deep blue (3.6.19)	6·50	1·7
	a. Bright blue	6·50	1·0
	ab. Wmk inverted	†	—
	aw. Wmk Crown to right of CA	50·00	20·0
45	20c. mauve and black (3.05)	10·00	1·2
	a. Chalk-surfaced paper	13·00	3·0
	w. Wmk Crown to right of CA	65·00	20·0
46	35c. scarlet/*pale yellow* (25.8.22)	5·50	12·0
47	50c. grey and orange (3.05)	70·00	8·0
	aw. Wmk Crown to right of CA	£160	55·0
	b. Wmk inverted	†	—
	c. Grey-brown and orange-brown (1906)	45·00	8·0
	caw. Wmk Crown to right of CA	†	—
	cb. Chalk-surfaced paper. *Grey-brown and orange-brown*	50·00	7·5
	cc. Grey and orange-brown	60·00	8·0
	cd. Black and orange-brown	85·00	15·0
	ce. Jet-black and orange-brown (1914)	£110	18·0
48	$1 grey-green and green (11.07)	60·00	42·0
	a. Green and pale green	80·00	42·0
	aw. Wmk inverted		
49	$2 green and carmine (4.12.07)	75·00	£11
	a. Printed on the gummed side		
	w. Wmk inverted		
50	$5 green and blue (1.08)	£160	£13
51	$25 green and orange (12.09)	£1100	£70
27/50 *Set of* 22		£475	£27
28s, 30s/1s, 33s/5s, 38s, 40s, 42s, 44s, 46s Optd "Specimen" *Set of* 11		£450	

*The normal sideways watermark shows Crown to left of CA, as seen from the back of the stamp.

Nos. 29/*b*, 30, 31, 33, 34/*b* and 35 were printed from single working plates and all the rest from double plates.

Most examples of No. 47b have fiscal cancellations, but at least one is known postally used.

1922–34. Wmk Mult Script CA (sideways* on *T* **3**). *Ordinary paper (1c. to 10c. (No. 66), 12c., 35c. (No. 72)) or chalk-surfaced paper (others).*

52 **3**	1c. deep brown (1.8.22)	1·50	3·2
	w. Wmk Crown to right of CA	42·00	42·0
53	1c. black (12.6.23)	75	2
54	2c. brown (5.8.25)	6·50	6·0
55	2c. green (15.6.26)	3·00	1
	a. Wmk upright	£200	
56	3c. grey (27.12.22)	1·75	7·5
	w. Wmk Crown to right of CA	50·00	50·0
57	3c. green (22.1.24)	1·25	1·5
58	3c. brown (31.5.27)	2·00	5
	a. Wmk upright	£200	
59	4c. carmine-red (Die II) (27.11.23)	3·50	5
	w. Wmk Crown to right of CA	35·00	16·0
60	4c. orange (9.11.26)	1·50	
	a. No watermark	£300	£2
	b. Wmk upright	£200	
61	5c. mauve/*pale yellow* (17.3.22)	1·00	2
	w. Wmk Crown to right of CA	42·00	32·0
62	5c. brown (1.3.32)	3·50	1
63	6c. orange (2.5.22)	1·00	4
	w. Wmk Crown to right of CA	75·00	
64	6c. scarlet (9.11.26)	1·50	
	a. Wmk upright		
65	10c. bright blue (23.10.23)	1·25	8·0
	w. Wmk Crown to right of CA		
66	10c. black and blue (18.1.24†)	2·00	7
67	10c. purple/*pale yellow* (14.7.31)	3·75	
68	12c. ultramarine (12.9.22)	1·25	
	w. Wmk Crown to right of CA	50·00	28·
	x. Wmk sideways reversed	£150	
69	20c. dull purple & black (*chalk-surfaced paper*) (3.4.23)	4·00	1·0
	a. Ordinary paper (29.12.26)	32·00	2·
	b. Wmk inverted	†	£1
70	25c. purple and bright magenta (3.9.29)	2·75	1·
71	30c. purple and orange-yellow (3.9.29)	3·25	3·
72	35c. scarlet/*pale yellow* (6.11.28)	3·25	22·0
73	35c. scarlet and purple (29.9.31)	13·00	14·0
74	50c. black and orange (24.4.24)	13·00	9·0
	aw. Wmk Crown to right of CA	£110	
	b. Black and orange-brown	28·00	5·0
75	50c. black/*green* (16.6.31)	4·00	2·
76 **4**	$1 pale green and green (2.2.26)	22·00	90·0
	a. Grey-green and emerald (5.10.26)	17·00	45·
77 **3**	$1 black and red/*blue* (10.3.31)	12·00	3·
78 **4**	$2 green and carmine (17.8.26)	19·00	70·
79 **3**	$2 green and red/*yellow* (6.2.34)	38·00	35·
80 **4**	$5 green and blue (24.2.25)	95·00	£1
	w. Wmk inverted	£750	
81 **3**	$5 green and red/*green* (7.34)	£140	£1
82 **4**	$25 green and orange (14.2.28)	£800	£6
	s. Optd "Specimen"	£180	
52/81 *Set of* 30		£350	£5
52s/81s Optd or Perf (No. 62s, 67s, 70s/1s, 73s, 77s, 79s, 81s) "Specimen" *Set of* 30		£1000	

*The normal sideways watermark shows Crown to left of CA, as seen from the back of the stamp.

†No. 66 was released in London by the Crown Agents some months earlier but this is the official date of issue in the States.

Nos. 52, 56 and 59 were printed from single working plates and the rest from double plates

No. 55 exists in coils constructed from normal sheets.

The 5c. mauve on white Script paper is the result of soaking early printings of No. 61 in water.

STAMP BOOKLETS

1909. *Black on pink (Nos. SB1/2) or black on buff (No. SB3) covers. Stapled.*
SB1 25c. booklet containing twenty-four 1c. (No. 29) in blocks of 6 . . . £20
a. Black on green cover (1917)
b. Black on blue cover . . . £20
SB2 73c. booklet containing twenty-four 3c. (No. 34) in blocks of 6 . . . £18
a. Black on red cover (1917)
b. Black on blue cover . . . £18
SB3 97c. booklet containing twenty-four 4c. (No. 36*d*) in blocks of 6 . . . £20

1919. *Black on green (No. SB4) or black on pink (No. SB5) covers. Stapled.*

SB4 49c. booklet containing twenty-four 2c. (No. 31) in blocks of 6 . . . £5000
SB5 97c. booklet containing twenty-four 4c. (No. 37) in blocks of 6 . . . £1800

1922. *Black on buff cover (No. SB7). Stapled.*

SB6 $1.21 booklet containing twenty-four 5c. (No. 61) in blocks of 6 . . . £2500
SB7 $1.45 booklet containing twenty-four 6c. (No. 63) in blocks of 6 . . . £2000

1926. *As Nos. SB4, SB3 and SB7, but sold at face value without premium. Black on green (No. SB8), black on pink (No. SB9) or black on buff (No. SB10) covers. Stapled.*

SB8 48c. booklet containing twenty-four 2c. (No. 55) in blocks of 6
SB9 96c. booklet containing twenty-four 4c. (No. 60) in blocks of 6 . . . £2000
SB10 $1.44 booklet containing twenty-four 6c. (No. 64) in blocks of 6 . . . £2000

1926. *Black on grey cover. Stapled.*

SB11 $1 booklet containing 4c. and 6c. (Nos. 60, 64) each in block of 10 . . . £2000

1927. *Black on bluish green cover. Stapled.*

SB12 $1.50 booklet containing 2c., 3c., 4c. and 6c. (Nos. 55, 58, 60, 64) each in block of 10 . . . £2500

1927–30. *Black on red (No. SB13), black on green (No. SB14) or black on blue (No. SB15) covers. Stapled.*

SB13 $1.20 booklet containing thirty 4c. (No. 60) in blocks of 10 . . . £2250
a. Black on orange cover (1930)
SB14 $1.20 booklet containing twenty 6c. (No. 64) in blocks of 10 (1928) . . . £2750
SB15 $1.20 booklet containing 2c., 4c. and 6c. (Nos. 55, 60, 64) each in block of 10 (1928) . . . £2250
a. Black on white cover (1930)

1934. *Black on buff cover. Stapled.*

SB16 $1 booklet containing twenty 5c. (No. 62) in blocks of 10 . . . £2500

POSTAGE DUE STAMPS

D 1

(Typo Waterlow)

1924 (1 Dec)–**26**. Wmk Mult Script CA (sideways*). P 15 × 14.

D1	D 1	1c. violet	4·75	28·00
		w. Wmk Crown to left of CA (1926)	15·00	22·00
D2		2c. black	1·75	4·25
		w. Wmk Crown to left of CA (1926)	4·00	3·25
D3		4c. green (wmk Crown to left of CA) (27.4.26)	2·25	5·00
D4		8c. red	5·50	28·00
		w. Wmk Crown to left of CA (1926)	15·00	18·00
D5		10c. orange	9·00	17·00
		w. Wmk Crown to left of CA (1926)	20·00	17·00
D6		12c. blue	9·00	26·00
		w. Wmk Crown to left of CA (1926)	15·00	14·00
D1/6 *Set of 6*			29·00	70·00
D1s/6s Optd "Specimen" *Set of 6*			£170	

*The normal sideways watermark shows Crown to right of CA, *as seen from the back of the stamp.*

The issues of the Federated Malay States were replaced by stamps for the individual States from 1935 onwards.

III. MALAYAN POSTAL UNION

The Malayan Postal Union was organised in 1934 and, initially, covered the Straits Settlements and the Federated Malay States. Stamps of the Straits Settlements together with issues for the individual States continued to be used, but Malayan Postal Union postage due stamps were introduced in 1936.

Following the end of the Second World War the use of these postage dues spread throughout Malaya and to Singapore.

PRICES FOR STAMPS ON COVER TO 1945	
Nos. D1/6	*from* × 10
Nos. D7/13	*from* × 4

POSTAGE DUE STAMPS

D 1

(Typo Waterlow until 1961, then D.L.R.)

1936 (June)–**38**. Wmk Mult Script CA. P 15 × 14.

D1	D 1	1c. slate-purple (4.38)	5·50	70
D2		4c. green (9.36)	18·00	1·00
D3		8c. scarlet	9·50	3·50
D4		10c. yellow-orange	14·00	30
D5		12c. pale ultramarine (9.36)	14·00	14·00
D6		50c. black (1.38)	28·00	6·00
D1/6 *Set of 6*			80·00	23·00
D1s/6s Perf "Specimen" *Set of 6*			£200	

For use in Negri Sembilan, Pahang, Perak, Selangor and Straits Settlements including Singapore.

1945–49. *New values and colours.* Wmk Mult Script CA. P 15 × 14.

D 7	D 1	1c. purple	3·25	2·00
D 8		3c. green	6·00	6·00
D 9		5c. scarlet	6·00	4·00
D10		8c. yellow-orange (1949)	16·00	16·00
		s. Perf "Specimen"	75·00	
D11		9c. yellow-orange	50·00	48·00
D12		15c. pale ultramarine	£150	35·00
D13		20c. blue (1948)	8·00	5·00
		s. Perf "Specimen"	75·00	
D7/13 *Set of 7*			£200	£100

1951 (8 Aug)–**63**. Wmk Mult Script CA. P 14.

D14	D 1	1c. violet (21.8.52)	70	1·60
D15		2c. deep slate-blue (16.11.53)	1·25	2·25
		a. Perf 12½ (15.11.60)	60	15·00
		ab. Chalk-surfaced paper (10.7.62)	85	8·00
		ac. Ditto. Imperf horiz (vert pair)	†	£10000
D16		3c. deep green (21.8.52)	24·00	12·00
D17		4c. sepia (16.11.53)	70	7·00
		a. Perf 12½ (15.11.60)	80	17·00
		ab. Chalk-surfaced paper. *Bistre-brown* (10.7.62)	80	14·00
D18		5c. vermilion	48·00	12·00
D19		8c. yellow-orange	2·25	4·50
D20		12c. bright purple (1.2.54)	1·25	6·00
		a. Perf 12½. Chalk-surfaced paper (10.7.62)	2·00	24·00
D21		20c. blue	5·50	6·50
		a. Perf 12½. *Deep blue* (10.12.57)	7·00	26·00
		ab. Chalk-surfaced paper (15.10.63)	3·50	38·00
D14/21 *Set of 8*			70·00	45·00

Nos. D7 to D21ab were for use in the Federation and Singapore.

IV. MALAYA (BRITISH MILITARY ADMINISTRATION)

Following the Japanese surrender on 2 September 1945 British troops landed in Malaya which was placed under a British Military Administration. The Director of Posts was ashore at Singapore on 6 September and had reached Kuala Lumpur by 13 September. Postal services in Singapore and Johore resumed on 17 September and had spread to the remainder of the country by 5 October. No stamps were initially available so all mail up to 1 oz. was carried free until the first overprinted stamps appeared on 19 October.

De La Rue had overprinted available stocks of pre-war Straits Settlements stamps earlier in 1945 and initial supplies of these London overprints were placed on sale from 19 October (Nos. 1, 2a, 4, 6a, 7 and 8a) with the 15c. and 25c. (Nos. 11 and 13a) issued later. A second consignment contained dollar values including the $5 purple and orange. Duplicate plates were subsequently sent to the Government Printing Office at Kuala Lumpur, where the overprinting of surviving local stocks of the 1c., 5c., 10c., 15c. (overprinted in black) and $5 green and red on emerald took place, and to Australia for those shipments which had been diverted there in 1941.

The stamps were used throughout all Malay States and in Singapore. From 1948 this general issue was gradually replaced by individual issues for each state. The last usage was in Kelantan where B M A overprints were not withdrawn until 10 July 1951.

BMA
MALAYA
(1)

1945 (19 Oct)–**48**. *T 58 of Straits Settlements from Die I (double-plate printing) or Die II (single-plate printing) optd with T 1.* Wmk Mult Script CA. *Chalk-surfaced paper.* P 14 or 15 × 14 (No. 11).

1	1c. black (I) (R.)	3·75	50
	a. Ordinary paper	10	30
2	2c. orange (II) (8.7.47)	5·00	60
	a. Ordinary paper (19.10.45)	20	10
	w. Wmk inverted	†	£1400
3	2c. orange (I) (*ordinary paper*) (9.46)	20·00	3·50
4	3c. yellow-green (II) (*ordinary paper*)	30	50
	a. Blue-green (27.1.47)	4·00	3·50
	b. Chalk-surfaced paper. *Blue-grn* (8.7.47)	14·00	1·00
5	5c. brown (II) (24.10.45)	70	1·00
6	6c. grey (II) (22.3.48)	18·00	3·25
	a. Ordinary paper (19.10.45)	30	20
7	8c. scarlet (II) (*ordinary paper*)	30	10
8	10c. purple (I) (12.45)	4·50	80
	a. Ordinary paper (19.10.45)	50	10
	b. Slate-purple (12.45)	4·00	30
	c. Magenta (22.3.48)	6·50	70
9	10c. purple (II) (28.7.48)	19·00	3·00
10	12c. bright ultramarine (I) (11.45)	1·75	6·00
11	15c. brt ultram (II) (*ordinary paper*) (11.45)	2·50	8·50
12	15c. bright ultramarine (II) (R.) (22.3.48)	28·00	1·00
	a. Ordinary paper (12.45)	75	20
	b. Blue (27.11.47)	60·00	85
	ba. Ordinary paper (8.7.47)	£120	14·00
13	25c. dull purple and scarlet (I) (22.3.48)	15·00	2·00
	a. Ordinary paper (12.45)	1·40	30
	ab. Opt double	£4500	
14	50c. black/*emerald* (I) (R.) (12.45)	27·00	2·25
	a. Ordinary paper	75	10
15	$1 black and red (I) (*ordinary paper*) (12.45)	2·00	10
16	$2 green & scar (I) (*ordinary paper*) (12.45)	2·75	75
17	$5 green and red/*emerald* (I) (11.45)	85·00	95·00
18	$5 pur & orge (I) (*ordinary paper*) (12.45)	3·75	3·00
1/18 *Set of 15*		90·00	95·00
1s/11s, 13s/16s, 18s Perf "Specimen" *Set of 14*		£425	

The 8c. grey with "BMA" opt was prepared but not officially issued (*Price £350 unused*).

Nos. 3 and 9 do not exist without the overprint.

Initial printings on ordinary paper were produced by Harrison and Sons in 1941 following bomb damage to the De La Rue works on 29 December 1940.

No. 8 with reddish purple medallion and dull purple frame is from a 1947 printing with the head in fugitive ink which discolours with moisture.

Postal forgeries of the 50c. value exist made by dyeing examples of the 1c. and then altering the face value to 50c.

In 1946 8c. and 15c. stamps in the Crown Colony Victory design were prepared for the Malayan Union, but not issued. Examples of the 8c. carmine from this issue exist from unofficial leakages (*Price £325 unused*).

V. MALAYAN STATES

PRINTERS. All Malayan States stamps were printed in typography by De La Rue and Co, Ltd, London, *unless otherwise stated.*

JOHORE

A British adviser was appointed to Johore in 1914. The state joined the Federation of Malaya on 1 February 1948.

Until 1 January 1899 mail for addresses outside Malaya had the external postage paid by stamps of the STRAITS SETTLEMENTS.

PRICES FOR STAMPS ON COVER TO 1945	
Nos. 1/2	—
Nos. 3/5	*from* × 15
No. 6	*from* × 20
Nos. 7/8	—
Nos. 9/15	*from* × 25
No. 16	—
Nos. 17/20	*from* × 15
Nos. 21/31	*from* × 10
Nos. 32/8	*from* × 15
Nos. 39/53	*from* × 8
Nos. 54/60	*from* × 6
Nos. 61/74	*from* × 8
Nos. 75/7	—
Nos. 78/87	*from* × 8
No. 88	*from* × 10
Nos. 89/102	*from* × 6
Nos. 103/25	*from* × 5
Nos. 126/8	—
Nos. 129/30	*from* × 6
Nos. D1/5	*from* × 5

(1)

1876 (July). *No. 11 of Straits Settlements handstamped with T 1.*

1 2c. brown . . . £11000 £4250

No. 1 is known with the handstamp double.

From September 1878 to August 1884 no overprinted stamps were supplied by Singapore to Johore.

JOHORE (2)

JOHORE (3) ("H" and "E" wide. "J" raised. Opt 16 mm long)
JOHORE (4) ("H" wide, "E" narrow. Opt 16 mm long)
JOHORE (5) ("H" and "E" wide. Opt 16¾ mm long)

JOHORE. (6)
JOHORE (7)
JOHORE (8)

1884 (June)–**86**. *No. 63 of Straits Settlements optd with T 2/8.*

2	2	2c. pale rose	£4750	
3	3	2c. pale rose (8.84)	£1400	£550
		a. Opt double	£3000	£1600
4	4	2c. pale rose (8.84)	£1700	£650
		a. Opt double		
5	5	2c. pale rose (8.84)	£1400	£550
		a. Opt double	—	£1600
6	6	2c. pale rose (3.85)	£170	£180
		a. Opt double	£1000	
7	7	2c. pale rose (1885)	£2500	
8	8	2c. pale rose (4.86)	85·00	£100

Nos. 3 to 7 were from triplet settings, either 3+4+5 or three examples of the same overprint. Nos. 2 and 8 are probably single unit handstamps.

JOHOR (9) (All letters narrow)
JOHOR (10)
JOHOR (11) ("H" wide)

JOHOR (12)
JOHOR (13)
JOHOR. (14)

JOHOR (15)
JOHOR (16)

1884 (Aug)–**91**. *Nos. 63/a of Straits Settlements optd with T 9/16.*

9	9	2c. pale rose	11·00	17·00
		a. Opt double	£750	

10 **10** 2c. pale rose (10.84) 11·00 7·50
a. Thin, narrow "J" (R. 6/6) £150 £110
b. Opt double £750
c. *Bright rose* (1890) 11·00 11·00
ca. Thin, narrow "J" (R. 6/6) £160 £170
cb. Opt double £800
11 **11** 2c. pale rose (2.85) 90·00 90·00
12 **12** 2c. pale rose (1886) 55·00 55·00
a. Opt double £750
13 **13** 2c. pale rose (1886) 40·00 42·00
14 **14** 2c. pale rose (1888) £130 55·00
a. Thin, narrow "J" £650 £350
b. Opt double £700
15 **15** 2c. bright rose (9.90) 14·00 14·00
16 **16** 2c. bright rose (1891) £7500

Settings:

No.	9 –	various triplets with the length of the overprint varying from 12 to 15 mm
No.	10 –	triplet or 60 (6 × 10)
No.	11 –	two types, length 13¾ mm and 14¾ mm, from separate printings, both triplets of 11+9+9
No.	12 –	triplet
No.	13 –	triplet
No.	14 –	30 (3 × 10)
No.	15 –	60 (6 × 10)
No.	16 –	not known. As no used examples are known it is possible that this stamp was not issued.

JOHOR Two CENTS (17)
JOHOR Two CENTS (18)
JOHOR Two CENTS (19)
JOHOR Two CENTS (20)

1891 (May). *No. 68 of Straits Settlements surch as T* **17/20**.
17 **17** 2c.on 24c. green 25·00 38·00
a. "CENST" (R. 5/4) £850 £450
b. Narrow "J" (R. 6/6) £375 £375
w. Wmk inverted £140 £140
18 **18** 2c.on 24c. green £130 £130
a. Narrow "J" (R. 6/6) £375 £375
w. Wmk inverted £375
19 **19** 2c.on 24c. green 40·00 55·00
w. Wmk inverted £200 £200
20 **20** 2c.on 24c. green £120 £120

Nos. 17/20 come from the same setting of 60. Type **17** occurs on horizontal rows 1 to 5, Type **18** on row 6, Type **19** on rows 7, 8 and 9 and Type **20** on row 10.

21 Sultan Aboubakar

3 cents. (22)

KEMAHKOTAAN (23)

1891 (16 Nov)–**94**. No wmk. P 14.
21 **21** 1c. dull purple and mauve (7.94) 50 50
22 2c. dull purple and yellow 50 1·50
23 3c. dull purple and carmine (7.94) 55 50
24 4c. dull purple and black 2·75 16·00
25 5c. dull purple and green 7·00 21·00
26 6c. dull purple and blue 8·00 21·00
27 $1 green and carmine 75·00 £160
21/7 *Set of* 7 85·00 £200

1894 (Mar). *Surch with T* **22**.
28 **21** 3c.on 4c. dull purple and black 2·50 50
a. No stop (R. 5/11) 80·00 65·00
29 3c.on 5c. dull purple and green 1·75 3·25
a. No stop (R. 5/11) £100 £130
b. "3 cents." spaced 3½ mm from bar £130 90·00
30 3c.on 6c. dull purple and blue 3·00 3·75
a. No stop (R. 5/11) £150 £170
31 3c.on $1 green and carmine 10·00 65·00
a. No stop (R. 5/11) £375 £650
28/31 *Set of* 4 16·00 65·00

No. 29b shows the surcharge spaced 3½ mm from the bar instead of the normal 7½ mm. It appears to come from a separate setting as a cancelled-to-order block of eight is known.

1896 (Mar). *Coronation of Sultan Ibrahim. Optd with T* **23**.
32 **21** 1c. dull purple and mauve 50 85
a. "KETAHKOTAAN" 3·75 5·00
33 2c. dull purple and yellow 50 1·00
a. "KETAHKOTAAN" 3·75 7·00
34 3c. dull purple and carmine 55 1·00
a. "KETAHKOTAAN" 8·50 10·00
35 4c. dull purple and black 80 2·25
a. "KETAHKOTAAN" 2·75 9·00
36 5c. dull purple and green 5·50 7·50
a. "KETAHKOTAAN" 3·50 7·50
37 6c. dull purple and blue 3·50 6·50
a. "KETAHKOTAAN" 6·00 8·50
38 $1 green and carmine 50·00 £110
a. "KETAHKOTAAN" 38·00 £160
32/8 *Set of* 7 55·00 £120
32a/8a *Set of* 7 60·00 £190

Stamps overprinted "KETAHKOTAAN" (= We mourn) come from the first overprinting. The overprint was subsequently changed to the intended "KEMAHKOTAAN" (= Coronation), but both were issued together some months after the Coronation of Sultan Ibrahim had taken place.

24 Sultan Ibrahim

25 Sultan Ibrahim

26

27

1896 (26 Aug)–**99**. W **27**. P 14.
39 **24** 1c. green 80 70
40 2c. green and blue 50 30
41 3c. green and purple 4·00 2·00
a. *Green and dull claret* 4·00 2·50
42 4c. green and carmine 1·00 1·00
43 4c. yellow and red (1899) 1·50 80
44 5c. green and brown 2·00 2·00
45 6c. green and yellow 2·00 3·00
46 **25** 10c. green and black (1898) 7·00 45·00
47 25c. green and mauve (1898) 9·00 40·00
48 50c. green and carmine (1898) 16·00 42·00
49 **24** $1 dull purple and green (1898) 32·00 75·00
50 **26** $2 dull purple and carmine (1898) 35·00 80·00
51 $3 dull purple and blue (1898) 35·00 £110
52 $4 dull purple and brown (1898) 35·00 85·00
53 $5 dull purple and yellow (1898) 75·00 £130
39/53 *Set of* 15 £225 £550

Nos. 42 and 43 were reissued in 1918 to meet a shortage of 4c. stamps.

3 cents. (28)

10 cents. (29)

1903 (Apr). *Surch with T* **28** *or* **29**.
54 **24** 3c.on 4c. yellow and red 60 1·10
a. Original value uncancelled 3·75 18·00
55 10c.on 4c. green and carmine 2·50 9·00
a. Tall "1" in "10" (R. 9/12) 75·00 £130
b. Original value uncancelled 20·00 65·00
ba. As b, with tall "1" in "10" (R. 9/12) £900 £1200

The bars on these stamps were ruled by hand with pen and ink.

50 Cents. (30)

One Dollar (31)

1903 (Oct). *Surch with T* **30** *or* **31**.
56 **26** 50c.on $3 dull purple and blue 30·00 80·00
57 $1on $2 dull purple and carmine 60·00 £110
a. "e" of "One" inverted (R. 7/9) £1500

10 CENTS. (32)

1904. *Surch as T* **32**.
58 **24** 10c.on 4c. yellow and red (Apr) 20·00 40·00
a. Surcharge double £6500
59 10c.on 4c. green and carmine (Aug) 9·50 45·00
60 **26** 50c.on $5 dull purple and yellow (May) 65·00 £150
58/60 *Set of* 3 85·00 £200

33

34

35 Sultan Sir Ibrahim

1904 (Sept)–**10**. W **27**. *Ordinary paper*. P 14.
61 **33** 1c. dull purple and green 2·00 40
a. Chalk-surfaced paper (10.09) 6·00 7·00
62 2c. dull purple and orange 3·00 3·75
a. Chalk-surfaced paper (10.10) 7·00 11·00
63 3c. dull purple and olive-black 4·75 60
a. Chalk-surfaced paper — £100
64 4c. dull purple and carmine 8·00 3·00
65 5c. dull purple and sage-green 2·50 3·00
66 **35** 8c. dull purple and blue 4·25 10·00
67 **34** 10c. dull purple and black 50·00 11·00
a. Chalk-surfaced paper (1910) 80·00 80·00
68 25c. dull purple and green 8·50 40·00
69 50c. dull purple and red 45·00 17·00
70 **33** $1 green and mauve 13·00 55·00
71 **35** $2 green and carmine 22·00 50·00
72 $3 green and blue 26·00 75·00
73 $4 green and brown 26·00 £10(
74 $5 green and orange 42·00 85·0(
75 **34** $10 green and black 65·00 £16(
76 $50 green and ultramarine £200 £30(
77 $100 green and scarlet £375 £55(
61/75 *Set of* 15 £300 £55(

1910–19. Wmk Mult Rosettes (vertical). *Chalk-surfaced paper*. P 14.
78 **33** 1c. dull purple and green (1912) 1·25 1[illegible]
79 2c. dull purple and orange (1912) 6·00 7[illegible]
80 3c. dull purple and olive-black (1912) 10·00 6[illegible]
a. Wmk horizontal (1910) 10·00 19·0[illegible]
81 4c. dull purple and carmine (1912) 9·00 1·0[illegible]
a. Wmk horizontal (1910) 20·00 48·0[illegible]
82 5c. dull purple and sage-green (1912) 5·00 2·0[illegible]
83 **35** 8c. dull purple and blue (1912) 4·00 6·5[illegible]
84 **34** 10c. dull purple and black (1912) 50·00 3·0[illegible]
a. Wmk horizontal (1911) 25·00 70·0[illegible]
85 25c. dull purple and green (1912) 12·00 35·0[illegible]
86 50c. dull purple and red (1919) 55·00 £12[illegible]
87 **33** $1 green and mauve (1918) 80·00 £11[illegible]
78/87 *Set of* 10 £190 £25[illegible]

3 CENTS. (36)

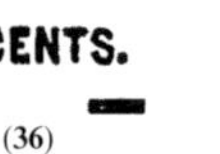

37 Sultan Sir Ibrahim and Sultana

1912 (Mar). *No. 66 surch with T* **36**.
88 3c.on 8c. dull purple and blue 3·25 7·5[illegible]
a. "T" of "CENTS" omitted £1200
b. Bars double

No. 88b shows the bars printed twice with the upper pair partl[illegible] erased.

1918–20. Wmk Mult Crown CA. *Chalk-surfaced paper*. P 14.
89 **33** 2c. dull purple and green (1919) 50 1·[illegible]
w. Wmk inverted † £2[illegible]
90 2c. purple and orange (1919) 1·00 3·[illegible]
91 4c. dull purple and red 1·75 [illegible]
92 5c. dull purple and sage-green (1920) 2·00 6·[illegible]
w. Wmk inverted £150
93 **34** 10c. dull purple and blue 2·00 1·[illegible]
94 21c. dull purple and orange (1919) 2·25 2·[illegible]
95 25c. dull purple and green (1920) 8·00 22·[illegible]
96 50c. dull purple and red (1920) 24·00 45·[illegible]
97 **33** $1 green and mauve 14·00 65·[illegible]
98 **35** $2 green and carmine 23·00 50·[illegible]
99 $3 green and blue 50·00 £1[illegible]
100 $4 green and brown 50·00 £1[illegible]
101 $5 green and orange 90·00 £1[illegible]
102 **34** $10 green and black £200 £3[illegible]
89/102 *Set of* 14 £425 £8[illegible]
89s/102s Optd "Specimen" *Set of* 14 £475

1922–40. Wmk Mult Script CA. *Chalk-surfaced paper*. P 14.
103 **33** 1c. dull purple and black 30
104 2c. purple and sepia (1924) 1·25 4·[illegible]
105 2c. green (1928) 50
106 3c. green (1925) 2·00 4·[illegible]
107 3c. purple and sepia (1928) 1·40 1·[illegible]
108 4c. purple and carmine (1924) 2·50
109 5c. dull purple and sage-green 50
w. Wmk inverted
110 6c. dull purple and claret 50
111 **34** 10c. dull purple and blue 16·00 32·[illegible]
w. Wmk inverted † £2[illegible]
112 10c. dull purple and yellow 50
113 **33** 12c. dull purple and blue 1·00 1·[illegible]
114 12c. ultramarine (1940) 42·00 4·[illegible]
115 **34** 21c. dull purple and orange (1928) 2·00 3·[illegible]
116 25c. dull purple and myrtle 3·75 1·[illegible]
117 **35** 30c. dull purple and orange (1936) 8·00 7·[illegible]
118 40c. dull purple and brown (1936) 8·00 7·[illegible]
119 **34** 50c. dull purple and red 3·75 1[illegible]
120 **33** $1 green and mauve 3·75 1·[illegible]
121 **35** $2 green and carmine (1923) 7·50 4·[illegible]
122 $3 green and blue (1925) 55·00 80·[illegible]
123 $4 green and brown (1926) 85·00 £1[illegible]
w. Wmk inverted
124 $5 green and orange 55·00 50·[illegible]
125 **34** $10 green and black (1924) £190 £3[illegible]
126 $50 green and ultramarine £650
s. Optd "Specimen" £170
127 $100 green and scarlet £1500
s. Optd "Specimen" £275
128 **35** $500 blue and red (1926) £17000
s. Optd "Specimen" £750
103/25 *Set of* 23 £450 £6[illegible]
103s/25s Optd or Perf (12c. ultram, 30c., 40c.) "Specimen" *Set of* 23 £650

It is believed that printings of various values were made in 19[illegible] by Williams, Lea & Co. Ltd. following bomb damage to the De Rue works on 29 December 1940. Of the ten values involv[illegible] examples of the 10c. and $2 have been reported used in Joh[illegible] during 1942.

(Recess Waterlow)

1935 (15 May). *50th Anniv of Treaty Relations with Great Brit[illegible]* Wmk Mult Script CA (sideways). P 12½.
129 **37** 8c. bright violet and slate 3·50 1[illegible]
s. Perf "Specimen" 50·00

38 Sultan Sir Ibrahim

39 Sultan Sir Ibrahim

(Recess D.L.R.)

940 (Feb). Wmk Mult Script CA. P 13½.
30 **38** 8c. black and pale blue . . . . 17·00 1·00
s. Perf "Specimen" . . . . 50·00

948 (1 Dec). *Royal Silver Wedding. As Nos. 112/13 of Antigua.*
31 10c. violet 20 75
32 $5 green . . . . 25·00 38·00

949 (2 May)–**55**. Wmk Mult Script CA. *Chalk-surfaced paper.* P 17½ × 18.
33 **39** 1c. black 50 10
34 2c. orange 20 20
a. Orange-yellow (22.1.52) . . . . 1·00 1·25
35 3c. green . . . . 50 1·00
a. Yellow-green (22.1.52) . . . . . 14·00 3·00
36 4c. brown 60 10
36*a* 5c. bright purple (1.9.52) 30 30
37 6c. grey 60 20
a. Pale grey (22.1.52) 60 50
ac. Error. St. Edward's Crown W 9*b* £1400 £1200
38 8c. scarlet . . . . 3·25 1·25
38*a* 8c. green (1.9.52) . . . . 4·00 2·25
39 10c. magenta 70 10
aa. Imperf (pair) £1900
39*a* 12c. scarlet (1.9.52) . . . . 4·00 4·50
40 15c. ultramarine . . . . 2·75 10
41 20c. black and green . . . . 50 1·00
41*a* 20c. bright blue (1.9.52) . . . . . . 1·00 10
42 25c. purple and orange . . . . . . 1·75 10
42*a* 30c. scarlet and purple (4.9.55) . . . 1·75 2·75
42*b* 35c. scarlet and purple (1.9.52) . . . 4·50 1·25
43 40c. red and purple . . . . 4·25 9·50
44 50c. black and blue . . . . 2·50 10
45 $1 blue and purple . . . . 5·00 2·00
46 $2 green and scarlet . . . . 14·00 5·00
47 $5 green and brown . . . . 40·00 11·00
33/47 *Set of* 21 . . . . 85·00 38·00

949 (10 Oct). *75th Anniv of U.P.U. As Nos. 114/17 of Antigua.*
48 10c. purple 30 40
49 15c. deep blue . . . . 1·75 1·00
50 25c. orange . . . . 65 3·00
51 50c. blue-black . . . . 1·25 3·50
48/51 *Set of* 4 . . . . 3·50 7·00

STAMP BOOKLETS

28. *Black on white card. Interleaved with tissue. Stapled.*
31 $2 booklet containing ten 1c. and 2c. (Nos. 103, 105), twenty 4c. (No. 108), each in blocks of 10and eighteen 5c. (No. 109) in blocks of 6 . . . .

29. *Black on pink cover. Stapled.*
32 $1 booklet containing 2c., 3c. and 5c. (Nos. 105, 107, 109) in blocks of 10 . . . .

30. *Black on buff cover. Stapled.*
33 $1 booklet containing ten 1c. and 5c. (Nos. 103, 109) and twenty 2c. (Nos. 105) in blocks of 10 . . . .

POSTAGE DUE STAMPS

D 1

(Typo Waterlow)

38 (1 Jan). Wmk Mult Script CA. P 12½.
D1 1c. carmine . . . . 14·00 40·00
4c. green . . . . 40·00 40·00
8c. orange . . . . 48·00 £140
10c. brown . . . . 48·00 48·00
12c. purple . . . . 55·00 £130
/5 *Set of* 5 . . . . £180 £350
s/5s Perf "Specimen" *Set of* 5 . . . . . . £140

KEDAH

Suzerainty over Kedah was transferred by Thailand to Great tain on 15 July 1909. A Treaty of Friendship between Great tain and Kedah was signed on 1 November 1923.

The state joined the Federation of Malaya on 1 Febuary 1948.

For stamps of THAILAND used in Kedah between 1887 and 1909 see SIAMESE POSTS IN NORTHERN MALAYA section.

Issues of the FEDERATED MALAY STATES were used in Kedah from 16 July 1909 until 15 June 1912.

PRICES FOR STAMPS ON COVER TO 1945	
Nos. 1/14	*from* × 15
Nos. 15/23	*from* × 10
Nos. 24/40	*from* × 8
Nos. 41/8	*from* × 12
Nos. 49/51	—
Nos. 52/9	*from* × 4
Nos. 60/8	*from* × 3
Nos. 68*a*/9	*from* × 4

1 Sheaf of Rice

2 Malay ploughing

3 Council Chamber, Alor Star

(Recess D.L.R.)

1912 (16 June). Wmk Mult Crown CA (sideways* on 10c. to $5). P 14.
1 **1** 1c. black and green 60 25
2 3c. black and red . . . . 4·50 30
3 4c. rose and grey . . . . 10·00 25
4 5c. green and chestnut . . . . . . 2·25 3·00
5 8c. black and ultramarine . . . . . 3·75 3·50
6 **2** 10c. blue and sepia . . . . 2·25 90
w. Wmk Crown to left of CA . . . . . † —
y. Wmk Crown to left of CA and reversed . . . . † £200
7 20c. black and green . . . . 4·75 4·00
x. Wmk reversed £150
8 30c. black and rose . . . . 3·00 11·00
9 40c. black and purple . . . . 3·50 14·00
10 50c. brown and blue . . . . 9·00 13·00
11 **3** $1 black and red/*yellow* . . . . . . 16·00 22·00
w. Wmk Crown to left of CA . . . . 42·00
x. Wmk reversed £225
y. Wmk Crown to left of CA and reversed . . . .
12 $2 green and brown . . . . 22·00 85·00
13 $3 black and blue/*blue* . . . . 75·00 £170
a. "A" of "CA" missing from wmk . . £1400
14 $5 black and red . . . . 75·00 £160
1/14 *Set of* 14 . . . . £200 £450
1s/14s Optd "Specimen" *Set of* 14 . . . . . . £300

*The normal sideways watermark shows the Crown to right of CA, *as seen from the back of the stamp.*

Due to an increase in postal rates 1c. and 4c. stamps of STRAITS SETTLEMENTS were used in Kedah for some months from March 1919.

Short sheaf (R. 10/1)

(i)

(ii)

DOUBLE AND SINGLE PLATES. (i) Printed from separate plates for frame and centre, with dotted shading extending close to the central sheaf. Soft impression of centre with little clear detail.

(ii) Printed from single plate, with white space around sheaf. Centre more deeply etched with sharp image.

1919 (June)–**21**. *New colours and values.* Wmk Mult Crown CA (sideways* on 21c., 25c.). P 14.
15 **1** 1c. brown (i) (18.8.19) 55 50
w. Wmk inverted . . . . 90·00
y. Wmk inverted and reversed . . . . † £200
18 2c. green (ii) 50 30
19 3c. deep purple (i) (1920) . . . . . . 65 1·00
x. Wmk reversed . . . .
y. Wmk inverted and reversed . . . . 80·00 £100
20 4c. rose (i) . . . . 3·75 20
21 4c. red (ii) (18.8.19) . . . . 3·25 75
a. Short sheaf . . . . £100 50·00
w. Wmk inverted . . . .
22 **2** 21c. mauve and purple (18.8.19) . . . . 5·50 55·00
a. "A" of "CA" missing from wmk . . — £500
w. Wmk Crown to left of CA £120 £150
x. Wmk reversed . . . .
y. Wmk Crown to left of CA and reversed £200
23 25c. blue and purple (1921) . . . . . . 1·75 24·00
a. "A" of "CA" missing from wmk . . £450
15/23 *Set of* 6 . . . . 10·50 70·00
15s/23s Optd "Specimen" *Set of* 6 . . . . . . £150

*The normal sideways watermark shows Crown to right of CA, *as seen from the back of the stamp.*

ONE
DOLLAR
(4)

MALAYA-
BORNEO
EXHIBITION.
(5)

(Surch by Ribeiro & Co, Penang)

1919 (Mar). *Surch as T* **4**.
24 **3** 50c.on $2 green and brown . . . . . . 70·00 75·00
a. "C" of "CENTS" inserted by handstamp (R. 6/4) £1200 £1300
25 $1on $3 black and blue/*blue* . . . . . 20·00 90·00

Nos. 24/5 were surcharged from settings of 30 (5 × 6).

Two types of centre plate for Type **2** wmkd Mult Script CA:

Type I (Plate 1) (produced by electrotyping)

Type II (Plate 2) (produced by transfer die)

A new common centre plate, 2, was prepared from the original die in 1926. Stamps from Plate 2, produced using a transfer die, show considerably more detail of the ground and have the oxen, ploughman's hat and his clothing much more deeply cut as illustrated in Type II above.

1921–32. Wmk Mult Script CA (sideways* on 10c. to $5). P 14.
26 **1** 1c. brown 70 20
w. Wmk inverted . . . . † £200
y. Wmk inverted and reversed . . . . † £200
27 2c. dull green (ii) (Type I) . . . . . . 1·50 20
28 3c. deep purple (ii) 80 70
w. Wmk inverted £250
29 4c. deep carmine (ii) . . . . 5·00 20
a. Short sheaf . . . . £150 30·00
30 **2** 10c. blue and sepia (I) . . . . 2·75 75
ay. Wmk Crown to left of CA and reversed . . . . 80·00
b. Type II (wmk Crown to left of CA) (1927) . . . . 42·00 3·25
by. Wmk Crown to right of CA and reversed £325 £200
31 20c. black and yellow-green (I) . . . . 4·00 2·00
32 21c. mauve and purple (I) . . . . . . 2·00 13·00
33 25c. blue and purple (I) . . . . 2·25 8·50
a. Type II (wmk Crown to left of CA) (1932) . . . . 70·00 4·00
34 30c. black and rose (I) (1922) . . . . . 3·00 10·00
a. Type II (wmk Crown to left of CA) (1927) . . . . 40·00 3·00
35 40c. black and purple (I) . . . . . . 4·25 48·00
aw. Wmk Crown to left of CA (1924) . . . . 32·00 45·00
b. Type II (wmk Crown to left of CA) (1932) . . . . 75·00 23·00
36 50c. brown and grey-blue (I) . . . . . . 2·50 14·00
aw. Wmk Crown to left of CA (1924) . . . . 28·00 17·00
b. Type II (wmk Crown to left of CA) (1932) . . . . 80·00 7·00
37 **3** $1 black and red/*yellow* (1924) . . . . 60·00 65·00
w. Wmk Crown to left of CA . . . . 6·50 9·00
38 $2 myrtle and brown . . . . 13·00 95·00
w. Wmk Crown to left of CA (1924) . . . . 29·00 85·00
39 $3 black and blue/*blue* . . . . 65·00 95·00
w. Wmk Crown to left of CA (1924) . . . . 85·00 80·00
40 $5 black and deep carmine . . . . . . 75·00 £150
w. Wmk Crown to left of CA (1926) . . . . 90·00 £150
26/40 *Set of* 15 . . . . £170 £350
26s/40s Optd "Specimen" *Set of* 15 . . . . . £300

*The normal sideways watermark shows Crown to right of CA, *as seen from the back of the stamp.*

Nos. 26/40 were produced by De La Rue using the "wet" method of recess-printing during which the stamps contracted when they were dried before gumming. From 1933 the firm adopted the "dry" method, using pre-gummed paper, with the result that stamps were up to 0.5 mm larger in size. Of the low values as Type **1** in this series only the 2c. was still current when the "dry" method was introduced.

Stamps as Type **1** can be found perforated either comb or line. The 1c. and 4c. come comb only, the 3c. line only and the 2c. either way.

Examples of Nos. 37/40 are known with part strikes of a forged Sungei Patang postmark dated "14 JY 1920".

For the 2c. Type II see No. 69.

OVERPRINT SETTINGS FOR NOS. 41/51. The low values in Type **1** were overprinted using Setting II as detailed under Straits Settlements. The three listed constant varieties from the original typeset block of 12 occur in the same positions for these Kedah stamps as does the No Stop variety from R. 1/5 of the left pane.

For the higher values in Type **2**, which were in sheets of 60 (5 × 12), a further setting was prepared using the first four vertical rows of the typeset block with each horizontal row completed by a single random impression of the overprint. This means that, in addition to their positions in the truncated typeset block, the Oval last "O" additionally occurs on R. 11/5 and the Raised stop on R. 5/5 of the sheet. In this setting, as for the low values, "BORNEO" was 14 mm long.

Further supplies were subsequently required of the 21, 25 and 50c. values and these were produced using a completely different setting of 20 (5 × 4), applied three times to each sheet, on which "BORNEO" was 15–15½ mm long.

1922 (Apr). *Malaya-Borneo Exhibition, Singapore. Optd as T* **5** *at Singapore.*

I. "BORNEO" *14 mm long.*

(a) Wmk Mult Crown CA *(Nos. 10, 18 and 22/3).*

41 **1** 2c. green (ii) . . . 3·50 24·00
b. Oval last "O" in "BORNEO" . . . 8·00 42·00
c. Raised stop after "EXHIBITION" . . . 8·00 42·00
d. Small second "A" in "MALAYA" . . . 8·00 42·00
f. No stop . . . 35·00
42 **2** 21c. mauve and purple . . . 27·00 80·00
b. Oval last "O" in "BORNEO" . . . 50·00 £130
c. Raised stop after "EXHIBITION" . . . 50·00 £130
43 25c. blue and purple . . . 27·00 80·00
a. Opt inverted . . . £1100
b. Oval last "O" in "BORNEO" . . . 50·00 £130
c. Raised stop after "EXHIBITION" . . . 50·00 £130
44 50c. brown and blue . . . 27·00 95·00
b. Oval last "O" in "BORNEO" . . . 50·00 £150
c. Raised stop after "EXHIBITION" . . . 50·00 £150

(b) Wmk Mult Script CA (Nos. 26 and 28/30).

45 **1** 1c. brown (ii) . . . 3·00 16·00
b. Oval last "O" in "BORNEO" . . . 6·50 28·00
c. Raised stop after "EXHIBITION" . . . 6·50 28·00
d. Small second "A" in "MALAYA" . . . 6·50 28·00
f. No stop . . . 29·00
46 3c. deep purple (ii) . . . 3·00 42·00
b. Oval last "O" in "BORNEO" . . . 7·00 65·00
c. Raised stop after "EXHIBITION" . . . 7·00 65·00
d. Small second "A" in "MALAYA" . . . 7·00 65·00
f. No stop . . . 32·00
47 4c. deep carmine (ii) . . . 3·00 25·00
a. Short sheaf . . . £110
b. Oval last "O" in "BORNEO" . . . 7·00 45·00
c. Raised stop after "EXHIBITION" . . . 7·00 45·00
d. Small second "A" in "MALAYA" . . . 7·00 45·00
f. No stop . . . 32·00
48 **2** 10c. blue and sepia (I) . . . 4·50 45·00
b. Oval last "O" in "BORNEO" . . . 9·50 70·00
c. Raised stop after "EXHIBITION" . . . 9·50 70·00
41/8 *Set of* 8 . . . 80·00 £350

II. "BORNEO" *15–15½ mm long.* Wmk Mult Crown CA *(Nos. 10 and 22/3).*

49 **2** 21c. mauve and purple . . . 23·00 £100
50 25c. blue and purple . . . 23·00 £120
51 50c. brown and blue . . . 50·00 £170
49/51 *Set of* 3 . . . 85·00 £350

Examples of all values are known with part strikes of the forged postmark mentioned after Nos. 26/40.

1922–40. *New colours, etc.* Wmk Mult Script CA (sideways* on 12, 35c.). P 14.

52 **1** 1c. black (ii) (Type I) . . . 1·00 10
53 3c. green (ii) (1924) . . . 2·25 90
54 4c. violet (ii) (1926) . . . 1·00 10
a. Short sheaf . . . 50·00 10·00
55 5c. yellow (ii) . . . 1·50 10
w. Wmk inverted . . . 85·00 £100
x. Wmk reversed . . . † £170
y. Wmk inverted and reversed . . . † £170
56 6c. carmine (ii) (1926) . . . 1·75 65
a. Carmine-red (1940) . . . 12·00 48·00
57 8c. grey-black (ii) (10.36) . . . 12·00 10
58 **2** 12c. black and indigo (II) (1926) . . . 4·00 4·00
59 35c. purple (II) (1926) . . . 8·00 28·00
52/9 *Set of* 8 . . . 28·00 30·00
52s/9s Optd or Perf (8c.) "Specimen" *Set of* 8 . . . £300

*The normal sideways watermark shows Crown to left of CA, *as seen from the back of the stamp.*

With the exception of the 6c. and 8c. the printing plates for the Type **1** values listed above were, as for the previous issue, produced by electrotyping with the face values added to the plates by pantograph. The plates for the 6c. and 8c. values were constructed by the more modern method of using a transfer die to enter each impression.

Printings after November 1933 were normally produced by the "dry" method as described beneath Nos. 26/40. There were late "wet" printings of the 1c. (No. 68*a*) and 2c. (No. 27) in August 1938. The 3c. only exists from a "wet" printing, the 6c. (No. 56*a*) and 8c. from dry printings and the remainder from either method.

Stamps as Type **1** can be found perforated either comb or line. The 3c. and 6c. (No. 56) come comb only, the 6c. (No. 56*a*) and 8c. line only and the 1, 4 and 5c. either way.

For the 1c. Type II see No. 68*a*.

6 Sultan Abdul Hamid Halimshah

(Recess Waterlow)

1937 (30 June). Wmk Mult Script CA. P 12½.

60 **6** 10c. ultramarine and sepia . . . 4·25 1·25
61 12c. black and violet . . . 38·00 9·00
a. "A" of "CA" missing from wmk
62 25c. ultramarine and purple . . . 7·50 4·50
63 30c. green and scarlet . . . 8·00 10·00
64 40c. black and purple . . . 4·00 16·00
65 50c. brown and blue . . . 6·50 4·50
66 $1 black and green . . . 4·00 10·00
67 $2 green and brown . . . £120 75·00
68 $5 black and scarlet . . . 32·00 £160
60/8 *Set of* 9 . . . £200 £250
60s/8s Perf "Specimen" *Set of* 9 . . . £250

I

II

I

II

1938 (May)–**40**. *As Nos. 52 and 27, but face values redrawn as Types II.*

68*a* **1** 1c. black . . . £100 3·00
69 2c. bright green (1940) . . . £200 6·50

1c. Type II. Figures "1" have square-cut corners instead of rounded, and larger top serif. Larger "C". Line perf. Produced from a new electrotyped Plate 2 with different engraved face values. Printings exist from either the "wet" or "dry" methods.

2c. Type II. Figures "2" have circular instead of oval drops and the letters "c" are thin and tall instead of thick and rounded. Produced from a new plate, made from a transfer die, and printed by the "dry" method.

1948 (1 Dec). *Royal Silver Wedding. As Nos. 112/13 of Antigua.*

70 10c. violet . . . 20 30
71 $5 carmine . . . 27·00 32·00

1949 (10 Oct). *75th Anniv of U.P.U. As Nos. 114/17 of Antigua.*

72 10c. purple . . . 25 75
73 15c. deep blue . . . 1·75 1·50
74 25c. orange . . . 65 1·50
75 50c. blue-black . . . 1·00 2·75
72/5 *Set of* 4 . . . 3·25 6·00

7 Sheaf of Rice

8 Sultan Badlishah

1950 (1 June)–**55**. Wmk Mult Script CA. *Chalk-surfaced paper.* P 17½ × 18.

76 **7** 1c. black . . . 50 30
77 2c. orange . . . 50 15
78 3c. green . . . 2·00 1·00
79 4c. brown . . . 75 10
79*a* 5c. bright purple (1.9.52) . . . 1·75 2·25
ab. Bright mauve (24.9.53) . . . 1·75 1·00
80 6c. grey . . . 70 15
81 8c. scarlet . . . 1·75 2·50
81*a* 8c. green (1.9.52) . . . 1·00 1·75
ab. Deep green (24.9.53) . . . 12·00 11·00
82 10c. magenta . . . 70 10
82*a* 12c. scarlet (1.9.52) . . . 1·00 2·50
83 15c. ultramarine . . . 1·25 35
84 20c. black and green . . . 1·25 2·50
84*a* 20c. bright blue (1.9.52) . . . 1·00 10
85 **8** 25c. purple and orange . . . 1·50 30
85*a* 30c. scarlet and purple (4.9.55) . . . 2·50 1·25
85*b* 35c. scarlet and purple (1.9.52) . . . 1·00 1·50
86 40c. red and purple . . . 2·75 6·00
87 50c. black and blue . . . 2·25 35
88 $1 blue and purple . . . 3·00 4·25
89 $2 green and scarlet . . . 20·00 23·00
90 $5 green and brown . . . 42·00 42·00
76/90 *Set of* 21 . . . 75·00 80·00

KELANTAN

Suzerainty over Kelantan was transferred by Thailand to Great Britain on 15 July 1909. A British adviser was appointed in 1923.

The state joined the Federation of Malaya on 1 February 1948.

For stamps of THAILAND used in Kelantan between 1895 and 1909 see SIAMESE POSTS IN NORTHERN MALAYA section.

From 1909 until the introduction of Kelantan stamps in 1911 the issues of the FEDERATED MALAY STATES to $2 were in use.

PRICES FOR STAMPS ON COVER TO 1945

Nos.	1/11	*from* × 30
No.	12	—
Nos.	14/23	*from* × 30
Nos.	30/8	*from* × 15
Nos.	39/*a*	*from* × 10
Nos.	40/8	*from* × 30
Nos.	49/52	*from* × 20
No.	53	*from* × 3
No.	54	—

1

MALAYA
BORNEO
EXHIBITION
(2)

1911 (Jan)–**15**. Wmk Mult Crown CA. *Ordinary paper* (1c. to 10c or *chalk-surfaced paper* (30c. to $25). P 14.

1 **1** 1c. yellow-green . . . 6·00 9
a. Blue-green . . . 4·75 3
2 3c. red . . . 4·25 1
3 4c. black and red . . . 1·50 1
4 5c. green and red/*yellow* . . . 10·00 8
w. Wmk inverted . . . † £40
5 8c. ultramarine . . . 5·50 1·
6 10c. black and mauve . . . 30·00 7
7 30c. dull purple and red . . . 11·00 2·
a. Purple and carmine . . . 27·00 14·
8 50c. black and orange . . . 8·00 2·
9 $1 green and emerald . . . 48·00 48·
9*a* $1 green and brown (5.15) . . . 48·00 2·
10 $2 green and carmine . . . 1·50 4·
11 $5 green and blue . . . 4·00 7·
12 $25 green and orange . . . 42·00 80·
1/12 *Set of* 13 . . . £200 £1
1s/12s Optd "Specimen" *Set of* 13 . . . £275

1921 (5 May)–**28**. Wmk Mult Script CA. *Ordinary paper* (1c. to 10c or *chalk-surfaced paper* (30c. to $1). P 14.

14 **1** 1c. dull green (7.21) . . . 4·25
15 1c. black (24.2.23) . . . 1·00
16 2c. brown (29.7.22) . . . 7·00 3·
16*a* 2c. green (24.7.26) . . . 3·50
16*b* 3c. brown (5.3.27) . . . 4·50 1·
ba. "C" of "CA" missing from wmk
17 4c. black and red (15.7.22) . . . 2·50
18 5c. green and red/*pale yellow* (12.22) . . . 1·50
19 6c. claret (29.7.22) . . . 3·50 1·
19*a* 6c. scarlet (26.5.28) . . . 4·00 5·
20 10c. black and mauve . . . 3·00
21 30c. purple and carmine (24.7.26) . . . 4·00 5·
22 50c. black and orange (21.3.25) . . . 6·50 45·
23 $1 green and brown (9.2.24) . . . 28·00 80·
14/23 *Set of* 13 . . . 65·00 £1
14s/23s Optd "Specimen" *Set of* 13 . . . £375

Examples of Nos. 22/3 are known showing part strikes of a forg Kota Bharu postmark dated "27 JUL 11".

For the 4c., 5c. and 6c. surcharged, see issues under "Japane Occupation".

OVERPRINT SETTINGS FOR NOS. 30/8. All values we overprinted using a triplet of three slightly different types. It is r known if this was applied to the sheets three stamps at a time or a forms to overprint a pane of 60 was constructed from it.

On the normal setting "MALAYA" is 13 mm long. The 5c. or is also known with "MALAYA" 14 mm from a different trip setting. It has been suggested that this was a trial overprint on c sheet which was subsequently included in postal stocks.

1922 (31 Mar). *Malaya-Borneo Exhibition, Singapore. Optd with* 7 ("MALAYA" *13 mm long) by Govt Survey Office, Kkota Bha*

(a) Wmk Mult Crown CA.

30 **1** 4c. black and red . . . 5·00 48
a. Opt double . . . £2500
31 5c. green and red/*pale yellow* . . . 6·00 48
a. "MALAYA" 14 mm long
32 30c. dull purple and red . . . 6·00 65
33 50c. black and orange . . . 8·50 70
34 $1 green and brown . . . 27·00 90
35 $2 green and carmine . . . 65·00 £1
36 $5 green and blue . . . £160 £3

(b) Wmk Mult Script CA.

37 **1** 1c. green . . . 3·50 48
a. Opt double . . . £2500
38 10c. black and mauve . . . 6·00 60
30/8 *Set of* 9 . . . £250 £8

Nos. 30a and 37a show all three lines of the overprint double

Examples of all values are known showing part strikes of forged postmark mentioned below Nos. 14/23.

3 Sultan Ismail

4 Sultan Ismail

(Recess Harrison (No. 39) or D.L.R. (No. 39a))

1928–35. Wmk Mult Script CA. P 12.

39 **3** $1 blue . . . 14·00 80
a. Perf 14 (1935) . . . 40·00 42
s. Perf "Specimen" . . . 85·00

(Recess B.W.)

937 (July)–**40**. Wmk Mult Script CA. P 12.

0 4 1c. grey-olive and yellow 50 55
1 2c. green . . . . 4·00 20
2 4c. scarlet . . . . 5·50 1·00
3 5c. red-brown . . . . 4·75 10
4 6c. lake (10.37) . . . . 11·00 8·00
5 8c. grey-olive . . . . 4·75 10
6 10c. purple (10.37) . . . . 22·00 2·75
7 12c. blue . . . . 3·50 6·00
8 25c. vermilion and violet . . . . 5·00 3·50
9 30c. violet and scarlet (10.37) . . . . 40·00 20·00
0 40c. orange and blue-green . . . . 8·50 26·00
1 50c. grey-olive and orange (10.37) . . . . 65·00 5·50
2 $1 violet and blue-green (10.37) . . . . 48·00 13·00
3 $2 red-brown and scarlet (3.40) £225 £180
4 $5 vermilion and lake (3.40) £375 £475
0/54 *Set of* 15 . . . . £750 £650
0s/54s Perf "Specimen" *Set of* 15 . . . . £500

For above issue surcharged see issues under "Japanese)ccupation".

948 (1 Dec). *Royal Silver Wedding. As Nos. 112/13 of Antigua.*
5 10c. violet . . . . 75 2·75
6 $5 carmine . . . . 26·00 48·00

949 (10 Oct). *75th Anniv of U.P.U. As Nos. 114/17 of Antigua.*
7 10c. purple 25 30
8 15c. deep blue . . . . 2·00 1·00
9 25c. orange . . . . 40 2·75
0 50c. blue-black . . . . 70 2·50
7/60 *Set of* 4 . . . . 3·00 6·00

Due to the exhaustion of certain B.M.A. values PERAK 3c., 4c., 20c. black and green, 25c., 40c. and 50c. stamps were used in Kelantan from 27 November 1950 until the issue of Nos. 61/81.

5 Sultan Ibrahim

Normal No. 62a Tiny stop (R. 1/2)

951 (11 July)–**55**. *Chalk-surfaced paper.* Wmk Mult Script CA. P $17\frac{1}{2} \times 18$.

5 1c. black 50 30
2c. orange . . . . 1·25 35
a. Tiny stop . . . . 25·00
b. Orange-yellow (11.5.55) . . . . 4·00 1·50
3c. green . . . . 4·00 1·25
4c. brown 75 15
5c. bright purple (1.9.52) . . . . 1·25 50
a. Bright mauve (9.12.53) . . . . 2·25 70
6c. grey 75 20
8c. scarlet . . . . 2·00 3·50
8c. green (1.9.52) . . . . 1·25 1·75
10c. magenta 50 10
12c. scarlet (1.9.52) . . . . 2·50 2·25
15c. ultramarine . . . . 4·25 60
20c. black and green . . . . 80 6·00
20c. bright blue (1.9.52) . . . . 1·00 25
25c. purple and orange . . . . 1·50 55
30c. scarlet and purple (4.9.55) . . . . 1·25 2·00
35c. scarlet and purple (1.9.52) . . . . 1·25 1·50
40c. red and purple . . . . 9·00 13·00
50c. black and blue . . . . 3·75 40
$1 blue and purple . . . . 7·50 5·00
$2 green and scarlet . . . . 27·00 27·00
$5 green and brown . . . . 48·00 40·00
a. Green and sepia (8.12.53) . . . . 85·00 90·00
/81 *Set of* 21 . . . . £110 95·00

STAMP BOOKLETS

27 (June). *Black on white (No. SB1) or black on grey (No. SB2) covers. Stapled.*
1 36c. booklet containing thirty-six 1c. (No. 15) in blocks of 6 . . . . £2250
2 96c. booklet containing twenty-four 4c. (No. 17) in blocks of 6 . . . . £2250

27 (Dec). *Black on white (No. SB3) or on grey (No. SB4) covers. Stapled.*
3 40c. booklet containing forty 1c. (No. 15) in blocks of 10 . . . . £2250
4 80c. booklet containing twenty 4c. (No. 17) in blocks of 10 . . . . £2250

MALACCA

One of the Straits Settlements which joined the Federation of alaya on 1 February 1948.

48 (1 Dec). *Royal Silver Wedding. As Nos. 112/13 of Antigua.*
10c. violet . . . . 30 1·75
$5 brown . . . . 28·00 38·00

49 (1 Mar)–**52**. *As T* **58** *of Straits Settlements, but inscr* "MALACCA" *at foot.* Wmk Mult Script CA. *Chalk-surfaced paper.* P $17\frac{1}{2} \times 18$.
1c. black 30 70
2c. orange 80 45
3c. green . . . . 30 1·75
4c. brown 30 10
5c. bright purple (1.9.52) . . . . 60 1·50
6c. grey 75 85
8c. scarlet . . . . 75 6·00
8c. green (1.9.52) . . . . 1·50 4·75
10c. purple 30 10
12c. scarlet (1.9.52) . . . . 1·50 6·00
15c. ultramarine . . . . 2·50 60
20c. black and green . . . . 50 7·00
20c. bright blue (1.9.52) . . . . 3·50 2·50

12 25c. purple and orange 50 70
12*a* 35c. scarlet and purple (1.9.52) . . . . 1·75 3·00
13 40c. red and purple . . . . 1·25 11·00
14 50c. black and blue . . . . 1·00 1·25
15 $1 blue and purple . . . . 8·50 20·00
16 $2 green and scarlet . . . . 21·00 21·00
17 $5 green and brown . . . . 42·00 35·00
3/17 *Set of* 20 . . . . 80·00 £110

1949 (10 Oct). *75th Anniv of U.P.U. As Nos. 114/17 of Antigua.*
18 10c. purple 30 50
19 15c. deep blue . . . . 2·00 1·75
20 25c. orange . . . . 40 4·75
21 50c. blue-black . . . . 60 4·75
18/21 *Set of* 4 . . . . 3·00 10·50

NEGRI SEMBILAN

A federation of smaller states reconstituted in 1886. Sungei Ujong, taken under British protection in 1874, was absorbed into Negri Sembilan by Treaty of 8 August 1895. The Negri Sembilan federation joined the Federated Malay States in 1896.

A. SUNGEI UJONG

Until 1 January 1899, when the Federated Malay States joined the U.P.U., mail for addresses outside Malaya was franked with the stamps of the STRAITS SETTLEMENTS.

PRICES FOR STAMPS ON COVER	
Nos. 1/14	—
Nos. 15/27	*from* × 25
Nos. 28/36	*from* × 8
Nos. 37/49	*from* × 10
Nos. 50/5	*from* × 25

(1)

1878. *No. 11 of Straits Settlements handstamped with T* **1**.
1 2c. brown £2250 £2500
This overprint on India No. 54 is bogus.

SUNGEI (**2**) (Narrow letters) SUNGEI (**3**) ("N" wide) SUNGEI (**4**) ("S" wide)

UJONG (**5**) ("N" wide) UJONG (**6**) (Narrow letters, "UJ" close together) UJONG (**7**) (Narrow letters, evenly spaced)

1881. *No. 11 of Straits Settlements optd with T* **2/7**.
2 **2+5** 2c. brown £3500 £2750
3 **3+5** 2c. brown £2250 £1900
4 **2+6** 2c. brown £275
a. Opt Type **6** double £1600
5 **4+6** 2c. brown £850
6 **2+7** 2c. brown £375

The two lines of this surcharge were applied as separate operations. On Nos. 2/3 "SUNGEI" was printed as a triplet, probably 2+3+3 "UJONG" being added by a single unit handstamp. Nos. 4 and 5 come from a similar triplet, 4+4+5, completed by another single unit handstamp. No. 6 comes from a single type triplet with the second line added as a triplet instead of by a single unit handstamp.

The 10c. slate overprinted Types **2** + **7** is bogus.

SUNGEI (**8**) ("N" and "E" wide) SUNGEI (**9**) ("SUN" and "E" wide) SUNGEI (**10**) ("SUN" wide)

SUNGEI (**11**) ("S" wide) SUNGEI (**12**) (Narrow letters)

UJONG (**13**) ("U" and "NG" wide) UJONG (**14**) (Narrow letters)

1881. *No. 11 of Straits Settlements optd with T* **8/14**.
7 **8+13** 2c. brown £250
8 **9+13** 2c. brown £275
9 **10+13** 2c. brown £250
10 **11+14** 2c. brown £250
a. "S" inverted £3000
11 **12+14** 2c. brown £160

Nos. 7/11 also had the two lines of the overprint applied at separate operations. "SUNGEI" as a triplet, either 7+8+9 or 10+11+11, and "UJONG" as a single unit.

S.U.

(**15**)

1882. *Nos. 50/1 of Straits Settlements optd as T* **15**.
12 2c. brown (with stops) £300
13 2c. brown (without stops) £275 £325
14 4c. rose (with stops) £2750 £3000

Each of the above was applied by a triplet setting.

Examples of Straits Settlements No. 11 with a similar overprint, including stops, are trials which were not issued.

SUNGEI (**16**) ("S" and "E" wide) SUNGEI (**17**) ("E" wide) UJONG (**18**) ("N" wide)

1882 (Dec)–**84**. *Nos. 12, 50, 52/3 and 63 of Straits Settlements optd with T* **11/12**, **14** *and* **16/18**.
15 **12+14** 2c. brown £650 £350
16 **11+14** 2c. brown £900 £500
17 **12+14** 2c. pale rose (1884) £180 £180
18 **11+14** 2c. pale rose (1884) £180 £180
a. Opt Type **14** double
19 **16+14** 2c. pale rose (1884) £100 £100
20 **17+14** 2c. pale rose (1884) £110 £120
21 **12+18** 2c. pale rose (1884) £110 £120
a. Opt Type **18** double £800
22 **12+14** 4c. rose £1200 £1300
23 **11+14** 4c. rose £2000 £2250
24 **12+14** 8c. orange £1400 £1100
25 **11+14** 8c. orange £2500 £2250
26 **12+14** 10c. slate £500 £475
27 **11+14** 10c. slate £800 £750

Nos. 15/27 had the two lines of the overprint applied by separate triplets. Settings so far identified are Nos. 15+16+15, 17+18+19, 19+20+21, 22+23+22, 24+25+24 and 26+27+26.

The 4c. rose overprinted Types **16** + **14** is now believed to be a trial.

UJONG. (**19**) (With stop. Narrow letters) UJONG. (**20**) (With stop. "N" wide) UJONG (**21**) (Without stop. Narrow letters)

1883–84. *Nos. 50 and 63/4 of Straits Settlements optd with T* **12**, **16/17** *and* **19/21**.
28 **12+19** 2c. brown . . . . 45·00 £100
29 **16+19** 2c. brown . . . . 45·00 £100
30 **12+20** 2c. brown . . . . 45·00 £100
a. Opt Type **12** double £1100
31 **16+21** 2c. pale rose (1884) . . . . 90·00 £100
32 **17+21** 2c. pale rose (1884) . . . . 90·00 £100
33 **12+21** 2c. pale rose (1884) . . . . 90·00 £100
34 **16+21** 4c. brown (1884) £225 £300
a. Opt Type **16** double
b. Opt Type **21** double £1600
35 **17+21** 4c. brown (1884) £225 £300
36 **12+21** 4c. brown (1884) £225 £300
a. Opt Type **21** double £3750

Nos. 28/36 had the two lines of the overprint applied by separate triplets. Settings were Nos. 28+29+30, 31+32+33 and 34+35+36.

The 8c. orange overprinted Types **12** + **19** is now believed to be a trial (*Price* £900 *unused*).

Sungei Ujong (**22**) SUNGEI UJONG (**23**) SUNGEI UJONG (**24**)

SUNGEI UJONG (**25**) SUNGEI UJONG (**26**) SUNGEI UJONG (**27**)

SUNGEI UJONG (**28**) SUNGEI UJONG. (**29**) SUNGEI UJONG (**30**)

1885–90. *Nos. 63/a of Straits Settlements optd with T* **22/30**.
37 **22** 2c. pale rose . . . . 75·00 85·00
a. Opt double £600 £600
38 **23** 2c. pale rose . . . . 29·00 60·00
a. Opt double £600
39 **24** 2c. pale rose (1886) . . . . 95·00 £110
40 **25** 2c. pale rose (1886) £140 £150
a. Opt double
41 **26** 2c. pale rose (1886) . . . . 80·00 90·00
a. Opt double
42 **27** 2c. pale rose (1887) . . . . 12·00 32·00
43 **28** 2c. pale rose (1889) . . . . 8·00 11·00
a. Narrow "E" (2 mm wide) (R. 3/4 and 4/3) . . . . 80·00
c. Opt double £1300
d. Bright rose (1890) . . . . 11·00 9·00
da. Narrow "E" (2 mm wide) (R. 3/4 and 4/3) . . . . 95·00
db. Antique "N" in "UJONG" (R. 10/6) £150
44 **29** 2c. pale rose (1889) . . . . 90·00 70·00
a. "UNJOG" (R. 7/3) £4250 £2750
45 **30** 2c. bright rose (1890) . . . . 32·00 15·00
a. Antique "G" in "SUNGEI" (R. 6/1) £275
b. Antique "G" in "UJONG" (R. 8/3) £275
c. Pale rose

All the above overprints had both lines applied at the same operation. Nos. 37/42 were from different triplet settings. The first printing of Type **28** was from a triplet (No. 43) but this was followed by two further settings of 60 (6 × 10), the first containing No. 43a and the second Nos. 43*d*/db. Nos. 44/5 were both from settings of 60.

SUNGEI UJONG Two CENTS (**31**) SUNGEI UJONG Two CENTS (**32**) SUNGEI UJONG Two CENTS (**33**)

SUNGEI UJONG Two CENTS (**34**)

1891. *No. 68 of Straits Settlements surch with T* **31/4**.
46 **31** 2c.on 24c. green . . . £700 £750
47 **32** 2c.on 24c. green . . . £275 £300
w. Wmk inverted . . . £450 £475
48 **33** 2c.on 24c. green . . . £700 £750
49 **34** 2c. on 24c. green . . . £150 £170
a. Antique "G" in "SUNGEI" (R. 6/1) . . . £900
b. Antique "G" in "UJONG" (R. 8/3) . . . £900
w. Wmk inverted . . . £325 £350

Nos. 46/9 come from the same setting of 60 on which "SUNGEI UJONG" was from the same type as No. 45. No. 46 occurs in row 1. No. 47 from rows 2 to 4, No. 48 from row 5 and No. 49 from rows 6 to 10.

35

3 CENTS
(36)

37

1891 (Nov)–**94**. Wmk Crown CA. P 14.
50 **35** 2c. rose . . . 29·00 27·00
51 2c. orange (12.94) . . . 1·75 4·25
52 5c. blue (3.93) . . . 5·00 6·50
50/2 *Set of* 3 . . . 32·00 35·00
50s/2s Optd "Specimen" *Set of* 3 . . . 60·00

1894 (Dec). *Surch as T* **36** *by De La Rue*. Wmk Mult Crown CA. P 14.
53 **35** 1c.on 5c. green . . . 1·00 70
54 3c. on 5c.rose . . . 2·50 4·75

1895 (Oct). Wmk Crown CA. P 14.
55 **37** 3c. dull purple and carmine . . . 9·50 3·00
53s/5s Optd "Specimen" *Set of* 3 . . . 60·00

B. NEGRI SEMBILAN

Stamps of the STRAITS SETTLEMENTS were used in Negri Sembilan during 1891, until replaced by the stamps listed below. Until the Federated Malay States joined the U.P.U. On 1 January 1899 Straits Settlements stamps continued to be used for mail to addresses outside Malaya.

PRICES FOR STAMPS ON COVER TO 1945

No.	1	*from* × 200
Nos.	2/4	*from* × 10
Nos.	5/14	*from* × 8
Nos.	15/20	*from* × 10
Nos.	21/49	*from* × 4

Negri
Sembilan
(1)

2

3

1891 (Aug?). *No. 63a of Straits Settlements optd with T* **1**.
1 2c. bright rose . . . 3·00 5·00

N.SEMBILAN

Short "N" in "SEMBILAN" (Top left pane R. 8/3)

1891 (Nov)–**94**. Wmk Crown CA. P 14.
2 **2** 1c. green (6.93) . . . 3·00 1·00
3 2c. rose . . . 3·25 7·50
a. Short "N" . . . 80·00
4 5c. blue (11.94) . . . 30·00 40·00
2/4 *Set of* 3 . . . 32·00 42·00
2s/4s Optd "Specimen" *Set of* 3 . . . 80·00

1895–99. Wmk Crown CA. P 14.
5 **3** 1c. dull purple and green (1899) . . . 9·50 5·00
6 2c. dull purple and brown (1898) . . . 35·00 £110
7 3c. dull purple and carmine . . . 14·00 1·00
8 5c. dull purple and orange-yellow (1897) . . . 8·50 8·00
9 8c. dull purple and ultramarine (1898) . . . 29·00 16·00
10 10c. dull purple and orange (1897) . . . 27·00 14·00
11 15c. green and violet (1896) . . . 42·00 75·00
12 20c. green and olive (1897) . . . 65·00 38·00
13 25c. green and carmine (1896) . . . 70·00 90·00
14 50c. green and black (1896) . . . 70·00 65·00
5/14 *Set of* 10 . . . £325 £375
5s/14s Optd "Specimen" *Set of* 10 . . . £225

Four cents.
(4)

Four cents.
(5)

1898 (Dec)–**1900**.

(a) Surch as T **4**.
15 **3** 1c.on 15c. green and violet (1900) . . . 95·00 £180
a. Raised stop (R. 5/1 and R. 10/1 of each pane) . . . £375 £650
16 **2** 4c.on 1c. green . . . 2·00 15·00
17 **3** 4c.on 3c. dull purple and carmine . . . 3·00 16·00
a. Horiz pair, one without surch . . . £5500 £4000
b. Surch double . . . £1800 £1000
ba. Ditto. "Four cents" albino . . . † £1000
c. Surch inverted . . . £1500 £1200
d. "cents" repeated at left . . . £1800 £1600
e. "Four" repeated at right . . . £1800 £1600
f. Without bar . . . £800 £650
g. Bar double . . . † £800
18 **2** 4c.on 5c. blue . . . 1·25 15·00

On Nos. 15 and 17 the bar is at the top of the stamp.
The surcharges were applied as a setting of 30 (6 × 5).

(b) Surch as T **5**.
19 **3** 4c.on 8c. dull purple & ultram (G.) (12.98) . . . 4·75 4·25
a. Vert pair, one without surch . . . £4500 £3500
b. Surch double . . . £1800 £1800
c. Surch double (G.+R.) . . . £800 £850
20 4c.on 8c. dull purple & ultramarine (Bk.) . . . £1100 £1200

Care should be taken in distinguishing the true black surcharge, No. 20, from very deep shades of the green surcharge, No. 19.

Pending the arrival of the permanent Federated Malay States issue the stamps of SELANGOR, FEDERATED MALAY STATES provisional overprints, STRAITS SETTLEMENTS and PERAK were used at various times between October 1899 and Aril 1901.
The general issues for FEDERATED MALAY STATES were used in Negri Sembilan from 29 April 1901 until 1935.

6 Arms of Negri Sembilan

7 Arms of Negri Sembilan

1935 (2 Dec)–**41**. Wmk Mult Script CA. *Ordinary paper* (6c. grey, 15c.) *or chalk-surfaced paper* (*others*). P 14.
21 **6** 1c. black (1.1.36) . . . 1·00 20
22 2c. green (1.1.36) . . . 1·00 20
23 2c. orange (11.12.41) . . . 4·25 65·00
24 3c. green (21.8.41) . . . 8·00 8·00
a. Ordinary paper . . . 17·00 8·00
25 4c. orange . . . 1·00 10
26 5c. brown (5.12.35) . . . 1·75 10
27 6c. scarlet (1.1.37) . . . 15·00 2·50
a. Stop omitted at right (R. 10/4) . . . £375 £100
28 6c. grey (18.12.41) . . . 4·75 75·00
a. Stop omitted at right (R. 10/4) . . . £160 £600
29 8c. grey . . . 2·00 10
30 10c. dull purple (1.1.36) . . . 1·00 10
31 12c. bright ultramarine (1.1.36) . . . 1·90 50
32 15c. ultramarine (1.10.41) . . . 10·00 50·00
33 25c. dull purple and scarlet (1.4.36) . . . 1·25 70
34 30c. dull purple and orange (1.1.36) . . . 3·50 2·00
35 40c. scarlet and dull purple . . . 2·00 2·00
36 50c. black/*emerald* (1.2.36) . . . 4·50 2·25
37 $1 black and red/*blue* (1.4.36) . . . 4·00 3·50
38 $2 green and scarlet (16.5.36) . . . 32·00 16·00
39 $5 green and red/*emerald* (16.5.36) . . . 21·00 60·00
21/39 *Set of* 19 . . . £110 £250
21s/39s Perf "Specimen" *Set of* 19 . . . £350

The stamps issued in 1941 were printed by Harrison and Sons following bomb damage to the De La Rue works on 29 December 1940. The used prices quoted for Nos. 23, 28 and 32 are for examples with clearly identifiable 1941 cancellations.
An 8c. scarlet was issued but only with opt during Japanese Occupation of Malaya. Unoverprinted specimens result from leakages.

During shortages in 1941 stamps of STRAITS SETTLEMENTS (2c. green, 25c., 30c.), SELANGOR (2c. green, 2c. orange (both perfs), 8c. grey, 25c.), PERAK (2c. orange, 25c., 50c.) and PAHANG (8c. scarlet) were issued in Negri Sembilan.

1948 (1 Dec). *Royal Silver Wedding. As Nos. 112/13 of Antigua.*
40 10c. violet . . . 15 50
41 $5 green . . . 19·00 28·00

1949 (1 Apr)–**55**. *Chalk-surfaced paper.* Wmk Mult Script CA. P $17\frac{1}{2}$ × 18.
42 **7** 1c. black . . . 20 10
43 2c. orange . . . 20 10
44 3c. green . . . 20 30
45 4c. brown . . . 20 10
46 5c. bright purple (1.9.52) . . . 30 50
a. Bright mauve (25.8.53) . . . 30 45
47 6c. grey . . . 1·00 10
a. Pale grey (25.8.53) . . . 5·00 1·25
48 8c. scarlet . . . 50 75
49 8c. green (1.9.52) . . . 1·75 1·60
50 10c. purple . . . 20 10
51 12c. scarlet (1.9.52) . . . 1·75 2·75
52 15c. ultramarine . . . 3·00 10
53 20c. black and green . . . 50 75
54 20c. bright blue (1.9.52) . . . 1·00 10
55 25c. purple and orange . . . 50 10
56 30c. scarlet and purple (4.9.55) . . . 1·25 2·50
57 35c. scarlet and purple (1.9.52) . . . 1·00 1·00
58 40c. red and purple . . . 1·50 4·75
59 50c. black and blue . . . 2·25 20
60 $1 blue and purple . . . 3·75 2·25
61 $2 green and scarlet . . . 12·00 17·00
62 $5 green and brown . . . 50·00 45·00
42/62 *Set of* 21 . . . 70·00 70·00

1949 (10 Oct). *75th Anniv of U.P.U. As Nos. 114/17 of Antigua.*
63 10c. purple . . . 20 10
64 15c. deep blue . . . 1·40 2·75
a. "A" of "CA" missing from wmk . . . £750
65 25c. orange . . . 30 2·2
66 50c. blue-black . . . 60 3·2
63/6 *Set of* 4 . . . 2·25 7·5

STAMP BOOKLETS

1935. *Stapled.*
SB1 $1 booklet containing twenty 5c. (No. 26) in blocks of 10 . . .
SB2 $1.30, booklet containing 5c. and 8c. (Nos. 26, 29), each in block of 10 . . .

PAHANG

The first British Resident was appointed in 1888. Pahang joine the Federated Malay States in 1896.

Until 1 January 1899, when the Federated Malay States joined the U.P.U., mail for addresses outside Malaya was franked with stamps of the STRAITS SETTLEMENTS.

PRICES FOR STAMPS ON COVER TO 1945

No.	1	*from* × 50
Nos.	2/3	—
No.	4	*from* × 100
No.	5	—
No.	6	*from* × 100
Nos.	7/10	*from* × 8
Nos.	11/13	*from* × 25
Nos.	14/16	*from* × 20
Nos.	17/*a*	—
Nos.	18/*d*	*from* × 6
Nos.	19/24	*from* × 8
No.	25	*from* × 20
Nos.	26/7	—
No.	28	*from* × 15
Nos.	29/46	*from* × 6

PAHANG
(1)

PAHANG
(2)

PAHANG
(**2a**) (Antique letters)

1889 (Jan). *Nos. 52/3 and 63 of Straits Settlements optd with T* **1**.
1 2c. pale rose . . . 95·00 50·
2 8c. orange . . . £1700 £15
3 10c. slate . . . £225 £2

All three values were overprinted from a triplet setting, but t 2c. also exists from a similar setting of 30 or 60.

1889. *No. 63 of Straits Settlements optd with T* **2**.
4 2c. pale rose . . . 12·00 16·
a. Bright rose . . . 4·50 8·
ab. Opt Type **2a**. Antique letters . . . £750

No. 4 was overprinted from a setting of 60. No. 4ab usua occurs on R. 10/1, but has also been found on R. 8/1 as the res of revision of the setting.

PAHANG
(3)

PAHANG
(4)

1890. *No. 63a of Straits Settlements optd.*
5 **3** 2c. bright rose . . . £4500 £14
6 **4** 2c. bright rose . . . 95·00 14·
w. Wmk inverted

No. 5 may have been overprinted from a triplet setting. No. was from a setting of 60.

PAHANG
Two
CENTS
(5)

PAHANG
Two
CENTS
(6)

PAHANG
Two
CENTS
(7)

PAHANG
Two
CENTS
(8)

1891. *No. 68 of Straits Settlements surch with T* **5/8**.
7 **5** 2c.on 24c. green . . . £150 £
8 **6** 2c.on 24c. green . . . £700 £
9 **7** 2c.on 24c. green . . . £250 £
10 **8** 2c.on 24c. green . . . £700 £

Nos. 7/10 come from one setting used to surcharge the panes sixty. No. 7 occurs in rows 1 to 5, No. 8 on row 6, No. 9 on rc 7 to 9 and No. 10 on row 10.

9

10

1891 (Nov)–**95**. Wmk Crown CA. P 14.
11 **9** 1c. green (3.95) . . . 4·25 3
12 2c. rose . . . 4·50 3
13 5c. blue (6.93) . . . 11·00 40
11/13 *Set of* 3 . . . 18·00 42
11s/13s Optd "Specimen" *Set of* 3 . . . 75·00

Following an increase of postage rates on 1 March 1894 1 cent stamps of STRAITS SETTLEMENTS were used in Pahang until the autumn of the following year.

1895–99. Wmk Crown CA. P 14.
4 **10** 3c. dull purple and carmine . . . . 6·50 2·75
5 4c. dull purple and carmine (1899) . . . 17·00 12·00
6 5c. dull purple and olive-yellow (1897) . . . . 25·00 21·00
4/16 *Set of* 3 . . . . 45·00 32·00
4s/16s Optd "Specimen" *Set of* 3 . . . . 65·00

897 (2 Aug). *No. 13 bisected, surch in red manuscript at Kuala Lipis and initialled "JFO".*

(a) Bisected horizontally.
7 2c.on half of 5c. blue (surch "2" and bar across "5") . . . . — £1600
7*a* 3c.on half of 5c. blue (surch "3") £4500 £1600

(b) Bisected diagonally.
8 2c.on half of 5c. blue (surch "2" and bar across "5") £1300 £375
a. Unsevered pair. Nos. 18 and 18d . . . £9000 £3750
b. Se-tenant pair. Nos. 18 and 18d . . . £3750 £1000
c. Surch in black manuscript . . . £7500 £3000
8*d* 3c.on half of 5c. blue (surch "3") . . . £1300 £375
dc. Surch in black manuscript . . . £7500 £3000

The initials are those of John Fortescue Owen, the District Treasurer at Kuala Lipis.

Nos. 17 and 18 only occur on the bottom half of the 5c. and Nos. 17*a* and 18*d* on the top half. No. 18a is a complete example of No. 13 showing the two surcharges. No. 18b is a *se-tenant* pair of bisects from adjoining stamps.

Pahang. (11) **Pahang.** (12)

898–99.

(a) Nos. 72/5 of Perak optd with T **11**.
9 10c. dull purple and orange (3.98) . . . . 18·00 25·00
0 25c. green and carmine . . . . 85·00 £150
1 50c. dull purple and greenish black £350 £375
2 50c. green and black (1899) £225 £275

(b) Nos. 76 and 79 of Perak optd with T **12**.
3 $1 green and pale green £350 £425
4 $5 green and ultramarine £1100 £1600

Pahang
Four cents
(13)

Four cents.
(14)

898.

(a) No. 71 of Perak surch with T **13**.
5 4c.on 8c. dull purple and ultramarine . . . 3·75 5·50
a. Surch inverted £2750 £1300
b. Surch double £750

(b) *T* **13** *on plain paper (no stamp), but issued for postage. Imperf.*
4c. black . . . . — £3000
5c. black £1900

No. 26 also exists pin-perforated.

899. *No. 16 surch with T* **14**.
10 4c.on 5c. dull purple and olive-yellow . . . . 16·00 55·00

Pending the arrival of the permanent Federated Malay States issue the stamps of SELANGOR, FEDERATED MALAY STATES provisional overprints and PERAK were used at various times between November 1899 and July 1902.

The general issues for the FEDERATED MALAY STATES were used in Pahang from July 1902 until 1935.

15 Sultan Sir Abu Bakar

16 Sultan Sir Abu Bakar

35 (2 Dec)–**41**. *Chalk-surfaced paper.* Wmk Mult Script CA. P 14.
15 1c. black (1.1.36) 15 40
2c. green (1.1.36) 80 50
3c. green (21.8.41) . . . . 15·00 15·00
a. Ordinary paper . . . . 32·00 4·25
4c. orange 50 50
5c. brown (5.12.35) 60 10
6c. scarlet (1.1.37) . . . . 13·00 1·75
8c. grey 60 10
8c. scarlet (11.12.41) . . . . 2·25 50·00
10c. dull purple (1.1.36) 60 10
12c. bright ultramarine (1.1.36) . . . . 1·75 1·25
15c. ultram (*ordinary paper*) (1.10.41) . . . 12·00 50·00
25c. dull purple and scarlet (1.4.36) . . . 80 1·50
30c. dull purple and orange (1.1.36) . . . 80 1·10
40c. scarlet and dull purple . . . . 75 2·00
50c. black/*emerald* (1.2.36) . . . . 2·75 1·50
$1 black and red/*blue* (1.4.36) . . . . 2·00 8·00
$2 green and scarlet (16.5.36) . . . . 19·00 28·00
$5 green and red/*emerald* (16.5.36) . . . 7·50 60·00
/46 *Set of* 18 . . . . 70·00 £190
s/46s Perf "Specimen" *Set of* 18 . . . . £350

The stamps issued during 1941 were printed by Harrison and Sons following bomb damage to the De La Rue works on December 1940. The used prices quoted for Nos. 36 and 39 are examples with clearly identifiable 1941 cancellations.

A 2c. orange and a 6c. grey were prepared but not officially issued. (*Price mint £4 each*).

During shortages in 1941 stamps of STRAITS SETTLEMENTS (2c., 25c.), SELANGOR (2c. orange, 3c., 8c.), NEGRI SEMBILAN (6c.) and PERAK (2c. orange) were issued in Pahang.

1948 (1 Dec). *Royal Silver Wedding. As Nos. 112/13 of Antigua.*
47 10c. violet 15 60
48 $5 green . . . . 24·00 40·00

1949 (10 Oct). *75th Anniv of U.P.U. As Nos. 114/17 of Antigua.*
49 10c. purple 30 20
50 15c. deep blue . . . . 1·10 1·25
51 25c. orange . . . . 35 1·25
52 50c. blue-black . . . . 70 2·00
49/52 *Set of* 4 . . . . 2·25 4·25

1950 (1 June)–**56**. Wmk Mult Script CA. *Chalk-surfaced paper.* P 17½ × 18.
53 **16** 1c. black 10 10
54 2c. orange 20 10
55 3c. green 30 80
56 4c. brown 80 10
a. Chocolate (24.3.54) . . . . 8·00 2·00
57 5c. bright purple (1.9.52) 50 70
a. Bright mauve (10.9.53) 50 15
58 6c. grey 30 30
59 8c. scarlet . . . . 50 1·50
60 8c. green (1.9.52) 85 75
61 10c. magenta 25 10
62 12c. scarlet (1.9.52) . . . . 85 1·25
63 15c. ultramarine 75 10
64 20c. black and green . . . . 50 2·75
65 20c. bright blue (1.9.52) . . . . 1·00 10
a. Ultramarine (8.3.56) . . . . 6·00 2·75
66 25c. purple and orange 50 10
67 30c. scarlet and brown-purple (4.9.55) . . . . 1·25 35
a. Scarlet and purple (8.3.56) . . . . 16·00 4·00
68 35c. scarlet and purple (1.9.52) 60 25
69 40c. red and purple . . . . 1·50 7·50
70 50c. black and blue . . . . 1·50 10
71 $1 blue and purple . . . . 2·75 2·75
72 $2 green and scarlet . . . . 13·00 21·00
73 $5 green and brown . . . . 55·00 70·00
a. Green and sepia (24.3.54) . . . . 90·00 90·00
53/73 *Set of* 21 . . . . 70·00 95·00

STAMP BOOKLETS

1935. *Black on buff covers. Stapled.*
SB1 $1 booklet containing twenty 5c. (No. 33) in blocks of 10
SB2 $1.30 booklet containing 5c. and 8c. (Nos. 33, 35) each to block of 10 and pane of airmail labels £2500

PENANG

One of the Straits Settlements which joined the Federation of Malaya on 1 February 1948.

1948 (1 Dec). *Royal Silver Wedding. As Nos. 112/13 of Antigua.*
1 10c. violet 30 20
2 $5 brown . . . . 30·00 28·00

1949 (21 Feb)–**52**. *As T* **58** *of Straits Settlements, but inscr* "PENANG" *at foot.* Wmk Mult Script CA. *Chalk-surfaced paper.* P 17½ × 18.
3 1c. black 20 20
4 2c. orange 85 20
5 3c. green . . . . 20 1·00
6 4c. brown 20 10
7 5c. bright purple (1.9.52) . . . . 2·00 2·75
8 6c. grey 30 20
9 8c. scarlet . . . . 60 3·25
10 8c. green (1.9.52) . . . . 1·50 1·75
11 10c. purple 20 10
12 12c. scarlet (1.9.52) . . . . 2·00 5·00
13 15c. ultramarine 50 30
14 20c. black and green . . . . 50 1·00
15 20c. bright blue (1.9.52) . . . . 55 1·25
16 25c. purple and orange . . . . 1·75 20
17 35c. scarlet and purple (1.9.52) . . . . 1·00 1·25
18 40c. red and purple . . . . 1·50 11·00
19 50c. black and blue . . . . 2·50 20
20 $1 blue and purple . . . . 17·00 2·00
21 $2 green and scarlet . . . . 22·00 2·00
22 $5 green and brown . . . . 48·00 3·00
3/22 *Set of* 20 . . . . 95·00 32·00

1949 (10 Oct). *75th Anniv of U.P.U. As Nos. 114/17 of Antigua.*
23 10c. purple 20 10
24 15c. deep blue . . . . 2·00 2·75
25 25c. orange . . . . 45 2·75
26 50c. blue-black . . . . 1·50 3·50
23/6 *Set of* 4 . . . . 3·75 8·00

PERAK

Perak accepted a British Resident in 1874, although he was later murdered.

The state joined the Federated Malay States in 1896.

The stamps of the STRAITS SETTLEMENTS were used in Perak during 1877/8.

Until 1 January 1899, when the Federated Malay States joined the U.P.U., mail for addresses outside Malaya was franked with stamps of the STRAITS SETTLEMENTS.

PRICES FOR STAMPS ON COVER TO 1945

No.	1	—
Nos.	2/9	*from* × 60
Nos.	10/13	*from* × 30
Nos.	14/16	*from* × 8
Nos.	17/22	*from* × 20
No.	23	—
Nos.	24/5	—
Nos.	26/8	*from* × 15
No.	29	*from* × 75
No.	30	*from* × 20
Nos.	31/2	—
Nos.	33/40	*from* × 15
Nos.	43/60	*from* × 6
Nos.	61/5	*from* × 20
Nos.	66/79	*from* × 12
No.	80	—
Nos.	81/7	*from* × 8
Nos.	88/102	*from* × 4
Nos.	103/21	*from* × 3

The Official stamps of Perak are rare used on cover.

(1)

1878. *No. 11 of Straits Settlements handstamped with T* **1**.
1 2c. brown £1600 £1200

PERAK (**2**) (14½ mm long) — PERAK (**3**) (11 mm long) — PERAK (**4**) (10¼ mm long)

PERAK (**5**) (17 mm long) — PERAK (**6**) ("RA" narrow) — PERAK (**7**) ("R" narrow)

PERAK (**8**) ("P" and "K" wide) — PERAK (**9**) (12 to 13½ mm long)

1880–81. *No. 11* (wmk Crown CC) *of Straits Settlements optd with T* **2/9**.
2 **2** 2c. brown £1600 £750
3 **3** 2c. brown £1400 £650
4 **4** 2c. brown £700 £550
5 **5** 2c. brown (1881) . . . . 28·00 55·00
6 **6** 2c. brown (1881) £190 £200
7 **7** 2c. brown (1881) £130 £150
8 **8** 2c. brown (1881) £450 £425
a. Opt double . . . . † £1600
9 **9** 2c. brown (1881) £130 £140

Of the above No. 2 is from a single unit overprint, No. 5 from a setting of sixty and the remainder from settings applied as horizontal strips of three. Nos. 6/8 come from mixed triplets, either 6+7+7 or 7+7+8. No. 4 is believed to come from a single unit overprint in addition to a triplet.

PERAK (**10**) ("A" wide) — PERAK (**11**) ("E" wide)

1882–83. *Nos. 50* (wmk Crown CA) *and 63 of Straits Settlements optd with T* **9/11**.
10 **9** 2c. brown . . . . 19·00 48·00
a. Opt double £600
11 2c. pale rose (1883) . . . . 23·00 42·00
a. Opt double £650
12 **10** 2c. pale rose (1883) . . . . 23·00 65·00
13 **11** 2c. pale rose (1883) . . . . 23·00 50·00
a. Opt double £650

The above were all overprinted as triplet settings. Those for the 2c. rose were 11+12+13, 13+11+11 and 13+11+12.

2 CENTS PERAK (**12**) — 2 CENTS (**13**)

1883 (July). *No. 51* (wmk Crown CA) *of Straits Settlements surch.*

(a) Surch with T **12**.
14 2c.on 4c. rose £2750
a. On Straits Settlements No. 12 (wmk Crown CC) £7500

(b) Optd as T **9** *or* **11** *and surch with T* **13**.
15 **11** 2c. on 4c. rose £950 £400
16 **9** 2c. on 4c. rose £550 £250

It is believed that No. 14 occurred on the top row of the sheet with the remaining nine rows surcharged with a triplet containing 15+16+16.

Only one unused example, with defects, of No. 14a is recorded.

PERAK (**14**) ("E" wide) — PERAK (**15**) ("E" narrow) — PERAK (**16**) (12½–13 mm long)

PERAK (**17**) (12–12½ mm long) — PERAK (**18**) (10½ mm long) — PERAK (**19**) (10 mm long)

PERAK (**20**) (13 mm long)

1884–91. *Nos. 63la of Straits Settlements optd with T* **14/20**.

17 **14** 2c. pale rose 3·00 2·25
a. Opt double £600 £600
b. Opt inverted £375 £475
c. Bright rose 4·50 1·75
18 **15** 2c. pale rose 65·00 65·00
b. Opt inverted £1300 £1400
c. Opt triple £1300
d. Bright rose
19 **16** 2c. pale rose (1886) £150 28·00
a. Bright rose (1891) 1·60 5·50
ab. Optd "FERAK" £350 £425
20 **17** 2c. pale rose (1886) 5·00 21·00
a. Opt double £1400
21 **18** 2c. pale rose (1886) £100 £110
a. Bright rose
22 **19** 2c. bright rose (1890) 14·00 45·00
23 **20** 2c. bright rose (1891) £3000

Settings:
Nos. 17/18 – triplets (either 17 + 17 + 17 or 18 + 17 + 17)
– 30 (3 × 10) (containing twenty-eight as No. 17 and two as No. 18)
– 60 (6 × 10) (containing either fifty-seven as No. 17 and three as No. 18 or all as No. 17)
No. 19 – 60 (6 × 10) (No. 19a occurs on one position of the setting, it is often found amended in manuscript)
No. 20 – triplet
No. 21 – triplet
No. 22 – 60 (6 × 10)
No. 23 – not known

1 CENT
(**21**)

1886. *No. 17 surch with T* **21**.

24 **14** 1c.on 2c. pale rose £2250 £2000

ONE CENT PERAK (**22**)
ONE CENT PERAK. (**23**)
ONE CENT PERAK. (**24**) ("N" wide in "ONE" and "CENT")

1886. *No. 63 of Straits Settlements surch with T* **22/4**.

25 **22** 1c.on 2c. pale rose £550 £600
26 **23** 1c.on 2c. pale rose 65·00 85·00
a. Surch double £900
27 **24** 1c.on 2c. pale rose £100 £120

Nos. 26/7 are from a triplet setting, Types **23-24-23**, in which the two Type **23**'s can be differentiated by the height of the "N", which is short on one. This triplet was used for the top nine rows of the sheet. Type **22** may have been used on the bottom row.

1 CENT PERAK (**25**)
One CENT PERAK (**26**)
ONE CENT PERAK (**27**)

1886. *No. 63 of Straits Settlements surch with T* **25**.

28 1c.on 2c. pale rose £120 £130
a. Surch double £1600 £1600

No. 28 comes from a triplet setting.

1886. *No. 63 of Straits Settlements surch with T* **26**.

29 1c.on 2c. pale rose 2·50 9·00
a. "One" inverted £2750
b. Surch double £1100

No. 29 comes from a triplet setting. It is believed that No. 29a occurred when the type was dropped and "One" replaced upside down.

1887. *No. 63 of Straits Settlements surch with T* **27** *in blue.*

30 1c.on 2c. pale rose 40·00 50·00
a. Optd in black £1800 £1300

No. 30 was printed from a setting of 60.

1 CENT PERAK (**28**)
1 CENT PERAK (**29**)

1887. *No. 63 of Straits Settlements surch with T* **28**.

31 1c.on 2c. pale rose £600 £600

No. 31 comes from a triplet setting

1887. *No. 63 of Straits Settlements surch with T* **29**.

32 1c.on 2c. pale rose £1800 £1900

The size of setting used for No. 32 is not known.

One CENT PERAK (**30**)
One CENT PERAK (**31**)
One CENT PERAK (**32**)
One CENT PERAK (**33**)
One CENT PERAK (**34**)
One CENT PERAK (**35**)
One CENT PERAK (**36**)
One CENT PERAK (**37**)

1887–89. *No. 63 of Straits Settlements surch with T* **30/7**.

33 **30** 1c.on 2c. pale rose 2·00 5·00
a. Surch double £1100
b. Bright rose 2·25 2·25
34 **31** 1c.on 2c. pale rose (1889) £120 £140
b. Bright rose
35 **32** 1c.on 2c. pale rose (1889) 11·00 35·00
a. "PREAK" (R. 6/1) £500 £600
b. Bright rose 16·00 35·00
ba. "PREAK" (R. 6/1) £700 £850
w. Wmk inverted £140
36 **33** 1c.on 2c. pale rose (1889) 6·50 13·00
b. Bright rose 4·50 13·00
37 **34** 1c.on 2c. pale rose (1889) 8·00 15·00
b. Bright rose 4·50 15·00
38 **35** 1c.on 2c. bright rose (1889) £600 £750
39 **36** 1c.on 2c. bright rose (1889) £300 £400
40 **37** 1c.on 2c. pale rose (1889) 15·00 30·00
b. Bright rose 15·00 27·00

Settings. No. 33 originally appeared as a triplet, then as a block of 30 (3 × 10) and, finally, as part of a series of composite settings of 60. Specialists recognise four such composite settings:

Setting I contained No. 33 in Rows 1 to 4, R. 5/1 to 5/5 and Row 7; No. 34 on R. 5/6, 6/1 and 6/2; No. 35 on R. 6/3–6; No. 36 on Row 8; No. 37 on Rows 9 and 10.

Setting II was similar, but had the example of No. 33 on R. 3/5 replaced by No. 38 and those on R. 7/4 and R. 7/6 by No. 39.

Setting III contained No. 33 in Rows 1 to 5; No. 35 in Row 6 with the "PREAK" error on the first position; No. 36 in Row 7; No. 37 in Rows 8 and 9; No. 40 in Row 10.

Setting IV was similar, but showed the "PREAK" error on R. 6/1 corrected.

ONE CENT. (**38**)
ONE CENT (**39**)

1889–90. *No. 17 surch with T* **38/9**.

41 **38** 1c.on 2c. bright rose £225 £130
42 **39** 1c.on 2c. bright rose (1890) — £250

PERAK *Two* CENTS (**40**)
PERAK *One* CENT (**41**)

1891. *Nos. 63a, 66 and 68 of Straits Settlements surch.*

(a) As T **30**, **32/4** *and* **37**, *but with "PERAK" at top and a bar through the original value.*

43 **30** 1c.on 6c. lilac 45·00 26·00
44 **32** 1c.on 6c. lilac £160 £150
45 **33** 1c.on 6c. lilac £160 £150
46 **34** 1c.on 6c. lilac 75·00 70·00
47 **37** 1c.on 6c. lilac £160 £150

(b) With T **40** *and as T* **32/4** *and* **37** *but with "PERAK" at top, all with a bar through the original value.*

48 **40** 2c.on 24c. green 14·00 9·50
49 **32** 2c.on 24c. green 90·00 60·00
w. Wmk inverted
50 **33** 2c.on 24c. green 90·00 60·00
51 **34** 2c.on 24c. green 55·00 27·00
52 **37** 2c.on 24c. green 90·00 60·00

(c) With T **41** *and as T* **30**, **34** *and* **37**, *but with "PERAK" at top.*

(i) Without bar over original value.

53 **30** 1c.on 2c. bright rose £170
a. Narrow "O" in "One" (R. 3/3) £1800
54 **41** 1c.on 2c. bright rose £750
55 **34** 1c.on 2c. bright rose £300
56 **37** 1c.on 2c. bright rose £750

(ii) With bar through original value.

57 **30** 1c.on 2c. bright rose 1·75 6·50
a. Narrow "O" in "One" (R. 3/3) 22·00 55·00
58 **41** 1c.on 2c. bright rose 6·00 25·00
59 **34** 1c.on 2c. bright rose 1·75 9·00
60 **37** 1c.on 2c. bright rose 6·00 25·00

Settings. Nos. 43/7 were arranged as Setting IV described under Nos. 33/40.

Nos. 48/52 were similar except that Type **40** replaced Type **30** on the first five rows.

The first printing of the 1c. on 2c. was without a bar through the original face value. Both printings, Nos. 53/60, were from the same setting with Type **30** on Rows 1 to 5, **41** on Row 6, **34** on Rows 7 to 9 and **37** on Row 10.

42

3 CENTS
(**43**)

1892 (1 Jan)–**95**. Wmk Crown CA. P 14.

61 **42** 1c. green 2·25 15
62 2c. rose 1·75 30
63 2c. orange (9.9.95) 50 3·25
64 5c. blue 3·25 7·50
61/4 *Set of* 4 7·00 10·00
61s/4s Optd "Specimen" *Set of* 4 £100

1895 (26 Apr). *Surch with T* **43**. Wmk Crown CA. P 14.

65 **42** 3c.on 5c. rose 3·00 2·25
s. Optd "Specimen" 30·00

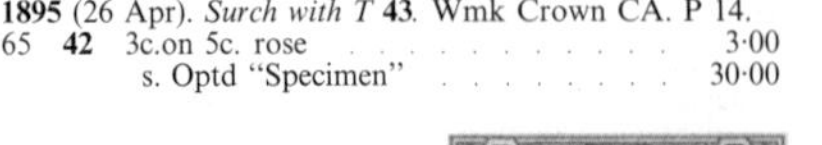

44

45

Malformed "C" in left value tablet (R. 9/3, left pane)

1895 (2 Sept)–**99**. P 14.

(a) Wmk Crown CA.

66 **44** 1c. dull purple and green 2·25 5
a. Malformed "C" £100 50·0
67 2c. dull purple and brown 2·25 5
68 3c. dull purple and carmine 2·50 5
69 4c. dull purple and carmine (1899) 11·00 4·7
70 5c. dull purple and olive-yellow 3·75 5
71 8c. dull purple and ultramarine 45·00 6
72 10c. dull purple and orange 13·00 5
73 25c. green and carmine (1897) £140 12·0
74 50c. dull purple and greenish black 48·00 29·0
75 50c. green and black (2.99) £180 £16

(b) Wmk Crown CC.

76 **45** $1 green and pale green (1896) £170 £18
77 $2 green and carmine (1896) £275 £30
78 $3 green and ochre (1898) £325 £37
79 $5 green and ultramarine (1896) £500 £50
80 $25 green and orange (1899?) £7000 £250
s. Optd "Specimen" £200
66/76 *Set of* 11 £550 £35
66s/79s Optd "Specimen" *Set of* 14 £400

Pending the arrival of the permanent Federated Malay States issue the stamps of FEDERATED MALAY STATES provisional overprints, SELANGOR and STRAITS SETTLEMENTS were used at various times between June 1900 and February 1901.

The general issues for the FEDERATED MALAY STATE were used in Perak from 1901 until 1935.

One Cent. (**46**)
ONE CENT. (**47**)

Three Cent. (**48**)
Three Cent. (**49**)

1900. *Stamps of 1895–99 surch.*

81 **46** 1c.on 2c. dull purple & brown (13 July*) 50 2
a. Antique "e" in "One" (R. 5/2) 55·00 £
b. Antique "e" in "Cent" (R. 9/4) 55·00 £
82 **47** 1c.on 4c. dull purple and carmine 75 10
a. Surch double £1000
83 **46** 1c.on 5c. dull purple & ol-yell (30 June*) 1·75 11
a. Antique "e" in "One" (R. 5/2) 80·00 £
b. Antique "e" in "Cent" (R. 9/4) 80·00 £
84 **48** 3c.on 8c. dull purple & ultram (26 Sept*) 3·75 8
a. Antique "e" in "Cent" (R. 9/4) £150 £
b. No stop after "Cent" (R. 9/5) £150 £
c. Surch double £450 £
85 3c.on 50c. green and black (31 Aug*) 2·25 5
a. Antique "e" in "Cent" (R. 9/4) £110 £
b. No stop after "Cent" (R. 9/5) £110 £
86 **49** 3c.on $1 green and pale green (21 Oct*) 55·00 £
a. Thinner "t" in "Cent" £300 £
b. Surch double £1400
w. Wmk inverted £375 £
87 3c.on $2 green and carmine (24 Oct*) 29·00 8
81/7 *Set of* 7 85·00 £2

*Earliest known postmark date.

With exception of No. 86a, whose sheet position is not know the remaining surcharge varieties all occur in the left-hand pane. (No. 86a the "t" is in a different font which is thinner than norm with a different curve to the foot.

No. 86b is also known showing the thinner "t" in "Cent" varie (*Price* £3750 *unused*).

50 Sultan Iskandar

51 Sultan Iskandar

Malformed "2c." (R. 10/10)

1935 (2 Dec)–**37**. *Chalk-surfaced paper.* Wmk Mult Script CA. P

88 **50** 1c. black (1.1.36) 1·00
89 2c. green (1.1.36) 1·00
90 4c. orange 1·50
91 5c. brown (5.12.35) 60
92 6c. scarlet (1.1.37) 11·00 4
93 8c. grey 1·00
94 10c. dull purple (1.1.36) 70
95 12c. bright ultramarine (1.1.36) 2·00 1
96 25c. dull purple and scarlet (1.4.36) 2·00 1
97 30c. dull purple and orange (1.1.36) 2·50 1

98 40c. scarlet and dull purple 4·25 4·50
99 50c. black/*emerald* (1.2.36) 4·50 1·25
00 $1 black and red/*blue* (1.4.36) 2·50 1·25
01 $2 green and scarlet (16.5.36) 20·00 8·50
02 $5 green and red/*emerald* (16.5.36) 90·00 40·00
38/102 *Set of* 15 £130 55·00
38s/102s Perf "Specimen" *Set of* 15 £275

No. 91 exists in coils constructed from normal sheets in 1936.

938 (2 May)–**41**. Wmk Mult Script CA. *Chalk-surfaced paper*. P 14.
03 **51** 1c. black (4.39) 9·00 10
04 2c. green (13.1.39) 4·25 10
05 2c. orange (30.10.41) 3·50 6·00
a. Malformed "2c" 75·00 25·00
b. Ordinary paper 4·50 17·00
ba. Malformed "2c"
06 3c. green (*ordinary paper*) (21.8.41) — 6·00
a. Chalk-surfaced paper (10.41) 2·75 4·50
07 4c. orange (5.39) 38·00 10
08 5c. brown (1.2.39) 6·00 10
09 6c. scarlet (12.39) 27·00 10
10 8c. grey (1.12.38) 24·00 10
11 8c. scarlet (18.12.41) 1·00 65·00
12 10c. dull purple (17.10.38) 26·00 10
13 12c. bright ultramarine (17.10.38) 20·00 1·00
14 15c. brt ultram (*ordinary paper*) (8.41) 4·00 13·00
15 25c. dull purple and scarlet (12.39) 60·00 3·25
16 30c. dull purple and orange (17.10.38) 9·50 2·25
17 40c. scarlet and dull purple 50·00 2·00
18 50c. black/*emerald* (17.10.38) 32·00 75
19 $1 black and red/*blue* (7.40) £130 16·00
20 $2 green and scarlet (9.40) £140 60·00
21 $5 green and red/*emerald* (1.41) £200 £275
03/21 *Set of* 19 £700 £400
03s/21s perf "Specimen" *Set of* 19 £375

No. 108 exists in coils constructed from normal sheets.

The stamps issued during 1941 were printed by Harrison and ons following bomb damage to the De La Rue works on 9 December 1940. The used price quoted for No. 111 is for an xample with clearly identifiable 1941 cancellation.

During shortages in 1941 stamps of STRAITS SETTLEMENTS (2c. green) and SELANGOR (2c. orange (both perfs), 3c.) were issued in Perak.

948 (1 Dec). *Royal Silver Wedding. As Nos. 112/13 of Antigua.*
22 10c. violet 15 10
23 $5 green 22·00 28·00

949 (10 Oct). *75th Anniv of U.P.U. As Nos. 114/17 of Antigua.*
24 10c. purple 15 10
25 15c. deep blue 1·50 2·00
26 25c. orange 30 1·75
27 50c. blue-black 1·25 3·50
24/7 *Set of* 4 2·75 6·50

52 Sultan Yussuf 'Izzuddin Shah

950 (17 Aug)–**56**. *Chalk-surfaced paper.* Wmk Mult Script CA. P $17\frac{1}{2}\times18$.
28 **52** 1c. black 10 10
29 2c. orange 20 10
30 3c. green 2·50 10
a. Yellowish green (15.11.51) 9·00 5·50
31 4c. brown 50 10
a. Yellow-brown (20.6.56) 6·50 10
32 5c. bright purple (1.9.52) 50 2·00
a. Bright mauve (10.11.54) 1·25 2·00
33 6c. grey 30 10
34 8c. scarlet 65 2·25
35 8c. green (1.9.52) 1·00 1·00
36 10c. purple 20 10
a. Brown-purple (20.6.56) 6·00 30
37 12c. scarlet (1.9.52) 1·00 4·00
38 15c. ultramarine 1·00 10
39 20c. black and green 1·00 65
40 20c. bright blue (1.9.52) 75 10
41 25c. purple and orange 50 10
42 30c. scarlet and purple (4.9.55) 1·50 20
43 35c. scarlet and purple (1.9.52) 1·00 25
44 40c. red and purple 2·75 6·00
45 50c. black and blue 2·75 10
46 $1 blue and purple 7·00 1·00
47 $2 green and scarlet 13·00 7·00
48 $5 green and brown 38·00 14·00
28/48 *Set of* 21 65·00 35·00

STAMP BOOKLETS

35.
31 $1 booklet containing twenty 5c. (No. 91) in blocks of 10
32 $1.30 booklet containing 5c. and 8c. (Nos. 91, 93), each in block of 10

38.
33 $1 booklet containing twenty 5c. (No. 108) in blocks of 10
34 $1.30 booklet containing 5c. and 8c. (Nos. 108, 110), each in block of 10

OFFICIAL STAMPS

P.G.S. (O 1) **Service.** (O 2)

1889 (1 Nov). *Stamps of Straits Settlements optd Type* O **1**. Wmk Crown CC (Nos. O6 and O8) or Crown CA (others).
O1 2c. bright rose 3·50 4·75
a. Opt double £750 £750
b. Wide space between "G" and "S" 55·00 70·00
c. No stop after "S" 55·00 70·00
O2 4c. brown 11·00 20·00
a. Wide space between "G" and "S" 80·00 £100
b. No stop after "S" £130 £150
c. Broken oval £200
w. Wmk inverted 80·00
O3 6c. lilac 23·00 45·00
a. Wide space between "G" and "S" £130 £170
O4 8c. orange 29·00 65·00
a. Wide space between "G" and "S" £160 £225
O5 10c. slate 75·00 75·00
a. Wide space between "G" and "S" £300 £300
O6 12c. blue (CC) £200 £250
a. Wide space between "G" and "S" £700
O7 12c. brown-purple (CA) £250 £325
a. Wide space between "G" and "S" £800
O8 24c. green (CC) £750 £850
a. Wide space between "G" and "S" £2250
O9 24c. green (CA) £180 £200
a. Wide space between "G" and "S" £650

Nos. O1/9 were overprinted from a setting of 30 (3 × 10). The variety "wide space between G and S" occurs on R. 10/3 and R. 10/6 of the original printing. A later printing of the 2c. and 4c. values had this variety corrected, but was without a stop after "S" on R. 10/1 and R. 10/4.

The broken oval flaw occurs on R. 10/5 (lower right pane) of the basic stamp. For illustration see Straits Settlements.

1894 (1 June). *No. 64 optd with Type* O **2**.
O10 5c. blue 70·00 1·00
a. Overprint inverted £850 £475

1897. *No. 70 optd with Type* O **2**.
O11 5c. dull purple and olive-yellow 2·25 50
a. Overprint double £550 £400

PERLIS

Suzerainty over Perlis was transferred by Thailand to Great Britain in 1909. A Treaty of Friendship between Great Britain and Perlis was signed on 28 April 1930.

The State joined the Federation of Malaya on 1 February 1948.

For stamps of THAILAND used in Perlis between 1894 and 1909 see SIAMESE POSTS IN NORTHERN MALAYA section.

Issues of the FEDERATED MALAY STATES were in use from 10 July 1909 until 1912 and these were replaced by the stamps of KEDAH between 1912 and 1941.

1948 (1 Dec). *Royal Silver Wedding. As Nos. 112/13 of Antigua.*
1 10c. violet 30 2·75
2 $5 brown 29·00 45·00

1949 (10 Oct). *75th Anniv of U.P.U. As Nos. 114/17 of Antigua.*
3 10c. purple 30 1·50
4 15c. deep blue 1·25 3·25
5 25c. orange 45 2·00
6 50c. blue-black 1·00 3·75
3/6 *Set of* 4 2·75 9·50

1 Raja Syed Putra

1951 (26 Mar)–**55**. *Chalk-surfaced paper.* Wmk Mult Script CA. P $17\frac{1}{2}\times18$.
7 **1** 1c. black 20 1·00
8 2c. orange 75 50
9 3c. green 1·50 2·75
10 4c. brown 1·25 30
11 5c. bright purple (1.9.52) 50 3·00
12 6c. grey 1·50 1·25
13 8c. scarlet 2·25 4·75
14 8c. green (1.9.52) 75 3·50
15 10c. purple 50 30
a. Error. St. Edward's Crown W **9***b* £3500
16 12c. scarlet (1.9.52) 75 2·50
17 15c. ultramarine 4·00 4·25
18 20c. black and green 2·25 6·50
19 20c. bright blue (1.9.52) 1·00 70
20 25c. purple and orange 1·75 1·75
21 30c. scarlet and purple (4.9.55) 1·75 9·00
22 35c. scarlet and purple (1.9.52) 75 4·00
23 40c. red and purple 3·25 18·00
24 50c. black and blue 4·00 4·25
25 $1 blue and purple 7·50 20·00
26 $2 green and scarlet 14·00 32·00
27 $5 green and brown 50·00 80·00
7/27 *Set of* 21 90·00 £180

SELANGOR

The first British Resident was appointed in 1874. Selangor joined the Federated Malay States in 1896.

The stamps of the STRAITS SETTLEMENTS were used in Selangor from 1879 until 1881.

Until 1 January 1899, when the Federated Malay States joined the U.P.U., mail for addresses outside Malaya was franked with stamps of the STRAITS SETTLEMENTS.

PRICES FOR STAMPS ON COVER TO 1945	
Nos. 1/8	—
Nos. 9/19	*from* × 10
Nos. 20/30	*from* × 12
Nos. 31/3	*from* × 25
Nos. 34/6	*from* × 20
Nos. 37/8	*from* × 15
Nos. 38*a*/40	—
Nos. 41/2	*from* × 8
Nos. 43	—
Nos. 44/8	*from* × 8
Nos. 49/53	*from* × 30
Nos. 54/66	*from* × 10
Nos. 66*a*/7	*from* × 4
Nos. 68/85	*from* × 3
Nos. 86/7	*from* × 4

The Straits Settlements 1867 2c. brown with Crown CC watermark (No. 11) has been known since 1881 overprinted in black with a cresent and star over a capital S, all within an oval, similar in style to the overprints listed for Perak and Sungei Ujong.

The status of this item remains unclear, but it may well represent the first issue of distinctive stamps for Selangor. This overprint should not be confused with a somewhat similar cancellation used on Selangor stamps of the same period. This cancellation differs in having a circular frame with the capital S shown above the cresent and star. It is usually struck in red.

A similar overprint in red on the Straits Settlements 2c. brown with Crown CA watermark also exists and may have been produced for sale to collectors (*Price* £275, *unused*).

SELANCOR (**1**) ("S" inverted and narrow letters) · SELANCOR (**2**) ("S" wide) · SELANCOR (**3**) (narrow letters)

SELANCOR (**4**) ("N" wide) · SELANCOR (**5**) ("SE" and "AN" wide) · SELANCOR (**6**) ("SEL" and "N" wide)

SELANCOR (**7**) ("SELAN" wide)

1881–82. *No. 11* (wmk Crown CC) *of Straits Settlements optd with T* **1/7**.
1 **1** 2c. brown £450 £475
2 **2** 2c. brown £160 £170
3 **3** 2c. brown £100 £100
4 **4** 2c. brown £5500 £2000
5 **5** 2c. brown (1882) £200 £200
6 **6** 2c. brown (1882) £200 £200
7 **7** 2c. brown (1882) £200 £200

Nos. 1/3 and 5/7 have been identified as coming from triplet settings, either Nos. 1+2+3, 2+3+3 or 5+6+7. The setting for No. 4 is unknown.

S. (**8**)

1882. *No. 50* (wmk Crown CA) *of Straits Settlements optd with T* **8**.
8 **8** 2c. brown — £2500

SELANGOR (**9**) ("SEL" and "NG" wide) · SELANGOR (**10**) ("E" and "ANG" wide) · SELANGOR (**11**) ("ELANG" wide)

SELANCOR (**12**) ("S" and "L" wide) · SELANCOR (**13**) ("S" and "A" wide) · SELANCOR (**14**) ("E" wide)

SELANCOR (**15**) ("EL" wide) · SELANCOR (**16**) ("SE" and "N" wide) · SELANCOR (**17**) ("S" and "N" wide)

1882–83. *No. 50* (wmk Crown CA) *of Straits Settlements optd with T* **2/3** *and* **9/17**.
9 **9** 2c. brown £250 £250
10 **10** 2c. brown £250 £250
11 **11** 2c. brown £250 £250
12 **2** 2c. brown (1883) £150 £120
13 **3** 2c. brown (1883) £275 £120
14 **12** 2c. brown (1883) — £3000
15 **13** 2c. brown (1883) £500 £450
16 **14** 2c. brown (1883) £350 £275
17 **15** 2c. brown (1883) £350 £275
18 **16** 2c. brown (1883) £160 £150
a. Opt double £900
19 **17** 2c. brown (1883) £160 £150

The above were all printed from triplet settings. Those so far identified are Nos. 9+10+11, 12 (with defective "G") +13+13, 15+16+17 and 18+12+19. No. 14 occurs as the first position of a triplet, but the second and third units are not yet known.

SELANCOR (**18**) ("E" and "A" wide) · SELANCOR (**19**) ("A" wide) · SELANCOR (**20**) ("L" wide)

SELANGOR (**21**) ("L" narrow) · SELANGOR (**22**) ("A" narrow) · SELANGOR (**23**) (wide letters)

1883–85. *No. 63 of Straits Settlements optd with T* **2**, **4**, **12**, **14/15** *and* **18/23**.
20 **12** 2c. pale rose £180 £150
21 **14** 2c. pale rose £120 £100
a. Opt double
22 **4** 2c. pale rose (1884) £180 £150
23 **15** 2c. pale rose (1884) £100 90·00
a. Opt double £800
b. Opt triple
24 **2** 2c. pale rose (1884) £120 90·00
25 **18** 2c. pale rose (1884) £120 90·00
26 **19** 2c. pale rose (1884) £325 £160
27 **20** 2c. pale rose (1884) £400 £190
28 **21** 2c. pale rose (1885) 95·00 85·00
29 **22** 2c. pale rose (1885) £170 £130
30 **23** 2c. pale rose (1885) £375 £180

The above come from triplet settings with Nos. 20+21+21, 22+22+23, 23+26 (with defective "A") +26, 24+25+23 and 28+29+28 so far identified. The triplets for Nos. 27 and 30 are not known.

SELANGOR (24) Selangor (25) SELANGOR (26)

SELANGOR (27) SELANGOR (28) SELANGOR (29) SELANGOR (30)

SELANGOR (31) SELANGOR (32) SELANGOR (33) SELANGOR (34)

1885–91. *Nos. 63/a of Straits Settlements optd with T* **24/34**.

No.	Type	Description	Unused	Used
31	24	2c. pale rose	10·00	21·00
		a. Opt double	£850	£750
		w. Wmk inverted	—	£250
32	25	2c. pale rose	£1100	£1200
33	26	2c. pale rose	32·00	38·00
34	27	2c. pale rose (1886)	50·00	50·00
		a. Opt double	†	£700
35	28	2c. pale rose (horiz opt without stop) (1887)	9·00	2·75
		a. Opt double	£700	
		b. Bright rose	10·00	2·25
36		2c. pale rose (horiz opt with stop) (1887)	90·00	65·00
		a. Bright rose		
37	29	2c. pale rose (1889)	£180	80·00
38	30	2c. pale rose (vert opt) (1889)	70·00	6·00
		a. Bright rose		
38*b*		2c. bright rose (horiz opt) (1889)	£3250	
39	31	2c. pale rose (diagonal opt) (1889)	£1800	
40	32	2c. pale rose (1889)	£475	27·00
41	28	2c. brt rose (vert opt without stop) (1890)	16·00	27·00
42	33	2c. bright rose (1890)	£110	3·00
		a. Opt double		
43	34	2c. bright rose (1891)	£325	£150

Settings:
Nos. 31/4 – each in triplet containing three examples of the same stamp
No. 35 – triplet or 60 (6 × 10)
No. 36 – 60 (6 × 10)
Nos. 37/8 – 60 (6 × 10) containing both overprints in an unknown combination, but with No. 38 predominating
Nos. 38*b*/9 – not known
Nos. 40/3 – each in 60 (6 × 10)

SELANGOR Two CENTS (35) SELANGOR Two CENTS (36) SELANGOR Two CENTS (37)

SELANGOR Two CENTS (38) SELANGOR Two CENTS (39)

1891. *No. 68 of Straits Settlements, surch with T* **35/9**, *each with bar obliterating old value.*

No.	Type	Description	Unused	Used
44	35	2c.on 24c. green	27·00	65·00
45	36	2c.on 24c. green	£170	£225
46	37	2c.on 24c. green	£170	£225
47	38	2c.on 24c. green	90·00	£130
		a. "SELANGCR"		
48	39	2c.on 24c. green	£170	£225

Nos. 44/8 come from the one setting used to surcharge the panes of sixty. No. 44 occurs in rows 1 to 5, No. 45 on row 6, No. 46 on row 7, No. 47 on rows 8 and 9, and No. 48 on row 10.

The error, No. 47a, occurs in the first printing only and is No. 45 (R.8/3) on the pane.

40

3 CENTS (41)

1891 (1 Nov)–**95**. Wmk Crown CA. P 14.

No.	Type	Description	Unused	Used
49	40	1c. green (5.93)	1·50	25
50		2c. rose	3·50	1·00
51		2c. orange (27.5.95)	2·50	80
52		5c. blue (8.92)	24·00	4·75
49/52 *Set of* 4			28·00	6·00
49s/52s Optd "Specimen" *Set of* 4			90·00	

1894 (Dec). *Surch with T* **41**. Wmk Crown CA. P 14.

No.	Type	Description	Unused	Used
53	40	3c.on 5c. rose	3·50	50
		s. Optd "Specimen"	35·00	

42

43

Dented frame above "A" of "SELANGOR" (left pane R. 4/5)

1895–99. Wmk Crown CA or Crown CC (dollar values). P 14.

No.	Type	Description	Unused	Used
54	42	3c. dull purple and carmine	6·50	30
55		5c. dull purple and olive-yellow	4·00	30
56		8c. dull purple and ultramarine (1898)	48·00	7·00
57		10c. dull purple and orange	9·00	1·75
58		25c. green and carmine (1896)	80·00	50·00
59		50c. dull purple and greenish black (1896)	60·00	22·00
		a. Dented frame	£375	
60		50c. green and black (1898)	£400	£120
		a. Dented frame		
61	43	$1 green and yellow-green	50·00	£130
62		$2 green and carmine (1897)	£200	£200
63		$3 green and ochre (1897)	£450	£350
64		$5 green and blue	£250	£300
65		$10 green and purple (1899)	£600	£750
		s. Optd "Specimen"	£120	
66		$25 green and orange (1899?)	£2500	
		s. Optd "Specimen"	£225	
54/62 *Set of* 9			£750	£475
54s/64s Optd "Specimen" *Set of* 11			£350	

Pending the arrival of the permanent Federated Malay States issue the stamps of STRAITS SETTLEMENTS and PERAK were used at various times between July 1900 and March 1901.

The general issues for the FEDERATED MALAY STATES were used in Selangor from 1901 until 1935.

One cent. (44) Three cents. (45)

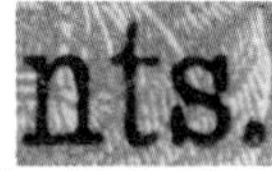
Antique "t" (R. 3/4 and 8/4)

1900 (Oct). *Nos. 55 and 59 surch with T* **44** *or* **45**.

No.	Type	Description	Unused	Used
66*a*	42	1c.on 5c. dull purple & ol-yell (31 Oct*)	60·00	£120
66*b*		1c.on 50c. green and black (22 Oct*)	2·50	21·00
		bc. "cent" repeated at left	£2000	
		bd. Dented frame	85·00	
67		3c.on 50c. green and black (30 Oct*)	4·00	21·00
		a. Antique "t" in "cents"	£300	£400
		b. Dented frame	£200	

*Earliest known postmark date.

It is believed that these stamps were surcharged from settings of 30, repeated four times to complete the sheet of 120.

No. 66bc occurred on two separate vertical strips of five stamps where two impressions of the setting overlapped.

46 Mosque at Palace, Klang

47 Sultan Suleiman

(Des E. J. McNaughton)

1935 (2 Dec)–**41**. Wmk Mult Script CA (sideways on *T* **46**). *Chalk-surfaced paper*. P 14 or 14 × 14½ (No. 70).

No.	Type	Description	Unused	Used
68	46	1c. black (1.1.36)	30	10
69		2c. green (1.1.36)	90	10
70		2c. orange (*ordinary paper*) (P 14 × 14½) (21.8.41)	3·50	75
		a. Perf 14. Ordinary paper (9.41)	20·00	2·00
71		3c. green (21.8.41)	16·00	2·75
		a. Ordinary paper	1·25	8·00
72		4c. orange	50	10
73		5c. brown (5.12.35)	70	10
74		6c. scarlet (1.1.37)	5·50	10
75		8c. grey	60	10
76		10c. dull purple (1.1.36)	60	10
77		12c. bright ultramarine (1.1.36)	1·00	10
78		15c. brt ultram (*ordinary paper*) (1.10.41)	12·00	32·00
79		25c. dull purple and scarlet (1.4.36)	1·00	60
80		30c. dull purple and orange (1.1.36)	1·00	85
81		40c. scarlet and dull purple	1·50	1·00
82		50c. black/*emerald* (1.2.36)	1·00	15
83	47	$1 black and rose/*blue* (1.4.36)	7·50	90
84		$2 green and scarlet (16.5.36)	23·00	8·00
85		$5 green and red/*emerald* (16.5.36)	65·00	23·00
68/85 *Set of* 18			£110	60·00
68s/85s Perf "Specimen" *Set of* 18			£350	

The stamps issued during 1941 were printed by Harrison and Sons following bomb damage to the De La Rue works on 29 December 1940.

No. 69 exists in coils constructed from normal sheets.

Supplies of an unissued 8c. scarlet were diverted to Australia in 1941. Examples circulating result from leakages of this supply (*Price* £500).

48 Sultan Hisamud-din Alam Shah

49 Sultan Hisamud-din Alam Shah

1941. Wmk Mult Script CA. *Chalk-surfaced paper*. P 14.

No.	Type	Description	Unused	Used
86	48	$1 black and red/*blue* (15.4.41)	15·00	6·0
87		$2 green and scarlet (7.7.41)	48·00	27·0
		s. Perf "Specimen"	70·00	

A $5 green and red on emerald, *T* **48**, was issued overprinted during the Japanese occupation of Malaya. Unoverprinted examples are known, but were not issued (*Price* £110).

During shortages in 1941 stamps of STRAITS SETTLEMENTS (2c.) and PERAK (25c.) were issued in Selangor.

1948 (1 Dec). *Royal Silver Wedding. As Nos. 112/13 of Antigua.*

No.	Description	Unused	Used
88	10c. violet	20	2
89	$5 green	26·00	16·0

1949 (12 Sept)–**55**. Wmk Mult Script CA. *Chalk-surfaced paper*. P 17½ × 18.

No.	Type	Description	Unused	Used
90	49	1c. black	10	6
91		2c. orange	10	7
92		3c. green	1·75	1·5
93		4c. brown	20	1
94		5c. bright purple (1.9.52)	30	2·0
		a. Bright mauve (17.9.53)	30	6
95		6c. grey	20	4
96		8c. scarlet	35	6
97		8c. green (1.9.52)	65	1·7
98		10c. purple	10	1
99		12c. scarlet (1.9.52)	80	3·5
		w. Wmk inverted	£325	
100		15c. ultramarine	4·00	1
101		20c. black and green	2·00	3
102		20c. bright blue (1.9.52)	80	1
103		25c. purple and orange	2·00	2
104		30c. scarlet and purple (4.9.55)	2·00	2·2
105		35c. scarlet and purple (1.9.52)	70	1·5
106		40c. scarlet and purple	7·00	6·0
107		50c. black and blue	2·25	1
108		$1 blue and purple	3·00	6
109		$2 green and scarlet	13·00	6
110		$5 green and brown	45·00	2·2
90/110 *Set of* 21			75·00	21·0

1949 (10 Oct). *75th Anniv of U.P.U. As Nos. 114/17 of Antigua.*

No.	Description	Unused	Used
111	10c. purple	30	
112	15c. deep blue	2·00	2·
113	25c. orange	35	3·2
114	50c. blue-black	1·00	3·2
111/14 *Set of* 4		3·25	8·(

STAMP BOOKLETS

1935. *Stapled.*

SB1 $1 booklet containing twenty 5c. (No. 73) in blocks of 10

SB2 $1.30 booklet containing 5c. and 8c. (Nos. 73, 75), each in block of 10

TRENGGANU

Suzerainty over Trengganu was transferred by Thailand to Great Britain in 1909. A British adviser was appointed in 1919.

The state joined the Federation of Malaya on 1 February 1948.

PRICES FOR STAMPS ON COVER TO 1945	
Nos. 1/17	*from* × 12
No. 18	—
Nos. 19/22	*from* × 10
Nos. 23/33	*from* × 12
Nos. 34/6	—
Nos. 37/47	*from* × 15
Nos. 48/60	*from* × 6
Nos. D1/4	—

1 Sultan Zain ul ab din

2 Sultan Zain ul ab din

RED CROSS 2c. (3)

1910 (14 Dec)–**19**. Wmk Mult Crown CA. *Ordinary paper* (1c. to 10c.) *or chalk-surfaced paper* (20c. to $25). P 14.

No.	Type	Description	Unused	Used
1	1	1c. blue-green	1·75	1·
		a. Green	2·75	1·
2		2c. brown and purple (1915)	1·00	
3		3c. carmine-red	2·25	2·
4		4c. orange	3·50	5·
5		4c. red-brown and green (1915)	2·00	3·
5*a*		4c. carmine-red (1919)	1·25	1·

No.	Type	Description	Unused	Used
6		5c. grey	1·25	3·25
7		5c. grey and brown (1915)	2·25	2·00
8		8c. ultramarine	1·25	9·00
9		10c. purple/*yellow*	5·00	13·00
		a. On pale yellow	3·25	5·00
10		10c. green and red/*yellow* (1915)	1·25	2·25
11		20c. dull and bright purple	3·50	4·25
12		25c. green and dull purple (1915)	8·00	32·00
13		30c. dull purple and black (1915)	6·50	55·00
14		50c. black/*green*	4·50	8·50
15		$1 black and carmine/*blue*	17·00	24·00
16		$3 green and red/*green* (1915)	£160	£325
17	2	$5 green and dull purple (1912)	£160	£450
18		$25 rose-carmine and green (1912)	£950	£1700
		s. Optd "Specimen"	£250	
1/17 *Set of* 18			£350	£850
1s/17s Optd "Specimen" *Set of* 18			£550	

The 8c. is known used bisected at Kretai in December 1918. Such use was not officially authorised.

1917 (June)–**18**. *Surch with T* **3**.

No.	Type	Description	Unused	Used
19	1	2c.on 3c. carmine-red	50	7·00
		a. Comma after "2c."	10·00	38·00
		b. "SS" in "CROSS" inverted	£325	£400
		c. "CSOSS" for "CROSS"	95·00	£190
		d. "2" in thick block type	22·00	60·00
		e. Surch inverted	£800	£850
		f. Pair, one without surch	£3250	£2750
		g. "RED CROSS" omitted	£275	
		h. "RED CROSS" twice	£350	
		i. "2c." omitted	£275	
		j. "2c." twice	£325	
20		2c.on 4c. orange	1·50	15·00
		a. Comma after "2c."	18·00	65·00
		b. "SS" in "CROSS" inverted	£1600	£1100
		c. "CSOSS" for "CROSS"	£170	£375
		d. Surch double	£900	
		e. "RED CROSS" omitted	£325	
		f. "RED CROSS" twice	£475	
		g. "2c." omitted	£325	
		h. "2c." twice	£425	
21		2c.on 4c. red-brown and green (1918)	3·25	38·00
		a. Pair, one without surch	£2000	
22		2c.on 8c. ultramarine (1917)	1·25	28·00
		a. Comma after "2c."	11·00	80·00
		b. "SS" in "CROSS" inverted	£700	
		c. "CSOSS" for "CROSS"	£150	£400
		d. "RED CROSS" omitted	£325	
		e. "RED CROSS" twice	£425	
		f. "2c." omitted	£325	
		g. "2c." twice	£400	

The surcharges on Nos. 19/22 were arranged in settings of 18 (6 × 3) applied three times to cover the top nine rows of the sheet with the tenth row completed by a further impression so that "RED CROSS" from the centre row of the setting appears on the bottom sheet margin. Specialists recognise six different settings:

Setting I	– Shows comma after "2" on both R. 1/3 and 1/5, "SS" inverted on R. 1/6 and "CSOSS" for "CROSS" on R. 2/1. Used for 4c. orange and 8c.
Setting Ia	– Inverted "SS" on R. 1/6 corrected. Other varieties as Setting I. Used for 3c., 4c. orange and 8c.
Setting II	– "CSOSS" on R. 2/1 corrected. Comma varieties as Setting I. Used for 3c., 4c. orange and 8c.
Setting III	– Both comma varieties now corrected. Used for 3c., both 4c. and 8c.
Setting IIIa	– "SS" inverted on R. 2/5. Used for 3c. only
Setting IV	– Thick block "2" on R. 2/2. Inverted "SS" on R. 2/5 corrected. Used for 3c. only.

Nos. 19g/j, 20e/h and 22d/g result from the misplacement of the surcharge.

During a temporary shortage between March and August 1921 2c., 4c. and 6c. stamps of the STRAITS SETTLEMENTS were authorised for use in Trengganu.

4 Sultan Suleiman

5 Sultan Suleiman

2 CENTS
(6)

1921–41. *Chalk-surfaced paper*. P 14.

(a) Wmk Mult Crown CA.

No.	Type	Description	Unused	Used
23	4	$1 purple and blue/*blue*	12·00	23·00
24		$3 green and red/*emerald*	£100	£225
25	5	$5 green and red/*pale yellow*	£110	£300
23/5 *Set of* 3			£200	£500
23s/5s Optd "Specimen" *Set of* 3			£140	

(b) Wmk Mult Script CA.

No.	Type	Description	Unused	Used
	4	1c. black (1926)	1·75	1·50
		a. Ordinary paper (1941)	—	30·00
		2c. green	1·25	2·00
		a. Ordinary paper (1941)	—	30·00
		3c. green (1926)	2·00	1·00
		3c. reddish brown (1938)	24·00	14·00
		a. Ordinary paper. *Chestnut* (1941)	—	20·00
		4c. rose-red	1·50	1·25
		a. Ordinary paper. *Scarlet-verm* (1941)	£225	25·00
		5c. grey and deep brown	2·00	5·00
		5c. purple/*yellow* (1926)	1·75	1·25
		a. Deep reddish purple/brt yellow (1939)	£225	5·00
		6c. orange (1924)	3·75	50
		a. Ordinary paper (1941)	—	35·00
		8c. grey (1938)	27·00	6·00
		a. Ordinary paper (1941)	—	23·00
		10c. bright blue	2·00	1·00
		12c. bright ultramarine (1926)	4·25	4·50
		20c. dull purple and orange	2·25	1·50
38		25c. green and deep purple	2·25	3·00
39		30c. dull purple and black	3·25	3·75
40		35c. carmine/*yellow* (1926)	4·75	8·00
41		50c. green and bright carmine	7·50	3·25
42		$1 purple and blue/*blue* (1929)	9·00	3·75
43		$3 green and lake/*green* (1926)	55·00	£150
		a. Green and brown-red/green (1938)	£140	
44	5	$5 green and red/*yellow* (1938)	£300	£1700
45		$25 purple and blue	£650	£1100
		s. Optd "Specimen"	£140	
46		$50 green and yellow	£1600	£2750
		s. Optd "Specimen"	£300	
47		$100 green and scarlet	£5000	£6000
		s. Optd "Specimen"	£550	
26/44 *Set of* 19			£400	£1800
26s/44s Optd or Perf (3c., 8c., $1, $5) "Specimen" *Set of* 19			£700	

The used price quoted for No. 44 is for an example with an identifiable cancellation from 1938–41.

Printings of the 2c. yellow-orange, 3c. blue-green, 4c. purple/*yellow*, 6c. slate-grey, 8c. rose, 15c. ultramarine and $1 black and red/*blue* on ordinary paper were despatched to Malaya in late 1941, but did not arrive before the Japanese occupation. Unused examples are known of the 2, 3, 6, 8 and 15c. (*Prices*, 3c. £350, *others* £160 *each, unused*).

OVERPRINT SETTINGS FOR NOS. 48/58. The low values in Types **1** and **4** were overprinted using Setting II as detailed under Straits Settlements. The three listed constant varieties from the original typeset block of 12 occur in the same positions for these Trengganu stamps as does the No stop variety from R. 1/5 of the left pane.

A separate setting, believed to be of 30 (6 × 5), was required for the $5 in the larger design. This was constructed by duplicating the second horizontal row of the original typeset block five times so that the raised stop after "EXHIBITION" variety occurs on all stamps in the second vertical row and the small second "A" in "MALAYA" on all stamps in the sixth.

1922 (Apr). *Malaya-Borneo Exhibition, Singapore. Optd as T* **56** *of Straits Settlements at Singapore.*

No.	Type	Description	Unused	Used
48	4	2c. green	4·75	27·00
		b. Oval last "O" in "BORNEO"	9·50	48·00
		c. Raised stop after "EXHIBITION"	9·50	48·00
		d. Small second "A" in "MALAYA"	9·50	48·00
		f. No stop		
49		4c. rose-red	6·50	35·00
		b. Oval last "O" in "BORNEO"	13·00	60·00
		c. Raised stop after "EXHIBITION"	13·00	60·00
		d. Small second "A" in "MALAYA"	13·00	60·00
		f. No stop		
50	1	5c. grey and brown	3·25	40·00
		b. Oval last "O" in "BORNEO"	7·00	65·00
		c. Raised stop after "EXHIBITION"	7·00	65·00
		d. Small second "A" in "MALAYA"	7·00	65·00
		f. No stop		
51		10c. green and red/*yellow*	5·50	32·00
		b. Oval last "O" in "BORNEO"	11·00	55·00
		c. Raised stop after "EXHIBITION"	11·00	55·00
		d. Small second "A" in "MALAYA"	11·00	55·00
		f. No stop		
52		20c. dull and bright purple	5·50	35·00
		b. Oval last "O" in "BORNEO"	11·00	60·00
		c. Raised stop after "EXHIBITION"	11·00	60·00
		d. Small second "A" in "MALAYA"	11·00	60·00
		f. No stop		
53		25c. green and dull purple	4·75	35·00
		b. Oval last "O" in "BORNEO"	9·50	60·00
		c. Raised stop after "EXHIBITION"	9·50	60·00
		d. Small second "A" in "MALAYA"	9·50	60·00
		f. No stop		
54		30c. dull purple and black	5·50	35·00
		b. Oval last "O" in "BORNEO"	11·00	60·00
		c. Raised stop after "EXHIBITION"	11·00	60·00
		d. Small second "A" in "MALAYA"	11·00	60·00
		f. No stop		
55		50 c. black/*green*	5·50	35·00
		b. Oval last "O" in "BORNEO"	11·00	60·00
		c. Raised stop after "EXHIBITION"	11·00	60·00
		d. Small second "A" in "MALAYA"	11·00	60·00
		f. No stop		
56		$1 black and carmine/*blue*	14·00	70·00
		b. Oval last "O" in "BORNEO"	24·00	£120
		c. Raised stop after "EXHIBITION"	24·00	£120
		d. Small second "A" in "MALAYA"	24·00	£120
		f. No stop		
57		$3 green and red/*green*	£140	£375
		b. Oval last "O" in "BORNEO"	£200	£550
		c. Raised stop after "EXHIBITION"	£200	£550
		d. Small second "A" in "MALAYA"	£200	£550
		f. No stop		
58	2	$5 green and dull purple	£250	£650
		c. Raised stop after "EXHIBITION"	£325	£800
		d. Small second "A" in "MALAYA"	£325	£800
48/58 *Set of* 11			£400	£1200

1941 (1 May). *Nos. 32a and 35 surch as T* **6**.

No.	Type	Description	Unused	Used
59	4	2c.on 5c. deep reddish purple/*brt yellow*	6·50	3·50
60		8c.on 10c. bright blue	7·00	4·00

1948 (2 Dec). *Royal Silver Wedding. As Nos. 112/13 of Antigua.*

No.	Description	Unused	Used
61	10c. violet	15	1·75
62	$5 carmine	24·00	40·00

1949 (10 Oct). *75th Anniv of U.P.U. As Nos. 114/17 of Antigua.*

No.	Description	Unused	Used
63	10c. purple	30	75
64	15c. deep blue	1·90	3·00
65	25c. orange	40	2·25
66	50c. blue-black	1·00	3·50
	a. "C" of "CA" missing from wmk		
63/6 *Set of* 4		3·25	8·50

7 Sultan Ismail

1949 (27 Dec)–**55**. Wmk Mult Script CA. *Chalk-surfaced paper*. P 17½ × 18.

No.	Type	Description	Unused	Used
67	7	1c. black	15	75
68		2c. orange	20	75
69		3c. green	1·00	3·25
70		4c. brown	20	60
71		5c. bright purple (1.9.52)	30	1·75
72		6c. grey	1·00	60
73		8c. scarlet	30	2·50
74		8c. green (1.9.52)	65	1·75
		a. Deep green (11.8.53)	9·00	9·00
75		10c. purple	30	30
76		12c. scarlet (1.9.52)	65	2·75
77		15c. ultramarine	2·00	30
78		20c. black and green	2·25	3·75
79		20c. bright blue (1.9.52)	80	40
80		25c. purple and orange	1·75	2·00
81		30c. scarlet and purple (4.9.55)	1·25	2·25
82		35c. scarlet and purple (1.9.52)	85	2·25
83		40c. red and purple	5·00	15·00
84		50c. black and blue	2·00	2·25
85		$1 blue and purple	7·00	8·00
86		$2 green and scarlet	27·00	24·00
87		$5 green and brown	50·00	55·00
67/87 *Set of* 21			95·00	£120

POSTAGE DUE STAMPS

D 1

1937 (10 Aug). Wmk Mult Script CA (sideways). P 14.

No.	Type	Description	Unused	Used
D1	D 1	1c. scarlet	7·50	55·00
D2		4c. green	9·50	60·00
D3		8c. yellow	55·00	£325
D4		10c. brown	£110	95·00
D1/4 *Set of* 4			£160	£475
D1s/4s Perf "Specimen" *Set of* 4			£140	

VI. SIAMESE POSTS IN NORTHERN MALAYA 1887–1909

The Thai monarchy exercised suzerainty over the northern states of the Malay Peninsula from the 16th century onwards. The extent of Thai involvement in the internal affairs of Kedah, Kelantan, Perlis and Trengganu was very variable, being dependent on the strength, or otherwise, of the Bangkok administration and the degree of co-operation of the local rulers.

The Thai public postal service, which had been inaugurated in 1883, gradually extended into the north of the Malay Peninsula from 1887 onwards and post offices were established in Kedah, Kelantan and Perlis. There is some evidence that Sultan Zainal Abidin III of Trengganu successfully blocked the use of Siamese stamps in his state.

Types of Thailand (Siam)

1 Att. 1 Att.

ราคา ๑ อัฐ (34) ราคา ๑ อัฐ (35) 1 Att. (36)

2 Atts. 10 Atts.

ราคา ๒ อัฐ (37) 2 Atts. (38) ราคา๑๐อัฐ (39)

4 Atts. (40) 4 Atts. (41)

1 Att.

ราคา ๑ อัฐ (42) 2 Atts. (44) 3 Atts. (45) 4 Atts. (46)

2 Atts. (48a)

1 Att.

49 50 ๑ อัฐ (51)

๔ อัฐ

1att. (56) 9 Atts (59)

The following types of postmark were used on Siamese stamps from the Malay tributary states:

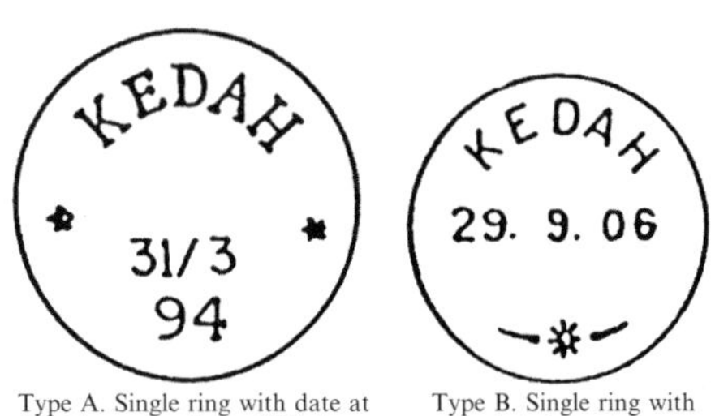

Type A. Single ring with date at foot (examples from 1900 show the year in manuscript)

Type B. Single ring with date in centre

Type C. Double ring. Bilingual

Type D. Double ring. English at top and ornament at foot

Type E. Double ring. English at top and bottom

PRICES are for stamps showing a large part of the postmark with the inscription clearly visible.

KEDAH

The Siamese post office at Alor Star was opened during 1887 with the first known postmark being dated 27 October. Further post offices at Kuala Muda (3 Oct 1907), Kulim (7 July 1907) and Langkawi (16 Feb 1908) followed.

A straight-line obliteration showing "KEDAH" between short vertical dashes is not believed to be genuine.

Alor Star

Stamps of SIAM *cancelled as Type* A *inscribed* "KEDAH".

1883. *(Nos. 1/5).*
Z2 1 1att. rose-carmine . . . £225
Z3 1sio. red . . . £425
Z4 2 1sik. yellow . . . £425

1887–91. *(Nos. 11/18).*
Z 6 9 1a. green . . . 80·00
Z 7 2a. green and carmine . . . 70·00
Z 8 3a. green and blue . . . 90·00
Z 9 4a. green and brown . . . 80·00
Z10 8a. green and yellow . . . 80·00
Z11 12a. purple and carmine . . . 70·00
Z12 24a. purple and blue . . . 80·00
Z13 64a. purple and brown . . . £130

1889–91. *Surch as T* **12** *(Nos. Z15, Z19), T* **17** *(No. Z21) or T* **18** *(No. Z22) (Nos. 20/30).*
Z15 9 1a.on 2a. green and carmine . . . 90·00
Z19 1a.on 3a. green and blue . . . £100
Z21 2a.on 3a. green and blue . . . £130
Z22 2a.on 3a. green and blue . . . £160

1892. *Surch as T* **24/5** *(with or without stop) and Siamese handstamp (Nos. 33/6).*
Z28 9 4a.on 24a. purple and blue (Type **24**) . . . 90·00
Z29 4a.on 24a. purple and blue (Type **25**) . . . £110
Z30 4a.on 24a. purple and blue (Type **24** with stop) . . . £110
Z31 4a.on 24a. purple and blue (Type **25** with stop) . . . £110

1894. *Surch as T* **27** *with variations of English figures as T* **28** *and* **33** *(Nos. 37/44).*
Z34 9 2a.on 64a. purple and brown (Type **28**) . . . 90·00
Z39 2a.on 64a. purple and brown (Type **33**) . . . 90·00

1894. *Surch with T* **34** *(No. 45).*
Z41 9 1a.on 64a. purple and brown . . . £110

1894–95. *Surch as T* **35** *with variations of English figures as T* **36/9** *(Nos. 46/50).*
Z42 9 1a.on 64a. purple and brown (Type **35**) . . . 90·00
Z43 1a.on 64a. purple and brown (Type **36**) . . . 90·00
Z44 2a.on 64a. purple and brown (Type **37**) . . . 90·00
Z45 2a.on 64a. purple and brown (Type **38**) . . . 90·00
Z46 10a.on 24a. purple and blue (Type **39**) . . . 90·00

1896. *Surch as T* **39** *(Siamese) and T* **40** *(English) (No. 51).*
Z47 9 4a.on 12a. purple and carmine . . . 90·00

1897. *Surch as T* **39** *(Siamese) and T* **41** *(English) (No. 52).*
Z48 9 4a.on 12a. purple and carmine . . . 90·00

1898–99. *Surch as T* **42** *with variations of English section as T* **44/6** *(Nos. 53/62).*
Z49 9 1a.on 12a. purple and carmine (Type **42**–11½ mm long) . . . £120
Z52 2a.on 64a. purple and brown (Type **44**) . . . £100
Z53 3a.on 12a. purple and carmine (Type **45**–13½ mm long) . . . 90·00
Z54 3a.on 12a. purple and carmine (Type **45**–11½ to 11¾ mm long) . . . 90·00
Z55 4a.on 12a. purple & carm (Type **46**–8 mm long) . . . 90·00
Z56 4a.on 12a. purple and carmine (Type **46**–8½ to 9 mm long) . . . 90·00

1899. *Surch in Siamese and English with T* **48a** *(Nos. 63/6).*
Z62 9 2a.on 64a. purple and brown . . . £100

1899–1904. *(Nos. 67/81).*
Z63 49 1a. olive-green (wide Siamese characters in face value) . . . 90·00
Z64 2a. grass-green . . . 70·00
Z65 3a. red and blue . . . 75·00
Z66 4a. carmine . . . 70·00
Z67 8a. deep green and orange . . . 70·00
Z69 12a. brown-purple and carmine . . . £110
Z70 24a. brown-purple and blue . . . £160
Z71 64a. brown-purple and chestnut . . . £130

1899. *(Nos. 82/6).*
Z72 50 1a. green . . . £275
Z73 2a. green and red . . . £425

Stamps of SIAM *cancelled as Type* B *inscr* "KEDAH" *(from* March 1901).

1887–91. *(Nos. 11/18).*
Z74 9 12a. purple and carmine . . . 70·00
Z75 24a. purple and brown . . . 70·00

1898–99. *Surch with T* **42** *with variations of English section as T* **45/6** *(Nos. 53/62).*
Z76 9 1a.on 12a. pur & carm (Type **42**–11½ mm long) . . . 90·00
Z81 3a.on 12a. purple and carmine (Type **45**–11½ to 11¾ mm long) . . . 70·00
Z83 4a.on 12a. purple and carmine (Type **46**–8½ to 9 mm long) . . . 70·00
Z84 4a.on 24a. purple and blue (Type **46**) . . . 75·00

1899–1904. *(Nos. 67/81).*
Z86 49 1a. olive-green (wide Siamese characters in face value) . . . 70·00
a. Narrow Siamese characters in face value . . . 65·00
Z87 2a. grass-green . . . 55·00
Z88 2a. scarlet and pale blue . . . 55·00
Z89 3a. red and blue . . . 65·00
Z90 3a. deep green . . . 65·00
Z91 4a. carmine . . . 55·00
Z92 4a. chocolate and pink . . . 60·00
Z93 8a. deep green and orange . . . 55·00
Z94 10a. ultramarine . . . 55·00
Z95 12a. brown-purple and carmine . . . 65·00
Z96 24a. brown-purple and blue . . . £13
Z97 64a. brown-purple and chestnut . . . £12

1905–09. *(Nos. 92/105).*
Z102 53 1a. green and orange . . . 55·0
Z103 2a. grey and deep violet . . . 55·0
Z104 3a. green . . . 65·0
Z105 4a. pale red and sepia . . . 55·0
Z106 5a. carmine . . . 65·0
Z107 8a. olive-bistre and dull black . . . 55·0
Z108 12a. blue . . . 65·0
Z109 24a. red-brown . . . £16
Z110 1t. bistre and deep blue . . . £16

Stamps of SIAM *cancelled as Type* C *inscr* "Kedah" *at foot (fro*
July 1907).

1887–91. *(Nos. 11/18).*
Z111 9 12a. purple and carmine . . . 80·0

1899–1904. *(Nos.67/81).*
Z112 49 1a. olive-green (wide Siamese characters in face value) . . . 65·
a. Narrow Siamese characters in face value . . . 60·
Z113 2a. scarlet and pale blue . . . 55·
Z114 3a. red and blue . . . 65·
Z116 8a. deep green and orange . . . 65·0
Z117 10a. ultramarine . . . 60·0
Z118 12a. brown-purple and carmine . . . 60·0

1905–09. *(Nos. 95/105).*
Z128 53 1a. green and orange . . . 55·
Z129 2a. grey and deep violet . . . 55·
Z130 3a. green . . . 65·
Z131 4a. pale red and sepia . . . 55·
Z132 4a. scarlet . . . 55·
Z133 5a. carmine . . . 65·
Z134 8a. olive-bistre and dull black . . . 55·
Z135 9a. blue . . . 55·
Z136 18a. red-brown . . . 90·
Z137 24a. red-brown . . . £1
Z138 1t. bistre and deep blue . . . £1

1907. *Surch with T* **56** *(No. 109).*
Z139 9 1a.on 24a. purple and blue . . . 65·

Kuala Muda

Stamps of SIAM *cancelled as Type* B *inscr* "KUALA MUDA" *(from* Oct 1907).

1887–91. *(Nos. 11/18).*
Z143 9 12a. purple and carmine . . . £3

1899–1904. *(Nos. 67/81).*
Z144 49 2a. scarlet and pale blue . . . £3
Z145 24a. brown-purple and blue . . . £3

1905–09. *(Nos. 92/105).*
Z146 53 1a. green and orange . . . £3
Z147 2a. grey and deep violet . . . £3
Z148 3a. green . . . £3
Z150 5a. carmine . . . £3
Z151 8a. olive-bistre and dull black . . . £3

Stamps of SIAM *cancelled as Type* C *inscr* "Kwala Muda" *at f*
(from 1907).

1887–91. *(Nos. 11/18).*
Z155 9 12a. purple and carmine . . . £1

1899–1904. *(Nos. 67/81).*
Z156 49 8a. deep green and orange . . . £1
Z157 10a. ultramarine . . . £1

1905–09. *(Nos. 92/105).*
Z158 53 1a. green and orange . . . £1
Z159 2a. grey and deep violet . . . £1
Z160 3a. green . . . £1
Z161 4a. pale red and sepia . . . £1
Z162 4a. scarlet . . . £1
Z163 5a. carmine . . . £2
Z164 8a. olive-bistre and dull black . . . £1
Z165 9a. blue . . . £1
Z166 24a. red-brown . . . £3

1907. *Surch with T* **56** *(No. 109)*.
Z167 **9** 1a.on 24a. purple and blue £150

Kulim

Stamps of SIAM *cancelled as Type* D *inscr* "KULIM" (*from* July 1907).

1887–91. *(Nos. 11/18)*.
Z173 **9** 12a. purple and carmine £325

1899–1904. *(Nos. 67/81)*.
Z174 **49** 8a. deep green and orange £325

1905–09. *(Nos. 92/105)*.
Z175 **53** 1a. green and orange £350
Z176 2a. grey and deep violet £350
Z177 3a. green £375
Z178 4a. pale red and sepia £325
Z179 4a. scarlet £325
Z180 5a. carmine £350
Z181 8a. olive-bistre and dull black £325
Z182 9a. blue £325

1907. *Surch with T* **56**. *(No. 109)*.
Z184 **9** 1a.on 24a. purple and blue £325

Stamps of SIAM *cancelled as Type* C *inscr* "Kulim" *at foot* (*from* Feb 1908).

1887–91. *(Nos. 11/18)*.
Z190 **9** 12a. purple and carmine £130

1899–1904. *(Nos. 67/81)*.
Z191 **49** 8a. deep green and orange £130
Z192 10a. ultramarine £140

1905–09. *(Nos. 92/105)*.
Z196 **53** 4a. pale red and sepia £130
Z197 4a. scarlet £130
Z198 5a. carmine £140
Z199 9a. blue £140
Z200 24a. red-brown £325
Z201 1t. bistre and deep blue £325

1907. *Surch with T* **56** *(No. 109)*.
Z202 **9** 1a.on 24a. purple and blue £140

Langkawi

Stamps of SIAM *cancelled as Type* D *inscr* "LANGKAWI" (*from* Feb 1908).

1899–1904. *(Nos. 67/81)*.
Z208 **49** 8a. deep green and orange £325
Z209 10a. ultramarine £325

1905–09. *(Nos. 92/105)*.
Z212 **53** 3a. green £350
Z213 4a. pale red and sepia £325
Z215 8a. olive-bistre and dull black £325

Stamps of SIAM *cancelled as Type* C *inscr* "Langkawi" *at foot* (*from* Nov 1908).

1887–91. *(Nos. 11/18)*.
Z219 **9** 12a. purple and carmine £140

1899–1904. *(Nos. 67/81)*
Z220 **49** 1a. olive-green (Type B) £150
Z221 8a. green and orange £140

1905–09. *(Nos. 92/105)*.
Z222 **53** 2a. grey and deep violet £140
Z223 3a. green £190
Z224 4a. pale red and sepia £140
Z225 4a. scarlet £150
Z226 8a. olive-bistre and dull black £140
Z228 24a. red-brown £375
Z229 1t. bistre and deep blue £375

1907. *Surch with T* **56** *(No. 109)*.
Z230 **9** 1a.on 24a. purple and blue £150

KELANTAN

The first Siamese post office in Kelantan opened at Kota Bharu in 1895. It appears that in the early years this office only accepted letters franked with stamps for delivery within Kelantan.

The initial cancellation, of which no complete example has been discovered, showed Thai characters only. Partial examples have been reported on the 1887–91 8a. and 1896 4a. on 12a.

The operations of the Duff Development Company in Kelantan from 1903 led to a considerable expansion of the postal service based on the company's river steamers. A further post office opened at Batu Mengkebang in 1908, but may have been preceded by manuscript endorsements of "B.M." and date known from early 1907 onwards.

Kota Bharu

Stamps of SIAM *cancelled as Type* B *inscr* "KALANTAN" (*from* March 1898).

1887–91. *(Nos. 11/18)*.
Z237 **9** 2a. green and carmine . . . . 90·00
Z238 3a. green and blue . . . . 95·00
Z239 4a. green and brown . . . . 95·00
Z240 8a. green and yellow . . . . 95·00
Z241 12a. purple and carmine . . . . 85·00
Z242 24a. purple and blue . . . . 90·00

1894. *Surch as T* **27** *with variation of English figures as T* **33** *(Nos. 37/44)*.
Z251 **9** 2a.on 64a. purple and brown £130

1894–95. *Surch as T* **35** *with variation of English figures as T* **36** *(Nos. 46/50)*.
Z255 **9** 1a.on 64a. purple and brown £110

1896. *Surch as T* **39** *(Siamese) and T* **40** *(English) (No. 51)*.
Z259 **9** 4a.on 12a. purple and carmine £110

1897. *Surch as T* **39** *(Siamese) and T* **41** *(English) (No. 52)*.
Z260 **9** 4a.on 12a. purple and carmine £110

1898–99. *Surch as T* **42** *with variation of English section as T* **46** *(Nos. 53/62)*.
Z266 **9** 3a.on 12a. (11½–11¾ mm long) . . . .
Z267 4a.on 12a. purple and carmine (8 mm long) £110

1899–1904. *(Nos. 67/81)*.
Z275 **49** 1a. olive-green (wide Siamese characters in face value) . . . . 90·00
Z276 2a. grass-green . . . . 85·00
Z277 2a. scarlet and pale blue . . . . 85·00
Z278 3a. red and blue . . . . 95·00
Z279 4a. carmine . . . . 85·00
Z280 4a. chocolate and pink . . . . 95·00
Z281 8a. deep green and orange . . . . 85·00
Z282 10a. ultramarine . . . . 90·00
Z283 12a. brown-purple and carmine . . . . 90·00
Z284 64a. brown-purple and chestnut £190

1905–09. *(Nos. 92/105)*.
Z293 **53** 1a. green and orange . . . . 85·00
Z294 2a. grey and deep violet . . . . 85·00
Z296 4a. pale red and sepia . . . . 85·00
Z297 4a. scarlet . . . . 85·00
Z298 5a. carmine £100
Z299 8a. olive-bistre and dull black . . . . 85·00
Z300 12a. blue £100
Z301 24a. red-brown £275
Z302 1t. bistre and deep blue £275

1907. *Surch with T* **56** *(No. 109)*.
Z303 **9** 1a.on 24a. purple and blue £110

Stamps of SIAM *cancelled as Type* E *inscr* "Kota Bahru/Kelantan" (*from* July 1908).

1887–91. *(Nos. 11/18)*.
Z307 **9** 12a. purple and carmine . . . . 85·00
Z308 24a. purple and blue £110

1899–1904. *(Nos. 67/81)*.
Z309 **49** 8a. deep green and orange . . . . 90·00
Z310 64a. brown-purple and chestnut £130

1905–09. *(Nos. 92/105)*.
Z311 **53** 1a. green and orange . . . . 90·00
Z312 2a. grey and deep violet . . . . 90·00
Z313 2a. pale yellow-green . . . . 90·00
Z314 4a. pale red and sepia . . . . 90·00
Z315 4a. scarlet . . . . 90·00
Z316 8a. olive-bistre and dull black . . . . 85·00
Z317 9a. blue . . . . 95·00
Z318 18a. red-brown £150

1907. *Surch with T* **56** *(No. 109)*.
Z320 **9** 1a.on 24a. purple and blue . . . . 90·00

1908. *Surch as T* **59** *(Nos. 110/12)*.
Z326 **9** 2a.on 24a. purple and blue £130
Z327 **53** 4a. on 5a. carmine £160
Z328 **49** 9a.on 10a. ultramarine £100

Batu Mengkebang

Stamps of SIAM *cancelled as Type* E *inscr* "Batu Menkebang/ Kelantan" (*from* July 1908).

1887–91. *(Nos. 11/18)*.
Z329 **9** 12a. purple and carmine £150

1899–1904. *(Nos. 67/81)*.
Z330 **49** 8a. deep green and orange £160

1905–09. *(Nos. 92/105)*.
Z331 **53** 1a. green and orange £150
Z332 2a. grey and deep violet £150
Z333 2a. pale yellow-green £160
Z334 4a. pale red and sepia £160
Z335 4a. scarlet £150
Z336 8a. olive-bistre and dull black £130
Z337 9a. blue £130
Z338 12a. blue £190
Z339 24a. red-brown £325
Z340 1t. bistre and deep blue £350

1907. *Surch with T* **56** *(No. 109)*
Z341 **9** 1a.on 24a. purple and blue £130

1908. *Surch as T* **59** *(Nos. 110/12)*.
Z347 **49** 9a.on 10a. ultramarine £190

PERLIS

The Siamese post office at Kangar is recorded as opening during 1894. It is believed that the initial cancellation showed Thai characters only, but no complete example has so far been discovered.

Stamps of SIAM *cancelled as Type* B *inscr* "PERLIS" (*from* July 1904).

1887–91. *(Nos. 11/18)*.
Z349 **9** 12a. purple and carmine £150
Z350 24a. purple and blue £200

1897. *Surch as T* **39** *(Siamese) and T* **41** *(English) (No. 52)*.
Z351 **9** 4a.on 12a. purple and carmine £275

1899–1904. *(Nos. 67/81)*.
Z352 **49** 1a. olive-green (wide Siamese characters in face value) £180
Z353 2a. grass-green £160
Z354 2a. scarlet and pale blue £160
Z355 3a. red and blue £250
Z356 4a. carmine £160
Z357 4a. chocolate and pink £160
Z358 8a. deep green and orange £160
Z359 10a. ultramarine £160
Z360 12a. brown-purple and carmine £150
Z361 24a. brown-purple and blue £300

1905–09. *(Nos. 97/105)*.
Z370 **53** 1a. green and orange £150
Z371 2a. grey and deep violet £150
Z372 3a. green £160
Z373 4a. pale red and sepia £150
Z374 5a. carmine £160
Z375 8a. olive-bistre and dull black £150
Z376 12a. blue £170
Z377 24a. red-brown £250

Stamps of SIAM *cancelled as Type* C *inscr* "Perlis" *at foot* (*from* Sept. 1907).

1887–91. *(Nos. 11/18)*.
Z379 **9** 12a. purple and carmine £170

1899–1904. *(Nos. 67/81)*.
Z380 **49** 1a. olive-green (narrow Siamese characters in face value) £180
Z381 8a. deep green and orange £170
Z382 10a. ultramarine £180

1905–09. *(Nos. 92/105)*.
Z383 **53** 1a. green and orange £180
Z384 2a. grey and deep violet £170
Z385 3a. green £180
Z386 4a. pale red and sepia £170
Z387 4a. scarlet £180
Z388 5a. carmine £180
Z389 8a. olive-bistre and dull black £180
Z390 9a. blue £170
Z391 24a. red-brown £300

1907. *Surch with T* **56** *(No. 109)*.
Z392 **9** 1a.on 24a. purple and blue £180

Siam transferred suzerainty over the four northern Malay states to Great Britain on 15 July 1909. Use of Siamese stamps in Kelantan and Perlis appears to have extended into early August 1909.

VII. JAPANESE OCCUPATION OF MALAYA

PRICES FOR STAMPS ON COVER		
Nos.	J1/55	*from* × 10
Nos.	J56/76	*from* × 12
Nos.	J77/89	*from* × 20
Nos.	J90/1	*from* × 15
Nos.	J92/115	*from* × 6
Nos.	J116/18	—
Nos.	J119/32	*from* × 12
Nos.	J133/45	*from* × 10
Nos.	J146/223	*from* × 6
Nos.	J224/58	*from* × 12
No.	J259	*from* × 15
Nos.	J260/96	*from* × 12
Nos.	J297/310	*from* × 20
Nos.	J311/17	—
Nos.	JD1/10	*from* × 30
Nos.	JD11/16	*from* × 12
Nos.	JD17/20	*from* × 30
Nos.	JD21/7	*from* × 20
Nos.	JD28/33	*from* × 30
Nos.	JD34/41	*from* × 60

Japanese forces invaded Malaya on 8 December 1941 with the initial landings taking place at Kota Bharu on the east coast. Penang fell, to a force which crossed the border from Thailand, on 19 December, Kuala Lumpur on 11 January 1942 and the conquest of the Malay peninsula was completed by the capture of Singapore on 15 February.

During the Japanese Occupation various small Dutch East Indies islands near Singapore were administered as part of Malaya. Stamps of the Japanese Occupation of Malaya were issued to the post offices of Dabo Singkep, Puloe Samboe, Tanjong Balei, Tanjong Batu, Tanjong Pinang and Terempa between 1942 and 1945. The overprinted issues were also used by a number of districts in Atjeh (Northern Sumatra) whose postal services were administered from Singapore until the end of March 1943.

Malayan post offices were also opened in October 1943 to serve camps of civilians working on railway construction and maintenance in Thailand. Overprinted stamps of the Japanese Occupation of Malaya were used at these offices between October 1943 and the end of the year after which mail from the camps was carried free. Their postmarks were inscribed in Japanese Katakana characters, and, uniquely, showed the Japanese postal symbol.

JOHORE

The postal service in Johore was reconstituted in mid-April 1942 using Nos. J146/60 and subsequently other general issues. Stamps of Johore overprinted "DAI NIPPON 2602" were, however, only used for fiscal purposes. Overprinted Johore postage due stamps were not issued for use elsewhere in Malaya.

POSTAGE DUE STAMPS

(1) (Upright)

大日本郵便

(2)

Second character sideways (R. 6/3)

1942 (1 Apr). *Nos. D1/5 of Johore optd as T* **1** *in brown.*

JD1	**D 1**	1c. carmine	50·00	85·00
		a. Black opt	20·00	70·00
JD2		4c. green	80·00	95·00
		a. Black opt	65·00	80·00
JD3		8c. orange	£140	£150
		a. Black opt	80·00	95·00
JD4		10c. brown	50·00	70·00
		a. Black opt	16·00	50·00
JD5		12c. purple	85·00	95·00
		a. Black opt	40·00	50·00

1943. *Nos. D1/5 of Johore optd with T* **2**.

JD 6	**D 1**	1c. carmine	6·50	26·00
		a. Second character sideways	£275	£475
JD 7		4c. green	6·50	28·00
		a. Second character sideways	£275	£475
JD 8		8c. orange	8·00	28·00
		a. Second character sideways	£350	£550
JD 9		10c. brown	7·50	35·00
		a. Second character sideways	£325	£550
JD10		12c. purple	9·00	50·00
		a. Second character sideways	£375	£650

KEDAH

Postal services resumed by 31 January 1942 using unoverprinted Kedah values from 1c. to 8c. which were accepted for postage until 13 May 1942.

During the Japanese occupation Perlis was administered as part of Kedah.

DAI NIPPON 2602

(3)

DAI NIPPON 2602

(4)

1942 (13 May)–**43**. *Stamps of Kedah* (Script wmk) *optd with T* **3** (1c. to 8c.) *or* **4** (10c. to $5), *both in red.*

J 1	**1**	1c. black (No. 68*a*)	5·00	8·50
J 2		2c. bright green (No. 69)	26·00	30·00
J 3		4c. violet	4·75	4·00
J 4		5c. yellow	4·75	4·25
		a. Black opt (1943)	£200	£225
J 5		6c. carmine (No. 56) (Blk.)	4·00	12·00
J 6		8c. grey-black	4·00	2·25
J 7	**6**	10c. ultramarine and sepia	12·00	12·00
J 8		12c. black and violet	28·00	40·00
J 9		25c. ultramarine and purple	9·00	13·00
		a. Black opt (1943)	£275	£250
J10		30c. green and scarlet	70·00	80·00
J11		40c. black and purple	35·00	50·00
J12		50c. brown and blue	35·00	50·00
J13		$1 black and green	£140	£150
		a. Opt inverted	£650	£750
J14		$2 green and brown	£170	£170
J15		$5 black and scarlet	65·00	90·00
		a. Black opt (1943)	£950	£900

Nos. J1/15 were gradually replaced by issues intended for use throughout Malaya. Kedah and Perlis were ceded to Thailand by the Japanese on 19 October 1943.

KELANTAN

Postal services resumed on 1 June 1942. Stamps used in Kelantan were overprinted with the personal seals of Sunagawa, the Japanese Governor, and of Handa, the Assistant Governor.

(5) Sunagawa Seal

(6) Handa Seal

40 CENTS

(7)

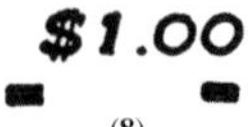

(8)

1 Cents

(9)

1942 (June). *Stamps of Kelantan surch.*

(a) As T **7** *or* **8** *(dollar values). Optd with T* **5** *in red.*

J16	**4**	1c.on 50c. grey-olive and orange	£225	£180
J17		2c.on 40c. orange and blue-green	£650	£300
J18		4c.on 30c. violet and scarlet	£1700	£1200
J19		5c.on 12c. blue (R.)	£225	£190
J20		6c.on 25c. vermilion and violet	£300	£190
J21		8c.on 5c. red-brown (R.)	£350	£140
J22		10c.on 6c. lake	75·00	£120
		a. "CENST" for "CENTS"	£4500	
J23		12c.on 8c. grey-olive (R.)	50·00	£110
J24		25c.on 10c. purple (R.)	£1200	£1300
J25		30c.on 4c. scarlet	£1800	£2000
J26		40c.on 2c. green (R.)	60·00	85·00
		a. Surch double (B.+R.)	£2750	
J27		50c.on 1c. grey-olive and yellow	£1400	£1300
J28	**1**	$1on 4c. black and red (R., bars Blk.)	50·00	80·00
J29		$2on 5c. green and red/*yellow*	50·00	80·00
J30		$5on 6c. scarlet	50·00	80·00
		a. Surch double	£400	

(b) As T **7**. *Optd with T* **6** *in red.*

J31	**4**	12c.on 8c. grey-olive	£170	£275
		a. Type **6** omitted (in horiz pair with normal)	£2750	

(c) As T **9**. *Optd with T* **5** *in red.*

J32	**4**	1c.on 50c. grey-olive and orange	£160	95·00
		a. "Cente" for "Cents" (R. 5/1)	£1800	£1100
J33		2c.on 40c. orange and blue-green	£140	£100
		a. "Cente" for "Cents" (R. 5/1)	£1400	£1100
J34		5c.on 12c. blue (R.)	£140	£130
		a. "Cente" for "Cents" (R. 5/1)	£1400	
J35		8c.on 5c. red-brown (R.)	£120	75·00
		a. "Cente" for "Cents" (R. 5/1)	£1200	£950
J36		10c.on 6c. lake	£325	£350
		a. "Cente" for "Cents" (R. 5/1)	£2500	

(d) As T **9**. *Optd with T* **6** *in red.*

J41	**4**	1c.on 50c. grey-olive and orange	95·00	£140
		a. "Cente" for "Cents" (R. 5/1)	£1200	
J42		2c.on 40c. orange and blue-green	£110	£150
		a. "Cente" for "Cents" (R. 5/1)	£1400	
J43		8c.on 5c. red-brown (R.)	65·00	£130
		a. "Cente" for "Cents" (R. 5/1)	£1200	
J44		10c.on 6c. lake	85·00	£150
		a. "Cente" for "Cents" (R. 5/1)	£1300	

As stamps of the above series became exhausted the equivalent values from the series intended for use throughout Malaya were introduced. Stamps as Nos. J28/30, J32/3 and J35/6, but without Type **5** or **6**, are from remainders sent to Singapore or Kuala Lumpur after the state had been ceded to Thailand (*Price from* £16 *each unused*). Nos. J19, J21, J23 and J25/6 have also been seen without Type **5** (*Price from* £60 *each unused*).

The 12c. on 8c., 30c. on 4c., 40c. on 2c. and 50c. on 1c. surcharged with Type **9**, formerly listed as Nos. J37/40, are now believed to exist only as remainders without the Type **5** red handstamp (*Price from* £20 *each, unused*).

Kelantan was ceded to Thailand by the Japanese on 19 October 1943.

MALACCA

Postal services from Malacca resumed on 21 April 1942, but there were no stamps available for two days.

PRICES. Those quoted are for single stamps. Blocks of four showing complete handstamp are worth from five times the price of a single stamp.

(**10**) "Military Administration Malacca State Government Seal"

1942 (23 Apr). *Stamps of Straits Settlements handstamped as T* **10**, *in red, each impression covering four stamps.*

			Single Un.	Used
J45	**58**	1c. black	85·00	70·00
J46		2c. orange	55·00	65·00
J47		3c. green	55·00	70·00
J48		5c. brown	£120	£130
J49		8c. grey	£180	£110
J50		10c. dull purple	80·00	90·00
J51		12c. ultramarine	90·00	£100
J52		15c. ultramarine	70·00	85·00
J53		40c. scarlet and dull purple	£550	£600
J54		50c. black/*emerald*	£850	£850
J55		$1 black and red/*blue*	£900	£850

The 30c., $2 and $5 also exist with this overprint, but these values were not available to the public. (*Price for set of 3 £5000 unused*)

POSTAGE DUE STAMPS

1942 (23 Apr). *Postage Due stamps of Malayan Postal Union handstamped as T* **10**, *in red, each impression covering four stamps.*

JD11	**D 1**	1c. slate-purple	£200	£180
JD12		4c. green	£225	£225
JD13		8c. scarlet	£2000	£1600
JD14		10c. yellow-orange	£425	£375
JD15		12c. ultramarine	£600	£500
JD16		50c. black	£1800	£1400

Nos. J45/55 and JD11/16 were replaced during May 1942 by the overprinted issues intended for use throughout Malaya.

PENANG

Postal services on Penang Island resumed on 30 March 1942 using Straits Settlements stamps overprinted by Japanese seals of the Government Accountant, Mr. A. Okugawa, and his assistant, Mr. Itchiburi.

(**11**) Okugawa Seal

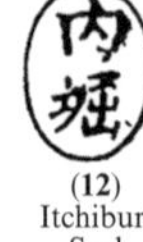

(**12**) Itchiburi Seal

DAI NIPPON 2602 PENANG

(**13**)

1942 (30 Mar). *Straits Settlements stamps optd.*

(a) As T **11** *(three forms of the seal).*

J56	**58**	1c. black	9·50	11·00
J57		2c. orange	24·00	22·00
		a. Pair, one without handstamp	£1100	
J58		3c. green	20·00	22·00
J59		5c. brown	24·00	25·00
J60		8c. grey	26·00	32·00
J61		10c. dull purple	50·00	50·00
J62		12c. ultramarine	30·00	48·00
J63		15c. ultramarine	50·00	50·00
J64		40c. scarlet and dull purple	90·00	£110
J65		50c. black/*emerald*	£200	£225
J66		$1 black and red/*blue*	£200	£250
J67		$2 green and scarlet	£600	£600
J68		$5 green and red/*emerald*	£1800	£1500

(b) With T **12**.

J69	**58**	1c. black	£140	£110
J70		2c. orange	£140	95·00
J71		3c. green	95·00	95·00
J72		5c. brown	£1800	£1800
J73		8c. grey	80·00	90·00
J74		10c. dull purple	£130	£140
J75		12c. ultramarine	90·00	£110
J76		15c. ultramarine	£100	£110

Straits Settlements 1, 2, 3, 4 and 5c. values exist with a similar but circular seal containing four characters, but these were not available to the public.

1942 (15 Apr). *Straits Settlements stamps optd with T* **13** *by Penang Premier Press.*

J77	**58**	1c. black (R.)	4·25	3·00
		a. Opt inverted	£425	£42
		b. Opt double	£300	£30
J78		2c. orange	4·25	4·0
		a. "PE" for "PENANG"	£100	85·0
		b. Opt inverted	£160	
		c. Opt double	£425	
J79		3c. green (R.)	4·75	3·7
		a. Opt double, one inverted	£375	
J80		5c. brown (R.)	2·75	6·5
		a. "N PPON"	£180	
		b. Opt double	£400	£37
J81		8c. grey (R.)	2·25	1·4
		a. "N PPON"	50·00	55·0
		b. Opt double, one inverted	£425	
J82		10c. dull purple (R.)	1·50	2·2
		a. Opt double	£375	£37
		b. Opt double, one inverted	£400	£40
J83		12c. ultramarine (R.)	3·75	14·0
		a. "N PPON"	£450	
		b. Opt double	£375	
		c. Opt double, one inverted	£500	£50
J84		15c. ultramarine (R.)	1·75	3·0
		a. "N PPON"	£100	£11
		b. Opt inverted	£400	£40
		c. Opt double	£475	£47
J85		40c. scarlet and dull purple	4·75	14·0
J86		50c. black/*emerald* (R.)	3·75	24·0
J87		$1 black and red/*blue*	6·00	32·0
		a. Opt inverted	£850	
J88		$2 green and scarlet	50·00	80·0
J89		$5 green and red/*emerald*	£475	£55

Nos. J77/89 were replaced by the overprinted issues intended for use throughout Malaya.

SELANGOR

Postal services resumed in the Kuala Lumpur area on 3 April 1942 and gradually extended to the remainder of the state. Stamps of the general overprinted issue were used, but the following commemorative set was only available in Selangor.

SELANGOR EXHIBITION DAI NIPPON 2602 MALAYA

(**14**)

1942 (3 Nov). *Selangor Agri-horticultural Exhibition. Nos. 294 and 283 of Straits Settlements optd with T* **14**.

J90	**58**	2c. orange	12·00	24·0
		a. "C" for "G" in "SELANGOR" (R. 1/9)	£375	£4
		b. Opt inverted	£300	£4
J91		8c. grey	13·00	24·
		a. "C" for "G" in "SELANGOR" (R. 1/9)	£375	£4
		b. Opt inverted	£300	£4

SINGAPORE

The first post offices re-opened in Singapore on 16 March 1942.

(**15**) "Malaya Military Government Division Postal Services Bureau Seal"

(Handstamped at Singapore)

1942 (16 Mar). *Stamps of Straits Settlements optd with T* **15** *in red.*

J92	**58**	1c. black	13·00	17·
J93		2c. orange	13·00	13·
		a. Pair, one without handstamp	£1900	
J94		3c. green	50·00	70·
J95		8c. grey	22·00	18·
J96		15c. ultramarine	15·00	15·

The overprint Type **15** has a double-lined frame, although the two lines are not always apparent, as in the illustration. Three chops were used, differing slightly in the shape of the characters, but forgeries also exist. It is distinguishable from Type **1**, used for the general issues, by its extra width, measuring approximately 14 mm against 12½ mm.

The 6, 10, 30, 40, 50c., $2 and $5 also exist with this overprint, but were not sold to the public.

Nos. J92/6 were replaced on the 3 May 1942 by the stamps overprinted with Type **1** which were intended for use throughout Malaya.

TRENGGANU

Postal services resumed in Trengganu on 5 March 1942 using unoverprinted stamps up to the 35c. value. These remained in use until September 1942.

1942 (Sept). *Stamps of Trengganu* (Script wmk) *optd as T* **1** *at Kuala Lumpur.*

No.	Type	Description	Unused	Used
97	**4**	1c. black (No. 26a)	90·00	90·00
		a. Chalk-surfaced paper (No. 26)	—	£130
		b. Red opt	£180	£200
		c. Brown opt (chalk-surfaced paper)	£450	£275
98		2c. green (No. 27a)	£140	£140
		a. Chalk-surfaced paper (No. 27)	—	£190
		b. Red opt	£250	£275
		c. Brown opt	£500	£325
99		2c.on 5c. deep reddish purple/*bright yellow* (No. 59)	40·00	40·00
		a. Red opt	50·00	70·00
100		3c. chestnut (No. 29a)	85·00	80·00
		a. Brown opt	£650	£450
101		4c. scarlet-vermilion (No. 30a)	£160	£140
102		5c. dp reddish purple/*brt yell* (No. 32*a*)	10·00	19·00
		a. Purple/yellow (No. 32)	£100	£120
		b. Red opt	25·00	
103		6c. orange (No. 33a)	9·00	25·00
		a. Red opt	£150	
		b. Brown opt	£600	£600
104		8c. grey (No. 34a)	9·00	13·00
		a. Chalk-surfaced paper (No. 34)	£130	
		b. Brown to red opt	55·00	70·00
105		8c.on 10c. bright blue (No. 60)	13·00	48·00
		a. Red opt	21·00	
106		10c. bright blue	22·00	38·00
		a. Red opt	£160	
		b. Brown opt	£600	£600
107		12c. bright ultramarine	8·00	40·00
		a. Red opt	27·00	55·00
108		20c. dull purple and orange	8·50	35·00
		a. Red opt	21·00	
109		25c. green and deep purple	7·50	42·00
		a. Red opt	22·00	
		b. Brown opt	£650	£650
110		30c. dull purple and black	8·50	35·00
		a. Red opt	29·00	55·00
111		35c. carmine/*yellow*	25·00	48·00
		a. Red opt	28·00	
112		50c. green and bright carmine	75·00	90·00
113		$1 purple and blue/*blue*	£3000	£3000
114		$3 green & brown-red/*green* (No. 43*a*)	60·00	£100
		a. Green and lake/green (No. 43)	£170	
		b. Red opt	65·00	
115	**5**	$5 green and red/*yellow*	£160	£200
116		$25 purple and blue	£1200	
		a. Red opt	£4000	
117		$50 green and yellow	£10000	
118		$100 green and scarlet	£1300	

DAI NIPPON

2602

MALAYA

(16)

1942 (Sept). *Stamps of Trengganu* (Script wmk) *optd with T* **16**.

No.	Type	Description	Unused	Used
119	**4**	1c. black (No. 26a)	12·00	12·00
120		2c. green (No. 27a)	£190	£200
121		2c.on 5c. deep reddish purple/*bright yellow* (No. 59)	6·00	8·00
122		3c. chestnut (No. 29a)	12·00	23·00
123		4c. scarlet-vermilion (No. 30a)	12·00	11·00
124		5c. dp reddish purple/*brt yell* (No. 32*a*)	5·50	13·00
125		6c. orange (No. 33a)	5·00	13·00
126		8c. grey (No. 34a)	80·00	27·00
127		8c.on 10c. bright blue (No. 60)	5·50	10·00
128		12c. bright ultramarine	5·00	25·00
129		20c. dull purple and orange	14·00	15·00
130		25c. green and deep purple	7·00	35·00
131		30c. dull purple and black	7·50	29·00
132		$3 green & brown-red/*green* (No. 43*a*)	75·00	£140

1943. *Stamps of Trengganu* (Script wmk) *optd with T* **2**.

No.	Type	Description	Unused	Used
133	**4**	1c. black	13·00	17·00
134		2c. green (No. 27a)	11·00	28·00
135		2c.on 5c. bright reddish purple/*bright yellow* (No. 59)	8·00	20·00
136		5c. brt reddish purple/*brt yell* (No. 32*a*)	9·50	28·00
137		6c. orange (No. 33a)	11·00	32·00
138		8c. grey (No. 34a)	60·00	£100
139		8c.on 10c. bright blue (No. 60)	23·00	50·00
140		10c. bright blue	90·00	£225
141		12c. bright ultramarine	15·00	45·00
142		20c. dull purple and orange	20·00	45·00
143		25c. green and deep purple	15·00	48·00
144		30c. dull purple and black	22·00	50·00
145		35c. carmine/*yellow*	22·00	55·00

POSTAGE DUE STAMPS

1942 (Sept). *Nos. D1/4 of Trengganu optd with T* **1** *sideways.*

No.	Type	Description	Unused	Used
JD17	**D 1**	1c. scarlet	50·00	85·00
JD18		4c. green	85·00	£120
		a. Brown opt	50·00	90·00
JD19		8c. yellow	14·00	50·00
JD20		10c. brown	14·00	50·00

The Trengganu 8c. postage due also exists overprinted with Type **16**, but this was not issued (*Price* £550 *unused*).

Trengganu was ceded to Thailand by the Japanese on 19 October 1943.

GENERAL ISSUES

The following stamps were produced for use throughout Malaya, except for Trengganu.

1942 (3 Apr). *Stamps optd as T* **1**.

(a) On Straits Settlements.

No.	Type	Description	Unused	Used
J146	**58**	1c. black (R.)	3·25	3·25
		a. Black opt	£375	£375
		b. Violet opt	£800	£600
J147		2c. green (V.)	£2500	£1800
J148		2c. orange (R.)	3·00	2·25
		a. Black opt	£120	£130
		b. Violet opt	£200	£200
		c. Brown opt	£750	£600
J149		3c. green (R.)	2·75	2·25
		a. Black opt	£325	£350
		b. Violet opt	£800	£700
J150		5c. brown (R.)	22·00	28·00
		a. Black opt	£500	£500
J151		8c. grey (R.)	4·25	2·25
		a. Pair, one without handstamp	†	£1600
		b. Black opt	£250	£250
J152		10c. dull purple (R.)	48·00	45·00
		a. Brown opt	£850	£700
J153		12c. ultramarine (R.)	80·00	£130
J154		15c. ultramarine (R.)	3·50	3·75
		a. Violet opt	£600	£500
J155		30c. dull purple and orange (R.)	£1900	£1900
J156		40c. scarlet and dull purple (R.)	90·00	95·00
		a. Brown opt	£650	£375
J157		50c. black/*emerald* (R.)	50·00	48·00
J158		$1 black and red/*blue* (R.)	75·00	75·00
J159		$2 green and scarlet (R.)	£130	£160
J160		$5 green and red/*emerald* (R.)	£170	£190

The 2c. green is known with the overprint in red, but this was not available to the public.

(b) On Negri Sembilan.

No.	Type	Description	Unused	Used
J161	**6**	1c. black (R.)	19·00	13·00
		a. Violet opt	22·00	20·00
		b. Brown opt	13·00	17·00
		c. Black opt	50·00	38·00
		d. Pair. Nos. J161/a	£275	
		e. Pair. Nos. J161 and J161b		
J162		2c. orange (R.)	26·00	18·00
		a. Violet opt	48·00	27·00
		b. Black opt	32·00	28·00
		c. Brown opt	60·00	48·00
J163		3c. green (R.)	35·00	20·00
		a. Violet opt	23·00	29·00
		c. Brown opt	£130	60·00
		d. Black opt	55·00	45·00
J164		5c. brown	35·00	21·00
		a. Pair, one without opt	£1600	
		b. Brown opt	17·00	15·00
		c. Red opt	15·00	11·00
		d. Violet opt	50·00	38·00
		e. Pair. Nos. J164c/d	£325	
J165		6c. grey	£140	£120
		a. Brown opt	£325	£325
J166		8c. scarlet	£110	95·00
J167		10c. dull purple	£170	£170
		a. Red opt	£300	£225
		b. Brown opt	£425	£325
J168		12c. bright ultramarine (Br.)	£1300	£1300
J169		15c. ultramarine (R.)	21·00	8·00
		a. Violet opt	75·00	28·00
		b. Brown opt	27·00	12·00
J170		25c. dull purple and scarlet	28·00	38·00
		a. Red opt	60·00	75·00
		b. Brown opt	£400	£325
J171		30c. dull purple and orange	£190	£170
		a. Brown opt	£950	£800
J172		40c. scarlet and dull purple	£950	£900
		a. Brown opt	£850	£800
J173		50c. black/*emerald*	£750	£750
J174		$1 black and red/*blue*	£200	£225
		a. Red opt	£170	£190
		b. Brown opt	£400	£400
J175		$5 green and red/*emerald*	£500	£600
		a. Red opt	£850	£900

(c) On Pahang.

No.	Type	Description	Unused	Used
J176	**15**	1c. black	50·00	45·00
		a. Red opt	55·00	48·00
		b. Violet opt	£325	£250
		c. Brown opt	£250	£200
J177		3c. green	£325	£300
		a. Red opt	£225	£275
		b. Violet opt	£650	£475
J178		5c. brown	14·00	12·00
		a. Red opt	£180	£110
		b. Brown opt	£225	£110
		c. Violet opt	£425	£250
		d. Pair. Nos. J178/b	£800	
J179		8c. grey	£750	£600
J180		8c. scarlet	20·00	8·00
		a. Red opt	£100	50·00
		b. Violet opt	£100	55·00
		c. Brown opt	£110	65·00
		d. Pair. Nos. J180a/c	£400	
J181		10c. dull purple	£275	£140
		a. Red opt	£225	£200
		b. Brown opt	£375	£250
J182		12c. bright ultramarine	£1500	£1500
		a. Red opt	£1200	£1200
J183		15c. ultramarine	£130	£110
		a. Red opt	£325	£250
		b. Violet opt	£650	£475
		c. Brown opt	£450	£325
J184		25c. dull purple and scarlet	21·00	29·00
J185		30c. dull purple and orange	12·00	28·00
		a. Red opt	£140	£170
J186		40c. scarlet and dull purple	20·00	32·00
		a. Brown opt	£375	£275
		b. Red opt	80·00	85·00
J187		50c. black/*emerald*	£750	£750
		a. Red opt	£800	£800
J188		$1 black and red/*blue* (R.)	£140	£150
		a. Black opt	£300	£300
		b. Brown opt	£650	£650
J189		$5 green and red/*emerald*	£650	£800
		a. Red opt	£900	£1000

(d) On Perak.

No.	Type	Description	Unused	Used
J190	**51**	1c. black	55·00	35·00
		a. Violet opt	£200	£100
		b. Brown opt	80·00	80·00
J191		2c. orange	30·00	20·00
		a. Violet opt	70·00	70·00
		b. Red opt	60·00	40·00
		c. Brown opt	55·00	55·00
J192		3c. green	26·00	28·00
		a. Violet opt	£450	£300
		b. Brown opt	£180	£150
		c. Red opt	£325	£250
J193		5c. brown	7·00	6·00
		a. Pair, one without opt	£1000	
		b. Brown opt	38·00	27·00
		c. Violet opt	£225	£200
		d. Red opt	£225	£200
J194		8c. grey	70·00	48·00
		a. Red opt	£350	£225
		b. Brown opt	£350	£250
J195		8c. scarlet	38·00	42·00
		a. Violet opt	£450	£275
J196		10c. dull purple	26·00	24·00
		a. Red opt	£325	£225
J197		12c. bright ultramarine	£225	£225
J198		15c. ultramarine	24·00	32·00
		a. Red opt	£225	£200
		b. Violet opt	£375	£300
		c. Brown opt	£375	£275
J199		25c. dull purple and scarlet	14·00	25·00
		a. Red opt	£250	
J200		30c. dull purple and orange	17·00	32·00
		a. Pair, one without opt	£1600	
		b. Brown opt	£500	£400
		c. Red opt	35·00	55·00
		ca. Pair, one without opt	£2000	
J201		40c. scarlet and dull purple	£375	£325
		a. Brown opt	£500	£425
J202		50c. black/*emerald*	40·00	50·00
		a. Red opt	50·00	60·00
		b. Brown opt	£425	£350
J203		$1 black and red/*blue*	£425	£400
		a. Brown opt	£450	£375
J204		$2 green and scarlet	£2750	£2750
J205		$5 green and red/*emerald*	£475	
		a. Brown opt	£1500	

(e) On Selangor.

No.	Type	Description	Unused	Used
J206	**46**	1c. black, S	12·00	24·00
		a. Red opt, SU	42·00	38·00
		b. Violet opt, SU	42·00	40·00
J207		2c. green, SU	£1300	£1100
		a. Violet opt, SU	£1600	£1200
J208		2c. orange (P 14 × 14½), S	85·00	60·00
		a. Red opt, U	£190	£170
		b. Violet opt, U	£225	£150
		c. Brown opt, S	75·00	80·00
J209		2c. orange (P 14), S	£100	80·00
		a. Red opt, U	£200	£170
		b. Violet opt, U	£325	£160
		c. Brown opt, S	—	£160
J210		3c. green, SU	23·00	15·00
		a. Red opt, SU	18·00	15·00
		b. Violet opt, SU	65·00	50·00
		c. Brown opt, SU	18·00	15·00
J211		5c. brown, SU	6·00	5·50
		a. Red opt, SU	12·00	16·00
		b. Violet opt, SU	21·00	22·00
		c. Brown opt, SU	60·00	50·00
J212		6c. scarlet, SU	£375	£375
		a. Red opt, S	£200	£250
		b. Brown opt, S	£800	£800
J213		8c. grey, S	17·00	17·00
		a. Red opt, SU	60·00	40·00
		b. Violet opt, U	35·00	35·00
		c. Brown opt, S	£160	70·00
J214		10c. dull purple, S	13·00	21·00
		a. Red opt, S	75·00	60·00
		b. Brown opt, S	£140	80·00
J215		12c. bright ultramarine, S	60·00	70·00
		a. Red opt, S	£120	£130
		b. Brown opt, S	£120	£120
J216		15c. ultramarine, S	16·00	22·00
		a. Red opt, SU	55·00	55·00
		b. Violet opt, U	£140	95·00
		c. Brown opt, S	90·00	65·00
J217		25c. dull purple and scarlet, S	75·00	95·00
		a. Red opt, S	60·00	80·00
J218		30c. dull purple and orange, S	11·00	24·00
		a. Brown opt, S	£425	£275
J219		40c. scarlet and dull purple, S	£140	£140
		a. Brown opt, S	£375	£200
		b. Red opt, S	£275	
J220		50c. black/*emerald*, S	£130	£140
		a. Red opt, S	£130	£140
		b. Brown opt, S	£450	£375
J221	**48**	$1 black and red/*blue*	30·00	45·00
		a. Red opt	£120	£150
J222		$2 green and scarlet	35·00	60·00
		a. Pair, one without opt	£1500	
		b. Red opt	£550	£600
J223		$5 green and red/*emerald*	65·00	90·00

Nos. J161a and J163a exist with the handstamped overprint sideways.

On *T* **46** the overprint is normally sideways (with "top" to either right or left), but on *T* **48** it is always upright.

S = Sideways

U = Upright
SU = Sideways or upright (our prices being for the cheaper).
Specialists recognise nine slightly different chops as Type **1**. Initial supplies with the overprint in red were produced at Singapore. Later overprintings took place at Kuala Lumpur in violet, red or brown and finally, black. No. J155 was from the Kuala Lumpur printing only. Except where noted, these overprints were used widely in Malaya and, in some instances, Sumatra.

The following stamps also exist with this overprint, but were not available to the public:
Straits Settlements (in red) 6, 25c.
Kelantan (in black) 10c.
Negri Sembilan 2c. green (Blk. or Brn.), 4c. (Blk.), 6c.scarlet (Blk.), 8c. grey (Blk.), 12c. (Blk.), $2 (Blk. or Brn.)
Pahang (in black, 2c. also in brown) 2, 4, 6c., $2
Perak 2c. green (R.), 6c. (Blk.)
Selangor 4c. (Blk.)

1942 (May). *Optd with T* **16**.

(a) On Straits Settlements.

J224 **58** 2c. orange . . . 1·75 60
a. Opt inverted . . . 10·00 19·00
b. Opt double, one inverted . . . 48·00 60·00
J225 3c. green . . . 50·00 65·00
J226 8c. grey . . . 5·00 2·50
a. Opt inverted . . . 15·00 29·00
J227 15c. blue . . . 13·00 8·50

(b) On Negri Sembilan.

J228 **6** 1c. black . . . 2·25 60
a. Opt inverted . . . 9·00 25·00
b. Opt double, one inverted . . . 35·00 50·00
J229 2c. orange . . . 6·00 50
J230 3c. green . . . 4·50 50
J231 5c. brown . . . 1·50 2·50
J232 6c. grey . . . 3·50 1·75
a. Opt inverted . . . — £1300
b. Stop omitted at right (R. 10/4) . . . 95·00 £100
J233 8c. scarlet . . . 5·00 1·25
J234 10c. dull purple . . . 3·00 2·50
J235 15c. ultramarine . . . 15·00 2·50
J236 25c. dull purple and scarlet . . . 4·00 14·00
J237 30c. dull purple and orange . . . 7·00 3·00
J238 $1 black and red/*blue* . . . 80·00 95·00

(c) On Pahang.

J239 **15** 1c. black . . . 2·50 2·75
a. Opt omitted (in pair with normal) . . . £500
J240 5c. brown . . . 1·25 70
J241 8c. scarlet . . . 25·00 2·50
a. Opt omitted (in pair with normal) . . . £1300
J242 10c. dull purple . . . 11·00 6·50
J243 12c. bright ultramarine . . . 2·25 13·00
J244 25c. dull purple and scarlet . . . 4·50 20·00
J245 30c. dull purple and orange . . . 2·50 9·00

(d) On Perak.

J246 **51** 2c. orange . . . 2·75 2·00
a. Opt inverted . . . 40·00 42·00
J247 3c. green . . . 1·25 1·25
a. Opt inverted . . . 14·00 25·00
b. Opt omitted (in pair with normal) . . . £500
J248 8c. scarlet . . . 70 50
a. Opt inverted . . . 4·50 7·00
b. Opt double, one inverted . . . £225 £250
c. Opt omitted (in horiz pair with normal) . . . £400
J249 10c. dull purple . . . 13·00 6·00
J250 15c. ultramarine . . . 6·00 2·00
J251 50c. black/*emerald* . . . 2·75 4·00
J252 $1 black and red/*blue* . . . £375 £425
J253 $5 green and red/*emerald* . . . 35·00 70·00
a. Opt inverted . . . £275 £350

(e) On Selangor.

J254 **46** 3c. green . . . 1·50 3·00
J255 12c. bright ultramarine . . . 1·10 12·00
J256 15c. ultramarine . . . 5·50 1·50
J257 40c. scarlet and dull purple . . . 2·00 4·00
J258 **48** $2 green and scarlet . . . 10·00 40·00

On *T* **46** the overprint is sideways, with "top" to left or right.

The following stamps also exist with this overprint, but were not available to the public.
Perak 1, 5, 30c. (*Price for set of* 3 £350 *unused*).
Selangor 1, 5, 10, 30c., $1, $5 (*Price for set of* 6 £650 *unused*).

DAI NIPPON
2602
MALAYA
2 Cents
(17)

DAI NIPPON
YUBIN
2 Cents
(18) "Japanese Postal Service"

1942 (Nov). *No. 108 of Perak surch with T* **17**.
J259 **51** 2c.on 5c. brown . . . 1·25 2·75
a. Inverted "s" in "Cents" (R. 3/5) . . .

1942 (Nov). *Perak stamps surch or opt only, as in T* **18**.
J260 **51** 1c. black . . . 4·50 9·00
a. Opt inverted . . . 19·00 40·00
J261 2c.on 5c. brown . . . 2·00 6·50
a. "DAI NIPPON YUBIN" inverted . . . 17·00 38·00
b. Ditto and "2 Cents" omitted . . . 45·00 65·00
c. Inverted "s" in "Cents" (R. 3/5) . . . 50·00
J262 8c. scarlet . . . 4·50 2·25
a. Opt inverted . . . 11·00 24·00

A similar overprint exists on the Selangor 3c. but this was not available to the public (*Price* £350 *unused*).

On 8 December 1942 contemporary Japanese 3, 5, 8 and 25s. stamps were issued without overprint in Malaya and the 1, 2, 4, 6, 7, 10, 30 and 50s. and 1y. values followed on 15 February 1943.

大日本郵便
(19)

6cts. (20) 6 cts. (21) 2 Cents (22)

6 cts. (23) $1.00 (24)

1942 (4 Dec)–**44**. *Stamps of various Malayan territories optd "Japanese Postal Service" in Kanji characters as T* **2** *or* **19**, *some additionally surch as T* **20** *to* **24**.

(a) Stamps of Straits Settlements optd with T **2**.

J263 **58** 8c. grey (Blk.) (1943) . . . 1·40 50
a. Opt inverted . . . 45·00 55·00
b. Opt omitted (in pair with normal) . . . £800
c. Red opt . . . 2·25 2·75
J264 12c. ultramarine (1943) . . . 1·25 9·50
J265 40c. scarlet and dull purple (1943) . . . 1·75 4·25

(b) Stamps of Negri Sembilan optd with T **2** *or surch also.*

J266 **6** 1c. black . . . 30 2·00
a. Opt inverted . . . 10·00 27·00
b. Sideways second character . . . 32·00 35·00
ba. Opt inverted with sideways second character . . . £750
J267 2c.on 5c. brown (surch as *T* **20**) . . . 80 1·00
J268 6c.on 5c. brown (surch *T* **21**) (1943) . . . 40 1·50
a. Opt Type **2** and surch as Type **21** both inverted . . . £225 £225
J269 25c. dull purple and scarlet (1943) . . . 1·10 14·00

(c) Stamp of Pahang optd with T **2** *and surch also.*

J270 **15** 6c.on 5c. brown (surch *T* **20**) (1943) . . . 50 75
J271 6c.on 5c. brown (surch *T* **21**) (1943) . . . 1·00 1·75

(d) Stamps of Perak optd with T **2** *or surch also.*

J272 **51** 1c. black . . . 1·00 70
a. Sideways second character . . . £200 £225
J273 2c.on 5c. brown (surch as *T* **20**) . . . 50 50
a. Opt Type **2** and surch Type **20** both inverted . . . 18·00 32·00
b. Opt Type **2** inverted . . . 18·00 32·00
c. Sideways second character . . . 50·00 50·00
J274 2c.on 5c. brown (surch *T* **22**) . . . 60 50
a. Surch Type **22** inverted . . . 18·00 32·00
b. Opt Type **2** and surch Type **22** both inverted . . . 20·00 35·00
c. Sideways second character . . . 25·00 32·00
ca. Surch Type **22** inverted . . . £1300
cb. Opt Type **2** with sideways second character and surch Type **22** both inverted . . . £1300
J275 5c. brown . . . 55 65
a. Opt inverted . . . 30·00 40·00
b. Sideways second character . . . £475 £375
J276 8c. scarlet . . . 55 1·50
a. Opt inverted . . . 15·00 27·00
b. Sideways second character . . . 50·00 65·00
ba. Opt inverted with sideways second character . . . £700
c. Opt omitted (in pair with normal) . . . £1000
J277 10c. dull purple (1943) . . . 60 50
J278 30c. dull purple and orange (1943) . . . 3·50 5·50
J279 50c. black/*emerald* (1943) . . . 3·25 18·00
J280 $5 green and red/emerald (1943) . . . 55·00 95·00

(e) Stamps of Selangor optd with T **2** *(sideways on T* **46**).

J281 **46** 1c. black (1943) . . . 1·00 2·25
J282 3c. green . . . 40 45
a. Sideways second character . . . 17·00 26·00
J283 12c. bright ultramarine . . . 45 1·60
a. Sideways second character . . . 50·00 65·00
J284 15c. ultramarine . . . 3·75 3·25
a. Sideways second character . . . 50·00 55·00
J285 **48** $1 black and red/*blue* . . . 3·00 20·00
a. Opt inverted . . . £225 £225
b. Sideways second character . . . £375 £400
J286 $2 green and scarlet (1943) . . . 10·00 48·00
J287 $5 green and red/*emerald* (1943) . . . 22·00 80·00
a. Opt inverted . . . £225 £275

(f) Stamps of Selangor optd with T **19** *or surch also.*

J288 **46** 1c. black (R.) (1943) . . . 35 50
J289 2c.on 5c. brown (surch as *T* **21**) (R.) (1943) . . . 40 50
J290 3c.on 5c. brown (surch as *T* **21**) (1943) . . . 30 4·00
a. "s" in "cts." inverted (R. 4/3) . . . 29·00 55·00
b. Comma after "cts" (R. 9/3) . . . 29·00 55·00
J291 5c. brown (R.) (1944) . . . 1·25 4·00
J292 6c.on 5c. brown (surch *T* **21**) (1944) . . . 50 1·75
J293 6c.on 5c. brown (surch *T* **23**) (1944) . . . 30 70
a. "6" inverted (R. 7/8) . . . £850
b. Full stop between "6" and "cts" (R. 8/6) . . .
c. Surch and opt double . . . £425
J294 15c. ultramarine . . . 4·00 4·00
J295 $1on 10c. dull purple (surch *T* **24**) (18.12.1944) . . . 40 1·00
J296 $1.50 on 30c. dull purple and orange (surch *T* **24**) (18.12.1944) . . . 40 1·00

The error showing the second character in Type **2** sideways occurred on R. 6/3 in the first of four settings only.

The 2c. orange, 3c. and 8c. grey of Perak also exist overprinted with Type **2**, but these stamps were not available to the public (*Price for set of* 3 £100 *unused*).

Examples of No. J275 are known postally used from the Shan States (part of pre-war Burma).

25 Tapping Rubber

26 Fruit

27 Japanese Shrine, Singapore

(Litho Kolff & Co, Batavia)

1943 (29 Apr–30 Oct). *T* **25/7** *and similar designs.* P 12½.
J297 **25** 1c. grey-green (30 Oct) . . . 1·00 5
J298 **26** 2c. pale emerald (1 June) . . . 75 2
J299 **25** 3c. drab (30 Oct) . . . 30 2
J300 – 4c. carmine-rose . . . 2·00 2
J301 – 8c. dull blue . . . 30 2
J302 – 10c. brown-purple (30 Oct) . . . 30 2
J303 **27** 15c. violet (30 Oct) . . . 60 3·5
J304 – 30c. olive-green (30 Oct) . . . 1·00 3
J305 – 50c. blue (30 Oct) . . . 3·25 3·5
J306 – 70c. blue (30 Oct) . . . 16·00 10·0
J297/306 *Set of* 10 . . . 23·00 17·0

Designs: *Vert*—4c. Tin dredger; 8c. War Memorial, Bukit Batok Singapore; 10c. Fishing village; 30c. Sago palms; 50c. Straits o Johore. *Horiz*—70c. Malay Mosque, Kuala Lumpur.

The 2c. and 4c. values exist, printed by typography, in pale shades either imperforate or rouletted. It is suggested that these ma have been available in Singapore at the very end of the Japanes Occupation.

28 Ploughman

29 Rice-planting

1943 (1 Sept). *Savings Campaign. Litho.* P 12½.
J307 **28** 8c. violet . . . 9·50 2·7
J308 15c. scarlet . . . 6·50 2·7

(Des Hon Chin. Litho)

1944 (15 Feb). *"Re-birth" of Malaya.* P 12½.
J309 **29** 8c. rose-red . . . 14·00 3·2
J310 15c. magenta . . . 4·00 3·2

大日本
マライ郵便
50 セント
(30)

大日本
マライ郵便
1 ドル
(31)

大日本
マライ郵便
1½ドル
(32)

1944 (16 Dec). *Stamps intended for use on Red Cross letters. Sur with T* **30/2** *in red.*

(a) On Straits Settlements.

J311 **58** 50c.on 50c. black/*emerald* . . . 10·00 24·
J312 $1on $1 black and red/*blue* . . . 19·00 35·
J313 $1.50on $2 green and scarlet . . . 29·00 70·

(b) On Johore.

J314 **29** 50c.on 50c. dull purple and red . . . 7·00 20·
J315 $1.50on $2 green and carmine . . . 4·00 12·

(c) On Selangor.

J316 **48** $1on $1 black and red/*blue* . . . 3·50 14·
J317 $1.50on $2 green and scarlet . . . 5·00 20·

Nos. J311/17 were issued in Singapore but were withdrawn aft one day, probably because supplies of Nos. J295/6 were receiv and issued on the 18 December.

A similar 6c. surcharge exists on the Straits Settlements 5c. b this was not available to the public (*Price* £475 *unused*).

STAMP BOOKLETS

1942. *Nos. SB3/4 of Perak and SB2 of Selangor with covers op with T* **1**.
SB1 $1 booklet containing twenty 5c. (No. J193) in blocks of 10 . . . £22
SB2 $1.30 booklet containing 5c. and 8c. (Nos. J193/4), each in block of 10 . . . £22
SB3 $1.30 booklet containing 5c. and 8c. (Nos. J211 and J213), each in block of 10 . . . £22

POSTAGE DUE STAMPS

Postage Due stamps of the Malayan Postal Union overprinted

1942 (3 Apr). *Handstamped as T* **1** *in black.*
JD21 **D 1** 1c. slate-purple . . . 12·00 24·
a. Red opt . . . £120 £1
b. Brown opt . . . £110 £1
JD22 3c. green . . . 60·00 65·
a. Red opt . . . £190 £2
JD23 4c. green . . . 48·00 32·
a. Red opt . . . 55·00 50·
b. Brown opt . . . £130 £1
JD24 8c. scarlet . . . 85·00 70·
a. Red opt . . . £130 £1
b. Brown opt . . . £160 £1
JD25 10c. yellow-orange . . . 25·00 42·
a. Red opt . . . £170 £1
b. Brown opt . . . 65·00 70
JD26 12c. ultramarine . . . 25·00 50
a. Red opt . . . £190 £1
JD27 50c. black . . . 60·00 80
a. Red opt . . . £375 £4

1942. *Optd with T* **16**.

JD28	D 1	1c. slate-purple	2·25	8·50
JD29		3c. green	14·00	20·00
JD30		4c. green	15·00	11·00
JD31		8c. scarlet	19·00	17·00
JD32		10c. yellow-orange	1·75	14·00
JD33		12c. ultramarine	1·75	28·00

The 9c. and 15c. also exist with this overprint, but these were not issued (*Price £500 each unused*).

1943–45. *Optd with T* **2**.

JD34	D 1	1c. slate-purple	1·75	4·00
JD35		3c. green	1·75	4·00
		a. Opt omitted (in pair with normal)	£650	
JD36		4c. green	55·00	40·00
JD37		5c. scarlet	1·50	4·50
JD38		9c. yellow-orange	80	7·00
		a. Opt inverted	20·00	28·00
JD39		10c. yellow-orange	1·75	7·50
		a. Opt inverted	65·00	65·00
JD40		12c. ultramarine	1·75	14·00
JD41		15c. ultramarine	2·00	7·50

VIII. THAI OCCUPATION OF MALAYA

Stamps issued for use in the Malay States of Kedah (renamed Syburi), Kelantan, Perlis and Trengganu, ceded by Japan to Thailand on 19 October 1943. British rule was restored on 9 (Kelantan), 18 (Perlis), 22 (Kedah) and 24 September 1945 (Trengganu). Nos TM1/6 continued to be used for postage until replaced by the overprinted B.M.A. Malaya issues on 10 October 1945.

PRICES FOR STAMPS ON COVER		
Nos.	TK1/5	*from* × 30
Nos.	TM1/6	*from* × 25
Nos.	TT1/35	—

KELANTAN

TK 1

(Typo Kelantan Ptg Dept, Khota Baru)

1943 (15 Nov). *Handstamped with State arms in violet. No gum.* P 11.

TK1	TK 1	1c. black	£200	£300
TK2		2c. black	£250	£250
		a. Handstamp omitted	£700	
TK3		4c. black	£250	£300
		a. Handstamp omitted	£850	
TK4		8c. black	£250	£250
		a. Handstamp omitted	£550	
TK5		10c. black	£300	£400

Nos. TK1/5 were printed in sheets of 84 (12 × 7) and have sheet watermarks in the form of "STANDARD" in block capitals with curved "CROWN" above and "AGENTS" below in double-lined capitals. This watermark occurs four times in the sheet.

Sheets were imperforate at top and left so that stamps exist imperforate at top, left or at top and left.

Genuine examples have a solid star at the top centre of the arms, as shown in Type TK **1**. Examples with a hollow outline star in this position are forgeries.

Similar stamps, but with red handstamps, were for fiscal use.

GENERAL ISSUE

TM **1** War Memorial

(Litho Defence Ministry, Bangkok)

1944 (15 Jan–4 Mar). *Thick opaque, or thin semi-transparent paper. Gummed or ungummed.* P $12\frac{1}{2}$.

TM1	TM 1	1c. yellow (4 Mar)	30·00	32·00
TM2		2c. red-brown	12·00	20·00
		a. Imperf (pair)	£850	
		b. Perf $12\frac{1}{2}$ × 11	20·00	20·00
TM3		3c. green (4 Mar)	20·00	38·00
		a. Perf $12\frac{1}{2}$ × 11	30·00	42·00
TM4		4c. purple (4 Mar)	14·00	28·00
		a. Perf $12\frac{1}{2}$ × 11	20·00	35·00
TM5		8c. carmine (4 Mar)	14·00	20·00
		a. Perf $12\frac{1}{2}$ × 11	20·00	20·00
TM6		15c. blue (4 Mar)	38·00	60·00
		a. Perf $12\frac{1}{2}$ × 11	42·00	60·00

5c. and 10c. stamps in this design were prepared, but never issued.

TRENGGANU

TRENGGANU
(TT 1)

(Overprinted at Trengganu Survey Office)

1944 (1 Oct). *Various stamps optd with Type TT* **1**.

(a) On Trengganu without Japanese opt.

TT1	4	1c. black (26a)		
TT2		30c. dull purple and black (39)		

(b) On Trengganu stamps optd as T **1** *of Japanese Occupation.*

TT2*a*	4	1c. black (J97)	—	£1200
TT3		8c. grey (J104)	£475	£350

(c) On stamps optd with T **16** *of Japanese Occupation.*

(i) Pahang.

TT4	15	12c. bright ultramarine (J243)	£375	£120

(ii) Trengganu.

TT5	4	2c.on 5c. deep reddish purple/*bright yellow* (J121)*	£450	£450
TT6		8c.on 10c. brt blue (J127) (inverted)	£375	£375
TT7		12c. brt ultramarine (J128) (inverted)	£375	£375

This is spelt "TRENGANU" with one "G".

(d) On stamps optd with T **2** *of Japanese Occupation.*

(i) Straits Settlements.

TT8	58	12c. ultramarine (J264)	£400	£400
TT9		40c. scarlet and dull purple (J265)	£400	£400

(ii) Negri Sembilan.

TT9*a*	6	25c. dull purple and scarlet (J269)	—	£1200

(iii) Pahang.

TT10	15	6c. on 5c. brown (J271)		

(iv) Perak.

TT11	51	1c. black (J272)		
TT12		10c. dull purple (J277)		
TT13		30c. dull purple and orange (J278)	£700	£400
TT13*a*		50c. black/*emerald* (J279)	—	£1200

(v) Selangor.

TT14	46	3c. green (J282)	£300	£300
TT15		12c. brt ultramarine (J283) (L. to R.)	£180	£110
TT16		12c. brt ultramarine (J283) (R. to L.)	£180	£110
		a. Sideways second character	£1800	£1800

(e) On Selangor stamps optd with T **19** *of Japanese Occupation.*

TT16*b*	46	1c. black (J288)	—	£1200
TT17		2c.on 5c. brown (J289)	£400	£400
TT18		3c.on 5c. brown (J290)	£400	£400

(f) On pictorials of 1943 (Nos. J297/306).

TT19	25	1c. grey-green	£300	£275
TT20	26	2c. pale emerald	£300	£150
TT21	25	3c. drab	£180	£120
TT22	–	4c. carmine-rose	£275	£150
TT23	–	8c. dull blue	£450	£425
TT24	–	10c. brown-purple	£900	£600
TT25	27	15c. violet	£275	£150
TT26	–	30c. olive-green	£400	£130
TT27	–	50c. blue	£400	£250
TT28	–	70c. blue	£800	£600

(g) On Savings Campaign stamps (Nos. J307/8).

TT29	28	8c. violet	£450	£450
TT30		15c. scarlet	£325	£160

(h) On stamps of Japan.

TT31	–	3s. green (No. 319)		
TT32	–	5s. claret (No. 396)	£400	£325
TT33	–	25c. brown and chocolate (No. 329)	£250	£110
TT34	–	30c. blue-green (No. 330)	£400	£160

(i) On Trengganu Postage Due stamp optd with T **1** *of Japanese Occupation.*

TT35	D 1	1c. scarlet (JD17)	£1600	£1600

Maldive Islands

PRICES FOR STAMPS ON COVER TO 1945		
Nos.	1/6	*from* × 10
Nos.	7/10	*from* × 50
Nos.	11/20	*from* × 20

BRITISH PROTECTORATE

(Currency. 100 cents = 1 Ceylon rupee)

MALDIVES
(1)

2 Minaret, Juma Mosque, Malé

3

1906 (9 Sept). *Nos. 277/9, 280a and 283/4 of Ceylon optd with T* **1**. Wmk Mult Crown CA. P 14.

1	44	2c. red-brown	15·00	38·00
2	45	3c. green	20·00	38·00
3		4c. orange and ultramarine	35·00	75·00
4	46	5c. dull purple	4·00	6·50
5	48	15c. blue	70·00	£140
6		25c. bistre	80·00	£150
1/6 *Set of* 6			£200	£400

Supplies of Nos. 1/6 were exhausted by March 1907 and the stamps of CEYLON were used until 1909. Overseas mail to destinations other than Ceylon or India continued to be franked with Ceylon stamps until 1967 when Maldive Islands joined the U.P.U.

(Recess D.L.R.)

1909 (May). *T* **2** ($18\frac{1}{2}$ × $22\frac{1}{2}$ mm). W **3**. P 14 × $13\frac{1}{2}$ (2c., 5c.) or $13\frac{1}{2}$ × 14 (3c., 10c.).

7	2	2c. orange-brown	2·25	3·00
		a. Perf $13\frac{1}{2}$ × 14	2·50	90
8		3c. deep myrtle	50	70
9		5c. purple	50	35
10		10c. carmine	7·50	80
7/10 *Set of* 4			9·50	2·50

These stamps perforated 14 × $13\frac{1}{2}$ (14 × 13.7) are from a line machine and those perforated $13\frac{1}{2}$ × 14 (13.7 × 13.9) from a comb machine.

4

(Photo Harrison)

1933. *T* **2** *redrawn (reduced to* 18 × $21\frac{1}{2}$ mm*)*. W **4**. P 15 × 14.

A. Wmk upright.

11A	2	2c. grey	2·75	2·00
12A		3c. red-brown	70	2·75
14A		5c. mauve	23·00	10·00
15A		6c. scarlet	1·50	5·50
16A		10c. green	85	55
17A		15c. black	6·50	14·00
18A		25c. brown	6·50	14·00
19A		50c. purple	6·50	16·00
20A		1r. deep blue	11·00	14·00
11A/20A *Set of* 9			50·00	70·00

B. Wmk sideways.

11B	2	2c. grey	5·00	4·50
12B		3c. red-brown	3·75	1·75
13B		5c. claret	35·00	32·00
15B		6c. scarlet	8·00	5·50
16B		10c. green	3·50	4·50
17B		15c. black	13·00	17·00
18B		25c. brown	11·00	17·00
19B		50c. purple	13·00	17·00
20B		1r. deep blue	14·00	3·25
11B/20B *Set of* 9			95·00	90·00

(New Currency. 100 larees = 1 rupee)

5 Palm Tree and Dhow

(Recess B.W.)

1950 (24 Dec). P 13.

21	5	2l. olive-green	2·25	1·25
22		3l. blue	10·00	50
23		5l. emerald-green	10·00	50
24		6l. red-brown	1·25	80
25		10l. scarlet	1·25	60
26		15l. orange	1·25	60
27		25l. purple	1·25	1·00
28		50l. violet	1·25	1·75
29		1r. chocolate	11·00	30·00
21/9 *Set of* 9			35·00	32·00

7 Fish

8 Native Products

1952. P 13.

30	7	3l. blue	2·00	60
31	8	5l. emerald	1·00	2·00

Malta

Early records of the postal services under the British Occupation are fragmentary, but it is known that an Island Postmaster was appointed in 1802. A British Packet Agency was established in 1806 and it later became customary for the same individual to hold the two appointments together. The inland posts continued to be the responsibility of the local administration, but the overseas mails formed part of the British G.P.O. system.

The stamps of Great Britain were used on overseas mails from September 1857. Previously during the period of the Crimean War letters franked with Great Britain stamps from the Crimea were cancelled at Malta with a wavy line obliterator. Such postmarks are known between April 1855 and September 1856.

The British G.P.O. relinquished control of the overseas posts on 31 December 1884 when Great Britain stamps were replaced by those of Malta.

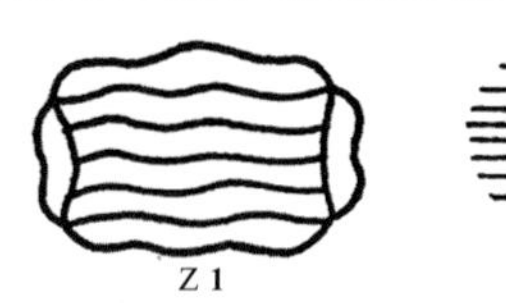
Z 1

Z 2

1855–1856. *Stamps of* GREAT BRITAIN *cancelled with wavy lines obliteration, Type Z* **1**.

Z1 1d. red-brown (1854), Die I, wmk Small Crown, perf 16 . . . £800
Z2 1d. red-brown (1855), Die II, wmk Small Crown, perf 14 . . . £800
a. Very blued paper
Z3 1d. red-brown (1855), Die II, wmk Large Crown, perf 16 . . . £800
Z3*a* 1d. red-brown (1855), Die II, wmk Large Crown, perf 14 . . . £800
Z4 2d. blue (1855), wmk Large Crown, perf 14
Plate No. 5
Z5 6d. (1854) embossed . . . £4000
Z6 1s. (1847) embossed . . . £4500

It is now established that this obliterator was sent to Malta and used on mail in transit emanating from the Crimea.

1857 (18 Aug)–**59**. *Stamps of* GREAT BRITAIN *cancelled "M", Type Z* **2**.

Z 7 1d. red-brown (1841) . . . £1400
Z 8 1d. red-brown, Die I, wmk Small Crown, perf 16 . . . £110
Z 9 1d. red-brown, Die II, wmk Small Crown, perf 16 . . . £800
Z10 1d. red-brown, Die II (1855), wmk Small Crown, perf 14 . . . £180
Z11 1d. red-brown, Die II (1855), wmk Large Crown, perf 14 . . . 70·00
Z12 1d. rose-red (1857), wmk Large Crown, perf 14 . . . 20·00
Z13 2d. blue (1841), imperf . . . £2500
Z14 2d. blue (1854) wmk Small Crown, perf 16 . . . £650
Plate No. 4.
Z15 2d. blue (1855), wmk Large Crown, perf 14 . . . *From* 50·00
Plate Nos. 5, 6.
Z16 2d. blue (1858), wmk Large Crown, perf 16 . . . £250
Plate No. 6.
Z17 2d. blue (1858) (Plate Nos. 7, 8, 9) . . . *From* 40·00
Z18 4d. rose (1857) . . . 35·00
a. Thick glazed paper . . . £170
Z19 6d. violet (1854), embossed . . . £3000
Z20 6d. lilac (1856) . . . 40·00
a. Thick paper . . . £190
Z21 6d. lilac (1856) (*blued paper*) . . . £850
Z22 1s. green (1856) . . . £120
a. Thick paper . . . £170

Z 3 Z 6 Z 4 Z 5 Z 7

1859–84. *Stamps of* GREAT BRITAIN *cancelled "A 25" as in Types Z* **3/7**.

Z23 ½d. rose-red (1870–79) . . . *From* 21·00
Plate Nos. 4, 5, 6, 8, 9, 10, 11, 12, 13, 14, 15, 19, 20.
Z24 1d. red-brown (1841), *imperf* . . . £2250
Z25 1d. red-brown (1854), wmk Small Crown, perf 16 . . . £275
Z26 1d. red-brown (1855), wmk Large Crown, perf 14 . . . 65·00
Z27 1d. rose-red (1857), wmk Large Crown, perf 14 . . . 7·50
Z28 1d. rose-red (1861), Alphabet IV . . . £450
Z30 1d. rose-red (1864–79) . . . *From* 14·00
Plate Nos. 71, 72, 73, 74, 76, 78, 79, 80, 81, 82, 83, 84, 85, 86, 87, 88, 89, 90, 91, 92, 93, 94, 95, 96, 97, 98, 99, 100, 101, 102, 103, 104, 105, 106, 107, 108, 109, 110, 111, 112, 113, 114, 115, 116, 117, 118, 119, 120, 121, 122, 123, 124, 125, 127, 129, 130, 131, 132, 133, 134, 135, 136, 137, 138, 139, 140, 141, 142, 143, 144, 145, 146, 147, 148, 149, 150, 151, 152, 153, 154, 155, 156, 157, 158, 159, 160, 161, 162, 163, 164, 165, 166, 167, 168, 169, 170, 171, 172, 173, 174, 175, 176, 177, 178, 179, 180, 181, 182, 183, 184, 185, 186, 187, 188, 189, 190, 191, 192, 193, 194, 195, 196, 197, 198, 199, 200, 201, 202, 203, 204, 205, 206, 207, 208, 209, 210, 211, 212, 213, 214, 215, 216, 217, 218, 219, 220, 221, 222, 223, 224.
Z31 1½d. lake-red (1870–79) (Plate Nos. 1, 3) . . . *From* £400
Z32 2d. blue (1841), *imperf* . . . £3500
Z33 2d. blue (1855) wmk Large Crown perf 14 . . . 60·00
Z34 2d. blue (1858–69) . . . *From* 15·00
Plate Nos. 7, 8, 9, 12, 13, 14, 15.
Z35 2½d. rosy mauve (1875) (*blued paper*) . . . *From* 65·00
Plate Nos. 1, 2.
Z36 2½d. rosy mauve (1875–76) . . . *From* 30·00
Plate Nos. 1, 2, 3.
Z37 2½d. rosy mauve (Error of Lettering) . . . £2250
Z38 2½d. rosy mauve (1876–79) . . . *From* 16·00
Plate Nos. 3, 4, 5, 6, 7, 8, 9, 10, 11, 12, 13, 14, 15, 16, 17.
Z39 2½d. blue (1880–81) . . . *From* 10·00
Plate Nos. 17, 18, 19, 20.
Z40 2½d. blue (1881) (Plate Nos. 21, 22, 23) . . . *From* 7·00
Z41 3d. carmine-rose (1862) . . . £100
Z42 3d. rose (1865) (Plate No. 4) . . . 60·00
Z43 3d. rose (1867–73) . . . *From* 22·00
Plate Nos. 4, 5, 6, 7, 8, 9, 10.
Z44 3d. rose (1873–76) . . . *From* 30·00
Plate Nos. 11, 12, 14, 15, 16, 17, 18, 19, 20.
Z45 3d. rose (1881) (Plate Nos. 20, 21) . . . *From* £850
Z46 3d.on 3d. lilac (1883) . . . £450
Z47 4d. rose (or rose-carmine) (1857) . . . 27·00
a. Thick glazed paper . . . £110
Z48 4d. red (1862) (Plate Nos. 3, 4) . . . *From* 30·00
Z49 4d. vermilion (1865–73) . . . *From* 16·00
Plate Nos. 7, 8, 9, 10, 11, 12, 13, 14.
Z50 4d. vermilion (1876) (Plate No. 15) . . . £160
Z51 4d. sage-green (1877) (Plate Nos. 15, 16) . . . *From* 85·00
Z52 4d. grey-brown (1880) wmk Large Garter . . . £120
Plate No. 17.
Z53 4d. grey-brown (1880) wmk Crown . . . *From* 42·00
Plate Nos. 17, 18.
Z54 6d. violet (1854), embossed . . . £2000
Z55 6d. lilac (1856) . . . 40·00
a. Thick paper
Z56 6d. lilac (1862) (Plate Nos. 3, 4) . . . *From* 32·00
Z57 6d. lilac (1865–67) (Plate Nos. 5, 6) . . . *From* 28·00
Z58 6d. lilac (1865–67) (Wmk error) . . . £1200
Z59 6d. lilac (1867) (Plate No. 6) . . . 32·00
Z60 6d. violet (1867–70) (Plate Nos. 6, 8, 9) . . . *From* 25·00
Z61 6d. buff (1872–73) (Plate Nos. 11, 12) . . . *From* £100
Z62 6d. chestnut (1872) (Plate No. 11) . . . 30·00
Z63 6d. grey (1873) (Plate No. 12) . . . 75·00
Z64 6d. grey (1873–80) . . . *From* 28·00
Plate Nos. 13, 14, 15, 16, 17.
Z65 6d. grey (1881–82) (Plate Nos. 17, 18) . . . *From* 50·00
Z66 6d.on 6d. lilac (1883) . . . £110
Z67 8d. orange (1876) . . . £325
Z68 9d. straw (1862) . . . £550
Z69 9d. bistre (1862) . . . £500
Z70 9d. straw (1865) . . . £500
Z71 9d. straw (1867) . . . £650
Z72 10d. red-brown (1867) . . . £130
Z73 1s. (1847), embossed . . . £2250
Z74 1s. green (1856) . . . 70·00
Z75 1s. green (1856) (*thick paper*) . . . £250
Z76 1s. green (1862) . . . 60·00
Z77 1s. green ("K" *variety*) . . . £2250
Z78 1s. green (1865) (Plate No. 4) . . . 40·00
Z79 1s. green (1867–73) (Plate Nos. 4, 5, 6, 7) . . . *From* 24·00
Z80 1s. green (1873–77) . . . *From* 38·00
Plate Nos. 8, 9, 10, 11, 12, 13.
Z81 1s. orange-brown (1880) (Plate No. 13) . . . £225
Z82 1s. orange-brown (1881) . . . *From* 65·00
Plate Nos. 13, 14.
Z83 2s. blue (*shades*) (1867) . . . *From* £120
Z84 2s. brown (1880) . . . £2000
Z85 5s. rose (1867–74) (Plate Nos. 1, 2) . . . *From* £300
Z86 5s. rose (1882) (Plate No. 4), *blue paper* . . . £1200
Z87 5s. rose (1882) (Plate No. 4), *white paper* . . . £1000
Z88 10s. grey-green (1878) . . . £1800

1880.

Z89 ½d. deep green . . . 11·00
Z90 ½d. pale green . . . 11·00
Z91 1d. Venetian red . . . 10·00
Z92 1½d. Venetian red . . . £350
Z93 2d. pale rose . . . 32·00
Z94 2d. deep rose . . . 32·00
Z95 5d. indigo . . . 55·00

1881.

Z96 1d. lilac (14 *dots*) . . . 20·00
Z97 1d. lilac (16 *dots*) . . . 7·00

1883–84.

Z 98 ½d. slate-blue . . . 12·00
Z 99 1½d. lilac
Z100 2d. lilac . . . 75·00
Z101 2½d. lilac . . . 10·00
Z102 3d. lilac
Z103 4d. dull green . . . £130
Z104 5d. dull green . . . £120
Z105 6d. dull green
Z106 9d. dull green
Z107 1s. dull green
Z108 5s. rose (*blued paper*) . . . £1100
Z109 5s. rose (*white paper*) . . . £800

POSTAL FISCALS

Z109*a* 1d. reddish lilac (Type F **8**) (1867) wmk Anchor
Z110 1d. purple (Type F **12**) (1871) wmk Anchor . . . £80(
Z111 1d. purple (Type F **12**) (1881) wmk Orb . . . £60(

PRICES FOR STAMPS ON COVER TO 1945		
Nos.	1/3	*from* × 4
Nos.	4/19	*from* × 5
Nos.	20/9	*from* × 6
No.	30	—
Nos.	31/3	*from* × 4
Nos.	34/7	*from* × 10
Nos.	38/88	*from* × 4
Nos.	92/3	*from* × 5
Nos.	97/103	*from* × 3
Nos.	104/5	—
Nos.	106/20	*from* × 3
No.	121	—
Nos.	122/38	*from* × 3
Nos.	139/40	—
Nos.	141/72	*from* × 4
Nos.	173/209	*from* × 3
Nos.	210/31	*from* × 2
Nos.	D1/10	*from* × 30
Nos.	D11/20	*from* × 15

CROWN COLONY

PRINTERS. Nos. 1/156. Printed by De La Rue; typographed *excep where otherwise stated.*

1

Type **1**

The first Government local post was established on 10 June 18 and, as an experiment, mail was carried free of charge. During 18 the Council of Government decided that a rate of ½d. per ½ ounc should be charged for this service and stamps in Type I were ordere for this purpose. Both the new rate and the stamps were introduce on 1 December 1860. Until 1 January 1885 the ½d stamps we intended for the local service only; mail for abroad being handle by the British Post Office on Malta, using G.B. stamps.

Specialists now recognise 29 printings in shades of yellow and or in green during the period to 1884. These printings can be linked the changes in watermark and perforation as follows:

Ptg 1—Blued paper without wmk. P 14.
Ptgs 2 and 3—White paper without wmk. P 14.
Ptgs 4 to 9, 11, 13 to 19, 22 to 24—Crown CC wmk. P 14.
Ptg 10—Crown CC wmk. P 12½ (rough).
Ptg 12—Crown CC wmk. P 12½ (clean-cut).
Ptgs 20 and 21—Crown CC wmk. P 14 × 12½.
Ptgs 25 to 28, 30—Crown CA wmk. P 14.
Ptg 29—In green (No. 20).

(Des E. Fuchs)

1860 (1 Dec)–**63**. No wmk. P 14.

(a) Blued paper.

1 ½d. buff (1.12.60) . . . £850 £4

(b) Thin, hard white paper.

2 ½d. brown-orange (11.61) . . . £800 £3
3 ½d. buff (1.63) . . . £550 £2
a. *Pale buff* . . . £550 £2

No. 1 is printed in fugitive ink. It is known imperforate but w not issued in that state (*Price* £9000 *unused*).

The printing on No. 2 gives a very blurred and muddy impressic on Nos. 3/3*a* the impression is clear.

Specks of carmine can often be detected with a magnifying gla on Nos. 2/3*a*, and also on No. 4. Examples also exist on which pa of the design are in pure rose, due to defective mixing of the ink

1863–81. Wmk Crown CC.

(a) P 14.

4 ½d. buff (6.63) . . . 80·00 50·
w. Wmk inverted . . . £275 £2
x. Wmk reversed . . . £750
5 ½d. bright orange (11.64) . . . £400 £1
w. Wmk inverted . . . † £5
6 ½d. orange-brown (4.67) . . . £300 80·
7 ½d. dull orange (4.70) . . . £180 65·
w. Wmk inverted . . . † £3
x. Wmk reversed . . . £700
8 ½d. orange-buff (5.72) . . . £130 55·
9 ½d. golden yellow (aniline) (10.74) . . . £250 £3
10 ½d. yellow-buff (9.75) . . . 60·00 55·
11 ½d. pale buff (3.77) . . . £150 55·
w. Wmk inverted . . . † £4
12 ½d. bright orange-yellow (4.80) . . . £150 80·
13 ½d. yellow (4.81) . . . 85·00 50·
w. Wmk inverted . . . † £3

(b) P 12½ *rough (No. 14) or clean-cut (No. 15).*

14 ½d. buff-brown (11.68) . . . £110 90·
15 ½d. yellow-orange (5.71) . . . £250 £1

(c) P 14 × 12½.

16 ½d. yellow-buff (7.78) . . . £150 85·
17 ½d. yellow (2.79) . . . £170 90·

Examples of No. 4 from the 1863 printing are on thin, surfac paper; later printings in the same shade were on unsurfaced pap

The ink used for No. 5 is mineral and, unlike that on No. 9, d not stain the paper.

Some variations of shade on No. 6 may be described as chestn The ink of No. 6 is clear and never muddy, although some examp are over-inked. Deeper shades of No. 4, with which examples No. 6 might be confused, have muddy ink.

It is believed that there are no surviving pairs of the buff-bro imperforate between variety previously listed.

The Royal Collection contains an unused horizontal pair of the yellow-buff perforated 12½ × 14.

882 (Mar)–**84**. Wmk Crown CA. P 14.
8 ½d. orange-yellow . . . . . 35·00 35·00
9 ½d. red-orange (9.84) . . . . . 17·00 48·00

2 3

4 5

885 (1 Jan)–**90**. Wmk Crown CA. P 14.
0 **1** ½d. green . . . . . 2·25 50
w. Wmk inverted . . . . . 90·00 75·00
1 **2** 1d. rose . . . . . 85·00 26·00
w. Wmk inverted £1000
2 1d. carmine (*shades*) (1890) . . . . . 4·00 35
w. Wmk inverted . . . . . † £900
3 **3** 2d. grey . . . . . 5·00 1·50
4 **4** 2½d. dull blue . . . . . 55·00 2·50
5 2½d. bright blue . . . . . 35·00 1·00
5 2½d. ultramarine . . . . . 35·00 1·00
7 **3** 4d. brown . . . . . 11·00 3·00
a. Imperf (pair) £4750 £4750
w. Wmk inverted £1000
3 1s. violet . . . . . 35·00 9·00
) 1s. pale violet (1890) . . . . . 55·00 19·00
w. Wmk inverted £550 £200
)/9 *Set of* 6 . . . . . 80·00 14·00
)s/8s Optd "Specimen" *Set of* 6 . . . . . £3250

Although not valid for postage until 1 January 1885 these stamps were available at the G.P.O., Valletta from 27 December 1884.

Three unused examples of the ½d. green, No. 20, are known line perforated 12. It is believed that these originated from proof books, the stamp not being issued for use with this perforation.

The Royal Collection includes an example of the 1d. carmine printed on the gummed side.

886 (1 Jan). Wmk Crown CC. P 14.
) **5** 5s. rose . . . . . £110 80·00
s. Optd "Specimen" £500
w. Wmk inverted £140 £110

6 Harbour of Valletta **7** Gozo Fishing Boat **8** Galley of Knights of St. John

9 Emblematic figure of Malta **10** Shipwreck of St. Paul

(T **6/10** recess)

99 (4 Feb)–**1901**. P 14.

(*a*) Wmk Crown CA (sideways* on ½d).
6 ½d. brown (4.1.01) . . . . . 3·75 2·50
a. Red-brown . . . . . 1·50 40
w. Wmk Crown to left of CA . . . . . 2·50 75
x. Wmk sideways reversed . . . . . 35·00 20·00
y. Wmk Crown to left of CA and reversed . . . . . 45·00 25·00
7 4½d. sepia . . . . . 17·00 11·00
8 5d. vermilion . . . . . 32·00 15·00
x. Wmk reversed £150 £150

(*b*) Wmk Crown CC.
9 2s.6d. olive-grey . . . . . 40·00 12·00
10 10s. blue-black . . . . . 90·00 65·00
x. Wmk reversed . . . . . — £375
y. Wmk inverted and reversed £350 £275
'5 *Set of* 5 . . . . . £160 90·00
s/5s Optd "Specimen" *Set of* 5 . . . . . £225

*The normal sideways watermark shows Crown to right of CA, *seen from the back of the stamp.*

One Penny
(**11**)

12

1902 (4 July). *Nos. 24 and 25 surch locally at Govt Ptg Office with T* **11**.
36 1d.on 2½d. dull blue . . . . . 1·00 1·25
a. Surch double £15000 £3750
b. "One Pnney" (R. 9/2) . . . . . 28·00 55·00
ba. Surch double, with "One Pnney" . . .
s. Optd "Specimen" . . . . . 70·00
37 1d.on 2½d. bright blue . . . . . 1·00 1·75
a. "One Pnney" (R. 9/2) . . . . . 30·00 55·00

(Des E. Fuchs)

1903 (12 Mar)–**04**. Wmk Crown CA. P 14.
38 **12** ½d. green . . . . . 8·00 85
39 1d. blackish brown and red (7.5.03) . . . . . 15·00 40
40 2d. purple and grey . . . . . 27·00 6·00
41 2½d. maroon and blue (9.03) . . . . . 20·00 4·50
42 3d. grey and purple (26.3.03) . . . . . 1·75 50
43 4d. blackish brown and brown (19.5.04) . . . . . 26·00 16·00
44 1s. grey and violet (6.4.03) . . . . . 16·00 7·00
38/44 *Set of* 7 . . . . . £100 32·00
38s/44s Optd "Specimen" *Set of* 7 . . . . . £130

1904–14. Wmk Mult Crown CA (sideways* on ½d.). P 14.
45 **6** ½d. red-brown (10.10.05) . . . . . 4·50 60
a. Deep brown (2.4.10†) . . . . . 2·50 10
aw. Wmk Crown to left of CA . . . . . 8·00 1·50
ax. Wmk reversed . . . . .
ay. Wmk Crown to left of CA and reversed . . . . .
47 **12** ½d. green (6.11.04) . . . . . 4·50 30
aw. Wmk inverted . . . . .
b. Deep green (1909) . . . . . 4·00 10
bw. Wmk inverted . . . . .
48 1d. black and red (24.4.05) . . . . . 17·00 20
49 1d. red (2.4.07) . . . . . 2·50 10
50 2d. purple and grey (22.2.05) . . . . . 8·50 2·25
51 2d. grey (4.10.11) . . . . . 3·25 5·50
52 2½d. maroon and blue (10.04) . . . . . 18·00 60
53 2½d. bright blue (15.1.11) . . . . . 5·50 2·75
54 4d. black and brown (1.4.06) . . . . . 11·00 5·50
w. Wmk inverted . . . . .
55 4d. black and red/*yellow* (21.11.11) . . . . . 4·00 3·50
57 **7** 4½d. brown (27.2.05) . . . . . 26·00 5·50
w. Wmk inverted £200 £180
58 4½d. orange (6.3.12†) . . . . . 4·50 3·50
59 **8** 5d. vermilion (20.2.05) . . . . . 27·00 5·00
60 5d. pale sage-green (1909) . . . . . 4·25 3·50
a. Deep sage-green (1914) . . . . . 11·00 14·00
61 **12** 1s. grey and violet (14.12.04) . . . . . 50·00 2·00
62 1s. black/*green* (15.3.11) . . . . . 7·50 2·75
63 5s. green and red/*yellow* (22.3.11) . . . . . 65·00 75·00
45/63 *Set of* 17 . . . . . £225 £100
45*a*s, 47*b*s, 49s, 51s, 53s, 55s, 58s, 60s, 62s/3s Optd "Specimen" *Set of* 10 . . . . . £325

*The normal sideways watermark shows Crown to right of CA, *as seen from the back of the stamp.*

†These are the earliest known dates of use.

13

14

15

1914–21. *Ordinary paper (½d. to 2½d., 2s.6d.) or chalk-surfaced paper (others).* Wmk Mult Crown CA. P 14.
69 **13** ½d. brown (2.1.14) . . . . . 1·00 10
a. Deep brown (1919) . . . . . 1·25 60
x. Wmk reversed . . . . . † £475
71 ½d. green (20.1.14) . . . . . 2·25 30
aa. Wmk sideways . . . . . † £4000
a. Deep green (1919) . . . . . 2·75 75
aw. Wmk inverted . . . . . † £200
73 1d. carmine-red (15.4.14) . . . . . 1·50 10
a. Scarlet (1915) . . . . . 1·50 40
w. Wmk inverted . . . . . † £200
75 2d. grey (12.8.14) . . . . . 9·00 3·50
aw. Wmk inverted . . . . . † £475
b. Deep slate (1919) . . . . . 9·00 12·00
77 2½d. bright blue (11.3.14) . . . . . 2·25 50
w. Wmk inverted . . . . . † £130
78 **14** 3d. purple/*yellow* (1.5.20) . . . . . 2·50 8·50
a. On orange-buff . . . . . 55·00 42·00
79 **6** 4d. black (21.8.15) . . . . . 15·00 3·25
a. Grey-black (28.10.16) . . . . . 27·00 8·00
80 **13** 6d. dull and bright purple (10.3.14) . . . . . 11·00 18·00
a. Dull purple and magenta (1918) . . . . . 14·00 18·00
w. Wmk inverted . . . . .
81 **14** 1s. black/*green* (*white back*) (2.1.14) . . . . . 13·00 25·00
a. On green, green back (1915) . . . . . 12·00 15·00
ab. Wmk sideways . . . . . † £1800
as. Optd "Specimen" . . . . . 48·00
b. On *blue-green, olive back* (1918) . . . . . 19·00 21·00
c. On *emerald surface* (1920) . . . . . 8·50 22·00
d. On *emerald back* (1921) . . . . . 28·00 65·00
86 **15** 2s. purple and bright blue/*blue* (15.4.14) . . . . . 50·00 30·00
a. Break in scroll £275
b. Broken crown and scroll £300
c. Nick in top right scroll £275
d. Dull purple and blue/blue (1921) . . . . . 75·00 50·00
da. Break in scroll £325
db. Broken crown and scroll £375
de. Break in lines below left scroll £325
df. Damaged leaf at bottom right £325
87 **9** 2s.6d. olive-green (1919) . . . . . 55·00 75·00
a. Olive-grey (1920) . . . . . 60·00 95·00
88 **15** 5s. green and red/*yellow* (21.3.17) . . . . . 80·00 95·00
a. Break in scroll £375
b. Broken crown and scroll £425
e. Break in lines below left scroll £375
f. Damaged leaf at bottom right £375
69/88 *Set of* 12 . . . . . £200 £200
69s/88s (*ex* 2s.6d.) Optd "Specimen" *Set of* 11 . . . . . £425

The design of Nos. 79/*a* differs in various details from that of Type **6**.

We have only seen one copy of No. 71aa; it is in used condition.

A 3d. purple on yellow on white back, Type **14**, was prepared for use but not issued. It exists overprinted "Specimen" (*Price* £250).

An example of the 2s.6d. olive-grey with bottom margin attached exists with the "A" omitted from "CA" in the watermark on the margin.

For illustrations of the varieties on Nos. 86 and 88 see above No. 51*b* of Bermuda.

(**16**)

17

18

1917–18. *Optd with T* **16** *by De La Rue.*
92 **13** ½d. deep green (14.12.17*) . . . . . 1·50 15
w. Wmk inverted £425
93 **12** 3d. grey and purple (15.2.18*) . . . . . 1·75 8·00
92s/3s Optd "Specimen" *Set of* 2 . . . . . £140

*These are the earliest known dates of use.

(T **17** recess)

1919 (6 Mar). Wmk Mult Crown CA. P 14.
96 **17** 10s. black £2500 £3500
s. Optd "Specimen" £750

Dark flaw on scroll (R. 2/4 1st state)

Lines omitted from scroll (R. 2/4 2nd state)

1921 (16 Feb)–**22**. *Chalk-surfaced paper (6d., 2s.) or ordinary paper (others).* Wmk Mult Script CA. P 14.
97 **13** ¼d. brown (12.1.22) . . . . . 2·50 28·00
98 ½d. green (19.1.22) . . . . . 3·00 19·00
99 1d. scarlet (24.12.21) . . . . . 2·75 1·60
w. Wmk inverted £475 £170
100 **18** 2d. grey . . . . . 4·50 1·75
101 **13** 2½d. bright blue (15.1.22) . . . . . 3·75 28·00
102 6d. dull purple & brt purple (19.1.22) . . . . . 29·00 70·00
103 **15** 2s. purple and blue/*blue* (19.1.22) . . . . . 60·00 £190
a. Break in scroll £225
b. Broken crown and scroll £225
c. Dark flaw on scroll £1700
d. Lines omitted from scroll £375
e. Break in lines below left scroll £225
f. Damaged leaf at bottom right £225
104 **17** 10s. black (19.1.22) £350 £650
97/104 *Set of* 8 . . . . . £400 £900
97s/104s Optd "Specimen" *Set of* 8 . . . . . £425

For illustrations of other varieties on No. 103 see above No. 51*b* of Bermuda.

Examples of all values are known showing a forged G.P.O. Malta postmark dated "MY 10 22".

(**19**)

(**20**)

1922 (12 Jan–Apr). *Optd with T* **19** *or T* **20** *(large stamps), at Govt Printing Office, Valletta.*

(*a*) *On No. 35.* Wmk Crown CC.
105 **10** 10s blue-black (R.) £190 £350

(*b*) *On Nos. 71, 77, 78a, 80, 81d, 86c, 87a and 88.* Wmk Mult Crown CA.
106 **13** ½d. green . . . . . 1·00 1·75
w. Wmk inverted . . . . . 80·00
107 2½d. bright blue . . . . . 8·50 29·00
108 **14** 3d. purple/*orange-buff* . . . . . 3·00 17·00
109 **13** 6d. dull and bright purple . . . . . 2·50 16·00
x. Wmk reversed . . . . . † £700
110 **14** 1s. black/*emerald* . . . . . 3·50 16·00
111 **15** 2s. purple and blue/*blue* (R.) £225 £450
a. Break in scroll £650
b. Broken crown and scroll £650
e. Break in lines below left scroll £650
f. Damaged leaf at bottom right £650
112 **9** 2s.6d. olive-grey . . . . . 22·00 45·00
a. "C" of "CA" missing from wmk £850

No.	Type	Description	Unused	Used
113	**15**	5s. green and red/*yellow*	50·00	80·00
		a. Break in scroll	£275	
		b. Broken crown and scroll	£275	
		c. Lines omitted from scroll	£300	
		e. Break in lines below left scroll	£275	
		f. Damaged leaf at bottom right	£275	
106/13 *Set of* 8			£275	£600

(c) On Nos. 97/104. Wmk Mult Script CA.

No.	Type	Description	Unused	Used
114	**13**	¼d. brown	30	75
		w. Wmk inverted		
115		½d. green (29.4)	2·00	6·00
116		1d. scarlet	1·00	20
117	**18**	2d. grey	2·25	45
118	**13**	2½d. bright blue (15.1)	1·10	1·00
119		6d. dull and bright purple (19.4)	11·00	32·00
120	**15**	2s. purple and blue/*blue* (R.) (25.1)	40·00	85·00
		a. Break in scroll	£200	
		b. Broken crown and scroll	£200	
		c. Lines omitted from scroll	£300	
		e. Break in lines below left scroll	£200	
		f. Damaged leaf at bottom right	£200	
121	**17**	10s. black (R.) (9.3)	£140	£200
114/21 *Set of* 8			£180	£300

Examples of all values are known showing a forged G.P.O. Malta postmark dated "MY 10 22".

One Farthing
(21)

22

23

1922 (15 Apr.). *No. 100 surch with T* **21**, *at Govt Printing Office, Valletta.*

No.	Type	Description	Unused	Used
122	**18**	¼d. on 2d. grey	85	30

(Des C. Dingli (*T* **22**) and G. Vella (**23**))

1922 (1 Aug)–**26**. Wmk Mult Script CA (sideways* on *T* **22**, except No. 140). P 14.

(a) Typo. Chalk-surfaced paper.

No.	Type	Description	Unused	Used
123	**22**	¼d. brown (22.8.22)	2·50	60
		a. Chocolate-brown	3·25	70
		w. Wmk Crown to right of CA	—	60·00
124		½d. green	2·50	15
		w. Wmk Crown to right of CA	—	60·00
125		1d. orange and purple	3·25	20
		w. Wmk Crown to right of CA	—	45·00
126		1d. bright violet (25.4.24)	3·25	80
127		1½d. brown-red (1.10.23)	4·25	15
128		2d. bistre-brown & turquoise (28.8.22)	2·75	1·25
		w. Wmk Crown to right of CA	—	85·00
129		2½d. ultramarine (16.2.26)	2·75	7·00
130		3d. cobalt (28.8.22)	3·75	1·50
		a. Bright ultramarine	3·25	1·50
131		3d. black/*yellow* (16.2.26)	3·00	13·00
132		4d. yellow and bright blue (28.8.22)	2·00	2·50
		w. Wmk Crown to right of CA	£140	
133		6d. olive-green and reddish violet	3·25	2·25
134	**23**	1s. indigo and sepia	7·00	2·50
135		2s. brown and blue	10·00	10·00
136		2s.6d. brt magenta & black (28.8.22)	11·00	15·00
137		5s. orange-yell & brt ultram (28.8.22)	21·00	42·00
138		10s. slate-grey and brown (28.8.22)	55·00	£150

(b) Recess.

No.	Type	Description	Unused	Used
139	**22**	£1 black and carmine-red (wmk sideways) (28.8.22)	£120	£300
140		£1 black and bright carmine (wmk upright) (14.5.25)	95·00	£300
123/40 *Set of* 17			£200	£500
123s/39s Optd "Specimen" *Set of* 17			£475	

*The normal sideways watermark shows Crown to left of CA, *as seen from the back of the stamp.*

Two pence halfpenny
(24)

POSTAGE
(25)

1925. *Surch with T* **24**, *at Govt Printing Office, Valletta.*

No.	Type	Description	Unused	Used
141	**22**	2½d.on 3d. cobalt (3 Dec)	1·75	3·75
142		2½d.on 3d. bright ultramarine (9 Dec)	1·75	3·50

1926 (1 Apr). *Optd with T* **25** *at Govt Printing Office, Valletta.*

No.	Type	Description	Unused	Used
143	**22**	¼d. brown	70	4·00
144		½d. green	70	15
		w. Wmk Crown to right of CA	70·00	
145		1d. bright violet	1·00	25
146		1½d. brown-red	1·00	60
147		2d. bistre-brown and turquoise	75	1·00
148		2½d. ultramarine	1·25	80
149		3d. black/*yellow*	75	80
		a. Opt inverted	£170	£475
150		4d. yellow and bright blue	7·00	17·00
151		6d. olive-green and violet	2·75	3·50
152	**23**	1s. indigo and sepia	5·50	11·00
153		2s. brown and blue	50·00	£140
154		2s.6d. bright magenta and black	13·00	35·00
155		5s. orange-yellow & brt ultramarine	9·00	35·00
156		10s. slate-grey and brown	7·00	18·00
143/56 *Set of* 14			90·00	£250

26

27 Valletta Harbour

28 St. Publius

33 St. Paul

(*T* **26** typo, others recess Waterlow)

1926 (6 Apr)–**27**. *T* **26/8**, **33** *and similar designs. Inscr* "POSTAGE". Wmk Mult Script CA. P 15 × 14 (*T* **26**) or 12½ (others).

No.	Type	Description	Unused	Used
157	**26**	¼d. brown	80	15
158		½d. yellow-green (5.8.26)	60	15
		a. Printed on the gummed side	£750	
		w. Wmk inverted	†	£500
159		1d. rose-red (1.4.27)	3·00	1·00
160		1½d. chestnut (7.10.26)	2·00	10
161		2d. greenish grey (1.4.27)	4·50	9·50
162		2½d. blue (1.4.27)	4·00	1·00
162*a*		3d. violet (1.4.27)	4·25	2·50
163		4d. black and red	3·25	9·50
164		4½d. lavender and ochre	3·50	2·75
165		6d. violet and scarlet (5.5.26)	4·25	3·75
166	**27**	1s. black	6·50	4·50
167	**28**	1s.6d. black and green	6·50	13·00
168	–	2s. black and purple	6·50	15·00
169	–	2s.6d. black and vermilion	15·00	48·00
170	–	3s. black and blue	17·00	30·00
171	–	5s. black and green (5.5.26)	22·00	60·00
172	**33**	10s. black and carmine (9.2.27)	55·00	£100
157/72 *Set of* 17			£140	£275
157s/72s Optd "Specimen" *Set of* 17			£300	

Designs: *Vert*—2s.6d. Gozo fishing boat; 3s. Neptune; *Horiz*—2s. Mdina (Notabile); 5s. Neolithic temple, Mnajdra.

AIR MAIL
(34)

POSTAGE AND REVENUE
(35)

POSTAGE AND REVENUE.
(36)

1928 (1 Apr). *Air. Optd with T* **34**.

No.	Type	Description	Unused	Used
173	**26**	6d. violet and scarlet	1·75	1·00

1928 (1 Oct–5 Dec). *As Nos. 157/72, optd.*

No.	Type	Description	Unused	Used
174	**35**	¼d. brown	1·50	10
175		½d. yellow-green	1·50	10
176		1d. rose-red	1·75	3·25
177		1d. chestnut (5.12.28)	4·50	10
178		1½d. chestnut	2·00	85
179		1½d. rose-red (5.12.28)	4·25	10
180		2d. greeenish grey	4·25	9·00
181		2½d. blue	2·00	10
182		3d. violet	2·00	80
183		4d. black and red	2·00	1·75
184		4½d. lavender and ochre	2·25	1·00
185		6d. violet and scarlet	2·25	1·50
186	**36**	1s. black (R.)	5·50	2·50
187		1s.6d. black and green (R.)	6·50	9·50
188		2s. black and purple (R.)	24·00	55·00
189		2s.6d. black and vermilion (R.)	17·00	23·00
190		3s. black and blue (R.)	19·00	30·00
191		5s. black and green (R.)	29·00	65·00
192		10s. black and carmine (R.)	55·00	90·00
174/92 *Set of* 19			£160	£250
174s/92s Optd "Specimen" *Set of* 19			£325	

1930 (20 Oct). *As Nos. 157/172, but inscr* "POSTAGE (&) REVENUE".

No.	Type	Description	Unused	Used
193		¼d. brown	60	10
194		½d. yellow-green	60	10
195		1d. chestnut	60	10
196		1½d. rose-red	70	10
197		2d. greenish grey	1·25	50
198		2½d. blue	2·00	10
199		3d. violet	1·50	20
200		4d. black and red	1·25	4·00
201		4½d. lavender and ochre	3·25	1·25
202		6d. violet and scarlet	2·75	1·25
203		1s. black	10·00	14·00
204		1s.6d. black and green	8·50	19·00
205		2s. black and purple	10·00	19·00
206		2s.6d. black and vermilion	17·00	48·00
207		3s. black and blue	27·00	55·00
208		5s. black and green	32·00	65·00
209		10s. black and carmine	75·00	£160
193/209 *Set of* 17			£170	£350
193s/209s Perf "Specimen" *Set of* 17			£325	

1935 (6 May). *Silver Jubilee. As Nos. 91/4 of Antigua, but printed by B.W.* P 11 × 12.

No.	Type	Description	Unused	Used
210		½d. black and green	50	50
		a. Extra flagstaff	22·00	35·00
		b. Short extra flagstaff	40·00	
		c. Lightning conductor	30·00	
211		2½d. brown and deep blue	2·50	4·50
		a. Extra flagstaff	£130	£160
		b. Short extra flagstaff	£160	
		c. Lightning conductor	£110	
212		6d. light blue and olive-green	7·00	4·50
		a. Extra flagstaff	£180	£200
		b. Short extra flagstaff	£250	
		c. Lightning conductor	£140	
213		1s. slate and purple	11·00	16·0
		a. Extra flagstaff	£425	£45
		b. Short extra flagstaff	£350	
		c. Lightning conductor	£250	
210/13 *Set of* 4			19·00	23·0
210s/13s Perf "Specimen" *Set of* 4			£140	

For illustrations of plate varieties see Omnibus section followin Zanzibar.

Sheets from the second printing of the ½d., 6d. and 1s. i November 1935 had the extra flagstaff partially erased from th stamp with a sharp point.

1937 (12 May). *Coronation. As Nos. 95/7 of Antigua, but printed b D.L.R..* P 14.

No.	Type	Description	Unused	Used
214		½d. green	10	2
215		1½d. scarlet	1·25	6
		a. Brown-lake	£550	£55
216		2½d. bright blue	1·00	8
214/16 *Set of* 3			2·00	1·5
214s/16s Perf "Specimen" *Set of* 3			70·00	

37 Grand Harbour, Valletta

38 H.M.S. *St. Angelo*

39 Verdala Palace

40 Hypogeum, Hal Saflieni

Broken cross (Right pane R. 5/7)

Extra windows (R. 2/7) (corrected in 1945)

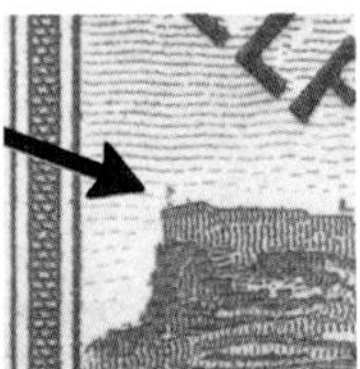
Flag on citadel (R. 5/8)

Damaged value tablet (R. 4/9)

Semaphore flaw (R. 2/7)

(Recess Waterlow)

1938 (17 Feb*)–**43**. *T* **37/40** *and similar designs.* Wmk Mult Scr CA (sideways on No. 217). P 12½.

No.	Type	Description	Unused	Used
217	**37**	¼d. brown	10	
218	**38**	½d. green	1·75	
218*a*		½d. red-brown (8.3.43)	55	
219	**39**	1d. red-brown	4·25	
219*a*		1d. green (8.3.43)	60	
220	**40**	1½d. scarlet	1·00	
		a. Broken cross	95·00	60
220*b*		1½d. slate-black (8.3.43)	30	
		ba. Broken cross	60·00	50
221	–	2d. slate-black	40	2
		a. Extra windows	45·00	
221*b*	–	2d. scarlet (8.3.43)	40	
		ba. Extra windows	45·00	
		bb. Flag on citadel	45·00	
222	–	2½d. greyish blue	75	
222*a*	–	2½d. dull violet (8.3.43)	60	
223	–	3d. dull violet	55	
223*a*	–	3d. blue (8.3.43)	30	
224	–	4½d. olive-green and yellow-brown	50	
225	–	6d. olive-green and scarlet	75	
226	–	1s. black	75	
227	–	1s.6d. black and olive-green	7·00	4
228	–	2s. green and deep blue	4·50	4
229	–	2s.6d. black and scarlet	8·00	5
		a. Damaged value tablet	£190	£

30 – 5s. black and green . . . 4·50 6·50
a. Semaphore flaw . . . 70·00
31 – 10s. black and carmine . . . 15·00 15·00
17/31 *Set of* 21 . . . 48·00 38·00
17s/31s Perf "Specimen" *Set of* 21 . . . £375

Designs: *Horiz (as T39)*—2d. Victoria and citadel, Gozo; 2½d. De Isle Adam entering Mdina; 4½d. Ruins at Mnajdra; 1s.6d. t. Publius; 2s. Mdina Cathedral; 2s.6d. Statue of Neptune. *Vert (as* **40)**—3d. St. John's Co-Cathedral; 6d. Statue of Manoel de 'ilhena; 1s. Maltese girl wearing faldetta; 5s. Palace Square, 'alletta; 10s. St. Paul.

*This is the local date of issue but the stamps were released in ondon on 15 February.

946 (3 Dec). *Victory. As Nos. 110/11 of Antigua, but inscr* "MALTA" *between Maltese Cross and George Cross.*
32 1d. green . . . 15 10
w. Wmk inverted . . . £550
33 3d. blue . . . 30 80
32s/3s Perf "Specimen" *Set of* 2 . . . 60·00

SELF-GOVERNMENT

(52)

"NT" joined (R. 4/10)

Halation flaw (Pl 2 R. 2/5) (ptg of 8 Jan 1953)

Cracked plate (Pl 2 R. 5/1) (ptg of 8 Jan 1953)

(Optd by Waterlow)

48 (25 Nov)–**53**. *New Constitution. As Nos. 217/31 but optd as T* **52**; *reading up on ½d. and 5s., down on other values, and smaller on ½d. value.*
4 **37** ½d. brown . . . 30 20
5 **38** ½d. red-brown . . . 30 10
a. "NT" joined . . . 19·00
6 **39** 1d. green . . . 30 10
6a 1d. grey (R.) (8.1.53) . . . 30 10
7 **40** 1½d. blue-black (R.) . . . 1·25 10
a. Broken cross . . . 80·00 40·00
7b 1½d. green (8.1.53) . . . 30 10
ba. Albino opt . . . † £10000
8 – 2d. scarlet . . . 1·25 10
a. Extra windows . . . 55·00
b. Flag on citadel . . . 55·00
8b – 2d. yellow-ochre (8.1.53) . . . 30 10
ba. Halation flaw . . . £120
bc. Cracked plate . . . £110
9 – 2½d. dull violet (R.) . . . 80 10
9a – 2½d. scarlet-vermilion (8.1.53) . . . 50 1·50
0 – 3d. blue (R.) . . . 1·25 15
0a – 3d. dull violet (R.) (8.1.53) . . . 50 15
1 – 4½d. olive-green and yellow-brown . . . 2·00 1·50
1a – 4½d. olive-grn & dp ultram (R.) (8.1.53) . . . 50 90
2 – 6d. olive-green and scarlet . . . 3·00 15
3 – 1s. black . . . 2·75 40
4 – 1s.6d. black and olive-green . . . 2·50 50
5 – 2s. green and deep blue (R.) . . . 5·00 2·50
6 – 2s.6d. black and scarlet . . . 12·00 2·50
a. Damaged value tablet . . . £600
7 – 5s. black and green (R.) . . . 20·00 3·50
a. "NT" joined . . . £200 £110
b. Semaphore flaw . . . — £2000
8 – 10s. black and carmine . . . 20·00 22·00
4/48 *Set of* 21 . . . 65·00 32·00

49 (4 Jan). *Royal Silver Wedding. As Nos. 112/13 of Antigua, but inscr* "MALTA" *between Maltese Cross and George Cross and with £1 ptd in recess.*
9 1d. green . . . 50 10
0 £1 indigo . . . 38·00 35·00

49 (10 Oct). *75th Anniv of U.P.U. As Nos. 114/17 of Antigua, but inscr* "MALTA" *in recess.*
1 2½d. violet . . . 30 10
2 3d. deep blue . . . 3·00 1·00
3 6d. carmine-red . . . 60 1·00
4 1s. blue-black . . . 60 2·50
1/4 *Set of* 4 . . . 4·00 4·25

53 Queen Elizabeth IIwhen Princess

54 "Our Lady of Mount Carmel" (attrib Palladino)

(*T* **53/4**. Recess B.W.)

1950 (1 Dec). *Visit of Princess Elizabeth to Malta.* Wmk Mult Script CA. P 12×11½.
255 **53** 1d. green . . . 10 15
256 3d. blue . . . 20 20
257 1s. black . . . 65 1·25
255/7 *Set of* 3 . . . 80 1·40

1951 (12 July). *Seventh Centenary of the Scapular.* Wmk Mult Script CA. P 12×11½.
258 **54** 1d. green . . . 15 15
259 3d. violet . . . 50 10
260 1s. black . . . 1·10 85
258/60 *Set of* 3 . . . 1·60 1·00

POSTAGE DUE STAMPS

D 1

D 2

1925 (16 Apr). *Typeset by Govt Printing Office, Valletta. Imperf*
D 1 **D 1** ½d. black . . . 1·25 7·00
a. *Tête-bêche* (horiz pair) . . . 5·00 18·00
D 2 1d. black . . . 3·25 3·00
a. *Tête-bêche* (horiz pair) . . . 10·00 12·00
D 3 1½d. black . . . 3·00 3·75
a. *Tête-bêche* (horiz pair) . . . 10·00 15·00
D 4 2d. black . . . 7·50 13·00
a. *Tête-bêche* (horiz pair) . . . 17·00 35·00
D 5 2½d. black . . . 2·75 2·75
a. "2" of "½" omitted . . . £800 £1200
b. *Tête-bêche* (horiz pair) . . . 12·00 15·00
D 6 3d. black/*grey* . . . 9·00 15·00
a. *Tête-bêche* (horiz pair) . . . 30·00 48·00
D 7 4d. black/*buff* . . . 5·00 9·50
a. *Tête-bêche* (horiz pair) . . . 17·00 38·00
D 8 6d. black/*buff* . . . 5·00 17·00
a. *Tête-bêche* (horiz pair) . . . 17·00 50·00
D 9 1s. black/*buff* . . . 7·50 22·00
a. *Tête-bêche* (horiz pair) . . . 25·00 60·00
D10 1s.6d. black/*buff* . . . 14·00 55·00
a. *Tête-bêche* (horiz pair) . . . 40·00 £140
D1/10 *Set of* 10 . . . 50·00 £130

Nos. D1/10 were each issued in sheets containing 4 panes (6×7) printed separately, the impressions in the two right-hand panes being inverted. Fourteen horizontal *tête-bêche* pairs occur from the junction of the left and right-hand panes.

No. D5a occurred on R. 4/4 of the last 2½d. pane position to be printed. Forgeries exist, but can be detected by comparison with a normal example under ultra-violet light. They are often found in pair with normal, showing forged cancellations of "VALLETTA AP20 25" or "G.P.O" MY 7 25".

(Typo B.W.)

1925 (20 July). Wmk Mult Script CA (sideways). P 12.
D11 **D 2** ½d. green . . . 1·25 60
D12 1d. violet . . . 1·25 45
D13 1½d. brown . . . 1·50 80
D14 2d. grey . . . 11·00 1·00
D15 2½d. orange . . . 2·00 1·25
x. Wmk reversed . . . 80·00
D16 3d. blue . . . 3·50 1·25
D17 4d. olive-green . . . 12·00 16·00
D18 6d. purple . . . 3·00 4·25
D19 1s. black . . . 6·50 12·00
D20 1s.6d. carmine . . . 8·50 29·00
D11/20 *Set of* 10 . . . 45·00 60·00
D11s/20s Optd "Specimen" *Set of* 10 . . . £200

Mauritius

GREAT BRITAIN STAMPS USED IN MAURITIUS. We no longer list the Great Britain stamps with obliteration "B 53" as there is no evidence that British stamps were available from the Mauritius Post Office

See under SEYCHELLES for stamps of Mauritius used at Victoria with "B 64" cancellations between 1861 and 1890.

A similar "B 65" cancellation was used on the island of Rodrigues, a dependency of Mauritius, from 11 December 1861 onwards.

PRICES FOR STAMPS ON COVER TO 1945

Nos.	1/5	*from* × 2
Nos.	6/9	*from* × 3
Nos.	10/15	*from* × 4
Nos.	16/25	*from* × 5
Nos.	26/9	*from* × 3
Nos.	30/1	*from* —
Nos.	32/5	*from* × 4
Nos.	36/44	*from* × 5
Nos.	46/72	*from* × 3
Nos.	76/82	*from* × 5
Nos.	83/91	*from* × 6
Nos.	92/100	*from* × 4
Nos.	101/11	*from* × 3
Nos.	117/24	*from* × 8
Nos.	127/32	*from* × 7
No.	133	*from* × 4
Nos.	134/5	*from* × 10
No.	136	*from* × 8
Nos.	137/56	*from* × 6
Nos.	157/63	*from* × 5
Nos.	164/221	*from* × 3
No.	222	—
Nos.	223/41	*from* × 3
Nos.	242/4	*from* × 10
Nos.	245/8	*from* × 3
Nos.	249/63	*from* × 2
Nos.	E1/6	*from* × 10
Nos.	D1/7	*from* × 40
Nos.	R1/3	*from* × 15

CROWN COLONY

Nos. 1/25*b* and 36/44 were printed in Mauritius.

1 ("POST OFFICE")

2 ("POST PAID")

(Engraved on copper by J. O. Barnard)

1847 (21 Sept). *Head of Queen on groundwork of diagonal and perpendicular lines. Imperf.*
1 **1** 1d. orange-red . . . — £450000
2 2d. deep blue . . . — £550000

A single plate contained one example of each value.

It is generally agreed that fifteen examples of No. 1 have survived (including two unused) and twelve of No. 2 (including four unused). Most are now in permanent museum collections.

NOTE. Our prices for early Mauritius are for stamps in very fine condition. Exceptional copies are worth more, poorer copies considerably less.

(Engraved on copper by J. O. Barnard)

1848 (June)–**59**. *Imperf.*

A. Earliest impressions. Design deep, sharp and clear. Diagonal lines predominate. Thick paper (Period of use: 1d. 1853–54, 2d. 1848–49).
3 **2** 1d. orange-vermilion/*yellowish* . . . £35000 £13000
4 2d. indigo-blue/*grey to bluish* . . . £30000 £15000
a. "PENOE" for "PENCE" (R. 3/1) . . . £60000 £23000
5 2d. deep blue/*grey to bluish* . . . £30000 £15000
a. "PENOE" for "PENCE" (R. 3/1) . . . £60000 £26000

B. Early impressions. Design sharp and clear but some lines slightly weakened. Paper not so thick, grey to yellowish white or bluish (Period of use:1d. 1853–55, 2d. 1849–54).
6 **2** 1d. vermilion . . . £15000 £5500
7 1d. orange-vermilion . . . £16000 £5000
8 2d. blue . . . £17000 £6000
a. "PENOE" for "PENCE" (R. 3/1) . . . £27000 £9500
9 2d. deep blue . . . £21000 £6500

C. Intermediate impressions. White patches appear where design has worn. Paper yellowish white, grey or bluish, of poorish quality (Period of use: 1d and 2d. 1854–57).
10 **2** 1d. bright vermilion . . . £8000 £2000
11 1d. dull vermilion . . . £8000 £2000
12 1d. red . . . £8000 £2000
13 2d. deep blue . . . £11000 £3000
14 2d. blue . . . £8000 £2250
a. "PENOE" for "PENCE" (R. 3/1) *from* . . . £14000 £4750
15 2d. light blue . . . £8000 £2250

D. Worn impressions. Much of design worn away but some diagonal lines distinct. Paper yellowish, grey or bluish, of poorish quality (Period of use: 1d. 1857–59, 2d. 1855–58).
16 **2** 1d. red/*yellowish or grey* . . . £2750 £475
17 1d. red-brown/*yellowish or grey* . . . £2750 £475
18 1d. red/*bluish* . . . £2000 £425
a. Doubly printed . . .
19 1d. red-brown/*bluish* . . . £2000 £425
20 2d. blue (*shades*)/*yellowish or grey* . . . £3000 £900
a. "PENOE" for "PENCE" (R. 3/1) . . . *from* — £1500
21 2d. grey-blue/*yellowish or grey* . . . £3250 £850
22 2d. blue (shades)/*bluish* . . . £3000 £850
a. Doubly printed . . .

E. Latest impressions. Almost none of design showing except part of Queens's head and frame. Paper yellowish, grey or bluish, of poorish quality (Period of use: 1d. 1859, 2d. 1856–58)
23 **2** 1d. red . . . £1700 £400
24 1d. red-brown . . . £1700 £400
25 2d. grey-blue/*bluish* . . . £2250 £600
a. "PENOE" for "PENCE" (R. 3/1) . . . £4000 £1000

Earliest known use of the 2d. value is on 19 June 1848, but the 1d. value is not known used before 27 September 1853.

There were separate plates for the 1d. and 2d. values, each of 12 (3×4).

3

(**4**)

5

(Eng G. Fairman. Recess P.B.)

1858*. *Surch with T* **4**. *Imperf.*
26 **3** 4d. green . . . £1000 £400

*Although originally gazetted for use from 8 April 1854, research into the archives indicates that No. 26 was not actually issued until 1858, when the stamps were mentioned in an ordinance of 30 April. The earliest dated postmark known is 27 March 1858.

PERKINS BACON "CANCELLED". For notes on these handstamps, showing "CANCELLED" between horizontal bars forming an oval, see Catalogue Introduction.

1858–62. *No value expressed. Imperf.*

27	**3**	(4d.) green	£425	£200
28		(6d.) vermilion	32·00	60·00
29		(9d.) dull magenta (1859)	£550	£200
		a. Reissued as (1d.) value (11.62)	†	£160

Prepared for use but not issued.

30	**3**	(No value), red-brown	15·00	
31		(No value), blue (H/S "CANCELLED" in oval £6000)	3·75	

Use of the dull magenta as a 1d. value can be confirmed by the presence of the "B 53" cancellation which was first introduced in 1861.

Remainders of Nos. 30/1, overprinted "L.P.E. 1890" in red, were perforated at the London Philatelic Exhibition and sold as souvenirs.

(Recess P.B.)

1859–61. *Imperf.*

32	**5**	6d. bl (H/S "CANCELLED" in oval £8000)	£600	38·00
33		6d. dull purple-slate (1861)	22·00	42·00
34		1s. vermilion (H/S "CANCELLED" in oval £4500)	£2000	45·00
35		1s. yellow-green (1861)	£500	£120

The 1859 printings had the colours transposed by mistake.

6

7

8

(Engraved on copper by J. Lapirot)

1859 (Mar–Nov). Imperf.

(a) Early impressions.

36	**6**	2d. deep blue	£5500	£2000
37		2d. blue	£4500	£1800

(b) Intermediate prints. Lines of background, etc, partly worn away (July).

38	**6**	2d. blue	£2750	£700

(c) Worn impressions, bluish-paper (Oct).

39	**6**	2d. blue	£1400	£450

(d) Retouched impression (Nov).

39*a*	**6**	2d. blue	†	—
		ab. "MAURITUIS" (R. 2/4)	†	£100000
		ac. "MAURITUS" (R. 3/1)	†	£100000

Nos. 36/9*a* were printed from a plate of 12 (4×3). The plate became worn through use, and was eventually extensively re-engraved. Only two pairs (one on cover) have been recorded from this re-touched impression. The errors made in the re-engraving of the inscriptions probably resulted in it being withdrawn from use.

(1848 plate re-engraved by R. Sherwin)

1859 (Oct). *Bluish paper. Imperf.*

40	**7**	2d. deep blue	£100000	£4000

The 1d. plate was also re-engraved, but was not put into use. Reprints in black were made in 1877 from both 1d. and 2d. re-engraved plates. Coloured autotype illustrations were prepared from these reprints and 600 were included in the R.P.S.L. handbook on *British Africa* in 1900. Further reprints in black were made in 1911 after the plates had been presented to the R.P.S.L. and defaced.

(Lithographed by L. A. Dardenne)

1859 (12 Dec). *White laid paper. Imperf.*

41	**8**	1d. deep red	£6500	£1500
41*a*		1d. red	£4750	£950
42		1d. dull vermilion	£3750	£800
43		2d. slate-blue	£4000	£750
43*a*		2d. blue	£2250	£550
44		2d. pale blue	£2000	£450
		a. Heavy retouch on neck	—	£1200
		b. Retouched below "TWO"	—	£650

The neck retouch shows a prominent curved white line running from the base of the chignon to the nape of the neck. No. 44b shows several diagonal lines in the margin below "TWO".

9

10

(Typo D.L.R.)

1860 (7 Apr)–**63**. No wmk. P 14.

46	**9**	1d. purple-brown	£180	20·00
47		2d. blue	£225	38·00
48		4d. rose	£225	27·00
49		6d. green (1862)	£650	£120
50		6d. slate (1863)	£250	90·00
51		9d. dull purple	£110	38·00
52		1s. buff (1862)	£250	80·00
53		1s. green (1863)	£550	£150

1862. Intermediate perf 14 to 16.

54	**5**	6d. slate	21·00	60·00
		a. Imperf between (horiz pair)	£5000	
55		1s. deep green	£1900	£325

1863–72. Wmk Crown CC. P 14.

56	**9**	1d. purple-brown	65·00	11·00
		w. Wmk inverted	85·00	24·00
		y. Wmk inverted and reversed		
57		1d. brown	85·00	7·00
58		1d. bistre (1872)	£110	9·00
		w. Wmk inverted		
59		2d. pale blue	70·00	8·00
		a. Imperf (pair)	£1400	£1800
		w. Wmk inverted	£120	23·00
		x. Wmk reversed		
		y. Wmk inverted and reversed		
60		2d. bright blue	80·00	8·00
61		3d. deep red	£140	24·00
61*a*		3d. dull red	50·00	11·00
		aw. Wmk inverted	£110	30·00
62		4d. rose	80·00	3·25
		w. Wmk inverted	£140	18·00
63		6d. dull violet	£200	27·00
		w. Wmk inverted		
		x. Wmk reversed		
64		6d. yellow-green (1865)	£150	13·00
65		6d. blue-green	£130	4·75
		w. Wmk inverted	£190	29·00
		y. Wmk inverted and reversed		
66		9d. yellow-green (1872)	£130	£200
		w. Wmk inverted		
67	**10**	10d. maroon (1872)	£250	35·00
		w. Wmk inverted		
68	**9**	1s. yellow	£190	21·00
		w. Wmk inverted	£250	40·00
69		1s. blue (1866)	£130	21·00
		w. Wmk inverted	—	45·00
		x. Wmk reversed	—	£110
70		1s. orange (1872)	£180	12·00
		w. Wmk inverted	£300	40·00
		y. Wmk inverted and reversed		
71		5s. rosy mauve	£160	55·00
		w. Wmk inverted	£300	
72		5s. bright mauve (1865)	£225	55·00
		w. Wmk inverted	£325	

HALF PENNY
(11)

½ d
HALF PENNY
(12)

1876.

(a) Nos. 51 and 67 surch with T **11** *locally.*

76	**9**	½d.on 9d. dull purple	8·50	13·00
		a. Surch inverted	£450	
		b. Surch double	—	£1400
77	**10**	½d.on 10d. maroon	1·75	18·00
		y. Wmk inverted and reversed		

(b) Prepared for use, but not issued. No. 51 surch with T **12**.

78	**9**	½d.on 9d. dull purple (R.)	£1700	
		a. "PRNNY"		
		b. Black surch	£2500	

HALF PENNY **(13)**   **One Penny** **(14)**   **OneShilling** **(15)**

Shill
Wrong fount "S"

1877 (Apr–Dec). *Nos. 62, 67 (colour changed) and 71/2 surch T* **13** *by D.L.R. or T* **14/15** *locally.*

79	**10**	½d.on 10d. rose	4·25	29·00
		w. Wmk inverted	60·00	
80	**9**	1d.on 4d. rose-carmine (6 Dec)	9·00	14·00
		w. Wmk inverted	—	60·00
81		1s.on 5s. rosy mauve (6 Dec)	£225	90·00
		w. Wmk inverted	£300	£120
82		1s.on 5s. bright mauve (6 Dec)	£200	£100
		a. Wrong fount "S"		
		w. Wmk inverted		

(New Currency. 100 cents = 1 rupee)

"CANCELLED" OVERPRINTS. Following the change of currency in 1878 various issues with face values in sterling were overprinted "CANCELLED" in serifed type and sold as remainders. The stamps involved were Nos. 51, 56/62, 65, 67/8, 71/2, 76, 78/b, 79 and 81/2. Examples of such overprints on stamps between Nos. 51 and 72 are worth about the same as the prices quoted for used, on Nos. 78/b they are worth 6% of the unused price, on No. 79 65% and on Nos. 81/2 20%.

2 CENTS **(16)**   **2Rs.50C.** **(17)**

1878 (3 Jan). *Surch as T* **16** *or* **17** *(No. 91).* Wmk Crown CC. P 14.

83	**10**	2c. dull rose (lower label blank)	7·50	5·00
		w. Wmk inverted	60·00	40·00
84	**9**	4c.on 1d. bistre	13·00	5·00
85		8c.on 2d. blue	70·00	1·75
		w. Wmk inverted		
86		13c.on 3d. orange-red	12·00	27·00
87		17c.on 4d. rose	£150	2·50
88		25c.on 6d. slate-blue	£200	5·00
89		38c.on 9d. pale violet	21·00	60·00
90		50c.on 1s. green	85·00	2·75
		w. Wmk inverted		
91		2r.50 on 5s. bright mauve	13·00	16·00
83/91 *Set of* 9			£500	£110

18

19

20

21

22

23

24

25

26

(Typo D.L.R.)

1879 (Mar)–**80**. Wmk Crown CC. P 14.

92	**18**	2c. Venetian red (1.80)	38·00	15·0
93	**19**	4c. orange	60·00	3·5
		w. Wmk inverted		
94	**20**	8c. blue (1.80)	17·00	2·5
		w. Wmk inverted	—	85·0
95	**21**	13c. slate (1.80)	£120	£16
96	**22**	17c. rose (1.80)	55·00	5·0
		w. Wmk inverted	—	£12
97	**23**	25c. olive-yellow	£300	8·5
98	**24**	38c. bright purple (1.80)	£150	£22
99	**25**	50c. green (1.80)	3·75	2·7
		w. Wmk inverted	90·00	
100	**26**	2r.50 brown-purple (1.80)	35·00	55·0
92/100 *Set of* 9			£700	£42

27

(Typo D.L.R.)

1883–94. Wmk Crown CA. P 14.

101	**18**	1c. pale violet (1893)	1·75	
102		2c. Venetian red	30·00	4·
103		2c. green (1885)	2·25	
104	**19**	4c. orange	70·00	3·
		w. Wmk inverted		
105		4c. carmine (1885)	2·75	
		w. Wmk inverted		
106	**20**	8c. blue (1891)	2·00	1·
		w. Wmk inverted		
		x. Wmk reversed		
107	**27**	15c. chestnut (1893)	4·00	1·
		w. Wmk inverted	—	90·
108		15c. blue (1894)	5·50	1·
109		16c. chestnut (1885)	4·00	1·
110	**23**	25c. olive-yellow	4·75	2·
		w. Wmk inverted	†	£1
111	**25**	50c. orange (1887)	28·00	8·
		w. Wmk inverted		
101/11 *Set of* 11			£140	22·
101s, 103s, 105s, 107s/9s, 111s Optd "Specimen" *Set of* 7			£475	

16 CENTS **(28)**   **16 CENTS** **(28a)**

1883 (26 Feb). *No. 96 surch with T* **28/a** *locally.*

112	**22**	16c.on 17c. rose (surch *T* **28**–14½ mm long)	£130	50
		a. Surch double	†	£1
		b. Horiz pair. Nos. 112/13	£450	£4
113		16c.on 17c. rose (surch *T* **28**–15½ mm long)	£140	50
		a. Surch double	†	£1
114		16c.on 17c. rose (surch *T* **28a**)	£275	£1

These stamps were surcharged using two different settings, ea of which produced three horizontal rows at a time.

The length of the surcharge in the first setting (Type **28**) is eit 14½ mm or 15½ mm and these exist in horizontal *se-tenant* pairs. Type **28** the height of the surcharge is 3.25 mm. On the secc setting (Type **28a**) the type differs, especially the numerals and " with the surcharge measuring 15-15½ mm long and 3 mm high.

SIXTEEN CENTS **(29)**   **2 CENTS** **(30)**   **2 CENTS** **(31)**

1883 (14 July). *Surch with T* **29** *by D.L.R.* Wmk Crown CA. P

115	**22**	16c.on 17c. rose	75·00	1
		w. Wmk inverted		

1886 (11 May). *No. 98 surch with T* **30** *locally.*

116	**24**	2c.on 38c. bright purple	£100	35
		a. Without bar	—	£
		b. Surch inverted	£650	£
		c. Surch double	£700	

1887 (6 July). *No. 95 surch with T* **31** *locally.*

117	**21**	2c.on 13c. slate (R.)	48·00	85
		a. Surch inverted	£150	£
		b. Surch double	£650	£
		c. Surch double, one on back of stamp	£650	
		d. Surch double, both inverted	†	£1

TWO CENTS **(32)**   **TWO CENTS** **(33)**

891 (10–16 Sept). *Nos. 88, 96, 98 and 105 surch locally as T* **32** *(Nos. 118/19, 121) or T* **33** *(No. 120).*

18	**19**	2c.on 4c. carmine (No. 105) (12 Sept)	1·50	60
		a. Surch inverted	70·00	
		b. Surch double	75·00	70·00
		c. Surch double, one inverted	75·00	70·00
19	**22**	2c.on 17c. rose (No. 96) (16 Sept)	95·00	£100
		a. Surch inverted	£325	
		b. Surch double	£600	£600
20	**9**	2c.on 38c. on 9d. pale violet (No. 89) (16 Sept)	3·00	3·75
		a. Surch inverted	£325	
		b. Surch double	£600	£600
		c. Surch double, one inverted	£130	£140
21	**24**	2c.on 38c. bright purple (No. 98)	4·00	5·00
		a. Surch inverted	£700	
		b. Surch double	£150	£160
		c. Surch double, one inverted	£160	£170

Minor varieties are also known with portions of the surcharge ıissing, due to defective printing.

ONE CENT (34)   ONE CENT (35)

893 (1–7 Jan). *Surch with T* **34** *by D.L.R. or T* **35** *locally.* Wmk Crown CA. P 14.

23	**18**	1c.on 2c. pale violet	1·25	50
		s. Optd "Specimen"	28·00	
24	**27**	1c.on 16c. chestnut (7 Jan)	1·25	2·75
		w. Wmk inverted	40·00	

36   37

(Typo D.L.R.)

95–99. Wmk Crown CA. P 14.

7	**36**	1c. dull purple and ultramarine (8.7.97)	75	1·50
8		2c. dull purple and orange (8.7.97)	3·00	50
9		3c. dull purple and deep purple	70	50
0		4c. dull purple and emerald (8.7.97)	3·75	50
1		6c. green and rose-red (1899)	4·50	4·00
2		18c. green and ultramarine (8.7.97)	10·00	3·50
7/32 *Set of* 6			20·00	9·50
7s/32s Optd "Specimen" *Set of* 6			95·00	

(Des L. Duvergé. Typo D.L.R.)

98 (15 Apr). *Diamond Jubilee.* Wmk CA over Crown (sideways). P 14.

3	**37**	36c. orange and ultramarine	11·00	18·00
		s. Optd "Specimen"	45·00	

6 CENTS (38)   15 CENTS (39)

99 (23–28 May). *Nos. 132/3 surcharged with T* **38/9** *locally.*

4	**36**	6c.on 18c. green and ultramarine (R.)	1·00	1·00
		a. Surch inverted	£450	£225
5	**37**	15c.on 36c. orge & ultram (B) (28 May)	1·40	1·75
		a. Bar of surch omitted	£300	

The space between "6" and "CENTS" varies from 2½ to 4 mm.

40 Admiral Mahé de Labourdonnais, Governor of Mauritius, 1735–46

4 Cents (41)

(Recess D.L.R.)

9 (13 Dec). *Birth Bicentenary of Labourdonnais.* Wmk Crown CC. P 14.

	40	15c. ultramarine	12·00	3·50
		s. Optd "Specimen"	70·00	
		w. Wmk inverted	70·00	

0. *No. 109 surch with T* **41** *locally.*

	27	4c. on 16c. chestnut	3·25	13·00

42   12 CENTS (43)

(Typo D.L.R.)

1900–05. *Ordinary paper.* Wmk Crown CC (1r.) or Crown CA (others) (sideways on 2r.50, 5r.). P 14.

138	**36**	1c. grey and black (1901)	50	10
139		2c. dull purple and bright purple (4.01)	75	20
140		3c. green and carmine/*yellow* (1902)	3·75	1·25
141		4c. purple and carmine/*yellow*	1·50	40
		w. Wmk inverted		
142		4c. grey-green and violet (1903)	75	2·00
		w. Wmk inverted		
143		4c. black and carmine/*blue* (14.10.04)	6·50	60
		w. Wmk inverted	16·00	16·00
144		5c. dull purple & brt pur/*buff* (8.10.02)	6·50	50·00
145		5c. dull purple and black/*buff* (2.03)	2·50	2·50
146		6c. purple and carmine/*red* (1902)	2·00	80
		w. Wmk inverted	21·00	16·00
147		8c. green and black/*buff* (16.7.02)	2·00	7·00
148		12c. grey-black and carmine (16.7.02)	1·75	2·25
149		15c. green and orange	13·00	6·00
		w. Wmk inverted		
150		15c. black and blue/*blue* (1905)	48·00	1·25
151		25c. green and carmine/*green* (1902)	10·00	25·00
		a. Chalk-surfaced paper	3·50	14·00
152		50c. dull green & dp green /*yellow* (1902)	16·00	42·00
153	**42**	1r. grey-black and carmine (1902)	50·00	50·00
		w. Wmk inverted	95·00	
154		2r.50 green and black/*blue* (1902)	18·00	85·00
155		5r. purple and carmine/*red* (1902)	65·00	85·00
138/55 *Set of* 18			£225	£325
138s/55s Optd "Specimen" *Set of* 18			£300	

Examples of Nos. 144 and 151/5 are known showing a forged Port Louis postmark dated "SP 29 10".

1902. *No. 132 surch with T* **43**.

156	**36**	12c.on 18c. green and ultramarine	2·00	5·00

The bar cancelling the original value seems in some cases to be one thick bar and in others two thin ones.

Postage & Revenue. (44)

1902 (7 July). *Various stamps optd with T* **44** *locally.*

157	**36**	4c. purple and carmine/*yellow* (No. 141)	1·25	20
158		6c. green and rose-red (No. 131)	1·25	2·75
159		15c. green and orange (No. 149)	2·50	75
160	**23**	25c. olive-yellow (No. 110)	3·25	2·75
161	**25**	50c. green (No. 99)	4·50	3·00
162	**26**	2r.50 brown-purple (No. 100)	90·00	£130
157/62 *Set of* 6			90·00	£130

Nos. 157/62 were overprinted to make surplus stocks of postage stamps available for revenue (fiscal) purposes also.

1902 (22 Sept). *No. 133 surch as T* **43**, *but with longer bar.*

163	**37**	12c.on 36c. orange and ultramarine	1·25	1·25
		a. Surch inverted	£475	£350

The note below No. 156 also applies to No. 163.

Forged double surcharge errors show a straight, instead of a curved, serif to the "1" of "12".

1904–07. *Ordinary paper (2c., 4c., 6c.) or chalk-surfaced paper (others).* Wmk Mult Crown CA. P 14.

164	**36**	1c. grey and black (1907)	8·00	3·75
165		2c. dull and bright purple (1905)	22·00	3·00
		a. Chalk-surfaced paper	22·00	1·75
166		3c. green and carmine/*yellow*	21·00	9·00
167		4c. black and carmine/*blue*	16·00	1·50
		a. Chalk-surfaced paper	3·50	10
168		6c. purple and carmine/*red*	9·00	30
		a. Chalk-surfaced paper	4·25	10
171		15c. black and blue/*blue* (1907)	4·00	35
174		50c. green and deep green/*yellow*	2·00	2·50
175	**42**	1r. grey-black and carmine (1907)	23·00	48·00
164/75 *Set of* 8			80·00	60·00

46   47

(Typo D.L.R.)

1910 (17 Jan). *Ordinary paper (1c. to 15c.) or chalk-surfaced paper (25c. to 10r.).* Wmk Mult Crown CA. P 14.

181	**46**	1c. black	2·75	30
182		2c. brown	2·75	10
183		3c. green	3·00	10
		a. "A" of "CA" missing from wmk	†	—
		w. Wmk inverted	25·00	
184		4c. pale yellow-green and carmine	3·50	10
		w. Wmk inverted	—	40·00
185	**47**	5c. grey and carmine	2·75	3·00
186	**46**	6c. carmine-red	2·25	20
		a. Pale red	3·00	1·25
		ab. "A" of "CA" missing from wmk	†	—
187		8c. orange	3·00	1·25
188	**47**	12c. greyish slate	2·25	2·75
189	**46**	15c. blue	17·00	20
190	**47**	25c. black and red/*yellow*	2·00	12·00
191		50c. dull purple and black	2·25	18·00
192		1r. black/*green*	6·50	12·00
193		2r.50 black and red/*blue*	13·00	70·00
194		5r. green and red/*yellow*	26·00	95·00
195		10r. green and red/*green*	95·00	£180
181/95 *Set of* 15			£170	£350
181s/95s Optd "Specimen" *Set of* 15			£300	

On Nos. 185, 191, 192, 193 and 194 the value labels are as in *T* **48**.

48   49

(Typo D.L.R.)

1913–22. *Die I. Ordinary paper (5c., 12c.) or chalk-surfaced paper (others).* Wmk Mult Crown CA. P 14.

196	**48**	5c. grey and carmine (1913)	1·75	4·00
		a. Slate-grey and carmine	10·00	10·00
198	**49**	12c. greyish slate (1914)	4·25	1·00
199		25c. black and red/*yellow* (1913)	40	1·40
		a. White back (1914)	80	16·00
		aw. Wmk inverted and reversed	30·00	
		b. On orange-buff (1920)	32·00	60·00
		c. On pale yellow (1921)	32·00	40·00
		cs. Optd "Specimen"	35·00	
		cw. Wmk inverted	95·00	
		d. Die II. *On pale yellow* (1921)	80	18·00
		ds. Optd "Specimen"	35·00	
200	**48**	50c. dull purple and black (1920)	38·00	80·00
201		1r. black/*blue-green (olive back)* (1917)	3·25	17·00
		a. On emerald (olive back) (1921)	7·50	48·00
		b. Die II. *On emerald (emerald back)* (1921)	2·25	7·50
		bs. Optd "Specimen"	35·00	
202		2r.50 black and red/*blue* (1916)	20·00	55·00
203		5r. green and red/*orange-buff* (1921)	85·00	£130
		a. On pale yellow (1921)	75·00	£130
		b. Die II. *On pale yellow* (1922)	48·00	£150
204	**49**	10r. grn & red/*grn* (*bl-grn back*) (1913)	70·00	£140
		a. On blue-green (*olive back*) (1919)	£750	
		b. On emerald (*olive back*) (1921)	80·00	£140
		c. On emerald (*emerald back*) (1921)	45·00	£130
		d. Die II. *On emerald* (*emerald back*) (1922)	26·00	£110
		ds. Optd "Specimen"	42·00	
196/204 *Set of* 8			£130	£350
196s/202s, 203as, 204s Optd "Specimen" *Set of* 8			£200	

Examples of Nos. 200/4d are known showing part strikes of the forged Port Louis postmark mentioned after Nos. 238/55.

1921–26. *Chalk-surfaced paper (50r).* Wmk Mult Script CA. P 14.

205	**46**	1c. black	1·00	1·00
		w. Wmk inverted	22·00	
206		2c. brown	1·00	10
		w. Wmk inverted		
207		2c. purple/*yellow* (1926)	1·00	30
		w. Wmk inverted	18·00	
208		3c. green (1926)	2·75	1·25
209		4c. pale olive-green and carmine	1·50	1·75
		x. Wmk reversed	60·00	
210		4c. green (1922)	1·00	10
		w. Wmk inverted		
		x. Wmk reversed		
211		4c. brown (1926)	2·75	1·50
212		6c. carmine	12·00	6·50
		x. Wmk reversed	70·00	
213		6c. bright mauve (1922)	1·25	10
214		8c. orange (1925)	2·25	17·00
215		10c. grey (1922)	2·00	3·25
216		10c. carmine-red (1926)	4·00	1·50
217		12c. carmine-red (1922)	1·50	40
218		12c. grey (1926)	1·75	3·50
219		15c. blue	5·50	4·75
		ax. Wmk reversed	70·00	
		b. Cobalt (1926)	75	25
220		20c. blue (1922)	2·00	80
221		20c. purple (1926)	8·50	10·00
222	–	50r. dull purple and green (1924)	£700	£1300
		s. Optd "Specimen"	£200	
205/21 *Set of* 17			42·00	42·00
205s/21s Optd "Specimen" *Set of* 17			£325	

No. 222 is as Type **46**, but measures 25 × 35 mm.

4c Normal   4c Open "C" (R. 9/6 of right pane)

MAURITIUS 12c A   MAURITIUS 12c B

Two types of duty plate in the 12c. In Type B the letters of "MAURITIUS" are larger; the extremities of the downstroke and the tail of the "2" are pointed, instead of square, and the "c" is larger.

1921–34. *Die II. Chalk-surfaced paper (25c. to 10r.).* Wmk Mult Script CA. P 14.

223	**49**	1c. black (1926)	80	1·25
224		2c. brown (1926)	70	10

225		3c. green (1926)	70	40
226		4c. sage-green and carmine (1926)	60	30
		a. Open "C"	38·00	
		b. Die I (1932)	6·50	42·00
		ba. Open "C"	£100	
226*c*		4c. green (Die I) (1932)	6·00	45
		ca. Open "C"	95·00	
227	**48**	5c. grey and carmine (1922)	90	10
		a. Die I (1932)	6·00	6·00
228	**49**	6c. sepia (1927)	2·00	60
229		8c. orange (1926)	75	10·00
230		10c. carmine-red (1926)	1·25	20
		a. Die I (1932)	7·00	9·00
231		12c. grey (Type A) (1922)	1·40	15·00
232		12c. carmine-red (Type A) (1922)	30	3·50
232*a*		12c. pale grey (Type A) (1926)	1·40	14·00
		as. Optd "Specimen"	38·00	
232*b*		12c. grey (Type B) (1934)	5·50	20
233		15c. Prussian blue (1926)	1·50	20
234		20c. purple (1926)	70	40
235		20c. Prussian blue (Die I) (1932)	9·50	90
		a. Die II (1934)	15·00	40
236		25c. black and red/*pale yellow* (1922)	60	15
		a. Die I (1932)	3·00	35·00
237	**48**	50c. dull purple and black (1921)	7·50	3·50
238		1r. black/*emerald* (1924)	3·50	50
		a. Die I (1932)	16·00	35·00
239		2r.50 black and red/*blue* (1922)	20·00	7·00
240		5r. green and red/*yellow* (1924)	28·00	70·00
241	**49**	10r. green and red/*emerald* (1924)	80·00	£200
223/41 *Set of* 20			£150	£275
223s/41s Optd or Perf (Nos. 226cs, 235s) "Specimen" *Set of* 20			£400	

3
Cents

(50)

51

1925 (25 Nov). *Nos. 210, 217 and 220 surch locally as T* **50**.

242	**46**	3c.on 4c. green	3·00	3·75
243		10c.on 12c. carmine-red	30	40
244		15c.on 20c. blue	55	20
242/4 *Set of* 3			3·50	4·00
242s/4s Optd "Specimen" *Set of* 3			80·00	

1935 (6 May). *Silver Jubilee. As Nos. 91/4 of Antigua.* P $13\frac{1}{2} \times 14$.

245	5c. ultramarine and grey	50	10
	f. Diagonal line by turret	48·00	25·00
	g. Dot to left of chapel	90·00	50·00
	h. Dot by flagstaff	90·00	50·00
246	12c. green and indigo	4·50	10
	f. Diagonal line by turret	95·00	40·00
	g. Dot to left of chapel	£170	60·00
247	20c. brown and deep blue	5·50	20
	f. Diagonal line by turret	£120	50·00
	g. Dot to left of chapel	£180	70·00
248	1r. slate and purple	29·00	42·00
	h. Dot by flagstaff	£400	£475
245/8 *Set of* 4		35·00	42·00
245s/8s Perf "Specimen" *Set of* 4		95·00	

For illustrations of plate varieties see Omnibus section following Zanzibar.

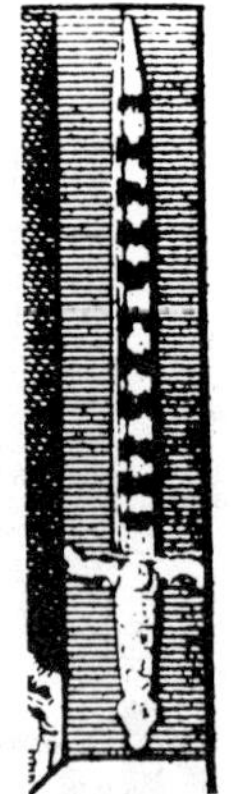
Line through sword (R. 2/2)

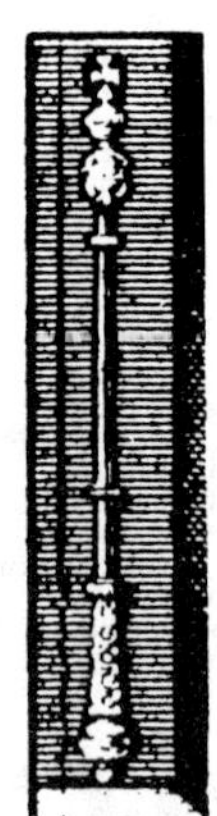
Line by sceptre (R. 5/3)

1937 (12 May). *Coronation. As Nos. 95/7 of Antigua, but printed by D.L.R.* P 14.

249	5c. violet	40	10
250	12c. scarlet	50	2·00
251	20c. bright blue	65	10
	a. Line through sword	60·00	35·00
	b. Line by sceptre	60·00	35·00
249/51 *Set of* 3		1·40	2·00
249s/51s Perf "Specimen" *Set of* 3		65·00	

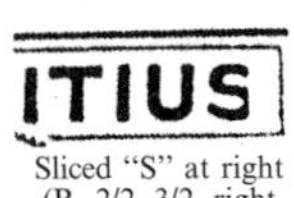

Sliced "S" at right (R. 2/2, 3/2, right pane)

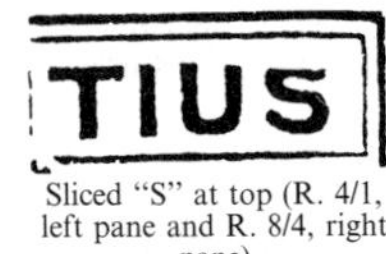

Sliced "S" at top (R. 4/1, left pane and R. 8/4, right pane)

Broken frame under "A" of "MAURITIUS" (R. 9/3 left pane, Key Plate 2)

"IJ" flaw (R. 3/6 of right pane)

Battered "A" (R. 6/1 of right pane)

(Typo D.L.R.)

1938–49. *T* **51** *and similar types. Chalk-surfaced paper (25c. to 10r.).* Wmk Mult Script CA. P 14.

252	2c. olive-grey (9.3.38)	30	10
	a. Perf 15 × 14 (1942)	1·00	10
253	3c. reddish purple and scarlet (27.10.38)	2·00	2·00
	a. Sliced "S" at right	80·00	80·00
	b. Reddish lilac and red (4.43)	3·50	3·50
	ba. Sliced "S" at right	£130	£130
254	4c. dull green (26.2.38)	3·25	2·00
	a. Open "C"	£110	80·00
	b. Deep dull green (4.43)	2·00	2·00
	ba. Open "C"	80·00	80·00
255	5c. slate-lilac (23.2.38)	9·50	85
	a. Pale lilac (*shades*) (4.43)	3·25	20
	b. Perf 15 × 14 (1942)	55·00	10
256	10c. rose-red (9.3.38)	2·75	30
	a. Sliced "S" at top	£130	40·00
	b. Deep reddish rose (*shades*) (4.43)	2·50	20
	ba. Sliced "S" at top	£110	30·00
	c. Perf 15 × 14. *Pale reddish rose* (1942)	28·00	1·25
	ca. Sliced "S" at top	£375	£100
257	12c. salmon (*shades*) (26.2.38)	1·00	20
	a. Perf 15 × 14 (1942)	55·00	75
258	20c. blue (26.2.38)	1·00	10
	a. Broken frame	£180	70·00
259	25c. brown-purple (2.3.38)	12·00	20
	a. "IJ" flaw	£275	50·00
	b. Ordinary paper (8.4.43)	6·00	10
	ba. "IJ" flaw	£150	40·00
260	1r. grey-brown (2.3.38)	27·00	2·00
	a. Battered "A"	£400	£130
	b. Ordinary paper (8.4.43)	19·00	1·25
	ba. Battered "A"	£325	£100
	c. Drab (4.49)	32·00	5·00
	ca. Battered "A"	£400	£160
261	2r.50 pale violet (2.3.38)	38·00	13·00
	a. Ordinary paper (8.4.43)	29·00	13·00
	b. Slate-violet (4.48)	50·00	28·00
262	5r. olive-green (2.3.38)	48·00	24·00
	a. Ordinary paper. *Sage-green* (8.4.43)	27·00	24·00
263	10r. reddish purple (*shades*) (2.3.38)	50·00	35·00
	a. Ordinary paper (8.4.43)	12·00	24·00
252/63a *Set of* 12		90·00	60·00
252s/63s Perf "Specimen" *Set of* 12		£200	

The stamps perf 15 × 14 were printed by Bradbury, Wilkinson from De La Rue plates and issued only in the colony in 1942. De La Rue printings of the 2c. to 20c. in 1943–45 were on thin, whiter paper. 1943–45 printings of the 25c. to 10r. were on unsurfaced paper.

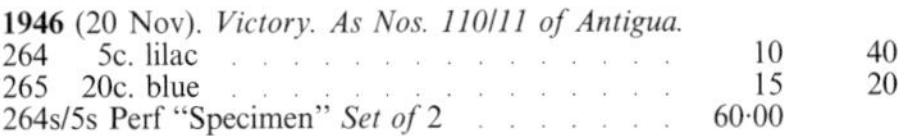

1946 (20 Nov). *Victory. As Nos. 110/11 of Antigua.*

264	5c. lilac	10	40
265	20c. blue	15	20
264s/5s Perf "Specimen" *Set of* 2		60·00	

52 1d. "Post Office" Mauritius and King George VI

(Recess B.W.)

1948 (22 Mar). *Centenary of First British Colonial Postage Stamp.* Wmk Mult Script CA. P $11\frac{1}{2} \times 11$.

266	**52**	5c. orange and magenta	10	40
267		12c. orange and green	15	20
268	–	20c. blue and light blue	15	10
269	–	1r. blue and red-brown	15	30
266/9 *Set of* 4			50	85
266s/9s Perf "Specimen" *Set of* 4			£100	

Design:—20c., 1r. As *T* **52** but showing 2d. "Post Office" Mauritius.

1948 (25 Oct). *Royal Silver Wedding. As Nos. 112/13 of Antigua.*

270	5c. violet	10	10
271	10r. magenta	11·00	24·00

1949 (10 Oct). *75th Anniv of U.P.U. As Nos. 114/17 of Antigua.*

272	12c. carmine	50	1·25
273	20c. deep blue	2·25	2·25
274	35c. purple	60	1·25
275	1r. sepia	50	20
272/5 *Set of* 4		3·50	4·50

53 Labourdonnais Sugar Factory

55 Aloe Plant

(Photo Harrison)

1950 (1 July). *T* **53**, **55** *and similar designs. Chalk-surfaced paper* Wmk Mult Script CA. P $13\frac{1}{2} \times 14\frac{1}{2}$ (horiz), $14\frac{1}{2} \times 13\frac{1}{2}$ (vert).

276	1c. bright purple	10	5
277	2c. rose-carmine	15	1
278	3c. yellow-green	60	2·7
279	4c. green	20	1·5
280	5c. blue	15	1
281	10c. scarlet	30	7
282	12c. olive-green	1·50	2·2
283	20c. ultramarine	1·00	1
284	25c. brown-purple	1·75	4
285	35c. violet	30	[illegible]
286	50c. emerald-green	2·75	5
287	1r. sepia	5·00	1
288	2r.50 orange	12·00	9·5
289	5r. red-brown	14·00	15·0
290	10r. dull blue	14·00	22·0
276/290 *Set of* 15		48·00	50·0

Designs: *Horiz*—2c. Grand Port; 5c. Rempart Mountain; 10c. Transporting cane; 12c. Mauritius Dodo and map; 35c. Government House, Reduit; 1r. Timor Deer; 2r.50, Port Louis; 5r. Beach scene; 10r. Arms of Mauritius. *Vert*—4c. Tamarind Falls; 20c. Legend of Paul and Virginie (inscr "VIRGINIA"); 25c. Labourdonnais statue; 50c. Pieter Both Mountain.

The latitude is incorrectly shown on No. 282. This was corrected before the same design was used for No. 302*a*.

EXPRESS DELIVERY STAMPS

EXPRESS
DELIVERY
15c.
(E 1)

EXPRESS
DELIVERY
(INLAND)
15c.
(E 2)

EXPRESS
DELIVERY
(INLAND)
15 c.
(E 3)

EXPRESS
DELIVERY
(INLAND)
15 c
(E 4)

Type E **2**. "(INLAND)" was inserted at a second printing on stamps already surcharged with Type E **1** (No. E1).
Type E **3**. New setting made at one printing. More space above and below "(INLAND)".
Type E **4**. New setting with smaller "15c" and no stop.

1903 (10 Aug)–**04**. *No. 136 surch locally in red.*

E1	E **1**	15c.on 15c. ultramarine	8·50	23
E2	E **2**	15c.on 15c. ultramarine (28.3.04)	40·00	55
		a. "A" inverted	£1100	£8
		b. "(INLAND)" inverted	†	£2?
E3	E **3**	15c.on 15c. ultramarine (4.04)	7·50	3
		a. Surch inverted	£750	£4
		aw. Surch and wmk inverted	—	£4
		b. Surch double, both inverted	£1300	£13
		c. Imperf between (vert pair)	£3500	
		w. Wmk inverted		
E4	E **4**	15c.on 15c. ultramarine (1904)	£500	£4
		a. Surch inverted	—	£12
		b. Surch double	—	£2
		c. Surch double, both inverted	—	£3
		d. "c" omitted	—	£1

(FOREIGN)
EXPRESS
DELIVERY
18 CENTS
(E 5)

1904. *T* **42** *(without value in label), surch with Type E* **5** *loca[lly].* Wmk Crown CC. P 14.

E5	18c. green	1·75	24
	a. Exclamation mark for "I" in "FOREIGN"	£475	

1904. *T* **42** *(without value in label) surch with Type E* **3** *locally.*

E6	15c. grey-green (R.)	4·25	4
	a. Surch inverted	£650	£
	b. Surch double	£450	£
	c. Surch double, one "LNIAND"	£550	£

AFFIX STAMP HERE

Gibbons Stamp Monthly
7 Parkside
Christchurch Road
RINGWOOD
HAMPSHIRE
ENGLAND
BH24 3SH

AFFIX STAMP HERE

Stanley Gibbons Mail Order
399 Strand
LONDON
ENGLAND
WC2R 0LX

AFFIX STAMP HERE

Stanley Gibbons Auctions
399 Strand
LONDON
ENGLAND
WC2R 0LX

POSTAGE DUE STAMPS

D 1

(Typo Waterlow)

33–54. Wmk Mult Script CA. P 15 × 14.
1 2c. black . . . 1·25 50
2 4c. violet . . . 50 65
3 6c. scarlet . . . 60 80
4 10c. green . . . 70 1·25
5 20c. bright blue . . . 50 1·50
6 50c. deep magenta (1.3.54) . . . 55 16·00
7 1r. orange (1.3.54) . . . 70 16·00
1/7 *Set of* 7 . . . 4·25 32·00
1s/5s Perf "Specimen" *Set of* 5 . . . 75·00

Stamps in a similar design on Black CA paper were issued tween 1966 and 1972.

FISCALS USED FOR POSTAGE

INLAND
REVENUE
(F 1)

INLAND
(F 2)

REVENUE

F 3

89. *T* **19**, wmk Crown CA, optd. P 14.
F **1** 4c. carmine . . . 16·00 5·00
F **2** 4c. lilac . . . 3·75 11·00

(Typo D.L.R.)

'6. Wmk Crown CA. P 14.
F **3** 4c. dull purple . . . 25·00 40·00

Montserrat

A local post office operated on Montserrat from 1702, although first recorded postal marking does not occur until 1791. A nch of the British G.P.O. was established at Plymouth, the island ital, in 1852.

The stamps of Great Britain were used from 1858 until the rseas postal service reverted to local control on 1 April 1860.

n the interim period between 1860 and the introduction of ntserrat stamps in 1876 No. CC1 and a similar "uncrowned" dstamp were again used.

PLYMOUTH

CROWNED-CIRCLE HANDSTAMPS

C 1

1 C **1** MONTSERRAT (R.) (15.7.1852)
Price on cover £3000

No. CC1 was used as an emergency measure, struck in black, ing 1886.

nps of GREAT BRITAIN *cancelled* "A 08" *as Type* Z **1** *of aica.*

8 (8 May)–**60**.
1d. rose-red (1857), *perf* 14 . . . £1100
4d. rose (1857) . . .
6d. lilac (1856) . . . £475
1s. green (1856) . . . £1400

PRICES FOR STAMPS ON COVER TO 1945	
Nos. 1/2	*from* × 50
No. 3	†
Nos. 4/5	*from* × 10
Nos. 6/13	*from* × 12
Nos. 14/22	*from* × 4
No. 23	—
Nos. 24/33	*from* × 4
Nos. 35/47	*from* × 3
No. 48	—
Nos. 49/59	*from* × 3
Nos. 60/2	*from* × 15
Nos. 63/83	*from* × 3
Nos. 84/93	*from* × 4
Nos. 94/7	*from* × 3
Nos. 98/100	*from* × 8
Nos. 101/12	*from* × 5

1

MONTSERRAT
(2)

3 (Die I)

(T **1** recess D.L.R.)

1876 (Sept)–**83**. *Stamps of Antigua optd with T* **2**. Wmk Crown CC. P 14.
1 **1** 1d. red . . . 24·00 16·00
a. Bisected (½d.) (1883) (on cover) . . . † £1400
b. Inverted "S" . . . £1000 £750
w. Wmk inverted . . . 50·00
x. Wmk reversed . . . 28·00 21·00
y. Wmk inverted and reversed . . . 45·00
2 6d. green . . . 65·00 42·00
a. Trisected (used as 2d.) (12.83) (on cover) . . . † £5500
b. Inverted "S" . . . £1500 £1000
x. Wmk reversed . . . — 85·00
3 6d. blue-green . . . £1100
a. Inverted "S" . . . £7000

Nos. 1/3 were overprinted either from a setting of 120 (12 × 10) or from a setting of 60 (6 × 10) applied twice to each sheet. This setting of 60 had an inverted "S" on R. 2/3. The same setting was subsequently used for some sheets of Nos. 6 and 8.

No. 1 was bisected and used for a ½d. in 1883. This bisected stamp is found surcharged with a small "½" in *black* and also in *red*; both were unofficial and they did not emanate from the Montserrat P.O.

The 6d. in blue-green is only known unused.

(T **3** typo D.L.R.)

1880 (Jan). Wmk Crown CC. P 14.
4 **3** 2½d. red-brown . . . £250 £180
5 4d. blue . . . £140 40·00
w. Wmk inverted . . . — £130
x. Wmk reversed . . . £325

1883 (Mar). Wmk Crown CA. P 12.
6 **1** 1d. red . . . 70·00 55·00
a. Inverted "S" . . . £2000 £1300
b. Bisected (½d.) (on cover) . . . † £1600
x. Wmk reversed . . . — 50·00

Top left triangle detached (Pl 2 R. 3/3 of right pane)

1884–85. Wmk Crown CA. P 14.
7 **3** ½d. dull green . . . 1·00 8·00
a. Top left triangle detached . . . £100
8 **1** 1d. red . . . 16·00 18·00
a. Inverted "S" . . . £850 £850
bx. Wmk reversed . . . — 25·00
c. Rose-red (1885) . . . 17·00 14·00
ca. Bisected vert (½d.) (on cover) . . . † £1300
cb. Inverted "S" . . . £1000 £950
ex. Wmk reversed . . . 20·00 20·00
9 **3** 2½d. red-brown . . . £225 65·00
10 2½d. ultramarine (1885) . . . 22·00 20·00
a. Top left triangle detached . . . £375
w. Wmk inverted . . . 95·00
11 4d. blue . . . £1800 £250
12 4d. mauve (1885) . . . 5·00 3·00
a. Top left triangle detached . . . £200
10s, 12s Optd "Specimen" *Set of* 2 . . . £375

The stamps for Montserrat were superseded by the general issue for Leeward Islands in November 1890, but the following issues were in concurrent use with the stamps inscribed "LEEWARD ISLANDS" until 1 July 1956, when Leeward Islands stamps were withdrawn and invalidated.

4 Device of the Colony

5

(Typo D.L.R.)

1903 (Aug).

(*a*) Wmk Crown CA. P 14.
14 **4** ½d. grey-green and green . . . 75 14·00
15 1d. grey-black and red . . . 75 40
w. Wmk inverted . . .
16 2d. grey and brown . . . 5·50 30·00
17 2½d. grey and blue . . . 1·50 1·75
18 3d. dull orange and deep purple . . . 4·25 32·00
19 6d. dull purple and olive . . . 5·00 48·00
20 1s. green and bright purple . . . 10·00 17·00
21 2s. green and brown-orange . . . 25·00 17·00
22 2s.6d. green and black . . . 19·00 38·00

(*b*) Wmk Crown CC. P 14.
23 **5** 5s. black and scarlet . . . £100 £150
14/23 *Set of* 10 . . . £150 £300
14s/23s Optd "Specimen" *Set of* 10 . . . £160

1904–08. *Ordinary paper (½d., 2d., 3d., 6d.) or chalk-surfaced paper (others)*. Wmk Mult Crown CA. P 14.
24 **4** ½d. grey-green and green . . . 5·50 2·00
a. Chalk-surfaced paper (3.06) . . . 80 1·25
25 1d. grey-black and red (11.07) . . . 15·00 24·00
26 2d. grey and brown . . . 1·00 6·00
a. Chalk-surfaced paper (5.06) . . . 2·25 1·25
27 2½d. grey and blue (12.05) . . . 2·50 6·50
28 3d. dull orange and deep purple . . . 7·00 7·00
a. Chalk-surfaced paper (5.08) . . . 9·50 2·50
29 6d. dull purple and olive . . . 4·25 24·00
a. Chalk-surfaced paper (5.08) . . . 10·00 5·50
30 1s. green and bright purple (5.08) . . . 10·00 7·00
31 2s. green and orange (5.08) . . . 32·00 42·00
32 2s.6d. green and black (5.08) . . . 42·00 48·00
33 **5** 5s. black and red (9.07) . . . 95·00 £110
24/33 *Set of* 10 . . . £190 £225

1908 (June)–**14**. *Ordinary paper (½d. to 2½d.) or chalk-surfaced paper (3d. to 5s.)*. Wmk Mult Crown CA. P 14.
35 **4** ½d. deep green (4.10) . . . 7·00 1·00
36 1d. rose-red . . . 1·40 30
38 2d. greyish slate (9.09) . . . 1·75 15·00
39 2½d. blue . . . 2·25 3·50
40 3d. purple/*yellow* (9.09) . . . 1·00 18·00
a. White back (1.14) (Optd S. £25) . . . 4·00 30·00
43 6d. dull and deep purple (9.09) . . . 6·50 50·00
a. Dull and bright purple (1914) . . . 10·00 50·00
44 1s. *black/green* (9.09) . . . 8·50 45·00
45 2s. purple and bright blue/*blue* (9.09) . . . 30·00 55·00
46 2s.6d. black and red/*blue* (9.09) . . . 30·00 70·00
47 **5** 5s. red and green/*yellow* (9.09) . . . 50·00 70·00
35/47 *Set of* 10 . . . £120 £275
35s/47s Optd "Specimen" *Set of* 10 . . . £190

Examples of most values are known showing forged Montserrat postmarks dated "OC 16 1909" or "NO 26 1910".

7

8

WAR STAMP
(9)

(T **7/8** typo D.L.R.)

1914. *Chalk-surfaced paper*. Wmk Mult Crown CA. P 14.
48 **7** 5s. red and green/*yellow* . . . 65·00 90·00
s. Optd "Specimen" . . . 75·00

1916 (10 Oct)–**22**. *Ordinary paper (½d. to 2½d.) or chalk-surfaced paper (3d. to 5s.)*. Wmk Mult Crown CA. P 14.
49 **8** ½d. green . . . 30 2·50
50 1d. scarlet . . . 1·00 75
a. Carmine-red . . . 20·00 7·00
51 2d. grey . . . 2·00 4·00
52 2½d. bright blue . . . 1·50 18·00
53 3d. purple/*yellow* . . . 1·25 10·00
a. On pale yellow (13.7.22) . . . 75 13·00
as. Optd "Specimen" . . . 24·00
54 4d. grey-black & red/*pale yell* (13.7.22) . . . 5·50 35·00
55 6d. dull and deep purple . . . 2·75 21·00
56 1s. black/*blue-green (olive back)* . . . 3·00 23·00
57 2s. purple and blue/*blue* . . . 14·00 30·00
58 2s.6d. black and red/*blue* . . . 22·00 55·00
59 5s. green and red/*yellow* . . . 38·00 55·00
49/59 *Set of* 11 . . . 80·00 £225
49s/59s Optd "Specimen" *Set of* 11 . . . £160

1917 (8 Oct)–**18**. *No. 49 optd with T* **9**.
60 **8** ½d. green (R.) . . . 10 1·50
a. Short opt (right pane R. 10/1) . . . 10·00
y. Wmk inverted and reversed . . . 50·00
61 ½d. green (Blk.) (5.18) . . . 75 2·75
a. Short opt (right pane R. 10/1) . . . 15·00
b. Deep green (10.18) . . . 15 1·75
ba. "C" and "A" missing from wmk . . .
bb. Short opt (right pane R. 10/1) . . . 10·00
w. Wmk inverted . . .

Nos. 60a, 61a, and 61bb show the overprint 2 mm high instead of 2½ mm.

No. 61ba shows the "C" omitted from one impression and the "A" missing from the next.

1919 (6 Mar). *T* **8**. *Special printing in orange. Value and "*WAR STAMP*" as T* **9** *inserted in black at one printing.*
62 1½d. black and orange . . . 10 30
60s/2s Optd "Specimen" *Set of* 3 . . . 80·00

1922 (13 July)–**29**. *Ordinary paper (¼d. to 3d.) (No. 73) or chalk-surfaced paper (others)*. Wmk Mult Script CA. P 14.
63 **8** ¼d. brown . . . 15 5·50
64 ½d. green (5.4.23) . . . 30 30
65 1d. bright violet (5.4.23) . . . 30 60
66 1d. carmine (1929) . . . 75 1·50
67 1½d. orange-yellow . . . 1·75 9·50
68 1½d. carmine (5.4.23) . . . 30 3·75
69 1½d. red-brown (1929) . . . 2·00 50
70 2d. grey . . . 50 2·00
71 2½d. deep bright blue . . . 8·00 16·00
a. Pale bright blue (17.8.26) . . . 60 90
as. Optd "Specimen" . . . 30·00
72 2½d. orange-yellow (5.4.23) . . . 1·25 19·00
73 3d. dull blue (5.4.23) . . . 60 16·00
74 3d. purple/*yellow* (2.1.27) . . . 1·10 4·75
75 4d. black and red/*pale yellow* . . . 60 12·00
76 5d. dull purple and olive . . . 3·75 10·00
77 6d. pale and bright purple (5.4.23) . . . 3·00 7·50
78 1s. black/*emerald* (5.4.23) . . . 3·00 7·00
79 2s. purple and blue/*blue* . . . 7·00 15·00
80 2s.6d. black and red/*blue* (5.4.23) . . . 12·00 50·00
81 3s. green and violet . . . 12·00 19·00

82 4s. black and scarlet . . . . 15·00 38·00
83 5s. green and red/*pale yellow* (6.23) . . 26·00 45·00
63/83 *Set of* 21 . . . . 80·00 £225
63s/83s Optd or Perf (Nos. 66s, 69s) "Specimen" *Set of* 21 . . . . £300

10 Plymouth

(Recess D.L.R.)

1932 (18 Apr). *300th Anniv of Settlement of Montserrat.* Wmk Mult Script CA. P 14.
84 **10** ½d. green . . . . 75 8·00
85 1d. scarlet . . . . 75 5·50
86 1½d. red-brown . . . . 1·25 2·50
87 2d. grey . . . . 1·50 16·00
88 2½d. ultramarine . . . . 1·25 15·00
89 3d. orange . . . . 1·50 17·00
90 6d. violet . . . . 2·25 28·00
91 1s. olive-brown . . . . 12·00 38·00
92 2s.6d. purple . . . . 48·00 70·00
93 5s. chocolate £100 £160
84/93 *Set of* 10 . . . . £150 £325
84s/93s Perf "Specimen" *Set of* 10 . . . . . . £225
Examples of all values are known showing a forged G.P.O. Plymouth postmark dated "MY 13 32".

1935 (6 May). *Silver Jubilee. As Nos. 91/4 of Antigua, but ptd by Waterlow & Sons.* P 11 × 12.
94 1d. deep blue and scarlet . . . . 85 3·25
95 1½d. ultramarine and grey . . . . 1·50 2·75
96 2½d. brown and deep blue . . . . 2·25 3·25
97 1s. slate and purple . . . . 3·00 14·00
94/7 *Set of* 4 . . . . 7·00 21·00
94s/7s Perf "Specimen" *Set of* 4 . . . . 85·00

1937 (12 May). *Coronation. As Nos. 95/7 of Antigua, but printed by D.L.R.* P 14.
98 1d. scarlet . . . . 30 1·25
99 1½d. yellow-brown 40 30
100 2½d. bright blue . . . . 40 1·25
98/100 *Set of* 3 . . . . 1·00 2·50
98s/100s Perf "Specimen" *Set of* 3 . . . . . . 60·00

11 Carr's Bay

12 Sea Island Cotton

13 Botanic Station

(Recess D.L.R.)

1938 (2 Aug)–**48**. Wmk Mult Script CA. P 12 (10s., £1) or 13 (others).
101 **11** ½d. blue-green . . . . 3·75 1·50
a. Perf 14 (1942) 15 20
102 **12** 1d. carmine . . . . 3·75 40
a. Perf 14 (1943) 50 30
103 1½d. purple . . . . 15·00 50
a. Perf 14 (1942) 50 50
ab. "A" of "CA" missing from wmk . . . .
104 **13** 2d. orange . . . . 15·00 60
a. Perf 14 (1942) . . . . 1·50 70
105 **12** 2½d. ultramarine . . . . 1·25 60
a. Perf 14 (1943) 50 30
106 **11** 3d. brown . . . . 3·25 50
a. Perf 14. *Red-brown* (1942) . . . . 2·00 40
ab. Deep brown (1943) . . . . 1·75 4·50
107 **13** 6d. violet . . . . 15·00 80
a. Perf 14 (1943) . . . . 2·50 60
108 **11** 1s. lake . . . . 16·00 70
a. Perf 14 (1942) . . . . 2·25 30
109 **13** 2s.6d. slate-blue . . . . 28·00 80
a. Perf 14 (1943) . . . . 17·00 2·50
110 **11** 5s. rose-carmine . . . . 35·00 8·00
a. Perf 14 (1942) . . . . 21·00 3·00
111 **13** 10s. pale blue (1.4.48) . . . . . . 13·00 19·00
112 **11** £1 black (1.4.48) . . . . 13·00 27·00
101a/12 *Set of* 12 . . . . 65·00 50·00
101s/12s Perf "Specimen" *Set of* 12 . . . . . . £250
Nos. 101/2 exist in coils constructed from normal sheets.

1946 (1 Nov). *Victory. As Nos. 110/11 of Antigua.*
113 1½d. purple 10 10
114 3d. chocolate 10 10
113s/14s Perf "Specimen" *Set of* 2 . . . . 60·00

1949 (3 Jan). *Royal Silver Wedding. As Nos. 112/13 of Antigua.*
115 2½d. ultramarine 10 10
116 5s. carmine . . . . 4·75 8·50

1949 (10 Oct). *75th Anniv of U.P.U. As Nos. 114/17 of Antigua.*
117 2½d. ultramarine . . . . 15 1·00
118 3d. brown . . . . 1·75 50
119 6d. purple 30 50
120 1s. purple 30 50
117/20 *Set of* 4 . . . . 2·25 2·25

(New Currency. 100 cents = 1 West Indies, later Eastern Caribbean dollar)

1961 (16 Feb). *Inauguration of B.W.I. University College. As Nos. 118/19 of Antigua.*
121 3c. black and purple . . . . 20 1·00
122 12c. black and violet . . . . 20 1·00

14 Government House

18 Badge of Presidency

(Recess B.W.)

1951 (17 Sept). *T* **14**, **18** *and similar horiz designs.* Wmk Mult Script CA. P 11½ × 11.
123 **14** 1c. black . . . . 10 2·00
124 – 2c. green 15 70
125 – 3c. orange-brown 30 70
126 – 4c. carmine 30 80
127 – 5c. reddish violet 30 70
128 **18** 6c. olive-brown 30 30
129 – 8c. deep blue . . . . 1·00 20
130 – 12c. blue and chocolate 50 30
131 – 24c. carmine and yellow-green . . . 1·25 30
132 – 60c. black and carmine . . . . . . 6·50 3·25
133 – $1.20 yellow-green and blue . . . . 6·50 6·00
134 – $2.40 black and green . . . . . . 8·00 12·00
135 **18** $4.80 black and purple . . . . . . 17·00 16·00
123/135 *Set of* 13 . . . . 38·00 38·00
Designs:—2c., $1.20, Sea Island cotton: cultivation; 3c. Map of colony; 4, 24c. Picking tomatoes; 5, 12c. St. Anthony's Church; 8, 60c. Sea Island cotton: ginning; $2.40, Government House.

Morocco Agencies

(British Post Offices)

With the growth of trade and commerce during the 19th century European powers opened post offices or postal agencies in various ports along the Moroccan coast from the early 1850's onwards. French and, in the north, Spanish influence eventually became predominant, leading to the protectorates of 1912. The British, who had inaugurated a regular postal service between Gibraltar and Tangier or Tetuan in May 1778, established their first postal agency in 1857. German offices followed around the turn of the century.

Before 1892 there was no indigenous postal service and those towns where there was no foreign agency were served by a number of private local posts which continued to flourish until 1900. In November 1892 the Sultan of Morocco established the Cherifian postal service, but this was little used until after its reorganization at the end of 1911. The Sultan's post was absorbed by the French postal service on 1 October 1913. Issues of the local posts and of the Sultan's post can occasionally be found used on cover in combination with stamps of Gibraltar or the Morocco Agencies.

In 1857 the first British postal agency was established at Tangier within the precincts of the Legation and was run by the official interpreter. From 1 March 1858 all letters for Great Britain sent via the British mail packets from Gibraltar required franking with Great Britain stamps.

In 1872 the Tangier office was relocated away from the Legation and the interpreter was appointed British Postal Agent. At the same time the agency was placed under the control of the Gibraltar postmaster. When the colonial posts became independent of the British G.P.O. on 1 January 1886 Gibraltar retained responsibility for the Morocco Agencies. Further offices, each under the control of the local Vice-Consul, were opened from 1886 onwards.

I. GIBRALTAR USED IN MOROCCO

Details of the various agencies are given below. Type C, the "A26" killer, is very similar to postmarks used at Gibraltar during this period. In addition to the town name, postmarks as Types A, B and D from Fez, Mazagan, Saffi and Tetuan were also inscribed "MOROCCO".

Postmark Types used on Gibraltar issues.

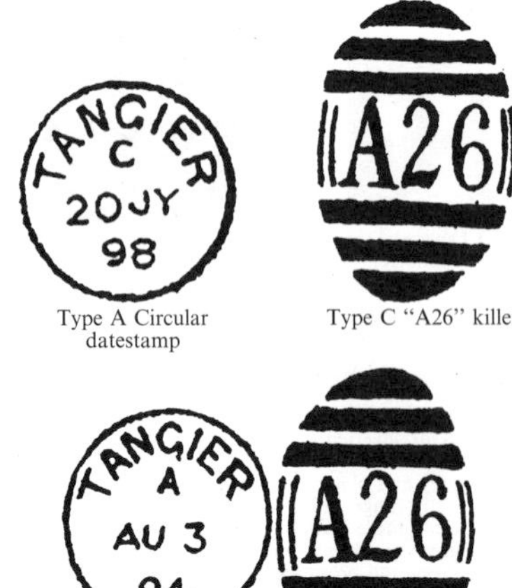

Type A Circular datestamp

Type C "A26" killer

Type B Duplex cancellation

Type D Registered oval

BISECTS. The 10c., 40c. and 50c. values of the 1889 surcha and of the 1889–96 issue are known bisected and used for half value from various of the Morocco Agencies. These bisects never authorised by the Gibraltar Post Office.

CASABLANCA

The British postal agency opened on 1 January 1887 and initially supplied with ½d., 4d. and 6d. stamps from the Gibra 1886 overprinted on Bermuda issue and 1d., 2d. and 2½d. va from the 1886–87 set.

Stamps of GIBRALTAR *cancelled with Types* A (*without coo code* "C"), B (*without code or code* "A") *or* D.

1886. *Optd on Bermuda (Nos. 1/7).*
Z1 ½d. dull green 6
Z2 4d. orange-brown . . . .
Z3 6d. deep lilac . . . .

1886–87. *Queen Victoria £sd issue (Nos. 8/14).*
Z 4 ½d. dull green 2
Z 5 1d. rose 3
Z 6 2d. brown-purple 7
Z 7 2½d. blue 4
Z 8 4d. orange-brown . . . .
Z10 1s. bistre . . . .

1889. *Surch in Spanish currency (Nos. 15/21).*
Z11 5c.on ½d. green 4
Z12 10c.on 1d. rose 4
Z13 25c.on 2d. brown-purple 6
Z14 25c.on 2½d. bright blue 3
Z15 40c.on 4d. orange-brown . . . .
Z16 50c.on 6d. bright lilac . . . .
Z17 75c.on 1s. bistre . . . .

1889–96. *Queen Victoria Spanish currency issue (Nos. 22/33).*
Z18 5c. green 1
Z19 10c. carmine 1
Z20 20c. olive-green and brown 3
Z22 25c. ultramarine 1
Z23 40c. orange-brown 3
Z24 50c. bright lilac 2
Z25 75c. olive-green 8
Z26 1p. bistre 7
Z28 1p. bistre and ultramarine 3
Z29 2p. black and carmine 5

FEZ

The British postal agency in this inland town opened 13 February 1892 and was initially supplied with stamps up to 50c. value from the Gibraltar 1889–96 issue.

Stamps of GIBRALTAR *cancelled with Types* A (*without code* D.

1889–96. *Queen Victoria Spanish currency issue (Nos. 22/33).*
Z31 5c. green 2
Z32 10c. carmine 3
Z33 20c. olive-green and brown 5
Z35 25c. ultramarine 4
Z36 40c. orange-brown 7
Z37 50c. bright lilac 5

LARAICHE

The British postal agency at Laraiche opened in March 1 although the first postmark, an "A26" killer, was not supplied May.

Stamps of GIBRALTAR *cancelled with Types* B (*without code* D.

1886. *Optd on Bermuda (Nos. 1/7).*
Z39 ½d. dull green . . . .
Z40 1d. rose-red . . . .
Z41 2½d. ultramarine . . . .

1886–87. *Queen Victoria £sd issue (Nos. 8/14).*
Z42 ½d. dull green 9
Z43 1d. rose 8
Z45 2½d. blue 9

1889. *Surch in Spanish currency (Nos. 15/21).*
Z47 5c.on ½d. green 6
Z48 10c.on 1d. rose . . . .
Z49 25c.on 2½d. bright blue . . . .
It is believed that the other surcharges in this series were supplied to Laraiche.

1889–96. *Queen Victoria Spanish currency issue (Nos. 22/33).*
Z50 5c. green 3
Z51 10c. carmine 4
Z52 20c. olive-green and brown . . . . . .
Z54 25c. ultramarine 4
Z55 40c. orange-brown . . . .
Z56 50c. bright-lilac 8
Z57 1p. bistre and ultramarine . . . . . .

MAZAGAN

This was the main port for the inland city of Marrakesh. British postal agency opened on 1 March 1888 and was ini supplied with stamps from the Gibraltar 1886–87 series.

Stamps of GIBRALTAR *cancelled with Types* A (*codes* "A" *or* "C") *or* D (*without code, code* "A" *or code* "C").

1886–87. *Queen Victoria £sd issue (Nos. 8/14).*
Z58 ½d. dull green . . . 30·00
Z59 1d. rose . . . 30·00
Z60 2d. brown-purple
Z61 2½d. blue . . . 38·00
Z62 4d. orange-brown . . . £110
Z63 6d. lilac . . . £130

1889. *Surch in Spanish currency (Nos. 15/21).*
Z64 5c. on ½d. green
Z65 10c. on 1d. rose
Z66 25c. on 2½d. bright blue

It is believed that the other surcharges in this series were not supplied to Mazagan.

1889–96. *Queen Victoria Spanish currency issue (Nos. 22/33).*
Z67 5c. green . . . 19·00
Z68 10c. carmine . . . 17·00
Z69 20c. olive-green and brown . . . 50·00
Z70 25c. ultramarine . . . 42·00
Z71 40c. orange-brown . . . 75·00
Z72 50c. bright lilac
Z74 1p. bistre and ultramarine
Z75 2p. black and carmine

MOGADOR

The British postal agency at this port opened on 1 April 1887 and was initially supplied with stamps from the Gibraltar 1886–87 series.

Stamps of GIBRALTAR *cancelled with Types* A (*code* "C"), B (*code* "C") *or* D.

1886–87. *Queen Victoria £sd issue (Nos. 8/14).*
Z76 ½d. dull green . . . 29·00
Z77 1d. rose . . . 38·00
Z78 2d. brown-purple . . . 70·00
Z79 2½d. blue . . . 38·00

1889. *Surch in Spanish currency (Nos. 15/21).*
Z80 5c.on ½d. green . . . 48·00
Z81 10c.on 1d. rose . . . 48·00
Z82 25c.on 2½d. bright blue . . . 48·00

It is believed that the other surcharges in this series were not supplied to Mogador.

1889–96. *Queen Victoria Spanish currency issue (Nos. 22/33).*
Z83 5c. green . . . 13·00
Z84 10c. carmine . . . 15·00
Z85 20c. olive-green and brown
Z87 25c. ultramarine . . . 19·00
Z88 40c. orange-brown . . . 32·00
Z89 50c. bright lilac . . . 32·00

RABAT

The British postal agency at this port on the north-west coast of Morocco opened in March 1886, although the first cancellation, an "A26" killer, was not supplied until May. The initial stock of stamps was from the Gibraltar 1886 overprinted on Bermuda issue.

Stamps of GIBRALTAR *cancelled with Types* B (*code* "O") *or* D.

1886. *Optd on Bermuda (Nos. 1/7).*
Z92 ½d. dull green
Z93 1d. rose-red
Z94 2½d. ultramarine . . . £130

1886–87. *Queen Victoria £sd issue (Nos. 8/14).*
Z 95 ½d. dull green . . . 29·00
Z 96 1d. rose . . . 29·00
Z 97 2d. brown-purple . . . 70·00
Z 98 2½d. blue . . . 40·00
Z101 1s. bistre . . . £350

1889. *Surch in Spanish currency (Nos. 15/21).*
Z102 5c.on ½d. green . . . 48·00
Z103 10c.on 1d. rose . . . 42·00
Z104 25c.on 2½d. bright blue . . . 48·00

It is believed that the other surcharges in this series were not supplied to Rabat.

1889–96. *Queen Victoria Spanish currency issue (Nos. 22/33).*
Z105 5c. green . . . 18·00
Z106 10c. carmine . . . 18·00
Z107 20c. olive-green and brown . . . 40·00
Z108 25c. ultramarine . . . 19·00
Z109 40c. orange-brown . . . 45·00
Z110 50c. bright lilac . . . 40·00

SAFFI

The British postal agency at this port opened on 1 July 1891 and was supplied with stamps from the Gibraltar 1889–96 series.

Stamps of GIBRALTAR *cancelled with Types* B (*code* "C") *or* D (*code* "C").

1889–96. *Queen Victoria Spanish currency issue (Nos. 22/33).*
Z111 5c. green . . . 19·00
Z112 10c. carmine . . . 19·00
Z113 20c. olive-green and brown . . . 45·00
Z115 25c. ultramarine . . . 21·00
Z116 40c. orange-brown . . . 75·00
Z117 50c. bright lilac . . . 55·00
Z118 1p. bistre and ultramarine . . . 60·00
Z119 2p. black and carmine . . . 70·00

TANGIER

The British postal agency in Tangier opened on 1 April 1857 and from 1 March of the following year letters from it sent via the packet service to Great Britain required franking with Great Britain stamps.

No identifiable postmark was supplied to Tangier until 1872 and all earlier mail was cancelled with one of the Gibraltar marks. In April 1872 a postmark as Type A was supplied on which the "N" of "TANGIER" was reversed. A corrected version, with code letter "A", followed in 1878, but both were used as origin or arrival marks and the Great Britain stamps continued to be cancelled with Gibraltar obliterators. The Type A postmarks generally fell into disuse after 1880 and very few identifiable marks occur on mail from Tangier until the introduction of Gibraltar stamps on 1 January 1886.

Stamps of GIBRALTAR *cancelled with Types* A (*codes* "A" *or* "C"), B (*code* "A") *or* D.

1886. *Optd on Bermuda (Nos. 1/7).*
Z120 ½d. dull green . . . 42·00
Z121 1d. rose-red . . . 65·00
Z122 2d. purple-brown . . . £140
Z123 2½d. ultramarine . . . 42·00
Z124 4d. orange-brown . . . £170
Z125 6d. deep lilac . . . £225
Z126 1s. yellow-brown . . . £500

1886–87. *Queen Victoria £sd issue (Nos. 8/14).*
Z127 ½d. dull green . . . 18·00
Z128 1d. rose . . . 18·00
Z129 2d. brown-purple . . . 48·00
Z130 2½d. blue . . . 27·00
Z131 4d. orange-brown . . . 80·00
Z132 6d. lilac . . . £120
Z133 1s. bistre . . . £275

1889. *Surch in Spanish currency (Nos. 15/21).*
Z134 5c.on ½d. green . . . 29·00
Z135 10c.on 1d. rose . . . 20·00
Z136 25c.on 2d. brown-purple . . . 38·00
Z137 25c.on 2½d. bright blue . . . 29·00
Z138 40c.on 4d. orange-brown . . . 95·00
Z139 50c.on 6d. bright lilac . . . 90·00
Z140 75c.on 1s. bistre . . . £120

1889–96. *Queen Victoria Spanish currency issue (Nos. 22/33).*
Z141 5c. green . . . 5·00
Z142 10c. carmine . . . 5·00
Z143 20c. olive-green and brown . . . 21·00
Z144 20c. olive-green . . . 55·00
Z145 25c. ultramarine . . . 8·00
Z146 40c. orange-brown . . . 13·00
Z147 50c. bright lilac . . . 12·00
Z148 75c. olive-green . . . 50·00
Z149 1p. bistre . . . 60·00
Z150 1p. bistre and ultramarine . . . 20·00
Z151 2p. black and carmine . . . 40·00
Z152 5p. slate-grey . . . £110

TETUAN

The British postal agency in this northern town opened on 1 April 1890 and was supplied with stamps from the Gibraltar 1889–96 series.

Stamps of GIBRALTAR *cancelled with Types* A (*code* "C"), B (*code* "C" *often inverted*) *or* D (*code* "C").

1889–96. *Queen Victoria Spanish currency issue (Nos. 22/33).*
Z153 5c. green . . . 24·00
Z154 10c. carmine . . . 28·00
Z155 20c. olive-green and brown . . . 50·00
Z157 25c. ultramarine . . . 32·00
Z158 40c. orange-brown . . . 60·00
Z159 50c. bright lilac . . . 60·00
Z161 1p. bistre and ultramarine

PRICES FOR STAMPS ON COVER TO 1945

Nos.	1/16	*from* × 7
Nos.	17/30	*from* × 3
Nos.	31/74	*from* × 3
Nos.	75/6	*from* × 4
Nos.	112/24	*from* × 4
No.	125	—
Nos.	126/35	*from* × 5
Nos.	136/42	*from* × 2
Nos.	143/59	*from* × 3
Nos.	160/75	*from* × 8
Nos.	191/9	*from* × 5
Nos.	200/1	*from* × 3
Nos.	202/11	*from* × 4
Nos.	212/15	*from* × 5
Nos.	216/24	*from* × 8
Nos.	225/6	*from* × 2
Nos.	227/30	*from* × 8
Nos.	231/52	*from* × 6

The above prices apply to stamps used on cover from Morocco. Examples of Nos. 31/76 & 231/52 used on cover in G.B. after 1950 have little value.

II. GIBRALTAR ISSUES OVERPRINTED

With the reversion of Gibraltar to sterling in 1898 it became necessary to provide separate issues for the Morocco Agencies which continued to use Spanish currency.

The following were used in all the British postal agencies.

Morocco Agencies (1) — Morocco Agencies (2)

Agencies — Inverted "V" for "A" (Right-hand pane R. 6/6)

Agencies — Long tail to "S" (Right-hand pane R. 8/2)

Broken "M" (Pl 2 R. 4/5)

CENTIMOS — Flat top to "C" (Pl 2 R. 4/4)

1898 (1 June)–**1900**. *Nos. 22/8 and 31/2 (Queen Victoria) of Gibraltar optd Typographically (No. 2e) or by lithography (others) with T* **1** *(wide "M" and ear of "g" projecting upwards), in black at Gibraltar Chronicle office.*

1	5c. green	2·50	2·50
	a. Inverted "V" for "A"	29·00	32·00
	b. Long tail to "S"	32·00	35·00
	c. Broken "M" in "CENTIMOS"	48·00	
2	10c. carmine	4·00	75
	b. Bisected (5c.) (on cover)	†	£1100
	c. Inverted "V" for "A"	£225	£275
	d. Long tail to "S"	£225	
	e. Lines of opt 5 mm apart (6.00)	4·50	3·00
	ea. Opt double	£500	
3	20c. olive-green and brown	7·50	1·75
	a. Inverted "V" for "A"	45·00	45·00
	b. Long tail to "S"	48·00	48·00
3*c*	20c. olive-green	8·50	5·50
	ca. Opt double	£450	£550
	cb. Inverted "V" for "A"	55·00	60·00
	cc. Long tail to "S"	60·00	65·00
	cd. Flat top to "C" in "CENTIMOS"	80·00	
4	25c. ultramarine	3·75	60
	a. Inverted "V" for "A"	£110	£120
	b. Long tail to "S"	£120	£130
5	40c. orange-brown (2.6.98)	6·00	3·25
	a. Inverted "V" for "A"	£160	£180
	b. Long tail to "S"	£170	£190
	c. Blue opt (7.98)	42·00	32·00
6	50c. bright lilac (2.6.98)	17·00	23·00
	a. Inverted "V" for "A"	£250	£300
	b. Long tail to "S"	£275	£300
	c. Blue opt (7.98)	12·00	12·00
7	1p. bistre and ultramarine (2.6.98)	17·00	27·00
	a. Inverted "V" for "A"	£225	£325
	b. Long tail to "S"	£250	£325
	c. Blue opt (7.98)	£150	£190
8	2p. black and carmine (4.6.98)	21·00	27·00
	a. Inverted "V" for "A"	£275	£325
	b. Long tail to "S"	£300	£325
1/8 *Set of* 8		65·00	65·00

The blue overprint can be easily distinguished by looking through the stamp in front of a strong light.

The listed varieties of overprint occur from the first litho setting. They were corrected on the second setting of July 1898, which produced Nos. 5c, 6c, 7c and further supplies of No 8. The corrected type was subsequently used to produce additional stocks of Nos. 1/2. Numerous more minor varieties exist from these settings.

No. 2e comes from two further printings in 1900 using a third setting on which the two lines of the overprint were 5 mm apart instead of the 4 mm space used previously and applied typographically.

Agencies — "CD" sideways flaw (Left-hand pane R. 1/5)

Morocco — Broad top to "M" (Left-hand pane R. 7/3)

Agencies — Hyphen between "nc" (Right-hand pane R. 3/5)

1899 (Feb)–**1902**. *Nos. 22/3, 25/8 and 31/2 (Queen Victoria) of Gibraltar optd typographically with T* **2** *(narrow "M" and ear of "g" horizontal), in black by D.L.R., London.*

9	5c. green (4.99)	50	75
	a. "CD" sideways	13·00	14·00
	b. Broad top to "M"	8·50	10·00
	c. Hyphen between "nc"	8·50	10·00
	d. Broken "M" in "CENTIMOS"	24·00	
10	10c. carmine	2·00	30
	a. "CD" sideways	15·00	14·00
	b. Broad top to "M"	9·50	9·50
	c. Hyphen between "nc"	9·50	9·50
	d. Opt double	£700	£700
11	20c. olive-green (5.02)	6·50	70
	b. Broad top to "M"	29·00	29·00
	c. Hyphen between "nc"	29·00	29·00
	d. Flat top to "C" in "CENTIMOS"	55·00	
12	25c. ultramarine (10.99)	9·50	90
	a. "CD" sideways	48·00	42·00
	b. Broad top to "M"	40·00	35·00
	c. Hyphen between "nc"	40·00	35·00
13	40c. orange-brown (3.02)	40·00	30·00
	b. Broad top to "M"	£200	£200
	c. Hyphen between "nc"	£200	£200
14	50c. bright lilac (4.99)	9·00	3·50
	b. Broad top to "M"	£100	£110
	c. Hyphen between "nc"	£100	£110
15	1p. bistre and ultramarine (4.99)	27·00	42·00
	b. Broad top to "M"	£150	£200
	c. Hyphen between "nc"	£150	£200
16	2p. black and carmine (3.01)	55·00	48·00
	b. Broad top to "M"	£300	£325
	c. Hyphen between "nc"	£300	£325
9/16 *Set of* 8		£130	£110
9s/16s Optd "Specimen" *Set of* 8		£190	

1903–05. *As Nos. 46/51 (King Edward VII) of Gibraltar, but with value in Spanish currency, optd with T* **2**. Wmk Crown CA. P 14.

17	5c. grey-green and green (1.03)	9·50	3·50
	a. "CD" sideways	48·00	45·00
	b. Broad top to "M"	45·00	42·00
	c. Hyphen between "nc"	45·00	42·00
18	10c. dull purple/*red* (8.03)	8·50	40
	a. "CD" sideways	42·00	35·00
	b. Broad top to "M"	40·00	35·00
	c. Hyphen between "nc"	40·00	35·00
	w. Wmk inverted	35·00	

19 20c. grey-green and carmine (9.04) 17·00 45·00
a. "CD" sideways 90·00 £150
b. Broad top to "M" 85·00 £150
c. Hyphen between "nc" 85·00 £150
20 25c. purple and black/*blue* (1.7.03) 8·00 30
a. "CD" sideways 48·00 40·00
b. Broad top to "M" 45·00 40·00
c. Hyphen between "nc" 45·00 40·00
21 50c. purple and violet (3.7.05) 90·00 £160
a. "CD" sideways £325 £550
b. Broad top to "M" £325 £550
c. Hyphen between "nc" £325 £550
22 1p. black and carmine (19.11.05) 40·00 £150
a. "CD" sideways £225 £475
b. Broad top to "M" £225 £475
c. Hyphen between "nc" £225 £475
23 2p. black and blue (19.11.05) 50·00 £120
a. "CD" sideways £250 £450
b. Broad top to "M" £250 £450
c. Hyphen between "nc" £250 £450
17/23 *Set of* 7 £200 £425
17s/23s Optd "Specimen" *Set of* 7 £190

Examples of Nos. 19 and 21/3 are known showing a forged Registered Mazagan postmark dated "15 SP 10".

1905 (Jan)–**06**. *As Nos. 17/23 but* wmk Mult Crown CA. *Ordinary paper (5, 10, 20c.) or chalk-surfaced paper (others).*

24 5c. grey-green and green (4.05) 8·50 3·00
a. "CD" sideways 48·00 40·00
b. Broad top to "M" 48·00 40·00
c. Hyphen between "nc" £750 £800
d. Chalk-surfaced paper (1.06) 8·00 4·25
da. "CD" sideways 45·00 42·00
db. Broad top to "M" 45·00 42·00
25 10c. dull purple/*red* 10·00 1·75
a. "CD" sideways 48·00 30·00
b. Broad top to "M" 48·00 30·00
cw. Wmk inverted 26·00 20·00
d. Chalk-surfaced paper (12.05) 5·00 1·75
da. "CD" sideways 32·00 30·00
db. Broad top to "M" 32·00 30·00
26 20c. grey-green and carmine (1.06) 4·75 29·00
a. "CD" sideways 45·00 £130
b. Broad top to "M" 45·00 £130
27 25c. purple and black/*blue* (6.06) 38·00 8·50
a. "CD" sideways £275 £140
b. Broad top to "M" £275 £140
28 50c. purple and violet (7.06) 7·00 42·00
a. "CD" sideways £140 £225
b. Broad top to "M" £140 £225
29 1p. black and carmine (11.05) 28·00 80·00
a. "CD" sideways £190 £300
b. Broad top to "M" £190 £300
30 2p. black and blue (11.05) 15·00 35·00
a. "CD" sideways £160 £225
b. Broad top to "M" £160 £225
24/30 *Set of* 7 95·00 £180

Examples of Nos. 26 and 28/30 are known showing a forged Registered Mazagan postmark dated "15 SP 10".

Control of the British postal agencies in Morocco returned to the G.P.O., London, from 1 January 1907.

All the following issues are overprinted on Great Britain

III. BRITISH CURRENCY

Stamps overprinted "MOROCCO AGENCIES" only were primarily intended for use on parcels (and later, air-mail correspondence), and were on sale at British P.Os throughout Morocco including Tangier, until 1937.

PRICES. Our prices for used stamps with these overprints are for specimens used in Morocco. These stamps were valid for postal purposes in Great Britain from the summer of 1950 onwards. Examples with G.B. postmarks are worth 50 per cent of the used prices quoted.

MOROCCO AGENCIES (4) MOROCCO AGENCIES (5) MOROCCO AGENCIES (6)

1907 (30 Apr)–**13**. *King Edward VII optd as T* **4** *or* **5** *(2s.6d.).*

(a) De La Rue printings. Ordinary paper (½d., 1d., 4d. (No. 35) or chalk-surfaced paper (others).

31 ½d. pale yellowish green (1.6.07) 2·25 8·50
32 1d. scarlet (5.5.07) 9·50 5·50
33 2d. pale grey-green and carmine-red 9·50 5·50
34 4d. green and chocolate-brown (29.10.07) 3·75 4·00
35 4d. pale orange (3.12) 11·00 11·00
a. Orange-red 10·00 11·00
36 6d. pale dull purple (5.5.07) 15·00 19·00
a. Dull purple 15·00 19·00
37 1s. dull green and carmine (5.5.07) 26·00 17·00
38 2s.6d. pale dull purple (5.5.07) 75·00 £110
a. Dull purple 75·00 £110
31/8 *Set of* 8 £130 £160
37s/8s Optd "Specimen" *Set of* 2 £140

(b) Harrison printing. Ordinary paper.

40 4d. bright orange (No. 286) (1913) 20·00 23·00

(c) Somerset House printing. Ordinary paper.

41 2s.6d. dull greyish purple (No. 315) (1913) 90·00 £170

1914–31. *King George V.*

(a) W **100** (Simple Cypher). Optd with *T* **4**.

42 ½d. green 3·00 50
43 1d. scarlet 85 20
44 1½d. red-brown (1921) 3·00 12·00
45 2d. orange (Die I) 3·50 60
46 3d. bluish violet (1921) 1·25 35
47 4d. grey-green (1921) 3·00 1·25
48 6d. reddish purple (*chalk-surfaced paper*) (1921) 4·75 15·00
49 1s. bistre-brown (1917) 5·50 1·25
a. Opt triple, two albino £120

(b) W **110** (Single Cypher). Optd with T **6**.

50 2s.6d. sepia-brown (*Waterlow ptg*) (No. 400) (1914) 45·00 55·00
a. Re-entry (R. 2/1) £750 £800
b. Opt double, one albino £160
51 2s.6d. yellow-brown (*D.L.R. ptg*) (No. 406) (1917) 48·00 30·00
a. Opt double £1600 £1100
b. Opt triple, two albino £200
c. Pale brown (No. 407) 38·00 50·00
53 2s.6d. chocolate-brown (*B.W. ptg*) (No. 414) 38·00 25·00
a. Opt double, one albino* £160
54 5s. rose-red (*B.W. ptg*) (No. 416) (1931) 55·00 90·00
a. Opt triple, two albino
42/54 *Set of* 10 £100 £130
49s/50s, 54s Optd "Specimen" *Set of* 3 £200

*The albino overprint is quite clear, with the "MOROCCO" appearing just below "AGENCIES" of the normal overprint and a little to the right as seen from the back. There is also a second faint albino impression just below the normal overprint.

MOROCCO AGENCIES S (7) (A) MOROCCO AGENCIES S (8) (B)

Type **7**: Opt 14 mm long; ends of "s" cut off diagonally.
Type **8**: Opt 15½ mm long; ends of "s" cut off horizontally

1925–36. *King George V (*W **111** (Block Cypher)*) optd with T* **8** *(4d.) or* **7** *(others).*

55 ½d. green 1·50 50
aw. Wmk inverted 75·00
b. Optd with Type **8** 7·50 38·00
56 1½d. chestnut (1931) 12·00 13·00
57 2d. orange 2·25 1·00
58 2½d. blue 2·25 5·00
a. Optd with Type **8** £100 30·00
59 4d. grey-green (1.36) 7·00 35·00
60 6d. purple (1931) 2·00 8·50
a. Opt double, one albino £100
b. Optd with Type **8** 1·00 60
61 1s. bistre-brown 17·00 5·00
as. Optd "Specimen" 60·00
b. Optd with Type **8** 55·00 55·00
55/61 *Set of* 7 38·00 55·00

1935 (8 May). *Silver Jubilee (Nos. 453/6) optd "*MOROCCO AGENCIES*" only, as in T* **17**.

62 ½d. green (B.) 1·25 6·50
63 1d. scarlet (B.) 1·25 6·50
64 1½d. red-brown (B.) 2·25 10·00
65 2½d. blue (R.) 2·50 2·50
62/5 *Set of* 4 6·50 23·00

1935–37. *King George V.*

(a) Harrison photo ptgs (Nos. 440/5 and 449). W **111** (Block Cypher). *Optd with T* **8**.

66 1d. scarlet (4.35) 3·25 13·00
67 1½d. red-brown (28.4.36) 3·25 16·00
68 2d. orange (1.5.36) 1·25 7·00
69 2½d. ultramarine (11.2.36) 1·75 4·25
70 3d. violet (2.3.36) 50 30
71 4d. deep grey-green (14.5.36) 50 30
72 1s. bistre-brown (31.8.36) 80 3·00
s. Optd "Specimen" 60·00

(b) Waterlow re-engraved ptgs. W **110** (Single Cypher) optd with *T* **6**.

73 2s.6d. chocolate-brown (No. 450) 40·00 60·00
s. Optd "Specimen" 70·00
74 5s. bright rose-red (No. 451) (2.3.37) 23·00 £100
66/74 *Set of* 9 65·00 £180

1936 (26 Oct)–**37**. *King Edward VIII, optd "*MOROCCO AGENCIES*" only, as in T* **18** *with "*MOROCCO*" 14¼ mm long.*

75 1d. scarlet 10 30
a. "MOROCCO" 15¼ mm long (5.1.37) 6·00 16·00
76 2½d. bright blue 10 15
a. "MOROCCO" 15¼ mm long (5.1.37) 1·00 4·25

The first two printings of both values showed all the stamps with the short overprint, Nos. 75/6.

On 5 January 1937 a further printing of both values was placed on sale in London which had the 24 stamps from the bottom two horizontal rows (Rows 19 and 20) with the long overprint, Nos. 75a/6a. Subsequent printings increased the number of long overprints in the sheet to 25 by the addition of R. 8/9, and, finally, to 31 (R. 1/7, R. 7/1, R. 8/1, R. 13/3, 4 and 10, R. 14/6, but without R. 8/9).

For the 1d. value all sheets from cylinder 2 show the first setting. Sheets from cylinder 6 were also used for the first, and for all subsequent settings. The 2½d. value was overprinted on sheets from cylinder 2 throughout.

From 3 June 1937 unoverprinted stamps of Great Britain were supplied to the post offices at Tangier and Tetuan (Spanish Zone) as local stocks of issues overprinted "MOROCCO AGENCIES" were exhausted.

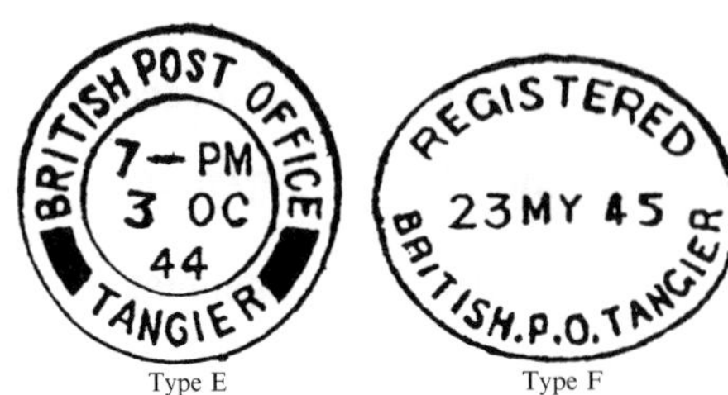

Type E Type F

Stamps of GREAT BRITAIN *cancelled as Types* E *or* F *at Tangier.*

1937. *King George V.*

Z170 1½d. red-brown (No. 441)
Z171 2d. orange (No. 442) 12·00
Z172 3d. violet (No. 444) 12·00
Z173 4d. deep grey-green (No. 445) 9·00
Z174 6d. purple (No. 426*a*) 9·00
Z175 1s. bistre-brown (No. 449) 32·00
Z176 2s.6d. chocolate-brown (No. 450) 70·00
Z177 5s. bright rose-red (No. 451)

1937–39. *King George VI (Nos. 462/75).*

Z178 ½d. green 13·00
Z179 1d. scarlet 13·00
Z180 1½d. red-brown 11·00
Z181 2d. orange 11·00
Z182 2½d. ultramarine 8·50
Z183 3d. violet 8·50
Z184 4d. grey-green 8·50
Z185 5d. brown 11·00
Z186 6d. purple 5·50
Z187 7d. emerald-green 9·00
Z188 8d. bright carmine 17·00
Z189 9d. deep olive-green 12·00
Z190 10d. turquoise-blue 17·00
Z191 1s. bistre-brown 5·50

1939–42. *King George VI (Nos. 476/8a).*

Z192 2s.6d. brown 42·00
Z193 2s.6d. yellow-green 13·00
Z194 5s. red 19·00
Z195 10s. dark blue 80·00
Z196 10s. ultramarine 35·00

1941–42. *King George VI pale colours (Nos. 485/90).*

Z197 ½d. pale green 8·50
Z198 1d. pale scarlet 8·50
Z199 1½d. pale red-brown 8·50
Z200 2d. pale orange 8·50
Z201 2½d. light ultramarine 7·50
Z202 3d. pale violet 5·50

1946. *Victory (Nos. 491/2).*

Z203 2½d. ultramarine 7·50
Z204 3d. violet 7·50

Type G

Stamps of GREAT BRITAIN *cancelled as Type* G *at Tetuan.*

1937. *King George V.*

Z208 4d. deep grey-green (No. 445) 20·00
Z209 6d. purple (No. 426*a*) 20·00
Z210 1s. bistre-brown (No. 449)

1937–39. *King George VI (Nos. 465/75).*

Z211 2d. orange 17·00
Z212 2½d. ultramarine
Z213 3d. violet
Z214 4d. grey-green 17·00
Z215 6d. purple 11·00
Z216 9d. deep olive-green
Z217 1s. bistre-brown 11·00

1939–42. *King George VI (Nos.476/7).*

Z218 2s.6d. brown
Z219 2s.6d. yellow-green 35·00
Z220 5s. red 45·00

1941. *King George VI pale colours (Nos. 485/90).*

Z221 ½d. pale green
Z222 2d. pale orange
Z223 2½d. light ultramarine
Z224 3d. pale violet 11·00

Other unoverprinted stamps of Great Britain are known wit[h] Morocco Agencies postmarks during this period, but it is believe[d] that only Nos. Z170/224 were sold by the local post offices.

The use of unoverprinted stamps in Tangier ceased with the issu[e] of Nos. 261/75 on 1 January 1949. Stamps overprinte[d] "MOROCCO AGENCIES" replaced the unoverprinted values a[t] Tetuan on 16 August 1949.

MOROCCO AGENCIES (9) MOROCCO AGENCIES (10)

1949 (16 Aug). *King George VI, optd with T* **9** *or* **10** *(2s.6d., 5s.).*

77 ½d. pale green 1·75 7·0[0]
78 1d. pale scarlet 2·75 9·0[0]
79 1½d. pale red-brown 2·75 8·5[0]
80 2d. pale orange 3·00 9·0[0]
81 2½d. light ultramarine 3·25 10·0[0]
82 3d. pale violet 1·50 1·7[5]
83 4d. grey-green 50 1·2[5]
84 5d. brown 3·00 15·0[0]
85 6d. purple 1·50 1·5[0]
86 7d. emerald-green 50 16·0[0]
87 8d. bright carmine 3·00 6·5[0]
88 9d. deep olive-green 50 11·0[0]
89 10d. turquoise-blue 50 6·5[0]
90 11d. plum 70 7·0[0]
91 1s. bistre-brown 2·75 6·0[0]
92 2s.6d. yellow-green 16·00 35·0[0]
93 5s. red 28·00 60·0[0]
77/93 *Set of* 17 60·00 £18[0]

1951 (3 May). *King George VI (Nos. 503/7, 509/10), optd with T* **9** *or* **10** *(2s.6d., 5s.).*

94 ½d. pale orange . . . 2·00 1·00
95 1d. light ultramarine . . . 2·00 1·40
96 1½d. pale green . . . 2·00 2·75
97 2d. pale red-brown . . . 2·25 4·00
98 2½d. pale scarlet . . . 2·00 4·25
99 2s.6d. yellow-green (H.M.S. *Victory*) . . 13·00 21·00
100 5s. red (Dover) . . . 13·00 22·00
94/100 *Set of* 7 . . . 32·00 50·00

IV. SPANISH CURRENCY

Stamps surcharged in Spanish currency were sold at British P.Os. throughout Morocco until the establishment of the French Zone and the Tangier International Zone, when their use was confined to the Spanish Zone.

During this period further British postal agencies were opened at Alcazar (1907–1916), Fez–Mellah (Jewish quarter) (1909), Marrakesh (1909), Marrakesh–Mellah (Jewish quarter) (1909–17) and Mequinez (1907–1916).

MOROCCO AGENCIES 5 CENTIMOS (11)

MOROCCO AGENCIES 6 PESETAS (12)

1907 (1 Jan)–**12**. *King Edward VII surch as T* **11** *(5c. to 1p.) or* **12** *(3p. to 12p.).*

(a) De La Rue printings. Ordinary paper (Nos. 112/13, 116, 118, 122/3) or chalk-surfaced paper (others).

112 5c.on ½d. pale yellowish green . . . 7·00 20
a. Yellowish green . . . 7·00 20
113 10c.on 1d. scarlet . . . 11·00 10
a. Bright scarlet . . . 11·00 10
114 15c.on 1½d. pale dull purple and green . . 4·50 80
a. Slate-purple and bluish green . . . 2·50 20
b. "1" of "15" omitted . . . £4500
115 20c.on 2d. pale grey-green and carmine-red . . . 2·25 20
a. Pale grey-green and scarlet . . . 2·75 70
116 25c.on 2½d. ultramarine . . . 2·50 20
a. Pale ultramarine . . . 1·50 20
117 40c.on 4d. green & chocolate-brn (29.10.07) . . . 1·00 2·75
a. Deep green and chocolate-brown . . . 1·75 1·75
118 40c.on 4d. pale orange (12.5.10) . . . 2·25 1·25
a. Orange-red . . . 1·00 60
119 50c.on 5d. dull purple and ultramarine . . 3·50 3·25
a. Slate-purple and ultramarine . . . 1·75 3·00
120 1p.on 10d. dull purple and carmine . . . 25·00 13·00
a. Slate-purple and carmine . . . 22·00 12·00
b. No cross on crown
121 3p.on 2s.6d. pale dull purple . . . 21·00 25·00
a. Dull purple . . . 21·00 25·00
122 6p.on 5s. bright carmine . . . 35·00 45·00
a. Deep bright carmine . . . 35·00 45·00
123 12p.on 10s. ultramarine (30.4.07) . . . 75·00 75·00
112/23 *Set of* 12 . . . £160 £140
117s, 123s Optd "Specimen" *Set of* 2 . . . £140

(b) Harrison printing Ordinary paper.

124 25c.on 2½d. bright blue (No. 283) (1912) . . 35·00 25·00
a. Dull blue . . . 25·00 25·00

(c) Somerset House printing. Ordinary paper.

125 12p.on 10s. blue (No. 319) (1912) . . . £160 £225

No. 114b occurred on stamps from the first vertical row of one sheet.

1912. *King George V (W* **49** *(Imperial Crown)) surch as T* **11**.

126 5c.on ½d. green (No. 339) . . . 3·00 20
127 10c.on 1d. scarlet (No. 342) . . . 1·00 10
a. No cross on crown . . . £110 55·00

MOROCCO AGENCIES 3 CENTIMOS (13)

MOROCCO AGENCIES 10 CENTIMOS (14)

MOROCCO AGENCIES 15 CENTIMOS (15)

MOROCCO AGENCIES 6 PESETAS (16)

1914–26. *King George V.*

(a) W **100** (Simple Cypher). *Surch as T* **11** *(5c.),* **13** *(3c. and 40c.)**, **15** *(15c.) and* **14** *(remainder).*

128 3c.on ½d. green (1917) . . . 1·00 4·25
129 5c.on ½d. green . . . 60 10
130 10c.on 1d. scarlet . . . 1·25 10
y. Wmk inverted and reversed . . . — £150
131 15c.on 1½d. red-brown (1915) . . . 1·00 10
a. Surch double, one albino . . . 80·00
132 20c.on 2d. orange (Die I) . . . 1·00 25
a. Surch double, one albino . . . 80·00
133 25c.on 2½d. blue (*shades*) . . . 1·75 25
a. Surch double, one albino . . . 60·00
w. Wmk inverted
134 40c.on 4d. grey-green (1917) . . . 2·75 4·00
a. Surch double, one albino
135 1p.on 10d. turquoise-blue . . . 3·00 6·50
a. Surch double, one albino . . . 80·00

*The surcharge on Nos. 134, 148 and 158 is as T **13** for the value and T **15** for "MOROCCO AGENCIES".

(b) W **110** (Single Cypher). *Surch as T* **16**.

(i) Waterlow printings.

136 6p.on 5s. rose-carmine . . . 29·00 48·00
a. Surch double, one albino . . . £130
b. Surch triple, two albino . . . £150
137 6p.on 5s. pale rose-carmine . . . £130 £180
a. Surch double, one albino . . . £180
138 12p.on 10s. indigo-blue (R.) . . . £100 £160
a. Surch double, one albino . . . £225
b. Surch triple, two albino
136s, 138s Optd "Specimen" *Set of* 2 . . . £180

(ii) De La Rue printings.

139 3p.on 2s.6d. grey-brown (1918) . . . 38·00 £110
a. Surch double, one albino
140 3p.on 2s.6d. yellow-brown . . . 30·00 £140
a. Surch double, one albino
141 12p.on 10s. blue (R.) . . . 90·00 £160
a. Surch double, one albino . . . £275

(iii) Bradbury Wilkinson printings.

142 3p. on 2s.6d. chocolate-brown (1926) . . . 23·00 75·00
128/42 *Set of* 11 . . . £140 £275

1925–31. *King George V (W* **111** *(Block Cypher)), surch as T* **11**, **13**, **14** *or* **15**.

143 5c.on ½d. green (1931) . . . 2·50 14·00
144 10c.on 1d. scarlet (1929) . . . 18·00 25·00
145 15c.on 1½d. red-brown . . . 7·50 23·00
146 20c.on 2d. orange (1931) . . . 3·00 8·50
a. Surch double, one albino . . . 85·00
147 25c.on 2½d. blue . . . 2·00 2·25
a. Surch double, one albino . . . 60·00
w. Wmk inverted . . . 50·00
148 40c.on 4d. grey-green (1930) . . . 2·00 2·25
a. Surch double, one albino
143/8 *Set of* 6 . . . 32·00 65·00

MOROCCO AGENCIES 10 CENTIMOS (17)

MOROCCO 10 AGENCIES CENTIMOS (18)

1935 (8 May). *Silver Jubilee (Nos. 453/6). Surch as T* **17**.

149 5c.on ½d. green (B.) . . . 1·00 80
150 10c.on 1d. scarlet (B.) . . . 2·75 2·25
a. Pair, one with "CENTIMES" . . . £1200 £1400
151 15c.on 1½d. red-brown (B.) . . . 5·50 17·00
152 25c.on 2½d. blue (R.) . . . 3·50 2·25
149/52 *Set of* 4 . . . 11·50 20·00

No. 150a occurred on R. 5/4 of a small second printing made in June 1935. The error can only be identified when *se-tenant* with a normal No. 150. Beware of forgeries.

1935–37. *King George V (Harrison photo ptgs) (Nos. 439/43, 445 and 448). Surch as T* **11**, **13**, **14** *or* **15**. W **111** (Block Cypher).

153 5c.on ½d. green (9.6.36) . . . 1·00 18·00
154 10c.on 1d. scarlet (11.36) . . . 2·50 9·00
155 15c.on 1½d. red-brown (4.35) . . . 5·50 3·25
156 20c.on 2d. orange (26.10.36) . . . 50 25
157 25c.on 2½d. ultramarine (8.9.36) . . . 1·25 4·25
158 40c.on 4d. deep grey-green (18.5.37) . . . 50 3·00
159 1p.on 10d. turquoise-blue (14.4.37) . . . 5·50 30
153/9 *Set of* 7 . . . 15·00 35·00

1936 (26 Oct)–**37**. *King Edward VIII surch as T* **18** *with* "MOROCCO" *14¼ mm long.*

160 5c.on ½d. green . . . 10 10
161 10c.on 1d. scarlet . . . 50 2·00
a. "MOROCCO" 15¼ mm long (5.1.37) . . . 3·50 13·00
162 15c.on 1½d. red-brown . . . 10 15
163 25c.on 2½d. bright blue . . . 10 10
160/3 *Set of* 4 . . . 65 2·00

The first three printings of the 10c. on 1d. (from cyls 4, 5 and 6) showed all stamps with the short surcharge (No. 161).

On 5 January 1937 a further printing was placed on sale in London which had 49 stamps in the sheet (R. 1/2 to 11, R. 2/1, 5 and 6, 8 and 9, R. 3/5, R. 4/5, R. 5/4 and 5, 10, R. 6/6 and 7, R. 7/8, R. 8/8, R. 9/8, R. 11/7, 9, R. 13/2 to 5, 7 and 8, R. 14/1, 7, R. 15/7, 11, R. 16/5, 10, R. 17/4, 10 and 11, R. 18/1, R. 19/2, R. 20/1 and 2, 3, 7, 9) with long surcharge (No. 161a). The next printing increased the number of long surcharges in the sheet to 50 (R. 10/2), but the final version, although retaining 50 long surcharges, showed them on R. 1/2 to 11, R. 17/5 to 8 and the entire rows 18, 19 and 20. The first two printings with long surcharges were from cylinder 6 and the last from cylinder 13.

MOROCCO 15 CENTIMOS AGENCIES (19)

1937 (13 May). *Coronation (No. 461), surch as T* **19**.

164 15c.on 1½d. maroon (B.) . . . 60 50

MOROCCO AGENCIES 10 CENTIMOS (20)

MOROCCO AGENCIES 10 CENTIMOS (21)

1937 (June)–**52**. *King George VI (Nos. 462/4, 466, 468, 471 and 474), surch as T* **20**.

165 5c.on ½d. green (B.) . . . 1·00 30
166 10c.on 1d. scarlet . . . 80 10
167 15c.on 1½d. red-brown (B.) (4.8.37) . . . 1·00 25
168 25c.on 2½d. ultramarine . . . 1·75 1·00
169 40c.on 4d. grey-green (9.40) . . . 30·00 13·00
170 70c.on 7d. emerald-green (9.40) . . . 1·50 13·00
171 1p.on 10d. turquoise-blue (16.6.52) . . . 2·25 3·50
165/71 *Set of* 7 . . . 35·00 28·00

1940 (6 May). *Centenary of First Adhesive Postage Stamps (Nos. 479/81 and 483), surch as T* **21**.

172 5c.on ½d. green (B.) . . . 30 2·25
173 10c.on 1d. scarlet . . . 3·50 2·25
174 15c.on 1½d. red-brown (B.) . . . 60 2·25
175 25c.on 2½d. ultramarine . . . 70 75
172/5 *Set of* 4 . . . 4·50 6·75

25 CENTIMOS MOROCCO AGENCIES (22)

45 PESETAS MOROCCO AGENCIES (23)

1948 (26 Apr). *Silver Wedding (Nos. 493/4), surch with T* **22** *or* **23**.

176 25c.on 2½d. ultramarine . . . 1·00 30
177 45p.on £1 blue . . . 17·00 22·00

1948 (29 July). *Olympic Games (Nos. 495/8), variously surch as T* **22**.

178 25c.on 2½d. ultramarine . . . 50 1·00
179 30c.on 3d. violet . . . 50 1·00
180 60c.on 6d. bright purple . . . 50 1·00
181 1p.20c. on 1s. brown . . . 60 1·00
a. Surch double . . . £750
178/81 *Set of* 4 . . . 1·90 3·50

1951 (3 May)–**52**. *King George VI (Nos. 503/5 and 507/8), surch as T* **20**.

182 5c.on ½d. pale orange . . . 2·00 4·00
183 10c.on 1d. light ultramarine . . . 3·25 7·00
184 15c.on 1½d. pale green . . . 1·75 16·00
185 25c.on 2½d. pale scarlet . . . 1·75 8·50
186 40c.on 4d. light ultramarine (26.5.52) . . . 60 9·50
182/6 *Set of* 5 . . . 8·50 40·00

V. FRENCH CURRENCY

For use in the British postal agencies at Casablanca (closed 14.8.37), Fez (closed 8.1.38), Fez–Mellah (closed after 1930), Marrakesh (closed 14.8.37), Mazagan (closed 14.8.37), Mogador (closed 31.10.33), Rabat (closed 8.1.38) and Saffi (closed 14.8.37).

MOROCCO AGENCIES 25 CENTIMES (24)

MOROCCO AGENCIES 1 FRANC (25)

1917–24. *King George V (W* **100** *(Simple Cypher)), surch as T* **24** *or* **25** *(1f.).*

191 3c.on ½d. green (R.) . . . 1·00 2·50
192 5c.on ½d. green . . . 40 20
193 10c.on 1d. scarlet . . . 3·25 40
194 15c.on 1½d. red-brown . . . 2·50 20
195 25c.on 2½d. blue . . . 2·00 20
196 40c.on 4d. slate-green . . . 2·50 1·50
197 50c.on 5d. yellow-brown (1923) . . . 80 2·75
198 75c.on 9d. olive-green (1924) . . . 1·00 75
199 1f.on 10d. turquoise-blue . . . 7·00 3·00
a. Surch double, one albino . . . 85·00
191/9 *Set of* 9 . . . 18·00 10·50

1924–32. *King George V (B.W. ptg).* W **110** (Single Cypher), *surch as T* **25**, *but closer vertical spacing.*

200 3f.on 2s.6d. chocolate-brown . . . 7·50 1·50
a. Major re-entry (R. 1/2) . . . £375 £375
b. Surch double, one albino
c. Reddish brown . . . 13·00 10·00
201 6f.on 5s. rose-red (1932) . . . 38·00 42·00
200s/1s Optd "Specimen" *Set of* 2 . . . £120

1925–34. *King George V (W* **111** *(Block Cypher)), surch as T* **24** *or* **25** *(1f.).*

202 5c.on ½d. green . . . 30 6·50
203 10c.on 1d. scarlet . . . 30 1·75
204 15c.on 1½d. red-brown . . . 1·00 1·75
205 25c.on 2½d. blue . . . 1·25 50
206 40c.on 4d. grey-green . . . 60 80
a. Surch double, one albino . . . 65·00
207 50c.on 5d. yellow-brown . . . 1·25 10
w. Wmk inverted . . . 75·00
208 75c.on 9d. olive-green . . . 3·00 15
w. Wmk inverted . . . — 75·00
209 90c.on 9d. olive-green . . . 15·00 7·00

210 1f.on 10d. turquoise-blue . . . . 1·00 10
a. Surch double, one albino £100
211 1f.50 on 1s. bistre-brown . . . . 9·50 2·25
s. Optd "Specimen" . . . . 50·00
202/11 *Set of* 10 . . . . 30·00 19·00

1935 (8 May). *Silver Jubilee (Nos. 453/6), surch as T* **17**, *but in French currency.*
212 5c.on ½d. green (B.) 15 15
213 10c.on 1d. scarlet (B.) . . . . 2·50 50
214 15c.on 1½d. red-brown (B.) 35 50
215 25c.on 2½d. blue (R.) 30 25
212/15 *Set of* 4 . . . . 3·00 1·25

1935–37. *King George V (Harrison photo ptgs.* W **111** (Block Cypher)*), surch as T* **24** *or* **25** *(1f.).*
216 5c.on ½d. green (10.35) . . . . 50 5·00
217 10c.on 1d. scarlet (2.3.36) 35 30
218 15c.on 1½d. red-brown . . . . 4·75 5·50
219 25c.on 2½d. ultramarine (25.9.36) 30 15
220 40c.on 4d. deep grey-green (2.12.36) 30 15
221 50c.on 5d. yellow-brown (15.9.36) 30 15
222 90c.on 9d. deep olive-green (15.2.37) . . . . 35 1·75
223 1f.on 10d. turquoise-blue (10.2.37) 30 30
224 1f.50 on 1s. bistre-brown (20.7.37) . . . . 75 3·25
s. Optd "Specimen" . . . . 50·00

1935–36. *King George V (Waterlow re-engraved ptgs.* W **100** (Single Cypher)*), surch as T* **25**, *but closer vertical spacing.*
225 3f.on 2s.6d. chocolate-brown (No. 450) . . 4·75 12·00
226 6f.on 5s. bright rose-red (No. 451) (17.6.36) . . . . 6·00 21·00
216/26 *Set of* 11 . . . . 17·00 45·00
225s/6s Optd "Specimen" *Set of* 2 . . . . . . £120

1936 (26 Oct). *King Edward VIII, surch as T* **18**, *but in French currency.*
227 5c.in ½d. green 10 15
a. Bar through "POSTAGE" £475
228 15c.on 1½d. red-brown 10 15

No. 227a involved R. 18/10 to 12 on a total of eight sheets. The bar, probably a printers rule, became progressively longer so that on four of the sheets it extends over all three stamps. Price quoted is for an example with the bar through the entire word.

1937 (13 May). *Coronation (No. 461), surch as T* **19**, *but in French currency.*
229 15c.on 1½d. maroon (B.) 30 20

1937 (June). *King George VI, surch as T* **20**, *but in French currency.*
230 5c.on ½d. green (B.) . . . . 2·25 2·25

Stamps surcharged in French currency were withdrawn from sale on 8 January 1938.

VI. TANGIER INTERNATIONAL ZONE

By an agreement between Great Britain, France and Spain, Tangier was declared an international zone in 1924. Stamps overprinted "Morocco Agencies" or surcharged in Spanish currency were used there until replaced by Nos. 231/4.

PRICES. Our note *re* U.K. usage (at beginning of Section III) also applies to "TANGIER" optd stamps.

TANGIER (26) TANGIER TANGIER (27)

1927. *King George V (*W **111** (Block Cypher)*), optd with T* **26**.
231 ½d. green . . . . 2·75 20
a. Opt double, one albino . . . . . .
232 1d. scarlet . . . . 3·00 25
a. Inverted "Q" for "O" (R. 20/3) . . . £800
233 1½d. chestnut . . . . 5·50 3·50
234 2d. orange . . . . 3·25 20
a. Opt double, one albino . . . . . . 80·00
231/4 *Set of* 4 . . . . 13·00 3·75

1934 (Dec)–**35**. *King George V (Harrison photo ptgs.* W **111** (Block Cypher)*), optd with T* **26**.
235 ½d. green (2.35) . . . . 1·25 1·60
236 1d. scarlet . . . . 3·75 2·50
237 1½d. red-brown 50 20
235/7 *Set of* 3 . . . . 5·00 3·75

1935 (8 May). *Silver Jubilee (Nos. 453/5), optd with T* **27**.
238 ½d. green (B.) . . . . 1·25 4·50
239 1d. scarlet . . . . 13·50 14·00
240 1½d. red-brown (B.) . . . . 1·25 1·00
238/40 *Set of* 3 . . . . 14·50 18·00

1936 (26 Oct). *King Edward VIII, optd with T* **26**.
241 ½d. green 10 20
242 1d. scarlet 10 10
243 1½d. red-brown 15 10
241/3 *Set of* 3 . . . . 30 30

TANGIER (28) TANGIER TANGIER (29)

1937 (13 May). *Coronation (No. 461), optd with T* **28**.
244 1½d. maroon (B.) 50 30

1937. *King George VI (Nos. 462/4), optd with T* **29**.
245 ½d. green (B.) (June) . . . . 2·25 1·25
246 1d. scarlet (June) . . . . 6·50 1·00
247 1½d. red-brown (B.) (4 Aug) . . . . 2·25 25
245/7 *Set of* 3 . . . . 10·00 2·25

TANGIER (30) TANGIER (31)

1940 (6 May). *Centenary of First Adhesive Postage Stamps (Nos. 479/81), optd with T* **30**.
248 ½d. green (B.) . . . . 30 4·50
249 1d. scarlet 45 50
250 1½d. red-brown (B.) . . . . 2·00 4·50
248/50 *Set of* 3 . . . . 2·50 8·50

1944. *King George VI pale colours (Nos. 485/6), optd with T* **29**.
251 ½d. pale green (B.) . . . . 10·00 3·50
252 1d. pale scarlet . . . . 10·00 2·75

1946 (11 June). *Victory (Nos. 491/2), optd as T* **31**.
253 2½d. ultramarine 50 50
254 3d. violet . . . . 50 1·75

The opt on No. 254 is smaller (23 × 2½ mm).

1948 (26 Apr). *Royal Silver Wedding (Nos. 493/4), optd with T* **30**.
255 2½d. ultramarine 50 15
a. Opt omitted (in vert pair with stamp optd at top) £3500
256 £1 blue . . . . 20·00 25·00

No. 255a comes from a sheet on which the overprint is misplaced downwards resulting in the complete absence of the opt from the six stamps of the top row. On the rest of the sheet the opt falls at the top of each stamp instead of at the foot (*Price* £250, *unused*, £350 *used*).

1948 (29 July). *Olympic Games (Nos. 495/8), optd with T* **30**.
257 2½d. ultramarine . . . . 1·00 1·75
258 3d. violet . . . . 1·00 1·75
259 6d. bright purple . . . . 1·00 1·75
260 1s. brown . . . . 1·00 1·00
257/60 *Set of* 4 . . . . 3·50 5·50

1949 (1 Jan). *King George VI, optd with T* **29**.
261 2d. pale orange . . . . 5·00 5·50
262 2½d. light ultramarine . . . . 1·75 5·00
263 3d. pale violet . . . . 70 1·25
264 4d. grey-green . . . . 11·00 10·00
265 5d. brown . . . . 3·75 18·00
266 6d. purple 70 30
267 7d. emerald-green . . . . 1·25 12·00
268 8d. bright carmine . . . . 3·75 10·00
269 9d. deep olive-green . . . . 1·25 12·00
270 10d. turquoise-blue . . . . 1·25 12·00
271 11d. plum . . . . 1·25 10·00
272 1s. bistre-brown . . . . 1·25 2·50
273 2s.6d. yellow-green . . . . 4·50 12·00
274 5s. red . . . . 13·00 38·00
275 10s. ultramarine . . . . 40·00 £100
261/75 *Set of* 15 . . . . 80·00 £225

1949 (10 Oct). *75th Anniv of U.P.U. (Nos. 499/502), optd with T* **30**.
276 2½d. ultramarine . . . . 70 2·50
277 3d. violet . . . . 70 1·50
278 6d. bright purple . . . . 70 1·00
279 1s. brown . . . . 70 3·00
276/9 *Set of* 4 . . . . 2·50 7·25

1950 (2 Oct)–**51**. *King George VI, optd with T* **29** *or* **30** *(shilling values).*
280 ½d. pale orange (3.5.51) . . . . 85 1·50
281 1d. light ultramarine (3.5.51) . . . . . 1·00 3·00
282 1½d. pale green (3.5.51) . . . . 1·00 14·00
283 2d. pale red-brown (3.5.51) . . . . . . 1·00 2·50
284 2½d. pale scarlet (3.5.51) . . . . 1·00 5·00
285 4d. light ultramarine . . . . 3·00 3·00
286 2s.6d. yell-grn (H.M.S. *Victory*) (3.5.51) . . . . 9·50 5·00
287 5s. red (Dover) (3.5.51) . . . . 15·00 17·00
288 10s. ultramarine (St. George) (3.5.51) . . . 20·00 17·00
280/8 *Set of* 9 . . . . 48·00 60·00

Muscat

An independent Arab Sultanate in Eastern Arabia with an Indian postal administration.

The Indian post office at Muscat town is officially recorded as having opened on 1 May 1864. Stamps of India were provided for its use, most surviving examples being of the ½a. value, although others to the 8a. are known.

The office was initially included in the Bombay Postal Circle and the first postmark, so far only recorded on stampless covers, was a single circle, 21½ mm in diameter, broken at the top by "MUSCAT" and with the date in two lines across the centre. This was followed by a cancellation showing the post office number, "309", within a diamond of 13, later 16, bars. It is believed that this was used in conjunction with a single ring date stamp inscribed "MUSCAT".

1864 Diamond

In 1869 the office was transferred to the Sind Circle, assigned new number, "23", and issued with a duplex cancellation. Maj reorganisation of the postal service in 1873 resulted in Musc becoming office "K-4". For ten years from 1873 the cancellatio do not, very confusingly, carry any indication of the year of use.

1869 Duplex

1873 Duplex

Muscat rejoined the Bombay Circle in 1879 and was issued wi a cancellation showing a "B" within a square of horizontal bar The date stamp used at this time was unique in that it carried t inscription "MASKAT", although the spelling reverted to the mo usual form by 1882. The square cancellation had been replaced b a similar circular mark by 1884.

Subsequent postmarks were of various circular types, all inscrib "MUSCAT".

There was only one Indian post office in Muscat, but a furth office did exist, from 12 April 1868, at the Muscat dependency Guadur, a port on the Mekran coast of Baluchistan.

No cancellations have been reported from Guadur before i transfer to the Sind Circle in 1869. Cancellations are all similar style to those for Muscat, Guadur being initially assigned numb "24", although an office in Southern India is also known to hav used this numeral. The 1869 duplex is interesting in that it inscribed "GWADUR". Under the 1873 reorganisation the offi became "4/K-1", this postmark using the "GUADUR" spelling.

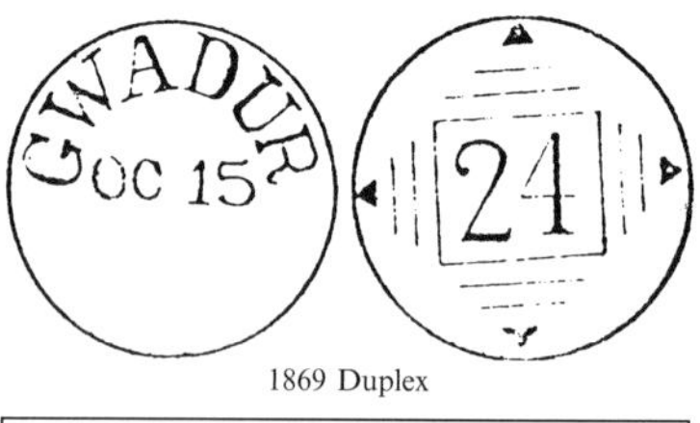

1869 Duplex

PRICES FOR STAMPS ON COVER	
Nos. 1/15	*from* × 50
Nos. O1/10	*from* × 75

(Currency 12 pies = 1 anna; 16 annas = 1 Indian rupee)

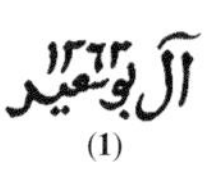

(1)

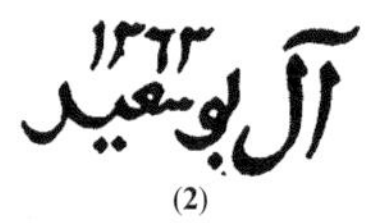

(2)

1944 (20 Nov). *Bicentenary of Al-Busaid Dynasty. Nos. 259/60, 265/ and 269a/77 (King George VI) of India optd ("*AL BUSAI *1363" in Arabic script) as T* **1** *or* **2** *(rupee values).*
1 3p. slate . . . . 30 6·0
w. Wmk inverted . . . . 5·00
2 ½a. purple . . . . 30 6·0
3 9p. green . . . . 30 6·0
4 1a. carmine . . . . 30 6·0
5 1½a. dull violet . . . . 30 6·0
6 2a. vermilion . . . . 40 6·0
w. Wmk inverted . . . .
7 3a. bright violet . . . . 1·00 6·0
w. Wmk inverted . . . . 5·00
8 3½a. bright blue . . . . 1·00 6·0
9 4a. brown . . . . 1·00 6·0
10 6a. turquoise-green . . . . 1·00 6·0
11 8a. slate-violet . . . . 1·25 6·0
12 12a. lake . . . . 1·25 6·0
13 14a. purple . . . . 4·00 9·5
14 1r. grey and red-brown . . . . 1·50 10·0
15 2r. purple and brown . . . . 3·00 16·0
1/15 *Set of* 15 . . . . 15·00 95·0

OFFICIAL STAMPS

1944 (20 Nov). *Bicentenary of Al-Busaid Dynasty. Nos. O138, O14 O144a/6 and 146b/50 of India optd as T* **1** *or* **2** *(1r.).*
O 1 3p. slate . . . . 50 11·0
O 2 ½a. purple . . . . 50 11·0
O 3 9p. green . . . . 50 11·0
O 4 1a. carmine . . . . 50 11·0
O 5 1½a. dull violet . . . . 50 11·0
O 6 2a. vermilion . . . . 70 11·0
O 7 2½a. bright violet . . . . 3·50 11·0
O 8 4a. brown . . . . 1·75 11·0
O 9 8a. slate-violet . . . . 3·75 13·0
O10 1r. grey and red-brown . . . . 2·50 21·0
O1/10 *Set of* 10 . . . . 13·00 £11

From December 1947 there was a Pakistani postal administration nd stamps of Pakistan were used until 31 March 1948. The ıbsequent British administration operated from 1 April 1948 to 9 April 1966 when the stamps of the BRITISH POSTAL GENCIES IN EASTERN ARABIA were used. Guadur, however, ontinued to use the stamps of Pakistan until the dependency was nally ceded to that country in 1953.

Natal
see **South Africa**

Nauru
see after **Australia**

Nevis
see **St. Kitts-Nevis**

New Brunswick
see **Canada**

Newfoundland
see **Canada**

New Guinea
see after **Australia**

New Hebrides

Stamps of NEW SOUTH WALES were used by various Postal Agencies in the New Hebrides from August 1891 onwards. From late 1892 the N.S.W. agency at Port Vila was run by the Australian New Hebrides Company who, from 1897, issued local 1d. and 2d. stamps for the carriage of mail on the Company's ships. These can be found used in combination with N.S.W. issues. Similar Postal Agencies supplying the stamps of NEW CALEDONIA were opened from 1903 onwards. The use of New South Wales and New Caledonia stamps was prohibited after 1 December 1908.

PRICES FOR STAMPS ON COVER TO 1945

Nos.	1/8 (F1/5)	*from* × 10
No.	9	*from* × 2
Nos.	10/16 (F6/10)	*from* × 8
Nos.	18/28 (F11/32)	*from* × 6
Nos.	30/4 (F33/7)	*from* × 4
No.	35 (F32*a*)	—
Nos.	36/9	*from* × 3
Nos.	40/2 (F38/41)	*from* × 4
Nos.	43/51 (F42/52)	*from* × 5
Nos.	52/63 (F53/64)	*from* × 3
Nos.	D1/5 (FD53/7)	*from* × 100
Nos.	D6/10 (FD65/9)	*from* × 8

ANGLO-FRENCH CONDOMINIUM

The New Hebrides, an island group in the south-west Pacific, were recognised as an area of joint Anglo-French influence in 1878. The position was regularised by the Convention of 20 October 1906 which created a Condominium, the two nations having equal rights and shares in the administration of the islands.

Stamps inscribed in English or French were issued concurrently and had equal validity throughout the islands. A common currency was reflected in the face values from 1938.

Where common designs were used, the main differences between stamps inscribed in English and those in French are as follows:

(a) Inscriptions in English or French.
(b) Position of cyphers. French issues normally have "RF" to the right or above the British royal cypher.
(c) French issues are without watermark, *unless otherwise stated.*

Inscriptions in English

Inscriptions in French

I. STAMPS INSCRIBED IN ENGLISH

NEW HEBRIDES. / CONDOMINIUM. (1)

NEWHEBRIDES / CONDOMINIUM (2)

1908 (29 Oct). *T* **23** *and* **24** *of Fiji optd with T* **1** *by Govt Printing Establishment, Suva. On the bicoloured stamps the word "FIJI" obliterated by a bar in the colour of the word.* P 14.

(*a*) Wmk Multiple Crown CA. *Ordinary paper* (*½d., 1d.*) *or chalk-surfaced paper* (*1s.*).

1	½d. green and pale green (No. 115)	3·75	15·00
1*a*	½d. green (No. 118)	40	7·00
2	1d. red	50	40
	a. Opt omitted (in vert pair with normal)	£5500	
3	1s. green and carmine	19·00	3·75

(*b*) Wmk Crown CA.

4	½d. green and grey-green	50·00	80·00
5	2d. dull purple and orange	60	70
6	2½d. dull purple and blue/*blue*	60	70
7	5d. dull purple and green	80	2·00
8	6d. dull purple and carmine	70	1·25
9	1s. green and carmine	£120	£250
1/9	*Set of* 9	£170	£300

1910 (15 Dec). *Types as last optd with T* **2** *by D.L.R. Ordinary paper* (*½d. to 2½d.*) *or chalk-surfaced paper* (*5d., 6d., 1s.*). Wmk Multiple Crown CA. P 14.

10	½d. green	3·50	24·00
11	1d. red	10·00	8·50
12	2d. grey	60	3·00
13	2½d. bright blue	65	4·25
14	5d. dull purple and olive-green	1·25	5·50
15	6d. dull and deep purple	1·00	5·00
16	1s. black/*green* (R.)	1·00	7·50
10/16	*Set of* 7	16·00	50·00
10s/16s	Optd "Specimen" *Set of* 7	£275	

3 Weapons and Idols

1d. (4)

(Des J. Giraud. Recess D.L.R.)

1911 (25 July). Wmk Mult Crown CA. P 14.

18	**3**	½d. green	85	1·75
19		1d. red	3·75	2·00
20		2d. grey	8·00	4·00
21		2½d. ultramarine	3·00	5·50
24		5d. sage-green	4·50	7·00
25		6d. purple	3·00	5·00
26		1s. black/*green*	2·75	13·00
27		2s. purple/*blue*	22·00	22·00
28		5s. green/*yellow*	35·00	48·00
18/28		*Set of* 9	75·00	95·00
18s/28s		*Set of* 9	£190	

1920 (June)–**21**. *Surch with T* **4** *at Govt Printing Establishment, Suva.*

(*a*) *On Nos. 24 and 26/8.*

30	**3**	1d.on 5d. sage-green (10.3.21)	7·00	60·00
		a. Surch inverted	£2000	
31		1d.on 1s. black/*green*	1·25	13·00
32		1d.on 2s. purple/*blue*	1·00	10·00
33		1d.on 5s. green/*yellow*	1·00	10·00

(*b*) *On No. F16.*

34	**3**	2d.on 40c. red/*yellow*	1·00	18·00

(*c*) *On No. F27.*

35	**3**	2d.on 40c. red/*yellow*	£120	£550

1921 (Sept–Oct). Wmk Mult Script CA. P 14.

36	**3**	1d. scarlet	2·50	14·00
37		2d. slate-grey	4·25	38·00
39		6d. purple	14·00	75·00
36/9		*Set of* 3	19·00	£110
36s/9s		Optd "Specimen" *Set of* 3	75·00	

1924 (1 May). *Surch as T* **4**, *at Suva.*

40	**3**	1d.on ½d. green (No. 18)	4·00	22·00
41		3d.on 1d. scarlet (No. 36)	4·00	11·00
42		5d.on 2½d. ultramarine (No. 21)	7·50	21·00
		a. Surch inverted	£1800	
40/2		*Set of* 3	14·00	48·00

5

(Recess D.L.R.)

1925 (June). Wmk Mult Script CA. P 14.

43	**5**	½d.(5c.) black	1·25	12·00
44		1d.(10c.) green	1·00	11·00
45		2d.(20c.) slate-grey	1·75	2·50
46		2½d.(25c.) brown	1·00	13·00
47		5d.(50c.) ultramarine	3·00	2·75
48		6d.(60c.) purple	3·50	12·00
49		1s.(1.25fr.) black/*emerald*	3·25	19·00
50		2s.(2.50fr.) purple/*blue*	6·00	22·00
51		5s.(6.25fr.) green/*yellow*	6·00	25·00
43/51		*Set of* 9	23·00	£110
43s/51s		Optd "Specimen" *Set of* 9	£190	

(New Currency. 100 gold centimes = 1 gold franc)

The currency used for the face values of issues to 1977 was an artificial, rather than an actual, monetary unit. The actual currencies in use were Australian dollars and the local franc.

6 Lopevi Is and Outrigger Canoe

(Des J. Kerhor. Eng J. G. Hall. Recess B.W.)

1938 (1 June). *Gold Currency.* Wmk Mult Script CA. P 12.

52	**6**	5c. blue-green	2·50	4·00
53		10c. orange	1·25	2·00
54		15c. bright violet	3·50	4·00
55		20c. scarlet	1·60	2·50
56		25c. reddish brown	1·60	2·50
57		30c. blue	2·25	2·50
58		40c. grey-olive	4·50	6·00
59		50c. purple	1·60	2·50
60		1f. red/*green*	4·00	8·50
61		2f. blue/*green*	30·00	17·00
62		5f. red/*yellow*	70·00	48·00
63		10f. violet/*blue*	£200	75·00
52/63		*Set of* 12	£300	£160
52s/63s		Perf "Specimen" *Set of* 12	£225	

(Recess Waterlow)

1949 (10 Oct). *75th Anniv of U.P.U. As No. 117 of Antigua.* Wmk Mult Script CA. P 13½ × 14.

64	10c. red-orange	30	75
65	15c. violet	30	75
66	30c. ultramarine	30	75
67	50c. purple	40	75
64/7	*Set of* 4	1·10	2·75

POSTAGE DUE STAMPS

POSTAGE DUE (D 1) POSTAGE DUE (D 2) POSTAGE DUE (D 3)

1925 (June). *Optd with Type D* **1**, *by D.L.R.*

D1	**5**	1d. (10c.) green	30·00	1·00
D2		2d. (20c.) slate-grey	35·00	1·00
D3		3d. (30c.) red	35·00	2·50
D4		5d. (50c.) ultramarine	40·00	4·50
D5		10d. (1f.) carmine/blue	45·00	5·50
D1/5		*Set of* 5	£170	13·00
D1s/5s		Optd "Specimen" *Set of* 5	£180	

1938 (1 June). *Optd with Type D* **2**, *by B.W.*

D 6	**6**	5c. blue-green	24·00	38·00
D 7		10c. orange	24·00	38·00
D 8		20c. scarlet	28·00	55·00
D 9		40c. grey-olive	35·00	65·00
D10		1f. red/*green*	45·00	75·00
D6/10		*Set of* 5	£140	£250
D6s/10s		Perf "Specimen" *Set of* 5	£130	

II. STAMPS INSCRIBED IN FRENCH

(Currency. 100 centimes = 1 French franc)

NOUVELLES HEBRIDES (F 1)

NOUVELLES-HEBRIDES (F 2)

1908 (21 Nov). *T* **15/17** *of New Caledonia. optd with Types F* **1** *or F* **2** *(1f.), by Govt Ptg Wks, Paris.*

F1	5c. green	4·75	4·75
F2	10c. carmine	6·00	3·50
F3	25c. blue/*greenish* (R.)	6·00	2·25
F4	50c. red/*orange*	7·00	4·75
F5	1f. blue/*green* (R.)	17·00	20·00
F1/5	*Set of* 5	38·00	30·00

CONDOMINIUM (F 3)

10c. (F 4)

1910 (Aug)–**11**. *Nos.* F **1/5** *further optd with Type* F **3**, *or larger (1f.), by Govt Ptg Wks, Paris.*

F 6	5c. green	2·75	3·00
F 7	10c. carmine	2·75	1·25
F 8	25c. blue/*greenish* (R.) (1911)	2·25	3·75
F 9	50c. red/*orange* (1911)	6·50	9·75
F10	1f. blue/*green* (R.)	14·00	22·00
F6/10 *Set of* 5		25·00	35·00

All the above were released in Paris on 16 March 1910. The 5c., 10c. and 1f. were issued in New Hebrides in August but the 25c. and 50c. were not received until 1911 after the issue of the definitive stamps and they were placed in reserve, although some may have been issued on request.

1911 (12 July). Wmk Mult Crown CA. P 14.

F11	**3**	5c. green	1·00	2·75
F12		10c. carmine	50	75
F13		20c. greyish slate	1·00	2·25
F14		25c. ultramarine	2·50	7·00
F15		30c. brown/*yellow*	6·50	5·25
F16		40c. red/*yellow*	1·40	3·75
F17		50c. sage-green	2·00	4·00
F18		75c. orange	7·00	23·00
F19		1f. red/*blue*	2·50	3·00
F20		2f. violet	8·50	22·00
F21		5f. red/*green*	12·00	35·00
F11/21 *Set of* 11			40·00	95·00

1913. As last but wmk "R F" in sheet or without wmk.

F22	**3**	5c. green	1·25	4·75
F23		10c. carmine	1·00	3·75
F24		20c. greyish slate	1·00	2·40
F25		25c. ultramarine	1·25	5·50
F26		30c. brown/*yellow*	1·90	10·00
F27		40c. red/*yellow*	22·00	70·00
F28		50c. sage-green	10·00	27·00
F29		75c. orange	9·00	40·00
F30		1f. red/*blue*	6·00	10·00
F31		2f. violet	9·00	40·00
F32		5f. red/*green*	22·00	48·00
F22/32 *Set of* 11			75·00	£225

The above were placed on sale in Paris on 29 April 1912.

1920–21. *Surch as Type* F **4**, *at Govt Printing Establishment, Suva, Fiji.*

(a) On stamps of 1908–11 (June 1920).

F32*a*		5c. on 50c. red/*orange* (F4)	£450	£450
F33		5c. on 50c. red/*orange* (F9)	2·40	11·00
F33*a*		10c. on 25c. blue/*greenish* (F8)	50	1·50

(b) On stamps of 1911–13 (10.3.21).

F34	**3**	5c.on 40c. red/*yellow* (F27)	27·00	95·00
F35		20c.on 30c. brown/*yellow* (F15)	11·00	65·00
F36		20c.on 30c. brown/*yellow* (F26)	6·50	70·00

(c) On Inscr in English (10.3.21).

F37	**3**	10c.on 5d. sage-green (24)	11·00	50·00

1924 (1 May). *Stamps of 1911–13 surch as Type* F **4**, *at Suva.*

F38	**3**	10c.on 5c. green (F22)	1·00	5·00
F39		30c.on 10c. carmine (F23)	1·00	2·50
F40		50c.on 25c. ultramarine (F14)	29·00	90·00
F41		50c.on 25c. ultramarine (F25)	2·50	24·00
F38/41 *Set of* 4			30·00	£110

F **5**

France Libre
(F **6**)

(Recess D.L.R.)

1925 (June). Wmk "R F" in sheet or without wmk. P 14.

F42	F **5**	5c.(½d.) black	75	10·00
F43		10c.(1d.) green	1·00	9·00
F44		20c.(2d.) greyish slate	1·75	2·75
F45		25c.(2½d.) brown	1·50	9·00
F46		30c.(3d.) red	1·50	8·00
F47		40c.(4d.) red/*yellow*	1·50	8·00
F48		50c.(5d.) ultramarine	1·50	1·75
F49		75c.(7½d.) yellow-brown	1·50	13·00
F50		1f.(10d.) carmine/*blue*	1·50	2·50
F51		2f.(1/8) violet	2·50	24·00
F52		5f.(4s.) carmine/*green*	3·50	24·00
F42/52 *Set of* 11			17·00	£100
F42s/52s Optd "Specimen" *Set of* 11			£250	

In July 1929 a batch of mail was carried by aircraft from Port Vila to the French cruiser *Tourville* for sorting and forwarding at Nouméa, New Caledonia. Stamps of the above issue (including those with English inscriptions) were affixed to covers and handstamped "PAR AVION" before cancellation.

(New Currency. 100 gold centimes = 1 gold franc)

1938 (1 June). *Gold Currency.* Wmk "R F" in sheet or without wmk. P 12.

F53	**6**	5c. blue-green	2·25	5·00
F54		10c. orange	1·75	1·40
F55		15c. bright violet	1·50	3·25
F56		20c. scarlet	1·90	3·00
F57		25c. reddish brown	4·50	3·50
F58		30c. blue	4·50	4·00
F59		40c. grey-olive	1·50	8·00
F60		50c. purple	1·50	2·50
F61		1f. lake/*pale green* (*shades*)	2·00	4·50
F62		2f. blue/*pale green* (*shades*)	27·00	28·00
F63		5f. red/*yellow*	50·00	45·00
F64		10f. violet/*blue*	£120	90·00
F53/64 *Set of* 12			£200	£180
F53s/64s Perf "Specimen" *Set of* 12			£300	

1941 (15 Apr). *Adherence to General de Gaulle. Optd with Type* F **6**, *at Nouméa, New Caledonia.*

F65	**6**	5c. blue-green	2·00	24·00
F66		10c. orange	3·25	23·00
F67		15c. bright violet	5·50	38·00
F68		20c. scarlet	16·00	30·00
F69		25c. reddish brown	19·00	40·00
F70		30c. blue	19·00	35·00
F71		40c. grey-olive	17·00	38·00
F72		50c. purple	17·00	35·00
F73		1f. lake/*pale green*	18·00	35·00
F74		2f. blue/*pale green*	16·00	35·00
F75		5f. red/*yellow*	16·00	35·00
F76		10f. violet/*blue*	16·00	35·00
F65/76 *Set of* 12			£150	£350

1949 (10 Oct). *75th Anniv of U.P.U. As Nos. 64/7.* Wmk "R F" in sheet or without wmk. P 13½.

F77	10c. red-orange	2·50	4·75
F78	15c. violet	3·75	8·50
F79	30c. ultramarine	5·50	11·00
F80	50c. purple	6·50	14·00
F77/80 *Set of* 4		16·00	35·00

POSTAGE DUE STAMPS

CHIFFRE TAXE	**CHIFFRE TAXE**	**TIMBRE-TAXE**
(FD **1**)	(FD **2**)	(FD **3**)

1925 (June). *Optd with Type* FD **1**, *by D.L.R.*

FD53	F **5**	10c.(1d.) green	50·00	3·00
FD54		20c.(2d.) greyish slate	55·00	3·00
FD55		30c.(3d.) red	55·00	3·00
FD56		50c.(5d.) ultramarine	48·00	3·00
FD57		1f.(10d.) carmine/*blue*	48·00	3·00
FD53/7 *Set of* 5			£225	13·50
FD53s/7s Optd "Specimen" *Set of* 5			£250	

Although on sale in Paris, the Postmaster would not issue any in unused condition for about a year and most copies are cancelled-to-order.

1938 (1 June). *Optd with Type* FD **2**, *by Bradbury, Wilkinson.*

FD65	**6**	5c. blue-green	14·00	50·00
FD66		10c. orange	17·00	50·00
FD67		20c. scarlet	23·00	55·00
FD68		40c. grey-olive	48·00	£110
FD69		1f. lake/*pale green*	48·00	£130
FD65/9 *Set of* 5			£130	£350
FD65s/9s Perf "Specimen" *Set of* 5			£200	

1941 (15 Apr). *Nos. FD65/9 optd with Type* F **6** *at Nouméa, New Caledonia.*

FD77	**6**	5c. blue-green	13·00	35·00
FD78		10c. orange	13·00	35·00
FD79		20c. scarlet	13·00	35·00
FD80		40c. grey-olive	17·00	35·00
FD81		1f. lake/*pale green*	16·00	35·00
FD77/81 *Set of* 5			65·00	£160

New Republic *see* South Africa

New South Wales *see* Australia

New Zealand

From 1831 mail from New Zealand was sent to Sydney, New South Wales, routed through an unofficial postmaster at Kororareka.

The first official post office opened at Kororareka in January 1840 to be followed by others at Auckland, Britannia, Coromandel Harbour, Hokianga, Port Nicholson, Russell and Waimate during the same year. New South Wales relinquished control of the postal service when New Zealand became a separate colony on 3 May 1841.

The British G.P.O. was responsible for the operation of the overseas mails from 11 October 1841 until the postal service once again passed under colonial control on 18 November 1848.

CC 1

CC 2

AUCKLAND

CROWNED-CIRCLE HANDSTAMPS

CC1 CC **1** AUCKLAND NEW ZEALAND (R.) (31.10.1846) *Price on cover* £27

NELSON

CROWNED-CIRCLE HANDSTAMPS

CC2 CC **1** NELSON NEW ZEALAND (R.) (31.10.1846) *Price on cover* £9

NEW PLYMOUTH

CROWNED-CIRCLE HANDSTAMPS

CC3 CC **1** NEW PLYMOUTH NEW ZEALAND (R. or Black) (31.10.1846) *Price on cover* £20

CC3*a* CC **2** NEW PLYMOUTH NEW ZEALAND (R. or Black) (1854) *Price on cover* £25

OTAGO

CROWNED-CIRCLE HANDSTAMPS

CC4 CC **2** OTAGO NEW ZEALAND (R.) (1851) *Price on cover* £18

PETRE

CROWNED-CIRCLE HANDSTAMPS

CC5 CC **1** PETRE NEW ZEALAND (R.) (31.10.1846) *Price on cover* £12

PORT VICTORIA

CROWNED-CIRCLE HANDSTAMPS

CC6 CC **2** PORT VICTORIA NEW ZEALAND (R.) (1851) *Price on cover* £10

RUSSELL

CROWNED-CIRCLE HANDSTAMPS

CC7 CC **1** RUSSELL NEW ZEALAND (R.) (31.10.1846) *Price on cover* £32

WELLINGTON

CROWNED-CIRCLE HANDSTAMPS

CC8 CC **1** WELLINGTON NEW ZEALAND (R.) (31.10.1846) *Price on cover* £3

A similar mark for Christchurch as Type CC **2** is only kno struck, in black, as a cancellation after the introduction of adhes stamps.

No. CC3*a* is a locally-cut replacement with the office na around the circumference, but a straight "PAID AT" in the cent

PRICES FOR STAMPS ON COVER TO 1945

Nos.	1/125	*from* × 2
Nos.	126/36	*from* × 3
Nos.	137/9	*from* × 2
No.	140	—
No.	141	*from* × 2
No.	142	—
Nos.	143/8	*from* × 2
Nos.	149/51	*from* × 10
Nos.	152/84	*from* × 2
Nos.	185/6	—
Nos.	187/203	*from* × 3
Nos.	205/7*e*	—
Nos.	208/13	*from* × 2
Nos.	214/16*j*	—
Nos.	217/58	*from* × 3
No.	259	—
Nos.	260/9	*from* × 3
No.	270	—
Nos.	271/6	*from* × 3
Nos.	277/307	*from* × 2
Nos.	308/16	*from* × 3
No.	317	—
Nos.	318/28	*from* × 3
Nos.	329/48	—
No.	349	*from* × 5
Nos.	350/1	—
No.	352	*from* × 5
Nos.	353/69	—
Nos.	370/86	*from* × 2
No.	387	*from* × 4
Nos.	388/99	*from* × 3
Nos.	400/666	*from* × 2
Nos.	E1/5	*from* × 5
No.	E6	*from* × 10
Nos.	D1/8	*from* × 3
Nos.	D9/16	*from* × 5
Nos.	D17/20	*from* × 3
Nos.	D21/47	*from* × 6
Nos.	O1/24	*from* × 12
Nos.	O59/66	*from* × 4
Nos.	O67/8	—
Nos.	O69/81	*from* × 5
Nos.	O82/7	—
Nos.	O88/93	*from* × 20
Nos.	O94/9	*from* × 12
Nos.	O100/11	*from* × 5

Nos.	O112/13	—
Nos.	O115/19	*from* × 15
Nos.	O120/33	*from* × 10
Nos.	O134/51	*from* × 4
Nos.	P1/7	*from* × 8
Nos.	L1/9	*from* × 10
Nos.	L9a/12	—
Nos.	L13/20	*from* × 15
Nos.	L21/3	—
Nos.	L24/41	*from* × 12
No.	F1	—
No.	F2	*from* × 5
Nos.	F3/144	—
Nos.	F145/58	*from* × 3
Nos.	F159/68	—
Nos.	F169/79	*from* × 3
Nos.	F180/6	—
Nos.	F187/90	*from* × 2
Nos.	F191/203	*from* × 3
Nos.	F204/11	—
Nos.	F212/18	*from* × 2
Nos.	A1/3	*from* × 2

CROWN COLONY

PERKINS BACON "CANCELLED". For notes on these handstamps, showing "CANCELLED" between horizontal bars forming an oval, see Catalogue Introduction.

1

2

(Eng by Humphreys. Recess P.B.)

1855 (18 July). Wmk Large Star, W w **1**. Imperf.

1	**1**	1d. dull carmine *(white paper)* (H/S "CANCELLED" in oval £16000)	£35000	£10000
2		2d. dull blue *(blued paper)* (H/S "CANCELLED" in oval £12000)	£14000	£550
3		1s. pale yellow-green *(blued paper)* (H/S "CANCELLED" in oval £11000)	£26000	£5000
		a. Bisected (6d.) (on cover)	†	£35000

The 2d. and 1s. on white paper formerly listed are now known to be stamps printed on blued paper which have had the bluing washed out. Nos. 3a and 6a were used at Dunedin between March 1857, when the rate for ½ oz. letters to Great Britain was reduced to 6d., and August 1859. All known examples are bisected vertically.

(Printed by J. Richardson, Auckland, N.Z.)

1855 (Dec). *First printing. White paper.* Wmk Large Star. Imperf.

3*b*	**1**	1d. orange	£18000	

1855 (Dec)–**57**. *Blue paper.* No wmk. Imperf.

4	**1**	1d. red	£8000	£1700
5		2d. blue (3.56)	£2750	£300
		a. Without value		
6		1s. green (9.57)	£24000	£3500
		a. Bisected (6d.) (on cover)	†	£22000

These stamps on blue paper may occasionally be found watermarked double-lined letters, being portions of the papermaker's name.

1857 (Jan). *White paper similar to the issue of July 1855.* Wmk Large Star.

7	**1**	1d. dull orange	†	£15000

This stamp is in the precise shade of the 1d. of the 1858 printing by Richardson on *no wmk* white paper. An unsevered pair is known with Dunedin cancellation on a cover front showing an Auckland arrival postmark of 19.1.1857.

1857–63. *Hard or soft white paper.* No wmk.

(a) Imperf.

8	**1**	1d. dull orange (1858)	£2000	£600
8*a*		2d. deep ultramarine (1858)	£1800	£800
9		2d. pale blue	£850	£180
10		2d. blue (12.57)	£850	£180
11		2d. dull deep blue	£1300	£275
12		6d. bistre-brown (8.59)	£2750	£500
13		6d. brown	£1600	£300
14		6d. pale brown	£1600	£300
15		6d. chestnut	£3000	£550
16		1s. dull emerald-green (1858)	£12000	£1500
17		1s. blue-green	£11000	£1500

(b) Pin-roulette, about 10 at Nelson (1860).

18	**1**	1d. dull orange	†	£5000
19		2d. blue	†	£3250
20		6d. brown	†	£4000
20*a*		1s. dull emerald-green	†	£6000
21		1s. blue-green	†	£6000

(c) Serrated perf about 16 or 18 at Nelson (1862).

22	**1**	1d. dull orange	†	£4500
23		2d. blue	†	£3250
24		6d. brown	†	£3000
25		6d. chestnut	†	£6000
26		1s. blue-green	†	£5500

(d) Rouletted 7 at Auckland (April 1859).

27	**1**	1d. dull orange	£6500	£4500
28		2d. blue	£6500	£3000
29		6d. brown	£6000	£2500
		a. Imperf between (pair)	£16000	£10000
30		1s. dull emerald-green	†	£4000
31		1s. blue-green	†	£4000

(e) P 13 *at Dunedin (1863).*

31*a*	**1**	1d. dull orange	†	£5000
31*b*		2d. pale blue	£3500	£2000
32		6d. pale brown	†	£5500

(f) "H" roulette 16 at Nelson.

32*a*	**1**	2d. blue	†	£4000
32*b*		6d. brown	†	£4250

(g) "Y" roulette 18 at Nelson.

32*c*	**1**	1d. dull orange	†	£4750
32*d*		2d. blue	†	£3500
32*e*		6d. brown	†	£4000
32*f*		6d. chestnut	†	£4000
32*g*		1s. blue-green	†	£6500

(h) Oblique roulette 13 at Wellington.

32*h*	**1**	1d. dull orange	†	£5000

The various separations detailed above were all applied by hand to imperforate sheets. The results were often poorly cut and badly aligned. Nos. 32*a*/*b* and 32*c*/*g* were produced using roulette wheels fitted with cutting edges in the shape of "H" or "Y".

(Printed by John Davies at the G.P.O., Auckland, N.Z.)

1862 (Feb–Dec). Wmk Large Star.

(a) Imperf.

33	**1**	1d. orange vermilion	£550	£200
34		1d. vermilion	£450	£200
35		1d. carmine-vermilion	£375	£225
36		2d. deep blue (Plate I)	£400	75·00
		a. Double print	—	£2750
37		2d. slate-blue (Plate I)	£1600	£180
37*a*		2d. milky blue (Plate I, worn)	—	£225
38		2d. pale blue (Plate I, worn)	£350	75·00
39		2d. blue (*to* deep) (Plate I, very worn)	£325	75·00
40		3d. brown-lilac (Dec 1862)	£350	£140
41		6d. black-brown	£1000	£110
42		6d. brown	£900	90·00
43		6d. red-brown	£800	90·00
44		1s. green	£1100	£250
45		1s. yellow-green	£1000	£275
46		1s. deep green	£1200	£325

The 2d. in a distinctive deep bright blue on white paper wmkd. Large Star is believed by experts to have been printed by Richardson in 1861 or 1862. This also exists doubly printed and with serrated perf.

No. 37 shows traces of plate wear to the right of the Queen's head. This is more pronounced on Nos. 37*a*/8 and quite extensive on No. 39.

(b) Rouletted 7 at Auckland (5.62).

47	**1**	1d. orange-vermilion	£4000	£800
48		1d. vermilion	£2500	£800
48*a*		1d. carmine-vermilion	£4000	£950
49		2d. deep blue	£2500	£450
50		2d. slate-blue	£3500	£800
51		2d. pale blue	£2000	£600
52		3d. brown-lilac	£2500	£750
53		6d. black-brown	£2750	£475
54		6d. brown	£2500	£600
55		6d. red-brown	£2500	£475
56		1s. green	£2750	£750
57		1s. yellow-green	£3750	£750
58		1s. deep green	£3750	£850

(c) Serrated perf 16 or 18 at Nelson (8.62).

59	**1**	1d. orange-vermilion	£7500	£1700
60		2d. deep blue	†	£1100
		a. Imperf between (pair)	£9500	£4250
61		2d. slate-blue		
62		3d. brown-lilac	£3500	£1600
63		6d. black-brown	†	£1700
64		6d. brown	†	£1900
65		1s. yellow-green	†	£3250

(d) Pin-perf 10 at Nelson (8.62).

66	**1**	2d. deep blue	†	£2500
67		6d. black-brown	†	£3500

(e) "H" roulette 16 at Nelson.

67*a*	**1**	2d. deep blue (Plate I)	†	£1900
67*b*		6d. black-brown	†	£1900
67*c*		1s. green	—	£3000

(f) "Y" roulette 18 at Nelson.

67*d*	**1**	1d. orange-vermilion	†	£1800
67*e*		2d. deep blue (Plate I)	†	£1800
67*f*		2d. slate-blue (Plate I)	†	£1800
67*g*		3d. brown-lilac	†	£2250
67*h*		6d. black-brown	†	£1800
67*i*		6d. brown	†	£1800
67*j*		1s. yellow-green	†	£3000

(g) Oblique roulette 13 at Wellington.

67*k*	**1**	2d. deep blue (Plate I)	†	£1900
67*l*		2d. slate-blue (Plate I)		
67*m*		3d. brown-lilac	†	£2500
67*n*		6d. black-brown	†	£1900

(h) Square roulette 14 at Auckland.

67*o*	**1**	1d. orange-vermilion	†	£1800
67*p*		2d. deep blue (Plate I)	†	£1800
67*q*		3d. brown-lilac	†	£2500
67*r*		6d. black-brown	†	£1900

(i) Serrated perf 13 at Dunedin.

67*s*	**1**	1d. orange-vermilion	†	£2250
67*t*		2d. deep blue (Plate I)	†	£1800
67*u*		3d. brown-lilac	£3250	£1700
67*v*		6d. black-brown	†	£1800
67*w*		1s. yellow-green	†	£3250

The dates put to above varieties are the earliest that have been met with.

1862. Wmk Large Star. P 13 (at Dunedin).

68	**1**	1d. orange-vermilion	£1200	£300
		a. Imperf between (horiz pair)	†	£7000
69		1d. carmine-vermilion	£1200	£300
70		2d. deep blue (Plate I)	£375	80·00
71		2d. slate-blue (Plate I)	†	£600
72		2d. blue (Plate I)	£300	60·00
72*a*		2d. milky blue (Plate I)	—	£500
73		2d. pale blue (Plate I)	£300	60·00
74		3d. brown-lilac	£1200	£375
75		6d. black-brown	£1000	£190
		a. Imperf between (horiz pair)		
76		6d. brown	£850	£110
77		6d. red-brown	£800	90·00
78		1s. dull green	£1200	£350
79		1s. deep green	£1300	£325
80		1s. yellow-green	£1300	£300

See also Nos. 110/25 and the note that follows these.

1862–63. *Pelure paper.* No wmk.

(a) Imperf.

81	**1**	1d. orange-vermilion (1863)	£7000	£2000
82		2d. ultramarine	£3750	£850
83		2d. pale ultramarine	£3500	£800
84		3d. lilac	£30000	†
85		6d. black-brown	£1700	£250
86		1s. deep green	£7500	£1000

The 3d. is known only unused.

(b) Rouletted 7 at Auckland.

87	**1**	1d. orange-vermilion	†	£4750
88		6d. black-brown	£2500	£475
89		1s. deep green	£8500	£1600

(c) P 13 *at Dunedin.*

90	**1**	1d. orange-vermilion	£11000	£3000
91		2d. ultramarine	£4750	£700
92		2d. pale ultramarine	£4750	£700
93		6d. black-brown	£3750	£400
94		1s. deep green	£8500	£1500

(d) Serrated perf 16 at Nelson.

95	**1**	6d. black-brown	—	£4500

(e) Serrated perf 13 at Dunedin.

95*a*	**9**	1d. orange-vermilion	†	£7000

1863 (early). *Thick soft white paper.* No wmk.

(a) Imperf.

96	**1**	2d. dull deep blue *(shades)*	£2500	£800

(b) P 13.

96*a*	**1**	2d. dull deep blue *(shades)*	£1700	£475

These stamps show slight beginnings of wear of the printing plate in the background to right of the Queen's ear, as one looks at the stamps. By the early part of 1864, the wear of the plate had spread, more or less, all over the background of the circle containing the head. The major portion of the stamps of this printing appears to have been consigned to Dunedin and to have been there perforated 13.

1864. Wmk "N Z", W **2**.

(a) Imperf.

97	**1**	1d. carmine-vermilion	£750	£275
98		2d. pale blue (Plate I worn)	£850	£225
99		6d. red-brown	£3250	£600
100		1s. green	£1100	£250

(b) Rouletted 7 at Auckland.

101	**1**	1d. carmine-vermilion	£4750	£2750
102		2d. pale blue (Plate I worn)	£1500	£750
103		6d. red-brown	£4750	£2750
104		1s. green	£3000	£1000

(c) P 13 *at Dunedin.*

104*a*	**1**	1d. carmine-vermilion	£7500	£5000
105		2d. pale blue (Plate I worn)	£600	£160
106		1s. green	£1300	£475
		a. Imperf between (horiz pair)	£10000	

(d) "Y" roulette 18 at Nelson.

106*b*	**1**	1d. carmine-vermilion	—	£5000

(e) P 12½ *at Auckland.*

106*c*	**1**	1d. carmine-vermilion	£7500	£4500
107		2d. pale blue (Plate I worn)	£250	55·00
108		6d. red-brown	£275	42·00
109		1s. yellow-green	£5000	£2250

1864–67. Wmk Large Star. P 12½ (at Auckland).

110	**1**	1d. carmine-vermilion (1864)	£130	30·00
111		1d. pale orange-vermilion	£160	30·00
		a. Imperf (pair)	£2750	£1800
112		1d. orange	£375	80·00
113		2d. pale blue (Plate I worn) (1864)	£160	22·00
114		2d. deep blue (Plate II) (1866)	£130	19·00
		a. Imperf vert (horiz pair)	†	£3250
115		2d. blue (Plate II)	£130	19·00
		a. Retouched (Plate II) (1867)	£200	48·00
		c. Imperf (pair) (Plate II)	£1700	£1500
		d. Retouched. Imperf (pair)	£2750	£3000
116		3d. brown-lilac (1864)	£1500	£600
117		3d. lilac	£100	30·00
		a. Imperf (pair)	£3250	£1700
118		3d. deep mauve	£450	70·00
		a. Imperf (pair)	£3250	£1700
119		4d. deep rose (1865)	£2250	£250
120		4d. yellow (1865)	£160	£100
121		4d. orange	£1800	£950
122		6d. red-brown (1864)	£180	25·00
122*a*		6d. brown	£200	38·00
		b. Imperf (pair)	£1600	£1700
123		1s. deep green (1864)	£700	£300
124		1s. green	£350	£120
125		1s. yellow-green	£160	90·00

The above issue is sometimes difficult to distinguish from Nos. 68/80 because the vertical perforations usually gauge 12¾ and sometimes a full 13. However, stamps of this issue invariably gauge 12½ horizontally, whereas the 1862 stamps measure a full 13.

Nos. 111a, 115c/d, 117a, 118a and 122b were issued during problems with the perforation machine which occurred in 1866–67, 1869–70 and 1871–73. Imperforate sheets of the 1s. were also released, but these stamps are very similar to Nos. 44/6.

The new plate of the 2d. showed signs of deterioration during 1866 and thirty positions in rows 13 and 16 to 20 were retouched by a local engraver.

The 1d., 2d. and 6d. were officially reprinted imperforate, without gum, in 1884 for presentation purposes. They can be distinguished from the errors listed by their shades which are pale orange, dull blue and dull chocolate-brown respectively, and by the worn state of the plates from which they were printed *(Prices £70 each unused)*.

71. Wmk Large Star.

(a) P 10.
6 1 1d. brown £500 £110

(b) P 12½ × 10.
7 1 1d. deep brown . . . . † £2750

(c) P 10 × 12½.
8 1 1d. brown . . . . £180 48·00
a. Perf 12½ comp 10 (1 side) £425 £150
9 2d. deep blue (Plate II) . . . . † £7500
a. Perf 10* . . . . † £13000
0 2d. vermilion . . . . £180 32·00
a. Retouched . . . . £300 50·00
b. Perf 12½ comp 10 (1 side) £1300 £425
c. Perf 10* . . . . † £13000
1 6d. deep blue £1600 £700
a. Blue £1100 £500
b. Imperf between (vert pair) . . . . — £6000
c. Perf 12½ comp 10 (1 side) £900 £425
ca. Imperf vert (horiz pair) . . . . † —

(d) P 12½.
2 1 1d. red-brown . . . . £120 35·00
a. Brown (shades, worn plate) . . . . £120 35·00
b. Imperf horiz (vert pair) . . . . — £4000
3 2d. orange . . . . £110 27·00
a. Retouched . . . . £170 48·00
4 2d. vermilion . . . . £140 30·00
a. Retouched . . . . £225 60·00
5 6d. blue . . . . £170 50·00
5 6d. pale blue . . . . £130 50·00

*Only one used copy each of Nos. 129a and 130c have been ported.

72. No wmk. P 12½.
7 1 1d. brown £650 £140
a. Watermarked (script letters)* £3500 £2250
b. Watermarked (double-lined capitals)* £1700 £550
3 2d. vermilion . . . . 95·00 50·00
a. Retouched . . . . £170 75·00
b. Watermarked (script letters)* £3250 £1300
c. Watermarked (double-lined capitals)* £1600 £750
4d. orange-yellow £150 £650
a. Watermarked (double-lined capitals)* £225

*In or about 1872, 1d., 2d. and 4d. stamps were printed on paper owing sheet watermarks of either "W. T. & Co." (Wiggins Teape Co.) in script letters or "T. H. Saunders" in double-lined capitals; tions of these letters are occasionally found on stamps.

72. Wmk "N Z", W 2. P 12½.
1 1d. brown . . . . † £4000
2d. vermilion £700 £275
a. Retouched £1000 £375

2. Wmk Lozenges, with "INVICTA" in double-lined capitals our times in the sheet. P 12½.
1 2d. vermilion £2750 £500
a. Retouched £4000 £750

3

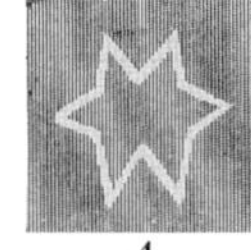
4

es John Davies. Die eng on wood in Melbourne. Printed from electrotypes at Govt Ptg Office, Wellington)

3 (1 Jan).

(a) Wmk "NZ", W 2.
3 ½d. pale dull rose (P 10) . . . . 75·00 42·00
½d. pale dull rose (P 12½) . . . . £180 65·00
½d. pale dull rose (P 12½ × 10) . . . . £110 65·00
a. Perf 10 × 12½ . . . . £130 75·00

(b) No wmk.
3 ½d. pale dull rose (P 10) . . . . £110 55·00
½d. pale dull rose (P 12½) . . . . £200 75·00
½d. pale dull rose (P 12½ × 10) . . . . £150 70·00
a. Perf 10 × 12½ . . . . £180 85·00

s the paper used for Nos. 143/5 was originally intended for fiscal nps which were more than twice as large, about one-third of the ressions fall on portions of the sheet showing no watermark, ng rise to varieties Nos. 146/8. In later printings of No. 151 a stamps in each sheet are without watermark. These can be inguished from No. 147 by the shade.

5 (Jan). Wmk Star, W 4.
3 ½d. pale dull rose (P 12½) . . . . 17·00 2·25
a. Imperf horiz (vert pair) £700 £400
b. Imperf between (horiz pair) . . . . † £600
c. Perf compound of 12½ and 10 . . . . † —
½d. dull pale rose (p *nearly* 12) . . . . 60·00 11·00

(May). Wmk "NZ and Star". W 12b. P 12½.
3 ½d. bright rose (shades) . . . . 10·00 1·40
a. No Wmk . . . . 15·00 8·50
w. Wmk inverted . . . . 50·00 30·00
x. Wmk reversed . . . . — 90·00

5

6

7

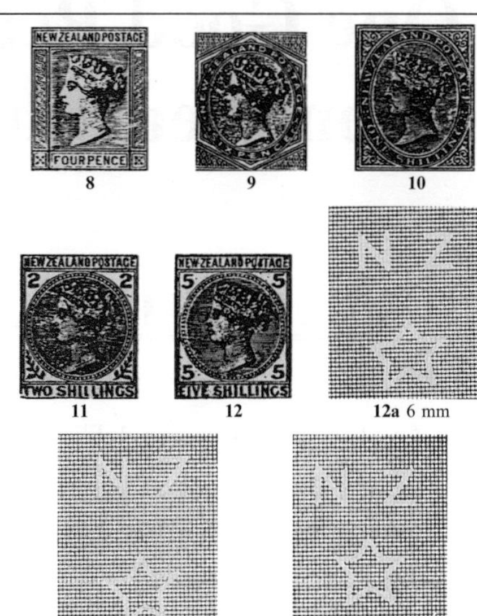

8 9 10
11 12 12a 6 mm
12b 7 mm 12c 4 mm

(*T* **5/10** eng De La Rue. *T* **11** and **12** des, eng & plates by W. R. Bock. Typo Govt Ptg Office, Wellington)

1874 (2 Jan)–**78**. *A. White paper.* W **12***a*.

(a) P 12½.
152 5 1d. lilac . . . . 55·00 5·00
a. Imperf £400
w. Wmk inverted . . . . † 42·00
x. Wmk reversed . . . . † 95·00
153 6 2d. rose . . . . 55·00 3·25
154 7 3d. brown . . . . £100 55·00
155 8 4d. maroon . . . . £275 65·00
w. Wmk inverted £475 £100
156 9 6d. blue . . . . £180 10·00
w. Wmk inverted . . . . — 55·00
x. Wmk reversed
157 10 1s. green . . . . £550 28·00
w. Wmk inverted . . . . — £275

(b) Perf nearly 12.
158 6 2d. rose (1878) £600 £180

(c) Perf compound of 12½ and 10.
159 5 1d. lilac . . . . £150 40·00
w. Wmk inverted . . . . — 65·00
160 6 2d. rose . . . . £200 80·00
w. Wmk inverted . . . . — £110
161 7 3d. brown . . . . £160 65·00
162 8 4d. maroon £400 £110
163 9 6d. blue . . . . £225 45·00
w. Wmk inverted . . . . — 80·00
164 10 1s. green £550 £110
a. Imperf between (vert pair) . . . . † £4250
bw. Wmk inverted . . . . † £275

(d) Perf nearly 12 × 12½.
164*c* 5 1d. lilac (1875) £650 £250
165 6 2d. rose (1878) £650 £190

B. Blued paper.

(a) P 12½.
166 5 1d. lilac . . . . 90·00 30·00
167 6 2d. rose . . . . £110 30·00
w. Wmk inverted . . . . — 55·00
x. Wmk reversed . . . . † 80·00
168 7 3d. brown . . . . £225 85·00
169 8 4d. maroon £425 £110
170 9 6d. blue . . . . £325 50·00
171 1s. green £1000 £190

(b) Perf compound of 12½ and 10.
172 5 1d. lilac . . . . £190 55·00
173 6 2d. rose . . . . £550 85·00
174 7 3d. brown . . . . £250 80·00
175 8 4d. maroon £500 £130
176 9 6d. blue . . . . £325 95·00
177 10 1s. green £1000 £225

1875. Wmk Large Star, W w **1**. P 12½.
178 5 1d. deep lilac £700 £110
179 6 2d. rose . . . . £300 22·00

1878. W **12***a*. P 12 × 11½ (comb).
180 5 1d. mauve-lilac . . . . 45·00 4·00
181 6 2d. rose . . . . 45·00 2·50
182 8 4d. maroon . . . . £140 42·00
183 9 6d. blue . . . . 80·00 10·00
184 10 1s. green . . . . £120 38·00
w. Wmk inverted . . . . † £325
185 11 2s. deep rose (1 July) £325 £275
186 12 5s. grey (1 July) £350 £275

This perforation is made by a horizontal "comb" machine, giving a gauge of 12 horizontally and about 11¾ vertically. Single specimens can be found apparently gauging 11½ all round or 12 all round, but these are all from the same machine. The perforation described above as "nearly 12" was from a single-line machine.

13

14

15

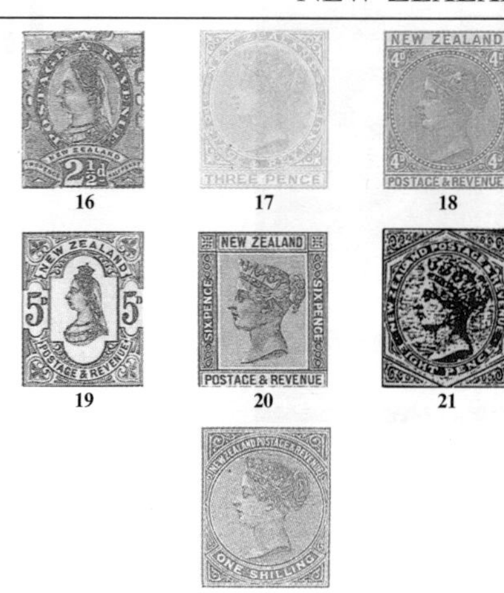

16 17 18
19 20 21
22

Description of Watermarks

W **12***a*. 6 mm between "N Z" and star; broad irregular star; comparatively wide "N"; "N Z" 11½ mm wide.
W **12***b*. 7 mm between "N Z" and star; narrower star; narrow "N"; "N Z" 10 mm wide.
W **12***c*. 4 mm between "N Z" and star; narrow star; wide "N"; "N Z" 11½ mm wide.

Description of Papers

1882–88. Smooth paper with horizontal mesh. W **12***a*.
1888–98. Smooth paper with vertical mesh. W **12***b*.
1890–91. Smooth paper with vertical mesh. W **12***c*.
1898. Thin yellowish toned, coarse paper with clear vertical mesh. W **12***b*. Perf 11 only.

In 1899–1900 stamps appeared on medium to thick white coarse paper but we do not differentiate these (except where identifiable by shade) as they are more difficult to distinguish.

PAPER MESH. This shows on the back of the stamp as a series of parallel grooves, either vertical or horizontal. It is caused by the use of a wire gauze conveyor-belt during paper-making.

Description of Dies

1d.

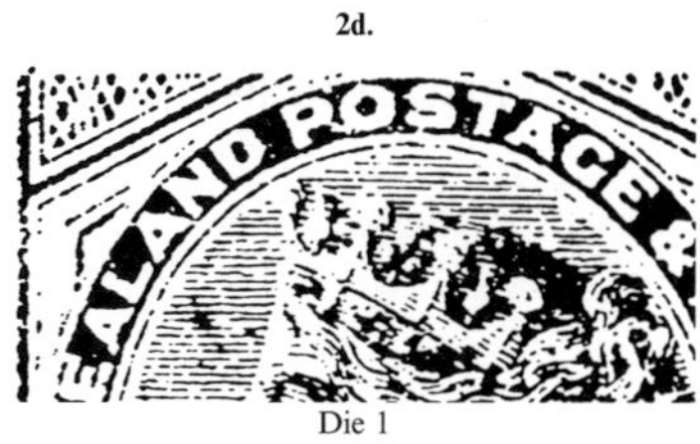
Die 1
Die 2
Die 3

1882. Die 1. Background shading complete and heavy.
1886. Die 2. Background lines thinner. Two lines of shading weak or missing left of Queen's forehead.
1889. Die 3. Shading on head reduced; ornament in crown left of chignon clearer, with unshaded "arrow" more prominent.

2d.

Die 1
Die 2

Die 3

882. Die 1. Background shading complete and heavy.
.886. Die 2. Weak line of shading left of forehead and missing shading lines below "TA".
889. Die 3. As Die 2 but with comma-like white notch in hair below "&".

6d.

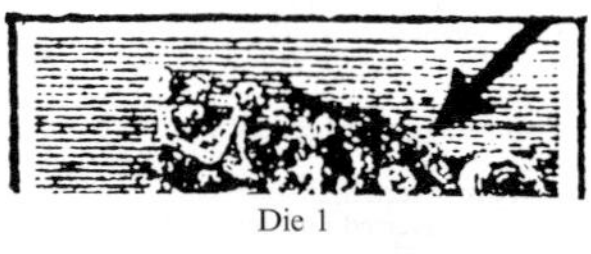

Die 1

Die 2

882. Die 1. Shading heavy. Top of head merges into shading. Second ornament from the right on the crown shows a line in its left portion.
392. Die 2. Background lines thinner. Shading on head more regular with clear line of demarcation between head and background shading. Second ornament from the right in the crown has small dots in its left portion. Most examples also show a break in the back line of the neck immediately above its base.

AMPS WITH ADVERTISEMENTS. During November 1891 New Zealand Post Office invited tenders for the printing of vertisements on the reverse of the current 1d. to 1s. stamps. The ntract was awarded to Messrs Miller, Truebridge & Reich and first sheets with advertisements on the reverse appeared in oruary 1893.

Different advertisements were applied to the backs of the ividual stamps within the sheets of 240 (four panes of 60).

On the first setting those in a vertical format were inverted in ation to the stamps and each of the horizontal advertisements d its base at the left-hand side of the stamp when seen from the k. For the second and third settings the vertical advertisements re the same way up as the stamps and the bases of those in the izontal format were at the right as seen from the back. The third ting only differs from the second in the order of the individual vertisements.

The experiment was not, however, a success and the contract was celled at the end of 1893.

Des F. W. Sears (½d.), A. E. Cousins (2½d.), A. W. Jones (5d.); hers adapted from 1874 issue by W. H. Norris. Dies eng A. E. Cousins (½d., 2½d., 5d.), W. R. Bock (others). Typo Govt Ptg Office)

2–1900. *Inscr "POSTAGE & REVENUE". A. Paper with horiz mesh (1.4.82–86).* W **12***a*.

(a) P 12 × 11½.

	14	1d. rose *to* rose-red (Die 1)	38·00	5·50
		a. Imperf (pair)	£450	
		b. Imperf between (vert pair)	£475	
		cw. Wmk inverted		
		d. Die 2. *Pale rose to carm-rose* (1886)	35·00	5·50
		dw. Wmk inverted	†	27·00
		dx. Wmk reversed	70·00	30·00
	15	2d. lilac *to* lilac-purple (Die 1)	48·00	4·00
		a. Imperf (pair)	£475	
		b. Imperf between (vert pair)	£475	
		cw. Wmk inverted	70·00	15·00
		d. Die 2. *Lilac* (1886)	55·00	8·50
	17	3d. yellow (1884)	55·00	8·50
	18	4d. blue-green	75·00	5·50
	20	6d. brown (Die 1)	80·00	3·75
		w. Wmk inverted	£160	28·00
	21	8d. blue	75·00	45·00
	22	1s. red-brown	95·00	14·00

(b) P 12½ (1884?).

a	14	1d. rose *to* rose-red (Die 1)	£190	90·00

B. Paper with vert mesh (1888–95) W **12***b*.

(a) P 12 × 11½ (1888–95).

	13	½d. black (1.4.95)	30·00	75·00
	14	1d. rose *to* rosine (Die 2)	42·00	3·50
		aw. Wmk inverted	£150	15·00
		b. Die 3. *Rose to carmine* (1889)	42·00	3·50
		bb. Red-brn advert (1st setting) (2.93)	80·00	14·00
		bc. Red advert (1st setting) (3.93)	80·00	14·00
		bd. Blue advert (2nd setting) (4.93)	90·00	40·00
		be. Mauve advert (2nd setting) (5.93)	70·00	8·50
		bf. Green advert (2nd setting) (6.93)		
		bg. Brn-red advert (3rd setting) (9.93)	70·00	8·50
		bw. Wmk inverted	65·00	15·00
		bx. Wmk reversed	75·00	20·00
196	15	2d. lilac (Die 2)	48·00	4·50
		a. Die 3. *Lilac to purple* (1889)	48·00	4·75
		ab. Red advert (1st setting) (3.93)	90·00	18·00
		ac. Mauve advert (2nd setting) (5.93)	80·00	18·00
		ad. Sepia advert (2nd setting) (5.93)	80·00	24·00
		ae. Green advert (2nd setting) (6.93)	—	75·00
		af. Brn-red advert (3rd setting) (9.93)	80·00	18·00
		aw. Wmk inverted	70·00	8·50
197	16	2½d. pale blue (1891)	65·00	5·50
		a. Brn-red advert (2nd setting) (4.93)	£110	18·00
		ax. Wmk reversed	£150	35·00
		b. *Ultramarine* (green advert. 2nd setting) (6.93)	£110	22·00
198	17	3d. yellow	45·00	7·00
		a. Brn-red advert (2nd setting) (4.93)	95·00	22·00
		b. Sepia advert (2nd setting) (5.93)	—	75·00
199	18	4d. green *to* bluish green	55·00	3·50
		a. Sepia advert (2nd setting) (5.93)	£100	14·00
		aw. Wmk inverted	†	£100
200	19	5d. olive-black (1.2.91)	50·00	14·00
		a. Imperf (pair)	£425	
		b. Brn-pur advert (3rd setting) (9.93)	£150	50·00
201	20	6d. brown (Die 1)	70·00	3·25
		a. Die 2 (1892)	£110	55·00
		ab. Sepia advert (2nd setting) (5.93)		
		ac. Brn-red advert (3rd setting) (9.93)	£275	£100
		ax. Wmk reversed	†	—
202	21	8d. blue	65·00	45·00
203	22	1s. red-brown	85·00	6·00
		a. Black advert (2nd setting) (5.93)	£350	£160
		b. Brn-pur advert (3rd setting) (9.93)	£170	18·00
		w. Wmk inverted	£160	20·00

(b) P 12 × 12½ (1888–91).

204	14	1d. rose (Die 2)	£190	90·00
		a. Die 3 (1889)		

(c) P 12½ (1888–89).

205	14	1d. rose (Die 3) (1889)	£170	£100
		a. Mauve advert (2nd setting) (5.93)		
		x. Wmk reversed	†	—
206	15	2d. lilac (Die 2)	£150	£100
		a. Die 3. *Deep lilac* (1889)	£100	75·00
		ab. Brn-red advert (3rd setting) (9.93)	£200	£110
207	16	2½d. blue (1891)	£180	£100

(d) Mixed perfs 12 × 11½ and 12½ (1891–93).

207*a*	14	1d. rose (Die 3) (brn-red advert. 3rd setting)	£100	60·00
207*b*	15	2d. lilac (Die 3)	†	£300
		ba. Brn-red advert (3rd setting) (9.93)	†	—
207*c*	18	4d. green	†	75·00
207*d*	19	5d. olive-black	†	£100
207*e*	20	6d. brown (Die I)	†	£110
		ea. Die 2	†	£160

C. Paper with vert mesh (1890). W **12***c*.

(a) P 12 × 11½.

208	14	1d. rose (Die 3)	75·00	12·00
209	15	2d. purple (Die 3)	75·00	11·00
		x. Wmk reversed		
210	16	2½d. ultramarine (27.12)	55·00	9·00
		x. Wmk reversed	†	40·00
211	17	3d. yellow	75·00	19·00
		a. Lemon-yellow	75·00	23·00
212	20	6d. brown (Die 1)	£120	25·00
213	22	1s. deep red-brown	£150	65·00

(b) P 12½.

214	14	1d. rose (Die 3)	£180	£110
215	15	2d. purple (Die 3)	£160	£110
216	16	2½d. ultramarine	£225	£110

(c) P 12 × 12½.

216*a*	20	6d. brown (Die 1)	£190	£150

D. Paper with vert mesh (1891–1900) Continuation of W **12***b*.

(a) P 10 × 12½ (1891–94).

216*b*	14	1d. rose (Die 3)	£180	£120
		ba. Perf 12½ × 10	£200	£130
		bb. Red-brn advert (1st setting) (2.93)	£275	£140
		bc. Brn-red advert (2nd setting) (4.93)	£275	£130
		bd. Mauve advert (2nd setting) (5.93)	£275	£130
		be. Green advert (2nd setting) (6.93)	£275	£150
216*c*	15	2d. lilac (Die 3)	£160	65·00
216*d*	16	2½d. blue (1893)	£140	70·00
		da. Perf 12½ × 10	£160	
216*e*	17	3d. yellow	£160	80·00
		ea. Perf 12½ × 10		
216*f*	18	4d. green	£180	£150
216*g*	19	5d. olive-black (1894)	£180	£170
		ga. Perf 12½ × 10	£225	£170
216*h*	20	6d. brown (Die 1)	£200	£200
		i. Die 2 (1892)	£150	£150
		ia. Brn-pur advert (3rd setting) (9.93)	£300	£190
216*j*	22	1s. red-brown	£170	£170
		ja. Perf 12½ × 10	†	—

(b) P 10 (1891–95).

217	13	½d. black (1895)	5·50	1·25
218	14	1d. rose (Die 3)	6·50	60
		a. Carmine	9·50	1·25
		b. Imperf (pair)	£375	£375
		c. Imperf between (pair)	£450	
		d. Imperf horiz (vert pair)	£375	
		e. Mixed perfs 10 and 12½	£250	£130
		f. Red-brn advert (1st setting) (2.93)	18·00	4·75
		g. Red advert (1st setting) (3.93)	18·00	6·50
		h. Brown-red advert (2nd and 3rd settings) (4.93)	13·00	3·00
		i. Blue advert (2nd setting) (4.93)	60·00	32·00
		j. Mauve advert (2nd setting) (5.93)	13·00	3·00
		k. Green advert (2nd setting) (6.93)	50·00	17·00
		l. Brn-pur advert (3rd setting) (9.93)	13·00	4·00
		w. Wmk inverted	30·00	12·00
		x. Wmk reversed	35·00	15·00
219	15	2d. lilac (Die 3)	14·00	1·00
		a. Purple	15·00	1·00
		b. Imperf between (pair)	£450	
		c. Mixed perfs 10 and 12½	—	£100
		d. Red-brn advert (1st setting) (2.93)	27·00	9·00
		e. Red advert (1st setting) (3.93)	27·00	6·50
		f. Brown-red advert (2nd and 3rd settings) (4.93)	17·00	3·25
		g. Sepia advert (2nd setting) (5.93)	19·00	3·75
		h. Green advert (2nd setting) (6.93)	40·00	11·00
		i. Brn-pur advert (3rd setting) (9.93)	17·00	3·25
		x. Wmk reversed	60·00	20·00
220	16	2½d. blue (1892)	50·00	3·50
		a. Ultramarine	50·00	4·00
		b. Mixed perfs 10 and 12½	£180	£100
		c. Mauve advert (2nd setting) (5.93)	£100	9·00
		d. Green advert (2nd setting) (6.93)	£110	11·00
		e. Brn-pur advert (3rd setting) (9.93)	£100	8·00
		ex. Wmk reversed	£140	35·00
221	17	3d. pale orange-yellow	48·00	8·50
		a. Orange	48·00	11·00
		b. Lemon-yellow	48·00	13·00
		c. Mixed perfs 10 and 12½	£170	£120
		d. Brown-red advert (2nd and 3rd settings) (4.93)	85·00	17·00
		e. Sepia advert (2nd setting) (5.93)	95·00	32·00
		f. Brn-pur advert (3rd setting) (9.93)	85·00	15·00
222	18	4d. green (1892)	50·00	3·75
		a. Blue-green	50·00	4·00
		b. Mixed perfs 10 and 12½	£200	85·00
		c. Brn-red advert (2nd setting) (4.93)	95·00	4·75
		d. Brn-pur advert (3rd setting) (9.93)	95·00	4·00
223	19	5d. olive-black (1893)	48·00	13·00
		a. Brn-pur advert (3rd setting) (9.93)	£130	22·00
		ab. Mixed perfs 10 and 12½	£140	85·00
224	20	6d. brown (Die 1)	90·00	26·00
		a. Mixed perfs 10 and 12½		
		b. Die 2 (1892)	55·00	7·50
		ba. Black-brown	55·00	7·50
		bb. Imperf (pair)	£450	
		bc. Mixed perfs 10 and 12½	£150	60·00
		bd. Sepia advert (2nd setting) (4.93)	£150	13·00
		be. Brn-red advert (3rd setting) (9.93)	£150	13·00
		bf. Brn-pur advert (3rd setting) (9.93)	£150	13·00
		bx. Wmk reversed (with brown-purple advert)	†	40·00
225	21	8d. blue (brown-purple advert. 3rd setting) (9.93)	70·00	45·00
226	22	1s. red-brown	80·00	7·00
		a. Imperf between (pair)	£750	
		b. Mixed perfs 10 and 12½	£200	£140
		c. Sepia advert (2nd setting) (5.93)	£150	21·00
		d. Black advert (2nd setting) (5.93)	£200	£110
		e. Brn-red advert (3rd setting) (9.93)	£150	21·00
		f. Brn-pur advert (3rd setting) (9.93)	£150	21·00

(c) P 10 × 11 (1895–97).

227	13	½d. black (1896)	3·25	50
		a. Mixed perfs 10 and 11	90·00	40·00
		b. Perf 11 × 10	30·00	13·00
228	14	1d. rose (Die 3)	4·75	15
		a. Mixed perfs10 and 11	£100	55·00
		b. Perf 11 × 10	55·00	9·50
		x. Wmk reversed	50·00	20·00
229	15	2d. purple (Die 3)	12·00	30
		a. Mixed perfs 10 and 11	65·00	50·00
230	16	2½d. blue (1896)	50·00	3·75
		a. Ultramarine	50·00	4·50
		b. Mixed perfs 10 and 11	—	85·00
231	17	3d. lemon-yellow (1896)	60·00	11·00
232	18	4d. pale green (1896)	70·00	12·00
		a. Mixed perfs 10 and 11	—	£110
233	19	5d. olive-black (1897)	50·00	10·00
234	20	6d. deep brown (Die 2) (1896)	65·00	7·50
		a. Mixed perfs 10 and 11		
		b. Perf 11 × 10	£160	50·00
235	22	1s. red-brown (1896)	75·00	9·00
		a. Mixed perfs 10 and 11	£160	75·00

(d) P 11 (1895–1900).

236	13	½d. black (1897)	4·00	15
		aw. Wmk inverted	40·00	15·00
		ax. Wmk reversed	50·00	20·00
		b. Thin coarse toned paper (1898)	27·00	3·50
		ba. Wmk sideways	—	£275

237	**14**	1d. rose (Die 3)	4·00	10
		a. Deep carmine	5·50	1·50
		b. Imperf between (pair)	£450	
		c. Dp carm/thin coarse toned (1898)	9·50	2·00
		ca. Wmk sideways	—	£250
		w. Wmk inverted	20·00	17·00
		x. Wmk reversed	35·00	17·00
		y. Wmk inverted and reversed	60·00	40·00
238	**15**	2d. mauve (Die 3)	11·00	40
		a. Purple	11·00	40
		b. Dp purple/thin coarse toned (1898)	12·00	2·50
		ba. Wmk sideways	£180	£250
		w. Wmk inverted	16·00	5·50
		x. Wmk reversed	60·00	20·00
239	**16**	2½d. blue (1897)	48·00	3·75
		a. Thin coarse toned paper (1898)	75·00	17·00
240	**17**	3d. pale yellow (1897)	50·00	6·50
		a. Pale dull yellow/thin coarse toned (1898)	65·00	15·00
		b. *Orange* (1899)	42·00	9·50
		c. Dull orange-yellow (1900)	48·00	16·00
241	**18**	4d. yellowish green	48·00	4·00
		a. Bluish green (1897)	48·00	3·75
		w. Wmk inverted	80·00	11·00
242	**19**	5d. olive-black/*thin coarse toned* (1899)	50·00	24·00
243	**20**	6d. brown (Die 2) (1897)	65·00	3·75
		a. Black-brown	65·00	3·75
		b. Brown/thin coarse toned (1898)	85·00	8·00
		x. Wmk reversed	†	30·00
244	**21**	8d. blue (1898)	65·00	45·00
245	**22**	1s. red-brown (1897)	75·00	7·00

Only the more prominent shades have been included.

Stamps perf compound of 11 and 12½ exist but we do not list them as there is some doubt as to whether they are genuine.

For the ½d. and 2d. with double-lined watermark, see Nos. 271/2.

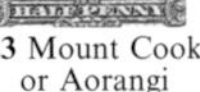

23 Mount Cook or Aorangi

24 Lake Taupo and Mount Ruapehu

25 Pembroke Peak, Milford Sound

26 Lake Wakatipu and Mount Earnslaw, inscribed "WAKITIPU"

27 Lake Wakatipu and Mount Earnslaw, inscribed "WAKATIPU"

28 Huia

29 White Terrace, Rotomahana

30 Otira Gorge and Mount Ruapehu

31 Brown Kiwi

32 Maori War Canoe

33 Pink Terrace, Rotomahana

34 Kea and Kaka

35 Milford Sound

36 Mount Cook

(Des H. Young (½d.), J. Gaut (1d.), W. Bock (2d., 3d., 9d., 1s.), E. Howard (4d., 6d., 8d.), E. Luke (others). Eng A. Hill (2½d., 1s.), J. A. C. Harrison (5d.), Rapkin (others). Recess Waterlow)

1898 (5 Apr). No Wmk. P 12 to 16.

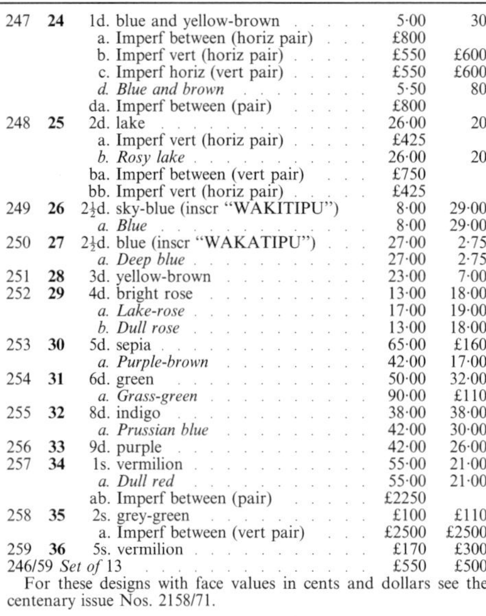

246	**23**	½d. purple-brown	6·00	1·00
		a. Imperf between (pair)	£950	£850
		b. Purple-slate	6·00	1·00
		c. Purple-black	8·00	2·75
247	**24**	1d. blue and yellow-brown	5·00	30
		a. Imperf between (horiz pair)	£800	
		b. Imperf vert (horiz pair)	£550	£600
		c. Imperf horiz (vert pair)	£550	£600
		d. Blue and brown	5·50	80
		da. Imperf between (pair)	£800	
248	**25**	2d. lake	26·00	20
		a. Imperf vert (horiz pair)	£425	
		b. Rosy lake	26·00	20
		ba. Imperf between (vert pair)	£750	
		bb. Imperf vert (horiz pair)	£425	
249	**26**	2½d. sky-blue (inscr "WAKITIPU")	8·00	29·00
		a. Blue	8·00	29·00
250	**27**	2½d. blue (inscr "WAKATIPU")	27·00	2·75
		a. Deep blue	27·00	2·75
251	**28**	3d. yellow-brown	23·00	7·00
252	**29**	4d. bright rose	13·00	18·00
		a. Lake-rose	17·00	19·00
		b. Dull rose	13·00	18·00
253	**30**	5d. sepia	65·00	£160
		a. Purple-brown	42·00	17·00
254	**31**	6d. green	50·00	32·00
		a. Grass-green	90·00	£110
255	**32**	8d. indigo	38·00	38·00
		a. Prussian blue	42·00	30·00
256	**33**	9d. purple	42·00	26·00
257	**34**	1s. vermilion	55·00	21·00
		a. Dull red	55·00	21·00
		ab. Imperf between (pair)	£2250	
258	**35**	2s. grey-green	£100	£110
		a. Imperf between (vert pair)	£2500	£2500
259	**36**	5s. vermilion	£170	£300
246/59		*Set of* 13	£550	£500

For these designs with face values in cents and dollars see the centenary issue Nos. 2158/71.

37 Lake Taupo and Mount Ruapehu

(Recess Govt Printer, Wellington)

1899 (May)–**03**. *Thick, soft ("Pirie") paper.* No Wmk. P 11.

260	**27**	2½d. blue (6.99)	13·00	3·50
		a. Imperf between (horiz pair)	£700	
		b. Imperf horiz (vert pair)	£400	
		c. Deep blue	13·00	3·50
261	**28**	3d. yellow-brown (5.00)	23·00	2·00
		a. Imperf between (pair)	£950	
		b. Imperf vert (horiz pair)	£450	
		c. Deep brown	23·00	2·00
		ca. Imperf between (pair)	£950	
262	**37**	4d. indigo and brown (8.99)	5·50	3·00
		a. Bright blue and chestnut	5·50	3·00
		b. Deep blue and bistre-brown	5·50	3·00
263	**30**	5d. purple-brown (6.99)	25·00	3·25
		a. Deep purple-brown	25·00	3·25
		ab. Imperf between (pair)	£1300	
264	**31**	6d. deep green	55·00	60·00
		a. Yellow-green	70·00	95·00
265		6d. pale rose (5.5.00)	35·00	4·00
		a. Imperf vert (horiz pair)	£400	
		b. Imperf between (horiz pair)	£800	
		c. Rose-red	35·00	4·00
		ca. Printed double	£475	£500
		cb. Imperf between (vert pair)	£800	
		cc. Imperf vert (horiz pair)	£275	
		cd. Showing part of sheet wmk (7.02)*	75·00	75·00
		d. Scarlet	55·00	12·00
		da. Imperf vert (horiz pair)	£475	
266	**32**	8d. indigo	28·00	12·00
		a. Prussian blue	28·00	11·00
267	**33**	9d. deep purple (8.99)	45·00	25·00
		a. Rosy purple	38·00	9·50
268	**34**	1s. red (5.00)	48·00	8·50
		a. Dull orange-red	50·00	4·00
		b. Dull brown-red	50·00	8·50
		c. Bright red	60·00	30·00
269	**35**	2s. blue-green (7.99)	80·00	38·00
		a. Laid paper (1.03)	£180	£200
		b. Grey-green	85·00	50·00
270	**36**	5s. vermilion (7.99)	£170	£225
		a. Carmine-red	£275	£325
260/70		*Set of* 11	£425	£325

*No. 265bd is on paper without general watermark, but showing the words "LISBON SUPERFINE" wmkd once in the sheet; the paper was obtained from Parsons Bros, an American firm with a branch at Auckland.

38

1900. *Thick, soft ("Pirie") paper.* Wmk double-lined "NZ" and Star, W **38** (sideways*). P 11.

271	**13**	½d. black	8·50	11·00
		x. Wmk reversed	75·00	60·00
272	**15**	2d. bright purple	20·00	9·50
		w. Wmk sideways inverted	30·00	15·00
		y. Wmk sideways inverted and reversed	—	55·00

*The normal sideways wmk on Nos. 271/2 shows the star to the right of NZ, *as seen from the back of the stamp.*

39 White Terrace, Rotomahana

41

40 Commemorative of the New Zealand Contingent in the South African War

(Des J. Nairn (1½d.). Recess Govt Printer, Wellington)

1900 (Mar–Dec). *Thick, soft ("Pirie") paper.* W **38**. P 11.

273	**23**	½d. pale yellow-green (7.3.00)	9·00	4·
		a. Yellow-green	6·50	1·
		b. Green	6·00	
		ba. Imperf between (pair)	£325	
		c. Deep green	6·00	
		w. Wmk inverted	20·00	10
		y. Wmk inverted and reversed	50·00	25
274	**39**	1d. crimson (7.3.00)	13·00	
		a. Rose-red	13·00	
		ab. Imperf between (pair)	£800	£8
		ac. Imperf vert (horiz pair)	£400	
		b. Lake	28·00	4
		w. Wmk inverted	†	£1
		x. Wmk reversed	†	
275	**40**	1½d. khaki (7.12.00)	£800	£5
		a. Brown	50·00	50
		ab. Imperf vert (horiz pair)	£600	
		ac. Imperf (pair)	£700	
		b. Chestnut	9·50	4
		ba. Imperf vert (horiz pair)	£600	
		bb. Imperf horiz (vert pair)	£750	
		c. Pale chestnut	9·50	4
		ca. Imperf (pair)	£700	
276	**41**	2d. dull violet (3.00)	9·50	
		a. Imperf between (pair)	£800	
		b. Mauve	11·00	1
		c. Purple	9·50	
		ca. Imperf between (pair)	£800	

The above ½d. stamps are slightly smaller than those of previous printing. A new plate was made to print 240 stamps inst of 120 as previously, and to make these fit the watermarked pap the border design was redrawn and contracted, the centre vign remaining as before. The 2d. stamp is also from a new p. providing smaller designs.

42

(Des G. Bach and G. Drummond. Eng J. A. C. Harrison. Rec Waterlow)

1901 (1 Jan). *Universal Penny Postage.* No Wmk. P 12 to 16.

277	**42**	1d. carmine	3·50	

All examples of No. 277 show a small dot above the upper corner of the value tablet which is not present on later printing

(Recess Govt Printer, Wellington)

1901 (Feb–Dec). *Thick, soft ("Pirie") paper.* W **38**.

(a) P 11.

278	**42**	1d. carmine	6·00	
		a. Imperf vert (horiz pair)	£275	
		b. Deep carmine	6·00	
		ba. Imperf vert (horiz pair)	£275	
		c. Carmine-lake	20·00	
		x. Wmk reversed	†	
		y. Wmk inverted and reversed	—	5

(b) P 14.

279	**23**	½d. green (11.01)	13·00	
280	**42**	1d. carmine	48·00	1
		a. Imperf vert (horiz pair)	£250	
		y. Wmk inverted and reversed	80·00	3

(c) P 14 × 11.

281	**23**	½d. green	8·00	
		a. Deep green	8·00	
		b. Perf 11 × 14	12·00	1
282	**42**	1d. carmine	£200	7
		a. Perf 11 × 14	£1200	

(d) P 11 and 14 mixed*.

283	**23**	½d. green	45·00	6
284	**42**	1d. carmine	£200	7

*The term "mixed" is applied to stamps from sheets which at first perforated 14, or 14 × 11, and either incompletely defectively perforated. These sheets were patched on the back strips of paper, and re-perforated 11 in those parts where original perforation was defective.

Nos. 278/84 were printed from new plates supplied by Water These were subsequently used for Nos. 285/307 with later print on Cowan paper showing considerable plate wear.

WATERMARK VARIETIES. The watermark on the Basted M version of the W **38** paper used for Nos. 285/92 oc indiscriminately normal, reversed, inverted etc.

(Recess Govt Printer, Wellington)

1901 (Dec). *Thin, hard ("Basted Mills") paper.* W **38**.

(a) P 11.
285 **23** ½d. green . . . 55·00 65·00
286 **42** 1d. carmine . . . 75·00 90·00

(b) P 14.
287 **23** ½d. green . . . 25·00 25·00
a. Imperf vert (horiz pair) . . . £325
288 **42** 1d. carmine . . . 14·00 4·25
a. Imperf vert (horiz pair) . . . £250
b. Imperf horiz (vert pair) . . . £250

(c) P 14 × 11.
289 **23** ½d. green . . . 22·00 55·00
a. Deep green . . . 22·00 55·00
b. Perf 11 × 14 . . . 20·00 50·00
290 **42** 1d. carmine . . . 22·00 9·00
a. Perf 11 × 14 . . . 12·00 3·25

(d) Mixed perfs.
291 **23** ½d. green . . . 55·00 65·00
292 **42** 1d. carmine . . . 75·00 75·00

(Recess Govt Printer, Wellington)

1902 (Jan). *Thin, hard ("Cowan") paper.* No Wmk.

(a) P 11.
293 **23** ½d. green . . . £120 £170

(b) P 14.
294 **23** ½d. green . . . 12·00 5·00
295 **42** 1d. carmine . . . 12·00 2·75

(c) P 14 × 11.
296 **23** ½d. green . . . 75·00 £140
a. Perf 11 × 14 . . . £110 £180
297 **42** 1d. carmine . . . £110 £120
a. Perf 11 × 14 . . . £110 £140

(d) Mixed perfs.
298 **23** ½d. green . . . £110 £140
299 **42** 1d. carmine . . . £120 £130

43 "Single" Wmk

SIDEWAYS WATERMARKS. In its sideways format the single NZ and Star watermark W **43**, exists indiscriminately sideways, sideways inverted, sideways reversed and sideways inverted plus reversed.

(Recess Govt Printer, Wellington)

1902 (Apr). *Thin, hard ("Cowan") paper.* W **43**.

(a) P 11.
300 **23** ½d. green . . . 60·00 85·00
301 **42** 1d. carmine . . . £650 £475

(b) P 14.
302 **23** ½d. green . . . 5·50 70
a. Imperf vert (horiz pair) . . . £190
b. Deep green . . . 5·50 1·00
ba. Imperf vert (horiz pair) . . . £190
c. Yellow green . . . 6·50 1·00
d. Pale yellow-green . . . 14·00 3·00
w. Wmk inverted . . . 22·00 13·00
x. Wmk reversed . . . 30·00 22·00
y. Wmk inverted and reversed . . . 42·00 28·00
303 **42** 1d. carmine . . . 3·00 10
a. Imperf horiz (vert pair) . . . £170
b. Booklet pane of 6 (21.8.02) . . . £200
c. Pale carmine . . . 3·00 10
ca. Imperf horiz (vert pair) . . . £170
cb. Booklet pane of 6 . . . £200
*d. Deep carmine** . . . 32·00 4·00
w. Wmk inverted . . . 60·00 35·00
x. Wmk reversed . . . 60·00 35·00
y. Wmk inverted and reversed . . . 35·00 15·00

(c) P 14 × 11.
304 **23** ½d. green . . . 19·00 95·00
a. Deep green . . . 25·00
b. Perf 11 × 14 . . . 20·00 75·00
305 **42** 1d. carmine . . . £100 £100
a. Perf 11 × 14 . . . £120 £120
*ab. Deep carmine** . . . £425 £425

(d) Mixed perfs.
306 **23** ½d. green . . . 25·00 50·00
a. Deep green . . . 32·00
307 **42** 1d. carmine . . . 24·00 42·00
a. Pale carmine . . . 24·00 42·00
*b. Deep carmine** . . . £275 £275
y. Wmk inverted and reversed

*Nos. 303*d*, 305*a* and 307*b* were printed from a plate made by Waterlow & Sons, known as the "Reserve" plate. The stamps do not show evidence of wearing and the area surrounding the upper part of the figure is more deeply shaded. This plate was subsequently used to produce Nos. 362, 364 and 366/9.

A special plate, made by W. R. Royle & Sons, showing a minute dot between the horizontal rows, was introduced in 1902 to print the booklet pane, No. 303b. A special characteristic of the booklet pane was that the pearl in the top left-hand corner was large. Some panes exist with the outer edges imperforate.

(Recess Govt Printer, Wellington)

1902 (28 Aug)–**09**. *Thin, hard ("Cowan") paper.* W **43** (sideways on 3d., 5d., 6d., 8d., 1s. and 5s.).

(a) P 11.
308 **27** 2½d. blue (5.03) . . . 11·00 12·00
a. Deep blue . . . 14·00 12·00
w. Wmk inverted . . . 85·00 50·00
x. Wmk reversed . . . 60·00 25·00
y. Wmk inverted and reversed . . . 75·00 40·00
309 **28** 3d. yellow-brown . . . 26·00 1·50
a. Bistre-brown . . . 27·00 1·50
b. Pale bistre . . . 35·00 4·00
310 **37** 4d. dp blue & dp brn/*bluish* (27.11.02) . . . 6·00 55·00
a. Imperf vert (horiz pair) . . . £450
311 **30** 5d. red-brown (4.03) . . . 28·00 9·00
a. Deep brown . . . 26·00 5·00
b. Sepia . . . 40·00 16·00
312 **31** 6d. rose (9.02) . . . 35·00 6·50
a. Rose-red . . . 35·00 7·50
ab. Wmk upright . . . £700 £450
b. Rose-carmine . . . 40·00 7·50
ba. Imperf vert (horiz pair) . . . £500
bb. Imperf horiz (vert pair)
c. Bright carmine-pink . . . 50·00 8·00
d. Scarlet . . . 60·00 16·00
313 **32** 8d. blue (2.03) . . . 28·00 11·00
a. Steel-blue . . . 28·00 11·00
ab. Imperf vert (horiz pair) . . . £800
ac. Imperf horiz (vert pair) . . . £800
314 **33** 9d. purple (5.03) . . . 48·00 12·00
w. Wmk inverted . . . 65·00 40·00
x. Wmk reversed . . . £100 85·00
y. Wmk inverted and reversed . . . £100 75·00
315 **34** 1s. brown-red (11.02) . . . 48·00 11·00
a. Bright red . . . 48·00 12·00
b. Orange-red . . . 48·00 4·50
ba. Error. Wmk W **12*b*** (inverted) . . . † £1400
c. Orange-brown . . . 60·00 13·00
316 **35** 2s. green (4.03) . . . 85·00 50·00
a. Blue-green . . . 75·00 45·00
x. Wmk reversed . . . £300
w. Wmk inverted . . . £275 70·00
317 **36** 5s. deep red (6.03) . . . £170 £225
a. Wmk upright . . . £200 £275
b. Vermilion . . . £170 £225
ba. Wmk upright . . . £200 £275
w. Wmk inverted . . . £550 £450

(b) P 14.
318 **40** 1½d. chestnut (2.07) . . . 18·00 50·00
319 **41** 2d. grey-purple (12.02) . . . 5·50 1·75
a. purple . . . 5·50 1·75
ab. Imperf vert (horiz pair) . . . £375 £550
ac. Imperf horiz (vert pair) . . . £400
b. Bright reddish purple . . . 6·50 2·50
320 **27** 2½d. blue (1906) . . . 15·00 3·50
a. Deep blue . . . 15·00 3·50
w. Wmk inverted . . . £100 75·00
x. Wmk reversed . . . † £100
y. Wmk inverted and reversed . . . £140 £100
321 **28** 3d. bistre-brown (1906) . . . 27·00 4·50
a. Imperf vert (horiz pair) . . . £550
b. Bistre . . . 27·00 4·50
c. Pale yellow-bistre . . . 48·00 13·00
322 **37** 4d. dp blue & dp brown/bluish (1903) . . . 6·50 3·00
a. Imperf vert (horiz pair) . . . £425
b. Imperf horiz (vert pair) . . . £400
c. Centre inverted
d. Blue and chestnut/bluish . . . 4·00 2·50
e. Blue and ochre-brown/bluish . . . 4·00 2·50
w. Wmk inverted . . . 22·00 9·00
x. Wmk reversed . . . 28·00 18·00
y. Wmk inverted and reversed . . . 40·00 15·00
323 **30** 5d. black-brown (1906) . . . 55·00 22·00
a. Red-brown . . . 30·00 10·00
324 **31** 6d. bright carmine-pink (1906) . . . 55·00 9·50
a. Imperf vert (horiz pair) . . . £500
b. Rose-carmine . . . 55·00 9·50
325 **32** 8d. steel-blue (1907) . . . 27·00 11·00
326 **33** 9d. purple (1906) . . . 27·00 8·00
w. Wmk inverted . . . 80·00 35·00
327 **34** 1s. orange-brown (1906) . . . 60·00 7·50
a. Orange-red . . . 55·00 7·50
b. Pale red . . . 90·00 48·00
328 **35** 2s. green (1.06) . . . 70·00 24·00
a. blue-green . . . 75·00 32·00
aw. Wmk inverted . . . £250 75·00
ax. Wmk reversed . . . † —
ay. Wmk inverted and reversed . . . £275 80·00
329 **38** 5s. deep red (1906) . . . £170 £200
a. Wmk upright . . . £200 £250
b. Dull red . . . £170 £200
ba. Wmk upright . . . £190 £250

(c) Perf compound of 11 and 14.
330 **40** 1½d. chestnut (1907) . . . £800
331 **41** 2d. purple (1903) . . . £300 £300
332 **28** 3d. bistre-brown (1906) . . . £600 £475
333 **37** 4d. blue and yellow-brown (1903) . . . £300 £325
334 **30** 5d. red-brown (1906) . . . £700 £700
335 **31** 6d. rose-carmine (1907) . . . £325 £225
336 **32** 8d. steel-blue (1907) . . . £700 £800
337 **33** 9d. purple (1906) . . . £1000 £1000
338 **36** 5s. deep red (1906) . . . £2000

(d) Mixed perfs.
339 **40** 1½d. chestnut (1907) . . . £800
340 **41** 2d. purple (1903) . . . £200 £225
341 **28** 3d. bistre-brown (1906) . . . £600 £475
342 **37** 4d. blue and chestnut/*bluish* (1904) . . . £250 £275
a. Blue and yellow-brown/bluish . . . £250 £275
343 **30** 5d. red-brown (1906) . . . £600 £600
344 **31** 6d. rose-carmine (1907) . . . £275 £225
a. Bright carmine-pink . . . £300 £225
345 **32** 8d. steel-blue (1907) . . . £700 £800
346 **33** 9d. purple (1906) . . . £900 £900
347 **35** 2s. blue-green (1906) . . . £1000 £1000
348 **36** 5s. vermilion (Wmk upright) (1906) . . . £1600
w. Wmk inverted

Two sizes of paper were used for the above stamps:—

(1) A sheet containing 240 wmks, with a space of 9 mm between each.

(2) A sheet containing 120 wmks, with a space of 24 mm between each vertical row.

Size (1) was used for the ½d., 1d., 2d., and 4d., and size (2) for 2½d., 5d., 9d., and 2s. The paper in each case exactly fitted the plates, and had the watermark in register, though in the case of the 4d., the plate of which contained only 80 stamps, the paper was cut up to print it. The 3d., 6d., 8d., and 1s. were printed on variety (1), but with watermark sideways: by reason of this, specimens from the margins of the sheets show parts of the words "NEW ZEALAND POSTAGE" in large letters, and some copies have no watermark at all. For the 1½d. and 5s. stamps variety (1) was also used, but two watermarks appear on each stamp.

The only known example of No. 322c, postmarked at Picton on 21 March 1904, was purchased for the New Zealand Post archive collection in 1998.

(Recess Govt Printer, Wellington)

1904 (Feb). *Printed from new "dot" plates made by W. R. Royle & Sons. Thin, hard ("Cowan") paper.* W **43**.

(a) P 14.
349 **42** 1d. rose-carmine . . . 8·00 50
a. Pale carmine . . . 8·00 50
w. Wmk inverted . . . 75·00 27·00
y. Wmk inverted and reversed . . . 85·00 35·00

(b) P 11 × 14.
350 **42** 1d. rose-carmine . . . £120 £120

(c) *Mixed perfs.*
351 **42** 1d. rose-carmine . . . 28·00 32·00
a. Pale carmine . . . 28·00 32·00

These plates have a minute dot in the horizontal margins between the rows, centred under each stamp, but it is frequently cut out by the perforations. However, they can be further distinguished by the notes below.

In 1906 fresh printings were made from four new plates, two of which, marked in the margin "W1" and "W2", were supplied by Waterlow Bros and Layton, and the other two, marked "R1" and "R2", by W. R. Royle & Son. The intention was to note which pair of plates wore the best and produced the best results. They can be distinguished as follows:—

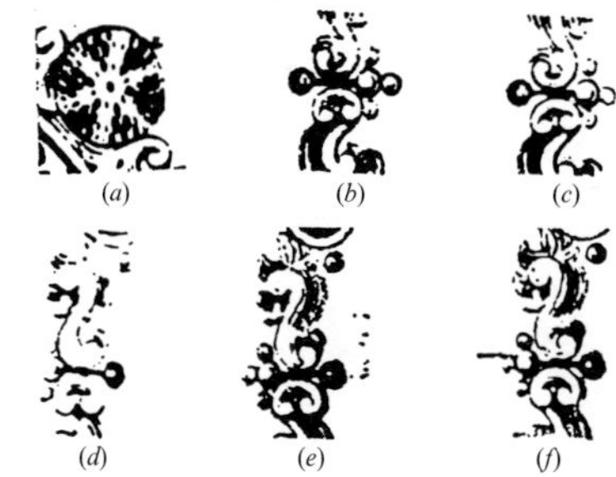

(a) Four o'clock flaw in rosette at top right corner. Occurs in all these plates but not in the original Waterlow plates.
(b) Pearl at right strong.
(c) Pearl at right weak.
(d) Dot at left and S-shaped ornament unshaded.
(e) S-shaped ornament with one line of shading within.
(f) As *(e)* but with line from left pearl to edge of stamp.

"Dot" plates comprise *(a)* and *(d)*.
Waterlow plates comprise *(a)*, *(b)* and *(e)*.
Royle plates comprise *(a)*, *(c)* and *(e)* and the line in *(f)* on many stamps but not all.

(Recess Govt Printer, Wellington)

1906. *Thin, hard ("Cowan") paper.* W **43**.

(a) Printed from new Waterlow plates.

(i) P 14.
352 **42** 1d. deep rose-carmine . . . 27·00 1·75
a. Imperf horiz (vert pair) . . . £200
b. Aniline carmine . . . 26·00 1·75
ba. Imperf vert (horiz pair) . . . £200
c. Rose-carmine . . . 26·00 1·75
y. Wmk inverted and reversed

(ii) P 11.
353 **42** 1d. aniline carmine . . . £600 £700

(iii) P 11 × 14.
354 **42** 1d. rose-carmine . . . £425 £475
a. Perf 14 × 11 . . . £425 £750

(iv) Mixed perfs.
355 **42** 1d. deep rose-carmine . . . £400 £400

(b) Printed from new Royle plates. (i) P 14.
356 **42** 1d. rose-carmine . . . 11·00 1·25
a. Imperf horiz (vert pair) . . . £225 £225
b. Bright rose-carmine . . . 12·00 1·40
w. Wmk inverted
y. Wmk inverted and reversed . . . — £150

(ii) P 11.
357 **42** 1d. bright rose-carmine . . . £100 £180

(iii) P 11 × 14.
358 **42** 1d. rose-carmine . . . £100
a. Perf 14 × 11 . . . £100 £150

(iv) Mixed perfs.
359 **42** 1d. rose-carmine . . . £100 £130

(v) P 14 × 14½ (comb).
360 **42** 1d. bright rose-carmine . . . 60·00 55·00
a. Rose-carmine . . . 60·00 55·00

Nos. 360/*a* are known both with and without the small dot. See also No. 386

1905 (15 June)–**06**. *Stamps supplied to penny-in-the-slot machines.*

(i) "Dot" plates of 1904.

(ii) Waterlow "reserve" plate of 1902.

(a) Imperf top and bottom; zigzag roulette 9½ on one or both sides, two large holes at sides.

361 **42** 1d. rose-carmine (*i*) . . . £140
362 1d. deep carmine (*ii*) . . . £160

(b) As last but rouletted 14½ (8.7.05).

363 **42** 1d. rose-carmine (*i*) . . . £150
364 1d. deep carmine (*ii*) . . . £300

(c) Imperf all round, two large holes each side (6.3.06).

365 **42** 1d. rose-carmine (*i*) . . . £120
366 1d. deep carmine (*ii*) . . . £120

(d) Imperf all round (21.6.06).

367 **42** 1d. deep carmine (*ii*) . . . £130

(e) Imperf all round. Two small indentations on back of stamp (1.06).

368 **42** 1d. deep carmine (*ii*) . . . £160 £140

(f) Imperf all round; two small pin-holes in stamp (21.6.06).

369 **42** 1d. deep carmine (*ii*) . . . £140 £140

No. 365 *only* exists from strips of Nos. 361 or 363 (resulting from the use of successive coins) which have been separated by scissors. Similarly strips of Nos. 362 and 364 can produce single copies of No. 366 but this also exists in singles from a different machine.

Most used copies of Nos. 361/7 are forgeries and they should only be collected on cover.

44 Maori Canoe, *Te Arawa*

(Des L. J. Steele. Eng W. R. Bock. Typo Govt Printer, Wellington)

1906 (1–17 Nov). *New Zealand Exhibition, Christchurch. T* **44** *and similar horiz designs.* W **43** (sideways). P 14.

370 ½d. emerald-green . . . 22·00 30·00
371 1d. vermilion . . . 16·00 16·00
a. Claret . . . £6000 £9000
372 3d. brown and blue . . . 48·00 75·00
373 6d. pink and olive-green (17.11) . . . £170 £250
370/3 *Set of* 4 . . . £225 £325

Designs:—1d. Maori art; 3d. Landing of Cook; 6d. Annexation of New Zealand.

The 1d. in claret was the original printing, which was considered unsatisfactory.

47 (T **28** reduced)

48 (T **31** reduced)

49 (T **34** reduced)

(New plates (except 4d.), supplied by Perkins Bacon. Recess Govt Printer, Wellington).

1907–**08**. *Thin, hard ("Cowan") paper.* W **43**.

(a) P 14 (line).

374 **23** ½d. green (1907) . . . 26·00 9·50
a. Imperf (pair) . . . £140
b. Yellow-green . . . 17·00 3·25
c. Deep yellow-green . . . 17·00 3·25
375 **47** 3d. brown (6.07) . . . 50·00 25·00
376 **48** 6d. carmine-pink (3.07) . . . 40·00 8·00
a. Red . . . 50·00 35·00

(b) P 14 × 13, 13½ (comb).

377 **23** ½d. green (1907) . . . 17·00 10·00
a. Yellow-green . . . 8·00 3·50
b. Imperf three sides (top stamp of vert pair) . . . £225
378 **47** 3d. brown (2.08) . . . 48·00 30·00
a. Yellow-brown . . . 48·00 30·00
379 **37** 4d. blue and yellow-brown/*bluish* (6.08) . . . 29·00 32·00
380 **48** 6d. pink (2.08) . . . £275 £110
381 **49** 1s. orange-red (12.07) . . . £120 48·00

(c) P 14 × 15 (comb).

382 **23** ½d. yellow-green (1907) . . . 8·00 1·00
a. Imperf three sides (top stamp of vert pair) . . . £225
y. Wmk inverted and reversed . . . — £160
383 **47** 3d. brown (8.08) . . . 35·00 15·00
a. Yellow-brown . . . 35·00 15·00
384 **48** 6d. carmine-pink (8.08) . . . 40·00 11·00
385 **49** 1s. orange-red (8.08) . . . £110 24·00
a. Deep orange-brown . . . £325 £550

The ½d. stamps of this 1907–8 issue have a minute dot in the margin between the stamps, where not removed by the perforation. (See note after No. 351*a*). Those perforated 14 can be distinguished from the earlier stamps, Nos. 302/*d*, by the absence of plate wear. This is most noticeable on the 1902 printings as a white patch at far left, level with the bottom of the "P" in "POSTAGE". Such damage is not present on the new plates used for Nos. 374/*c*.

Stamps of *T* **47**, **48** and **49** also have a small dot as described in note after No. 351*a*.

TYPOGRAPHY PAPERS. 1908–30. De La Rue paper is chalk-surfaced and has a smooth finish. The watermark is as illustrated. The gum is toned and strongly resistant to soaking.

Jones paper is chalk-surfaced and has a coarser texture, is poorly surfaced and the ink tends to peel. The outline of the watermark commonly shows on the surface of the stamp. The gum is colourless or only slightly toned and washes off readily.

Cowan paper is chalk-surfaced and is white and opaque. The watermark is usually smaller than in the "Jones" paper and is often barely visible

Wiggins Teape paper is chalk-surfaced and is thin and hard. It has a vertical mesh with a narrow watermark, whereas the other papers have a horizontal mesh and a wider watermark.

50

(Typo Govt Printer, Wellington, from Perkins Bacon plate).

1908 (1 Dec). *De La Rue chalk-surfaced paper.* W **43**. P 14 × 15 (comb).

386 **50** 1d. carmine . . . 22·00 1·75
w. Wmk inverted . . . — 50·00

The design of Type **50** differs from Type **42** by alterations in the corner rosettes and by the lines on the globe which are diagonal instead of vertical.

51

52

53

(Eng. P.B. Typo Govt Printer, Wellington)

1909 (8 Nov)–**12**. *De La Rue chalk-surfaced paper with toned gum.* W **43**. P 14 × 15 (comb).

387 **51** ½d. yellow-green . . . 4·25 50
aa. Deep green . . . 4·25 50
a. Imperf (pair) . . . £170
b. Booklet pane. Five stamps plus label in position 1 (4.10) . . . £600
c. Ditto, but label in position 6 (4.10) . . . £600
d. Booklet pane of 6 (4.10) . . . £170
e. Ditto, but with coloured bars on selvedge (5.12) . . . £160
w. Wmk inverted . . . † £325

Stamps with blurred and heavy appearance are from booklets.

(Eng W. R. Royle & Son, London. Recess Govt Printer, Wellington)

1909 (8 Nov)–**16**. *T* **52** *and similar portraits.*

(a) W **43**. P 14 × 14½ (comb).

388 2d. mauve . . . 9·50 6·50
a. Deep mauve . . . 18·00 6·50
w. Wmk inverted . . . † —
389 3d. chestnut . . . 23·00 1·25
390 4d. orange-red . . . 26·00 27·00
a. Orange-yellow (1912) . . . 6·00 6·50
aw. Wmk inverted . . . £275 75·00
391 5d. brown (1910) . . . 17·00 3·00
a. Red-brown . . . 17·00 3·00
w. Wmk inverted . . . † —
392 6d. carmine (1910) . . . 40·00 1·25
a. Deep carmine (29.10.13) . . . 45·00 3·00
393 8d. indigo-blue . . . 10·00 1·50
a. Deep bright blue . . . 13·00 1·50
w. Wmk inverted . . . 45·00 24·00
394 1s. vermilion (1910) . . . 48·00 2·75
w. Wmk inverted . . . £160 60·00
388/94 *Set of* 8 . . . £160 45·00

(b) W **43**. P 14 (line)*.

395 3d. chestnut (1910) . . . 45·00 10·00
396 4d. orange (1910) . . . 20·00 14·00
397 5d. brown . . . 26·00 4·50
a. Red-brown (15.9.11) . . . 26·00 5·00
w. Wmk inverted
398 6d. carmine . . . 40·00 10·00
399 1s. vermilion . . . 55·00 13·00
395/9 *Set of* 5 . . . £170 45·00

(c) W **43** (sideways) (paper with widely spaced wmk as used for Nos. 308 and 320 – see note below No. 348). P 14 (line)*.

400 8d. indigo blue (8.16) . . . 22·00 55·00
a. No wmk . . . 60·00 £140

(d) W **43**. P 14 × 13½ (comb)†.

401 3d. chestnut (1915) . . . 60·00 75·00
a. Vert pair. P 14 × 13½ and 14 × 14½ . . . £225 £275
w. Wmk inverted . . . £140 £140
402 5d. red-brown (1916) . . . 19·00 3·00
a. Vert pair. P 14 × 13½ and 14 × 14½ . . . 50·00 70·00
403 6d. carmine (1915) . . . 70·00 75·00
a. Vert pair. P 14 × 13½ and 14 × 14½ . . . £225 £275
404 8d. indigo-blue (3.16) . . . 26·00 3·00
a. Vert pair. P 14 × 13½ and 14 × 14½ . . . 50·00 70·00
b. Deep bright blue . . . 29·00 3·25
ba. Vert pair. P 14 × 13½ and 14 × 14½ . . . 55·00 75·00
w. Wmk inverted . . . 45·00 24·00
401/4 *Set of* 4 . . . £150 £140

*In addition to showing the usual characteristics of a line perforation, these stamps may be distinguished by their vertical perforation which measures 13.8. Nos. 388/94 generally measure vertically 14 to 14.3. An exception is 13.8 one vertical side but 14 the other.

†The 3d. and 6d. come in full sheets perf 14 × 13½. The 3d., 5d. and 6d. values also exist in two combinations: *(a)* five top rows perf 14 × 13½ with five bottom rows perf 14 × 14½ and *(b)* four top rows perf 14 × 13½ with six bottom rows perf 14 × 14½. The 8d. perf 14 × 13½ only exists from combination *(b)*.

(Eng P.B. Typo Govt Printer, Wellington)

1909 (8 Nov)–**26**. P 14 × 15 (comb).

(a) W **43**. *De La Rue chalk-surfaced paper with toned gum.*

405 **53** 1d. carmine . . . 1·75 10
a. Imperf (pair) . . . £300
b. Booklet pane of 6 (4.10) . . . £140
c. Ditto, but with coloured bars on selvedge (5.12) . . . £110
w. Wmk inverted . . . 28·00 23·00
y. Wmk inverted and reversed

Examples of No. 405 with a blurred and heavy appearance a from booklets.

(b) W **43**. *Jones chalk-surfaced paper with white gum.*

406 **53** 1d. deep carmine (6.24) . . . 13·00 6·
a. On unsurfaced paper. *Pale carmine* . . . £350
b. Booklet pane of 6 with bars on selvedge (1.12.24) . . . £100
w. Wmk inverted . . . 40·00 28·

No. 406a comes from a sheet on which the paper coating w missing from the right-hand half.

(c) W **43**. *De La Rue unsurfaced medium paper with toned gum*

407 **53** 1d. rose-carmine (4.25) . . . 32·00 £1

(d) W **43** (sideways). *De La Rue chalk-surfaced paper with ton gum.*

408 **53** 1d. bright carmine (4.25) . . . 9·00 45·
a. No Wmk . . . 20·00 60·
b. Imperf (pair) . . . 60·00

Many stamps from the sheets of No. 408 were without waterma or showed portions of "NEW ZEALAND POSTAGE" in doub lined capitals.

(e) No Wmk, but bluish "NZ" and Star lithographed on back. A paper.

409 **53** 1d. rose-carmine (7.25) . . . 2·50 3·
a. "NZ" and Star in black . . . 13·00
b. "NZ" and Star colourless . . . 24·00

(f) W **43**. *Cowan thick, opaque, chalk-surfaced paper with white g*

410 **53** 1d. deep carmine (8.25) . . . 5·00 1·
a. Imperf (pair) . . . 85·00 £1
b. Booklet pane of 6 with bars and adverts on selvedge . . . £100
w. Wmk inverted . . . 35·00 25·
x. Wmk reversed (1926) . . . 8·00 2·
y. Wmk inverted and reversed (1926) . . . 40·00 28·

(g) W **43**. *Wiggins Teape thin, hard, chalk-surfaced paper with wh gum.*

411 **53** 1d. rose-carmine (6.26) . . . 27·00 18·
w. Wmk inverted . . . 40·00 25·

AUCKLAND EXHIBITION, 1913.

(**59**)

60

1913 (1 Dec). *Auckland Industrial Exhibition. Nos. 387aa, 389, 3 and 405 optd with T* **59** *by Govt Printer, Wellington.*

412 **51** ½d. deep green . . . 13·00 48·
413 **53** 1d. carmine . . . 19·00 40·
414 **52** 3d. chestnut . . . £130 £2
415 6d. carmine . . . £160 £3
412/15 *Set of* 4 . . . £275 £5

These overprinted stamps were only available for letters in Ne Zealand and to Australia.

(Des H. L. Richardson. Recess Govt Printer, Wellington, from plates made in London by P.B.)

1915 (30 July)–**30**. W **43**. P 14 × 13½ (comb) (see notes below).

(a) Cowan unsurfaced paper.

416 **60** 1½d. grey-slate . . . 3·00 1·
a. Perf 14 × 14½ (1915) . . . 3·50 1·
aw. Wmk inverted . . . 40·00 35·
b. Vert pair. Nos. 416/a . . . 35·00 80·
417 2d. bright violet . . . 7·50 42·
a. Perf 14 × 14½ . . . 7·00 35·
b. Vert pair. Nos. 417/a . . . 24·00 £1
418 2d. yellow (15.1.16) . . . 7·00 30·
a. Perf 14 × 14½ . . . 7·00 30·
b. Vert pair. Nos. 418/a . . . 18·00 £2
419 2½d. blue . . . 3·25 5·
a. Perf 14 × 14½ (1916) . . . 9·50 25·
b. Vert pair. Nos. 419/a . . . 35·00 £1
420 3d. chocolate . . . 12·00 1·
aw. Wmk inverted . . . £110 65·
ax. Wmk reversed
b. Perf 14 × 14½ . . . 12·00 2·
bw. Wmk inverted . . . £110 65·
bx. Wmk reversed . . . £225
c. Vert pair. Nos. 420 and 420b . . . 40·00 £1
cw. Wmk inverted
cx. Wmk reversed
421 4d. yellow . . . 4·25 50·
a. Re-entry (Pl 20 R. 1/6) . . . 32·00
b. Re-entry (Pl 20 R. 4/10) . . . 38·00
c. Perf 14 × 14½ . . . 4·25 55·
d. Vert pair. Nos. 421 and 421c . . . 26·00 £1
422 4d. bright violet (7.4.16) . . . 9·00
a. Imperf (horiz pair) . . . £1000
b. Re-entry (Pl 20 R. 1/6) . . . 38·00 20·
c. Re-entry (Pl 20 R. 4/10) . . . 42·00 24·
dx. Wmk reversed
e. Perf 14 × 14½ . . . 7·00
ew. Wmk inverted . . . †
ex. Wmk reversed . . . — £1
f. Vert pair. Nos. 422 and 422e . . . 55·00 £1
fx. Wmk reversed
423 4½d. deep green . . . 12·00 23·
a. Perf 14 × 14½ (1915) . . . 12·00 42·
b. Vert pair. Nos. 423/a . . . 50·00 £1
424 5d. light blue (4.22) . . . 6·50 1·
a. Imperf (pair) . . . £140 £1
bw. Wmk inverted . . . — £1
c. Perf 14 × 14½ . . . 12·00 38·
d. Pale ultramarine (5.30) . . . 10·00 10·
da. Perf 14 × 14½ . . . 14·00 21·
db. Vert pair. Nos. 424d/da . . . 60·00 £1

6d. carmine . . . . . . 8·00 50
a. Imperf three sides (top stamp of vert pair) £1500
bw. Wmk inverted . . . . £120 65·00
bx. Wmk reversed . . . . — £120
by. Wmk inverted and reversed . . .
c. Carmine-lake (11.27) £500 £275
d. Perf 14 × 14½ (1915) . . . . 8·00 60
dw. Wmk inverted . . . . 50·00 40·00
e. Vert pair. Nos. 425 and 425d . . 65·00 £130
7½d. red-brown . . . . 10·00 23·00
a. Perf 14 × 14½ (10.20) . . . . 11·00 50·00
b. Vert pair. Nos. 426/a . . . . 45·00 £190
8d. indigo-blue (19.4.21) . . . . 11·00 50·00
a. Perf 14 × 14½ . . . . 11·00 50·00
b. Vert pair. Nos. 427/a . . . . 38·00 £170
8d. red-brown (3.22) . . . . 18·00 1·50
9d. sage-green . . . . 17·00 2·75
a. Imperf (pair) £1000
b. Imperf three sides (top stamp of vert pair) £1500
c. Yellowish olive (12.25) . . . . 20·00 15·00
d. Perf 14 × 14½ . . . . 17·00 16·00
e. Vert pair. Nos. 429 and 429d . . 75·00 £190
1s. vermilion . . . . 13·00 2·25
a. Imperf (pair) £2250
bw. Wmk inverted £225 £130
c. Perf 14 × 14½ (1915) . . . . 14·00 50
ca. Pale orange-red (4.24) . . . . 30·00 20·00
cb. Imperf (pair) £325
cc. Orange-brown (1.2.28) £500 £250
cw. Wmk inverted £225
d. Vert pair. Nos. 430 and 430c . . 75·00 £225
dw. Wmk inverted . . . .
30 *Set of* 15 . . . . £120 £200
3 (sideways on 2d., 3d. and 6d.). P 14 × 13¾ (comb) (see notes w) (1½d.) or 14 (line) (others).

Thin paper with widely spaced watermark as used for Nos. 308 and 320 (see note below No. 348).

60 1½d. grey-slate (3.16) . . . . 2·75 7·50
a. No wmk . . . . 3·75 16·00
b. Perf 14 × 14½ . . . . 2·75 7·50
ba. No wmk . . . . 3·75 16·00
by. Wmk inverted and reversed . . .
c. Vert pair. Nos. 431 and 431b . . 20·00 80·00
ca. Vert pair. Nos. 431a and 431ba . . . . 40·00 £110
2d. yellow (6.16) . . . . 5·00 55·00
a. No wmk . . . . 42·00 £110
3d. chocolate (6.16) . . . . 7·00 32·00
a. No wmk . . . . 42·00 85·00
6d. carmine (6.16) . . . . 8·00 65·00
a. No wmk . . . . 65·00 £150
4 *Set of* 4 . . . . 20·00 £140

he 1½d., 2½d., 4½d. and 7½d. have value tablets as shown in e 60. For the other values the tablets are shortened and the amental border each side of the crown correspondingly extended.

Vith the exception of Nos. 432/4 stamps in this issue were comb-orated 14 × 13¾, 14 × 14½ or a combination of the two.

he 1½d. (No. 416), 2½d., 4d. (both), 4½d., 5d., 6d., 7½d., 8d. red-wn, 9d. and 1s. are known to have been produced in sheets orated 14 × 13¾ throughout with the 4d. bright violet, 5d., 6d. 1s. known perforated 14 × 14½ throughout.

n the sheets showing the two perforations combined, the top rows are usually perforated 14 × 13¾ and the bottom six 14½. Combination sheets are known to have been produced in form for the 1½d. (Nos. 416 and 431), 2d. (both), 2½d., 3d., 4d. h), 4½d., 6d., 7½d., 8d. indigo-blue, 9d. and 1s. On a late printing he 4d. bright violet and 5d. pale ultramarine the arrangement is erent with the top five rows perforated 14 × 14½ and the bottom 14 × 13¾.

Vith the exception of Nos. 432/4 any with perforations measuring 14 or nearly must be classed as 14 × 14½, this being an gularity of the comb machine, and not a product of the 14-line hine.

During the laying-down of plate 20 for the 4d., from the roller-which also contained dies of other values, an impression of the . value was placed on R. 1/6 and of the 2½d. on R. 4/10. These rs were subsequently corrected by re-entries of the 4d. ression, but on R. 1/6 traces of the original impression can be nd in the right-hand value tablet and above the top frame line, le on R. 4/10 the foot of the "2" is visible in the left-hand value et with traces of "½" to its right.

61

62

WAR STAMP
(63)

'ype 62 (from local plates) can be identified from Type 61 pared by Perkins Bacon) by the shading on the portrait. This is gonal on Type 62 and horizontal on Type 61.

e eng W. R. Bock. Typo Govt Printer, Wellington, from plates made by P.B. (*T* 61) or locally (*T* 62))

5 (30 July)–33. W 43. P 14 × 15.

(a) De La Rue chalk-surfaced paper with toned gum.

61 ½d. green . . . . 1·25 20
a. Booklet pane of 6 with bars on selvedge £110
b. Yellow-green . . . . 3·75 1·40
ba. Booklet pane of 6 with bars on selvedge . . . . 90·00
c. Very thick, hard, highly surfaced paper with white gum (12.15) . . 12·00 40·00
w. Wmk inverted . . . . 35·00 70·00
x. Wmk reversed . . . . — 60·00
y. Wmk inverted and reversed . . . — 60·00
62 1½d. grey-black (4.16) . . . . 8·00 1·25
a. Black . . . . 9·00 1·40
y. Wmk inverted and reversed . . . — £130
61 1½d. slate (5.9.16) . . . . 6·50 20
w. Wmk inverted . . . . — £130
1½d. orange-brown (9.18) . . . . 2·25 20
w. Wmk inverted . . . . £120 85·00
x. Wmk reversed . . . . † —
y. Wmk inverted and reversed . . . £140 90·00

439 2d. yellow (9.16) . . . . 2·25 20
a. Pale yellow . . . . 3·75 70
w. Wmk inverted . . . . 85·00
440 3d. chocolate (5.19) . . . . 7·00 75
435/40 *Set of* 6 . . . . 25·00 2·50

(b) W 43. *Jones chalk-surfaced paper with white gum.*

441 61 ½d. green (10.24) . . . . 8·50 9·00
a. Booklet pane of 6 with bars on selvedge (1.12.24) £100
w. Wmk inverted . . . . 45·00 25·00
442 2d. dull yellow (7.24) . . . . 7·00 29·00
w. Wmk inverted . . . . 35·00
443 3d. deep chocolate (3.25) . . . . 21·00 17·00
441/3 *Set of* 3 . . . . 32·00 50·00

(c) No Wmk, but bluish "NZ" and Star lithographed on back. Art paper.

444 61 ½d. apple-green (4.25) . . . . 2·50 3·25
a. "NZ" and Star almost colourless . . . . 4·50
445 2d. yellow (7.25) . . . . 6·50 55·00

(d) W 43. *Cowan thick, opaque, chalk-surfaced paper with white gum.*

446 61 ½d. green (8.25) . . . . 1·25 30
a. Booklet pane of 6 with bars and adverts on selvedge . . . . 90·00
ab. Booklet pane of 6 with bars on selvedge (1928) £250
bw. Wmk inverted . . . . 40·00 40·00
bx. Wmk reversed (1926) . . . . 4·00 2·25
by. Wmk inverted and reversed (1926) . . . . 40·00 25·00
c. Perf 14 (1927) . . . . 1·25 35
ca. Booklet pane of 6 with bars on selvedge (1928) . . . . 85·00
cb. Booklet pane of 6 with bars and adverts on selvedge (1928) . . . . 85·00
cc. Imperf three sides (horiz pair) . . £500
cw. Wmk inverted . . . . 42·00 38·00
447 1½d. orange-brown (P 14) (8.29) . . . 8·50 22·00
a. Perf 14 × 15 (7.33) . . . . 35·00 75·00
448 2d. yellow (8.25) . . . . 7·00 50
ax. Wmk reversed (1927) . . . . 11·00 60·00
ay. Wmk inverted and reversed (1927) £120
b. Perf 14 (1929) . . . . 2·75 20
bw. Wmk inverted . . . . 40·00 28·00
449 3d. chocolate (8.25) . . . . 7·50 65
aw. Wmk inverted . . . . 60·00
b. Perf 14 (1929) . . . . 7·50 2·75
446/9 *Set of* 4 . . . . 17·00 22·00

(e) W 43. *Wiggins Teape thin, hard, chalk-surfaced paper.*

450 61 1½d. orange-brown (P 14) (1930) . . . 35·00 70·00
451 2d. yellow (5.26) . . . . 8·00 19·00
aw. Wmk inverted . . . . 26·00 26·00
b. Perf 14 (10.27) . . . . 7·50 19·00
bw. Wmk inverted . . . . 35·00 35·00

The designs of these stamps also differ as described beneath No. 434.

Stamps from booklet panes often have blurred, heavy impressions. Different advertisements can be found on the listed booklet panes.

Examples of No. 446cc, which occur in booklet panes, show the stamps perforated at top.

The ½d. and 2d. (Nos. 446c and 448b) are known showing ½d. and 1d. local surcharges from 1932 applied diagonally in blue to stamps previously stuck on to envelopes or cards at Christchurch (½d.) or Wellington (1d.).

1915 (24 Sept). *No. 435 optd with T* 63.

452 61 ½d. green . . . . 2·00 50

64 "Peace" and Lion

65 "Peace" and Lion

(Des and typo D.L.R. from plates by P.B., Waterlow and D.L.R.)

1920 (27 Jan). *Victory. T* 64/5 *and similar designs. De La Rue chalk-surfaced paper.* W 43 (sideways on ½d., 1½d., 3d. and 1s.). P 14.

453 ½d. green . . . . 3·00 2·50
a. Pale yellow-green . . . . 26·00 27·00
454 1d. carmine-red . . . . 4·50 60
a. Bright carmine . . . . 6·00 70
w. Wmk inverted . . . . 15·00 7·50
x. Wmk reversed . . . . 48·00 16·00
455 1½d. brown-orange . . . . 3·00 50
456 3d. chocolate . . . . 12·00 14·00
457 6d. violet . . . . 13·00 17·00
a. Wmk sideways . . . . † £400
w. Wmk inverted . . . . — £120
458 1s. orange-red . . . . 20·00 48·00
453/8 *Set of* 6 . . . . 50·00 75·00

Designs: *Horiz* (as *T* 65)—1½d. Maori chief. (As *T* 64)—3d. Lion; 1s. King George V. *Vert* (as *T* 64)—6d. "Peace" and "Progress".

The above stamps were placed on sale in London in November, 1919.

2d. 2d.

TWOPENCE
(68)

69

1922 (Mar). *No. 453 surch with T* 68.

459 64 2d.on ½d. green (R.) . . . . 3·50 1·40

(Des and eng W. R. Bock, Typo Govt Printer, Wellington)

1923 (1 Oct)–25. *Restoration of Penny Postage.* W 43. P 14 × 15.

(a) De La Rue chalk-surfaced paper with toned gum.

460 69 1d. carmine . . . . 3·00 60

(b) Jones chalk-surfaced paper with white gum.

461 69 1d. carmine (3.24) . . . . 7·00 5·00
a. Wmk sideways . . . . † —
w. Wmk inverted . . . . 55·00 45·00

(c) Cowan unsurfaced paper with very shiny gum.

462 69 1d. carmine-pink (4.25) . . . . 27·00 27·00

The paper used for No. 462 is similar to that of Nos. 416/30.

70 Exhibition Buildings

(Des H. L. Richardson. Eng and typo Govt Printer, Wellington)

1925 (17 Nov). *Dunedin Exhibition. Cowan chalk-surfaced paper.* W 43. P 14 × 15.

463 70 ½d. yellow-green/*green* . . . . 3·00 11·00
w. Wmk inverted £120 £100
464 1d. carmine/*rose* . . . . 3·50 5·50
w. Wmk inverted £120 £100
465 4d. mauve/*pale mauve* . . . . 30·00 70·00
a. "POSTAGF" at right (R. 1/2, R. 10/1) £100 £170
463/5 *Set of* 3 . . . . 32·00 80·00

71

72

(Des H. L. Richardson; plates by B.W. (1d. from sheets), P.B. (1d. from booklets), Royal Mint, London (others). Typo Govt Printer, Wellington)

1926 (12 July)–34. W 43. P 14.

(a) Jones chalk-surfaced paper with white gum.

466 72 2s. deep blue . . . . 48·00 55·00
w. Wmk inverted . . . . 48·00 55·00
467 3s. mauve . . . . 70·00 £150
w. Wmk inverted . . . . 70·00 £150

(b) Cowan thick, opaque, chalk-surfaced paper with white gum.

468 71 1d. rose-carmine (15.11.26) 75 20
a. Imperf (pair) £120
b. Booklet pane of 6 with bars on selvedge (1928) . . . . 75·00
c. Booklet pane of 6 with bars and adverts on selvedge (1928) . . . . 75·00
dw. Wmk inverted . . . . 24·00 14·00
e. Perf 14 × 15 (3.27) 65 50
ea. Booklet pane of 6 with bars and adverts on selvedge (1934) . . . . 85·00
ew. Wmk inverted . . . . 24·00 14·00
ex. Wmk reversed . . . . 10·00
469 72 2s. light blue (5.27) . . . . 50·00 23·00
470 3s. pale mauve (9.27) . . . . 85·00 £140
468/70 *Set of* 3 . . . . £120 £150

(c) Wiggins Teape thin, hard, chalk-surfaced paper with white gum.

471 71 1d. rose-carmine (6.30) . . . . 15·00 11·00
w. Wmk inverted . . . . 55·00 24·00

No. 468ex exists in a range of colours including scarlet and deep carmine to magenta but we have insufficient evidence to show that these were issued.

Following the reduction of the postage rate to ½d. on 1 June 1932 the firm of R. H. White & Co. Ltd. of Stratford returned a quantity of envelopes stamped with 1d. stamps (No. 468) to the New Plymouth post office who surcharged the stamps "HALFPENNY" in purple using a handstamp. The covers were then returned to the firm for normal use. Similar local surcharges were applied diagonally to 1d. stamps stuck onto postcards or lettercards at Dunedin, Greymouth and Invercargill in blue or at Palmerston North in purple. With the exception of the Greymouth provisional, where forty mint examples were acquired by a stamp dealer, these local surcharges are only found unused, no gum, or used.

73 Nurse

74 Smiling Boy

(Typo Govt Printing Office, Wellington)

1929–30. *Anti-Tuberculosis Fund. T* 73 *and similar design.* W 43. P 14.

*(a) Inscribed "*HELP STAMP OUT TUBERCULOSIS*".*

544 1d.+1d. scarlet (11.12.29) . . . . 11·00 18·00
w. Wmk inverted £200 £160

*(b) Inscribed "*HELP PROMOTE HEALTH*".*

545 1d.+1d. scarlet (29.10.30) . . . . 20·00 32·00

(Des L. C, Mitchell. Dies eng and plates made Royal Mint, London (1d.), Govt Ptg Office, Wellington from W. R. Bock die (2d.). Typo Govt Ptg Office, Wellington)

1931 (31 Oct). *Health Stamps.* W **43** (sideways). P 14½ × 14.

546	**74**	1d.+1d. scarlet	75·00	75·00
547		2d.+1d. blue	75·00	60·00

75 New Zealand Lake Scenery

FIVE PENCE
(**76**)

(Des L. C. Mitchell. Plates, Royal Mint, London. Typo Govt Ptg Office)

1931 (10 Nov)–**35**. *Air.* W **43**. P 14 × 14½.

548	**75**	3d. chocolate	24·00	15·00
		a. Perf 14 × 15 (4.35)	£130	£425
549		4d. blackish purple	24·00	19·00
550		7d. brown-orange	27·00	9·00
548/50 *Set of* 3			65·00	38·00

1931 (18 Dec). *Air. Surch with T* **76**. W **43**. P 14 × 14½.

551	**75**	5d.on 3d. green (R.)	10·00	8·00

77 Hygeia, Goddess of Health

78 The Path to Health

(Des R. E. Tripe and W. J. Cooch. Eng H. T. Peat. Recess Govt Printing Office, Wellington)

1932 (18 Nov). *Health Stamp.* W **43**. P 14.

552	**77**	1d.+1d. carmine	20·00	27·00
		w. Wmk inverted	£225	£120
		x. Wmk reversed	†	£275

(Des J. Berry. Eng H. T. Peat. Recess Govt Printing Office, Wellington)

1933 (8 Nov). *Health Stamp.* W **43**. P 14.

553	**78**	1d.+1d. carmine	13·00	17·00
		w. Wmk inverted	£160	£110

TRANS-TASMAN
AIR MAIL
"FAITH IN AUSTRALIA."
(**79**)

80 Crusader

1934 (17 Jan). *Air. T* **75** *in new colour optd with T* **79**. W **43**. P 14 × 14½.

554	**75**	7d. light blue (B.)	35·00	40·00

(Des J. Berry. Recess D.L.R.)

1934 (25 Oct). *Health Stamp.* W **43** (sideways). P 14 × 13½.

555	**80**	1d.+1d. carmine	11·00	17·00

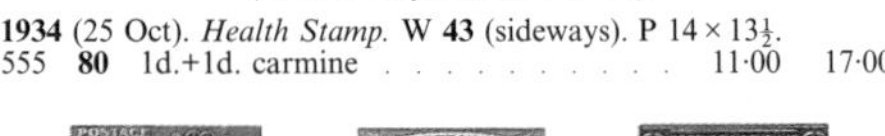

81 Collared Grey Fantail

82 Brown Kiwi

83 Maori Woman

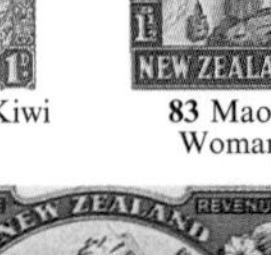

84 Maori Carved House

85 Mt Cook

86 Maori Girl

87 Mitre Peak

88 Striped Marlin

89 Harvesting

90 Tuatara Lizard

91 Maori Panel

92 Parson Bird

93 Capt. Cook at Poverty Bay

94 Mt Egmont

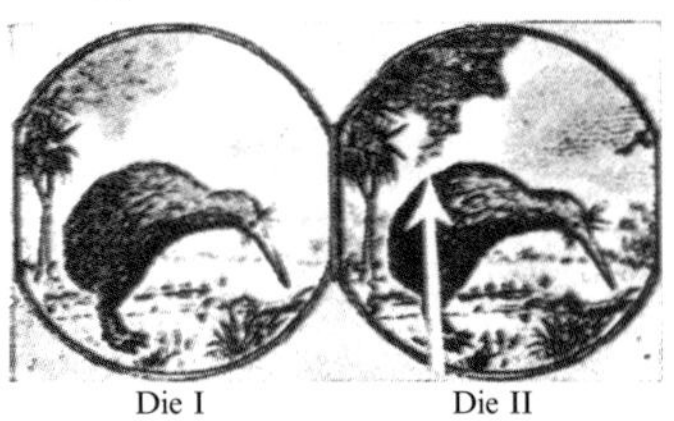

Die I

Die II

"Captain Coqk" (R. 1/4)

(Des J. Fitzgerald (½d., 4d.), C. H. and R. J. G. Collins (1d.) M. Matthews (1½d.), H. W. Young (2d.), L. C. Mitchell (2½d., 3d., 8d., 1s., 3s.), W. J. Cooch and R. E. Tripe (5d.), T. I. Archer (6d.), I. F. Calder (9d.) and I. H. Jenkins (2s.). Litho Waterlow (9d.). Recess D.L.R. (remainder))

1935 (1 May)–**36**. W **43** (sideways on. 8d.).

556	**81**	½d. bright green, P 14 × 13½	1·50	1·00
		w. Wmk inverted	2·25	2·75
557	**82**	1d. scarlet (Die I), P 14 × 13½	1·75	75
		aw. Wmk inverted	2·75	2·50
		b. Perf 13½ × 14 (1936)	75·00	48·00
		c. Die II. Perf 14 × 13½ (1935)	5·50	3·00
		ca. Booklet pane of 6 with adverts on selvedge	40·00	
		cw. Wmk inverted	12·00	3·50
558	**83**	1½d. red-brown, P 14 × 13½	8·00	12·00
		a. Perf 13½ × 14 (1935)	6·00	7·00
		ay. Wmk inverted and reversed (2.36)	18·00	24·00
559	**84**	2d. orange, P 14 × 13½	4·00	1·00
		w. Wmk inverted	£100	24·00
560	**85**	2½d. chocolate and slate, P 13-14 × 13½	5·50	27·00
		aw. Wmk inverted	20·00	40·00
		b. Perf 13½ × 14 (11.35)	4·50	20·00
		bx. Wmk reversed	†	£550
561	**86**	3d. brown, P 14 × 13½	12·00	2·75
		w. Wmk inverted	£375	£140
562	**87**	4d. black and sepia, P 14	3·75	2·00
		w. Wmk inverted	£250	95·00
563	**88**	5d. ultramarine, P 13-14 × 13½	23·00	27·00
		aw. Wmk inverted	†	£120
		b. Perf 13½ × 14	25·00	40·00
564	**89**	6d. scarlet, P 13½ × 14	7·00	6·50
		w. Wmk inverted	£225	75·00
565	**90**	8d. chocolate, P 14 × 13½	9·50	11·00
566	**91**	9d. scarlet and black, P 14 × 14½	11·00	3·25
567	**92**	1s. deep green, P 14 × 13½	20·00	13·00
		w. Wmk inverted	—	90·00
568	**93**	2s. olive-green, P 13-14½ × 13½	42·00	40·00
		a. "CAPTAIN COQK"	90·00	
		bw. Wmk inverted	85·00	50·00
		c. Perf 13½ × 14 (1935)	50·00	50·00
		ca. "CAPTAIN COQK"	95·00	
569	**94**	3s. choc & yell-brn, P 13-14 × 13½	17·00	48·00
		a. Perf 13½ × 14 (11.35)	19·00	48·00
		aw. Wmk inverted	†	£200
		ay. Wmk inverted and reversed (1936)	£350	£375
556/69 *Set of* 14			£150	£170

Some stamps from sheets perforated 14 × 13½ by De La Rue sometimes show the horizontal perforations nearer 13½.

In the 2½d., 5d., 2s. and 3s. perf 13-14 × 13½ the horizontal perforations of each stamp are in two sizes, one half of each horizontal side measuring 13 and the other 14.

See also Nos. 577/90 and 630/1.

95 Bell Block Aerodrome

96 King George V and Queen Mary

(Des J. Berry. Eng Stamp Printing Office, Melbourne. Recess Govt Printing Office, Wellington)

1935 (4 May). *Air.* W **43**. P 14.

570	**95**	1d. carmine	1·00	7
		w. Wmk inverted	65·00	40·0
571		3d. violet	5·00	3·0
		w. Wmk inverted	80·00	45·0
572		6d. blue	9·50	3·0
		w. Wmk inverted	95·00	60·0
570/2 *Set of* 3			14·00	6·0

(Frame by J. Berry. Recess B.W.)

1935 (7 May). *Silver Jubilee.* W **43**. P 11 × 11½.

573	**96**	½d. green	75	1·0
574		1d. carmine	1·00	8
575		6d. red-orange	17·00	26·0
573/5 *Set of* 3			17·00	26·0

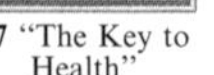

97 "The Key to Health"

98 "Multiple Wmk"

(Des S. Hall. Recess John Ash, Melbourne)

1935 (30 Sept). *Health Stamp.* W **43**. P 11.

576	**97**	1d.+1d. scarlet	2·50	2·7

WATERMARKS. In W **43** the wmk units are in vertical colum[n]s widely spaced and the sheet margins are unwatermarked or wmk "NEW ZEALAND POSTAGE" in large letters.

In W **98** the wmk units are arranged alternately in horizontal row[s] closely spaced and are continued into the sheet margins.

Stamps with W **98** sideways show the star to the left of NZ, *a[s] seen from the back*. Sideways inverted varieties have the star to righ[t] *as seen from the back*.

(Litho Govt Ptg Office, Wellington (9d). Recess Waterlow or D.L.R.(others))

1936–42. W **98**.

577	**81**	½d. bright green, P 14 × 13½	3·00	[illegible]
		w. Wmk inverted	5·50	1·
578	**82**	1d. scarlet (Die II), P 14 × 13½ (4.36)	2·50	[illegible]
		w. Wmk inverted	7·00	2·
579	**83**	1½d. red-brown, P 14 × 13½ (6.36)	11·00	5·
580	**84**	2d. orange, P 14 × 13½ (3.36)	30	[illegible]
		aw. Wmk inverted	90·00	32·
		b. Perf 12½† (6.41)	4·50	[illegible]
		bw. Wmk inverted		
		c. Perf 14 (6.41)	25·00	[illegible]
		d. Perf 14 × 15 (6.41)	38·00	22·
581	**85**	2½d. chocolate and slate, P 13–14 × 13½	7·50	18·
		aw. Wmk inverted	24·00	38·
		b. Perf 14 (11.36)	6·00	1·
		bw. Wmk inverted	16·00	19·
		c. Perf 14 × 13½ (11.42)	50	4·
582	**86**	3d. brown, P 14 × 13½	35·00	
		w. Wmk inverted	60·00	38·
583	**87**	4d. black and sepia, P 14 × 13½	6·00	
		aw. Wmk inverted	15·00	9·
		b. Perf 12½* (1941)	29·00	12·
		bw. Wmk inverted	†	
		c. Perf 14, line (1941)	65·00	£1
		d. Perf 14 × 14½ comb (7.42)	1·00	
		dw. Wmk inverted	90·00	40·
584	**88**	5d. ultramarine, P 13–14 × 13½ (8.36)	18·00	2·
		aw. Wmk inverted	35·00	15·
		b. Perf 12½*† (7.41)	17·00	3·
		c. Perf 14 × 13½ (11.42)	2·00	1·
		cw. Wmk inverted	95·00	75·
585	**89**	6d. scarlet, P 13½ × 14 (8.36)	16·00	1·
		aw. Wmk inverted	40·00	6·
		b. Perf 12½* (10.41)	3·00	3·
		c. Perf 14½ × 14 (6.42)	1·25	
		cw. Wmk inverted	£225	£1
586	**90**	8d. choc, P 14 × 13½ (wmk sideways)	11·00	3·
		aw. Wmk sideways inverted	25·00	10·
		b. Wmk upright (7.39)	4·00	3·
		bw. Wmk inverted		
		c. Perf 12½* (wmk sideways) (7.41)	3·75	1·
		d. Perf 14 × 14½ (wmk sideways) (7.42)	3·75	
		dw. Wmk sideways inverted	—	40·
587	**91**	9d. red and grey, P 14 × 15 (wmk sideways)	45·00	3·
		ay. Wmk sideways inverted and reversed	—	£1
		b. Wmk upright. *Red and grey-black*, P 13½ × 14 (1.3.38)	55·00	3·
		bw. Wmk inverted	95·00	35
588	**92**	1s. deep green, P 14 × 13½	2·50	
		aw. Wmk inverted	55·00	12
		b. Perf 12½* (11.41)	65·00	19
589	**93**	2s. olive-green, P 13–14 × 13½ (8.36)	38·00	7
		a. "CAPTAIN COQK"	65·00	
		bw. Wmk inverted	£140	60
		c. Perf 13½ × 14 (3.39)	£275	3
		ca. "CAPTAIN COQK"	£275	
		d. Perf 12½*† (7.41)	19·00	8
		da. "CAPTAIN COQK"	60·00	
		e. Perf 14 × 13½ (10.42)	5·50	1
		ea. "CAPTAIN COQK"	85·00	
		ew. Wmk inverted	—	90·

590 **94** 3s. chocolate & yellow-brown, P 13–14 × 13½ . . . . . 48·00 8·00
aw. Wmk inverted . . . . . 70·00 17·00
b. Perf 12½* (1941) . . . . . 80·00 48·00
c. Perf 14 × 13½ (1942) . . . . . 3·50 2·25
577/90c *Set of* 14 . . . . . £100 14·00

*†Stamps indicated with an asterisk were printed and perforated by Waterlow; those having a dagger were printed by D.L.R. and perforated by Waterlow. No. 580d was printed by D.L.R. and perforated by Harrison and No. 583c was printed by Waterlow and perforated by D.L.R. These are all known as "Blitz perfs" because De La Rue were unable to maintain supplies after their works were damaged by enemy action. All the rest, except the 9d., were printed and perforated by D.L.R.

On stamps printed and perforated by De La Rue the perf 14 × 13½ varies in the sheet and is sometimes nearer 13½. 2d. perf 14 × 15 is sometimes nearer 14 × 14½.

2½d., 5d., 2s. and 3s. In perf 13–14 × 13½ one half the length of each horizontal perforation measures 13 and the other 14. In perf 14 × 13½ the horizontal perforation is regular.

4d. No. 583c. is line-perf measuring 14 exactly and has a blackish sepia frame. No. 583d is a comb-perf measuring 14 × 14.3 or 14 × 14.2 and the frame is a warmer shade.

2s. No. 589c is comb-perf and measures 13.5 × 13.75.

For 9d. typographed, see Nos. 630/1.

99 N.Z. Soldier at Anzac Cove

100 Wool

(Des L. C. Mitchell. Recess John Ash, Melbourne)

1936 (27 Apr). *Charity. 21st Anniv of "Anzac" Landing at Gallipoli.* W **43**. P 11.
591 **99** ½d.+½d. green . . . . . 60 1·75
592 1d.+1d. scarlet . . . . . 60 1·40

(Des L. C. Mitchell. Recess John Ash, Melbourne)

1936 (1 Oct). *Congress of British Empire Chambers of Commerce, Wellington. Industries Issue. T* **100** *and similar horiz designs.* W **43** (sideways). P 11½.
593 ½d. emerald-green 30 30
594 1d. scarlet 30 20
595 2½d. blue . . . . . 1·25 8·00
596 4d. violet . . . . . 1·00 5·50
597 6d. red-brown . . . . . 2·50 4·50
593/7 *Set of* 5 . . . . . 4·75 17·00

Designs:—1d. Butter; 2½d. Sheep; 4d. Apples; 6d. Exports.

105 Health Camp

106 King George VI and Queen Elizabeth

(Des J. Berry. Recess John Ash, Melbourne)

1936 (2 Nov). *Health Stamp.* W **43** (sideways). P 11.
598 **105** 1d.+1d. scarlet . . . . . 1·75 3·75

(Recess B.W.)

1937 (13 May). *Coronation.* W **98**. P 14 × 13½.
599 **106** 1d. carmine 30 10
600 2½d. Prussian blue . . . . . 80 2·50
601 6d. red-orange . . . . . 1·10 2·25
599/601 *Set of* 3 . . . . . 2·00 4·25

107 Rock climbing

108 King George VI

108a King George VI

(Des G. Bull and J. Berry. Recess John Ash, Melbourne)

1937 (1 Oct). *Health Stamp.* W **43**. P 11.
602 **107** 1d.+1d. scarlet . . . . . 3·00 3·75

Broken ribbon flaw (R. 6/6 of Pl 8)

(Des W. J. Cooch. Recess B.W.)

1938–44. W **98**. P 14 × 13½.
603 **108** ½d. green (1.3.38) . . . . . 6·50 10
w. Wmk inverted . . . . . 16·00 2·75
604 ½d. orange-brown (10.7.41) 20 40
w. Wmk inverted . . . . .
605 1d. scarlet (1.7.38) . . . . . 5·00 10
a. Broken ribbon . . . . . 60·00
w. Wmk inverted . . . . . 16·00 2·75
606 1d. green (21.7.41) 20 10
w. Wmk inverted . . . . . 35·00 18·00
607 **108a** 1½d. purple-brown (26.7.38) . . . . . 26·00 2·50
w. Wmk inverted . . . . . 38·00 4·25
608 1½d. scarlet (1.2.44) 20 60
w. Wmk inverted . . . . . — 60·00
609 3d. blue (26.9.41) 20 10
w. Wmk inverted . . . . . — 45·00
603/9 *Set of* 7 . . . . . 35·00 3·25

For other values see Nos. 680/9.

109 Children playing

110 Beach Ball

(Des J. Berry. Recess B.W.)

1938 (1 Oct). *Health Stamp.* W **98**. P 14 × 13½.
610 **109** 1d.+1d. scarlet . . . . . 6·50 3·00

(Des S. Hall. Recess Note Printing Branch, Commonwealth Bank of Australia, Melbourne)

1939 (16 Oct). *Health Stamps. Surcharged with new value.* W **43**. P 11.
611 **110** 1d.on ½d.+½d. green . . . . . 4·75 4·50
612 2d.on 1d.+1d. scarlet . . . . . 4·75 4·50

111 Arrival of the Maoris, 1350

115 Signing Treaty of Waitangi, 1840

(Des L. C. Mitchell (½d., 3d., 4d.); J. Berry (others). Recess BW.)

1940 (2 Jan–8 Mar). *Centenary of Proclamation of British Sovereignty. T* **111, 115** *and similar designs.* W **98**. P 14 × 13½ (2½d.), 13½ × 14 (5d.) or 13½ (others).
613 ½d. blue-green 30 10
614 1d. chocolate and scarlet . . . . . 2·75 10
615 1½d. light blue and mauve 30 60
616 2d. blue-green and chocolate . . . . . 1·50 10
617 2½d. blue-green and blue . . . . . 2·00 1·00
618 3d. purple and carmine . . . . . 3·75 1·00
619 4d. chocolate and lake . . . . . 13·00 1·50
620 5d. pale blue and brown . . . . . 7·00 3·75
621 6d. emerald-green and violet . . . . . 11·00 1·25
622 7d. black and red . . . . . 1·50 4·00
623 8d. black and red (8.3) . . . . . 11·00 3·00
624 9d. olive-green and orange . . . . . 7·50 2·00
625 1s. sage-green and deep green . . . . . 13·00 3·75
613/25 *Set of* 13 . . . . . 65·00 19·00

Designs: *Horiz (as T***111***)*—1d. *Endeavour*, Chart of N.Z., and Capt. Cook; 1½d. British Monarchs; 2d. Tasman with his ship and chart; 3d. Landing of immigrants, 1840; 4d. Road, Rail, Sea and Air Transport; 6d. *Dunedin* and "Frozen Mutton Route" to London; 7d., 8d. Maori council; 9d. Gold mining in 1861 and 1940. (*As T* **115**)—5d. H.M.S. *Britomar* at Akaroa, 1840. *Vert* (*as T* **111**)—1s. Giant Kauri tree.

1940 (1 Oct). *Health Stamps. As T* **110**, *but without extra surcharge.* W **43**. P 11.
626 **110** 1d.+½d. blue-green . . . . . 14·00 16·00
627 2d.+1d. brown-orange . . . . . 14·00 16·00

1ᴰ 1ᴰ ■ ■ (123)

2ᴰ Inserted "2"

1941 (124)

1941. *Nos. 603 and 607 surch as T* **123**.
628 **108** 1d.on ½d. green (1.5.41) . . . . . 1·75 10
629 **108a** 2d.on 1½d. purple-brown (4.41) . . . . . 1·75 10
a. Inserted "2" £550 £300

The surcharge on No. 629 has only one figure, at top left, and there is only one square to obliterate the original value at bottom right.

The variety "Inserted 2" occurs on the 10th stamp, 10th row. It is identified by the presence of remnants of the damaged "2", and by the spacing of "2" and "D" which is variable and different from the normal.

(Typo Govt Printing Office, Wellington)

1941. *As T* **91**, *but smaller (17½ × 20½ mm). Chalk-surfaced paper.* P 14 × 15.

(a) W **43**.
630 **91** 9d. scarlet and black (5.41) . . . . . 95·00 27·00
w. Wmk inverted . . . . . † £200

(b) W **98**.
631 **91** 9d. scarlet and black (29.9.41) . . . . . 3·50 3·00
w. Wmk inverted £140 £100

1941 (4 Oct). *Health Stamps. Nos. 626/7 optd with T* **124**.
632 **110** 1d.+½d. blue-green . . . . . 50 2·25
633 2d.+1d. brown-orange . . . . . 50 2·25

125 Boy and Girl on Swing

126 Princess Margaret

(Des S. Hall. Recess Note Printing Branch, Commonwealth Bank of Australia, Melbourne)

1942 (1 Oct). *Health Stamps.* W **43**. P 11.
634 **125** 1d.+½d. blue-green . . . . . 30 1·25
635 2d.+1d. orange-red . . . . . 30 1·25

(Des J. Berry. Recess B.W.)

1943 (1 Oct). *Health Stamps. T* **126** *and similar triangular design.* W **98**. P 12.
636 1d.+½d. green . . . . . 20 1·50
a. Imperf between (vert pair) £7000
637 2d.+1d. red-brown 20 25
a. Imperf between (vert pair) £9000 £9000

Design:— 2d. Queen Elizabeth II as Princess.

TENPENCE (128)

1944 (1 May). *No. 615 surch with T* **128**.
662 10d.on 1½d. light blue and mauve 15 20

129 Queen Elizabeth II as Princess and Princess Margaret

130 Statue of Peter Pan, Kensington Gardens

(Recess B.W.)

1944 (9 Oct). *Health Stamps.* W **98**. P 13½.
663 **129** 1d.+½d. green 30 40
664 2d.+1d. blue 30 30

(Des J. Berry. Recess B.W.)

1945 (1 Oct). *Health Stamps.* W **98**. P 13½.
665 **130** 1d.+½d. green and buff 15 20
w. Wmk inverted . . . . . 50·00 40·00
666 2d.+1d. carmine and buff 15 20
w. Wmk inverted . . . . . 95·00 60·00

131 Lake Matheson

132 King George VI and Parliament House, Wellington

133 St. Paul's Cathedral

139 "St. George" (Wellington College War Memorial Window)

Printer's guide mark (R. 12/3) Completed rudder (R. 2/4 of Pl 42883 and R. 3/2 of Pl 42796)

(Des J. Berry. Photo Harrison (1½d. and 1s.). Recess B.W. (1d. and 2d.) and Waterlow (others))

1946 (1 Apr). *Peace issue. T* **131/3**, **139** *and similar designs.* W **98** (sideways on 1½d.). P 13 (1d., 2d.), 14 × 14½ (1½d., 1s.), 13½ (others)

667	½d. green and brown	20	65
	a. Printer's guide mark	12·00	
	w. Wmk inverted	60·00	45·00
668	1d. green	10	10
	w. Wmk inverted	40·00	23·00
669	1½d. scarlet	10	50
	w. Wmk sideways inverted	10	10
670	2d. purple	15	10
671	3d. ultramarine and grey	30	15
	a. Completed rudder	8·50	
672	4d. bronze-green and orange	20	20
	w. Wmk inverted	£100	45·00
673	5d. green and ultramarine	40	65
674	6d. chocolate and vermilion	15	30
675	8d. black and carmine	15	30
676	9d. blue and black	15	30
677	1s. grey-black	15	40
667/77	*Set of* 11	1·75	3·25

Designs: *Horiz* (*as T***132**)—2d. The Royal Family. (*As T* **131**)—3d. R.N.Z.A.F. badge and airplanes; 4d. Army badge, tank and plough; 5d. Navy badge, H.M.N.Z.S. *Achilles* (cruiser) and *Dominion Monarch* (liner); 6d. N.Z. coat of arms, foundry and farm; 9d. Southern Alps and Franz Josef Glacier. *Vert* (*as T* **139**)—1s. National Memorial Campanile.

142 Soldier helping Child over Stile

(Des J. Berry. Recess Waterlow)

1946 (24 Oct). *Health Stamps.* W **98**. P 13½.

678	**142**	1d.+½d. green and orange-brown	15	15
		a. Yellow-green and orange-brown	4·50	5·00
		w. Wmk inverted	18·00	18·00
679		2d.+1d. chocolate and orange-brown	15	15

144 King George VI

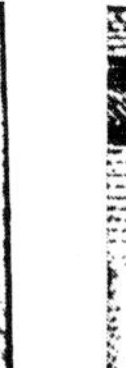

145 Statue of Eros

Plate 1 Plate 2

(Des W. J. Cooch. Recess *T* **108***a*, B.W.; *T* **144**, D.L.R.)

1947–52. W **98** (sideways on "shilling" values).

(a) P 14 × 13½..

680	**108a**	2d. orange	15	10
		w. Wmk inverted	80·00	
681		4d. bright purple	70	50
682		5d. slate	50	90
683		6d. carmine	50	10
		w. Wmk inverted	80·00	16·00
684		8d. violet	65	50
685		9d. purple-brown	1·75	50
		w. Wmk inverted	38·00	12·00

(b) P 14.

686	**144**	1s. red-brown and carmine (Plate 1)	1·40	80
		aw. Wmk sideways inverted	14·00	9·00
		b. Wmk upright (Plate 1)	50	80
		c. Wmk upright (Plate 2)	2·25	1·25
		cw. Wmk inverted	60·00	23·00
687		1s.3d. red-brown and blue (Plate 2)	1·25	1·25
		aw. Wmk sideways inverted	9·50	6·00
		b. Wmk upright (14.1.52)	2·25	4·50
		bw. Wmk inverted	†	—
688		2s. brown-orange and green (Plate 1)	3·75	2·50
		aw. Wmk sideways inverted	16·00	12·00
		b. Wmk upright (Plate 1)	5·50	8·00
689		3s. red-brown and grey (Plate 2)	3·50	3·50
		w. Wmk sideways inverted	30·00	16·00
680/9		*Set of* 10	12·00	9·50

In head-plate 2 the diagonal lines of the background have been strengthened and result in the upper corners and sides appearing more deeply shaded.

(Des J. Berry. Recess Waterlow)

1947 (1 Oct). *Health Stamps.* W **98** (sideways). P 13½.

690	**145**	1d.+½d. green	15	15
		w. Wmk sideways inverted	40·00	40·00
691		2d.+1d. carmine	15	15
		w. Wmk sideways inverted	60·00	60·00

146 Port Chalmers, 1848

148 First Church, Dunedin

(Des J. Berry. Recess B.W.)

1948 (23 Feb). *Centennial of Otago. T* **146**, **148** *and similar designs.* W **98** (sideways on 3d.). P 13½.

692	1d. blue and green	25	35
	w. Wmk inverted	50·00	50·00
693	2d. green and brown	25	35
694	3d. purple	30	60
695	6d. black and rose	30	60
	w. Wmk inverted	—	£170
692/5	*Set of* 4	1·00	1·75

Designs: *Horiz*—2d. Cromwell, Otago; 6d. University of Otago.

150 Boy Sunbathing and Children Playing

151 Nurse and Child

(Des E. Linzell. Recess B.W.)

1948 (1 Oct). *Health Stamps.* W **98**. P 13½.

696	**150**	1d.+½d. blue and green	15	20
		w. Wmk inverted	40·00	30·00
697		2d.+1d. purple and scarlet	15	20

1949 ROYAL VISIT ISSUE. Four stamps were prepared to commemorate this event: 2d. Treaty House, Waitangi; 3d. H.M.S. *Vanguard*; 5d. Royal portraits; 6d. Crown and sceptre. The visit did not take place and the stamps were destroyed, although a few examples of the 3d. later appeared on the market. A similar set was prepared in 1952, but was, likewise, not issued.

(Des J. Berry. Photo Harrison)

1949 (3 Oct). *Health Stamps.* W **98.** P 14 × 14½.

698	**151**	1d.+½d. green	25	20
699		2d.+1d. ultramarine	25	20
		a. No stop below "D" of "1D." (R. 1/2)	6·50	16·00

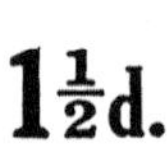

(152)

153 Queen Elizabeth IIand Prince Charles

1950 (28 July). *As Type F* **6**, *but without value, surch with T* **152**. *Chalk-surfaced paper.* W **98** (inverted). P 14.

700	**F 6**	1½d. carmine	40	30
		w. Wmk upright	3·00	3·75

(Des J. Berry and R. S. Phillips. Photo Harrison)

1950 (2 Oct). *Health Stamps.* W **98.** P 14 × 14½.

701	**153**	1d.+½d. green	25	20
		w. Wmk inverted	5·00	5·00
702		2d.+1d. plum	25	20
		w. Wmk inverted	25·00	30·00

154 Christchurch Cathedral

155 Cairn on Lyttleton Hills

(Des L. C. Mitchell (2d.), J. A. Johnstone (3d.) and J. Berry (others). Recess B.W.)

1950 (20 Nov). *Centennial of Canterbury, N.Z. T* **154/5** *and similar designs.* W **98** (sideways on 1d. and 3d.). P 13½.

703	1d. green and blue	35	55
704	2d. carmine and orange	35	55
705	3d. dark blue and blue	35	75
706	6d. brown and blue	45	75
707	1s. reddish purple and blue	45	1·00
703/7	*Set of* 5	1·75	3·25

Designs: *Vert* (*as T***154**)—3d. John Robert Godley. *Horiz* (*as T* **155**)—6d. Canterbury University College; 1s. Aerial view of Timaru.

159 "Takapuna" class Yachts

(Des J. Berry and R. S. Phillips. Recess B.W.)

1951 (1 Nov). *Health Stamps.* W **98**. P 13½.

708	**159**	1½d.+½d. scarlet and yellow	25	1·00
709		2d.+1d. deep green and yellow	25	2
		w. Wmk inverted	45·00	45·0

STAMP BOOKLETS

Nos. SB1 to SB19 are stapled.

Nos. SB1/5 were sold at ½d. above the face value of the stamps to cover the cost of manufacture.

1901 (1 Apr). *White card covers with postage rates.*

SB1	1s. ½d. booklet containing twelve 1d. (No. 278) in blocks of 6	£225
SB2	2s. 6½d. booklet containing thirty 1d. (No. 278) in blocks of 6	£300

Original printings of Nos. SB1/2 showed the face value on the cover in small figures. Subsequent printings show large figures of value on the covers and the prices quoted are for this type.

1902 (21 Aug)–**05**. *White card covers with postage rates.*

SB3	1s. ½d. booklet containing twelve 1d. in panes of 6 (Nos. 303b or 303cb)	£180
SB4	2s. ½d. booklet containing twenty-four 1d. in panes of 6 (Nos. 303b or 303cb) (21.3.05)	£200
SB5	2s. 6½d. booklet containing thirty 1d. in panes of 6 (Nos. 303b or 303cb)	£275

1910 (Apr). *White card cover with postage rates*

SB6	2s. booklet containing eleven ½d. in pane of 5 with 1 label (Nos. 387b or 387c) and pane of 6 (No. 387d), and eighteen 1d. in three panes of 6 (No. 405b)	£375

1912 (May). *White card cover.*

SB7	2s. booklet containing twelve ½d. and eighteen 1d. in panes of 6 with bars on the selvedge (Nos. 387e, 405c)	£275
	a. Blue cover	

1915 (Feb). *Red card cover.*

SB8	2s. booklet containing twelve ½d. and eighteen 1d. in panes of 6 with bars on the selvedge (Nos. 435a or 435ba, 405c)	£150
	a. Grey cover	
	b. Blue cover	
	c. Yellow-buff cover	
	d. Purple-buff cover	

1924 (1 Dec)–**25**. *Cover inscription within frame.*

SB 9	2s. booklet containing twelve ½d. and eighteen 1d. in panes of 6 with bars on the selvedge (Nos. 441a, 406b) (lilac cover)	£16
	a. Grey cover	
SB10	2s. booklet containing twelve ½d. and eighteen 1d. in panes of 6 with bars and advertisements on the selvedge (Nos. 446a, 410b) (yellow-buff cover) (1925)	£18
	a. Grey-green cover	£18
	b. Grey-buff cover	
	c. Grey-pink cover	£20

1928–34.

SB11	2s. booklet containing twelve ½d. (P 14 × 15) and eighteen 1d. in panes of 6 with bars on the selvedge (Nos. 446ab, 468b)	£20
	a. As No. SB11, but ½d. (P 14) (Nos. 446ca, 468b)	£15
	b. As No. SB11 but panes with bars and advertisements on the selvedge (Nos. 446cb, 468c)	£15
SB12	2s. booklet containing twenty-four 1d (P 14) in panes of 6 with bars and advertisements on the selvedge (No.468c) (1930)	£15
	a. As No. SB12, but 1d. (P 14 × 15) (No. 468ea) (1934)	£14

1935.
SB15 2s. booklet containing twenty-four 1d, in panes of 6 with advertisements on the selvedge (No. 557ca) . . . £375

1936.
SB16 2s. booklet containing twenty-four 1d. (No. 578) in blocks of 6 . . . £250

B 1

1938 (1 July). *Cream cover as Type* **B 1**.
SB17 2s. booklet containing twenty-four 1d. (No. 605) in blocks of 6 . . . £325

1938 (Nov). *Cream (No. SB18) or blue (No. SB19) covers as Type* **B 1**.
SB18 2s. booklet containing twelve ½d. and eighteen 1d. (Nos. 603, 605) in blocks of 6 . . . £425
SB19 2s.3d. booklet containing eighteen 1½d. (No. 607) in blocks of 6 . . . £375

EXPRESS DELIVERY STAMPS

E 1

(Typo Govt Printing Office, Wellington)

1903 (9 Feb). *Value in first colour.* W **43** (sideways). P 11.
E1 **E 1** 6d. red and violet . . . 38·00 23·00

1926–36. *Thick, white, opaque chalk-surfaced "Cowan" paper.* W **43**.
(a) P 14 × 14½.
E2 **E 1** 6d. vermilion and bright violet . . . 42·00 25·00
w. Wmk inverted . . . £130
(b) P 14 × 15 (1936).
E3 **E 1** 6d. carmine and bright violet . . . 55·00 60·00

1937–39. *Thin, hard, chalk-surfaced "Wiggins Teape" paper.*
(a) P 14 × 14½.
E4 **E 1** 6d. carmine and bright violet . . . 85·00 48·00
(b) P 14 × 15 (1939).
E5 **E 1** 6d. vermilion and bright violet . . . £150 £250

E 2 Express Post Delivery Car

Des J. Berry. Eng Stamp Ptg Office, Melbourne Recess Govt Ptg Office, Wellington)

1939 (16 Aug). W **43**. P14.
E6 **E 2** 6d. violet . . . 1·50 1·75
w. Wmk inverted . . . 80·00

POSTAGE DUE STAMPS

D 1 (I)

(II)

3D. 5D.
(a) Large "D" (b) Small "D"

(Typo Govt Printing Office, Wellington)

1899 (1 Dec). *Coarse paper.* W **12b**. P 11.
Type I. Circle of 14 ornaments, 17 dots over "N.Z.", "N.Z." large.
(a) Large "D".
D1 **D 1** ½d. carmine and green . . . 16·00 27·00
a. No stop after "D" (Right pane R. 2/3) . . . 85·00 £140
D2 8d. carmine and green . . . 60·00 75·00
a. Carmine "8D." printed double
D3 1s. carmine and green . . . 65·00 85·00
D4 2s. carmine and green . . . £120 £140
D1/4 *Set of* 4 . . . £225 £275

To avoid further subdivision the 1s. and 2s. are placed with the *pence* values, although the two types of "D" do not apply to the higher values.

(b) Small "D".
D6 **D 1** 5d. carmine and green . . . 22·00 24·00
D7 6d. carmine and green . . . 29·00 29·00
D8 10d. carmine and green . . . 70·00 85·00
D6/8 *Set of* 3 . . . £110 £120

II. Type II. Circle of *13 ornaments, 15* dots over *"N.Z.", "N.Z." small.*
(a) Large "D".
D 9 **D 1** ½d. vermilion and green . . . 3·00 16·00
a. No stop after "D" (Right pane R. 2/3) . . . 55·00 95·00
D10 1d. vermilion and green . . . 12·00 2·00
D11 2d. vermilion and green . . . 48·00 9·00
D12 3d. vermilion and green . . . 13·00 3·50
D9/12 *Set of* 4 . . . 70·00 27·00
(b) Small "D".
D14 **D 1** 1d. vermilion and green . . . 15·00 1·50
D15 2d. vermilion and green . . . 45·00 6·00
D16 4d. vermilion and green . . . 32·00 9·00
D14/16 *Set of* 3 . . . 85·00 15·00

Nos. D9/16 were printed from a common frame plate of 240 (4 panes of 60) used in conjunction with centre plates of 120 (2 panes of 60) for the ½d. and 4d. or 240 for the other values. Sheets of the ld. and 2d. each contained two panes with large "D" and two panes with small "D".

D 2 D 3

(Des W. R. Bock. Typo Govt Printing Office)

1902 (28 Feb). No wmk. P 11.
D17 **D 2** ½d. red and deep green . . . 1·75 7·00

1904–08. *"Cowan" unsurfaced paper.* W **43** (sideways).
(a) P 11.
D18 **D 2** ½d. red and green (4.04) . . . 1·75 2·00
a. Imperf between (horiz pair) . . . £600
D19 1d. red and green (5.12.05) . . . 9·50 3·50
D20 2d. red and green (5.4.06) . . . 90·00 £100
D18/20 *Set of* 3 . . . 90·00 £100
(b) P 14.
D21 **D 2** 1d. carmine and green (12.06) . . . 14·00 1·50
a. Rose-pink and green (9.07) . . . 13·00 1·50
D22 2d. carmine and green (10.06) . . . 9·00 6·00
a. Rose-pink and green (6.08) . . . 5·50 2·00

1919 (Jan)–**20**. *"De La Rue" chalky paper. Toned gum.* W **43**. P 14 × 15.
D23 **D 2** ½d. carmine and green (6.19) . . . 3·25 3·75
D24 1d. carmine and green . . . 7·00 50
w. Wmk inverted . . . † —
D25 2d. carmine and green (8.20) . . . 13·00 2·75
D23/5 *Set of* 3 . . . 21·00 6·25

1925 (May). *"Jones" chalky paper. White gum.* W **43**. P 14 × 15.
D26 **D 2** ½d. carmine and green . . . 35·00 42·00

1925 (July). No wmk, but bluish "N Z" and Star lithographed on back. P 14 × 15.
D27 **D 2** ½d. carmine and green . . . 2·00 23·00
D28 2d. carmine and green . . . 3·50 23·00

1925 (Nov)–**35**. *"Cowan" thick, opaque chalky paper.* W **43**.
(a) P 14 × 15.
D29 **D 2** ½d. carmine and green (12.26) . . . 1·75 8·50
D30 1d. carmine and green . . . 3·75 80
D31 2d. carmine and green (6.26) . . . 19·00 4·25
x. Wmk reversed . . . 30·00 20·00
D32 3d. carmine and green (1.35) . . . 48·00 55·00
D29/32 *Set of* 4 . . . 65·00 60·00
(b) P 14.
D33 **D 2** ½d. carmine and green (10.28) . . . 48·00 30·00
D34 1d. rose and pale yellow-green (6.28) . . . 4·00 1·25
D35 2d. carmine and green (10.29) . . . 7·00 3·00
D36 3d. carmine and green (5.28) . . . 15·00 42·00
D33/6 *Set of* 4 . . . 65·00 70·00

1937–38. *"Wiggins Teape" thin, hard chalky paper.* W **43**. P 14 × 15.
D37 **D 2** ½d. carmine and yellow-green (2.38) . . . 25·00 35·00
D38 1d. carmine and yellow-green (1.37) . . . 11·00 3·75
D39 2d. carmine and yellow-green (6.37) . . . 38·00 13·00
D40 3d. carmine and yellow-green (11.37) . . . 95·00 70·00
D37/40 *Set of* 4 . . . £150 £110

(Des J. Berry. Typo Govt Printing Office, Wellington)

1939–49. P 15 × 14.
(a) W **43** (sideways inverted) (16.8.39).
D41 **D 3** ½d. turquoise-green . . . 5·00 5·00
D42 1d. carmine . . . 2·75 50
w. Wmk sideways . . . £150 4·00
D43 2d. bright blue . . . 6·00 2·75
D44 3d. orange-brown . . . 23·00 25·00
w. Wmk sideways
D41/4 *Set of* 4 . . . 32·00 30·00

(b) W **98** (sideways (1d.), sideways inverted (2d.) or upright (3d.).
D45 **D 3** 1d. carmine (4.49) . . . 16·00 5·50*
D46 2d. bright blue (12.46) . . . 8·00 1·40
w. Wmk sideways (4.49) . . . 2·75 9·00
D47 3d. orange-brown (1943) . . . 50·00 32·00
a. Wmk sideways inverted (6.45) . . . 20·00 5·50
aw. Wmk sideways (28.11.49) . . . 9·00 9·00
D45/7 *Set of* 3 . . . 25·00 11·00*

*The use of Postage Due stamps ceased on 30 September 1951, our used price for No. D45 being for stamps postmarked after this date (*price for examples clearly cancelled* 1949–51, £27).

OFFICIAL STAMPS

1891 (Dec)–**1906**. *Contemporary issues handstamped "O.P.S.O." diagonally.*

(a) Stamps of 1873 type. W **12b**. P 12½.
O 1 **3** ½d. rose (V.) . . . — £500

(b) Stamps of 1882–97 optd in rose or magenta. W**12b**.
O 2 **13** ½d. black (P 10) . . . — £225
a. Violet opt . . . — £275
O 3 ½d. black (P 10 × 11) . . . — £225
O 4 **14** 1d. rose (P 12 × 11½) . . . — £225
O 5 1d. rose (P 11) . . . — £225
O 6 **15** 2d. purple (P 11) . . . — £375
O 7 2d. mauve-lilac (P 10) . . . — £375
a. Violet opt
O 8 **16** 2½d. blue (P 11) . . . — £275
O 9 2½d. ultramarine (P 10) . . . — £275
O10 2½d. ultramarine (P 10 × 11) . . . — £275
O11 **19** 5d. olive-black (P 12 × 11½) . . . — £425
O12 **20** 6d. brown (P 12 × 11½) . . . — £600

(c) Stamps of 1898–1903 optd in violet. P 11.
(i) No wmk.
O13 **23** ½d. green (P 14) (No. 294) . . . — £225
O14 **26** 2½d. blue (P 12–16) (No. 249*a*) . . . — £450
O15 **27** 2½d. blue (No. 260) . . . — £375
O16 **37** 4d. indigo and brown (No. 262) . . . — £425
O17 **30** 5d. purple-brown (No. 263) . . . — £450
a. Green opt . . . — £425
O18 **32** 8d. indigo (No. 266) . . . — £550
(ii) W**38**.
O19 **42** 1d. carmine (No. 278) . . . — £250
(iii) W**43** (sideways on 3d., 1s.).
O20 **42** 1d. carmine (P 14) (No. 303) . . . — £250
a. Green opt . . . — £250
O21 **27** 2½d. blue (No. 308) . . . — £325
O22 **28** 3d. yellow-brown (No 309) . . . — £450
O23 **34** 1s. orange-red (No. 315*b*) . . . — £900
O24 **36** 2s. green (No. 316) . . . — £1400

The letters signify "On Public Service Only", and stamps so overprinted were used by the Post Office Department at Wellington on official correspondence to foreign countries.

Unused examples with the "O.P.S.O." handstamp are generally considered to be reprints.

(O 3)

1907–11. *Stamps of 1902–6 optd with Type* **O 3** *(vertically, upwards).* W **43** (sideways on 3d., 6d., 1s. and 5s.). P 14.
O59 **23** ½d. yellow-green . . . 9·00 60
a. Perf 11 × 14 . . . £110
b. Mixed perfs . . . £110
O60 **42** 1d. carmine (No. 303) (1.7.07*) . . . 7·50 12·00
a. Booklet pane of 6 . . . 42·00
ab. Imperf horiz (booklet pane of 6) . . . £1400
O60*b* 1d. rose-carmine (Waterlow) (No. 352) . . . 10·00 50
ba. Perf 11 × 14 . . . — £250
bb. Mixed perfs . . . — £250
O60*c* 1d. carmine (Royle) . . . 21·00 50
ca. Perf 11 × 14 . . . £225
cb. Mixed perfs . . . £225
O61 **41** 2d. purple . . . 9·00 1·75
a. Bright reddish purple . . . 8·50 1·60
ab. Mixed perfs . . . £190 £200
O63 **28** 3d. bistre-brown . . . 45·00 1·75
O64 **31** 6d. bright carmine-pink . . . £140 20·00
a. Imperf vert (horiz pair) . . . £800
b. Mixed perfs . . . £500 £450
O65 **34** 1s. orange-red . . . 85·00 15·00
O66 **35** 2s. blue-green . . . 70·00 75·00
a. Imperf between (pair) . . . £1700
b. Imperf vert (horiz pair) . . . £1400
w. Wmk inverted . . . £275 £275
O67 **36** 5s. deep red . . . £150 £170
a. Wmk upright (1911) . . . £700 £750

*Though issued in 1907 a large quantity of booklets was mislaid and not utilized until they were found in 1930.

1908–09. *Optd as Type* **O 3**. W **43**.
O69 **23** ½d. green (P 14 × 15) . . . 7·50 2·75
O70 **50** 1d. carmine (P 14 × 15) . . . 65·00 2·75
O71 **48** 6d. pink (P 14 × 13, 13½) . . . £140 45·00
O72 6d. pink (P 14 × 15) (1909) . . . £130 35·00
O72*a* **F 4** £1 rose-pink (P 14) (No. F89) . . . £500 £400

1910. *No. 387 optd with Type* **O 3**.
O73 **51** ½d. yellow-green . . . 5·00 30
a. Opt inverted (reading downwards) . . . † £1400

1910–16. *Nos. 389 and 392/4 optd with Type* O **3**. P 14 × 14½.
O74 **52** 3d. chestnut . . . 14·00 80
a. Perf 14 × 13½ (1915) . . . 60·00 75·00
ab. Vert pair. Nos. O74/a . . . £300 £400
O75 – 6d. carmine . . . 19·00 5·50
a. Perf 14 (line) (No. 398) . . . † —
b. Deep carmine . . . 25·00 5·50
w. Wmk inverted . . .
O76 – 8d. indigo-blue (R.) (5.16) . . . 12·00 18·00
aw. Wmk inverted . . . 38·00 38·00
b. Perf 14 × 13½ . . . 12·00 18·00
bw. Wmk inverted . . . 32·00 32·00
c. Vert pair, Nos. O76 and O76b . . 45·00 80·00
cw. Wmk inverted . . . £100 £130
O77 1s. vermilion . . . 48·00 15·00
O74/7 *Set of* 4 . . . 85·00 35·00

1910–26. *Optd with Type* O **3**.
(a) W **43**. *De La Rue chalk-surfaced paper with toned gum.*
O78 **53** 1d. carmine (No. 405) . . . 3·25 10
y. Wmk inverted and reversed . . .
(b) W **43**. *Jones chalk-surfaced paper with white gum.*
O79 **53** 1d. deep carmine (No. 406) (1925) . . 10·00 6·50
(c) No wmk, but bluish "NZ" and Star lithographed on back. Art paper.
O80 **53** 1d. rose-carmine (No. 409) (1925) . . 6·00 17·00
(d) W**43**. *Cowan thick, opaque, chalk-surfaced paper with white gum.*
O81 **53** 1d. deep carmine (No. 410) (1925) . . 8·00 1·25
x. Wmk reversed (1926) . . . 28·00 20·00

1913–25. *Postal Fiscal stamps optd with Type* O **3**.
(i) Chalk-surfaced De La Rue paper.
(a) P 14 (1913–14).
O82 **F 4** 2s. blue (30.9.14) . . . 48·00 45·00
O83 5s. yellow-green (13.6.13) . . . 75·00 90·00
O84 £1 rose-carmine (1913) . . . £550 £550
O82/4 *Set of* 3 . . . £600 £600
(b) P 14½ × 14, comb (1915).
O85 **F 4** 2s. deep blue (Aug) . . . 55·00 45·00
a. No stop after "OFFICIAL" . . £120 £100
O86 5s. yellow-green (Jan) . . . 65·00 80·00
a. No stop after "OFFICIAL" . . £200 £250
(ii) Thick, white, opaque chalk-surfaced Cowan paper. P 14½ × 14 (1925).
O87 **F 4** 2s. blue . . . 80·00 75·00
a. No stop after "OFFICIAL" . . £190 £190

The overprint on these last, and on Nos. O69 and O72*a* is from a new set of type, giving a rather sharper impression than Type O **3**, but otherwise resembling it closely.

1915 (12 Oct)–**34**. *Optd with Type* O 3. P 14 × 15.
(a) On Nos. 435/40 (De La Rue chalk-surfaced paper with toned gum).
O88 **61** ½d. green . . . 1·25 20
O89 **62** 1½d. grey-black (6.16) . . . 7·00 2·50
O90 **61** 1½d. slate (12.16) . . . 5·00 1·00
O91 1½d. orange-brown (4.19) . . . 5·00 30
O92 2d. yellow (4.17) . . . 5·00 20
O93 3d. chocolate (11.19) . . . 11·00 90
O88/93 *Set of* 6 . . . 30·00 4·50
(b) On Nos. 441 and 443 (Jones chalk-surfaced paper with white gum).
O94 **61** ½d. green (1924) . . . 4·50 3·50
O95 3d. deep chocolate (1924) . . . 38·00 9·50
(c) On Nos. 446/7 and 448a/9 (Cowan thick, opaque, chalk surfaced paper with white gum).
O96 **61** ½d. green (1925) . . . 1·50 10
ax. Wmk reversed (1927) . . . 12·00 13·00
ay. Wmk inverted and reversed (1927) . . . 35·00 24·00
b. Perf 14 (1929) . . . 3·50 40
ba. No stop after "OFFICIAL" . . 25·00 32·00
O97 1½d. orange-brown (P 14) (1929) . . 10·00 12·00
a. No stop after "OFFICIAL" . . 55·00 65·00
b. Perf 14 × 15 (1934) . . . 25·00 30·00
O98 2d. yellow (P 14) (1931) . . . 2·50 50
a. No stop after "OFFICIAL" . . 40·00 45·00
O99 3d. chocolate (1925) . . . 5·00 50
a. No stop after "OFFICIAL" . . 65·00 45·00
b. Perf 14 (1930) . . . 38·00 1·75
ba. No stop after "OFFICIAL" . . £120 55·00
O96/9 *Set of* 4 . . . 17·00 13·00

1915 (Dec)–**27**. *Optd with type* O **3**. P 14 × 13½.
(a) Nos. 420, 422, 425, 428 and 429/30 (Cowan unsurfaced paper).
O100 **60** 3d. chocolate . . . 4·50 1·50
aw. Wmk inverted . . . 15·00 4·50
b. Perf 14 × 14½ . . . 4·50 1·75
bw. Wmk inverted . . . 15·00 4·50
c. Vert pair, Nos. O100 and O100b . . . 35·00 85·00
cw. Wmk inverted . . . 75·00 £110
O101 4d. bright violet (4.25) . . . 14·00 3·75
a. Re-entry (Pl 20 R. 1/6) . . . 45·00 22·00
b. Re-entry (Pl 20 R. 4/10) . . . 50·00 30·00
c. Perf 14 × 14½ (4.27) . . . 27·00 1·00
O102 6d. carmine (6.16) . . . 5·00 75
aw. Wmk inverted . . . 90·00
b. Perf 14 × 14½ . . . 5·00 1·25
c. Vert pair, Nos. O102 and O102b . . . 55·00 £120
O103 8d. red-brown (8.22) . . . 65·00 £160
O104 9d. sage-green (4.25) . . . 40·00 38·00
O105 1s. vermilion (9.16) . . . 18·00 13·00
aw. Wmk inverted . . . £180 £120
b. Perf 14 × 14½ . . . 7·00 2·00
ba. Pale orange-red . . . 15·00 20·00
bw. Wmk inverted . . . £180 £180
c. Vert pair. Nos. O105 and O105b . . . 65·00 £150
cw. Wmk inverted . . . £450
O100/5 *Set of* 6 . . . £120 £170
(b) No. 433 (Thin paper with widely spaced sideways wmk).
O106 **60** 3d. chocolate (P 14) (7.16) . . . 3·00 12·00
a. No wmk . . . 35·00 55·00

1927–33. *Optd with Type* O **3**. W **43**. P 14.
O111 **71** 1d. rose-carmine (No. 468) . . . 2·00 20
a. No stop after "OFFICIAL" . . 28·00 60·00
bw. Wmk inverted . . . † 30·00
c. Perf 14 × 15 . . . 2·50 20
O112 **72** 2s. light blue (No. 469) (2.28) . . 70·00 £100
O113 **F 6** 5s. green (1933) . . . £250 £300
O111/13 *Set of* 3 . . . £300 £350

Official (O **4**)   Official (O **5**)

1936–61. *Pictorial issue optd horiz or vert (2s.) with Type* O **4**.
(a) W **43** (Single "N Z" and Star).
O115 **82** 1d. scarlet (Die I) (P 14 × 13½) . . 3·75 1·25
a. Perf 13½ × 14 . . . 80·00 65·00
O116 **83** 1½d. red-brown (P 13½ × 14) . . . 25·00 27·00
a. Perf 14 × 13½ . . . £6000
O118 **92** 1s. deep green (P 14 × 13½) . . . 28·00 45·00
w. Wmk inverted . . . † £110
O119 **F 6** 5s. green (P 14) (12.38) . . . £130 45·00
O115/19 *Set of* 4 . . . £170 £110

The watermark of No. O119 is almost invisible.

Only four examples of No. O116a exist. The error occurred when a sheet of No. 558a was found to have a block of four missing. This was replaced by a block of No. 558 and the sheet was then sent for overprinting.

(b) W**98** (Mult "N Z" and Star).
O120 **81** ½d. bright green, P 14 × 13½ (7.37) . . . 7·50 4·50
O121 **82** 1d. scar (Die II), P 14 × 13½ (11.36) . . . 5·50 50
w. Wmk inverted . . . 13·00 11·00
O122 **83** 1½d. red-brown, P 14 × 13½ (7.36) . . . 21·00 4·75
O123 **84** 2d. orange, P 14 × 13½ (1.38) . . . 3·75 10
aw. Wmk inverted . . . — £120
b. Perf 12½ (1942) . . . £190 55·00
c. Perf 14 (1942) . . . 50·00 15·00
O124 **85** 2½d. chocolate & slate, P 13-14 × 13½ (26.7.38) . . . 55·00 85·00
a. Perf 14 (1938) . . . 14·00 21·00
O125 **86** 3d. brown, P 14 × 13½ (1.3.38) . . 48·00 3·50
w. Wmk inverted . . . — 65·00
O126 **87** 4d. black and sepia, P 14 × 13½ (8.36) . . . 9·50 1·10
a. Perf 14 (8.41) . . . 9·50 4·50
b. Perf 12½ (1941) . . . 7·50 6·50
c. Perf 14 × 14½ (10.42) . . . 4·50 1·00
cw. Wmk inverted . . . — 90·00
O127 **89** 6d. scarlet, P 13½ × 14 (12.37) . . 19·00 80
aw. Wmk inverted . . . † —
b. Perf 12½ (1941) . . . 15·00 5·50
c. Perf 14½ × 14 (7.42) . . . 10·00 30
O128 **90** 8d. chocolate, P 12½ (wmk sideways) (1942) . . . 15·00 17·00
a. Perf 14 × 14½ (wmk sideways) (1945) . . . 8·50 16·00
b. Perf 14 × 13½ . . . † £2000
O129 **91** 9d. red & grey-black (G.) (No. 587*a*), P 13½ × 14 (1.3.38) . . . 75·00 38·00
O130 9d. scar & blk (*chalk-surfaced paper*) (Blk.) (No. 631), P 14 × 15 (1943) . . . 20·00 22·00
O131 **92** 1s. deep green, P 14 × 13½ (2.37) . . . 50·00 1·50
aw. Wmk inverted . . . — 95·00
b. Perf 12½ (1942) . . . 25·00 1·75
O132 **93** 2s. olive-green, P 13-14 × 13½ (5.37) . . . 80·00 35·00
a. "CAPTAIN COQK" . . . £110
b. Perf 13½ × 14 (1939) . . . £180 6·50
ba. "CAPTAIN COQK" . . . £200
c. Perf 12½ (1942) . . . 80·00 22·00
ca. "CAPTAIN COQK" . . . £110
d. Perf 14 × 13½ (1944) . . . 42·00 7·50
da. "CAPTAIN COQK" . . . £250
O133 **F 6** 5s. green (*chalk-surfaced paper*), P 14 (3.43) . . . 42·00 6·00
aw. Wmk inverted . . . 40·00 6·00
b. Perf 14 × 13½. Yellow-green (*ordinary paper*) (10.61) . . . 17·00 32·00
O120/33 *Set of* 14 . . . £275 £110

The opt on No. O127a was sometimes applied at the top of the stamp, instead of always at the bottom as on No. O127.

All examples of No. O128b were used by a government office in Whangerei.

The 5s. value on ordinary paper perforated 14 × 13½ does not exist without the "Official" overprint.

See notes on perforations after No. 590b.

1938–51. *Nos. 603 etc., optd with Type* O **4**.
O134 **108** ½d. green (1.3.38) . . . 19·00 2·25
O135 ½d. brown-orange (1946) . . . 1·60 3·50
O136 1d. scarlet (1.7.38) . . . 19·00 15
O137 1d. green (10.7.41) . . . 3·00 10
O138 **108a** 1½d. purple-brown (26.7.38) . . . 75·00 18·00
O139 1½d. scarlet (2.4.51) . . . 9·00 6·00
O140 3d. blue (16.10.41) . . . 3·00 10
O134/40 *Set of* 7 . . . £110 27·00

1940 (2 Jan–8 Mar). *Centennial. Nos. 613, etc., optd with Type* O **5**.
O141 ½d. blue-green (R.) . . . 2·50 35
a. "ff" joined, as Type O **4** . . . 50·00 60·00
O142 1d. chocolate and scarlet . . . 5·00 10
a. "ff" joined, as Type O **4** . . . 50·00 60·00
O143 1½d. light blue and mauve . . . 3·50 2·00
O144 2d. blue-green and chocolate . . . 5·00 10
a. "ff" joined, as Type O **4** . . . 60·00 60·00
O145 2½d. blue-green and ultramarine . . . 4·75 2·75
a. "ff" joined, as Type O **4** . . . 50·00 65·00
O146 3d. purple and carmine (R.) . . . 8·00 1·00
a. "ff" joined, as Type O **4** . . . 42·00 48·00
O147 4d. chocolate and lake . . . 40·00 1·50
a. "ff" joined, as Type O **4** . . . £120 90·00
O148 6d. emerald-green and violet . . . 25·00 1·50
a. "ff" joined, as Type O **4** . . . 70·00 70·00
O149 8d. black and red (8.3) . . . 30·00 17·00
a. "ff" joined, as Type O **4** . . . 70·00 £100
O150 9d. olive-green and vermilion . . . 11·00 5·00
O151 1s. sage-green and deep green . . . 48·00 3·00
O141/51 *Set of* 11 . . . £160 30·00

For this issue the Type O **4** overprint occurs on R. 4/3 of the 2½d. and on R. 1/10 of the other values.

1947–49. *Nos. 680, etc., optd with Type* O **4**.
O152 **108a** 2d. orange . . . 2·25 10
O153 4d. bright purple . . . 4·25 2·50
O154 6d. carmine . . . 13·00 50
O155 8d. violet . . . 8·00 6·50
O156 9d. purple-brown . . . 9·00 6·50
O157 **144** 1s. red-brown and carmine (wmk upright) (Plate 1) . . . 17·00 1·00
a. Wmk sideways (Plate 1) (1949) . . . 8·50 9·00
aw. Wmk sideways inverted . . . 35·00 15·00
b. Wmk upright (Plate 2) . . . 24·00 7·00
bw. Wmk inverted . . . 65·00 28·00
O158 2s. brown-orange and green (wmk sideways) (Plate 1) . . . 27·00 16·00
a. Wmk upright (Plate 1) . . . 32·00 48·00
O152/8 *Set of* 7 . . . 65·00 30·00

STAMP BOOKLET

1907 (1 July). *White card cover.*
OB1 10s. booklet containing one hundred and twenty 1d. in panes of 6 (No. O60a) . . . £1000

PROVISIONALS ISSUED AT REEFTON AND USED BY THE POLICE DEPARTMENT

1907 (Jan). *Current stamps of 1906, optd "Official", in red manuscript and handstamped with a circular "Greymouth—PAID—3".* P 14.
P1 **23** ½d. green . . . £1000 £1200
P2 **40** 2d. carmine . . . £1100 £1100
P3 **38a** 2d. purple . . . £1300 £1500
P4 **28** 3d. bistre . . . £1800
P5 **31** 6d. pink . . . £1800
P6 **34** 1s. orange-red . . . £2250
P7 **35** 2s. green . . . £6500

Only the ½d., 1d. and 2d. are known postally used, cancelled with the Reefton squared circle postmark. The 3d. and 6d. were later cancelled by favour at Wanganui.

LIFE INSURANCE DEPARTMENT

L **1** Lighthouse   L **2** Lighthouse

(Des W. B. Hudson and J. F. Rogers; Eng. A. E. Cousins. Typo Govt Printing Office, Wellington)

1891 (2 Jan)–**98**.
A. W**12***c*. P 12 × 11½.
L 1 **L 1** ½d. bright purple . . . 65·00 6·0
a. Mixed perf 12 × 11 and 12½ . . . † –
x. Wmk reversed . . . † –
L 2 1d. blue . . . 55·00 4·0
ax. Wmk reversed . . .
ay. Wmk inverted and reversed . . . † 35·0
b. Wmk **12***b* . . . 90·00 20·0
bx. Wmk reversed . . . † –
L 3 2d. brown-red . . . 85·00 7·5
ax. Wmk reversed . . . † 85·0
b. Wmk **12***b* . . . 95·00 14·0
L 4 3d. deep brown . . . £170 22·0
L 5 6d. green . . . £275 60·0
L 6 1s. rose . . . £500 £12
L1/6 *Set of* 6 . . . £1000 £20
B. W**12***b* (1893–98).
(a) P 10 (1893).
L 7 **L 1** ½d. bright purple . . . 65·00 9·0
L 8 1d. blue . . . 55·00 1·5
L 9 2d. brown-red . . . 80·00 3·7
L7/9 *Set of* 3 . . . £170 13·0
(b) P 11 × 10.
L10 **L 1** ½d. bright purple (1896) . . . 90·00 27·0
a. Perf 10 × 11 . . . £160 65·0
L11 1d. blue (1897) . . . † 40·0
a. Perf 10 × 11 . . . 60·00 13·0
(c) Mixed perfs 10 and 11 (1897).
L12 **L 1** 2d. brown-red . . . £650 £65
(d) P 11 (1897–98).
L13 **L 1** ½d. bright purple . . . 55·00 3·7
a. Thin coarse toned paper (1898) . . . 80·00 5·5
L14 1d. blue . . . 55·00
a. Thin coarse toned paper (1898) . . . 75·00 2·5
x. Wmk reversed . . . £120 13·
y. Wmk inverted and reversed . . . £120 24·
L15 2d. brown-red . . . 80·00 3·
a. Chocolate . . . £110 24·
b. Thin coarse toned paper (1898) . . . £140 3·
L13/15 *Set of* 3 . . . £170 7·

1902–04. W **43** (sideways).
(a) P 11.
L16 **L 1** ½d. bright purple (1903) . . . 55·00 6·
L17 1d. blue (1902) . . . 55·00 1·
L18 2d. brown-red (1904) . . . 95·00 9·
L16/18 *Set of* 3 . . . £180 15·
(b) P 14 × 11.
L19 **L 1** ½d. bright purple (1903) . . . £1400
L20 1d. blue (1904) . . . 95·00 11·

Nos. L16/17 and L20 are known without watermark from the margins of the sheet.

1905–06. *Redrawn, with "V.R." omitted.* W **43** (sideways).

(a) P 11.

L21	L **2**	2d. brown-red (12.05)	£1000	90·00

(b) P 14.

L22	L **2**	1d. blue (7.06)	£160	30·00

(c) P 14 × 11.

L23	L **2**	1d. blue (7.06)	£475	£150
		a. Mixed perfs	†	£400

Between January 1907 and the end of 1912 the Life Insurance Department used ordinary Official stamps.

1913 (2 Jan)–**37**. *New values and colours.* W **43**.

(a) "De La Rue" paper. P 14 × 15.

L24	L **2**	½d. green	14·00	2·00
		a. Yellow-green	14·00	2·00
L25		1d. carmine	8·50	1·00
		a. Carmine-pink	15·00	1·40
L26		1½d. black (1917)	40·00	8·00
L27		1½d. chestnut-brown (1919)	1·50	2·75
L28		2d. bright purple	48·00	28·00
		w. Wmk inverted	†	90·00
L29		2d. yellow (1920)	5·50	2·00
L30		3d. yellow-brown	45·00	26·00
L31		6d. carmine-pink	35·00	23·00
L24/31 *Set of* 8			£180	85·00

(b) "Cowan" paper. (i) P 14 × 15.

L31*a*	L **2**	½d. yellow-green (1925)	32·00	4·50
L31*b*		1d. carmine-pink (1925)	32·00	3·50
		bw. Wmk inverted	40·00	5·50

(ii) P 14.

L32	L **2**	½d. yellow-green (1926)	10·00	2·75
		w. Wmk inverted	†	15·00
L33		1d. scarlet (1931)	7·50	2·00
		w. Wmk inverted	14·00	3·25
L34		2d. yellow (1937)	7·00	6·00
		w. Wmk inverted	32·00	26·00
L35		3d. brown-lake (1931)	18·00	23·00
L36		6d. pink (1925)	35·00	38·00
L32/6 *Set of* 5			70·00	65·00

(c) "Wiggins Teape" paper. P 14 × 15.

L36*a*	L **2**	½d. yellow-green (3.37)	8·00	12·00
L36*b*		1d. scarlet (3.37)	15·00	3·25
L36*c*		6d. pink (7.37)	35·00	40·00
L36*a/c Set of* 3			50·00	50·00

For descriptions of the various types of paper, see after No. 385. In the 1½d. the word "POSTAGE" is in both the side-labels instead of at left only.

1944–47. W **98**. P 14 × 15.

L37	L **2**	½d. yellow-green (7.47)	5·50	9·00
L38		1d. scarlet (6.44)	3·25	2·00
L39		2d. yellow (1946)	12·00	16·00
L40		3d. brown-lake (10.46)	17·00	38·00
L41		6d. pink (7.47)	13·00	35·00
L37/41 *Set of* 5			45·00	90·00

L **3** Castlepoint Lighthouse

N.Z. GOVERNMENT LIFE INSURANCE OFFICE
CAPE CAMPBELL
2½d POSTAGE

L **6** Cape Campbell Lighthouse

(Des J. Berry. Recess B.W.).

1947 (1 Aug)–**65**. *Type* L **3**, L **6** *and similar designs.* W **98** (sideways inverted on 1d., 2d., sideways on 2½d.). P 13½.

L42	½d. grey-green and orange-red	1·50	70
L43	1d. olive-green and pale blue	1·75	1·25
L44	2d. deep blue and grey-black	1·00	1·00
L45	2½d. black and bright blue (*white opaque paper*) (4.11.63)	9·50	13·00
L46	3d. mauve and pale blue	3·25	1·00
L47	4d. brown and yellow-orange	4·25	1·75
	a. Wmk sideways (*white opaque paper*) (13.10.65)	4·00	14·00
L48	6d. chocolate and blue	4·00	2·50
L49	1s. red-brown and blue	4·00	3·25
L42/49 *Set of* 8		26·00	22·00

Designs: *Horiz (as Type* L **3**)—1d. Taiaroa lighthouse; 2d. Cape Palliser lighthouse; 6d. The Brothers lighthouse. *Vert (as Type* L **6**)—3d. Eddystone lighthouse; 4d. Stephens Island lighthouse; 1s. Cape Brett lighthouse.

POSTAL FISCAL STAMPS

As from 1 April 1882 fiscal stamps were authorised for postal use and conversely postage stamps became valid for fiscal use. Stamps in the designs of 1867 with "STAMP DUTY" above the Queen's head were withdrawn and although some passed through the mail quite legitimately they were mainly "philatelic" and we no longer list them. The issue which was specifically authorised in 1882 was the one which had originally been put on sale for fiscal use in 1880.

Although all fiscal stamps were legally valid for postage, only values between 2s. and £1 were stocked at ordinary post offices. Other values could only be obtained by request from the G.P.O., Wellington or from offices of the Stamp Duties Department. Later the Arms types above £1 could also be obtained from the head post offices in Auckland, Christchurch, Dunedin and also a branch post office at Christchurch North where there was a local demand for them.

It seems sensible to list under Postal Fiscals the Queen Victoria stamps up to the £1 value and the Arms types up to the £5 because by 1931 the higher values were genuinely needed for postal purposes. Even the £10 was occasionally used on insured airmail parcels.

Although 2s. and 5s. values were included in the 1898 pictorial issue, it was the general practice for the Postal Department to limit the postage issues to 1s. until 1926 when the 2s. and 3s. appeared. These were then dropped from the fiscal issues and when in turn the 5s. and 10s. were introduced in 1953 and the £1 in 1960 no further printings of these values occurred in the fiscal series.

FORGED POSTMARKS. Our prices are for stamps with genuine postal cancellations. Beware of forged postmarks on stamps from which fiscal cancellations have been cleaned off.

Many small post offices acted as agents for government departments and it was the practice to use ordinary postal date-stamps on stamps used fiscally, so that when they are removed from documents they are indistinguishable from postally used specimens unless impressed with the embossed seal of the Stamp Duties Department.

Date-stamps very similar to postal date-stamps were sometimes supplied to offices of the Stamp Duties Department and it is not clear when this practice ceased. Prior to the Arms types the only sure proof of the postal use of off-cover fiscal stamps is when they bear a distinctive duplex, registered or parcel post cancellation, but beware of forgeries of the first two.

F **1**

F **2**

F **3**

(Die eng W. R. Bock. Typo Govt Ptg Office)

1882 (Feb). W **12***a*. P 12 × 11½.

F1	F **1**	1d. lilac	£250	£325
F2		1d. blue	£120	25·00
		w. Wmk inverted		

The 1d. fiscal was specifically authorised for postal use in February 1882 owing to a shortage of the 1d. Type **5** and pending the introduction of the 1d. Type **14** on 1 April.

The 1d. lilac fiscal had been replaced by the 1d. blue in 1878 but postally used copies with 1882 duplex postmarks are known although most postally used examples are dated from 1890 and these must have been philatelic.

1882 (early). W **12***a*. P 12 × 11½.

F3	F **2**	1s. grey-green		
F4	F **3**	1s. grey-green and red		
F4*a*		2s. rose and blue		

Examples of these are known postally used in 1882 and although not specifically authorised for postal use it is believed that their use was permitted where there was a shortage of the appropriate postage value.

WMK TYPE F 5. The balance of the paper employed for the 1867 issue was used for early printings of Type F **4** introduced in 1880 before changing over to the "N Z" and Star watermark. The values we list with this watermark are known with 1882–83 postal date stamps. Others have later dates and are considered to be philatelic but should they be found with 1882–83 postal dates we would be prepared to add them to the list.

In the following list the 4d., 6d., 8d. and 1s. are known with early 1882 postal date-stamps and, like Nos. F3/4, it is assumed that they were used to meet a temporary shortage of postage stamps.

F **4**

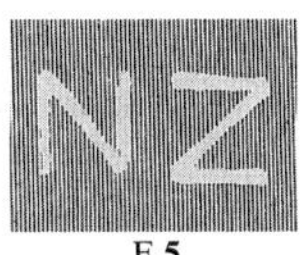

F **5**

The 12s.6d. value has the head in an oval (as Type **10**), and the 15s. and £1 values have it in a broken circle (as Type **7**).

(Dies eng W.R. Bock. Typo Govt Ptg Office)

1882 (1 Apr). *Type* F **4** *and similar types. "De La Rue" paper.*

A. W **12***a* (6 mm).

(a) P 12 (1882).

F 5	4d. orange-red (Wmk F **5**)	—	£170
F 6	6d. lake-brown	—	£170
F 7	8d. green (Wmk F **5**)		
F 8	1s. pink		
	a. Wmk F **5**		
F 9	2s. blue	50·00	4·50
F10	2s.6d. grey-brown	85·00	4·50
	a. Wmk F **5**		
F11	3s. mauve	£110	6·00
F12	4s. brown-rose	£110	11·00
	a. Wmk F **5**		
F13	5s. green	£140	12·00
	a. Yellow-green	£140	12·00
F14	6s. rose	£150	29·00
F15	7s. ultramarine	£160	50·00
F16	7s.6d. bronze-grey	£250	85·00
F17	8s. deep blue	£170	60·00
F18	9s. orange	£190	55·00
F19	10s. brown-red	£140	20·00
	a. Wmk F **5**		
F20	15s. green	£250	85·00
F21	£1 rose-pink	£190	50·00

(b) P 12½ (1886).

F22	2s. blue	50·00	4·50
F23	2s.6d. grey-brown	85·00	4·50
F24	3s. mauve	£110	6·00
F25	4s. purple-claret	£110	11·00
	a. Brown-rose	£110	11·00
F26	5s. green	£140	12·00
	a. Yellow-green	£140	12·00
F27	6s. rose	£150	29·00
F28	7s. ultramarine	£160	50·00
F29	8s. deep blue	£170	60·00
F30	9s. orange	£190	55·00
F31	10s. brown-red	£140	20·00
F32	15s. green	£250	85·00
F33	£1 rose-pink	£190	50·00

B. W**12***b* (7 mm). P 12½ (1888).

F34	2s. blue	45·00	4·50
F35	2s. 6d. grey-brown	80·00	4·50
F36	3s. mauve	£100	6·00
F37	4s. brown-rose	£100	11·00
	a. Brown-red	£100	11·00
F38	5s. green	£130	12·00
	a. Yellow-green	£130	12·00
F39	6s. rose	£150	29·00
F40	7s. ultramarine	£160	50·00
F41	7s.6d. bronze-grey	£250	85·00
F42	8s. deep blue	£170	60·00
F43	9s. orange	£190	55·00
F44	10s. brown-red	£140	18·00
	a. Maroon	£140	18·00
F45	£1 pink	£190	50·00

C. W**12***c* (4 mm). P 12½ (1890).

F46	2s. blue	75·00	11·00
F46*a*	2s.6d. grey-brown	£110	13·00
F47	3s. mauve	£150	27·00
F48	4s. brown-red	£120	15·00
F49	5s. green	£140	13·00
F50	6s. rose	£160	29·00
F51	7s. ultramarine	£170	50·00
F52	8s. deep blue	£180	60·00
F53	9s. orange	£200	65·00
F54	10s. brown-red	£150	20·00
F55	15s. green	£275	£100

D. Continuation of W**12***b*. P 11 (1895–1901).

F56	2s. blue	27·00	5·50
F57	2s.6d. grey-brown	80·00	4·50
	a. Inscr "COUNTERPART" (1901)*	£160	£180
F58	3s. mauve	£100	6·00
F59	4s. brown-red	£100	10·00
F60	5s. yellow-green	£130	13·00
F61	6s. rose	£140	29·00
F62	7s. pale blue	£160	50·00
F63	7s.6d. bronze-grey	£250	85·00
F64	8s. deep blue	£170	60·00
F65	9s. orange	£190	55·00
	a. Imperf between (horiz pair)	£900	
F66	10s. brown-red	£140	18·00
	a. Maroon	£140	18·00
F67	15s. green	£250	85·00
F68	£1 rose-pink	£190	50·00

*The plate normally printed in yellow and inscribed "COUNTERPART" just above the bottom value panel, was for use on the counterparts of documents but was issued in error in the colour of the normal fiscal stamp and accepted for use.

E. W**43** *(sideways).*

(i) Unsurfaced "Cowan" paper.

(a) P 11 (1903).

F69	2s.6d. grey-brown	80·00	4·50
F70	3s. mauve	£100	6·00
F71	4s. orange-red	£100	10·00
F72	6s. rose	£140	29·00
F73	7s. pale blue	£160	50·00
F74	8s. deep blue	£170	60·00
F75	10s. brown-red	£130	20·00
	a. Maroon	£130	20·00
F76	15s. green	£250	85·00
F77	£1 rose-pink	£170	50·00

(b) P 14 (1906).

F78	2s.6d. grey-brown	80·00	4·50
F79	3s. mauve	£100	6·00
F80	4s. orange-red	£100	7·50
F81	5s. yellow-green	90·00	8·50
F82	6s. rose	£140	29·00
F83	7s. pale blue	£150	50·00
F84	7s.6d. bronze-grey	£250	85·00
F85	8s. deep blue	£170	60·00
F86	9s. orange	£180	55·00
F87	10s. maroon	£130	18·00
F88	15s. green	£250	85·00
F89	£1 rose-pink	£170	50·00

(c) P 14½ × 14, comb (clean-cut) (1907).

F90	2s. blue	25·00	4·00
F91	2s.6d. grey-brown	80·00	4·50
F92	3s. mauve	£100	6·00
F93	4s. orange-red	90·00	7·50
F94	6s. rose	£140	29·00
F95	10s. maroon	£130	18·00
F96	15s. green	£250	85·00
F97	£1 rose-pink	£170	50·00

(ii) Chalk-surfaced "De la Rue" paper.

(a) P 14 (1913).

F 98	2s. blue	25·00	4·00
F 99	2s.6d. grey-brown	27·00	4·50
F100	3s. purple	70·00	6·00
F101	4s. orange-red	70·00	7·00
F102	5s. yellow-green	70·00	8·50
F103	6s. rose	£110	15·00
F104	7s. pale blue	£120	25·00
F105	7s.6d. bronze-grey	£250	85·00
F106	8s. deep blue	£150	30·00
F107	9s. orange	£180	55·00
F108	10s. maroon	£130	16·00
F109	15s. green	£250	85·00
F110	£1 rose-carmine	£170	50·00

(b) P 14½ × 14, comb (1913–21).

F111	2s. deep blue	25·00	4·00
F112	2s.6d. grey-brown	27·00	4·50
F113	3s. purple	70·00	6·00
F114	4s. orange-red	70·00	7·00
F115	5s. yellow-green	70·00	8·50
F116	6s. rose	£110	15·00
F117	7s. pale blue	£120	25·00
F118	8s. deep blue	£150	30·00
F119	9s. orange	£170	55·00
F120	10s. maroon	£130	16·00
F121	12s.6d. deep plum (1921)	£4000	£1600
F122	15s. green	£250	85·00
F123	£1 rose-carmine	£170	50·00

The "De La Rue" paper has a smooth finish and has toned gum which is strongly resistant to soaking.

(iii) Chalk-surfaced "Jones" paper. P 14½ × 14, comb (1924).

F124 2s. deep blue 30·00 5·00
F125 2s.6d. deep grey-brown 32·00 5·50
F126 3s. purple 80·00 6·50
F127 5s. yellow-green 80·00 9·00
F128 10s. brown-red £140 16·00
F129 12s.6d. deep purple £4000 £1600
F130 15s. green £275 95·00

The "Jones" paper has a coarser texture, is poorly surfaced and the ink tends to peel. The outline of the watermark commonly shows on the surface of the stamp. The gum is colourless or only slightly toned and washes off readily.

(iv) Thick, opaque, chalk-surfaced "Cowan" paper. P 14½ × 14, comb (1925–30).

F131 2s. blue 27·00 5·00
F132 2s.6d. deep grey-brown 30·00 5·50
F133 3s. mauve £100 10·00
F134 4s. orange-red 70·00 10·00
F135 5s. yellow-green 70·00 12·00
x. Wmk reversed (1927) £100 20·00
F136 6s. rose £110 18·00
F137 7s. pale blue £120 25·00
F138 8s. deep blue £150 30·00
a. Error. Blue (as 2s.) (1930) £500
F139 10s. brown-red £130 16·00
x. Wmk reversed (1927) £200 £150
F140 12s.6d. blackish purple £4000 £1600
F141 15s. green £275 95·00
F142 £1 rose-pink £170 50·00

The "Cowan" paper is white and opaque and the watermark, which is usually smaller than in the "Jones" paper, is often barely visible.

(v) Thin, hard, chalk-surfaced "Wiggins Teape" paper. P 14½ × 14, comb (1926).

F143 4s. orange-red 80·00 13·00
F144 £1 rose-pink £180 95·00

The "Wiggins Teape" paper has a horizontal mesh, in relation to the design, with narrow watermark, whereas other chalk-surfaced papers with this perforation have a vertical mesh and wider watermark.

ONE SHILLING
AND THREEPENCE

F 6

35/-

(F 7)

(Des H. L. Richardson. Typo Govt Ptg Office)

1931–40. *As Type* F **6** *(various frames).* W **43**. P 14.

(i) Thick, opaque, chalk-surfaced "Cowan" paper, with horizontal mesh (1931–35).

F145 1s.3d. lemon (4.31) 6·00 40·00
F146 1s.3d. orange-yellow 7·00 8·50
F147 2s.6d. deep brown 14·00 4·50
F148 4s. red 15·00 6·50
F149 5s. green 19·00 12·00
F150 6s. carmine-rose 32·00 13·00
F151 7s. blue 28·00 23·00
F152 7s.6d. olive-grey 65·00 80·00
F153 8s. slate-violet 28·00 32·00
F154 9s. brown-orange 30·00 29·00
F155 10s. carmine-lake 24·00 9·00
F156 12s.6d. deep plum (9.35) £130 £130
F157 15s. sage-green 60·00 38·00
F158 £1 pink 65·00 19·00
F159 25s. greenish blue £325 £425
F160 30s. brown (1935) £250 £140
F161 35s. orange-yellow £2500 £2750
F162 £2 bright purple £300 60·00
F163 £2 10s. red £300 £350
F164 £3 green £375 £190
F165 £310s. rose (1935) £1300 £1200
F166 £4 light blue (1935) £350 £150
F167 £410s. deep olive-grey (1935) £1000 £1100
F168 £5 indigo-blue £325 £100

(ii) Thin, hard 'Wiggins Teape" paper with vertical mesh (1936–40).

(a) Chalk-surfaced (1936–39).

F169 1s.3d. pale orange-yellow 19·00 3·50
F170 2s.6d. dull brown 65·00 3·75
F171 4s. pale red-brown 80·00 7·50
F172 5s. green 80·00 7·00
w. Wmk inverted
F173 6s. carmine-rose 80·00 29·00
F174 7s. pale blue £110 30·00
F175 8s. slate-violet £130 48·00
F176 9s. brown-orange £140 70·00
F177 10s. pale carmine-lake £140 7·00
F178 15s. sage-green £200 50·00
F179 £1 pink £160 26·00
F180 30s. brown (1.39) £400 £160
F181 35s. orange-yellow £3250 £3500
F182 £2 bright purple (1937) £650 £100
w. Wmk inverted
F183 £3 green (1937) £700 £300
F184 £5 indigo-blue (1937) £900 £200

(b) Unsurfaced (1940).

F185 7s.6d. olive-grey £170 75·00

Not all values listed above were stocked at ordinary post offices as some of them were primarily required for fiscal purposes but all were valid for postage.

1939. *No.* F161 *surch with Type* F **7**.

F186 35/- on 35s. orange-yellow £450 £225

Because the 35s. orange-yellow could so easily be confused with the 1s.3d. in the same colour, it was surcharged.

1940 (June). *New values surch as Type* F **7**. *"Wiggins Teape" chalk-surfaced paper.* W **43**. P 14.

F187 3/6on 3s.6d. grey-green 55·00 19·00
F188 5/6on 5s.6d. lilac 95·00 50·00
F189 11/- on 11s. yellow £170 £130
F190 22/-on 22s. scarlet £400 £300
F187/90 *Set of* 4 £650 £450

These values were primarily needed for fiscal use.

1940–58. *As Type* F **6** *(various frames).* W **98** P 14.

(i) "Wiggins Teape" chalk-surfaced paper with vertical mesh (1940–56).

F191 1s.3d. orange-yellow 10·00 2·00
w. Wmk inverted
F192 1s.3d. yellow and black (wmk inverted) (14.6.55) 2·00 1·25
aw. Wmk upright (9.9.55) 32·00 32·00
b. Error. Yellow and blue (wmk inverted) (7.56) 4·50 5·50
F193 2s.6d. deep brown 8·50 70
w. Wmk inverted (3.49) 8·50 70
F194 4s. red-brown 16·00 1·25
w. Wmk inverted (3.49) 18·00 1·50
F195 5s. green 18·00 1·00
w. Wmk inverted (1.5.50) 22·00 1·00
F196 6s. carmine-rose 32·00 3·25
w. Wmk inverted (1948) 32·00 3·25
F197 7s. pale blue 32·00 5·50
F198 7s.6d. ol-grey (wmk inverted) (21.12.50) 60·00 50·00
F199 8s. slate-violet 50·00 17·00
w. Wmk inverted (6.12.50) 50·00 18·00
F200 9s. brown-orange (1.46) 22·00 42·00
w. Wmk inverted (9.1.51) 55·00 42·00
F201 10s. carmine-lake 32·00 2·25
w. Wmk inverted (4.50) 32·00 2·50
F202 15s. sage-green 42·00 19·00
w. Wmk inverted (8.12.50) 60·00 26·00
F203 £1 pink 28·00 3·75
w. Wmk inverted (1.2.50) 42·00 4·25
F204 25s. greenish blue (1946) £375 £375
w. Wmk inverted (7.53) £475 £475
F205 30s. brown (1946) £225 £100
w. Wmk inverted (9.49) £225 £100
F206 £2 bright purple (1946) 85·00 22·00
w. Wmk inverted (17.6.52) 90·00 22·00
F207 £2 10s. red (wmk inverted) (9.8.51) £250 £275
F208 £3 green (1946) £140 48·00
w. Wmk inverted (17.6.52) £130 48·00
F209 £3 10s. rose (11.48) £1500 £1100
w. Wmk inverted (5.52) £1600 £1100
F210 £4 light blue (wmk inverted) (12.2.52) £140 £120
w. Wmk upright † —
F211 £5 indigo-blue £300 60·00
w. Wmk inverted (11.9.50) £170 45·00
F191/211 *Set of* 21 £2750 £2000

THREE SHILLINGS

THREE SHILLINGS

3s.6d.

Type I. Broad serifed capitals

Type II. Taller capitals, without serifs

Surcharged as Type F **7**.

F212 3/6on 3s.6d. grey-green (I) (1942) 20·00 7·00
w. Wmk inverted (12.10.50) 38·00 10·00
F213 3/6on 3s.6d. grey-green (II) (6.53) 14·00 38·00
w. Wmk inverted (6.53) 45·00 45·00
F214 5/6on 5s.6d. lilac (1944) 48·00 18·00
w. Wmk inverted (13.9.50) 60·00 18·00
F215 11/-on 11s. yellow (1942) 75·00 48·00
F216 22/-on 22s. scarlet (1945) £275 £130
w. Wmk inverted (1.3.50) £300 £140
F212/16 *Set of* 5 £375 £200

(ii) P 14 × 13½. *"Wiggins Teape" unsurfaced paper with horizontal mesh (1956–58).*

F217 1s.3d. yellow and black (11.56) 2·25 2·75
w. Wmk inverted 22·00 22·00
F218 £1 pink (20.10.58) 35·00 12·00

No. F192b had the inscription printed in blue in error but as many as 378,000 were printed.

From 1949 53 inferior paper had to be used and for technical reasons it was necessary to feed the paper into the machine in a certain way which resulted in whole printings with the watermark inverted for most values.

ANTARCTIC EXPEDITIONS

VICTORIA LAND

These issues were made under authority of the New Zealand Postal Department and, while not strictly necessary, they actually franked correspondence to New Zealand. They were sold to the public at a premium.

1908 (15 Jan). *Shackleton Expedition. T* **42** *of New Zealand (*P 14*), optd "*King Edward VII Land*", in two lines, reading up, by Coulls, Culling and Co., Wellington.*

A1 1d. rose-carmine (No. 356 Royle) (G.) £400 35·00
a. Opt double † £1500
A1*b* 1d. rose-carmine (No. 352*c* Waterlow) (G.) £1300 £800

Nos. A1/1*b* were used on board the expedition ship, *Nimrod*, and at the Cape Royds base in McMurdo Sound. Due to adverse conditions Shackleton landed in Victoria Land rather than King Edward VII Land, the intended destination.

1911 (9 Feb)–**13**. *Scott Expedition. Stamps of New Zealand optd "*VICTORIA LAND.*", in two lines by Govt Printer, Wellington.*

A2 **51** ½d. deep green (No. 387*aa*) (18.1.13) £550 £650
A3 **53** 1d. carmine (No. 405) 45·00 85·00
a. No stop after "LAND" (R. 7/5) £275 £600

Nos. A2/3 were used at the Cape Evans base on McMurdo Sound or on the *Terra Nova*.

AITUTAKI

The island of Aitutaki, under British protection from 1888, was annexed by New Zealand on 11 June 1901.

NEW ZEALAND DEPENDENCY

Stamps of COOK ISLANDS were used in Aitutaki from 1892 until 1903.

PRICES FOR STAMPS ON COVER TO 1945	
Nos. 1/7	*from* × 4
Nos. 9/14	*from* × 3
Nos. 15/29	*from* × 4
Nos. 30/2	*from* × 6

Stamps of New Zealand overprinted or surcharged. For illustrations of watermarks and definitive types see New Zealand.

AITUTAKI.

(1)

Ava Pene.

(2) ½d.

Tai Pene.

(3) 1d.

Rua Pene Ma Te Ava.

(4) 2½d.

Toru Pene.

(5) 3d.

Ono Pene.

(6) 6d.

Tai Tiringi.

(7) 1s.

1903 (29 June)–**11**. *T* **23**, **27/8**, **31**, **34** *and* **42** *surch with T* **1** *at to[p] and T* **2** *to* **7** *at foot. Thin, hard Cowan paper.* W **43**.

(a) P 14.

1 ½d. green (No. 302) (R.) 4·50 6·5[0]
2 1d. carmine (No. 303) (B.) 4·75 5·5[0]
3 2½d. deep blue (No. 320*a*) (R.) (9.11) 8·00 18·0[0]
a. "Ava" without stop £150 £19[0]
1/3 *Set of* 3 15·00 27·0[0]

(b) P 11.

4 2½d. blue (No. 308) (R.) 11·00 12·0[0]
5 3d. yellow-brown (No. 309) (B.) 18·00 15·0[0]
6 6d. rose-red (No. 312*a*) (B.) 30·00 25·0[0]
7 1s. bright red (No. 315*a*) (B.) 50·00 85·0[0]
a. "Tiringi" without stop (R. 7/12) £550 £70[0]
b. Orange-red 65·00 95·0[0]
ba. "Tiringi" without stop (R. 7/12) £650 £80[0]
4/7 *Set of* 4 £100 £12[0]

Nos. 1/2 and 4/7 were placed on sale in Auckland on 12 Jun[e] 1903. There were four states of the overprint used for No. 3. On th[e] first the "no stop" variety (No. 3a) occurs on R. 6/8, on the secon[d] it appears on R. 1/4, 2/4 and 6/8, on the third on R. 5/8 and 6/8 and on the fourth all stops are present.

AITUTAKI.

Ono Pene.

(8)

1911–16. *T* **51** *and* **53** *surch with T* **1** *at top and T* **2** *or* **3** *at fo[ot] and T* **52** *surch as T* **8**. P 14 × 15 (½d., 1d.) or 14 × 14½ (others).

9 ½d. green (No. 387) (R.) (9.11) 1·00 3·5[0]
10 1d. carmine (No. 405) (B.) (2.13) 3·00 10·0[0]
11 6d. carmine (No. 392) (B.) (23.5.16) 45·00 £1[..]
12 1s. vermilion (No. 394) (B.) (9.14) 50·00 £1[..]
9/12 *Set of* 4 90·00 £2[..]

1916–17. *T* **60** *(recess) surch as T* **8**. W **43**. P 14 × 13½.

13 6d. carmine (No. 425) (B.) (6.6.16) 12·00 50·[..]
a. Perf 14 × 14½ 7·50 27·[..]
b. Vert pair. Nos. 13/13a 50·00 £1[..]
14 1s. vermilion (No. 430) (B.) (3.17) 17·00 90·[..]
a. Perf 14 × 14½ 20·00 90·[..]
ab. "Tai" without dot (R. 8/9, 9/12, 10/12) £225 £4[..]
ac. "Tiringi" without dot on second "i" (R. 8/12, 10/7) £275 £5[..]
ad. "Tiringi" without dot on third "i" (R. 8/11) £375 £6[..]
b. Vert pair. Nos. 14/14a £120 £3[..]

1917–18. *T* **60** *(recess) optd "*AITUTAKI*" only, as in T* **8**. W **4[3]**. P 14 × 13½.

15 2½d. blue (No. 419) (R.) (12.18) 2·00 17·[..]
a. Perf 14 × 14½ 1·75 15·[..]
b. Vert pair. Nos. 15/15a 30·00 £1[..]
16 3d. chocolate (No. 420) (B.) (1.18) 1·75 25·[..]
a. Perf 14 × 14½ 1·50 24·[..]
b. Vert pair. Nos. 16/16a 30·00 £1[..]
17 6d. carmine (No. 425) (B.) (11.17) 6·00 21·[..]
a. Perf 14 × 14½ 4·75 21·[..]
b. Vert pair. Nos. 17/17a 40·00 £1[..]
18 1s. vermilion (No. 430) (B.) (11.17) 14·00 40·[..]
a. Perf 14 × 14½ 12·00 32·[..]
b. Vert pair. Nos. 18/18a 65·00 £1[..]
15/18 *Set of* 4 18·00 85·[..]

1917–20. *T* **53** *and* **61** *(typo) optd "*AITUTAKI*" only, as in T* **8**. [W] **43**. P 14 × 15.

19 ½d. green (No. 435) (R.) (2.20) 1·00 6·[..]
20 1d. carmine (No. 405) (B.) (5.20) 4·00 28·[..]
21 1½d. slate (No. 437) (R.) (11.17) 3·75 30·[..]
22 1½d. orange-brown (No. 438) (R.) (2.19) 80 7·[..]
23 3d. chocolate (No. 440) (B.) (6.19) 3·50 17·[..]
19/23 *Set of* 5 11·50 80·[..]

(Des and recess Perkins, Bacon & Co)

1920 (23 Aug). *T* **9/14** *of Cook Islands, but inscr "*AITUTAKI*"*. No wmk. P 14.

24 ½d. black and green . . . . 3·50 25·00
25 1d. black and dull carmine . . . . 3·50 17·00
a. Double derrick flaw (R.2/8, 3/6 or 5/2) . . . . 11·00
26 1½d. black and sepia . . . . 6·00 12·00
27 3d. black and deep blue . . . . 2·50 14·00
28 6d. red-brown and slate . . . . 5·50 14·00
29 1s. black and purple . . . . 9·50 16·00
24/9 *Set of* 6 . . . . 27·00 90·00

(Recess Govt Printing Office, Wellington)

1924–27. *T* **9/10** *and* **16** *of Cook Islands, but inscr "*AITUTAKI*"*. W **43** of New Zealand. P 14.

30 ½d. black and green (5.27) . . . . 2·00 13·00
31 1d. black and deep carmine (10.24) . . . . 6·00 7·00
a. Double derrick flaw (R.2/8, 3/6 or 5/2) . . . . 15·00
32 2½d. black and dull blue (10.27) . . . . 7·50 55·00
30/2 *Set of* 3 . . . . 14·00 65·00

Cook Islands stamps superseded those of Aitutaki on 15 March 1932. Separate issues were resumed in 1972.

COOK ISLANDS

This group of fifteen islands was originally also known as the Hervey Islands. A British Protectorate was declared over the group by the local Vice-Consul on 20 September 1888.

Before the introduction of the Cook Islands Post Office, mail was forwarded via Auckland, New Zealand.

PRICES FOR STAMPS ON COVER TO 1945	
Nos. 1/4	*from* × 5
Nos. 5/74	*from* × 4
Nos. 75/145	*from* × 3

BRITISH PROTECTORATE

1

2 Queen Makea Takau

3 White Tern or Torea

(Des F. Moss. Typo Govt Printing Office, Wellington)

1892 (19 Apr). No wmk. *Toned or white paper*. P 12½.

1 **1** 1d. black . . . . 27·00 26·00
a. Imperf between (vert pair) £8500
1½d. mauve . . . . 40·00 38·00
a. Imperf (pair) £9000
2½d. blue . . . . 40·00 38·00
10d. carmine £140 £130
1/4 *Set of* 4 . . . . £200 £200

Nos. 1/4 were printed in sheets of 60 (6 × 10) from plates constructed from a matrix of 6 slightly different types.

(Eng A. E. Cousins. Typo Govt Printing Office, Wellington)

1893 (28 July)–**1900**. W **12**b of New Zealand (N Z and Star wide apart) (sideways on *T* **3**).

(a) P 12 × 11½.

5 **2** 1d. brown . . . . 40·00 45·00
6 1d. blue (3.4.94) . . . . 9·00 2·00
a. Perf 12 × 11½ and 12½ mixed . . . . † £1100
7 1½d. mauve . . . . 8·50 6·50
8 2½d. rose . . . . 38·00 23·00
a. Rose-carmine . . . . 60·00 48·00
ab. Perf 12 × 11½ and 12½ mixed £1800
9 5d. olive-black . . . . 17·00 13·00
10d. green . . . . 70·00 48·00
5/10 *Set of* 6 . . . . £160 £120

(b) P 11 (July 1896–1900).

3 ½d. steel blue (1st setting) (11.99) . . . . 32·00 45·00
a. Upper right "d" omitted £1500
b. Second setting . . . . 20·00 22·00
ba. Deep blue (1900) . . . . 4·50 6·00
2 1d. blue . . . . 5·00 4·50
1d. deep brown/*cream* (4.99) . . . . 16·00 16·00
a. Wmk sideways
b. Bistre-brown (1900) . . . . 19·00 20·00
1½d. deep lilac . . . . 9·00 6·50
a. Deep mauve (1900) . . . . 9·00 6·50
3 2d. brown/*thin toned* (7.98) . . . . 11·00 6·50
a. Deep brown (1900) . . . . 8·50 6·50
2 2½d. pale rose . . . . 48·00 38·00
a. Deep rose (1900) . . . . 16·00 9·00
5d. olive-black . . . . 24·00 17·00
3 6d. purple/*thin toned* (7.98) . . . . 25·00 29·00
a. Bright purple (1900) . . . . 19·00 23·00
2 10d. green . . . . 18·00 48·00
3 1s. red/*thin toned* (7.98) . . . . 60·00 70·00
a. Deep carmine (1900) . . . . 48·00 48·00
/20a *Set of* 10 . . . . £150 £160

Examples of the 1d., 1½d., 2½d. and 5d. perforated 11 and on laid paper are perforation trials. On the 1st setting of the ½d. the face values are misplaced in each corner. As corrected in the second setting the face values are correctly positioned in each corner.

ONE
HALF
PENNY
(4)

(5)

1899 (24 Apr). *No. 12 surch with T* **4** *by Govt Printer, Rarotonga.*

21 **2** ½d.on 1d. blue . . . . 32·00 42·00
a. Surch inverted £850 £900
b. Surch double £1000 £850

NEW ZEALAND TERRITORY

On 8 and 9 October 1900 the chiefs of all the main islands, except Aitutaki, ceded their territory to the British Crown. On 11 June 1901 all the islands, including Aitutaki, were transferred by Great Britain to New Zealand control.

1901 (8 Oct). *No. 13 optd with T* **5** *by Govt Printer, Rarotonga.*

22 **2** 1d. brown £180 £140
a. Crown inverted £1800 £1400
c. Optd with crown twice £1600 £1600

1902. No wmk. P 11.

(a) Medium white Cowan paper (Feb).

23 **3** ½d. blue-green . . . . 6·50 7·00
a. Imperf horiz (vert pair) £1200
24 **2** 1d. dull rose . . . . 9·00 13·00

(b) Thick white Pirie paper (May).

25 **3** ½d. yellow-green . . . . 4·25 4·25
26 **2** 1d. rose-red . . . . 12·00 11·00
a. Rose-lake . . . . 11·00 6·50
27 2½d. dull blue . . . . 13·00 21·00

NEW ZEALAND WATERMARKS. In W **43** the wmk units are in vertical columns widely spaced and the sheet margins are unwatermarked or wmkd "NEW ZEALAND POSTAGE" in large letters.

In W **98** the wmk units are arranged alternately in horizontal rows closely spaced and are continued into the sheet margins. Stamps with W **98** sideways show the star to the left of NZ, *as seen from the back*. Sideways inverted varieties have the star to the right, *as seen from the back*.

1902 (Sept). W **43** of New Zealand (single-lined NZ and Star, close together; sideways on *T* **2**). P 11.

28 **3** ½d. yellow-green . . . . 2·75 3·25
a. Grey-green . . . . 19·00 48·00
29 **2** 1d. rose-pink . . . . 4·00 3·00
30 1½d. deep mauve . . . . 4·00 8·50
31 **3** 2d. deep brown . . . . 5·00 10·00
a. No figures of value £2000 £2750
b. Perf 11 × 14 . . . . £1500
32 **2** 2½d. deep blue . . . . 3·75 7·00
33 5d. olive-black . . . . 35·00 48·00
34 **3** 6d. purple . . . . 32·00 28·00
35 **2** 10d. green . . . . 48·00 95·00
36 **3** 1s. carmine . . . . 48·00 70·00
a. Perf 11 × 14 . . . . £1700
28/36 *Set of* 9 . . . . £150 £225

Stamps in Type **3** were printed from a master plate with the value added by a series of separate duty plates. One sheet of the 2d. missed this second pass through the press and was issued without value.

For Nos. 28/36 Type **2** exists with the watermark in equal quantities either upright or inverted and for Type **3**, on which the watermark is sideways, in equal quantities with the star to the right or left of NZ.

1909–11. W **43** of New Zealand.

37 **3** ½d. green (P 14½ × 14) (1911) . . . . 6·00 8·00
38 **2** 1d. deep red (P 14) . . . . 35·00 29·00
a. Wmk sideways (24.12.09) . . . . 14·00 7·00

For Nos. 37/8 the watermark is either upright or inverted. For No. 38a it is sideways, either with star to right or left of NZ.

1913–19. W **43** of New Zealand (sideways on *T* **3**). *Chalk-surfaced paper.*

39 **3** ½d. deep green (P 14) (1915) . . . . 4·75 15·00
a. Wmk upright . . . . 6·00 11·00
40 **2** 1d. red (P 14) (7.13) . . . . 4·75 4·25
41 1d. red (P 14 × 14½) (1914) . . . . 5·50 6·00
42 1½d. deep mauve (P 14) (1915) . . . . 75·00 40·00
43 1½d. deep mauve (P 14 × 15) (1916) . . . . 8·50 4·00
44 **3** 2d. deep brown (P 15 × 14) (1919) . . . . 5·00 45·00
45 **2** 10d. green (P 14 × 15) (1918) . . . . 16·00 90·00
46 **3** 1s. carmine (P 15 × 14) (1919) . . . . 27·00 90·00
39/46 *Set of* 6 . . . . 60·00 £225

RAROTONGA

APA PENE
(8)

1919 (Apr–July). *Stamps of New Zealand surch as T* **8**.

(a) T **53**. **W 43**. *De La Rue chalk-surfaced paper.* P 14 × 15.

47 1d. carmine (No. 405) (B.) (June) . . . . 1·00 3·00

(b) T **60** *(recess)*. W **43**. *Cowan unsurfaced paper.* P 14 × 13½.

48 2½d. blue (No. 419) (R.) (June) . . . . 2·25 6·50
a. Perf 14 × 14½ . . . . 2·00 2·25
b. Vert pair. Nos. 48/a . . . . 20·00 45·00
49 3d. chocolate (No. 420) (B.) . . . . 2·00 8·00
a. Perf 14 × 14½ . . . . 2·25 2·00
b. Vert pair. Nos. 49/a . . . . 22·00 50·00
50 4d. bright violet (No. 422) (B.) . . . . 2·00 5·50
a. Re-entry (Pl 20 R. 1/6) . . . . 60·00
b. Re-entry (Pl 20 R. 4/10) . . . . 60·00
c. Perf 14 × 14½ . . . . 1·75 4·25
d. Vert (pair Nos 50 and 50c) . . . . 20·00 55·00
51 4½d. deep green (No. 423) (B.) . . . . 2·00 7·00
a. Perf 14 × 14½ . . . . 1·75 8·00
b. Vert pair. Nos. 51/a . . . . 20·00 65·00
52 6d. carmine (No. 425) (B.) (June) . . . . 3·00 8·50
a. Perf 14 × 14½ . . . . 1·75 5·50
b. Vert pair. Nos. 52/a . . . . 38·00 80·00
53 7½d. red-brown (No. 426a) (B.) . . . . 1·50 5·50
54 9d. sage-green (No. 429) (R.) . . . . 3·25 15·00
a. Perf 14 × 14½ . . . . 2·00 15·00
b. Vert pair. Nos. 54/a . . . . 38·00 £100
55 1s. vermilion (No. 430) (B.) (June) . . . . 11·00 30·00
a. Perf 14 × 14½ . . . . 2·75 18·00
b. Vert pair. Nos. 55/a . . . . 48·00 £110

(c) T **61** *(typo)*. W **43**. *De La Rue chalk-surfaced paper.* P 14 × 15.

56 ½d. green (No. 435) (R.) (June) . . . . 40 1·00
57 1½d. orange-brown (No. 438) (R.) (June) 50 75
58 2d. yellow (No. 439) (R.) . . . . 1·50 1·75
59 3d. chocolate (No. 440) (B.) (July) . . . . 2·75 13·00
47/59 *Set of* 13 . . . . 19·00 70·00

9 Capt. Cook landing

10 Wharf at Avarua

11 "Capt. Cook" (Dance)

12 Palm Tree

13 Huts at Arorangi

14 Avarua Harbour

R. 2/8

R. 3/6 Double derrick flaws

R. 5/2

(Des, eng and recess Perkins, Bacon & Co)

1920 (23 Aug). No wmk. P 14.

70 **9** ½d. black and green . . . . 4·00 19·00
71 **10** 1d. black and carmine-red . . . . 4·75 19·00
a. Double derrick flaw (R. 2/8, 3/6 or 5/2) . . . . 12·00
72 **11** 1½d. black and dull blue . . . . 8·50 8·50
73 **12** 3d. black and chocolate . . . . 2·25 5·50
74 **13** 6d. brown and yellow-orange . . . . 3·00 8·50
75 **14** 1s. black and violet . . . . 5·00 17·00
70/5 *Set of* 6 . . . . 24·00 70·00

Examples of the 1d. and 1s. with centre inverted were not supplied to the Post Office.

RAROTONGA
(15)

RAROTONGA
Trimmed overprint (R. 1/6 and R. 3/7)

1921 (Oct)–**23**. *Postal Fiscal stamps as Type* **F 4** *of New Zealand optd with T* **15**. W **43** (sideways). *Chalk-surfaced "De La Rue" paper*. P 14½ × 14.

76 2s. deep blue (No. F111) (R.) . . . . 27·00 55·00
a. Trimmed opt £100
b. Carmine opt (1923) £150 £170
ba. Trimmed opt £425
77 2s.6d. grey-brown (No. F112) (B.) . . . . 19·00 50·00
a. Trimmed opt . . . . 80·00
78 5s. yellow-green (No. F115) (R.) . . . . 27·00 65·00
a. Trimmed opt £100
79 10s. maroon (No. F120) (B.) . . . . 65·00 £100
a. Trimmed opt £170
80 £1 rose-carmine (No. F123) (B.) £100 £180
a. Trimmed opt £300
76/80 *Set of* 5 . . . . £200 £400

See also Nos. 85/9.

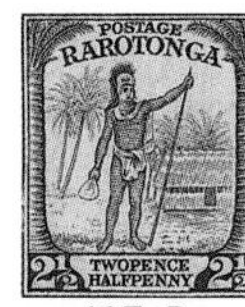

16 Te Po, Rarotongan Chief

17 Harbour, Rarotonga and Mt. Ikurangi

(2½d. from a print; 4d. des A. H. Messenger. Plates by P.B. Recess Govt Ptg Office, Wellington)

1924–27. W **43** of New Zealand. P 14.

81 **9** ½d. black and green (13.5.26) . . . . 4·50 8·50
82 **10** 1d. black and deep carmine (10.11.24) . . . . 6·00 2·25
a. Double derrick flaw (R. 2/8, 3/6 or 5/2) . . . . 16·00
x. Wmk reversed £150

83 **16** 2½d. red-brown and steel blue (15.10.27) . . . . 5·00 24·00
84 **17** 4d. green and violet (15.10.27) . . . . 8·00 16·00
81/4 *Set of* 4 . . . . 21·00 45·00

1926 (Feb–May). *As Nos. 76/80, but on thick, opaque white chalk-surfaced "Cowan" paper.*
85 2s. blue (No. F131) (C.) £130 £180
a. Trimmed opt £375
86 2s.6d. deep grey-brown (No. F132) (B.) . . 75·00 £110
87 5s. yellow-green (No. F135) (R.) (May) . . 75·00 £100
a. Trimmed opt £180
88 10s. brown-red (No. F139) (B.) (May) . . 80·00 £130
89 £1 rose-pink (No. F142) (B.) (May) . . £110 £180
a. Trimmed opt £350
85/9 *Set of* 5 . . . . £425 £600

1926 (Oct)–**28**. *T* **72** *of New Zealand, overprinted with T* **15**.
(a) Jones chalk-surfaced paper.
90 2s. deep blue (No. 466) (R.) . . . . 10·00 40·00
w. Wmk inverted . . . .
(b) Cowan thick, opaque chalk-surfaced paper.
91 2s. light blue (No. 469) (R.) (18.6.27) . . 15·00 40·00
92 3s. pale mauve (No. 470) (R.) (30.1.28) . . 16·00 42·00
90/2 *Set of* 3 . . . . 38·00 £110

TWO PENCE (18)   **COOK ISLANDS.** (19)

1931 (1 Mar). *Surch with T* **18**. P 14.
(a) No wmk.
93 **11** 2d.on 1½d. black and blue (R.) . . . . 9·50 2·75
(b) W **43** of New Zealand.
94 **11** 2d.on 1½d. black and blue (R.) . . . . 4·75 11·00

1931 (12 Nov)–**32**. *Postal Fiscal stamps as Type F* **6** *of New Zealand.* W **43**. *Thick, opaque, white chalk-surfaced "Cowan" paper.* P 14.
(a) Optd with T **15**.
95 2s.6d. deep brown (No. F147) (B.) . . . . 10·00 22·00
96 5s. green (No. F149) (R.) . . . . 18·00 55·00
97 10s. carmine-lake (No. F155) (B.) . . . . 38·00 95·00
98 £1 pink (No. F158) (B.) . . . . 90·00 £150
(b) Optd with T **19** *(3.32).*
98*a* £3 green (No. F164) (R.) £275 £475
98*b* £5 indigo-blue (No. F168) (R.) £180 £325
The £3 and £5 values were mainly used for fiscal purposes.

20 Capt. Cook landing

21 Capt. Cook

22 Double Maori Canoe

23 Natives working Cargo

24 Port of Avarua

25 R.M.S. *Monowai*

26 King George V

(Des L. C. Mitchell. Recess P.B.)

1932 (15 Mar–2 May). No wmk. P 13.
99 **20** ½d. black and deep green . . . . 3·50 16·00
a. Perf 14 . . . . 28·00 90·00
100 **21** 1d. black and lake . . . . 6·50 4·50
a. Centre inverted £2750 £2750
b. Perf compound of 13 and 14 . . £180 £200
c. Perf 14 . . . . 15·00 21·00
101 **22** 2d. black and brown . . . . 3·00 5·50
a. Perf 14 . . . . 9·00 20·00
102 **23** 2½d. black and deep blue . . . . 11·00 50·00
a. Perf 14 . . . . 14·00 50·00
103 **24** 4d. black and bright blue . . . . 20·00 60·00
a. Perf 14 . . . . 10·00 50·00
b. Perf 14 × 13 . . . . 30·00 £100
c. Perf compound of 14 and 13 . . 50·00 £110
104 **25** 6d. black and orange . . . . 24·00 48·00
a. Perf 14 . . . . 4·25 15·00
105 **26** 1s. black and violet (P 14) (2 May) . . . . 8·50 22·00
99/105 *Set of* 7 . . . . 42·00 £140
Nos. 100b and 103c come from sheets reperforated 14 on arrival at Wellington. No. 100b comes from the first vertical column of a sheet and has 14 at left and No. 103c from the third or fourth vertical column with 13 at left or right.

Other major errors exist on this issue, but these are not listed as they originated from printer's waste which appeared on the market in 1935.

(Recess from P.B. plates at Govt Printing Office, Wellington)

1933–**36**. W **43** of New Zealand (Single N Z and Star). P 14.
106 **20** ½d. black and deep green . . . . 1·00 4·50
w. Wmk inverted . . . . — 75·00
107 **21** 1d. black and scarlet (1935) . . . . 1·25 2·00
w. Wmk inverted and reversed . .
108 **22** 2d. black and brown (1936) . . . . 1·50 50
w. Wmk inverted . . . .
109 **23** 2½d. black and deep blue . . . . 1·50 2·25
110 **24** 4d. black and bright blue . . . . 1·50 50
111 **25** 6d. black and orange-yellow (1936) . . . . 1·75 2·25
112 **26** 1s. black and violet (1936) . . . . 27·00 38·00
106/12 *Set of* 7 . . . . 32·00 45·00

SILVER JUBILEE OF KING GEORGE V. 1910-1935. (27)

Normal Letters: **B K E N**
B K E N Narrow Letters

1935 (7 May). *Silver Jubilee. Optd with T* **27** *(wider vertical spacing on 6d.). Colours changed.* W **43** of New Zealand. P 14.
113 **21** 1d. red-brown and lake . . . . 60 1·40
a. Narrow "K" in "KING" . . . . 2·75 5·00
b. Narrow "B" in "JUBILEE" . . 6·50 10·00
114 **23** 2½d. dull and deep blue (R.) . . . . 1·00 2·50
a. Narrow first "E" in "GEORGE" . . . . 3·50 6·00
115 **25** 6d. green and orange . . . . 3·50 6·00
a. Narrow "N" in KING" . . . . 13·00 20·00
113/15 *Set of* 3 . . . . 4·50 9·00

1936 (15 July)–**44**. *Stamps of New Zealand optd with T* **19**. W **43**. P 14.
(a) T **72**. *Cowan thick, opaque chalk-surfaced paper.*
116 2s. light blue (No. 469) . . . . 13·00 45·00
117 3s. pale mauve (No. 470) . . . . 13·00 70·00
(b) Type F **6**. *Cowan thick, opaque chalk-surfaced paper.*
118 2s.6d. deep brown (No. F147) . . . . 18·00 70·00
119 5s. green (No. F149) (R.) . . . . 23·00 90·00
120 10s. carmine-lake (No. F155) . . . . 48·00 £170
121 £1 pink (No. F158) . . . . 75·00 £190
118/21 *Set of* 4 . . . . £150 £475
(c) Type F **6**. *Thin, hard, chalk-surfaced Wiggins Teape paper.*
122 2s.6d. dull brown (No. F170) (12.40) . . 95·00 £100
123 5s. green (No. F172) (R.) (10.40) £375 £350
123*a* 10s. pale carmine-lake (No. F177) (11.44) £130 £180
123*b* £3 green (No. F183) (R.) (date?) £375 £600
122/3b *Set of* 4 . . . . £900 £1100

COOK IS'DS. (28)   **IS'DS.** Small second "S" (R. 1/2)

1937 (1 June). *Coronation. Nos. 599/601 of New Zealand (inscr "12th MAY 1937") optd with T* **28**.
124 1d. carmine 40 60
a. Small second "S" . . . . 13·00
125 2½d. Prussian blue 80 70
a. Small second "S" . . . . 22·00
126 6d. red-orange 80 35
a. Small second "S" . . . . 22·00
124/6 *Set of* 3 . . . . 1·75 1·50

29 King George VI

30 Native Village

31 Native Canoe

32 Tropical Landscape

(Des J. Berry (2s., 3s., and frame of 1s.). Eng B.W. Recess Govt Ptg. Office, Wellington)

1938 (2 May). W **43** of New Zealand. P 14.
127 **29** 1s. black and violet . . . . 8·50 12·00
128 **30** 2s. black and red-brown . . . . 18·00 13·00
w. Wmk inverted . . . .
129 **31** 3s. greenish blue and green . . . . 48·00 35·00
127/9 *Set of* 3 . . . . 65·00 55·00

(Recess B.W.)

1940 (2 Sept). *Surch as in T* **32**. W **98** of New Zealand. P 13½ × 14.
130 **32** 3d.on 1½d. black and purple 60 60
Type **32** was not issued without surcharge.

1943–**54**. *Postal Fiscal stamps as Type F* **6** *of New Zealand optd with T* **19**. W **98**. *Wiggins Teape chalk-surfaced paper.* P 14.
131 2s.6d. dull brown (No. F193) (3.46) . . . . 55·00 65·00
w. Wmk inverted (2.4.51) . . . . 20·00 23·00
132 5s. green (No. F195) (R.) (11.43) . . . . 9·50 22·00
w. Wmk inverted (5.54) . . . . 23·00 26·00
133 10s. pale carmine-lake (No. F201) (10.48) . . . . 65·00 95·00
w. Wmk inverted (10.51) . . . . 55·00 80·00
134 £1 pink (No. F203) (11.47) . . . . 60·00 90·00
w. Wmk inverted (19.5.54) . . . . 65·00 95·00
135 £3 green (No. F208) (R.) (1946?) £600 £800
w. Wmk inverted (28.5.53) . . . . 60·00 £160
136 £5 indigo-blue (No. F211) (R.) (25.10.50) £275 £400
w. Wmk inverted (19.5.54) £250 £375
131/6 *Set of* 6 . . . . £400 £650
The £3 and £5 were mainly used for fiscal purposes.

(Recess Govt Ptg Office, Wellington)

1944–**46**. W **98** of New Zealand (sideways on ½d. 1d., 1s., and 2s.). P 14.
137 **20** ½d. black and deep green (11.44) . . 1·75 4·00
w. Wmk sideways inverted . . . . 5·00 9·00
138 **21** 1d. black and scarlet (3.45) . . . . 2·00 1·00
w. Wmk sideways inverted . . . . 7·00 2·50
x. Wmk sideways reversed . . . .
139 **22** 2d. black and brown (2.46) . . . . 1·75 7·00
140 **23** 2½d. black and deep blue (5.45) . . 75 2·00
141 **24** 4d. black and blue (4.44) . . . . 4·50 12·00
y. Wmk inverted and reversed . . 40·00 40·00
142 **25** 6d. black and orange (6.44) . . . . 2·50 2·00
143 **29** 1s. black and violet (9.44) . . . . 2·50 2·50
144 **30** 2s. black and red-brown (8.45) . . 35·00 45·00
145 **31** 3s. greenish blue and green (6.45) . . 35·00 32·00
w. Wmk inverted . . . . 95·00
137/45 *Set of* 9 . . . . 75·00 95·00
The normal sideways watermark shows the star to the right of NZ *as seen from the back of the stamp.*

COOK ISLANDS (33)

1946 (4 June). *Peace. Nos. 668, 670, 674/5 of New Zealand optd with T* **33** *(reading up and down at sides on 2d.).*
146 1d. green (Parliament House) 40 1
147 2d. purple (Royal family) (B.) 40 5
148 6d. chocolate and vermilion (Coat of arms, foundry and farm) 70 6
149 8d. black and carmine ("St. George") (B.) 70 6
146/9 *Set of* 4 . . . . 2·00 1·6

34 Ngatangiia Channel, Rarotonga

41 Map and Statue of Capt. Cook

(Des J. Berry. Recess Waterlow)

1949 (1 Aug)–**61**. *T* **34**, **41** *and similar designs.* W **98** of New Zealand (sideways on shilling values). P 13½ × 13 (horiz) or 13 × 13½ (vert).
150 ½d. violet and brown . . . . 10 1·
151 1d. chestnut and green . . . . 3·50 2·
152 2d. reddish brown and scarlet . . . . 2·00 2·
153 3d. green and ultramarine . . . . 2·00 2·
aw. Wmk inverted £100
b. Wmk sideways (white opaque paper) (22.5.61) . . . . 3·75 2·
154 5d. emerald-green and violet . . . . 6·00 1·
155 6d. black and carmine . . . . 5·50 2·
156 8d. olive-green and orange . . . . 55 3·
w. Wmk inverted . . . . £100 50·
157 1s. light blue and chocolate . . . . 4·25 3·
158 2s. yellow-brown and carmine . . . . 3·00 13·
w. Wmk sideways inverted . . . .
159 3s. light blue and bluish green . . . . 10·00 24·
150/9 *Set of* 10 . . . . 32·00 50·
Designs: *Horiz*—1d. Capt. Cook and map of Hervey Islands; 2d. Rarotonga and Revd. John Williams; 3d. Aitutaki and palm trees; 5d. Rarotonga Airfield; 6d. Penrhyn village; 8d. Native hut. *Vert*—2s. Native hut and palms; 3s. *Matua* (inter-island freighter).

NIUE

Niue became a British Protectorate on 20 April 1900 and was transferred to New Zealand control on 11 June 1901. There was considerable local resentment at attempts to incorporate Niue into the Cook Islands and, in consequence, the island was recognised as a separate New Zealand dependency from 1902.

PRICES FOR STAMPS ON COVER TO 1945

No. 1	*from* × 3
Nos. 2/5	*from* × 8
Nos. 6/7	—
Nos. 8/9	*from* × 30
Nos. 10/12	—
Nos. 13/31	*from* × 3
Nos. 32/7c	—
Nos. 38/47	*from* × 5
Nos. 48/9	—
No. 50	*from* × 15
Nos. 51/4	—
Nos. 55/61	*from* × 8
Nos. 62/8	*from* × 12
Nos. 69/71	*from* × 3
Nos. 72/4	*from* × 10
Nos. 75/8	*from* × 8
Nos. 79/88	—
Nos. 89/97	*from* × 2

NEW ZEALAND DEPENDENCY

Stamps of New Zealand overprinted

NIUE
(1)

1902 (4 Jan). *Handstamped with T* **1**. *in green or bluish green. Pirie paper.* Wmk double-lined "N Z" and Star, W **38** of New Zealand. P 11.
42 1d. carmine . . . £300 £300

A few overprints were made with a *greenish violet* ink. These occurred only in the first vertical row and part of the second row of the first sheet overprinted owing to violet ink having been applied to the pad (*Price* £1400 *un*).

NIUE. ½ PENI. (2) NIUE. TAHA PENI. (3) 1d. NIUE. 2½ PENI. (4)

1902 (4 Apr). *Type-set surcharges. T* **2**, **3**, *and* **4**.

(i) Pirie paper. No wmk. P 11.
27 2½d. blue (R.) . . . 1·25 4·00
a. No stop after "PENI" . . . 26·00 50·00
b. Surch double . . . £2500

(ii) Basted Mills paper. Wmk double-lined "N Z" and Star, W **38** of New Zealand.

(a) P 14.
23 ½d. green (R.) . . . 2·50 4·50
a. Spaced "U" and "E" (R. 3/3, 3/6, 8/3, 8/6) . . . 13·00 21·00
b. Surch inverted . . . £325 £550
c. Surch double . . . £950
42 1d. carmine (B.) . . . 23·00 25·00
a. Spaced "U" and "E" (R.3/3, 3/6, 8/6) . . . £120 £130
b. No stop after "PENI" (R. 9/3) . . . £300 £325
c. Varieties a. and b. on same stamp (R. 8/3) . . . £300 £325

(b) P 11 × 14.
42 1d. carmine (B.) . . . 1·75 2·50
b. Spaced "U" and "E" (R. 3/3, 3/6, 8/6) . . . 12·00 16·00
c. No stop after "PENI (R. 9/3) . . . 32·00 48·00
d. Varieties b. and c. on same stamp (R. 8/3) . . . 32·00 48·00

(c) Mixed perfs.
23 ½d. green (R.) . . . £1100
42 1d. carmine (B.) . . . £700

1902 (2 May). *Type-set surcharges, T* **2**, **3**. *Cowan paper.* Wmk single-lined "N Z" and Star, W **43** of New Zealand.

(a) P 14.
23 ½d. green (R.) . . . 1·00 1·00
a. Spaced "U" and "E" (R. 3/3, 3/6, 8/3, 8/6) . . . 7·50 9·50
42 1d. carmine (B.) . . . 60 1·00
a. Surch double . . . £1400 £1500
b. Spaced "U" and "E" (R. 3/3, 3/6, 8/6) . . . 9·50 16·00
c. No stop after "PENI" (R. 5/3, 7/3, 9/3, 10/3, 10/6) . . . 9·00 15·00
d. Varieties b. and c. on same stamp (R. 8/3) . . . 30·00 45·00
e. "I" of "NIUE" omitted (R. 6/5 from end of last ptg) . . .

(b) P 14 × 11.
23 ½d. green (R.) . . .

(c) Mixed perfs.
23 ½d. green (R.) . . . £1000
42 1d. carmine (B.) . . . £180
a. Spaced "U" and "E" (R. 3/3, 3/6, 8/3, 8/6) . . . £475
b. No stop after "PENI" (R. 5/3, 7/3, 9/3, 10/3, 10/6) . . . £475

NIUE. (5) Tolu e Pene. (6) 3d.
Ono e Pene. (7) 6d. Taha e Sileni. (8) 1s.

1903 (2 July). *Optd with name at top, T* **5**, *and values at foot, T* **6/8**, *in blue.* W **43** of New Zealand (sideways). P 11.
28 3d. yellow-brown . . . 9·50 5·00
31 6d. rose-red . . . 12·00 11·00
34 1s. brown-red ("Tahae" joined) . . . £650
a. Surch double, one albino . . . £850
1s. bright red . . . 35·00 35·00
a. Orange-red . . . 45·00 48·00
?/16 *Set of* 3 . . . 50·00 45·00

NIUE. ½ PENI. (9) NIUE. 2½ PENI. (9a) NIUE. (10)

1911 (30 Nov). ½*d. surch with T* **9**, *others optd at top as T* **5** *and values at foot as T* **7**, **8**. W **43** of New Zealand. P 14 × 15 (½d.) or 14 × 14½ (others).
51 ½d. green (C.) . . . 50 50
52 6d. carmine (B.) . . . 2·00 7·00
1s. vermilion (B.) . . . 6·50 48·00
?/19 *Set of* 3 . . . 8·00 50·00

1915 (Sept). *Surch with T* **9a**. W **43** of New Zealand. P 14.
27 2½d. deep blue (C.) . . . 15·00 35·00

1917 (Aug). *1d. surch as T* **3**, *3d. optd as T* **5** *with value as T* **6**. W **43** of New Zealand.
21 **53** 1d. carmine (P 14 × 15) (Br.) . . . 12·00 5·50
a. No stop after "PENI" (R. 10/16) . . . £375
22 **60** 3d. chocolate (P 14 × 14½) (B.) . . . 42·00 80·00
a. No stop after "Pene" (R. 10/4) . . . £800
b. Perf 14 × 13½ . . . 55·00 90·00
c. Vert pair, Nos. 22/b . . . £160

1917–21. *Optd with T* **10**. W **43** of New Zealand.

(a) P 14 × 15.
23 **61** ½d. green (R.) (2.20) . . . 70 2·50
24 **53** 1d. carmine (B.) (10.17) . . . 10·00 8·50
25 **61** 1½d. slate (R.) (11.17) . . . 1·00 2·25
26 1½d. orange-brown (R.) (2.19) . . . 70 4·50
27 3d. chocolate (B.) (6.19) . . . 1·40 27·00

(b) P 14 × 13½.
28 **60** 2½d. blue (R.) (10.20) . . . 3·00 8·00
a. Perf 14 × 14½ . . . 1·25 6·00
ab. Opt double, one albino . . .
b. Vert pair, Nos. 28/a . . . 18·00 48·00
29 3d. chocolate (B.) (10.17) . . . 1·60 2·00
a. Perf 14 × 14½ . . . 1·25 1·50
b. Vert pair, Nos. 29/a . . . 22·00 45·00
30 6d. carmine (B.) (8.21) . . . 6·50 24·00
a. Perf 14 × 14½ . . . 4·75 24·00
b. Vert pair, Nos. 30/a . . . 32·00 90·00
31 1s. vermilion (B.) (10.18) . . . 8·50 25·00
a. Perf 14 × 14½ . . . 5·50 25·00
b. Vert pair, Nos. 31/a . . . 38·00 95·00
23/31 *Set of* 9 . . . 24·00 90·00

1918–29. *Postal Fiscal stamps as Type* F **4** *of New Zealand optd with T* **10**. W **43** of New Zealand (sideways).

(i) Chalk-surfaced "De La Rue" paper.

(a) P 14.
32 5s. yellow-green (R.) (7.18) . . . £100 £110

(b) P 14½ × 14, comb.
33 2s. deep blue (R.) (9.18) . . . 16·00 32·00
34 2s.6d. grey-brown (B.) (2.23) . . . 21·00 48·00
35 5s. yellow-green (R.) (10.18) . . . 25·00 50·00
36 10s. maroon (B.) (2.23) . . . £100 £140
37 £1 rose-carmine (B.) (2.23) . . . £140 £190
33/7 *Set of* 5 . . . £275 £425

(ii) Thick, opaque, white chalk-surfaced "Cowan" paper. P 14½ × 14.
37*a* 5s. yellow-green (R.) (10.29) . . . 27·00 60·00
37*b* 10s. brown-red (B.) (2.27) . . . 90·00 £130
37*c* £1 rose-pink (B.) (2.28) . . . £140 £190
37*a/c Set of* 3 . . . £225 £350

11 Landing of Captain Cook

12 Landing of Captain Cook

R. 2/8 R. 3/6

R. 5/2

Double derrick flaws

(Des, eng and recess P.B.)

1920 (23 Aug). *T* **11** *and similar designs.* No wmk. P 14.
38 ½d. black and green . . . 3·75 3·75
39 1d. black and dull carmine . . . 2·00 1·25
a. Double derrick flaw (R. 2/8, 3/6 or 5/2) . . . 6·50 6·50
40 1½d. black and red . . . 2·50 8·50
41 3d. black and blue . . . 75 14·00
42 6d. red-brown and green . . . 1·75 18·00
43 1s. black and sepia . . . 1·75 18·00
38/43 *Set of* 6 . . . 11·00 55·00

Designs: *Vert*—1d. Wharf at Avarua; 1½d. "Capt Cook (Dance)"; 3d. Palm tree. *Horiz*—6d. Huts at Arorangi; 1s. Avarua Harbour.

Examples of the 6d. with inverted centre were not supplied to the Post Office.

1925–27. *As Nos. 38/9 and new values.* W **43** of New Zealand. P 14.
44 ½d. black and green (1927) . . . 1·50 8·00
45 1d. black and deep carmine (1925) . . . 1·75 1·00
a. Double derrick flaw (R. 2/8, 3/6 or 5/2) . . . 5·50 4·50
46 2½d. black and blue (10.27) . . . 4·25 11·00
47 4d. black and violet (10.27) . . . 7·00 20·00
44/7 *Set of* 4 . . . 13·00 35·00

Designs: *Vert*—2½d. Te Po, Rarotongan chief. *Horiz*—4d. Harbour, Rarotonga, and Mount Ikurangi.

1927–28. *Admiral type of New Zealand optd as T* **10**. W **43** of New Zealand. P 14.

(a) "Jones" paper (wmk inverted).
48 **72** 2s. deep blue (2.27) (R.) . . . 15·00 48·00

(b) "Cowan" paper.
49 **72** 2s. light blue (R.) (2.28) . . . 18·00 32·00

1931 (1 Apr). *No. 40 surch as T* **18** *of Cook Is.*
50 2d.on 1½d. black and red . . . 2·25 1·00

1931 (12 Nov). *Postal Fiscal stamps as Type* F **6** *of New Zealand optd as T* **10**. W **43** of New Zealand. *Thick, opaque, chalk-surfaced "Cowan" paper.* P 14.
51 2s.6d. deep brown (B.) . . . 4·00 11·00
52 5s. green (R.) . . . 35·00 70·00
53 10s. carmine-lake (B.) . . . 35·00 £100
54 £1 pink (B.) . . . 60·00 £140
51/4 *Set of* 4 . . . £120 £275

See also Nos. 79/82 for different type of overprint.

(Des L. C. Mitchell. Recess P.B.)

1932 (16 Mar). *T* **12** *and similar designs inscr "*NIUE*" and "*COOK ISLANDS*".* No wmk. P 13.
55 ½d. black and emerald . . . 9·50 22·00
a. Perf 13 × 14 × 13 × 13 . . . £250
56 1d. black and deep lake . . . 1·00 50
57 2d. black and red-brown . . . 2·50 4·00
a. Perf 14 × 13 × 13 × 13 . . . £100 £160
58 2½d. black and slate-blue . . . 8·00 75·00
59 4d. black and greenish blue . . . 14·00 60·00
a. Perf 14 . . . 16·00 55·00
60 6d. black and orange-vermilion . . . 2·50 2·00
61 1s. black and purple (P 14) . . . 2·25 5·00
55/61 *Set of* 7 . . . 35·00 £150

Designs: *Vert*—1d. Capt. Cook; 1s. King George V. *Horiz*—2d. Double Maori canoe; 2½d. Islanders working cargo; 4d. Port of Avarua; 6d. R.M.S. *Monowai.*

Examples of the 2½d. with inverted centre were not supplied to the Post Office.

Nos. 55a and 57a are mixed perforations, each having one side perforated 14 where the original perforation, 13, was inadequate.

(Recess from Perkins Bacon's plates at Govt Ptg Office, Wellington, N.Z.)

1932–36. *As Nos. 55/61, but* W **43** of New Zealand. P 14.
62 ½d. black and emerald . . . 50 3·25
63 1d. black and deep lake . . . 50 1·50
w. Wmk inverted . . . 45·00
64 2d. black and yellow-brown (1.4.36) . . . 50 1·50
w. Wmk inverted . . . 25·00 45·00
65 2½d. black and slate-blue . . . 50 4·25
w. Wmk inverted . . . 45·00
66 4d. black and greenish blue . . . 1·75 4·00
w. Wmk inverted . . .
67 6d. black and red-orange (1.4.36) . . . 70 75
68 1s. black and purple (1.4.36) . . . 8·50 24·00
62/8 *Set of* 7 . . . 11·50 35·00

Imperforate proofs of No. 65 are known used on registered mail from Niue postmarked 30 August 1945 or 29 October 1945.

See also Nos. 89/97.

SILVER JUBILEE OF KING GEORGE V 1910-1935.
(13)

Normal Letters
B K E N
B K E N
Narrow Letters

1935 (7 May). *Silver Jubilee. Designs as Nos. 63, 65 and 67 (colours changed) optd with T* **13** *(wider vertical spacing on 6d.).* W **43** of New Zealand. P 14.
69 1d. red-brown and lake . . . 60 3·50
a. Narrow "K" in "KING" . . . 2·75 9·00
b. Narrow "B" in "JUBILEE" . . . 2·75 9·00
70 2½d. dull and deep blue (R.) . . . 3·25 7·50
a. Narrow first "E" in "GEORGE" . . . 4·00 13·00
71 6d. green and orange . . . 3·25 6·00
a. Narrow "N" in "KING" . . . 15·00 35·00
69/71 *Set of* 3 . . . 6·50 15·00

Examples of No. 70 imperforate horizontally are from proof sheets not issued through the Post and Telegraph Department (*Price* £250 *for vert pair*).

NIUE (14) NIUE Short opt (R. 9/4)

1937 (13 May). *Coronation. Nos. 599/601 of New Zealand optd with T* **14**.
72 1d. carmine . . . 30 10
a. Short opt . . . 8·00
73 2½d. Prussian blue . . . 40 1·25
a. Short opt . . . 10·00
74 6d. red-orange . . . 40 20
a. Short opt . . . 10·00
72/4 *Set of* 3 . . . 1·00 1·40

15 King George VI

16 Tropical Landscape

1938 (2 May). *T* **15** *and similar designs inscr "*NIUE COOK ISLANDS*".* W **43** of New Zealand. P 14.
75 1s. black and violet . . . 10·00 8·00
76 2s. black and red-brown . . . 12·00 17·00
77 3s. blue and yellowish green . . . 35·00 17·00
75/7 *Set of* 3 . . . 50·00 38·00

Designs: *Vert*—2s. Island village. *Horiz*—3s. Cook Islands canoe.

1940 (2 Sept). *Unissued stamp surch as in T* **16**. W **98** of New Zealand. P 13½ × 14.
78 3d.on 1½d. black and purple . . . 75 20

NIUE.
(17)

1941–67. *Postal Fiscal stamps as Type F* **6** *of New Zealand with thin opt, T* **17**. P 14.

(i) Thin, hard, chalk-surfaced "Wiggins Teape" paper with vertical mesh (1941–43).

(a) W **43** of New Zealand.

79 2s.6d. deep brown (B.) (4.41) 75·00 80·00
80 5s. green (R.) (4.41) £275 £200
81 10s. pale carmine-lake (B.) (6.42) £120 £200
82 £1 pink (B.) (2.43?) £190 £300
79/82 *Set of* 4 £600 £700

(b) W **98** of New Zealand (1944–54).

83 2s.6d. deep brown (B.) (3.45) 3·50 10·00
w. Wmk inverted (11.51) 12·00 16·00
84 5s. green (R.) (11.44) 7·50 11·00
w. Wmk inverted (19.5.54) 7·50 13·00
85 10s. carmine-lake (B.) (11.45) 55·00 £100
w. Wmk inverted 60·00 £100
86 £1 pink (B.) (6.42) 42·00 60·00
83/6 *Set of* 4 95·00 £160

(ii) Unsurfaced "Wiggins Teape" paper with horizontal mesh. W **98** of New Zealand (1957–67).

87 2s.6d. deep brown (P 14 × 13½) (1.11.57) 9·00 10·00
88 5s. pale yellowish green (wmk sideways) (6.67) 20·00 75·00

No. 88 came from a late printing made to fill demands from Wellington, but no supplies were sent to Niue. It exists in both line and comb perf.

1944–46. *As Nos. 62/7 and 75/7, but* W **98** of New Zealand (sideways on ½d., 1d., 1s. and 2s.).

89 **12** ½d. black and emerald 50 2·25
90 – 1d. black and deep lake 50 1·50
91 – 2d. black and red-brown 5·50 6·50
92 – 2½d. black and slate-blue (1946) 60 1·25
93 – 4d. black and greenish blue 4·25 1·00
w. Wmk inverted and reversed 16·00
94 – 6d. black and red-orange 2·25 1·40
95 **15** 1s. black and violet 1·50 85
96 – 2s. black and red-brown (1945) 8·50 3·00
97 – 3s. blue and yellowish green (1945) 15·00 7·00
89/97 *Set of* 9 35·00 22·00

1946 (4 June). *Peace. Nos. 668, 670, 674/5 of New Zealand optd as T* **17** *without stop (twice, reading up and down on 2d.).*

98 1d. green (Blk.) 30 10
99 2d. purple (B.) 30 10
100 6d. chocolate and vermilion (Blk.) 30 70
a. Opt double, one albino £225
101 8d. black and carmine (B.) 40 70
98/101 *Set of* 4 1·10 1·40

Nos. 102/112 are no longer used.

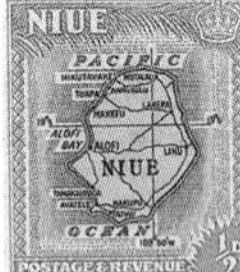

18 Map of Niue

19 H.M.S. *Resolution*

23 Bananas

24 Matapa Chasm

(Des J. Berry. Recess B.W.)

1950 (3 July). *T* **18/19**, **23/24** *and similar designs.* W **98** of New Zealand (sideways inverted on 1d., 2d., 3d., 4d., 6d. and 1s.). P 13½ × 14 (horiz) or 14 × 13½ (vert).

113 ½d. orange and blue 10 60
114 1d. brown and blue-green 2·25 1·75
115 2d. black and carmine 1·00 1·25
116 3d. blue and violet-blue 10 15
117 4d. olive-green and purple-brown 10 15
118 6d. green and brown-orange 60 1·00
119 9d. orange and brown 10 1·25
120 1s. purple and black 10 15
121 2s. brown-orange and dull green 1·50 4·25
122 3s. blue and black 4·50 4·25
113/22 *Set of* 10 9·00 13·00

Designs: *Horiz* (as *T* **19**)—2d. Alofi landing; 3d. Native hut; 4d. Arch at Hikutavake; 6d. Alofi bay; 1s. Cave, Makefu. *Vert* (as *T* **18**)—9d. Spearing fish.

PENRHYN ISLAND

Stamps of COOK ISLANDS were used on Penrhyn Island from late 1901 until the issue of the surcharged stamps in May 1902.

PRICES FOR STAMPS ON COVER TO 1945

No.	1	*from* × 25
No.	3	—
Nos.	4/5	*from* × 25
Nos.	6/8	—
Nos.	9/10	*from* × 50
Nos.	11/13	—
Nos.	14/18	*from* × 3
Nos.	19/23	*from* × 2
Nos.	24/37	*from* × 3
Nos.	38/40	*from* × 5

NEW ZEALAND DEPENDENCY

The island of Penrhyn, under British protection from 20 September 1888, was annexed by New Zealand on 11 June 1901.

Stamps of New Zealand overprinted or surcharged. For illustrations of New Zealand watermarks and definitive types see the beginning of Cook Islands.

PENRHYN ISLAND.
½ PENI.
(1)

PENRHYN ISLAND.
TAI PENI.
(2) 1d.

PENRHYN ISLAND.
2½ PENI.
(3)

1902 (5 May). *T* **23**, **27** *and* **42** *surch with T* **1**, **2** *and* **3**.

(a) Thick, soft Pirie paper. No wmk. P 11.

1 2½d. blue (No. 260) (R.) 3·00 8·00
a. "½" and "P" spaced (all stamps in 8th vert row) 16·00 32·00

(b) Thin, hard Basted Mills paper. W **38** of New Zealand.

(i) P 11.

3 1d. carmine (No. 286) (Br.) £850 £900

(ii) P 14.

4 ½d. green (No. 287) (R.) 80 6·00
a. No stop after "ISLAND" £150 £200
5 1d. carmine (No. 288) (Br.) 3·25 15·00

(iii) Perf compound of 11 and 14.

6 1d. carmine (No. 290) (Br.) £850 £900

(iv) Mixed perfs.

7 ½d. green (No. 291) (R.) £1200
8 1d. carmine (No. 292) (Br.) £1400

(c) Thin, hard Cowan paper. W **43** of New Zealand.

(i) P 14.

9 ½d. green (No. 302) (R.) 2·00 6·00
a. No stop after "ISLAND" (R. 10/6) £140 £190
10 1d. carmine (No. 303) (B.) 1·25 4·00
a. No stop after "ISLAND" (R. 10/6) 48·00 85·00

(ii) Perf compound of 11 and 14.

11 1d. carmine (No. 305) (B.) £7000

(iii) Mixed perfs.

12 ½d. green (No. 306) (R.) £1300 £1400
13 1d. carmine (No. 307) (B.) £650 £700

PENRHYN ISLAND.
(4)

Toru Pene.
(5) 3d.

Ono Pene.
(6) 6d.

Tahi Silingi.
(7) 1s.

1903 (28 Feb). *T* **28**, **31** *and* **34** *surch with name at top, T* **4**, *and values at foot, T* **5/7**. *Thin, hard Cowan paper.* W **43** (sideways) of New Zealand. P 11.

14 3d. yellow-brown (No. 309) (B.) 10·00 22·00
15 6d. rose-red (No. 312*a*) (B.) 15·00 35·00
16 1s. brown-red (No. 315) (B.) 55·00 55·00
a. Bright red 42·00 42·00
b. Orange-red 55·00 55·00
14/16*a Set of* 3 60·00 90·00

1914 (May)–**15**. *T* **51/2** *surch with T* **1** *(½d.) or optd with T* **4** *at top and surch with T* **6/7** *at foot.*

19 ½d. yellow-green (No. 387) (C.) (5.14) 80 8·00
a. No stop after "ISLAND" 25·00 75·00
b. No stop after "PENI" (R. 3/17) 90·00 £160
c. Vermilion opt (1.15) 80 8·00
ca. No stop after "ISLAND" 10·00 45·00
cb. No stop after "PENI" (R. 3/5, 3/17) 40·00 £100
22 6d. carmine (No. 393) (B.) (8.14) 23·00 70·00
23 1s. vermilion (No. 394) (B.) (8.14) 42·00 95·00
19/23 *Set of* 3 60·00 £150

The "no stop after ISLAND" variety occurs on R. 1/4, 1/10, 1/16, 1/22, 6/4, 6/10, 6/16 and 6/22 of the carmine surcharge, No. 19, and on these positions plus R. 1/12, 1/24, 6/12 and 6/24 for the vermilion, No. 19c.

1917 (Nov)–**20**. *Optd as T* **4**.

(a) T **60** *(recess).* W **43** of New Zealand. P 14 × 13½.

24 2½d. blue (No. 419) (R.) (10.20) 3·00 9·50
a. Perf 14 × 14½ 2·00 7·00
ab. No stop after "ISLAND" (R. 10/8) £190 £325
b. Vert pair. Nos. 24/4a 45·00 85·00
25 3d. chocolate (No. 420) (B.) (6.18) 12·00 70·00
a. Perf 14 × 14½ 9·50 70·00
b. Vert pair. Nos. 25/5a 70·00 £200
26 6d. carmine (No. 425) (B.) (1.18) 8·00 25·00
a. Perf 14 × 14½ 5·00 19·00
ab. No stop after "ISLAND" (R. 10/8) £425 £600
b. Vert pair. Nos. 26/6a 55·00 £130
27 1s. vermilion (No. 430) (B.) (12.17) 15·00 42·00
a. Perf 14 × 14½ 12·00 32·00
ab. No stop after "ISLAND" (R. 10/8) £475 £650
b. Vert pair. Nos. 27/7a £100 £200
24/7 *Set of* 4 25·00 £110

(b) T **61** *(typo).* W **43** of New Zealand. P 14 × 15.

28 ½d. green (No. 435) (R.) (2.20) 1·00 2·00
a. No stop after "ISLAND" (R. 2/24) £120 £170
b. Narrow spacing 6·50 11·00
29 1½d. slate (No. 437) (R.) 6·50 18·00
a. Narrow spacing 18·00 40·00
30 1½d. orange-brown (No. 438) (R.) (2.19) 60 18·00
a. Narrow spacing 5·00 40·00
31 3d. chocolate (No. 440) (B.) (6.19) 3·50 22·00
a. Narrow spacing 16·00 55·00
28/31 *Set of* 4 10·50 55·00

The narrow spacing variety occurs on R. 1/5–8, 4/21–4, 7/5–8 and 9/21–4.

(Recess P.B.)

1920 (23 Aug). *As T* **9/14** *of Cook Islands, but inscr* "PENRHYN". No wmk. P 14.

32 ½d. black and emerald 1·00 16·0
a. Part imperf block of 4 £1400
33 1d. black and deep red 1·50 15·0
a. Double derrick flaw (R. 2/8, 3/6 or 5/2) 5·50 45·0
34 1½d. black and deep violet 6·50 19·0
35 3d. black and red 2·50 8·5
36 6d. red-brown and sepia 3·25 20·0
37 1s. black and slate-blue 10·00 26·0
32/7 *Set of* 6 22·00 95·0

No. 32a comes from sheets on which two rows were imperforat between horizontally and the second row additionally imperforat vertically.

Examples of the ½d. and 1d. with centre inverted were nc supplied to the Post Office.

(Recess Govt Printing Office, Wellington)

1927–29. *As T* **9/10** *and* **16** *of Cook Islands, but inscr* "PENRHYN". W **43**. P 14.

38 ½d. black and green (5.29) 5·50 21·0
39 1d. black and deep carmine (14.3.28) 5·50 18·0
a. Double derrick flaw (R. 2/8, 3/6 or 5/2) 16·00
40 2½d. red-brown and dull blue (10.27) 3·50 27·0
38/40 *Set of* 3 13·00 60·0

Cook Islands stamps superseded those of Penrhyn Island c 15 March 1932.

TOKELAU ISLANDS

Formerly known as the Union Islands, and administered as pa of the Gilbert & Ellice Islands Colony, Tokelau was transferred t New Zealand on 4 November 1925 and administered with Wester Samoa. The Islands were finally incorporated in New Zealand c 1 January 1949 and became a dependency. The name Tokelau wa officially adopted on 7 May 1946.

Stamps of GILBERT AND ELLICE ISLANDS were used in Tokelau from Febuary 1911 until June 1926 when they were replaced by those of SAMOA. These were current until 1948.

The post office on Atafu opened in 1911, but the cancellations for the other two islands, Fakaofo and Nukunono, did not appear until 1926.

NEW ZEALAND ADMINISTRATION

1 Atafu Village and Map

(Des J. Berry from photographs by T. T. C. Humphrey. Recess B.W.)

1948 (22 June). *T* **1** *and similar horiz designs.* Wmk *T* **98** of Ne Zealand (Mult N Z and Star). P 13½.

1 ½d. red-brown and purple 15
2 1d. chestnut and green 15
w. Wmk inverted £275
3 2d. green and ultramarine 15
1/3 *Set of* 3 40 1·

Designs:—1d. Nukunono hut and map; 2d. Fakaofo village a map.

Covers are known postmarked 16 June 1948, but this was in err for 16 July.

WESTERN SAMOA

PRICES FOR STAMPS ON COVER TO 1945

Nos. 1/20 are very rare used on cover.

Nos.	21/40	*from* × 20
Nos.	41/8	*from* × 100
Nos.	49/56	*from* × 4
Nos.	57/64	*from* × 12
Nos.	65/8	*from* × 2
Nos.	69/97	*from* × 20
Nos.	101/9	*from* × 3
Nos.	110/14	—
Nos.	115/21	*from* × 3
Nos.	122/32	—
Nos.	134/64	*from* × 3
Nos.	165/76	—
Nos.	177/214	*from* × 2

INDEPENDENT KINGDOM OF SAMOA

The first postal service in Samoa was organised by C. L. Griffi who had earlier run the *Fiji Times* Express post in Suva. In b instances the principal purpose of the service was the distribut of newspapers of which Griffiths was the proprietor. The first is of the *Samoa Times* (later the *Samoa Times and South Sea Gaze* appeared on 6 October 1877 and the newspaper continued in wee publication until 27 August 1881.

Mail from the Samoa Express post to addresses overseas v routed via New South Wales, New Zealand or U.S.A. and recei additional franking with stamps of the receiving country on landi

Cancellations, inscribed "APIA SAMOA", did not arrive u March 1878 so that examples of Nos. 1/9 used before that date w cancelled in manuscript.

1

A 2nd State (Nos. 4/9)

B 3rd State (Nos. 10/19)

(Des H. H. Glover. Litho S. T. Leigh & Co, Sydney, N.S.W.)

877 (1 Oct)–**80**.

1st state: white line above "X" in "EXPRESS" not broken. P 12½..

No.	Type	Description	Unused	Used
	1	1d. ultramarine	£250	£120
		3d. deep scarlet	£300	£130
		6d. bright violet	£300	£110
		a. Pale lilac	£325	£110

2nd state: white line above "X" broken by a spot of colour, and dot between top of "M" and "O" of "SAMOA". P 12½ *(1878–79).*

No.	Type	Description	Unused	Used
	1	1d. ultramarine	90·00	95·00
		3d. bright scarlet	£325	£130
		6d. bright violet	£190	90·00
		1s. dull yellow	£150	90·00
		a. Line above "X" not broken	£180	£120
		b. Perf 12 (1879)	80·00	95·00
		c. Orange-yellow	95·00	£100
		2s. red-brown	£275	£200
		a. Chocolate	£300	£350
		5s. green	£900	£1100
		a. Line above "X" not broken	£1200	£1400

3rd state: line above "X" repaired, dot merged with upper right serif of "M" (1879).

(a) P 12½..

No.	Type	Description	Unused	Used
	1	1d. ultramarine	90·00	90·00
		3d. vermilion	£120	£120
		6d. lilac	£120	85·00
		2s. brown	£250	£250
		a. Chocolate	£250	£250
		5s. green	£500	£500
		a. Line above "X" not repaired (R. 2/3)	£650	

(b) P 12.

No.	Type	Description	Unused	Used
	1	1d. blue	24·00	40·00
		a. Deep blue	32·00	70·00
		b. Ultramarine	28·00	40·00
		3d. vermilion	48·00	75·00
		a. Carmine-vermilion	48·00	85·00
		6d. bright violet	40·00	48·00
		a. Deep violet	40·00	80·00
		2s. deep brown	£150	£250
		5s. yellow-green	£400	£600
		a. Deep green	£375	£550
		b. Line above "X" not repaired (R. 2/3)	£500	

4th state: spot of colour under middle stroke of "M". P 12 *(1880).*

No.	Type	Description	Unused	Used
	1	9d. orange-brown	60·00	£120

Originals exist imperf, but are not known used in this state.

On sheets of the 1d., 1st state, at least eight stamps have a stop er "PENNY". In the 2nd state, three stamps have the stop, and the 3rd state, only one.

In the 1st state, all the stamps, 1d., 3d. and 6d., were in sheets of (5 × 4) and also the ld. in the 3rd state.

All values in the 2nd state, all values except the 1d. in the 3rd te and No. 20 were in sheets of 10 (5 × 2).

As all sheets of all printings of the originals were imperf at the ter edges, the only stamps which can have perforations on all four es are Nos. 1 to 3*a*, 10 and 15 to 15*b*, all other originals being perf on one or two sides.

The perf 12 stamps, which gauge 11.8, are generally very rough t later the machine was repaired and the 1d., 3d. and 6d. are own with clean-cut perforations.

Remainders of the 1d., unissued 2d. rose, 6d. (in sheets of 21 × 3), 3d., 9d., 1s. (in sheets of 12 (4 × 3)) and of the 2s. and 5s. eet format unknown) were found in the Samoan post office when service closed down in 1881. The remainders are rare in complete ets, but of very little value as singles, compared with the ginals.

Reprints of all values, in sheets of 40 (8 × 5), were made after the ginals had been withdrawn from sale. These are practically rthless.

The majority of both reprints and remainders are in the 4th state the 9d. with the spot of colour under the middle stroke of the ", but a few stamps (both remainders and reprints) do not show , while on some it is very faint.

There are three known types of forgery, one of which is rather dangerous, the others being crude.

The last mail despatch organised by the proprietors of the Samoa Express took place on 31 August 1881, although one cover is recorded postmarked 24 September 1881.

After the withdrawal of the Samoa Express service it would appear that the Apia municipality appointed a postmaster to continue the overseas post. Covers are known franked with U.S.A. or New Zealand stamps in Samoa, or routed via Fiji.

In December 1886 the municipal postmaster, John Davis, was appointed Postmaster of the Kingdom of Samoa by King Malietoa. Overseas mail sent via New Zealand was subsequently accepted without the addition of New Zealand stamps, although letters to the U.S.A. continued to require such franking until August 1891.

2 Palm Trees

3 King Malietoa Laupepa

4a 6 mm

4b 7 mm

4c 4 mm

Description of Watermarks

(These are the same as W **12***a*/*c* of New Zealand)

W **4***a*. 6 mm between "N Z" and star; broad irregular star; comparatively wide "N"; "N Z" 11½ mm wide.

W **4***b*. 7 mm between "N Z" and star; narrower star; narrow "N"; "N Z" 10 mm wide.

W **4***c*. 4 mm between "N Z" and star; narrow star; wide "N"; "N Z" 11 mm wide.

(Des A. E. Cousins (*T* **3**). Dies eng W. R. Bock and A. E. Cousins (*T* **2**) or A. E. Cousins (*T* **3**). Typo Govt Ptg Office, Wellington)

1886–1900.

(i) W **4***a*.

(a) P 12½ (Oct–Nov 1886).

No.	Type	Description	Unused	Used
21	**2**	½d. purple-brown	23·00	55·00
22		1d. yellow-green	9·50	12·00
23		2d. dull orange	28·00	10·00
24		4d. blue	48·00	10·00
25		1s. rose-carmine	65·00	11·00
		a. Bisected (2½d.) (on cover)*	†	£325
26		2s.6d. reddish lilac	55·00	75·00

(b) P 12 × 11½ (July–Nov 1887).

No.	Type	Description	Unused	Used
27	**2**	½d. purple-brown	70·00	80·00
28		1d. yellow-green	£100	27·00
29		2d. yellow	95·00	£140
30		4d. blue	£250	£200
31		6d. brown-lake	29·00	14·00
32		1s. rose-carmine	—	£190
33		2s.6d. reddish lilac	£350	

(ii) W **4***c*. P 12 × 11½ (May 1890).

No.	Type	Description	Unused	Used
34	**2**	½d. purple-brown	75·00	30·00
35		1d. green	55·00	40·00
36		2d. brown-orange	80·00	40·00
37		4d. blue	£140	5·00
38		6d. brown-lake	£300	11·00
39		1s. rose-carmine	£350	13·00
		x. Wmk reversed	†	32·00
40		2s.6d. reddish lilac	£450	8·50

(iii) W **4***b*.

(a) P 12 × 11½ (1890–92).

No.	Type	Description	Unused	Used
41	**2**	½d. pale purple-brown	4·25	4·25
		a. Blackish purple	4·25	4·25
42		1d. myrtle-green (5.90)	26·00	1·40
		a. Green	26·00	1·40
		b. Yellow-green	26·00	1·40
43		2d. dull orange (5.90)	35·00	1·75
44	**3**	2½d. rose (11.92)	75·00	3·75
		a. Pale rose	75·00	3·75
45	**2**	4d. blue	£225	19·00
46		6d. brown-lake	£110	9·00
47		1s. rose-carmine	£225	5·00
48		2s.6d. slate-lilac	—	8·50

(b) P 12½ (Mar 1891–92).

No.	Type	Description	Unused	Used
49	**2**	½d. purple-brown		
50		1d. green		
51		2d. orange-yellow	—	£160
52	**3**	2½d. rose (1.92)	26·00	4·50
53	**2**	4d. blue	—	£450
54		6d. brown-purple	£2750	£1300
55		1s. rose-carmine	—	£450
56		2s.6d. slate-lilac		

(c) P 11 (May 1895–1900).

No.	Type	Description	Unused	Used
57	**2**	½d. purple-brown	2·75	1·75
		a. Deep purple-brown	2·25	1·75
		b. Blackish purple (1900)	2·25	35·00
58		1d. green	7·50	1·75
		a. Bluish green (1897)	7·50	1·75
		b. Deep green (1900)	2·75	22·00
59		2d. pale yellow	40·00	40·00
		a. Orange (1896)	40·00	40·00
		b. Bright yellow (1.97)	13·00	6·00
		c. Pale ochre (10.97)	5·00	1·50
		d. Dull orange (1900)	7·50	
60	**3**	2½d. rose	2·75	4·50
		a. Deep rose-carmine (1900)	2·25	42·00
61	**2**	4d. blue	9·50	2·00
		a. Deep blue (1900)	1·25	50·00
62		6d. brown-lake	9·50	3·00
		a. Brown-purple (1900)	1·75	60·00
63		1s. rose	10·00	3·75
		a. Dull rose-carmine/toned (5.98)	3·25	35·00
		b. Carmine (1900)	1·50	
64		2s.6d. purple	55·00	10·00
		a. Reddish lilac (wmk inverted) (1897)	11·00	8·00
		b. Deep purple/toned (wmk reversed) (5.98)	4·75	9·50
		ba. Imperf between (vert pair)	£400	
		c. Slate-violet	£120	

*Following a fire on 1 April 1895 which destroyed stocks of all stamps except the 1s. value perf 12½, this was bisected diagonally and used as a 2½d. stamp for overseas letters between 24 April and May 1895, and was cancelled in blue. Fresh supplies of the 2½d. did not arrive until July 1895, although other values were available from 23 May.

Examples of the 1s. rose perforated 11, No. 63, were subsequently bisected and supplied cancelled-to-order by the post office to collectors, often with backdated cancellations. Most of these examples were bisected vertically and all were cancelled in black (*Price* £7).

The dates given relate to the earliest dates of printing in the various watermarks and perforations and not to issue dates.

The perf 11 issues (including those later surcharged or overprinted), are very unevenly perforated owing to the large size of the pins. Evenly perforated copies are extremely hard to find.

For the 2½d. black, see Nos. 81/2 and for the ½d. green and 1d. red-brown, see Nos. 88/9.

FIVE PENCE **(5)** FIVE PENCE **(6)** 5d **(7)**

1893 (Nov–Dec). *Handstamped singly, at Apia.*

(a) In two operations.

No.	Type	Description	Unused	Used
65	**5**	5d.on 4d. blue (37)	55·00	45·00
		a. Bars omitted	£500	£400
66		5d.on 4d. blue (45)	70·00	£100
67	**6**	5d.on 4d. blue (37)	£100	£110
68		5d.on 4d. blue (45)	£100	

(b) In three operations (Dec).

No.	Type	Description	Unused	Used
69	**7**	5d.on 4d. blue (37) (R.)	26·00	32·00
		a. Stop after "d"	£250	65·00
		b. Bars omitted	—	£400
70		5d.on 4d. blue (45) (R.)	29·00	50·00

In Types **5** and **6** the bars obliterating the original value vary in length from 13½ to 16½ mm and can occur with either the thick bar over the thin one or vice versa.

Double handstamps exist but we do not list them.

No. 69a came from a separate handstamp which applied the "5d." at one operation. Where the "d" was applied separately its position in relation to the "5" naturally varies.

8

Surcharged 1½d. **(9)** R 3d. **(10)**

The "R" in Type **10** indicates use for registration fee

(Des and die eng A. E. Cousins. Typo New Zealand Govt Ptg Office)

1894–1900. W **4***b* (sideways).

(a) P 11½ × 12.

No.	Type	Description	Unused	Used
71	**8**	5d. dull vermilion (3.94)	32·00	2·75
		a. Dull red	32·00	3·75

(b) P 11.

No.	Type	Description	Unused	Used
72	**8**	5d. dull red (1895)	19·00	7·00
		a. Deep red (1900)	3·00	15·00

1895–1900. W **4***b*.

(i) Handstamped with T **9** *or* **10**.

(a) P 12 × 11½ (26.1.95).

No.	Type	Description	Unused	Used
73	**2**	1½d.on 2d. dull orange (B.)	16·00	8·00
74		3d.on 2d. dull orange	48·00	13·00

(b) P 11 (6.95).

No.	Type	Description	Unused	Used
75	**2**	1½d. on 2d. orange (B.)	3·00	7·00
		a. Pair, one without handstamp		
		b. On 2d. yellow	75·00	60·00
76		3d.on 2d. orange	8·00	10·00
		a. On 2d. yellow	75·00	60·00

*(ii) Surch printed**. P 11.

No.	Type	Description	Unused	Used
77	**2**	1½d.on 2d. orange-yellow (B.)	£100	

(iii) Handstamped as T **9** *or* **10**.† P 11 (1896).

No.	Type	Description	Unused	Used
78	**2**	1½d.on 2d. orange-yellow (B.)	3·00	23·00
79		3d.on 2d. orange-yellow	3·75	48·00
		a. Imperf between (vert pair)	£425	
		b. Pair, one without handstamp		

(iv) Surch typo as T **10**. P 11 (Feb 1900).

No.	Type	Description	Unused	Used
80	**2**	3d.on 2d. deep red-orange (G.)	1·50	£130

*It is believed that this was type-set from which clichés were made and set up in a forme and then printed on a hand press. This would account for the clear indentation on the back of the stamp and the variation in the position on the stamps which probably resulted from the clichés becoming loose in the forme.

†In No. 78 the "2" has a serif and the handstamp is in pale greenish blue instead of deep blue. In No. 79 the "R" is slightly narrower. In both instances the stamp is in a different shade.
A special printing in a distinctly different colour was made for No. 80 and the surcharge is in green.
Most of the handstamps exist double.

1896 (Aug). *Printed in the wrong colour.* W **4***b*.
(a) P 10 × 11.
81 **3** 2½d. black . . . 1·50 3·00
(b) P 11.
82 **3** 2½d. black . . . 50·00 65·00
a. Mixed perfs 10 and 11 . . . £375

Surcharged 2½d. (11) — PROVISIONAL GOVT. (12)

1898–99. W **4***b*. P 11.
(a) Handstamped as T **11** (10.98).
83 **2** 2½d.on 1s. dull rose-carmine/*toned* . . . 48·00 50·00
(b) Surch as *T* **11** (1899).
84 **2** 2½d.on 1d. bluish green (R.) . . . 75 3·00
a. Surch inverted . . . — £350
85 2½d.on 1s. dull rose-carmine/*toned* (R.) . . . 7·50 13·00
a. Surch double . . . £350
86 2½d.on 1s. dull rose-carmine/*toned* (Blk.) . . . 7·50 13·00
a. Surch double . . . £450
87 2½d.on 2s.6d. deep purple/*toned* . . . 8·50 17·00
The typographed surcharge was applied in a setting of nine, giving seven types differing in the angle and length of the fractional line, the type of stop, etc.

1899. *Colours changed.* W **4***b*. P 11.
88 **2** ½d. dull blue-green . . . 1·60 2·25
a. Deep green . . . 1·60 2·25
89 1d. deep red-brown . . . 2·25 2·25

1899–1900. *Provisional Government. New printings optd with T* **12** *(longer words and shorter letters on 5d.).* W **4***b*. P 11.
90 **2** ½d. dull blue-green (R.) . . . 1·75 3·50
a. Yellowish green (1900) . . . 1·75 5·00
91 1d. chestnut (B.) . . . 2·50 8·50
92 2d. dull orange (R.) . . . 2·50 7·50
a. Orange-yellow (1900) . . . 2·25 8·50
93 4d. deep dull blue (R.) . . . 70 9·50
94 **8** 5d. dull vermilion (B.) . . . 3·00 9·00
a. Red (1900) . . . 2·75 9·00
95 **2** 6d. brown-lake (B.) . . . 1·50 8·50
96 1s. rose-carmine (B.) . . . 1·50 27·00
97 2s.6d. reddish purple (R.) . . . 4·75 21·00
90/7 *Set of* 8 . . . 16·00 85·00

The Samoan group of islands was partitioned on 1 March 1900: Western Samoa (Upolu, Savaii Apolima and Manono) to Germany and Eastern Samoa (Tutuila, the Manu'a Is and Rose Is) to the United States. German issues of 1900–14 will be found listed in Part 7 (*Germany*) of this catalogue, there were no U.S. issues.
The Samoan Kingdom post office run by John Davis was suspended in March 1900.

NEW ZEALAND OCCUPATION

The German Islands of Samoa surrendered to the New Zealand Expeditionary Force on 30 August 1914 and were administered by New Zealand until 1962.

G.R.I. 1d. (13) — G.R.I. 1 Shillings. (14)

SETTINGS. Nos. 101/9 were surcharged by a vertical setting of ten, repeated ten times across the sheet. Nos. 110/14 were from a horizontal setting of four repeated five times in the sheet.
Nos. 101b, 102a and 104a occurred on position 6. The error was corrected during the printing of No. 102.
Nos. 101c, 102c, 104d and 105b are from position 10.
Nos. 101d, 102e and 104b are from position 1.
No. 108b is from position 9.

(Surch by *Samoanische Zeitung*, Apia)

1914 (3 Sept). *German Colonial issue (ship)* (no wmk) *inscr* "SAMOA" *surch as T* **13** *or* **14** *(mark values).*
101 ½d.on 3pf. brown . . . 35·00 9·00
a. Surch double . . . £650 £500
b. No fraction bar . . . 60·00 32·00
c. Comma after "I" . . . £600 £400
d. "1" to left of "2" in "½" . . . 60·00 32·00
102 ½d.on 5pf. green . . . 50·00 13·00
a. No fraction bar . . . £120 55·00
c. Comma after "I" . . . £350 £170
d. Surch double . . . £650 £500
e. "1" to left of "2" in "½" . . . £100 40·00
103 1d.on 10pf. carmine . . . 95·00 40·00
a. Surch double . . . £750 £600
104 2½d.on 20pf. ultramarine . . . 40·00 10·00
a. No fraction bar . . . 75·00 38·00
b. "1" to left of "2" in "½" . . . 75·00 38·00
c. Surch inverted . . . £900 £800
d. Comma after "I" . . . £450 £325
e. Surch double . . . £650 £550
105 3d.on 25pf. black and red/*yellow* . . . 55·00 40·00
a. Surch double . . . £850 £700
b. Comma after "I" . . . £4750 £1000
106 4d.on 30pf. black and orange/*buff* . . . £110 60·00
107 5d.on 40pf. black and carmine . . . £110 70·00
108 6d.on 50pf. black and purple/*buff* . . . 60·00 35·00
a. Surch double . . . £950 £900
b. Inverted "9" for "6" . . . £170 £100
109 9d.on 80pf. black and carmine/*rose* . . . £200 £100
110 "1shillings" on 1m. carmine . . . £3250 £3500
111 "1shilling" on 1m. carmine . . . £10000 £7000
112 2s.on 2m. blue . . . £3000 £2750
113 3s.on 3m. violet-black . . . £1400 £1200
a. Surch double . . . £8000 £9000
114 5s.on 5m. carmine and black . . . £1100 £1000
a. Surch double . . . £11000 £11000
No. 108b is distinguishable from 108, as the "d" and the "9" are not in a line, and the upper loop of the "9" turns downwards to the left.

UNAUTHORISED SURCHARGES. Examples of the 2d. on 20pf., 3d. on 30pf., 3d. on 40pf., 4d. on 40pf., 6d. on 80pf., 2s. on 3m. and 2s. on Marshall Islands 2m., together with a number of errors not listed above, were produced by the printer on stamps supplied by local collectors. These were not authorised by the New Zealand Military Administration.

SAMOA. (15)

1914 (29 Sept)–**15.** *Stamps of New Zealand. T* **50**, **51**, **52** *and* **27**, *optd as T* **15**, *but opt only 14 mm long on all except 2½d.* Wmk "N Z" and Star, W **43** of New Zealand.
115 ½d. yellow-green (R.) (P 14 × 15) . . . 1·00 30
116 1d. carmine (B.) (P 14 × 15) . . . 1·00 10
117 2d. mauve (R.) (P 14 × 14½) (10.14) . . . 1·00 1·00
118 2½d. deep blue (R.) (P 14) (10.14) . . . 1·75 1·75
w. Wmk inverted
119 6d. carmine (B.) (P 14 × 14½) (10.14) . . . 1·75 1·75
a. Perf 14 × 13½ . . . 17·00 23·00
b. Vert pair. Nos. 119/a (1915) . . . 48·00 80·00
120 6d. pale carmine (B.) (P 14 × 14½) (10.14) . . . 10·00 10·00
121 1s. vermilion (B.) (P 14 × 14½) (10.14) . . . 5·50 19·00
115/21 *Set of* 6 . . . 11·00 21·00

1914–24. *Postal Fiscal stamps as Type* F **4** *of New Zealand optd with T* **15**. W **43** of New Zealand (sideways). *Chalk-surfaced "De La Rue" paper.*
(a) P 14 (Nov 1914–17).
122 2s. blue (R.) (9.17) . . . 95·00 £100
123 2s.6d. grey-brown (B.) (9.17) . . . 5·50 9·00
124 5s. yellow-green (R.) . . . 12·00 11·00
125 10s. maroon (B.) . . . 26·00 28·00
126 £1 rose-carmine (B.) . . . 65·00 45·00
(b) P 14½ × 14, comb (1917–24).
127 2s. deep blue (R.) (3.18) . . . 5·50 5·50
128 2s.6d. grey-brown (B.) (10.24) . . . £275 £150
129 3s. purple (R.) (6.23) . . . 16·00 50·00
130 5s. yellow-green (R.) (9.17) . . . 16·00 15·00
131 10s. maroon (B.) (11.17) . . . 65·00 45·00
132 £1 rose-carmine (B.) (3.18) . . . 75·00 70·00
We no longer list the £2 value as it is doubtful if this was used for postal purposes.
See also Nos. 165/6*e*.

1916–19. *King George V stamps of New Zealand optd as T* **15**, *but 14 mm long.*
(a) Typo. P 14 × 15.
134 **61** ½d. yellow-green (R.) . . . 60 1·25
135 1½d. slate (R.) (1917) . . . 50 25
136 1½d. orange-brown (R.) (1919) . . . 30 50
137 2d. yellow (R.) (14.2.18) . . . 1·50 20
138 3d. chocolate (B.) (1919) . . . 1·75 15·00
(b) Recess. P 14 × 13½.
139 **60** 2½d. blue (R.) . . . 60 50
a. Perf 14 × 14½ . . . 1·25 60
b. Vert pair. Nos. 139/a . . . 15·00 24·00
140 3d. chocolate (B.) (1917) . . . 50 1·00
a. Perf 14 × 14½ . . . 50 1·00
b. Vert pair. Nos. 140/a . . . 15·00 27·00
141 6d. carmine (B.) (5.5.17) . . . 1·50 3·25
a. Perf 14 × 14½ . . . 1·50 1·25
b. Vert pair. Nos. 141/a . . . 17·00 32·00
142 1s. vermilion (B.) . . . 2·00 1·50
a. Perf 14 × 14½ . . . 4·75 9·00
b. Vert pair. Nos. 142/a . . . 22·00 45·00
134/42 *Set of* 9 . . . 8·25 19·00

LEAGUE OF NATIONS MANDATE

Administered by New Zealand.

1920 (July). *Victory. Nos. 453/8 of New Zealand optd as T* **15**, *but 14 mm long.*
143 ½d. green (R.) . . . 3·75 9·50
144 1d. carmine (B.) . . . 2·75 9·00
145 1½d. brown-orange (R.) . . . 1·50 8·50
146 3d. chocolate (B.) . . . 8·00 9·00
147 6d. violet (R.) . . . 4·50 7·00
148 1s. orange-red (B.) . . . 13·00 11·00
143/8 *Set of* 6 . . . 30·00 48·00

16 Native Hut

SILVER JUBILEE OF KING GEORGE V 1910 - 1935. (17)

(Eng B.W. Recess-printed at Wellington, NZ)

1921 (23 Dec). W **43** of New Zealand.
(a) P 14 × 14½.
149 **16** ½d. green . . . 2·25 7·00
150 1d. lake . . . 3·25 40
151 1½d. chestnut . . . 1·00 1
152 2d. yellow . . . 2·25
149/52 *Set of* 4 . . . 8·00 2
(b) P 14 × 13½.
153 **16** ½d. green . . . 4·50
154 1d. lake . . . 5·00
155 1½d. chestnut . . . 10·00
156 2d. yellow . . . 13·00
157 2½d. grey-blue . . . 1·75
158 3d. sepia . . . 1·75
159 4d. violet . . . 1·75
160 5d. light blue . . . 1·75
161 6d. bright carmine . . . 1·75
162 8d. red-brown . . . 1·75 1
163 9d. olive-green . . . 2·00 2
164 1s. vermilion . . . 1·75 2
153/64 *Set of* 12 . . . 42·00 9

1925–28. *Postal Fiscal stamps as Type* F **4** *of New Zealand with T* **15**. W **43** of New Zealand (sideways). P 14½ × 14.
(a) Thick, opaque, white chalk-surfaced "Cowan" paper.
165 2s. blue (R.) (12.25) . . . £160
166 2s.6d. deep grey-brown (B.) (10.28) . . . 65·00
166*a* 3s. mauve (R.) (9.25) . . . 60·00 8
166*b* 5s. yellow-green (R.) (11.26) . . . 18·00 4
ba. Opt at top of stamp . . . £1100
166*c* 10s. brown-red (B.) (12.25) . . . £160
166*d* £1 rose-pink (B.) (11.26) . . . 70·00 9
165/6*d* *Set of* 6 . . . £475
(b) Thin, hard, chalk-surfaced "Wiggins Teape" paper.
166*e* £1 rose-pink (B.) (1928) . . . —

1926–27. *T* **72** *of New Zealand, optd with T* **15**, *in red.*
(a) "Jones" paper.
167 2s. deep blue (11.26) . . . 5·00 1
168 3s. mauve (10.26) . . . 17·00 4
w. Wmk inverted . . . 17·00 4
(b) "Cowan" paper.
169 2s. light blue (10.11.27) . . . 6·00 4
170 3s. pale mauve (10.11.27) . . . 48·00 9

1932 (Aug). *Postal Fiscal stamps as Type F* **6** *of New Zealand with T* **15**. W **43** of New Zealand. *Thick, opaque, white ch surfaced "Cowan" paper.* P 14.
171 2s.6d. deep brown (B.) . . . 16·00 4
172 5s. green (R.) . . . 26·00 5
173 10s. carmine-lake (B.) . . . 45·00
174 £1 pink (B.) . . . 70·00
175 £2 bright purple (R.) . . . £750
176 £5 indigo-blue (R.) . . . £1900
The £2 and £5 values were primarily for fiscal use.

1935 (7 May). *Silver Jubilee. Optd with T* **17**. P 14 × 13½.
177 **16** 1d. lake . . . 30
a. Perf 14 × 14½ . . . 85·00
178 2½d. grey-blue . . . 60
179 6d. bright carmine . . . 2·75
177/9 *Set of* 3 . . . 3·25

18 Samoan Girl

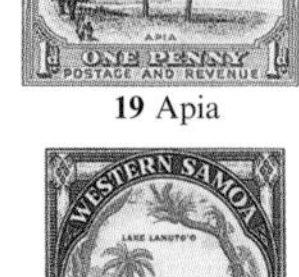
19 Apia

21 Chief and Wife

25 Lake Lanuto'o

(Recess D.L.R.)

1935 (7 Aug). *T* **18/19**, **21**, **25** *and similar designs.* W **43** of N Zealand ("N Z" and Star). P 14 × 13½ (½d., 2½d., 2s., 3s.), 14 (or 13½ × 14 (others).
180 ½d. green . . . 10
w. Wmk inverted
181 1d. black and carmine . . . 10
182 2d. black and orange . . . 3·50
aw. Wmk inverted
b. Perf 13½ × 14 . . . 4·00
bw. Wmk inverted
183 2½d. black and blue . . . 10
184 4d. slate and sepia . . . 70
185 6d. bright magenta . . . 50
186 1s. violet and brown . . . 30
187 2s. green and purple-brown . . . 80
188 3s. blue and brown-orange . . . 1·50
180/8 *Set of* 9 . . . 6·50
Designs: *Horiz*—2d. River scene; 4d. Canoe and house; 6d. R Stevenson's home "Vailima"; 1s. Stevenson's Tomb. *Vert* (a **25**)—3s. Falefa Falls.
See also Nos. 200/3.

WESTERN SAMOA. (27)

1935–42. *Postal Fiscal stamps as Type F* **6** *of New Zealand with T* **27**. W **43** of New Zealand. P 14.
(a) Thick, opaque chalk-surfaced "Cowan" paper (7.8.35).
189 2s.6d. deep brown (B.) . . . 6·00 1
190 5s. green (B.) . . . 12·00 2
191 10s. carmine-lake (B.) . . . 55·00 7
192 £1 pink (B.) . . . 55·00

93 £2 bright purple (R.) £160 £350
94 £5 indigo-blue (R.) £225 £450

(b) Thin, hard chalk-surfaced "Wiggins Teape" paper (1941–42).

94*a* 5s. green (B.) (6.42) . . . . 90·00 £110
94*b* 10s. pale carmine-lake (B.) (6.41) £130 £140
94*c* £2 bright purple (R.) (2.42) £450 £700
94*d* £5 indigo-blue (R.) (2.42) £1000 £1300

The £2 and £5 values were primarily for fiscal use.
See also Nos. 207/14.

28 Coastal Scene

31 Robert Louis Stevenson

Des J. Berry (1d. and 1½d.). L. C. Mitchell (2½d. and 7d.). Recess B.W.)

939 (29 Aug). *25th Anniv of New Zealand Control. T* **28**, **31** *and similar horiz designs.* W **98** of New Zealand. P 13½ × 14 or 14 × 13½ (7d.).

95 1d. olive-green and scarlet 60 25
96 1½d. light blue and red-brown . . . . . . 1·00 75
97 2½d. red-brown and blue . . . . 1·00 75
98 7d. violet and slate-green . . . . 7·50 3·50
95/8 *Set of* 4 . . . . 9·00 4·75

Designs:—1½d. Map of Western Samoa; 2½d. Samoan dancing party.

32 Samoan Chief

33 Apia Post Office

(Recess B.W.)

940 (2 Sept). W **98** of New Zealand (Mult "N Z" and Star). P 14 × 13½.

99 **32** 3d.on 1½d. brown 75 10

T **32** was not issued without surcharge.

(*T* **33**. Des L. C. Mitchell. Recess B.W.)

44–49. *As Nos. 180, 182/3 and T* **33**. W **98** of New Zealand (Mult "N Z" and Star) (sideways on 2½d.). P 14 or 13½ × 14 (5d.)

0 ½d. green . . . . 30 17·00
2 2d. black and orange . . . . 3·00 5·50
3 2½d. black and blue (1948) . . . . 4·75 30·00
5 5d. sepia and blue (8.6.49) . . . . 1·50 50
0/5 *Set of* 4 . . . . 8·75 48·00

45–53. *Postal Fiscal stamps as Type F* **6** *of New Zealand optd with T* **27**. W **98** of New Zealand. *Thin hard, chalk-surfaced "Wiggins Teape" paper.* P 14.

7 2s.6d. deep brown (B.) (6.45) . . . . . . 7·00 14·00
w. Wmk inverted . . . . 9·00 11·00
8 5s. green (B.) (5.45) . . . . 14·00 15·00
w. Wmk inverted . . . . 15·00 16·00
9 10s. carmine-lake (B.) (4.46) . . . . . . 20·00 17·00
w. Wmk inverted . . . . 27·00 29·00
0 £1 pink (B.) (6.48) £110 £170
w. Wmk inverted
1 30s. brown (8.48) £180 £300
w. Wmk inverted £375 £500
2 £2 bright purple (R.) (11.47) £190 £275
w. Wmk inverted £300 £400
3 £3 green (8.48) £225 £375
w. Wmk inverted £400 £650
4 £5 indigo-blue (R) (1946) £350 £450
w. Wmk inverted (5.53) £350 £450
7/10 *Set of* 4 . . . . £140 £190

The £2 to £5 values were mainly used for fiscal purposes.
The 5s., 10s., £1 and £2 were reissued in 1955 with a larger erprint, omitting the stop after "SAMOA".

WESTERN
SAMOA
(34)

46 (4 June). *Peace Issue. Nos. 668, 670 and 674/5 of New Zealand optd with T* **34** *(reading up and down at sides on 2d.).*

5 1d. green 40 15
w. Wmk inverted £140
5 2d. purple (B.) 40 15
7 6d. chocolate and vermilion 40 15
3 8d. black and carmine (B.) 40 15
5/18 *Set of* 4 . . . . 1·40 55

Nigeria

LAGOS

A British Consul was established at Lagos during 1853 as part of the anti-slavery policy, but the territory was not placed under British administration until occupied by the Royal Navy in August 1861. From 19 February 1866 Lagos was administered with Sierra Leone and from July 1874 as part of Gold Coast. It became a separate colony on 13 January 1886.

Although a postal service had been established by the British G.P.O. in April 1852 no postal markings were supplied to Lagos until 1859. The British G.P.O. retained control of the postal service until June 1863, when it became the responsibility of the colonial authorities.

CROWNED-CIRCLE HANDSTAMPS

CC 1

CC1 CC **1** LAGOS (19.12.1859) . . *Price on cover* £2500

First recorded use of No. CC1 is 12 December 1871. It is later known used as a cancellation.

PRICES FOR STAMPS ON COVER		
Nos.	1/9	*from* × 10
Nos.	10/26	*from* × 8
Nos.	27/9	—
Nos.	30/8	*from* × 10
Nos.	39/41	—
No.	42	*from* × 20
Nos.	44/50	*from* × 8
Nos.	51/3	—
Nos.	54/60	*from* × 8
Nos.	61/3	—

PRINTERS. All the stamps of Lagos were typographed by D.L.R.

1

1874 (10 June)–**75**. Wmk Crown CC. P 12½.

1 **1** 1d. lilac-mauve . . . . 55·00 32·00
2 2d. blue . . . . 55·00 28·00
3 3d. red-brown (2.75) . . . . 85·00 42·00
5 4d. carmine . . . . 85·00 40·00
6 6d. blue-green . . . . 95·00 12·00
8 1s. orange (value 15½ mm) (2.75) £450 £140
a. Value 16½ mm long (7.75) . . . . . £275 60·00
1/8a *Set of* 6 . . . . £550 £180

1876–79. Wmk Crown CC. P 14.

10 **1** 1d. lilac-mauve . . . . 38·00 18·00
11 2d. blue . . . . 42·00 13·00
12 3d. red-brown . . . . £100 18·00
13 3d. chestnut . . . . £110 35·00
14 4d. carmine . . . . £190 11·00
a. Wmk sideways £1100 £130
15 6d. green . . . . 95·00 6·00
16 1s. orange (value 16½ mm long) (1879) . . . £600 85·00
10/16 *Set of* 6 . . . . £950 £130

1882 (June). Wmk Crown CA. P 14.

17 **1** 1d. lilac-mauve . . . . 19·00 10·00
18 2d. blue . . . . £150 4·75
19 3d. chestnut . . . . 15·00 5·00
20 4d. carmine . . . . £140 12·00
17/20 *Set of* 4 . . . . £275 29·00

1884 (Dec)–**86**. *New values and colours.* Wmk Crown CA. P 14.

21 **1** ½d. dull green (1885) . . . . 2·00 80
22 1d. rose-carmine . . . . 2·00 80
w. Wmk inverted . . . . £100 90·00
23 2d. grey . . . . 60·00 5·50
24 4d. pale violet . . . . £100 8·50
25 6d. olive-green . . . . 8·00 40·00
26 1s. orange (3.85) . . . . 7·00 20·00
27 2s.6d. olive-black (1886) £275 £250
28 5s. blue (1886) £500 £425
29 10s. purple-brown (1886) £1300 £950
21/9 *Set of* 9 . . . . £2000 £1500
27s/9s Optd "Specimen" *Set of* 3 . . . . . £425

We would warn collectors against clever forgeries of Nos. 27 to 29 on genuinely watermarked paper.

2½ PENNY

A

2½ PENNY

B

1887 (Mar)–**1902**. Wmk Crown CA. P 14.

30 **1** 2d. dull mauve and blue . . . . 3·25 2·00
31 2½d. ultramarine (A) (1891) . . . . . . 3·50 1·75
a. Larger letters of value (B) . . . . . 22·00 17·00
b. Blue (A) . . . . 80·00 50·00
32 3d. dull mauve and chestnut (4.91) . . . 2·50 3·25
33 4d. dull mauve and black . . . . 2·25 1·75
34 5d. dull mauve and green (2.94) . . . . 2·00 11·00
35 6d. dull mauve and mauve . . . . 4·75 3·00
a. Dull mauve and carmine (10.02) . . . 5·00 12·00
36 7½d. dull mauve and carmine (2.94) . . . 2·25 29·00
37 10d. dull mauve and yellow (2.94) . . . 3·25 13·00
38 1s. yellow-green and black . . . . . . 5·50 24·00
a. Blue-green and black . . . . 5·00 25·00
39 2s.6d. green and carmine . . . . 23·00 80·00
40 5s. green and blue . . . . 40·00 £150
41 10s. green and brown . . . . 75·00 £200
30/41 *Set of* 12 . . . . £150 £475
30s/41s Optd "Specimen" *Set of* 12 . . . . . £250

HALF PENNY

(2)

3

1893 (2 Aug). *No. 33 surch with T* **2** *locally.*

42 **1** ½d. on 4d. dull mauve and black . . . . 4·25 2·50
a. Surch double . . . . 55·00 55·00
b. Surch treble £120
c. Error. ½d. on 2d. (No. 30) . . . . . — £15000

There were two separate settings of No. 42. The most common, of which there were five separate printings, shows "HALF PENNY" 16 mm long and was applied as a horizontal pair or triplet. The scarcer setting, also applied as a triplet, shows "HALF PENNY" 16½ mm long.

Three examples of No. 42c are known, two unused and one used. Only the latter is in private hands.

1904 (22 Jan–Nov). Wmk Crown CA. P 14.

44 **3** ½d. dull green and green . . . . 1·50 5·50
45 1d. purple and black/*red* . . . . 1·00 15
46 2d. dull purple and blue . . . . 6·00 6·00
47 2½d. dull purple and blue/*blue* (B) . . . 1·00 1·50
aw. Wmk inverted . . . . — 75·00
b. Smaller letters of value as A . . . . 4·50 8·50
bw. Wmk inverted £130 £130
48 3d. dull purple and brown . . . . 2·25 1·75
49 6d. dull purple and mauve . . . . 35·00 10·00
50 1s. green and black . . . . 35·00 42·00
51 2s.6d. green and carmine . . . . 90·00 £200
52 5s. green and blue £130 £275
53 10s. green and brown (Nov) £275 £750
44/53 *Set of* 10 . . . . £500 £1200
44s/53s Optd "Specimen" *Set of* 10 . . . . . £180

1904–06. *Ordinary paper.* Wmk Mult Crown CA. P 14.

54 **3** ½d. dull green and green (30.10.04) . . . 7·50 2·50
a. Chalk-surfaced paper (12.3.06) . . . 10·00 1·75
w. Wmk inverted
55 1d. purple and black/*red* (22.10.04) . . . 7·00 10
a. Chalk-surfaced paper (21.9.05) . . . 1·50 10
aw. Wmk inverted . . . . — 75·00
56 2d. dull purple and blue (2.05) . . . . . 2·25 2·00
a. Chalk-surfaced paper (25.9.06) . . . 13·00 10·00
aw. Wmk inverted £100
57 2½d. dull purple and blue/*blue* (B) (*chalk-surfaced paper*) (13.10.05) . . . . . 1·75 16·00
a. Smaller letters of value as A . . . . 55·00 £120
58 3d. dull purple and brown (27.4.05) . . . 3·50 1·25
a. Chalk-surfaced paper (2.8.06) . . . . 15·00 1·75
w. Wmk inverted
59 6d. dull purple and mauve (31.10.04) . . . 6·50 2·25
a. Chalk-surfaced paper (1.3.06) . . . . 4·25 1·50
60 1s. green and black (15.10.04) . . . . . 13·00 19·00
a. Chalk-surfaced paper (4.06) . . . . . 23·00 2·25
w. Wmk inverted
61 2s.6d. green and carmine (3.12.04) . . . . 16·00 55·00
a. Chalk-surfaced paper (21.10.06) . . . 35·00 50·00
62 5s. green and blue (1.05) . . . . 22·00 95·00
a. Chalk-surfaced paper (21.10.06) . . . 65·00 £160
63 10s. green and brown (3.12.04) . . . . . 60·00 £200
a. Chalk-surfaced paper (12.3.06) . . . 75·00 £190
54/63 *Set of* 10 . . . . £120 £325

Lagos was incorporated into the Colony and Protectorate of Southern Nigeria, previously formed from Niger Coast Protectorate and part of the Niger Company territories, on 16 February 1906. Stamps of Lagos were then authorised for use throughout Southern Nigeria.

NIGER COAST PROTECTORATE

OIL RIVERS PROTECTORATE

A British consulate for the Bights of Benin and Biafra was established in 1849 on the off-shore Spanish island of Fernando Po. In 1853 the appointment was divided with a consul for the Bight of Benin at Lagos. The consulate for the Bight of Biafra was transferred to Old Calabar in 1882.

A British protectorate was proclaimed over the coastal area, with the exceptions of the colony of Lagos and the centre of the Niger delta, on 5 June 1885. It was not, however, until July 1891 that steps were taken to set up an administration with a consul-general at Old Calabar and consuls at some of the river ports.

The consulate-general at Old Calabar and the vice-consulates at Benin, Bonny, Brass, Forcados and Opobo acted as collection and distribution centres for mail from November 1891, but were not recognised as post offices until 20 July 1892.

For a few months from July 1892 local administrative handstamps, as Type Z **1**, were in use either as obliterators or in conjunction with the c.d.s.

Z 1

These oval handstamps are usually found on the 1892 overprinted issue, but the following are known on unoverprinted stamps of Great Britain:

1892

BENIN

Stamps of GREAT BRITAIN *cancelled with oval postmark, Type Z* **1**, *inscribed "BENIN".*

Z1 2½d. purple/*blue* (V.) £1000

BONNY

Stamps of GREAT BRITAIN *cancelled with oval postmark, Type Z* **1**, *inscribed "BONNY".*

Z2 2½d. purple/*blue* (V.) £1000

BRASS RIVER

Stamps of GREAT BRITAIN *cancelled with oval postmark, Type Z* **1**, *inscribed "BRASS".*

Z3 2½d. purple/*blue* (Blk.) £750

OLD CALABAR RIVER

Stamps of GREAT BRITAIN *cancelled with oval postmark, Type Z* **1**, *inscribed "OLD CALABAR".*

Z4 2d. purple/*blue* (Blk.) £750

Stamps of GREAT BRITAIN *cancelled "*BRITISH VICE-CONSULATE OLD CALABAR*" within double-lined circle.*

Z5 2½d. purple/*blue* (V.) £450
Z6 5d. dull purple and blue (V.) . . . .

For later use of Type Z **1** and the circular Vice-Consulate marks see note beneath No. 6.

Z 2

Unoverprinted stamps of Great Britain remained officially valid for postage in the Protectorate until 30 September 1892, but were available from post offices in the Niger Company Territories up to the end of 1899. The two areas were so closely linked geographically that offices in the Protectorate continued to accept letters franked with Great Britain stamps until the reorganisation of 1900. The listing below covers confirmed examples, known on cover or piece, the prices quoted being for the latter.

1892–99.

Stamps of GREAT BRITAIN *cancelled with circular postmarks as Type Z* **2**.

BENIN RIVER

Z 7 2d. green and carmine . . . .
Z 8 2½d. purple/*blue* £550
Z 9 3d. purple/*yellow* £550
Z10 5d. dull purple and blue . . . .
Z11 1s. green . . . .

BONNY RIVER

Z12 ½d. vermilion £375
Z12*a* 1d. lilac £325
Z13 2½d. purple/*blue* £275
Z14 5d. dull purple and blue £375
Z15 6d. deep purple/*red* £375

BRASS RIVER

Z16 1½d. dull purple and green £800
Z17 2½d. purple/*blue* £700
Z17*a* 2½d. purple/*blue* (squared-circle cancellation) . . . £850
Z18 6d. purple/*red* £750

FORCADOS RIVER

Z19 1d. lilac £600
Z20 2½d. purple/*blue* . . . .
Z21 5d. dull purple and blue (m/s cancellation) . . . .
Z22 10d. dull purple and carmine . . . .

OLD CALABAR RIVER

Z23 ½d. vermilion £325
Z24 1d. lilac £275
Z25 1½d. dull purple and green £375
Z26 2d. green and vermilion £375
Z27 2½d. purple/*blue* £275
Z28 5d. dull purple and blue £375
Z29 6d. purple/*red* £375
Z30 1s. green £475

OPOBO RIVER

Z31 2½d. purple/*blue* £300
Z32 10d. dull purple and carmine £600

Some later covers are known franked with G.B. stamps, but the origin of the stamps involved is uncertain.

PRICES FOR STAMPS ON COVER		
Nos.	1/6	*from* × 12
Nos.	7/36	*from* × 4
Nos.	37/44	—
Nos.	45/50	*from* × 10
Nos.	51/6	*from* × 12
Nos.	57/65	*from* × 3
Nos.	66/73	*from* × 12

BRITISH PROTECTORATE

OIL RIVERS

(1)

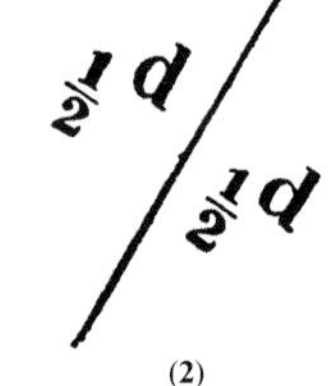

(2)

1892 (20 July)–**94**. *Nos. 172, 197, 200/1, 207a and 211 of Great Britain optd by D.L.R. with T* **1**.

		Unused	Used
1	½d. vermilion	10·00	7·00
2	1d. lilac	6·00	7·50
	a. Opt reversed "OIL RIVERS" at top	£4500	
	b. Bisected (½d.) (on cover)	†	£2500
3	2d. grey-green and carmine	23·00	8·00
	a. Bisected (1d.) (on cover)	†	£2500
4	2½d. purple/*blue*	6·50	2·25
5	5d. dull purple and blue (Die II (No. 207*a*))	9·00	6·50
	a. On Die I (No. 207)		
6	1s. dull green	55·00	75·00
1/6	*Set of* 6	£100	95·00
1s/6s	H/S "Specimen" *Set of* 6	£275	

Nos. 2b and 3a were used at Bonny River during August and September 1894.

Die II of the 5d. shows thin vertical lines to the right of "5d.". On Die I there are square dots in this position.

OVAL HANDSTAMPS. In addition to Nos. Z1/4 postmarks as Type Z **1** are also known used on the 1892–94 overprinted issue from the following offices:

Bakana (Nos. 2, 4/6)
Benin (Nos. 1/6)
Bonny (No. 2)
Brass (Nos. 3/5)
Buguma (Nos. 4 and 6)
Old Calabar (No. 4)
Opobo (Nos. 1/3)
Sombreiro River (Nos. 1/6)

The Vice-Consulate marks, as Nos. Z5/6, are also known struck on examples of No. 4 from Bonny, Forcados or Old Calabar.

Nos. 2 to 6 surcharged locally

1893 (3 Sept). *Issued at Old Calabar. Surch with T* **2** *and then bisected.*

		Unused	Used
7	½d. on half of 1d. (R.)	£150	£140
	a. Unsevered pair	£450	£425
	ab. Surch inverted and dividing line reversed (unsevered pair)	—	£11000
	b. Surch reversed (dividing line running from left to right) (unsevered pair)	—	£11000
	c. Straight top to "1" in ½	£350	£350
	d. "½" omitted		
	e. Surch double (unsevered pair with normal)	—	£1600
	f. Vert *se-tenant* pair. Nos. 7a/8a	—	£14000
8	½d. on half of 1d. (V.)	£4250	£4000
	a. Unsevered pair	£11000	£10000
	b. Surch double (pair)	£17000	

The surcharge was applied in a setting covering one horizontal row at a time. Violet ink was used for the top row in the first sheet, but was then replaced with red.

HALF PENNY.

(3)

HALF PENNY.

(4)

In T **3** "HALF" measures 9½ mm and "PENNY" 12½ mm with space 1½ mm between the words. Bar 14½ mm ending below the stop. The "F" is nearly always defective.

In T **4** "HALF" is 8½ mm, "PENNY" 12½ mm, spacing 2½ mm, and bar 16 mm, extending beyond the stop.

HALF PENN.Y

5 (Stop after "N")

HALF PENNY

6 (No stop after "N")

In T **5** the "P" and "Y" are raised, and the space between the words is about 4 mm. Bar is short, approx 13½ mm. T **6** is similar but without the stop after "N".

Half Penny

(7)

Half Penny

(8)

In T **7** the "a" and "e" are narrow and have a short upwarc terminal hook. The "1" has a very small hook. The letters "nny" have curved serifs, and the distance between the words is 5½ mm.

In T **8** the "a" and "e" are wider. The "1" has a wider hook. The letters "nny" have straight serifs, and the distance between the words is 4½ mm.

HALF PENNY.

(9)

HALF PENNY

(10)

1893 (Dec). *Issue at Old Calabar. Nos. 3/4 handstamped.*

(a) With T **3**.

		Unused	Used
9	½d. on 2d. (V.)	£500	£30
	a. Surch inverted	£5500	
	b. Surch diagonal (up or down)	£3500	
	c. Surch vertical (up or down)	£4000	
10	½d. on 2½d. (Verm.)	£9000	
10*a*	½d. on 2½d. (C.)	£22000	

(b) With T **4**.

		Unused	Used
11	½d. on 2½d. (G.)	£250	£25
	a. Surch double	£2500	£250
	b. Surch diagonally inverted	£3500	
12	½d. on 2½d. (Verm.)	£800	£30
13	½d. on 2½d. (C.)	£375	£40
	a. Surch omitted (in pair)		
14	½d. on 2½d. (B.)	£325	£40
15	½d. on 2½d. (Blk.)	£4000	
	a. Surch inverted	£6500	
	b. Surch diagonal inverted (up or down)	£5000	
16	½d. on 2½d. (B.-Blk.)	£4000	

(c) With T **5**.

		Unused	Used
17	½d. on 2½d. (Verm.)	£650	£2
	a. Surch double	—	£140
	b. Surch vertical (up)	—	£32

(d) With T **6**.

		Unused	Used
18	½d. on 2d. (V.)	£650	£3
19	½d. on 2½d. (Verm.)	£300	£3
	a. Surch inverted	£2750	
	b. Surch double	—	£16
	c. Surch diagonal (up or down)	£1600	
	d. Surch omitted (in strip of 3)	£13000	
	e. Surch vertical (up or down)	£2250	
	f. Surch diagonal, inverted (up or down)	£2250	

(e) With T **7**.

		Unused	Used
20	½d. on 2d. (V.)	£325	£2
	a. Surch double	—	£60
	b. Surch vertical (up or down)	£3000	
	c. Surch diagonal (up or down)	£2500	
	d. Surch diagonal (inverted)	£3750	
	e. Surch inverted		
21	½d. on 2½d. (Verm.)	£300	£1
	a. Surch double	£4500	
	b. Surch vertical (up or down)	£2250	
	c. Surch inverted	£2750	
	d. Surch diagonal (up or down)	£1500	
	e. Surch diagonal, inverted (up)	£3750	
22	½d. on 2½d. (B.)	£10000	£100
23	½d. on 2½d. (C.)	£9000	
24	½d. on 2½d. (V.)	£6500	

(f) With T **8**.

		Unused	Used
25	½d. on 2½d. (Verm)	£425	£6
	a. Surch diagonal (up)	£2250	
26	½d. on 2½d. (B.)	£22000	
27	½d. on 2½d. (G.)	£425	£4
	a. Surch double	£5500	
28	½d. on 2½d. (C.)	£16000	£160

(g) With T **9**.

		Unused	Used
29	½d. on 2d. (V.)	£325	£3
30	½d. on 2d. (B.)	£1500	£7
	a. Surch double		
31	½d. on 2½d. (Verm.)	£475	£5
	a. Surch double		
32	½d. on 2½d. (B.)	£350	£3
33	½d. on 2½d. (G.)	£375	£4
	a. Surch double (G.)	£1800	
	b. Surch double (G. + Verm.)		
34	½d. on 2½d. (V.)	£5500	

(h) With T **10**.

		Unused	Used
35	½d. on 2½d. (G.)	£425	£4
36	½d. on 2½d. (Verm.)	£6500	

Various types of surcharges on Nos. 9 to 36 were printed on the same sheet, and different types in different colours may be fou *se-tenant* (*Prices, from* £2000 *per pair, unused*).

One Shilling

(11)

5/-

(12)

1893 (Dec). *Issued at Old Calabar. Nos. 3 and 5/6 handstamped.*

(a) With T **11**.

37 1s. on 2d. (V.) . . . £425 £350
a. Surch inverted . . . £4750
b. Surch vertical (up or down) . . . £3750
c. Surch diagonal (up or down) . . . £2750
d. Surch diagonal, inverted (up or down) . . . £4500
e. Pair, Nos. 37 and 38 . . . £2250
38 1s. on 2d. (Verm.) . . . £600 £3750
a. Surch inverted . . . £6500
b. Surch diagonal (up or down) . . . £4500
c. Surch vertical (up or down) . . . £6500
39 1s. on 2d. (Blk.) . . . £5500
a. Surch inverted . . . £11000
b. Surch vertical (up or down) . . . £9000
c. Surch diagonal (up) . . . £7000

(b) As T **12**.

40 5s. on 2d. (V.) . . . £9000 £10000
a. Surch inverted . . . £18000
b. Surch vertical (up or down) . . . £18000 £18000
c. Surch diagonal (down) . . . £18000
41 10s. on 5d. (Verm.) . . . £6000 £8000
a. Surch inverted . . . £17000
b. Surch vertical (up or down) . . . £17000
c. Surch diagonal (down) . . .
42 20s. on 1s. (V.) . . . £70000
a. Surch inverted . . . £90000
43 20s. on 1s. (Verm.) . . . £70000
44 20s. on 1s. (Blk.) . . . £70000

There are two main settings of the "One Shilling" surcharge:—

Type A. The "0" is over the "hi" of "Shilling" and the downstrokes on the "n" in "One", if extended, would meet the "ll" of "Shilling". The "g" is always raised. Type A is known in all three colours from one sheet of 120.

Type B. The "O" is over the first "i" of "Shilling" and the downstrokes of the "n" would meet the "li" of "Shilling". Type B is known in violet (two sheets) and vermilion (one sheet).

NIGER COAST PROTECTORATE

The protectorate was extended into the interior and the name changed to Niger Coast Protectorate on 12 May 1893.

PERFORATION. There are a number of small variations in the perforation of the Waterlow issues of 1893 to 1898 which were due to irregularity of the pins rather than different perforators.

In the following lists, stamps perf 12, 12½, 13 or compound are described as perf 12–13, stamps perf 13½, 14 or compound are described as perf 13½–14 and those perf 14½, 15 or compound are listed as perf 14½–15. In addition the 13½–14 perforation exists compound with 14½–15 and with 12–13, whilst perf 15½–16 comes from a separate perforator.

13

14

(Des G. D. Drummond. Recess Waterlow)

1894 (1 Jan). *T* **13** *(with* "OIL RIVERS" *obliterated and* "NIGER COAST" *in top margin). Various frames. Thick and thin papers.* No wmk. P 14½–15.

45 ½d. vermilion . . . 4·00 4·00
a. Perf 13½–14 . . . 7·00 8·50
46 1d. pale blue . . . 6·00 3·25
a. Bisected (½d.) (on cover) . . . † £550
b. Dull blue . . . 3·75 3·25
ba. Bisected (½d.) (on cover) . . . † £450
c. Perf 13½–14 . . . 4·00
d. Perf 13½–14, comp 12–13 . . .
e. Perf 12–13 . . . — 35·00
47 2d. green . . . 29·00 25·00
a. Imperf between (horiz pair) . . . † £8500
b. Bisected (1d.) (on cover) . . . † £700
c. Perf 14½–15, comp 12–13 . . .
d. Perf 13½–14 . . . 19·00 13·00
e. Perf 13½–14, comp 12–13 . . . 42·00 29·00
f. Perf 12–13 . . .
48 2½d. carmine-lake . . . 8·50 3·50
a. Perf 13½–14 . . . 13·00 11·00
b. Perf 13½–14, comp 12–13 . . .
c. Perf 12–13 . . .
49 5d. grey-lilac . . . 17·00 12·00
a. Lilac (1894) . . . 14·00 18·00
b. Perf 13½–14 . . . 14·00 13·00
50 1s. black . . . 14·00 12·00
a. Perf 14½–15, comp 12–13 . . .
b. Perf 13½–14 . . . 28·00 22·00
c. Perf 13½–14, comp 12–13 . . . 28·00
d. Perf 14½–15, comp 13½–14 . . . — 38·00
45/50 *Set of* 6 . . . 55·00 42·00

There were three printings of each value, in November 1893, Jan 1894 and March 1894.

Nos. 46a, 46ba and 47b were used at Bonny River during August and September 1894.

(Recess Waterlow)

1894 (May). *T* **14** *(various frames).* No wmk. P 14½–15.

51 ½d. yellow-green . . . 4·75 4·75
a. Deep green . . . 5·50 5·50
b. Perf 14½–15, comp 13½–14 . . .
c. Perf 13½–14 . . . 8·50 8·00
d. Perf 13½–14, comp 12–13 . . . 22·00
52 1d. orange-vermilion . . . 16·00 10·00
a. Vermilion . . . 13·00 8·00
b. Bisected diagonally (½d.) (on cover) . . . † £500
c. Perf 15½–16 . . .
d. Perf 13½–14 . . . 22·00
e. Perf 13½–14, comp 12–13 . . . — 16·00
53 2d. lake . . . 30·00 6·50
a. Bisected diagonally (1d.) (on cover) . . .
b. Perf 13½–14 . . . 35·00 8·00
c. Perf 13½–14, comp 12–13 . . . 45·00

54 2½d. blue . . . 14·00 3·75
a. Pale blue . . . 8·50 7·50
b. Perf 13½–14 . . . 22·00
55 5d. purple . . . 6·50 5·50
a. Deep violet . . . 6·00 5·50
56 1s. black . . . 42·00 15·00
a. Perf 13½–14 . . . 42·00 7·00
b. Perf 13½–14, comp 12–13 . . . 50·00
51/6 *Set of* 6 . . . 90·00 32·00

Nos. 52b and 53a were used at Bonny River during August and September 1894

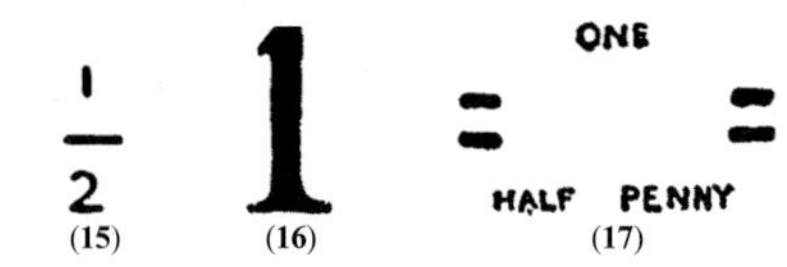

(15) (16) (17)

1894. *Provisionals. Issued at Opobo.*

(a) Nos. 46b and 46 bisected vertically and surch with T **15** *(May–June).*

57 "½" on half of 1d. dull blue (R.) (May) . . . £1200 £425
a. Surch inverted (in strip of 3 with normals) . . . £11000
58 "½" on half of 1d. pale blue (R.) (June) . . . £750 £300
a. Surch *tête-bêche* (pair) . . .
b. Surcharge inverted . . . £4250

(b) No. 3 bisected vertically and surch.

(i) With T **16** *(12 mm high) (June–Oct).*

59 "1" on half of 2d. (Verm.) . . . £1500 £325
a. Surch double . . . £2500 £1200
b. Surch inverted . . . — £1600
c. Unsevered pair . . . † —

(ii) Smaller "1" (4¾ mm high).

60 "1" on half of 2d. (C.) . . . — £5000

(iii) Smaller "1" (3¾ mm high).

61 "1" on half of 2d. (C.) . . .

Nos. 60 and 61 exist *se-tenant*. (*Price* £22000 *used*)

(c) No. 52a bisected, surch with T **15** *(Aug–Sept).*

62 "½" on half of 1d. vermilion (Blk.) . . . £3750 £950
63 "½" on half of 1d. vermilion (V.) . . . £2750 £600
64 "½" on half of 1d. vermilion (B.) . . . £2000 £400
a. "½" double . . . — £2500

The stamp is found divided down the middle and also diagonally.

1894 (10 Aug). *Issued at Old Calabar. No. 54 surch with T* **17** *and two bars through value at foot.*

65 ½d. on 2½d. blue . . . £350 £225
a. Surch double . . . £3500 £1500
b. "OIE" for "ONE" . . . £1500 £1000
c. Ditto. Surch double . . . — £5000

There are eight types in the setting of Type **17**, arranged as a horizontal row. No. 65b occurred on No. 8 in the setting at some point during surcharging.

(Recess Waterlow)

1897 (Mar)–**98**. *As T* **14** *(various frames).* Wmk Crown CA. P 14½–15.

66 ½d. green (7.97) . . . 3·50 1·50
a. Sage-green . . . 4·25 2·25
b. Perf 13½–14 . . . 3·25 3·00
c. Perf 15½–16 . . . 12·00 6·50
d. Perf 13½–14, comp 12–13 . . . 22·00
x. Wmk reversed . . . 80·00
67 1d. orange-vermilion . . . 4·50 1·50
a. Vermilion . . . 4·50 1·50
b. Imperf vert (horiz pair) . . . £6500
c. Perf 15½–16 . . . 8·50 7·00
d. Perf 13½–14 . . . 2·50 2·75
e. Perf 13½–14, comp 12–13 . . . — 11·00
68 2d. lake (7.97) . . . 1·75 1·75
a. Perf 15½–16 . . . 4·00 2·25
b. Perf 13½–14 . . . 4·00 3·75
c. Perf 13½–14, comp 12–13 . . . 24·00
x. Wmk reversed . . . 80·00 80·00
69 2½d. slate-blue (8.97) . . . 7·50 2·00
a. Deep bright blue . . . 8·50 2·00
b. Perf 13½–14 . . . 6·00 4·00
c. Perf 15½–16 . . . — 30·00
w. Wmk inverted . . .
70 5d. red-violet (p 13½–14) (1898) . . . 9·00 65·00
a. Purple . . . 9·00 70·00
b. Perf 13½–14, comp 12–13 . . . 19·00
71 6d. yellow-brown (6.98) . . . 7·00 6·50
a. Perf 13½–14 . . . 8·50
b. Perf 15½–16 . . . — 18·00
x. Wmk reversed . . .
72 1s. black (1898) . . . 15·00 29·00
a. Perf 13½–14 . . . 14·00 30·00
b. Perf 13½–14, comp 12–13 . . . 40·00
73 2s.6d. olive-bistre (6.98) . . . 50·00
a. Perf 15½–16 . . . 50·00
b. Perf 13½–14 . . . 22·00 80·00
74 10s. deep violet (6.98) . . . 95·00 £170
a. Bright violet . . . 95·00 £170
b. Perf 13½–14 . . . 80·00 £160
ba. Bright violet . . . 80·00 £160
c. Perf 13½–14, comp 12–13 . . . £160
66/74 *Set of* 9 . . . £130 £300
71s, 73s/4s Optd "Specimen" *Set of* 3 . . . £250

Owing to temporary shortages in Southern Nigeria, the above issue was again in use at various times from 1902 until 1907.

On 1 January 1900 the Niger Coast Protectorate together with the southern portion of the Niger Company Territories became the protectorate of Southern Nigeria.

NIGER COMPANY TERRITORIES

Following the development of trade along the Niger, British commercial interests formed the United African Company in 1879 which became the National African Company in 1882 and the Royal Niger Company in 1886. A charter was granted to the Company in the same year to administer territory along the Rivers Niger and Benue over which a British protectorate had been proclaimed in June 1885. The Company's territories extended to the Niger delta to provide access to the interior.

Post Offices were opened at Akassa (1887), Burutu (1896), Lokoja (1899) and Abutshi (1899). The stamps of Great Britain were used from 1888.

On the establishment of postal services in 1887 the Company arranged with the British G.P.O. that unstamped mail marked with their handstamps would be delivered in Great Britain, the recipients only being charged the normal rate of postage from West Africa. This system was difficult to administer, however, so the British authorities agreed in 1888 to the supply of G.B. stamps for use at the Company post offices.

Initially the stamps on such covers were left uncancelled until the mail arrived in the United Kingdom, the Company handstamp being struck elsewhere on the address side. This method continued to be used until early 1896, although a number of covers from the twelve months prior to that date do show the Company handstamp cancelling the stamps. Some of these covers were later recancelled on arrival in Great Britain. From May 1896 the postage stamps were cancelled in the Niger Territories.

In the following listings no attempt has been made to cover the use of the Company marks on the reverse of envelopes.

Dates given are those of earliest known postmarks. Colour of postmarks in brackets. Where two or more colours are given, price is for cheapest. Illustrations are reduced to two-thirds linear of the actual size.

Stamps of GREAT BRITAIN *cancelled as indicated below.*

ABUTSHI

1899. *Cancelled as T* **8**, *but inscribed* "THE ROYAL NIGER CO. C. & L. ABUTSHI" *with* "CUSTOMS (date) OFFICE" *in central oval.*

Z1 ½d. vermilion (V.) . . . £600
Z2 1d. lilac (V.) . . . £425
Z3 2½d. purple/*blue* (V.) . . . £600
Z4 5d. dull purple and blue (V.) . . . £650
Z5 10d. dull purple and carmine (V.) . . . £750
Z6 2s.6d. deep lilac (V.) . . . £850

AKASSA

The listings for Nos. Z7/15*a* are for *covers* on which the Akassa handstamp appears on the front, but is *not* used as a cancellation for the G.B. stamps. Examples of Nos. Z16/26 occur, from 1895–96, with the handstamp struck on the front of the cover away from the stamps, or, from 1896, used as a cancellation. The prices quoted are for *single stamps* showing the cancellation; covers from either period being worth considerably more. On Nos. Z29/42*b* the handstamp was used as a cancellation and the prices quoted are for *single stamps*.

1

2

1888–90. *Cancelled as T* **3**, *but with Maltese cross each side of* "AKASSA". *Size 36 × 22 mm.*

Z7 6d. deep purple/*red* (V.) . . . £1200

1889–94. *Size 39 × 24 mm.*

Z 8 **1** 2½d. purple/*blue* (V.) . . . £650
Z 9 3d. purple/*yellow* (V.) . . .
Z10 5d. dull purple and blue (V.) . . .
Z11 6d. deep purple/*red* (V.) . . . £425
Z12 10d. dull purple and carmine (V.) . . .
Z12*a* 1s. green (V.) . . .
Z13 2s.6d. lilac (V.) . . .

1894–95.

Z14 **2** 1d. lilac (V.) . . . £425
Z15 2½d. purple/*lilac* (V.) . . .
Z15*a* 2s.6d. lilac (V.) . . .

3

4

1895. *Size 39 × 25 mm.*

Z16 **3** 2½d. purple/*blue* (V.) . . .

1895–99.

Z17 **4** ½d. vermilion (V.) . . . 80·00
Z18 1d. lilac (V.) . . . 75·00
Z19 2d. green and carmine (V.) . . . £425
Z20 2½d. purple/*blue* (V.) . . . 40·00
Z21 3d. purple/*yellow* (V.) . . . £300
Z22 5d. dull purple and blue (V.) . . . 60·00
Z23 6d. deep purple/*red* (V.) . . . £300
Z24 9d. dull purple and blue (V.) . . . £375
Z25 10d. dull purple and carmine (V.) . . . 95·00
Z26 2s.6d. deep lilac (V.) . . . £250

THE ROYAL NIGER COMPANY,
CHARTERED & LIMITED.
4 NOV.1899
POST OFFICE,
AKASSA.

5

1897–99.
Z29 **5** ½d. vermilion (V.) . . . 60·00
Z30 1d. lilac (V.) . . . 50·00
a. "RECD" for year in postmark . . . £600
Z31 2d. green and carmine (V.) . . . £225
Z32 2½d. purple/*blue* (V.) . . . 60·00
a. "RECD" for year in postmark (1898) . . . £1000
Z33 3d. purple/*yellow* (V.) . . . £200
Z34 4d. green and brown (V.) . . . £250
Z35 4½d. green and carmine (V.) . . . £850
Z36 5d. dull purple and blue (V.) . . . 75·00
Z37 6d. deep purple/*red* (V.) . . . £250
Z38 9d. dull purple and blue (V.) . . . £400
Z39 10d. dull purple and carmine (V.) . . . £180
Z40 1s. green (V.) . . . £750
Z41 2s.6d. deep lilac (V.) . . . £350

1899. *Cancelled as T* **7** *but inscribed* "AKASSA".
Z42 5d. dull purple and blue (V.) . . . £1000

1899. *Cancelled as T* **4**, *but* "CUSTOMS DEPT" *in place of* "POST OFFICE".
Z42*a* 1d. lilac (V.) . . . £650
Z42*b* 2½d. purple/*blue* (V.) . . . £650

BURUTU

THE ROYAL NIGER COMPANY
CHARTERED & LIMITED.
31 MAR 1898
POST OFFICE.
BURUTU.

6

1896–99. *Cancelled as T* **6**, "BURUTU" *in sans-serif caps. Size 44 × 24 mm.*
Z43 **6** ½d. vermilion (V., Blk) . . . 95·00
Z44 1d. lilac (V.) . . . 85·00
Z45 1½d. dull purple and green (V.) . . . £375
Z46 2d. green and carmine (V.) . . . £225
Z47 2½d. purple/*blue* (V., Blk.) . . . 38·00
Z48 3d. purple/*yellow* (V., Blk) . . . £225
Z49 4d. green and brown (V.) . . . £225
Z50 5d. dull purple and blue (V., Blk.) . . . 80·00
Z51 6d. deep purple/*red* (V.) . . . £275
Z52 9d. dull purple and blue (V.) . . . £400
Z53 10d. dull purple and carmine (V., Blk.) . . . £140
Z54 1s. green (V.) . . . £700
Z55 2s.6d. lilac (V.) . . . £300

1898–99. *Cancelled as T* **4**, *but inscribed* "BURUTU" *in serifed caps. Size 44 × 27 mm.*
Z56 ½d. vermilion (V., Blk) . . . 65·00
Z57 1d. lilac (V., Blk.) . . . 48·00
Z58 2d. green and carmine (V.) . . . £325
Z59 2½d. purple/*blue* (V., Blk.) . . . 50·00
Z60 3d. purple/*yellow* (V.) . . . £275
Z61 4d. green and brown (V.) . . . £275
Z62 4½d. green and carmine (V.) . . . £850
Z63 5d. dull purple and blue (V.) . . . 80·00
Z64 6d. deep purple/*red* (V.) . . . £300
Z65 9d. dull purple and blue (V.) . . . £425
Z66 10d. dull purple and carmine (V., Blk) . . . £130
Z67 2s.6d. lilac (V., Blk.) . . . £350

7

1898–99.
Z68 **7** 1d. lilac (V.)
Z69 2½d. purple/*blue* (V.) . . . £325

1899. *Cancelled as T* **4**, *but inscribed* "CUSTOM DEPT. BURUTU".
Z70 1d. lilac (V.)

LOKOJA

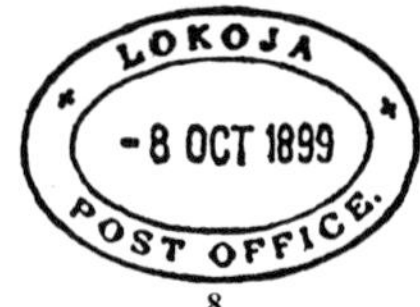

8

1899.
Z71 **8** ½d. vermilion (V.) . . . £110
Z72 1d. lilac (V.) . . . 80·00
Z73 2½d. purple/*blue* (V.) . . . £250
Z74 5d. dull purple and blue (V.) . . . £400
Z75 10d. dull purple and carmine (V.) . . . £450
Z76 2s.6d. deep lilac (V.) . . . £550

AGENT GENERAL NIGER TERRITORIES

The listings for Nos. Z78/9 are for covers showing a handstamp struck on the address side, but *not* used as a cancellation for the G.B. stamp.

1894–99. *Cancelled as T* **8**, *but inscribed* "AGENT GENERAL NIGER TERRITORIES".
Z77 1d. lilac (V.)
Z78 2½d. purple/*blue* (V.) . . . £1200

1895–96. *Cancelled as T* **7**, *but inscribed as Nos. Z77/8.*
Z79 2½d. purple/*blue* (V.) . . . £1200
Z80 5d. dull purple and blue (V.)
Z81 10d. dull purple and carmine (V.)
Z82 2s.6d. deep lilac (V.)

It is now believed that these cancellations may have been used at Asaba. They all occur on covers with Akassa handstamps, often of different dates.

The British Government purchased the Royal Niger Company territories and from 1 January 1900 they were incorporated into the protectorates of Northern and Southern Nigeria. Of the post offices listed above, only Lokoja was then situated in Northern Nigeria, the remainder joining Niger Coast in forming Southern Nigeria.

Issues for Northern Nigeria did not reach Lokoja until sometime in March 1900 and the post office there continued to use unoverprinted stamps of Great Britain until these supplies arrived.

NORTHERN NIGERIA

The protectorate of Northern Nigeria was formed on 1 January 1900 from the northern part of the Niger Company Territories. Only one post office existed in this area, at Lokoja, and this continued to use unoverprinted stamps of GREAT BRITAIN until the arrival of Nos. 1/9 during April 1900.

PRICES FOR STAMPS ON COVER		
Nos.	1/7	*from* × 6
Nos.	8/9	—
Nos.	10/16	*from* × 5
Nos.	17/19	—
Nos.	20/6	*from* × 5
No.	27	—
Nos.	28/37	*from* × 5
Nos.	38/9	—
Nos.	40/9	*from* × 5
Nos.	50/2	—

PRINTERS. All issues were typographed by De La Rue & Co.

1 2

1900 (Apr). Wmk Crown CA. P 14.
1 **1** ½d. dull mauve and green . . . 2·75 13·00
2 1d. dull mauve and carmine . . . 3·50 3·75
3 2d. dull mauve and yellow . . . 12·00 42·00
4 2½d. dull mauve and ultramarine . . . 9·00 38·00
5 **2** 5d. dull mauve and chestnut . . . 22·00 45·00
6 6d. dull mauve and violet . . . 19·00 29·00
7 **1** 1s. green and black . . . 24·00 65·00
8 2s.6d. green and ultramarine . . . 95·00 £400
9 10s. green and brown . . . £225 £550
1/9 *Set of* 9 . . . £350 £1000
1s/9s Optd "Specimen" *Set of* 9 . . . £180

Examples of all values are known showing a forged Northern Nigeria postmark dated "AU 14 1900".

3 4

1902 (1 July). Wmk Crown CA. P 14.
10 **3** ½d. dull purple and green . . . 2·00 1·00
w. Wmk inverted . . . † £200
11 1d. dull purple and carmine . . . 2·25 75
12 2d. dull purple and yellow . . . 2·00 3·00
13 2½d. dull purple and ultramarine . . . 1·50 9·00
14 **4** 5d. dull purple and chestnut . . . 2·75 5·00
15 6d. dull purple and violet . . . 7·50 4·50
16 **3** 1s. green and black . . . 3·50 6·00
17 2s.6d. green and ultramarine . . . 8·00 45·00
18 10s. green and brown . . . 48·00 55·00
10/18 *Set of* 9 . . . 70·00 £110
10s/18s Optd "Specimen" *Set of* 9 . . . £150

1904 (Apr). Wmk Mult Crown CA. P 14.
19 **4** £25 green and carmine . . . £38000

No. 19, although utilising the "POSTAGE & REVENUE" Key type, was intended to pay the fiscal fee for liquor licences.

1905 (Aug)–**07**. *Ordinary paper.* Wmk Mult Crown CA. P 14.
20 **3** ½d. dull purple and green (10.05) . . . 19·00 8·00
a. Chalk-surfaced paper (1906) . . . 5·50 5·00
21 1d. dull purple and carmine . . . 19·00 1·00
a. Chalk-surfaced paper (1906) . . . 5·50 1·25
22 2d. dull purple and yellow (10.05) . . . 14·00 32·00
a. Chalk-surfaced paper (1907) . . . 19·00 25·00
23 2½d. dull purple and ultramarine (10.05) . . . 6·50 8·00
24 **4** 5d. dull purple and chestnut (10.05) . . . 24·00 65·00
a. Chalk-surfaced paper (1907) . . . 35·00 65·00
25 6d. dull purple and violet (10.05) . . . 27·00 50·00
a. Chalk-surfaced paper (1906) . . . 38·00 38·00
26 **3** 1s. green and black (10.05) . . . 55·00 90·00
a. Chalk-surfaced paper (1906) . . . 22·00 48·00
27 2s.6d. green and ultramarine (10.05) . . . 48·00 50·00
a. Chalk-surfaced paper (1906) . . . 30·00 48·00
20/7 *Set of* 8 . . . £120 £200

1910 (30 Jan)–**11**. *Ordinary paper (½d. to 2½d.) or chalk-surfaced paper (others).* Wmk Mult Crown. CA. P 14.
28 **3** ½d. green (15.4.10) . . . 2·00 1·25
29 1d. carmine . . . 2·00 1·25
30 2d. grey (26.10.11) . . . 4·50 2·25
31 2½d. blue (10.10) . . . 2·25 7·00
32 **4** 3d. purple/*yellow* (10.9.11) . . . 3·50 75
34 5d. dull purple and olive-green (26.2.11) . . . 4·00 12·00
35 6d. dull purple and purple (10.11.10) . . . 6·00 16·00
a. Dull and bright purple (1911) . . . 5·00 6·00
36 **3** 1s. black/*green* (10.11.10) . . . 2·25 75
37 2s.6d. black and red/*blue* (15.3.11) . . . 10·00 29·00
38 **4** 5s. green and red/*yellow* (10.9.11) . . . 23·00 75·00
39 **3** 10s. green and red/*green* (15.3.11) . . . 42·00 48·00
28/39 *Set of* 11 . . . 90·00 £160
28s/39s Optd "Specimen" *Set of* 11 . . . £225

5 6

1912. *Ordinary paper (½d., 1d., 2d.) or chalk-surfaced paper (others).* Wmk Mult Crown CA. P 14.
40 **5** ½d. deep green . . . 1·50 6
41 1d. red . . . 1·50 6
42 2d. grey . . . 3·00 7·5
43 **6** 3d. purple/*yellow* . . . 2·25 1·2
44 4d. black and red/*yellow* . . . 1·25 2·2
45 5d. dull purple and olive–green . . . 4·00 10·0
46 6d. dull and bright purple . . . 4·00 4·2
47 9d. dull purple and carmine . . . 2·00 12·0
48 **5** 1s. black/*green* . . . 4·50 2·2
49 2s.6d. black and red/*blue* . . . 7·00 40·0
50 **6** 5s. green and red/*yellow* . . . 20·00 80·0
51 **5** 10s. green and red/*green* . . . 38·00 48·0
52 **6** £1 purple and black/*red* . . . £170 £11
40/52 *Set of* 13 . . . £225 £27
40s/52s Optd "Specimen" *Set of* 13 . . . £200

Examples of most values are known showing forged postmark of Lokoja dated "MR 22 12" or Minna dated "JN 16 1913". Thes forged postmarks have also been seen on examples of earlier issue

On 1 January 1914 Northern Nigeria became part of Nigeria.

SOUTHERN NIGERIA

The Colony and Protectorate of Southern Nigeria was formed o 1 January 1900 by the amalgamation of Niger Coast Protectora with the southern part of the Niger Territories. Lagos wa incorporated into the territory on 1 May 1906.

The stamps of NIGER COAST PROTECTORATE were used in Southern Nigeria until the introduction of Nos. 1/9, and also during a shortage of these values in mid-1902. The issues of LAGOS were utilized throughout Southern Nigeria after 1 May 1906 until supplies were exhausted.

PRICES FOR STAMPS ON COVER		
Nos.	1/7	*from* × 8
Nos.	8/9	—
Nos.	10/18	*from* × 4
Nos.	19/20	—
Nos.	21/30	*from* × 4
Nos.	31/2	—
Nos.	33/42	*from* × 4
Nos.	43/4	—
Nos.	45/53	*from* × 4
Nos.	55/6	—

PRINTERS. All issues of Southern Nigeria were typographed b De La Rue & Co, Ltd, London.

1 2 3

1901 (Mar)–**02**. Wmk Crown CA. P 14.
1 **1** ½d. black and pale green . . . 1·75 2·
a. Sepia and green (1902) . . . 2·25 2·
2 1d. black and carmine . . . 1·40 1·
a. Sepia and carmine (1902) . . . 2·25 1·
3 2d. black and red-brown . . . 3·25 3·
4 4d. black and sage-green . . . 2·75 17·
5 6d. black and purple . . . 2·75 6·
6 1s. green and black . . . 8·00 26·
7 2s.6d. black and brown . . . 45·00 80·
8 5s. black and orange-yellow . . . 48·00 £1
9 10s. black and purple/*yellow* . . . 90·00 £1
1/9 *Set of* 9 . . . £190 £4
1s/9s Optd "Specimen" *Set of* 9 . . . £150

1903 (Mar)–**04**. Wmk Crown CA. P 14.
10 **2** ½d. grey-black and pale green . . . 1·00
w. Wmk inverted
11 1d. grey-black and carmine . . . 1·25
12 2d. grey-black and chestnut . . . 6·50 1·
13 2½d. grey-black and blue (1904) . . . 2·00
14 4d. grey-black and olive-green . . . 2·75 5·

15 6d. grey-black and purple 4·25 8·00
16 1s. green and black 29·00 19·00
17 2s.6d. grey-black and brown 28·00 60·00
18 5s. grey-black and yellow 65·00 £150
19 10s. grey-black and purple/*yellow* 29·00 90·00
20 £1 green and violet £325 £650
10/20 *Set of* 11 £450 £900
10s/20s Optd "Specimen" *Set of* 11 £200

Two Dies of Head Plate:

A

B

In Head A the fifth line of shading on the king's cheek shows as a line of dots and the lines of shading up to the king's hair are broken in places. In Head B the lines of shading are more regular, especially the fifth line.

1904 (June)–**09**. *Head Die A. Ordinary paper.* Wmk Mult Crown CA. P 14.
21 **2** ½d. grey-black and pale green 60 10
a. Chalk-surfaced paper (1905) 1·25 90
22 1d. grey-black and carmine 12·00 20
a. Chalk-surfaced paper (1905) 12·00 10
23 2d. grey-black and chestnut (1905) 2·50 45
a. Pale grey and chestnut (Head Die B) (1907) 4·50 40
24 2½d. grey-black and bright blue (9.09) 1·00 1·00
25 3d. orange-brown & bright purple (*chalk-surfaced paper*) (Head Die B) (18.8.07) 9·50 1·25
s. Optd "Specimen" 20·00
26 4d. grey-black and olive-green (12.05) 14·00 25·00
a. Chalk-surfaced paper (1906) 26·00 30·00
ab. Grey-black and pale olive-green (Head Die B) (1907) 38·00 35·00
27 6d. grey-black and bright purple (12.05) 13·00 3·50
a. Chalk-surfaced paper (1906) 13·00 6·00
ab. Head Die B (1907) 18·00 2·25
28 1s. grey-green and black (19.9.07) 3·25 3·50
a. Chalk-surfaced paper (Head Die B) (1907) 38·00 3·25
29 2s.6d. grey-black and brown (30.4.06) 24·00 17·00
a. Chalk-surfaced paper (1906) 38·00 13·00
ab. Head Die B (1907) 38·00 16·00
30 5s. grey-black and yellow (10.12.07) 40·00 75·00
a. Chalk-surfaced paper (Head Die B) (1908) 55·00 75·00
31 10s. grey-black and purple/*yellow* (*chalk-surfaced paper*) (Head Die B) (9.08) £100 £170
32 £1 green and violet (19.3.06) £200 £225
a. Chalk-surfaced paper (1906) £200 £250
ab. Head Die B (1907) £160 £200
21/32 *Set of* 12 £325 £425

I

II

Die I. Thick "1", small "d". (double working plate).
Die II. Thinner "1", larger "d" (single working plate).

1907–11. *Colours changed. Head Die B. Ordinary paper (½d. to 2½d.) or chalk-surfaced paper (others).* Wmk Mult Crown CA. P 14.
3 **2** ½d. pale green (1907) 2·00 20
a. Head Die A 7·50 80
b. Blue-green (1910) 2·25 20
4 1d. carmine (I) (12.8.07) 3·75 60
a. Head Die A 11·00 1·25
ab. Die II. *Carmine-red* (1910) 75 10
5 2d. greyish slate (9.09) 2·50 70
6 2½d. blue (9.09) 2·00 3·75
7 3d. purple/*yellow* (7.09) 2·00 30
8 4d. black and red/*yellow* (9.09) 2·25 80
9 6d. dull purple and purple (9.09) 25·00 3·25
a. Dull purple and bright purple (1911) 26·00 3·25
aw. Wmk inverted
0 1s. black/*green* (7.09) 7·00 40
1 2s.6d. black and red/*blue* (9.09) 5·00 1·00
2 5s. green and red/*yellow* (9.09) 38·00 48·00
3 10s. green and red/*green* (9.09) 65·00 95·00
4 £1 purple and black/*red* (9.09) £190 £225
3/44 *Set of* 12 £300 £350
3s/44s Optd "Specimen" *Set of* 12 £250

912. Wmk Mult Crown CA. P 14.
5 **3** ½d. green 2·25 10
6 1d. red 2·00 10
w. Wmk inverted £140 £130
7 2d. grey 75 85
8 2½d. bright blue 2·75 2·75
9 3d. purple/*yellow* 1·00 30
0 4d. black and red/*yellow* 1·25 2·00
1 6d. dull and bright purple 1·25 1·25
2 1s. black/*green* 2·75 75
3 2s.6d. black and red/*blue* 8·00 32·00
4 5s. green and red/*yellow* 20·00 75·00
5 10s. green and red/*green* 45·00 90·00
6 £1 purple and black/*red* £170 £225
5/56 *Set of* 12 £225 £375
5s/56s Optd "Specimen" *Set of* 12 £200

STAMP BOOKLETS

1904. *Black on red cover. Stapled.*
SB1 2s.1d. booklet containing twenty-four 1d (No. 11) in blocks of 6

1905 (1 June)–**06**. *Black on red cover. Stapled.*
SB2 2s.1d. booklet containing twenty-four 1d. (No. 22) in blocks of 6 £1800
a. As No. SB2 but containing No. 22a (1906) £1500

1907 (7 Oct). *Black on red cover. Stapled.*
SB3 2s.1d. booklet containing twenty-four 1d (No. 34) in blocks of 6 £2000

1910 (19 Sept). *Black on red cover. Stapled.*
SB4 2s. booklet containing eleven ½d. and eighteen 1d. (Nos. 33*b*, 34ab) in blocks of 6 or 5

1912 (Oct). *Black on red cover. Stapled.*
SB5 2s. booklet containing twelve ½d. and eighteen 1d. (Nos. 45/6) in blocks of 6 £1500

On 1 January 1914 Southern Nigeria became part of Nigeria.

NIGERIA

Nigeria was formed on 1 January 1914 from the former protectorates of Northern and Southern Nigeria.

PRICES FOR STAMPS ON COVER TO 1945	
Nos. 1/10	*from* × 3
Nos. 11/12	—
Nos. 15/28	*from* × 3
Nos. 29/a	—
Nos. 30/3	*from* × 3
Nos. 34/59	*from* × 2

CROWN COLONY

1

2

(Typo D.L.R.)

1914 (1 June)–**29**. *Die I. Ordinary paper (½d. to 2½d.) or chalk-surfaced paper (others).* Wmk Mult Crown CA. P 14.
1 **1** ½d. green 4·50 70
2 1d. carmine-red 4·75 10
a. Scarlet (1916) 7·00 20
w. Wmk inverted 90·00 £100
3 2d. grey 8·00 1·75
a. Slate-grey (1918) 9·00 75
4 2½d. bright blue 6·50 2·75
a. Dull blue (1915) 12·00 4·25
5 **2** 3d. purple/*yellow* (*white back*) 3·25 10·00
a. Lemon back (19.8.15) 1·50 2·75
b. On deep yellow (*yellow back*) (*thick paper*) (1915) 30·00 7·50
bs. Optd "Specimen" 42·00
c. On orange-buff (1920) 9·00 22·00
d. On buff (1920) 11·00
e. On pale yellow (1921) 11·00 15·00
6 4d. black and red/*yellow* (*white back*) 1·40 10·00
a. Lemon back (19.8.15) 1·00 4·25
b. On deep yellow (*yellow back*) (*thick paper*) (1915) 30·00 8·00
bs. Optd "Specimen" 42·00
c. On orange-buff (1920) 11·00 10·00
d. On buff (1920) 11·00
e. On pale yellow (1921) 10·00 17·00
7 6d. dull purple and bright purple 9·00 10·00
8 **1** 1s. black/*blue-green* (*white back*) 1·50 23·00
a. On yellow-green (*white back*) (1915) £150
b. Yellow-green back (19.8.15) 35·00 35·00
c. Blue-green back (1915) 1·00 9·50
cs. Optd "Specimen" 42·00
d. Pale olive back (1917) 27·00 27·00
dw. Wmk inverted
e. On emerald (*pale olive back*) (1920) 8·00 32·00
f. On emerald (*emerald back*) (1920) 1·25 15·00
9 2s.6d. black and red/*blue* 16·00 6·50
10 **2** 5s. green and red/*yellow* (*white back*) 13·00 50·00
a. Lemon back (19.8.15) 21·00 50·00
b. On deep yellow (*yellow back*) (*thick paper*) (1915) 50·00 65·00
bs. Optd "Specimen" 45·00
c. On orange-buff (1920) 42·00 80·00
d. On buff (1920) 50·00
e. On pale yellow (1921) 65·00 £130
11 **1** 10s. green and red/*blue-green* (*white back*) 45·00 £140
a. Blue-green back (19.8.15) 48·00 85·00
as. Optd "Specimen" 50·00
b. Pale olive back (1917) £800 £1400
c. On emerald (*pale olive back*) (1920) £100 £150
d. On emerald (*emerald back*) (1921) 35·00 £100
12 **2** £1 deep purple and black/*red* £170 £200
a. Purple and black/red (1917) £170 £200
b. Die II. *Dp purple & blk/red* (19.1.27) £180 £275
ba. Purple and black/red (1929) £180 £275
1/12 *Set of* 12 £250 £325
1s/12s Optd "Specimen" *Set of* 12 £325

The ½d. and 1d. were printed in sheets of 240 using two plates one above the other.

1921–32. *Ordinary paper (½d. to 3d.) or chalk-surfaced paper (others).* Wmk Mult Script CA. P 14.
15 **1** ½d. green (Die I) (1921) 1·25 40
aw. Wmk inverted 80·00 80·00
b. Die II (1925) 3·75 85
c. Vert gutter pair. Die I and Die II. Nos. 15/b (1925) £190
16 1d. rose-carmine (Die I) (1921) 3·25 30
aw. Wmk inverted 75·00 75·00
b. Die II (1925) 1·75 55
c. Vert gutter pair. Die I and Die II. Nos. 16/b (1925) £190
17 **2** 1½d. orange (Die II) (1.4.31) 4·25 15
18 **1** 2d. grey (Die I) (1921) 1·50 5·00
a. Die II (1924) 7·50 40
19 2d. chestnut (Die II) (1.10.27) 4·50 1·00
20 2d. chocolate (Die II) (1.7.28) 1·25 15
a. Die I (1932) 5·50 75
21 2½d. bright blue (Die I) (1921) 1·00 6·00
22 **2** 3d. bright violet (Die I) (1924) 5·00 3·25
a. Die II (1925) 10·00 1·00
23 3d. bright blue (Die II) (1.4.31) 6·00 1·00
24 4d. black & red/*pale yellow* (Die II) (1923) 65 55
a. Die I (1932) 5·50 7·00
25 6d. dull purple & brt purple (Die I) (1921) 12·00 20·00
a. Die II (1923) 7·00 8·00
aw. Wmk inverted 90·00
26 **1** 1s. black/*emerald* (Die II) (1924) 1·25 2·00
27 2s.6d. black and red/*blue* (Die II) (1925) 6·50 26·00
a. Die I (1932) 40·00 65·00
28 **2** 5s. green & red/*pale yellow* (Die II) (1926) 15·00 65·00
a. Die I (1932) 65·00 £180
29 **1** 10s. green and red/*green* (Die II) (1925) 60·00 £180
a. Die I (1932) £100 £400
15/29 *Set of* 15 £100 £250
15s/29s (ex 2d. chocolate) Optd or Perf (1½d., 3d. blue) "Specimen" *Set of* 14 £400

The ½d. and 1d., together with the 1½d. from 1932, were printed in sheets of 240 using two plates one above the other. Nos. 15c and 16c come from printings in November 1924 which combined Key Plate No. 7 (Die I) above Key Plate No. 12 (Die II).

1935 (6 May). *Silver Jubilee. As Nos. 91/4 of Antigua, but ptd by Waterlow.* P 11 × 12.
30 1½d. ultramarine and grey 80 1·00
31 2d. green and indigo 1·50 1·00
k. Kite and vertical log 75·00
32 3d. brown and deep blue 3·00 13·00
33 1s. slate and purple 3·00 29·00
30/3 *Set of* 4 7·50 40·00
30s/3s Perf "Specimen" *Set of* 4 80·00

For illustration of plate variety see Omnibus section following Zanzibar.

3 Apapa Wharf

4 Fishing Village

5 Victoria-Buea Road

(Recess D.L.R.)

1936 (1 Feb). *Designs as T* **3/5**. Wmk Mult Script CA.

(a) P 11½ × 13.
34 ½d. green 1·50 1·40
35 1d. carmine 50 40
36 1½d. brown 2·00 40
a. Perf 12½ × 13½ 55·00 4·00
37 2d. black 50 80
38 3d. blue 2·00 1·50
a. Perf 12½ × 13½ £100 24·00
39 4d. red-brown 2·00 2·00
40 6d. dull violet 50 60
41 1s. sage-green 1·75 4·75

(b) P 14.
42 2s.6d. black and ultramarine 3·75 23·00
43 5s. black and olive-green 7·00 28·00
44 10s. black and grey 48·00 70·00
45 £1 black and orange 75·00 £150
34/45 *Set of* 12 £130 £250
34s/45s Perf "Specimen" *Set of* 12 £225

Designs: *Vert as T* **3/4**—1d. Cocoa; 1½d. Tin dredger; 2d. Timber industry; 4d. Cotton ginnery; 6d. Habe minaret; 1s. Fulani Cattle. *Horiz as T* **5**—5s. Oil Palms; 10s. River Niger at Jebba; £1, Canoe pulling.

1937 (12 May). *Coronation. As Nos. 95/7 of Antigua.* P 11 × 11½.
46 1d. carmine 60 2·50
47 1½d. brown 1·60 2·75
48 3d. blue 1·60 2·75
46/8 *Set of* 3 3·50 7·25
46s/8s Perf "Specimen" *Set of* 3 65·00

15 King George VI

16 Victoria-Buea Road

(Recess B.W. (T **15**), D.L.R. (others))

1938 (1 May)–**51**. *Designs as T* **15/16**. Wmk Mult Script CA. P 12 (*T* **15**) or 13 × 11½ (others).
49 **15** ½d. green . . . 10 10
 a. Perf 11½ (15.2.50) . . . 1·50 20
50 1d. carmine . . . 19·00 2·50
 a. Rose-red (*shades*) (1940) . . . 75 30
 ab. "A" of "CA" missing from wmk
50*b* 1d. bright purple (1.12.44) . . . 10 20
 ba. Perf 11½ (15.2.50) . . . 30 50
 bw. Wmk inverted (P 12)
51 1½d. brown . . . 20 10
 a. Perf 11½ (15.11.50) . . . 10 10
52 2d. black . . . 10 1·25
52*a* 2d. rose-red (1.12.44) . . . 10 1·00
 ab. Perf 11½ (15.2.50) . . . 10 50
52*b* 2½d. orange (4.41) . . . 10 1·00
53 3d. blue . . . 10 10
 a. Wmk sideways . . . † £3000
53*b* 3d. black (1.12.44) . . . 15 75
54 4d. orange . . . 48·00 3·00
54*a* 4d. blue (1.12.44) . . . 15 1·75
55 6d. blackish purple . . . 40 10
 a. Perf 11½ (17.4.51) . . . 1·50 60
56 1s. sage-green . . . 60 10
 a. Perf 11½ (15.2.50) . . . 30 10
57 1s.3d. light blue (1940) . . . 90 30
 a. Perf 11½ (14.6.50) . . . 80 70
 ab. Wmk sideways . . . † £2750
58 **16** 2s.6d. black and blue . . . 60·00 15·00
 a. Perf 13½ (6.42) . . . 3·75 4·25
 ab. Black and deep blue (1947) . . . 55·00 55·00
 b. Perf 14 (1942) . . . 2·25 3·50
 c. Perf 12 (15.8.51) . . . 2·00 4·25
59 – 5s. black and orange . . . £110 12·00
 a. Perf 13½ (8.42) . . . 5·50 4·50
 b. Perf 14 (1948) . . . 7·00 3·00
 c. Perf 12 (19.5.49) . . . 5·50 4·00
49/59c *Set of* 16 . . . 55·00 13·00
49s/59s (*ex* 2½d.) Perf "Specimen" *Set of* 15 . . . £250
Design: *Horiz as T* **16**—5s. R. Niger at Jebba.
The 1d., No. 50ba, exists in coils constructed from normal sheets.

1946 (21 Oct). *Victory. As Nos. 110/11 of Antigua*
60 1½d. chocolate . . . 35 10
61 4d. blue . . . 35 2·00
60s/1s Perf "Specimen" *Set of* 2 . . . 55·00

1948 (20 Dec). *Royal Silver Wedding. As Nos. 112/13 of Antigua.*
62 1d. bright purple . . . 35 30
63 5s. brown-orange . . . 5·50 9·50

1949 (10 Oct). *75th Anniv of U.P.U. As Nos. 114/17 of Antigua.*
64 1d. bright reddish purple . . . 15 25
65 3d. deep blue . . . 1·25 3·00
66 6d. purple . . . 30 3·00
67 1s. olive . . . 50 2·00
64/7 *Set of* 4 . . . 2·00 7·50

STAMP BOOKLETS

1915. *Crimson cover.*
SB1 2s. booklet containing twelve ½d. and eighteen 1d. (Nos. 1/2) in blocks of 6

1921–26. *Black on scarlet cover. Stapled.*
SB2 4s. booklet containing twelve 1d. and eighteen 2d. grey (both Die I) (Nos. 16, 18) in blocks of 6 . . . £1800
 a. Containing Nos. 16 and 18a (Die II) (1924) . . . £1600
 b. Containing Nos. 16b and 18a (both Die II) (1926)

1928. *Scarlet cover.*
SB5 4s. booklet containing twelve 1d. (Die II) and eighteen 2d. chestnut (Nos. 16b, 19) in blocks of 6

1929.
SB6 4s. booklet containing twelve 1d. (Die II) and eighteen 2d. chocolate (Nos. 16b, 20) in blocks of 6 . . . £1500

1931 (Jan).
SB7 4s. booklet containing twelve 1d. and twenty-four 1½d. (Nos. 16a, 17) in blocks of 6

Niue
see after New Zealand

Norfolk Island
see after Australia

North Borneo

PRICES FOR STAMPS ON COVER TO 1945

No.	1	*from* × 100
Nos.	2/3	*from* × 10
Nos.	4/5	—
Nos.	6/19	*from* × 10
Nos.	19*b*/21*b*	—
Nos.	22/8	*from* × 50
Nos.	29/35	—
Nos.	36/44	*from* × 100
Nos.	45/50	—
Nos.	51/2	*from* × 10
No.	54	—
Nos.	55/65	*from* × 10
Nos.	66/79	*from* × 4
Nos.	81/6	—
Nos.	87/91	*from* × 12
Nos.	92/111	*from* × 4
Nos.	112/26	*from* × 10
Nos.	127/40	*from* × 6
Nos.	141/5	—
Nos.	146/57	*from* × 5
Nos.	158/79	*from* × 8
Nos.	181/5	—
Nos.	186/8	*from* × 10
Nos.	189/230	*from* × 4
Nos.	231/4	—
Nos.	235/49	*from* × 3
Nos.	250/2	—
Nos.	253/75	*from* × 12
Nos.	276/92	*from* × 7
Nos.	293/4	—
Nos.	295/300	*from* × 6
Nos.	301/2	—
Nos.	303/17	*from* × 3
Nos.	318/19	*from* × 20
Nos.	320/34	*from* × 3
Nos.	D1/30	*from* × 25
Nos.	D31/6	*from* × 12
No.	D37	—
Nos.	D38/84	*from* × 40
Nos.	D85/9	*from* × 8

BRITISH NORTH BORNEO COMPANY ADMINISTRATION

PRINTERS. The stamps of this country up to 1894 were designed by T. Macdonald and printed in lithography by Blades, East and Blades, London.

1

8 Cents
(2)

EIGHT CENTS
(3)

1883 (Mar). P 12.
1 **1** 2c. red-brown . . . 27·00 60·00
 a. Imperf between (horiz pair)
The figure "2" varies in size.

1883 (June). *No. 1 surch as T* **2** *or* **3**.
2 **2** 8c.on 2c. red-brown . . . £950 £650
3 **3** 8c.on 2c. red-brown . . . £450 £190
 a. Surch double . . . † £4000
Type **2** was handstamped and stamps without stop are generally forgeries. Type **3** was a setting of 50 (10 × 5) providing ten varieties; it normally has a stop which sometimes failed to print.

CANCELLED-TO-ORDER—Prices are separately indicated in a third price column, for stamps showing the recognisable black bars remainder cancellation. The issues since 1916 have not been thus cancelled.
It should be noted, however, that a postmark of this form was in use for postal purposes up to this period, and was used at one or two of the smaller post-offices until 1949. A small oval with five bars was used to mark railway mail during 1945/55 and also as a paquebot mark at Jesselton *c.* 1950.

4

5

and Revenue
(6)

1883. P 14.
4 **4** 50c. violet . . . £130 — 25·00
 a. Inverted "L" for first "F" in "FIFTY" (R. 5/2) . . . £900 — £170
5 **5** $1 scarlet . . . £110 — 12·00

1883 (July). P 12.
6 **1** 4c. pink . . . 48·00 55·00
 a. Imperf (horiz pair) . . . † —
7 8c. green . . . 80·00 60·00

1886. P 14.
8 **1** ½c. magenta . . . 95·00 £180
9 1c. orange . . . £180 £325
 a. Imperf (pair) . . . £275 £275
 b. Imperf horiz (vert pair) . . . £950
10 2c. brown . . . 26·00 25·00
 a. Imperf between (horiz pair) . . . £600
11 4c. pink . . . 17·00 50·00
12 8c. green . . . 19·00 50·00
 a. Imperf between (horiz pair) . . . £800
13 10c. blue . . . 29·00 50·00
 a. Imperf (pair) . . . £325
8/13 *Set of* 6 . . . £325 £600
Imperforate examples of the 4c. pink are listed under No. 6a.

1886 (Sept). *Nos. 8 and 13 optd with T* **6**.
14 ½c. magenta . . . £120 £200
15 10c. blue . . . £170 £200

3 CENTS
(7)

5 CENTS
(8)

3 CENTS
Small "3" variety (R. 3/1, 3/4, 3/7)

(Surchd by *North Borneo Herald*, Sandakan)

1886 (Sept). *T* **1** *surch as T* **7/8**.

(a) P 12.
16 **7** 3c.on 4c. pink . . . £180 £250
 a. Small "3" . . . — £5500
17 **8** 5c. on 8c. green . . . £200 £250

(b) P 14.
18 **7** 3c. on 4c. pink . . . 95·00 £110
 a. Small "3" . . . £1700
19 **8** 5c.on 8c. green . . . £100 £110
 a. Surch inverted . . . £2250

9

10

11

12

13

1886–87.

(a) P 14.
21*b* **9** ½c. magenta . . . 15·00 50·0
22 ½c. rose . . . 3·00 13·0
 a. Imperf (pair) . . . 35·00
23 1c. orange-yellow . . . 10·00 28·0
 a. Imperf between (vert pair) . . . £325
 b. Imperf (pair) . . . 42·00
24 1c. orange . . . 2·00 8·0
 a. Imperf (pair) . . . 32·00
25 2c. brown . . . 2·00 8·5
 a. Imperf (pair) . . . 32·00
26 4c. pink . . . 3·00 10·0
 a. Imperf (pair) . . . 35·00
 b. Imperf between (horiz or vert pair) . . . £275
 c. Imperf vert (horiz pair) . . . £275
 d. Error. 1c. pink (R. 2/3) (centre stamp of strip of 3) . . . £225 £55
 da. Imperf between (pair)
 db. Imperf (pair) . . . £4000
27 8c. green . . . 11·00 19·0
 a. Imperf (pair) . . . 32·00
28 10c. blue . . . 7·00 26·0
 a. Imperf between (vert pair) . . . £350
 b. Imperf (pair) . . . 32·00
29 **10** 25c. indigo . . . £190 13·0
 a. Imperf between (vert pair)
 b. Imperf (pair) . . . £300 28·0
30 **11** 50c. violet . . . £275 15·0
 a. Imperf (pair) . . . £375 28·0
31 **12** $1 scarlet . . . £300 13·0
 a. Imperf (pair) . . . £375 28·0

32	**13**	$2 sage-green	£375	19·00
		a. Imperf (pair)	£275	30·00
22/32 *Set of* 10			£1000	£130

(b) P 12.

34	**9**	½c. magenta	£180	£375
35		1c. orange	£150	£190

Nos. 21*b*/32 are known to have been sold as cancelled remainders, but these are difficult to distinguish from postally used. Values above 10c. are infrequently found postally used so that the used prices quoted are for the remainders.

14

15

16

17

18

1888–92. *T* **14** *(as T* **9** *but inscr* "POSTAGE & REVENUE"*) and T* **15/18** *(T* **10/13** *redrawn)*. P 14.

36	**14**	½c. magenta (1889)	4·00	25·00	2·00
		a. Imperf vert (horiz pair)	†	†	£225
		b. Rose	1·50	4·25	60
		ba. Imperf between (horiz pair)	£375		
		c. Imperf (pair)	32·00	—	10·00
37		1c. orange (1892)	2·25	4·25	50
		a. Imperf vert (horiz pair)	£325		
		b. Imperf (pair)	32·00	—	9·00
38		2c. brown (1889)	8·50	14·00	90
		a. Imperf between (horiz pair)	†	†	£375
		b. Lake-brown	3·75	14·00	50
		c. Imperf (pair)	32·00	—	8·50
39		3c. violet (1889)	2·50	12·00	50
		b. Imperf (pair)	24·00	—	8·50
40		4c. rose-pink (1889)	6·00	32·00	50
		a. Imperf between (pair)	—	£200	—
		b. Imperf (pair)	32·00	—	9·00
41		5c. slate (1889)	2·75	21·00	50
		a. Imperf between (pair)			
		b. Imperf (pair)	32·00	—	9·00
42		6c. lake (1892)	8·00	21·00	50
		a. Imperf (pair)	32·00	—	11·00
43		8c. blue-green (1891)	25·00	30·00	1·00
		a. Yellow-green	19·00	25·00	50
		c. Imperf (pair)	32·00	—	11·00
44		10c. blue (1891)	8·00	28·00	1·00
		a. Imperf between (vert pair)	†	†	£225
		b. Dull blue	6·50	21·00	50
		ba. Imperf between (horiz pair)			
		d. Imperf (pair)	32·00	—	10·00
45	**15**	25c. indigo	60·00	80·00	75
		a. Imperf (pair)	£200	†	16·00
		b. Imperf vert (horiz pair)	†	†	£275
46	**16**	50c. violet	85·00	£130	75
		a. Imperf (pair)	£300	†	16·00
		b. Chalky blue	†	£120	†
47	**17**	$1 scarlet	27·00	£110	75
		a. Imperf (pair)	£200	†	16·00
48	**18**	$2 dull green	£130	£180	1·50
		a. Imperf (pair)	£350	†	18·00
36*b*/48 *Set of* 13			£325	£600	7·50

Nos. 39, 43 and 44 showing stamps printed double or triple, one inverted, are from waste sheets subsequently sold by the British North Borneo Company to collectors.

These stamps to the 10c. value were forged on several occasions. Most forgeries of the ½c. value can be identified by the presence of a diagonal line joining the top two horizontal strokes of the uppermost Chinese character.

The new 25c. has the inscription "BRITISH NORTH BORNEO" in taller capitals. In the 50c. the "0" of the numerals "50" in the two upper corners is square-shaped at the top and bottom instead of being oval. The 1 dollar has 14 pearls instead of 13 at each side, and on the 2 dollars the word "BRITISH" measures 10½ to 11 mm in length in place of 12 mm.

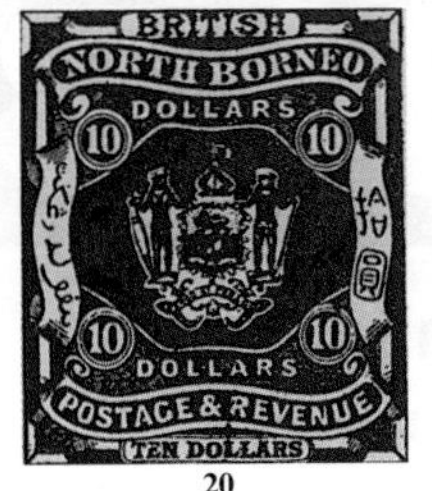

19 **20**

1889. P 14.

49	**19**	$5 bright purple	£180	£190	8·50
		a. Imperf (pair)	£450	†	35·00
50	**20**	$10 brown	£250	£325	12·00
		a. Imperf (pair)	£600	†	40·00
		b. "DOLLAPS" for "DOLLARS" (R. 2/1)	£1200	£1500	£325
		ba. Ditto. Imperf (pair)	£2500	†	£700

Two Cents. (21) **6 cents.** (22) **1 cent.** (23)

1890 (Dec). *Surch as T* **21**, *in red.*

51	**15**	2c.on 25c. indigo	70·00	90·00
		a. Surch inverted	£400	£400
52		8c.on 25c. indigo	95·00	£110

The first printing of Nos. 51/2 had the two lines of the surcharge 3.5 mm apart. On a second printing of both values this gap widened to 5 mm.

1891–92. *Surch with T* **22**.

54	**9**	6c.on 8c. green (1892)	£8000	£4250
		a. Large "s" in "cents"	£14000	
55	**14**	6c.on 8c. yellow-green	22·00	10·00
		a. Surch inverted	£400	£450
		b. Inverted "c" in "cents" (R. 5/4)	£450	£500
		c. "cetns." for "cents" (R. 3/7)	£450	£500
		d. Large "s" in "cents" (R. 2/9 or 3/7)	£190	£190
56	**9**	6c.on 10c. blue	60·00	21·00
		a. Surch inverted	£250	£250
		b. Surch double		
		c. Surch treble	£450	
		d. Large "s" in "cents"	£275	£160
57	**14**	6c.on 10c. blue	£150	26·00
		a. Large "s" in "cents"	£550	£190

Unused examples of Nos. 55 and 57 are normally without gum.

There were three settings of the surcharge for No. 55. On the first two the large "s" in "cents" occurred on R. 2/9 with the other two listed varieties also included. Nos. 55b/c were corrected on the third setting and the large "s" in cents occurred on R. 3/7.

1892 (Mar–Nov). *Surch as T* **23** *("Cents." with capital "C" as in T* **21** *on No. 65), in red.*

63	**14**	1c.on 4c. rose-pink	23·00	14·00
		a. Surch double	£1200	
		b. Surch on back and on front	—	£600
		ba. As b, but with surch double on front		
64		1c.on 5c. slate (Nov)	7·00	6·00
65	**15**	8c.on 25c. indigo (date?)	£140	£160

Unused examples of Nos. 63/5 are normally without gum.

24 Dyak Chief

25 Sambar Stag (*Cervus unicolor*)

26 Sago Palm

27 Great Argus Pheasant

28 Arms of the Company

29 Malay Dhow

30 Estuarine Crocodile

31 Mount Kinabalu

32 Arms of the Company with Supporters

PERFORATION. There are a number of small variations in the perforation of the Waterlow issues of 1894 to 1922 which we believe were due to irregularity of the pins rather than different perforators.

In the following lists, stamps perf 12, 12½, 13 or compound are described as perf 12–13, stamps perf 13½, 14 or compound are described as perf 13½–14 and those perf 14½, 15 or compound are listed as perf 14½–15. In addition the 13½–14 perforation exists compound with 14½–15 and with 12–13, whilst perf 15½–16 comes from a separate perforator.

(Recess Waterlow)

1894 (Feb). P 14½–15.

66	**24**	1c. black and olive-bistre	1·25	9·50	50
		a. Imperf between (horiz or vert pair)	£650		
		b. Perf 13½–14	1·75	11·00	50
		c. Perf 13½–14, comp 14½–15	42·00	55·00	—
		d. Perf 13½–14, comp 12–13	23·00	50·00	—
		e. Perf 12–13			
67		1c. black and bistre-brown	1·75	13·00	50
		a. Perf 13½–14	2·50	13·00	50
		b. Perf 13½–14, comp 12–13	26·00	55·00	—
		c. Perf 12–13			
68	**25**	2c. black and rose-lake	5·50	4·75	50
		a. Imperf between (horiz or vert pair)	£650	£650	†
		b. Perf 13½–14	38·00	42·00	—
69		2c. black and lake	5·50	4·75	50
		a. Perf 13½–14	40·00	40·00	1·50
		b. Perf 13½–14, comp 12–13	29·00	30·00	—
		c. Imperf between (horiz pair)			
70	**26**	3c. olive-green and dull purple	2·75	8·50	50
		a. Imperf between (horiz pair)	—	£650	†
		b. Bronze-green and dull purple	5·00	—	50
		c. Perf 13½–14			
71		3c. olive-green & violet (P 13½–14)	17·00	50·00	—
		a. Imperf between (horiz pair)			
72	**27**	5c. black and vermilion	14·00	11·00	60
		a. Imperf between (horiz or vert pair)	£550		
		b. Perf 13½–14	45·00	60·00	1·25
		c. Perf 13½–14, comp 12–13	—	65·00	5·50
		d. Perf 13½–14, comp 14½–15			
		e. Perf 12-13			
73	**28**	6c. black and bistre-brown	60·00	80·00	60
		a. Perf 13½–14	4·50	18·00	60
		b. Perf 13½–14, comp 12–13	—	65·00	5·50
		c. Perf 13½–14, comp 14½–15	60·00		
		d. Imperf between (horiz pair)			
74	**29**	8c. black and dull purple	6·50	11·00	60
		a. Imperf between (vert pair)	£550		
		b. Perf 13½–14	9·00	35·00	80
		ba. Imperf between (vert pair)	£425	†	£300
		d. Perf 13½–14, comp 12–13			
75	**30**	12c. black and blue	28·00	85·00	2·50
		a. Perf 13½–14	28·00	80·00	2·50
		b. Imperf between (horiz pair)	£900	†	£500
76		12c. black and ultramarine	42·00	85·00	3·00
		a. Perf 13½–14	40·00	85·00	3·00
		b. Imperf between (pair)			
78	**31**	18c. black and deep green	27·00	50·00	2·00
		a. Perf 13½–14	28·00	50·00	2·00
79	**32**	24c. blue and rose-lake	23·00	80·00	2·00
		a. Imperf between (vert pair)	—	—	£375
		b. Imperf between (vert strip of 3)	†	†	£500
		c. Perf 13½–14	23·00	70·00	2·00
		d. Perf 13½–14, comp 14½–15			
66/79 *Set of* 9			£100	£225	9·00

32a

32b

32c

32d

(Litho Blades, East & Blades, London)

1894 (Feb). *T* **32a** *to* **32d** *and T* **19/20**, *but inscribed* "THE STATE OF NORTH BORNEO". P 14.

81	25c. indigo	9·00	30·00	1·00
	a. Imperf (pair)	38·00	†	8·50
	b. Imperf between (horiz or vert pair)	£700	—	95·00
82	50c. deep slate-purple	22·00	60·00	2·00
	a. Imperf (pair)	—	†	8·50
	b. Imperf between (horiz pair)			
	d. Chalky blue	—	60·00	—
83	$1 scarlet	12·00	24·00	1·25
	a. Perf 14 × 11	£250		
	b. Imperf (pair)	35·00	†	8·50
84	$2 dull green	20·00	75·00	2·50
	a. Imperf (pair)	—	†	13·00
85	$5 bright purple	£225	£300	16·00
	a. Imperf (pair)	£375	†	40·00
	b. Dull purple	£200	£275	8·00
86	$10 brown	£225	£325	15·00
	a. Imperf (pair)	£375	†	40·00
81/6	*Set of* 6	£450	£700	27·00
81s/6s	Optd "Specimen" *Set of* 6	£150		

For Nos. 81 to 83 in other colours, see Labuan 80*a*, 81*a* and 82*a*.

Nos. 81/4 showing stamps printed double, double, one inverted, or on both sides, are from waste sheets subsequently sold by the British North Borneo Company to collectors.

4
CENTS

(**33** (3½ mm between lines of surcharge))

(Surcharged by Waterlow)

1895 (June). *No.* 83 *surch as T* **33**.

87	**32c** 4cents on $1 scarlet	6·50	1·50	50
	a. Surch double, one diagonal	£900		
88	10cents on $1 scarlet	19·00	1·75	50
89	20cents on $1 scarlet	40·00	17·00	50
90	30cents on $1 scarlet	29·00	27·00	50
91	40cents on $1 scarlet	29·00	48·00	50
87/91	*Set of* 5	£110	85·00	2·25
87s/91s	Optd "Specimen" *Set of* 5	85·00		

For 4c. on $1 with wider spacing see No. 121.

No. 88 exists with the figures of the surcharge 2½ mm away from "CENTS". The normal setting has a space of 3½ mm. Examples of the narrow setting have, so far, only been seen on cancelled-to-order stamps.

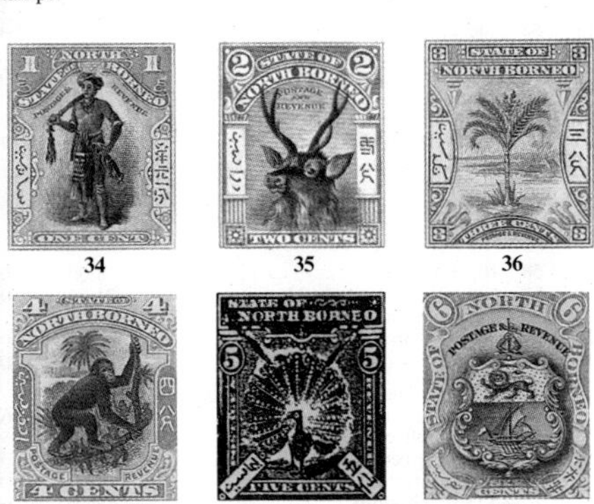

34 35 36

37 Orang-Utan 38 39

40 41 Sun Bear

42 43 Borneo Railway Train

44 45

(Recess Waterlow)

1897 (Mar)–**1902**. *T* **34** *to* **45**. *New frames*. P 13½–14.

92	1c. black and bistre-brown	12·00	3·75	40
	aa. Perf 16			
	a. Perf 14½–15	11·00	2·75	40
	b. Perf 13½–14, comp 12–13	65·00	50·00	—
	c. Imperf between (horiz pair)	†	†	£475
93	1c. black and ochre	50·00	14·00	50
	a. Perf 14½–15	30·00	11·00	50
	ab. Imperf between (horiz pair)	†	†	£475
	b. Perf 13½–14 comp 12–13			
94	2c. black and lake	35·00	3·50	40
	a. Perf 14½–15	22·00	3·00	40
	ab. Imperf between (horiz pair)	†	†	£500
	b. Perf 13½–14, comp 12–13	—	16·00	1·25
	c. Perf 12–13			
	d. Imperf between (vert pair)	†	†	£550
95	2c. black and green (1900)	48·00	2·00	60
	a. Perf 14½–15	90·00	15·00	—
	b. Perf 13½–14, comp 12–13	£110	26·00	—
	c. Perf 12–13			
	d. Imperf between (vert pair)	—	£800	†
96	3c. green and rosy mauve	48·00	11·00	40
	a. Perf 14½–15	55·00	50·00	1·00
	b. Perf 13½–14, comp 12–13	75·00	75·00	—
97	3c. green & dull mauve (P 14½–15)	18·00	3·00	50
98	4c. black and green (1900)	9·00	—	1·50
	a. Perf 13½–14, comp 12–13			
99	4c. black and carmine (1900)	35·00	8·00	50
	a. Perf 16	75·00	45·00	50
	b. Perf 14½–15	55·00	2·25	50
	c. Perf 13½–14, comp 12–13	38·00	45·00	—
	d. Perf 12–13			
100	5c. black and orange-vermilion	95·00	3·50	50
	a. Perf 14½–15	95·00	3·00	50
	ab. Imperf between (horiz pair)	†	£1200	†
	b. Perf 13½–14, comp 12–13	95·00	14·00	60
	c. Perf 12–13			
101	6c. black and bistre-brown	48·00	22·00	50
	a. Perf 14½–15	28·00	4·00	50
102	8c. black and brown-purple	75·00	50·00	—
	a. Perf 16	£110	17·00	70
	ab. Imperf between (vert pair)	£375	£375	—
	b. Perf 14½–15	40·00	2·75	60
103	8c. black and brown	12·00	28·00	75
	a. Perf 14½–15	65·00	80·00	—
	b. Perf 16			
104	10c. brown and slate-lilac (1902)	90·00	42·00	2·75
	a. Imperf between (vert pair)			
105	10c. brown and slate-blue (1902)	£200	85·00	1·50
106	12c. black and dull blue	£120	48·00	1·75
	a. Imperf between (vert pair)	†	†	£500
	b. Perf 14½–15	90·00	35·00	1·50
	c. Perf 13½–14, comp 12–13	£150	55·00	—
	d. Perf 12–13			
107	16c. green and chestnut (1902)	£130	90·00	3·25
	a. Perf 14½–15	£150	£140	10·00
108	18c. black and green (P 16)	22·00	75·00	1·50
	a. Imperf vert (horiz pair)	†	†	85·00
	b. Imperf between (vert pair)	†	†	£325
	c. Imperf (pair)	†	†	£180
109	24c. blue and lake	20·00	90·00	1·75
	a. Perf 13½–14, comp 12–13	40·00	£100	1·75
	b. Perf 12–13	£120		
92/109	(*one of each value*) *Set of* 12	£500	£300	11·00
92s/109s	(*excl* 93, 97, 103, 105) Optd "Specimen" *Set of* 14	£300		

No. 98 was printed in an incorrect frame colour and it is doubtful if it was issued for postal purposes in North Borneo. Used examples come from dealers' stock sent to the territory for cancellation.

In the above the 18c. has "POSTAL REVENUE" instead of "POSTAGE AND REVENUE" and the 24c. has those words omitted. These stamps were replaced by others with corrected inscriptions; see Nos. 110 and 111.

46

47

1897. *Corrected inscriptions*. P 13½–14.

110	**46** 18c. black and green	95·00	26·00	1·75
	a. Imperf between (horiz pair)	†	†	£475
	b. Perf 14½–15	70·00	12·00	1·50
	c. Perf 13½–14, comp 12–13	—	—	2·75
111	**47** 24c. blue and lake	75·00	40·00	2·25
	a. Perf 16	£130	£110	2·00
	b. Perf 14½–15	45·00	55·00	2·50
	c. Perf 13½–14, comp 12–13	—	—	2·75
	d. Perf 12–13			
110s/11s	Optd "Specimen" *Set of* 2	50·00		

BRITISH

4
CENTS

(**48**) (4½ mm between lines of surcharge)

PROTECTORATE.

(**49**)

4
cents

(**50**)

1899 (22 July–Oct). *Surch with T* **48**.

(*a*) *4½ mm between lines of surch (Nos. 112/17) or 14 (Nos. 118/24)*. P 14½–15.

112	4c.on 5c. (No. 100a)	42·00	48·00
	a. Perf 13½–14	25·00	10·00
	b. Perf 13½–14, comp 12–13	35·00	32·00
113	4c.on 6c. (No. 101a) (date?)	19·00	24·00
	a. Perf 13½–14	18·00	48·00
114	4c.on 8c. (No. 102b) (Oct)	15·00	10·00
115	4c.on 12c. (No. 106b) (Oct)	22·00	13·00
	a. Imperf between (horiz pair)	£600	
	b. Imperf between (vert pair)	—	£650
	c. Perf 13½–14	40·00	
	d. Perf 12–13		
	e. Perf 13½–14, comp 12–13	35·00	35·00
116	4c.on 18c. (No. 110a) (Oct)	10·00	14·00
	a. Perf 13½–14	27·00	32·00
117	4c.on 24c. (No. 111b) (Oct)	22·00	18·00
	a. Perf 16	50·00	50·00
	b. Perf 13½–14	18·00	38·00
	c. Perf 13½–14, comp 12–13	32·00	38·00
	d. Perf 12–13	50·00	70·00
118	4c.on 25c. indigo (No. 81)	5·50	8·50
	a. Imperf between (horiz strip of 3)	£900	
119	4c.on 50c. deep slate-purple (No. 82)	9·00	16·00
	a. Chalky blue	28·00	38·00
121	4c.on $1 scarlet (No. 83)	5·50	12·00
122	4c.on $2 dull green (No. 84)	5·50	13·00
123	4c.on $5 bright purple (No. 85)	£150	£225
	a. Dull purple	£225	£250
124	4c.on $10 brown (No. 86)	£110	£225
112/24	*Set of* 12	£350	£500
112s/24s	Optd "Specimen" *Set of* 12	£190	

(*b*) *8½ mm between lines of surch*. P 14.

125	4c. on $5 (No. 85)	6·50	14·00
126	4c. on $10 (No. 86)	6·50	14·00

No. 121 differs only from No. 87 in having the "4" and "cents" wider apart.

Examples of the Kudat postmark dated "AU 15 1899" struck on Nos. 112/24 are generally considered to be faked.

A new setting of the surcharge, with 2½ mm between "4" and "CENTS" for values to $2 and 3½ mm on the $5 and $10, was used for the Specimen overprints, including unissued surcharges on the 1c., 2c. and 3c. values (*price* £110 *the set of three*).

(Optd by Waterlow)

1901 (8 Oct)–**05**. *Optd as T* **49**.

(*a*) P 13½–14.

127	1c. (No. 92) (R.)	3·50	1·50	30
	a. Perf 14½–15	2·50	1·75	30
128	2c. (No. 95) (R.)	3·75	1·25	30
	a. Perf 16	3·50	12·00	30
	b. Perf 14½–15	12·00	12·00	30
129	3c. (No. 96)	1·75	5·50	30
	a. Imperf between (vert pair)	†	†	£850
	b. Perf 14½–15	9·00	2·75	30
	c. Perf 13½–14, comp 14½–15	50·00		
130	4c. (No. 99) (G.)	9·00	1·50	30
	a. Perf 14½–15	22·00	1·50	30
131	5c. (No. 100) (G.)	45·00	3·50	30
	a. Perf 14½–15	14·00	2·50	30
132	6c. (No. 101) (R.)	50·00	65·00	1·25
	a. No stop after "Protectorate"	75·00	75·00	1·25
	b. Perf 16	4·00	15·00	70
133	8c. (No. 103) (B.)	3·75	3·75	50
	a. No stop after "Protectorate"	3·00	24·00	1·50
	b. Perf 13½–14, comp 12–13	60·00	24·00	—
	c. Imperf horiz (vert pair)	†	†	£350
134	10c. (No. 104) (R.) (7.02)	50·00	5·00	1·00
	a. Perf 14½–15	95·00	32·00	1·75
	c. Perf 13½–14. No stop after "Protectorate"	£170	—	8·50
	d. Opt double	£650	†	£275
	e. On 10c. (No. 105)	£180	—	1·00
	f. Imperf vert (horiz pair)	†	†	£475
135	12c. (No. 106) (R.)	48·00	12·00	1·50
136	16c. (No. 107) (7.02)	£130	24·00	2·25
	a. Perf 14½–15	£130	50·00	2·25
	b. Perf 13½–14 comp 12–13	£180	70·00	—
137	18c. (No. 110) (R.)	11·00	25·00	1·25
	a. No stop after "Protectorate"			
	b. Perf 13½–14, comp 12–13	—	—	1·50
138	24c. (No. 111)	16·00	40·00	1·50
	a. Perf 14½–15	60·00	90·00	1·75
	b. Imperf between (horiz pair)			

(*b*) P 14.

139	25c. (No. 81) (R.)	2·00	10·00	50
	a. No stop after "Protectorate"	£160	£180	24·00
	b. Overprints *tête-bêche* (horiz pair)			
	c. Overprint inverted	£450		
140	50c. (No. 82) (R.)	2·75	11·00	55
	a. No stop after "Protectorate"	80·00	£140	—
	b. Chalky blue			
141	$1 (No. 83) (R.) (1.04)	10·00	65·00	—
142	$1 (No. 83)	6·50	38·00	2·50
	a. Imperf horiz (vert pair)	£600		
	b. Opt double	†	†	£350
	c. Opt treble			
143	$2 (No. 84) (R.) (1903)	30·00	95·00	3·50
	a. Opt double	£1100	†	£400
144	$5 (No. 85*b*) (R.) (2.05)	£200	£450	8·00
145	$10 (No. 86) (R.) (2.05)	£375	£700	11·00
	a. Opt inverted	£1600	†	£400
127/45	*Set of* 18	£850	£1300	30·00
127s/40s	Optd "Specimen" *Set of* 14	£275		

There was more than one setting of the overprint for some of the values. Full sheets of the 6c. and 8c. are known, without stop throughout.

1904–05. *Surch locally with T* **50**.

(*a*) P 14½–15.

146	4c.on 5c. (No. 100a)	32·00	48·00	12·00
	a. Surch omitted (in pair with normal)			
147	4c.on 6c. (No. 101a)	7·00	21·00	12·00
	a. Surch inverted	£225		
148	4c.on 8c. (No. 102b)	13·00	26·00	12·00
	a. Surch inverted	£300		
149	4c.on 12c. (No. 106b)	26·00	40·00	12·00
	a. Perf 13½–14	48·00	60·00	12·00
	b. Perf 13½–14 comp 12–13	26·00	60·00	—
	c. Surch omitted (in pair with normal)			
150	4c.on 18c. (No. 110b)	14·00	38·00	12·00
	a. Perf 13½–14			

151 4c.on 24c. (No. 111b) . . . 21·00 50·00 12·00
a. Perf 16 . . . 17·00 50·00 12·00
b. Perf 13½–14 . . . 22·00 50·00 12·00
c. Perf 12–13

(b) P 14.

152 4c.on 25c. (No. 81) . . . 4·25 25·00 12·00
153 4c.on 50c. (No. 82) . . . 4·75 38·00 12·00
154 4c.on $1 (No. 83) . . . 6·00 48·00 12·00
155 4c.on $2 (No. 84) . . . 6·00 48·00 12·00
156 4c.on $5 (No. 85) . . . 12·00 48·00 12·00
a. Surch on No. 85*b* . . . 30·00 50·00 —
157 4c.on $10 (No. 86) . . . 12·00 48·00 12·00
a. Surch inverted . . . £1500
b. Surch omitted (in pair with normal)
146/57 *Set of* 12 . . . £130 £425 £130

51 Malayan Tapir

52 Travellers' Tree

53 Jesselton Railway Station

54 The Sultan of Sulu, his staff and W. C. Cowie, Managing Director of the Company

55 Indian Elephant

56 Sumatran Rhinoceros

57 Ploughing with Buffalo

58 Wild Boar

59 Palm Cockatoo

60 Rhinoceros Hornbill

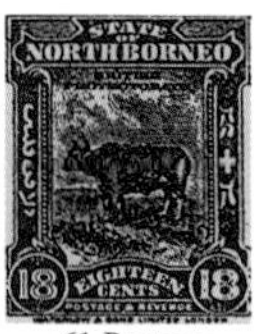

61 Banteng

62 Dwarf Cassowary

(Recess Waterlow)

1909 (1 July)–**23**. *Centres in black.* P 13½–14.

158 **51** 1c. chocolate-brown . . . 7·00 1·25 30
a. Perf 14½–15 . . . 40·00 13·00 40
159 1c. brown . . . 15·00 1·60 30
a. Perf 14½–15 . . . 30·00 3·75 30
b. Imperf between (vert pair) . . . £1300
160 **52** 2c. green . . . 1·00 70 30
a. Imperf between (pair)
b. Perf 14½–15 . . . 2·25 70 30
161 **53** 3c. lake . . . 3·25 2·75 30
162 3c. rose-lake . . . 2·75 2·75 40
a. Perf 14½–15 . . . 32·00 — 55
163 3c. green (1923) . . . 19·00 1·50 —
164 **54** 4c. scarlet . . . 2·75 30 30
a. Imperf between (vert pair)
b. Perf 14½–15 . . . 15·00 2·00 35
165 **55** 5c. yellow-brown . . . 9·50 6·50 40
a. Perf 14½–15
166 5c. dark brown . . . 19·00 5·50 —
167 **56** 6c. olive-green . . . 8·00 1·75 30
a. Perf 14½–15 . . . 70·00 6·50 60
168 6c. apple-green . . . 32·00 3·50 60
169 **57** 8c. lake . . . 4·00 1·75 60
a. Perf 14½–15 . . . — — 10·00
170 **58** 10c. greyish blue . . . 45·00 8·00 1·25
a. Perf 14½–15 . . . 85·00 32·00 —
171 10c. blue . . . 50·00 3·75 —
172 10c. turquoise-blue . . . 30·00 2·00 1·25
a. Perf 14½–15 . . . 60·00 5·50 —
173 **59** 12c. deep blue . . . 26·00 3·50 1·00
a. Perf 14½–15 . . . — — 10·00
b. Imperf between (horiz pair) . . . † † £500
173*c* 12c. deep bright blue
174 **60** 16c. brown-lake . . . 26·00 7·00 1·00
175 **61** 18c. blue-green . . . 90·00 32·00 1·00
176 **62** 24c. deep rose-lilac . . . 28·00 3·50 1·75
a. Deep lilac . . . — 6·00 —
158/76 *Set of* 13 . . . £225 55·00
158s/76s Optd "Specimen" *Set of* 13 . . . £275

For this issue perf 12½ see Nos. 277, etc.

20

CENTS

(63)

64

65

1909 (7 Sept). *No. 175 surch with T* **63** *by Waterlow.* P 13½–14.
177 20c.on 18c. blue-green (R.) . . . 7·00 1·00 30
a. Perf 14½–15 . . . £190 60·00 —
s. Optd "Specimen" . . . 42·00

(Recess Waterlow)

1911 (7 Mar). P 13½–14.
178 **64** 25c. black and yellow-green . . . 10·00 4·75 2·00
a. Perf 14½–15 . . . 12·00 38·00 —
b. Imperf (pair) . . . 50·00
178*c* 25c. black and blue-green . . . 42·00
179 50c. black and steel-blue . . . 10·00 4·50 2·25
a. Perf 14½–15 . . . 19·00 20·00 —
ab. Imperf between (horiz pair) . . . £2000
c. Imperf (pair) . . . 85·00
180 $1 black and chestnut . . . 17·00 4·00 2·75
a. Perf 14½–15 . . . 48·00 15·00 6·00
b. Imperf (pair) . . . £140
181 $2 black and lilac . . . 65·00 17·00 4·75
182 **65** $5 black and lake . . . £100 £110 30·00
a. Imperf (pair) . . . £180
183 $10 black and brick-red . . . £350 £400 65·00
a. Imperf (pair) . . . £375
178/83 *Set of* 6 . . . £500 £500 95·00
178s/83s Optd "Specimen" *Set of* 6 . . . £275

BRITISH

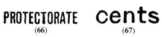

PROTECTORATE

(66)

2

cents

(67)

(68)

1912 (July). *Nos. 85b and 86 optd with T* **66**.
184 $5 dull purple (R.) . . . £1000 £1200 8·50
185 $10 brown (R.) . . . £1400 — 8·50
a. Opt inverted . . . † † —

1916 (Feb). *Nos. 162, 167 and 173 surch as T* **67** *by Govt Printing Office, Sandakan.* P 13½–14.
186 **53** 2c.on 3c. black and rose-lake . . . 24·00 15·00
a. "s" inverted (R. 2/5) . . . £100 95·00
b. Surch double . . . £1400
187 **56** 4c.on 6c. black and olive-green (R.) . . . 19·00 17·00
a. "s" inverted (R. 2/5) . . . 95·00 95·00
b. "s" inserted by hand . . . — £850
c. Perf 14½–15 . . . £150 £150
ca. "s" inverted
188 **59** 10c.on 12c. black and deep blue (R.) . . . 50·00 65·00
a. "s" inverted (R. 2/5) . . . £150 £160
b. "s" inserted by hand . . . £1000
186/8 *Set of* 3 . . . 85·00 85·00
186s/8s Optd "Specimen" *Set of* 3 . . . £120

Nos. 186/8 were surcharged from a setting of 25 (5 × 5) on which the required face values were inserted.

1916 (May). *Stamps of 1909–11 optd with T* **68** *by Waterlow. Centres in black.* P 13½–14.

(a) Cross in vermilion (thick shiny ink).

189 **51** 1c. brown . . . 7·50 35·00
190 **52** 2c. green . . . 45·00 75·00
a. Perf 14½–15 . . . 32·00 80·00
ab. Opt double, one albino . . . £250
191 **53** 3c. rose-lake . . . 27·00 48·00
a. Nos. 191 and 204 *se-tenant* (vert pair) . . . £2250
192 **54** 4c. scarlet . . . 5·50 32·00
a. Perf 14½–15 . . . £200 £150
193 **55** 5c. yellow-brown . . . 35·00 55·00
a. Perf 14½–15
194 **56** 6c. apple-green . . . 55·00 60·00
a. Perf 14½–15 . . . £190 £190
195 **57** 8c. lake . . . 23·00 60·00
196 **58** 10c. blue . . . 40·00 70·00
197 **59** 12c. deep blue . . . 90·00 90·00
198 **60** 16c. brown-lake . . . 90·00 90·00
199 **61** 20c.on 18c. blue-green . . . 38·00 85·00
200 **62** 24c. dull mauve . . . £100 £100
a. Imperf between (vert pair)
201 **64** 25c. green (P 14½–15) . . . £325 £400
189/201 *Set of* 13 . . . £750 £1100

(b) Cross in shades of carmine (matt ink).

202 **51** 1c. brown . . . 26·00 65·00
a. Perf 14½–15 . . . £200
203 **52** 2c. green . . . 27·00 50·00
b. Perf 14½–15 . . . £170
ba. Opt double . . . † £1200
204 **53** 3c. rose-lake . . . 38·00 65·00
204*a* **54** 4c. scarlet . . . £700 £800
205 **55** 5c. yellow-brown . . . 55·00 70·00
206 **56** 6c. apple-green . . . 48·00 65·00
a. Perf 14½–15 . . . £170 £190
207 **57** 8c. lake . . . 25·00 55·00
208 **58** 10c. blue . . . 48·00 70·00
209 **59** 12c. deep blue . . . 85·00 £110
210 **60** 16c. brown-lake . . . 90·00 £110
211 **61** 20c.on 18c. blue-green . . . 80·00 £100
212 **62** 24c. dull mauve . . . 95·00 £140
213 **64** 25c. green . . . £750
a. Perf 14½–15 . . . £425 £475
202/13 (*ex* 4c.) *Set of* 12 . . . £900 £1200

The British North Borneo Company donated a proportion of the above issue to be sold by the National Philatelic War Fund for the benefit of the Red Cross and St. John's Ambulance Brigade.

RED CROSS

TWO CENTS

(69)

FOUR CENTS

(70)

1918 (Aug). *Stamps of 1909–11 surch as T* **69**. P 13½–14.

(a) Lines of surcharge 9 mm apart.

214 **51** 1c.+2c. brown . . . 3·50 12·00
a. Imperf between (horiz pair) . . . £1900
215 **52** 2c.+2c. green . . . 1·00 8·50
a. Imperf between (horiz or vert pair) . . . £2250
b. Imperf (pair)
c. Perf 14½–15
216 **53** 3c.+2c. rose-red . . . 14·00 19·0
a. Imperf between (horiz pair) . . . £2250
b. Perf 14½–15 . . . 25·00 65·0
217 3c.+2c. dull rose-carmine . . . £150
a. Perf 14½–15 . . . £190
218 **54** 4c.+2c. scarlet . . . 70 5·0
a. Surch inverted . . . £400
219 **55** 5c.+2c. deep brown . . . 8·00 22·0
220 5c.+2c. pale brown . . . 8·50 28·0
221 **56** 6c.+2c. olive-green . . . 5·00 24·0
a. Perf 14½–15 . . . £170 £19
221*b* 6c.+2c. apple-green
c. Perf 14½–15 . . . £275
222 **57** 8c.+2c. lake . . . 5·50 11·0
a. Inverted figure "3" for "C" in "CENTS"
223 **58** 10c.+2c. blue . . . 8·00 24·0
224 **59** 12c.+2c. deep bright blue . . . 21·00 45·0
a. Surch inverted . . . £650
225 **60** 16c.+2c. brown-lake . . . 22·00 45·0
226 **62** 24c.+2c. mauve . . . 22·00 45·0

(b) Lines of surch 13–14 mm apart.

227 **52** 2c.+2c. green . . . 85·00 £16
228 **56** 6c.+2c. olive-green . . . £425 £75
229 **64** 25c.+2c. green . . . 10·00 42·0
230 50c.+2c. steel-blue . . . 12·00 42·0
231 $1+2c. chestnut . . . 45·00 50·0
232 $2+2c. lilac . . . 75·00 95·0
233 **65** $5+2c. lake . . . £350 £50
234 $10+2c. brick-red . . . £375 £50
214/34 *Set of* 17 . . . £850 £130

The above stamps were dispatched from London in thre[e] consignments, of which two were lost through enemy action at sea.

Only one sheet was found of No. 228.

These stamps were sold at a premium of 2c. per stamp, whic[h] went to the Red Cross Society.

1918 (Oct). *Stamps of 1909–11 surch with T* **70**, *in red.* P 13½–14.
235 **51** 1c.+4c. chocolate . . . 60 5·0
a. Imperf between (horiz pair) . . . £1800
236 **52** 2c.+4c. green . . . 65 8·0
237 **53** 3c.+4c. rose-lake . . . 1·00 3·7
238 **54** 4c.+4c. scarlet . . . 40 4·7
239 **55** 5c.+4c. brown . . . 2·00 22·0
240 **56** 6c.+4c. apple-green . . . 1·90 12·0
a. Imperf between (vert pair) . . . £1600
241 **57** 8c.+4c. lake . . . 1·25 9·5
242 **58** 10c.+4c. turquoise-blue . . . 3·75 12·0
242*a* 10c.+4c. greenish blue . . . 8·50 40·0
243 **59** 12c.+4c. deep blue . . . 14·00 14·0
a. Surch double . . . £1000
244 **60** 16c.+4c. brown-lake . . . 8·00 16·0
245 **62** 24c.+4c. mauve . . . 11·00 20·0
246 **64** 25c.+4c. yellow-green . . . 6·00 50·0
247 25c.+4c. blue-green . . . 26·00 75·0
248 50c.+4c. steel-blue . . . 15·00 45·0
a. Perf 14½–15 . . . 60·00
249 $1+4c. chestnut . . . 15·00 60·0
a. Perf 14½–15 . . . £110
250 $2+4c. lilac . . . 48·00 80·0
251 **65** $5+4c. lake . . . £275 £40
252 $10+4c. brick-red . . . £300 £40
235/52 *Set of* 17 . . . £650 £100

Nos. 235/52 were sold at face, plus 4c. on each stamp for Re[d] Cross Funds.

Examples of a double-ring "SANDAKAN N. BORNEO" postmark dated "1 NOV 1918" on these stamps are generall[y] considered to be faked.

THREE

MALAYA-BORNEO

EXHIBITION

1922.

(71)

CENTS

(72)

1922 (31 Mar). *Malaya-Borneo Exhibition, Singapore. Stamps of 1909–22 some in different shades, optd as T* **71** *by Govt Printing Office, Sandakan.* P 13½–14.

253 **51** 1c. brown (R.) 12·00 60·00
a. "BORHEO" £300 £400
b. "BORNEQ" £450 £600
c. Stop after "EXHIBITION." 75·00
d. Raised stop after "1922" £500
e. "EXHIBITICN." with stop £550
f. Perf 14½–15 27·00 70·00
fa. "BORHEO" £475
fb. "BORNEQ" £700
fc. Raised stop after "1922" £700
fd. "EXHIBITICN." with stop £800
fe. "MHLAYA" and stop after "EXHIBITION" £2500
ff. Stop after "EXHIBITION." £120
53*g* 1c. brown (B.) (P 14½–15) £1100
ga. Vert pair, with and without opt £4500
gb. Raised stop after "1922." £3000
gc. "BORHEO" £2500
gd. "BORNEQ" £3250
gf. "EXHIBITICN." with stop £3250
gg. "MHLAYA" and stop after "EXHIBITION"
54 1c. orange-brown (R.) 27·00 65·00
55 **52** 2c. green (R.) 2·00 21·00
a. Stop after "EXHIBITION." 30·00
56 **53** 3c. rose-lake (B.) 14·00 55·00
a. Stop after "EXHIBITION." 75·00
b. "EXHIBITICN." with stop £2500
c. Raised stop after "1922" £1700
57 **54** 4c. scarlet (B.) 2·25 38·00
a. Stop after "EXHIBITION." 32·00
b. Perf 14½–15 75·00
ba. Stop after "EXHIBITION." £325
58 **55** 5c. orange-brown (B.) 9·00 55·00
a. Imperf between (vert pair) £1200 £1300
b. Stop after "EXHIBITION." 65·00
c. Opt double £1800
d. Opt double (with stop) £4250
59 5c. chestnut (B.) 19·00 60·00
a. Stop after "EXHIBITION." 90·00
60 **56** 6c. apple-green (R.) 8·50 60·00
a. Stop after "EXHIBITION." 55·00
b. Opt double £1800
c. Opt double (with stop) £4250
1 **57** 8c. dull rose (B.) 5·00 42·00
a. Stop after "EXHIBITION." 65·00
2 8c. deep rose-lake (B.) 6·00 48·00
a. Stop after "EXHIBITION." 70·00
3 **58** 10c. turquoise-blue (R.) 11·00 55·00
a. Stop after "EXHIBITION." 75·00
b. Perf 14½–15 35·00
ba. Stop after "EXHIBITION." £170
4 10c. greenish blue (R.) 11·00 70·00
a. Stop after "EXHIBITION." 75·00
5 **59** 12c. deep blue (R.) 7·00 21·00
a. Stop after "EXHIBITION." 70·00 £150
6 12c. deep bright blue (R.) 32·00
a. Stop after "EXHIBITION." £180
7 **60** 16c. brown-lake (B.) 18·00 60·00
a. Stop after "EXHIBITION." 95·00
b. Opt in red £6000
8 **61** 20c.on 18c. blue-green (B.) 18·00 75·00
a. Stop after "EXHIBITION." £160
9 20c.on 18c. blue-green (R.) 20·00 £130
a. Stop after "EXHIBITION." £225 £350
0 **62** 24c. mauve (R.) 32·00 60·00
a. Stop after "EXHIBITION." £160 £300
1 24c. lilac (R.) 32·00 60·00
a. Stop after "EXHIBITION." £160
2 24c. reddish lilac (R.) 40·00 70·00
a. Stop after "EXHIBITION." £180
3 **64** 25c. blue-green (R.) 18·00 65·00
a. Stop after "EXHIBITION." £150
4 25c. yellow-green (R.) 6·50 55·00
a. Stop after "EXHIBITION." £110
b. Opt double £2500
c. Perf 14½–15 13·00 65·00
ca. Stop after "EXHIBITION." £200
cb. Opt double £2750
5 50c. steel-blue (R.) 9·50 55·00
a. Stop after "EXHIBITION." £130
b. Perf 14½–15 21·00 75·00
ba. Stop after "EXHIBITION." £170
3/75 *Set of* 14 £140 £650
3s/75s Optd "Specimen" *Set of* 14 £450

These overprints were applied from a number of settings covering 20, 25 or 30 stamps at a time.

Of the ten settings known for the horizontal stamps the earliest were only used for the 1c. on which most of the varieties occur. Of the others the vast majority come from settings of 20 (10 × 2) with stop after "EXHIBITION" variety on R. 2/7, or 25 (5 × 5) on which the same variety can be found on R. 5/4. In addition the 3c. comes from a different setting of 20 (10 × 2) on which there is a raised stop after "1922" on R. 2/8 and "EXHIBITICN." on R. 2/9.

The 1c. sequence is complicated, but additionally includes a setting of 10 with "BORHEO" on stamps 3 and 10, BORNEQ" on stamp 4, raised stop on stamp 8 and "EXHIBITICN." on stamp 9. A setting of 20 repeats this sequence on its bottom line as does one of 30, although in this instance "MHLAYA" replaces "EXHIBITICN" as the variety on stamp 9.

For the vertical stamps (2, 6, 10, 12, 16 and 20c. on 18c.) the settings were of 20 (10 × 2) or 25 (5 × 5). The stop after "EXHIBITION" occurs on R. 2/7 of the former and R. 5/4 of the latter.

The 25c. and 50c. high values were overprinted from a setting of 20 (10 × 2), with the stop after "EXHIBITION" on R. 2/7, or 25 (5 × 5).

1923 (Oct). *T* **54** *surch with T* **72**.
276 3c.on 4c. black and scarlet 1·25 6·00
a. Surch double £900
s. Optd "Specimen" 50·00

1925–28. *Designs as 1909–22 issue with centres in black and some frame colours changed.* P 12½.
277 **51** 1c. chocolate-brown 1·00 70
a. Imperf between (horiz pair) £1000
278 **52** 2c. claret 85 60
a. Imperf between (vert pair) — £850
b. Imperf between (horiz pair)
279 **53** 3c. green 3·00 75
a. Imperf between (horiz pair) † £1100
280 **54** 4c. scarlet 50 10
a. Imperf between (vert pair) £275 £375
b. Imperf between (horiz pair) £750
c. Imperf between (vert strip of three) £1000
281 **55** 5c. yellow-brown 5·00 2·75
a. Imperf between (vert pair) £900
282 **56** 6c. olive-green 6·00 90
283 **57** 8c. carmine 3·25 50
a. Imperf between (vert pair) £475
b. Imperf between (horiz pair)
c. Imperf between (vert strip of four) £1400
284 **58** 10c. turquoise-blue 3·75 90
a. Imperf between (horiz pair) £800 £1000
b. Imperf between (vert pair)
285 **59** 12c. deep blue 21·00 80
286 **60** 16c. red-brown 28·00 £150
287 **61** 20c.on 18c. blue-green (R.) 8·00 3·00
288 **62** 24c. violet 48·00 £120
289 **64** 25c. green 8·50 4·25
290 50c. steel-blue 12·00 14·00
291 $1 chestnut 18·00 £275
292 $2 mauve 60·00 £325
293 **65** $5 lake (1928) £150 £750
294 $10 orange-red (1928) £350 £850
277/94 *Set of* 18 £650 £2250

Examples of No. 278 were supplied for U.P.U. distribution punched with a 3½ mm diameter hole.

Examples of the 16c., 24c., $1, $2, $5 and $10 in this perforation were not supplied to the territory for postal purposes. Used examples exist from covers prepared by stamp dealers.

73 Head of a Murut

76 Mount Kinabalu

(Eng J. A. C. Harrison. Recess Waterlow)

1931 (1 Jan). *50th Anniv of British North Borneo Company. T* **73**, **76** *and similar designs.* P 12½.
295 3c. black and blue-green 1·25 80
296 6c. black and orange 16·00 3·25
297 10c. black and scarlet 4·25 13·00
298 12c. black and ultramarine 4·75 8·00
299 25c. black and violet 38·00 35·00
300 $1 black and yellow-green 27·00 £100
301 $2 black and chestnut 48·00 £110
302 $5 black and purple £150 £425
295/302 *Set of* 8 £250 £600
295s/302s Optd "Specimen" *Set of* 8 £300

Designs: *Vert*—6c. Orang-Utan; 10c. Dyak warrior; $1 Badge of the Company; $5 Arms of the Company. *Horiz*—25c. Clouded Leopard; $2 Arms of the Company.

Examples of all values are known showing a forged Jesselton postmark dated "22 AUG 1931".

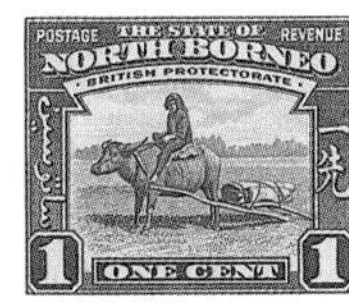

81 Buffalo Transport

82 Palm Cockatoo

(Eng J. A. C. Harrison. Recess Waterlow)

1939 (1 Jan). *T* **81/2** *and similar designs.* P 12½.
303 1c. green and red-brown 3·25 1·75
304 2c. purple and greenish blue 5·00 1·75
305 3c. slate-blue and green 3·75 2·00
306 4c. bronze-green and violet 7·00 50
307 6c. deep blue and claret 6·50 8·00
308 8c. scarlet 10·00 1·50
309 10c. violet and bronze-green 38·00 6·00
310 12c. green and royal blue 27·00 6·00
a. Green and blue 50·00 7·50
311 15c. blue-green and brown 23·00 8·00
312 20c. violet and slate-blue 15·00 4·00
313 25c. green and chocolate 20·00 11·00
314 50c. chocolate and violet 22·00 8·50
315 $1 brown and carmine 80·00 19·00
316 $2 violet and olive-green £120 £100
317 $5 indigo and pale blue £300 £200
303/17 *Set of* 15 £600 £350
303s/17s Perf "Specimen" *Set of* 15 £350

Designs: *Vert*—3c. Native; 4c. Proboscis Monkey; 6c. Mounted Bajaus; 10c. Orang-Utan; 15c. Dyak; $1, $2 Badge of the Company. *Horiz*—8c. Eastern Archipelago; 12c. Murut with blowpipe; 20c. River scene; 25c. Native boat; 50c. Mt Kinabalu; $5 Arms of the Company.

Examples of most values are known showing forged Jesselton postmarks dated "22 AUG 1941" or "15 JA 48".

WAR TAX

(96)

WAR TAX

(97)

1941 (24 Feb). *Nos. 303/4 optd at Sandakan with T* **96/7**.
318 1c. green and red-brown 1·75 3·50
a. Optd front and back £400
319 2c. purple and greenish blue 7·00 4·00

The 1c. was for compulsory use on internal mail and the 2c. on overseas mail, both in addition to normal postage.

BRITISH MILITARY ADMINISTRATION

North Borneo, including Labuan, was occupied by the Japanese in January 1942. Australian forces landed on Labuan on 10 June 1945 and by the end of the war against Japan on 14 August had liberated much of western North Borneo. The territory was placed under British Military Administration on 5 January 1946.

BMA

(98)

(99)

1945 (17 Dec). *Nos. 303/17 optd with T* **98**.
320 1c. green and red-brown 7·00 2·00
321 2c. purple and greenish blue 14·00 2·00
a. Opt double £5500
322 3c. slate-blue and green 1·25 1·25
323 4c. bronze-green and violet 16·00 16·00
324 6c. deep blue and claret 1·25 1·25
325 8c. scarlet 3·00 75
326 10c. violet and bronze-green 3·00 40
327 12c. green and blue 6·00 2·75
a. Green and royal blue 9·00 1·25
328 15c. blue-green and brown 1·50 1·00
329 20c. violet and slate-blue 4·25 1·25
330 25c. green and chocolate 6·50 1·50
331 50c. chocolate and violet 3·00 1·75
332 $1 brown and carmine 48·00 40·00
333 $2 violet and olive-green 48·00 32·00
a. Opt double £3000
334 $5 indigo and pale blue 20·00 14·00
320/34 *Set of* 15 £160 £100

These stamps and the similarly overprinted stamps of Sarawak were obtainable at all post offices throughout British Borneo (Brunei, Labuan, North Borneo and Sarawak), for use on local and overseas mail.

CROWN COLONY

North Borneo became a Crown Colony on 15 July 1946.

Lower bar broken at right (R. 8/3)

Lower bar broken at left (R. 8/4)

1947 (1 Sept–22 Dec). *Nos. 303 to 317 optd with T* **99** *and bars obliterating words "THE STATE OF" and "BRITISH PROTECTORATE".*
335 1c. green and red-brown (15.12) 15 1·00
b. Lower bar broken at right 18·00 35·00
c. Lower bar broken at left 18·00 35·00
336 2c. purple and greenish blue (22.12) 1·75 90
337 3c. slate-blue and green (R.) (22.12) 15 90
338 4c. bronze-green and violet 70 90
339 6c. deep blue and claret (R.) (22.12) 25 20
340 8c. scarlet 30 20
b. Lower bar broken at right 21·00 21·00
341 10c. violet and bronze-green (15.12) 1·50 40
342 12c. green and royal blue (22.12) 2·00 2·75
a. Green and blue 7·50 6·00
343 15c. blue-green and brown (22.12) 2·25 30
344 20c. violet and slate-blue (22.12) 2·50 85
b. Lower bar broken at right 38·00 30·00
345 25c. green and chocolate (22.12) 2·75 50
b. Lower bar broken at right 55·00 30·00
346 50c. chocolate and violet (22.12) 2·75 85
b. Lower bar broken at right 55·00 30·00
c. Lower bar broken at left 55·00 30·00
347 $1 brown and carmine (22.12) 5·50 1·75
348 $2 violet and olive-green (22.12) 14·00 17·00
349 $5 indigo and pale blue (R.) (22.12) 22·00 17·00
b. Lower bar broken at right £140 £140
335/49 *Set of* 15 50·00 40·00
335/49 Perf "Specimen" *Set of* 15 £250

1948 (1 Nov). *Royal Silver Wedding. As Nos. 112/13 of Antigua.*
350 8c. scarlet 30 80
351 $10 mauve 22·00 35·00

1949 (10 Oct). *75th Anniv of U.P.U. As Nos. 114/17 of Antigua.*
352 8c. carmine 60 30
353 10c. brown 3·25 1·00
354 30c. orange-brown 1·25 1·75
355 55c. blue 1·25 2·50
352/5 *Set of* 4 5·50 5·00

100 Mount Kinabalu

102 Coconut Grove

(Photo Harrison)

1950 (1 July)–**52**. *T* **100**, **102** *and similar designs. Chalk-surfaced paper.* Wmk Mult Script CA. P 13½ × 14½ (horiz), 14½ × 13½ (vert).

356 1c. red-brown 15 1·25
357 2c. blue 15 50
358 3c. green 15 15
359 4c. bright purple 15 10
360 5c. violet 15 10
361 8c. scarlet 75 85
362 10c. maroon 1·25 15
363 15c. ultramarine 2·00 65
364 20c. brown 1·25 10
365 30c. olive-brown 3·50 20
366 50c. rose-carmine ("JESSLETON") 85 3·25
366*a* 50c. rose-carmine ("JESSELTON") (1.5.52) 8·00 2·25
367 $1 red-orange 3·75 1·00
368 $2 grey-green 5·50 14·00
369 $5 emerald-green 15·00 21·00
370 $10 dull blue 40·00 55·00
356/70 *Set of* 16 75·00 90·00

Designs: *Horiz*—2c. Native musical instrument; 8c. Map; 10c. Log pond; 15c. Malay prau, Sandakan; 20c. Bajau Chief; $2 Murut with blowpipe; $5 Net-fishing; $10 Arms of North Borneo. *Vert*—4c. Hemp drying; 5c. Cattle at Kota Belud; 30c. Suluk river canoe, Lahad Datu; 50c. Clock tower, Jesselton; $1 Bajau horsemen.

POSTAL FISCALS

Three Cents. Revenue
(F **1**) (Raised stop)

Ten Cents. Revenue
(F **2**)

1886. *Regular issues surch as Type* F **1** *or* F **2**.

F1 **1** 3c.on 4c. pink (No. 6) £120 £170
a. Raised stop after "Cents" £100 £160
F2 5c.on 8c. green (No. 7) £120 £170
a. Raised stop after "Cents" £100 £160
F3 **4** 10c.on 50c. violet (No. 4) £160 £180
a. Surch double — £1100
b. No stop after "Cents" and stop after "Revenue." £450 £500
c. Inverted "L" for first "F" in "FIFTY" (R. 5/2) — £800

It is believed that Nos. F1/2 were each surcharged from a horizontal setting of five so that the raised stop variety occurs on every stamp in the first, second, third, sixth, seventh and eighth vertical columns in the sheets of 50 (10 × 5).

POSTAGE DUE STAMPS

POSTAGE DUE
(D **1**)

1895 (1 Aug)–**97**. *Nos. 68/79 optd with Type* D **1** *horizontally (8, 12, 18 and 24c.) or vertically, reading upwards (others).* P 14½–15.

D1 **25** 2c. black and rose-lake 20·00 40·00 2·75
a. Opt double* † † £300
b. Opt vertical, reading downwards* † † £350
D2 2c. black and lake 16·00 24·00 2·00
a. Perf 13½–14
b. Perf 13½–14, comp 12–13* † † 10·00
c. Opt omitted (in vert pair with normal)* † † £1500
D3 **26** 3c. olive-green and dull purple 6·00 16·00 1·00
a. Bronze-green and dull purple
b. Opt vertical, reading downwards* † † —
D4 3c. olive-green and violet
a. Perf 13½–14
b. Opt double* † † £425
D5 **27** 5c. black and vermilion 55·00 25·00 3·00
a. Printed double † — —
b. With stop after "DUE" in opt (1897) £180
c. Opt double £600 £650 †
d. Perf 13½–14 — 50·00 2·50
e. Perf 13½–14, comp 12–13 — 55·00 —
D6 **28** 6c. black and bistre-brown 55·00 70·00 2·50
a. Perf 13½–14 14·00 48·00 2·50
b. Perf 12–13* † † —
c. Perf 13½–14, comp 12–13
d. Opt vertical, reading downwards* † †
D7 **29** 8c. black and dull purple 48·00 50·00 2·75
a. Opt double* † † £350
b. Perf 13½–14
ba. Opt inverted* † † £190
c. Perf 13½–14, comp 12–13 65·00
D8 **30** 12c. black and blue — 50·00 2·50
a. Opt double* † † £375
b. Perf 13½–14 70·00 50·00 2·50
c. Perf 13½–14, comp 14½–15
D9 12c. black & ultram (P 13½–14) 80·00 60·00 —
D10 **31** 18c. black and deep green 70·00 60·00 4·00
a. Opt inverted £325 £400 †
b. Perf 13½–14 75·00 80·00 4·00
ba. Opt double* † † £300
c. Opt vertical, reading upwards (1897) 75·00 95·00 4·25
ca. Opt vertical, reading downwards £425 £325 †
D11 **32** 24c. blue and rose-lake 70·00 85·00 4·00
a. Opt double* † † £325
b. Perf 13½–14 27·00 55·00 4·00
c. Perf 13½–14, comp 14½–15
D3s, D5s, D8s, D10cs, D11s Optd "Specimen" *Set of* 5 £150

There were two local overprintings of these stamps which show variations in the distance between the two words. Further overprints were produced in London for sale to dealers by the British North Borneo Company. Those listings marked with an * only exist from the London overprinting and are usually only known cancelled-to-order.

No. D5b comes from at least one sheet which was included in a later overprinting.

1897–99. *Nos. 94/7, 99/103, 106, 108/11 optd with Type* D **1** *horizontally (8c.) or vertically reading upwards (others).* P 14½–15.

D12 **35** 2c. black and lake (1898) 8·50 9·00 1·50
a. Perf 13½–14 29·00
b. Opt horizontal* £120
s. Optd "Specimen" 27·00
D13 2c. black and green (P 13½–14)* 50·00 † 70
a. Perf 13½–14, comp 12–13* — † 90
b. Perf 16*
c. Perf 12–13*
d. Opt vertical, reading downwards*
e. Opt horizontal* £120
D14 **36** 3c. green and rosy mauve* 18·00 † 50
a. Perf 13½–14* 30·00 † 1·00
b. Perf 13½–14, comp 14½–15*
c. Opt double*
D15 3c. green and dull mauve 17·00 35·00 †
D16 **37** 4c. black and carmine * — † 85
a. Perf 13½–14 40·00 † 50
D17 **38** 5c. black & orange-verm (1899) 60·00 60·00 90
a. Perf 13½–14 20·00 45·00 1·75
D18 **39** 6c. black and bistre-brown 5·00 30·00 70
a. Perf 13½–14 — 35·00 50
b. Perf 13½–14, comp 12–13* — † 2·00
s. Optd "Specimen" 27·00
D19 **40** 8c. black & brown-purple (1898) 65·00 80·00 †
a. Opt vertical, reading upwards (P 16)* † † £225
s. Optd "Specimen" 27·00
D20 8c. blk & brn (opt vert, reading upwards)* 6·00 † 50
a. Opt vertical, reading downwards* † † £550
b. Perf 13½–14*
D21 **42** 12c. black and dull blue* — † 5·00
a. Perf 13½–14* 95·00 † 4·00
D22 **44** 18c. black and green (P 16)* † † £650
D23 **46** 18c. black and green (P 13½–14)* 50·00 † 4·00
a. Perf 13½–14, comp 12–13* 95·00 † 4·00
D24 **45** 24c. blue and lake* — † £325
D25 **47** 24c. blue and lake* 23·00 † 2·25
a. Perf 13½–14*

In addition to local overprints, stamps from the 1897–1902 series were also overprinted by Waterlow on two occasions for sale by the British North Borneo Company to dealers from London. These Waterlow overprints were not supplied to North Borneo for postal purposes and are indicated by an * in the above listing.

1901–02. *Nos. 96/7, 100 and 102/3 optd locally as Type* D **1**, *but with stop after "DUE", horizontally (8c.) or vertically reading upwards (others).* P 13½–14.

D26 **36** 3c. green and rosy mauve (1902) 50·00 70·00
a. Opt double £250
D27 3c. green & dull mve (P 14½–15) (1902) 50·00 70·00
a. Opt double £250 £275
D28 **38** 5c. black & orange-verm (P 14½–15) 60·00
D29 **40** 8c. black and brown-purple 22·00 75·00
D30 8c. black and brown (P 14½–15) £150 £180

1902 (10 Oct)–**12**. *Stamps of 1901–05 (optd "*BRITISH PROTECTORATE*") further optd with Type* D **1** *locally (No. D31) or by Waterlow (others).* P 13½–14.

(a) Optd horizontally showing stop after "DUE".

D31 **34** 1c. black and bistre-brown 4·50 55·00
a. With raised stop after "DUE" 4·75 60·00

(b) Optd vertically reading upwards.

D32 **35** 2c. black and green (P 16) £350 £180
D33 **36** 3c. green and rosy mauve 95·00 £110
D34 **38** 5c. black & orange-verm (P 14½–15) £160 £110
D35 **40** 8c. black and brown £140 90·00
D36 **47** 24c. blue and lake £180 95·00

(c) Optd horizontally at centre of stamp.

D37 **34** 1c. black and bistre-brown* — † 28·00
a. Perf 14½–15* £200 † 28·00
D38 **35** 2c. black and green (1909) 13·00 3·75 30
a. Perf 14½–15 (1903) 50·00 45·00 †
D39 **36** 3c. green and rosy mauve (1912) 4·75 3·25 30
a. Perf 14½–15 (1904) 48·00 35·00 †
ab. Type D **1** opt double £425
D40 **37** 4c. black and carmine (1912) 11·00 6·50 30
a. Type D **1** opt double* £500 † £140
b. Perf 14½–15 (1.3.03) 6·50 15·00 50
D41 **38** 5c. black & orange-verm (1905) 23·00 4·50 30
a. Perf 14½–15 (1905) 65·00 26·00 †
D42 **39** 6c. black & bistre-brown (1912) 16·00 11·00 40
a. Type D **1** opt inverted* £425 † £100
b. Type D **1** opt double £600 — —
c. No stop after "PROTECTORATE" (1912)
d. Perf 16 (1906) 70·00 38·00 †
D43 **40** 8c. black and brown (1912) 20·00 4·25 40
a. No stop after "PROTECTORATE" (1903) 50·00 60·00
D44 **41** 10c. brown and slate-lilac (1906) £180 65·00 3·75
a. No stop after "PROTECTORATE" (1906) — —
D45 10c. brown and slate-blue (1912) 80·00 18·00 1·4
D46 **42** 12c. black and dull blue (2.12.10) 24·00 15·00 2·0
D47 **43** 16c. green and chestnut (2.12.10) 42·00 20·00 2·0
D48 **46** 18c. black and green (2.12.10) 9·50 19·00 1·5
a. Type D **1** opt double* £475 † 60·0
b. Imperf between (vert pair) — † £60
D49 **47** 24c. blue and lake (1906) 11·00 24·00 2·0
a. Perf 14½–15 (1909) — —
b. Type D **1** opt double* £275 † 85·0

(d) Optd horizontally at top of stamp.

D50 **35** 2c. black and green (P 16) (1907) 85·00 40·0
a. Perf 14½–15 (1908) 70·00 45·0
D51 **37** 4c. black and carmine (1906) 65·00 22·0

Items marked * only occur in stocks obtained from the British North Borneo Company in London.

POSTAGE DUE
(D **2**)

POSTAGE DUE
(D **3**)

Type D **2**. Thick letters. Ends of "S" and top of "G" straight. Pointed beard to "G".
Type D **3**. Thinner letters. Ends of "S" and top of "G" slanted. Square beard to "G".

1918–30. *Opt with Type* D **2** *locally.*

(a) On stamps of 1909–23. P 13½–14.

D52 **52** 2c. black and green (opt at foot) (1.24) 11·00 75·
a. Perf 14½–15 19·00 80·
s. Optd "Specimen" 28·00
D53 **53** 3c. black and green (opt at foot) (1.9.23) 4·50 42·
D54 **54** 4c. black and scarlet (opt at top) (10.18) 90·00 17·
D55 4c. black and scarlet (opt at foot) (1.22) 1·00 1·
D56 4c. black & scarlet (opt in centre) (5.23) — 12·
D57 **55** 5c. black & yell-brn (opt at foot) (1.22) 9·00 22·
D58 5c. blk & yell-brn (opt in centre) (1.23) 9·50 22
D59 **56** 6c. black & ol-grn (opt at foot) (1.9.23) 9·50 9·
D60 6c. black & ol-grn (opt in centre) (6.23) 13·00 7·
D61 – 6c. blk & apple-grn (opt at foot) (1.9.23) 10·00 16
D62 **57** 8c. blk & rose-lake (opt at foot) (1.9.23) 1·50 1·
a. Opt double £800
D63 **58** 10c. black & turq-bl (opt at foot) (1.8.24) 13·00 19
a. Perf 14½–15 75·00 £1
D64 **59** 12c. black and deep blue (1.8.24) 55·00 48
a. Horiz pair, one without opt £11000
D65 **60** 16c. black and brown-lake (2.29)
a. Black and red-brown 19·00 50
s. Optd "Specimen" 30·00

(b) On stamps of 1925–28 with opt at foot. P 12½ (1928–30).

D66 **52** 2c. black and claret (3.30) 75 1
D67 **53** 3c. black and green (1926) 7·50 25
D68 **54** 4c. black and scarlet (1926) 1·50 1
D69 **55** 5c. black and yellow-brown (1926) 7·50 90
D70 **56** 6c. black and olive-green (3.28) 5·00 2
D71 **57** 8c. black and carmine (2.28) 3·50 16
D72 **58** 10c. black and turquoise-blue (1926) 10·00 90
D73 **59** 12c. black and deep blue (1926) 30·00 £

Dates given as month and year only indicate first known postmark where recorded.

1930–38. *Optd with Type* D **3**, *locally, at foot of stamp.*

(a) On stamps of 1909–23. P 13½–14.

D74 **57** 8c. black and carmine (1931) —
D75 **60** 16c. black and brown-lake (11.31) 17·00 75
a. Black and red-brown 6·50

(b) On stamps of 1925–28. P 12½.

D76 **52** 2c. black and claret (5.31) 50
D77 **53** 3c. black and green (11.38) 7·00 2
D78 **54** 4c. black and scarlet (6.36) —
D79 **55** 5c. black and yellow-brown 12·00
D80 **56** 6c. black and olive-green (12.30) 4·75
D81 **57** 8c. black and carmine (9.31) 3·25 1
D82 **58** 10c. black and turquoise-blue (12.32) 12·00 9
D83 **59** 12c. black and deep blue 35·00
D84 **60** 16c. black and red-brown 60·00 £

Dates given are those of earliest postmark where recorded.

D 4 Crest of the Company

(Recess Waterlow)

939 (1 Jan). P 12½.
)85 D 4 2c. brown . . . 6·50 75·00
)86 4c. scarlet . . . 6·50 £100
)87 6c. violet . . . 22·00 £130
)88 8c. green . . . 23·00 £225
)89 10c. blue . . . 50·00 £350
)85/9 *Set of* 5 . . . £100 £800
)85s/9s Perf "Specimen" *Set of* 5 . . . £150

LABUAN

CROWN COLONY

The island of Labuan, off the northern coast of Borneo, was ›ded to Great Britain by the Sultan of Brunei in December 1846.

Stamps of STRAITS SETTLEMENTS were used from 1867 until 1879. Covers of 1864 and 1865 are known from Labuan franked with stamps of INDIA or HONG KONG.

PRICES FOR STAMPS ON COVER

Nos. 1/4		—
Nos. 5/10	*from*	× 50
Nos. 11/13		—
Nos. 14/21	*from*	× 40
Nos. 22/5		—
Nos. 26/35	*from*	× 50
Nos. 36/8		—
Nos. 39/47	*from*	× 100
Nos. 49/50	*from*	× 15
Nos. 51/7	*from*	× 60
Nos. 62/74	*from*	× 15
Nos. 75/9	*from*	× 40
Nos. 80/8	*from*	× 20
Nos. 89/97	*from*	× 15
Nos. 98/116	*from*	× 10
Nos. 117/28	*from*	× 30
Nos. 129/37	*from*	× 10
Nos. 138/42		—
Nos. D1/9	*from*	× 30

1

(2)

(3)

(Recess D.L.R.)

79 (May). Wmk CA over Crown, sideways. P 14.
1 2c. blue-green . . . £950 £700
6c. orange-brown . . . £190 £170
a. No dot at upper left (R. 2/4) . . . £425 £375
12c. carmine . . . £1500 £600
a. No right foot to second Chinese character (R. 2/3) . . . £2500 £1000
16c. blue . . . 60·00 £120

This watermark is always found sideways, and extends over two ›mps, a single specimen showing only a portion of the Crown or letters CA, these being tall and far apart. This paper was chiefly d for long fiscal stamps.

80 (Jan)–**82**. Wmk Crown CC (reversed on 8c.). P 14.
1 2c. yellow-green . . . 21·00 29·00
x. Wmk reversed . . . 42·00 50·00
y. Wmk inverted and reversed . . . 70·00 70·00
6c. orange-brown . . . £100 £110
a. No dot at upper left . . . £225 £225
w. Wmk inverted . . . £180
8c. carmine (4.82) . . . £100 £100
a. No dot at lower left (R. 2/5) . . . £200 £200
x. Wmk normal (not reversed) . . . £225 £225
10c. brown . . . £150 85·00
w. Wmk inverted . . . £120 90·00
x. Wmk reversed
12c. carmine . . . £250 £325
a. No right foot to second Chinese character . . . £450 £500
w. Wmk inverted . . . £350
x. Wmk reversed . . . £250 £325
y. Wmk inverted and reversed
16c. blue (1881) . . . 80·00 80·00
w. Wmk inverted . . . £160 £160
x. Wmk reversed . . . £130 £140
y. Wmk inverted and reversed . . . £190
) *Set of* 6 . . . £600 £650

1880 (Aug).

(a) No. 9 surch with T **2** *in black and with the original value obliterated by manuscript bar in red or black.*
11 8c.on 12c. carmine . . . £1200 £750
a. Type **2** inverted . . . £1400 £800
b. "12" not obliterated . . . £1900 £1300
c. As b. with Type **2** inverted
d. No right foot to second Chinese character . . . £1900 £1200
x. Wmk reversed . . . £1100 £700

(b) No. 4 surch with two upright figures and No. 9 surch with two at right angles as T **3**.
12 6c.on 16c. blue (R.) . . . £2000 £850
a. With one "6" only
13 8c.on 12c. carmine . . . £1400 £950
a. Both "8's" upright
b. Upright "8" inverted . . . £1500 £1000
c. No right foot to second Chinese character . . . £2000 £1500
w. Wmk inverted . . . † £1400
x. Wmk reversed . . . £1400 £950
y. Wmk inverted and reversed

EIGHT CENTS (4) Eight Cents (5) One Dollar A.S.H. (6)

1881 (Mar). *No. 9 handstamped with T* **4**.
14 8c.on 12c. carmine . . . £325 £375
a. No right foot to second Chinese character . . . £600 £700
w. Wmk inverted . . . £400
x. Wmk reversed . . . £325 £375

1881 (June). *No. 9 surch with T* **5**.
15 8c.on 12c. carmine . . . £110 £120
a. Surch double . . . £1600 £1600
b. Surch inverted . . . £10000
c. "Eighr" . . . £16000
d. No right foot to second Chinese character . . . £225 £275
w. Wmk inverted . . . £225
x. Wmk reversed . . . £110 £120

The error "Eighr" occurred on R. 2/1 of the first printing, but was soon corrected.

Only one sheet of 10 has been reported of No. 15b, which also shows wmk inverted and reversed.

1883. Wmk Crown CA (reversed on 8c.). P 14.
17 **1** 2c. yellow-green . . . 18·00 27·00
a. Imperf between (horiz pair) . . . £8500
w. Wmk inverted . . . 50·00
x. Wmk reversed . . . 19·00 40·00
y. Wmk inverted and reversed
18 8c. carmine . . . £250 95·00
a. No dot at lower left . . . £450 £180
19 10c. yellow-brown . . . 29·00 40·00
w. Wmk inverted . . . 70·00 80·00
x. Wmk reversed . . . 70·00 80·00
20 16c. blue . . . 95·00 £180
21 40c. amber . . . 16·00 £100
x. Wmk reversed . . . 24·00 £100
17/21 *Set of* 5 . . . £350 £400

1883 (May). *No. 10 surch "One Dollar A.S.H." by hand as T* **6**.
22 **1** $1 on 16c. blue (R.) . . . £3250

The initials are those of the postmaster, Mr. A. S. Hamilton.

2 CENTS (7) 2 Cents (8) 2 Cents (9)

1885 (June). *Nos. 18 and 10 handstamped as T* **7**.
23 **1** 2c.on 8c. carmine . . . £200 £400
a. No dot at lower left . . . £400
24 2c.on 16c. blue . . . £950 £850
w. Wmk inverted . . . £1000
x. Wmk reversed . . . † £850

1885 (July). *No. 20 surch as T* **8**.
25 **1** 2c.on 16c. blue . . . £110 £160
a. Surch double . . . † £4250
b. "2" inserted . . . £1600
w. Wmk inverted

No. 25b shows a second "2" applied by a separate handstamp to correct indistinct impressions of Type **8**.

1885 (Sept). *No. 18 handstamped diag as T* **9**.
26 **1** 2c.on 8c. carmine . . . 65·00 £100
a. No dot at lower left . . . £130 £225
x. Wmk normal (not reversed) . . . £120

1885 (Sept)–**86**. Wmk Crown CA. P 14.
30 **1** 2c. rose-red . . . 2·50 10·00
a. Pale rose-red (1886) . . . 2·50 9·00
x. Wmk reversed . . . 6·50
31 8c. deep violet . . . 22·00 7·00
a. No dot at lower left . . . 50·00 20·00
b. Mauve (1886) . . . 25·00 8·00
ba. No dot at lower left . . . 60·00 22·00
bw. Wmk inverted . . . 65·00
32 10c. sepia (1886) . . . 9·50 38·00
w. Wmk inverted . . . 38·00
x. Wmk reversed . . . 23·00
33 16c. grey (1886) . . . £120
x. Wmk reversed . . . £100 £160
30/3 *Set of* 4 . . . £110 £190
30s/3s Optd "Specimen" *Set of* 4 . . . £425

ISSUES OF BRITISH NORTH BORNEO COMPANY

From 1 January 1890 while remaining a Crown Colony, the administration of Labuan was transferred to the British North Borneo Co, which issued the following stamps.

6 Cents (10) Two CENTS (11) Six CENTS (12)

1891 (July)–**92**. *Handstamped with T* **10**.
34 **1** 6c.on 8c. deep violet (No. 31) . . . £120 £100
a. Surch inverted . . . £190 £180
b. Surch double . . . £475
c. Surch double, one inverted . . . £850
d. "Cents" omitted . . . £425 £425
f. Pair, one without surch, one surch inverted . . . £1400
g. No dot at lower left . . . £250 £225
35 6c.on 8c. mauve (No. 31*b*) . . . 9·00 8·00
a. Surch inverted . . . 65·00 65·00
b. Surch double, one inverted . . . £750
c. Surch double, both inverted . . . £750
d. "6" omitted . . . £450
e. Pair, one without surcharge . . . £1200 £1200
f. Surch inverted with "Cents" omitted . . . £450
g. Pair, one without surch, one surch inverted . . . £1400 £1400
h. Surch double . . . £325
i. No dot at lower left . . . 22·00 22·00
j. Imperf between (horiz pair)
w. Wmk inverted . . . 45·00 45·00
x. Wmk reversed . . . 30·00
36 6c.on 8c. mauve (R.) (No. 31*b*) (2.92) . . . £850 £425
a. Surch inverted . . . £1200 £600
37 6c.on 16c. blue (No. 4) (3.92) . . . £2000 £1800
a. Surch inverted . . . £7500 £5500
38 6c.on 40c. amber (No. 21) . . . £8000 £4250
a. Surch inverted . . . £7000 £6500

There are two different versions of Type **10** with the lines of the surcharge either 1 mm or 2 mm apart.

(Recess D.L.R.)

1892–**93**. No wmk. P 14.
39 **1** 2c. rose-lake . . . 4·25 3·50
40 6c. bright green . . . 8·00 4·50
a. No dot at upper left . . . 20·00 15·00
41 8c. violet . . . 4·00 9·00
a. Pale violet (1893) . . . 4·25 9·00
43 10c. brown . . . 11·00 8·00
a. Sepia-brown (1893) . . . 11·00 14·00
45 12c. bright blue . . . 5·50 6·50
a. No right foot to second Chinese character . . . 15·00 18·00
46 16c. grey . . . 6·00 9·50
47 40c. ochre . . . 20·00 32·00
a. Brown-buff (1893) . . . 42·00 25·00
39/47 *Set of* 7 . . . 50·00 60·00

The 6c., 12c., 16c. and 40c. are in sheets of 10, as are all the earlier issues. The other values are in sheets of 30.

1892 (Dec). *Nos. 47 and 46 surch locally as T* **11** *or* **12**.
49 **1** 2c.on 40c. ochre (13 December) . . . £160 90·00
a. Surch inverted . . . £375 £500
50 6c.on 16c. grey (20 December) . . . £350 £150
a. Surch inverted . . . £475 £275
b. Surch sideways . . . £475 £275
c. Surch "Six Cents" . . . £1600

There are 10 slightly different versions of each of these surcharges which were applied in settings of 5 × 2, although instances of single handstamps are known.

A "SIX CENTS" handstamp with Roman "I" in "SIX" (without dot) is a clandestine surcharge, although it can be found with genuine postmarks. It also exists sideways or inverted.

The "Six Cents" surcharge of No. 50c was handstamped onto examples where the Type **12** surcharge had failed to print or where it was partially or completely albino.

CANCELLED-TO-ORDER. Prices are separately indicated, in a third price column, for stamps showing the recognisable black bars remainder cancellation. Earlier issues of the Company administration were also so treated, but, as postal cancellations were used, these cannot be identified.

(Litho D.L.R.)

1894 (Apr). No wmk. P 14.
51 **1** 2c. carmine-pink . . . 1·40 12·00 50
52 6c. bright green . . . 13·00 30·00 50
a. Imperf between (horiz pair) . . . £5500
b. No dot at upper left . . . 26·00 70·00 1·25
53 8c. bright mauve . . . 12·00 30·00 50
54 10c. brown . . . 42·00 45·00 50
55 12c. pale blue . . . 20·00 60·00 60
a. No right foot to second Chinese character . . . 45·00 £100 1·25
56 16c. grey . . . 25·00 £100 50
57 40c. orange-buff . . . 50·00 £110 50
51/7 *Set of* 7 . . . £150 £325 3·25
51s/7s H/S "Specimen" *Set of* 7 . . . £110

Collectors are warned against forgeries of this issue.

PERFORATION. There are a number of small variations in the perforation of the Waterlow issues of 1894 to 1905 which we believe to be due to irregularity of the pins rather than different perforators.

In the following lists, stamps perf 12, 12½, 13 or compound are described as perf 12–13, stamps perf 13½, 14 or compound are described as perf 13½–14 and those perf 14½, 15 or compound are listed as perf 14½–15. In addition the 13½–14 perforation exists compound with 14½–15 and with 12–13, whilst perf 16 comes from a separate perforator.

13

LABUAN
40
CENTS
(14)

1894 (May)–**96**. *T* **24/32** *of North Borneo (colours changed), with "LABUAN" engraved on vignette plate as T* **13** *(8, 12, 24c.) or horizontally (others)*. P 14½–15.

(a) Name and central part of design in black.

62 **24** 1c. grey-mauve 1·50 8·50 50
b. Perf 13½–14 9·50 9·50 —
ba. Imperf between (vert pair) £800 — £400
c. Perf 13½–14, comp 14½–15 24·00
d. Perf 13½–14, comp 12–13 23·00 11·00 90
e. Perf 12–13
63 **25** 2c. blue 2·50 8·00 50
a. Imperf (pair) £600
b. Perf 13½–14 4·00 8·00 —
c. Perf 13½–14, comp 14½–15 27·00
d. Perf 13½–14, comp 12–13 80·00
e. Perf 12–13
64 **26** 3c. ochre 3·75 17·00 50
a. Perf 13½–14 8·50 9·00 —
b. Perf 13½–14, comp 14½–15
c. Perf 13½–14, comp 12–13 40·00
d. Perf 12–13
65 **27** 5c. green 32·00 24·00 65
a. Perf 13½–14 38·00 14·00 —
ab. Imperf between (horiz pair) £1100
b. Perf 13½–14, comp 12–13 50·00
c. Perf 12–13 90·00
67 **28** 6c. brown-lake 2·50 15·00 50
a. Imperf (pair) £550 † £300
b. Perf 13½–14 — — 1·50
c. Perf 13½–14, comp 14½–15 — — 90
d. Perf 13½–14, comp 12–13
e. Perf 12–13
68 **29** 8c. rose-red 22·00 26·00 50
a. Perf 13½–14 26·00 42·00 —
69 8c. pink (1896) 7·00 23·00 50
a. Perf 13½–14 27·00 32·00 50
70 **30** 12c. orange-vermilion 23·00 48·00 50
a. Imperf between (vert pair) † † £1900
b. Perf 13½–14 65·00 70·00 2·00
c. Perf 12–13
d. Perf 13½–14, comp 12–13 — 85·00 —
71 **31** 18c. olive-brown 22·00 55·00 50
a. Perf 13½–14 70·00
72 18c. olive-bistre (1896) 55·00 70·00 50
a. Perf 13½–14 27·00 65·00 —
b. Perf 13½–14, comp 12–13
c. Imperf between (vert pair) † † £1100
d. Perf 13½–14, comp 14½–15 † † 1·50

(b) Name and central part in blue.

73 **32** 24c. pale mauve 22·00 55·00 50
a. Perf 13½–14 21·00 50·00 —
74 24c. dull lilac (1896) 15·00 45·00 50
a. Perf 13½–14 13·00 45·00 50
62/74 *Set of* 9 95·00 £200 4·00
62s/74s Optd "Specimen" *Set of* 9 £150

1895 (June). *No. 83 of North Borneo ($1 inscr "STATE OF NORTH BORNEO") surch as T* **14**.

75 **32c** 4c.on $1 scarlet 1·25 2·00 40
76 10c.on $1 scarlet 4·00 1·40 40
77 20c.on $1 scarlet 28·00 10·00 40
78 30c.on $1 scarlet 32·00 40·00 40
79 40c.on $1 scarlet 28·00 30·00 40
75/9 *Set of* 5 85·00 75·00 1·75
75s/9s Optd "Specimen" *Set of* 5 80·00

No. 76 exists with the figures of the surcharge 2½ mm away from "CENTS". The normal setting has a space of 4 mm. Examples of the narrow setting have, so far, only been seen on cancelled-to-order stamps (*Price* £18 *c.t.o.*).

LABUAN (15)

1846 JUBILEE 1896 (16)

4 CENTS (17)

1896. *T* **32a** *to* **32c** *of North Borneo (as Nos. 81 to 83, but colours changed) optd with T* **15**.

80 25c. green 25·00 29·00 60
a. Opt omitted 22·00 — 1·25
b. Imperf (pair) — — 60·00
ba. Opt omitted 42·00
81 50c. maroon 25·00 29·00 60
a. Opt omitted 20·00 — 1·25
b. Imperf (pair) — — 60·00
ba. Opt omitted 40·00
82 $1 blue 60·00 55·00 60
a. Opt omitted 29·00 — 1·25
b. Imperf (pair) — — 60·00
ba. Opt omitted 45·00
80s/2s Optd "Specimen" *Set of* 3 60·00

Nos. 80/1 showing stamps either printed double or double, one inverted, are from waste sheets subsequently sold by the British North Borneo Company to collectors.

1896 (24 Sept). *Jubilee of Cession of Labuan to Gt Britain. Nos. 62 to 68 optd with T* **16**. P 14½–15.

83 1c. black and grey-mauve 18·00 22·00 80
b. Opt in orange £190 £190 20·00
c. "JEBILEE" (R. 8/7) £950 £500 £300
d. "JUBILE" (R. 3/10) £1600
e. Perf 13½–14 24·00 22·00 —
ea. Opt double £325 £325 —
eb. Opt in orange £225 £190 †
f. Perf 13½–14, comp 12–13 29·00 18·00 —
fa. Opt in orange — £190 †
g. Perf 12–13
84 2c. black and blue 38·00 23·00 80
a. Imperf horiz (vert pair) £700 £800 †
b. "JEBILEE" (R. 8/7) £1100 £1100 —
c. "JUBILE" (R. 3/10) £1900
d. Perf 13½–14 38·00 15·00 —
e. Perf 13½–14, comp 14½–15 — 38·00 —
f. Perf 13½–14 comp 12–13 45·00
85 3c. black and ochre 35·00 22·00 80
a. "JEBILEE" (R. 8/7) £1400 £1400 £700
b. "JUBILE" (R. 3/10)
d. Perf 13½–14 40·00 28·00 90
db. Opt treble £650
e. Perf 13½–14, comp 14½–15
f. Perf 13½–14, comp 12–13
fa. Opt double £350 £350 £150
fb. Opt treble £650
86 5c. black and green 55·00 16·00 90
a. Opt double £550 £475 —
b. Perf 13½–14 60·00 22·00 90
c. Perf 13½–14, comp 12–13
87 6c. black and brown-lake 27·00 21·00 80
a. Opt double £650 £475 †
b. "JUBILE" (R. 3/10) £1900
c. Perf 13½–14, comp 14½–15
d. Perf 13½–14 — 70·00 —
88 8c. black and pink 45·00 13·00 80
a. Opt double † £2250 †
b. Perf 13½–14 40·00 11·00 80
c. Perf 13½–14, comp 14½–15 50·00 18·00 —
83/8 *Set of* 6 £190 95·00 4·50
83s/8s Optd "Specimen" *Set of* 6 £150

The normal overprint on the 1c. varies in appearance from pure black to brownish black due to a mixing of the inks. The orange overprint on this value is in a clear, bright, unadulterated ink.

No. 84b is known in a vertical strip of 3 imperf horizontally except at the base of the bottom stamp (*Price* £5000 *unused*).

1897 (Apr)–**1901**. *T* **34/45** *of North Borneo (colours changed), with "LABUAN" engraved on vignette plate as T* **13** *(8, 10, 12, 24c.) or horizontally (others). Name and central part in black (24c. in blue)*. P 13½–14.

89 **34** 1c. dull claret (P 14½–15) 4·00 4·75 50
a. Perf 13½–14, comp 14½–15
b. Brown (1901) 16·00 18·00 65
ba. Perf 14½–15 3·00
bb. Perf 16 13·00 13·00 —
90 **35** 2c. blue 14·00 4·25 65
a. Imperf between (vert pair) † † £600
b. Imperf between (horiz pair) † † £650
c. Perf 14½–15 22·00 — 75
d. Perf 13½–14, comp 12–13 38·00 18·00 —
e. Perf 16 — — 7·00
91 **36** 3c. ochre 12·00 25·00 50
a. Imperf between (vert pair) £750 † £500
b. Perf 14½–15 8·50 6·50 50
c. Perf 13½–14, comp 12–13 26·00 30·00 1·00
92 **38** 5c. green 55·00 55·00 70
a. Perf 14½–15 48·00 55·00 —
b. Perf 13½–14, comp 12–13
93 **39** 6c. brown-lake 9·50 32·00 50
b. Perf 14½–15 6·50 21·00 50
ba. Imperf between (vert pair) † † £600
c. Perf 13½–14, comp 12–13 — — 6·00
94 **40** 8c. rose-red 50·00 — 50
a. Perf 14½–15 18·00 12·00 —
b. Perf 13½–14, comp 12–13 32·00 — 2·75
c. Vermilion 16·00 — 50
ca. Perf 16 — — 4·50
95 **42** 12c. vermilion 80·00 90·00 1·00
a. Perf 14½–15 42·00 50·00 80
96 **44** 18c. olive-bistre 70·00 70·00 70
a. Imperf between (vert pair) † † —
b. Perf 16 16·00 45·00 50
97 **45** 24c. grey-lilac 45·00 75·00 75
a. Perf 14½–15 14·00 50·00 50
89/97 *Set of* 9 £150 £225 4·75
89s/97s Optd "Specimen" *Set of* 9 £160

The 12, 18 and 24c. above were errors; in the 12c., "LABUAN" is over the value at the top; the 18c. has "POSTAL REVENUE" instead of "POSTAGE AND REVENUE", and the 24c. is without "POSTAGE AND REVENUE".

1897 (Nov)–**98**.

(a) Types of North Borneo (colours changed), with "LABUAN" engraved on the vignette plate as in T **13**. P 13½–14.

98 **42** 12c. black and vermilion (3.98) † — 3·2
a. Perf 14½–15 42·00 50·00 —
b. Perf 13½–14, comp 14½–15
c. Perf 16 55·00 60·00 —
99 **46** 18c. black and olive-bistre
a. Perf 14½–15 80·00 60·00 2·0
b. Perf 13½–14, comp 12–13
c. Perf 16 † — 8·5
100 **47** 24c. blue and lilac-brown 29·00 55·00 2·0
a. Perf 14½–15 29·00 55·00 —
b. Perf 13½–14, comp 12–13 — 65·00 —
c. Perf 16 32·00
d. Blue and ochre (P 14½–15) — — 3·0

In the 12c. "LABUAN" is now correctly placed at foot of stam… The 18c. and 24c. have the inscriptions on the stamps corrected, b… the 18c. still has "LABUAN" *over* the value at foot, and was furth… corrected as follows.

(b) As No. 99, but "LABUAN" at top.

101 **46** 18c. black and olive-bistre (3.98) 60·00 60·00 –
a. Perf 14½–15 27·00 70·00 2·7
b. Perf 13½–14, comp 12–13 38·00 55·00 –
c. Perf 12–13
98s, 100s/1as Optd "Specimen" *Set of* 3 70·00

1899 (July). *Surch with T* **17**.

(a) P 14½–15.

102 **38** 4c.on 5c. (No. 92a) 35·00 26·
103 **39** 4c.on 6c. (No. 93b) 23·00 19·
a. Perf 13½–14 32·00 38·
b. Perf 13½–14 comp 12–13 50·00 60·
104 **40** 4c.on 8c. (No. 94a) 60·00 40·
a. Perf 13½–14 30·00 32·
b. Perf 13½–14, comp 12–13 29·00 35·
c. Perf 12–13
105 **42** 4c.on 12c. (No. 98a) 38·00 35·
a. Perf 13½–14 38·00 42·
b. Perf 16 38·00 40·
c. Perf 13½–14, comp 12–13 55·00 65·
106 **46** 4c. on 18c. (No. 101a) 26·00 18·
a. Surch double £400 £4
107 **47** 4c.on 24c. (No. 100a) 25·00 30·
a. Perf 13½–14 20·00 25·
b. Perf 13½–14, comp 12–13 30·00 30·
c. Perf 16 45·00 48·

(b) P 14.

108 **32a** 4c.on 25c. (No. 80) 6·00 7
109 **32b** 4c.on 50c. (No. 81) 6·50 7
110 **32c** 4c.on $1 (No. 82) 6·50 7
102/10 *Set of* 9 £170 £
102s/10s Optd "Specimen" *Set of* 9 £150

A new setting of the surcharge with closer spacing (2½ m… between "4" and "CENTS" was used for the Specimen overpri… including unissued surcharges on the 1c., 2c. and 3c. values (*pr… £140 for the set of three*).

1900–02. *Types of North Borneo with "LABUAN" engraved on vignette plate as in T* **13**, *in green on 16c*. P 13½–14.

111 **35** 2c. black and green 3·75 2·50
a. Imperf between (horiz pair) £2250
b. Perf 13½–14, comp 12–13
112 **37** 4c. black and yellow-brown 8·50 42·00
a. Imperf between (vert pair) £950
b. Perf 13½–14, comp 12–13 32·00
113 4c. black and carmine (8.1900) 12·00 2·75
a. Perf 14½–15 6·50 9·50
b. Perf 13½–14, comp 12–13 32·00 8·00
c. Perf 16
114 **38** 5c. black and pale blue 29·00 18·00
a. Perf 13½–14, comp 12–13 — 85·00
b. Perf 12–13 £110
115 **41** 10c. brown & slate-lilac (P 14½–15) (1902) 50·00 80·00
116 **43** 16c. green and chestnut (1902) 50·00 £110
a. Perf 13½–14, comp 12–13 85·00 £110
b. Perf 12–13 £190
c. Perf 14½–15 £110
111/16 *Set of* 6 £130 £225
111s/16s Optd "Specimen" *Set of* 6 £150

No. 112 was printed in an incorrect frame colour and was issued for postal purposes in Labuan. Used examples come f… dealers' stock sent to the island for cancellation.

18

Line through "B" (R. 5/10)

(Recess Waterlow)

902 (Sept)–**03**. P 13½–14.
17 **18** 1c. black and purple (10.03) 4·00 7·00 50
a. Perf 14½–15 80·00 7·50 —
b. Perf 13½–14 comp 12–13 75·00 50·00
c. Line through "B" 60·00 85·00 6·50
18 2c. black and green 3·75 4·75 30
a. Perf 14½–15 £100 5·00 —
b. Line through "B" 55·00 70·00 6·50
19 3c. black and sepia (10.03) 3·25 12·00 30
a. Line through "B" 55·00 90·00 6·50
20 4c. black and carmine 3·25 3·50 30
a. Perf 14½–15 6·00 8·00 —
b. Perf 13½–14 comp 12–13 65·00 50·00 —
c. Line through "B" 55·00 60·00 6·50
21 8c. black and vermilion 9·00 9·00 50
a. Perf 14½–15 7·50
b. Line through "B" 80·00 95·00 6·50
22 10c. brown and slate-blue 3·25 12·00 30
b. Perf 14½–15 4·75 13·00 50
ba. Imperf between (vert pair) † † £700
c. Line through "B" 55·00 £110 6·50
23 12c. black and yellow 6·00 14·00 30
a. Imperf between (vert strip of 3) † † £2500
b. Perf 16 6·00 18·00 50
c. Line through "B" 70·00 £120 6·50
24 16c. green and brown 4·75 18·00 30
a. Imperf between (vert pair) † — £1600
b. Line through "B" 75·00 £140 6·50
25 18c. black and pale brown 3·25 22·00 30
a. Line through "B" 60·00 £160 6·00
26 25c. green and greenish blue 7·50 18·00 50
a. Perf 14½–15 15·00 30·00 60
b. Error. Black and greenish blue — † £425
c. Line through "B" 90·00 £170 7·50
27 50c. dull purple and lilac 10·00 42·00 80
a. Perf 13½–14 comp 12–13 16·00 48·00 —
b. Line through "B" £160 £350 10·00
8 $1 claret and orange 8·50 50·00 80
a. Perf 14½–15 10·00 — 80
b. Line through "B" £130 £375 11·00
7/28 *Set of* 12 60·00 £200 4·75
7s/28s Optd "Specimen" *Set of* 12 £190

4
cents
(19)

04 (Dec). *Issues of 1895 and 1897–8 surch with T* **19**.

(a) P 14½–15.
9 **38** 4c.on 5c. (No. 92a) 40·00 40·00 14·00
0 **39** 4c.on 6c. (No. 93b) 12·00 38·00 14·00
1 **40** 4c.on 8c. (No. 94a) 25·00 42·00 14·00
2 **42** 4c.on 12c. (No. 98a) 19·00 42·00 14·00
a. Perf 16 27·00 45·00 —
3 **46** 4c.on 18c. (No. 101) (P 13½–14) 23·00 45·00 14·00
a. Perf 13½–14, comp 12–13 27·00 45·00 —
b. Perf 12–13
4 **47** 4c.on 24c. (No. 100a) 16·00 50·00 14·00
a. Perf 13½–14 27·00 38·00 —
b. Perf 13½–14, comp 12–13 35·00 48·00 —
c. Perf 16 26·00 40·00 14·00

(b) P 14.
32a 4c.on 25c. (No. 80) 8·50 24·00 14·00
32b 4c.on 50c. (No. 81) 8·50 24·00 14·00
a. Surch double £275
32c 4c.on $1 (No. 82) 8·50 24·00 14·00
/37 *Set of* 9 £140 £300 £110

No. 136a usually shows one complete surcharge and parts of two ther examples due to the position of the second impression.

The barred cancels can be found used on "philatelic" covers of issue.

LABUAN **(20)** **LABUAN** **(21)**

4 (12 Oct)–**05**. *Nos. 81, 83 (in Labuan colour), and 84/6 of North Borneo optd locally with T* **20** *(25c.. $2) or* **21** *(others).*
32a 25c. indigo (2.05) £1100 † £900
32c $1 blue (2.05) † † £800
32d $2 dull green £2750 £2750 —
14 $5 bright purple (2.05) £5500 £6000 £1100
15 $10 brown (11.05) £25000 † £8000

Dangerous forgeries exist.

The overprint on No. 140 is 12 mm long.

POSTAGE DUE STAMPS

POSTAGE DUE
(D 1)

. *Optd with Type* D **1**, *reading vertically upwards.* P 13½–14.
35 2c. black and green (111) 15·00 23·00 50
a. Opt double £350
b. Perf 13½–14, comp 12–13 70·00 75·00 10·00
36 3c. black and ochre (91) 18·00 80·00 70
a. Perf 13½–14, comp 12–13 70·00 — 2·00

D3 **37** 4c. black and carmine (113) 32·00 — 1·00
a. Opt double † † £650
b. Perf 14½–15 32·00 80·00 50
D4 **38** 5c. black and pale blue (114) 50·00 95·00 75
a. Perf 14½–15 — — 1·00
b. Perf 13½–14, comp 12–13 70·00 £130 —
D5 **39** 6c. black and brown-lake (93) 26·00 90·00 75
a. Perf 14½–15 40·00 80·00 —
b. Perf 16 48·00 — 65
D6 **40** 8c. black and vermilion (94c) 55·00 85·00 1·25
b. Perf 14½–15 65·00 £110 85
ba. Frame inverted † † £8000
c. Perf 16 65·00 85·00 —
d. Black and rose-red (94) 70·00 £100 —
da. Perf 14½–15 90·00 — 7·00
db. Perf 13½–14, comp 12–13 90·00
D7 **42** 12c. black and vermilion (98) 85·00 — 3·75
a. Opt reading downwards † † £550
b. Perf 14½–15 80·00 £100 12·00
D8 **46** 18c. black and olive-bistre (101) (P 14½–15) 21·00 95·00 1·25
D9 **47** 24c. blue and lilac-brown (100) 42·00 £100 5·00
a. Perf 13½–14, comp 12–13 65·00
b. Perf 14½–15 29·00
ba. Blue and ochre 65·00 — 1·25
c. Perf 16 45·00 80·00 —
D1/9 *Set of* 9 £300 £650 9·00

No. D6ba only comes cancelled-to-order. About 20 examples exist, many having been found in 6d. stamp packets sold to collectors.

The administration of Labuan reverted to Colonial Office control, as part of an agreement with Brunei on 1 January 1906. By Letters Patent dated 30 October 1906 Labuan was incorporated with Straits Settlements and ceased issuing its own stamps. In 1946 it became part of the Colony of North Borneo.

JAPANESE OCCUPATION OF NORTH BORNEO

Japanese forces landed in Northern Borneo on 15 December 1941 and the whole of North Borneo had been occupied by 19 January 1942.

Brunei, North Borneo, Sarawak and, after a short period, Labuan, were administered as a single territory by the Japanese. Until 12 December 1942, previous stamp issues, without overprint, continued to be used in conjunction with existing postmarks. From November 1942 onwards unoverprinted stamps of Japan were made available and examples can be found used from the area for much of the remainder of the War. Japanese Occupation issues for Brunei, North Borneo and Sarawak were equally valid throughout the combined territory but not, in practice, equally available.

PRICES FOR STAMPS ON COVER	
Nos. J1/17	*from* × 5
Nos. J18/19	*from* × 6
Nos. J20/32	*from* × 25
Nos. J33/4	*from* × 2
Nos. J35/48	*from* × 12

(1)

2 Mt. Kinabalu

3 Borneo Scene

1942 (30 Sept). *Stamps of North Borneo handstamped with T* **1**.

(a) In violet on Nos. 303/17.
J 1 1c. green and red-brown £160 £225
a. Black opt £250 £200
ab. Pair, one without opt £2750
J 2 2c. purple and greenish blue £160 £225
a. Black opt £300 £225
J 3 3c. slate-blue and green £130 £225
a. Black opt £325 £275
J 4 4c. bronze-green and violet £160 £250
a. Black opt 50·00 £120
J 5 6c. deep blue and claret £130 £250
a. Black opt £325 £275
J 6 8c. scarlet £160 £190
a. Pair, one without opt £2750
b. Black opt £250 £190
J 7 10c. violet and bronze-green £150 £250
a. Black opt £300 £250
J 8 12c. green and bright blue £170 £400
a. Black opt £475 £400
J 9 15c. blue-green and brown £160 £400
a. Pair, one without opt £2750
b. Black opt £500 £400
J10 20c. violet and slate-blue £190 £450
a. Black opt £600 £450
J11 25c. green and chocolate £190 £450
a. Black opt £600 £450
J12 50c. chocolate and violet £275 £500
a. Black opt £700 £500
J13 $1 brown and carmine £275 £650
a. Black opt £800 £650
J14 $2 violet and olive-green £425 £850
a. Pair, one without opt £3750
b. Black opt £1000 £850
J15 $5 indigo and pale blue £500 £900
a. Black opt £1300 £1000

(b) In black on Nos. 318/19 ("WAR TAX").
J16 1c. green and red-brown £475 £275
a. Pair, one without opt † £3000
b. Violet opt — £600
J17 2c. purple and greenish blue £1200 £450
a. Violet opt — £750

(Litho Kolff & Co., Batavia)

1943 (29 Apr). P 12½.
J18 **2** 4c. red 17·00 40·00
J19 **3** 8c. blue 15·00 40·00

本日大
便郵國帝
オネルボ北
(4)

本日大
便郵國帝
貳
弗
(5)

("Imperial Japanese Postal Service North Borneo")

1944 (30 Sept). *Nos. 303/15 of North Borneo optd with T* **4** *at Chinese Press, Kuching.*
J20 1c. green and red-brown 5·00 12·00
J21 2c. purple and greenish blue 7·50 9·00
a. Optd on No. J2 £425
J22 3c. slate-blue and green 4·50 9·00
a. Optd on No. J3 £425
J23 4c. bronze-green and violet 7·50 15·00
J24 6c. deep blue and claret 5·50 6·50
J25 8c. scarlet 7·50 17·00
a. Optd on No. J6 £425
J26 10c. violet and bronze-green 8·50 13·00
a. Optd on No. J7 £425
b. Optd on No. J7a £200 £375
J27 12c. green and bright blue 9·50 13·00
a. Optd on No. J8 £425
J28 15c. blue-green and brown 9·50 16·00
a. Optd on No. J9 £425
J29 20c. violet and slate-blue 22·00 45·00
a. Optd on No. J10 £1400
J30 25c. green and chocolate 22·00 45·00
a. Optd on No. J11 £1400
J31 50c. chocolate and violet 65·00 £120
a. Optd on No. J12 £1900
J32 $1 brown and carmine 90·00 £150
J20/32 *Set of* 13 £225 £425

The spacing between the second and third lines of the overprint is 12 mm on the horizontal stamps, and 15 mm on the upright.

1944 (11 May). *No. J1 surch with T* **5**.
J33 **81** $2 on 1c. green and red-brown £4500 £3750

本日大
五
弗
便郵國帝
(6)

7 Girl War-worker

オネルボ北
(8) ("North Borneo")

1944 (11 May). *North Borneo No. 315 surch with T* **6**.
J34 $5on $1 brown and carmine £4000 £2750
a. Surch on No. J13 £5500 £4250

1944 (2 Oct)–**45**. *Contemporary stamps of Japan as T* **7** *(various subjects) optd with T* **8** *at Chinese Press, Kuching.*
J35 1s. red-brown (No. 391) (1.45) 8·00 20·00
J36 2s. scarlet (No. 318) (10.44) 7·00 17·00
J37 3s. emerald-green (No. 319) (8.45) 6·50 20·00
J38 4s. yellow-green (No. 395) (10.44) 9·50 18·00
J39 5s. claret (No. 396) (1.45) 9·00 21·00
J40 6s. orange (No. 322) (8.45) 10·00 22·00
a. Opt double, one inverted £400 £400
J41 8s. violet (No. 324) (11.44) 6·50 22·00
a. Opt double £350
J42 10s. carmine and pink (No. 399) (1.45) 7·00 22·00
J43 15s. blue (No. 401) (11.44) 9·00 22·00
J44 20s. blue-slate (No. 328) (11.44) 80·00 90·00
J45 25s. brown and chocolate (No. 329) (2.45) 55·00 70·00
J46 30s. turquoise-blue (No. 330) £170 95·00
J47 50s. olive and bistre (No. 331) (8.45) 60·00 70·00
J48 1y. red-brown & chocolate (No. 332) (5.45) 60·00 95·00
J35/48 *Set of* 14 £450 £550

Designs:—2s. General Nogi; 3s. Hydro-electric Works; 4s. Hyuga Monument and Mt Fuji; 5s. Admiral Togo; 6s. Garambi Lighthouse, Formosa; 8s. Meiji Shrine; 10s. Palms and map of S.E. Asia; 15s. Airman; 20s. Mt Fuji and cherry blossoms; 25s. Horyu Temple; 30s. Torii, Itsukushima Shrine at Miyajima; 50s. Kinkaku Temple; 1y. Great Buddha, Kamakura.

Examples of some values have been found with hand-painted forged overprints.

POSTAGE DUE STAMPS

1942 (30 Sept). *Nos. D66/7 and D69 of North Borneo handstamped with T* **1** *in black.*
JD1 D **2** 2c. brown — £2750
JD2 4c. scarlet — £2750
JD3 8c. green — £2750

Northern Nigeria *see* Nigeria

Northern Rhodesia

The north-eastern and north-western provinces of Rhodesia, previously administered by the British South Africa Company, became a Crown Colony on 1 April 1924.

The current stamps of Rhodesia (the "Admiral design" first issued in 1913) remained in use until 31 March 1925 and continued to be valid for postal purposes until 30 September of that year.

PRICES FOR STAMPS ON COVER TO 1945		
Nos.	1/21	*from* × 2
Nos.	22/4	*from* × 5
Nos.	25/45	*from* × 2
Nos.	D1/4	*from* × 15

1

2

(Des W. Fairweather. Eng J. A. C. Harrison. Recess Waterlow)

1925 (1 April)–**29**. Wmk Mult Script CA. P 12½.

No.	Type	Description	Unused	Used
1	**1**	½d. green	1·75	80
2		1d. brown	1·75	10
3		1½d. carmine-red	1·75	30
4		2d. yellow-brown	2·00	10
5		3d. ultramarine	2·00	1·25
6		4d. violet	4·00	50
7		6d. slate-grey	4·25	40
8		8d. rose-purple	3·75	45·00
9		10d. olive-green	4·25	40·00
10	**2**	1s. yellow-brown and black	3·75	1·75
11		2s. brown and ultramarine	15·00	23·00
12		2s.6d. black and green	15·00	8·00
13		3s. violet and blue (1929)	23·00	19·00
14		5s. slate-grey and violet	30·00	17·00
15		7s.6d. rose-purple and black	£100	£150
16		10s. green and black	70·00	70·00
17		20s. carmine-red and rose-purple	£150	£170
1/17 *Set of* 17			£375	£475
1s/17s Optd or Perf (3s.) "Specimen" *Set of* 17			£750	

A used example of the 4d. exists imperforate between the stamp and a fragment of another below it.

1935 (6 May). *Silver Jubilee. As Nos. 91/4 of Antigua.* P 13½ × 14.

No.	Description	Unused	Used
18	1d. light blue and olive-green	80	1·50
	f. Diagonal line by turret	50·00	70·00
	h. Dot by flagstaff	90·00	£120
	i. Dash by turret	90·00	£120
19	2d. green and indigo	80	1·50
	f. Diagonal line by turret	65·00	85·00
	g. Dot to left of chapel	£110	£140
20	3d. brown and deep blue	2·50	5·50
	f. Diagonal line by turret	£100	£150
	g. Dot to left of chapel	£190	£250
21	6d. slate and purple	3·75	1·50
	a. Frame printed double, one albino	£1800	
	h. Dot by flagstaff	£225	£170
18/21 *Set of* 4		7·00	9·00
18s/21s Perf "Specimen" *Set of* 4		£120	

For illustrations of plate varieties see Omnibus section following Zanzibar.

THERN_RHODE

Hyphen between "NORTHERN" AND "RHODESIA" (R. 9/6)

1937 (12 May). *Coronation. As Nos. 95/7 of Antigua.* P 11 × 11½.

No.	Description	Unused	Used
22	1½d. carmine	30	35
23	2d. buff	40	35
24	3d. blue	60	1·25
	a. Hyphen flaw	£160	
22/4 *Set of* 3		1·10	1·75
22s/4s Perf "Specimen" *Set of* 3		85·00	

3

4

"Tick bird" flaw (Pl 1 R. 7/1 of ptgs from Sept 1938 onwards)

(Recess Waterlow)

1938 (1 Mar)–**52**. Wmk Mult Script CA. P 12½.

No.	Type	Description	Unused	Used
25	**3**	½d. green	10	10
		a. "C" of "CA" missing from wmk		
26		½d. chocolate (15.11.51)	75	1·50
		a. Perf 12½ × 14 (22.10.52)	1·40	6·00
27		1d. brown	20	20
		a. Chocolate (1948)	1·75	75
28		1d. green (15.11.51)	75	1·50
29		1½d. carmine-red	45·00	75
		a. Imperf between (horiz pair)	£13000	
		b. "Tick bird" flaw	£2500	£225
30		1½d. yellow-brown (10.1.41)	30	10
		b. "Tick bird" flaw	65·00	30·00
31		2d. yellow-brown	45·00	1·75
32		2d. carmine-red (10.1.41)	30	50
33		2d. purple (1.12.51)	45	1·50
34		3d. ultramarine	40	30
35		3d. scarlet (1.12.51)	50	2·75
36		4d. dull violet	30	40
37		4½d. blue (5.5.52)	55	6·00
38		6d. grey	30	10
39		9d. violet (5.5.52)	55	4·25
40	**4**	1s. yellow-brown and black	3·25	60
41		2s.6d. black and green	7·00	3·50
42		3s. violet and blue	13·00	8·00
43		5s. grey and dull violet	13·00	8·50
44		10s. green and black	15·00	13·00
45		20s. carmine-red and rose-purple	40·00	48·00
25/45 *Set of* 21			£170	90·00
25s/45s Perf "Specimen" *Set of* 15			£300	

Nos. 26a and 28 exist in coils, constructed from normal sheets.

1946 (26 Nov). *Victory. As Nos. 110/11 of Antigua.* P 13½ × 14.

No.	Description	Unused	Used
46	1½d. red-orange	20	20
	a. Perf 13½	14·00	12·00
47	2d. carmine	10	50
46s/7s Perf "Specimen" *Set of* 2		70·00	

The decimal perforation gauge for Nos. 46/7 is 13.7 × 14.1 and for No. 46a 13.7 × 13.4.

1948 (1 Dec). *Royal Silver Wedding. As Nos. 112/13 of Antigua, but 20s. ptd in recess.*

No.	Description	Unused	Used
48	1½d. orange	30	10
49	20s. brown-lake	45·00	48·00

1949 (10 Oct). *75th Anniv of U.P.U. As Nos. 114/17 of Antigua..*

No.	Description	Unused	Used
50	2d. carmine	20	30
51	3d. deep blue	1·50	1·75
52	6d. grey	55	1·75
53	1s. red-orange	55	1·00
50/3 *Set of* 4		2·50	4·25

POSTAGE DUE STAMPS

D 1

1929 (June)–**52**. *Ordinary paper.* Wmk Mult Script CA. P 14.

No.	Type	Description	Unused	Used
D1	**D 1**	1d. grey-black	2·50	2·50
		a. Chalk-surfaced paper. *Blk* (22.1.52)	23·00	75·00
		ab. Error. St. Edward's Crown, **W9*b***	£1900	
D2		2d. grey-black	3·00	3·00
D3		3d. grey-black	3·00	26·00
		a. Chalk-surfaced paper. *Blk* (22.1.52)	7·00	65·00
		ab. Error. Crown missing, **W9*a***	£325	
		ac. Error. St. Edward's Crown, **W9*b***	£180	
D4		4d. grey-black	9·50	30·00
D1/4 *Set of* 4			16·00	55·00
D1s/4s Perf "Specimen" *Set of* 4			95·00	

The 2d. is known bisected and used as a 1d. at Luanshya or Nkana on various dates between 1937 and 1951 and on understamped letters from South Africa at Chingola in May 1950 (*Price on cover* £500).

North-West Pacific Islands *see* New Guinea *after* Australia

Nova Scotia *see* Canada

Nyasaland

PRICES FOR STAMPS ON COVER TO 1945		
Nos.	1/9*a*	*from* × 15
Nos.	10/19	—
No.	20	*from* × 10
Nos.	21/6	*from* × 5
Nos.	27/31	—
Nos.	32/7	*from* × 6
Nos.	38/42	—
Nos.	43/7	*from* × 12
Nos.	48/52	—
No.	53	*from* × 15
No.	54	*from* × 2
No.	55	*from* × 4
Nos.	55*b*/7*a*	*from* × 7
Nos.	57*d*/63	*from* × 6
Nos.	64/71	—
Nos.	72/9	*from* × 5
Nos.	80/2	—
Nos.	83/95	*from* × 4
Nos.	96/9	—
Nos.	100/57	*from* × 2

By 1891 the territory west of Lake Nyasa was recognised as b under British protection and the southern, eastern and nort borders had been delineated with the Portuguese and Ger governments.

BRITISH CENTRAL AFRICA

A protectorate under the name "Nyassaland Districts" declared on 14 May 1891, the title being changed to the "Br Central Africa Protectorate" on 22 February 1893. Suc description had been in use for some time previously and handwritten notice of 20 July 1891, announcing the introductic postal services, described the area as "British Central Africa".

Until 1895 the British South Africa Company contributed to revenues of the protectorate administration which, in re governed North-eastern Rhodesia. Stamps of the British S Africa Company overprinted "B.C.A.", in addition to use in Br Central Africa, were issued to post offices at Fife, Fort Rose Katwe, Johnston Falls, Rhodesia (later Kalungwisi) Tanganyika (later Abercorn) in North-eastern Rhodesia from until 1899.

B.C.A.
(1)

B.C.A. FOUR SHILLINGS.
(2)

ONE PENNY.
(3)

1891 (20 July)–**95**. *Stamps of Rhodesia optd as T* **1**. P 14, 14½.

No.	Type	Description	Unused	Used
1	**1**	1d. black	5·00	
2	**4**	2d. sea-green and vermilion	5·00	
		a. Bisected (1d.) (on cover) (1895)	†	£
3		4d. reddish chestnut and black	5·50	
4	**1**	6d. ultramarine	50·00	
5		6d. deep blue	8·00	
6	**4**	8d. rose-lake and ultramarine	14·00	
6*a*		8d. red and ultramarine	25·00	
7	**1**	1s. grey-brown	15·00	
8		2s. vermilion	26·00	
9		2s.6d. grey-purple	65·00	
9*a*		2s.6d. lilac	65·00	
10	**4**	3s. brown and green (1895)	65·00	
11		4s. grey-black and vermilion (2.93)	60·00	
12	**1**	5s. orange-yellow	70·00	
13		10s. deep green	£140	
14	**2**	£1 deep blue	£700	
15		£2 rose-red	£900	
16		£5 sage-green	£1500	
17		£10 brown	£3250	£
1/14 *Set of* 13			£1000	£

The overprint varies on values up to 10s. Sets may be made *thin* or *thick* letters.

The bisected 2d, No. 2a, was authorised for use at Blan Chiromo and Zomba in July and October 1895.

1892 (Aug)–**93**. *Stamps of Rhodesia surch as T* **2**.

No.	Type	Description	Unused	Used
18	**4**	3s.on 4s. grey-black and vermilion (10.93)	£325	
19	**1**	4s.on 5s. orange-yellow	70·00	

1895. *No. 2 surch at Cape Town with T* **3**.

No.	Type	Description	Unused	Used
20	**4**	1d.on 2d. sea-green and vermilion	9·00	
		a. Surch double	£4000	£

Specimens are known with double surcharge, without stop "PENNY". These are from a trial printing made at Blantyre, b is believed that they were not issued to the public (*Price* £550

5 Arms of the Protectorate

6 Arms of the Protectorate

(Des Sir Harry Johnston. Litho D.L.R.)

895. No wmk. P 14.

1	**5**	1d. black	14·00	10·00
2		2d. black and green	24·00	12·00
3		4d. black and reddish buff	48·00	35·00
4		6d. black and blue	65·00	7·50
5		1s. black and rose	75·00	29·00
6	**6**	2s.6d. black and bright magenta	£200	£300
7		3s. black and yellow	£130	50·00
8		5s. black and olive	£160	£190
9		£1 black and yellow-orange	£900	£375
0		£10 black and orange-vermilion	£4500	£3750
1		£25 black and blue-green	£8000	
1/8 *Set of* 8			£650	£550
1s/9s Optd "Specimen" *Set of* 9			£375	

Cancellations inscribed "BRITISH CENTRAL AFRICA" within double-circle and with the name of a town across the centre or at oot were intended for use on stamps presented for the payment of ne hut tax. Such marks can be found in black, violet or blue and re without date. Stamps with such fiscal obliterations are of little alue. Prices quoted are for postally used.

896 (Feb). Wmk Crown CA (T **5**) or CC (sideways) (T **6**). P 14.

2	**5**	1d. black	3·25	4·75
		y. Wmk inverted and reversed	†	£325
3		2d. black and green	15·00	5·00
4		4d. black and orange-brown	23·00	17·00
5		6d. black and blue	26·00	13·00
6		1s. black and rose	26·00	15·00
7	**6**	2s.6d. black and magenta	£140	£130
8		3s. black and yellow	£100	55·00
9		5s. black and olive	£150	£180
)		£1 black and blue	£850	£475
		£10 black and orange	£5000	£3500
		s. Optd "Specimen"	£180	
		£25 black and green	£9500	
		s. Optd "Specimen"	£325	
/9 *Set of* 8			£425	£375
s/40s Optd "Specimen" *Set of* 9			£375	

7

8

(Typo D.L.R.)

97 (Aug)–**1900**. T **7** (wmk Crown CA) and **8** (wmk Crown CC). P 14.

	7	1d. black and ultramarine	3·25	1·25
		w. Wmk inverted	£160	£225
		2d. black and yellow	2·00	2·00
		4d. black and carmine	6·50	1·50
		6d. black and green	45·00	4·25
		1s. black and dull purple	11·00	7·00
	8	2s.6d. black and ultramarine	48·00	42·00
		3s. black and sea-green	£190	£225
		4s. black and carmine	70·00	80·00
a		10s. black and olive-green (1900)	£140	£150
		£1 black and dull purple	£275	£160
		£10 black and yellow	£4500	£1700
		s. Optd "Specimen"	£200	
'51 *Set of* 10			£700	£600
s/51s Optd "Specimen" *Set of* 10			£275	

ONE

PENNY

(9)

10

7 (31 Dec). *No. 49 surch with T* **9**, *in red.*

	8	1d.on 3s. black and sea-green	6·00	9·50
		a. "PNNEY" (R. 4/2)	£2750	£2500
		b. "PENN"	£1700	£1400
		c. Surch double	£475	£750

lo. 53b shows an albino impression of the "Y".

1898 (11 Mar). Imperf.

(a) Setting I. The vertical frame lines of the stamps cross the space between the two rows of the sheet.

(i) With the initials "J.G." or "J.T.G." on the back in black ink.

54	**10**	1d. vermilion and grey-blue	£6500	£800
		a. Without the initials	£3250	
		b. Without the initials and centre inverted	£12000	

(ii) With a control number and letter or letters, printed in plain relief at the back.

55	**10**	1d. vermilion and grey-blue	—	£475

(b) Setting II. The vertical frame lines do not cross the space between the rows except at the extreme ends of the sheet. Control as No. 55.

55*b*	**10**	1d. vermilion and pale ultramarine	—	£100
		c. Control on face	—	£3250
		d. Centre omitted (vert pair with normal)	£14000	
56		1d. vermilion and deep ultramarine	—	£100
		a. Without Control at back	£2500	£160
		b. Control doubly impressed	—	£425

1898 (June). *Setting* II. *Control as No. 55.* P 12.

57	**10**	1d. vermilion and pale ultramarine	£2500	21·00
57*a*		1d. vermilion and deep ultramarine	—	38·00
		ab. Without Control at back	£2500	85·00
		ac. Two different Controls on back	—	£600
		ad. Control printed in black	£3500	

The two different settings of these stamps are each in 30 types, issued without gum.

1901. Wmk Crown CA. P 14.

57*d*	**7**	1d. dull purple and carmine-rose	2·50	50
57*e*		4d. dull purple and olive-green	8·50	11·00
58		6d. dull purple and brown	3·75	3·00
57*d*/8 *Set of* 3			13·00	13·00
57*d*s/8s Optd "Specimen" *Set of* 3			60·00	

11

12

(Typo D.L.R.)

1903–04. T **11** (Wmk Crown CA) and **12** (Wmk Crown CC). P 14.

59	**11**	1d. grey and carmine	7·00	1·75
60		2d. dull and bright purple	3·50	1·00
61		4d. grey-green and black	2·50	9·00
62		6d. grey and reddish buff	3·25	2·00
		aw. Wmk inverted	£120	
62*b*		1s. grey and blue	3·50	11·00
63	**12**	2s.6d. grey-green and green	48·00	75·00
64		4s. dull and bright purple	65·00	80·00
		w. Wmk inverted	£650	
65		10s. grey-green and black	£120	£200
66		£1 grey and carmine	£275	£180
67		£10 grey and blue	£4500	£3250
		s. Optd "Specimen"	£350	
59/66 *Set of* 9			£450	£500
59s/66s Optd "Specimen" *Set of* 9			£325	

1907. *Chalk-surfaced paper.* Wmk Mult Crown CA. P 14.

68	**11**	1d. grey and carmine	4·75	2·75
69		2d. dull and bright purple	£10000	
70		4d. grey-green and black	£10000	
71		6d. grey and reddish buff	27·00	45·00

Nos. 69/70 were prepared, but not issued in Nyasaland due to the Protectorate's name being changed. It is estimated that no more than a dozen examples of each remain in collectors' hands.

NYASALAND PROTECTORATE

The title of the Protectorate was changed again from 6 July 1907.

13

14

POSTAGE

Serif on "G" (R. 4/5. All ptgs of £1 Duty plate)

(Typo D.L.R.)

1908 (22 July)–**11**. P 14.

(a) Wmk Crown CA. Chalk-surfaced paper.

72	**13**	1s. black/*green*	2·75	11·00

(b) Wmk Mult Crown CA. Ordinary paper (½d., 1d.) or chalk-surfaced paper (others).

73	**13**	½d. green	1·75	2·00
74		1d. carmine	4·00	1·00
75		3d. purple/*yellow*	1·50	4·25
		w. Wmk inverted	£180	
76		4d. black and red/*yellow*	1·50	1·50
		w. Wmk inverted	£110	£120
77		6d. dull purple and bright purple	3·75	11·00

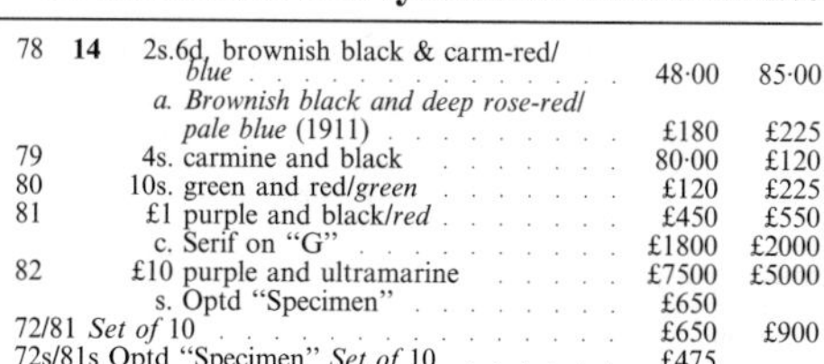

78	**14**	2s.6d. brownish black & carm-red/*blue*	48·00	85·00
		a. Brownish black and deep rose-red/pale blue (1911)	£180	£225
79		4s. carmine and black	80·00	£120
80		10s. green and red/*green*	£120	£225
81		£1 purple and black/*red*	£450	£550
		c. Serif on "G"	£1800	£2000
82		£10 purple and ultramarine	£7500	£5000
		s. Optd "Specimen"	£650	
72/81 *Set of* 10			£650	£900
72s/81s Optd "Specimen" *Set of* 10			£475	

15

16

"Bullet holes" flaw (R. 5/2. March 1919 ptgs)

Triangle flaw (R. 3/5. March 1919 ptg of 4s.)

1913 (1 Apr)–**19**. Wmk Mult Crown CA. *Ordinary paper (½d. to 2½d.) or chalk-surfaced paper (others).* P 14.

83	**15**	½d. green	1·25	1·50
84		½d. blue-green (1918)	1·50	1·75
85		1d. carmine-red	1·50	2·00
86		1d. scarlet (1916)	2·75	90
87		2d. grey (1916)	2·75	1·00
88		2d. slate	6·00	2·50
89		2½d. bright blue	2·25	7·00
90		3d. purple/*yellow* (1914)	4·50	4·50
		a. On pale yellow	4·25	9·50
		w. Wmk inverted		
91		4d. black and red/*yellow* (*shades*)	2·00	2·50
		a. On pale yellow	6·00	8·00
92		6d. dull and bright purple	3·50	9·50
92*a*		6d. dull purple and bright violet	10·00	10·00
93		1s. black/*green*	1·75	8·50
		a. On blue-green, olive back	5·50	1·50
		aw. Wmk inverted	£110	£150
		b. On emerald back	3·75	6·50
		bs. Optd "Specimen"	55·00	
94	**16**	2s.6d. black and red/*blue*	11·00	13·00
		a. Break in scroll	£160	
		b. Broken crown and scroll	£200	
		c. Nick in top right scroll	£170	
		f. Damaged leaf at bottom right	£170	
		h. "Bullet-holes" flaw	£275	
		x. Wmk reversed	†	£1100
95		4s. carmine and black	14·00	50·00
		a. Break in scroll	£180	
		b. Broken crown and scroll	£225	
		d. Nick in top right scroll	£190	
		f. Damaged leaf at bottom right	£190	
		h. "Bullet-holes" flaw	£300	
		i. Triangle flaw	£300	
96		10s. pale green and deep scarlet/*green*	80·00	£100
		d. Nick in top right scroll	£450	
		e. Green and deep scarlet/green (1919)	80·00	£100
		ea. Break in scroll	£425	
		eb. Broken crown and scroll	£425	
		ef. Damaged leaf at bottom right	£425	
		eh. "Bullet holes" flaw	£500	
98		£1 purple and black/*red*	£180	£140
		a. Break in scroll	£650	
		b. Broken crown and scroll	£650	
		c. Nick in top right scroll	£700	
		e. Break in lines below left scroll	£750	
		f. Damaged leaf at bottom right	£650	
		h. "Bullet holes" flaw	£1000	
		i. Serif on "G"	£700	£550

99 £10 purple and dull ultramarine . . . £4500
c. Nick in top right scroll . . . .
e. Purple and royal blue (1919) . . . £2750 £1700
ea. Break in scroll £4500 £3000
eb. Broken crown and scroll £4500
ef. Damaged leaf at bottom right . .
eh. "Bullet holes" flaw . . . .
s. Optd "Specimen" £400
83/98 *Set of* 12 . . . . £275 £300
83s/98s Optd "Specimen" *Set of* 12 . . . . . . £450

For illustrations of the other varieties on Nos. 94/9 see above Bermuda No. 51*b*.

For stamps overprinted "N.F." see TANZANIA.

Damaged crown (R. 4/1. 2s.6d. ptg of June 1924)

1921–30. Wmk Mult Script CA. *Ordinary paper (½d. to 2d.) or chalk-surfaced paper (others)*. P 14.
100 **15** ½d. green . . . . 1·50 50
w. Wmk inverted . . . . — £150
101 1d. carmine . . . . 2·25 50
102 1½d. orange . . . . 3·25 17·00
103 2d. grey . . . . 1·00 50
105 3d. purple/*pale yellow* . . . . . . 10·00 3·25
106 4d. black and red/*yellow* . . . . . 3·00 11·00
107 6d. dull and bright purple . . . . . 3·00 3·25
108 1s. black/*emerald* (1930) . . . . . 9·00 4·50
109 **16** 2s. purple and blue/*blue* (1926) . . . 15·00 12·00
a. Break in scroll £140 £140
b. Broken crown and scroll £140 £140
d. Break through scroll (Oct 1933 ptg only) £225 £225
e. Break in lines below left scroll . . £140 £140
f. Damaged leaf at bottom right . . £140 £140
g. Gash in fruit and leaf (Oct 1933 ptg only) £225 £225
h. Breaks in scrolls at right (Oct 1933 ptg only) £225 £225
110 2s.6d. black and red/*blue* (1924) . . . 20·00 16·00
a. Break in scroll £150 £150
b. Broken crown and scroll £150 £150
c. Nick in top right scroll £150 £150
d. Break through scroll (Oct 1933 ptg only) £250 £250
e. Break in lines below left scroll . . £150 £150
f. Damaged leaf at bottom right . . £150 £150
g. Gash in fruit and leaf (Oct 1933 ptg only) £250 £250
h. Breaks in scrolls at right (Oct 1933 ptg only) £250 £250
i. Damaged crown £300 £300
111 4s. carmine and black (1927) . . . . 19·00 27·00
a. Break in scroll £150
b. Broken crown and scroll £150
c. Nick in top right scroll £150
e. Break in lines below left scroll . . £150
f. Damaged leaf at bottom right . . £150
112 5s. green and red/*yellow* (1929) . . . 38·00 75·00
a. Break in scroll £250
b. Broken crown and scroll £250
c. Nick in top right scroll £250
e. Break in lines below left scroll . . £250
f. Damaged leaf at bottom right . . £250
113 10s. green and red/*pale emerald* (1926) . . . . 85·00 95·00
a. Break in scroll £375 £425
b. Broken crown and scroll £375 £425
c. Nick in top right scroll £375 £425
e. Break in lines below left scroll . . £375 £425
f. Damaged leaf at bottom right . . £375 £425
g. green and scarlet/*emerald* (1927) £425 £600
ga. Break in scroll £1200
gb. Broken crown and scroll £1200
ge. Break in lines below left scroll . . £1200
gf. Damaged leaf at bottom right . . £1200
100/13 *Set of* 13 . . . . £190 £225
100s/13s Optd or Perf (1s., 5s.) "Specimen" *Set of* 13 . . . . £400

For illustrations of the other varieties on Nos. 109/13 see above Bermuda No. 51*b*.

17 King George V and Symbol of the Protectorate

(Des Major H. E. Green. Recess Waterlow)

1934 (June)–**35**. Wmk Mult Script CA. P 12½.
114 **17** ½d. green . . . . 75 1·25
115 1d. brown 75 75
116 1½d. carmine . . . . 75 3·00
117 2d. pale grey . . . . 80 1·25
118 3d. blue . . . . 2·50 1·75
119 4d. bright magenta (20.5.35) . . . . 2·50 3·50
120 6d. violet . . . . 2·50 50
121 9d. olive-bistre (20.5.35) . . . . . . 6·00 9·00
122 1s. black and orange . . . . 8·50 14·00
114/22 *Set of* 9 . . . . 23·00 32·00
114s/22s Perf "Specimen" *Set of* 9 . . . . . . £200

1935 (6 May). *Silver Jubilee. As Nos. 91/4 of Antigua, but ptd by Waterlow.* P 11 × 12.
123 1d. ultramarine and grey . . . . . . 1·00 2·00
k. Kite and vertical log £100
m. "Bird" by turret £140
124 2d. green and indigo . . . . 1·00 1·25
m. "Bird" by turret £140
125 3d. brown and deep blue . . . . . . 7·00 16·00
k. Kite and vertical log £225
126 1s. slate and purple . . . . 17·00 42·00
k. Kite and vertical log £300
123/6 *Set of* 4 . . . . 23·00 55·00
123s/6s Perf "Specimen" *Set of* 4 . . . . . . £110

For illustrations of plate varieties see Omnibus section following Zanzibar.

1937 (12 May). *Coronation. As Nos. 95/7 of Antigua* P 11 × 11½.
127 ½d. green . . . . 30 1·00
128 1d. brown . . . . 50 1·00
129 2d. grey-black . . . . 50 2·00
127/9 *Set of* 3 . . . . 1·10 3·50
127s/9s Perf "Specimen" *Set of* 3 . . . . . . 75·00

18 Symbol of the Protectorate

19

(T **18** recess Waterlow; T **19** typo D.L.R.)

1938 (1 Jan)–**44**. *Chalk-surfaced paper (2s. to £1).* P 12½ (T **18**) or 14 (T **19**).

(a) Wmk Mult Script CA.
130 **18** ½d. green . . . . 30 1·50
130*a* ½d. brown (12.12.42) . . . . 10 1·75
131 1d. brown . . . . 2·75 30
131*a* 1d. green (12.12.42) 30 75
132 1½d. carmine . . . . 4·75 4·50
132*a* 1½d. grey (12.12.42) . . . . 30 5·00
133 2d. grey . . . . 8·00 1·25
133*a* 2d. carmine (12.12.42) . . . . . . 30 1·75
134 3d. blue 60 50
135 4d. bright magenta . . . . 2·75 1·25
136 6d. violet . . . . 2·75 1·25
137 9d. olive-bistre . . . . 2·75 2·75
138 1s. black and orange . . . . 3·50 1·50
139 **19** 2s. purple and blue/*blue* . . . . . 10·00 10·00
140 2s.6d. black and red/*blue* . . . . . 12·00 12·00
141 5s. pale green and red/*yellow* . . . 42·00 20·00
a. Ordinary paper. *Green and red/pale yellow* (3.44) . . . . 80·00 £100
142 10s. emerald and deep red/*pale green* . . . . 50·00 42·00
a. Ordinary paper. *Bluish green and brown-red/pale green* (1.38) . . . £350 £300

(b) Wmk Mult Crown CA.
143 **19** £1 purple and black/*red* . . . . . . 35·00 28·00
c. Serif on "G" £700 £500
130/43 *Set of* 18 . . . . £160 £120
130s/43s Perf "Specimen" *Set of* 18 . . . . . £650

No. 141a has a yellow surfacing often applied in horizontal lines giving the appearance of laid paper.

The printer's archives record the despatch of No. 142a to Nyasaland in January 1938, but no examples have been reported used before 1945. The paper coating on this printing varied considerably across the sheet. It is reported that some examples show a faint reaction to the silver test.

20 Lake Nyasa

21 King's African Rifles

(Recess B.W.)

1945 (1 Sept). *T* **20/1** *and similar designs.* Wmk Mult Script CA (sideways on horiz designs). P 12.
144 ½d. black and chocolate 50 10
145 1d. black and emerald 20 70
146 1½d. black and grey-green 30 50
147 2d. black and scarlet . . . . 1·50 85
148 3d. black and light blue 20 30
149 4d. black and claret . . . . 1·75 80
150 6d. black and violet . . . . 1·50 90
151 9d. black and olive . . . . 1·50 3·00
152 1s. indigo and deep green . . . . . 1·50 20
153 2s. emerald and maroon . . . . . . 4·50 4·75
154 2s.6d. emerald and blue . . . . . . 7·50 4·75
155 5s. purple and blue . . . . 4·50 6·50
156 10s. claret and emerald . . . . . . 14·00 14·00
157 20s. scarlet and black . . . . 18·00 27·00
144/57 *Set of* 14 . . . . 50·00 60·00
144s/57s Perf "Specimen" *Set of* 14 . . . . . £300

Designs: *Horiz*—1½d., 6d. Tea estate; 2d., 1s., 10s. Map of Nyasaland; 4d., 2s.6d. Tobacco; 9d. Type **20**; 5s., 20s. Badge of Nyasaland. *Vert*—3d., 2s. Fishing Village.

1946 (16 Dec). *Victory. As Nos. 110/11 of Antigua.*
158 1d. green 10 30
159 2d. red-orange 30 10
158s/9s Perf "Specimen" *Set of* 2 . . . . . . 65·00

26 Symbol of the Protectorate

27 Arms in 1891 and 1951

(Recess B.W.)

1947 (20 Oct). Wmk Mult Script CA. P 12.
160 **26** 1d. red-brown and yellow-green . . . 50 2
a. Perf "Specimen" . . . . 48·00

1948 (15 Dec). *Royal Silver Wedding. As Nos. 112/13 of Antigua.*
161 1d. green 15 1
162 10s. mauve . . . . 15·00 26·0

1949 (21 Nov). *75th Anniv of U.P.U. As Nos. 114/17 of Antigua.*
163 1d. blue-green 30 2
a. "A" of "CA" missing from wmk . . . £600
164 3d. greenish blue . . . . 2·00 3·0
165 6d. purple 50 5
166 1s. ultramarine 30 5
163/6 *Set of* 4 . . . . 2·75 3·7

As on other examples of this variety, No. 163a shows traces of the left leg of the "A".

(Des C. Twynam. Recess B.W.)

1951 (15 May). *Diamond Jubilee of Protectorate.* Wmk Mult Script CA. P 11 × 12.
167 **27** 2d. black and scarlet . . . . 1·25 1·5
168 3d. black and turquoise-blue . . . . 1·25 1·5
169 6d. black and violet . . . . 1·25 2·0
170 5s. black and indigo . . . . 3·75 7·0
167/70 *Set of* 4 . . . . 6·75 11·0

POSTAGE DUE STAMPS

D 1

(Typo D.L.R.)

1950 (1 July). Wmk Mult Script CA. P 14.
D1 **D 1** 1d. scarlet . . . . 3·75 23·
D2 2d. ultramarine . . . . 11·00 23·
D3 3d. green . . . . 11·00 6·
D4 4d. purple . . . . 20·00 42·
D5 6d. yellow-orange . . . . 27·00 £1
D1/5 *Set of* 5 . . . . 65·00 £1

Orange Free State *see* South Africa

Pakistan

(Currency. 12 pies = 1 anna; 16 annas = 1 rupee)

DOMINION

PAKISTAN (1) **PAKISTAN** (2)

1947 (1 Oct). *Nos. 259/68 and 269a/77 (King George VI) of India optd by litho at Nasik, as T* **1** *(3p. to 12a.) or* **2** *(14a. and rupee values).*
1 3p. slate 10
2 ½a. purple 10
3 9p. green 10
4 1a. carmine 10
5 1½a. dull violet 10
w. Wmk inverted . . . .
6 2a. vermilion 10
7 3a. bright violet 10
8 3½a. bright blue 65 2
9 4a. brown 20
10 6a. turquoise-green . . . . 1·00
11 8a. slate-violet 30
12 12a. lake . . . . 1·00
13 14a. purple . . . . 2·75
14 1r. grey and red-brown . . . . 1·75
w. Wmk inverted . . . . 60·00
15 2r. purple and brown . . . . 3·25

16		5r. green and blue	4·00	4·00
17		10r. purple and claret	4·00	2·75
18		15r. brown and green	48·00	80·00
19		25r. slate-violet and purple	55·00	45·00
/19 *Set of* 19			£110	£130

Numerous provisional "PAKISTAN" overprints, both handstamped and machine-printed, in various sizes and colours, on Postage and Official stamps, also exist.

These were made under authority of Provincial Governments, District Head Postmasters or Local Postmasters and are of considerable philatelic interest.

The 1a.3p. (India No. 269) exists only as a local issue (*Price*, Karachi opt 90*p. unused*; £1.75 *used*).

The 12a., as No. 12 but overprinted at Karachi, exists with overprint inverted (*Price* £60 *unused*).

The 1r. value with Karachi local overprint exists with overprint inverted (*Price* £150 *unused*) or as a vertical pair with one stamp without overprint (*Price* £600 *unused*).

3 Constituent Assembly Building, Karachi

6 Crescent and Stars

(Des A. Chughtai (1r.). Recess D.L.R.)

1948 (9 July). *Independence. T* **3**, **6** *and similar horiz designs.* P 13½ × 14 or 11½ (1r.).

0		1½a. ultramarine	1·00	70
1		2½a. green	1·00	20
2		3a. purple-brown	1·00	35
3		1r. scarlet	1·00	70
		a. Perf 14 × 13½	4·75	16·00
0/3 *Set of* 4			3·50	1·75

Designs:—2½a. Karachi Airport entrance; 3a. Gateway to Lahore Fort.

7 Scales of Justice

8 Star and Crescent

9 Lloyds Barrage

10 Karachi Airport

13 Khyber Pass

(Des M. Suharwardi (T **8**). Recess Pakistan Security Ptg Corp Ltd, Karachi (P 13 and 13½), D.L.R. (others))

48 (14 Aug)–**56?**. *T* **7/10**, **13** *and similar designs.* P 13½ × 14 or 11½ (1r.).

	7	3p. red (P 12½)	10	10
		a. Perf 13½ (1954?)	60	1·00
		6p. violet (P 12½)	80	10
		a. Perf 13½ (1954?)	3·00	2·25
		9p. green (P 12½)	50	10
		a. Perf 13½ (1954?)	1·50	1·75
	8	1a. blue (P 12½)	10	50
		1½a. grey-green (P 12½)	10	10
		2a. red (P 12½)	1·00	50
	9	2½a. green (P 14 × 13½)	2·75	6·50
	10	3a. green (P 14)	7·50	1·00
	9	3½a. bright blue (P 14 × 13½)	3·50	5·50
		4a. reddish brown (P 12½)	50	10
	–	6a. blue (P 14 × 13½)	70	50
	–	8a. black (P 12)	50	70
	10	10a. scarlet (P 14)	4·75	7·00
	–	12a. scarlet (P 14 × 13½)	7·50	1·00
	–	1r. ultramarine (P 14)	5·50	10
		a. Perf 13½ (1954?)	16·00	4·75
	–	2r. chocolate (P 14)	20·00	60
		a. perf 13½ (1954?)	26·00	2·00
	–	5r. carmine (P 14)	17·00	70
		a. Perf 13½ (7.53)	12·00	20
	13	10r. magenta (P 14)	10·00	18·00
		a. Perf 12	80·00	6·00
		b. Perf 13 (1951)	18·00	1·25
		15r. blue-green (P 12)	18·00	14·00
		a. Perf 14	18·00	42·00
		b. Perf 13 (1956?)	21·00	13·00
		25r. violet (P 14)	55·00	80·00
		a. Perf 12	30·00	30·00
		b. Perf 13 (1954)	45·00	27·00
/43 *Set of* 20			£110	60·00

Designs: *Vert* (*as T*7)—6a., 8a., 12a. Karachi Port Trust. (*As* 0)—1r., 2r., 5r. Salimullah Hostel, Dacca.

For 25r. with W **98**, see No. 210.

14 Star and Crescent

15 Karachi Airport

(Recess Pakistan Security Ptg Corp (P 13½), D.L.R. (others).

1949 (Feb)–**53?**. *Redrawn. Crescent moon with points to left as T* **14**/**15**.

44	**14**	1a. blue (P 12½)	4·00	85
		a. Perf 13½ (1953?)	3·75	10
45		1½a. grey-green (P 12½)	3·75	85
		a. Perf 13½ (1952?)	3·00	10
		ab. Printed on the gummed side	55·00	
46		2a. red (P 12½)	4·50	10
		a. Perf 13½ (1953?)	3·50	10
47	**15**	3a. green (P 14)	12·00	1·00
48	–	6a. blue (as No. 34) (P 14 × 13½)	9·00	1·25
49	–	8a. black (as No. 35) (P 12½)	7·00	1·50
50	**15**	10a. scarlet (P 14)	17·00	2·00
51	–	12a. scarlet (as No. 37) (P 14 × 13½)	22·00	50
44/51 *Set of* 8			70·00	5·50

16

(Recess D.L.R.)

1949 (11 Sept). *First Death Anniv of Mohammed Ali Jinnah. T* **16** *and similar design.* P 14.

52	**16**	1½a. brown	2·00	1·25
53		3a. green	2·00	1·25
54	–	10a. black	6·00	8·00
52/4 *Set of* 3			9·00	9·50

Design:—10a. Similar inscription reading "QUAID-I-AZAM/MOHAMMAD ALI JINNAH" etc.

17 Pottery

18 Aeroplane and Hourglass

Two Types of 3½a.:

I

II

19 Saracenic Leaf Pattern

20 Archway and Lamp

(Des A. Chughtai. Recess D.L.R., later printings, Pakistan Security Ptg Corp)

1951 (14 Aug)–**56**. *Fourth Anniv of Independence.* P 13.

55	**17**	2½a. carmine	1·75	1·25
56	**18**	3a. purple	1·00	10
57	**17**	3½a. blue (I)	1·25	3·75
57*a*		3½a. blue (II) (12.56)	3·50	5·00
58	**19**	4a. green	75	10
59		6a. brown-orange	1·00	10
60	**20**	8a. sepia	4·50	25
61		10a. violet	2·00	1·25
62	**18**	12a. slate	2·00	10
55/62 *Set of* 9			16·00	10·50

The above and the stamps issued on the 14 August 1954, 1955 and 1956, are basically definitive issues, although issued on the Anniversary date of Independence.

OFFICIAL STAMPS

PAKISTAN
(O 1)

1947. *Nos. O138/41 and O143/50 (King George VI) of India, optd as Type* O **1** *(Nos. O1/9) or as T* **2** *(Nos. O10/13) both in litho by Nasik.*

O 1	3p. slate	1·50	75
O 2	½a. purple	30	10
O 3	9p. green	5·00	2·75
O 4	1a. carmine	30	10
O 5	1½a. dull violet	30	10
	w. Wmk inverted	20·00	
O 6	2a. vermilion	30	10
O 7	2½a. bright violet	7·00	8·50
O 8	4a. brown	1·25	60
O 9	8a. slate-violet	1·75	1·50
O10	1r. grey and red-brown	80	1·50
O11	2r. purple and brown	4·25	3·75
O12	5r. green and blue	18·00	32·00
O13	10r. purple and claret	48·00	90·00
O1/13 *Set of* 13		80·00	£130

See note after No. 19. The 1a.3p. (India No. O146*a*) exists as a local issue (*Price*, Karachi opt, £6.50 *mint*, £21 *used*).

SERVICE
(O 2)

SERVICE
(O 3)

NOTE. Apart from a slight difference in size, Types O **2** and O **3** can easily be distinguished by the difference in the shape of the "c".

PRINTERS. Type O **2** was overprinted by De La Rue and Type O **3** by the Pakistan Security Ptg Corp.

1948 (14 Aug)–**54?**. *Optd with Type* O **2**.

O14	**7**	3p. red (No. 24)	10	10
O15		6p. violet (No. 25) (R.)	10	10
O16		9p. green (No. 26) (R.)	10	10
O17	**8**	1a. blue (No. 27) (R.)	3·75	10
O18		1½a. grey-green (No. 28) (R.)	3·50	10
O19		2a. red (No. 29)	1·50	10
O20	**10**	3a. green (No. 31)	26·00	8·00
O21	**9**	4a. reddish brown (No. 33)	1·00	10
O22	–	8a. black (No. 35) (R.)	2·25	8·50
O23	–	1r. ultramarine (No. 38)	1·00	10
O24	–	2r. chocolate (No. 39)	14·00	9·50
O25	–	5r. carmine (No. 40)	38·00	9·50
O26	**13**	10r. magenta (No. 41)	15·00	45·00
		a. Perf 12 (10.10.51)	19·00	50·00
		b. Perf 13 (1954?)	13·00	55·00
O14/26 *Set of* 13			95·00	75·00

1949. *Optd with Type* O **2**.

O27	1a. blue (No. 44) (R.)	1·75	10
O28	1½a. grey-green (No. 45) (R.)	75	10
	a. Opt inverted	£250	40·00
O29	2a. red (No. 46)	1·25	10
	a. Opt omitted (in pair with normal)	—	£140
O30	3a. green (No. 47)	26·00	5·50
O31	8a. black (No. 49) (R.)	42·00	17·00
O27/31 *Set of* 5		65·00	20·00

1951 (14 Aug). *4th Anniv of Independence. As Nos. 56, 58 and 60, but inscr "SERVICE" instead of "PAKISTAN POSTAGE".*

O32	**18**	3a. purple	7·50	9·50
O33	**19**	4a. green	2·00	10
O34	**20**	8a. sepia	8·00	3·75
O32/4 *Set of* 3			16·00	12·00

1953. *Optd with Type* O **3**.

O35	3p. red (No. 24a)	10	10
O36	6p. violet (No. 25a) (R.)	10	10
O37	9p. green (No. 26a) (R.)	10	10
O38	1a. blue (No. 44a) (R.)	10	10
O39	1½a. grey-green (No. 45a) (R.)	10	10
O40	2a. red (No. 46a) (1953?)	15	10
O41	1r. ultramarine (No. 38a)	10·00	3·75
O42	2r. chocolate (No. 39a)	4·25	20
O43	5r. carmine (No. 40a)	38·00	16·00
O44	10r. magenta (No. 41b) (date?)	22·00	48·00
O35/44 *Set of* 10		65·00	60·00

BAHAWALPUR

Bahawalpur, a former feudatory state situated to the west of the Punjab, was briefly independent following the partition of India on 15 August 1947 before acceding to Pakistan on 3 October of the same year.

East India Company and later Indian Empire post offices operated in Bahawalpur from 1854. By a postal agreement of 1879 internal mail from the state administration was carried unstamped, but this arrangement was superseded by the issue of Official stamps in 1945.

These had been preceded by a series of pictorial stamps prepared in 1933–34 on unwatermarked paper. It was intended that these would be used as state postage stamps, but permission for such use was withheld by the Indian Government so they were used for revenue purposes. The same designs were utilised for the 1945 Official series, Nos. O1/6, on paper watermarked Star and Crescent. Residual stocks of the unwatermarked 1a., 8a., 1r. and 2r. were used for the provisional Officials, Nos. O7 and O11/13.

A commemorative 1a. Receipt stamp was produced to mark the centenary of the alliance with Great Britain. This may not have been ready until 1935, but an example of this stamp is known used on cover from Deh Rawal to Sadiq Garh and postmarked 14 August 1933. Both this 1a. and the same value from the unwatermarked set also exist with Official Arabic overprint in black. These were not issued for postal purposes although one used example of the latter has been recorded postmarked 22 February 1933 also from Deh Rawal.

Stamps of India were overprinted in the interim period between 15 August and 3 October 1947. After the state joined Pakistan postage stamps were issued for internal use until 1953.

PRICES FOR STAMPS ON COVER

The postage and Official stamps of Bahawalpur are rare used on cover.

Nawab (from 1947 Amir) Sadiq Mohammad Khan Abbasi V, 1907–1966

(1)

1947 (15 Aug). *Nos. 265/8, 269a/77 and 259/62 (King George VI) of India optd locally with T* **1**.

No.	Description	Unused
1	3p. slate (R.)	20·00
2	½a. purple	20·00
3	9p. green (R.)	20·00
4	1a. carmine	20·00
5	1½a. dull violet (R.)	20·00
6	2a. vermilion	20·00
	a. Opt double	£1100
7	3a. bright violet (R.)	20·00
8	3½a. bright blue (R.)	20·00
9	4a. brown	20·00
10	6a. turquoise-green (R.)	20·00
	a. Opt double	£1100
11	8a. slate-violet (R.)	20·00
12	12a. lake	20·00
13	14a. purple	60·00
14	1r. grey and red-brown	23·00
	a. Opt double, one albino	£300
15	2r. purple and brown (R.)	£1200
16	5r. green and blue (R.)	£1200
17	10r. purple and claret	£1200
1/17 *Set of* 17		£3500

Nos. 1/17 were issued during the interim period, following the implementation of the Indian Independence Act, during which time Bahawalpur was part of neither of the two Dominions created. The Amir acceded to the Dominion of Pakistan on 3 October 1947 and these overprinted stamps of India were then withdrawn.

The stamps of Bahawalpur only had validity for use within the state. For external mail Pakistan stamps were used.

PRINTERS. All the following issues were recess-printed by De La Rue & Co, Ltd, London.

2 Amir Muhammad Bahawal Khan I Abbasi

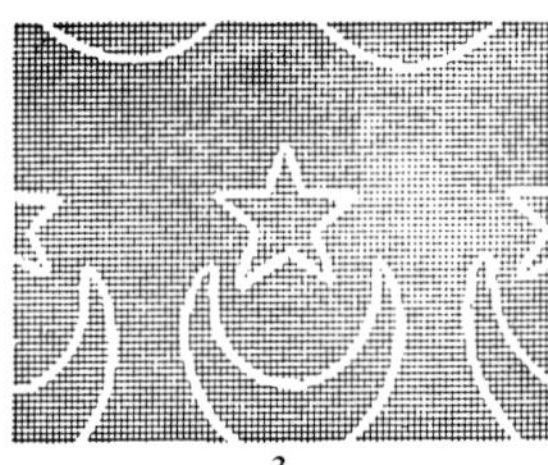

3

1947 (1 Dec). *Bicentenary Commemoration.* W **3** (sideways). P 12½ × 11½.

No.	Type	Description	Unused	Used
18	**2**	½a. black and carmine	2·50	3·00

4 H.H. the Amir of Bahawalpur

5 The Tombs of the Amirs

6 Mosque in Sadiq-Garh

7 Fort Derawar from the Lake

8 Nur-Mahal Palace

9 The Palace, Sadiq-Garh

10 H.H. the Amir of Bahawalpur

11 Three Generations of Rulers; H.H. the Amir in centre

1948 (1 Apr). W **3** (sideways on vert designs). P 12½ (T **4**), 11½ × 12½ (T **5**, **7**, **8** and **9**), 12½ × 11½ (T **6** and **10**) or 13½ × 14 (T **11**).

No.	Type	Description	Unused	Used
19	**4**	3p. black and blue	1·75	20·00
20		½a. black and claret	1·75	20·00
21		9p. black and green	1·75	20·00
22		1a. black and carmine	1·75	20·00
23		1½a. black and violet	1·75	16·00
24	**5**	2a. green and carmine	2·00	20·00
25	**6**	4a. orange and brown	2·25	20·00
26	**7**	6a. violet and blue	2·25	20·00
27	**8**	8a. carmine and violet	2·25	20·00
28	**9**	12a. green and carmine	2·75	30·00
29	**10**	1r. violet and brown	19·00	42·00
30		2r. green and claret	45·00	70·00
31		5r. black and violet	45·00	85·00
32	**11**	10r. scarlet and black	32·00	£100
19/32 *Set of* 14			£140	£450

12 H.H. The Amir of Bahawalpur and Mohammed Ali Jinnah

13 Soldiers of 1848 and 1948

1948 (3 Oct). *First Anniv of Union of Bahawalpur with Pakistan.* W **3**. P 13.

No.	Type	Description	Unused	Used
33	**12**	1½a. carmine and blue-green	1·50	3·00

1948 (15 Oct). *Multan Campaign Centenary.* W **3**. P 11½.

No.	Type	Description	Unused	Used
34	**13**	1½a. black and lake	1·25	9·00

1948. *As Nos. 29/32, but colours changed.*

No.	Type	Description	Unused	Used
35	**10**	1r. deep green and orange	1·50	18·00
36		2r. black and carmine	1·75	22·00
37		5r. chocolate and ultramarine	1·90	40·00
38	**11**	10r. red-brown and green	2·00	45·00
35/8 *Set of* 4			6·50	£110

14 Irrigation

17 U.P.U. Monument, Berne

1949 (3 Mar). *Silver Jubilee of Accession of H.H. the Amir of Bahawalpur. T* **14** *and similar horiz designs.* W **3**. P 14.

No.	Description	Unused	Used
39	3p. black and ultramarine	10	8·00
40	½a. black and brown-orange	10	8·00
41	9p. black and green	10	8·00
42	1a. black and carmine	10	8·00
39/42 *Set of* 4		30	29·00

Designs:—½a. Wheat; 9p. Cotton; 1a. Sahiwal bull.

Nos. 39/42 exist imperforate (*Prices, £16 per pair, unused*).

1949 (10 Oct). *75th Anniv of Universal Postal Union.* W **3**. P 13.

No.	Type	Description	Unused	Used
43	**17**	9p. black and green	20	1·25
		a. Perf 17½ × 17	1·25	17·00
44		1a. black and magenta	20	1·25
		a. Perf 17½ × 17	1·25	17·00
45		1½a. black and orange	20	1·25
		a. Perf 17½ × 17	1·25	17·00
46		2½a. black and blue	20	1·25
		a. Perf 17½ × 17	1·25	17·00
43/6 *Set of* 4			70	4·50
43a/6a *Set of* 4			4·50	60·00

Nos. 43/6 exist imperforate (*Prices, £10 per pair, unused*).

OFFICIAL STAMPS

O 1 PanjnadWeir

O 2 Dromedary and Calf

O 3 Blackbuck

O 4 Eastern White Pelicans

O 5 Friday Mosque, Fort Derawar

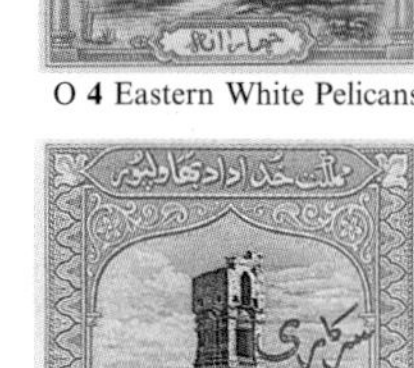

O 6 Temple at Pattan Munara

1945 (1 Mar). *Various horizontal pictorial designs, with red Arabi[c] opt.* W **3**. P 14.

No.	Type	Description	Unused	Used
O1	O **1**	½a. black and green	3·75	13·0
O2	O **2**	1a. black and carmine	3·75	7·5
		a. Opt omitted	†	£90
O3	O **3**	2a. black and violet	3·25	11·0
O4	O **4**	4a. black and olive-green	12·00	26·0
O5	O **5**	8a. black and brown	22·00	15·0
O6	O **6**	1r. black and orange	22·00	15·0
O1/6 *Set of* 6			60·00	80·0

Permission for the introduction of Nos. O1/6 was granted by th[e] Imperial Government as from 1 January 1945, but the stamps wer[e] not used until 1 March. First Day covers exist showing the Januar[y] date.

Examples of No. O2a come from a sheet used at Rahimya Khan.

It is believed that examples of Nos. O1/2 in different shades an[d] with white gum appeared in 1949 and were included in the Silve[r] Jubilee Presentation Booklet.

O 7 Baggage Camels

(**O 8**)

1945 (10 Mar). *Revenue stamp with red Arabic opt.* No wmk. P 14.

No.	Type	Description	Unused	Used
O7	O **7**	1a. black and brown	40·00	55·0

1945 (Mar–June). *Surch as Type* O **8** *(at Security Printing Pres[s] Nasik) instead of red Arabic opt.* No wmk. P 14.

No.	Type	Description	Unused	Used
O11	O **5**	½a.on 8a. black and purple	5·50	4·5
O12	O **6**	1½a.on 1r. black and orange	40·00	11·0
O13	O **1**	1½a.on 2r. black and blue (1 June)	£120	8·0
O11/13 *Set of* 3			£150	21·0

The stamps used as a basis for Nos. O7 and O11/13 were part [of] the Revenue series issued in 1933–34.

SERVICE

(**O 9**)

O 10 H.H. the Amir of Bahawalpur

1945. *Optd with Type* O **9** *(by D.L.R.) instead of red Arabic op[t].* No wmk. P 14.

No.	Type	Description	Unused	Used
O14	O **1**	½a. black and carmine	1·25	11·
O15	O **2**	1a. black and carmine	2·00	13·
O16	O **3**	2a. black and orange	3·25	45·
O14/16 *Set of* 3			6·00	60·

1945. P 14.

No.	Type	Description	Unused	Used
O17	O **10**	3p. black and blue	3·50	8·
O18		1½a. black and violet	20·00	8·

O 11 Allied Banners

(Des E. Meronti. Recess, background litho)

1946 (1 May). *Victory.* P 14.

No.	Type	Description	Unused	Used
O19	O **11**	1½a. green and grey	3·00	4·

1948. *Nos. 19, 22, 24/5 and 35/8 optd as Nos. O1/6.*

No.	Type	Description	Unused	Used
O20	**4**	3p. black and blue (R.)	80	12·
O21		1a. black and carmine (Blk.)	80	11·
O22	**5**	2a. green and carmine (Blk.)	80	12·
O23	**6**	4a. orange and brown (Blk.)	80	16·
O24	**10**	1r. deep green and orange (R.)	80	18·
O25		2r. black and carmine (R.)	80	24·
O26		5r. chocolate and ultramarine (R.)	80	40·
O27	**11**	10r. red-brown and green (R.)	80	40·
O20/7 *Set of* 8			5·75	£1

1949 (10 Oct). *75th Anniv of Universal Postal Union. Nos. 43/6 optd as Nos. O1/6.*

O28 **17** 9p. black and green . . . 15 4·50
aw. Wmk inverted . . . † £190
b. Perf 17½ × 17 . . . 2·50 29·00
O29 1a. black and magenta . . . 15 4·50
b. Perf 17½ × 17 . . . 2·50 29·00
O30 1½a. black and orange . . . 15 4·50
b. Perf 17½ × 17 . . . 2·50 29·00
O31 2½a. black and blue . . . 15 4·50
b. Perf 17½ × 17 . . . 2·50 29·00
O28/31 *Set of* 4 . . . 55 16·00
O28b/31b *Set of* 4 . . . 9·00 £100

Nos. O28/31 exist imperforate (*Prices, £10 per pair, unused*)

From 1947 stamps of Pakistan were used on all external mail. Bahawalpur issues continued to be used on internal mail until 1953.

Palestine

The stamps of TURKEY were used in Palestine from 1865.

In addition various European Powers, and Egypt, maintained post offices at Jerusalem (Austria, France, Germany, Italy, Russia), Jaffa (Austria, Egypt, France, Germany, Russia) and Haifa (Austria, France) using their own stamps or issues specially prepared for Levant post offices. All foreign post offices had closed by the time of the British Occupation.

PRICES FOR STAMPS ON COVER TO 1945

No.	1	*from* × 6
No.	2	*from* × 4
Nos.	3/4	*from* × 5
Nos.	5/15	*from* × 4
Nos.	16/29	*from* × 3
Nos.	30/42	*from* × 2
No.	43	—
Nos.	44/57	*from* × 2
Nos.	58/9	—
Nos.	60/8	*from* × 3
Nos.	69/70	—
Nos.	71/89	*from* × 3
Nos.	90/103	*from* × 4
Nos.	104/11	*from* × 8
Nos.	D1/5	*from* × 30
Nos.	D6/20	*from* × 10

BRITISH MILITARY OCCUPATION

British and allied forces invaded Palestine in November 1917 apturing Gaza (7 November), Jaffa (16 November) and Jerusalem) December). The front line then stabilised until the second British ffensive of September 1918.

Nos. 1/15 were issued by the British military authorities for use y the civilian population in areas they controlled previously part f the Ottoman Empire. Before the issue of Nos. 1/2 in February 918, civilian mail was carried free. In addition to Palestine the amps were available from E.E.F. post offices in Syria (including hat subsequently became Transjordan) from 23 September 1918 23 February 1922, Lebanon from 21 October 1918 to September 920 and Cilicia from 2 September 1919 to 16 July 1920. Use in the llowing post offices outside Palestine is recorded in *British Empire ampaigns and Occupations in the Near East, 1914–1924* by John irebrace:

Adana, Cilicia
Akkari ("Akkar"), Syria
Aleppo ("Alep, Halep"), Syria
Aleih ("Alie"), Lebanon
Alexandretta, Syria
Antakie, Syria
Ba'abda, Lebanon
Baalbek, Lebanon
Bab, Syria
Babitoma, Syria
Behamdoun, Lebanon
Beit ed Dine, Lebanon
Bekaa, Lebanon
Beyrouth, Lebanon
Beit Mery, Beyrouth Lebanon
Bouzanti, Syria
Broumana, Lebanon
Damascus ("Damas"), Syria
Damour ("Damor"), Lebanon
Der'a ("Deraa"), Syria
Deurt-Yol, Syria
Djey Han, Syria
Djezzin ("Djezzine"), Lebanon
Djon, Lebanon
Djounie, Lebanon
Djubeil, Lebanon
Douma, Syria
Edleb, Syria
eke, Turkey
Habib Souk, Syria
Hajjin ("Hadjin"), Cilicia
Hama, Syria
Hasbaya, Lebanon
Hasine, Cilicia
Hommana, Lebanon
Homs, Syria
Kozan, Cilicia
Lattakia ("Laskie, Lattaquie"), Syria
Massel el Chouf ("Moussalc"), Lebanon
Merdjajoun Lebanon
Mersina ("Mersine"), Cilicia
Mounboudje, Syria
Nabatti, Lebanon
Nebk ("Nebik"), Syria
Payass, Syria
Racheya, Lebanon
Safita, Syria
Savour, Tyre, Lebanon
Selimie, Syria
Sidan ("Saida (Echelle)"), Lebanon
Suweidiya ("Suvedie"), Syria
Talia, Syria
Tarsous, Cilicia
Tartous, Syria
Tibnin, Lebanon
Tripoli, Syria
Zahle, Lebanon
Zebdani, Syria

This information is reproduced here by permission of the blishers, Robson Lowe Publications.

(Currency. 10 milliemes = 1 piastre)

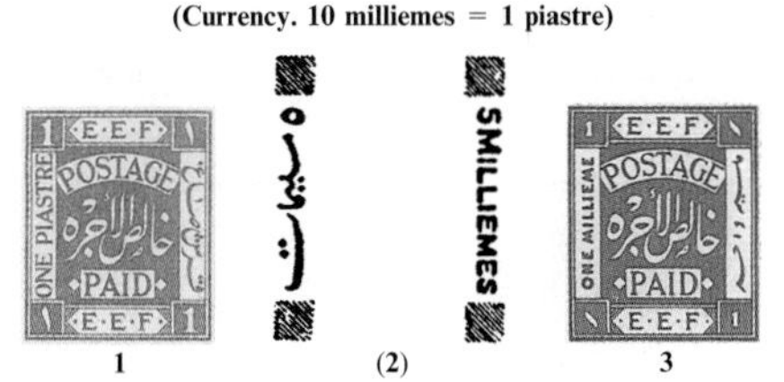

1 (2) 3

"E.E.F." = Egyptian Expeditionary Force

W **100** of Great Britain

(Des G. Rowntree. Litho Typographical Dept, Survey of Egypt, Giza, Cairo)

1918 (10 Feb). Wmk Royal Cypher in column (W **100** of Great Britain). *Ungummed. Roul 20.*

1 **1** 1p. indigo . . . £180 £100
a. Deep blue . . . £150 90·00
b. Blue . . . £150 90·00
s. Optd "Specimen" . . . £300

Control: A 18 (*Prices, corner block of* 4; No. 1 £850. No. 1*a*, £750. No. 1*b*, £850).

1918 (16 Feb). *As last (ungummed) surch with T* **2**.

2 **1** 5m.on 1p. cobalt-blue . . . 90·00 £475
a. "MILLILMES" (R. 1/10) . . . £3250 £9000
s. Optd "Specimen" . . . £300
w. Wmk inverted

Control: B 18 A (*Corner block*, £1100)

1918 (5 Mar). *As No. 1 but colour changed. With gum.*

3 **1** 1p. ultramarine (*shades*) . . . 2·00 2·00
a. Crown missing from wmk . . . 40·00
b. Printed on the gummed side
w. Wmk inverted . . . £180 £225

Control: C 18. (*Corner block*, £70).

1918 (5 Mar–13 May). *No. 3 surch with T* **2**.

4 **1** 5m.on 1p. ultramarine . . . 4·00 2·75
a. Arabic surch wholly or partly missing (R. 1/11) . . . £300 £400
b. Crown missing from wmk . . . 60·00
w. Wmk inverted . . . £250

Controls: C 18 B (Mar). (*Corner block*, £700).
D 18 C (May). (*Corner block*, £200).

(Typo Stamping Dept, Board of Inland Revenue, Somerset House, London)

1918 (16 July–27 Dec). Wmk Royal Cypher in column (W **100** of Great Britain). P 15 × 14.

5 **3** 1m. sepia . . . 30 40
a. Deep brown . . . 40 40
6 2m. blue-green . . . 30 45
a. Deep green . . . 1·50 80
7 3m. yellow-brown (17 Dec) . . . 35 35
a. Chestnut . . . 13·00 6·00
8 4m. scarlet . . . 35 40
9 5m. yellow-orange (25 Sept) . . . 1·75 30
a. Orange . . . 65 30
b. Crown missing from wmk . . . £140
w. Wmk inverted . . . — £1500
10 1p. deep indigo (9 Nov) . . . 35 25
a. Crown missing from wmk . . . £120
w. Wmk inverted . . . £150 £160
11 2p. pale olive . . . 1·00 60
a. Olive . . . 1·75 1·10
12 5p. purple . . . 1·75 2·25
13 9p. ochre (17 Dec) . . . 3·75 4·75
14 10p. ultramarine (17 Dec) . . . 3·00 3·25
w. Wmk inverted . . . £400
15 20p. pale grey (27 Dec) . . . 11·00 16·00
a. Slate-grey . . . 16·00 22·00
5/15 *Set of* 11 . . . 22·00 26·00

There are two sizes of the design of this issue:
19 × 23 mm. 1, 2, and 4m., and 2 and 5p.
18 × 21½ mm. 3 and 5m., and 1, 9, 10 and 20p.

There are numerous minor plate varieties in this issue, such as stops omitted in "E.E.F.", malformed Arabic characters, etc.

CIVIL ADMINISTRATION UNDER BRITISH HIGH COMMISSIONER

Palestine was placed under civil administration by a British High Commissioner on 1 July 1920.

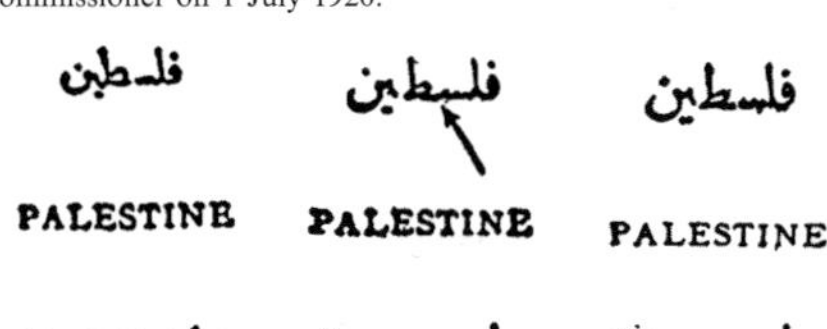

(4) (5) (6)

Differences:—
T **5**. 20 mm vert and 7 mm between English and Hebrew.
T **6**. 19 mm and 6 mm respectively.

Two settings of Type **4**:

Setting I (used for Nos. 16/26). This consisted of two horizontal rows of 12 of which the first setting row appeared on Rows 1, 3/7, 15, 17/18 and 20 of the sheet and the second on Rows 2, 8/14, 16 and 19.

On the first position in the top setting row the Arabic "t" (third character from the left) is incorrectly shown as an Arabic "z" by the addition of a dot to its right. On the eleventh position in the same row the first two letters in the Hebrew overprint were transposed so that " character appears first. On row 12 stamp 1 the final "E" of "PALESTINE" appears as a "B" on certain values. Once the errors were noticed vertical columns one and eleven were removed from the remaining sheets.

Setting II (used for Nos. 16/29). This consisted of a single horizontal row of 12 reproduced to overprint the complete sheet of 240. The order in which the horizontal rows were used was changed several times during overprinting. During one such re-arrangement a damaged impression was replaced by one from Setting I showing the Arabic "z" error. (R. 14/8 for 1, 2, 3, 4, 5 (P 14) 20p.). The "B" error also occurs in the second setting, once in each sheet on either R. 17/8, 18/8 or 19/8.

(Optd at Greek Orthodox Convent, Jerusalem)

1920 (1 Sept). *Optd with T* **4** *(Arabic 8 mm long).*

(a) P 15 × 14.

16 **3** 1m. sepia . . . 3·50 1·90
b. Arabic "z" (Settings I and II) . . . £1000
c. Hebrew characters transposed (I) . . . £1000
d. "PALESTINB" (II) . . . 75·00
17 2m. blue-green . . . 6·50 4·50
b. "Arabic "z" (Settings I and II) . . . £850
c. Hebrew characters transposed (I) . . . £850
d. "PALESTINB" (II) . . . 85·00
18 3m. chestnut . . . 7·50 4·75
a. Opt inverted . . . £450 £600
b. Arabic "z" (Settings I and II) . . . £1500
c. Hebrew characters transposed (I) . . . £1500
d. "PALESTINB" (II) . . . 45·00
19 4m. scarlet . . . 1·75 1·25
b. Arabic "z" (Settings I and II) . . . £1500
c. Hebrew characters transposed (I) . . . £1500
d. PALESTINB" (II) . . . 45·00
20 5m. yellow-orange . . . 15·00 4·25
c. Hebrew characters transposed (I) . . . † £2500
d. "PALESTINB" (II) . . . 85·00
21 1p. deep indigo (Sil.) . . . 3·00 80
d. "PALESTINB" (II) . . . 20·00
w. Wmk inverted . . . £120 £130
22 2p. deep olive . . . 2·50 1·90
a. Crown missing from wmk . . . £500
b. Arabic "z" (I) . . . £180
c. Hebrew characters transposed (I) . . . £180
d. "PALESTINB" (Settings I and II) . . . 90·00
23 5p. deep purple . . . 16·00 21·00
b. Arabic "z" (I) . . . £900
c. Hebrew characters transposed (I) . . . £500
d. "PALESTINB" (Setting I and II) . . . £140
24 9p. ochre . . . 9·00 20·00
b. Arabic "z" (I) . . . £400
c. Hebrew characters transposed (I) . . . £450
d. "PALESTINB" (Settings I and II) . . . £160
25 10p. ultramarine . . . 10·00 17·00
b. Arabic "z" (I) . . . £300
c. Hebrew characters transposed (I) . . . £400
d. "PALESTINB" (Settings I and II) . . . £200
26 20p. pale grey . . . 25·00 42·00
b. Arabic "z" (Settings I and II) . . . £800
c. Hebrew characters transposed (I) . . . £900
d. "PALESTINB" (Settings I and II) . . . £1800

(b) P 14.

27 **3** 2m. blue-green . . . 1·40 1·40
d. "PALESTINB" (II) . . . 30·00
28 3m. chestnut . . . 55·00 55·00
29 5m. orange . . . 2·25 65
d. "PALESTINB" (II) . . . 70·00
16/29 *Set of* 14 . . . £140 £150

Faulty registration of the overprint in this issue has resulted in numerous misplaced overprints, either vertically or horizontally, which are not of great importance with the exception of Nos. 21 and 29 which exist with the overprint out of sequence, i.e. Hebrew/Arabic/English or English/Arabic/Hebrew or English/Hebrew only. Also all values are known with Arabic/English only.

1920 (Dec)–**21**. *Optd with T* **5*** *(Arabic 10 mm long).*

(a) P 15 × 14.

30 **3** 1m. sepia (27.12.20) . . . 1·25 1·00
a. Opt inverted . . . £400 †
31 2m. blue-green (27.12.20) . . . 6·00 4·00
a. Opt double
32 3m. yellow-brown (27.12.20) . . . 2·50 1·00
33 4m. scarlet (27.12.20) . . . 3·00 1·25
34 5m. yellow-orange . . . 2·25 75
35 1p. deep indigo (Silver) (21.6.21) . . . £425 26·00
36 2p. olive (21.6.21) . . . 60·00 26·00
37 5p. deep purple (21.6.21) . . . 38·00 9·50

(b) P 14.

38 **3** 1m. sepia . . . £500 £700
39 2m. blue-green . . . 3·00 4·00
40 4m. scarlet . . . 55·00 75·00
41 5m. orange . . . 85·00 9·00
a. Yellow-orange . . . 6·00 1·10
42 1p. deep indigo (Silver) . . . 48·00 1·25
43 5p. purple . . . £200 £450

*In this setting the Arabic and Hebrew characters are badly worn and blunted, the Arabic "S" and "T" are joined (i.e. there is no break in the position indicated by the arrow in our illustration); the letters of "PALESTINE" are often irregular or broken; and the space between the two groups of Hebrew characters varies from 1 mm to over 1¾ mm. The " character in the left-hand Hebrew word extends above the remainder of the line (*For clear, sharp overprint, see Nos. 47/59.*)

The dates of issue given are irrespective of the perforations, i.e. one or both perfs could have been issued on the dates shown.

Nos. 31 and 39 exist with any one line of the overprint partly missing.

1920 (6 Dec). *Optd with T* **6**.

(a) P 15 × 14.

44 **3** 3m. yellow-brown . . . . 45·00 32·00
44*a* 5m. yellow-orange £14000 £12000

(b) P 14.

45 **3** 1m. sepia . . . . 45·00 32·00
46 5m. orange . . . . £350 30·00

فلسطين PALESTINE פלשתינה א״י (6a)
فلسطين PALESTINE פלשתינה א״י (7)
فلسطين PALESTINE פלשתינה א״י (8)

1921 (29 May–4 Aug). *Optd as T* **6a**.

(a) P 15 × 14.

47 **3** 1m. sepia (23.6) . . . . 10·00 3·50
48 2m. blue-green (18.6) . . . . 18·00 5·50
49 3m. yellow-brown (23.6) . . . . 26·00 3·00
50 4m. scarlet (23.6) . . . . 28·00 3·50
51 5m. yellow-orange . . . . 50·00 1·00
52 1p. deep indigo (Silver) (1.7) . . . . 18·00 75
53 2p. olive (4.8) . . . . 23·00 6·00
54 5p. purple (4.8) . . . . 25·00 8·00
55 9p. ochre (4.8) . . . . 50·00 90·00
56 10p. ultramarine (4.8) . . . . 55·00 14·00
57 20p. pale grey (4.8) . . . . 85·00 50·00
47/57 *Set of* 11 . . . . £350 £160

(b) P 14.

58 **3** 1m. sepia . . . . — £2000
59 20p. pale grey £12000 £2500

In this setting the Arabic and Hebrew characters are sharp and pointed and there is usually a break between the Arabic "S" and "T", though this is sometimes filled with ink. The space between the two groups of Hebrew characters is always 1¾ mm. The top of the " character in the Hebrew aligns with the remainder of the word.

The 3m. with "PALESTINE" omitted is an essay (*Price* £2500 *unused*).

1921 (26 Sept)–**22**. *Optd with T* **7** *("PALESTINE" in sans-serif letters) by Stamping Dept, Board of Inland Revenue, Somerset House, London.* Wmk Royal Cypher in column (W **100** of Great Britain). P 15 × 14.

60 **3** 1m. sepia (5.10.21) . . . . 1·25 30
61 2m. blue-green (11.10.21) . . . . . . 1·50 30
62 3m. yellow-brown (17.10.21) . . . . . 1·50 30
63 4m. scarlet (15.10.21) . . . . 1·75 60
64 5m. yellow-orange . . . . 1·50 30
65 1p. bright turquoise-blue (14.11.21) . . 1·50 35
66 2p. olive (7.12.21) . . . . 2·25 40
67 5p. deep purple (11.12.21) . . . . . . 6·00 5·00
68 9p. ochre (10.3.22) . . . . 14·00 14·00
69 10p. ultramarine (10.3.22) . . . . . . 19·00 £500
w. Wmk inverted . . . . † —
70 20p. pale grey (10.3.22) . . . . 50·00 £1200
60/70 *Set of* 11 . . . . 90·00

Dates quoted are of earliest known postmarks.

(Printed and optd by Waterlow & Sons from new plates)

1922 (Sept–Nov). *T* **3** *(redrawn), optd with T* **8**. Wmk Mult Script CA.

(a) P 14.

71 **3** 1m. sepia 85 30
a. Deep brown . . . . 1·00 30
b. Opt inverted . . . . — £12000
c. Opt double £225 £425
w. Wmk inverted . . . . 35·00 25·00
72 2m. yellow . . . . 1·00 30
a. Orange-yellow . . . . 3·50 50
b. Wmk sideways . . . . † £1500
w. Wmk inverted . . . . 30·00 30·00
73 3m. greenish blue . . . . 1·50 15
w. Wmk inverted . . . . 30·00 30·00
74 4m. carmine-pink . . . . 1·50 20
w. Wmk inverted . . . . 38·00 38·00
75 5m. orange . . . . 1·75 30
w. Wmk inverted . . . . 50·00 38·00
76 6m. blue-green . . . . 1·50 30
w. Wmk inverted . . . . 40·00 40·00
77 7m. yellow-brown . . . . 1·50 30
w. Wmk inverted £200 £200
78 8m. scarlet . . . . 1·50 30
w. Wmk inverted . . . . 45·00 50·00
79 1p. grey . . . . 2·00 30
w. Wmk inverted . . . . 50·00 50·00
80 13m. ultramarine . . . . 2·00 15
w. Wmk inverted . . . . 30·00 20·00
81 2p. olive . . . . 2·50 35
a. Opt inverted £300 £500
b. Ochre . . . . £120 6·50
w. Wmk inverted £180 £140
82 5p. deep purple . . . . 4·75 1·25
aw. Wmk inverted . . . . † £550
82*b* 9p. ochre £900 £200
83 10p. light blue . . . . 55·00 12·00
a. "E.F.F." for "E.E.F." in bottom panel (R. 10/3) £600 £400
84 20p. bright violet . . . . £130 95·00

(b) P 15 × 14.

86 **3** 5p. deep purple . . . . 50·00 4·00
87 9p. ochre . . . . 9·00 9·00
88 10p. light blue . . . . 7·50 2·50
a. "E.F.F." for "E.E.F." in bottom panel (R. 10/3) £375 £275
w. Wmk inverted £425 £225
89 20p. bright violet . . . . 9·00 5·50
71s/89s Optd "Specimen" *Set of* 15 . . . . £400

Most values can be found on thin paper.

In this issue the design of all denominations is the same size, 18 × 21¾ mm. Varieties may be found with one or other of the stops between "E.E.F." missing.

BRITISH MANDATE TO THE LEAGUE OF NATIONS

The League of Nations granted a mandate to Great Britain for the administration of Palestine on 29 September 1923.

(New Currency. 1,000 mils = 1 Palestine pound)

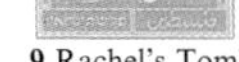

9 Rachel's Tomb

10 Dome of the Rock

11 Citadel, Jerusalem

12 Sea of Galilee

(Des F. Taylor. Typo Harrison)

1927 (1 June)–**45**. Wmk Mult Script CA. P 13½ × 14½ (2m. to 20m.) or 14.

90 **9** 2m. greenish blue (14.8.27) 75 10
w. Wmk inverted . . . . † £500
91 3m. yellow-green 75 10
w. Wmk inverted . . . . — £225
92 **10** 4m. rose-pink (14.8.27) . . . . . . 4·50 1·25
93 **11** 5m. orange (14.8.27) . . . . 1·75 10
a. From coils. Perf 14½ × 14 (1936) . . . . 14·00 18·00
ac. Yellow. From coils. Perf 14½ × 14 (1945) . . . . 30·00 28·00
aw. Wmk inverted . . . . 16·00 25·00
b. Yellow (12.44) . . . . 1·50 15
w. Wmk inverted . . . . 25·00 27·00
94 **10** 6m. pale green (14.8.27) . . . . . 3·50 1·75
a. Deep green 75 20
95 **11** 7m. scarlet (14.8.27) . . . . 5·50 60
96 **10** 8m. yellow-brown (14.8.27) . . . . 12·00 6·00
97 **9** 10m. slate (14.8.27) . . . . 1·00 10
a. Grey. From coils. Perf 14½ × 14 (11.38) . . . . 20·00 24·00
aw. Wmk inverted . . . .
b. Grey (1944) . . . . 1·25 10
98 **10** 13m. ultramarine . . . . 6·00 30
99 **11** 20m. dull olive-green (14.8.27) . . . 1·75 15
a. Bright olive-green (12.44) . . 1·25 15
w. Wmk inverted . . . . — £325
100 **12** 50m. deep dull purple (14.8.27) . . . 1·50 30
a. Bright purple (12.44) . . . . 2·25 30
x. Wmk reversed . . . . — £350
101 90m. bistre (14.8.27) . . . . 55·00 60·00
102 100m. turquoise-blue (14.8.27) . . . . 2·25 70
103 200m. deep violet (14.8.27) . . . . . 8·00 5·00
a. Bright violet (1928) . . . . . 28·00 16·00
b. Blackish violet (12.44) . . . 7·50 3·50
90/103*b Set of* 14 . . . . 90·00 65·00
90s/103s Handstamped "Specimen" *Set of* 14 . . £325

Three sets may be made of the above issue; one on thin paper, one on thicker paper with a ribbed appearance, and another on thick white paper without ribbing.

2m. stamps in the grey colour of the 10m., including an example postmarked in 1935, exist as do 50m. stamps in blue, but it has not been established whether they were issued.

Nos. 90/1 and 93 exist in coils, constructed from normal sheets.

1932 (1 June)–**44**. *New values and colours*. Wmk Mult Script CA. P 13½ × 14½ (4m. to 15m.) or 14.

104 **10** 4m. purple (1.11.32) . . . . 1·00 10
w. Wmk inverted . . . . † £400
105 **11** 7m. deep violet 60 10
106 **10** 8m. scarlet . . . . 1·25 20
w. Wmk inverted . . . . † £500
107 13m. bistre (1.8.32) . . . . 1·00 10
108 15m. ultramarine (1.8.32) . . . . . 3·00 10
a. Grey-blue (12.44) . . . . . . 2·25 40
b. Greenish blue . . . . 2·25 40
w. Wmk inverted . . . . † £500
109 **12** 250m. brown (15.1.42) . . . . 4·00 1·75
110 500m. scarlet (15.1.42) . . . . 4·50 3·00
111 £P1 black (15.1.42) . . . . 6·00 3·50
104/11 *Set of* 8 . . . . 19·00 8·00
104s/11s Perf "Specimen" *Set of* 8 . . . . . £375

No. 108 exists in coils, constructed from normal sheets.

STAMP BOOKLETS

1929. *Blue cover inscr* "PALESTINE POSTAGE STAMP BOOKLET" *and contents in English. Without advertisements on front. Stitched.*

SB1 150m. booklet containing twelve 2m., 3m. and eighteen 5m. (Nos. 90/1, 93) in blocks of 6 . . . . £2000
a. As No. SB1, but stapled £1600

1933. *Blue cover inscr* "PALESTINE POSTS & TELEGRAPHS POSTAGE STAMP BOOKLET" *and contents all in English, Arabic and Hebrew. Without advertisements on front. Stapled.*

SB2 150m. booklet. Contents as No. SB1 . . . . . .

1937–38. *Red cover inscr* "POSTAGE STAMP BOOKLET" *and contents in English, Hebrew and Arabic. With advertisements on front. Stapled.*

SB3 150m. booklet containing 2m., 3m., 5m. and 15m. (Nos. 90/1, 93, 108) in blocks of 6 . . . . . £1600
a. Blue cover (1938) £1600

1939. *Pink cover inscr* "POSTAGE STAMP BOOKLET" *and contents in English, Hebrew and Arabic. With advertisements on front. Stapled.*

SB4 120m. booklet containing six 10m. and twelve 5m. (Nos. 93, 97) in blocks of 6 . . . . £1500

POSTAL FISCALS

Type-set stamps inscribed "O.P.D.A." (= Ottoman Public Debt Administration) or "H.J.Z." (Hejaz Railway); British 1d. stamps of 1912–24 and Palestine stamps overprinted with one or other of the above groups of letters, or with the word "Devair", with or without surcharge of new value, are fiscal stamps. They are known used as postage stamps, alone, or with other stamps to make up the correct rates, and were passed by the postal authorities, although they were not definitely authorised for postal use.

POSTAGE DUE STAMPS

D 1

D 2 (MILLIEME)

D 3 (MIL)

(Typo Greek Orthodox Convent Press, Jerusalem)

1923 (1 Apr). P 11.

D1 **D 1** 1m. yellow-brown . . . . 15·00 25·0
a. Imperf (pair) £300
b. Imperf between (horiz pair) . . £1100
D2 2m. blue-green . . . . 10·00 10·0
a. Imperf (pair) £400
D3 4m. scarlet . . . . 10·00 10·0
D4 8m. mauve . . . . 7·00 7·0
a. Imperf (pair) £120
b. Imperf between (horiz pair) . . † £180
D5 13m. steel blue . . . . 6·00 6·0
a. Imperf between (horiz pair) . . £850
D1/5 *Set of* 5 . . . . 42·00 50·0

Perfectly centred and perforated stamps of this issue are wort considerably more than the above prices, which are for averag specimens.

(Types D **2/3**. Typo D.L.R.)

1924 (3 Oct). Wmk Mult Script CA. P 14.

D 6 **D 2** 1m. deep brown . . . . 90 2·0
D 7 2m. yellow . . . . 2·25 1·7
w. Wmk inverted . . . . † £40
D 8 4m. green . . . . 2·00 1·2
D 9 8m. scarlet . . . . 3·00 9
D10 13m. ultramarine . . . . 2·75 2·5
D11 5p. violet . . . . 8·50 1·7
D6/11 *Set of* 6 . . . . 17·00 9·0
D6s/11s Optd "Specimen" *Set of* 6 . . . . . £275

1928 (1 Feb)–**45**. Wmk Mult Script CA. P 14.

D12 **D 3** 1m. brown 50 8
a. Perf 15 × 14 (1944) . . . . . 35·00 70·0
D13 2m. yellow . . . . 1·00 6
w. Wmk inverted . . . . † £40
D14 4m. green . . . . 1·25 1·6
a. Perf 15 × 14 (1945) . . . . . 60·00 85·0
D15 6m. orange-brown (10.33) . . . . 15·00 5·0
D16 8m. carmine . . . . 1·75 1·0
D17 10m. pale grey . . . . 1·25 6
D18 13m. ultramarine . . . . 1·75 1·7
D19 20m. pale olive-green . . . . . . 1·75 1·2
D20 50m. violet . . . . 2·50 1·2
D12/20 *Set of* 9 . . . . 24·00 14·0
D12s/20s Optd or Perf (6m.) "Specimen" *Set of* 9 . . . . £300

Nos. D12a and D14a were printed and perforated by Harris and Sons following bomb damage to the De La Rue works c 29 December 1940.

The British Mandate terminated on 14 May 1948. Later issues stamps and occupation issues will be found listed under Gaza, Isra and Jordan in Part 19 (*Middle East*) of this catalogue.

Papua
see after Australia

Penrhyn Island
see after New Zealand

Pitcairn Islands

CROWN COLONY

The settlement of Pitcairn Island by the *Bounty* mutineers in 1790 was not discovered until the American whaler *Topaz*, Capt. Mayhew Folger, called there in 1808. A visit by two Royal Navy frigates followed in 1814 and reports from their captains resulted in considerable interest being taken in the inhabitants' welfare by religious and philanthrophic circles in Great Britain.

Due to overcrowding the population was resettled on Tahiti in 1831, but many soon returned to Pitcairn which was taken under British protection in 1838. The island was again evacuated in 1856, when the inhabitants were moved to Norfolk Island, but a number of families sailed back to their original home in 1859 and 1864.

The earliest surviving letter from the island is dated 1849. Before 1921 the mail service was irregular, as it depended on passing ships, and mail for the island was often sent via Tahiti. Some covers, purportedly sent from Pitcairn between 1883 and 1890 are known handstamped "Pitcairn Island" or "PITCAIRN ISLAND", but these are now believed to be forgeries.

In 1920 a regular mail service was introduced. As there were no stamps available, letters were allowed free postage as long as they carried a cachet, or manuscript endorsement, indicating their origin. Illustrations of Cachets I/VI, VIII, VIIIa, X and XIII are taken from *Pitcairn Islands Postal Markings 1883–1991*, published by the Pitcairn Islands Study Group, and are reproduced by permission of the author, Mr. Cy Kitching. Cachets I to XIII are shown three-quarter size.

POSTED IN PITCAIRN
NO STAMPS AVAILABLE
Cachet I

Cat No. *Value on cover*

C1 **1920–25.** Cachet I (62 × 8 *mm*) (*violet or black*) . . £3000

POSTED AT PITCAIRN ISLAND
NO STAMPS AVAILABLE.
Cachet II

C2 **1921–25.** Cachet II (*violet or red*) £2500

POSTED AT PITCAIRN ISLAND
NO STAMPS AVAILABLE.
Cachet III

C3 **1922–28.** Cachet III (49 × 8½ *mm*) (*vio, pur or blk*) £1800

POSTED IN PITCAIRN ISLAND
1923 NO STAMPS AVAILABLE
Cachet IV

C4 **1923.** Cachet IV (*black*) £2500

Posted at Pitcairn
Island no Stamps
Available
Cachet IVa

C4*a* **1923.** Cachet IVa (73½ × 22 *mm*) (*red*) £2500

POSTED AT PITCAIRN ISLAND
NO STAMPS AVAILABLE
Cachet V

C5 **1923–28.** (Aug). Cachet V (47 × 9 *mm*) (*red, violet or black*) £1700

C5*a* **1925–26.** As Cachet V, but second line shown as "No Stamps Available" (*black*) . . . .

POSTED AT PITCAIRN ISLAND.
NO STAMPS AVAILABLE.
NOT TO BE SURCHARGED.
Cachet VI

C6 **1923.** Cachet VI (*blue-green or red*) . . . . . .

C7 **1923.** As Cachet V, but in three lines (*red*) . . .

POSTED AT PITCAIRN ISLAND
NO STAMPS AVAILABLE.
Cachet VII

C8 **1923–27.** Cachet VII (*violet*) £1700

C9 **1924.** As Cachet IV, but dated "1924" (*black*) £2250

POSTED AT PITCAIRN ISLAND.
NO STAMPS AVAILABLE.
Cachet VIII

C10 **1924–26.** Cachet VIII (36 × 8 *mm*) (*vio, blk or red*) £2250

POSTED AT PITCAIRN
NO STAMPS AVAILABLE
Cachet VIIIa

C10*a* **1924–26.** Cachet VIIIa (36 × 8¾ *mm*) (*vio or blk*) £1800

POSTED AT PITCAIRN ISLAND
NO STAMPS AVAILABLE.
Cachet IX

C11 **1924.** (Feb)–**25**. Cachet IX (63 × 7 *mm*) (*vio or blk*) £2500

POSTED·IN·PITCAIRN·
NO'STAMPS·AVAILABLE
Cachet IXa

C11*a* **1924–26.** Cachet IXa (58 × 8½ *mm*) (*vio or blk*) . . . .

C12 **1925.** (Sept). As Cachet IV, but dated "1925" (*blk*) £2250

POSTED IN PITCAIRN
NO STAMPS AVAILABLE.
Cachet X

C13 **1925.** Cachet X (48 × 5 *mm*) £1900

POSTED AT PITCAIRN ISLAND,
NO STAMPS AVAILABLE.
Cachet XI

C14 **1925–26.** Cachet XI (50 × 10 *mm*) (*violet or blk*) £2250

Posted at PITCAIRN ISLAND
No Stamps Available
Cachet XII

C15 **1925.** Cachet XII (55 × 7½ *mm*) (*violet*) . . . . .

POSTED IN PITCAIRN
NO STAMPS AVAILABLE.
Cachet XIII

C16 **1926.** (Jan). Cachet XIII (64 × 8 *mm*) (*pur or blk*) . . . .

The New Zealand Government withdrew the free postage concession on 12 May 1926, but after representations from the islanders, opened a postal agency on Pitcairn using New Zealand stamps cancelled with Type Z **1**. Some impressions of this postmark appear to show a double ring, but this is the result of heavy or uneven use of the handstamp. The postal agency operated from 7 June 1927 until 14 October 1940.

PRICES. Those quoted for Nos. Z1/72 and ZF1 are for examples showing a virtually complete strike of Type Z **1**. Due to the size of the cancellation such examples will usually be on piece.

Z 1

Stamps of New Zealand cancelled with Type Z **1**.

1915–29. *King George V (Nos. 419, 422/6, 428/31 and 446/9).*

Z 1	½d. green	24·00
Z 2	1½d. grey-slate	50·00
Z 3	1½d. orange-brown	42·00
Z 4	2d. yellow	38·00
Z 5	2½d. blue	70·00
Z 6	3d. chocolate	75·00
Z 7	4d. bright violet	70·00
Z 8	4½d. deep green	85·00
Z 9	5d. light blue	70·00
Z10	6d. carmine	85·00
Z11	7½d. red-brown	90·00
Z12	8d. red-brown	£120
Z13	9d. yellowish olive	£120
Z14	1s. vermilion	£120

1926–27. *King George V in Admiral's uniform (Nos. 468/9).*

Z15	1d. rose-carmine	24·00
Z16	2s. light blue	£180

1929. *Anti-Tuberculosis Fund (No. 544).*

Z17	1d.+1d. scarlet	£110

1931. *Air (No.548).*

Z18	3d. chocolate	£190

1932. *Health (No. 552).*

Z21	1d.+1d. carmine	£110

1935. *Pictorials (Nos. 556/8 and 560/9).* W **43**.

Z22	½d. bright green	55·00
Z23	1d. scarlet	35·00
Z24	1½d. red-brown	80·00
Z26	2½d. chocolate and slate	70·00
Z27	3d. brown	80·00
Z28	4d. black and sepia	90·00
Z29	5d. ultramarine	95·00
Z30	6d. scarlet	90·00
Z31	8d. chocolate	95·00
Z32	9d. scarlet and black	95·00
Z33	1s. deep green	85·00
Z34	2s. olive-green	£180
Z35	3s. chocolate and yellow-brown	£225

1935. *Silver Jubilee (Nos. 573/5).*

Z36	½d. green	38·00
Z37	1d. carmine	38·00
Z38	6d. red-orange	70·00

1935. *Health (No. 576).*

Z39	1d.+1d. scarlet	60·00

1936. *Pictorials (Nos. 577/82).* W **98**.

Z40	½d. bright green	42·00
Z41	1d. scarlet	14·00
Z42	1½d. red-brown	70·00
Z43	2d. orange	55·00
Z44	2½d. chocolate and slate	60·00
Z45	3d. brown	65·00

1936. *21st Anniv of "Anzac" Landing at Gallipoli (Nos. 591/2).*

Z46	½d.+½d. green	40·00
Z47	1d.+1d. scarlet	40·00

1936. *Congress of British Empire Chambers of Commerce (Nos. 593/7).*

Z48	½d. emerald-green	38·00
Z49	1d. scarlet	38·00
Z50	2½d. blue	42·00
Z51	4d. violet	65·00
Z52	6d. red-brown	65·00

1936. *Health (No. 598).*

Z53	1d.+1d. scarlet	60·00

1937. *Coronation (Nos. 599/601).*

Z54	1d. carmine	28·00
Z55	2½d. Prussian blue	30·00
Z56	6d. red-orange	30·00

1937. *Health (No. 602).*

Z57	1d.+1d. scarlet	60·00

1938. *King George VI (Nos. 603, 605, 607).*

Z58	½d. green	60·00
Z59	1d. scarlet	60·00
Z60	1½d. purple-brown	70·00

1940. *Centenary of British Sovereignty (Nos. 613/22, 624/5).*

Z61	½d. blue-green	30·00
Z62	1d. chocolate and scarlet	35·00
Z63	1½d. light blue and mauve	38·00
Z64	2d. blue-green and chocolate	38·00
Z65	2½d. blue-green and blue	40·00
Z66	3d. purple and carmine	40·00
Z67	4d. chocolate and lake	60·00
Z68	5d. pale blue and brown	65·00
Z69	6d. emerald-green and violet	65·00
Z70	7d. black and red	85·00
Z71	9d. olive-green and orange	85·00
Z72	1s. sage-green and deep green	85·00

POSTAL FISCAL STAMPS

1932. *Arms (No. F147).*

ZF1	2s.6d. deep brown	£225

PRICES FOR STAMPS ON COVER TO 1945	
Nos. 1/8	*from* × 10

1 Cluster of Oranges **2** Christian on *Bounty* and Pitcairn Island

(Recess B.W. (1d., 3d., 4d., 8d. and 2s.6d.), and Waterlow (others))

1940 (15 Oct)–**51**. *T* **1/2** *and similar horiz designs.* Wmk Mult Script CA. P 11½ × 11 (1d., 3d., 4d., 8d. and 2s.6d.) or 12½ (others).

1	½d. orange and green	40	60
2	1d. mauve and magenta	55	70
3	1½d. grey and carmine	55	50
4	2d. green and brown	1·75	1·40

5	3d. yellow-green and blue	1·25	1·40
	aw. Wmk inverted	£3250	
5b	4d. black and emerald-green (1.9.51)	15·00	11·00
6	6d. brown and grey-blue	5·00	1·50
6a	8d. olive-green and magenta (1.9.51)	16·00	7·00
7	1s. violet and grey	3·00	2·00
8	2s.6d. green and brown	8·00	3·75
1/8	*Set of* 10	45·00	26·00
1s/8s	(*ex* 4d., 8d.) Perf "Specimen" *Set of* 8	£1000	

Designs:—1½d. John Adams and his house; 2d. Lt. Bligh and H.M.S. *Bounty*; 3d. Pitcairn Islands and Pacific Ocean; 4d. *Bounty* Bible; 6d. H.M.S. *Bounty*; 8d. School, 1949; 1s. Fletcher Christian and Pitcairn Island; 2s.6d. Christian on H.M.S. *Bounty* and Pitcairn Coast.

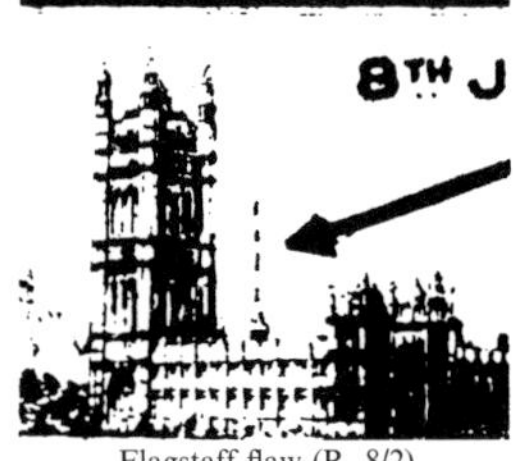

Flagstaff flaw (R. 8/2)

1946 (2 Dec). *Victory. As Nos. 110/11 of Antigua.*

9	2d. brown	60	15
10	3d. blue	60	15
	a. Flagstaff flaw	30·00	
9s/10s	Perf "Specimen" *Set of* 2	£250	

1949 (1 Aug). *Royal Silver Wedding. As Nos. 112/13 of Antigua.*

11	1½d. scarlet	2·00	1·00
12	10s. mauve	35·00	50·00

1949 (10 Oct). *75th Anniv of U.P.U. As Nos. 114/17 of Antigua.*

13	2½d. red-brown	1·00	4·25
14	3d. deep blue	8·00	4·25
15	6d. deep blue-green	4·00	4·25
16	1s. purple	4·00	4·25
13/16	*Set of* 4	15·00	15·00

STAMP BOOKLETS

1940 (15 Oct). *Black on deep green cover. Stapled.*

SB1 4s.8d. booklet containing one each ½d., 1d., 1½d., 2d., 3d., 6d., 1s. and 2s.6d. (Nos. 1/5, 6, 7/8) £2750

Genuine examples of No. SB1 are interleaved with ordinary kitchen wax-paper, which frequently tones the stamps, and are secured with staples 17 mm long.

The status of other booklets using different size staples or paper fasteners is uncertain although it is believed that some empty booklet covers were available on the island.

Prince Edward Island *see* Canada

Queensland *see* Australia

Rhodesia

Stamps of BECHUANALAND (see BOTSWANA) were used in Matabeleland on the runner post between Gubulawayo and Mafeking (Bechuanaland) from 9 August 1888 until 5 May 1894. Such stamps were cancelled "GUBULAWAYO" or by the barred oval "678" obliteration.

Between 27 June 1890 and 13 May 1892 external mail from Mashonaland sent via Bechuanaland was franked with that territory's stamps. A similar arrangement, using the stamps of MOZAMBIQUE existed for the route via Beira inaugurated on 29 August 1891. In both instances the stamps were cancelled by the post offices receiving the mail from Mashonaland. From 14 May until 31 July 1892 letters via Bechuanaland were franked with a combination of B.S.A Company and Bechuanaland issues.

Rhodesia joined the South African Postal Union on 1 August 1892 when its stamps became valid for international mail. Combination frankings with Mozambique stamps continued to be required until April 1894.

For the use of British Central Africa overprints in North-eastern Rhodesia from 1893 to 1899 see MALAWI (NYASALAND).

PRICES FOR STAMPS ON COVER TO 1945

Nos.	1/7	*from* × 5
Nos.	8/13	—
Nos.	14/17	*from* × 2
Nos.	18/24	*from* × 10
Nos.	25/6	—
Nos.	27/8	*from* × 7
Nos.	29/35	*from* × 10
Nos.	36/7	—
Nos.	41/6	*from* × 6
Nos.	47/50	—
Nos.	51/3	*from* × 2
Nos.	58/64	*from* × 3
Nos.	66/72	*from* × 8
Nos.	73/4	—
Nos.	75/87	*from* × 6
Nos.	88/93*a*	—
Nos.	94/9	*from* × 3
Nos.	100/10	*from* × 5
Nos.	111/13*e*	—
Nos.	114/18	*from* × 7
Nos.	119/60*a*	*from* × 10
Nos.	160*b*/6*b*	—
Nos.	167/78	*from* × 6
Nos.	179/81*a*	—
Nos.	182/5*a*	*from* × 4
Nos.	186/208	*from* × 8
Nos.	209/41	*from* × 8
Nos.	242/54*a*	—
Nos.	255/77	*from* × 8
Nos.	278/9*c*	—
Nos.	280/1	*from* × 15
Nos.	282/310	*from* × 8
Nos.	311/22	—

A. ISSUES FOR THE BRITISH SOUTH AFRICA COMPANY TERRITORY

1

2

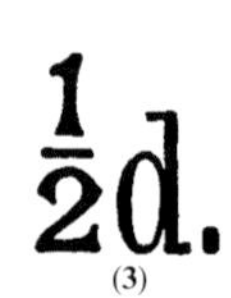

(3)

(Recess B.W.)

1892 (2 Jan*)–**93**. *Thin wove paper.* P 14, 14½.

1	**1**	1d. black	10·00	2·75
2		6d. ultramarine	50·00	24·00
3		6d. deep blue (1893)	27·00	3·75
4		1s. grey-brown	38·00	8·00
5		2s. vermilion	42·00	25·00
6		2s.6d. grey-purple	30·00	38·00
7		2s.6d. lilac (1893)	48·00	40·00
8		5s. orange-yellow	65·00	50·00
9		10s. deep green	80·00	£100
10	**2**	£1 deep blue	£180	£130
11		£2 rose-red**	£400	£150
12		£5 sage-green	£1600	£450
13		£10 brown	£2750	£700
1/10		*Set of* 8	£400	£300

Great caution is needed in buying the high values in either used or unused condition, many stamps offered being revenue stamps cleaned and re-gummed or with forged postmarks.

*Printing of stamps in Types **1**, **2** and **4** commenced in 1890, although none were used for postal purposes before 2 January 1892 when the route to the East Coast was inaugurated.

**For later printings of the £2 see No. 74.

The following sheet watermarks are known on Nos. 1/26: (1) William Collins, Sons & Co's paper watermarked with the firm's monogram, and "PURE LINEN WOVE BANK" in double-lined capitals (1890 and 1891 ptgs). (2) As (1) with "EXTRA STRONG" and "139" added (1892 ptgs). (3) Paper by Wiggins Teape & Co, watermarked "W T & Co" in script letters in double-lined wavy border (1893 ptgs). (4) The same firm's paper, watermarked "1011" in double-lined figures (1894 ptgs except ½d.). (5) "WIGGINS TEAPE & CO LONDON" in double-lined block capitals (1894 ptg of No. 18). Many values can also be found on a slightly thicker paper without wmk, but single specimens are not easily distinguishable.

1892 (2 Jan). *Nos. 2 and 4 surch as T* **3**.

14	**1**	½d. on 6d. ultramarine	£100	£300
15		2d. on 6d. ultramarine	£110	£425
16		4d. on 6d. ultramarine	£140	£500
17		8d. on 1s. grey-brown	£140	£550
14/17		*Set of* 4	£450	£1600

Caution is needed in buying these surcharges as both forged surcharges and forged postmarks exist.

4

5 (ends of scrolls behind legs of springboks)

(T **4**. Centre recess; value B.W.)

1892 (2 Jan)–**94**. *Thin wove paper (wmks as note after No. 13).* P 14, 14½.

18	**4**	½d. dull blue and vermilion	2·50	3·00
19		½d. deep blue and vermilion (1893)	2·75	4·50
20		2d. deep dull green and vermilion	19·00	2·50
21		3d. grey-black and green (8.92)	11·00	3·75
22		4d. chestnut and black	22·00	2·50
23		8d. rose-lake and ultramarine	11·00	11·00
24		8d. red and ultramarine (1892)	10·00	11·00
25		3s. brown and green (1894)	£140	75·00
26		4s. grey-black and vermilion (1893)	32·00	50·00
18/26		*Set of* 7	£200	£130

(Recess P.B. from the Bradbury, Wilkinson plates)

1895. *Thick soft wove paper.* P 12½.

27	**4**	2d. green and red	22·00	11·00
28		4d. yellow-brown and black	22·00	13·00
		a. Imperf (pair)	£1800	

(Centre recess; value typo P.B.)

1896–97. *Wove paper.* P 14.

(a) Die I. Plates 1 and 2. Small dot to the right of the tail of the right-hand supporter in the coat of arms. Body of lion only partly shaded.

29	**5**	1d. scarlet and emerald	13·00	4·50
		a. Carmine-red and emerald		
30		2d. brown and mauve	22·00	2·00
31		3d. chocolate and ultramarine	3·75	1·75
32		4d. ultramarine and mauve	50·00	
		a. Imperf between (pair)		
		b. Blue and mauve	24·00	15·00
33		6d. mauve and pink	80·00	17·00
34		8d. green and mauve/*buff*	5·00	60
		a. Imperf between (pair)		
		b. Imperf (pair)	£2500	
35		1s. green and blue	15·00	2·75
36		3s. green and mauve/*blue*	65·00	32·00
		a. Imperf (pair)	£6500	
37		4s. orange-red and blue/*green*	48·00	2·75
29/37		*Set of* 9	£250	70·00

(b) Die II. Plates 3 and 4. No dot. Body of lion heavily shaded all over.

41	**5**	½d. slate and violet	2·50	3·25
42		1d. scarlet and emerald	3·50	3·75
43		2d. brown and mauve	8·50	4·50
44		4d. ultramarine and mauve	75·00	12·00
		a. Blue and mauve	9·00	50
46		6d. mauve and rose	7·00	75
47		2s. indigo and green/*buff*	23·00	8·50
48		2s.6d. brown and purple/*yellow*	70·00	50·00
49		5s. chestnut and emerald	45·00	9·00
50		10s. slate and vermilion/*rose*	90·00	60·00
41/50		*Set of* 9	£225	£130

One Penny

(6)

THREE

PENCE.

(7)

(Surchd by *Bulawayo Chronicle*)

1896 (April). *Matabele Rebellion provisionals. Surch with T* **6** *and* **7**

51	**6**	1d.on 3d. (No. 21)	£475	£50
		a. "P" in "Penny" inverted	£25000	
		b. "y" in "Penny" inverted		
52		1d.on 4s. (No. 26)	£250	£27
		a. "P" in "Penny" inverted	£21000	
		b. "y" in "Penny" inverted	£21000	
		c. Single bar through original value	£1000	£120
53	**7**	3d.on 5s. (No. 8)	£170	£22
		a. "R" in "THREE" inverted	£21000	
		b. "T" in "THREE" inverted	£25000	

Nos. 51 and 52 occur in two settings, one with 9¾ mm betwee value and upper bar, the other with 11 mm between value and uppe bar.

BRITISH

SOUTH AFRICA

COMPANY.

(8)

9 (Ends of scrolls between legs of springboks)

1896 (22 May Aug). *Cape of Good Hope stamps optd by Arg Printing Co, Cape Town, with T* **8**. Wmk Anchor (3d. wmk Crow CA). P 14.

58	**6**	½d. grey-black (No. 48*a*)	11·00	17·
59	**17**	1d. rose-red (No. 58)	13·00	18·
60	**6**	2d. deep bistre (No. 50*a*)	16·00	9·
61		3d. pale claret (No. 40)	50·00	70·
62		4d. blue (No. 51)	18·00	18·
		a. "COMPANY," omitted	£8500	
63	**4**	6d. deep purple (No. 52*a*)	50·00	65·
64	**6**	1s. yellow-ochre (No. 65) (Aug)	£140	£1
58/64		*Set of* 7	£250	£3

No. 62 also exists with "COMPANY" partially omitte Examples with the word completely omitted, as No. 62a, occur positions 1 to 6 of the setting.

Forgeries of this overprint show a narrow final "A" "AFRICA" and have a rectangular full stop. On the genui overprint both "As" are the same and the stop is oval.

(Eng J. A. C. Harrison (vignette), Bain or Rapkin (£1) (frames) Recess Waterlow)

1897. P 13½ to 16.

66	**9**	½d. grey-black and purple	2·50	4·
67		1d. scarlet and emerald	3·00	4·
68		2d. brown and mauve	7·00	1·
69		3d. brown-red and slate-blue	2·50	
		a. Imperf between (vert pair)	£2750	
70		4d. ultramarine and claret	10·00	1·
		a. Imperf between (horiz pair)	£10000	£100
71		6d. dull purple and pink	6·50	3·
72		8d. green and mauve/*buff*	11·00	
		a. Imperf between (vert pair)	†	£25
73		£1 black and red-brown/*green*	£350	£2

(Recess Waterlow, from the Bradbury plate)

1897 (Jan). P 15.

74	**2**	£2 rosy red	£1700	£4

10 11 12

(Recess Waterlow)

1898–1908. P 13½ to 15½.

No.	Type	Description	Unused	Used
75	10	½d. dull bluish green	4·00	1·00
		a. Yellow green (1904)	2·25	1·00
		aa. Imperf vert (horiz pair)	£650	
		ab. Imperf (pair)	£700	
		ac. Imperf between (vert pair)	£800	
76		½d. deep green (*shades*) (1908)	24·00	1·25
77		1d. rose (*shades*)	3·50	50
		a. Imperf (pair)	£650	£750
		b. Imperf between (vert pair)	£500	
78		1d. red (*shades*) (1905)	4·50	50
		a. Imperf vert (horiz pair)	£350	£400
		ab. Imperf horiz (vert pair)	£850	
		b. Imperf (pair)	£500	£600
		c. Imperf between (horiz pair)	†	£450
		d. Imperf between (vert strip of 4)	£1500	
79		2d. brown	2·75	60
80		2½d. dull blue (*shades*)	4·50	80
		a. Imperf vert (horiz pair)	£800	£900
		b. Grey-blue (*shades*) (1903)	12·00	1·00
81		3d. claret	4·00	80
		a. Imperf between (vert pair)	£700	
82		4d. olive	4·25	30
		a. Imperf between (vert pair)	£700	
83		6d. reddish purple	10·00	1·75
		a. Reddish mauve (1902)	15·00	5·50
84	11	1s. bistre	15·00	2·25
		a. Imperf between (vert pair)	£2750	
		ab. Imperf between (horiz pair)	£3000	
		b. Deep olive-bistre (1907)	£275	
		bc. Imperf (pair)	£2750	
		bd. Imperf between (horiz pair)	£3750	
		c. Bistre-brown (1908)	50·00	13·00
		d. Brownish yellow (1908)	17·00	6·50
85		2s.6d. bluish grey (11.06)	45·00	75
		a. Imperf between (vert pair)	£1000	£500
86		3s. deep violet (1902)	14·00	1·75
		a. Deep bluish violet (1908)	55·00	10·00
87		5s. brown-orange	38·00	10·00
88		7s.6d. black (11.01)	65·00	18·00
89		10s. grey-green	24·00	1·00
90	12	£1 greyish red-purple (p 15½) (7.01)	£225	85·00
		a. Perf 14. *Blackish purple* (1902)	£400	85·00
91		£2 brown (5.08)	75·00	6·50
92		£5 deep blue (7.01)	£3000	£2250
93		£10 lilac (7.01)	£3250	£2250
93a		£20 yellow-bistre (1901?)	£14000	
75/90 *Set of* 14			£400	£110
80s/1s, 85s/6s, 88s/93s Perf "Specimen" *Set of* 10			£900	

A £100 cherry-red, perf 13½, was ordered in June 1901, a number of mint, together with several examples showing fiscal cancellations being known.

13 Victoria Falls

(14)

(Recess Waterlow)

1905 (13 July). *Visit of British Association and Opening of Victoria Falls Bridge.* P 13½ to 15.

No.	Type	Description	Unused	Used
94	13	1d. red	3·50	4·50
95		2½d. deep blue	8·00	6·00
96		5d. claret	22·00	48·00
		sa. Optd "Specimen"	£150	
97		1s. blue-green	24·00	38·00
		a. Imperf (pair)	£19000	
		b. Imperf between (horiz pair)	£25000	
		c. Imperf between (vert pair)	£25000	
		d. Imperf vert (horiz pair)	£20000	
98		2s.6d. black	£100	£150
99		5s. violet	85·00	40·00
94/9 *Set of* 6			£200	£250
94s/9s Optd or Perf (5d.) "Specimen" *Set of* 6			£375	

1909 (15 Apr)–**12**. *Optd as T* **14**. P 13½ to 15.

No.	Type	Description	Unused	Used
100	10	½d. green *to* deep green	1·75	1·25
		a. No stop	48·00	30·00
		b. Yellow-green (1911)	35·00	27·00
101		1d. carmine-rose	2·75	75
		a. No stop	60·00	25·00
		b. Imperf between (horiz pair)	£400	
		c. Deep carmine-rose	2·75	75
		cd. Imperf between (horiz pair)	£400	
102		2d. brown	1·60	3·50
		a. No stop	90·00	65·00
103		2½d. pale dull blue	1·25	70
		a. No stop	38·00	24·00
104		3d. claret	1·60	60
		a. No stop	£150	65·00
		b. Opt inverted	†	15·00
105		4d. olive	3·25	1·25
		a. No stop	65·00	55·00
		b. Opt inverted	†	15·00
106		6d. reddish purple	5·00	4·00
		a. No stop	60·00	
		b. Reddish mauve		
		c. Dull purple	16·00	4·25
		ca. No stop	80·00	45·00
107	11	1s. bistre	18·00	
		a. No stop	£150	
		b. Bistre-brown		
		ba. No stop		
		c. Deep brownish bistre	8·50	3·25
		ca. No stop	80·00	38·00
108		2s.6d. bluish grey	18·00	9·00
		a. No stop	85·00	55·00
		b. Opt inverted	†	20·00
109		3s. deep violet	15·00	8·50
110		5s. orange	25·00	32·00
		a. No stop	95·00	95·00
111		7s.6d. black	90·00	19·00
112		10s. dull green	32·00	12·00
		a. No stop	£250	£180
113	12	£1 grey-purple	£140	75·00
		a. Vert pair, lower stamp without opt	£25000	
		b. Opt in violet	£350	£180
113c		£2 brown	£4000	£300
113d		£2 rosy brown (*bluish paper*) (P 14½ × 15) (1912)	£3250	£275
113e		£5 deep blue (*bluish paper*)	£6500	£3000
100/13 *Set of* 14			£300	£150
100s/13s Perf "Specimen" *Set of* 14			£325	

In some values the no stop variety occurs on every stamp in a vertical row of a sheet, in other values only once in a sheet. Other varieties, such as no serif to the right of apex of "A", no serif to top of "E", etc., exist in some values.

No. 113a comes from a sheet with the overprint omitted from the bottom row.

RHODESIA. 5d

(15)

RHODESIA. TWO SHILLINGS.

(16)

1909 (April)–**11**. *Surch as T* **15** *and* **16** *(2s.) in black.*

No.	Type	Description	Unused	Used
114	10	5d.on 6d. reddish purple	6·50	12·00
		a. Surcharge in violet	90·00	
		b. Reddish mauve		
		c. Dull purple	14·00	12·00
116	11	7½d.on 2s.6d. bluish grey	3·50	3·75
		a. Surcharge in violet	17·00	9·00
		ab. Surch double	†	£6500
117		10d.on 3s. deep violet	13·00	16·00
		a. Surcharge in violet	4·00	3·75
118		2s.on 5s. orange	12·00	7·50
114s/18s Perf "Specimen" *Set of* 4			£180	

In the 7½d. and 10d. surcharges the bars are spaced as in T **16**.

17

18

(Recess Waterlow)

1910 (11 Nov)–**13**.

(a) P 14.

No.	Type	Description	Unused	Used
119	17	½d. yellow-green	10·00	1·75
		a. Imperf between (horiz pair)	£18000	
120		½d. bluish green	20·00	2·75
		a. Imperf (pair)	£11000	£4500
121		½d. olive-green	27·00	2·75
122		½d. dull green	65·00	50·00
123		1d. bright carmine	18·00	2·00
		a. Imperf between (vert pair)	£15000	£10000
		b. Imperf between (horiz pair)		
124		1d. carmine-lake	42·00	2·00
125		1d. rose-red	20·00	2·00
126		2d. black and grey	48·00	9·00
127		2d. black-purple and slate-grey	£160	£750
128		2d. black and slate-grey	50·00	6·00
129		2d. black and slate	65·00	7·50
130		2d. black and grey-black	75·00	13·00
131		2½d. ultramarine	21·00	6·00
131a		2½d. bright ultramarine	20·00	6·00
132		2½d. dull blue	24·00	7·00
133		2½d. chalky blue	18·00	14·00
134		3d. purple and ochre	28·00	28·00
135		3d. purple and yellow-ochre	35·00	12·00
136		3d. magenta and yellow-ochre	£130	12·00
137		3d. violet and ochre	£100	75·00
138		4d. greenish black and orange	85·00	85·00
139		4d. brown-purple and orange	65·00	50·00
140		4d. black and orange	35·00	12·00
141		5d. purple-brown and olive-green	25·00	42·00
141a		5d. purple-brown and olive-yellow	25·00	50·00
		ab. Error. Purple-brown and ochre	£550	£150
143		5d. lake-brown and olive	£250	60·00
143a		5d. lake-brown and green (9.12)	£19000	£1600
144		6d. red-brown and mauve	32·00	32·00
145		6d. brown and purple	30·00	14·00
145a		6d. bright chestnut and mauve	£650	60·00
146		8d. black and purple	£4750	
147		8d. dull purple and purple	£160	90·00
148		8d. greenish black and purple	£130	90·00
149		10d. scarlet and reddish mauve	32·00	48·00
150		10d. carmine and deep purple	£600	60·00
151		1s. grey-black and deep blue-green	38·00	18·00
151a		1s. black and deep blue-green	£140	26·00
152		1s. black and pale blue-green	42·00	11·00
152a		1s. purple-black and blue-green	£225	45·00
153		2s. black and ultramarine	75·00	50·00
154		2s. black and dull blue	£1000	60·00
154a		2s. purple-black and ultramarine	£3000	£225
155		2s.6d. black and lake	£300	£325
155a		2s.6d. black and crimson	£300	£275
156		2s.6d. sepia and deep crimson	£400	£325
156a		2s.6d. bistre-brown and crimson	£1000	£550
157		2s.6d. black and rose-carmine	£275	£300
158		3s. green and violet (*shades*)	£150	£150
158a		3s. bright green and magenta	£1100	£600
159		5s. vermilion and deep green	£250	£300
160		5s. scarlet and pale yellow-green	£275	£180
160a		5s. crimson and yellow-green	£225	£180
160b		7s.6d. carmine and pale blue	£600	£425
161		7s.6d. carmine and light blue	£650	£700
162		7s.6d. carmine and bright blue	£2000	£950
163		10s. deep myrtle and orange	£600	£250
164		10s. blue-green and orange	£375	£375
165		£1 carmine-red and bluish black	£1000	£475
166		£1 rose-scarlet and bluish black	£1100	£350
166a		£1 crimson and slate-black	£1300	£850
		b. Error. Scarlet and reddish mauve	£9000	

(b) P 15.

No.	Type	Description	Unused	Used
167	17	½d. blue-green	£275	13·00
168		½d. yellow-green	£325	11·00
169		½d. apple-green	£550	27·00
170		1d. carmine	£275	8·50
170a		1d. carmine-lake	£400	14·00
170b		1d. rose-carmine	£300	11·00
171		2d. black and grey-black	£850	30·00
171a		2d. black and grey	£850	30·00
171b		2d. black and slate	£950	30·00
172		2½d. ultramarine (*shades*)	70·00	35·00
173		3d. purple and yellow-ochre	£5000	70·00
173a		3d. claret and pale yellow-ochre	£2500	50·00
174		4d. black and orange (*shades*)	45·00	60·00
175		5d. lake-brown and olive	£700	75·00
176		6d. brown and mauve	£800	60·00
177		1s. black and blue-green (*shades*)	£1000	55·00
178		2s. black and dull blue	£1800	£325
179		£1 red and black	£15000	£3000

(c) P 14 × 15 (½d., 3d., 1s.) or 15 × 14 (1d., 4d.).

No.	Type	Description	Unused	Used
179a	17	½d. yellow-green	†	£2750
179b		1d. carmine	†	£5000
180		3d. purple and ochre	£5500	£225
181		4d. black and orange	£425	
181a		1s. black and blue-green	£21000	£2500

(d) P 13½.

No.	Type	Description	Unused	Used
182	17	½d. yellow-green	£275	40·00
182a		½d. green	£325	40·00
183		1d. bright carmine	£1800	48·00
184		2½d. ultramarine (*shades*)	35·00	60·00
185		8d. black and purple (*shades*)	60·00	£250
185a	17	8d. grey-purple and dull purple	£375	£450
119s/85s Optd "Specimen" (all perf 14 except 2½d. and 8d. perf 13½) *Set of* 18			£3250	

Plate varieties in T **17** are:—½d., double dot below "D" in right-hand value tablet (R. 3/9) (*from* £500 *un.* £350 *used*); 2d. to £1 excluding 2½d., straight stroke in Queen's right ear known as the "gash in ear" variety (R. 1/2) (*from* 3 *to* 5 *times normal*).

Stamps from the above and the next issue are known compound perf with 14 or 15 on one side only or on adjoining sides but we no longer list them.

Examples of some values are known with a forged registered Bulawayo postmark dated "JA 10 11".

(Recess Waterlow)

1913 (1 Sept)–**22**. No wmk.

(i) From single working plates.

(a) P 14.

No.	Type	Description	Unused	Used
186	18	½d. blue-green	5·50	1·50
187		½d. deep green	4·50	1·50
		a. Imperf horiz (vert pair)	£700	
		b. Imperf between (vert strip of 5)	£2000	
188		½d. yellow-green	11·00	1·50
		a. Imperf between (horiz pair)	£750	
188b		½d. dull green	8·00	1·50
		ba. Imperf vert (horiz pair)	£750	£750
189		½d. bright green	17·00	1·50
		a. Imperf between (vert pair)	£1200	
190		1d. rose-carmine	5·00	1·50
		a. Imperf between (horiz pair)	£750	£650
191		1d. carmine-red (*shades*)	9·00	1·50
		a. Imperf between (pair)	£1000	
192		1d. brown-red	3·50	1·50
193		1d. red	4·50	1·50
		a. Imperf between (horiz pair)	£700	
194		1d. scarlet	13·00	1·75
		a. Imperf between (horiz pair)	£850	
195		1d. rose-red	8·00	1·50
		a. Imperf between (horiz pair)	£600	
		b. Imperf between (vert pair)	£1700	
196		1d. rosine	£500	19·00
197		1½d. brown-ochre (1919)	3·50	1·50
		a. Imperf between (horiz pair)	£600	£600
198		1½d. bistre-brown (1917)	3·50	1·50
		a. Imperf between (horiz pair)	£650	£650
199		1½d. drab-brown (1917)	4·00	1·50
		a. Imperf between (horiz pair)	£600	
		b. Imperf between (vert pair)	£1700	
200		2½d. deep blue	4·25	24·00
201		2½d. bright blue	4·25	24·00

(b) P 15.

No.	Type	Description	Unused	Used
202	18	½d. blue-green	8·50	15·00
203		½d. green	14·00	14·00
204		1d. rose-red	£550	22·00
		a. Imperf between (horiz pair)	£12000	
205		1d. brown-red	3·00	5·00
206		1½d. bistre-brown (1919)	27·00	7·00
		a. Imperf between (horiz pair)	£15000	
206b		1½d. brown-ochre (1917)	35·00	10·00
207		2½d. deep blue	19·00	40·00
208		2½d. bright blue	16·00	38·00

(c) P 14 × 15.

No.	Type	Description	Unused	Used
208a	18	½d. green	£5500	£170

(d) P 15 × 14.

No.	Type	Description	Unused	Used
208b	18	½d. green	£5500	£325
208c		1½d. drab-brown		

(e) P 13½.

No.	Type	Description	Unused	Used
208d	18	1d. red (1914)	†	£500

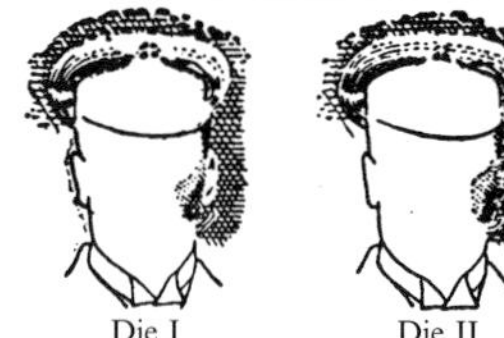

Die I Die II Die III

The remaining values were printed from double, i.e. head and duty, plates. There are at least four different head plates made from three different dies, which may be distinguished as follows:—

Die I. The King's left ear is neither shaded nor outlined; no outline to top of cap. Shank of anchor in cap badge is complete.

Die II. The ear is shaded all over, but has no outline. The top of the cap has a faint outline. Anchor as Die I.

Die III. The ear is shaded and outlined; a heavy continuous outline round the cap. Shank of anchor is broken just below the lowest line which crosses it.

(ii) Printed from double plates. Head Die I.

(a) P 14.

209 18 2d. black and grey . . . 10·00 7·00
210 3d. black and yellow . . . 70·00 7·50
211 4d. black and orange-red . . . 6·50 27·00
212 5d. black and green . . . 4·00 11·00
213 6d. black and mauve . . . £190 23·00
213*a* 8d. violet and green . . . £5000
214 2s. black and brown . . . 90·00 75·00

(b) P 15.

215 18 3d. black and yellow . . . 4·75 17·00
216 4d. black and orange-red . . . £130 17·00
217 6d. black and mauve . . . 5·00 6·00
217*a* 8d. violet and green . . . £18000 £20000
218 2s. black and brown . . . 10·00 32·00

(iii) Head Die II.

(a) P 14.

219 18 2d. black and grey . . . 13·00 3·00
220 2d. black and brownish grey . . . 42·00 5·50
221 3d. black and deep yellow . . . 27·00 5·00
222 3d. black and yellow . . . 60·00 5·00
223 3d. black and buff . . . 7·50 5·00
224 4d. black and orange-red . . . 18·00 7·00
225 4d. black and deep orange-red . . . 10·00 7·00
226 5d. black and grey-green . . . 13·00 28·00
227 5d. black and bright green . . . 11·00 28·00
228 6d. black and mauve . . . 27·00 3·00
229 6d. black and purple . . . 70·00 4·00
230 8d. violet and green . . . 11·00 48·00
231 10d. blue and carmine-red . . . 17·00 40·00
232 1s. black and greenish blue . . . 50·00 42·00
233 1s. black and turquoise-blue . . . 9·00 9·50
234 2s. black and brown . . . 70·00 8·50
235 2s. black and yellow-brown . . . £300 27·00
236 2s.6d. indigo and grey-brown . . . 45·00 29·00
236*a* 2s.6d. pale blue and brown . . . £850 50·00
236*b* 3s. brown and blue . . . 80·00 95·00
237 3s. chestnut and bright blue . . . 75·00 £100
238 5s. blue and yellow-green . . . £110 60·00
239 5s. blue and blue-green . . . 50·00 55·00
240 7s.6d. blackish purple and slate-black . . . £275 £300
241 10s. crimson and yellow-green . . . £170 £275
242 £1 black and purple . . . £375 £500
243 £1 black and violet . . . £325 £550

(b) P 15.

244 18 2d. black and grey . . . 6·50 6·50
245 4d. black and deep orange-vermilion . . . £1100 £250
246 8d. violet and green . . . £180 £150
247 10d. blue and red . . . 7·50 27·00
248 1s. black and greenish blue . . . 50·00 10·00
249 2s.6d. indigo and grey-brown . . . 38·00 70·00
250 3s. chocolate and blue . . . £600 £250
251 5s. blue and yellow-green . . . £120 £130
251*a* 5s. blue and blue-green . . . £1500
252 7s.6d. blackish purple and slate-black . . . £120 £170
253 10s. red and green . . . £170 £375
a. Frame double, one albino . . . £500
254 £1 black and purple . . . £1200 £1300
254*a* £1 black and deep purple . . . £3000 £2500

186s, 190s, 198s, 208s, 209s, 211s/12s, 215s, 217s/18s, 230s, 232s, 237s/8s, 240s/2s, 247s, 249s Optd "Specimen" *Set of* 19 . . . £2000

(iv) Head Die III (1919). Toned paper, yellowish gum.

(a) P 14.

255 18 2d. black and brownish grey . . . 9·00 4·75
256 2d. black and grey-black . . . 7·00 2·75
a. Imperf between (horiz pair) . . . £4500
b. Imperf between (horiz strip of 3) . . . £8500
c. Imperf vert (horiz pair) . . . £4000 £4000
257 2d. black and grey . . . 8·50 3·50
258 2d. black and sepia . . . 38·00 7·50
259 3d. black and yellow . . . 8·50 2·00
260 3d. black and ochre . . . 8·50 2·00
261 4d. black and orange-red . . . 11·00 4·75
262 4d. black and dull red . . . 10·00 6·00
263 5d. black and pale green . . . 6·00 28·00
a. Imperf between (horiz strip of 3) . . . £15000
264 5d. black and green . . . 6·00 28·00
265 6d. black and reddish mauve . . . 6·00 5·50
a. Imperf between (horiz pair) . . . £12000
266 6d. black and dull mauve . . . 6·00 5·50
267 8d. mauve and dull blue-green . . . 18·00 50·00
268 8d. mauve and greenish blue . . . 17·00 48·00
a. Imperf vert (horiz pair) . . . £9500
269 10d. indigo and carmine . . . 13·00 45·00
270 10d. blue and red . . . 12·00 45·00
271 1s. black and greenish blue . . . 8·50 6·50
272 1s. black and pale blue-green . . . 7·00 6·00
272*a* 1s. black and light blue . . . 9·50 13·00
272*b* 1s. black and green . . . 70·00 27·00
273 2s. black and brown . . . 12·00 15·00
aa. Imperf between (vert pair) . . . † £24000
273*a* 2s. black and yellow-brown . . . £2500 £120
274 2s.6d. dp ultramarine & grey-brn . . . 30·00 55·00
274*a* 2s.6d. pale blue and pale bistre-brown (*shades*) . . . 90·00 60·00
274*b* 3s. chestnut and light blue . . . £200 £140
275 5s. deep blue and blue-green (*shades*) . . . 70·00 50·00
276 5s. blue & pale yell-grn (*shades*) . . . 90·00 55·00
276*a* 7s.6d. maroon and slate-black . . . £750 £1100
277 10s. carmine-lake and yellow-green . . . £300 £180
278 £1 black and bright purple . . . £400 £550
279 £1 black and deep purple . . . £425 £550
279*a* £1 black and violet-indigo . . . £475 £650
279*b* £1 black and deep violet . . . £500 £650

(b) P 15.

279*c* 18 2d. black and brownish grey . . . £5500 £500

Half Penny (19) **Half-Penny.** (20)

1917 (15 Aug). *No. 190 surch at the Northern Rhodesian Administrative Press, Livingstone, with T* **19**, *in violet or violet-black.*

280 18 ½d.on 1d. rose-carmine (*shades*) . . . 2·50 7·00
a. Surch inverted . . . £1400 £1500
b. Letters "n n" spaced wider . . . 11·00 26·00
c. Letters "n y" spaced wider . . . 7·50 21·00

The setting was in two rows of 10 repeated three times in the sheet.

The two colours of the surcharge occur on the same sheet.

1917 (22 Sept). *No. 190 surch as T* **20** *(new setting with hyphen, and full stop after "Penny"), in deep violet.*

281 18 ½d. on 1d. rose-carmine (*shades*) . . . 1·75 7·00

1922–24. *New printings on white paper with clear white gum.*

(i) Single working plates.

(a) P 14.

282 18 ½d. dull green (1922) . . . 5·50 5·50
a. Imperf between (vert pair) . . . £1900 £1400
283 ½d. deep blue-green (1922) . . . 5·50 6·00
284 1d. bright rose (1922) . . . 8·00 5·50
285 1d. bright rose-scarlet (1923) . . . 8·00 5·50
a. Imperf between (horiz pair) . . . £1600
286 1d. aniline red (8.24) . . . 20·00 7·50
287 1½d. brown-ochre (1923) . . . 7·00 6·50
a. Imperf between (vert pair) . . . £2250 £1300

(b) P 15.

288 18 ½d. dull green (1923) . . . 42·00
289 1d. bright rose-scarlet (1923) . . . 48·00
290 1½d. brown-ochre (1923) . . . 48·00

(ii) Double plates. Head Die III.

(a) P 14.

291 18 2d. black and grey-purple (1922) . . . 6·00 3·75
292 2d. black and slate-purple (1923) . . . 6·00 4·50
293 3d. black and yellow (1922) . . . 10·00 25·00
294 4d. black & orange-vermilion (1922–3) . . . 11·00 30·00
295 6d. jet-black and lilac (1922–3) . . . 4·75 3·75
296 8d. mauve and pale blue-green (1922) . . . 30·00 70·00
297 8d. violet and grey-green (1923) . . . 32·00 70·00
298 10d. bright ultramarine and red (1922) . . . 10·00 55·00
299 10d. brt ultramarine & carm-red (1923) . . . 16·00 60·00
300 1s. black and dull blue (1922–3) . . . 7·50 9·50
a. Imperf between (horiz pair) . . . £10000
b. Imperf between (vert pair) . . . £12000
301 2s. black and brown (1922–3) . . . 19·00 42·00
302 2s.6d. ultramarine and sepia (1922) . . . 38·00 70·00
303 2s.6d. violet-blue & grey-brown (1923) . . . 48·00 70·00
304 3s. red-brown & turquoise-bl (1922) . . . 80·00 95·00
305 3s. red-brown and grey-blue (1923) . . . £100 £120
306 5s. brt ultramarine and emerald (1922) . . . 90·00 £110
307 5s. deep blue and bright green (1923) . . . 95·00 £110
308 7s.6d. brown-purple and slate (1922) . . . £190 £275
309 10s. crimson and brt yellow-green (1922) . . . £170 £200
310 10s. carmine and yellow-green (1923) . . . £180 £250
311 £1 black and magenta (1922) . . . £550 £750
311*a* £1 black and deep magenta (1923) . . . £500 £750

(b) P 15 (1923).

312 18 2d. black and slate-purple . . . 38·00
313 4d. black and orange-vermilion . . . 40·00
314 6d. jet-black and lilac . . . 50·00
315 8d. violet and grey-green . . . 55·00
316 10d. bright ultramarine & carmine-red . . . 60·00
317 1s. black and dull blue . . . 70·00
318 2s. black and brown . . . 95·00
319 2s.6d. violet-blue and grey-brown . . . £110
320 3s. red-brown and grey-blue . . . £140
321 5s. deep blue and bright green . . . £180
322 £1 black and deep magenta . . . £800

The 1922 printing shows the mesh of the paper very clearly through the gum. In the 1923 printing the gum is very smooth and the mesh of the paper is not so clearly seen. Where date is given as "(1922–23)" two printings were made, which do not differ sufficiently in colour to be listed separately.

Nos. 288/90 and 312/22 were never sent out to Rhodesia, but only issued in London. Any used copies could, therefore, only have been obtained by favour.

Southern Rhodesia, that part of the Company's territory south of the River Zambesi, became a self-governing colony on 1 October 1923. British South Africa Company rule continued in Northern Rhodesia until the administration was transferred to the Colonial Office on 1 April 1924.

The current stamps of Rhodesia, the Admiral series first issued in 1913, continued to be used in Southern Rhodesia until 1 April 1924 (invalidated 1 May 1924) and in Northern Rhodesia until 1 April 1925 (invalidated 30 September 1925).

St. Christopher *see* St. Kitts-Nevis

St. Helena

CROWN COLONY

PRICES FOR STAMPS ON COVER TO 1945		
Nos.	1/5	*from* × 12
Nos.	6/30	*from* × 10
Nos.	34/45	*from* × 15
Nos.	46/52	*from* × 6
Nos.	53/67	*from* × 5
No.	71	—
Nos.	72/86	*from* × 5
Nos.	87/8	*from* × 12
Nos.	89/95	*from* × 5
No.	96	—
Nos.	97/110	*from* × 5
Nos.	111/13	—
Nos.	114/40	*from* × 4

PERKINS BACON "CANCELLED". For notes on these handstamps, showing "CANCELLED" between horizontal bars forming an oval, see Catalogue Introduction.

1

ONE PENNY (2) **FOUR PENCE** (3)

(Recess P.B.)

1856 (1 Jan). Wmk Large Star, W w **1**. Imperf.

1 1 6d. bl (H/S "CANCELLED" in oval £6000) . . . £500 £1[illegible]

1861 (April (?)). Wmk Large Star, W w **1**.

(a) Clean-cut perf 14 to 16.

2 1 6d. blue . . . £1700 £[illegible]

(b) Rough perf 14 to 16.

2*a* 1 6d. blue . . . £400 £1[illegible]

NOTE: The issues which follow consist of 6d. stamps, T **1**, printed in various colours and (except in the case of the 6d. values) surcharged with a new value, as T **2** to **10**, *e.g.* stamps described as "1d." are, in fact, 1d. on 6d stamps, and so on.

The numbers in the Type column below refer to the *types of the lettering* of the surcharged value.

(Printed by D.L.R. from P.B. plate)

Two Types of Bar on 1d. value:
A. Bar 16–17 mm long.
B. Bar 18½–19 mm long.

1863 (July). *Surch as T* **2/3** *with thin bar approximately the sa[illegible] length as the words.* Wmk Crown CC. Imperf.

3 2 1d. lake (Type A) . . . £110 £1[illegible]
a. Surch double . . . £5000 £30[illegible]
b. Surch omitted . . . £15000
w. Wmk inverted . . . £275
4 1d. lake (Type B) . . . £120 £1[illegible]
a. Vert pair. Nos. 3/4 . . . £8000
5 3 4d. carmine (*bar* 15½–16½ mm) . . . £500 £2[illegible]
a. Surch double . . . £12000 £90[illegible]

ONE PENNY (4 (A)) **ONE PENNY** (4 (B)) **ONE PENN[illegible]** (4 (C))

TWO PENCE (5) **THREE PENCE** (6) **FOUR PENC[illegible]** (7)

ONE SHILLING **FIVE SHILLINGS**

(8) (9)

Three Types of Bar:
A. Thin bar (16½ to 17 mm) nearly the same length as the words.
B. Thick bar (14 to 14½ mm) much shorter than the words, except on the 2d. (Nos. 9, 22, 28) where it is nearly the same length.
C. Long bar (17 to 18 mm) same length as the words.

1864–80. *6d. as T* **1**, *without surcharge.* Wmk Crown CC.

(a) P 12½ (1864–73).

6 **4** 1d. lake (Type A) (1864) 45·00 24·00
a. Surch double £7500
7 1d. lake (Type B) (1868) £140 50·00
a. Surch double
b. Imperf £2250
w. Wmk inverted — £110
8 **4** 1d. lake (Type C) (1871) 90·00 17·00
a. Surch in blue-black £1000 £550
x. Wmk reversed £140
y. Wmk inverted and reversed £190
9 **5** 2d. yellow (Type B) (1868) £160 60·00
a. Imperf £10000
x. Wmk reversed £250
0 2d. yellow (Type C) (1873) 90·00 40·00
a. Surch in blue-black £4000 £2250
b. Surch double, one albino
x. Wmk reversed £130 70·00
1 **6** 3d. deep dull purple (Type B) (1868) 75·00 50·00
a. Surch double — £6000
b. Imperf £800
c. Light purple £2750 £750
x. Wmk reversed £140
2 3d. deep dull purple (Type A) (1873) 90·00 55·00
3 **7** 4d. carmine (Type A) (*words* 17 *mm long*) (1864) £130 48·00
a. Surch double † £5500
4 4d. carmine (Type B) (*words* 18 *mm long*) (1868) 90·00 50·00
a. Surch double † £5000
b. Surch double (18+19 *mm widths*) £19000 £9000
c. Imperf £10000
x. Wmk reversed £150 80·00
5 4d. carmine-rose (Type B) (*words* 19 *mm long*) (1868) £200 £120
a. Surch omitted † —
6 – 6d. dull blue (1871) £650 £100
a. Ultramarine (1873) £375 80·00
x. Wmk reversed † £150
7 **8** 1s. deep yellow-green (Type A) (1864) £250 26·00
a. Surch double † £19000
w. Wmk inverted — 55·00
8 1s. deep yellow-green (Type B) (1868) £550 £130
a. Surch double £13000
b. Imperf £13000
c. Surch omitted* £13000
9 1s. deep green (Type C) (1871) £450 16·00
a. Surch in blue-black
x. Wmk reversed £500 55·00
) **9** 5s. orange (Type B) (1868) 48·00 60·00
a. Yellow £450 £375
x. Wmk reversed £120 £140

(b) P 14 × 12½ (1876).

4 1d. lake (Type B) 70·00 15·00
w. Wmk inverted £120
2 **5** 2d. yellow (Type B) 90·00 50·00
3 3d. purple (Type B) £190 70·00
4 4d. carmine (Type B) (*words* 16½ *mm long*) £100 60·00
y. Wmk inverted and reversed £100 60·00
5 – 6d. milky blue £350 48·00
5 **8** 1s. deep green (Type C) £600 22·00

(c) P 14 (1880).

7 **4** 1d. lake (Type B) 80·00 16·00
3 **5** 2d. yellow (Type B) £100 28·00
) – 6d. milky blue £375 50·00
x. Wmk reversed † £100
8 1s. yellow-green (Type B) 20·00 12·00
y. Wmk inverted and reversed — 75·00

Two used examples of No. 15a are known, one being in the Royal ollection and the other damaged at bottom right.

*No. 18c is from a sheet of the 1s. with surcharge misplaced, the th row of 12 stamps being thus doubly surcharged and the tenth w without surcharge.

2½d

(10)

11

12

84–94. *T* **1** *surch. Bars similar to Type B above (except 2½d., T* **10**, *and the 1s., in which the bar is nearly the same length as the words). The 6d. as before without surcharge.* Wmk Crown CA. P 14.

– ½d. emerald (*words* 17 *mm*) (1884) 10·00 14·00
a. "N" and "Y" spaced £800
b. Surch double £1200 £1300
ba. Ditto. "N" and "Y" spaced £11000
– ½d. green (*words* 17 *mm*) (1885) 7·50 14·00
a. "N" and "Y" spaced £375 £550
x. Wmk reversed 8·50 16·00
– ½d. green (*words* 14½ *mm*) (1893) 2·00 2·25
a. "N" and "Y" spaced £1500
4 1d. red (1887) 4·00 3·25
x. Wmk reversed 4·25 4·00
1d. pale red (1890) 4·50 2·50
x. Wmk reversed 5·50 3·50
5 2d. yellow (1894) 2·00 6·00
10 2½d. ultramarine (1893) 2·50 5·50
a. Surch double £16000
b. Stamp doubly printed £8000
w. Wmk inverted 20·00
6 3d. deep mauve (1887) 6·50 9·50
a. Surch double — £9000

42 3d. deep reddish lilac (1887) 4·25 4·50
a. Surch double £8500 £6000
w. Wmk reversed 5·50 4·00
43 **7** 4d. pale brn (*words* 16½ *mm*) (1890) 19·00 23·00
a. Additional thin bar in surch (R. 7/4) £550
by. Wmk inverted and reversed 27·00
43*c* 4d. sepia (*words* 17 *mm*) (1894) 22·00 15·00
cx. Wmk reversed 25·00
44 – 6d. grey (1887) 19·00 4·50
x. Wmk reversed 26·00 4·25
45 **8** 1s. yellow-green (1894) 45·00 23·00
a. Surch double £4250
34/45 *Set of* 8 90·00 55·00
40s/1s, 43bys, 44s Optd "Specimen" *Set of* 4 £180

Examples of the above are sometimes found showing no watermark; these are from the bottom row of the sheet, which had escaped the watermark, the paper being intended for stamps of a different size to Type **1**.

Some are found without bar and others with bar at top of stamp, due to careless overprinting.

Nos. 34a and 35a occur on R. 18/12 and show a minimum space between the letters of 0.8 mm. Normal examples are spaced 0.5 mm, but some stamps show intermediate measurements due to loose type, On No. 34ba only one impression of the surcharge shows "N" and "Y" spaced. On the reset surcharge, No. 36, a similar variety occurs on R. 5/9.

Of the 2½d. with double surcharge only six copies exist, and of the 2½d. double printed, one row of 12 stamps existed on one sheet only.

CANCELLATIONS. Nos. 40/5 and No. 20 were sold as remainders in 1904 cancelled with a violet diamond-shaped grill with four interior bars extending over two stamps. These cannot be considered as *used* stamps, and they are consequently not priced in the list.

This violet obliteration is easily removed and many of these remainders have been cleaned and offered as unused; some are repostmarked with a date and name in thin type rather larger than the original, a usual date being "Ap.4.01."

(Typo D.L.R.)

1890–97. *Plate I for the 1½d. Plate II for the other values (for differences see Seychelles).* Wmk Crown CA. P 14.

46 **11** ½d. green (1897) 2·75 5·50
47 1d. carmine (1896) 14·00 1·25
48 1½d. red-brown and green (1890) 4·50 7·00
49 2d. orange-yellow (1896) 5·00 12·00
50 2½d. ultramarine (1896) 12·00 12·00
51 5d. mauve (1896) 11·00 28·00
52 10d. brown (1896) 23·00 60·00
46/52 *Set of* 7 65·00 £110
46s/52s Optd "Specimen" *Set of* 7 £300

The note below No. 45a *re* violet diamond-shaped grill cancellation also applies to Nos. 48/52.

1902. Wmk Crown CA. P 14.

53 **12** ½d. green (Mar) 1·50 2·25
54 1d. carmine (24 Feb) 6·00 70
53s/4s Optd "Specimen" *Set of* 2 75·00

13 Government House

14 The Wharf

(Typo D.L.R.)

1903 (May). Wmk Crown CC. P 14.

55 **13** ½d. brown and grey-green 2·00 3·25
w. Wmk inverted £110 £140
56 **14** 1d. black and carmine 1·50 35
57 **13** 2d. black and sage-green 6·50 1·25
58 **14** 8d. black and brown 22·00 32·00
59 **13** 1s. brown and brown-orange 23·00 40·00
60 **14** 2s. black and violet 48·00 85·00
55/60 *Set of* 6 90·00 £150
55s/60s Optd "Specimen" *Set of* 6 £225

A printing of the 1d. value in Type **14** in red only on Mult Crown CA paper was made in 1911, but not sold to the public. Examples are known overprinted "SPECIMEN" (*Price* £325).

15

(Typo D.L.R.)

1908 (May)–**11**. *Ordinary paper (2½d.) or chalk-surfaced paper (4d., 6d.).* P 14.

(a) Wmk Mult Crown CA.

64 **15** 2½d. blue 1·50 1·50
66 4d. black and red/*yellow* 6·00 17·00
a. Ordinary paper (1911) 3·00 17·00
67 6d. dull and deep purple 12·00 26·00
a. Ordinary paper (1911) 4·25 14·00

(b) Wmk Crown CA. Chalk-surfaced paper.

71 **15** 10s. green and red/*green* £180 £250
64/71 *Set of* 4 £180 £250
64s/71s Optd "Specimen" *Set of* 4 £250

Examples of Nos. 58/60 and 66/71 are known showing a forged St. Helena postmark dated "JY 28 1".

16

17

(Typo D.L.R.)

1912–16. Wmk Mult Crown CA. P 14.

72 **16** ½d. black and green 2·25 10·00
73 **17** 1d. black and carmine-red 4·75 1·75
a. Black and scarlet (1916) 12·00 20·00
74 1½d. black and dull orange (1913) 3·50 5·50
75 **16** 2d. black and greyish slate 4·50 1·75
76 **17** 2½d. black and bright blue 3·50 5·50
77 **16** 3d. black and purple/*yellow* (1913) 3·50 5·00
78 **17** 8d. black and dull purple 7·00 50·00
79 **16** 1s. black/*green* 9·00 35·00
80 **17** 2s. black and blue/*blue* 40·00 80·00
81 3s. black and violet (1913) 55·00 £130
72/81 *Set of* 10 £120 £275
72s/81s Optd "Specimen" *Set of* 10 £300

No. 73*a* is on thicker paper than 73.

18

19

Split "A" (R. 8/3 of left pane)

(Typo D.L.R.)

1912. *Chalk-surfaced paper.* Wmk Mult Crown CA. P 14.

83 **18** 4d. black and red/*yellow* 11·00 24·00
84 6d. dull and deep purple 4·00 5·00
83s/4s Optd "Specimen" *Set of* 2 85·00

1913. Wmk Mult Crown CA. P 14.

85 **19** 4d. black and red/*yellow* 8·00 2·75
a. Split "A" £225
86 6d. dull and deep purple 14·00 27·00
a. Split "A" £375
85s/6s Optd "Specimen" *Set of* 2 85·00

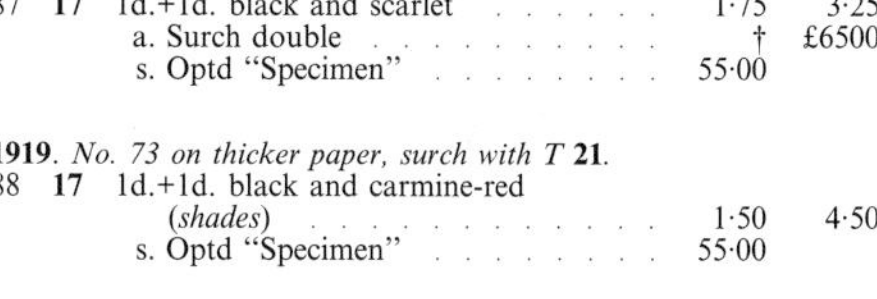

(20) (21)

1916 (Sept). *As No. 73a, on thin paper, surch with T* **20**.

87 **17** 1d.+1d. black and scarlet 1·75 3·25
a. Surch double † £6500
s. Optd "Specimen" 55·00

1919. *No. 73 on thicker paper, surch with T* **21**.

88 **17** 1d.+1d. black and carmine-red (*shades*) 1·50 4·50
s. Optd "Specimen" 55·00

1922 (Jan). *Printed in one colour.* Wmk Mult Script CA. P 14.

89 **17** 1d. green 1·75 28·00
w. Wmk inverted £150
y. Wmk inverted and reversed £150
90 1½d. rose-scarlet 10·00 28·00
91 **16** 3d. bright blue 19·00 55·00
y. Wmk inverted and reversed £160
89/91 *Set of* 3 28·00 £100
89s/91s Optd "Specimen" *Set of* 3 95·00

22 Badge of St. Helena

PLATE FLAWS ON THE 1922–37 ISSUE. Many constant plate varieties exist on both the vignette and duty plates of this issue. The three major varieties are illustrated and listed below.

a. Broken mainmast. Occurs on R. 2/1 of all sheets from the second printing onwards. It does not appear on Nos. 93/6 and 112/13 as these stamps only exist from the initial printing invoiced in May 1922.

b. Torn flag. Occurs on R. 4/6 of all sheets from printings up to and including that invoiced in December 1922. The flaw was retouched for the printing invoiced in December 1926 and so does not occur on Nos. 99*e*, 103 and 107/10.

c. Cleft rock. Occurs on R. 5/1 of all sheets from the second printing onwards. It does not appear on Nos. 93/6 and 112/13 as these stamps only exist from the initial printing invoiced in May 1922.

(Des T. Bruce. Typo D.L.R.)

1922 (June)–**37**. P 14

(*a*) Wmk Mult Crown CA. *Chalk-surfaced paper.*

92 **22** 4d. grey and black/*yellow* (2.23) . . 11·00 6·00
a. Broken mainmast . . £150 £160
b. Torn flag . . £150 £160
c. Cleft rock . . £130 £150
93 1s.6d. grey and green/*blue-green* . . 22·00 55·00
b. Torn flag . . £375
94 2s.6d. grey and red/*yellow* . . 25·00 55·00
b. Torn flag . . £425
95 5s. grey and green/*yellow* . . 38·00 85·00
b. Torn flag . . £550
96 £1 grey and purple/*red* . . £375 £450
b. Torn flag . . £1900
92/6 *Set of* 5 . . £400 £600
92s/6s Optd "Specimen" *Set of* 5 . . £500

The paper of No. 93 is bluish on the surface with a full green back.

(*b*) Wmk Mult Script CA. *Ordinary paper (1s.6d., 2s.6d., 5s.) or chalk-surfaced paper (others).*

97 **22** ½d. grey and black (2.23) . . 2·25 2·25
a. Broken mainmast . . 45·00 65·00
b. Torn flag . . £140 £180
c. Cleft rock . . 40·00 65·00
dw. Wmk inverted . . £300 £325
e. Grey-black and black (1937) . . 6·00 4·00
ea. Broken mainmast . . £110 £120
ec. Cleft rock . . £100 £110
98 1d. grey and green . . 2·50 1·60
a. Broken mainmast . . 50·00 65·00
b. Torn flag . . £120 £160
c. Cleft rock . . 45·00 65·00
99 1½d. rose-red (*shades*) (2.23) . . 2·75 13·00
a. Broken mainmast . . 75·00 £140
b. Torn flag . . 75·00 £140
c. Cleft rock . . 70·00 £140
dw. Wmk inverted . . £750
e. Deep carmine-red (1937) . . 80·00 85·00
ea. Broken mainmast . . £650 £750
ec. Cleft rock . . £650 £750
100 2d. grey and slate (2.23) . . 3·75 2·00
a. Broken mainmast . . 90·00 95·00
b. Torn flag . . £160 £190
c. Cleft rock . . 85·00 95·00
101 3d. bright blue (2.23) . . 2·00 4·00
a. Broken mainmast . . 85·00 £120
b. Torn flag . . 90·00 £120
c. Cleft rock . . 70·00 £110
x. Wmk reversed . . £375
103 5d. green and deep carmine/*green* (1927) . . 3·00 5·50
a. Broken mainmast . . £140 £190
c. Cleft rock . . £130 £190
d. Green and carmine-red/green (1936) . . 3·00 5·50
da. Broken mainmast . . £140 £190
dc. Cleft rock . . £130 £190
104 6d. grey and bright purple . . 4·50 8·00
a. Broken mainmast . . £170 £250
b. Torn flag . . £190 £275
c. Cleft rock . . £150 £250
105 8d. grey and bright violet (2.23) . . 3·75 7·00
a. Broken mainmast . . £150 £225
b. Torn flag . . £150 £225
c. Cleft rock . . £130 £225
106 1s. grey and brown . . 6·50 9·00
a. Broken mainmast . . £200 £250
b. Torn flag . . £250 £300
c. Cleft rock . . £180 £225
107 1s.6d. grey and green/*green* (1927) . . 15·00 45·00
a. Broken mainmast . . £275
c. Cleft rock . . £250
108 2s. purple and blue/*blue* (1927) . . 17·00 42·00
a. Broken mainmast . . £275
c. Cleft rock . . £250
109 2s.6d. grey and red/*yellow* (1927) . . 14·00 55·00
a. Broken mainmast . . £275
c. Cleft rock . . £250
110 5s. grey and green/*yellow* (1927) . . 38·00 75·00
a. Broken mainmast . . £425
c. Cleft rock . . £400
111 7s.6d. brownish grey and yellow-orange . . 75·00 £120
b. Torn flag . . £700 £1200
d. Blackish brown and orange (1937) . . £550 £650
da. Broken mainmast . . £3750
dc. Cleft rock . . £3750
112 10s. grey and olive-green . . £110 £170
b. Torn flag . . £1100
113 15s. grey and purple/*blue* . . £800 £1500
b. Torn flag . . £3500 £5000
97/112 *Set of* 15 . . £275 £500
97s/113s Optd "Specimen" *Set of* 16 . . £1000

Examples of all values are known showing a forged St. Helena postmark dated "DE 18 27".

23 Lot and Lot's Wife

24 The "Plantation"

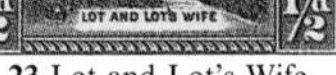

30 St. Helena

32 Badge of St. Helena

(Recess B.W.)

1934 (23 April). *Centenary of British Colonisation. T* **23/4**, **30**, **32** *and similar horiz designs.* Wmk Mult Script CA. P 12.

114 ½d. black and purple . . 1·00 80
115 1d. black and green . . 65 85
116 1½d. black and scarlet . . 2·50 3·25
117 2d. black and orange . . 2·25 1·25
118 3d. black and blue . . 1·40 4·50
119 6d. black and light blue . . 3·25 3·00
120 1s. black and chocolate . . 6·50 18·00
121 2s.6d. black and lake . . 35·00 48·00
122 5s. black and chocolate . . 75·00 80·00
123 10s. black and purple . . £225 £250
114/23 *Set of* 10 . . £325 £375
114s/23s Perf "Specimen" *Set of* 10 . . £375

Design:—1½d. Map of St. Helena; 2d. Quay at Jamestown; 3d. James Valley; 6d. Jamestown; 1s. Munden's Promontory; 5s. High Knoll.

Examples of all values are known showing a forged St. Helena postmark dated "MY 12 34".

1935 (6 May). *Silver Jubilee. As Nos. 91/4 of Antigua.* P 13½ × 14.

124 1½d. deep blue and carmine . . 1·00 5·50
f. Diagonal line by turret . . 75·00 £150
125 2d. ultramarine and grey . . 1·50 90
f. Diagonal line by turret . . 90·00
g. Dot to left of chapel . . £130
126 6d. green and indigo . . 6·50 3·25
a. Frame printed double, one albino . . £1500
f. Diagonal line by turret . . £170
h. Dot by flagstaff . . £275
127 1s. slate and purple . . 12·00 14·00
h. Dot by flagstaff . . £350
i. Dash by turret . . £350
124/7 *Set of* 4 . . 19·00 21·00
124s/7s Perf "Specimen" *Set of* 4 . . £120

For illustrations of plate varieties see Omnibus section following Zanzibar.

1937 (19 May). *Coronation. As Nos. 95/7 of Antigua, but ptd by D.L.R.* P 14.

128 1d. green . . 40 60
129 2d. orange . . 55 35
130 3d. bright blue . . 80 50
128/30 *Set of* 3 . . 1·60 1·25
128s/30s Perf "Specimen" *Set of* 3 . . 70·00

33 Badge of St. Helena

(Recess Waterlow)

1938 (12 May)–**44**. Wmk Mult Script CA. P 12½.

131 **33** ½d. violet . . 10 65
132 1d. green . . 9·00 2·25
132*a* 1d. yellow-orange (8.7.40) . . 20 30
133 1½d. scarlet . . 20 40
134 2d. red-orange . . 20 15
135 3d. ultramarine . . 80·00 18·00
135*a* 3d. grey (8.7.40) . . 30 30
135*b* 4d. ultramarine (8.7.40) . . 2·00 80
136 6d. light blue . . 2·00 80
136*a* 8d. sage-green (8.7.40) . . 3·25 9
b. Olive-green (24.5.44) . . 4·50 4·0
137 1s. sepia . . 1·00 3
138 2s.6d. maroon . . 17·00 6·5
139 5s. chocolate . . 18·00 12·0
140 10s. purple . . 18·00 18·0
131/40 *Set of* 14 . . £130 50·0
131s/40s Perf "Specimen" *Set of* 14 . . £325

See also Nos. 149/51.

1946 (21 Oct). *Victory. As Nos. 110/11 of Antigua.*

141 2d. red-orange . . 20 2
142 4d. blue . . 20 2
141s/2s Perf "Specimen" *Set of* 2 . . 70·00

1948 (20 Oct). *Royal Silver Wedding. As Nos. 112/13 of Antigua.*

143 3d. black . . 30 2
144 10s. violet-blue . . 24·00 29·0

1949 (10 Oct). *75th Anniv of U.P.U. As Nos. 114/17 of Antigua.*

145 3d. carmine . . 25 7
146 4d. deep blue . . 3·00 1·2
147 6d. olive . . 45 1·5
148 1s. blue-black . . 35 1·1
145/8 *Set of* 4 . . 3·50 4·0

1949 (1 Nov). Wmk Mult Script CA. P 12½.

149 **33** 1d. black and green . . 1·00 1·2
150 1½d. black and carmine . . 1·00 1·2
151 2d. black and scarlet . . 1·00 1·5
149/51 *Set of* 3 . . 2·75 3·5

St. Kitts-Nevis

ST. CHRISTOPHER

From 1760 the postal service for St. Christopher was organise by the Deputy Postmaster General on Antigua. It was not until Ma 1779 that the first postmaster was appointed to the island and th use of postmarks on outgoing mail commenced.

Stamps of Great Britain were used between May 1858 and th end of March 1860 when control of the postal services passed t the local authorities. In the years which followed, prior to th introduction of St. Christopher stamps in April 1870, a circul "PAID" handstamp was used on overseas mail.

BASSETERRE

Stamps of GREAT BRITAIN *cancelled* "A 12" *as Type* Z **1** *Jamaica.*

1858–60.

Z1 1d. rose-red (1857), perf 14 . . £6
Z2 2d. blue (1858) (Plate No. 7) . . £9
Z3 4d. rose (1857) . . £3
Z4 6d. lilac (1856) . . £2
Z5 1s. green (1856) . . £15

PRICES FOR STAMPS ON COVER		
Nos. 1/9	*from* × 25	
Nos. 11/21	*from* × 30	
Nos. 22/6	*from* × 25	
No. 27	—	
No. 28	*from* × 30	
Nos. R1/6	—	

1

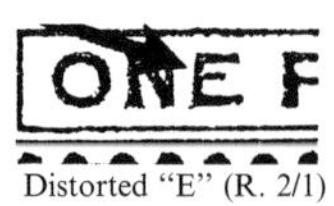

Distorted "E" (R. 2/1)

1870 (1 Apr)–**79**. Wmk Crown CC.

(*a*) P 12½.

1 **1** 1d. dull rose . . 85·00 48·
a. Wmk sideways . . £225 £1
w. Wmk inverted
2 1d. magenta (*shades*) (1871) . . 70·00 30·
a. Wmk sideways . . † £5
w. Wmk inverted . . £100 65·
x. Wmk reversed
4 6d. yellow-green . . £120 19·
w. Wmk inverted
5 6d. green (1871) . . £120 7·

(*b*) P 14.

6 **1** 1d. magenta (*shades*) (1875) . . 65·00 7·
a. Bisected diag or vert (½d.) (on cover) (3.82) . . † £17
w. Wmk inverted
7 2½d. red-brown (11.79) . . £180 £2
8 4d. blue (11.79) . . £180 15·
a. Wmk sideways . . £950 £1
w. Wmk inverted . . £325 45
9 6d. green (1876) . . 55·00 5·
a. Imperf between (pair)
b. Wmk sideways . . £550 £1
x. Wmk reversed . . £180

The magenta used for the 1d. was a fugitive colour which rea to both light and water.

No. 6a was authorised for use between March and June 1882 make up the 2½d. letter rate and for ½d. book post.

1882 (June)–**90**. Wmk Crown CA. P 14.

11 **1** ½d. dull green . . 1·50 1
a. Wmk sideways . . £275
x. Wmk reversed

2 1d. dull magenta £550 70·00
a. Bisected diagonally (½d.) (on cover)
3 1d. carmine-rose (2.84) 1·25 2·25
a. Bisected (½d.) (on cover)
b. Distorted "E" 16·00
x. Wmk reversed
4 2½d. pale red-brown £180 60·00
5 2½d. deep red-brown £190 65·00
6 2½d. ultramarine (2.84) 1·75 1·50
7 4d. blue £450 20·00
w. Wmk inverted
8 4d. grey (10.84) 1·25 1·00
9 6d. olive-brown (3.90) 85·00 £350
w. Wmk inverted
20 1s. mauve (6.86) 90·00 65·00
w. Wmk inverted — £130
21 1s. bright mauve (1890) 85·00 £160
9s/20s Optd "Specimen" *Set of* 2 £120

FOUR PENCE (2) Halfpenny (3)

884 (Dec). *No. 9 surch with T* **2** *by* The Advertiser Press.
2 1 4d.on 6d. green 65·00 50·00
a. Full stop after "PENCE" 65·00 50·00
b. Surch double — £2250
No. 22a occurred on alternate stamps.

885 (Mar). *No. 13 bisected and each half diagonally surch with T* **3**.
3 1 ½d.on half of 1d. carmine-rose 25·00 40·00
a. Unsevered pair £120 £120
ab. Ditto, one surch inverted £400 £275
b. Surch inverted £225 £110
ba. Ditto, unsevered pair £1000
c. Surch double

ONE PENNY. (4) 4d. (5)

886 (June). *No. 9 surch with T* **4** *or* **5** *each showing a manuscript line through the original value.*
4 1 1d.on 6d. green 20·00 30·00
a. Surch inverted £7000
b. Surch double — £1400
5 4d.on 6d. green 48·00 90·00
a. No stop after "d" £190 £275
b. Surch double £1700 £1800
No. 24b is only known penmarked with dates between 21 July and 3 August 1886, or with violet handstamp.

887 (May). *No. 11 surch with T* **4** *showing a manuscript line through the original value.*
5 1 1d. on ½d. dull green 35·00 42·00

ONE PENNY. (7)

888 (May). *No. 16 surch.*

(a) With T **4**. *Original value unobliterated.*
1 1d. on 2½d. ultramarine £15000 £10000

(b) With T **7** *showing a manuscript line through the original value.*
1 1d.on 2½d. ultramarine 65·00 65·00
a. Surch inverted £12000 £7000

The 1d. of Antigua was used provisionally in St. Christopher between February and March 1890 during a shortage of 1d. stamps. Such use can be distinguished by the postmark, which is "A 12" in place of "A02" (*price from* £130 *used*).

REVENUE STAMPS USED FOR POSTAGE

Saint Christopher (R 1) SAINT KITTS NEVIS REVENUE (R 2)

83. *Nos. F6 and F8 of Nevis optd with Type* R **1**, *in violet.* Wmk Crown CA. P 14.
1d. lilac-mauve £275
2 6d. green 75·00 £130

85. *Optd with Type* R **2**. Wmk Crown CA. P 14.
3 1 1d. rose 2·25 14·00
4 3d. mauve 14·00 65·00
5 6d. orange-brown 8·50 50·00
6 1s. olive 2·50 42·00
Other fiscal stamps with overprints as above also exist, but none of these were ever available for postal purposes.

The stamps for St. Christopher were superseded by the general issue for Leeward Islands on 31 October 1890.
Stamps for St. Kitts, issued from 1980 onwards will be found listed after those for the combined colony.

NEVIS

Little is known concerning the early postal affairs of Nevis, although several covers exist from the island in the 1660s. It is recorded that the British G.P.O. was to establish a branch office on the island under an Act of Parliament of 1710, although arrangements may not have been finalised for a number of years afterwards. Nevis appears as "a new office" in the P.O. Accounts of 1787.

Stamps of Great Britain were used on the island from May 1858 until the colonial authorities assumed control of the postal service on 1 May 1860. Between this date and the introduction of Nevis stamps in 1861 No. CC1 was again used on overseas mail.

CHARLESTOWN

CROWNED-CIRCLE HANDSTAMPS

CC 1

CC1 CC **1** NEVIS (R.) (9.1852)
Price on cover £3500
No. CC1, struck in black or red (1882) was later used on several occasions up to 1882 when there were shortages of adhesive stamps.

Stamps of GREAT BRITAIN *cancelled* "A 09" *as Type* Z **1** *of Jamaica.*

1858–60.
Z1 1d. rose-red (1857), perf 14 £450
Z2 2d. blue (1858) (Plate Nos. 7, 8) £1700
Z3 4d. rose (1857) £375
Z4 6d. lilac (1856) £300
Z5 1s. green (1856)

PRICES FOR STAMPS ON COVER		
Nos. 5/22	*from* × 20	
Nos. 23/4	*from* × 10	
Nos. 25/34	*from* × 20	
Nos. 35/6	*from* × 10	
Nos. F1/8	*from* × 30	

NEVIS ONE PENNY 1 NEVIS FOUR PENCE 2 NEVIS SIX PENCE 3 NEVIS ONE SHILLING 4

The designs on the stamps refer to a medicinal spring on the island

(Recess Nissen & Parker, London)

1861. *Greyish paper.* P 13.
5 1 1d. dull lake 75·00 48·00
a. On blued paper £250 £120
6 2 4d. rose £100 60·00
a. On blued paper £750 £170
7 3 6d. grey-lilac £100 50·00
a. On blued paper £600 £225
8 4 1s. green £250 70·00
a. On blued paper £900 £190
Nos. 5/8 and later printings of Types **1/4** were in sheets of 12 (3 × 4).

1866–76. *White paper.* P 15.
9 1 1d. pale red 42·00 40·00
10 1d. deep red 42·00 40·00
11 2 4d. orange £100 21·00
12 4d. deep orange £100 21·00
13 4 1s. blue-green £225 29·00
14 1s. yellow-green (1876) £850 £110
a. Vertically laid paper £15000 £5000
b. No. 9 on sheet with crossed lines on hill £3500 £500
c. Ditto. On laid paper † £11000
Examples of the 4d. exist showing part of a papermakers watermark reading "A. COWAN & SONS EXTRA SUPERFINE".

(Lithographed by transfer from the engraved plates Nissen and Parker, London)

1876–78.

(a) P 15.
15 1 1d. pale rose-red 20·00 15·00
a. Imperf (pair) £700
16 1d. deep rose-red 29·00 25·00
17 1d. vermilion-red 25·00 25·00
a. Bisected (½d.) (on cover) † £2000
18 2 4d. orange-yellow (1878) £160 29·00
a. Imperf between (vert pair) £4500
19 3 6d. grey (1878) £200 £180
20 4 1s. pale green (1878) 85·00 £100
a. Imperf
b. Imperf between (horiz strip of three) £6000
c. No. 9 on sheet with crossed lines on hill £225
21 1s. deep green 95·00 £130
c. No. 9 on sheet with crossed lines on hill £850

(b) P 11½.
22 1 1d. vermilion-red (1878) 45·00 50·00
a. Bisected (½d.) (on cover) † £2000
b. Imperf (pair) £450
c. Imperf between (horiz pair)
No. 21c occurs on a small part of the deep green printing only.

RETOUCHES. 1d. Lithograph.

i. No. 1 on sheet. Top of hill over kneeling figure redrawn by five thick lines and eight small slanting lines £140 £150
ii. No. 1 on sheet. Another retouch. Three series of short vertical strokes behind the kneeling figure £140 £150
iii. No. 3 on sheet. Right upper corner star and border below star retouched £140 £150
iv. No. 9 on sheet. Retouch in same position as on No. 3 but differing in detail £160 £170
v. No. 12 on sheet. Dress of standing figure retouched by a number of horizontal and vertical lines £140 £150

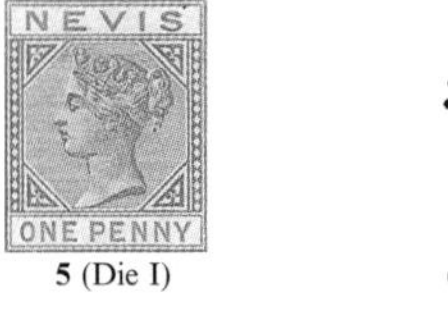

5 (Die I) (6)

(Typo D.L.R.)

1879–80. Wmk Crown CC. P 14.
23 5 1d. lilac-mauve (1880) 70·00 32·00
a. Bisected (½d.) (on cover) † £950
w. Wmk inverted
24 2½d. red-brown £110 85·00

1882–90. Wmk Crown CA. P 14.
25 5 ½d. dull green (11.83) 4·75 13·00
a. Top left triangle detached £170
26 1d. lilac-mauve 90·00 28·00
a. Bisected (½d.) on cover (1883) † £700
27 1d. dull rose (11.83) 24·00 16·00
a. Carmine (1884) 9·00 9·00
ab. Top left triangle detached £250
28 2½d. red-brown £110 50·00
29 2½d. ultramarine (11.83) 17·00 16·00
a. Top left triangle detached £425
30 4d. blue £300 50·00
31 4d. grey (1884) 9·50 3·50
a. Top left triangle detached £350 £325
32 6d. green (11.83) £375 £350
33 6d. chestnut (10.88) 22·00 60·00
a. Top left triangle detached £475
34 1s. pale violet (3.90) £100 £180
a. Top left triangle detached £1100
33s/4s Optd "Specimen" *Set of* 2 £110
For illustration of the "top left triangle detached" variety, which occurs on Plate 2 R. 3/3 of the right pane, see below Montserrat No. 5.

1883 (4 Sept). *No. 26 bisected vertically and surch with T* **6**, *reading upwards or downwards.*
35 ½d.on half 1d. lilac-mauve (V.) £850 45·00
a. Surch double — £300
b. Surch on half "REVENUE" stamp No. F6 — £550
36 ½d.on half 1d. lilac-mauve £1000 42·00
a. Surch double — £300
b. Unsevered pair £3500 £550
c. Surch on half "REVENUE" stamp No. F6 — £550

FISCALS USED FOR POSTAGE

Revenue (F 1) REVENUE (F 2)

1882.

(a) Stamps of 1876–78 optd with Type F **1**.
F1 1 1d. bright red 55·00
F2 2 1d. rose 55·00 22·00
F3 4d. orange 95·00
F4 3 6d. grey £160
F5 4 1s. green £180
a. No. 9 on sheet with crossed lines on hill

(b) Nos. 26, 30 and 32 optd with Type F **2**.
F6 5 1d. lilac-mauve 55·00 50·00
a. Bisected (½d.) (on cover)
F7 4d. blue 32·00 55·00
F8 6d. green 20·00 60·00
Nos. F1/5 were produced from fresh transfers. Similar "REVENUE" handstamps, both with and without stop, were also applied to postage issues.

The stamps of Nevis were superseded by the general issue for Leeward Islands on 31 October 1890.

ST. KITTS-NEVIS

CROWN COLONY

Stamps for the combined colony were introduced in 1903, and were used concurrently with the general issues of Leeward Islands until the latter were withdrawn on 1 July 1956.

PRICES FOR STAMPS ON COVER TO 1945	
Nos. 1/9	*from* × 3

No.	10	—
Nos.	11/20	*from* × 3
No.	21	—
Nos.	22/3	*from* × 15
Nos.	24/34	*from* × 3
Nos.	35/6	—
Nos.	37/47	*from* × 2
Nos.	47*a*/*b*	—
Nos.	48/57	*from* × 2
Nos.	58/60	—
Nos.	61/4	*from* × 2
Nos.	65/7	*from* × 5
Nos.	68/77	*from* × 2

1 Christopher Columbus

2 Medicinal Spring

(Typo D.L.R.)

1903. Wmk Crown CA. P 14.

No.	Type			
1	**1**	½d. dull purple and deep green	1·75	70
2	**2**	1d. grey-black and carmine	4·75	20
3	**1**	2d. dull purple and brown	2·25	11·00
4		2½d. grey-black and blue	17·00	4·25
5	**2**	3d. deep green and orange	13·00	27·00
6	**1**	6d. grey-black and bright purple	4·25	35·00
7		1s. grey-green and orange	6·00	11·00
8	**2**	2s. deep green and grey-black	12·00	20·00
9	**1**	2s.6d. grey-black and violet	18·00	42·00
10	**2**	5s. dull purple and sage-green	55·00	55·00
1/10 *Set of* 10			£120	£180
1s/10s Optd "Specimen" *Set of* 10			£130	

1905–18. *Chalk-surfaced paper (1d. (No. 13), 5s.) or ordinary paper (others).* Wmk Mult Crown CA. P 14.

No.	Type			
11	**1**	½d. dull purple and deep green	6·00	5·50
12		½d. grey-green (1907)	1·00	60
		a. Dull blue-green (1916)	50	1·75
13	**2**	1d. grey-black and carmine (1906)	1·75	25
14		1d. carmine (1907)	2·25	15
		a. Scarlet (1916)	70	20
15	**1**	2d. dull purple and brown	9·00	8·00
		a. Chalk-surfaced paper (1906)	6·50	8·00
16		2½d. grey-black and blue (1907)	14·00	3·25
17		2½d. bright blue (1907)	2·50	50
18	**2**	3d. deep green and orange	7·00	8·50
		a. Chalk-surfaced paper (1906)	2·75	2·75
19	**1**	6d. grey-black and deep violet	22·00	42·00
		a. Chalk-surfaced paper. *Grey-black and deep purple* (1908)	15·00	25·00
		ab. Grey-black and bright purple (1916)	5·50	25·00
20		1s. grey-green and orange (1909)	22·00	38·00
		a. Chalk-surfaced paper	3·50	30·00
21	**2**	5s. dull purple and sage-green (11.18)	32·00	75·00
11/21 *Set of* 11			65·00	£130
12s, 14s, 17s Optd "Specimen" *Set of* 3			60·00	

WAR TAX (**3**)

WAR STAMP (**3a**)

1916 (Oct). *Optd with T* **3**. Wmk Mult Crown CA. P 14.

No.	Type			
22	**1**	½d. dull blue-green (No. 12*a*)	1·00	50
		a. Deep green	1·00	50
		s. Optd "Specimen"	40·00	
		x. Wmk reversed	35·00	

No. 22*a* was a special printing produced for this overprint.

1918 (Aug). *Optd with T* **3a**. Wmk Mult Crown CA. P 14.

No.	Type			
23	**1**	1½d. orange	80	80
		a. Short opt (right pane R. 10/1)	17·00	
		s. Optd "Specimen"	45·00	

No. 23 was a special printing produced for this overprint.
No. 23a shows the overprint 2 mm high instead of 2½ mm.

4

5

(Typo D.L.R.)

1920–22. *Ordinary paper (½d. to 2½d.) or chalk-surfaced paper (others).* Wmk Mult Crown CA (sideways*). P 14.

No.	Type			
24	**4**	½d. blue-green	3·75	5·50
25	**5**	1d. scarlet	2·25	6·00
26	**4**	1½d. orange-yellow	1·25	1·75
		x. Wmk sideways reversed	75·00	
		y. Wmk sideways inverted and reversed		
27	**5**	2d. slate-grey	3·00	3·75
28	**4**	2½d. ultramarine	2·00	9·00
		a. "A" of "CA" missing from wmk	£350	
29	**5**	3d. purple/*yellow*	1·75	11·00
30	**4**	6d. dull purple and bright mauve	3·50	11·00
31	**5**	1s. grey and black/*green*	3·50	4·00
32	**4**	2s. dull purple and blue/*blue*	15·00	22·00
		x. Wmk sideways reversed	£150	
33	**5**	2s.6d. grey and red/*blue*	5·00	30·00
		y. Wmk sideways inverted and reversed	£150	
34	**4**	5s. green and red/*pale yellow*	5·00	40·00
		x. Wmk sideways reversed	£100	
35	**5**	10s. green and red/*green*	12·00	48·00
36	**4**	£1 purple and black/*red* (1922)	£225	£300
24/36 *Set of* 13			£250	£400
24s/36s Optd "Specimen" *Set of* 13			£300	

*The normal sideways watermark shows Crown to left of CA, *as seen from the back of the stamp.*

Examples of most values are known showing a forged St. Kitts postmark dated "8 DE 23".

1921–29. *Chalk-surfaced paper (2½d. (No. 44), 3d. (No. 45a) and 6d. to 5s.) or ordinary.* Wmk Mult Script CA (sideways*). P 14.

No.	Type			
37	**4**	½d. blue-green	2·25	1·50
		a. Yellow-green (1922)	1·50	80
38	**5**	1d. rose-carmine	65	15
		sa. Perf "Specimen" (1929)	70·00	
39		1d. deep violet (1922)	3·75	90
		a. Pale violet (1929)	7·00	1·50
40	**4**	1½d. red (1925)	2·50	2·75
40*a*		1½d. red-brown (1929)	1·00	30
41	**5**	2d. slate-grey (1922)	50	60
42	**4**	2½d. pale bright blue (1922)	3·00	2·25
43		2½d. brown (1922)	2·25	9·00
44		2½d. ultramarine (1927)	1·50	2·25
45	**5**	3d. dull ultramarine (1922)	1·00	4·25
45*a*		3d. purple/*yellow* (1927)	75	4·50
46	**4**	6d. dull and bright purple (1924)	5·00	5·50
		aw. Wmk Crown to right of CA	4·00	5·00
46*b*	**5**	1s. black/*green* (1929)	3·75	6·50
47	**4**	2s. purple and blue/*blue* (1922)	8·00	23·00
47*a*	**5**	2s.6d. black and red/*blue* (1927)	15·00	29·00
47*b*	**4**	5s. green and red/*yellow* (1929)	40·00	70·00
37/47*b* *Set of* 16			75·00	£150
37s/47*b*s Optd or Perf (1½d. red-brown, 1s., 5s.) "Specimen" *Set of* 16			£350	

*The normal watermark shows Crown to left of CA, *as seen from the back of the stamp.*

6 Old Road Bay and Mount Misery

(Typo D.L.R.)

1923. *Tercentenary of Colony. Chalk-surfaced paper.* P 14.

(*a*) Wmk Mult Script CA (sideways).

No.	Type			
48	**6**	½d. black and green	2·25	7·00
49		1d. black and bright violet	4·50	1·50
50		1½d. black and scarlet	4·50	10·00
51		2d. black and slate-grey	3·75	1·50
52		2½d. black and brown	6·00	32·00
53		3d. black and ultramarine	3·75	15·00
54		6d. black and bright purple	9·50	32·00
55		1s. black and sage-green	14·00	32·00
56		2s. black and blue/*blue*	40·00	55·00
57		2s.6d. black and red/*blue*	48·00	70·00
58		10s. black and red/*emerald*	£250	£375

(*b*) Wmk Mult Crown CA (sideways).

No.	Type			
59	**6**	5s. black and red/*pale yellow*	70·00	£170
60		£1 black and purple/*red*	£700	£1300
48/60 *Set of* 13			£1000	£1900
48s/60s Optd "Specimen" *Set of* 13			£650	

Examples of all values are known showing a forged St. Kitts postmark dated "8 DE 23."

1935 (6 May). *Silver Jubilee. As Nos. 91/4 of Antigua, but ptd by Waterlow.* P 11 × 12.

No.			
61	1d. deep blue and scarlet	1·00	70
	k. Kite and vertical log	70·00	
	l. Kite and horizontal log	£100	
62	1½d. ultramarine and grey	75	75
	k. Kite and vertical log	65·00	70·00
63	2½d. brown and deep blue	1·00	80
64	1s. slate and purple	5·50	15·00
	k. Kite and vertical log	£200	
	l. Kite and horizontal log	£225	
61/4 *Set of* 4		7·50	15·00
61s/4s Perf "Specimen" *Set of* 4		85·00	

For illustrations of plate varieties see Omnibus section following Zanzibar.

1937 (12 May). *Coronation. As Nos. 95/7 of Antigua, but ptd by D.L.R.* P 14.

No.			
65	1d. scarlet	30	20
66	1½d. buff	40	10
67	2½d. bright blue	60	60
65/7 *Set of* 3		1·10	80
65s/7s Perf "Specimen" *Set of* 3		65·00	

Nos. 61/7 are inscribed "ST. CHRISTOPHER AND NEVIS".

7 King George VI

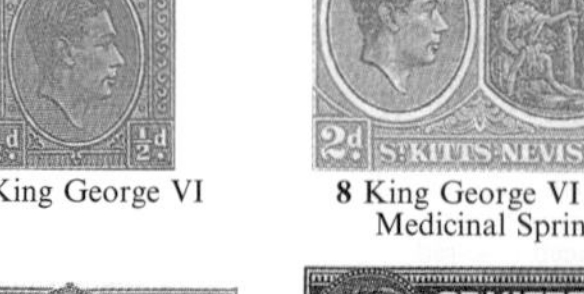

8 King George VI and Medicinal Spring

9 King George VI and Christopher Columbus

10 King George VI and Anguilla Island

Break in value tablet (R. 12/5) (1947 ptg only)

Break in oval (R. 12/1) (1938 ptg only)

Break in value tablet frame (R. 3/2)

Break in value tablet frame (R. 12/3) (ptgs between 1941 and 1945)

Break in frame above ornament (R. 2/4) (ptgs between 1941 and 1950)

Break in oval at foot (R. 12/5) (ptgs between 1941 and 1945 only). Sometimes touched-in by hand painting)

Break in oval at left (R. 7/1) (ptgs between 1941 and 1945 only)

(Typo; centre litho (T **10**). D.L.R.)

1938 (15 Aug)–**50**. *Chalk-surfaced paper (10s., £1).* Wmk Mu[lt] Script CA (sideways on T **8** and **9**). P 14 (T **7** and **10**) or 13 × [12] (T **8/9**).

No.	Type			
68	**7**	½d. green	4·00	
		a. Blue-green (5.4.43)	10	
69		1d. scarlet	6·00	
		a. Carmine (5.43)	1·50	
		b. Carmine-pink (4.47)	60·00	16·
		c. Rose-red (7.47)	1·50	
70		1½d. orange	20	
71	**8**	2d. scarlet and grey	21·00	2·
		a. Chalk-surfaced paper. *Carmine and deep grey* (5.41*)	55·00	10·
		b. Perf 14. *Scarlet & pale grey* (6.43*)	1·25	1·
		ba. Scarlet and deep grey (6.42*)	23·00	5·
		c. Perf 14. Chalk-surfaced paper. *Scarlet and pale grey* (2.50*)	2·75	3·
72	**7**	2½d. ultramarine	3·50	
		a. Bright ultramarine (5.4.43)	70	
73	**8**	3d. dull reddish purple and scarlet	17·00	4·
		a. Chalk-surfaced paper. *Brown-purple and carmine-red* (1940)	21·00	5·
		b. Perf 14. Chalk-surfaced paper. *Dull reddish purple & carm-red* (6.43*)	35·00	3·
		c. Perf 14. Ordinary paper. *Reddish lilac and scarlet* (8.46*)	3·75	12
		d. Perf 14. Ordinary paper. *Purple and bright scarlet* (1.46*)	12·00	7·
		da. Break in value tablet	£150	
		e. Perf 14. Chalk-surfaced paper. *Deep purple and scarlet* (12.47*)	75·00	19
		f. Perf 14. Ordinary paper. *Rose-lilac and bright scarlet* (1.49*)	9·00	9·
		g. Perf 14. Chalk-surfaced paper. *Deep reddish purple & brt scarlet* (8.50*)	5·50	5
74	**9**	6d. green and bright purple	6·50	2
		a. Break in oval	£130	
		b. Perf 14. Chalk-surfaced paper. *Green and deep claret* (17.5.43*)	55·00	11
		c. Perf 14. Ordinary paper. *Green and purple* (10.44*)	5·00	1
		d. Perf 14. Chalk-surfaced paper. *Green and purple* (11.48*)	5·00	3
75	**8**	1s. black and green	12·00	1
		a. Break in value tablet frame	£190	
		b. Perf 14 (8.43*)	4·00	
		ba. Break in value tablet frame	£100	
		c. Perf 14. Chalk-surfaced paper (7.50*)	5·00	5
		ca. Break in value tablet frame	£110	
76		2s.6d. black and scarlet	32·00	9
		a. Perf 14. Chalk-surfaced paper (12.43*)	16·00	6
		ab. Ordinary paper (5.45*)	12·00	3
77	**9**	5s. grey-green and scarlet	65·00	19
		a. Perf 14. Chalk-surfaced paper (25.10.43*)	£130	28
		ab. Break in value tablet frame	£650	£
		ac. Break in frame above ornament	£650	£
		ad. Break in oval at foot	£650	£

ae. Break in oval at left £650 £250
b. Perf 14. Ordinary paper. *Bluish green and scarlet* (7.11.45*) . . . 24·00 12·00
ba. Break in value tablet frame . . . £275 £150
bb. Break in frame above ornament £300 £160
bc. Break in oval at foot £250 £140
bd. Break in oval at left £275 £150
c. Perf 14. Chalk-surfaced paper. *Green & scarlet-vermilion* (10.50*) . . . . 42·00 48·00
cb. Break in frame above ornament £350
7e 10 10s. black and ultramarine (1.9.48) . . 12·00 19·00
7f £1 black and brown (1.9.48) . . . . 12·00 23·00
›8/77f *Set of* 12 . . . . 70·00 60·00
›8s/77s Perf "Specimen" *Set of* 10 . . . . £190

*Earliest postmark date. Many printings were supplied to St. Kitts-Nevis considerably earlier. Details of many of the dates are taken, with permission, from *A Study of the King George VI Stamps of St. Kitts-Nevis* by P. L. Baldwin (2nd edition 1997).

946 (1 Nov). *Victory. As Nos. 110/11 of Antigua.*
8 1½d. red-orange 10 10
9 3d. carmine 10 10
8s/9s Perf "Specimen" *Set of* 2 . . . . 70·00

949 (3 Jan). *Royal Silver Wedding. As Nos. 112/13 of Antigua.*
) 2½d. ultramarine 10 50
1 5s. carmine . . . . 6·50 2·75

949 (10 Oct). *75th Anniv of U.P.U. As Nos. 114/17 of Antigua.*
2 2½d. ultramarine 15 20
3 3d. carmine-red . . . . 1·50 1·00
4 6d. magenta 20 50
5 1s. blue-green 20 30
a. "A" of "CA" missing from wmk . . . — £500
2/5 *Set of* 4 . . . . 1·90 1·75

ANGUILLA ANGUILLA

TERCENTENARY 1650-1950 (11) TERCENTENARY 1650—1950 (12)

950 (10 Nov). *Tercentenary of British Settlement in Anguilla. Nos. 69c, 70 and 72a (*perf 14*) optd as T* **11** *and new ptgs of T* **8***/9 on chalk-surfaced paper* perf 13 × 12½ *optd as T* **12**.
7 1d. rose-red 10 20
1½d. orange 10 35
a. Error. Crown missing, W **9***a* . . . £1700
b. Error. St. Edward's Crown, W **9***b* £900
2½d. bright ultramarine 15 20
8 3d. dull purple and scarlet 15 60
9 6d. green and bright purple 15 20
8 1s. black and green (R.) 60 25
a. Break in value tablet frame . . . . 12·00
/91 *Set of* 6 . . . . 1·00 1·60

Nos. 87a/b occur on a row in the watermark, in which the crowns and letters "CA" alternate.

(New Currency. 100 cents = 1 West Indian dollar)

51 (16 Feb). *Inauguration of B.W.I. University College. As Nos. 118/19 of Antigua.*
3c. black and yellow-orange 30 15
12c. turquoise-green and magenta . . . . . 30 1·00

ST. CHRISTOPHER, NEVIS AND ANGUILLA

LEGISLATIVE COUNCIL

13 Bath House and Spa, Nevis

14 Map of the Islands

(Recess Waterlow)

52 (14 June). *Vert designs as T* **14** *(3, 12c.) or horiz as* **13** *(others).* Wmk Mult Script CA. P 12½.
1c. deep green and ochre . . . . 15 1·25
2c. green . . . . 1·00 1·00
3c. carmine-red and violet . . . . 30 1·25
4c. scarlet 20 20
5c. bright blue and grey 30 10
6c. ultramarine 30 15
12c. deep blue and reddish brown . . . . 1·25 10
24c. black and carmine-red 30 10
48c. olive and chocolate . . . . 2·00 2·50
60c. ochre and deep green . . . . 1·50 3·00
$1.20 deep green and ultramarine . . . . 6·50 2·75
$4.80 green and carmine . . . . 13·00 18·00
'105 *Set of* 12 . . . . 24·00 27·00

Designs:—2c. Warner Park; 4c. Brimstone Hill; 5c. Nevis from sea, North; 6c. Pinney's Beach, Nevis; 12c. Sir Thomas Warner's tomb; 24c. Old Road Bay; 48c. Sea Island cotton, Nevis; 60c. The Treasury; $1.20, Salt pond, Anguilla; $4.80, Sugar factory.

St. Lucia

Although a branch office of the British G.P.O. was not opened at Castries, the island capital, until 1844 some form of postal arrangements for overseas mails existed from at least 1841 when the issue of a Ship Letter handstamp is recorded.

The stamps of Great Britain were used on the island from May 1858 until the end of April 1860 when the local authorities assumed responsibility for the postal service. No. CC1 was again used on overseas mail between 1 May and the introduction of St. Lucia stamps in December 1860.

CASTRIES

CROWN-CIRCLE HANDSTAMPS

CC 1

CC1 CC **1** ST. LUCIA (R.) (1.5.1844) *Price on cover* £750

No. CC1 was utilised, struck in black, during a shortage of 1d. stamps in late April and early May 1904. *Price on cover* £325

Stamps of GREAT BRITAIN *cancelled* "A 11" *as Type* Z **1** *of Jamaica.*

1858–60.
Z1 1d. rose-red (1857), *perf* 14 . . . . £1000
Z2 2d. blue (1855) . . . .
Z3 4d. rose (1857) £425
Z4 6d. lilac (1856) £225
Z5 1s. green (1856) £1200

PRICES FOR STAMPS ON COVER TO 1945		
Nos.	1/3	*from* × 60
Nos.	5/8	*from* × 30
Nos.	9/10	†
Nos.	11/24	*from* × 15
Nos.	25/30	*from* × 10
Nos.	31/6	*from* × 6
Nos.	39/42	*from* × 10
Nos.	43/50	*from* × 15
Nos.	51/2	—
Nos.	53/62	*from* × 6
No.	63	*from* × 15
Nos.	64/75	*from* × 4
Nos.	76/7	—
Nos.	78/88	*from* × 3
No.	89	*from* × 4
No.	90	*from* × 20
Nos.	91/112	*from* × 3
Nos.	113/24	*from* × 2
Nos.	125/7	*from* × 10
Nos.	128/41	*from* × 2
Nos.	D1/6	*from* × 10
Nos.	F1/28	—

CROWN COLONY

PERKINS BACON "CANCELLED". For notes on these handstamps, showing "CANCELLED" between horizontal bars forming an oval, see Catalogue Introduction.

1

Half penny (2)

(Recess P.B.)

1860 (18 Dec). Wmk Small Star, W w **2**. P 14 to 16.
1 **1** (1d.) rose-red (H/S "CANCELLED" in oval £5000) . . . . 90·00 65·00
a. Imperf vert (horiz pair) . . . . . .
b. Double impression £1800
2 (4d.) blue (H/S "CANCELLED" in oval £6000) £200 £150
a. Deep blue . . . .
b. Imperf vert (horiz pair) . . . . . .
3 (6d.) green (H/S "CANCELLED" in oval £6000) £275 £200
a. Imperf vert (horiz pair) . . . . . .
b. Deep green £325 £225

(Recess D.L.R.)

1863. Wmk Crown CC. P 12½.
5 **1** (1d.) lake . . . . 70·00 85·00
ax. Wmk reversed . . . . 65·00 80·00
b. Brownish lake . . . . 80·00 80·00
bx. Wmk reversed . . . .
7 (4d.) indigo £110 £120
x. Wmk reversed . . . .
8 (6d.) emerald-green £160 £160
w. Wmk inverted . . . .
x. Wmk reversed £170 £160

Prepared for use, but not issued. Surch as T **2**.
9 **1** ½d.on (6d.) emerald-green . . . . 70·00
x. Wmk reversed . . . . 75·00
10 6d.on (4d.) indigo £1100

All three values exist imperforate from proof sheets.

1864 (19 Nov)–**76**. Wmk Crown CC.

(a) P 12½.
11 **1** (1d.) black . . . . 20·00 12·00
a. Intense black . . . . 19·00 11·00
ax. Wmk reversed . . . . 25·00 15·00
12 (4d.) yellow . . . . £160 32·00
b. Lemon-yellow £1500
c. Chrome-yellow . . . . £180 32·00
d. Olive-yellow . . . . £325 80·00
w. Wmk inverted . . . .
x. Wmk reversed . . . . £200 42·00
y. Wmk inverted and reversed . . . .
13 (6d.) violet . . . . £110 29·00
a. Mauve . . . . £170 29·00
b. Deep lilac . . . . £130 32·00
x. Wmk reversed £130
14 (1s.) brown-orange . . . . £300 26·00
b. Orange . . . . £225 26·00
c. Pale orange . . . . £180 26·00
ca. Imperf between (horiz pair) . . . .
x. Wmk reversed £200

(b) P 14.
15 **1** (1d.) black (6.76) . . . . 26·00 16·00
a. Imperf between (horiz pair) . . . .
x. Wmk reversed . . . . — 16·00
16 (4d.) yellow (6.76) . . . . 95·00 19·00
a. Olive-yellow . . . . £250 85·00
w. Wmk inverted . . . .
x. Wmk reversed . . . .
17 (6d.) mauve (6.76) . . . . 95·00 32·00
a. Pale lilac . . . . 95·00 18·00
b. Violet . . . . £225 65·00
x. Wmk reversed . . . .
18 (1s.) orange (10.76) . . . . £200 22·00
a. Deep orange . . . . £130 16·00
w. Wmk inverted . . . .
x. Wmk reversed . . . . — 22·00

All four values exist imperforate from proof sheets.

HALFPENNY (3) 2½ PENCE (4) ST. LUCIA THREE PENCE 5

1881 (Sept). *Surch with T* **3** *or* **4**. Wmk Crown CC. P 14.
23 **1** ½d. green . . . . 60·00 80·00
x. Wmk reversed . . . .
24 2½d. brown-red . . . . 30·00 22·00

The 1d. black is known surcharged "1d." in violet ink by hand, but there is no evidence that this was done officially.

1882–84. *Surch as T* **3**. Wmk Crown CA.

(a) P 14.
25 **1** ½d. green (1882) . . . . 18·00 27·00
26 1d. black (C.) . . . . 26·00 9·00
a. Bisected (on cover) . . . . † —
27 4d. yellow . . . . £275 18·00
28 6d. violet . . . . 28·00 27·00
29 1s. orange £275 £170

(b) P 12.
30 **1** 4d. yellow . . . . £275 28·00

Deep blue stamps, wmk Crown CA, perf 14 or 12 are fiscals from which the overprint "THREE PENCE—REVENUE", or "REVENUE", has been fraudulently removed.

(Typo D.L.R.)

1883 (6 July)–**86**. *Die I*. Wmk Crown CA. P 14.
31 **5** ½d. dull green . . . . 7·50 4·00
a. Top left triangle detached £225
32 1d. carmine-rose . . . . 35·00 9·50
33 2½d. blue . . . . 38·00 2·00
a. Top left triangle detached £550 £130
34 4d. brown (1885) . . . . 28·00 1·00
a. Top left triangle detached . . . . £550 95·00
35 6d. lilac (1886) £250 £200
36 1s. orange-brown (1885) £375 £140

The 4d. and 6d. exist imperforate from proof sheets.

For illustration of "top left triangle detached" variety on this and the following issue see above No. 6 of Montserrat.

1886–87. *Die I*. Wmk Crown CA. P 14.
39 **5** 1d. dull mauve . . . . 6·00 6·00
a. Top left triangle detached £170
40 3d. dull mauve and green . . . . . . £120 17·00
a. Top left triangle detached . . . . — £400
41 6d. dull mauve and blue (1887) . . . . 3·75 9·00
a. Top left triangle detached £150
42 1s. dull mauve and red (1887) . . . . £110 25·00
a. Top left triangle detached £800
39/42 *Set of* 4 . . . . £200 50·00
39s/42s Optd "Specimen" *Set of* 4 . . . . . £180

The 1d. exists imperforate from proof sheets.

1891–98. *Die II*. Wmk Crown CA. P 14.
43 **5** ½d. dull green . . . . 2·00 1·00
44 1d. dull mauve . . . . 3·25 30

45 2d. ultramarine and orange (1898) 3·00 1·00
46 2½d. ultramarine 4·00 1·00
47 3d. dull mauve and green 4·25 5·50
48 4d. brown 2·50 2·25
49 6d. dull mauve and blue 24·00 24·00
50 1s. dull mauve and red 5·50 5·00
51 5s. dull mauve and orange 50·00 £130
52 10s. dull mauve and black 85·00 £140
43/52 *Set of* 10 £170 £275
45s, 51s/2s Optd "Specimen" *Set of* 3 £120

For description and illustration of differences between Die I and Die II see Introduction.

ONE HALF PENNY (6)   ½d (7)   ONE PENNY (8)

N Normal "N"   N Thick "N"

Three types of T8

I. All letters "N" normal.
II. Thick diagonal stroke in first "N".
III. Thick diagonal stroke in second "N".

1891–92.

(a) Stamps of Die I surch.

53 **6** ½d.on 3d. dull mauve and green £140 70·00
a. Small "A" in "HALF" £350 £150
b. Small "O" in "ONE" £350 £150
c. Top left triangle detached £850
54 **7** ½d.on half 6d. dull mauve and blue 22·00 3·25
a. No fraction bar £200 £130
b. Surch sideways £1000
c. Surch double £550 £550
d. "2" in fraction omitted £450 £500
e. Thick "1" with sloping serif £200 £120
f. Surch triple £1000
g. Figure "1" used as fraction bar £475 £275
h. Top left triangle detached — £275
55 **8** 1d.on 4d. brown (I) (12.91) 4·50 3·50
a. Surch double £200
b. Surch inverted £750 £650
c. Type II 23·00 20·00
ca. Surch double £350
cb. Surch inverted — £750
d. Type III 22·00 20·00
e. Top left triangle detached £150 £150

(b) Stamp of Die II surch.

56 **6** ½d.on 3d. dull mauve and green 70·00 22·00
a. Surch double £750 £600
b. Surch inverted £1700 £600
c. Surch both sides — £700
d. Small "O" in "ONE" £170 90·00
e. Small "A" in "HALF" £170 90·00
f. "ONE" misplaced ("O" over "H") £170 90·00

9   10

(Typo D.L.R.)

1902–03. Wmk Crown CA. P 14.
58 **9** ½d. dull purple and green 2·75 1·50
59 1d. dull purple and carmine 5·00 50
60 2½d. dull purple and ultramarine 21·00 5·50
61 **10** 3d. dull purple and yellow 6·00 8·50
62 1s. green and black 10·00 27·00
58/62 *Set of* 5 40·00 38·00
58s/62s Optd "Specimen" *Set of* 5 £100

11 The Pitons

(Recess D.L.R.)

1902 (15 Dec). *400th Anniv of Discovery by Columbus.* Wmk Crown CC (sideways). P 14.
63 **11** 2d. green and brown 8·50 1·75
s. Optd "Specimen" 60·00

This stamp was formerly thought to have been issued on 16 December but it has been seen on a postcard clearly postmarked 15 December.

1904–10. *Chalk-surfaced paper (Nos. 71, 73/5 and 77) or ordinary paper (others).* Wmk Mult Crown CA. P 14.
64 **9** ½d. dull purple and green 4·25 60
a. Chalk-surfaced paper 4·25 1·25
65 ½d. green (1907) 1·75 1·00
66 1d. dull purple and carmine 6·00 1·25
a. Chalk-surfaced paper 3·25 1·25
67 1d. carmine (1907) 4·25 30
68 2½d. dull purple and ultramarine 15·00 1·25
a. Chalk-surfaced paper 11·00 4·50
69 2½d. blue (1907) 3·75 1·75
70 **10** 3d. dull purple and yellow 5·00 3·00
71 3d. purple/*yellow* (1909) 2·75 12·00
72 6d. dull purple and violet (1905) 15·00 19·00
a. Chalk-surfaced paper 20·00 25·00
ab. *Dull purple and bright purple* (1907) 8·50 27·00
73 6d. dull purple (1910) 50·00 65·00
74 1s. green and black (1905) 32·00 25·00
75 1s. black/*green* (1909) 4·75 8·00
76 5s. green and carmine (1905) 70·00 £170
77 5s. green and red/*yellow* (1907) 60·00 70·00
64/77 *Set of* 14 £225 £350
65s, 67s, 69s, 71s/2s, 72abs and 75s/7s Optd "Specimen" *Set of* 9 £225

Examples of Nos. 71/7 are known with a forged Castries postmark dated "JA 21 09".

12   13   14   15   16

(Typo D.L.R.)

1912–21. *Die I. Chalk-surfaced paper (3d. to 5s.).* Wmk Mult Crown CA. P 14.
78 **12** ½d. deep green 70 50
a. Yellow-green (1916) 75 30
79 1d. carmine-red 1·90 10
a. Scarlet (1916) 3·25 10
b. Rose-red 7·00 1·00
80 **13** 2d. grey 1·50 4·25
a. Slate-grey (1916) 17·00 13·00
81 **12** 2½d. ultramarine 3·75 2·75
a. Bright blue 2·25 2·75
b. Deep bright blue (1916) 10·00 10·00
82 **15** 3d. purple/*yellow* 1·25 2·25
b. Die II. *On pale yellow* (1921) 10·00 38·00
bw. Wmk inverted
83 **14** 4d. black and red/*yellow* 1·00 2·00
a. White back 70 1·50
as. Optd "Specimen" 25·00
84 **15** 6d. dull and bright purple 2·00 11·00
a. Grey-purple and purple (1918) 16·00 17·00
85 1s. black/*green* 3·25 5·00
a. On blue-green (olive back) (1918) 8·00 8·00
86 1s. orange-brown (1920) 9·00 45·00
87 **16** 2s.6d. black and red/*blue* 22·00 35·00
88 **15** 5s. green and red/*yellow* 24·00 75·00
78/88 *Set of* 11 60·00 £160
78s/88s Optd "Specimen" *Set of* 11 £200

WAR TAX (17)   WAR TAX (18)

1916 (1 June). *No. 79a optd locally with T* **17**.
89 **12** 1d. scarlet 9·00 9·00
a. Opt double £425 £425
b. Carmine-red 60·00 38·00

For overprinting with Type **17** the sheets were vertically divided to the left of the centre margin and the top margin of the sheet was folded beneath the top row of stamps so that the marginal examples from this row show an inverted albino impression of the overprint in the top margin.

Examples are also recorded of similar albino overprints in the right-hand and bottom margins but it is unclear if some sheets had all margins folded under before overprinting.

1916 (Sept). *No. 79a optd in London with T* **18**.
90 **12** 1d. scarlet 1·00 30
s. Optd "Specimen" 40·00

1921–30. *Die II. Chalk-surfaced paper (3d. (No. 100) to 5s.).* Wmk Mult Script CA. P 14.
91 **12** ½d. green 75 50
92 1d. rose-carmine 8·50 14·00
93 1d. deep brown (1922) 1·40 15
94 **14** 1½d. dull carmine (1922) 75 2·50
95 **13** 2d. slate-grey 75 15
96 **12** 2½d. bright blue 3·75 2·75
97 2½d. orange (1925) 11·00 50·00
98 2½d. dull blue (1926) 3·25 2·50
99 **15** 3d. bright blue (1922) 5·00 16·00
a. Dull blue (1924) 2·50 11·00
100 3d. purple/*pale yellow* (1926) 1·00 12·00
a. Deep purple/pale yellow (1930) 14·00 12·00
101 **14** 4d. black and red/*yellow* (1924) 1·25 2·50
102 **15** 6d. grey-purple and purple 2·00 4·75
103 1s. orange-brown 2·25 3·25
104 **16** 2s.6d. black and red/*blue* (1924) 18·00 27·00
105 **15** 5s. green and red/*pale yellow* (1923) 45·00 75·00
91/105 *Set of* 15 90·00 £190
91s/105s Optd "Specimen" *Set of* 15 £275

1935 (6 May). *Silver Jubilee. As Nos. 91/4 of Antigua.* P 13½ × 14.
109 ½d. black and green 20 75
f. Diagonal line by turret 29·00
110 2d. ultramarine and grey 50 90
f. Diagonal line by turret 45·00
111 2½d. brown and deep blue 1·00 1·25
a. Frame printed double, one albino † —
f. Diagonal line by turret 65·00
g. Dot to left of chapel 95·00
112 1s. slate and purple 6·50 8·50
h. Dot by flagstaff £250
109/12 *Set of* 4 7·50 10·00
109s/12s Perf "Specimen" *Set of* 4 85·00

For illustrations of plate varieties see Omnibus section following Zanzibar.

19 Port Castries

20 Columbus Square, Castries (inscr "COLOMBUS SQUARE" in error)

21 Ventine Falls

25 The Badge of the Colony

(Recess D.L.R.)

1936 (1 Mar–Apr). *T* **19/21**, **25** *and similar designs.* Wmk Mult Scri[p]
CA. P 14 or 13 × 12 (1s. and 10s.).
113 **19** ½d. black and bright green 30 5
a. Perf 13 × 12 (8.4.36) 2·25 11·(
114 **20** 1d. black and brown 40 1
a. Perf 13 × 12 (8.4.36) 2·75 2·5
115 **21** 1½d. black and scarlet 55 3
a. Perf 12 × 13 7·00 2·2
116 **19** 2d. black and grey 50 2
117 **20** 2½d. black and blue 50 1
118 **21** 3d. black and dull green 1·25 7
119 **19** 4d. black and red-brown 50 1·
120 **20** 6d. black and orange 1·00 1·(
121 – 1s. black and light blue 1·25 2·5
122 – 2s.6d. black and ultramarine 8·50 14·(
123 – 5s. black and violet 8·50 20·(
124 **25** 10s. black and carmine 45·00 70·(
113/24 *Set of* 12 60·00 £1(
113s/24s Perf "Specimen" *Set of* 12 £180

Designs: *Vert (as T***21***)*—2s.6d. Inniskilling monument. *Horiz (*
*T***19***)*—1s. Fort Rodney, Pigeon Island; 5s. Government House.

Examples of most values are known with a forged Castri
postmark dated "1 MR 36".

1937 (12 May). *Coronation. As Nos. 95/7 of Antigua.* P 11 × 11½.
125 1d. violet 30
126 1½d. carmine 55
127 2½d. blue 55 1·
125/7 *Set of* 3 1·25 1·
125s/7s Perf "Specimen" *Set of* 3 65·00

26 King George VI

27 Columbus Square

28 Government House

31 Device of St. Lucia

(Des E. Crafer (T **26**), H. Fleury (5s.). Recess Waterlow (½d. t
3½d., 8d., 3s., 5s., £1), D.L.R. (6d., 1s.) and B.W. (2s., 10s.))

1938 (22 Sept)–**48**. *T* **26/8**, **31** *and similar designs.* Wmk Mult Scr
CA (sideways on 2s.).
128 **26** ½d. green (P 14½ × 14) 1·50
a. Perf 12½ (1943) 10
129 1d. violet (P 14½ × 14) 2·00
a. Perf 12½ (1938) 10
129*b* 1d. scarlet (P 12½) (1947) 50
c. Perf 14½ × 14 (1948) 10
130 1½d. scarlet (P 14½ × 14) 1·75
a. Perf 12½ (1943) 1·25 1
131 2d. grey (P 14½ × 14) 2·50 1
a. Perf 12½ (1943) 10
132 2½d. ultramarine (P 14½ × 14) 3·75
a. Perf 12½ (1943) 10
132*b* 2½d. violet (P 12½) (1947) 70
133 3d. orange (P 14½ × 14) 1·00
a. Perf 12½ (1943) 10
133*b* 3½d. ultramarine (P 12½) (1947) 70
134 **27** 6d. claret (P 13½) 5·00
a. Carmine-lake (P 13½) (1945) 2·50
b. Perf 12. *Claret* (1948) 2·00 1
134*c* **26** 8d. brown (P 12½) (1946) 3·50
135 **28** 1s. brown (P 13½) 55
a. Perf 12 (1948) 75
136 – 2s. blue and purple (P 12) 3·50 1
136*a* **26** 3s. bright purple (P 12½) (1946) 8·00 1
137 – 5s. black and mauve (P 12½) 14·00 7

138 **31** 10s. black/*yellow* (P 12) . . . . . . 7·50 9·00
141 **26** £1 sepia (P 12½) (1946) . . . . . . 11·00 8·00
128a/41 *Set of* 17 . . . . 45·00 27·00
128s/41s Perf "Specimen" *Set of* 17 . . . . . . £325
Designs: *Horiz* (*as* **T28**)—2s. The Pitons; 5s. *Lady Hawkins* loading bananas.

1946 (8 Oct). *Victory. As Nos. 110/11 of Antigua.*
142 1d. lilac 10 10
143 3½d. blue 10 10
142s/3s Perf "Specimen" *Set of* 2 . . . . 60·00

1948 (26 Nov). *Royal Silver Wedding. As Nos. 112/13 of Antigua.*
144 1d. scarlet 15 10
145 £1 purple-brown . . . . 15·00 35·00

(New Currency. 100 cents = 1 West Indian dollar)

32 King George VI

33 Device of St. Lucia

(Recess Waterlow (**32**), B.W. (**33**))

1949 (1 Oct)–**50**. *Value in cents or dollars.* Wmk Mult Script CA. P 12½ (1c. to 16c.), 11 × 11½ (others).
146 **32** 1c. green 25 10
a. Perf 14 (1949) . . . . 2·25 40
147 2c. magenta 75 10
a. Perf 14½ × 14 (1949) . . . . 2·50 1·00
148 3c. scarlet . . . . 75 1·75
149 4c. grey 75 10
a. Perf 14½ × 14 . . . . † £7500
150 5c. violet 75 10
151 6c. orange . . . . 75 2·00
152 7c. ultramarine . . . . 2·75 2·50
153 12c. claret . . . . 5·50 2·50
a. Perf 14½ × 14 (1950) £500 £375
154 16c. brown . . . . 3·25 50
155 **33** 24c. light blue 50 10
156 48c. olive-green . . . . 1·50 1·25
157 $1.20, purple . . . . 2·25 8·00
158 $2.40, blue-green . . . . 3·25 17·00
159 $4.80, rose-carmine . . . . 8·50 18·00
146/159 *Set of* 14 . . . . 28·00 48·00
Most examples of Nos. 146a and 147a were produced as coils, but a few sheets in these perforations were distributed and blocks of four are scarce.
No genuine mint example of No. 149a is known. Photographic forgeries do, however, exist.

1949 (10 Oct). *75th Anniv of U.P.U. As Nos. 114/17 of Antigua.*
160 5c. violet 15 50
161 6c. orange . . . . 1·40 1·75
a. "A" of "CA" missing from wmk . . . £500
162 12c. magenta 20 20
163 24c. blue-green 30 20
160/3 *Set of* 4 . . . . 1·90 2·40

1951 (16 Feb). *Inauguration of B.W.I. University College. As Nos. 118/19 of Antigua.*
164 3c. black and scarlet 45 50
165 12c. black and deep carmine 65 50

34 Phoenix rising from Burning Buildings

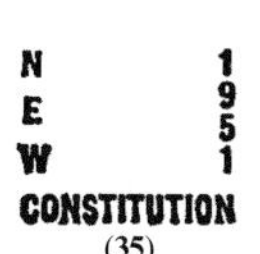

(**35**)

(Flames typo, rest recess B.W.)

1951 (19 June). *Reconstruction of Castries.* Wmk Mult Script CA. P 13½ × 13.
166 **34** 12c. red and blue 25 80

1951 (25 Sept). *New Constitution. Nos. 147, 149/50 and 153 optd with T* **35** *by Waterlow.* P 12½.
167 **32** 2c. magenta 15 70
168 4c. grey 15 60
169 5c. violet 15 60
170 12c. claret 70 50
167/70 *Set of* 4 . . . . 1·00 2·25

POSTAGE DUE STAMPS

D 1

No. Normal   **No.** Wide fount

(Type-set Government Printing Office)

1930. *Each stamp individually handstamped with different number. No gum.* No wmk. Rough perf 12.

(a) Horizontally laid paper.
D1 **D 1** 1d. black/*blue* . . . . 4·50 15·00
b. Wide, wrong fount "No." . . . . 16·00 38·00
c. Missing stop after "ST" £100 £160
d. Missing stop after "LUCIA" . . £100 £160
e. Handstamped number double . . £500
f. Handstamped number triple . . .
g. Incorrect number with correction above . . . .
h. Two different numbers on same stamp £650
i. Number omitted £1800

(b) Wove paper.
D2 **D 1** 2d. black/*yellow* . . . . 12·00 40·00
a. Imperf between (vert pair) . . . £4750
b. Wide, wrong fount "No." . . . . 35·00 95·00
c. Missing stop after "ST" £200 £375
d. Missing stop after "LUCIA" . . £300
g. Incorrect number with correction above £900
h. Two different numbers on same stamp £1000

Nos. D1/2 were produced in sheets of 60 (6 × 10) usually with imperforate outer edges at the top, at right and at foot. It would appear that the sheets were bound into books from which they could be detached using the line of perforations along the left-hand side.

There were three printings of each value, utilising the same basic type. The paper for the first two printings of the 1d. and the first printing of the 2d. showed papermaker's watermarks, that for the 1d. being "KINGSCLERE" in double-lined capitals below a crown with parts occurring on between ten and fourteen stamps in each sheet.

Details of the printings are as follows:

1d.
First printing. On paper with sheet watermark. Shows wide fount "No." on R. 10/3–6 and missing stop after "ST" on R. 5/3
Second printing. On paper with sheet watermark. Shows wide fount "No." on R. 10/2–6 and missing stop after "ST" on R. 5/3. The first two printings of the 1d. were numbered together as 1 to 12000.
Third printing. On paper without watermark. Shows wide fount "No." on all stamps in Row 10. Missing stop after "ST" on R. 5/3 corrected, but missing stop after "LUCIA" occurs on R. 9/2. Numbered 12001 to 24000.

2d.
First printing. On paper with sheet watermark. Shows wide fount "No." on R. 10/2–6 and missing stop after "ST" on R. 5/3 (as 1d. second printing). Numbered 1 to 4800.
Second printing. On paper without watermark. Shows wide fount "No." on all stamps in Row 10. Missing stop after "ST" corrected (printed *before* 1d. third printing). Numbered 4801 to 14820.
Third printing. On paper without watermark. Shows wide fount "No." on all stamps in Row 10. Missing stop after "ST" corrected, but missing stop after "LUCIA" occurs on R. 4/4 and 9/2 (printed *after* 1d. third printing). Numbered 14821 to 16800.

The handstamped numbers were applied at the Post Office using a numbering machine. Mistakes in the numbering on the 1d. were sometimes partially erased and then corrected with a second strike, either of the complete number or of incorrect digits, using a machine with a smaller font.

D 2

D 3

(Typo D.L.R.)

1933–47. Wmk Mult Script CA. P 14.
D3 **D 2** 1d. black . . . . 4·75 6·00
D4 2d. black . . . . 19·00 8·00
D5 4d. black (28.6.47) . . . . 5·50 42·00
D6 8d. black (28.6.47) . . . . 5·50 50·00
D3/6 *Set of* 4 . . . . 32·00 95·00
D3s/6s Perf "Specimen" *Set of* 4 . . . . . . £130

1949 (1 Oct)–**52**. *Value in cents. Typo.* Wmk Mult Script CA. P 14.
D7 **D 3** 2c. black . . . . 1·75 27·00
a. Chalk-surfaced paper (27.11.52) . . . . 10 8·50
ab. Error. Crown missing, W **9***a* . . £120
ac. Error. St. Edward's Crown, W **9***b* . . . . 32·00
D8 4c. black . . . . 3·50 21·00
a. Chalk-surfaced paper (27.11.52) . . . . 50 11·00
ab. Error. Crown missing, W **9***a* . . £170
ac. Error. St. Edward's Crown, W **9***b* . . . . 45·00
D9 **D 3** 8c. black . . . . 3·25 25·00
a. Chalk-surfaced paper (27.11.52) . . . . 3·00 38·00
ac. Error. St. Edward's Crown, W **9***b* £325
D10 16c. black . . . . 15·00 65·00
a. Chalk-surfaced paper (27.11.52) . . . . 4·50 50·00
ac. Error. St. Edward's Crown, W **9***b* £425
D7/10 *Set of* 4 . . . . 21·00 £120
D7a/10a *Set of* 4 . . . . 7·25 95·00
The 2c. and 4c. watermarked Block CA were issued in 1965.

POSTAL FISCAL STAMPS

Nos. F1/28 were authorised for postal use from 14 April 1885.

CANCELLATIONS. Many used examples of the Postal Fiscal stamps have had previous pen cancellations removed before being used postally.

SHILLING STAMP (F 1)   One Penny Stamp (F 2)   HALFPENNY Stamp (F 3)

1881. Wmk Crown CC. P 14.

(a) Surch as Type F **1**.
F1 **1** ONE PENNY STAMP, black (C.) . . 55·00 48·00
a. Surch inverted £700 £700
b. Surch double £650 £700
F2 FOUR PENNY STAMP, yellow . . 90·00 70·00
a. Bisected (2d.) (on cover) . . . . . .
F3 SIX PENCE STAMP, mauve £150 £130
F4 SHILLING STAMP, orange . . . . 85·00 65·00
a. "SHILEING" £650 £600
b. "SHILDING" £650 £600

(b) Surch as Type F **2**.
F7 **1** One Penny Stamp, black (R.) . . . 55·00 48·00
a. Surch double £700
w. Wmk inverted . . . .
F8 Four Pence Stamp, yellow . . . . . 90·00 65·00
x. Wmk reversed . . . .
F9 Six Pence Stamp, mauve . . . . . 90·00 65·00
F10 Shilling Stamp, orange . . . . . . 95·00 85·00

(c) Surch as Type F **3**.
F11 **1** Halfpenny Stamp, green . . . . . . 65·00 55·00
a. "Stamp" double £450 £450
F12 One Shilling Stamp, orange (wmk Crown CA) . . . . £100 75·00
a. "Stamp" double £450 £500
A fiscally used example of No. F1b is known showing one red and one black surcharge.

FOUR PENCE REVENUE (F 4)   Revenue (F 5)   REVENUE (F 6)

1882. *Surch as Type* F **4**. Wmk Crown CA.

(a) P 14.
F13 **1** 1d. black (C.) . . . . 40·00 22·00
F14 2d. pale blue . . . . 26·00 10·00
F15 3d. deep blue (C.) . . . . 75·00 45·00
F16 4d. yellow . . . . 30·00 4·00
F17 6d. mauve . . . . 50·00 26·00

(b) P 12.
F18 **1** 1d. black (C.) . . . . 40·00 24·00
F19 3d. deep blue (C.) . . . . 55·00 20·00
F20 1s. orange . . . . 60·00 13·00
The 1d. and 2d. exist as imperforate proofs.

1883. *Nos. 25, 26, 30 and 32 optd locally as Type* F **5**.

(a) Word 11 mm long.
F21 1d. black (C.) . . . . 32·00 40·00
a. Opt inverted . . . .
b. Opt double £275 £350

(b) Word 13 mm
F22 1d. black (C.) . . . . — 65·00

(c) Word 15½ mm
F23 ½d. green . . . . — 55·00
a. "Revenue" double . . . . — £250
F24 1d. black (C.) . . . . 32·00 10·00
a. "Revenue" double £140
b. "Revenue" triple £275
c. "Revenue" double, one inverted . . . £250 £300
F25 1d. rose (No. 32) . . . . — 60·00
F26 4d. yellow . . . . — 70·00

1884–85. *Optd with Type* F **6**. Wmk Crown CA. P 14.
F27 **5** 1d. slate (C.) . . . . 23·00 14·00
F28 1d. dull mauve (Die I) (1885) . . . . . 23·00 7·50
No. F27 exists as an imperforate proof.

St. Vincent

Although postal markings for St. Vincent are recorded as early as 1793 it was not until 1852 that the British G.P.O. opened a branch office at Kingstown, the island's capital.

The stamps of Great Britain were used between May 1858 and the end of April 1860. From 1 May in that year the local authorities assumed responsibility for the postal services and fell back on the use of No. CC 1 until the introduction of St. Vincent stamps in 1861.

ST. VINCENT

KINGSTOWN

CROWNED-CIRCLE HANDSTAMPS

CC 1

CC1 CC **1** ST. VINCENT (R.) (30.1.1852)
Price on cover £800

Stamps of GREAT BRITAIN *cancelled* "A 10" *as Type* Z **1** *of Jamaica.*

1858–60.
Z1 1d. rose-red (1857), perf 14 . . . . £650
Z2 2d. blue (1855) . . . . —
Z3 4d. rose (1857) £400
Z4 6d. lilac (1856) £300
Z5 1s. green (1856) £1300

PRICES FOR STAMPS ON COVER TO 1945		
Nos.	1/7	*from* × 15
No.	8	—
No.	9	*from* × 15
No.	10	—
Nos.	11/19	*from* × 10
Nos.	20/1	*from* × 6
Nos.	22/5	*from* × 10
Nos.	26/8	—
Nos.	29/31	*from* × 12
No.	32	—
Nos.	33/4	*from* × 10
No.	35	—
Nos.	36/8	*from* × 8
Nos.	39/41	*from* × 15
Nos.	42/5	*from* × 8
No.	46	*from* × 15
Nos.	47/54	*from* × 4
Nos.	55/8	*from* × 8
No.	59	*from* × 10
No.	60	*from* × 6
Nos.	61/3	*from* × 8
Nos.	67/75	*from* × 3
Nos.	76/84	*from* × 2
Nos.	85/92	*from* × 3
No.	93	—
Nos.	94/8	*from* × 3
Nos.	99/107	*from* × 2
Nos.	108/19	*from* × 3
No.	120	—
No.	121	*from* × 3
No.	122	*from* × 5
No.	123	—
No.	124	*from* × 5
Nos.	126/9	*from* × 10
Nos.	131/45	*from* × 3
Nos.	146/8	*from* × 6
Nos.	149/59	*from* × 2

CROWN COLONY

1

(2)

3

(T **1**, **3** and **7** recess P.B)

1861 (8 May). No Wmk. Rough to intermediate perf 14 to 16.
1 **1** 1d. rose-red . . . . 45·00 14·00
a. Imperf vert (horiz pair) £300
b. Imperf (pair) £250
2 6d. deep yellow-green £6500 £200

The perforations on the 1d. are usually rough, but individual examples can be found on which some, or all, of the holes have the appearance of the intermediate perforations. All examples of the 6d. show intermediate perforations.

Imperforate examples, possibly proofs, exist of the 1d. rose-red and 6d. deep green handstamped "CANCELLED" in oval of bars (see note on Perkins Bacon "CANCELLED" in Catalogue Introduction). (*Price* 1d. £5500, 6d. £6500)

1862 (Sept). No wmk. Rough perf 14 to 16.
4 **1** 6d. deep green . . . . 55·00 18·00
a. Imperf between (horiz pair) £5000 £5500
b. Imperf (pair) £850

1863–68. No wmk.

(a) P 11 to 12½.
5 **1** 1d. rose-red (3.63) . . . . 35·00 15·00
6 4d. deep blue (*shades*) (1866) £275 £110
a. Imperf between (horiz pair) . . . . † —
7 6d. deep green (7.68) . . . . £200 75·00
8 1s. slate-grey (8.66) £1900 £900

(b) P 14 to 16.
9 **1** 1s. slate-grey (*shades*) (8.66) £300 £140

(c) P 11 to 12½ × 14 to 16.
10 **1** 1d. rose-red (1866) £3250 £1100
11 1s. slate-grey (*shades*) (8.66) £225 £120

1869 (Apr–Sep). *Colours changed.* No wmk. P 11 to 12½.
12 **1** 4d. yellow (9.69) £350 £160
13 1s. indigo . . . . £325 90·00
14 1s. brown (9.69) £450 £160

1871 (Apr). Wmk Small Star, W w **2**. Rough perf 14 to 16.
15 **1** 1d. black . . . . 50·00 10·00
a. Imperf between (vert pair) £7500
16 6d. deep green . . . . £275 70·00
a. Wmk sideways . . . . — 85·00

1872 (June). *Colour changed.* W w **2** (sideways). P 11 to 12½.
17 **1** 1s. deep rose-red £750 £140

1872–75. W w **2** (sideways).

(a) Perf about 15.
18 **1** 1d. black (*shades*) (11.72) . . . . 48·00 8·50
a. Wmk upright . . . . 55·00 9·50
19 6d. dull blue-green (*shades*) (1873) . . . . £950 48·00
b. Deep blue-green (1875) . . . . £650 45·00
c. Wmk upright

(b) P 11 to 12½ × 15.
20 **1** 1s. lilac-rose (1873) £5000 £350

1875. *Colour changed.* W w **2** (sideways). P 11 to 12½.
21 1s. claret £600 £250

1875–78. W w **2** (sideways).

(a) P 11 to 12½ × 15.
22 **1** 1d. black (*shades*) (4.75) . . . . 70·00 9·50
a. Imperf between (horiz pair) . . . . † £7000
b. Wmk upright . . . . — 50·00
23 6d. pale green (1877) . . . . £600 50·00
24 1s. vermilion (2.77) . . . . £900 85·00
a. Imperf vert (horiz pair)

(b) P 11 to 12½.
25 **1** 4d. deep blue (7.77) . . . . £475 90·00

(c) Perf about 15.
26 **1** 6d. pale green (3.77) £1500 £450
a. Wmk upright. *Lt yellow-green* (1878) . . . . £650 25·00
27 1s. vermilion (1878?) . . . . † £13000
a. Imperf . . . . † £7000

1880 (May). *No. 19b divided vertically by a line of perforation gauging 12, and surch locally with T* **2** *in red.*
28 **1** 1d.on half 6d. deep blue-green £450 £325
a. Unsevered pair £1600 £1100

1880 (June). W w **2** (sideways). P 11 to 12½.
29 **1** 1d. olive-green . . . . £130 4·00
30 6d. bright green . . . . £375 70·00
31 1s. bright vermilion . . . . £650 55·00
a. Imperf between (horiz pair) £8500
32 **3** 5s. rose-red £1000 £1300
a. Imperf £4250

d
1
½
(4)

ONE PENNY
(5)

4d
(6)

1881. *Nos. 30/1 surch locally. No. 33 is divided vertically as No. 28.*
33 **4** ½d.on half 6d. bright green (R.) (1.9) £160 £160
a. Unsevered pair £425 £425
b. Fraction bar omitted (pair with and without bar) £4000 £4500
34 **5** 1d.on 6d. bright green (30.11) £450 £325
35 **6** 4d.on 1s. bright vermilion (28.11) £1500 £800

No. 33 exists showing the "1" of "½" with a straight serif. Some examples come from a constant variety on R. 6/20, but others are the result of faulty type.

It is believed that Type **4** was applied as a setting of 36 (6 × 6) surcharges repeated three times on each sheet across rows 1 to 9. The missing fraction bar occurs on R. 6/3 of the setting.

The tenth vertical row of stamps appears to have been surcharged from a separate setting of 12 (2 × 6) on which the constant "straight serif" flaw occurs on the bottom right half-stamp.

Three unused single copies of No. 33 are known with the surcharge omitted.

It is believed that Nos. 34 and 35 were surcharged in settings of 30 (10 × 3).

No. 34 was only on sale between the 30 November and 3 December when supplies of No. 37 became available.

7

2½ PENCE
(8)

1d
2½ PENCE
(9)

1881 (Dec). W w **2**. P 11 to 12½.
36 **7** ½d. orange (*shades*) . . . . 7·00 4·00
37 **1** 1d. drab (*shades*) . . . . £550 8·50
38 4d. bright blue £1200 £110
a. Imperf between (horiz pair)

(Recess D.L.R. from Perkins, Bacon plates)

1882 (Nov)–**83**. *No. 40 is surch with T* **8**. Wmk Crown CA. P 14.
39 **1** 1d. drab . . . . 48·00 2·0
x. Wmk reversed . . . . 80·00 10·0
40 2½d.on 1d. lake (1883) . . . . 16·00 7
w. Wmk inverted
x. Wmk reversed . . . . 25·00 5·0
y. Wmk inverted and reversed
41 4d. ultramarine . . . . £425 38·0
a. Dull ultramarine £950 £35
w. Wmk inverted
x. Wmk reversed . . . . £425 38·0
y. Wmk inverted and reversed

1883–84. Wmk Crown CA. P 12.
42 **7** ½d. green (1884) . . . . 80·00 26·0
x. Wmk reversed
43 **1** 4d. ultramarine-blue . . . . £400 24·0
a. Grey-blue £1000 £25
w. Wmk inverted
x. Wmk reversed . . . . £400 22·0
y. Wmk inverted and reversed
44 6d. bright green £150 £30
x. Wmk reversed £200
45 1s. orange-vermilion . . . . £120 60·0
x. Wmk reversed

The ½d. orange, 1d. rose-red, 1d. milky blue (without surcharge and 5s. carmine-lake which were formerly listed are now considere to be colour trials. They are, however, of great interest (*Prices ur* ½d. £900, 1d. red £900, 1d. blue £1200, 5s. £1700).

1885 (Mar). *No. 40 further surch locally as in T* **9**.
46 **1** 1d.on 2½d. on 1d. lake . . . . 22·00 16·0
w. Wmk inverted
x. Wmk reversed . . . . 22·00 16·0

Stamps with three cancelling bars instead of two are considere to be proofs.

1885–93. *No. 49 is surch with T* **8**. Wmk Crown CA. P 14.
47 **7** ½d. green . . . . 1·00 6
a. Deep green . . . . 2·50 6
w. Wmk inverted
x. Wmk reversed
48 **1** 1d. rose-red . . . . 3·00 1·
a. Rose (1886) . . . . 4·75 1·
b. Red (1887) . . . . 1·60 8
c. Carmine-red (1889) . . . . 24·00 3·
w. Wmk inverted
x. Wmk reversed . . . . 5·00 1·
49 2½d.on 1d. milky blue (1889) . . . . 23·00 5·
x. Wmk reversed
50 4d. red-brown . . . . £850 22·
x. Wmk reversed
51 4d. purple-brown (1886) . . . . 60·00 7
a. Chocolate (1887) . . . . 60·00 1·
w. Wmk inverted
x. Wmk reversed
y. Wmk inverted and reversed
52 6d. violet (1888) £140 £1
w. Wmk inverted £150 £1
ws. Optd "Specimen" . . . . 75·00
x. Wmk reversed
53 **3** 5s. lake (1888) . . . . 27·00 50·
a. Printed both sides £4500
b. Brown-lake (1893) . . . . 30·00 50·
w. Wmk inverted
49s, 51s/2s Optd "Specimen" *Set of* 3 . . . . £180

2½d.
(10)

5
PENCE
(11)

1890 (Aug). *No. 51a surch locally with T* **10**.
54 **1** 2½d.on 4d. chocolate . . . . 80·00 £1
a. No fraction bar (R. 1/7, 2/4) £375 £4

1890–93. *No. 55 is surch with T* **8**. *Colours changed.* Wmk Cro CA. P 14.
55 **1** 2½d.on 1d. grey-blue (1890) . . . . 18·00
a. Blue (1893) . . . . 1·50
w. Wmk inverted
56 4d. yellow (1893) . . . . 1·60 8·
s. Optd "Specimen" . . . . 30·00
57 6d. dull purple (1891) . . . . 2·25 13
58 1s. orange (1891) . . . . 5·50 11
a. Red-orange (1892) . . . . 11·00 17

1892 (Nov). *No. 51a surch locally with T* **11**, *in purple.*
59 **1** 5d.on 4d. chocolate . . . . 19·00 30·
s. Optd "Specimen" . . . . 30·00
sa. Error. "Spicemen" £550

Some letters are known double due to loose type, the best kno being the first "E", but they are not constant.

FIVE PENCE
(12)

13

14

Short "F" (R. 5/1)

1893–94. *Surch with T* 12. Wmk Crown CA. P 14.

50	1	5d.on 6d. carmine-lake	20·00	30·00
		a. Deep lake (1893)	1·00	1·75
		b. Lake (1894)	1·75	4·25
		c. Surch double	£4500	£3000
		d. Short "F"	25·00	30·00
		s. Optd "Specimen"	45·00	

(Recess D.L.R.)

1897 (13 July). *New values.* Wmk Crown CA. P 14.

61	1	2½d. blue	4·00	1·75
62		5d. sepia	5·50	21·00
61s/2s Optd "Specimen" *Set of* 2			60·00	

1897 (6 Oct). *Surch as T* 12. Wmk Crown CA. P 14.

63	1	3d.on 1d. mauve	5·00	17·00
		a. Red-mauve	10·00	28·00
		s. Optd "Specimen"	40·00	

(Typo D.L.R.)

1899 (1 Jan). Wmk Crown CA. P 14.

67	13	½d. dull mauve and green	2·75	2·50
68		1d. dull mauve and carmine	4·50	1·25
		w. Wmk inverted	£250	
69		2½d. dull mauve and blue	4·00	2·00
70		3d. dull mauve and olive	4·00	13·00
71		4d. dull mauve and orange	4·00	17·00
72		5d. dull mauve and black	7·00	13·00
73		6d. dull mauve and brown	13·00	35·00
74	14	1s. green and carmine	13·00	48·00
75		5s. green and blue	75·00	£140
67/75 *Set of* 9			£110	£225
67s/75s Optd "Specimen" *Set of* 9			£170	

15

16

(Typo D.L.R)

1902. Wmk Crown CA. P 14.

76	15	½d. dull purple and green	3·00	70
77		1d. dull purple and carmine	4·25	30
78	16	2d. dull purple and black	2·50	2·25
79	15	2½d. dull purple and blue	5·00	3·50
80		3d. dull purple and olive	5·00	3·25
81		6d. dull purple and brown	11·00	30·00
82	16	1s. green and carmine	24·00	55·00
83	15	2s. green and violet	25·00	55·00
84	16	5s. green and blue	70·00	£120
76/84 *Set of* 9			£130	£225
76s/84s Optd "Specimen" *Set of* 9			£120	

1904–11. *Ordinary paper (½d., 1d., 1s.) or chalk-surfaced paper (others).* Wmk Mult Crown CA. P 14.

85	15	½d. dull purple and green (1905)	7·50	3·25
		a. Chalk-surfaced paper	1·25	1·25
86		1d. dull purple and carmine	24·00	1·50
		a. Chalk-surfaced paper	20·00	1·50
88		2½d. dull purple and blue (1906)	16·00	42·00
89		6d. dull purple and brown (1905)	16·00	42·00
90	16	1s. green and carmine (1906)	18·00	48·00
		a. Chalk-surfaced paper	11·00	55·00
91	15	2s. purple and bright blue/*blue* (3.09?)	23·00	42·00
92	16	5s. green and red/*yellow* (3.09?)	17·00	50·00
93		£1 purple and black/*red* (22.7.11)	£275	£325
85/93 *Set of* 8			£350	£475
91s/3s Optd "Specimen" *Set of* 3			£190	

Examples of most values are known showing a forged Kingstown postmark code letter "O", dated "JA 7 10" or a forged Calliaqua postmark dated "SP 20 09". Both have also been seen on some values of the 1899 and 1902 issues.

17

18

(Recess D.L.R.)

1907–08. Wmk Mult Crown CA. P 14.

94	17	½d. green (2.7.07)	3·25	2·25
95		1d. carmine (26.4.07)	3·50	15
96		2d. orange (5.08)	1·50	6·50
97		2½d. blue (8.07)	28·00	8·50
98		3d. violet (1.6.07)	8·00	15·00
94/8 *Set of* 5			40·00	29·00
94s/8s Optd "Specimen" *Set of* 5			£110	

1909. *No dot below "d".* Wmk Mult Crown CA. P 14.

99	18	1d. carmine (3.09)	1·25	30
100		6d. dull purple (16.1.09)	5·50	32·00
101		1s. black/*green* (16.1.09)	4·25	8·50
99/101 *Set of* 3			10·00	38·00
99s/101s Optd "Specimen" *Set of* 3			70·00	

1909 (Nov)–**11.** *T* 18, *redrawn (dot below "d", as in T* 17*).* Wmk Mult Crown CA. P 14.

102		½d. green (31.10.10)	1·50	60
		w. Wmk inverted	95·00	
103		1d. carmine	1·50	20
104		2d. grey (3.8.11)	4·00	8·50
105		2½d. ultramarine (25.7.10)	8·00	3·50
106		3d. purple/*yellow*	2·50	7·00
107		6d. dull purple	10·00	5·00
102/7 *Set of* 6			25·00	22·00
102s, 104s/6s Optd "Specimen" *Set of* 4			85·00	

19

ONE

PENNY.

(20)

(Recess D.L.R.)

1913 (1 Jan)–**17.** Wmk Mult Crown CA. P 14.

108	19	½d. green	75	20
109		1d. red	80	75
		a. Rose-red	1·00	75
		b. Scarlet (1.17)	14·00	5·00
		w. Wmk inverted		
		y. Wmk inverted and reversed	85·00	
110		2d. grey	7·00	29·00
		a. Slate	3·00	29·00
111		2½d. ultramarine	50	75
		x. Wmk reversed	£120	
112		3d. purple/*yellow*	80	5·00
		a. On lemon	2·75	12·00
		aw. Wmk inverted		
		ax. Wmk reversed		
		b. On pale yellow	2·50	9·00
113		4d. red/*yellow*	80	2·00
114		5d. olive-green (7.11.13)	2·25	14·00
		x. Wmk reversed		
115		6d. claret	2·00	4·50
116		1s. black/*green*	1·50	3·75
117		1s. bistre (1.5.14)	4·00	23·00
118	18	2s. blue and purple	4·75	25·00
119		5s. carmine and myrtle	13·00	48·00
		x. Wmk reversed	£190	
120		£1 mauve and black	85·00	£160
108/20 *Set of* 13			£110	£275
108s/20s Optd "Specimen" *Set of* 13			£250	

Nos. 118/20 are from new centre and frame dies, the motto "PAX ET JUSTITIA" being slightly over 7 mm long, as against just over 8 mm in Nos. 99 to 107. Nos. 139/41 are also from the new dies.

Examples of several values are known showing part strikes of the forged postmarks mentioned below Nos. 85/93.

1915. *No.* 116 *surch with T* 20.

121	19	1d.on 1s. black/*green* (R.)	7·50	26·00
		a. "ONE" omitted	£900	£800
		b. "ONE" double	£650	
		c. "PENNY" and bar double	£650	£650

The spacing between the two words varies from 7¾ mm to 10 mm.

WAR STAMP. (21) WAR STAMP. (22) WAR STAMP (24)

1916 (June). *No.* 109 *optd locally with T* 21.

(a) First and second settings; words 2 to 2½ mm apart.

122	19	1d. red	6·50	9·00
		a. Opt double	£160	£160
		b. Comma for stop	8·50	17·00
		w. Wmk inverted		

In the first printing every second stamp has the comma for stop. The second printing of this setting has full stops only. These two printings can therefore only be distinguished in blocks or pairs.

(b) Third setting; words only 1½ mm apart.

123	19	1d. red	80·00	
		a. Opt double	£1100	

Stamps of the first setting are offered as this rare one. Care must be taken to see that the distance between the lines is not over 1½ mm.

(c) Fourth setting; optd with T 22*. Words* 3½ *mm apart.*

124	19	1d. carmine-red	3·00	13·00
		a. Opt double	£225	
		w. Wmk inverted		
		y. Wmk inverted and reversed		

1916 (Aug)–**18.** *T* 19, *from new printings, optd with T* 24.

126		1d. carmine-red	30	80
		s. Optd "Specimen"	60·00	
		w. Wmk inverted		
		x. Wmk reversed		
127		1d. pale rose-red	80	80
		w. Wmk inverted	60·00	
		x. Wmk reversed		
128		1d. deep rose-red	65	80
129		1d. pale scarlet (1918)	30	80

1921–32. Wmk Mult Script CA. P 14.

131	19	½d. green (3.21)	1·75	30
132		1d. carmine (6.21)	1·00	80
		a. Red	2·50	15
132*b*		1½d. brown (1.12.32)	3·25	15
133		2d. grey (3.22)	2·50	80
133*a*		2½d. bright blue (12.25)	1·25	1·25
134		3d. bright blue (3.22)	1·00	6·00
135		3d. purple/*yellow* (1.12.26)	1·00	1·50
135*a*		4d. red/*yellow* (9.30)	1·75	6·00
136		5d. sage-green (8.3.24)	1·00	6·50
137		6d. claret (1.11.27)	1·50	3·50
138		1s. bistre-brown (9.21)	6·00	25·00
		a. Ochre (1927)	3·25	17·00
139	18	2s. blue and purple (8.3.24)	7·50	13·00
140		5s. carmine and myrtle (8.3.24)	18·00	32·00
141		£1 mauve and black (9.28)	90·00	£130
131/41 *Set of* 14			£120	£200
131s/41s Optd or Perf (1½d., 4d., £1) "Specimen" *Set of* 14			£300	

Examples of Nos. 140/1 are known with forged postmarks, including part strikes of those mentioned above, and others from Kingstown dated "6 MY 35" and "16 MY 41 ".

1935 (6 May). *Silver Jubilee. As Nos.* 91/4 *of Antigua, but ptd by Waterlow.* P 11 × 12.

142	1d. deep blue and scarlet	40	2·25
143	1½d. ultramarine and grey	1·00	3·50
144	2½d. brown and deep blue	1·90	3·50
145	1s. slate and purple	2·00	3·50
	l. Kite and horizontal log	£325	
142/5 *Set of* 4		4·75	11·50
142s/5s Perf "Specimen" *Set of* 4		80·00	

For illustration of plate variety see Omnibus section following Zanzibar.

1937 (12 May). *Coronation. As Nos.* 95/7 *of Antigua.* P 11 × 11½.

146	1d. violet	35	1·00
147	1½d. carmine	40	1·00
148	2½d. blue	45	2·00
146/8 *Set of* 3		1·10	3·50
146s/8s Perf "Specimen" *Set of* 3		60·00	

25

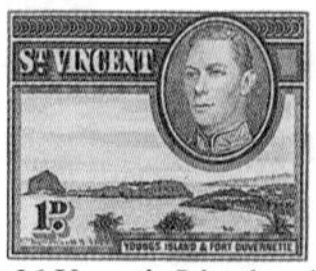

26 Young's Island and Fort Duvernette

27 Kingstown and Fort Charlotte

28 Bathing Beach at Villa

29 Victoria Park, Kingstown

NEW CONSTITUTION 1951

(29a)

(Recess B.W.)

1938 (11 Mar)–**47.** Wmk Mult Script CA. P 12.

149	25	½d. blue and green	20	10
150	26	1d. blue and lake-brown	20	10
151	27	1½d. green and scarlet	20	10
152	25	2d. green and black	40	35
153	28	2½d. blue-black and blue-green	20	40
153*a*	29	2½d. green and purple-brown (1947)	40	20
154	25	3d. orange and purple	20	10
154*a*	28	3½d. blue-black and blue-green (1947)	40	2·50
155	25	6d. black and lake	1·00	40
156	29	1s. purple and green	1·00	80
157	25	2s. blue and purple	6·00	75
157*a*		2s.6d. red-brown and blue (1947)	1·25	3·50
158		5s. scarlet and deep green	10·00	2·50
158*a*		10s. violet and brown (1947)	4·00	9·00
		aw. Wmk inverted	£4500	£1500
159		£1 purple and black	16·00	15·00
149/59 *Set of* 15			35·00	30·00
149s/59s Perf "Specimen" *Set of* 15			£275	

1946 (15 Oct). *Victory. As Nos.* 110/11 *of Antigua.*

160	1½d. carmine	10	10
161	3½d. blue	10	10
160s/1s Perf "Specimen" *Set of* 2		60·00	

1948 (30 Nov). *Royal Silver Wedding. As Nos.* 112/13 *of Antigua.*

162	1½d. scarlet	10	10
163	£1 bright purple	16·00	19·00

No. 163 was originally printed in black, but the supply of these was stolen in transit. A few archive examples exist, some perforated "Specimen".

(New Currency. 100 cents = 1 West Indian dollar)

1949 (26 Mar)–**52.** *Value in cents and dollars.* Wmk Mult Script CA. P 12.

164	25	1c. blue and green	20	1·75
164*a*		1c. green and black (10.6.52)	30	2·50
165	26	2c. blue and lake-brown	15	50
166	27	3c. green and scarlet	50	1·00
166*a*	25	3c. orange and purple (10.6.52)	30	2·50
167		4c. green and black	35	20
167*a*		4c. blue and green (10.6.52)	30	20
168	29	5c. green and purple-brown	15	10
169	25	6c. orange and purple	50	1·25
169*a*	27	6c. green and scarlet (10.6.52)	30	2·25
170	28	7c. blue-black and blue-green	5·50	1·50
170*a*		10c. blue-black and blue-green (10.6.52)	50	20
171	25	12c. black and lake	35	15
172	29	24c. purple and green	35	55
173	25	48c. blue and purple	2·75	2·75
174		60c. red-brown and blue	2·00	4·00
175		$1.20, scarlet and deep green	4·25	4·25
176		$2.40, violet and brown	6·00	10·00
177		$4.80, purple and black	12·00	20·00
164/77 *Set of* 19			32·00	48·00

1949 (10 Oct). *75th Anniv of U.P.U. As Nos.* 114/17 *of Antigua.*

178	5c. blue	20	15
179	6c. purple	1·25	1·90
180	12c. magenta	20	1·90
181	24c. blue-green	20	75
178/81 *Set of* 4		1·60	4·25

1951 (16 Feb). *Inauguration of B.W.I. University College. As Nos. 118/19 of Antigua.*
182 3c. deep green and scarlet . . . 30 50
183 12c. black and purple . . . 30 1·50

1951 (21 Sept). *New Constitution. Optd with T* **29a** *by B.W.*
184 **27** 3c. green and scarlet . . . 20 1·75
185 **25** 4c. green and black . . . 20 40
186 **29** 5c. green and purple-brown . . . 20 40
187 **25** 12c. black and lake . . . 1·25 1·00
184/7 *Set of* 4 . . . 1·60 3·25

Samoa
see after New Zealand

Sarawak

Sarawak was placed under British protection in 1888. It was ceded to Great Britain on 1 July 1946 and was administered as a Crown Colony until 16 September 1963 when it became a state of the Federation of Malaysia.

From 1859 letters from Sarawak to overseas addresses, other than to other British possessions in Borneo and Singapore, were franked by stamps of INDIA and, after 1867, STRAITS SETTLEMENTS, a stock of which was kept by the Sarawak Post Office. The stamps of Sarawak continued to have this limited validity until 1 July 1897 when the country joined the U.P.U.

PRICES FOR STAMPS ON COVER TO 1945		
No.	1	—
Nos.	2/7	*from* × 50
Nos.	8/21	*from* × 8
Nos.	22/6	*from* × 6
No.	27	*from* × 40
Nos.	28/35	*from* × 6
Nos.	36/47	*from* × 8
No.	48	†
No.	49	*from* × 10
Nos.	50/61	*from* × 6
No.	62	†
Nos.	63/71	*from* × 4
Nos.	72/3	*from* × 8
Nos.	74/5	—
Nos.	76/90	*from* × 7
Nos.	91/105	*from* × 5
Nos.	106/25	*from* × 3
Nos.	126/45	*from* × 2

BROOKE FAMILY ADMINISTRATION

Sir James Brooke. 1842–11 June 1868
Sir Charles Brooke. 11 June 1868–17 May 1917

UNUSED PRICES. Nos. 1/7, 27 and 32/5 in unused condition are normally found to be without gum. Prices in the unused column are for stamps in this state. Examples of these issues with original gum are worth considerably more.

1 Sir James Brooke

2 Sir Charles Brooke

The initials in the corners of T **1** and **2** stand for "James (Charles) Brooke, Rajah (of) Sarawak".

(T **1** and **2**. Die eng Wm. Ridgeway. Litho Maclure, Macdonald & Co, Glasgow)

1869 (1 Mar). P 11.
1 **1** 3c. brown/*yellow* . . . 48·00 £225

Similar stamps are known printed from the engraved die in orange-brown on orange surface-coloured paper, and perf 12. These are specimens submitted to the Sarawak authorities and exist both with and without obliterations.

1871 (1 Jan). P 11 (irregular).
2 **2** 3c. brown/*yellow* . . . 1·75 3·50
a. Stop after "THREE" . . . 45·00 55·00
b. Imperf between (vert pair) . . . £500
c. Imperf between (horiz pair) . . . £800

The "stop" variety, No. 2a, which occurs on R. 10/7 is of no more philatelic importance than any of the numerous other variations, such as narrow first "A" in "SARAWAK" (R. 2/7) and "R" with long tail in left lower corner (R. 9/10), but it has been accepted by collectors for many years, and we therefore retain it. The papermaker's wmk "L N L" appears once or twice in sheets of No. 2.

Specimens are known, recess-printed, similar to those mentioned in the note after No. 1.

TWO CENTS

Copies of No. 2 surcharged as above were first reported in 1876 but following the discovery of dies for forgeries and faked postmarks in 1891 it was concluded that the issue was bogus, especially as the availability of the 2c. of 1875 made it unnecessary to issue a provisional. It has now been established that a 2c. postal rate was introduced from 1 August 1874 for the carriage of newspapers. Moreover four examples are known with a stop after "CENTS." and showing other minor differences from the forgery illustrated. This version could be genuine and if others come to light we will reconsider listing it.

1875 (1 Jan). P 11½–12.
3 **2** 2c. mauve/*lilac* (*shades*) . . . 5·50 17·00
4 4c. red-brown/*yellow* . . . 3·25 3·00
a. Imperf between (vert pair) . . . £700
5 6c. green/*green* . . . 3·50 3·50
6 8c. bright blue/*blue* . . . 3·50 3·50
7 12c. red/*pale rose* . . . 7·00 6·50
3/7 *Set of* 5 . . . 21·00 30·00

Nos. 3, 4, 6 and 7 have the watermark "L N L" in the sheet, as No. 2. No. 5 is watermarked "L N T".

All values exist imperf and can be distinguished from the proofs by shade and impression. Stamps rouletted, pin-perf, or roughly perf 6½ to 7 are proofs clandestinely perforated.

The 12c. "laid" paper, formerly listed, is not on a true laid paper, the "laid" effect being accidental and not consistent.

The lithographic stones for Nos. 3 to 7 were made up from strips of five distinct impressions hence there are five types of each value differing mainly in the lettering of the tablets of value. There are flaws on nearly every individual stamp, from which they can be plated.

4 Sir Charles Brooke

(Typo D.L.R.)

1888 (10 Nov)–**97**. No wmk. P 14.
8 **4** 1c. purple and black (6.6.92) . . . 1·75 50
9 2c. purple and carmine (11.11.88) . . . 2·75 1·50
a. Purple and rosine (1897) . . . 9·00 3·75
10 3c. purple and blue (11.11.88) . . . 3·00 2·75
11 4c. purple and yellow . . . 17·00 50·00
12 5c. purple and green (12.6.91) . . . 12·00 2·50
13 6c. purple and brown (11.11.88) . . . 14·00 55·00
14 8c. green and carmine (11.11.88) . . . 9·50 3·00
a. Green and rosine (1897) . . . 21·00 15·00
15 10c. green and purple (12.6.91) . . . 38·00 14·00
16 12c. green and blue (11.11.88) . . . 8·50 8·50
17 16c. green and orange (28.12.97) . . . 42·00 75·00
18 25c. green and brown (19.11 88) . . . 40·00 38·00
19 32c. green and black (28.12.97) . . . 29·00 55·00
20 50c. green (26.7.97) . . . 40·00 85·00
21 $1 green and black (2.11.97) . . . 70·00 80·00
8/21 *Set of* 14 . . . £300 £425

Prepared for use but not issued.
21*a* $2 green and blue . . . £650
21*b* $5 green and violet . . . £650
21*c* $10 green and carmine . . . £650

On No. 21 the value is in black on an uncoloured ground.

The tablet of value in this and later similar issues is in the second colour given.

One Cent. (5) **one cent.** (6)

2c. (7) **5c** (8) **5c.** (9)

1889 (3 Aug)–**92**. *T* **4** *surch.* P 14.
22 **5** 1c. on 3c. purple and blue (12.1.92) . . . 42·00 29·00
a. Surch double . . . £600 £500
23 **6** 1c. on 3c. purple and blue (2.92) . . . 3·00 2·75
a. No stop after "cent" (R. 2/6) . . . £160
24 **7** 2c. on 8c. green and carmine (3.8.89) . . . 3·00 5·50
a. Surch double . . . £400
b. Surch inverted . . . £2500
c. Surch omitted (in pair with normal) . . . £4500
25 **8** 5c. on 12c. green and blue (with stop after "C") (17.2.91) . . . 24·00 45·00
a. No stop after "C" . . . 26·00 48·00
b. "C" omitted . . . £400 £400
c. Surch double . . . £1000
d. Surch double, one vertical . . . £2750
e. Surch omitted (in pair with normal) . . . £7500
26 **9** 5c. on 12c. green and blue (17.2.91) . . . £110 £170
a. No stop after "C" . . . 90·00 £110
b. "C" omitted . . . £550 £600
c. Surch double . . . £1200

ONE CENT

(10)

1892 (23 May). *No. 2 surch with T* **10**.
27 **2** 1c. on 3c. brown/*yellow* . . . 1·40 2·00
a. Stop after "THREE." . . . 38·00 40·00
b. Imperf between (vert pair) . . . £650
c. Imperf horiz (vert pair) . . . £600
d. Bar omitted (1st ptg) . . . £200
e. Bar at top and bottom (1st ptg) . . . £275
f. Surch double (2nd ptg) . . . £400 £425

No. 27 was surcharged with a setting of 100 (10 × 10). It was originally intended that there should be no bar at foot, but this was then added at a second operation before the stamps were issued. Subsequent supplies were surcharged with "ONE CENT" and bar at one operation.

Varieties with part of the surcharge missing are due to gum on the face of the unsurcharged stamps receiving part of the surcharge, which was afterwards washed off.

11

12

13 Sir Charles Brooke 14

(Die eng Wm. Ridgeway. Recess P.B.)

1895 (12 Feb–Sept). No wmk. P 11½–12.
28 **11** 2c. brown-red . . . 8·00 9·0
a. Imperf between (vert pair) . . . £425
b. Imperf between (horiz pair) . . . £350
c. Second ptg. Perf 12½ (Sept) . . . 9·50 4·5
ca. Perf 12½. Imperf between (horiz pair) . . . £450
29 **12** 4c. black . . . 8·00 3·5
a. Imperf between (horiz pair) . . . £550
30 **13** 6c. violet . . . 9·00 9·0
31 **14** 8c. green . . . 27·00 6·0
28/31 *Set of* 4 . . . 48·00 21·0

Stamps of these types, printed in wrong colours, are trials and these, when surcharged with values in "pence", are from wast sheets that were used by Perkins, Bacon & Co as trial paper whe preparing an issue of stamps for British South Africa.

(15)

16

1899 (29 June–16 Nov). *Surch as T* **15**.
32 **2** 2c. on 3c. brown/*yellow* (19 Sept) . . . 1·40 1·7
a. Stop after "THREE" . . . 55·00 55·0
b. Imperf between (vert pair) . . . £900
33 2c. on 12c. red/*pale rose* . . . 2·75 3·(
a. Surch inverted . . . £800 £12(
34 4c. on 6c. green/*green* (R.) (16 Nov) . . . 26·00 65·(
35 4c. on 8c. bright blue/*blue* (R.) . . . 3·50 7·
32/5 *Set of* 4 . . . 30·00 70·(

A variety of surcharge with small "S" in "CENTS" may be foun in the 2c. on 12c. and 4c. on 8c. and a raised stop after "CENTS on the 4c. on 6c.

The omission of parts of the surcharge is due to gum on th surface of the stamps (see note after No. 27).

A block of 50 of No. 35 from the right of the pane is known lir perforated 12.7 between the stamps and the margins at top ar right.

(Typo D.L.R.)

1899 (10 Nov)–**1908**. *Inscribed* "POSTAGE POSTAGE." No wm P 14.
36 **4** 1c. grey blue and rosine (1.1.01) . . . 1·25 1·
a. Grey-blue and red . . . 4·50 1·
b. Ultramarine and rosine . . . 7·50 2·
c. Dull blue and carmine . . . 15·00 4·
37 2c. green (16.12.99) . . . 2·00
38 3c. dull purple (1.2.08) . . . 8·50
39 4c. rose-carmine (10.11.99) . . . 8·50 2·
a. Aniline carmine . . . 2·50
40 8c. yellow and black (6.12.99) . . . 1·75
41 10c. ultramarine (10.11.99) . . . 2·50 1·
42 12c. mauve (16.12.99) . . . 4·50 4·
a. Bright mauve (1905) . . . 24·00 8·
43 16c. chestnut and green (16.12.99) . . . 3·00 1·
44 20c. bistre and bright mauve (4.00) . . . 5·50 3·
45 25c. brown and blue (16.12.99) . . . 5·00 5·
46 50c. sage-green and carmine (16.12.99) . . . 20·00 25·
47 $1 rose-carmine and green (16.12.99) . . . 50·00 £1
a. Rosine and pale green . . . 70·00 £1
36/47 *Set of* 12 . . . 95·00 £1

Prepared for use but not issued.
48 **4** 5c. olive-grey and green . . . 12·00

The figures of value in the $1 are in colour on an uncolour ground.

1902. *Inscribed* "POSTAGE POSTAGE". W **16**. P 14.
49 **4** 2c. green . . . 23·00 14·

Sir Charles Vyner Brooke. 17 May 1917–1 June 1946

17 Sir Charles Vyner Brooke

(18)

(Typo D.L.R.)

918 (24 Mar–Apr). *Chalk-surfaced paper*. No wmk. P 14.

0	17	1c. slate-blue and red	2·25	2·50
		a. Dull blue and carmine	2·25	2·50
1		2c. green	2·50	1·50
2		3c. brown-purple (Apr)	3·25	2·75
3		4c. rose-carmine (Apr)	4·00	3·00
		a. Rose-red	4·75	3·00
4		8c. yellow and black (Apr)	12·00	60·00
5		10c. blue (*shades*) (Apr)	3·00	3·25
5		12c. purple (Apr)	11·00	27·00
7		16c. chestnut and green (Apr)	5·50	7·50
3		20c. olive and violet (*shades*) (Apr)	7·00	6·50
)		25c. brown and bright blue (Apr)	4·00	13·00
)		50c. olive-green and carmine (Apr)	10·00	15·00
		$1 bright rose and green (Apr)	18·00	28·00
)/61 *Set of* 12			75·00	£150
)s/61s Optd "Specimen" *Set of* 12			£275	

Prepared for use but not issued.

2	17	1c. slate-blue and slate	22·00	

On the $1 the figures of value are in colour on an uncoloured round.

Most values are known with part strikes of a forged Kuching ostmark dated "12 MAR 90".

922 (Jan)–**23**. *New colours and values. Chalk-surfaced paper*. No wmk. P 14.

3	17	2c. purple (5.3.23)	2·00	2·75
4		3c. dull green (23.3.22)	1·50	1·25
5		4c. brown-purple (10.4.23)	1·50	85
5		5c. yellow-orange	1·75	90
7		6c. claret	1·50	1·40
3		8c. bright rose-red (1922)	4·50	32·00
		10c. black (1923)	2·00	4·00
)		12c. bright blue (12.22)	10·00	18·00
		a. Pale dull blue	9·50	19·00
		30c. ochre-brown and slate	3·75	4·25
3/71 *Set of* 9			25·00	60·00

23 (Jan). *Surch as T* **18**.

(a) First printing. Bars $1\frac{1}{4}$ mm apart.

2	17	1c. on 10c. dull blue	10·00	55·00
		a. "cnet" for "cent" (R. 9/5)	£375	£850
		2c. on 12c. purple	6·50	42·00
		a. Thick, narrower "W" in "TWO"	19·00	90·00

(b) Second printing. Bars $\frac{3}{4}$ mm apart.

	17	1c. on 10c. dull blue	£300	
		b. "cnet" for "cent" (R. 9/5)	£12000	
		c. Bright blue	£120	£350
		ca. "en" of "cent" scratched out and "ne" overprinted (R. 9/5)	£4500	
		2c. on 12c. purple	70·00	£200
		a. Thick, narrower "W" in "TWO"	£150	

In the 2c. on 12c. the words of the surcharge are about $7\frac{1}{2}$ mm om the bars.

The "cnet" error occurred on R. 9/5 of all sheets from the first inting of the 1c. on 10c. A single example of the error, No. 74b, known from the second printing, but the error was then corrected, shown by the evidence of a surviving plate block, only to have correct spelling scratched out by a local employee, and "ne" bstituted (No. 74ca).

The thick "W" variety occurs on all stamps of the last two rizontal rows of the first printing (12 stamps per sheet), and in last two vertical rows of the second (20 stamps per sheet).

28 (7 Apr)–**29**. *Chalk-surfaced paper*. W **16** (Multiple). P 14.

	17	1c. slate-blue and carmine	1·50	35
		2c. bright purple	1·75	1·25
		3c. green	2·00	5·00
		4c. brown-purple	1·75	10
		5c. yellow-orange (7.8.29)	11·00	5·00
		6c. claret	1·25	30
		8c. bright rose-red	3·25	16·00
		10c. black	1·75	1·25
		12c. bright blue	3·25	23·00
		16c. chestnut and green	3·25	4·00
		20c. olive-bistre and violet	3·25	5·50
		25c. brown and bright blue	5·50	8·50
		30c. bistre-brown and slate	4·50	10·00
		50c. olive-green and carmine	5·50	14·00
		$1 bright rose and green	15·00	24·00
'90 *Set of* 15			60·00	£110
s/90s Optd or Perf (5c.) "Specimen" *Set of* 15			£275	

In the $1 the value is as before.

19 Sir Charles Vyner Brooke

20

(Recess Waterlow)

32 (1 Jan). W **20**. P $12\frac{1}{2}$.

	19	1c. indigo	80	1·00
		2c. green	1·00	1·50
		3c. violet	3·25	1·00
		4c. red-orange	1·75	75
		5c. deep lake	8·00	1·25

96		6c. scarlet	8·50	9·50
97		8c. orange-yellow	5·50	8·50
98		10c. black	2·25	3·25
99		12c. deep ultramarine	4·00	9·50
100		15c. chestnut	7·50	8·50
101		20c. red-orange and violet	6·00	8·00
102		25c. orange-yellow and chestnut	14·00	22·00
103		30c. sepia and vermilion	9·50	24·00
104		50c. carmine-red and olive-green	14·00	13·00
105		$1 green and carmine	22·00	35·00
91/105 *Set of* 15			95·00	£130
91s/105s Perf "Specimen" *Set of* 15			£325	

21 Sir Charles Vyner Brooke

BMA

(22)

(Recess B.W.)

1934 (1 May)–**41**. No wmk. P 12.

106	21	1c. purple	1·25	10
107		2c. green	1·50	10
107*a*		2c. black (1.3.41)	3·25	1·60
108		3c. black	1·25	10
108*a*		3c. green (1.3.41)	6·00	4·50
109		4c. bright purple	1·25	15
110		5c. violet	1·75	10
111		6c. carmine	2·75	60
111*a*		6c. lake-brown (1.3.41)	6·50	8·00
112		8c. red-brown	2·25	10
112*a*		8c. carmine (1.3.41)	7·50	10
113		10c. scarlet	2·25	40
114		12c. blue	3·00	25
114*a*		12c. orange (1.3.41)	5·00	4·75
115		15c. orange	3·50	10·00
115*a*		15c. blue (1.3.41)	7·50	15·00
116		20c. olive-green and carmine	3·50	1·25
117		25c. violet and orange	4·00	1·50
118		30c. red-brown and violet	4·00	2·50
119		50c. violet and scarlet	4·00	75
120		$1 scarlet and sepia	1·50	75
121		$2 bright purple and violet	13·00	11·00
122		$3 carmine and green	28·00	30·00
123		$4 blue and scarlet	28·00	50·00
124		$5 scarlet and red-brown	32·00	50·00
125		$10 black and yellow	22·00	55·00
106/25 *Set of* 26			£180	£225
106s/25s Perf "Specimen" *Set of* 26			£475	

For the 3c. green, wmkd Mult Script CA, see No. 152a.

BRITISH MILITARY ADMINISTRATION

Following the Japanese surrender, elements of the British Military Administration reached Kuching on 11 September 1945. From 5 November 1945 current Australian 1d., 3d., 6d. and 1s. stamps were made available for civilian use until replaced by Nos. 126/45. Other Australian stamps were also accepted as valid for postage during this period.

1945 (17 Dec). *Optd with T* **22**.

126	21	1c. purple	1·25	60
127		2c. black (R.)	1·25	1·25
		a. Opt double	†	£5000
128		3c. green	1·25	1·50
129		4c. bright purple	1·50	30
		a. Opt double, one albino	£1700	
130		5c. violet (R.)	2·25	1·00
131		6c. lake-brown	2·75	75
132		8c. carmine	13·00	13·00
133		10c. scarlet	1·25	70
134		12c. orange	1·75	3·75
135		15c. blue	3·50	40
136		20c. olive-green and carmine	2·50	2·50
137		25c. violet and orange (R.)	2·75	2·75
138		30c. red-brown and violet	6·00	2·75
139		50c. violet and scarlet	1·25	35
140		$1 scarlet and sepia	2·50	1·25
141		$2 bright purple and violet	9·00	10·00
142		$3 carmine and green	17·00	60·00
143		$4 blue and scarlet	25·00	45·00
144		$5 scarlet and red-brown	£150	£180
145		$10 black and yellow (R.)	£140	£190
126/45 *Set of* 20			£350	£475

These stamps, and the similarly overprinted stamps of North Borneo, were obtainable at all post offices throughout British Borneo (Brunei, Labuan, North Borneo and Sarawak), for use on local and overseas mail.

The administration of Sarawak was returned to the Brooke family on 15 April 1946, but the Rajah, after consulting the inhabitants, ceded the territory to Great Britain on 1 June 1946. Values from the 1934–41 issue were used until replaced by Nos. 150/64.

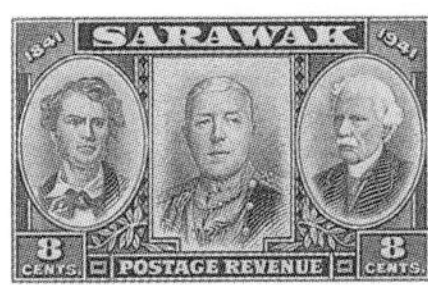

23 Sir James Brooke, Sir Charles Vyner Brooke and Sir Charles Brooke

(24)

(Recess B.W.)

1946 (18 May). *Centenary Issue*. P 12.

146	23	8c. lake	1·50	1·00
147		15c. blue	1·50	2·00
148		50c. black and scarlet	1·75	2·50
149		$1 black and sepia	2·50	19·00
146/9 *Set of* 4			6·50	22·00
146s/9s Perf "Specimen" *Set of* 4			£120	

CROWN COLONY

1947 (16 Apr). *Optd with T* **24**, *typo by B.W. in blue-black or red*. Wmk Mult Script CA. P 12.

150	21	1c. purple	15	30
151		2c. black (R.)	15	15
152		3c. green (R.)	15	15
		a. Albino opt	£4500	
153		4c. bright purple	15	15
154		6c. lake-brown	20	90
155		8c. carmine	75	10
156		10c. scarlet	20	20
157		12c. orange	20	90
158		15c. blue (R.)	20	40
159		20c. olive-green and carmine (R.)	1·75	50
160		25c. violet and orange (R.)	40	30
161		50c. violet and scarlet (R.)	40	40
162		$1 scarlet and sepia	75	90
163		$2 bright purple and violet	1·60	3·25
164		$5 scarlet and red-brown	3·00	3·25
150/64 *Set of* 15			9·00	10·50
150s/64s Perf "Specimen" *Set of* 15			£300	

No. 152a shows an uninked impression of T **24**.

1948 (25 Oct). *Royal Silver Wedding. As Nos. 112/13 of Antigua.*

165	8c. scarlet	30	30
166	$5 brown	30·00	38·00

1949 (10 Oct). *75th Anniv of U.P.U. As Nos. 114/17 of Antigua.*

167	8c. carmine	1·25	60
168	15c. deep blue	3·00	2·50
169	25c. deep blue-green	2·00	1·50
170	50c. violet	2·00	5·00
167/70 *Set of* 4		7·50	8·75

25 *Trogonoptera brookiana*

26 Western Tarsier

(Recess; Arms typo B.W.)

1950 (3 Jan). *T* **25/6** *and similar designs*. Wmk Mult Script CA. P $11\frac{1}{2}\times11$ (horiz) or $11\times11\frac{1}{2}$ (vert).

171	1c. black	40	30
172	2c. red-orange	20	40
173	3c. green	20	60
174	4c. chocolate	20	20
175	6c. turquoise-blue	20	15
176	8c. scarlet	20	30
177	10c. orange	1·00	4·00
178	12c. violet	3·50	1·50
179	15c. blue	2·50	15
180	20c. purple-brown and red-orange	1·75	30
181	25c. green and scarlet	3·00	30
182	50c. brown and violet	3·50	25
183	$1 green and chocolate	20·00	4·50
184	$2 blue and carmine	26·00	15·00
185	$5 black, yellow, red and purple	19·00	15·00
171/85 *Set of* 15		70·00	38·00

Designs: *Horiz*—8c. Dayak dancer; 10c. Malayan Pangolin; 12c. Kenyah boys; 15c. Fire-making; 20c. Kelemantan rice barn; 25c. Pepper vines; $1 Kelabit smithy; $2 Map of Sarawak; $5 Arms of Sarawak. *Vert*—3c. Kayan tomb; 4c. Kayan girl and boy; 6c. Bead work; 50c. Iban woman.

40 Map of Sarawak

(Recess B.W.)

1952 (1 Feb). Wmk Mult Script CA. P $11\frac{1}{2}\times11$.

186	40	10c. orange	1·75	50

JAPANESE OCCUPATION OF SARAWAK

Japanese forces landed in North Borneo on 16 December 1941 and Sarawak was attacked on 23 December 1941.

Brunei, North Borneo, Sarawak and after a short period, Labuan, were administered as a single territory by the Japanese. Until September–October 1942, previous stamp issues, without overprint, continued to be used in conjunction with existing postmarks. From 1 October 1942 onwards unoverprinted stamps of Japan were made available and examples can be found used from the area for much of the remainder of the War. Japanese Occupation issues for Brunei, North Borneo and Sarawak were equally valid throughout the combined territory but not, in practice, equally available.

PRICES FOR STAMPS ON COVER	
Nos. J1/21	*from* × 8
Nos. J22/6	—

府政國帝本日大

(1) ("Imperial Japanese Government")

1942 (Oct). *Stamps of Sarawak handstamped with T* **1** *in violet.*

J1	21	1c. purple	32·00	75·00
		a. Pair, one without opt	£1700	
J2		2c. green	95·00	£170
		a. Black opt	95·00	
J3		2c. black	90·00	£110
		a. Black opt	£130	£150

J4 3c. black . . . £350 £350
J5 3c. green . . . 50·00 90·00
a. Black opt . . . £110
J6 4c. bright purple . . . 70·00 90·00
a. Black opt . . . £110
J7 5c. violet . . . 80·00 90·00
a. Black opt . . . £110
J8 6c. carmine . . . £130 £130
J9 6c. lake-brown . . . 80·00 90·00
a. Black opt . . . £110 £120
J10 8c. red-brown . . . £350 £350
a. Black opt . . . £475
J11 8c. carmine . . . 75·00 £120
a. Black opt . . . £200 £275
J12 10c. scarlet . . . 75·00 95·00
a. Black opt . . . £110
J13 12c. blue . . . £150 £170
a. Black opt . . . £200
J14 12c. orange . . . £150 £180
J15 15c. orange . . . £350 £350
a. Black opt . . . £400
J16 15c. blue . . . 95·00 £110
J17 20c. olive-green and carmine . . . 60·00 95·00
a. Black opt . . . £110
J18 25c. violet and orange . . . 90·00 95·00
a. Black opt . . . £120
J19 30c. red-brown and violet . . . 65·00 95·00
a. Black opt . . . £110
J20 50c. violet and scarlet . . . 70·00 95·00
a. Black opt . . . £200
b. Blue opt . . . £400
J21 $1 scarlet and sepia . . . 95·00 £130
a. Blue opt . . . £275
J22 $2 bright purple and violet . . . £190 £275
a. Blue opt . . . £325
J23 $3 carmine and green . . . £1400 £1500
a. Black opt . . . £1900
J24 $4 blue and scarlet . . . £225 £350
J25 $5 scarlet and red-brown . . . £250 £350
J26 $10 black and yellow . . . £250 £350

The overprint, being handstamped, exists inverted or double on some values. Those on Nos. J20b, J21a and J22a are diagonal. The remainder are horizontal.

Stamps of T **21** optd with Japanese symbols within an oval frame are revenue stamps, while the same stamps overprinted with three Japanese characters between two vertical double rules, were used as seals.

"Nos. J1/26 have been extensively forged. Recent research indicates that complete or part sets on cover cancelled by Japanese circular postmarks in violet dated "17 11 21" (21 Nov 1942) or "18 3 1" (1 Mar 1943) have forged overprints."

Seychelles

Seychelles was administered as a dependency of Mauritius from 1810 until 1903, although separate stamp issues were provided from April 1890 onwards.

The first post office was opened, at Victoria on Mahé, on 11 December 1861 and the stamps of Mauritius were used there until 1890. No further post offices were opened until 1901.

Z 1

Stamps of MAURITIUS *cancelled with Type* Z **1**.

1848–59.
Z1 2d. blue (intermediate impression) (No. 14) . . . £9000

1859–61
Z2 6d. blue (No. 32) . . . £800
Z3 6d. dull purple-slate (No. 33) . . . £1700
Z4 1s. vermilion (No. 34) . . . £1300

1860–63. *(Nos. 46/53).*
Z 5 1d. purple-brown . . . £180
Z 6 2d. blue . . . £225
Z 7 4d. rose . . . £190
Z 8 6d. green . . . £800
Z 9 6d. slate . . . £500
Z10 9d. dull purple . . . £110
Z11 1s. buff . . . £300
Z12 1s. green . . . £600

1862.
Z13 6d. slate (No. 54) . . . £800

1863–72. *(Nos. 56/72).*
Z14 1d. purple-brown . . . £110
Z14*a* 1d. brown . . . 95·00
Z15 1d. bistre . . . £100
Z16 2d. pale blue . . . £120
Z17 2d. bright blue . . . £120
Z18 3d. deep red . . . £140
Z19 3d. dull red . . . 85·00
Z20 4d. rose . . . 48·00
Z21 6d. dull violet . . . £225
Z22 6d. yellow-green . . . £110
Z23 6d. blue-green . . . 75·00
Z24 9d. yellow-green . . . £1300
Z25 10d. maroon . . . £325
Z26 1s. yellow . . . £100
Z27 1s. blue . . . £275
Z28 1s. orange . . . £110
Z29 5s. rosy mauve . . . £800
Z30 5s. bright mauve . . . £800

1876. *(Nos. 76/7).*
Z31 ½d.on 9d. dull purple . . . £275
Z32 ½d.on 10d. maroon . . . £275

1877. *(Nos. 79/82).*
Z33 ½d. on 10d. rose . . . £500
Z34 1d. on 4d. rose-carmine . . .
Z35 1s. on 5s. rosy mauve . . .
Z36 1s. on 5s. bright mauve . . .

1878. *(Nos. 83/91).*
Z37 2c. dull rose (lower label blank) . . . 85·00
Z38 4c.on 1d. bistre . . . £375
Z39 8c.on 2d. blue . . . 40·00
Z40 13c.on 3d. orange-red . . . £120
Z41 17c.on 4d. rose . . . 40·00
Z42 25c.on 6d. slate-blue . . . £100
Z43 38c.on 9d. pale violet . . . £475
Z44 50c.on 1s. green . . . £110
Z45 2r.50 on 5s. bright mauve . . . £475

1879–80. *(Nos. 92/100).*
Z46 2c. Venetian red . . . £130
Z47 4c. orange . . . £130
Z48 8c. blue . . . 40·00
Z49 13c. slate . . . £1100
Z50 17c. rose . . . 90·00
Z51 25c. olive-yellow . . . £190
Z52 38c. bright purple . . . £1600
Z53 50c. green . . . £800
Z54 2r.50 brown-purple . . . £750

1883–90.
Z55 2c. Venetian red (No. 102) . . . 95·00
Z56 2c. green (No. 103) . . . £160
Z57 4c. orange (No. 104) . . . 65·00
Z58 4c. carmine (No. 105) . . . 95·00
Z59 16c. chestnut (No. 109) . . . 55·00
Z60 25c. olive-yellow (No. 110) . . . £110
Z61 50c. orange (No. 111) . . . £900

1883.
Z62 16c. on 17c. rose (No. 112) . . . £120

1883.
Z63 16c. on 17c. rose (No. 115) . . . 45·00

1885.
Z64 2c. on 38c. bright purple (No. 116) . . .

1887.
Z65 2c. on 13c. slate (No. 117) . . .

POSTAL FISCAL

1889.
ZR1 4c. lilac (No. R2) . . . £850

Mauritius stamps are occasionally found cancelled with the "SEYCHELLES" cds. Examples are known dated between 25 and 29 February 1884 when it seems that Type Z **1** may have been mislaid (*Price from* £325).

We no longer list the G.B. 1862 6d. lilac with this obliteration as there is no evidence that the stamps of Great Britain were sold by the Victoria post office.

PRICES FOR STAMPS ON COVER TO 1945

Nos.	1/8	*from* × 20
Nos.	9/24	*from* × 30
No.	25	*from* × 10
No.	26	*from* × 20
No.	27	*from* × 10
Nos.	28/32	*from* × 20
No.	33	*from* × 5
No.	34	*from* × 30
Nos.	35/6	—
Nos.	37/40	*from* × 40
Nos.	41/2	*from* × 25
Nos.	43/5	*from* × 10
Nos.	46/50	*from* × 30
Nos.	51/4	*from* × 10
Nos.	55/6	—
Nos.	57/9	*from* × 10
Nos.	60/7	*from* × 20
Nos.	68/70	—
Nos.	71/81	*from* × 10
Nos.	82/131	*from* × 5
Nos.	132/4	*from* × 10
Nos.	135/49	*from* × 3

(Currency: 100 cents = 1 Mauritius, later Seychelles rupee)

DEPENDENCY OF MAURITIUS

PRINTERS. Nos. 1 to 123 were typographed by De La Rue & Co.

1

Die I

Die II

In Die I there are lines of shading in the middle compartment of the diadem which are absent from Die II.

Normal

Malformed "S"

Repaired "S"

The malformed "S" occurs on R. 7/3 of the left pane from Ke Plate 2. It is believed that the repair to it took place in mid-189 Both states may occur on other stamps in Types **1** and **4**. Stamp subsequently printed from Key Plate 3 showed the "S" normal.

1890 (5 April)–**92**. Wmk Crown CA. P 14.

(i) Die I.
1 **1** 2c. green and carmine . . . 3·00 9·
2 4c. carmine and green . . . 26·00 11·
3 8c. brown-purple and blue . . . 9·00 3·
4 10c. ultramarine and brown . . . 7·00 18·
5 13c. grey and black . . . 6·00 11·
6 16c. chestnut and blue . . . 6·00 4·
7 48c. ochre and green . . . 20·00 10·
8 96c. mauve and carmine . . . 55·00 48·
1/8 *Set of* 8 . . . £120 £1
1s/8s Optd "Specimen" *Set of* 8 . . . £190

(ii) Die II (1892).
9 **1** 2c. green and rosine . . . 2·50
10 4c. carmine and green . . . 2·50 1·
11 8c. brown-purple and ultramarine . . . 7·50 1·
12 10c. bright ultramarine and brown . . . 9·00 3·
a. Malformed "S" . . .
13 13c. grey and black . . . 3·25 1·
14 16c. chestnut and ultramarine . . . 42·00 11·
a. Malformed "S" . . .
9/14 *Set of* 6 . . . 60·00 17·

The 10c. Die I also exists in ultramarine and chestnut, but has far only been found with "SPECIMEN" overprint (*Price* £475).

3
cents
(2)

18 CENTS
(3)

4

1893 (1 Jan). *Surch locally as T* **2**.
15 3c.on 4c. (No. 10) . . . 1·10 1·
a. Surch inverted . . . £300 £3
b. Surch double . . . £475
c. Surch omitted (in horiz pair with normal) . . . £9000
16 12c.on 16c. (No. 6) . . . 1·75 3·
a. Surch inverted . . . £450
b. Surch double . . . £12000 £90
17 12c.on 16c. (No. 14) . . . 12·00 2·
a. Surch double . . . £4500 £45
b. Surch omitted (in pair with normal) . . .
18 15c.on 16c. (No. 6) . . . 9·00 13·
a. Surch inverted . . . £325 £3
b. Surch double . . . £1200 £12
19 15c.on 16c. (No. 14) . . . 14·00 3·
a. Surch inverted . . . £900 £9
b. Surch double . . . £650 £7
c. Surch triple . . . £4250
20 45c.on 48c. (No. 7) . . . 24·00 5·
21 90c.on 96c. (No. 8) . . . 55·00 32·
a. Wide "O" (3½ mm wide instead of 3 mm) (R. 1/1, 2/1 of setting) . . . £250 £2
15/21 *Set of* 7 . . . £100 55

Nos. 15/21 were each produced from settings of 30.

Nos. 15, 16, 18, 19 and 20 exist with "cents" omitted and w "cents" above value due to misplacement of the surcharge.

Some examples of No. 15b occur in the same sheet as No. with the double surcharge on stamps from the last vertical row the left pane and the surcharge omitted on stamps from the l vertical row of the right pane.

Most examples of the inverted surcharge error No. 16a w officially defaced with a red vertical ink line (*Price* £200, *unuse* Similarly examples of No. 19a exist defaced with a horizontal line (*Price* £400, *unused*).

1893 (Nov). *New values. Die II.* Wmk Crown CA. P 14.
22 **1** 3c. dull purple and orange . . . 1·50
23 12c. sepia and green . . . 2·50
24 15c. sage-green and lilac . . . 4·50 2
25 45c. brown and carmine . . . 23·00 35
22/5 *Set of* 4 . . . 28·00 35
22s/5s Optd "Specimen" *Set of* 4 . . . 95·00

1896 (1 Aug). *No. 25 surch locally as T* **3**.
26 **1** 18c.on 45c. brown and carmine . . . 7·00 2
a. Surch double . . . £1400 £1
b. Surch triple . . . £2000
27 36c.on 45c. brown and carmine . . . 8·00 50
a. Surch double . . . £1600
26s/7s Optd "Specimen" *Set of* 2 . . . 70·00

1897–1900. *Colours changed and new values. Die II.* Wmk Cro CA. P 14.
28 **1** 2c. orange-brown and green (1900) . . . 2·00 1
a. Repaired "S" . . . £225 £
29 6c. carmine (1900) . . . 3·50
a. Repaired "S" . . . £300 £
30 15c. ultramarine (1900) . . . 4·75
a. Repaired "S" . . . £325 £

18c. ultramarine 4·50 1·00
36c. brown and carmine 25·00 4·50
4 75c. yellow and violet (1900) 55·00 70·00
a. Repaired "S" £475
1r. bright mauve and deep red 13·00 4·25
1r.50 grey and carmine (1900) 70·00 85·00
a. Repaired "S" £500
2r.25 bright mauve and green (1900) £100 85·00
a. Repaired "S" £700
6 *Set of* 9 £250 £225
36s Optd "Specimen" *Set of* 9 £250

3 cents

(5)

6 cents

(5a)

(21 June–Oct). *Surch locally with T* **5** *or* **5a**.
3c.on 10c. bright ultramarine and brown (No. 12) (9.01) 1·25 60
a. Surch double £800
b. Surch triple £1800
c. Malformed "S" £200
3c.on 16c. chestnut and ultramarine (No. 14) (8.01) 2·50 4·00
a. Surch inverted £650 £650
b. Surch double £500 £550
c. "3 cents" omitted £550 £550
d. Malformed "S" £250 £300
3c.on 36c. brown and carmine (No. 32) 50 80
a. Surch double £750 £850
b. "3 cents" omitted £650 £700
6c.on 8c. brn-pur & ultram (No. 11) (7.01) 1·50 3·00
a. Surch inverted £650 £750
0 *Set of* 4 5·25 7·50
40s H/S "Specimen" *Set of* 4 £100

2 (June). *Surch locally as T* **5**.
1 2c.on 4c. carmine and green (No. 10) 1·75 2·75
4 30c.on 75c. yellow and violet (No. 33) 1·50 4·00
a. Narrow "0" in "30" (R. 3/6, 5/2-4) 8·00 45·00
b. Repaired "S" £250
30c.on 1r. bright mauve & dp red (No. 34) 5·50 28·00
a. Narrow "0" in "30" (R. 3/6, 5/2-4) 24·00 90·00
b. Surch double £1400
45c.on 1r. bright mauve & dp red (No. 34) 3·50 30·00
45c.on 2r.25 brt mauve & grn (No. 36) 42·00 90·00
a. Narrow "5" in "45" (R. 4/1) £200 £375
b. Repaired "S" £550 £800
Set of 5 48·00 £140
5s Optd "Specimen" *Set of* 5 £120

6

7

3 cents

(8)

Dented frame (R. 1/6 of left pane)

3 (26 May). Wmk Crown CA. P 14.
6 2c. chestnut and green 1·75 2·00
a. Dented frame 95·00 £120
3c. dull green 1·00 1·25
a. Dented frame 85·00 95·00
6c. carmine 2·75 1·25
a. Dented frame £130 £110
12c. olive-sepia and dull green 2·75 2·50
a. Dented frame £130 £140
15c. ultramarine 4·00 2·50
a. Dented frame £180 £150
18c. sage-green and carmine 4·25 6·50
a. Dented frame £180 £250
30c. violet and dull green 7·00 11·00
a. Dented frame £225 £325
45c. brown and carmine 7·00 11·00
a. Dented frame £275 £325
w. Wmk inverted £300 £350
7 75c. yellow and violet 10·00 28·00
a. Dented frame £275
1r.50 black and carmine 45·00 70·00
a. Dented frame £550 £750
2r.25 purple and green 32·00 85·00
a. Dented frame £475 £750
56 *Set of* 11 £100 £200
/56s Optd "Specimen" *Set of* 11 £200

3. *Surch locally with T* **8**.
6 3c.on 15c. ultramarine (3.7) 1·00 3·25
a. Dented frame £160
3c.on 18c. sage-green and carmine (2.9) 2·75 38·00
a. Dented frame £250 £750
3c.on 45c. brown and carmine (21.7) 3·00 3·25
a. Dented frame £250
9 *Set of* 3 6·00 40·00
/9s H/S "Specimen" *Set of* 3 80·00

CROWN COLONY

The Seychelles became a Seperate Crown Colony by Letters Patent dated 31 August 1903.

1906. Wmk Mult Crown CA. P 14.
60 **6** 2c. chestnut and green 1·50 4·25
a. Dented frame 85·00 £140
61 3c. dull green 1·50 1·50
a. Dented frame 95·00 £110
62 6c. carmine 2·00 80
a. Dented frame £110 85·00
63 12c. olive-sepia and dull green 3·00 3·25
a. Dented frame £150 £160
64 15c. ultramarine 3·00 2·00
a. Dented frame £140 £140
65 18c. sage-green and carmine 3·00 6·50
a. Dented frame £140 £225
66 30c. violet and dull green 6·00 8·00
a. Dented frame £250 £275
67 45c. brown and carmine 3·00 6·50
a. Dented frame £225 £275
68 **7** 75c. yellow and violet 8·50 55·00
a. Dented frame £300
69 1r.50 black and carmine 55·00 60·00
a. Dented frame £550 £550
70 2r.25 purple and green 35·00 60·00
a. Dented frame £475
60/70 *Set of* 11 £110 £180

9

10

1912 (Apr)–**16**. Wmk Mult Crown CA. P 14.
71 **9** 2c. chestnut and green 70 5·00
a. Split "A" 70·00 £150
72 3c. green 2·00 60
a. Split "A" 85·00 75·00
73 6c. Carmine-red (6.13) 4·25 70
a. Aniline-carmine(1916) 13·00 4·50
b. Split "A" £150 75·00
74 12c. olive-sepia and dull green (1.13) 1·25 4·00
a. Split "A" £100 £150
75 15c. ultramarine 3·75 75
a. Split "A" £150 75·00
76 18c. sage-green and carmine (1.13) 3·25 5·50
a. Split "A" £140 £200
77 30c. violet and green (1.13) 5·00 1·25
a. Split "A" £180 £110
78 45c. brown and carmine (1.13) 2·75 35·00
a. Split "A" £160
79 **10** 75c. yellow and violet (1.13) 2·75 5·50
a. Split "A" £160 £225
80 1r.50 black and carmine (1.13) 7·50 1·00
a. Split "A" £275 £110
81 2r.25 dp magenta & grn (*shades*) (1.13) 50·00 2·50
a. Split "A" £550 £170
71/81 *Set of* 11 75·00 55·00
71s/81s Optd "Specimen" *Set of* 11 £225
For illustration of "Split "A" flaw see above St. Helena No. 83.

11

12

13

1917–22. *Die I. Chalk-surfaced paper (18c. to 5r.).* Wmk Mult Crown CA. P 14.
82 **11** 2c. chestnut and green 50 2·75
83 3c. green 2·00 1·25
84 **12** 5c. deep brown (1920) 2·25 6·50
85 **11** 6c. carmine 2·00 1·50
a. Rose (1919) 4·75 2·50
86 12c. grey (1919) 1·00 1·00
87 15c. ultramarine 1·75 1·50
88 18c. purple/*yellow* (1919) 3·50 24·00
a. On orange-buff (1920) 14·00 55·00
b. On buff (1920)
c. Die II. *On pale yellow* (1922) 1·25 17·00
89 **13** 25c. black and red/*buff* (1920) 1·75 32·00
a. On orange buff (1920) 40·00 75·00
b. Die II. *On pale yellow* (1922) 1·75 9·50
90 **11** 30c. dull purple and olive (1918) 1·50 8·50
91 45c. dull purple and orange (1919) 3·00 35·00
92 **13** 50c. dull purple and black (1920) 5·50 27·00
93 75c. black/*blue-green* (*olive back*) (1918) 1·60 15·00
a. Die II. *On emerald back* (1922) 1·40 20·00
94 1r. dull purple and red (1920) 11·00 45·00
95 1r.50 reddish purple & blue/*blue* (1918) 9·00 50·00
a. Die II. *Blue-pur & blue/blue* (1922) 12·00 32·00
96 2r.25 yellow-green and violet (1918) 48·00 £130
97 5r. green and blue (1920) 85·00 £225
82/97 *Set of* 16 £160 £500
82s/97s Optd "Specimen" *Set of* 16 £300
Examples of most values are known showing forged postmarks. These include part strikes of Seychelles postmarks dated "24 AP 93" and "AU 6 1903", and Victoria postmarks dated "NO 27" or "MY 6 35".

1921–32. *Die II. Chalk-surfaced paper (18c. and 25c. to 5r.).* Wmk Mult Script CA. P 14.
98 **11** 2c. chestnut and green 25 15
99 3c. green 1·75 15
100 3c. black (1922) 1·00 30
101 4c. green (1922) 1·00 2·50
102 4c. sage-green and carmine (1928) 6·50 17·00
103 **12** 5c. deep brown 75 5·50
104 **11** 6c. carmine 2·75 9·00
w. Wmk inverted £140
105 6c. deep mauve (1922) 60 10
106 **13** 9c. red (1927) 3·25 4·25
107 **11** 12c. grey 2·75 20
a. Die I (1932) 13·00 65
108 12c. carmine-red (1922) 1·25 30
110 15c. bright blue 2·00 55·00
111 15c. yellow (1922) 1·00 2·75
112 18c. purple/*pale yellow* (1925) 2·50 12·00
113 **13** 20c. bright blue (1922) 1·50 35
a. Dull blue (1924) 8·00 55
114 25c. black and red/*pale yellow* (1925) 2·75 15·00
115 **11** 30c. dull purple and olive 1·25 15·00
w. Wmk inverted
116 45c. dull purple and orange 1·25 5·00
117 **13** 50c. dull purple and black 2·50 2·25
118 75c. black/*emerald* (1924) 8·00 21·00
119 1r. dull purple and red 14·00 18·00
a. Die I (1932) 12·00 35·00
121 1r.50 purple and blue/*blue* (1924) 14·00 22·00
122 2r.25 yellow-green and violet 12·00 14·00
123 5r. yellow-green and blue 80·00 £170
98/123 *Set of* 24 £150 £350
98s/123s Optd "Specimen" *Set of* 24 £400
The 3c. green and 12c. grey (Die II) were reissued in 1927. "Specimen" overprints on these printings are 15.5 × 1.75 mm instead of the 14.5 × 2.5 mm of the original issue. (*Price*, 3c. £150, 12c. £110).
Examples of most values are known showing the forged postmarks mentioned above.

1935 (6 May). *Silver Jubilee. As Nos. 91/4 of Antigua, but ptd by B.W.* P 11 × 12.
128 6c. ultramarine and grey-black 1·00 2·00
a. Extra flagstaff £225 £300
b. Short extra flagstaff £200 £250
c. Lightning conductor £300
d. Flagstaff on right-hand turret £300 £250
e. Double flagstaff £325 £250
129 12c. green and indigo 2·50 1·50
a. Extra flagstaff £3250 £2750
b. Short extra flagstaff £350 £250
c. Lightning conductor £1800
d. Flagstaff on right-hand turret £425
e. Double flagstaff £425
130 20c. brown and deep blue 2·25 2·50
a. Extra flagstaff £350 £375
b. Short extra flagstaff £250
c. Lightning conductor £375 £375
d. Flagstaff on right-hand turret £375
e. Double flagstaff £375
131 1r. slate and purple 6·00 14·00
a. Extra flagstaff £180 £250
b. Short extra flagstaff £350
c. Lightning conductor £200
d. Flagstaff on right-hand turret £450
128/31 *Set of* 4 10·50 18·00
128s/31s Perf "Specimen" *Set of* 4 £120
For illustrations of plate varieties see Omnibus section following Zanzibar.
Examples are known showing forged Victoria "B MY 6 35" postmarks.

1937 (12 May). *Coronation. As Nos. 95/7 of Antigua.* P 11 × $11\frac{1}{2}$.
132 6c. sage-green 35 15
133 12c. orange 50 40
134 20c. blue 70 80
132/4 *Set of* 3 1·40 1·25
132s/4s Perf "Specimen" *Set of* 3 70·00

14 Coco-de-mer Palm

15 Giant Tortoise

16 Fishing Pirogue

"Handkerchief" on oar flaw (R. 6/2)

(Photo Harrison)

1938 (1 Jan)–**49**. Wmk Mult Script CA. *Chalk-surfaced paper.* P $14\frac{1}{2}$ × $13\frac{1}{2}$ (vert) or $13\frac{1}{2}$ × $14\frac{1}{2}$ (horiz).
135 **14** 2c. purple-brown (10.2.38) 1·50 40
a. Ordinary paper (18.11.42) 30 1·75
136 **15** 3c. green 8·50 1·50
136*a* 3c. orange (8.8.41) 1·25 65
ab. Ordinary paper (18.11.42) 55 1·50

137 **16** 6c. orange . . . . . 8·50 3·00
137*a* 6c. greyish green (8.8.41) . . . . . 4·00 1·00
aw. Wmk inverted £650
b. Ordinary paper. *Green* (18.11.42) . . . . . 55 2·00
c. Green (5.4.49) . . . . . 5·50 1·00
138 **14** 9c. scarlet (10.2.38) . . . . . 10·00 2·25
138*a* 9c. grey-blue (8.8.41) . . . . . 10·00 40
ab. Ordinary paper (18.11.42) . . . 12·00 1·50
ac. Ordinary paper. *Dull bl* (19.11.45) . . . . . 6·00 2·00
ad. Dull blue (5.4.49) . . . . . 14·00 6·00
aw. Wmk inverted
139 **15** 12c. reddish violet . . . . . 42·00 1·25
139*a* 15c. brown-carmine (8.8.41) . . . . 11·00 40
ab. Ordinary paper. *Brn-red* (18.11.42) . . . . . 6·00 2·50
139*c* **14** 18c. carmine-lake (8.8.41) . . . . 9·00 60
ca. Ordinary paper (18.11.42) . . . 6·00 2·50
cb. Rose-carmine (5.4.49) . . . . . 16·00 11·00
140 **16** 20c. blue . . . . . 42·00 5·50
140*a* 20c. brown-ochre (8.8.41) . . . . 9·00 50
ab. Ordinary paper (18.11.42) . . . 2·50 2·75
ac. "Handkerchief" flaw . . . . £130 75·00
141 **14** 25c. brown-ochre . . . . . 50·00 14·00
142 **15** 30c. carmine (10.2.38) . . . . . 50·00 9·50
142*a* 30c. blue (8.8.41) . . . . . 9·00 50
ab. Ordinary paper (18.11.42) . . . 2·25 3·25
143 **16** 45c. chocolate (10.2.38) . . . . . 18·00 1·75
a. Ordinary paper. *Pur-brn* (18.11.42) . . . . . 2·75 1·75
b. Purple-brown (5.4.49) . . . . . 20·00 10·00
144 **14** 50c. deep reddish violet (10.2.38) . . 10·00 60
a. Ordinary paper (18.11.42) . . . 1·75 3·25
144*b* 50c. bright lilac (13.6.49) . . . . . 2·25 1·75
145 **15** 75c. slate-blue (10.2.38) . . . . . 85·00 38·00
145*a* 75c. deep slate-lilac (8.8.41) . . . . 11·00 1·75
ab. Ordinary paper (18.11.42) . . . 2·25 2·75
146 **16** 1r. yellow-green (10.2.38) . . . . £100 50·00
146*a* 1r. grey-black (8.8.41) . . . . . 19·00 2·00
ab. Ordinary paper (18.11.42) . . . 1·50 3·00
147 **14** 1r.50 ultramarine (10.2.38) . . . . 25·00 3·00
a. Ordinary paper (18.11.42) . . . 4·50 7·00
aw. Wmk inverted £1700
148 **15** 2r.25 olive (10.2.38) . . . . . 35·00 7·00
a. Ordinary paper (18.11.42) . . . 18·00 20·00
149 **16** 5r. red (10.2.38) . . . . . 11·00 7·50
a. Ordinary paper (18.11.42) . . . 18·00 24·00
135/49 *Set of* 25 . . . . . £425 £140
135s/49s (*ex* 50c. bright lilac) Perf "Specimen" *Set of* 24 . . . . . £450

Examples of most values are known showing forged Victoria postmarks dated "NO 27", "SP 17 41", "DE 12 41", "SP 14 42", "DE 21 42" or "NO 16 43".

Lamp on mast flaw (R. 1/5)

1946 (23 Sept). *Victory. As Nos. 110/11 of Antigua.*
150 9c. light blue 10 10
151 30c. deep blue 20 10
a. Lamp on mast flaw . . . . . 23·00
150s/1s Perf "Specimen" *Set of* 2 . . . . . 60·00

Line by crown (R. 1/3)

1948 (5 Nov). *Royal Silver Wedding. As Nos. 112/13 of Antigua.*
152 9c. ultramarine 15 50
a. Line by crown . . . . . 23·00
153 5r. carmine . . . . . 12·00 28·00

Examples are known showing forged Victoria "C 11 NOV 48" postmarks.

1949 (10 Oct). *75th Anniv of U.P.U. As Nos. 114/17 of Antigua, but inscribed "SEYCHELLES" in recess.*
154 18c. bright reddish purple 15 25
155 50c. purple . . . . . 1·75 1·00
156 1r. grey 25 20
157 2r.25 olive . . . . . 30 1·00
154/7 *Set of* 4 . . . . . 2·25 2·25

17 Sailfish

18 Map of Indian Ocean

(Photo Harrison)

1952 (3 Mar). *Various designs as T* **14/16** *but with new portrait and crown as in T* **17/18**. *Chalk-surfaced paper.* Wmk Mult Script CA. P 14½ × 13½ (vert) or 13½ × 14½ (horiz).
158 **17** 2c. lilac 60 70
a. Error. Crown missing, W **9***a* . . . £550
b. Error. St. Edward's Crown, W **9***b* £130 £170
159 **15** 3c. orange 60 30
a. Error. Crown missing, W **9***a* . . . £425 £425
b. Error. St. Edward's Crown, W **9***b* £140 £130
160 **14** 9c. chalky blue . . . . . 60 1·50
a. Error. Crown missing, W **9***a* . . . £800
b. Error. St. Edward's Crown, W **9***b* £250
161 **16** 15c. deep yellow-green 50 75
a. Error. Crown missing, W **9***a* . . . £550
b. Error. St. Edward's Crown, W **9***b* £225 £275
162 **18** 18c. carmine-lake . . . . . 1·25 20
a. Error. Crown missing, W **9***a* . . . £800
b. Error. St. Edward's Crown, W **9***b* £300 £275
163 **16** 20c. orange-yellow . . . . . 1·00 1·25
a. Error. Crown missing, W **9***a* . . . £850 £850
b. Error. St. Edward's Crown, W **9***b* £350 £375
164 **15** 25c. vermilion . . . . . 70 1·25
a. Error. Crown missing, W **9***a* . . . £950
b. Error. St. Edward's Crown, W **9***b* £375
165 **17** 40c. ultramarine . . . . . 1·00 1·00
a. Error. Crown missing, W **9***a* . . . £1000
b. Error. St. Edward's Crown, W **9***b* £500
166 **16** 45c. purple-brown 70 30
a. Error. Crown missing, W **9***a* . . . £1100
b. Error. St. Edward's Crown, W **9***b* £450
167 **14** 50c. reddish violet . . . . . 1·25 1·50
a. Error. Crown missing, W **9***a* . . . £1200 £1200
b. Error. St. Edward's Crown, W **9***b* £500 £550
168 **18** 1r. grey-black . . . . . 3·00 2·50
b. Error. St. Edward's Crown, W **9***b* £950
169 **14** 1r.50 blue . . . . . 7·00 11·00
b. Error. St. Edward's Crown, W **9***b* £1600
170 **15** 2r.25 brown-olive . . . . . 10·00 11·00
b. Error. St. Edward's Crown, W **9***b* £1100
171 **18** 5r. red . . . . . 10·00 13·00
b. Error. St. Edward's Crown, W **9***b* £900
172 **17** 10r. green . . . . . 18·00 29·00
158/72 *Set of* 15 . . . . . 50·00 65·00

See *Introduction* re the watermark errors.

POSTAGE DUE STAMPS

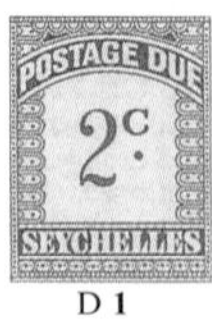

D 1

(Frame recess, value typo B.W.)

1951 (1 Mar). Wmk Mult Script CA. P 11½.
D1 **D 1** 2c. scarlet and carmine . . . . . 80 1·50
D2 3c. scarlet and green . . . . . 2·00 1·50
D3 6c. scarlet and bistre . . . . . 2·00 1·25
D4 9c. scarlet and orange . . . . . 2·00 1·25
D5 15c. scarlet and violet . . . . . 1·75 12·00
D6 18c. scarlet and blue . . . . . 1·75 12·00
D7 20c. scarlet and brown . . . . . 1·75 12·00
D8 30c. scarlet and claret . . . . . 1·75 7·50
D1/8 *Set of* 8 . . . . . 12·50 45·00

The 2c. and 3c. were issued on Block CA watermark in 1964–65.

Sierra Leone

PRICES FOR STAMPS ON COVER TO 1945		
Nos.	1/15	*from* × 10
Nos.	16/26	*from* × 15
Nos.	27/34	*from* × 20
Nos.	35/7	*from* × 10
No.	38	—
No.	39	*from* × 15
Nos.	41/52	*from* × 8
No.	53	—
No.	54	*from* × 40
Nos.	55/63	*from* × 5
Nos.	64/71	—
Nos.	73/84	*from* × 4
No.	85	—
Nos.	86/97	*from* × 4
No.	98	—
Nos.	99/110	*from* × 4
No.	111	—
Nos.	112/26	*from* × 2
Nos.	127/30	—
Nos.	131/45	*from* × 2
Nos.	146/8	—
Nos.	155/66	*from* × 2
No.	167	—
Nos.	168/78	*from* × 2
Nos.	179/80	—
Nos.	181/4	*from* × 6
Nos.	185/7	*from* × 5
Nos.	188/200	*from* × 2

CROWN COLONY AND PROTECTORATE

The first settlement in Sierra Leone intended as a home repatriated Africans, and subsequently those released by the R Navy from slave ships, was established in 1787. The Sierra Le Company was created by Act of Parliment in 1791, but its cha was surrendered in 1808 and the coastal settlements then becar Crown Colony. The inland region was proclaimed a Br protectorate on 21 August 1896.

A post office was established in 1843 but, until the inclusio Freetown in the British Post Office packet system in 1850, over mail was carried at irregular intervals by passing merchant or n vessels.

The stamps of GREAT BRITAIN were not sold at Sierra Le post offices, although examples from ships of the West Afr Squadron do exist with local cancellations.

PRINTERS. All issues of Sierra Leone until 1932 were typograp by De La Rue & Co. Ltd, London.

1

2

HALF
PENNY

(3)

Dot after "SIX" and break in octagonal frame (R. 19/11)

1859 (21 Sept)–**74**. No wmk. P 14.
1 **1** 6d. dull purple £200
a. Dot after "SIX" £900
2 6d. grey-lilac (1865) £250
a. Dot after "SIX" . . . . . —
3 6d. reddish violet (P 12½) (1872) £375
a. Dot after "SIX . . . . . —
4 6d. reddish lilac (1874) . . . . . 50·00
a. Dot after "SIX" £300

Imperforate proofs exist.

The paper used for the 6d. value often shows varying degree blueing, caused by a chemical reaction.

The 6d. plate contained 240 stamps arranged in panes of 20 (4 with the sheets containing 12 such panes in four horizontal row three.

1872–73. Wmk Crown CC. P 12½.

(a) Wmk sideways (April 1872).
7 **2** 1d. rose-red . . . . . 75·00
8 3d. buff £130
9 4d. blue £170
10 1s. green £450

(b) Wmk upright (Sept 1873).
11 **2** 1d. rose-red £130
w. Wmk inverted £180
12 2d. magenta £120
13 3d. saffron-yellow £500
14 4d. blue £250
15 1s. green £425

1876. Wmk Crown CC. P 14.
16 **2** ½d. brown . . . . . 2·50
w. Wmk inverted £120
17 1d. rose-red . . . . . 50·00
18 1½d. lilac (Nov) . . . . . 48·00
19 2d. magenta . . . . . 65·00
20 3d. buff . . . . . 50·00
w. Wmk inverted
21 4d. blue £170
w. Wmk inverted
22 1s. green . . . . . 55·00
16/22 *Set of* 7 . . . . . £400

1883 (June–19 Sept). Wmk Crown CA. P 14.

No.	Type	Description	Unused	Used
23	2	½d. brown	23·00	50·00
24		1d. rose-red (19.9.83*)	£200	35·00
25		2d. magenta	50·00	8·50
26		4d. blue	£900	28·00

*Earliest known postmark date.

1884 SIERRA 5s. LEONE SURCHARGE. From 2 June 1884 the administration decided that, as a temporary measure, revenue and fiscal duties were to be paid with ordinary postage stamps. At that time there was no postage value higher than 1s., so a local surcharge, reading "SIERRA 5s. LEONE", was applied to No. 22 (*Price* £200 *unused*). Until withdrawal on 1 March 1885 this surcharge was valid for both fiscal and postal purposes, although no genuine postal cover or piece has yet been found. One mint example is known with overprint inverted (*Price* £750).

Remainders of the surcharge were cancelled by a horizontal red brush stroke (*Price* £32 *with upright surcharge*, £160 *with inverted surcharge*).

1884 (July)–**91**. Wmk Crown CA. P 14.

No.	Type	Description	Unused	Used
27	2	½d. dull green	2·50	1·75
		w. Wmk inverted	£180	£120
28		1d. carmine	4·25	1·00
		a. Rose-carmine (1885?)	28·00	8·50
		aw. Wmk inverted	†	£120
29		1½d. pale violet (1889)	3·00	6·50
30		2d. grey	32·00	2·50
31		2½d. ultramarine (1891)	9·00	1·00
32		3d. yellow (1889)	3·00	10·00
33		4d. brown	1·75	1·50
		w. Wmk inverted	£190	
34		1s. red-brown (1888)	20·00	11·00
27/34 *Set of* 8			65·00	32·00
27s/34s (*ex* 1½d., 3d.) Optd "Specimen" *Set of* 6			£600	
27sa/8sa, 30sa, 33sa Optd "Specimen" (perf 12) *Set of* 4			£1000	

1885–96. Wmk Crown CC. P 14.

No.	Type	Description	Unused	Used
35	1	6d. dull violet (1885)	60·00	23·00
		a. Bisected (3d.) (on cover)	†	£2500
		b. Dot after "SIX"	—	£160
36		6d. brown-purple (1890)	17·00	14·00
		a. Dot after "SIX"	£120	£100
		s. Optd "Specimen"	70·00	
		w. Wmk inverted		
37		6d. purple-lake (1896)	2·50	6·50
		a. Dot after "SIX"	48·00	70·00

Proofs of the 6d. brown-purple exist from 1889 on Crown CA watermark and perforated 12 (*Price* £1500, *unused*).

1893 (8 Jan). *Surch with T* **3** *by Govt Printer, Freetown.*

(a) On No. 18. Wmk Crown CC.

No.	Type	Description	Unused	Used
38	2	½d.on 1½d. lilac	£475	£700
		a. "PFNNY"(R.3/1)	£2750	£3750

(b) On No. 29. Wmk Crown CA.

No.	Type	Description	Unused	Used
39	2	½d.on 1½d. pale violet	4·00	3·00
		a. Surch inverted	£110	£110
		b. "PFNNY" (R. 3/1)	75·00	75·00
		ba. Ditto. Surch inverted	£2500	£5000

On Nos. 38/9 the surcharge and the cancelling bars were often applied separately using a separate forme. When the bar missed its intended position across the value tablet, second, or even third bars were added, sometimes by pen or brush. No. 39a exists with the bars either normal or inverted with the rest of the surcharge. No. 39c shows the bars normal.

Forged surcharges with "HALF PENNY" shown on one line were prepared by employees of the printer. It is believed that only a single example of this forgery still exists.

The 6d. fiscal, inscribed "STAMP DUTY" as Type **6** surcharged "ONE-PENNY" is known used for postage between May and August 1894, but no official sanction for such usage has been found.

4

5

1896–97. Wmk Crown CA. P 14.

No.	Type	Description	Unused	Used
41	4	½d. dull mauve and green (1897)	2·25	2·75
42		1d. dull mauve and carmine	3·25	1·75
43		1½d. dull mauve and black (1897)	4·00	19·00
44		2d. dull mauve and orange	2·50	5·00
45		2½d. dull mauve and ultramarine	2·25	1·25
46	5	3d. dull mauve and slate	8·00	7·00
47		4d. dull mauve and carmine (1897)	9·50	13·00
48		5d. dull mauve and black (1897)	13·00	13·00
49		6d. dull mauve (1897)	8·00	22·00
50		1s. green and black	6·00	18·00
51		2s. green and ultramarine	25·00	55·00
52		5s. green and carmine	60·00	£170
53		£1 purple/*red*	£160	£425
41/53 *Set of* 13			£275	£650
41s/53s Optd "Specimen" *Set of* 13			£225	

Examples of most values are known showing forged oval registered postmarks dated "16 JUL 11" or "4 SP 11".

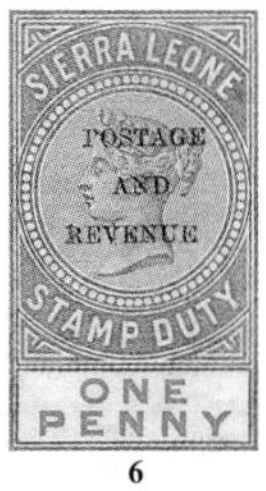

6

POSTAGE
AND
REVENUE
(7)

2½d. (8) 2½d. (9) 2½d. (10)

2½d. (11) 2½d. (12) 2½d. (13)

POSTAGE AND REVENUE (14)

REVENUE
Italic "N" (R. 3/4 of the setting)

1897. *Fiscal stamps as T* **6**. Wmk CA over Crown, w **7**. P 14.

(a) Optd with T **7** *(26 Feb*).*

No.	Type	Description	Unused	Used
54		1d. dull purple and green	3·75	3·00
		a. Opt double	£1500	£1500

(b) Optd with T **7** *and surch T* **8**, **10**, **11** *(with square stop) or* **12** *with six thin bars across the original face value (27 Feb)*.*

No.	Type	Description	Unused	Used
55	8	2½d.on 3d. dull purple and green	11·00	13·00
		a. Surch double	£24000	
		b. Surch double (Types **8+10**)	£20000	
		c. Surch double (Types **8+11**)	£30000	
		d. Bars omitted		
56	10	2½d.on 3d. dull purple and green	55·00	65·00
57	11	2½d.on 3d. dull purple and green	£160	£180
58	12	2½d.on 3d. dull purple and green	£325	£400
59	8	2½d.on 6d. dull purple and green	8·50	13·00
60	10	2½d.on 6d. dull purple and green	42·00	55·00
61	11	2½d.on 6d. dull purple and green	£110	£130
62	12	2½d.on 6d. dull purple and green	£250	£300

Nos. 55/8 and 59/62 were surcharged from a setting of 30 (10 × 3) which contained twenty-two examples of Type **8** (including three with square stops), five of Type **10**, two of Type **11** and one of Type **12**.

Two examples are known of No. 55a, five of No. 55b (of which two are in the Royal Collection) and two of No. 55c (one in the Royal Collection). A unique example of a double surcharge on No. 55 showing Types **8+12** is also in the Royal Collection.

No. 55d comes from the top row of a setting and was caused by the downward displacement of the overprint. Stamps in the lower rows show the overprint transposed with the obliterating bars at the top of the stamp.

(c) Optd with T **14** *and surch T* **8**, **9**, **10**, **11** *(with round stop) or* **13** *with five thin bars across the original face value (1 Mar).*

No.	Type	Description	Unused	Used
63	8	2½d.on 1s. dull lilac	85·00	65·00
64	9	2½d.on 1s. dull lilac	£1300	£1200
65	10	2½d.on 1s. dull lilac	£750	£700
66	11	2½d.on 1s. dull lilac	£400	£400
		a. Italic "N"	£1200	£1200
66*b*	13	2½d.on 1s. dull lilac	£1300	£1200
67	8	2½d.on 2s. dull lilac	£1600	£1900
68	9	2½d.on 2s. dull lilac	£32000	£38000
69	10	2½d.on 2s. dull lilac	£14000	
70	11	2½d.on 2s. dull lilac	£8000	£9000
		a. Italic "N"	£16000	£16000
71	13	2½d.on 2s. dull lilac	£32000	£38000

*Earliest known postmark date.

The setting of 30 (10 × 3) used for both Nos. 63/6*b* and 67/71 contained twenty-two examples of Type **8** (including one with square stop), one of Type **9**, two of Type **10**, four of Type **11** (including one with italic "N") and one of Type **13**.

Most examples of Nos. 63/6*b* are water-stained. Stamps in this condition are worth about 30% of the price quoted.

15

16

1903. Wmk Crown CA. P 14.

No.	Type	Description	Unused	Used
73	15	½d. dull purple and green	3·00	4·50
74		1d. dull purple and rosine	2·00	1·00
75		1½d. dull purple and black	1·25	10·00
76		2d. dull purple and brown-orange	3·75	16·00
77		2½d. dull purple and ultramarine	4·50	8·00
78	16	3d. dull purple and grey	9·50	13·00
79		4d. dull purple and rosine	7·00	14·00
80		5d. dull purple and black	8·00	32·00
81		6d. dull purple	11·00	17·00
82		1s. green and black	16·00	50·00
83		2s. green and ultramarine	48·00	60·00
84		5s. green and carmine	70·00	£100
85		£1 purple/*red*	£225	£250
73/85 *Set of* 13			£350	£500
73s/85s Optd "Specimen" *Set of* 13			£180	

1904–05. *Ordinary paper (1d.) or chalk-surfaced paper (others).* Wmk Mult Crown CA. P 14.

No.	Type	Description	Unused	Used
86	15	½d. dull purple and green (1905)	5·00	4·50
87		1d. dull purple and rosine	1·50	1·00
		a. Chalk-surfaced paper (1905)	4·25	1·50
88		1½d. dull purple and black (1905)	3·00	13·00
89		2d. dull purple and brown-orange (1905)	4·25	4·00
90		2½d. dull purple and ultramarine (1905)	4·50	2·00
91	16	3d. dull purple and grey (1905)	38·00	3·50
		w. Wmk inverted	42·00	30·00
92		4d. dull purple and rosine (1905)	7·00	7·00
		w. Wmk inverted	£100	
93		5d. dull purple and black (1905)	12·00	26·00
94		6d. dull purple (1905)	4·00	3·25
95		1s. green and black (1905)	7·50	9·00
96		2s. green and ultramarine (1905)	22·00	27·00
97		5s. green and carmine (1905)	30·00	50·00
98		£1 purple/*red* (1905)	£225	£250
86/98 *Set of* 13			£300	£325

1907–12. *Ordinary paper (½d. to 2½d.) or chalk-surfaced paper (others).* Wmk Mult Crown CA. P 14.

No.	Type	Description	Unused	Used
99	15	½d. green	1·00	50
100		1d. carmine	11·00	75
		a. Red	6·50	60
101		1½d. orange (1910)	1·25	2·00
102		2d. greyish slate (1909)	1·25	1·50
103		2½d. blue	3·75	3·00
104	16	3d. purple/*yellow* (1909)	7·50	2·75
		a. Ordinary paper (1912)	12·00	12·00
105		4d. black and red/*yellow* (1908)	2·25	1·60
106		5d. purple and olive-green (1908)	9·00	5·00
107		6d. dull and bright purple (1908)	9·00	8·00
108		1s. black/*green* (1908)	5·50	5·00
109		2s. purple and bright blue/*blue* (1908)	15·00	19·00
110		5s. green and red/*yellow* (1908)	40·00	55·00
111		£1 purple and black/*red* (1911)	£250	£180
99/111 *Set of* 13			£325	£250
99s/111s Optd "Specimen" *Set of* 13			£300	

Most values from the 1903, 1904–05 and 1907–12 issues are known with forged postmarks. These include oval registered examples dated "16 JUL 11" or "4 SP 11".

USED HIGH VALUES. The £2 and £5 values of the King George V series were intended for fiscal use only. Before the introduction of the airmail service at the end of 1926 there was no postal rate for which they could be used. Under the airmail rates used between 1926 and 1932 it is just possible that a very heavy letter may have required a £2 value. Postmarks on the £5 and on the £2 before December 1926 can only have been applied "by favour" or, in the case of the cds type, are on stamps removed from telegraph forms. Used prices quoted for Nos. 129/30 and 147/8 are for "by favour" cancellations.

17

18

19

20

1912–21. *Die I. Chalk-surfaced paper (3d. and 6d. to £5).* Wmk Mult Crown CA. P 14.

No.	Type	Description	Unused	Used
112	17	½d. blue-green	3·00	2·50
		a. Yellow-green (1914)	3·00	2·50
		b. Deep green (1919)	4·75	2·75
113		1d. carmine-red	2·00	30
		a. Scarlet (1916)	4·50	1·00
		b. Rose-red (1918)	4·50	80
		bw. Wmk inverted	†	£140
		bx. Wmk reversed	£130	£130
114		1½d. orange (1913)	2·00	2·50
		a. Orange-yellow (1919)	5·00	1·00
115		2d. greyish slate	1·25	20
		a. "A" of "CA" missing from wmk		
		w. Wmk inverted	35·00	35·00
116		2½d. deep blue	10·00	2·50
		a. Ultramarine (1917)	1·00	80
116*b*	20	3d. purple/*yellow*	3·00	3·25
		ba. On pale yellow (1921)	3·25	3·25
117	18	4d. black and red/*yellow*	2·75	8·50
		a. On lemon (1915)	4·00	6·50
		b. Die II. *On pale yellow* (1921)	4·25	5·50
118		5d. purple and olive-green	1·25	6·50
119		6d. dull and bright purple	3·25	6·00
120	19	7d. purple and orange	3·00	8·50
121		9d. purple and black	5·00	12·00
122	18	10d. purple and red	3·00	18·00
124	20	1s. black/*green*	4·50	4·50
		a. On blue-green, green back	4·50	3·25
		w. Wmk inverted	50·00	50·00
125		2s. blue and purple/*blue*	13·00	5·50
126		5s. red and green/*yellow*	13·00	26·00
127		10s. red and green/*green*	70·00	£120
		a. Carmine and blue-green/green	90·00	£140
		b. Carmine and yellow-green/green	£100	£160
128		£1 black and purple/*red*	£150	£225
129		£2 blue and dull purple	£475	£650
		s. Optd "Specimen"	£110	
130		£5 orange and green	£1300	£1800
		s. Optd "Specimen"	£250	
112/28 *Set of* 17			£250	£400
112s/28s Optd "Specimen" *Set of* 17			£300	

Examples of Nos. 127/8 are known with part strikes of the forged postmarks mentioned after Nos. 99/111.

1921–27. *Die II. Chalk-surfaced paper (6d. to £5).* Wmk Mult Script CA. P 14.

No.	Type	Description	Unused	Used
131	17	½d. dull green	1·25	1·00
		a. Bright green	3·50	1·50
132		1d. bright violet (Die I) (1924)	1·75	2·25
		a. Die II (1925)	3·00	20
133		1½d. scarlet (1925)	1·75	1·25
134		2d. grey (1922)	1·25	20
135		2½d. ultramarine	1·50	9·00
136	18	3d. bright blue (1922)	1·25	1·25
137		4d. black and red/*pale yellow* (1925)	1·75	3·25
138		5d. purple and olive-green	1·25	1·25
139		6d. grey-purple and bright purple	1·25	2·50
		y. Wmk inverted and reversed		
140	19	7d. purple and orange (1927)	2·75	21·00
141		9d. purple and black (1922)	2·75	15·00
142	18	10d. purple and red (1925)	3·25	26·00
143	20	1s. black/*emerald* (1925)	8·50	7·00
144		2s. blue and dull purple/*blue*	9·50	10·00
		w. Wmk inverted	£110	£120
145		5s. red and green/*yellow* (1927)	9·50	50·00
146		10s. red and green/*green* (1927)	90·00	£180

147 £2 blue and dull purple (1923) . . . £450 £650
s. Optd "Specimen" £110
148 £5 orange and green (1923) £1100 £1700
s. Optd "Specimen" £250
131/46 *Set of* 16 . . . . £120 £300
131s/46s Optd "Specimen" *Set of* 16 . . . . . . £300

21 Rice Field

22 Palms and Cola Tree

(Eng J.A.C. Harrison (T **21**))

1932 (1 Mar). Wmk Mult Script CA.

(a) Recess Waterlow. P 12½.

155 **21** ½d. green 20 30
156 1d. violet 30 30
157 1½d. carmine . . . . 30 1·25
a. Imperf between (horiz pair) . . .
158 2d. brown 30 30
159 3d. blue . . . . 60 1·75
160 4d. orange . . . . 60 7·50
161 5d. bronze-green . . . . 85 3·50
162 6d. light blue . . . . 60 3·00
163 1s. lake . . . . 2·50 6·50

(b) Recess B.W. P 12.

164 **22** 2s. chocolate . . . . 5·00 5·50
165 5s. deep blue . . . . 12·00 19·00
166 10s. green . . . . 60·00 £120
167 £1 purple £110 £190
155/67 *Set of* 13 . . . . £170 £325
155s/67s Perf "Specimen" *Set of* 13 . . . . . . £180

23 Arms of Sierra Leone

24 Old Slave Market. Freetown

27 African Elephant

28 King George V

(Des Father F. Welsh. Recess B.W.)

1933 (2 Oct). *Centenary of Abolition of Slavery and of Death of William Wilberforce. T* **23/4**, **27/8** *and similar designs.* Wmk Mult Script CA (sideways on horiz designs). P 12.

168 ½d. green . . . . 1·00 1·25
169 1d. black and brown 65 10
170 1½d. chestnut . . . . 4·50 4·50
171 2d. purple . . . . 3·00 20
172 3d. blue . . . . 3·00 1·75
173 4d. brown . . . . 6·50 10·00
174 5d. green and chestnut . . . . 7·00 13·00
175 6d. black and brown-orange . . . . . . 8·00 8·00
176 1s. violet . . . . 4·75 18·00
177 2s. brown and light blue . . . . 22·00 40·00
178 5s. black and purple £150 £170
179 10s. black and sage-green £180 £275
180 £1 violet and orange £350 £425
168/80 *Set of* 13 . . . . £650 £850
168s/80s Perf "Specimen" *Set of* 13 . . . . . £500

Designs: *Vert*—1d. "Freedom"; 1½d. Map of Sierra Leone; 4d. Government sanatorium. *Horiz*—3d. Native fruit seller; 5d. Bullom canoe; 6d. Punting near Banana; 1s. Government buildings; 2s. Bunce Island; £1 Freetown harbour.

1935 (6 May). *Silver Jubilee. As Nos. 91/4 of Antigua, but ptd by B.W.* P 11 × 12.

181 1d. ultramarine and grey-black . . . . . 1·00 2·50
a. Extra flagstaff . . . . 50·00 75·00
b. Short extra flagstaff £140
c. Lightning conductor . . . . 42·00
182 3d. brown and deep blue . . . . 1·25 8·50
a. Extra flagstaff . . . . 70·00 £100
b. Short extra flagstaff £325
c. Lightning conductor . . . . 80·00
183 5d. green and indigo . . . . 1·75 14·00
a. Extra flagstaff £110 £180
b. Short extra flagstaff £400
c. Lightning conductor £110
184 1s. slate and purple . . . . 8·00 5·00
a. Extra flagstaff £325 £250
b. Short extra flagstaff £350
c. Lightning conductor £300 £250
181/4 *Set of* 4 . . . . 11·00 27·00
181s/4s Perf "Specimen" *Set of* 4 . . . . . . 90·00

For illustrations of plate varieties see Omnibus section following Zanzibar.

1937 (12 May). *Coronation. As Nos. 95/7 of Antigua.* P 11 × 11½.

185 1d. orange . . . . 70 1·00
186 2d. purple . . . . 90 1·00
187 3d. blue . . . . 1·50 3·75
185/7 *Set of* 3 . . . . 2·75 5·25
185s/7s Perf "Specimen" *Set of* 3 . . . . . . 65·00

30 Freetown from the Harbour

31 Rice Harvesting

(Recess Waterlow)

1938 (1 May)–**44**. Wmk Mult Script CA (sideways). P 12½.

188 **30** ½d. black and blue-green 15 40
189 1d. black and lake 40 60
a. Imperf between (vert pair) . . . † —
190 **31** 1½d. scarlet . . . . 20·00 1·00
190*a* 1½d. mauve (1.2.41) 30 60
191 2d. mauve . . . . 40·00 2·25
191*a* 2d. scarlet (1.2.41) . . . . 30 2·00
192 **30** 3d. black and ultramarine 40 50
193 4d. black and red-brown (20.6.38) . . . . 80 4·50
194 **31** 5d. olive-green (20.6.38) . . . . . 5·00 4·00
195 6d. grey (20.6.38) 75 50
196 **30** 1s. black and olive-green (20.6.38) . . . . 2·00 70
196*a* **31** 1s.3d. yellow-orange (1.7.44) . . . 50 60
197 **30** 2s. black and sepia (20.6.38) . . . . 4·50 2·50
198 **31** 5s. red-brown (20.6.38) . . . . . 10·00 8·00
199 10s. emerald-green (20.6.38) . . . . 17·00 9·00
200 **30** £1 deep blue (20.6.38) . . . . . 17·00 21·00
188/200 *Set of* 16 . . . . £100 50·00
188s/200s Perf "Specimen" *Set of* 16 . . . . . . £275

1946 (1 Oct). *Victory. As Nos. 110/11 of Antigua.*

201 1½d. lilac 20 10
202 3d. ultramarine 20 10
201s/2s Perf "Specimen" *Set of* 2 . . . . . . 65·00

1948 (1 Dec). *Royal Silver Wedding. As Nos. 112/13 of Antigua.*

203 1½d. bright purple 15 15
204 £1 indigo . . . . 18·00 17·00

1949 (10 Oct). *75th Anniv of U.P.U. As Nos. 114/17 of Antigua.*

205 1½d. purple 20 50
206 3d. deep blue . . . . 1·50 3·75
207 6d. grey . . . . 35 3·75
208 1s. olive . . . . 35 1·00
205/8 *Set of* 4 . . . . 2·25 8·00

STAMP BOOKLETS

1929.

SB1 1s. booklet containing twelve 1d. (No. 132a) . . .
SB2 2s. booklet containing twelve 2d. (No. 134) . . .

Singapore

A Crown Colony until the end of 1957. From 1 August 1958, an internally self-governing territory designated the State of Singapore. From 16 September 1963, part of the Malaysian Federation until 9 August 1965, when it became an independent republic within the Commonwealth.

Stamps in the Crown Colony Victory design with face values of 8c. and 15c. were prepared for Singapore in 1946, but were not issued.

(Currency. 100 cents = 1 Malayan, dollar)

CROWN COLONY

(Typo D.L.R.)

1948 (1 Sept)–**52**. *As T* **58** *of Malaysia (Straits Settlements), but inscribed "SINGAPORE" at foot. Chalk-surfaced paper.* Wmk Mult Script CA.

(a) P 14.

1 1c. black . . . . 15 1·00
2 2c. orange 15 50
3 3c. green 50 75
4 4c. brown . . . . 20 1·25
5 6c. grey 40 70
6 8c. scarlet (1.10.48) 50 70
7 10c. purple 20 10
8 15c. ultramarine (1.10.48) . . . . . . 11·00 10
9 20c. black and green (1.10.48) . . . . . 4·50 30
10 25c. purple and orange (1.10.48) . . . . 6·00 15
11 40c. red and purple (1.10.48) . . . . . 8·50 5·00
12 50c. black and blue (1.10.48) . . . . . 3·25 10
13 $1 blue and purple (1.10.48) . . . . . 10·00 3·25
14 $2 green and scarlet (25.10.48) . . . . 48·00 4·25
15 $5 green and brown (1.10.48) . . . . . £120 5·50
1/15 *Set of* 15 . . . . £180 21·00

(b) P 17½ × 18

16 1c. black (21.5.52) . . . . 1·25 3·50
17 2c. orange (31.10.49) . . . . 1·25 1·25
19 4c. brown (1.7.49) . . . . 1·50 10
19*a* 5c. bright purple (1.9.52) . . . . . . 2·50 1·50
21 6c. grey (10.12.52) . . . . 2·00 1·25
21*a* 8c. green (1.9.52) . . . . 6·50 3·25
22 10c. purple (9.2.50) 50 10
22*a* 12c. scarlet (1.9.52) . . . . 8·00 9·00
23 15c. ultramarine (9.2.50) . . . . 17·00 10
24 20c. black and green (31.10.49) . . . . . 6·00 3·50
24*a* 20c. bright blue (1.9.52) . . . . 4·00 10
25 25c. purple and orange (9.2.50) . . . . . 1·00 10
25*a* 35c. scarlet and purple (1.9.52) . . . . . 4·25 1·00
26 40c. red and purple (30.4.51*) . . . . . 38·00 14·00
27 50c. black and blue (9.2.50) . . . . . . 8·50 10
28 $1 blue and purple (31.10.49) . . . . . 17·00 20
a. Error. St. Edward's Crown, W **9***b* . . £6000 £3000
29 $2 green and scarlet (24.5.51) . . . . . 90·00 1·25
a. Error. St. Edward's Crown. W **9***b* . . £6000
w. Wmk inverted . . . .
30 $5 green and brown (19.12.51) . . . . . £180 1·50
w. Wmk inverted . . . .
16/30 *Set of* 18 . . . . £350 38·00

*Earliest known postmark date.

Single-colour values were from single plate printings (Die II) and all bi-colour, except the 25c., from separate head and duty plates (Die I). For differences between the Dies see after Nos. 278/98 of Malaysia (Straits Settlements). The 25c. is unique in this series in that it combines a Die II frame with a separate head plate.

Nos. 28a and 29a occur on rows in the watermark in which the crowns and letters "CA" alternate.

Postal forgeries of the 50c., $1 and $2 exist on unwatermarked paper and perforated 14 × 14½.

1948 (25 Oct). *Royal Silver Wedding. As Nos. 112/13 of Antigua.*

31 10c. violet 75 60
32 $5. brown . . . . £110 38·00

1949 (10 Oct). *75th Anniv of U.P.U. As Nos. 114/17 of Antigua.*

33 10c. purple 75 50
34 15c. deep blue . . . . 6·00 2·75
35 25c. orange . . . . 6·00 2·75
36 50c. blue-black . . . . 6·00 3·00
33/6 *Set of* 4 . . . . 17·00 8·00

Somaliland Protectorate

Egyptian post offices were opened in Somaliland during 1876 and the stamps of Egypt were used there until the garrisons were withdrawn in 1884.

Cancellations for these offices have been identified as follows (for illustrations of postmark types see SUDAN).

BARBARA (Berbera). Open 1876 to 1 November 1884. Circular datestamp as Sudan Type I.

ZEILA. Open 1876 to 1 November 1884. Circular datestamp as Sudan Types G and I, sometimes inscr ZEJLA. One example with seal type cancellation as Sudan Type B is also known.

Stamps of India were used at the two post offices from 1 January 1887 until 1903 usually cancelled with circular datestamps or the "B" obliterator used by all offices controlled from Bombay.

The Protectorate Post Office was established on 1 June 1903, when control of British Somaliland was transferred from the Indian Government to the British Foreign Office.

PRICES FOR STAMPS ON COVER TO 1945		
Nos.	1/11	*from* × 25
Nos.	12/13	—
Nos.	18/22	*from* × 12
Nos.	23/4	—
Nos.	25/30	*from* × 30
Nos.	32/59	*from* × 12
Nos.	60/92	*from* × 6
Nos.	93/104	*from* × 3
Nos.	105/16	*from* × 4
Nos.	O1/13	*from* × 8
Nos.	O14/15	—

(Currency. 12 pies = 1 anna; 16 annas = 1 rupee)

BRITISH SOMALILAND
(1)

2

3

SETTINGS OF TYPE 1

In all printings the ½, 1, 2, 2½, 3, 4, 8, 12a. and 1r. values we[re] overprinted from a setting of 240 (2 panes 12 × 10, one above th[e] other), covering the entire sheet at one operation.

The 6a., which was in sheets of 320 (4 panes, each 8 × 10), had modified setting of 160, applied twice to each sheet.

The high values were overprinted in sheets of 96 (8 panes, eac[h] 4 × 3).

The settings for the low value stamps contained two slight[ly] different styles of overprint, identified by the position of "B" [in] "BRITISH". Type A shows this letter over the "M" [of] "SOMALILAND" and Type B over the "OM".

For the first printing with the overprint at the top of the desig[n] the 240 position setting showed all the stamps in the upper pan[e] and 63 in the lower as Type A, with the remaining 57 as Type [B]. When the setting was used for the printing with overprint at foot was amended slightly so that one of the Type A examples in th[e] upper pane became a Type B.

The 6a. value with overprint at top shows 250 examples [of] Type A and 70 as Type B in each sheet. This proportion altered the printing with overprint at foot to 256 as Type A and 64 [as] Type B.

OVERPRINT VARIETIES

Missing second "I" in "BRITISH"—Occurs on the stamps with overprint at top from R. 2/6 of the upper pane and R. 5/1 of the lower, although it is believed that the example on the 2½a. (No. 4a) only occurs from the second position. On the later printing with overprint at foot a similar error can be found on R. 7/12 of the upper pane. Some examples of both these errors show traces of the letter remaining, but the prices quoted are for stamps with it completely omitted.

Figure "1" for first "I" in "BRITISH"—Occurs on R. 6/4 of the upper pane for all printings of the 240 impression setting. In addition it has been reported from R. 7/12 of the Queen Victoria 2½, 12a. and 1r. with overprint at foot. Both versions of the 6a. show the variety on R. 6/4 of the upper left and upper right panes.

Curved overprint—Occurs on R. 3/4 of the top right-hand pane of the high values.

"SUMALILAND"—Occurs on R. 2/9 of the upper pane for all low values with the overprint at foot, except the 6a. A similar variety occurs on the high values from the same series on R. 1/3 of the top left pane.

"SOMAL.LAND"—Occurs on R. 7/5 of the lower pane from the 240 impression setting with the overprint at foot. In addition the Edwardian values of this series also have an example on R. 6/7. The 6a. has examples of the flaw on R. 6/9 and R. 7/5 of both the lower right and left panes. A similar variety occurs on the high values from the same series at R. 3/4 of the third pane in the left-hand column.

903 (1 June). *Nos. 80, 94, 96, 98, 100, 106/9, 114/16 and 118 of India (Queen Victoria) optd with T* **1**, *at top of stamp, in Calcutta.* Wmk Elephant Head (6a.) or Star (others).

1 ½a. yellow-green 2·75 4·00
a. "BRIT SH" £170
2 1a. carmine 2·75 3·75
a. "BRIT SH" £190 £275
b. "BR1TISH" £140
3 2a. pale violet 2·25 1·50
a. "BRIT SH" £300 £375
b. "BR1TISH" £275
c. Opt double £650
4 2½a. ultramarine 2·00 1·75
a. "BRIT SH" £475
b. "BR1TISH" £300
5 3a. brown-orange 3·25 3·00
a. "BRIT SH" £600
b. "BR1TISH" £325 £350
6 4a. slate-green 3·50 2·75
a. "BR1TISH" £325 £350
7 6a. olive-bistre 5·00 4·50
a. "BR1TISH" £225 £250
8 8a. dull mauve 3·75 5·00
a. "BR1TISH" £325
12a. purple/*red* 3·25 7·00
a. "BR1TISH" £325 £425
0 1r. green and aniline carmine 7·00 10·00
a. "BR1TISH" £375
2r. carmine and yellow-brown 26·00 42·00
a. Curved opt £300
2 3r. brown and green 22·00 48·00
a. Curved opt £300
3 5r. ultramarine and violet 38·00 55·00
a. Curved opt £350
13 *Set of* 13 £110 £170

903 (1 Sept–2 Nov). *Stamps of India optd with T* **1**, *at bottom of stamp, in Calcutta.*

(a) On Nos. 80, 100, 106/9 and 118 (Queen Victoria).

2½a. ultramarine (2.11) 3·25 6·50
a. "BR1TISH" £180
b. "SUMALILAND" £225
c. "SOMAL.LAND" £225
6a. olive-bistre (2.11) 6·00 5·50
a. "BR1TISH" £250
b. "SOMAL.LAND" £150
12a. purple/*red* (2.11) 7·00 12·00
a. "BR1TISH" £225
b. "SUMALILAND" £300
c. "SOMAL.LAND" £300
1r. green and aniline carmine (2.11) 3·50 11·00
a. "BR1TISH" £275
b. "SUMALILAND" £375
c. "SOMAL.LAND" £375
2r. carmine and yellow-brown (2.11) 80·00 £120
a. Curved opt £450
b. "SUMALILAND" £450
c. "SOMAL.LAND" £450
3r. brown and green (2.11) 80·00 £130
a. Opt double, both inverted with one albino £600
b. Curved opt £550
c. "SUMALILAND" £550
d. "SOMAL.LAND" £550
5r. ultramarine and violet (2.11) 75·00 £100
a. Curved opt £450
b. "SUMALILAND" £450
c. "SOMAL.LAND" £450

(b) On Nos. 122/4, 127/8 and 133 (King Edward VII).

½a. green 2·25 55
a. "BRIT SH" £375
b. "BR1TISH" 85·00
c. "SUMALILAND" 85·00
d. "SOMAL.LAND" 48·00 50·00
1a. carmine (8.10) 1·25 30
a. "BRIT SH" £250
b. "BR1TISH" 85·00 85·00
c. "SUMALILAND" 85·00
d. "SOMAL.LAND" 45·00 45·00
2a. violet (2.11) 1·75 2·50
a. "BRIT SH" £950
b. "BR1TISH" £170
c. "SUMALILAND" £170
d. "SOMAL.LAND" 85·00
3a. orange-brown (2.11) 2·50 2·50
a. "BR1TISH" £180 £225
b. "SUMALILAND" £180
c. "SOMAL.LAND" 85·00
4a. olive (2.11) 1·50 4·00
a. "BR1TISH" £170
b. "SUMALILAND" £170
c. "SOMAL.LAND" 85·00

30 8a. purple (2.11) 1·75 2·25
a. "BR1TISH" £225
b. "SUMALILAND" £225
c. "SOMAL.LAND" £120
18/30 *Set of* 13 £225 £350

(Typo D.L.R.)

1904 (15 Feb–3 Sept).

(a) Wmk Crown CA. P 14.

32 **2** ½a. dull green and green 1·50 4·25
33 1a. grey-black and red (3.9) 10·00 3·25
34 2a. dull and bright purple (3.9) 1·75 2·25
35 2½a. bright blue (3.9) 3·25 3·75
36 3a. chocolate and grey-green (3.9) 1·75 2·50
37 4a. green and black (3.9) 1·75 4·75
38 6a. green and violet (3.9) 4·25 17·00
39 8a. grey-black and pale blue (3.9) 3·50 5·50
40 12a. grey-black and orange-buff (3.9) 6·50 11·00

(b) Wmk Crown CC. P 14.

41 **3** 1r. green (3.9) 12·00 40·00
42 2r. dull and bright purple (3.9) 40·00 75·00
43 3r. green and black (3.9) 40·00 85·00
44 5r. grey-black and red (3.9) 40·00 85·00
32/44 *Set of* 13 £150 £300
32s/44s Optd "Specimen" *Set of* 13 £180

1905 (July)–**11**. *Ordinary paper.* Wmk Mult Crown CA. P 14.

45 **2** ½a. dull green and green 1·25 7·50
46 1a. grey-black and red (10.7.05) 12·00 4·50
a. Chalk-surfaced paper (1906) 10·00 1·60
47 2a. dull and bright purple 7·50 9·00
a. Chalk-surfaced paper (1909) 10·00 12·00
48 2½a. bright blue 3·00 10·00
49 3a. chocolate and grey-green 2·00 14·00
a. Chalk-surfaced paper (1911) 9·50 25·00
50 4a. green and black 4·00 14·00
a. Chalk-surfaced paper (1911) 12·00 32·00
51 6a. green and violet 3·00 24·00
a. Chalk-surfaced paper (1911) 24·00 45·00
52 8a. grey-black and pale blue 6·00 9·00
a. Chalk-surfaced paper. *Black and blue* (27.1.11) 27·00 70·00
53 12a. grey-black and orange-buff 6·50 10·00
a. Chalk-surfaced paper. *Black and orange-brown* (9.11.11) 17·00 60·00

1909 (30 Apr–May). Wmk Mult Crown CA. P 14.

58 **2** ½a. bluish green (May) 23·00 26·00
59 1a. red 2·50 2·00
s. Optd "Specimen" 28·00
45/59 *Set of* 11 60·00 £110

4

5

(Typo D.L.R.)

1912 (Sept)–**19**. *Chalk-surfaced paper (2a. and 3a. to 5r.).* Wmk Mult Crown CA. P 14.

60 **4** ½a. green (11.13) 65 8·00
w. Wmk inverted 15·00 60·00
61 1a. red 2·50 50
a. Scarlet (1917) 3·00 1·25
62 2a. dull and bright purple (12.13) 3·50 15·00
a. Dull purple and violet-purple (4.19) 22·00 32·00
63 2½a. bright blue (10.13) 1·00 8·50
64 3a. chocolate and grey-green (10.13) 2·25 6·50
w. Wmk inverted 85·00
65 4a. green and black (12.12) 2·50 10·00
66 6a. green and violet (4.13) 2·50 5·00
67 8a. grey-black and pale blue (10.13) 3·50 15·00
68 12a. grey-black and orange-buff (10.13) 3·50 21·00
69 **5** 1r. green (11.12) 11·00 16·00
70 2r. dull purple and purple (4.19) 18·00 65·00
71 3r. green and black (4.19) 60·00 £120
72 5r. black and scarlet (4.19) 55·00 £160
60/72 *Set of* 13 £150 £400
60s/72s Optd "Specimen" *Set of* 13 £180

1921. *Chalk-surfaced paper (2a. and 3a. to 5r.).* Wmk Mult Script CA. P 14.

73 **4** ½a. blue-green 2·75 11·00
74 1a. carmine-red 3·50 70
75 2a. dull and bright purple 4·25 1·00
76 2½a. bright blue 1·00 4·50
77 3a. chocolate and green 2·50 7·50
78 4a. green and black 2·50 7·50
79 6a. green and violet 1·50 13·00
80 8a. grey-black and pale blue 2·00 5·50
81 12a. grey-black and orange-buff 8·50 15·00
82 **5** 1r. dull green 8·50 48·00
83 2r. dull purple and purple 23·00 50·00
84 3r. dull green and black 35·00 £100
85 5r. black and scarlet 65·00 £170
73/85 *Set of* 13 £130 £375
73s/85s Optd "Specimen" *Set of* 13 £180

Examples of most values are known showing a forged Berbera postmark dated "21 OC 1932".

1935 (6 May). *Silver Jubilee. As Nos. 91/4 of Antigua. but ptd by Waterlow.* P 11 × 12.

86 1a. deep blue and scarlet 2·25 3·25
m. "Bird" by turret 90·00
87 2a. ultramarine and grey 2·75 3·00
k. Kite and vertical log 70·00
88 3a. brown and deep blue 2·25 13·00
k. Kite and vertical log £100
l. Kite and horizontal log 90·00
89 1r. slate and purple 7·00 13·00
k. Kite and vertical log £140
l. Kite and horizontal log £140
86/9 *Set of* 4 13·00 29·00
86s/9s Perf "Specimen" *Set of* 4 80·00

For illustrations of plate varieties see Omnibus section following Zanzibar.

1937 (13 May). *Coronation. As Nos. 95/7 of Antigua. but ptd by D.L.R.* P 14.

90 1a. scarlet 15 20
91 2a. grey-black 55 1·75
92 3a. bright blue 85 75
90/2 *Set of* 3 1·40 2·40
90s/2s Perf "Specimen" *Set of* 3 65·00

6 Berbera Blackhead Sheep

7 Lesser Kudu

8 Somaliland Protectorate

(Des H. W. Claxton. Recess Waterlow)

1938 (10 May). *Portrait to left.* Wmk Mult Script CA. P 12½.

93 **6** ½a. green 40 5·00
94 1a. scarlet 40 1·75
95 2a. maroon 2·00 2·25
96 3a. bright blue 9·00 11·00
97 **7** 4a. sepia 4·75 9·00
98 6a. violet 8·00 12·00
99 8a. grey 1·50 12·00
100 12a. red-orange 7·50 16·00
101 **8** 1r. green 8·50 55·00
102 2r. purple 17·00 55·00
103 3r. bright blue 18·00 32·00
104 5r. black 20·00 32·00
a. Imperf between (horiz pair) £16000
93/104 *Set of* 12 85·00 £225
93s/104s Perf "Specimen" *Set of* 12 £170

Examples of most values are known showing a forged Berbera postmark dated "15 AU 38".

Following the Italian Occupation, from 19 August 1940 until 16 March 1941, the stamps of ADEN were used at Berbera from 1 July 1941 until 26 April 1942.

9 Berbera Blackhead Sheep

5 Cents
(**10**)

1 Shilling
(**11**)

(Recess Waterlow)

1942 (27 Apr). *As T* **6/8** *but with full-face portrait of King George VI, as in T* **9**. Wmk Mult Script CA. P 12½.

105 **9** ½a. green 20 40
106 1a. scarlet 20 10
107 2a. maroon 50 20
108 3a. bright blue 2·00 20
109 **7** 4a. sepia 3·00 30
110 6a. violet 3·00 20
111 8a. grey 3·25 20
112 12a. red-orange 3·25 40
113 **8** 1r. green 1·75 70
114 2r. purple 1·75 4·50
115 3r. bright blue 2·75 8·00
116 5r. black 7·50 7·50
105/16 *Set of* 12 26·00 20·00
105s/16s Perf "Specimen" *Set of* 12 £170

1946 (15 Oct). *Victory. As Nos. 110/11 of Antigua.*

117 1a. carmine 10 10
a. Perf 13½ 14·00 45·00
118 3a. blue 10 10
117s/18s Perf "Specimen" *Set of* 2 55·00

1949 (28 Jan). *Royal Silver Wedding. As Nos. 112/13 of Antigua.*

119 1a. scarlet 10 10
120 5r. black 3·50 3·25

1949 (24 Oct*). *75th Anniv of U.P.U. As Nos. 114/17 of Antigua. Surch with face values in annas.*

121 1a. on 10c. carmine 20 20
122 3a. on 30c. deep blue (R.) 1·25 1·00
123 6a. on 50c. purple 35 1·25
124 12a. on 1s. red-orange 35 70
121/4 *Set of* 4 1·90 2·75

*This is the local date of issue. The Crown Agents released these stamps in London on 10 October.

(New Currency. 100 cents = 1 shilling)

1951 (1 Apr). *1942 issue surch as T* **10/11**.

No.	Description	Unused	Used
125	5c.on ½a. green	30	1·25
126	10c.on 2a. maroon	30	50
127	15c.on 3a. bright blue	1·75	1·25
128	20c.on 4a. sepia	2·00	20
129	30c.on 6a. violet	1·75	60
130	50c.on 8a. grey	2·50	20
131	70c.on 12a. red-orange	4·00	4·00
132	1s.on 1r. green	1·50	50
133	2s.on 2r. purple	5·50	13·00
134	2s.on 3r. bright blue	6·50	5·00
135	5s.on 5r. black (R.)	7·00	7·50
125/35	*Set of* 11	30·00	30·00

OFFICIAL STAMPS

SERVICE

BRITISH
SOMALILAND
(O 1)

BRITISH
SOMALILAND
(O 2)

O.H.M.S.
(O 3)

SETTING OF TYPE O 1

The 240 impression setting used for the Official stamps differs considerably from that on the contemporary postage issue with overprint at foot, although the "BR1TISH" error can still be found on R. 6/4 of the upper pane. The Official setting is recorded as consisting of 217 overprints as Type A and 23 as Type B.

OVERPRINT VARIETIES

Figure "1" for first "I" in "BRITISH"—Occurs on R. 6/4 of the upper pane as for the postage issue.
"BRITIS H"—Occurs on R. 8, stamps 4 and 10 of the lower pane.

1903 (1 June). *Nos. O45, O48, O49a and O50/1 of India (Queen Victoria optd "O.H.M.S".) additionally optd with Type* **O 1** *in Calcutta.*

No.	Description	Unused	Used
O1	½a. yellow-green	6·50	48·00
	a. "BR1TISH"	£275	
	b. "BRITIS H"	£130	
O2	1a. carmine	15·00	8·50
	a. "BR1TISH"	£300	£275
	b. "BRITIS H"	£150	
O3	2a. pale violet	8·00	48·00
	a. "BR1TISH"	£350	
	b. "BRITIS H"	£170	
O4	8a. dull mauve	10·00	£375
	a. "BR1TISH"	£850	
	b. "BRITIS H"	£400	
	c. Stop omitted after "M" of "O.H.M.S." (lower pane R. 12/10)	£1800	
O5	1r. green and carmine	10·00	£550
	a. "BR1TISH"	£850	
	b. "BRITIS H"	£400	
O1/5	*Set of* 5	45·00	£900

No. O4c was caused by an attempt to correct a minor spacing error of the "O.H.M.S." overprint which is known on the equivalent India Official stamp.

SETTING OF TYPE O 2

This 240 impression setting of "BRITISH SOMALILAND" also differs from that used to prepare the postage issue with overprint at foot, although many of the errors from the latter still occur in the same positions for the Official stamps. The setting used for Nos. O6/9*f* contained 180 overprints as Type A and 60 as Type B.

OVERPRINT VARIETIES

Missing second "I" in "BRITISH"—Occurs R. 7/12 of upper pane as for the postage issue.
Figure "1" for first "I" in "BRITISH"—Occurs R. 6/4 of upper pane as for the postage issue.
"SUMALILAND"—Occurs R. 2/9 of the upper pane as for the postage issue.
"SOMAL.LAND"—Occurs R. 6/7 of the lower pane as for the postage issue.

SERVICE
(O **2a**)

"SERVICE" in wrong fount (Type O **2a**)—Occurs R. 1/7 of lower pane.

1903. *Prepared for use but not issued. Nos. 106, 122/4 and 133 of India (1r. Queen Victoria, rest King Edward VII), optd with Type* **O 2** *in Calcutta.*

No.	Description	Unused
O6	½a. green	40
	a. "BRIT SH"	65·00
	b. "BR1TISH"	48·00
	c. "SUMALILAND"	48·00
	d. "SOMAL.LAND"	38·00
	e. "SERVICE" as Type O **2a**	42·00
O7	1a. carmine	40
	a. "BRIT SH"	65·00
	b. "BR1TISH"	48·00
	c. "SUMALILAND"	48·00
	d. "SOMAL.LAND"	38·00
	e. "SERVICE" as Type O **2a**	42·00
O8	2a. violet	70
	a. "BRIT SH"	95·00
	b. "BR1TISH"	75·00
	c. "SUMALILAND"	75·00
	d. "SERVICE" as Type O **2a**	55·00
O9	8a. purple	4·00
	a. "BRIT SH"	£1600
	b. "BR1TISH"	£600
	c. "SUMALILAND"	£600
	d. "SERVICE" as Type O **2a**	£600
O9*f*	1r. green and aniline carmine	17·00
	fa. "BRIT SH"	£1600
	fb. "BR1TISH"	£600
	fc. "SUMALILAND"	£600
	fd. "SOMAL.LAND"	£600
	fe. "SERVICE" as Type O **2a**	£600
O6/9*f*	*Set of* 5	20·00

Used examples of Nos. O6/9*f* are known, but there is no evidence that such stamps did postal duty.

SETTING OF TYPE O 3

The anna values were overprinted in sheets of 120 (2 panes 6 × 10) from a setting matching the pane size. The full stop after the "M" on the fifth vertical column was either very faint or completely omitted. The prices quoted are for stamps with the stop missing; examples with a partial stop are worth much less.

The 1r. value was overprinted from a separate setting of 60 which did not show the "missing stop" varieties.

1904 (1 Sept)–**05**. *Stamps of Somaliland Protectorate optd with Type* O **3**.

No.	Type	Description	Unused	Used
		(a) Wmk Crown CA. P 14.		
O10	**2**	½a. dull green and green	3·75	48·00
		a. No stop after "M"	£275	
O11		1a. grey-black and carmine	3·25	7·00
		a. No stop after "M"	£200	£275
O12		2a. dull and bright purple	£180	65·00
		a. No stop after "M"	£1900	£700
O13		8a. grey-black and pale blue	60·00	£140
		a. No stop after "M"	£475	£600
		(b) Wmk Mult Crown CA.		
O14	**2**	2a. dull and bright purple, **O** (7.05?)	80·00	£800
		a. No stop after "M"	£1900	
		(c) Wmk Crown CC.		
O15	**3**	1r. green	£170	£600
O10s/13s, O15s		Optd "Specimen" *Set of* 5	£130	

South Africa

South Africa as a nation, rather than a geographical term, came into being with the creation of the Union of South Africa on 31 May 1910.

The development, both political and philatelic, of the area is very complex and the method adopted by the catalogue is to first list, in alphabetical order, the various colonies and republics which formed this federation, followed by stamps for the Union of South Africa.

The section is divided as follows:

I. CAPE OF GOOD HOPE. British Kaffraria. Mafeking Siege Stamps. Vryburg
II. GRIQUALAND WEST
III. NATAL
IV. NEW REPUBLIC
V. ORANGE FREE STATE. Orange River Colony
VI. TRANSVAAL. Pietersburg. Local British Occupation Issues
VII. ZULULAND
VIII. BRITISH ARMY FIELD OFFICES DURING SOUTH AFRICAN WAR
IX. UNION OF SOUTH AFRICA

I. CAPE OF GOOD HOPE

PRICES FOR STAMPS ON COVER

Nos.	1/4	*from* × 4
Nos.	5/14	*from* × 3
Nos.	18/21	*from* × 5
No.	22	—
Nos.	23/6	*from* × 5
Nos.	27/31	*from* × 8
Nos.	32/3	*from* × 10
No.	34	*from* × 25
No.	35	*from* × 20
No.	36	*from* × 10
Nos.	37/8	*from* × 25
Nos.	39/45	*from* × 10
Nos.	46/7	*from* × 12
Nos.	48/54	*from* × 10
Nos.	55/6	*from* × 25
No.	57	*from* × 50
Nos.	58/69	*from* × 10
Nos.	70/8	*from* × 6

PRICES. Our prices for early Cape of Good Hope are for stamps in very fine condition. Exceptional copies are worth more, poorer copies considerably less.

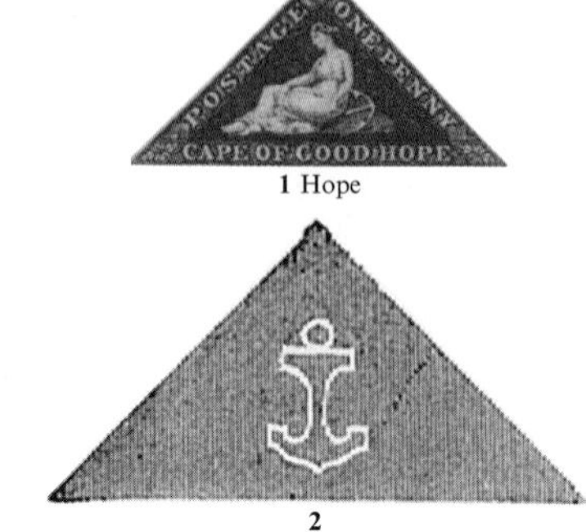

1 Hope

2

(Des Charles Bell, Surveyor-General. Eng W. Humphrys. Recess P.B.)

1853 (1 Sept). W **2**. Imperf.

No.	Type	Description	Unused	Used
		(a) Paper deeply blued.		
1	**1**	1d. pale brick-red	£3500	£30
		a. Deep brick-red	£5000	£32
		b. Wmk sideways	†	£40
2		4d. deep blue	£2000	£16
		a. Wmk sideways	£3000	£25

Plate proofs of the 4d. in a shade similar to the issued stamp exis on ungummed watermarked paper. The blueing on the reverse o these proofs is uneven giving a blotchy appearance.

No.	Type	Description	Unused	Used
		(b) Paper slightly blued (blueing not pronounced at back).		
3	**1**	1d. brick-red	£3000	£20
		a. Brown-red	£3250	£22
		b. Wmk sideways	†	£32
4		4d. deep blue	£1300	£11
		a. Blue	£1400	£15
		b. Wmk sideways	†	£27

PERKINS BACON "CANCELLED". For notes on thes handstamps showing "CANCELLED" between horizontal bar forming an oval, see Catalogue Introduction.

1855–63. W **2**.

No.	Type	Description	Unused	Used
		(a) Imperf.		
5	**1**	1d. brick-red/*cream toned paper* (1857)	£5000	£90
		a. Rose (1858) (H/S "CANCELLED" in oval £10000)	£450	£20
		ab. Wmk sideways	—	£40
		b. Deep rose-red	£650	£25
		ba. Wmk sideways	—	£40
6		4d. deep blue/*white paper* (1855)	£600	45·0
		a. Blue (H/S "CANCELLED" in oval £10000)	£425	45·0
		b. Bisected (on cover)	†	£350
		c. Wmk sideways	†	£16
7		6d. pale rose-lilac/*white paper* (18.2.58) (H/S "CANCELLED" in oval £8000)	£750	£20
		a. Wmk sideways	†	£85
		b. Deep rose-lilac/white paper	£1700	£30
		c. Slate-lilac/blued paper (1862)	£4250	£45
		d. Slate-purple/blued paper (1863)	£3500	£100
		e. Bisected (on cover)	†	–
8		1s. brt yellow-green/*white paper* (18.2.58) (H/S "CANCELLED" in oval £10000)	£2500	£18
		a. Wmk sideways	†	£85
		b. Deep dark green (1859)	£250	£50

The method adopted for producing the plate of the 4d., 6d ar 1s. stamps involved the use of two dies, so that there are two typ of each of these values differing slightly in detail, but produced equal numbers.

The 1d. value in dull rose on ungummed watermarked paper wi the watermark sideways is a plate proof.

The 4d. is known bisected in 1858 and used with two other 4 values to pay the inland registered fee. The 6d. is known bisect and used with 1d. for 4d. rate.

The paper of No. 5 is similar to that of Nos. 1/4, but is witho the blueing. It is much thicker than the white paper used for la printings of the 1d. The evolution of the paper on these Cape Good Hope stamps is similar to that on the line-engraved issues Great Britain. Examples of the 6d. slate-lilac apparently on wh paper have had the blueing washed out.

The 4d. value is known printed in black on white watermark paper. Twelve authenticated copies have been recorded, the majori of which show cancellations or, at least, some indication that th have been used.

It was, at one time, believed that these stamps came from a sm supply printed. in black to mark the death of the Prince Conso but references to examples can be found in the philatelic press bef news of this event reached Cape Town.

It is now thought that these stamps represent proof shee possibly pressed into service during a shortage of stamps in 1861 There is, however, no official confirmation of this theory. (*Pr* £35000 *un*, £30000 *with obliteration*).

No.	Type	Description	Unused	Used
		(b) Unofficially rouletted.		
9	**1**	1d. brick-red	†	£30
10		4d. blue	†	£22
11		6d. rose-lilac	†	£15
12		1s. bright yellow-green	†	£32
		a. Deep dark green	†	£35

These rouletted stamps are best collected on cover.

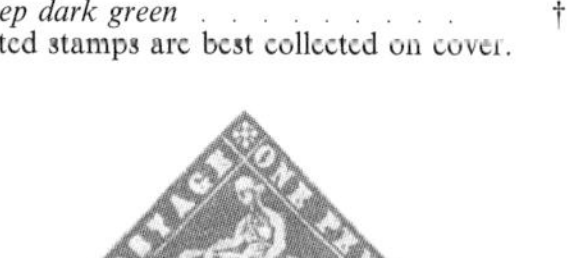

3 Hope

(Local provisional (so-called "wood-block") issue. Engraved o steel by C. J. Roberts. Printed from stereotyped plates by Sau Solomon & Co, Cape Town)

1861 (Feb–Apr). *Laid paper.* Imperf.

No.	Type	Description	Unused	Used
13	**3**	1d. vermilion (27 February)	£14000	£2
		a. Carmine (7 March)	£24000	£3
		b. Brick-red (10 April)	£35000	£4
		c. Error. Pale milky blue	£150000	£28
		ca. Pale bright blue	—	£30
14		4d. pale milky blue (23 February)	£10000	£1
		aa. Retouch or repair to rt-hand corner	—	£5
		a. Pale grey-blue (March?)	£11000	£1
		b. Pale bright blue (March?)	£11000	£1
		ba. Retouch or repair to rt-hand corner	—	£5
		c. Deep bright blue (12 April)	£95000	£4
		d. Blue	£15000	£3
		e. Error. Vermilion	£150000	£40
		ea. Carmine	—	£95
		f. Sideways *tête-bêche* (pair)	†	£100

Nos. 13/14 were each issued in *tête-bêche* pairs normally joi at edges bearing the same inscription ("POSTAGE" aga "POSTAGE", etc). No. 14f, of which only one used exampl known, comes from the first printing and shows the right-h stamp misplaced so that "FOUR PENCE" adjoins "POSTAG

Nos. 13c/ca and 14e/ea were caused by the inclusion of incorrect clichés in the plates of the 1d. or 4d. values.
Both values were officially reprinted in March 1883, on wove paper. The 1d. is in deep red, and the 4d. in a deeper blue than that of the deepest shade of the issued stamp.
Specimens of the reprints have done postal duty, but their use thus was not intended. There are no reprints of the errors or of the retouched 4d.
Further reprints were made privately but with official permission, in 1940/41, in colours much deeper than those of any of the original printings, and on thick carton paper.
Examples of the 4d. are known unofficially rouletted.
Early in 1863, Perkins Bacon Ltd handed over the four plates used for printing the triangular Cape of Good Hope stamps to De La Rue & Co, Ltd, who made all the subsequent printings.

(Printed from the P.B. plates by D.L.R.)

1863–64. Imperf.

(a) W **2**.

18	**1**	1d. deep carmine-red (1864)	£140	£225
		a. Wmk sideways	£300	£300
		b. Deep brown-red	£375	£250
		ba. Wmk sideways	£500	£300
		c. Brownish red	£375	£225
		ca. Wmk sideways	£500	£275
19		4d. deep blue (1864)	£140	50·00
		a. Blue	£150	60·00
		b. Slate-blue	£2000	£500
		c. Steel-blue	£2000	£250
		d. Wmk sideways	£450	£180
20		6d. bright mauve (1864)	£180	£450
		a. Wmk sideways	†	£1000
21		1s. bright emerald-green	£375	£450
		a. Pale emerald-green	£1000	

(b) Wmk Crown CC (sideways).

22	**1**	1d. deep carmine-red	£15000	

No. 22 was a trial printing, and is only known unused.
Our prices for the 4d. blue are for stamps which are blue by comparison with the other listed shades. An exceptionally pale shade is recognised by specialists and is rare.
With the exception of the 4d., these stamps may be easily distinguished from those printed by Perkins Bacon by their colours, which are quite distinct.
The De La Rue stamps of all values are less clearly printed, the figure of Hope and the lettering of the inscriptions standing out less boldly, while the fine lines of the background appear blurred and broken when examined under a glass. The background as a whole often shows irregularity in the apparent depth of colour, due to wear of the plates.
For note regarding the two dies of the 4d., 6d., and 1s. values, see after No. 8.
All the triangular stamps were demonetised as from 1 October 1900.

4 "Hope" seated, with vine and ram. (With outer frame-line)

Four Pence.

(**5**)

(Des Charles Bell. Die engraved on steel and stamps typo by D.L.R.)

1864–77. *With outer frame-line surrounding the design.* Wmk Crown CC. P 14.

23	**4**	1d. carmine-red (5.65)	85·00	23·00
		a. Rose-red	80·00	22·00
		w. Wmk inverted	£275	£120
24		4d. pale blue (8.65)	£100	2·75
		a. Blue	£100	2·75
		b. Ultramarine	£250	55·00
		c. Deep blue (1872)	£150	3·50
		w. Wmk inverted	£400	£130
25		6d. pale lilac (before 21.3.64)	£110	21·00
		a. Deep lilac	£200	6·50
		b. Violet (to bright) (1877)	£130	1·50
		w. Wmk inverted	†	£225
26		1s. deep green (1.64)	£500	18·00
		a. Green	£110	3·00
		ax. Wmk reversed		
		b. Blue-green	£120	4·25
		w. Wmk inverted	£600	£130

The 1d. rose-red, 6d. lilac, and 1s. blue-green are known imperf, probably from proof sheets.
The 1d. and 4d. stamps of this issue may be found with side and/or top outer frame-lines missing, due to wear of the plates.
See also Nos. 44 and 52/3.

(Surch by Saul Solomon & Co, Cape Town)

1868 (17 Nov). *No. 25a surch with T* **5**.

27	**4**	4d.on 6d. deep lilac (R.)	£225	16·00
		a. "Peuce" for "Pence"	£1800	£700
		b. "Fonr" for "Four"	—	£700
		w. Wmk inverted	—	£275

Specimens may also be found with bars omitted or at the top of the stamp, due to misplacement of the sheet.
The space between the words and bars varies from 12½ to 16 mm, stamps with spacing 15½ and 16 mm being rare. There were two printings, one of 120,000 in November 1868 and another of 1,000,000 in December. Stamps showing widest spacings are probably from the earlier printing.

6 (No outer frame-line)

(Die re-engraved. Typo D.L.R.)

1871–76. *Outer frame-line removed.* Wmk Crown CC. P 14.

28	**6**	½d. grey-black (*shades*) (12.75)	16·00	7·00
		w. Wmk inverted	—	85·00
29		1d. carmine-red (*shades*) (2.72)	29·00	60
		w. Wmk inverted	£275	£110
30		4d. dull blue (*shades*) (12.76)	£100	75
		b. Ultramarine	£200	50·00
		w. Wmk inverted	£325	85·00
31		5s. yellow-orange (25.8.71)	£350	16·00

The ½d., 1d. and 5s. are known imperf, probably from proof sheets.
See also Nos. 36, 39, 40/3, 48/51, 54, 61/2 and 64/8.

ONE PENNY (**7**) **THREE PENCE** (**8**)

(Surch by Saul Solomon & Co, Cape Town)

1874–76. *Nos. 25a and 26a surch with T* **7**.

32	**4**	1d.on 6d. deep lilac (R.) (1.9.74)	£475	90·00
		a. "E" of "PENNY" omitted	—	£1000
33		1d.on 1s. green (11.76)	70·00	45·00

These provisionals are found with the bar only, either across the centre of the stamp or at top, with value only; or with value and bar close together, either at top or foot. Such varieties are due to misplacement of sheets during surcharging.

1879 (1 Nov). *No. 30 surch with T* **8**.

34	**6**	3d.on 4d. blue (R.)	£100	1·75
		a. "PENCB" for "PENCE"	£1600	£225
		b. "THE.EE" for "THREE"	£1900	£275
		c. Surch double	£7500	£2750
		d. Variety b. double		

The double surcharge must also have existed showing variety a. but only variety b. is known.
There are numerous minor varieties, including letters broken or out of alignment, due to defective printing and use of poor type.
The spacing between the bar and the words varies from 16½ to 18 mm.

THREEPENCE (**9**) **3** (**10**) **3** (**11**)

(Surch by D.L.R.)

1880 (Feb). *Special printing of the 4d. in new colour, surch, with T* **9**. Wmk Crown CC.

35	**6**	3d.on 4d. pale dull rose	70·00	1·75
		w. Wmk inverted	—	£140

A minor constant variety exists with foot of "P" in "PENCE" broken off, making the letter appear shorter.

1880 (1 July). Wmk Crown CC. P 14.

36	**6**	3d. pale dull rose	£190	23·00
		w. Wmk inverted	—	£275

(Surch by Saul Solomon & Co, Cape Town)

1880 (Aug). *No. 36 surch.*

37	**10**	"3"on 3d. pale dull rose	75·00	1·50
		a. Surch inverted	£800	40·00
		b. Vert pair. Nos. 37/8	£850	£350
		w. Wmk inverted	—	£110
38	**11**	"3"on 3d. pale dull rose	£180	6·00
		a. Surch inverted	£7000	£900
		w. Wmk inverted	—	£300

The "3" (T **10**) is sometimes found broken. Vert pairs are known showing the two types of surcharge *se-tenant*, and vertical strips of three exist, the top stamp having surcharge T **10**, the middle stamp being without surcharge, and the lower stamp having surcharge T **11** (*Price for strip of* 3 £4000 *un.*).

1881 (Jan). Wmk Crown CC. P 14.

39	**6**	3d. pale claret	£120	2·50
		a. Deep claret	£110	2·25
		w. Wmk inverted		

This was a definite colour change made at the request of the Postmaster-General owing to the similarity between the colours of the 1d. stamp and the 3d. in pale dull rose. Imperf copies are probably from proof sheets.
Proofs of this value were printed in brown, on unwatermarked wove paper and imperf, but the colour was rejected as unsuitable.

1882 (July)–**83**. Wmk Crown CA. P 14.

40	**6**	½d. black (1.9.82)	23·00	1·75
		a. Grey-black	19·00	1·75
		w. Wmk inverted	—	£130
41		1d. rose-red	48·00	1·00
		a. Deep rose-red	50·00	1·00
		w. Wmk inverted	—	£130
42		2d. pale bistre (1.9.82)	80·00	50
		a. Deep bistre	85·00	50
		w. Wmk inverted	—	£130
43		3d. pale claret	6·50	1·00
		a. Deep claret	10·00	75
		aw. Wmk inverted	—	90·00
44	**4**	6d. mauve (to bright) (8.82)	90·00	70
45	**6**	5s. orange (8.83)	£800	£200

Imperf pairs of the ½d., 1d. and 2d. are known, probably from proof sheets.

One Half-penny. (**12**)

13 "Cabled Anchor"

(Surch by Saul Solomon & Co, Cape Town)

1882 (July). *Nos. 39a and 43a surch with T* **12**.

46	**6**	½d.on 3d. deep claret (Wmk CC)	£2750	£130
		a. Hyphen omitted	—	£3250
47		½d.on 3d. deep claret (Wmk CA)	25·00	3·25
		a. "p" in "penny" omitted	£2000	£700
		b. "y" in "penny" omitted	£1000	£600
		c. Hyphen omitted	£650	£350
		w. Wmk inverted	—	£250

Varieties also exist with broken and defective letters, and with the obliterating bar omitted or at the top of the stamp.

1884–90. W **13**. P 14.

48	**6**	½d. black (1.86)	4·00	10
		a. Grey-black	4·00	10
		w. Wmk inverted		
49		1d. rose-red (12.85)	4·00	10
		a. Carmine-red	4·00	10
		w. Wmk inverted	—	80·00
50		2d. pale bistre (12.84)	23·00	80
		a. Deep bistre	6·00	10
		w. Wmk inverted	—	£110
51		4d. blue (6.90)	9·50	50
		a. Deep blue	9·50	50
52	**4**	6d. reddish purple (12.84)	60·00	1·60
		a. Purple (shades)	8·50	20
		b. Bright mauve	10·00	50
		w. Wmk inverted	—	£190
53		1s. green (12.85)	£140	4·75
		a. Blue-green (1889)	80·00	40
		w. Wmk inverted	—	£300
54	**6**	5s. orange (7.87)	85·00	4·75
48/54 *Set of* 7			£180	5·50

All the above stamps are known in imperf pairs, probably from proof sheets.
For later shade and colour changes, etc., see Nos. 61, etc.

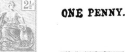

2½d (**14**) **15** **ONE PENNY.** (**16**)

(Surch by D.L.R.)

1891 (Mar). *Special printing of the 3d. in new colour, surch with T* **14**.

55	**6**	2½d.on 3d. pale magenta	5·00	1·00
		a. Deep magenta	3·25	20
		b. "1" with horiz serif	50·00	32·00

No. 55b occurs on two stamps (Nos. 8 and 49) of the pane of 60.
Two types of "d" are found in the surcharge, one with square end to serif at top, and the other with pointed serif.

1892 (June). W **13**. P 14.

56	**15**	2½d. sage-green	8·00	10
		a. Olive-green	10·00	55

See also No. 63.

(Surch by W. A. Richards & Sons, Cape Town)

1893 (Mar). *Nos. 50/a surch with T* **16**.

57	**6**	1d.on 2d. pale bistre	4·00	1·00
		a. Deep bistre	2·50	50
		b. No stop after "PENNY"	50·00	11·00
		c. Surch double	—	£400

No. 57b occurs on stamp No. 42 of the upper left-hand pane, and on No. 6 of the lower right-hand pane.
Minor varieties exist showing broken letters and letters out of alignment or widely spaced. Also with obliterating bar omitted, due to misplacement of the sheet during surcharging.

17 "Hope" standing. Table Bay in background

18 Table Mountain and Bay with Arms of the Colony

(Des Mr. Mountford. Typo D.L.R.)

1893 (Oct)–**1902**. W **13**. P 14.

58	**17**	½d. green (9.98)	2·00	10
59		1d. rose-red	3·00	1·00
		a. Carmine	1·25	10
		aw. Wmk inverted	†	£100
60		3d. magenta (3.02)	4·00	1·50

The 1d. is known in imperf pairs, probably from proof sheets.

1893–98. *New colours, etc.* W **13**. P 14.

61	**6**	½d. yellow-green (12.96)	1·50	50
		a. Green	2·75	50
62		2d. chocolate-brown (3.97)	2·00	40
63	**15**	2½d. pale ultramarine (3.96)	4·00	15
		a. Ultramarine	4·00	10
64	**6**	3d. bright magenta (9.98)	7·00	85
65		4d. sage-green (3.97)	4·00	1·75
66		1s. blue-green (12.93)	60·00	3·75
		a. Deep blue-green	70·00	7·50
67		1s. yellow-ochre (5.96)	8·00	1·00
68		5s. brown-orange (6.96)	65·00	3·50
61/8 *Set of* 8			£140	11·00

(Des E. Sturman. Typo D.L.R.)

1900 (Jan). W **13**. P 14.
69 **18** 1d. carmine . . . . 2·50 10
w. Wmk inverted . . . . — £100

19 20 21

22 23 24

25 26 27

(Typo D.L.R.)

1902 (Dec)–**04**. W **13**. P 14.
70 **19** ½d. green . . . . 2·25 10
71 **20** 1d. carmine . . . . 2·00 10
w. Wmk inverted . . . .
y. Wmk inverted and reversed . . .
72 **21** 2d. brown (10.04) . . . . . . 9·50 80
w. Wmk inverted . . . .
73 **22** 2½d. ultramarine (3.04) . . . . . 2·75 6·50
74 **23** 3d. magenta (4.03) . . . . . . 7·00 75
75 **24** 4d. olive-green (2.03) . . . . . 8·00 65
76 **25** 6d. bright mauve (3.03) . . . . . 15·00 30
77 **26** 1s. yellow-ochre . . . . 12·00 80
78 **27** 5s. brown-orange (2.03) . . . . . 75·00 13·00
70/8 *Set of* 9 . . . . £120 21·00

All values exist in imperf pairs, from proof sheets.

The ½d. exists from coils constructed from normal sheets for use in stamp machines introduced in 1911.

STAMP BOOKLET

1905 (Dec). *Black on red cover. Stapled.*
SB1 2s.7d. booklet containing thirty 1d. (No. 71) in blocks of 6 . . . . £2000

OFFICIAL STAMPS

The following stamps, punctured with a double triangle device, were used by the Stationery and Printed Forms Branch of the Cape of Good Hope Colonial Secretary's Department between 1904 and 1906. Later South Africa issues may have been similarly treated, but this has not been confirmed.

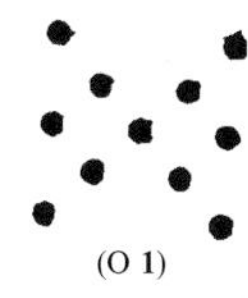

(O 1)

1904. *Various issues punctured as Type* O **1**.

(a) Nos. 50 and 52a.
O1 **6** 2d. pale bistre . . . . 16·00
O2 **4** 6d. purple . . . . 18·00

(b) Nos. 58 and 60.
O3 **17** ½d. green . . . . 19·00
O4 3d. magenta . . . . 15·00

(c) Nos. 62 and 64/5.
O5 **6** 2d. chocolate-brown . . . . . . 15·00
O6 3d. bright magenta . . . . . . 20·00
O7 4d. sage-green . . . . 19·00

(d) No. 69.
O8 **18** 1d. carmine . . . . 16·00

(e) Nos. 70/2 and 74/8.
O9 **19** ½d. green . . . . 20·00
O10 **20** 1d. carmine . . . . 12·00
O11 **21** 2d. brown . . . . 20·00
O12 **23** 3d. magenta . . . . 15·00
O13 **24** 4d. olive-green . . . . 16·00
O14 **25** 6d. bright mauve . . . . 16·00
O15 **26** 1s. yellow-ochre . . . . 19·00
O16 **27** 5s. brown-orange . . . . 50·00

Nos. O1/16 are only known used.

Cape of Good Hope became a province of the Union of South Africa on 31 May 1910.

BRITISH KAFFRARIA

The history of the Cape eastern frontier was punctuated by a series of armed conflicts with the native population, known as the Kaffir Wars. After a particularly violent outbreak in 1846 the Governor, Sir Harry Smith, advanced the line of the Cape frontier to the Keikama and Tyumie Rivers. In the area between the new frontier and the Kei River a buffer state, British Kaffraria, was established on 17 December 1847. This area was not annexed to the Cape, but was administered as a separate Crown dependency by the Governor of Cape Colony in his capacity as High Commissioner for South Africa.

The territory, with its administration based on King William's Town, used the stamps of the Cape of Good Hope from 1853 onwards, the mail being sent via Port Elizabeth or overland from the Cape. Covers from British Kaffraria franked with the triangular issues are rare.

The first postal marking known from British Kaffraria is the 1849 type octagonal numeral No 47 from Port Beaufort. Oval post-marks of the 1853 type were used at Alice, Aliwal North, Bedford, Fort Beaufort, King William's Town and Queenstown. In 1864 numeral cancellations were issued to all post offices within the Cape system and it is known that the following numbers were initially assigned to post towns in Kaffraria: 4 (King William's Town), 7 (Bedford), 11 (Queenstown), 29 (East London), 32 (Fort Beaufort), 38 (Aliwal North) and 104 (Cathcart).

It is believed that post offices may have also existed at Adelaide, Barkly East, Sterkstoom and Stutterheim, but, to date, no examples of handstamps or cancellations are known from them during the British Kaffraria period.

Following the decimation by famine of the Xhosa tribes in 1857 British Kaffraria was annexed to Cape Colony in 1865. The area eventually formed the basis of the Ciskei independent "homeland".

MAFEKING SIEGE STAMPS

PRICES FOR STAMPS ON COVER	
Nos. 1/16	*from* × 12
Nos. 17/18	*from* × 25
Nos. 19/20	*from* × 15
Nos. 21/2	*from* × 12

23 MARCH to 17 MAY 1900

There are numerous forgeries of the Mafeking overprints, many of which were brought home by soldiers returning from the Boer War.

MAFEKING,
3d.
BESIEGED.
(1)

MAFEKING
3d.
BESIEGED.
(2)

(Surcharged by Townsend & Co, Mafeking)

1900 (23 Mar–28 Apr). *Various stamps surch as T* **1** *and* **2**.

(a) Cape of Good Hope stamps surch as T **1** *(23 Mar).*
1 **6** 1d.on ½d. green . . . . £180 65·00
2 **17** 1d.on ½d. green (24.3) . . . . . . £225 75·00
3 3d.on 1d. carmine . . . . £200 50·00
4 **6** 6d.on 3d. magenta (24.3) £26000 £250
5 1s.on 4d. sage-green (24.3) £6000 £325

A variety in the setting of each value exists without comma after "MAFEKING".

(b) Nos. 59 and 61/3 of Bechuanaland Protectorate (previously optd on Great Britain) surch as T **1**.
6 1d.on ½d. vermilion (28.3) . . . . . . £180 60·00
a. Surch inverted . . . . † £4250
b. Vert pair, surch *tête-bêche* . . . . . † £22000
7 3d.on 1d. lilac (4.4) . . . . £850 90·00
a. Surch double . . . . † £16000
8 6d.on 2d. green and carmine (6.4) . . . . £1700 75·00
9 6d.on 3d. purple/*yellow* (30.3) £4750 £275
a. Surch inverted . . . . † £22000
b. Surch double . . . .

(c) Nos. 12 and 35 of British Bechuanaland (4d. previously optd on Great Britain) surch as T **1**.
10 6d.on 3d. lilac and black (27.3) . . . . . £350 65·00
11 1s.on 4d. green and purple-brown (29.3) . . £1200 80·00
a. Surch double (both Type **1**) . . . . . † £16000
ab. Surch double (Type **1** and Type **2**) . . . £7000 £4500
b. Surch treble . . . . † £16000
c. Surch double, one inverted . . . . . † £16000

(d) Nos. 61/2 and 65 of Bechuanaland Protectorate (previously optd on Great Britain) surch as T **2**.
12 3d.on 1d. lilac (1 Apr) . . . . £900 75·00
a. Surch double . . . . † £6500
13 6d.on 2d. green and carmine (25 Apr) . . . £1100 75·00
14 1s.on 6d. purple/*rose-red* (12 Apr) . . . . £4250 90·00

(e) Nos. 36/7 of British Bechuanaland (previously optd on Great Britain) surch as T **2**.
15 1s. on 6d. purple/*rose-red* (28 Apr) . . . £14000 £700
16 2s. on 1s. green (13 Apr) £7500 £375

On the stamps overprinted "BECHUANALAND PROTECTORATE" and "BRITISH BECHUANALAND" the local surcharge is so adjusted as not to overlap the original overprint.

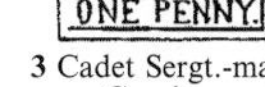

3 Cadet Sergt.-major Goodyear

4 General Baden-Powell

(Des Dr. W. A. Hayes (T **3**), Capt. H. Greener (T **4**))

1900 (6–11 Apr). *Produced photographically by Dr. D. Taylor. Horiz laid paper with sheet wmk* "OCEANA FINE". P 12.

(a) 18½ mm wide. (b) 21 mm wide.
17 **3** 1d. pale blue/*blue* (7.4) £800 £275
18 1d. deep blue/*blue* £800 £275
19 **4** 3d. pale blue/*blue (a)* £1200 £400
a. Reversed design £50000 £35000
20 3d. deep blue/*blue (a)* £1200 £350
a. Imperf between (horiz pair) . . . . . † £50000
b. Double print . . . . † £16000
21 3d. pale blue/*blue (b)* (11.4) £7000 £800
a. Vert laid paper £9000
22 3d. deep blue/*blue (b)* (11.4) £7500 £950

These stamps vary a great deal in colour from deep blue to pale grey.

No. 18 imperforate and without gum is believed to be a proof (*Price for unused pair* £16000).

No. 19a comes from a sheet of 12 printed in reverse of which nine, three mint and six used, are known to have survived.

VRYBURG

PRICES FOR STAMPS ON COVER	
Nos. 1/4	*from* × 5
Nos. 11/12	*from* × 2

BOER OCCUPATION

Vryburg was occupied by Boer forces on 15 October 1899. Unoverprinted stamps of Transvaal were used initially. Nos. 1/4 were only available from 24 to 29 November. The Boers evacuated the town on 7 May 1900.

½ PENCE

Z.A.R.
(1)

1899 (24 Nov). *Cape stamps surch as T* **1**. *Surch 12 mm high on No. 3 and 10 mm on all other values.*
1 **6** ½PENCE green . . . . £200 80·00
a. Italic "Z" £1700 £700
b. Surch 12 mm high £1700 £700
2 **17** 1PENCE rose £225 £100
a. Italic "Z" £1900 £800
b. Surch 12 mm high £1900 £800
c. "I" for "1" £1200 £500
3 **4** 2PENCE on 6d. mauve £2000 £500
a. Italic "Z" £10000 £4250
4 **15** 2½PENCE on 2½d. blue £1700 £425
a. Italic "Z" £10000 £4250
b. Surch 12 mm high £10000 £4250

The "2 PENCE" on 6d. shows the surcharge 12 mm high. It is possible that this was the first value surcharged as the remaining three show the height reduced to 10 mm with the exception of one position in the second vertical row of the setting. The italic "Z" occurs on one position in the sixth vertical row. It is believed that the setting was of 60 (6 × 10).

BRITISH REOCCUPATION

(2)

1900 (16 May). *Provisionals issued by the Military Authorities. Stamps of Transvaal handstamped with T* **2**.
11 **30** ½d. green . . . . — £2000
11*a* 1d. rose-red (No. 206) . . . . . .
12 1d. rose-red and green (No. 217) . . £8500 £4000
13 2d. brown and green . . . . . .
14 2½d. dull blue and green . . . . .

No. 11 is known used with double handstamp and Nos. 11/12 with the overprint reading downwards

II. GRIQUALAND WEST

Griqualand West was situated to the North of Cape Colony, bounded on the north by what became British Bechuanaland and on the east by the Orange Free State.

The area was settled the early nineteenth century by the Griqua tribal group, although many members of the tribe, including the paramount chief, migrated to Griqualand East (between Basutoland and the east coast of South Africa) in 1861–63. There was little European involvement in Griqualand West before 1866, but in that year the diamond fields along the Vaal River were discovered. Sovereignty was subsequently claimed by the Griqua Chief, the Orange Free State and the South African Republic (Transvaal). In 1871 the British authorities arbitrated in favour of the Griqua Chief who promptly ceded his territory to Great Britain. Griqualand West became a separate Crown Colony in January 1873.

During the initial stages of the prospecting boom, mail was passed via the Orange Free State, but a post office connected to the Cape Colony postal system was opened at Klip Drift (subsequently Barkly) in late 1870. Further offices at De Beer's New Rush (subsequently Kimberley), Douglas and Du Toit's Pan (subsequently Beaconsfield) were open by September 1873.

Cape of Good Hope stamps to the 5s. value were in use from October 1871, but those originating in Griqualand West can only be identified after the introduction of Barred Oval Diamond Numeral cancellations in 1873. Numbers known to have been issued in the territory are:

1 De Beers N.R. (New Rush) (subsequently Kimberley)
3 Junction R. & M. (Riet and Modder Rivers)
4 Barkly
6 or 9 Du Toit's Pan (subsequently Beaconsfield)
8 Langford (transferred to Douglas)
10 Thornhill

PRICES FOR STAMPS ON COVER The stamps of Griqualand West are worth from × 10 the price quoted for used stamps, when on cover from the territory.

FORGED OVERPRINTS. Many stamps show forged overprints. Great care should be taken when purchasing the scarcer items.

Stamps of the Cape of Good Hope, **Crown CC, perf 14, overprinted.**

1874 (Sept). *No. 24a of Cape of Good Hope surch "1d." in red manuscript by the Kimberley postmaster.*
1 1d. on 4d. blue £1200 £2000

G. W.
(1)

1877 (Mar). *Nos. 29/30 of Cape of Good Hope optd with T* **1**.
2 1d. carmine-red . . . £500 85·00
a. Opt double . . . † £2000
3 4d. dull blue (R.) . . . £400 75·00

G G G G G G
(1a) (2) (3) (4) (5) (6)
G G G G G
(7) (8) (9) (10) (11)
G G G
(12) (13) (14)

1877 (Mar)–**78**. *Nos. 24a, 25a, 26a and 28/31 Cape of Good Hope optd with capital "G".*

(a) First printing. Optd with T **1a**/**6** *and* **8** *in black (1d.) or red (others).*

4 ½d. grey-black
a. Opt Type **1a** . . . 19·00 23·00
b. Opt Type **2** . . . 45·00 55·00
c. Opt Type **3** . . . 25·00 30·00
d. Opt Type **4** . . . 45·00 55·00
e. Opt Type **5** . . . 50·00 65·00
f. Opt Type **6** . . . 23·00 27·00
g. Opt Type **8** . . . £400 £450
5 1d. carmine-red
a. Opt Type **1a** . . . 20·00 15·00
b. Opt Type **2** . . . 48·00 32·00
c. Opt Type **3** . . . 25·00 21·00
d. Opt Type **4** . . . 48·00 32·00
e. Opt Type **5** . . . 55·00 40·00
f. Opt Type **6** . . . 20·00 15·00
g. Opt Type **8** . . . *
6 4d. blue (with frame-line) (No. 24*a*)
a. Opt Type **1a** . . . £200 32·00
b. Opt Type **2** . . . £550 90·00
c. Opt Type **3** . . . £375 45·00
d. Opt Type **4** . . . £550 90·00
e. Opt Type **5** . . . £650 £110
f. Opt Type **6** . . . £275 42·00
g. Opt Type **8** . . . £1800 £550
7 4d. dull blue (without frame-line) (No. 30)
a. Opt Type **1a** . . . £150 21·00
b. Opt Type **2** . . . £400 60·00
c. Opt Type **3** . . . £250 28·00
d. Opt Type **4** . . . £375 60·00
e. Opt Type **5** . . . £450 75·00
f. Opt Type **6** . . . £225 26·00
g. Opt Type **8** . . . £1500 £400
8 6d. deep lilac
a. Opt Type **1a** . . . £110 23·00
b. Opt Type **2** . . . £250 65·00
c. Opt Type **3** . . . £170 32·00
d. Opt Type **4** . . . £250 65·00
e. Opt Type **5** . . . £325 80·00
f. Opt Type **6** . . . £150 30·00
g. Opt Type **8** . . . £1300 £475
9 1s. green
a. Opt Type **1a** . . . £140 20·00
ab. Opt inverted . . . — £425
b. Opt Type **2** . . . £325 45·00
ba. Opt inverted . . . — £700
c. Opt Type **3** . . . £225 26·00
d. Opt Type **4** . . . £325 45·00
da. Opt inverted . . . — £700
e. Opt Type **5** . . . £400 55·00
f. Opt Type **6** . . . £200 23·00
fa. Opt inverted . . . — £475
g. Opt Type **8** . . . £2250 £475
10 5s. yellow-orange
a. Opt Type **1a** . . . £500 25·00
b. Opt Type **2** . . . £850 50·00
c. Opt Type **3** . . . £700 29·00
d. Opt Type **4** . . . £850 50·00
e. Opt Type **5** . . . £1200 65·00
f. Opt Type **6** . . . £650 28·00
g. Opt Type **8** . . . £2250

*The 1d. with overprint Type **8** from this setting can only be distinguished from that of the second printing when *se-tenant* with overprint Type **3**.

Nos. 4/10 were overprinted by a setting of 120 covering two panes of 60 (6 × 10). This setting contained 41 examples of Type **1***a*, 10 of Type **2**, 23 of Type **3**, 10 of Type **4**, 8 of Type **5**, 27 of Type **6** and 1 of Type **8**. Sub-types of Types **1***a* and **2** exist. The single example of Type **8** occurs on R.7/4 of the right-hand pane.

It is believed that there may have been an additional setting used for the 5s. which was in considerable demand to cover the postage and registration on diamond consignments. It is also possible that single panes of this value and of the 1s. were overprinted using the right-hand half of the normal 120 setting.

(b) Second printing. Optd with T **6**/**14** *in black (1878).*

11 1d. carmine-red
a. Opt Type **6** . . . *
b. Opt Type **7** . . . 22·00 16·00
c. Opt Type **8** . . . 45·00 27·00
d. Opt Type **9** . . . 23·00 17·00
e. Opt Type **10** . . . 65·00 60·00
f. Opt Type **11** . . . 50·00 38·00
g. Opt Type **12** . . . 60·00 55·00
h. Opt Type **13** . . . 95·00 85·00
i. Opt Type **14** . . . £325 £275
12 4d. dull blue (without frame-line) (No. 30)
a. Opt Type **6** . . . £275 50·00
b. Opt Type **7** . . . £100 21·00
c. Opt Type **8** . . . £250 45·00
d. Opt Type **9** . . . £120 22·00
e. Opt Type **10** . . . £325 70·00
f. Opt Type **11** . . . £275 55·00
g. Opt Type **12** . . . £300 65·00
h. Opt Type **13** . . . £475 £140
i. Opt Type **14** . . . £1600 £400
13 6d. deep lilac
a. Opt Type **6** . . . £400 80·00
b. Opt Type **7** . . . £190 45·00
ba. Opt double
c. Opt Type **8** . . . £375 75·00
d. Opt Type **9** . . . £225 50·00
da. Opt double . . . — £700
e. Opt Type **10** . . . £450 £120
ea. Opt double . . . — £850
f. Opt Type **11** . . . £400 85·00
g. Opt Type **12** . . . £400 £110
h. Opt Type **13** . . . £650 £190
i. Opt Type **14** . . . £1600 £500

*The 1d. with overprint Type **6** from this setting can only be distinguished from that of the first printing when *se-tenant* with Types **11**, **12** or **13**.

Nos. 11/13 were overprinted by another double-pane setting of 120 in which only Types **6** and **8** were repeated from that used for the first printing. The second printing setting contained 12 examples of Type **6**, 30 of Type **7**, 13 of Type **8**, 27 of Type **9**, 9 of Type **10**, 11 of Type **11**, 11 of Type **12**, 6 of Type **13** and 1 of Type **14**. Sub-types of Types **7** and **12** exist.

G G G
(15) (16) (17)

1878 (June). *Nos. 24a, 25a and 28/30 of Cape of Good Hope optd with small capital "G", T* **15**/**16**.
14 **15** ½d. grey-black (R.) . . . 8·00 9·50
a. Opt inverted . . . 9·50 9·50
b. Opt double . . . 38·00 48·00
c. Opt double, both inverted . . . 70·00 90·00
d. Black opt . . . £160 85·00
da. Opt inverted . . . £160
db. Opt double, one inverted in red . . . £325
dc. Opt double, one inverted (Type **16**) in red . . . 90·00
15 **16** ½d. grey-black (R.) . . . 9·50 9·50
a. Opt inverted . . . 9·50 11·00
b. Opt double . . . 65·00 65·00
c. Opt double, both inverted
d. Black opt . . . 38·00 38·00
da. Opt inverted . . . 38·00 38·00
db. Opt double, one inverted (Type **15**) in red . . . £130
16 **15** 1d. carmine-red . . . 9·00 6·00
a. Opt inverted . . . 9·00 9·00
b. Opt double . . . £150 38·00
c. Opt double, both inverted . . . £150 55·00
d. Opt double, both inverted with one in red . . . 32·00 32·00
e. Opt double, both inverted with one (Type **16**) in red
17 **16** 1d. carmine-red . . . 9·00 9·00
a. Opt inverted . . . 70·00 25·00
b. Opt double . . . — 75·00
c. Opt double, both inverted . . . — 90·00
d. Opt double, both inverted with one in red . . . 70·00 70·00
18 **15** 4d. blue (with frame-line) (No. 24a) . . . — £120
19 **16** 4d. blue (with frame-line) (No. 24a) . . . — £120
20 **15** 4d. dull blue (without frame-line) (No. 30) . . . £110 23·00
a. Opt inverted . . . £170 70·00
b. Opt double . . . — £160
c. Opt double, both inverted . . . — £225
d. Red opt . . . £275 85·00
da. Opt inverted . . . £800 65·00
21 **16** 4d. dull blue (without frame-line) (No. 30) . . . £130 10·00
a. Opt inverted . . . £180 25·00
b. Opt double . . . — £170
c. Opt double, both inverted . . . — £225
d. Red opt . . . — 70·00
da. Opt inverted . . . £275 70·00
22 **15** 6d. deep lilac . . . £110 22·00
23 **16** 6d. deep lilac . . . — 22·00

Nos. 14/23 were also overprinted using a double-pane setting of 120. Based on evidence from surviving ½d. and 1d. sheets all overprints in the left-hand pane were roman, Type **15**, and all those in the right-hand pane italic, Type **16**, except for R.1/6, 4/5, 6/6, 7/6, 8/6, 9/6 and 10/6 which were Type **15**. There is considerable evidence to suggest that after the ½d. value had been overprinted the setting was amended to show a Type **15**, instead of a Type **16**, on R.10/5 of the right-hand pane. Two strikes of the setting were required to overprint the sheets of 240 and it would appear that on many sheets the bottom two panes had the overprints inverted.

1879. *Nos. 25b, 26b and 28/31 of Cape of Good Hope optd with small capital "G", T* **17**.
24 ½d. grey-black . . . 12·00 6·50
a. Opt double . . . £350 £225
25 1d. carmine-red . . . 13·00 4·00
a. Opt inverted . . . — 80·00
b. Opt double . . . — £130
c. Opt treble . . . — £180
26 4d. dull blue . . . 25·00 4·00
a. Opt double . . . — £100
27 6d. violet . . . £120 7·00
a. Opt inverted . . . — 28·00
b. Opt double . . . £550 £150
28 1s. green . . . £100 4·50
a. Opt double . . . £300 85·00
29 5s. yellow-orange . . . £350 8·50
a. Opt double . . . £450 75·00
b. Opt treble . . . — £275

Nos. 24/9 were also overprinted using a setting of 120 which contained a number of minor type varieties.

Griqualand West was merged with Cape Colony in October 1880. The remaining stock of the overprinted stamps was returned from Kimberley to Cape Town and redistributed among various post offices in Cape Colony where they were used as ordinary Cape stamps.

III. NATAL

PRICES FOR STAMPS ON COVER		
Nos.	1/7	*from* × 2
Nos.	9/25	*from* × 3
Nos.	26/56	*from* × 4
Nos.	57/8	—
Nos.	59/73	*from* × 5
Nos.	76/84	*from* × 4
Nos.	85/93	*from* × 3
Nos.	96/103	*from* × 6
Nos.	104/5	*from* × 5
Nos.	106/25	*from* × 6
Nos.	127/42	*from* × 4
Nos.	143/5*a*	—
Nos.	146/57	*from* × 4
No.	162	—
Nos.	165/71	*from* × 3
No.	F1	—
Nos.	O1/6	*from* × 10

1 2 3 4 5

(Embossed in plain relief on coloured wove paper)

1857 (26 May)–**61**. Imperf.
1 **1** 1d. blue (9.59) . . . — £1
2 1d. rose (1859) . . . — £1
3 1d. buff (1861) . . . — £1(
4 **2** 3d. rose . . . — £
a. *Tête-bêche* (pair) . . . — £32(
5 **3** 6d. green . . . — £1
6 **4** 9d. blue . . . — £7(
7 **5** 1s. buff . . . — £5

All the above have been reprinted more than once, and the ea reprints of some values cannot always be distinguished w certainty from originals.

Stamps on surface-coloured paper with higher face values a perforated 12½ are fiscals.

NOTE. The value of the above stamps depends on their dimensio and the clearness of the embossing, but our prices are for fine us

PERKINS BACON "CANCELLED". For notes on th handstamps showing "CANCELLED" between horizontal b forming an oval, see Catalogue Introduction.

6

7

(Eng C. H. Jeens. Recess P.B.)

1859–60. No wmk. P 14.
9 **6** 1d. rose-red (1860) (H/S "CANCELLED" in oval £6500) . . . £130 70
10 3d. blue . . . £160 42
a. Imperf between (vert pair) . . . † £6

No. 10a is only known from a cover of 1867 franked with t such pairs.

The 3d. also exists with "CANCELLED" in oval, but examples are believed to be in private hands.

1861. No wmk. Intermediate perf 14 to 16.
11 **6** 3d. blue . . . £225 65

1861–62. No wmk. Rough perf 14 to 16.
12 **6** 3d. blue . . . £110 32
a. Imperf between (horiz pair) . . . £3500
b. Imperf (pair) . . . — £3(
13 6d. grey (1862) . . . £170 50

1862. Wmk Small Star. Rough perf 14 to 16.
15 **6** 1d. rose-red . . . £140 65

The 1d. without watermark and the 3d. watermark Small S both imperforate, are proofs.

(Recess D.L.R.)

1863. *Thick paper.* No wmk. P 13.
18 **6** 1d. lake . . . 90·00 27
19 1d. carmine-red . . . 90·00 27

863–65. Wmk Crown CC. P 12½.
0 6 1d. brown-red £140 38·00
y. Wmk inverted and reversed
1 1d. rose 90·00 35·00
x. Wmk reversed 90·00 35·00
2 1d. bright red 90·00 38·00
x. Wmk reversed 90·00 38·00
3 6d. lilac 65·00 17·00
4 6d. violet 50·00 28·00
x. Wmk reversed 50·00 28·00

(Typo D.L.R.)

867 (Apr). Wmk Crown CC. P 14.
5 7 1s. green £140 28·00
w. Wmk inverted — £250

POSTAGE (7a) Postage. (7b) Postage. (7c)
Postage. (7d) POSTAGE. (7e)

869 (23 Aug). *Optd horiz in Natal.* No wmk (3d.), wmk Crown CC (others). P 14 or 14–16 (3d.), 12½ (1d., 6d) or 14 (1s.).

(a) With T 7a (tall capitals without stop).
5 6 1d. rose £375 80·00
x. Wmk reversed £375 80·00
7 1d. bright red £325 70·00
x. Wmk reversed — 70·00
8 3d. blue (No. 10) £2000 £600
3a 3d. blue (No. 11) £600 £250
3b 3d. blue (No. 12) £475 90·00
) 6d. lilac £500 70·00
) 6d. violet £450 80·00
x. Wmk reversed £450 80·00
7 1s. green £7000 £1200

(b) With T 7b (12¾ mm long).
6 1d. rose £350 75·00
1d. bright red £300 65·00
a. Opt double † £1200
x. Wmk reversed £300 65·00
3d. blue (No. 10) — £300
a 3d. blue (No. 11) £550 £200
b 3d. blue (No. 12) £450 80·00
6d. lilac £475 65·00
6d. violet £400 75·00
x. Wmk reversed £400 75·00
7 1s. green £5000 £900

(c) With T 7c (13¾ mm long).
6 1d. rose £700 £200
1d. bright red £750 £180
x. Wmk reversed — £180
3d. blue (No. 10)
a 3d. blue (No. 11) — £700
b 3d. blue (No. 12) £1500 £350
6d. lilac £1600 £150
6d. violet £1500 £140
x. Wmk reversed — £160
7 1s. green — £1800

(d) With T 7d (14½ to 15½ mm long).
6 1d. rose £600 £170
1d. bright red £600 £150
3d. blue (No. 10)
a 3d. blue (No. 11) — £450
b 3d. blue (No. 12) — £275
6d. lilac — £100
6d. violet £1200 95·00
7 1s. green £13000 £1600

(e) With T 7e (small capitals with stop).
6 1d. rose 90·00 40·00
x. Wmk reversed 90·00 40·00
1d. bright red £150 40·00
x. Wmk reversed £150 40·00
3d. blue (No. 10) £275 70·00
3d. blue (No. 11) £150 45·00
3d. blue (No. 12) £180 40·00
a. Opt double † £900
6d. lilac £180 60·00
6d. violet £140 50·00
x. Wmk reversed £140 50·00
7 1s. green £200 65·00

It is believed that there were two settings of these overprints.
e first setting, probably of 240, contained 60 examples of Type 7a, of Type 7b, 20 of Type 7c, 28 of Type 7d and 60 of Type 7e.
e second, probably of 60 (6 × 10), contained Type 7e only.

POSTAGE (8)

70. *No. 25 optd with T 8 by De La Rue.*
7 1s. green (C.) — £3250
1s. green (Blk.) £2250 £1200
a. Opt double — £2250
1s. green (G.) 75·00 10·00
For 1s. orange, see No. 108.

POSTAGE (9) POSTAGE (10) POSTAGE POSTAGE (11)

0–73. *Optd with T 9 by De La Rue.* Wmk Crown CC. P 12½.
6 1d. bright red 75·00 13·00
x. Wmk reversed 75·00 13·00
3d. bright blue (R.) (1872) 80·00 13·00
x. Wmk reversed 80·00 13·00
6d. mauve (1873) £160 25·00

1873 (July). *Fiscal stamp optd locally with T 10.* Wmk Crown CC. P 14.
63 7 1s. purple-brown £190 19·00

1874 (July). *No. 21 optd locally with T 11.*
65 6 1d. rose £225 70·00
a. Opt double
x. Wmk reversed — 70·00

12 13 14
15 16

(Typo D.L.R.)

1874 (Jan)–**99**. Wmk Crown CC (sideways on 5s.). P 14.
66 12 1d. dull rose 23·00 2·75
67 1d. bright rose 23·00 2·75
68 13 3d. blue £100 19·00
a. Perf 14 × 12½ £1500 £850
69 14 4d. brown (1878) £110 11·00
aw. Wmk inverted £350 £100
b. Perf 12½ £325 65·00
70 15 6d. bright reddish violet 48·00 6·00
w. Wmk inverted † £150
71 16 5s. maroon (1882) £170 48·00
a. Perf 15½ × 15 (1874) £300 80·00
72 5s. rose 75·00 29·00
73 5s. carmine (H/S S. £160) 70·00 28·00
a. Wmk upright (1899)

POSTAGE (17) POSTAGE (18) ½ HALF (19)

1875–76. Wmk Crown CC. P 14 (1s.) or 12½ (others).

(a) Optd locally with T 17.
76 6 1d. rose £110 50·00
a. Opt double £900 £425
x. Wmk reversed £110 50·00
77 1d. bright red £100 60·00
x. Wmk reversed £100 60·00

(b) Optd locally with T 18 (14½ mm long, without stop).
81 6 1d. rose (1876) 85·00 50·00
a. Opt inverted £950 £425
x. Wmk reversed 85·00 50·00
82 1d. yellow (1876) 70·00 70·00
a. Opt double, one albino £200
x. Wmk reversed 80·00 80·00
83 6d. violet (1876) 55·00 6·50
a. Opt double — £550
b. Opt inverted £650 £150
w. Wmk inverted — £100
x. Wmk reversed 55·00 6·50
84 7 1s. green (1876) 80·00 6·00
a. Opt double — £325

TYPE 19. There are several varieties of this surcharge, of which T 19 is an example. They may be divided as follows:

(*a*) "½" 4½ mm high, "2" has straight foot.
(*b*) As last but "½" is 4 mm high.
(*c*) As last but "2" has curled foot.
(*d*) "½" 3½ mm. high, "2" has straight foot.
(*e*) As last but "2" has curled foot.
(*f*) As last but "2" smaller.

As the "½" and "HALF" were overprinted separately, they vary in relative position, and are frequently overlapping.

1877 (13 Feb). *No. 66 surch locally as T 19.*
85 12 ½d.on 1d. rose (*a*) 26·00 65·00
a. "½" double
86 ½d.on 1d. rose (*b*) £120
87 ½d.on 1d. rose (*c*) £100
88 ½d.on 1d. rose (*d*) 60·00 90·00
89 ½d.on 1d. rose (*e*) 65·00
90 ½d.on 1d. rose (*f*) 75·00

POSTAGE Half-penny (21) 23 ONE HALF-PENNY. (24)

1877 (7 Oct)–**79**. *T 6 (wmk Crown CC. P 12½) surch locally as T 21.*
91 ½d.on 1d. yellow 8·00 13·00
a. Surch inverted £275 £190
b. Surch double £250 £180
c. Surch omitted (lower stamp, vertical pair) £2250 £1300
d. "POSTAGE" omitted (in pair with normal) £1500
e. "S" of "POSTAGE" omitted (R. 8/3) £250 £190
f. "T" of "POSTAGE" omitted £250 £250
x. Wmk reversed 8·00 13·00
92 1d.on 6d. violet (10.10.77) 50·00 9·00
a. "S" of "POSTAGE" omitted (R. 8/3) £375 £150
x. Wmk reversed — 9·00
93 1d.on 6d. rose (12.2.79) 95·00 40·00
a. Surch inverted £550 £300
b. Surch double — £250
c. Surch double, one inverted £250 £200
d. Surch four times £375 £200
e. "S" of "POSTAGE" omitted (R. 8/3) £500 £300
x. Wmk reversed — 40·00
No. 93c. is known with one surcharge showing variety "S" of "POSTAGE" omitted.
Other minor varieties exist in these surcharges.

(Typo D.L.R.)

1880 (13 Oct). Wmk Crown CC. P 14.
96 23 ½d. blue-green 12·00 18·00
a. Imperf between (vert pair)

1882 (20 Apr)–**89**. Wmk Crown CA. P 14.
97 23 ½d. blue-green (23.4.84) 90·00 16·00
a. Dull green (10.4.85) 2·75 75
99 12 1d. rose (*shades*) (1.84) 3·00 10
a. Carmine 3·25 20
w. Wmk inverted † £150
100 13 3d. blue (23.4.84) £100 17·00
101 3d. grey (11.89) 3·75 1·25
102 14 4d. brown 4·50 75
103 15 6d. mauve 4·00 1·00
w. Wmk inverted † £100
97*a*/103 *Set of* 6 £110 19·00
97*as*, 99*as*, 101*s*/3*s* H/S "Specimen" *Set of* 5 £250

1885 (26 Jan). *No. 99 surch locally with T 24.*
104 12 ½d.on 1d. rose 16·00 11·00
a. No hyphen after "HALF" 60·00 42·00

TWO PENCE (25) 26 TWOPENCE HALFPENNY (27)

1886 (7 Jan). *No. 101 surch with T 25 by D.L.R.*
105 13 2d. on 3d. grey 18·00 5·50

(Typo D.L.R.)

1887 (Sept)–**89**. Wmk Crown CA. P 14.
106 26 2d. olive-green (Die I*) 30·00 2·00
a. Top left triangle detached — £190
s. Optd "Specimen" 75·00
107 2d. olive-green (Die II) (1889) 2·75 1·40
s. Handstamped "Specimen" 60·00
The differences between Dies I and II are shown in the introduction.
For illustration of "top left triangle detached" variety see above No. 21 of Antigua.

1888 (16 Mar). *As No. 25, but colour changed and* wmk Crown CA, *optd with T 8 by D.L.R.*
108 7 1s. orange (C.) 4·00 1·00
a. Opt double — £1500
s. Handstamped "Specimen" £100

1891 (22 Apr). *Surch locally with T 27.*
109 14 2½d.on 4d. brown 10·00 10·00
a. "TWOPENGE" 50·00
b. "HALFPENN" £225 £180
c. Surch double £250 £180
d. Surch inverted £350 £275
s. Handstamped "Specimen" 50·00

(28) POSTAGE. Half-Penny (29) POSTAGE. Varieties of long-tailed letters

(Typo D.L.R.)

1891 (June). Wmk Crown CA. P 14.
113 28 2½d. bright blue 5·00 75
s. Handstamped "Specimen" 60·00

1895 (12 Mar). *No. 24 surch locally with T 29 in carmine.*
114 ½d.on 6d. violet 1·75 3·75
a. "Ealf-Penny" 20·00 28·00
b. "Half-Pennv" and long "P" 18·00 28·00
ba. "Half Pennv" and long "T" and "A" 18·00 28·00
c. No stop after "POSTAGE" and long "P", "T" and "A" 18·00 28·00
d. Long "P" 2·25 4·75
e. Long "T" 2·25 4·75
f. Long "A" 3·25 6·50
g. Long "P" and "T" 2·25 4·75

h. Long "P" and "A" . . . . 2·25 4·75
i. Long "T" and "A" . . . . 3·00 6·00
k. Long "P", "T" and "A" . . . . . . 3·00 6·00
ka. Long "P", "T" and "A" with comma after "POSTAGE" . . . . 7·50 12·00
l. Surch double £250
la. Surch double, one vertical £250
m. "POSTAGE" omitted £1000
s. Handstamped "Specimen" . . . . . . 50·00
x. Wmk reversed . . . . 1·75 3·50

The surcharge was applied as a setting of 60 (12 × 5) which contained seventeen normals, one each of Nos. 114a, 114b, 114ba, 114c, six of No. 114d, six of 114e, three of 114f, six of 114g, seven of 114h, five of No. 114i, four of No. 114k and two of No. 114ka.

(30)

31

32

1895 (18 Mar). *No. 99 surch locally with T* **30**.
125 HALFon 1d. rose (*shades*) . . . . 2·00 1·50
a. Surch double £350 £350
b. "H" with longer left limb . . . . . 26·00
c. Pair, one without surcharge . . . .
s. Handstamped "Specimen" . . . . 50·00

No. 125b, in which the "A" also has a short right leg, occurs on the second, fourth, sixth etc., stamps of the first vertical column of the right-hand pane of the first printing only.

In the second printing what appears to be a broken "E" (with the top limb removed) was used instead of "L" in "HALF" on the last stamp in the sheet (*Price* £30), No. 125c also comes from this second printing.

(Typo D.L.R)

1902–03. *Inscr "*POSTAGE REVENUE*"*. Wmk Crown CA. P 14.
127 **31** ½d. blue-green . . . . 2·50 20
128 1d. carmine . . . . 6·50 15
129 1½d. green and black . . . . 3·00 2·25
130 2d. red and olive-green . . . . . . 1·75 25
131 2½d. bright blue . . . . 1·25 3·00
132 3d. purple and grey . . . . 1·00 1·25
133 4d. carmine and cinnamon . . . . . 3·75 16·00
134 5d. black and orange . . . . 2·00 2·75
w. Wmk inverted . . . . £130 75·00
135 6d. green and brown-purple . . . . 2·00 2·00
136 1s. carmine and pale blue . . . . . 2·75 2·50
137 2s. green and bright violet . . . . 48·00 9·00
138 2s.6d. purple . . . . 40·00 12·00
139 4s. deep rose and maize . . . . . 65·00 70·00
a. Imperf between (horiz pair) . . .
127/39 *Set of* 13 . . . . £160 £110
127s/39s Optd "Specimen" *Set of* 13 . . . . . . £160

No. 139a is also imperforate between stamp and left-hand margin.

(Typo D.L.R.)

1902. Wmk Crown CC. P 14.
140 **32** 5s. dull blue and rose . . . . 26·00 9·50
141 10s. deep rose and chocolate . . . . 65·00 26·00
142 £1 black and bright blue . . . . . £170 55·00
143 £1 10s. green and violet . . . . . £375 95·00
s. Optd "Specimen" . . . . 65·00
144 £5 mauve and black £2500 £600
s. Optd "Specimen" £100
145 £10 green and orange £6500 £2500
as. Optd "Specimen" £200
145*b* £20 red and green £14000 £6500
bs. Optd "Specimen" £325
140s/2s Optd "Specimen" *Set of* 3 . . . . £100

USED HIGH VALUES. Collectors are warned against fiscally used high value Natal stamps with penmarks cleaned off and forged postmarks added.

1904–08. *Chalk-surfaced paper (£1 10s.)*. Wmk Mult Crown CA. P 14.
146 **31** ½d. blue-green . . . . 4·50 15
147 1d. rose-carmine . . . . 4·75 15
a. Booklet pane of 6, one stamp optd "NOT FOR USE" (1907) £275
148 1d. deep carmine . . . . 7·50 30
w. Wmk inverted . . . . † 80·00
149 2d. red and olive-green . . . . . . 7·50 3·25
152 4d. carmine and cinnamon . . . . . 2·75 1·25
153 5d. black and orange (1908) . . . . 4·25 4·00
155 1s. carmine and pale blue . . . . . 75·00 7·00
156 2s. dull green and bright violet . . . 55·00 35·00
157 2s.6d. purple . . . . 50·00 35·00
162 **32** £1 10s. brown-orange & dp pur (1908) £1100 £1800
s. Optd "Specimen" £180
146/57 *Set of* 9 . . . . £190 75·00

1908–09. *Inscr "*POSTAGE POSTAGE*"*. Wmk Mult Crown CA. P 14.
165 **31** 6d. dull and bright purple . . . . . 4·50 2·75
166 1s. black/*green* . . . . 6·00 2·00
167 2s. purple and bright blue/*blue* . . . 15·00 3·00
168 2s.6d. black and red/*blue* . . . . . 25·00 3·00
169 **32** 5s. green and red/*yellow* . . . . . 19·00 22·00
170 10s. green and red/*green* . . . . . 70·00 70·00
171 £1 purple and black/*red* £250 £225
165/71 *Set of* 7 . . . . £350 £300
165s/71s Optd "Specimen" *Set of* 7 . . . . . . £225

STAMP BOOKLETS

1906. *Black on red cover. Stapled.*
SB1 2s.7d. booklet containing thirty 1d. (No. 147) in blocks of 6 . . . .

1907. *Black on red cover. Stapled.*
SB2 2s.6d. booklet containing thirty 1d. (No. 147) in blocks of 6 . . . . £2000

The first stamp of the first pane in No. SB2 was overprinted "NOT FOR USE" (No. 147a), the additional penny being used to defray the cost of production.

FISCALS USED FOR POSTAGE

1869. *Embossed on coloured wove, surfaced paper.* P 12½.
F1 **1** 1d. yellow . . . . 50·00 80·00

Examples of 1d. yellow and 6d. rose values as Type **6**, 1s. purple-brown as Type **7** and various values between 5s, and £10 in the design illustrated above are believed to exist postally used, but, as such use was not authorised, they are not now listed.

OFFICIAL STAMPS

OFFICIAL
(O 1)

1904. *T* **31**, wmk Mult Crown CA, *optd with Type* O **1**. P 14.
O1 ½d. blue-green . . . . 3·00 35
O2 1d. carmine . . . . 3·50 70
O3 2d. red and olive-green . . . . 22·00 10·00
O4 3d. purple and grey . . . . 12·00 4·00
O5 6d. green and brown-purple . . . . . . 42·00 55·00
O6 1s. carmine and pale blue £130 £190
O1/6 *Set of* 6 . . . . £190 £225

The use of stamps overprinted as above was discontinued after 30 May 1907. Stamps perforated with the letters "N.G.R." were for use on Government Railways.

Natal became a province of the Union of South Africa on 31 May 1910.

IV. NEW REPUBLIC

During the unrest following the death of Cetshwayo, the Zulu king, in 1884, a group of Boers from the Transvaal offered their support to his son, Dinizulu. The price for this support was the cession of a sizeable portion of Zulu territory to an independent Boer republic. The New Republic, centred on Vryheid, was proclaimed on 16 August 1884 with the remaining Zulu territory becoming a protectorate of the new administration. The first reference to an organised postal service occurs in December 1884.

Alarmed by these developments the British authorities annexed the southernmost part of the land grant, around St. Lucia Bay, to prevent access to the Indian Ocean. The remainder of the New Republic was, however, recognised as independent on 22 October 1886. Zululand was annexed by the British on 22 May 1887.

Difficulties beset the New Republic, however, and its Volksraad voted for union with the South African Republic (Transvaal). The two republics united on 21 July 1888. In 1903 the territory of the former New Republic was transferred to Natal.

Mail from Vryheid in 1884–85 was franked with issues of Transvaal (for dispatches made via Utrecht) or Natal (for those sent via Dundee from August 1885 onwards). Issues of the New Republic were never accepted as internationally valid by these administrations so that all external mail continued to show Transvaal or Natal stamps used in combination with those of the republic.

PRICES FOR STAMPS ON COVER		
No.	1	—
Nos.	2/5	*from* × 50
Nos.	6/25	—
Nos.	26/9	*from* × 50
Nos.	30/47	—
Nos.	48/50	*from* × 50
No.	51	—
Nos.	52/3	*from* × 50
Nos.	72/5	*from* × 50
Nos.	76/7*b*	—
Nos.	78/80	*from* × 50
Nos.	81/95	—

1

Printed with a rubber handstamp on paper bought in Europe and sent out ready gummed and perforated.

1886 (7 Jan)–**87**. *Various dates indicating date of printing.* P 11½.

A. Without Arms. (i) Yellow paper.
1 **1** 1d. black (9.1.86) . . . . † £3000
2 1d. violet (9.1.86) . . . . 11·00 13·00
a. "1d." omitted (in pair with normal) (24.4.86) £1500
3 2d. violet (9.1.86) . . . . 11·00 16·00
a. "d" omitted (13.10.86) £3000
4 3d. violet (13.1.86) . . . . 25·00 27·00
a. "d" omitted (13.10.86) £3000
b. *Tête-bêche* (pair) (13.10.86) . . . .
5 4d. violet (30.8.86) . . . . 38·00
6 6d. violet (20.2.86) . . . . 32·00 35·00
a. "6d." omitted (in pair with normal) (2.7.86) . . . .
7 9d. violet (13.1.86) . . . . 32·00
8 1s. violet (30.8.86) . . . . 70·00
a. "1s." omitted (in pair with normal) (6.9.86) . . . .
9 1/s. violet (13.10.86) £500
10 1/6 violet (30.8.86) . . . . 70·00
11 1s.6d. violet (13.1.86) £400
a. *Tête-bêche* (pair) (6.9.86) . . . .
b. "d" omitted (13.10.86) . . . . . . 90·00
12 2s. violet (30.8.86) . . . . 40·00
a. *Tête-bêche* (pair) (6.9.86) £475
13 2/6 violet (13.1.86) £150
14 2s.6d. violet (1.86) £100
15 4/s. violet (17.1.87) £400
16 5s. violet (1.86) . . . . 30·00 32·0
a. "s" omitted (in pair with normal) (7.3.86) £2000
17 5/6 violet (20.2.86) . . . . 38·00
18 5s.6d. violet (13.1.86) £160
19 7/6 violet (13.1.86) £170
20 7s.6d. violet (24.5.86) £100
21 10s. violet (13.1.86) £100 £11
a. *Tête-bêche* (pair) (2.7.86) . . . .
22 10s.6d. violet (1.86) £170
a. "d" omitted (1.86) . . . . 50·00
23 13s. violet (24.11.86) £400
24 £1 violet (13.1.86) £120
a. *Tête-bêche* (pair) (13.10.86) . . . .
25 30s. violet (13.1.86) £100
a. *Tête-bêche* (pair) (24.11.86) £500

(ii) Blue granite paper.
26 **1** 1d. violet (20.1.86) . . . . 14·00 15·0
a. "d" omitted (24.11.86) £375
b. "1" omitted (in pair with normal) (24.11.86) . . . .
27 2d. violet (24.1.86) . . . . 14·00 15·0
a. "d" omitted (24.4.86) £750
b. "2d." omitted (in pair with normal) (24.4.86) . . . .
28 3d. violet (13.10.86) . . . . 18·00 20·0
a. *Tête-bêche* (pair) (13.10.86) £300
29 4d. violet (24.5.86) . . . . 14·00 17·0
30 6d. violet (7.3.86) . . . . 27·00 23·0
a. "6" omitted in pair with normal (24.5.86) £1500
31 9d. violet (6.9.86) . . . . 26·00
32 1s. violet (1.86) . . . . 30·00 32·0
a. *Tête-bêche* (pair) (21.5.86) £325
b. "1s." omitted (in pair with normal) (29.4.86) £1500
33 1s.6d. violet (2.7.86) . . . . 38·00
a. *Tête-bêche* (pair) (6.9.86) £475
34 1/6 violet (6.9.86) £150
35 2s. violet (21.5.86) £120
a. "2s." omitted (in pair with normal) (24.5.86) £1500
36 2s.6d. violet (19.8.86) £140
37 2/6 violet (19.8.86) £180
38 4/s. violet (17.1.87) £200
39 5/6 violet (13.1.86) £200
a. "/" omitted (13.1.87) . . . . . .
40 5s.6d. violet (13.1.86) £170
41 7/6 violet (13.1.86) £200
41*a* 7s.6d. violet (13.1.86) . . . .
42 10s. violet (1.86) £200 £2
a. *Tête-bêche* (pair) (2.7.86) £425
b. "s" omitted (13.1.86) . . . . . .
43 10s.6d. violet (1.86) £200
a. *Tête-bêche* (pair) (13.1.86) . . . .
b. "d" omitted (1.86) £450
44 12s. violet (13.1.86) £300
45 13s. violet (17.1.87) £475
46 £1 violet (13.1.86) £250
47 30s. violet (13.1.86) £250

B. With embossed Arms of New Republic.

(i) Yellow paper.
48 **1** 1d. violet (20.1.86) . . . . 14·00 16·
a. Arms inverted (20.1.86) . . . . . . 27·00 27·
b. Arms *tête-bêche* (pair) (14.4.86) . . . £100 £1
c. *Tête-bêche* (pair) (3.11.86) £800
49 2d. violet (30.8.86) . . . . 14·00 16·
a. Arms inverted (24.11.86) . . . . . 25·00 30·
50 4d. violet (2.12.86) . . . . 20·00 24
a. Arms inverted (12.86) . . . . . . £100 70·
b. Arms *tête-bêche* (pair) (12.86) . . . £250
51 6d. violet (2.12.86) . . . . 48·00

(ii) Blue granite paper.
52 **1** 1d. violet (20.1.86) . . . . 15·00 17·
a. Arms inverted (10.2.86) . . . . . . 38·00 42·
b. Arms *tête-bêche* (pair) (3.11.86) . . . £500
53 2d. violet (24.5.86) . . . . 15·00 17·
a. Arms inverted (30.8.86) . . . . . . 50·00
b. Arms *tête-bêche* (pair) (2.12.86) . . . £500 £5

Stamps as Type **1** were produced as and when stocks w[ere] required, each printing including in its design the date on which [it] was prepared. The dates quoted above for Nos. 1/53 are those [on] which the various stamps first appeared. Details of the vario[us] printing dates are given below. From these dates it can be seen t[hat] some values share common printing dates, and, it is believed, t[hat] the different values were produced *se-tenant* within the same she[et] at least in some instances. A reported proof sheet in the Preto[ria] Postal Museum, on yellow paper and embossed, contains [...] examples of the 6d. value and 3 each of the 3d., 4d., 9d., 1s., [...] 2/-, 2/6, 3s., 4s., 5s., 5/6, 7/6, 10/-, 10/6, £1 and 30/-.

The significance, if any, of the two coloured papers and the [...] of the embossing machine have never been satisfactorily explain[ed]. Both the different papers and the embossing machine w[ere] introduced in January 1886, and occur throughout the period t[hat] the stamps with dates were used.

PRINTINGS

Date	*Paper*	*Face value*	*Cat. No.*	*Un.*	
Jan 86	*Yellow*	5s.	16	30·00	32
		10s.6d.	22	£170	
		10s.6d.	22a	85·00	
	Blue	1s.	32		
		10s.	42	£200	£
		10s.6d.	43	£200	
		10s.6d.	43b	£450	
7 Jan 86	*Yellow*	10s.6d.	22	£160	
	Blue	10s.	42		
		10s.6d.	43	£475	

9 Jan 86	*Yellow*	1d. blk	1	†	£3000
		1d. vio	2	11·00	13·00
		2d.	3	11·00	16·00
13 Jan 86	*Yellow*	1d.	2	38·00	
		2d.	3	15·00	16·00
		3d.	4	42·00	
		9d	7	£200	
		1s.6d.	11	£400	
		2/6	13	£160	
		2s.6d.	14	£100	
		5s.6d.	18		
		7/6	19	£170	
		10s.	21		
		£1	24	£130	
		30s.	25	£100	
	Blue	5/6	39	£200	
		5s.6d.	40	£170	
		7/6	41	£200	
		7s 6d.	41*a*		
		10s.	42	£400	
		10s.	42b		
		10s.6d.	43	£200	
		10s.6d.	43a		
		12s.	44	£300	
		£1	46	£250	
		30s.	47	£250	
20 Jan 86	*Yellow*	1d.	2		
	Blue	1d.	26	£250	
	Yellow, embossed	1d.	48	35·00	
		1d.	48a	50·00	
	Blue, embossed	1d.	52	£100	
Jan 20 86	*Blue*	1d.	26	25·00	
	Yellow, embossed	1d.	48a		
	Blue, embossed	1d.	52	£100	
24 Jan 86	*Blue*	1d.	26	20·00	
		2d.	27	32·00	
10 Feb 86	*Yellow*	1d.	2		
	Yellow, embossed	1d.	48		
		1d.	48a	50·00	
	Blue, embossed	1d.	52	£130	
		1d.	52a	38·00	
20 Feb 86	*Yellow*	6d.	6		
		1s.6d.	11		
		2s.6d.	14	£130	
		5/6	17	£120	
		5s.6d.	18		
7 Mar 86	*Yellow*	1d.	2	£110	
		2/6	13		
		2s.6d.	14	£100	
		5s.	16	£200	90·00
		5s.	16a		
		5/6	17	38·00	
		5s.6d.	18	£160	
	Blue	2d.	27	£100	
		6d.	30		
		1s.	32		
17 Mar 86	*Yellow*	1d.	2	£100	
	Yellow, embossed	1d.	48	50·00	
	Blue, embossed	1d.	52	£100	
		1d.	52a	85·00	
6 Mar 86	*Blue, embossed*	1d.	52a	£130	
4 Apr 86	*Yellow*	1d.	2		
	Yellow, embossed	1d.	48	25·00	
		1d.	48a	£120	
		1d.	48b	£100	£120
	Blue, embossed	1d.	52	48·00	
		1d.	52a		
4 Apr 86	*Yellow*	1d.	2	£100	
		1d.	2a	£1500	
		5s.	16		
	Blue	2d.	27	30·00	
		2d.	27a	£750	
		2d.	27b		
9 Apr 86	*Blue*	1s.	32	£110	
		1s.	32b		
1 May 86	*Yellow*	6d.	6	£130	
	Blue	1d.	26	90·00	
		1s.	32	30·00	32·00
		1s.	32a	£325	
		1s.	32b	£1500	
		2s.	35	£275	
3 May 86	*Blue, embossed*	1d.	52a	£100	
4 May 86	*Yellow*	1d.	2	£100	
		2d.	3	£120	
		5s.	16	75·00	
		7/6	19	£170	
		7s.6d.	20	£100	
	Blue	1d.	26	14·00	15·00
		2d.	27	£300	£300
		4d.	29	90·00	
		6d.	30	£120	
		6d.	30a		
		1s.	32	£200	
		1s.	32b		
		2s.	35	£120	
		2s.	35a	£1500	
	Blue, embossed	2d.	53		
6 May 86	*Yellow*	1d.	2		
	Blue	1d.	26	£110	
	Yellow, embossed	1d.	48	£250	
		1d.	48a	£100	
	Blue, embossed	1d.	52	£130	
		1d.	52a	50·00	55·00
8 May 86	*Yellow, embossed*	1d.	48	35·00	
un 30 86	*Blue*	1d.	26	16·00	17·00
	Yellow, embossed	1d.	48	15·00	17·00
		1d.	48a	27·00	30·00
		1d.	48b	£200	£225
	Blue, embossed	1d.	52	48·00	42·00
Jul 86	*Yellow*	6d.	6	£200	
		6d.	6a		
		9d	7	£100	£100
		10s.	21		
		10s.	21a		
	Blue	1s.6d.	33	38·00	
		10s.	42	£200	
		10s.	42a	£425	
		10s.6d.	43		
		10s.6d.	43b	£450	
Jul 86	*Blue*	10s.	42		
ul 7 86	*Yellow*	1d.	2		
	Blue	1d.	26		
	Yellow, embossed	1d.	48	27·00	
		1d.	48a	£100	£100
	Blue, embossed	1d.	52	15·00	17·00
		1d.	52a	60·00	42·00
4 Aug 86	*Yellow*	1d.	2		
	Yellow, embossed	1d.	48	60·00	
	Blue, embossed	1d.	52	38·00	
		1d.	52a		
19 Aug 86	*Yellow*	2/6	13		
		2s.6d.	14	£140	
	Blue	2s.6d.	36	£140	
		2/6	37	£180	
30 Aug 86	*Yellow*	1d.	2	11·00	13·00
		2d.	3	12·00	
		3d.	4	25·00	
		4d.	5	50·00	
		6d.	6	35·00	
		9d.	7	50·00	
		1s.	8	70·00	
		1/6	10	70·00	
		2s.	12	£100	
		2/6	13	£150	
	Blue	2d.	27	14·00	15·00
	Yellow, embossed	2d.	49		
	Blue, embossed	2d.	53	45·00	
		2d.	53a	£110	
6 Sep 86	*Yellow*	1d.	2	13·00	
		2d.	3	11·00	16·00
		3d.	4	40·00	
		4d.	5	42·00	
		6d.	6	32·00	
		9d.	7	32·00	
		1s.	8	£100	
		1s.	8a		
		1/6	10	75·00	
		1s.6d.	11	£400	
		1s.6d.	11a		
		2s.	12	£100	
		2s.	12a	£475	
		2/6	13	£150	
		2s.6d.	14		
		5s.	16	£140	
		7s.6d.	20	£200	
		10s.	21	£100	
		£1	24	£120	
	Blue	6d.	30	22·00	23·00
		9d.	31	£110	
		1s.	32	70·00	
		1s.6d.	33	£140	
		1s.6d.	33a	£475	
		1/6	34		
		2s.6d.	36		
		2/6	37	£400	
		10s.6d.	43		
13 Sep 86	*Yellow*	1d.	2		
	Yellow, embossed	1d.	48	50·00	
		1d.	48a	50·00	
	Blue, embossed	1d.	52	90·00	
6 Oct 86	*Yellow*	1d.	2		
	Blue	1d.	26	90·00	
	Yellow, embossed	1d.	48	25·00	20·00
		1d.	48a		
	Blue, embossed	1d.	52	48·00	20·00
		1d.	52a	90·00	
13 Oct 86	*Yellow*	1d.	2	13·00	13·00
		2d.	3	11·00	16·00
		2d.	3a	£3000	
		3d.	4	25·00	27·00
		3d.	4a	£3000	
		3d.	4b		
		4d.	5	38·00	
		6d.	6	32·00	35·00
		9d.	7	38·00	
		1s.	8	75·00	
		1/s	9	£500	
		1/6	10	£150	
		1s.6d.	11b	90·00	
		2s.	12	40·00	
		2/6	13	£160	
		5s.	16	45·00	
		10s.	21	£100	£110
		10s.6d.	22a	50·00	
		£1	24	£120	
		£1	24a		
	Blue	2d.	27	14·00	15·00
		3d.	28	18·00	20·00
		3d.	28a	£300	
		4d.	29	30·00	30·00
		1s.	32	30·00	
		1/6	34	£150	
		2s.	35	£120	
3 Nov 86	*Yellow*	1d.	2	30·00	
	Blue	1d.	26		
	Yellow, embossed	1d.	48	14·00	16·00
		1d.	48a	27·00	30·00
		1d.	48b	£100	£120
		1d.	48c	£800	
	Blue, embossed	1d.	52	15·00	
		1d.	52a	38·00	42·00
		1d.	52b	£500	
13 Nov 86	*Yellow*	1d.	2	38·00	
24 Nov 86	*Yellow*	1d.	2	15·00	
		2d.	3	11·00	16·00
		3d.	4	32·00	35·00
		1/6	10		
		10s.	21	£200	
		13s.	23	£400	
		30s.	25	£100	
		30s.	25a	£500	
	Blue	1d.	26	40·00	18·00
		1d.	26a	£375	
		1d.	26b		
		2d.	27	20·00	
		2d.	27a		
		4d.	29	14·00	17·00
		6d.	30	22·00	23·00
		9d.	31	26·00	
		1s.	32	48·00	50·00
		1/6	34	£160	
		2s.	35	£140	
		2s.	35a	£3000	
	Yellow, embossed	2d.	49	£160	
		2d.	49a		
26 Nov 86	*Yellow*	1/6	10	£140	
2 Dec 86	*Yellow*	1d.	2		
		2d.	3		
	Blue	2d.	27		
	Yellow, embossed	1d.	48	14·00	16·00
		1d.	48a	£160	
		2d.	49	14·00	16·00
		2d.	49a	25·00	30·00
		4d.	50	85·00	
		6d.	51	48·00	
	Blue, embossed	1d.	52	30·00	
		1d.	52a	£160	
		2d.	53	15·00	17·00
		2d.	53a	50·00	
		2d.	53b	£500	£500
3 Dec 86	*Yellow, embossed*	6d.	51		
Dec 86	*Yellow*	6d.	6		
	Blue	4d.	29		
	Yellow, embossed	4d.	50	20·00	24·00
		4d.	50a	£100	65·00
		4d.	50b	£250	
		6d.	51	45·00	
4 Jan 87	*Yellow*	1d.	2	38·00	
		2d.	3	35·00	
		13s.	23	£450	
	Blue	1d.	26	14·00	15·00
		2d.	27	17·00	15·00
	Blue, embossed	2d.	53	45·00	
13 Jan 87	*Blue*	5/6	39	£450	
		5/6	39a		
		7/6	41	£500	
17 Jan 87	*Yellow*	1d.	2	40·00	
		2d.	3	32·00	
		3d.	4	48·00	
		4/s.	15	£200	
	Blue	1d.	26	80·00	
		4/s.	38	£200	
		13s.	45	£475	
		30s.	47	£250	
20 Jan 87	*Blue*	2d.	27	35·00	
	Yellow, embossed	2d.	49	55·00	
		2d.	49a	£140	
	Blue, embossed	2d.	53	45·00	
		2d.	53a	£100	
Jan 20 87	*Yellow, embossed*	1d.	48a	£400	

1887 (Jan–Mar). *As T* **1**, *but without date. With embossed Arms.*

(a) Blue granite paper.

72 1d. violet 15·00 15·00
a. Imperf between (pair)
b. Stamps *tête-bêche* (pair) £375
c. Arms *tête-bêche* (pair)
d. Arms inverted 25·00 25·00
e. Arms omitted £110 £110
f. Arms sideways
73 2d. violet 9·00 9·00
a. Stamps *tête-bêche* (pair) £325
b. Arms inverted 25·00 25·00
c. Arms omitted £110 £100
d. Arms *tête-bêche* (pair)
74 3d. violet 14·00 14·00
a. Stamps *tête-bêche* (pair) £375
b. Arms *tête-bêche* (pair)
c. Arms inverted 50·00 50·00
75 4d. violet 14·00 14·00
a. Stamps *tête-bêche* (pair) £325
b. Arms *tête-bêche* (pair) £275
c. Arms inverted 85·00
76 6d. violet 14·00 14·00
a. Arms inverted 85·00
77 1/6 violet 15·00 15·00
a. Arms inverted 80·00
b. Arms *tête-bêche* (pair) £350
77*c* 2/6 violet † £750

(b) Yellow paper (March 1887).

78 2d. violet (*arms omitted*) 14·00
79 3d. violet 14·00 14·00
a. Imperf between (pair)
b. Stamps *tête-bêche* (pair) £325 £375
c. Arms *tête-bêche* (pair) £200
d. Arms inverted 25·00 25·00
80 4d. violet 14·00 14·00
a. Arms inverted 15·00 15·00
81 6d. violet 8·50 8·50
a. Arms *tête-bêche* (pair) £350
b. Arms inverted 45·00 45·00
c. Arms omitted 80·00
82 9d. violet 9·00 9·00
a. Arms inverted £200
b. Arms *tête-bêche* (pair) £350
83 1s. violet 9·00 9·00
a. Arms inverted 70·00
84 1/6 violet 18·00 15·00
85 2s. violet 19·00 17·00
a. Arms inverted 55·00 50·00
b. Arms omitted 70·00
86 2/6 violet 25·00 25·00
a. Arms inverted 30·00 30·00
87 3s. violet 45·00 45·00
a. Arms inverted 48·00 48·00
b. Stamps *tête-bêche* (pair) £450
88 4s. violet 12·00 12·00
a. Arms omitted £180
88*b* 4/s violet 95·00
ba. Arms omitted £130
89 5s. violet 14·00 14·00
a. Imperf between (pair)
b. Arms inverted — 80·00
90 5/6 violet 13·00 13·00
91 7/6 violet 15·00 18·00
a. Arms *tête-bêche* (pair)
a. Arms inverted 48·00
92 10s. violet 13·00 13·00
a. Imperf between (pair)
b. Arms *tête-bêche* (pair) £120
c. Arms inverted 25·00
d. Arms omitted £110 48·00
93 10/6 violet 17·00 17·00
a. Imperf between (pair)
b. Arms inverted
94 £1 violet 48·00 48·00
a. Stamps *tête-bêche* (pair) £300 £350
b. Arms inverted 60·00
95 30s. violet £120

A £15 value as Nos. 78/95 exists, but is only known fiscally used (*Price* £4000).

Many values exist with double impressions of the handstamp.

New Republic united with the South African Republic (Transvaal) on 21 July 1888. In 1903 the territory of the former New Republic was transferred to Natal.

V. ORANGE FREE STATE

PRICES FOR STAMPS ON COVER

Nos. 1/9	*from* × 20
Nos. 10/13	*from* × 30
Nos. 18/19	*from* × 20
No. 20	—
Nos. 21/42	*from* × 40
Nos. 48/51	*from* × 25
Nos. 52/138	*from* × 10
Nos. 139/51	*from* × 7
Nos. F1/17	—
Nos. PF1/3	*from* × 20
No. M1	*from* × 20

Supplies of Cape of Good Hope stamps were available at Bloemfontein and probably elsewhere in the Orange Free State, from mid-1856 onwards for use on mail to Cape Colony and beyond. Such arrangements continued after the introduction of Orange Free State stamps in 1868. It is not known if the dumb cancellations used on the few surviving covers were applied in the Free State or at Cape Town.

1

(Typo D.L.R.)

1868 (1 Jan)–**94**. P 14.
1 **1** 1d. pale brown 12·00 1·00
2 1d. red-brown 10·00 45
3 1d. deep brown 13·00 45
4 6d. pale rose (1868) 48·00 8·00
5 6d. rose (1871) 17·00 5·50
6 6d. rose-carmine (1891) 16·00 12·00
7 6d. bright carmine (1894) 10·00 2·00
8 1s. orange-buff 70·00 6·00
9 1s. orange-yellow 32·00 1·50
a. Double print — £3000

4 4 4 4
(**2**) (*a*) (*b*) (*c*) (*d*)

1877. *No. 5 surcharged T* **2** *(a) to (d).*
10 **1** 4d.on 6d. rose (*a*) £325 55·00
a. Surch inverted — £550
b. Surch double (*a* + *c*)
c. Surch double. one inverted (*a* + *c* inverted) † £2750
d. Surch double, one inverted (*a* inverted + *c*) † £4500
11 4d.on 6d. rose (*b*) £1200 £180
a. Surch inverted — £1100
b. Surch double (*b* + *d*)
12 4d.on 6d. rose (*c*) £180 25·00
a. Surch inverted — £350
b. Surch double
13 4d.on 6d. rose (*d*) £225 35·00
a. Surch inverted £1100 £375
b. Surch double, one inverted (*d* + *c* inverted) † £3000

The setting of 60 comprised nine stamps as No. 10, four as No. 11, twenty-seven as No. 12 and twenty as No. 13.

1878 (July). P 14.
18 **1** 4d. pale blue 17·00 2·75
19 4d. ultramarine 4·00 2·50
20 5s. green 9·00 11·00

1d. 1d. 1d. 1d. 1d. 1d.
(**3**) (*a*) (*b*) (*c*) (*d*) (*e*) (*f*)

Type **3**: (*a*) Small "1" and "d." (*b*) Sloping serif. (*c*) Same size as (*b*), but "1" with straighter horizontal serif. (*d*) Taller "1" with horizontal serif and antique "d". (*e*) Same size as (*d*) but with sloping serif and thin line at foot. (*f*) as (*d*) but with Roman "d".

1881 (19 May). *No. 20 surch T* **3** *(a) to (f) with heavy black bar cancelling the old value.*
21 **1** 1d.on 5s. green (*a*) 85·00 19·00
22 1d.on 5s. green (*b*) 50·00 19·00
a. Surch inverted — £750
b. Surch double — £1000
23 1d.on 5s. green (*c*) £170 70·00
a. Surch inverted — £1100
b. Surch double — £1300
24 1d.on 5s. green (*d*) 70·00 19·00
a. Surch inverted £1500 £750
b. Surch double — £1000
25 1d.on 5s. green (*e*) £425 £225
a. Surch inverted † £2000
b. Surch double † £2000
26 1d.on 5s. green (*f*) 70·00 19·00
a. Surch inverted — £700
b. Surch double — £800

No. 21 was the first printing in one type only. Nos. 22 to 25 constitute the second printing about a year later, and are all found on the same sheet; and No. 26 the third printing of which about half have the stop raised.

Owing to defective printing, examples of Nos. 22 and 24/5 may be found with the obliterating bar at the top of the stamps or, from the top row, without the bar.

½d
(**4**)

1882 (Aug). *No. 20 surch with T* **4** *and with a thin black line cancelling old value.*
36 **1** ½d.on 5s. green 14·00 3·75
a. Surch double £400 £325
b. Surch inverted £1200 £800

3d 3d 3d 3d 3d
(**5**) (*a*) (*b*) (*c*) (*d*) (*e*)

1882. *No. 19 surch with T* **5** *(a) to (e) with thin black line cancelling value.*
38 **1** 3d.on 4d. ultramarine (*a*) 70·00 23·00
a. Surch double † £1200
39 3d.on 4d. ultramarine (*b*) 70·00 18·00
a. Surch double † £1200
40 3d.on 4d. ultramarine (*c*) 29·00 16·00
a. Surch double † £1200
41 3d.on 4d. ultramarine (*d*) 70·00 19·00
a. Surch double † £1200
42 3d.on 4d. ultramarine (*e*) £190 60·00
a. Surch double † £2750

Examples of Nos. 39 and 41/2 exist without the cancelling bar due to the misplacement of the surcharge.

1883–84. P 14.
48 **1** ½d. chestnut 2·00
49 2d. pale mauve 12·00
50 2d. bright mauve 12·00
51 3d. ultramarine 2·50

For 1d. purple, see No. 68.

2d 2d 2d
(**6**) (*a*) (*b*) (*c*)

1888 (Sept–Oct). *No. 51 surch with T* **6** *(a), (b) or (c).*

(a) Wide "2". (b) Narrow "2".

52 **1** 2d.on 3d. ultramarine (*a*) (Sept) 50·00
a. Surch inverted —
53 2d.on 3d. ultramarine (*b*) 30·00
a. Surch inverted —
b. "2" with curved foot (*c*) £1200

1d 1d Id
(**7**) (*a*) (*b*) (*c*)

1890 (Dec)–**91**. *Nos. 51 and 19 surch with T* **7** *(a) to (c).*
54 **1** 1d.on 3d. ultramarine (*a*) 4·50
a. Surch double 80·00
c. "1" and "d" wide apart £140
d. Dropped "d" (Right pane R. 5/6) £100
55 1d.on 3d. ultramarine (*b*) 19·00
a. Surch double £225
57 1d.on 4d. ultramarine (*a*) 25·00
a. Surch double £130
b. Surch double (*a* + *b*) £375
c. Surch triple —
d. Raised "1" (Left pane R. 3/1)
58 1d.on 4d. ultramarine (*b*) 75·00
a. Surch double £400
59 1d.on 4d. ultramarine (*c*) £1400
a. Surch double

The settings of the 1d. on 3d. and on 4d. are not identical. variety (*c*) does not exist on the 3d.

2½d. (**8**)

2½d. Printers leads after surcharge (Lower right pane No. 43)

1892 (Oct). *No. 51 surch with T* **8**.
67 **1** 2½d.on 3d. ultramarine 12·00
a. No stop after "d" 75·00
b. Printers leads after surcharge —

1894 (Sept). *Colour changed.* P 14.
68 **1** 1d. purple 2·75

½d ½d ½d
(**9**) (*a*) (*b*) (*c*)

½d ½d ½d ½d
(*d*) (*e*) (*f*) (*g*)

Types (*a*) and (*e*) differ from types (*b*) and (*f*) respectively, in serifs of the "**1**", but owing to faulty overprinting this distinctio not always clearly to be seen.

1896 (Sept). *No. 51 surch with T* **9** *(a) to (g).*
69 **1** ½d.on 3d. ultramarine (*a*) 3·50
70 ½d.on 3d. ultramarine (*b*) 8·00
71 ½d.on 3d. ultramarine (*c*) 7·00
72 ½d.on 3d. ultramarine (*d*) 7·00
73 ½d.on 3d. ultramarine (*e*) 7·00
74 ½d.on 3d. ultramarine (*f*) 9·00
75 ½d.on 3d. ultramarine (*g*) 5·50
a. Surch double 13·00
b. Surch triple 60·00

The double and triple surcharges are often different types, but always type (*g*), or in combination with type (*g*).

Double surcharges in the same type, but without the "d" and b also exist, probably from a trial sheet prepared by the printer. B mint and used examples are known.

Halve Penny.
(**10**)

2½
(**11**)

1896. *No. 51 surch with T* **10**.
77 **1** ½d. on 3d. ultramarine 65

(i) Errors in setting.
78 **1** ½d. on 3d. (no stop) 13·00
79 ½d. on 3d. ("Peuny") 13·00

(ii) Surch inverted.
81 **1** ½d. on 3d. 55·00
81*a* ½d. on 3d. (no stop)
81*b* ½d. on 3d. ("Peuny") £1500

(iii) Surch double, one inverted.
81*c* **1** ½d. on 3d. (Nos. 77 and 81) £180
81*d* ½d. on 3d. (Nos. 77 and 81*a*) £750
81*e* ½d. on 3d. (Nos. 77 and 81*b*) £850
81*f* ½d. on 3d. (Nos. 81 and 78) —
82 ½d. on 3d. (Nos. 81 and 79) —

Examples from the top horizontal row can be found without bar due to the surcharge being misplaced.

Nos. 69 to 75 also exist surcharged as last but they are considered not to have been issued with authority (*Prices from £30 each, unused*).

1897 (1 Jan). *No. 51 surch with T* **11**. *(a) As in illustration. (b) With Roman "1" and antique "2" in fraction.*

83 **1** 2½d. on 3d. ultramarine (*a*) . . . 5·50 80
83*a* 2½d. on 3d. ultramarine (*b*) . . . £140 90·00

1897. P 14.

84 **1** ½d. yellow (March) . . . 2·00 35
85 ½d. orange . . . 2·00 35
87 1s. brown (Aug) . . . 18·00 1·50

The 6d. blue was prepared for use in the Orange Free State, but had not been brought into use when the stamps were seized in Bloemfontein. A few have been seen without the "V.R.I." overprint but they were not authorized or available for postage (*Price* £60).

BRITISH OCCUPATION

V. R. I. V. R. I. V. R. I.

4d ½d ½d

31 (Level stops) (**32**) Thin "V" (Raised stops) (**33**) Thick "V"

V. R. I.
Inserted "R"

(Surch by Curling & Co, Bloemfontein)

1900. *T* **1** *surch as T* **31/33** *(2½d. on 3d. optd "V.R.I." only).*

(a) First printings surch as T **31** *with stops level (March).*

101 ½d.on ½d. orange . . . 2·50 3·00
a. No stop after "V" . . . 18·00 22·00
b. No stop after "I" . . . £160 £160
c. "½" omitted . . . £170 £170
d. "I" omitted . . . £190 £190
e. "V.R.I." omitted . . . £160
f. Value omitted . . . £100
g. Small "½" . . . 50·00 50·00
h. Surch double . . . £170

102 1d.on 1d. purple . . . 2·50 1·25
a. Surch on 1d. deep brown (No. 3) . . . £600 £400
b. No stop after "V" . . . 14·00 10·00
c. No stop after "R" . . . £150 £160
d. No stop after "I"
e. "1" omitted . . . £170 £180
f. "I" omitted . . . £300 £300
g. "I" and stop after "R" omitted . . . £300 £300
h. "V.R.I." omitted . . . £140 £150
i. "d" omitted . . . £300 £300
j. Value omitted . . . 80·00 85·00
k. Inverted stop after "R" . . . £200
l. Wider space between "1" and "d" . . . £100 £100
m. "V" and "R" close . . . £150
n. Pair, one without surch . . . £425
o. "V" omitted . . . £800

103 2d.on 2d. bright mauve . . . 1·75 80
a. No stop after "V" . . . 12·00 14·00
b. No stop after "R" . . . £250
c. No stop after "I" . . . £250
d. "V.R.I." omitted . . . £300
e. Value omitted . . . £300

104 2½d.on 3d. ultramarine (*a*) . . . 13·00 10·00
a. No stop after "V" . . . 80·00 80·00

105 2½d.on 3d. ultramarine (*b*) . . . £180 £180

106 3d.on 3d. ultramarine . . . 1·75 1·50
a. No stop after "V" . . . 16·00 14·00
b. Pair, one without surch . . . £400
c. "V.R.I." omitted . . . £250
d. Value omitted . . . £250

107 4d.on 4d. ultramarine . . . 6·50 13·00
a. No stop after "V" . . . 55·00 60·00

108 6d.on 6d. bright carmine . . . 38·00 35·00
a. No stop after "V" . . . £250 £275
b. "6" omitted . . . £300 £300

109 6d.on 6d. blue . . . 6·00 3·25
a. No stop after "V" . . . 35·00 38·00
b. "6" omitted . . . 70·00 75·00
c. "V.R.I." omitted . . . — £300

110 1s.on 1s. brown . . . 7·00 2·75
a. Surch on 1s. orange-yellow (No. 9) . . . £3500 £2500
b. No stop after "V" . . . 40·00 30·00
c. "1" omitted . . . £120 £120
ca. "1" inserted by hand . . . † £1000
d. "1" omitted and spaced stop after "s" . . . £130 £140
e. "V.R.I." omitted . . . £160 £160
f. Value omitted . . . £160 £160
g. Raised stop after "s" . . . 15·00 11·00
h. Wider space between "1" and "s" . . . £150 £150

111 5s.on 5s. green . . . 17·00 38·00
a. No stop after "V" . . . £225 £275
b. "5" omitted . . . £950 £1000
c. Inverted stop after "R" . . . £700 £700
d. Wider space between "5" and "s" . . . £130 £140
e. Value omitted . . . £375

All values are found with a rectangular, instead of an oval, stop after "R". Misplaced surcharges (upwards or sideways) occur.

No. 110ca shows the missing "1" replaced by a handstamp in a different type face.

(b) Subsequent printings.

(i) Surch as T **32**.

112 ½d.on ½d. orange . . . 30 20
a. Raised and level stops mixed . . . 2·00 2·00
b. Pair, one with level stops . . . 10·00 14·00
c. No stop after "V" . . . 2·75 3·00
d. No stop after "I" . . . 26·00 27·00
e. "V" omitted . . . £550
f. Small "½" . . . 14·00 16·00
g. As a, and small "½" . . . 14·00 16·00
i. Space between "V" and "R"
j. Value omitted . . . £120

113 1d.on 1d. purple . . . 30 20
a. Raised and level stops mixed . . . 1·60 2·25
b. Pair, one with level stops . . . 19·00 20·00
c. No stop after "V" . . . 3·25 6·00
d. No stop after "R" . . . 15·00 16·00
e. No stop after "I" . . . 15·00 16·00
f. No stops after "V" and "I" . . . £300
g. Surch inverted . . . £300
h. Surch double . . . £110 £100
i. Pair, one without surch . . . £225
j. Short figure "1" . . . £100 £100
k. Space between "V" and "R" . . . 50·00 55·00
l. Space between "R" and "I" . . . £110
m. Space between "1" and "d" . . . £180
n. Inserted "R" . . . £325
o. Inserted "V" . . . £700

114 2d.on 2d. bright mauve . . . 1·00 30
a. Raised and level stops mixed . . . 4·50 4·50
b. Pair, one with level stops . . . 8·00 8·50
c. Surch inverted . . . £300 £300
d. "1" raised . . . 75·00
e. Pair, one without surch . . . £300
f. No stop after "V" . . . £1000
g. No stop after "I"

115 2½d.on 3d. ultramarine (*a*) . . . £200 £180
a. Raised and level stops mixed . . . £550

116 2½d.on 3d. ultramarine (*b*) . . . £1200

117 3d.on 3d. ultramarine . . . 60 30
a. Raised and level stops mixed . . . 6·50 6·50
b. Pair, one with level stops . . . 17·00 18·00
c. No stop after "V" . . . £140 £140
d. No stop after "R" . . . £350 £450
e. "I" omitted . . . £400
f. Surch double . . . £400
g. Surch double, one diagonal . . . £375
h. Ditto, diagonal surch with mixed stops . . . £6500
n. Inserted "R"
o. Space between "3" and "d" . . . £140

118 4d.on 4d. ultramarine . . . 2·00 2·50
a. Raised and level stops mixed . . . 9·00 12·00
b. Pair, one with level stops . . . 20·00 27·00

119 6d.on 6d. bright carmine . . . 35·00 48·00
a. Raised and level stops mixed . . . £140 £140
b. Pair, one with level stops . . . £200 £250

120 6d.on 6d. blue . . . 70 40
a. Raised and level stops mixed . . . 7·50 7·50
b. Pair, one with level stops . . . 19·00 20·00
c. No stop after "V" . . . £500
d. No stop after "R" . . . £300
e. Value omitted . . . £450

121 1s.on 1s. brown . . . 4·00 45
a. Surch on 1s. orange-yellow (No. 9) . . . £1300 £1300
b. Raised and level stops mixed . . . 18·00 18·00
c. Pair, one with level stops . . . 35·00 35·00
f. "s" omitted . . . £250
g. "V.R.I." omitted . . . £400

122 5s.on 5s. green . . . 7·00 8·50
a. Raised and level stops mixed . . . £300 £300
b. Pair, one with level stops . . . £950
c. Short top to "5" . . . 60·00 70·00
s. Handstamped "Specimen" . . . 50·00

(ii) Surch as T **33**.

123 ½d.on ½d. orange . . . 3·25 2·25
124 1d.on 1d. purple . . . 3·50 35
a. Inverted "1" for "I" . . . 18·00 18·00
b. No stops after "R" and "I" . . . 90·00 70·00
c. No stop after "R" . . . 40·00 45·00
d. Surch double . . . £325 £325
n. Inserted "R" . . . £400 £400

125 2d.on 2d. bright mauve . . . 7·00 9·00
a. Inverted "1" for "I" . . . 26·00 29·00

126 2½d.on 3d. ultramarine (*a*) . . . £600 £700
127 2½d.on 3d. ultramarine (*b*) . . . £3500
128 3d.on 3d. ultramarine . . . 4·75 9·50
a. Inverted "1" for "I" . . . 65·00 75·00
b. Surch double . . . £550
ba. Surch double, one diagonal . . . £550

129 6d.on 6d. bright carmine . . . £425
130 6d.on 6d. blue . . . 9·50 21·00
131 1s.on 1s. brown . . . 18·00 7·50
132 5s.on 5s. green . . . 50·00 48·00
s. Handstamped "Specimen" . . . £150

Stamps with thick "V" occur in certain positions in *later* settings of the type with stops above the line (T **32**). *Earlier* settings with stops above the line have all stamps with thin "V".

Some confusion has previously been caused by the listing of certain varieties as though they occurred on stamps with thick "V" in fact they occur on stamps showing the normal thin "V", included in the settings which also contained the thick "V".

For a short period small blocks of unsurcharged Free State stamps could be handed in for surcharging so that varieties occur which are not found in the complete settings. Nos. 102a, 110a and 121a also occur from such stocks.

The inserted "R" variety occurs on positions 6 (T **32**) and 12 (T **33**) of the forme. The "R" of the original surcharge failed to print and the "R", but not the full stop, was added by the use of a handstamp. Traces of the original letter are often visible. The broken "V" flaw, also shown in the illustration, does not appear on No. 124n.

ORANGE RIVER COLONY

CROWN COLONY

ORANGE RIVER COLONY. 4d E. R. I. 6d

(**34**) (**35**) (**36**)

1900 (10 Aug)–**02**. *Nos. 58a, 61a and 67 of Cape of Good Hope (wmk Cabled Anchor. P 14) optd with T* **34** *by W. A. Richards and Sons, Cape Town.*

133 ½d. green (13.10.00) . . . 40 10
a. No stop . . . 7·00 14·00
b. Opt double . . . £650 £700
134 1d. carmine (May 1902) . . . 1·00 10
a. No stop . . . 14·00 20·00
135 2½d. ultramarine . . . 1·00 35
a. No stop . . . 60·00 70·00
133/5 *Set of* 3 . . . 2·25 50

In the ½d. and 2½d., the "no stop" after "COLONY" variety was the first stamp in the left lower pane. In the 1d. it is the twelfth stamp in the right lower pane on which the stop was present at the beginning of the printing but became damaged and soon failed to print.

1902 (14 Feb). *Surch with T* **35** *by "Bloemfontein Express".*

136 4d.on 6d. on 6d. blue (No. 120) (R.) . . . 1·50 75
a. No stop after "R" . . . 32·00 38·00
b. No stop after "I" . . . £1200
c. Surch on No. 130 (Thick "V") . . . 2·00 5·50
ca. Inverted "1" for "I" . . . 6·00 15·00

1902 (Aug). *Surch with T* **36**.

137 **1** 6d.on 6d. blue . . . 3·50 9·50
a. Surch double, one inverted
b. Wide space between "6" and "d" (R. 4/2) . . . 60·00 90·00

One Shilling
*
(**37**)

38 King Edward VII, Springbok and Gnu

1902 (Sept). *Surch with T* **37**.

138 **1** 1s.on 5s. green (O.) . . . 7·00 12·00
a. Thick "V" . . . 15·00 32·00
b. Short top to "5" . . . 70·00 80·00
c. Surch double

(Typo D.L.R.)

1903 (3 Feb)–**04**. Wmk Crown CA. P 14.

139 **38** ½d. yellow-green (6.7.03) . . . 8·00 1·25
w. Wmk inverted . . . — 85·00
140 1d. scarlet . . . 4·50 10
w. Wmk inverted . . . — 75·00
141 2d. brown (6.7.03) . . . 4·75 80
142 2½d. bright blue (6.7.03) . . . 1·60 50
143 3d. mauve (6.7.03) . . . 7·00 90
144 4d. scarlet and sage-green (6.7.03) . . . 32·00 2·00
a. "IOSTAGE" for "POSTAGE" . . . £800 £450
145 6d. scarlet and mauve (6.7.03) . . . 8·00 1·00
146 1s. scarlet and bistre (6.7.03) . . . 26·00 1·75
147 5s. blue and brown (31.10.04) . . . 75·00 22·00
139/47 *Set of* 9 . . . £150 27·00
139s/47s Optd "Specimen" *Set of* 9 . . . £150

No. 144a occurs on R. 10/2 of the upper left pane.

The 2d. exists from coils constructed from normal sheets for use in stamp machines introduced in 1911.

Several of the above values are found with the overprint "C.S.A.R.", in black, for use by the Central South African Railways. Examples also exist perforated "CSAR" or "NGR".

1905 (Nov)–**09**. Wmk Mult Crown CA. P 14.

148 **38** ½d. yellow-green (28.7.07) . . . 9·00 50
149 1d. scarlet . . . 8·50 30
150 4d. scarlet and sage-green (8.11.07) . . . 4·50 2·50
a. "IOSTAGE" for "POSTAGE" . . . £180 £150
151 1s. scarlet and bistre (2.09) . . . 40·00 14·00
148/51 *Set of* 4 . . . 55·00 15·00

POSTCARD STAMPS

From 1889 onwards the Orange Free State Post Office sold postcards franked with adhesives as Type **1**, some subsequently surcharged, over which the State Arms had been overprinted.

There are five known dies of the Arms overprint which can be identified as follows:

(a) Shield without flags. Three cows (two lying down, one standing) at left. Point of shield complete.
(b) Shield with flags. Four cows (two lying down, two standing) at left (*illustrated*).
(c) Shield with flags. Three cows (one lying down, two standing) at left.
(d) Shield without flags. Three cows (one lying down, two standing) at left.
(e) Shield without flags. Three cows (two lying down, one standing) at left. Point of shield broken.

There are also other differences between the dies.

PRICES. Those in the left-hand column are for unused examples on complete postcard; those on the right for used examples off card. Examples used on postcard are worth more.

1889 (Feb). *No. 2 (placed sideways on card) optd Shield Type (a).*

P1 **1** 1d. red-brown . . . 85·00 38·00
a. Optd Shield Type (b) . . . 30·00 7·00

1891 (Aug). *No. 48 optd Shield Type (b).*
P2 **1** ½d. chestnut . . . . 5·00 1·75
a. Optd Shield Type (c) . . . . 12·00 4·25
b. Optd Shield Type (d) . . . . 5·50 2·25
c. Optd Shield Type (e) . . . . 13·00 5·00

1892 (June). *No. 54 optd Shield Type (b).*
P3 **1** 1d.on 3d. ultramarine . . . . 85·00 45·00
a. Optd Shield Type (c) . . . . 14·00 3·00

1½d. 1½d. 1½d.
(P 1) (P 2) (P 3)

1892 (Sept)–**95**. *Nos. 50/1 optd Shield Type (b) or (d) (No. P6) and surch with Types P 1/3.*
P4 **1** 1½d.on 2d. bright mauve (Type **P 1**) (11.92) . . . . 7·50 3·75
P5 1½d.on 2d. bright mauve (Type **P 2**) (9.93) . . . . 5·50 1·75
a. Surch inverted . . . .
P6 1½d.on 2d. brt mauve (Type **P 3**) (R.) (6.95) . . . . 12·00 4·25
P7 1½d.on 3d. ultramarine (Type **P 1**) . . . 7·00 2·25

No. P5a shows the stamp affixed to the card upside down with the surcharge correctly positioned in relation to the card.

½d.
(P 4)

1895 (Aug). *No. 48 optd Shield Type (e) and surch with Type P 4.*
P8 **1** ½d. on ½d. chestnut . . . . 12·00 2·75

1½d. 1½d.
(P 5) (P 6)

1895 (Dec)–**97**. *No. 50 optd Shield Type (e) and surch with Types P 5/6.*
P9 **1** 1½d.on 2d. bright mauve (Type **P 5**) . . 6·00 2·75
P10 1½d.on 2d. brt mauve (Type **P 6**) (12.97) . . . . 7·00 3·25
P11 1½d.on 2d. bright mauve (as Type **P 6**, but without stop) (12.97) . . . . 7·00 3·25

1897 (Mar). *No. 85 optd Shield Type (d).*
P12 **1** ½d. orange . . . . 12·00 1·75
a. Optd Shield Type (e) . . . . 13·00 2·75

V.R.I.
(P 7)

1900. *Nos. P10/11 optd as T* **31/2** *or with Type P 7.*
P13 **1** 1½d.on 2d. bright mauve (No. P10) (**T 31**) . . . . 26·00 5·50
P14 1½d.on 2d. bright mauve (No. P11) (**T 31**) . . . . 26·00 5·50
P15 1½d.on 2d. bright mauve (No. P10) (**T 32**) . . . . 26·00 5·50
P16 1½d.on 2d. bright mauve (No. P11) (**T 32**) . . . . 26·00 5·50
P17 1½d.on 2d. brt mve (No. P10) (Type **P 7**) . . . . 38·00 10·00
P18 1½d.on 2d. brt rove (No. P11) (Type **P 7**) . . . . 38·00 10·00

POLICE FRANK STAMPS

The following frank stamps were issued to members of the Orange Free State Mounted Police ("Rijdende Dienst Macht") for use on official correspondence.

PF **1** (eight ornaments at left and right)

PF **2**

1896. P 12.
PF1 PF **1** (–) Black £200

No. PF1 was printed in horizontal strips of 5 surrounded by wide margins.

1898. *As Type* PF **1**, *but with nine ornaments at left and right.* P 12.
PF2 (–) Black £140 £170

No. PF2 was printed in blocks of 4 (2 × 2) surrounded by wide margins.

1899. P 12.
PF3 PF **2** (–) Black/*yellow* £130 £130
a. No stop after "V" £550

No. PF3 was printed in sheets of 24 (6 × 4) with the edges of the sheet imperforate. It is believed that they were produced from a setting of 8 (2 × 4) repeated three times. No. PF3a occurs on R. 1/1 of the setting.

Examples of No. PF3 are known postmarked as late as 28 April 1900. The O.F.S. Mounted Police were disbanded by the British authorities at the end of the following month.

MILITARY FRANK STAMP

M 1

(Typeset Curling & Co, Bloemfontein)

1899 (15 Oct). P 12.
M1 **M 1** (–) Black/*bistre-yellow* . . . . 13·00 45·00

Supplies of No. M1 were issued to members of the Orange Free State army on active service during the Second Boer War. To pass free through the O.F.S. fieldpost system, letters had to be franked with No. M1 or initialled by the appropriate unit commander. The franks were in use between October 1899 and February 1900.

No. M1 was printed in sheets of 20 (5 × 4) using a setting of five different types in a horizontal row. The colour in the paper runs in water.

Typeset forgeries can be identified by the appearance of 17 pearls, instead of the 16 of the originals, in the top and bottom frames. Forgeries produced by lithography omit the stops after "BRIEF" and "FRANKO".

FISCAL STAMPS USED FOR POSTAGE

The following were issued in December 1877 (Nos. F1 and F3 in 1882) and were authorised for postal use between 1882 and 1886.

F 1

F 2

F 3

(Typo D.L.R.)

1882–86. P 14.
F 1 **F 1** 6d. pearl-grey . . . . 8·50 12·00
F 2 6d. purple-brown . . . . 29·00 18·00
F 3 **F 2** 1s. purple-brown . . . . 9·50 14·00
F 4 1s. pearl-grey . . . . 45·00 48·00
F 5 1s.6d. blue . . . . 18·00 12·00
F 6 2s. magenta . . . . 18·00 12·00
F 7 3s. chestnut . . . . 23·00 48·00
F 8 4s. grey . . . .
F 9 5s. rose . . . . 24·00 20·00
F10 6s. green . . . . — 55·00
F11 7s. violet . . . .
F12 10s. orange . . . . 50·00 32·00
F13 **F 3** £1 purple . . . . 60·00 38·00
a. "VRY-STAAT" (R. 1/5) . . .
F14 £2 red-brown . . . . 70·00
a. "VRY-STAAT" (R. 1/5) . . .
F14*b* £4 carmine . . . .
ba. "VRY-STAAT" (R. 1/5) . . .
F15 £5 green . . . . 95·00 48·00
a. "VRY-STAAT" (R. 1/5) . . .

Die proofs of Type **F 3** showed a hyphen in error between "VRY" and "STAAT". This was removed from each impression on the plate before printing, but was missed on R. 1/5.

A fiscally used example of No. F2 exists showing "ZES PENCE" double, one inverted.

The 8s. yellow was prepared but we have no evidence of its use postally without surcharge Type **F 3**.

ZES PENCE.
(F 4)

1886. *Surch with Type F 4.*
F16 **F 2** 6d. on 4s. grey . . . .
F17 6d. on 8s. yellow £225

Postage stamps overprinted for use as Telegraph stamps and used postally are omitted as it is impossible to say with certainty which stamps were genuinely used for postal purposes.

Orange Free State became a province of the Union of South Africa on 31 May 1910.

VI. TRANSVAAL

(*formerly* South African Republic)

From 1852 mail from the Transvaal was forwarded to the Cape of Good Hope, via the Orange Free State, by a post office at Potchefstroom. In 1859 the Volksraad voted to set up a regular postal service and arrangements were made for letters sent to the Cape and for overseas to be franked with Cape of Good Hope stamps.

The Potchefstroom postmaster placed his first order for these on 23 August 1859 and examples of all four triangular values are known postmarked there. From 1868 mail via the Orange Free State required franking with their issues also.

A similar arrangement covering mail sent overseas via Natal was in operation from 9 July 1873 until the first British Occupation. Such letters carried combinations of Transvaal stamps, paying the rate to Natal, and Natal issues for the overseas postage. Such Natal stamps were sold, but not postmarked, by Transvaal post offices.

PRICES FOR STAMPS ON COVER

Nos. 1/6 are rare used on cover.

Nos.	7/80	*from* × 20
Nos.	86/155	*from* × 3
Nos.	156/62	*from* × 6
Nos.	163/9	*from* × 5
Nos.	170/225	*from* × 10
Nos.	226/34	*from* × 20
Nos.	235/7	—
Nos.	238/43	*from* × 12
Nos.	244/55	*from* × 4
Nos.	256/7	*from* × 6
Nos.	258/9	—
Nos.	260/76	*from* × 20
Nos.	F1/5	*from* × 5
Nos.	D1/7	*from* × 20

The issues for Pietersburg, Lydenburg, Rustenburg, Schweizer Renecke and Wolmaransstad are very rare when on cover. are very rare when on cover.

1 (Eagle with spread wings)

2

3

(Typo Adolph Otto, Gustrow, Mecklenburg-Schwerin)

1870 (1 May). *Thin paper, clear and distinct impressions.*

(a) Imperf.
1 **1** 1d. brown-lake £350
a. *Orange-red* £350 £35
2 6d. bright ultramarine £130 £13
a. *Pale ultramarine* £150 £16
3 1s. deep green £550 £55
a. *Tête-bêche* (pair) . . . .

(b) Fine roulette, 15½ to 16.
4 **1** 1d. brown-lake . . . . 85·00
a. *Brick-red* . . . . 65·00
b. *Orange-red* . . . . 65·00
c. *Vermilion* . . . . 65·00
5 6d. bright ultramarine . . . . 60·00 60·0
a. *Pale ultramarine* . . . . 70·00
6 1s. deep green £130 £13
a. *Yellow-green* . . . . £100 95·0
b. *Emerald-green* . . . . 80·00 80·0

Examples of Nos. 1/6 may have been sold to dealers at some stag between their arrival in Transvaal during August 1869 and the sa of stamps to the public for postal purposes on 1 May 1870.

PLATES. The German printings of the 1d., 6d. and 1s. in Type were from two pairs of plates, each pair printing sheets of 80 in tw panes of five horizontal rows of eight.

One pair of plates, used for Nos. 4*a*, 4*c*, 5*a* and 6/*a*, produce stamps spaced 1¼ to 1½ mm apart with the rouletting close to th design on all four sides. The 1d. from these "narrow" plates show a gap in the outer frame line at the bottom right-hand corner. Th second pair, used for Nos. 1/3, 4, 4*b*, 5/*a* and 6*b*, had 2¼ to 3¼ m between the stamps. These "wide" plates were sent to the Transva in 1869 and were used there to produce either single or double pa printings until 1883.

The 6d. and 1s. "wide" plates each had an inverted *cliché*. Whe printed these occurred on right-hand pane R. 4/1 of the 6d. an right-hand pane R.1/1 of the 1s. These were never corrected an resulted in *tête-bêche* pairs of these values as late as 1883.

REPRINTS AND IMITATIONS. A number of unauthoris printings were made of these stamps by the German printer. Ma of these can be identified by differences in the central arms, unusu colours or, in the case of the 1d., by an extra frame around th numeral tablets at top.

Genuine stamps always show the "D" of "EENDRAGT" high than the remainder of the word, have no break in the border abo "DR" and depict the flagstaff at bottom right, behind "MAGT stopping short of the central shield. They also show the eagle's e as a clear white circle. On the forgeries the eye is often blurred.

The most difficult of the reprints to detect is the 1s. yellow-gre which was once regarded as genuine, but was subsequen identified, by J. N. Luff in *The Philatelic Record* 1911–12, as comi from an unauthorised plate of four. Stamps from this plate sh either a white dot between "EEN" and "SHILLING" or a wh flaw below the wagon pole.

(Typo M. J. Viljoen, Pretoria)

1870 (1 May–4 July).

I. Thin gummed paper from Germany. Impressions coarse and defective.

(a) Imperf.

8 **1** 1d. dull rose-red . . . 70·00
a. Reddish pink . . . 60·00
b. Carmine-red . . . 55·00 65·00
9 6d. dull ultramarine . . . £250 60·00
a. *Tête-bêche* (pair) . . .

(b) Fine roulette, 15½ to 16.

10 **1** 1d. carmine-red . . . £700 £250
11 6d. dull ultramarine . . . £180 90·00
a. Imperf between (vert pair) . . . £600

(c) Wide roulette, 6½.

12 **1** 1d. carmine-red . . . — £850

II. Thick, hard paper with thin yellow smooth gum (No. 15) or yellow streaky gum (others).

(a) Imperf.

13 **1** 1d. pale rose-red . . . 60·00
a. Carmine-red . . . 60·00 70·00
14 1s. yellow-green . . . 85·00 75·00
a. *Tête-bêche* (pair) . . . £14000
b. Bisected (6d.) (on cover) . . . † £1300

(b) Fine roulette, 15½ to 16.

15 **1** 1d. carmine-red (24 May) . . . 80·00
16 6d. ultramarine (10 May) . . . 80·00 80·00
a. *Tête-bêche* (pair) . . . £22000 £17000
17 1s. yellow-green . . . £550 £550

III. Medium paper, blotchy heavy printing and whitish gum. Fine roulette 15½ to 16 (4 July).

18 **1** 1d. rose-red . . . 60·00 75·00
a. Carmine-red . . . 40·00 45·00
b. Crimson. From over-inked plate . . . £130
19 6d. ultramarine . . . 75·00 65·00
a. *Tête-bêche* (pair) . . .
b. Deep ultram. From over-inked plate . . . £400 £150
20 1s. deep green . . . £100 65·00
a. From over-inked plate . . . £450 £150

The rouletting machine producing the wide 6½ gauge was not ntroduced until 1875.

Nos. 18*b*, 19*b* and 20a were printed from badly over-inked plates giving heavy blobby impressions.

(Typo J. P. Borrius, Potchefstroom)

1870 (Sept)–**71**. *Stout paper, but with colour often showing through, whitish gum.*

(a) Imperf.

21 **1** 1d. black . . . £120 £100

(b) Fine roulette, 15½ to 16.

22 **1** 1d. black . . . 17·00 25·00
a. Grey-black . . . 17·00 25·00
23 6d. blackish blue (7.71) . . . £120 60·00
a. Dull blue . . . 90·00 75·00

(Typo Adolph Otto, Gustrow, Mecklenburg-Schwerin)

871 (July). *Thin paper, clear and distinct impressions. Fine roulette, 15½ to 16.*

24 **2** 3d. pale reddish lilac . . . 80·00 90·00
a. Deep lilac . . . 85·00 95·00
b. Vert laid paper . . .

No. 24 and later printings in the Transvaal were produced from pair of plates in the same format as the 1869 issue. All genuine tamps have a small dot on the left leg of the eagle.

Imperforate examples in the issued shade, without the dot on agle's leg, had been previously supplied by the printer, probably as ssays, but were not issued for postal purposes. (*Price* £750 *unused*). hey also exist *tête-bêche* (*Price for un pair* £3250).

Imperforate and rouletted stamps in other colours are reprints.

(Typo J. P. Borrius, Potchefstroom)

872–74. *Fine roulette, 15½ to 16.*

(a) Thin transparent paper.

5 **1** 1d. black . . . £170 £550
6 1d. bright carmine . . . £140 50·00
7 6d. ultramarine . . . £100 40·00
8 1s. green . . . £120 55·00

(b) Thinnish opaque paper, clear printing (Dec 1872).

9 **1** 1d. reddish pink . . . 55·00 38·00
a. Carmine-red . . . 55·00 38·00
0 **2** 3d. grey-lilac . . . 85·00 45·00
1 **1** 6d. ultramarine . . . 55·00 27·00
a. Pale ultramarine . . . 65·00 29·00
2 1s. yellow-green . . . 70·00 38·00
a. Green . . . 70·00 38·00
aa. Bisected (6d.) (on cover) . . . † £1500

(c) Thickish wove paper (1873–74).

3 **1** 1d. dull rose . . . £400 70·00
a. Brownish rose . . . £475 £110
b. Printed on both sides . . .
4 6d. milky blue . . . £140 45·00
a. Deep dull blue . . . 85·00 40·00
aa. Imperf (pair) . . . £600
ab. Imperf between (horiz pair) . . . £650
ac. Wide roulette 6½ . . .

(d) Very thick dense paper (1873–74).

5 1d. dull rose . . . £500 £120
a. Brownish rose . . . £375 95·00
6 6d. dull ultramarine . . . £170 65·00
a. Bright ultramarine . . . £180 60·00
7 1s. yellow-green . . . £750 £550

(Typo P. Davis & Son, Pietermaritzburg)

1874 (Sept). P 12½.

(a) Thin transparent paper.

38 **1** 1d. pale brick-red . . . 80·00 35·00
a. Brownish red . . . 75·00 35·00
39 6d. deep blue . . . £120 50·00

(b) Thicker opaque paper.

40 **1** 1d. pale red . . . £130 65·00
41 6d. blue . . . £100 45·00
a. Imperf between (pair) . . .
b. Deep blue . . . £100 45·00

(Typo Adolph Otto, Gustrow, Mecklenburg-Schwerin)

1874 (Oct). *Thin smooth paper, clearly printed. Fine roulette 15½ to 16.*

42 **3** 6d. bright ultramarine . . . 60·00 24·00
a. Bisected (3d.) (on cover) . . . † £1200

Stamps in other shades of blue, brown or red, often on other types of paper, are reprints.

(Typo J. F. Celliers on behalf of Stamp Commission, Pretoria)

1875 (29 Apr)–**77**.

I. Very thin, soft opaque (semi-pelure) paper.

(a) Imperf.

43 **1** 1d. orange-red . . . £120 45·00
a. Pin-perf . . . £500 £250
44 **2** 3d. lilac . . . 80·00 45·00
45 **1** 6d. blue . . . 75·00 38·00
a. Milky blue . . . £120 40·00
aa. *Tête-bêche* (pair) . . . £9500
ab. Pin-perf . . . — £250

(b) Fine roulette, 15½ to 16.

46 **1** 1d. orange-red . . . £400 £130
47 **2** 3d. lilac . . . £425 £140
48 **1** 6d. blue . . . £400 £130

(c) Wide roulette, 6½.

49 **1** 1d. orange-red . . . — £150
50 **2** 3d. lilac . . . £550 £225
51 **1** 6d. blue . . . — £120
a. Bright blue . . . — £120
b. Milky blue . . . — £120

II. Very thin, hard transparent (pelure) paper (1875–76).

(a) Imperf.

52 **1** 1d. brownish red . . . 48·00 27·00
a. Orange-red . . . 38·00 22·00
b. Dull red . . . 42·00 42·00
ba. Pin-perf . . . £425 £250
53 **2** 3d. lilac . . . 45·00 38·00
a. Pin-perf . . . — £250
b. Deep lilac . . . 55·00 38·00
54 **1** 6d. pale blue . . . 45·00 45·00
a. Blue . . . 45·00 38·00
ab. *Tête-bêche* (pair) . . .
ac. Pin-perf . . . — £225
b. Deep blue . . . 50·00 42·00

(b) Fine roulette 15½ to 16.

55 **1** 1d. orange-red . . . £250 £120
a. Brown-red . . . £250 £120
56 **2** 3d. lilac . . . £325 £110
57 **1** 6d. blue . . . £150 95·00
a. Deep blue . . . £150 £110

(c) Wide roulette, 6½.

58 **1** 1d. orange-red . . . £700 £160
a. Bright red . . . — £140
59 **2** 3d. lilac . . . £600 £190
60 **1** 6d. deep blue . . . £700 90·00

III. Stout hard-surfaced paper with smooth, nearly white, gum (1876).

(a) Imperf.

61 **1** 1d. bright red . . . 22·00 16·00
62 **2** 3d. lilac . . . £300 £100
63 **1** 6d. bright blue . . . 90·00 22·00
a. *Tête-bêche* (pair) . . .
b. Pale blue . . . 90·00 22·00
c. Deep blue (deep brown gum) . . . 55·00 18·00
ca. *Tête-bêche* (pair) . . . — £14000

(b) Fine roulette, 15½ to 16.

64 **1** 1d. bright red . . . £400 £150
65 **2** 3d. lilac . . . £275
66 **1** 6d. bright blue . . . — £110
a. Deep blue (deep brown gum) . . . £600 £250

(c) Wide roulette, 6½.

67 **1** 1d. bright red . . . £450 £140
68 6d. pale blue . . . — £200
a. Deep blue (deep brown gum) . . . £500 £250

IV. Coarse, soft white paper (1876–77).

(a) Imperf.

69 **1** 1d. brick-red . . . £100 50·00
70 6d. deep blue . . . £160 50·00
a. Milky blue . . . £275 90·00
71 1s. yellow-green . . . £275 £100
a. Bisected (6d.) (on cover) . . . † £1300

(b) Fine roulette, 15½ to 16.

72 **1** 1d. brick-red . . . — £250
73 6d. deep blue . . . — £130
74 1s. yellow-green . . . £550 £275

(c) Wide roulette, 6½.

75 **1** 1d. brick-red . . . — £300
76 6d. deep blue . . . — £750
77 1s. yellow-green . . . — £800

(d) Fine × wide roulette.

78 **1** 1d. brick-red . . . £550 £250

V. Hard, thick, coarse yellowish paper (1876–77).

79 **1** 1d. brick-red (imperf) . . . — £200
80 1d. brick-red (*wide roulette*) . . . — £300

The pin-perforated stamps have various gauges and were probably produced privately or by one or more post offices other than Pretoria.

On Nos. 63*c*/ca, 66*a* and 68*a* the brown gum used was so intense that it caused staining of the paper which is still visible on used examples.

See also Nos. 171/4.

FIRST BRITISH OCCUPATION

By 1876 conditions in the Transvaal had deteriorated and the country was faced by economic collapse, native wars and internal dissension. In early 1877 Sir Theophilus Shepstone, appointed Special Commissioner to the South African Republic by the British Government, arrived in Pretoria and on 12 April annexed the Transvaal with the acquiesence of at least part of the European population.

V. R. V. R.

TRANSVAAL. TRANSVAAL.
(4) (5)

T **4** is the normal overprint, but Setting I No. 11 (R. 2/3) has a wider-spaced overprint as T **5**.

1877 (Apr). *Optd with T* **4** *in red.*

(a) Imperf.

86 **2** 3d. lilac (*semi-pelure*) (No. 44) . . . £1100 £250
a. Opt Type **5** . . .
87 3d. lilac (*pelure*) (No. 53) . . . £1100 £170
a. Opt Type **5** . . . £3500 £1400
b. Opt on back . . . £3000 £3000
c. Opt double, in red and in black . . . £4750
88 **1** 6d. milky blue (No. 70) . . . £1300 £170
a. Opt inverted . . . — £4250
b. Opt double . . . £3500 £750
c. Opt Type **5** . . . £4250
d. Deep blue . . . — £225
89 1s. yellow-green (No. 71) . . . £475 £170
a. Bisected (6d.) (on cover) . . . † £1400
b. Opt inverted . . . — £3250
c. Opt Type **5** . . . £3000 £750
d. *Tête-bêche* (pair) . . .

(b) Fine roulette, 15½ to 16.

90 **2** 3d. lilac (*pelure*) (No. 56) . . . — £1100
91 **1** 6d. deep blue (No. 73) . . . — £1100
92 1s. yellow-green (No. 74) . . . £1100 £500
a. Opt Type **5** . . .

(c) Wide roulette, 6½.

93 **2** 3d. lilac (*pelure*) (No. 59) . . . — £1100
a. Opt Type **5** . . .
94 **1** 6d. deep blue (No. 76) . . . — £1100
a. Opt Type **5** . . .
95 1s. yellow-green (No. 77) . . . £2750 £1000
a. Opt inverted . . . — £3500

Nos. 88a, 89b and 95a occurred on the inverted *cliché* of the basic stamps.

1877 (June). *Optd with T* **4** *in black.*

I. Very thin, hard transparent (pelure) paper.

96 **1** 1d. orange-red (imperf) (No. 52*a*) . . . £170 95·00
97 1d. orange-red (*fine roulette*) (No. 55) . . . — £1000

II. Stout hard-surfaced paper with smooth, nearly white, gum.

98 **1** 1d. bright red (imperf) (No. 61) . . . 21·00 21·00
a. Opt inverted . . . £475 £400
b. Opt Type **5** . . . £550 £600
99 1d. bright red (*fine roulette*) (No. 64) . . . £140 45·00
a. Opt inverted . . .
b. Opt double . . . — £750
c. Imperf between (horiz pair) . . . £650
100 1d. bright red (*wide roulette*) (No. 67) . . . £475 £140
100*a* 1d. bright red (*fine × wide roulette*) (No. 78) . . .

III. New ptgs on coarse, soft white paper.

(a) Imperf.

101 **1** 1d. brick-red (5.77) . . . 21·00 21·00
a. Opt double . . . — £900
b. Opt Type **5** . . . £600
102 **2** 3d. lilac . . . 70·00 38·00
a. Opt inverted . . .
b. Deep lilac . . . £140 80·00
103 **1** 6d. dull blue . . . 85·00 32·00
a. Opt double . . . £2750 £1500
b. Opt inverted . . . £1200 £150
d. Opt Type **5** . . . — £750
da. Opt Type **5** inverted . . .
e. Blue (bright to deep) . . . £150 27·00
ea. Bright blue, opt inverted . . . — £475
f. Pin-perf . . . — £450
104 1s. yellow-green . . . 90·00 45·00
a. Opt inverted . . . £950 £180
b. *Tête-bêche* (pair) . . . £15000 £15000
c. Opt Type **5** . . . £2750 £900
d. Bisected (6d.) (on cover) . . . † £1100

(b) Fine roulette, 15½ to 16.

105 **1** 1d. brick-red . . . 65·00 65·00
a. Imperf horiz (vert strip of 3) . . .
b. Imperf between (horiz pair) . . . † £600
106 **2** 3d. lilac . . . £140 55·00
107 **1** 6d. dull blue . . . £160 45·00
a. Opt inverted . . . — £550
b. Opt Type **5** . . . £3500
108 1s. yellow-green . . . £160 85·00
a. Opt inverted . . . £850 £375
b. Opt Type **5** . . . — £2500

(c) Wide roulette, 6½.

109 **1** 1d. brick-red . . . £550 £140
a. Opt Type **5** . . . — £650
110 **2** 3d. lilac . . . — £550
111 **1** 6d. dull blue . . . — £1100
a. Opt inverted . . . — £3000
112 1s. yellow-green . . . £350 £120
a. Opt inverted . . . £1100 £475

1877 (31 Aug). *Optd with T* **4** *in black.*
113 **1** 6d. blue/*rose* (imperf) 70·00 45·00
a. Bisected (3d.) (on cover)
b. Opt inverted 85·00 45·00
c. *Tête-bêche* (pair)
d. Opt omitted £2750 £2000
114 6d. blue/*rose* (*fine roulette*) £150 60·00
a. Opt inverted £425 60·00
b. *Tête-bêche* (pair)
c. Opt omitted
d. Bisected (3d.) (on cover)
115 6d. blue/*rose* (*wide roulette*)
a. Opt inverted
b. Opt omitted

Nos. 113/15 were overprinted from a setting of 40 which was applied upright to one pane in each sheet and inverted on the other.

V. R. Transvaal (6) V. R. Transvaal (7)

1877 (28 Sept)–**79**. *Optd with T* **6** *in black.*

(a) *Imperf.*
116 **1** 1d. red/*blue* 48·00 26·00
a. "Transvral" (Right pane R. 2/3) £4000 £2000
b. Opt double £3000
c. Opt inverted £600 £300
d. Opt omitted
117 1d. red/*orange* (6.12.77) 17·00 16·00
a. Pin-perf
b. Printed both sides
c. Opt double £2500
d. Optd with Type **7** (15.4.78) 45·00 38·00
e. Pair. Nos. 117 and 117d £110
118 **2** 3d. mauve/*buff* (24.10.77) 38·00 24·00
a. Opt inverted — £550
b. Pin-perf
c. Bisected (1½d) (on cover) † —
d. Optd with Type **7** (15.4.78) 55·00 32·00
da. Pin-perf £550 £550
e. Pair. Nos. 118 and 118d £140
119 3d. mauve/*green* (18.4.79) £140 42·00
a. Pin-perf
b. Opt inverted — £1500
c. Opt double
d. Printed both sides † —
e. Optd with Type **7** 95·00 35·00
ea. Opt inverted — £1500
eb. Printed both sides
f. Opt omitted — £2750
g. Pair. Nos. 119 and 119e £325
120 **1** 6d. blue/*green* (27.11.77) 75·00 35·00
a. Deep blue/green 90·00 38·00
b. Broken "Y" for "V" in "V.R." (Left pane R. 3/7) — £550
c. Small "v" in "Transvaal" (Left pane R. 5/2) — £550
d. "V.R." (Right pane R. 3/4) — £550
e. *Tête-bêche* (pair) — £14000
f. Opt inverted — £700
g. Pin-perf
h. Bisected (3d.) (on cover) † —
121 6d. blue/*blue* (20.3.78) 48·00 24·00
a. *Tête-bêche* (pair)
b. Opt inverted — £700
c. Opt omitted — £1600
d. Opt double — £2500
e. Pin-perf
f. Bisected (3d.) (on cover) † £700
g. Optd with Type **7** 95·00 27·00
ga. *Tête-bêche* (pair) £11000
gb. Opt inverted — £400
gc. Bisected (3d.) (on cover) † —
h. Pair. Nos. 121 and 121g £225

(b) *Fine roulette, 15½ to 16.*
122 **1** 1d. red/*blue* 75·00 35·00
a. "Transvral" (Right pane R. 2/3) — £2250
123 1d. red/*orange* (6.12.77) 30·00 24·00
a. Imperf between (pair) £500
b. Optd with Type **7** (15.4.78) £130 £110
c. Pair. Nos. 123 and 123b £250
124 **2** 3d. mauve/*buff* (24.10.77) 85·00 25·00
a. Imperf horiz (vert pair) £600
b. Opt inverted — £2500
c. Optd with Type **7** (15.4.78) £130 95·00
ca. Imperf between (pair)
d. Pair. Nos. 124 and 124c £350
125 3d. mauve/*green* (18.4.79) £550 £150
a. Optd with Type **7** £500 £150
b. Pair. Nos. 125 and 125a
126 **1** 6d. blue/*green* (27.11.77) 70·00 25·00
a. "V..R" (Right pane R. 3/4) — £1000
b. *Tête-bêche* (pair)
c. Opt inverted — £500
d. Opt omitted — £3000
e. Bisected (3d.) (on cover) † £550
127 6d. blue/*blue* (20.3.78) £180 48·00
a. Opt inverted — £900
b. Opt omitted — £2500
c. Imperf between (pair)
d. Bisected (3d.) (on cover) † £600
e. Optd with Type **7** £300 £100
ea. Opt inverted — £800

(c) *Wide roulette, 6½.*
128 **1** 1d. red/*orange* (15.4.78) £250 £100
a. Optd with Type **7** — £250
129 **2** 3d. mauve/*buff* (24.10.77) — £100
a. Optd with Type **7** (15.4.78) — £300
130 3d. mauve/*green* (18.4.79) £375 £275
a. Optd with Type **7** — £300
131 **1** 6d. blue/*green* (27.11.77) — £850
132 6d. blue/*blue* (20.3.78) — £250
a. Opt inverted
b. Optd with Type **7** — £300
ba. Opt inverted.

(d) *Fine × wide roulette.*
132*c* **1** red/*orange*

Nos. 116/32c were overprinted from various settings covering sheets of 80 or panes of 40 (8 × 5). Initially these settings contained Type **6** only, but from March 1878 settings also contained examples of Type **7**. Details of these mixed settings are as follows:
1d. red/*orange* (sheets of 80): all Type **6** except for 16 Type **7**.
3d. mauve/*buff* (panes of 40): 16 Type **7**.
3d. mauve/*green* (panes of 40): uncertain, some panes at least contained 27 Type **7**.
6d. blue/*blue* (sheets of 80): either 24 or 27 Type **7**.

9

(Recess B.W.)

1878 (26 Aug)–**80**. P 14, 14½.
133 **9** ½d. vermilion (1880) 19·00 70·00
134 1d. pale red-brown 10·00 3·50
a. Brown-red 9·50 3·00
135 3d. dull rose 13·00 3·75
a. Claret 17·00 5·00
136 4d. sage-green 18·00 4·50
137 6d. olive-black 9·00 3·50
a. Black-brown 11·00 3·00
138 1s. green £100 32·00
139 2s. blue £140 65·00

The above prices are for specimens perforated on all four sides. Stamps from margins of sheets, with perforations absent on one or two sides, can be supplied for about 30% less.

The used price quoted for No. 139 is for an example with telegraphic cancel, a 23.5 mm circular datestamp of Pretoria (or more rarely Heidelberg or Standerton). Postally used examples are worth much more.

1 Penny (10) 1 Penny (11) 1 Penny (12)
1 Penny (13) 1 Penny (14)
1 PENNY (15) 1 Penny (16)

1879 (22 Apr). *No. 137a surch with T* **10** *to* **16** *in black.*
140 **10** 1d.on 6d. 70·00 40·00
a. Surch in red £190 £130
141 **11** 1d.on 6d. £170 75·00
a. Surch in red £475 £275
142 **12** 1d.on 6d. £170 75·00
a. Surch in red £475 £275
143 **13** 1d.on 6d. 75·00 45·00
a. Surch double
b. Surch in red £225 £150
144 **14** 1d.on 6d. £450 £140
a. Surch in red — £1500
145 **15** 1d.on 6d. 38·00 22·00
a. Surch in red £120 65·00
146 **16** 1d.on 6d. £160 70·00
a. Surch in red £425 £250

Nos. 140/6 were surcharged from a setting of 60 containing eleven examples of Type **10**, four of Type **11**, four of Type **12**, nine of Type **13**, two of Type **14** (although there may have been only one in the first two ptgs), twenty-five of Type **15** and five of Type **16**.

The red surcharges may have been produced first.

V. R. Transvaal (16a)

1879 (Aug–Sept). *Optd with T* **16***a in black.*

(*a*) Imperf.
147 **1** 1d. red/*yellow* 40·00 35·00
a. Small "T" £225 £150
b. Red/orange 35·00 25·00
ba. Small "T" £160 £150
148 **2** 3d. mauve/*green* (Sept) 35·00 20·00
a. Small "T" £160 85·00
149 3d. mauve/*blue* (Sept) 42·00 25·00
a. Small "T" £170 85·00

(*b*) *Fine roulette 15½ to 16.*
150 **1** 1d. red/*yellow* £350 £200
a. Small "T" £800 £550
b. Red/orange £750 £375
ba. Small "T"
151 **2** 3d. mauve/*green* £700 £225
a. Small "T"
152 3d. mauve/*blue* — £160
a. Small "T" — £600

(*c*) *Wide roulette 6½.*
153 **1** 1d. red/*yellow* £600 £600
a. Small "T"
b. Red/orange
154 **2** 3d. mauve/*green*
a. Small "T"
155 3d. mauve/*blue*

(*d*) Pin-perf about 17.
156 **1** 1d. red/*yellow* — £450
a. Small "T"
157 **2** 3d. mauve/*blue* — £600

SECOND REPUBLIC

Following the first Boer War the independence of the South African Republic was recognised by the Convention of Pretoria from 8 August 1881.

Nos. 133/9 remained valid and some values were available for postage until 1885.

EEN PENNY (17)

1882 (11 Aug). *No. 136 surch with T* **17**.
170 **9** 1d.on 4d. sage-green 11·00 4·2
a. Surch inverted £300 £20

Used examples of a similar, but larger, surcharge (width 20 mm) are known. These were previously considered to be forgeries, but it is now believed that some, at least, may represent a trial printing of the "EEN PENNY" surcharge.

(Typo J. F. Celliers)

1883 (20 Feb). *Re-issue of T* **1** *and* **2**. P 12.
171 **1** 1d. grey (*to* black) (Apr) 4·25 1·5
a. Imperf vert (horiz pair) £250
b. Imperf horiz (vert pair) £500 £32
172 **2** 3d. grey-black (*to* black)/*rose* 21·00 4·0
a. Bisected (1d.) (on cover) † £55
173 3d. pale red (Mar) 8·00 2·0
a. Bisected (1d.) (on cover) † £55
b. Imperf horiz (vert pair) † £100
c. Chestnut 22·00 3·5
ca. Imperf between (horiz pair) † —
d. Vermilion 22·00 4·5
174 **1** 1s. green (*to* deep) (July) 45·00 3·0
a. Bisected (6d.) (on cover) † £42
b. *Tête-bêche* (pair) £700 £12

Reprints are known of Nos. 172, 173, 173*b* and 173*c*. The paper of the first is *bright rose* in place of *dull rose*, and the impression is brownish black in place of grey-black to deep black. The reprints on white paper have the paper thinner than the originals, and the gum yellowish instead of white. The colour is a dull deep orange-red.

The used price quoted for No. 174b is for an example with telegraphic cancel. Postally used examples are worth much more. (See note below No. 139).

18

PERFORATIONS. Stamps perforated 11½ × 12 come from the first vertical row of sheets of the initial printing otherwise perforated 12½ × 12.

REPRINTS. Reprints of the general issues 1885–93, 1894–95, 1895–96 and 1896–97 exist in large quantities produced using the original plates from 1911 onwards. They cannot readily be distinguished from genuine originals except by comparison with used stamps, but the following general characteristics may be noted. The reprints are all perf 12½, large holes; the paper is whiter and thinner than that usually employed for the originals and the colours lack the lustre of those of the genuine stamps.

Forged surcharges have been made on these reprints.

(Des J. Vurtheim. Typo Enschedé)

1885 (13 Mar)–**93**. P 12½.
175 **18** ½d. grey (30.3.85) 40
a. Perf 13½ 4·75
b. Perf 12½ × 12 1·75
ba. Perf 11½ × 12 20·00 6·
176 1d. carmine 40
a. Perf 12½ × 12 70
aa. Perf 11½ × 12 12·00 2·
b. Rose 30
ba. Perf 12½ × 12 65
177 2d. brown-purple (P 12½ × 12) (9.85) 1·75 2·
178 2d. olive-bistre (14.4.87) 80
a. Perf 12½ × 12 3·75
179 2½d. mauve (*to* bright) (8.93) 1·75
180 3d. mauve (*to* bright) 1·75
a. Perf 12½ × 12 6·00
aa. Perf 11½ × 12 27·00 17·

4d. bronze-green 3·00 70
a. Perf 13½ 6·00 1·00
b. Perf 12½ × 12 13·00 80
ba. Perf 11½ × 12 £160 60·00
6d. pale dull blue 3·75 2·25
a. Perf 13½ 4·50 80
b. Perf 12½ × 12 5·50 30
ba. Perf 11½ × 12
1s. yellow-green 2·50 50
a. Perf 13½ 22·00 5·50
b. Perf 12½ × 12 7·50 55
2s.6d. orange-buff (*to* buff) (2.12.85) 4·25 1·75
a. Perf 12½ × 12 15·00 4·00
5s. slate (2.12.85) 6·00 3·00
a. Perf 12½ × 12 30·00 4·75
10s. dull chestnut (2.12.85) 30·00 6·50
a. yellow-brown (1891)
£5 dp grn (3.92)* (Optd "Monster" £150) £3250 £180

ingles of the 6d. pale dull blue imperforate have been reported d in 1893.

Most examples of No. 187 on the market are either forgeries or rints.

HALVE PENNY

(19)

5 (22 May–Aug). *Surch with T* **19**. *Reading up or down.*
2 ½d.on 3d. (No. 173) 3·75 9·00
1 ½d.on 1s. (No. 174) (Aug) 19·00 45·00
a. Tête-bêche (pair) £650 £300

Nos. 188/9 were surcharged by a setting of 40. After the left pane d been surcharged reading down, the sheets were turned so that right pane had the surcharges reading up.

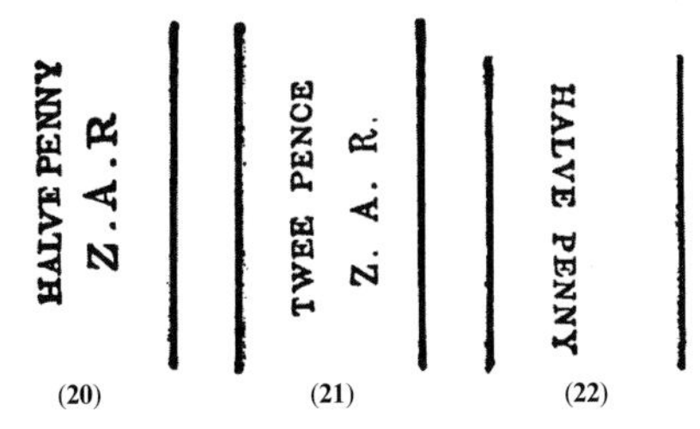

(20) (21) (22)

5 (1 Sept). *No. 137a surch with T* **20/1** *in red.*
9 ½d. on 6d. black-brown 50·00 80·00
2d. on 6d. black-brown 4·25 9·50

5 (28 Sept). *No. 180a surch with T* **22**.
18 ½d.on 3d. mauve 3·50 3·50
a. "PRNNY" (R. 6/6) 35·00 50·00
b. 2nd "N" inverted (R. 3/8) 75·00 90·00
c. Perf 11½ × 12 10·00 10·00

2d 2d

(23) (24)

7 (15 Jan). *No. 180a surch with T* **23/4**.
3 **18** 2d.on 3d. mauve (Type **23**) 6·50 6·50
a. Surch double — £225
b. Perf 11½ × 12 20·00 10·00
4 2d.on 3d. mauve (Type **24**) 1·25 2·50
a. Surch double — £160
b. Perf 11½ × 12 5·00 7·00

Nos. 193/4 were surcharged from the same setting of 60 (10 × 6) ich showed Type **24** on the top five horizontal rows and Type **23** the sixth horizontal row.

Halve Penny (25) 1 Penny (26)

2½ Pence (27) 2½ Pence (28)

Two types of surcharge:
A. Vertical distance between bars 12½ mm.
B. Distance 13½ mm.

1893. *T* **18** *surch.* P 12½.

(a) In red.

195 **25** ½d.on 2d. olive-bistre (A) (27 May) 80 1·25
a. Surch inverted 2·00 1·75
b. Surch Type B 1·50 1·75
ba. Surch inverted 4·75 8·00

(b) In black.

196 **25** ½d.on 2d. olive-bistre (A) (2 July) 85 1·00
a. Surch inverted 4·00 5·00
b. Extra surch on back inverted £150
c. Surch Type B 1·10 1·50
ca. Surch inverted 17·00 14·00
cb. Extra surch on back inverted £250
197 **26** 1d.on 6d. blue (A) (26 Jan) 50 60
a. Surch double 50·00 40·00
b. Surch inverted 1·40 1·75
c. Surch treble
d. Surch Type B 70 85
da. Surch inverted 4·50 3·25
db. Surch double — 70·00
e. Pair, one without surch £200
198 **27** 2½d.on 1s. green (A) (2 Jan) 1·00 3·00
a. "2/½d" for "2½" (R. 1/10) 30·00 40·00
b. Surch inverted 6·50 7·50
ba. Surch inverted and "2/½d" for "2½" £325 £275
c. Extra surch on back inverted £400 £400
d. Surch double, one inverted £600
e. Surch Type B 1·50 3·25
ea. Surch inverted 7·50 16·00
199 **28** 2½d.on 1s. green (A) (24 June) 3·75 3·75
a. Surch double 45·00 40·00
b. Surch inverted 7·00 7·00
c. Surch Type B 7·00 7·50
ca. Surch double 70·00 80·00
cb. Surch inverted 16·00 16·00

Surcharge Types **25/8** all show a similar setting of the horizontal bars at top and bottom. On horizontal rows 1 to 4 and 6, the bars are 12½ mm apart and on row 5 the distance is 13½ mm.

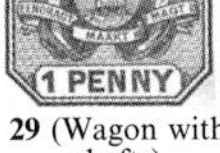

29 (Wagon with shafts)

30 (Wagon with pole)

1894 (July). P 12½.
200 **29** ½d. grey 60 30
201 1d. carmine 1·00 10
202 2d. olive-bistre 1·00 10
203 6d. pale dull blue 1·75 40
204 1s. yellow-green 9·50 12·00
For note *re* reprints, see below T **18**.

1895 (16 Mar)–**96**. P 12½.
205 **30** ½d. pearl-grey (1895) 60 10
a. Lilac-grey 60 10
206 1d. rose-red 60 10
207 2d. olive-bistre (1895) 70 10
208 3d. mauve (1895) 1·25 40
209 4d. olive-black (1895) 2·00 80
210 6d. pale dull blue (1895) 2·00 60
211 1s. yellow-green (18.3.95) 2·50 1·00
212 5s. slate (1896) 13·00 21·00
212*a* 10s. pale chestnut (1896) 13·00 4·25
205s/8s, 211s Optd "Monster" *Set of* 5 £150
For note *re* reprints, see below T **18**.

Halve Penny

(31)

1d. 1d.

(**32**—Round dot) (**32***a*—Square dot)

1895 (July–Aug). *Nos. 211 and 179 surch with T* **31/2**.
213 **30** ½d.on 1s. green (R.) 70 10
a. Surch spaced 1·50 1·00
b. "Pennij" for "Penny" (R. 6/6) 42·00 50·00
c. Surch inverted 3·75 4·50
d. Surch double 60·00 85·00
214 **18** 1d.on 2½d. bright mauve (G.) 50 10
a. Surch inverted 18·00 14·00
b. Surch double 60·00 60·00
c. Surch on back only 70·00
d. Surch Type **32***a* 1·50 1·25
da. Surch inverted 60·00
e. Surch treble £500

The normal space between "Penny" and the bars is 3 mm. On No. 213a, which comes from the fifth horizontal row of the setting, this is increased to 4 mm. Copies may be found in which one or both of the bars have failed to print.

Type **32***a* with square stop occurred on R. 3/3-4, 3/6-8, 4/4-5, 4/7-8, 4/10, 6/3, 6/7-8 and 6/10 of the setting of 60.

33

34

1895 (July). *Fiscal stamp optd* "POSTZEGEL". P 11½.
215 **33** 6d. bright rose (G.) 1·00 1·75
a. Imperf between (pair)
b. Opt inverted

(Litho The Press Printing and Publishing Works, Pretoria)

1895 (6 Sept). *Introduction of Penny Postage.* P 11.
215*c* **34** 1d. red (pale *to* deep) 1·50 1·75
ca. Imperf between (pair) 80·00 85·00
cb. Imperf vert (horiz pair)
cc. Imperf (pair)

1896–97. P 12½.
216 **30** ½d. green (1896) 60 10
217 1d. rose-red and green (1896) 60 10
218 2d. brown and green (2.97) 60 10
219 2½d. dull blue and green (6.96) 80 10
220 3d. purple and green (3.97) 1·50 1·75
221 4d. sage-green and green (3.97) 1·50 1·75
222 6d. lilac and green (11.96) 80 1·00
223 1s. ochre and green (3.96) 1·25 30
224 2s.6d. dull violet and green (6.96) 1·50 2·00
For note *re* reprints, see below T **18**.

SECOND BRITISH OCCUPATION

The Second Boer War began on 11 October 1899 and was concluded by the Peace of Vereeniging on 31 May 1902. Pretoria was occupied by the British on 5 June 1900 and a civilian postal service began operating thirteen days later.

FORGERIES. The forgeries of the "V.R.I." and "E.R.I." overprints most often met with can be recognised by the fact that the type used is perfect and the three stops are always in alignment with the bottom of the letters. In the genuine overprints, which were made from old type, it is impossible to find all three letters perfect and all three stops perfect and in exact alignment with the bottom of the letters.

V. R. I. (35) E. R. I. (36) E. R. I. Half Penny (37)

1900 (18 June). *Optd with T* **35**.
226 **30** ½d. green 30 20
a. No stop after "V" 10·00 10·00
b. No stop after "R" 8·00 8·00
c. No stop after "I" 6·50 6·50
d. Opt inverted 8·50 10·00
e. Opt double
f. "V.I.R." (R. 4/4) £500
227 1d. rose-red and green 30 20
a. No stop after "V" 10·00 10·00
b. No stop after "R" 8·00 8·00
c. No stop after "I" 5·00 5·00
d. Opt inverted 8·50 15·00
e. Opt double 60·00 75·00
f. No stops after "R" and "I" 65·00 65·00
g. Opt omitted (in pair with normal) £250
228 2d. brown and green 2·00 1·50
a. No stop after "V" 23·00 23·00
c. No stop after "I" 27·00 27·00
d. Opt inverted 15·00 17·00
e. Opt double
f. "V.I.R." (R. 4/4) £500 £550
g. Opt albino
229 2½d. dull blue and green 1·00 1·50
a. No stop after "V" 17·00 19·00
b. No stop after "R" 40·00 45·00
c. No stop after "I" 13·00 15·00
d. Opt inverted 9·00 10·00
230 3d. purple and green 1·00 1·25
a. No stop after "V" 20·00 22·00
b. No stop after "R" 40·00 45·00
c. No stop after "I" 26·00 29·00
d. Opt inverted 60·00 70·00
231 4d. sage-green and green 2·25 80
a. No stop after "V" 35·00 35·00
b. No stop after "R" 45·00 45·00
c. No stop after "I" 30·00 30·00
d. Opt inverted 22·00 25·00
f. "V.I.R." (R. 4/4) £500
232 6d. lilac and green 2·25 1·25
a. No stop after "V" 16·00 16·00
b. No stop after "R" 22·00 22·00
c. No stop after "I" 22·00 22·00
d. Opt inverted 24·00 28·00
233 1s. ochre and green 2·25 2·25
a. No stop after "V" 17·00 20·00
b. No stop after "R" 17·00 20·00
c. No stop after "I" 29·00 35·00
d. Opt inverted 28·00 35·00
e. Opt double 65·00 75·00
234 2s.6d. dull violet and green 3·00 7·50
a. No stop after "V" 30·00
b. No stop after "R" 65·00
c. No stop after "I" — £400
235 5s. slate 5·50 9·50
a. No stop after "V" 90·00
236 10s. pale chestnut 7·50 12·00
a. No stop after "V" 75·00
c. No stop after "I" 75·00

237 **18** £5 deep green* £1800 £750
a. No stop after "V" . . . .
234s/7s Optd "Specimen" *Set of* 4 . . . . £200

*Many examples of No. 237 on the market are forgeries and the stamps should only be purchased if accompanied by a recent expert committee certificate.

The error "V.I.R." occurred on R. 4/4 in the first batch of stamps to be overprinted—a few sheets of the ½d., 2d. and 4d. The error was then corrected and stamps showing it are very rare.

A number of different settings were used to apply the overprint to Nos. 226/37. The missing stop varieties listed above developed during overprinting and occur on different positions in the various settings.

1901 (Jan)–**02**. *Optd with T* **36**.

No.	Type	Description	Unused	Used
238	**30**	½d. green	50	85
		a. Opt double		
239		1d. rose-red and green (20.3.01)	50	10
		a. "E" of opt omitted	70·00	
240		3d. purple and green (6.02)	2·25	3·00
241		4d. sage-green and green (6.02)	2·25	3·00
242		2s.6d. dull violet and green (10.02)	7·50	15·00

1901 (July). *Surch with T* **37**.

No.	Type	Description	Unused	Used
243	**30**	½d.on 2d. brown and green	65	65
		a. No stop after "E" (R. 4/6)	45·00	

38 (POSTAGE REVENUE)

39 (POSTAGE POSTAGE)

(Typo D.L.R.)

1902 (1 Apr)–**03**. Wmk Crown CA. P 14.

No.	Type	Description	Unused	Used
244	**38**	½d. black and bluish green	1·50	20
		w. Wmk inverted	80·00	55·00
245		1d. black and carmine	1·25	15
		w. Wmk inverted	60·00	45·00
246		2d. black and purple	3·00	50
247		2½d. black and blue	5·50	1·25
		w. Wmk inverted	55·00	30·00
248		3d. black and sage-green (17.12.02)	5·50	50
249		4d. black and brown (17.12.02)	4·25	75
250		6d. black and orange-brown	3·75	60
251		1s. black and sage-green	10·00	8·50
252		2s. black and brown	35·00	38·00
253	**39**	2s.6d. magenta and black	14·00	9·50
254		5s. black and purple/*yellow*	23·00	24·00
255		10s. black and purple/*red*	50·00	26·00
244/55 *Set of* 12			£140	£100
244s/55s (*inc* 247ws) Optd "Specimen" *Set of* 12			£130	

The colour of the "black" centres varies from brownish grey or grey to black.

1903 (1 Feb). Wmk Crown CA. P 14.

No.	Type	Description	Unused	Used
256	**39**	1s. grey-black and red-brown	13·00	2·25
257		2s. grey-black and yellow	15·00	10·00
258		£1 green and violet	£180	£120
259		£5 orange-brown and violet	£1300	£600
256s/9s Optd "Specimen" *Set of* 4			£180	

1904–**09**. *Ordinary paper*. Wmk Mult Crown CA. P 14.

No.	Type	Description	Unused	Used
260	**38**	½d. black and bluish green	6·50	2·50
		w. Wmk inverted	85·00	55·00
		y. Wmk inverted and reversed	85·00	30·00
261		1d. black and carmine	3·75	20
262		2d. black and purple (*chalk-surfaced paper*) (1906)	8·00	75
263		2½d. black and blue (1905)	10·00	5·00
		a. Chalk-surfaced paper	10·00	2·25
264		3d. black & sage-green (*chalk-surfaced paper*) (1906)	3·50	30
265		4d. black and brown (*chalk-surfaced paper*) (1906)	4·75	70
		w. Wmk inverted	75·00	55·00
266		6d. black and orange (1905)	7·50	1·50
		a. Chalk-surfaced paper. *Black and brown-orange* (1906)	2·75	50
		w. Wmk inverted	85·00	65·00
267	**39**	1s. black and red-brown (1905)	6·50	50
268		2s. black and yellow (1906)	20·00	5·50
269		2s.6d. magenta and black (1909)	42·00	4·00
270		5s. black and purple/*yellow*	18·00	1·50
271		10s. black and purple/*red* (1907)	45·00	2·75
272		£1 green and violet (1908)	£180	26·00
		a. Chalk-surfaced paper	£170	16·00
260/72 *Set of* 13			£300	32·00

There is considerable variation in the "black" centres as in the previous issue.

1905–**09**. Wmk Mult Crown CA. P 14.

No.	Type	Description	Unused	Used
273	**38**	½d. yellow-green	1·75	10
		a. Deep green (1908)	2·50	20
		w. Wmk inverted	£110	65·00
274		1d. scarlet	1·25	10
		aw. Wmk inverted	—	£250
		b. Wmk Cabled Anchor, T **13** of Cape of Good Hope	—	£325
275		2d. purple (1909)	3·50	50
276		2½d. bright blue (1909)	12·00	4·50
273/6 *Set of* 4			17·00	4·50
273s/6s Optd "Specimen" *Set of* 4			60·00	

A 2d. grey, T **38**, was prepared for use but not issued. It exists overprinted "Specimen", *price* £130.

The monocoloured ½d. and 1d. are printed from new combined plates. These show a slight alteration in that the frame does not touch the crown.

The ½d., 1d. and 2d. exist from coils constructed from normal sheets for use in stamp machines introduced in 1911. These coils were originally joined horizontally but the 1d. was subsequently issued joined vertically.

Many of the King's Head stamps are found overprinted or perforated "C.S.A.R.", for use by the Central South African Railways.

STAMP BOOKLETS

1905 (July). *Black on red cover showing arms. Stapled.*
SB1 2s.7d. booklet containing thirty 1d. (No. 261) in blocks of 6 . . . . £2000

1905. *Black on red cover. Stapled.*
SB2 2s.7d. booklet containing thirty 1d. (No. 274) in blocks of 6 . . . . £2250

1909. *Black on red cover. Stapled.*
SB3 2s.6d. booklet containing ten ½d. (No. 273) in block of 6 and block of 4, and twenty-four 1d. (No. 274) in blocks of 6 . . . . £2750

Stocks of No. SB3 were supplied containing twelve examples of the ½d., it being intended that the postal clerks would remove two stamps before the booklets were sold. In some instances this did not occur.

POSTAL FISCAL STAMPS

1900–**02**. *Fiscal stamps as in T* **33**, *but optd with T* **35**. P 11½.

No.	Description	Unused	Used
F1	1d. pale blue	—	45·00
F2	6d. dull carmine	—	60·00
F3	1s. olive-bistre	—	75·00
F4	1s.6d. brown	—	90·00
F5	2s.6d. dull purple	—	£100

Nos. F1/5, previously listed as Nos. 1/5 of Volksrust, are fiscal issues which are known postally used from various Transvaal post offices between June 1900 and June 1902.

Other fiscal stamps are found apparently postally used, but these were used on telegrams not on postal matter.

POSTAGE DUE STAMPS

D 1

(Typo D.L.R.)

1907. Wmk Mult Crown CA. P 14.

No.	Type	Description	Unused	Used
D1	**D 1**	½d. black and blue-green	3·25	1·25
D2		1d. black and scarlet	4·00	85
D3		2d. brown-orange	4·00	1·25
D4		3d. black and blue	7·50	4·00
D5		5d. black and violet	2·00	12·00
		a. Inverted "p" for "d" (Right pane R. 10/6)	50·00	
D6		6d. black and red-brown	4·25	12·00
D7		1s. scarlet and black	9·00	8·50
D1/7 *Set of* 7			30·00	35·00

Transvaal became a province of the Union of South Africa on 31 May 1910.

PIETERSBURG

After the fall of Pretoria to the British in June 1900 the Transvaal government withdrew to the north of the country. Those post offices in areas not occupied by the British continued to function, but by early the following year supplies of stamps were exhausted. The following stamps were then authorised by the State Secretary and remained in use in some towns to early May 1901. Pietersburg itself was taken by British forces on 9 April.

PRICES. Genuinely used examples are very rare. Stamps cancelled by favour exist and are worth the same as the unused prices quoted.

The issued stamps are initialled by the Controller J. T. de V. Smit. All values exist without his signature and these are believed to come from remainders abandoned when the Boers evacuated Pietersburg.

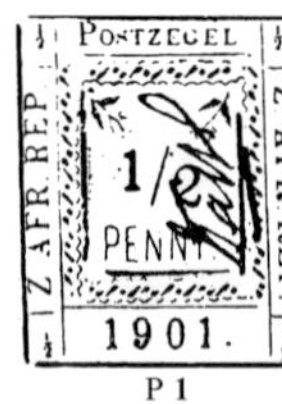

P 1

P 2

P 3

TYPES P 1/3. Each value was printed in sheets of 24 (6×4) of which the first two horizontal rows were as Type **P 1**, the third row as Type **P 2** and the fourth as Type **P 3**. The stamps were issued to post offices in blocks of 12.

(Type-set *De Zoutpansberg Wachter* Press, Pietersburg)

1901 (20 Mar (1d.)–3 Apr (others)). A. Imperf.

(a) Controller's initials in black.

No.	Type	Description	Unused
1	**P 1**	½d. black/*green*	15·00
		e. Controller's initials omitted	95·00
2	**P 2**	½d. black/*green*	45·00
		d. Controller's initials omitted	95·00
3	**P 3**	½d. black/*green*	45·00
		d. Controller's initials omitted	95·00
4	**P 1**	1d. black/*red*	3·50
5	**P 2**	1d. black/*red*	5·50
6	**P 3**	1d. black/*red*	7·00
7	**P 1**	2d. black/*orange*	6·00
8	**P 2**	2d. black/*orange*	14·00
9	**P 3**	2d. black/*orange*	22·00
10	**P 1**	4d. black/*blue*	5·50
11	**P 2**	4d. black/*blue*	9·50
12	**P 3**	4d. black/*blue*	32·00
13	**P 1**	6d. black/*green*	9·50
14	**P 2**	6d. black/*green*	15·00
15	**P 3**	6d. black/*green*	40·00
16	**P 1**	1s. black/*yellow*	8·00
17	**P 2**	1s. black/*yellow*	14·00
18	**P 3**	1s. black/*yellow*	25·00

(b) Controller's initials in red.

No.	Type	Description	Unused
19	**P 1**	½d. black/*green*	15·00
20	**P 2**	½d. black/*green*	35·00
21	**P 3**	½d. black/*green*	40·00

B. P 11½.

(a) Controller's initials in red.

No.	Type	Description	Unused
22	**P 1**	½d. black/*green*	5·50
		c. Imperf vert (horiz pair)	95·00
23	**P 2**	½d. black/*green*	17·00
		c. Imperf vert (horiz pair)	£120
24	**P 3**	½d. black/*green*	12·00
		b. Imperf vert (horiz pair)	£120

(b) Controller's initials in black.

No.	Type	Description	Unused
25	**P 1**	1d. black/*red*	2·00
		m. Imperf vert (horiz pair)	55·00
		n. Imperf between (vert pair: No. 25 + No. 26)	75·00
		o. Imperf horiz (vert pair)	55·00
26	**P 2**	1d. black/*red*	2·75
		f. Imperf vert (horiz pair)	80·00
		g. Imperf horiz (vert pair: No. 26 + No. 27)	60·00
27	**P 3**	1d. black/*red*	4·00
		f. Imperf vert (horiz pair)	80·00
28	**P 1**	2d. black/*orange*	5·50
29	**P 2**	2d. black/*orange*	8·00
30	**P 3**	2d. black/*orange*	14·00

For the ½d. the First printing had initials in either black or rec those of the Second printing had them in black and all of the Thir were in red.

CONSTANT VARIETIES

Rows 1 *and* 2 *are as Type* **P 1**, *Row* 3 *as Type* **P 2** *and Row* 4 *a Type* **P 3**.

½d. value
First printing—Imperf

Position	Variety	No.	Price
R.1/1	& 4 Top left "½" inverted, no stop after right "AFR"	(No. 19c)	70·(
R.1/2	Top right "½" inverted	(No. 19d)	90·(
R.1/3	"$\frac{1}{1}$" at lower right	(No. 19e)	90·(
R.1/5	"POSTZFGEL"	(No. 19f)	90·(
R.1/6	Left spray inverted, "AFB" at right	(No. 19g)	90·(
R.2/1	"REB" at left, left side of inner frame 3 mm too high	(No. 19h)	90·(
R.2/2	"BEP" at left	(No. 19i)	90·(
R.2/3	"POSTZEOEL"	(No. 19j)	90·(
R.2/4	"AER" at right, left side of inner frame 2 mm too high	(No. 19k)	90·(
R.2/5	No stop after date	(No. 19l)	90·(
R.2/6	No stop after "PENNY"	(No. 19m)	
R.3/1	"$\frac{1}{1}$" at top left, "PE" of "PENNY" spaced	(No. 20c)	90·(
R.3/2	Right spray inverted	(No. 20d)	90·(
R.3/3	Top left "½" inverted	(No. 20e)	90·(
R.3/4	No stop after "2" at left	(No. 20f)	
R.3/5	Centre figures "½" level	(No. 20g)	
R.3/6	"POSTZEGFL", no stop after right"AFR"	(No. 20h)	
R.4/3	"$\frac{1}{1}$" at top right	(No. 21b)	90·(
R.4/4	Lower left "½" inverted	(No. 21c)	90·(
R.4/5	"¼" at top left	(No. 21d)	90·(
R.4/6	Left spray inverted, "901" for "1901"	(No. 21e)	

This printing was produced first and was then adapted for th higher values.

Second printing

Position	Variety		No.	Price
R.1/2	No stop after left "AFR"	Imperf	(No. 1a)	60·(
R.1/3	"$\frac{1}{1}$" at top left, no bar over lower right"½"	Imperf	(No. 1b)	60·
R.1/6	No stop after date	Imperf	(No. 1c)	60·
R.2/5	"BEP" at left, no stop after date	Imperf	(No. 1d)	60·
R.3/3	"AFB" at left	Imperf	(No. 2a)	60·
		Perf	(No. 23a)	
R.3/4	"POSTZEGEI"	Imperf	(No. 2b)	60·
		Perf	(No. 23b)	
R.3/6	No bar over lower right "½"	Imperf	(No. 2c)	60·
R.4/1	No stop after right "AFR"	Imperf	(No. 3a)	60·
R.4/4	No stop after left "Z", no bar under top right "½"	Imperf	(No. 3b)	60·
		Perf	(No. 23c)	
R.4/5	"POSTZECEL AER" at left	Imperf	(No. 3c)	60·

rd printing

/4 No stop after right "AFR" . . . . Imperf (No. 19a) 70·00
Perf (No. 22a) 40·00
/1 Left side of inner frame too high Imperf (No. 19b) 70·00
Perf (No. 22b) 40·00
/5 Centre figures "½" level . . Imperf (No. 20a) 70·00
Perf (No. 23d) 40·00
/6 No stop after right "AFR" . . . . Imperf (No. 20b) 70·00
Perf (No. 23e) 40·00
/6 Hyphen between right "AFR" and "REP" . . . . Imperf (No. 21a) 70·00
Perf (No. 24a) 40·00

value
st printing

1/2 Inverted "1" at lower left, first "1" of date dropped . . . . . Imperf (No. 4a) 35·00
Perf (No. 25a) 22·00
1/3 No bar under top left "1" . . . . Imperf (No. 4b) 35·00
Perf (No. 25b) 22·00
1/4 No bar over lower right "1" . . . . Imperf (No. 4c) 35·00
Perf (No. 25c) 22·00
1/5 "POSTZFGEL" . . . . . Imperf (No. 4d) 35·00
Perf (No. 25d) 22·00
1/6 "AFB" at right . . . . . Imperf (No. 4e) 35·00
Perf (No. 25e) 22·00
2/1 "REB" at left . . . . . . Imperf (No. 4f) 35·00
Perf (No. 25f) 22·00
2/2 "BEP" at left . . . . . . Imperf (No. 4g) 35·00
Perf (No. 25g) 22·00
2/3 "POSTZEOEL" . . . . . Imperf (No. 4h) 35·00
Perf (No. 25h) 22·00
2/4 "AER" at right . . . . . Imperf (No. 4i) 35·00
Perf (No. 25i) 22·00
2/5 No stop after date . . . . Imperf (No. 4j) 35·00
Perf (No. 25j) 22·00
2/6 No stop after "PENNY" Imperf (No. 4k) 35·00
Perf (No. 25k) 22·00
3/2 Right spray inverted . . . Imperf (No. 5a) 35·00
Perf (No. 26a) 22·00
3/3 No bar over lower left "1" . . . . Imperf (No. 5b) 35·00
Perf (No. 26b) 22·00
3/4 No stop after left "Z" . . . Imperf (No. 5c) 35·00
Perf (No. 26c) 22·00
3/6 "POSTZEGFL", no stop after right "AFR" . . . . Imperf (No. 5d) 35·00
Perf (No. 26d) 22·00
4/1 No stop after right "AFR" . . . . Imperf (No. 6a) 35·00
Perf (No. 27a) 22·00
4/2 & 6 Left spray inverted . . Imperf (No. 6b) 22·00
Perf (No. 27b) 13·00
4/3 "POSTZEGEI" . . . . . Imperf (No. 6c) 35·00
Perf (No. 27c) 22·00
4/4 No bar under top right "1" . . . . Imperf (No. 6d) 35·00
Perf (No. 27d) 22·00

ond printing

/2 First "1" in date dropped Imperf (No. 4l) 35·00
Perf (No. 25l) 22·00
/6 No stop after right "AFR" . . . . Imperf (No. 5e) 35·00
Perf (No. 26e) 22·00
/5 Dropped "P" in "PENNY" . . . . Imperf (No. 6e) 35·00
Perf (No. 27e) 22·00

t has been suggested that there may have been a third printing.

value
st printing—Imperf

/1 "1" at lower right . . . . (No. 7a) 45·00
/2 No stop after left "AFR" (*on small part of printing*) . . . . (No. 7b) 90·00
/3 No bar over lower right "2" (*on small part of printing*) . . . . (No. 7c) 90·00
/3 "PENNY" for "PENCE" . . . . (No. 7d) 45·00
/5 "POSTZFGEL" . . . . (No. 7e) 45·00
/6 "AFB" at right . . . . (No. 7f) 45·00
2/1 "REB" at left . . . . (No. 7g) 45·00
2/2 "AFB" at left . . . . (No. 7h) 45·00
2/3 "POSTZEOEL" . . . . (No. 7i) 45·00
2/4 "AER" at right . . . . (No. 7j) 45·00
2/5 No stop after date . . . . . . (No. 7k) 45·00
2/6 No stop after date, vertical line after "POSTZEGEL" . . . . (No. 7l) 45·00
3/2 Right spray inverted . . . . . (No. 8a) 45·00
3/3 No bar over lower left "2" . . . . (No. 8b) 45·00
3/4 Centre "2" inverted, no stop after left "Z" . . . . (No. 8c) 45·00
3/6 "POSTZEGFL", no stop after right "AFR" . . . . (No. 8d) 45·00
4/1 Centre "2" wider, no stop after right "AFR" (*occurs on second printing also*) . . . . (No. 9a) 38·00
4/2 Centre "2" wider, left spray inverted . . . . (No. 9b) 45·00
4/3 "POSTZEGEI" . . . . (No. 9c) 45·00
4/4 No bar under top right "2" . . . . (No. 9d) 45·00
4/5 "1" at lower left, "P" in "PENCE" dropped . . . . (No. 9e) 45·00
4/6 Left spray inverted . . . . (No. 9f) 45·00

ond printing

/2 First "1" in date dropped Imperf (No. 7m) 45·00
Perf (No. 28a) 30·00
2/1 No stop after left "REP" Imperf (No. 7n) 45·00
Perf (No. 28b) 30·00
3/4 No stop after left "Z" . . . Imperf (No. 8e) 45·00

R.3/6 No stop after right "AFR" . . . . Imperf (No. 8f) 45·00
Perf (No. 29a) 30·00
R.4/1 Centre 2 wider, no stop after right "AFR" (*occurs on first printing also*) Imperf (No. 9a) 38·00
Perf (No. 30a) 30·00
R.4/2 Centre "2" wider . . . . . Imperf (No. 9g) 45·00
Perf (No. 30b) 30·00
R.4/5 "P" in "PENCE" dropped . . . . Imperf (No. 9h) 45·00
Perf (No. 30c) 30·00

It has been suggested that there was a third printing of this value.

4d. value
First printing

R.1/2 No stop after left "AFR" . . . . . (No. 10a) 45·00
R.1/3 No bar over lower right "4" . . . . (No. 10b) 45·00
R.1/3 "PENNY" for "PENCE" (*on small part of printing*) . . . . (No. 10c) 90·00
R.1/5 "POSTZFGEL" . . . . (No. 10d) 45·00
R.1/6 "AFB" at right . . . . (No. 10e) 45·00
R.2/1 "REB" at left . . . . (No. 10f) 45·00
R.2/2 "AFB" at left . . . . (No. 10g) 45·00
R.2/3 "POSTZEOEL" . . . . (No. 10h) 45·00
R.2/4 "AER" at right . . . . (No. 10i) 45·00
R.2/5 No stop after date . . . . (No. 10j) 45·00
R.3/2 Right spray inverted . . . . . . (No. 11a) 45·00
R.3/3 No bar over lower left "4" (*on small part of printing*) . . . . (No. 11b) 90·00
R.3/4 No stop after left "Z" . . . . . . (No. 11c) 45·00
R.3/6 "POSTZEGFL" . . . . (No. 11d) 45·00
R.4/1 Centre "4" wider, no stop after right "AFR" . . . . (No. 12a) 45·00
R.4/2 Centre "4" wider, left spray inverted . . . . (No. 12b) 45·00
R.4/3 "POSTZEGEI" . . . . (No. 12c) 45·00
R.4/4 No bar under top right "4" . . . . (No. 12d) 45·00
R.4/5 "AER" at left, "P" in "PENCE" dropped . . . . (No. 12e) 45·00
R.4/6 Left spray inverted . . . . (No. 12f) 45·00

Second printing

R.2/1 Left inner frame too high . . . . (No. 10k) 45·00
R.4/1–2 Centre "4" wider . . . . (No. 12g) 35·00
R.4/5 "P" in "PENCE" dropped . . . . (No. 12h) 45·00

6d. value
First printing

R.1/2 No stop after left "AFR" . . . . . (No. 13a) 55·00
R.1/3 No bar over lower right "6" . . . . (No. 13b) 55·00
R.1/3 "PENNY" for "PENCE" (*on small part of printing*) . . . . (No. 13c) £100
R.1/5 "POSTZFGEL" . . . . (No. 13d) 55·00
R.1/6 "AFB" at right . . . . (No. 13e) 55·00
R.2/1 "REB" at left . . . . (No. 13f) 55·00
R.2/2 "AFB" at left . . . . (No. 13g) 55·00
R.2/3 "POSTZEOEL" . . . . (No. 13h) 55·00
R.2/4 "AER" at right . . . . (No. 13i) 55·00
R.2/5 No stop after date . . . . (No. 13j) 55·00
R.3/2 Right spray inverted . . . . . . (No. 14a) 55·00
R.3/4 Centre "6" inverted, no stop after left "Z" (*on small part of printing*) . . . (No. 14b) £100
R.3/4 No stop after left "Z" . . . . . . (No. 14c) 55·00
R.3/6 "POSTZEGFL" . . . . (No. 14d) 55·00
R.4/1 Centre "6" wider, no stop after right "AFR" . . . . (No. 15a) 55·00
R.4/2 Centre "6" wider, left spray inverted . . . . (No. 15b) 55·00
R.4/3 "POSTZEGEI" . . . . (No. 15c) 55·00
R.4/4 No bar under top right "6" . . . . (No. 15d) 55·00
R.4/5 "AER" at left. "P" in "PENCE" dropped . . . . (No. 15e) 55·00
R.4/6 Left spray inverted . . . . (No. 15f) 55·00

Second printing

R.2/1 Left inner frame too high, no stop after left "REP" . . . . (No. 13k) 55·00
R.4/1–2 Centre "6" wider . . . . (No. 15g) 40·00
R.4/5 "P" in "PENCE" dropped . . . (No. 15h) 55·00

1s. value

R.1/2 No stop after left "AFR" . . . . . (No. 16a) 40·00
R.1/3 No bar over lower right "1" . . . . (No. 16b) 40·00
R.2/5 No stop after date . . . . (No. 16c) 40·00
R.3/3 Centre "1" inverted (*on small part of printing*) . . . . (No. 17a)
R.3/4 "POSTZEGEI", no stop after left "Z" . . . . (No. 17b) 40·00
R.4/1 No stop after right "AFR" . . . . . (No. 18a) 40·00
R.4/4 No bar under top right "1" . . . . (No. 18b) 40·00
R.4/5 "AER" at left . . . . (No. 18c) 40·00

LOCAL BRITISH OCCUPATION ISSUES DURING THE SOUTH AFRICAN WAR 1900–2

Stamps of the Transvaal Republic, unless otherwise stated, variously overprinted or surcharged.

LYDENBURG

Lydenburg fell to the British on 6 September 1900.

V.R.I.
3d.
(L 1)

1900 (Sept). *Nos. 215b and 217 surch as Type* L **1**, *others optd "V.R.I." only.*

1	**30**	½d. green	£110	£120
2		1d. rose-red and green	£100	£100
2*a*	**34**	1d.on 1d. red		
3	**30**	2d. brown and green	£1000	£750
4		2½d. blue and green	£1900	£850
5		3d.on 1d. rose-red and green	85·00	80·00
6		3d. purple and green		
7		4d. sage-green and green	£2500	£750
8		6d. lilac and green	£2000	£700
9		1s. ochre and green	£3750	£2500

The above were cancelled by British Army postal service postmarks. These overprints with Transvaal cancellations are believed to be forgeries.

RUSTENBURG

The British forces in Rustenburg, west of Pretoria, were besieged by the Boers during June 1900. When relieved on the 22 June 1900 no "V.R.I" stamps were available so a local handstamp was applied.

V.R.
(R 1)

1900 (23 June). *Handstamped with Type* R **1** *in violet.*

1	**30**	½d. green	£130	95·00
2		1d. rose-red and green	95·00	75·00
3		2d. brown and green	£275	£110
4		2½d. blue and green	£160	95·00
5		3d. purple and green	£200	£120
6		6d. lilac and green	£1000	£325
7		1s. ochre and green	£1500	£700
8		2s.6d. dull violet and green	£8500	£4250
		a. Handstamp in black	†	£7500

Nos. 2 and 5 exist with the handstamp inverted.

SCHWEIZER RENECKE

BESIEGED
(SR 1)

1900 (Sept). *Handstamped with Type* SR **1** *in black, reading vert up or down.*

(a) On stamps of Transvaal.

1	**30**	½d. green	†	£250
2		1d. rose-red and green	†	£250
3		2d. brown and green	†	£325
4		6d. lilac and green	†	£900

(b) On stamps of Cape of Good Hope.

5	**17**	½d. green	†	£425
6		1d. carmine	†	£425

Schweizer Renecke, near the Bechuanaland border, was under siege from 1 August 1900 to 9 January 1901. The British commander authorised the above stamps shortly after 19 August. All stamps were cancelled with the dated circular town postmark ("Schweizer Renecke, Z.A.R."), usually after having been stuck on paper before use. Unused, without the postmark, do not exist.

No. 4 exists with double handstamp.

WOLMARANSSTAD

A British party occupied this town in the south-west of the Transvaal from 15 June to 27 July 1900. Transvaal stamps, to a face value of £5 2s.6d., were found at the local firm of Thos. Leask and Co. and surcharged as below. The first mail left on 24 June and the last on 21 July.

Cancelled **V-R-I.** (L 3)   *Cancelled* **V-R-I.** (L 4)

1900 (24 June). *Optd with Type* L **3**.

1	**30**	½d. green (B.)	£225	£350
		a. Opt inverted	£700	
		b. Opt in black		
1*c*		½d.on 1s. green (B.)		
2		1d. rose-red and green (B.)	£150	£250
		a. Opt in green	£1800	
		b. Opt in black		
3		2d. brown and green (B.)	£1800	£1800
		a. Opt in black	£3000	
4		2½d. blue and green (R.)	£1800	
		a. Opt in blue	£2750	£2750
		b. Opt in black		
5		3d. purple and green (B.)	£3000	£3250
6		4d. sage-green and green (B.)	£3750	£4250
7		6d. lilac and green (B.)	£4000	£4250
8		1s. ochre and green (B.)	—	£7500

The two lines of the overprint were handstamped separately. The ½d. exists with two impressions of the "Cancelled" handstamp, the 2½d. with two impressions of "V-R-I", one in red and one in blue and the 3d. with "Cancelled" in green and "V.R.I." in blue.

1900 (24 June). *Optd with Type* L **4**.

9	**34**	1d. red (B.)	£150	£275

The ½d., 1d. and 3d. in Type **30** are also known with this overprint.

VII. ZULULAND

Zululand remained an independent kingdom until annexed by Great Britain on 19 May 1887 when it was declared a Crown Colony.

The first European postal service was operated by a Natal postal agency at Eshowe opened in 1876 which cancelled Natal stamps with a "No. 56 P.O. Natal" postmark. The agency closed during the Zulu War of 1879 and did not re-open until 1885 when a Eshowe postmark was provided. "ZULULAND" was added to the cancellation in 1887 and stamps of Natal continued to be used until replaced by the overprinted series on 1 May 1888.

PRICES FOR STAMPS ON COVER		
Nos.	1/2	*from* × 100
Nos.	3/10	*from* × 20
No.	11	—
Nos.	12/16	*from* × 20
Nos.	20/3	*from* × 30
No.	24	*from* × 20
Nos.	25/6	*from* × 12
Nos.	27/9	—
No.	F1	*from* × 100

ZULULAND (1) ZULULAND. (2)

1888 (1 May)–**93**.

(a) Nos. 173, 180, 197, 200/2, 205a, 207a/8, 209 and 211 of Great Britain (Queen Victoria) optd with T **1** *by D.L.R.*

1	½d. vermilion (11.88)	3·25	2·50
2	1d. deep purple	25·00	3·75
3	2d. grey-green and carmine	13·00	25·00
4	2½d. purple/*blue* (9.91)	22·00	20·00
5	3d. purple/*yellow*	25·00	22·00
6	4d. green and deep brown	42·00	55·00
7	5d. dull purple and blue (3.93)	90·00	£120
	w. Wmk inverted	†	—
8	6d. purple/*rose-red*	13·00	17·00
9	9d. dull purple and blue (4.92)	90·00	90·00
10	1s. dull green (4.92)	£110	£130
11	5s. rose (4.92)	£500	£600
1/11 *Set of* 11		£800	£950
1s/11s (*ex* 1d.) H/S "Specimen" *Set of* 10		£600	

(b) No. 97a of Natal optd with T **2** *at Pietermaritzburg*

12	½d. dull green (with stop) (7.88)	55·00	75·00
	a. Opt double	£1000	£1100
	b. Opt inverted	£1200	
	d. Opt omitted (vert pair with normal)	£5500	
13	½d. dull green (without stop)	23·00	38·00
	a. Opt double	£1400	£1500

1893 (29 Nov*). *T* **15** *of Natal optd with T* **1** *by D.L.R. (*Wmk Crown CA. P 14*).*
16 6d. dull purple . . . 55·00 55·00
*Earliest known date of use. No. 16 was, apparently, originally supplied in 1889 for fiscal purposes.

3 4

(Typo D.L.R.)

1894 (18 Apr)–**96**. Wmk Crown CA. P 14.

20	**3**	½d. dull mauve and green	3·25	4·25
		w. Wmk inverted	£130	£140
21		1d. dull mauve and carmine	5·00	1·75
22		2½d. dull mauve and ultramarine	14·00	8·50
23		3d. dull mauve and olive-brown	8·00	3·00
24	**4**	6d. dull mauve and black	20·00	20·00
25		1s. green	38·00	38·00
26		2s.6d. green and black (2.96)	75·00	85·00
27		4s. green and carmine	£110	£150
28		£1 purple/*red*	£450	£550
29		£5 purple and black/*red*	£4500	£1500
		s. Optd "Specimen"	£400	
20/8 *Set of* 9			£650	£750
20s/8s Optd "Specimen" *Set of* 9			£350	

Dangerous forgeries exist of the £1 and £5.

FISCAL STAMP USED FOR POSTAGE

1891 (5 May*). *Fiscal stamp of Natal optd with T* **1**. Wmk Crown CA. P 14.

F1	1d. dull mauve	3·00	3·00
	a. Top left triangle detached	£110	£110
	s. Handstamped "Specimen"	60·00	

*Earliest known date of postal use. A proclamation published in the *Natal Government Gazette* on 27 June 1891 authorised the use of this stamp for postal purposes, but it is clear from the wording that such use had already commenced.

For illustration of "top left triangle detached" variety see above No. 21 of Antigua.

Other values, 1s. to £20 as No. F1 exist apparently with postmarks, but, as these were never authorised for postal use, they are no longer listed.

Zululand was annexed to Natal on 31 December 1897 and its stamps were withdrawn from sale on 30 June 1898.

VIII. BRITISH ARMY FIELD OFFICES DURING SOUTH AFRICAN WAR, 1899–1902

Z 1

Z 2

Stamps of GREAT BRITAIN *used by British Army Field Offices in South Africa cancelled as Types* Z **1**, Z **2** *or similar postmarks.*

1881. *Stamp of Queen Victoria.*
Z1 1d. lilac (16 *dots*) . . . 5·00

1883–84. *Stamps of Queen Victoria*

Z1*a*	2s.6d lilac	£200
Z2	5s. rose	£200
Z2*a*	10s. ultramarine	£400

1887–92. *Stamps of Queen Victoria.*

Z3	½d. vermilion	6·00
Z4	1½d. dull purple and green	20·00
Z5	2d. grey-green and carmine	14·00
Z6	2½d. purple/*blue*	6·00
Z7	3d. purple/*yellow*	12·00
Z8	4d. green and brown	16·00
Z9	4½d. green and carmine	48·00
Z10	5d. dull purple and blue (Die II)	14·00
Z11	6d. purple/*rose-red*	11·00
Z12	9d. dull purple and blue	50·00
Z13	10d. dull purple and carmine	48·00
Z14	1s. dull green	70·00
Z15	£1 green	£750

1900. *Stamps of Queen Victoria.*

Z16	½d. blue-green	6·00
Z17	1s. green and carmine	£130

1902. *Stamps of King Edward VII.*

Z18	½d. blue-green	7·00
Z19	1d. scarlet	5·00
Z20	1½d. purple and green	
Z21	2d. yellowish green and carmine-red	
Z22	2½d. ultramarine	10·00
Z23	3d. purple/*orange-yellow*	
Z24	4d. green and grey-brown	
Z25	5d. dull purple and ultramarine	
Z26	6d. pale dull purple	15·00
Z27	9d. dull purple and ultramarine	
Z28	10d. dull purple and carmine	
Z29	1s. dull green and carmine	

ARMY OFFICIAL STAMPS

1896–1901. *Stamps of Queen Victoria optd "*ARMY OFFICIAL*".*

ZO1	½d. vermilion	£100
ZO2	½d. blue-green	£100
ZO3	1d. lilac (16 *dots*)	85·00
ZO4	6d. purple/*rose-red*	

IX. UNION OF SOUTH AFRICA

The province continued to use their existing issues until the introduction of Nos. 3/17. From 19 August 1910 the issues of any province were valid for use throughout the Union until they were demonetised on 31 December 1937.

PRICES FOR STAMPS ON COVER TO 1945		
Nos.	1/15	*from* × 4
Nos.	16/17	—
Nos.	18/21	*from* × 6
Nos.	26/32	*from* × 2
No.	33	*from* × 4
Nos.	34/110	*from* × 1
Nos.	D1/7	*from* × 4
Nos.	D8/33	*from* × 6
Nos.	O1/33	*from* × 4

1

(Des H. S. Wilkinson. Recess D.L.R.)

1910 (4 Nov). *Opening of Union Parliament. Inscribed bilingually.* Wmk Multiple Rosettes. P 14.

1	**1**	2½d. deep blue	3·00	3·00
		s. Handstamped "Specimen"	£350	
2		2½d. blue	1·75	1·40

The deep blue shade is generally accompanied by a blueing of the paper.

No. 1s. has the overprint in italic capital and lower case letters which measure 12½ mm in length.

2

3

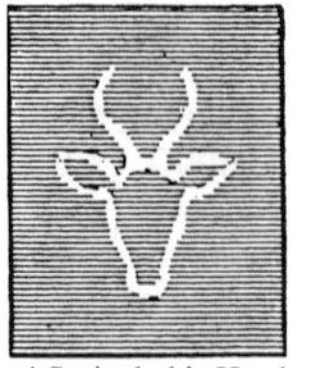
4 Springbok's Head

(Typo D.L.R.)

1913 (1 Sept)–**24**. *Inscribed bilingually.* W **4**.

(a) P 14.

3	**2**	½d. green	1·25	30
		a. Stamp doubly printed	£10000	
		b. Blue-green	2·00	20
		c. Yellow-green	2·50	80
		d. Printed on the gummed side	£600	
		w. Wmk inverted	2·00	70
4		1d. rose-red (*shades*)	1·50	
		a. Carmine-red	2·25	
		b. *Scarlet* (*shades*)	2·50	
		c. Printed on the gummed side	£600	
		w. Wmk inverted	2·50	
5		1½d. chestnut (*shades*) (23.8.20)	80	
		a. *Tête-bêche* (pair)	1·75	
		b. Printed on the gummed side	£650	
		c. Wmk sideways	†	£1
		w. Wmk inverted	80	
6	**3**	2d. dull purple	1·75	
		a. Deep purple	2·50	
		b. Printed on the gummed side	£650	
		w. Wmk inverted	3·25	
7		2½d. bright blue	3·75	
		a. Deep blue	5·50	
		w. Wmk inverted	65·00	
8		3d. black and orange-red	9·50	
		a. Black and dull orange-red	10·00	
		w. Wmk inverted	17·00	
9		3d. ultramarine (*shades*) (4.10.22)	3·50	
		w. Wmk inverted	9·00	
10		4d. orange-yellow and olive-green	9·00	
		a. Orange-yellow and sage-green	6·50	
		w. Wmk inverted	8·00	
11		6d. black and violet	5·50	
		a. Black and bright violet	9·00	
		aw. Wmk inverted	16·00	
12		1s. orange	16·00	
		a. Orange-yellow	25·00	
		w. Wmk inverted	18·00	
13		1s.3d. violet (*shades*) (1.9.20)	13·00	
		w. Wmk inverted	90·00	
14		2s.6d. purple and green	55·00	
15		5s. purple and blue	£110	
		a. Reddish purple and light blue	£110	
		w. Wmk inverted	£2750	£1
16		10s. deep blue and olive-green	£180	
		w. Wmk inverted	£4000	£1
17		£1 green and red (7.16)	£600	
		a. Pale olive-green and red (1924)	£800	£1
3/17 *Set of* 15			£900	
3s/8s, 10s/17s Optd or H/S (1½d. and 1s.3d. in violet, £1 in green) "Specimen" *Set of* 14			£1300	

(b) Coil stamps. P 14 × imperf.

18	**2**	½d. green	6·00	
		w. Wmk inverted	£450	
19		1d. rose-red (13.2.14)	10·00	
		a. Scarlet	14·00	
		w. Wmk inverted	£450	
20		1½d. chestnut (15.11.20)	11·00	
		w. Wmk inverted		†
21	**3**	2d. dull purple (7.10.21)	13·00	
18/21 *Set of* 4			35·00	

The 6d. exists with "Z" of "ZUID" wholly or partly missing to wear of plate (*Price wholly missing*, £80 *un*, £38 *us*).

5 De Havilland D.H.9 Biplane

(Eng A. J. Cooper. Litho *Cape Times* Ltd)

1925 (26 Feb). *Air. Inscr bilingually.* P 12.

26	**5**	1d. carmine	3·75
27		3d. ultramarine	7·00
28		6d. magenta	9·00
29		9d. green	23·00
26/9 *Set of* 4			38·00

Beware of forgeries of all values perforated 11, 11½ or 13.

INSCRIPTIONS. From 1926 until 1951 most issues were inscri in English and Afrikaans alternately throughout the sheets.

PRICES for Nos. 30/135 are for unused horizontal pairs, used horizontal pairs and used singles (either inscription), *unless otherwise indicated.* Vertical pairs are worth between 25% and 40% of the prices quoted for horizontal pairs.

6 Springbok

7 *Dromedaris*(Van Riebeeck's ship)

8 Orange Tree

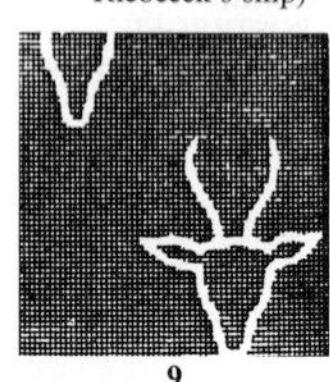
9

(Typo Waterlow until 1927, thereafter Govt Printer, Pretoria

1926 (2 Jan)–**27**. W **9**. P 14½ × 14.

			Un pair	Used pair	Used single
30	6	½d. black and green	3·00	4·00	10
		a. Missing "1" in "½"	£2000		
		b. Centre omitted (in pair with normal)	£1400		
		cw. Wmk inverted	4·00	4·25	
		d. Frame printed double	£2000		
		e. Perf 13½ × 14 (1927)	60·00	60·00	4·00
		ea. *Tête-bêche* (pair)	£850		
		ew. Wmk inverted	60·00	60·00	
31	7	1d. black and carmine	2·00	50	10
		a. Imperf (vert pair)*	£650		
		b. Imperf 3 sides (vert pair)*	£650	£700	
		cw. Wmk inverted	5·00	1·50	
		d. Perf 13½ × 14 (1927)	85·00	70·00	4·00
		da. *Tête-bêche* (pair)	£950		
		dw. Wmk inverted	85·00	70·00	
		e. Wmk sideways	£2000	£2000	
32	8	6d. green and orange (1.5.26)	38·00	42·00	1·50
		w. Wmk inverted	70·00	75·00	
30/2		*Set of* 3	40·00	42·00	1·50

No. 30a exists in Afrikaans only. Nos. 30e and 31d were only issued in booklets.

No. 30d occurred on the bottom left-hand corner of one sheet and included the bottom four stamps in the first vertical row and the bottom two in the second. As listed No. 30d shows the left-hand stamp with the frame completely double and the right-hand stamp with two-thirds of the frame double.

*Both Nos. 31a and 31b occur in blocks of four with the other vertical pair imperforate at left.

For ½d. with pale grey centre, see No. 126.

For rotogravure printing see Nos. 42, etc.

10 "Hope"

(Recess B.W.)

1926 (2 Jan). *T* **10**. *Inscribed in English or Afrikaans.* W **9** (upright or inverted in equal quantities).

		Single stamps	
33	4d. grey-blue (English inscr) (*shades*)	1·75	1·25
	a. Inscr in Afrikaans	1·75	1·25

In this value the English and Afrikaans inscriptions are on separate sheets.

This stamp is known with private perforations or roulettes.

11 Union Buildings, Pretoria

12 Groot Schuur

12a A Native Kraal

13 Black and Blue Wildebeest

14 Ox-wagon inspanned

15 Ox-wagon outspanned

16 Cape Town and Table Bay

(Recess B.W.)

1927 (1 Mar)–**30**. W **9**. P 14.

			Un pair	Used Pair	Used single
	11	2d. grey and maroon	11·00	21·00	60
		aw. Wmk inverted	£350	£400	
		b. Perf 14 × 13½ (2.30)	24·00	24·00	70
	12	3d. black and red	15·00	26·00	60
		a. Perf 14 × 13½ (1930)	55·00	60·00	80
	12a	4d. brown (23.3.28)	24·00	50·00	1·00
		bw. Wmk inverted	£500	£450	
		c. Perf 14 × 13½ (1930)	42·00	55·00	1·25
	13	1s. brown and deep blue	29·00	55·00	1·00
		a. Perf 14 × 13½ (1930)	55·00	70·00	1·25
	14	2s.6d. green and brown	£110	£325	17·00
		a. Perf 14 × 13½ (1930)	£250	£400	22·00
	15	5s. black and green	£225	£650	35·00
		a. Perf 14 × 13½ (1930)	£350	£750	40·00
	16	10s. bright blue and brown	£150	£130	10·00
		a. Centre inverted (*single stamp*)	£9500		
		b. Perf 14 × 13½ (1930)	£180	£150	11·00
9		*Set of* 7	£500	£1100	55·00
/9s		H/S "Specimen" *Set of* 7	£850		

17 De Havilland D.H.60 Cirrus Moth

(Typo Govt Ptg Wks, Pretoria)

1929 (16 Aug). *Air. Inscribed bilingually.* No wmk. P 14 × 13½.

			Un single	Us single
40	**17**	4d. green	5·50	2·50
41		1s. orange	16·00	13·00

PRINTER. All the following issues, except *where stated otherwise*, are printed by rotogravure (the design having either plain lines or a dotted screen) by the Government Printer, Pretoria.

I

II

The two types of the 1d. differ in the spacing of the horizontal lines in the side panels:—Type I close; Type II wide. The Afrikaans had the spacing of the words POSSEEL-INKOMSTE close in Type I and more widely spaced in Type II.

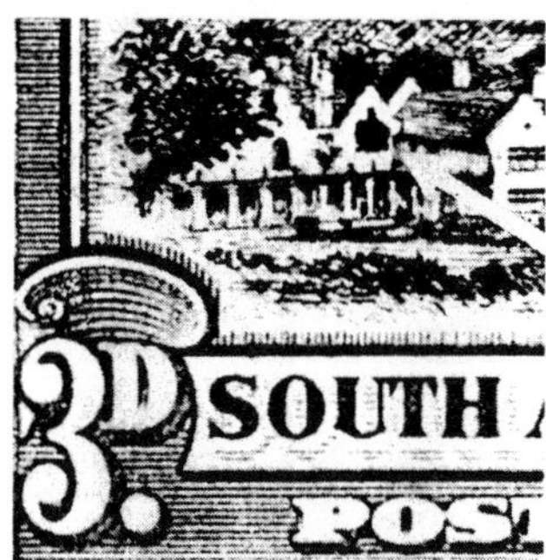

Window flaw (R. 20/4 on all ptgs before 1937)

Spear flaw (R. 9/2)

"Monkey" in tree (R. 2/2)

Twisted horn (Cyl 7020 R. 1/5)

1930–45. *T* **6** *to* **8** *and* **11** *to* **14** *redrawn, "SUIDAFRIKA" (in one word) on Afrikaans stamps.* W **9**. P 15 × 14 (½d., 1d., and 6d.) or 14.

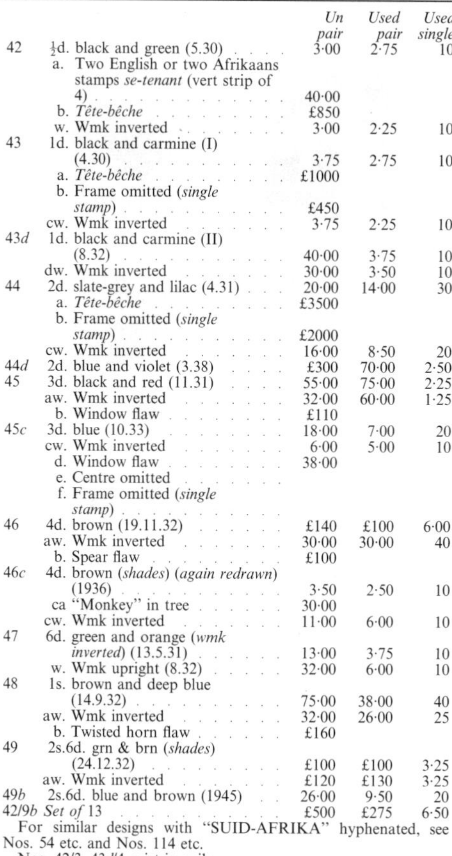

		Un pair	Used pair	Used single
42	½d. black and green (5.30)	3·00	2·75	10
	a. Two English or two Afrikaans stamps *se-tenant* (vert strip of 4)	40·00		
	b. *Tête-bêche*	£850		
	w. Wmk inverted	3·00	2·25	10
43	1d. black and carmine (I) (4.30)	3·75	2·75	10
	a. *Tête-bêche*	£1000		
	b. Frame omitted (*single stamp*)	£450		
	cw. Wmk inverted	3·75	2·25	10
43*d*	1d. black and carmine (II) (8.32)	40·00	3·75	10
	dw. Wmk inverted	30·00	3·50	10
44	2d. slate-grey and lilac (4.31)	20·00	14·00	30
	a. *Tête-bêche*	£3500		
	b. Frame omitted (*single stamp*)	£2000		
	cw. Wmk inverted	16·00	8·50	20
44*d*	2d. blue and violet (3.38)	£300	70·00	2·50
45	3d. black and red (11.31)	55·00	75·00	2·25
	aw. Wmk inverted	32·00	60·00	1·25
	b. Window flaw	£110		
45*c*	3d. blue (10.33)	18·00	7·00	20
	cw. Wmk inverted	6·00	5·00	10
	d. Window flaw	38·00		
	e. Centre omitted			
	f. Frame omitted (*single stamp*)			
46	4d. brown (19.11.32)	£140	£100	6·00
	aw. Wmk inverted	30·00	30·00	40
	b. Spear flaw	£100		
46*c*	4d. brown (*shades*) (*again redrawn*) (1936)	3·50	2·50	10
	ca "Monkey" in tree	30·00		
	cw. Wmk inverted	11·00	6·00	10
47	6d. green and orange (*wmk inverted*) (13.5.31)	13·00	3·75	10
	w. Wmk upright (8.32)	32·00	6·00	10
48	1s. brown and deep blue (14.9.32)	75·00	38·00	40
	aw. Wmk inverted	32·00	26·00	25
	b. Twisted horn flaw	£160		
49	2s.6d. grn & brn (*shades*) (24.12.32)	£100	£100	3·25
	aw. Wmk inverted	£120	£130	3·25
49*b*	2s.6d. blue and brown (1945)	26·00	9·50	20
42/9*b*	*Set of* 13	£500	£275	6·50

For similar designs with "SUID-AFRIKA" hyphenated, see Nos. 54 etc. and Nos. 114 etc.

Nos. 42/3, 43*d*/4 exist in coils.

No. 42a comes from the coil printing on the cylinder for which two horizontal rows were incorrectly etched so that two Afrikaans-inscribed stamps were followed by two English. This variety is normally without a coil join, although some examples do occur showing a repair join.

The 1d. (Type I) exists without watermark from a trial printing (*Price* £25 *un*).

Although it appears to be printed in one colour No. 45*c* was produced from vignette and frame cylinders in the same way as the bicoloured version. The clouds in the background, which are present on No. 45e, were printed from the frame cylinder.

Nos. 45b, 45d, 46b and 48b all occur on printings with either upright or inverted watermark. The price quoted is for the cheapest version in each instance.

The Rotogravure printings may be distinguished from the preceding Typographed and Recess printed issues by the following tests:—

TYPO — ROTO

RECESS — ROTO

2d.

3d.

No. 35*b* — No. 46 — No. 46*c*

4d.

1s.

2s.6d.

5s.

ROTOGRAVURE:

½d. 1d. and 6d. Leg of "R" in "AFR" ends squarely on the bottom line.

2d. The newly built War Memorial appears to the left of the value.

3d. Two fine lines have been removed from the top part of the frame.

4d. No. 46. The scroll is in solid colour.

No. 46*c*. The scroll is white with a crooked line running through it. (No. 35*b*. The scroll is shaded by the diagonal lines.)

1s. The shading of the last "A" partly covers the flower beneath.

2s.6d. The top line of the centre frame is thick and leaves only one white line between it and the name.

5s. (Nos. 64/*b*). The leg of the "R" is straight. Rotogravure impressions are generally coarser.

18 Church of the Vow

19 "The Great Trek" (C. Michell)

20 A Voortrekker

21 Voortrekker Woman

Blurred "SOUTH AFRICA" and red "comet" flaw (Cyls 6917/6922 R. 2/7)

(Des J. Prentice (½d., 2d., 3d.)

1933 (3 May)–**36**. *Voortrekker Memorial Fund.* W **9** (sideways). P 14.

50	**18**	½d.+½d. black and green (16.1.36)	3·50	4·50	50
51	**19**	1d.+½d. grey-black and pink	2·75	1·50	25
		a. Blurred "SOUTH AFRICA" and red "comet" flaw	40·00		
52	**20**	2d.+1d. grey-green and purple	3·50	4·00	55
53	**21**	3d.+1½d. grey-green and blue	5·50	5·00	70
50/3 *Set of* 4			14·00	13·50	1·75

22 Gold Mine

22a Groot Schuur

Dies of 6d.

I

II

III

23 Groot Constantia

"Falling ladder" flaw (R. 5/10)

1933–48. *"SUID-AFRIKA" (hyphenated) on Afrikaans stamps.* W **9**. P 15 × 14 (½d., 1d. and 6d.) or 14 (others).

54	**6**	½d. grey and green (*wmk inverted*) (9.35)	4·00	1·75	10
		aw. Wmk upright (1936)	8·00	2·00	10
		b. Coil stamp. Perf 13½ × 14 (1935)	32·00	55·00	1·00
		bw. Wmk upright	32·00	55·00	1·00
		c. Booklet pane of 6 (with adverts on margins) (*wmk upright*)	25·00		
56	**7**	1d. grey & car (*shades*) (19.4.34)	1·50	1·50	10
		a. Imperf (pair) (*wmk inverted*)	£150		
		b. Frame omitted (*single stamp*)	£250		
		cw. Wmk inverted	1·50	1·50	10
		d. Coil stamp. Perf 13½ × 14 (1935)	35·00	60·00	1·40
		dw. Wmk inverted	35·00	60·00	1·40
		e. Booklet pane of 6 (with adverts on margins) (1935)	14·00		
		f. Booklet pane of 6 (with blank margins) (1937)	15·00		
		h. Booklet pane of 6 (with postal slogans on margins) (1948)	4·00		
		i. Grey & brt rose-carm (7.48)	70	2·00	10
57	**22**	1½d. green & brt gold (12.11.36)	3·25	2·00	10
		a. Shading omitted from mine dump (in pair with normal)	£180	£140	
		bw. Wmk inverted	1·50	1·50	10
		c. Blue-grn & dull gold (8.40)	6·50	3·00	10
58	**11**	2d. blue and violet (11.38)	70·00	32·00	75
58*a*		2d. grey and dull purple (5.41)	48·00	75·00	1·25
59	**22a**	3d. ultramarine (2.40)	9·00	2·25	10
61	**8**	6d. green & vermilion (I) (10.37)	70·00	25·00	70
		a. "Falling ladder" flaw	£190	£225	
61*b*		6d. green & vermilion (II) (6.38)	35·00	1·00	10
61*c*		6d. grn & red-orge (III) (11.46)	19·00	75	10
62	**13**	1s. brown & chalky blue (2.39)	50·00	10·00	10
		a. Frame omitted (*single stamp*)	£2500		
64	**15**	5s. black and green (10.33)	55·00	65·00	1·75
		aw. Wmk inverted	£110	£120	3·00
		b. Black and blue-green (9.44)	38·00	15·00	35
64*c*	**23**	10s. blue and sepia (8.39)	65·00	14·00	70
		ca. Blue & blackish brn (8.39)	42·00	5·50	30
54/9, 61*c*/64*ca* *Set of* 10			£250	£130	2·50

The ½d. and 1d. coil stamps may be found in blocks emanating from the residue of the large rolls which were cut into sheets and distributed to Post Offices.

Nos. 54 and 56 also exist in coils.

1d. Is printed from Type II. Frames of different sizes exist due to reductions made from time to time for the purpose of providing more space for the perforations.

3d. In No. 59 the frame is unscreened and composed of solid lines. Centre is diagonally screened. Scrolls above "3d." are clear lined, light in the middle and dark at sides.

6d. Die I. Green background lines faint. "SUID-AFRIKA" 16¼ mm long.

Die II. Green background lines heavy. "SUID-AFRIKA" 17 mm long. "S" near end of tablet. Scroll open.

Die III. Scroll closed up and design smaller (18 × 22 mm).

Single specimens of the 1933–48 issue inscribed in English may be distinguished from those of 1930–45 as follows:—

½d. and 1d. Centres in grey instead of varying intensities of black.

2d. The letters of "SOUTH AFRICA" are narrower and thinner.

3d. The trees are taller and the sky is without lines.

6d. The frame is vermilion.

1s. The frame is chalky blue.

For similar designs, but printed in screened rotogravure, see Nos. 114 to 122a.

BOOKLET PANES. Booklets issued in 1935 contained ½d. and 1d. stamps in panes with advertisements in the top and bottom margins and no margin at right (Nos. 54b and 56d). These were replaced in 1937 by editions showing blank margins on all four sides (Nos. 56e and 75ba). Following a period when the booklet panes were without margins a further 3s. booklet was issued in 1948 which had four margins on the panes and postal slogans at top and bottom (Nos. 56h, 87b and 114a).

24

JIPEX
1936
(24a)

"Cleft skull" flaw (R. 14/2)

(Des J. Booysen)

1935 (1 May). *Silver Jubilee. Inscr bilingually.* W **9**. P 15 × 14.

65	**24**	½d. black and blue-green	2·50	12·00	1(
		a. "Cleft skull" flaw	6·50		
66		1d. black and carmine	2·50	5·00	1(
		a. "Cleft skull" flaw	6·50		
67		3d. blue	14·00	55·00	2·2
		a. "Cleft skull" flaw	35·00		
68		6d. green and orange	27·00	75·00	3·2
		a. "Cleft skull" flaw	55·00		
65/8 *Set of* 4			42·00	£130	5·0

In stamps with English at top the ½d., 3d. and 6d. have "SILWEF JUBILEUM" to left of portrait, and "POSTAGE REVENUE" o "POSTAGE" (3d. and 6d.) in left value tablet. In the 1d., "SILVEF JUBILEE" is to the left of portrait. In alternate stamps the position of English and Afrikaans inscriptions are reversed.

1936 (2 Nov). *Johannesburg International Philatelic Exhibition. Opt with T* **24a**.

		Un sheet	*U shee*
MS69 **6**	½d. grey and green (No. 54)	3·50	10·0
MS70 **7**	1d. grey and carmine (No. 56)	2·75	7·0

Issued each in miniature sheet of six stamps with margina advertisements.

25

"Mouse" flaw (R. 4/1)

(Des J. Prentice)

1937 (12 May). *Coronation.* W **9** (sideways*). P 14.

71	**25**	½d. grey-black and blue-green	80	1·25	
		w. Wmk horns pointing to left	80	1·25	
72		1d. grey-black and carmine	80	1·00	
		w. Wmk horns pointing to left	80	1·00	
73		1½d. orange and greenish blue	80	80	
		a. "Mouse" flaw	6·50		
		w. Wmk horns pointing to left	80	80	
74		3d. ultramarine	1·50	3·00	
		w. Wmk horns pointing to left	1·50	3·00	
75		1s. red-brown and turquoise-blue	2·25	5·00	
		a. Hyphen on Afrikaans stamp omitted (R. 2/13)	55·00		
		bw. Wmk horns pointing to left	2·25	5·00	
71/5 *Set of* 5			5·50	10·00	

*The normal sideways watermark shows the horns of t springbok pointing to the right, *as seen from the back of the stan*

No. 75a shows the hyphen completely omitted and the top of t "K" damaged. A less distinct flaw, on which part of the hyphen still visible and with no damage to the "K", occurs on R. 4/17.

25a

"Tick" flaw on ear and spot on nose (multipositive flaw (occurring in 1947) (R. 3/4 or 3/1 on some ptgs of No. 114)

1937–40. W **9**. P 15 × 14.

75*c*	**25a**	½d. grey and green	9·00	1·75
		ca. Booklet pane of 6 (with blank margins) (1937)	48·00	
		cd. Grey and blue green (1940)	6·50	1·00
		ce. "Tick" flaw and spot on nose	55·00	

The lines of shading in T **25a** are all horizontal and thicker th in T **6**. In Nos. 75*c* and 75*cd* the design is composed of solid lir For stamps with designs composed of dotted lines, see No. 1 Later printings of No. 75*cd* have a smaller design.

26 Voortrekker Ploughing

27 Wagon crossing Drakensberg

28 Signing of Dingaan–Retief Treaty

29 Voortrekker Monumer

(Des W. Coetzer and J. Prentice)

8 (14 Dec). *Voortrekker Centenary Memorial Fund.* W **9**. P 14 (Nos. 76/7) or 15 × 14 (others).

26	½d.+½d. blue and green	12·00	4·50	30
27	1d.+1d. blue and carmine	13·00	5·50	40
28	1½d.+1½d. chocolate & blue-grn	17·00	8·00	80
29	3d.+3d. bright blue	18·00	9·00	1·00
	Set of 4	55·00	24·00	2·25

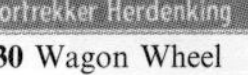

30 Wagon Wheel **31** Voortrekker Family

Three bolts in wheel rim (R. 15/5)

(Des W. Coetzer and J. Prentice)

8 (14 Dec). *Voortrekker Commemoration.* W **9**. P 15 × 14.

30	1d. blue and carmine	6·50	3·50	30
	a. Three bolts in wheel rim	32·00		
31	1½d. greenish blue and brown	8·50	3·50	30

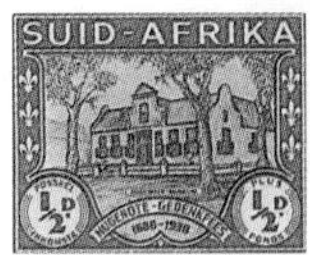

32 Old Vicarage, Paarl, now a museum **33** Symbol of the Reformation

34 Huguenot Dwelling, Drakenstein Mountain Valley

(Des J. Prentice)

9 (17 July). *250th Anniv of Huguenot Landing in South Africa and Huguenot Commemoration Fund.* W **9**. P 14 (Nos. 82/3) or 15 × 14 (No. 84).

32	½d.+½d. brown and green	4·75	6·00	30
33	1d.+1d. green and carmine	11·00	6·50	30
34	1½d.+1½d. blue-green and purple	26·00	13·00	1·00
	Set of 3	38·00	23·00	1·40

34a Gold Mine

1 (Aug)–**48**. W **9** (sideways). P 14 × 15.

34a	1½d. blue-grn and yellow-buff (*shades*)	1·75	1·00	10
	a. Yellow-buff (centre) omitted	£2000	£1300	
	b. Booklet pane of 6 (with postal slogans on margins) (1948)	8·00		

35 Infantry **36** Nurse and Ambulance **37** Airman

38 Sailor, Destroyer and Lifebelts **39** Women's Auxiliary Services

40 Artillery

41 Electric Welding

42 Tank Corps **42a** Signaller

"Stain" on uniform (R. 14/11)

"Cigarette" flaw (R. 18/2)

1941–46. *War Effort.* W **9** (sideways on 2d., 4d., 6d.). P 14 (2d., 4d., 6d.) or 15 × 14 (others).

(a) Inscr alternately.

88	**35**	½d. green (19.11.41)	1·50	2·25	10
		a. Blue-green (7.42)	3·50	2·50	10
89	**36**	1d. carmine (3.10.41)	2·00	2·25	10
		a. "Stain" on uniform flaw	20·00		
90	**37**	1½d. myrtle-green (12.1.42)	1·50	1·75	10
91	**39**	3d. blue (1.8.41)	22·00	30·00	70
		a. "Cigarette" flaw	75·00		
92	**40**	4d. orange-brown (20.8.41)	21·00	19·00	15
		a. Red-brown (6.42)	35·00	32·00	1·25
93	**41**	6d. red-orange (3.9.41)	12·00	13·00	15
94	**42a**	1s.3d. olive-brown (2.1.43)	12·00	8·00	20
		a. Blackish brown (5.46)	4·00	8·00	20

(b) Inscr bilingually.

			Un single	*Us single*
95	**38**	2d. violet (15.9.41)	1·00	50
96	**42**	1s. brown (27.10.41)	3·50	75
88/96		*Set of* 7 *pairs and* 2 *singles*	60·00	70·00

43 Infantry **44** Nurse **45** Airman **46** Sailor

47 Women's Auxiliary Services **48** Electric Welding

49 Heavy Gun in Concrete Turret

50 Tank Corps

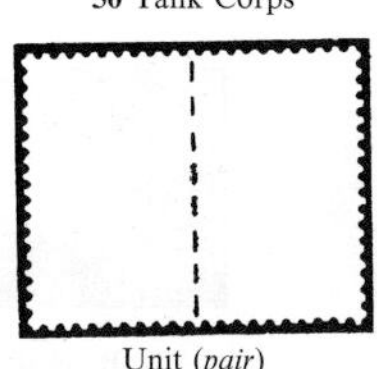

Unit (*pair*)

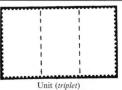

Unit (*triplet*)

Ear Flap flaw (Cyl 43 R. 13/3)

Apostrophe flaw (Cyl 6931 R. 19/1) (later corrected)

Line on Cap (Cyl 39 R. 12/11)

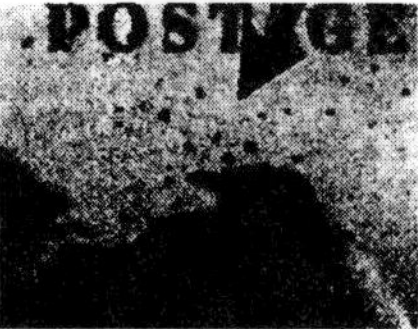

"Bursting Shell" (Cyl 46 R. 11/20) Smoking "L" (Cyl 46 R. 8/2)

1942–44. *War Effort. Reduced sizes.* In pairs perf 14 (P) or strips of three, perf 15 × 14 (T), subdivided by roulette 6½. W **9** (sideways* on 3d., 4d. and 1s.).

(a) Inscr alternately.

			Un unit	*Used unit*	*Used single*
97	**43**	½d. blue-green (T) (10.42)	1·75	1·50	10
		a. Green (3.43)	2·75	2·00	10
		b. Greenish blue (7.44)	2·00	1·50	10
		c. Roulette omitted	£700		
98	**44**	1d. carmine-red (T) (5.1.43)	1·50	1·25	10
		a. Bright carmine (3.44)	1·00	1·00	10
		b. Both roulettes omitted	£550	£600	
		ba. Left-hand roulette omitted	£700		
99	**45**	1½d. red-brown (P) (9.42)	65	2·00	10
		a. Roulette 13 (8.42)	1·50	4·00	15
		b. Roulette omitted	£250	£275	
		c. Ear flap flaw	15·00		
100	**46**	2d. violet (P) (2.43)	90	1·75	10
		a. Reddish violet (6.43)	1·50	65	10
		b. Roulette omitted	£475		
		c. Apostrophe flaw	50·00		
		d. Line on cap	50·00		
101	**47**	3d. blue (T) (10.42)	7·00	16·00	10
102	**48**	6d. red-orange (P) (10.42)	2·00	1·75	10
		(b) Inscr bilingually.			
103	**49**	4d. slate-green (T) (10.42)	18·00	9·00	10
104	**50**	1s. brown (P) (11.42)	15·00	3·50	10
		a. "Bursting shell"	70·00		
		b. Smoking "L"	65·00		
97/104		*Set of* 8	40·00	32·00	65

*The sideways watermark shows springbok horns pointing to left on the 3d. and 1s., and to right on the 4d., *all as seen from the back of the stamp.*

52 **53**

1943. *Coil stamps. Redrawn. In single colours with plain background.* W **9**. P 15 × 14.

			Un pair	*Used pair*	*Used single*
105	**52**	½d. blue-green (18.2.43)	2·25	4·25	20
106	**53**	1d. carmine (9.43)	3·25	3·50	15

Quoted prices are for *vertical* pairs.

54 Union Buildings, Pretoria

1945–46. *Redrawn.* W **9**. P 14.

107	**54**	2d. slate and violet (3.45)	12·00	2·50	10
		a. *Slate & brt vio* (*shades*) (10.46)	3·25	9·00	15

In Nos. 107 and 107*a* the Union Buildings are shown at a different angle from Nos. 58 and 58*a*. Only the centre is screened i.e., composed of very small square dots of colour arranged in straight diagonal lines. For whole design screened and colours changed, see No. 116. No. 107*a* also shows "2" of "2d." clear of white circle at top.

55 "Victory"

56 "Peace"

57 "Hope"

1945 (3 Dec). *Victory.* W **9**. P 14.

108	**55**	1d. brown and carmine	20	1·00	10
109	**56**	2d. slate-blue and violet	20	1·00	10
110	**57**	3d. deep blue and blue	20	1·40	10
108/10 *Set of* 3			55	3·00	25

58 King George VI

59 King George VI and Queen Elizabeth

60 Queen Elizabeth II as Princess, and Princess Margaret

"Bird" on "2" (Cyl 6912 R. 10/6)

(Des J. Prentice)

1947 (17 Feb). *Royal Visit.* W **9**. P 15 × 14.

111	**58**	1d. black and carmine	10	25	10
112	**59**	2d. violet	15	45	10
		a. "Bird" on "2" flaw	3·75		
113	**60**	3d. blue	15	45	10
111/13 *Set of* 3			35	1·00	20

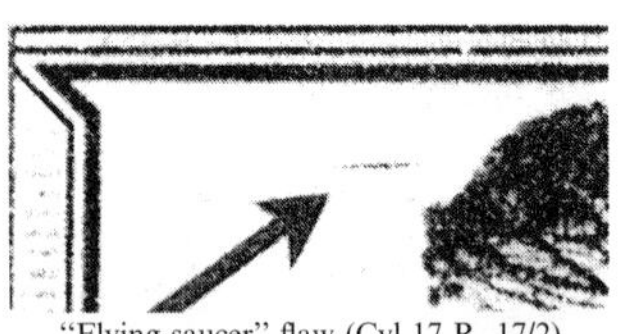

"Flying saucer" flaw (Cyl 17 R. 17/2)

I

II

5s.

1947–54. *"SUID-AFRIKA" hyphenated on Afrikaans stamps. Printed from new cylinders with design in screened rotogravure.* W **9**. P 15 × 14 (½d., 1d. and 6d.) or 14 (others).

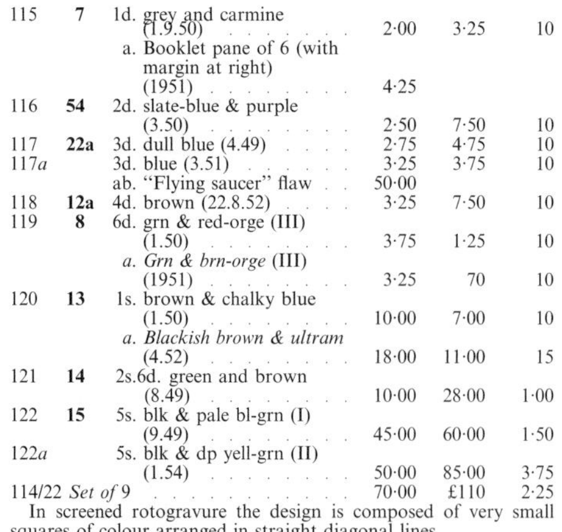

114	**25**	½d. grey and green (frame only screened) (1947)	2·00	3·00	10
		a. Booklet pane of 6 (with postal slogans on margins) (1948)	3·50		
		b. "Tick" flaw and spot on nose	38·00		
		c. Entire design screened (2.49)	2·00	3·25	10
		ca. Booklet pane of 6 (with margin at right) (1951)	3·75		
115	**7**	1d. grey and carmine (1.9.50)	2·00	3·25	10
		a. Booklet pane of 6 (with margin at right) (1951)	4·25		
116	**54**	2d. slate-blue & purple (3.50)	2·50	7·50	10
117	**22a**	3d. dull blue (4.49)	2·75	4·75	10
117*a*		3d. blue (3.51)	3·25	3·75	10
		ab. "Flying saucer" flaw	50·00		
118	**12a**	4d. brown (22.8.52)	3·25	7·50	10
119	**8**	6d. grn & red-orge (III) (1.50)	3·75	1·25	10
		a. Grn & brn-orge (III) (1951)	3·25	70	10
120	**13**	1s. brown & chalky blue (1.50)	10·00	7·00	10
		a. Blackish brown & ultram (4.52)	18·00	11·00	15
121	**14**	2s.6d. green and brown (8.49)	10·00	28·00	1·00
122	**15**	5s. blk & pale bl-grn (I) (9.49)	45·00	60·00	1·50
122*a*		5s. blk & dp yell-grn (II) (1.54)	50·00	85·00	3·75
114/22 *Set of* 9			70·00	£110	2·25

In screened rotogravure the design is composed of very small squares of colour arranged in straight diagonal lines.

½d. Size 17¾ × 21¾ mm. Early printings have only the frame screened.

1d. Size 18 × 22 mm. For smaller, redrawn design, see No. 135.

2d. For earlier issue with centre only screened, and in different colours, see Nos. 107/*a*.

3d. No. 117. Whole stamp screened with irregular grain. Scrolls above "3d." solid and toneless. Printed from two cylinders.

No. 117*a*. Whole stamp diagonally screened. Printed from one cylinder. Clouds more pronounced. Late printings were often in deep shades.

4d. Two groups of white leaves below name tablet and a clear white line down left and right sides of stamp.

61 Gold Mine

62 King George VI and Queen Elizabeth

1948 (1 Apr). In pair, perf 14, sub-divided by roulette 6½. W **9** (sideways).

			Un unit of 4	*Us unit*	*Used single*
124	**61**	1½d. blue-green and yellow-buff	2·50	3·75	10

(Des J. Booysen and J. Prentice)

1948 (26 Apr). *Silver Wedding.* W **9**. P 14.

			Un pair	*Used pair*	*Used single*
125	**62**	3d. blue and silver	50	1·00	10

(Typo Government Printer, Pretoria)

1948 (July). W **9**. P 14½ × 14.

126	**6**	½d. pale grey and blue-green	1·50	9·00	70

This was an economy printing made from the old plates of the 1926 issue for the purpose of using up a stock of cut paper. For the original printing in black and green, see No. 30.

63 *Wanderer* (emigrant ship) entering Durban

Extended rigging on mainmast (R. 14/2)

(Des J. Prentice)

1949 (2 May). *Centenary of Arrival of British Settlers in Natal.* W **9**. P 15 × 14.

127	**63**	1½d. claret	80	70	10
		a. Extended rigging	7·00		

64 Hermes

65 Wagons approaching Bingham's Berg

Serif on "C" (R. 1/1)

"Lake" in East Africa (R. 2/19)

(Des J. Booysen and J. Prentice)

1949 (1 Oct). *75th Anniv of Universal Postal Union. As T* **64** *i* "UNIVERSAL POSTAL UNION" *and* "WERELDPOSUN *alternately.* W **9** (sideways). P 14 × 15.

128	**64**	½d. blue-green	50	1·00
129		1½d. brown-red	50	1·00
130		3d. bright blue	60	1·00
		a. Serif on "C"	28·00	
		b. "Lake" in East Africa	32·00	
128/30 *Set of* 3			1·40	2·75

(Des W. Coetzer and J. Prentice)

1949 (1 Dec). *Inauguration of Voortrekker Monument, Pretoria.* *and similar horiz designs.* W **9**. P 15 × 14.

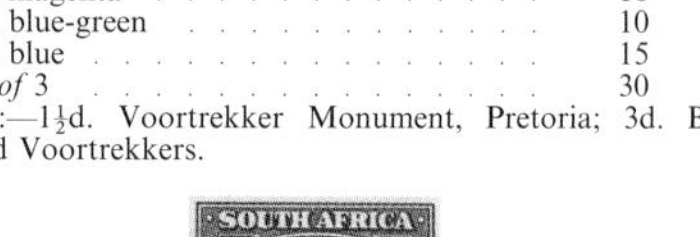

		Un single	*si*
131	1d. magenta	10	
132	1½d. blue-green	10	
133	3d. blue	15	
131/3 *Set of* 3		30	

Designs:—1½d. Voortrekker Monument, Pretoria; 3d. B candle and Voortrekkers.

68 Union Buildings, Pretoria

1950 (Apr)–**51**. W **9** (sideways). P 14 × 15.

			Un pair	*Used pair*	*U si*
134	**68**	2d. blue and violet	40	65	
		a. Booklet panes of 6 (with margin at right) (1951)	4·00		

1951 (22 Feb). *As No. 115, but redrawn with the horizon cle defined. Size reduced to 17¾ × 21¼ mm.*

135	**7**	1d. grey and carmine	1·40	2·50

STAMP BOOKLETS

1913. *Black on red cover. With* "UNION OF SOUTH AFRIC *at top and* "UNIE VAN ZUID AFRIKA" *at foot. Stapled.*
SB1 2s.6d. booklet containing twelve ½d. and twenty-four 1d. (Nos. 3/4) in blocks of 6 . . . £5

1913–20. *Black on red cover with* "UNION OF SOUTH AFRIC *and* "UNIE VAN ZUID AFRIKA" *both at top. Stapled.*
SB2 2s.6d. booklet containing twelve ½d. and twenty-four 1d. (Nos. 3/4) in blocks of 6 . . . £5
a. Black on pink cover (1920) . . . £5

1921. *Black on salmon pink cover with* "UNION OF SOU AFRICA" *and* "UNIE VAN ZUID AFRIKA" *either sid arms and telegraph rates beneath. Stapled.*
SB3 3s. booklet containing twelve ½d., 1d. and 1½d. (Nos. 3/5) in blocks of 6 . . . £

1922. *Black on salmon-pink cover as No. SB3 surch. Stapled.*
SB4 3s.6d. on 3s. booklet containing twelve ½d., 1d. and 2d. (Nos. 3/4, 6) in blocks of 6 . . . £1

1926. *Black on salmon-pink cover as No. SB3. Stitched.*
SB5 2s.6d. booklet containing twelve ½d. and twenty-four 1d. (Nos. 30/1) . . . £1

1927. *Black on salmon-pink cover as No. SB3, but inscr* "Unio South Africa" *and* "Unie van Suidafrika". *Stitched.*
SB6 2s.6d. booklet containing twelve ½d. and twenty-four 1d. (Nos. 30e, 31d) . . . £4

1930. *Black on pink cover as No. SB6, but with advertisement at instead of telegraph rates. Stitched.*
SB7 2s.6d. booklet containing twelve ½d. and twenty-four 1d. (Nos. 42/3) in blocks of 6 . . . £1

1931. *Black on pink cover. Smaller inscr and advertisement on f cover. Stitched.*
SB8 3s. booklet containing twelve 1d. (No. 43) in blocks of 6 and twelve 2d. (No. 44) in blocks of 4 . . . £1

1935. *Black on lemon cover. Advertisement on front cover. Stitch*
SB9 2s.6d. booklet containing two panes of six ½d. (No. 54c) and four panes of six 1d. (No. 56e), all with adverts on margins . . . £

1937. *Black on lemon cover. Advertisement on front cover. Stitched.*
SB10 2s.6d. booklet containing two panes of six ½d. (No. 75ba) and four panes of six 1d. (No. 56f), all with blank margins £500

1937. *Machine vended booklets. Red cover. Stitched.*
SB11 6d. booklet containing four ½d. and 1d. (Nos. 75c, 56) in pairs . . . . . . 7·00

1938. *Machine vended booklets. Blue cover. Stitched.*
SB12 3d. booklet containing ½d. and 1d. (Nos. 75c, 56), each in pair . . . . . . 40·00

1938. *Black on buff cover. Union arms at top left with advertisement at foot. Stitched.*
SB13 2s.6d. booklet containing twelve ½d. and twenty-four 1d. (Nos. 75c, 56) in blocks of 6 . . . . £450

1939. *Black on buff cover. Union arms centred at top with advertisement at foot. Stitched.*
SB14 2s.6d. booklet containing twelve ½d. and twenty-four 1d. (Nos. 75c, 56) in blocks of 6 . . . . £375

1939–40. *Green on buff cover. Union arms centred at top with large advertisement at bottom left. Stitched.*
SB15 2s.6d. booklet containing twelve ½d. and twenty-four 1d. (Nos. 75c, 56) in blocks of 6 . . . . £2250
a. Blue on buff cover (1940) . . . . . . 90·00

1941. *Blue on buff cover as No. SB15. Stitched.*
SB17 2s.6d. booklet containing twelve ½d. and 1d. (Nos. 75c, 56) in blocks of 6 and 1½d. (No. 57) in block of 4 . . . . . . £140

1948. *Black on buff cover. With advertisement. Stitched.*
SB18 3s. booklet containing two panes of six ½d., 1d. and 1½d. (Nos. 114a, 56h, 87b), all with postal slogans on margins, and pane of air mail labels . . . . . . 30·00

1951. *Black on buff cover. Stitched.*
SB19 3s.6d. booklet containing two panes of six ½d., 1d. and 2d. (Nos. 114ca, 115a, 134a), each with margins at right . . . . . . 13·00

POSTAGE DUE STAMPS

D 1

UNION OF SOUTH AFRICA (A) UNION OF SOUTH AFRICA (B)

(Typo D.L.R.)

1914–22. *Inscribed bilingually. Lettering as A.* W **4**. P 14.

			Un single	Used single
D1	D 1	½d. black and green (19.3.15)	2·25	3·75
D2		1d. black and scarlet (19.3.15)	2·25	15
		a. Black ptd double	£1500	
		w. Wmk inverted	80·00	
D3		2d. black and reddish violet (12.12.14)	6·50	50
		a. Black and bright violet (1922)	7·00	60
		w. Wmk inverted	£130	
D4		3d. black and bright blue (2.2.15)	2·25	60
		w. Wmk inverted	25·00	
D5		5d. black and sepia (19.3.15)	4·00	24·00
D6		6d. black and slate (19.3.15)	7·00	30·00
D7		1s. red and black (19.3.15)	60·00	£150
D1/7 *Set of* 7			75·00	£180

There are interesting minor varieties in some of the above values, e.g. ½d. to 3d., thick downstroke to "d"; 1d., short serif to "1"; raised "d"; 2d., forward point of "2" blunted; 3d., raised "d"; very thick "d".

(Litho Govt Printer, Pretoria)

1922. *Lettering as A.* No wmk. *Rouletted.*

D8	D 1	½d. black and bright green (6.6.22)	1·50	13·00
D9		1d. black and rose-red (3.10.22)	1·00	1·00
D10		1½d. black and yellow-brown (3.6.22)	1·25	1·75
D8/10 *Set of* 3			3·25	14·00

(Litho Govt Printer, Pretoria)

1922–26. *Type* D **1** *redrawn. Lettering as B.* P 14.

D11	½d. black and green (1.8.22)	80	1·75
D12	1d. black and rose (16.5.23)	90	15
D13	1½d. black and yellow-brown (12.1.24)	1·00	1·25
D14	2d. black and pale violet (16.5.23)	1·00	70
	a. Imperf (pair)	£225	£300
	b. Black and deep violet	11·00	2·00
D15	3d. black and blue (3.7.26)	8·00	21·00
D16	6d. black and slate (9.23)	12·00	3·50
D11/16 *Set of* 6		21·00	25·00

The locally printed stamps, perf 14, differ both in border design and in figures of value from the rouletted stamps. All values except the 3d. and 6d. are known with closed "G" in "POSTAGE" usually referred to as the "POSTADE" variety. This was corrected in later printings.

D 2

D 3

D 4

Blunt "2" (R. 3/6, 8/6)

(Typo Pretoria)

1927–28. *Inscribed bilingually.* No wmk. P 13½ × 14.

D17	D 2	½d. black and green	1·00	3·25
		a. Blunt "2"	11·00	
D18		1d. black and carmine	1·25	30
D19		2d. black and mauve	1·25	30
		a. Black and purple	16·00	80
D20		3d. black and blue	8·50	24·00
D21		6d. black and slate	21·00	3·50
D17/21 *Set of* 5			30·00	28·00

1932–42. *Type* D **2** *redrawn.* W **9**. P 15 × 14.

(a) Frame roto, value typo.

D22	½d. black and blue-green (1934)	2·75	1·75
	w. Wmk inverted	2·25	1·60
D23	2d. black and deep purple (10.4.33)	9·00	2·50
	w. Wmk inverted	9·00	2·50

(b) Whole stamp roto.

D25	1d. black & carmine (wmk inverted) (3.34)	2·25	10
D26	2d. black and deep purple (1940)	24·00	10
	a. Thick (double) "2d." (R. 5/6, R. 18/2)	£250	20·00
	w. Wmk inverted	24·00	10
D27	3d. black and Prussian blue (3.8.32)	25·00	14·00
D28	3d. dp blue & blue (wmk inverted) (1935)	8·00	30
	a. Indigo and milky blue (wmk inverted) (1942)	70·00	3·25
	w. Wmk upright	42·00	1·00
D29	6d. green and brown-ochre (wmk inverted) (7.6.33)	25·00	5·00
	a. Green & brt orge (wmk inverted) (1938)	13·00	3·00
D22/9a *Set of* 7		75·00	19·00

In No. D26 the value is screened, whereas in No. D23 the black of the value is solid.

1943–44. *Inscr bilingually. Roto.* W **9**. In units of three, perf 15 × 14 subdivided by roulette 6½.

			Un unit	Us unit	Us single
D30	D 3	½d. blue-green (1944)	11·00	42·00	30
D31		1d. carmine	10·00	5·50	10
D32		2d. dull violet	6·50	11·00	15
		a. Bright violet	16·00	45·00	65
D33		3d. indigo (1943)	48·00	80·00	1·25
D30/3 *Set of* 4			65·00	£120	1·90

Split "D" (R. 7/5 on every fourth sheet)

1948–49. *New figure of value and capital "D". Whole stamp roto.* W **9**. P 15 × 14.

D34	D 4	½d. black and blue-green	6·00	12·00
D35		1d. black and carmine	13·00	5·50
D36		2d. black and violet (1949)	13·00	7·00
		a. Thick (double) "2D." (R. 15/5-6, R. 16/5-6)	55·00	28·00
D37		3d. deep blue and blue	15·00	17·00
		a. Split "D"	£160	£170
D38		6d. green and bright orange (1949)	25·00	8·00
D34/8 *Set of* 5			65·00	45·00

1950–58. *As Type* D **4**, *but "SUID-AFRIKA" hyphenated. Whole stamp roto.* W **9**. P 15 × 14.

D39	1d. black and carmine (5.50)	70	30
D40	2d. black and violet (4.51)	50	20
	a. Thick (double) "2D." (R. 15/5-6, R. 16/5-6)	8·00	7·00
	b. Black and reddish violet (12.52)	1·00	20
	ba. Thick (double) "2D."	9·50	7·00
	bb. Black (value) omitted	£2000	
D41	3d. deep blue and blue (5.50)	4·50	2·25
	a. Split "D"	85·00	50·00
D42	4d. deep myrtle-green and emerald (2.58)	12·00	15·00
D43	6d. green and bright orange (3.50)	7·00	9·00
D44	1s. black-brown and purple-brown (2.58)	12·00	15·00
D39/44 *Set of* 6		32·00	38·00

No. D40bb occurs in horizontal pair with a normal.

OFFICIAL STAMPS

OFFICIAL. OFFISIEEL. OFFISIEEL OFFICIAL

(O 1) (O 2)

(Approximate measurements of the space between the two lines of overprint are quoted in millimetres, either in the set headings or after individual listings)

1926 (1 Dec). *Optd with Type* O **1** *(reading upwards with stops and 12½ mm between lines of opt).*

(a) On 1913 issue (No. 6).

O1	3	2d. purple	20·00	1·75	

(b) On 1926 issue (Nos. 30/2).

			Un pair	Used pair	Used single
O2	6	½d. black and green	7·00	15·00	1·50
O3	7	1d. black and carmine	3·75	6·50	50
O4	8	6d. green and orange	£550	75·00	10·00
		w. Wmk inverted	£900	£350	30·00

The overprint occurs on both the London and Pretoria printings of Nos. 30/2. For the lower two values the overprinted London printings are scarcer than the Pretoria, but for the 6d. the ratio is reversed.

1928–30. *Nos. 32 and 34 optd as Type* O **1** *(reading upwards without stops).*

O5	11	2d. grey & maroon (P 14) (17½ *mm*)	5·50	20·00	2·00
		a. Lines of opt 19 mm apart (1929)	5·50	15·00	1·50
		ab. On No. 34a (P 14 × 13½) (1930)	26·00	40·00	5·00
O6	8	6d. green and orange (11½–12 *mm*)	19·00	35·00	2·75

1929–31. *Optd with Type* O **2**.

(a) On 1926 (Typo) issue (Nos. 30/2) (13½–15 mm between lines of opt).

O7	6	½d. black and green	2·50	3·75	35
		a. Stop after "OFFISIEEL" on English inscr stamp (1930)	32·00	32·00	3·25
		b. Ditto, but on Afrikaans inscr stamp (1930)	42·00	42·00	3·25
O8	7	1d. black and carmine	3·00	4·50	45
O9	8	6d. green and orange	9·50	35·00	3·25
		a. Stop after "OFFISIEEL" on English inscr stamp (1930)	65·00	£110	10·00
		b. Ditto, but on Afrikaans inscr stamp (1930)	75·00	£120	12·00

(b) On 1927 (Recess) issue (Nos. 36a/7) (17½–19 mm between lines of opt).

O10	13	1s. brown and deep blue (1931)	38·00	90·00	9·50
		a. Stop after "OFFICIAL" on Afrikaans inscr stamp (R. 10/1, 10/7)	£110	£225	
		b. Lines of opt 22 mm apart	£250	£350	
O11	14	2s.6d. green and brown (1931)	60·00	£150	19·00
		a. Stop after "OFFICIAL" on Afrikaans inscr stamp (R. 10/1)	£275	£475	
O7/11 *Set of* 5			£100	£250	29·00

The "stop" varieties for the ½d., and 6d. occur on R. 5/3, 5/11, 8/12, 15/3, 15/11, 18/12 with English inscriptions and R. 9/10, 9/12, 19/10, 19/12 with Afrikaans on the 1930 overprinting only.

As only the left-hand panes of the 2s.6d. were overprinted in 1931 the stop variety only occurs once. A further overprinting in 1932 was on both panes, but did not include No. O11a.

1930–47. *Nos. 42/4 and 47/9 ("SUIDAFRIKA" in one word) optd with Type* O **2**.

O12	6	½d. black and green (9½–12½ *mm*) (1931)	2·25	4·75	40
		a. Stop after "OFFISIEEL" on English inscr stamp	38·00	45·00	4·00
		b. Ditto, but on Afrikaans inscr stamp	32·00	40·00	3·50
		w. Wmk inverted (1934)	5·50	8·50	60
O13	7	1d. black & carm (I) (12½ *mm*)	4·50	5·00	55
		a. Stop after "OFFISIEEL" on English inscr stamp	48·00	50·00	4·00
		b. Ditto, but on Afrikaans inscr stamp	35·00	40·00	3·50
		cw. Wmk inverted (1931)	4·50	5·00	55
		d. On Type II (No. 43d) (12½–13½ *mm*) (1933)	13·00	9·00	90
		da. Opt double	£275	£300	
O14	11	2d. slate-grey and lilac (20½–22½ *mm*) (1931)	7·00	11·00	1·50
		w. Wmk inverted (1934)	50·00	85·00	8·00
O15		2d. blue and violet (20½–22½ *mm*) (1938)	£120	£100	9·00
O16	8	6d. green & orange (12½–13½ *mm*) (*wmk inverted*) (1931)	8·00	8·50	85
		a. Stop after "OFFISIEEL" on English inscr stamp	85·00	90·00	6·50
		b. Ditto, but on Afrikaans inscr stamp	70·00	75·00	5·50
		c. "OFFISIEEL" reading upwards (R. 17/12, 18/12, 19/12, 20/12) (1933)	£500		
		w. Wmk upright (1935)	55·00	85·00	7·00

O17 **13** 1s. brown and deep blue (19 *mm*) (*wmk inverted*) (1932) . . . 45·00 85·00 8·50
a. Twisted horn flaw . . . £225
b. Lines of opt 21 mm apart (*wmk inverted*) (1933) . . 48·00 80·00 7·50
ba. Twisted horn flaw . . . £225
bw. Wmk upright (1936) . . 60·00 £110 10·00

O18 **14** 2s.6d. green and brown (17½–18½ *mm*) (1933) . . 75·00 £140 15·00
a. Lines of opt 21 mm apart (1934) . . . . 48·00 75·00 8·50
aw. Wmk inverted (1937) . . £200 £275

O19 2s.6d. blue and brown (19½–20 *mm*) (11.47) . . 40·00 85·00 6·50
a. Diaeresis over second "E" of "OFFISIEEL" on Afrikaans inscr stamp (R. 6/2) £900 £1000
b. Ditto, but on English inscr stamp (R. 6/3) . . . £900 £1000

The stop varieties for the ½d., 1d. and 6d. occur on R. 9/10, 9/12, 19/10, 19/12 with English inscriptions and R. 5/3, 5/11, 8/12, 15/3, 15/11, 18/12 with Afrikaans on the 1930 and 1931 overprintings only.

OFFICIAL OFFISIEEL
(O 3)

OFFISIEEL OFFICIAL
(O 4)

1935–49. *Nos.* 54, 56/8, 61/2 *and* 64a/b ("SUID-AFRIKA" *hyphenated*) *optd.*

(*a*) *With Type* O **2** (*reading downwards with* "OFFICIAL" *at right*).

O20 **6** ½d. grey and green (12½ *mm*) (*wmk inverted*) (1936) . . 5·00 24·00 1·75
w. Wmk upright (1937) . . 6·50 25·00 1·75

O21 **7** 1d. grey and carmine (11½–13 *mm*) (*wmk inverted*) . . . . 3·50 3·75 35
aw. Wmk upright (1937) . . 2·50 3·00 20
b. Grey & bright rose-carmine (No. 56*i*) (1949) . . . . 2·75 3·75 30

O22 **22** 1½d. green and bright gold (20 *mm*) (*wmk inverted*) (1937) . . . . 40·00 25·00 1·75
aw. Wmk upright (1939) . . 27·00 21·00 1·00
b. Blue-green and dull gold (No. 57*c*) (1941) . . . 45·00 11·00 1·10

O23 **11** 2d. blue & violet (20 *mm*) (1939) . . . . £120 26·00 2·25

O24 **8** 6d. green and vermilion (I) (11½–13 *mm*) (1937) . . 80·00 45·00 3·75
a. "Falling ladder" flaw . . £375
b. Die II (No. 61*b*) (1938) . . . . 11·00 12·00 1·25
c. Die III *Green & red-orange* (No. 61*c*) (11.47) . . . . 4·00 8·50 85

O25 **13** 1s. brown and chalky blue (20 *mm*) (1939) . . . 80·00 38·00 2·25
a. Diaeresis over second "E" of "OFFISIEEL" on both English and Afrikaans inscr stamps (1941) £1500 £1000
b. Ditto, but on English inscr stamp only (11.47) £1200 £850

O26 **15** 5s. black and blue-green (20 *mm*) (6.48) . . . . . . 65·00 £150 13·00

O27 **23** 10s. blue and blackish brown (No. 64*ba*) (20 *mm*) (6.48) . . . . £100 £250 23·00

(*b*) *With Type* O **3** (*reading downwards with* "OFFICIAL" *at left and 18–19 mm between lines of opt*).

O28 **15** 5s. black and blue-green (1940) . . . . 85·00 £120 12·00
O29 **23** 10s. blue and sepia (1940) . . £400 £400 38·00

(*c*) *With Type* O **4** (*reading upwards with* "OFFICIAL" *at right and 18½ mm between lines of opt.*

O30 **11** 2d. grey and dull purple (No. 58*a*) (1941) . . . 14·00 27·00 2·25

No. O25a first appeared in the 1941 overprinting where the variety occurs on stamps 5 and 6 of an unidentified row. The variety reappears in the November 1947 overprinting where the stamps involved are R. 6/1 and 2. No. O25b occurs on R. 6/3 of the same overprinting.

Horizontal rows of 6 of the 1s. exist with "OFFICIAL" twice on the first stamp and "OFFISIEEL" twice on the last stamp. Such rows are believed to come from two half sheets which were overprinted in 1947, but not placed into normal stock (*Price for row of* 6, £2250, *unused*).

OFFICIAL OFFISIEEL
(O 5)

OFFICIAL OFFISIEEL
(O 6)

1937–44. *No. 75c (redrawn design) optd.*

(*a*) *With Type* O **2** (*reading downwards with* "OFFICIAL" *at right and 11–12½ mm between lines of opt*).

O31 **25a** ½d. grey and green . . . . 16·00 16·00 1·25
a. Grey and blue-green (No. 75*cd*) (1944) . . . 2·25 9·00 60

(*b*) *With Type* O **5** (*reading up and down with* "OFFICIAL" *at left and diaeresis over the second* "E" *of* "OFFISIEEL". *10 mm between lines of opt*).

O32 **25a** ½d. grey and blue-green (No. 75*cd*) (1944) . . . 28·00 25·00 2·00

1944–50. *Nos.* 87 *and* 134 *optd.*

(*a*) *With Type* O **2** (*reading downwards with* "OFFICIAL" *at right*).

O33 **34a** 1½d. blue-green and yellow-buff (14½ *mm*) . . . . 2·50 10·00 80
a. With diaeresis over second "E" of "OFFISIEEL" . . . . £475 £225 20·00
b. Lines of opt 16½ mm apart (6.48) . . . . . 2·25 10·00 50

(*b*) *With Type* O **6** (*reading upwards with* "OFFICIAL" *at left and 16 mm between lines of opt*).

O34 **34a** 1½d. bl-green & yell-buff (1949) . . . . 50·00 50·00 4·00
O35 **68** 2d. blue and violet (1950) £2000 £2500 £170

Two different formes were used to overprint Type **34a** between 1944 and 1946. The first, applied to the left halves of sheets only, had a diaeresis over the second "E" of "OFFISIEEL" on all positions of the setting, except for R. 1/2, 2/2 and 3/2. The second form, from which the majority of the stamps came, was applied twice to overprint complete sheets, had no diaeresis.

1947 (Nov)–**49**. *No. 107 optd with Type* O **2** (*reading downwards with* "OFFICIAL" *at right and 20 mm between lines of opt*).

O36 **54** 2d. slate and violet . . . . . 5·50 23·00 1·90
a. With diaeresis over second "E" of "OFFISIEEL" (R. 1/5-6, 11/5-6) £425 £650
b. Slate-purple and bright violet (No. 107*a*) (1949) . . . . 6·50 15·00 1·60

1949–50. *Nos. 114 and 120 optd with Type* O **2** (*reading downwards with* "OFFICIAL" *at right*).

O37 **25a** ½d. grey and green (11 *mm*) . . . . 3·00 7·50 70
a. "Tick" flaw and spot on nose . . . . . . 35·00
O38 **13** 1s. brown and chalky blue (17½–18½ *mm*) (1950) . . 9·50 28·00 2·50

OFFISIEEL OFFICIAL
(O 7)

1950 (June)–**54**. *Optd as Type* O **7** *using stereo blocks measuring either 10 (½d., 1d., 6d.), 14½ (1½d., 2d.) or 19 mm (others) between the lines of opt.*

O39 **25a** ½d. grey and green (No. 114*c*) (6.51) . . . 70 1·50 15
O41 **7** 1d. grey & bright rose-carmine (No. 56*i*) . . . 1·00 6·00 50
O42 1d. grey & car (No. 115) (3.51) . . . . 1·00 3·25 20
O43 1d. grey & car (No. 135) (6.52) . . . . 1·25 2·00 20
O44 **34a** 1½d. blue-green and yellow-buff (No. 87) (3.51) . . 1·40 4·50 30
O45 **68** 2d. blue and violet (No. 134) . . . . . . 1·00 2·00 20
a. Opt inverted £1000
O46 **8** 6d. green & red-orge (No. 119) . . . . . . 1·00 4·00 35
a. Green and brown-orange (No. 119*a*) (6.51) . . . 1·50 3·50 35
O47 **13** 1s. brn & chalky bl (No. 120) . . . . . . 5·50 18·00 2·00
a. Blackish brown and ultram (No. 120*a*) (2.53) . . . . £150 £160 18·00
O48 **14** 2s.6d. green & brn (No. 121) . . . . . . 8·50 35·00 3·50
O49 **15** 5s. black and blue-green (No. 64*a*) (3.51) . . . £180 £100 9·00
O50 5s. black and pale blue-green (I) (No. 122) (2.53) . . . . . . 65·00 80·00 6·50
a. Black & deep yellow-green (II) (No. 122*a*) (1.54) . . . . 75·00 95·00 9·00
O51 **23** 10s. blue and blackish brown (No. 64*ca*) . . . 75·00 £225 22·00

The use of the official stamps ceased in January 1955.

South Australia
see Australia

Southern Nigeria
see Nigeria

Southern Rhodesia

PRICES FOR STAMPS ON COVER TO 1945
Nos. 1/61 *from* × 2

SELF-GOVERNMENT

The southern part of Rhodesia, previously administered by the British South Africa Company, was annexed by the British Government and granted the status of a self-governing colony from 1 October 1923.

The existing stamps of Rhodesia (the "Admiral" design first issued in 1913) remained in use until 31 March 1924 and continued to be valid for postal purposes until 30 April of that year.

1

2 King George V

3 Victoria Falls

(Recess Waterlow)

1924 (1 Apr)–**29**. P 14.

1 **1** ½d. blue-green . . . . 2·00 1
a. Imperf between (horiz pair) £700 £80
b. Imperf between (vert pair) £700 £80
c. Imperf vert (horiz pair) £800
2 1d. bright rose . . . . 1·75 1
a. Imperf between (horiz pair) £650 £75
b. Imperf between (vert pair) £1100
c. Perf 12½ (coil) (1929) . . . . 2·75 80·0
3 1½d. bistre-brown . . . . 2·00 8
a. Imperf between (horiz pair) £7500
b. Imperf between (vert pair) £4500
c. Printed double, once albino £325
4 2d. black and purple-grey . . . . 2·25 7
a. Imperf between (horiz pair) £9500
5 3d. blue . . . . 2·25 2·7
6 4d. black and orange-red . . . . 2·50 2·7
7 6d. black and mauve . . . . 2·00 3·7
a. Imperf between (horiz pair) £30000
8 8d. purple and pale green . . . . 11·00 42·(
a. Frame double, once albino . . . .
9 10d. blue and rose . . . . 11·00 48·(
10 1s. black and light blue . . . . 5·00 5·5
11 1s.6d. black and yellow . . . . 19·00 32·(
12 2s. black and brown . . . . 17·00 17·(
13 2s.6d. blue and sepia . . . . 30·00 60·
14 5s. blue and blue-green . . . . 60·00 £1
1/14 *Set of* 14 . . . . £150 £3:

Prices for "imperf between" varieties are for adjacent stamps fro[m] the same pane and not for those separated by wide gutter margi[ns] between vertical or horizontal pairs, which come from the junctio[n] of two panes.

(T **2** recess by B.W.; T **3** typo by Waterlow)

1931 (1 April)–**37**. *T* **2** (line perf 12 unless otherwise stated and (comb perf 16 × 14). (The 11½ perf is comb.).

15 **2** ½d. green . . . . 85 1·
a. Perf 11½ (1933) 65
b. Perf 14 (1935) . . . . 1·60
16 1d. scarlet . . . . 1·00
a. Pert 11½ (1933) . . . . 1·75
b. Perf 14 (1935) 50
16*c* 1½d. chocolate (3.3.33) . . . . 55·00 42·
d. Perf 11½ (1.4.32) . . . . 2·50
17 **3** 2d. black and sepia . . . . 4·00 1·
18 3d. deep ultramarine . . . . 10·00 11·
19 **2** 4d. black and vermilion . . . . 1·25 1·
a. Perf 11½ (1935) . . . . 17·00 5·
b. Perf 14 (10.37) . . . . 32·00 48·
20 6d. black and magenta . . . . 2·25 3·
a. Perf 11½ (1933) . . . . 15·00 1
b. Perf 14 (1936) . . . . 7·00
21 8d. violet and olive-green . . . . 1·75 3·
a. Perf 11½ (1934) . . . . 17·00 32
21*b* 9d. vermilion and olive-green (1.9.34) . . . . 6·00 9
22 10d. blue and scarlet . . . . 7·00 2·
a. Perf 11½ (1933) . . . . 6·00 13
23 1s. black and greenish blue . . . . 2·00 2·
a. Perf 11½ (1935) £100 60
b. Perf 14 (10.37) £200 £1
24 1s.6d. black and orange-yellow . . . . 10·00 16
a. Perf 11½ (1936) . . . . 50·00 £1
25 2s. black and brown . . . . 21·00 6
a. Perf 11½ (1933) . . . . 35·00 30
26 2s.6d. blue and drab . . . . 32·00 35
a. Perf 11½ (1933) . . . . 28·00 30
27 5s. blue and blue-green . . . . 48·00 48
a. Printed on gummed side £4000
15/27 *Set of* 15 . . . . £130 £1

No. 16c was only issued in booklets.

PRINTERS. All stamps from Types **4** to **29** were recess-printed by Waterlow and Sons, Ltd, London, except where otherwise stated.

4

932 (1 May). P 12½.

9	**4**	2d. green and chocolate	3·75	1·00
0		3d. deep ultramarine	4·00	1·75
		a. Imperf horiz (vert pair)	£7000	£9000
		b. Imperf between (vert pair)	£16000	

5 Victoria Falls

935 (6 May). *Silver Jubilee.* P 11 × 12.

1	**5**	1d. olive and rose-carmine	3·25	1·75
2		2d. emerald and sepia	5·50	5·00
3		3d. violet and deep blue	5·50	10·00
4		6d. black and purple	8·00	14·00
1/4 *Set of* 4			20·00	28·00

935–34. *Inscr "POSTAGE AND REVENUE".*

5	**4**	2d. green and chocolate (P 12½)	3·00	10·00
		a. Perf 14 (1941)	1·75	10
5*b*		3d. deep blue (P 14) (1938)	3·75	30

6 Victoria Falls and Railway Bridge

7 King George VI

937 (12 May). *Coronation.* P 12½.

	6	1d. olive and rose-carmine	60	60
		2d. emerald and sepia	60	1·50
		3d. violet and blue	3·25	7·00
		6d. black and purple	1·75	3·25
/9 *Set of* 4			5·50	11·00

937 (25 Nov). P 14.

	7	½d. green	50	10
		1d. scarlet	50	10
		1½d. red-brown	1·00	30
		4d. red-orange	1·50	10
		6d. grey-black	1·50	50
		8d. emerald-green	2·00	2·25
		9d. pale blue	1·50	70
		10d. purple	2·25	2·75
		1s. black and blue-green	1·75	10
		a. Frame double, one albino	£1300	
		1s.6d. black and orange-yellow	10·00	2·25
		2s. black and brown	14·00	55
		2s.6d. ultramarine and purple	9·00	4·75
		5s. blue and blue-green	18·00	2·25
/52 *Set of* 13			55·00	15·00

Nos. 40/1 exist in coils, constructed from normal sheets.

On No. 48a the frame appears blurred and over-inked.

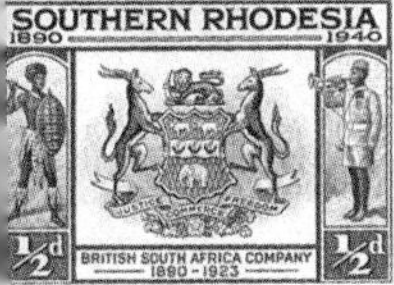

8 British South Africa Co's Arms

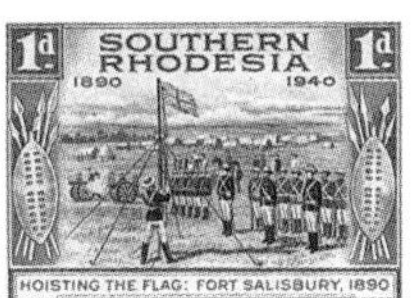

9 Fort Salisbury, 1890

10 Cecil John Rhodes (after S. P. Kendrick)

15 Lobengula's Kraal and Govt House, Salisbury

Recut shirt collar (R. 6/1)

"Cave" flaw (R. 6/6)

(Des Mrs. L. E. Curtis (½d., 1d., 1½d., 3d.), Mrs I. Mount (others))

1940 (3 June). *British South Africa Company's Golden Jubilee. T* **8**/**10**, **15** *and similar designs.* P 14.

53	½d. slate-violet and green	10	65
54	1d. violet-blue and scarlet	10	10
55	1½d. black and red-brown	15	80
	a. Recut shirt collar	20·00	35·00
56	2d. green and bright violet	30	70
57	3d. black and blue	30	1·50
	a. Cave flaw	35·00	
58	4d. green and brown	2·00	2·50
59	6d. chocolate and green	60	2·00
60	1s. blue and green	60	2·00
53/60 Set of 8		3·75	9·00

Designs: *Horiz (as T* **8**)—2d. Fort Victoria; 3d. Rhodes makes peace. *Vert (as T* **10**)—4d. Victoria Falls Bridge; 6d. Statue of Sir Charles Coghlan.

16 Mounted Pioneer

Hat brim retouch (Pl 1B R. 1/8)

Line under saddlebag (Pl 1B R. 6/10)

(Roto South African Govt Printer, Pretoria)

1943 (1 Nov). *50th Anniv of Occupation of Matabeleland.* W **9** of South Africa (Mult Springbok) sideways. P 14.

61	**18**	2d. brown and green	20	85
		a. Hat brim retouch	17·00	
		b. Line under saddlebag	17·00	

17 Queen Elizabeth II when Princess and Princess Margaret

1947 (1 Apr). *Royal Visit. T* **17** *and similar horiz design.* P 14.

62	½d. black and green	25	60
63	1d. black and scarlet	25	60

Design:—1d. King George VI and Queen Elizabeth.

19 Queen Elizabeth

20 King George VI

21 Queen Elizabeth II when Princess

22 Princess Margaret

Damage to right-hand frame (R. 1/10)

1947 (8 May). *Victory.* P 14.

64	**19**	1d. carmine	10	10
65	**20**	2d. slate	10	10
		a. Double print	£1100	
		b. Damaged frame	30·00	
66	**21**	3d. blue	65	75
67	**22**	6d. orange	30	1·25
64/7 *Set of* 4			1·00	1·75

(Recess B.W.)

1949 (10 Oct). *76th Anniv of U.P.U. As Nos. 115/16 of Antigua.*

68	2d. slate-green	70	20
69	3d. blue	80	3·25

23 Queen Victoria, Arms and King George VI

1950 (12 Sept). *Diamond Jubilee of Southern Rhodesia.* P 14.

70	**23**	2d. green and brown	50	1·00

STAMP BOOKLETS

1928 (1 Jan). *Black on blue cover. Stitched.*

SB1 2s.6d. booklet containing twelve ½d. and twenty four 1d. (Nos. 1/2) in blocks of 6 . . . £3500

1931. *Black on blue cover. Stitched.*

SB2 2s.6d. booklet containing twelve ½d. and twentyfour 1d. (Nos. 15/16) in blocks of 6 . . . £5000

1933 (3 Mar). *Black on red cover, size 69 × 53 mm. Stitched.*

SB3 3s. booklet containing twelve ½d., 1d. and 1½d. (Nos. 15, 16, 16c) in blocks of 6 . . . £2750

The 1½d. postage rate was reduced to 1d. eight weeks after No. SB3 was issued. Postal officials were instructed to detach the 1½d. panes and use them for other purposes. The remaining stocks of the booklet were then sold for 1s.6d.

1938 (Oct)–**45**. *Black on yellow cover. Stitched.*

SB4 2s.6d. booklet containing twenty-four ½d. and eighteen 1d. (Nos. 40/1) in blocks of 6 with postage rates on inside front cover . . . £225
a. Label with new rates affixed to inside front cover (1945)
b. Inside front cover blank . . . £250

No. SB4b was issued sometime between 1945 and 1949

POSTAGE DUE STAMPS

SOUTHERN

RHODESIA

(D 1)

1951 (1 Oct). *Postage Due stamps of Great Britain optd with Type* D 1.

D1	D 1	½d. emerald (No. D27)	3·25	16·00
D2		1d. violet-blue (No. D36)	3·00	2·00
D3		2d. agate (No.D29)	2·50	1·75
D4		3d. violet (No. D30)	2·75	2·75
D5		4d. blue (No. D38)	1·75	3·50
D6		4d. dull grey-green (No. D31)	£180	£550
D7		1s. deep blue (No. D33)	2·50	4·00
D1/5, 7 *Set of* 6			14·00	27·00

No. D6 is reported to have been issued to Fort Victoria and Gwelo main poet offices only.

South West Africa

The stamps of Germany were used in the colony from July 1886 until the introduction of issues for GERMAN SOUTH-WEST AFRICA in May 1897. Following occupation by South African forces in 1914–15 the issues of SOUTH AFRICA were used, being replaced by the overprinted issues in 1923.

Walvis (or Walfish) Bay, the major anchorage on the South West Africa coast, was claimed by Great Britain as early as 1796. In 1878 the 430 sq mile area around the port, together with a number of offshore islands, was annexed to Cape Province, passing to the Union of South Africa in 1910.

Stamps of the Cape of Good Hope and South Africa were used at Walfish Bay, often cancelled with numeral obliterator 300, until the enclave was transferred to the South West Africa administration on 1 October 1922.

The Walfish Bay territory reverted to South Africa on 30 August 1977 and from that date the stamps of South Africa were, once again, in use.

PRICES FOR STAMPS ON COVER TO 1945

Nos.	1/40*a*	*from* × 6
Nos.	41/133	*from* × 2
Nos.	D1/5	*from* × 10
Nos.	D6/51	*from* × 20
Nos.	O1/4	*from* × 3
Nos.	O5/20	*from* × 15
No.	O21	*from* × 2
No.	O22	*from* × 15

INSCRIPTIONS. Most of the postage stamps up to No. 140 are inscribed alternately in English and Afrikaans throughout the sheets and the same applies to all the Official stamps and to Nos. D30/33.

PRICES for Nos. 1/140 are for unused horizontal pairs, used horizontal pairs or used singles (either inscr), *unless otherwise indicated.*

OVERPRINT SETTINGS. Between 1923 and 1928 the King George V definitives of South Africa, Types **2** and **3**, and the various postage due stamps were issued overprinted for use in South West Africa. A number of overprint settings were used:

- Setting I – Overprint Types **1** and **2** ("Zuid-West Afrika"). 14 mm between lines of overprint. See Nos. 1/12 and D1/9
- Setting II – As Setting I, but 10 mm between lines of overprint. See Nos. 13/15 and D10/13
- Setting III – Overprint Types **3** ("Zuidwest" Afrika") and **4**. "South West" 14 mm long. "Zuidwest" 11 mm long. 14 mm between lines of overprint. See Nos. 16/27 and D14/17
- Setting IV – As Setting III, but "South West" 16 mm long, "Zuidwest" 12 mm long and 14 mm between lines of overprint. See Nos. 28 and D17*a*/20
- Setting V – As Setting IV, but 12 mm between lines of overprint. See Nos. D21/4
- Setting VI – As Setting IV, but 9½ mm between lines of overprint. See Nos. 29/40 and D25/32.

South West / **Africa.** (1) **Zuid-West** / **Afrika.** (2)

1923 (1 Jan–17 June). *Nos. 3/4, 6 and 9/17 of South Africa optd alternately with T* **1** *and* **2** *by typography.*

(a) Setting I (14 mm between lines of opt).

		Un Pair	*Us pair*	*Us single*
1	½d. green	2·50	9·00	1·00
	a. "Wes" for "West" (R. 20/8)	85·00	£130	
	b. "Afr ica" (R. 20/2)	£120		
	c. Litho opt in shiny ink (17 June)	9·00	50·00	4·75
2	1d. rose-red	3·25	9·00	1·00
	a. Opt inverted	£500		
	b. "Wes" for "West" (R. 12/2)	£160		
	c. "Af.rica" for "Africa" (R. 20/6)	£160	£200	
	d. Opt double	£900		
	e. "Afr ica" (R. 20/2)	£120		
	f. "Afrika" without stop (R. 17/8)	£275		
3	2d. dull purple	4·25	12·00	1·50
	a. Opt inverted	£600	£650	
	b. "Wes" for "West" (R. 20/8)	£250		
	c. Litho opt in shiny ink (30 Mar)	38·00	£100	10·00
4	3d. ultramarine	7·50	16·00	2·75
5	4d. orange-yellow and sage-green	13·00	45·00	4·00
	a. Litho opt in shiny ink (19 Apr)	35·00	70·00	8·00
6	6d. black and violet	8·00	45·00	4·00
	a. Litho opt in shiny ink (19 Apr)	35·00	75·00	7·50
7	1s. orange-yellow	23·00	48·00	5·00
	a. Litho opt in shiny ink (19 Apr)	60·00	£110	11·00
	b. "Afrika" without stop (R. 17/8)			
8	1s.3d. pale violet	30·00	55·00	5·50
	a. Opt inverted	£350		
	b. Litho opt in shiny ink (19 Apr)	75·00	£140	14·00
9	2s.6d. purple and green	60·00	£130	18·00
	a. Litho opt in shiny ink (19 Apr)	£130	£275	35·00
10	5s. purple and blue	£140	£325	50·00
11	10s. blue and olive-green	£1300	£2500	£400
12	£1 green and red	£700	£1700	£250
1/12 *Set of* 12		£2000	£4250	£650
1s/12s Optd "Specimen" *Set of* 12 *singles*		£1300		

Nos. 1/12 were overprinted in complete sheets of 240 (4 panes 6 × 10).

No. 3b shows traces of a type spacer to the right of where the "t" should have been. This spacer is not visible on Nos. 1a and 2b.

Minor varieties, such as broken "t" in "West", were caused by worn type. Stamps showing one line of overprint only or with the lower line above the upper line due to overprint misplacement may also be found. All values exist showing a faint stop after "Afrika" on R. 17/8, but only examples of the 1d. and 1s. have been seen with it completely omitted.

(b) Setting II (10 mm between lines of opt) (31 Mar).

13	5s. purple and blue	£140	£250	45·00
	a. "Afrika" without stop (R. 6/1)	£1000	£1100	£225
14	10s. blue and olive-green	£500	£850	£140
	a. "Afrika" without stop (R. 6/1)	£2250	£2750	£550
15	£1 green and red	£1000	£1400	£200
	a. "Afrika" without stop (R. 6/1)	£4000	£5000	£1000
13/15 *Set of* 3		£1500	£2250	£350

Nos. 13/15 were overprinted in separate panes of 60 (6 × 10).

Examples of most values are known showing a forged Windhoek postmark dated "30 SEP 24".

Zuidwest / **Afrika.** (3) **South West** / **Africa.** (4)

1923 (15 July)–**26**. *Nos. 3/4, 6 and 9/17 of South Africa optd as T* **3** *("Zuidwest" in one word, without hyphen) and* **4** *alternately.*

(a) Setting III ("South West" 14 mm long, "Zuidwest" 11 mm long, 14 mm between lines of opt).

16	½d. green (5.9.24)	6·50	35·00	3·75
	a. "outh" for "South" (R. 1/1)	£1600		
17	1d. rose-red (28.9.23)	5·50	9·00	1·40
	a. "outh" for "South" (R. 1/1)	£1600		
18	2d. dull purple (28.9.23)	6·00	9·00	1·25
	a. Opt double	£1000		
19	3d. ultramarine	5·00	10·00	1·25
20	4d. orange-yellow and sage-green	6·00	21·00	2·75
	w. Wmk inverted	†	†	—
21	6d. black and violet (28.9.23)	14·00	45·00	5·00
22	1s. orange-yellow	14·00	45·00	5·00
23	1s.3d. pale violet	29·00	45·00	5·50
24	2s.6d. purple and green	45·00	80·00	10·00
25	5s. purple and blue	60·00	£130	18·00
26	10s. blue and olive-green	£160	£250	40·00
27	£1 green and red (28.9.23)	£300	£400	60·00
16/27 *Set of* 12		£600	£1000	£140

Nos. 16/27 were overprinted in complete sheets of 240 (4 panes 6 × 10).

Two sets may be made with this overprint, one with bold lettering, and the other from September 1924, with thinner lettering and smaller stops.

(b) Setting IV ("South West" 16 mm long, "Zuidwest" 12 mm long, 14 mm between lines of opt).

28	2s.6d. purple and green (29.6.24)	80·00	£150	28·00

No. 28 was overprinted on two panes of 60 horizontally side by side.

(c) Setting VI ("South West" 16 mm long, "Zuidwest" 12 mm long, 9½ mm between lines of opt).

29	½d. green (16.12.25)	7·00	40·00	5·00
30	1d. rose-red (9.12.24)	3·25	10·00	1·40
	a. Opt omitted (in pair with normal)	£1400		
31	2d. dull purple (9.12.24)	5·00	22·00	1·75
32	3d. ultramarine (31.1.26)	4·50	29·00	2·75
	a. Deep bright blue (20.4.26)	42·00	95·00	12·00
33	4d. orge-yellow & sage-grn (9.12.24)	6·50	45·00	4·00
34	6d. black and violet (9.12.24)	9·00	48·00	5·00
35	1s. orange-yellow (9.12.24)	11·00	48·00	5·00
36	1s.3d. pale violet (9.12.24)	15·00	48·00	5·00
37	2s.6d. purple and green (9.12.24)	29·00	70·00	10·00
38	5s. purple and blue (31.1.26)	42·00	£100	14·00
39	10s. blue and olive-green (9.12.24)	70·00	£130	20·00
40	£1 green and red (9.1.26)	£250	£925	55·00
	a. Pale olive-green and red (8.11.26)	£250	£425	65·00
29/40*a* *Set of* 12		£400	£900	£120
35s, 39s/40s H/S "Specimen" *Set of* 3		£500		

Nos. 29/40 were overprinted in complete sheets of 240 (4 panes of 6 × 10) with, initially, "South West Africa" 16½ mm long on the upper two panes and 16 mm long on the lower two. This order was subsequently reversed. For printings from 8 November 1926 all four panes showed the 16½ mm measurement. No. 40*a* only comes from this printing.

Examples of most values are known showing a forged Windhoek postmark dated "30 SEP 24".

Suidwes / **Afrika.** (5) **South West** / **Africa.** (6)

1926 (1 Jan–1 May). *Nos. 30/2 of South Africa optd with T* **5** *(on stamps inscr in Afrikaans) and* **6** *(on stamps inscr in English) sideways, alternately in black.*

41	½d. black and green	4·00	9·00	1·00
42	1d. black and carmine	3·25	8·00	80
43	6d. green and orange (1 May)	25·00	48·00	7·00
41/3 *Set of* 3		29·00	60·00	8·00

SOUTH WEST AFRICA (7) **SUIDWES-AFRIKA** (8)

1926. *No. 33 of South Africa, imperf optd.*

(a) With T **7** *(English).*

		Single stamps	
44A	4d. grey-blue	75	3·00

(b) With T **8** *(Afrikaans).*

44B	4d. grey-blue	75	3·00

1927. *As Nos. 41/3, but Afrikaans opt on stamp inscr in English and vice versa.*

45	½d. black and green	1·75	7·00	80
	a. "Africa" without stop (R. 13/8)	£160		
46	1d. black and carmine	2·25	2·50	50
	a. "Africa" without stop (R. 13/8)	£300		
47	6d. green and orange	11·00	28·00	3·00
	a. "Africa" without stop (R. 13/8)	£180		
45/7 *Set of* 3		13·50	35·00	3·75

SOUTH WEST AFRICA (9) **S.W.A.** (10) **S.W.A.** (11)

1927. *As No. 44A, but overprint T* **9**.

		Single stamp	
48	4d. grey-blue	6·00	19·0
	s. Handstamped "Specimen"	70·00	

1927 (Apr). *Nos. 34/9 of South Africa optd alternately as T* **5** *and* **6** *in blue, but with lines of overprint spaced 16 mm.*

49	2d. grey and purple	4·75	15·00	1·7
50	3d. black and red	4·75	27·00	2·5
51	1s. brown and blue	15·00	32·00	4·0
52	2s.6d. green and brown	35·00	85·00	13·0
53	5s. black and green	75·00	£170	20·0
54	10s. blue and bistre-brown	65·00	£140	20·0
49/54 *Set of* 6		£180	£425	50·0
49s/51s, 54s H/S "Specimen" *Set of* 4		£350		

A variety of Nos. 49, 50, 51 and 54 with spacing 16½ mm between lines of overprint, occurs in the third vertical row of each sheet.

1927. *As No. 44, but perf 11½ by John Meinert Ltd, Windhoek.*

(a) Optd with T **7** *(English).*

		Single stamp	
55A	4d. grey-blue	80	4·2
	a. Imperf between (pair)	35·00	70·0
	s. Handstamped "Specimen"	70·00	

(b) Optd with T **8** *(Afrikaans).*

55B	4d. grey-blue	80	4·2
	a. Imperf between (pair)	35·00	70·0
	s. Handstamped "Specimen"	70·00	

1927 (Aug)–**30**. *Optd with T* **10**.

(a) On Nos. 13 and 17a of South Africa.

		Single stamp	
56	1s.3d. pale violet	1·25	6·5
	a. Without stop after "A" (R. 3/4)	£100	
	s. Handstamped "Specimen"	75·00	
57	£1 pale olive-green and red	90·00	£16
	a. Without stop after "A" (R. 3/4)	£1400	£225

(b) On Nos. 30/2 and 34/9 of South Africa.

		Un pair	*Us pair*	*U single*
58	½d. black and green	2·25	6·50	8
	a. Without stop after "A"	40·00	75·00	
	b. "S.W.A." opt above value	2·75	15·00	2·2
	c. As b, in vert pair, top stamp without opt	£550		
59	1d. black and carmine	1·25	3·25	5
	a. Without stop after "A"	40·00	75·00	
	b. "S.W.A." opt at top (30.4.30)	1·75	14·00	1·6
	c. As b, in vert pair, top stamp without opt	£475		
60	2d. grey and maroon	9·00	25·00	1·
	c. Perf 14 × 13½	16·00	32·00	
	ca. Without stop after "A"	75·00	£110	
	cb. Opt double, one inverted	£700	£900	
61	3d. black and red	6·00	23·00	3·2
	a. Without stop after "A"	75·00	£120	
	b. Perf 14 × 13½	11·00	38·00	
	ba. Without stop after "A"	80·00	£130	
	bb. Without stop after "W"	£170		
62	4d. brown (4.28)	15·00	40·00	7·
	a. Without stop after "A"	85·00	£130	
	b. Perf 14 × 13½	23·00	48·00	
63	6d. green and orange	11·00	23·00	2·
	a. Without stop after "A"	£110		
64	1s. brown and deep blue	20·00	48·00	5·
	b. Perf 14 × 13½	42·00	80·00	
	ba. Without stop after "A"	£1300	£1500	£3
65	2s.6d. green and brown	40·00	85·00	12·
	a. Without stop after "A"	£160	£275	
	b. Perf 14 × 13½	70·00	£120	
	ba. Without stop after "A"	£190	£325	
66	5s. black and green	60·00	£120	18·
	a. Without stop after "A"	£225	£375	
	b. Perf 14 × 13½	90·00	£150	
	ba. Without stop after "A"	£225	£375	
67	10s. bright blue and brown	£100	£190	28·
	a. Without stop after "A"	£350	£550	
58/67 *Set of* 10		£225	£500	70·
58s/61s, 63s/7s H/S "Specimen" *Set of* 9		£550		

On the ½d., 1d. and 6d. the missing stop variety occurs three tim on each sheet, R. 1/7, 13/4 and one position not yet identified. F the other values it comes on R. 2/3 of the right pane and, for t 2s.6d., 5s. and 10s., on R. 8/1 of the left pane.

The missing stop after "W" on the 3d. occurs on R. 10/5 of t right pane.

The overprint is normally found at the base of the ½d., 1d., 6 1s.3d. and £1 values and at the top of the remainder.

Examples of all values are known showing a forged Windho postmark dated "20 MAR 31".

1930–**31**. *Nos. 42 and 43 of South Africa (rotogravure printing) op with T* **10**.

68	½d. black and green (1931)	9·00	28·00	2·
69	1d. black and carmine	7·50	27·00	2·

1930 (27 Nov–Dec). *Air. Nos. 40/1 of South Africa optd.*

(a) As T **10**.

		Un single	*sin*
70	4d. green (*first printing*)	10·00	28·
	a. No stop after "A" of "S.W.A."	65·00	£1
	b. Later printings	7·00	28·
71	1s. orange (*first printing*)	70·00	£1
	a. No stop after "A" of "S.W.A."	£425	£5
	b. Later printings	11·00	50·

First printing: Thick letters, blurred impression. Stops w rounded corners.

Later printings: Thinner letters, clear impression. Clean c square stops.

(b) As T **11** *(12.30).*

72	4d. green	1·25	6
	a. Opt double	£170	
	b. Opt inverted	£170	
73	1s. orange	3·75	15
	a. Opt double	£500	

12 Kori Bustard

13 Cape Cross

14 Bogenfels

15 Windhoek

16 Waterberg

17 Luderitz Bay

18 Bush Scene

19 Elands

20 Mountain Zebra and Blue Wildebeests

21 Herero Huts

22 Welwitschia Plant

23 Okuwahaken Falls

24 Monoplane over Windhoek

25 Biplane over Windhoek

(Recess B.W.)

931 (5 Mar). *T* **12** *to* **25** *(inscr alternately in English and Afrikaans).* W **9** of South Africa. P 14 × 13½.

(a) Postage.

4 ½d. black and emerald . . . 2·25 2·50 10
5 1d. indigo and scarlet . . . 2·25 2·50 10
6 2d. blue and brown . . . 70 4·00 15
w. Wmk inverted . . . £375
7 3d. grey-blue and blue . . . 70 4·25 15
8 4d. green and purple . . . 1·75 7·00 20
9 6d. blue and brown . . . 1·50 9·00 20
0 1s. chocolate and blue . . . 1·50 10·00 25
1 1s.3d. violet and yellow . . . 7·50 11·00 50
2 2s.6d. carmine and grey . . . 20·00 24·00 1·75
3 5s. sage-green and red-brown . . . 16·00 40·00 2·75
4 10s. red-brown and emerald . . . 45·00 50·00 6·00
5 20s. lake and blue-green . . . 70·00 80·00 10·00

(b) Air.

6 3d. brown and blue . . . 25·00 30·00 2·50
7 10d. black and purple-brown . . . 35·00 65·00 5·00
4/87 *Set of* 14 . . . £200 £300 27·00

Examples of most values are known showing a forged Windhoek ostmark dated "20 MAR 31".

26

(Recess B.W.)

935 (1 May). *Silver Jubilee. Inscr bilingually.* W **9** of South Africa. P 14 × 13½.

Un single *Us single*

8 **26** 1d. black and scarlet . . . 1·00 25
2d. black and sepia . . . 1·00 25
3d. black and blue . . . 7·50 19·00
6d. black and purple . . . 3·00 10·00
/91 *Set of* 4 . . . 11·00 27·00

935–36. *Voortrekker Memorial Fund. Nos. 50/3 of South Africa optd with T* **10**.

½d.+½d. black and green . . . 1·50 5·50 75
a. Opt inverted . . . £275
1d.+½d. grey-black and pink . . . 1·50 3·25 40

94 2d.+1d. grey-green and purple . . . 5·50 6·00 80
a. Without stop after "A" . . . £200 £225
b. Opt double . . . £225
95 3d.+1½d. grey-green and blue . . . 16·00 32·00 4·00
a. Without stop after "A" . . . £250 £300
92/5 *Set of* 4 . . . 22·00 42·00 5·50

27 Mail Train

28

Re-entry (R. 6/3)

(Recess B.W.)

1937 (1 Mar). W **9** of South Africa. P 14 × 13½.

96 **27** 1½d. purple-brown . . . 23·00 3·25 25

(Recess B.W.)

1937 (12 May). *Coronation.* W **9** of South Africa (sideways). P 13½ × 14.

97 **28** ½d. black and emerald . . . 40 15 10
98 1d. black and scarlet . . . 40 15 10
99 1½d. black and orange . . . 40 15 10
100 2d. black and brown . . . 40 15 10
101 3d. black and blue . . . 50 15 10
102 4d. black and purple . . . 50 20 10
a. Re-entry . . . 15·00
103 6d. black and yellow . . . 50 2·75 20
104 1s. black and grey-black . . . 55 3·00 25
97/104 *Set of* 8 . . . 3·25 6·00 65

On. No. 102a the frame and leaves at lower left are doubled. The stamp is inscribed in Afrikaans.

1938 (14 Dec). *Voortrekker Centenary Memorial. Nos. 76/9 of South Africa optd as T* **11**.

105 ½d.+½d. blue and green . . . 8·00 18·00 1·75
106 1d.+1d. blue and carmine . . . 20·00 12·00 1·00
107 1½d.+1½d. chocolate & blue-green . . . 22·00 23·00 2·75
108 3d.+3d. bright blue . . . 45·00 60·00 6·50
105/8 *Set of* 4 . . . 85·00 £100 11·00

1938 (14 Dec). *Voortrekker Commemoration. Nos. 80/1 of South Africa optd as T* **11**.

109 1d. blue and carmine . . . 10·00 18·00 1·50
a. Three bolts in wheel rim . . . 45·00
110 1½d. greenish blue and brown . . . 14·00 20·00 1·75

1939 (17 July). *250th Anniv of Landing of Huguenots in South Africa and Huguenot Commemoration Fund. Nos. 82/4 of South Africa optd as T* **11**.

111 ½d.+½d. brown and green . . . 14·00 13·00 1·10
112 1d.+1d. green and carmine . . . 17·00 13·00 1·25
113 1½d.+1½d. blue-green and purple . . . 25·00 13·00 1·25
111/13 *Set of* 3 . . . 50·00 35·00 3·25

SWA (29) **SWA** (30) **SWA** (31) **S W A** (32)

1941 (1 Oct)–**43**. *War Effort. Nos. 88/96 of South Africa optd with T* **29** *or* **30** *(3d. and 1s.).*

(a) Inscr alternately.

114 ½d. green (1.12.41) . . . 75 4·00 25
a. Blue-green (1942) . . . 65 2·25 15
115 1d. carmine (1.11.41) . . . 55 3·00 15
a. "Stain" on uniform . . . 7·00
116 1½d. myrtle-green (21.1.42) . . . 55 3·25 15
117 3d. blue . . . 22·00 22·00 1·00
a. Cigarette flaw . . . 60·00
118 4d. orange-brown . . . 6·50 14·00 1·00
a. Red-brown . . . 18·00 24·00 3·00
119 6d. red-orange . . . 2·50 4·00 50
120 1s.3d. olive-brown (15.1.43) . . . 12·00 18·00 1·25

(b) Inscr bilingually.

Un single *Us single*

121 2d. violet . . . 50 80
122 1s. brown (17.11.41) . . . 60 80
114/22 *Set of 7 pairs and 2 singles* . . . 42·00 60·00

1943–44. *War Effort (reduced sizes). Nos. 97/104 of South Africa, optd with T* **29** *(1½d. and 1s., No. 130), or T* **31** *(others).*

(a) Inscr alternately.

Un unit *Us unit* *Used single*

123 ½d. blue-green (T) . . . 50 3·75 10
a. Green . . . 4·50 5·50 15
b. Greenish blue . . . 4·00 4·75 10
124 1d. carmine-red (T) . . . 2·25 3·75 10
a. Bright carmine . . . 2·50 4·25 10
125 1½d. red-brown (P) . . . 50 1·00 10
126 2d. violet (P) . . . 7·00 4·50 10
a. Reddish violet . . . 8·50 4·50 10
b. Apostrophe flaw . . . 24·00
127 3d. blue (T) . . . 3·25 16·00 45
128 6d. red-orange (P) . . . 5·50 2·75 30
a. Opt inverted . . . £475

(b) Inscr bilingually.

129 4d. slate-green (T) . . . 2·00 17·00 45
a. Opt inverted . . . £600 £375 50·00
130 1s. brown (opt T **29**) (P) . . . 11·00 24·00 2·00
a. Opt inverted . . . £475 £325
b. Opt T **31**(1944) . . . 4·00 5·00 30
c. Opt T **31** inverted . . . £425 £300 40·00
d. "Bursting shell" . . . 30·00
123/30*b* *Set of* 8 . . . 22·00 48·00 1·75

The "units" referred to above consist of pairs (P) or triplets (T).

No. 128 exists with another type of opt as Type **31**, but with broader "s", narrower "w" and more space between the letters.

1945. *Victory. Nos. 108/10 of South Africa optd with T* **30**.

131 1d. brown and carmine . . . 25 65 10
a. Opt inverted . . . £250 £275
132 2d. slate-blue and violet . . . 30 65 10
133 3d. deep blue and blue . . . 1·25 1·40 10
131/3 *Set of* 3 . . . 1·60 2·40 20

1947 (17 Feb). *Royal Visit. Nos. 111/13 of South Africa optd as T* **31**, *but 8½ × 2 mm.*

134 1d. black and carmine . . . 10 10 10
135 2d. violet . . . 10 40 10
a. "Bird" on "2" . . . 6·00
136 3d. blue . . . 15 25 10
134/6 *Set of* 3 . . . 30 70 15

1948 (26 Apr). *Royal Silver Wedding. No. 125 of South Africa, optd as T* **31**, *but 4 × 2 mm.*

137 3d. blue and silver . . . 1·00 35 10

1949 (1 Oct). *75th Anniv of U.P.U. Nos. 128/30 of South Africa optd as T* **30**, *but 13 × 4 mm.*

138 ½d. blue-green . . . 75 2·00 25
139 1½d. brown-red . . . 75 1·50 15
140 3d. bright blue . . . 1·00 1·00 25
a. Serif on "C" . . . 28·00
b. "Lake" in East Africa . . . 32·00
138/40 *Set of* 3 . . . 2·50 4·00 60

1949 (1 Dec). *Inauguration of Voortrekker Monument, Pretoria. Nos. 131/3 of South Africa optd with T* **32**.

Un single *Us single*

141 1d. magenta . . . 10 10
142 1½d. blue-green . . . 10 10
143 3d. blue . . . 15 45
141/3 *Set of* 3 . . . 30 60

POSTAGE DUE STAMPS

PRICES for Nos. D1/39 are for unused horizontal pairs, used horizontal pairs and used singles.

1923 (1 Jan–July). *Optd with T* **1** *and* **2** *alternately.*

(a) Setting I (14 mm between lines of overprint).

(i) On Nos. D5/6 of Transvaal.

D1 5d. black and violet . . . 4·00 50·00 11·00
a. "Wes" for "West" (R. 8/6, 10/2 left pane) . . . £150
b. "Afrika" without stop (R. 6/1) . . . 95·00
D2 6d. black and red-brown . . . 17·00 50·00 11·00
a. "Wes" for "West" (R. 10/2) . . . £300
b. "Afrika" without stop (R. 6/1, 7/2) . . . £170

(ii) On Nos. D3/4 and D6 of South Africa (De La Rue printing).

D3 2d. black and violet . . . 27·00 48·00 10·00
a. "Wes" for "West" (R. 10/2) . . . £190 £275
b. "Afrika" without stop (R. 6/1, 7/2) . . . £190
D4 3d. black and blue . . . 15·00 48·00 10·00
a. "Wes" for "West" (R. 8/6, 10/2) . . . £140
D5 6d. black and slate (20 Apr) . . . 26·00 55·00 13·00
a. "Wes" for "West" (R. 8/6) . . . £170

(iii) On Nos. D9/10, D11 and D14 of South Africa (Pretoria printings).

D6 ½d. black and green (P 14) . . . 6·00 29·00 5·50
a. Opt inverted . . . £450
b. Opt double . . . £850 £900
c. "Wes" for "West" (R. 10/2) . . . 90·00
d. "Afrika" without stop (R. 6/1, 7/2) . . . 90·00
D7 1d. black and rose (*roul*) . . . 7·00 30·00 6·00
a. "Wes" for "West" (R. 10/2) . . . 95·00 £225
b. "Afrika" without stop (R. 6/1) . . . 95·00
c. Imperf between (horiz pair) . . . £1200
D8 1½d. black and yellow-brown (*roul*) . . . 1·25 14·00 2·75
a. "Wes" for "West" (R. 8/6, 10/2) . . . 75·00
b. "Afrika" without stop (R. 6/1) . . . 80·00
D9 2d. black and violet (P 14) (21 June) . . . 3·50 25·00 5·00
a. "Wes" for "West" (R. 8/6) . . . 90·00
b. "Afrika" without stop (R. 6/1) . . . £110

Nos. D1/9 were initially overprinted as separate panes of 60, but some values were later done as double panes of 120.

A variety of Nos. D1, D4/5 and D9 with 15 mm between the lines of overprint occurs on four positions in each pane from some printings.

(b) Setting II (10 mm between lines of overprint).

(i) On No. D5 of Transvaal.

D10 5d. black and violet (20 Apr) . . 55·00 £150

(ii) On Nos. D3/4 of South Africa (De La Rue printing).

D11 2d. black and violet (20 Apr) . . 17·00 45·00 9·00
a. "Afrika" without stop (R. 6/1) . . . £170
D12 3d. black and blue (20 Apr) . . . 7·50 28·00 5·50
a. "Afrika" without stop (R. 6/1) . . . 85·00

(iii) On No. D9 of South Africa (Pretoria printing). Roul.

D13 1d. black and rose (July) . . . . £8500 — £1500

1923 (30 July)–**26**. *Optd as T* **3** *("Zuidwest" in one word without hyphen) and* **4**.

(a) Setting III ("South West" 14 mm long, "Zuidwest" 11 mm long and 14 mm between lines of overprint).

(i) On No. D6 of Transvaal.

D14 6d. black and red-brown . . . . 21·00 85·00 20·00

(ii) On Nos. D9 and D11/12 of South Africa (Pretoria printing).

D15 ½d. black and green (P 14) . . . 11·00 32·00 5·50
D16 1d. black and rose (*roul*) . . . . 4·25 32·00 5·50
D17 1d. black and rose (P 14) (2.8.23) . . . . 16·00 32·00 5·50

(b) Setting IV ("South West" 16 mm long, "Zuidwest" 12 mm long and 14 mm between lines of overprint).

(i) On No. D5 of Transvaal.

D17*a* 5d. black and violet (1.7.24) . . £450 £900

(ii) On Nos. D11/12 and D16 of South Africa (Pretoria printing). P 14.

D18 ½d. black and green (1.7.24) . . . 7·50 29·00 5·50
D19 1d. black and rose (1.7.24) . . . 6·00 29·00 5·50
D20 6d. black and slate (1.7.24) . . . 2·25 42·00 9·00
a. "Africa" without stop (R. 9/5) £120

(c) Setting V (12 mm. between lines of overprint).

(i) On No. D5 of Transvaal.

D21 5d. black and violet (6.8.24) . . . 4·00 50·00 9·00

(ii) On No. D4 of South Africa (De La Rue printing).

D22 3d. black and blue (6.8.24) . . . 16·00 50·00 11·00

(iii) On Nos. D11 and D13 of South Africa (Pretoria printing). P 14.

D23 ½d. black and green (6.8.24) . . 3·00 29·00 6·50
D24 1½d. black & yellow-brown (6.8.24) . . . . 5·00 42·00 7·50

(d) Setting VI (9½ mm between lines of overprint).

(i) On No. D5 of Transvaal.

D25 5d. black and violet (7.9.24) . . . 2·75 19·00 3·50
a. "Africa" without stop (R. 9/5) . . . . 75·00

(ii) On No. D4 of South Africa (De La Rue printing).

D26 3d. black and blue (3.2.26) . . . 7·00 55·00 11·00

(iii) On Nos. D11/16 of South Africa (Pretoria printing). P 14.

D27 ½d. black and green (1.3.26) . . 9·50 35·00 7·50
D28 1d. black and rose (16.3.25) . . 2·00 11·00 1·60
a. "Africa" without stop (R. 9/5 right pane) . . . . 80·00
D29 1½d. black & yellow-brown (1.10.26) . . . . . . 4·50 32·00 6·50
a. "Africa" without stop (R. 9/5 right pane) . . . . 85·00
D30 2d. black and violet (7.9.24) . . 2·50 18·00 3·50
a. "Africa" without stop (R. 9/5) right pane) . . . 70·00
D31 3d. black and blue (6.5.26) . . . 4·50 19·00 3·75
a. "Africa" without stop (R. 9/5) right pane) . . . 75·00
D32 6d. black and slate (1.10.26) . . 9·00 50·00 14·00
a. "Africa" without stop (R. 9/5 right pane) £140
D27/32 *Set of* 6 . . . . 29·00 £150 32·00

For Setting VI the overprint was applied to sheets of 120 (2 panes of 60) of the 1d., 3d. and 6d., and to individual panes of 60 for the other values. The two measurements of "South West", as detailed under No. 40, also occur on the postage dues. Nos. D25 and D31/2 show it 16 mm long, No. 27 16½ mm long and the other stamps can be found with either measurement. In addition to the complete panes the 16½ mm long "South West" also occurs on R. 2/4 in the 16 mm left pane for Nos. D28 and D30/2.

Suidwes **Afrika.** (D 1)   **South West** **Africa.** (D 2)

1927 (14 May–27 Sept). *Optd as Types D* **1** *and D* **2**, *alternately, 12 mm between lines of overprint.*

(a) On No. D5 of Transvaal.

D33 5d. black and violet (27 Sept) . . 19·00 85·00 23·00

(b) On Nos. D13/16 of South Africa (Pretoria printing). P 14.

D34 1½d. black and yellow-brown . . 1·00 19·00 3·50
D35 2d. black and pale violet (27 Sept) . . . . 4·75 15·00 3·25
a. Black and deep violet . . . . 8·00 16·00 3·50
D37 3d. black and blue (27 Sept) . . 13·00 45·00 11·00
D38 6d. black and slate (27 Sept) . . 7·50 35·00 8·50

(c) On No. D18 of South Africa (Pretoria printing). P 14.

D39 1d. black and carmine . . . . . 1·00 11·00 2·25
D33/9 *Set of* 6 . . . . 42·00 £200 45·00

No. D33 was overprinted in panes of 60 and the remainder as complete sheets of 120.

Examples of all values can be found with very small or very faint stops from various positions in the sheet.

1928–29. *Optd with T* **10**.

(a) On Nos. D15/16 of South Africa.

		Un Single	Us Single
D40	3d. black and blue	1·50	15·00
	a. Without stop after "A" (R. 3/6)	32·00	
D41	6d. black and slate	6·00	28·00
	a. Without stop after "A" (R. 3/6)	£130	

(b) On Nos. D17/21 of South Africa.

D42	½d. black and green	50	8·00
D43	1d. black and carmine	50	3·25
	a. Without stop after "A" (R. 3/6)	40·00	
D44	2d. black and mauve	50	4·50
	a. Without stop after "A" (R. 3/6)	55·00	
D45	3d. black and blue	2·25	26·00
D46	6d. black and slate	1·50	20·00
	a. Without stop after "A" (R. 3/6)	50·00	£180
D42/6	*Set of* 5	4·75	55·00

D 3

(Litho B.W.)

1931 (23 Feb). *Inscribed bilingually.* W **9** of South Africa. P 12.

D47	D 3	½d. black and green	1·00	9·00
D48		1d. black and scarlet	1·00	1·25
D49		2d. black and violet	1·00	2·75
D50		3d. black and blue	4·25	17·00
D51		6d. black and slate	13·00	27·00
D47/51		*Set of* 5	18·00	50·00

OFFICIAL STAMPS

OFFICIAL South West Africa. (O 1)   **OFFISIEEL Suidwes Afrika.** (O 2)

1926 (Dec). *Nos. 30, 31, 6 and 32 of South Africa optd with Type* O **1** *on English stamp and* O **2** *on Afrikaans stamp alternately.*

		Un pair	Us pair	Us single
O1	½d. black and green	75·00	£180	30·00
O2	1d. black and carmine	75·00	£180	30·00
O3	2d. dull purple	£170	£300	45·00
O4	6d. green and orange	95·00	£170	30·00
O1/4	*Set of* 4	£375	£750	£120

OFFICIAL S.W.A. (O 3)   **OFFISIEEL S.W.A.** (O 4)

1929 (May). *Nos. 30, 31, 32 and 34 of South Africa optd with Type* O **3** *on English stamp and* O **4** *on Afrikaans stamp.*

O5	½d. black and green	1·00	15·00	2·75
O6	1d. black and carmine	1·00	15·00	2·75
	w. Wmk inverted	£200		
O7	2d. grey and purple	1·50	20·00	3·50
	a. Pair, one stamp without stop after "OFFICIAL"	5·50	45·00	
	b. Pair, one stamp without stop after "OFFISIEEL"	5·50	45·00	
	c. Pair, comprising a and b	16·00	85·00	
O8	6d. green and orange	2·00	20·00	3·75
O5/8	*Set of* 4	5·00	65·00	11·50

Types O 3 and O 4 are normally spaced 17 mm between lines on all except the 2d. value, which is spaced 13 mm.

Except on No. O7, the words "OFFICIAL" or "OFFISIEEL" normally have no stops after them.

OFFICIAL S.W.A. (O 5)   **OFFISIEEL S.W.A.** (O 6)

OFFICIAL. S.W.A. (O 7)   **OFFISIEEL. S.W.A.** (O 8)

1929 (Aug). *Nos. 30, 31 and 32 of South Africa optd with Types* O **5** *and* O **6**, *and No. 34 with Types* O **7** *and* O **8**, *languages to correspond.*

O 9	½d. black and green	75	15·00	2·75
O10	1d. black and carmine	1·00	15·00	2·75
O11	2d. grey and purple	1·00	15·00	3·25
	a. Pair, one stamp without stop after "OFFICIAL"	3·75	40·00	
	b. Pair, one stamp without stop after "OFFISIEEL"	3·75	40·00	
	c. Pair, comprising a and b	18·00	90·00	
O12	6d. green and orange	2·50	27·00	6·50
O9/12	*Set of* 4	4·75	65·00	13·50

Examples of Nos. O1/12 are known showing forged Windhoek postmarks dated "30 SEP 24" or "20 MAR 31".

OFFICIAL (O 9)   **OFFISIEEL** (O 10)

1931. *English stamp optd with Type* O **9** *and Afrikaans stamp with Type* O **10** *in red.*

O13	12	½d. black and emerald	11·00	18·00	3·50
O14	13	1d. indigo and scarlet	1·00	18·00	3·50
O15	14	2d. blue and brown	2·25	10·00	2·25
O16	17	6d. blue and brown	3·25	14·00	3·25
O13/16		*Set of* 4	16·00	55·00	11·50

OFFICIAL (O 11)   **OFFISIEEL** (O 12)

1938 (1 July). *English stamp optd with Type* O **11** *and Afrikaans stamp with Type* O **12** *in red.*

O17	27	1½d. purple-brown	25·00	45·00	6·00

OFFICIAL (O 13)   **OFFISIEEL** (O 14)

1945–50. *English stamp optd with Type* O **13**, *and Afrikaans stamp with Type* O **14** *in red.*

O18	12	½d. black and emerald	13·00	27·00	5·00
O19	13	1d. indigo and scarlet (1950)	6·50	16·00	3·25
		a. Opt double	£425		
O20	27	1½d. purple-brown	35·00	45·00	6·50
O21	14	2d. blue and brown (1947?)	£475	£600	£100
O22	17	6d. blue and brown	17·00	48·00	7·00
O18/20, O22		*Set of* 4	65·00	£120	20·00

OFFICIAL (O 15)   **OFFISIEEL** (O 16)

1951 (16 Nov)–**52**. *English stamp optd with Type* O **15** *and Afrikaans stamp with Type* O **16**, *in red.*

O23	12	½d. black and emerald (1952)	14·00	22·00	4·5
O24	13	1d. indigo and scarlet	5·00	16·00	1·7
		a. Opts transposed	80·00	£160	
O25	27	1½d. purple-brown	24·00	25·00	5·0
		a. Opts transposed	70·00	80·00	
O26	14	2d. blue and brown	1·50	17·00	3·5
		a. Opts transposed	50·00	£160	
O27	17	6d. blue and brown	2·75	40·00	7·5
		a. Opts transposed	22·00	£110	
O23/7		*Set of* 5	42·00	£110	20·0

The above errors refer to stamps with the English overprint on Afrikaans stamp and *vice versa.*

The use of official stamps ceased in January 1955.

Sudan

ANGLO-EGYPTIAN CONDOMINIUM

An Egyptian post office was opened at Suakin in 1867 and the stamps of Egypt, including postage dues and the official (No. O64) were used in the Sudan until replaced by the overprinted "SOUDAN" issue of 1897.

Cancellations have been identified from eleven post offices, using the following postmark types:

A B C D E F

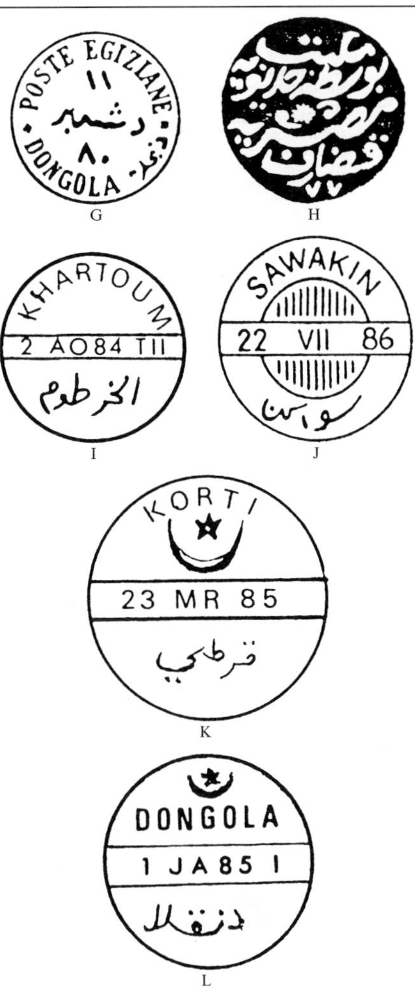

G H I J K L

BERBER (*spelt* BARBAR). *Open* 1 October 1873 *to* 20 May 1884. *Postmark type* G.
DABROUSSA. *Open* 1891 *onwards. Postmark as type* J *but with* 11 *bars in arcs.*
DONGOLA. *Open* 1 October 1873 *to* 13 June 1885 *and* 1896 *onwards. Postmark types* F, G, K, L.
GEDAREF. *Open* August 1878 *to* April 1884. *Postmark type* H.
KASSALA. *Open* 15 May 1875 *to* 30 July 1885. *Postmark type* G.
KHARTOUM. *Open* 1 October 1873 *to* 14 December 1885. *Postmark types* E (*spelt* KARTUM), G (*spelt* HARTUM), I (*with or without line of Arabic above date*).
KORTI. *Open* January *to* March 1885 *and* 1897. *Postmark type* K.
SUAKIN. *Open* November 1867 *onwards. Postmark types* A, B, C (*spelt* SUAKIM), D (*spelt* SUAKIM *and also with year replaced by concentric arcs*), I (*spelt* SOUAKIN), J (*spelt* SAWAKIN, *number of bars differs*).
TANI. *Open* 1885. *Postmark type* K.
TOKAR. *Open* 1891 *onwards. Postmark type* J (7 *bars in arcs*).
WADI HALFA. *Open* 1 October 1873 *onwards. Postmark types* F (*spelt* WADI HALFE), G (*spelt* WADI HALFE), I, J (*number of bars differs*).
WADI HALFA CAMP. *Open* 1896 *onwards. Postmark type* I.

Official records also list post offices at the following locations, but no genuine postal markings from them have yet been reported: Chaka, Dara, Debeira, El Abiad, El Fasher, El Kalabat, Faras, Fashoda, Fazogl, Ishkeit, Kalkal, Karkok, Mesellemia, Sara, Sennar and Taoufikia (not to be confused with the town of the same name in Egypt).

M

The post office at Kassala was operated by Italy from 1894 until 1896, using stamps of Eritrea cancelled with postmark type M.

From the last years of the nineteenth century that part of Sudan lying south of the 5 degree North latitude line was administered by Uganda (the area to the east of the Nile) (until 1912) or by Belgium (the area to the west of the Nile, known as the Lado Enclave) (until 1910).

Stamps of Uganda or East Africa and Uganda were used at Gondokoro and Nimuli between 1901 and 1911, usually cancelled with circular date stamps or, probably in transit at Khartoum, by a lozenge-shaped grid of 18 × 17 dots.

Stamps of Belgian Congo were used from the Lado Enclave between 1897 and 1910, as were those of Uganda (1901–10) and Sudan (1902–10), although no local postmarks were supplied, examples being initially cancelled in manuscript.

Stamps of Sudan were used at Gambeila (Ethiopia) between 1910 and 10 June 1940 and from 22 March 1941 until 15 October 1956. Sudan stamps were also used at Sabderat (Eritrea) between March 1910 and 1940.

PRICES FOR STAMPS ON COVER TO 1945	
Nos. 1/9	*from* × 20
Nos. 10/17	*from* × 6
Nos. 18/29	*from* × 5
Nos. 30/95	*from* × 2
Nos. D1/11	*from* × 30
Nos. O1/3	*from* × 10
Nos. O4/22	*from* × 15
Nos. A1/16	*from* × 6

(Currency. 10 milliemes = 1 piastre. 100 piastres = £1 Sudanese)

السودان
SOUDAN
(1)

1897 (1 Mar). *Nos. 54b, 55a, 57la, 58a, 59, 60, 62a and 63 of Egypt optd as T* **1** *by Govt Ptg Wks, Blaq, Cairo.*

1	1m. pale brown	2·00	2·00
	a. Opt inverted	£200	
	b. Opt omitted (in vert pair with normal)	£1000	
	c. Deep brown	2·00	2·25
	w. Wmk inverted		
3	2m. green	1·25	1·75
4	3m. orange-yellow	1·40	1·50
5	5m. rose-carmine	2·00	70
	a. Opt inverted	£200	£225
	b. Opt omitted (in vert pair with normal)	£1100	
6	1p. ultramarine	7·00	2·00
7	2p. orange-brown	50·00	16·00
8	5p. slate	48·00	18·00
	a. Opt double	£4000	
	b. Opt omitted (in vert pair with normal)	£4000	
9	10p. mauve	30·00	40·00
1/9 *Set of* 8		£130	75·00

Numerous forgeries exist including some which show the characteristics of the varieties mentioned below.

There are six varieties of the overprint on each value. Vertical strips of 6 showing them are worth a premium.

Four settings of the overprint were previously recognised by specialists, but one of these is now regarded as an unauthorised reprint from the original type. Here reprints can only be detected when in multiples. The 2p. with inverted watermark only exists with this unauthorised overprint so it is not listed.

In some printings the large dot is omitted from the left-hand Arabic character on one stamp in the pane of 60.

Only two examples, one unused and the other used (in the Royal Collection), are known of No. 8a. In both instances one impression is partially albino.

PRINTERS. All stamps of Sudan were printed by De La Rue & Co, Ltd, London, *except where otherwise stated.*

2 Arab Postman

3

(Des E. A. Stanton. Typo)

1898 (1 Mar). W **3**. P 14.

10	**2**	1m. brown and pink	65	2·25
11		2m. green and brown	2·00	2·75
12		3m. mauve and green	2·00	2·25
13		5m. carmine and black	1·75	1·50
14		1p. blue and brown	5·50	4·00
15		2p. black and blue	24·00	7·50
16		5p. brown and green	30·00	15·00
17		10p. black and mauve	25·00	2·25
10/17 *Set of* 8			80·00	32·00

4

5 Milliemes
(5)

1902–21. *Ordinary paper.* W **4**. P 14.

18	**2**	1m. brown and carmine (5.05)	1·25	65
19		2m. green and brown (11.02)	1·75	10
20		3m. mauve and green (3.03)	2·25	25
21		4m. blue and bistre (20.1.07)	1·50	2·50
22		4m. vermilion and brown (10.07)	1·50	75
23		5m. scarlet and black (12.03)	2·00	10
		w. Wmk inverted	†	£100
24		1p. blue and brown (12.03)	2·25	30
25		2p. black and blue (2.08)	24·00	1·75
26		2p. purple & orge-yellow (*chalk-surfaced paper*) (22.12.21)	3·75	10·00
27		5p. brown and green (2.08)	22·00	30
		a. Chalk-surfaced paper	32·00	4·00
28		10p. black and mauve (2.11)	22·00	3·75
		a. Chalk-surfaced paper	28·00	9·00
18/28 *Set of* 11			75·00	18·00

1903 (Sept). *No. 16 surch at Khartoum with T* **5**, *in blocks of 30.*

29	**2**	5m.on 5 pi. brown and green	6·50	9·50
		a. Surch inverted	£250	£225

6

7

1921–23. *Chalk-surfaced paper. Typo.* W **4**. P 14.

30	**6**	1m. black and orange (4.2.22)	80	4·25
31		2m. yellow-orange and chocolate (1922)	9·00	11·00
		a. Yellow and chocolate (1923)	11·00	11·00
32		3m. mauve and green (25.1.22)	2·50	9·00
33		4m. green and chocolate (21.3.22)	6·00	4·50
34		5m. olive-brown and black (4.2.22)	2·25	10
35		10m. carmine and black (1922)	3·00	10
36		15m. bright blue and chestnut (14.12.21)	2·75	1·00
30/36 *Set of* 7			24·00	27·00

1927–41. *Chalk-surfaced paper.* W **7**. P 14.

37	**6**	1m. black and orange	70	10
		a. Ordinary paper (1941)	70	10
38		2m. orange and chocolate	75	10
		a. Ordinary paper (1941)	1·50	10
39		3m. mauve and green	70	10
		a. Ordinary paper (1941)	2·75	30
40	**6**	4m. green and chocolate	60	10
		a. Ordinary paper (1941)	3·50	30
		aw. Wmk inverted	75·00	75·00
41		5m. olive-brown and black	60	10
		a. Ordinary paper (1941)	2·50	10
42	**6**	10m. carmine and black	1·50	10
		a. Ordinary paper (1941)	3·00	10
43		15m. bright blue and chestnut	1·75	10
		a. Ordinary paper (1941)	1·50	10
44	**2**	2p. purple and orange-yellow	1·75	10
		a. Ordinary paper (1941)	4·00	10
44*b*		3p. red-brown and blue (1.1.40)	2·75	10
		ba. Ordinary paper (1941)	17·00	10
44*c*		4p. ultramarine and black (2.11.36)	3·50	10
45		5p. chestnut and green	1·25	10
		a. Ordinary paper (1941)	5·00	1·75
45*b*		6p. greenish blue and black (2.11.36)	6·00	1·25
		ba. Ordinary paper (1941)	32·00	1·75
45*c*		8p. emerald and black (2.11.36)	6·00	2·75
		ca. Ordinary paper (1941)	42·00	4·00
46		10p. black and reddish purple	3·75	10
		a. Ordinary paper. *Black and bright mauve* (1941)	8·50	70
46*b*		20p. pale blue and blue (17.10.35)	4·50	10
		ba. Ordinary paper (1941)	5·50	10
37/46*b Set of* 15			32·00	4·00

The ordinary paper of this issue is thick, smooth and opaque and was a wartime substitute for chalk-surfaced paper.

For similar stamps, but with different Arabic inscriptions, see Nos. 96/111.

AIR MAIL (8) **AIR MAIL** (9) **AIR** Extended foot to "R" (R. 5/12)

1931 (15 Feb–Mar). *Air. Nos. 41/2 and 44 optd with T* **8** *or* **9** *(2p.).*

47	**6**	5m. olive-brown and black (Mar)	35	70
48		10m. carmine and black	85	11·00
49	**2**	2p. purple and orange-yellow	85	7·50
		a. Extended foot to "R"	25·00	
47/9 *Set of* 3			1·90	16·00

2½ 2½

10 Statue of Gen. Gordon

AIR MAIL
(11)

1931 (1 Sept)–**37**. *Air. Recess.* W **7** (sideways*). P 14.

49*b*	**10**	3m. green and sepia (1.1.33)	2·50	6·50
50		5m. black and green	1·00	10
51		10m. black and carmine	1·00	20
52		15m. red-brown and sepia	40	10
		aw. Wmk top of G to right		
		b. Perf 11½ × 12½ (1937)	4·50	10
53		2p. black and orange	30	10
		ax. Wmk reversed		
		b. Perf 11½ × 12½ (1937)	4·50	15·00

53*c* 2½p. magenta and blue (1.1.33) 3·50 10
d. Perf 11½ × 12½ (1936) 3·00 10
da. Aniline magenta and blue 7·50 3·50
dx. Wmk reversed
dy. Wmk sideways inverted (top of G to right) and reversed
54 3p. black and grey 60 15
a. Perf 11½ × 12½ (1937) 85 35
55 3½p. black and violet 1·50 80
a. Perf 11½ × 12½ (1937) 2·50 12·00
ay. Wmk sideways inverted (top of G to right) and reversed † —
56 4½p. red-brown and grey 10·00 15·00
57 5p. black and ultramarine 1·00 30
a. Perf 11½ × 12½ (1937) 3·75 35
57*b* 7½p. green and emerald (17.10.35) 9·50 5·00
by. Wmk sideways inverted (top of G to right) and reversed £100
c. Perf 11½ × 12½ (1937) 4·00 10·00
57*d* 10p. brown and greenish blue (17.10.35) 9·00 1·75
e. Perf 11½ × 12½ (1937) 4·00 20·00
ey. Wmk sideways inverted (top of G to right) and reversed
49*b*/57*d* *Set of* 12 (P 14) 35·00 26·00
52b/7e *Set of* 8 (P 11½ × 12½) 24·00 50·00

*The normal sideways watermark shows the top of the G pointing left *as seen from the back of the stamp.*

1932 (18 July). *Air. No. 44 surch with T* **11**.
58 **2** 2½p.on 2p. purple and orange-yellow 1·40 3·50

12 Gen. Gordon (after C. Ouless)

13 Gordon Memorial College, Khartoum

14 Gordon Memorial Service, Khartoum (after R. C. Woodville)

1935 (1 Jan). *50th Death Anniv of General Gordon. Recess.* W **7**. P 14.
59 **12** 5m. green 35 10
60 10m. yellow-brown 85 25
61 13m. ultramarine 85 10·00
62 15m. scarlet 1·75 25
63 **13** 2p. blue 1·25 20
64 5p. orange-vermilion 1·25 40
65 10p. purple 7·50 8·50
66 **14** 20p. black 22·00 50·00
67 50p. red-brown 80·00 £110
59/67 *Set of* 9 £100 £160

7½ PIASTRES
٧ ١/٢ قروش
(15)

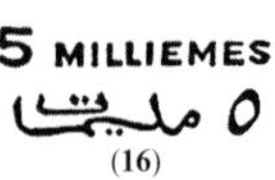

(16)

1935. *Air. Nos. 49b/51 and 56 surch as T* **15** *at Khartoum.*
68 **10** 15m.on 10m. black and carmine (Apr) 40 10
a. Surch double £650 £750
69 2½p.on 3m. green and sepia (Apr) 85 5·50
a. Second arabic letter from left missing 50·00 £100
b. Small "½" 2·25 21·00
70 2½p.on 5m. black and green (Apr) 50 1·50
a. Second Arabic letter from left missing 25·00 55·00
b. Small "½" 1·25 8·00
c. Surch inverted £700 £800
d. Ditto with variety a. £3500
e. Ditto with variety b. £1400 £1500
71 3p.on 4½p. red-brown and grey (Apr) 1·75 17·00
72 7½p.on 4½p. red-brown and grey (Mar) 6·50 48·00
73 10p.on 4½p. red-brown and grey (Mar) 6·50 48·00
68/73 *Set of* 6 15·00 £110

Nos. 69a and 70a occur in position 49 of the sheet of 50; the small "½" variety occurs in positions 17, 27, 32, 36, 41, 42 and 46.

The 15m. on 10m. surcharged in red and the 2½p. on 3m. and 2½p., on 5m. in green are from proof sheets; the latter two items being known cancelled (*Price*, £200 *each, unused*).

There were four proof sheets of the 7½p. on 4½p, two in red and two in black. The setting on these proof sheets showed three errors subsequently corrected before No. 72 was surcharged. Twelve positions showed an Arabic "¹" instead of "½", one an English "¼" for "½" and another one of the Arabic letters inverted.

1938 (1 July). *Air. Nos. 53d, 55, 57b and 57d surch as T* **16** *by De La Rue.*
74 **10** 5m.on 2½p. mag & bl (P 11½ × 12½) 3·50 10
w. Wmk top of G to right
x. Wmk reversed
75 3p.on 3½p. black and violet (P 14) 35·00 48·00
a. Perf 11½ × 12½ £450 £550
76 3p.on 7½p. green and emerald (P 14) 7·00 6·50
ax. Wmk reversed
ay. Wmk sideways inverted (top of G to right) and reversed 50·00
b. Perf 11½ × 12½ £450 £550
77 5p.on 10p. brown & greenish bl (P 14) 1·75 4·75
a. Perf 11½ × 12½ £450 £550
74/7 *Set of* 4 42·00 55·00

A 5p. on 2½p., perf 11½ × 12½ exists either mint or cancelled from a trial printing (*Price* £350 *unused*).

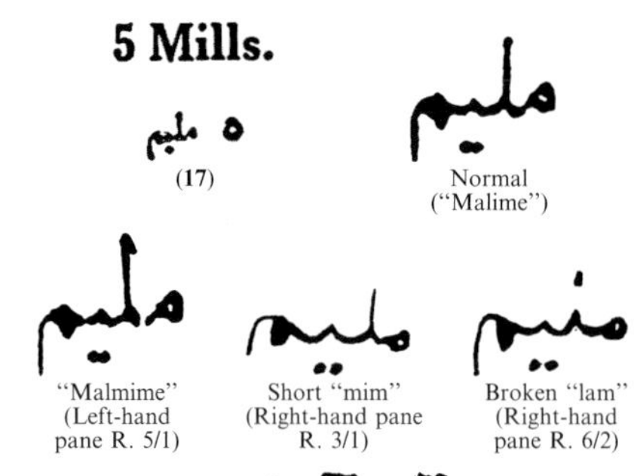

5 Mills.
(17)
Normal ("Malime")
"Malmime" (Left-hand pane R. 5/1)
Short "mim" (Right-hand pane R. 3/1)
Broken "lam" (Right-hand pane R. 6/2)

5 M

Inserted "5" (Bottom right-hand pane R. 4/5)

1940 (25 Feb). *No. 42 surch with T* **17** *by McCorquodale (Sudan) Ltd, Khartoum.*
78 **6** 5m.on 10m. carmine and black 60 30
a. "Malmime" 60·00 70·00
b. Two dots omitted (Right-hand pane R. 8/6) 60·00 70·00
c. Short "mim" 60·00 70·00
d. Broken "lam" 60·00 70·00
e. Inserted "5" £160

4½
PIASTRES
(18)

4½
Piastres
٤ ١/٢ قرش
(19)

1940–41. *Nos. 41 and 45c surch as T* **18** *or* **19** *at Khartoum.*
79 **6** 4½p.on 5m. olive-brown & blk (9.2.41) 48·00 6·00
80 **2** 4½p.on 8p. emerald and black (12.12.40) 40·00 9·00

20 Tuti Island, R. Nile, near Khartoum

21 Tuti Island, R. Nile near Khartoum

(Des Miss H. M. Hebbert. Litho Security Printing Press, Nasik, India)

1941 (25 Mar–10 Aug). P 14 × 13½ (T **20**) or P 13½ × 14 (T **21**).
81 **20** 1m. slate and orange (10.8) 1·50 4·00
82 2m. orange and chocolate (10.8) 1·50 4·00
83 3m. mauve and green (10.8) 1·75 20
84 4m. green and chocolate (10.8) 80 60
85 5m. olive-brown and black (10.8) 30 10
86 10m. carmine and black (10.8) 8·00 2·25
87 15m. bright blue and chestnut 1·00 10
88 **21** 2p. purple and orange-yellow (10.8) 6·50 60
89 3p. red-brown and blue 1·00 10
90 4p. ultramarine and black 1·50 10
91 5p. chestnut and green (10.8) 5·00 9·00
92 6p. greenish blue and black (10.8) 18·00 40
93 8p. emerald and black (10.8) 14·00 45
94 10p. slate and purple (10.8) 60·00 75
95 20p. pale blue and blue (10.8) 55·00 32·00
81/95 *Set of* 15 £160 48·00

22

23

1948 (1 Jan–June). *Arabic inscriptions below camel altered. Typo. Ordinary paper (8, 10, 20p.) or chalk-surfaced paper (others).* W **7**. P 14.
96 **22** 1m. black and orange 35 3·50
97 2m. orange and chocolate 80 4·50
98 3m. mauve and green 30 4·50
99 4m. deep green and chocolate 50 30
100 5m. olive-brown and black 5·50 2·00
w. Wmk inverted 75·00
101 10m. rose-red and black 5·50 10
a. Centre inverted † —
102 15m. ultramarine and chestnut 5·00 10
103 **23** 2p. brown-orange and orange-yellow 8·00 2·50
104 3p. red-brown and deep blue 7·00 30
105 4p. ultramarine and black 4·00 1·75
106 5p. brown-orange and deep green 4·00 2·50
107 6p. greenish blue and black 4·50 3·00
108 8p. bluish green and black 4·50 3·00
109 10p. black and mauve 11·00 4·50
a. Chalk-surfaced paper (June) 38·00 5·50
110 20p. pale blue and deep blue 4·50 30
a. Perf 13. Chalk-surfaced paper (June) 50·00 £170
111 50p. carmine and ultramarine 6·50 2·50
96/111 *Set of* 16 60·00 32·00

A single used example is known of No. 101a.

For similar stamps, but with different Arabic inscriptions, see Nos. 37/46*b*.

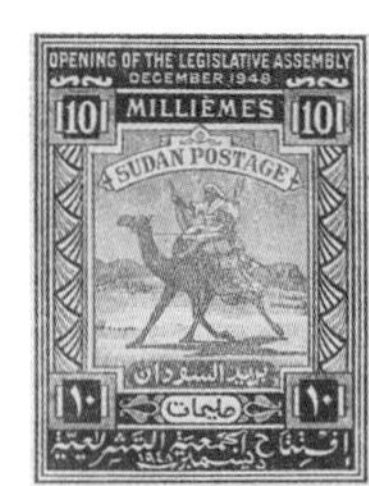

24 **25**

1948 (1 Oct). *Golden Jubilee of "Camel Postman" design. Chalk-surfaced paper. Typo.* W **7**. P 13.
112 **24** 2p. black and light blue 20 1(

1948 (23 Dec). *Opening of Legislative Assembly. Chalk-surfaced paper. Typo.* W **7**. P 13.
113 **25** 10m. rose-red and black 50 1(
114 5p. brown-orange and deep green 1·00 1·5

26 Blue Nile Bridge, Khartoum

(Des Col. W. L. Atkinson (2½p., 6p.), G. R. Wilson (3p.), others from photographs. Recess)

1950 (1 July). *Air. T* **26** *and similar horiz designs.* W **7**. P 12.
115 2p. black and blue-green 4·50 1·5
116 2½p. light blue and red-orange 75 1·2
117 3p. reddish purple and blue 3·00 1·2
118 3½p. purple-brown and yellow-brown 2·50 3·0
119 4p. brown and light blue 1·50 2·7
120 4½p. black and ultramarine 2·50 3·7
a. Black and steel-blue 10·00 6·5
121 6p. black and carmine 2·25 3·2
122 20p. black and purple 2·25 5·5
115/122 *Set of* 8 17·00 20·0

Designs:—2½p. Kassala Jebel; 3p. Sagia (water wheel); 3½p. Po[r] Sudan 4p. Gordon Memorial College; 4½p. *Gordon Pasha* (Nile ma[il] boat); 6p. Suakin; 20p. G.P.O., Khartoum.

34 Ibex

35 Cotton Picking

(Des Col. W. L. Atkinson (1m., 2m., 4m., 5m., 10m., 3p., 3½p., 20p.), Col. E. A. Stanton (50p.) others from photographs. Typo

1951 (1 Sept)–**62**?. *Designs as T* **34/5**. *Chalk-surfaced paper.* W
P 14 (millieme values) or 13 (piastre values).
123 1m. black and orange 1·50 1·
124 2m. black and bright blue 1·75 1·(
125 3m. black and green 6·50 3·
126 4m. black and yellow-green 1·50 3·
127 5m. black and purple 2·25
a. Black and reddish purple (11.61*) 6·00
128 10m. black and pale blue 30
129 15m. black and chestnut 3·50
a. Black and brown-orange (1961*) 4·50
130 2p. deep blue and pale blue 30
a. Deep blue and very pale blue (1960*) 4·00
131 3p. brown and dull ultramarine 7·50
a. Brown and deep blue (1960*) 9·00 1·
132 3½p. bright green and red-brown 2·00
a. Light emerald and red-brown (11.61*) 4·00
133 4p. ultramarine and black 1·25
a. Deep blue and black (7.59*) 7·00
134 5p. orange-brown and yellow-green 50
135 6p. blue and black 8·50 2·
a. Deep blue and black (1962?) 16·00 6·
136 8p. blue and brown 14·00 3·
a. Deep blue and brown (1962?) 16·00 3·
137 10p. black and green 1·50
138 20p. blue-green and black 5·00 2·
139 50p. carmine and black 13·00 2·
123/39 *Set of* 17 60·00 18·

Designs: *Vert as T* **34**—2m. Whale-headed Stork; 3m. Giraffe; 4m. Baggara girl; 5m. Shilluk warrior; 10m. Hadendowa; 15m. Policeman. *Horiz as T* **35**—3p. Ambatch reed canoe; 3½p. Nuba wrestlers; 4p. Weaving; 5p. Saluka farming; 6p. Gum tapping; 8p. Darfur chief 10p. Stack Laboratory; 20p. Nile Lechwe. *Vert as T* **35**—50p. Camel postman.
*Earliest known postmark date.

STAMP BOOKLETS

Nos. SB1/4 have one cover inscribed in English and one in Arabic. Listings are provided for booklets believed to have been issued, with prices quoted for those known to still exist.

1912 (Dec). *Black on pink cover, size 74 × 29 mm. Stapled.*
SB1 100m. booklet containing twenty 5m. (No. 23) in pairs . . . £650

1924. *Black on pink cover, size 45 × 50 mm. Stapled.*
SB2 105m. booklet containing twenty 5m. (No. 34) in blocks of 4 . . .

1930. *Black on pink cover, size 45 × 50 mm. Stapled.*
SB3 100m. booklet containing twenty 5m. (No. 41) in blocks of 4 . . . £1200
Some supplies of No. SB3 included a page of air mail labels.

POSTAGE DUE STAMPS

1897 (1 Mar). *Type* D **24** *of Egypt, optd with T* **1** *at Blaq.*
D1 2m. green . . . 1·75 5·00
a. Opt omitted (in horiz pair with normal) . . . £2250
D2 4m. maroon . . . 1·75 5·00
a. Bisected (2m.) (on cover) . . . † —
D3 1p. ultramarine . . . 10·00 3·50
D4 2p. orange . . . 10·00 7·00
a. Bisected (1p.) (on cover) . . . † £1200
D1/4 *Set of* 4 . . . 21·00 18·00
In some printings the large dot is omitted from the left-hand Arabic character on one stamp in the pane.
No. D1 has been recorded used as a bisect.

D 1 Gunboat *Zafir* D 2

1901 (1 Jan)–**26**. *Typo. Ordinary paper.* W **4** (sideways). P 14.
D5 D **1** 2m. black and brown . . . 55 60
a. Wmk upright (1912) . . . £150 60·00
b. Chalk-surfaced paper (6.24*) . . . 75 5·00
D6 4m. brown and green . . . 2·00 90
a. Chalk-surfaced paper (9.26*) . . . 5·50 2·25
D7 10m. green and mauve . . . 3·75 3·75
a. Wmk upright (1912) . . . £100 50·00
b. Chalk-surfaced paper (6.24*) . . . 10·00 9·00
D8 20m. ultramarine and carmine . . . 3·25 3·25
D5/8 *Set of* 4 . . . 8·00 7·50
*Dates quoted for the chalk-surfaced paper printings are those of the earliest recorded postal use. These printings were despatched to the Sudan in March 1922 (10m.) or September 1922 (others).
The 4 m is known bisected at Khartoum or Omdurman in November/December 1901 and the 20m. at El Obeid in 1904–05.

1927–30. *Chalk-surfaced paper.* W **7**. P 14.
D9 D **1** 2m. black and brown (1930) . . . 2·50 2·50
D10 4m. brown and green . . . 1·00 80
D11 10m. green and mauve . . . 1·25 1·60
a. Ordinary paper . . . 18·00
D9/11 *Set of* 3 . . . 4·25 4·50

1948 (1 Jan). *Arabic inscriptions at foot altered. Chalk-surfaced paper. Typo.* W **7**. P 14.
D12 D **2** 2m. black and brown-orange . . . 1·00 35·00
D13 4m. brown and green . . . 2·00 35·00
D14 10m. green and mauve . . . 18·00 20·00
D15 20m. ultramarine and carmine . . . 18·00 32·00
D12/15 *Set of* 4 . . . 35·00 £110
The 10 and 20m. were reissued in 1980 on Sudan arms watermarked paper.

OFFICIAL STAMPS

1900 (8 Feb). *5 mils of 1897 punctured "S G" by hand. The "S" has 14 and the "G" 12 holes.*
O1 5m. rose-carmine . . . 48·00 16·00

1901 (Jan). *1m.* wmk Quatrefoil, *punctured as No. O1.*
O2 1m. brown and pink . . . 42·00 30·00
Nos. O1/2 are found with the punctured "SG" inverted, reversed or inverted and reversed.

O.S.G.S. **O.S.G.S.**
(O 1) (O 2)
("On Sudan Government Service")

1902. *No. 10 optd at Khartoum as Type* O **1** *in groups of 30 stamps.*
O3 **2** 1m. brown and pink . . . 2·00 8·50
a. Oval "O" (No. 19) . . . 40·00 £110
b. Round stops. (Nos. 25 to 30) . . . 7·50 40·00
c. Opt inverted . . . £250 £350
d. Ditto and oval "O" . . . £2500 £3000
e. Ditto and round stops . . . £600 £750
f. Opt double . . . £350
g. Ditto and round stops . . . £800
h. Ditto and oval "O" . . .

1903–12. *T* **2** *optd as Type* O **2**, *by D.L.R. in sheets of 120 stamps.*
(i) Wmk Quatrefoil (3.06).
O4 10p. black and mauve . . . 13·00 25·00
a. Malformed "O" . . . £120
(ii) Wmk Mult Star and Crescent.
O 5 1m. brown and carmine (9.04) . . . 50 10
a. Opt double . . .
b. Malformed "O" . . . 19·00
O 6 3m. mauve and green (2.04) . . . 2·50 15
a. Opt double . . . £850 £850
b. Malformed "O" . . . 42·00
O 7 5m. scarlet and black (1.1.03) . . . 2·50 10
a. Malformed "O" . . . 42·00
O 8 1p. blue and brown (1.1.03) . . . 2·50 10
a. Malformed "O" . . . 42·00
O 9 2p. black and blue (1.1.03) . . . 22·00 20
a. Malformed "O" . . . £150
O10 5p. brown and green (1.1.03) . . . 2·00 30
a. Malformed "O" . . . 45·00
O11 10p. black and mauve (9.12) . . . 4·00 55·00
a. Malformed "O" . . . 65·00
O4/11 *Set of* 8 . . . 45·00 70·00
The malformed "O" is slightly flattened on the left-hand side and occurs on position 7 of the lower pane.

1913 (Jan)–**22**. *Nos. 18/20 and 23/8 punctured "SG" by machine. The "S" has 12 holes and the "G" 13.*
O12 **2** 1m. brown and carmine . . . 8·00 25
O13 2m. green and brown (1915) . . . 8·00 7·50
O14 3m. mauve and green . . . 13·00 70
O15 5m. scarlet and black . . . 4·50 15
O16 1p. blue and brown . . . 6·50 35
O17 2p. black and blue . . . 14·00 65
O18 2p. purple and orange-yellow (*chalk-surfaced paper*) (1922) . . . 5·50 8·00
O19 5p. brown and green . . . 29·00 1·50
a. Chalk-surfaced paper . . . 29·00 4·25
O20 10p. black and mauve (1914) . . . 38·00 32·00
a. Chalk-surfaced paper . . . 38·00 32·00
O12/20 *Set of* 9 . . . £110 45·00

1922. *Nos. 32/5 punctured "SG" by machine. The "S" has 9 holes and the "G" 10.*
O21 **6** 3m. mauve and green . . . 16·00 14·00
O22 4m. green and chocolate . . . 19·00 9·00
O23 5m. olive-brown and black . . . 2·50 1·50
O24 10m. carmine and black . . . 2·50 1·50
O21/4 *Set of* 4 . . . 35·00 23·00

1927–30. *Nos. 39/42, 44, 45 and 46 punctured "SG" by machine. Nos. O25/8 have 9 holes in the "S" and 10 in the "G"; Nos. O29/31 12 holes in the "S" and 13 in the "G".*
O25 **6** 3m. mauve and green (1928) . . . 13·00 3·50
O26 4m. green and chocolate (1930) . . . 70·00 48·00
O27 5m. olive-green and black . . . 5·00 10
O28 10m. carmine and black . . . 15·00 35
O29 **2** 2p. purple and orange-yellow . . . 17·00 1·00
O30 5p. chestnut and green . . . 18·00 3·50
O31 10p. black and reddish purple . . . 35·00 10·00
O25/31 *Set of* 7 . . . £160 60·00
The use of Nos. O25/31 on internal official mail ceased in 1932, but they continued to be required for official mail to foreign destinations until replaced by Nos. O32/46 in 1936.

S.G. **S.G.** **S.G.**
(O 3) (O 4) (O 4a)

1936 (19 Sept)–**46**. *Nos. 37a, 38a, 39/43 optd with Type* O **3**, *and 44, 44ba, 44c, 45, 45ba, 45ca, 46 and 46ba with Type* O **4**. W **7**. P 14.
O32 **6** 1m. black and orange (22.11.46) . . . 2·50 9·50
a. Opt double . . . † £150
O33 2m. orange and chocolate (*ordinary paper*) (4.45) . . . 1·00 4·50
a. Chalk-surfaced paper . . . — 70·00
O34 3m. mauve and green (*chalk-surfaced paper*) (1.37) . . . 3·00 10
O35 4m. green and chocolate (*chalk-surfaced paper*) . . . 3·50 2·75
a. Ordinary paper . . .
O36 5m. olive-brown and black (*chalk-surfaced paper*) (3.40) . . . 2·25 10
a. Ordinary paper . . . 20·00 40
O37 10m. carmine and black (*chalk-surfaced paper*) (6.46) . . . 1·00 10
O38 15m. bright blue and chestnut (*chalk-surfaced paper*) (21.6.37) . . . 7·50 30
a. Ordinary paper . . . 50·00 2·25
O39 **2** 2p. purple and orange-yellow (*chalk-surfaced paper*) (4.37) . . . 14·00 10
a. Ordinary paper . . . 35·00 2·50
O39*b* 3p. red-brown and blue (4.46) . . . 6·50 2·75
O39*c* 4p. ultramarine and black (*chalk-surfaced paper*) (4.46) . . . 28·00 4·50
ca. Ordinary paper . . . 60·00 4·00
O40 5p. chestnut and green (*chalk-surfaced paper*) . . . 17·00 10
a. Ordinary paper . . . 65·00 4·50
O40*b* 6p. greenish blue and black (4.46) . . . 8·00 7·00
O40*c* 8p. emerald and black (4.46) . . . 5·50 29·00
O41 10p. black and reddish purple (*chalk-surfaced paper*) (10.37) . . . 30·00 11·00
a. Ordinary paper. *Black and bright mauve* (1941) . . . 50·00 4·00
O42 20p. pale blue and blue (6.46) . . . 28·00 23·00
O32/42 *Set of* 15 . . . £140 80·00

1948 (1 Jan). *Nos. 96/102 optd with Type* O **3**, *and 103/111 with Type* O **4**.
O43 **22** 1m. black and orange . . . 30 3·75
O44 2m. orange and chocolate . . . 1·25 10
O45 3m. mauve and green . . . 3·25 6·50
O46 4m. deep green and chocolate . . . 3·25 4·25
O47 5m. olive-brown and black . . . 3·25 10
O48 10m. rose-red and black . . . 3·25 1·50
O49 15m. ultramarine and chestnut . . . 3·25 10
O50 **23** 2p. purple and orange-yellow . . . 3·25 10
O51 3p. red-brown and deep blue . . . 3·25 10
O52 4p. ultramarine and black . . . 3·25 10
a. Perf 13 (optd Type O **4*a***) . . . 13·00 15·00
O53 5p. brown-orange and deep green . . . 4·00 10
O54 6p. greenish blue and black . . . 3·25 10
O55 8p. bluish green and black . . . 3·25 2·50
O56 10p. black and mauve . . . 5·00 20
O57 20p. pale blue and deep blue . . . 4·50 25
O58 50p. carmine and ultramarine . . . 65·00 60·00
O43/58 *Set of* 16 . . . £100 70·00

1950 (1 July). *Air. Optd with Type* O **4a**.
O59 2p. black and blue-green (R.) . . . 15·00 3·25
O60 2½p. light blue and red-orange . . . 1·50 1·75
O61 3p. reddish purple and blue . . . 80 1·00
O62 3½p. purple-brown and yellow-brown . . . 80 7·50
O63 4p. brown and light blue . . . 80 7·50
O64 4½p. black and ultramarine (R.) . . . 4·00 17·00
a. Black and steel-blue . . . 9·00 18·00
O65 6p. black and carmine (R.) . . . 1·00 4·25
O66 20p. black and purple (R.) . . . 4·00 12·00
O59/66 *Set of* 8 . . . 25·00 48·00

1951 (1 Sept)–**62?**. *Nos. 123/9 optd with Type* O **3**, *and 130/9 with Type* O **4a**.
O67 1m. black and orange (R.) . . . 40 3·75
O68 2m. black and bright blue (R.) . . . 50 1·00
O69 3m. black and green (R.) . . . 4·00 15·00
O70 4m. black and yellow-green (R.) . . . 10 5·50
O71 5m. black and purple (R.) . . . 10 10
O72 10m. black and pale blue (R.) . . . 10 10
O73 15m. black and chestnut (R.) . . . 30 10
O74 2p. deep blue and pale blue . . . 10 10
a. Opt inverted . . . £500
b. Deep blue and very pale blue (1962?) . . . 1·25 10
O75 3p. brown and dull ultramarine . . . 8·50 10
a. Brown and deep blue (1962?) . . . 8·50 1·75
O76 3½p. bright green and red-brown . . . 25 10
a. Light emerald & red-brown (1962?) . . . 3·50 2·00
O77 4p. ultramarine and black . . . 1·00 10
a. Deep blue and black (1961) . . . 2·25 10
O78 5p. orange-brown and yellow-green . . . 25 10
O79 6p. blue and black . . . 50 2·75
a. Deep blue and black (1962?) . . . 9·00 6·50
O80 8p. blue and brown . . . 55 10
a. Deep blue and brown (1962?) . . . 4·50 2·25
O81 10p. black and green (R.) . . . 50 10
O81*a* 10p. black and green (Blk.) (1958) . . . 13·00 2·00
O82 20p. blue-green and black . . . 1·25 30
a. Opt inverted . . . — £700
O83 50p. carmine and black . . . 3·50 1·25
O67/83 *Set of* 18 . . . 30·00 27·00
The 5, 10 and 15m. values were later reissued with a thinner overprint.

ARMY SERVICE STAMPS

ARMY OFFICIAL / ARMY OFFICIAL / Army Service
(A 1) (A 2) (A 3)

1905 (1 Jan). *T* **2** *optd at Khartoum as Types* A **1** *or* A **2**. Wmk Mult Star and Crescent.
(i) "ARMY" *reading up.*
A1 1m. brown and carmine (A **1**) . . . 2·50 2·00
a. "!" for "1" . . . 55·00 32·00
b. Opt Type A **2** . . . 40·00 24·00
c. Pair. Types A **1** and A **2** *se-tenant* . . . 75·00
(ii) Overprint horizontal.
A2 1m. brown and carmine (A **1**) . . . £325
a. "!" for "1" . . . £3500
b. Opt Type A **2** . . . £2000
The horizontal overprint exists with either "ARMY" or "OFFICIAL" reading the right way up. It did not fit the stamps, resulting in misplacements where more than one whole overprint appears, or when the two words are transposed.
(iii) "ARMY" reading down.
A3 1m. brown and carmine (A **1**) . . . 80·00 65·00
a. "!" for "1" . . . £750 £750
b. Opt Type A **2** . . . £650 £450

1905 (Nov). *As No. A1, but* wmk Quatrefoil, W **3**.
A4 1m. brown and pink (A **1**) . . . £130 £140
a. "!" for "1" . . . £3000 £1700
b. Opt Type A **2** . . . £1400 £1400
c. Pair. Types A **1** and A **2** *se-tenant* . . . £3000
The setting used for overprinting Nos. A1/4 was 30 (6 × 5). The "!" for "1" variety occurs on R. 5/4 and overprint Type A **2** on R. 1/6 and 2/6 of the setting.

Two varieties of the 1 millieme.

A. 1st Ptg. 14 mm between lines of opt.
B. Later Ptgs. 12 mm between lines.
All other values are Type B.

1906 (Jan)–**11**. *T* **2** *optd as Type A* **3**.
(i) Wmk Mult Star and Crescent, W **4**.
A 5 1m. brown and carmine (Type A) . . . £325 £250
a. Opt double, one albino . . . £350
A 6 1m. brown and carmine (Type B) . . . 1·50 20
a. Opt double, one diagonal . . . † £750
b. Opt inverted . . . £400 £425
c. Pair, one without opt . . . † £4000
d. "Service" omitted . . . † £3500
e. "" for "A" in "Army" . . . £150 £150
A 7 2m. green and brown . . . 12·00 1·00
a. Pair, one without opt . . . £2500
b. "Army" omitted . . . £3000 £3000
A 8 3m. mauve and green . . . 17·00 40
a. Opt inverted . . . £1900

A 9 5m. scarlet and black . . . 1·50 10
a. Opt. double . . . £190 £190
ab. Opt double, one diagonal . . . £200
b. Opt inverted . . . † £200
c. "Amry" . . . † £2250
d. "" for "A" in "Army" . . . — £250
e. Opt double, one inverted . . . £800 £375
A10 1p. blue and brown . . . 13·00 15
a. "Army" omitted . . . † £2000
A11 2p. black and blue (1.09) . . . 55·00 13·00
a. Opt double . . . † £3000
A12 5p. brown and green (5.08) . . . £120 65·00
A13 10p. black and mauve (5.11) . . . £475 £600
A6s/10s Optd "Specimen" *Set of* 5 . . . £110

There were a number of printings of these Army Service stamps; the earlier are as Type A **3**; the 1908 printing has a narrower "A" in "Army" and the 1910–11 printings have the tail of the "y" in "Army" much shorter.

(ii) Wmk Quatrefoil, W **3**.

A14 2p. black and blue . . . 65·00 10·00
A15 5p. brown and green . . . 90·00 £180
A16 10p. black and mauve . . . £130 £375
A14/16 *Set of* 3 . . . £250 £500
A14s/16s Optd "Specimen" *Set of* 3 . . . £100

1912 (1 Jan)–**22**. *Nos. 18/20 and 23/8 punctured "AS" by machine. The "A" has 12 holes and the "S" 11.*

A17 **2** 1m. brown and carmine . . . 27·00 3·75
A18 2m. green and brown . . . 6·50 70
A19 3m. mauve and green . . . 42·00 3·00
A20 5m. scarlet and black . . . 9·00 50
a. On No. 13
A21 1p. blue and brown . . . 22·00 75
A22 2p. black and blue . . . 48·00 4·25
A23 2p. purple and orange-yellow (*chalk-surfaced paper*) (1922) . . . 55·00 55·00
A24 5p. brown and green . . . 55·00 27·00
a. Chalk-surfaced paper . . . 55·00 27·00
A25 10p. black and mauve (1914) . . . £400 £225
A17/25 *Set of* 9 . . . £600 £275

1922–24. *Nos. 31a and 34/5 punctured "AS" by machine. The "A" has 8 holes and the "S" 9.*

A26 **6** 2m. yellow and chocolate (1924) . . . 65·00 42·00
A27 5m. olive-brown and black (4.2.22) . . . 11·00 4·00
A28 10m. carmine and black . . . 17·00 4·75
A26/8 *Set of* 3 . . . 85·00 45·00

The use of Nos. A17/28 on internal Army mail ceased when the Egyptian units were withdrawn at the end of 1924, but existing stocks continued to be used on Army mail to foreign destinations until supplies were exhausted.

Swaziland

PRICES FOR STAMPS ON COVER TO 1945		
Nos.	1/10	*from* × 40
Nos.	11/20	*from* × 4
Nos.	21/4	*from* × 5
Nos.	25/7	*from* × 10
Nos.	28/38	*from* × 4
Nos.	39/41	*from* × 5
Nos.	D1/2	*from* × 30

TRIPARTITE GOVERNMENT

Following internal unrest and problems caused by the multitude of commercial concessions granted by the Swazi king the British and Transvaal governments intervened during 1889 to establish a tripartite administration under which the country was controlled by their representatives, acting with the agent of the Swazi king.

The Pretoria government had previously purchased the concession to run the postal service and, on the establishment of the tripartite administration, provided overprinted Transvaal stamps for use from a post office at Embekelweni and later at Bremersdorp and Darkton.

Swazieland
(**1**)

1889 (18 Oct)–**90**. *Stamps of Transvaal (South African Republic) optd with T* **1**, *in black.*

(a) P 12½ × 12.

1 **18** 1d. carmine . . . 17·00 16·00
a. Opt inverted . . . £700 £650
2 2d. olive-bistre . . . 85·00 22·00
a. Opt inverted . . . — £1100
b. "Swazielan" . . . £1000 £650
3 1s. green . . . 10·00 13·00
a. Opt inverted . . . £600 £450

(b) P 12½.

4 **18** ½d. grey . . . 9·00 18·00
a. Opt inverted . . . £850 £650
b. "Swazielan" . . . £1100 £700
c. "Swazielan" inverted . . . — £4000
5 2d. olive-bistre . . . 17·00 15·00
a. Opt inverted . . . £700 £450
b. "Swazielan" . . . £475 £400
c. "Swazielan" inverted . . . £3750 £3500
d. Opt double . . . £2250
6 6d. blue . . . 21·00 42·00
7 2s.6d. buff (20.10.90) . . . £225 £250
8 5s. slate-blue (20.10.90) . . . £140 £180
a. Opt inverted . . . £1600 £1800
b. "Swazielan" . . . £4250
c. "Swazielan" inverted
9 10s. dull chestnut (20.10.90) . . . £5000 £3000

The variety without "d" occurs on the left-hand bottom corner stamp in each sheet of certain printings.

A printing of the ½d, 1d., 2d. and 10s. yellow-brown with stop after "Swazieland" was made in July 1894, but such stamps were not issued.

It is possible that the dates quoted above were those on which the overprinting took place in Pretoria and that the stamps were issued slightly later in Swaziland itself.

1892 (Aug). *Optd in carmine.* P 12½.

10 **18** ½d. grey . . . 7·50 16·00
a. Opt inverted . . . £500
b. Opt double . . . £450 £450
c. Pair, one without opt . . . — £1700

No. 10 was overprinted in Pretoria during August 1892 when Swaziland was under quarantine due to smallpox. It is unlikely that it saw much postal use before all the overprints were withdrawn, although cancelled-to-order examples are plentiful.

It appears likely that no further supplies of stamps overprinted "Swazieland" were provided by Pretoria after December 1892, although stocks held at post offices were used up. The overprinted stamps were declared to be invalid from 7 November 1894. They were replaced by unoverprinted issues of the Transvaal (South African Republic).

Stamps of TRANSVAAL (SOUTH AFRICAN REPUBLIC) *used in Swaziland between* December 1892 *and* January 1900.

1885–93. *(Nos. 175/87).*

Z1 ½d. grey . . . 28·00
Z2 1d. carmine . . . 28·00
Z3 2d. olive-bistre . . . 14·00
Z4 2½d. mauve . . . 28·00
Z5 3d. mauve . . . 28·00
Z6 4d. bronze-green . . . 28·00
Z9 2s. 6d. orange-buff

1893. *(Nos.195/9).*

Z10 ½d.on 2d. olive-bistre (Type A surch in red)
Z11 ½d.on 2d. olive-bistre (Type A surch in black)
Z12 1d.on 6d. blue (Type A surch) . . . 30·00
a. Surch Type B . . . 30·00
Z13 2½d.on 1s. green ("2½ Pence" in one line) (Type A surch) . . . 30·00
a. Surch Type B . . . 30·00

1894. *(Nos. 200/4).*

Z16 1d. carmine . . . 28·00
Z17 2d. olive-bistre . . . 28·00

1895–96. *(Nos. 205/12a)*

Z20 ½d. pearl-grey . . . 28·00
Z21 1d. rose-red . . . 14·00
Z22 2d. olive-bistre . . . 14·00
Z25 6d. pale dull blue . . . 28·00

1895. *(Nos. 213/14).*

Z27 ½d.on 1s. green

1895. *Introduction of Penny Postage (No. 215b)*

Z29 1d. red . . . 38·00

1896–97. *(Nos. 216/24).*

Z30 ½d. green . . . 28·00
Z31 1d. rose-red and green . . . 14·00
Z35 4d. sage-green and green . . . 28·00
Z36 6d. lilac and green . . . 28·00
Z37 1s. ochre and green . . . 55·00

Prices are for clear and fairly complete postmarks. Examples dated in 1892 and 1893 are worth a premium. For list of post offices open during this period see boxed note below. Most known examples are from Bremersdorp (squared circle inscr "SWAZIEL" later replaced by "Z.A.R." or c.d.s.) or Darkton (c.d.s.).

Shortly after the outbreak of the Boer War in 1899 the Transvaal administration withdrew from Swaziland, although the post office at Darkton, which was on the border, was still operating in early 1900. There was, however, no further organised postal service in Swaziland until the country became a British Protectorate in March 1902. From that date, until the introduction of the 1933 definitives, the stamps of Transvaal and subsequently South Africa were in use.

The following post offices or postal agencies existed in Swaziland before 1933. Dates given are those on which it is generally accepted that the offices were first opened. Some were subsequently closed before the end of the period.

Bremersdorp (1890)	Mankaiana (1913)
Darkton (1891)	Mbabane (*previously*
Dwaleni (1918)	Embabaan) (1905)
Embabaan (1895)	M'dimba (1898)
Embekelweni (1889)	Mhlotsheni (1910)
Ezulweni (1910)	Mooihoek (1918)
Forbes Reef (1906)	Motshane (1929)
Goedgegun (1925)	Nomahasha (1904)
Hlatikulu (1903)	Nsoko (1927)
Hluti (1912)	Piggs Peak (1899)
Ivy (1912)	Sandhlan (1903)
Kubuta (1926)	Sicunusa (1913)
Mahamba (1899)	Stegi (1910)
Malkerns (1914)	Umkwakweni (1898)
Malomba (1928)	White Umbuluzi (1925)

BRITISH PROTECTORATE

2 King George V

3 King George VI

(Des Rev. C. C. Tugman. Recess D.L.R.)

1933 (2 Jan). Wmk Mult Script CA. P 14.

11 **2** ½d. green . . . 30 30
12 1d. carmine . . . 30 20
13 2d. brown . . . 30 4
14 3d. blue . . . 45 2·7
15 4d. orange . . . 2·75 3·2
16 6d. bright purple . . . 1·25 1·0
17 1s. olive . . . 1·50 2·7
18 2s.6d. bright violet . . . 15·00 22·0
19 5s. grey . . . 30·00 48·0
20 10s. sepia . . . 80·00 £10
11/20 *Set of* 10 . . . £120 £15
11s/20s Perf "Specimen" *Set of* 10 . . . £225

The ½d, 1d., 2d. and 6d. values exist overprinted "OFFICIAL" but authority for their use was withdrawn before any were actuall used. However, some stamps had already been issued to th Secretariat staff before instructions were received to invalidate thei use (*Price* £12000 *per set un*).

1935 (4 May). *Silver Jubilee. As Nos. 91/4 of Antigua, but ptd b B.W.* P 11 × 12.

21 1d. deep blue and scarlet . . . 50 1·5
a. Extra flagstaff . . . £225 £30
b. Short extra flagstaff . . . £325
c. Lightning conductor . . . £325
d. Flagstaff on right-hand turret . . . £100
e. Double flagstaff . . . £100
22 2d. ultramarine and grey-black . . . 50 1·5
a. Extra flagstaff . . . £100
b. Short extra flagstaff . . . £120
c. Lightning conductor . . . 90·00
23 3d. brown and deep blue . . . 55 5·0
a. Extra flagstaff . . . 75·00
b. Short extra flagstaff . . . 90·00 £15
c. Lightning conductor . . . 85·00
24 6d. slate and purple . . . 65 2·0
a. Extra flagstaff . . . 90·00
b. Short extra flagstaff . . . 95·00
c. Lightning conductor . . . £100
21/4 *Set of* 4 . . . 2·00 9·0
21s/4s Perf "Specimen" *Set of* 4 . . . 95·00

For illustrations of plate varieties see Omnibus section followin Zanzibar.

1937 (12 May). *Coronation. As Nos. 95/7 of Antigua.* P 11 × 11½.

25 1d. carmine . . . 50 1·7
26 2d. yellow-brown . . . 50 2
27 3d. blue . . . 50 6
25/7 *Set of* 3 . . . 1·40 2·2
25s/7s Perf "Specimen" *Set of* 3 . . . 75·00

(Recess D.L.R.)

1938 (1 Apr)–**54**. Wmk Mult Script CA. P 13½ × 13.

28 **3** ½d. green . . . 2·50 1·2
a. Perf 13½ × 14 (1.43) . . . 30 2·7
b. Perf 13½ × 14. *Bronze-green* (2.50) . . . 1·75 6·0
29 1d. rose-red . . . 2·75 1·2
a. Perf 13½ × 14 (1.43) . . . 1·00 1·7
30 1½d. light blue . . . 4·25 7
a. Perf 14 (1941) . . . 2·75 1·0
b. Perf 13½ × 14 (1.43) . . . 30 1·0
ba. Printed on the gummed side . . . £2500
31 2d. yellow-brown . . . 2·50 1·2
a. Perf 13½ × 14 (1.43) . . . 30 5
32 3d. ultramarine . . . 11·00 1·7
a. Deep blue (10.38) . . . 16·00 1·7
b. Perf 13½ × 14 *Ultramarine* (1.43) . . . 3·75 5·0
c. Perf 13½ × 14 *Light ultram* (10.46) . . . 21·00 14·0
d. Perf 13½ × 14 *Deep blue* (10.47) . . . 11·00 12·0
33 4d. orange . . . 5·50 1·7
a. Perf 13½ × 14 (1.43) . . . 50 1·4
34 6d. deep magenta . . . 15·00 2·7
a. Perf 13½ × 14 (1.43) . . . 4·50 4·5
b. Perf 13½ × 14. *Reddish purple* (*shades*) (7.44) . . . 4·50 1·5
c. Perf 13½ × 14. *Claret* (13.10.54) . . . 7·00 5·5
35 1s. brown-olive . . . 15·00 2·
a. Perf 13½ × 14 (1.43) . . . 1·25
36 2s.6d. bright violet . . . 25·00 4·
a. Perf 13½ × 14. *Violet* (1.43) . . . 15·00 2·5
b. Perf 13½ × 14. *Reddish violet* (10.47) . . . 15·00 9·0
37 5s. grey . . . 55·00 14·0
a. Perf 13½ × 14. *Slate* (1.43) . . . 55·00 50·0
b. Perf 13½ × 14. *Grey* (5.44) . . . 27·00 14·0
38 10s. sepia . . . 55·00 6·0
a. Perf 13½ × 14 (1.43) . . . 6·50 6·0
28/38a *Set of* 11 . . . 55·00 28·0
28s/38s Perf "Specimen" *Set of* 11 . . . £225

The above perforations vary slightly from stamp to stamp, b the average measurements are respectively: 13.3 × 13.2 com (13½ × 13), 14.2 line (14) and 13.3 × 13.8 comb (13½ × 14).

Swaziland
(**4**)

1945 (3 Dec). *Victory. Nos. 108/10 of South Africa optd with T* **4**.

	Un pair	*Us pair*	*sing*
39 1d. brown and carmine	55	80	
40 2d. slate-blue and violet	55	80	
41 3d. deep blue and blue	55	2·50	
39/41 *Set of* 3	1·50	3·50	

1947 (17 Feb). *Royal Visit. As Nos. 32/5 of Basutoland.*

Un
42 1d. scarlet . . . 10
43 2d. green . . . 10
44 3d. ultramarine . . . 10
45 1s. mauve . . . 10
42/5 *Set of* 4 . . . 30
42s/5s Perf "Specimen" *Set of* 4 . . . 85·00

1948 (1 Dec). *Royal Silver Wedding. As Nos. 112/13 of Antigua.*

46 1½d. ultramarine . . . 50
47 10s. purple-brown . . . 24·00 28·

1949 (10 Oct). *75th Anniv of U.P.U. As Nos. 114/17 of Antigua.*

48 1½d. blue . . . 15
a. "A" of "CA" missing from wmk
49 3d. deep blue . . . 2·00 2·

50 6d. magenta 30 60
51 1s. olive 30 1·00
48/51 *Set of* 4 2·50 4·00

POSTAGE DUE STAMPS

D 1

(Typo D.L.R.)

1933 (2 Jan)–**57**. Wmk Mult Script CA. P 14.
D1 **D 1** 1d. carmine 30 9·00
a. Chalk-surfaced paper. *Dp carmine* (24.10.51) 20 14·00
ac. Error. St Edward's Crown, W **9***b* £250
D2 2d. pale violet 2·00 24·00
a. Chalk-surfaced paper (22.2.57) 4·75 32·00
ab. Large "d" 50·00
D1/2 Perf "Specimen" *Set of* 2 42·00

For illustrations of No. D2ab see above No. D1 of Basutoland.

Tanganyika

The stamps of GERMANY were used in the colony between October 1890 and July 1893 when issues for GERMAN EAST AFRICA were provided.

PRICES FOR STAMPS ON COVER TO 1945

The Mafia Island provisionals (No. M1/52) are very rare used on cover.

Nos.	N1/5	*from* × 8
Nos.	45/59	*from* × 6
Nos.	60/2	—
Nos.	63/73	*from* × 6
Nos.	74/86	*from* × 8
Nos.	87/8	—
Nos.	89/92	*from* × 6
Nos.	93/106	*from* × 3
No.	107	—

MAFIA ISLAND

BRITISH OCCUPATION

Mafia Island was captured by the British from the Germans in January 1915. Letters were first sent out unstamped, then with stamps handstamped with Type M **1**. Later the military were supplied with handstamps by the post office in Zanzibar. These were used to produce Nos. M11/52.

(Currency. 100 heller = 1 rupee)

(M 1)

(M 3)

1915 (Jan). *German East Africa Yacht types, handstamped with Type* M **1**. Wmk Lozenges, or no wmk (1r., 2r.). *A. In black (2½h. in blackish lilac). B. In deep purple. C. In reddish violet.*

		A	B	C
M1	2½h. brown	£475	†	£200
	a. Pair, one without handstamp	†	†	£2500
M2	4h. green	£550	£800	£275
	a. Pair, one without handstamp	†	†	£2500
M3	7½h. carmine	£400	£475	£100
	a. Pair, one without handstamp	£4000	†	£2000
M4	15h. ultramarine	£450	£650	£160
	a. Pair, one without handstamp	†	†	£2000
M5	20h. black and red/*yellow*	£600	£750	£325
	a. Pair, one without handstamp	†	£3500	£2500
M6	30h. black and carmine	£700	£1000	£350
	a. Pair, one without handstamp	£4500	†	£2500
M7	45h. black and mauve	£700	£950	£425
	a. Pair, one without handstamp	£4500	†	£3000
M8	1r. carmine	£7000	†	£5000
M9	2r. green	£8000	†	£5500
M10	3r. blue-black and red	£9000	†	£6500

Prices are for unused examples.

A few contemporary Zanzibar stamps (1, 3, 6 and 15c.) and India I.E.F. ½a and 1a are known with the above handstamp.

(Currency. 100 cents = 1 rupee)

1915 (May). *German East Africa Yacht types with handstamped four-line surcharge* "G.R.—POST—6 CENTS—MAFIA" *in black, green or violet.* Wmk Lozenges or no wmk (1r., 2r.).
M11 6c.on 2½h. brown £1200 £1400
a. Pair, one without handstamp † £4500
M12 6c.on 4h. green £1200 £1400
a. Pair, one without handstamp £4500
M13 6c.on 7½h. carmine £1200 £1500
a. Pair, one without handstamp
M14 6c.on 15h. ultramarine £1200 £1500
M15 6c.on 20h. black and red/*yellow* £1400 £1800
M16 6c.on 30h. black and carmine £2000 £2250
M17 6c.on 45h. black and mauve £2000 £2250
a. Pair, one without handstamp
M18 6c.on 1r. carmine £11000
M19 6c.on 2r. green £12000
M20 6c.on 3r. blue-black and red £13000

The 5, 20 and 40 pesa values of the 1901 Yacht issue are also known with the above surcharge as are the contemporary 1c. and 6c. Zanzibar stamps.

1915 (Sept). *(a) German East African fiscal stamps.* "Statistik des Waaren-Verkehrs" *(Trade Statistical Charge) handstamped in bluish green or violet,* "O.H.B.M.S. Mafia" *in a circle, as Type* M **3**.
M21 24pesa, vermilion/*buff* £700 £850
M22 12½heller, drab £750 £950
a. Pair, one without handstamp £4500
M23 25heller, dull green £750 £950
M24 50heller, slate £750 £950
a. Pair, one without handstamp £4500
M25 1rupee, lilac £750 £950

(b) German East African "Ubersetzungs- Gebühren" *(Fee) stamp, overprinted as before.*
M26 25heller, grey £750 £950

G. R
POST
MAFIA
(M 4)

G. R.
Post
MAFIA.
(M 5)

(c) Stamps as above, but with further opt as Type M **4**, *in bluish green or violet.*
M27 24pesa, vermilion/*buff* £950
M28 12½heller, drab £950
M29 25heller, dull green £950
M30 50heller, slate £950
M31 1rupee, lilac £950
M32 25heller, grey (No. M26) £950
a. Pair, one without handstamp Type M **4** £4500

Type M **3** is also known handstamped on the 7½h., 20h. and 30h. values of German East Africa 1905 Yacht issue and also on contemporary 1, 3, 6 and 25c. Zanzibar stamps.

(Currency. 12 pies = 1 anna. 16 annas = 1 rupee)

1915 (Sept). *Nos. E1/2, E4/9, E11 and E13 of Indian Expeditionary Forces (India King George V optd* "I.E.F."*) with a further opt Type* M **4** *handstruck in green, greenish black or dull blue.*
M33 3p. grey 32·00 75·00
a. Pair, one stamp without handstamp — £1500
M34 ½a. light green 50·00 80·00
a. Pair, one stamp without handstamp † £1500
M35 1a. aniline carmine 55·00 80·00
M36 2a. purple 85·00 £130
M37 2½a. ultramarine £110 £160
M38 3a. orange £110 £170
a. Pair, one stamp without handstamp † £2250
M39 4a. olive-green £140 £190
M40 8a. deep magenta £250 £325
a. Pair, one stamp without handstamp † £2500
M41 12a. carmine-lake £300 £425
M42 1r. red-brown and deep blue-green £350 £450
M33/42 *Set of* 10 £1300 £1900

All values exist with the overprint inverted, and several are known with overprint double or sideways.

1916 (Oct). *Nos. E1/2, E4/9, E11 and E13 of Indian Expeditionary Forces (India King George V optd* "I.E.F."*) with further opt Type* M **5** *handstruck in green, greenish black, dull blue or violet.*
M43 3p. grey £120 £140
M44 ½a. light green £130 £130
a. Pair, one without handstamp † £2500
M45 1a. aniline carmine 95·00 £110
M46 2a. purple £160 £160
M47 2½a. ultramarine £170 £180
M48 3a. orange £170 £180
M49 4a. olive-green £275 £275
M50 8a. deep magenta £350 £375
M51 12a. carmine-lake £375 £450
M52 1r. red-brown and deep blue-green £425 £450
M43/52 *Set of* 10 £2000 £2250

Stamps with handstamp inverted are known.

Used examples of Nos. M43/52 with black double-ring backdated postmarks of "JA 23 1915" are worth about 60% of the prices quoted.

NYASALAND-RHODESIAN FORCE

This issue was sanctioned for use by the Nyasaland-Rhodesian Force during operations in German East Africa, Mozambique and Nyasaland. Unoverprinted Nyasaland stamps were used by the Force prior to the introduction of Nos. N1/5 and, again, in 1918.

N. F.
(N 1)

1916 (7 Aug–18 Sept*). *Nos. 83, 86, 90/1 and 93 of Malawi (Nyasaland) optd with Type* N **1** *by Govt Printer, Zomba.*
N1 ½d. green 1·50 8·00
N2 1d. scarlet 1·50 3·25
N3 3d. purple/*yellow* (15 Sept*) 9·00 17·00
a. Opt double † £9000
N4 4d. black and red/*yellow* (13 Sept*) 30·00 40·00
N5 1s. black/*green* (18 Sept*) 32·00 42·00
N1/5 *Set of* 5 65·00 £100
N1s/5s Optd "Specimen" *Set of* 5 £200

* Earliest known dates of use.

Of No. N3a only six copies were printed, these being the bottom row on one pane issued at M'bamba Bay F.P.O., German East Africa in March 1918.

This overprint was applied in a setting of 60 (10 rows of 6) and the following minor varieties occur on all values: small stop after "N" (R.1/1); broken "F" (R. 4/3); very small stop after "F" (R. 6/5); no serifs at top left and bottom of "N" (R. 10/1).

TANGANYIKA

BRITISH OCCUPATION OF GERMAN EAST AFRICA

Following the invasion of German East Africa by Allied forces civilian mail was accepted by the Indian Army postal service, using Indian stamps overprinted "I.E.F.". Some offices reverted to civilian control on 1 June 1917 and these used stamps of East Africa and Uganda until the "G.E.A." overprints were ready. The last field post offices, in the southern part of the country, did not come under civilian control until 15 March 1919.

(Currency. 100 cents = 1 rupee)

G.E.A. (1) G. E. A. (2) G.E.A. (3)

1917 (Oct)–**21**. *Nos. 44/5, 46a/51, 52b, 53/9 and 61 of Kenya, Uganda and Tanganyika optd with T* **1** *and* **2**. *Ordinary paper (1c. to 15c.) or chalk-surfaced paper (others).* Wmk Mult Crown CA.
45 1c. black (R.) 15 80
aw. Wmk inverted £160
ay. Wmk inverted and reversed 95·00
b. Vermilion opt 20·00 16·00
47 3c. green 15 15
48 6c. scarlet 15 10
a. Wmk sideways £1800 £1800
w. Wmk inverted † £180
49 10c. yellow-orange 50 60
y. Wmk inverted and reversed £140
50 12c. slate-grey 50 2·25
y. Wmk inverted and reversed £110
51 15c. bright blue 80 2·25
w. Wmk inverted £130
52 25c. black and red/*yellow* 80 3·50
a. On pale yellow (1921) 1·40 14·00
as. Optd "Specimen" 40·00
53 50c. black and lilac 80 3·25
54 75c. black/*blue-green, olive back* (R.) 1·00 4·50
a. On emerald back (1921) 3·25 45·00
as. Optd "Specimen" 50·00
55 1r. black/*green* (R.) 3·00 7·00
a. On emerald back (1919) 6·50 55·00
56 2r. red and black/*blue* 9·50 45·00
x. Wmk reversed
57 3r. violet and green 13·00 80·00
58 4r. red and green/*yellow* 17·00 90·00
59 5r. blue and dull purple 38·00 90·00
60 10r. red and green/*green* 75·00 £325
a. On emerald back 90·00 £350
61 20r. black and purple/*red* £190 £400
62 50r. carmine and green £475 £800
s. Optd "Specimen" £180
45/61 *Set of* 16 £325 £950
45s/61s Optd "Specimen" *Set of* 16 £400

Early printings of the rupee values exist with very large stop after the "E" in "G.E.A." (R. 5/3). There are round stops after "E" varieties, which in one position of later printings became a small stop.

The only known used example of No. 48a is cancelled at Tanga in August 1918.

Examples of Nos. 45/55 can also be found handstamped with Type M **5**, but these were not issued.

1921. *Nos. 69/74 of Kenya, Uganda and Tanganyika optd with T* **1** *or* **2**. *Chalk-surfaced paper (50c. to 5r.).* Wmk Mult Script CA.
63 12c. slate-grey 6·50 95·00
64 15c. bright blue 2·25 4·25
65 50c. black and dull purple 9·00 85·00
66 2r. red and black/*blue* 32·00 £120
67 3r. violet and green 60·00 £170
68 5r. blue and dull purple 85·00 £200
63/8 *Set of* 6 £180 £600
63s/8s Optd "Specimen" *Set of* 6 £225

1922. *Nos. 65 and 68 of Kenya, Uganda and Tanganyika optd by the Government Printer at Dar-es-Salaam with T* **3**. Wmk Mult Script CA.
72 1c. black (R.) 80 17·00
73 10c. orange 80 14·00
y. Wmk inverted and reversed £110

No. 73 is known with the overprint inverted, but this is of clandestine origin.

BRITISH MANDATED TERRITORY

(New Currency. 100 cents = 1 shilling)

4 Giraffe

5 Giraffe

(Recess B.W.)

1922–**24**. *Head in black.*

(a) Wmk Mult Script CA. P 15 × 14.
74 **4** 5c. slate-purple 2·25 20
75 10c. green 2·25 85
76 15c. carmine-red 2·00 10
77 20c. orange 1·75 10
78 25c. black 5·50 6·50
79 30c. blue 5·00 5·00
80 40c. yellow-brown 2·75 4·50
81 50c. slate-grey 2·00 1·50

82		75c. yellow-bistre	3·25	18·00
		(b) Wmk Mult Script CA (sideways). P 14.		
83	5	1s. green	3·75	14·00
		a. Wmk upright (1923)	2·50	11·00
84		2s. purple	5·50	15·00
		a. Wmk upright (1924)	4·50	23·00
85		3s. black	15·00	28·00
86		5s. scarlet	27·00	85·00
		a. Wmk upright (1923)	14·00	75·00
87		10s. deep blue	£110	£190
		a. Wmk upright (1923)	50·00	95·00
88		£1 yellow-orange	£170	£325
		a. Wmk upright (1923)	£150	£300
74/88		*Set of* 15	£225	£500
74s/88s		Optd "Specimen" *Set of* 15	£450	

On the £1 stamp the words of value are on a curved scroll running across the stamp above the words "POSTAGE AND REVENUE".

Nos. 83/8 are known showing a forged Dodoma postmark, dated "16 JA 22".

1925. *As 1922. Frame colours changed.*

89	4	5c. green	2·50	1·50
90		10c. orange-yellow	4·00	1·50
91		25c. blue	4·00	17·00
92		30c. purple	4·00	12·00
89/92		*Set of* 4	13·00	29·00
89s/92s		Optd "Specimen" *Set of* 4	70·00	

6

7

(Typo D.L.R.)

1927–31. *Head in black. Chalk-surfaced paper (5s., 10s., £1).* Wmk Mult Script CA. P 14.

93	6	5c. green	1·50	10
94		10c. yellow	2·00	10
95		15c. carmine-red	1·50	10
96		20c. orange-buff	2·50	10
97		25c. bright blue	3·50	2·00
98		30c. dull purple	2·75	2·50
98*a*		30c. bright blue (1931)	24·00	30
99		40c. yellow-brown	2·00	4·50
100		50c. grey	2·25	1·00
101		75c. olive-green	2·00	13·00
102	7	1s. green	4·00	2·75
103		2s. deep purple	17·00	4·50
104		3s. black	17·00	50·00
105		5s. carmine-red	17·00	17·00
		a. Ordinary paper		
106		10s. deep blue	55·00	95·00
107		£1 brown-orange	£140	£250
93/107		*Set of* 16	£250	£400
93s/107s		Optd or Perf (No. 98as) "Specimen" *Set of* 16	£250	

Examples of Nos. 104/7 are known showing a forged Dar-es-Salaam postmark dated "20 NO 1928".

Tanganyika became part of the joint East African postal administration on 1 January 1933 and subsequently used the stamps of KENYA, UGANDA AND TANGANYIKA.

STAMP BOOKLETS

1922–25. *Black on red cover.*

SB1	3s. booklet containing 5c., 10c., 15c. and 20c. (Nos. 74/7), each in block of 6	
	a. As No. SB1, but contents changed (Nos. 89/90, 76/7) (1925)	

1922–26. *Black on red cover. Stapled.*

SB2	3s. booklet containing six 10c., and twelve 5c. and 15c. (Nos. 74/6) in blocks of 6	
	a. As No. SB2, but contents changed (Nos. 74, 90, 76) (1925)	
	b. As No. SB2, but contents changed (Nos. 89/90, 76) (1926)	£1400

1927. *Black on red covers. Stapled.*

SB3	3s. booklet containing six 10c., and twelve 5c. and 15c. (Nos. 93/5) in blocks of 6	£1000
SB4	3s. booklet containing 5c., 10c. and 15c. (Nos. 93/5), each in block of 10	

Tasmania *see* Australia

see Australia

Tobago *see* Trinidad and Tobago

Togo

The stamps of GERMANY were used in the colony from March 1888 until June 1897 when issues for TOGO were provided.

PRICES FOR STAMPS ON COVER

Nos.	H1/7	*from* × 6
No.	H8	—
No.	H9	*from* × 6
No.	H10	*from* × 2
No.	H11	—
Nos.	H12/13	*from* × 6
Nos.	H14/16	—
Nos.	H17/19	*from* × 12
Nos.	H20/6	—
Nos.	H27/8	*from* × 20
No.	H29	—
Nos.	H30/1	*from* × 6
Nos.	H32/3	—
Nos.	H34/58	*from* × 6

ANGLO-FRENCH OCCUPATION

French forces invaded southern Togo on 8 August 1914 and the British landed at Lomé on 12 August. The German administration surrendered on 26 August 1914.

The territory was jointly administered under martial law, but was formally divided between Great Britain and France, effective 1 October 1920. League of Nations mandates were issued for both areas from 20 July 1922.

(Currency. 100 pfennig = 1 mark)

Stamps of German Colonial issue Yacht Types 1900 and 1909–14 (5pf. and 10pf.)

TOGO Anglo-French Occupation
(1)

Half penny
(2)

SETTINGS. Nos. H1/33 were all overprinted or surcharged by the Catholic Mission, Lomé.

The initial setting for the 3pf. to 80pf. was of 50 (10 × 5), repeated twice on each sheet of 100. Overprints from this setting, used for Nos. H1/9, had the lines of type 3 mm apart.

Nos. H1/2 were subsequently surcharged, also from a setting of 50, to form Nos. H12/13. The surcharge setting showed a thin dropped "y" with small serifs on R. 1/1–2, 2/1, 3/1, 4/1 and 5/1–2.

The type from the overprint and surcharge was then amalgamated in a new setting of 50 on which the lines of the overprint were only 2 mm apart. On this amalgamated setting, used for Nos. H27/8, the thin "y" varieties were still present and R. 4/7 showed the second "O" of "TOGO" omitted.

The surcharge was subsequently removed from this "2 mm" setting which was then used to produce Nos. H17/19. The missing "O" was spotted and corrected before any of the 30pf. stamps were overprinted.

The remaining low values of the second issue, Nos. H14/16 and H20/2, were overprinted from settings of 25 (5 × 5), either taken from the last setting of 50 or from an amended version on which there was no space either side of the hyphen. This slightly narrower overprint was subsequently used for Nos. H29/33. It shows the top of the second "O" broken so that it resembles a "U" on R. 1/5.

The mark values were overprinted from settings of 20 (5 × 4), showing the same differences in the spacing of the lines as on the low values.

It is believed that odd examples of some German colonial values were overprinted from individual settings in either spacing.

1914 (17 Sept*). *Optd with T* **1** *by Catholic Mission, Lomé. Wide setting. Lines 3 mm apart.*

H 1	3pf. brown	£110	95·00
H 2	5pf. green	£100	95·00
H 3	10pf. carmine (Wmk Lozenges)	£120	£100
	a. Opt inverted	£7500	£3000
	b. Opt *tête-bêche* in vert pair	†	£8000
	c. No wmk	†	£5500
H 4	20pf. ultramarine	28·00	40·00
H 5	25pf. black and red/*yellow*	28·00	30·00
H 6	30pf. black and orange/*buff*	30·00	48·00
H 7	40pf. black and carmine	£225	£250
H 8	50pf. black and purple/*buff*	£9000	£7500
H 9	80pf. black and carmine/*rose*	£225	£275
H10	1m. carmine	£5000	£2500
H11	2m. blue	£8000	£9000
	a. "Occupation" double	£13000	£11000
	b. Opt inverted	£10000	

*The post office at Lomé was open for four hours on 17 September, before closing again on instructions from Accra. It finally reopened on 24 September.

The *tête-bêche* overprint on the 10pf. is due to the sheet being turned round after the upper 50 stamps had been overprinted so that vertical pairs from the two middle rows have the overprint *tête-bêche*.

1914 (1 Oct). *Nos. H1 and H2 surch as T* **2**.

H12	½d.on 3pf. brown	£160	£140
	a. Thin "y" in "penny"	£400	£350
H13	1d.on 5pf. green	£160	£140
	a. Thin "y" in "penny"	£400	£350

TOGO Anglo-French Occupation
(3)

TOGO Anglo-French Occupation Half penny
(4)

1914 (Oct). *(a) Optd with T* **3**. *Narrow Setting. Lines 2 mm apart. "Anglo-French" measures 16 mm.*

H14	3pf. brown	£4500	£900
H15	5pf. green	£1100	£700
H16	10pf. carmine	†	£2750
H17	20pf. ultramarine	18·00	12·00
	a. "TOG"	£4000	£4000
	b. Nos. H4 and H17 *se-tenant* (vert pair)	£6500	
H18	25pf. black and red/*yellow*	24·00	30·00
	a. "TOG"	£12000	
H19	30pf. black and orange/*buff*	19·00	29·00
H20	40pf. black and carmine	£4500	£1500
H21	50pf. black and purple/*buff*	†	£6000
H22	80pf. black and carmine/*rose*	£1800	£1800
H23	1m. carmine	£7000	£4000
H24	2m. blue	†	£9000
H25	3m. violet-black	†	£40000
H26	5m. lake and black	†	£40000
	(b) Narrow setting, but including value, as T **4**.		
H27	½d.on 3pf. brown	35·00	26·0C
	a. "TOG"	£425	£30C
	b. Thin y" in "penny"	60·00	60·0C
H28	1d.on 5pf. green	4·25	4·2
	a. "TOG"	£130	£11C
	b. Thin "y" in "penny"	12·00	15·0C

In the 20pf. one half of a sheet was overprinted with the wide setting (3 mm), and the other half with the narrow setting (2 mm) so that vertical pairs from the middle of the sheet show the two varieties of the overprint.

TOGO Anglo-French Occupation
(6)

TOGO ANGLO-FRENCH OCCUPATION
(7)

TOGO ANGLO-FRENCH OCCUPATION
(8)

1915 (7 Jan). *Optd as T* **6**. *The words "Anglo-French" measur 15 mm instead of 16 mm as in T* **3**.

H29	3pf. brown	£7500	£250
H30	5pf. green	£200	£13
	a. "Occupation" omitted	£12000	
H31	10pf. carmine	£200	£13
	a. No wmk	†	£700
H32	20pf. ultramarine	£1400	£50
H32*a*	40pf. black and carmine	†	£750(
H33	50pf. black and purple/*buff*	£12000	£950(

This printing was made on another batch of German Tog stamps, found at Sansane-Mangu.

Stamps of Gold Coast overprinted

1915 (May). *Nos. 70/81, 82a and 83/4 of Gold Coast (Kin George V) optd at Govt Press, Accra, with T* ("OCCUPATION" *14½ mm long).*

H34	½d. green	30	1·2
	a. Small "F" in "FRENCH"	1·50	4·0
	b. Thin "G" in "TOGO"	3·25	8·0
	c. No hyphen after "ANGLO"	3·25	8·0
	e. "CUPATION" for "OCCUPATION"	95·00	
	f. "CCUPATION" for "OCCUPATION"	55·00	
H35	1d. red	30	5
	a. Small "F" in "FRENCH"	1·75	3·2
	b. Thin "G" in "TOGO"	5·00	8·5
	c. No hyphen after "ANGLO"	5·00	8·5
	f. "CCUPATION" for "OCCUPATION"	£150	
	g. Opt double	£325	£45
	h. Opt inverted	£170	£25
	ha. Ditto. "TOGO" omitted	£6500	
H36	2d. grey	30	1·2
	a. Small "F" in "FRENCH"	1·75	4·5
	b. Thin "G" in "TOGO"	5·50	12·(
	c. No hyphen after "ANGLO"	80·00	
	d. Two hyphens after "ANGLO"	48·00	
	f. "CCUPATION" for "OCCUPATION"	£150	
H37	2½d. bright blue	1·25	3·2
	a. Small "F" in "FRENCH"	2·75	9·(
	b. Thin "G" in "TOGO"	9·50	24·(
	c. No hyphen after "ANGLO"	42·00	
	d. Two hyphens after "ANGLO"	50·00	
	f. "CCUPATION" for "OCCUPATION"	£130	
H38	3d. purple/*yellow*	1·25	1·
	a. Small "F" in "FRENCH"	2·75	5·
	b. Thin "G" in "TOGO"	11·00	18·
	c. No hyphen after "ANGLO"	42·00	
	f. "CCUPATION" for "OCCUPATION"	£150	
	g. White back	4·00	17·
	ga. Small "F" in "FRENCH"	21·00	50·
	gb. Thin "G" in "TOGO"	60·00	95·
H40	6d. dull and bright purple	1·00	1·
	a. Small "F" in "FRENCH"	4·25	11·
	b. Thin "G" in "TOGO"	12·00	25·
	f. "CCUPATION" for "OCCUPATION"	£200	
H41	1s. black/*green*	1·50	4·
	a. Small F" in "FRENCH"	4·25	15·
	b. Thin "G" in "TOGO"	13·00	38·
	f. "CCUPATION" for "OCCUPATION"	£120	
	g. Opt double	£1000	
H42	2s. purple and blue/*blue*	9·00	13·
	a. Small "F" in "FRENCH"	26·00	45·
	b. Thin "G" in "TOGO"	60·00	85·
	c. No hyphen after "ANGLO"	£160	
	f. "CCUPATION" for "OCCUPATION"	£350	
H43	2s.6d. black and red/*blue*	4·50	21·
	a. Small "F" in "FRENCH"	18·00	65·
	b. Thin "G" in "TOGO"	48·00	£1
	c. No hyphen after "ANGLO"	£150	
	f. "CCUPATION" for "OCCUPATION"	£500	

H44 5s. green and red/*yellow* (*white back*) 8·00 15·00
a. Small "F" in "FRENCH" 42·00 65·00
b. Thin "G" in "TOGO" 70·00 £140
c. No hyphen after "ANGLO" £190
f. "CCUPATION" for "OCCUPATION" £350
H45 10s. green and red/*green* 35·00 60·00
a. Small "F" in "FRENCH" 85·00
b. Thin "G" in "TOGO" £180
f. "CCUPATION" for "OCCUPATION" £475
H46 20s. purple and black/*red* £130 £150
a. Small "F" in "FRENCH" £325
b. Thin "G" in "TOGO" £550
f. "CCUPATION" for "OCCUPATION" £750
H34/46 *Set of* 12 £170 £250

Varieties (*Nos. indicate positions in pane*).
a. Small "F" in "FRENCH" (25, 58 and 59).
b. Thin "G" in "TOGO" (24).
c. No hyphen after "ANGLO" (5).
d. Two hyphens after "ANGLO" (5).
e. "CUPATION" for "OCCUPATION" (33).
f. "CCUPATION" for "OCCUPATION" (57).

Varieties c and e also occur together on position 28 of the ½d. value only.

The 1d. opt inverted (No. H35h) exists with small "F" (*Price* £1400 *unused*), thin "G" (*Price* £4000 *unused*) and "No hyphen" (*Price* £4000 *unused*).

Examples of all values, and especially the varieties, are known showing a forged Lomé postmark dated "22 1 15".

1916 (Apr)–**20**. *Nos. 70/84 of Gold Coast (King George V) optd in London with T* **8** *("OCCUPATION" 15 mm long). Heavy type and thicker letters showing through on back.*
H47 ½d. green 30 2·50
H48 1d. red 30 85
H49 2d. grey 50 70
H50 2½d. bright blue 50 1·50
H51 3d. purple/*yellow* 2·00 70
H52 6d. dull and bright purple 1·75 1·00
w. Wmk inverted 95·00 £130
H53 1s. black/*green* 2·50 5·00
a. On blue-green (olive back) (1918) 5·50 14·00
b. On emerald-green (olive back) (1920) £500
c. On emer-grn (emer-grn back) (1920) £275 £600
H54 2s. purple and blue/*blue* 4·50 8·50
a. Wmk sideways £2000 £2000
H55 2s.6d. black and red/*blue* 4·50 7·00
H56 5s. green and red/*yellow* 15·00 26·00
a. On orange-buff (1919) 13·00 42·00
b. On buff (1920)
H57 10s. green and red/*green* 24·00 65·00
a. On blue-green (olive back) (1920) 16·00 60·00
H58 20s. purple and black/*red* £140 £160
H47/58 *Set of* 12 £170 £250
H47s/58s Optd "Specimen" *Set of* 12 £325

Nos. H47/58 were withdrawn in October 1920 when Gold Coast stamps were introduced.

The mandates were transferred to the United Nations in January 1946. The inhabitants of the British mandate voted to join Ghana in 1957.

Tokelau
see after New Zealand

Tonga

The Tongan Post Office was established in 1885 and FIJI 2d. and 6d. stamps are recorded in use until the arrival of Nos. 1/4.

PRICES FOR STAMPS ON COVER TO 1945		
Nos.	1/4	*from* × 60
Nos.	5/9	*from* × 20
Nos.	10/28	*from* × 8
Nos.	29/31	*from* × 7
Nos.	32/7	*from* × 6
Nos.	38/54	*from* × 5
Nos.	55/63	*from* × 6
Nos.	64/70	*from* × 3
Nos.	71/87	*from* × 2
Nos.	O1/10	*from* × 25

PROTECTORATE KINGDOM
King George I, 1845–93

1 King George I

2

(Eng Bock and Cousins. Plates made and typo Govt Ptg Office, Wellington)

1886–88. W **2**. P 12½ (line) or 12 × 11½ (comb)*.
1 **1** 1d. carmine (P 12½) (27.8.86) £400 6·00
a. Perf 12½ × 10
b. Perf 12 × 11½ (15.7.87) 10·00 3·25
ba. Pale carmine (P 12 × 11½) 16·00 8·50
2 2d. pale violet (P 12½) (27.8.86) 50·00 10·00
a. Bright violet 70·00 3·50
b. Perf 12 × 11½ (15.7.87) 30·00 2·75
ba. Bright violet (P 12 × 11½) 45·00 3·00
3 6d. blue (P 12½) (9.10.86) 60·00 2·25
a. Perf 12 × 11½ (15.10.88) 50·00 2·25
ab. Dull blue (P 12 × 11½) 27·00 2·25
4 1s. pale green (P 12½) (9.10.86) 90·00 4·50
a. Deep green (P 12½) £100 2·25
b. Perf 12 × 11½ (15.10.88) 55·00 6·00
ba. Deep green (P 12 × 11½) 55·00 3·25

*See note after New Zealand, No. 186.

FOUR PENCE. (3) EIGHT PENCE. (4)

(Surch Messrs Wilson & Horton, Auckland, N.Z.)

1891 (10 Nov). *Nos. 1b and 2b surch.*
5 **3** 4d.on 1d. carmine 3·00 11·00
a. No stop after "PENCE" 50·00 £110
6 **4** 8d.on 2d. violet 35·00 90·00
a. Short "T" in "EIGHT" £170 £300

No. 5a occurred on R. 6/8 and 9, R. 10/11, all from the right-hand pane.

1891 (23 Nov). *Optd with stars in upper right and lower left corners.* P 12½.
7 **1** 1d. carmine 45·00 50·00
a. Three stars £400
b. Four stars £500
c. Five stars £750
d. Perf 12 × 11½ £300
da. Three stars £500
db. Four stars £650
dc. Five stars £900
8 2d. violet 70·00 38·00
a. Perf 12 × 11½ £375

1892 (15 Aug). W **2**. P 12 × 11½.
9 **1** 6d. yellow-orange 16·00 26·00

5 Arms of Tonga

6 King George I

Damaged "O" in "TONGA" (R. 1/1, later corrected)

(Dies eng A. E. Cousins. Typo at Govt Printing Office, Wellington, N.Z.)

1892 (10 Nov). W **2**. P 12 × 11½.
10 **5** 1d. pale rose 12·00 18·00
a. Bright rose 12·00 18·00
b. Bisected diag (½d.) (1893) (on cover) † £850
c. Damaged "O" £100
11 **6** 2d. olive 17·00 16·00
12 **5** 4d. chestnut 48·00 70·00
13 **6** 8d. bright mauve 55·00 £170
14 1s. brown 80·00 £110
10/14 *Set of* 5 £190 £350

No. 10b was used from 31 May 1893 to provide a 2½d. rate before the arrival of No. 15, and on subsequent occasions up to 1895.

½d. (7) 2½d. (8) FIVE PENCE. (9) 7½d. (10)

1893. *Printed in new colours and surch with T* **7/10** *by Govt Printing Office, Wellington.*

(a) In carmine. P 12½ (21 Aug).
15 **5** ½d.on 1d. bright ultramarine 23·00 27·00
a. Surch omitted
16 **6** 2½d.on 2d. green 14·00 12·00
17 **5** 5d.on 4d. orange 4·00 6·50
18 **6** 7½d.on 8d. carmine 24·00 80·00

(b) In black. P 12 × 11½ (Nov).
19 **5** ½d.on 1d. dull blue 45·00 48·00
20 **6** 2½d.on 2d. green 17·00 17·00
a. Surch double £1800 £1800
b. Fraction bar completely omitted (R. 3/3)

King George II, 1893–1918

SURCHARGE. HALF-PENNY (11) SURCHARGE, 2½d. (12) HALF-PEI Small "F" in "HALF"

(Surch at the *Star* Office, Auckland, N.Z.)

1894 (June–Nov). *Surch with T* **11** *or* **12**.
21 **5** ½d.on 4d. chestnut (B.) (Nov) 2·00 7·00
a. "SURCHARCE" 9·00 20·00
b. Small "F" 9·00 20·00
22 **6** ½d.on 1s. brown 2·50 11·00
a. "SURCHARCE" 10·00 40·00
b. Small "F" 10·00 40·00
c. Surch double £275
d. Surch double with "SURCHARCE" £900
e. Surch double with small "F" £750
23 2½d.on 8d. mauve 5·00 8·00
a. No stop after "SURCHARGE" 32·00 55·00
24 2½d.on 1s. deep green (No. 4*a*) (Nov) 55·00 25·00
a. No stop after "SURCHARGE" £170
b. Perf 12 × 11½ 15·00 42·00
ba. No stop after "SURCHARGE" 55·00

Nos. 21/4 were surcharged in panes of 60 (6 × 10) with No. 21a occurring on R. 2/6, 4/6, 5/6, 8/6 and 10/6, No. 21b on R. 1/4, 3/4, 6/4, 7/4 and 9/4, No. 22a on R. 1/6, 3/6, 5/6, 8/6 and 10/6, No. 22b on R. 2/4, 4/4, 6/4, 7/4 and 9/4 (both after the setting had been rearranged), No. 23a on R. 3/1–3 and Nos. 24a and 24ba on R. 6/3 and R. 7/3 or R. 7/1–2.

Sheets used for these provisionals were surcharged with the remains of the tissue interleaving still in place. This sometimes subsequently fell away taking parts of the surcharge with it.

Deformed "E" in "PENI" (R. 2/2)

(Design resembling No. 11 litho and surch at *Star* Office Auckland, N.Z.)

1895 (22 May*). *As T* **6** *surch as T* **11** *and* **12**. No wmk. P 12.
25 **11** 1d.on 2d. pale blue (C.) 45·00 23·00
a. Deformed "E" £110
26 **12** 1½d.on 2d. pale blue (C.) 60·00 29·00
a. Deformed "E" £150
b. Perf 12 × 11 48·00 29·00
ba. Deformed "E" £110
27 2½d.on 2d. pale blue (C.)† 40·00 45·00
a. No stop after "SURCHARGE" £225 £225
b. Deformed "E" £110
28 7½d.on 2d. pale blue (C.) £400
a. Deformed "E"
b. Perf 12 × 11 60·00 45·00
ba. Deformed "E" £150

*Earliest known date of use.

†The 2½d. on 2d. is the only value which normally has a stop after the word "SURCHARGE".

No. 27a occurs on R. 1/3 of the right-hand pane.

12a King George II

13 King George II

Half Penny VAHE OE PENI (14)

"BU" joined (R. 1/1)

Missing eyebrow (R. 2/4)

"7" for "1" in "½d." (R. 2/1)

1895 (20 June*). *Unissued stamp surch as in T* **12a**. No wmk. P 12.

No.	Type	Description	Unused	Used
29	**11**	½d.on 2½d. vermilion	30·00	32·00
		a. "BU" joined	75·00	
		b. "SURCHARCE"	70·00	
		c. Missing eyebrow	75·00	
		d. Stop after "POSTAGE" (R. 2/5)	75·00	
		e. "7" for "1" in "½d."	75·00	
30		1d.on 2½d. vermilion	60·00	40·00
		a. "BU" joined	£110	
		c. Missing eyebrow	£110	
		d. Stop after "POSTAGE" (R. 2/5)	£110	
		e. "7" for "1" in "½d."	£110	
31	**12**	7½d.on 2½d. vermilion	55·00	60·00
		a. "BU" joined	£100	
		c. Missing eyebrow	£100	
		d. Stop after "POSTAGE" (R. 2/5)	£100	
		e. "7" for "1" in "½d."	£100	

*Earliest known date of use.

No. 29b occurs on R. 1/6 and 3/6 of both the right and the left pane.

In the ½d. surcharge there is a stop after "SURCHARGE" and not after "PENNY". In the 1d. and 7½d. the stop is after the value only.

"Black Eye" flaw (Rt pane R. 2/4)

(Litho *Star* Office, Auckland, N.Z.)

1895 (9 July–Sept). No wmk. P 12.

No.	Type	Description	Unused	Used
32	**13**	1d. olive-green	20·00	26·00
		a. Bisected diagonally (½d.) (on cover) (9.95)	†	£750
		b. Imperf between (horiz pair)	—	£6000
33		2½d. rose	20·00	13·00
		a. Stop (flaw) after "POSTAGE" (R.4/5)	60·00	60·00
34		5d. blue	23·00	50·00
		a. "Black eye" flaw	60·00	
		b. Perf 12 × 11	23·00	50·00
		ba. "Black eye" flaw	65·00	
		c. Perf 11	£350	
		ca. "Black eye" flaw		
35		7½d. orange-yellow	30·00	48·00
		a. Yellow	30·00	48·00

1896 (May). *Nos. 26b and 28b with typewritten surcharge* "Half-Penny-", *in violet, and Tongan surcharge, in black, as T* **14**.

A. Tongan surch reading downwards (right panes).

No.	Type	Description	Unused	Used
36A	**6**	½d.on 1½d. on 2d.	£450	
		a. Perf 12	£425	£425
		e. "Halef"	£5500	
		f. "H" over "G"		
		g. "Pen?y"	£4500	
37A		½d.on 7½d. on 2d.	85·00	£110
		a. "Hafl" for "Half"	£2250	£2500
		b. "Hafl" ("Penny" omitted)	£4000	
		c. "PPenny"	£750	
		d. Stops instead of hyphens	£1000	
		e. "Halyf"		
		f. "Half-Penny-" inverted	£2250	
		g. No hyphen after "Penny"		
		i. No hyphen after "Half"	£1000	
		l. Capital "P" over small "p"		
		m. Hyphen after "Penny" over capital "Y"	£2250	
		p. Perf 12	£800	
		pa. No hyphen after "Half"		

B. Tongan surch reading upwards (left panes).

No.	Type	Description	Unused	Used
36B	**6**	½d.on 1½d. on 2d.	£450	£450
		a. Perf 12	£475	£475
		ab. "Haalf"	£2500	
		c. "H" double		
		d. Tongan surch omitted	£5000	
		e. "Penyny"	£2500	
37B		½d.on 7½d. on 2d.	85·00	£110
		d. Stops instead of hyphens	£1000	
		f. "Half-Penny-" inverted	£3500	
		g. Comma instead of hyphen after "Penny"	£750	
		h. "Hwlf"		
		i. No hyphen after "Half"	£1500	
		j. "Penny" double		
		k. "Penny" twice, with "Half" on top of upper "Penny"	£3750	
		m. "Half H"	£1000	
		n. Tongan surch double	£1500	
		o. Two hyphens between "Half" and "Penny"		
		p. Perf 12	£800	

Nos. 26b and 28b were in sheets of 48 (2 panes 6 × 4). The panes were separated before the surcharges were applied.

There are variations in the relative positions of the words "Half" and "Penny", both vertically and horizontally.

15 Arms

16 Ovava Tree, Kana-Kubolu

17 King George II

18 Prehistoric Trilith at Haamonga

19 Bread Fruit

20 Coral

21 View of Haapai

22 Red Shining Parrot

23 View of Vavau Harbour

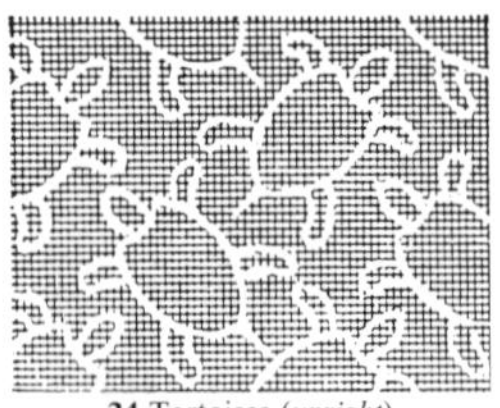
24 Tortoises (*upright*)

Types of Type **17**:

Type I. Top of hilt showing

Type II. No sword hilt

Normal

Lopped branch (R. 8/5) (ptgs from 1934 onwards)

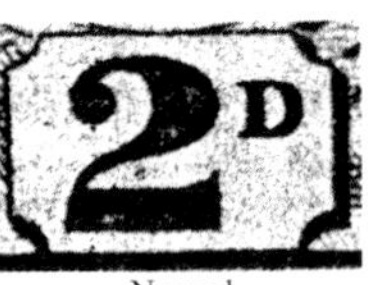
Normal

Small "2" (R. 1/2, 1/4–5, 2/8, 4/4, 5/4 and 6/1)

Normal

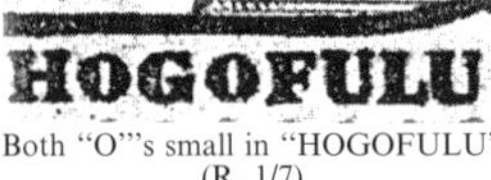

Both "O"'s small in "HOGOFULU" (R. 1/7)

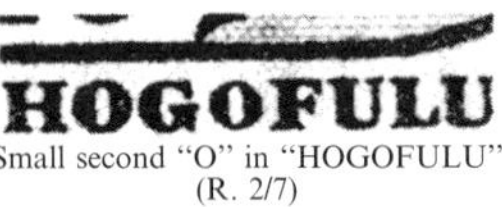

Small second "O" in "HOGOFULU" (R. 2/7)

WATERMARKS. Stamps with W **24** upright show all the tortois heads pointing upwards, or downwards if inverted. On stamps wit sideways watermark the heads point upwards or downwarc alternately.

(Recess D.L.R.)

1897 (1 June). W **24**. P 14.

No.	Type	Description	Unused	Used
38	**15**	½d. indigo	4·25	2·7
		a. Wmk sideways	70	3·(
39	**16**	1d. black and scarlet	80	8
		a. Wmk sideways	6·50	3·5
		b. Lopped branch	45·00	
40	**17**	2d. sepia and bistre (I)	17·00	5·5
		a. Wmk sideways	14·00	3·5
		b. Small "2"	35·00	15·(
41		2d. sepia and bistre (II)	32·00	9·(
		a. Wmk sideways	22·00	9·(
		b. Small "2"	55·00	25·(
42		2d. grey and bistre (II)	32·00	3·2
		a. Wmk sideways	16·00	3·
		b. Small "2"	38·00	5·
43		2½d. black and blue	6·00	1·
		a. No fraction bar in "½" (R. 2/10)	£100	60·
		b. Wmk sideways	4·00	1·
		ba. No fraction bar in "½" (R. 2/10)	70·00	60·
44	**18**	3d. black and yellow-green	3·50	9·
		a. Wmk sideways	2·50	6·
45	**19**	4d. green and purple	3·75	4·
		a. Wmk sideways	4·00	4·
46	**17**	5d. black with orange (II)	32·00	14·
		a. Wmk sideways		
47	**20**	6d. red	13·00	6·
		a. Wmk sideways	8·50	5·
48	**17**	7½d. black and green (II)	16·00	23·
		a. Centre inverted	£4250	
49		10d. black and lake (II)	45·00	48·
		a. Wmk sideways		
		b. Both "O"'s small	£225	£2
		c. Small second "O"	£225	£2
50		1s. black and red-brown (II)	14·00	7·
		a. No hyphen before "TAHA" (R. 3/5)	£140	£1
		b. Wmk sideways		
51	**21**	2s. black and ultramarine	60·00	65
		a. Wmk sideways	20·00	28
52	**22**	2s.6d. deep purple	50·00	30
		a. Wmk sideways	65·00	50
53	**23**	5s. black and brown-red	48·00	48
		a. Wmk sideways	26·00	32
38a/53a		*Set of* 14	£200	£1

The 1d., 3d. and 4d. are known bisected and used for half th value.

T - L

1 June, 1899.

(25)

26 Queen Salote

1899 (1 June). *Royal Wedding. No. 39a optd with T* **25** *at "St Office, Auckland, N.Z.*

No.	Type	Description	Unused	Used
54	**16**	1d. black and scarlet (hyphen 2 mm long)	28·00	55
		a. "1889" for "1899" (R. 8/1, 8/4)	£225	£
		b. Hyphen 3 mm long	45·00	80
		c. Wmk upright	50·00	85
		ca. "1889" for "1899" (R. 8/1, 8/4)	£400	£
		cb. Hyphen 3 mm long	75·00	£

The letters "T L" stand for Taufa'ahau, the King's family name, and Lavinia, the bride.

No. 54 was overprinted from a setting of 30 (3 × 10) applied twice to the sheets of 60. The setting contains twenty-one examples of the 2 mm hyphen and nine of the 3 mm.

Queen Salote, 1918–65

Dies of the 2d.:

Die I (As used for 1897 issue)

Die II

Normal

"2½" recut (note lines on "2" and different "½") (R. 1/1)

Retouched (small) hyphen (R. 3/5)

(Recess D.L.R.)

1920 (Apr)–**35**. W **24** (sideways). P 14.

5	**15**	½d. yellow-green (1934)	1·00	1·25
		a. Wmk upright	22·00	32·00
6	**26**	1½d. grey-black (1935)	50	3·00
7		2d. agate and aniline violet (Die I)	9·00	13·00
		a. Wmk upright	20·00	40·00
		b. Small "2"	60·00	85·00
		c. Black and slate-violet (1924)	9·00	2·25
		ca. Wmk upright		
		cb. Small "2"	55·00	20·00
		d. Black and deep purple (1925)	10·00	3·00
		db. Small "2"	65·00	25·00
7*e*		2d. black & blackish lilac (Die II) (1932)	4·50	7·00
8		2½d. black and blue (3.21)	4·75	40·00
9		2½d. bright ultramarine (1934)	2·00	1·00
		a. Recut "2½"	20·00	9·50
		5d. black and orange-vermilion (1921)	3·25	4·75
		7½d. black and yellow-green (1922)	1·75	1·75
2		10d. black and lake (1922)	2·50	4·75
		a. Both "O"'s small	28·00	45·00
		b. Small second "O"	28·00	45·00
		c. Black and aniline carmine (9.25)	7·00	
		ca. Both "O"'s small	75·00	
		cb. Small second "O"	75·00	
		1s. black and red-brown (1922)	1·25	2·50
		a. Retouched (small) hyphen	15·00	24·00
		b. Wmk upright	26·00	26·00
		ba. Retouched (small) hyphen	£130	£130
/63 *Set of* 10			26·00	55·00
s/63s Optd or Perf (Nos. 55s/6s and 59s) "Specimen" *Set of* 9			£180	

In Die II the ball of the "2" is larger and the word "PENI-E-UA" is re-engraved and slightly shorter; the "U" has a spur on the left side.

For illustration of No. 62a see above No. 38.

TWO PENCE **TWO PENCE**

PENI-E-UA (27) **PENI-E-UA** (28)

1923 (20 Oct)–**24**. *Nos. 46, 48/9, 50, 51/2 and 53a surch as T* **27** *(vert stamps) or* **28** *(horiz stamps).*

	17	2d.on 5d. black and orange (II) (B.)	1·00	85
		a. Wmk sideways	9·50	6·50
		2d.on 7½d. black and green (II) (B.)	19·00	28·00
		a. Wmk sideways	55·00	65·00
		2d.on 10d. black and lake (II) (B.)	13·00	50·00
		a. Wmk sideways	40·00	70·00
		b. Both "O"'s small	75·00	
		c. Small second "O"	75·00	
		2d.on 1s. black and red-brown (II) (B.)	50·00	22·00
		a. No hyphen before "TAHA" (R. 3/5)	£325	£200
		b. Wmk sideways	65·00	55·00
	21	2d.on 2s. black and ultramarine (R)	21·00	22·00
		a. Wmk sideways	11·00	5·00
	22	2d.on 2s.6d. deep purple (R.)	32·00	6·50
		a. Wmk sideways	£100	55·00

70	**23**	2d.on 5s. black and brown-red (R.)	15·00	15·00
		a. Wmk sideways	3·25	2·50
64/70a *Set of* 7			£120	£100

29 Queen Salote

(Recess D.L.R.)

1938 (12 Oct). *20th Anniv of Queen Salote's Accession. Tablet at foot dated* "1918–1938". W **24** (sideways). P 13½.

71	**29**	1d. black and scarlet	1·00	4·00
72		2d. black and purple	9·00	3·00
73		2½d. black and ultramarine	9·00	3·50
71/3 *Set of* 3			17·00	9·50
71s/3s Perf "Specimen" *Set of* 3			70·00	

For Silver Jubilee issue in a similar design, see Nos. 83/7.

Further die of 2d.:

Die III

(Recess D.L.R.)

1942–49. Wmk Mult Script CA (sideways on 5s.). P 14.

74	**15**	½d. yellow-green	30	3·00
		a. "A" of "CA" missing from wmk	£500	
75	**16**	1d. black and scarlet	2·50	3·00
		a. Lopped branch	55·00	
76	**26**	2d. black and purple (Die II)	7·00	2·75
		a. Die III (4.49)	4·00	8·00
77		2½d. bright ultramarine	1·75	2·00
		a. Recut "2½"	32·00	
78	**18**	3d. black and yellow-green	65	4·00
79	**20**	6d. red	3·50	2·25
80	**26**	1s. black and red-brown	3·75	3·50
		a. Retouched (small) hyphen	38·00	38·00
81	**22**	2s.6d. deep purple (1943)	30·00	22·00
82	**23**	5s. black and brown-red (1943)	16·00	48·00
74/82 *Set of* 9			55·00	80·00
74s/82s Perf "Specimen" *Set of* 9			£170	

In Die III the foot of the "2" is longer than in Die II and extends towards the right beyond the curve of the loop; the letters of "PENI-E-UA are taller and differently shaped.

Damage to the "2" on R. 4/9 of No. 77 was frequently corrected by hand-painting.

For illustration of No. 75a see above No. 38 and of No. 77a see above No. 55.

The ½d. 1d., 3d. and 1s. exist perforated from either line or comb machines. The other values only come line perforated.

UANIMA TA'U 'OE PULE 'A 'ENE 'AFIO 1918-1943

30

(Recess D.L.R.)

1944 (25 Jan). *Silver Jubilee of Queen Salote's Accession. As T* **29**, *but inscr* "1918–1943" *at foot, as T* **30**. Wmk Mult Script CA. P 14.

83	1d. black and carmine	15	1·25
84	2d. black and purple	15	1·25
85	3d. black and green	15	1·25
86	6d. black and orange	1·00	2·00
87	1s. black and brown	75	2·00
83/7 *Set of* 5		2·00	7·00
83s/7s Perf "Specimen" *Set of* 5		75·00	

1949 (10 Oct). *75th Anniv of U.P.U. As Nos. 114/17 of Antigua.*

88	2½d. ultramarine	20	1·00
89	3d. olive	1·60	3·25
90	6d. carmine-red	20	50
91	1s. red-brown	25	50
88/91 *Set of* 4		2·00	4·75

31 Queen Salote

33 Queen Salote

32 Queen Salote

(Photo Waterlow)

1950 (1 Nov). *Queen Salote's Fiftieth Birthday.* Wmk Mult Script CA. P 12½.

92	**31**	1d. carmine	70	2·25
93	**32**	5d. green	70	2·50
94	**33**	1s. violet	70	2·75
92/4 *Set of* 3			1·90	6·75

34 Map

35 Palace, Nuku'alofa

(Recess Waterlow)

1951 (2 July). *50th Anniv of Treaty of Friendship between Great Britain and Tonga. T* **34/5** *and similar designs.* Wmk Mult Script CA. P 12½ (3d.), 13 × 13½ (½d.), 13½ × 13 (others).

95	½d. green	20	2·75
96	1d. black and carmine	15	2·75
97	2½d. green and brown	30	2·75
98	3d. yellow and bright blue	2·50	3·00
99	5d. carmine and green	1·75	1·00
100	1s. yellow-orange and violet	1·40	1·25
95/100 *Set of* 6		5·50	12·00

Designs: *Horiz*—2½d. Beach scene; 5d. Flag; 1s. Arms of Tonga and G.B. *Vert*—3d. H.M.N.Z.S. *Bellona.*

OFFICIAL STAMPS

G.F.B. (O 1) **1D ½** (O 2)

(G.F.B. = Gaue Faka Buleaga = On Government Service)

1893 (13 Feb). *Optd with Type* O **1** *by Govt Printing Office, Wellington, N.Z.* W **2**. P 12 × 11½.

O1	**5**	1d. ultramarine (C.)	11·00	50·00
		a. Bisected diagonally (½d.) (on cover)		
O2	**6**	2d. ultramarine (C.)	28·00	55·00
O3	**5**	4d. ultramarine (C.)	48·00	95·00
O4	**6**	8d. ultramarine (C.)	90·00	£170
O5		1s. ultramarine (C.)	£110	£200
O1/5 *Set of* 5			£250	£500

Above prices are for stamps in good condition and colour. Faded and stained stamps from the remainders are worth much less.

1893 (Dec). *Nos. O1 to O5 variously surch with new value, sideways as Type* O **2**.

O 6	**5**	½d.on 1d. ultramarine	19·00	50·00
O 7	**6**	2½d.on 2d. ultramarine	25·00	45·00
O 8	**5**	5d.on 4d. ultramarine	25·00	45·00
O 9	**6**	7½d.on 8d. ultramarine	25·00	80·00
		a. "D" of "7½D." omitted	£1200	
		b. Surch double	£2000	
O10		10d.on 1s. ultramarine	28·00	85·00
O6/10 *Set of* 5			£110	£275

Transjordan

PRICES FOR STAMPS ON COVER

Nos.	1/88*a*	*from* × 10
Nos.	89/142	*from* × 5
Nos.	143/243	*from* × 3
Nos.	D112/24	*from* × 5
Nos.	D159/248	*from* × 3
Nos.	O117	*from* × 5

Transjordan was part of the Turkish Empire from 1516 to 1918.

Turkish post offices are known to have existed at Ajlun ("Adjiloun"), Amman ("Omman"), Amman Station, Kerak ("Kerek"), Ma'an ("Mohan" or "Maan"), Qatrana, Salt and Tafila ("Tafile"). Stamps cancelled "Ibin" may have been used at Ibbin.

The area was overrun by British and Arab forces, organised by Colonel T. E. Lawrence, in September 1918, and as Occupied Enemy Territory (East), became part of the Syrian state under the Emir Faisal, who was king of Syria from 11 March to 24 July 1920. During 1920 the stamps of the Arab Kingdom of Syria were in use. On 25 April 1920 the Supreme Council of the Allies assigned to the United Kingdom a mandate to administer both Palestine and Transjordan, as the area to the east of the Jordan was called. The mandate came into operation on 29 September 1923.

E.E.F. post offices, using the stamps of Palestine, operated in the area from September 1918.

BRITISH MANDATED TERRITORY

(Currency. 1000 milliemes = 100 piastres = £1 Egyptian)

"EAST". Where the word "East" appears in Arabic overprints it is not use in its widest sense but as implying the land or government "East of Jordan".

شرقي الاردن (**1**) ("East of Jordan")

شرقي الا ردن (**1a**)

(Optd at Greek Orthodox Convent, Jerusalem)

1920 (Nov). *T* **3** *of Palestine optd with T* **1**.

(a) P 15 × 14.

No.	Type	Description	Unused	Used
1	**1**	1m. sepia	70	1·75
		a. Opt inverted	£130	£250
2		2m. blue-green	9·00	11·00
		a. Silver opt		
3		3m. yellow-brown	1·10	1·25
		a. Opt Type **1a**	£1100	
4		4m. scarlet	1·25	1·25
5		5m. yellow-orange	2·50	1·25
5a		1p. deep indigo (Silver)	£2000	
6		2p. olive	4·25	7·00
		a. Opt Type **1a**	£850	
7		5p. deep purple	27·00	38·00
		a. Opt Type **1a**	£1400	
8		9p. ochre	£800	£1400
1/7 (*ex 5a*)		*Set of* 7	42·00	55·00

(b) P 14.

No.	Type	Description	Unused	Used
9	**1**	1m. sepia	1·25	1·60
		a. Opt inverted	£160	
10		2m. blue-green	60	80
		a. Silver opt	£550	£600
11		3m. yellow-brown	16·00	17·00
12		4m. scarlet	15·00	21·00
13		5m. orange	2·00	1·00
14		1p. deep indigo (Silver)	1·50	1·75
15		2p. deep olive	3·75	3·00
16		5p. purple	2·50	6·50
17		9p. ochre	3·50	23·00
18		10p. ultramarine	6·50	23·00
19		20p. pale grey	8·50	40·00
9/19		*Set of* 11	55·00	£120

Nos. 1/9 were surcharged from five different settings of 120 (12 × 10) which produced eight sub-types of Type **1**. Type **1a** occurred on R. 8/12 from one setting. The 9p. also exists with this overprint, but no example appears to have survived without further overprint or surcharge.

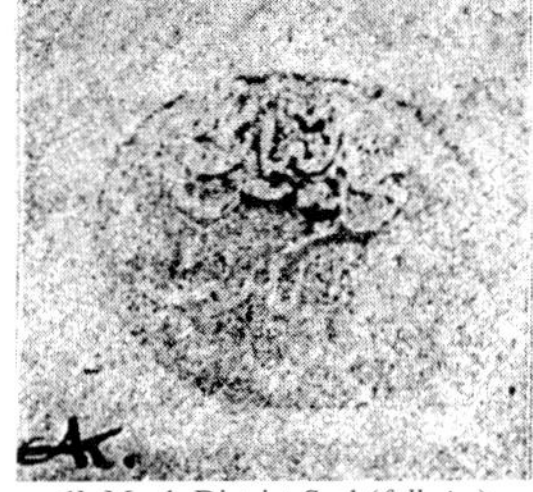

1b Moab District Seal (*full size*)

1920 (Nov). *Issued at Kerak. Handstamped. Manuscript initials "AK" in violet.* Imperf.

No.	Type	Description	Unused	Used
19*a*	**1b**	(1p.) pale blue	£3500	£4000

No. 19*a* was issued in November 1920 by the political officer for Moab District, Captain (later Sir) Alex Kirkbride, and was used until supplies of Nos. 1/19 reached the area in March 1921. The local Turkish canceller was used as a postmark.

Emir Abdullah, 1 April 1921–22 May 1946

Abdullah, a son of the King of the Hejaz, was made Emir of Transjordan in 1921. On 26 May 1923 Transjordan was recognised as an autonomous state and on 20 February 1928 it was accorded a degree of independence.

(2) ("Tenth of a piastre")

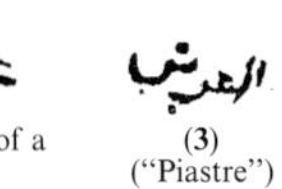

(3) ("Piastre")

(4) ("Arab Government of the East, April 1921")

1922 (Nov). *Nos. 1/19 additionally handstamped with steel dies at Amman as T* **2** *or* **3**.

(a) P 15 × 14.

No.	Type	Description	Unused	Used
20	**2**	$\frac{1}{10}$p.on 1m. sepia	25·00	45·00
		a. Red surch	70·00	70·00
		b. Violet surch	70·00	70·00
21		$\frac{2}{10}$p.on 2m. blue-green	28·00	28·00
		a. Error. Surch "$\frac{3}{10}$" for "$\frac{2}{10}$"	£110	£100
		b. Red surch	80·00	80·00
		c. Violet surch	£100	£100
		ca. Error. "$\frac{3}{10}$" for "$\frac{2}{10}$"		
22		$\frac{3}{10}$p.on 3m. yellow-brown	10·00	10·00
		a. Pair, one without surch	£750	
		b. Opt Type **1a**	£1200	£1200
		c. Error. "$\frac{2}{10}$" for "$\frac{3}{10}$"		
		d. Violet surch	£150	£150
		da. Opt Type **1a**	£2750	
23		$\frac{4}{10}$p.on 4m. scarlet	50·00	50·00
		a. Violet surch		
24		$\frac{5}{10}$p.on 5m. yellow-orange	£180	£100
		a. Pair, one without surch		
		b. Violet surch	£250	£225
25	**3**	2p.on 2p. olive	£250	75·00
		a. Opt Type **1a**	£1300	
		b. Red surch	£325	80·00
		ba. Opt Type **1a**		
		c. Violet surch	£300	90·00
26		5p.on 5p. deep purple	50·00	70·00
		a. Opt Type **1a**	£1500	
		b. Violet surch		
27		9p.on 9p. ochre	£300	£350
		a. Red surch	£130	£140
		b. Violet surch		

(b) P 14.

No.	Type	Description	Unused	Used
28	**2**	$\frac{1}{10}$p.on 1m. sepia	20·00	25·00
		a. Pair, one without surch	£1500	
		b. Red surch	60·00	60·00
		c. Violet surch	£250	£300
29		$\frac{2}{10}$p.on 2m. blue-green	25·00	25·00
		a. Pair, one without surch	£1500	
		b. Error. Surch "$\frac{3}{10}$" for "$\frac{2}{10}$"	£100	£100
		c. Red surch	80·00	80·00
		ca. Error. Surch "$\frac{3}{10}$" for "$\frac{2}{10}$"		
		d. Violet surch	80·00	80·00
30		$\frac{5}{10}$p.on 5m. orange	£225	£100
		a. Pair, one without surch	†	£2000
		b. Violet surch	£275	
31	**3**	1p.on 1p. deep indigo (R.)	£200	60·00
		a. Pair, one without surch	£1800	
		b. Violet surch	£400	
32		9p.on 9p. ochre (R.)	£500	£500
		a. Violet surch		
33		10p.on 10p. ultramarine	£850	£1000
		a. Violet surch inverted		
34		20p.on 20p. pale grey	£650	£850
		a. Violet surch	£900	£950

T **3** *of Palestine* (perf 15 × 14) *similarly surch.*

No.	Type	Description	Unused	Used
35	**3**	10p.on 10p. ultramarine	£1800	£2500
36		20p.on 20p. pale grey	£2500	£3000
		a. Violet surch		

T **2** reads "tenths of a piastre" and T **3** "the piastre", both with Arabic figures below. These surcharges were applied in order to translate the Egyptian face values of the stamps into the currency of the Arab Kingdom of Syria, but the actual face value of the stamps remained unchanged.

Being handstamped the surcharge may be found either at the top or bottom of the stamp, and exists double on most values.

1922 (Dec). *Stamps of 1920 handstamped with a steel die as T* **4** *in red-purple, violet or black.**

(a) P 15 × 14.

No.	Type	Description	Unused	Used
37	**4**	1m. sepia (R.P.)	25·00	25·00
		a. Violet opt	28·00	28·00
		b. Black opt	22·00	22·00
38		2m. blue-green (R.P.)	22·00	22·00
		a. Violet opt	20·00	20·00
		b. Black opt	18·00	18·00
39		3m. yellow-brown (R.P.)	40·00	40·00
		a. Opt Type **1a**	£1600	
		b. Violet opt	7·00	7·00
		ba. Pair, one without opt	£1200	
		bb. Opt Type **1a**	£1500	£2000
		c. Black opt	8·00	8·00
		ca. Opt Type **1a**		
40		4m. scarlet (R.P.)	45·00	50·00
		b. Violet opt	45·00	50·00
		c. Black opt	45·00	50·00
41		5m. yellow-orange (R.P.)	35·00	10·00
		a. Violet opt	15·00	10·00
42		2p. olive (R.P.)	55·00	40·00
		a. Opt Type **1a**	£1500	
		b. Violet opt	20·00	15·00
		ba. Opt Type **1a**	£1500	£1300
		c. Black opt	12·00	10·00
43		5p. deep purple (R.P.)	£100	£120
		a. Pair, one without opt	£1500	
		b. Violet opt	60·00	80·00
		c. Black opt		
44		9p. ochre (R.P.)	£400	£450
		a. Violet opt	£200	£250
		ab. Opt Type **1a**	£2250	
		b. Black opt	65·00	80·00

(b) P 14.

No.	Type	Description	Unused	Used
45	**4**	1m. sepia (R.P.)	12·00	15·00
		a. Pair, one without opt	£1200	
		b. Violet opt	22·00	20·00
		c. Black opt	18·00	18·00
46		2m. blue-green (R.P.)	25·00	25·00
		a. Violet opt	8·00	8·00
		b. Black opt	10·00	10·00
46*c*		3m. yellow-brown (V.)	£800	£350
47		5m. orange (R.P.)	£300	75·00
		a. Violet opt	25·00	20·00
48		1p. deep indigo (R.P.)	25·00	15·00
		a. Violet opt	15·00	9·00
49		2p. deep olive (V.)	75·00	80·00
50		5p. purple (R.P.)	90·00	£100
		a. Violet opt	£100	£110
		b. Black opt		
51		9p. ochre (V.)	£900	£1000
52		10p. ultramarine (R.P.)	£1800	£1900
		a. Violet opt	£1100	£1600
		b. Black opt		
53		20p. pale grey (R.P.)	£1600	£2000
		a. Violet opt	£1100	£1800
		b. Black opt		

*The ink of the "black" overprint is not a true black, but is caused by a mixture of inks from different ink-pads. The colour is, however, very distinct from either of the others.

Most values are known with inverted and/or double overprints.

(5) ("Arab Government of the East, April 1921")

1923 (1 Mar). *Stamps of 1920, with typographed overprint, T* **5** *applied by Govt Printing Press, Amman.*

(a) P 15 × 14.

No.	Type	Description	Unused	Used
54	**5**	1m. sepia (Gold)	£1500	£1800
55		2m. blue-green (Gold)	20·00	22·00
56		3m. yellow-brown (Gold)	12·00	15·0
		a. Opt double	£500	
		b. Opt inverted	£550	
		c. Black opt	75·00	85·0
57		4m. scarlet	10·00	12·0
58		5m. yellow-orange	50·00	45·0
		a. Opt Type **1** albino	£1200	£140
59		2p. olive (Gold)	15·00	15·0
		a. Opt Type **1a**	£1200	£100
		b. Black opt	£250	£25
		ba. Opt Type **1a**		
60		5p. deep purple (Gold)	60·00	80·0
		a. Opt inverted	£225	
		b. Opt Type **1a**	£2000	
		ba. Opt inverted	£2500	
		c. Black opt inverted	£1500	

(b) P 14.

No.	Type	Description	Unused	Used
62	**5**	1m. sepia (Gold)	16·00	24·0
		a. Opt inverted	£600	
63		2m. blue-green (Gold)	14·00	18·0
		a. Opt inverted	£350	£35
		b. Opt double	£300	
		c. Black opt	£300	
		ca. Opt double	£1500	
64		5m. orange	10·00	12·0
65		1p. deep indigo (Gold)	10·00	14·0
		a. Opt double	£450	£47
		b. Black opt	£800	£85
66		9p. ochre	75·00	£10
		a. Gold opt	£3000	
67		10p. ultramarine (Gold)	70·00	£10
68		20p. pale grey (Gold)	70·00	£10
		a. Opt inverted	£375	
		b. Opt double	£450	
		c. Opt double, one inverted	£450	
		e. Opt double, one gold, one black, latter inverted	£750	
		f. Opt treble, one inverted	£1100	
		g. Black opt	£850	
		ga. Opt inverted	£1100	
		gb. Opt double, one inverted	£1300	

The gold overprints were created by sprinkling gold dust on w black ink.

There are numerous constant minor varieties in this overprint all values.

The 9p. perforated 15 × 14 was also prepared with this overprin but the entire stock was used for No. 85.

The 20p. exists with top line of overprint only or with the lin transposed, both due to misplacement.

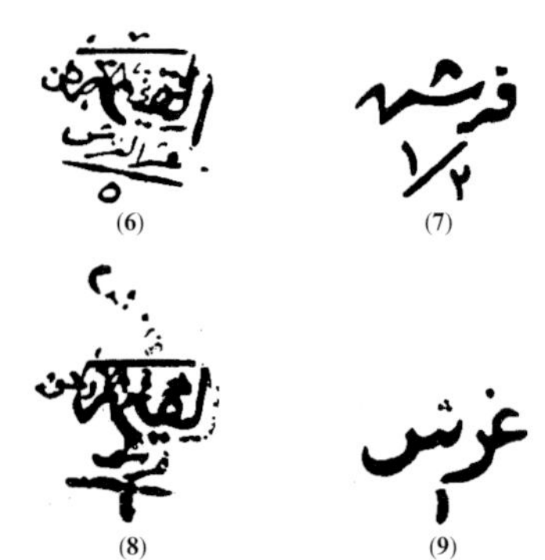

(6) (7)

(8) (9)

1923 (Apr–Oct). *Stamps of the preceding issues further surch means of handstamps.*

(a) Issue of Nov 1920.

No.	Type	Description	Unused	Used
70	–	2½/10thsp. on 5m. (13) (B.–Blk.)	£160	£1
		a. Black surch	£160	£1
		b. Violet surch	£160	£1
70*c*	**6**	$\frac{5}{10}$p.on 3m. (3)	†	£50
70*d*		$\frac{5}{10}$p.on 5m. (13)		
70*e*	**9**	2p.on 20p. (19)		

(b) Stamp of Palestine.

No.	Type	Description	Unused	Used
71	**6**	$\frac{5}{10}$p.on 3m. (P 15 × 14)	£3000	

(c) Issue of Nov 1922.

No.	Type	Description	Unused	Used
72	**6**	$\frac{5}{10}$p.on 3m. (22)	£7000	
		a. Pair, one without surch	£7500	
73		$\frac{5}{10}$p.on 5p. (26) (V.)	70·00	80
		a. Black surch		
		ab. Opt Type **3** omitted	£1200	
73*b*		$\frac{5}{10}$p.on 9p. (27a)	£1200	
74	**7**	½p.on 5p. (26)	70·00	80
		a. Pair, one without surch	£750	
75		½p.on 9p. (27)	£3500	
		a. On No. 27a	£350	£4
		ab. Opt Type **1a**	£3500	
76		½p.on 9p. (32)	—	£80
77	**8**	1p.on 5p. (26)	80·00	£1

(d) Issue of Dec 1922.

No.	Type	Description	Unused	Used
78	**6**	$\frac{5}{10}$p.on 3m. (39) (V.)	85·00	£1
		a. Black surch	£750	
		ab. Opt Type **1a**		
		b. On No. 39v	40·00	50
		ba. Pair, one without surch	£1400	
		bb. Without numeral of value		
		bc. Black surch		
79		$\frac{5}{10}$p.on 5p. (43b) (Blk.)	8·00	14
		a. Opt Type **1a**	£2000	
		b. Pair, one without surch	£500	
		c. Violet surch		
79*d*		$\frac{5}{10}$p.on 9p. (44b)	—	£1
		da. On No. 44a. Violet surch	—	£1
80	**7**	½p.on 2p. (42)	£100	£1
		a. Opt Type **1a**	£2000	
		b. On No. 42b	80·00	£
		c. On No. 42c	60·00	£
		ca. Pair, one without surch	£1000	
		w. Wmk inverted		
81		½p.on 5p. (43)	£3000	
		a. On No. 43b	£1000	
82		½p.on 5p. (50)	£2000	
		a. On No. 50a	£2500	

83	8	1p.on 5p. (43)	£3750	
		b. On No. 43b	£2000	£2250
83c		1p.on 5p. (50)	£2500	

(e) Issue of 1 March 1923.

84	6	⅛p.on 3m. (56)	25·00	30·00
		a. On No. 56c	£700	
85	7	½p.on 9p. (P 15 × 14)	90·00	£150
		a. Pair, one without surch	£5000	
86		½p.on 9p. (66)	£150	
87	9	1p.on 10p. (67)	£2250	£2500
		a. Violet surch	£2750	
88		2p.on 20p. (68)	60·00	80·00
88a		2p.on 20p. (68g)	£2000	

The handstamp on Nos. 70c, 88 and 88a has an Arabic "2" in place of the "1" shown in the illustration of Type **9**.

Being handstamped many of the above exist inverted or double.

TYPES OF SAUDI ARABIA. The following illustrations are repeated here for convenience from Saudi Arabia.

11

20

21

22

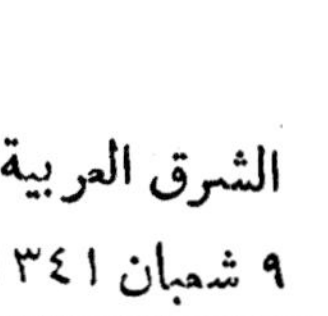

(**10**) ("Arab Government of the East, 9 Sha'ban 1341")

(**11**) ("Arab Government of the East. Commemoration of Independence, 25 May 1923")

It should be noted that as Arabic is read from right to left, the overprint described as reading downwards appears to the English reader as though reading upwards. Our illustration of Type **11** shows the overprint reading downwards

1923 (April). *Stamps of Saudi Arabia. T* **11**, *with typographed opt, T* **10**.

	10	⅛p. chestnut	2·25	1·75
		a. Opt double	£200	
		b. Opt inverted	£110	
		½p. scarlet	2·25	1·75
		a. Opt inverted		
		1p. blue	1·75	1·00
		a. Opt inverted	£120	£140
		1½p. lilac	1·75	1·75
		a. Opt double	£150	
		b. Top line omitted	—	£250
		c. Pair, one without opt	£250	
		d. Imperf between (horiz pair)	£150	
		2p. orange	2·25	6·50
		3p. brown	3·25	9·00
		a. Opt inverted	£225	
		b. Opt double	£225	£250
		c. Pair, one without opt	£375	
		5p. olive	5·50	10·00
/95 *Set of 7*			17·00	28·00

… same stamps, surcharged with new values (Saudi Arabia, Nos. 47 and 49).

	10	¼p.on ⅛p. chestnut	4·50	6·00
		a. Opt and surch inverted	£150	
		b. Ditto but 2nd and 3rd lines of opt omitted	£200	
		c. Opt double	†	£200
		10p.on 5p. olive	15·00	22·00
		a. Top line omitted	£350	

In this setting the third line of the overprint measures 19–21 mm. …n 35 stamps out of the setting of 36 the Arabic "9" (right-hand …aracter in bottom line) is widely spaced from the rest of the …scription. Minor varieties of this setting exist on all values.

For later setting, varying from the above, see Nos. 121/4.

٩٢٣ ٩٣٣

Normal. "923" Error. "933"

An error reading "933" instead of "923" occurs as No. 3 in the …ting of 24 on all values. Only 24 stamps are believed to have been …erprinted for each of Nos. 103A, 108A, 105B and 107B so that … these stamps only one example of the error can exist. No …ample has yet been confirmed for Nos. 103A or 105B.

1923 (25 May). *T* **3** *of Palestine optd with T* **11**, *reading up or down, in black or gold by Govt Press, Amman, in a setting of 24 (12 × 2).*

A. Reading downwards.

98A	1m. (Blk)	17·00	17·00
	a. Opt double, one inverted (Blk.)	£650	£650
	b. Arabic "933"	85·00	
	c. Gold opt	£150	£160
	ca. Opt double, one inverted (Gold)	£900	
	cb. Opt double (Blk.+Gold)	£900	£900
	cc. Arabic "933"	£300	
99A	2m. (Blk)	29·00	35·00
	a. Arabic "933"	£160	
100A	3m. (Blk.)	10·00	12·00
	a. Arabic "933"	70·00	
101A	4m. (Blk.)	10·00	12·00
	a. Arabic "933"	70·00	
102A	5m. (Blk.)	50·00	60·00
	a. Arabic "933"	£300	
103A	1p. (Gold)	£650	£750
	a. Opt double	£750	£850
104A	2p. (Blk.)	50·00	70·00
	a. Arabic "933"	£275	
105A	5p. (Gold)	60·00	70·00
	a. Opt double (Gold)	£650	
	b. Arabic "933"	£300	
	c. Opt double (Blk.)	£1500	
106A	9p. (Blk.)	70·00	90·00
	a. Arabic "933"	£325	
107A	10p. (Blk)	60·00	80·00
	a. Arabic "933"	£300	
108A	20p. (Blk.)	£750	
	a. Arabic "933"	£2750	

B. Reading upwards.

98B	1m. (Blk.)	90·00	£110
	b. Arabic "933"	£250	
	c. Gold opt	£150	£160
	cc. Arabic "933"	£350	
99B	2m. (Blk.)	45·00	50·00
	a. Arabic "933"	£250	
100B	3m. (Blk.)	90·00	£110
	a. Arabic "933"	£250	
101B	4m. (Blk.)	26·00	32·00
	a. Arabic "933"	£130	
103B	1p. (Gold)	50·00	60·00
	a. Opt double	£600	
	b. Black opt		
	c. Arabic "933"	£300	
105B	5p. (Gold)	£750	£600
	a. Opt double		
106B	9p. (Blk.)	50·00	60·00
	a. Arabic "933"	£275	
107B	10p. (Blk.)	£600	
	a. Arabic "933"	£2500	
108B	20p. (Blk.)	70·00	90·00
	a. Arabic "933"	£325	

The 9 and 10p. are perf 14, all the other values being perf 15 × 14.

No. 107A surch with T **9**.

109	1p.on 10p. ultramarine	£6000	

نصف قرش

(**12**)

1923 (Sept). *No. 92 surch with T* **12**.

(a) Handstamped.

110	12	½p.on 1½p. lilac	7·00	7·50
		a. Surch and opt inverted	55·00	
		b. Opt double	75·00	
		c. Opt double, one inverted	90·00	£100
		d. Pair, one without opt	£150	

This handstamp is known inverted, double and double, one inverted.

(b) Typographed.

111	12	½p.on 1½p. lilac	50·00	50·00
		a. Surch inverted	£150	
		b. Surch double	£180	
		c. Pair, one without surch	£500	

حكومة / الشرق العربية / ٩ شعبان ١٣٤١

(**13a**) (**13b**)

("Arab Government of the East, 9 Sha'ban, 1341")

These two types differ in the spacing of the characters and in the position of the bottom line which is to the left of the middle line in T **13a** and centrally placed in T **13b**.

1923 (Oct). *T* **11** *of Saudi Arabia handstamped as T* **13a** *or* **13b**.

112	13a	½p. scarlet	6·50	8·50
113	13b	½p. scarlet	6·50	8·50

No. 112 exists with handstamp inverted.

د ٠ ق ٠ ج

ملك العرب

١١ ج ٠ ث ٣٤٢

15 ("Arab Government of the East")

(**16**) ("Commemorating the coming of His Majesty the King of the Arabs" and date)

1924 (Jan). *T* **11** *of Saudi Arabia with typographed opt T* **15**.

114	15	½p. scarlet	6·50	8·50
		a. Opt inverted	£180	
115		1p. blue	£300	£200
116		1½p. lilac	£350	
		a. Pair, one without opt	£1500	

The ½p. exists with thick, brown gum, which tints the paper, and with white gum and paper.

The 2p. in the same design was also overprinted, but was not issued without the subsequent Type **16** overprint.

1924 (18 Jan). *Visit of King Hussein of Hejaz. Nos. 114/16 and unissued 2p. with further typographed opt T* **16** *in black.*

117	16	½p. scarlet	1·00	1·25
		a. Type **15** omitted	£150	
		b. Type **16** inverted	£150	
		c. Imperf between (pair)	£110	
		d. Type **16** in gold	2·00	2·25
		dc. Imperf between (pair)	£250	
118		1p. blue	1·25	1·50
		a. Type **15** omitted	£150	
		b. Both opts inverted	£200	
		c. Imperf between (pair)		
		d. Type **16** in gold	2·00	2·25
		db. Both opts inverted	£300	
		dc. Imperf between (pair)	£225	
119		1½p. lilac	2·00	2·25
		a. Type **15** omitted		
		b. Type **15** inverted	£130	
		d. Type **16** in gold	3·00	3·25
		da. Type **15** inverted	£150	
120		2p. orange	4·00	4·25
		d. Type **16** in gold	6·00	6·50

The spacing of the lines of the overprint varies considerably, and a variety dated "432" for "342" occurs on the twelfth stamp in each sheet (*Price* £75 *un*).

حكومة / الشرق العربية / ٩ شعبان ١٣٤١

(**16a**)

شعبان — "Shaban" (normal)

شعبال — "Shabal" (R. 4/6)

شعبن — "Shabn" (R. 5/3)

1924 (Mar–May). *T* **11** *of Saudi Arabia optd with T* **16a** *(new setting of Type* **10***).*

121	⅛p. chestnut	14·00	9·50
	a. Opt inverted	£100	
122	½p. scarlet	3·75	3·50
	a. "Shabal"	50·00	
	b. "Shabn"	50·00	
	c. Opt inverted	£120	
123	1p. blue	7·00	2·00
	a. "Shabal"	75·00	
	b. "Shabn"	75·00	
	c. Opt double	£120	
	d. Imperf between (horiz pair) with opt double	£500	
124	1½p. lilac	11·00	13·00
	a. "Shabal"	90·00	
	b. "Shabn"	90·00	

This setting is from fresh type with the third line measuring 18¾ mm.

On all stamps in this setting (except Nos. 1, 9, 32 and 33) the Arabic "9" is close to the rest of the inscription.

The dots on the character "Y" (the second character from the left in the second line) are on many stamps vertical (:) instead of horizontal (..).

On some sheets of the ⅛p. and ½p. the right-hand character, "H", in the first line, was omitted from the second stamp in the first row of the sheet.

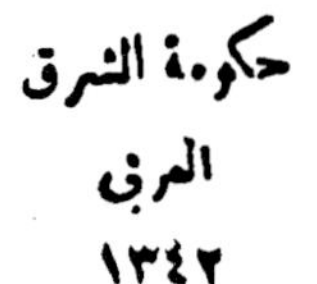

(**17**) ("Government of the Arab East, 1342")

(**18**) ("Government of the Arab East, 1343")

"Hukumat" (normal)

"Jakramat" (R. 2/1)

١٣٤٢	١٣٤٣	١٢٤٢
"1342" (normal)	"1343" (R. 4/2)	"1242" (R. 6/1)

1924 (Sept–Nov). *T* **11** *of Saudi Arabia with type-set opt as T* **17** *by Govt Press, Amman.*

No.	Type	Description	Unused	Used
125	**17**	½p. chestnut	50	50
		a. Opt inverted	£130	
		b. "Jakramat"	25·00	
		c. "1242"	25·00	
126		½p. green	50	50
		a. *Tête-bêche* (pair, both opts normal)	7·50	10·00
		b. Opt inverted	85·00	
		c. *Tête-bêche* (pair, one with opt inverted)	£300	
		d. "Jakramat"	25·00	
		e. "1242"	25·00	
127		½p. bright scarlet	50	50
		a. Deep rose-red		
		b. "1343"	25·00	
129		1p. blue	3·00	1·50
		a. Imperf between (horiz pair)	£130	
		b. Opt inverted		
		c. "Jakramat"	35·00	
		d. "1242"	35·00	
130		1½p. lilac	3·00	3·00
		a. "1343"	50·00	
131		2p. orange	2·25	2·50
		a. Opt double		
		b. "1343"	50·00	
132		3p. brown-red	1·75	2·00
		a. Opt inverted	£100	
		b. Opt double	£100	
		c. "1343"	75·00	
133		5p. olive	2·25	3·00
		a. "Jakramat"	60·00	
		b. "1242"	60·00	
134		10p. brown-purple and mauve (R.)	4·75	6·50
		a. Centre inverted	£2000	
		b. Black opt	£200	
		c. "Jakramat"	90·00	
		d. "1242"	90·00	
125/34 *Set of* 9			17·00	18·00

Type **11** of Saudi Arabia was printed in sheets of 36 (6 × 6). The ½p. value had the bottom three rows inverted, giving six vertical *tête-bêche* pairs. A few sheets were overprinted with the normal setting of Type **17**, with the result that the overprints on the bottom rows were inverted in relation to the stamp, including on one of the stamps in the *tête-bêche* pair (No. 126c). A corrected setting with the overprint inverted on the lower rows was used for the majority of the printing giving *tête-bêche* pairs with the overprints both normal in relation to the stamps (No. 126a).

1925 (2 Aug). *T* **20/2** *of Saudi Arabia with lithographed opt T* **18** *applied in Cairo.*

No.	Type	Description	Unused	Used
135	**18**	½p. chocolate	30	1·25
		a. Imperf between (horiz pair)	£120	£140
		b. Opt inverted	60·00	
136		½p. ultramarine	30	1·25
		a. Opt inverted	60·00	
137		½p. carmine	50	40
		a. Opt inverted	60·00	
138		1p. green	40	40
139		1½p. orange	1·00	2·25
		a. Opt inverted	60·00	
140		2p. blue	1·50	2·75
		a. Opt treble	£150	£200
141	**18**	3p. sage-green (R.)	2·00	3·75
		a. Imperf between (horiz pair)	£120	£160
		b. Opt inverted	80·00	
		c. Black opt	£120	£150
142		5p. chestnut	2·25	8·50
		a. Opt inverted	80·00	
135/42 *Set of* 8			7·50	18·00

All values exist imperforate.

No. 141 imperforate with gold overprint comes from a presentation sheet for the Emir.

(**19**) ("East of the Jordan")

22 Emir Abdullah

23 Emir Abdullah

(Opt typo by Waterlow)

1925 (1 Nov)–**26**. *Stamps of Palestine, 1922 (without the three-line Palestine opt), optd with T* **19**. Wmk Mult Script CA. P 14.

No.	Type	Description	Unused	Used
143	**19**	1m. deep brown	15	1·75
144		2m. yellow	15	30
145		3m. greenish blue	60	70
146		4m. carmine-pink	50	1·50
147		5m. orange	1·00	40
		a. Yellow-orange	35·00	20·00
148		6m. blue-green	60	1·00
149		7m. yellow-brown	60	1·00
150		8m. scarlet	60	60
151		1p. grey	60	50
152		13m. ultramarine	60	80
153		2p. olive	2·00	2·25
		a. Olive-green	£100	25·00
154		5p. deep purple	3·00	5·00
155		9p. ochre	6·00	10·00
		a. Perf 15 × 14 (1926)	£850	£1200
156		10p. light blue	14·00	18·00
		a. Error. "E.F.F." in bottom panel (R.10/3)	£750	£800
		b. Perf 15 × 14 (1926)	75·00	85·00
157		20p. light violet	20·00	32·00
		a. Perf 15 × 14 (1926)	£850	£850
143/57 *Set of* 15			45·00	70·00
143s/57s Optd "Specimen" *Set of* 15			£170	

(New Currency. 1000 milliemes = £1 Palestinian)

(Recess Perkins, Bacon & Co)

1927 (1 Nov)–**29**. *New Currency.* Wmk Mult Script CA. P 14.

No.	Type	Description	Unused	Used
159	**22**	2m. greenish blue	20	30
160		3m. carmine-pink	1·50	1·50
161		4m. green	1·50	1·75
162		5m. orange	65	30
163		10m. scarlet	80	1·75
164		15m. ultramarine	80	30
165		20m. olive-green	80	1·25
166	**23**	50m. purple	2·50	5·00
167		90m. bistre	6·00	16·00
168		100m. blue	8·00	12·00
169		200m. violet	17·00	28·00
170		500m. brown (5.29)	60·00	85·00
171		1000m. slate-grey (5.29)	£100	£140
159/71 *Set of* 13			£180	£275
159s/71s Optd or Perf (500, 1000m.) "Specimen" *Set of* 13			£190	

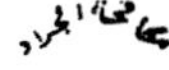

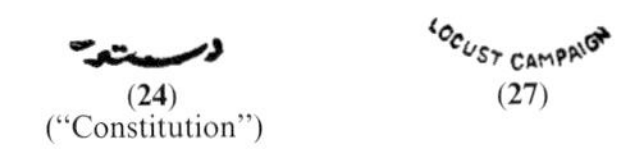

(**24**) ("Constitution") (**27**)

1928 (1 Sept). *New Constitution of 20 February 1928. Optd with T* **24** *by Atwood, Morris & Co, Cairo.*

No.	Type	Description	Unused	Used
172	**22**	2m. greenish blue	1·50	2·75
173		3m. carmine-pink	1·50	3·75
174		4m. green	1·75	5·00
175		5m. orange	1·75	2·75
176		10m. scarlet	2·00	4·50
177		15m. ultramarine	2·00	2·50
178		20m. olive-green	3·75	9·50
179	**23**	50m. purple	6·00	10·00
180		90m. bistre	16·00	50·00
181		100m. blue	22·00	60·00
182		200m. violet	65·00	£130
172/82 *Set of* 11			£110	£250

1930 (1 Apr). *Locust Campaign. Optd as T* **27** *by Whitehead, Morris & Co, Alexandria.*

No.	Type	Description	Unused	Used
183	**22**	2m. greenish blue	1·75	5·00
		a. Opt inverted	£225	£500
184		3m. carmine-pink	1·75	6·50
185		4m. green	1·75	7·50
186		5m. orange	17·00	14·00
		a. Opt double	£325	£500
		b. Vert pair, top stamp opt double. Lower stamp without bottom line of opt	£1100	
187		10m. scarlet	1·75	4·00
188		15m. ultramarine	1·75	2·25
		a. Opt inverted	£190	£350
189		20m. olive-green	1·75	4·00
190	**23**	50m. purple	5·00	11·00
191		90m. bistre	10·00	45·00
192		100m. blue	12·00	45·00
193		200m. violet	30·00	85·00
194		500m. brown	75·00	£200
		a. "C" of "LOCUST" omitted (R. 5/3)	£700	£900
183/94 *Set of* 12			£140	£375

No. 186a was sold at Kerak.

28

29

(Re-engraved with figures of value at left only. Recess Perkins, Bacon)

1930 (1 June)–**39**. Wmk Mult Script CA. P 14.

No.	Type	Description	Unused	Used
194*b*	**28**	1m. red-brown (6.2.34)	1·25	1·00
		c. Perf 13½ × 13 (1939)	4·75	3·50
195		2m. greenish blue	50	50
		a. Perf 13½ × 13. *Bluish grn* (1939)	8·50	2·00
196		3m. carmine-pink	60	70
196*a*		3m. green (6.2.34)	2·50	85
		b. Perf 13½ × 13 (1939)	15·00	4·25
197		4m. green	60	2·50
197*a*		4m. carmine-pink (6.2.34)	2·75	1·00
		b. Perf 13½ × 13 (1939)	65·00	23·00
198		5m. orange	50	40
		a. Coil stamp. Perf 13½ × 14 (29.2.36)	21·00	17·00
		b. Perf 13½ × 13 (1939)	65·00	3·00
199		10m. scarlet	1·25	15
		a. Perf 13½ × 13 (1939)	95·00	4·25
200		15m. ultramarine	1·00	20
		a. Coil stamp. Perf 13½ × 14 (29.2.36)	21·00	16·00
		b. Perf 13½ × 13 (1939)	40·00	4·00
201		20m. olive-green	1·25	35
		a. Perf 13½ × 13 (1939)	65·00	12·00
202	**29**	50m. purple	2·00	1·25
203		90m. bistre	2·50	4·25
204		100m. blue	3·75	4·25
205		200m. violet	9·00	14·00
206		500m. brown	21·00	42·00
207		£P1 slate-grey	48·00	80·00
194*b*/207 *Set of* 16			85·00	£130
194*b*s/207s Perf "Specimen" *Set of* 16			£190	

For stamps perf 12 see Nos. 230/43, and for T **28** lithographed, perf 13½, see Nos. 222/9.

30 Mushetta

31 Threshing Scene

32 The Khazneh at Petra

33 Emir Abdullah

(Vignettes from photographs; frames des Yacoub Sukker. Recess Bradbury, Wilkinson)

1933 (1 Feb). *As T* **30** *(various designs) and T* **31/3**. Wmk Mul Script CA. P 12.

No.	Description	Unused	Used
208	1m. black and maroon	70	1·40
209	2m. black and claret	1·25	1·00
210	3m. blue-green	1·50	1·60
211	4m. black and brown	1·75	2·2
212	5m. black and orange	2·50	1·2
213	10m. carmine	2·50	3·00
214	15m. blue	2·50	1·2
215	20m. black and sage-green	3·50	5·0
216	50m. black and purple	12·00	12·0
217	90m. black and yellow	15·00	29·0
218	100m. black and blue	15·00	29·0
219	200m. black and violet	45·00	70·0
220	500m. scarlet and red-brown	£140	£18
221	£P1 black and yellow-green	£350	£55
208/21 *Set of* 14		£550	£80
208s/21s Perf "Specimen" *Set of* 14		£500	

Designs: *As T* **30**—2m. Nymphaeum, Jerash; 3m. Kasr Kharana 4m. Kerak Castle; 5m. Temple of Artemis, Jerash; 10m. Ajlu Castle; 20m. Allenby Bridge over the Jordan.

The 90m., 100m. and 200m. are similar to the 3m., 5m. and 10m respectively, but are larger (33½ × 23½ mm). The 500m. is simila to T **32**, but larger (23½ × 33½ mm).

34

(Litho Survey Dept, Cairo)

1942 (18 May). *T* **28**, *but with Arabic characters above portrait an in top left circle modified as in T* **34**. No wmk. P 13½.

No.	Type	Description	Unused	Used
222	**34**	1m. red-brown	80	3·2
223		2m. green	1·50	1·5
224		3m. yellow-green	2·25	2·7
225		4m. carmine-pink	2·25	3·5
226		5m. yellow-orange	3·25	1·0
227		10m. scarlet	3·75	2·7
228		15m. blue	8·00	1·7
229		20m. olive-green	16·00	13·0
222/9 *Set of* 8			35·00	27·0

Forgeries of the above exist on whiter paper with roug perforations.

(Recess Bradbury, Wilkinson)

1943 (1 Jan)–**46**. Wmk Mult Script CA. P 12.

No.	Type	Description	Unused	Used
230	**28**	1m. red-brown	20	
231		2m. bluish green	1·75	
232		3m. green	2·00	1·
233		4m. carmine-pink	1·75	1·
234		5m. orange	1·75	
235		10m. red	3·00	1·
236		15m. blue	3·00	
237		20m. olive-green (26.8.46)	3·00	1·
238	**29**	50m. purple (26.8.46)	3·00	1·
239		90m. bistre (26.8.46)	4·75	4·
240		100m. blue (26.8.46)	5·00	1·
241		200m. violet (26.8.46)	9·00	7·
242		500m. brown (26.8.46)	13·00	12·
243		£P1 slate-grey (26.8.46)	24·00	22·
230/43 *Set of* 14			65·00	48·

Nos. 237/43 were released in London by the Crown Agents May 1944, but were not put on sale in Transjordan until 26 Augu 1946.

Printings of the 3, 4, 10, 15 and 20m. in changed colours, togeth with a new 12m. value, were released on 12 May 1947.

POSTAGE DUE STAMPS

مستحق

(D **12** "Due")

حكومة
مستحق
الشرق العربية
٩ شعبان ١٣٤١

(D **13**)

1923 (Sept). *Issue of April, 1923, with opt T* **10** *with further typographed opt Type* D **12** *(the 3p. with handstamped surch as T* **12** *at top).*

D112 ½p.on 3p. brown . . . . . 17·00 21·00
a. "Due" inverted . . . . . 50·00 55·00
b. "Due" double . . . . . 50·00 60·00
ba. "Due" double, one inverted £150
c. Arabic "t" & "h" transposed (R. 1/2) £100
ca. As c, inverted £350
d. Surch at foot of stamp . . . . . 26·00
da. Ditto, but with var. c £120
e. Surch omitted £200
D113 1p. blue . . . . . 10·00 12·00
a. Type **10** inverted . . . . . 80·00
b. "Due" inverted . . . . . 45·00 40·00
c. "Due" double . . . . . 50·00
d. "Due" double, one inverted £150
e. Arabic "t" & "h" transposed (R. 1/2) . . . . . 70·00
f. "Due" omitted (in vertical pair with normal) £200
D114 1½p. lilac . . . . . 12·00 13·00
a. "Due" inverted . . . . . 45·00 45·00
b. "Due" double . . . . . 50·00
ba. "Due" double, one diagonal . . . . 75·00
c. Arabic "t" & "h" transposed (R. 1/2) . . . . . 70·00
ca. As c, inverted £275
d. "Due" omitted (in pair with normal) £200
D115 2p. orange . . . . . 14·00 15·00
a. "Due" inverted . . . . . 60·00 60·00
b. "Due" double . . . . . 65·00
ba. "Due" double, one diagonal £100
c. "Due" treble £150
d. Arabic "t" & "h" transposed (R. 1/2) . . . . . 70·00
e. Arabic "h" omitted . . . . . 90·00

The variety, Arabic "t" and "h" transposed, occurred on R. 1/2 of all values in the first batch of sheets printed. The variety, Arabic "h" omitted, occurred on every stamp in the first three rows of at least three sheets of the 2p.

Handstamped in four lines as Type D **13** *and surch as on No. D112*

D116 ½p.on 3p. brown . . . . . 50·00 55·00
a. Opt and surch inverted £200
b. Opt double £200
c. Surch omitted £225
d. Opt inverted. Surch normal, but at foot of stamp £150
e. Opt omitted and opt inverted (pair) £300
f. "Due" double, one inverted £160
h. Surch double £250

(D 14)

(D 20) ("Due. East of the Jordan")

1923 (Oct). *T* **11** *of Saudi Arabia handstamped with Type* D **14**.

D117 ½p. scarlet . . . . . 1·50 3·25
D118 1p. blue . . . . . 3·25 3·50
a. Pair, one without handstamp
D119 1½p. lilac . . . . . 2·50 4·25
D120 2p. orange . . . . . 4·00 4·75
D121 3p. brown . . . . . 7·00 9·50
a. Pair, one without handstamp . . . £500
D122 5p. olive . . . . . 8·00 15·00
D117/22 *Set of* 6 . . . . . 24·00 35·00

There are three types of this handstamp, differing in some of the Arabic characters. They occur inverted, double etc.

1923 (Nov). *T* **11** *of Saudi Arabia with opt similar to Type* D **14** *but first three lines typo and fourth handstruck.*

D123 1p. blue . . . . . 55·00
D124 5p. olive . . . . . 10·00
a. Imperf between (vert pair)

(Opt typo by Waterlow)

1925 (Nov). *Stamps of Palestine 1922 (without the three-line Palestine opt), optd with Type* D **20**. P 14.

D159 1m. deep brown . . . . . 1·40 6·50
D160 2m. yellow . . . . . 2·00 4·25
D161 4m. carmine-pink . . . . . 3·00 8·00
D162 8m. scarlet . . . . . 4·00 11·00
D163 13m. ultramarine . . . . . 4·50 11·00
D164 5p. deep purple . . . . . 5·50 15·00
a. Perf 15 × 14 . . . . . 40·00 55·00
D159/64 *Set of* 6 . . . . . 18·00 50·00
D159s/64s Optd "Specimen" *Set of* 6 . . . . . 65·00

Stamps as No. D164, but with a different top line to overprint Type D **20**, were for revenue purposes.

(D 21) (1m.) (2m.) (4m.)

(8m.) (13m.) (5p.)

(Surch typo at Jerusalem)

1926 (Feb–May). *Postage stamps of 1 November 1925, surch* "Due" *and new value as Type* D **21** *by Greek Orthodox Printing Press, Jerusalem. Bottom line of surcharge differs for each value as illustrated.*

D165 1m. on 1m. deep brown . . . . . 5·00 6·00
a. Red opt £100
D166 2m.on 1m. deep brown . . . . . 4·25 6·00
D167 4m. on 3m. greenish blue . . . . . 4·50 7·00
D168 8m. on 3m. greenish blue . . . . . 4·50 7·00
D169 13m. on 13m. ultramarine . . . . . 7·00 8·00
D170 5p. on 13m. ultramarine . . . . . 8·00 12·00
D165/70 *Set of* 6 . . . . . 30·00 42·00

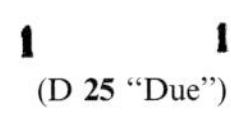

(D **25** "Due")

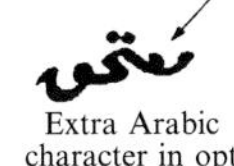

Extra Arabic character in opt (R. 4/10)

1929 (1 Jan). *Nos. 159 etc. optd only or surch in addition as Type* D **25** *by Whitehead, Morris & Co, Alexandria.*

D183 **22** 1m.on 3m. carmine-pink . . . . . 1·00 6·00
a. Extra Arabic character . . . . 25·00
D184 2m. greenish blue . . . . . 1·25 6·00
a. Pair, one without opt £325
D185 4m.on 15m. ultramarine . . . . . 1·25 7·00
a. Surch inverted £130 £190
D186 10m. scarlet . . . . . 2·25 7·00
D187 **23** 20m.on 100m. blue . . . . . 3·75 15·00
a. Vert pair, one without surch . . . £400
D188 50m. purple . . . . . 4·75 19·00
a. Horiz pair, one without opt . . £425
D183/8 *Set of* 6 . . . . . 13·00 55·00

D **26**

D **35**

(Recess Perkins, Bacon)

1929 (1 Apr)–**39**. Wmk Mult Script CA. P 14.

D189 D **26** 1m. red-brown . . . . . 1·00 5·00
a. Perf 13½ × 13 (1939) . . . . 80·00 50·00
D190 2m. orange-yellow . . . . . 1·50 4·50
D191 4m. green . . . . . 2·25 6·00
D192 10m. scarlet . . . . . 4·00 6·00
D193 20m. olive-green . . . . . 7·50 12·00
D194 50m. blue . . . . . 9·50 20·00
D189/94 *Set of* 6 . . . . . 23·00 48·00
D189s/94s Perf "Specimen" *Set of* 6 . . . . . 70·00

(Litho Survey Dept, Cairo)

1942 (22 Dec). *Redrawn. Top line of Arabic in taller lettering.* No wmk. P 13½.

D230 D **35** 1m. red-brown . . . . . 2·00 15·00
D231 2m. orange-yellow . . . . . 11·00 9·00
D232 10m. scarlet . . . . . 15·00 6·00
D230/2 *Set of* 3 . . . . . 25·00 27·00

Forgeries of the above exist on whiter paper with rough perforations.

(Recess Bradbury, Wilkinson)

1944–49. Wmk Mult Script CA. P 12.

D244 D **26** 1m. red-brown . . . . . 70 3·00
D245 2m. orange-yellow . . . . . 70 3·50
D246 4m. green . . . . . 70 4·50
D247 10m. carmine . . . . . 1·75 6·00
D248 20m. olive-green (1949) . . . . . 42·00 55·00
D244/8 *Set of* 5 . . . . . 42·00 65·00

OFFICIAL STAMP

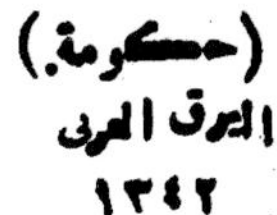

(O **16**) ("Arab Government of the East, 1342" = 1924)

1924. *T* **11** *of Saudi Arabia with typographed opt, Type* O **16**.

O117 ½p. scarlet . . . . . 22·00 £100
a. Arabic "1242" (R. 2/2, 3/6, 4/5, 4/6) £150

By treaty of 22 March 1946 with the United Kingdom, Transjordan was proclaimed an independent kingdom on 25 May 1946.

Later issues are listed under JORDAN in Part 19 (*Middle East*) of this catalogue.

Transvaal *see* South Africa

Trinidad and Tobago

TRINIDAD

CROWN COLONY

The first post office was established at Port of Spain in 1800 to deal with overseas mail. Before 1851 there was no post office inland service, although a privately-operated one along the coast did exist, for which rates were officially fixed (see No. 1). During 1851 the colonial authorities established an inland postal system which commenced operation on 14 August. Responsibility for the overseas mails passed to the local post authorities in 1858.

No. CC1 is recorded in the G.P.O. Record Book on 21 March 1852, but no examples have been recorded used on cover before February 1858. The prepayment of postage on mail to Great Britain was made compulsory from 9 October 1858. From March 1859 it was used with the early Britannia 1d. stamps to indicate prepayment of the additional overseas rate in cash or, later, to show that letters were fully franked with adhesive stamps. This is the normal usage of the handstamp and commands little, if any premium over the cover price quoted below for the stamps involved. The use of the handstamp without an adhesive is rare.

PORT OF SPAIN

CROWNED-CIRCLE HANDSTAMPS

CC 1

CC1 CC **1** TRINIDAD (R.) (*without additional adhesive stamp*) (21.3.52) *Price on cover* £2500

PRICES FOR STAMPS ON COVER		
No.	1	*from* × 2
Nos.	2/12	*from* × 10
Nos.	13/20	*from* × 4
Nos.	25/9	*from* × 10
No.	30	—
Nos.	31/44	*from* × 4
No.	45	—
Nos.	46/59	*from* × 4
Nos.	60/3	*from* × 5
Nos.	64/8	*from* × 4
Nos.	69/74	*from* × 20
Nos.	75/8	*from* × 50
No.	79	—
No.	87	*from* × 20
Nos.	98/102	*from* × 6
No.	103	—
Nos.	104/5	*from* × 20
Nos.	106/12	*from* × 12
No.	113	—
Nos.	114/21	*from* × 4
Nos.	122/4	—
No.	125	*from* × 10
Nos.	126/30	*from* × 5
No.	131	—
Nos.	132/43	*from* × 3
Nos.	144/5	—
Nos.	146/8	*from* × 3
Nos.	D1/17	*from* × 15

1

2 Britannia

1847 (16 Apr). *Litho.* Imperf.

1 **1** (5c.) blue £25000 £10000

The "LADY McLEOD" stamps were issued in April 1847, by David Bryce, owner of the S.S. *Lady McLeod*, and sold at five cents each for the prepayment of the carriage of letters by his vessel between Port of Spain and San Fernando.

The price quoted for used examples of No. 1 is for pen-cancelled. Stamps cancelled by having a corner skimmed-off are worth less.

(Recess P.B.)

1851 (14 Aug)–**56**. *No value expressed.* Imperf. *Blued paper.*

2 **2** (1d.) purple-brown (1851) . . . . . 12·00 75·00
3 (1d.) blue *to* deep blue (12.51) . . . . . 12·00 60·00
4 (1d.) deep blue (1852)* . . . . . £150 80·00
5 (1d.) grey (11.52) . . . . . 70·00 65·00
6 (1d.) brownish grey (1853) . . . . . 42·00 75·00
7 (1d.) brownish red (1853) . . . . . £300 65·00
8 (1d.) brick-red (1856) . . . . . £160 70·00

*No. 4 shows the paper deeply and evenly blued, especially on the back. It has more the appearance of having been printed on blue paper rather than on white paper that has become blued.

1854–57. Imperf. *White paper.*

9 **2** (1d.) deep purple (1854) . . . . . 24·00 85·00
10 (1d.) dark grey (1854) . . . . . 38·00 80·00
12 (1d.) rose-red (1857) . . . . . £1700 65·00

PRICES. Prices quoted for the unused of most of the above issues and Nos. 25 and 29 are for "remainders" with original gum, found in London. Old colours that have been out to Trinidad are of much greater value.

3 Britannia

4 Britannia

The following provisional issues were lithographed in the Colony (from die engraved by Charles Petit), and brought into use to meet shortages of the Perkins Bacon stamps during the following periods: (1) Sept 1852–May 1853; (2) March 1855–June 1855; (3) Dec 1856–Jan 1857; (4) Oct 1858–Jan 1859; (5) March 1860–June 1860.

1852–60. *No value expressed.* Imperf.

A. First Issue (Sept 1852). Fine impression; lines of background clear and distinct.

(i) Yellowish paper.

13	3	(1d.) blue	£8500	£1600

(ii) Bluish cartridge paper (Feb 1853).

14	3	(1d.) blue	—	£1800

B. Second issue (March 1855). Thinner paper. Impression less distinct than before.

15	3	(1d.) pale blue *to* greenish blue	—	£900

C. Third issue (August 1856). Background often of solid colour, but with clear lines in places.

16	3	(1d.) bright blue *to* deep blue	£4500	£1000

D. Fourth issue (October 1858). Impression less distinct, and rarely showing more than traces of background lines.

17	3	(1d.) very deep greenish blue	—	£650
18		(1d.) slate-blue	£4000	£650

E. Fifth issue (March 1860). Impression shows no (or hardly any) background lines.

19	3	(1d.) grey to bluish grey	£4000	£400
20		(1d.) red (*shades*)	14·00	£600

In the worn impression of the fourth and fifth issues, the impression varies according to the position on the stone. Generally speaking, stamps of the fifth issue have a flatter appearance and cancellations are often less well defined. The paper of both these issues is thin or very thin. In all issues except 1853 (Feb) the gum tends to give the paper a toned appearance.

Stamps in the slate-blue shade (No. 18) also occur in the fifth issue, but are not readily distinguishable.

PERKINS BACON "CANCELLED". For notes on these handstamps, showing "CANCELLED" between horizontal bars forming an oval, see Catalogue Introduction.

(Recess P.B.)

1859 (9 May). Imperf.

25	4	4d. grey-lilac (H/S "CANCELLED" in oval £6500)	95·00	£325
28		6d. deep green (H/S "CANCELLED" in oval £6500)	—	£425
29		1s. indigo	95·00	£350
30		1s. purple-slate	£6500	

"CANCELLED" examples of No. 25 are in lilac rather than grey-lilac.

No. 30 may be of unissued status.

1859 (Sept).

(a) Pin-perf $12\frac{1}{2}$.

31	2	(1d.) rose-red	£1500	55·00
32		(1d.) carmine-lake	£1800	50·00
33	4	4d. dull lilac	—	£900
34		4d. dull purple	£6000	£900
35		6d. yellow-green	£2750	£200
36		6d. deep green	£2750	£200
37		1s. purple-slate	£6500	£1300

(b) Pin-perf $13\frac{1}{2}$–14.

38	2	(1d.) rose-red	£140	24·00
39		(1d.) carmine-lake	£275	23·00
40	4	4d. dull lilac	£1200	80·00
40*a*		4d. brownish purple	£120	£110
41		4d. dull purple	£350	£110
42		6d. yellow-green	£500	75·00
43		6d. deep green	£500	70·00
43*a*		6d. bright yellow-green	£120	£110
		b. Imperf between (vert pair)	£4750	
44		1s. purple-slate	£6500	£800

(c) Compound pin-perf $13\frac{1}{2}$–14 × $12\frac{1}{2}$.

45	2	(1d.) carmine-lake	†	£3500
45*a*	4	4d. dull purple	†	—

PRICES. The Pin-perf stamps are very scarce with perforations on all sides and the prices quoted above are for good average specimens.

The note after No. 12 also applies to Nos. 38, 40*a*, 43*a*, 46, 47 and 50.

1860 (Aug). Clean-cut perf 14–$16\frac{1}{2}$.

46	2	(1d.) rose-red	£120	55·00
		a. Imperf vert (horiz pair)	£1100	
47	4	4d. brownish lilac	£130	80·00
48		4d. lilac	—	£300
49		6d. bright yellow-green	£400	90·00
50		6d. deep green	£225	£140

1861 (June). Rough perf 14–$16\frac{1}{2}$.

52	2	(1d.) rose-red (H/S "CANCELLED" in oval £6500)	£110	27·00
53		(1d.) rose	£110	24·00
54	4	4d. brownish lilac	£225	70·00
55		4d. lilac	£600	80·00
		a. Imperf		
56		6d. yellow-green	£225	80·00
57		6d. deep green	£400	70·00
58		1s. indigo	£800	£275
59		1s. dp bluish purple (H/S "CANCELLED" in oval £6500)	£1300	£425

(Recess D.L.R.)

1862–63. *Thick paper.*

(a) P $11\frac{1}{2}$, 12.

60	2	(1d.) crimson-lake	£100	18·00
61	4	4d. deep purple	£150	60·00
62		6d. deep green	£1000	85·00
63		1s. bluish slate	£2000	90·00

(b) P $11\frac{1}{2}$, 12, compound with 11.

63*a*	2	(1d.) crimson-lake	£1600	£475
63*b*	4	6d. deep green	—	£6500

(c) P 13 (1863).

64	2	(1d.) lake	38·00	18·00
65	4	6d. emerald-green	£450	55·00
67		1s. bright mauve	£4000	£275

(d) P $12\frac{1}{2}$ (1863).

68	2	(1d.) lake	42·00	18·00

1863–80.

(a) Wmk Crown CC. P $12\frac{1}{2}$.

69	2	(1d.) lake	48·00	5·00
		a. Wmk sideways	£120	14·00
		b. Rose	48·00	2·00
		ba. Imperf (pair)		
		c. Scarlet	48·00	2·00
		d. Carmine	48·00	2·25
		w. Wmk inverted	†	55·00
		x. Wmk reversed	50·00	2·50
		y. Wmk inverted and reversed	—	65·00
70	4	4d. bright violet	£100	10·00
		a. Pale mauve	£180	14·00
		b. Dull lilac	£140	14·00
		w. Wmk inverted	£225	55·00
		x. Wmk reversed	£110	12·00
71		4d. grey (1872)	£110	4·75
		a. Bluish grey	£100	5·00
		ax. Wmk reversed	£100	7·00
		w. Wmk inverted	—	65·00
72		6d. emerald-green	80·00	13·00
		a. Deep green	£375	7·50
		b. Yellow-green	75·00	4·00
		c. Apple-green	70·00	5·00
		d. Blue-green	£130	7·00
		x. Wmk reversed	90·00	6·00
73		1s. bright deep mauve	£140	7·00
		a. Lilac-rose	£110	7·00
		b. Mauve (aniline)	95·00	4·50
		bw. Wmk inverted		
		bx. Wmk reversed	—	6·00
74		1s. chrome-yellow (1872)	£130	1·25
		x. Wmk reversed	—	6·00

(b) P 14 (1876).

75	2	(1d.) lake	23·00	1·00
		a. Bisected ($\frac{1}{2}$d.) (on cover)	†	£550
		b. Rose-carmine	23·00	1·00
		c. Scarlet	42·00	1·00
		x. Wmk reversed	27·00	1·00
76	4	4d. bluish grey	£100	70
		y. Wmk inverted and reversed	†	80·00
77		6d. bright yellow-green	90·00	1·25
		a. Deep yellow-green	£110	1·25
		w. Wmk inverted	†	70·00
		x. Wmk reversed		
78		1s. chrome-yellow	£110	2·75

(c) P 14 × $12\frac{1}{2}$ (1880).

79	4	6d. yellow-green	†	£5500

The 1s. perforated $12\frac{1}{2}$ in purple-slate is a colour changeling.

5

(Typo D.L.R.)

1869. Wmk Crown CC. P $12\frac{1}{2}$.

87	5	5s. rose-lake	£160	75·00

HALFPENNY (6) **ONE PENNY** (7)

1879–82. *Surch with T* **6** *or* **7**. P 14.

(a) Wmk Crown CC (June 1879).

98	2	$\frac{1}{2}$d. lilac	11·00	7·50
		w. Wmk inverted	£100	32·00
		x. Wmk reversed	11·00	7·50
99		$\frac{1}{2}$d. mauve	11·00	7·50
		a. Wmk sideways	50·00	50·00
		w. Wmk inverted	†	—

(b) Wmk Crown CA (1882).

100	2	$\frac{1}{2}$d. lilac (wmk reversed)	£180	70·00
101		1d. rosy carmine	29·00	1·00
		a. Bisected ($\frac{1}{2}$d.) (on cover)	†	£550
		x. Wmk reversed	29·00	1·40

1882. Wmk Crown CA. P 14.

102	4	4d. bluish grey	£170	7·00
		x. Wmk reversed		

(**8**) Various styles

1882 (9 May). *Surch by hand in various styles as T* **8** *in red or b[lack] ink and the original value obliterated by a thick or thin bar or b[ars] of the same colour.*

103	1d. on 6d. (No. 77) (Bk.)	—	£1
104	1d.on 6d. (No. 77) (R.)	8·00	
	x. Wmk reversed	12·00	
105	1d.on 6d. (No. 77*a*) (R.)	8·00	
	a. Bisected ($\frac{1}{2}$d.) (on cover)	†	£

10

11 Britannia

12 Britannia

(Typo D.L.R.)

1883–94. P 14.

(a) Wmk Crown CA.

106	10	$\frac{1}{2}$d. dull green	4·25	
107		1d. carmine	10·00	
		a. Bisected ($\frac{1}{2}$d.) (on cover)	†	£
		w. Wmk inverted	†	£
108		$2\frac{1}{2}$d. bright blue	11·00	
110		4d. grey	2·50	
		w. Wmk inverted	†	£
111		6d. olive-black (1884)	3·50	
112		1s. orange-brown (1884)	4·00	

(b) Wmk Crown CC.

113	5	5s. maroon (1894)	55·00	8
106/13 *Set of* 7			80·00	9
106s/12s Optd "Specimen" *Set of* 6			£475	

Two types of 1d. value:

ONE PENNY (I) (round "o") **ONE PENNY** (II) (oval "o")

(Typo D.L.R.)

1896 (17 Aug)–**1906**. P 14.

(a) Wmk Crown CA.

114	11	$\frac{1}{2}$d. dull purple and green	3·25	
115		1d. dull purple and rose (I)	3·50	
116		1d. dull purple and rose (II) (1900)	£325	
117		$2\frac{1}{2}$d. dull purple and blue	4·75	
118		4d. dull purple and orange	6·50	1
119		5d. dull purple and mauve	7·00	1
120		6d. dull purple and black	7·50	
121		1s. green and brown	7·00	

(b) Wmk CA over Crown. *Ordinary paper.*

122	12	5s. green and brown	42·00	7
123		10s. green and ultramarine	£160	£
124		£1 green and carmine	£140	£
		a. Chalk-surfaced paper (1906)	£200	
114/24 *Set of* 10			£350	£
114s/24s Optd "Specimen" *Set of* 10			£160	

No. 119, surcharged "3d." was prepared for use in 1899 but [not] issued (*Price* £2750 *unused*). It also exists overprinted "Specim[en]" (*Price* £75).

Collectors are warned against apparently postally used copie[s of] this issue which bear "REGISTRAR-GENERAL" obliterati[ons] and are of very little value.

13 Landing of Columbus

(Recess D.L.R.)

1898 (31 July). *400th Anniv of Discovery of Trinidad.* Wmk Cr[own] CC. P 14.

125	13	2d. brown and dull violet	2·50	1
		s. Optd "Specimen"	50·00	

1901–06. *Colours changed. Ordinary paper.* Wmk Crown CA or [CA] over Crown (5s.). P 14.

126	11	$\frac{1}{2}$d. grey-green (1902)	65	2
127		1d. black/*red* (II)	1·25	
		a. Value omitted	£27000	
		w. Wmk inverted	†	£
128		$2\frac{1}{2}$d. purple and blue/*blue* (1902)	15·00	
129		4d. green and blue/*buff* (1902)	1·75	15
		a. Chalk-surfaced paper	3·50	14
130		1s. black and blue/*yellow* (1903)	18·00	5
131	12	5s. lilac and mauve	45·00	65
		a. Chalk-surfaced paper. *Deep purple and mauve* (1906)	65·00	80
126/31 *Set of* 6			75·00	80
126s/31s Optd "Specimen" *Set of* 6			£120	

pane of sixty of No. 127a was found at the San Fernando post e of which fifty-one were subsequently returned to London and troyed. Only three mint examples, one of which is in the Royal ection, are now thought to survive.

-09. *Ordinary paper (½d., 1d., 2½d. (No. 137)) or chalk-surfaced per (others).* Wmk Mult Crown CA. P 14.

11	½d. grey-green		2·75	1·00
		a. Chalk-surfaced paper	4·75	2·25
	½d. blue-green (1906)		9·00	2·50
	1d. black/*red* (II)		3·75	10
		a. Chalk-surfaced paper	5·50	10
	1d. rose-red (1907)		1·25	10
	2½d. purple and blue/*blue*		22·00	90
	2½d. blue (1906)		2·75	15
	4d. grey and red/*yellow* (1906)		1·50	8·00
		a. Black and red/yellow	9·00	21·00
	6d. dull purple and black (1905)		15·00	15·00
	6d. dull and bright purple (1906)		7·00	9·50
	1s. black and blue/*yellow*		20·00	8·00
	1s. purple and blue/*golden yellow*		10·00	14·00
	1s. black/*green* (1906)		1·75	1·25
12	5s. deep purple and mauve (1907)		42·00	80·00
	£1 green and carmine (1907)		£130	£225

45 *Set of* 13 . . . £225 £325
s/43s (*ex* Nos. 136, 139, 141) Optd
ecimen" *Set of* 6 . . . £120

o. 135 is from a new die, the letters of "ONE PENNY" being t and thick, while the point of Britannia's spear breaks the ermost horizontal line of shading in the background.

14

15

16

(Typo D.L.R.)

9. Wmk Mult Crown CA. P 14.

14	½d. green	3·50	10
15	1d. rose-red	3·50	10
16	2½d. blue	11·00	3·25
/8 *Set of* 3		16·00	3·25
s/8s Optd "Specimen" *Set of* 3		70·00	

TOBAGO

Although a Colonial Postmaster was appointed in January 1765 as not until 1841 that the British G.P.O established a branch ce at Scarborough, the island capital, to handle the overseas l.

The stamps of Great Britain were in use from May 1858 to the of April 1860 when the control of the postal service passed to local authorities.

From April 1860 Nos. CC1/2 were again used on overseas mail, ding the introduction of Tobago stamps in 1879.

SCARBOROUGH

CROWNED-CIRCLE HANDSTAMPS

CC 1

CC 2

1 CC **1** TOBAGO (R.) (31.10.1851) . . . *Price on cover* £800
2 CC **2** TOBAGO (R.) (1875) . . . *Price on cover* £3000

mps of GREAT BRITAIN cancelled "A 14" as Type Z 1of naica.

8–60.

1d. rose-red (1857), perf 14	£750
4d. rose (1857)	£325
6d. lilac (1856)	£250
1s. green (1856)	£1300

PRICES FOR STAMPS ON COVER

Nos. 1/4	*from* × 25
Nos. 5/7	—
Nos. 8/12	*from* × 10
Nos. 13/19	*from* × 6
Nos. 20/4	*from* × 40
Nos. 26/33	*from* × 25

NCELLATIONS. Beware of early stamps of Tobago with fiscal lorsements removed and forged wide "A 14" postmarks added.

1

2

2½ PENCE
(3)

(T **1** and **2** Typo D.L.R.)

1879 (1 Aug). *Fiscal stamps issued provisionally pending the arrival of stamps inscr* "POSTAGE". Wmk Crown CC. P 14.

1	**1**	1d. rose	85·00	65·00
2		3d. blue	85·00	50·00
3		6d. orange	40·00	55·00
		w. Wmk inverted	90·00	£100
4		1s. green	£400	65·00
		a. Bisected (6d.) (on cover)	†	—
5		5s. slate	£700	£650
6		£1 mauve	£4000	

The stamps were introduced for fiscal purposes on 1 July 1879.

Stamps of T **1**, watermark Crown CA, are fiscals which were never admitted to postal use.

1880 (Nov). *No. 3 bisected vertically and surch with pen and ink.*

7	**1**	1d.on half of 6d. orange	£4750	£800
		w. Wmk inverted		

1880 (20 Dec). Wmk Crown CC. P 14.

8	**2**	½d. purple-brown	40·00	65·00
9		1d. Venetian red	£110	60·00
		a. Bisected (½d.) (on cover)	†	£2000
10		4d. yellow-green	£225	27·00
		a. Bisected (2d.) (on cover)	†	£2000
		b. Malformed "CE" in "PENCE"	£1400	£400
		w. Wmk inverted	—	£140
11		6d. stone	£325	£110
12		1s. yellow-ochre	65·00	75·00
		w. Wmk inverted	£150	

For illustration of Nos. 10b, 18a, 22b, 30a, 31a and 33b see above No. 4 of Dominica.

1883 (Apr). *No. 11 surch with T* **3**.

13	**2**	2½d.on 6d. stone	50·00	50·00
		a. Surch double	£3000	£1500
		b. Large "2" with long tail	£120	£130

"SLASH" FLAW. Stamps as Type **2** were produced from Key and Duty plates. On the Key plate used for consignments between 2 October 1892 and 16 December 1896, damage in the form of a large cut or "slash" shows after the "E" of "POSTAGE" on R. 1/4.

After 1896 an attempt was made to repair the "slash". This resulted in its disappearance, but left an incomplete edge to the circular frame at right.

1882–84. Wmk Crown CA. P 14.

14	**2**	½d. purple-brown (1882)	1·50	13·00
15		1d. Venetian red (1882)	3·25	2·00
		a. Bisected diag (½d.) (on cover)		
16		2½d. dull blue (1883)	32·00	1·60
		a. Bright blue	6·00	75
		b. Ultramarine	6·00	75
		c. "Slash" flaw	48·00	40·00
		ca. "Slash" flaw repaired	90·00	
18		4d. yellow-green (1882)	£180	90·00
		a. Malformed "CE" in "PENCE"	£1200	£475
19		6d. stone (1884)	£550	£475

1885–96. *Colours changed and new value.* Wmk Crown CA. P 14.

20	**2**	½d. dull green (1886)	2·00	85
		a. "Slash" flaw	27·00	32·00
		ab. "Slash" flaw repaired	50·00	
		w. Wmk inverted		
21		1d. carmine (1889)	2·50	1·00
		a. "Slash" flaw	35·00	35·00
		ab. "Slash" flaw repaired	65·00	
22		4d. grey (1885)	2·50	1·75
		a. Imperf (pair)	£1700	
		b. Malformed "CE" in "PENCE"	50·00	80·00
		c. "Slash" flaw	85·00	£120
		ca. "Slash" flaw repaired	£120	
23		6d. orange-brown (1886)	2·25	5·00
		a. "Slash" flaw	95·00	£150
		ab. "Slash" flaw repaired	£130	
24		1s. olive-yellow (1894)	2·50	17·00
		a. Pale olive-yellow	7·00	
		b. "Slash" flaw	£110	£225
		ba. "Slash" flaw repaired	£140	
24*c*		1s. orange-brown (1896)	8·50	70·00
		ca. "Slash" flaw	£150	
20s/3s (*ex* 4d.) Optd "Specimen" *Set of* 3			£170	

No. 24*c* was printed in the colour of the 6d. by mistake.

½d

½ PENNY
(4)

2½ PENCE
(5)

POSTAGE
(6)

1886–89. *Nos. 16, 19 and 23 surch as T* **4**.

26		½d.on 2½d. dull blue (4.86)	5·00	13·00
		a. Figure further from word	24·00	55·00
		b. Surch double	£2000	£1600
		c. Surch omitted. Vert pair with No. 26	£11000	
		d. Ditto with No. 26a	£18000	
27		½d.on 6d. stone (1.86)	3·00	20·00
		a. Figure further from word	26·00	£110
		b. Surch inverted	£2000	
		c. Surch double	£2500	
28		½d.on 6d. orange-brown (8.87)	£100	£130
		a. Figure further from word	£300	£325
		b. Surch double	—	£2000
29		1d.on 2½d. dull blue (7.89)	65·00	17·00
		a. Figure further from word	£170	80·00

The surcharge is in a setting of 12 (two rows of 6) repeated five times in the pane. Nos. 7, 9 and 10 in the setting have a raised "P" in "PENNY", and No. 10 also shows the wider spacing between figure and word.

1891–92. *No. 22 surch with T* **4** *or* **5**.

30		½d.on 4d. grey (3.92)	15·00	50·00
		a. Malformed "CE" in "PENCE"	£225	£425
		b. Surch double	£2500	
31		2½d.on 4d. grey (8.91)	7·00	7·00
		a. Malformed "CE" in "PENCE"	£140	£200
		b. Surch double	£2500	£2500

1896. *Fiscal stamp (T* **1**, *value in second colour,* wmk Crown CA, *P 14), surch with T* **6**.

33		½d.on 4d. lilac and carmine	60·00	32·00
		a. Space between "½" and "d"	£130	75·00
		b. Malformed "CE" in "PENCE"	£600	£500

Tobago became a ward of Trinidad on 1 January 1899. Stamps of Trinidad were used until issues inscribed "TRINIDAD AND TOBAGO" appeared in 1913.

TRINIDAD AND TOBAGO

PRICES FOR STAMPS ON COVER

Nos. 149/55	*from* × 3
Nos. 156/7	—
Nos. 174/89	*from* × 10
Nos. 206/56	*from* × 2
Nos. D18/25	*from* × 12

17

18

(Typo D.L.R.)

1913–23. *Ordinary paper (½d. to 4d. and 1s.) or chalk-surfaced paper (others).* Wmk Mult Crown CA. P 14.

149	**17**	½d. green	3·00	10
		a. Yellow-green (1915)	3·50	20
		b. Blue-green (thick paper) (1917)	7·00	1·00
		ba. Wmk sideways	†	£1300
		c. Blue-green/bluish (3.18)	14·00	12·00
		w. Wmk inverted		
150		1d. bright red	1·50	10
		a. Red (thick paper) (1916)	3·25	30
		b. Pink (1918)	22·00	3·00
		c. Carmine-red (5.18)	2·50	10
		w. Wmk inverted		
151		2½d. ultramarine	6·50	50
		a. Bright blue (thick paper) (1916)	6·50	50
		b. Bright blue (thin paper) (1918)	8·00	50
152		4d. black and red/*yellow*		
		a. Chalk-surfaced paper	70	6·00
		b. White back (12.13)	1·75	10·00
		bs. Optd "Specimen"	22·00	
		c. On lemon (1917)	10·00	
		d. On pale yellow (1923)	5·00	9·00
		ds. Optd "Specimen"	26·00	
153		6d. dull and reddish purple	9·50	7·00
		a. Dull and deep purple (1918)	10·00	4·00
		b. Dull purple and mauve (2.18)	10·00	8·00
154		1s. black/*green*	1·75	4·50
		a. White back	1·00	6·50
		as. Optd "Specimen"	22·00	
		b. On blue-green, olive back	8·00	9·00
		c. On emerald back	1·50	3·00
		cs. Optd "Specimen"	26·00	
155	**18**	5s. dull purple and mauve (1914)	55·00	90·00
		a. Deep purple and mauve (1918)	55·00	90·00
		b. Lilac and violet	85·00	£120
		c. Dull purple and violet	90·00	£130
		d. Brown-purple and violet	50·00	90·00
156		£1 grey-green and carmine (1914)	£140	£180
		a. Deep yellow-green & carmine (1918)	£120	£170
149/56 *Set of* 8			£170	£250
149s/56s Optd "Specimen" *Set of* 8			£170	

No. 156*a* is from a plate showing background lines very worn.

18a

1914 (18 Sept). *Red Cross Label authorised for use as ½d. stamp. Typo.* P 11–12.

157	**18a**	(½d.) Red	11·00	£190

The above was authorised for internal use on one day only, to raise funds for the Red Cross. The used price is for stamp on cover.

21. 10. 15.
(19)

19. 10. 16.

(19a)

1915 (21 Oct). *Optd with T* **19**. *Cross in red with outline and date in black.*
174 **17** 1d. red . . . . 1·50 1·50
a. Cross 2 mm to right . . . . 20·00 25·00
b. "1" of "15" forked foot . . . . 11·00 17·00
c. Broken "0" in "10" . . . . 12·00 17·00

The varieties occur in the following positions on the *pane* of 60: a. No. 11. b. No. 42. c. No. 45. Variety a. is only found on the right-hand pane.

1916 (19 Oct). *Optd with T* **19a**. *Cross in red with outline and date in black.*
175 **17** 1d. scarlet . . . . 50 2·00
a. No stop after "16" . . . . 9·00 26·00
b. "19.10.16" omitted . . . .
c. Red shading on cross omitted . . . .

No. 175a appears on stamp No. 36 on the right-hand pane only.

FORGERIES. Beware of forgeries of the "War Tax" errors listed below. There are also other unlisted errors which are purely fakes.

WAR TAX (19b) | WAR TAX (20) | WAR TAX (21) | WAR TAX (22)

1917 (2 Apr). *Optd with T* **19b**.
176 **17** 1d. red . . . . 2·25 2·75
a. Opt inverted £200 £275
b. Scarlet . . . . 2·25 2·75
w. Wmk inverted . . . .

1917 (May). *Optd with T* **20**.
177 **17** ½d. green 10 20
a. Pair, one without opt £500
178 1d. red . . . . 75 1·75
a. Pair, one without opt £500 £1000
b. Scarlet . . . . 3·00 80
ba. Opt double £130

The varieties without overprint were caused by the type being shifted over towards the left so that one stamp in the lowest row of each pane escaped.

1917 (21 June). *Optd with T* **21**.
179 **17** ½d. yellow-green . . . . 1·40 7·50
a. Pale green . . . . 10 6·50
b. Deep green . . . . 1·25 7·50
180 1d. red 10 75
a. Pair, one without opt . . . .

No. 180a was caused by a shifting of the type to the left-hand side, but only a few stamps on the right-hand vertical row escaped the overprint and such pairs are very rare.

1917 (21 July–Sept). *Optd with T* **22**.
181 **17** ½d. yellow-green . . . . 4·00 6·00
a. Deep green . . . . 10 3·00
aw. Wmk inverted £100
182 1d. red (Sept) . . . . 3·25 1·00

WAR TAX (23) | WAR TAX (24) | WAR TAX (25)

1917 (1 Sept). *Optd with T* **23** *(closer spacing between lines of opt).*
183 **17** ½d. deep green . . . . 10 2·50
a. Pale yellow-green . . . .
184 1d. red . . . . 35·00 27·00

1917 (31 Oct). *Optd with T* **24**.
185 **17** 1d. scarlet . . . . 60 1·00
a. Opt inverted £110

1918 (7 Jan). *Optd with T* **25**.
186 **17** 1d. scarlet . . . . 1·50 15
a. Opt double £200 £200
b. Opt inverted £120 £120

War Tax (26) | War Tax (26a)

27

1918 (13 Feb–May). *Optd with T* **26**.
187 **17** ½d. bluish green . . . . 10 1·75
a. Pair, one without opt £1000
188 1d. scarlet . . . . 1·25 1·25
a. Opt double £110
b. Rose-red (1.5.18) 10 60

The ½d. exists with "TAX" omitted caused by a paper fold.

1918 (14 Sept). *New printing as T* **26**, *but 19 stamps on each sheet have the letters of the word "Tax" wider spaced, the "x" being to the right of "r" of "War" as T* **26a**. *Thick bluish paper.*
189 **17** 1d. scarlet ("Tax" spaced) . . . . 60 5·50
a. Opt double £200
b. Pair, one without opt £1000
c. Opt inverted on back £1000

The varieties 189b and 189c are caused by a paper fold.

1921–22. *Chalk-surfaced paper (6d. to £1).* Wmk Mult Script CA. P 14.
206 **17** ½d. green . . . . 2·00 2·25
207 1d. scarlet 60 30
208 1d. brown (17.2.22) . . . . 60 1·50
209 2d. grey (17.2.22) . . . . 1·00 1·25
210 2½d. bright blue . . . . 80 14·00
211 3d. bright blue (17.2.22) . . . . 3·00 3·00
212 6d. dull and bright purple . . . . 2·00 16·00
213 **18** 5s. dull purple and purple (1921) . . 50·00 £130
214 5s. deep purple and purple (1922) . . 50·00 £130
215 £1 green and carmine . . . . 90·00 £225
206/15 *Set of* 9 . . . . £130 £350
206s/15s Optd "Specimen" *Set of* 9 . . . . £225

(Typo D.L.R.)

1922–28. *Chalk-surfaced paper (4d. to £1).* P 14.

(a) Wmk Mult Crown CA.
216 **27** 4d. black and red/*pale yellow* . . . . 3·25 7·50
217 1s. black/*emerald* . . . . 3·50 9·50

(b) Wmk Mult Script CA.
218 **27** ½d. green 50 10
219 1d. brown 50 10
w. Wmk inverted . . . . 32·00
220 1½d. bright rose . . . . 2·25 20
aw. Wmk inverted . . . . 65·00
b. Scarlet . . . . 1·75 30
bw. Wmk inverted . . . .
222 2d. grey . . . . 50 1·25
223 3d. blue . . . . 50 1·25
224 4d. black and red/*pale yellow* (1928) . . . . 3·25 3·25
225 6d. dull purple and bright magenta . . . . 2·25 25·00
226 6d. green and red/*emerald* (1924) . . 1·25 60
227 1s. black/*emerald* . . . . 5·50 1·75
228 5s. dull purple and mauve . . . . 22·00 38·00
229 £1 green and bright rose £100 £200
216/29 *Set of* 13 . . . . £130 £250
216s/29s Optd "Specimen" *Set of* 13 . . . . £250

(New Currency. 100 cents = 1 West Indian dollar)

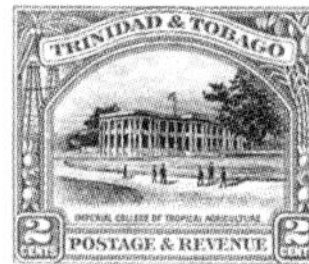
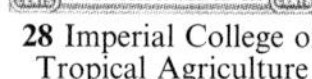
28 Imperial College of Tropical Agriculture

29 Discovery of Lake Asphalt

(Recess B.W.)

1935 (1 Feb)–**37**. *T* **28/9** *and similar horiz designs.* Wmk Mult Script CA (sideways). P 12.
230 1c. blue and green 40 85
a. Perf 13 × 12½ (1936) 30 10
231 2c. ultramarine and yellow-brown . . . . 75 1·00
a. Perf 13 × 12½ (1936) . . . . 1·00 10
232 3c. black and scarlet . . . . 1·00 30
a. Perf 13 × 12½ (1936) . . . . 2·50 30
233 6c. sepia and blue . . . . 4·25 2·50
a. Perf 13 × 12½ (1937) . . . . 6·00 3·75
234 8c. sage-green and vermilion . . . . 3·75 3·50
235 12c. black and violet . . . . 3·25 1·75
a. Perf 13 × 12½ (1937) . . . . 6·50 5·00
236 24c. black and olive-green . . . . 2·75 1·50
a. Perf 13 × 12½ (1937) . . . . 12·00 8·00
237 48c. deep green . . . . 8·50 15·00
238 72c. myrtle-green and carmine . . . . 28·00 30·00
230/8 *Set of* 9 . . . . 45·00 48·00
230s/8s Perf "Specimen" *Set of* 9 . . . . £130

Designs:—1c. First Boca; 3c. Mt Irvine Bay, Tobago; 8c. Queen's Park, Savannah; 12c. Town Hall, San Fernando; 24c. Government House; 48c. Memorial Park; 72c. Blue Basin.

1935 (6 May). *Silver Jubilee. As Nos. 91/4 of Antigua, but ptd by B.W.* P 11 × 12.
239 2c. ultramarine and grey-black 30 75
a. Extra flagstaff . . . . 35·00 50·00
b. Short extra flagstaff . . . . 50·00
c. Lightning conductor . . . . 40·00
d. Flagstaff on right-hand turret . . . . 65·00
240 3c. deep blue and scarlet . . . . 30 1·25
a. Extra flagstaff . . . . 60·00
c. Lightning conductor . . . . 55·00
241 6c. brown and deep blue . . . . 1·50 2·50
a. Extra flagstaff . . . . 90·00
b. Short extra flagstaff £120
c. Lightning conductor . . . . 90·00
242 24c. slate and purple . . . . 5·50 16·00
a. Extra flagstaff £140
c. Lightning conductor £140
d. Flagstaff on right-hand turret £180
e. Double flagstaff £190
239/42 *Set of* 4 . . . . 7·00 18·00
239s/42s Perf "Specimen" *Set of* 4 . . . . 85·00

For illustrations of plate varieties see Omnibus section following Zanzibar.

1937 (12 May). *Coronation. As Nos. 95/7 of Antigua, but ptd by D.L.R.* P 14.
243 1c. green 15 40
244 2c. yellow-brown 35 15
245 8c. orange . . . . 90 2·00
243/5 *Set of* 3 . . . . 1·25 2·25
243s/5s Perf "Specimen" *Set of* 3 . . . . 75·00

37 First Boca

47 King George VI

(Recess B.W.)

1938 (2 May)–**44**. *T* **37** *and similar horiz designs, and T* **47**. W Mult Script CA (sideways on 1c. to 60c.).

(a) P 11½ × 11.
246 1c. blue and green . . . . 1·00
247 2c. blue and yellow-brown . . . . 1·25
248 3c. black and scarlet . . . . 11·00
248*a* 3c. green and purple-brown (1941) 30
ab. "A" of "CA" missing from wmk . . . .
249 4c. chocolate . . . . 25·00
249*a* 4c. scarlet (1941) 50
249*b* 5c. magenta (1.5.41) 50
250 6c. sepia and blue . . . . 2·75
251 8c. sage-green and vermilion . . . . 2·75
252 12c. black and purple . . . . 18·00
a. Black and slate-purple (1944) . . . . 2·75
253 24c. black and olive-green . . . . 2·00
254 60c. myrtle-green and carmine . . . . 8·50

(b) T **47**. P 12.
255 $1.20, blue-green (1.40) . . . . 11·00
256 $4.80, rose-carmine (1.40) . . . . 23·00 3
246/56 *Set of* 14 . . . . 80·00 3
246s/56s (*ex* 5c.) Perf "Specimen" *Set of* 13 . . . . £250

Designs:—2c. Imperial College of Tropical Agriculture; 3c. Irvine Bay, Tobago; 4c. Memorial Park; 5c. G.P.O. and Treas 6c. Discovery of Lake Asphalt; 8c. Queen's Park, Savannah; Town Hall, San Fernando; 24c. Government House; 60c. Basin.

1946 (1 Oct). *Victory. As Nos. 110/11 of Antigua.*
257 3c. chocolate 10
258 6c. blue 10
257s/8s Perf "Specimen" *Set of* 2 . . . . 60·00

1948 (22 Nov). *Royal Silver Wedding. As Nos. 112/13 of Anti but $4.80 in recess.*
259 3c. red-brown 10
260 $4.80 carmine . . . . 20·00 2

1949 (10 Oct). *75th Anniv of U.P.U. As Nos. 114/17 of Antigua*
261 5c. bright reddish purple 35
262 6c. deep blue . . . . 1·75
263 12c. violet 40
264 24c. olive 45
261/4 *Set of* 4 . . . . 2·75

1951 (16 Feb). *Inauguration of B.W.I. University College. Nos. 118/19 of Antigua.*
265 3c. green and red-brown 20
266 12c. black and reddish violet 30

STAMP BOOKLETS

1925.
SB1 2s. booklet containing eight ½d., 1d. and 1½d. (Nos. 218/20) in blocks of 4 . . . .

1931–32. *Black on pink covers.*
SB2 1s.8d. booklet containing eight ½d. and sixteen 1d. (Nos. 218/19) in blocks of 8 . . . .
SB3 2s. booklet containing eight ½d., 1d. and 1½d. (Nos. 218/20) in blocks of 8 (1932) . . . .

1935.
SB4 48c. booklet containing eight 1, 2 and 3c. (Nos. 230/2) in blocks of 4 . . . .

POSTAGE DUE STAMPS

D 1

1/- Row 4 | 1/- Row 5

The degree of inclination of the stroke on the 1s. value varies each vertical column of the sheet: Columns 1, 2 and 6 104°, Colu 3 108°, Column 4 107° and Column 5 (Nos. D9a, D17a, D25a) 1

(Typo D.L.R.)

1885 (1 Jan). Wmk Crown CA. P 14.
D1 **D 1** ½d. slate-black . . . . 15·00 4
D2 1d. slate-black . . . . 5·50
D3 2d. slate-black . . . . 26·00
D4 3d. slate-black . . . . 48·00
D5 4d. slate-black . . . . 29·00
D6 5d. slate-black . . . . 23·00
D7 6d. slate-black . . . . 38·00
D8 8d. slate-black . . . . 55·00
D9 1s. slate-black . . . . 60·00
a. Upright stroke £110 1
D1/9 *Set of* 9 . . . . £250 5

1905–06. Wmk Mult Crown CA. P 14.

D10	**D 1**	1d. slate-black	4·00	20
D11		2d. slate-black	23·00	20
		w. Wmk inverted	†	£170
D12		3d. slate-black	11·00	2·75
		w. Wmk inverted	—	£120
D13		4d. slate-black	11·00	12·00
		w. Wmk inverted		
D14		5d. slate-black	11·00	12·00
D15		6d. slate-black	6·00	10·00
D16		8d. slate-black	12·00	14·00
D17		1s. slate-black	12·00	35·00
		a. Upright stroke	25·00	75·00
D10/17 *Set of* 8			80·00	75·00

1923–45. Wmk Mult Script CA. P 14.

D18	**D 1**	1d. black	1·25	2·00
D19		2d. black	2·50	1·50
D20		3d. black (1925)	2·50	2·75
D21		4d. black (1929)	3·00	22·00
D22		5d. black (1944)	35·00	95·00
D23		6d. black (1945)	55·00	38·00
D24		8d. black (1945)	45·00	£160
D25		1s. black (1945)	65·00	£120
		a. Upright stroke	£130	£200
D18/25 *Set of* 8			£190	£400
D18s/25s Optd or Perf (5d. to 1s.) "Specimen" *Set of* 8			£150	

1947 (1 Sept)–**61**. *Values in cents. Ordinary paper.* Wmk Mult Script CA. P 14.

D26	**D 1**	2c. black	2·50	3·50
		a. Chalk-surfaced paper (20.1.53)	20	3·75
		ab. Error. Crown missing. W **9***a*	85·00	
		ac. Error. St. Edward's Crown. W **9***b*	28·00	
D27		4c. black	1·00	3·00
		a. Chalk-surfaced paper (10.8.55)	3·25	4·50
D28		6c. black	1·90	6·00
		a. Chalk-surfaced paper (20.1.53)	30	7·50
		ab. Error. Crown missing. W **9***a*	£250	
		ac. Error. St. Edward's Crown. W **9***b*	65·00	
D29		8c. black	1·10	24·00
		a. Chalk-surfaced paper (10.9.58)	35	23·00
D30		10c. black	1·10	4·25
		a. Chalk-surfaced paper (10.8.55)	3·50	12·00
D31		12c. black	1·25	19·00
		a. Chalk-surfaced paper (20.1.53)	40	18·00
		ab. Error. Crown missing. W **9***a*	£325	
		ac. Error. St. Edward's Crown. W **9***b*	£110	
D32		16c. black	2·00	42·00
		a. Chalk-surfaced paper (22.8.61)	10·00	55·00
D33		24c. black	7·50	8·00
		a. Chalk-surfaced paper (10.8.55)	4·25	40·00
D26/33 *Set of* 8			16·00	£100
D26a/33a *Set of* 8			20·00	£150
D26s/33s Perf "Specimen" *Set of* 8			£140	

"TOO LATE" STAMPS

A handstamp with the words "TOO LATE" was used upon letters on which a too-late fee had been paid, and was sometimes used for cancelling the stamps on such letters.

OFFICIAL STAMPS

O S (O 1) **OFFICIAL** (O 2) **OFFICIAL** (O 3)

1894. *Optd with Type* O **1**.

(a) On Nos. 106/12. Wmk Crown CA. P 14.

O1	**10**	½d. dull green	35·00	55·00
O2		1d. carmine	38·00	60·00
O3		2½d. bright blue	45·00	90·00
O4		4d. grey	48·00	95·00
O5		6d. olive-black	48·00	95·00
O6		1s. orange-brown	65·00	£130

(b) On No. 87. Wmk Crown CC. P 12½.

O7	**5**	5s. rose-lake	£160	£475

1909. *Nos. 133 and 135 optd with Type* O **2**. Wmk Mult Crown CA. P 14.

O8	**11**	½d. blue-green	1·00	6·50
O9		1d. rose-red	1·00	6·50
		a. Opt double	—	£300
		b. Opt vertical	£100	£120
		c. Opt inverted	£750	£225

1910. *No. 148 optd with Type* O **2**. Wmk Mult Crown CA. P 14.

O10	**14**	½d. green	4·50	6·50

1913. *No. 149 optd with Type* O **3** *by lithography.*

O11	**17**	½d. green	1·00	7·00
		a. Opt vertical		

OFFICIAL (O 4) **OFFICIAL** (O 5) **OFFICIAL** (O 6)

1914. *No. 149 optd with Type* O **4**.

O12	**17**	½d. green	1·75	13·00

1914–17. *No. 149 optd with Type* O **5** *(without stop).*

O13	**17**	½d. green	3·00	13·00
		a. Blue-green (*thick paper*) (1917)	50	6·50

1916. *No. 149a optd with Type* O **5** *(with stop).*

O14	**17**	½d. yellow-green	1·50	3·25
		a. Opt double	28·00	

1917 (22 Aug). *No. 149 optd with Type* O **6**.

O15	**17**	½d. green	3·00	16·00
		a. Yellow-green	3·75	19·00
		b. Blue-green (*thick paper*)	1·50	17·00

Tristan Da Cunha

Although first settled in 1817 no surviving mail is known from Tristan da Cunha until two whaler's letters written in 1836 and 1843, these being carried home in other whaling ships. Then there is a long gap until the late 1800's when other letters are known—surprisingly only some seven in number, up to 1908 when the first of the island cachet handstamps came into use.

The collecting of postal history material from 1908 to 1952, when Tristan's first stamps were issued, revolves around the numerous cachets of origin which were struck on mail from the island during these 44 years. The handstamps producing these cachets were supplied over the years by various people particularly interested in the island and the islanders, and were mostly used by the clergymen who volunteered to go and serve as the community's ministers.

The postal cachets are illustrated below. The use of the different cachets on mail frequently overlapped, at one period in 1930 there were five different types of handstamp in use. As there was no official source for providing them they appeared on the island from various donors; then disappeared without trace once they became worn out. Only one of these early rubber handstamps has apparently survived, Cachet Va.

Covers bearing the cachets are recognised collector's items, but are difficult to value in general terms. As elsewhere the value is discounted by poor condition of the cover, and may be increased by use on a scarce date or with additional postal markings.

Cachet Types V and VII on cover are the commonest, Type Va, used only for three months, and Type IVa are the scarcest, equalling the scarcest use of Type I examples. All cacheted covers, particularly if non-philatelic, are desirable forerunner items. Even a philatelic cover of Type V is, at present, worth in the region of £35.

Dates given are of the first recorded use.

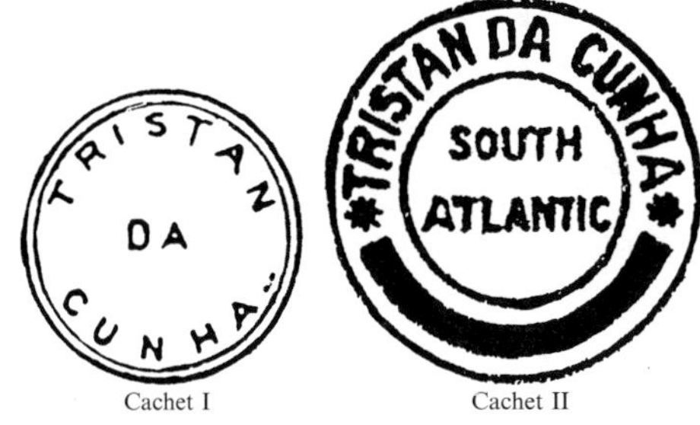

Cachet I Cachet II

Cat. No. *Value on cover*

C1	**1908** (May). Cachet I	*from*	£4000
C2	**1919** (31 July). Cachet II	*from*	£425

Cachet III

C3	**1921** (8 Feb). Cachet III	*from*	£275

Cachet IVa

C4	**1927** (1 Oct). Cachet IV (*as* IVa, *but without centre label*)	*from*	£800
C5	**1928** (28 Oct). Cachet IVa	*from*	£5500

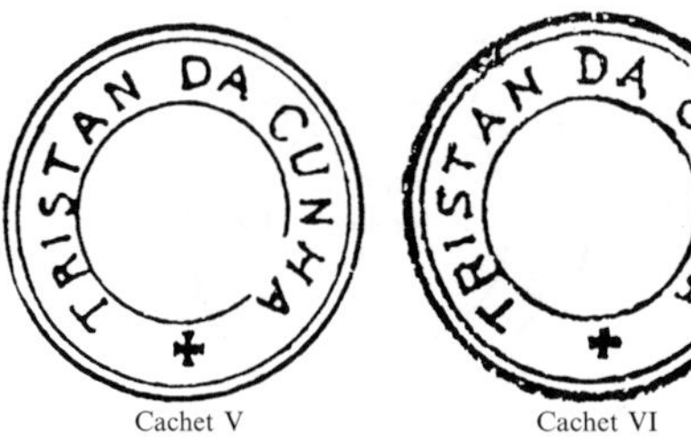

Cachet V Cachet VI

C6	**1929** (24 Feb). Cachet V	*from*	35·00
C7	**1929** (15 May). Cachet Va (*as* V, *but without break in inner ring. Shows* "T" "C" *and* "N" *damaged*)	*from*	£6500
C8	**1936** (Aug). Cachet VI	*from*	60·00

Cachet VII

C9	**1936** (1 Feb). Cachet VII	*from*	22·00

During World War II there was little mail from the island as its function as a meteorological station was cloaked by security. Such covers as are known are generally struck with the "tombstone" naval censor mark and postmarked "maritime mail" or have South African postal markings. A few philatelic items from early in the war bearing cachets exist, but this usage was soon stopped by the military commander and the handstamps were put away until peace returned. Covers from the period would be worth from £75 to, at least, £350.

Cachet VIII

C10	**1946** (8 May). Cachet VIII	*from*	85·00

Cachet IX

C11	**1948** (2 Feb). Cachet IX	*from*	45·00

This cachet with "A.B.C." below the date was in private use between 1942 and 1946.

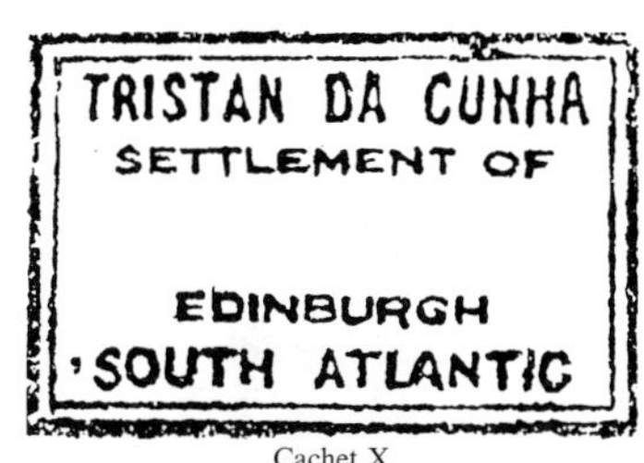

Cachet X

C12	**1948** (29 Feb). Cachet X	*from*	55·00

Cachet XIII

Cachets XI to XIII from the 1961/63 "volcano eruption" and "return to the island" period vary in value from £30 to £120, due to philatelic usage on the one hand and scarce mailings from the small survey parties on shore during this period on the other.

TRISTAN
DA CUNHA
(1)

1952 (1 Jan). *Nos. 131, 135a/40 and 149/51 of St. Helena optd with T* **1**.

No.	Description	Unused	Used
1	½d. violet	15	2·00
2	1d. black and green	70	1·50
3	1½d. black and carmine	70	1·50
4	2d. black and scarlet	70	1·50
5	3d. grey	1·00	1·50
6	4d. ultramarine	4·00	2·50
7	6d. light blue	4·25	2·50
8	8d. olive-green	4·00	6·00
9	1s. sepia	4·25	2·00
10	2s.6d. maroon	19·00	13·00
11	5s. chocolate	21·00	20·00
12	10s. purple	40·00	30·00
1/12	*Set of* 12	90·00	75·00

Turks and Caicos Islands

TURKS ISLANDS

DEPENDENCY OF JAMAICA

A branch of the British Post Office opened at Grand Turk on 11 December 1854 replacing an earlier arrangement under which mail for the islands was sorted by local R.M.S.P. agents.

No. CC 1 is known used between 22 October 1857 and 20 April 1862.

GRAND TURK

CROWNED-CIRCLE HANDSTAMPS

CC 1

CC1 CC **1** TURKS-ISLANDS (Oct 1857)
Price on cover £5500

PRICES FOR STAMPS ON COVER TO 1945

Nos.		
Nos.	1/5	*from* × 30
No.	6	—
Nos.	7/20	*from* × 50
Nos.	20a/48	—
Nos.	49/52	*from* × 12
Nos.	53/7	*from* × 10
Nos.	58/65	*from* × 20
Nos.	66/9	*from* × 5
Nos.	70/2	*from* × 10
Nos.	101/9	*from* × 8
Nos.	110/26	*from* × 6
Nos.	129/39	*from* × 4
Nos.	140/53	*from* × 12
Nos.	154/90	*from* × 3
Nos.	191/3	*from* × 10
Nos.	194/205	*from* × 2

1

Throat flaw (R. 3/4)

(Recess P.B.)

1867 (4 Apr). No wmk. P 11–12.

No.	Type	Description	Unused	Used
1	**1**	1d. dull rose	55·00	55·00
		a. Throat flaw	£190	£225
2		6d. black	90·00	£120
3		1s. dull blue	90·00	60·00

1873–79. Wmk Small Star. W w **2** (sideways on Nos. 5 and 6). P 11–12 × 14½–15½.

No.	Type	Description	Unused	Used
4	**1**	1d. dull rose-lake (7.73)	50·00	50·00
		a. Throat flaw	£180	£200
		b. Wmk sideways	85·00	85·00
		ba. Throat flaw	£300	£325
5		1d. dull red (1.79)	55·00	60·00
		a. Imperf between (horiz pair)	£17000	
		b. Throat flaw	£200	£225
		c. Wmk upright		
6		1s. lilac (1.79)	£5000	£2000

1881 (1 Jan). *Stamps of the preceding issues surcharged locally, in black.*

There are twelve different settings of the ½d., nine settings of the 2½d., and six settings of the 4d.

(2) (3)

Setting 1. *T* **2**. *Long fraction bar. Two varieties repeated fifteen times in the sheet.*

No.	Description	Unused	Used
7	½ on 6d. black	75·00	£120

Setting 2. *T* **3**. *Short fraction bar. Three varieties in a vertical strip repeated ten times in sheet.*

Setting 3. *Similar to setting 2, but the middle stamp of the three varieties has a longer bar.*

No.	Description	Unused	Used
8	½on 6d. black (*setting 2 only*)	70·00	£100
9	½on 1s. dull blue	95·00	£160
	a. Surch double	£5000	

(4) (5) (6)

Three varieties in a vertical strip repeated ten times in sheet.
Setting 4. *Types* **4**, **5**, **6**.
Setting 5. *Types* **4** *(without bar)*, **5**, **6**.
Setting 6. *Types* **4**, **5**, **6** *(without bar)*.
Setting 7. *Types* **4** *(shorter thick bar)*, **6**, **6**.

No.	Description	Unused	Used
10	½on 1d. dull red (*setting 7 only*) (T **6**)		
	a. Type **4** (shorter thick bar)	£9000	
11	½on 1s. dull blue (*setting 6 and 7*) (T **4**)	£1300	
	a. Type **4** (shorter thick bar)	£1600	
	b. Type **5**	£950	
	c. Type **6**	£850	
	d. Type **6** (without bar)	£1400	
	e. Surch double (T **4**)	£6500	
	f. Surch double (T **5**)	£6500	
	g. Surch double (T **6** without bar)		
12	½on 1s. lilac (T **4**)	£250	£375
	a. Without bar	£500	
	b. With short thick bar	£475	
	c. Surch double	£3000	
	cb. Surch double and short thick bar	£6500	
13	½on 1s. lilac (T **5**)	£120	£200
	a. Surch double	£2750	
14	½on 1s. lilac (T **6**)	£120	£200
	a. Without bar	£550	
	b. Surch double	£4500	
	ba. Surch double and without bar	£6500	

Care should be taken in the identification of Types **6** and **7** which are very similar. For the 1s. value some varieties of No. 9 are often confused with Nos. 11b/c.

(7) (8) (9) (10)

Setting 8. *T* **7**. *Three varieties in a vertical strip. All have a very short bar.*

No.	Description	Unused	Used
15	½on 1d. dull red	60·00	£100
	a. Throat flaw	£250	

Setting 9. *T* **8**. *Three varieties in a vertical strip. Bars long and thick and "1" leaning a little to left.*

No.	Description	Unused	Used
16	½ on 1d. dull red	£180	£250
	a. Surch double	£3750	
	b. Throat flaw	£550	

Setting 10. *T* **9** *and* **10**. *Fifteen varieties repeated twice in a sheet. Ten are of T* **9** *(Rows 1 and 2), five of T* **10** *(Row 3).*

No.	Description	Unused	Used
17	½on 1d. dull red (T **9**)	50·00	£110
	a. Surch double	£4500	
18	½on 1d. dull red (T **10**)	80·00	£160
	a. Surch double	£6500	
	b. Throat flaw	£275	
19	½on 1s. lilac (T **9**)	90·00	£170
20	½on 1s. lilac (T **10**)	£160	£325
20*a*	½on 1s. dull blue (T **9**)	£8000	
20*b*	½on 1s. dull blue (T **10**)	£13000	

Types **9** and **11**. The difference is in the position of the "2" in relation to the "1". In setting 10 the "2" is to the left of the "1" except on No. 10 (where it is directly below the "1") and in setting 11 it is to the right except on No. 2 (where it is to the left, as in setting 10).

(11) (12) (13) (14)

Setting 11. *T* **9** *and* **11** *to* **14**. *Fifteen varieties repeated twice in a sheet. Nine of T* **11**, *three of T* **12**, *and one each of T* **9**, **13** *and* **14**.

Setting 12. *Similar to last, but T* **13** *replaced by another T* **12**.

No.	Description	Unused	Used
21	½on 1d. dull red (T **11**)	£100	£18
22	½on 1d. dull red (T **12**)	£225	
	a. Throat flaw	£1100	
23	½on 1d. dull red (T **13**)	£1000	
	a. Throat flaw	£1000	
24	½on 1d. dull red (T **14**)	£550	
24*a*	½on 1s. dull blue (T **11**)	£12000	

Type **9** from these settings, where it occurs on position 2, can only be distinguished from similar stamps from setting 10 when *se tenant* with Type **11**.

(15) (16)

Setting 1. *T* **15**. *Fraction in very small type.*

No.	Description	Unused	Used
25	2½on 6d. black	£8500	

Setting 2. *T* **16**. *Two varieties repeated fifteen times in a sheet. Large "2" on level with top of the "1", long thin bar.*

No.	Description	Unused	Used
26	2½on 6d. black	£325	£40
	a. Imperf between (horiz pair)	£17000	
	b. Surch double	£8500	

(17) (18) (19)

Setting 3. *T* **17**. *As T* **16**, *but large "2" not so high up.*

No.	Description	Unused	Used
27	2½on 1s. lilac	£2250	

Setting 4. *T* **18**. *Three varieties in a vertical strip repeated ten times in sheet. Large "2" placed lower and small bar.*

No.	Description	Unused	Used
28	2½on 6d. black	£150	£2
	a. Surch double	£8500	

Setting 5. *T* **19**. *Three varieties in a vertical strip repeated ten times in sheet "2" further from "½", small fraction bar.*

No.	Description	Unused	Used
29	2½on 1s. lilac	£550	£8

(20) (21)

Setting 6. *T* **20** *and* **21**. *Fifteen varieties. Ten of T* **20** *and five of T* **21** *repeated twice in a sheet.*

No.	Description	Unused	Used
30	2½on 1s. lilac (T **20**)	£8500	
31	2½on 1s. lilac (T **21**)	£13000	

(22) (23) (24)

Setting 7. T **22**. *Three varieties in a vertical strip, repeated ten times in a sheet.*

32 2½on 6d. black . . . £7500
33 2½on 1s. dull blue . . . £13000

Setting 8. T **23** *and* **24**. *Fifteen varieties. Ten of T* **23** *and five of T* **24** *repeated twice in a sheet.*

34 2½on 1d. dull red (T **23**) . . . £600
35 2½on 1d. dull red (T **24**) . . . £1300
a. Throat flaw . . . £3000
36 2½on 1s. lilac (T **23**) . . . £550 £700
a. Surch "½" double . . . £3000
37 2½on 1s. lilac (T **24**) . . . £1200
a. Surch "½" double . . . £5000

(25) (26) (27)

Setting 9. T **25**, **26**, *and* **27**. *Fifteen varieties. Ten of T* **25**, *three of T* **26**, *one of T* **26** *without bar, and one of T* **27**, *repeated twice in a sheet.*

8 2½on 1s. dull blue (T **25**) . . . £750
9 2½on 1s. dull blue (T **26**) . . . £1900
0 2½on 1s. dull blue (T **26**) (without bar) . . . £7000
1 2½on 1s. dull blue (T **27**) . . . £7000

(28) (29) (30)

Setting 1. T **28**. *"4" 8 mm high, pointed top.*

2 4on 6d. black . . . £425 £300

Settings 2-6. T **29** *and* **30**.

3 4on 6d. black (T **29**) . . . 75·00 £100
4 4on 6d. black (T **30**) . . . £325 £425
5 4on 1s. lilac (T **29**) . . . £400 £550
a. Surch double
6 4on 1s. lilac (T **30**) . . . £2250
a. Surch double
7 4on 1d. dull red (T **29**) . . . £750 £475
8 4on 1d. dull red (T **28**) . . . £850 £550

The components of these settings can only be distinguished when in blocks. Details are given in the handbook by John J. Challis.

31

One Penny
(32)

(Typo D.L.R.)

81. Wmk Crown CC (sideways* on T **1**). P 14.
1 1d. brown-red (Oct) . . . 60·00 85·00
a. Throat flaw . . . £225 £275
31 4d. ultramarine (Die I) (Aug) . . . £120 60·00
1 6d. olive-black (Oct) . . . £100 £150
1s. slate-green (Oct) . . . £150 £120

*The normal sideways watermark shows Crown to right of CC, *seen from the back of the stamp.*

Nos. 49 and 51/2 also exist showing Crown to left of CC, but due the position of the watermark such varieties are difficult to detect single stamps.

82–85. Wmk Crown CA (reversed on 1d.). P 14.
31 ½d. blue-green (Die I) (2.82) . . . 9·00 22·00
a. Pale green (12.85) . . . 2·25 3·50
b. Top left triangle detached . . . £160
1 1d. orange-brown (10.83) . . . 65·00 30·00
a. Bisected (½d.) (on cover) . . . † £4250
b. Throat flaw . . . £225 £130
x. Wmk normal (not reversed) . . . £100
31 2½d. red-brown (Die I) (2.82) . . . 20·00 10·00
4d. grey (Die I) (10.84) . . . 17·00 2·50
a. Bisected (2d.) (on cover) . . . † £4250

For illustration of "top left triangle detached" variety see above o. 6 of Montserrat.

87 (July)–**89**. Wmk Crown CA.

(a) P 12.
1 1d. crimson-lake . . . 18·00 4·25
a. Imperf between (horiz pair) . . . £16000
b. Throat flaw . . . 48·00 13·00
x. Wmk reversed . . . 12·00 2·75

(b) P 14.
1 6d. yellow-brown (2.89) . . . 2·75 3·25
s. Optd "Specimen" . . . 60·00
1s. sepia . . . 4·25 3·00

During a shortage of 1d. stamps a supply of JAMAICA No. 27 was sent to the Turks and Caicos Islands in April 1889 and used until replaced by No. 61. *Price from* £225 *used.*

89 (May). *Surch at Grand Turk with T* **32**.
31 1d.on 2½d. red-brown . . . 7·50 9·50
a. "One" omitted . . . £1600
b. Bisected (½d.) (on cover) . . . † £4750

No. 61a was caused by misplacement of the surcharge. Stamps from the same sheet can be found with the surcharge reading "Penny One".

Neck flaw (R. 3/2)

1889–93. Wmk Crown CA. P 14.
62 **1** 1d. crimson-lake (7.89) . . . 3·50 3·75
a. Bisected (½d.) (on cover) . . . † £4250
b. Throat flaw . . . 16·00 18·00
c. Neck flaw . . . 22·00 24·00
x. Wmk reversed . . . 42·00
63 1d. lake . . . 2·75 2·75
a. Bisected (½d.) (on cover) . . . † £4250
b. Throat flaw . . . 11·00 11·00
c. Neck flaw . . . 16·00 17·00
64 1d. pale rosy lake . . . 2·75 4·50
b. Throat flaw . . . 11·00 20·00
c. Neck flaw . . . 16·00 25·00
65 **31** 2½d. ultramarine (Die II) (4.93) . . . 2·50 2·50
s. Optd "Specimen" . . . 55·00

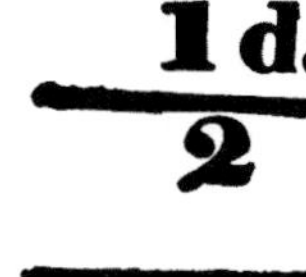
(33)

34

1893 (10 June). *No. 57 surch at Grand Turk with T* **33**.

Setting 1. Bars between "1d." and "2" separate, instead of continuous across the rows of stamps.

66 ½d.on 4d. grey . . . £2250 £1000

Setting 2. Continuous bars. Thin and thick bar 10¾ mm apart. "2" under the "1".

67 ½d.on 4d. grey . . . £180 £130

Setting 3. As last, but bars 11¾ mm apart.

68 ½d.on 4d. grey . . . £140 £160

Setting 4. Bars 11 mm apart. Five out of the six varieties in the strip have the "2" below the space between the "1" and "d".

69 ½d.on 4d. grey . . . £180 £160

There is a fifth setting, but the variation is slight.

(Typo D.L.R.)

1893–95. Wmk Crown CA. P 14.
70 **31** ½d. dull green (Die II) (12.93) . . . 2·50 1·75
71 4d. dull purple & ultram (Die II) (5.95) . . . 9·50 13·00
72 **34** 5d. olive-green and carmine (6.94) . . . 4·00 13·00
a. Bisected (2½d.) (on cover) . . . † £3750
70/2 *Set of* 3 . . . 14·00 23·00
71s/2s Optd "Specimen" *Set of* 2 . . . £100

TURKS AND CAICOS ISLANDS

35 Badge of the Islands 36

The dates on the stamps have reference to the political separation from Bahamas.

(Recess D.L.R.)

1900 (10 Nov)–**04**. Wmk Crown CA (½d. to 1s.) or Wmk Crown CC (2s., 3s.). P 14.
101 **35** ½d. green . . . 2·75 4·00
x. Wmk reversed
102 1d. red . . . 3·50 75
w. Wmk inverted . . . 75·00
103 2d. sepia . . . 1·00 1·25
w. Wmk inverted
x. Wmk reversed . . . 95·00
104 2½d. blue . . . 7·50 16·00
a. Greyish blue (1904) . . . 1·75 1·00
aw. Wmk inverted . . . 75·00
ay. Wmk inverted and reversed . . . — £120
105 4d. orange . . . 3·75 7·00
106 6d. dull mauve . . . 2·50 6·50
107 1s. purple-brown . . . 3·25 18·00
108 **36** 2s. purple . . . 40·00 55·00
109 3s. lake . . . 55·00 75·00
101/9 *Set of* 9 . . . £100 £150
101s/9s Optd "Specimen" *Set of* 9 . . . £225

1905–08. Wmk Mult Crown CA. P 14.
110 **35** ½d. green . . . 5·00 15
111 1d. red . . . 16·00 50
w. Wmk inverted
112 3d. purple/*yellow* (1908) . . . 2·25 6·00
s. Optd "Specimen" . . . 50·00
w. Wmk inverted
110/12 *Set of* 3 . . . 21·00 6·00

37 Turk's-head Cactus

38

(Recess D.L.R.)

1909 (2 Sept)–**11**. Wmk Mult Crown CA. P 14.
115 **37** ¼d. rosy mauve (1910) . . . 1·75 1·00
w. Wmk inverted
116 ¼d. red (1911) . . . 60 40
w. Wmk inverted
117 **38** ½d. yellow-green . . . 75 40
w. Wmk inverted
x. Wmk reversed . . . 50·00
y. Wmk inverted and reversed
118 1d. red . . . 1·25 40
119 2d. greyish slate . . . 2·50 1·40
120 2½d. blue . . . 2·75 3·75
w. Wmk inverted
x. Wmk reversed . . . 60·00 65·00
121 3d. purple/*yellow* . . . 2·50 2·00
122 4d. red/*yellow* . . . 3·25 7·00
123 6d. purple . . . 7·00 7·00
124 1s. black/*green* . . . 7·00 8·50
w. Wmk inverted
125 2s. red/*green* . . . 32·00 48·00
126 3s. black/*red* . . . 32·00 40·00
115/26 *Set of* 12 . . . 85·00 £110
115s/26s Optd "Specimen" *Set of* 12 . . . £200

See also Nos. 154 and 162.

39

WAR TAX
(40)

1913 (1 Apr)–**21**. Wmk Mult Crown CA. P 14.
129 **39** ½d. green . . . 50 1·75
w. Wmk inverted
130 1d. red . . . 1·00 2·25
a. Bright rose-scarlet . . . 1·10 2·00
ax. Wmk reversed . . . 48·00
b. Rose-carmine (1918) . . . 3·75 5·50
131 2d. greyish slate . . . 2·25 3·50
132 2½d. ultramarine . . . 2·25 3·00
aw. Wmk inverted
b. Bright blue (1918) . . . 4·00 2·75
133 3d. purple/*yellow* . . . 2·25 11·00
a. On lemon . . . 16·00
b. On yellow-buff . . . 4·00 9·50
c. On orange-buff . . . 1·75
cx. Wmk reversed . . . 75·00
d. On pale yellow . . . 2·25 8·50
134 4d. red/*yellow* . . . 1·00 9·50
a. On orange-buff . . . 1·60 7·50
ab. "A" of "CA" missing from wmk
as. Optd "Specimen" . . . 48·00
b. Carmine on pale yellow . . . 7·50 16·00
135 5d. pale olive-green (18.5.16) . . . 6·50 22·00
136 6d. dull purple . . . 2·50 3·50
w. Wmk inverted
x. Wmk reversed
137 1s. brown-orange . . . 1·50 5·00
w. Wmk inverted
138 2s. red/*blue-green* . . . 7·50 26·00
a. On greenish white (1919) . . . 24·00 70·00
b. On emerald (3.21) . . . 48·00 70·00
bs. Optd "Specimen" . . . 48·00
bx. Wmk reversed . . . £150
139 3s. black/*red* . . . 15·00 26·00
129/39 *Set of* 11 . . . 35·00 95·00
129s/39s Optd "Specimen" *Set of* 11 . . . £180

1917 (3 Jan). *Optd with T* **40** *at bottom of stamp.*
140 **39** 1d. red . . . 10 1·50
a. Opt double . . . £180 £250
ab. Opt double (in horiz pair with normal) . . . £350
b. "TAX" omitted
c. "WAR TAX" omitted in vert pair with normal . . . £475
d. Opt inverted at top . . . 65·00 85·00
e. Opt double, one inverted . . . £110
f. Opt inverted only, in pair with No. 140e . . . £500
141 3d. purple/*yellow-buff* . . . 1·00 4·25
a. Opt double . . . 90·00
b. Purple/lemon . . . 2·00 6·50
ba. Opt double . . . 90·00 £110
bb. Opt double, one inverted . . . £325

The overprint was in a setting of 60, applied twice to the sheets of 120. One sheet of the 1d. exists with the right-hand impression of the setting misplaced one row to the left so that stamps in vertical row 6 show a double overprint (No. 140ab). It appears that the right-hand vertical row on this sheet had the overprint applied at a third operation.

In Nos. 140e/f the inverted overprint is at foot and reads "TAX WAR" owing to displacement. No. 140e also exists with "WAR" omitted from the inverted overprint.

In both values of the first printings the stamp in the bottom left-hand corner of the sheet has a long "T" in "TAX", and on the first stamp of the sixth row the "X" is damaged and looks like a reversed "K".

1917 (Oct). *Second printing with overprint at top or in middle of stamp.*

143	**39**	1d. red	10	1·25
		a. Inverted opt at bottom or centre	45·00	
		c. Opt omitted (in pair with normal)	£450	
		d. Opt double, one at top, one at bottom	55·00	
		e. As d., but additional opt in top margin	£120	
		f. Horiz pair, one as d., the other normal	£275	
		g. Pair, one opt inverted, one normal	£450	
		h. Double opt at top (in pair with normal)	£250	
		i. Opt double	42·00	48·00
144		3d. purple/*yellow*	60	1·75
		a. Opt double	42·00	
		b. Opt double, one inverted	£325	
		c. Purple/lemon	3·50	

1918. *Overprinted with T* **40**.

145	**39**	3d. purple/*yellow* (R.)	8·50	24·00
		a. Opt double	£300	

WAR / **TAX** (41) W A R / TAX (42) W A R / TAX (43)

1918. *Optd with T* **41** *in London by D.L.R.*

146	**39**	1d. rose-carmine	20	1·25
		a. Bright rose-scarlet	15	1·25
		aw. Wmk inverted	65·00	
147		3d. purple/*yellow*	1·75	3·75
146/7 Optd "Specimen" *Set of* 2			80·00	

1919. *Optd with T* **41** *in London by D.L.R.*

148	**39**	3d. purple/*orange-buff* (R.)	10	2·00
		s. Optd "Specimen"	40·00	

1919. *Local overprint. T* **40**, *in violet.*

149	**39**	1d. bright rose-scarlet	30	3·25
		a. "WAR" omitted	£150	
		b. Opt double	21·00	
		c. Opt double in pair with normal	£120	
		d. Opt double, one inverted		
		e. Rose-carmine	6·50	14·00
		ea. Opt double		
		w. Wmk inverted	32·00	

1919. *Optd with T* **42**.

150	**39**	1d. scarlet	10	1·00
		a. Opt double	£140	£170
		b. Opt double, one albino and reversed		
151		3d. purple/*orange-buff*	30	2·75
		w. Wmk inverted	32·00	
		x. Wmk reversed	32·00	

1919 (17 Dec). *Optd with T* **43**.

152	**39**	1d. scarlet	20	2·50
		a. Opt inverted		
153		3d. purple/*orange-buff*	50	2·75
		w. Wmk inverted	30·00	
		x. Wmk reversed	25·00	
		y. Wmk inverted and reversed	12·00	

The two bottom rows of this setting have the words "WAR" and "TAX" about 1 mm further apart.

1921 (23 Apr). Wmk Mult Script CA. P 14.

154	**37**	¼d. rose-red	2·50	13·00
155	**39**	½d. green	2·75	5·50
156		1d. carmine-red	1·00	5·50
157		2d. slate-grey	1·00	19·00
		y. Wmk inverted and reversed	55·00	
158		2½d. bright blue	1·75	7·50
159		5d. sage-green	8·00	48·00
160		6d. purple	6·50	48·00
		w. Wmk inverted		
		x. Wmk reversed	60·00	
161		1s. brown-orange	6·50	27·00
154/61 *Set of* 8			26·00	£160
154s/61s Optd "Specimen" *Set of* 8			£140	

44

45

(Recess D.L.R.)

1922 (20 Nov)–**26**. P 14.

(a) Wmk Mult Script CA.

162	**37**	¼d. black (11.10.26)	80	1·00
163	**44**	½d. yellow-green	2·00	3·00
		a. Bright green	2·00	3·00
		b. Apple-green	5·50	10·00
164		1d. brown	50	3·25
165		1½d. scarlet (24.11.25)	6·50	15·00
166		2d. slate	50	5·00
167		2½d. purple/*pale yellow*	50	1·75
168		3d. bright blue	50	5·00
169		4d. red/*pale yellow*	1·25	16·00
		ax. Wmk reversed	55·00	
		b. Carmine/pale yellow	4·50	16·00
170		5d. sage-green	85	22·00
		y. Wmk inverted and reversed	60·00	
171		6d. purple	70	5·50
		x. Wmk reversed	65·00	
172		1s. brown-orange	80	17·00
173		2s. red/*emerald*	2·00	9·00

(b) Wmk Mult Crown CA.

174	**44**	2s. red/*emerald* (24.11.25)	25·00	70·00
175		3s. black/*red* (24.11.25)	5·00	27·00
162/75 *Set of* 14			42·00	£180
162s/75s Optd "Specimen" *Set of* 14			£200	

1928 (1 Mar). *Inscr* "POSTAGE & REVENUE". Wmk Mult Script CA. P 14.

176	**45**	½d. green	75	50
177		1d. brown	75	70
178		1½d. scarlet	75	3·25
179		2d. grey	75	50
180		2½d. purple/*yellow*	75	5·00
181		3d. bright blue	75	6·50
182		6d. purple	75	7·50
183		1s. brown-orange	3·75	7·50
184		2s. red/*emerald*	6·00	35·00
185		5s. green/*yellow*	11·00	35·00
186		10s. purple/*blue*	50·00	£100
176/86 *Set of* 11			70·00	£180
176s/86s Optd "Specimen" *Set of* 11			£140	

1935 (6 May). *Silver Jubilee. As Nos. 91/4 of Antigua, but ptd by Waterlow.* P 11 × 12.

187	½d. black and green	30	75
	k. Kite and vertical log	38·00	
	l. Kite and horizontal log	27·00	
188	3d. brown and deep blue	2·75	4·50
	k. Kite and vertical log	80·00	£110
189	6d. light blue and olive-green	1·75	4·75
	k. Kite and vertical log	80·00	£110
190	1s. slate and purple	1·75	3·25
	k. Kite and vertical log	80·00	
187/90 *Set of* 4		6·00	12·00
187s/90s Perf "Specimen" *Set of* 4		80·00	

For illustrations of plate varieties see Omnibus section following Zanzibar.

1937 (12 May). *Coronation. As Nos. 95/7 of Antigua, but ptd by D.L.R.* P 14.

191	½d. myrtle-green	10	10
	a. Deep green	40·00	
192	2d. grey-black	65	50
193	3d. bright blue	65	50
191/3 *Set of* 3		1·25	1·00
191s/3s Perf "Specimen" *Set of* 3		65·00	

46 Raking Salt

47 Salt Industry

(Recess Waterlow)

1938 (18 June)–**45**. Wmk Mult Script CA. P 12½.

194	**46**	¼d. black	20	10
195		½d. yellowish green	4·00	15
		a. Deep green (6.11.44)	1·50	70
196		1d. red-brown	75	10
197		1½d. scarlet	75	15
198		2d. grey	1·00	30
199		2½d. yellow-orange	4·50	80
		a. Orange (6.11.44)	2·25	1·75
200		3d. bright blue	70	30
201		6d. mauve	14·00	1·75
201*a*		6d. sepia (9.2.45)	50	20
202		1s. yellow-bistre	4·75	8·00
202*a*		1s. grey-olive (9.2.45)	50	20
203	**47**	2s. deep rose-carmine	42·00	14·00
		a. Bright rose-carmine (6.11.44)	17·00	17·00
204		5s. yellowish green	48·00	17·00
		a. Deep green (6.11.44)	35·00	21·00
205		10s. bright violet	12·00	7·50
194/205 *Set of* 14			80·00	45·00
194s/205s Perf "Specimen" *Set of* 14			£200	

1946 (4 Nov). *Victory. As Nos. 110/11 of Antigua.*

206	2d. black	10	10
207	3d. blue	15	10
206s/7s Perf "Specimen" *Set of* 2		60·00	

1948 (13 Sept). *Royal Silver Wedding. As Nos. 112/13 of Antigua.*

208	1d. red-brown	15	10
209	10s. mauve	8·00	11·00

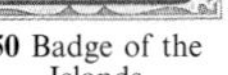
50 Badge of the Islands

53 Queen Victoria and King George VI

(Recess Waterlow)

1948 (14 Dec). *Centenary of Separation from Bahamas. T* **50**, **53** *and similar designs.* Wmk Mult Script CA. P 12½.

210	**50**	½d. blue-green	1·25	1
211		2d. carmine	1·25	1
212	–	3d. blue	1·75	1
213	–	6d. violet	1·00	3
214	**53**	2s. black and bright blue	1·25	1·0
215		5s. black and green	1·25	4·0
216		10s. black and brown	1·25	4·0
210/16 *Set of* 7			8·00	8·7

Designs: *Horiz*—3d. Flag of Turks and Caicos Islands; 6d. Ma of islands.

1949 (10 Oct). *75th Anniv of U.P.U. As Nos. 114/17 of Antigua.*

217	2½d. red-orange	20	1·4
218	3d. deep blue	2·00	6
219	6d. brown	20	6
220	1s. olive	20	3
217/20 *Set of* 4		2·40	2·7

65 Bulk Salt Loading

66 Dependency's Badge

(Recess Waterlow)

1950 (1 Aug). *T* **65** *and similar horiz designs, and T* **66**. Wmk Mu Script CA. P 12½.

221	½d. green	85	4
222	1d. red-brown	80	7
223	1½d. deep carmine	1·25	5
224	2d. red-orange	1·00	4
225	2½d. grey-olive	1·25	5
226	3d. bright blue	60	4
227	4d. black and rose	2·75	7
228	6d. black and blue	2·00	5
229	1s. black and blue-green	1·00	4
230	1s.6d. black and scarlet	8·50	3·2
231	2s. emerald and ultramarine	3·00	4·5
232	5s. blue and black	18·00	8·5
233	10s. black and violet	18·00	18·0
221/33 *Set of* 13		50·00	35·0

Designs:—1d. Salt Cay; 1½d. Caicos mail; 2d. Grand Turk; 2½ Sponge diving; 3d. South Creek; 4d. Map; 6d. Grand Turk Ligh 1s. Government House; 1s.6d. Cockburn Harbour; 2s. Governme Offices; 5s. Loading salt.

Uganda

PRICES FOR STAMPS ON COVER TO 1945

The type-written stamps of Uganda, Nos. 1/53, are very rare used on cover.

Nos. 54/60	*from* × 20	
No. 61	—	
Nos. 70/5	*from* × 12	
No. 76	—	
Nos. 84/90	*from* × 20	
No. 91	—	
Nos. 92/3	*from* × 40	

PROTECTORATE

Following a period of conflict between Islamic, Protestant a Roman Catholic factions, Uganda was declared to be in the Brit sphere of influence by the Anglo-German Agreement of July 18 The British East Africa Company exercised a variable degree control until 27 August 1894 when the country was declared British Protectorate.

Before the introduction of Nos. 84/91 the stamps of Uganda w only valid for internal postage. Letters for overseas were frank with British East Africa issues on arrival at Mombasa.

(Currency. 200 cowries = 1 rupee)

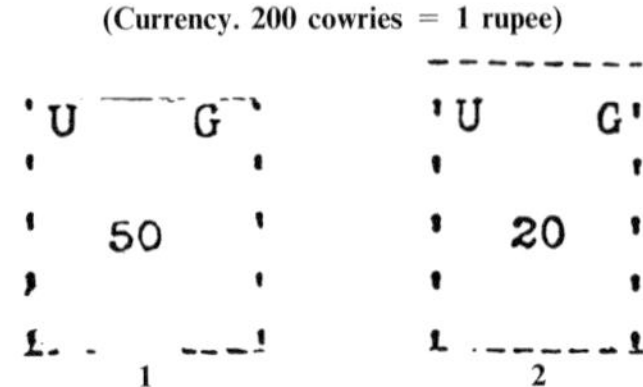

1 2

TYPE-WRITTEN STAMPS. Nos. 2/53 were type-written by Revd. E. Millar at Mengo for the Uganda administration. For "printings" a thin laid paper was used, and all issues w imperforate and ungummed. The laid lines are invariably horizon with the exception of No. 20a.

The original typewriter used had wide letters, but in late April, 895 Millar obtained a new machine on which the type face was in narrower fount.

Each sheet was made up of whatever values were required at the ime, so that different values can be found *se-tennant* or *tête-bêche*. These last were caused by the paper being inverted in the machine o that space at the foot could be utilised.

For the first issue the sheets were of 117 (9 × 13), but with the ntroduction of the narrower width (Nos. 17 onwards) a larger umber of stamps per sheet, 143 (11 × 13), was adopted.

The manuscript provisionals, Nos. 9*a*/16 come from the Mission t Ngogwe, most of the manuscript surchages including the initials of the Revd. G. R. Blackledge stationed there.

1895 (20 Mar). *Wide letters. Wide stamps, 20 to 26 mm wide.*

No.	Type		Unused	Used
	1	10 (c.) black	£2750	£1200
		20 (c.) black	£4500	£1200
		a. "U A" for "U G"	†	£2750
		30 (c.) black	£1400	£1400
		40 (c.) black	£2500	£1200
		50 (c.) black	£1200	£1000
		a. "U A" for "U G"	†	£4500
		60 (c.) black	£1700	£1700

It is now believed that the 5, 15 and 25 cowries values in this width, previously Nos. 1, 3 and 5, do not exist.

A strip of three of No. 2 is known on cover of which one stamp as the value "10" altered to "5" in manuscript and initialled E.M.".

895 (May). *Wide stamps with pen-written surcharges, in black.*

No.	Type		Unused	Used
9*a*	**1**	10 on 30 (c.) black	†	£32000
0		10 on 50 (c.) black	†	£32000
1		15 on 10 (c.) black	†	£23000
2		15 on 20 (c.) black	†	£27000
3		15 on 40 (c.) black	†	£27000
4		15 on 50 (c.) black	†	£32000
5		25 on 50 (c.) black	†	£32000
6		50 on 60 (c.) black	†	£32000

895 (April). *Wide letters. Narrow stamps, 16 to 18 mm wide.*

No.	Type		Unused	Used
7	**1**	5 (c.) black	£1500	£950
8		10 (c.) black	£1500	£1000
9		15 (c.) black	£1000	£1000
		20 (c.) black	£1500	£650
		a. Vertically laid paper	†	£1500
1		25 (c.) black	£950	£950
2		30 (c.) black	£8000	£8000
3		40 (c.) black	£7500	£7500
4		50 (c.) black	£3250	
5		60 (c.) black	£6000	

A single used example of No. 20a has been seen. Nos. 2/53 therwise show the laid lines horizontal.

895 (May). *Narrow letters. Narrow stamps 16 to 18 mm wide.*

No.	Type		Unused	Used
	2	5 (c.) black	£850	
		10 (c.) black	£850	
		15 (c.) black	£850	
		20 (c.) black	£650	
		25 (c.) black	£850	
		30 (c.) black	£850	
		40 (c.) black	£900	
		50 (c.) black	£750	
		60 (c.) black	£1600	

95 (Nov). *Narrow letters. Narrow stamps, 16–18 mm wide. Change of colour.*

No.	Type		Unused	Used
	2	5 (c.) violet	£500	£500
		10 (c.) violet	£475	£475
		15 (c.) violet	£600	£425
		20 (c.) violet	£375	£275
		a. "G U" for "U G"		
		25 (c.) violet	£750	£750
		30 (c.) violet	£1000	£750
		40 (c.) violet	£850	£850
		50 (c.) violet	£850	£900
		100 (c.) violet	£2500	£2500

Stamps of 35 (c.) and 45 (c.) have been recorded in violet, on rtically laid paper. They were never prepared for postal use, and d not represent a postal rate, but were type-written to oblige a cal official. (*Price* £2500 *each, unused*)

'V.96.R'

25

'Uganda'

3

96 (June).

No.	Type		Unused	Used
	3	5 (c.) violet	£475	£500
		10 (c.) violet	£425	£400
		15 (c.) violet	£475	£500
		20 (c.) violet	£275	£200
		25 (c.) violet	£450	
		30 (c.) violet	£500	£650
		40 (c.) violet	£550	£650
		50 (c.) violet	£600	£650
		60 (c.) violet	£1500	
		100 (c.) violet	£1400	£1500

(New Currency. 16 annas = 1 rupee)

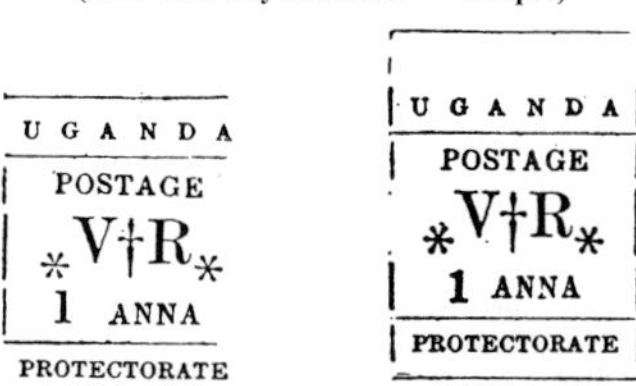

4 (Thin "1") 5 (Thick "1")

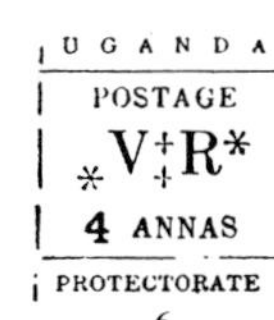

6

7

In the 2a. and 3a. the dagger points upwards; the stars in the 2a. are level with the top of "VR". The 8a. is as T **6** but with left star at top and right star at foot. The 1r. has three stars at foot. The 5r. has central star raised and the others at foot.

(Type-set by the Revd. F. Rowling at Lubwa's, in Usoga)

1896 (7 Nov). *Thick white wove paper (Nos. 54/8) or thin yellowish paper ruled with vertical lines 9 mm apart (Nos. 59/61).*

(a) Types **4/6**.

No.	Type		Unused	Used
54	**4**	1a. black	£110	95·00
		a. Small "o" in "POSTAGE"	£550	£500
55	**5**	1a. black	18·00	23·00
		a. Small "o" in "POSTAGE"	75·00	90·00
56	**6**	2a. black	24·00	28·00
		a. Small "o" in "POSTAGE"	95·00	£110
57		3a. black	26·00	30·00
		a. Small "o" in "POSTAGE"	£100	£130
58		4a. black	25·00	29·00
		a. Small "o" in "POSTAGE"	95·00	£120
59		8a. black	29·00	30·00
		a. Small "o' in "POSTAGE"	£110	£130
60		1r. black	75·00	95·00
		a. Small "o" in "POSTAGE"	£300	£400
61		5r. black	£225	£350
		a. Small "o" in "POSTAGE"	£700	£900

(b) Optd "L", in black as in T **7** *for local use, by a postal official, R. R. Racey, at Kampala.*

No.	Type		Unused	Used
70	**4**	1a. black	£190	£160
		a. Small "o" in "POSTAGE"	£1000	£850
71	**6**	2a. black	95·00	£110
		a. Small "o" in "POSTAGE"	£375	£425
72		3a. black	£225	£250
		a. Small "o" in "POSTAGE"	£1100	£1200
73		4a. black	£100	£150
		a. Small "o" in "POSTAGE"	£450	
74		8a. black	£190	£225
		a. Small "o" in "POSTAGE"	£950	£1100
75		1r. black	£375	£425
		a. Small "o" in "POSTAGE"	£1400	
76		5r. black	£12000	£12000

Tête-bêche pairs of all values may be found owing to the settings of 16 (4 × 4) being printed side by side or above one another. They are worth a premium. The variety with small "O" occurs on R. 3/1.

8

9

UGANDA
(10)

(Recess D.L.R.)

1898 (Nov)–**1902**. P 14.

(a) Wmk Crown CA.

No.	Type		Unused	Used
84	**8**	1a. scarlet	1·75	2·00
		a. Carmine-rose (1902)	2·00	1·00
86		2a. red-brown	2·50	7·00
87		3a. pale grey	10·00	26·00
		a. Bluish grey	11·00	13·00
88		4a. deep green	4·75	6·50
89		8a. pale olive	7·00	24·00
		a. Grey-green	10·00	29·00

(b) Wmk Crown CC.

No.	Type		Unused	Used
90	**9**	1r. dull blue	38·00	42·00
		a. Bright blue	45·00	50·00
91		5r. brown	70·00	£100
84/91		*Set of* 7	£120	£180
84s/91s		Optd "Specimen" *Set of* 7	£160	

On 1 April 1901 the postal administrations of British East Africa and Uganda were merged. Subsequent issues to 1962 are listed under KENYA, UGANDA and TANGANYIKA.

1902 (Feb). *T* **11** *of British East Africa (Kenya, Uganda, and Tanganyika) optd with T* **10**.

No.		Unused	Used
92	½a. yellow-green	2·00	1·40
	a. Opt omitted (in pair with normal)	£4000	
	b. Opt inverted (at foot)	£1600	
	c. Opt double	£1800	
	x. Wmk reversed		
93	2½a. deep blue (R.)	2·75	3·00
	a. Opt double	£600	
	b. Inverted "S" (R. 1/1)	65·00	80·00

The Eastern Province of Uganda was transferred to British East Africa on 1 April 1902.

Victoria *see* Australia

Virgin Islands

CROWN COLONY

Apart from the 1951 Legislative Council issue, the word "BRITISH" did not appear regularly on the stamps until 1968 when it was introduced to avoid confusion with the nearby Virgin Islands of the United States (the former Danish West Indies).

Most mail from the early years of the islands' history was sent via the Danish island of St. Thomas.

It is not known exactly when the first post office, or agency, was established on Tortola, but an entry in a G.P.O. account book suggest that it was operating by 1787 and the earliest letter postmarked "TORTOLA" dates from June of that year. The stamps of Great Britain were used from 1858 to May 1860, when the colonial authorities assumed responsibility for the overseas mails from the British G.P.O.

For illustrations of the handstamp and postmark types see BRITISH POST OFFICES ABROAD notes, following GREAT BRITAIN.

TORTOLA

CROWNED-CIRCLE HANDSTAMPS

CC1 **CC 1** TORTOLA (R.) (15.12.1842) *Price on cover* £4750

CC2 **CC 5** TORTOLA (R.) (21.6.1854) *Price on cover* £8000

No. CC2 is known used as an Official Paid mark during the years 1900 to 1918. *Price on cover* £1200.

Stamps of GREAT BRITAIN *cancelled* "A 13" *as Type* **2**.

1858–60.

No.		Price
Z1	1d. rose-red (1857), perf 14	£3750
Z2	4d. rose (1857)	£3750
Z3	6d. lilac (1856)	£1400
Z4	1s. green (1856)	

PRICES FOR STAMPS ON COVER TO 1945

Nos.		
Nos.	1/7	*from* × 30
Nos.	8/9	*from* × 40
No.	10	—
No.	11	*from* × 10
No.	12	*from* × 30
No.	13	—
Nos.	14/b	*from* × 10
Nos.	15/17	*from* × 30
Nos.	18/19	*from* × 40
No.	20	—
Nos.	21/b	*from* × 20
Nos.	22/b	*from* × 30
Nos.	24/31	*from* × 25
Nos.	32/4	*from* × 50
Nos.	35/7	*from* × 30
Nos.	38/41	*from* × 15
No.	42	*from* × 20
Nos.	43/50	*from* × 8
Nos.	54/77	*from* × 6
Nos.	78/81	*from* × 6
Nos.	82/101	*from* × 3
Nos.	103/6	*from* × 4
Nos.	107/9	*from* × 6
Nos.	110/21	*from* × 2

1 St. Ursula

2 St. Ursula

(Litho Nissen & Parker from original dies by Waterlow)

1866 (Dec). No wmk. P 12.

(a) White wove paper.

No.	Type		Unused	Used
1	**1**	1d. green	45·00	60·00
2		1d. deep green	55·00	65·00
3	**2**	6d. rose	90·00	£110
		a. Large "V" in "VIRGIN" (R. 2/1)	£375	£475
4		6d. deep rose	£130	£140
		a. Large "V" in "VIRGIN" (R. 2/1)	£425	£500

(b) Toned paper.

No.	Type		Unused	Used
5	**1**	1d. green	48·00	60·00
		a. Perf 15 × 12	£5000	£6500
6		1d. deep green	£100	£120
7	**2**	6d. rose-red	60·00	90·00
		a. Large "V" in "VIRGIN" (R. 2/1)	£275	£375

The above were printed in sheets of 25.

6d. stamps showing part of the papermaker's watermark ("A. Cowan & Sons Extra Superfine A. C. & S.") are worth 50% more.

Beware of fakes of No. 5a made from perf 12 stamps.

3

4

VIRGIN ISLANDS

Normal

Variety

1s. Long-tailed "S" in "ISLANDS" (R. 3/1)

(Litho and typo (figure of the Virgin) (1s.) or litho (others) Nissen and Parker from original dies by Waterlow)

1867–70. No wmk. P 15. *1s. with double-lined frame.*

(a) White wove paper.
8 **1** 1d. yellow-green (1868) . . . 80·00 80·00
9 1d. blue-green (1870) . . . 65·00 70·00
10 **2** 6d. pale rose . . . £550 £550
11 **4** 1s. black and rose-carmine . . . £250 £350
a. Long-tailed "S" . . . £750 £900

(b) Greyish (No. 14) or toned paper (others).
12 **1** 1d. yellow-green (1868) . . . 85·00 80·00
13 **2** 6d. dull rose (1868) . . . £275 £325
14 **4** 1s. black & rose-carmine (*greyish paper*) . . . £250 £350
a. Long-tailed "S" . . . £750 £900
14*b* 1s. black and rose-carmine (*toned paper*) . . . £325 £350
ba. Long-tailed "S" . . . £800 £900

(c) Pale rose paper.
15 **3** 4d. lake-red . . . 50·00 70·00

(d) Buff paper.
16 **3** 4d. lake-red . . . 40·00 60·00
17 4d. lake-brown . . . 40·00 60·00

The thin lines of the frame on the 1s. are close together and sometimes merge into one.

The 1d. from the 1868 printing was in sheets of 20 (5 × 4) with narrow margins between the stamps. Later printings were in sheets of 12 (3 × 4) with wider margins. The 4d. was in sheets of 25; and the remaining two values in sheets of 20 (5 × 4).

The greyish paper used for Nos. 14 and 20 often shows traces of blue.

1867. *Nos. 11 and 14b with crimson frames superimposed extending into margins.* P 15.
18 **4** 1s. black and rose-carmine (*white paper*) . . . 55·00 65·00
a. Long-tailed "S" . . . £180 £200
b. Figure of Virgin omitted . . . £75000
19 1s. black and rose-carmine (*toned paper*) . . . 55·00 65·00
a. Long-tailed "S" . . . £180 £200
20 1s. black and rose-carmine (*greyish paper*) . . . £750 £900
a. Long-tailed "S" . . . £1800 £2000

1868. *Nos. 11 and 14b with frame lines retouched so as to make them single lines. Margins remain white.* P 15.
21 **4** 1s. black and rose-carmine (*white paper*) . . . £140 £170
a. Long-tailed "S" . . . £425 £500
21*b* 1s. black and rose-carmine (*toned paper*) . . . £140 £170
ba. Long-tailed "S" . . . £425 £500

(Litho D.L.R.)

1878. Wmk Crown CC (sideways). P 14.
22 **1** 1d. green . . . 80·00 £100
a. Yellow-green . . . £170 £130
b. Wmk upright . . . 90·00 £120

6 (Die I)

(**7**)

(Typo D.L.R.)

1879–80. Wmk Crown CC. P 14.
24 **6** 1d. emerald-green (1880) . . . 70·00 85·00
25 2½d. red-brown . . . 95·00 £120

1883 (June)–**84**. Wmk Crown CA. P 14.
26 **6** ½d. yellow-buff . . . 85·00 85·00
27 ½d. dull green (*shades*) (11.83) . . . 4·75 9·00
b. Top left triangle detached . . . £180 £250
29 1d. pale rose (15.9.83) . . . 25·00 29·00
a. Deep rose (1884) . . . 55·00 60·00
31 2½d. ultramarine (9.84) . . . 2·75 14·00
b. Top left triangle detached . . . £160
w. Wmk inverted

For illustration of "top left triangle detached" variety see above No. 21 of Antigua.

(Litho D.L.R.)

1887–89. Wmk Crown CA. P 14.
32 **1** 1d. red (5.89) . . . 2·25 7·00
x. Wmk reversed . . . £110
33 1d. rose-red . . . 2·25 7·00
34 1d. rose . . . 5·00 14·00
35 **3** 4d. chestnut . . . 35·00 65·00
x. Wmk reversed . . . £160
36 4d. pale chestnut . . . 35·00 65·00
37 4d. brown-red . . . 45·00 70·00
38 **2** 6d. dull violet . . . 15·00 48·00
39 6d. deep violet . . . 14·00 42·00
40 **4** 1s. sepia (2.89) . . . 80·00 £100
41 1s. brown *to* deep brown . . . 45·00 70·00
34s/40s Optd "Specimen" *Set of* 4 . . . £300

The De La Rue transfers of T **1** to **4** are new transfers and differ from those of Messrs. Nissen and Parker, particularly T **4**.

1888 (July). *Nos. 18/19. Surch with T* **7**, *in violet, in Antigua.*
42 **4** 4d.on 1s. black & rose-car (*toned paper*) . . . £130 £160
a. Surch double . . . £6500
b. Surch inverted (in pair with normal) . . . £40000
c. Long-tailed "S" . . . £450 £550
42*d* 4d.on 1s. black & rose-car (*white paper*) . . . £170 £225
dc. Long-tailed "S" . . . £550 £700

The special issues for Virgin Islands were superseded on 31 October 1890, by the general issue for Leeward Islands. In 1899, however, a new special issue, Nos. 43/50, appeared; it did not supersede the general issue for Leeward Islands, but was used concurrently, as were all subsequent issues, until 1 July 1956 when the general Leeward Islands stamps were withdrawn.

8

9

10

(Recess D.L.R.)

1899 (Jan). Wmk Crown CA. P 14.
43 **8** ½d. yellow-green . . . 1·75 55
a. Error. "HALFPFNNY" (R. 10/1) . . . 80·00 £120
b. Error. "HAL PENNY" (R. 8/2) . . . 80·00 £120
c. Imperf between (horiz pair) . . . £7500
44 1d. brick-red . . . 2·75 2·50
45 2½d. ultramarine . . . 12·00 2·75
46 4d. brown . . . 4·00 18·00
a. Error "FOURPENCF" (R.10/3) . . . £750 £1100
47 6d. dull violet . . . 4·50 3·00
48 7d. deep green . . . 8·00 6·00
49 1s. brown-yellow . . . 22·00 35·00
50 5s. indigo . . . 70·00 85·00
43/50 *Set of* 8 . . . £110 £140
43s/50s Optd "Specimen" *Set of* 8 . . . £160

Nos. 43a/b and 46a were corrected after the first printing.

(Typo D.L.R.)

1904 (1 June). Wmk Mult Crown CA. P 14.
54 **9** ½d. dull purple and green . . . 75 40
55 1d. dull purple and scarlet . . . 2·50 35
56 **10** 2d. dull purple and ochre . . . 6·00 3·50
57 **9** 2½d. dull purple and ultramarine . . . 2·00 2·00
58 **10** 3d. dull purple and black . . . 3·50 2·50
59 **9** 6d. dull purple and brown . . . 2·75 2·50
60 **10** 1s. green and scarlet . . . 4·00 5·00
61 2s.6d. green and black . . . 23·00 55·00
62 **9** 5s. green and blue . . . 48·00 65·00
54/62 *Set of* 9 . . . 80·00 £120
54s/62s Optd "Specimen" *Set of* 9 . . . £140

11

12

(Typo D.L.R.)

1913 (Feb)–**19**. *Die I. Chalk-surfaced paper (3d. to 5s.).* Wmk Mult Crown CA. P 14.
69 **11** ½d. green . . . 1·50 4·00
a. Yellow-green (8.16) . . . 2·75 12·00
b. Blue-green and deep green (3.19) . . . 1·25 6·00
70 1d. deep red . . . 8·50 11·00
a. Deep red and carmine (10.17) . . . 2·25 14·00
b. Scarlet (10.17) . . . 2·25 14·00
c. Carmine-red (3.19) . . . 48·00 27·00
71 **12** 2d. grey . . . 4·00 23·00
a. Slate-grey (1919) . . . 4·25 27·00
72 **11** 2½d. bright blue . . . 5·50 9·00
73 **12** 3d. purple/*yellow* . . . 2·75 6·50
74 **11** 6d. dull and bright purple . . . 5·00 11·00
75 **12** 1s. black/*blue-green* . . . 3·25 9·00
76 2s.6d. black and red/*blue* . . . 48·00 50·00
77 **11** 5s. green and red/*yellow* . . . 35·00 £110
69/77 *Set of* 9 . . . 95·00 £200
69s/77s Optd "Specimen" *Set of* 9 . . . £180

Stock of the original printing of the ½d., No. 69 was exhausted by January 1916 and Leeward Islands ½d. stamps were used until the yellow-green printing, No. 69*a*, arrived in August 1916.

14

WAR STAMP
(**13**)

1916 (20 Oct)–**19**. *Optd with T* **13**.
78 **11** 1d. carmine . . . 1·75 18·00
a. Watermark sideways . . . £1100
b. Pale red/bluish . . . 50 7·00
bw. Wmk inverted . . . 55·00
by. Wmk inverted and reversed
c. Scarlet (11.3.19) . . . 30 3·75
d. Short opt (right pane R.10/1) . . . 21·00
79 **12** 3d. purple/*yellow* . . . 2·25 15·00
a. Purple/lemon (12.3.17) . . . 3·00 12·00
b. Purple/buff-yellow (11.3.19) . . . 3·00 19·00
bw. Wmk inverted . . . 10·00 45·00
by. Wmk inverted and reversed
c. Short opt (right pane R. 10/1) . . . 38·00
78s/9s Optd "Specimen" *Set of* 2 . . . 70·00

Nos. 78d and 79c show the overprint 2 mm high instead of 2½ mm.

1921 (18 Nov). *As 1913–19, but Die II and* wmk Mult Script CA.
80 **11** ½d. green . . . 3·75 28·00
w. Wmk inverted
81 1d. scarlet and deep carmine . . . 2·75 23·00
80s/1s Optd "Specimen" *Set of* 2 . . . 70·00

(Typo D.L.R.)

1922 (Mar)–**28**. P 14.

(a) Wmk Mult Crown CA. *Chalk surfaced paper.*
82 **14** 3d. purple/*pale yellow* (15.6.22) . . . 65 17·0(
83 1s. black/*emerald* (15.6.22) . . . 75 14·0(
84 2s.6d. black and red/*blue* (15.6.22) . . . 5·50 11·0(
85 5s. green and red/*pale yellow* (15.6.22) . . . 30·00 £10
82/5 *Set of* 4 . . . 32·00 £13
82s/5s Optd "Specimen" *Set of* 4 . . . 90·00

(b) Wmk Mult Script CA. *Chalk-surfaced paper (5d. to 5s.).*
86 **14** ½d. dull green . . . 85 2·7
87 1d. rose-carmine . . . 60 6
88 1d. bright violet (1.27) . . . 1·00 3·5
89 1d. scarlet (12.28) . . . 14·00 14·0
90 1½d. carmine-red (1.27) . . . 1·50 2·5
91 1½d. Venetian red (11.28) . . . 1·75 1·5
92 2d. grey . . . 1·00 6·0
93 2½d. pale bright blue . . . 1·50 17·0
94 2½d. dull orange (1.9.23) . . . 1·25 1·5
95 2½d. bright blue (1.27) . . . 3·50 3·5
96 3d. purple/*pale yellow* (2.28) . . . 2·25 11·0
97 5d. dull purple and olive (6.22) . . . 5·50 45·0
98 6d. dull and bright purple (6.22) . . . 1·50 6·5
99 1s. black/*emerald* (2.28) . . . 2·50 14·0
100 2s.6d. black and red/*blue* (2.28) . . . 19·00 48·0
101 5s. green and red/*yellow* (1.9.23) . . . 19·00 70·0
86/101 *Set of* 16 . . . 65·00 £22
86s/101s Optd or Perf (Nos. 89, 91) "Specimen" *Set of* 16 . . . £275

In the 1½d. stamps the value is in colour on a white ground.

1935 (6 May). *Silver Jubilee. As Nos. 91/4 of Antigua but printed b Waterlow.* P 11 × 12.
103 1d. deep blue and scarlet . . . 1·25 4·0
k. Kite and vertical log . . . 75·00
l. Kite and horizontal log . . . 80·00
104 1½d. ultramarine and grey . . . 1·25 3·7
k. Kite and vertical log . . . 80·00
l. Kite and horizontal log . . . 90·00
m. "Bird" by turret . . . £130 £1
105 2½d. brown and deep blue . . . 1·50 3·7
k. Kite and vertical log . . . 90·00
l. Kite and horizontal log . . . £100
106 1s. slate and purple . . . 8·00 18·0
k. Kite and vertical log . . . £180
l. Kite and horizontal log . . . £170
103/6 *Set of* 4 . . . 11·00 27·(
103s/6s Perf "Specimen" *Set of* 4 . . . 95·00

For illustrations of plate varieties see Omnibus section followir Zanzibar.

1937 (12 May). *Coronation. As Nos. 95/7 of Antigua.* P 11 × 11½.
107 1d. carmine . . . 20 1·
108 1½d. yellow-brown . . . 50 2·
109 2½d. blue . . . 45 1·
107/9 *Set of* 3 . . . 1·10 5·
107s/9s Perf "Specimen" *Set of* 3 . . . 65·00

15 King George VI and Badge of Colony

16 Map

(Photo Harrison)

1938 (1 Aug)–**47**. *Chalk-surfaced paper.* Wmk Mult Script CA. P
110 **15** ½d. green . . . 2·50 2·
a. Ordinary paper (10.43) . . . 30 1·
111 1d. scarlet . . . 3·25 1·
a. Ordinary paper (10.43) . . . 30
112 1½d. red-brown . . . 5·50 5·
a. Ordinary paper (10.43) . . . 1·00 1·
w. Wmk inverted . . . † £10
113 2d. grey . . . 4·75 2·
a. Ordinary paper (10.43) . . . 1·25
114 2½d. ultramarine . . . 4·00 1·
a. Ordinary paper (10.43) . . . 70 2·
115 3d. orange . . . 5·50
a. Ordinary paper (10.43) . . . 70
116 6d. mauve . . . 4·25 1·
a. Ordinary paper (10.43) . . . 2·00
117 1s. olive-brown . . . 11·00 3·
a. Ordinary paper (8.42) . . . 1·50
118 2s.6d. sepia . . . 35·00 6
a. Ordinary paper (8.42) . . . 15·00 3
119 5s. carmine . . . 50·00 6·
a. Ordinary paper (8.42) . . . 13·00 4
120 10s. blue (1.12.47) . . . 6·00 8
121 £1 black (1.12.47) . . . 8·00 20
110a/21 *Set of* 12 . . . 45·00 38
110s/21s Perf "Specimen" *Set of* 12 . . . £225

The ordinary paper, used as a substitute for the chalk-surfa for printings between 1942 and 1945, is thick, smooth and opaq

1946 (1 Nov). *Victory. As Nos. 110/11 of Antigua.*
122 ½d. lake-brown . . . 10
123 3d. orange . . . 10
122s/3s Perf "Specimen" *Set of* 2 . . . 65·00

1949 (3 Jan). *Royal Silver Wedding. As Nos. 112/13 of Antigua.*

124	2½d. ultramarine	10	10
125	£1 black	13·00	16·00

1949 (10 Oct). *75th Anniv of U.P.U. As Nos. 114/17 of Antigua.*

126	2½d. ultramarine	30	55
127	3d. orange	1·25	2·50
128	6d. magenta	35	40
129	1s. olive	35	50
126/9	*Set of* 4	2·00	3·50

(New Currency. 100 cents = 1 B.W.I. dollar)

1951 (16 Feb–10 Apr). *Inauguration of B.W.I. University College. As Nos. 118/19 of Antigua.*

130	3c. black and brown-red (10 Apr)	40	1·75
131	12c. black and reddish violet	60	1·75

Issue of the 3c. value was delayed when the supplies were sent to Puerto Rico by mistake.

(Recess Waterlow)

1951 (2 Apr). *Restoration of Legislative Council.* Wmk Mult Script CA. P 14½ × 14.

132	**16**	6c. orange	40	1·50
133		12c. purple	40	50
134		24c. olive	40	50
135		$1.20 carmine	1·00	1·00
132/5		*Set of* 4	2·00	3·25

17 Sombrero Lighthouse

18 Map of Jost Van Dyke

(Recess D.L.R.)

1952 (15 Apr). *T* **17/18** *and similar designs.* Wmk Mult Script CA. P 12½ × 13 (vert) or 13 × 12½ (horiz).

36	1c. black	80	1·75
37	2c. deep green	70	30
38	3c. black and brown	80	1·25
39	4c. carmine-red	70	1·50
40	5c. claret and black	1·50	50
41	8c. bright blue	70	1·25
42	12c. dull violet	80	1·40
43	24c. deep brown	70	50
44	60c. yellow-green and blue	4·00	11·00
45	$1.20 black and bright blue	4·75	12·00
46	$2.40 yellowish green and red-brown	11·00	16·00
47	$4.80 bright blue and carmine	12·00	16·00
36/47	*Set of* 12	32·00	55·00

Designs: *Horiz*—3c. Sheep industry; 4c. Map of Anegada; 5c. Cattle industry; 8c. Map of Virgin Gorda; 12c. Map of Tortola; 60c. Dead Man's Chest; $1.20, Sir Francis Drake Channel; $2.40, Road Town; $4.80, Map of Virgin Islands. *Vert*—24c. Badge of the Presidency.

Western Australia *see* Australia

Western Samoa *see after* New Zealand

Zanzibar

An Indian post office opened in Zanzibar in November 1868, but was closed for political reasons on 1 April of the following year. Little has survived from this period. Subsequently mail was forwarded via Seychelles or, later, Aden.

Stamps of INDIA were used in Zanzibar from 1 October 1875 until 10 November 1895, when the administration of the postal service was transferred from India to British East Africa. Seperate cancellations for Zanzibar are known from 1 June 1878.

Z 1

Stamps of INDIA *cancelled with Type* Z **1** (1878–79)

1865. *(Nos. 54/65).*

Z1	1a. deep brown	£160
Z2	2a. orange	£160

1866–78. *(Nos. 69/72).*

Z3	4a. blue-green (Die II)	£140

1873. *(Nos. 75/6).*

Z4	½a. blue (Die II)	£140

Surviving covers show that Type Z **1** was normally used as a datestamp, struck clear of the stamps which were obliterated by a rhomboid of bars, but examples of the c.d.s. used as a cancel are known.

Z 2

Stamps of INDIA *cancelled with Type* Z **2** (1879–82).

1865. *(Nos. 54/65).*

Z10	8p. mauve	£160
Z11	1a. deep brown	18·00
Z12	2a. orange	18·00

1866–78. *(Nos. 69/72).*

Z13	4a. green (Die I)	£100
Z14	4a. blue-green (Die II)	27·00

1868. *(Nos. 73/4).*

Z15	8a. rose (Die II)	70·00

1873. *(Nos. 75/6).*

Z16	½a. blue (Die II)	18·00

1874. *(Nos. 77/9).*

Z17	1r. slate	£170

1876. *(Nos. 80/2).*

Z18	6a. pale brown	70·00
Z19	12a. Venetian red	£110

1882. *(No. 90).*

Z19*a*	1a.6p. sepia	£110

OFFICIAL STAMPS

1874–82. *(Nos. O31/7).*

Z19*b*	1a. brown	£170
Z20	2a. orange	£160
Z21	4a. green (Die I)	£180
Z22	8a. rose (Die II)	£180

Z 3

Stamps of INDIA *cancelled with Type* Z **3** (1882–84)

1865. *(Nos. 54/65).*

Z25	1a. deep brown	38·00
Z26	2a. brown-orange	30·00

1866–78. *(Nos. 69/72).*

Z27	4a. blue-green (Die II)	38·00

1868. *(Nos. 73/4).*

Z28	8a. rose (Die II)	48·00

1873. *(Nos. 75/6).*

Z29	½a. blue (Die II)	28·00

1874. *(Nos. 77/9).*

Z29*a*	1r. slate	£110

1876. *(Nos. 80/2).*

Z30	6a. pale brown	45·00
Z31	12a. Venetian red	90·00

1882–83. *(Nos. 84/101).*

Z32	1a. brown-purple	30·00
Z33	1a.6p. sepia	35·00
Z34	3a. orange	38·00

Z 4 Z 5

Stamps of INDIA *cancelled with Type* Z **4** (June 1884–May 1887) (*between* January *and* September 1885 *the postmark was used without year numerals*).

1865. *(Nos. 54/65).*

Z39	1a. deep brown	70·00
Z40	2a. brown-orange	35·00

1866–78. *(Nos. 69/72).*

Z41	4a. blue-green (Die I)	£110
Z41*a*	4a. blue-green (Die II)	32·00

1868. *(Nos. 73/4).*

Z42	8a. rose (Die II)	35·00

1873. *(Nos. 75/6).*

Z43	½a. blue (Die II)	30·00

1874. *(Nos. 77/9).*

Z44	1r. slate	£120

1876. *(Nos. 80/2).*

Z45	6a. pale brown	60·00
Z45*a*	12a. Venetian red	£110

1882–86. *(Nos.84/101).*

Z46	½a. blue-green	15·00
Z47	1a. brown-purple	26·00
Z48	1a.6p. sepia	21·00
Z49	2a. blue	42·00
Z50	3a. orange	15·00
Z51	4a. olive-green	45·00
Z52	4a.6p. yellow-green	20·00
Z53	8a. dull mauve	42·00
Z54	1r. slate	42·00

OFFICIAL STAMPS

1867–73. *(Nos. O20/30a).*

Z55	2a. orange	£160

1874–82. *(Nos.O31/7).*

Z55*a*	½a. blue	£110
Z56	1a. brown	90·00

1883–95. *(Nos. O37a/48).*

Z57	1a. brown-purple	95·00

Stamps of INDIA *cancelled with Type* Z **5** (1887–94).

1876. *(Nos. 80/2).*

Z60	6a. pale brown	18·00
Z61	12a. Venetian red	48·00

1882–90. *(Nos. 84/101).*

Z62	½a. blue-green	6·50
Z63	9p. aniline carmine	42·00
Z64	1a. brown-purple	6·00
Z65	1a.6p. sepia	8·50
Z66	2a. blue	7·00
Z67	3a. orange	9·00
Z68	3a. brown-orange	7·50
Z69	4a. olive-green	38·00
Z70	4a.6p. yellow-green	12·00
Z71	8a. dull mauve	20·00
Z72	12a. purple/*red*	42·00
Z73	1r. slate	16·00

1891. *(No. 102).*

Z74	2½a. on 4a.6p. yellow-green	8·00

1892–95. *(Nos. 103/6).*

Z75	2a.6p. yellow-green	6·00

OFFICIAL STAMPS

1874–82. *(Nos. O31/71.*

Z76	½a. blue	85·00
Z77	1a. brown	85·00
Z78	2a. yellow	£150

Z 6

Z 7

Stamps of INDIA *cancelled with Type* Z **6** (1888–95).

1876. *(Nos. 80/2)*.

Z80	6a. pale brown	19·00
Z80*a*	12a. venetian red	£110

1882–90. *(Nos. 84/101)*.

Z81	½a. blue-green	30·00
Z82	9p. aniline carmine	48·00
Z83	1a. brown-purple	9·00
Z84	1a.6p. sepia	8·50
Z85	2a. blue	9·50
Z86	3a. orange	20·00
Z87	3a. brown-orange	16·00
Z88	4a. olive-green	16·00
Z89	4a.6p. yellow-green	15·00
Z90	8a. dull mauve	21·00
Z91	12a. purple/*red*	45·00
Z92	1r. slate	18·00

1891. *(No. 102)*.

Z93	2½a. on 4a.6p. yellow-green	22·00

1892–95. *(Nos. 103/6)*.

Z94	2a.6p. yellow-green	19·00

Stamps of INDIA *cancelled with Type* Z 7 (1894–95).

1876. *(Nos. 80/2)*.

Z95	6a. pale brown	55·00

1882–90. *(Nos. 84/101)*.

Z100	½a. blue-green	20·00
Z101	9p. aniline carmine	60·00
Z102	1a. brown-purple	28·00
Z103	1a.6p. sepia	42·00
Z104	2a. blue	20·00
Z105	3a. brown-orange	40·00
Z106	4a. olive-green	40·00
Z107	8a. dull mauve	55·00
Z108	12a. purple/*red*	60·00
Z109	1r. slate	50·00

1892–95. *(Nos.103/6)*.

Z110	2a.6p. yellow-green	12·00

1895. *(Nos. 107/9)*.

Z111	2r. carmine and yellow-brown	£250

A French post office was opened on the island in January 1889 and this service used the stamps of FRANCE until 1894 when specific stamps for this office were provided. The French postal service on the island closed on 31 July 1904 and it is known that French stamps were again utilised during the final month.

A German postal agency operated in Zanzibar between 27 August 1890 and 31 July 1891, using stamps of GERMANY.

PRICES FOR STAMPS ON COVER TO 1945

Nos.	1/2	—
Nos.	3/16	*from* × 30
No.	17	*from* × 8
No.	18	*from* × 25
Nos.	19/21	—
No.	22	*from* × 40
Nos.	23/5	—
No.	26	*from* × 40
Nos.	27/40	—
Nos.	41/6	*from* × 25
Nos.	156/68	*from* × 15
Nos.	169/77	—
Nos.	178/87	*from* × 20
Nos.	188/204	*from* × 15
Nos.	205/9	*from* × 20
Nos.	210/38	*from* × 15
Nos.	239/45	—
Nos.	246/59	*from* × 8
Nos.	260/*f*	—
Nos.	261/330	*from* × 4
Nos.	D1/3	*from* × 8
No.	D4	*from* × 1
No.	D5	*from* × 15
No.	D6	—
No.	D7	*from* × 1
Nos.	D8/12	*from* × 15
No.	D13	*from* × 1
No.	D14	—
Nos.	D15/16	*from* × 6
No.	D17	*from* × 4
Nos.	D18/24	*from* × 15
Nos.	D25/30	*from* × 30

PROTECTORATE

(Currency. 12 pies = 1 anna. 16 annas = 1 rupee)

Zanzibar
(1)

1895 (14 Nov)–**96**. *Nos. 81, 85, 90/6, 98/101, 103 and 106/9 of India (Queen Victoria) optd with T* **1** *by Zanzibar Gazette.*

(a) In blue.

No.	Type	Description	Unused	Used
		½a. blue-green	£13000	£4000
		1a. plum	£2250	£500
		j. "Zanzidar" (R. 4/6, 8/5)	†	£15000

(b) In black.

No.	Type	Description	Unused	Used
3		½a. blue-green	3·75	3·50
		j. "Zanzidar" (R. 4/6, 8/5)	£1200	£650
		k. "Zanibar" (R. 7/2)	£1200	£1600
		l. Diaeresis over last "a" (R. 10/5)	£1300	£1300
		m. Opt double, one albino	£225	
4		1a. plum	4·00	3·50
		j. "Zanzidar" (R. 4/6, 8/5)	—	£2750
		k. "Zanibar" (R. 7/2)	£1500	£1700
		l. Diaeresis over last "a" (R. 10/5)	£2750	
5		1a.6p. sepia	4·50	3·25
		j. "Zanzidar" (R. 4/6, 8/5)	£3250	£950
		k. "Zanibar" (R. 7/2)	£1400	£1500
		l. "Zanizbar" (R. 1/9)		
		m. Diaeresis over last "a" (R. 10/5)	£1200	
6		2a. pale blue	4·75	4·50
7		2a. blue	5·00	4·75
		j. "Zanzidar" (R. 4/6, 8/5)	£3750	£1800
		k. "Zanibar" (R. 7/2)	£3750	£1800
		l. Diaeresis over last "a" (R. 10/5)	£1800	
		m. Opt double	£250	
		n. Opt double, one albino	£250	
8		2½a. yellow-green	7·50	4·75
		j. "Zanzidar" (R. 4/6, 8/5)	£3250	£1600
		k. "Zanibar" (R. 7/2)	£600	£1100
		l. "Zapzibar"		
		n. Diaeresis over last "a" (R.10/5)	£1600	£1300
		o. Second "z" italic (R. 10/1)	£250	£375
		p. Opt double, one albino	£250	
10		3a. brown-orange	11·00	9·50
		j. "Zanzidar" (R. 4/6, 8/5)	£750	£1400
		k. "Zanizbar" (R. 1/9)	£3500	£4000
11		4a. olive-green	18·00	15·00
		j. "Zanzidar" (R. 4/6, 8/5)	£6000	£3750
12		4a. slate-green	11·00	13·00
		l. Diaeresis over last "a" (R. 10/5)	£2750	
13		6a. pale brown	18·00	11·00
		j. "Zanzidar" (R. 4/6, 8/5)	£6000	£3500
		k. "Zanibar" (R. 7/2)	£650	£1200
		l. "Zanzibarr"	£3750	£3500
		m. Opt double		
		n. Opt double, one albino	£140	
		o. Opt triple, two albino	£180	
14		8a. dull mauve	24·00	20·00
		j. "Zanzidar" (R 4/6, 8/5)	£6000	£6000
15		8a. magenta (7.96)	16·00	22·00
16		12a. purple/*red*	16·00	10·00
		j. "Zanzidar" (R.4/6, 8/5)	£5500	£3750
17		1r. slate	75·00	70·00
		j. "Zanzidar" (R 4/6, 8/5)	£5500	£4250
18		1r. green and aniline carmine (7.96)	16·00	24·00
		j. Opt vert downwards	£425	
19		2r. carmine and yellow-brown	55·00	80·00
		j. "r" omitted	£7500	
		k. "r" inverted	£3750	£3750
20		3r. brown and green	48·00	60·00
		j. "r" omitted	£7500	
		k. "r" inverted	£3750	£4000
		l. Opt double, one albino	£800	
21		5r. ultramarine and violet	55·00	75·00
		j. "r" omitted	£7500	
		k. "r" inverted	£3250	£4000
		l. Opt double, one inverted	£850	
		m. Opt double, one albino	£800	
3/21 *Set of* 15			£300	£350

There were a number of different settings for this overprint. Values to 1r. were initially overprinted from settings of 120 (12 × 10) including one which showed "Zanzidar" on R. 4/6 and R. 8/5 (soon corrected) and "Zanizbar" on R. 1/9 (also soon corrected). Later supplies of these values were overprinted from settings of 80 (8 × 10) for the 6a. only or 60 (6 × 10) for the others. One of these settings included "Zanibar" on R. 7/2. Another late setting, size unknown, showed a diaeresis over last "a" on R. 10/5.

Many forgeries of this overprint exist and also bogus errors.

Forged examples of the blue overprints, Nos. 1/2, can be found on piece with genuine cancellations as type Z 7, dated "13 FE 97".

MINOR VARIETIES. The following minor varieties of type exist on Nos. 1/21:

A. First "Z" antique (all values)
B. Broken "p" for "n" (all values to 1r.)
C. Tall second "z" (all values)
D. Small second "z" (all values)
E. Small second "z" and inverted "q" for "b" (all values)
F. Second "z" Gothic (½a. to 12a. and 1r.) (No. 18) (black opts only)
G. No dot over "i" (all values to 1r.)
H. Inverted "q" for "b" (all values to 1r.)
I. Arabic "2" for "r" (all values to 1r.) (black opts only)

Varieties D and E are worth the same as normal examples, A (2, 3, 5r.) and C normal plus 50%, G and I from 3 times normal, A (values to 1r.), F and H from 4 times normal and B from 5 times normal.

2½ (2) 2½ (3) 2½ (4) 2½ (5)

1895–98. *Provisionals. I. Stamps used for postal purposes.*

(a) No. 5 surch in red (30.11.95).

No.	Type	Description	Unused	Used
22	**2**	2½on 1½a. sepia	50·00	40·00
		j. "Zanzidar"	£1300	£1200
		k. "Zanizbar"	£3750	£1900
		l. Inverted "1" in "½"	£1100	£900

(b) No. 4 surch in black (11.5.96).

No.	Type	Description	Unused	Used
23	**3**	2½on 1a. plum	£150	£100
24	**4**	2½on 1a. plum	£400	£275
		j. Inverted "1" in "½"	£2250	
25	**5**	2½on 1a. plum	£160	£110

2½ (6) 2½ (7) 2½ (8)

(c) No. 6 surch in red (15.8.96).

No.	Type	Description	Unused	Used
26	**6**	2½on 2a. pale blue	50·00	30·00
		j. Inverted "1" in "½"	£425	£275
		k. Roman "I" in "½"	£225	£150
		l. "Zanzibar" double, one albino	£140	
27	**7**	2½on 2a. pale blue	£150	90·00
		j. "2" of "½" omitted	£8500	
		k. "22" for "2½"	£11000	
		l. "1" of "½" omitted	£8500	£5000
		m. Inverted "1" in "½"	£2000	£1500
		n. "Zanzibar" double, one albino	£325	
28	**8**	2½on 2a. pale blue	£4500	£1900

No. 28 only exists with small "z" and occurs on R. 2/2 in the setting of 60.

(d) No. 5 surch in red (15.11.96).

No.	Type	Description	Unused	Used
29	**6**	2½on 1½a. sepia	£130	£100
		j. Inverted "1 in "½"	£1100	£950
		k. Roman "I" in "½"	£800	£750
		l. Surch double, one albino	£250	
30	**7**	2½on 1½a. sepia	£375	£325
		l. Surch double, one albino	£700	
31	**8**	2½on 1½a. sepia	£12000	£8000

No. 31 only exists with small "z" and occurs on R. 2/2 in the setting of 60.

II. Stamps prepared for official purposes. Nos. 4, 5 and 7 surch as before in red (1.98).

No.	Type	Description	Unused	Used
32	**3**	2½on 1a. plum	£225	£600
33	**4**	2½on 1a. plum	£425	£900
34	**5**	2½on 1a. plum	£250	£600
35	**3**	2½on 1½a. sepia	75·00	£180
		j. Diaeresis over last "a"	£4500	
36	**4**	2½on 1½a. sepia	£180	£425
37	**5**	2½on 1½a. sepia	£110	£250
38	**3**	2½on 2a. dull blue	95·00	£250
39	**4**	2½on 2a. dull blue	£190	£450
40	**5**	2½on 2a. dull blue	£110	£300

It is doubtful whether Nos. 32/40 were issued to the public.

1896. *Nos. 65/6, 68 and 71/3 of British East Africa (Queen Victoria), optd with T* **1**.

No.	Description	Unused	Used
41	½a. yellow-green (23 May)	30·00	17·00
42	1a. carmine-rose (1 June)	26·00	16·00
	j. Opt double	£750	£850
	k. Opt double, one albino	£300	
43	2½a. deep blue (R.) (24 May)	75·00	45·00
44	4½a. orange-yellow (12 Aug)	45·00	50·00
45	5a. yellow-bistre (12 Aug)	50·00	32·00
	j. "r" omitted	—	£2500
46	7½a. mauve (12 Aug)	38·00	50·00
41/6 *Set of* 6		£225	£190

MINOR VARIETIES. The various minor varieties of type detailed in the note below No. 21 also occur on Nos. 22 to 46 as indicated below:

A. Nos. 23, 25, 27, 30, 35, 38, 41/6
B. Nos. 22/3, 26, 29/30, 32/3, 36, 39, 44/6
C. Nos. 22, 25/6, 32, 36, 38, 40/6
D. Nos. 22/46
E. Nos. 22/46
F. Nos. 22, 25/6, 29, 41/6
G. Nos. 25/6, 29, 35, 37/8, 40/6
H. Nos. 22, 41/6 (on the British East Africa stamps this variety occurs in the same position as variety C)
I. Nos. 26, 29, 35, 38, 41/6

The scarcity of these varieties on the surcharges (Nos. 22/40) is similar to those on the basic stamps, but examples on the British East Africa values (Nos. 41/6) are more common.

PRINTERS. All Zanzibar stamps up to Type **37** were printed by De La Rue & Co.

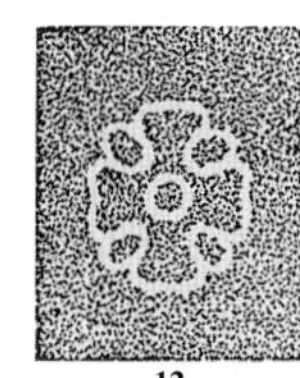
12

13

14 Sultan Seyyid Hamed-bin-Thwain

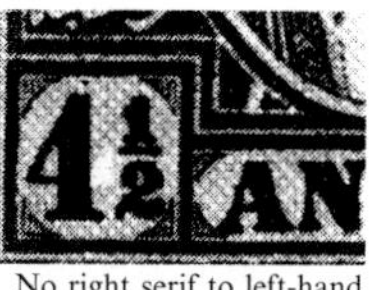
No right serif to left-hand "4" (R. 1/1)

1896 (Dec). *Recess. Flags in red on all values.* W **12**. P 14.

No.	Type	Description	Unused	Used
156	**13**	½a. yellow-green	3·75	1·75
157		1a. indigo	2·50	1·50
158		1a. violet-blue	4·50	4·25
159		2a. red-brown	2·75	75
160		2½a. bright blue	10·00	1·50
161		2½a. pale blue	11·00	1·50
162		3a. grey	9·00	5·00
163		3a. bluish grey	11·00	7·00
164		4a. myrtle-green	6·00	2·75
165		4½a. orange	4·50	4·75
		a. No right serif to left-hand "4"	£100	£110
		b. No fraction bar at right (R. 2/1)	£100	£110
166		5a. bistre	3·75	2·50
		a. Bisected (2½a.) (on cover)	†	£3250
167		7½a. mauve	3·50	2·75
168		8a. grey-olive	9·50	7·00
169	**14**	1r. blue	13·00	9·00
170		1r. deep blue	18·00	13·00
171		2r. green	23·00	9·50
172		3r. dull purple	23·00	9·50
173		4r. lake	18·00	13·00
174		5r. sepia	24·00	13·00
156/74 *Set of* 15			£140	75·00
156s/74s Optd "Specimen" *Set of* 15			£200	

The ½, 1, 2, 2½, 3 and 8a. are known without wmk, these being from edges of the sheets.

ZANZIBAR

1897 (5 Jan). *No. 164 surch as before, in red.*

175	**3**	2½ on 4a. myrtle-green	60·00	40·00
176	**4**	2½ on 4a. myrtle-green	£190	£170
177	**5**	2½ on 4a. myrtle-green	75·00	50·00
175/7 *Set of* 3			£300	£225

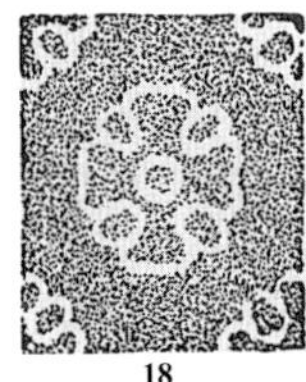
18

1898 (May). *Recess.* W **18**. P 14.

178	**13**	½a. yellow-green	1·50	35
179		1a. indigo	2·00	55
		a. Greenish black	4·25	1·50
180		2a. red-brown	4·00	1·00
		a. Deep brown	5·00	1·75
181		2½a. bright blue	2·50	30
182		3a. grey	5·50	60
183		4a. myrtle-green	3·25	1·00
184		4½a. orange	7·00	80
		a. No right serif to left-hand "4"	£150	55·00
		b. No fraction bar at right (R. 2/1)	£150	55·00
185		5a. bistre	14·00	1·75
		a. Pale bistre	14·00	2·00
186		7½a. mauve	8·50	2·75
187		8a. grey-olive	11·00	2·25
178/87 *Set of* 10			55·00	10·00

19

20 Sultan Seyyid Hamoud-bin-Mohammed bin Said

1899 (June)–**1901**. *Recess. Flags in red.* W **18** (Nos. 188/99) or W **12** (others). P 14.

188	**19**	½a. yellow-green	2·00	60
		a. Wmk sideways	11·00	4·50
189		1a. indigo	4·50	20
		a. Wmk sideways	25·00	1·25
190		1a. carmine (1901)	2·00	20
191		2a. red-brown	2·25	50
192		2½a. bright blue	2·25	60
193		3a. grey	2·75	2·25
194		4a. myrtle-green	3·25	1·50
195		4½a. orange	11·00	3·50
196		4½a. blue-black (1901)	14·00	12·00
197		5a. bistre	3·00	1·25
198		7½a. mauve	3·25	3·75
199		8a. grey-olive	3·25	4·50
200	**20**	1r. blue	18·00	15·00
201		2r. green	18·00	18·00
202		3r. dull purple	30·00	35·00
203		4r. lake	48·00	55·00
204		5r. sepia	55·00	65·00
188/204 *Set of* 17			£200	£200
188s/204s Optd "Specimen" *Set of* 17			£200	

One	Two & Half	Two & Half	Two & Half
(21)	(22)	(22a) Thin open "w" (R. 2/2, 3/4)	(22b) Serif to foot of "f" (R. 3/1)

1904. *Nos. 194/6 and 198/9 surch as T* **21** *and* **22**, *in black or lake (L.) by Zanzibar Gazette in setting of 30 (6 × 5).*

205	**19**	1 on 4½a. orange	4·00	4·75
206		1 on 4½a. blue/black (L.)	4·50	18·00
207		2 on 4a. myrtle-green (L.)	14·00	18·00
208		2½ on 7½a. mauve	13·00	20·00
		a. Opt Type **22a**	80·00	£100
		b. Opt Type **22b**	£130	£170
		c. "Hlaf" for "Half"	£11000	
209		2½ on 8a. grey-olive	16·00	30·00
		a. Opt Type **22a**	£110	£160
		b. Opt Type **22b**	£170	£275
		c. "Hlaf" for "Half"	£10000	£8000
205/9 *Set of* 5			48·00	80·00

23

24

Monogram of Sultan Seyyid Ali bin Hamoud bin Naherud

1904 (8 June). *Typo. Background of centre in second colour.* W **18**. P 14.

210	**23**	½a. green	1·50	90
211		1a. rose-red	1·50	10
212		2a. brown	1·50	45
213		2½a. blue	2·50	35
214		3a. grey	2·50	2·25
215		4a. deep green	2·25	1·60
216		4½a. black	3·00	2·50
217		5a. yellow-brown	3·50	1·25
218		7½a. purple	4·25	7·00
219		8a. olive-green	3·75	2·75
220	**24**	1r. blue and red	21·00	12·00
		a. Wmk sideways	80·00	35·00
221		2r. green and red	23·00	38·00
		a. Wmk sideways	£150	£190
222		3r. violet and red	40·00	75·00
223		4r. claret and red	48·00	90·00
224		5r. olive-brown and red	48·00	95·00
210/24 *Set of* 15			£180	£275
210s/24s Optd "Specimen" *Set of* 15			£140	

25

26

27 Sultan Ali bin Hamoud

28 View of Port

1908 (May)–**09**. *Recess.* W **18** (sideways on 10r. to 30r.). P 14.

225	**25**	1c. pearl-grey (10.09)	2·25	30
226		3c. yellow-green	5·00	10
		a. Wmk sideways	5·00	1·25
227		6c. rose-carmine	9·00	10
		a. Wmk sideways	9·00	2·25
228		10c. brown (10.09)	2·50	2·00
229		12c. violet	14·00	3·00
		a. Wmk sideways	12·00	1·25
230	**26**	15c. ultramarine	11·00	40
		a. Wmk sideways	10·00	6·00
231		25c. sepia	3·25	1·00
232		50c. blue-green	5·50	4·25
233		75c. grey-black (10.09)	10·00	12·00
234	**27**	1r. yellow-green	24·00	12·00
		a. Wmk sideways	55·00	9·00
235		2r. violet	18·00	14·00
		a. Wmk sideways	£140	65·00
236		3r. orange-bistre	25·00	48·00
237		4r. vermilion	45·00	75·00
238		5r. steel-blue	40·00	55·00
239	**28**	10r. blue-green and brown	£130	£250
		s. Optd "Specimen"	35·00	
240		20r. black and yellow-green	£275	£450
		s. Optd "Specimen"	45·00	
241		30r. black and sepia	£325	£600
		s. Optd "Specimen"	55·00	
242		40r. black and orange-brown	£450	
		s. Optd "Specimen"	75·00	
243		50r. black and mauve	£400	
		s. Optd "Specimen"	75·00	
244		100r. black and steel-blue	£650	
		s. Optd "Specimen"	£130	
245		200r. brown and greenish black	£1000	
		s. Optd "Specimen"	£170	
225/38 *Set of* 14			£190	£200
225s/38s Optd "Specimen" *Set of* 14			£180	

29 Sultan Kalif bin Harub

30 Sailing Canoe

31 Dhow

1913. *Recess.* W **18** (sideways on 75c. and 10r. to 200r.). P 14.

246	**29**	1c. grey	40	20
247		3c. yellow-green	50	20
248		6c. rose-carmine	1·50	20
249		10c. brown	1·10	1·90
250		12c. violet	1·00	20
251		15c. blue	1·25	30
252		25c. sepia	1·00	1·00
253		50c. blue-green	2·00	4·00
254		75c. grey-black	2·00	2·75
		a. Wmk upright	£150	
		as. Optd "Specimen"	95·00	
255	**30**	1r. yellow-green	7·00	9·00
256		2r. violet	11·00	25·00
257		3r. orange-bistre	13·00	40·00
258		4r. scarlet	26·00	65·00
259		5r. steel-blue	35·00	35·00
260	**31**	10r. green and brown	£110	£190
260*b*		20r. black and green	£160	£350
		bs. Optd "Specimen"	35·00	
260*c*		30r. black and brown	£170	£425
		cs. Optd "Specimen"	45·00	
260*d*		40r. black and vermilion	£350	£600
		ds. Optd "Specimen"	70·00	
260*e*		50r. black and purple	£325	£600
		es. Optd "Specimen"	70·00	
260*f*		100r. black and blue	£400	
		fs. Optd "Specimen"	95·00	
260*g*		200r. brown and black	£650	
		gs. Optd "Specimen"	£130	
246/60 *Set of* 15			£180	£325
246s/60as Optd "Specimen" *Set of* 15			£190	

1914–22. Wmk Mult Crown CA (sideways on 10r.). P 14.

261	**29**	1c. grey	80	25
262		3c. yellow-green	1·25	10
		a. Dull green	4·75	15
		w. Wmk inverted	†	£110
263		6c. deep carmine	85	10
		a. Bright rose-carmine	85	10
		aw. Wmk inverted	†	£110
264		8c. purple/*pale yellow* (1922)	75	3·50
265		10c. myrtle/*pale yellow* (1922)	75	30
266		15c. deep ultramarine	1·10	5·00
268		50c. blue-green	4·50	4·00
269		75c. grey-black	3·00	23·00
270	**30**	1r. yellow-green	4·00	3·50
271		2r. violet	5·00	8·00
272		3r. orange-bistre	16·00	32·00
273		4r. scarlet	16·00	85·00
		y. Wmk inverted and reversed	£110	
274		5r. steel-blue	16·00	65·00
		w. Wmk inverted	£110	
275	**31**	10r. green and brown	£110	£400
261/75 *Set of* 14			£160	£550
261s/75s Optd "Specimen" *Set of* 14			£200	

1921–29. Wmk Mult Script CA (sideways on 10r. to 30r.). P 14.

276	**29**	1c. slate-grey	20	7·0
277		3c. yellow-green	50	3·2
278		3c. yellow (1922)	30	1
		w. Wmk inverted		
279		4c. green (1922)	50	6
280		6c. carmine-red	30	5
281		6c. purple/*blue* (1922)	35	1
		w. Wmk inverted	†	£18
282		10c. brown	70	8·5
283		12c. violet	40	3
		w. Wmk inverted		
284		12c. carmine-red (1922)	40	4
285		15c. blue	55	8·5
286		20c. indigo (1922)	1·00	3
287		25c. sepia	75	10·0
288		50c. myrtle-green	1·25	3·7
		y. Wmk inverted and reversed	£110	
289		75c. slate	2·50	50·0
290	**30**	1r. yellow-green	4·25	3·5
291		2r. deep violet	3·25	8·5
292		3r. orange-bistre	4·25	7·5
293		4r. scarlet	12·00	35·0
294		5r. Prussian blue	19·00	65·0
		w. Wmk inverted	£160	
295	**31**	10r. green and brown	95·00	£25
296		20r. black and green	£190	£40
		s. Optd "Specimen"	80·00	
297		30r. black and brown (1929)	£180	£50
		s. Perf "Specimen"	85·00	
276/95 *Set of* 20			£130	£40
276s/95s Optd "Specimen" *Set of* 20			£250	

32 Sultan Kalif bin Harub **33**

1926–27. *T* **32** *("CENTS" in serifed capitals). Recess.* Wmk Mu Script CA. P 14.

299	**32**	1c. brown	50	
300		3c. yellow-orange	20	
301		4c. deep dull green	20	
302		6c. violet	20	
303		8c. slate	1·00	4·
304		10c. olive-green	1·00	4
305		12c. carmine-red	1·50	
306		20c. bright blue	50	
307		25c. purple/*yellow* (1927)	4·25	2·
308		50c. claret	1·75	
309		75c. sepia (1927)	17·00	22·
299/309 *Set of* 11			25·00	27·
299s/309s Optd "Specimen" *Set of* 11			£120	

(New Currency. 100 cents = 1 shilling)

1936 (1 Jan). *T* **33** *("CENTS" in sans-serif capitals), and T* **30** *but values in shillings. Recess.* Wmk Mult Script C P 14 × 13½–14.

310	**33**	5c. green	10	
311		10c. black	10	
312		15c. carmine-red	10	1·
313		20c. orange	10	
314		25c. purple/*yellow*	10	
315		30c. ultramarine	10	
316		40c. sepia	15	
317		50c. claret	30	
318	**30**	1s. yellow-green	50	
319		2s. slate-violet	75	1·
320		5s. scarlet	11·00	6·
321		7s.50 light blue	23·00	25·
322	**31**	10s. green and brown	24·00	22·
310/22 *Set of* 13			55·00	50·
310s/22s Perf "Specimen" *Set of* 13			£130	

36 Sultan Kalif bin Harub

1936 (9 Dec). *Silver Jubilee of Sultan. Recess.* Wmk Mult Script CA. P 14.

323	**36**	10c. black and olive-green	2·25	30
324		20c. black and bright purple	4·50	1·00
325		30c. black and deep ultramarine	9·00	35
326		50c. black and orange-vermilion	9·50	4·00
323/6 *Set of* 4			23·00	5·00
323s/6s Perf "Specimen" *Set of* 4			75·00	

37 *Sham Alam* (Sultan's dhow)

(**38**)

1944 (20 Nov). *Bicentenary of Al Busaid Dynasty. Recess.* Wmk Mult Script CA. P 14.

327	**37**	10c. ultramarine	85	2·50
		a. "C" of "CA" missing from wmk	£450	
328		20c. red	85	3·25
		a. "C" of "CA" missing from wmk	£450	
329		50c. blue-green	85	30
330		1s. dull purple	85	65
		a. "A" of "CA" missing from wmk		
327/30 *Set of* 4			3·00	6·00
327s/30s Perf "Specimen" *Set of* 4			75·00	

1946 (11 Nov). *Victory. Nos. 311 and 315 optd with T* **38**.

331	**33**	10c. black (R.)	20	50
332		30c. ultramarine (R.)	20	50
331s/2s Perf "Specimen" *Set of* 2			48·00	

1949 (10 Jan). *Royal Silver Wedding. As Nos. 112/13 of Antigua.*

333	20c. orange	30	1·50
334	10s. brown	18·00	28·00

1949 (10–13 Oct). *75th Anniv of UPU. As Nos. 114/17 of Antigua.*

335	20c. red-orange (13 Oct)	30	3·00
336	30c. deep blue	1·75	1·00
	a. "C" of "CA" missing from wmk	£750	
337	50c. magenta	1·00	2·50
338	1s. blue-green (13 Oct)	1·00	4·50
335/8 *Set of* 4		3·50	10·00

POSTAGE DUE STAMPS

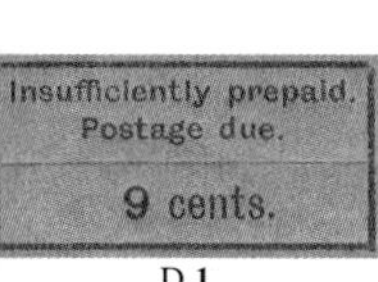

D **1**

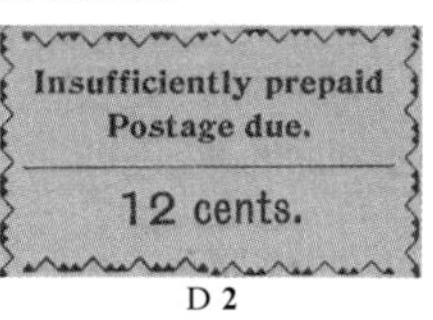

D **2**

(Types D **1** and D **2** typo by the Government Printer)

1926–30. *Rouletted 10, with imperf sheet edges. No gum.*

D1	D **1**	1c. black/*orange*	11·00	£100
D2		2c. black/*orange*	4·50	50·00
D3		3c. black/*orange*	5·00	42·00
		a. "cent.s" for "cents."	£120	
D4		6c. black/*orange*	—	£7000
		a. "cent.s" for "cents."	—	£16000
D5		9c. black/*orange*	2·75	22·00
		a. "cent.s" for "cents."	20·00	80·00
D6		12c. black/*orange*	£9000	£8500
		a. "cent.s" for "cents."		
D7		12c. black/*green*	£1400	£600
		a. "cent.s" for "cents."	£3750	£1700
D8		15c. black/*orange*	2·75	24·00
		a. "cent.s" for "cents."	20·00	85·00
D9		18c. black/*salmon*	4·25	40·00
		a. "cent.s" for "cents."	38·00	£120
D10		18c. black/*orange*	17·00	65·00
		a. "cent.s" for "cents."	65·00	£180
D11		20c. black/*orange*	4·00	55·00
		a. "cent.s" for "cents."	40·00	£160
D12		21c. black/*orange*	3·50	32·00
		a. "cent.s" for "cents."	32·00	£110
D13		25c. black/*magenta*	£2750	£1300
		a. "cent.s" for "cents."	£6500	£3750
D14		25c. black/*orange*	£10000	£10000
D15		31c. black/*orange*	9·50	75·00
		a. "cent.s" for "cents."	50·00	
D16		50c. black/*orange*	21·00	£150
		a. "cent.s" for "cents."	95·00	
D17		75c. black/*orange*	65·00	£325
		a. "cent.s" for "cents."	£250	

Initial printings, except the 1c. and 2c., contained the error "cent.s" for "cents" on R. 4/1 in the sheets of 10 (2 × 5). The error was corrected on subsequent supplies of the 3c., 9c. and 15c.

It is known that examples of these stamps used before early 1929 were left uncancelled on the covers. Uncancelled examples of Nos. D4, D6/7 and D13/14 which are not in very fine condition, must be assumed to have been used.

1930–33. *Rouletted 5. No gum.*

D18	D **2**	2c. black/*salmon*	15·00	29·00
D19		3c. black/*rose*	3·00	48·00
D21		6c. black/*yellow*	3·00	32·00
D22		12c. black/*blue*	4·00	26·00
D23		25c. black/*rose*	9·00	75·00
D24		25c. black/*lilac*	14·00	50·00
D18/24 *Set of* 6			45·00	£225

D **3**

(Typo D.L.R.)

1936 (1 Jan)–**62**. Wmk Mult Script CA. P 14.

D25	D **3**	5c. violet	4·25	8·50
		a. Chalk-surfaced paper (18.7.56)	35	15·00
D26		10c. scarlet	3·50	2·75
		a. Chalk-surfaced paper (6.3.62)	35	7·00
D27		20c. green	2·25	4·25
		a. Chalk-surfaced paper (6.3.62)	35	18·00
D28		30c. brown	8·50	18·00
		a. Chalk-surfaced paper (18.7.56)	35	13·00
D29		40c. ultramarine	8·50	25·00
		a. Chalk-surfaced paper (18.7.56)	60	30·00
D30		1s. grey	8·50	29·00
		a. Chalk-surfaced paper (18.7.56)	1·00	21·00
D25/30 *Set of* 6			32·00	80·00
D25a/30a *Set of* 6			2·75	95·00
D25s/30s Perf "Specimen" *Set of* 6			70·00	

Zululand
see South Africa

Set Prices For British Empire Omnibus Issues

The composition of these sets is in accordance with the tables on the following pages. Only such items considered basic stamps are included; varieties such as shades, perforation changes and watermark changes are excluded.

1935 SILVER JUBILEE

1935. *Silver Jubilee. Complete set of 250 stamps*

	Price *Un*	Price *Used*
	£950	£1300

Country	*Catalogue Nos.*	*Stamps*
Great Britain	453/6	4
Antigua	91/4	4
Ascension	31/4	4
Australia	156/8	3
Nauru	40/3	4
New Guinea	206/7	2
Papua	150/3	4
Bahamas	141/4	4
Barbados	241/4	4
Basutoland	11/14	4
Bechuanaland	111/14	4
Bermuda	94/7	4
British Guiana	301/4	4
British Honduras	143/6	4
British Solomon Islands	53/6	4
Canada	335/40	6
Newfoundland	250/3	4
Cayman Islands	108/11	4
Ceylon	379/82	4
Cyprus	144/7	4
Dominica	92/5	4
Egypt-British Forces	A10	1
Falkland Islands	139/42	4
Fiji	242/5	4
Gambia	143/6	4
Gibraltar	114/17	4
Gilbert and Ellice Islands	36/9	4
Gold Coast	113/16	4
Grenada	145/8	4
Hong Kong	133/6	4
India	240/6	7
Jamaica	114/17	4
Kenya, Uganda and Tanganyika	124/7	4
Leeward Islands	88/91	4
Malaya-Straits Settlements	256/9	4
Malta	210/13	4
Mauritius	245/8	4
Montserrat	94/7	4
Morocco Agencies		
British Currency	62/5	4
Spanish Currency	149/52	4
French Currency	212/15	4
Tangier	238/40	3
New Zealand	573/5	3
Cook Islands	113/15	3
Niue	69/71	3
Western Samoa	177/9	3
Nigeria	30/3	4
Northern Rhodesia	18/21	4
Nyasaland	123/6	4
St. Helena	124/7	4
St. Kitts-Nevis	61/4	4
St. Lucia	109/12	4
St. Vincent	142/5	4
Seychelles	128/31	4
Sierra Leone	181/4	4
Somaliland Protectorate	86/9	4
South Africa	65/8	4×2
Southern Rhodesia	31/4	4
South West Africa	88/91	4
Swaziland	21/4	4
Trinidad and Tobago	239/42	4
Turks and Caicos Islands	187/9	4
Virgin Islands	103/6	4
Total		250

The concept initiated by the 1935 Silver Jubilee omnibus issue has provided a pattern for a series of Royal commemoratives over the past 50 years which have introduced countless collectors to the hobby.

The Crown Colony Windsor Castle design by Harold Fleury is, surely, one of the most impressive produced to the 20th-century and its reproduction in the recess process by three of the leading stamp-printing firms of the era has provided a subject for philatelic research which has yet to be exhausted.

Each of the three, Bradbury, Wilkinson & Co. and Waterless and Sons, who both produced fifteen issues, together with De La Rue & Co. who printed fourteen, used a series of vignette (centre) plates coupled with individual frame plates for each value. All were taken from dies made by Waterlow. Several worthwhile varieties exist on the frame plates but most interest has been concentrated on the centre plates, each of which was used to print a considerable number of different stamps.

Sheets printed by Bradbury, Wilkinson were without printed plate numbers, but research has now identified eleven centre plates which were probably used in permanent pairings. A twelfth plate awaits confirmation. Stamps from some of these centre plates have revealed a number of prominent plate flaws, the most famous of which, the extra flagstaff, has been eagerly sought by collectors for many years.

Extra flagstaff (Plate "1" R. 9/1)

Short extra flagstaff (Plate "2" R. 2/1)

Lightning conductor (Plate "3" R. 2/5)

Flagstaff on right-hand turret (Plate "5" R. 7/1)

Double flagstaff (Plate "6" R. 5/2)

De La Rue sheets were initially printed with plate numbers, but in many instances these were subsequently trimmed off. Surviving examples do, however, enable a positive identification of six centre plates, 2A, 2B, (2A), (2B), 4 and 4/ to be made. The evidence of sheet markings and plate flaws clearly demonstrates that there were two different pairs of plates numbered 2A 2B. The second pair is designated (2A) (2B) by specialist collectors to avoid further confusion. The number of major plate flaws is not so great as on the Bradbury, Wilkinson sheets, but four examples are included in the catalogue.

Diagonal line by turret (Plate 2A R. 10/1 and 10/2)

Dot to left of chapel (Plate 2B R. 8/3)

Dot by flagstaff (Plate 4 R. 8/4)

Dash by turret (Plate 4/ R. 3/6)

Much less is known concerning the Waterlow centre plate system as the sheets did not show plate numbers. Ten individual plates have. so far, been identified and it is believed that these were used in pairs. The two versions of the kite and log flaw from plate "2" show that this plate exists in two states.

Damaged turret (Plate "1" R. 5/6)

Kite and vertical log (Plate "2A" R. 10/6)

Kite and horizontal log (Plate "2B" R. 10/6)

Bird by turret (Plate "7" R. 1/5)

1937 CORONATION

1937. *Coronation. Complete set of 202 stamps* £120 £16

Country	*Catalogue Nos.*	*Stamp*
Great Britain	461	
Aden	13/15	
Antigua	95/7	
Ascension	35/7	
Australia		
Nauru	44/7	
New Guinea	208/11	
Papua	154/7	
Bahamas	146/8	
Barbados	245/7	
Basutoland	15/17	
Bechuanaland	115/17	
Bermuda	107/9	
British Guiana	305/7	
British Honduras	147/9	
British Solomon Islands	57/9	
Canada	356	
Newfoundland	254/6, 257/67	
Cayman Islands	112/14	
Ceylon	383/5	
Cyprus	148/50	
Dominica	96/8	
Falkland Islands	143/5	
Fiji	246/8	
Gambia	147/9	
Gibraltar	118/20	
Gilbert and Ellice Islands	40/2	
Gold Coast	117/19	
Grenada	149/51	
Hong Kong	137/9	
Jamaica	118/20	
Kenya, Uganda and Tanganyika	128/30	
Leeward Islands	92/4	
Malaya-Straits Settlements	275/7	
Malta	214/16	
Mauritius	249/51	
Montserrat	98/100	
Morocco Agencies		
Spanish Currency	164	
French Currency	229	
Tangier	244	
New Zealand	599/601	
Cook Islands	124/6	
Niue	72/4	
Nigeria	46/8	
Northern Rhodesia	22/4	
Nyasaland	127/9	
St. Helena	128/30	
St. Kitts-Nevis	65/7	
St. Lucia	125/7	
St. Vincent	146/8	
Seychelles	132/4	
Sierra Leone	185/7	
Somaliland Protectorate	91/2	
South Africa	71/5	5
Southern Rhodesia	36/9	
South West Africa	97/104	8
Swaziland	25/7	

Trinidad and Tobago	243/5	3
Turks and Caicos Islands	191/3	3
Virgin Islands	107/9	3
Total		202

1945–46 VICTORY

1945–46. *Victory. Complete set of 164 stamps* 42·00 62·00

Country	*Catalogue Nos.*	*Stamps*
Great Britain	491/2	2
Aden	28/9	2
Seiyun	12/13	2
Shihr and Mukalla	12/13	2
Antigua	110/11	2
Ascension	48/9	2
Australia	213/15	3
Bahamas	176/7	2
Barbados	262/3	2
Basutoland	29/31	3 × 2
Bechuanaland	129/31	3 × 2
Bermuda	123/4	2
British Guiana	320/1	2
British Honduras	162/3	2
British Solomon Islands	73/4	2
Burma	64/7	4
Cayman Islands	127/8	2
Ceylon	400/1	2
Cyprus	164/5	2
Dominica	110/11	2
Falkland Islands	164/5	2
Falkland Islands Dependencies	617/18	2
Fiji	268/9	2
Gambia	162/3	2
Gibraltar	132/3	2
Gilbert and Ellice Islands	55/6	2
Gold Coast	133/4	2
Grenada	164/5	2
Hong Kong	169/70	2
India	278/81	4
Hyderabad	53	1
Jamaica	141/2	2
Kenya, Uganda and Tanganyika	155/6	2
Leeward Islands	115/16	2
Malta	232/3	2
Mauritius	264/5	2
Montserrat	113/14	2
Morocco Agencies		
Tangier	253/4	2
New Zealand	667/77	11
Cook Islands	146/9	4
Niue	98/101	4
Western Samoa	215/18	4
Nigeria	60/1	2
Northern Rhodesia	46/7	2
Nyasaland	158/9	2
Pakistan		
Bahawalpur	O19	1
Pitcairn Islands	9/10	2
St. Helena	141/2	2
St. Kitts-Nevis	78/9	2
St. Lucia	142/3	2
St. Vincent	160/1	2
Seychelles	150/1	2
Sierra Leone	201/2	2
Somaliland Protectorate	117/18	2
South Africa	108/10	3 × 2
Southern Rhodesia	64/7	4
South West Africa	131/3	3 × 2
Swaziland	39/41	3 × 2
Trinidad and Tobago	257/8	2
Turks and Caicos Islands	206/7	2
Virgin Islands	122/3	2
Zanzibar	331/2	2
Total		164

1948 ROYAL SILVER WEDDING

1948–49. *Royal Silver Wedding. Complete set of 138 stamps* £1700 £1800

Country	*Catalogue Nos.*	*Stamps*
Great Britain	493/4	2
Aden	30/1	2
Seiyun	14/15	2
Shihr and Mukalla	14/15	2
Antigua	112/13	2
Ascension	50/1	2
Bahamas	194/5	2
Bahrain	61/2	2
Barbados	265/62	2
Basutoland	36/7	2
Bechuanaland	136/7	2
Bermuda	125/6	2
British Guiana	322/3	2
British Honduras	164/5	2
British Postal Agencies in Eastern Arabia	25/6	2
British Solomon Islands	75/6	2
Cayman Islands	129/30	2
Cyprus	166/7	2
Dominica	112/13	2
Falkland Islands	166/7	2
Falkland Islands Dependencies	G19/20	2
Fiji	270/1	2
Gambia	164/5	2
Gibraltar	134/5	2
Gilbert and Ellice Islands	57/8	2
Gold Coast	147/8	2
Grenada	166/7	2
Hong Kong	171/2	2
Jamaica	143/4	2
Kenya, Uganda and Tanganyika	157/8	2
Kuwait	74/5	2
Leeward Islands	117/18	2
Malaya		
Johore	131/2	2
Kedah	70/1	2
Kelantan	55/6	2
Malacca	1/2	2
Negri Sembilan	40/1	2
Pahang	47/8	2
Penang	1/2	2
Perak	122/3	2
Perlis	1/2	2
Selangor	88/9	2
Trengganu	61/2	2
Malta	249/50	2
Mauritius	270/1	2
Montserrat	115/16	2
Morocco Agencies		
Spanish Currency	176/7	2
Tangier	255/6	2
Nigeria	62/3	2
North Borneo	350/1	2
Northern Rhodesia	48/9	2
Nyasaland	161/2	2
Pitcairn Islands	11/12	2
St. Helena	143/4	2
St. Kitts-Nevis	80/1	2
St. Lucia	144/5	2
St. Vincent	162/3	2
Sarawak	165/6	2
Seychelles	152/3	2
Sierra Leone	203/4	2
Singapore	31/2	2
Somaliland Protectorate	119/20	2
South Africa	125	1 × 2
South West Africa	137	1x2
Swaziland	46/7	2
Trinidad and Tobago	259/60	2
Turks and Caicos Islands	208/9	2
Virgin Islands	124/5	2
Zanzibar	333/4	2
Total		138

1949 75th ANNIVERSARY OF U.P.U.

1949. *U.P.U. 75th Anniversary Complete set of 310 stamps* £275 £400

Country	*Catalogue Nos.*	*Stamps*
Great Britain	449/502	4
Aden	32/5	4
Seiyun	16/19	4
Shihr and Mukalla	16/19	4
Antigua	114/17	4
Ascension	52/5	4
Australia	232	1
Bahamas	196/9	4
Bahrain	67/70	4
Barbados	267/70	4
Basutoland	38/41	4
Bechuanaland	138/41	4
Bermuda	130/3	4
British Guiana	324/7	4
British Honduras	172/5	4
British Postal Agencies in Eastern Arabia	31/4	4
British Solomon Islands	77/80	4
Brunei	96/9	4
Cayman Islands	131/4	4
Ceylon	410/12	3
Cyprus	168/71	4
Dominica	114/17	4
Falkland Islands	168/71	4
Falkland Islands Dependencies	631/4	4
Fiji	272/5	4
Gambia	166/9	4
Gibraltar	136/9	4
Gilbert and Ellice Islands	59/62	4
Gold Coast	149/52	4
Grenada	168/71	4
Hong Kong	173/6	4
India	325/8	4
Jamaica	145/8	4
Kenya, Uganda and Tanganyika	159/62	4
Kuwait	80/3	4
Leeward Islands	119/22	4
Malaya		
Johore	148/51	4
Kedah	72/5	4
Kelantan	57/60	4
Malacca	18/21	4
Negri Sembilan	63/6	4
Pahang	49/52	4
Penang	23/6	4
Perak	124/7	4
Perlis	3/6	4
Selangor	111/14	4
Trengganu	63/6	4
Malta	251/4	4
Mauritius	272/5	4
Montserrat	117/20	4
Morocco Agencies		
Tangier	276/9	4
New Hebrides	64/7, F77/80	4+4
Nigeria	64/7	4
North Borneo	352/5	4
Northern Rhodesia	50/3	4
Nyasaland	163/6	4
Pakistan		
Bahawalpur	43/6, O28/31	4+4
Pitcairn Islands	13/16	4
St. Helena	145/8	4
St. Kitts-Nevis	82/5	4
St. Lucia	160/3	4
St. Vincent	178/81	4
Sarawak	167/70	4
Seychelles	154/7	4
Sierra Leone	205/8	4
Singapore	33/6	4
Somaliland Protectorate	121/4	4
South Africa	128/30	3 × 2
Southern Rhodesia	68/9	2
South West Africa	138/40	3 × 2
Swaziland	48/51	4
Tonga	88/91	4
Trinidad and Tobago	261/4	4
Turks and Caicos Islands	217/20	4
Virgin Islands	126/9	4
Zanzibar	335/8	4
Total		310

1951 INAUGURATION OF B.W.I. UNIVERSITY COLLEGE

1951. *B.W.I. University College Complete set of 28 stamps* 10·00 22·00

Country	*Catalogue Nos.*	*Stamps*
Antigua	118/19	2
Barbados	283/4	2
British Guiana	328/9	2
British Honduras	176/7	2
Dominica	118/19	2
Grenada	185/6	2
Jamaica	149/50	2
Leeward Islands	123/4	2
Montserrat	121/2	2
St. Kitts-Nevis	92/3	2
St. Lucia	164/5	2
St. Vincent	182/3	2
Trinidad and Tobago	265/6	2
Virgin Islands	130/1	2
Total		28

Index

BUILD YOUR COMMONWEALTH ONE COUNTRY CATALOGUE COLLECTION

Other titles in our popular One Country catalogue range include:-

Stanley Gibbons Canada Catalogue

Features revised content and prices, new issues up to the end of 2002, including Canadian Provinces.

Item 2874(03) **Black & White** **£9.95**

Item 2874(03)c **Colour** **£19.95**

Loose leaf format*

Stanley Gibbons St. Helena & Dependencies Catalogue

Features detailed, fully updated priced listings of all issues from SG1 to the end of 2002, including stamps issued during the present reign. All prices carefully revised in line with the current market in stamps from the ever popular islands of Ascension, St. Helena and Tristan da Cunha.

Item 2875(03) **Black & White** **£7.95**

Item 2875(03)c **Colour** **£14.95**

Loose leaf format*

Stanley Gibbons New Zealand Catalogue

A new style, bound A4 catalogue, with illustrations predominantly in colour, including express delivery stamps, postage dues, officials, booklets and postal fiscals, the Antarctic Expedition issues, Ross Dependency and Tokelau.

Item 2876(03)c **Colour** **£12.95**

Stanley Gibbons Australia Catalogue

The second edition of this popular catalogue covers issues up to October 2003. Includes Cocos (Keeling) Islands, Christmas Island, Norfolk Island and Australian Antarctic Territory, as well as States and Dependencies.

Item 2871(04) **Colour** **£19.95**

Stanley Gibbons Hong Kong Catalogue

Includes postage dues, postcard stamps, postal fiscals, stamp booklets, Japanese occupation stamps and stamps used in the British Post Offices in China and Japan. Plus the stamps of the Special Administrative region of the People's Republic of China up to the end of 2003.

Item 2877(04) **Colour** **£9.95**

Stanley Gibbons Falkland Islands Catalogue

Includes priced listings of Falkland Island stamps used in the Dependencies, as well as the issues of the Falkland Island Dependencies, British Antarctic Territory, South Georgia and the South Sandwich Islands to early 2004.

Item 2872(04) **Colour** **£9.95**

Stanley Gibbons India (including Feudatory States) Catalogue

Includes issues up to mid-2003, as well as the stamps of the Indian Convention States & Feudatory States, and there are notes on Indian Stamps used abroad. Lists and prices, booklets and officials for India and the Indian States, and also lists the stamps overprinted for the Indian Expeditionary Forces and for Indian forces in Korea, the Congo, Gaze, and Indo-China.

Item 2873(04) **Colour** **£19.95**

New titles added throughout the year—contact us for details
postage rates apply—please enquire

Stanley Gibbons Publications
7 Parkside, Christchurch Road,
Ringwood, Hants BH24 3SH
Fax: +44 (0) 1425 470247

Freephone (UK only) 0800 611 622
Overseas telephone +44 (0)1425 472363
Email: sales@stanleygibbons.co.uk

www.stanleygibbons.com

COLLECT COMMONWEALTH STAMPS

Condition	Country	SG No.	Description	Price
			SUB TOTAL	£
			POSTAGE & PACKAGING	£3.60
			GRAND TOTAL	£

Please complete payment, name and address details overleaf